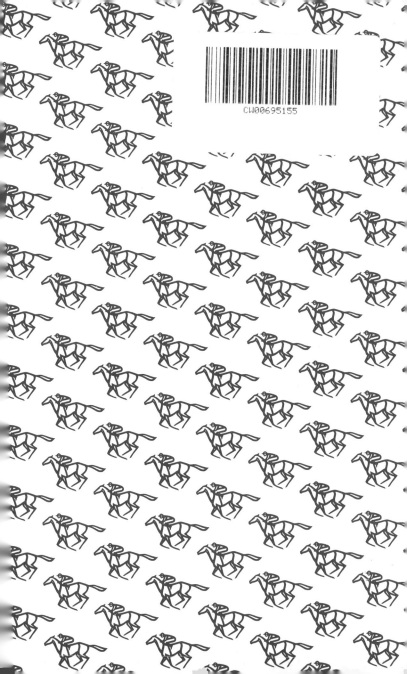

CW00695155

RACEHORSES
OF 1997

Price £67.00

A TIMEFORM PUBLICATION

AGE, WEIGHT & DISTANCE TABLE

Timeform's scale of weight-for-age for the flat

Dist	Age	Jan 1-16	Jan 17-31	Feb 1-16	Feb 17-28	Mar 1-16	Mar 17-31	Apr 1-16	Apr 17-30	May 1-16	May 17-31	June 1-16	June 17-30
5f	4	10–0	10–0	10–0	10–0	10–0	10–0	10–0	10–0	10–0	10–0	10–0	10–0
	3	9–5	9–5	9–6	9–7	9–7	9–8	9–8	9–9	9–9	9–10	9–10	9–11
	2						8–0	8–1	8–3	8–4	8–5	8–6	8–7
6f	4	10–0	10–0	10–0	10–0	10–0	10–0	10–0	10–0	10–0	10–0	10–0	10–0
	3	9–2	9–3	9–4	9–5	9–5	9–6	9–7	9–7	9–8	9–8	9–9	9–9
	2									8–0	8–2	8–3	8–4
7f	4	9–13	9–13	10–0	10–0	10–0	10–0	10–0	10–0	10–0	10–0	10–0	10–0
	3	9–0	9–1	9–2	9–3	9–4	9–4	9–5	9–6	9–6	9–7	9–8	9–8
	2											7–13	8–1
1m	4	9–13	9–13	9–13	9–13	10–0	10–0	10–0	10–0	10–0	10–0	10–0	10–0
	3	8–12	8–13	9–0	9–1	9–2	9–2	9–3	9–4	9–5	9–5	9–6	9–7
	2												
9f	4	9–12	9–12	9–12	9–13	9–13	9–13	9–13	9–13	10–0	10–0	10–0	10–0
	3	8–10	8–11	8–12	8–13	9–0	9–1	9–2	9–2	9–3	9–4	9–5	9–5
	2												
1¼m	4	9–11	9–12	9–12	9–12	9–13	9–13	9–13	9–13	9–13	10–0	10–0	10–0
	3	8–8	8–9	8–10	8–11	8–12	8–13	9–0	9–1	9–2	9–2	9–3	9–4
	2												
11f	4	9–10	9–11	9–11	9–12	9–12	9–12	9–13	9–13	9–13	9–13	9–13	10–0
	3	8–6	8–7	8–8	8–9	8–10	8–11	8–12	8–13	9–0	9–1	9–2	9–2
1½m	4	9–10	9–10	9–10	9–11	9–11	9–12	9–12	9–12	9–13	9–13	9–13	9–13
	3	8–4	8–5	8–6	8–7	8–8	8–9	8–10	8–11	8–12	8–13	9–0	9–1
13f	4	9–9	9–9	9–10	9–10	9–11	9–11	9–11	9–12	9–12	9–12	9–13	9–13
	3	8–2	8–3	8–4	8–5	8–7	8–8	8–9	8–10	8–11	8–12	8–13	9–0
1¾m	4	9–8	9–8	9–9	9–9	9–10	9–10	9–11	9–11	9–12	9–12	9–12	9–13
	3	8–0	8–2	8–3	8–4	8–5	8–6	8–7	8–8	8–9	8–10	8–11	8–12
15f	4	9–7	9–8	9–8	9–9	9–9	9–10	9–10	9–11	9–11	9–11	9–12	9–12
	3	7–13	8–0	8–1	8–2	8–4	8–5	8–6	8–7	8–8	8–9	8–10	8–11
2m	4	9–6	9–7	9–7	9–8	9–9	9–9	9–10	9–10	9–11	9–11	9–11	9–12
	3	7–11	7–12	7–13	8–1	8–2	8–3	8–4	8–5	8–6	8–7	8–8	8–9
2¼m	4	9–5	9–5	9–6	9–7	9–7	9–8	9–9	9–9	9–10	9–10	9–10	9–11
	3	7–8	7–9	7–11	7–12	7–13	8–0	8–2	8–3	8–4	8–5	8–6	8–7
2½m	4	9–3	9–4	9–5	9–6	9–6	9–7	9–7	9–8	9–9	9–9	9–10	9–10
	3	7–5	7–7	7–8	7–9	7–11	7–12	7–13	8–1	8–2	8–3	8–4	8–5

For 5-y-o's and older, use 10-0 in all cases
Race distances in the above tables are shown only at 1 furlong intervals.
For races over odd distances, the nearest distance shown in the table should be used:
thus for races of 1m to 1m 109 yards, use the table weights for 1m;
for 1m 110 yards to 1m 219 yards use the 9f table

AGE, WEIGHT & DISTANCE TABLE
Timeform's scale of weight-for-age for the flat

Dist	Age	July 1-16	July 17-31	Aug 1-16	Aug 17-31	Sept 1-16	Sept 17-30	Oct 1-16	Oct 17-31	Nov 1-16	Nov 17-30	Dec 1-16	Dec 17-31
5f	4	10–0	10–0	10–0	10–0	10–0	10–0	10–0	10–0	10–0	10–0	10–0	10–0
	3	9–11	9–12	9–12	9–12	9–13	9–13	9–13	9–13	10–0	10–0	10–0	10–0
	2	8–8	8–9	8–10	8–11	8–12	8–13	9–0	9–1	9–2	9–2	9–3	9–4
6f	4	10–0	10–0	10–0	10–0	10–0	10–0	10–0	10–0	10–0	10–0	10–0	10–0
	3	9–10	9–10	9–11	9–11	9–12	9–12	9–12	9–13	9–13	9–13	9–13	10–0
	2	8–5	8–6	8–7	8–8	8–9	8–10	8–11	8–12	8–13	9–0	9–1	9–2
7f	4	10–0	10–0	10–0	10–0	10–0	10–0	10–0	10–0	10–0	10–0	10–0	10–0
	3	9–9	9–9	9–10	9–10	9–11	9–11	9–11	9–12	9–12	9–12	9–13	9–13
	2	8–2	8–3	8–4	8–5	8–6	8–7	8–9	8–10	8–11	8–12	8–13	9–0
1m	4	10–0	10–0	10–0	10–0	10–0	10–0	10–0	10–0	10–0	10–0	10–0	10–0
	3	9–7	9–8	9–8	9–9	9–9	9–10	9–10	9–11	9–11	9–12	9–12	9–12
	2			8–2	8–3	8–4	8–5	8–6	8–7	8–8	8–9	8–10	8–11
9f	4	10–0	10–0	10–0	10–0	10–0	10–0	10–0	10–0	10–0	10–0	10–0	10–0
	3	9–6	9–7	9–7	9–8	9–8	9–9	9–9	9–10	9–10	9–11	9–11	9–12
	2					8–1	8–3	8–4	8–5	8–6	8–7	8–8	8–9
1¼m	4	10–0	10–0	10–0	10–0	10–0	10–0	10–0	10–0	10–0	10–0	10–0	10–0
	3	9–5	9–5	9–6	9–7	9–7	9–8	9–8	9–9	9–9	9–10	9–10	9–11
	2						8–0	8–1	8–2	8–4	8–5	8–6	8–7
11f	4	10–0	10–0	10–0	10–0	10–0	10–0	10–0	10–0	10–0	10–0	10–0	10–0
	3	9–3	9–4	9–5	9–5	9–6	9–7	9–7	9–8	9–8	9–9	9–9	9–10
1½m	4	10–0	10–0	10–0	10–0	10–0	10–0	10–0	10–0	10–0	10–0	10–0	10–0
	3	9–2	9–2	9–3	9–4	9–5	9–5	9–6	9–7	9–7	9–8	9–9	9–9
13f	4	9–13	9–13	10–0	10–0	10–0	10–0	10–0	10–0	10–0	10–0	10–0	10–0
	3	9–0	9–1	9–2	9–3	9–4	9–4	9–5	9–6	9–6	9–7	9–8	9–8
1¾m	4	9–13	9–13	9–13	10–0	10–0	10–0	10–0	10–0	10–0	10–0	10–0	10–0
	3	8–13	9–0	9–1	9–2	9–3	9–3	9–4	9–5	9–5	9–6	9–7	9–7
15f	4	9–12	9–13	9–13	9–13	9–13	10–0	10–0	10–0	10–0	10–0	10–0	10–0
	3	8–12	8–13	9–0	9–1	9–1	9–2	9–3	9–4	9–4	9–5	9–6	9–6
2m	4	9–12	9–12	9–13	9–13	9–13	9–13	10–0	10–0	10–0	10–0	10–0	10–0
	3	8–10	8–11	8–12	8–13	9–0	9–1	9–2	9–3	9–3	9–4	9–5	9–5
2¼m	4	9–11	9–12	9–12	9–12	9–13	9–13	9–13	9–13	10–0	10–0	10–0	10–0
	3	8–8	8–9	8–10	8–11	8–12	8–13	9–0	9–1	9–2	9–2	9–3	9–4
2½m	4	9–10	9–11	9–11	9–12	9–12	9–12	9–13	9–13	9–13	9–13	10–0	10–0
	3	8–6	8–7	8–8	8–9	8–10	8–11	8–12	8–13	9–0	9–1	9–2	9–3

For 5-y-o's and older, use 10-0 in all cases
Race distances in the above tables are shown only at 1 furlong intervals.
For races over odd distances, the nearest distance shown in the table should be used:
thus for races of 1m to 1m 109 yards, use the table weights for 1m;
for 1m 110 yards to 1m 219 yards use the 9f table

CONTENTS

Compiled and produced by

G. Greetham, B.A. (Director); S. D. Rowlands, B.A. (Editor); C. S. Williams (Deputy Editor & Handicapper); S. N. Copeland, G. J. North, B.Sc. (Handicappers); R. J. C. Austen, B.A., J. Ingles, B.A., E. K. Wilkinson (Essays); P. Morrell, R. J. O'Brien, B.A., S. L. Walker (Short Commentaries); O. C. Pennant Jones, B.A. (Foreign); D. Holdsworth, W. Muncaster, D. Smith, C. Wright, B.A. (Production)

© **Portway Press Limited 1998**   ISBN 0 900599 99 5

Racehorses of 1997

Introduction

After shaping up into a largely uneventful year in racing politics, 1997 produced a sting in the tail. Sheikh Mohammed's Gimcrack speech in early-December proved a turning point, focussing attention on the massive contribution that owners make to British racing and providing a backdrop to a wildly optimistic plan presented at around the same time to the British Horseracing Board. The report by the BHB's Levy Review Group, chaired by Peter Savill, was adopted, with some revisions, as the Financial Plan for British Racing, the main thrust being that racing needs an additional £105m (including £80m from government) to put it on a firm financial basis. On the eve of the presentation of the plan to the annual Industry Forum in January, there was a further twist when Lord Wakeham resigned the BHB chairmanship saying that 'the plan is unrealistic in the current economic circumstances.'

The speech by the winning owner at the Gimcrack dinner at York is traditionally expected to let off a few crackers, but Sheikh Mohammed's exploded a bombshell. He used the occasion, in a speech delivered on his behalf by Michael Osborne, to announce that he and his brothers, the biggest spenders in British racing, might 'massively reduce' their operation unless racing's finances underwent radical change. The speech was scathing about the government for 'taking out', in betting tax, six times the amount that finds its way back to racing via the betting levy, and was fiercely critical of the bookmakers, who 'must laugh at us as they make their way to the bank with ever-increasing profits.' The Maktoum family, it was said, could 'no longer escape the stark fact that our racing operation in Britain is a luxury that we can no longer sustain—and just as that applies to us, so, logically, it must also apply to the major international players and all

Sheikh Mohammed and his brother Hamdan—finding it difficult to look on the bright side

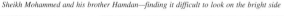

too many home-based owner-breeders as well.' The Sheikh's speech made the point that he and his brothers were not asking for a subsidy—it would be ludicrous to 'pretend we were down to our last three camels'—but they feared the underfunding of British racing would force them to move elsewhere where the sport is more rewarding. It used to be a byword in sport that 'no player is bigger than the game', but there can be little argument that the Maktoums, who have already divested themselves of *Racing Post*, would be an enormous loss to British racing. Between them, the brothers had over five hundred individual *runners* on the flat in Britain in the latest season and a sizeable number in training which didn't make the racecourse. As well as the impact on employment in some stables and studs, the Maktoums' withdrawal would rob British racing in years to come of a valuable quota of the finest racehorses in the world.

Sheikh Mohammed's speech emphasised the attractions of owning horses in Britain. 'Nowhere else in the world can come close to matching its wonderful history, its traditions or its incomparable prestige . . . the variety of the courses and the splendid settings are unique . . . it has a general racing public who understand what they are watching, value the horse and provide the most enthusiastic following in the world . . . racing is part of the British heritage.' Perhaps that's the reason British racing has never been short of people prepared to pay for the pleasure they get from having a racehorse—collectively, owners are estimated to have paid over £150m for their fun in the latest season. The philosophy was further articulated by others, including Nigel Payne ('I don't think prize money is quite the critical thing people make it out to be. It is the thrill of the win and taking part') and David Abell ('Racing is a hobby and I have not yet found any hobbies that don't cost money . . . anybody who is in racing to make money is a fool'). Their position reflects that of the majority of racehorse owners, but not, apparently, that of BHB director Peter Savill, whose presentation of the Financial Plan included the assertion that owners not in the Sheikhs' league 'have to look at it from a commercial standpoint.' The plan presents owners in the role of altruistic providers of a product for the 'betting industry', a scenario so ludicrously false as to be laughable. Currently, owners collectively recoup 24% of training costs through prize money, 'too low a return in relation to our international competition' according to the BHB, whose plan establishes a target of a 50% return 'which would place Britain just ahead of France and the United States.' This requires a doubling of prize money and, together with extra for marketing, breeders' premiums, training and research, appearance money and reduction in race-entry costs, is where the BHB's figure of £105m comes from.

The predicted result of this additional funding, according to the plan's findings, would be an increase in the number of horses in training by 3,400 and an expansion of the fixture list by 8% to 10%; this would lead to an increase in betting turnover which, with additional jobs created in racing and betting, conveniently would mean that the government would get back the £80m it would give to racing (the other £25m was to come from 'self-help'). Whether treasury officials will accept this argument looks very doubtful. The plan assumes a rise in betting turnover on horseracing of £450m, or just under 10%, but that wasn't even achieved when SIS pictures were first beamed into betting shops, a much bigger innovation than anything in the BHB's plan, one of the main consequences of which would

Peter Savill—
architect of the Financial Plan for British Racing

be an expansion in racing at the lowest tier, of which there is too much already. The indications are that the government is unlikely to be influenced by the questionable international comparisons which form the basis of the BHB's assessment of British racing's financial needs; the list of countries chosen for international comparison shows a low percentage of betting turnover 'returned to racing' in Britain, where owners contribute a bigger percentage of the cost of staging racing than in most other major racing nations (Japanese owners, who need to be nationals, recover over 80% of their costs).

The need to improve the lot of owners in Britain seems to have become an article of faith with the BHB, yet, collectively, owners are faring better than in practically any previous era. A study by the Racegoers Club, for example, into the ten years from 1985 showed that prize money as a whole rose by 240% and the Levy Board's contribution to prize money by 314%, against the rate of inflation in the same period of 55%. Notwithstanding Levy Board cuts in the short period since then, a BHB press release in December pointed out that owners still raced for a record £60m in 1997, when, among other things, the growth in the contribution by racecourses themselves went up by over 10% and race-sponsorship set a new record, growing by around 8%. Figures can, of course, be used to prove almost anything—and these would seem to indicate a sport making striking progress! Racing has also enjoyed beneficial government measures in recent years, including two reductions in the rate of betting duty, the long-overdue introduction of Sunday racing with betting, and evening opening of betting shops, and, directly for owners, the surprising 1993 concession on VAT estimated by the BHB to be worth about £20m a year. The government is also likely to take a dim view of the fact that when the BHB made its submission for the last Conservative budget it argued that racing needed an additional £23m to meet the target at that time for prize money—to cover 35% of owners' costs (the aim then was that a horse winning three class E races should recover its training costs). Little wonder the Financial Plan for British Racing was headlined 'The plan from Planet Zonk' over a scathing article by David Ashforth in *The Sporting Life*.

The plan succeeded, however, in producing what one BHB director called 'a united board and a united industry' in the aftermath of Lord Wakeham's resignation. Wakeham, by contrast, claimed that he had found the chairmanship an 'impossible' job because the BHB's structure produces a board made up of 'different barons representing different interests.' 'In every other job I have done, people wanted a solution,' he said. 'I think these people want a posture.' The fate of the BHB's Financial Plan rests with the government, and it was Wakeham's acute differences over the

7

likely government response that led to his departure. For our part, whether Lord Wakeham is proved right or wrong, the BHB has picked the wrong ground on which to fight its battle with government. The 'Sheikh Mohammed versus the British government' billing is unfortunate as it diverts attention away from the issues and on to individuals, which always suits the media best but cannot possibly help racing's case with government. There is a strong argument, as Sheikh Mohammed says, that the government raises too much from betting tax compared to the amount that finds its way back to racing through the 1¼% levy on individual bets. The BHB's Financial Plan is careful not to specify the means by which government might deliver another £80m to racing, but it has been suggested that a cut in the betting tax of 1¾% (to 5%) would provide the amount being sought—if it is was diverted directly to racing. However, no responsible government could consent to that. As we have said before, owners may or may not have a case for a better deal, but it is impossible to justify that their lot should be rectified at the expense of punters who pay a penal rate of tax on bets placed off course. Money raised from betting tax is the punters' money in the first place—not racing's—and, should the government decide that the imposition of betting tax is still too high, it is the punters who should be the principal beneficiaries.

The main thrust of racing's argument should be that the true rate of betting tax on horse racing—betting money is bet and rebet so that the rate, in real terms, is 33%—is unfairly high compared to that levied on the lottery at 24% and the pools at 26%, for example. This argument would be more just, especially if the BHB, supporting the bookmakers, was seen to back the principle that the money should be returned to the punter. That cash would then be recycled—much of it returning to the government anyway—and racing would enjoy the indirect benefit (through the levy) arising from the anticipated increase in turnover. If the BHB was lucky, the government might even be persuaded to transfer a fraction—it transferred ¼% in 1992—of such a cut in betting duty directly to the levy!

The subsidy racing receives from punters via the levy is invaluable—indeed, racing is lucky to have it—and everything should be done to nurture and increase it by pressing for a betting set-up that gives the punter a fair chance of beating the odds in the long run if he or she is skilful enough. The penal rate of betting tax has contributed to a steady decline, in real terms, in betting turnover on horse-racing down the years. The indexation of turnover at the end of the 'sixties suggests that it should now be around £9,500m a year; in fact it's about half that sum, £4,800m. In the same period the number of licensed betting shops—the engine room of British racing—has continued to decline sharply (roughly a thousand have closed in the 'nineties) to around 8,600, further illustrating the fact that the high take-out from betting on horses, coupled with a growth in the range of gambling alternatives, has historically alienated punters by reducing the prospect of winning the battle with bookmakers. The government takes around £300m a year in tax on horserace betting turnover, a sum that roughly equates to the total contribution made to the cost of staging racing in Britain by owners, racecourses, sponsors and the Levy Board combined.

The BHB's Financial Plan acknowledges the importance of betting's contribution and calls for betting on horseracing to be allowed by law in outlets other than betting shops, something that would have serious repercussions for the betting chains. The ownership of a good proportion of Britain's betting shops changed hands in 1997, Nomura, a Japanese bank, acquiring William Hill (1530 shops) for £700m from its troubled parent company Brent Walker, and Ladbroke (1900 shops) taking over Corals (890) for £375m. Corals, the third biggest betting chain, came on the market when its parent company Bass failed in its bid for William Hill. Ladbroke announced a plan to sell 130 Coral shops to the Tote, which would then have 340, placing it fourth behind Ladbroke, Hill and Stanley (570). The new Tote chairman Peter Jones explained that the long-term strategy was to increase its share of the off-course betting market 'to improve its profitability and its contribution to racing.' If the Corals takeover is formally approved, Ladbroke will have 30% of the outlets and (because of the distribution of high turnover shops) an even higher percentage of the turnover, the consequences of which kept the letters columns of the trade papers plentifully supplied. A general complaint that punters will have less choice—true in the field of morning odds, ante-post prices and sports betting—has to be seen in the light of the general preference for starting-price betting (80% of bets on horseracing are at SP). All the betting chains—who compete mainly on location and service—adopt a similar approach when it comes to the rules and terms offered to punters. That the concentration of market share has the potential to increase Ladbroke's influence on the racecourse betting market (and thereby the SP) is another concern that was expressed, along with the potential to influence pool bets placed through Tote Direct (owned by the Tote, Corals and Ladbroke).

Before succeeding Lord Wyatt (who died shortly after relinquishing the Tote chairmanship), Peter Jones had chaired the BHB's Off-Course Betting Development Group, whose report in September came as a breath of fresh air and provided a blueprint offering real hope. Defying the BHB's obduracy in the face of criticism of the dullness of so many of its race programmes, the group emphasised the need to produce races attractive to punters. There was particular emphasis on working closely with terrestrial TV (Channel 4 Racing's Andrew Franklin was a member of the group) to make the best of this invaluable shop window. Television means big money for sport these days—Sky Sports' £675m deal is the bedrock of football's Premier League—but for racing its im-

Peter Jones—chaired the Off-Course Betting Development Group which produced an important blueprint

portance is primarily in its significant influence on betting turnover. The group recommended strengthening the races shown on TV, with forty-eight-hour declarations allowing more late flexibility in race timing to ensure that the most attractive events are televised. The quality of Sunday racing, the least popular day with the off-course market, should also be improved and every weekday afternoon should have a 'showcase race' worth at least £10,000. The 'showcase' initiative has been implemented for 1998, financed in part by £425,000-worth of sponsorship from the major bookmakers under the banner of their 49's numbers game. Racing and the bookmakers, the group said, had a mutual interest in promoting the sport to the new audience brought into the shops by the introduction of lottery-style betting, especially as horseracing has lost market share and now accounts for around 70% of off-course betting with bookmakers, compared to over 75% at the start of the 'nineties. The bookmakers, of course, might also have the motive of promoting numbers betting (on which the margins are much higher) to its traditional racing audience. The introduction of a new 'superbet', offering the opportunity to win a significant sum for a small stake on Saturday TV races, recommended by the group, is pencilled in for 1999.

Whatever the future involvement of the Maktoum family in British racing, the racing year 1997 emphasised their current dominance. Sheikh Mohammed was leading owner for the ninth time—no owner outside the Maktoum family has filled that position since Robert Sangster in 1984—with his brothers Hamdan Al Maktoum and Maktoum Al Maktoum and the family's Godolphin operation also in the top five. **Singspiel** was the most successful horse to carry the Sheikh Mohammed colours, covering himself in glory by winning the second running of his owner's brainchild, the Dubai World Cup, before winning two championship races in Britain, the Coronation Cup and the International. Singspiel's victory at Nad Al Sheba, coupled with the Irish Champion and Japan Cup victories of his admirable stable-companion **Pilsudski** once again put Michael Stoute, who also won the domestic trainers' championship, way out in front as the leading British-based trainer overseas. British-trained horses enjoyed another outstanding year with their raids abroad (though, unusually, there

Sheikh Mohammed raises the Dubai World Cup after Singspiel's success

was no Irish or French classic victory for them). All told, 126 races were won by British horses on foreign soil, earning, according to figures produced by the International Racing Bureau, total prize money of £10,911,644, a little short of the record set the previous year. Clive Brittain and John Gosden both topped the £1m-mark abroad. Brittain's wins included the equivalent of the Italian and German Two Thousand Guineas with **Air Express**, who went on to establish himself as one of the leading three-year-old milers in Europe with a victory in the Queen Elizabeth II Stakes. That race saw the final racecourse appearance of the Two Thousand Guineas winner **Entrepreneur**, who was such a disappointment when odds on for the Derby, which went to the Gosden-trained **Benny The Dip**. Derby Day itself saw the beginnings of a revival after a period in the doldrums, and sponsors Vodafone renewed their commitment to the big race with a two-year extension worth over £2m; the Guineas meeting will, however, have a new sponsor, Wafic Said's Sagitta Asset Management signing a £2m deal covering the next three years. Mr Said's **Bosra Sham** looked as if she might carry all before her when winning in scintillating style at Royal Ascot, but she will also be remembered for her performance in the Coral-Eclipse, in which Henry Cecil's new stable-jockey, Kieren Fallon, got into hot water after she managed only third to Pilsudski and Benny The Dip. Fallon had joked at the start of the season that there would be spread betting on how long he would survive with Cecil—but he flourished as the season went on, the highlights of his first championship including British classic victories on the three-year-old fillies **Sleepytime** and **Reams of Verse** and a Sussex Stakes triumph on the high-class miler **Ali-Royal**. The second and third in the Sussex, the St James's Palace winner **Starborough** and Queen Anne winner **Allied Forces**, had helped Frankie Dettori to win the trophy for the top jockey at Royal Ascot (the essay on Allied Forces assesses his career so far). Dettori also had the dubious distinction of losing two races in the stewards room on one afternoon, as discussed in the essay on one of them, **Cape Cross**.

Unusually, none of the winners of the British classics went on to further success, though **Silver Patriarch**, beaten a whisker in the Derby, upheld the classic form when taking the St Leger and providing Pat Eddery with his 4,000th British winner. Eddery becomes the third jockey, after Gordon Richards and Lester Piggott, to reach the landmark. In fourth place, with 3,828 domestic winners, is Willie Carson, who announced his retirement in March. Carson won five jockeys' championships and seventeen British classics, a good proportion of them with Dick Hern, who announced his retirement from training at the end of the season. Hern won every British classic at least twice—saddling sixteen in all—and was champion trainer four times. Other retirements included former French champion Freddie Head (mentioned in the essay on **Always Loyal**) and two members of the 'thousand winners club' Tony Ives and Mark Birch, among the jockeys, and Reg Akehurst, Bill Watts and Paul Kelleway among the trainers. Sadly, trainer David Morley, who won the Gold Cup with **Celeric** and the Middle Park with **Hayil**, died suddenly in January, 1998. Carson, who handed over the ride on Celeric to Pat Eddery (who rode a vintage race on him at Royal Ascot), is carving out a television career with the BBC, whose coverage has been given a fresh look by a new producer. Peter O'Sullevan collected his knighthood in October and bowed out of television on Hennessy Gold

*Two notable retirements—four-times champion trainer Dick Hern and Willie Carson,
fourth in the all-time list of winning flat jockeys in Britain*

Cup day at Newbury in November, followed a month later by BBC TV's
long-serving racing correspondent Julian Wilson.

Swain pulled off a surprise under dramatically-changed conditions in
the King George VI and Queen Elizabeth Diamond Stakes. The short-priced
favourite **Helissio** managed only third at Ascot and failed to reproduce his
sparkling performance of the previous year when attempting a second
victory in the Prix de l'Arc de Triomphe at Longchamp. The Arc winner
Peintre Celebre put up the performance of the European racing year,
slamming a clutch of top older horses. The only other three-year-old in the
first seven was the German filly **Borgia**, who went on to finish second in
the Breeders' Cup Turf (a race robbed of its 'star' when Singspiel was seriously injured in the build-up to the race). The European challenge at the
Breeders' Cup was spearheaded by French-trained **Spinning World**, whose
victory in the Mile crowned a fine season after his earlier achievements
had established him as clearly the best horse over the distance in Europe.

Making his first appearance among the top ten owners in Britain was
Michael Tabor, whose colours were carried to classic success by Entrepreneur. **Desert King**'s two classic victories in Ireland helped him to top
the table there, the feats of his trainer Aidan O'Brien dominating the year
in that country. Another horse to carry the Tabor colours with distinction
in Britain was the three-year-old **Danetime**, who landed a big gamble in
the Stewards' Cup before graduating to pattern company and showing
himself not far removed from the best sprinters when placed behind the
leading four-year-old **Royal Applause** in the Haydock Sprint Cup. Royal
Applause built up a good record in the top sprints, though he went down
to a shock defeat at the hands of **Compton Place** in the July Cup and was
just beaten by the three-year-old fillies **Carmine Lake** and **Pas de Reponse**

in the Prix de l'Abbaye. Danetime and Compton Place will face tough opposition in the top sprints in 1998 from the impressive Diadem winner **Elnadim**, who, like Danetime, came through the ranks of the handicappers. Another horse to cause quite a stir in handicaps was **Pasternak** who landed the gamble of the season in the Cambridgeshire. Seeing smart performers contesting valuable handicaps is less common than it used to be, but adds much to the variety of British racing, and we have sought to recognise this with a broader range of essays in this edition. Other handicappers featured in essay form include Royal Ascot winners **Zaralaska**, who brought the effectiveness of the punishment of 'non-triers' into focus, and **Fly To The Stars**, whose owner Peter Savill receives some light-hearted advice. Not all top handicappers have a wide choice of opportunities when it comes to stepping up to pattern company. The essay on **Dashing Blue**, winner of the Portland under top weight, points out that the horse was denied the chance to contest the Prix de l'Abbaye because of French racing's prejudice against geldings, who are still excluded from most championship races. That doesn't apply so much in Britain, where the most dramatic race of the year, the Nunthorpe at York's Ebor meeting, produced a dead-heat between the geldings **Coastal Bluff** and **Ya Malak**, the former's jockey, Kevin Darley, performing heroics and the latter's, Alex Greaves, becoming the first woman to ride a Group 1 winner in Britain.

The two-year-old scene was dominated by the exceptional performance of French-trained **Xaar** in the Dewhurst. Not every champion two-year-old lives up to the highest expectations at three, but his return to Newmarket for the Two Thousand Guineas is a mouth-watering prospect. France's top two-year-old race, the Grand Criterium at Longchamp, was staged as part of a severely-truncated programme after a protest by stable staff prevented many of the day's intended runners from leaving the training centre at Chantilly. Those racegoers who hung around in the hope of some racing saw Irish raider **Second Empire** maintain his unbeaten record. The O'Brien stable also housed two other Group 1-winning two-year-olds, **Saratoga Springs** (Racing Post Trophy) and the much-vaunted **King of Kings** (National Stakes). The Maktoum family strengthened its classic hand when Godolphin purchased the smart **Central Park** out of the Cole stable for a rumoured £1m in December. Sheikh Mohammed's Cheveley Park winner **Embassy** will also carry the Godolphin colours in 1998, joining her Lowther conqueror **Cape Verdi**, one of four two-year-olds purchased from Robert Sangster in a reported £3m deal in September. Newmarket staged a trial for its new sectional timing equipment on Cheveley Park day, an innovation discussed in the essay on **Tamarisk**, winner of the Tattersalls Houghton Sales Stakes on the same card.

As usual, all the horses highlighted in this introduction are among those dealt with in essays in the main body of the book. The Timeform 'Top Horses Abroad' feature in the back section has been further expanded this year to include short reviews of racing in Dubai, Hong Kong and Japan. And, finally, we should record the retirement of our editor-in-chief Dave Newton whose work on the Timeform annuals down the years earned him the utmost respect of everyone who worked closely with him. As a writer Dave produced more words for Timeform than anyone in the history of the company, and his influence as an editor will be a lasting legacy.

February 1998

THE TIMEFORM 'TOP HUNDRED'

Here are listed the 'Top 100' two-year-olds, three-year-olds and older horses in the annual.

Two Year Olds

132	Xaar
122p	Second Empire
117	Central Park
117	Muhtathir
116	Charge d'Affaires
115	King of Kings
114p	Lend A Hand
114	Daggers Drawn
114	Embassy
113p	Tamarisk
113	Mudeer
113	Saratoga Springs
112p	Thief of Hearts
111p	Mutamam
111+	Arkadian Hero
111	Princely Heir
110p	Cape Verdi
110p	Loving Claim
109p	Glorosia
109p	Special Quest
109	Bold Fact
109	Docksider
109	Halmahera
108p	Croco Rouge
108p	Daymarti
108p	Pinmix
108p	Teapot Row
108p	Woodland Melody
108+	Asfurah
108+	Midnight Line
108	Alboostan
108	Anna Palariva
108	Asakir
108	Harbour Master
108	Hayil
107P	Fleetwood
107p	Chester House
107p	Isle de France
107p	Jibe
107p	Setteen
107p	Zalaiyka
107	Crazee Mental
107	Desert Prince
107	La-Faah
107	Merlin's Ring
107	Mijana
107	Nadwah
107	Trans Island
106p	Bahr
106p	Gulland
106p	Haami

106p	Impressionist
106	Carrowkeel
106	Greenlander
106	Mantles Star
106	Speedfit Too
106	Tippitt Boy
105p	Bintang
105p	City Honours
105p	Rabi
105+	Land of Dreams
105	Designer
105	Heeremandi
105	Little Indian
105	Lord Kintyre
105	Name of Love
105	Prolix
105	Regal Revolution
104p	Alborada
104p	Arnaqueur
104p	Ashraakat
104p	Craigsteel
104p	Duck Row
104+	Kilimanjaro
104	Almutawakel
104	Royal Shyness
104	Silent Tribute
104	Tracking
103p	Altibr
103p	Celtic Cavalier
103p	Exclusive
103p	Ikhteyaar
103p	Wren
103	Baltic State
103	Hopping Higgins
103	Jimmy Too
103	Lady In Waiting
103	Linden Heights
103	Mountain Song
103	Quiet Assurance
103	Sensory
102P	Grazia
102p	Dr Fong
102p	Fruits of Love
102p	Mahboob
102p	Tarascon
102+	Lady Alexander
102	Flawless
102	Mutawwaj
102	Sharp Play

Three Year Olds

137	Peintre Celebre
129	Desert King
127	Benny The Dip
126p	Elnadim
126	Starborough
125	Air Express
125	Caitano
125	Compton Place
125	Silver Patriarch
124	Borgia
124	Daylami
123	Entrepreneur
123	Magellano
122	Dr Johnson
122	Ebadiyla
122	Loup Sauvage
122	Oscar
122	Rebecca Sharp
121p	One So Wonderful
121	Astarabad
121	Bahhare
121	Faithful Son
121	Reams of Verse
121	Revoque
121	Ryafan
121	Sleepytime
120p	Stowaway
120	Cape Cross
120	Carmine Lake
120	Kingfisher Mill
120	Kool Kat Katie
120	Que Belle
120	Vereva
120	Vertical Speed
119p	Among Men
119p	Danetime
119	Fahris
119	Queen Maud
119	The Fly
118p	Kahal
118	Crimson Tide
118	Kaliana
118	Kirkwall
118	Mousse Glacee
118	Pas de Reponse
118	Poteen
118	Rajpoute
118	Tomba
118	Verglas
118	Yashmak
118§	Maylane

15

TIMEFORM CHAMPIONS OF 1997

HORSE OF THE YEAR
BEST THREE-YEAR-OLD COLT
BEST MIDDLE-DISTANCE HORSE
RATED AT 137
PEINTRE CELEBRE

BEST TWO-YEAR-OLD FILLY RATED AT 114
EMBASSY

BEST TWO-YEAR-OLD COLT RATED AT 132
XAAR

BEST THREE-YEAR-OLD FILLY RATED AT 124
BORGIA

BEST OLDER MALES RATED AT 134
PILSUDSKI
SWAIN

BEST OLDER FEMALE RATED AT 130
BOSRA SHAM

BEST SPRINTER RATED AT 126p
ELNADIM

BEST MILER RATED AT 130
SPINNING WORLD

BEST STAYING PERFORMANCE RATED AT 126
CLASSIC CLICHE

BEST PERFORMANCE IN A HANDICAP IN BRITAIN
CENTRE STALLS
ran to 119
won Grosvenor Casinos Hambleton Rated Stakes at York

BEST PERFORMANCE ON ALL-WEATHER IN BRITAIN
CHEWIT
ran to 112
won Tote Jackpot Handicap at Wolverhampton

1997 STATISTICS

The following tables show the leading owners, trainers, jockeys, sires of winners and horses on the flat in Britain during 1997 (Jan 1–Dec 31). The prize-money statistics, compiled by *Timeform*, relate to first-three prize money and win-money. Win money was traditionally used to decide the trainers' championship, until in 1994 the BHB and the National Trainers' Federation established a championship decided by total prize-money as determined by *Racing Post*. The jockeys' championship has traditionally been decided by the number of winners ridden during the year, though in 1997 the Jockeys' Association recognised a championship that ran for the turf season (Mar–Nov).

OWNERS (1,2,3 earnings)	Horses	Indiv'l Wnrs	Races Won	Runs	%	Stakes
1 Sheikh Mohammed	137	65	87	477	18.2	1,401,229
2 Mr Hamdan Al Maktoum	191	86	135	723	18.6	1,245,827
3 Mr K. Abdulla	91	37	49	283	17.3	1,130,005
4 Godolphin	71	32	40	156	25.6	1,085,961
5 Maktoum Al Maktoum	81	37	55	304	18.0	849,067
6 Mr Landon Knight	2	1	2	5	40.0	743,842
7 Lord Weinstock	18	9	13	74	17.5	641,025
8 Mr M. Tabor & Mrs John Magnier	18	10	19	62	30.6	614,372
9 Mr R. E. Sangster	46	20	28	156	17.9	579,887
10 Mr Peter S. Winfield	4	3	5	16	31.2	492,915
11 H. R. H. Prince Fahd Salman	50	19	27	156	17.3	380,446
12 Mr A. E. Oppenheimer	18	11	20	93	21.5	378,721

OWNERS (win-money, £½m+)	Horses	Indiv'l Wnrs	Races Won	Runs	%	Stakes
1 Sheikh Mohammed	137	65	87	477	18.2	1,060,589
2 Mr Hamdan Al Maktoum	191	86	135	723	18.6	888,289
3 Mr K. Abdulla	91	37	49	283	17.3	813,095
4 Godolphin	71	32	40	156	25.6	783,759
5 Mr Landon Knight	2	1	2	5	40.0	674,440
6 Maktoum Al Maktoum	81	37	55	304	18.0	524,751

TRAINERS (1,2,3 earnings)	Horses	Indiv'l Wnrs	Races Won	Runs	%	Stakes
1 M. R. Stoute	122	69	84	431	19.4	2,009,436
2 J. H. M. Gosden	145	62	91	471	19.3	1,764,657
3 H. R. A. Cecil	106	57	78	326	23.9	1,535,500
4 J. L. Dunlop	138	61	97	560	17.3	1,349,317
5 Saeed bin Suroor	73	33	41	159	25.7	1,098,389
6 L. M. Cumani	88	46	66	312	21.1	976,357
7 B. W. Hills	137	60	79	574	13.7	970,560
8 M. Johnston	137	68	123	790	15.5	878,823
9 D. R. Loder	94	39	56	316	17.7	734,677
10 P. F. I. Cole	116	42	60	472	12.7	708,082
11 R. Hannon	177	71	94	941	9.9	682,337
12 P. W. Chapple-Hyam	72	29	37	236	15.6	620,236

TRAINERS (win-money, £½m+)	Horses	Indiv'l Wnrs	Races Won	Runs	%	Stakes
1 J. H. M. Gosden	145	62	91	471	19.3	1,417,993
2 M. R. Stoute	122	69	84	431	19.4	1,410,695
3 H. R. A. Cecil	106	57	78	326	23.9	1,175,537
4 J. L. Dunlop	138	61	97	560	17.3	804,907
5 Saeed bin Suroor	73	33	41	159	25.7	796,187
6 L. M. Cumani	88	46	66	312	21.1	705,139
7 M. Johnston	137	68	123	790	15.5	634,583
8 B. W. Hills	137	60	79	574	13.7	598,578
9 P. F. I. Cole	116	42	60	472	12.7	560,155
10 D. R. Loder	94	39	56	316	17.7	524,987

Note: M. Johnston was the only trainer to saddle 100 winners

JOCKEYS (by winners)	1st	2nd	3rd	Unpl	Total Mts	%
1 K. Fallon	202	147	119	478	946	21.3
2 L. Dettori	176	115	94	395	780	22.5
3 K. Darley	128	108	96	509	841	15.2
4 Pat Eddery	116	87	65	362	630	18.4
5 J. Reid	110	105	97	511	823	13.3
6 S. Sanders	105	126	113	600	944	11.1
7 D. Holland	104	96	77	442	719	14.5
8 J. Weaver	101	88	70	393	652	15.4
9 R. Hills	85	72	86	281	524	16.2
10 T. Sprake	84	71	87	503	745	11.2
11 M. Hills	84	64	73	342	563	14.9
12 G. Duffield	79	76	59	427	641	12.3

Note: K. Fallon was leading jockey in the turf season with 196 winners

JOCKEYS (1,2,3 earnings of £1m+)	Races Won	Rides	%	Stakes £
1 K. Fallon	202	946	21.3	2,555,315
2 L. Dettori	176	780	22.5	2,519,054
3 Pat Eddery	116	630	18.4	1,912,675
4 J. Reid	110	823	13.3	1,725,469
5 M. Hills	84	563	14.9	1,424,843
6 M. J. Kinane	23	160	14.3	1,341,300
7 W. Ryan	66	588	11.2	1,173,833
8 O. Peslier	29	152	19.0	1,157,503
9 R. Hills	85	524	16.2	1,001,605

JOCKEYS (win-money of £1m+)	Races Won	Rides	%	Stakes £
1 L. Dettori	176	780	22.5	1,902,209
2 K. Fallon	202	946	21.3	1,863,997
3 Pat Eddery	116	630	18.4	1,288,182
4 J. Reid	110	823	13.3	1,137,622

APPRENTICES (by winners)	1st	2nd	3rd	Unpl	Total Mts	%
1 R. Ffrench	77	67	64	423	631	12.3
2 Martin Dwyer	57	66	53	425	601	9.5
3 C. Lowther	53	35	43	317	448	11.8

4	D. Sweeney	40	20	31	215	306	13.0
5	P. Fessey	39	53	35	380	507	7.6
6	F. Lynch	37	53	56	335	481	7.6

SIRES OF WINNERS	Races			Stakes
(1,2,3 earnings of £500,000+)	Won	Runs	%	£
1 Silver Hawk (by Roberto)	15	143	10.4	899,249
2 Polish Precedent (by Danzig)	21	168	12.5	695,355
3 Sadler's Wells (by Northern Dancer)	44	309	14.2	688,359
4 Efisio (by Formidable)	71	555	12.7	582,323
5 Danehill (by Danzig)	48	386	12.4	573,216
6 Nashwan (by Blushing Groom)	30	151	19.8	551,686
7 In The Wings (by Sadler's Wells)	20	151	13.2	542,374
8 Soviet Star (by Nureyev)	20	163	12.2	522,185
9 Fairy King (by Northern Dancer)	37	326	11.3	520,670
10 Machiavellian (by Mr Prospector)	26	148	17.5	516,909
11 Saddlers' Hall (by Sadler's Wells)	12	128	9.3	516,612
12 Royal Academy (by Nijinsky)	34	283	12.0	508,577

		Indiv'l	Races	Stakes
SIRES OF WINNERS (by win-money)	Horses	Wnrs	Won	£
1 Silver Hawk (by Roberto)	28	11	15	735,894
2 Polish Precedent (by Danzig)	43	13	21	524,073
3 Sadler's Wells (by Northern Dancer)	72	34	44	483,262
4 In The Wings (by Sadler's Wells)	31	14	20	460,888
5 Nashwan (by Blushing Groom)	37	19	30	459,239
6 Soviet Star (by Nureyev)	37	12	20	448,204
7 Efisio (by Formidable)	83	36	71	436,814
8 Generous (by Caerleon)	43	24	37	387,742
9 Danehill (by Danzig)	69	28	48	364,006
10 Cadeaux Genereux (by Young Generation)	58	28	49	354,295
11 Mtoto (by Busted)	39	17	28	344,029
12 Royal Academy (by Nijinsky)	52	22	34	337,068

	Races			Stakes
LEADING HORSES (1,2,3 earnings)	Won	Runs	%	£
1 Benny The Dip 3 b.c Silver Hawk – Rascal Rascal	2	6	33.3	776,623
2 Pilsudski 5 b. h. Polish Precedent – Cocotte	2	4	50.0	516,062
3 Silver Patriarch 3 gr.c. Saddlers' Hall – Early Rising	2	5	40.0	467,482
4 Singspiel 5 b.h. In The Wings – Glorious Song	2	3	66.6	316,047
5 Swain 5 b.h. Nashwan – Love Smitten	1	3	33.3	312,380
6 Air Express 3 b.c Salse – Ibtisamm	1	4	25.0	238,234
7 Rebecca Sharp 3 b.f. Machiavellian – Nuryana	2	6	33.3	215,520
8 Reams of Verse 3 ch.f. Nureyev – Modena	2	5	40.0	214,156
9 Royal Applause 4 b.c. Waajib – Flying Melody	4	5	80.0	184,947
10 Starborough 3 ch.c. Soviet Star – Flamenco Wave	2	4	50.0	179,957
11 Celeric 5 b.g. Mtoto – Hot Spice	2	6	33.3	178,447
12 Ali-Royal 4 b.c. Royal Academy – Alidiva	3	6	50.0	163,673

THE JOCKEYS' CHAMPIONSHIP

Champion jockeys are a rare breed. Periods of domination by the likes of Steve Donoghue, Sir Gordon Richards, Lester Piggott and Pat Eddery have meant that only sixteen different riders have taken the title going back as far as the First World War. The number of winners ridden is the time-honoured way of recognising the champion. Kieren Fallon beat Frankie Dettori to the latest title amid calls for first prize-money won to become the deciding factor, calls heightened when Dettori followed former National Hunt champion Richard Dunwoody's example two years earlier in announcing that he'd pursue the championship with less vigour in future. 'When the championships are irrelevant to the two best jockeys in Britain, there must be something fundamentally wrong with the way they are decided,' wrote John Randall in *Racing Post*. 'Championships should be about quality, not quantity, and it cannot be right that a win in a seller counts for just as much as a win in the Derby or the Grand National.' The Jockeys' Association, which has toyed with the idea of basing its championship on prize-money, departed from tradition in the latest season by restricting the championship to the number of winners ridden in the turf season (March-November). Although Timeform has never commented on how the various titles should be decided, there is some validity in the argument, probably supported by most punters, that riding winners day-in-day-out has stood the test of time as the truest measure of a champion jockey. The Timeform Annuals include tables both by winners and by earnings.

Kieren Fallon's ratio of winners to rides was around 21%, a bit behind Dettori's and comfortably ahead of those of any other leading rider. Blind faith in him to a level stake was repaid with more than one hundred points profit, an incredible return considering the vast majority of riders show a massive loss each season. Fallon partnered a winner on all bar two turf tracks, and rides as though far more alive than most jockeys to the wide variety of course and draw biases that prevail. Front running, however, has so far played little part in his success. Tactically, his typical ride sees him taking up a good position in the pack, seizing the initiative at the most opportune time and using his strength in a finish. He was willing publicly to concede style marks to Dettori in the latest season, but he cuts a powerful figure in the saddle next to most.

Kieren Fallon—champion jockey for the first time

It is big-race mounts and mistakes, real or perceived, which come in for closest scrutiny, and can alter the course of a jockey's career, however. 1997 provided Fallon with his first classic successes on Sleepytime and Reams of Verse, both trained by Henry Cecil. Plenty of criticism came Fallon's way, too, notably over Cecil's Bosra Sham. It's worth remembering, however, that, despite being thirty-two, Fallon was inexperienced at the highest level at the beginning of the year, and relatively so on the tracks where most of the top prizes are decided. Set-backs haven't daunted him to date. He rode out the storm over Bosra Sham with a stream of winners, effectively securing the title with forty-one more successes in September alone. His six-month ban in 1994 now reads like a turning point. He rode a career-best ninety-two winners the following season and one hundred and thirty-six before Cecil, to most people's surprise, appointed him stable jockey towards the end of 1996.

Only Joe Mercer and Michael Roberts have failed to add to their first jockeys' title since 1946, and it's hard to see Kieren Fallon not being champion again. Only Dettori got near his one hundred and ninety-six winners during the latest turf season. Pat Eddery, champion eleven times, kept pace with them for a while before back trouble reduced his mounts and eventually cut short his season. Seb Sanders is a rider on the up among the younger brigade, and champion Royston Ffrench will be hoping to further the good recent record of leading apprentices in making a successful fully-fledged rider. Fergus Sweeney had a notably good strike rate among the other most successful apprentices in 1997 and Gyles Parkin and Paul Fessey were young riders to catch the eye.

THE TRAINERS' CHAMPIONSHIP

The trainers' title and over £4½m in prize money earned across the globe gave Stoute another year to remember. Defining the best as opposed to the most successful is largely subjective. There's no sure way of knowing which trainer is getting the most out of their string in relation to their horses' ability. The *Timeform Statistical Review* measures the quality of each trainer's string by calculating a median rating for their horses as a whole. The leaders in this table are usually at the top of the prize-money table which decides the trainers' championship, though weight of numbers can make a difference. Discrepancies between a trainer's placing in the two lists arguably say more than the prize-money table alone.

Win and place money now decides the domestic trainers' title in most people's eyes. Had it still been determined by win money alone, John Gosden would have pipped Michael Stoute in 1997. Had number of winners counted Mark Johnston would have been champion, as he would have been in 1996. Johnston was the only trainer to top a hundred winners in 1997, and needed help from the all-weather to do so. John Dunlop trained most winners during the turf season with ninety-seven. Pick your own champion! Times are changing for trainers. Richard Hannon had one hundred and eighty-two winners (all bar two on the turf) in the first year of the BHB's competitive racing initiative in 1993, but, as the structure has bedded down, so the totals among the leading trainers have withered. Few have the range of horses to dominate at both ends of the ever-widening scale of races. Henry Cecil's strike rate of over 40% when training a hundred and eighty winners in 1987 is virtually out of the question nowadays. Two-year-olds are, for example, much harder to place for a string of victories.

Michael Stoute—
took his fifth trainers' championship

Michael Stoute had eighty-four winners in 1997. Three-year-olds provided the bulk of his successes, but, following a trend in the 'nineties, it was the older horses which flew the stable's flag highest and most often. Racehorse of the Year Pilsudski and Singspiel were largely responsible for Stoute regaining the trainers' title he'd last won in 1994, between them winning four Group 1 prizes at home to add to Entrepreneur's success in the Two Thousand Guineas, the stable's first British classic winner since Musical Bliss in 1989. Stoute sandwiched fourteen European pattern-race successes between Singspiel's Dubai World Cup and Pilsudski's Japan Cup (a second consecutive one for the yard) in 1997, giving him one fewer than Henry Cecil. Andre Fabre, who was champion trainer in France, led the way, as usual, with twenty-six, while the now-retired Bruno Schutz in Germany had sixteen. Aidan O'Brien was level with Cecil on fifteen, which included three classics in Ireland, where he predictably ran away with the trainers' title. Indeed, an aggregate of British and Irish prize money left O'Brien only just behind Stoute in 1997, and he's champion National Hunt trainer in Ireland, too! Winning the trainers' title from a base outside Britain, as his compatriots Paddy Prendergast and Vincent O'Brien did in a different era, seems less likely for O'Brien, but at the age of twenty-eight his influence on British racing seems sure to continue to grow.

Breaking into the upper band of trainers isn't easy. Most of those near the top of the tree in Britain have held a licence for twenty years or more. Owners' patronage is obviously important, and it would be interesting to see how the trainers' table would look should Sheikh Mohammed and his brothers disappear from the scene. Cecil, of course, doesn't train for Sheikh Mohammed now, and Richard Hannon, for example, has never done so. One-time Godolphin man Jeremy Noseda begins his British training career in 1998, while Gerard Butler, a former assistant to D Wayne Lukas in America, will be trying to make a mark too. Among the up-and-coming trainers, David Nicholls and Gay Kelleway have increased their tallies of winners each season, and it will be no surprise to see them progress again in 1998. Tim Easterby, Sir Mark Prescott and Geoff Wragg are others we fancy could have a particularly good year.

EXPLANATORY NOTES

'Racehorses of 1997' deals individually, in alphabetical sequence, with every horse that ran on the flat in Britain in 1997 (including on the all-weather tracks), plus many foreign-trained horses that did not race here. For each of these horses is given (1) its age, colour and sex, (2) its breeding, and, where this information has not been given in a previous Racehorses Annual, a family outline (3) a form summary giving details of its performances during the last two seasons, together, where applicable, with the horse's rating in 1996, which appears at the start of the form summary, (4) a rating of its merit in 1997 (which appears in the margin), (5) a Timeform commentary on its racing or general characteristics as a racehorse, with some suggestions, perhaps, regarding its prospects for 1998, and (6) the name of the trainer in whose charge it was on the last occasion it ran. For each two-year-old the foaling date is also given.

The book is published with a twofold purpose. Firstly, it is intended to have permanent value as a review of the exploits and achievements of the more notable of the flat-racing thoroughbreds in 1997. Thus, while the commentaries upon the vast majority of the horses are, of necessity, in note form, the best horses are more critically examined, and the essays upon them are illustrated by half-tone portraits and photographs of some of the races in which they ran. Secondly, the book is designed to help the punter to analyse races, and the notes which follow contain instructions for using the data. The attention of foreign buyers of British bloodstock, and others who are concerned with Timeform Ratings as a measure of absolute racing class in terms of a standard scale, is particularly drawn to the section headed 'The Level of the Ratings'.

TIMEFORM RATINGS

The Timeform Rating of a horse is simply the merit of the horse expressed in pounds and is arrived at by careful examination of its running against other horses using a scale of weight for distance beaten which ranges from around 3 lb a length at five furlongs and 2 lb a length at a mile and a quarter to 1 lb at two miles. Timeform maintains a 'running' handicap of all horses in training throughout the season.

THE LEVEL OF THE RATINGS

At the close of each season all the horses that have raced are re-handicapped from scratch, and each horse's rating is revised. It is also necessary to adjust the general level of the handicap, so that all the ratings are kept at the same standard level from year to year. This explains why, in this book, the ratings are, in general, different from those in the final issue of the 1997 Timeform Black Book.

RATINGS AND WEIGHT-FOR-AGE

The reader has, in the ratings in this book, a universal handicap embracing all the horses in training it is possible to weigh up, ranging from tip-top classic performers, with ratings from 130 to 145, down to the meanest selling platers, rated around the 20 mark. All the ratings are at weight-for-age, so that equal ratings mean horses of equal merit: perhaps it would be clearer if we said that the universal rating handicap is really not a single handicap, but four handicaps side by side: one for two-year-olds, one for three-year-olds, one for four-year-olds and one for older horses. Thus, a three-year-old rated, for argument's sake, at 117 is deemed to be identical in point of 'merit' with a four-year-old also rated at 117: but for them to have equal chances in, say, a mile race in May, the three-year-old would need to be receiving 9 lb from the four-year-old, which is the weight difference specified by the Age, Weight and Distance Tables on pages 2 and 3.

USING THE RATINGS

In using Timeform Ratings with a view to discovering which horses in any race have the best chances at the weights, we have two distinct cases, according to whether the horses taking part are of the same age or of different ages. Here is the procedure in each case:-

A. Horses of the Same Age

If the horses all carry the same weight there are no adjustments to be made, and the horses with the highest ratings have the best chances. If the horses carry different weights, jot down their ratings, and to the rating of each horse add one point for every pound the horse is set to carry less than 10 st, or subtract one point for every pound it has to carry more than 10 st. When the ratings have been adjusted in this way the highest resultant figure indicates the horse with the best chance at the weights.

Example (any distance: any week of the season)

2 Good Girl (9-6)	....	Rating 119	....	add 8	....	127
2 Paulinus (9-4)	....	Rating 113	....	add 10	....	123
2 Abilene (8-11)	....	Rating 107	....	add 17	....	124
2 Bob's Joy (8-7)	....	Rating 108	....	add 21	....	129
2 Time Warp (8-2)	....	Rating 100	....	add 26	....	126
2 Eagle Eye (7-7)	....	Rating 92	....	add 35	....	127

Bob's Joy (129) has the best chance strictly on form;
Good Girl (127) and Eagle Eye (127) are the next best

B. Horses of Different Ages

Take no notice of the weight any horse receives from any other. Instead, consult the Age, Weight and Distance Tables on pages 2 and 3. Treat each horse separately, and compare the weight it has to carry with the weight prescribed for it in the tables, according to the age of the horse, the distance of the race and the time of the year. Then, add one point to the rating for each pound the horse has to carry less than the weight given in the tables: or, subtract one point from the rating for every pound it has to carry more than the weight prescribed by the tables. The highest resultant figure indicates the horse most favoured by the weights.

Example (1½ miles on June 30th)

(Table Weights: 5-y-o 10-0; 4-y-o 9-13; 3-y-o 9-1)

6 Nimitz (10-2)	....	Rating 115	....	subtract 2	....	113
4 Red Devil (9-9)	....	Rating 114	....	add 4	....	118
6 Sweet Cindy (9-5)	....	Rating 115	....	add 9	....	124

3 Jailhouse (9-2)	....	Rating 120	....	subtract 1	....	119
4 Haakon (8-11)	....	Rating 101	....	add 16	....	117
3 Fine Strike (8-7)	....	Rating 108	....	add 8	....	116

Sweet Cindy (124) has the best chance at the weights,
with 5 lb in hand of Jailhouse

TURF AND ALL-WEATHER RATINGS

When a horse has raced on turf and on all-weather and its form on one is significantly different from the other, the two ratings are given, the all-weather set out below the turf preceded by 'a'.

Thus with FREE FOR ALL 47
a55

the top figure, 47, is the rating to be used in turf races, and the one below, a55, is for use in all-weather races. Where there is only one rating, that is to be used for both turf and all-weather.

NOTE ON RIDERS' ALLOWANCES

For the purposes of rating calculations it is assumed that the allowance a rider is able to claim is nullified by his or her inexperience. The adjustments to the ratings *should therefore be calculated on the weight allotted by the handicapper, or determined by the conditions of the race.* No extra 7lb should be added to the rating when a rider claims 7lb. This is the general routine procedure; but of course, after the usual adjustments have been made the quality of jockeyship is still an important factor to be considered when deciding between horses with similar chances.

WEIGHING UP A RACE

The ratings tell you which horses in a particular race are most favoured by the weights; but complete analysis demands that the racing character of each horse, as set out in the commentary upon it, is also studied carefully to see if there is any reason why the horse might be expected not to run up to its rating or indeed might improve on it. It counts for little that a horse is thrown in at the weights if it has no pretensions whatever to staying the distance, or is unable to act on the prevailing going.

These two matters, suitability of distance and going, are no doubt the most important points to be considered. But there are others. For example, the ability of a horse to accommodate itself to the conformation of the track. Then there is the matter of temperament and behaviour: nobody would be in a hurry to take a short price about a horse with whom it is always an even chance whether it will give its running.

A few minutes spent checking up on these matters in the commentaries upon the horses concerned will sometimes put a very different complexion on a race from that which is put upon it by the ratings alone. We repeat, therefore, that the correct way to use Timeform, or this annual volume, in the analysis of individual races is, first to use the ratings to discover which horses are most favoured by the weights, and second, to check through the comments on the horse to discover what factors other than weight might also affect the outcome of the race.

25

THE FORM SUMMARIES

The form summary enclosed in the brackets shows for each individual horse the distance, the state of the going and where the horse finished in each of its races on the flat during the last two seasons. Performances are in chronological sequence, the earliest being given first.

The distance of each race is given in furlongs, fractional distances being expressed in decimal notation to the nearest tenth of a furlong. Races on an all-weather surface are prefixed by letter 'a'.

The going is symbolised as follows: h=hard; f=firm (turf) or fast (all-weather); m=good to firm; g=good (turf) or standard (all-weather); d= good to soft/dead; s=soft (turf) or slow (all-weather); v=heavy.

Placings are indicated, up to sixth place, by the use of superior figures, an asterisk being used to denote a win.

Thus [1996 81: 10s* 12f³ 1997 11.7g a11g² Sep 7] signifies that the horse was rated 81 in 1996, when winning over 10 furlongs on soft going first time out and finishing third over twelve furlongs on firm going next time out. In 1997 he finished out of the first six over 11.7 furlongs on good going, then second over eleven furlongs on standard going on an all-weather track. The date of his last run was September 7.

Included in the pedigree details are the highest Timeform Annual ratings during their racing careers of the sires, dams and sires of dams of all horses, where the information is available.

Where sale prices are considered relevant F denotes the price as a foal, Y the price as a yearling, 2-y-o as a two-year-old, and so on. These are given in guineas unless prefixed by IR (Irish guineas), $ (American dollars) or accompanied by francs (French francs). Other currencies are converted approximately into guineas or pounds sterling at the prevailing exchange rate.

THE RATING SYMBOLS

The following symbols, attached to the ratings, are to be interpreted as stated:-

p   likely to improve.

P   capable of *much* better form.

+   the horse may be better than we have rated it.

d   the horse appears to have deteriorated, and might no longer be capable of running to the rating given.

§   unreliable (for temperamental or other reasons).

§§   so temperamentally unsatisfactory as not to be worth a rating.

?   the horse's rating is suspect. If used without a rating the symbol implies that the horse can't be assessed with confidence, or, if used in the in-season Timeform publications, that the horse is out of form.

RACEHORSES OF 1997

Horse	Commentary	Rating

AARDWOLF 6 b.g. Dancing Brave (USA) 140 – Pretoria 100 (Habitat 134) 63
[1996 NR 1997 21.6g² 16g³ 22.2d⁵ Jun 20] second foal: half-brother to useful 1¼m
and 13.4f winner Nassma (by Sadler's Wells): dam 7f and 1¼m winner: fair maiden
at 3 yrs for M. Kauntze in Ireland: fairly useful hurdler/chaser: modest form on return
to flat at 6 yrs: thorough stayer: visored last start: acts on dead ground. *C. P. E. Brooks*

ABAJANY 3 b.g. Akarad (FR) 130 – Miss Ivory Coast (USA) (Sir Ivor 135) [1996 83
57: 10g⁵ 1997 12s³ 8g 8m³ 8d² 8m⁵ 8d⁵ 8g* 8.1s⁵ 8.1m* 8.1m⁵ 8v Oct 11]
sturdy colt: fairly useful handicapper: won at Leicester in August and Sandown in
September: thought to have gone lame penultimate start, last of 16 final one: should
stay 1¼m: acts on good to firm and soft ground: tends to wander in front, but is game.
M. R. Channon

ABBEY THEATRE (IRE) 3 b.c. Sadler's Wells (USA) 132 – Altiyna 109 (Troy –
137) [1996 NR 1997 10g 11.7g 10.2m 17.2g⁴ Aug 7] 2,000 2-y-o: compact colt:
half-brother to winners around 1½m by Shernazar and Darshaan: dam, 2-y-o 7f
winner who stayed 14.6f, half-sister to Aliysa: of little account. *M. Salaman*

ABDUCTION 4 ch.g. Risk Me (FR) 127 – Spirit Away 54 (Dominion 123) [1996 –
NR 1997 7.1g Aug 3] poor maiden: tried visored (possibly temperamental).
R. T. Juckes

ABERKEEN 2 ch.c. (May 3) Keen 116 – Miss Aboyne 64 (Lochnager 132) [1997 78
6g⁴ 6m* 6m⁵ 5.9g² 6m² Aug 2] 5,000Y, 15,000 2-y-o: workmanlike colt: first foal:
dam, 5f and 1m winner at 4/5 yrs, seemed to stay 1¼m: won 3-runner minor event at
Pontefract in June: best effort in nursery at Newcastle final start: should stay 1m.
M. Dods

ABLE LASS (IRE) 3 ch.f. Classic Music (USA) – Miami Life (Miami Springs –
121) [1996 NR 1997 6m⁵ 8.5g a8g⁵ Nov 25] half-sister to two 1½m winners by Be
My Native: dam unraced: little promise in maidens. *R. W. Armstrong*

ABLE PLAYER (USA) 10 b. or br.g. Solford (USA) 127 – Grecian Snow 39
(CAN) (Snow Knight 125) [1996 NR 1997 12m³ 15g⁵ Aug 9] poor handicapper:
should stay beyond 15f. *K. J. Drewry, Isle of Man*

ABLE SHERIFF 5 gr.g. Doulab (USA) 115 – Rich Lass (Broxted 120) [1996 65: 67
5g² 5g 5g 5f* 5f 5m³ 5m⁵ 5m² 5g³ 6f⁴ 5f² 5.1d 5m* 5m⁶ 5g 5m⁴ 1997 5g 5m² 5m² 5g
May 16] close-coupled gelding: had a round action: fair handicapper: brought down
fatally at Thirsk in May: best efforts at 5f: acted on good to firm and soft ground:
usually blinkered. *M. W. Easterby*

ABOO HOM 3 b.c. Sadler's Wells (USA) 132 – Maria Waleska (Filiberto (USA) 74
123) [1996 NR 1997 8d 12d⁵ 11.5s⁴ 12m 13.4g³ 14.1s⁵ Oct 15] 290,000Y: tall,
useful-looking colt: brother to 4-y-o Mazurek, closely related to 3 winners by
Danzig, notably high-class sprinter Polish Patriot, and half-brother to 3 winners
abroad: dam won Oaks d'Italia and Gran Premio d'Italia: fair maiden: probably stays
13f: well beaten on good to firm going: sold (to join M. Pipe) 10,000 gns after final
start. *A. C. Stewart*

ABOU ZOUZ (USA) 3 b.c. Miswaki (USA) 124 – Bold Jessie (Never So Bold 100
135) [1996 109: 5m* 6d² 6m* 7m⁴ 1997 5g 7d⁶ 6g* 6m⁵ 6m 5.5g⁵ Dec 22] imposing,
well-made colt: won Gimcrack Stakes at York at 2 yrs: only useful form at best in
1997: won 4-runner minor event at Doncaster (hung left) in July: below form in
better company afterwards, leaving D. Loder after penultimate start: best form at 6f:
yet to race on extremes of going: has swished tail in preliminaries: reportedly has
broken blood vessels. *B. Cecil, USA*

ABOVE BOARD 2 b.g. (Jan 29) Night Shift (USA) – Bundled Up (USA) 67 p
(Sharpen Up 127) [1997 6g 5.1m³ Jul 25] 32,000Y: sturdy gelding: fourth foal:

brother to fair 5f winner Midnight Spell and half-brother to 2 winners, including 4-y-o Rififi: dam won over 9.7f at 2 yrs in France: running-on third of 10 in maiden at Nottingham: subsequently gelded and joined J. Hanson: unimpressive to post and very green on debut: should do better. *B. Cecil USA*

A BREEZE   3 br.g. Precocious 126 – Wasimah 84 (Caerleon (USA) 132) [1996 75:   70
6m⁶ 6m 5g⁴ 5m* 6m⁶ 6s 1997 a6g a7g 7m 6m 6s⁴ 8g 6f⁴ 6g Jun 16] compact gelding: fair handicapper at best: rather disappointing after fourth start: barely stays 7f: acts on good to firm ground: visored (raced too freely) final 2-y-o start. *D. Morris*

ABREEZE (USA)   2 b.c. (Mar 5) Danzig (USA) – Priceless Pearl (USA) 101   96
(Alydar (USA)) [1997 7.1m* 7m 7d⁴ Oct 17] strong, close-coupled colt: fourth foal: closely related to fairly useful 6f winner Pearl d'Azur (by Dayjur) and useful 6f and 7f winner Isla Del Rey (by Nureyev): dam, 7f winner at 2 yrs, sister to Saratoga Six and half-sister to Dunbeath: 5-length winner of maiden at Sandown in September, quickening from 2f out despite edging left: only seventh of 8 to Haami in listed contest then fair fourth of 6 to Lucayan Indian in minor event (cruised up 2f out, hung right, found little), both at Newmarket following month: should stay 1m. *Saeed bin Suroor*

ABSALOM'S LAD   2 gr.c. (Jan 22) Absalom 128 – Rose Bouquet 78 (General   69 p
Assembly (USA)) [1997 7m³ 8s Nov 8] sturdy, angular colt: fifth foal: half-brother to 6-y-o Rising Spray: dam, 2-y-o 6f winner, out of smart filly (stayed 1m) Premier Rose: some promise in autumn maidens at Brighton and Doncaster: likely to stay at least 1¼m: should do better. *P. W. Harris*

ABSENTEE   2 br.f. (Feb 13) Slip Anchor 136 – Meliora 73 (Crowned Prince   – p
(USA) 128) [1997 8.2g Oct 4] closely related to useful 1¾m winner Krius (by Shirley Heights) and half-sister to several winners, notably very smart stayer Weld (by Kalaglow): dam 7f winner: 11/1, well-held eighth of 13 in maiden at Nottingham, chasing leaders over 5f: should improve given test of stamina. *W. Jarvis*

ABSOLUTE CHARLIE   3 ch.g. Prince Daniel (USA) – Absolutely Blue 42   –
(Absalom 128) [1996 –: 7g 1997 7m 10g May 12] leggy, short-backed gelding: no sign of ability. *C. W. Fairhurst*

ABSOLUTE LIBERTY (USA)   3 ch.g. Gold Alert (USA) – Mutterfly (USA)   68
(Muttering (USA)) [1996 62?: 6f⁴ 7.6d 7.9g 1997 a8.5g* 7f⁵ 10d* 10m⁴ a8.5g² 10.4s   a77
10m 11.8d 10.3g Oct 24] sparely-made gelding: fair performer: won maiden at Wolverhampton in May and apprentice handicap at Lingfield in June: well below form last 4 starts: stays 1¼m: acts on dead ground and fibresand: blinkered (raced too freely) penultimate start, visored on last: sold after final start and sent to Holland. *S. P. C. Woods*

ABSOLUTELY ABSTONE   3 gr.f. Petong 126 – Odilese 82 (Mummy's Pet   –
125) [1996 44: 5g⁴ 5g³ 5m⁴ 1997 7f a6g Nov 14] leggy, angular filly: poor form early in season at 2 yrs: well beaten in 1997. *P. D. Evans*

ABSOLUTELY FAYRE   6 ch.g. Absalom 128 – June Fayre (Sagaro 133) [1996   –
–: a14.8g 1997 10g 8m⁵ 10d 8.5d⁴ 10m Jul 28] one-time fair performer: no worthwhile form at 6 yrs: stays 10.8f: acts on good to firm ground and soft, no form on all-weather. *V. Soane*

ABSOLUTELYSTUNNING   4 br.f. Aragon 118 – Dramatic Mood (Jalmood   63 d
(USA) 126) [1996 63: 10.2g 10m⁶ 10m* 10g 8.2m 10g² 10m 11.4m⁶ 10.3g² 12g a10g⁴ a10g* a10g 1997 a7g a8g⁵ a10g 10m² 10d 10m 10m 10m 11.1m 10m 10.3d a12g Nov 18] sparely-made filly: modest handicapper: only form at 4 yrs when runner-up in April: stays 11.4f: acts on good to firm going and on equitrack: tried visored. *Mrs Barbara Waring*

ABSOLUTE MAGIC   7 b.g. Doulab (USA) 115 – Trickster 92 (Major Portion   –
129) [1996 85: 7.6d⁵ 8m 6d⁵ 7g* 8.1s* a8.5g⁵ 1997 a8g a8g Feb 14] sturdy gelding: poor mover: fairly useful performer: lightly raced last 2 seasons (has reportedly had foot problems) and well beaten in claimers both starts in 1997: stays 8.5f: acts on good to firm and heavy ground and fibresand. *W. J. Haggas*

ABSOLUTE UTOPIA (USA)   4 b.g. Mr Prospector (USA) – Magic Gleam   69
(USA) 122 (Danzig (USA)) [1996 69: 8.2d⁵ 8g⁶ 10.2g 8g⁶ 10m⁵ 8.5m⁴ 9m 8s 1997 8d 9m⁴ 8g 8m² 8m* 10.2d⁴ 8m⁵ 10m* Oct 1] tall gelding: has been hobdayed and had

soft-palate operation: fair handicapper: won 18-runner races at Bath in August and Salisbury (improved form, first time ridden by L. Dettori) in October: seems better at 1¼m than shorter: acts on good to firm and dead ground. *N. E. Berry*

ABSOLUTLY SPARKLIN   2 b.c. (Mar 5) Midyan (USA) 124 – Tino-Ella 73   86
(Bustino 136) [1997 7s⁵ 7m⁵ 7d⁴ Oct 14] 26,000Y: compact colt: good walker: fifth foal: half-brother to an Italian 2-y-o 7f winner by Warning and a 1¾m winner by Distant Relative: dam 1¼m winner out of half-sister to Teenoso: won maiden at York in September by 4 lengths from Equity Princess: no improvement in minor events at Ascot (much firmer going) and Leicester: will probably stay at least 1¼m: sold 26,000 gns after final start and sent to USA. *L. M. Cumani*

ABSTONE PET GIRL   2 b.f. (Mar 13) Absalom 128 – Peters Pet Girl (Norwick   –
(USA) 125) [1997 a5g a5g a8.5g⁴ a8.5g 7.1s a6g⁴ a6g a8g Dec 10] 3,000Y: half-sister to 4-y-o Lancashire Legend and 1m winner A Million Watts (both by Belfort): little sign of ability, including in sellers. *P. D. Evans*

ABSTONE QUEEN   3 b.f. Presidium 124 – Heavenly Queen (Scottish Reel 123)   55
[1996 66, a48: a5g³ 5m³ a6g³ a7g³ 7m³ a7g³ 7g² a6g³ 6g* 6m³ 7g* 6f⁴ 6m* 6g⁵ 6m⁴   a40
7m⁴ a7g⁴ 6d³ 6m 7g* 7g 6m⁵ 1997 a7g⁴ a7g⁶ a6g⁵ 7g* 8.2m 7g⁴ 7f⁶ 7m 8d⁶ 6m 7g 7g² a6g a7g a7g Dec 10] leggy filly: modest performer: won seller at Catterick in March: needs further than 6f, and should stay 1m: acts on good to firm and dead ground, poor form on the all-weather: usually blinkered or visored. *P. D. Evans*

ABTAAL   7 b.g. Green Desert (USA) 127 – Stufida (Bustino 136) [1996 52, a–:   55 §
a7g⁵ a7g a6g 7f 10.8f 10m 11.6g⁵ 10d⁵ 10g 1997 8d⁴ 8g² 8m 6.9m 7m* 7s 7d 6.9m⁵   a– §
6g³ 7.1g⁴ 7.1g Sep 11] good-bodied gelding: modest performer: won selling handicap at Lingfield in June: best form up to 1m: acts on good to firm and soft going (used to act on fibresand): unreliable. *R. J. Hodges*

ABU CAMP   2 b.c. (Feb 15) Indian Ridge 123 – Artistic Licence (High Top 131)   – p
[1997 7d Oct 14] 24,000F, 35,000Y: close-coupled colt: sixth foal: half-brother to 3-y-o Around Fore Alliss: dam, stayed 1¼m, out of half-sister to Oaks winner Circus Plume: 33/1 and backward, not knocked about when behind in Leicester maiden: should do better. *M. J. Heaton-Ellis*

ABUHAIL (USA)   2 b. or br.c. (Apr 20) Silver Hawk (USA) 123 – Bank Key   85
(USA) (Key To The Mint (USA)) [1997 7m* 8.1s² 10d³ Oct 13] $170,000Y: angular colt: has fluent, rather round action: second foal: dam won up to 9f in USA: won maiden at Redcar in July: 8 lengths second of 4 to Kilimanjaro in minor event at Sandown following month: off course 6 weeks, tailed-off last of 3 in minor race at Leicester: should stay at least 1¼m: sent to UAE. *D. Morley*

ABUSAMRAH (USA)   2 b.c. (Apr 23) Riverman (USA) 131 – Azayim 111 (Be   77 p
My Guest (USA) 126) [1997 6m⁵ Oct 31] sixth foal: brother to useful 1993 2-y-o 6f winner Watani and 7f and 1¼m winner Mufarej: dam 8.5f and 1¼m winner: 12/1, 6 lengths fifth of 14 to Tussle in steadily-run maiden at Newmarket, soon prominent after slow start, not unduly knocked about: should stay 1m: sure to do better. *R. W. Armstrong*

ACADEMY HOUSE (IRE)   4 b.c. Sadler's Wells (USA) 132 – Shady Leaf   –
(IRE) 56 (Glint of Gold 128) [1996 13g 17f⁴ 16m* 16g⁴ 16s⁴ 1997 14m 20m Jun 17] 220,000Y: small ex-Irish colt: first foal: dam, lightly-raced maiden, from good family: fairly useful handicapper (rated 81) for A. O'Brien in 1996 (sold 20,000 gns at end of year): tailed off at Sandown and Royal Ascot (didn't look keen) in 1997: a stayer: best form on good going or firmer. *R. Åkehurst*

ACADEMY (IRE)   2 ch.g. (Apr 28) Archway (IRE) 115 – Dream Academy   –
(Town And Country 124) [1997 6m 7d 7g Oct 27] IR 7,200Y, 10,000 2-y-o: close-coupled gelding: second foal: dam winning hurdler: signs of just a little ability in maidens at Windsor and Leicester. *Andrew Turnell*

ACADEMY STAR   3 b.f. Royal Academy (USA) 130 – Startino 111 (Bustino   71 ?
136) [1996 65p: 7d 1997 8g⁴ 10.1g 10d⁵ Sep 13] unfurnished filly: seemingly best effort in maidens when unseating rider due to badly slipping saddle inside final 1f at Yarmouth in August, challenging eventual winner Grand Splendour for lead at time: better at 1¼m than shorter. *J. R. Fanshawe*

ACCESS ADVENTURER (IRE)   6 b.g. Al Hareb (USA) 123 – Olwyn 109   –
(Relko 136) [1996 78d: a10g⁴ a10g³ a8g⁶ 10m² 10.1m³ 10f 8m 12g 8m 10f⁵ 1997
10g 10m Sep 25] big, close-coupled gelding: fair performer at 1¼m in first half of
1996: has lost his form: blinkered once. *R. Boss*

ACCOMMODATE YOU   4 br.f. Precocious 126 – Time For Joy 42 (Good
Times (ITY)) [1996 NR 1997 8.1g 10.1f a6g Nov 14] second reported foal: half-
sister to 6f seller winner Joyful Times (by Doc Marten): dam stayed 6f: little sign of
ability. *J. M. Bradley*

ACCYSTAN   2 ch.g. (Apr 12) Efisio 120 – Amia (CAN) (Nijinsky (CAN) 138)   50 ?
[1997 7m a7g a6g⁵ Nov 21] 10,000Y: first foal: dam (unraced) from family of 2 very
smart French stayers: dropped in class, appeared to show some ability in seller at
Wolverhampton final start. *P. C. Haslam*

ACEBO LYONS (IRE)   2 b.f. (May 14) Waajib 121 – Etage (Ile de Bourbon   69
(USA) 133) [1997 6m⁵ 7g⁶ 8.1m⁴ 7.3g² Oct 25] IR 1,500Y: leggy filly: half-sister to
4-y-o Magic Combination and unreliable 1¼m and 1½m winner Tirolette (by Tirol):
dam winner in Germany: fair maiden: good second of 14 to Flying Bold in nursery at
Newbury, though flashing tail and edging left under amateur: will stay at least 1m.
A. P. Jarvis

ACERBUS DULCIS   6 ch.g. Hadeer 118 – Current Pattie (USA) 102 (Little   35
Current (USA)) [1996 –: a16g a11g 1997 a11s a12g a12g² a12g⁵ a16g⁶ a11g a11g⁵
8.2g 10.1f⁴ 10.1f³ 12g³ 10.1s 14.1m⁴ 11.5m* 14.1g a11g Dec 8] poor performer: won
4-runner maiden handicap at Yarmouth in August: stays 1½m: acts on firm going and
fibresand: tried blinkered: none too consistent. *M. C. Chapman*

ACHARNE   4 ch.c. Pharly (FR) 130 – Sibley 84 (Northfields (USA)) [1996 113:   112 d
8s* 8d⁵ 11.5f⁶ 12m 12f² 10g² 10.5m 10s³ 8m 1997 9g⁵ 8.1g⁵ 8d 10g⁴ 10m⁵ 10.3m⁵
10m⁴ 8.9s⁴ 10d⁵ 7g a10g³ a8g⁴ Dec 4] well-made colt: has a quick action: smart
performer at best: disappointing at 4 yrs after close fifth to Wixim in Sandown Mile
on second start: effective at 1m to 1½m: acts on firm ground and soft, well below
form on equitrack: tends to hang left. *C. E. Brittain*

ACHILLES   2 ch.c. (Apr 29) Deploy 131 – Vatersay (USA) (Far North (CAN)   88
120) [1997 6m³ 8m² 7.9s² 8s³ Nov 8] 9,200Y, 15,000 2-y-o: third foal: dam third
over 1m from 3 starts in Ireland: fairly useful maiden: close second at Goodwood in
September and York in October: edged left when below form final start: should be
suited by at least 1¼m. *R. Akehurst*

ACID TEST   2 ch.c. (May 4) Sharpo 132 – Clunk Click 72 (Star Appeal 133)   72
[1997 6m 5.1g 5.7g 6m* 6g 7g* 7.3m² 8g⁵ 7.3d² 6g Sep 26] 15,000Y: good-bodied
colt: half-brother to several winners, including French sprinter Touch And Love (by
Green Desert) and 6f/7f winner Crazy Paving (by Danehill), both useful: dam,
maiden, stayed 1½m: fair performer: won seller at Lingfield in July and nursery at
Newmarket in August: seems better over 7f/
1m than 6f: acts on good to firm and dead ground. *W. R. Muir*

ACQUITTAL (IRE)   5 b.g. Danehill (USA) 126 – Perfect Alibi (Law Society   40
(USA) 130) [1996 48: a16g a14.8g⁵ 10m 10m 8f⁴ 8.1m 8.3m 8m 10f² 1997 10g³ 10g²
10m 10.8g 10m Sep 26] poor handicapper: stays 1½m: acts on any ground: visored
nowadays: none too consistent. *A. Streeter*

ACROSS THE WATER   3 b.f. Slip Anchor 136 – Stara (Star Appeal 133) [1996   52
NR 1997 10m⁵ 12m⁶ 10d Jun 24] 2,500Y: second foal: dam twice-raced sister to
Oaks winner Madam Gay: modest form at best in maidens: should stay beyond 1¼m.
C. A. Cyzer

ACT DEFIANT (USA)   2 br.c. (Apr 27) Nureyev (USA) 131 – Alydariel (USA)   79
(Alydar (USA)) [1997 7m⁵ 8.1s⁴ 8f⁵ Oct 29] $200,000Y: leggy, useful-looking colt:
sixth foal: brother to 2 winners abroad, notably smart French/US 1m/1¼m winner
Jeune Homme: dam, minor stakes winner at about 1m in USA, half-sister to Royal
Academy: fair form in maidens at Leicester and Yarmouth in October: disappointing
in between: should stay 1¼m: carries head awkwardly. *P. F. I. Cole*

ACTION JACKSON   5 ch.g. Hadeer 118 – Water Woo (USA) 102 (Tom Rolfe)   56
[1996 58, a–: 8m 8.3g⁴ 8g² 10m* 12m 10d⁴ 10g* 10.1m 10f 1997 10.1g 10g² 10g²   a–
10g³ 16.4m⁴ 10m 10g⁵ 10m³ 14.1g² 16.4g Sep 2] close-coupled, angular gelding:

modest handicapper: seems best at 1¼m (given good test) to 1¾m: acts on firm and dead going: tried tongue tied. *B. J. McMath*

ACTION STATIONS   3 b.g. High Estate 127 – Toast (IRE) (Be My Guest (USA) –
126) [1996 NR 1997 8m 12m⁴ 10d⁵ a14g⁴ 12m 11.9f Oct 1] 21,000Y: quite good-
topped gelding: unimpressive mover: first foal: dam lightly-raced Irish maiden: little
sign of ability: tried visored. *C. A. Cyzer*

ACT OF FOLLY   2 b.f. (Jan 31) Midyan (USA) 124 – Height of Folly 81 (Shirley – p
Heights 130) [1997 7m Sep 22] sixth foal: half-sister to several winners, including
6-y-o Charity Crusader and 4-y-o Opalette: dam stayer: 33/1, towards rear in
steadily-run 14-runner maiden at Kempton, slowly away: will be suited by 1¼m+:
likely to do better. *Lady Herries*

ADAMTON   5 b.g. Domynsky 110 – Berwyn (Sharpo 132) [1996 75p: a6g⁶ 6f –
10.1m* a10s* a11g² a10g* 1997 a10g Dec 2] lightly-raced gelding: progressive form
late on at 4 yrs, making all in 3 handicaps: well beaten only outing in 1997: stays 11f:
acts on good to firm ground and all-weather surfaces: has swished tail, but is game.
Mrs J. Cecil

ADESTE FIDELES   2 b.f. (Mar 18) Groom Dancer (USA) 128 – Decided Air 78 p
(IRE) (Sure Blade (USA) 130) [1997 7.9s 7m³ a8.5g* Oct 6] 6,200Y: second foal:
dam, French 1¼m winner, half-sister to Poule d'Essai des Poulains winner Vettori,
and daughter of Air Distingue: progressive form: won maiden auction at Wolverhampton in October by ½ length from Gralmano: will be suited by 1¼m/1½m:
swished tail throughout preliminaries and slowly away on debut: has been bandaged
off hind: likely to do better. *M. Bell*

ADILOV   5 b.g. Soviet Star (USA) 128 – Volida 105 (Posse (USA) 130) [1996 56d: –
8.3m³ 8.1d 7g a8g 10m 8m 11.5m 8m a10g a16g⁵ a13g⁴ 1997 a13g a12g Dec 19]
rangy gelding: no form on flat for long time: winning selling hurdler. *J. J. Bridger*

ADJUTANT   2 b.c. (Mar 15) Batshoof 122 – Indian Love Song 68 (Be My Guest 76
(USA) 126) [1997 6m³ 8.1d³ 7.1s⁶ Oct 15] 14,500F: tall, useful-looking colt: rather
weak at 2 yrs: has knee action: fifth foal: half-brother to 3-y-o Tomba and 7f and 1m
winner Indian Rhapsody (by Rock City): dam, maiden, stayed 1½m: fair form in
maidens at Haydock in August and September: below that level final start: stays 1m:
may make a better 3-y-o. *B. J. Meehan*

ADMIRALS FLAME (IRE)   6 b.g. Doulab (USA) 115 – Fan The Flame 69 76
(Grundy 137) [1996 84, a–: 8m 8s² 8g⁴ 8m⁴ 8m³ 8.3d* 8g 8d 1997 8m 8g⁵ 8d 8m⁴ a–
8.3m Aug 23] leggy gelding: fairly useful handicapper: easily best effort at 6 yrs on
second start: stays 8.3f well: has form on firm ground, very best on going softer than
good: ran poorly when sweating: wears bandages. *C. F. Wall*

ADMIRALS SECRET (USA)   8 ch.g. Secreto (USA) 128 – Noble Mistress 57
(USA) (Vaguely Noble 140) [1996 64: 13.8s³ 14.1s 12d⁴ 12g 11.8m 11.5f⁴ 12m⁵
1997 11.6g 12d 12s⁵ 12m⁵ 11.6m* 13.8g 12g⁶ 12m⁶ 12d a12g Nov 18] good-
quartered gelding: carries condition: has a round action: modest handicapper:
confidently ridden to win at Windsor in July: below form afterwards: effective at
1½m to 1¾m: acts on any turf going and on equitrack: normally held up. *C. F. Wall*

ADMIRE   2 b.f. (Apr 19) Last Tycoon 131 – Belle Isis (USA) 77 (Sir Ivor 135) 77
[1997 6.9m 8.1d* 8f 7.3g Oct 25] 3,500Y, 21,000 2-y-o: sturdy filly: second foal:
dam lightly-raced 1¼m winner out of half-sister to Oaks winner Jet Ski Lady: easy
winner of maiden at Chepstow in August: seemed amiss subsequently, tailed off in
May Hill Stakes at Doncaster and listed race at Newbury: should stay at least 1¼m:
acts on good to soft ground. *Miss Gay Kelleway*

ADRENALIN   2 ch.g. (Jan 2) Risk Me (FR) 127 – High Cairn (FR) 74 53 d
(Ela-Mana-Mou 132) [1997 5m³ 5d⁵ 5d 6g 5m Jul 12] 6,000Y: good-topped gelding:
brother to an ungenuine 2-y-o 5f winner and a 1m to 11.5f winner in Sweden: dam
2-y-o 6f winner: disappointing sprint maiden: visored third start: gelded after final
one and joined T. Clement. *Mrs J. R. Ramsden*

ADVANCE EAST   5 b.g. Polish Precedent (USA) 131 – Startino 111 (Bustino 50
136) [1996 61: 12g 14m⁴ 14.1m 11.9m⁶ 12f 11.9m 10f⁴ 10.3m⁴ 10m³ 8g³ 9m⁶ 10.1m⁵
1997 9f⁶ 8g 8g 14.1m⁶ 13.1g⁴ 12.5d⁴ Jun 24] big, good-topped gelding: unimpressive

mover: modest maiden: best form up to 1½m: acts on firm and dead ground: has been equipped with tongue grip: held up: tried visored: often finds little. *M. Dods*

ADVANCE REPRO   3 b.f. Risk Me (FR) 127 – Sunday Sport Gem 42 (Lomond (USA) 128) [1996 56, a61: 6d 5f 5f* a5g² a6g* a7g a6g* 1997 a7g⁶ a6g a6g³ a6g⁴ a6g* 6.1d a6g⁵ a7g Jun 7] good-quartered filly: poor mover: modest performer: won seller at Southwell in April: poor efforts afterwards: stays 6f: acts on firm ground and fibresand: usually blinkered: temperament under suspicion: sold (to go to Kuwait) in September. *J. Akehurst*   –   a61

AEGEAN   3 b.g. Rock Hopper 124 – Sayulita 67 (Habitat 134) [1996 NR 1997 8f⁴ 10.2m 10m 16.4m⁶ a16g Aug 28] tall gelding: third foal: half-brother to winner at 11f and 13f in Italy by Rambo Dancer: dam maiden (stayed 1½m) out of half-sister to Gift Wrapped, dam of Royal Lodge winner Reach: little promise: left R. Hannon after third start: tried blinkered. *K. T. Ivory*

AEGEAN BREEZE   2 b.g. (Mar 11) Pharly (FR) 130 – Rich Pickings 44 (Dominion 123) [1997 5m 7.5m 7g Aug 6] 5,600F, 12,000Y: small gelding: first foal: dam, 2¼m winner at 4 yrs, also successful over hurdles: no form in maidens. *Miss Gay Kelleway*   –

AEGEAN DAWN   2 ch.f. (Feb 1) Anshan 119 – Midnight Owl (FR) (Ardross 134) [1997 5.3f² 7m Jul 24] third reported foal: dam lightly raced: close second in weak maiden at Brighton: last in similar event there 8 days later. *R. Hannon*   68

AEGEAN SOUND   3 b.f. Distant Relative 128 – Imperatrice (USA) (Kings Lake (USA) 133) [1996 71: 6m⁵ 5.1f² 6g* 6d³ 6m² 6s a6g 1997 6m 7f 8.3m 10g 7m 6.1m 7f a7g a7g² a7s a6g a7g Dec 19] leggy filly: fair winner for R. Hannon at 2 yrs: poor in 1997, trained by H. Akbary on reappearance: stays 7f: acts on good to firm and dead ground, best 3-y-o form on equitrack: well beaten in blinkers. *K. T. Ivory*   47

AEOLINA (FR)   3 gr.f. Kaldoun (FR) 122 – Folia 83 (Sadler's Wells (USA) 132) [1996 NR 1997 11.1g² 13.4g⁴ 10m⁵ 13.8s⁶ 11m³ a11g* Nov 24] 7,000 3-y-o: first foal: dam, 1¼m winner, out of sister to very smart middle-distance stayer High Hawk, herself dam of In The Wings: modest performer: well backed when winning minor event at Southwell in November: stays 1¾m: acts on good to firm and soft ground and on fibresand. *S. E. Kettlewell*   60

AERLEON PETE (IRE)   3 b.c. Caerleon (USA) 132 – Bristle 96 (Thatch (USA) 136) [1996 79p: 7m 7f³ 1997 8g⁶ 10.1m 10.1s 10g² 10m* 12d* 11.9g³ 12d Oct 16] fairly useful performer: won maiden at Windsor in August and minor event (by 6 lengths) at Goodwood in September: best effort when third to Marsul in handicap at Haydock penultimate start, staying on from poor position in steadily-run race: probably better at 1½m than shorter: acts on good to firm and dead ground: sold 82,000 gns after final start, and ran over hurdles in Ireland for C. Roche. *M. R. Stoute*   94

AFAAN (IRE)   4 ch.c. Cadeaux Genereux 131 – Rawaabe (USA) 87 (Nureyev (USA) 131) [1996 NR 1997 a8g⁵ a7g² a6g² a6g² a5g³ a5g 5d² 6.1g³ 6m* a5g 6d² a6g a6g 5m 6d 5d* 5m* 8s a5g² a5g* Dec 18] first foal: dam, 5f winner, closely related to smart sprinter Doulab: fairly useful performer: won amateurs maiden handicap at Redcar in May, handicap at Pontefract in October, minor event at Redcar in November and apprentice handicap at Southwell in December: probably best at 5f/6f: acts on good to firm and dead going and on fibresand: best form in visor/blinkers: usually races prominently: tough and consistent. *R. F. Marvin*   82

AFICIONADO (IRE)   3 b.g. Marju (IRE) 127 – Haneena 118 (Habitat 134) [1996 73d: 6g³ 6m³ 5f 6m³ 6m 6m⁶ 7m⁵ 8g* a8.5g⁴ 1997 8.2m² 9.7m² 11.6s 8f 8f 10g 10d Nov 3] workmanlike gelding: fluent mover: fair performer: well held last 5 starts: probably needs further than 1m and stays 1¼m: acts on good to firm ground and fibresand: blinkered twice. *R. J. Hodges*   67

AFON ALWEN   4 ch.f. Henbit (USA) 130 – Brenig 68 (Horage 124) [1996 61: a9.4g³ 10f* 10m³ 10f 1997 11.7m 11.8m³ 14g³ 11.9m⁴ 12d² Sep 2] angular filly: fair performer: stays 1¾m: acts on firm and dead ground, yet to race on softer: tends to carry head high: sold 14,500 gns in December. *S. C. Williams*   67

AFRICAN-PARD (IRE)   5 b.g. Don't Forget Me 127 – Petite Realm 95 (Realm 129) [1996 66, a59: 10.8f a9.4g³ 8m⁵ 8.3g 7.1m³ 7.1m² 7g⁵ 8m a9.4g a7s 1997 a8g a9.4g a11g² a12g³ 10g a12f³ 10m* 10m 10.2d* 10.2g a10g a12g⁴ Dec 6] good-   72   a46 topped gelding: fair handicapper: successful at Nottingham and Chepstow in the summer, coming from well back each time: seems ideally suited by around 1¼m: acts on good to firm and soft ground, poor form on fibresand: ran creditably in blinkers/visor at 4 yrs: none too consistent. *D. Haydn Jones*

AFRICAN SUN (IRE) 4 b.g. Mtoto 134 – Nuit d'Ete (USA) 90 (Super Con- 45 d
corde (USA) 128) [1996 –: 9m a8.5g⁵ 12m 10m⁴ 10m⁵ 1997 a12g a11g 7f 10.3d²
11.9g 10g 10.1f 8g 10d⁶ 14.1s 10g 11.8d 11.5m⁶ Oct 22] close-coupled, workmanlike
gelding: shows knee action: poor and disappointing maiden handicapper: best around
1¼m: possibly needs good to soft going or softer. *M. C. Chapman*

AFTER DAWN (IRE) 2 b.f. (Apr 20) Brief Truce (USA) 126 – Faakirah –
(Dragonara Palace (USA) 115) [1997 5.1m 5g 6m⁶ 6.9s 6m 10g 8g Oct 7] IR 4,000Y:
leggy filly: sixth reported foal: half-sister to several winners, including fairly useful
1996 Irish 2-y-o 5f winner Klinsman (by Danehill) and fair 7f to 1¼m winner Upper
Grosvenor (by Alzao): dam unraced sister to smart juvenile sprinter Crime of
Passion: little sign of ability. *Mrs P. N. Dutfield*

AFTER EIGHT 2 b.c. (Mar 22) Presidium 124 – Vickenda 52 (Giacometti 130) 62
[1997 7g 6g 7d 6m a7g³ Nov 25] 1,800F, 16,500Y: smallish colt: fourth foal: dam 7f
winner at 4 yrs: modest maiden: best effort when third of 11 at Lingfield: should stay
1m: acts on equitrack: blinkered fourth start. *R. W. Armstrong*

AFTER HOURS 3 b.f. Polar Falcon (USA) 126 – Tarasova (USA) (Green Forest –
(USA) 134) [1996 –: 7.1s 1997 8d 8f⁵ 10m 9.7d Oct 21] leggy, unfurnished filly: no
worthwhile form. *D. J. S. ffrench Davis*

AFTER THE RAIN 2 ch.c. (Feb 11) Sanglamore (USA) 126 – Rainy Sky 82
(Rainbow Quest (USA) 134) [1997 6g⁶ 7m⁴ 7m⁴ 8g² 8f 8m⁴ 8d Oct 17] leggy,
good-topped colt: first foal: dam French 1½m winner, sister to smart French winner
up to 1½m Bonash: fairly useful maiden: neck second of 16 in valuable nursery at
Newcastle in August: not discredited subsequently: will prove well suited by 1¼m/
1½m: sold 42,000 gns after final start. *B. W. Hills*

AGAINST THE CLOCK 5 b.g. Puissance 110 – Sara Sprint (Formidable –
(USA) 125) [1996 –: a16g 1997 11.6m Aug 11] modest maiden at 3 yrs in Ireland:
tailed off both starts in Britain. *P. Bowen*

AGAMI (USA) 2 b.f. (Feb 27) Nureyev (USA) 131 – Agacerie (USA) (Exclusive – p
Native (USA)) [1997 8.2g Sep 23] $275,000Y: seventh foal: sister to winners in
France (at 13.5f) and Japan and half-sister to 3 winners in USA: dam won 9 races in
USA, including Grade 3 1½m event: 16/1, behind in 14-runner maiden at
Nottingham, weakening quickly from 3f out: sent to France: bred to do much better.
D. R. Loder

AGANON 2 b.c. (Mar 27) Aragon 118 – Plain Tree 71 (Wolver Hollow 126) [1997 76 p
6d⁶ 6g 6d⁵ Nov 7] 14,500Y: leggy colt: eighth foal: brother and half-brother to
several poor winners and to useful sprinter Plain Fact (by Known Fact): dam 7f
winner from good French family: tenderly handled at long odds in autumn maidens,
particularly catching eye when around 3 lengths fifth of 21 to Masha-Il at Doncaster,
going on well finish: should stay beyond 6f: seems sure to do better. *M. R. Channon*

AGENT 4 ch.g. Anshan 119 – Maria Cappuccini 70 (Siberian Express (USA) 125) a55
[1996 62, a70: a7g² a8g³ a6g³ 8f⁴ 6d 6.1d⁶ 7m 8.2s² a8.5g² a8.5g³ 1997 a7g* 7m a7g
10.3d 8g a8g Jul 21] leggy gelding: modest performer: won maiden at Lingfield in
February: disappointing afterwards and sold cheaply after last outing: stays 8.5f: acts
on all-weather and on soft ground: sometimes unruly at start. *J. L. Eyre*

AGENT MULDER 3 b.g. Kylian (USA) – Precious Caroline (IRE) 60 (The 61
Noble Player (USA) 126) [1996 –: 7d 1997 a7g⁵ a8g 8m² 8.3g* 8f⁴ Jun 10] modest
handicapper: won at Windsor (18 ran) in June: sweating, ran well at Salisbury 8 days
later: will stay 1¼m: acts on firm going. *P. D. Cundell*

AGIFT 3 b.f. Cadeaux Genereux 131 – Aspark (Sparkler 130) [1996 NR 1997 6m⁶
8g 7m 6.1d Jul 5] tall filly: half-sister to fairly useful winners Amidst (up to 1m, by
Midyan) and Arturian (unreliable sprinter, by Vaigly Great): dam little form: signs of
ability on debut, little afterwards. *R. F. Johnson Houghton*

AGONY AUNT 3 b.f. Formidable (USA) 125 – Loch Clair (IRE) 53 (Lomond 81
(USA) 128) [1996 75: 7.1d^4 8.2g 8g^5 1997 10m^4 10d^4 12.3d^5 10m* 10d 12d^3 10.5g^3
10.5s Oct 15] robust filly: fairly useful performer: won maiden at Sandown in July:
creditable third twice after: stays 1½m: acts on good to firm going and dead, ran
poorly on soft: races prominently. *Mrs J. Cecil*

AGWA 8 b.g. Local Suitor (USA) 128 – Meissarah (USA) (Silver Hawk (USA) –
123) [1996 73d: a6g^6 a7g a8g 6f* 6f 6g 6m 5f^6 a7g a7g 1997 5.3f^6 6m 5.7g 8m 8g
Sep 3] small, sturdy gelding: has shown little since winning claimer in April, 1996:
has broken blood vessel. *J. J. Bridger*

AHLIYAT (USA) 3 ch.f. Irish River (FR) 131 – Alimana 74 (Akarad (FR) 130) 55
[1996 NR 1997 10g^6 12.5s 9d^2 8.3s^2 a8.5g* Dec 26] third foal: half-sister to winners
in France at 1½m+ by Alleged and Shahrastani: dam, 2-y-o 9f winner (only start),
half-sister to Aliysa: second twice in French Provinces for A. de Royer Dupre before
winning 6-runner maiden at Wolverhampton: should stay beyond 9f: acts on soft
ground. *J. W. Hills*

AILLEACHT (USA) 5 b. or br.m. Chief's Crown (USA) – Poster Beauty (USA) 108
(Codex (USA)) [1996 111: 5s^3 5m^2 5g^2 5f 6m^6 5m* 5m 6g 6d* 5m^2 5d 6s^5 1997 5m^4
5d^3 5g^2 6g 5m^5 6m^3 6g^4 5g^3 Sep 13] useful performer: best efforts of 1997 on first,
third (second in Ballyogan Stakes at Leopardstown) and fifth starts: last in Cork And
Orrery Stakes at Royal Ascot on fourth: best at 5f/6f: acted on good to firm ground
and soft: raced prominently: sent to USA and has been retired. *J. S. Bolger, Ireland*

AIR ATTACHE (USA) 2 b.c. (Mar 11) Sky Classic (CAN) – Diplomatic Cover 82 p
(USA) (Roberto (USA) 131) [1997 7m^2 7.1g^4 Sep 11] tall, useful-looking colt: has
scope: good walker: second foal: dam, winning sprinter at 4 yrs in USA, half-sister
to South African Grade 1 winner Fools Holme: sire (by Nijinsky) high-class North
American middle-distance horse: in frame in maidens at Newmarket in August and
Chepstow in September: should stay at least 1m: should do better at 3 yrs. *G. Lewis*

AIRBORNE HARRIS (IRE) 4 ch.g. Persian Heights 129 – Excuse Slip (USA) –
(Damascus (USA)) [1996 68: 7.1g^5 a8g 1997 a7g 8m a8.5g 9.9g a10g Sep 9] no form
since debut: raced freely in visor/blinkers last 2 starts. *A. Bailey*

AIR EXPRESS (IRE) 3 b.c. Salse (USA) 128 – Ibtisamm (USA) 71 125
(Caucasus (USA) 127) [1996 112: 6m^2 6g^3 7m^4 7.1g^3 6m* 8g^6 7g^3 1997 8m^4
8g* 8d* 8m^2 8m 8g* Sep 27]
A programme in Channel 4's *Cutting Edge* series, shown in November,
focussed on the role of the Jockey Club and its stewards of meetings. Much of
the footage was shot on Timeform Day at Sandown in August but the producers
must have wished they had chosen York's May meeting instead. It was there
that the York steward John Jenyns delivered his much-publicised admonish-
ment of two Channel 4 executives, telling them, after they had requested a seat
while discussing a detail of TV coverage, to 'stand up and take your hands out
of your pockets!' With their One Thousand and Two Thousand Guineas, in
particular, it has sometimes been all too easy for observers in the major
European racing countries to regard the Italian and German classics in a
similarly condescending manner. Until the last fifteen years in Italy and the
current decade in Germany, these events were local affairs and the winners
nearly always remained local phenomena. Among recent home winners of the
Premio Parioli and Mehl-Mulhens-Rennen, the likes of Poliuto, Dancer Mitral
and Manzoni did little to boost the image, but Royal Abjar and Lavirco, in
particular, established big reputations in Germany, and such as Misil, Pelder,
Platini and Royal Abjar went on to make an impact outside their own countries.
The Parioli has been prey to British and Irish raiders, who won nine renewals
from 1983 to 1996, whereas Flying Brave's 1991 victory was the only win in the
German Two Thousand. However, the latest Premio Parioli winner, Air
Express, stepped up to take the Mehl-Mulhens-Rennen as well, and went on to
prove himself one of the highest-rated three-year-olds over the distance in the
whole of Europe.

To extend the metaphor involving that notorious steward and the browbeaten men from Channel 4, Clive Brittain, the trainer of Air Express, does not strike us as the type who has ever risked much criticism for keeping his hands in his pockets or asking for a chair. His energy and enthusiasm are legendary, not least for seeking out ambitious targets and conquering the demons of international competition. Both traits were manifest in his handling of Air Express, and he gained a rich reward. For much of Air Express' two-year-old career, it seemed that ambition was overambition, with, for instance, Air Express contesting three pattern events before the end of August and before he had even got off the mark. But a narrowly-beaten third of eight at 50/1 in the Dewhurst showed that the trainer had not after all been so far wide of the target. A respectable fourth in the Craven on his reappearance saw Air Express travel strongly for a long way but then carry his head high. Fortunately, it was the former rather than the latter that became the chief feature of his 1997 season. If he was going to shirk the issue, the Premio Parioli ten days after the Craven gave him every opportunity, but Air Express got home in front by a nose. Three weeks after that, the show had moved from Rome to Mulheim and Air Express won by a length and a quarter. Who did he beat in his two classics? Risiat, Gianky Gioffry and Golden Biscayne filled the frame in Italy; Is Tirol, Fine Fellow and Icemoon did so in Germany.

Perhaps British pundits, oddsmakers and backers could be excused for allowing Air Express to go off at 20/1 in the St James's Palace Stakes at Royal Ascot the following month. Air Express was up against some far more familiar names from the European mainstream, all but one of which he beat—Daylami, Desert King and Poteen were his closest pursuers, four lengths adrift and more. Entering the straight and through the next furlong, it looked as if Air Express might take the measure of Starborough as well, but Dettori had kept something in reserve on the winner for the last hundred yards. Brittain ensured that British racegoers saw plenty more of his charge by aiming him at the two biggest remaining events for milers in the British calendar, the Sussex Stakes and the Queen Elizabeth II Stakes. The Sussex, however, proved a disappointment, with Air Express racing wide from a low draw and never threatening much better than his eventual seventh of nine, his trainer later saying that he 'might

Queen Elizabeth II Stakes, Ascot—Air Express (left) just holds the unlucky-in-running Rebecca Sharp

have been a little bit kind on him' in his preparation and that the colt had not acted on the camber. Brittain was required to repeat these explanations immediately after the Queen Elizabeth, this time to a throng of reporters and the Ascot stewards. With Frankie Dettori, on Allied Forces, returning to the scene of his seven-out-of-seven, and the likes of Revoque, Entrepreneur and Bahhare also in the line-up, there was not much room for Air Express in the pre-publicity, but in the event none of those big names posed a threat. Rebecca Sharp was a different matter altogether, but, with consummate performances from horse and jockey, Air Express and Olivier Peslier were able to manoeuvre themselves from the rear into an ideal position and then get first run on the filly one and a half furlongs out. With Rebecca Sharp taking time to get herself sorted out and the remainder mastered quickly, Air Express had enough in hand to hang on by a short head, despite flagging in the last half furlong. In his two visits to Ascot, he had beaten Daylami, Desert King and Entrepreneur—the Guineas winners from France, Ireland and Britain. Immediately after the Queen Elizabeth, Brittain announced that he would like Air Express to run in the Hong Kong International Bowl, but in the end the horse was allowed to spend the winter resting on his laurels. We are sure that there will be very little of that in store for him in the next season.

		Topsider	Northern Dancer
	Salse (USA)	(b 1974)	Drumtop
	(b 1985)	Carnival Princess	Prince John
Air Express (IRE)		(ch 1974)	Carnival Queen
(b.c. 1994)		Caucasus	Nijinsky
	Ibtisamm (USA)	(b 1972)	Quill
	(ch 1981)	Lorgnette	High Hat
		(ch 1964)	Mlle Lorette

An angular, good-topped colt, Air Express acts on good to firm going and good to soft; he has not yet encountered anything more extreme. His head tends to go rather high under pressure, but he is both game and consistent. Salse as a sire of middle-distance horses and stayers has become somewhat to be

Mr Mohamed Obaida's "Air Express"

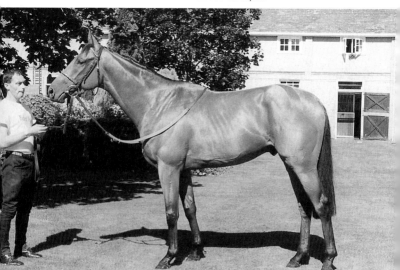

expected, but here is a colt who is most unlikely to stay beyond a mile. That is an additional surprise, perhaps, given that his dam's sire is the 1975 Irish St Leger winner Caucasus (who does not figure in many good pedigrees). But that dam, Ibtisamm, was a miler. She wasn't a very good one, but her win in a Warwick maiden was one more win than achieved by her own dam, the significantly more talented Lorgnette. Lorgnette stayed a mile and a quarter and is a granddaughter of the top-class American performer Gallorette. Another of Lorgnette's daughters, Au Printemps, produced the Breeders' Cup Juvenile winner Success Express, while the best of Ibtisamm's four winners (she also had three unraced foals) before Air Express was the useful middle-distance performer Aljazzaf (by Mtoto). A brother to Air Express will be two years old in 1998. *C. E. Brittain*

AIR QUEST   4 b.c. Rainbow Quest (USA) 134 – Aryenne (FR) 125 (Green Dancer (USA) 132) [1996 95+: 11d* 12.3g⁵ 1997 12g 14d³ May 21] tall colt: has a markedly round action: brother to Derby winner Quest For Fame and smart stayer Silver Rainbow: useful performer, lightly raced: not seen out after staying-on third in handicap at Goodwood in May: will be suited by 2m+: raced only on good and dead going: evidently difficult to train. *R. Charlton*   105

AIX EN PROVENCE (USA)   2 b.c. (May 11) Geiger Counter (USA) – Low Hill (Rousillon (USA) 133) [1997 6g* 6g 6f⁴ 6m* 7m³ 8d Oct 20] 15,000Y, 21,000 2-y-o: leggy, useful-looking colt: third foal: half-brother to a winner in USA by Ela-Mana-Mou: dam, 5f winner in Italy at 2 yrs, half-sister to smart winner up to 1½m Beldale Star: useful form: won maiden at Ayr in June and minor event at Ripon in August: easily best effort when about 3 lengths third to Haami in listed race at Newmarket: tailed off final start: should stay 1m: form only on good ground or firmer. *M. Johnston*   98

AJAYIB (USA)   3 b.f. Riverman (USA) 131 – Maplejinsky (USA) (Nijinsky (CAN) 138) [1996 73: 7g² 7m² 8.1g* 1997 9.9m² 12.1g⁵ 10d 10.5g² 10.9s³ 11m⁶ Nov 4] lengthy, good-topped filly: fairly useful handicapper: stayed 1¼m: acted on soft ground, probably good to firm: blinkered last 3 starts: ran well when sweating: stud. *J. L. Dunlop*   84

AJCOMBE (IRE)   4 b.g. Ajraas (USA) 88 – Whichcombe 79 (Huntercombe 133) [1996 NR 1997 11.7g 14m 14m³ 14.4m 16m Sep 25] IR 2,800F: 9,200Y: half-brother to several winners, including Chart Cross (9f seller, by Millfontaine): dam second over 6f at 2 yrs on only start: fair maiden: stays 1¾m: raced only on good/good to firm going. *Lady Herries*   68

AJEEBAH (IRE)   3 b.f. Mujtahid (USA) 118 – Saffron (FR) (Fabulous Dancer (USA) 124) [1996 NR 1997 8m⁵ 10.1g⁶ 8g Jul 23] IR 13,500Y: second living foal: half-sister to fairly useful 1m/1¼m winner Roman Gold (by Petorius): dam French 12.5f winner: well beaten in sellers after fifth in maiden on debut. *W. J. Haggas*   –

AJIG DANCER   2 b.f. (Mar 1) Niniski (USA) 125 – Gloire (Thatching 131) [1997 6s² 7g 6g 5.1g* 6g Sep 19] 5,000F, 11,500Y: leggy, useful-looking filly: first foal: dam unraced sister to smart sprinter Puissance: fairly useful form: easily won maiden at Bath in September: highly tried previous 2 starts and on final outing (reportedly lame): stays 6f: yet to race on ground firmer than good. *M. R. Channon*   86

AJKUIT (IRE)   4 b.g. Persian Heights 129 – Hazar (IRE) 75 (Thatching 131) [1996 –: 10g 8g a8g 1997 a8g⁶ a8g Mar 13] no worthwhile form. *J. J. Sheehan*   –

AKALIM   4 b.g. Petong 126 – Tiszta Sharok 81 (Song 132) [1996 –: 6m 6m⁶ 6f 5m 1997 6d 5d 5.7f⁴ 6m⁴ 7.1g³ 8m 6.1s³ a7g³ Oct 27] good-topped gelding: has a quick action: modest handicapper: generally creditable efforts at 4 yrs: stays 7f: acts on firm and soft ground and equitrack: tried blinkered. *L. G. Cottrell*   64

AKARITA (IRE)   2 b.f. (May 18) Akarad (FR) 130 – Safita 117 (Habitat 134) [1997 7g⁶ 7.5f⁴ 7.1s³ Oct 15] leggy filly: half-sister to several winners, notably smart performer up to 1m Safawan (by Young Generation) and useful 7f to 9f winner Sadapour (by Auction Ring): dam smart up to 1¼m in France: fair form in autumn maidens at Salisbury, Beverley and Haydock: will stay 1¼m. *B. A. McMahon*   69

AKDARIYA (IRE) 3 b.f. Shirley Heights 130 – Akishka (Nishapour (FR) 125) 103
[1996 7s² 1997 12g² 12d* 12g² 12.3m⁵ Jul 14] rangy, unfurnished filly: third living
foal: half-sister to useful Akhiyar (probably stayed 1¼m, by Doyoun) and lightly-
raced 9.6f winner Akilara (by Kahyasi): dam unraced daughter of Arc winner
Akiyda: useful performer: simple task when winning maiden at Fairyhouse in May:
ran well when 9 lengths second to Yashmak in Ribblesdale Stakes at Royal Ascot:
will stay beyond 1½m. *J. Oxx, Ireland*

AL ABRAQ (IRE) 4 b.g. Reprimand 122 – Dazzling Maid (IRE) 64 (Tate 68
Gallery (USA) 117) [1996 92: 8.1g⁶ 8f 8m⁴ 10m 1997 8g 7.6g 8.1m³ May 27]
good-bodied colt: fairly useful handicapper in 1996: best form at best at 4 yrs: best
up to 1m: acts on firm and dead ground: sold 10,500 gns in June, and sent to Italy.
J. W. Hills

ALAFLAK (IRE) 6 b.h. Caerleon (USA) 132 – Safe Haven (Blakeney 126) 75
[1996 84: 10.9m 8f⁶ 10.2g² 10.2m* 10m⁵ 11.9m 12m 1997 10d⁴ 10.2f⁴ Jul 23] good-
bodied horse: fair performer: pulled up final start in 1996 and well below best final
one of 1997: should stay beyond 1¼m: acts on good to firm and dead going: has been
bandaged and tongue tied. *Major W. R. Hern*

ALAGNA 3 b.f. Unfuwain (USA) 131 – Spica (USA) 76§ (Diesis 133) [1996 NR 48
1997 a7g⁶ a8.5g 6.9m⁴ 12d³ 14.1m² a14.8g² a12g 15.4s⁵ a14.8g⁶ 16g⁴ 11.9f⁶ 12m
Oct 31] third foal: half-sister to 1m winner Danico (by Most Welcome): dam, 1m
winner, wasn't one to trust: poor maiden handicapper: stays 2m: acts on good to firm
and dead ground and on fibresand: blinkered/visored last 3 starts: none too
consistent. *S. C. Williams*

ALAKDAR (CAN) 3 ch.c. Green Dancer (USA) 132 – Population (General 81
Assembly (USA)) [1996 NR 1997 10.3d 10m³ 10g 14m 14.4m³ 16g 12s* 11m Nov
4] $220,000Y: third foal: half-brother to 1997 Racing Post Trophy winner Saratoga
Springs: dam Irish maiden from good family: fairly useful form: won maiden at
Catterick in October: bought out of A. Stewart's stable 27,000 gns later in month:
unenterprisingly ridden final start: should stay beyond 1¾m: acts on good to firm
ground, best effort on soft: spooked and unseated rider at start (tapes) fourth outing.
R. Champion

ALAMEIN (USA) 4 ch.g. Roi Danzig (USA) – Pollination 100 (Pentotal) [1996 88
87: 6m³ 7g* 7f* 8f⁶ 7.1m³ 1997 8m⁶ 7g² 6g 7g⁴ 7m 8m Aug 26] workmanlike gelding: fairly useful handicapper: tailed off last 2 starts: best at 7f/1m: acts on firm
ground, unraced on softer than good: usually blinkered nowadays, but effective when
not: sometimes sweating: tends to carry head high and isn't a straightforward ride:
sold 10,000 gns in October. *W. J. Haggas*

ALAMODE 3 b.f. Statoblest 120 – Alo Ez 100 (Alzao (USA) 117) [1996 NR 1997 59
5m* 5g⁶ 5m Sep 22] good-quartered filly: second living foal: sister to 5-y-o Mousehole: dam sprinter: won maiden at Doncaster in May, easily despite being green: little
show in minor event and handicap after. *J. G. Smyth-Osbourne*

ALANA'S BALLAD (IRE) 4 b.f. Be My Native (USA) 122 – Radalgo (Ballad –
Rock 122) [1996 –: 10.5d 10.8g 1997 a11s a8.5g a8g a8g a10g Feb 18] of little
account. *B. P. J. Baugh*

ALARABY (IRE) 5 b.m. Caerleon (USA) 132 – Circo 77 (High Top 131) [1996 –
–: 14.1g 1997 16s⁶ Jul 26] lengthy mare: 1¾m winner in 1995: tailed off both starts
for current stable. *Martyn Wane*

ALARICO (FR) 4 ch.g. Kadrou (FR) 126 – Calabria (FR) (Vitiges (FR) 132) 66
[1996 –: 10g 10s 1997 a10g* a10g³ 14g⁶ 12d 14m³ 14m² 14.1m Aug 6] strong gelding: fair performer: easy winner of Lingfield maiden in January: mostly creditable
efforts after: takes good hold but stays 1¾m: acts on equitrack and on good to firm
going: carries head high. *I. P. Williams*

ALARMING MOTOWN 2 b.f. (Jan 28) Warning 136 – Sweet Soul Dream – p
(USA) 61 (Conquistador Cielo (USA)) [1997 6g Oct 24] leggy filly: second foal:
half-sister to a winner in Japan by Capote: dam maiden half-sister to top-class
sprinter Committed: 20/1 and carrying plenty of condition, around 9 lengths tenth of
24 to Mister Rambo in maiden at Newbury, losing touch 2f out and not knocked
about: sold 30,000 gns later in October: should do better. *I. A. Balding*

38

ALARMIST 3 b.g. Warning 136 – Wryneck 89 (Niniski (USA) 125) [1996 NR 1997 10g³ 10s³ 10m 11.7m 11.5d 10.2g 10m Oct 1] eighth foal: closely related to fair 1½m winner Strategic Ploy (by Deploy) and half-brother to several other winners, including 5-y-o Myrtle Quest: dam 7f winner at 2 yrs on only start: didn't go on after third in maidens at Goodwood: visored sixth start: sold 12,000 gns in October and joined G. Richards. *R. Charlton* **81 d**

AL AVA CONSONANT 3 b.f. Reprimand 122 – Dragonist 82 (Dragonara Palace (USA) 115) [1996 63?: 5m⁶ 5m³ 6m 7g 1997 a7g 7.5d 8g 10f 12g⁶ 9.2g 8g⁵ 9m a10s⁶ a14g Dec 18] tall, unfurnished filly: poor performer: probably stays 1m: tried in visor. *J. D. Bethell* **37**

ALAZAN 2 ch.c. (Apr 9) Risk Me (FR) 127 – Gunnard 62 (Gunner B 126) [1997 7g 7f⁵ 8g⁵ Oct 25] 900Y: workmanlike colt: half-brother to 11f winner by Hotfoot and 1½m seller winner by Relkino: dam won 1m/1¼m sellers: tailed off in listed race and 2 minor events. *D. M. Hyde* **–**

AL AZHAR 3 b.c. Alzao (USA) 117 – Upend 120 (Main Reef 126) [1996 92P: 7m² 8.1g* 8m* 1997 10.4d⁶ 10m 9g² 8m³ 9m 12g* 12s⁵ Nov 8] well-made colt: has reportedly had knee trouble: useful handicapper: won 17-runner race at Doncaster by 1½ lengths from Veridian, quickening well having had plenty of trouble getting a run: respectable fifth (on much softer going) to Sabadilla in November Handicap there 2 weeks later: seems suited by 1½m: best effort on good going: open to further improvement at 4 yrs. *I. A. Balding* **103 p**

ALBAHA (USA) 4 br.g. Woodman (USA) 126 – Linda's Magic (USA) 114 (Far North (CAN) 120) [1996 81: 9g 7m⁵ 7g 6d² 6m 6f³ 10m⁴ 8.5m 10m 12g a12g* 1997 a11g² a12g* a12g* 12g 10g 12g³ 10.9s Oct 13] big, robust gelding: fairly useful performer: won minor event at Southwell in January and handicap at Wolverhampton in March: gambled on, easily best run on turf afterwards when third in handicap at Thirsk in August: stays easy 1½m: acts on good to firm and dead ground, goes well on fibresand: blinkered 3 times as 3-y-o. *J. E. Banks* **76 a90**

ALBARAHIN (USA) 2 b.c. (Jan 28) Silver Hawk (USA) 123 – My Dear Lady (USA) (Mr Prospector (USA)) [1997 8d² 8m² Oct 31] $425,000F: strong, deep-girthed, attractive colt: fluent mover: half-brother to several winners abroad, including minor stakes winners and French 5f to 7.5f winner Le Vivarois (by Local Talent): dam stakes winner up to 9f in USA: fairly useful form when runner-up to Border Arrow in 22-runner maiden and to Rabah (beaten a neck) in 3-runner minor event, both at Newmarket in October: will be well suited by at least 1¼m: good sort, seems sure to win races at 3 yrs. *Saeed bin Suroor* **94 p**

ALBERICH (IRE) 2 b.c. (Mar 21) Night Shift (USA) – Tetradonna (IRE) 102 (Teenoso (USA) 135) [1997 7.5d⁵ 8.5g* 8.1s³ Oct 15] 14,000Y: sturdy, good-bodied colt: has scope: good mover: first living foal: dam second in Nell Gwyn but disappointing afterwards, stayed 1½m: won maiden at Beverley in August: eased quickly once held when 9 lengths third of 4 to Close Up in minor event at Haydock nearly 2 months later: stays 8.5f: very much the type to improve at 3 yrs, and should make useful handicapper. *M. Johnston* **85 p**

ALBERT THE BEAR 4 b.g. Puissance 110 – Florentynna Bay 61 (Aragon 118) [1996 80: 6g 5.7m² 7m* 7f² 7m⁵ 7d³ 1997 6s³ 7.6v* 7d 7m* 6g 7.1g⁵ 7.6m⁴ 7m⁶ 7m² 7d 7.6s 8m 6g⁵ 6g² a7g Nov 1] tall gelding: easy mover: fairly useful handicapper: usually goes well at Chester, and won there in May and June: best of last 6 efforts when fifth of 29 to Wildwood Flower in Ayr Gold Cup: needs thorough test at 6f, but seemed to stay strongly-run 1m beyond him: acts on any turf ground, has shown nothing on fibresand: blinkered last 3 starts. *J. Berry* **94 a–**

ALBOOSTAN 2 b.c. (Feb 20) Sabrehill (USA) 120 – Russian Countess (USA) 104 (Nureyev (USA) 131) [1997 7.5m* 7g² 8d* 8s³ Oct 12] 13,000F, 105,000Y: good-bodied colt: has scope: good mover: fifth foal: closely related to useful 7f and 8.5f winner Romanzof (by Kris) and half-brother to 3 winners, notably 3-y-o Crown of Light: dam 2-y-o 1m winner in France: useful form: won maiden at Beverley in July and 5-runner listed race at Goodwood in September, beating odds-on Almutawakel a length in latter: very good 4½ lengths third of 5 to Second Empire in Grand Criterium at Longchamp: should stay 1¼m: won on good to firm ground, **108**

Hamdan Al Maktoum's "Alboostan"

better form on good to soft/soft: front runner: genuine: to be trained in 1998 by B. Hills. *D. Morley*

ALBORADA 2 gr.f. (Mar 8) Alzao (USA) 117 – Alouette 105 (Darshaan 133)   104 p
[1997 6.1m³ 7m³ 7.5f* 7d* Oct 4] smallish filly: first foal: dam Irish 1m (at 2 yrs) and 1½m winner, sister to Irish middle-distance stayer Arrikala and half-sister to 1m/ 1¼m filly Last Second (by Alzao), both at least smart: progressive filly: won maiden at Beverley in September and C. L. Weld Park Stakes at the Curragh in October, beating Winona 2 lengths in latter: will stay at least 1m: remains capable of better. *Sir Mark Prescott*

ALBRIGHTON 2 b.g. (Mar 21) Terimon 124 – Bright-One 78 (Electric 126)   –
[1997 6d 6d Nov 7] 5,000Y: lengthy, workmanlike gelding: fifth foal: dam, maiden miler, successful over hurdles: only a little sign of ability in late-season maidens at Pontefract and Doncaster. *B. S. Rothwell*

ALCALALI (USA) 3 ch.f. Septieme Ciel (USA) 123 – Princess Verna (USA) (Al   96 ?
Hattab (USA)) [1996 94p: 10s 1997 10g² 10.4g⁶ 7d 10m⁴ 12g⁴ 11.9g 12d⁴ 11.9g 8.1s⁴ 12v Oct 11] long-backed filly: highly tried on occasions, including when appearing to excel herself when fourth to Yashmak in Ribblesdale Stakes at Royal Ascot fifth start: disappointing in maidens: likely to stay beyond 1½m: sold 20,000 gns (to join M. Hammond) after final start. *P. A. Kelleway*

ALCAYDE 2 ch.c. (Feb 13) Alhijaz 122 – Lucky Flinders 77 (Free State 125)   73 p
[1997 7.1g⁴ Sep 27] 20,000Y: rather sparely-made colt: fourth foal: half-brother to a winning sprint 2-y-o by Mazilier: dam stayed 1m: 12/1, ridden with little enterprise and nearest finish when 5 lengths fourth of 12 to Last Christmas in maiden at Haydock: should stay 1¼m: can do better. *J. L. Dunlop*

ALCIAN BLUE 6 b.g. Tina's Pet 121 – Rhiannon 65 (Welsh Pageant 132) [1996   36
NR 1997 16.2m⁶ 21.6g Apr 28] sturdy gelding: poor handicapper: stays 2¼m: acts on any going. *M. D. Hammond*

40

ALCONLEIGH 2 ch.c. (Jan 22) Pursuit of Love 124 – Serotina (IRE) 73 (Mtoto 93
134) [1997 5d³ 6d* 6d² 6m² 7g* 7g² 8d 8.2d⁴ 7s² Nov 8] 9,400Y: strong, lengthy
colt: has scope: dam 9f winner from family of Waajib: fairly useful performer: won
maiden at Ripon in May and minor event at Thirsk in July: ran well 3 of 4 starts in
nurseries: likely to prove best up to 1m: acts on good to firm and soft ground: tends
to wander: usually a front runner: consistent. *M. Johnston*

ALDWYCH ARROW (IRE) 2 ch.g. (Mar 26) Rainbows For Life (CAN) – 62
Shygate (Shy Groom (USA)) [1997 6d⁶ 5d 7m⁶ 8g 10g Sep 23] IR 16,000Y: third
foal: dam Irish 1½m winner: modest form in maidens first 3 starts: should stay 1m
(though seemed not to get 1¼m). *M. Bell*

ALEZAL 3 b.c. Anshan 119 – Dance On The Stage (Dancing Brave (USA) 140) 109
[1996 81p: 7m² 1997 8g² 8.3s* 8.1d* 8m 10.3m² 10v* Oct 11] close-coupled colt:
has a roundish action: useful performer: won maiden at Hamilton (long odds on),
£21,200 handicap at Haydock in May and rated stakes at Ascot in October: had hard
race at Ascot, leading early in straight then wandering, holding Cugina by ½ length:
stays 1¼m well: acts on good to firm and heavy ground: races prominently. *W. Jarvis*

ALFAHAAL (IRE) 4 b.c. Green Desert (USA) 127 – Fair of The Furze 112 68
(Ela-Mana-Mou 132) [1996 –: 7g 1997 10g 8m 6.1g⁵ 6g 8m* 8m 8g⁵ 7m³ 7.1m 10m
8d* 8s² a8g⁴ a9.4g Dec 6] robust colt: fair performer: won handicap at Doncaster in
July and minor event at Leicester (final start for R. F. J. Houghton) in October: ran
well in frame in November: likely to prove best at 7f/1m: acts on good to firm and
soft going and on equitrack: has been bandaged: well suited by waiting tactics.
C. A. Dwyer

ALFANNAN 3 b.c. Lear Fan (USA) 130 – Connecting Link (USA) (Linkage –
(USA)) [1996 NR 1997 8g Apr 16] 500,000Y: big, strong colt with plenty of scope:
sixth foal: half-brother to 1994 2-y-o 6f winner Fiendish (by Devil's Bag) and 1m
winner Link River (by Gone West), later successful in Grade 1 9f event in USA: dam
maiden from family of Ajdal and Arazi: weak 11/2 and decidedly burly, signs of
ability when well held in newcomers race at Newmarket: moved well to post.
J. H. M. Gosden

Miss K. Rausing's "Alborada"

AL-FATEH (IRE) 2 b.c. (May 2) Caerleon (USA) 132 – Filia Ardross 121   80 p
(Ardross 134) [1997 7d⁶ 7d³ Nov 7] 42,000Y: close-coupled colt: second foal:
half-brother to smart Irish 1m to 1¾m winner French Ballerina (by Sadler's Wells):
dam top filly in Germany at 3 yrs and winner twice in Britain at 5 yrs, effective from
7f to 1½m: better effort in autumn when about 1½ lengths third of 18, staying on
strongly, behind High-Rise in maiden at Doncaster: should be well suited by 1¼m+:
lethargic in preliminaries at Doncaster: sure to improve again and win races.
J. L. Dunlop

ALFIGLIA 2 b.f. (Apr 21) Alhijaz 122 – Saraswati 55 (Mansingh (USA) 120)   83
[1997 5g* 5g⁵ 5.1m³ 6m⁶ 7d Sep 12] 15,500Y: smallish, lightly-made filly: second
foal: dam, ran only at 2 yrs, closely related to Norfolk Stakes winner Petillante: fairly
useful form first 3 starts: won minor event at Windsor in June: about 3 lengths fifth to
Asfurah in Windsor Castle Stakes at Royal Ascot: tailed off last 2 starts, in blinkers
on final outing: should stay beyond 5f: sold (to go to Sweden) only 1,500 gns in
October. *P. J. Makin*

ALFREDO ALFREDO (USA) 5 b.g. Miswaki (USA) 124 – Alleged Queen   63
(USA) (Alleged (USA) 138) [1996 71p: 8m⁴ 7m⁶ 10d⁵ 1997 10m Apr 11] sturdy
gelding: lightly raced but showed ability all starts: bandaged only one of 1997:
retired. *J. L. Dunlop*

ALGALEB 2 ch.c. (Feb 7) Alhijaz 122 – Brise de Mer (USA) (Bering 136) [1997   66
6g a7g⁴ 6.1g Sep 28] 15,000Y: lengthy colt: second foal: dam French 1m winner,
half-sister to Halling: fourth of 12 to wide-margin winner Confirmation in maiden at
Southwell (had to be led to post) in September: well held on turf (bandaged on
debut): should stay at least 1m: sent to UAE. *H. Akbary*

ALGEBRA 2 b.g. (Feb 16) Statoblest 120 – Alghabrah 70 (Lomond (USA) 128)   58 ?
[1997 5m 6.1g 6.9d 6.1d a6g Nov 13] 12,500Y: fourth foal: half-brother to a winner
in Italy by Dominion: dam stayed 1m: best effort when mid-division in maiden at
Nottingham second start: sold 3,300 gns after final start. *R. Hannon*

AL HAAL (USA) 8 b.g. Northern Baby (CAN) 127 – Kit's Double (USA)   –
(Spring Double) [1996 –: a12g a13g⁵ 1997 a12g⁵ a16g a16.2g a13g⁶ Jan 30] poor
maiden. *R. J. O'Sullivan*

ALHAARTH (IRE) 4 b.c. Unfuwain (USA) 131 – Irish Valley (USA) (Irish   121
River (FR) 131) [1996 123: 8m² 8m⁴ 12m⁵ 12m 8m³ 8g³ 8d* 1997 10m² 8d*
8m 10g³ 9.8m* Oct 4]
    A winter in Dubai and a change of trainer didn't bring about any
improvement in Alhaarth, but nor did they do him harm and once again he
showed very smart form, winning two of his five starts. Those wins came in the

*Prix Dollar, Longchamp—Alhaarth's racing career ends on a winning note;
Lord Cromby is his nearest pursuer*

Budweiser American Bowl International Stakes over a mile at the Curragh and the Prix Dollar over virtually a mile and a quarter at Longchamp, the latter setting the seal on a racing career probably best summed up as being very successful in terms of races and prize-money won, yet ultimately disappointing in that in his second and third seasons Alhaarth failed to fulfil the abundant promise of his first.

Alhaarth had been the leading two-year-old in 1995, unbeaten in five starts, including the Dewhurst Stakes, and was installed as favourite for both the Two Thousand Guineas and Derby. He was to fail in both those races and in four others as well before gaining his only success as a three-year-old on his final start for Dick Hern, in the Prix du Rond-Point at Longchamp. A tendency to race lazily had resulted in Alhaarth's being fitted with blinkers on three occasions, including in the Rond-Point, but they were dispensed with at the start of his four-year-old campaign, which began at Royal Ascot in June. Although no match at all for Bosra Sham in the Prince of Wales's Stakes, Alhaarth acquitted himself well in finishing a clear second, and twelve days later he went one better at the Curragh in a race in which all five runners were trained in Britain. Settled in second behind a strong pace, Alhaarth responded to pressure to edge ahead entering the final furlong and pull a length clear of Gothenberg. A return to Group 1 company saw Alhaarth run well below his

Alhaarth (IRE) (b.c. 1993)	Unfuwain (USA) (b 1985)	Northern Dancer (b 1961)	Nearctic
			Natalma
		Height of Fashion (b 1979)	Bustino
			Highclere
	Irish Valley (USA) (ch 1982)	Irish River (ch 1976)	Riverman
			Irish Star
		Green Valley (br 1967)	Val de Loir
			Sly Pola

Godolphin's "Alhaarth"

ALH

best in both the Sussex Stakes at Goodwood and the Champion Stakes at Leopardstown, in the latter left a long way behind in the straight by both Pilsudski and Desert King. Following those lack-lustre performances it came as no surprise to see Alhaarth fitted with a visor in the Group 2 Prix Dollar. One of three British-trained runners in the eight-runner field, along with Desert Story, with whom he was coupled for betting purposes, and Handsome Ridge, the heavily-bandaged Alhaarth was able to make all the running, just as he'd done over the same course twelve months earlier. Lord Cromby ran on the best of his rivals in the straight, but Alhaarth always looked like holding him and had a length to spare at the line.

Alhaarth is to stand at the Derrinstown Stud at a fee of IR 7,000 guineas and has plenty to recommend him as a stallion in addition to his form. A strong, well-made individual, he invariably took the eye in the paddock and also on the way to post, being a good mover with a powerful action, and his pedigree stands close inspection, too. His sire Unfuwain was an impeccably-bred top-class mile-and-a-half horse, while his dam Irish Valley, though a disappointment on the racecourse, is from a very good family. Irish Valley's dam, the unraced Green Valley, a daughter of the Prix de l'Abbaye winner Sly Pola, has produced numerous winners, most notably the triple Group 1 winner (Observer Gold Cup, French Guineas and Prix Lupin) and good stallion Green Dancer. Irish Valley herself has produced three winners besides Alhaarth, including a couple by Nijinsky named Gaelic Myth and Green Pola. The former showed useful form on the Flat and over hurdles, while the latter, who raced only at two years, won both her starts, including the Group 3 Prix du Calvados. Alhaarth is the sixth foal of Irish Valley. Her seventh, a two-year-old by Sadler's Wells named Dalayil, has yet to race. Alhaarth, who has run well when sweating, acted on firm and good to soft ground. Although a staying-on fifth in the Derby on the first of two runs at a mile and a half, he showed better form at shorter distances. *Saeed bin Suroor*

ALHARIR (USA) 2 b. or br.f. (Mar 2) Zafonic (USA) 130 – Thawakib (IRE) 108 (Sadler's Wells (USA) 132) [1997 7g³ 7m* 8f⁵ Sep 11] good-topped filly: first foal: dam Ribblesdale Stakes winner, half-sister to Celestial Storm: stormed clear to beat some fair subsequent winners by very wide margin in maiden at Redcar in August: below that form when under 7 lengths fifth of 9 to Midnight Line in May Hill Stakes at Doncaster, tending to edge left and stride out poorly (possibly unsuited by firm going) having gone smoothly in rear: should stay 1m: likely to make a better 3-y-o. *J. L. Dunlop* 101 p

ALHAWA (USA) 4 ch.c. Mt Livermore (USA) – Petrava (NZ) (Imposing (AUS)) [1996 83: 7.6m* 10d 8f 10m⁶ 8m 8.1g 8d 1997 8.1g⁴ 8g 8d³ 8m Jul 31] leggy, unfurnished colt: fair handicapper: creditable efforts first and third starts at 4 yrs: slowly away last one: probably stays 1¼m: acts on firm and dead ground: blinkered final start at 3 yrs. *R. Akehurst* 78

AL HELAL 5 b.h. In The Wings 128 – Rosia Bay 102 (High Top 131) [1996 59d: 10g 12g³ 16d 12g 16g 9g⁴ 9g⁴ a12g⁶ 1997 a11g⁶ a13g³ a12g⁴ a12g² a13g² a12g Feb 4] poor maiden: broke leg at Lingfield in February: stayed 13f: acted on equitrack, probably on fibresand: sometimes blinkered. *J. R. Jenkins* 45

ALHOSAAM 3 b.c. Belmez (USA) 131 – Leipzig 107 (Relkino 131) [1996 NR 1997 11g 10s 12.1g 11.6s³ 12m* 15.9g⁴ Sep 24] big colt: half-brother to 4 winners, including fairly useful Namoodaj (stays 1½m, by Polish Precedent) and useful miler Pfalz (by Pharly): dam 6f and 1m winner: progressive form first 5 starts: fitted with tongue strap, won 20-runner handicap at Kempton by a neck from Renzo, coming from off strong pace: seemed not quite to stay 2m later in September: may prove best at 1½m/1¾m: sold (to join G. L. Moore) 30,000 gns in October. *Major W. R. Hern* 88

ALIFANDANGO (IRE) 3 b.f. Alzao (USA) 117 – Fandangerina (USA) (Grey Dawn II 132) [1996 –p: 1997 10g 8m* 9m 11.6m⁶ Aug 18] angular filly: fair performer: led near finish when winning maiden at Yarmouth in June: well held in handicaps afterwards: needs good pace at 1m, should stay further. *A. C. Stewart* 78

ALIGNMENT (IRE)   2 b.f. (May 20) Alzao (USA) 117 – Scots Lass 79 (Shirley 98
Heights 130) [1997 7.1m² 7g² 8g Sep 28] leggy filly: fluent mover: sixth foal:
half-sister to several winners, including smart middle-distance stayer Bonny Scot (by
Commanche Run): dam 13f winner: useful form: runner-up in maiden at Sandown
and Prestige Stakes at Goodwood in July, caught final stride by Midnight Line in
latter: ran too freely in front when well beaten in Fillies' Mile at Ascot: bred to stay
1¼m+, but seems headstrong. *M. R. Stoute*

ALIKHLAS   3 b. or br.f. Lahib (USA) 129 – Mathaayl (USA) 79 (Shadeed (USA) 78
135) [1996 81: 6m² 6m 1997 7m³ 7d⁵ 7.5m² 8m* 8g³ 6.9g 7.1m⁶ 7.1g Sep 27] leggy,
lengthy filly: has a quick action: fair performer: won 3-runner maiden at Brighton in
July: stayed in form, having no luck in running last 2 starts: stays 1m, at least when
conditions aren't testing: unraced on extremes of going: sold 18,000 gns in
December. *Major W. R. Hern*

ALIMERJAM   3 b.f. Thowra (FR) – Sicilian Vespers 44 (Mummy's Game 120) –
[1996 –: 5g 5s⁴ 6g⁵ 6m 6g 8f⁶ a8g⁶ a10g 1997 a10g⁶ a10g⁴ 12.5m⁴ 14.1d 16f⁵ May
28] good-topped filly: little worthwhile form: usually blinkered. *J. White*

ALI-ROYAL (IRE)   4 b.c. Royal Academy (USA) 130 – Alidiva 105 (Chief 127
Singer 131) [1996 118: 8m³ 7g* 7m⁵ 8m 7m² 8f² 8d* 8g* 1997 9g* 10d³ 8d²
8m³ 7.9g* 8m* Jul 30]
   Outstanding horses have been thin on the ground in the rarefied
atmosphere of Britain's highest racecourse Bath since the legendary Tudor
Minstrel won his Guineas trial there in 1947. However, racegoers at the course
probably witnessed something pretty special on September 30th 1996 when
Ali-Royal bolted up in the Morris Dancer Conditions Stakes. On the book
Ali-Royal's trouncing of the smart Nijo and four other useful performers by
twelve lengths and more could be made a performance right out of the top
drawer. But Timeform was not alone in treating this back-end form with a large
pinch of salt at the time, a view that seemed justified when Ali-Royal beat Nijo
by only a length and a quarter (admittedly in a tactical race) in a listed event at
Newmarket on his only subsequent start of 1996.
   Twelve months on and a literal interpretation of the Bath form has much
more credibility. Ali-Royal took most of the best milers around in 1997,
and, in winning the Sussex Stakes at Goodwood on his final start, showed form
surpassed in that division only by Spinning World and First Island. The
impression that Ali-Royal was some way removed from the top of the tree had
persisted in the first half of 1997. He won the Group 3 Earl of Sefton Stakes at
Newmarket on his reappearance by two lengths from Wixim, but, in a muddling
affair, a number of useful performers finished fairly close up. Ali-Royal was
then third behind Sasuru in the Gordon Richards Stakes at Sandown, though in
his defence he seemed not quite to see out the mile and a quarter. Back at a mile
Ali-Royal put up a far more convincing performance in the Lockinge Stakes,
finishing one and a half lengths second to First Island, with five lengths back to
Spinning World and Decorated Hero among others. A good effort, yes. But
exactly *how* good was still open to debate. Ali-Royal received an enterprising
ride, his rider kicking on soon after halfway, and he and First Island seemed at
something of an advantage in racing towards the centre. A subsequent defeat in
the Queen Anne Stakes at Royal Ascot (keeping-on third to Allied Forces) and
a fairly hollow victory in a minor event at York (his only serious rival, Kahal,
failed to give his running) hardly made the Lockinge form look any better.
   The 1997 renewal of the Sussex Stakes wasn't a strong one; besides the
now-deceased First Island, the absentees included Spinning World, Bosra
Sham, Entrepreneur and Ali-Royal's sister, the One Thousand Guineas winner
Sleepytime. All the same, Ali-Royal went off at 13/2 fourth favourite in a field
of nine, behind the St James's Palace Stakes winner Starborough, Allied Forces
and the Jersey Stakes winner Among Men. Ali-Royal won decisively, the only
plausible excuses for his rivals being that Starborough had to go a strong pace
in order to adopt his customary front-running tactics and that despite this the

Sussex Stakes, Goodwood—Ali-Royal takes the measure of Starborough and Allied Forces

inexperienced Among Men refused to settle. The strong pace certainly seemed to suit Ali-Royal, who was niggled along in the early stages but made steady progress in the straight to throw down a challenge approaching the final furlong. Starborough fought back but the only other horse in the firing line by this stage, the Irish One Thousand Guineas winner Classic Park, was soon beaten off. Ali-Royal stayed on dourly to cross the line three quarters of a length to the good over Starborough, with Allied Forces staying on well the same distance further back in third. That proved to be it with Ali-Royal. He reportedly returned with a slight leg problem after Goodwood that didn't clear up in time for him to run in the Queen Elizabeth II Stakes at Ascot in September. Shortly after that race he was retired.

		Nijinsky	Northern Dancer
	Royal Academy (USA)	(b 1967)	Flaming Page
	(b 1987)	Crimson Saint	Crimson Satan
Ali-Royal (IRE)		(ch 1969)	Bolero Rose
(b.c. 1993)		Chief Singer	Ballad Rock
	Alidiva	(b 1981)	Principia
	(b 1987)	Alligatrix	Alleged
		(br 1980)	Shore

Ali-Royal returns to the stud, Coolmore, where he was foaled and raised and where his own sire stood until recently. Royal Academy had a stint in Japan in 1996 and reportedly is to stand next at the American base of Coolmore, Ashford Stud. The July Cup and Breeders' Cup Mile winner Royal Academy has made a creditable start to his stallion career, with winners over a wide range of distances. Oscar Schindler has won two Irish St Legers as well as finishing in the frame in a King George VI and Queen Elizabeth Diamond Stakes and two Arcs, while Carmine Lake landed the 1997 Prix de l'Abbaye. Obviously, Sleepytime is another good winner of his, while his two-year-olds of 1997 included the useful pair Impressionist and Royal Shyness. Ali-Royal's dam has the notable distinction of having produced Group 1 winners with all of her first three foals. Further details of this remarkable family can be found in the essays on Sleepytime and Taipan.

Ali-Royal is a rather leggy colt, not an especially prepossessing individual (then neither are Taipan nor Sleepytime). Nor was he all that precocious,

46

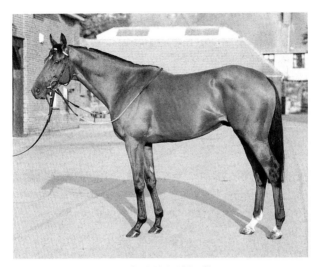

Greenbay Stables' "Ali-Royal"

though he did win a maiden at Warwick as a two-year-old and a listed race at Newmarket early the following season. He seemed well suited by around a mile and showed that he acted on going ranging from firm to good to soft (he didn't race on softer). He sometimes sweated, but was genuine. His stud fee will be IR 6,000 guineas. *H. R. A. Cecil*

ALISADARA   3 b.f. Nomination 125 – Nishara (Nishapour (FR) 125) [1996 –: a5g⁴ 6g⁴ 6d⁴ 6m 7m 6g⁵ 6m⁶ 7d 1997 6m⁴ 5m 6g 8.2d 7g 8g⁴ 7g⁴ 10m 5f 7m Oct 7] bad maiden: tried blinkered. *N. Bycroft*   23

ALISURA   4 br.f. Lead On Time (USA) 123 – Iosifa 108 (Top Ville 129) [1996 65: 10m⁵ 11.5g⁵ 12f³ 16m 14d a12g 1997 a10g 12g 16d 8m 14.1g Aug 21] sparely-made filly: modest maiden at best: soundly beaten last 6 starts: blinkered/visored last 2. *D. T. Thom*   –

ALJAZ   7 b.g. Al Nasr (FR) 126 – Santa Linda (USA) (Sir Ivor 135) [1996 52: 5s a6g⁴ a5g* a6g⁵ 5.1g a6g a5g² a5g⁵ 1997 a6g³ a5f² a6g⁶ a6g⁶ a5g² a6g a5g a5g² 6.1s a5g² Nov 29] modest handicapper: effective at 5f to 7f: acts on the all-weather and heavy ground: tried blinkered. *Miss Gay Kelleway*   60

AL JINN   6 ch.g. Hadeer 118 – Mrs Musgrove (Jalmood (USA) 126) [1996 NR 1997 a12g Jan 24] no longer of any account. *Martyn Wane*   –

ALLASELLA (IRE)   2 b.f. (Apr 17) Persian Bold 123 – Silks Princess 96 (Prince Tenderfoot (USA) 126) [1997 5d⁵ 5m 5.7m 5m⁴ 5.3g⁵ 6.1m 5.1g Oct 4] 9,500F: third foal: dam effective at 6f to 1m: disappointing maiden: fair form fifth and sixth starts, but finished last final 2. *B. Palling*   69 ?

ALLATON (IRE)   2 ch.g. (Mar 11) Shalford (IRE) 124§ – Confirmed Friend (Wolverlife 115) [1997 6d 5.1s⁶ 7.6d Aug 28] 10,000 2-y-o: second foal: dam unraced: well beaten in maidens. *Mrs P. Sly*   –

47

ALL

ALL DONE   4 ch.f. Northern State (USA) 91 – Doogali 93 (Doon 124) [1996 NR   –
1997 12m 12.1g May 26] sixth living foal: half-sister to 3 winners, including 5-y-o
Debutante Days and fairly useful stayer Mount Nelson (by Morston): dam won 9
times from 1m to 1¼m: placed all 3 starts in bumpers, but soundly beaten in maidens
in May. *S. Mellor*

ALLEMANDE (IRE)   5 b.h. Nashwan (USA) 135 – Dance Festival 101   –
(Nureyev (USA) 131) [1996 a7g³ a7f⁵ 1997 7g Oct 24] useful winner in 1995 for J.
Gosden: well beaten since, in Dubai in 1996. *Ronald Thompson*

ALLEZ CYRANO (IRE)   6 b.g. Alzao (USA) 117 – Miss Bergerac (Bold Lad   –
(IRE) 133) [1996 71: a7g* a7g⁴ a16g⁶ 8d² 6.9f 7d 1997 a12g⁵ a7g a8g⁶ Feb 28] leggy
gelding: triple 7f winner: no form in 1997. *O. O'Neill*

ALLEZ PABLO   7 b.g. Crisp 87 – Countess Mariga (Amboise 113) [1996 –: 8.1d   –
10f 9.7g⁶ 14m 14d 1997 a16g Mar 4] of little account. *R. Rowe*

ALL GIRLS FORGET   3 ch.f. Rock Hopper 124 – Happydrome (Ahonoora   –
122) [1996 NR 1997 10.5g⁵ 12s 11m Oct 28] first reported foal: dam unraced from
family of smart filly and good broodmare Triple First: well beaten in maiden and
claimers. *J. D. Bethell*

ALLGRIT (USA)   2 b.c. (Apr 22) Shadeed (USA) 135 – Arsaan (USA) 106   73 p
(Nureyev (USA) 131) [1997 7m 8m⁵ 8d Oct 16] tall, rangy colt with plenty of scope:
has a round action: fifth foal: dam 7f and listed 1m winner: showed ability in maidens
at Leicester and Goodwood in September and Newmarket (never placed to challenge): should still do better, probably in handicaps. *E. A. L. Dunlop*

ALLIED ACADEMY   3 ch.g. Royal Academy (USA) 130 – Tsungani 64 (Cure   57
The Blues (USA)) [1996 67p: 8g⁶ 6m⁶ 1997 a8.5g⁵ 8.2m⁶ 10m⁵ 11g Jun 20]
short-backed gelding: modest maiden: ran badly final start: stays 1m. *S. C. Williams*

ALLIED FORCES (USA)   4 ch.c. Miswaki (USA) 124 – Mangala (USA)   123
(Sharpen Up 127) [1996 8.5f* a9.5f 8.5f³ 8.5f* 9.5g 8.5f 9s 8.5s* 8.5f* 1997
8m* 10d⁴ 8m³ 10g⁶ 8g⁶ Sep 27]

Ten years on from riding his first winner in Britain, Frankie Dettori has
little left to prove but plenty he can still achieve. Three or even four decades in
the saddle is commonplace among other riders to have reached the top of the
tree in the post-war era, but Dettori has achieved a far higher profile than the
vast majority of them with his career still in its infancy by comparison. In the
wake of his 'Magnificent Seven' he has become a nationally-recognisable
celebrity. 1997 saw him turning on the Christmas lights in Regent Street as well
as appearing regularly on prime-time television.

On the track, Dettori was leading money earner for the third time in four
seasons but failed for the second time to regain the jockeys title he ran away
with in 1994 and 1995 (when his tallies made him only the third rider ever to
top two hundred winners in a season more than once). Kieren Fallon was
champion jockey. Dettori started the season 6/1-on to regain the title he lost
after injury in 1996, but international commitments and suspension hampered
his challenge. A sixth riding offence of the season, in a Newmarket maiden on
October 31st—coincidentally scheduled to be his last day's riding on turf in
Britain anyway—saw Dettori referred to Portman Square. Under the current
totting-up procedure, once a rider has accumulated fifteen days or more in local
bans (other than for misuse of the whip) the next offence automatically
becomes a matter for higher powers; Dettori had eighteen before Newmarket.
The Disciplinary Committee imposed a further fourteen-day ban to stand
worldwide. Had they applied it to British-racing days only, Dettori in effect
would have been banned merely from a period on the all-weather. Hardly a
punishment at all, considering he planned to be elsewhere. Instead, he missed
the Japan Cup and the lucrative Super Jockeys Series held there a week later.
He also had hanging over him a seven-day ban suspended for six months to
come into play should he reoffend in the interim. The stewards' decision was
considered harsh by some in the sporting press and contrasted with the leniency

shown by Formula One motor racing's governing body to Michael Schumacher after his collision with Jacques Villeneuve in the deciding race of the world drivers' championship. As Schumacher is to motor racing, Dettori is one of racing's most valuable assets, far better on the track than on the side-lines. But would the stewards' legitimate use of previously-agreed guidelines have batted many eye-lids had it been a less well-known jockey in front of them? Suspensions are part and parcel of racing for most jockeys, and the 8/1 offered about Dettori avoiding one in 1998 underestimates their frequency considerably.

Careless/irresponsible riding was at the root of Dettori's suspensions in the latest season. Press quotes suggested those closest to him felt he was in danger of 'burning out'. 'Riding in races is not an easy job. And a lot of the jockeys end up like zombies. They have to be extremely fit and the travelling is very taxing. And they do it all on an inadequate food diet,' said John Gosden. Five riders took more mounts in Britain during the season, including Fallon, but Dettori's contract with Sheikh Mohammed and his standing internationally added to his workload. He rode abroad more than thirty times during the British turf season. The day after his disqualification for irresponsible riding from Cape Cross in the Tripleprint Celebration Mile at Goodwood he rode in the Arlington Million in Chicago. In between he'd been at Windsor's Saturday night fixture, and he rode at Chepstow on the Monday! Dettori was still level-pegging with Fallon for the title at the time of his Cape Cross suspension, but five days for that offence and five more for a similarly-rash manoeuvre on the same course the following month saw him concede defeat before the closing weeks of the season. By all accounts, the championship won't be such a high priority for Dettori in 1998.

The vast majority of Dettori's twenty-two successes in European pattern races in 1997 (a total surpassed only by Olivier Peslier) were provided by Sheikh Mohammed or his Godolphin operation. Owner and jockey didn't fare at all well in the classics, however. Shamikh, Moonlight Paradise, Siyadah, Bold Demand and Haltarra finished no better than ninth between them. Dettori's career classic haul stands at five, one Two Thousand Guineas, two Oaks and two St Legers. Piggott had only eight at the same age—he rode the bulk of his classic winners in his 'thirties and early-'forties—but had to ride on until he was forty-eight to beat Frank Buckle's record on Commanche Run and was fifty-six when Rodrigo de Triano gave him his thirtieth and final success.

Queen Anne Stakes, Royal Ascot—
Allied Forces makes a successful return at the chief expense of Centre Stalls (blaze)

Dettori isn't so renowned as Piggott was for whip-cracking finishes, but the rules don't allow the whip to play the same part as in Piggott's day. Dettori's approach is very much the future of race-riding anyway, with the whip as a last resort, and though his crouching style isn't yet the dominant approach among leading riders, the latest season's champion apprentice Royston Ffrench—attached to the Cumani stable, as was Dettori as an apprentice—is in a similar mould.

A one-day suspension which fell on the Friday of the meeting made Dettori a relative outsider to be top jockey at Royal Ascot, but he belied his odds of 10/1 to take the London Clubs Charity Trophy for the first time with four winners. Allied Forces got him off to the ideal start in the opening Queen Anne Stakes. British racegoers hadn't seen Allied Forces since he'd shown smart form for Henry Cecil in four races as a two-year-old. In the meantime, he'd won four of eight races on turf for Godolphin trainer Kieran McLaughlin in the USA—he was down the field in the Preakness Stakes on dirt. None of his American successes came outside Grade 2 and Grade 3 events, and he looked to face a stiff task on his reappearance at Ascot, where he was penalized 3 lb. In a field of eleven, Lockinge Stakes runner-up Ali-Royal was favourite at 9/4, with Guineas disappointment Hidden Meadow at 5/1 and Wixim at 11/2. Allied Forces was at 10/1, but Dettori gave him a typically-astute ride, making his move first among the principals two furlongs out, and the pair held on all out by a neck from Centre Stalls with Ali-Royal, who'd stumbled when switched, just over another length back. Allied Forces was a first British pattern-race winner of the season for the Godolphin operation. He kept Group 1 company subsequently. His best placing was third in the Sussex Stakes at Goodwood, where he couldn't confirm the form with Ali-Royal, but kept on well to be beaten only a length and a half. In between, he ran respectably to be fourth of five in the Eclipse at Sandown, held up in a steadily-run race then plugging on without threatening the big guns He tried a mile and a quarter again on medication in the Arlington Million in Chicago, but could manage only sixth behind Marlin. He was probably past his best for the season when a fading sixth in the Queen Elizabeth II Stakes at Ascot's Festival of Racing.

		Mr Prospector	Raise A Native
	Miswaki (USA)	(b 1970)	Gold Digger
	(ch 1978)	Hopespringseternal	Buckpasser
Allied Forces (USA)		(ch 1971)	Rose Bower
(ch.c. 1993)		Sharpen Up	Atan
	Mangala (USA)	(ch 1969)	Rocchetta
	(ch 1982)	Meadow Blue	Raise A Native
		(ch 1975)	Gay Hostess

There isn't much to add to the details in *Racehorses of 1995* of Allied Forces' pedigree; his dam Mangala's three-year-old filly by Siberian Express won at around a mile in the USA in the latest season. He's easily one of the best products of his sire Miswaki, along with the Arc winner Urban Sea and the Breeders' Cup Classic winner Black Tie Affair. Allied Forces often takes the eye, but can tend to get on edge and sweat, and ran well when doing so markedly at Goodwood. He acts on firm and soft ground, and is probably best at around a mile, though as we've said he's not been discredited over a mile and a quarter. A good mover with a long stride, he's probably best with waiting tactics. He stays in training. *Saeed bin Suroor*

ALL IN LEATHER 3 b.f. Saddlers' Hall (IRE) 126 – Ivana (IRE) 82 (Taufan –
(USA) 119) [1996 76: 6g³ 7.6m³ 7f³ 1997 a9.4g* 10m⁴ 9s Aug 29] easily best effort a85
when very easy winner of weak Wolverhampton maiden in August: very disappointing back on turf later in month: stays 9.4f: sold 10,500 gns in October. *W. J. Haggas*

ALLINSON'S MATE (IRE) 9 b.g. Fayruz 116 – Piney Pass (Persian Bold 123) 70
[1996 70: a6g⁶ a7g⁴ a7g a7g⁵ 7s⁵ 7.5m 8g 7g 7.1g 7g⁴ 7g⁴ 7m⁶ 7m 8.1g⁴ 7.1g*
7.1m³ 7m⁶ 7m 7m⁴ 8g⁴ 7g⁶ 7g* 7g⁵ a8g³ a7g 1997 a8g⁶ 7g⁵ 7d 6.9d* 7s⁶ 7m* 6.9f⁴

7g² 6.9m³ 7s 7g 7m² 7.5g 6.9f⁶ 7m⁴ 7f 7s Oct 17] small, robust gelding: carries condition: unimpressive mover: fair performer: successful at Carlisle (claimer) and Doncaster (apprentices handicap) in May: effective at 7f to 8.5f: acts on firm ground, dead and the all-weather: effective blinkered/visored or not: held up, and suited by strongly-run race: usually ridden by claimers Victoria Appleby/Kimberley Hart: tough. *T. D. Barron*

ALL IS FAIR   3 b.f. Selkirk (USA) 129 – Allegra 73 (Niniski (USA) 125) [1996   91
79p: 6m³ 6f* 7g 1997 7g² 7f⁵ 7.3d⁴ 7m⁵ 7s⁶ Oct 20] good-topped filly: fairly useful performer: in frame in handicaps and creditable efforts in listed events in second half of 1997: has raced freely, but should stay 1m: acts on firm and dead going, probably on soft. *Sir Mark Prescott*

ALL MADE UP (USA)   2 b.c. (Mar 18) Sheikh Albadou 128 – Mascara Miss   70
(USA) (Fio Rito (USA)) [1997 8s⁵ 8d Oct 28] tall colt: has scope: fourth foal: dam minor winner of 3 races in USA: burly, slow-starting fifth of 17 to Mantusis in maiden at Leicester: behind in similar event there later in month. *M. Bell*

ALLMAITES   2 b.g. (Feb 13) Komaite (USA) – Darling Miss Daisy 77 (Tina's   59 +
Pet 121) [1997 5m 5.1m⁵ 7g 6s 5g³ Sep 15] 1,200F, 8,000Y: workmanlike gelding: has a round action: first foal: dam 2-y-o 5f winner: modest maiden: best effort in nursery at Musselburgh final start: should prove as effective at 6f as 5f. *D. Nicholls*

ALL ON   6 ch.m. Dunbeath (USA) 127 – Fresh Line 60 (High Line 125) [1996 37,   60
a59: 16.2m⁵ a12g² a12g* 12g⁵ a14g 1997 16.1g³ a14g a14.8g² 21.6g* 12m* 13s³ 14.1s* a12g³ 16.1m⁵ 18d³ 14.6g³ 16s Nov 6] workmanlike mare: modest handicapper: in cracking form in the spring, winning at Pontefract, Musselburgh and Carlisle within space of 12 days: had a couple of lengthy breaks afterwards, best effort when third of 22 at Doncaster penultimate outing: stays extremely well: acts on good to firm and soft going as well as fibresand (unraced on equitrack): front runner/races prominently: tough and genuine. *J. Hetherton*

ALL OUR BLESSINGS (IRE)   2 b.f. (Apr 16) Statoblest 120 – Zenga (Try My   –
Best (USA) 130) [1997 6s 5m 7m Nov 4] IR 5,500F, 21,000Y: smallish filly: seventh foal: closely related to Nell Gwyn winner A-To-Z (by Ahonoora) and half-sister to a winner abroad: dam Italian 5f to 7f winner: no promise in autumn maidens. *P. C. Haslam*

ALL STAND   4 ch.f. Dominion 123 – Now In Session (USA) (Diesis 133) [1996   –
58: 7d 7m⁵ 7f 10s 1997 8.3s May 12] angular filly: modest maiden: ran poorly only outing in 1997: should stay beyond 7f. *Major D. N. Chappell*

ALLSTARS DANCER   4 b.f. Primo Dominie 121 – Danzig Harbour (USA)   –
(Private Account) [1996 35: a7g⁵ a6g⁴ 7.6m 6m 5g 1997 a6g⁵ a7g² a6g⁴ a5g²   a37
a5g a6g⁶ 5.3m 7g⁶ a5g⁶ Dec 22] poor handicapper: stays 7f: acts on equitrack. *T. J. Naughton*

ALLSTARS EXPRESS   4 b.g. Rambo Dancer (CAN) 107 – Aligote (Nebbiolo   –
125) [1996 70: 7g a8g³ 8g³ 10f* 9f³ 10g⁵ 10f² 10.8f* 11.5f⁴ 10f³ 8f⁴ 8.5g⁶ 11.5m⁴ a12g⁵ a12g³ a10g² 1997 9.7m Apr 10] fair handicapper at 3 yrs for T. J. Naughton: below form only outing in 1997: stays 1½m: acts on firm and equitrack: consistent, but tends to wander under pressure and has found little. *K. C. Bailey*

ALLWIGHT THEN (IRE)   6 gr.g. Dancing Dissident (USA) 119 – Abergwrle   –
(Absalom 128) [1996 69d, a–: a5g 5g 5.3f² 5.1g 5m⁵ 5.1m 5m 5.1d 6m⁴ 6d⁵ a6g 6m 1997 5m 5m Jun 19] neat, good-quartered gelding: has a quick action: fair handicapper at best: well beaten both starts in 1997: stays 6f: acts on firm ground: blinkered (no improvement) twice at 4 yrs: often a front runner: inconsistent. *T. D. Barron*

AL MABROOK (IRE)   2 b.c. (Mar 28) Rainbows For Life (CAN) – Sky Lover   75 +
(Ela-Mana-Mou 132) [1997 6m 6.1g⁶ 6g⁵ 5.3m² Aug 16] 4,000 2-y-o: leggy colt: closely related to fairly useful Irish 3-y-o 1½m winner Rainbow Warrior (by Imperial Frontier): dam Irish 2-y-o 5f winner: fair maiden: best effort when fifth at Newmarket, hanging left: probably found trip too short when second at Brighton 2 weeks later: should stay beyond 6f. *K. Mahdi*

ALMANDAB (IRE)   2 b. or br.c. (Feb 8) Last Tycoon 131 – Fortune Teller (Troy   97 P
137) [1997 8m⁵ 8.2d* Oct 30] IR 65,000Y: big, rangy colt with scope: sixth foal:

half-brother to 1m winner Water Gypsy (by Dowsing): dam unraced half-sister to 2 Galtres Stakes winners and daughter of another: highly promising colt: needed experience badly on debut, and later in month won maiden at Nottingham most impressively by 9 lengths from Free As The Wind, slowly away but soon going strongly behind good pace and quickening clear immediately 3f out, still green and kept up to work: will be well suited by 1¼m+: almost certainly has a deal more improvement in him, and could develop into a classic contender. *J. H. M. Gosden*

ALMASI (IRE)   5 b.m. Petorius 117 – Best Niece 84 (Vaigly Great 127) [1996 72: 7s 6.1g 6.1m* 6g² 6g* 6g³ 6d⁴ 6m² 6m 6d³ 6m 7m 1997 6.1g 7d 6.1g² 6g* 6s* 6g² 6m² 6m* 6d* 6g² 6m³ Oct 3] sparely-made mare: impresses in appearance: useful performer, better than ever: won handicaps at Doncaster and Salisbury in June and Newbury (apprentice) in August and minor event at Haydock in September: good second in Ayr Silver Cup (to Perryston View) and third in handicap at Newmarket last 2 starts: suited by 6f: acts on good to firm and soft ground: sometimes slowly away, and comes from behind: tough and consistent. *C. F. Wall*   96

AL MASROOR (USA)   3 b.c. Red Ransom (USA) – Gaye's Delight (USA) (Imperial Falcon (CAN)) [1996 65p: 7.1m 7m 6.1m⁵ 1997 7g 7m⁵ 7d 8m* 8g² 8m⁶ 7.1m³ 8d³ 8.1s 8.1m 7.1g² 7m Nov 1] tall, well-made colt: has a round action: fairly useful handicapper: won at Ripon in June: mostly creditable efforts after: effective at 7f and 1m: acts on good to firm going and dead. *J. W. Payne*   80

ALMATY (IRE)   4 b.c. Dancing Dissident (USA) 119 – Almaaseh (IRE) 63 (Dancing Brave (USA) 140) [1996 110: 5g⁴ 5f³ 5m 1997 5.1m³ 5m* 5d 5m 5d 5m² 5.2g 5m⁶ Oct 2] well-made ex-Irish colt: smart performer on his day: made all in well-contested listed race at Kempton (beat Compton Place by 2½ lengths) in May: good second to Bollin Joanne in listed race at Doncaster in September: ran badly all other starts in 1997, leaving J. Gosden after seventh: speedy: acts on firm going, below form on dead: visored (reportedly lame) final 3-y-o outing and on penultimate start: has worn tongue strap: can't be relied on. *W. R. Muir*   113 §

Britain's Fastest Railway Park Stakes, Doncaster—
Almushtarak is hard pressed by Decorated Hero (left) and Samara

ALMAZHAR (IRE) 2 b.c. (Apr 20) Last Tycoon 131 – Mosaique Bleue (Shirley – p
Heights 130) [1997 8m Sep 22] IR 44,000Y: third foal: half-brother to fairly useful
Irish 3-y-o 9f winner Poker School (by Night Shift): dam unraced half-sister to Prix
Royal-Oak winner Mersey and Prix Saint-Alary winner Muncie: 12/1, towards rear
in 17-runner maiden at Kempton, never dangerous after very slow start, not knocked
about: should do better, particularly over more than 1m. *E. A. L. Dunlop*

ALMOND ROCK 5 b.g. Soviet Star (USA) 128 – Banket 120 (Glint of Gold 100
128) [1996 101: 8.1g² 8m² 8d* 10g⁵ 9m 1997 8g⁴ 8g 9s³ 8g 7.6s⁵ 8d Sep 20] strong,
lengthy gelding: takes the eye in appearance: shows a rather round action: useful
handicapper: best effort at 5 yrs, despite being forced to race wide throughout, when
fifth of 18 at Chester in August: probably stays 1¼m: has form on firm going, raced
mainly on good ground and softer nowadays: usually held up. *J. R. Fanshawe*

AL MUALLIM (USA) 3 b.c. Theatrical 128 – Gerri N Jo Go (USA) (Top 98 p
Command (USA)): 6m⁴ 6g* 1997 6g⁴ 6m* 7m³ 7f² 7m* Oct 3] compact
colt: lightly-raced handicapper, useful already: won at Lingfield in August and
Newmarket in October, in latter always close up in slowly-run race and quickening
well to beat Madly Sharp 1¾ lengths: effective at 6f/7f: acts on firm going, yet to race
on ground softer than good: should do well again in 1998. *J. W. Payne*

ALMUHIMM (USA) 5 ch.g. Diesis 133 – Abeesh (USA) 77 (Nijinsky (CAN) 89
138) [1996 92: 7m³ 7m² 6d⁵ 7m* 7m* 7m⁴ 8m 7m 7g⁶ 7m 1997 7g 7m⁵ 7m* 7g⁵ 6g
7f Sep 11] big, rangy gelding: fairly useful handicapper: won at Ayr in July: left T. D.
Barron after penultimate start: best at 7f/1m: best form on good to firm going: keen
sort, often slowly away and usually held up. *M. W. Easterby*

ALMUHTARAM 5 b.g. Rambo Dancer (CAN) 107 – Mrs Mainwaring (FR) 64 64 d
(Home Guard (USA) 129) [1996 72, a80: a9.4g⁴ a10g² a10g² a10g⁵ 12g⁴ 10f⁴ 10g
12.1m⁴ 11f* 10m⁴ 11.6g 11f² 11m³ 12g⁴ᵈⁱˢ 12g² a12g² 1997 12m 12.3m 12m³ 12.3v
12g 11.9f³ 14.1g 14m⁵ 11.5g⁵ Aug 2] strong, good-bodied gelding: good mover:
modest form at best at 5 yrs: stays 1½m: acts on firm ground and the all-weather:
usually blinkered nowadays: has been bandaged: sent to Italy. *G. Lewis*

ALMUROOJ 2 b.f. (Apr 16) Zafonic (USA) 130 – Al Bahathri (USA) 123 – p
(Blushing Groom (FR) 131) [1997 6m Oct 4] compact filly: eighth foal: half-sister to
several winners up to 1m, including 3-y-o Za-Im, useful Goalwah (stayed 1¼m, by
Sadler's Wells) and smart Hasbah (by Kris): dam won Lowther Stakes and Irish 1000
Guineas: 11/2 from 3/1, gave impression something amiss when ninth of 10 in
maiden at Newmarket, tracking pace until losing action around 2f out: should prove
capable of better. *B. W. Hills*

ALMUSHTARAK (IRE) 4 b.c. Fairy King (USA) – Exciting (Mill Reef (USA) 112
141) [1996 108: 7m* 7m³ 7m⁴ 7.6f* 7m 1997 8.5g⁵ 6g 7d² 8.1g 7.3m⁵ 6m³ 8.5g² 8f*
7d 7g Oct 18] good-quartered colt: smart performer: 25/1, gained a deserved win
under good ride from R. Cochrane in Britain's Fastest Railway Park Stakes at
Doncaster in September, beating Decorated Hero (gave 4 lb) by a neck: likely to
prove best up to 8.5f: acts on firm and dead ground, yet to race on anything softer:
usually held up: game. *K. Mahdi*

ALMUTAWAKEL 2 b.c. (Jan 19) Machiavellian (USA) 123 – Elfaslah (IRE) 104
107 (Green Desert (USA) 127) [1997 7.1d* 7g* 8d² 8g⁵ Sep 28] tall, angular colt:
has scope: third foal: half-brother to fairly useful 7f and 1¼m winner Mawjud (by
Mujtahid): dam, winner 3 times around 1¼m, half-sister to White Muzzle: useful
form: won maiden at Sandown in July and 2-runner minor event at Newmarket (from
Mijana) in August: second in 5-runner listed race won by Alboostan at Goodwood
and fifth of 8 in Royal Lodge Stakes won by Teapot Row at Ascot, beaten only about
a length in latter: will probably be suited by further than 1m. *Saeed bin Suroor*

ALOSAILI 10 ch.g. Kris 135 – Vaison La Romaine 100 (Arctic Tern (USA) 126) –
[1996 NR 1997 a12g Jan 18] probably of no account nowadays. *J. Cullinan*

ALPEN WOLF (IRE) 2 ch.g. (Feb 5) Wolfhound (USA) 126 – Oatfield 69 68
(Great Nephew 126) [1997 5d⁵ 5d⁶ 6g 5.1m⁵ 5m 5m⁶ 6m Sep 9] 17,000Y: sturdy,
rather dipped-backed gelding: half-brother to numerous winners, including 4-y-o
Oatey and smart pair by Kalaglow, Munwar (up to 11.5f) and Hateel (middle-

distance stayer): dam out of half-sister to High Line: fair maiden: best efforts at 5f: visored sixth/seventh starts, running well first time. *W. R. Muir*

ALPHABET 3 b.f. Saddlers' Hall (IRE) 126 – A-To-Z (IRE) 101 (Ahonoora 122) 87 [1996 80+: 7g² 8.1m² 8.2g 1997 7m 8.3g* 8.3m⁴ 7f Sep 11] smallish, good-topped filly: fairly useful performer: won maiden at Windsor in August: fitted with net muzzle, disappointing final start: stays 1m: raced only on good going or firmer: often bandaged behind: sold (to go to USA) 30,000 gns in October. *M. R. Stoute*

ALPHA WHISKY (GER) 2 gr.f. (Mar 26) Wolfhound (USA) 126 – Alsiba 68 67 (Northfields (USA)) [1997 5g⁵ 5.7m³ 5.2m⁵ 6d² 6.1m 5.7f³ Sep 29] leggy filly: has a round action: seventh foal: half-sister to 2 winners, including fairly useful 1¼m and 1½m winner Smart Blade (by Elegant Air): dam, stayer, half-sister to dam of Oscar Schindler: fair maiden: should stay further than 6f: acts on good to soft and good to firm ground (hung right throughout on firm final start): sold (to go to Holland) 7,000 gns in October. *I. A. Balding*

ALPHETON PRINCE 4 b.g. Prince of Cill Dara – Batsam Lady (Battle Hymn – 103) [1996 –: a8g a6g 8.2d⁵ 9.9g 1997 a8g 10g⁶ May 17] small gelding: bad mover: little sign of ability. *John A. Harris*

ALPINA (USA) 3 b.f. El Prado (IRE) 119 – Aspara (USA) 58 (Crimson Satan) 69 [1996 NR 1997 10g⁶ 12.3g⁶ 10.1s⁵ 12g Aug 22] $55,000Y: big, good-topped filly: half-sister to several winners, including useful Hot Princess (up to 9f, by Hot Spark), later the dam of Rodrigo de Triano: dam sprint maiden: fair form: may prove best short of 1½m. *J. H. M. Gosden*

ALPINE HIDEAWAY (IRE) 4 b.g. Tirol 127 – Arbour (USA) 76 (Graustark) 80 [1996 80: 7.1g² 6.9f² 7.6g 6m² 7m 6d³ 7m² 6m⁵ 8m⁶ 7f* 7g 1997 6d³ 8d 8m³ 8g 7s a7g* 7m³ a7g 7m⁶ 8m* 12f 8.1g 8m² 8m³ 8s Nov 6] useful-looking gelding: has a round action: fair performer: won claimers at Southwell and Ripon (claimed out of B. Hanbury's stable) in the summer: best effort for present trainer when third of 25 in handicap at Redcar in October: stays 1m, not 1½m: acts on firm and dead ground and fibresand: ran poorly blinkered: has been bandaged: races keenly. *M. W. Easterby*

ALPINE MUSIC (IRE) 3 b.g. Tirol 127 – Holy Devotion (Commanche Run – 133) [1996 –: 7.1f 5.7d 1997 6.1d 8.2g 6.1m 8g 6.1d⁶ 7.1m Jul 25] no form: tried blinkered. *J. M. Bradley*

ALPINE PANTHER (IRE) 4 b.g. Tirol 127 – Kentucky Wildcat 64 (Be My 66 Guest (USA) 126) [1996 65: 7s⁶ 7g 6.9m 10m³ 9g³ 1997 10g⁵ 8g⁶ 8d 10.9d 14g² 14.1g 16s Nov 6] tall gelding: modest maiden: stays 1¾m: acts on good to firm ground. *Mrs M. Reveley*

ALPINE TIME (IRE) 3 b.f. Tirol 127 – Millie Musique (Miller's Mate 116) 85 [1996 80: 5m* 6g² 6m* 6m⁴ 1997 7.1g⁴ 8d 8g Jul 10] leggy filly: good mover: fairly useful performer: off course over 11 months before reappearance: very disappointing both subsequent starts: bred to stay at least 1m: acts on good to firm ground. *D. R. Loder*

ALRABYAH (IRE) 2 br.c. (Apr 20) Brief Truce (USA) 126 – Bean Siamsa – (Solinus 130) [1997 6s 7g Oct 24] IR 45,000Y: compact colt: half-brother to several winners, including a fairly useful 2-y-o 5f winner by Bluebird and smart Irish 9f and 1¼m winner Cherry Grove Lad (by Caerleon): dam unraced: well beaten in maidens at York and Doncaster (swished tail in paddock). *P. T. Walwyn*

AL REET (IRE) 6 b.m. Alzao (USA) 117 – Reet Petite (Thatching 131) [1996 –: 58 8s 6g 7m 8.5m 8.1d 7g 1997 a5g 6.1d a5g⁶ 6.1g 7g a6g³ 7d⁴ 8g² a7g⁵ a6g 7.5g 8.2d 8d 6g 8.2d³ a7g a8g⁵ Nov 17] sturdy mare: modest handicapper nowadays: won at Doncaster in June: in-and-out form after: stays 1m: acts on good to firm and soft ground and on fibresand: tried blinkered and visored. *S. R. Bowring*

ALSAHIB (USA) 4 b.g. Slew O' Gold (USA) – Khwlah (USA) 99 (Best Turn 64 (USA)) [1996 73: 8m 10.5d⁵ 10m⁴ 10.5v 8d² 8g 1997 8f⁶ 8m 8s⁶ a9.4g²* a8.5f⁶ 10s³ a81 10.5g 10g a8.5g a12g² Nov 29] big, robust gelding: fairly useful handicapper on the all-weather, just modest on turf: won at Wolverhampton in June: good second on same course final start: stays 1½m: acts on firm and soft ground and on fibresand: has had tongue tied. *W. R. Muir*

AL'S ALIBI   4 b.c. Alzao (USA) 117 – Lady Kris (IRE) (Kris 135) [1996 82:   80
10.3s⁶ 10g⁵ 12d* 12.3g 12d⁵ 1997 11.9s⁴ 12g 11.9s² 16s⁶ 12d 12m* 12g 12.3d⁴ 13.1d
12g Sep 28] sturdy colt: has pronounced knee action: fairly useful handicapper:
in-and-out form at 4 yrs, winning at Carlisle in August: seems best around 1½m: acts
on good to firm and soft going: sold 8,500 gns in October. *W. R. Muir*

AL'S FELLA (IRE)   2 br.c. (Feb 21) Alzao (USA) 117 – Crystal Cross (USA) 88   68
(Roberto (USA) 131) [1997 5d³ 7d⁴ 7m⁶ 7d⁶ 8g 8d 8.2d² a8g⁶ Nov 18] IR 42,000Y:
workmanlike colt: first foal: dam, 11.6f to 1¾m winner, half-sister to very smart 6f/
7f performer Iktamal: fair maiden: should be suited by at least 1¼m: has ungainly
head carriage and doesn't look easiest of rides. *P. F. I. Cole*

AL SHAATI (FR)   7 b.m. Lead On Time (USA) 123 – With You All (Free Round   –
(USA) [1996 37: a6g a8g a6g 7g 5.1f⁴ a6g a7g 1997 a7g Jan 9] poor handicapper:
stayed 1m: acted on firm and soft ground, and on equitrack: tried blinkered: dead.
R. J. O'Sullivan

ALTHIB (IRE)   2 ch.c. (Feb 25) Wolfhound (USA) 126 – Sure Enough (IRE)   83 d
(Diesis 133) [1997 6s² 6m⁴ 6.1s⁶ 5m⁵ Sep 16] 75,000Y: rangy colt: good mover:
second foal: half-brother to 3-y-o Sarabi: dam (unraced) from family of Sure Blade
and Sure Sharp: odds on, second of 6 in maiden at Yarmouth on debut: disappointing
afterwards, twice finding little: visored final start: sold 28,000 gns in October.
M. R. Stoute

ALTIBR (USA)   2 ch.c. (Mar 1) Diesis 133 – Love's Reward (Nonoalco (USA)   103 p
131) [1997 7g* Oct 27] $300,000F: big, strong, rangy colt: fluent mover, though
shows knee action: brother to 2 winners, notably very smart sprinter Keen Hunter,
and half-brother to 2 others: dam lightly-raced half-sister to Bassenthwaite: paddock
pick, landed the odds with plenty in hand in 13-runner Leicester maiden, though
looked very green (almost to point of waywardness), edging right when asked to
quicken clear then propping near post but still beating Lonesome Dude by 2 lengths
(rated value 4): will probably prove best up to 1m: has deal of physical scope, and
should go on to better things if his temperament holds. *Saeed bin Suroor*

ALTITUDE (IRE)   2 b.c. (May 5) Alzao (USA) 117 – Elevate 98 (Ela-Mana-Mou   – p
132) [1997 7m 8f⁶ 9m Sep 26] IR 35,000Y: good-topped colt: sixth foal: half-brother
to several winners, including fair 6f winner Hoist (by Bluebird) and French 1½m
winner Upper Gallery (by Sadler's Wells): dam, 1½m winner, half-sister to Sun
Princess and Saddlers' Hall: well beaten in maidens, but has scope and should do
better. *Sir Mark Prescott*

ALUMISIYAH (USA)   3 b. or br.f. Danzig (USA) – Mathkurh (USA) 97   93
(Riverman (USA) 131) [1996 80p: 5.3f* 6f³ 1997 6s² 6m 6g 6s* 6g³ 6s Nov 8]
close-coupled, deep-girthed filly: fairly useful handicapper: won 22-runner event at
Haydock in October, leading halfway: staying-on third of 20 at Newcastle week later,
racing in disadvantageous centre: stiff task final outing: raced only at 5f/6f (not bred
to stay much further): acted on firm and soft ground: visits Zafonic. *R. W. Armstrong*

ALVILDE   3 b.f. Alzao (USA) 117 – Volida 105 (Posse (USA) 130) [1996 70: 5m⁵   65 d
6.1m⁶ 5g⁵ 1997 a7g² a8g² a7g⁴ a8.5g⁴ a8g⁵ 8.2m⁶ Apr 11] small filly: fluent mover:
fair maiden at best: well below form after reappearance: should prove best up to 7f:
has had tongue tied: sent to Czech Republic. *D. J. S. Cosgrove*

ALWARQA   4 b.f. Old Vic 136 – Ostora (USA) 83 (Blushing Groom (FR) 131)   55 d
[1996 69: 8.2d 12m⁶ 11.6m⁵ 17.2g² 14.1f* 14.1f² 12f³ 12m a12g⁶ 17.5m 17.1m* 18g
1997 16d 18g 16.1g⁶ 16m⁴ 16.2m 16m 16m⁵ 12f⁵ 15.8m a14g⁶ a14g Nov 17] sturdy
filly: carries condition: has a long stride: on the downgrade in 1997, capable of modest form only on occasions: trained on reappearance by Miss J. Bower and second to
ninth starts by M. Wane: out-and-out stayer: best form on good to firm/firm going:
pulled up only try in blinkers. *N. P. Littmoden*

ALWAYS ALIGHT   3 ch.g. Never So Bold 135 – Fire Sprite 83 (Mummy's Game   87
120) [1996 60: 5.1m 7g a6g 6.9d 6g³ 6v³ 1997 7m 6.1m² 6g² 6.1d 6s⁴ 6m* 6f² 6d*
6m³ 7m 6g³ 6g⁶ 6s⁵ 6g* 6m³ Nov 4] good-bodied gelding: fairly useful handicapper:
had good season, winning at Newbury in May, Goodwood in June and Newcastle in
October, and running well most other starts: best form at 6f: acts on any turf ground:

has been blinkered (not after fourth start): tough and genuine: could go on again at 4 yrs. *K. R. Burke*

ALWAYS GRACE 5 b.m. Never So Bold 135 – Musical Sally (USA) (The Minstrel (CAN) 135) [1996 64, a54: a6g⁶ a6g⁵ 6.1g⁵ 6m 6f 6g* 7f³ 6m 6m* 6f⁵ 7m⁶ 7f 1997 6m⁶ 5.3f⁴ 6m⁴ 7.1m⁶ 6m Oct 1] strong mare: shows knee action: modest performer: mostly disappointing at 5 yrs: stays 7f: acts on all-weather and firm ground, well beaten on heavy: inconsistent. *Miss Gay Kelleway*   58 a–

ALWAYS HAPPY 4 ch.f. Sharrood (USA) 124 – Convivial 81 (Nordance (USA)) [1996 73: 10g⁶ 8.5g 10.8f⁶ 8m* 1997 a12g² a10g⁶ 8f⁶ May 23] unfurnished filly: has a fluent, round action: fair performer: likely to prove best at 1¼m/1½m: acts on equitrack, raced only on good going or firmer on turf: none too consistent. *Miss Gay Kelleway*   75

ALWAYS LOYAL (USA) 3 b. or br.f. Zilzal (USA) 137 – Balbonella (FR) 120 (Gay Mecene (USA) 128) [1996 98p: 7.5s* 1997 8g* 8d* 10.5d⁶ 9.5g⁵ 9.3f Oct 5]   113

After thirty-four years in the saddle, during which time he rode nearly three thousand winners and was champion jockey in France on numerous occasions, Freddie Head announced his surprise decision to retire after winning the Prix de Tourgeville at Deauville in August on Marathon, a colt trained by his sister Criquette for their father Alec. Freddie had won all the top French races at least once, including the Arc (on Bon Mot in 1966, San San in 1972, Ivanjica in 1976 and Three Troikas in 1979), the Prix du Jockey-Club and Prix de Diane on four occasions each and the Prix Jacques Le Marois six times, twice with Miesque. The partnership with Miesque also brought two Breeders' Cup Miles and the One Thousand Guineas, the jockey's third English classic after Zino in the 1982 Two Thousand Guineas and Ma Biche in the One Thousand a year later. Head's name was at one time most readily associated in Britain with his steering problems on Lyphard at Tattenham Corner in the 1972 Derby. But he gained further wins in the best company on this side of the channel with Green Dancer in the 1974 Observer Gold Cup, Ma Biche in the 1982 Cheveley Park Stakes, Pas de Reponse in the same race in 1996 and the same year's July Cup with Anabaa.

It was Anabaa's half-sister Always Loyal who provided Freddie Head with the final Group 1 winner of his career in the Poule d'Essai des Pouliches. The latest running was a poor one by classic standards, certainly compared to some of the contests won by Head's seven previous winners which included the

Dubai Poule d'Essai des Pouliches, Longchamp—
Always Loyal (right) edges ahead of Seebe (noseband) and Red Camellia

top-class fillies Ivanjica, Three Troikas and Miesque. Only one other French-trained filly, Mousse Glacee, joined Always Loyal in the seven-runner line-up. Always Loyal had won her only start at two, a seven-and-a-half furlong event at Saint-Cloud in November, and despite having had a head to spare over Mousse Glacee on their reappearances in the Prix de La Grotte over the Poule d'Essai course and distance three weeks beforehand, it was the latter who started favourite. Always Loyal was coupled in the betting with the Godolphin pair Nightbird and Star Profile but it was the three other British fillies who came closest to spoiling Always Loyal's unbeaten record. Never far away, she battled gamely and nosed ahead near the line to beat Seebe a head with Red Camellia and Dances With Dreams only a length or so back.

Always Loyal failed to make the frame in her three remaining starts. She ran up to her best on her next two outings but it was good enough only to see her into sixth place in the Prix de Diane (Mousse Glacee, who'd finished sixth in the Poule d'Essai, taking second this time) and fifth place behind the very smart American fillies Memories of Silver and Maxzene in the Beverly D Stakes at Arlington. Always Loyal's season ended back at Longchamp in the autumn when she finished seventh in a competitive Prix de L'Opera, performing a little below her best.

		Nureyev	Northern Dancer
Always Loyal (USA) (b. or br.f. 1994)	Zilzal (USA) (ch 1986)	(b 1977)	Special
		French Charmer (ch 1978)	Le Fabuleux / Bold Example
	Balbonella (FR) (b or br 1984)	Gay Mecene (b 1975)	Vaguely Noble / Gay Missile
		Bamieres (br 1978)	Riverman / Bergamesque

Maktoum Al Maktoum's "Always Loyal"

ALW

Always Loyal, a tall filly who impressed in appearance when we saw her at Longchamp in both the spring and the autumn, stayed ten and a half furlongs and probably acted on any ground. Her emergence on the classic scene wasn't entirely unheralded; that win as a two-year-old earned her a mention in Anabaa's essay in *Racehorses of 1996* where full details of her breeding may be found. Her dam Balbonella won the Prix Robert Papin at two, was fourth in Miesque's Poule d'Essai des Pouliches at three (when her best form was at short of a mile) but was successful in a Grade 3 eight-and-a-half furlong handicap in the United States at four. Balbonella's first foal, Key of Luck (by Chief's Crown), showed high-class form again in the latest season as a six-year-old when fourth to Singspiel in the Dubai World Cup a year after winning the main supporting race on the same card by twenty lengths. Balbonella's latest foals, Country Belle (a two-year-old filly by Seattle Slew) and a yearling sister to champion sprinter Anabaa (by Danzig) have a bright future if the achievements of the rest of the family are anything to go by. The same can be said of Freddie Head in his new career as a trainer. *Mme C. Head, France*

ALWAYS LUCKY 2 gr.f. (May 4) Absalom 128 – Petitesse 55 (Petong 126) 71 d [1997 5m³ 5f⁵ a5g* 5m² 5g³ 5m² a6g* 5d² 5m⁵ a6g⁴ Oct 18] 10,000Y: third foal: dam, 5f and 6f winner, sister to Paris House: fair performer: won maiden in May and claimer in July, both at Southwell: below form last 3 starts: stays 6f: acts on good to firm ground and fibresand: front runner. *J. Berry*

ALWAYS ON MY MIND 3 b.f. Distant Relative 128 – Fleur Rouge 71 (Pharly 91 p (FR) 130) [1996 75p: 6m⁴ 1997 7m 6m² 6s* 6g* 6g* 6d 6m* Nov 1] tall filly: fairly useful and progressive performer: successful in maiden at Warwick and handicaps at Newmarket and Doncaster in July and minor event at Newmarket (made all, beating Distinctive Dream by 1¼ lengths) in November: stays 6f (pulled hard at 7f): acts on good to firm ground and soft: carries head high but genuine: races prominently: capable of better still. *P. J. Makin*

ALWAYS TRYING 2 b.g. (Apr 5) Always Fair (USA) 121 – Bassita (Bustino 47 136) [1997 6d 8.3g² 8m Nov 1] 65,000 francs Y, 6,400 2-y-o: brother to French 3-y-o 10.5f and 1½m winner Baldaccini: dam unraced half-sister to Pebbles: remote second in maiden at Hamilton in September: well beaten in seller at Newmarket 5 weeks later. *M. Johnston*

ALZAHRA 2 ch.f. (May 1) Interrex (CAN) – Flirty Lady (Never So Bold 135) – [1997 7g Oct 27] second reported foal: dam unraced: 33/1, backward and never on terms (tenderly handled) in Leicester maiden: may do better. *J. G. Smyth-Osbourne*

ALZOTIC (IRE) 4 b.g. Alzao (USA) 117 – Exotic Bride (USA) (Blushing 35 Groom (FR) 131) [1996 –: 7d 10.3m 10g 12s⁶ 14.1m 15.8g 1997 16m 14g⁴ 12s Oct 16] sturdy gelding: poor maiden: tried visored at 3 yrs. *J. Norton*

AMABEL (USA) 2 b.f. (May 7) Silver Hawk (USA) 123 – Routilante 96 95 (Rousillon (USA) 133) [1997 6m 7g 7d* 7m⁶ 7.3g² Oct 25] smallish, useful-looking filly: has a round action: second foal: dam 2-y-o 6f winner, stayed 7f, probably ungenuine: useful form: won minor event at Newbury in September: better effort when length second of 13 to Ffestiniog in listed event at same course: will stay 1m: best form on good/good to soft going: flashes tail. *I. A. Balding*

AMADOUR (IRE) 4 b.g. Contract Law (USA) 108 – Truly Flattering (Hard – Fought 125) [1996 71: 8d² 9f² 10g³ 11.4m⁵ 11.9g* 11.9g 1997 a12g* 12m 16g a10g⁵ a72 11.6g⁵ Jun 2] workmanlike gelding: fair handicapper: won at Lingfield in February: should stay beyond 1½m: best form on equitrack and good going. *P. Mitchell*

AMANY (IRE) 5 b.m. Waajib 121 – Treeline 59 (High Top 131) [1996 NR 1997 – 9.2d 6.1g May 23] probably no longer of any account. *D. Burchell*

AMARELLA (IRE) 3 ch.f. Soviet Lad (USA) 94 – Eight Mile Rock 76 – (Dominion 123) [1996 67?: 6g 7m 7g⁴ 1997 7.1m⁶ 8.3m 7m Sep 21] small filly: poor mover: showed nothing at 3 yrs. *M. J. Haynes*

AMAZING BAY 4 b.f. Mazilier (USA) 107 – Petriece 64 (Mummy's Pet 125) 91 [1996 100: 6g 5f 5.1m² 5m 5g² 5d 5m² 5.2m³ 5g 1997 5.2g 5m 5g 5g Jun 7] angular,

58

lightly-made filly: unimpressive mover: useful performer at 3 yrs: ninth in Palace House Stakes at Newmarket, second and best effort in 1997: won at 6f at 2 yrs, raced mostly at 5f: acted on good to firm going, possibly unsuited by ground softer than good: held up: in foal to Cadeaux Genereux. *I. A. Balding*

AMAZING SAIL (IRE)   4 b.g. Alzao (USA) 117 – Amazer (USA) 122 (Vaguely Noble 140) [1996 9m 12g⁶ 13g 1997 a12g a16g Jan 27] closely related to smart French filly Delighter (by Lypheor), successful up to 12.5f, and half-brother to several winners, including Oaks and Irish Oaks third Oakmead (by Lomond): dam won up to 12.5f in France and USA: modest at best in 4 runs in Ireland for D. Weld: no form in 2 runs on all-weather in Britain: won selling hurdle in April. *Miss M. K. Milligan*

AMAZONIAN   2 b.c. (Mar 25) Formidable (USA) 125 – Red Rose Garden 87   – (Electric 126) [1997 7s⁶ a7g a8.5g Dec 13] 15,000Y: sixth foal: half-brother to 3-y-o Handsome Ridge and fairly useful stayer Red Bustaan (by Aragon): dam Irish 1½m winner: well beaten in maidens. *C. W. Thornton*

AMBER FORT   4 gr.g. Indian Ridge 123 – Lammastide 93 (Martinmas 128)   82 [1996 82: 5d⁵ 7m⁵ 6m 8.5m⁴ 7f⁵ a7g* 8m 7m² 7m² 7g³ 7s* 7g⁶ 1997 a8.5g 8.1g 8g⁵ 7m² 8.1g 8.5m 8g³ 7s* Jun 27] tall gelding: fairly useful handicapper: won apprentice event at Goodwood: effective at 7f/1m: acts on firm and soft ground and on equi-track: not an easy ride, and tends to wander: has been blinkered, visored nowadays. *D. R. C. Elsworth*

AMBER REGENT   2 ch.g. (Apr 13) King's Signet (USA) 110 – Silly Sally   64 ? (Music Boy 124) [1997 5m 5f 5g a5g Nov 14] 9,000Y, 8,000 2-y-o: strong, workman-like gelding: first foal: dam looked temperamental: easily best effort in maidens when eighth of 16 at Beverley (slowly away) on second outing. *P. C. Haslam*

AMBER VALLEY (USA)   6 ch.g. Bering 136 – Olatha (USA) (Miswaki (USA)   – 124) [1996 NR 1997 a8.5f Jan 11] fair jumper: always behind in Wolverhampton handicap on first outing on flat for nearly 2 years. *D. L. Williams*

AMBIDEXTROUS (IRE)   5 b.h. Shareef Dancer (USA) 135 – Amber Fizz   66 (USA) (Effervescing (USA)) [1996 57: a12g⁵ 10d⁶ 12.3g⁵ 10g 12.1g⁵ 11.1f* 11.1f*   a50 11.1g² 11.1g³ 11.1m³ 10m 11.1m³ 11.9m⁴ 12.1f⁴ 12.1m* 10f 1997 a11g⁶ a12g³ a12g² a12g⁵ 9.9m 12d³ 10.3m⁵ 12g* 12d³ 10.5g² 10.3m* 10m 10.5m⁴ 10.3d⁶ 12g⁵ Sep 15] good-bodied horse: fair handicapper: successful at Musselburgh in June and Chester in July: stays 1½m well: acts on firm and dead ground, modest form on fibresand: tried visored: held up: tough. *E. J. Alston*

AMBIGUOUS   2 ch.c. (Mar 26) Arazi (USA) 135 – Vaguely 92 (Bold Lad (IRE)   – p 133) [1997 7.1m 7m 8s Oct 14] 190,000Y: close-coupled colt: has a markedly round action: half-brother to several winners, notably high-class 1¼m performer Shady Heights (by Shirley Heights): dam 1m and 1¼m winner: behind in maidens at Haydock, Newmarket and Leicester, never placed to challenge nor knocked about on last-named course: likely to do better. *D. R. Loder*

AMBITIOUS   2 b.f. (Feb 15) Ardkinglass 114 – Ayodhya (IRE) (Astronef 116)   72 p [1997 6m 6m² 6m⁴ Sep 2] 11,000Y: fifth foal: dam French 2-y-o 6f and 7f winner: progressive form: in frame in maidens at Lingfield and Folkestone, travelling well both times: should stay 7f: likely to improve again. *J. R. Fanshawe*

AMBUSCADE (USA)   11 ch.g. Roberto (USA) 131 – Gurkhas Band (USA)   – (Lurullah) [1996 NR 1997 18d⁵ 17.5d 16s 18d Oct 20] modest handicapper in 1995: showed nothing at 11 yrs. *Mrs J. Jordan*

AMEENA (USA)   2 b.f. (Mar 28) Irish River (FR) 131 – London Pride (USA) 106   – (Lear Fan (USA) 130) [1997 7m Sep 9] second foal: half-sister to a German 3-y-o 1m winner (by Shadeed): dam 1m winner and third in Fred Darling: 20/1 from 8/1, ninth of 15 to Jibe in maiden at Lingfield, prominent until halfway: sold 4,800 gns in November. *P. F. I. Cole*

AMEER ALFAYAAFI (IRE)   4 b.g. Mujtahid (USA) 118 – Sharp Circle (IRE)   – 83 (Sure Blade (USA) 130) [1996 55: 7g 8d 7f 7.1m⁶ 7f⁵ 8g 10f⁶ 9.7d 1997 6.9g 8.2m Apr 8] small, sturdy gelding: carries condition: well beaten at 4 yrs, sold cheaply after final start: seems to stay 1¼m: acts on firm ground: tried blinkered. *B. J. Meehan*

AME

AMELIA JANE   3 ch.f. Efisio 120 – Blue Jane 81 (Blue Cashmere 129) [1996   –
NR 1997 6m 5m a7g⁵ a6g⁶ a8g Dec 4] sister to a few winners, including 8-y-o
Eastleigh (multiple winner up to 1m, fair at best), and half-sister to smart sprinter
Ever Sharp (by Sharpo): dam 6f winner: little sign of ability. *L. Montague Hall*

AMERICAN COUSIN   2 b.g. (Feb 6) Distant Relative 128 – Zelda (USA)   63
(Sharpen Up 127) [1997 6d 6s³ 6d³ a6g³ 6m Aug 18] 24,000Y: third living foal:
half-brother to 1996 2-y-o 6f winner Spaniards Inn (by Dominion): dam once-raced
half-sister to Moorestyle: modest maiden: will stay beyond 6f: ran poorly in blinkers
final start, then gelded. *B. J. Meehan*

AMERICAN HERO   9 ch.g. Persian Bold 123 – American Winter (USA) 78   –
(Lyphard (USA) 132) [1996 NR 1997 13s May 4] useful chaser, winner of all 3 starts
in 1997: very lightly raced on flat since 5 yrs and no form. *R. Allan*

AMERICAN WHISPER   3 b.c. Dixieland Band (USA) – Only A Rumour 115   92
(Ela-Mana-Mou 132) [1996 76: 7g³ 7.1f⁶ 1997 8m 8s 10g* 10.1m* 10m 10.3g* Oct
24] leggy, unfurnished colt: has a quick action: improved into fairly useful
handicapper: won at Goodwood and Yarmouth in June and Doncaster (beat Secret
Ballot 3 lengths) in October: will stay further than 1¼m: acts on good to firm going.
P. W. Harris

AMIARGE   7 b.g. Reference Point 139 – Scotia Rose (Tap On Wood 130) [1996   54
53: 12.4d⁵ 14g⁴ 16.5g⁵ 14.6g 16m⁵ 16g⁶ 16.4g 15.9g² 17.9g* 18g a16g 1997 16m⁵
16.2m⁵ 14.1m 14.6d* 16.2v⁴ 14.8m 16.1m⁴ 16.2d⁵ 16m* 14.6g Oct 24] small
gelding: modest handicapper: won at Doncaster in June and Ripon in August: stays
2¼m: acts on firm and soft going: effective visored/blinkered or not: inconsistent,
but game in a finish. *M. Brittain*

AMIASAPPHIRE   2 ch.f. (Apr 24) Safawan 118 – Amethystine (USA) 69   –
(Barachois (CAN)) [1997 5.1m 5.7g Jun 28] 900Y: first foal: dam sprinter/miler: no
promise. *R. J. Hodges*

AMICO   3 b.c. Efisio 120 – Stormswept (USA) 74 (Storm Bird (CAN) 134) [1996   59
52: 6g 7.1v a6g⁵ 1997 a7g² a8g* a10g² 12g³ Mar 26] leggy colt: has a round action: a66
modest performer: won 5-runner maiden at Lingfield in February: better effort next
time: stays 1¼m: acts on equitrack. *C. W. Thornton*

AMID ALBADU (USA)   3 b.c. Sheikh Albadou 128 – Dream Play (USA)   109
(Blushing Groom (FR) 131) [1996 89: 6g² 6m² 7d* 7f* 1997 8g* 8g² 8.5g⁴ 10.1d²
10g⁵ 10.1d* 10d⁴ 9d² Oct 17] quite good-topped colt: has a round action: useful
performer: won 18-runner handicap at Newbury in April and slowly-run minor event
(easily) at Epsom in August: ran well behind Fahris in Group 3 event at Goodwood
and listed race at Newmarket final 2 starts: stays 1¼m: acts on firm and dead going:
blinkered last 3 starts: consistent: sent to race in UAE. *J. L. Dunlop*

AMID THE STARS   3 b.f. Midyan (USA) 124 – Celebrity 101 (Troy 137) [1996   –
61: 7g⁴ 7m 1997 7g³ 8.3d⁴ Aug 13] modest maiden: well held in small fields in
August: bred to stay at least 1m. *M. Johnston*

A MILLION WATTS   6 b.g. Belfort (FR) 89 – Peters Pet Girl (Norwick (USA)   –
125) [1996 –: a8g 1997 a12g a11g Jan 20] one-time fair handicapper on all-weather,
very much on the downgrade. *G. M. McCourt*

AMINGTON GIRL   2 b.f. (Mar 16) Tragic Role (USA) – Millfields House 70   39
(Record Token 128) [1997 5f⁵ 5m³ 5d⁶ 6g⁶ Aug 15] fourth foal: half-sister to 4-y-o
Amington Lass: dam maiden who appeared to stay 1¼m: poor maiden: stays 6f:
visored fourth start. *P. D. Evans*

AMINGTON LASS   4 ch.f. Cree Song 99 – Millfields House 70 (Record Token   48
128) [1996 70: 7.9g⁶ 5.2m⁴ a5g* 1997 a5g⁴ a5g Jan 8] leggy, workmanlike filly: fair
winner at 3 yrs: disappointing in 2 starts in January: should stay 6f. *P. D. Evans*

AMNESTY BAY   5 b.m. Thatching 131 – Sanctuary Cove (Habitat 134) [1996 –:   –
6.1g 7m 10d 8.1g 10.2m 1997 a8g a12g a9.4g 5.7d 6m 10.2m 8d⁴ 8g 8m Jul 18]
light-framed mare: poor maiden handicapper: tried visored. *M. D. I. Usher*

AMOEBA (IRE)   4 b.f. Distinctly North (USA) 115 – Lady Ingrid (Taufan (USA)   47
119) [1996 51: a6g* a6g⁵ a7g⁶ 6g⁵ 5.9f² 7f 5.9f⁴ 1997 5f⁵ a5g a5g⁴ 5g⁶ 7.1d Jul 3]

60

workmanlike filly: poor handicapper: best at 6f/stiff 5f: acts on fibresand and firm ground: blinkered last 3 starts. *A. Bailey*

AMONG ISLANDS   6 b.m. Jupiter Island 126 – Queen of The Nile (Hittite Glory   –
125) [1996 NR 1997 11.9s Oct 15] of little account. *R. Lee*

AMONG MEN (USA)   3 b.c. Zilzal (USA) 137 – Questionablevirtue (USA)   119 p
(Key To The Mint (USA)) [1996 NR 1997 8m* 8g* 7m* 8m⁴ 8g* Aug 23]
    Here is a horse whose most important success to date owed little to his own efforts. Among Men's 'victory' in the Tripleprint Celebration Mile at Goodwood in August came only after the deliberations of the stewards. He had to finish second, of course, in order to benefit from Dettori's brainstorm on the two-and-a-half length winner Cape Cross, but it was a four-runner race and Among Men's only other serious opponent, Polar Prince, was even further below form than he was. Starting at 11/8-on but failing to settle and clearly running below his best, Among Men was not affected by Dettori's rash manoeuvre over three furlongs out. Less charitable towards the Italian than they had been after the rated stakes two races earlier—when the verdict on his first-past-the-post, Swiss Law, had been 'accidental interference'—the stewards again demoted his mount but this time banned him for 'irresponsible riding'.
    Among Men did not appear again, returning from Goodwood lame behind after pulling a muscle, but he will be back in 1998 and will surely be a major contender in the top races over seven furlongs and a mile. The way in which he began 1997, completing his first three races unbeaten, persuaded many that he might reach the top a bit sooner. He stood out in appearance and ability among a field of maidens at Newmarket on One Thousand Guineas day, and then showed he has courage as well when upped markedly in class in the listed Crawley Warren Heron Stakes at Kempton and the Jersey Stakes at Royal Ascot. At 11/10-on, Among Men came between Amid Albadu and Green Card to take the Heron Stakes by a short head. 4/1 favourite in the Jersey, he won by

Jersey Stakes, Royal Ascot—Among Men rallies splendidly to overhaul Kahal

Tripleprint Celebration Mile, Goodwood—
Cape Cross is first past the post but Among Men is awarded the race

half a length, going on three furlongs out, losing the lead to Kahal approaching the furlong marker and grabbing it back again close home. Put into a Group 1 race for the first time in the Sussex Stakes at Goodwood, Among Men started co-favourite and was beaten two and a half lengths into fourth of nine behind Ali-Royal, but he had shown improved form again, and that despite obvious signs of inexperience, pulling hard and taking time to get balanced on the track. That remains his best form, but it could look pretty meagre by the end of 1998. So far, he has been raced only on good ground or good to firm.

		Nureyev	Northern Dancer
	Zilzal (USA)	(b 1977)	Special
	(ch 1986)	French Charmer	Le Fabuleux
Among Men (USA)		(ch 1978)	Bold Example
(b.c. 1994)		Key To The Mint	Graustark
	Questionablevirtue (USA)	(b 1969)	Key Bridge
	(b 1987)	Propositioning	Mr Prospector
		(ch 1980)	Stay Over

Among Men is a big, lengthy, most imposing individual, a surprise perhaps for one whose price as a yearling, 55,000 dollars at Keeneland in September, was about 8,000 dollars less than the average that year for a Zilzal and 5,000 less than Zilzal's 1993 covering fee. The type to do well from three to four, Among Men has always impressed us in appearance, although he was sweating before the Sussex Stakes. Since being returned to Britain for the 1996 covering season, Zilzal has been standing for a fee of £10,000. The likes of Always Loyal, Faithful Son and Haltarra were good adverts in Europe in the latest season, while Kammtarra started the year in fine style in Dubai. Among Men is the second foal of the unraced dam Questionablevirtue. Both the second and third dams, Propositioning and Stay Over, won three races, the former in France (two wins at seven furlongs, one at a mile) where she was also runner-up in the Prix du Rond-Point. Propositioning's 1988 colt Deposit Ticket was a high-class sprinting two-year-old in the United States. *M. R. Stoute*

AMRAK AJEEB (IRE)   5 b.h. Danehill (USA) 126 – Noble Dust (USA) (Dust   108
Commander (USA)) [1996 112: 7m 10m 8m⁶ 8s* 9.8g² 8m 8m⁵ 10.4m 10.4m* 8.9g

62

8g* 10g⁶ 1997 8m⁴ 9g³ 10d⁵ 8m 8d³ 8.1g 10s 10.1d⁵ 10d⁵ Sep 19] leggy, good-topped horse: takes the eye: useful performer: over 2 lengths third of 11 to Ali-Royal in Earl of Sefton Stakes at Newmarket in April: mostly disappointing after: effective at 1m to 10.5f: acts on good to firm and soft going: has run well when sweating: sometimes taken early/last to post: has edged left: takes good hold, and is usually held up: none too consistent: sent to UAE. *B. Hanbury*

AMRON   10 b.g. Bold Owl 101 – Sweet Minuet (Setay 105) [1996 67: 7g 6g⁶ 6m 6d² 6d 6m 6m 5d³ 6m 6m 6s⁵ 5m³ 6m 6m² 1997 5g* 5m⁶ 5.9g² 6s⁶ 5.9d² 6s 6g² 5.9g⁶ 6m³ 6g 6g⁴ 6d 5d Sep 18] sparely-made gelding: fair handicapper: often goes well fresh, and gained first success for 3 years at Newcastle in March: form after only when in frame: stays 6f: acts on any ground: usually held up: inconsistent. *J. Berry*   67

AMY   3 b.f. Timeless Times (USA) 99 – Rion River (IRE) (Taufan (USA) 119) [1996 –: 5.1g⁶ 5m⁵ 5g 5f 7d a5g 1997 a7g a8g Jan 6] small filly: no sign of ability: tried blinkered. *C. Smith*   –

AMYAS (IRE)   3 b.c. Waajib 121 – Art Duo 86 (Artaius (USA) 129) [1996 85: 6g⁵ 7m⁶ 6g* 6g* 6m 1997 8.1d* 8.1d⁶ 8m 10g⁴ 10m 10.4g* Aug 20] sturdy colt: useful handicapper: won at Sandown in April and York (quite valuable event) in August, coming from off very strong pace when beating Sandmoor Chambray 1½ lengths in latter: better around 1¼m than shorter: possibly unsuited by going firmer than good: usually held up: sent to UAE. *B. W. Hills*   108

AMY LEIGH (IRE)   4 b.f. Imperial Frontier (USA) 112 – Hollyberry (IRE) (Runnett 125) [1996 62d: 5d⁵ 5g 5d 5.1f 5.1g 5.1g 6m a5g⁶ a5g⁴ a7s a5g⁶ 1997 a5g* a6g⁴ a5g a6g* 6.1d a5g² 5g a5g⁶ 6d a6g a6g a7g a7g Dec 18] small, sturdy filly: modest at best in 1997, form only on fibresand: successful at Wolverhampton in January (claimer) and March (selling handicap): effective at 5f and 6f: usually blinkered/visored: inconsistent. *Capt. J. Wilson*   –
a62 d

ANAKELA BAY (IRE)   2 b.f. (Apr 12) Fairy King (USA) – Natuschka (Authi 123) [1997 7m Jul 31] IR 28,000Y: smallish, angular filly: closely related to smart 7f (at 2 yrs) to 1½m winner Surrealist (by Tate Gallery) and half-sister to several winners, including Derby third Blues Traveller (by Bluebird): dam won from 9f to 2m in Ireland: 33/1 and blinkered, tailed off in maiden at Goodwood: sent to New Zealand. *B. W. Hills*   –

ANAK-KU   4 ch.g. Efisio 120 – City Link Lass 92 (Double Jump 131) [1996 73: a8g⁶ a8g² a10g³ 8.5m⁵ 7m² 7f³ 8.1g* 10f² 1997 a10g* 10g⁵ 10.3d 9m² 10.2m* 10m* 10.2m² 10m* 10.2g² 10.1g Sep 5] leggy gelding: fairly useful performer: improved in 1997, winning handicaps at Lingfield, Chepstow and Windsor and (on sixth start) minor event at Ripon: gave trouble to post and didn't lead when running poorly final start: unlikely to stay much beyond 1¼m: acts on equitrack and firm ground, well beaten only start on dead: effective in blinkers/visor earlier in career: usually makes running: game. *Miss Gay Kelleway*   87

ANCHORED IN LOVE   3 b.f. Alzao (USA) 117 – Lyndonville (IRE) (Top Ville 129) [1996 NR 1997 7g 8g⁵ 7d 10g⁶ Jun 16] 30,000F: close-coupled filly: fluent mover: second foal: dam Irish 1¾m winner: fair maiden: disappointing favourite final start: should stay at least 1¼m. *R. Charlton*   66

ANCHORENA   5 b.m. Slip Anchor 136 – Canna (Caerleon (USA) 132) [1996 62, a48: a12g a12g⁶ a16g a11g a11g 9.9d² 10g⁵ 9.9m⁴ 12g* a11g² 12m 14.1f 12f³ a14g a12g⁴ 1997 13.8g 16.2m⁴ 16m² 13s⁶ 16.2s 16m³ 14.1f⁴ 14.1g⁵ 16g 16m Aug 26] tall, angular mare: poor handicapper: well below form last 2 starts: stays 2m: acts on good to firm and fibresand, seemingly not on ground softer than good: effective visored (rarely tried these days): used to flash tail and hang. *D. W. Barker*   48
a–

ANCHOR VENTURE   4 b.g. Slip Anchor 136 – Ski Michaela (USA) (Devil's Bag (USA)) [1996 61: 12m⁴ 12.3g⁵ 12f⁵ a16g⁴ 14.1f³ 14g 1997 12m 12d a10g³ 12m⁵ 10m* 10.1s³ Jul 3] rangy gelding: modest performer: dropped in class, landed gamble in seller at Pontefract (bought in 11,000 gns) in June: should stay further than 1½m: acts on firm and soft ground, and equitrack. *S. P. C. Woods*   55

ANCIENT QUEST   4 b.g. Rainbow Quest (USA) 134 – Racquette 120 (Ballymore 123) [1996 78: 10.3g 12g²² 13.1d² 12m⁶ 1997 12m 14g⁴ 13.3g⁵ 12d* 12d* 11.6s⁴ Jun 30] tall, workmanlike gelding: fairly useful handicapper: improved in   91

1997, winning at Newmarket and Epsom (by 9 lengths) in June: not discredited final start: suited by a good test at 1½m, and should stay at least 1¾m: acts on soft ground, ran poorly both starts on good to firm. *N. A. Callaghan*

ANDALISH 2 b.f. (Feb 27) Polish Precedent (USA) 131 – Risanda (Kris 135) – p [1997 7m Sep 9] first foal: dam unraced half-sister to Cheveley Park winner Prophecy out of Lancashire Oaks winner Andaleeb: 10/1 from 3/1, showed ability, racing alone and not unduly knocked about, in 16-runner maiden at Lingfield: will do better. *B. W. Hills*

ANDITZ (IRE) 2 b.f. (Mar 3) Soviet Lad (USA) 94 – Miss Fortunate (IRE) 53 (Taufan (USA) 119) [1997 5f 5g⁵ 6s 8m Nov 4] IR 2,200Y: first foal: dam, unraced, from good family: only form when fifth of 14 in maiden at Catterick: should stay at least 6f. *J. L. Eyre*

ANDREYEV (IRE) 3 ch.c. Presidium 124 – Missish (Mummy's Pet 125) [1996 105 101: 6f⁴ 5m* 6.1d* 6m⁴ 6m 7d* 7.3s⁶ 1997 7g⁴ 7g* 7m 6f Jul 19] tall colt: impresses in appearance: useful performer: showed good turn of foot to win slowly-run 6-runner listed event at Newmarket in May by ¾ length from Royal Aty: well below form after: not sure to stay much beyond 7f: acts on good to firm and dead ground: game. *R. Hannon*

ANEMOS (IRE) 2 ch.c. (Mar 12) Be My Guest (USA) 126 – Frendly Persuasion 74 p (General Assembly (USA)) [1997 7m 7d³ Nov 7] 65,000Y: good-topped colt: type to carry condition: second foal: dam fairly useful up to 1½m in Ireland: much better effort in autumn maidens when 6½ lengths third of 19 behind Scorned at Doncaster, held up and keeping on: trained by M. Tompkins on debut: should stay at least 1¼m: should improve again. *M. A. Jarvis*

ANETTA 3 ch.f. Aragon 118 – Pronetta (USA) (Mr Prospector (USA)) [1996 –: 56 6g 7f 1997 5m 6m 6m 7.1d³ 8.2g* 8.2m⁶ 7m 8s Nov 6] unfurnished filly: modest handicapper: won at Nottingham in July: ran poorly last 2 starts: stays 1m (not sure to get much further): acts on good to firm and dead ground, below form on extremes. *Miss S. E. Hall*

ANGEL CHIMES 4 ch.f. Most Welcome 131 – Bell Toll 87 (High Line 125) 74 + [1996 77: 7m* 1997 7m 10g 7g⁶ 7.3d 9m 7g Oct 18] smallish, workmanlike filly: has a markedly round action: fair handicapper: probably flattered when seventh in Cambridgeshire at Newmarket fifth start, stealing early march on rivals: best up to 9f: acts on firm and dead going: visored last 2 starts: usually comes from behind. *J. E. Banks*

ANGEL FACE (USA) 4 b.f. Zilzal (USA) 137 – Touching Love 109 (Touching 85 + Wood (USA) 127) [1996 75: 7.6m⁴ 7f 6.1m a10g* a8g² a9.4g² a10g* a10g 1997 a9.4g* 10.3m 10.8m* 8g* 8m a9.4g³ 10m³ 9f⁶ Aug 2] fairly useful handicapper in Britain: won at Wolverhampton, Warwick (gamely) and Thirsk and good third in Zetland Gold Cup at Redcar (final start for P. D. Evans) in the spring: appeared to run very well when sixth of 7 in Grade 1 event at Del Mar: effective at 1m to 11f: acts on firm ground and the all-weather: tends to be unruly in preliminaries. *D. Vienna, USA*

ANGEL HILL 2 ch.f. (Feb 28) King's Signet (USA) 110 – Tawny 81 (Grey Ghost 74 98) [1997 5m* 5m² 5m³ 6m⁴ 5m³ 6m⁵ 6g⁴ 6d Oct 6] strong filly: progressed physically: third living foal: half-sister to Italian 3-y-o 7.5f winner Patsy Jo (by Absalom): dam 2-y-o 5f and 6f winner: fair performer: won maiden at Newcastle in May: ran creditably most subsequent starts: stays 6f: acts on good to firm ground, below form on good to soft. *T. D. Barron*

ANGELINA 2 b.f. (Mar 7) Most Welcome 131 – Mystic Crystal (IRE) 85 63 p (Caerleon (USA) 132) [1997 6m⁵ 6m³ Sep 2] third foal: half-sister to 4-y-o Siberian Mystic: dam 7f winner at 2 yrs: some promise in maidens at Haydock (green and bit backward) then Folkestone: will stay at least 1m: should progress again. *P. Howling*

ANGELIQUE 2 ch.f. (Feb 14) Soviet Star (USA) 128 – Lady Habitat (Habitat 53 134) [1997 5g⁵ 5d⁵ 6d Jun 21] tall filly: has a fluent action: half-sister to several winners, including Italian 9f winner Big Reef (by Mill Reef) and fairly useful middle-distance stayer The Gaelcharn (by Prince Bee): dam 5f (at 2 yrs) to 7.5f winner in Italy: modest form first 2 starts, though green: stiff task final outing: should stay at least 6f: sold 2,400 gns in December. *M. J. Haynes*

ANGEL ONE FIVE   3 b.f. Allazzaz – Watch Her Go (Beldale Flutter (USA) 130)   –
[1996 NR 1997 10g Oct 24] workmanlike filly: fifth reported foal: dam ran once at 2
yrs: sire (by Mill Reef) of little account: tailed off in Newbury maiden. *P. R. Hedger*

ANGIE MINOR   2 b.f. (Apr 20) Mazilier (USA) 107 – Angelica Park 57 (Simply   –
Great (FR) 122) [1997 a5g⁶ a6g⁶ 7g a7g Dec 18] first foal: dam stayer: well beaten in
maidens and a seller. *J. Wharton*

ANGLESEY SEA VIEW   8 gr.m. Seymour Hicks (FR) 125 – Lexham View 72   a47
(Abwah 118) [1996 62: 16.2g⁶ 14.9d 18.7g 16g⁴ 14d⁴ 20f 15.9m 16.5m⁴ 16g⁵ 15.9d⁵
16g⁵ 15.1s² a16g 1997 a16.2g³ a16g⁴ Jan 27] leggy, angular mare: poor handicapper:
should stay further than 2m: acts on good to firm and soft ground and on fibresand:
ran well only try in blinkers. *A. Bailey*

ANGRY ALBERT   2 ch.c. (May 17) Clantime 101 – Croft Original (Crofthall   39
110) [1997 a5g 6.1g 5.2m⁵ 5s⁴ 5d⁵ 6g Aug 11] 5,000Y, 4,500 2-y-o: brother to a poor
maiden: dam probably ungenuine: poor maiden: best efforts at 5f: visored last 3
starts: dead. *C. Smith*

ANGSTROM (IRE)   2 b.g. (May 27) Alzao (USA) 117 – Anna Petrovna (FR) 90   91 p
(Wassl 125) [1997 7m 8m* 8d² Nov 7] sturdy, angular gelding: good mover: fourth
foal: half-brother to 1996 Italian 2-y-o 5f and 7f winner Sophia Antipolis (by
Nordico) and 5-y-o Annus Mirabilis: dam 1¼m winner who stayed 1½m: fairly
useful form: ran as though something amiss on debut: won maiden at Brighton in
October by 4 lengths from Hadith, making all: hung left when first put under pressure
when 1¾ lengths second of 5 to Derryquin in minor event at Doncaster: will be suited
by at least 1¼m: has potential if temperament holds. *M. R. Stoute*

ANGUS-G   5 br.g. Chief Singer 131 – Horton Line 89 (High Line 125) [1996 89:   98 p
8g⁵ 8m³ 10m 10f³ 10f* 10m* 10m² 10.3m² 9m³ 1997 12g* 11.9g* May 13] big,
useful-looking gelding: impresses in appearance: progressive handicapper: ran just
twice early as 5-y-o, justifying favouritism at Newmarket (third win there) in April
and York (something to spare) in May: better at 1½m than shorter, and likely to stay
further (settles well): shaped well on dead ground on debut, raced on good ground or
firmer since: held up and tends to idle in front: due to return in 1998, and could well
improve further. *Mrs M. Reveley*

ANISTOP   5 b.h. Nomination 125 – Pounelta 91 (Tachypous 128) [1996 50, a59:   –
a10g⁵ a12g² a12g⁵ a12g² 12d a12g² 10m³ a12g 11.1g 1997 a14g⁶ 9.9m 10g a12g Apr
28] sparely-made horse: modest performer: well beaten in 1997: stays 1½m: acts on
all-weather and firm ground: often soon off bridle. *J. L. Eyre*

ANITA AT DAWN (IRE)   2 br.f. (Feb 11) Anita's Prince 126 – Dawn Is   73
Breaking (Import 1) [1997 5.1m³ 6.1d* 7s² 6g 7.3g Oct 25] 6,000F: sparely-made
filly: half-sister to several winners, including useful Italian sprinter Sotabrasciet (by
Danehill) and 5-y-o Thaljanah: dam Irish 2-y-o 5f winner: fair form: won maiden at
Nottingham in June: good second at Chester 2 months later, easily best nursery effort:
stays 7f: best efforts on dead/soft going: races prominently. *B. Palling*

ANITA IN WALES (IRE)   3 b.f. Anita's Prince 126 – Regal Charmer (Royal   –
And Regal (USA)) [1996 NR 1997 a7g Dec 22] IR 5,500Y: sister to 4 winners,
including Irish 1994 2-y-o 6.5f winner Anita's Galaxy and Irish 1¼m winner Galaxy
High: dam Irish 1½m winner: behind in maiden at Lingfield. *P. Eccles*

ANITA MARIE (IRE)   2 b.f. (Apr 20) Anita's Prince 126 – Fandangerina (USA)   –
(Grey Dawn II 132) [1997 7g Oct 18] 10,000F: half-sister to several winners,
including 1987 2-y-o 6f and 7f winner Western Gun (by Lypheor) and 7f (at 2 yrs) to
12.2f winner Ocean Air (by Elegant Air), both useful: dam won up to 1m in USA:
14/1, well held in Redcar maiden, prominent to 2f out. *M. Johnston*

ANITA'S CONTESSA (IRE)   5 b.m. Anita's Prince 126 – Take More (GER)   a58
(Frontal 122) [1996 56, a60: 6m 6f a6g³ a6g 7f a6g⁶ a6g² a7g⁵ a7g⁵ 1997 a6s⁵
a6g* a7g⁴ a7g³ a6g³ a7g³ Feb 27] leggy, sparely-made mare: modest handicapper:
won at Southwell in January: effective at 6f and 7f: acts on dead ground and all-
weather. *B. Palling*

ANJOU   5 b.g. Saumarez 132 – Bourbon Topsy 108 (Ile de Bourbon (USA) 133)   68
[1996 –: a16.2g⁴ a16g⁵ 1997 11.8d⁵ 11.5m* 14.1f² a16g² a14.8g³ Dec 13] rangy
gelding: fair performer: absent for 20 months before reappearance: won selling

ANK

handicap at Yarmouth in October, and placed all 3 starts afterwards: effective at 11.5f to easy 2m: acts on firm ground and the all-weather: usually held up. *J. Pearce*

ANKA LADY 2 b.f. (Apr 19) Precocious 126 – Hicklam Millie 49 (Absalom 128) 44 ? [1997 5g⁶ 5d³ 6g 8.3g⁶ 6s⁴ 7.1s⁵ Nov 6] 3,500Y: leggy filly: fourth foal: related to 2 winners in Italy: dam (maiden) stayed 1¼m: poor form at best. *D. Moffatt*

ANLACE 8 b.m. Sure Blade (USA) 130 – Ascot Strike (USA) 85 (Mr Prospector (USA)) [1996 NR 1997 a14.8g Dec 13] modest handicapper at 6 yrs: well beaten in seller only start in 1997. *S. Mellor*

ANNA 2 b.f. (Feb 16) Ela-Mana-Mou 132 – Anna Rella (IRE) (Danehill (USA) 69 p 126) [1997 6.9m³ Jul 14] 7,000Y: first foal: dam, unraced, from family of Fred Darling winner Sueboog and Oaks/Irish Oaks winner Fair Salinia: 7/2, 1¾ lengths third of 8 to Country Garden in maiden at Folkestone, staying on: will probably be suited by 1¼m+: should do better. *C. E. Brittain*

ANNABA (IRE) 4 ch.f. In The Wings 128 – Anna Matrushka (Mill Reef (USA) 114 141) [1996 120: 10m⁵ 10m³ 11.9m⁵ 10.1m⁵ 12.5d* 12d* 1997 12.5m⁴ 12m⁵ 12s⁴ Nov 8] workmanlike filly: very smart performer at 3 yrs: not quite so good in 3 runs late in 1997, best effort when fifth of 9 to Caitano in Gran Premio del Jockey Club at Milan: should stay beyond 12.5f: best efforts on dead going: free-going sort. *J. H. M. Gosden*

ANNALETTA 3 b.f. Belmez (USA) 131 – A Priori (GER) (Prince Ippi (GER)) 89 [1996 NR 1997 13.8g³ 12m* 11m² 14g³ Sep 14] half-sister to several winners, including fairly useful Francfurter (1¼m, would have stayed further, by Legend of France): dam placed 3 times from 5 starts in Germany: refused to enter stalls intended debut: won maiden at Rochefort-sur-Loire in August on final outing for J. Pearce: best effort when 2½ lengths third of 6 in listed race at Krefeld final start: stayed 1¾m: sold IR 54,000 gns in November, in foal to Kris. *H. Pantall, France*

ANNA PALARIVA (IRE) 2 ch.f. (May 18) Caerleon (USA) 132 – Anna of 108 Saxony 111 (Ela-Mana-Mou 132) [1997 8g* 8d* 8f Oct 5] leggy, unfurnished filly: first foal: dam 11.5f to 14.6f (Park Hill Stakes) winner, half-sister to very smart middle-distance filly Annaba: won 5-runner minor event at Deauville in August and 9-runner Prix d'Aumale at Chantilly (beat Fairly Grey a neck, making all) in September: favourite but edgy, very slowly away when well beaten in 10-runner Prix Marcel Boussac on much firmer ground at Longchamp final start, never going well: bred to be well suited by further than 1m: tail swisher: did not move well to post at Longchamp. *A. Fabre, France*

ANNIE HALL 2 b.f. (Apr 24) Saddlers' Hall (IRE) 126 – Rainbow Fleet 66 – (Nomination 125) [1997 7s Jun 26] 10,500Y: first foal: dam 5f (at 2 yrs) and 6f winner: 33/1, behind in maiden at Salisbury. *Martyn Meade*

ANNIEMITCHELLSLASS 2 b.f. (Apr 19) Noble Patriarch 115 – Fair Janet 39 (Feelings (FR)) [1997 6d⁶ 7.1m² 8g⁶ Sep 15] first reported foal: dam placed in NH Flat race: poor form in sellers and a claimer: should be well suited by 1¼m+. *D. Moffatt*

ANNO LUCE 4 ch.f. Old Vic 136 – Anna Paola (GER) (Prince Ippi (GER)) [1996 107 105: 10.5g* 11v² 11v³ 11s² 12g² 12m* 14d 1997 12f⁵ 12d³ 12m* 14.6m Sep 10] useful ex-German filly: won 10-runner listed race at Newmarket in July under fine ride from L. Dettori, beating Kaliana by 2 lengths: ran no sort of race in Park Hill Stakes at Doncaster 2 months later: should stay beyond 1½m: acts on good to firm and heavy ground: usually blinkered or visored: has been reluctant at stalls: sent to USA. *J. H. M. Gosden*

ANNOUNCING 3 b. or br.g. Old Vic 136 – D'Azy 91 (Persian Bold 123) [1996 70 d NR 1997 10d 11.5m³ 10.1g² 11.7g 16.1m 14d Oct 17] big, rangy gelding: fourth foal: half-brother to very smart 1m to 13.3f winner Presenting (by Mtoto) and 2 other winners: dam, 2-y-o 7f winner, half-sister to smart middle-distance performer Sirk: fair form in maidens second and third starts: gave impression something amiss last 3 outings: should stay beyond 11.5f: tried visored: sold (joined G. L. Moore) 21,000 gns in October. *J. H. M. Gosden*

ANNOUNCING PEACE 2 b.f. (Feb 22) Danehill (USA) 126 – Remoosh (Glint – of Gold 128) [1997 10m 7d⁶ 8s⁶ a8g Nov 24] 9,200F: seventh foal: sister to fairly

Winter Hill Stakes, Windsor—Annus Mirabilis wins this event for the second year running; Even Top (rails) and Fahris take the minor honours

useful 1½m winner Mount Pleasant and half-sister to 3 winners, including fairly useful 7f and 1m winner Moorish (also smart hurdler, by Dominion): dam poor half-sister to Nomination: well beaten in maidens and seller: blinkered second start. *C. A. Dwyer*

ANN'S MUSIC   4 b.f. Clantime 101 – An-Go-Look (Don't Look 107) [1996 –: a6g 1997 a11g a8g Jan 20] of little account. *J. M. Jefferson*   –

ANNUS MIRABILIS (FR)   5 b.h. Warning 136 – Anna Petrovna (FR) 90 (Wassl 125) [1996 120: a8s⁴ 10d³ 12f² 12g³ 12m⁵ 10d* 9f* 1997 10m³ 10g* 10m* 11f⁵ 9m Dec 14] tall horse: very smart performer: length third of 14 to London News in Queen Elizabeth II Cup at Sha Tin in April: off course nearly 4 months before winning minor event at Newmarket and Winter Hill Stakes at Windsor (for second year running, beat Even Top 3½ lengths) in August: raced on medication when creditable fifth of 10 to Influent in Man O'War Stakes at Belmont on penultimate start: stays 1½m: acts on firm and soft ground, possibly not on sand: visored 7 of last 8 starts: usually held up: tends to come off a true line under pressure: consistent. *Saeed bin Suroor*   120

ANOKATO   3 b.g. Tina's Pet 121 – High Velocity 53 (Frimley Park 109) [1996 66: 6g⁶ 5.7m³ 5.2g⁴ 5.7m³ 6d⁶ 5m 5f³ 5m* 5m³ 1997 5m⁴ 5.1m 5.1d⁶ 5d 5.3f* 5.3f³ 5.1m⁶ 5m⁶ 5.1m³ 5m⁶ 5m⁴ 6m 6g 5.2m 5m 5m⁶ a7g a5g* a5g⁶ a6g³ a7g Dec 10] good-topped gelding: has a round action: fair handicapper: in good form for most of 1997, and won at Brighton in May and Lingfield in November: best form at 5f/6f on ground firmer than good or on equitrack: best blinkered nowadays: sometimes looks irresolute. *K. T. Ivory*   68 a73

ANONYM (IRE)   5 b.g. Nashamaa 113 – Bonny Bertha (Capistrano 120) [1996 67: 6s 6g 7m 8g 8g⁴ 8f⁵ 7m 7s⁴ 7.1m* 7g² 8f³ 8f⁶ 8s 8g⁴ 8m⁴ 7f³ 8.2g⁵ 8g⁵ a7g⁶ a7g 1997 a7s* a8.5f* a7g² a9.4g a8.5g 8m⁵ 8.5d a8.5g* a9.4g³ 8d⁵ 7m² 7.5d 8m 8g 8s Nov 8] leggy, lengthy gelding: has a quick action: fair performer: won claimer at Southwell and handicap at Wolverhampton in January for D. Nicholls and amateurs handicap at Wolverhampton in May on fourth start for new yard: well below form last 4 starts: best at 7f to 8.5f: best turf form on good going or firmer, goes well on fibresand: usually blinkered: often edgy. *J. L. Eyre*   67 a74

ANOTHERANNIVERSARY   4 gr.f. Emarati (USA) 74 – Final Call 79 (Town Crier 119) [1996 NR 1997 5m⁶ 5.1m 5g³ 5m⁴ 6g⁶ Aug 10] good-topped filly: fairly useful performer: off course 21 months prior to reappearance: best efforts of 1997 when in frame in handicaps at Epsom (Vodac 'Dash') and Newmarket in the summer: best at 5f: raced only on good going or firmer: often wears bandages: sold 20,000 gns in December. *G. Lewis*   94

ANOTHER BATCHWORTH   5 b.m. Beveled (USA) – Batchworth Dancer 67 (Ballacashtal (CAN)) [1996 72: 6m² 5f² 6g 5g 5.3m² 5m 5.3m³ a6g 5.1m² 5.1g* 5m* 5.1g² a5g² a5g³ a5g⁶ 1997 5d 5m 5g⁵ 5m 5.1m⁵ 5m² 5.3f⁴ 5g³ a5g³ a5g Dec 2]   68 §

67

Tattersalls Breeders Stakes, the Curragh—
Another Fantasy gives her trainer his second successive win in this event

lengthy mare: fair handicapper: effective at 5f (best form) and 6f: acts on firm and soft ground and the all-weather: blinkered: often early to post: usually a front runner, but tends to give trouble in stalls and sometimes ruins chance by starting slowly: not one to trust. *E. A. Wheeler*

ANOTHER EPISODE (IRE)   8 b.g. Drumalis 125 – Pasadena Lady (Captain   56
James 123) [1996 –: 5g 5g 5m 5g 5f 6m 1997 5f 5d⁵ 5m 5s² 5g Oct 22] leggy, lengthy gelding: just a modest handicapper nowadays: raced mainly at 5f: successful on both all-weather, easily best recent turf efforts on dead/soft going: ran poorly in visor. *Miss L. A. Perratt*

ANOTHER FANTASY (IRE)   2 b.f. (Apr 19) Danehill (USA) 126 – Ariadne   97 +
79 (Bustino 136) [1997 5g* 5.2d⁴ 6g³ 6m² 6d 6m⁵ 6g* Aug 30] IR 23,000Y: good-topped filly: good walker: half-sister to several winners, including fairly useful sprinter Denham Green (by Dominion): dam, 2m winner, is sister to Italian Group 1 winner Stufida: useful performer: won maiden at Kempton in May and valuable 28-runner Tattersalls Breeders Stakes at the Curragh in August, improved form to beat Law Library by 2½ lengths in latter: second to Dance Trick in listed event at Epsom, best effort in between: will probably stay at least 1m: best efforts on good ground or firmer. *R. Hannon*

ANOTHER FIDDLE (IRE)   7 b.g. Waajib 121 – Elmar 87 (Lord Gayle (USA)   –
124) [1996 –: 9.7m⁴ a10g 1997 8f 10m 10d⁶ 9.7g 11.6m 14m⁴ 12g 11.9f⁵ 11.5f Oct 3] fair handicapper in 1995: has deteriorated considerably: tried blinkered. *J. E. Long*

ANOTHER MONK (IRE)   6 br.g. Supreme Leader 123 – Royal Demon   –
(Tarboosh (USA)) [1996 NR 1997 a12g² a16g* a12s* Nov 28] modest handicapper: a54
impressive winner of 2 of 3 starts at Lingfield in November, second an amateurs race: stays 2m: acts on equitrack. *R. Ingram*

ANOTHER NIGHT (IRE)   3 ch.c. Waajib 121 – Little Me (Connaught 130)   87
[1996 77: 7g² 7f² 7m³ 1997 7m 8.1m* 8s⁵ 10.1d 10m⁶ 10.3m 11.9m Sep 21] leggy, good-topped colt: fluent mover: fairly useful performer: comfortably won maiden at Haydock in June: also ran creditably third and fifth starts: stays 1¼m: acts on firm and soft going: has hinted at temperament: sold 20,000 gns in October. *R. Hannon*

ANOTHER NIGHTMARE (IRE)   5 b.m. Treasure Kay 114 – Carange   56
(Known Fact (USA) 135) [1996 59: 6d 5d 5m 5g⁴ 5f 7.1g 5d⁴ 6m⁵ 5m² 7g³ 7g 6f* 7g⁶   a46
5m⁵ 6s* 6f² 6.1m⁴ 6m⁶ 6d 6d 6m 6m 8.1s a6g 1997 a6g* a6g 5s a6g⁶ 5.9g 5s⁵ 6m 6g⁴ 5s* 6d⁵ 5m⁴ 5m⁶ 5m 6g* 6g 5m⁶ 6d 6d 5d 8.3g 5s Oct 14] leggy, sparely-made mare:

ANT

modest handicapper: made all in amateurs events at Wolverhampton, Hamilton (has
gained 3 of her 6 wins there) and Thirsk (seller): best at 5f/6f: acts on firm and soft
ground and on fibresand: sometimes hangs right: often forces pace: none too
consistent. *R. M. McKellar*

ANOTHERONE TO NOTE 6 ch.g. Beveled (USA) – Dame Nellie 84
(Dominion 123) [1996 42: a8g³ a8g a7g a11g⁴ a12g⁵ 1997 10.2m 8g Jun 28] poor
maiden handicapper: no form in 1997. *A. J. Chamberlain*

ANOTHER QUARTER (IRE) 4 b.f. Distinctly North (USA) 115 – Numidia
(Sallust 134) [1996 47, a61: 8.2m 8g⁶ 10.2g³ a8.5g⁴ 10m² 9.7g⁴ 10.1f² a12g* 12m*
15.8g a14g⁵ 1997 a12g⁴ a12g a12g a14g⁵ 18g⁶ 14.1g Jun 21] sturdy filly: won 2
sellers at 1½m for S. Woods in 1996: no worthwhile form at 4 yrs. *M. C. Chapman*

ANOTHER TIME 5 ch.g. Clantime 101 – Another Move 69 (Farm Walk 111) 98
[1996 84: 10s 10m² 10.8g⁶ 10m* 10g⁵ 10m* 10v 10.2f³ 9m⁴ 10s⁵ 1997 8m* 10m⁵
8.1g⁵ 8m 10.4m 9f* 10m² 10m⁴ 9m 10v 9g Oct 25] neat gelding: poor mover: useful
handicapper: won at Pontefract in April and Newbury in July: well beaten last 3
starts: best at 1m to 1¼m: acts on any going except heavy: usually held up, and suited
by strongly-run race. *S. P. C. Woods*

ANOTHER VICTIM 3 ch.g. Beveled (USA) – Ragtime Rose (Ragstone 128)
[1996 NR 1997 8d May 19] leggy gelding: half-brother to several winners, including
sprinter Supreme Rose (by Frimley Park) and 7f winner Mel's Rose (by Anfield),
both fairly useful: dam ran 3 times: tailed-off last in maiden at Bath: moved poorly to
post. *M. Blanshard*

ANOTHER WYN-BANK 2 b.f. (Apr 6) Presidium 124 – Wyn-Bank (Green 50
God 128) [1997 5f⁴ 5g 7m⁴ 8m Nov 4] 1,100Y: one of many foals (none winner on
flat) out of dam who won from 6f to 1¼m and over hurdles: poor form in maidens
first 3 starts: should stay at least 1m. *J. G. FitzGerald*

ANSELLMAN 7 gr.g. Absalom 128 – Grace Poole (Sallust 134) [1996 89: 5s 5g 93
5.1g* 5.1f⁶ 6d 5.1f* 6.1m² 6m³ᵈⁱˢ 6g 5.6m 5d⁵ 5s² 5g 5g⁵ a5g³ 1997 a5g⁴ 5g* a5g⁴ 5d
5d² 5m 5g 5.1s⁵ a5g² 5.7f³ 5.1g² 5d 5m* 5g² 5v² 5d³ 5g Oct 25] sturdy gelding:
carries condition: has a round action: fairly useful performer: won claimer at Ripon
in April and handicap at Leicester in September: effective at 5f and 6f: acts on any
turf/all-weather: tried visored, nearly always blinkered nowadays: tough and consistent. *J. Berry*

ANSTAND 2 b.c. (May 4) Anshan 119 – Pussy Foot 83 (Red Sunset 120) [1997 5d 65 p
5d⁵ 5m⁶ Oct 28] 25,000Y: useful-looking colt: good walker: fourth foal: half-brother
to 3-y-o German 9f winner Plentymore (by Sanglamore) and 1995 2-y-o 5f and 6f
winner Top Cat (by Be My Chief), later successful in Scandinavia: dam 5f performer,
granddaughter of Ribblesdale winner Catalpa: shaped with definite promise in
maidens in autumn, eating up ground at finish when sixth of 16 to Mary Jane at
Redcar: should stay at least 6f: considerably handled to date, and sure to do better
and win races at 3 yrs. *Mrs J. R. Ramsden*

ANSWERS-TO-THOMAS 4 b.g. Komaite (USA) – Launde Abbey 75 52 d
(Absalom 128) [1996 51: 6g³ 5.9f 5.9f 1997 a7g⁶ a6g⁵ a6g⁶ a6g a6g⁶ 5m 5d 8m 5m
5m⁶ Jul 21] lengthy gelding: modest maiden handicapper: well below form last 4
starts (blinkered final one): stays 6f: acts on firm and dead ground and on fibresand.
J. M. Jefferson

ANTARCTIC STORM 4 b.g. Emarati (USA) 74 – Katie Scarlett 70 (Lochnager 74
132) [1996 62: 8.2d 6.9f 8.3m* 8m 7m 1997 6s 5m³ 6d 5m⁴ 6g⁵ 7.6m³ 8g* 8g² 8.3g*
8m 8m⁵ 8g⁵ 8m* Nov 6] strong, close-coupled gelding: fair handicapper: better than
ever in 1997, winning at Ayr in August, Hamilton in September and Musselburgh in
November: stays 8.3f: acts on good to firm and soft ground: usually edgy in
preliminaries, and has got loose: front runner, best dominating. *R. A. Fahey*

ANTARES 3 b.g. Governor General 116 – Eucharis 41 (Tickled Pink 114) [1996 –
54: 5g 5d 5g³ 5m 5f 5f² 5f 6m a5g 1997 a6g 6.1g Apr 21] strong gelding: modest
sprint maiden: well beaten in 1997: tried blinkered. *N. Tinkler*

ANTARTICTERN (USA) 7 b.g. Arctic Tern (USA) 126 – False Image (USA) – §
79 (Danzig (USA)) [1996 –: a12g⁴ 12d 10g 11m 1997 12.3m 10.1f May 28]

69

ANT

good-bodied gelding: no form on Flat since 1995: tried blinkered/visored: probably ungenuine. *G. R. Oldroyd*

ANTIGUAN JANE   4 b.f. Shirley Heights 130 – Dabbiana (CAN) (Fappiano (USA)) [1996 71: 10g 1997 10g a12g⁴ 12s 12g Jul 9] good-topped filly: lightly-raced maiden: showed little in handicaps in 1997: blinkered last 2 outings: tail flasher. *R. W. Armstrong*

ANTITHESIS (IRE)   4 b.f. Fairy King (USA) – Music of The Night (USA)   60 d
(Blushing Groom (FR) 131) [1996 7s 7m 7g 5m⁵ 5m² 5m³ 5d* 5s³ 5g⁶ 5g⁵ 5s⁶ 1997 5g⁴ 5s 5g⁶ 5m⁵ 5g 7.1g⁵ 6m 5g Oct 18] ex-Irish filly: half-sister to several winners, including 5-y-o At Liberty: dam unraced half-sister to Champion Stakes second Prima Voce: fair winner (rated 75) for T. Stack in 1996: disappointing for new connections: seems best at 5f: acts on soft and good to firm ground: blinkered (at 7f) once. *J. S. Haldane*

ANTONIA'S CHOICE   3 ch.f. Music Boy 124 – Mainly Sunset (Red Sunset   63
120) [1996 73: 5g³ 5.1g* 1997 5f 5m 6m⁵ 6.1m Sep 15] strong, lengthy filly: fluent mover: off course for a year after making all on final 2-y-o start: just modest form in handicaps in 1997, though shaped quite well over 6f last 2 starts: will prove best at 5f: yet to race on ground softer than good. *J. Berry*

ANTONIA'S DOUBLE   2 ch.f. (Apr 14) Primo Dominie 121 – Mainly Sunset   74 +
(Red Sunset 120) [1997 5m⁴ 5g³ 5.1v⁶ May 8] 88,000Y: strong, lengthy filly: easy mover: fifth foal: half-sister to 4 winning sprinters, including 3-y-o Antonia's Choice and fairly useful Irish performer Musical Sunset (both by Music Boy): dam once-raced half-sister to useful sprinters Tod and Great Chaddington: fair form in early-season maidens at Newcastle and Thirsk: soon floundering final start: speedy. *J. Berry*

ANTONIAS MELODY   4 b.f. Rambo Dancer (CAN) 107 – Ayodessa 78   60
(Lochnager 132) [1996 86d: 6g⁶ 6g* 7.3d 6m² 6m 6v 6g 7m a5g a8.5s 1997 a6g*   a83
a7g* a5g 6m 5d⁶ 6g⁶ 6d 5g 5d 8m 7s⁵ 6g⁶ 7m a8.5g a5g Dec 18] good-topped filly: fairly useful handicapper: clearly best form in 1997 on the all-weather, winning twice at Southwell in February: mostly disappointing afterwards: likely to prove best at 6f/7f: acts on good to firm and dead ground, goes well on fibresand: tried blinkered, no improvement: often a front runner. *S. R. Bowring*

ANTONIO JOLI   2 b.g. (Apr 2) Prince Sabo 123 – Revisit 86 (Busted 134) [1997   –
a7g 8.2m 6m 8m Nov 4] sixth living foal: brother to modest 12.5f winner Peter Monamy and half-brother to 3-y-o Venetian Scene and 4-y-o Samuel Scott: dam stayer: well held in maidens and nursery: likely to need 1½m+. *P. F. I. Cole*

ANVIL (USA)   2 ch.g. (Jan 18) Strike The Gold (USA) – Matilda The Hun (USA)   78
(Young Bob (USA)) [1997 5m⁵ 6s² 7g⁶ 7m 6f⁵ 6g³ Oct 22] $43,000F: close-coupled gelding: fluent mover: fifth foal: half-brother to several winners abroad, including Drummer Boy (by Steady Beat), placed in Grade 3 9f event: dam ran 4 times in USA: fair maiden: placed at Newbury in May and Newcastle (blinkered) in October: should stay beyond 6f: acts on soft ground. *G. Lewis*

ANYAR REEM   6 b.g. Slip Anchor 136 – Alruccaba 83 (Crystal Palace (FR) 132)   70
[1996 NR 1997 a11g² 10.3d* a12g⁴ Jul 26] fair performer: looked ungenuine as 3-y-o: off course 3 years before reappearance: gained first success in amateurs handicap at Doncaster in June: ran poorly final start: effective at 1¼m, probably 1¾m: acts on good to firm and soft ground and fibresand: often has tongue tied: wears bandages. *D. Shaw*

APACHE PARK (USA)   4 b.g. Alleged (USA) 138 – Fairly Magic (USA) (Raise   –
A Native) [1996 6m 8g⁵ 8d 9g 1997 a12g Apr 28] $50,000Y: ex-Irish gelding: third foal: half-brother to a minor winner in USA by Fast Play: dam never ran: no worthwhile form at 3 yrs for D. Weld or in one start in Britain: won claiming hurdle in June, and joined A. Streeter. *D. Burchell*

APACHE RED (IRE)   2 ch.c. (Mar 29) Indian Ridge 123 – Moonlight Partner   84
(IRE) (Red Sunset 120) [1997 5m⁴ 6d³ 5d 7m 6d 8d⁴ 8g⁴ 9s⁶ Nov 9] 40,000Y: first foal: dam Irish 5f winner, sister to smart Irish 1½m winner Dancing Sunset: fairly useful form: won maiden at Leopardstown in October: down field in valuable sales

70

race at Newmarket fourth start: stays 1m (well beaten over 9f): unraced on extremes of going: blinkered (stiff task) third start. *J. S. Bolger, Ireland*

APACHE STAR   3 b.f. Arazi (USA) 135 – Wild Pavane (Dancing Brave (USA) 140) [1996 80p: 7f² 7d* 1997 10g⁴ 11.4s³ 10g 10.2s³ 7m³ 9m* 8g* 8.1s³ 8d 8g Oct 18] big filly: useful performer: won handicaps at Goodwood and Pontefract in the summer: good third to One So Wonderful in listed race at Sandown next start: best efforts at 1m/9f: acts on good to firm and soft ground: visored last 6 starts. *G. Wragg*   96

APARTMENTS ABROAD   4 b.f. Prince Sabo 123 – La Graciosa (Comedy Star (USA) 121) [1996 43, a46: a8g⁴ a8g a10g⁴ a8g⁶ a8g³ 8.1g⁵ 8g 7.1m⁵ 7.5m⁶ 8.1m 6g 6.9d⁶ a12g 1997 10g May 17] leggy filly: poor performer: well beaten only 4-y-o start: stays 1m: headstrong, and has found little. *K. McAuliffe*   –

APICULATE (IRE)   3 b.g. Exactly Sharp (USA) 121 – Reine de Chypre (FR) (Habitat 134) [1996 –: 5s⁵ 5g⁶ 5g⁵ 7f 7.1g² 7.1m⁴ 7g⁶ 8g⁶ 7.5m 7m 1997 a11g⁶ a12g⁵ a7g⁶ 7.5s May 11] no worthwhile form: tried blinkered. *S. R. Bowring*   –

APOLLONO   5 b.g. Cyrano de Bergerac 120 – Daima (Dominion 123) [1996 79: 7f² 7.6g 8.5m 10.1f² 10m⁵ 10m⁵ 12m⁶ 10f⁵ 10.4g⁵ 8.2g a10g 1997 11.9f May 23] angular gelding: fairly useful handicapper at 1m/1¼m at 4 yrs for J. Fanshawe: well beaten both starts for new stable. *R. Lee*   –

APOLLO RED   8 ch.g. Dominion 123 – Woolpack (Golden Fleece (USA) 133) [1996 63, a69: a6g a8g³ a6g⁴ a7g³ a6g 6f³ 5.3f* 7f* 7g a7g a7g* a7g* 1997 a7g⁴ a6g⁴ a7g³ a6g* a6g³ a6g² a6g³ a6g² a6g* 6f² 6.9m³ 7m* 6d 7m³ 6g 8f 7.6m² 6g⁵ 8f⁵ a6s* a7g a6g* Dec 19] sturdy gelding: useful handicapper on all-weather, fair on turf: won at Lingfield in February and April, Brighton in May, and back at Lingfield in November and December (seventh win on all-weather at course): effective at 6f, probably doesn't quite stay 1m: goes well on equitrack, and acts on firm and dead ground: used to be effective in visor (hasn't worn one since 1995): usually races prominently: tough and consistent. *G. L. Moore*   78 a96

APPEAL AGAIN (IRE)   4 br.g. Mujtahid (USA) 118 – Diva Encore 74 (Star Appeal 133) [1996 43: 8.5d 8g 9.9m⁴ 12m⁶ 1997 a8g⁵ a11g⁶ a6g 8g a7g May 12] leggy gelding: poor maiden: little form in 1997, including in blinkers: has pulled hard and looked temperamental. *D. Burchell*   –

APPEARANCE MONEY (IRE)   6 b.m. Dancing Dissident (USA) 119 – Fussy Budget (Wolver Hollow 126) [1996 –: 9.9m a14g 1997 a12g 8d Apr 26] modest maiden (rated 53) at 3 yrs in Ireland: no form on flat in Britain: won chase in May. *F. Murphy*   –

APPIAN DAME (IRE)   2 b.f. (May 18) Mukaddamah (USA) 125 – Apapa Port 80 (My Swanee 122) [1997 6s a5s⁶ a6g Nov 17] 10,000Y: closely related to useful sprinter Sea Gazer (by Magical Wonder) and half-sister to 3 winners here and abroad: dam 5f mudlark: well beaten in maidens. *D. J. G. Murray Smith*   –

APPLE SAUCE   2 b.f. (Apr 14) Prince Sabo 123 – Mrs Bacon 82 (Balliol 125) [1997 5.7f 5m⁴ 5g⁵ 5m 7.6m Sep 9] strong, good-bodied filly: carries plenty of condition: closely related to 5f winner (probably stayed 1m) Presently (by Cadeaux Genereux) and half-sister to smart sprinter Sizzling Melody (by Song): dam 2-y-o 5f winner who didn't train on: modest form in maidens then well held in 2 nurseries: speedily bred. *J. R. Arnold*   52

APPLETON'S FANCY   3 ch.g. Thowra (FR) – Rota 58 (Reliance II 137) [1996 NR 1997 8g 5d⁶ 6m 6g 7.8m 10.3g Oct 25] 6,600 2-y-o: brother to a 2-y-o winner in Italy, and half-brother to 6f winner Kings Touch (by Tachypous): dam 1¼m winner: little sign of ability, trained first 5 starts in Ireland by W. P. Browne: tried blinkered. *A. Bailey*   –

APPREHENSION   3 b.c. In The Wings 128 – First Kiss 84 (Kris 135) [1996 95p: 7.1f* 1997 10.4g⁶ 10.3m³ 11.9g⁴ 12s Sep 14] strong, close-coupled colt: fluent mover: useful performer: best effort when 6¼ lengths fourth of 5 to Stowaway in Great Voltigeur Stakes at York: beat only one in 11-runner Stockholm Cup at Taby final start, but reportedly broke blood vessel: seems better at 1½m than shorter. *D. R. Loder*   109

APPYABO 2 ch.g. (May 25) Never So Bold 135 – Cardinal Palace 85 (Royal 71
Palace 131) [1997 6g 6.9m⁴ 7m⁵ 6m² 7.1m³ a7g² Dec 12] 6,500Y: brother to Irish
1¼m/11f winner Bold Habibti and half-brother to several winners, including
sprinters by Rudimentary and Music Boy: dam won from 9.4f to 1½m: fair maiden:
strong-finishing second of 19 at Newcastle in August: left M. Channon and gelded
after next start, then respectable effort at Lingfield 4 months later: should prove as
effective at 7f as 6f. *M. Quinn*

APRIL IN PARIS 3 b.f. Inca Chief (USA) – Plectrum 58 (Adonijah 126) [1996 –
–: 5.1m 6g 1997 8.2m Jul 19] no form. *C. James*

APRIL JACKSON 3 b.f. Petong 126 – Raintree Venture (Good Times (ITY)) –
[1996 –: 6.1m⁵ 6m 6.1m 1997 8m 6.1d Apr 29] no form. *P. T. Dalton*

AQUADO 8 b.g. Green Desert (USA) 127 – Meliora 73 (Crowned Prince (USA) §§
128) [1996 61§: a7g⁵ a8g⁴ a7g a6g a8g 6g⁶ 7g 5g* 6g² 6m⁵ 6.1m 5m⁵ 5m⁵ 7f² 6g 6f
1997 6g 5s a7g May 12] formerly modest up to 1m: refused or virtually refused to
race on 3 of last 4 starts, and one to leave alone. *D. Shaw*

AQUARELA 2 b.f. (Mar 13) Shirley Heights 130 – Mardi Gras Belle (USA) 65§ – p
(Masked Dancer (USA)) [1997 7m Sep 9] fifth foal: dam, highly strung, stayed 1¼m:
20/1 from 8/1, some promise in midfield in 15-runner Lingfield maiden won by Jibe,
never dangerous and not knocked about: should improve over 1¼m+. *M. R. Stoute*

AQUATIC QUEEN 3 b.f. Rudimentary (USA) 118 – Aquarula 88 (Dominion 58
123) [1996 –: 7f 8g a6g⁶ 1997 a6g 7m 5.1m⁶ 6.1g³ 8.2d⁵ 6.1d⁵ 7f⁶ 6d⁵ 6.1d² 6m* 6m³ a–
6g 6d 7f a7s Nov 28] lengthy filly: modest performer: trained until after ninth start by
R. Weaver: well drawn, made winning debut for new trainer in maiden handicap at
Ripon in July: only form after on next start: likely to prove best at 6f/7f: acts on good
to firm and dead ground, no form on all-weather: well beaten in blinkers. *C. A. Dwyer*

AQUAVITA 3 b. or gr.f. Kalaglow 132 – Aigua Blava (USA) (Solford (USA) 127) 47
[1996 –: 8m 1997 10d 8g 11.9f⁴ 10g 9.7g 14.1d a12g⁴ a12g² Dec 19] leggy filly: poor
maiden: trained until after fifth start by R. Hannon: stays 1½m (stiff task over 1¾m):
acts on firm and dead ground and on equitrack. *J. S. Moore*

ARAB GOLD 2 b.g. (Mar 31) Presidium 124 – Parklands Belle 73 (Stanford 67 +
121§) [1997 6d 7m⁴ 6d Oct 20] 6,800Y: tall, leggy gelding: third foal: dam 6f (at 2
yrs) and 1m winner: best effort in maidens when fourth of 11 at Newcastle, driven
clear halfway but tiring: sweating and probably feeling effects of that race next time:
should stay 1m. *Miss S. E. Hall*

ARABIAN STORY 4 gr.c. Sharrood (USA) 124 – Once Upon A Time 77 114
(Teenoso (USA) 135) [1996 104: 8g² 11.6g* 12m⁶ 12g* 11.9g* 12g 12m² 1997 9s⁶
12g* 10f* 12m² 11g² 16m⁶ Nov 4] tall, angular colt: shows knee action: smart
performer: won valuable rated stakes at Epsom in June and 4-runner listed race at
Newbury (confidently ridden to beat Germano a neck) in July: also second in listed
races at Klampenborg and Newbury (beaten short head by Posidonas) and sixth on
final start to Might And Power in Melbourne Cup at Flemington: stays 2m: acts on
firm going (showed promise only run on ground softer than good): wears bandages:
genuine. *Lord Huntingdon*

ARABOYBILL 6 b.g. Aragon 118 – Floral 82 (Floribunda 136) [1996 55d: a8g⁵ 42 §
a9.4g a12g⁶ a7g⁴ a10g⁴ 10f² 10f⁵ 10.2g⁶ 10m 10.8f a11g⁵ a12g 1997 10g 10f³ 12.1d⁴
16.4g Sep 2] workmanlike gelding: poor performer: stays 1½m: acts on any turf
going, and fibresand: usually blinkered: inconsistent and not one to trust. *J. Neville*

ARANA 2 b.f. (May 10) Noble Patriarch 115 – Pod's Daughter (IRE) 43 (Tender –
King 123) [1997 a5g a6g Dec 4] 720F, 500Y: small, leggy filly: second foal: dam
2-y-o 5f seller winner: well beaten in seller and maiden. *D. M. Hyde*

ARANTXA 3 b.f. Sharpo 132 – Amalancher (USA) 85 (Alleged (USA) 138) –
[1996 72p: 6s 6v* 1997 7g Oct 24] small, good-bodied filly: won maiden at
Folkestone at 2 yrs: off course a year before well held in handicap at Newbury:
should stay beyond 6f. *M. Bell*

ARAWAK CAY (IRE) 2 b.g. (Mar 2) Common Grounds 118 – Alaroos (IRE) 101
(Persian Bold 123) [1997 6d* 5g³ 7g³ 7m⁴ Jul 30] 15,500F, 26,000Y: lengthy, good-
topped gelding: third foal: half-brother to 5-y-o Persian Conquest: dam unraced:

useful form: won maiden at Newmarket in June: in frame in Norfolk Stakes at Royal Ascot, listed race at Newmarket and Lanson Champagne Vintage Stakes at Goodwood, beaten 5¼ lengths behind Central Park in last named (subsequently gelded): stays 7f: sent to Hong Kong. *D. R. Loder*

ARBENIG (IRE)   2 b.f. (Mar 31) Anita's Prince 126 – Out On Her Own (Superlative 118) [1997 5.1m⁵ 6m³ 6m a6g⁴ 6m⁵ a6g⁴ a7g⁵ Dec 13] neat filly: second reported live foal: dam Irish 2-y-o 6f winner: modest performer: made all in maiden at Wolverhampton in October: below form afterwards: stays 6f. *B. Palling*   60 a64

ARBOREAL (USA)   3 b.f. Green Forest (USA) 134 – Saddle Bow 87 (Sadler's Wells (USA) 132) [1996 NR 1997 8m⁶ 6.9g 12g⁶ 9.9d⁴ 12d⁴ 10g May 26] sparely-made filly: second live foal: half-sister to a winner in USA by Elmaamul: dam winning miler: poor maiden: probably stays 1¼m: tried visored. *Mrs L. Stubbs*   42

ARCADY   4 b.f. Slip Anchor 136 – Elysian 94 (Northfields (USA)) [1996 67, a64: 10.2g³ 10d⁵ 12g 11.5f² 14m⁵ 11.7f³ 11.9f³ 16s 13.1m* a14.8g² a12g² 15.8g³ a12g a14.8g* 1997 9.7m 14.1g 14.1d 16.2s 16g² 14m* 20m³ 16.1g⁴ 20m 16.1g* 16.2v⁶ Oct 10] leggy filly: fair handicapper: won at Sandown in May and Newmarket (sweating and bandaged) in August: effective at 1¾m to 2½m: acts on firm ground and fibresand, below form on ground softer than good: often ridden by claimer. *J. L. Harris*   69

ARCANE STAR (IRE)   2 b.g. (Apr 23) Arcane (USA) – Chatsworth Bay (IRE) (Fairy King (USA)) [1997 7.1g 6d⁵ 8d 7m a6g 6.1d Nov 3] IR 7,000Y: sturdy gelding: first foal: dam unraced: modest maiden: no form after second start. *A. P. Jarvis*   61 d

ARCATURA   5 b.g. Beveled (USA) – Bar Gold 80 (Lucky Brief 128) [1996 54: a9.4g 10g⁵ 8g⁶ 10m³ 11.6d⁴ 10.8m 12m 8m² a10g⁴ a10g* 1997 a10g* 10d⁶ 8.1m a8.5f⁴ 8s Jul 4] workmanlike gelding: modest on all-weather, poor on turf: won claimer at Lingfield in January: below that form after: best form up to 1¼m: tried blinkered, but not in 1997. *C. James*   43 a61

ARCH ANGEL (IRE)   4 ch.f. Archway (IRE) 115 – Saintly Guest (What A Guest 119) [1996 55d: a8g² a8g² a8g a8g² a11g⁵ a8g⁵ a8g a8.5g 6.9d 1997 a16g⁶ May 14] light-framed, dipped-backed filly: modest performer at best up to 1m at 3 yrs: tailed off over 2m only start in 1997. *G. F. H. Charles-Jones*   –

ARCHELLO (IRE)   3 b.f. Archway (IRE) 115 – Golden Room (African Sky 124) [1996 69: 5m² 6f³ 1997 5m³ 5m³ 5s² 5m² 6g² 5v⁴ 6g³ 5m* 5m 6.1m 5g⁶ Oct 22] robust filly: fair performer: gained deserved success after making frame 9 times in a row in maiden at Ripon in August: stays 6f: acts on firm and soft going, ran poorly (only time visored) on heavy. *G. R. Oldroyd*   67

ARCO COLORA   3 b.f. Rainbow Quest (USA) 134 – Bella Colora 119 (Bellypha 130) [1996 64p: 7g⁵ 1997 7g 8.1s 10d⁴ 8d Oct 16] leggy filly: modest maiden: left M. Stoute after reappearance: stays 1¼m: found little second start. *D. R. C. Elsworth*   60

ARCTIC AIR   2 br.f. (Feb 13) Polar Falcon (USA) 126 – Breadcrumb 111 (Final Straw 127) [1997 7m² 7d⁶ 7.3g Oct 25] 24,000Y: lengthy, rather unfurnished filly: sixth foal: half-sister to 3 winners, including useful 1990 2-y-o 5f and 6f winner Heard A Whisper (by Bellypha) and fairly useful 7f winner Khubza (by Green Desert): dam 6f and 7f winner from sprinting family: won maiden at Ayr in September by 1¼ lengths from Set Trail: gone in coat, well beaten in listed race at Newbury: likely to prove best up to 1m: should do better again at 3 yrs. *E. Weymes*   79 p

ARCTIC FANCY (USA)   4 ch.g. Arctic Tern (USA) 126 – Fit And Fancy (USA) (Vaguely Noble 140) [1996 85: 12g³ 14d² 14d* 12m 13.3f² 14m 13.9g 1997 13.9g 14m³ 13.9d⁵ 16.1s 14.8m 14s³ 14.4m Sep 21] big, good-topped gelding: fair handicapper: should stay beyond 1¾m: acts on firm and soft going: tends to carry head high, and reluctant to race third start: not to be trusted. *P. W. Harris*   80 §

ARCTIC OWL   3 b.g. Most Welcome 131 – Short Rations (Lorenzaccio 130) [1996 NR 1997 10g* 10.1g⁴ 12g² 11.9s* 12g³ 12s Nov 8] 10,000Y: workmanlike gelding: shows knee action: half-brother to numerous winners here and abroad, including useful stayer Patience Camp (by Bustino) and a Grade 1 2m winner in Australia by Mill Reef: dam Italian 2-y-o 5f winner: useful form: won maiden at Windsor in June and handicap at York (beaten short head by Honourable, but   100 p

ARC

hampered and awarded race) in September: fast-finishing third to demoted Taufan's
Melody in Tote Sunday Special Handicap at Ascot penultimate start, but ran poorly
final one: will stay at least 1¾m: yet to race on going firmer than good: generally
progressive and should do well in handicaps in 1998. *J. R. Fanshawe*

ARCTIC STAR 2 b.g. (Apr 27) Polar Falcon (USA) 126 – Three Stars 93 (Star 66 p
Appeal 133) [1997 7m 7d 6g 7m⁶ 7.3g⁴ 8m⁶ Nov 4] 42,000Y: leggy, unfurnished
gelding: seventh live foal: half-brother to several winners at 1¼m+, notably Irish
Oaks winner Bolas and 3-y-o One For Baileys (both by Unfuwain): dam 1½m winner
from staying family: fair form: good efforts in nurseries at Newbury and Redcar last
2 starts: will prove well suited by 1¼m+: should do better. *M. R. Channon*

ARCTIC THUNDER (USA) 6 b.g. Far North (CAN) 120 – Flying Cloud 78 +
(USA) (Roberto (USA) 131) [1996 93: 13.3d⁵ 12m⁶ 14m³ 1997 12g a12g 10g
a12g⁵ Nov 29] leggy, workmanlike gelding: shows knee action: one-time useful
handicapper: signs of retaining ability in 1997 only on final start: effective at 1½m
and 1¾m: acts on good to firm and dead ground, probably on fibresand: sometimes
bandaged and has tongue tied. *B. Palling*

ARCTIC TRIUMPH 6 b.g. Arctic Lord 114 – Borotown (Treboro (USA) 114) –
[1996 NR 1997 14m⁶ Jul 12] first foal: dam winning selling hurdler: NH Flat race
winner: fair hurdler, winner 3 times in 1997: reluctant stalls, tailed off in maiden at
Lingfield on flat debut. *M. Bradstock*

ARCTIID (USA) 4 b. or br.g. Silver Hawk (USA) 123 – Arctic Eclipse (USA) –
(Northern Dancer) [1996 93p: 10d⁴ 10g* 10.3g² 10.4m³ 1997 10g 10s 10.1g Sep 5]
big, good-topped gelding: fairly useful handicapper, lightly raced: no worthwhile
form in 1997: bred to be well suited by 1½m+: sold approx. £32,000 in Dubai in
November. *J. H. M. Gosden*

ARCUS (IRE) 4 ch.g. Archway (IRE) 115 – Precision Chop (Hard Fought 125) –
[1996 70d: 6d 7s 7v⁶ 5m⁴ 5d³ 5d⁶ 8d⁶ a7g a8g a7s 1997 a7g Feb 3] fair maiden at best
in Ireland: well beaten all 4 starts in Britain (all on all-weather), including in blinkers.
W. R. Muir

ARDARROCH PRINCE 6 b.g. Chief Singer 131 – Queen's Eyot 79 (Grundy 62
137) [1996 NR 1997 12.1s⁵ 10g⁴ 12.3g 15.8g² Aug 15] half-brother to fair stayers
Island Blade (by Sure Blade) and Persuasive (by Sharpo): dam suited by 1¼m: fair
form in NH Flat races (winner) and novice hurdles: modest performer on flat: beaten
head in handicap at Catterick on final start: will prove suited by test of stamina: often
gives trouble at stalls (refused to enter then once) and starts slowly. *Mrs M. Reveley*

ARDENT 3 b.g. Aragon 118 – Forest of Arden (Tap On Wood 130) [1996 –: 6s 56
1997 7g⁵ 7m 8f 8d⁶ 9.7d⁶ 8.2d Oct 30] well-made gelding: modest handicapper:
tailed off final start: seems to stay 9.7f: acts on firm and dead ground. *C. J. Benstead*

ARDLEIGH CHARMER 2 ch.c. (Mar 3) Theatrical Charmer 114 – Miss –
Adventure 69 (Adonijah 126) [1997 8f 8f Oct 29] third foal: dam 1½m winner: well
beaten in autumn maidens at Yarmouth. *C. A. Dwyer*

AREISH (IRE) 4 b.f. Keen 116 – Cool Combination 76 (Indian King (USA) 128) –
[1996 44?: 8m a7g 11.6g⁶ 10f⁵ a7g⁵ a10g 1997 a10g 10g⁶ 11.9f a12g⁴ a12g⁴ Dec 19] a46
poor maiden: stays 1¼m: tried blinkered. *J. Ffitch-Heyes*

ARETHUSA 3 ch.f. Primo Dominie 121 – Downeaster Alexa (USA) (Red Ryder 97
(USA)) [1996 101: 5m* 5.2g² 5m 6m² 6m* 6m⁵ 1997 7.3g 5.7d² 6m⁵ May 31] big,
leggy filly: useful performer: easily best 3-y-o effort when staying-on second of 7 to
Royale Figurine in listed race at Bath: may prove best at 6f: acts on good to firm and
dead ground: sometimes bandaged in front: held up. *R. Hannon*

ARE YER THERE 2 gr.g. (May 24) Terimon 124 – Indian Swallow (FR) –
(Shirley Heights 130) [1997 5s 5m 5g 7g 7.5v 7g Aug 1] 4,800Y: strong gelding:
second foal: dam lightly-raced novice hurdler out of useful German winner Swift
And Sure: no worthwhile form, including in seller. *M. W. Easterby*

ARGUMENTATIVE 2 b.g. (Mar 1) Mujadil (USA) 119 – Dusky Nancy 65 (Red 50
Sunset 120) [1997 6d 6d 6s 6d 6.9g⁴ 7.3d 7m Oct 23] 9,500F, 23,000Y: good-
quartered gelding: fourth reported foal: dam won 1m seller: modest maiden: stays 7f:
acts on soft ground (badly hampered on good to firm). *S. Dow*

74

AR HYD Y KNOS 3 b.f. Alzao (USA) 117 – Top Table 65 (Shirley Heights 130) 36
[1996 –p: 6g 6m 1997 8.2d 8m 6.9m² 7f a7g Jun 28] neat filly: poor maiden: left
R. Charlton after second in claimer at Folkestone: should stay 1m. *G. L. Moore*

ARIAN DA 2 ch.f. (Feb 20) Superlative 118 – Nell of The North (USA) (Canadian 81
Gil (CAN)) [1997 5f² 5.2g² 5m 5m³ 6f⁴ 5d² 6m 5.1g² 5m* 5m² 5d⁴ 5.2f³ Oct 29]
8,000Y: strong filly: sister to 5-y-o Super High and half-sister to several winners,
including 3-y-o Superbelle: dam won up to 9f in USA: fairly useful performer:
gained overdue success in maiden at Sandown in September: ran well in nurseries
afterwards: best at 5f: acts on firm and good to soft going: has been taken early to
post: front runner: tough and consistent. *B. Palling*

ARIAN SPIRIT (IRE) 6 b.m. High Estate 127 – Astral Way (Hotfoot 126) [1996 55
56, a–: a16g 16.1s* 16.2m² 21.6m⁵ 16m* 14.1m* 16.5m² 15d* 16d³ 18g⁶ 15.1s a51
a14.8g 1997 14.9m 15.8m⁵ 18g 16d⁵ 16.2m* a16.2g³ 16.5g² 15g* 17.1g 17.5d³ 15.8g
a14.8g Oct 6] small mare: modest handicapper: won at Beverley and Ayr (amateurs)
in the summer: stays 2¼m: acts on good to firm and soft ground and the all-weather:
blinkered (ran poorly) once at 3 yrs, visored last 5 starts: tail swisher. *J. L. Eyre*

ARIANT (USA) 2 ch.c. (Feb 2) Mr Prospector (USA) – Six Months Long (USA) 93
(Northern Dancer) [1997 6m* 6g Aug 20] $675,000Y: lengthy, good-topped colt: has
a quick action: half-brother or closer to several good winners, notably smart 6f and 7f
winner Half Term (brother) and top-class miler Half A Year (by Riverman): dam won
twice up to 1m in USA: long odds on, overcame greenness to win steadily-run minor
event at Newbury in July by neck from Sabhaan, quickening on over 2f out: tailed-off
last of 7 in Gimcrack Stakes at York month later, too free and dropping away tamely
from 2f out: should stay 1m: seems well regarded, but has presumably had problems.
J. H. M. Gosden

ARIES BOY 2 ch.c. (Apr 16) Risk Me (FR) 127 – Fancy Pages 67 (Touch Paper –
113) [1997 5m 6m a7g a6g Nov 1] 1,850Y: sixth foal: half-brother to a 2-y-o 5f
winner by Today And Tomorrow: dam 2-y-o 5f seller winner: no sign of ability.
D. C. O'Brien

ARIF (IRE) 5 b. or br.g. Try My Best (USA) 130 – Sable Royale (USA) (Real 42
Value (USA)) [1996 12m⁵ 16g 12m 11d⁶ 10g 10f 1997 12m⁶ 12s* 10.1s 14.1s* a14g⁵
16s 11.8d 11.5m² Oct 22] 29,000Y: strong ex-Irish gelding: fifth foal: brother to
French 1m winner Rudyard: dam, placed, half-sister to high-class miler Brinkmanship: modest maiden (rated 51) at 4 yrs for D. Weld: poor form here, winning
weakly-contested handicaps at Folkestone and Nottingham (seller, final run for
B. Curley) in the summer: good effort final start: stays 1¾m: acts on firm and soft
ground: usually blinkered in Ireland: has had tongue tied. *John A. Harris*

ARISAIG (IRE) 3 ch.g. Ela-Mana-Mou 132 – Glasson Lady (GER) 108 59
(Priamos (GER) 123) [1996 –: 7.9g 8s 1997 12.4m⁶ 12g³ 14.1m⁶ 17.2m² 16.2m 16m⁵
16g³ Sep 23] modest maiden handicapper: thorough stayer: acts on good to firm
ground: blinkered (went in snatches) final start: looks a difficult ride. *P. Calver*

ARJAN (IRE) 2 gr.f. (Apr 25) Paris House 123 – Forest Berries (IRE) (Thatching 72
131) [1997 5.1g 5d 5g 5d* Oct 17] IR 14,000Y: third foal: half-sister to 3-y-o Tycoon
Girl: dam unraced half-sister to smart middle-distance colt Pencader: easily best
effort when winning maiden at Catterick by 2½ lengths from Odette, breaking well
and making all: very slowly away first 2 starts, refused to race next time: speedy:
clearly has her quirks. *J. Berry*

ARKADIAN HERO (USA) 2 ch.c. (Jan 29) Trempolino (USA) 135 – 111 +
Careless Kitten (USA) (Caro 133) [1997 7g⁵ 6m* 6g* 6d* 6m⁴ Oct 2]
　　　Since Formidable won both races in 1977, eight winners of the Mill
Reef Stakes at Newbury have attempted to follow up in the Middle Park Stakes
and all have failed, including Kahir Almaydan, Indian Rocket and Arkadian
Hero in the last three years. This trio, who had also won the Champion Two
Yrs Old Trophy at Ripon, failed to do themselves justice at Newmarket, in
Arkadian Hero's case the after-effects of a hard race on softish ground at
Newbury twelve days earlier being the most probable explanation for his
performance. Arkadian Hero started at odds on for the Middle Park but he could

75

Ripon Champion Two Yrs Old Trophy—Arkadian Hero wins impressively from Land of Dreams

make no further impression on the leaders going into the final furlong and finished quite tired in fourth, almost three lengths behind Hayil. Kahir Almaydan and Indian Rocket have so far failed to add to their two-year-old successes, but we'll be disappointed if Arkadian Hero doesn't put his one disappointing effort behind him and win races at three years. A strong, rangy individual with plenty of scope, he certainly looks the type to train on.

Arkadian Hero had got off the mark at the second attempt, in a maiden at Goodwood in July, and he improved significantly again when justifying

Mr M. Tabor & Mrs John Magnier's "Arkadian Hero"

favouritism in the six-runner Champion Trophy at Ripon, making all and quickening clear when shaken up over a furlong out to score apparently with something to spare by two and a half lengths and one and a half lengths from Land of Dreams and Mijana. The second and third went on to take the Flying Childers Stakes and Sirenia Stakes respectively on their next starts, while Arkadian Hero went on to complete his hat-trick, without running up to his Ripon form, in the Bonusprint Mill Reef Stakes. Mijana took on Arkadian Hero again at Newbury and was sent off second favourite in a race where none of the five other runners looked much out of the ordinary. Yet Arkadian Hero made very hard work of disposing of them, allowed to bowl along in the lead approaching halfway having missed the break and taken a strong hold, and all out to hold on by a neck from Jimmy Too after looking as though he might be swallowed up going into the final furlong. It was the first time that Arkadian Hero, who is a fluent mover, had encountered ground softer than good, and it could well be that it doesn't suit him ideally. The pleasing aspect of Arkadian Hero's performance was the manner in which he responded to strong pressure, and his willingness to put his head down and battle (despite having swished his tail for his first win) is another reason to be enthusiastic about his prospects.

		Sharpen Up	Atan
	Trempolino (USA)	(ch 1969)	Rocchetta
	(ch 1984)	Trephine	Vice Regal
Arkadian Hero (USA)		(b 1977)	Quiriquina
(ch.c. Jan 29, 1995)		Caro	Fortino II
	Careless Kitten (USA)	(gr 1967)	Chambord
	(gr 1980)	T. C. Kitten	Tom Cat
		(ch 1969)	Needlebug

Raced only at six furlongs following a promising debut over seven, Arkadian Hero is bred to stay a good deal further—his sire won the Prix de l'Arc de Triomphe while his dam won at up to nine furlongs—but his free-running style suggests that he is unlikely to do so. In this respect he's not unlike another of the stable's sons of Trempolino, Blue Goblin. Arkadian Hero's dam Careless Kitten, from a good American family, is a half-sister to the dams of the 1996 Belmont Stakes winner Editor's Note and the fillies Family Style and Lost Kitty, both Grade 1 winning two-year-olds. Careless Kitten produced four winners (plus a maiden in Japan to the end of 1996) from six foals prior to Arkadian Hero, a 110,000-dollar yearling originally named Crystal Kouger. These included the minor stakes winner Adversarial (by Fit To Fight) who was successful at up to ten furlongs. Her first foal Masnun (by Nureyev) also won at that trip but he was much better known as a sprinter, a useful one in his prime. *L. M. Cumani*

ARLETTY 3 b.f. Rainbow Quest (USA) 134 – Mixed Applause (USA) 101   63
(Nijinsky (CAN) 138) [1996 NR 1997 10.5s[6] 11.8m[4] 10.2m[5] 12g 10d 11.1m[2] 10g[5]
12s[3] 12m Oct 31] good-topped filly: half-sister to several winners, including
high-class miler Shavian (by Kris) and Gold Cup winner Paean (by Bustino): dam
won up to 7f at 2 yrs: modest maiden: stays 1½m: acts on good to firm and soft going:
blinkered seventh (respectable effort) and ninth starts. *H. R. A. Cecil*

ARM AND A LEG (IRE)   2 ch.c. (Mar 31) Petardia 113 – Ikala (Lashkari 128)   68 ?
[1997 5f[6] 5d 6g[5] 5.2f* 7f[2] 7m[6] 7m 6g[5] 7.1s[6] 8m[3] 9m[4] 7d[3] Oct 16] IR 13,000Y: leggy,
close-coupled colt: third foal: half-brother to 2 winners by Fayruz, including 5f (at 2
yrs in Italy) and 7.5f winner Coyote Bluff: dam fourth in Irish 2½m bumpers: fair
performer: won seller at Yarmouth in May: appeared to run very well when third of
29 in similar event at Newmarket final start: stays 1m: acts on firm and soft ground:
has looked none too keen on occasions (visored twice). *C. A. Dwyer*

ARMSTON   5 ch.g. Rock City 120 – Silka (ITY) (Lypheor 118) [1996 NR 1997   50
a14.8g 11.8d[6] 11.5m[5] Oct 22] quite good-topped gelding: lightly-raced handicapper,
only poor nowadays: stays 14.8f: acts on good to firm and dead ground and on
fibresand: usually held up. *J. Wharton*

ARNAQUEUR (USA) 2 b.c. Miswaki (USA) 124 – All Along (FR) 134   104 p
(Targowice (USA) 130) [1997 8d* 8g³ Sep 23] eighth foal: half-brother to smart
French 1m (at 2 yrs) and 10.5f winner Along All (by Mill Reef) and French 1m
winner Aquitaine (by Nureyev): dam top-class middle-distance mare: won 11-runner
newcomers event at Chantilly in September by 8 lengths: odds on, 1¾ lengths third
of 4 to Pinmix in Prix La Rochette there 3 weeks later: should prove capable of better.
A. Fabre, France

ARNIE (IRE) 5 b.g. Double Schwartz 128 – The Moneys Gone (Precocious 126)   48 ?
[1996 NR 1997 5g⁵ a6g² 6m 5m 5.7d 6.9m 6s* 6s 6m 7d⁴ a7g a6g Nov 21] good-
topped gelding: 33/1, easily best 5-y-o effort when gaining first win in apprentice
handicap at Goodwood in June, though probably flattered in coming through late
against favoured stand rail: stays 6f: acts on soft ground: often blinkered. *Jamie
Poulton*

AROUND FORE ALLISS 3 b.g. Reprimand 122 – Artistic Licence (High Top   60
131) [1996 69, a66: 7f⁵ 6m⁵ 6m a8g² 1997 a10g a8g⁴ a10g² a10g³ 10g⁴ 8m 8.3g⁵   a72
a8g* 8.2s 8m⁵ Jul 24] fair handicapper: won at Lingfield in June: barely stays 1¼m:
best recent form on equitrack: takes good hold: inconsistent, and possibly none too
genuine. *T. G. Mills*

ARPEGGIO 2 b.c. (Feb 22) Polar Falcon (USA) 126 – Hilly 96 (Town Crier 119)   87
[1997 5m² 6d² 6m⁴ May 31] 4,000F, 30,000Y: good-topped colt: has scope: has a
quick action: sixth foal: half-brother to a 13f NH Flat race winner by Hadeer: dam
2-y-o 6f winner: fairly useful early-season form in minor event and maidens at
Newmarket and Goodwood: mulish at start and missed break on final occasion:
should prove better at 6f than 5f. *R. Hannon*

ARRASAS LADY 7 ch.m. Arrasas (USA) 100 – Sharelle 67 (Relko 136) [1996   – §
NR 1997 a7g³ a8g³ a7g³ 8.1g a8.5g² a8.5g Sep 30] poor maiden: best form at 7f   a38 §
to 8.5f on fibresand: blinkered (well beaten) twice: refused to race once at 5 yrs:
untrustworthy. *Jamie Poulton*

ARRIVING 3 br.f. Most Welcome 131 – Affirmation 75 (Tina's Pet 121) [1996   77
67p: 7g⁴ 1997 8.2d⁶ 8d⁶ 11.4g* 11.5d² 12.3m³ 12g⁴ 11.8g³ 10m² 10g* 10.5g⁶ 10d
Oct 25] leggy, workmanlike filly: fair handicapper: won at Sandown in June and
Newbury (came from last to first) in September: very stiff task in listed race at
Gelsenkirchen final start: stays 1½m: acts on good to firm and dead going. *J. W. Hills*

ARRUHAN (IRE) 3 b.f. Mujtahid (USA) 118 – Wakayi 87 (Persian Bold 123)   87
[1996 78+: 5m* 6m³ 6f⁴ 1997 6m⁶ 6m³ 7g 7.1g² 7g³ 7m⁵ 7m* 7g Oct 18] tall, useful-
looking filly: fairly useful performer: won 5-runner minor event at Newcastle in
October: should stay 1m: acts on firm ground, yet to race on going softer than good:
has sweated and given trouble at stalls: sent to UAE. *P. T. Walwyn*

ARRY MARTIN 2 b.c. (Apr 14) Aragon 118 – Bells of St Martin 89 (Martinmas   – p
128) [1997 6m Oct 31] half-brother to several winners, including 4-y-o Longwick
Lad and 5-y-o Princess Danielle: dam 2-y-o 5f winner: 33/1, remote tenth of 14,
racing freely and never dangerous, in maiden won by Tussle at Newmarket: should
do better. *W. R. Muir*

ARTAN (IRE) 5 br.h. Be My Native (USA) 122 – Cambridge Lodge 65 (Tower   118
Walk 130) [1996 119: 11d⁴ 11d³ 8g⁴ 10d⁶ 10m* 10g* 10g⁴ 10g* 1997 10f* 11f⁵
Jun 1] smart German horse: won Premio Presidente della Repubblica at Rome in
May by 2½ lengths from Needle Gun, needing only to be pushed out after going on
in straight: conceding weight all round, not discredited behind Oxalagu in Group 2
race at Baden-Baden: stays 1½m, at least as effective at 1¼m: possibly suited by
good ground or firmer: has turn of foot: consistent: suffered injury problems
(including to a pastern) in second half of year, but may return in 1998. *M. Rolke,
Germany*

ARTERXERXES 4 b.g. Anshan 119 – Hanglands (Bustino 136) [1996 83: 7g⁵   87
6.9f* 8.3m⁵ 7f² 7m² 7f² 7m³ 7m 1997 7f² 7m⁴ 8d⁵ 8m 7.9g 7.1m⁶ 7g* Aug 21]
lengthy gelding: fairly useful handicapper: fourth in Victoria Cup at Ascot in April:
won at Yarmouth in August: barely stays 1m: acts on firm and dead ground: front
runner: genuine and consistent. *M. J. Heaton-Ellis*

ARTFUL DANE (IRE) 5 b.h. Danehill (USA) 126 – Art Age (Artaius (USA) 79
129) [1996 76: 8.2d 7g⁴ a8.5g 8.1m 8.2m 8m* 8.1m 8f 8g 8m* 8d⁵ 8g³ 8g⁶ 1997
8m* 8g 7m⁵ 8g 8s² 8m 7.9s 8d 8g 8m⁴ Nov 1] strong, good-quartered horse: fair
handicapper: won Spring Mile at Doncaster in March: ran well after only when in
frame: best around 1m: acts on firm and soft going: visored: takes strong hold:
inconsistent. *M. J. Heaton-Ellis*

ARTHUR'S SEAT 3 b.c. Salse (USA) 128 – Abbey Strand (USA) 78 (Shadeed –
(USA) 135) [1996 –: 6g 1997 10.2m⁶ 10g⁶ 8s Jun 26] good-bodied colt: no
worthwhile form. *Lord Huntingdon*

ARTIC COURIER 6 gr.g. Siberian Express (USA) 125 – La Reine de France 86
(Queen's Hussar 124) [1996 87: 12g⁵ 14.9d 12m* 12m⁴ 12g² 11.8g⁴ 12m² 12g⁵ 12m³
12g² 12g 1997 12m³ 12m 12g⁴ 12s⁴ 12g⁶ 12g 12g³ 14.4m⁵ 14.1d Oct 30] good-
topped gelding: fairly useful handicapper: seems suited by 1½m/1¾m: acts on firm
and soft going: tried blinkered, not in 1997: sometimes wanders under pressure:
normally held up. *D. J. S. Cosgrove*

ARZANI (USA) 6 ch.h. Shahrastani (USA) 135 – Vie En Rose (USA) (Blushing 61
Groom (FR) 131) [1996 59: 6.9g 8.2g 10g a10g* a10g* a10s a10g a10g⁶ 1997 a10g⁴ a56
a9.4g⁴ a12g⁴ 9.7g⁴ 8.2m 10d³ a12g 10g* 10g² 9.7s⁴ 10.8g* 12.5m² 11.6m a10g 10m⁵
10d a10g⁶ Nov 25] plain horse: modest handicapper: won sellers at Leicester in May
and Warwick in July: stays 1½m, at least in steadily-run race: acts on good to firm
and soft ground and on equitrack. *D. J. S. Cosgrove*

ASAD 2 ch.c. (Apr 8) Lion Cavern (USA) 117 – Negligent 118 (Ahonoora 122) 93 p
[1997 7f* Oct 29] second foal: half-brother to 1995 2-y-o Shawanni (by Shareef
Dancer), 7f winner on debut but then showed temperament: dam, won Rockfel
Stakes and third in 1000 Guineas, half-sister to smart stayer Ala Hounak: 5/2, won
steadily-run maiden at Yarmouth by 1½ lengths (pair clear) from Great Dane,
dictating pace and running on strongly: will stay 1m: seems sure to improve. *Saeed
bin Suroor*

ASAKIR 2 ch.c. (Apr 7) Nashwan (USA) 135 – Yaqut (USA) 77 (Northern 108
Dancer) [1997 8.2m* 10d* 10d² Nov 1] rangy colt: has scope: fluent mover with long
stride: seventh foal: half-brother to 3 winners, including useful 1¼m/1½m winner
Estimraa (by Bustino): dam 2-y-o 7f winner from family of Alydar and smart 1997
2-y-o (in USA) Grand Slam: useful form: won 17-runner maiden at Nottingham in
September and 3-runner minor event at Leicester (beat St Helensfield 1½ lengths) in
October: much better form when neck second of 7 to Special Quest in blanket finish
to Criterium de Saint-Cloud: will be at least as effective over 1½m+. *Saeed bin
Suroor*

ASAS 3 b.c. Nashwan (USA) 135 – Oumaldaaya (USA) 111 (Nureyev (USA) 131) –
[1996 95: 8m* 8g 1997 10.4g⁶ 10m 12d Oct 16] tall, rangy colt: fine mover: made
winning debut at 2 yrs, well beaten since: left Saeed bin Suroor after second 3-y-o
start: should stay at least 1¼m: sold 9,000 gns after final start. *J. L. Dunlop*

ASBESTASWECAN 2 ch.c. (Mar 13) Faustus (USA) 118 – Lady Chaser (Posse 58
(USA) 130) [1997 6m 6g⁵ 7g Sep 5] useful-looking colt: fourth foal: brother to a
winner in Belgium: dam unraced: modest form when fifth of 19 in valuable seller at
York in August: not knocked about in maiden at Epsom next time: should stay
beyond 6f: slowly away all starts: sent to Norway. *W. Jarvis*

ASCOT CYCLONE (USA) 2 ch.f. (Mar 7) Rahy (USA) 115 – Dabaweyaa 118 90
(Shareef Dancer (USA) 135) [1997 5.7f* 5m 7g⁴ 6.5m² 6g⁶ Sep 19] smallish, lengthy
filly: fifth foal: closely related to useful performer up to 7f Bin Nashwan (by
Nashwan) and half-sister to 3 winners, including smart 4-y-o 1m and 1¼m winner
Magellan (now in USA, by Hansel): dam 7f/1m winner second in 1000 Guineas:
fairly useful performer: won maiden at Bath in May: excellent head second of 18 to
Branston Berry in valuable nursery at Doncaster in September: well held in Queen
Mary and listed events otherwise: should stay 7f: raced only on good ground or
firmer. *B. W. Hills*

ASEF ALHIND 3 ch.c. Indian Ridge 123 – Willowbed 66 (Wollow 132) [1996 86
NR 1997 8m 8d⁵ 8.5m* 8m 10d 7.1m³ 8.5g⁶ Aug 10] 40,000Y: close-coupled, good-
bodied colt: half-brother to several winners, including modest stayer White Jasmin

ASF

Charles Heidsieck Champagne Cherry Hinton Stakes, Newmarket—
Asfurah (left) shows further improvement in beating Crazee Mental

(by Jalmood) and fair 1987 2-y-o 6f winner Lord's Wood (by Dominion), later winner up to 11f in Italy: dam 1¼m winner: fairly useful performer: won maiden at Beverley in June despite flashing tail: ran well in handicaps next 3 starts: likely to prove best at 7f/1m: acts on good to firm and dead ground. *B. Hanbury*

ASFURAH (USA)   2 b. or br.f. (Apr 19) Dayjur (USA) 137 – Mathkurh (USA) 97   108 + (Riverman (USA) 131) [1997 5m² 5g* 6g* 6m² Aug 10] quite good-topped filly: has a quick action: third foal: closely related to 3-y-o Alumisiyah and half-sister to 4-y-o 1¼m winner (in Dubai) Mutamanni (by Caerleon): dam sprinter: progressive form: won Windsor Castle Stakes at Royal Ascot (by neck from Cortachy Castle) and Charles Heidsieck Champagne Cherry Hinton Stakes at Newmarket (by length from Crazee Mental): favourite, head second of 9 to Princely Heir in Phoenix Stakes at Leopardstown on final start, changing legs repeatedly and not quite getting up: shapes as though will stay beyond 6f: genuine. *Saeed bin Suroor*

ASHANGEM   2 ch.g. (Apr 14) Risk Me (FR) 127 – Dancing Belle 80 (Dance In   – Time (CAN)) [1997 5.1g 5d 6d Oct 28] 5,800Y: fifth foal (all by Risk Me): brother to 2-y-o winners Dances With Risk (at 5f) and Circa (at 6f and 7.3f), latter useful: dam sprinter: no promise in maidens. *Bob Jones*

ASHBY HILL (IRE)   6 ch.m. Executive Perk 120 – Petite Deb (Cure The Blues   72 (USA)) [1996 74: 12f* 10g⁵ 12.1d 9.7m* 8.1m⁴ 10g 10m³ 10m³ 10g* 10m⁶ 8g* 8d* 8g 1997 10g³ 10m⁶ 8s⁵ 9.7m⁵ 7g 7.1m 10m⁶ Oct 1] compact mare: fair handicapper: has won at 1½m, but best at 1m to 1¼m: probably acts on any going: held up and suited by good gallop. *R. Rowe*

ASHGORE   7 b.g. Efisio 120 – Fair Atlanta 73 (Tachypous 128) [1996 88d: a7g*   48 a7g a7g² a7g³ a7g² a7g² 7.5m⁴ a8g³ 6m 7m a8.5g 1997 a6g a7g² a7g a9.4g a8g Dec 8] good-topped gelding: has reportedly had leg problems: fairly useful on the all-weather early in 1996, only poor nowadays: effective at 6f to 7.5f. *T. H. Caldwell*

ASHJAJON   2 b.f. (Apr 26) Lugana Beach 116 – Dondale Rose (Nishapour (FR)   – 125) [1997 5m 5.2f⁶ May 28] first reported foal: dam unraced from family of Oaks winner Polygamy: well beaten in sellers. *J. White*

Godolphin's "Asfurah"

ASHKERNAZY (IRE) 6 ch.m. Salt Dome (USA) – Eskaroon (Artaius (USA) 48
129) [1996 50: 5.7g a5g 5m* 5f 5.1f² 5m a5g⁶ 1997 5m⁶ 5.1m 5m⁵ 5.1m* 5g 5m Sep
24] sparely-made mare: poor handicapper: won at Chepstow in July: stays 6f, races
mostly at 5f nowadays: acts on fibresand and firm ground, unraced on going softer
than good: has been visored/blinkered, not for long time: races prominently: game.
N. E. Berry

ASHRAAKAT (USA) 2 b.f. (May 2) Danzig (USA) – Elle Seule (USA) 122 104 p
(Exclusive Native (USA)) [1997 6m² 7m* 8f Oct 5] lengthy, attractive filly: good
mover: seventh foal: sister to 3-y-o Elnadim and closely related to fairly useful
sprinter Jawlaat (by Dayjur) and very smart miler Mehthaaf (by Nureyev): dam very
smart French 1m to 1¼m winner: promising performer: won maiden at Newmarket
in August by 1¾ lengths from Shimaal, making all: under 3 lengths seventh of 10 to
Loving Claim in Prix Marcel Boussac at Longchamp, racing freely on outer and
going second only briefly in straight: may well prove at least as effective returned to
shorter than 1m: should progress. *J. L. Dunlop*

ASINBOX (IRE) 2 ch.g. (May 17) Persian Bold 123 – Traveling Dancer (FR) –
(Lomond (USA) 128) [1997 6g 7.6d 7.1m Sep 16] 21,000Y: sixth foal: half-brother
to winners in USA and Italy by Jade Hunter: dam unraced: well beaten in maidens.
B. J. Meehan

AS-IS 3 b.g. Lomond (USA) 128 – Capriati (USA) 83 (Diesis 133) [1996 55: 7m⁵ 67
7.1d 6m⁶ 1997 a8s⁵ a8g* a8g² a10g* a12g² a12g* 10.3m⁶ 12.5m² 12m* a12g 12d²
11.8g⁶ 14.1m a12g a13g Dec 12] sturdy gelding: shows knee action: fair performer:
won seller and 2 claimers (second one an apprentice race) at Lingfield in January/
February and handicap at Musselburgh in April: should stay beyond 1½m: acts on
the all-weather and on good to firm and dead ground. *M. Johnston*

81

A S JIM 6 b.g. Welsh Captain 113 – Cawston's Arms (Cawston's Clown 113) – [1996 NR 1997 a8.5g a11g Jan 17] fourth foal: dam never ran: well beaten in sellers on fibresand, blinkered second time: modest hurdler, winner 4 times in 1997. *O. O'Neill*

ASKERN 6 gr.g. Sharrood (USA) 124 – Silk Stocking 109 (Pardao 120) [1996 79: 10g 10m³ 10.9d 13g² 10.2m³ 10.2f³ 11.7f² 11.1m* 11.1m* 11.9m 12m 10m⁶ 11.1d² 12g 10g 10f* 1997 10.8m 10.8m 9.9g² 9.2g 10.2m⁴ 9.2m* 10m⁵ 10.2g 10.5m² Aug 8] tall, good-topped gelding: has a round action: fair handicapper: landed gamble at Hamilton in July: mostly below that form otherwise in 1997 (reportedly suffered from heart irregularity fourth start): effective at 9f, and probably 1¾m: acts on firm and dead ground: blinkered (out of form) once: tends to hang when in front: mounted on track and early to post final start. *D. Haydn Jones* 66

ASKING 5 b.g. Skyliner 117 – Ma Famille 90 (Welsh Saint 126) [1996 NR 1997 10.8m 10s⁶ 12s⁶ Jul 2] poor maiden on flat: tried visored. *J. A. Bennett* 31

ASK SPEEDY SNAPS 2 ch.g. (Feb 19) Librate 91 – Miss Moody 67 (Jalmood – (USA) 126) [1997 5d 6m 6.1m Aug 6] first reported foal: dam, poor maiden on flat, winning hurdler: soundly beaten in sellers. *J. M. Bradley* –

ASPECTO LAD (IRE) 3 ch.g. Imp Society (USA) – Thatcherite (Final Straw – 127) [1996 43: 5m a6g 6g a8g³ a8g 1997 a8g* a8g² a8g² a10g³ a9.4g a12g² a8g² 10g a9.4g Sep 30] sturdy gelding: modest performer: won seller at Southwell in January: left M. Johnston after seventh start: no form for new yard: stays 1½m: form only on the all-weather: blinkered fifth and sixth (ran well) starts, visored final one. *D. L. Williams* a61

ASPEN (IRE) 2 br.f. (Feb 14) Scenic 128 – All In White (FR) (Carwhite 127) [1997 5.7f⁶ 6g³ Jun 16] IR 13,500Y: half-sister to 1990 2-y-o 6f winner Sail Past (by No Pass No Sale) and a winner in Germany: dam French 10.5f winner, half-sister to 2 smart middle-distance winners: better effort in maidens when close third at Pontefract: should be better suited by 1m+. *R. Hannon* 65

ASPIRANT DANCER 2 b.g. (Feb 6) Marju (IRE) 127 – Fairy Ballerina (Fairy – King (USA)) [1997 7m 7m 6m Sep 25] 15,000Y: heavy-topped gelding: third foal: dam Irish 2-y-o 7f winner: well beaten in maidens. *M. Bell* –

ASPRILLA (IRE) 2 b.g. (Apr 29) Sharp Victor (USA) 114 – Aspire (Nebbiolo – 125) [1997 5m 5g 5.9f 5m Sep 26] 4,000 2-y-o: related to several winners in USA one listed placed: dam Irish 7f (at 2 yrs) and 9f winner: not a patch on his footballing namesake. *B. Ellison* –

ASSAILABLE 3 b.c. Salse (USA) 128 – Unsuitable (Local Suitor (USA) 128) [1996 NR 1997 8m⁵ 8m⁴ Oct 22] 16,000Y: sturdy colt: fourth foal: brother to 1m and 1¼m winner Sistar Act and half-brother to Italian 5f winner Lady Unsuitable (by Warrshan): dam unraced daughter of half-sister to good milers Final Straw and Achieved: fair form in maidens at Newmarket in May and Yarmouth in October: sold to N. Callaghan 34,000 gns after latter. *A. C. Stewart* 78

ASSET MANAGER 2 b.c. (Apr 20) Night Shift (USA) – Hud Hud (USA) (Alydar (USA)) [1997 8m 8m⁵ 7m Oct 22] IR 50,000Y: lengthy colt: has scope: third foal: half-brother to 3-y-o 5f (at 2 yrs) and 7f (in UAE) winner Hula Prince (by Lead On Time) and a winner abroad by Great Commotion: dam, thrice-raced, from family of leading American sprinter Mr Nickerson: fair form in steadily-run autumn maidens at Pontefract, Newcastle and Yarmouth: type to do better, probably up to 1m. *M. Johnston* 68 p

ASSIGNMENT 11 b.g. Known Fact (USA) 135 – Sanctuary (Welsh Pageant 132) – [1996 41d: a6g⁴ a6g a7g⁶ a6g 6f 5m 7f 6m 1997 6g 5f May 29] no longer of any account. *Mrs L. Stubbs*

ASSUME (USA) 3 br.c. Known Fact (USA) 135 – Free Spirit (USA) (Avatar – (USA)) [1996 80+: 6g² 5f² 1997 a8g* 7m a7g² a6.5f⁵ Dec 14] strong, useful-looking colt: fairly useful performer: easily made all in 4-runner maiden at Lingfield in March on penultimate start for J. W. Hills: off course over 5 months (and running on medication), second then fifth in allowance races at Hollywood Park in November: likely to prove best up to 1m. *R. Frankel, USA* 80

ASSURED GAMBLE   3 b.g. Rock Hopper 124 – Willowbank 66 (Gay   88
Fandango (USA) 132) [1996 NR 1997 12g³ 12g* 16.2m 11.9g 14m 12m 12m⁵ 14d
Oct 17] lengthy, good-bodied individual: third foal: dam 1½m winner who stayed
well: fairly useful performer: easy winner of maiden at Newmarket in May:
creditable efforts 4 of 6 subsequent starts: stays 2m: acts on good to firm ground:
awkward at start and tailed off fourth outing: sweating last 2: gelded after final one.
C. E. Brittain

ASTARABAD (USA)   3 b.c. Alleged (USA) 138 – Anaza 100 (Darshaan 133)   121
[1996 8g* 1997 10.5m² 10.5g² 10.5d⁴ 12m³ 9.8m⁴ 9.5s* 12m⁶ Nov 23] tall colt:
fourth foal: half-brother to 3 winners, notably useful 1996 Irish 3-y-o winner Asmara
(up to 1¼m, by Lear Fan): dam 1m winner in France at 2 yrs, only season to race:
very smart performer: won newcomers event at Deauville as 2-y-o: in frame
first 6 starts in 1997, best form in Prix du Jockey Club (2½ lengths third to
Peintre Celebre, leading on bit early in straight) at Chantilly, then off course 4
months: won Group 3 race at Bordeaux in October by 1½ lengths from Keep Playing:
back to very best when around 2 lengths sixth to Pilsudski in Japan Cup: stays 1½m:
acts on good to firm and soft ground: held up for turn of foot. *A. de Royer Dupre,
France*

ASTERIX   9 ch.g. Prince Sabo 123 – Gentle Gael 97 (Celtic Ash) [1996 47: 6f 6.1g   42 d
8f 8g 8g 7f³ 7.1g 6.1m⁵ 8.1m* 8.1f² 8.3g 7m 7.1m 9.9m⁴ 1997 8m 8d 8g 6.9m⁴ 8f
7.1m³ 8.1s⁶ 8.1m 7d 8.1g⁵ 8.3g 8m Aug 11] smallish, lengthy gelding: unimpressive
mover: poor handicapper, steadily on the downgrade: effective at 6f to easy 1m: acts
on any going: used to be visored, blinkered nowadays: often partnered by
inexperienced rider. *J. M. Bradley*

ASTRAC (IRE)   6 b.g. Nordico (USA) – Shirleen (Daring Display (USA) 129)   96
[1996 115: 7m⁶ 6m 6f 7.1d⁵ 6m 5g⁶ 6g⁴ 6.1s* 6s* 6s* 1997 6m 6s⁶ 6g 5d 6g³ 6s 5.6m
6g 6g⁵ a7g⁵ 6s a7g Dec 6] sturdy gelding: impresses in appearance: formerly smart,
only useful at best in 1997, leaving Miss G. Kelleway after fourth start: very best
form at 6f: has won on firm ground and fibresand, but probably ideally suited by soft:
well beaten only try in blinkers. *N. Tinkler*

ASTRAL CROWN (IRE)   3 b.f. Astronef 116 – Current Bay (Tyrant (USA))   –
[1996 NR 1997 5.1m 5s 5m 5m⁴ 5d 5d Jun 30] 5,000Y: ninth foal: sister to Italian
sprinter Dia, closely related to a 1¼m winner in France by What A Guest, and
half-sister to 2 winners, including fairly useful Katzakeena (seemed to stay 1m, by
Gorytus): dam 6.5f to 1m winner in Italy/France: seems of little account. *J. Berry*

ASTRAL INVADER (IRE)   5 ch.g. Astronef 116 – Numidia (Sallust 134) [1996   54 d
54: 6g 5d³ 6g⁵ 6m 5.1f³ 6m 5.1m² 5.7f⁵ 7f³ 7.6m⁴ 8f 7.1f a7g 1997 a6g a7g⁴ a6g³ a7g   a36
a7g⁵ a6g² a6g 7m* 6m 7f 6m a7g⁵ 6s⁶ 5.1m a8g Nov 17] leggy gelding: poor
performer: won seller at Leicester in March, making virtually all: well below form
afterwards: stays 7.6f: acts on any turf/all-weather: tried visored, including when
successful: inconsistent. *M. S. Saunders*

ASTRAL INVASION (USA)   6 ch.g. Risen Star (USA) – Santiki 116 (Be My   –
Guest (USA) 126) [1996 NR 1997 a14.8f Jan 11] modest 1½m winner in 1994:
showed nothing only start since: sometimes blinkered/visored: won twice over
fences for T. Wall in December. *G. M. McCourt*

ASTRAL WEEKS (IRE)   6 ch.g. Astronef 116 – Doon Belle (Ardoon 124)   –
[1996 66: 10.1s* 11.1d² 12.1d³ 12.4d 12.1d 1997 12m 11.6s Jun 30] rangy gelding:
fair at best, well held in 1997. *M. J. Bolton*

ASTRAPI   2 b.f. (Feb 23) Last Tycoon 131 – Graecia Magna (USA) 109 (Private   80 p
Account (USA)) [1997 6m⁵ 7d² 7g² Oct 22] lengthy, good-topped filly: sixth foal:
sister to fairly useful 1¼m winner Polydamas and half-sister to 3 winners, including
smart performer up to 1m Thourios (by Green Desert): dam 7f and 1½m winner: fair
form in autumn in minor event at Ascot and maidens at Leicester and Newcastle,
outpaced near finish by Fraud on last-named course: will be suited by at least 1m:
should make a better 3-y-o. *M. R. Stoute*

ASTROJOY (IRE)   5 ch.m. Astronef 116 – Pharjoy (FR) 85 (Pharly (FR) 130)   –
[1996 –: a12g 1997 11.7g Sep 8] disappointing maiden: tried blinkered. *G. A. Ham*

'Bet Compelling Timeform Commentaries' Maiden Stakes, Newcastle—
Atlantic Viking easily upsets the odds laid on Shegardi

ASTROLABE   5 b.g. Rainbow Quest (USA) 134 – Sextant 98 (Star Appeal 133) [1996 –: 14.9d 14.1g 16m 1997 10g 7g 11.9f May 29] leggy gelding: fairly useful staying handicapper at 3 yrs: no form last 2 seasons. *J. M. Bradley* –

ASTROLFELL (IRE)   2 ch.f. (Mar 11) River Falls 113 – Indian Starlight (Kafu 120) [1997 5.1m Mar 31] 2,000Y: first living foal: dam Irish maiden: tailed off throughout in seller at Nottingham. *J. S. Moore* –

ASTROLOGER   2 b.c. (Jan 25) Soviet Star (USA) 128 – Taalif 73 (Last Tycoon 131) [1997 6d³ 7d² Oct 17] 13,000Y: tall, lengthy colt: has plenty of scope: shows knee action: first foal: dam, 6f winner from 3 starts, half-sister to 6-y-o Averti out of sister to Reesh: promising maiden: third of 18 at Newbury (finished strongly under hands and heels) then length second of 6 to Lucayan Indian in steadily-run minor event at Newmarket following month (on toes, free to post and early in race): will be as effective back at 6f as 7f: sure to improve, and win a race or two. *W. R. Muir* 90 p

ASYAAD (USA)   2 br.c. (Feb 25) Zilzal (USA) 137 – Shihama (USA) 88 (Shadeed (USA) 135) [1997 6g³ 6m⁴ 6s⁴ Oct 8] tall, rather unfurnished colt: third foal: half-brother to 3-y-o Bint Shihama: dam, 6f winner at 2 yrs, sister to Sayyedati: shaped better than distance beaten all 3 starts in maidens, best work at finish in first and not at all knocked about at York final start: should stay 1m: type to win races at 3 yrs, particularly handicaps. *B. W. Hills* 78 p

ATH CHEANNAITHE (FR)   5 ch.g. Persian Heights 129 – Pencarreg 87 (Caerleon (USA) 132) [1996 –: 8.3m 1997 a8.5g Apr 8] fair form in Ireland at 3 yrs: tailed off (in blinkers and visor) on flat in Britain: won over hurdles in April and May. *J. Neville* –

ATIENZA (USA)   4 ch.f. Chief's Crown (USA) – Hattab Voladora (USA) (Dewan (USA)) [1996 56: 7m 12.3g 12g⁵ 13.8s³ 12.1g² a14g⁶ 16m⁵ 11.9g 17.9g 1997 15.4m Apr 22] sparely-made filly: modest maiden handicapper: ran badly last 3 starts: stays 2m: acts on good to firm ground: inconsistent. *S. C. Williams* –

ATLANTA   2 b.f. (Jan 19) Rock City 120 – Olympic Run 56 (Salse (USA) 128) [1997 6d⁴ 6g⁶ 5d³ a5g² a5g Dec 8] 1,000Y: lengthy, unfurnished filly: first foal: dam, ran 4 times at 2 yrs, out of half-sister to Electric: fair maiden: trained first 3 starts by J. Dunlop: below form in nursery final outing: bred to stay beyond 6f, but is headstrong. *G. Woodward* 67

ATLANTIC DESIRE (IRE) 3 b.f. Ela-Mana-Mou 132 – Bold Miss (Bold Lad 100 (IRE) 133) [1996 86: 7f 8.5m* 10f² 10g⁵ 1997 9m⁵ 8f² 9g² 8d³ 10.1g* 10g 8m 10m³ 9m* 8d* Aug 8] workmanlike filly: useful performer: won minor event at Newcastle in June and handicap at Ripon and minor event at Salisbury (did well to overcome drop back in trip) in August: should prove better at 1¼m than 1m: acts on firm ground and dead: effective from front or held up: has gone early to post: tough and genuine. *M. Johnston*

ATLANTIC MIST 4 ch.g. Elmaamul (USA) 125 – Overdue Reaction (Be My 57 Guest (USA) 126) [1996 64: 12s⁴ 14.1g²ᵈⁱˢ 12d⁶ 11.6m⁶ 11.4d* 10.2g³ 11.6g 14m⁶ 11.6m² 11.9m 11.4m 1997 10m⁶ 12g² 12m³ 12.5m 12.1m Jul 11] close-coupled gelding: modest handicapper: stays 1½m: acts on good to firm ground and dead: headstrong, and has worn crossed noseband: hung right third start. *B. R. Millman*

ATLANTIC VIKING (IRE) 2 b.c. (Apr 9) Danehill (USA) 126 – Hi Bettina 96 101 p (Henbit (USA) 130) [1997 6g 5f* 5.5d⁶ 5d² 5m³ Oct 31] IR 40,000Y: well-made colt: sixth foal: brother to useful Italian sprinter Fred Bongusto and half-brother to 3 winners: dam Irish sprinter: useful form: won maiden at Newcastle in June: placed in minor event at Ripon (paid for setting strong pace and caught near finish) and nursery at Newmarket: well beaten in Prix Robert Papin third start: almost certainly a sprinter: acts on firm and dead ground: should go on again. *M. Johnston*

AT LARGE (IRE) 3 b.g. Night Shift (USA) – Lady Donna 92 (Dominion 123) 84 [1996 NR 1997 5m⁴ 6m² 5s³ 5g 5s³ 5f² 6.1g* 7g⁴ Oct 18] 25,000F: small, stocky gelding: sixth foal: half-brother to 2 winners in Australasia: dam, 2-y-o 5f winner, half-sister to Tirol: fairly useful handicapper: won at Nottingham then ran well in big field at Newmarket in October: effective at 5f to 7f: acts on good to firm and soft ground: sold 25,000 gns after final start. *J. R. Fanshawe*

AT LIBERTY (IRE) 5 b.h. Danehill (USA) 126 – Music of The Night (USA) 80 d (Blushing Groom (FR) 131) [1996 89: 10g 12m 10m⁶ 12m 12m³ 11.9g 13.3f 8m* 11.9m 10m⁵ 12g 12m⁶ 12s 1997 a12g a10g⁴ 8m a12g* 12g a12g² 12.3v 11.9f⁴ 12m⁴ 11.6m³ 11.9f⁴ 12m 12g⁶ a12g³ Nov 6] sturdy horse: has a quick action: fairly useful at best in 1997: below form after winning claimer at Lingfield in March: stays 1½m: acts on good to firm and soft going and on equitrack: blinkered once. *R. Hannon*

ATNAB (USA) 3 b. or br.f. Riverman (USA) 131 – Magic Slipper 97 (Habitat 64 134) [1996 62: 6m 7.1s 1997 7m 10.2s 12m* 12g³ 14m⁴ 16.4g⁵ Sep 2] sturdy filly: modest handicapper: won at Doncaster in July: ran well next 2 starts: should have stayed at least 2m: acted on good to firm ground: stud. *P. T. Walwyn*

ATOMIC SHELL (CAN) 4 ch.c. Geiger Counter (USA) – In Your Sights 74 (USA) (Green Dancer (USA) 132) [1996 –p: 8.3m 1997 8d 8.1g⁴ 10m Jun 9] leggy colt: fair maiden, lightly raced: clearly best effort on second start: should stay 1¼m. *C. F. Wall*

ATOURS (USA) 9 b.g. Chief's Crown (USA) – Ataire (USA) (What A Pleasure – (USA)) [1996 NR 1997 16g Oct 24] big, good sort: high-class hurdler in 1995/6: has twice suffered off-hind pastern injury: first run of any sort since and in need of race when last in handicap at Newbury: should stay at least 2m. *D. R. C. Elsworth*

ATRAF 4 b.c. Clantime 101 – Flitteriss Park 62§ (Beldale Flutter (USA) 130) 116 [1996 116: 6d⁵ 6m² 6g² 6m* 6m* 7m 6d² 6g 6g 1997 a6f³ a6f⁴ a6f* a7s* 8f 8f Jul 19] smallish, well-made colt: smart performer: won 3 times in 1996 for D. Morley, notably Cork and Orrery Stakes at Royal Ascot: won listed race at Nad Al Sheba in April by short head from Rasas and Grade 3 event at Belmont in May by a neck from Mighty Forum: soundly beaten afterwards: stayed 7f: acted on good to firm and dead ground (below form on firm, at 2 yrs), and on sand: usually raced prominently: tough and game: to stand at Tweenhills Farm, Gloucestershire (fee £1,500, Oct 1st). *K. P. McLaughlin, USA*

ATTARIKH (IRE) 4 b.g. Mujtahid (USA) 118 – Silly Tune (IRE) (Coquelin 50 (USA) 121) [1996 74: 7d⁵ 8f⁴ 10m⁶ 8.1m³ 1997 6m 7f 8.1g⁶ 8m 6d 5.9g⁵ 8m 7d 8g³ 8f 8f⁵ Sep 29] lengthy, angular gelding: has been hobdayed: just a modest maiden handicapper in 1997: stays 1m: acts on firm going, probably on dead: no improvement in visor/blinkers: has carried head awkwardly. *Mrs A. L. M. King*

Kyoto Sceptre Stakes, Doncaster—Aunty Jane (No. 1) just holds off Dazzle (right) and Miss Riviera

ATTITRE (FR)   3 b.f. Mtoto 134 – Aquaglow 84 (Caerleon (USA) 132) [1996 88: 8m 8.2m* 7m⁵ 10g⁴ 1997 7.3g 10m² 11m² 12m 11.9g³ 11.9g 12g⁶ Sep 28] sturdy filly: useful performer: best efforts when placed in listed race at Newmarket, Oaks d'Italia at Milan (beaten length by Nicole Pharly) and Lancashire Oaks at Haydock (1¼ lengths third to Squeak): well beaten all other starts, including in the Oaks: should stay beyond 1½m: raced only on good and good to firm going: visored final start: tends to get on toes and sometimes gives trouble at stalls (refused to enter them once at 2 yrs). *C. E. Brittain*   105

ATTITUDE   3 b.g. Priolo (USA) 127 – Parfum d'Automne (FR) (Sharpen Up 127) [1996 83p: 7.1m 7f* 1997 10.3m 8g³ 8g⁵ 8.1s 9d 8m* Oct 5] workmanlike gelding: fairly useful handicapper: best effort when winning at Leicester in October: seems best at 1m: acts on firm ground. *H. Candy*   92

ATTRIBUTE   3 b.f. Warning 136 – Victoriana (USA) (Storm Bird (CAN) 134) [1996 69: 6m⁴ 5m 7f 7m² 7g 1997 a7g⁴ a7g Jan 23] fair maiden at 2 yrs for R. Charlton: modest at best on the all-weather early in 1997: should stay further than 7f. *R. Guest*   56

ATUF (USA)   2 b.f. (Apr 20) Danzig (USA) – Alchaasibiyeh (USA) 85 (Seattle Slew (USA)) [1997 6m⁶ 6m² 6d* Oct 17] round-actioned filly: fifth foal: sister to useful 1993 2-y-o 6f winner Alami, later 1m winner in Dubai, and closely related to 1990 2-y-o 6f and 1m winner Fraar (by Topsider), later Group 1 1½m winner in Australia, and 6-y-o Ethbaat: dam placed from 6f to 1m is out of a smart sprinter: narrowly beaten in minor event at Ascot prior to justifying favouritism in maiden at Newmarket by head from Swing Along, going smoothly to front then ridden right out: likely to prove best up to 1m: tends to wander: should still do better. *Saeed bin Suroor*   88 p

AUCHINLECK JUDGE   4 b.g. Precious Metal 106 – Pharly Rose (Pharly (FR) 130) [1996 –: a8g 1997 7m 7f 10g 8f Jun 5] tall gelding: no sign of ability. *J. L. Harris*   –

AUDEEN   2 ch.f. (Mar 15) Keen 116 – Aude La Belle (FR) 81 (Ela-Mana-Mou 132) [1997 8.1d Aug 25] first foal: dam winning stayer: tailed off in maiden at Chepstow. *S. G. Knight*   –

AUGUSTAN   6 b.g. Shareef Dancer (USA) 135 – Krishnagar (Kris 135) [1996 57: 10g 10.8g⁵ 10.1m⁵ 12m⁵ 11.9m³ 10m³ 14.6g⁶ 11m² 11f⁶ 10f⁴ 12.1m* 12m⁵ 10g 10f 1997 9.9m⁴ 10g³ 12d* 11.9g 12m⁴ 12f² 12g³ 12g⁶ 14.6d 12m³ 12.1m² 12g⁶ 10m* 11g³ 12d⁴ 12f³ 10g³ 10g 14.6g Oct 24] heavy-bodied gelding: has a markedly round action: fair handicapper: won at Doncaster in May and Pontefract (amateurs) in   65

August: effective at 1¼m/1½m: acts on firm and soft going: tried in visor, not in 1997: has started slowly, and usually held up: tough and consistent. *S. Gollings*

AUNT DAPHNE 3 b.f. Damister (USA) 123 – Forbearance 77 (Bairn (USA) – 126) [1996 –: 7.1s 1997 13.8m² 11.1s⁶ Jul 1] signs of ability, looking a stayer, but no worthwhile form. *B. A. McMahon*

AUNT SADIE 2 ch.f. (Apr 16) Pursuit of Love 124 – Piney River 63 (Pharly (FR) 71 130) [1997 6g⁶ 6d 5.7m² Jul 7] 6,000F: fifth foal: half-sister to fairly useful 1996 2-y-o 5f winner Eye Shadow (by Mujtahid), and 1m winner Gushing (by Formidable): dam maiden from family of Bassenthwaite: best effort in maidens when length second of 14 to Hill Magic at Bath. *R. Charlton*

AUNTY JANE 4 b.f. Distant Relative 128 – Aloha Jane (USA) 57 (Hawaii) [1996 105 92: 7d² 7g*⁸ 8.5m 8g*ᵈⁱˢ 7g 8g⁶ 1997 8.1g 8.1d² 8d* 8g 7f* 8g* 8m⁶ 7s Nov 9] tall, good-bodied filly: impresses in appearance: has a quick action: useful performer: won handicap at Ascot in July and listed races at Doncaster (beat unlucky-in-running Dazzle by head) and Cologne (by ½ length from Big Flower) in September: stayed 1m: acted on firm and dead ground: in foal to Celtic Swing. *J. L. Dunlop*

AURELIAN 3 ch.g. Ron's Victory (USA) 129 – Rive-Jumelle (IRE) 78 (M 64 Double M (USA)) [1996 59: 6m 7f³ 6g⁴ 8f 1997 10d 11.6s 14.1m* 14.1m* 14.1m⁴ 16m 16.1m 14.1g³ Sep 23] lengthy, sparely-made gelding: modest handicapper: won at Redcar (hung left) in May and Yarmouth in June: stays 2m: acts on firm ground, well beaten both starts on going softer than good: sold 1,200 gns in November. *M. Bell*

AURIGNY 2 b.f. (Mar 18) Timeless Times (USA) 99 – Dear Glenda 66 (Gold 99 Song 112) [1997 5d³ 5.3m* 5.1d⁶ 5g³ 5d³ 5d³ 5.5d² 5.2m* 5m Sep 13] 6,600Y: sturdy filly: fifth living foal: sister to 4-y-o Tymeera and half-sister to winner up to 1m (including in Belgium) by Belfort: dam sprinter: useful performer: won maiden at Brighton in May and listed race at Newbury in August, confidently ridden to beat Banningham Blade a head in latter: also placed in Windsor Castle Stakes at Royal Ascot and Prix Robert Papin at Maisons-Laffitte (short-neck second to Greenlander): speedy, and raced only around 5f: yet to race on extremes of ground: sometimes slowly away: best waited with: tough. *S. Dow*

AURORA BAY (IRE) 3 b.f. Night Shift (USA) – Dimmer 108 (Kalaglow 132) – [1996 NR 1997 8g a7g 8.3s 8g Aug 11] second reported living foal: dam, effective from 1m to 1¼m, half-sister to high-class (at 1¼m) Shady Heights: no worthwhile form. *M. Bell*

AUTUMN COVER 5 gr.g. Nomination 125 – Respray 64 (Rusticaro (FR) 124) 83 d [1996 78: a8g³ 8f* 8f* 8m⁴ 8.1m* 8.5m 10m² 8m* 8d 9g* 8g⁴ 9m a7g a10g 1997 8g* 10.1g⁶ 9f 10m 8.3m Aug 23] strong, lengthy gelding: fairly useful handicapper: 33/1-winner at Kempton in May, battling on well: below form all 4 subsequent starts: effective at 1m and 1¼m: acts on firm ground, below form on fibresand and going softer than good: no improvement in blinkers: often bandaged: often makes running. *P. R. Hedger*

AUTUMN TIME (IRE) 3 b.f. Last Tycoon 131 – Cochineal (USA) 52 (Vaguely 66 Noble 140) [1996 NR 1997 12g⁶ 13.9g⁵ 12m² 13.1g⁶ 12s Oct 16] tall sparely-made filly: second foal: half-sister to fairly useful 1995 2-y-o 1m winner Ski Academy (by Royal Academy), disappointing at 3 yrs: dam stayed at least 11.7f: fair maiden: well below form last 2 starts: should stay 1¾m: joined H. Alexander. *P. W. Chapple-Hyam*

AVANT HUIT 5 ch.m. Clantime 101 – Apres Huit 66 (Day Is Done 115) [1996 –: – a5g a6g a5g 5m a6g a6g a5g a5g 1997 a5g a6g⁶ Jan 14] workmanlike mare: sprint maiden, no form since 1995. *Mrs N. Macauley*

AVANTI BLUE 3 b.g. Emarati (USA) 74 – Dominion Blue 66 (Dominion 123) 53 [1996 –: 1.1f 7f 1997 a8g a6g⁵ 5m⁴ a8g³ a8.5g⁶ a12g² a10g³ a14g² a12g⁵ Dec 13] modest maiden: stays 1¾m: acts on all-weather: no improvement blinkered or visored: sometimes hangs left. *K. McAuliffe*

AVERHAM STAR 2 ch.g. (Mar 20) Absalom 128 – Upper Sister (Upper Case – (USA)) [1997 5s a5g 6g⁵ a6g Jun 6] 8,200Y: half-brother to 6-y-o Shuttlecock, and several winners in Italy, where dam winning sprinter: no worthwhile form, including in sellers: blinkered final start. *D. Shaw*

King George Stakes, Goodwood—
Averti storms through on the rail to catch Cathedral (centre)

AVERTI (IRE) 6 b.h. Warning 136 – Imperial Jade 105 (Lochnager 132) 117
[1996 104: 6f⁴ 6d* 6f 5.2m⁶ 6m 6g 6s⁵ 6s 1997 5.1m* 6g⁴ 5g⁴ 5d⁴ 6f⁵ 5m* 5d³
6d⁴ 6m³ 5f⁵ Oct 5]
    Averti spent the first two years of his racing career being confused with
another 1991 foal, a Henry Cecil-trained filly, now at stud, who carried the
USA suffix. There wasn't much to choose between the pair in terms of ability
in those days, but Willie Muir's charge left his previous form well behind in the
latest season, ensuring that he'll be the one better remembered for his exploits
on the racecourse. The third win of his career, gained in a minor event at Bath
on his reappearance, isn't worth expanding on, but his fourth certainly is. That
came in the King George Stakes at Goodwood in July, and it provided Muir
with his first pattern-race winner, repaying the faith he'd kept in the horse
despite various setbacks. Muir recalled that when Averti first arrived in his yard
the horse reared up and landed on the trainer's wife, breaking her knee, and that
his first reaction was 'How's the horse?' rather than 'How's the wife?' As had
been the case with Hever Golf Rose and Rambling Bear in the previous two
runnings of the King George, Averti came from a fair way off a very fast pace,
bursting through under the stand rail to lead in the last fifty yards or so. He was
followed over the line by the three-year-olds Cathedral and Indian Rocket, the
pair beaten half a length and a length respectively, with about a length covering
the next five home. Averti didn't add to that success, but he went on to run well
in good company at both five and six furlongs. He finished just a head behind
dead-heaters Coastal Bluff and Ya Malak when third, storming home after a
tardy start, in the Nunthorpe Stakes at York, then came fourth behind Royal
Applause in the Haydock Park Sprint, third to Elnadim in the Diadem Stakes at
Ascot and fifth to Carmine Lake in the Prix de l'Abbaye de Longchamp. If his
form in previous seasons had been somewhat in-and-out, it was hard to fault
Averti's consistency in 1997.
    Averti, by the miler Warning, is the fourth foal of the useful sprinter
Imperial Jade. Imperial Jade herself was a sister to another notable sprinter in
Reesh, whose six wins included three Group 3 events, namely the Greenlands
Stakes, Palace House Stakes and Temple Stakes. There are plenty of other
speedy animals in the family, including Imperial Jade's half-sister Tadwin who,
like Averti, finished third in the Diadem Stakes. Tadwin's daughter Nadwah
won the Queen Mary in the latest season. Averti's third dam Lady Jester, a
winner seven times over five furlongs, is the grandam of yet another of the
family's smart sprinters, namely Jester. Imperial Jade has produced six winners
besides Averti, all either fair or fairly useful performers.

88

Mr D. J. Deer's "Averti"

		Known Fact	In Reality
	Warning	(b 1977)	Tamerett
	(b 1985)	Slightly Dangerous	Roberto
Averti (IRE)		(b 1979)	Where You Lead
(b.c. 1991)		Lochnager	Dumbarnie
	Imperial Jade	(br 1972)	Miss Barbara
	(b 1982)	Songs Jest	Song
		(b 1976)	Lady Jester

Averti, a robust, attractive horse, acts on firm and good to soft ground, and probably on soft. He's improved with age, and there seems no reason why he shouldn't continue to show smart form in 1998. *W. R. Muir*

AVIVA LADY (IRE) 2 ch.f. (Apr 18) Mac's Imp (USA) 116 – Flying Beauty – (Super Concorde (USA) 128) [1997 5.1g⁵ 5m 5g⁴ 7g a6g Oct 6] 10,000 2-y-o: half-sister to Irish 1½m winner Master Glaze (by Camden Town): dam showed a little ability at 2 yrs in Ireland: little worthwhile form. *C. A. Dwyer*

AVRO AVIAN 3 b.f. Ardross 134 – Tremellick 87 (Mummy's Pet 125) [1996 NR – 1997 10g 10m 7g 16.2m Jul 21] shows plenty of knee action: sister to fair stayer/smart jumper Avro Anson and half-sister to 2 modest winners: dam won 3 times over 5f: no worthwhile form in northern maidens and handicap. *M. J. Camacho*

AWAFEH 4 b.g. Green Desert (USA) 127 – Three Piece (Jaazeiro (USA) 127) – [1996 49: a6g² a8g² a8g a8g⁵ a7g a7g 1997 a7g a8g Feb 22] tall gelding: poor maiden: well beaten in 1997. *S. Mellor*

AWASHA (IRE) 5 b.m. Fairy King (USA) – Foliage (Thatching 131) [1996 68: – a6g² a6g³ a6g³ a5g² a5g* 5g* 5g⁵ 5g⁴ 1997 5g Jul 8] good-topped mare: fair handicapper in first half of 1996 for Miss G. Kelleway: ran as if something amiss over a year later. *K. Mahdi*

AWASSI (IRE)   4 b.c. Fairy King (USA) – Phantom Row 37 (Adonijah 126) [1996   71
7m 1997 8.2d 6s² 7g³ 8m 6g⁵ 7m Nov 1] 42,000F, 75,000Y: ex-Irish colt: second
foal: dam, unplaced, out of Irish 1000 Guineas winner Front Row: bought out of D.
Weld's stable 900 gns in 1996 after only start in Ireland: fair form in Warwick
maidens second and third starts: failed to repeat it: best with testing conditions at 6f,
and stays 7f: acts on soft ground. *K. Mahdi*

AWESOME POWER   11 b.g. Vision (USA) – Majestic Nurse 80 (On Your Mark   –
125) [1996 –, a55: a10g⁶ a10g a12g² a10g* 10m 10m a10g³ a10g² a12g a10g* a10g⁵   a55
1997 a10g² a10g² a10g* a10g* a10g a12g a12g a10s a10g² Dec 12] strong gelding:
veteran who races almost exclusively on equitrack at Lingfield: successful 10 times
there, including in seller in March: stays 1¼m: tried blinkered earlier in career.
J. W. Hills

AWESOME VENTURE   7 b.g. Formidable (USA) 125 – Pine Ridge 80 (High   36
Top 131) [1996 55, a83: a7g² a6g² a6g⁴ a6g² a7g a6g⁴ a6g² a7g² a6g² a7g²   a76 d
a6g³ 7s⁴ a8g* a6g³ 8m a8g* 7m a7g³ a7g* 7.5m³ 7.5f⁵ 7m⁵ 8g⁴ 7f² 7g² 8m⁶ 7m⁵
7f 7m 6m 8f² 9m 1997 a7s² a8g a6g² a7g a6g⁶ a8g a8g 5g⁵ a8g 6m a7g⁴ a6g⁵ a8g 7g
8m⁵ 8m a8g a8g³ a8g a8g⁴ Dec 18] big gelding: fair handicapper on fibresand,
modest on turf: well below form after fifth start: effective at 6f to 1m: acts on any
ground: effective visored (not tried since 1995): well beaten both tries in blinkers.
M. C. Chapman

AWESOME WELLS (IRE)   3 b.c. Sadler's Wells (USA) 132 – Shadywood 96   86
(Habitat 134) [1996 NR 1997 12g⁵ 14m² 12.3g² 11.5m² 11.5m* 12m⁵ Sep 22] big,
lengthy colt: eighth foal: closely related to 1991 2-y-o 6f winner Sun And Shade (by
Ajdal), later successful in USA, and half-brother to very smart 9f to 14.6f winner
Madame Dubois (by Legend of France): dam Lancashire Oaks second from excellent
family of middle-distance stayers: fairly useful performer: won maiden at Lingfield
in September: ran as though something amiss later in month: should stay at least
1¾m: raced only on good/good to firm going. *H. R. A. Cecil*

AWESTRUCK   7 b.g. Primo Dominie 121 – Magic Kingdom 76 (Kings Lake   –
(USA) 133) [1996 –: a14.8g 1997 a14.8g a16.2g⁵ Jun 18] sturdy gelding: lightly
raced and no form last 2 seasons. *B. Preece*

AXEMAN (IRE)   5 b.g. Reprimand 122 – Minnie Tudor (Tudor Melody 129)   47
[1996 –: 7g 7g⁴ 8f 7.9g 1997 7d 7g 7.5g 6d 7m 7f² 8.3g 8.2d Oct 8] leggy, good-
topped gelding: just a poor handicapper nowadays: trained by Miss J. Bower on
reappearance: stays 7f: best form on good ground and firmer: tried blinkered, but not
for a long time. *Martyn Wane*

AYBEEGIRL   3 b.f. Mazilier (USA) 107 – So It Goes 73 (Free State 125) [1996   52
66?: 5m² 5d 6f⁵ 5.1m³ 5f⁴ 5.1m* 5g 5.3f⁶ 6.1m² 7g⁴ 6m 1997 6.9g 6.1d a6g 7m³ 7f⁵
7g Oct 24] close-coupled filly: modest handicapper: well beaten most starts in 1997:
may prove a sprinter: acts on firm ground: no improvement visored: sold only 850
gns in October. *Mrs J. Cecil*

AYE READY   4 ch.g. Music Boy 124 – Cindy's Princess (Electric 126) [1996 –:   –
6s a6g 5s⁴ 5g 5g⁶ 7.1f 7s 7m 6m 1997 5s 6m 9m Jul 19] of little account. *D. A. Nolan*

AZIZZI   5 ch.g. Indian Ridge 123 – Princess Silca Key 61 (Grundy 137) [1996 100:   101
7m* 7.6f² 1997 6s² 7g 6m² 6g⁴ 5v 5g Oct 25] stocky gelding: useful performer,
lightly raced: easily best 5-y-o efforts when second in listed race at Newcastle and
Phoenix Sprint Stakes at Leopardstown and fourth to Wildwood Flower in Gold Cup
at Ayr: has form at 7.6f, but at least as good at 6f: acts on firm and soft ground.
C. R. Egerton

AZORES   3 b.c. Polish Precedent (USA) 131 – Shirley Superstar 94 (Shirley   83
Heights 130) [1996 NR 1997 10g 14.1g⁴ 10m⁵ 11.6m³ 9s* 12d⁵ Sep 12] 31,000Y:
quite good-topped colt: has a round action: fourth living foal: half-brother to Oaks
winner Lady Carla (by Caerleon): dam lightly-raced 7f winner (at 2 yrs) out of smart
filly up to 1¾m Odeon: fairly useful performer: won strongly-run claimer at
Sandown in August, getting up near finish: needs testing conditions at 9f, and
stays 11.6f: acts on good to firm and soft ground: sold 20,000 gns in October.
P. F. I. Cole

AZTEC FLYER (USA)   4 b.g. Alwasmi (USA) 115 – Jetta J (USA) (Super   64
Concorde (USA) 128) [1996 56: 14.1m³ 15m⁴ 16.1m 1997 a14.8g⁵ 10d⁴ 12.5d⁵   a52
14.1m* 16m* 16.1d* 17.5d⁵ 18g a16g⁴ a16g⁵ Dec 10] tall, narrow gelding: modest
handicapper: won at Yarmouth, Nottingham and Warwick in the summer: stays
2m: acts on good to firm, dead ground and equitrack: probably best in blinkers.
C. E. Brittain

AZULINO (IRE)   2 gr.f. (May 8) Bluebird (USA) 125 – Page Blanche (USA)   –
(Caro 133) [1997 6m 7d Oct 27] 50,000Y: good-topped, useful-looking filly:
half-sister to a French 2-y-o 6f winner by Last Tycoon and one over 7f by Sadler's
Wells: dam useful 1m winner from good family: well beaten in maidens at Newbury
(very green) and Lingfield. *J. W. Hills*

B

BAAHETH (USA)   3 ch.g. Seeking The Gold (USA) – Star Glimmer (USA)   68 d
(General Assembly (USA)) [1996 78?: 7d⁵ 8m a8.5g 1997 a8g² a10g³ 10m 12m³
10.8s 11s⁴ 8m 9.9g a10g Sep 9] small gelding: fair maiden: ran poorly after reappearance: blinkered/visored last 3 starts. *S. C. Williams*

BAAJIL   2 b.c. (Feb 4) Marju (IRE) 127 – Arctic River (FR) (Arctic Tern (USA)   85 p
126) [1997 6m² Oct 31] 30,000F, 70,000Y: fifth foal: half-brother to French 9f
winner Springmelt (by Lead On Time) and French 9f to 10.5f winner Melting (by
Antheus): dam French 1¼m winner out of sister to Arc winner Gold River: 5/1,
plenty of promise when 2 lengths second of 14 to Tussle in steadily-run maiden at
Newmarket, short of room until switched and running on well despite holding head
awkwardly and edging right under pressure: will stay at least 1m: should win races at
3 yrs. *L. M. Cumani*

BABA AU RHUM (IRE)   5 b.g. Baba Karam 117 – Spring About (Hard Fought   80
125) [1996 63: 15g 9g 8.1f 8g⁶ 8d 8.2g⁴ 8m³ 1997 8.2g² 8m 8.1g* 8.1d⁴ 8m 8.1m*
Aug 8] tall gelding: fairly useful handicapper: won at Sandown in June and Haydock
(allowed to set pace) in August: unlikely to stay much beyond 1m: acts on dead
going, very best form on good ground or firmer: won over fences in September.
I. P. Williams

BABANINA   2 b.f. (Feb 27) Night Shift (USA) – Babita 107 (Habitat 134) [1997   73
6g⁶ 5.2m⁶ 5m Sep 2] robust filly: fifth foal: half-sister to 1½m winner Bambara and
1995 2-y-o 7f winner (later useful at 1½m) Babinda (both by Old Vic): dam best at 6f
at 2 yrs: 5¼ lengths sixth of 13 in maiden at Newmarket on debut, leading over 4f:
disappointing both subsequent starts. *C. E. Brittain*

BABA SADHU   3 b.g. Mazilier (USA) 107 – La Jambalaya 65 (Reform 132)   –
[1996 NR 1997 8d 8.1g 10d Nov 3] fifth foal: half-brother to a winner in Belgium by
Absalom: dam 7.5f winner suited by soft ground: signs of a little ability on debut,
well beaten in sellers after. *P. J. Makin*

BABE (IRE)   3 b.f. Treasure Kay 114 – Nujoom (USA) 61 (Halo (USA)) [1996 –:   –
7m⁶ 7g 7g 1997 6m Jun 3] well beaten in maidens. *M. H. Tompkins*

BABSY BABE   4 b.f. Polish Patriot (USA) 128 – Welcome Break (Wollow 132)   88
[1996 94: 6m⁴ 5m⁴ 6m⁵ 6m⁶ 6d⁶ 6m 6m 1997 7g 6s 6m⁶ 6m⁴ 6m 6d⁶ Sep 5] tall,
angular filly: fairly useful handicapper: best effort at 4 yrs when fourth at Ripon in
August: should stay 7f: acts on good to firm and dead ground: has flashed tail under
pressure: none too consistent. *J. J. Quinn*

BABY GRAND (IRE)   2 b.f. (Apr 3) Mukaddamah (USA) 125 – Samriah (IRE)   91
(Wassl 125) [1997 5f³ 5d⁴ 5m* 5m* 5g* 5m 5g* 5d* 5d⁵ Sep 18] 3,000Y:
leggy filly: first foal: dam unraced: fairly useful performer: won maiden at
Catterick and minor events at Catterick and Ayr in early summer, then nursery
at Thirsk and minor event at Ripon in August: best effort when catching Atlantic

Viking near finishat last-named track: well held in 2 listed races: should stay 6f: acts on firm and good to soft going: usually ridden by apprentice Kimberley Hart (unable to claim last 3 starts): tough: sold 38,000 gns in October. *T. D. Barron*

BABY JANE 3 b.f. Old Vic 136 – Sutosky 78 (Great Nephew 126) [1996 63p: 6m⁴ 7g⁵ 8.1g⁵ 1997 a8.5g³ a8g⁶ a9.4g² 12g* 12m* 12.4g⁴ 12f 11.1s² 10m Jul 19] angular filly: modest performer: won seller at Pontefract and claimer at Musselburgh (simple task, claimed out of R. Guest's stable) in space of 5 days in the spring: headstrong but stays 1½m: acts on good to firm ground, soft and fibresand (ran poorly on equitrack). *B. Mactaggart* — 64

BABY SPICE 2 ch.f. (May 24) Then Again 126 – Starawak 68 (Star Appeal 133) [1997 6d 7g 7s Oct 16] sister to 5-y-o Fame Again and half-sister to 3-y-o Brand New Dance and useful middle-distance stayer Army of Stars (by Posse): dam 1½m winner: has shown even less talent than her pop-star namesake, but may do better with another year on her back. *M. R. Channon* —

BABY'S TIARA (IRE) 2 b.f. (Mar 1) Chief's Crown (USA) – Baby Diamonds (Habitat 134) [1997 5m⁶ 6d 6g Jul 10] 60,000Y: plain filly: half-sister to several winners in North America, including Grade 2 1m winner Gem Master (by Green Dancer) and Grade 3 9.5f winner Madame Adolphe (by Criminal Type): dam 6f winner at 2 yrs in USA (only season to race), sister to smart 1982 2-y-o sprinter Tatibah: fair form at best in maidens: dead. *R. Akehurst* — 65

BACCHUS 3 b.c. Prince Sabo 123 – Bonica 56 (Rousillon (USA) 133) [1996 NR 1997 6s⁴ 6g* 6m⁶ 6m 7g 7g Oct 24] 29,000Y: workmanlike colt: first foal: dam, lightly-raced maiden, half-sister to smart 1990 2-y-o 6f winner (later stayed 1m) Chipaya: fairly useful performer: carried head high when winning maiden at Newmarket in July: below that form in handicaps afterwards: seems not to stay 7f: sold 16,000 gns after final start. *A. C. Stewart* — 82

BACHELORS PAD 3 b.g. Pursuit of Love 124 – Note Book 94 (Mummy's Pet 125) [1996 94: 6m² 6m* 7m⁵ 1997 8d⁶ 7g⁴ 7m 7d³ 7m 8.2d⁶ Nov 3] leggy gelding: has plenty of knee action: useful performer: best efforts at 3 yrs when in frame in minor event at Leicester in May and handicap at Goodwood in September: bandaged fore-joints, well held final start: stays 7f: yet to race on extremes of going: blinkered second and third starts. *W. Jarvis* — 95

BACKHANDER (IRE) 5 b.g. Cadeaux Genereux 131 – Chevrefeuille 87 (Ile de Bourbon (USA) 133) [1996 56d: a8g a6g² 7.1g² 7m⁴ a6g⁵ 8.2m 7g² 6f⁴ 8.1g⁴ 6.9f 6m⁶ 7m⁴ 9f 6f 1997 a9.4g 7m² 6f 7.1g⁶ a8.5g 6.9m 8f Sep 29] sturdy gelding: poor maiden: effective at 6f to 1m: acts on firm ground and fibresand: usually blinkered nowadays: has hung under pressure. *R. T. Phillips* — 45 d

BACK ROW 3 b.f. In The Wings 128 – Temple Row (Ardross 134) [1996 NR 1997 10g 12d⁵ 10m 12g² 12s² 12m³ 12s Nov 6] small filly: fourth foal: half-sister to useful Mount Row (stays 13.4f, by Alzao) and a winner in USA by Salse: dam unraced half-sister to smart sprinter Colmore Row, out of Irish 1000 Guineas winner Front Row: fair maiden: trained by L. Cumani first 5 starts (ran well next time): should stay beyond 1½m: acts on good to firm and soft going. *J. Hetherton* — 66

BACKVIEW 5 ch.g. Backchat (USA) 98 – Book Review (Balidar 133) [1996 –, a77: a14.8g a16.2g⁵ a12g³ a12g* a12g a14.8g* a12g³ 14.9d⁵ a14.8g³ 12.3m⁴ 14.9m a14g a12g 1997 a12g⁵ Feb 21] short-backed gelding: fair handicapper: well held only outing at 5 yrs: stays 14.8f: acts on fibresand and firm going: tried blinkered. *B. J. Llewellyn* —

BADAWI (FR) 7 ch.g. Script Ohio (USA) – Beautiful Bedouin (USA) (His Majesty (USA)) [1996 –, a49: a14.8g³ a16g* a16g 1997 14.9m⁵ 16.1m* 14.9d⁴ Jun 24] poor handicapper: off course well over a year before reappearance: made all in weak event at Warwick in June: stays 2m well: acts on the all-weather and firm and dead ground: tried blinkered/visored. *N. M. Babbage* — 44 a–

BADENOCH (IRE) 3 b. or br.c. Ela-Mana-Mou 132 – Highland Ball 73 (Bold Lad (IRE) 133) [1996 NR 1997 12.1g³ 12.3g⁵ Aug 25] IR 90,000Y: workmanlike colt: fifth foal: brother to a winner (including at middle distances) in Italy and — 74

half-brother to 11f winner Ceilidh Star (by Soviet Star): dam, second at 1½m, out of1000 Guineas winner Full Dress II: 7½ lengths third of 13 to Prairie Falcon in maiden at Chepstow: tailed off in similar event at Ripon 3 months later: sold approx. £13,000 in Dubai in November. *J. H. M. Gosden*

BADGE OF FAME (IRE) 3 gr.g. Caerleon (USA) 132 – Infamy 123 (Shirley Heights 130) [1996 NR 1997 10s 12d* 14g⁴ 13.9s Sep 3] 2,200,000 francs Y: lengthy gelding: fourth foal: half-brother to winners Kamikaze (1¾m) and Simy (11f in Italy), both by Kris: dam middle-distance performer out of half-sister to good stayer High Hawk, herself dam of In The Wings: fairly useful performer: won maiden at Newmarket in June: withdrawn after getting loose then attacking another horse next intended outing: best effort when fourth in handicap at Sandown in August, running a bit in snatches: stays 1¾m: well beaten both starts on soft going: sold to join K. Bailey 27,000 gns in October and gelded. *L. M. Cumani* 87

BADGER BAY (IRE) 4 b.f. Salt Dome (USA) – Legit (IRE) (Runnett 125) [1996 64§, a54§: a6g⁴ a7g² a7g⁴ a6g⁶ 6m 6m 8f³ 7g 8f² 7m⁶ 7.6m⁴ 1997 7d 6.1d 8g 8g Jul 16] leggy filly: unreliable maiden: well beaten at 4 yrs. *C. A. Dwyer* – §

BADLESMERE (USA) 3 b.c. Geiger Counter (USA) – Arising (USA) 72 (Secreto (USA) 128) [1996 87p: 8s² 1997 8g* 12m* 12f⁴ May 25] tall colt: has scope: won maiden at Kempton and falsely-run 4-runner minor event at Salisbury in May: smart form (easily best effort) when around a length fourth of 16 to Single Empire in Derby Italiano later in month, disputing lead much of straight: stays 1½m: acts on firm ground, shaped promisingly on soft. *P. F. I. Cole* 114

BAD NEWS 5 ch.m. Pharly (FR) 130 – Phylae (Habitat 134) [1996 44, a–: a8g⁶ 8d³ 10.8f 8.2m³ 8m 8m 10.8m 8.3m a8g a9.4g 1997 a8.5g 8g 8.2g 10.1f 8g Jun 18] of no account nowadays. *J. M. Bradley* –

BADRINATH (IRE) 3 b.g. Imperial Frontier (USA) 112 – Badedra (Kings Lake (USA) 133) [1996 NR 1997 a9.4g a7g 7g a5g⁴ 5g a6g a7s² a7g³ Dec 10] half-brother to fairly useful maiden Bawardi (by Doyoun): dam unraced half-sister to Arc second Behera: poor maiden: stays 7f: best efforts on the all-weather. *H. J. Collingridge* 46

BAFFIN BAY 2 b.c. (Apr 28) Bustino 136 – Surf Bird (Shareef Dancer (USA) 135) [1997 8d 8d* Oct 28] good-topped colt: has scope: fifth foal: half-brother to 3-y-o Epic Stand and 5-y-o Break The Rules: dam thrice-raced daughter of Oaks third Britannia's Rule: too green to do himself justice on debut at Newmarket, and later in month won maiden at Leicester by ½ length from Banker Dwerry, under pressure 2f out but keeping on strongly: will be well suited by 1¼m+: looks a useful prospect at the least. *H. R. A. Cecil* 83 p

BAG AND A BIT 4 b.f. Distant Relative 128 – Vaigrant Wind 75 (Vaigly Great 127) [1996 51: 5.1d 5.1g 5m⁵ 7f* 8m⁶ 7g² 6f³ 1997 7m⁴ Mar 27] small filly: modest winner: fourth in seller at Leicester only outing in 1997: best efforts at 7f: acts on firm ground: hung left sixth 3-y-o start. *N. M. Babbage* 34

BAGSHOT 6 b.h. Rousillon (USA) 133 – Czar's Bride (USA) 78 (Northern Dancer) [1996 68§, a61§: 8s 7f⁵ 8.3m⁴ 8.1d⁶ a10g² a7g⁵ a10g² 1997 a8g⁶ a10g* a8g* a8g² 9.7g a8g³ 8g 7m a7g a10g a7g a8g Dec 2] good-topped horse: fair performer at best nowadays: form in 1997 only on the all-weather, winning claimer and seller at Lingfield in January and February: stays 1¼m: tried blinkered/visored: normally held up: unreliable. *G. L. Moore* – § a65 d

BAHAMIAN BEAUTY (USA) 3 b.f. Lord At War (ARG) – Ever (USA) (What Luck (USA)) [1996 NR 1997 7g³ 9s⁶ 6g⁵ 5g* 5g* 6d³ 5.2m Sep 16] $37,000Y: angular ex-Irish filly: sixth foal: sister to 2 minor winners in North America and half-sister to 2 others: dam won up to 7f in North America: fairly useful performer: trained first 2 starts by C. Collins in Ireland: won maiden at Newcastle (easily) and quite valuable handicap at York in summer: best form when ¾-length third to Almasi in minor event at Haydock: should prove best at 5f/6f: acts on dead ground, ran poorly on good to firm: sold 27,000 gns in October. *D. R. Loder* 92

BAHAMIAN BOUNTY 3 ch.c. Cadeaux Genereux 131 – Clarentia 111 (Ballad Rock 122) [1996 116: 6m² 5.2f* 6g* 6m* 7g⁴ 1997 8d⁶ 6g⁴ Jul 10] quite good-topped 113

colt: not best of walkers: fluent mover: smart performer: trained at 2 yrs by D. Loder, successful in Prix Morny and Middle Park Stakes: in marvellous shape, 5 lengths fourth of 9 to Compton Place in July Cup at Newmarket, tracking leaders then unable to quicken from 2f out: a sprinter (didn't stay 1m in Poule d'Essai des Poulains): acted on firm ground: retired to National Stud, Newmarket (fee £4,500, Oct 1st). *Saeed bin Suroor*

BAHAMIAN KNIGHT (CAN)   4 b. or br.c. Ascot Knight (CAN) 130 – Muskoka Command (USA) (Top Command (USA)) [1996 110: 8m² 10m² 10.4m 12m* 12m 12m 10f 1997 10g⁶ 12m⁶ 12g⁶ 12m³ 15.5d Oct 26] quite attractive colt: useful performer at 3 yrs, winning Derby Italiano at Rome: rather disappointing in 1997, leaving D. Loder after second start: stays 1½m: acts on good to firm going: visored once at 3 yrs: blinkered last 2 starts: sold 26,000 gns in October. *R. Akehurst*   **100**

BAHAMIAN MELODY (USA)   2 b.c. (Apr 30) Rubiano (USA) – Song of Syria (USA) (Damascus (USA)) [1997 6g⁶ 6m 5g 6m* 7f 8m Oct 22] $35,000Y: rather leggy colt: looks on weak side: fifth foal: half-brother to 3 minor winners in USA: dam, won twice in USA, half-sister to smart sprinter Doulab: fair form: twice considerably handled before winning maiden at Lingfield in September: disappointing in nurseries last 2 starts: should stay beyond 6f: visored last 3 starts: has high head carriage: looks untrustworthy: sold 11,500 gns after final start. *D. R. Loder*   **72 §**

BAHAMIAN SUNSHINE (USA)   6 ch.h. Sunshine Forever (USA) – Pride of Darby (USA) (Danzig (USA)) [1996 96: 14.4m² 16.4d⁵ 22.2f⁴ 13.9m⁴ 18g⁴ 1997 14d² 22.2d 12m* 14g³ Sep 4] tall, lengthy horse: useful performer: won 7-runner listed handicap at Goodwood by 3½ lengths from Bright Water: soundly beaten in minor event at Salisbury month later: effective at 1½m to 2¾m: acts on any going: sold 30,000 gns in October, and sent to USA. *R. Akehurst*   **103**

BAHHARE (USA)   3 b.c. Woodman (USA) 126 – Wasnah (USA) 96 (Nijinsky (CAN) 138) [1996 122p: 7g* 7m* 7f* 1997 8m² 8g⁴ 10g³ Oct 18]   **121**

Winter classic hope Bahhare didn't make his seasonal debut until the St Leger meeting, a stress fracture of the pelvis, sustained on the gallops in April, having ruled him out of a classic campaign. A slow recovery prompted concern that the colt was suffering from so-called 'Kentucky fever' an ailment affecting the nervous system associated with horses foaled in that State (stablemate Nwaamis had contracted it) and would be out for the season. But such fears proved unfounded, and by September Bahhare had made sufficient progress to be sent to Doncaster on trial for the Queen Elizabeth II Stakes. The result of the three-runner minor race was not really conclusive, with Revoque —a rival for the title 'champion two-year-old' the previous year—holding Bahhare in a sustained duel. After some deliberation, Bahhare lined up at Ascot, a 15/2-shot in a field of nine. Paddock inspection was none too encouraging as Bahhare worked himself into a lather and, in the race itself, he was being niggled along in rear rounding the home turn. He finally found his stride in the final furlong, however, running on to finish just over two lengths behind the winner, Air Express, with Revoque over five lengths further back in eighth place. Having given the firm impression that a mile and a quarter might well be within his compass, Bahhare was sent next for the Dubai Champion Stakes at Newmarket three weeks later. As at Ascot, he sweated profusely, and again he ran on strongly after taking closer order three furlongs out, seeing out the trip well to finish a respectable four lengths behind Pilsudski. This was the final outing of an all-too-brief campaign for Bahhare, but connections made the welcome announcement soon afterwards that he would remain in training as a four-year-old.

Bahhare's breeding was covered in detail in *Racehorses of 1996*. Since him, Wasnah has produced Winsa, a maiden filly who has shown fairly useful form up to a mile. Though not fulfilling his full potential at three years, Bahhare should make a mark in 1998 in company just short of top-class at a mile to a

		Mr Prospector	Raise A Native
	Woodman (USA)	(b 1970)	Gold Digger
	(ch 1983)	Playmate	Buckpasser
Bahhare (USA)		(ch 1975)	Intriguing
(b.c. 1994)		Nijinsky	Northern Dancer
	Wasnah (USA)	(b 1967)	Flaming Page
	(b 1987)	Highest Trump	Bold Bidder
		(b 1972)	Dear April

mile and a quarter, and there is a chance that he'll stay a mile and a half. A rangy, attractive colt with a fluent action, Bahhare has yet to race on ground softer than good, though it's worth noting that a good proportion of his sire's progeny go well under such conditions. *J. L. Dunlop*

BAHIA BLANCA SUN (IRE)   2 b.g. (Apr 28) Tirol 127 – Wild Applause (IRE)   –
71 (Sadler's Wells (USA) 132) [1997 8g Oct 18] 4,000F: second foal: half-brother to useful 1996 2-y-o 7f winner Great Ovation (by High Estate): dam 1½m winner, closely related to high-class miler The Noble Player: 25/1, last of 15 in Redcar maiden, hampered halfway. *J. L. Eyre*

BAHR   2 ch.f. (Apr 19) Generous (IRE) 139 – Lady of The Sea 86 (Mill Reef   106 p
(USA) 141) [1997 7d* 7m* Aug 15]
We don't know a great deal about Bahr just yet, but if the bookmakers are to be believed we'll be hearing plenty more of her as a three-year-old. Although Bahr didn't contest any of the major two-year-old fillies races Ladbrokes have her the 14/1 joint-favourite (with Jibe) for the Oaks at the time of writing. Bahr's claims rest principally on two wins out of two in the summer and the fact that she should prove well suited by further than a mile. Bahr's form can't be rated particularly highly. She gained an impressive debut win in a maiden at Doncaster in June despite going off at 8/1 in a field of seven, storming clear to beat Dazilyn Lady by eight lengths in a fairly good time. However, the nine-length third, Light Step, was beaten twice in ordinary company subsequently and none of the others seem to be anything special. Bahr took on better opposition in the listed Grosvenor Casinos Washington Singer Stakes at Newbury two months later and justified favouritism. Bahr had to work hard briefly, however, before accounting for Quiet Assurance by three quarters of a length, with Fruits of Love and City Honours (making his debut) quite close behind. Quiet Assurance and City Honours won maidens subsequently as well as finishing respectively fifth in the Racing Post Trophy and third in a bunched finish for the Royal Lodge Stakes, while Fruits of Love was second in the Futurity Stakes at the Curragh. Bahr's form, then, is useful but no better, and she would need to improve on it to the tune of about a stone to win an average Oaks.
That's a tall order but not out of the question. Bahr doesn't possess abundant physical scope (we describe her as compact) but she does seem a genuine filly with good prospects of being a better horse when tried at a mile and a quarter plus at three years. Her sire, Generous, has proved a consistent producer of above-average individuals, most of them ultimately suited by at least a mile and a quarter, even though in his short time at stud he's yet to sire a really good performer. Bahr's dam, Lady of The Sea, is a daughter of the great Mill Reef and the champion New Zealand filly La Mer (her ten wins included the country's Oaks over a mile and a half) and fetched 335,000 guineas as a yearling. Lady of The Sea won only once (over a mile) from seven starts but has produced five winners from five foals of racing age, the four before Bahr being Cypriot (by Sure Blade, and a winner several times around a mile in Belgium), Green Palm Tree (a two-year-old five-furlong winner, by Green Desert), Nereus (a mile-and-a-quarter winner, by Shareef Dancer) and Clerio. Of these, Bahr's year-older half-sister Clerio (by Soviet Star), a winner of the Group 3 Trusted Partner Matron Stakes over a mile at the Curragh in the latest season, is by far the best.

Sheikh Ahmed Al Maktoum's "Bahr"

		Caerleon	Nijinsky
	Generous (IRE)	(b 1980)	Foreseer
	(ch 1988)	Doff The Derby	Master Derby
Bahr		(b 1981)	Margarethen
(ch.f. Apr 19, 1995)		Mill Reef	Never Bend
	Lady of The Sea	(b 1968)	Milan Mill
	(ch 1986)	La Mer	Copenhagen
		(ch 1973)	La Balsa

Bahr has been acquired by Godolphin and will winter in Dubai. There are probably better Oaks prospects around, but not many, and we'll be in a much better position to judge her classic prospects after she has reappeared at three. *B. W. Hills*

BAHR ALSALAAM (USA)   3 b. or br.f. Riverman (USA) 131 – Trolley Song –
(USA) (Caro 133) [1996 NR 1997 10d Apr 26] fifth foal: half-sister to Breeders' Cup
Juvenile and Florida Derby winner Unbridled's Song (by Unbridled): dam, winner at
2 yrs in North America, half-sister to smart 6f/7f winner Merlins Charm out of very
smart winner up to 9f Lucky Spell: 25/1, well-beaten eighth of 9 in maiden at Ripon:
sent to USA. *J. H. M. Gosden*

BAILIEBOROUGH BOY (IRE)   3 ch.g. Shalford (IRE) 124§ – Salique   68
(Sallust 134) [1996 61: 5m³ 5m³ 6g a6g⁴ 1997 a6g a7g² a8g² a7g* a8.5g* a8g* a8g³
a8g⁶ Mar 14] fair performer: completed quick hat-trick in February, in sellers at
Southwell and Wolverhampton and claimer at Southwell: effective at 7f and 1m: acts
well on all-weather: blinkered last 5 starts: sold 2,500 gns in October. *T. D. Barron*

BAILIWICK   4 b.g. Dominion 123 – Lady Barkley (Habitat 134) [1996 –, a54: –
a8g* a7g³ a8.5g³ a8.5g² 11.6m 11.8d a12g 1997 a12g a12g⁵ a9.4g Apr 26] workmanlike gelding: modest handicapper: well beaten in 1997: stays 8.5f: acts on
fibresand: usually blinkered: races prominently. *N. A. Graham*

BAIRN ATHOLL 4 ch.f. Bairn (USA) 126 – Noble Mistress 80 (Lord Gayle 41
(USA) 124) [1996 –: 6m 6.9d 1997 8f 6.1m 5g² 5.1m 5.7g⁴ 8m 5m² 6.1m Sep 15]
sturdy filly: poor maiden handicapper: probably a sprinter: acts on good to firm
going: has looked a difficult ride. *R. J. Hodges*

BAJAN (IRE) 6 b.g. Taufan (USA) 119 – Thatcherite (Final Straw 127) [1996 –: –
10m 12d 1997 a10g⁵ Jan 23] lengthy gelding: one-time fair handicapper: lightly
raced and no form last 2 seasons: often visored (not on only start in 1997). *Lady
Herries*

BAJAN ROSE 5 b.m. Dashing Blade 117 – Supreme Rose 95 (Frimley Park 109) 76
[1996 89: 6g 6s² 5.1m* 5m⁴ 6.1m 5.2m³ 5m 6m 6m² 6g³ 6s³ 6f 1997 6m 6d⁶ 5d 6f⁵
5d⁴ 5.1s 6s 5m³ Nov 4] leggy mare: only fair handicapper at 5 yrs: stays 6f: acts on
firm and soft ground: blinkered fifth (ran creditably) and sixth starts. *M. Blanshard*

BAKED ALASKA 3 b.f. Green Desert (USA) 127 – Snowing (USA) (Icecapade 93
(USA)) [1996 90p: 6g* 1997 7g⁶ 7s² 8.5m⁵ 8d⁶ 7g Jul 8] good-topped filly: fairly
useful performer: best effort when 2 lengths second, running in snatches, to Supercal
in listed event at Lingfield in May: should stay beyond 7f: acts on soft going: visored
(finished last) final start: one to treat with caution. *A. C. Stewart*

BAKERS DAUGHTER 5 ch.m. Bairn (USA) 126 – Tawnais 80 (Artaius (USA) 64
129) [1996 57, a61: a8g² a8g a8g³ a8g³ a8g 8.1m³ 8m³ 8.3g³ 10g* a10g* 10m⁵ 10.2f a48
10d⁵ a10g³ a10g 1997 a12g a8g⁴ a10g² a10g 10s² 10g⁴ 9.7s² a10g⁴ 10m* 8.1g⁶ 10m
10m⁴ 10s 10d Oct 28] sparely-made mare: modest handicapper on turf: mainly in
good form in summer, gaining repeat success in 18-runner race at Windsor in July:
only poor form on all-weather at 5 yrs: suited by around 1¼m: acts on good to firm
and soft ground: blinkered (ran well) once in 1996. *J. R. Arnold*

BALA 2 ch.f. (Mar 28) Casteddu 111 – Baladee (Mummy's Pet 125) [1997 5g⁶ 5m³ 60
5.1m 5.1g⁴ 5s⁵ Oct 16] 11,500Y: lengthy, unfinished filly: half-sister to fairly useful
1995 2-y-o 5.2f winner Kandavu (by Safawan) and a winner abroad by Dunbeath:
dam unraced: modest maiden: raced only at 5f: shows tendency to hang. *H. Morrison*

BALACLAVA (IRE) 2 b.g. (Mar 9) Balla Cove 119 – Little Cynthia 76 (Wolver 74
Hollow 126) [1997 7m 7g² 7g³ 8f 7g⁶ 7v Oct 10] IR 5,600F, IR 22,000Y: workmanlike gelding: good mover: half-brother to numerous winners, including sprinters
Hinari Disk Deck (by Indian King) and Hinari Video (by Sallust): dam stayer: fair
form in maidens when placed at Newcastle and Kempton in summer: disappointing
in nurseries: sold (7,500 gns) and gelded after end of season: stays 7f: may be worth
a try in headgear. *E. A. L. Dunlop*

BALAITINI (IRE) 2 b.f. (Apr 24) Lion Cavern (USA) 117 – Balwa (USA) 101 71 p
(Danzig (USA)) [1997 7m⁶ Sep 9] third foal: half-sister to 1½m winner Laazim
Afooz (by Mtoto): dam 5f (at 2 yrs) and 7f winner from very good family: 16/1 from
7/1, some promise when under 3 lengths sixth of 16 to Vocation in Lingfield maiden,
drawn wide but improving halfway and keeping on: should stay at least 1m: will
improve. *A. C. Stewart*

BALALAIKA 4 b.f. Sadler's Wells (USA) 132 – Bella Colora 119 (Bellypha 130) 108
[1996 106: 9m* 10m⁵ 12m² 11.9m 10.1m² 12g⁵ 10g⁴ 1997 9m* 8d⁴ 10m⁶ 8.9s³ 9.3f⁴
8m² Nov 1] strong, rangy filly: has a powerful, round action: useful performer: won
listed race at Newmarket in May: in frame in similar events at Goodwood, York and
Newmarket and Prix de l'Opera (best effort when 1¾ lengths fourth of 17 to Clodora)
at Longchamp after: stayed 1½m: acted on firm and dead going: sometimes bandaged: stud. *L. M. Cumani*

BALANCE OF POWER 5 b.g. Ballacashtal (CAN) – Moreton's Martha (Derry- 56
lin 115) [1996 76: 6f 6d 7m 7f³ 7g* 7g 8m* 7f² 8.5m⁶ 8d 8.2g 1997 8f⁵ 8.5m 7m 10g
8.1g 7d⁴ 7f Jul 15] useful-looking gelding: modest performer: fell fatally at Brighton:
effective at 7f/1m: best efforts on good going or firmer: tried blinkered, no
improvement. *S. Dow*

BALANCE THE BOOKS 2 b.f. (Mar 10) Elmaamul (USA) 125 – Psylla 96 75
(Beldale Flutter (USA) 130) [1997 5g* 7g 6g 7g⁵ 8f 6m⁶ Oct 6] 11,500F, 44,000Y:
rangy, unfinished filly: eighth foal: half-sister to several winners, including fair
1¼m winners Akayid (by Old Vic) and Kabayil (by Dancing Brave): dam, 9f and
1¼m winner, from family of Kris and Diesis: fair form: won minor event at York in

May: good fifth in nursery at Newmarket in August: had excuses final 2 starts: bred to stay beyond 7f: sold 20,000 gns in October. *R. Hannon*

BALANITA (IRE) 2 b.g. (Mar 8) Anita's Prince 126 – Ballybannon 76 (Bally- 70 more 123) [1997 6.1g 5g⁶ 6s⁶ 5.1m 6m 7m* a7g⁴ Nov 14] 40,000Y: eighth foal: half-brother to Irish 1½m winner Indian Desire (by Indian King) and 2 other winners: dam, 1m and 1¼m winner in Ireland, sister to Irish Oaks third Racquette, the family of Ardross: fair performer: made all in 18-runner nursery at Brighton in October: well beaten in similar event at Southwell after: stays 7f: acts on good to firm ground (fair effort on soft): tends to sweat and give trouble at stalls. *B. Palling*

BALERIENA (BEL) 4 br.f. Bacalao (USA) – Regendinoa (FR) (Prince Regent – (FR) 129) [1996 NR 1997 8s Jul 4] Belgian-bred filly: showed little in Warwick maiden on debut. *J. M. Plasschaert, Belgium*

BALFOUR LADY 3 gr.f. Absalom 128 – Pearl Cove 63 (Town And Country 66 124) [1996 NR 1997 7g⁶ 8.3s 6s⁵ 8.3m 7d 10m⁶ 10m³ 12s Oct 16] 7,200Y: seventh foal: sister to 7f winner St Louis Lady and half-sister to several winners, including 4-y-o Prospector's Cove: dam lightly raced: fair maiden: form only on sixth and seventh starts: should stay beyond 1¼m: acts on good to firm ground. *J. A. R. Toller*

BALI DANCE 2 br.f. (Mar 28) Rambo Dancer (CAN) 107 – Baliana 75 (Midyan 64 ? (USA) 124) [1997 6g³ 6f⁵ 6g³ 7g³ 7s³ 7g 7m⁵ 8d 8m 7s⁴ a7g⁵ a7g* Dec 12] 6,000Y: close-coupled filly: first foal: dam unreliable sprinter: modest performer: made all in maiden at Lingfield in December: should stay 1m: acts on firm and soft ground and equitrack: blinkered twice, running creditably first time: possibly ungenuine. *C. B. B. Booth*

BALINSKY (IRE) 4 b.f. Skyliner 117 – Ballinacurra (King's Troop 118) [1996 – 55: 7s 7f³ 7g 7f⁴ a8.5g⁴ a7g³ a8s⁵ a8.5g⁶ 1997 a6g a6g⁴ Feb 14] angular filly: poor maiden: showed little in visor/blinkers at 4 yrs: stays 7f. *J. Berry*

BALI PARADISE (USA) 3 b.g. Red Ransom (USA) – Dream Creek (USA) 100 (The Minstrel (CAN) 135) [1996 95: 5d* 6d³ 7g⁶ 7.3m* 7.3s⁵ 1997 8.2m⁴ 10.4g⁵ 10m⁵ 10.1s⁴ 8g⁶ 10m⁵ 10m² 10d⁵ 12m Sep 30] tall, workmanlike gelding: useful handicapper: ran best races at Newbury in August (neck second to Song of Freedom) and September (fifth to Sharp Consul in Courage Handicap): stays 10.4f: acts on good to firm and soft ground: races prominently: consistent: sold 45,000 gns in October, to go to Saudi Arabia. *P. F. I. Cole*

BALI-PET 3 b.g. Tina's Pet 121 – Baligay 84 (Balidar 133) [1996 ?, a57: a7g⁶ 43 d a7g² 7f⁵ a7g 10f a8.5g² a8g* a7g² 1997 a8s⁵ a8g⁵ 10m 7g 9.9d 7m⁶ 8.2d a11g³ a9.4g 8g 8.5d 10m 7m a8g a8g Dec 18] leggy gelding: has a round action: poor performer: left W. G. M. Turner after second outing: stays 8.5f: acts on fibresand: often blinkered: inconsistent. *J. Parkes*

BALLA D'AIRE (IRE) 2 b. or br.g. (Mar 4) Balla Cove 119 – Silius (Junius 72 (USA) 124) [1997 6d⁴ 6m 7d Oct 14] 15,000Y: leggy gelding: fifth foal: half-brother to useful Irish 5f performer Dairine's Delight (by Fairy King): dam Irish 4-y-o 1m and 9.5f winner: fair form in maiden at Newmarket in June: well below that level in 2 subsequent starts 3 months apart, failing to settle final one. *R. Boss*

BALLADARA (IRE) 3 b.c. Ballad Rock 122 – Mochara (Last Fandango 125) – [1996 NR 1997 6g⁵ 7m 7.1g⁶ 6.1d 8g 8f a8.5g Sep 30] IR 17,000Y: close-coupled colt: sixth reported foal: half-brother to 2 winners, notably 6-y-o Cool Edge: dam second over 5f at 2 yrs in Ireland: little worthwhile form, including blinkered. *R. Hannon*

BALLANTRAE BOY 3 ch.g. Safawan 118 – Romany Home (Gabitat 119) – [1996 NR 1997 7d 7m 9.2g Sep 29] third foal: dam unraced: no sign of ability in maidens, trained first start by R. McKellar. *J. S. Goldie*

BALLARD LADY (IRE) 5 ch.m. Ballad Rock 122 – First Blush (Ela-Mana- 53 Mou 132) [1996 49: 8s³ 8g⁵ 8.3s a8g 8m⁴ 8m⁴ 7g 7.1d* 7.6m⁴ 6d* 7g⁵ 6.1m 6m⁵ 6m⁴ 7g a6g³ 1997 a6s* a6g⁵ a7g⁵ a6g 8g 6.1d⁶ 5.1g⁴ 5g² 6g 7.1d² 7.6m³ 8g⁵ 6g* 5g 6.1m Sep 15] big mare: shows traces of stringhalt: has a round action: modest handicapper: won at Southwell in January and Hamilton (idled) in August: effective at 5f to 7.6f (had form over as far as 1½m in 1995): acts on good to firm ground, dead and on fibresand: visored once at 2 yrs. *J. S. Wainwright*

BALLASILLA   2 b.f. (Mar 4) Puissance 110 – Darussalam 78 (Tina's Pet 121)   55
[1997 5m⁵ 5.1d 7m⁶ a6g⁴ a5g⁶ Nov 14] 5,500Y: first foal: dam winning sprinter: a59
modest maiden: best effort at Wolverhampton fourth start: stays 6f. *B. Palling*

BALLERINA'S DREAM   3 b.f. Suave Dancer (USA) 136 – Our Reverie (USA)   –
(J O Tobin (USA) 130) [1996 –p: 6f 1997 a5g⁵ a6g⁶ a8.5g Mar 29] sparely-made
filly: no worthwhile form. *Martyn Meade*

BALLET DE COUR   4 b.g. Thowra (FR) – Chaleureuse (Final Straw 127) [1996   35 d
–: 10m 12g⁵ 13.8g⁴ 1997 a12g a12g a8.5g³ a7g a8g 8m 9f 11.1s³ 16m 13g 14.1s⁴
13m³ 14.1m Jul 19] poor maiden: stays 1½m: acts on good to firm and soft ground:
often blinkered/visored. *T. J. Etherington*

BALLET RAMBERT   2 b.f. (Apr 22) Rambo Dancer (CAN) 107 – Kind   69
Thoughts 71 (Kashmir II 125) [1997 5.1m* 6f⁶ 6d⁴ 7f 5.7m 8m 7.3d 8m⁶ 8m Oct 22]
2,600Y: close-coupled filly: half-sister to several winners here and abroad, including
useful 6f (at 2 yrs) and 7f winner Kayus (by Junius), later successful in USA, and
stayer Penny Forum (by Pas de Seul): dam staying sister to high-class sprinter Blue
Cashmere: fair performer: won maiden at Bath in April: in-and-out form in minor
events and nurseries: stays 1m: acts on good to firm ground, probably on good to soft.
M. J. Heaton-Ellis

BALL GOWN   7 b.m. Jalmood (USA) 126 – Relatively Smart 76 (Great Nephew   –
126) [1996 98, a–: 10m* 10.4f⁶ 10f 10g 10m⁵ 10m⁴ 10m⁴ 10d* 11.1m⁶ 1997 10.4g³
10d 10.4m 12m 10d 9m Oct 4] small mare: tough, genuine and useful handicapper in
1996: signs of retaining ability but no worthwhile form as 7-y-o (faced several stiff
tasks): stays 1½m: possibly best on ground from good to firm to good to soft (no form
in 3 races on all-weather): needs to be held up. *D. T. Thom*

BALLPOINT   4 ch.g. Indian Ridge 123 – Ballaquine 56 (Martinmas 128) [1996   78
77: 7m 8.1m² 10g 8g³ 8g⁴ 10.1g* 8.9g⁴ 11.5m² 11f 1997 12* 12.4m⁵ 16.1f⁴ 12m
13.8g⁴ 12.3m Aug 16] small gelding: poor mover: fair handicapper: won at Catterick
in April: pulled up lame final start: likely to prove best up to 1¾m: acts on good to
firm ground: held up. *G. M. Moore*

BALLYDINERO (IRE)   3 b.g. Ballacashtal (CAN) – Nutwood Emma (Henbit   –
(USA) 130) [1996 43: 5m 5.9g 5.9f⁴ 7.1g⁵ 7m 7g 10f⁵ a8.5g 1997 12g a12g⁵ 11.1s
12v a12g³ 11s 8.1m Aug 15] maiden, no form as 3-y-o: visored last start, blinkered
previous two. *Capt. J. Wilson*

BALLYKISSANGEL   4 ro.g. Hadeer 118 – April Wind 91 (Windjammer (USA))   –
[1996 –: a6g⁶ 8g 6m 8.3m 7g 12.1g a8g 1997 a6g Jan 10] tall gelding: little worthwhile form. *N. Bycroft*

BALLYKISSANN   2 ch.g. (Mar 19) Ballacashtal (CAN) – Mybella Ann (Anfield   67
117) [1997 8m 8m⁵ Oct 23] leggy gelding: second foal: dam out of 1½m winner and
successful hurdler, little sign of ability: fair form in maidens at Salisbury (not
knocked about) and Brighton in October: may do better. *D. J. S. ffrench Davis*

BALLYMOTE   3 b.g. Chilibang 120 – Be My Honey (Bustino 136) [1996 74: 5d   76
5.1m⁴ 5m² 5f* 5f⁵ 6g 5m* 1997 5m⁵ 5g² 5d⁴ 5m⁴ 5m 5d 5m Nov 4] tall gelding: fair
handicapper at best: lost his form after third start at 3 yrs, off course 4 months after
fourth one: races keenly and form only at 5f: acts on firm ground and dead, unraced
on anything softer. *J. Berry*

BALLYRANTER   8 ch.g. Bold Owl 101 – Whipalash 73 (Stephen George 102)   49
[1996 NR 1997 10s⁶ 10g Jun 2] strong gelding: poor handicapper: stays 1½m:
acts on equitrack and any turf going, except heavy: used to be best in a visor.
H. J. Collingridge

BALLY SOUZA (IRE)   3 b.f. Alzao (USA) 117 – Cheese Soup (USA) (Spec-   87
tacular Bid (USA)) [1996 70: 6.1m 7g³ 7m⁵ 1997 8g⁶ 10g² 11.5d⁴ 11.9d³ 11m* 12g*
12.4m³ 11.9m³ 11.9s⁴ Sep 4] close-coupled filly: fairly useful handicapper: won at
Redcar and Thirsk within space of 6 days in July: will probably stay beyond 1½m:
acts on good to firm ground and dead, possibly not soft: sold IR 18,000 gns in
December. *M. Johnston*

BALLY WONDER   5 b.m. Music Boy 124 – Salacious (Sallust 134) [1996 NR   –
1997 7g 10.4s Sep 4] bad maiden. *H. J. Collingridge*

BAL

BALTIC STATE (USA) 2 b.c. (May 12) Danzig (USA) – Kingscote 118 (Kings   103
Lake (USA) 133) [1997 6f* 7g* 7m⁵ Jul 30] good-bodied colt: has a round action:
eighth foal: half-brother to 3-y-o Sambac and very smart French/US 1m winner Rainbow Corner (by Rainbow Quest): dam 2-y-o 5f and 6f (including Lowther Stakes)
winner from good family, failed to train on: useful form: odds on, won maiden at
Yarmouth in June and falsely-run 4-runner listed race at Newmarket (all out, by head
from Silent Tribute) in July: moved scratchily to post and failed to progress again
when just over 5 lengths fifth of 6 to Central Park in Lanson Champagne Vintage
Stakes at Goodwood (found to be jarred after): will probably stay 1m. *H. R. A. Cecil*

BANBURY (USA) 3 b.c. Silver Hawk (USA) 123 – Sugar Hollow (USA) (Val de   93
L'Orne (FR) 133) [1996 NR 1997 7.1s³ 10d³ 10g* 12d 10.1m Aug 3] small colt:
closely related to 2 winners by Lear Fan, notably very smart performer around 1¼m
Cruachan: dam unraced: won maiden at Redcar in May: ran poorly in handicaps at
Royal Ascot (tongue tied, upset in preliminaries) and Newcastle afterwards: should
be suited by 1½m. *J. W. Watts*

BANDBOX (IRE) 2 ch.c. (Feb 7) Imperial Frontier (USA) 112 – Dublah (USA)   79
(Private Account (USA)) [1997 5d 5g⁵ 5.1s³ 5g 6.1g² 5g⁴ 5.1d² 5m² 6g² 5d² 6d*
Oct 28] IR 5,000F, 8,200Y: third foal: half-brother to 5f winner Happy Partner (by
Nabeel Dancer): dam unraced: fair performer: won maiden at Leicester by ½ length
from Double Brandy: stays 6f: acts on good to firm and good to soft ground:
consistent. *S. Mellor*

BAND ON THE RUN 10 ch.h. Song 132 – Sylvanecte (FR) 70 (Silver Shark   90 d
129) [1996 98d: 8d⁶ 8d⁶ 7.1d³ 7.9m⁶ 8.1d² 7.1d⁴ 7.1d² 8m⁵ 7.3m 7.6d 8m 8g 1997
8m³ 8g 8m 8m 8.1m* 8.9d 7.1g⁶ 7.9g⁴ 8.1m 7.6s 8m 8.1g 8g Oct 18] good-topped
horse: carries condition: poor mover: veteran handicapper: not quite so good at 10
yrs, though still won at Haydock in June: below best last 5 starts: effective at 7f/1m:
acts on good to firm and dead ground: has won in blinkers, but not tried for long time.
B. A. McMahon

BANDORE (IRE) 3 ch.g. Salse (USA) 128 – Key Tothe Minstrel (USA) 108   –
(The Minstrel (CAN) 135) [1996 81p: 7.1m⁵ 7.6m* 7m 1997 12s 9.7m 9.9g⁴ 11.5d
16g Sep 23] good-topped gelding: has a quick action: fair winning 2-y-o: little show
in handicaps in 1997: should stay 1¼m: sold 14,000 gns in October. *D. R. Loder*

BANKER DWERRY (FR) 2 b.c. (Feb 25) Unfuwain (USA) 131 – Tartique   79 p
Twist (USA) 78 (Arctic Tern (USA) 126) [1997 8m⁶ 8d² Oct 28] 28,000Y: good-
topped colt: fourth foal: closely related to 2m winner Tabdeel (by Warrshan), 1¼m
winner in UAE in 1997, and half-brother to 3-y-o Barnwood Crackers: dam 1¾m and
2m winner from family of good French performers Salpinx and L'Emigrant: better
effort in autumn maidens when ½-length second of 13 to Baffin Bay at Leicester,
tracking leaders, switched wide and staying on: likely to be suited by at least 1½m:
open to further improvement. *S. P. C. Woods*

BANKERS ORDER 3 b.c. Prince Sabo 123 – Bad Payer 72 (Tanfirion 110)   –
[1996 –: 6d 1997 a5g 5f Sep 17] good-quartered colt: no form. *T. D. Easterby*

BANK ON HIM 2 b.g. (Mar 30) Elmaamul (USA) 125 – Feather Flower 74   52
(Relkino 131) [1997 8s a7g⁶ a7g⁶ Dec 10] 15,000F: unfurnished gelding: half-
brother to several winners, including 1995 2-y-o 5f winner Maggi For Margaret (by
Shavian), later useful up to 1m in France, and fairly useful 1½m winner Meavy (by
Kalaglow): dam second at 1¼m here before winning at 1½m in France: only sign of
ability in maidens at Lingfield second start. *G. L. Moore*

BANNERET (USA) 4 b.g. Imperial Falcon (CAN) – Dashing Partner 71 (Form-   –
idable (USA) 125) [1996 62: 8d 8g⁴ 1997 12.1s 10.8s 12g 8m 11m Oct 28]
good-bodied gelding: maiden, no form in 1997 (trained by J. A. Harris on reappearance): blinkered last 2 starts. *J. O'Reilly*

BANNINGHAM BLADE 2 b.f. (Apr 9) Sure Blade (USA) 130 – High Velocity   94
53 (Frimley Park 109) [1997 5m 5f* 5.3f* 5.3f* 5m³ 5d* 5m² 6m⁴ 5m⁴ 6d⁶ 5.2f³ 5m⁴
5.2m² 5d³ 5m⁵ 6d⁶ 5v Oct 11] 600Y: leggy filly: half-sister to 3-y-o Anokato and
4-y-o Mindrace: dam 5f performer: very tough youngster, and fairly useful: won
maiden at Lingfield and minor events at Brighton (2) and Windsor: already having
ninth outing when fourth in Queen Mary Stakes at Royal Ascot and subsequently

100

fourth in Molecomb Stakes at Goodwood and second (beaten head by Aurigny) in listed race at Newbury: continued to run well until final start: best form at 5f: acts on firm and good to soft ground: tremendously game and genuine, and a credit to her trainer. *K. T. Ivory*

BANZHAF (USA) 4 ch.g. Rare Performer (USA) – Hang On For Effer (USA) (Effervescing (USA)) [1996 74, a82: a7g* a8g* a8g⁴ 6m 6f⁵ 7g 7m² 7f³ 7m⁶ 1997 a8g 7f a8g² 8d 8m⁵ 7.6m⁵ 7.1m* 8.3m 6.9g² 6.9m⁴ 7f³ a8s³ a8g* Dec 12] big gelding: fairly useful on the all-weather, fair on turf: won claimer at Sandown in July and handicap at Lingfield in December: best at 7f/easy 1m: acts on firm going and on equitrack. *G. L. Moore* — 73 / a91

BAPSFORD 3 b.g. Shalford (IRE) 124§ – Bap's Miracle (Track Spare 125) [1996 61d: 5g⁶ 5f 5.1m⁴ 6g⁵ 6g⁵ 7m 6.9v 1997 a6g 7m a8g⁴ a9.4g⁵ a10g³ a10g* a8.5g* a7g⁵ a9.4g² Dec 6] neat gelding: modest performer: won selling handicap at Lingfield in August and apprentice claimer at Wolverhampton following month: effective at 1m to 1¼m: best form on the all-weather: visored twice at 2 yrs. *M. Waring* — – / a65

BAPTISMAL ROCK (IRE) 3 ch.g. Ballad Rock 122 – Flower From Heaven (Baptism 119) [1996 5s 5m 5m⁵ 5m⁵ 7g 5m² 5g 1997 a6g a7g 6f 8.2m 6.1g 5g 5m Jun 6] IR 11,000Y: compact ex-Irish gelding: poor mover: fifth foal: half-brother to 2 winners, notably fairly useful 5-y-o Angel From Heaven (stays 1¼m, by Bob Back): dam sprinter: fair maiden (rated 68) for T. Stack in 1996: well beaten in Britain, including in sellers. *B. J. Curley* — –

BARANOV (IRE) 4 b.g. Mulhollande (USA) 107 – Silojoka 95 (Home Guard (USA) 129) [1996 64: a8g⁵ a7g² a7g⁵ a7g² a7g⁵ 6.9m 7f 10.8m* 9.7m³ 10.8f⁴ 12.1s 1997 a10g 10.8m 9.7s 12s Oct 16] modest winner: soundly beaten at 4 yrs. *D. J. G. Murray Smith* — –

BARATO 6 ch.g. Efisio 120 – Tentraco Lady 65 (Gay Fandango (USA) 132) [1996 72: 5s³ 6g 6.1g³ 5.9d 5.9m² 6.1m³ 6d⁶ 5m⁴ 6m 5.9f² 6m 7g 6m 6g³ 6d³ 6f⁴ 6m⁵ 6f 1997 6m 5m 5g 6g Apr 28] sturdy gelding: just modest form in 1997: effective at 5f to 7f: acted on firm and soft going: effective visored or not: dead. *Mrs J. R. Ramsden* — 60

BARBA PAPA (IRE) 3 b.c. Mujadil (USA) 119 – Baby's Smile 68 (Shirley Heights 130) [1996 ?: 8s² 1997 6.9m* 9.9s³ 9d* 10f* 8d⁵ 10m 9d⁵ 9m Oct 4] smallish colt: good mover: useful performer: won apprentice maiden at Folkestone in April (by 7 lengths) and small-field minor events at Milan in May and June: creditable efforts in face of stiff tasks in handicaps last 3 starts: will probably stay beyond 1¼m: acts on firm and dead ground. *L. M. Cumani* — 98

BARBARA'S JEWEL 5 b.g. Rakaposhi King 119 – Aston Lass 66 (Headin' Up) [1996 –: 8s 8m⁶ 10d 1997 a7g a7g³ a9.4g* a8g a8.5g a14.8g 11.1s⁵ a12g² 13.1g⁵ 10.5m⁴ Jun 6] poor performer: won maiden at Wolverhampton in March: stayed 13.1f: acted on good to firm ground and fibresand: dead. *A. Bailey* — 49

BARBASON 5 ch.g. Polish Precedent (USA) 131 – Barada (USA) (Damascus (USA)) [1996 –, a61: a10g³ a7g* a7g a7g⁵ 6m 10g⁵ a8g³ a8g⁴ a8g⁴ a7g³ 1997 a6g³ a7g⁴ a7g a7g* a7g* a8g* 7f* 7f* 8f⁵ 6m³ 7f* 7f⁶ a7g⁴ a7g³ a8g³ a8g⁵ Dec 12] compact gelding: fair performer: had a good year, successful 3 times on equitrack at Lingfield (2 handicaps and a minor event) in February/March before winning handicaps on turf at Lingfield and Brighton in April and again at Brighton in July: stays easy 1m: acts on firm ground and equitrack: usually held up: tough and consistent: a credit to his trainer. *G. L. Moore* — 75

BARBRALLEN 5 b.m. Rambo Dancer (CAN) 107 – Barrie Baby 86 (Import 127) [1996 38: 8.3m 6.9m⁵ 8.2d 7.1m a6g a8g 1997 8.1m 6.9m 9.7s 6.9s 6.9m Aug 5] of little account. *Mrs L. C. Jewell* — –

BARBURY BALLAD (IRE) 3 b.c. Ballad Rock 122 – Eeduff (Auction Ring (USA) 123) [1996 NR 1997 7g 8.3s 8f³ 6f 5g³ 7g 6m⁴ 6f Sep 18] IR 13,500Y: second foal: dam, Irish maiden, half-sister to Diomed winner Mr Martini: no worthwhile form: sent to Germany. *M. J. Heaton-Ellis* — –

BARDON HILL BOY (IRE) 5 br.g. Be My Native (USA) 122 – Star With A Glimer (Montekin 125) [1996 96: a8g⁴ a10g³ a10g⁶ 10.2f* 12s² 12f² 11.9m⁶ 12.4m²⁺ 16.1g 10m* 10d⁴ 10.1m 10m 1997 a9.4g³ a12g⁶ a10g⁴ 10.3d 8.5d⁵ 10.1g 10s⁴ 12.3m³ 10m² 10g Aug 2] leggy, lengthy gelding: fairly useful handicapper: best effort at 5 — 88 yrs when second at Sandown in July: best around 1¼m to 1½m: yet to race on heavy going, acts on any other turf/all-weather. *B. Hanbury*

BARGASH 5 ch.g. Sharpo 132 – Anchor Inn 48 (Be My Guest (USA) 126) [1996 69d, a45: 7s* 6.1g³ 7.1g 7m⁵ 7g⁴ 7g⁵ 6d 7s 6d a7g⁶ a7g³ 1997 a7g⁴ Jan 4] sturdy gelding: formerly fair winner: poor form only start at 5 yrs: stays 7f: acts on firm and soft ground: tried blinkered/visored: none too consistent. *P. D. Evans*   – a45

BARITONE 3 b.g. Midyan (USA) 124 – Zinzi (Song 132) [1996 70: 6g³ 6m³ 6g³ 6s 1997 7m⁶ 8g² 7m 7g 6d 7v⁵ 7s⁵ Jul 3] close-coupled colt: fair maiden handicapper: probably best at 7f/1m: acts on good to firm ground, probably soft: respectable effort in blinkers fifth start: looked none too keen final start: joined S. Kettlewell. *J. W. Watts*   75

BARKSTON WARRIOR 3 b.g. Totem (USA) 118 – Bold Difference 66 (Bold Owl 101) [1996 NR 1997 8m 11.8d 8d Oct 28] small, compact gelding: third foal: dam won from 6f (at 2 yrs) to 1¼m: no sign of ability in a maiden and claimers. *D. Shaw*   –

BARNBURGH BOY 3 ch.g. Shalford (IRE) 124§ – Tuxford Hideaway 102 (Cawston's Clown 113) [1996 70p: 5m⁵ 6d⁵ 6g⁶ 5f⁴ 6m⁴ 1997 5.1m³ 6g⁵ 6g⁴ 7g² 8g² 8m² 8g³ 8d³ 8m 7m² 8m² 8g Oct 18] close-coupled gelding: fairly useful maiden handicapper: left T. D. Barron after eighth outing: stays 1m: acts on good to firm and dead ground, yet to race on softer: genuine and consistent: winning hurdler. *T. D. Easterby*   87

BARNUM SANDS 3 b.c. Green Desert (USA) 127 – Circus Plume 124 (High Top 131) [1996 101: 7m⁴ 7.6d* 8.1m* 8d² 8g² 1997 9m⁴ 10.3v² 9d² 10g⁵ 10m* 10d⁴ Oct 16] angular colt: useful performer: in frame in listed races at Newmarket and Chester in the spring on first 2 starts: made all in 5-runner minor event at Kempton in September, beating Haltarra a neck: stays 1¼m: acts on good to firm and dead going: blinkered fourth start (below form): often forces pace: sold 50,000 gns and sent to Saudi Arabia. *J. L. Dunlop*   106

BARNWOOD CRACKERS 3 ch.g. Be My Chief (USA) 122 – Tartique Twist (USA) 78 (Arctic Tern (USA) 126) [1996 58: 6m 6f* 7f* 8d⁶ 7.1m⁶ a8g 1997 a8g⁵ a10g⁴ 11.6m 12g³ 16.4m Aug 19] sturdy gelding: modest form at 2 yrs and on reappearance: left Miss G. Kelleway after next start, off course 6 months and only a little subsequent form: pulled up lame final start: should be suited by further than 1m: acts on firm ground and equitrack: fractious type: tended to hang left at 2 yrs. *M. R. Channon*   53 d

BARONESS NOBLE 2 b.f. (Mar 28) Noble Patriarch 115 – Baroness Gymcrak 53§ (Pharly (FR) 130) [1997 6m Jun 2] third foal: dam, ungenuine sprint maiden, half-sister to smart Domynsky: last in seller at Thirsk. *T. D. Easterby*   –

BARON FERDINAND 7 ch.g. Ferdinand (USA) – In Perpetuity 90 (Great Nephew 126) [1996 NR 1997 10m Oct 31] strong, lengthy gelding: fine mover: made into a smart performer at 5 yrs (rated 114), though met with a setback final start: 7 lengths seventh of 9 to Saafeya in steadily-run listed event at Newmarket over 2 years later: should prove as effective at 1½m as 1¼m: acts on good to firm ground: wears crossed noseband and sometimes bandages: held up and has turn of foot: pulled up over hurdles in December. *R. Charlton*   99

BAROON 3 ch.c. Rainbow Quest (USA) 134 – Dreamawhile 85 (Known Fact (USA) 135) [1996 7g⁵ 7g² 1997 11g* 11g* 11v 12g² 12g* Aug 10] 120,000Y: third foal: half-brother to 5-y-o Struggler: dam, 7f winner, is half-sister to Derby Italiano winner My Top: smart performer: won in minor company at Dusseldorf and Bremen in the spring: neck second of 20 to Borgia in Deutsches Derby at Hamburg in July then won very valuable 6-runner Group 2 event at Hoppegarten (beat Borgia ½ length) in August: stayed 1½m: well beaten on heavy ground: injured a tendon and at stud in South Africa. *A. Wohler, Germany*   117

BAROSSA VALLEY (IRE) 6 b.g. Alzao (USA) 117 – Night of Wind 101 (Tumble Wind (USA)) [1996 84: a7g² a8g³ a8g² a10g* a10g* 1997 a10g⁶ 8m 7m 8m Jun 6] fairly useful at best: disappointing in 1997: stays 1¼m: acts on firm ground, went well on equitrack at 5 yrs: effective in blinkers, but not tried since 1995: often front runner. *P. Butler*   –

BARRACK YARD   4 b.c. Forzando 122 – Abbotswood (Ahonoora 122) [1996   57
62p: 7m 8.3m a8g* 8.3g⁵ a7g* 1997 a6g* 7d⁵ 7.3g 7s a6g⁵ 7s Oct 17] lengthy colt: a77
easily best effort when winning handicap at Wolverhampton in April: modest form
at best on turf (well beaten at 4 yrs all bar second start): effective at 6f to 1m: acts
on dead ground, goes well on fibresand: sold 3,800 gns, and sent to Sweden.
A. C. Stewart

BARRANAK (IRE)   5 b.g. Cyrano de Bergerac 120 – Saulonika 94 (Saulingo   68
122) [1996 64: 6m 5m³ 5m 6m 10g 6m³ 5m 5m⁴ 5g* 5d⁴ 5m 5f⁶ 1997 5g⁶ 5g
6m⁵ 5.1g 5f² 5m* 5g* 5d² 5d⁴ 5.1m² 5m 5g⁵ 5s⁴ 5m 5m 6.1s Oct 15] compact
gelding: fair handicapper: won at Salisbury and Lingfield in June: effective at 5f
and 6f: unraced on heavy going, acts on any other: blinkered (ran poorly) once.
G. M. McCourt

BARRELBIO (IRE)   2 b.g. (Apr 14) Elbio 125 – Esther (Persian Bold 123)   60
[1997 5g⁴ 5s 5m⁶ 6g 7s 5s* Nov 6] 6,400 2-y-o: first foal: dam, unraced, from family
of Bustino: won selling nursery at Musselburgh, comfortably despite wandering:
probably a sprinter: acts on soft going. *J. J. O'Neill*

BARREL OF HOPE   5 b.g. Distant Relative 128 – Musianica 92 (Music Boy   61 §
124) [1996 82, a73: a8g³ a8g⁶ 8s 7g² 6m* 7g³ 6m 6m 7m 6v⁴ 7g 7s a7g³ a9.4g*   a70 §
a8g³ 1997 a9.4g⁴ a7g² a8g⁶ a7g⁶ 8m 6g 6g May 16] sturdy gelding: fair handicapper:
typically inconsistent at 5 yrs: acts on good to firm and heavy ground and
on all-weather: usually blinkered/visored nowadays: often makes running: moody.
J. L. Eyre

BARRESBO   3 br.g. Barrys Gamble 102 – Bo' Babbity 75 (Strong Gale 116)   69
[1996 55, a?: 5.9f 6m⁶ 6g⁴ 6m 7g a6g⁵ a6g a5g 1997 8.2m⁴ 8.3d³ 8.2d⁵ 10g 8m²   a–
10f 7.1d² 8g 7g* 8m⁴ 7.1g Sep 27] strong, lengthy gelding: has a quick action: fair
handicapper: best effort when winning at Newcastle in July: stays 7f: blinkered once
at 2 yrs. *C. W. Fairhurst*

BARRIER RIDGE   3 ch.g. Lycius (USA) 124 – Star Ridge (USA) (Storm Bird   86
(CAN) 134) [1996 NR 1997 8.2m² 9d³ 8f* Jun 2] good-topped gelding: unim-
pressive mover: fifth foal: half-brother to minor winners in USA by In Fijar and
Siberian Express (2): dam, ran twice in France, half-sister to Grade 1 placed Bee A
Scout: fairly useful form: won maiden at Thirsk by a length from Dantesque, making
all: may prove best up to 1m: sold 8,000 gns in October and joined G. L. Moore.
H. R. A. Cecil

BARROW CREEK   3 ch.c. Cadeaux Genereux 131 – Breadcrumb 111 (Final   64
Straw 127) [1996 NR 1997 6.1g⁶ 7d Oct 13] 135,000Y: quite attractive colt: fifth
foal: half-brother to 3 winners, including useful 1990 2-y-o 5f and 6f winner Heard A
Whisper (by Bellypha): dam 6f and 7f winner from sprinting family: green and not
knocked about when sixth of 10 at Nottingham, better effort in maidens. *G. Wragg*

BARWELL BOY   3 b.g. Clantime 101 – Kasu 35 (Try My Best (USA) 130) [1996   43
NR 1997 a7g a6g⁴ a6g² 6g⁵ a6g⁵ a6g⁶ Apr 28] third reported foal: dam staying
maiden: poor form: seems a sprinter. *J. L. Harris*

BASHFUL BRAVE   6 ch.g. Indian Ridge 123 – Shy Dolly 74 (Cajun 120) [1996   56
76d: 6f* 6m 6m⁵ 6f³ 5m 5m⁵ 5g 6d a7g a5g⁶ a5g⁶ a5g 1997 5m 5m² 5g 5m* 5g⁶ a5g³   a48
5m⁶ a6g⁵ a5g a5g Dec 8] smallish gelding: modest performer nowadays: won selling
handicap at Ripon in August: stays 6f: acts on the all-weather, possibly needs good
going or firmer on turf: tried blinkered and visored. *B. P. J. Baugh*

BASIC STYLE   2 b.g. (Apr 23) Alhijaz 122 – Turbo Rose 81 (Taufan (USA) 119)   –
[1997 5d 5g⁶ 6d 7d⁵ a6g Dec 22] 15,000Y: close-coupled gelding: sixth foal: half-
brother to 3 winners, including 3-y-o Wait For Rosie and 1993 2-y-o 6f winner Co
Pilot (by Petorius): dam miler: little worthwhile form in maidens, though signs of
ability: gelded and off course 6 months before final start. *N. A. Callaghan*

BASMAN (IRE)   3 b.c. Persian Heights 129 – Gepares (IRE) (Mashhor Dancer   102
(USA)) [1996 51p: 8.2g 1997 11g² 11.5s³ 10g² 12g⁵ 10s* 12s Nov 8] big, unfurnished colt, still weak: has been fired: useful performer: 9 lengths third of 5 to
Silver Patriarch in Lingfield Derby Trial in May and 6 lengths fifth of 6 to Maylane
in steadily-run September Stakes at Epsom: 9/2 on, wide-margin winner of maiden at

Nottingham in October: probably stays 1½m: acts on soft going: has taken strong hold. *B. Smart*

BATAAN (USA)   6 b.h. Manila (USA) – Comtesse de Loir (FR) 131 (Val de Loir   46
133) [1996 a9.3g* a9.3g* a9.3g* 9.5f⁵ 9f⁴ 10s² 8.3g³ 8g a7g* a7g* 8s 1997 8d⁶ 9.7m 10.5s
8d 9g a9.3g² 10g⁶ 5g a9.3g² 8s⁶ a7.5g* a10g Dec 2] Belgian-trained horse: won
handicap at Sterrebeek in November: well held both British starts in 1997. *Alex
Vanderhaeghen, Belgium*

BATABANOO   8 ch.g. Bairn (USA) 126 – For Instance (Busted 134) [1996 NR   61
1997 a12g³ a16g⁴ 13.8m³ 14.1m⁵ 16.2m³ 16.1m* 16g⁴ 16m² 14.1f⁶ Oct 29] leggy,   a64
sparely-made gelding: modest performer nowadays: won handicap at Newcastle
in August: reportedly finished lame final outing: stays 2m: acts on firm ground
and fibresand, respectable effort on dead: held up and suited by strong gallop.
Mrs M. Reveley

BATALEUR   4 b.g. Midyan (USA) 124 – Tinkerbird 76 (Music Boy 124) [1996   60
63: 6f 5m³ 5g 6d* 7g 1997 5.9g⁶ 6.1d 6.1g 6d 5m 6m 6g³ Oct 27] angular,
good-quartered gelding: modest handicapper: trained by Miss J. Bower until after
third start: stays 6f, poorly drawn at 7f: acts on dead going, probably on good to firm:
blinkered twice at 4 yrs (ran well). *G. Woodward*

BATCHWORTH BELLE   2 b.f. (May 19) Interrex (CAN) – Treasurebound 63   65 +
(Beldale Flutter (USA) 130) [1997 5d a8g⁴ a7g² a6g* a6g² a6g³ Dec 22] lengthy,
good-topped filly: has some scope: closely related to winning sprinter Batchworth
Bound (by Ballacashtal): dam, placed over 6f at 4 yrs, daughter of smart 6f/7f
performer Miss Tweedie: fair form: won maiden at Lingfield in December: ran well
in nurseries there afterwards: speedy, and should prove effective at 5f. *E. A. Wheeler*

BATHE IN LIGHT (USA)   3 ch.f. Sunshine Forever (USA) – Ice House 89   64
(Northfields (USA)) [1996 66p: 6m⁶ 7.1m 1997 6.9g⁶ 9g 10m³ 10.2m² 12g⁶ 11.9g²
Sep 3] modest maiden handicapper: seems to stay 1½m: raced only on good ground
or firmer: has worn near-side pricker. *Lord Huntingdon*

BATH KNIGHT   4 b.g. Full Extent (USA) 113 – Mybella Ann (Anfield 117) –
[1996 –, a65d: a10g³ a10g² a10g² a10g⁴ a8.5g 11.9f² 9f⁶ a10g 8m a8.5g 1997 a10g
a12g⁵ a13g Jan 30] strong, lengthy gelding: maiden, formerly fair: no form at 4 yrs:
visored once as 2-y-o. *D. J. S. ffrench Davis*

BATOUTOFTHEBLUE   4 br.g. Batshoof 122 – Action Belle (Auction Ring   47
(USA) 123) [1996 65, a70: 8s⁴ 10g⁵ 12g⁴ 11.9m³ 12.3m⁴ 12m a14g* a14.8g* 14.1m⁵   a70
1997 14s 13.9g 16s 16.1m 16.2d a14.8g² Sep 30] big, strong gelding: poor walker:
fair handicapper on all-weather, poor on turf: gambled on, back-to-form second at
Wolverhampton: should be well suited by 2m: goes well on fibresand: not easiest of
rides. *W. W. Haigh*

BATSMAN   3 b.g. Batshoof 122 – Lady Bequick 81 (Sharpen Up 127) [1996 66p: 53
5m² 5m 1997 6g 6m 6d 8.3g 6g² 5s 7g Oct 24] close-coupled gelding: modest
handicapper: best effort of 1997 when strong-finishing second of 21 at Windsor in
July: stays 6f. *W. J. Musson*

BATSWING   2 b.c. (Mar 1) Batshoof 122 – Magic Milly 60 (Simply Great (FR)   91
122) [1997 5d 5m² 6m 5d* 6f⁶ 7g⁴ 7.3m 5d 7v² 7.3g Oct 24] quite good-topped colt:
third foal: half-brother to 4-y-o Westcourt Magic and 6f (at 2 yrs) to 10.8f winner
Folly Finesse (by Joligeneration): dam 2-y-o 1m winner: fairly useful performer:
won maiden at Lingfield in June: good second in minor event at Ascot in October:
stays 7f: best form on dead ground or softer: best efforts in blinkers: none too
consistent: often sweats: sold 20,000 gns after final start. *Martyn Meade*

BATTLE GROUND (IRE)   3 b.g. Common Grounds 118 – Last Gunboat 50   51
(Dominion 123) [1996 59d, a47: 5m⁶ 6g³ a6g 6m⁶ 5f 7m³ 6d⁵ 6.9v a7g⁴ 1997 6f⁵
a9.4g⁵ 8f⁵ 7m 8.2d⁵ 9.7s³ 9.7g* a10f⁴ a8g³ a6.7f² a10g² a6g⁴ a10g Dec 13] modest
handicapper: won selling event at Folkestone for N. Callaghan: in frame first 5 starts
in Sweden: stays 1¼m: acts on any ground, except possibly heavy: blinkered (not
discredited) final 2-y-o start. *O. Stenstrom, Sweden*

BATTLESHIP BRUCE   5 b.g. Mazilier (USA) 107 – Quick Profit 78 (Form-   –
idable (USA) 125) [1996 67, a–: 6.9s⁴ 8.2d² 10g 10s³ 10.2g⁶ 10m⁶ a8g 1997 8.3s Jun
30] sturdy gelding: unimpressive mover: fair performer: poor effort only start of

1997: stays 1¼m: acts on soft ground and equitrack (well beaten both starts on fibresand): blinkered (below form) once: usually bandaged behind: pulled up lame over hurdles in August. *P. Bowen*

BATTLE SPARK (USA)   4 b.g. Gold Seam (USA) 124 – Flick Your Bick (USA)   –
(Bicker (USA)) [1996 75: 8d 7g⁴ 10d⁵ 8.1d³ 8m³ 9m⁴ a9.4g 1997 a10g Mar 24] tall, angular gelding: has a round action: fair maiden at 3 yrs: well held only outing in 1997: seems to stay 1¼m: acts on good to firm ground and dead: sold 7,000 gns and sent to Qatar. *C. A. Cyzer*

BATTLE WARNING   2 b.c. (Mar 2) Warning 136 – Royal Ballet (IRE) (Sadler's   –
Wells (USA) 132) [1997 8f Oct 29] first foal: dam twice-raced sister to high-class winner up to 1½m King's Theatre and half-sister to high-class 1988 2-y-o High Estate: 14/1, little promise in 10-runner maiden at Yarmouth: has joined H. Candy. *H. R. A. Cecil*

BAUBIGNY (USA)   3 b.g. Shadeed (USA) 135 – Pearl Essence (USA) 54   60 d
(Conquistador Cielo (USA)) [1996 76?: 8m 8d 8s⁵ 1997 10.3m 10m⁶ 8.2d 11.6s⁶ 14m⁵ 7g⁴ 9g⁴ 8f Sep 18] tall, rangy gelding: modest performer: bred to stay beyond 1m (seemed not to stay 1¾m). *M. R. Channon*

BAWARA (IRE)   3 b.g. Slip Anchor 136 – Alwatar (USA) 64 (Caerleon (USA)   75
132) [1996 NR 1997 14f³ 14.1s Oct 15] angular gelding: first foal: dam, twice-raced maiden who should have stayed 1½m, granddaughter of disqualified Irish Oaks winner Sorbus: looked slow in back-end maidens, much better effort third at Lingfield: sold and joined L. Lungo. *M. R. Channon*

BAWSIAN   2 b.c. (Apr 2) Persian Bold 123 – Bawaeth (USA) 72 (Blushing Groom   79 p
(FR) 131) [1997 5g³ 7g 7m 7m 8d⁶ 8m* a8g² Nov 18] IR 7,500Y, 17,000 2-y-o: smallish, close-coupled colt: first foal: dam middle-distance maiden half-sister to useful 7f/1m winner Ruznama, out of Oaks third Last Feather: fair performer: twice caught early before winning 27-runner nursery at Redcar in November: good second of 9 in similar event at Lingfield fortnight later: will be well suited by 1¼m+: type to go on improving and should make a fairly useful handicapper. *J. L. Eyre*

BAYFORD THRUST   3 ro.g. Timeless Times (USA) 99 – Gem of Gold 52   77 §
(Jellaby 124) [1996 83: 5d² 5g* 5g* 5m² 6g⁵ 6m 1997 5.1d 5m 6.1m³ 6g² 6g² 6g³ 5.1m⁵ 5m² 5g 6g 6m Sep 22] sparely-made gelding: capable of fair form but ruined his chance with slow start last 3 outings: effective at 5f/6f: yet to race on extremes of going: blinkered ninth start: not to be trusted. *J. Berry*

BAYIN (USA)   8 b.g. Caro 133 – Regatela (USA) (Dr Fager) [1996 79: 6m 6d 6d⁴   72
6g² 6m³ 6m² 6f* 6m⁴ 6m 6.1d 6m 5f³ 6g 5g 6m 6m* 1997 6m 6f 6d 6s 6m⁶ 6d 5.7g* 6m⁶ 5m 6g 6m 5.7g² 6d 6f⁶ 6m⁶ 6m 6g Oct 27] tall, lengthy gelding: usually impresses in appearance: has round action: fair performer: won minor event at Bath in June: some respectable efforts in handicaps otherwise: stays 6f well: yet to race on heavy going, acts on any other: blinkered (raced too freely) once: often bandaged: often slowly away and set plenty to do. *M. D. I. Usher*

BAYLEAF   2 ch.f. (Feb 5) Efisio 120 – Bayonne 72 (Bay Express 132) [1997   97 p
5.2m* 5m⁴ Sep 13] quite attractive filly: second foal: sister to fairly useful 1995 2-y-o 5f winner Baize: dam suited by 5f: won maiden at Newbury in August by head from Cloudberry: highly tried considering inexperience when 3½ lengths fourth of 7 to Land of Dreams in Flying Childers Stakes at Doncaster, no extra final 1f: speedy: should improve again. *R. F. Johnson Houghton*

BAYLHAM   2 b.g. (Mar 11) Risk Me (FR) 127 – So Beguiling (USA) 49 (Wood-   58 d
man (USA) 126) [1997 7g⁴ 6m² 8.3g⁵ 6g 6g 8s 8m Nov 4] second foal: brother to an unsatisfactory maiden: dam 7f seller winner at 2 yrs: disappointing maiden: stays 1m. *J. S. Goldie*

BAY OF DELIGHT   2 ch.f. (Apr 25) Cadeaux Genereux 131 – Zawaahy (USA)   – p
89 (El Gran Senor (USA) 136) [1997 7g 7.1s Oct 15] good-topped filly: second foal: half-sister to UAE 3-y-o 7f and 1m winner As Friendly (by Arazi): dam 1m winner, closely related to Golden Fleece: well held in maidens at Doncaster (green and edgy) and Haydock (very much in need of race, considerably handled) 2½ months apart: likely to do better. *E. A. L. Dunlop*

BAY

BAY OF ISLANDS 5 b.g. Jupiter Island 126 – Lawyer's Wave (USA) (Advocator) 86 [1996 NR 1997 10g 10m⁵ 10s⁵ 10.3m* 10g³ 10.4m 10g⁴ Aug 2] strong gelding: fairly useful handicapper: won at Chester in June: ran creditably all subsequent starts: well worth a try at 1½m: acts on good to firm going, probably soft. *D. Morris*

BAY PRINCE (IRE) 2 b.c. (Mar 19) Mujadil (USA) 119 – Kingston Rose (Tudor 98 Music 131) [1997 5m 5g* 5g* 6g⁴ 5s 6g Oct 18] IR 21,000Y: lengthy colt: half-brother to several winners, including a 4-y-o Kings Harmony: dam Irish 5f winner: useful performer: won maiden at Pontefract in August and listed race at York 3 days later, beating Yorkies Boy by 1¾ lengths in latter: creditable fourth of 6 in Group 2 event at Baden-Baden: below form last 2 starts: speedy, but stays 6f: has been taken early to post (mounted on track at York): races prominently. *M. R. Channon*

BAYRAK (USA) 7 b.g. Bering 136 – Phydilla (FR) 126 (Lyphard (USA) 132) – [1996 74d: 11.8g² 13s 12.1g* 12g³ 11.6m³ 12.3m 11.6g³ 11.4g 11.8m⁴ 12.1m a14g⁴ a14.8g 12v 1997 a12g a12g May 1] compact, good-bodied gelding: fair performer up to 1¾m at best: tailed off in 1997. *P. A. Kelleway*

BAY WATCH (IRE) 2 ch.c. (Mar 11) Priolo (USA) 127 – Life Watch (USA) – (Highland Park (USA)) [1997 6.1m⁶ Jul 25] 25,000Y: first foal: dam twice-raced sister to Poule d'Essai des Pouliches runner-up Duckling Park: green, sixth of 7 in maiden at Chepstow: sold 3,000 gns in October. *I. A. Balding*

BEACH BUOY (IRE) 3 ch.g. Orchestra 118 – Seapoint (Major Point) [1996 NR 62 d 1997 9m³ 8g 8g² 12g 14g 10s Oct 8] IR 4,200Y: half-brother to a fairly useful winner in Hong Kong (up to 1m) by The Noble Player: dam, Irish 7f/1m winner, out of Irish Cesarewitch winner Orofino: signs of ability all 3 starts in maidens: disappointing in handicaps (reportedly lame on first occasion): likely to prove a stayer. *Capt. J. Wilson*

BEACON BLAZE 2 ch.f. (Feb 11) Rudimentary (USA) 118 – Beacon Hill 81 – p (Bustino 136) [1997 8g Oct 24] big, lengthy filly: sixth living foal: half-sister to several winners, including useful 1m and (in UAE) 1½m winner Clever Cliche (by Danehill) and stayers Mountain Ballet (by Shareef Dancer) and Rhodes (by Pharly): dam, sister to Height of Fashion, second over 1¼m from 3 starts: 20/1 and distinctly backward, never-dangerous tenth of 18 in maiden at Doncaster: should do better with time and distance. *D. R. Loder*

BEACON SILVER 3 b.f. Belmez (USA) 131 – Nettle 106 (Kris 135) [1996 NR 75 1997 8d⁵ 8d³ 10m⁴ 10.5g² Sep 26] fifth foal: sister to fair 1m winner Stinging Reply: dam, 2-y-o 6f and 7.3f winner, appeared to stay 1½m: fair maiden: stays 10.5f: yet to race on extremes of ground. *Lord Huntingdon*

BEANO SCRIPT 4 b.g. Prince Sabo 123 – Souadah (USA) (General Holme 60 (USA) 128) [1996 73: 8m 7f³ 8m 1997 8g² 8m⁴ 8g 7d 9m⁴ 10m⁵ Aug 7] strong, lengthy gelding: modest maiden: should prove best up to 1m: acts on firm going: upset in stalls and withdrawn once. *J. Hanson*

BEAR HUG 4 b.g. Polar Falcon (USA) 126 – Tender Loving Care 105 (Final 78 Straw 127) [1996 72p: 8.3g⁴ 1997 10s⁴ 10m 9.7m² 10m 10m Sep 30] big, lengthy gelding: fair maiden: well below form last 2 starts: best up to 1¼m: acts on good to firm ground: sold only 1,800 gns in October and joined M. Sheppard. *Lady Herries*

BEAR TO DANCE 4 b.f. Rambo Dancer (CAN) 107 – Pooh Wee 71 (Music Boy – 124) [1996 –: a7g⁴ a10g 7f 1997 7f 7d 5.2s⁵ Jul 2] of little account. *P. Howling*

BEA'S RUBY (IRE) 3 b.f. Fairy King (USA) – Beautiful Secret (USA) (Secreto 86 (USA) 128) [1996 77+: 6m⁴ 7.1v³ 6m² 1997 7s* 8s* 8s⁴ 8.2d 10.3d Nov 7] leggy filly: fairly useful performer: won maiden at Chester and minor event at Ayr (made all) in May: below form after 5-month absence last 3 starts: better at 1m than shorter: acts on good to firm and heavy going: visored penultimate start, bandaged final one: front runner. *A. Bailey*

BEAU BRUNO 4 b.g. Thatching 131 – Lady Lorelei 105 (Derring-Do 131) [1996 – 76: 8m² 8.3m 8d 7m³ a7g³ 6m⁶ 1997 a7m² a6g⁴ a7g Feb 4] leggy, workmanlike gelding: fair maiden at 7f at 3 yrs: well beaten in 1997: visored last start. *M. Bell*

BEAUCATCHER (IRE) 3 b.f. Thatching 131 – Gale Warning (IRE) (Last 55 Tycoon 131) [1996 NR 1997 6s 7g⁶ 6g⁵ 6.1g 9m Oct 31] 17,000F: second foal: half-sister to 1995 2-y-o Irish 7f and 8.5f winner Common Spirit (by Common

Grounds): dam, French 2-y-o 6f winner, half-sister to smart sprinter Bold Apparel: modest maiden: best effort second start. *M. J. Heaton-Ellis*

BEAUCHAMP JADE   5 gr.m. Kalaglow 132 – Beauchamp Buzz 85 (High Top 131) [1996 105: 10g⁴ 12m* 12g* 12m⁴ 11.8g* 13.9m² 14.6m³ 12g⁶ 1997 12g 12m³ 12m⁵ 13.4s⁵ 13.3d² 14.6d⁵ Nov 7] lengthy mare: fluent mover: useful performer: best efforts in 1997 when placed in listed race at Newmarket in July and £14,300 handicap at Newbury (reportedly strained a joint) in September: stays 14.6f: acts on firm and good to soft ground: sometimes gives trouble at stalls: held up. *H. Candy*   101

BEAUCHAMP KING   4 gr.c. Nishapour (FR) 125 – Afariya (FR) (Silver Shark 129) [1996 117: 8m* 8m⁵ 8d³ 8f⁴ 10g 8g 1997 8.1g⁶ 8d 8m 8g* 8g Aug 16] angular colt: has a rather round action: won Racing Post Trophy as 2-y-o and Craven Stakes as 3-y-o: only useful form in 1997, winning minor event at Doncaster in July by head from Jamrat Jumairah, quickening well having been short of room 2f out: should stay beyond 1m: acts on any ground: sometimes keen/edgy in preliminaries: usually held up: failed to reach reserve at December Sales. *J. L. Dunlop*   107

BEAUCHAMP KNIGHT   4 ch.g. Chilibang 120 – Beauchamp Cactus 86 (Niniski (USA) 125) [1996 67?: 8m 8g 10m 1997 14.1g 17.2f Jul 23] big gelding: disappointing maiden. *H. Candy*   –

BEAUCHAMP LION   3 ch.g. Be My Chief (USA) 122 – Beauchamp Cactus 86 (Niniski (USA) 125) [1996 –p: 7m 8.2m 8f 1997 11.6s 11.8g⁴ 11.8g⁴ 14.1g 14m 16s Oct 8] leggy, useful-looking gelding: fair maiden handicapper: disappointing last 3 starts (then gelded): should be suited by further than 1½m: probably unsuited by soft ground. *J. L. Dunlop*   65

BEAUCHAMP MAGIC   2 b.g. (Jun 3) Northern Park (USA) 107 – Beauchamp Buzz 85 (High Top 131) [1997 7m 7g 7g Oct 7] sixth foal: half-brother to 5-y-o Beauchamp Jade: dam, stayed 1m, half-sister to very smart middle-distance horse Beauchamp Hero: sire (by Northern Dancer) useful French winner up to 1½m who stayed 2m: showed promise in large fields of maidens at Newbury and Warwick, finishing well from rear, not knocked about, on latter course final start: type to do better in handicaps at 1¼m+. *J. L. Dunlop*   – p

BEAUMAN   7 b.g. Rainbow Quest (USA) 134 – Gliding 94 (Tudor Melody 129) [1996 66: a9.4g² a8g⁴ a11g³ a11g⁶ a12s⁵ 1997 a9.4g⁴ a8.5f a11g⁶ Jan 13] leggy gelding: has a round action: modest handicapper: sold only 580 gns in March: subsequently won in Austria: stays 1½m: acts on good to firm ground and fibresand, used to go particularly well on soft: tried blinkered/visored (not for long time). *P. D. Evans*   54

BEAU MATELOT   5 ch.g. Handsome Sailor 125 – Bellanoora 60 (Ahonoora 122) [1996 –: 10m 1997 a12g Jan 6] leggy, angular gelding: modest maiden handicapper at 1¼m/1½m in 1995: only twice raced on flat since and no form. *Miss M. K. Milligan*   –

BEAUMONT (IRE)   7 br.g. Be My Native (USA) 122 – Say Yes (Junius (USA) 124) [1996 75: a11g⁶ a12g* a12g² 10.8f² 12f² 12m⁵ 13.9g³ 15.9g* 13.9g* 14.6g⁴ 1997 a14.8g⁵ a14g⁶ 14.8m* 16.1g⁴ 15.9g⁵ 14.1d³ 16.5s⁵ Nov 8] compact gelding: usually impresses in appearance: fairly useful handicapper: first start for well over 3 months, won at Newmarket in July: ran well in frame after: stays 2m well: acts on fibresand and any turf ground: below form tried in blinkers: normally held up. *J. E. Banks*   80 a–

BEAU ROBERTO   3 b.g. Robellino (USA) 127 – Night Jar 102 (Night Shift (USA)) [1996 51: 7.5m³ 7m 7.1f⁶ 8m 1997 8d 8d 9.2g³ 7g³ 7m⁶ 9.2g⁵ 10m⁵ 10.4s⁶ 10.9d 9s 8g Oct 22] small, strong gelding: shows knee action: modest maiden: left M. Johnston after third start and mostly below form after: stays 9.2f well: acts on firm ground: twice blinkered, running creditably first occasion. *J. S. Goldie*   52 d

BEAU TUDOR (IRE)   3 b.g. Aragon 118 – Sunley Silks 80 (Formidable (USA) 125) [1996 NR 1997 7.1d 6g 5g⁶ 5m 5f 8.2g⁶ Sep 23] IR 13,500F, 21,000Y: workmanlike gelding: first foal: half-brother to an Italian 2-y-o 5f winner by Mujadil: dam 5f winner (stayed 7f) out of half-sister to dam of Sonic Lady: no promise in maidens. *Miss L. C. Siddall*   –

BEAU VENTURE (USA) 9 ch.h. Explodent (USA) – Old Westbury (USA) 75
(Francis S) [1996 75, a–: 5g⁶ 5m 5g 5.7m* 5f⁴ 5m² 5m⁶ 5.1m 5.2m 5.1d 5m 5.1g 6m² a–
a6g a6g 1997 6.1m² 5m* 5.1m 5.1g 5.1m⁴ 6g 5g² 6d 5.7f⁶ 5.1m² 5g 5.1m 5g⁴ 5m⁶
5m* 5d a5g Dec 2] quite good-topped horse: poor mover: fair performer: won minor
event at Folkestone in April and handicap at Goodwood in September: ran well most
other starts: effective at 5f/6f: acts on firm and dead ground, well below form on the
all-weather: blinkered twice, not since 1993: has run well sweating. *B. Palling*

BEAU VIENNA 2 b.f. (Apr 25) Superpower 113 – Waltz On Air 86 (Doc Marten –
104) [1997 7.1m⁶ Aug 20] 2,600Y: third reported foal: dam 6f winner: 33/1, sixth of
8 in maiden at Musselburgh. *A. R. Dicken*

BECKENHAM INSIGHT 3 b.f. Efisio 120 – Capel Lass (The Brianstan 128) –
[1996 NR 1997 7m a6g⁶ Jul 25] 500Y: half-sister to a 2-y-o 5f winner by Today And
Tomorrow: dam unraced: showed nothing in maidens. *D. C. O'Brien*

BEDAZZLE 6 b.g. Formidable (USA) 125 – Wasimah 84 (Caerleon (USA) 132) 40
[1996 41: 8.1g* 7.1g⁶ 7d 8.1g 8m² 8m⁶ 7.5m² 8m 8.1m⁶ 8.2d 1997 8m 8.2m² 8m²
8d³ 8g 8.3s 9m 10m² 8g² 10v⁴ 9.2m⁵ 10m 10m⁶ 12m 10.1g Oct 22] small gelding:
poor handicapper: largely creditable efforts in 1997 until last 2 starts: stays 1¼m
when conditions aren't testing: acts on firm and dead ground: blinkered (well beaten)
once at 5 yrs. *M. Brittain*

BEDEVILLED 2 ch.c. (Feb 25) Beveled (USA) – Putout 69 (Dowsing (USA) 76
124) [1997 6.1g² 6d³ Oct 28] 12,000 2-y-o: first foal: dam, 5f winner, half-sister to
smart French sprinter Pole Position out of sister to Precocious: fair form in large-field
maidens at Nottingham (¾-length second to easy winner Sky Rocket) and Leicester
(2¼ lengths third to Bandbox) in October: sprint bred. *M. J. Heaton-Ellis*

BEDOUIN HONDA 3 b. or br.c. Mtoto 134 – Bedouin Veil (USA) (Shareef 71
Dancer (USA) 135) [1996 –: 7.1m 1997 10g 10d 10f³ 10g 10.1m 10d a10g² Nov 18]
fair maiden: stays 1¼m: acts on good to firm and dead ground and equitrack: ran
respectably only try in blinkers: sold 13,000 gns after final start. *C. E. Brittain*

BEDOUIN PRINCE (USA) 10 b.g. Danzig (USA) – Regal Heiress 81 (English 43
Prince 129) [1996 NR 1997 a12g³ a16g⁴ a12g³ 12m² 11.9f² 11.9m 12g5 a13g* a47
14.1m⁶ a16g Aug 9] poor handicapper: won selling event at Lingfield in June: stays
2m: acts on firm going and all-weather: effective with or without visor or blinkers.
Mrs L. Stubbs

BEDTIME STORY 2 b.f. (Apr 22) Fairy King (USA) – Prima Domina (FR) 89 42 p
(Dominion 123) [1997 a7g⁵ Dec 18] 4,600F, IR 15,000Y: sixth foal: half-sister to 6f
(at 2 yrs) to 1¾m winner Primo Figlio (by Assert): dam sprinting sister to Primo
Dominie: 5/1, fifth in seller at Southwell, keeping on and not given a hard race:
should improve. *R. Guest*

BEECHWOOD QUEST (IRE) 2 b.f. (Mar 30) River Falls 113 – Egalite (IRE) 57 +
(Fools Holme (USA)) [1997 a5g³ 6g 6g 5s² a5g* 5g³ a5g* 5g⁴ 5m Aug 26] 3,000 a65
2-y-o: leggy filly: first foal: dam poor Irish maiden: fair on all-weather, modest on
turf: made all in sellers at Southwell in July and August: speedy: acts on soft ground
and fibresand: usually equipped with blinkers and eyeshields. *B. S. Rothwell*

BEE DEE BEST (IRE) 6 b.g. Try My Best (USA) 130 – Eloquent Charm (USA) –
(Private Account (USA)) [1996 37: 6m³ 1997 5m 6m Aug 16] leggy gelding: poor
maiden handicapper: well beaten in 1997. *J. P. Smith*

BEE HEALTH BOY 4 b.g. Superpower 113 – Rekindle 70 (Relkino 131) [1996 72
72: 6m6g 6s* 6f⁵ 6m* 5g² 6d* 6m 6m 6m 5m 1997 5m² 5s⁶ 5d³ a5g 6g³ 6s⁶ 6d³ a–
6m 6g 7g⁵ 7m 5d 6s Oct 15] lengthy, good-topped gelding: fair handicapper: in good
form most of 1997 until last 3 starts: effective at 5f to 7f: acts on good to firm and soft
ground, unsuited by fibresand: blinkered nowadays (2 of 3 wins as 3-y-o when not):
successful when sweating: usually races prominently. *M. W. Easterby*

BEGORRAT (IRE) 3 ch.g. Ballad Rock 122 – Hada Rani (Jaazeiro (USA) 127) 71
[1996 77: 6m⁴ 7g 1997 8.5m⁴ 9g 10s 8m³ 10.8m⁵ 8.2g⁴ 8.1m* 7.9s⁴ 8d 10.9s* 8m
Nov 1] rangy, angular gelding: fair performer: won seller at Haydock (sold out of
B. Meehan's stable) in August and 5-runner claimer at Ayr (hung left) in October:
stays 11f: acts on good to firm and soft going: blinkered last 5 starts. *D. Moffatt*

BEGUINE (USA) 3 br.f. Green Dancer (USA) 132 – La Papagena (Habitat 134) –
[1996 77p: 7g 1997 8g 10m 11.1m Sep 22] big filly: shaped promisingly only start at
2 yrs but showed little in 1997. *W. Jarvis*

BEHAVIOUR 5 b.h. Warning 136 – Berry's Dream 101 (Darshaan 133) [1996 106
106: 10g 8m² 7.9m 8.5m² 7.9g³ 10m* 10d⁵ 10.9m³ 9g 1997 9g⁴ 10.1m³ 10g⁶ 10m⁵
10.1f³ Oct 29] sturdy horse: has a quick action: useful performer: best efforts at 5 yrs
on first 2 starts, in Earl of Sefton Stakes at Newmarket (3½ lengths fourth to
Ali-Royal) and handicap at Epsom (off course 3½ months after latter): effective at
1m to 10.9f: acts on firm going: usually held up and has turn of foot: sent to USA.
Mrs J. Cecil

BEHIND THE SCENES 3 ch.g. Kris 135 – Free Guest 125 (Be My Guest 70
(USA) 126) [1996 NR 1997 8g 10.3d 9d* 10g 12d 12m⁴ 14m a16g² Aug 2] 20,000Y:
strong, angular gelding: sixth live foal: brother to Oaks second Shamshir and
half-brother to 4-y-o Freequent and useful winner Fern (by Shirley Heights): dam,
high-class 7f to 1½m winner, won 9 of 15 starts: awarded maiden at Goodwood in
May: only other form when second in handicap at Lingfield on all-weather debut:
stays 2m: acts on dead ground and equitrack. *C. A. Cyzer*

BEHIND THE VEIL 2 ch.f. (Feb 28) Forzando 122 – Karonga (Main Reef 126) –
[1997 5m 7g 6d Jul 1] 3,500Y: small, close-coupled filly: sixth foal: half-sister to
winners abroad by Nicholas and Salse: dam French 9f winner: seems of little
account. *Mrs M. Reveley*

BEHOLD 2 ch.f. (Jan 25) Prince Sabo 123 – Be My Lass (IRE) (Be My Guest 92
(USA) 126) [1997 6m* 7s² Jul 3] first foal: dam unraced half-sister to smart
middle-distance winners Bonne Ile and Ile de Nisky: won maiden at Redcar in May:
better effort when ½-length second of 5 to Mazboon in steadily-run minor event at
Yarmouth: should stay 1m: slowly away both starts. *J. R. Fanshawe*

BELBAY STAR 4 b.f. Belfort (FR) 89 – Gavea (African Sky 124) [1996 53d: 7m⁴ 35
9m⁶ 7f 7g 7g 7g a6g⁶ 1997 6m⁶ 7m 6.9m⁵ 5m² 6m a6g Dec 4] poor maiden handicapper: probably a sprinter: no improvement in blinkers. *J. L. Eyre*

BEL CANTO (IRE) 3 b.c. Sadler's Wells (USA) 132 – Fair of The Furze 112 78
(Ela-Mana-Mou 132) [1996 NR 1997 10.4s³ 10m 10m* 12v Oct 10] IR 210,000Y:
good-bodied colt: half-brother to 3 winners, including useful Elfaslah (1¼m, by
Green Desert) and high-class White Muzzle (up to 1½m, by Dancing Brave): dam
Irish 1m and 1¼m winner who stayed 1½m: fair form: best effort when staying on to
win maiden at Goodwood in September: well held in handicap on heavy going at
Ascot 2 weeks later: should stay at least 1½m: sold approx. £104,000 in Dubai in
November. *J. H. M. Gosden*

BELDRAY PARK (IRE) 4 b. or br.g. Superpower 113 – Ride Bold (USA) (J O –
Tobin (USA) 130) [1996 72d: 6s* 6d⁶ 6m 6s 7m 1997 6.9g 6g 6g 6d 7.1m 10g Sep
28] angular gelding: fair winner: has lost his form: tried visored. *Mrs A. L. M. King*

BELINDA BLUE 5 b.m. Belfort (FR) 89 – Carrula (Palm Track 122) [1996 50d, –
a55d: 5g 5g² 6.1m a5g² 5f⁴ a6g⁵ a5g⁶ a6g 5g a6g⁶ 1997 a6s⁴ a5f³ a5g Jan 22] big, a38
lengthy mare: maiden sprint handicapper: just poor form in January at 5 yrs: stays 6f:
acts on firm ground and fibresand: tried visored: often slowly away. *R. A. Fahey*

BELLA DANIELLA 3 br.f. Prince Daniel (USA) – Danse d'Esprit 54 (Lidhame –
109) [1996 –: 7m 7.9g 1997 8g⁶ a14.8g a12g 12v Jun 30] small filly: no form.
T. T. Clement

BELLADERA (IRE) 2 b.f. (Apr 27) Alzao (USA) 117 – Reality 88 (Known Fact 82
(USA) 135) [1997 6g* 6g 7g² 7m⁶ 8f Sep 11] IR 30,000Y: leggy, unfurnished filly:
seventh foal: half-sister to several winners, including Italian 3-y-o 1m winner Regal
Dynasty (by Royal Academy) and useful 5f (at 2 yrs) to 7f winner Silca Blanka (by
Law Society): dam, 7f and 1m winner, half-sister to smart 7f performer Unblest:
fairly useful form: won maiden at York in May: second in minor event at Thirsk in
July: stiffer tasks otherwise, tailed off final start: should stay at least 1m. *N. Tinkler*

BELLAGRANA 3 ch.f. Belmez (USA) 131 – Nafis (USA) (Nodouble (USA)) 58
[1996 NR 1997 7g 8.3s⁵ 8f 10m 10g² 10.2g² 11.5d 11.9f⁵ 12m Oct 31] 10,500Y:
workmanlike filly: third foal: half-sister to fairly useful 1m winner Milford Sound

(by Batshoof): dam unraced: modest maiden: should stay beyond 1¼m: best efforts on good ground. *M. J. Fetherston-Godley*

BELLARA 5 b.m. Thowra (FR) – Sicilian Vespers 44 (Mummy's Game 120) 51 [1996 65: 14.1s* 14m* 16.1m⁵ 17.2d 1997 16.2s⁵ a16.2g 14s³ 13.9g May 14] small mare: modest handicapper: should stay beyond 1¾m: acts on good to firm ground and soft, well beaten both starts on all-weather. *N. M. Babbage*

BELLARULA 3 gr.f. Belfort (FR) 89 – Carrula (Palm Track 122) [1996 NR 1997 50 6g 6f³ 6.1g 6m 5m Jun 26] tall filly: has markedly round action: half-sister to winners abroad by Dublin Taxi and Marching On: dam unraced: only worthwhile form when third in seller at Leicester in April: usually soon off bridle. *M. Dods*

BELLAS GATE BOY 5 b.g. Doulab (USA) 115 – Celestial Air 96 (Rheingold 54 137) [1996 65d: 9.7s² a8.5g 9m 10.1g 8m 7m 10f 10.9m⁴ 1997 a8g a8g⁵ 8d⁶ 7m* a– 12g² 7.1m⁴ a8.5g 10.1s⁴ 10g 8.1g 10.1g² 10g⁶ Sep 3] leggy gelding: modest handicapper: usually runs in amateurs/ladies races, winning one of latter at Lingfield in May: finds 7f a minimum, barely stays 1½m: acts on soft and good to firm ground, no form in 4 races on all-weather: blinkered once: often slowly away of late: inconsistent. *J. Pearce*

BELLA'S LEGACY 4 b.f. Thowra (FR) – Miss Lawsuit (Neltino 97) [1996 48: 45 6m 7d 7f 6m 6g 6g³ 7g⁴ 6m 1997 6g 6m 6.1m 8.2g² 8g³ 10d Nov 3] sparely-made filly: poor maiden: stays 1m: best efforts on good ground. *K. R. Burke*

BELLE BIJOU 3 ch.f. Midyan (USA) 124 – Pushkar (Northfields (USA)) [1996 61 –p: 8s 1997 a10g* 10m 8.3g⁶ 11.1s³ 12.1s² 13d³ 17.5d 9s Oct 13] leggy filly: modest performer: awarded weak maiden at Lingfield in February: ran in handicaps after, giving impression something amiss final start: stayed 13f: acted on soft ground and equitrack: has wandered and gone in snatches: sold IR 48,000 gns in December: stud. *M. Johnston*

BELLE DE MONTFORT 2 b.f. (Mar 19) Presidium 124 – Judys Girl (IRE) – (Simply Great (FR) 122) [1997 5.7m 7m 7g Sep 3] 2,700Y: third foal: half-sister to 3-y-o Grate Times: dam of little account: well beaten, including in a seller. *J. L. Spearing*

BELLE DE NUIT (IRE) 2 b.f. (Feb 27) Statoblest 120 – Elminya (IRE) (Sure 85 Blade (USA) 130) [1997 5.2m⁶ 5.1m 6m* 6.5m 7m* 7m² 7g Oct 18] 12,500Y: workmanlike filly: third foal: closely related to 4-y-o Pleasureland and half-sister to 3-y-o Soden: dam unraced half-sister to Ruby Tiger: fairly useful performer: won maiden at Windsor in August and nursery at Yarmouth in September: excellent second to Golden Fortune in valuable nursery at Newmarket, making most: stiff task final start: will stay at least 1m: has raced only on good/good to firm ground: genuine, but seems rather lazy and suited by strong handling. *B. J. Meehan*

BELLOW (IRE) 2 b.g. (Mar 23) Petorius 117 – Kristen Belle (Viking (USA)) 67 [1997 5.1m 6.1s⁵ 7g* 7m Aug 2] 8,200Y: compact gelding: fluent mover: fifth foal: dam maiden daughter of Irish 1000 Guineas runner-up Annerbelle, herself sister to Irish Oaks winner Aurabella: won seller at Newmarket in July, making all despite flashing tail: folded quickly in nursery following month: should stay 1m: sent to Macau. *H. Morrison*

BELLROI (IRE) 6 b.g. Roi Danzig (USA) – Balela (African Sky 124) [1996 49: – 18m⁴ 17.1m* 16d 1997 14.1s Jul 2] poor handicapper: tailed off only outing in 1997: stays 2¼m: acts on good to firm ground, well beaten on dead: tried visored. *M. H. Tompkins*

BELMARITA (IRE) 4 ch.f. Belmez (USA) 131 – Congress Lady 93 (General 64 Assembly (USA)) [1996 76: 14m³ 14.4g⁴ 14g³ 13.8g² 12m² 12m⁴ 13.9g 14m² 14g⁵ 1997 14.1d 14m 12m⁶ Oct 2] good-bodied filly: fluent mover: modest maiden: first run for over 4 months, only form in 1997 when sixth in claimer at Newmarket: will stay beyond 1¾m: raced almost solely on good going or firmer: fair winning hurdler. *G. A. Hubbard*

BELMONT BUCCANEER 5 ch.g. Forzando 122 – Sharp Celine (Sharpo 132) – [1996 NR 1997 a6g Nov 14] of little account. *J. O'Reilly*

BELUSHI   3 b.f. Risk Me (FR) 127 – Trigamy 112 (Tribal Chief 125) [1996 NR   36
1997 a8g a7g³ a7g⁶ Feb 7] sister to fairly useful 1m/1¼m performer Risk Master and
half-sister to several winners, including fairly useful 7f performer Mango Manila (by
Martinmas): dam 5f performer: poor form in Southwell sellers. *D. Morley*

BELZAO   4 b.g. Alzao (USA) 117 – Belle Enfant 87 (Beldale Flutter (USA) 130)   –
[1996 63: 7m⁵ 11.7m⁴ 7m 7.1s⁵ 8.2s⁴ a7g⁵ 1997 6g 8m 7g 12s⁴ a12g⁶ Dec 6] sturdy
gelding: has been hobdayed: disappointing maiden handicapper: no form at 4 yrs:
trained on reappearance by T. Hind: blinkered final start. *R. Simpson*

BEMSHA SWING (IRE)   2 b. or br.c. (Jan 19) Night Shift (USA) – Move It   97
Baby (IRE) (Thatching 131) [1997 6g⁶ 6m² 6d⁵ 6m² 6m* 6m⁶ Oct 2] 18,500Y:
sturdy, well-made colt: fluent mover: first foal: dam unraced: useful performer:
generally contested above-average maidens before winning one at Newmarket in
August by neck from Ikhteyaar: not discredited when sixth of 8 to Hayil in Middle
Park Stakes on same course: likely to prove best up to 1m: acts on good to firm
ground (disappointed on good to soft). *R. Hannon*

BE MY GIRL   2 ch.f. (Feb 3) Be My Guest (USA) 126 – Kaprisky (IRE) (Red   –
Sunset 120) [1997 6m 7g 6f⁶ Sep 17] 23,000Y: first foal: dam German 6f (at 2 yrs)
and 7f winner: no worthwhile form in maidens: sold and sent to Holland. *C. F. Wall*

BE MY WISH   2 b.f. (Mar 15) Be My Chief (USA) 122 – Spinner 59 (Blue   79 ?
Cashmere 129) [1997 5.1v³ 5d⁴ 5m⁴ 5.2f Jul 19] 15,000Y: sturdy filly: good mover:
half-sister to several winning sprinters, including 3-y-o Nervous Rex and fairly
useful Resolute Bay (by Crofthall): dam sprinter: shaped with promise in maidens,
then probably put up fair effort when never-dangerous eighth of 23 to Lord Kintyre
in Super Sprint at Newbury (heavily bandaged behind): will be well suited by 6f.
Miss Gay Kelleway

BENATOM (USA)   4 gr.g. Hawkster (USA) – Dance Til Two (USA) (Sovereign   100
Dancer (USA)) [1996 102: 12m* 12.3g⁵ 14d⁴ 16.2m 16.1g* 14f* 15.9m⁶ 14g 1997
14d⁵ 13.9d⁴ 16.1s 13.9m* 14m³ Jul 29] well-made gelding: has a quick action: useful
handicapper: won 7-runner listed rated stakes at York in July by 1½ lengths from
Willie Conquer: creditable third to Media Star at Goodwood final start, keeping on
strongly: stays 2m: acts on firm going and dead: visored (edgy) third 4-y-o start.
H. R. A. Cecil

BEND WAVY (IRE)   5 ch.g. Kefaah (USA) 124 – Prosodie (FR) (Relko 136)   –
[1996 88: 8.3m² 10m³ 8.5m* 8m 1997 a9.4g 10.5m 10.4d 11.9s⁶ 8s Nov 8] big
gelding: fairly useful at 4 yrs for L. Cumani: showed nothing in 1997. *T. H. Caldwell*

BENEVENTUS   2 b.c. (Apr 28) Most Welcome 131 – Dara Dee 87 (Dara Mon-   79
arch 128) [1997 7m³ 7g⁴ 7.1m⁴ Sep 16] 20,000Y: good-bodied colt: second foal: dam
7f/1m winner: fair form in maidens at Salisbury, Newcastle and Sandown: will stay
at least 1m: joined J. Dunlop. *Major W. R. Hern*

BEN GUNN   5 b.g. Faustus (USA) 118 – Pirate Maid (Auction Ring (USA) 123)   75
[1996 60: 7g 6g 7s 7g 8s a7g³ a7g a10g² 1997 a10g³ a10g⁵ 7m* 7.3g⁶ 8.2g⁴ 8.3s² 8g*
8m 8g 8d 8g⁴ Oct 18] good-bodied gelding: fair handicapper: won in big fields at
Salisbury in May and Newmarket in July: good fourth of 30 to Gulf Shaadi at
Newmarket final start: effective at 7f (given good test) to easy 1¼m: well beaten on
heavy going, acts on any other turf and all-weather: visored (well beaten) second
start: best held up in strongly-run race. *P. T. Walwyn*

BENICIA BOY   5 ch.g. Grey Desire 115 – Fabia (FR) 51 (Faunus (FR)) [1996 NR   –
1997 7.1g 8.1g Sep 11] third reported foal: dam poor plater at 2 yrs: no sign of ability.
J. C. McConnochie

BENIN (USA)   2 b.c. (Feb 25) Sky Classic (CAN) – Battle Drum (USA) (Alydar   88 P
(USA)) [1997 7m* Oct 5] $250,000Y: half-brother to fairly useful stayer Blaze Away
(by Polish Navy), 7f and 1m winner at 2 yrs: dam won around 1m at 3 yrs: sire (by
Nijinsky) high-class North American middle-distance horse: 7/4, won maiden at
Leicester by ½ length from Rainbow Ways, making virtually all and looking better
the further he went, first 2 clear: will be well suited by at least 1¼m: held pattern
entries at 2 yrs, and should leave form well behind in 1998. *H. R. A. Cecil*

BENJAMIN FRANK   2 b.g. (Apr 8) Tragic Role (USA) – Flower Princess (Slip   – p
Anchor 136) [1997 7.9s⁶ Oct 8] 30,000Y: neat gelding: second foal: brother to 3-y-o

Beryllium: dam unraced daughter of Fillies' Mile winner Nepula: 14/1, green and backward, well-beaten sixth of 15 in York maiden, passing tired rivals late on: should stay at least 1¼m: should do better. *S. P. C. Woods*

BENJAMINS LAW 6 b. or br.g. Mtoto 134 – Absaloute Service 96 (Absalom 128) [1996 49, a70: a9.4g⁵ a8g² a8g* a8g⁴ a12g⁴ 8g⁶ 8f⁴ 12m 9f⁵ 8m⁴ 10f 1997 a8g³ 10m² 10g 11.5d² 10g² 16.2m² 16m³ 15.9d Aug 29] rangy, workmanlike gelding: fair handicapper on fibresand (not so good on equitrack), modest on turf: generally good efforts at 6 yrs until final outing: seems fully effective from 1m to 2m: acts on good to firm and dead ground. *J. A. Pickering*   53   a71

BENNY THE DIP (USA) 3 b. or br.c. Silver Hawk (USA) 123 – Rascal Rascal (USA) (Ack Ack (USA)) [1996 112: 7.1m² 7g* 7m* 8g* 8g³ 1997 10d² 10.4g* 12g* 10d² 10.4g³ 10g⁶ Oct 18]   127

Like the Boat Race, Trooping The Colour and the announcement of another Rolling Stones world tour, Derby Day remains a reassuring ritual for the older generation in a changing world. There was even a glimmer of hope with the latest edition that a flavour of the good old days might be returning for the race once regarded as 'London's favourite day out.' Epsom's recognition that the tradition of staging the Derby on the first Wednesday in June was contributing to a decline led to the race being switched to Saturday in 1995. The move has been controversial, but the Epsom management received a boost when the third successive Saturday Derby—the first two faced strong competition from sporting alternatives—produced significant increases over the previous year in attendances at the track, television viewing figures and betting turnover. A massive promotional exercise mounted by Epsom recovered from a shaky start, featuring a much-ridiculed 'celebrity conga', to yield a crowd of 72,000 (including an estimate for the non-paying crowd on the Downs), a terrestrial television audience of 5.6 million—making the Derby Channel 4's top-rated sports event—and an encouraging rise in betting turnover on the race itself of around twenty percent. The Downs seemed more vital and colourful than in recent years, while bookings for open-topped buses—a traditional feature of Derby Day—went up after a reduction in charges. With Epsom and the Derby's sponsors Vodafone—whose continued support of the race was rumoured to be in some doubt before the latest running—committed to showing the same drive in their marketing efforts over the next two years, Derby Day looks to be on the way to regaining at least some of its lost popular appeal. Problems remain, however, that are out of Epsom's control, one of the most pressing being the need to rationalise the programme of fixtures on Derby Day. Six other meetings take place at present, on the biggest day of the sporting week when racing already faces intense competition for space in the newspapers. The Derby has to compete for attention, not only with the rest of the weekend sport, but also against competition of the British Horseracing Board's own making, including second-rate meetings at Southwell, Wolverhampton and Worcester!

The emergence of a potentially outstanding champion in any sport creates a following and there was a feeling that the wide anticipation of a Derby victory for the much-vaunted Two Thousand Guineas winner Entrepreneur played a part in the record advance bookings for Epsom (corporate hospitality facilities for the revamped two-day fixture were sold out ten days beforehand). The latest Derby, the first to carry total prize money of a million pounds, looked a one-horse race to many from the moment Entrepreneur lived up to his lofty home reputation, justifying a sustained ante-post gamble over the winter in the process, by taking the first colts' classic on his seasonal reappearance from the Grand Criterium winner Revoque. Entrepreneur seemed to have all the qualities looked for in a Derby candidate and the bookmakers took no chances with him, installing him at around evens for Epsom straight after Newmarket. As for the places—the claims of other Derby candidates were apt to be considered a side issue at the time—it seemed difficult to get away from the solid

*Grosvenor Casinos Dante Stakes, York—Benny The Dip gallops on strongly
to maintain his advantage over Desert Story, Musalsal and Kingfisher Mill (blaze)*

performances of Silver Patriarch and Benny The Dip in two of the recognised trials, the Tripleprint Derby Trial at Lingfield (which Silver Patriarch won by seven lengths) and the Grosvenor Casinos Dante Stakes at York.

Benny The Dip won the Dante, traditionally the most influential of the Derby trials over more than a mile, with a front-running performance that saw him maintain a clear advantage for most of the straight. The Craven Stakes winner Desert Story, sixth in the Guineas, chased home Benny The Dip at York, never looking like closing the gap over the final furlong and eventually going down by two and a half lengths, just holding off the promising pair Musalsal and Kingfisher Mill.

Musalsal was the only other runner in the Dante to take his place in the Derby field, in which Silver Patriarch (6/1) and Benny The Dip (easing from 8/1 to 11/1) were the only ones, apart from Entrepreneur (heavily backed on the day to 6/4-on), to start at shorter than 12/1. Benny The Dip, winner of the Royal Lodge Stakes on his fourth start as a two-year-old before finishing third when favourite for the Racing Post Trophy, had his fifth jockey at Epsom in as many races. Walter Swinburn rode him in the Royal Lodge and John Reid in the Racing Post Trophy, before Frankie Dettori came second on him in the Classic Trial at Sandown on his reappearance and Olivier Peslier gave him a splendid ride at York. With Dettori and Peslier retained for other Derby runners, Willie Ryan took the mount. After partnering Benny The Dip in a gallop three days before the Derby, Ryan was reported to have told John Gosden that the horse was 'the laziest, most moronic horse I've ever ridden.'

Benny The Dip belied that piece of work with a thoroughly game and genuine display at Epsom. He was soon travelling sweetly close to the pace, set by the outsider Crystal Hearted, came down the hill beautifully and was sent for home in earnest soon after rounding Tattenham Corner. He'd built up a five- or six-length lead by the two-furlong marker and then held on tenaciously as the strong-finishing Silver Patriarch, who'd been off the bridle practically from the start, made ground hand-over-fist in the final furlong. The pair went past the post together, five lengths clear of the rest. As cliffhangers go, there can have been few Derby finishes to rival this one. If Benny The Dip had won it was by the skin of his teeth—Silver Patriarch was clearly in front a stride past the post —though Channel 4 chose correctly in despatching their mounted interviewer, Lesley Graham, to the winner. Ryan scarcely had time to catch his breath—and the photo-finish had still to be announced—when a microphone was thrust under his nose. The question 'How do you feel?' was met with an understand-able 'I don't know yet.' Ryan deserved credit for retaining his dignity in the face of an intrusion that many felt was ill-timed and unnecessary. Shouldn't jockeys, in any case, be left to report first to the owner and trainer, not to mention the small matter of weighing in, before giving media interviews?

Apart from discussion of the outcome of a pulsating finish, the other burning issue at the end of the Derby was the baffling display by the favourite. Beaten over eight and a half lengths into fourth—a place behind the Irish Two Thousand Guineas third Romanov—Entrepreneur had had his backers worried from early on and was never travelling with the freedom or zest that characterised his Guineas win. He was finished too far from home—'he never did much of anything' reported his rider—for lack of stamina to be considered the sole reason for a most disappointing performance. It was later reported that he'd suffered a hamstring strain.

Neither Benny The Dip nor Entrepreneur won another race, Benny The Dip ending his career on a low note with a rare below-form effort in the Dubai Champion Stakes at Newmarket after creditable performances in the Coral-Eclipse and the Juddmonte International. Ryan, who rode him in all his races after Epsom, dictated only a steady pace at Sandown, where Benny The Dip was the only three-year-old in a field of five. Splitting the winner Pilsudski and the odds-on Bosra Sham, who met trouble in running, probably represented an effort on a par with his Derby form, and his third to Singspiel, another of the season's outstanding batch of older horses, and the Irish Derby winner Desert King at York, confirmed the belief that Benny The Dip was a run-of-the-mill Derby winner. He was retired at the end of the season and will stand at Claiborne Farm, Kentucky, in 1998 at a fee of 25,000 dollars. The good-bodied, attractive Benny The Dip was a much better mover in his faster paces, a very well balanced galloper, than at the walk. He acted on good to firm and good to soft ground. A tendency to sweat and a reputation for excitability characterised the early part of his career—earning him the nickname 'Benny The Drip'—but he took the Derby preliminaries well and remained calm before each of his subsequent starts. There can be no denying that he was a consistent and thoroughly resolute racehorse overall.

*Vodafone Derby Stakes, Epsom—the post comes just in time for Benny The Dip
as the grey Silver Patriarch closes; Romanov and Entrepreneur (rails) come next*

The bold forcing tactics employed on Benny The Dip in the Derby came despite some closest to him, including his owner, thinking he wouldn't stay a mile and a half, but Gosden had no doubts about the best way to ride him at Epsom. 'If he wasn't going to stay, he wouldn't get home however he was ridden. He goes best from the front, so we decided to make a dash for glory.' Any pedigree doubts about Benny The Dip's ability to cope with the distance did not stem from his sire Silver Hawk, who was third in the Derby and runner-up in the Irish Derby. Benny The Dip's dam Rascal Rascal showed plenty of speed in her eight-race career, though she won at up to nine furlongs, and there was an abundance of sprinting influences on the distaff side, including Benny The Dip's grandam Savage Bunny, a three-parts sister to the smart sprinter-miler Distinctive. Savage Bunny gained all four of her wins at sprint distances, while her dam Tudor Jet was a minor stakes winner at four and a half furlongs. Rascal Rascal's seven previous foals to reach the racecourse—six of which won—also had records that suggested speed in excess of stamina, including the sometimes-excitable Horris Hill winner Beggarman Thief (by Arctic Tern) who was never raced beyond a mile. Even a mating with the stamina-packed Alleged had produced the seven-furlong winner Key Suspect. A report that Rascal Rascal's two-year-old Cryptic Rascal (by Cryptoclearance), a winner of the nine-furlong Grade 3 Pilgrim Stakes on turf at Aqueduct in October, would join Gosden for his three-year-old career seems to have been mistaken. Rascal Rascal's sire Ack Ack was a speedy individual with enough stamina to win top races at a mile and a quarter.

Benny The Dip (USA) (b. or br.c. 1994)	Silver Hawk (USA) (b 1979)	Roberto (b 1969)	Hail To Reason Bramalea
		Gris Vitesse (gr 1966)	Amerigo Matchiche II
	Rascal Rascal (USA) (b or br 1981)	Ack Ack (b 1966)	Battle Joined Fast Turn
		Savage Bunny (b or br 1974)	Never Bend Tudor Jet

Mr Landon Knight's "Benny The Dip"

The name Benny The Dip, incidentally, aroused comment during the season, including in the final interview before his death with the irascible columnist Jeffrey Bernard who said 'there should be a law against folk who give noble creatures the most awful names like Benny The Dip . . . there is also the unpleasantly named The Fly who is a stable-companion of The Glow Worm.' It had been thought that Benny The Dip took his name from a character in a Damon Runyon story but, after the Derby, the colt's owner referred to the name as being 'of that genre'. Ian Carnaby in *The Sporting Life* produced a theory that the horse was named after a 1951 film starring Freddie Bartholomew called *St Benny The Dip* in which, according to the film's publicity, 'gamblers learn to escape the law by dressing as priests, but circumstance converts them to good works.' There was no book of that title and, claimed Carnaby, no connection with Damon Runyon. In any event, Benny The Dip wasn't the only Derby Day character with some mystery about his identity. In an incident that could well have come from a Damon Runyon novel, a self-styled bookmaker calling himself John Batten—unknown to any of the bookmakers' organisations—set himself up on the Epsom Hill and disappeared with an estimated £40,000 during the running of the Derby. He had been offering 6/4 against Entrepreneur! *J. H. M. Gosden*

BEN RINNES 2 ch.c. (Feb 3) Ardkinglass 114 – Magical Veil 73 (Majestic Light (USA)) [1997 6s 6m 6d* 6f 5.7m 7.9s² 8d Oct 17] 17,000Y: has a round action: third foal: half-brother to 3-y-o Myrtlebank: dam 11.6f winner: fair form: won maiden at Windsor in June: good second in nursery at York in September: will stay beyond 1m: easily best form on good to soft/soft ground: has sweated: sold 7,500 gns in October. *R. F. Johnson Houghton* — 78

BENROCK (IRE) 2 ch.g. (May 17) Ballad Rock 122 – Madame Champvert (IRE) (Cardinal Flower 101) [1997 a5g⁵ 6d 6g Oct 7] 3,800Y: first foal: dam pulled up in Irish bumper, half-sister to dam of smart sprinter Stack Rock (by Ballad Rock): only form in maidens at Southwell on debut in May. *Capt. J. Wilson* — 44

BEN'S RIDGE 3 b.c. Indian Ridge 123 – Fen Princess (IRE) 72 (Trojan Fen 118) [1996 78, a71: 5m 5d³ 6g³ 7m³ a6g⁴ 7.5f⁴dis a7g* 8g² 8m 7.1m* 8.3g⁴ a8.5g a8.5g⁶ 1997 a7g⁴ a7g⁵ 8f³ 8.5f* 8.5f* 8.5f² 8f⁵ 9f² 8f* 8.5f⁵ 8f³ Nov 8] close-coupled colt: fair winner at 2 yrs: left P. Haslam after second start: did well for 3 different trainers in California, winning 2 claimers at Hollywood Park for P. Aguirre (later claimed for $80,000) and a minor stakes race at Bay Meadows and finishing good fifth of 7 in Grade 3 race on latter course: stays 9f: acts on firm and dead ground and on fibresand: raced on medication in USA. *R. Hess, jnr, USA* — 103

BENTICO 8 b.g. Nordico (USA) – Bentinck Hotel 74 (Red God 128§) [1996 58, a80: a8g² a8g³ a9.4g a8g⁶ 8m 8m 10f⁶ a8.5g* a9.4g⁶ 8m⁵ 7.6m⁵ a8.5g² 9g 8m⁵ a9.4g³ 8.5m⁶ 8f³ a7g² 8f² 7g a8.5g³ a8g² a9.4g⁵ a9.4g 1997 a7g⁴ a8g⁶ a9.4g⁴ 10d a8g³ a7g³ a7g* a8g² a8.5f² a8g* 8.3s⁵ a8g a9.4g⁵ a8g² 8.2d a8g⁴ a8g* a8.5g⁴ Dec 26] lengthy, well-made gelding: carries condition: poor mover: fair on all-weather, modest on turf: easily won claimer at Wolverhampton and minor event at Lingfield in June and claimer at Southwell in December: effective at 7f to 1¼m: best turf form on good going or firmer: has been blinkered, best form in 1997 visored: sometimes bandaged. *Mrs N. Macauley* — 52, a73

BENTNOSE 3 b.c. Saddlers' Hall (IRE) 126 – Blonde Prospect (USA) (Mr Prospector (USA)) [1996 –: 8m a8.5g 1997 a8s 10m Apr 8] well beaten in maidens and seller: pulled too hard in blinkers final outing. *D. Morris* — –

BENT RAIWAND (USA) 4 b.f. Cadeaux Genereux 131 – Raiwand 106 (Tap On Wood 130) [1996 67d: 8d 6m⁴ 8f 5m 6m 6m a6g a6g⁵ 1997 a6g a5g 5g 6d a8g 6g 8.3d³ 8f Aug 27] well-made filly: has a round action: disappointing maiden: stays 1m: acts on dead ground. *Don Enrico Incisa* — 32

BENZOE (IRE) 7 b.g. Taufan (USA) 119 – Saintly Guest (What A Guest 119) [1996 86: 5s 6g 6g 7m 6g* 6m² 5m 6f³ 6m³ 6f² 6f* 6m 6m 6v 6g 7m 1997 6m 6d 6s 6g³ 6s³ 5m* 6d 6g⁶ 5d 6m² 6g* 6g³ 6g⁵ 6g 6.1g 6s 6m Nov 4] tall gelding: has a — 86

116

round action: fairly useful handicapper: won at Thirsk in June and July (fifth course success): below best last 4 starts: stays 6f: acts on any ground: has worn blinkers/visor, but not for long time: sometimes slowly away and looks less than hearty. *Mrs J. R. Ramsden*

BEQUEATH 5 ch.h. Rainbow Quest (USA) 134 – Balabina (USA) 110 (Nijinsky 105
(CAN) 138) [1996 118: 12f² 12g* 12g⁵ 1997 10d⁵ 13.3s⁵ 10g³ 10.3m³ Jun 7] rather unfurnished horse: impressive winner of listed race at Newmarket in 1996, when not seen out after July: bandaged and only useful form as 5-y-o, third in minor events at Newbury and Doncaster (1¾ lengths behind Poseidon): stays 1½m: has won on firm ground (has clearly had problems and may not prove suited by it), seems to act on dead: has flashed tail under pressure: sold 16,500 gns in October and sent to Australia. *H. R. A. Cecil*

BERGEN (IRE) 2 b.c. (May 3) Ballad Rock 122 – Local Custom (IRE) (Be My 78 p
Native (USA) 122) [1997 6m* 7d⁵ Sep 19] 18,500Y: second foal: dam Irish maiden half-sister to Middle Park winner Balla Cove (by Ballad Rock): won 17-runner maiden at Pontefract in July by 1¼ lengths from Panama House: absent 2 months, only fifth of 6 to Confirmation in minor event at Ayr, racing freely and weakening over 1f out: possibly a sprinter: can probably do better. *J. Hanson*

BERING GIFTS (IRE) 2 b.g. (Mar 24) Bering 136 – Bobbysoxer 79 (Valiyar 82
129) [1997 7s³ 8d³ Oct 16] 100,000Y: tall, rangy, good sort: first foal: dam, 1¼m and 1½m winner, half-sister to Queen's Vase winner Stelvio and Fillies' Mile runner-up Safa: fair form in maidens at York and Newmarket, 6½ lengths third of 22 to Border Arrow on latter course, keeping on despite flashing tail: should stay at least 1½m: twice refused to enter stalls: has scope to go on, but clearly has a temperament problem (gelded at end of season). *P. F. I. Cole*

BERLIN BLUE 4 b.g. Belmez (USA) 131 – Blue Brocade 91 (Reform 132) 83 d
[1996 84: 10g 8.1d⁶ 8m⁵ 12.3m* 15m* 13.9m 1997 16d⁶ 11.9g⁴ 12m 14g 16.1g 14.6m⁶ Sep 10] robust gelding: fairly useful handicapper: below form after second start: stays 15f: best efforts on good/good to firm going: has found little, and best treated with caution: joined C. Brooks. *J. W. Watts*

BERMUDA BOY 2 b.g. (Apr 30) Robellino (USA) 127 – Bermuda Lily 78 89
(Dunbeath (USA) 127) [1997 7m² 7m 6m* Aug 21] 17,000Y: well-made gelding: fourth foal: half-brother to 3-y-o Sir Talbot, 4-y-o Sawa-Id and 1994 2-y-o 5f winner Dee-Lady (by Deploy): dam 2-y-o 5f winner: shaped well before winning maiden at Salisbury by 1¼ lengths from Cease Fire, leading halfway: should stay at least 7f: sent to Hong Kong. *B. J. Meehan*

BERMUDA TRIANGLE (IRE) 2 b.f. (Apr 11) Conquering Hero (USA) 116 – 63 d
Bermuda Princess (Lord Gayle (USA) 124) [1997 6m² 6f⁶ 6.9m⁶ 7m⁵ 6g* 6g² 6g⁵ 6f a7g⁶ Nov 18] IR 1,400Y: leggy, short-backed filly: half-sister to 5f winner The Dream Maker (by Cyrano de Bergerac): dam Irish maiden: modest performer: won seller at Lingfield in August: lost her way after next start: should stay 7f: raced only on good going or firmer on turf. *M. J. Haynes*

BERNARDO BELLOTTO (IRE) 2 b.g. (Feb 17) High Estate 127 – Naivity 79
(IRE) (Auction Ring (USA) 123) [1997 5g² 5.1m² 5m⁴ a6g² 7d² 6d² 6g* 7g 6g³ Sep 5] IR 8,000F, IR 34,000Y: smallish, workmanlike gelding: unimpressive mover: first foal: dam Irish 2-y-o 7f winner: fair performer: won maiden at Epsom in August: good third in nursery there final start: should stay 1m: acts on good to firm ground, good to soft and fibresand: usually races prominently: consistent. *M. Bell*

BERNARD SEVEN (IRE) 5 b.g. Taufan (USA) 119 – Madame Nureyev (USA) 66 d
(Nureyev (USA) 131) [1996 85d: a9.4g* a10g a9.4g a12g a10g 10m 8.5m 8f² 8.1m 8m 8.1d 8.5m 10.3g² 1997 a8g³ a9.4g³ a10g³ a8g 8g 10.3d a8g 8f 7g 10.8d⁴ 10g³ 8m⁶ 9.2d³ 10.1g⁶ Oct 22] neat gelding: has deteriorated considerably, fair form on all-weather early at 5 yrs but beaten in sellers late on: stays 1¼m: acts on firm and soft ground and all-weather: visored at 3 yrs, usually blinkered: modest winning hurdler: ungenuine. *M. Dods*

BERNIE'S STAR (IRE) 3 b. or br.g. Arcane (USA) – Abaca (USA) (Manila –
(USA)) [1996 NR 1997 7.1s 7d⁵ 10.3d 8m 16g Sep 23] IR 3,600Y, 4,600 2-y-o:

angular gelding: first foal: dam unraced half-sister to a useful American sprinter: no worthwhile form. *N. Bycroft*

BERYLLIUM 3 b.g. Tragic Role (USA) – Flower Princess (Slip Anchor 136) 70 [1996 86: 7g 7g 7.1f³ 7g* 7g³ 8g 1997 10m⁶ 10.5m 8g 9s² Aug 29] leggy, sparely-made gelding: fair performer: best effort at 3 yrs when second in claimer at Sandown, drifting right and caught close home: claimed to join M. Pipe £12,000 and won over hurdles in November: stays 9f: yet to race on heavy going, acts on any other. *R. Hannon*

BE SATISFIED 4 ch.g. Chilibang 120 – Gentalyn (Henbit (USA) 130) [1996 – 55d: a8g² a8g⁵ 6.9m a10g a6g a8g 1997 a8g Feb 22] well beaten since 3-y-o reappearance. *G. L. Moore*

BESIEGE 3 b.c. Rainbow Quest (USA) 134 – Armeria (USA) 79 (Northern 83 Dancer) [1996 108+: 8.5g* 8.1f* 8g³ 8g⁴ 1997 10d⁶ 14.6m 11.9s⁴ 11.8g² Oct 27] tall colt: has a fluent action: useful at 2 yrs, winner twice and in frame in Royal Lodge Stakes and Racing Post Trophy: very disappointing in 1997, reportedly breaking a bone in hind joint on reappearance and well below best when second of 5 to Wahiba Sands in steadily-run minor event at Leicester: bred to stay well: stays in training. *H. R. A. Cecil*

BEST ATTEMPT 2 ch.g. (Mar 10) Beveled (USA) – Sheznice (IRE) 58 (Try – My Best (USA) 130) [1997 6g⁶ Jul 9] 7,400Y: second foal: half-brother to 4-y-o Matthias Mystique: dam twice-raced: well-held sixth of 9 in maiden at Folkestone. *J. Neville*

BEST BEFORE DAWN (IRE) 6 b.g. Try My Best (USA) 130 – Pistol Petal 108 (Pitskelly 122) [1996 5s⁶ 6d⁶ 5g⁴ 5m* 5g³ 5m* 5m* 6g* 5m⁶ 6g⁶ 5d 5g⁵ 6g⁵ 6g³ 5g* 6f 5s* 1997 6g⁴ 5g* 5m² 5d* 6g 5m 6d³ 6g² 5g⁶ 6d Sep 20] half-brother to a prolific winner in Holland by Shack: dam won at 1¼m in Ireland: useful Irish performer: much improved in 1996 and again in 1997: won handicaps at the Curragh in April and June: also ninth in Wokingham Handicap at Royal Ascot and good second (beaten head by Poker-B) in August in listed race at Leopardstown: a sprinter: acts on good to firm ground and soft: below form in blinkers penultimate start: often slowly away. *A. P. O'Brien, Ireland*

BESTELINA 3 b.f. Puissance 110 – Brittle Grove 79 (Bustino 136) [1996 –: 44 6.1m⁶ 7g a7g⁴ a7g⁶ 1997 5.3f⁴ 5.3f 5m Jul 14] poor maiden handicapper: should be suited by further than 5f. *D. J. S. Cosgrove*

BESTEMOR 3 b.f. Selkirk (USA) 129 – Lillemor (Connaught 130) [1996 NR 60 1997 8.1s⁶ 7m 8d 8.2d⁶ Oct 30] sturdy, close-coupled filly: unimpressive mover: fifth foal: half-sister to 3 winners, including fairly useful 7f/1m performer Caleman (by Daring March): dam (ran twice) out of half-sister to Steel Heart: modest maiden: best effort final start. *H. Candy*

BEST KEPT SECRET 6 b.g. Petong 126 – Glenfield Portion 86 (Mummy's Pet 44 § 125) [1996 56§: a6g⁴ a7g⁶ a7g⁶ a8g a5g⁵ a6g³ 7.1g⁵ 6d² 5s² 5m 7g⁵ 8f 5.9f³ 6d³ 7.6m 7f 6f 7f⁶ 7m² 8f a7g 1997 a7g 10.5m 6.1d 8s 7.6m⁵ 6m⁵ Aug 8] neat gelding: has a quick action: poor performer nowadays: stays 7f: probably acts on any going: often blinkered/visored: none too resolute. *L. J. Barratt*

BEST OF ALL (IRE) 5 b.m. Try My Best (USA) 130 – Skisette (Malinowski 77 (USA) 123) [1996 70: 8s 8d 7m³ 10d 7m 7.1d⁴ 8.3m³ 7g⁵ a8g 8d 7.1s 7g⁵ 7m² 8.1s a7g² a8g* a9.4g 1997 8.3d⁶ 8g³ 8.3s a8g 8f* 8g* 8d² 9.2m⁴ 9m 8m⁶ 10d 8d Sep 20] fair handicapper: won at Redcar and Musselburgh in June: stays 9f: acts on firm and soft ground and on fibresand: effective blinkered or not: fairly useful winning hurdler. *J. Berry*

BEST OF OUR DAYS 2 b.c. (May 30) Clantime 101 – Uptown Girl 65 (Caruso 66 112) [1997 a6g 5m⁴ a5g² Dec 22] 16,500Y: fifth foal: brother to fair 5f winner Charterhouse Xpres and half-brother to 3-y-o Suite Factors: dam sprinter: modest form when in frame in maidens at Redcar and Lingfield: should stay 6f. *C. W. Thornton*

BEST QUEST 2 b.c. (Apr 24) Salse (USA) 128 – Quest For The Best (Rainbow 67 + Quest (USA) 134) [1997 6f⁶ 7s 7d Nov 7] 34,000Y: small colt: poor mover: first foal: dam thrice-raced half-sister to useful 1988 2-y-o 6f/7f winner Life At The Top: promising sixth in maiden at Lingfield: well beaten on soft/good to soft ground next 2 starts: likely to need at least 1m. *J. H. M. Gosden*

BESWEETOME   4 b.f. Mtoto 134 – Actraphane (Shareef Dancer (USA) 135)   81
[1996 –: 7d 1997 a8g* Feb 22] strong, lengthy filly: has been fired: favourite, emphatic winner of weak maiden at Lingfield: should have stayed at least 1¼m: in foal to Lion Cavern. *J. Pearce*

BE TRUE   3 b.g. Robellino (USA) 127 – Natchez Trace 52 (Commanche Run 133)   64
[1996 54: 5f 7f 6m⁶ 6f³ 7f 1997 a7g⁶ a8g⁶ 9.7m 10m⁶ 8m 12g³ 11.9f* 11.9m* a10s   a54
a16g⁵ a16g⁶ Dec 4] modest handicapper: won twice at Brighton in October, by 14 lengths on first occasion and when 8 lb out of handicap (apprentices) on second: probably stays 2m: acts on firm going and equitrack: well held in visor. *G. L. Moore*

BETTER OFFER (IRE)   5 b.g. Waajib 121 – Camden's Gift (Camden Town   100
125) [1996 110: 10m 14s⁵ 12m* 12m³ 13.9m 12g* 18g 12s 1997 12m 13.9m⁶ 12m⁴
13.9g 12g⁴ 12d Oct 16] tall gelding: useful handicapper: best effort at 5 yrs when staying-on fourth to demoted Taufan's Melody in Tote Sunday Special Handicap (won in 1996, seems to save best for Ascot nowadays): suited by good test at 1½m and stays 1¾m (probably not 2¼m): acts on soft ground and good to firm: effective sweating: carries head high and has wandered under pressure: held up: fairly useful hurdler. *Mrs A. J. Perrett*

BETTRON   2 b.g. (May 8) Alnasr Alwasheek 117 – Aigua Blava (USA) (Solford   84
(USA) 127) [1997 6m 7f* 7g² 7m 7.3g³ Oct 25] 5,000Y: second foal: dam, tailed off only start, half-sister to 1994 Cesarewitch winner Captain's Guest: fairly useful performer: won claimer at Brighton in July: good efforts when placed in minor event at Redcar and nursery at Newbury: may prove best up to 1m: slowly away first 2 starts, swerving sharply right and unseating rider on debut. *R. Hannon*

BE VALIANT   3 gr.g. Petong 126 – Fetlar (Pharly (FR) 130) [1996 NR 1997 8.3s   –
May 19] 11,000Y: third foal: half-brother to 2 winners, notably useful Be Mindful (up to 1¼m, by Warning): dam unraced half-sister to Jersey Stakes winner Ardkinglass: weak 16/1, slowly away and little promise in maiden at Windsor. *J. R. Fanshawe*

BEVELED CRYSTAL   3 ro.f. Beveled (USA) – Countess Mariga (Amboise   37
113) [1996 –: 6m 1997 6.9m 7.1m⁶ 6s⁵ 6m 6g 6.9d Oct 21] sparely-made filly: poor maiden. *C. James*

BEVIER   3 b.c. Nashwan (USA) 135 – Bevel (USA) (Mr Prospector (USA)) [1996   70
NR 1997 12m⁶ 10m 8f* 8m 10g 10.3d 8m⁶ Oct 5] leggy, unfurnished colt: first foal: dam, French 1m winner, out of half-sister to Ajdal, Formidable and the dam of Arazi: fair form: favourite, made all in steadily-run 4-runner maiden at Yarmouth in June: easily best effort in handicaps final start: should be suited by further than 1m: sold 13,000 gns and joined Mrs J. Cecil. *C. E. Brittain*

BEWARE   2 br.c. (Apr 5) Warning 136 – Dancing Spirit (IRE) 72 (Ahonoora 122)   81
[1997 6s⁶ 6m³ 7.5d⁶ 7d⁴ 6m² 6f³ 7d⁶ 6g* Oct 25] 20,000Y: smallish colt: first foal: dam 6f winner from family of Law Society: fairly useful performer: won 19-runner nursery at Newbury by ½ length from Who Nose, despite hanging badly right into whip: better form at 6f than 7f: usually races prominently. *R. W. Armstrong*

BE WARNED   6 b.g. Warning 136 – Sagar 74 (Habitat 134) [1996 72d: 7d 7m   59
7.3s³ 6d 6m 6m⁴ 6g 6m⁵ 7m 6d 6f 1997 a7g⁶ 7m⁴ 6d⁴ 6g² 7d 7s 6g a7g 6m 6m⁴
7m a7g² a8g⁵ 6f* 6m a8.5g⁵ 7f a7g⁴ a7g³ a8g a7g² Dec 18] good-topped gelding: unimpressive mover: modest handicapper: trained by M. Dods first 12 starts: won at Yarmouth in September on second start for new yard: effective at 6f, seemingly 1m: acts on firm ground, soft and fibresand: usually blinkered/visored: held up (often slowly away), and suited by strong pace. *J. Pearce*

BEWITCHING LADY   3 ch.f. Primo Dominie 121 – Spirit of India (Indian   49
King (USA) 128) [1996 60: 5.2f 6m³ 6g⁶ 6m 7.3s 1997 7g⁴ 8.5s 10m 10.1m⁶ 11.5m²
12g 12g 11.9m³ a16g 11.5m* 11.9f² 11.9m⁶ Oct 23] lengthy filly: poor performer: won claimer at Yarmouth in September: stays 1½m: acts on firm going: visored (ran creditably) eighth start. *D. W. P. Arbuthnot*

BEYOND CALCULATION (USA)   3 ch.c. Geiger Counter (USA) – Placer   73
Queen (Habitat 134) [1996 79: 6m^4 1997 7m^4 7g 7g^3 7.1m^5 a6g^2 6m* 6s Oct 15]
rather unfurnished colt: fair performer: won 5-runner maiden at Redcar in October:
stiff task and not well drawn final start: effective at 6f/7f: acts on good to firm going
and fibresand: has been bandaged: consistent. *P. W. Harris*

BIANCA NERA   3 b.f. Salse (USA) 128 – Birch Creek (Carwhite 127) [1996   93
107+: 5f* 6m* 7g* 8d^4 1997 7.3g^6 8m May 4] good-bodied filly: has a quick action:
useful juvenile, gaining last 2 wins in Lowther Stakes and Moyglare Stud Stakes:
disappointing in Fred Darling Stakes at Newbury and 1000 Guineas at Newmarket at
3 yrs: should stay beyond 1m. *D. R. Loder*

BIBA (IRE)   3 ch.f. Superlative 118 – Fahrenheit 69 (Mount Hagen (FR) 127)   –
[1996 –: a6g 6g 6m 1997 6.1m a10g May 9] poor maiden. *R. Boss*

BICTON PARK   3 b.g. Distant Relative 128 – Merton Mill 68 (Dominion 123)   –
[1996 61+: 6m 7.1d 7m^4 6d 1997 9m 10m 5.7g a6g Oct 4] workmanlike gelding:
modest maiden at 2 yrs: showed nothing in 1997: sometimes blinkered.
K. C. Comerford

BIFF-EM (IRE)   3 ch.g. Durgam (USA) – Flash The Gold (Ahonoora 122) [1996   –
68: 5d 6d^3 5g* 1997 6s 6s 9.2g^6 5s 7g 9.2g 9s Oct 13] rather leggy gelding: not seen
after winning in June at 2 yrs: no worthwhile form in 1997: should stay 7f: raced only
on good ground or softer. *Miss L. A. Perratt*

BIG BANG   3 b.g. Superlative 118 – Good Time Girl 65 (Good Times (ITY))   –
[1996 56: 8.1g^6 8.1s 1997 a8.5g^3 a9.4g* 10.8m a9.4g 11.6s a12g* a12g^3 16m a14g   a64
a14.8g Nov 15] modest performer: won maiden at Wolverhampton in March and
handicap at Southwell in June: well beaten last 3 starts, including in blinkers: stays
1½m: best on the all-weather. *M. Blanshard*

BIG BEN   3 ch.c. Timeless Times (USA) 99 – Belltina 41 (Belfort (FR) 89) [1996   62
87: 6g 5m* 5f* 5m^4 5s^3 6d^5 5v^5 1997 6g 6.1s 8g^3 7m* 7d a7g* a6g^4 6m^5 7.1m^4 7m^3 a69
a7g Aug 28] small, leggy colt: poor mover: fair on all-weather, modest on turf: won
claimers at Goodwood (3 ran) and Lingfield in June: stays 7f: best turf form on good
to firm/firm going. *R. Hannon*

BIG PAT   8 b.g. Backchat (USA) 98 – Fallonetta 41 (Tachypous 128) [1996 NR 1997   –
10g 11.9d^6 Jul 4] lightly raced and no worthwhile form since 1994. *J. G. M. O'Shea*

BIG TARGET (IRE)   3 b.g. Suave Dancer (USA) 136 – Prima Domina (FR) 89   75
(Dominion 123) [1996 NR 1997 8g 8m^5 10.2d^4 14.1s^6 Oct 15] 63,000F, 60,000Y:
useful-looking gelding: not best of movers: fifth foal: half-brother to 6f (at 2 yrs)
to 1¾m winner Primo Figlio (by Assert): dam sprinting sister to Primo Dominie:
encouraging debut in midfield for newcomers event at Newmarket: failed to
progress: off course 5 months before final start, sold 16,000 gns after it and joined R.
Allan. *M. R. Stoute*

BIJOU D'INDE   4 ch.c. Cadeaux Genereux 131 – Pushkar (Northfields (USA))   120
[1996 127: 8m^3 8d^4 8f* 10g^2 10.4m^3 8m^6 1997 a9f^4 a10f 8m 8g^5 10g 9m Dec 14]
big, quite good-topped colt: high-class performer at 3 yrs, winning St James's Palace
Stakes and in frame in 2000 Guineas, Irish 2000 Guineas, Eclipse Stakes and
International Stakes: easily best effort in 1997 when 2½ lengths fifth to Air Express
in Queen Elizabeth II Stakes at Ascot: reportedly injured a tendon when brought
down in Dubai World Cup (well beaten at time) second start and suffered recurrence
of that injury in Hong Kong International Cup on final outing: effective at 1m to
1¼m: used to go very well on good going or firmer: front runner/raced prominently:
retired to Elsenham Stud, Hertfordshire (fee £6,000, Oct 1st). *M. Johnston*

BILKO   3 gr.g. Risk Me (FR) 127 – Princess Tara 85 (Prince Sabo 123) [1996 88+:   84
5d* 5m^2 1997 6g^5 5d 5.1m Jun 4] fairly useful form very early at 2 yrs: shaped well
on reappearance, tailed off in handicaps at Sandown (reportedly broke blood vessel)
and Chester (early to post and sweating) after: may prove best at 5f: yet to race on
extremes of going: joined D. Nicholls. *G. Lewis*

BILLADDIE   4 b.g. Touch of Grey 90 – Young Lady (Young Generation 129)   55
[1996 60: a8g* a10g^3 a8g^4 1997 a8.5g^6 a7g^6 a10g a10g^3 a10g^3 Dec 19] modest

performer: best effort of 1997 on final start: stays 1¼m: acts on equitrack (not raced on turf since 1995). *R. M. Flower*

BILLIONAIRE 2 b.c. (May 1) Distant Relative 128 – Miss Plum 86 (Ardross 134) [1997 7d Nov 7] tall, unfurnished colt: first foal: dam, thorough stayer, also successful over hurdles: 3/1 favourite but thoroughly green, midfield in 19-runner maiden at Doncaster, slowly away and soon off bit: should do better, particularly with time and distance. *D. R. Loder* — p

BILLY BUSHWACKER 6 b.g. Most Welcome 131 – Secret Valentine 71 (Wollow 132) [1996 97: 8s 10.3m² 10m² 9.2g² 10.4m 10m⁶ 10m 10.4m 10.3m³ 9m 1997 10m² 10.3d³ 10m⁵ 10g² 10.1g² 9.9d⁴ 8m⁵ 10.3m 11.9g² 11.9s 10.3g³ Oct 25] workmanlike gelding: fairly useful performer: generally ran well in 1997, but isn't easy to win with: stays 1½m: acts on good to firm and dead going: occasionally blinkered, at least as good when not: held up, and suited by a strong pace. *Mrs M. Reveley* 94

BILLYCAN (IRE) 3 b.c. Mac's Imp (USA) 116 – Sassalin (Sassafras (FR) 135) [1996 –: 6m 6d⁶ a7g 7g 6m 1997 a8s a8g Jan 6] of no account. *B. P. J. Baugh* –

BILLY NOMAITE 3 ch.g. Komaite (USA) – Lucky Monashka (Lucky Wednesday 124) [1996 NR 1997 8f³ 10m² 10d² 10m⁶ 10g Aug 25] 800Y: tall, workmanlike gelding: fourth foal: dam unraced: fair form in maidens first 3 starts: not sure to stay beyond 1¼m: front runner. *Mrs S. J. Smith* 69

BILLY OWL (IRE) 2 ch.c. (May 21) Shalford (IRE) 124§ – Ounavarra 100 (Homeric 133) [1997 7.1m Aug 20] 5,000 2-y-o: seventh foal: half-brother to a winner in Italy by Trojan Fen: dam staying mudlark: 25/1, behind in maiden at Musselburgh. *J. O'Reilly* –

BIMSEY (IRE) 7 b.h. Horage 124 – Cut It Out (Cut Above 130) [1996 NR 1997 14g⁶ 14m⁴ 13.9g Aug 20] high-class hurdler (has won on firm and heavy going), winner of Martell Aintree Hurdle in April, 1997: lightly raced on flat: fairly useful form at 7 yrs: has joined C. Mann: will be very well suited by a good test of stamina, and may yet do better. *R. Akehurst* 81

BINA GARDENS 3 b.f. Shirley Heights 130 – Balabina (USA) 110 (Nijinsky (CAN) 138) [1996 NR 1997 11.5s⁶ 10m⁴ 12m⁴ 10d* 10.2g* Sep 11] big, good-topped filly: has a quick action: sixth foal: sister to smart 7f (at 2 yrs) and 1¼m winner Bal Harbour and half-sister to 3 winners by Rainbow Quest, including 5-y-o Bequeath: dam, 1½m winner, from excellent family: useful and generally progressive performer: odds on, easy winner of maiden at Ripon: much improved to win 5-runner minor event at Chepstow following month by 2 lengths from Cugina: should stay beyond 1¼m: tail flasher: stays in training and can do better again. *H. R. A. Cecil* 106 p

BIN CYCLONE (USA) 3 b.c. Shadeed (USA) 135 – Dubian 120 (High Line 125) [1996 NR 1997 8g 8.3m⁴ 7m³ 7g 8m a7f² Dec 18] strong, angular colt: sixth foal: brother to 2 winners, notably 1000 Guineas and Sussex Stakes winner Sayyedati: dam winner from 7f (at 2 yrs) to 1½m and third in Oaks and Irish Oaks: fair maiden: trained by C. Brittain first 5 starts: tried blinkered. *P. L. Rudkin, UAE* 68

BIN ROSIE 5 b.g. Distant Relative 128 – Come On Rosi 77 (Valiyar 129) [1996 120: 7g⁴ 7g³ 8m² 8g* 7.3m* 8m² 8d³ 1997 8.1g³ 8d 8m⁶ 8g⁵ 7.3m² 7.1d* 8d* 8m⁶ 8f Oct 18] smallish good-quartered gelding: smart performer: won Hungerford Stakes at Newbury as 4-y-o: didn't get best of runs when length second to Decorated Hero in same race at 5 yrs: won minor event at Chepstow later in August and Newbury in September: disappointing last 2 starts: effective at 7f/1m: acts on good to firm ground and dead: has been visored, blinkered nowadays: carries head awkwardly and sometimes hangs: goes well covered up in strongly-run race: to race in USA. *D. R. Loder* 113

BINT ALBAADIYA (USA) 3 ch.f. Woodman (USA) 126 – Pixie Erin 110 (Golden Fleece (USA) 133) [1996 7pp: 6m* 1997 6d* 6s* 6g* 7g⁴ Sep 18] angular filly: useful performer: won minor events at Doncaster in May and Newmarket in June and listed race at York (led final strides to beat Bollin Joanne a neck despite carrying head high) in July: lost unbeaten record but ran respectably when fourth to 108

Singapore Summer Stakes, York—Bint Albaadiya (left) catches Bollin Joanne close home

Russian Revival in another listed race at Newbury final start (first for over 2 months): probably stays 7f: acts on soft going (unraced on firmer than good since debut). *M. R. Stoute*

BINTANG (IRE) 2 ch.c. (Jan 27) Soviet Star (USA) 128 – Brush Away (Aho-   105 p
noora 122) [1997 6d* 6m* 7m² Oct 3] 50,000Y: good-topped colt: half-brother to several winners, including useful Irish performer up to 7f, Takwim (by Taufan): dam unraced half-sister to useful stayer Princess Genista: won valuable maiden at York (by 8 lengths) in August and minor event at Doncaster (by 1¼ lengths from Sky Rocket) in September: 1½ lengths second of 8 to Haami in listed contest at Newmarket, keeping on despite carrying head awkwardly: likely to prove best up to 1m: wears dropped noseband: joined Godolphin: has scope to go on if remaining tractable. *P. F. I. Cole*

BINTANG TIMOR (USA) 3 ch.c. Mt Livermore (USA) – Frisky Kitten (USA)   70
(Isopach (USA)) [1996 77: 6d² 7g⁴ 1997 6m⁴ 10d⁴ 7m May 31] close-coupled colt: unimpressive mover: fair maiden: headstrong, but seems to stay 1¼m: yet to race on extremes of going: sold only 1,000 gns in December. *P. F. I. Cole*

BINT BALADEE 3 b.f. Nashwan (USA) 135 – Sahara Baladee (USA) 79   101
(Shadeed (USA) 135) [1996 94d: 7d² 8m⁴ 7.3s⁶ 7d³ 1997 8g* 12m 10s* 10.2m² 10g⁴ 12s⁴ Oct 9] unfurnished filly: good mover: useful performer: won maiden at Kempton in May and minor event at Windsor in June: subsequently in frame in listed races at Chepstow (short-headed by Fiji), Salisbury (final outing for Saeed bin Suroor) and Longchamp: very best efforts around 1¼m, though not discredited at 1½m: acts on good to firm and soft going: blinkered last 2 starts as 2-y-o: none too easy ride: sent to USA. *N. Clement, France*

BINT KALDOUN (IRE) 2 b.f. (Feb 5) Kaldoun (FR) 122 – Shy Danceuse (FR)   71 p
(Groom Dancer (USA) 128) [1997 7m⁴ Sep 22] 1,400,000 francs Y: second foal: sister to German 1996 2-y-o 5f and 6f winner Shy Lady: dam, French 1m winner, half-sister to very smart 6f/7f performer Diffident: 16/1, 4½ lengths fourth of 14 to Elsurur in maiden at Kempton, tracking pace until fading near finish: should do better. *D. R. Loder*

BINT NADIA 2 b.f. (May 13) Deploy 131 – Faisalah (Gay Mecene (USA) 128)   50
[1997 6m⁶ 6g⁵ 7g³ 7g* 8g 7.5f⁴ 8m Oct 5] leggy, workmanlike filly: has a round action: fifth foal: half-sister to a 5f seller winner by Prince Sabo and untrustworthy

8.5f winner Tabriz (by Persian Heights): dam unraced: won seller at Catterick in August: some way below form in nurseries after: stays 7f: raced only on good going or firmer: sold to join Miss J. Craze. *J. D. Bethell*

BINT ROSIE   3 b.f. Exit To Nowhere (USA) 122 – Butterfly Rose (USA) (Iron   35
Ruler (USA)) [1996 –: 7d 1997 11g 10m 15.4s 12d⁶ 12g Aug 13] tall filly: poor
maiden: probably stays 1½m. *M. J. Fetherston-Godley*

BINT SHIHAMA (USA)   3 b.f. Cadeaux Genereux 131 – Shihama (USA) 88   78
(Shadeed (USA) 135) [1996 NR 1997 8f⁴ 7.1g³ 8m² 7.1d* 7g⁵ 7g Sep 4] second foal:
dam, winner at 2 yrs who should have stayed beyond 6f, sister to Sayyedati: fair
performer: won maiden at Chepstow in July: stiff tasks and last afterwards, pulling
hard penultimate outing: stays 1m: acts on dead ground, probably firm: sold 25,000
gns in December. *C. E. Brittain*

BIRCHWOOD SUN   7 b.g. Bluebird (USA) 125 – Shapely Test (USA)   56
(Elocutionist (USA)) [1996 –: 7.5d 7g 6g 6s 5.9m 6.9g 6g 1997 7m 5.9g⁵ 5.9d* 7m
6.9f 6d 7m 7m 8m⁴ 7d² 8g 8.2d Nov 3] compact gelding: poor mover: modest
handicapper: won at Carlisle in May: second at Leicester in October: stays 1m: acts
on any ground: best in blinkers: comes from behind: none too consistent. *M. Dods*

BISHOPS COURT   3 ch.g. Clantime 101 – Indigo 86 (Primo Dominie 121)   110
[1996 81p: 5m³ 5g* 1997 5m³ 5d³ 6.1s* 5g³ 6d³ 5d² 5.1m² 5m⁴ 5m² 5d⁴ Oct 26] big,
good-quartered gelding: powerful type with plenty of scope: quickly made into a
smart sprinter, though gained just one win at 3 yrs, in handicap at Chester in May: in
frame all 7 starts afterwards, including in listed and pattern company: best effort
when beaten neck by Dashing Blue at Newmarket penultimate start: effective at 5f
and 6f: acts on good to firm and soft ground: has edged left closing stages: held up,
travels very strongly and sometimes finds less than expected. *Mrs J. R. Ramsden*

BISON BELTING   3 b.g. Full Extent (USA) 113 – Sylvan Song (Song 132) [1996   51 d
NR 1997 a7g⁴ a8g⁵ 6.1d a7g 10m 8g 8g Oct 27] 2,000Y: fourth reported foal:
half-brother to 5-y-o Chewit: dam poor sister to smart (up to 9f) Shark Song, and to
dam of Prince Sabo: well beaten after debut: dead. *J. A. Glover*

BISQUET-DE-BOUCHE   3 ch.f. Most Welcome 131 – Larive 80 (Blakeney   47
126) [1996 –: 7.1s 8s 1997 12g 14.1d⁴ 14.1g³ 15.4s⁶ 14.9g Jul 12] shallow-girthed
filly: poor handicapper: should be suited by 2m+. *R. Dickin*

BIT OF A LAD   2 br.c. (Mar 14) Touch of Grey 90 – Lingfield Lass (USA) 60   –
(Advocator) [1997 a5s a7s Nov 28] second reported foal: dam 1¼m winner, half-
sister to very smart 1986 2-y-o 6f and 7f winner (also useful 1¼m winner at 3 yrs)
Genghiz: well beaten in maiden and minor event at Lingfield. *R. M. Flower*

Great North Eastern Railway Conditions Stakes, Doncaster—
Bintang is confidently ridden to beat Sky Rocket and Hayil

BIT ON THE SIDE (IRE)   8 b.m. Vision (USA) – Mistress (USA) (Damascus   87
(USA)) [1996 86: 10.8d* 12s 12g 10s⁴ 1997 10g³ 10g⁴ 12g³ 12s Nov 8] leggy,
lengthy mare: fairly useful handicapper: lightly raced of late, and ran poorly final
start: stays 1¾m: seems ideally suited by good going or softer: sometimes sweats and
gets on toes: lacks turn of foot, and suited by sound pace. *N. E. Berry*

BIYA (IRE)   5 ch.g. Shadeed (USA) 135 – Rosie Potts 83 (Shareef Dancer (USA)   –
135) [1996 NR 1997 a14.8f⁵ a12g³ a10g* a8g⁴ a8.5g a12g May 1] modest handi-   a50
capper: won amateurs race at Lingfield in January: below form after: should stay
further than 1¼m: acts on all-weather (twice-raced on turf): blinkered final start
(tailed off). *D. McCain*

BLACK ICE BOY (IRE)   6 b.g. Law Society (USA) 130 – Hogan's Sister   45
(USA) (Speak John) [1996 NR 1997 21.6g 17.2m* 16.2v* 16.2m⁶ a16.2g⁴ 15g 18d
Oct 20] tall, workmanlike gelding: poor handicapper: won at Carlisle in June and
Beverley in July: below form last 3 starts: needs at least 2m: acts on good to firm
going and heavy: blinkered once at 4 yrs and last 6 starts: front runner. *R. Bastiman*

BLACK JET   2 b.g. (Mar 22) Durgam (USA) – Blazing Sunset 55 (Blazing   –
Saddles (AUS)) [1997 5g 7s a6g⁴ a6g⁶ 8d a8.5g⁵ a8.5g Dec 13] 8,000 2-y-o 4f   a50 +
foal: dam winning sprinter, including at 2 yrs: modest maiden: stays 8.5f: best form
on fibresand. *N. P. Littmoden*

BLACK WEASEL (IRE)   2 br.c. (Apr 3) Lahib (USA) 129 – Glowlamp (IRE)   ?
93 (Glow (USA)) [1997 7m³ Sep 27] IR 14,000F, IR 30,000Y: second foal:
half-brother to 3-y-o Mr Paradise: dam 2-y-o 9f winner: 3 lengths third of 11 to
Sottvus in maiden at Milan: should stay at least 1¼m: difficult to assess. *J. L. Dunlop*

BLAKESET   2 ch.c. (Feb 6) Midyan (USA) 124 – Penset (Red Sunset 120) [1997   88
5.1m³ 5m* 6.1m² 6g⁵ 6m³ Oct 4] 8,000F, IR 42,000Y: sturdy colt: did well physically: fifth foal: dam unraced: fairly useful performer: won maiden at Newmarket in
April: good efforts after in minor event at Chepstow and nurseries at Epsom and
Newmarket (bandaged near-hind): should stay 7f: raced only on good/good to firm
going. *R. Hannon*

BLANCHE THE ALMOND   2 ch.f. (Apr 7) Northern Park (USA) 107 –   –
Gaucherie (USA) (Sharpen Up 127) [1997 8.2m 6.1g 8.2d a8.5g 8m Nov 1] IR
6,000Y: half-sister to several winners, including useful sprinter Green's Canaletto
(by Hagley): dam won up to 7f in USA: little sign of ability: tried visored. *C. A. Smith*

BLANE WATER (USA)   3 b.f. Lomond (USA) 128 – Triode (USA) 105   83
(Sharpen Up 127) [1996 93: 6m* 7m⁶ 6m⁴ 7.3s 1997 8g⁶ 8d 7g⁶ 7f 8m Sep 27] small
filly: fluent mover: fairly useful performer: stiff tasks in listed races and handicaps in
1997, showing form on third and fourth starts: likely to prove best short of 1m: acts
on firm ground, possibly unsuited by soft. *J. R. Fanshawe*

BLARNEY PARK   2 b.f. (Mar 5) Never So Bold 135 – Walking Saint 73   50d
(Godswalk (USA) 130) [1997 5g a5g⁵ 5.1m³ 5m 5.1m³ 6g³ 5g 6m 6d Oct 21] 1,500Y:
good-bodied filly: first foal: dam 7f (at 2 yrs) to 8.5f winner: some modest form, but
largely disappointing, particularly so last 2 starts: visored final one. *C. A. Dwyer*

BLATANT OUTBURST   7 b.g. War Hero 116 – Miss Metro 65 (Upper Case   –
(USA)) [1996 81d: 8.2m⁴ 11.5g⁴ 9f² 10g² 10.1m⁶ 7.6d 8g⁴ 8m⁴ 8g 1997 14.1g⁵ 14s
16m Aug 6] rangy gelding: disappointing maiden: tried blinkered: won novice hurdle
in September. *Miss S. J. Wilton*

BLAZE OF OAK (USA)   6 ch.g. Green Forest (USA) 134 – Magic Robe (USA)   46 d
(Grey Dawn II 132) [1996 53: 10.8d 10.2f 10.1m³ 8f 10.8f 1997 10g⁴ 9f 10g 11.9f
12f Jun 10] tall gelding: poor maiden handicapper: well held after reappearance:
stays 1¼m: acts on firm and dead ground: takes keen hold: carries head high:
inconsistent. *J. M. Bradley*

BLAZE OF SONG   5 ch.g. Jester 119 – Intellect (Frimley Park 109) [1996 82d:
8.1g 8d² 8m 10m 8.1m⁶ 8.1d⁶ 8m 8.1d 9m 8g a10g⁶ 1997 10s 10d⁵ Oct 28] lengthy
gelding: on the downgrade and no form in 1997: tried blinkered/visored. *R. Hannon*

BLAZER'S BABY   3 ch.f. Norton Challenger 111 – Qualitair Blazer 55 (Blazing   51 d
Saddles (AUS)) [1996 NR 1997 7m 7m⁵ 8d 10.1g⁴ 10m* 10.1m 10g 10.8g 8d a12g
Dec 26] lengthy, angular filly: first reported foal: dam 1½m winner: won seller at

Nottingham for J. Fanshawe in July: no form after: stays 1¼m: acts on good to firm going. *Mrs N. Macauley*

BLAZING BILLY 2 ch.c. (May 16) Anshan 119 – Worthy Venture 76 (North- –
fields (USA)) [1997 6d Oct 28] half-brother to several winners, including 8-y-o
Canovas Heart and Marbella Silks (both useful sprinters by Balidar): dam placed
over 5f at 2 yrs: little promise in maiden at Leicester. *C. A. Dwyer*

BLAZING CASTLE 3 gr.g. Vague Shot 108 – Castle Cary 69 (Castle Keep 121) 60 d
[1996 73: 5d³ a6g⁴ 5m* 5g 5.3f² 5.7m 1997 7m a6g 6.1g⁴ 6.1d 5.1f⁶ 5m⁴ 7.1m⁵ 7m
Jul 24] leggy gelding: just a modest performer at best in 1997: stays 6f: acts on firm
and dead ground and on fibresand: often claimer ridden: sometimes wanders.
W. G. M. Turner

BLAZING IMP (USA) 4 ch.g. Imp Society (USA) – Marital (USA) (Marine 51
Patrol (USA)) [1996 –: 7m⁵ 8m 6g³ 6m 1997 7m 5d* 5g 5g 5g⁶ 5g 5g 5s 5g 5m⁶ Nov
4] modest performer: won maiden at Musselburgh in June: shaped better than results
suggest afterwards, stiff tasks last 2 starts: a sprinter: acts on good to firm and dead
ground. *Mrs J. Jordan*

BLENHEIM TERRACE 4 b.g. Rambo Dancer (CAN) 107 – Boulevard Girl 80 62
(Nicholas Bill 125) [1996 69: 12m 10m⁴ 10m⁴ 11.1g* 14.1m² 12m² 11.8g² 12.1m²
13.9g 1997 12.1d² 12d 12m 12m⁴ 12g* 11.9g⁴ Sep 26] sturdy gelding: modest
handicapper: won at Musselburgh in September: stays 1¾m: acts on good to firm and
dead ground: tends to idle markedly in front. *C. B. B. Booth*

BLESSED SPIRIT 4 ch.f. Statoblest 120 – Kukri (Kris 135) [1996 84: 6s² 6f³ 96
6m⁴ 7g² 7s⁶ 8.3m² 8m* 8.1g² 8.1m⁵ 8m⁴ 1997 8g² 9m⁶ 8.3m² 8d⁶ 8m⁴ 8s* 7.1m³ 8g
8v³ Oct 10] tall filly: useful performer: won ladies race at Ascot in July by neck from
Cape Cross: sweating, good third to Jafn in listed race there final start: stays 1m: has
form on firm going, goes well on dead ground or softer: held up (usually travels well)
and best in strongly-run race: sent to USA. *C. F. Wall*

BLESS 'IM 2 b.c. (Mar 28) Presidium 124 – Saint Systems 68 (Uncle Pokey 116) 68
[1997 6g⁵ 8.1d 6d² Oct 20] 7,200Y: tall, angular colt: second foal: dam sprinter: fair
maiden: running-on length second of 13 to Sharp Cracker at Pontefract: should stay
7f (well held over 1m). *R. Hannon*

BLESSINGINDISGUISE 4 b.g. Kala Shikari 125 – Blowing Bubbles 72 103
(Native Admiral (USA)) [1996 84d: 6g 6g⁴ 6m 6d⁴ 6m 5m 7.1d 6g⁵ 7g 1997 5g 5g 6g
5d² 5g² 5m* 6d 5m* 5g² 5g* 5m* 5m* 5m³ 6g 5m 6g 5m³ Sep 26] strong gelding:
useful handicapper: had a splendid 1997, winning at Redcar in May, Ripon in June
and at Haydock, Ayr and Ascot (by 1½ lengths from Surprise Mission) in July: even
better efforts when third in competitive races at Haydock (to Moon Strike) and York
(behind Plaisir D'Amour) in August: effective at 5f/6f: acts on good to firm and dead
going: best in blinkers: usually races prominently: ducked and unseated rider leaving
stalls fifteenth start: tough and consistent. *M. W. Easterby*

BLEWBURY HILL (IRE) 3 gr.c. Kenmare (FR) 125 – Greatest Pleasure (Be 73
My Guest (USA) 126) [1996 NR 1997 8d 7m⁴ 7g⁴ 6d⁶ 8m² 8g 8.1s 7.3d³ 10m⁶ 8g*
8d⁵ Oct 28] 13,000Y: very tall, workmanlike colt: sixth foal: half-brother to Irish
1993 2-y-o 7f winner Doherty (by Entitled): dam unraced half-sister to Lancashire
Oaks winner Sing Softly (dam of Top Cees): fair performer: set strong pace and clear
from turn (drifted right final 1f) when 6-length winner of minor event at Warwick in
October: ran well in handicap next time, then sold 36,000 gns following day and sent
to USA: keen sort, best at 7f/1m: acts on good to firm and dead going. *R. F. Johnson
Houghton*

BLISS (IRE) 2 b.f. (May 3) Statoblest 120 – Moira My Girl (Henbit (USA) 130) 75 p
[1997 5g⁶ 5.1m 5.1m⁶ 5d⁴ 5g 5.3g* 5m* 5m* Oct 2] IR 3,500Y: half-sister to
Irish 5f winner Dieci Anno (by Classic Music) and 3 winners up to 7f by Fayruz: dam
third over 1¼m in Ireland: progressive performer: won nurseries at Brighton and
Sandown in September and Newmarket in October, quickening as soon as gap
appeared to beat Shawdon comfortably by ½ length on last-named course: speedy:
genuine: should make fairly useful handicapper. *Mrs P. N. Dutfield*

BLITZ 2 b.f. (Mar 29) Casteddu 111 – Lake Mistassiu 86 (Tina's Pet 121) [1997 –
5m⁶ 5m 5g 5m 5d⁵ 7g a5g Sep 8] 1,200Y: first reported living foal: dam 5f performer:
looks of little account. *M. W. Easterby*

BLOCKADE (USA)   8 b.g. Imperial Falcon (CAN) – Stolen Date (USA) (Sadair)   63
[1996 64: 7g 8m³ 8m³ 8g* 8m 7f* 1997 8g 7g 10.1f* 10.8f 10m* 10.1m⁴ 10.1s⁵
11.5g⁶ Jul 16] close-coupled gelding: tubed: modest performer: won apprentice
events at Yarmouth (handicap) in May and Nottingham (minor event) in June: stays
1¼m, probably not 11.5f: acts on firm and dead going: sometimes sweats: none too
consistent. *M. Bell*

BLOOD ORANGE   3 ch.c. Ron's Victory (USA) 129 – Little Bittern (USA) 73   –
(Riva Ridge (USA)) [1996 –: 6g 6g⁵ 1997 6m⁶ 7m a8g a8.5g⁶ Dec 26] good-topped
colt: signs of a little ability but no worthwhile form. *G. G. Margarson*

BLOOMING AMAZING   3 b.g. Mazilier (USA) 107 – Cornflower Blue   80
(Tyrnavos 129) [1996 71: 7g² 7m⁶ 7.9g 6g 1997 8.5m* 8g³ 8m⁴ 8g⁵ 7g 7.1g⁵ a7g   a60
10g⁶ 8.2d² a8g⁶ Dec 8] tall, plain gelding: fairly useful handicapper on turf, modest
on all-weather: made all at Beverley in April: ran well when placed afterwards: stays
8.5f, possibly not 1¼m: acts on good to firm, dead ground and fibresand: has been
bandaged behind: often front runner. *J. L. Eyre*

BLOT   3 b.c. Warning 136 – Rattle Along 80 (Tap On Wood 130) [1996 NR 1997   88
8g³ 8m 8.1m³ 8g* Aug 1] 19,000Y: leggy, sparely-made colt: fifth foal: half-brother
to several winners in Italy, including smart 6f to 1m performer Night Manoeuvres (by
Night Shift), successful in Britain at 2/3 yrs: dam 1¼m winner: fairly useful form:
justified favouritism in maiden at Thirsk in August: raced only at 1m: bandaged
behind: ran as though something amiss second start. *Mrs J. Cecil*

BLOWING AWAY (IRE)   3 b. or br.f. Last Tycoon 131 – Taken By Force   70 d
(Persian Bold 123) [1996 –: 7g 1997 8f³ 9s³ 8g⁵ 10m⁶ 8.3m 7f 10m 8d* 8.2d Nov 3]
leggy filly: fair performer: well below form after third start, including when winning
claimer at Leicester in October: stays 1m (pulled hard at 1¼m): best efforts on good
going or firmer: ran poorly in visor. *M. H. Tompkins*

BLUE ANCHOR   2 b.c. (Feb 23) Robellino (USA) 127 – Fair Seas 72 (General   –
Assembly (USA)) [1997 6g 6d 5d⁴ 6g 7.1g⁶ Aug 28] small colt: second foal: dam
lightly-raced maiden, best at 1¼m: no worthwhile form. *Mrs M. Reveley*

BLUE AND ROYAL (IRE)   5 b.g. Bluebird (USA) 125 – Cat Girl (USA) (Grey   –
Dawn II 132) [1996 –: a12g² 17.9g 1997 a12g⁵ a16g⁴ a16g 12g⁶ a12g 11.6g 12f Jun
10] rangy gelding: poor maiden: no form in 1997. *V. Soane*

BLUEBELL MISS   3 b.f. High Kicker (USA) – Mio Mementa 61 (Streak 119)   61
[1996 72d: 6d 6d* 6d 6g 7m 1997 8m 8.3g³ 10.8d² 9.7g² 10.1g* a12g³ Jul 26] leggy,
unfurnished filly: modest performer: won seller at Yarmouth in July: claimed to join
A. Streeter final start: stays 1½m: acts on dead ground and fibresand. *M. J. Ryan*

BLUEBERRY   2 b.f. (Feb 12) Batshoof 122 – Always A Lady 66 (Dominion 123)   63
[1997 6d 6m 7m⁴ 7m Aug 2] sturdy filly: fourth reported foal: dam soft-ground
sprinter: 3 lengths fourth of 11 in maiden at Brighton in July: no other form. *S. Dow*

BLUE CALVINE   3 b.g. Silver Kite (USA) 111 – Calvanne Miss 48 (Martinmas   –
128) [1996 NR 1997 8d 8.1g a5g 8f Sep 29] 2,800F: strong, lengthy gelding: second
foal: dam sprinter: no sign of ability. *C. J. Hill*

BLUE CHEESE   3 gr.f. Mystiko (USA) 124 – Legal Sound 85 (Legal Eagle 126)   –
[1996 NR 1997 6.1d a7g a7g a5g⁶ 7f Oct 3] 5,400Y, 2,000 2-y-o: good-topped filly:
seventh foal: half-sister to 2 winners up to 7f: dam 6f winner: no worthwhile form:
left Mrs. N. Macauley after fourth outing. *J. R. Jenkins*

BLUE DAWN (IRE)   2 ch.f. (Jan 29) Bluebird (USA) 125 – Spring Carnival   65
(USA) (Riverman (USA) 131) [1997 7g⁵ 7m 7d⁴ Oct 13] IR 10,500Y: leggy filly:
fourth foal: half-sister to a useful German 1m winner and a French 1m to 10.5f
winner (both by Cricket Ball): dam unraced: fair form in maidens at Doncaster,
Kempton and Leicester: bred to stay 1m. *E. A. L. Dunlop*

BLUE DESERT   2 ch.g. (Apr 14) Elmaamul (USA) 125 – Shehana (USA) 86   66
(The Minstrel (CAN) 135) [1997 5d⁵ 5m⁵ 6m 8.2d² 8d 8m⁵ a7g⁶ a8g³ Dec 8] 6,000Y: a57
smallish, good-bodied gelding: half-brother to several winners, including useful
1995 2-y-o 6f winner React (by Reprimand) and 1½m winner Legion of Honour (by
Ahonoora): dam 2-y-o 9f winner, apparently stayed 1½m: fair form on turf: won
seller at Nottingham in October by 8 lengths on final start for M. Bell: modest form

on fibresand, third in similar event at Southwell: stays 1m: joined S. R. Bowring. *G. Lewis*

BLUE DOMAIN   6 b.g. Dominion 123 – Blue Rag 70 (Ragusa 137) [1996 –: a6g   38
1997 a11g 9.9m Apr 5] strong gelding: poor performer, lightly raced on flat
nowadays: stays 1¼m: acts on good to firm ground and fibresand. *R. Craggs*

BLUE DUSTER (USA)   4 b.f. Danzig (USA) – Blue Note (FR) 122 (Habitat   105
134) [1996 118: 7f* 6.5d⁵ 6f² 1997 6g³ 6g Jun 19] compact filly: good walker: smart
at 2 (won Cheveley Park Stakes) and 3 (won July Cup): effective at 5f to 7f:
Royal Applause in Duke of York Stakes and Cork And Orrery Stakes at Royal Ascot
in 1997: successful at 7f, best form at 6f: acted on firm and dead ground: stud. *Saeed
bin Suroor*

BLUE FLYER (IRE)   4 b.g. Bluebird (USA) 125 – Born To Fly (IRE) 57 (Last   73 §
Tycoon 131) [1996 78, a84: a10g⁶ a8g² a8g* a8g* a8g² 6m⁵ 7m 7f* 8m 7.1m⁵ 7.6m³   a85 §
8d a7g a8g⁴ a7g 1997 a7g* a8g⁶ a6g a8g 8.5d 7m³ 7.1m 7m⁵ 7m 7g² 8f 8m Sep 28]
workmanlike gelding: has a quick action: fairly useful handicapper on all-weather,
fair on turf: best effort to win Ladbroke All-Weather Trophy (Final) at Lingfield in
January: suited by 7f/1m: best efforts on equitrack/firm ground, has shown nothing
on soft: effective blinkered or not: usually races prominently: unreliable. *R. Ingram*

BLUE GENTIAN (USA)   2 b.f. (Feb 25) Known Fact (USA) 135 – Caithness   96 p
(USA) (Roberto (USA) 131) [1997 7g* 7d³ Sep 19] tall, attractive filly: has scope:
second living foal: half-sister to French 6f (at 2 yrs in 1996 in Britain) and 1½m
winner Sinecure (by Explodent): dam, French 11f winner, half-sister to very smart
performer around 7f Condrillac: pulled hard when winning 15-runner maiden at
Salisbury by 2 lengths from Red Rabbit: failed to show expected
progress when 4 lengths third of 5 to Amabel in minor event at Newbury 15 days
later: should stay at least 1m: almost certainly remains capable of better. *R. Charlton*

BLUE GOBLIN (USA)   3 gr.c. Trempolino (USA) 135 – Blue Daisy (USA) 108   112
(Shahrastani (USA) 135) [1996 88: 6g² 7d³ 7.1f² 7d⁴ 7g⁵ 1997 7m⁴ 7g³ 6m³ 6m*
6m* 6g² 6g 6m Aug 22] strong, close-coupled colt: smart performer: won maiden at

Sheikh Mohammed's "Blue Goblin"

127

Lingfield and £22,500 Coral Sprint (Handicap) at Newmarket in May: best effort when 1½ lengths second of 23 to Royal Applause in Cork And Orrery Stakes at Royal Ascot: disappointing in July Cup and listed race (sweating) at Newmarket afterwards: seems suited by 6f: acts on firm and dead ground: often on toes: blinkered (best efforts at the time) second and third starts: sent to Dubai. *L. M. Cumani*

BLUE HAVANA 5 br.m. Cigar 68 – Welsh Bluebell (Manado 130) [1996 NR – 1997 a8.5f 5d 8g Sep 3] first foal: dam poor novice hurdler: no sign of ability. *Graeme Roe*

BLUE HOPPER 3 b.f. Rock Hopper 124 – Kimble Blue 56 (Blue Refrain 121) – [1996 58: 7m³ 7g² 7g 1997 8m 11.6s 10f 10g⁴ a9.4g Dec 13] workmanlike filly: modest maiden as 2-y-o: no form in 1997, including in visor: left M. Channon after fourth start. *M. Quinn*

BLUE IMPERIAL (FR) 3 gr.c. Bluebird (USA) 125 – Real Gold 113 (Yankee 76 Gold 115) [1996 –: 7d 7f 1997 6.9m 8m* 8f* 8m² 8f* 9m 8m Aug 21] strong colt: fair handicapper: made all at Salisbury and Bath in May, and always up with leaders when winning back at Bath in July: had hard race for final success, and well beaten last 2 starts: should stay further than 1m: has raced mainly on ground firmer than good: sent to Hong Kong. *J. W. Hills*

BLUE IRIS 4 b.f. Petong 126 – Bo' Babbity 75 (Strong Gale 116) [1996 105: 5m 102 5m³ 5m⁴ 6g 5m* 5m⁴ 5m² 5d⁵ 1997 5.7d³ 5g⁵ 5.1m 5m 5m* 5m Oct 2] strong, lengthy filly: unimpressive mover: useful performer: rather disappointing after reappearance until tried in tongue strap and patiently ridden in minor event at Leicester in September, beating Crofters Ceilidh by ¾ length: well held only subsequent outing: stays 6f: acts on firm and dead ground: bandaged behind fourth start: sold 36,000 gns in December. *M. A. Jarvis*

BLUE ISLAND (IRE) 3 br.g. Contract Law (USA) 108 – Bluebutton 65 (Blue – Cashmere 129) [1996 NR 1997 8.5m 8d 10m a12g Oct 20] 11,500Y: leggy, sparely-made gelding: seventh foal: half-brother to 5 winners, notably useful sprinter Call Me I'm Blue (by Reasonable): dam second over 5f at 2 yrs: no sign of ability: trained by I. Campbell first 2 starts. *N. P. Littmoden*

BLUE JAY (IRE) 3 b. or br.g. Bluebird (USA) 125 – Alpine Spring 95 (Head For – Heights 125) [1996 NR 1997 8g 7g Aug 11] third foal: half-brother to fair 1m to 1¼m winner Pennine Pink (by Pennine Walk): dam, Irish 2-y-o 7f winner, seemed best up to 1¼m: no sign of ability. *R. Hannon*

BLUE JUMBO (IRE) 4 b.f. Bluebird (USA) 125 – Finalist 78 (Star Appeal 133) 43 [1996 –: 7d 6m 8m 1997 a8g a13g⁶ 10g⁴ 12d* Nov 1] tall, lengthy filly: little form in Britain for W. Musson: won handicap at Clonmel in November on first start for new stable: stays 1½m. *M. J. P. O'Brien, Ireland*

BLUE KITE 2 ch.c. (Apr 7) Silver Kite (USA) 111 – Gold And Blue (IRE) 80 (Bluebird (USA) 125) [1997 a5g² a5g² a6g² 6g⁶ 6m² 5d⁶ a5g* 6d 6.1d⁵ Oct 30] 9,000 2-y-o: small, stocky colt: unimpressive mover: first foal: dam lightly-raced Irish maiden: fairly useful performer: runner-up in varied events, including nursery, prior to winning maiden at Wolverhampton in September: stiffish tasks last 2 starts: should stay beyond 6f: acts on fibresand and good to firm ground. *N. P. Littmoden*

BLUE LAMP (USA) 3 ch.f. Shadeed (USA) 135 – Matter of Time (Habitat 134) 56 [1996 68: 6g 1997 8d⁵ 7d 5m² 5g 5v 6f⁵ 5g⁴ 5m⁴ 5.1g a6g² a5g⁵ a7g⁶ Dec 22] unfurnished filly: modest maiden: trained by M. Jarvis before final start: stays 6f: acts on equitrack, best turf form on good ground or firmer: no improvement in blinkers. *R. Ingram*

BLUE LUGANA 5 b.g. Lugana Beach 116 – Two Friendly 54 (Be Friendly 130) 41 [1996 –: a6g a6g⁴ a6g 5g 7d 6m⁶ 5f⁶ 6g 5d⁵ 5m 5g 6s 1997 a8g⁵ a6g² a6g² a6g³ a6g² a6g a6g 6g⁶ a6g Apr 26] big gelding: poor maiden handicapper: stays 6f: acts on all-weather and firm ground: tried blinkered, at least as effective when not. *N. Bycroft*

BLUE MONK (IRE) 2 ch.c. (Apr 5) Bluebird (USA) 125 – High Habit 79 (Slip 69 Anchor 136) [1997 7m 7.1g 8m Oct 1] big, strong colt: third foal: half-brother to a 1¼m to 13f winner in Norway by Robellino: dam, second over 11.5f, half-sister to smart sprinter Blue Siren: sweating, easily best effort in maidens when seventh of 12

at Chepstow on second start: should stay at least 1m: sold 13,000 gns after final start.
I. A. Balding

BLUEPRINT (IRE) 2 b.c. (Apr 3) Generous (IRE) 139 – Highbrow 112§ (Shirley 80 p
Heights 130) [1997 7m 8d⁵ Sep 19] big, rangy colt: has scope: shows knee action:
fifth foal: half-brother to 3-y-o Ghillies Ball and fairly useful 1¼m/1½m winner
Beyond Doubt (by Belmez): dam, 2-y-o 1m winner later second in Ribblesdale
Stakes, from family of Height of Fashion: too green and backward to do himself
justice in maiden and minor event (10 lengths last of 5 to Duck Row) at Newbury:
will be well suited by 1½m+: useful prospect in long term. *Lord Huntingdon*

BLUE RIDGE 3 ch.c. Indian Ridge 123 – Souadah (USA) (General Holme 80
(USA) 128) [1996 95: 6m 5f* 6m⁶ 6g⁵ 5d 1997 7m⁵ 6f 5d⁵ 5.6m Sep 10] leggy colt:
fluent mover: fairly useful performer: trained at 2 yrs by R. Hannon, reappearance in
Ireland by D. Weld: stays 6f: acts on firm ground, possibly unsuited by dead: sent to
USA. *V. Soane*

BLUERIDGE DANCER (IRE) 2 gr.c. (Apr 30) Bluebird (USA) 125 – 94
Maraquiba (FR) (Kenmare (FR) 125) [1997 5m* 5m* 5m⁵ 6m 6g⁴ 5v 6g Oct 18] IR
7,500F, 18,000Y: tall, unfurnished colt: half-brother to ungenuine 1m to 1½m winner
Harken Premier (by Hard Fought) and a winner in Germany up to 12.5f by Don't
Forget Me: dam won over 7.5f at 2 yrs in France: won minor events at Doncaster
and Ascot in spring: had run of things when just over 5 lengths fourth of 8 to Bold
Fact in July Stakes at Newmarket, and largely disappointing subsequently: stays 6f:
blinkered last 3 outings: edgy sort, has gone steadily to post: sold 25,000 gns after
final start. *B. J. Meehan*

BLUE RIVER (IRE) 3 ch.c. River Falls 113 – Royal Resident 86 (Prince Regent 100
(FR) 114) [1996 88+: 7.1g⁵ 7.1m⁴ 7m* 8d* 8g⁵ 8d⁵ 1997 10m⁵ 10.4g³ 11.8d² 12s⁵
12m Jul 29] strong, rangy colt: fluent mover: useful performer: best efforts when
placed in handicap at York and minor event (beaten 2 lengths by Ghataas) at
Leicester: finished last final 2 outings: stays 1½m, at least in steadily-run race: acts
on good to firm and dead ground. *T. G. Mills*

BLUE SHADOW 2 gr.c. (Jan 29) Pips Pride 117 – Lingdale Lass 60 (Petong 126) 59
[1997 6s 5.2m⁶ 5.1m 6m⁵ 6m 5m a5g³ a5s⁴ a6g⁵ a6g* Dec 22] 14,000Y: strong, a65
good-bodied colt: first foal: dam 2-y-o 6f winner: modest performer: best effort to
win nursery at Lingfield in December, making all: stays 6f: blinkered last 3 starts on
turf. *R. Hannon*

BLUES MAGIC (IRE) 3 ch.g. Imp Society (USA) – Fairy Folk (IRE) 81 (Fairy 62
King (USA)) [1996 NR 1997 a6g² a6g⁴ a5g² a5g³ a5g² Mar 4] IR 16,500Y: second
foal: half-brother to Irish 5f winner Cuddles (by Taufan): dam lightly-raced Irish 6f
winner: modest maiden: best form at 5f: raced only on equitrack: no improvement in
visor. *M. Bell*

BLUES QUEEN 3 b.f. Lahib (USA) 129 – Queens Welcome 60 (Northfields 80 d
(USA)) [1996 85+: 5.2f³ 5.1m⁴ 5.1m² 6.5m⁵ 6m* 7m 6m 7.3s 1997 7.3g 6g⁶ 6g⁵
6.1s⁶ 6g⁵ 6m⁶ 6m 7g⁵ 5.7g 6m a5g Sep 8] fairly useful performer on her day: long
way below form last 3 starts: should stay 7f: acts on good to firm ground, seems
unsuited by soft: tried visored: sometimes slowly away: not one to trust implicitly.
M. R. Channon

BLUEWAIN LADY 2 b.f. (Feb 3) Unfuwain (USA) 131 – Blue Guitar 88 (Cure 76
The Blues (USA)) [1997 7.1m³ 8m⁴ 7m⁶ Sep 22] IR 20,000Y: tall filly: half-sister to
several winners, including 1994 2-y-o 6f winner Wicken Wonder (by Distant
Relative) and middle-distance stayer Dime Bag (by High Line): dam suited by 1m:
fair form in maidens at Sandown, Leicester and Kempton: should stay at least 1¼m:
hung final start. *P. W. Harris*

BLUEYGREEN 3 b.f. Green Desert (USA) 127 – Bluebook (USA) 120 (Secret- 79
ariat (USA)) [1996 67: 6m 7g 1997 7d² 8f² 7g* 7m 7m⁶ Sep 25] quite attractive filly:
good mover: fair performer: favourite, won maiden at Yarmouth in July: stiff tasks
afterwards: effective at 7f/1m: acts on firm and dead ground: races freely and
prominently: sent to USA. *P. W. Chapple-Hyam*

BLUE ZOLA (IRE) 2 b.f. (Feb 2) Alzao (USA) 117 – Lady of Shalott 61 (Kings 73 d
Lake (USA) 133) [1997 6m 7g² a7g⁴ 7d⁵ 7.5f³ 7d 8m² a8g Nov 14] 12,500Y: small

filly: poor mover: sixth foal: half-sister to 3 winners, including 3-y-o Meliksah, and 1m seller winner Irrepressible (by Don't Forget Me): dam maiden who stayed 1m, half-sister to Head For Heights: fair maiden: second at Brighton (best effort) and Newmarket (seller): stays 1m: acts on firm ground, good to soft and fibresand. *M. Bell*

BLUNDELL LANE (IRE) 2 ch.c. (Apr 7) Shalford (IRE) 124§ – Rathbawn 77 Realm (Doulab (USA) 115) [1997 6m² 6f⁵ 6g 6m* 6.1d⁵ Nov 3] 20,000 2-y-o: third foal: half-brother to a winner in Holland by Simply Great: dam Irish 5f (at 2 yrs) and 7f winner: fair performer: won 16-runner nursery at Redcar in October: not discredited in similar event final start: will stay 7f: acts on good to firm ground. *A. P. Jarvis*

BLURRED (IRE) 4 ch.g. Al Hareb (USA) 123 – I'll Take Paris (USA) 103 – (Vaguely Noble 140) [1996 85p: 10g³ 9.9m³ 8d⁶ 12.3m⁶ 10.3m² 10m 10f³ 10.3g* 11f⁴ 1997 10m 10m 12d Oct 16] big, heavy-topped gelding: made into a fairly useful handicapper around 1¼m at 3 yrs: well beaten in 1997 (looked in need of race all starts), not striding out to post on final outing§. *M. H. Tompkins*

BLUSH 3 b.f. Gildoran 123 – Rather Warm 103 (Tribal Chief 125) [1996 50p: 10f³ 57 1997 11.6m* 10s⁶ 11.9f⁴ 10.2d 10m 8d Oct 28] modest performer: won claimer at Windsor in June: had inadequate test of stamina most starts afterwards: likely to stay long distances: acts on good to firm going: blinkered/visored last 2 starts. *M. C. Pipe*

BLUSHING DESERT 3 b.f. Green Desert (USA) 127 – Blushing Storm (USA) 62 102 (Blushing Groom (FR) 131) [1996 –p: 6d⁵ 1997 7s 7m³ 8.2g a7g² Nov 6] modest maiden: stays 7f, possibly not 1m: acts on good to firm ground and equitrack: sold 16,000 gns in December. *R. Hannon*

BLUSHING GRENADIER (IRE) 5 ch.g. Salt Dome (USA) – La Duse 66 – (Junius (USA) 124) [1996 55: 8d 6f 6m⁶ 6g* 7m 7m 7g 7.1f 6d a7s² 1997 a6g³ a7g a55 a8g² 7m 6d 6.9s 8.1m 8.3g Aug 4] leggy gelding: modest handicapper: trained on reappearance only by P. Cundell: effective at 6f to 1m: form in 1997 only on all-weather: often blinkered/visored: inconsistent. *M. J. Fetherston-Godley*

BLUSHING VICTORIA 2 b.f. (Jan 17) Weldnaas (USA) 112 – Bollin Victoria 74 d 51 (Jalmood (USA) 126) [1997 5.1m* 5.1d⁵ 6m⁶ 6m⁴ a6g 6g Aug 20] 4,000 2-y-o: leggy filly: second foal: dam, ran only at 2 yrs, third over 7f: won maiden at Nottingham in April: lost her form after: should stay beyond 5f. *Martyn Meade*

BOATER 3 b.g. Batshoof 122 – Velvet Beret (IRE) (Dominion 123) [1996 74: 7f 74 6.1s a7s³ 1997 8f* 7.5m⁴ 8s² 8f³ 8m⁵ Jun 19] well-made gelding: fair handicapper: won at Brighton in April: creditable efforts all subsequent starts: stays 1m: acts on firm and soft ground and on equitrack: has high head carriage, but seems genuine enough: races up with pace: joined R. Frost. *D. Morley*

BOAT O'BRIG 4 b.g. Slip Anchor 136 – Advie Bridge 90§ (High Line 125) – [1996 NR 1997 14.1s Oct 15] second foal: dam, stayed 1½m, not one to trust: 33/1, very slowly away and well held in Nottingham maiden. *J. G. Smyth-Osbourne*

BOBBITT 3 b.f. Reprimand 122 – Pleasuring 68 (Good Times (ITY)) [1996 –: 48 7.1m 7f 7d 1997 8g⁶ 10.1f 8.5s³ 8.2m⁶ a11g⁶ 10.1f⁴ 11.8d Oct 14] poor maiden: stays 1¼m, seemingly not 1½m: acts on firm and soft going: blinkered last 2 starts: sold and sent to Saudi Arabia. *W. Jarvis*

BOBBYDAZZLE 2 ch.f. (Apr 16) Rock Hopper 124 – Billie Blue 63 (Ballad 76 Rock 122) [1997 6g 7g² 7g⁶ 7m⁴ 8g* 8f Sep 11] angular, workmanlike filly: fourth foal: half-sister to 3 winners, including 3-y-o Tumbleweed Pearl and 4-y-o Tumbleweed Ridge: dam second over 7f on only start: fair form: won valuable nursery at Newcastle in August gamely by neck from After The Rain: not at all discredited in similar event at Doncaster following month, racing on unfavoured side: should stay beyond 1m: yet to race on ground softer than good. *Dr J. D. Scargill*

BOBBY'S DREAM 5 b.m. Reference Point 139 – Kiralyi (FR) (Kings Lake 25 (USA) 133) [1996 42: a12g a16g 14.1s 15.8g³ 16m 16m 12m 18g⁵ 14.1g² 16.4v⁶ 1997 13.8m 16d 16g 14m² 12g⁴ 11.8d Oct 14] small, sturdy mare: poor maiden handicapper: stays 2¼m: acts on good to firm ground, seems unsuited by heavy: tried visored. *M. H. Tompkins*

BOB KNOWS 3 br.g. Robellino (USA) 127 – Snowline (Bay Express 132) [1996 —
NR 1997 7.9s 8d 10s⁵ 12d Oct 21] third reported foal: dam unraced: no form.
R. F. Johnson Houghton

BOB'S SAINTLY AIM 3 b.f. Mazilier (USA) 107 – Great Aim (Great Nephew —
126) [1996 NR 1997 10.1f Sep 17] 1,000Y: fourth foal: half-sister to a winner in Italy
by Formidable and in Belgium by Statoblest: dam (maiden) seemed to stay 1m: last
of 15 in Yarmouth seller. *B. J. McMath*

BOCCOLINO 2 b.g. (Jan 21) Robellino (USA) 127 – Brockton Dancer 85 (Fairy —
King (USA)) [1997 5.1m⁵ 5s a7g Jul 21] 5,200Y: first foal: dam winner around 6f,
including at 2 yrs: no worthwhile form, including in sellers. *T. D. Barron*

BODANTREE 6 b.g. Rambo Dancer (CAN) 107 – Snow Tree 86 (Welsh Pageant 43
132) [1996 NR 1997 12.1g³ Aug 3] fair hurdler, winner in June: poor maiden on flat:
stayed 1½m: tried blinkered/visored: dead. *N. M. Babbage*

BODFARIDISTINCTION (IRE) 2 b.f. (May 7) Distinctly North (USA) 115 – 69 +
Brave Louise 76 (Brave Shot) [1997 5g⁴ 5.1v* 5.2d⁵ 5m 6.1m⁶ 6.1d⁶ Aug 29]
9,000Y: leggy filly: half-sister to Italian 1¼m and 11f winner Schubert (by Masterclass) and 9f to 1½m winner Torghia (by Taufan): dam 6f to 1½m winner: won
maiden under extreme conditions at Chester in May: fair at best judged on other
form: should stay 6f: blinkered final start. *A. Bailey*

BODFARI PRIDE (IRE) 2 b.g. (Mar 23) Pips Pride 117 – Renata's Ring (IRE) 71 +
(Auction Ring (USA) 123) [1997 6g³ 7m Aug 3] 12,500Y: strong, lengthy gelding:
half-brother to fairly useful 1996 2-y-o 5f winner Joint Venture (by Common
Grounds), also successful abroad at 3 yrs: dam placed at 7f in Ireland: burly and
green, 7 lengths third of 14 in maiden at Haydock: gave impression amiss following
month (moved poorly to post both starts). *A. Bailey*

BODFARI WREN 3 b.f. Handsome Sailor 125 – My Valentine Card (USA) 57§ —
(Forli (ARG)) [1996 NR 1997 8g⁴ 8d⁶ Aug 25] half-sister to a poor 7f winner by
Dreams To Reality: dam, maiden (stayed 1¼m), became temperamental: little
worthwhile form in maidens. *A. Bailey*

BODYGUARD 2 ch.c. (Jan 19) Zafonic (USA) 130 – White Wisteria (Ahonoora 101
122) [1997 5m⁵ 6g* 5g⁴ 5d* 6m³ Jul 31] 54,000F, 165,000Y: compact colt: third
foal: half-brother to fairly useful Italian 1m winner White Gulch (by Gulch): dam

Grosvenor Casino Sheffield Conditions Stakes, York—
Bodyguard wins the first six-furlong race of the season for two-year-olds

unraced: useful performer: won maiden at Newmarket and minor event at York in May and 3-runner listed race at Sandown (held Daunting Lady by a neck in slowly-run affair) in July: in frame in Norfolk Stakes at Royal Ascot and Richmond Stakes at Goodwood: may prove best at 5f: yet to race on extremes of going. *P. F. I. Cole*

BOFFY (IRE) 4 ch.c. Mac's Imp (USA) 116 – No Dowry (Shy Groom (USA)) –
[1996 –, a75d: a6g^4 a5g* a6g^2 a5g* a5g^2 a5g^5 6.1d 5d 6d 6.1m a6g a6g^6 5m^5 5m a6g   a55 d
6m a6g a6g a6s a5g^2 1997 a5g^3 a5g a5f^4 a5g^6 a5g^4 a5g^5 a5g^4 a5g a5g^4 6g 5s a5g Jun
6] modest at best on all-weather nowadays (lightly raced and little form on turf): best
at 5f: tried blinkered and visored. *B. P. J. Baugh*

BOGAN (IRE) 3 b.c. Caerleon (USA) 132 – Belize Tropical (IRE) (Baillamont   70
(USA) 124) [1996 NR 1997 a10g^4 10d 10g 8g^4 a7g* a7g* Oct 6] 15,000Y: second
foal: half-brother to Irish 1995 2-y-o 6f winner Orange Walk (by Alzao): dam, French
2-y-o 7.3f winner, half-sister to Scenic: fair performer: dropped in distance and
visored last 2 starts, winning handicaps at Lingfield in August and Wolverhampton
in October: best efforts at 7f on all-weather: sold 9,000 gns after final start. *Lord
Huntingdon*

BOGART 6 gr.g. Belfort (FR) 89 – Larnem 43 (Meldrum 112) [1996 –: a8g a8g 7g   51 ?
a7s 1997 a7g^3 a9.4g a7g^3 a7g^6 a7g 9.9m Apr 5] tall, angular gelding: modest performer: stays 7f: acts on all-weather and on firm ground, possibly not on soft: tried
visored, no improvement. *C. W. Fairhurst*

BO'JUST 5 b.m. Bold Fort 100 – Just Blair (Prince Tenderfoot (USA) 126) [1996   –
NR 1997 a7g Dec 22] second foal: dam of no account: last of 15 in Lingfield maiden.
P. Hayward

BOLD APPEAL (IRE) 5 b.g. Caerleon (USA) 132 – La Bella Fontana (Lafon-   –
taine (USA) 117) [1996 NR 1997 8s^6 8g^6 10.1g Jul 26] workmanlike gelding: lightly
raced and little sign of ability. *W. Storey*

BOLD ARISTOCRAT (IRE) 6 b.g. Bold Arrangement 127 – Wyn Mipet   –
(Welsh Saint 126) [1996 –, a63: a6g a6g a6g* a6g^6 a6g^5 a6g^3 a6g* a6g a6g^5 5.9d a6g   a67
a5g^4 a6g^2 a6g a6g^3 a6g^3 a6g^2 a6s a6g^3 1997 a6g^5 a7g^3 a7g^2 a7g^5 a6g a6g* a6g^6 a6g^2
a6g^4 a6g^5 a6g^3 a7g^2 a7g a6g* a7g^3 a7g^6 a7g^4 a5g^4 a7g a6g^3 a7g^5 a6g^3 a6g^4 a8g^5 Dec
18] fair on the all-weather (poor and seldom raced nowadays on turf): won selling
handicap in February and minor event in June, both at Southwell: suited by 6f/7f: has
worn pricker near side: usually held up: tends to carry head high. *R. Hollinshead*

BOLD BECKY 3 b.f. Never So Bold 135 – Princess Silca Key 61 (Grundy 137)   69
[1996 NR 1997 8f^3 May 30] fifth foal: half-sister to 5-y-o Azizzi and fairly useful
sprinter Silca-Cisa (by Hallgate): dam lightly-raced 7f winner: 40/1, third of 10 in
maiden at Bath. *A. P. Jones*

BOLD BRIEF 3 b.g. Tina's Pet 121 – Immodest Miss 73 (Daring Display (USA)   54
129) [1996 65: 5m 5d^6 5m^5 5m* 6g^6 5g^5 6g 1997 7m 7g 6m 6m^5 5m 5.9m^2 5g^2 5.9m^4
Aug 4] leggy gelding: has a round action: modest handicapper: stays 6f: acts on good
to firm ground: effective blinkered or not. *Denys Smith*

BOLD BUSTER 4 b.g. Bustino 136 – Truly Bold 76 (Bold Lad (IRE) 133) [1996   77
–p: 10s 1997 14m^4 10g 11.5d* 10.9d^4 16.2v^3 14.1d^2 Nov 3] good-topped gelding:
fair handicapper: won at Lingfield in August: best efforts last 2 starts: stays 2m well:
acts on heavy going. *I. A. Balding*

BOLD CHARLIE 5 ch.g. Weldnaas (USA) 112 – Flirty Lady (Never So Bold   –
135) [1996 NR 1997 a11g Jan 3] little sign of ability: tried visored. *S. Mellor*

BOLD DEMAND 3 b.c. Rainbow Quest (USA) 134 – Dafrah (USA) 78 (Danzig   101
(USA)) [1996 72p: 8d^4 1997 12m^2 10m* 12g 11.9g^6 Jul 5] rangy, good sort: useful
performer: won maiden at Sandown in May: beaten 25 lengths when ninth in the
Derby at Epsom: best effort when 5 lengths last of 6 to Ivan Luis in falsely-run listed
event at Haydock final start: should stay beyond 1½m: yet to race on extremes of
going: flashed tail under pressure on reappearance. *Saeed bin Suroor*

BOLD EDGE 2 ch.c. (Apr 1) Beveled (USA) – Daring Ditty (Daring March 116)   94
[1997 6s* 6m 6f^3 6m^5 6d^5 6m^3 5v Oct 11] rangy colt: has plenty of scope: has a round
action: fifth foal: brother to 6-y-o Brave Edge and half-brother to 1¼m/1½m winner

Sparky's Song (by Electric): dam twice-raced daughter of useful sprinter Dawn Ditty: fairly useful performer: won maiden at Newbury in May: highly tried in the main afterwards, third in listed event on same course, then not discredited when fifth in Richmond Stakes at Goodwood and Mill Reef Stakes (under 4 lengths fifth to Arkadian Hero) at Newbury: stays 6f: acts on firm and soft ground: edgy last 3 starts. *R. Hannon*

BOLD EFFORT (FR) 5 b.g. Bold Arrangement 127 – Malham Tarn (Riverman 101 (USA) 131) [1996 92+: 7m 6f 6f 7.1d^6 6f 6m 8d* 5g^3 5.6m 6s* 5g 6d a6g* 1997 a7g^2 a6g^6 a5g^2 6m^6 5.2g 7m 6d a6g* 6g 6s^2 8g 5g^5 5g^{4dis} 5.6m^4 6g 5d 6g a7g 6s Nov 17] good-quartered, dipped-backed gelding: poor mover: useful handicapper on his day: won at Wolverhampton in May: good fourth in the Portland at Doncaster fourteenth start: effective at 5f to 1m: acts on firm and soft ground and the all-weather: usually blinkered/visored: none too consistent. *K. O. Cunningham-Brown*

BOLD ELECT 9 b.g. Electric 126 – Famous Band (USA) (Banderilla (USA)) 56 [1996 54: a14.8g 16.2m 17.1g 13s 12m^3 12.3m^2 14.1f* 15.1g* 1997 15.9m 16m^2 20m^6 Jul 30] sturdy gelding: modest handicapper: effective at 1½m to 2½m: acted on any going: usually held up: dead. *E. J. Alston*

BOLD ENGAGEMENT 3 b.f. Never So Bold 135 – Diamond House (Habitat – 134) [1996 –: 7m 1997 6m 7f May 1] well beaten in claimer/sellers. *M. Dods*

BOLD ET NOIR 3 b.g. Never So Bold 135 – Mill d'Art (Artaius (USA) 129) 40 [1996 NR 1997 a8g 10s 8.3s 8.3g 9.7g^6 14.1m a10g Aug 9] fourth reported foal: half-brother to a modest winning hurdler by Faustus: dam lightly raced: poor maiden handicapper: stays 9.7f. *W. Jarvis*

BOLD FACT (USA) 2 b.c. (May 13) Known Fact (USA) 135 – Sookera 109 (USA) 117 (Roberto (USA) 131) [1997 6m* 6m^3 6g* 6g^2 Aug 20]

The second day of Newmarket's July meeting is one that owner Khalid Abdulla will long remember; he had runners in five of the seven races and all were successful. Three were trained by Henry Cecil and ridden by Kieren Fallon, who themselves had four winners apiece, among them the winner of the TNT International Aviation July Stakes, Bold Fact. The evens favourite in an eight-runner field, Bold Fact could well have been on a hat-trick. He had won a maiden at Goodwood on his debut, but then forfeited his chance in the Coventry Stakes at Royal Ascot by hanging markedly right after taking the lead, travelling strongly, well over a furlong out, eventually finishing two lengths third to Harbour Master. At Newmarket Bold Fact was fitted with a special bit to help keep him straight, but it made not a jot of difference. On this occasion, though, Bold Fact's superiority was such that the ground and momentum lost proved immaterial. Waited with in a steadily-run race, he moved through easily to lead approaching the final furlong and maintained his effort to beat Linden Heights by two lengths, despite again veering right and ending up under the stand rail. There were no corrective aids evident when Bold Fact made his next appearance, in the Gimcrack Stakes at York, and this time he did keep a straight line under pressure. That was the positive side of his performance. On the negative side he looked to be beaten on merit, seeming to have his limitations exposed. Once again Bold Fact quickened to the front over a furlong out, but he was unable to hold the renewed challenge of Carrowkeel who, in receipt of 3 lb, beat him by three quarters of a length. That was Bold Fact's last outing of the season. He was due to contest the Middle Park Stakes in October, but a pulled muscle forced his withdrawal on the eve of the race.

Bold Fact, a strong, attractive colt with a quick action, was some way below the top as a two-year-old, but it's possible he'll progress and in time turn out as good as his full brother So Factual. So Factual, beaten a short head in the Coventry Stakes, won the seven-furlong Free Handicap at three years and then went on to show very smart form over sprint distances, winning the Cork And Orrery Stakes and the Nunthorpe Stakes as a five-year-old. Their dam Sookera, who won the 1977 Cheveley Park Stakes on her final racecourse appearance, has produced several other winners, including Field Dancer (by Northfields),

Mr K. Abdulla's "Bold Fact"

		In Reality	Intentionally
	Known Fact (USA)	(b 1964)	My Dear Girl
	(b 1977)	Tamerett	Tim Tam
Bold Fact (USA)		(b or br 1962)	Mixed Marriage
(b.c. May 13, 1995)		Roberto	Hail To Reason
	Sookera (USA)	(b 1969)	Bramalea
	(br 1975)	Irule	Young Emperor
		(gr 1968)	Iaround

who was very useful at around a mile, and Soothfast (by Riverman), a winner on the flat in France before showing fairly useful form over hurdles. The next dam, Irule, was a minor winner at up to a mile in the States, and is a half-sister to the smart I'm A Pleasure, successful eight times at up to seven furlongs there. Bold Fact, who looked in magnificent shape on each of his last three starts, seems likely to take after his brother by proving best up to seven furlongs. Ground firmer than good suited So Factual ideally. Bold Fact has raced only on good and good to firm to date. *H. R. A. Cecil*

BOLD FAITH 4 b.f. Warning 136 – Bold And Beautiful 105 (Bold Lad (IRE) 58 133) [1996 9.5g* 8d² 8s 1997 a10g⁴ a7g 8.3s 9.7s* 8.2g⁴ 8d⁴ 8.2d* Nov 3] ex-French filly: half-sister to useful 1¼m winner Besotted (by Shirley Heights) and French 1m winner (including in listed event) Silly Bold (by Rousillon): dam, suited by 1m, out of half-sister to very smart pair Western Jewel and Mr Fluorocarbon: won minor race at Chateauroux at 3 yrs for A. Fabre, then sold 5,500 gns: modest handicapper in Britain, winning at Folkestone (well backed) in June and Nottingham in November:

stays 9.7f: acts on soft ground, yet to race on going firmer than good: held up. *W. J. Musson*

BOLD FRONTIER 5 gr.g. Chief Singer 131 – Mumtaz Flyer (USA) (Al Hattab (USA)) [1996 –: a6g 1997 a5g⁵ a6g² a6g³ a6g² a5g* Mar 8] fairly useful handicapper on all-weather (formerly modest on turf): won in good style at Wolverhampton in March: effective at 5f/6f: effective blinkered/visored or not. *K. T. Ivory* — a84

BOLD GAYLE 3 ch.f. Never So Bold 135 – Storm Gayle (IRE) (Sadler's Wells (USA) 132) [1996 49p: 5g⁵ 5m 1997 5.1m³ 6m 6g Apr 26] modest maiden: likely to prove best at 5f: twice slowly away. *Mrs J. R. Ramsden* — 57

BOLD HABIT 12 ch.g. Homing 130 – Our Mother 95 (Bold Lad (IRE) 133) [1996 44: 7f 8g 8m 6.9m a9.4g a8g 6.9g⁶ 8.2g a10g⁵ a11g⁴ 1997 a10g* a8g² a8g³ a7g³ a6g⁵ a8g 8.2m 8m⁴ a11g Jun 19] sturdy gelding: poor handicapper: deteriorated after winning at Lingfield in January: stays 1¼m: acts on all-weather, best turf form on ground no softer than dead: blinkered/visored once each, and below form: held up. *J. Pearce* — 46 d

BOLD JOKER 6 b.g. Jester 119 – Bold Difference 66 (Bold Owl 101) [1996 –: a8g⁶ 10m 14.1f 15.1m a14g 1997 a12g⁶ a8.5g Feb 21] of no account. *G. R. Oldroyd* — —

BOLD KING 2 br.c. (Apr 4) Anshan 119 – Spanish Heart 86 (King of Spain 121) [1997 6d² 6.1d² 6m² 7.3m Aug 16] well-grown colt: fourth foal: half-brother to 1995 2-y-o 7f winner Spanish Luck (by Mazilier): dam effective from 7f to 9f: fair form: runner-up in maidens at Leicester, Chepstow and Ayr: below form in nursery at Newbury final start: should stay at least 1m. *J. W. Hills* — 78

BOLD LEGACY (IRE) 2 ch.c. (May 3) Mujtahid (USA) 118 – Lagrion (USA) (Diesis 133) [1997 7g 7d a8g⁵ Nov 13] 32,000F, 16,000Y: sturdy, lengthy colt: second foal: dam, Irish maiden who stayed 1½m, sister to smart 1988 2-y-o 6f winner Pure Genius: best effort in maidens at Lingfield final start. *W. R. Muir* — 59

BOLD ORIENTAL (IRE) 3 b.g. Tirol 127 – Miss Java 78 (Persian Bold 123) [1996 79: 6s 6d² 6f³ 6m 7f⁴ 6g⁶ 5.3f² 8m 8m* 1997 9g 10m 10.2m* 9g³ 7.9g 8m 10s⁵ 10g⁶ 10g Jul 18] fairly useful handicapper: won at Bath in April: creditable efforts most starts afterwards: stays 1¼m: acts on good to firm and soft ground: ran poorly when blinkered at 2 yrs: joined C. Brooks. *N. A. Callaghan* — 90

BOLD PATRIOT (IRE) 4 b.c. Polish Patriot (USA) 128 – Don't Be Cruel (Persian Bold 123) [1996 79: 6.9m⁵ 8d* 8g⁶ 1997 8d May 18] fair at 3 yrs for J. Hills: finished badly lame only start in 1997. *Bob Jones* — —

BOLD SAINT (IRE) 3 b.c. Persian Bold 123 – St Clair Star (Sallust 134) [1996 61?: 7f⁶ 8g 1997 8g 10.3d 8f 10m⁴ 10s a9.4g⁵ 11.5m³ a12g* a16g Aug 28] good-bodied colt: poor handicapper: won at Wolverhampton (apprentice maiden) in August: stays 1½m, not 2m: acts on firm ground and all-weather, possibly unsuited by soft: blinkered last 6 starts: front runner. *P. W. Harris* — 46

BOLD SPRING (IRE) 3 b.g. Never So Bold 135 – Oasis (Valiyar 129) [1996 77: 6s 6.1g⁴ 6.1m³ 5.7m⁶ 6g² 7d 6.1s a7g² a6g³ 1997 6m⁵ 6m⁵ 6m⁶ 6g⁵ 7f³ 6.1d a6g³ Jul 11] tall, good-topped gelding: modest maiden: stays 7f: best turf form on good ground or firmer, and acts on equitrack: tried blinkered/visored. *R. Hannon* — 63

BOLD STREET (IRE) 7 ch.g. Shy Groom (USA) – Ferry Lane (Dom Racine (FR) 121) [1996 68: 6d² 5g⁴ 6d a6g⁶ a6g a6g² 7.1s a7g⁴ a7g⁴ 1997 6d 6s⁶ 6g⁵ 7.5v a6g a7g³ a8g Sep 8] workmanlike gelding: modest handicapper at best nowadays: should stay 7f: acts on all-weather and soft going: often blinkered/visored: inconsistent. *G. M. Moore* — 55

BOLD TINA (IRE) 3 b.f. Persian Bold 123 – Tinas Image (He Loves Me 120) [1996 68: 5.1m² 5f³ 5.1m³ 6m⁵ 7f 1997 6m³ 6d 6.1g 8.3m 6g⁶ 6m² 7g* 6.1m⁶ 7f* 7g Oct 24] fair performer: won minor event at Brighton in September and handicap at Lingfield in October: likely to prove best at 6f/7f: acts on firm ground (stiff task on dead). *R. Hannon* — 70

BOLD TOP 5 ch.g. Bold Owl 101 – Whirlygigger 69 (Taufan (USA) 119) [1996 43: 12d³ 12.3g 16.2m 14.1m 12f³ 12f 10m² 9.9g 10g³ 10m⁵ 12m 10.1m a11g 1997 10m 12g³ 12m⁵ 10m² 10g³ 10m³ 16.2d 12g* 10d 15.8m 10d Oct 20] close-coupled gelding: modest handicapper: gained only win in 5-runner seller at Pontefract in — 50

August, dictating pace: stays 1½m (stiff task over 2m): acts on firm ground and dead, ran poorly on fibresand: usually blinkered/visored. *B. S. Rothwell*

BOLD WORDS (CAN) 3 ch.c. Bold Ruckus (USA) – Trillium Woods (CAN) 112
(Briartic (CAN)) [1996 90p: 7g 7m 8d* 8g* 10g 1997 9m* 9m⁵ 8.1g² 8m 8.1g⁴ 8d
Aug 3] strong, lengthy colt: fluent mover: smart performer: won minor event at
Ripon in April: good efforts in frame in 2 handicaps at Sandown afterwards: up with
good pace throughout when 1¼ lengths second to Insatiable in Whitsun Cup in May
and when 1¾ lengths fourth of 18 to Hawksley Hill in Hong Kong Jockey Club
Trophy in July: likely to prove best around 1m: winner on dead ground, best efforts
on good/good to firm. *E. A. L. Dunlop*

BOLERO KID 2 b.c. (Apr 20) Rambo Dancer (CAN) 107 – Barrie Baby 86 82 +
(Import 127) [1997 5d a5g⁴ 5m⁶ a5g³ 7s* 7.5d² Aug 14] 5,000Y: lengthy, good-
quartered colt: has scope: sixth foal: brother to fairly useful 1996 2-y-o 5f winner
(best at 6f/7f) Bolero Boy: dam 7f to 9f winner: fairly useful form: won nursery at
Redcar in July: bandaged, strong-finishing second in similar event at Beverley: will
stay at least 1m: acts on soft going, probably on fibresand. *M. W. Easterby*

BOLIVAR (IRE) 5 b.g. Kahyasi 130 – Shuss (USA) (Princely Native (USA)) 78
[1996 77: 12m 14d 16m⁴ 16.2f* 16.2m* 14.8d⁵ 1997 16g 16g 16.2s* 16.2m⁶ 16.1g⁶
Aug 8] well-made gelding: carries condition: fair handicapper: goes well at Ascot,
and gained third win there gamely in June: tailed off at Newmarket final start: will
stay beyond 2m: acts on firm and soft ground: usually blinkered. *R. Akehurst*

BOLLERO (IRE) 3 b.f. Topanoora 118 – Charo (Mariacci (FR) 133) [1996 61: 54
5s² a5g³ 5g² 6g* 6m 6g⁴ 6g 6m 1997 7.5d⁶ 10g 10f⁶ 8g 8.1s* 6.9g* 6m⁶ 7.5m² a7g⁴
8g⁵ 8.1m² 8f⁶ 7m a8.5g 8d Oct 28] tall filly: modest performer: won seller at
Chepstow and claimer at Carlisle in July: well below form last 3 starts: effective at
7f/1m: acts on soft and firm ground: front runner. *J. Berry*

BOLLIN ANN 2 b.f. (Mar 16) Anshan 119 – Bollin Zola 90 (Alzao (USA) 117) 60 p
[1997 6m 8.1d 7.5f⁶ Sep 17] good-quartered filly: fifth foal: half-sister to 3-y-o
Bollin Terry and 4-y-o Bollin Joanne: dam 5f (at 2 yrs) and 7f winner: distinct
promise in maidens, catching the eye at Beverley on final start, improving smoothly
from rear halfway then not at all knocked about, rated as finishing third (connections'
explanations recorded rather than accepted): sure to make a better 3-y-o, probably up
to 1m. *T. D. Easterby*

BOLLIN DOROTHY 4 b.f. Rambo Dancer (CAN) 107 – Bollin Harriet 59
(Lochnager 132) [1996 60: 8g 6g 7s* 7m 6m⁵ 6d 6f⁶ 7.1s⁵ 1997 7g 6g⁵ 5f⁴ 5.9d 6g²
6d² 7m 7g⁴ 6m³ 7g³ 6d⁶ 7m 7m Sep 20] strong filly: modest handicapper: effective at
5f to 7f: acts on firm and soft ground. *T. D. Easterby*

BOLLIN ETHOS 2 b.c. (Apr 26) Precocious 126 – Bollin Harriet (Lochnager – p
132) [1997 5d Sep 5] close-coupled, good-topped colt: fourth foal: half-brother to
4-y-o Bollin Dorothy and 5-y-o Bollin Harry: dam never ran: 33/1, burly and green,
in rear in 22-runner maiden at Haydock: should do better. *T. D. Easterby*

BOLLIN FRANK 5 b.g. Rambo Dancer (CAN) 107 – Bollin Emily 82 (Loch- 75
nager 132) [1996 75: 8m⁵ 8m² 8.5g² 8.1d* 8.1d⁵ 10f⁵ 7.9g 9g³ 8d² 8m 8g 1997 8m⁴
8.1m² 8m² 8.5v⁶ 8g⁶ 8g⁵ 8m 8d Sep 20] good-topped horse: fair handicapper: best up
to 9f: acts on firm and dead ground, well below form on heavy: blinkered (bit below
form) once at 3 yrs: sometimes hangs: often a front runner: game. *T. D. Easterby*

BOLLINGER ROSE (IRE) 2 b.f. (May 12) Fayruz 116 – Gobolino (Don 128) 60 ?
[1997 6m 6s⁴ 5m 6g 8s a7g⁶ Oct 20] IR 13,000Y: sister to a useful Italian 2-y-o 5f and
7f winner and half-sister to 2 winners, including 4-y-o Golden Ace: dam won at 7f at
2 yrs in Ireland: modest maiden: has run in sellers: best effort at 6f on soft going.
J. J. O'Neill

BOLLIN HARRY 5 b.h. Domynsky 110 – Bollin Harriet (Lochnager 132) [1996 74 d
82: 5s² 5g⁵ 6.1g* 6m² 6m 6m* 6g⁵ 5m 6m 6m 6v 5g 1997 6m⁴ 6g 6m 6g⁴ 6s 6d 6g
5m⁶ 6m 5m Oct 1] robust horse: impresses in appearance: has been hobdayed: fair
handicapper: well below form after fourth start, visored on final one: better form at
6f than 5f: acts on good to firm and soft ground: races prominently: has choked and
worn tongue strap. *T. D. Easterby*

Stanley Racing Sprint Trophy Rated Stakes (Handicap), York—
Bollin Joanne makes an excellent start to the season; Tumbleweed Ridge gives her most to do

BOLLIN JOANNE 4 b.f. Damister (USA) 123 – Bollin Zola 90 (Alzao (USA) 109
117) [1996 100: 6g² 7g⁴ 6m² 7.9m² 7.1d³ 6g* 6m* 6g⁵ 6m 6g* 1997 6g* 6g³ 6g² 6m²
5m* 5.2g³ 6d² Oct 17] close-coupled filly: useful performer: ran well on every start
in 1997, winning valuable handicap at York in May and listed race at Doncaster (beat
Almaty 1¼ lengths) in September: placed in listed races at Newbury and Newmarket
(led over 1f out, collared near finish by My Best Valentine) last 2 starts: has form at
1m, but best at 5f/6f: acts on good to firm and dead ground, yet to race on extremes:
bandaged: thoroughly genuine and consistent. *T. D. Easterby*

BOLLIN TERRY 3 b.c. Terimon 124 – Bollin Zola 90 (Alzao (USA) 117) [1996 79
58p: 7m 6g⁵ 8.1m⁵ 1997 7m⁴ 8m² 7.6d³ 7.9g 8f* Jun 4] tall, good-topped colt: fair
handicapper: returned lame after winning at Newcastle in June by 3 lengths: likely to
stay beyond 1m: acts on firm and dead going: keen-going type, probably suited by
waiting tactics. *T. D. Easterby*

BOLSHAYA 2 gr.f. (Mar 10) Cadeaux Genereux 131 – Mainly Dry (The Brian- 55 p
stan 128) [1997 6m 6m⁶ 6g Oct 22] 47,000Y: lengthy, unfurnished filly: half-sister
to several winning sprinters, including useful performers Great Chaddington (by
Crofter) and Tod (by Petorius): dam unraced: some promise, never
on terms nor knocked about, in maidens at Haydock, Catterick and Newcastle:
should do better. *J. Berry*

BOLSHOI (IRE) 5 br.g. Royal Academy (USA) 130 – Mainly Dry (The 109
Brianstan 128) [1996 103: 6s 6m⁴ 5m* 5g² 6m² 6f⁵ 5g⁴ 5m* 5m 5m* 6m⁴ 6g⁴ 5.6m⁵
6m 5g* 5d⁴ 5g 1997 5m* 5m⁴ 5g³ 5g³ 5d 5d 5.1m⁵ 5m⁴ 5d 5m 5m⁵ 6g Oct 24] tall,
lengthy gelding: useful performer: won minor event at Beverley in April: mostly ran
creditably afterwards, in frame in Palace House Stakes at Newmarket, Temple Stakes
at Sandown, Ballyogan Stakes at Leopardstown and King George Stakes at
Goodwood: effective at 5f and 6f: acts on good to firm and dead ground: usually
blinkered: best held up (ridden by Emma O'Gorman for last 4 successes): tough.
J. Berry

BOMB ALASKA 2 br.g. (May 9) Polar Falcon (USA) 126 – So True 116 (So 66 p
Blessed 130) [1997 6g 7d⁵ Nov 7] rangy gelding: sixth foal: half-brother to 4-y-o
Phonetic and 1m/9f winner Keep Your Word (by Castle Keep): dam 5f (at 2 yrs) and

1m winner, suited by 1½m: better effort in late-season maidens (burly on debut) when about 11 lengths fifth of 19 to Scorned at Doncaster: should prove suited by 1m+: has plenty of scope, and sure to make a better 3-y-o. *G. B. Balding*

BOMBASTIC   2 ch.c. (Mar 10) Polish Precedent (USA) 131 – Fur Hat (Habitat   75 p
134) [1997 7.1m 8m² 7d² Oct 14] big, good-topped colt with plenty of scope: seventh foal: half-brother to several winners, including 4-y-o Trilby and 5-y-o Merit: dam unraced half-sister to Teenoso: promising efforts in maidens: runner-up at Newcastle and Leicester, going on well at finish on latter course: will be well suited by 1¼m+: sort to thrive from 2 to 3 yrs, and should be worth following once upped in trip. *B. W. Hills*

BOMBAZINE (IRE)   3 ch.f. Generous (IRE) 139 – Brocade 121 (Habitat 134)   97
[1996 NR 1997 8m² 10d* 10.1m³ 12v⁵ 10.5d⁶ Oct 28] leggy, useful-looking filly: eighth foal: half-sister to 4 winners, 3 of them at least smart, notably Breeders Cup Mile winner Barathea (by Sadler's Wells): dam 7f/1m winner: useful performer: won maiden at Newmarket in June: best efforts when third in listed race at Yarmouth (3 lengths behind Entice) and fifth in Princess Royal Stakes at Ascot (edgy, beaten 8 lengths by Delilah): stayed 1½m: acted on good to firm and heavy ground: stud. *L. M. Cumani*

BONANZA PEAK (USA)   4 b.c. Houston (USA) – Bunnicula (USA) (Shadeed   74
(USA) 135) [1996 –: 10.4g⁶ 10s 1997 10m 10m 10.1m 10m³ 10.2g* 10s² 10d² 10d³ Nov 3] sturdy colt: fair handicapper: won apprentice maiden event at Bath in August: good efforts afterwards: will stay 1½m: acts on good to firm and soft ground. *Mrs J. Cecil*

BONGO   3 b.g. Efisio 120 – Boo Hoo 68 (Mummy's Pet 125) [1996 NR 1997 6m²   62
a8.5g⁵ Dec 26] leggy, unfurnished gelding: bad mover: third reported foal: half-brother to 1994 2-y-o 1m winner Lucidity (stayed 1½m, by Vision): dam probably stayed 1½m: better effort in maidens 7 months apart when second at Redcar: got behind both times. *C. W. Thornton*

BON GUEST (IRE)   3 ch.g. Kefaah (USA) 124 – Uninvited Guest 57 (Be My   59
Guest (USA) 126) [1996 64?: 5m 6m 7f 1997 a6g⁴ a6g³ a7g⁶ a5g² a5g⁴ 6.1g⁵ 5.1m 7m⁵ 8.2g* 8f 7f⁶ 8g⁵ a8.5f² 11.5s⁵ a9.4g² 8.2m³ a9.4g³ 10.1m³ a8.5g⁵ 11.5f Oct 3] small gelding: poor mover: modest performer: won apprentice maiden handicap at Nottingham in May: claimed out of T. J. Naughton's stable £8,000 after fifteenth start, trained next 4 by J. O'Shea: stays 1¼m: probably acts on any all-weather/turf: well beaten only try in blinkers: tends to get behind. *Miss B. Sanders*

BONJOUR   7 br.g. Primo Dominie 121 – Warm Welcome 89 (General Assembly   –
(USA)) [1996 NR 1997 a12g Dec 6] fair winner in 1992 for J. Gosden: subsequently placed in UAE for E. Charpy and over hurdles for C. Mann: well beaten on return to flat. *I. Semple*

BON LUCK (IRE)   5 ch.g. Waajib 121 – Elle Va Bon (Tanfirion 110) [1996 75:   69
7s⁵ 8.1m² 8.5m² 8.1d⁴ 8m⁴ 1997 6.9m⁴ 8.5d 8.2g Jun 18] fair handicapper: ran as if amiss last 2 starts: stays 8.5f: acts on any going: blinkered twice at 2 yrs. *J. A. Bennett*

BONNE VILLE   3 gr.f. Good Times (ITY) – Ville Air 85 (Town Crier 119) [1996   –
58: 8.1m 10.2d⁵ a8.5g* a8.5g a8g² 1997 a11g³ a12g⁴ 11.8g a12g² a14g⁵ 12d a12g⁴   a61
a9.4g⁶ a12g⁶ a12g² Nov 15] modest handicapper: stays 1½m: acts on fibresand, no form on turf: blinkered (poor effort) seventh start. *B. Palling*

BONNIE LASSIE   3 gr.f. Efisio 120 – Normanby Lass 100 (Bustino 136) [1996   52
69, a74: 5g⁵ 6m³ 7g³ a8g⁵ 1997 a8g⁵ a8g² 8m³ a12g 9s a8g Dec 18] leggy filly: fair   a65
on all-weather, modest on turf: stays 1m (not sure to stay 1½m): acts on fibresand and good to firm going. *C. W. Thornton*

BON SECRET (IRE)   5 b.g. Classic Secret (USA) 91 – Bon Retour (Sallust 134)   46
[1996 –, a71: a7g a8g* a10g³ a10g³ 1997 a8.5g³ a10g² a8g a7g⁴ 6m 7m³ 7m Jun 14]   a55
sturdy gelding: modest handicapper: probably stays 1¼m: acts on all-weather and on good to firm ground: inconsistent. *T. J. Naughton*

BONSIEL   3 b.f. Skyliner 117 – Shawiniga 58 (Lyphard's Wish (FR) 124) [1996   39
43: a5g a7g² a6g⁶ 6m 1997 7d 6g Jul 7] poor maiden handicapper: died in stalls at Folkestone in July. *K. Mahdi*

Mr R. M. Cyzer's "Book At Bedtime"

BON SIZZLE   2 b.c. (Apr 1) Sizzling Melody 117 – Bonne de Berry (Habitat 134)   56
[1997 6g 6d 6d Oct 28] 7,000Y: leggy colt: has quick action: brother to winning
sprinters Breakfast Boogie and Major Quality, latter useful, and half-brother to a
winner in France by Vayrann: dam French 1¼m winner: only form in maidens when
about 9 lengths eighth of 21 at Leicester final start. *J. R. Fanshawe*

BONYALUA MILL   3 gr.f. Chilibang 120 – Candesco 72 (Blushing Scribe   44
(USA) 107) [1996 NR 1997 a6g* 5g⁴ a6g 6g a7g Dec 18] first foal: dam 1m winner:
poor form: won maiden at Southwell in March: probably a sprinter: visored final
start. *A. Streeter*

BOOJUM   3 b.f. Mujtahid (USA) 118 – Haboobti (Habitat 134) [1996 101: 6.1m*   –
7m² 7g⁴ 7m 7.3s* 6.5d⁶ 1997 10m 10d³ 8.1s 10.5m⁶ 8m Nov 1] lengthy filly: useful
at 2 yrs: little form in 1997, including in pattern company and when visored.
B. W. Hills

BOOK AT BEDTIME (IRE)   3 b.f. Mtoto 134 – Akila (FR) (Top Ville 129)   114
[1996 NR 1997 10g⁴ 11.5s² 12m 16.2m³ 14d* 14.8g³ 15d² 11.9d³ 14g³ 14.6m*
14.6m⁴ Sep 13] 4,200Y: big, plain filly: half-sister to several 1¼m+ winners in
France and to useful Irish 4-y-o 2m winner Winged Hussar (by In The Wings): dam
unraced half-sister to Acamas, Akiyda and Akarad: smart performer: easily landed
odds in maiden at Sandown in July: improved efforts last 2 starts, winning Park Hill
Stakes at Doncaster (by a neck from The Faraway Tree) and under 5 lengths fourth to
Silver Patriarch in St Leger there just 3 days later: really needs further than 1½m, and
stays 2m: acts on good to firm and soft going: didn't handle descents at Lingfield and
Epsom (eighth in Oaks) at all well: tough and game. *C. A. Cyzer*

BOOKCASE   10 b.g. Siberian Express (USA) 125 – Colourful (FR) 97 (Gay   –
Mecene (USA) 128) [1996 NR 1997 10.8m⁵ Apr 12] fair handicapper at 1¼m to
1¾m in 1995: well below form only 10-y-o start. *D. R. C. Elsworth*

BORANI   2 b.c. (Apr 13) Shirley Heights 130 – Ower (IRE) 71 (Lomond (USA)   84 p
128) [1997 7m⁶ 8d³ Sep 13] 21,000Y: strong, lengthy colt: third foal: dam, 7f winner,

half-sister to smart middle-distance colts Weigh Anchor and Dr Massini: still not fully wound up, 3½ lengths third of 13 to Wales in maiden at Goodwood (moved poorly down), headed 1f out: should stay 1¼m+: edgy on debut: should improve further and win races at 3 yrs. *I. A. Balding*

BORDER ARROW 2 ch.c. (Feb 21) Selkirk (USA) 129 – Nibbs Point (IRE) 107   97 P
(Sure Blade (USA) 130) [1997 8d* Oct 16] 28,000Y: second foal: half-brother to 3-y-o Pen Friend: dam, 1¼m and 1½m winner, stayed 2m: 33/1, won 22-runner maiden at Newmarket most impressively by 3 lengths from Albarahin, last of principals to be asked for effort and storming clear up hill to score going away: will be better suited by 1¼m and will almost certainly stay 1½m: showed markedly round action to post: smart prospect (at least) for 1998, and should make his mark in listed/pattern races. *I. A. Balding*

BORDER FALCON 3 ch.g. Polar Falcon (USA) 126 – Tender Loving Care 105   68
(Final Straw 127) [1996 NR 1997 8g Apr 19] 22,000Y: big, strong gelding: seventh foal: half-brother to 1990 2-y-o 7f winner Noble Destiny (by Dancing Brave): dam 2-y-o 7f winner: burly, eighth of 15 in maiden at Newbury in April: sold 14,000 gns in October. *I. A. Balding*

BOREAS HILL (IRE) 2 b.g. (Apr 13) Petardia 113 – Salonniere (FR) 88 (Bikala   –
134) [1997 7m 8m⁶ Oct 23] 12,000Y: fourth foal: half-brother to 3-y-o Braveheart, a 2-y-o 6f seller winner by Red Sunset and fairly useful 1¼m winner Kissair (by Most Welcome), also winner of Triumph Hurdle: dam 1¼m winner: well held in maidens at Salisbury (backward, bandaged near hind) and Brighton. *J. R. Arnold*

BORGIA (GER) 3 b.f. Acatenango (GER) 127 – Britannia (GER) (Tarim)   124
[1996 7g² 7s³ 1997 10.3v* 10.5s* 11s* 11s² 12g* 12g² 12g* 12f³ 12f² Nov 8]
Her name may have suggested Italian origins, and she may have been partnered by a British-based Irishman in her most noteworthy races, but it was Germany's cause that Borgia was furthering abroad in the latest season. Success for German-trained horses elsewhere on the Continent is no longer that much of a rarity. But for a German horse—particularly a three-year-old filly—to be placed in two of the great international races, the Prix de l'Arc de Triomphe and the Breeders' Cup Turf, is an achievement that deserves plenty of recognition. Plenty of credit, too, for her connections, who campaigned Borgia in nine races from March to November without her finishing out of the first three.

German runners in the Arc have been few and far between, and none since the 1975 winner Star Appeal, who won at 119/1, had made the first three until Borgia in the latest running. Two of those to try in the meantime had been Borgia's sire and dam; Acatenango's winning run of twelve was brought to an end when seventh to Dancing Brave in 1986 and Britannia was ninth to Carroll House three years later. Borgia ran an excellent race in the Arc, despite giving the impression she'd have been suited by an even more severe test, not-withstanding the track record-breaking pace. Still with just two horses behind her starting the sweeping run towards the final straight, Borgia responded gamely to snatch third place from Oscar Schindler and Predappio on the post. She had no chance with the brilliant winner Peintre Celebre of course, but we made the distance she was beaten more like six lengths than the official seven and a half. Borgia followed Lando (fourth in the 1995 Arc) as just the second German runner at the Breeders' Cup when she contested the Turf. Lando had beaten only one home in his attempt, and, judging from the scant coverage she got in previews of the meeting in the major American racing publications, the locals weren't expecting much of a show from Borgia either. But she became the main European hope in the Turf, despite her stable's fears that she'd gone over the top and was beginning to grow her winter coat, after Singspiel's injury in training two days before the race.

The Formula One motor racing championship had resolved itself in a battle between Germany (Michael Schumacher) and Canada (Jacques Ville-neuve) in the final Grand Prix of the season, and less than a week later the

Breeders' Cup Turf was fought out by horses from the same countries. The result of both contests went the way of Canada, in the Turf to the favourite Chief Bearhart. Borgia handled the turns of Hollywood Park better than Schumacher did those at Jerez to be beaten three quarters of a length. Both Chief Bearhart and Borgia had been held up and made their moves on the home turn at the same time, Borgia finding space on the inner, Chief Bearhart taking a wider course, and it was only in the last seventy-five yards that Borgia was held. The other European runners, Majorien for France and Dance Design for Ireland, filled the last two places. Lando had gone on to give Germany its biggest international success by winning the Japan Cup after running in the Turf. Borgia was invited to Japan, but understandably was considered to have done enough for the year and the stable was represented instead by Caitano who ran a fine race in fourth.

Borgia's domestic achievements earlier in the season had already secured her a place in German racing history, as no filly had won either the German Derby or the Grosser Preis von Baden since the 'fifties. She was placed in both her starts at two and began her three-year-old career by winning a maiden at Dortmund and a minor event and a listed race at Mulheim. In the Preis der Diana (German Oaks) at Mulheim in June she'd had to give best to the Henkel Rennen (German One Thousand Guineas) winner Que Belle who was later to join Borgia in the Arc field and finish a good eighth. At Hamburg the following month Borgia was the only filly in a twenty-strong field for the BMW Deutsches Derby, five of which came from Borgia's stable, including favourite Caitano, the mount of stable-jockey Andrasch Starke (rider of Borgia in all but one of her previous starts). The ride on Borgia went to Olivier Peslier, and in a finish which prompted a stewards' inquiry the combination got the better of one of the outsiders, Baroon, by a neck. Caitano was fourth and Irish raider Zafarabad fifth, with the British runners Yorkshire and Conon Falls in mid-division. Baroon got his revenge to the tune of half a length in the

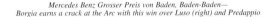

Mercedes Benz Grosser Preis von Baden, Baden-Baden—
Borgia earns a crack at the Arc with this win over Luso (right) and Predappio

Breeders' Cup Turf, Hollywood Park—Borgia (far side) gives best only to Chief Bearhart

all-German BMW EuropaChampionat at Hoppegarten in August, but Borgia was back in the winner's enclosure after the Grosser Preis von Baden a month before the Arc. Borgia was taking on older opposition for the first time and beat the high-class British-trained pair Luso and Predappio decisively in a steadily-run race. Kieren Fallon rode Borgia for the first time at Baden-Baden, and in the absence of a runner from the Cecil stable in both the Arc and the Breeders' Cup Turf, the partnership was maintained for the rest of her campaign.

		Surumu	Literat
	Acatenango (GER)	(ch 1974)	Surama
	(ch 1982)	Aggravate	Aggressor
Borgia (GER)		(b 1966)	Raven Locks
(b.f. 1994)		Tarim	Tudor Melody
	Britannia (GER)	(br 1969)	Tamerella
	(b 1985)	Bonna	Salvo
		(b 1978)	Birgit

Borgia's family is free of the intrigue and infamy associated with her historical Italian namesakes. It's a highly respectable German one in fact, and typically stoutly bred, with sire, grandsire and sire of the dam all German Derby winners and dam, Britannia, a German St Leger winner. Britannia's own Arc bid has already been mentioned. A year earlier she'd finished fourth in the French St Leger, the Prix Royal-Oak, and she'd also been successful in the Group 3 Oleander-Rennen, a two-mile event named in honour of the only other German horse, apart from Star Appeal and Borgia, to reach a place in the Arc (she was third in 1929). The next dams, Bonna and Birgit, won in lesser company in Germany but both bred good winners. Bonna is also the dam of the German Group 2 eleven-furlong winner Buenos, while Birgit's offspring include an Austrian Derby winner and a German St Leger runner-up. Borgia is Britannia's second foal. Her third, a full sister to Borgia named Bougainvillea, made 600,000 marks (just over £200,000) at the latest Baden-Baden Yearling Sales on the eve of Borgia's Grosser Preis win, thereby almost doubling the previous record sale price for a yearling in Germany.

The rangy Borgia not surprisingly proved better at a mile and a half than shorter in the latest season, and while she's sure to stay further, the big prizes at that trip will be on the agenda once more in 1998. She reportedly has the Arc as her main objective again and it's likely she'll be seen in Britain at some stage during the summer. Borgia acts on any going, and it goes almost without saying that she's tough, genuine and consistent. She was the best three-year-old filly in Europe in 1997, though her own stable had a colt of around the same ability in the aforementioned Caitano. They'll be trained in 1998 by Andreas Schutz who takes over from his father Bruno, who retired at the end of the year. *B. Schutz, Germany*

BORN A LADY   4 ch.f. Komaite (USA) – Lucky Candy 61 (Lucky Wednesday   42
124) [1996 53: a5g⁴ a5g⁶ a6g³ 6.1g 6.1m a5g 5g 8f 8m 8.2m³ 8m³ 8.5m⁵ 8f³ 8f⁴
a6g 10d 8.5m 10f⁴ 1997 a8g 13.8g 7f 6g⁴ a6g⁴ 7m 8f⁵ 7.5v a7g 8m Aug 11] poor
performer: effective at 6f to 1m: acts on firm ground and fibresand: tried blinkered/
visored: sometimes reluctant at stalls: usually races prominently. *Mrs V. A. Aconley*

BORN ON THE WILD   4 b.f. Golden Lahab (USA) – First Born 43 (Be My   –
Native (USA) 122) [1996 –: 6g 7g 1997 8g 8g Jun 21] angular filly: no worthwhile
form. *S. E. Kettlewell*

BORRADOR   3 b.g. Full Extent (USA) 113 – Wild Jewel (Great Heron (USA)   –
127) [1996 NR 1997 8.3s 7.6m 6g 10m Oct 1] leggy, sparely-made gelding: half-
brother to fairly useful sprinter Singing Star (by Crooner) and modest winning stayer
Mirador (by Town And Country): dam never ran: always behind in maidens and
handicap. *R. Curtis*

BOSRA SHAM (USA)   4 ch.f. Woodman (USA) 126 – Korveya (USA) 116   130
(Riverman (USA) 131) [1996 132: 7.3d* 8m* 8m² 10g* 1997 10m* 10m* 10d³
10.4g⁴ Aug 19]
It is inevitable, but those things which we value most are also those which risk providing the most disappointment. The value that Henry Cecil placed on Bosra Sham became clear enough when he stated that she was the best horse he had ever trained.

Going into the latest season, Bosra Sham was indisputably the best filly of her generation still in training, and by a huge margin. On the evidence of her three-year-old campaign, in which she had won the One Thousand Guineas and Champion Stakes and suffered the first defeat of her career at the hands of Mark of Esteem in the Queen Elizabeth II Stakes, she was also a good deal better than any filly of her generation now out of training. Her rating of 132 in *Racehorses of 1996* had been 5 lb above that of the American filly Yanks Music and 9 lb above that of any other three-year-old filly in North America or Europe. The next best in Europe were Kistena, Lady Carla, Shake The Yoke, Last Second, Annaba, Dance Design, La Blue, Luna Wells, Wurftaube, Blue Duster and Key Change. Amazingly, this top dozen were all due to race again in 1997. However, you do not have to proceed far down that list before appreciating that not all of these decisions received their reward.

Bosra Sham's campaign began in thoroughly satisfactory style in the Brigadier Gerard Stakes at Sandown at the end of May. She accomplished nothing that was not fully expected of her, indeed her starting price of 5/1-on in a five-runner race indicates that rather more was expected than victory by half a length. But Bosra Sham was some way off peak fitness and the runner-up, Predappio, went on to beat Pilsudski in the Hardwicke Stakes at Royal Ascot. Three days before the Hardwicke, Bosra Sham showed that she did not need the efforts of Predappio to prove her well-being. An eight-length win in the Prince of Wales's Stakes did not leave much room for doubt. Victory in itself was no surprise—this time she was sent off at 11/4-on—but Bosra Sham could not have been more imperious in storming clear in the last two furlongs, her nearest pursuer, Alhaarth, himself finishing five lengths and more in front of the other four runners, headed by South African challenger London News and 13/2 second-favourite Even Top. 'Bosra Sham is a great filly, one of the best we've seen for a long, long time,' stated Henry Cecil. 'As we are going to see her racing through the season, let's appreciate her and enjoy her, because we might not get another like her for a long time.' In the heady aftermath to those first two races of the season, Bosra Sham was the subject of glowing quotes from all connected with her. 'She's unbelievable to ride and does everything for you,' said Kieren Fallon. 'She makes my job very easy.'

Some quotes come back to haunt you. In this case, it took less than a month, when Bosra Sham started 7/4-on with four opponents in the Eclipse Stakes at Sandown. Her stop-start three-year-old campaign had illustrated that Bosra Sham was not that easy to train, and the Eclipse that riding her would not always be plain sailing either. A small field often results in a falsely-run race, and a falsely-run race in a false result. In the Eclipse, as widely forecast, the Derby winner Benny The Dip made the running, and did so at a very steady pace—hardly a new ploy when attempting to steal a march on better-fancied rivals, but, as this race proved, still a very effective one. Fallon was conceding an advantage in holding up Bosra Sham—she had also been held up in nearly all her previous races—but her effectiveness in a test of finishing speed was not something that had been questioned much before. More worrying was the lack of racing room, with Benny The Dip and Pilsudski in front of her and Sasuru close on the outside keeping her boxed in. To extricate Bosra Sham when the race began in earnest entering the straight, Fallon opted to send her for a temporary gap (the running rail temporarily kinking inwards) between Benny The Dip and the rails. He found out very swiftly that this had been a mistake. The gap closed and, as Michael Kinane was sending Pilsudski into the lead, Bosra Sham lost ground (about a length) and momentum. Switched to the outside as Sasuru's role in the race came to an end, Bosra Sham had about three lengths to make up and she could not do it. The case for Bosra Sham as an unlucky loser would have been more persuasive had she been a strong-finishing second, but, as it was, having gone marginally ahead of Benny The Dip, she then lost second place to him again just before the line. Pilsudski won by a length and a quarter, appearing to idle a little. There is no conclusive evidence that Bosra Sham would have beaten Pilsudski in this three-furlong sprint had she not encountered interference. She might have done, but it is just as likely that Fallon's unfortunate pathfinding served only to make her defeat more dramatic.

Dramatic, though, it certainly was. 'Bosra Shambles' was how *Racing Post* described it on their front page, as commentators examined the race again and again, as Cecil opened his heart to reporters, as Fallon lost the ride on Bosra Sham and Wafic Said's other star filly Lady Carla, and as speculation mounted as to whether he would lose other important rides for Warren Place, possibly all of them. Cecil's analysis of the race, as told to the Press Association on the

Prince of Wales's Stakes, Royal Ascot—a breathtaking performance from Bosra Sham

Sunday, was that: 'Everyone has a pair of eyes. It was appalling, and if people couldn't see what happened then they shouldn't go racing but go to the theatre instead . . . They went a crawl and she likes to go a decent gallop. If she dictated the race she would have won six lengths.' Fallon's appointment as Cecil's stable jockey from the start of the latest season had been a big surprise to those who knew the Irishman only by reputation, as the partner of Top Cees and as the assailant of fellow jockey Stuart Webster after a race at Beverley in 1994. There were also, however, those who knew him for his determination and tactical astuteness in a multitude of races in the North, and Fallon responded to the disappointment of Bosra Sham with both dignity and a series of barn-storming performances in the saddle that must have swelled the ranks of his admirers hugely. Among the most timely of those performances were fifteen winners during the week following the Eclipse, eleven of them for Cecil, including a four-timer at the Newmarket July meeting where the two men were the centre of a media-feeding frenzy. The Bosra Sham affair was the most extreme case in a year in which the performances of jockeys and the rivalries between them (Peslier and Asmussen, Kinane and Fallon spring to mind) came under intense scrutiny. But, well before the season was over, Fallon had established a reputation for effort and reliability that was second to none. When the season ended, 202 wins (196 during the turf season) had secured him the jockeys' championship, 947 rides (more than any other jockey, with the exception of Jimmy Quinn, who took 15 more rides) had demonstrated his popularity with the trainers, and punters could reflect that he was the only top jockey to have shown a level-stakes profit.

Sadly, the ride on Bosra Sham after the Eclipse had no bearing on any of the statistics. Pat Eddery was reunited with her in the Juddmonte International at York in August, but, six days before the race, she also became reacquainted with injury. Problems with her near-fore foot had dogged Bosra Sham's three-year-old career, and had also affected her at two. Now she returned from her penultimate gallop before the International and the same foot had been bruised. Bosra Sham was able to take her place in the field at York, heavily backed to 5/4-on, but she soon looked laboured in the straight and finished last of four, four and a quarter lengths behind the winner Singspiel and clearly some way below her best. A likely explanation became apparent when television replays highlighted an incident about six furlongs from home when one of Bosra Sham's shoes flew off, narrowly missing Michael Kinane who was following her on Desert King. Losing a shoe is mentioned often enough in connection with a disappointing effort—only a very small percentage of trainers will allow their horse to run without one of its plates if it is lost before the start—and it is not hard to imagine Bosra Sham hurting given that she had lost the special 'egg bar' shoe which was protecting her fragile near-fore. The Champion Stakes and Breeders' Cup Turf were the next reported targets, while Eddery's early end to the season with a back injury offered the fascinating possibility that the search for a replacement would end again with Fallon. But it was always the health reports that mattered most with Bosra Sham and on September 23rd it was announced that she had been retired, 'due to recurring foot problems'. She will visit Rainbow Quest in 1998.

Those foot problems meant that in three seasons at the top Bosra Sham ran only ten times. She had been a star long before that, though. At birth, she was already the sister of one classic winner, Hector Protector, and the three-parts sister of another, Shanghai (by Procida). At 530,000 guineas, she was the highest-priced yearling in Britain or Ireland in 1994 and that year's highest-priced yearling filly in the world; the underbidder—a man who has been determined not to lose out much since—was Michael Tabor. Korveya's 1994 colt, Great Success (by Nureyev), is a winner in Japan, and her 1995 filly, Maria Isabella (by Kris), was in training in 1997 with Luca Cumani but did not run. A colt by Mr Prospector failed to meet his engagement at the Keeneland July Yearling Sale.

Mr Wafic Said's "Bosra Sham"

		Mr Prospector (b 1970)	Raise A Native
	Woodman (USA) (ch 1983)		Gold Digger
		Playmate (ch 1975)	Buckpasser
Bosra Sham (USA) (ch.f. 1993)			Intriguing
		Riverman (b 1969)	Never Bend
	Korveya (USA) (ch 1982)		River Lady
		Konafa (b 1973)	Damascus
			Royal Statute

Bosra Sham showed top-class form at a mile and a mile and a quarter. She acted on good to firm ground and on good to soft, never encountering anything more extreme. A strong, rangy, attractive filly and a good mover, Bosra Sham did well from three to four years. When weight for age is taken into account, though, her highest rating is still that for her two-and-a-half length victory over Halling in the 1996 Champion Stakes, a win that also played a huge part in Cecil's rare duel with Saeed bin Suroor for the trainers' championship. Put her successes alongside the trauma of her training problems and the Eclipse, and it is easy to understand why Cecil said: 'She has given us thrills, pleasure and heartache beyond all measure.' However, while it cannot be said that Cecil was wrong to believe that Bosra Sham was the best horse he has ever trained, several other horses he has had through his stable have shown better form on the racecourse. For the record, we rated Reference Point at 139, Slip Anchor and Old Vic at 136, Le Moss and Kris at 135, Bolkonski and Ardross at 134, Buckskin and Indian Skimmer at 133. Most of those were very different types to Bosra Sham. Indian Skimmer is the only filly in that list, and

146

there are not many fillies or mares from any British stable that we have ever rated more highly. Of those that stayed in training beyond their classic year, Bosra Sham is worthy of comparison with Petite Etoile, Park Top and Pebbles. Bosra Sham's Eclipse was reminiscent to Park Top's shock defeat in the same race twenty-eight years earlier. On that occasion Park Top failed to find a clear run under Geoff Lewis; later in the 1969 season Lester Piggott was blamed for her defeat in the Arc, and the following year for those in the Coronation Cup and Prix de Royallieu. Lewis would soon be riding the horse for which his name will always be remembered, Mill Reef, while Piggott had to console himself with the likes of Nijinsky and Alleged. If the remainder of 1997 is anything to go by, Kieren Fallon will not go begging for good rides either. *H. R. A. Cecil*

BOSS LADY (IRE)   3 b.f. Last Tycoon 131 – Queen Helen 112 (Troy 137) [1996   80
NR 1997 8g⁶ 8.3s² 8f* 10m² 10g³ 10.5s⁵ 11m Nov 4] lengthy, useful-looking filly: fifth foal: half-sister to 11f winner Helen's Bower (by Bellypha) and a winner in Denmark: dam won up to 14.6f, but best at shorter: fairly useful performer: idled when winning maiden at Bath in May: creditable efforts in handicaps next 3 starts: should stay beyond 10.5f: acts on firm and soft going. *R. Charlton*

BOULEVARD ROUGE (USA)   2 b.f. (Feb 10) Red Ransom (USA) –   70
Beetwentysix (USA) (Buckaroo (USA)) [1997 5g³ 6m³ 6m⁵ 7.1g² 7g 7s a7g a8g Dec 10] IR 22,000Y: sixth foal: sister to 1995 2-y-o 5f winner Red Stream and a winner in USA, closely related to a winner by Silver Hawk and half-sister to a winner by Green Forest (both also in USA): dam, French 9f and 1¼m winner, from family of Lear Fan: fair maiden: poor efforts last 4 starts, unseating rider leaving stalls final one: should stay beyond 7f. *M. Johnston*

BOUNDLESS SHAPE (IRE)   2 ch.c. (Feb 17) Petardia 113 – Burren Breeze   –
(IRE) (Mazaad 106) [1997 8s Nov 14] IR 25,000Y: second foal: half-brother to 3-y-o Khamsin: dam unraced half-sister to smart 7f performer Braddells: well beaten in minor event at Milan in November. *L. M. Cumani*

BOUND TO PLEASE   2 b.g. (Mar 9) Warrshan (USA) 117 – Hong Kong Girl 94   71
(Petong 126) [1997 5d⁵ 6d 5m² 5m 5s⁴ a6g⁴ 7.3g Oct 25] neat gelding: third reported   a65 +
foal: half-brother to 6f winner Jersey Belle (by Distant Relative): dam best at 5f: fair maiden: second at Windsor in July: fly-jumped, hit rail and unseated rider next start: not sure to stay beyond 6f: acts on soft ground and good to firm, and on fibresand: sold 9,200 gns in December. *P. J. Makin*

BOUT   3 br.f. Batshoof 122 – Reyah 83 (Young Generation 129) [1996 65: 7m 8.1d⁶   –
1997 a8.5g a8g 8m 8.3d 14.1m 10.9d 8g 12.1g Sep 1] good-bodied filly: well beaten in 1997: tried in a visor. *R. M. McKellar*

BOW BELLS   2 b.f. (Apr 26) Absalom 128 – Dancing Chimes (London Bells   59
(CAN) 109) [1997 6d a7g⁵ Dec 12] 10,000Y: sixth foal: half-sister to several winners at up to 7f, including 3-y-o Simple Logic and 3-y-o Palacegate Touch: dam unraced: showed a little promise when mid-division in 21-runner maiden at Doncaster: slowly away in similar event at Lingfield month later. *C. F. Wall*

BOWCLIFFE   6 b.g. Petoski 135 – Gwiffina 87 (Welsh Saint 126) [1996 51:   70
12.3g 10.9d 8.1g* 8.1f 8.1m 10.4g 7g 8.1s 1997 8.3s 8g³ 8g³ 8m* 8m⁵ 8g* 8m⁶ 9m² 9m³ 8m⁶ 8.5f⁶ 9m⁴ 8g³ 8m⁵ Oct 28] good-topped gelding: fair handicapper: successful at Pontefract and Carlisle in the summer: suited by 1m/9f: acts on firm and dead ground, seems unsuited by soft: tried blinkered/visored earlier in career: goes well with waiting tactics: consistent. *E. J. Alston*

BOWCLIFFE COURT (IRE)   5 b.g. Slip Anchor 136 – Res Nova (USA)   78
(Blushing Groom (FR) 131) [1996 75: 14.1g⁵ 13.9m 15.8g² 16.4g² 16m 16s⁶ 15.9g⁴ 16s* 16.5s³ 1997 14.9m* 18.7s 16.4d³ 14g Jul 16] close-coupled gelding: unimpressive mover: fair handicapper: well ridden by T. Quinn to win steadily-run event at Warwick in April: tailed off final start: stays 16.5f: acts on good to firm and soft ground: usually held up: sometimes hangs fire under pressure. *R. Akehurst*

BOWCLIFFE GRANGE (IRE)   5 b.g. Dominion Royale 112 – Cala-Vadella   55
110 (Mummy's Pet 125) [1996 56: a6g a6g⁶ 5.9d 5s⁶ 6m² a6g⁶ 5f* 5f³ 5f* 5f³ 5d 5g*

5m* 5m³ 5m a5g⁵ 5.3m⁶ 1997 a5g⁴ a5g⁴ a5g a5g 5m 5f⁵ 5g⁶ 5g 5g³ 5g 5m Sep 22] good-topped gelding: modest handicapper: suited by sharp 5f: acts on firm ground and the all-weather: often blinkered at 4 yrs, only on penultimate start (well beaten) in 1997: has run well sweating: has blistering early speed. *D. W. Chapman*

BOWDEN ROSE   5 ch.m. Dashing Blade 117 – Elegant Rose 72 (Noalto 120)   100 [1996 98: 5.2d 6m 6d⁴ 5m² 6m 5m⁴ 5.1f² 5m⁶ 6m⁵ 5g* 5d² 6g 5.2m 5g 5g 5g 1997 5.2g 5.1v³ 6d 5m 5g 5m* 5m 6.1g* 6g* 6m⁴ 6g 5.6m 5m⁴ 6m* 5d 6g⁶ 6.1d Oct 30] angular, shallow-girthed mare: useful handicapper: better than ever in 1997, winning at Lingfield in June, Nottingham in July, Epsom in August and Newmarket (by 1¼ lengths from Plaisir D'Amour) in October: effective at 5f and 6f: acts on firm and dead ground: wears blinkers: somewhat wayward (may be best kept away from other horses), but has won for apprentice: none too consistent. *M. Blanshard*

BOWLED OVER   4 b.g. Batshoof 122 – Swift Linnet (Wolver Hollow 126)   73 d [1996 86: 8.2d² 10m 10.3g³ 12.1d³ 11.9m* 12m³ 15d⁵ 13.9m 10.3d 10.3m⁴ 13.3m 10.4g 1997 10m 12g⁴ 14.1d a12g 11.9f 12m a8g a10g Dec 2] workmanlike gelding: has a round action: disappointing handicapper, mostly well beaten in 1997: stays 1½m: acts on good to firm and dead ground: visored (took strong hold, tailed off) once: not one to trust implicitly. *C. A. Cyzer*

BOWLERS BOY   4 ch.g. Risk Me (FR) 127 – Snow Wonder (Music Boy 124)   81 [1996 78: 5m³ 6g 6d⁵ 6g 5m² a5g³ 6m* 6d 6g² 5m* 6g 1997 5g 6g⁴ 5d 6g⁵ 6m 5g² 5v* 6g² 5m 7s³ 6g 5d⁶ 5g⁵ 6d* 5g² 5.7g² 6.1g 5d² 6g 5d Nov 7] workmanlike gelding: fairly useful handicapper: in good form for much of 1997, and won at Beverley and Ripon (apprentices) in the summer: effective at 5f (on stiff track) to 7f: acts on good to firm and heavy ground: carries head high. *J. J. Quinn*

BOW PEEP (IRE)   2 b. or br.f. (Apr 21) Shalford (IRE) 124§ – Gale Force Seven   57 (Strong Gale 116) [1997 5m⁵ 5g⁴ a5g⁴ 5g⁴ Aug 1] IR 4,600Y: fifth foal: dam unraced from family of Cheveley Park winner Pass The Peace: modest form in varied events: will be suited by further than 5f: blinkered third start. *M. W. Easterby*

BRADBURY FALLS (IRE)   2 ch.f. (Apr 6) River Falls 113 – Asturiana (Julio   35 Mariner 127) [1997 5g 5s³ a5g 6g Jul 28] IR 1,500Y: sparely-made filly: half-sister to 5f winner (including at 2 yrs) Twice In Bundoran (by Bold Arrangement) and a winner in Italy by Gallic League: dam, half-sister to a Musidora winner, lightly raced: poor form in sellers. *D. J. S. Cosgrove*

BRAGANZA (USA)   2 ch.c. (Apr 15) Rahy (USA) 115 – Blue Daisy (USA) 108   67 p (Shahrastani (USA) 135) [1997 Oct 3] small colt: second foal: half-brother to 3-y-o Blue Goblin: dam 7f/1m winner, including in Ireland at 2 yrs, from good Canadian family: favourite, but easy to back and better for race, around 1½ lengths fourth of 6 in maiden at Lingfield, soon pushed along: sold approx. £21,000 in Dubai in November. *D. R. Loder*

BRAMBLE BEAR   3 b.f. Beveled (USA) – Supreme Rose 95 (Frimley Park 109)   72 [1996 71d: 5f⁵ 5m 5.1m³ 5.1f* 5m 5g 5m⁶ 1997 5m 5d* 5m* 5d 5.1m⁴ 5m⁵ 5g² 5m⁴ 5g 6m 5m Oct 2] leggy, unfurnished filly: fair 5f handicapper: won at Windsor and Catterick in May: below form last 3 starts: acts on firm and dead going. *M. Blanshard*

BRAMBLES WAY   8 ch.g. Clantime 101 – Streets Ahead 67 (Ovid 95) [1996 55:   56 7s 6.9d 6.9m³ 8g² 6.9g⁴ 8m 8f 9.2f⁵ 10f* 10.1m⁵ 10f a11g 1997 9.9m* 11f 8.3s⁶ 11g⁵ 10.9d 10g⁶ 10.1g* Oct 22] strong, lengthy gelding: modest handicapper: won at Beverley in April and Newcastle in October: may be best around 1¼m: acts on firm ground, probably on dead, well held on fibresand: effective visored/blinkered or not. *Mrs M. Reveley*

BRAND NEW DANCE   3 b.g. Gildoran 123 – Starawak 68 (Star Appeal 133)   82 [1996 68p: 8s⁵ 1997 a12g* 13.3g⁴ 14d⁶ 14m 14m² Aug 14] quite good-topped gelding: fairly useful performer: won maiden at Wolverhampton in April: best effort in handicap at Sandown final start: stays 1¾m: acts on good to firm ground: takes a strong hold. *D. W. P. Arbuthnot*

BRANDON FRANK   2 ch.g. (Mar 18) Beveled (USA) – Island Desert (IRE) 55   77 (Green Desert (USA) 127) [1997 5.1m 5m³ 6m² 5.7g* 5.2f 6.1g Jul 30] 5,000Y: leggy gelding: first foal: dam placed over 11f and 1½m: fair form: won maiden at Bath in June: ran creditably in Super Sprint at Newbury (stirred up in paddock) next time: stays 6f: yet to race on going softer than good: sent to Macau. *I. A. Balding*

BRANDON JACK 3 ch.g. Cadeaux Genereux 131 – Waitingformargaret 78   78
(Kris 135) [1996 81: 6.1m³ 7f³ 6.1d* 7g* 7g³ 1997 8m 9g 7.9g 10m 9g⁵ 9s* 10.3m⁵
10m⁶ 10m* 10.3d³ 9d Sep 12] angular, lengthy gelding: fair performer: won
handicap at Goodwood in June and minor event at Sandown in August: gelded after
final start: stays 1¼m: acts on good to firm and soft going. *I. A. Balding*

BRANDON MAGIC 4 ch.c. Primo Dominie 121 – Silk Stocking 109 (Pardao   88
120) [1996 97: 7m⁵ 8s⁵ 8.5m 8f 8.1g⁵ 8m 10m² 11.9g⁵ 10m 10m 1997 10.3d⁶ 10.4g
13.9d² 14s³ 11.9g 12m⁴ 12d² Aug 25] good-topped, lengthy colt: fairly useful
handicapper: has failed to win since 1995: barely stays 1¾m: acts on soft ground,
probably on firm: blinkered (refused to settle) once: sold 15,000 gns in October.
I. A. Balding

BRANDONVILLE 4 b.c. Never So Bold 135 – Enduring (Sadler's Wells (USA)   65
132) [1996 –: 6m⁵ 8d 8g 7m⁵ 7g⁴ 9f 1997 a7g 7s* 8g⁶ 7g 7.1d* Jul 3] big colt: fair
handicapper: won at Ayr in May and Haydock (apprentices) in July: should stay 1m:
acts on soft ground. *N. Tinkler*

BRANSTON BERRY (IRE) 2 ch.f. (Apr 23) Mukaddamah (USA) 125 – Food   80
of Love 109 (Music Boy 124) [1997 a5g² 5s* 5g³ 5m³ 5v² 5m 6.5m* 6g² 6d 7s Nov 8]
7,500Y: close-coupled filly: second foal: dam 5f performer: fairly useful performer:
claimed from M. Johnston debut: won maiden at Beverley in May and valuable
nursery at Doncaster in September: very good second in Haydock nursery later in
September: may prove best at 6f/7f: acts on good to firm and soft going: tends to
sweat and get on edge, and sometimes early to post. *J. L. Eyre*

BRAVE EDGE 6 b.g. Beveled (USA) – Daring Ditty (Daring March 116) [1996   108
108: 5.2d⁵ 6m⁵ 5m² 5m* 5m⁶ 6f 5m 5m 6m 5d⁴ 5m³ 5m⁴ 5s² 1997 5m³ 5m 5g² 5m⁶
5d 5d 6g⁴ 5m³ 5g⁴ 6s⁵ 5m⁶ 5m⁶ 5.2g 6g* 6g² 6.1d⁴ 6s Nov 8] good-topped gelding:
useful performer: good efforts when ¾-length second to Croft Pool in Temple Stakes
at Sandown and close fourth to Monaassib in Prix de Ris-Orangis at Deauville

Horris Vale Racing Partnerships' "Brave Edge"

seventh start: didn't need to be at best to win minor event at Hamilton in September: back to form when 1¾ lengths second to My Best Valentine in handicap at Newbury in October: effective at 5f/6f: acts on firm and soft ground: usually held up. *R. Hannon*

BRAVE ENVOY   3 b.g. High Estate 127 – Restless Anna (Thatching 131) [1996   69
–: 7d 1997 6f* 7g² 8m 8f⁵ 8.3g⁵ 7m⁵ 8d⁵ 8.2d* Oct 30] sturdy gelding: fair performer: won seller at Leicester (visored, well backed) in April and handicap at Nottingham in October: stays 1m well: acts on firm and dead ground. *M. J. Heaton-Ellis*

BRAVEHEART (IRE)   3 br.g. Mujadil (USA) 119 – Salonniere (FR) 88 (Bikala   76
134) [1996 79+: 5g⁴ 5g* 5m² 5.1g³ 5g⁴ 6.1d³ 6m⁵ 1997 10.5s 8g 6s 5.1s 7m⁵ 6d⁴ 7m² 8s Nov 8] lengthy gelding: fair handicapper: likely to prove best at 7f/1m: acts on good to firm and dead going. *M. R. Channon*

BRAVE KRIS (IRE)   3 b.f. Kris 135 – Famosa (Dancing Brave (USA) 140)   101
[1996 82: 7f 8.2g² 8g³ 1997 8m 8m* 8d* 7.6f⁵ Jul 12] well-made filly: has a round action: useful handicapper: won quite valuable events at Newmarket in May and Ascot (listed event, by 2½ lengths from Dancing Drop) in June: got worked up final start: stays 1m: acts on good to firm and dead ground: takes good hold, and suited by waiting tactics. *L. M. Cumani*

BRAVE MAPLE   2 b.c. (Jan 31) Petong 126 – Hazy Kay (IRE) 77 (Treasure Kay   –
114) [1996 7m 7s Oct 14] 15,000Y: small colt: first foal: dam disappointing maiden from family of Steel Heart and Chilibang: well beaten in maidens. *J. M. P. Eustace*

BRAVE MONTGOMERIE   3 ch.c. Most Welcome 131 – Just Precious 77   74
(Ela-Mana-Mou 132) [1996 77p: 6m² 7s³ 7m* 1997 8s² 8f⁴ 9g⁴ 10m⁶ Jul 19] fair performer: should stay 1¼m, well beaten when tried: acts on firm and soft ground. *Miss L. A. Perratt*

BRAVE NOBLE (USA)   2 ch.c. (Mar 25) Woodman (USA) 126 – Badge of   77 p
Courage (USA) (Well Decorated (USA)) [1997 7d 8d³ Oct 28] $15,000Y: tall colt with scope: closely related to an Irish 2-y-o 7f and 1m winner by Miswaki, also successful in USA, and half-brother to 2 winners, notably useful 7f (at 2 yrs) and 1¼m winner True Hero (by The Minstrel): dam unraced half-sister to Known Fact: much better effort in maidens at Leicester in October when keeping-on 4½ lengths third of 14 to Himself: should stay beyond 1m: should improve further. *E. A. L. Dunlop·*

BRAVE REWARD (USA)   2 b.c. (Mar 11) Lear Fan (USA) 130 – A Tad Better   89 p
(USA) (Northern Prospect (USA)) [1997 7d* 8m³ Oct 31] $90,000F, $160,000Y: leggy, quite attractive colt: second foal: dam maiden half-sister to top-class French middle-distance filly Northern Trick: 3/1 and better for race, won maiden at Leicester by 1½ lengths from Celtic Pageant, patiently ridden and quickening well: failed to settle behind slow pace when just over 4 lengths last of 3 to Rabah minor event at Newmarket later in October: should stay 1m: will do better. *M. R. Stoute*

BRAVE SPY   6 b.g. Law Society (USA) 130 – Contralto 100 (Busted 134) [1996   –
–: a12g⁵ a14.8g 11.8d a12g³ a16g a16g a13g 1997 a13g Jan 7] no longer of any account. *C. A. Cyzer*

BRAWLING SPRINGS   3 b.g. Belfort (FR) 89 – Oyster Gray 61 (Tanfirion 110)   –
[1996 –: 5m⁶ 5m⁵ 5f 1997 5g Aug 5] leggy gelding: well beaten in varied events. *J. J. O'Neill*

BREAK FOR PEACE (IRE)   2 b.f. (Mar 5) Brief Truce (USA) 126 – Run   –
Bonnie (Runnett 125) [1997 6m Sep 10] IR 23,000Y: unfurnished filly: third foal: half-sister to an Irish 2-y-o 5f and 6.5f winner by Common Grounds and useful Irish 2-y-o 5f winner Soreze (by Gallic League): dam Irish 6f winner: 20/1, last of 20 in maiden at Kempton: unimpressive to post. *Sir Mark Prescott*

BREAKIN EVEN   2 ch.g. (Feb 22) Chilibang 120 – Bee Dee Dancer (Balla-   –
cashtal (CAN)) [1997 7.1s 7m a6g a7g Dec 18] lengthy gelding: second foal: dam well beaten only start: little sign of ability: blinkered last 3 starts. *J. L. Eyre*

BREAK THE RULES   5 b.g. Dominion 123 – Surf Bird (Shareef Dancer (USA)   85
135) [1996 76: 9.2d⁴ 10m 8g³ 10m² 11.1g² 12.3m* 10v⁴ 12g 12.1d⁴ 10.5v² 12g³ 10.3g* 1997 10.3m* 10.3d* 11.9d⁴ 10.3s* 10d⁶ 10m 12.3m 10.3m 9d² 12m 12s⁶ 10g

10.3g⁴ Oct 25] neat gelding: fairly useful performer: won handicaps at Doncaster (ladies) and Chester and claimer back at Chester (claimed £15,000 from M. Pipe) in first half of season: mostly below form afterwards: effective at 1¼m to 1½m: acts on any going: has carried head high under pressure, and not the most straightforward of rides. *D. Nicholls*

BRECON 4 b. or br.c. High Estate 127 – No Can Tell (USA) (Clev Er Tell (USA)) [1996 –: a8g a8.5g⁴ 1997 13.1g⁴ a12g⁶ 13.8s⁴ a16g³ a16g Dec 10] modest handicapper: stays 2m: acts on good to firm and soft ground and on equitrack. *W. R. Muir* **61**

BRECONGILL LAD 5 b.g. Clantime 101 – Chikala 81 (Pitskelly 122) [1996 73: 6s 6g 6m 5m 6m 6d 6m⁵ 5f* 5m² 6m 5g⁶ 5g⁴ 5s 1997 5m 6m³ 6d⁶ 5d 6.1g² 5m² 5d³ 5g³ 5d 5m³ 5d Oct 8] tall gelding: fair handicapper: placed 6 times in 1997: probably best at 6f/stiff 5f: acts on firm and dead going: often blinkered earlier in career, seems effective with or without visor: tends to hang and carry head high: races prominently. *Miss S. E. Hall* **70**

BREEZED WELL 11 b.g. Wolverlife 115 – Precious Baby (African Sky 124) [1996 40: a8g a7g 10g⁵ 7f 8g 7.1g 7.5f³ 12m 8f⁴ 11.5m 1997 10g a8.5g a8.5g 9.9v* 9.9m 8.1g³ 10.1g⁴ 7.5d³ᵈⁱˢ 12d Sep 19] smallish, sparely-made gelding: poor mover: modest handicapper: usually contests amateurs events, and won one at Beverley in July: effective at 1m to 11.5f: acts on any going: blinkered (below form) once at 3 yrs. *K. G. Wingrove* **51**

BREFFNI (IRE) 3 b.f. Mac's Imp (USA) 116 – Bon Retour (Sallust 134) [1996 47: 6g 5.2f³ 6g² 6f² a5g⁴ 6.1m 6f⁵ 1997 5m⁶ 6m 5g a5g⁶ Aug 8] seems of little account. *R. Dickin* **–**

BRESIL (USA) 8 ch.g. Bering 136 – Clever Bidder (USA) (Bold Bidder) [1996 35, a–: 14.1s⁴ a12g 12d 12m 12f⁵ 14.1f² 13.1f⁵ 14.1f⁵ 14m⁴ 14.1m 14d 1997 15.4m⁶ 11.9f 13.1m 12.5m Jul 19] no longer of any account. *J. J. Bridger* **–**

BREYDON 4 ch.g. Be My Guest (USA) 126 – Palmella (USA) 89 (Grundy 137) [1996 50: 8.2d 8.2s 10g 12m⁶ 13g³ a14g² 12m³ 11.1m² 1997 11.1d 16m³ 11.1s 12d 14d⁶ 16m 12.1g⁴ Aug 2] angular, plain gelding: winning hurdler: poor maiden handicapper on flat: barely stays 2m: best form on ground no softer than good: inconsistent. *P. Monteith* **43 d**

BRIDE'S REPRISAL 3 b.f. Dunbeath (USA) 127 – Matching Lines 72 (Thatching 131) [1996 87: 5f³ 5f 5g² 5g* 6m³ 6m³ 5.2m⁵ 6f⁶ 1997 8.1d 5.7d May 11] workmanlike filly: fairly useful on good going or firmer at 2 yrs: tailed off on dead ground on return. *M. R. Channon* **–**

BRIDGE 2 b.f. (Apr 29) Batshoof 122 – The Strid (IRE) 53 (Persian Bold 123) [1997 8.2s 8m Nov 1] 11,000Y: second foal: sister to fair 1996 2-y-o winner around 7f Stride: dam ran once at 2 yrs: showed ability in maiden at Nottingham in October, but well beaten in Newmarket seller next time. *D. Morley* **58**

BRIDIE'S PRIDE 6 b.g. Alleging (USA) 120 – Miss Monte Carlo 75 (Reform 132) [1996 NR 1997 a16.2g 17.2d³ 16g⁵ 16.2s⁶ 18s² 18d* 16.1g Oct 7] sparely-made gelding: modest handicapper: won maiden event at Chepstow in July, making most: off course 3 months before well beaten only subsequent start: stays 2¼m: raced mostly on good ground or softer: front runner: genuine. *G. A. Ham* **57**

BRIDLINGTON BAY 4 b.g. Roscoe Blake 120 – City Sound 63 (On Your Mark 125) [1996 –: a8g a8g 11.1d 1997 8m Mar 31] of no account. *B. Ellison* **–**

BRIERY MEC 2 b.c. (Apr 24) Navy's Victory (USA) 129 – Briery Fille 81 (Sayyaf 121) [1997 6d a7g Nov 25] tall colt: looks weak: second reported foal: dam 5f (at 2 yrs) to 1¼m winner: little promise in maidens. *H. J. Collingridge* **–**

BRIGAND (IRE) 3 b.g. Common Grounds 118 – Strike It Rich (FR) (Rheingold 137) [1996 NR 1997 7.9s² 8d² 8f* Sep 29] IR 34,000Y: angular gelding: shows plenty of knee action: eighth foal: half-brother to 4 winners, including useful 1m to 1½m winner Lady Bentley (by Bellypha): dam, Irish 1¼m winner, half-sister to smart stayer Yawa: shaped well in maidens at York and Newbury before comfortably landing odds in 4-runner similar event at Bath: will stay beyond 1m: sold approx. £26,000 in Dubai in November: should improve. *D. R. Loder* **89 p**

Prix Saint-Alary, Longchamp—Brilliance is being eased
as Fleeting Glimpse (near side) and Gazelle Royale battle it out for second

BRIGGS TURN 3 b.g. Rudimentary (USA) 118 – Turnabout (Tyrnavos 129) – [1996 –: 7d 1997 10g 11.5m Jul 22] big gelding: well beaten in maidens. *W. Jarvis*

BRIGHSTONE 4 ch.c. Cadeaux Genereux 131 – High Fountain 102 (High Line 70 125) [1996 –: 10g 8d 7g⁶ 1997 10d 10.2m* 10.1d⁵ 11.6m* 8.9s* 9d 8.2s* 10.3g 10d² Nov 3] sturdy colt: has a quick action: has been tubed: fair performer at best these days: won claimer at Bath (claimed out of D. Elsworth's stable £10,000), 11.6f seller (unimpressive) at Windsor and claimers at York and Nottingham between June and October: best efforts up to 1¼m: acts on firm and soft going: front runner. *M. C. Pipe*

BRIGHT DESERT 4 b.g. Green Desert (USA) 127 – Smarten Up 119 (Sharpen Up 127) [1996 –: 8.5m 10d 1997 12.4m 10.1f 7g a6g Nov 14] strong gelding: no form: left R. McKellar after reappearance. *Martyn Wane*

BRIGHTER BYFAAH (IRE) 4 ch.g. Kefaah (USA) 124 – Bright Landing 78 51 (Sun Prince 128) [1996 47: 11.1g⁶ 12m 14.1m⁶ 14.1m* a16g 1997 14.1m 14.1m 17.2f* Jul 23] well-made gelding: modest handicapper: best effort when narrowly winning at Bath in July: suited by good test of stamina: acts on firm ground and equitrack: blinkered (took fierce hold) once at 3 yrs. *N. A. Graham*

BRIGHT FOUNTAIN (IRE) 3 ch.f. Cadeaux Genereux 131 – High Fountain 47 102 (High Line 125) [1996 NR 1997 10.2d⁶ 9s⁶ 8.1g⁴ 10m³ Sep 22] small, sparely-made filly: second foal: sister to 4-y-o Brighstone: dam 1¼m and 16.5f winner out of once-raced half-sister to Royal Palace: poor maiden: in frame in sellers: seems one paced. *H. Candy*

BRIGHT GOLD 3 ch.g. Clantime 101 – Miss Brightside 41 (Crofthall 110) – [1996 53: 6m 5m⁶ 6d 1997 5m 8g 6g 5m Aug 16] sturdy gelding: modest maiden: well beaten in 1997, including in blinkers. *A. Smith*

BRIGHT HERITAGE (IRE) 4 b.g. Ela-Mana-Mou 132 – Mother of The Wind 89 82 (Tumble Wind (USA)) [1996 NR 1997 10g⁴ 10g⁵ 8.1m² 8m* 8.3m⁵ Aug 23] strong, lengthy gelding: fairly useful performer: hacked up when long odds on in very weak Pontefract maiden in July: likely to prove best short of 1¼m: acts on good to firm and heavy ground: often a front runner: sold 12,000 gns in October and sent to Switzerland. *D. R. Loder*

BRIGHT PARAGON (IRE) 8 b. or br.g. Treasure Kay 114 – Shining Bright 45 (USA) (Bold Bidder) [1996 –: 5g a5g⁶ 1997 a6g a6g a6g⁵ a8g 5.3f⁴ 5.1m⁶ 5m* 5m⁵ a– 6m⁴ 5g 5.1m² 5m 5.3m² 5g³ 5.3g⁵ 6f⁵ 5m Sep 24] workmanlike gelding: poor handicapper: won seller at Lingfield in May: effective at 5f/6f: acts on any turf going, no recent form on the all-weather: tried visored. *K. T. Ivory*

BRIGHT SAPPHIRE 11 b.g. Mummy's Pet 125 – Bright Era 79 (Artaius (USA) – 129) [1996 NR 1997 a16g Jun 14] of little account on flat. *P. Butler*

BRIGHT WATER 4 b.c. Caerleon (USA) 132 – Shining Water 111 (Kalaglow 110 132) [1996 110: 11d⁴ 10m* 10g 1997 10.3m* 12m² 12m³ Aug 15] well-made colt:

152

Ecurie Skymarc Farm's "Brilliance"

smart performer: won minor event at Chester in July by 2 lengths from Maralinga despite seeming ill-at-ease on track: seemed to run well in listed rated stakes at Goodwood (3½ lengths second to Bahamian Sunshine) and 3-runner minor event at Newbury after: stays 1½m: acts on firm ground, well held on dead: reportedly choked on 3-y-o reappearance, and has had tongue tied: flashes tail under pressure: stays in training. *H. R. A. Cecil*

BRILLIANCE (FR) 3 b.f. Priolo (USA) 127 – Briesta (USA) (Cresta Rider (USA) 124) [1996 7g 7.5d² 1997 10.5d* 10.5g* 10d* 10.5d³ 12m³ 12m³ 10m⁴ Oct 19] third foal: half-sister to French winners by Roi Danzig (11f) and Zalazl (up to 9f, and over hurdles): dam, placed, half-sister to smart sprinter/miler Dictator's Song: smart performer: won minor event and slowly-run Prix Penelope (beat Darashandeh by a neck) at Saint-Cloud and Prix Saint-Alary (by 4 lengths from Fleeting Glimpse) at Longchamp in the spring: in frame in Prix de Diane (3½ lengths behind Vereva) at Chantilly, Irish Oaks (3 lengths behind Ebadiyla) at the Curragh, Prix Vermeille (beaten length by Queen Maud) at Longchamp and E P Taylor Stakes (won by Kool Kat Katie) at Woodbine afterwards: stays 1½m: acts on good to firm and dead ground: genuine and most consistent. *P. Bary, France*   117

BRILLIANT RED 4 b.g. Royal Academy (USA) 130 – Red Comes Up (USA) (Blushing Groom (FR) 131) [1996 94: 7.3f⁶ 8m⁵ 10m 1997 a10g² 8d³ 7.6m* 8m⁶ 8d⁴ 7g 8m⁶ 8m³ a7g⁴ Dec 6] tall, lengthy gelding: has a long stride: useful performer on turf, fair on the all-weather: won minor event at Lingfield in July: also good third in handicaps at Goodwood in June and Newmarket in November: stays easy 1¼m: acts on good to firm and dead ground: front runner/races prominently. *P. R. Hedger*   97 a81

BRIMMING 2 ch.c. (Feb 6) Generous (IRE) 139 – Rainbow Lake 113 (Rainbow Quest (USA) 134) [1997 7f² 8s³ Oct 14] close-coupled, useful-looking colt: first foal: dam won Lancashire Oaks: fair form in maidens at Yarmouth (odds on) and   83 p

153

Leicester, making most when 5½ lengths third of 17 to Mantusis: will be well suited by 1½m+: capable of better. *H. R. A. Cecil*

BRIMSTONE (IRE) 2 ch.c. (Feb 16) Ballad Rock 122 – Blazing Glory (IRE) 83 p (Glow (USA)) [1997 6d 5d⁶ 5m* 5.7m² Aug 12] 16,500Y: tall colt: second foal: half-brother to 3-y-o Prince Dome: dam Irish 5f winner, including at 2 yrs: progressive form: won maiden comfortably at Sandown in July: possibly unlucky when second in nursery at Bath, going well in lead until stumbling halfway then staying on again: probably a sprinter: presumably had a set-back, but should make a useful handicapper if all is well. *D. R. C. Elsworth*

BRIN-LODGE (IRE) 4 b.f. Doubletour (USA) – Nordico's Dream (Nordico – (USA)) [1996 –: a7g 8g a6g 5m a5g 5m 1997 5m³ 6d 5g a5g⁶ 5m Jul 19] leggy filly: little worthwhile form: tried blinkered. *K. S. Bridgwater*

BRISKA (IRE) 3 b.f. River Falls 113 – Calash (Indian King (USA) 128) [1996 44 69: 6m⁵ 6g³ 7f* 7m⁶ 7m 1997 7g 6.9g 8m 8d⁴ a10g Nov 13] lengthy filly: fair winner at 2 yrs, disappointing in 1997: stays 7f: acts on firm going. *R. Akehurst*

BRISTOL CHANNEL 2 b.f. (Feb 20) Generous (IRE) 139 – Shining Water 111 94 p (Kalaglow 132) [1997 8m* 7.3g⁴ Oct 25] sturdy filly: unimpressive mover: seventh foal: closely related to 3-y-o River Usk, 4-y-o Bright Water and Grand Criterium and Dante winner Tenby (all by Caerleon) and half-sister to 2 winners: dam, won Solario Stakes and stayed well as 3-y-o: won maiden at Leicester in September by ½ length from Rambling Rose: about 5 lengths fourth of 13 to Ffestiniog in listed race at Newbury following month: likely to need at least 1¼m at 3 yrs: should still do better. *B. W. Hills*

BRISTOL GOLD 4 b.g. Golden Heights 82 – The Bristol Flyer (True Song 95) – [1996 NR 1997 13.8m May 30] first foal: dam winning pointer: tailed off in seller only flat outing. *P. S. Felgate*

BRITANNIA MILLS 6 gr.m. Nordico (USA) – May Fox 67 (Healaugh Fox) – [1996 NR 1997 a11g a8g Jan 17] no longer of any account on flat. *M. C. Chapman*

BROADGATE FLYER (IRE) 3 b.g. Silver Kite (USA) 111 – Fabulous Pet 54 (Somethingfabulous (USA)) [1996 60, a?: 6m⁶ 7m⁵ 6g 7g³ a6s⁴ 1997 a7g² a7g² a6g a7g⁴ 6f⁶ 9.2s⁴ 7.5s⁵ 11g⁶ Jun 20] modest maiden: below form after reappearance: should stay beyond 7f: acts on good to firm ground and equitrack: blinkered (ran poorly) fourth start: joined D. Lamb, and won over hurdles in October. *Mrs L. Stubbs*

BROAD RIVER (USA) 3 b.c. Broad Brush (USA) – Monture Creek (USA) 78 (Stop The Music (USA)) [1996 –p: 6g 1997 7g⁵ 7f* 7d⁶ 6g 8g Jul 8] angular colt: has a round action: fair performer: landed odds in maiden at Redcar in May: harshly treated in handicaps afterwards: should stay 1m: acts on firm ground: sold and sent to Macau. *E. A. L. Dunlop*

BROADSTAIRS BEAUTY (IRE) 7 ch.g. Dominion Royale 112 – Holy Water 78 (Monseigneur (USA) 127) [1996 73, a–: 5s⁵ 5g 5g 1997 a6g a6g² a5g⁴ a6g³ a5g⁶ 5m² a83 5g³ 5g² 5d⁵ a6f 5d⁶ a5g² 5m³ 6d⁶ 6g² 5d a5g³ Dec 18] workmanlike gelding: has a quick action: fairly useful handicapper: placed 9 times in 1997: has won at 7f, better form at shorter: acts on good to firm and heavy ground and on fibresand: usually blinkered/visored: bandaged: suitable mount for claimer: tough, consistent and game. *D. Shaw*

BROADWAY MELODY 3 b.f. Beveled (USA) – Broadway Stomp (USA) 58 63 (Broadway Forli (USA)) [1996 NR 1997 7.5d⁵ a6g* 6m⁴ 5g 6g a5g⁵ Aug 8] fourth reported foal: dam poor maiden: modest form at best: won maiden at Wolverhampton in July: probably a sprinter. *A. P. Jarvis*

BROCTUNE GOLD 6 b.g. Superpower 113 – Golden Sunlight (Ile de Bourbon 73 (USA) 133) [1996 73: 7d² 7g* 7m 7.1f* 7s⁵ 8.1m* 10m 8.5f* 8m⁵ 8m³ 8.1s² 1997 6.9g² 6.9d⁵ 7.1d² 8f 7.1g* 8d³ 7.1g* a8g⁵ 8.5d² 7g Aug 21] leggy, workmanlike gelding: easy mover: fair performer: made all in Musselburgh claimers in June and July, fourth course success in latter: claimed out of Mrs M. Reveley's yard after ninth start: effective at 7f to 8.5f: acts on firm and soft ground, below form on the all-weather: sometimes has tongue tied: goes well forcing pace. *B. W. Hills*

BROCTUNE LINE   3 ch.g. Safawan 118 – Ra Ra (Lord Gayle (USA) 124) [1996   47
43: 5.9f 7m⁵ 7d 7f 6s⁶ 8f a7g⁴ 1997 a8g* a9.4g⁵ 12g⁴ a11g* a12g 8.3g 10.1g³ Oct 22]   a59
close-coupled gelding: modest handicapper on the all-weather, poor on turf: won at
Southwell in January and April: should stay 1½m: acts on fibresand, best turf form
on good ground or firmer. *Mrs M. Reveley*

BRODESSA   11 gr.g. Scallywag 127 – Jeanne du Barry 74 (Dubassoff (USA))   62
[1996 62: 16m² 16m* 14.1m² 16.2f* 1997 12m 17.1m 13s² 14.1m⁶ 16d* 16d³
14.1m² 16.2d² a14.8g* a14g Dec 8] big gelding: modest performer: won claimers at
Nottingham in June and Wolverhampton in November: needs further than 1½m, and
stays 2m: acts on firm and soft ground and on fibresand: suitable mount for amateur.
Mrs M. Reveley

BRONHALLOW   4 b.g. Belmez (USA) 131 – Grey Twig 68 (Godswalk (USA)   39
130) [1996 –: 10g 8g 10d 14m 11.6g 10m 1997 a12g a8g 10d⁴ 12s² 12.1m 10g 14m
14g Sep 27] good-bodied gelding: poor maiden handicapper: needs good test at 1¼m,
and stays 1½m: acts on soft going: visored (best efforts) third and fourth starts,
blinkered next 3. *Mrs Barbara Waring*

BRONZE MAQUETTE (IRE)   7 b.m. Ahonoora 122 – Working Model 99 (Ile   –
de Bourbon (USA) 133) [1996 39: 11.9f 11.7g³ 10m⁵ 10m 12g⁴ 11.5f 12m⁵ 9.7g⁶
1997 11.7m⁵ 12.1s⁴ 11.9f May 23] long-backed mare: poor handicapper: no form in
1997. *R. Simpson*

BRONZINO   2 ch.g. (May 2) Midyan (USA) 124 – Indubitable 87 (Sharpo 132)   64
[1997 6g 7.6d⁶ 7m 8m 8m⁵ Nov 4] third foal: half-brother to 3-y-o Cugina: dam
stayed 1¾m: modest form, including in nurseries: should stay at least 1¼m: below
form on dead going: may do better at 3 yrs. *G. B. Balding*

BROOKHOUSE LADY (IRE)   2 b.f. (Mar 17) Polish Patriot (USA) 128 –   60 ?
Honagh Lee (Main Reef 126) [1997 5g⁴ 6m 5m 5m 6m 8m⁴ 6m 7s⁶ Nov 8] 4,800Y:
leggy, angular filly: closely related to a winner in Italy by Roi Danzig and half-sister
to 3-y-o First Chance and 2 other winners: dam never ran: modest maiden: stays 1m:
good effort only outing on soft ground. *R. Hollinshead*

BROOKSEES DREAM   3 ch.f. Glacial Storm (USA) 127 – Good Holidays 60   –
(Good Times (ITY)) [1996 NR 1997 a8g Dec 10] second foal: dam stayed 7f:
hampered and fell soon after start, only outing. *B. Palling*

BROOKSIE   2 b.g. (Apr 20) Efisio 120 – Elkie Brooks 82 (Relkino 131) [1997 7d   –
7g 6d Nov 7] 18,000Y: strong, sturdy gelding: brother to 3 winners, notably smart
sprinter Pip's Pride and fairly useful 7f/1m performer Sunday's Hill, and half-brother
to a 2-y-o 6f seller winner by Another Realm: dam, second over 6f at 2 yrs, didn't
train on: backward, down field in late-season maidens at Leicester and Doncaster.
J. W. Hills

BROTHER ROY   4 b.g. Prince Sabo 123 – Classic Heights (Shirley Heights 130)   –
[1996 –: 10m⁵ 8m⁵ 8.2g 9g 12v 1997 a12g a10g Jan 16] little worthwhile form.
T. G. Mills

BROUGHTONS ERROR   3 ch.g. Most Welcome 131 – Eloquent Charm (USA)   53
(Private Account (USA)) [1996 67: 5g⁵ 7g 6g⁴ 6d 6m 7g* a8g⁴ 1997 7g⁶ 8.3g 8.1g
Jun 14] workmanlike gelding: fair performer at 2 yrs: modest at best in 1997: should
stay at least 1m: best turf form on good ground, respectable effort on equitrack:
gelded after final start. *W. J. Musson*

BROUGHTONS FORMULA   7 b.g. Night Shift (USA) – Forward Rally 84   –
(Formidable (USA) 125) [1996 51, a56: a13g 12m 12m 11.6m 12d 16.4g 16m*   a64 d
15.8g³ 16.1f³ 13.6m⁶ 16g a16g⁶ a13g⁴ a16g² a13g² 1997 a13g⁶ a16g* a16g* a16g⁶
a14.8g a14.8g 14.1g a16s a16g³ a16g⁶ Dec 10] compact gelding: modest
handicapper: won at Lingfield in January and February: well beaten most starts
afterwards: stays 2m: acts on the all-weather, ran only once on turf in 1997: usually
blinkered nowadays: quirky, and often gets well behind. *W. J. Musson*

BROUGHTONS LURE (IRE)   3 ch.f. Archway (IRE) 115 – Vaal Salmon   –
(IRE) (Salmon Leap (USA) 131) [1996 NR 1997 8.3g 8m 8.3m Jul 28] IR 2,000Y:
first foal: dam unraced: well held in maidens. *W. J. Musson*

BROUGHTONS MILL 2 ch.c. (Mar 10) Ron's Victory (USA) 129 – Sandra's 66
Desire (Grey Desire 115) [1997 6m⁶ Jul 19] 1,500Y: first foal: dam unraced: 66/1,
under 9 lengths sixth of 12, slowly away, to Hayil in maiden at Newmarket.
W. J. Musson

BROUGHTON'S PRIDE (IRE) 6 b.m. Superpower 113 – French Quarter (Ile 55
de Bourbon (USA) 133) [1996 56: 9.9d⁶ 9.9m 8.2m* 8f 8f 8g 8.9g⁵ 7g³ 8.1s² 1997
a8g* a8g² a8g a8g² a7g* a8g⁴ a8g 8.3s² 8g⁴ 8g⁶ 8g³ a8.5g⁴ a11g Dec 8] rangy mare:
modest handicapper: won at Southwell in January (apprentices) and February
(amateurs): left J. L. Eyre before final start: effective at 7f to 1¼m: acts on good to
firm and soft ground and on fibresand: well beaten only time visored. *Ronald
Thompson*

BROUGHTONS RELISH 4 b.f. Nomination 125 – Mosso 81 (Ercolano (USA) –
118) [1996 –: a8g a8g 1997 a8g a12g a13g a16g⁶ Feb 13] of no account. *W. J. Musson*

BROUGHTONS TURMOIL 8 b.g. Petorius 117 – Rustic Stile (Rusticaro (FR) 81
124) [1996 81, a–: 8s 8m⁶ 7m³ 7m³ 7m⁴ 7g³ 7.6m³ 7g* 8m 8g 7m² 7g⁶ 7g⁵ 1997 7m² a71
8m 8m* 8d³ a8.5f³ 8g 8d 8m 8d⁵ 8m 7m² Oct 4] lengthy, workmanlike gelding: fairly
useful handicapper on turf, fair on all-weather: claimed from W. Musson on
reappearance: won 28-runner event at Ascot in April: good efforts in big fields last 3
starts: effective at 7f/1m: acts on firm and dead ground and all-weather: usually held
up. *B. R. Millman*

BROWNING 2 b.g. (Mar 28) Warrshan (USA) 117 – Mossy Rose 78 (King of 61
Spain 121) [1997 6d 7g 7m⁴ a8g⁵ Dec 10] third foal: half-brother to 3-y-o Farley
Mount: dam stayed 1m: modest form at best in maidens and nursery: should stay
1¼m+. *Lord Huntingdon*

BRUME LA VOILE 4 b.g. Puissance 110 – Bali Lady 79 (Balidar 133) [1996 –
NR 1997 11.6m a12g 18d Jul 5] lightly raced and no form. *J. G. Smyth-Osbourne*

BRUMON (IRE) 6 b.g. Sadler's Wells (USA) 132 – Loveliest (USA) (Tibaldo) –
[1996 NR 1997 18m 13d Apr 10] workmanlike gelding: fair handicapper at 4 yrs:
winning hurdler: well beaten on return to flat. *D. Moffatt*

BRUTAL FANTASY (IRE) 3 b.g. Distinctly North (USA) 115 – Flash Donna 87
(USA) 70 (Well Decorated (USA)) [1996 64: 5g* 5f² 6g² 6g³ 6m 5g 1997 a6g* a6g⁵
a5g* 5m* 5g* 5d 6d 6g³ 5.1m⁶ 5m² 6m Aug 16] good-quartered gelding: fairly
useful handicapper: successful at Southwell in January, Wolverhampton in February,
Doncaster in March and Catterick in April: effective at 5f/6f: acts on fibresand and
firm ground, seemingly not at best on dead: races prominently: has run well for
apprentice: game and genuine. *J. L. Eyre*

BRUZ 6 b.g. Risk Me (FR) 127 – My Croft 64 (Crofter (USA) 124) [1996 29: 13m⁴ 28
13g⁶ 1997 16s⁵ 11.1s⁶ 12m 10.9d² 17.2m 11.1d 15.8m Sep 20] lengthy gelding: poor
handicapper: stays 11f: acts on soft ground: tried visored, no improvement. *L. Lungo*

BRYNKIR 3 b.g. Batshoof 122 – Felinwen (White Mill 76) [1996 61: 8d⁶ 8.1s 8g –
1997 8.2d 8m a12g⁴ 12m Oct 6] sturdy gelding: modest form in 2-y-o maidens, none
in 1997. *D. J. G. Murray Smith*

BRYONY BRIND (IRE) 2 ch.f. (Feb 9) Kris 135 – Bayadere (USA) 61 (Green – p
Dancer (USA) 132) [1997 7m⁶ Oct 22] second foal: dam staying maiden out of
half-sister to smart French middle-distance winner Anitra's Dance: 33/1, never
dangerous when well-beaten sixth of 13 in maiden at Yarmouth: should do better
over further. *J. R. Fanshawe*

BUBBLE WINGS (FR) 5 b.m. In The Wings 128 – Bubble Prospector (USA) 80
(Miswaki (USA) 124) [1996 77: a8.5g⁵ 7f² 8g* 8.2m⁵ 8g* 8f³ 8.1f³ 10m² 10.1m²
1997 a10g⁶ 10m⁵ 9m⁴ 10m 10.2g² 10m* 9m 10g⁴ 12s⁶ Nov 8] workmanlike mare:
unimpressive mover: fairly useful performer: won minor event at Pontefract in
September: ran well in competitive handicaps at Newmarket (Cambridgeshire) and
Newbury (best of those coming from off steady pace) next 2 starts: should stay
beyond 1¼m: acts on equitrack, raced mainly on good going or firmer on turf: has an
awkward head carriage. *S. P. C. Woods*

BUBBLY 3 b.c. Rudimentary (USA) 118 – Champagne Season (USA) 54 (Vaguely 75
Noble 140) [1996 74p: 7m⁵ 1997 8m⁴ 6.9m* 9g 7d 10g⁴ 8.1m 7f² 6d Oct 21]

good-bodied colt: fair performer: won maiden at Folkestone in April: ran well after only when in frame: barely stays 1¼m: acts on firm going: usually races prominently. *J. L. Dunlop*

BUDDY MARVEL (IRE) 3 b.c. Law Society (USA) 130 – Rosa Van Fleet 106 (Sallust 134) [1996 8d⁶ 8g³ 9s* 9d² 1997 12g* 10d⁵ 14g⁶ 12d* 14g³ 14s⁴ 12d⁵ 12g Oct 25] IR 12,000Y: good-topped colt: third reported foal: half-brother to 2 winners, notably fairly useful Rossmore Girl (up to 11f, by Scenic): dam Irish maiden half-sister to To-Agori-Mou: useful performer: won minor event at Gowran Park in May and handicap at Galway in August: stiff task in St Simon Stakes at Newbury final start: stays 1¾m: yet to race on going firmer than good, and acts on soft: promising juvenile hurdler. *John J. McLoughlin, Ireland*

BUDDY'S FRIEND (IRE) 9 ch.h. Jester 119 – Hasta (Skymaster 126) [1996 –: – 8d a8g 10m 8m 8m⁶ 8m⁶ 1997 a8g a8g a10g Feb 4] formerly fair winner around 1m, very much on the downgrade. *R. J. R. Williams*

BUENA VISTA 3 b.f. Be My Chief (USA) 122 – Florentynna Bay 61 (Aragon – 118) [1996 NR 1997 18,500Y: fifth foal: half-sister to 3 winners, one of them 4-y-o Albert The Bear: dam 2-y-o 5f winner: always rear in maiden at Southwell. *C. W. Thornton*

BUFFALO RIVER 7 b.g. Robellino (USA) 127 – Strapless 84 (Bustino 136) – [1996 NR 1997 10m Apr 11] of little account. *K. A. Morgan*

BULLFINCH 4 ch.g. Anshan 119 – Lambay 88 (Lorenzaccio 130) [1996 90: 8g – 8.1g⁵ 7.9f 8.1d 8f 1997 10m⁶ Jun 11] leggy gelding: fairly useful for P. Walwyn in 1995 (won at 7f) and 1996: well beaten only 4-y-o start. *R. T. Phillips*

BULLION 2 b.f. (Apr 15) Sabrehill (USA) 120 – High And Bright 95 (Shirley 85 p Heights 130) [1997 7g⁵ 8.1d* 7.3d³ Sep 19] unfurnished filly: fifth foal: dam, twice-raced 1¼ mile winner, closely related to Main Reef: won maiden at Haydock in September by 3½ lengths from Eco Friendly: good third of 17 to Sunley Seeker in nursery at Newbury, staying on: will be very well suited by 1¼m+: free to post at Newbury: useful handicapper in making. *B. W. Hills*

BULSARA 5 b.g. Dowsing (USA) 124 – Taiga 69 (Northfields (USA)) [1996 65: 59 8m⁶ 8.1f⁴ 8f³ 10f* 10.1m* 10.1f⁴ 9g 9.2g⁵ 9m 1997 8g⁵ 9m 9.9m 8f⁴ 8m 8m 10.1g⁶ Jul 26] strong gelding: modest handicapper: stayed 1¼m: acted on firm and dead ground: visored (ran well) once: dead. *C. W. Fairhurst*

BUNNIES OWN 2 b.f. (Apr 17) Flockton's Own 98 – Walsham Witch 61 (Music 56 Maestro 119) [1997 a8g³ a8.5g⁴ Dec 13] first reported foal: dam 2-y-o 6f winner who probably stayed 2m: third in seller at Southwell and fourth in maiden at Wolverhampton (better effort) late in year. *J. L. Harris*

BURDEN OF PROOF (IRE) 5 b.h. Fairy King (USA) – Belle Passe (Be My 118 Guest (USA) 126) [1996 7s² 6d 7g² 8m⁵ 7g³ 7g⁴ 6s² 7d* 7d⁶ 1997 8d* 6d* 6g 8m² 7m⁵ 6s* Oct 18] tall horse: smart performer: won listed race at Leopardstown and

Weatherbys Ireland Greenlands Stakes, the Curragh—
Burden of Proof beats the blinkered runners Catch The Blues and Lucayan Prince

Weatherbys Ireland Greenlands Stakes at the Curragh (beat Catch The Blues ½ length) in May: well beaten in Cork And Orrery Stakes at Royal Ascot: seemingly easily best effort afterwards to win listed race at the Curragh in October by neck from Alarme Belle: effective at 6f to 1m: very best form on dead/soft going: usually held up. *Charles O'Brien, Ireland*

BURLESQUE 3 b.g. Old Vic 136 – Late Matinee 84 (Red Sunset 120) [1996 60+: – 7d⁶ 8g 1997 8m 10.3d 8d 11.1d Aug 13] leggy gelding: well beaten since debut: tried blinkered. *J. D. Bethell*

BURNDEN DAYS (IRE) 2 ch.g. (Apr 28) Fayruz 116 – Monaco Lady 83   51
(Manado 130) [1997 5m 6d a6g a5g⁴ Dec 22] 10,000 2-y-o: strong gelding: half-brother to several winners, including 9f/1¼m winner Twice The Groom (by Digamist): dam placed over 1m: trained on debut by J. Hetherton: first form when fourth in maiden at Lingfield. *Miss J. F. Craze*

BURNING COST 7 br.m. Lochnager 132 – Sophie Avenue (Guillaume Tell – (USA) 121) [1996 –: a14g a14g a14.8g 1997 a11g⁵ 11.5d 12m 6g a7g⁵ 10g a12s Nov 28] no worthwhile form for long time. *R. E. Peacock*

BURNING FLAME 4 b.f. Robellino (USA) 127 – No Islands (Lomond (USA) – 128) [1996 42: 7d 7m 8g 9.7g 12m⁴ a16g 10m 11.9g 9g⁶ a10s 1997 a12g⁶ a11g 10m⁶ 10g 8f Jun 5] poor maiden handicapper: well beaten in 1997. *R. M. Flower*

BURNING LOVE 2 b.f. (Apr 29) Forzando 122 – Latest Flame (IRE) 66 (Last   46
Tycoon 131) [1997 5.2g 6s 6f Jun 10] 2,000Y: close-coupled filly: first foal: dam 2-y-o 7.5f winner who stayed 1¼m: well held in maidens at Newbury and Salisbury. *J. S. Moore*

BURNING TRUTH (USA) 3 ch.c. Known Fact (USA) 135 – Galega (Sure   80
Blade (USA) 130) [1996 57p: 7d 1997 8m³ 8m³ 8.1d² 9m² 8.2m³ 8.2g² Sep 23] angular colt: fluent mover: fairly useful maiden: stays 9f: yet to race on extremes of going: consistent: sold 18,000 gns in October. *R. Charlton*

BURNING (USA) 5 b.g. Bering 136 – Larnica (USA) (Alydar (USA)) [1996 –:   81
10g 12m 12m 10m 12m 9d⁵ 1997 11.5g² 14m 11.9m⁵ 11.5d Aug 28] big, rangy gelding: fairly useful handicapper: best effort in 1997 on reappearance: seems suited by around 1½m: acts on firm ground, seemingly not on softer than good: well held in blinkers: held up: sold 5,000 gns in October. *W. J. Haggas*

BURNLEY BELLE 5 b.m. Dominion 123 – Ulla Laing 107 (Mummy's Pet 125) – [1996 NR 1997 8d 8.2g Sep 23] sister to useful sprinter Domulla and closely related to 1½m winner (stayed 2m) Belafonte (by Derrylin): dam 2-y-o 5f winner who stayed at least 7f: well beaten in maidens. *M. R. Channon*

BURN OUT 5 b.g. Last Tycoon 131 – Obertura (USA) 100 (Roberto (USA) 131)   68
[1996 NR 1997 12m⁶ 11.9f⁵ 10m 20m 16.1g Jul 9] tall, gelding: sixth foal: half-brother to 3 winners at 1½m+, including 6-y-o Opera Buff: dam useful stayer: useful NH Flat race winner in 1996: fair form on flat, not beaten far in Ascot Stakes fourth start: out-and-out stayer: visored (edgy and well beaten) final outing. *J. Pearce*

BURNT OFFERING 4 b.c. Old Vic 136 – Burnt Amber (Balidar 133) [1996 79:   71
a12g³ a10g* 10.3d 12.3m³ 12g⁴ 12d⁴ 10.1m⁵ 10g 1997 10.1m 10.3d⁶ 14m² 20m 16.1s 16.2m 12.5m 12g Sep 20] close-coupled colt: fair handicapper: trained by C. Brittain before final start: stays 2m (ridden too forcefully over 2½m): acts on good to firm and soft ground and on equitrack: thrice blinkered. *S. Wattel, France*

BURNT YATES (IRE) 2 b.g. (Feb 19) Distinctly North (USA) 115 – Ibda   74
(Mtoto 134) [1997 5m 5m⁵ 6g³ 5.9m⁵ 5d⁵ 6m⁴ 6g 6d 5d⁴ 7g* 8s 7g⁶ 8m Nov 4] 26,000Y: smallish gelding: first foal: dam, Irish 2-y-o 7f winner, from family of Danzig: fair performer: won nursery at Chester in September: will probably prove best over 7f/1m: blinkered once. *M. W. Easterby*

BURSUL LADY 4 b.f. Be My Chief (USA) 122 – Neverdown 50 (Never So Bold – 135) [1996 –: 10m 11.6d⁶ a16g 1997 11.5m Sep 9] of no account. *Miss B. Sanders*

BURUNDI (IRE) 3 b.g. Danehill (USA) 126 – Sofala 103 (Home Guard (USA)   70
129) [1996 76: 8m 7f² 1997 7m 12.3s⁶ 12d 10.5g 10d a11g* Nov 17] tall gelding: fair performer on his day: trained first 4 starts by P. Chapple-Hyam: landed gamble in seller at Southwell in November by 12 lengths (performance referred to Jockey

Club): stays 11f: acts on fibresand and firm ground: well beaten all 3 starts on going softer than good: tried visored. *A. W. Carroll*

BUSHWHACKER   3 b.g. Green Desert (USA) 127 – Missed Again 84 (High   63
Top 131) [1996 NR 1997 7.1d⁴ Jul 3] good-topped gelding: second foal: half-brother to 4-y-o Failed To Hit: dam 1¼m winner: staying-on fourth of 14 in maiden at Haydock only start. *C. R. Egerton*

BUSTINGOUTALLOVER (USA)   3 ch.f. Trempolino (USA) 135 – June   –
Bride (USA) (Riverman (USA) 131) [1996 NR 1997 a6g a7g 8g Jun 21] 4,000Y: half-sister to fair 1½m winner Kaher (by Our Native) and several winners in France/USA: dam 1½m winner in USA: tailed off in maidens. *C. W. Thornton*

BUSTOPHER JONES   3 b.g. Robellino (USA) 127 – Catkin (USA) (Sir Ivor   –
135) [1996 NR 1997 7.1d a9.4g⁵ 7d Oct 13] 30,000Y: big, strong gelding: third foal: brother to fair but ungenuine 1¼m winner Kilcoran Bay: dam, ran 3 times, from good American family: signs of just a little ability in maidens. *C. R. Egerton*

BUSY FLIGHT   4 b.c. Pharly (FR) 130 – Bustling Nelly 94 (Bustino 136) [1996   120
119p: 10g⁶ 12m 12.3d* 12f* 12m* 1997 12m² 12s³ 12g 12m* 12m* 12f 12g³ Oct 25] quite attractive colt: has a free, round action: very smart performer: won minor event at Newbury in August and listed race (by 3 lengths from Memorise) at Doncaster in September: creditable tenth in Arc de Triomphe at Longchamp on penultimate start and at least respectable efforts when placed in Jockey Club Stakes at Newmarket (beaten ¾ length by Time Allowed), Prix Jean de Chaudenay at Saint-Cloud and St Simon Stakes at Newbury: stays 1½m: has form on soft ground, very best efforts on firmer than good: free-running sort, and usually a front runner: genuine. *B. W. Hills*

BUTRINTO   3 ch.g. Anshan 119 – Bay Bay 101 (Bay Express 132) [1996 NR   77
1997 8g 6m³ 6m⁶ 6g⁶ 6g* 5g⁴ 5.7g Sep 8] tall gelding: good mover: fourth foal: half-brother to 5-y-o Great Bear (formerly fairly useful) and 1993 2-y-o 5f winner Baskerville (by Night Shift): dam 7.6f winner: fair performer: made all in Salisbury maiden in August: ran creditably in handicap next start: likely to prove best at 5f/6f: raced only on good/good to firm going: blinkered (below form) fourth start: sold 18,000 gns in October. *Major W. R. Hern*

BUZZ   2 b.c. (Mar 30) Anshan 119 – Ryewater Dream 72 (Touching Wood (USA)   80
127) [1997 6g⁴ 7.1d* 5d⁵ 8f 7d⁴ 8d Oct 17] 16,500Y: second foal: dam 11.7f winner:

O & K Troy Stakes, Doncaster—
Busy Flight is impressive in landing this event for the second consecutive year

fair form: won minor event at Musselburgh in June: well held in nurseries fourth and final starts: should stay at least 1m: acts on good to soft ground. *C. W. Thornton*

BUZZBY BABE 3 b.f. Presidium 124 – Aposse Ad Esse (Record Run 127) [1996 –: 6m a7g 1997 a10g a8g a8g⁶ a11g⁴ 11.6m 17.2g Jun 28] little worthwhile form. *A. G. Foster*

BUZZING (IRE) 2 ch.c. (Apr 14) Ballad Rock 122 – Buzzing Around (Prince Bee 128) [1997 6g Oct 24] IR 7,000F, IR 15,000Y: fifth foal: dam Irish 7f winner from family of Time Charter: 20/1, slowly away and green, in rear in 24-runner maiden at Newbury. *R. Hannon*

BUZZ THE AGENT 2 b.c. (Feb 28) Prince Sabo 123 – Chess Mistress (USA) 59 (Run The Gantlet (USA)) [1997 6m 7g⁶ 5m 7m Sep 20] 900Y: good-topped colt: third reported foal: dam 1½m winner in France at 4 yrs: little sign of ability. *M. W. Easterby*

BYHOOKORBYCROOK (IRE) 5 b.m. Cardinal Flower 101 – Frisky Matron (On Your Mark 125) [1996 NR 1997 14m Jul 12] half-sister to several winners, none better than fairly useful: dam half-sister to Night Nurse: tailed off in Lingfield maiden. *K. C. Comerford*

BY JAY (IRE) 3 b.f. Last Tycoon 131 – Tomona (Linacre 133) [1996 5f⁵ 7g 7m⁴ 52 d 7m⁵ 7g 8.5m 6m⁴ 7g 1997 9d⁴ 8f⁵ 12g 7f 7d 10d a6g Nov 17] workmanlike ex-Irish filly: closely related to useful 1990 2-y-o 7f winner Full of Pluck (by Try My Best) and half-sister to Irish 1¼m winner Hegemonic (by Godswalk): dam won at 1½m and over hurdles in Ireland: trained by A. Leahy until after third start, showing modest form on several occasions: no show in Britain. *B. J. Curley*

BYZANTIUM 3 b.c. Shirley Heights 130 – Dulceata (IRE) (Rousillon (USA) 81 133) [1996 NR 1997 8g* 7d⁶ 10m 10m Aug 15] 27,000Y: good-bodied colt: second foal: dam once-raced daughter of half-sister to Al Hareb: won maiden at Kempton in May: well beaten in minor event and 2 handicaps afterwards: bred to stay beyond 1m. *Lord Huntingdon*

C

CABARET (IRE) 4 b.f. Sadler's Wells (USA) 132 – Chamonis (USA) 101 – (Affirmed (USA)) [1996 103: 9g* 10m⁴ 11.9g 10.1m⁵ 8m 10.8s² 10v⁴ 1997 12m 10g Aug 23] big, rangy filly: has scope: useful at 3 yrs: tailed off in listed events at 4 yrs: should be suited by further than 11f: acts on good to firm and soft ground. *P. W. Chapple-Hyam*

CABCHARGE BLUE 5 b.m. Midyan (USA) 124 – Mashobra 75 (Vision 47 (USA)) [1996 57d: a12g⁴ a12g a8g* a7g a8g⁴ a8g⁴ a8.5g⁶ a7g 1997 8.3s 8.1m 8.2m a10g 8m³ 10m* 8.2d⁶ a9.4g Dec 6] angular mare: poor performer nowadays: won 20-runner selling handicap at Brighton in October: stays 1¼m: acts on fibresand and on good to firm and soft ground: tends to hang, and is a tricky ride. *T. J. Naughton*

CABCHARGE GLORY 3 ch.f. Executive Man 119 – Clipsall 57 (Petitioner – 83) [1996 NR 1997 7f⁴ 7m⁶ 8.3s 10f 14.1g Jul 30] fourth reported foal: dam 7f and 1m seller winner: of little account. *G. G. Margarson*

CADBURY CASTLE 3 b.f. Midyan (USA) 124 – Orange Hill 75 (High Top 43 131) [1996 56: 8g⁴ 8d 1997 8.2d 11.6s 14.1g⁵ 11.8m 15.4s³ 16m a14g Aug 15] small filly: has a round action: poor maiden: seems suited by 1¾m+: acts on soft going, ran poorly on good to firm and fibresand. *M. Blanshard*

CADDY'S FIRST 5 b.g. Petong 126 – Love Scene (Carwhite 127) [1996 –: 8.3d – 8.2d a7g⁶ a8g 1997 a8g⁴ Jan 6] little worthwhile form since 1995: sometimes blinkered/visored. *S. Mellor*

CADEAUX CHER 3 ch.g. Cadeaux Genereux 131 – Home Truth 98 (Known 88 Fact (USA) 135) [1996 78+: 5g 5.1m² 5f² 5m⁴ 1997 6m* 5d⁴ 6m⁶ 6d 5g 6m⁴ Nov 4] lengthy gelding: unimpressive mover: fairly useful performer: won maiden at

Doncaster in March: best effort when fourth of 25 in handicap at Redcar final start: stays 6f: twice hung left at 2 yrs: wears bandages. *B. W. Hills*

CADEAUX TRYST 5 b.h. Cadeaux Genereux 131 – Trystero (Shareef Dancer 109 (USA) 135) [1996 106: 8d⁵ 8d³ 8m² 8m⁶ 8m⁴ 8m* 8d⁴ 1997 8g 7m 7g³ 8m³ 7.6f* 7.3m Aug 15] robust horse: shows knee action: useful performer: third in handicaps at Newmarket and Royal Ascot (Royal Hunt Cup) prior to career-best effort to win rated stakes at Lingfield in July by 2 lengths from Tregaron: best at 7f/1m: acts on firm ground and dead, unraced on anything softer: usually bandaged: normally held up. *E. A. L. Dunlop*

CADFORD JEWEL 4 gr.g. Distant Relative 128 – Fast Car (FR) (Carwhite 127) – [1996 NR 1997 6f a6g May 8] fifth foal: half-brother to 5-y-o Squire Corrie: dam French 8.5f winner: well beaten in claimer and seller. *W. G. M. Turner*

CADILLAC JUKEBOX (USA) 2 b. or br.c. (Feb 7) Alleged (USA) 138 – – p Symphonic Music (USA) (Al Nasr (FR) 126) [1997 8.2d Oct 30] $90,000Y: third foal: dam unraced half-sister to US Grade 2 9f winner Gulls Cry, herself dam of St Leger fourth Nemain (by Alleged): 16/1 and green, behind in 13-runner maiden at Nottingham: likely to do better at 1½m+. *J. W. Hills*

CADMAX (IRE) 2 b.g. (May 12) Second Set (IRE) 127 – Stella Ann (Ahonoora – 122) [1997 8.2s Oct 15] IR 8,000Y: sixth foal: half-brother to 5-y-o Indrapura: dam best at around 7f in Ireland: 50/1, behind in maiden at Nottingham. *K. R. Burke*

CA'D'ORO 4 ch.g. Cadeaux Genereux 131 – Palace Street (USA) 103 (Secreto 69 (USA) 128) [1996 60: 5d 6m 7g⁵ 6g 8m* 8m⁶ 8g 7m⁴ 7m⁴ 7s³ 1997 8.3d 8d 8g* 8s* 8d 8m⁵ 8.1g⁴ 8.1g⁵ 8g 8d³ 8.2d* 8s² Nov 8] small gelding: fair handicapper: won at Newbury (apprentices) and Goodwood (idled) in June and Nottingham in October: good second of 23 in ladies race at Doncaster final start: needs good test at 1m, and well worth a try over 9f/1¼m: acts on good to firm and soft ground. *G. B. Balding*

CAERFILLY DANCER 3 ch.f. Caerleon (USA) 132 – Darnelle 83 (Shirley 83 Heights 130) [1996 89: 6m* 6m 7m⁴ 1997 7g 6g⁵ 5d Jun 21] small, sturdy filly: has a quick action: fairly useful performer: best effort at 3 yrs when seventh in valuable handicap at Ascot final start: stays 7f. *R. Akehurst*

CAERNARFON BAY (IRE) 2 ch.c. (May 1) Royal Academy (USA) 130 – 67 p Bay Shade (USA) 90 (Sharpen Up 127) [1997 6g⁴ Oct 24] IR 80,000Y: sixth foal: half-brother to useful 7f (at 2 yrs) and 11.4f (Cheshire Oaks) winner Abury (by Law Society) and a winner in Norway by Green Desert: dam 2-y-o 7f winner, later won listed 1m event in Italy: 12/1 and not fully wound up, under 7 lengths fourth of 24 to Mister Rambo in maiden at Newbury, prominent until over 1f out: should stay at least 1m: sure to do better. *P. F. I. Cole*

CAGE AUX FOLLES (IRE) 2 b.c. (May 14) Kenmare (FR) 125 – Ivory 71 Thread (USA) (Sir Ivor 135) [1997 7m 7.1m³ 7m⁶ 8g Aug 25] IR 45,000Y: good-topped colt: sixth reported foal: dam won at 1¾m in Ireland at 4 yrs: fair form in maidens at Sandown and Chester second and third starts: ran poorly final outing: should prove suited by at least 1¼m: had tongue tied last 3 starts. *J. W. Hills*

CAIRN DHU 3 ch.g. Presidium 124 – My Precious Daisy (Sharpo 132) [1996 53: 60 d 6m⁵ 5f⁵ 5g 6m 6d⁴ 1997 6.1m 6.1g* 6m 6m⁴ 5.9g⁴ 8g 8.2d a7g Dec 18] robust gelding: modest performer: made all against favoured stand rail in seller at Nottingham in April: trained by Mrs J. Ramsden until after next start: tailed off last 2 outings: stays 6f: best efforts on good going: blinkered and didn't impress with attitude on reappearance. *D. W. Barker*

CAITANO 3 b.c. Niniski (USA) 125 – Eversince (USA) (Foolish Pleasure 125 (USA)) [1996 7v* 9.5g² 8d² 1997 11g² 11v* 12g⁴ 12m* 12g⁵ 12m* 12m⁴ Nov 23]

Timing is everything. Caitano was first past the post in four pattern events in 1997, yet his name will not be recognised by many. Success in the Aral-Pokal and Italy's Gran Premio del Jockey Club e Coppa d'Oro did not make up for failure in the Deutsches Derby and the Grosser Preis von Baden, Germany's two most prestigious races. The filly Borgia won both of them, and subsequent placings in the Arc and the Breeders' Cup Turf have made her well known outside her home country. Caitano's fourth in the Japan Cup, by contrast, caused barely a ripple in the British Press—Pilsudski was the story that day. The fact that there is little between Caitano and Borgia on form is incidental. In 'the fame game' it is not so much how well you run, but the time and the place you do it that counts.

Caitano's two-year-old career was short. He won a seven-furlong maiden at Gelsenkirchen on his debut and was second twice at Cologne, beaten a head by Ungaro in a listed race over nine and a half furlongs, then a length and a quarter by champion juvenile Eden Rock in the leading German two-year-old race, the Preis des Winterfavoriten. Not surprisingly, Caitano began 1997 at middle distances, and he was first past the post in Group 2 events at Munich (a race he lost in the stewards room) and Cologne. That form saw him sent off favourite for the German Derby, but he could finish no better than fourth behind Borgia, beaten four and a half lengths. Two of his next three starts resulted in Group 1 wins, but defeats of the ultra-consistent Luso by a length and three quarters in both the Aral-Pokal at Gelsenkirchen in August and the Gran Premio del Jockey Club e Coppa d'Oro at Milan in October sandwiched another moderate display behind Borgia in the Grosser Preis von Baden, in which Luso finished second, beaten a length and a half. Caitano's subsequent win in Italy was worth more money than Borgia's in the Grosser Preis von Baden, but simply didn't carry the same kudos.

Headlines or not, Caitano's performance in the Japan Cup confirmed that he is a high-class colt. He finished fourth, best of the three-year-olds and just a length and three quarters behind Pilsudski, short of room as the winner went for a gap early in the straight, then staying on dourly to the line. Connections seem keen to target the Japan Cup again in 1998, reportedly having turned down an offer of one and a half million dollars for the colt before the 1997 renewal. How well Caitano will fare overall as a four-year-old is open to debate. Though he is among the leaders of his generation at a mile and a half, he is a long way behind Peintre Celebre, and on form is vulnerable even if the new crop of three-year-olds proves only average.

		Nijinsky	Northern Dancer
	Niniski (USA)	(b 1967)	Flaming Page
	(b 1976)	Virginia Hills	Tom Rolfe
Caitano		(b 1971)	Ridin' Easy
(b.c. 1994)		Foolish Pleasure	What A Pleasure
	Eversince (USA)	(b 1972)	Fool-Me-Not
	(b 1983)	Eternity	Luthier
		(ch 1977)	El Mina

Caitano was an excellent buy at 21,000 guineas at the 1995 Tattersalls October Yearling Sales. He is the fourth live foal out of listed-placed Eversince, a winner over a mile and then at five and a half furlongs in France in the mid-'eighties. Preceding him as winners were the one-time useful six- and seven-furlong performer Everset (by Green Desert), and Lady Lodger (by Be My Guest) whose wins include a mile and a quarter handicap at Yarmouth and a Grade 3 race over a mile in America. There is a good deal of stamina further back on the distaff side. Caitano's grandam Eternity was a listed winner over a mile and a half and her best foal, Artic Envoy, was second in the Italian Derby. Great grandam El Mina was third to Allez France in the 1973 Prix Vermeille. Caitano's sire Niniski was retired from stallion duties in 1995. He proved a strong influence for stamina, as expected from one who had won the Irish St Leger and Prix Royal-Oak. His was not an outstanding stud career, but he did produce seven other winners at the highest level in Petoski (rated 135), Minster Son (130), Kala Dancer (129), Lomitas (129), Hernando (127), Sapience (124), Louis Cyphre (122) and Assessor (121)—all of them colts.

Caitano cannot produce instant acceleration, but responds to pressure and keeps on well. He will stay a mile and three quarters, and probably two miles, if required. He acts on good to firm and heavy ground, and inasmuch as we believe he is essentially a stayer, testing conditions may see him at his most effective in top company.

Stablemates Borgia and Caitano are owned by different parties and there is every chance they will meet on the track again. Caitano's connections will be hoping that this time he'll produce his very best when the racing world is watching. *B. Schutz, Germany*

CALAMANDER (IRE)   3 b.f. Alzao (USA) 117 – Local Custom (IRE) (Be My Native (USA) 122) [1996 55: 5.7g 6.9g⁴ 5.1m⁶ 7f 1997 8.2d 7.3s³ 8f² 8.2g² 8.3m³ 7g 8g 8m Sep 22] smallish filly: fair maiden handicapper: ran poorly last 3 starts: stays 1m: acts on firm and dead ground, below form on soft. *W. R. Muir*   66

CALANDRELLA   4 b.f. Sizzling Melody 117 – Maravilla 73 (Mandrake Major 122) [1996 46: 8.3g 8.3m 7m 6m⁵ 6.1m 8d 1997 6.1g 7m 6s 6s 8.3m Jul 14] little worthwhile form. *G. B. Balding*   46

CALCHAS (IRE)   2 b.g. (Mar 3) Warning 136 – Nassma (IRE) 95 (Sadler's Wells (USA) 132) [1997 a6g* 7d* 6g 7.5m² 7g³ Jul 31] sturdy gelding: has had shins fired: first foal: dam 1¼m and 13.4f winner: useful form: won maiden at Wolverhampton and minor event at Epsom in June: ran well when placed in minor events behind Lend A Hand at Beverley and Haami at Doncaster: should stay 1m. *Sir Mark Prescott*   98

CALCHOU   3 gr.f. Barrys Gamble 102 – Ping Pong 65 (Petong 126) [1996 ?, a65: 5g a5g³ 5g⁵ a5g* 5g⁶ a5g 1997 a5g a5g⁴ a5g Feb 5] fair 5f winner at 2 yrs: tailed off in 1997: visored final start. *C. W. Fairhurst*   –

CALDER KING   6 ch.g. Rakaposhi King 119 – Name The Game 66 (Fair Season 120) [1996 68, a75: a11g² a11g² a8g² a12g³ 10.3d 11.1d* 12.1d⁴ 10m 11.1s* 8.3s 10g⁵ 12f⁴ 12g² 12.3m⁶ 10.4g³ 10.9m² 11.9d 10.4g 10g 10f⁴ 1997 a11g⁵ a11g* a11g* a12g² 9.2d³ Apr 2] stocky, lengthy gelding: fair performer: won 2 sellers at Southwell in January: subsequently left J. L. Eyre: stays 1½m: acts on firm and soft going, very best form on fibresand: usually visored/blinkered (latter in 1997). *Mrs M. Reveley*   63 a69

CALEDONIAN EXPRESS   2 b.f. (Apr 1) Northern Park (USA) 107 – New Edition 72 (Great Nephew 126) [1997 7m 7d⁶ 7d Oct 27] rangy filly: eighth foal: closely related to 3-y-o Night Express and half-sister to 7.5f winner Arabian King (by Sayf El Arab): dam, 2-y-o 5f winner, appeared to stay 7f: fair form in maidens at Kempton and Leicester first 2 starts: will be suited by at least 1m: has scope to do better. *J. L. Dunlop*   64 p

CALENDULA   4 b.f. Be My Guest (USA) 126 – Sesame 117 (Derrylin 115) [1996 62: 12m 10s⁵ 11.5m⁵ 10.5s 12g 1997 a12g a12g⁵ a12g* a13g² a12g* a14.8g³ a10g a10g² a12g⁶ 10g³ 11.8m⁴ 10.1s* 10m² 10s⁴ 10d* Oct 28] sturdy, lengthy filly: un-impressive mover: fair handicapper on turf, successful at Yarmouth (lady riders) in July and Leicester (best effort, led close home) in October: modest on all-weather, winning at Southwell in January and Wolverhampton in February: effective at 1¼m to 14.8f: acts on the all-weather and good to firm and soft going: joined G. Balding. *D. Morley*   75 a60

CALLALOO   4 b.g. Mtoto 134 – Catawba 98 (Mill Reef (USA) 141) [1996 –: 10m a9.4g 1997 a8g⁶ Feb 15] leggy gelding: very lightly raced and no show since 2 yrs. *R. Harris*   –

CALLIRAM   2 b.f. (Apr 5) Petardia 113 – Sheesha (USA) (Shadeed (USA) 135) [1997 5m⁴ 5d 6f³ 7m³ 6g⁴ 6m⁵ 5m³ 6g 6m⁵ 7g a8g Dec 8] unfurnished filly: first reported foal: dam once-raced close relative of 4-y-o Samraan: poor maiden: stays 7f: acts on firm ground. *M. Blanshard*   41

CALL ME VERA   2 ch.f. (May 9) Beveled (USA) – Cee Beat § (Bairn (USA) 126) [1997 5m 5.1g 5m 5m Sep 26] first foal: dam temperamental half-sister to useful winner at around 7f Sharpalto: no worthwhile form in maidens. *E. A. Wheeler*   –

CALLONESCY (IRE)   5 b.g. Royal Academy (USA) 130 – Take Your Mark (USA) (Round Table) [1996 –: a10g⁵ a13g⁴ a10g³ a16g a12g a10s 1997 a10g a12g a8g Jan 23] little worthwhile form at Lingfield since 3 yrs: tried blinkered. *D. C. O'Brien*   –

CALL TO ORDER 2 b.c. (Mar 15) Reprimand 122 – Gena Ivor (USA) (Sir Ivor 91
135) [1997 5m⁴ 6m² 5m³ 5m* 6g⁴ Oct 18] 16,500Y: second foal: half-brother to
4-y-o Ivor's Deed: dam won at up to 9f in USA: fairly useful form: landed odds in
maiden at Folkestone in September: showed deal of improvement when 3 lengths
fourth of 26 to Grazia in Two-Year-Old Trophy at Redcar: probably a sprinter: raced
only on good/good to firm going. *C. F. Wall*

CALYPSO GRANT (IRE) 3 b.f. Danehill (USA) 126 – Why So Silent (Mill 98
Reef (USA) 141) [1996 91p: 7f² 7g² 8g* 1997 8g* 7.3g 10.4g 10g 10m⁴ 7.9d⁶ 9d 12d
Oct 16] compact filly: useful performer on her day: won listed race (comfortably) at
Kempton in March: clearly best subsequent effort when fourth of 18 to Future Perfect
in £35,000 handicap at Goodwood in August: stays 1¼m: best form on good going or
firmer: bandaged near hind final start. *P. W. Harris*

CALYPSO LADY (IRE) 3 ch.f. Priolo (USA) 127 – Taking Steps 100 (Gay 72
Fandango (USA) 132) [1996 88: 6m* 7m³ 1997 10m⁵ 7.9g 8.3m 10.2s 8.1m⁴ 8g 10g
Oct 24] unfurnished filly: only fair form at best at 3 yrs: stays 1m: acts on good to
firm ground: sold 15,000 gns in October after final start. *R. Hannon*

CAMBRIDGE BALL (IRE) 3 b.f. Royal Academy (USA) 130 – Boat Race –
(USA) (Seattle Slew (USA)) [1996 64: 6m² 7g⁴ 6.1d² 5f⁵ 6g⁵ 1997 10.1m 10.1g⁶
a11g Sep 8] leggy filly: modest maiden: well beaten at 3 yrs: should stay 1m, not
certain to get much further: acts on firm ground and dead. *M. Johnston*

CAMBRIDGE BLUE (USA) 3 gr.g. Sheikh Albadou 128 – Fit And Ready 61
(USA) (Fit To Fight (USA)) [1996 NR 1997 6f⁴ 5m 6m 5.1f 8.3g a9.4g a8g Dec 18]
$45,000F: 38,000Y: useful-looking gelding: unimpressive mover: first foal: dam
won 7 times at up to 1m in USA: modest maiden: left G. Lewis after fifth start: stays
1m: acts on fibresand, raced only on good going or firmer on turf: blinkered fourth
start, visored (ran well) final one. *I. Semple*

CAMIONNEUR (IRE) 4 b.g. Cyrano de Bergerac 120 – Fact of Time (Known 59
Fact (USA) 135) [1996 53: 6g 7.5g⁴ 6m 7.5m 7.5f⁶ 5.9f⁴ 6g⁴ 6s⁴ 6m³ 5m² 6m* 5m³
6m⁴ 5g 6s 5.1m⁴ 5m 6f⁶ 6m⁴ 1997 5m⁴ 5.9g 5m⁶ 5d⁶ 5m² 6m 5m 5m* 5d Oct 8]
workmanlike gelding: modest handi-
capper: dead-heated for first with Grand Chapeau at Redcar in August: effective at 5f
and 6f: acts on any turf going: usually blinkered: pulls hard and tends to carry head
awkwardly: often slowly away and comes from behind: consistent. *T. D. Easterby*

CAMPAIGN 6 b.g. Sure Blade (USA) 130 – Just Cause (Law Society (USA) 130) –
[1996 NR 1997 13.9g 14.1d⁶ Nov 3] sturdy gelding: has markedly round action: very
lightly raced on flat since 3 yrs: well held in 1997: fairly useful staying hurdler.
M. D. Hammond

CAMPARI (IRE) 2 b.f. (Mar 4) Distinctly North (USA) 115 – Foolish Flight 70
(IRE) (Fools Holme (USA)) [1997 6.9s⁴ 7m³ 8.1d⁴ 8m³ 8g⁵ Oct 18] 9,500F:
sparely-made filly: first foal: dam lightly raced in Ireland: fair maiden: stays 1m: acts
on good to firm and dead going: has hung and carried head awkwardly. *M. A. Jarvis*

CAMPASPE 5 b.m. Dominion 123 – Lady River (FR) (Sir Gaylord) [1996 60, a–: 79
12m* 14.1g³ 14.1m 12m² 12g² 12.3m² a12g⁵ 12.1m³ 12m* 13.6m⁶ 1997 12s² a–
14.1m* 12.1m³ 12m² 12.3m* 12d³ 14g* 12f* 15.9g 14.6g⁴ Oct 24] leggy mare: fair
handicapper: had good season, winning at Redcar in May, Ripon and Musselburgh in
August and Beverley (third course-and-distance success) in September: stayed on
when good fourth final outing: effective at 1½m and should stay 2m: yet to race on
heavy ground, acts on any other turf going, no form on fibresand: seems suited by a
good gallop. *J. G. FitzGerald*

CAMP DAVID (GER) 7 b.h. Surumu (GER) – Capitolina (FR) (Empery (USA) 116
128) [1996 116: 16g* 16g* 15m* 16g* 20d⁴ 1997 16s³ 16g* 20g 16g² Sep 3] strong,
good-topped horse: smart performer: won Oleander-Rennen at Baden-Baden in May
for second year running by 1½ lengths and a neck from Sweetness Herself and Lord
Jim: below best in Gold Cup at Royal Ascot (held when badly hampered on home
turn) and listed race at Baden-Baden afterwards: stayed 2½m: acted on good to firm
and dead ground, seemingly not on soft or heavy: retired to Gestut Quenhorn.
A. Wohler, Germany

CAMP FOLLOWER   4 b.g. Warrshan (USA) 117 – House Maid 95 (Habitat   –
134) [1996 89: 10g² 11.8g³ 14m⁴ 1997 8.3s 12m May 31] neat gelding: good mover:
fairly useful at 3 yrs: showed nothing in 1997. *D. C. O'Brien*

CAMPHAR   4 ch.f. Pharly (FR) 130 – Camomilla (Targowice (USA) 130) [1996   –
–: 7d 1997 a8g a7g 10g Jul 7] of no account. *R. M. Flower*

CAMPIONE (IRE)   2 b.c. (May 11) Common Grounds 118 – Kyrenia 53 (Zino   –
127) [1997 6m 6m⁵ 7m Oct 5] 15,000Y: first foal: dam third over 13f at 4 yrs in
Ireland: little sign of ability in maidens. *M. H. Tompkins*

CAMPORESE (IRE)   4 b.f. Sadler's Wells (USA) 132 – Campestral (USA) 97   112
(Alleged (USA) 138) [1996 111: 10.5d* 12m⁴ 13.5g² 12.5d⁶ 1997 11s* 11.9g⁵ 12.5s²
15.5d⁶ Oct 26] rather leggy filly: shows traces of stringhalt: smart performer: won
7-runner Prix Corrida at Lyon Parilly in May by 5 lengths: best subsequent effort
when length second of 4 to Taipan in Grand Prix de Deauville in August: stays 13.5f:
has form on good to firm ground, goes well on soft. *P. W. Chapple-Hyam*

CANADIAN FANTASY   3 b.g. Lear Fan (USA) 130 – Florinda (CAN) (Vice   76
Regent (CAN)) [1996 76: 6.1m³ 6m² 6m² 6m⁴ 7m² 10m³ 1997 a9.4g² 12m 12.1s
a8g* a9.4g² 9.2s* 9.2m 8m a8.5g Aug 8] strong, lengthy gelding: unimpressive
mover: fair performer: won maiden at Southwell in June and handicap at Hamilton in
July: ran poorly last 3 starts: stays 1¼m: acts on good to firm and soft ground, and
fibresand: blinkered (ran to form) once: flashes tail, and has gone early to post.
M. Johnston

CANADIAN JIVE   4 b.f. Dominion 123 – Ural Dancer (Corvaro (USA) 124)   –
[1996 –: 10m 1997 10s 10.2d 10s Jun 26] smallish filly: no form in maidens or
handicap. *D. W. P. Arbuthnot*

CANADIAN PUZZLER (USA)   2 gr.c. (Jan 29) With Approval (CAN) – Puzzle   83 p
Book (USA) (Text (USA)) [1997 7g⁴ 7m⁴ 8.2g³ 8d⁴ Oct 17] $40,000Y: angular colt:
has a quick action: sixth foal: half-brother to 3 winners in North America, including
smart Canadian mare up to 9f Mysteriously and Canadian Grade 3 8.5f winner Brock
Street (both by Afleet): dam, minor stakes winner up to 9f, closely related to Alphabatim: sire high-class middle-distance performer: progressive form, third in maiden
at Nottingham and good fourth of 28 (set lot to do and finished strongly behind The
Glow-Worm) in nursery at Newmarket: free-going sort, but should stay beyond 1m:
should do better again at 3 yrs. *P. W. Harris*

CANARY BLUE (IRE)   6 b.m. Bluebird (USA) 125 – Norfolk Bonnet (Morston   –
(FR) 125) [1996 –: 15.8g 17.2m 1997 a14g Nov 17] workmanlike mare: no form on
flat since modest maiden at 3 yrs. *P. W. Hiatt*

CANARY FALCON   6 ch.g. Polish Precedent (USA) 131 – Pumpona (USA)   –
(Sharpen Up 127) [1996 52, a64: a11g a10g a8g³ a10g a8g⁶ 9.7s 7.5m 11.5f⁶ 10g⁵   a61
11m⁶ a12g* 1997 a14.8g³ a12g Jan 29] compact gelding: good mover: modest
handicapper: stays 14.8f: acts on good to firm ground and the all-weather: often
blinkered/visored. *R. J. O'Sullivan*

CAN CAN CHARLIE   7 gr.g. Vaigly Great 127 – Norton Princess 76 (Wolver   –
Hollow 126) [1996 –: a10g a10g⁵ a12g 1997 a10g² a10g Jan 30] big gelding: modest   a57
handicapper: stays 1¼m: acts on good to firm ground, soft and all-weather: tried
blinkered: none too consistent. *J. Pearce*

CAN CAN LADY   3 ch.f. Anshan 119 – Agama (USA) 44 (Nureyev (USA) 131)   82
[1996 71: 5.9f⁴ 5.9f* 6m⁴ 6m 6.5m 8m* 8m⁵ 1997 7.5m³ 8m* 9.9d² 9g* 9s 8m 10.1g⁵
10.1f⁶ 8m⁵ Oct 5] tall, unfurnished filly: fairly useful handicapper: won at Newcastle
(made all) in May and Ayr in June: ran creditably last 3 starts: effective at 1m to 1¼m,
not sure to stay much further: acts on firm and dead ground, never going well on soft:
usually races prominently: game. *M. Johnston*

CANDY TWIST   2 b.f. (Mar 28) Deploy 131 – Simply Candy (IRE) 42 (Simply   43
Great (FR) 122) [1997 5m 5f⁶ 5s⁵ 5m 6.1m³ 6m⁴ 7.5f a8.5g Oct 18] 400Y: second
foal: dam, maiden, stayed 11f: poor maiden: sold 500 gns after final start: should stay
well beyond 6f. *Ronald Thompson*

CANNY CHRONICLE   9 b. or br.g. Daring March 116 – Laisser Aller (Sagaro   –
133) [1996 NR 1997 12.1g Sep 29] one-time fairly useful handicapper (and useful
hurdler): very lightly raced and no recent form on flat. *P. Monteith*

CANON CAN (USA)   4 ch.g. Green Dancer (USA) 132 – Lady Argyle   117
(USA) (Don B (USA)) [1996 104: 10m³ 12m⁴ 16.1m* 18g* 18g³ 1997 16g*
18.7s⁴ 22.2d* 16m 18f* 18g⁴ Oct 18]

Canon Can's rise towards the top of the staying division has been steady
yet relentless, an equally apt description of his racing style which carried him
to hard-fought wins in the Queen Alexandra Stakes and the Doncaster Cup in
the latest season. As a two-year-old he'd been in danger of getting labelled 'one
of his stable's lesser lights', already earning the nickname 'Canon Can't' in his
own yard. A step up to two miles or more at three saw him improve into a useful
performer with a win in the Phil Bull Trophy at Pontefract and third place in the
Cesarewitch.

That progress was maintained at four, beginning with a reappearance
win over Top Cees in a handicap at Newbury over two miles, Canon Can looking stronger the further he went. That seemed to augur well for his chances in
the Chester Cup for which he started favourite, but, running on soft ground for
the first time, Canon Can was beaten fully half a mile out, finishing a well-
beaten fourth in a strung-out field behind Top Cees. Ground softer than good
turned out to be the least of concerns come Royal Ascot. Canon Can had spread
a plate and pricked his foot three days before the Queen Alexandra and had
been swimming in the interim to maintain fitness. Then, in the race itself, there
were further problems for Canon Can, ridden by Kieren Fallon, when they were
hampered by Old Rouvel and Mick Kinane as the field converged on the far rail
to seek better ground under the trees coming out of Swinley Bottom. Still only
fifth rounding the home turn, Canon Can stayed on dourly to get the better of
Old Rouvel by a neck after a tremendous struggle which saw them pull
twenty-seven lengths clear of the third horse. As Canon Can had come out on
top anyway the incident around seven furlongs out would probably soon have

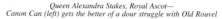

Queen Alexandra Stakes, Royal Ascot—
Canon Can (left) gets the better of a dour struggle with Old Rouvel

Great North Eastern Railway Doncaster Cup—
two views of the finish as Canon Can holds off Persian Punch and the grey Further Flight

been forgotten had it not been for an angry, headline-making reaction by Canon Can's trainer to Kinane's manoeuvre and to the same jockey's riding of Pilsudski earlier in the afternoon in the Hardwicke Stakes, in which the Fallon-ridden and Cecil-trained Lady Carla had been squeezed out on the home turn. The stewards took no action over either incident, though gave Kinane the benefit of the doubt in the Queen Alexandra where the wide course steered by the whole field meant that 'the cameras weren't lined up in the right position to give the stewards a clear picture.'

Canon Can's first venture into pattern company was as a 25/1-shot in the Goodwood Cup, in which he ran as well as could have been expected to finish seventh to Double Trigger. But it was a different story for the pair's next clash in the Great North Eastern Railway Doncaster Cup in September, when Canon Can was backed from 10/1 to 6/1 in a field of five. Showing further improvement, Canon Can put up another game display, challenging Double Trigger early in the straight and holding the persistent Persian Punch to win by a length and a quarter, with the 1992 winner Further Flight third and the odds-on Double Trigger, seeking a hat-trick in the race, only fourth. Canon Can's win (which broke Double Trigger's course record) earned him a second crack at the Cesarewitch. His first attempt had been when third under 7-13 (corresponding to a BHB mark of 84); as a measure of the improvement he'd shown in twelve months, he was set to carry 10-0 (a mark of 106) in the latest season. The return to handicap company after winning a pattern race is an unusual move these days but, run at the local course of the East Anglian-based firm whose advertising slogan Canon Can carries, the Cesarewitch had been 'a long-standing corporate plan' in the words of their managing director. Canon Can ran his usual game race in fourth, giving 32 lb to the winner Turnpole and over a stone to the placed horses Top Cees and Mawared.

When Canon Can was bought for just IR 15,500 guineas as a yearling at the Goffs October Sales his pedigree gave little clue that he'd be a thorough stayer, still less a potentially smart one. Green Dancer has been responsible for other good stayers, including Samraan and Tarator, but Canon Can's family is a modest and far-from-stoutly-bred American one. Grandam Fleet Polly was the

167

only mare in the bottom line of his pedigree to race and was twice successful at around a mile as a four-year-old. Much the best of her six winning foals was Truffles, a full sister to Canon Can's dam, who was successful in minor stakes races at around nine furlongs at four and five and finished fourth in a couple of Grade 1 handicaps—the Santa Margarita Invitational and the Santa Ana. Canon Can is Lady Argyle's second foal and first winner.

		Nijinsky	Northern Dancer
	Green Dancer (USA)	(b 1967)	Flaming Page
	(b 1972)	Green Valley	Val de Loir
Canon Can (USA)		(br 1967)	Sly Pola
(ch.g. 1993)		Don B	Fleet Nasrullah
	Lady Argyle (USA)	(b 1965)	Early Frames
	(b 1987)	Fleet Polly	Fleet Discovery
		(ch 1969)	Wardoura

A tall, good-topped gelding and a fluent mover, the game and genuine Canon Can acts on firm and dead ground. Canon Can may not have stopped improving yet, and looks a leading contender for the Cup races in 1998; the Queen Alexandra Stakes is reportedly on the agenda again but he already looks worth his place in the Gold Cup field. *H. R. A. Cecil*

CANONIZE (IRE)   2 b.f. (May 7) Alzao (USA) 117 – Cecina 100 (Welsh Saint   75
126) [1997 6g³ 6m 6m⁶ Sep 25] 14,000Y: angular filly: third foal: half-sister to 1m (at 2 yrs) and 1¼m winner What's The Verdict (by Law Society): dam useful maiden at 2 yrs in Ireland, best form at 1m, later won 4 races in USA: shaped well when third of 22 in maiden at Windsor in August: well below that form at Salisbury (bolted to post) and Pontefract (tongue tied): should stay at least 1m. *J. W. Hills*

CANOVAS HEART   8 b.g. Balidar 133 – Worthy Venture 76 (Northfields (USA))   96
[1996 81, a–: 5g⁴ 6g³ 5s⁵ 5m* 5m* 5m 5m 5g⁶ 5.2m* 1997 5d* 5g 5m 6m⁶ 6g 5d*   a68
5g⁶ a5g⁶ Dec 18] neat gelding: has a quick action: useful form, modest on all-weather: won at Ripon (made all, winning first time out for third consecutive season) in May and York (career-best effort) in October: ideally suited by 5f: acts on good to firm ground, soft and fibresand: usually races prominently: genuine. *Bob Jones*

CAN SHE CAN CAN   5 b.m. Sulaafah (USA) 119 – Dominance (Dominion 123)   –
[1996 –: a16g a16g 12d⁵ 12.3g 16.2g 14.1g⁶ 16m 17.2m 1997 16.2m Jul 15] workmanlike mare: no worthwhile form for long time: tried blinkered. *C. Smith*

CANTINA   3 b.f. Tina's Pet 121 – Real Claire (Dreams To Reality (USA) 113)   74
[1996 NR 1997 a9.4g³ 7m* 7.1g 7g Oct 24] leggy filly: second foal: half-sister to NH Flat winner by Scottish Reel: dam never ran: confirmed debut promise when making all in 15-runner maiden at Catterick in September: well held in handicaps afterwards, forcing too strong a gallop next time: stays 7f. *A. Bailey*

CANTONESE (USA)   2 b.f. (Apr 21) Easy Goer (USA) – Queen of Song (USA)   68
(His Majesty (USA)) [1997 7g 6.9m⁵ 7g³ 7g a7g* Nov 15] sturdy, angular filly: sister   a76 +
to 3-y-o Easy Song and 5-y-o Easy Listening and half-sister to several winners, notably useful Private Song (by Private Account, stays 1½m): dam twice graded winner over 8.5f at 5 yrs: fair form: best effort when making all in 10-runner maiden at Wolverhampton (beat Freedom Quest 2½ lengths) in November: should be well suited by further than 7f: sold 70,000 gns in December. *R. Charlton*

CANTON RON   3 ch.g. Ron's Victory (USA) 129 – Briery Fille 81 (Sayyaf 121)   –
[1996 53: 8.2m a6g⁵ 6g² a7g 1997 8d 7m 6m 7f a8g⁵ a6g⁴ 11.5m⁴ 12m Aug 19] big   a44
gelding: poor form at best on all-weather in 1997: left C. Dwyer after sixth start: best form at 6f: no form on turf: tried blinkered: sold 900 gns in November. *H. J. Collingridge*

CANTON VENTURE   5 ch.g. Arctic Tern (USA) 126 – Ski Michaela (USA)   80
(Devil's Bag (USA)) [1996 80: a12g² a11g* 12m* 12.5f* 12m* 12.3m² 12.4m*   a86
12.1m⁶ 11.9f* 11.5f³ 11.9f* 11.9m² 12g 12m⁶ 1997 a12g* a12g⁵ 12g² 11.9f⁶ 12g²
12g⁶ 12m⁶ a14g Nov 24] lengthy, angular gelding: fairly useful handicapper: won at

Lingfield in May: should stay further than 12.5f: acts on firm going (unraced on softer than good) and all-weather: blinkered (ran badly) once: front runner/races prominently: fairly useful hurdler: tough and genuine. *S. P. C. Woods*

CAN'T SAY (IRE) 5 br.g. Gallic League 119 – Mixed Feelings (Junius (USA) – 124) [1996 NR 1997 8.1g Aug 3] of no account. *J. M. Bradley*

CANYON CREEK (IRE) 4 b.c. Mr Prospector (USA) – River Memories 99 (USA) 123 (Riverman (USA) 131) [1996 87p: 8m* 1997 8m* 8m Apr 9] leggy colt: reportedly has had knee problems: impressive when showing useful form to win 6-runner listed race at Doncaster in March by 4 lengths from Yeast: 5/4 on, last of 8 in Group 3 at Saint-Cloud 3 weeks later: likely to stay beyond 1m: raced solely on good to firm going: had looked sure to go on again, but is clearly difficult to train: sent to USA. *J. H. M. Gosden*

CAPE CROSS (IRE) 3 b.c. Green Desert (USA) 127 – Park Appeal 122 120 (Ahonoora 122) [1996 88p: 7d⁴ 8f* 1997 8m³ 8m 8s² 8m* 8.1g² 8g*ᵈⁱˢ Aug 23]
One winner at Goodwood in the afternoon and two at Windsor in the evening would have made Saturday August 23rd a red-letter day for most jockeys, but for Frankie Dettori it's one he'd probably rather forget. Dettori had the misfortune to be on board two John Gosden-trained horses who were disqualified after passing the post first at Goodwood, and he'll be aware that a rare error of judgement on his part was responsible for Cape Cross, without doubt the winner on merit, losing the Group 2 Tripleprint Celebration Mile. While the knives had been out for Kieren Fallon following his riding of Bosra Sham in the Coral-Eclipse, criticism of Dettori's performance on Cape Cross was muted, leaving little room to doubt where the loyalties of certain sections of the Press lay at that time as the pair battled it out for the championship. Even the best make mistakes, and the fact that Dettori had dropped a clanger shouldn't have been glossed over.
The field for the Celebration Mile was disappointing, the four-year-old Polar Prince, no more than a smart performer, opposed by three three-year-olds, one of which, Peartree House, looked to be way out of his depth. Among Men, fourth in the Sussex Stakes over the course and distance on his previous start, was sent off favourite at 11/8-on, with Cape Cross third in the betting at 7/2. Cape Cross also had a good run to his credit over the course and distance, getting off the mark for the season in the Vodafone Stakes three weeks earlier, beating Dragonada by two and a half lengths. That was followed by a narrow defeat for Cape Cross at the hands of Hirasah, giving the winner 13 lb, at Sandown, and he went on to show further improvement on his return to Goodwood only to be left with little to show for his efforts. Cape Cross travelled strongly in behind as Among Men cut out the running (harried by Peartree House) but was needlessly asked to barge his way out at the three-furlong marker, bumping Peartree House who in turn hampered Polar Prince as he was poised to begin his challenge. Just over a furlong later Cape Cross took the lead off Among Men then went on to beat him by two and a half lengths, with a further five lengths back to third-placed Polar Prince. It was inevitable that Cape Cross would be disqualified and placed last, while Dettori, deemed guilty of irresponsible riding, was given a five-day suspension. Although Cape Cross's two main rivals had both been below their best, the horse was clearly thriving at this stage of the season and it was disappointing that he wasn't seen out again. All being well he'll be back in action in 1998, racing for the Godolphin team.
Cape Cross has had just eight outings to date, the first couple at two years when he was successful in a one-mile maiden at Doncaster. He was raced solely over that trip as a three-year-old, allowed to take his chance in the Two Thousand Guineas at Newmarket following a promising length third to Desert Story in the Craven Stakes there on his reappearance, but failing to do himself justice in finishing eighth. Cape Cross looked to have been set an easy task when next seen out nearly three months later in a valuable ladies' race at Ascot

Sheikh Mohammed's "Cape Cross"

but, sent off at odds on, he was beaten a neck by Blessed Spirit, his jockey, the experienced Lydia Pearce, on this occasion seeming not to get the best out of her mount. It's true, though, that this was the softest going Cape Cross has encountered.

		Danzig	Northern Dancer
	Green Desert (USA)	(b 1977)	Pas de Nom
	(b 1983)	Foreign Courier	Sir Ivor
Cape Cross (IRE)		(b 1979)	Courtly Dee
(b.c. 1994)		Ahonoora	Lorenzaccio
	Park Appeal	(b 1975)	Helen Nicholls
	(br 1982)	Balidaress	Balidar
		(gr 1973)	Innocence

Cape Cross is the fifth foal and fourth winner produced by Park Appeal, following on from Pastorale (by Nureyev) and Arvola and Lord of Appeal (both by Sadler's Wells), the last-named, a useful French mile-and-a-half winner, the pick of that trio. Park Appeal, unbeaten in four starts at two years, including in the Cheveley Park Stakes, finished seventh in the Poule d'Essai des Pouliches on her only outing at three but won over a mile in the States the following season. A half-sister to another Cheveley Park winner in Desirable and to the Irish Oaks winner Alydaress, Park Appeal is a daughter of Balidaress, a mare who won from seven to ten furlongs as well as being placed over hurdles. The next dam, twice successful over nine furlongs, died after producing Balidaress. A mile is likely to prove the optimum trip for Cape Cross, a big colt who carries condition and often looks lethargic in the preliminaries. He wears bandages behind. *J. H. M. Gosden*

CAPE HOPE 2 b.c. (Apr 1) Risk Me (FR) 127 – Bernstein Bette 76 (Petong 126) 61
[1997 5.1g 5v³ 6g 5m 5m 6d⁴ 5m a5g⁴ Nov 14] 5,400Y: small colt: first foal: dam
best up to 7f: modest maiden: should stay beyond 6f: acts on good to soft ground and
fibresand. *R. Boss*

CAPE PIGEON (USA) 12 ch.g. Storm Bird (CAN) 134 – Someway Somehow 63
(USA) (What Luck (USA)) [1996 70: 8d 8.3m* 8.3m⁵ 8.3g² 8.3g* 8.3d³ 9g⁴ 8.1f³
1997 8.3s 8d* 8f³ 8.3m⁶ Aug 11] big gelding: carries plenty of condition: modest
performer: has won a race or 2 in each of last 7 seasons: easy winner of 15-runner
claimer at Salisbury in June: stays 8.3f: acts on any going: has been blinkered,
visored nowadays: usually races prominently: sometimes finds little. *L. G. Cottrell*

CAPERCAILLIE 2 ch.g. (May 8) Deploy 131 – Tee Gee Jay 63 (Northern 46
Tempest (USA) 120) [1997 8m a8g⁵ Dec 8] 1,050Y: first foal: dam, 2-y-o 6f winner,
became irresolute: better effort in sellers when fifth at Southwell. *D. Morris*

CAPE SIREN 3 b.f. Warning 136 – Cape Race (USA) 88 (Northern Dancer) –
[1996 NR 1997 10m 10s⁶ 8m Oct 22] half-sister to several winners, including useful
pair Raiwand (probably stayed 1½m, by Tap On Wood) and 1981 2-y-o 5f and 7f
winner Final Strike (by Artaius): dam, 1m winner, is half-sister to very smart colts
Lord Gayle and Never Return: no worthwhile form in maidens. *M. J. Ryan*

CAPE VERDI (IRE) 2 b.f. (Feb 3) Caerleon (USA) 132 – Afrique Bleu Azur 110 p
(USA) (Sagace (FR) 135) [1997 6m* 7g² 6g* 6m⁴ Sep 30]
　　　　Oh dear, oh dear! It seems a tough life being a multi-millionaire these
days. Owner Robert Sangster explained his decision to sell four of his best
juveniles, including the then-favourite for the One Thousand Guineas Cape
Verdi, to Godolphin at the end of September as 'purely commercial', lamenting
the 'pitiful' level of prize money in Britain. Another of racing's wealthiest
owners Peter Savill was quick to leap to Sangster's defence, describing the
move as 'yet another condemnation of the current financial state of British
racing.' The pair, looking from their own perspective, have a point about the
relative well-being of owners in British racing, but it's difficult to sympathise
with their view in this specific instance. Poor prize money or not, if Sangster
were indeed made 'an offer he couldn't refuse' then, by definition, he couldn't
turn it down. Like (proverbially) 'all men', presumably all horses have their
price. In recent years Sangster has sold the likes of the Arc winner Carnegie,
the dual classic winner Balanchine and the Derby winner Dr Devious before
they reached their peak. But he's not always come off worse. In 1981 he struck
arguably one of the bloodstock deals of all time when reportedly selling a
seventy-five per cent stake in Storm Bird for a sum that put a total value on
the horse of an incredible 30,000,000 dollars. At the time Storm Bird was
unbeaten; shortly afterwards he'd flopped in his Arc trial and was retired.

Stakis Casinos Lowther Stakes, York—Cape Verdi (left) just gains the upper hand as Embassy stumbles

As it happens Sangster may seem to have done rather nicely out of the Cape Verdi deal, too, whatever the precise sum involved might have been. The day after his remarks were made the filly finished only fourth to Embassy in the Cheveley Park Stakes at Newmarket, beaten five lengths, and was pushed right out in the betting for the One Thousand. Such a conclusion could prove to be premature, though. Experience has shown that it is frequently worth forgiving a horse one poor run when the rest of the evidence is in its favour. What's more, Cape Verdi's stable was under something of a cloud at the time, failing to send out a single winner in Britain (though there were two in France) between September 17th and October 14th. Take out the Cheveley Park run and Cape Verdi has good prospects for the One Thousand, better than her odds at the time of writing suggest.

Cape Verdi's three runs before the Cheveley Park resulted in two wins. She went off the 2/1 favourite in a field of twelve for the Chesham Stakes at Royal Ascot on the back of an impressive debut success in a maiden at Newmarket in May, but went down by one and a half lengths to Central Park, the pair four lengths clear. The form looked useful at the time, and even better after Central Park comprehensively landed the Champagne Vintage Stakes at Goodwood the following month. Cape Verdi herself next ran in the Stakis Casinos Lowther Stakes at York. Her main rival on form looked to be Embassy, who had won the Princess Margaret Stakes at Ascot, and they dominated the betting, too, Cape Verdi the 7/4 favourite and Embassy 11/4. Receiving 3 lb from Embassy, Cape Verdi had to battle hard to prevail by a short head. Cape Verdi travelled strongly but on the opposite side of the field to Embassy and was suddenly left with a length or two to make up as that filly kicked on over a furlong out. Cape Verdi really knuckled down inside the final furlong and, with Embassy stumbling and edging left in the last few strides, gamely forced her head in front on the line. The Queen Mary Stakes winner Nadwah was a staying-on third, one and a half lengths away, with the six other runners well beaten off. Our enthusiasm for Cape Verdi as the better long-term prospect was enhanced by the belief that she'd be better suited by a longer trip than would Embassy. So, when they met over six furlongs once more in the Cheveley Park, there looked likely to be little in it. The writing was on the wall at an early stage for Cape Verdi, however, as she was soon niggled along and never looked likely to play a part. There's every reason to expect a much better showing from her on the course in May, on her return from a winter in Dubai.

		Nijinsky	Northern Dancer
	Caerleon (USA)	(b 1967)	Flaming Page
	(b 1980)	Foreseer	Round Table
Cape Verdi (IRE)		(b or br 1969)	Regal Gleam
(b.f. Feb 3, 1995)		Sagace	Luthier
	Afrique Bleu Azur (USA)	(b 1980)	Seneca
	(b or br 1987)	Albertine	Irish River
		(b 1981)	Almyre

On breeding it's surprising that Cape Verdi has shown such speed and precocity. Her sire, the Prix du Jockey Club winner Caerleon, has produced some smart two-year-olds (he himself was one) but is better known for winners at a mile and a quarter plus. His most famous son is Generous, who won a substandard Dewhurst at two then showed himself to be a true top-notcher at a mile and a half at three. Cape Verdi's dam, Afrique Bleu Azur, didn't even run at two years, but won in the French Provinces over eleven and a half furlongs at three and four. Afrique Bleu Azur is a very well-related mare. Her brother Arcangues won the Breeders' Cup Classic and her half-sister Agathe was second in the Poule d'Essai des Pouliches and third in the Prix de Diane. Their dam, Albertine, was smart at up to a mile and a quarter and a half-sister to the good middle-distance performers Ashmore and Acoma. Cape Verdi is a second reported foal, following the Saint Cyrien colt L'Africain Bleu, a useful mile and a half winner, including in the latest season.

Mr R. E. Sangster's "Cape Verdi"

All in all, the leggy Cape Verdi is bred much more to be an Oaks filly than a Guineas one, but she clearly possesses plenty of speed and the likely limit of her stamina is probably best reviewed after the One Thousand. Her claims for that race seem every bit as strong as those of Harayir at the end of 1994. Harayir won the Lowther Stakes and went on to win the One Thousand having been written off by some when finishing only third in the Cheveley Park. *P. W. Chapple-Hyam*

CAPILANO PRINCESS 4 b.f. Tragic Role (USA) – Lady Capilano 87 (Nebbiolo 125) [1996 79, a–: 8m 7.3d* 8g² 8f 8m⁶ 8.1g 1997 10d⁵ 10d* 8d 8d 10.2d* 10.3g* 10d* 12g 12s Nov 8] workmanlike filly: fairly useful performer: won minor event at Nottingham in May and handicaps at Chepstow and Doncaster in July and Ayr in September: will prove best at 1¼m/1½m: acts on good to firm and soft going, modest form on fibresand at 2 yrs. *D. Haydn Jones*   93

CAPITAL PRINCE (FR) 2 b.c. (Feb 26) Alzao (USA) 117 – Sudah (USA) (Rainbow Quest (USA) 134) [1997 7m⁴ Oct 22] 3,500,000 francs Y: first foal: dam French 2-y-o 9f winner, half-sister to Grade 1 Laurel Futurity winner Luge, a smart 2-y-o in 1988: second favourite, 6¾ lengths fourth of 13 to Misbah in maiden at Yarmouth, not knocked about when outpaced over 1f out: should do better over 1m+. *Saeed bin Suroor*   75 p

CAP JULUCA (IRE) 5 b.g. Mtoto 134 – Tabyan (USA) 68 (Topsider (USA)) [1996 –: 10f 1997 8m³ 10g* 8.5g³ 10.1d* Jun 25] strong gelding: fluent mover: most progressive in 1995 (rated 117p, won Cambridgeshire): beset by training troubles   112

173

since, but still capable of smart form: won 5-runner minor event at Newbury in May and 3-runner listed contest (beat Amid Albadu by 1¼ lengths despite carrying head awkwardly) at Epsom in June: stays 1¼m: acts on firm and dead ground: tongue tied and also difficult at stalls at Epsom: front runner: gelded after final start. *R. Charlton*

CAPLAW SKEEN   2 b.g. (Apr 7) Sure Blade (USA) 130 – Mary From Dunlow   –
49 (Nicholas Bill 125) [1997 6g 8s Nov 6] 3,800Y: third foal: half-brother to 3-y-o Smokey From Caplaw and a winner in Denmark, by Clantime: dam 2-y-o 5f winner, later had form at 1m: well held in maidens. *J. L. Eyre*

CAPRI   2 ch.c. (May 10) Generous (IRE) 139 – Island Jamboree (USA) (Explodent   75 p
(USA)) [1997 8.2d² Oct 30] big, rangy colt: third foal: half-brother to 3-y-o Fiji: dam, won 10 times from 6f to 8.5f in USA (also second in Grade 1 9f event at 5 yrs), from family of Cacoethes: 9/4, head second of 12 to Eliza Acton in maiden at Nottingham, soon recovering from slow start, edging left when first ridden, rallying close home: will be well suited by at least 1¼m: seems sure to make a fair bit better 3-y-o. *H. R. A. Cecil*

CAPSOFF (IRE)   4 b.f. Mazaad 106 – Minerstown (IRE) (Miner's Lamp 114)   70
[1996 NR 1997 10m 10g 11.5s³ 12g 14s 11.1m Sep 22] strong filly: third foal: dam unraced: modest form in NH Flat races: clearly best effort when third in maiden at Yarmouth in July: should stay beyond 11.5f. *G. A. Hubbard*

CAPTAIN BLISS   2 b.g. (Apr 10) Rambo Dancer (CAN) 107 – Edwins' Princess   52
75 (Owen Dudley 121) [1997 5d⁴ 5m³ 5g⁴ 5m⁴ 7g⁴ 6s² 7.1m* 6g⁴ 6.9m⁴ 7g⁵ a7g⁶ Sep 20] 6,500Y: good-quartered gelding: sixth foal: half-brother to several winners, including 8-y-o Pageboy and 5-y-o Royal Expression: dam, 2-y-o 5f winner, disappointing but stayed 1m: modest performer: won seller at Musselburgh in July: should stay beyond 7f: acts on good to firm and soft ground (well held on fibresand): blinkered: consistent. *N. Tinkler*

CAPTAIN BRADY (IRE)   2 ch.g. (Mar 25) Soviet Lad (USA) 94 – Eight Mile   56
Rock 76 (Dominion 123) [1997 5m 5d⁴ a5g³ a5g 5.3g 5.1d Oct 8] IR 16,000Y: lengthy, workmanlike gelding: sixth foal: brother to 3-y-o Amarella and half-brother to 1m (at 2 yrs) to 1¾m winner World Express (by Jareer) and useful French 9f and 1½m winner Macruby (by High Estate): dam 7f winner: modest maiden: should be suited by further than 5f: blinkered final start: has got on edge and played up in stalls. *W. G. M. Turner*

CAPTAIN CARAT   6 gr.g. Handsome Sailor 125 – Gem of Gold 52 (Jellaby 124)   64
[1996 70: 5s⁴ 5g⁴ 5g* 6m 6m⁶ 5g* 6d⁵ 6m 6m⁶ 5f² 6g⁶ 5m⁴ 5m³ 6.1m⁵ 5m³ 5f 5m 6g⁶ 5m² 5m 5g a5g⁴ 1997 a6g³ a6g⁴ a6g 6g⁴ 5m⁵ 5g 5m³ 5g⁴ 6.1g 5m* 5f⁵ 5g⁵ 5m 5d 5g⁴ 5g² 5.1g⁶ 6f 5d Nov 7] tall gelding: modest performer: dead-heated in claimer at Catterick in May: left D. Nicholls cheaply before final start: effective at 5f/6f: acts on any going: usually blinkered: has run well sweating: has won for claimer, as well as given trouble in stalls: best held up in strongly-run race. *Ronald Thompson*

CAPTAIN CARPARTS   3 b.c. Hubbly Bubbly (USA) – Choir (High Top 131)   60
[1996 –p: 8.5g 7.1v 1997 a6g³ a6g² 7g³ 7.1m⁵ 6.1g 7m³ 6g⁶ 8m* 8g Jul 7] leggy colt: a37
modest performer on turf: dictated pace to win 6-runner handicap at Carlisle in June: stays 1m: acts on good to firm ground, poor form on fibresand: best form without visor: inconsistent. *J. L. Eyre*

CAPTAIN COLLINS (IRE)   3 gr.c. El Gran Senor (USA) 136 – Kanmary (FR)   103
117 (Kenmare (FR) 125) [1996 99p: 7g² 8s³ 1997 6m* 7d* 7m⁴ 7g³ 7.3m⁴ 8f Sep 11] lengthy, angular colt: useful performer: won maiden at Newmarket in April and handicap at Goodwood in May: good efforts in frame in Jersey Stakes at Royal Ascot, Beeswing Stakes at Newcastle (beaten 6 lengths by Wizard King) and Hungerford Stakes at Newbury (2¼ lengths behind Decorated Hero): stays 7f (pulled too hard at 1m): acts on good to firm ground and dead: sometimes wanders: sent to USA. *P. W. Chapple-Hyam*

CAPTAIN FLINT   3 b. or br.g. Bedford (USA) 109 – Sun Yat Chen (Chou Chin   46
Chow 99) [1996 –: 5s⁵ 7m 10f a7g a8g 1997 10m 12g 12v* Jun 30] leggy gelding: 20/1, only worthwhile form when winning selling handicap by 15 lengths at Pontefract in June: will stay further than 1½m: clearly revels on heavy going. *A. Smith*

CAPTAIN HORATIUS (IRE) 8 b.h. Taufan (USA) 119 – One Last Glimpse 108
73 (Relko 136) [1996 114: 10g³ 10d⁵ 10s* 10m⁴ 10.5m³ 1997 10m⁴ 10d 12g³ 11.6m⁴
Aug 23] tall horse: unimpressive mover: half-brother to several winners, none
anywhere near so good as himself: dam maiden: smart and thoroughly likeable
campaigner at his best: won 11 races in 4 different countries (often campaigned
overseas), including Group 2 events in Germany and Turkey as 3-y-o: well below
form after reappearance at 8 yrs: suited by 1¼m/1½m: acted on good to firm and
heavy ground: held up for turn of foot: tough and genuine: to stand at Ridgebarn
Farm Stud, Buckinghamshire (fee £1,250, Oct 1st). *J. L. Dunlop*

CAPTAIN JACK 7 b.g. Salse (USA) 128 – Sanctuary (Welsh Pageant 132) [1996 92
NR 1997 16g⁴ 16m* 18g⁵ 16g Oct 24] big gelding: has been fired: lightly raced on
flat but still capable of fairly useful form: won handicap at Newbury in July: best of
those who raced up with pace when fifth in Cesarewitch at Newmarket: stays well:
acts on good to firm ground and dead: has won with blinkers and without: suited by
forcing pace (though set too strong gallop final start). *M. C. Pipe*

CAPTAIN JONES (IRE) 2 ch.c. (Mar 3) Imp Society (USA) – Thatcherite 61
(Final Straw 127) [1997 5.1d 6f³ 7g a7g⁶ Jul 10] IR 25,000Y: sturdy colt: has scope: a?
fluent mover: sixth foal: brother to 3-y-o Aspecto Lad and half-brother to 3 winners,
including 4-y-o Unconditional Love: dam unraced half-sister to Kampala: only form
in maidens when third at Haydock in June: should stay beyond 6f. *B. J. Meehan*

CAPTAIN LOGAN (IRE) 2 b.c. (Jun 11) Fairy King (USA) – Heaven High 78 p
(High Line 125) [1997 6m 7m⁴ Oct 22] useful-looking colt: half-brother to several
winners, including Irish 3-y-o God Forbid (by Caerleon), 7f winner at 2 yrs, and
fairly useful stayer Miss Plum (by Ardross): dam, lightly raced, probably stayed
1½m: better effort in maidens when over 2 lengths fourth of 13 to Jila at Yarmouth,
keeping on: will stay 1m: should improve further. *D. R. Loder*

CAPTAIN MARMALADE 8 ch.g. Myjinski (USA) – Lady Seville 64 (Orange 43
Bay 131) [1996 –, a48: a16g² a16g a13g⁴ a16g⁶ 10.3d a16g* 15.4m a12g⁵ 16m⁹⁹ a38
a12g⁴ a12g⁶ a12g a10g⁴ a16g 16.1g 10g² 10.1s 10m 10g a10g⁵ 9d 10g³ Sep 28]
workmanlike gelding: poor handicapper: effective at 1¼m to 2m: acts on good to
firm going, soft and all-weather: effective visored or not: usually gets well behind.
D. T. Thom

CAPTAIN MCCLOY (USA) 2 ch.g. (Apr 8) Lively One (USA) – Fly Me First 60
(USA) (Herbager 136) [1997 6m³ 7g⁶ 7.5m⁶ 7m 6g⁵ 8f⁴ 8g⁵ Oct 24] $55,000Y:
lengthy gelding: half-brother to several winners in USA, notably smart performer at
around 1m Flying Chevron (by Carson City): dam unraced: modest maiden: probably
stays 1m: visored fourth start: often slowly away, and may not have ideal
temperament: sold after final start. *Mrs J. R. Ramsden*

CAPTAIN PICARD 3 b.c. Today And Tomorrow 78 – Nimble Dancer (Northern –
Wizard 100) [1996 –: a5g 6m 1997 7m Jul 24] no sign of ability. *D. C. O'Brien*

CAPTAIN SCOTT (IRE) 3 b.g. Polar Falcon (USA) 126 – Camera Girl (Kala- 87
glow 132) [1996 NR 1997 a8g* 8m³ 7.9g⁵ 10m* 7.6s Aug 30] tall, lengthy gelding:
has scope: third foal: half-brother to lightly-raced Irish maiden Instamatic, useful at
1m, and to 1997 Italian 2-y-o 7.5f winner Night Answer (both by Night Shift): dam
unraced granddaughter of 1000 Guineas second Photo Flash: fairly useful form: won
maiden at Southwell in March: reportedly badly struck into third start: returned to
win handicap at Ayr in July, having to work harder than seemed likely: will probably
prove better at 1¼m than shorter: acts on fibresand and good to firm going, ran poorly
on soft. *J. A. Glover*

CAPTAIN'S DAY 5 ch.g. Ballacashtal (CAN) – Seymour Ann (Krayyan 117) –
[1996 70d: 10.8d 7s 8f⁶ 8m a8g 8.2m 9f 8.1f⁵ 8m 1997 a8g³ a8g⁶ a10g* a10g* 9.7g a58 d
a9.4g⁶ 10m 10g a9.4g a10s⁶ a10g⁵ a10g a10g Dec 19] sparely-made gelding:
poor mover: modest performer: won minor event and handicap at Lingfield in
February/March: generally poor efforts afterwards: better at 1¼m than 1m: clearly
best recent efforts on equitrack, no form for long time on turf: well held in visor.
H. J. Collingridge

CAPTAIN'S GUEST (IRE) 7 b.g. Be My Guest (USA) 126 – Watership (USA) 90
(Foolish Pleasure (USA)) [1996 –: 11.6d⁶ 16m⁵ 18g 1997 12d⁶ 14.8m³ Jul 19] tall

gelding: won Cesarewitch in 1994 (rated 100): best effort since when third in Newmarket handicap, running on strongly after none too clear a run: stays 2¼m: acts on firm and dead ground. *Mrs A. J. Perrett*

CAPTAIN SINBAD   5 b.g. Welsh Captain 113 – Lane Patrol (Hopton Lane 70)   42
[1996 NR 1997 5m² 5.1g 5m a5g 5g 5m Jul 19] tall gelding: poor maiden: wears visor/blinkers. *K. S. Bridgwater*

CAPTAIN TANDY (IRE)   8 ch.g. Boyne Valley 107 – Its All A Dream (Le   –
Moss 135) [1996 –: 8g a8g 1997 a12g a16g Jun 6] of no account. *C. Smith*

CAPTAIN TIM   2 ch.c. (Mar 4) Lion Cavern (USA) 117 – Monaiya (Shareef   82 p
Dancer (USA) 135) [1997 6.1m² 6m 7m³ Oct 22] R 290,000Y: tall, unfurnished colt: fourth foal: half brother to 3 winners, including 3-y-o Fiametta and Oaks/Irish Oaks fourth Musetta (by Cadeux Genereux), 7f winner at 2 yrs: dam French 7.5f and 1m winner: fairly useful form in maidens at Nottingham and Yarmouth, racing freely and carrying head high when ridden at latter course: highly tried when 9 lengths seventh of 8 in Middle Park Stakes at Newmarket in between: should stay 1m: likely to do better. *D. R. Loder*

CAPTIVATING (IRE)   2 b.f. (Mar 29) Wolfhound (USA) 126 – Winning   63
Appeal (FR) 62 (Law Society (USA) 130) [1997 5d 7m 6.9m⁶ Aug 19] unfurnished filly: first foal: dam maiden who stayed 1¼m, half-sister to smart French 1¼m performer D'Arros out of sister to El Gran Senor: modest form in maidens at Goodwood and Folkestone last 2 starts: should stay at least 1m. *R. Hannon*

CAPTIVE FACT (USA)   2 ch.c. (Mar 28) Known Fact (USA) 135 – Bold   –
Captive (USA) (Boldnesian) [1997 6m Jul 14] brother to smart French/US performer at up to 7f Nidd and half-brother to numerous winners, including Breeders' Cup Classic winner Skywalker (by Relaunch): dam American sprinter: 10/1, slowly away and always behind in maiden at Folkestone: sold 5,000 gns in October, to go to Sweden. *Mrs A. J. Perrett*

CARADOC   2 ch.c. (Feb 15) Bustino 136 – Hathaway (Connaught 130) [1997 8.2s   64
8d a8g Dec 19] third reported living foal: half-brother to useful miler Curtain Call   a?
(by Final Straw): dam poor maiden: best effort in maidens at Leicester on second start: should stay 1¼m+. *S. C. Williams*

CARAMBO   2 b.f. (Feb 21) Rambo Dancer (CAN) 107 – Light The Way 72   68
(Nicholas Bill 125) [1997 5m² 5m⁶ 5d² 5g² 6g a6g* 6g a7g* Oct 6] unfurnished filly: a83
fifth reported foal: sister to 1995 2-y-o 5f winner Rambo Delight: dam won 1m seller: fairly useful performer on the all-weather, fair on turf: won nurseries at Wolverhampton in July and October: should stay at least 1m. *J. L. Eyre*

CARATI   3 b.f. Selkirk (USA) 129 – Clytie (USA) 73 (El Gran Senor (USA) 136)   80
[1996 86: 6f⁴ 6.1m* 6f² 6m 1997 8g 6g⁴ 6m 6m⁵ 6g 7m Aug 23] tall filly: easy mover with a long stride: fairly useful performer: best effort of 1997 on second start: should stay 7f: raced only on good going or firmer: blinkered (raced freely) final outing: sold 8,500 gns in December. *R. Boss*

CARAWAY   2 b.f. (May 7) Shadeed (USA) 135 – Massorah (FR) 108 (Habitat 134)   –
[1997 7g 7g Sep 4] 44,000Y: lengthy filly: sister to a winner in Germany and half-sister to several winners, including fairly useful 6f winner Massiba (by Shareef Dancer): dam French sprinter: no worthwhile form in maidens: sold 12,500 gns in October. *R. Charlton*

CARBON   2 b.g. (Feb 9) Batshoof 122 – Reyah 83 (Young Generation 129) [1997   83
6d* 6d⁴ 6m³ 7g⁵ Aug 19] close-coupled gelding: half-brother to several winners, including useful 7f (at 2 yrs) and 1m winner Abs (by Nureyev) and 1991 2-y-o 5f winner Isdar (by Known Fact): dam 6f and 1m winner: fairly useful form: won maiden at York in June: creditable efforts afterwards, in nurseries at Newcastle and York last 2 starts: should stay at least 1m: carried head high first 2 starts: sold 18,000 gns in October. *D. Morley*

CARBURTON   4 b.c. Rock City 120 – Arminda (Blakeney 126) [1996 86: 8d³   79
8.1g 8g a7g 1997 a8g 8m 6m 7d 8g² 10g* 10m² 10m² Jun 19] well-made colt: fair handicapper: won 23-runner contest at Windsor in June: good second afterwards: stays 1¼m: acts on good to firm and soft ground, seemingly not on fibresand: blinkered second start at 4 yrs, visored third. *J. A. Glover*

CAREFUL TIMING   2 b.f. (Apr 30) Caerleon (USA) 132 – By Charter 104   71 p
(Shirley Heights 130) [1997 8g Oct 24] tall filly: fourth foal: closely related to 1994
2-y-o 7f winner Magna Carta (by Royal Academy) and half-sister to 1995 2-y-o 7f
winner Green Charter (by Green Desert): dam, seemed to stay 1¼m, sister to smart
stayer Zinaad out of Time Charter: 16/1 and bandaged behind, around 8 lengths
eighth of 18 to Merciless in maiden at Doncaster, not knocked about closing stages:
should prove suited by 1½m+: swished tail repeatedly in paddock and at start
(enstalled last): should do fair bit better if temperament holds. *M. R. Stoute*

CARIBBEAN MONARCH (IRE)   2 b.c. (Mar 27) Fairy King (USA) – Whos   – p
The Blonde (Cure The Blues (USA)) [1997 7g Aug 20] tall colt: third foal: half-
brother to 3-y-o Caribbean Star: dam Irish 7f winner out of sister to Bitty Girl and
Hot Spark: 8/1 and green, well held in maiden at Kempton, pulling hard and
weakening from 2f out: should do better. *M. R. Stoute*

CARIBBEAN STAR   3 b.f. Soviet Star (USA) 128 – Whos The Blonde (Cure   81
The Blues (USA)) [1996 72: 6d³ 6m⁴ 7g² 7.1v⁶ 1997 8m 7.1g 7g³ 7g* 7m⁴ 7.1m⁴
7.1g Sep 27] good-topped filly: fairly useful performer: won maiden at Thirsk in
July: ran well afterwards, persistently denied a run when favourite for handicap on
final one (bandaged near-hind): should stay 1m: acts on good to firm ground, not
discredited on heavy: edgy sort, sometimes attended by 2 handlers in paddock:
visored last 4 outings: races prominently. *M. R. Stoute*

CARIBBEE BEACH (IRE)   3 ch.f. Magical Strike (USA) 114 – Madam John   –
105 (Ballad Rock 122) [1996 –: 5.3f⁶ 1997 8f 10.8m 6.9s Jul 2] of little account.
G. G. Margarson

CARINTHIA (IRE)   2 br.f. (Apr 28) Tirol 127 – Hot Lavender (CAN) 67   63 p
(Shadeed (USA) 135) [1997 6m² Aug 23] second foal: dam (maiden) raced only at
5f: 14/1, neck second of 16 to Belle de Nuit in maiden at Windsor, making most and
keeping on: likely to do better. *C. F. Wall*

CARISBROOKE   3 b.c. Kahyasi 130 – Dayanata (Shirley Heights 130) [1996   99 p
NR 1997 12.3g² 12m* 14.6d⁴ Nov 7] 22,000Y: leggy, lengthy colt: had chipped bone
in knee: fourth foal: half-brother to useful Irish 6f (at 2 yrs) to 1m winner Daryabad
(by Thatching) and Irish 1¾m winner Dayadan (by Shernazar): dam unraced sister to
Darshaan: won maiden at Kempton in September by 5 lengths from Sabadilla,
staying on very strongly despite hanging left: favourite, bit more improvement when
under 5 lengths fourth of 7 to Sweetness Herself in minor event at Doncaster, leading
to over 3f out: will stay 2m: type to do well at 4 yrs. *H. R. A. Cecil*

CARLASANTA (IRE)   2 ch.f. (Mar 31) Imp Society (USA) – Ski Slope (Niniski   –
(USA) 125) [1997 6m 7.1g 10d Oct 13] 2,300Y: tall, workmanlike filly: half-sister to
1m winner in Germany by Mac's Imp: dam lightly raced: signs of only a little ability
in seller final start. *A. G. Newcombe*

CARLTON (IRE)   3 ch.g. Thatching 131 – Hooray Lady 92 (Ahonoora 122)   60
[1996 –: 6m⁶ 6m 5v 1997 8.2m 8d⁴ 7.5d* 8g³ a7g 7d 6.9g 7f Oct 3] sturdy gelding:
modest handicapper: well backed when winning at Beverley in May: gelded and off
course nearly 3 months after sixth outing: never placed to challenge or knocked about
final start: stays 1m: acts on dead ground. *G. Lewis*

CARLYS QUEST   3 ch.g. Primo Dominie 121 – Tuppy (USA) (Sharpen Up 127)   63
[1996 60?: a7g 7f⁴ a8.5g 8f 1997 8f³ 9f⁵ 8m³ 9.7m⁶ 10g⁴ 10m⁵ 10d Jun 23] modest
maiden: stays 1¼m: acts on firm going. *J. Neville*

CARMINE LAKE (IRE)   3 ch.f. Royal Academy (USA) 130 – Castilian   120
Queen (USA) 82 (Diesis 133) [1996 107?: 5m* 5.1g³ 5m* 6m⁴ 5d⁵ 1997 5m³
5f* a6f Nov 8]
     Racing over five furlongs on firm ground seems an unsuitable task for a
filly suffering from arthritis in her knees, yet Carmine Lake accomplished it in
a faster time, 56.9 seconds to be precise, than any of the eleven other runners in
the Prix de l'Abbaye de Longchamp in October. The field for the Prix de
l'Abbaye was far from vintage, but it still required a much-improved performance from Carmine Lake to win it. Fifth in the race twelve months earlier on
her final start as a two-year-old, her condition already causing problems, she

Prix de l'Abbaye de Longchamp—a career-best effort from Carmine Lake,
who leads close home to beat Pas de Reponse (far side), Royal Applause and Kistena

wasn't seen out until September in the latest season, when running an encouraging race to finish third behind Bollin Joanne in the Scarborough Stakes at Doncaster. Carmine Lake faced much stiffer opposition at Longchamp, where her rivals included the Prix de Meautry winner Pas de Reponse, Royal Applause, successful in the Haydock Park Sprint Cup on his previous start, the King's Stand Stakes winner Don't Worry Me and Kistena. The last-named was having only her second outing since winning the race in 1996, when she had ended an eighteen-year domination of the race by British and Irish stables. Apart from Carmine Lake, Kistena's victims had included Hever Golf Rose and Eveningperformance, both again in the line-up.

It was Eveningperformance, Pas de Reponse and the Italian-trained runner Late Parade who fought for the lead in the early stages, with Carmine Lake, drawn one and racing next to the rail, just behind them. Pas de Reponse, having seen off both the other pacesetters before the final furlong, was then challenged by Royal Applause and Carmine Lake. She just managed to repel the former but couldn't hold Carmine Lake, who quickened well to lead close home (despite appearing to hang fire for a stride or two) and win by half a length. It was very nearly a one-two-three for the fillies, with Kistena just failing to overhaul Royal Applause. Carmine Lake had one more outing, in the Breeders' Cup Sprint at Hollywood Park. It was the first time she'd encountered a dirt track, and the first time she'd raced at six furlongs since finishing fourth in the Lowther Stakes as a two-year-old, and she ran a long way below her best, fading out of contention turning into the straight.

Carmine Lake is the first foal of Castilian Queen, a winner over six furlongs at two years who showed fair form over seven furlongs at three. Her second foal, Star of Grosvenor (by Last Tycoon), won a seven-furlong maiden at Folkestone in August. Closely related to Regal Sabre (by Sharpen Up), a useful performer at up to a mile and a quarter, Castilian Queen is a daughter of the high-class miler Royal Heroine. A tough and genuine sort who won the Prix de l'Opera for Michael Stoute, Royal Heroine went on to even greater success in the States where she was trained by John Gosden, winning the Breeders' Cup Mile at Hollywood Park as a four-year-old. Carmine Lake's third dam My Sierra Leone was quite a well-bred filly, by a Derby winner out of a useful sprinter, but she showed little in two starts.

		Nijinsky	Northern Dancer
	Royal Academy (USA)	(b 1967)	Flaming Page
	(b 1987)	Crimson Saint	Crimson Satan
Carmine Lake (IRE)		(ch 1969)	Bolero Rose
(ch.f. 1994)		Diesis	Sharpen Up
	Castilian Queen (USA)	(ch 1980)	Doubly Sure
	(ch 1989)	Royal Heroine	Lypheor
		(br 1980)	My Sierra Leone

Carmine Lake, a lengthy filly, has form at six furlongs and on good to soft ground, but easily her best performance was put up over five furlongs on firm. She was awkward at the stalls at both Doncaster, where she also carried her head a bit high under pressure, and Longchamp. *P. W. Chapple-Hyam*

CARMOSA (USA) 4 ch.f. Blushing John (USA) 120 – Bobbinette (Whitstead 125) [1996 53: 7s 7.1g⁵ 8.1g² 7g³ 8.1f 12f 1997 a8.5g⁵ a7g a8g a7g Jan 29] lengthy filly: very much on the downgrade: tried blinkered. *D. Nicholls* —

CARNATION KING 2 b.c. (May 26) King's Signet (USA) 110 – Primrose Way 59 (Young Generation 129) [1997 5g Apr 19] 1,800Y: small colt: seventh foal: half-brother to 4-y-o Sweet Amoret and an 11f and 12.5f winner in Holland by Emarati: dam middle-distance maiden: last in claimer only outing: dead. *W. G. M. Turner* —

CARNIVAL OF LIGHT 5 b.m. Squill (USA) 122 – June Fayre (Sagaro 133) [1996 ?: 5.1g a6g 1997 a6g Feb 14] won 2 sprints in Czech Republic at 3 and 4 yrs: no form in Britain. *J. S. Moore* —

CAROL AGAIN 5 b.m. Kind of Hush 118 – Lady Carol 42 (Lord Gayle (USA) 124) [1996 –, a48: a8g² a11g² a11g⁴ a8g a8g² a12g³ a8g⁵ a11g* a12g* a12g a11g⁵ a11g 8m 12.1s a11g a11g² 1997 a8g a11g⁵ a12g a12g² a11g* a12g⁴ a11g² a12g⁵ 12.1d⁵ 12.3m a11g⁶ 13m³ a11g⁴ 10.9d Jun 21] close-coupled mare: poor handicapper: won at Southwell in February: below form last 6 starts: should stay beyond 1½m: acts on fibresand, no worthwhile form on turf: blinkered final start. *N. Bycroft* — a48

CAROL GRIMES 2 b.f. (May 14) Beveled (USA) – Come To Good (Swing Easy (USA) 126) [1997 5m⁶ 5g³ Mar 26] 6,200 2-y-o: workmanlike filly: first reported foal: dam seemed of little account: poor form in early-season maidens. *J. S. Moore* 49

CAROLINE'S PET (IRE) 2 b.f. (May 2) Contract Law (USA) 108 – Princess Roxanne 68 (Prince Tenderfoot (USA) 126) [1997 6g 6m 6m 7.1g Sep 27] 6,200Y: second foal: dam effective from 1m to 1½m: behind in minor event and maidens. *A. Bailey* —

CAROL'S DREAM (USA) 5 ch.h. Risen Star (USA) – Merle Halton (USA) (Rattle Dancer) [1996 75: a10g* a7g 1997 10.8m a12g⁵ a16g³ 12m 12m⁵ 17.2g Jun 28] good-bodied horse: has had soft palate operation: fair handicapper: trained by Miss J. Bower second start only: form in 1997 only on next outing: seems to stay 2m: acts on equitrack (and on firm ground as 3-y-o): inconsistent: joined M. Pitman. *J. W. Hills* — a72

CAROL SINGER (USA) 2 b.f. (Jan 12) Geiger Counter (USA) – Wake Up Noel (USA) (Nureyev (USA) 131) [1997 5d 5d³ 5g³ 5s² 5.2f² 5d a6g⁴ a5g a6g⁶ Dec 12] fair sort, looks on the weak side: first reported foal: dam unraced daughter of US Grade 1 1½m winner Anka Germania: fair maiden: second in nurseries at Catterick and Yarmouth in October: well below form afterwards though ran better than position suggests first start on all-weather: best at 5f: acts on firm and soft ground: has high head carriage. *M. Johnston* 71 a59

CAROUSE 2 br.g. (Feb 23) Petong 126 – Merry Rous 66 (Rousillon (USA) 133) [1997 6d⁵ 6m 7m 7m 8m Nov 1] 23,000Y: useful-looking gelding: fourth foal: 57

half-brother to 1994 2-y-o 5f winner Bruton Stream (by Taufan) and 5f (at 2 yrs) and 7.5f winner Clincher Club (by Polish Patriot): dam, 2-y-o 6f winner, half-sister to smart sprinter Tina's Pet: modest form in maidens second and third starts: well beaten in seller final outing: stays 7f: has carried head high. *M. R. Channon*

CARRANITA (IRE) 7 br.m. Anita's Prince 126 – Take More (GER) (Frontal 122) [1996 111: 5d* 6m* 6m⁴ 7f² 7.1d³ 6m⁴ 6g* 7m 6d* 6m 6g 6s⁴ 6s⁴ 1997 7m² 6g⁴ 6m³ 6g 6s⁵ 6g 6.1d* 6s Nov 8] angular mare: has a markedly round action: useful form at 7 yrs: best effort 1½ lengths third to Cyrano's Lad in rated stakes at Newmarket in May: won minor event at Nottingham in October: tailed off in listed race final outing: effective at 6f/7f: has form on any going, very best efforts on good going or softer: game. *B. Palling*   107

CARREAMIA 4 b.f. Weldnaas (USA) 112 – Carribean Tyme 85 (Tyrnavos 129) [1996 62: 6m⁵ a8.5g³ a8.5g 1997 7g 6m⁴ 6.1d 6d⁴ 6m⁵ 7g³ Aug 1] lengthy filly: has a short, round action: modest maiden handicapper: should stay 1m: acts on dead going and fibresand. *J. L. Eyre*   56

CARRICK VIEW (IRE) 2 b.c. (May 11) Posen (USA) – Linda's Fantasy 108 (Raga Navarro (ITY) 119) [1997 6g 6g⁴ 6d 7m Sep 20] IR 10,000Y: leggy, lengthy colt: half-brother to several winners, including 9f and 11f winner Priceless Fantasy (by Dunbeath) and fairly useful 1¼m winner Anafi (by Slip Anchor): dam 6f to 1m winner: no worthwhile form: sold and sent to Denmark. *P. Calver*   –

CARRIE'S FANTASY 3 ch.f. Formidable (USA) 125 – Caress 84 (Godswalk (USA) 130) [1996 NR 1997 a6g 7m Jun 9] second foal: dam, easily best form at 2 yrs, sprint winner: tailed off in seller and claimer. *A. G. Newcombe*   –

CARROLLS MARC (IRE) 9 b.g. Horage 124 – Rare Find (Rarity 129) [1996 53: a12g* a12g* a13g² a12g⁵ a12g⁶ a12g 1997 a12g a12g a12g⁴ a12g a12g a12g* a14g⁶ a11g⁶ a16g* a13g⁵ Jun 28] angular gelding: poor mover: poor performer: won claimer at Southwell in April and seller (easily) at Lingfield in May: effective at 1½m to 2m: acts on good to firm (possibly not firm) ground, dead and the all-weather: held up: inconsistent. *C. Murray*   48

Scottish Equitable Gimcrack Stakes, York—Carrowkeel shows much improved form in beating Bold Fact

Sheikh Marwan Al Maktoum's "Carrowkeel"

CARROWKEEL (IRE)   2 b.c. (May 16) Waajib 121 – Par Un Nez (IRE)   106
(Cyrano de Bergerac 120) [1997 5d* 6m⁴ 6g* 7m⁴ 6m² 8s⁴ Oct 12] IR 28,000Y: tall
colt, rather unfurnished at 2 yrs: first foal: dam unraced: useful performer: won
maiden at Windsor in May and Scottish Equitable Gimcrack Stakes at York in
August, latter by ¾ length from Bold Fact, dictating pace and rallying when headed:
in frame afterwards in Champagne Stakes at Doncaster, Middle Park Stakes at
Newmarket (again rallying up hill when beaten ¾ length by Hayil) and Grand
Criterium at Longchamp: may well prove better over 7f/1m than 6f: acts on good to
firm and soft ground: sent to UAE. *B. W. Hills*

CARRY THE FLAG   2 b.c. (Apr 14) Tenby 125 – Tamassos 67 (Dance In Time   92 p
(CAN)) [1997 6m⁴ 7g* 7.9s⁶ 8g* Oct 7] leggy colt: seventh foal: half-brother to
several winners, notably 5-y-o Posidonas: dam, 1¼m winner, half-sister to Ile de
Chypre: progressive form: won maiden at Thirsk in June and nursery at Warwick in
October, going clear under hands and heels and eased on latter course: should be well
suited by 1¼m+: well held on soft ground (when bandaged): should make a useful
3-y-o. *P. F. I. Cole*

CARTOUCHE   3 gr.g. Terimon 124 – Emblazon 91 (Wolver Hollow 126) [1996   63
66p: 7m 7f⁵ 7m 1997 a8g² 8d a8g² 9s* 11.5m Jul 11] fair on all-weather, modest on   a75
turf: runner-up in 2 maidens at Southwell before winning similar event at Lingfield
in June, dictating steady pace: disappointing on much firmer ground next time:
should be well suited by 1¼m+: acts on soft ground, goes well on fibresand. *Sir Mark
Prescott*

CARVER DOONE   2 b.c. (Mar 21) Tragic Role (USA) – Miss Milton (Young   –
Christopher 119) [1997 6m 6d Sep 20] sixth reported foal: half-brother to Molecomb
winner Poets Cove (by Bay Express): dam lightly raced on flat: little promise in
maidens at Folkestone and Newbury. *Major D. N. Chappell*

181

CARVER JOHN 2 ch.g. (May 5) Sure Blade (USA) 130 – Dawn Ditty 100 (Song 132) [1997 5.1d⁵ May 19] leggy, lightly-made gelding: half-brother to 3 winners, including sprinter How's Yer Father and 7f/1m winner The Can Can Man (both fairly useful and by Daring March): dam sprinter: 12/1 and very green, well-held fifth of 6 in minor event at Bath. *P. D. Cundell* –

CASA ROSA 2 b.f. (Apr 28) Casteddu 111 – Kasarose (Owen Dudley 121) [1997 5g 5.1m⁵ 6f⁴ Jun 16] 6,200Y: half-sister to 6f winner Double Matt (by Double Schwartz): dam showed temperament and little ability at 2 yrs: poor maiden. *R. Hannon* 39

CASCATELLE BLEUE (IRE) 4 b.f. Bluebird (USA) 125 – Wuthering Falls (Wind And Wuthering (USA) 132) [1996 7d⁴ 7.8d⁶ 9m³ 9g³ 10g³ 12v 1997 12m 10m 7.1g 8g Jun 20] 24,000Y: lengthy ex-Irish filly: third dam, Irish 7f winner, is half-sister to Baronet from family of Katies: fair maiden (rated 69) up to 1¼m in 1996 for J. Oxx: showed nothing as 4-y-o: tried blinkered/visored. *M. H. Tompkins* –

CASHAPLENTY 4 ch.g. Ballacashtal (CAN) – Storm of Plenty (Billion (USA) 120) [1996 –: a12g⁵ a8.5g 1997 a12g* a12g 10d a12g Nov 21] lightly raced: modest performer: well backed when winning maiden at Wolverhampton in February: showed little in handicaps afterwards. *N. P. Littmoden* a53

CASHMERE LADY 5 b.m. Hubbly Bubbly (USA) – Choir (High Top 131) [1996 77, a91: a7g² a8g⁵ a8.5g* 8m⁴ 7m⁴ a8.5g² 8.3g⁵ 8m² 8g³ 8.3m⁴ 8d⁴ 7m⁵ 8.9g 1997 a7g 8m 8g a9.4g⁴ 10g⁴ 12f⁵ 8g* a8.5f* 8d² 7.9g 8g⁴ 8g* 7.9s 8m 8m 8g 8s a8.5g⁶ Nov 15] tall mare: fairly useful handicapper: won at Thirsk and Wolverhampton (best effort) in June and Redcar in August: had excuses most starts after: needs true test/forcing tactics at 1m and stays 1¼m: acts on good to firm and dead ground, goes well on fibresand. *J. L. Eyre* 83 a94

CASHMIRIE 5 b.m. Domynsky 110 – Betrothed (Aglojo 119) [1996 NR 1997 12.3m 11f³ 10v* 10g* 12m² 9.9m² Jul 29] modest handicapper: won apprentice event and ladies race at Pontefract in summer: best effort at Beverley final start: effective at 1¼m to 1½m: acts on any turf going, well beaten on all-weather. *J. L. Eyre* 53

CASHTAL LACE 4 ch.f. Ballacashtal (CAN) – Chantilly Lace (FR) 69 (Carwhite 127) [1996 NR 1997 11.7g 10.8g Oct 7] lightly raced and no sign of ability. *B. J. Llewellyn* –

CASINO ACE (IRE) 2 b.f. (Feb 6) Scenic 128 – Aces Full (USA) (Round Table) [1997 8.1d² 8.1d⁵ a8.5g² 8g⁴ 10s³ a10s³ Nov 28] neat filly: unimpressive mover: half-sister to several winners, notably Irish St Leger winner Petite Ile (by Ile de Bourbon), Grade 2 winner at 11f/1½m in USA: fair maiden: will be suited by 1½m+: acts on fibresand (ran poorly on equitrack final start), yet to race on ground firmer than good on turf: sold 23,000 gns in December. *P. W. Chapple-Hyam* 74

CASINO KING (IRE) 2 b.c. (Feb 28) Fairy King (USA) – Justsayno (USA) (Dr Blum (USA)) [1997 7.1g* 7m³ 9s⁶ Nov 16] IR 38,000Y: leggy, angular colt: fifth foal: closely related to a winner in Germany by Be My Guest and half-brother to 12.5f winner Tintara (by Caerleon) and Italian middle-distance winner Spus (by Alzao): dam 5f winner at 2 yrs and later smart at around 1m: fairly useful form: won maiden at Chepstow in September: third in £12,000 event at Ascot (beaten 5½ lengths by Mudeer) and 5¾ lengths sixth of 10 to Special Nash in Group 2 race at Rome after: will stay at least 1¼m. *P. W. Chapple-Hyam* 93

CASPIAN MORN 3 b.f. Lugana Beach 116 – Parijoun (Manado 130) [1996 63d: 6m³ 6f* 6g 7g 7f 6m⁴ 1997 5.3f⁴ 5g a7g a5g⁵ 6m Aug 16] well-made filly: has a quick action: disappointing handicapper: stays 6f: raced only on good going or firmer and on fibresand: visored (ran well) once at 2 yrs. *W. G. M. Turner* 50

CASTEL ROSSELO 7 br.h. Rousillon (USA) 133 – On The House (FR) 125 (Be My Guest (USA) 126) [1996 60: a9.4g 8s 9.2d⁵ 7m 8g 7.6m⁶ 6d 8.2m 6g 1997 8d³ 7m⁵ 7g* 6.9s³ Jul 2] smallish horse: usually impresses in appearance: fair performer: best effort since 1995 when winning 16-runner handicap at Thirsk in June: stays 1m: acts on good to firm and soft ground and on fibresand: tried blinkered. *I. Campbell* 69

CASTLE ASHBY JACK 3 gr.g. Chilibang 120 – Carly-B (IRE) 42 (Commanche Run 133) [1996 67: a5g² 5m³ 5m 5.1m³ 5f³ 6m 5.2f² 1997 a6g³ a6g² a5g² 5m 5.1m⁵ a6g⁴ 6f⁵ a8g a5g² a6g² a6g³ 6.1m⁴ 6m a7s⁶ a7g a7g² Dec 22] strong, lengthy gelding: modest maiden: races freely but probably stays 7f: acts on all-weather and firm going, yet to race on softer than good: usually blinkered/visored before final 3 starts: sometimes wanders. *P. Howling* 48 a60

CASTLE COURAGEOUS 10 b.g. Castle Keep 121 – Peteona 97 (Welsh Saint 126) [1996 NR 1997 16g 14m⁴ 16.5m⁴ 14g⁵ 16g⁴ 14m⁶ 17.2m⁵ 16.4s⁵ Aug 29] useful stayer at best, on downgrade. *Lady Herries* 81 d

CASTLE FRIEND 2 b.g. (Mar 23) Durgam (USA) – Furry Friend (USA) (Bold Bidder) [1997 5g 6g 6m⁶ 7m Sep 20] 10,500Y: strong gelding: brother to 4-y-o Thorntoun Estate and half-brother to 1990 2-y-o 6f winner Russian Mink (by L'Emigrant): dam lightly raced: poor form in varied events. *P. C. Haslam* 46

CASTLES BURNING (USA) 3 b. or br.g. Minshaanshu Amad (USA) 91§ – Major Overhaul (Known Fact (USA) 135) [1996 56, a73: 6g⁴ 6m 7g 8.1g 7.6m⁴ 8m 7m³ 6d² 8f³ a10g² a7g³ 1997 a8g* 10m⁴ 8.2d a8g⁴ a9.4g⁴ a8.5g⁵ 10m³ 10g 11.9m* 14m a14.8g⁴ a10g* a10g⁶ a12g Nov 18] compact gelding: fair handicapper on all-weather, modest on turf: won at Lingfield in March and October and Brighton in August: effective at 1m to 1½m: acts on firm and dead ground, and all-weather: none too consistent. *C. A. Cyzer* 60 a74

CASTLE SECRET 11 b.g. Castle Keep 121 – Baffle 87 (Petingo 135) [1996 59: a16g² 17.2m² 18f² 1997 a16.2g 21.6g⁵ a16.2g* a16.2g² a16.2g⁵ a14.8g⁵ a14g Nov 14] modest handicapper: won at Wolverhampton in May: thorough stayer: acts on any going, except possibly soft: blinkered (ran well) and hooded earlier in career. *D. Burchell* 57

CASUAL MAGIC 2 ch.c. (Apr 26) Magic Ring (IRE) 115 – Unsuitable (Local Suitor (USA) 128) [1997 6g 6.9d Oct 21] 3,200F, 13,000 2-y-o: fifth foal: half-brother to 1m and 1¼m winner Sistar Act (by Salse) and a winner in Italy by Warrshan: dam unraced daughter of half-sister to good milers Final Straw and Achieved: slowly away and always behind in maidens. *Major D. N. Chappell* –

CASUAL WATER (IRE) 6 b.g. Simply Great (FR) 122 – Top Nurse (High Top 131) [1996 73: 11.9m 12m⁵ 12m 11.9g⁶ 14.8m⁴ 12m* 12g³ 1997 14m⁵ 14m⁴ 12.5m⁶ 14.9d 13.3f⁵ 12m 12d 14m⁵ 14.1g Oct 4] lengthy, angular gelding: poor mover: fair handicapper: effective at 1½m to 15f: acts on firm and dead ground: tried visored/blinkered at 3 yrs: usually held up, and suited by strongly-run race: none too consistent. *A. G. Newcombe* 70

CATCHABLE 3 b.c. Pursuit of Love 124 – Catawba 98 (Mill Reef (USA) 141) [1996 83p: 8m⁶ 8m² 1997 11g⁵ 12s⁵ 12g* 14.8g⁶ 12m 14.1m⁴ Sep 26] good-topped colt: fluent mover: fairly useful form: won 3-runner maiden at Goodwood in June, soon off bridle: stiffer tasks afterwards, looking short of pace: should be suited by 1¾m+: acts on good to firm going, possibly unsuited by soft: sold 50,000 gns in October. *H. R. A. Cecil* 87

CATCHMENT 3 ch.g. Persian Bold 123 – Cachou (USA) 74 (Roberto (USA) 131) [1996 NR 1997 10d 12m⁶ 10m Oct 5] 15,000 2-y-o: compact gelding: first foal: dam 8.9f winner out of half-sister to smart middle-distance performers Tralos and Polemic: well held in maidens, pulling hard last 2 starts. *Mrs A. J. Perrett* –

CATCH THE BLUES (IRE) 5 b.m. Bluebird (USA) 125 – Dear Lorraine (FR) (Nonoalco (USA) 131) [1996 115: 5g⁵ 6g³ 6d² 6m² 5m* 5g⁵ 5m⁵ 6f³ 5m³ 1997 6d² 5g* 6g³ Jun 19] big mare: smart performer: won Ballyogan Stakes at Leopardstown in June by ½ length from Ailleacht, leading close home: good 1½ lengths third of 23 to Royal Applause in Cork And Orrery Stakes at Royal Ascot, staying on well having been soon off bridle: best up to 7f: acts on firm and soft ground: wears visor/blinkers: reportedly pulled a ligament in near-fore early July. *A. P. O'Brien, Ireland* 115

CATCH THE LIGHTS 4 b.f. Deploy 131 – Dream Chaser 92 (Record Token 128) [1996 86: 7m 7m 8m⁴ 8.1m* 8m* 7.1m* 9m 8m 7f⁴ 8m 8g 1997 8.3m⁵ Jun 9] lengthy, angular filly: fairly useful handicapper at 7f/1m for R. Hannon at 3 yrs: well below that form only start in 1997. *Miss C. Johnsey* –

CATCH THE RAINBOW 2 ch.f. (Feb 24) Deploy 131 – Sing A Rainbow 56 (IRE) 68 (Rainbow Quest (USA) 134) [1997 6.1g⁵ 5.9f 7d a7g³ 7.1s³ 10g Sep 23] 9,500Y: sturdy filly: first foal: dam, maiden who stayed 1¼m, half-sister to smart middle-distance horse Alriffa: modest maiden: should be much better suited by 1¼m+ than shorter: acts on soft ground: sold, to go to Austria. *J. G. Smyth-Osbourne*

CATFOOT LANE 2 b.f. (Apr 28) Batshoof 122 – T Catty (USA) 62 (Sensitive 46 Prince (USA)) [1997 5v a6g⁴ 6d a6g Sep 30] leggy, unfurnished filly: shows knee action: fourth reported foal: half-sister to 1¼m seller winner (stayed 2m) St Kitts (by Tragic Role): dam, maiden stayed 1½m, sister to smart performer around 7f Condrillac: poor maiden: disappointing in seller final start. *W. G. M. Turner*

CATHEDRAL (IRE) 3 b.g. Prince Sabo 123 – Choire Mhor 100 (Dominion 109 123) [1996 83: 5.2s³ 1997 5.1m² 5m* 5d 5d³ 5m² 5d² Aug 28] lengthy, workmanlike gelding: has a splayed action: quickly developed into a useful performer: easily landed the odds in maiden at Beverley in April: best efforts when ½-length second to Averti in King George Stakes at Goodwood, leading briefly inside final 1f, and to My Melody Parkes in 5-runner minor event at Lingfield on last 2 starts: speedy, and raced only at 5f: acts on good to firm and dead ground, shaped well on soft. *B. J. Meehan*

CATHERINES SONG 2 b.f. (Feb 8) Aragon 118 – Songstead 92 (Song 132) 60 [1997 6g 5.2m* 5g⁴ 5.2f 6g² Aug 20] 7,500Y: fifth foal: sister to winning sprinter Arasong and half-sister to 3 other winners, including 4-y-o Songsteed: dam 6f winner from family of Crews Hill: won seller at Yarmouth in June: below-form second in similar event at Leicester: should stay 6f: has been bandaged. *C. A. Dwyer*

CATHERSTON LUCKY 3 b.f. Liboi (USA) 76 – Buckhurst 85 (Gulf Pearl – 117) [1996 NR 1997 8f 8s 8.3m Jul 28] half-sister to several winners, including 7f (at 2 yrs) and 1½m winner Winning Line (by Master Willie): dam stayed 7f: well beaten in maidens. *G. B. Balding*

CATIENUS (USA) 3 b. or br.c. Storm Cat (USA) – Diamond City (USA) 104 109 (Mr Prospector (USA)) [1996 93: 7g⁵ 7m³ 7.1v* 8d* 1997 8s⁶ 10.3m⁴ 10g⁴ 8.9s⁶ Sep 4] strong, close-coupled colt: has a round action: useful performer: won 4-runner minor event at Thirsk in May: good effort when close fourth to King Alex in Group 3 race at the Curragh in August 2 starts later: ran badly final outing: stays 1¼m: almost certainly suited by good going or softer (acts on heavy): usually a front runner: sent to USA. *M. R. Stoute*

CATRIA (IRE) 3 br.f. Caerleon (USA) 132 – Embla 121 (Dominion 123) [1996 – 76: 6m⁶ 6m 7.1s² 7f⁶ a6g⁶ 1997 6s Jul 4] well-bred filly (dam won Cheveley Park Stakes but didn't train on): fair maiden at 2 yrs: showed nothing only run of 1997: sold 55,000 gns in December. *J. H. M. Gosden*

CATS BOTTOM 5 ch.m. Primo Dominie 121 – Purple Fan (Dalsaan 125) [1996 59 d 59: 6f 7g 8m⁴ 7m⁶ 8m 10.2m 8f 7m 8m² 8f² 8m⁵ a7s⁶ a8g* 1997 a8g³ a9.4g² a8g a8g* a7g³ a8g a8g 8f 8g⁵ 8.3m 8m⁶ 8.3m a8.5g 8.2d a8g Nov 24] angular mare: unimpressive mover: modest handicapper: won at Southwell (apprentices) in March: below form last 6 starts: stays 9.4f: acts on firm and dead ground, and on fibresand: blinkered at 3 yrs: sometimes slowly away. *A. G. Newcombe*

CATWALK GIRL 4 b.f. Skyliner 117 – Pokey's Pet 56 (Uncle Pokey 116) [1996 – –: 7g⁶ 6m 7.5m 7g 1997 8g 7g 9.2m Aug 18] workmanlike filly: no worthwhile form since 1995: often visored/blinkered. *R. A. Fahey*

CAUDA EQUINA 3 gr.g. Statoblest 120 – Sea Fret 96 (Habat 127) [1996 74: 5g³ 82 5g 6g 1997 5.1m* 5.1d* 5d 5.1s⁴ 6g* 5.1m⁴ᵈⁱˢ 6m 5m⁶ 5m 6g Aug 25] good-topped gelding: unimpressive mover: has been hobdayed: fairly useful performer: won seller and minor event at Bath in the spring and handicap at Ripon in July: stays 6f: acts on good to firm and soft going. *M. R. Channon*

CAUDILLO (IRE) 4 b.f. Nordico (USA) – Over Swing (FR) (Saint Cyrien (FR) 63 128) [1996 8d³ 10m² 8d* 10g⁶ 8f 1997 a8.5g⁶ 8m 10m 16g 8.3s² 10g 7.1m² 6s² 7.1d⁴ 6m 6g⁴ 7.1g 8v 7g³ a7g* a7g Dec 18] small, strong filly: second foal: dam placed at 2 yrs in France: modest handicapper: won at Wolverhampton in November, rallying gamely: effective at 6f to 1¼m: acts on good to firm ground, soft and fibresand. *Mrs P. N. Dutfield*

184

CAUTION 3 b.f. Warning 136 – Fairy Flax (IRE) 97 (Dancing Brave (USA) 140) 78
[1996 78p: 5s² 5m³ 6m* 1997 7.9g 6.1m* 7.5m* 6g⁴ 6g³ 6m 7d 5.1g² 5m 6.1g 5d Oct
20] small, unfurnished filly: fair performer: won claimers at Chester and Beverley
for Mrs J. R. Ramsden in summer: effective at 5f (given really strong pace) to 7.5f:
acts on good to firm going, possibly not on softer than good. *S. Gollings*

CAVERSFIELD 2 ch.c. (Mar 27) Tina's Pet 121 – Canoodle 66 (Warpath 113) 75 p
[1997 5.1d² 5m 6g 6f 6m* 7g* Oct 27] 9,200Y: workmanlike colt: seventh foal:
brother to fairly useful stayer Satin Lover and half-brother to several winners,
including 5-y-o Kemo Sabo, fairly useful 6f (at 2 yrs) and 1m winner: dam 1½m to
2m winner: progressive performer: won nurseries at Windsor and Leicester 2 months
apart, soon travelling strongly but needing to rally gamely on latter course: should
stay 1m: acts on good to firm ground, shaped well on good to soft: should make a
fairly useful handicapper. *R. Hannon*

CAVIAR ROYALE (IRE) 3 ch.c. Royal Academy (USA) 130 – Petite 103
Liqueurelle (IRE) (Shernazar 131) [1996 94: 5m² 5m* 6m³ 5f⁵ 6m² 6d² 1997 8g³
10.4g 8.1d³ 8m 8g 8g* 7.9d 7.6s Aug 30] strong, lengthy colt: fluent mover: useful
handicapper: improved form to win strongly-run race at Thirsk in August: well
beaten afterwards: should prove as effective at 1¼m as 1m: acts on firm and
dead ground: has joined M. W. Easterby. *T. D. Barron*

CAYMAN KAI (IRE) 4 ch.c. Imperial Frontier (USA) 112 – Safiya (USA) 107
(Riverman (USA) 131) [1996 114: 7m³ 8g⁴ 8f⁵ 8m 1997 6g⁵ 6s² 8d 6g 6g³ 7.3m⁵ Jul
18] sturdy, good-quartered colt: takes the eye in appearance: tends to move short to
post nowadays: only useful form at best in 1997, best effort when fifth (to
Monaassib) in Abernant Stakes at Newmarket on reappearance: stays 1m: acts on
firm ground and dead: has had tongue tied: held up. *R. Hannon*

CD NEWSROUND (IRE) 2 b.f. (Apr 9) Mujadil (USA) 119 – Coffee Bean –
(Doulab (USA) 115) [1997 5.1m 6m 5.1g 5d 7f Oct 3] 10,500Y: workmanlike filly:
poor mover: fourth foal: half-sister to 3 winners up to 1¼m by Red Sunset, including
5-y-o Java Red: dam poor Irish maiden: no worthwhile form, including in seller:
visored final start: sold, and sent to Austria. *M. R. Channon*

CEANOTHUS (IRE) 3 ch.f. Bluebird (USA) 125 – Golden Bloom (Main Reef 61
126) [1996 –p: 7f 8g 1997 6m⁶ 7.1d² 10m⁴ 10m⁴ a12g² a11g⁴ a14.8g Sep 20] leggy,
sparely-made filly: modest performer: stays 1½m (well beaten over 14.8f): acts on
good to firm going and fibresand. *W. J. Haggas*

CEASE FIRE (IRE) 2 b.f. (Apr 29) Brief Truce (USA) 126 – Lisa's Favourite 86
(Gorytus (USA) 132) [1997 6m³ 6m² 6d² 6g Oct 18] 9,000Y: neat filly: fifth foal:
half-sister to 1993 2-y-o 7f winner Majestic Heights (by High Estate): dam Irish
maiden bred around 1m: fairly useful maiden: best effort eighth to Grazia in
Two-Year-Old Trophy at Redcar: should stay 1m: has been bandaged: sent to USA.
Mrs J. Cecil

CEDEZ LE PASSAGE (FR) 6 br.h. Warning 136 – Microcosme 100 (Golden 69
Fleece (USA) 133) [1996 73, a80: 8s 10g 12m 8m 10g 10d⁵ 10d a10s⁵ a9.4g* a9.4g⁶ a–
a10g³ a9.4g⁴ 1997 a9.4g⁶ a10g⁵ a12g a8g 12m⁶ 10.3d 10s³ 10.5s 10g² 10g⁴ 11g⁴ 8d³
10.5d 8v⁶ Dec 1] close-coupled horse: fair performer: stays 1½m: acts on firm and
soft ground and the all-weather: usually blinkered nowadays: trained by K. Cunningham-Brown until after eighth start, and has had 3 trainers in France: inconsistent.
P. Tual, France

CEE-JAY-AY 10 gr.g. Free State 125 – Raffinrula 75 (Raffingora 130) [1996 59: 50 d
a7g 7.5d⁶ 10.8g 8m 8.5m 8g⁵ 6.9g⁵ 10.3m⁵ 8f 8f² 7.6m³ 8m 6.9f* 7.5f² 7.5g⁶ 6.9m⁴
8.5m 8f³ 9m³ 8m⁴ 8m² 1997 7g 8g 8g⁴ 8g 8g 6.9f 8f³ 7.5g 6.9m 7.6m 8.1g 7.5d³ 8.3g
Sep 29] smallish gelding: modest form only on occasions at 10 yrs, well beaten last 6
starts: seems to stay 1¼m: acts on any going: blinkered (below form) once at 4 yrs:
usually ruins chance by starting slowly. *J. Berry*

CEE-N-K (IRE) 3 b.c. Thatching 131 – Valois (Lyphard (USA) 132) [1996 65+, 77
a77: 6g 6m⁴ a6g² a6g⁶ a6g² a8g* 1997 a8.5g a7g⁴ 7.5m⁴ 11.6s 10g⁶ 7.5m* 7.5m 8m⁵
7d 7.1g 8m 8g² 8d a8g a8.5g⁶ Dec 26] fair handicapper: won at Beverley in July:
below form after second at Redcar in October: seems best at 7f/1m: acts on good to

firm going and all-weather, below form on dead: blinkered last 5 starts: often a front runner. *M. Johnston*

CELANDINE 4 b.f. Warning 136 – Silly Bold (Rousillon (USA) 133) [1996 –: a6g^6 a5g^6 5g 6m 1997 6g 7g 8g 6m^6 6d^2 6m^3 7m^6 7m^3 Sep 20] leggy filly: has a quick action: modest handicapper: stays 7f: acts on firm and dead going. *Andrew Turnell*   56

CELEBRANT 3 b.f. Saddlers' Hall (IRE) 126 – Cathedra (So Blessed 130) [1996 66: 6.1m^2 6m^4 6d^5 1997 10d 10m 11.1m Sep 22] workmanlike filly: fair maiden in 1996: well beaten in handicaps at 3 yrs: bred to stay beyond 6f. *A. Hide*   –

CELEBRATION 2 br.f. (Jan 11) Selkirk (USA) 129 – No Restraint 84 (Habitat 134) [1997 7d Nov 7] 31,000Y: rangy, unfurnished filly: half-sister to 3 winners, including useful Spanish middle-distance stayer Alexandrovich (by Mtoto): dam, 1m and 1¼m winner, half-sister to very smart Sorbus: 20/1, about 9 lengths eighth of 18 to High-Rise in maiden at Doncaster, held up and nearest finish: should stay 1¼m+: type to do a fair bit better. *I. A. Balding*   61 p

CELEBRATION CAKE (IRE) 5 b.g. Mister Majestic 122 – My Louise 54 (Manado 130) [1996 81: 8.1m 8.3m^2 8.3m* 8d^2 8.1m* 7.9g 8m^5 7m* 9.2g 1997 9.9m 8g 8.3g 8.3m^6 7d 8d^6 8.1g 8m Oct 28] workmanlike gelding: reportedly operated on for his wind: just fair at best at 5 yrs, best effort on sixth start: stays 1m: acts on firm and dead going, below form on soft: visored (below form) once as 3-y-o: joined Mrs M. Reveley. *Miss L. A. Perratt*   71

CELERIC 5 b.g. Mtoto 134 – Hot Spice (Hotfoot 126) [1996 116+: 12m^6 13.9m* 13.9m^2 16.1m* 13.9m* 15.9m* 18m^2 16m* 1997 12m^4 13.9g* 16.4g^2 20g* 12g^5 15.9g^4 20m^2 Oct 4]   121

Former champion jockey Pat Eddery was riding as well as ever in 1997 until a back injury forced him to curtail his season in September, and his handling of Celeric in the Gold Cup at Royal Ascot in June provided a marvellous example of his artistry in the saddle. Indeed, the performance of both horse and rider ensured that the Gold Cup would be remembered as one of the races of the season. A race which had come to be regarded by many as an anachronism has enjoyed something of a revival in recent years, and the latest running will have done much to restore its popularity still further.

Although lacking an outstanding performer, the staying ranks in 1997 did have strength in depth, and no fewer than thirteen took part in the Gold Cup, the largest field for the race since Sadeem was placed first following the disqualification of Royal Gait in 1988. The race had a very open look to it. Even

Yorkshire Cup, York—Celeric (striped sleeves) idles as Mons rallies. Whitewater Affair (left) finishes third

*Gold Cup, Royal Ascot—Pat Eddery times his challenge to perfection
as Celeric wins a thrilling race from Classic Cliche and the visored Election Day*

Heron Island, the longest-priced runner in the field at 33/1, was by no means a
no-hoper. On his previous start he'd been beaten only two and a half lengths
when fifth behind Persian Punch in the Henry II Stakes at Sandown, and the
latter was the favourite for the Gold Cup at 9/2. Next in the betting at 11/2 came
Celeric, beaten three quarters of a length into second at Sandown where a
steady pace hadn't been ideal for him, and now meeting his conqueror on terms
2 lb better taking into account weight for age. Prior to Sandown, Celeric had
beaten Mons by a short head in the Yorkshire Cup, with the previous year's
Gold Cup winner Classic Cliche tailed-off last. Classic Cliche, having his first
race since York, was 6/1 to complete the double, while the 1995 Gold Cup
winner Double Trigger was a 20/1-shot. Celeric had demonstrated in the
Yorkshire Cup, run over a mile and three quarters, that he'd not only retained
his good turn of foot but also his habit of idling once he hits the front. Aware of
this and also of the fact that his mount was unproven over a distance beyond
two and a quarter miles, Eddery set out to conserve Celeric's energy and
produce him as late as possible. He dropped Celeric out in last place as Grey
Shot set a sound gallop, making his ground gradually approaching the turn
where Double Eclipse now led, pressed by Classic Cliche. Celeric, travelling
strongly on the wide outside, was switched inside for some cover as Classic
Cliche took command early in the straight, an audacious move by Eddery who
then showed remarkable composure by steadying Celeric a furlong out. A few
strides later, deciding the time was now right, Eddery asked Celeric for his
effort and the horse responded with a fine turn of speed to overhaul Classic
Cliche in the last fifty yards or so and win by three quarters of a length. Election
Day, staying on strongly, was a further length back in third, five lengths clear of
fourth-placed Heron Island. It was a thrilling finish to a magnificent race, and
one which must have been nerve-wracking for the connections of the winner to
watch!

Celeric didn't manage to add to his Gold Cup success, but he did acquit
himself well enough in his three remaining races without reproducing his best
form. A steadily-run mile and a half wasn't in Celeric's favour in the Princess
of Wales's Stakes at Newmarket, where he finished fifth behind Shantou, while
he had plenty on at the weights and didn't look his usual bright self in the
paddock prior to finishing fourth behind Double Eclipse in the Lonsdale Stakes

at York. Returned to two and a half miles and reunited with Frankie Dettori, who'd partnered him at Sandown, Celeric ended his season by failing narrowly to land the odds in the Prix du Cadran at Longchamp, where paddock inspection revealed that he was going in his coat. Brought with a smooth challenge to lead just inside the final furlong, Celeric was caught and beaten a neck by the rallying Chief Contender. Celeric has won eleven races all told, five of them as a four-year-old when he made remarkable progress, and although he's unlikely to improve any further, he's still going to prove a force to reckon with in the top staying races. After the sad death of his trainer, he will be with John Dunlop in 1998.

		Busted	Crepello
	Mtoto	(b 1963)	Sans Le Sou
	(b 1983)	Amazer	Mincio
Celeric		(b 1967)	Alzara
(b.g. 1992)		Hotfoot	Firestreak
	Hot Spice	(br 1966)	Pitter Patter
	(b 1978)	Persian Market	Taj Dewan
		(br 1972)	Londonderry Air

Hot Spice, the dam of Celeric, was put down in February after suffering complications with her pregnancy. Also trained by David Morley, she achieved little on the racecourse but it was a different story at stud. It will be interesting to see what name is given to the last of her offspring, a yearling filly by Cadeaux Genereux, the names of Hot Spice's other produce having had a spicy or culinary theme to them. They include the winners Turmeric (by Alias Smith), Sesame (by Derrylin) and Zucchini (by Absalom), easily the best of them the smart mile-and-a-half performer Sesame. Celeric's second dam, Persian Market, showed useful form and was awarded the eight-and-a-half furlong Princess Elizabeth Stakes at Epsom on the demotion of Juliette Marny.

Mr Christopher Spence's "Celeric"

The tall, close-coupled Celeric, a good walker with a quick action, usually impresses a good deal in appearance, though he does tend to get on his toes in the preliminaries. His connections were very worried by the rain which arrived at Ascot on Gold Cup day, fearing it could make the ground too soft for him, but it was no softer than good by the time the race was run. Apart from when showing promise on good to soft as a two-year-old, Celeric has raced only on good ground or firmer. *D. Morley*

CELESTIAL BAY (IRE) 2 b.f. (Apr 4) Star de Naskra (USA) – Kandara (FR) 62 + 88 (Dalsaan 125) [1997 7.1d³ 7.1g 6g³ 6.9m⁴ Aug 19] 3,400F: workmanlike filly: third foal: dam, 5f/6f winner at 2 yrs, half-sister to high-class US 1m/1¼m performer In Excess: modest maiden: rather headstrong, and may prove best up to 1m: has been edgy and swished tail. *A. G. Foster*

CELESTIAL CHOIR 7 b.m. Celestial Storm (USA) 132 – Choir (High Top 94 131) [1996 94: a10g* a12g* a9.4g⁴ a12g⁴ 8s⁵ 8g² 8g 10g 11.9m² 10.3g³ 12.3m² 10.3m* 11.9m* 10.3m 10m³ 12s 1997 a9.4g² a12g⁶ 11.9d 10.1g³ 11.9g 12m* 11.9g 12m⁵ 11.9g 11.9s* 12d 12s Nov 8] angular mare: fairly useful performer: won handicap at Pontefract in August and minor event at York in October: stays 1½m: acts on good to firm and soft ground and the all-weather: tried blinkered/visored, no improvement: has run well sweating: suited by strongly-run race: tough, but is becoming an increasingly hard ride (usually soon off bridle nowadays): useful hurdler, and won over fences in December. *J. L. Eyre*

CELESTIAL KEY (USA) 7 br.g. Star de Naskra (USA) – Casa Key (USA) 102 (Cormorant (USA)) [1996 106: 8.9g⁵ 7g⁴ 9m³ 7m 7g² 8.1s⁶ 7g³ 8g⁴ a9.4g 1997 a9g³ a8g² a10g 8s⁵ 8g⁵ 7.9g 8m 8g* 8g* 7.9s 8.2d Nov 3] close-coupled, good-topped gelding: impresses in appearance: has a quick action: useful performer: won minor events at Dielsdorf in Switzerland in August/September: below best all 4 starts in Britain in 1997: effective at 7f to 9f: acts on good to firm and dead ground and on fibresand: soundly beaten both starts in blinkers. *M. Johnston*

CELESTIAL RIDGE (IRE) 3 ch.f. Indian Ridge 123 – Orion Dream (Skyliner – 117) [1996 NR 1997 7.1g⁶ Sep 26] IR 22,000Y: second foal: dam Irish 1m winner: 33/1 and bandaged, tailed off in maiden at Haydock: sold 500 gns in November. *J. M. Carr*

CELESTIAL WELCOME 2 b.f. (May 17) Most Welcome 131 – Choral – Sundown 81 (Night Shift (USA)) [1997 6d 7m 6d⁶ 8m Nov 4] 3,000Y: strong, workmanlike filly: second foal: sister to 3-y-o Night Chorus: dam effective from 1m to 1½m: little worthwhile form. *Mrs M. Reveley*

CELIA'S RAINBOW 4 gr.f. Belfort (FR) 89 – Mrs Skinner 53 (Electric 126) – [1996 –: 8g 9g⁶ 1997 5m 8f 8m 8.5d 8g a8g Nov 17] of little account. *R. M. Whitaker*

CELTIC CAVALIER (IRE) 2 b.c. (Mar 3) Caerleon (USA) 132 – Irish Arms 103 p (FR) (Irish River (FR) 131) [1997 7m* 7.1s⁵ 8d² Sep 21] 2,200,000 francs Y: quite good-topped colt: half-brother to several winners in France, including useful stayer Lady Slave (by In The Wings): dam French 12.5f winner: won maiden at Gowran Park in August: ¾-length second of 9 to King of Kings in National Stakes at the Curragh, running on well: will be well suited by 1¼m+: visored (soon beaten in Solario Stakes at Sandown) second start: should improve further. *A. P. O'Brien, Ireland*

CELTIC COMFORT 2 ch.g. (Apr 29) Executive Man 119 – Annacando 48 66 (Derrylin 115) [1997 5m 7s² 5.9g* a7g³ a6g 8m a7g Nov 21] 2,200 2-y-o: a71 workmanlike gelding: brother to a winner in Italy and half-brother to 2 winners, including 9.7f winner Daring King (by King of Spain): dam 2-y-o 6f seller winner: fair performer: won minor event at Carlisle in July: good third in nursery at Wolverhampton following month but well below form afterwards: should stay 1m: acts on fibresand and soft ground. *P. C. Haslam*

CELTIC CROSS 2 b.f. (Apr 23) Selkirk (USA) 129 – Abbey Strand (USA) 78 93 p (Shadeed (USA) 135) [1997 6m⁴ 7m² Sep 10] tall, useful-looking filly: second foal: dam, 1m winner, half-sister to smart 6f to 10.5f winner Church Parade and smart middle-distance stayer Castle Rising: shaped promisingly both starts, beaten 1¾ lengths by Exclusive in minor event at Kempton on second of them, free in front but sticking well to task when headed 2f out: will stay 1m: open to further improvement, and well able to win races. *Lord Huntingdon*

CELTIC PAGEANT   2 b.c. (Apr 4) Tenby 125 – Certain Story (Known Fact   93 ?
(USA) 135) [1997 6m⁶ 7m² 7g³ 6m 7d² 7d⁵ Oct 27] leggy, useful-looking colt: half-brother to several winners, including 7f winner Fairy Story (by Persian Bold) and useful middle-distance performer Pharly Story (by Pharly): dam unraced half-sister to dam of Shaamit: fairly useful maiden: placed at Ascot (best effort), Epsom and Leicester: highly tried fourth outing: free-going sort, may prove best up to 1m: acts on good to firm and dead ground: hung left when well below form final start. *R. Akehurst*

CELTIC VENTURE   2 ch.g. (Mar 26) Risk Me (FR) 127 – Celtic River (IRE)   53
(Caerleon (USA) 132) [1997 5.1g 6m⁶ 6g² Aug 25] 14,000Y: second foal: dam French 1m winner, half-sister to Yorkshire Oaks winner and St Leger second Hellenic: easily best effort in sellers when short-head second at Ripon (claimed to join Mrs L. Stubbs £6,000): should stay at least 1m. *M. R. Channon*

CENSOR   4 b.g. Kris 135 – Mixed Applause (USA) 101 (Nijinsky (CAN) 138)   –
[1996 92: 8.1g⁵ 9s⁶ 8m³ 8m⁵ 1997 8m a9.4g 8.9d 10m 12g 8g Aug 17] big gelding: fairly useful in 1996 for H. Cecil: showed little at 4 yrs: backed at long odds but too free final start: stays 1¼m: acts on good to firm going. *D. Nicholls*

CENTRAL COMMITTEE (IRE)   2 ch.g. (Mar 22) Royal Academy (USA)   82 p
130 – Idle Chat (USA) 93 (Assert 134) [1997 7.5f* 7m⁴ Sep 24] 12,000Y: first living foal: dam, 2-y-o 1m winner who stayed 11.5f (later successful in Australia), half-sister to useful 1991 2-y-o Musicale out of half-sister to Committed: odds on, won 16-runner maiden at Beverley by 3 lengths from Long Bond: favourite, only fourth in minor event at Goodwood week later, though running on again in steadily-run affair having been bumped: will be suited by 1m+: remains capable of better. *P. W. Chapple-Hyam*

CENTRAL PARK (IRE)   2 ch.c. (Mar 20) In The Wings 128 – Park Special   117
(Relkino 131) [1997 6g⁴ 6f* 7g* 7m* 7g Oct 18]
  The partnership of Richard Quinn and Central Park cut no ice in the Dewhurst Stakes at Newmarket in October. For various reasons Quinn, first jockey to Central Park's stable, had missed out on riding the horse in all four of his previous races (he's unlikely to ride him again as the colt was bought by Godolphin for a rumoured £1m in December), and he must have been relishing the prospect of teaming up with one of the season's best two-year-olds in such an important event. It was to prove a bitterly disappointing experience, Central Park dropping away three furlongs out and trailing in last of seven, thirty lengths behind the winner Xaar. Although he'd taken the eye in the paddock, it's clear that Central Park, who'd missed two possible targets the previous

Lanson Champagne Vintage Stakes, Goodwood—Central Park is well on top near the finish

month due to an infection, was far from right. It can only be hoped the race hasn't left its mark, for Central Park looked to have the potential to develop into a very smart performer.

Engagements at other meetings caused Quinn to miss out on Central Park's first two races, the second of which, a maiden at Haydock, Central Park won by ten lengths. Despite such an impressive performance, when Central Park and his once-raced stable-companion Wales met in the Chesham Stakes at Royal Ascot it was the latter who was preferred by Quinn. Approaching the final furlong in the Chesham it was clear he'd made the wrong choice, for Central Park, who'd been prominent from the start, and the favourite Cape Verdi were beginning to draw away from Wales and the nine other runners. Central Park, finding plenty for Frankie Dettori, got the better of the battle in the last hundred yards to win by one and a half lengths. With Quinn injured and Dettori suspended, Pat Eddery came in for the ride on Central Park in the horse's next race, the Lanson Champagne Vintage Stakes at Goodwood in July. Though not so strongly contested as some recent renewals, this Group 3 event still provided a good test for Central Park, who, in winning it by three lengths, put up the performance of a smart two-year-old and showed himself still very much on the upgrade. Central Park tracked the leader Arawak Cay until ridden along to take up the running under two out, and ran on strongly to draw clear in the final furlong.

		Sadler's Wells	Northern Dancer
	In The Wings	(b 1981)	Fairy Bridge
	(b 1986)	High Hawk	Shirley Heights
Central Park (IRE)		(b 1980)	Sunbittern
(ch.c. Mar 20, 1995)		Relkino	Relko
	Park Special	(b 1973)	Pugnacity
	(b 1984)	Balilla	Balidar
		(b 1976)	Fighting

Central Park, a 42,000 guineas yearling, is by Singspiel's sire In The Wings, winner of the Coronation Cup, Grand Prix de Saint-Cloud and Breeders' Cup Turf, out of a mare who won a mile-and-a-quarter maiden in Ireland. Park Special has produced a couple of other winners, namely Majal (by Caerleon) and Velvet Moon (by Shaadi), the former a fair handicapper on the flat at up to one and a half miles and over hurdles, the latter winner of the Lowther Stakes at two and a listed event over a mile and a quarter at three. A half-sister to the useful miler Careafolie, the Horris Hill winner Gouriev and the smart French 1985 two-year-old Pantile, Park Special comes from a speedy family. Her dam Balilla won at five furlongs as a two-year-old and is a granddaughter of the sprinter Pelting, who appears in the extended pedigree of numerous pattern-race winners, including the Middle Park winner Bassenthwaite and the Prix de l'Abbaye winner Keen Hunter.

Central Park, who shows knee action, has raced only on good ground or firmer. A tall, lengthy colt with plenty of scope, he is sometimes on his toes in the preliminaries and does race freely, as did Velvet Moon. Central Park has yet to race beyond seven furlongs but will be suited by doing so and should stay a mile and a quarter, possibly more. *P. F. I. Cole*

CENTRE COURT 2 ch.f. (Feb 2) Second Set (IRE) 127 – Raffle 82 (Balidar 133) [1997 5d⁴ 5g* 5m 5.2d Sep 20] 8,000Y: small filly: half-sister to 3 winners, including useful 7f winner Rasan (by Dominion) and 9-y-o Top Prize: dam 6f winner, half-sister to Mummy's Pet: won maiden at Windsor in July: stiffish task in nurseries at Goodwood (unimpressive to post) and Newbury: may prove to be a sprinter. *R. Hannon*   **74**

CENTRE STALLS (IRE) 4 b.c. In The Wings 128 – Lora's Guest 99 (Be My Guest (USA) 126) [1996 117: 8g² 9m 8.1m* 8g* 8d 8g 1997 8.1g 7.9g* 10m³ 8m² 7g³ 8g a9.4g Dec 6]   **119**

The Queen Elizabeth II Stakes at Ascot has provided trainer Fulke Johnson Houghton with some happy memories; he won it with Romulus in

Grosvenor Casinos Hambleton Rated Stakes (Handicap), York—
an excellent weight-carrying performance from Centre Stalls. Prince Babar is second

1962 and Rose Bowl in both 1975 and 1976. But he'll have been disappointed that his latest representative in the race failed to do himself justice, Centre Stalls pulling too hard in a steadily-run contest and finishing last of nine. Few good horses have come Johnson Houghton's way in recent years and Centre Stalls himself isn't up to the standard of his Queen Elizabeth II winners, but two of the horse's performances in the latest season showed that he deserved his place in the field.

A hard puller who is suited by a strong pace, Centre Stalls had the race run to suit him in both the Grosvenor Casinos Hambleton Handicap, a listed event at York in May, and the Group 2 Queen Anne Stakes at Royal Ascot. Centre Stalls put up the best handicap performance of the season at York under top weight of 9-7, making headway over two furlongs out, leading entering the final furlong and being ridden clear to win by two and a half lengths from Prince Babar. He sweated that day but looked in superb shape before the Queen Anne, in which he finished a neck second to Allied Forces, who was conceding 3 lb, staying on strongly despite tending to carry his head awkwardly.

Centre Stalls's pedigree suggests he could stay beyond a mile, but he'll need to be taught to settle to have any chance of doing so. Tried at a mile and a quarter in the Brigadier Gerard Stakes at Sandown on his third start, Centre Stalls was left well behind by both Bosra Sham and Predappio in the last two furlongs of a slowly-run race; and he was probably unsuited by the fibresand when well below form over an extended nine furlongs at Wolverhampton on his final outing. By the high-class mile-and-a-half performer In The Wings, Centre Stalls is out of a mare whose only other winner, the quite useful Nawahil (by Shirley Heights), was suited by a test of stamina. The dam, Lora's Guest, showed useful form over seven furlongs and a mile for Johnson Houghton, is from a very good family. Her sister, On The House, won the One Thousand Guineas and Sussex Stakes, and her great grandam Tessa Gillian finished second in the former event. Lora's Guest's grandam, Courtessa, an unraced

192

Mr Anthony Pye-Jeary's "Centre Stalls"

sister to the good two-year-old Test Case, produced five winners, notably the high-class sprinter D'Urberville. This is also the family of the 1997 Coronation Stakes winner Rebecca Sharp.

		Sadler's Wells	Northern Dancer
Centre Stalls (IRE) (b.c. 1993)	In The Wings (b 1986)	(b 1981)	Fairy Bridge
		High Hawk (b 1980)	Shirley Heights
			Sunbittern
	Lora's Guest (ch 1984)	Be My Guest (ch 1974)	Northern Dancer
			What A Treat
		Lora (b 1972)	Lorenzaccio
			Courtessa

Centre Stalls, a strong, good-bodied colt, won on good to soft going as a two-year-old but has done virtually all of his racing since on good and good to firm. He should win more races kept away from the very best. *R. F. Johnson Houghton*

CERBERA 8 b.g. Caruso 112 – Sealed Contract 76 (Runnymede 123) [1996 –: a6g⁴ a5g⁵ a6g a6g 1997 a12g 7m Mar 27] little worthwhile form: tried blinkered. *J. P. Smith* —

CERISETTE (IRE) 2 b.f. (Jan 15) Polar Falcon (USA) 126 – Crimson Conquest (USA) 85 (Diesis 133) [1997 7f* Jul 12] third foal: closely related to 3-y-o China-berry: dam 2-y-o 6f winner who stayed 1¼m, half-sister to a Grade 2 2-y-o winner in USA: 20/1, won minor event at Lingfield by 3½ lengths from Mahboob, soon leading and striding clear from under 2f out despite carrying head on one side: should stay at least 1m: should make a useful filly if all is well. *C. E. Brittain* 94 p

CER

CERTAIN DANGER (IRE)   2 b.f. (Apr 2) Warning 136 – Please Believe Me 93   – p
(Try My Best (USA) 130) [1997 7m Nov 1] second foal: half-sister to 3-y-o
Storyteller: dam 2-y-o 5f winner out of Princess Royal Stakes winner Believer: 40/1,
never dangerous in 18-runner maiden at Newmarket: has joined N. Callaghan:
should do better. *R. Hannon*

CERTAIN MAGIC   3 ch.c. Faustus (USA) 118 – Dependable (Formidable   60
(USA) 125) [1996 64: 6g⁵ 6s* 7.3m⁶ 1997 10.8m 11.8d⁴ 11.6s 8f 11.6s 12s a14.8g*
11.9d* a14.8g³ Oct 6] strong, lengthy colt: modest handicapper: won at Wolverhampton (apprentices) and Haydock (amateurs) in September: effective at 1½m to
15f: acted on soft ground and fibresand: not the most straightforward of rides: tried
visored: dead. *W. R. Muir*

CERTAIN SURPRISE   3 b.f. Grey Desire 115 – Richesse (FR) (Faraway Son   –
(USA) 130) [1996 NR 1997 8d 10g 10m⁵ 12g Aug 13] leggy filly: half-sister to a
2-y-o 1m winner by Sonnen Gold, and a 9.4f winner by Mandrake Major: dam ran
once: signs of only a little ability in maidens and a handicap. *M. Madgwick*

CERTAINTY   3 br.f. Belmez (USA) 131 – La Carlotta (USA) (J O Tobin (USA)   –
130) [1996 NR 1997 a8g 10m 8s Jul 3] fourth reported foal: dam, French 9f winner,
is sister to smart French 5f to 1m winner L'Orangerie out of half-sister to Irish River:
well beaten in maidens and claimer. *J. R. Fanshawe*

CHABROL (CAN)   4 b.c. El Gran Senor (USA) 136 – Off The Record (USA)   67
(Chas Conerly (USA)) [1996 82d: 8m⁶ 10.3g⁵ 9s⁴ 10m 10.1m* 9g 10.1m 10.3g 9g
1997 12m⁵ 14.1m³ 14.1d³ 16s⁴ 14.1f² 20m 14.9s² 12g⁵ 11.6g Aug 4] leggy colt: fair
handicapper: left T. Clement after fifth start: suited by test of stamina: acts on any
going: tongue tied: fairly useful winning hurdler for John Berry. *R. Harris*

CHADLEIGH LANE (USA)   5 ch.g. Imp Society (USA) – Beauty Hour (USA)   –
(Bold Hour) [1996 –, a69: a7g⁶ a8g* a7g* a8g⁴ a7g³ a7g⁴ a8.5g* a7g⁵ a8.5g³ a8g⁵   a69 d
a9.4g⁴ a8g a9.4g⁴ a8g* 1997 a8g⁶ a8g* a8g² a8g³ a9.4g² 10.1g a8g a8g a9.4g⁶ a8g⁶
8.3d⁴ a8g a8g³ a11g a9.4g⁴ a9.4g² Dec 26] modest handicapper on fibresand: won at
Southwell in January on penultimate start for R. Hollinshead: not so good in second
half of season, though second at Wolverhampton final start: very lightly raced on turf
nowadays: stays 9.4f: seems effective visored or not. *A. B. Mulholland*

CHADWELL HALL   6 b.h. Kala Shikari 125 – Cherrywood Blessin (Good   71
Times (ITY)) [1996 73, a84: a5g² a5g⁴ a5g* a5g² a5g 5g² 5g* 5.1m⁵ 6m⁴ 5m* 6m   a76
5m 5.2m⁶ 5.1d 5m 5m⁶ 5.1g³ 5g⁶ 5s² a5g a6g* a6s² 1997 a6g⁴ a5g a5g⁵ a6g a5g²
6.1m⁵ 5g³ 5m 5g May 16] plain horse: had a round action: fair sprint handicapper:
broke leg at Thirsk in May: acted on good to firm and dead ground and on fibresand:
usually blinkered or visored: usually bandaged off-hind/had tongue tied: front
runner: game and consistent: dead. *S. R. Bowring*

CHAIN REACTION (IRE)   3 b.f. Fayruz 116 – Timiya (High Top 131) [1996   54
63: 6g³ 5g³ 5m⁵ 6m* 7m 1997 7m 6m 8.3s 8m³ 6.9m Aug 5] angular filly: modest
handicapper: stayed 1m: acted on good to firm ground: sold 6,500 gns in December,
in foal to Most Welcome. *M. A. Jarvis*

CHAIRMANS CHOICE   7 ch.g. Executive Man 119 – Revida Girl 63 (Habat   60
127) [1996 65, a–: a9.4g 8m³ 8s⁴ 7f* 7m³ 8m 1997 10m 8.3s⁵ 8d 8f³ 8.2m³ 9m³ 8d
8m 8s⁶ a10s* Nov 28] leggy gelding: has a screw in his knee: modest performer:
made all in seller at Lingfield in November: stays 1¼m: acts on firm ground and
all-weather, possibly not soft: edgy sort: ridden up with pace. *A. P. Jarvis*

CHAIRMANS DAUGHTER   3 b.f. Unfuwain (USA) 131 – Ville Sainte (FR)   68
(Saint Estephe (FR) 123) [1996 60: 6f⁴ 7g 6.9m 8f* 10m² 8f 8f 1997 12g⁶ 16.4m*
Aug 19] tall filly: has round action: fair performer: best effort when winning
apprentice handicap at Folkestone: stays 16.4f: acts on firm going: visored once,
successful both starts in blinkers. *J. Pearce*

CHAI-YO   7 b.g. Rakaposhi King 119 – Ballysax Lass (Main Reef 126) [1996 –p: 86
8.1s 1997 12m⁵ 8v² 9g Oct 25] close-coupled gelding: useful winning hurdler: lightly
raced on flat: best effort when second in minor event at Ascot: last but one in
handicap later in October: keen sort, likely to prove best short of 1½m. *J. A. B. Old*

CHAKRA   3 gr.g. Mystiko (USA) 124 – Maracuja (USA) (Riverman (USA) 131)   49
[1996 –: 6s 1997 7g 8g 6m 6g 6g 5.3m⁶* 6g 5.1g Sep 11] big gelding: only form when
winning handicap at Brighton in July: should stay 6f. *S. Dow*

194

CHALICE   4 b.f. Governor General 116 – Eucharis 41 (Tickled Pink 114) [1996   –
69: 6m⁶ a6g⁴ a5g 5g* 5m 5m⁴ 5g 5m 5m 1997 6.9g⁶ 6g 6g Aug 2] unfurnished filly:
fair handicapper at 3 yrs: well beaten in 1997: best efforts at 5f: acts on good to firm
and soft ground, below form on fibresand. *Mrs A. Swinbank*

CHALKY DANCER   5 br.g. Adbass (USA) 102 – Tiny Feet (Music Maestro   35
119) [1996 38, a–: a8g 7f 8m⁵ 8m² 8f a10g a8g a7g 1997 8m 8m⁶ 8.2g² 7f 8g³ 9.7g⁵   a–
7.5d 8m a8g⁶ a11g Nov 24] sturdy gelding: poor mover: poor maiden handicapper:
stays 1m: acts on firm ground, no form on all-weather: tried blinkered/visored:
inconsistent. *H. J. Collingridge*

CHALLENGER (IRE)   4 b.g. Nordico (USA) – Sweet Miyabi (JPN) (Royal Ski   –
(USA)) [1996 –: 7g 8g 9f⁵ 10g 1997 9.7g 8.3s 11.6m 9g 14m⁶ 10g 14m 16m Sep 25]
little sign of ability: left J. Sheehan after fourth start. *L. Wells*

CHALUZ   3 b.g. Night Shift (USA) – Laluche (USA) 100 (Alleged (USA) 138)   43
[1996 54p: 5m⁶ 6m 8g a8.5g² 1997 10m³ 9.7m 8s 9g 5.3g 7f a8.5g⁴ a7g* a7g⁴ a6g⁵   a60
a7g³ Dec 18] small, well-made gelding: type to carry condition: fluent mover:
modest handicapper on the all-weather, poor on turf: made all at Southwell in
November: creditable efforts afterwards: keen sort, best form at 7f: has had tongue
tied. *K. R. Burke*

CHAMELI   2 b.f. (Mar 1) Nordico (USA) – Try Vickers (USA) 72 (Fuzzbuster   49 +
(USA)) [1997 6.1s⁴ 6.1g Jul 30] 5,000 2-y-o: fifth foal: sister to fair winning sprinter
Nordico Princess, closely related to 3-y-o Hurgill Dancer and half-sister to winners
abroad by Primo Dominie and Pharly: dam, maiden, stayed 1¼m: poor form in
maiden and minor event at Nottingham in July. *Mrs L. Stubbs*

CHAMPAGNE GOLD   10 ch.g. Bairn (USA) 126 – Halkissimo 61 (Khalkis   –
127) [1996 NR 1997 12.1m Jul 25] lightly raced and no form for long time.
J. C. McConnochie

CHAMPAGNE N DREAMS   5 b.m. Rambo Dancer (CAN) 107 – Pink   46
Sensation 69 (Sagaro 133) [1996 47: 9m⁶ 8m⁶ 8m³ 8m 8.1m 12f³ 12.3g 1997 8g 9.9m
8m⁴ 8g³ 8m⁵ Aug 4] sturdy mare: poor handicapper: stays 1½m: acts on firm ground,
below form only outing on soft: blinkered (below form) once at 4 yrs. *D. Nicholls*

CHAMPAGNE ON ICE   3 b.f. Efisio 120 – Nip In The Air (USA) 114   43
(Northern Dancer) [1996 46: 5g 5.1g 6.1m 6.1m² 6m⁴ 7f 6s 1997 8s³ 8.2m⁵ 6.9d a7g⁴
a8g⁴ a9.4g⁶ Jun 18] small filly: poor maiden: should stay 1¼m: acts on soft going and
fibresand, probably on good to firm: inconsistent. *P. D. Evans*

CHAMPAGNE PRINCE   4 b.c. Prince Sabo 123 – Champagne Season (USA)   101
54 (Vaguely Noble 140) [1996 92: 8m⁵ 7m⁵ 10m 10.3d³ 10.1m⁴ 9m 10s 1997

*London Car Telephones Handicap, Epsom—Champagne Prince continues in corking form;
Star Manager (extreme left), Fahs (third left) and Conspicuous fill the minor placings*

CHA

9.9m⁴ 10.1m² 10m* 10m* 10.1g* 10m³ 10.4g 10d Sep 20] smallish colt: useful handicapper: well ridden by claimer C. Lowther when winning at Newmarket and Redcar (Zetland Gold Cup) in May and valuable event at Epsom in June: ran well in William Hill Cup at Goodwood next time, had excuses last 2 starts: stays 1¼m: acts on good to firm ground and dead, below form on soft: front runner/races prominently: upset in stalls and withdrawn fourth intended start: genuine: sold (to go to USA) 68,000 gns in October. *P. W. Harris*

CHAMPAGNE WARRIOR (IRE) 4 b.f. Waajib 121 – Late Swallow (My   53
Swallow 134) [1996 48: 10g⁶ 12m² 12m³ a12g⁴ 12s² 12.1m⁵ 13.8g⁴ 1997 12m*   a61
12.3m⁶ a12g* 12g a11g² a11g³ 11.8d a11g⁵ Nov 17] good-bodied filly: has lost off-side eye: modest performer: won seller at Beverley and claimer at Southwell in April: ran well when placed in June: should stay beyond 1½m: acts on good to firm ground, soft and on fibresand: blinkered (below form) once at 3 yrs. *M. J. Camacho*

CHANCANCOOK 4 ch.f. Hubbly Bubbly (USA) – Majuba Road (Scottish Rifle   –
127) [1996 –: 13.8g⁵ 11.8f a14g a11g 1997 14.1m⁵ 11.1d 11m Oct 28] no worthwhile form. *J. L. Eyre*

CHANDLER'S HALL 3 b.g. Saddlers' Hall (IRE) 126 – Queen's Visit (Top   –
Command (USA)) [1996 NR 1997 9d⁵ 10s⁴ 12m⁶ 10s 10d Oct 20] 11,000F, 23,000Y: sturdy gelding: seventh foal: half-brother to fairly useful 5f winner Bryan Robson (by Topsider): dam, maiden suited by 1¼m, half-sister to very smart 1984 2-y-o stayer Khozaam: only a little sign of ability in maidens and handicaps. *M. J. Heaton-Ellis*

CHANGE 3 b.c. North Briton 67 – Karminski 70 (Pitskelly 122) [1996 NR 1997   –
8d 8g May 27] sparely-made colt: half-brother to a winner in Norway by Blazing Saddles: dam middle-distance stayer: soundly beaten in maiden and claimer. *C. E. Brittain*

CHANGED TO BAILEYS (IRE) 3 b.g. Distinctly North (USA) 115 – Blue   –
Czarina (Sandhurst Prince 128) [1996 58: 5d 5m⁵ 5g³ 5g³ 5m⁵ 1997 5m⁵ 6m 5.9f Jun 12] leggy, sparely-made gelding: sprint maiden: little show at 3 yrs: tried blinkered. *J. Berry*

CHANGE FOR A BUCK (USA) 3 ch.f. Time For A Change (USA) – Pearl   83
Bracelet (USA) 118 (Lyphard (USA) 132) [1996 NR 1997 7g³ 8.2d* Apr 29] deep-girthed, lengthy filly: fourth foal: half-sister to 2 winners in USA, including one by Woodman: dam (ran twice) won Poule d'Essai des Pouliches: sire very smart 7f to 9f winner: evens after encouraging debut, won maiden at Nottingham by ½ length: keen type, but stays 1m: last and quietly to post both starts. *H. R. A. Cecil*

CHANSON D'AMOUR (IRE) 3 b.f. High Estate 127 – Wind of Change (FR)   –
(Sicyos (USA) 126) [1996 –: 5g⁴ 5m³ 5g⁶ 7.1m 7m 8.1m 8.3d 1997 10.9d 8.3s 8g 7g 8m⁴ 12.1g 7g⁶ 8.3d⁵ 11.1g⁴ 9d Sep 19] of little account. *Miss L. A. Perratt*

CHARBERTSAM 4 b.g. Rabdan 129 – Harts Mead (Posse (USA) 130) [1996   –
NR 1997 10g 14m Aug 17] first known foal: dam ran twice at 2 yrs: tailed off both starts. *R. Rowe*

CHARCOL 4 b.f. Nicholas Bill 125 – Dutch Princess 70 (Royalty 130) [1996 –:   –
10m 1997 10d 8s a12g 10.8g Oct 7] no sign of ability. *J. E. Banks*

CHARDANIA (IRE) 2 ch.f. (Apr 23) Rainbows For Life (CAN) – Far From   34
Home 73 (Habitat 134) [1997 5g⁴ a5g a5g⁶ 6g 6g⁴ 5m⁶ 6d⁶ 8g a8.5g Oct 6] 5,500Y: workmanlike filly: third foal: half-sister to useful Irish 3-y-o 6f and 7.8f winner Poker-B (by Shalford): dam, 6f winner, half-sister to smart 6f and 1m winner Missed Blessing: poor maiden. *Capt. J. Wilson*

CHARGE D'AFFAIRES 2 b.c. (Apr 13) Kendor (FR) 122 – Lettre de   116
Cachet (USA) (Secreto (USA) 128) [1997 5.5g* 5s³ 6g² 6g* 7g² 8s² Oct 12]
        Charge d'Affaires holds the distinction of being the only horse so far to beat Xaar, a feat he achieved in the Prix Morny Piaget over six furlongs at Deauville in August and one which we very much doubt he'll be able to repeat should the pair meet as three-year-olds. Indeed, provided Xaar lives up to expectations, Charge d'Affaires, smart colt though he is, could end up best remembered for that one performance. The pair had met for the first time in the Prix de Cabourg over the same course and distance three weeks earlier, Charge

196

Prix Morny Piaget, Deauville—
Charge d'Affaires (near side) is the only horse to get the better of Xaar in 1997

d'Affaires finishing one and a half lengths second. There seemed no reason why the tables should be turned in the Prix Morny, for which Xaar was sent off at odds on and Charge d'Affaires at 10/1. Of the five other runners in the field, two were overseas challengers, both of them beaten favourites at Royal Ascot on their previous starts, Desert Prince having finished second in the Coventry and Heeremandi sixth in the Queen Mary. Once again, though, it was Charge d'Affaires and Xaar who dominated the finish, the former produced late to win a tactical race by a head, the pair a length and a half clear of third-placed Heeremandi, with Desert Prince just behind in fifth. The seven-furlong Prix de la Salamandre at Longchamp was the deciding rubber in the challenge, and well though he ran, pulling five lengths and more clear of the remainder, Charge d'Affaires was distinctly second-best in a truly-run race. Both horses made their efforts early in the straight, but it was Xaar who produced much the better finishing speed to win by three lengths. Charge d'Affaires was stepped up to a mile for his final run of the season and turned in another good performance in finishing one and a half lengths second to Second Empire in the Grand Criterium at Longchamp, sticking gamely to his task but never looking likely to peg back the winner.

Charge d'Affaires won over an extended five furlongs at Chantilly on his debut, but he required further later in the season and there's no reason why he shouldn't stay a mile and a quarter as a three-year-old. His sire, Kendor, showed his best form at a mile, winning the Poule d'Essai des Poulains, but he would probably have been just as effective over further had he not raced so freely. Nevertheless, Kendor did finish a close second in the nine-furlong Prix Jean Prat and fourth, beaten little more than two lengths, in the ten-furlong Grand Prix de Paris. Charge d'Affaires' dam, Lettre de Cachet, successful over eleven furlongs in France as a four-year-old less than fourteen months before foaling him, is a sister to Secret Haunt, who showed smart form at up to a mile and a half, and a half-sister to Trigger Finger, a useful performer at a mile to a mile and a quarter in France. His grandam, Royal Suite, was a stakes winner in

Marquesa de Moratalla's "Charge d'Affaires"

Charge d'Affaires (b.c. Apr 13, 1995)	Kendor (FR) (gr 1986)	Kenmare (gr 1975)	Kalamoun
			Belle of Ireland
		Belle Mecene (b 1982)	Gay Mecene
			Djaka Belle
	Lettre de Cachet (USA) (ch 1990)	Secreto (b 1981)	Northern Dancer
			Betty's Secret
		Royal Suite (ch 1977)	Majestic Prince
			Nature

the States at two years, her only season to race. Charge d'Affaires, raced only on good and soft ground, seems genuine and consistent, and he should win races outside the best company as a three-year-old. *A. de Royer Dupre, France*

CHARISSE DANCER   4 b.f. Dancing Dissident (USA) 119 – Cadisa 82 (Top   43
Ville 129) [1996 52: 6m⁵ 5g³ 7m³ 8.3d⁴ 10f⁴ 8m 1997 8m 8g a8g⁴ 9m⁶ a12g Dec 6]
sparely-made filly: poor maiden handicapper: stays 1m, possibly 1¼m: acts on firm
and dead ground and on fibresand. *C. W. Thornton*

CHARITY CRUSADER   6 b.g. Rousillon (USA) 133 – Height of Folly 81   42
(Shirley Heights 130) [1996 NR 1997 12m⁵ 14.1s⁵ 16m² 14.1g³ 14d² 16m⁴ 14.1m*
14.1g² Aug 23] formerly useful, only poor on flat nowadays: won weak claimer at
Redcar in August: stays 2m: acts on firm and dead ground: usually blinkered: modest
hurdler, successful 3 times in 1997. *Mrs M. Reveley*

CHARLIE BIGTIME   7 b.g. Norwick (USA) 125 – Sea Aura 89 (Roi Soleil   46 §
125) [1996 52d: a12g³ a14.8g⁵ 12.1d a12g³ 14g a12g 12m 12m⁶ a12g³ a12g 11.9m⁴   a– §
11.9f⁵ a14.8g⁴ 14s⁶ a12g a12g 1997 a14g 12.1m³ 12.1g⁶ a14g⁵ 16s⁶ 11.5m³ Oct 22]
sturdy gelding: unimpressive mover: poor handicapper: probably stays 2m: acts on
good to firm ground and on fibresand: effective visored/blinkered or not: sometimes
bandaged: has looked reluctant: inconsistent. *I. Campbell*

198

CHARLIE CHANG (IRE) 4 b.g. Don't Forget Me 127 – East River (FR) 37
(Arctic Tern (USA) 126) [1996 73: 7m⁴ 7.9f⁴ 8s⁵ 8g 7.1m⁶ 8.2m² 7m⁶ 10.5m⁴ 8m
8.2g 1997 12f⁵ 10d³ a8g a12g Oct 27] close-coupled gelding: only poor form in 1997:
left D. W. Barker after third start: likely to prove best up to 1¼m: acts on firm going
and on equitrack, seemingly unsuited by soft: blinkered (raced too freely) once as
3-y-o. *B. J. Llewellyn*

CHARLIE'S GOLD 2 b.g. (Feb 12) Shalford (IRE) 124§ – Ballet 61 (Sharrood –
(USA) 124) [1997 7m 8m Nov 1] 21,000Y: first foal: dam, should have been suited
by at least 6f, half-sister to May Hill winner Satinette: last in maiden and a seller.
I. Campbell

CHARLIE SILLETT 5 ch.g. Handsome Sailor 125 – Bystrouska (Gorytus 92 §
(USA) 132) [1996 89: 7m 6d⁶ 7m⁶ 6v 7g 6.1s* 7g 1997 6m 7m 6g 6d 6.1s* 6s 6m 6m
6m Nov 4] tall gelding: fairly useful handicapper on his day: won at Chester in June:
effective at testing 6f to 7f: has form once good to firm going, goes extremely well on
soft: usually slowly away and has carried head high: nervy sort, usually early to post:
unreliable. *B. W. Hills*

CHARLIES LAD (IRE) 2 b.g. (Mar 26) Petardia 113 – Brigadina (Brigadier 62
Gerard 144) [1997 5m³ a5g² 5g⁴ 5.2f 6g* 6g² a5g³ 7g² Sep 3] IR 4,800Y: good-
topped gelding: half-brother to 3 winners, including 1994 2-y-o 7f winner Judge
Advocate (by Contract Law): dam ran twice in Ireland at 2 yrs: modest performer:
won seller at Yarmouth in July: probably stays 7f: has hung left and flashed tail:
doesn't always look keen: inconsistent: sent to Macau. *R. Guest*

CHARLOTTE CORDAY 4 b.f. Kris 135 – Dancing Rocks 118 (Green Dancer 105
(USA) 132) [1996 86: 7m³ 7g² 8g* 10g⁴ 1997 8m² 10.4g² 8.5m² 10.1d³ 8g Jul 9]
angular filly: useful performer: runner-up in minor race at Ascot and in listed events
at York (beaten ½ length by Papering) in May and Epsom (1½ lengths behind
Samara, having had poor run) in June: below form last 2 starts: stays 10.4f: acts on
good/good to firm going: tends to sweat, and often on toes: genuine. *G. Wragg*

CHARLTON IMP (USA) 4 b.f. Imp Society (USA) – Percentage (USA) 49
(Vaguely Noble 140) [1996 59: 7d⁶ 8d 6m 6.1d 8.3m⁵ 10m 8.1f* 8.3m 8m* 8.2d² 7f⁶
8m 1997 8f³ 8d 8d 8.2m³ 9d 8s 8.1m 6g⁴ 8.1g 8m 8g⁶ Sep 8] workmanlike filly: poor
handicapper: inconsistent in 1997: stays 1m: acts on firm and dead ground (tailed off
on soft): blinkered (ran respectably) seventh outing. *R. J. Hodges*

CHARLTON SPRING (IRE) 3 ch.f. Masterclass (USA) 116 – Relankina –
(IRE) (Broken Hearted 124) [1996 70: 5m² 5.1m 6m⁶ 6g² 6d* 7m 6g 1997 6f 6.1g⁶
7m 7g 6.1m Sep 15] leggy, sparely-made filly: fair winner in 1996: little worthwhile
form at 3 yrs, off course nearly 4 months after second start: best effort at 6f on dead
ground. *R. J. Hodges*

CHARMING ADMIRAL (IRE) 4 b.g. Shareef Dancer (USA) 135 – Lilac 62
Charm 87 (Bustino 136) [1996 71: 10g 12m⁵ 11.6m 13.1m³ 14d² 14d² a10g 11g²
1997 a12f⁶ 11f⁵ a10f⁴ a12f⁵ 12m a9f 14m 14.1m² 14.1d⁴ Nov 3] workmanlike
gelding: modest handicapper: left C. Wall after eighth start: stays 1¾m: acts on good
to soft ground, probably good to firm: tried blinkered, no improvement.
Mrs A. Swinbank

CHARNWOOD JACK (USA) 4 ch.c. Sanglamore (USA) 126 – Hyroglyph 69
(USA) (Northern Dancer) [1996 –: 8m 10g 10m 1997 10f⁵ 12m² 14.1d⁴ 11.9f 14.1f*
14.1s⁴ 14m⁴ a12g a12g³ Dec 6] strong, close-coupled colt: fair performer: won
5-runner minor event at Yarmouth in June: twice ran well in handicaps after: stays
1¾m: unraced on heavy going, acts on fibresand and any other turf ground.
I. Campbell

C-HARRY (IRE) 3 ch.c. Imperial Frontier (USA) 112 – Desert Gale (Taufan 65
(USA) 119) [1996 61, a67: 5s⁴ 5g³ 5.1d 5d² a5g³ a6g* 5m² 5d* 6.1s a6g² a7g² a7s⁴ a70
1997 a6g a7g* a6g* 6.1m 5m⁵ 6g⁵ 7.5d 6m³ 6.1m² 6g² 7g* 7g 6m⁵ 7g a6g Nov 15]
small, workmanlike colt: unimpressive mover: fair handicapper: won at Wolverhampton in February and March and Ayr (idled) in July: effective at 6f/7f: acts on
good to firm ground, dead and fibresand (yet to race on equitrack): has won in visor
but not worn one since eighth 2-y-o start. *R. Hollinshead*

CHARTER 6 b.g. Reference Point 139 – Winter Queen 60 (Welsh Pageant 132) 63
[1996 –: 14.1g^{4} 11.7f^{2} 10d 10m 1997 a16g a12g 16g 16m^{6} 12m 11.9d 14.6d^{4} 17.2m^{2}
16.1m 16g^{2} 15.8m^{6} Sep 20] sturdy gelding: modest handicapper: trained by T. J.
Naughton first 2 starts: stays 17f: acts on firm and dead ground: a difficult ride (has
hung markedly left): visored last 3 starts. *W. Storey*

CHASETOWN CAILIN 2 b.f. (Apr 11) Suave Dancer (USA) 136 – Kilvarnet 59 ?
78 (Furry Glen 121) [1997 5.1m^{6} a6g^{5} Jun 18] 8,000 2-y-o: half-sister to 3 winners,
including 6-y-o McGillycuddy Reeks and 7f (at 2 yrs) to 1¼m winner Ferdia (by
Petorius): dam 5f (at 2 yrs) and 7.6f winner: probably better effort in maidens when
fifth at Wolverhampton: should stay well beyond 6f. *R. Hollinshead*

CHASETOWN FLYER (USA) 3 b.c. Thorn Dance (USA) 107 – Thought 66
Provoker (USA) (Exceller (USA) 129) [1996 49: 5.9g 5.1m 6g^{6} a6g^{6} a8g^{3} a7g a7g^{2}
1997 a8s^{4} a8g^{5} a6g^{6} a6g^{4} a7g^{2} 6.1m^{6} a6g 8f* 8.3g* 8.3g^{3} 8g 8d 8m 7f Oct 3]
workmanlike colt: fair handicapper: trained by R. Hollinshead first 4 starts: won
18-runner events at Salisbury and Windsor within a week in June: should stay beyond
1m: acts on firm, dead ground and the all-weather. *N. E. Berry*

CHASKA 2 b.f. (Apr 23) Reprimand 122 – Royal Passion 78 (Ahonoora 122) [1997 59
6.1d 6g^{4} 6m^{5} 6m* 7.9s 8d a7g Oct 6] unfurnished filly: second living foal: half-sister
to 4-y-o Tadeo: dam winner 3 times around 1¼m: won claimer at Hamilton in August
(claimed out of M. Johnston's stable £10,000): well beaten afterwards: form only
over 6f: best efforts on good to firm ground: visored penultimate start. *A. Bailey*

CHATEAUHERAULT (IRE) 3 b.g. Contract Law (USA) 108 – Secret 61
Hideaway (USA) (Key To The Mint (USA)) [1996 50: 6m 7m 6m 10m^{4} 1997 a10g*
a9.4f^{2} a10g^{3} a10g^{3} 13d^{4} 14.1g Aug 23] tall gelding: modest handicapper: won at
Lingfield in January: off course 6 months before penultimate start: stays 13f: acts on
good to firm ground, dead and all-weather: visored (not discredited) once: carries
head awkwardly, and is difficult ride: sold, to go to Macau. *P. C. Haslam*

CHATHAM ISLAND 9 ch.g. Jupiter Island 126 – Floreal 68 (Formidable –
(USA) 125) [1996 77, a–: a12g^{6} 12g 11.8g 12f^{2} 12m^{2} 12g^{3} 11.5f^{2} 12m 14.1m* 1997
12m 14.8d^{6} 14.1s 14.1m^{6} Aug 6] rangy gelding: impresses in appearance: formerly
fairly useful up to 1¾m: well held at 9 yrs. *C. E. Brittain*

CHATTAN 2 b.c. (Feb 24) Lycius (USA) 124 – Chanzi (USA) 109 (El Gran Senor 88 p
(USA) 136) [1997 7m^{3} 7m^{2} Oct 22] round-actioned colt: first foal: dam Irish 7f and
1m winner, including at 2 yrs, from family of Nonoalco: placed in maidens at
Salisbury (pulled hard) and Yarmouth 3½ months apart, 1½ lengths second to Misbah
in latter: should stay 1m: can improve again. *B. W. Hills*

CHAYANEE'S ARENA (IRE) 2 b.f. (Feb 24) High Estate 127 – Arena 86 –
(Sallust 134) [1997 6.1g^{5} 7m 6m 7g Oct 27] 11,000Y: close-coupled filly: has a round
action: half-sister to several winners, including Wakil (up to 9.7f, by Tate Gallery)
and Gladiatorial (13f in Ireland, by Mazaad): dam lightly raced: signs of a little
ability in maidens and a nursery. *A. G. Newcombe*

CHECK THE BAND (USA) 3 gr.c. Dixieland Band (USA) – Check Bid (USA) 105
(Grey Dawn II 132) [1996 105: 5s^{4} 5d* 6m^{2} 6g^{5} 6m^{2} 6g 6g^{3} 5g* 6g* 5d^{2} 1997 5d^{2}
5g^{5} 5d Jun 20] strong, lengthy colt: useful performer: creditable second in listed
race at Tipperary in May: towards rear in King's Stand Stakes at Royal Ascot final
start: a sprinter: acted on good to firm and dead going: blinkered 3 times: dead.
A. P. O'Brien, Ireland

CHEEK TO CHEEK 3 b.f. Shavian 125 – Intoxication 73 (Great Nephew 126) 65
[1996 –: 7g 1997 8.2d 7d 10.1m^{2} 11.5d^{5} 11.9f^{2} 11.9m^{3} 11.1m^{6} 10f^{5} Oct 1] workmanlike filly: unimpressive mover: fair maiden: likely to prove suited by 1½m+: flashes
tail under pressure. *C. A. Cyzer*

CHEEKY CHAPPY 6 b.g. Sayf El Arab (USA) 127 – Guilty Guest (USA) 59 –
(Be My Guest (USA) 126) [1996 78, a63: a5g* a5g^{2} a5g^{5} a5g a5g^{6} a5g^{2} a5g 5g^{6} 5s^{5}
5m* a5g 5g^{3} 6.1m* 6g^{3} 6g^{2} 6g* 5m* 5m^{5} 6m^{3} 6g* 6f^{3} 6.1m* 6g^{4} 6f^{3} 6d a6g 6m a6g
5m 6f 5m a6g^{3} a6g 6m a6g* a6g^{5} a5g^{4} a5g a6g^{5} a7g a5g^{4} a6g^{3} a7s a5g a5g 1997 a5f
a5g Apr 1] tough and fairly useful sprint handicapper at his best: acted on hard
ground and all-weather, possibly unsuited by heavy: nearly always blinkered: dead.
D. W. Chapman

CHEERFUL GROOM (IRE)   6 ch.g. Shy Groom (USA) – Carange (Known   –
Fact (USA) 135) [1996 48, a41: a6g a8g a7g² a6g⁶ a8g a7g⁵ 7m* 6.9g 7.5m 1997 a7g   a34
a6g⁶ a7g a6g⁴ a7g a7g a6g⁶ a6g³ 7g Mar 26] sturdy gelding: poor handicapper: stays
7f: acts on fibresand and any turf going: visored (out of form) once as 3-y-o. *D. Shaw*

CHEMCAST   4 ch.g. Chilibang 120 – Golden October 62 (Young Generation   73
129) [1996 68, a72: a6g a5g* a5g* 5d 5f⁴ 5.1m⁵ 5f* 5s⁴ 5m 5m⁶ 5m⁴ 5m³ 5m 5s a5g*
a5g⁴ 1997 a5g² a5g² a5g⁶ a5g a5g⁵ 5s* 5g 5g 5m 5m⁴ 5g 5m 5g 5g Aug 28] lengthy
gelding: fair handicapper: won at Musselburgh in March: generally below form
afterwards: speedy, and best at 5f: probably acts on any turf/all-weather: effective
blinkered or not: races prominently. *J. L. Eyre*

CHERISHED (IRE)   2 b.f. (Apr 23) Distinctly North (USA) 115 – Key Partner   57 d
(Law Society (USA) 130) [1997 5.7f⁵ 5m 6.1g⁴ 8m 8m 8g³ 8.2d⁴ a8.5g³ a8.5g Nov
1] IR 38,000Y: close-coupled filly: third foal: half-sister to 3-y-o Iechyd-Da: dam
Irish 6f (at 2 yrs) to 12.5f (and hurdles) winner: modest maiden at best: trained first 5
starts by P. Cole: stays 8.5f: acts on fibresand: blinkered/visored sixth to eighth starts.
N. Tinkler

CHEROKEE BAND (USA)   2 b.c. (Feb 20) Dixieland Band (USA) – Cherokee   60 p
Darling (USA) (Alydar (USA)) [1997 7m 7g Sep 24] smallish, sturdy colt: sixth foal:
half-brother to 3 minor winners in USA: dam half-sister to two Grade 3 winners out
of Grade 2 7f winner Cherokee Frolic: not knocked about in maidens won by
stable-companions Sensory at Leicester and Pure Nobility at Chester: likely to need
1m+: moved fluently to post on debut: should do better. *B. W. Hills*

CHEROKEE CHARLIE   2 ch.g. (May 3) Interrex (CAN) – Valentine Song 63   –
(Pas de Seul 133) [1997 5g⁶ 5.9m 5m Jul 19] 1,500Y: seventh foal: dam 1m winner:
well held in minor event and maidens. *R. Craggs*

CHEROKEE FLIGHT   3 b.g. Green Desert (USA) 127 – Totham 84 (Shernazar   72
131) [1996 65: 5m⁴ 5m⁴ 5.1m* 7m 6m 6d⁵ 1997 7m 7.1g⁴ 7m⁶ 7d⁵ 8d a7g⁶ a9.4g*
8g³ 8.1g³ a9.4g* 10m² a12g⁵ a9.4g Dec 13] strong, good-bodied gelding: fair
handicapper: won at Wolverhampton in July and August: best effort when second
in apprentice event at Leicester in September: effective at 1m to 1¼m: acts on
fibresand, unraced on extremes of turf ground: raced too freely in visor once at 2 yrs.
S. Mellor

CHERRY BLOSSOM (IRE)   3 br.f. Primo Dominie 121 – Varnish 85 (Final   –
Straw 127) [1996 84: 5.2d* 5m⁴ 1997 6m 5.1d 6m May 31] leggy filly: fairly useful
winner in 1996: no form at 3 yrs: dead. *R. Hannon*

CHERRYMENTARY   3 b.f. Rudimentary (USA) 118 – Beaute Fatale (Hello   –
Gorgeous (USA) 128) [1996 NR 1997 8d 10g Oct 24] tall, angular filly: fourth foal:
dam twice-raced granddaughter of 1000 Guineas/Oaks winner Sweet Solera: no
promise in maidens: refused to enter stalls once. *K. O. Cunningham-Brown*

CHESTER HOUSE (USA)   2 b.c. (Feb 1) Mr Prospector (USA) – Toussaud   107 p
(USA) 120 (El Gran Senor (USA) 136) [1997 7m* 7g² Aug 19] good-bodied colt:
easy mover: first foal: dam 6f/7f winner here, later Grade 1 9f winner in USA: odds
on, won maiden at Goodwood by ½ length from Just In Time: favourite again, 5
lengths equal-second of 9 to Saratoga Springs in Acomb Stakes at York 18 days later,
missing break then keeping on well: shapes as though he'll stay at least 1¼m: raced
lazily long way on both starts (also lethargic in paddock on debut): well-regarded,
and probably still capable of fair bit better. *H. R. A. Cecil*

CHEVAL ROC   3 ch.c. Keen 116 – Gentle Gain 58 (Final Straw 127) [1996 67:   49
6m 6m 7d a8g 1997 a7g² a7g⁴ 7m 7d a8.5g Sep 30] close-coupled colt: poor maiden:
stays 7f: sold 600 gns in October. *R. Hannon*

CHEWIT   5 gr.g. Beveled (USA) – Sylvan Song (Song 132) [1996 88+, a99: a6g*   89
a6g* 6g 6f⁶ 6f⁵ 5m⁴ 5m 7m* 7.6m* 7m a7g³ 1997 a8g² a7g² 7m⁵ 7.6g³ 6.1m² 7g*   a112
7m⁶ 7g 8m⁵ a8.5g³ a7g* Dec 6] tall gelding: smart handicapper on all-weather, fairly
useful on turf: won at Ascot in August and Wolverhampton in December: gambled
on and best effort in latter, beating State of Caution in good style by 1¾ lengths:
effective at 6f to easy 8.5f: needs good going or firmer on turf: visored (below form)
once at 4 yrs: held up: usually ridden by Candy Morris (not at Wolverhampton).
G. L. Moore

CHEZ CATALAN   6 b.h. Niniski (USA) 125 – Miss Saint-Cloud 102 (Nonoalco   39
(USA) 131) [1996 –: a12g a13g 16.4m⁵ 15.4g a12g 1997 a13g² a13g⁵ a16g⁶ 16.4m
11.9m 15.4m Sep 26] compact horse: poor performer: stays 2m: acts on firm ground
and equitrack, twice well beaten on soft: best in blinkers. *R. Akehurst*

CHICAGO'S BEST   10 gr.g. Try My Best (USA) 130 – Maryville Bick   –
(Malacate (USA) 131) [1996 NR 1997 14.9g Jul 12] poor and lightly-raced maiden
on flat. *K. C. Comerford*

CHICKAWICKA (IRE)   6 b.h. Dance of Life (USA) – Shabby Doll 69   97
(Northfields (USA)) [1996 90: 7g⁴ 8g³ 7.6g⁴ 7.1m 8m 7g* 7m² 7d⁵ 7m 7g⁵ 8.1s⁵
a7g 1997 7g* 7m 7g⁵ 7m⁶ 7s² 7g 7m 7g 6g 7m 8.2d Nov 3] lengthy horse: useful
handicapper: won 18-runner event at Newmarket in April: good second at Epsom in
July: in-and-out form after: stays 1m: probably acts on any turf ground, well beaten
only start on fibresand: effective blinkered/visored or not: usually front runner.
B. Palling

CHIEF BLADE   2 ch.g. (Apr 30) Be My Chief (USA) 122 – Nagida 94 (Skyliner   63
117) [1997 6m 7.1m⁵ 6m 6.9g* 7f Oct 3] 16,000Y: smallish gelding: poor mover:
first foal: dam won Wokingham: improved markedly on nursery debut to win
15-runner event at Folkestone in September: well held in similar event at Lingfield
month later: will probably stay 1m: much better form on good ground than firmer:
has joined Miss G. Kelleway. *R. Akehurst*

CHIEF CASHIER   2 b.g. (Jan 16) Persian Bold 123 – Kentfield (Busted 134)   72
[1997 6g⁶ 7g 7.1g³ 7v Oct 10] close-coupled gelding: fourth foal: half-brother to
useful middle-distance stayer Saleel (by Salse): dam once-raced half-sister to
Puissance: fair form in maidens at Newbury and Chepstow first and third starts: races
freely, but should stay 1m. *G. B. Balding*

CHIEF CONNECTIONS   4 b.c. Inca Chief (USA) – Ballafort 73 (Ballacashtal   –
(CAN)) [1996 NR 1997 8d 8g 7.5m⁵ 6d 8g Jul 7] strong colt: second foal:
half-brother to Polly Particular (by Beveled), 5f winner at 2 yrs: dam 6f winner who
stayed 1¼m: no sign of ability. *M. P. Bielby*

CHIEF CONTENDER (IRE)   4 b.c. Sadler's Wells (USA) 132 – Minnie   120
Hauk (USA) 100 (Sir Ivor 135) [1996 114: 12m 12m* 12m* 12m 12s* 12m²
15g³ 15d³ 12s 1997 12g 15g³ 15.5m³ 20m* Oct 4]
      Prior to the latest Autumn Sales the highest price paid for a horse in
training there stood at 160,000 guineas, a record held jointly by the then
two-year-olds Take A Left in 1995 and Further Outlook a year later. As this pair
were no more than useful it looked very much as though the record would be
shattered when Chief Contender, a very well bred four-year-old who had won
the Group 1 Prix du Cadran at Longchamp twenty-three days earlier, came
under the hammer at Newmarket on October 27th. So it proved! It took a bid of
225,000 guineas to secure Chief Contender, and his future, whether it be on the
racecourse or at stud, lies in Australia.

Prix du Cadran, Longchamp—Chief Contender stays on too well for Celeric and Persian Punch

The journey there shouldn't bother him. Chief Contender is a seasoned traveller who has run almost as many times in France as he has in Britain. One of his three wins as a three-year-old was gained there, in a listed event at Nantes, and apart from on his reappearance he ran only in France in 1997, finishing third in the Prix Kergorlay and Prix Gladiateur before putting up a career-best performance in the Cadran. Unraced beyond two miles previously, Chief Contender lowered the record for the two-and-a-half-mile course at Longchamp, where tactics were changed at the last minute. Chief Contender's trainer, having left instructions for the horse to make the running, considered on a delayed journey to the course that others in the field would help by vying for the lead, and he arrived just in time to tell the rider to hold him up. It was one of the three other British-trained challengers in the field, Persian Punch, who did set the pace, with Chief Contender racing in third. Chief Contender, brought wide to deliver his challenge early in the straight, took a while to get the better of Persian Punch, and no sooner had he done so than he was headed by Celeric entering the final furlong. The last-named was not quite able to sustain his effort as Chief Contender stayed on strongly and regained the advantage close home to win by a neck; Persian Punch was three quarters of a length back in third.

		Northern Dancer	Nearctic
	Sadler's Wells (USA)	(b 1961)	Natalma
	(b 1981)	Fairy Bridge	Bold Reason
Chief Contender (IRE)		(b 1975)	Special
(b.c. 1993)		Sir Ivor	Sir Gaylord
	Minnie Hauk (USA)	(b 1965)	Attica
	(b 1975)	Best In Show	Traffic Judge
		(ch 1965)	Stolen Hour

Mrs J. Magnier's "Chief Contender"

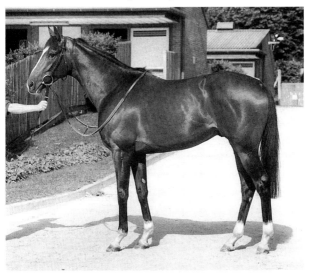

203

CHI

Chief Contender, a tall, lengthy colt with a short action, is from a family which has produced a host of good winners over the years. He himself is closely related to Aviance (by Northfields), a smart racemare and dam of the Coronation Stakes winner Chimes of Freedom and grandam of the top miler Spinning World. Chief Contender's brother Tafrah was a fair winner over a mile and a quarter, while he's a half-brother to winners in the States by Kings Lake and Chief's Crown. Their dam, Minnie Hauk, a useful winner at seven furlongs and a mile at three years in Ireland, is a daughter of the first-class broodmare Best In Show, whose progeny include the brothers Malinowski and Gielgud, winners of the Craven Stakes and Laurent Perrier Champagne Stakes respectively, and Monroe, the dam of 1997's top two-year-old, Xaar. Best In Show's half-sisters include Blushing With Pride, very smart at up to eleven furlongs in the States, and Sex Appeal, dam of El Gran Senor, Try My Best and Solar and the grandam of the 1997 Irish Derby runner-up Dr Johnson.

Chief Contender, well suited by a thorough test of stamina, acts on good to firm and soft ground. He does look none too easy a ride, tending to carry his head awkwardly under pressure, but is effective making the running or waited with. *P. W. Chapple-Hyam*

CHIEF MONARCH 3 b.c. Be My Chief (USA) 122 – American Beauty 74 (Mill Reef (USA) 141) [1996 NR 1997 8g 8g³ 10.2d² 10.1m⁵ 8s⁵ 8.1m* 10m⁵ 10.3m Sep 13] tall colt: half-brother to several winners, including smart Stephany's Dream (up to 9f in France, by Reform) and fair 1½m winner Candane (by Danehill): dam, second twice over 1¼m, out of Oaks second: fairly useful performer: didn't need to be at best to win maiden at Sandown in July: ran well in handicap at Newbury next time: stays 1¼m: acts on good to firm and dead going, possibly not soft: sold 21,000 gns in December. *B. Smart*   90

CHIEF MOUSE 4 b.g. Be My Chief (USA) 122 – Top Mouse (High Top 131) [1996 68: a8.5g* 10g 12.5f⁶ 1997 16m⁶ 14m⁶ Aug 9] sturdy gelding: good mover: fair winner at 3 yrs, and over hurdles early in 1997: behind in handicaps on return to flat: should stay beyond 8.5f: visored final 3-y-o start. *F. Jordan*   –

CHIEF PREDATOR (USA) 3 ch.c. Chief's Crown (USA) – Tsavorite (USA) (Halo (USA)) [1996 ?, a68: 7.1f 7d 7d a8g³ a8g² 1997 a10g³ 10.8m 9.7m 8.3s⁴ 10.8m³ 12f⁴ 10g² 12d 11.6m⁴ 16.4g Sep 2] close-coupled colt: modest maiden: trained by R. Hannon before final start: stays 1½m: acts on firm and soft ground and equitrack (unraced on fibresand): blinkered 3 starts prior to final one. *Miss K. M. George*   51 a64

CHIEF'S LADY 5 b.m. Reprimand 122 – Pussy Foot 83 (Red Sunset 120) [1996 39: a7g a7g a6g⁴ a6g 6f 6f⁴ 6m 6m⁴ 8m 8m 8f 8.3m 1997 a6g 5.1g³ 6m 6m² 5m 5g⁶ 5.1m 6g a6g a7s a7g Dec 19] smallish mare: poor maiden handicapper: effective at 5f to 7f: acts on firm ground, probably equitrack, well beaten on good to soft/soft going. *J. S. Moore*   45 d

CHIEF'S SONG 7 b.g. Chief Singer 131 – Tizzy 79 (Formidable (USA) 125) [1996 –: 16g 12d 1997 16m Sep 25] tall gelding: useful winning hurdler/chaser: still a maiden handicapper on flat: tried visored. *S. Dow*   –

CHIEF'S SPIRIT 3 b.g. Inca Chief (USA) – Country Spirit (Sayf El Arab (USA) 127) [1996 NR 1997 5.9m⁶ 6.1m² 8.1m Aug 15] 3,100Y: close-coupled gelding: first foal: dam unraced: poor form when second in weak auction event: well beaten in seller next time. *G. M. Moore*   48

CHIEFTAIN (IRE) 2 b.c. (Feb 18) Indian Ridge 123 – Legit (IRE) (Runnett 125) [1997 5m⁴ 5m³ 5m² 5g Aug 20] IR 135,000Y: big, strong, imposing colt: has scope: has a short action: third foal: half-brother to unreliable maiden Badger Bay (by Salt Dome): dam Irish maiden: appeared to show himself useful colt when 2 lengths third to Lady Alexander in Molecomb Stakes at Goodwood, finishing well from rear: well below that form subsequently in minor event at Lingfield and listed race at York: should be at least as effective over 6f. *N. A. Callaghan*   95 ?

CHIEFTAIN'S CROWN (USA) 6 ch.g. Chief's Crown (USA) – Simple Taste (USA) 93 (Sharpen Up 127) [1996 42: 10m 10.1f* 10f² 9.7g 1997 a12g 10g Jun 2]   –

204

strong, good-bodied gelding: poor handicapper: no show at 6 yrs: stays 1¼m: acts on firm going: often blinkered, including last 5 starts. *T. Hind*

CHIEF WHIP (USA) 2 b.c. (May 3) Premiership (USA) – Merci Mouillet 86 (USA) (Bob's Dusty (USA)) [1997 7.5m 6g⁴ 6d⁴ 6g² 7.5g* 8s² Nov 14] $47,000Y: tall colt: has scope: second foal: dam won at up to 9f in USA, including in minor stakes: sire (by Exclusive Native) useful sprinter: fair form in maidens in Britain before winning minor event at Milan in October, making all: second in another minor event at Milan final start: stays 1m: acts on soft going. *L. M. Cumani*

CHIKAL 2 b.g. (Mar 9) Nalchik (USA) – Ty-With-Belle 67 (Pamroy 99) [1997 47 6m 6.1m⁴ 8.1d 10g Sep 23] seventh foal: brother to fair 8.5f (at 2 yrs) and 12.5f winner Belle's Boy and half-brother to a 2-y-o 5f seller winner by Starch Reduced: dam fair maiden at 2 yrs: poor maiden. *B. Palling*

CHIKAPENNY 2 b.f. (Jan 16) Mon Tresor 113 – Arabian Nymph 49 (Sayf El 59 Arab (USA) 127) [1997 5m 5f³ 5g³ 5m⁶ 5m⁴ 6m³ 6g³ 5g³ 5m⁶ a5g⁶ Dec 22] 1,900Y: sister to a German 6.5f winner and a 6f seller winner: dam sprint plater at 2 yrs: modest maiden: stays 6f: well beaten on equitrack, raced only on good going or firmer on turf: usually blinkered/visored. *Mrs L. Stubbs*

CHIKA SHAN (IRE) 2 ch.c. (Apr 28) Archway (IRE) 115 – Judy's Pinch (Bally- 38 more 123) [1997 6f⁶ a6g⁵ 6g 7f⁵ a7g Dec 12] IR 1,000Y: half-brother to 3 winners, including a fairly useful 2-y-o 5f to 7f winner by Taufan and a 1m and 1¼m winner in Ireland by Vision: dam unraced: poor maiden: trained first 4 starts by B. Smart. *S. Mellor*

CHILD PRODIGY (IRE) 2 br.f. (Feb 5) Ballad Rock 122 – Minnie Habit 87 (Habitat 134) [1997 5g³ 5m 6m* 5.2m Aug 16] IR 32,000Y: second foal: half-sister to fairly useful 4-y-o Irish 1¾m winner Blue Bit (by Bluebird): dam, Irish 4-y-o 9f winner, closely related to the dam of Tropical and Shake The Yoke: won maiden at Ayr in July: ran very well when just over 5 lengths seventh in Queen Mary Stakes at Royal Ascot, but well below that form when behind in listed race at Newbury final start: may prove best at 5f: sent to USA. *J. W. Watts*

CHILDREN'S CHOICE (IRE) 6 b.m. Taufan (USA) 119 – Alice Brackloon 65 (USA) (Melyno 130) [1996 60: a12g 12m⁵ 14.1m* 14.1d² 13.9g 12m⁴ 14s³ 16.1f⁵ 13.8g⁶ 14.1s 1997 a13g 16g 14.1s³ 14m 16g* 16m² 16m⁵ 14.4m⁶ 14.1g* 12m 16s⁵ Nov 6] workmanlike mare: fair handicapper: won at Yarmouth in July and Notting- ham in October: stays 2m: probably acts on any turf going, well beaten on all- weather: blinkered (ran creditably) once at 5 yrs: usually held up: none too consistent. *W. J. Musson*

CHILIBANG BANG 4 b.f. Chilibang 120 – Quenlyn (Welsh Pageant 132) – [1996 –, a68d: a7g⁵ a7g* a6g⁵ a7g* a6g² a7g 6s⁴ 7g a7g a8.5s 1997 a7s a8g⁵ Jan 27] angular filly: has lost her form: twice visored. *J. Berry*

CHILI BOUCHIER (USA) 3 br.f. Stop The Music (USA) – Low Approach – (Artaius (USA) 129) [1996 –: 6m⁵ 1997 8f 7d⁵ 7m a8.5g Sep 20] tall filly: little sign of ability. *D. Marks*

CHILI CONCERTO 3 gr.f. Chilibang 120 – Whirling Words 75 (Sparkler 130) 88 d [1996 76: 5m² 5g* 1997 a6g 5d² 5d 5.1m 5.1g 6.1g 6.9d a6g⁶ a6g Dec 2] workmanlike filly: easily best effort when second in handicap at Windsor in May: very disappointing afterwards: tried blinkered. *P. J. Makin*

CHI-LIN 2 b.f. (Mar 4) Precocious 126 – Cool Combination 76 (Indian King 51 (USA) 128) [1997 7m a7g⁵ a7s³ Nov 28] fifth reported foal: half-sister to 3 winners, including sprinters by Jalmood and Midyan: dam 2-y-o 6f winner: best effort when third of 10 in minor event at Lingfield, keeping on. *J. Ffitch-Heyes*

CHILLED WINE 3 gr.f. Chilibang 120 – Persian Joy 45 (Persian Bold 123) – [1996 43: 5s⁵ a5g⁶ 5.1g³ 5m⁴ 5m a5g 5m 1997 6g 7f 7g 6m 5m May 30] robust filly: no form at 3 yrs. *G. P. Kelly*

CHILLI BOOM 3 gr.f. Chilibang 120 – Silent Sun 90 (Blakeney 126) [1996 –: – 5g 6f 6g 7g 1997 10m⁵ a8g⁵ Dec 10] no form. *R. Simpson*

CHILLING 3 gr.f. Chilibang 120 – Appealing 49 (Star Appeal 133) [1996 60d, 47 a40: 5.7g² 6.1m⁶ 5m 5.7m a6g a6g⁵ a6g³ 1997 a6g⁴ a6g* a6g⁵ a5g* a6g⁵ a5g⁴ 6g a62 d

CHI

a5g⁵ a5g⁴ a6g* 5g³ 6m 6.1m a6g a6g a5g a5g a7g Dec 18] sturdy filly: modest on all-weather at best, poor on turf: ridden by 7-lb claimer, won sellers at Wolverhampton in January (for P. Murphy) and February (handicap), and Southwell in May: well beaten last 6 outings: effective at 5f and 6f: best form on fibresand (unraced on equitrack), raced only on good/good to firm going on turf: has had tongue tied: blinkered last 10 starts. *N. Tinkler*

CHILL WIND 8 gr.g. Siberian Express (USA) 125 – Springwell 73 (Miami Springs 121) [1996 NR 1997 12m 12.1m⁶ 16m Sep 15] modest winning hurdler/chaser: lightly raced on flat nowadays and little sign of ability. *N. Bycroft*

CHILLY LAD 6 ch.g. High Kicker (USA) – Miss Poll Flinders (Swing Easy (USA) 126) [1996 55d: 9.9d³ 10g 8.3s⁵ 12d 10d⁶ a11g⁶ a11g 10m 11.5m a10g 12s a10g⁵ a11g 1997 a11g a14.8f Jan 11] tall gelding: has badly scarred near-fore: no worthwhile form since 5-y-o reappearance (has reportedly bled from nose): usually blinkered/visored: won selling hurdle in September. *R. T. Juckes* –

CHILTERN EMERALD 2 b.f. (Mar 9) Thowra (FR) – Treasure Time (IRE) 65 (Treasure Kay 114) [1997 5m 5m 6.1m 6g Aug 2] first foal: dam winning sprinter: soundly beaten, including in seller. *K. R. Burke* –

CHIMBORAZO 6 ch.g. Salse (USA) 128 – Pale Gold (FR) (New Chapter 106) [1996 NR 1997 14.4m 14g 17.1m⁴ Oct 6] poor staying maiden: acts on good to firm and soft ground. *B. J. McMath* 48

CHIM CHIMINEY 2 b.f. (Mar 15) Sabrehill (USA) 120 – William's Bird (USA) 104 (Master Willie 129) [1997 7m⁶ 8m⁵ 7.9s* 8d⁶ Oct 20] lengthy, useful-looking filly: fourth foal: half-sister to a winner in Malaysia by Hadeer: dam, 5f and 7f winner at 2 yrs, ran only once at 3 yrs: won maiden at York in October by a neck from Achilles (pair clear), staying on gamely: stiffish task in listed event at Pontefract final start: likely to prove suited by at least 1¼m: acts on soft ground. *B. W. Hills* 84

CHIMES OF PEACE 2 b.f. (Feb 1) Magic Ring (IRE) 115 – Leprechaun Lady 57 (Royal Blend 117) [1997 7.5f⁵ 6m 7s 6m Oct 28] fifth foal: half-sister to 3-y-o Ginny Wossername and winner at up to 13.8f Goodbye Millie (by Sayf El Arab): dam stayer: modest form in maidens and a nursery, not knocked about last 2 starts: will be well suited by 1m+: may do better at 3 yrs. *J. L. Eyre* 64

CHINABERRY 3 b.f. Soviet Star (USA) 128 – Crimson Conquest (USA) 85 (Diesis 133) [1996 NR 1997 7d⁴ 7m⁵ 7.6m⁴ 8g Jul 30] small, sturdy filly: second foal: dam 2-y-o 6f winner who stayed 1¼m: fair maiden: should stay 1m. *C. E. Brittain* 75

CHINA CASTLE 4 b.g. Sayf El Arab (USA) 127 – Honey Plum 57 (Kind of Hush 118) [1996 56, a76: a7g* a10g* a8.5g* a10g⁴ a8g⁴ a11g* a12g³ 10.3d a9.4g 8m a8.5g³ 12.1f³ a9.4g a9.4g a12g⁴ a9.4g⁴ 1997 a11g* a11g* a12g³ a11g² a12g⁴ a12g³ a12g⁵ a8g a12g a8.5g a14g a8g Dec 8] good-topped gelding: fairly useful handicapper on all-weather: won 3 times at Southwell in January: below form final 6 starts: may stay beyond 1½m: sometimes soon off bridle, and suited by strong gallop. *P. C. Haslam* a90 –

CHINA GIRL (IRE) 3 b.f. Danehill (USA) 126 – Chamonis (USA) 101 (Affirmed (USA)) [1996 91: 5m* 6m 5f* 1997 6g 6g⁵ 6g⁴ Aug 10] well-made filly: has a quick action: fairly useful winner at 2 yrs: stiff tasks in Cork And Orrery Stakes at Royal Ascot and listed race at York: asked to go too fast final start: speedy: acts on firm ground: sent to Australia. *P. W. Chapple-Hyam* 87

CHINAIDER (IRE) 2 b.f. (Mar 28) Mujadil (USA) 119 – We Two (Glenstal (USA) 118) [1997 a5g* a5g³ 6m* 6g* 6d² 8f⁶ 7m Sep 30] 5,000 2-y-o: lengthy filly: fifth foal: half-sister to Irish 1½m winner Saltonio (by Salt Dome): dam unraced: fair performer: won sellers at Southwell in June and Redcar (for J. J. O'Neill) and York in August, last-named valuable 19-runner event: claimed out of M. Pipe's yard £20,000 after fifth start: stffish tasks in nurseries subsequently: should stay 7f: acts on fibresand, best turf efforts on good ground or softer: consistent. *D. Nicholls* 73

CHINA MAIL (IRE) 5 b.g. Slip Anchor 136 – Fenney Mill 99 (Levmoss 133) [1996 NR 1997 16.1m⁵ 18d 14.1m Jul 19] ungenuine winning staying hurdler: little encouragement on return to flat. *J. A. Bennett* –

206

CHINA RED (USA) 3 br.g. Red Ransom (USA) – Akamare (FR) (Akarad (FR) 130) [1996 86: 6m⁴ 6m² 7g⁴ 1997 8.2m* 8m 7.6m⁵ 9f 8.1g Sep 26] tall gelding: has a fluent, round action: fairly useful form: made virtually all to win steadily-run maiden at Nottingham in April: subsequently off course 2 months and below form: stays 1m: raced only on good going or firmer. *J. W. Hills* 88

CHINGACHGOOK 3 b.g. Superlative 118 – Petomania 34 (Petong 126) [1996 61: 6.1m⁴ 6m 7d 5.3f⁵ 6m⁵ 1997 6.1m 8.3g² 8.3g 8s 8m⁶ a10g³ Dec 22] fair maiden handicapper: off course 5 months and left P. W. Harris before final start: stays 1¼m: acts on firm going and equitrack: well beaten in blinkers penultimate outing. *S. Dow* 65

CHINOUR (IRE) 9 b.g. Dalsaan 125 – Chishtiya 74 (Try My Best (USA) 130) [1996 NR 1997 a6g 7g 8m⁴ 8m 7m⁴ 8d⁶ 7g 8g⁶ 6.9m⁵ 8m 8m³ 8g² 8.2d Nov 3] good-topped gelding: modest handicapper: stays 1m: acts on good to firm and heavy ground and on fibresand: visored (ran badly) once as 6-y-o: sometimes slowly away, usually held up. *E. J. Alston* 50

CHIPS (IRE) 2 ch.c. (Jan 26) Common Grounds 118 – Inonder 31 (Belfort (FR) 89) [1997 5.2g³ 5m* 5d² 6g* 6m 7.5g* 7g 7v³ 6g Oct 18] 30,000Y: big, good-topped colt: has plenty of scope: first foal: dam poor maiden from family of smart French sprinter Three For Fantasy (by Common Grounds): fairly useful performer: won minor events at Salisbury and Kempton in May and listed race at Baden-Baden in August: well held facing stiff tasks last 3 starts: likely to prove best up to 1m: well beaten only try in visor: races prominently: has high head carriage and sometimes finds little. *D. R. C. Elsworth* 94

CHIPSTEAD BAY (IRE) 3 b.g. Ballad Rock 122 – Express Account 78 (Carr de Naskra (USA)) [1996 5g 5g³ 5m 5m⁴ 1997 5d⁶ 6g 6s⁶ 5d 7m 5d a6g* a7g* a5g* a6g Dec 19] IR 13,000Y: leggy, workmanlike ex-Irish gelding: second foal: dam, effective from 1¼m to 1½m, half-sister to smart middle-distance colt Diaghilef: left J. Coogan after sixth start: fair handicapper for new stable: won 3 times at Lingfield in space of 9 days in December: effective at 5f to 7f: acts on equitrack, probably on good to firm going (below form on softer than good): blinkered fourth start. *K. T. Ivory* 67

CHIST (USA) 2 b. or br.c. (May 30) Lear Fan (USA) 130 – Morna 82 (Blakeney 126) [1997 7m⁴ Nov 4] IR 29,000Y: brother to 2 winners in USA, including Grade 3 8.5f winner Casual Lies, placed in Kentucky Derby and Preakness Stakes, and half-brother to several winners in USA: dam, lightly raced, shaped like a stayer: 11/2, promising 3½ lengths fourth of 18 to Gypsy Passion in Redcar maiden, green when pace quickened then going on well: should stay at least 1¼m: sure to improve and win a race. *M. H. Tompkins* 78 p

CHLOE NICOLE (USA) 3 b.f. Personal Flag (USA) – Balakhna (FR) (Tyrant (USA)) [1996 67: 5.2f⁴ 1997 8.2d 6g 5.3f⁵ 6.1m Jun 13] tall filly: disappointing maiden: bred to stay much further than 5f but takes good hold. *P. F. I. Cole* 52

CHLOE'S ANCHOR 4 b.f. Slip Anchor 136 – Mademoiselle Chloe 106 (Night Shift (USA)) [1996 NR 1997 8.2d⁵ Jun 23] second foal: half-sister to 7f winner Cloette (by Damister): dam sprinter, won only at 2 yrs: pulled hard when fifth in maiden at Nottingham only start. *W. A. O'Gorman* –

CHLO-JO 2 b.f. (May 9) Belmez (USA) 131 – Shaadin (USA) 80 (Sharpen Up 127) [1997 6m 7g⁴ 8m 8d 7s Nov 8] 500F: leggy filly: fourth foal: dam maiden sister to Pebbles: fair form in maiden at Leicester second start: disappointing after. *A. G. Foster* 65

CHOCOLATE BOX 2 ch.f. (May 9) Most Welcome 131 – Short Rations (Lorenzaccio 130) [1997 7d³ 7.1s⁴ Nov 6] sister to 3-y-o Arctic Owl and half-sister to numerous winners, including useful stayer Patience Camp (by Bustino) and a Grade 1 winner in Australia by Mill Reef: dam Italian 2-y-o 5f winner: slow-starting third in maiden at Leicester in October: favourite, well below that form in similar event at Musselburgh: should stay at least 1½m. *W. J. Haggas* 70

CHOCOLATE ICE 4 b.g. Shareef Dancer (USA) 135 – Creake 80 (Derring-Do 131) [1996 70d: 8.2s 10g³ 12g³ 14m⁵ 12.3m 12.3m³ 16f⁴ 11.9f⁴ a16g⁵ 10.1g⁴ 13.1m 11.5m⁴ 12g a16g 1997 a12g⁶ 10.8s Jul 4] sturdy gelding: disappointing maiden on flat: tried blinkered: won over hurdles in July and (for J. O'Shea) August. *R. J. O'Sullivan*

CHOCOLATE (IRE) 2 b.f. (Feb 22) Brief Truce (USA) 126 – Vian (USA) (Far 77 Out East (USA)) [1997 6g⁵ 7d⁶ 6m² 7m² 8m 7s² 7d⁶ Oct 27] 115,000Y: seventh foal: half-sister to several winners, including useful sprinter Wavian (by Warning): dam unraced half-sister to Optimistic Lass: fair form at best: well below it last 3 starts, all in blinkers: should stay 1m: best efforts on good to firm ground: sold 20,000 gns in December. *J. L. Dunlop*

CHOICE LADY 3 b.f. Shavian 125 – Elarrih (USA) (Sharpen Up 127) [1996 NR – 1997 10m 14f Oct 3] workmanlike filly: third foal: dam unraced: no show in maidens. *J. L. Harris*

CHOPIN (IRE) 3 b.g. Classic Music (USA) – La Toulzanie (FR) (Sanctus II 132) 45 [1996 54?: 5.1d⁵ 5.3f⁴ 7f 6.9m 5g 8f 1997 7m⁴ 10g 8f 7m 10g⁴ 11.9m³ Aug 15] unfurnished gelding: poor maiden: stays 1¼m: has raced mainly on good going or firmer: often blinkered: won over hurdles in August: inconsistent. *R. F. Johnson Houghton*

CHORUS SONG (USA) 3 b.f. Alleged (USA) 138 – Performing Arts 104 (The 57 Minstrel (CAN) 135) [1996 70: 6m⁵ 7m² 7.1d 7.3s 1997 8g⁴ 6m 8f 10f Jun 10] modest maiden: better at 1¼m than 1m: acts on good to firm ground, well beaten on dead/soft: sent to Australia. *P. W. Chapple-Hyam*

CHRIS'S LAD 6 b.g. Thowra (FR) – Stockline (Capricorn Line 111) [1996 69, 70 d a55: 16.1f⁶ 20f a16.2g⁴ 14g* a16g² 16d² 16.4g* 18g 1997 14.1m 21.6g 16.2s⁶ 14m 12g* 14g 16.4d 12m 13.3f 12.1m³ 12g³ 14.1g⁶ 14.4m Sep 10] close-coupled gelding: fair handicapper: won 26-runner lady riders event at Newmarket in June: failed to reproduce that form: effective at 1½m to 2m: has won on good to firm going, better form on good or softer: wears blinkers: tends to run in snatches: won over hurdles after final start, then joined J. Jenkins: inconsistent. *B. J. Meehan*

CHRYSALIS 2 b.f. (Mar 2) Soviet Star (USA) 128 – Vivienda 93 (Known Fact 63 (USA) 135) [1997 5.2g³ 5.3m³ 6g⁵ May 26] smallish, sturdy filly: fifth live foal: half-sister to a winner in Denmark by Belmez and winning 2-y-o sprinters by Sharpo and Shavian: dam winning sprinter at 2 yrs: modest form in early-season maidens: bandaged on debut. *P. F. I. Cole*

CHRYSOLITE (IRE) 2 ch.c. (Feb 6) Kris 135 – Alamiya (IRE) (Doyoun 124) 73 [1997 7g 7m⁴ 7d³ Oct 27] IR 43,000Y: first foal: dam unraced half-sister to Prix du Jockey-Club runner-up Altayan, the family of Aliysa: in frame in maidens at Leicester (best effort) then Lingfield in October: should be well suited by 1¼m+. *B. W. Hills*

CHUCKLESTONE 14 b.g. Chukaroo 103 – Czar's Diamond 66 (Queen's – Hussar 124) [1996 38: 17.2m 17.2f⁴ 17.2m* 16d 1997 17.2m⁶ Jun 14] sturdy gelding: veteran staying handicapper: 8 times a winner at Bath, but well held there only 14-y-o start. *J. S. King*

CHUNITO 2 b.c. (Feb 19) Beveled (USA) – Wasimah 84 (Caerleon (USA) 132) 69 [1997 5.2g⁵ 5.1s³ 5m⁶ May 24] leggy colt: fourth foal: half-brother to 3-y-o A Breeze and 6-y-o Bedazzle: dam 2-y-o 5f winner: third in maiden at Chester, best effort early in season. *P. W. Chapple-Hyam*

CHURCHILL'S SHADOW (IRE) 3 b.c. Polish Precedent (USA) 131 – Shy 53 Princess (USA) 117 (Irish River (FR) 131) [1996 NR 1997 7g⁵ 7.3s 7.6m 5.7g 5m 7f² a64 9.7d a7g* a7s* a7g² Dec 19] 2,800 2-y-o: strong colt: easy mover: fifth foal: half-brother to 3 winners, notably 5-y-o Diffident: dam French 6f to 7f winner: modest handicapper: won 2 strongly-run events at Lingfield in November: stays 7f: acts on firm going and equitrack: headstrong, and suited by coming from off pace. *B. A. Pearce*

CHURLISH CHARM 2 b.c. (Feb 3) Niniski (USA) 125 – Blushing Storm (USA) – p 102 (Blushing Groom (FR) 131) [1997 7m Aug 16] good-bodied colt: second foal: dam (maiden) third in Ribblesdale and Lancashire Oaks, would have stayed further than 1½m: 33/1, behind in 19-runner maiden at Newbury, green throughout: sort to do better over much further in time. *R. Hannon*

CIM BOM BOM (IRE) 5 b.h. Dowsing (USA) 124 – Nekhbet 74 (Artaius 85
(USA) 129) [1996 74, a96: 8d 7.1d 8.3m⁶ 8.1d⁵ 8m 7g³ 6g* 6m³ 6f⁵ 6m³ 6d a6g*   a99
a7g* 1997 a7g² a7g* 6m⁴ 5g 7d a6g² 6m 6g* 5m³ 8f Sep 13] strong, heavy-bodied
horse: carries condition: reportedly has screws in near-fore: useful on the all-weather,
successful in minor event at Wolverhampton in February: not so good on turf, but
still won handicap at Pontefract in July: out of depth in valuable event in Turkey in
September, and reported to have stayed there: best at 6f/7f: acts on firm and dead
ground: visored nowadays. *M. Bell*

CIMMERIAN 3 ch.f. Aragon 118 – Relatively Easy 70 (Relkino 131) [1996 50:   57
6.1m 6f⁵ 6g 7m 1997 11m 8f 8.2d² 8g a11g 12d Sep 2] tall, sparely-made filly:
modest maiden: trained by M. Johnston first 3 starts: subsequently well below form:
stays 1m. *M. E. Sowersby*

CINDER HILLS 2 ch.f. (Mar 8) Deploy 131 – Dame du Moulin 81 (Shiny Tenth   50
120) [1997 5d 5m a5g Jun 19] 5,600Y: workmanlike filly: has scope: half-sister to a
German 7f/1m winner by Superlative: dam, 2-y-o 7f winner, is half-sister to useful
middle-distance fillies Rollrights and Rollfast: signs of ability only on debut: bred to
need much further than 5f: slowly away all starts. *M. W. Easterby*

CINDERS GIRL 7 b.m. Presidium 124 – Salinas 65 (Bay Express 132) [1996   –
NR 1997 5f 8d May 18] of little account. *Mrs M. Reveley*

CINDY KATE (IRE) 4 br.f. Sayf El Arab (USA) 127 – Marton Maid 74 (Silly   –
Season 127) [1996 49: a6g a6g³ 6s⁵ 6m 1997 a6g⁶ a7g 6.1d Apr 29] leggy, sparely-
made filly: poor maiden: soundly beaten in 1997. *W. R. Muir*

CINEMA PARADISO 3 b.g. Polar Falcon (USA) 126 – Epure (Bellypha 130)   94
[1996 83: 6f* 8.1m² 10g 1997 8d³ 7g⁵ 8.5m 8s* 10g 12m 10m 8.1m Sep 21] tall
gelding: has a round action: fairly useful handicapper: won at Salisbury in June: well
held afterwards: best with testing conditions at 1m, and should stay 1¼m: winner on
firm going, but goes very well on dead and soft: sold 25,000 gns in October and
joined G. Richards. *P. F. I. Cole*

CINNAMON STICK (IRE) 4 ch.g. Don't Forget Me 127 – Gothic Lady (Gods-   –
walk (USA) 130) [1996 –: 6.1d 9.9g⁶ a11g 8.2m 1997 8.2m 7f 10g May 17]
close-coupled gelding: little worthwhile form. *P. S. Felgate*

CIRCLED (USA) 4 gr.f. Cozzene (USA) – Hold The Hula (USA) (Hawaii) [1996   73
–: 14g⁵ 10m 14.6g⁵ 1997 a12g² a12g Jan 29] tall filly: has a quick action: fair
performer, lightly raced nowadays: easily better 4-y-o effort on reappearance: stays
1½m: acts on fibresand, best turf efforts on dead or soft ground. *John A. Harris*

CIRCLE OF MAGIC 3 gr.f. Midyan (USA) 124 – Miss Witch 59 (High Line   50
125) [1996 53: 5.1m 6m⁵ 6d 6.1m 8g a7g 1997 7m⁵ 8.2d 8.1m⁵ 8g* Jul 23]
unfurnished filly: modest performer: best efforts in 1997 in blinkers last 2 starts,
winning seller at Leicester in July: winning selling hurdler for M. Pipe: likely to stay
1¼m: acts on good to firm ground, possibly unsuited by dead: has given trouble
stalls. *P. J. Makin*

CIRCUITEER (IRE) 2 ch.g. (Apr 14) Pips Pride 117 – Day Dress (Ashmore   65 ?
(FR) 125) [1997 5g 6f⁶ 6g 6m³ 6g³ 6f² Oct 13] IR 11,000Y: lengthy gelding: half-
brother to 5f (at 2 yrs) to 1m winner Old Hook (by Digamist), also successful in
Belgium, and 2 other winners abroad: dam never ran: modest maiden: appeared to
run very well in claimer final start: stays 6f: yet to race on ground softer than good:
ran too freely in blinkers third outing. *J. Berry*

CIRCUMNAVIGATE 2 b.f. (Jan 24) Slip Anchor 136 – Circe 73 (Main Reef   41
126) [1997 a8g⁵ a8g Dec 8] 7,500Y: fourth foal: half-sister to 3 winners, including
6-y-o My Learned Friend: dam 1m winner (stayed 1¼m) from very good family:
poor form when mid-division in sellers at Southwell. *M. Johnston*

CIRCUS 2 b.c. (Apr 21) Caerleon (USA) 132 – Circo 77 (High Top 131) [1997   74 p
7.1d 7m⁴ 7m Sep 30] 74,000Y: fifth foal: brother to fair 1¾m winner Alaraby, closely
related to 3-y-o Topton and a winner in Italy (both by Royal Academy) and
half-brother to fairly useful sprinter Robin Lake (by Thatching): dam, second over
1m at 2 yrs, later placed in France: fair form when fourth in minor event at Yarmouth
then tenth in valuable sales race at Newmarket: will stay at least 1¼m: should still do
better. *C. E. Brittain*

CIRCUS COLOURS 7 b.g. Rainbow Quest (USA) 134 – Circus Plume 124   –
(High Top 131) [1996 NR 1997 a10g a16g May 24] fair handicapper at 4 yrs: well
beaten on equitrack in 1997. *J. R. Jenkins*

CIRO'S PEARL (IRE) 3 b.f. Petorius 117 – Cut It Fine (USA) (Big Spruce   85
(USA)) [1996 76: 6.1m⁵ 7g² 6g 1997 8.2d³ 10m* 12g* 12d³ 12.1m⁴ 13.9g 10s 12.1g⁴
11.9m⁴ Oct 23] smallish, good-bodied filly: fairly useful handicapper: won at
Lingfield (apprentices) in May and Goodwood in June: excellent third of 20 to
Heritage in King George V Stakes at Royal Ascot: only respectable efforts last 2
starts: should stay further than 1½m: acts on good to firm and dead going: usually
races prominently. *M. H. Tompkins*

CITADEL 2 b.f. (Mar 4) Emarati (USA) 74 – Round Tower 93 (High Top 131)   –
[1997 6g a7g Dec 10] half-sister to several winners, including useful 1986 2-y-o 7f
winner Roundlet (by Roberto) and fairly useful 1½m winner Moat Garden (by
Sportin' Life): dam 1¼m winner out of half-sister to Highclere: well beaten in
maidens at Leicester and Lingfield. *J. G. Smyth-Osbourne*

CITRUS EXPRESS (SWE) 2 br.c. (Jan 27) Mango Express 106 – Thilda (IRE)   –
(Roi Danzig (USA)) [1997 8.2g 7m 8m Nov 1] first foal: dam unraced: no form,
including in a seller: sent to Norway. *P. Mooney*

CITTERN 7 b.g. Ela-Mana-Mou 132 – Seattle Serenade (USA) 82 (Seattle Slew   59
(USA)) [1996 NR 1997 11.1s a14g 16.1m⁶ 16g⁴ Sep 15] ran in Britain in 1993 then
in Dubai (winner there): modest handicapper in 1997 on return to Britain: reportedly
lame final start: probably suited by a test of stamina. *Mrs M. Reveley*

CITY DANCE 2 b. or br.f. (May 15) Rock City 120 – Fen Dance (IRE) 82 (Trojan   –
Fen 118) [1997 6d a6g Oct 6] first foal: dam 7f winner, should have stayed further:
well beaten in claimer and seller. *P. J. Makin*

CITY GAMBLER 3 b.f. Rock City 120 – Sun Street 73 (Ile de Bourbon (USA)   74
133) [1996 71: 6m³ 6m⁴ 7m 8f² 1997 10m 12.5m³ 8g³ 10g⁴ 9g 7.6g* 8g* 8g⁴ 8d 10f⁵
8g Oct 7] rangy filly: fair performer: won maiden at Lingfield and handicap at
Leicester in August: best at 1m to easy 1¼m: acts on firm ground, well beaten on
dead. *G. C. Bravery*

CITY HALL (IRE) 3 gr.c. Generous (IRE) 139 – City Fortress (Troy 137) [1996   87
66p: 8m 8g⁵ 1997 10g 16g² 14m³ 18.2f³ 17.2f* 16.2v⁴ 16s² Oct 15] big colt: fairly
useful handicapper: won at Bath in September: ran well at Ascot and Nottingham
after: needs good test of stamina: acts on any ground: effective visored or not: sold
50,000 gns and joined Mrs V. Ward. *M. R. Stoute*

CITY HONOURS (USA) 2 b.c. (Apr 23) Darshaan 133 – Ikebana (IRE) 93   105 p
(Sadler's Wells (USA) 132) [1997 7m⁴ 8m* 8g³ Sep 28]
    About one and a half lengths covered the first six home in the Royal
Lodge Stakes, but it would be wrong to dismiss those involved for that reason
alone when it comes to assessing their prospects as three-year-olds. Collectively the Royal Lodge field was a good-looking one, the blanket finish wasn't
due to a falsely-run event—the pace was sound—and plenty of the principals
had the looks and pedigree to suggest they'll come into their own only over
further than a mile in their second season.
    That last point applies particularly to the third horse City Honours
whose sire and the sire of his dam, Darshaan and Sadler's Wells, fought out the
finish of the 1984 Prix du Jockey-Club. A strong, well-made colt, City Honours
looked in smashing shape at Ascot, impressing as a really good walker and
moving easily in his faster paces. City Honours needed chasing along in last
place right from the off and was still virtually last of the closely-grouped field
of eight with a furlong to run, but finished strongly to be beaten three-quarters
of a length and a head by Teapot Row and Prolix. A degree of laziness had also
characterised City Honours' win in a mile maiden at the Doncaster St Leger
meeting earlier in the month when he'd got up in the last stride to beat Prolix a
short head. That had followed a very promising introduction when clearly
green at Newbury in August, on that occasion City Honours finishing just over
two lengths fourth to the filly Bahr in the listed Washington Singer Stakes. The

AMCO Corporation Maiden Stakes, Doncaster—
City Honours produces a late thrust on the rail to beat Prolix with Mutawwaj (partially hidden) third

Criterium de Saint-Cloud was talked of as a likely target after his Doncaser win—the ten-furlong trip there would have suited him very well—but shortly after the Royal Lodge it was announced that City Honours had been purchased by Godolphin from Robert Sangster along with three stable companions, none of whom raced again at two. An offer had apparently first been made for the two-year-olds in late-August and was accepted after an increase in the asking price thanks to City Honours' prominent showing in the Royal Lodge.

City Honours (USA) (b.c. Apr 23, 1995)	Darshaan (br 1981)	Shirley Heights (b 1975)	Mill Reef
			Hardiemma
		Delsy (br 1972)	Abdos
			Kelty
	Ikebana (IRE) (b 1988)	Sadler's Wells (b 1981)	Northern Dancer
			Fairy Bridge
		Miss Toshiba (ch 1972)	Sir Ivor
			Royal Warrant

City Honours' dam showed fairly useful form in just three starts, following an impressive win in a mile-and-a-quarter maiden at Sandown with placed efforts in minor events at around a mile and a half. City Honours is her third foal and second winner after close relative Asari (by High Estate). Asari was another to be sold to warmer climes; he won a seven and a half furlong event in Seville, Spain, as a four-year-old early in the year having begun his career in Norway. Ikebana is one of eight winners out of Miss Toshiba. They include Youm Jadeed, a useful full sister at up to a mile and a half in France, and the Yorkshire Oaks third and Park Hill runner-up Guilty Secret. Miss Toshiba's seven wins began with a seven-furlong maiden at Ayr as a two-year-old and ended with a Grade 1 victory in the Vanity Handicap over nine furlongs at Hollywood Park at four. She'd displayed more stamina in between however, including a win in the Pretty Polly Stakes at the Curragh and a good sixth in Bruni's St Leger. She was another to race for Robert Sangster, as was the family's best performer, the high-class sprinter Committed, who's out of a half-sister to Miss Toshiba. *P. W. Chapple-Hyam*

211

CITY RUN (USA) 5 b.h. Mehmet (USA) – Sable Sham (USA) (Sham (USA)) –
[1996 NR 1997 a13g a8g Feb 7] of no account. *D. J. S. Cosgrove*

CIVIL LIBERTY 4 b.g. Warning 136 – Libertine 114 (Hello Gorgeous (USA) 70
128) [1996 93: 7g² 7g² 8f 8.3m* 10m⁴ 7g 8.5m⁴ 1997 8m 7d 7s 7m 8m 8.5d 7m⁵
10g* 11.5f² 12v⁴ 12g Oct 25] well-made sort: just a fair handicapper in 1997: won
amateurs event at Nottingham in September: stays 11.5f (not quite 1½m in testing
conditions): acts on any ground: blinkered (well beaten) twice: sold 25,000 gns in
October. *G. Lewis*

CLAIRESWAN (IRE) 5 ch.g. Rhoman Rule (USA) – Choclate Baby (Kashiwa –
115) [1996 –: 11.9g 18g 1997 13.8s Oct 17] workmanlike gelding: fair handicapper
at 3 yrs: lightly raced and no form on flat since, but won over hurdles in December.
M. H. Tompkins

CLAN BEN (IRE) 5 ch.h. Bluebird (USA) 125 – Trina's Girl (Nonoalco (USA) 110
131) [1996 101: 8d 8m² 7.9m³ 10m⁵ 10.4m⁵ 10.1m² 10m 9m 8.1s* 1997 10m⁶ 10.4g⁴
10m 8.1d* 8.1g 10m 10d* Sep 19] lengthy horse: good mover: smart
performer: won handicap at Sandown in July and minor event at Newbury (easily
best effort, beat Crimson Tide ¾ length in 5-runner race) in September: stays 10.4f:
acts on good to firm and soft going: effective blinkered or not: tends to edge left
under pressure: sold (to go to Saudi Arabia) 52,000 gns in October. *H. R. A. Cecil*

CLANBLUE CHICK 2 b.f. (May 7) Clantime 101 – Lavenham Blue 40
(Streetfighter 120) [1997 5g 5m a5s⁵ Nov 10] sixth reported foal: half-sister to a
2-y-o 5f and 7f winner by Sayf El Arab and 9-y-o Miss Aragon (modest 6f winner at
best): dam poor maiden: poor form in maidens. *J. Berry*

CLAN CHIEF 4 b.g. Clantime 101 – Mrs Meyrick 42 (Owen Dudley 121) [1996 82
87p: 5m⁵ 5f² 5.2m² 5m* 5m* 5m* 5m² 6m* 1997 6g⁴ 5d⁵ 5m 6m 5.2m Aug 16]
sparely-made gelding: fairly useful handicapper: progressive at 3 yrs: rather
disappointing in 1997: stays 6f: acts on firm and dead ground: usually bandaged
behind: has won sweating. *J. R. Arnold*

CLAPHAM COMMON (IRE) 2 b.c. (Apr 28) Common Grounds 118 – West 96
of Eden (Crofter (USA) 124) [1997 8m* 8d³ Oct 20] IR 9,000F, 24,000Y: sixth foal:
half-brother to fairly useful 5f performer Cindora (by Fairy King): dam unraced:
useful form: won minor event at Milan in September: 9½ lengths third to Gulland in
listed event at Pontefract: shapes as though will stay further than 1m. *L. M. Cumani*

CLAQUE 5 ch.g. Kris 135 – Mixed Applause (USA) 101 (Nijinsky (CAN) 138) –
[1996 –, a70d: a12g a10g a13g* a16g⁴ a13g* a11g* a12g 10.3d 9.9d 10g 13s a12g* a44
a12g² 15d⁶ a14.8g a14g a12g a14g a14g a13g⁴ a12s⁶ 1997 a10g³ 10g Apr 18] angular
gelding: has reportedly had back problems: poor handicapper at best in 1997: stays
13f: blinkered since third 4-y-o start: sold 3,000 gns in May. *D. W. Chapman*

CLARITY (IRE) 2 b.f. (Apr 10) Scenic 128 – Cristalga 90 (High Top 131) [1997 76 d
7g³ 7.1m 7m 8d 7d Nov 7] sturdy, lengthy filly: half-sister to useful 1¼m winner
General Sikorski (by Petoski) and a 1¼m seller winner by Song: dam won at 1¼m:
fair form in maidens and a nursery though didn't go on as expected, and disappointed
final start: should stay at least 1m. *A. P. Jarvis*

CLASH OF SWORDS 4 b.g. Shaadi (USA) 126 – Swept Away 106 (Kris 135) 54
[1996 58§: 10g 10m 10.1g 10m 12.3m⁵ 12.3m⁶ 15.8g² 17.2m⁶ 15.8g 1997 13s⁵ 16m
13.8g⁶ 15.8g* Aug 15] good-bodied gelding: modest handicapper: won maiden event
at Catterick in August, showing more resolution than on occasions in the past: stays
2m: acts on good to firm ground, probably on soft: well beaten both tries in blinkers:
sold 1,600 gns in November. *P. Calver*

CLASS DISTINCTION (IRE) 3 ch.c. Masterclass (USA) 116 – Brook's 50
Dilemma 80 (Known Fact (USA) 135) [1996 71+: 5g 5f² 5m* 7m³ 5.2f 6m 6g 1997
6d 6m 7m⁶ 6m 6m 6.9d Oct 21] fair winning juvenile: only modest form in 1997:
may prove best at 6f: acts on firm ground: sold, to go to Norway. *R. Hannon*

CLASSIC ACCOUNT 9 ch.g. Pharly (FR) 130 – Money Supply (Brigadier –
Gerard 144) [1996 NR 1997 a16.2g⁴ a16g⁵ a16g⁵ a12g³ a13g⁵ Mar 4] just a poor a41
handicapper on the all-weather nowadays: stays 2m. *J. L. Eyre*

CLASSICAL DANCE (IRE)   3 b.g. Classic Music (USA) – Eyre Square (IRE)   52
(Flash of Steel 120) [1996 NR 1997 10m 10m 10.3d 11.1d³ 11.9d⁴ 16.1m⁶ Oct 1] IR
4,000Y: rangy, good-topped gelding: second foal: brother to 1m seller winner She's
A Winner: dam (raced twice around 1¾m in Ireland) half-sister to Stayers' Hurdle
winner Galmoy: modest maiden: seems to stay 2m: yet to race on extremes of going.
Mrs M. Reveley

CLASSIC BALLET (FR)   4 b.f. Fabulous Dancer (USA) 124 – Tyranesque   68
(USA) (Key To The Mint (USA)) [1996 68: 9g⁴ 10g³ 11.6m³ 11.8d⁴ 8f* 10.1f⁴ 8m⁶   a73
10.1m 8.5g 8.2g a12g⁴ 1997 8.2g 10g 8.2g⁶ 8.3d² 12m* a12g* 12.4g² a10g³ a12g*
14g⁴ 12g² 12.1g³ a12g⁵ 12m Oct 31] sturdy filly: fair performer: won minor event at
Musselburgh and 2 handicaps at Southwell in the summer: suited by around 1½m:
acts on firm and soft ground and probably both all-weather: consistent. *R. Guest*

CLASSIC BEAUTY (IRE)   4 b.f. Fairy King (USA) – Working Model 99 (Ile   52 §
de Bourbon (USA) 133) [1996 65: a10g³ a8.5g⁴ a9.4g⁴ 7m² 7g⁶ 7f³ a9.4g 7m 11.1m*
12m⁶ 8g⁵ 7g 1997 9.9m³ a10g May 9] sturdy filly: modest handicapper: stays 11f:
acts on firm ground and equitrack: finds little: unreliable. *S. C. Williams*

CLASSIC CLICHE (IRE)   5 b.h. Salse (USA) 128 – Pato 90 (High Top 131)   126
[1996 128: 13.9f* 20m* 12m² 12d 1997 13.9g 20g² 16m² 15g* 14d Sep 20]
        Classic Cliche ended the season as he began it, in inglorious isolation,
on this occasion last of seven in the Irish St Leger, and one day later the end of
his racing career was announced. The judge at the Curragh did not tax himself
by working out the distance between Classic Cliche and the second-last horse,
but in the Yorkshire Cup four months earlier it had been measured at eighteen
lengths. Enough was enough for his connections as well as for Classic Cliche.
As Godolphin racing manager Simon Crisford explained: 'Yesterday he just
told us he's not enjoying his racing as much as he used to. You could see
he didn't really fancy it.' When connections go so far as to say this about their
own horse, and such a horse as this, you have to believe them.
        Of course, there was precious little to apologise about with Classic
Cliche. It is not that difficult to see where the Godolphin talent scouts are
coming from with most of their two-year-old purchases, but remember that, by

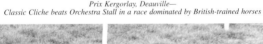

Prix Kergorlay, Deauville—
Classic Cliche beats Orchestra Stall in a race dominated by British-trained horses

their standards, Classic Cliche as a two-year-old was a dark horse. When the Godolphin team took everything by storm in 1995, however, Classic Cliche was in the vanguard, winning the Dante Stakes and St Leger. The Cup races nowadays are a place where the connections of classic winners generally fear to tread, and huge credit is due to those of Classic Cliche as well as to the horse himself for that four-year-old campaign in which the horse followed victory in the Yorkshire Cup with another in the Gold Cup itself. It was the first time since 1945 that one of the previous season's classic winners had gone on to win the Gold Cup, and Classic Cliche went on to demonstrate that those who line up in the staying races need not be labelled automatically as dyed-in-the-wool sluggards by beating all but Pentire in the King George VI and Queen Elizabeth Diamond Stakes.

In hindsight, trailing a tame fifteenth of sixteen in the Arc on his only other start of 1996 was a good hint that the King George would prove the pinnacle of Classic Cliche's achievements. However, although concurring with Crisford in suggesting that Classic Cliche never showed the same form again, we reckon that in 1997 he came pretty close. There is no denying that the Yorkshire Cup was an appalling start, but he made a fine attempt to register a repeat success in the Gold Cup five weeks later. With a somewhat wary public this time allowing him to drift from 4/1-favourite to 6/1-third favourite, Classic Cliche moved smoothly forward five furlongs out and kicked a couple of lengths clear early in the straight, but, stalked in ominous fashion by Celeric, he was overtaken in the last fifty yards and went down by three quarters of a length. As in 1996, he went on to show even better form the following month while having to settle for the runner-up spot, this time in the Goodwood Cup. Classic Cliche was waited with a little longer than at Royal Ascot, coming through to dispute the lead approaching the final furlong, but the concession of 5 lb to a battling Double Trigger proved beyond him and he was beaten by a length and a half, a performance that nonetheless, by our reckoning, deserves to be recognised as the best of 1997 by a horse over two miles or more. With the weights in his favour, though, Classic Cliche was still capable of keeping his head in front. The opportunity presented itself in the Prix Kergorlay at Deauville in August and he led home a British-trained one-two-three. Subsequent big-race winners Orchestra Stall and Chief Contender were the placed horses and Classic Cliche beat them by two lengths and another two and a half. At the time, the Irish St Leger was still being talked about as a stepping stone towards the Melbourne Cup.

		Topsider	Northern Dancer
	Salse (USA)	(b 1974)	Drumtop
	(b 1985)	Carnival Princess	Prince John
Classic Cliche (IRE)		(ch 1974)	Carnival Queen
(b.c. 1992)		High Top	Derring-Do
	Pato	(br 1969)	Camenae
	(b 1982)	Patosky	Skymaster
		(b 1969)	Los Patos

Classic Cliche stayed two and a half miles and his very best form was shown over a strongly-run mile and a half. He did not race on soft ground, but acted on any other. His record was tarnished a little in the latest season when the reluctance he frequently showed at the stalls appeared to spread to the race itself, but in essence his was a career to celebrate, a retirement well earned. It took a while for the details of his new home to be announced—perhaps connections had been taken a little by surprise—but he has been sold and will stand at the Wood Farm Stud in Shropshire at a fee of £2,500 (October 1st). From the third crop of Salse, Classic Cliche was one of the first to alert us to his sire's previously unsuspected ability to sire stayers, something of an extra surprise in Classic Cliche's case given that the best-known member of his dam Pato's family was her brother the very smart sprinter Crews Hill. As far as Pato at stud is concerned, My Emma (by Marju) demonstrated again in the latest

CLA

season that Classic Cliche is no flash in the pan. Classic Cliche is a good-topped, attractive horse who carried condition, a striking individual to look at, and if he gets many of his progeny in the same mould then his stud career should be a success. *Saeed bin Suroor*

CLASSIC COLOURS (USA)   4 ch.g. Blushing John (USA) 120 – All Agleam   – §
(USA) (Gleaming (USA)) [1996 68§: 8.2d⁴ 9.9m² 10.3m² 10d⁵ 10m³ 10g 11m⁴ a8g
1997 10s 10d 8.2d Nov 3] strong, compact gelding: no worthwhile form in 1997:
carries head high, and none too genuine. *G. H. Yardley*

CLASSIC DAISY   4 b.f. Prince Sabo 123 – Bloom of Youth (IRE) (Last Tycoon   –
131) [1996 –: a7g a7g⁵ 8.2m 8.2m a11g 1997 a11g Jan 10] of little account.
R. C. Spicer

CLASSIC DAME (FR)   4 gr.f. Highest Honor (FR) 124 – Reem El Fala (FR)   67
(Fabulous Dancer (USA) 124) [1996 72: 7f⁶ 9m³ 11.5m³ 10.5v 1997 10m 12m⁴ 11.9g
a12g Nov 6] leggy filly: fair maiden at best: trained by I. Campbell on reappearance:
stays 1½m: acts on good to firm ground, finished last on heavy: tends to pull hard:
inconsistent: sold 1,300 gns in December. *S. Dow*

CLASSIC DEFENCE (IRE)   4 b.g. Cyrano de Bergerac 120 – My Alanna   –
(Dalsaan 125) [1996 75: 8.1g* 8m 8g³ 10m* 10.2f² 9f 9g 1997 10m Sep 30] leggy
gelding: fair handicapper at 3 yrs: burly, bandaged and tailed off only start in 1997.
J. W. Hills

CLASSIC EAGLE   4 b.g. Unfuwain (USA) 131 – La Lutine 95 (My Swallow   –
134) [1996 88: 8m 12.3g⁶ 12m 12m 7.1g⁶ 14.1f⁴ 14.6g 1997 a12g 10.1m Oct 22]
close-coupled, workmanlike gelding: formerly fairly useful up to 1½m: showed
nothing in handicaps in 1997, but won over hurdles in December. *I. Campbell*

CLASSIC FAN (USA)   3 b.f. Lear Fan (USA) 130 – Miss Boniface 112 (Tap On   –
Wood 130) [1996 NR 1997 10g 10g⁵ 12.3s² 16g 12s⁶ Oct 16] $30,000Y, 6,000 2-y-o:
leggy, unfurnished filly: third foal: dam won Ribblesdale Stakes: only a little sign of
ability. *M. R. Channon*

CLASSIC FIND (USA)   4 br.g. Lear Fan (USA) 130 – Reve de Reine (USA) 97   76
(Lyphard (USA) 132) [1996 94: 10g 10m* 12m³ 1997 12g 12m 12m⁶ 12d 14g³
14.8m 10s 10m² 10m³ a10g² a10g* Dec 22] good-bodied gelding: fair handicapper:
trained first 6 starts by I. Campbell: won at Lingfield in December: effective at 1¼m,
probably 1¾m: acts on good to firm ground, dead and equitrack: often bandaged: has
worn tongue strap: has flashed tail. *Pat Mitchell*

CLASSIC FLYER (IRE)   4 b.f. Alzao (USA) 117 – Sea Harrier (Grundy 137)   72
[1996 78, a82: 10m⁵ 12g² a9.4g⁶ 10.3m⁶ 10.5s 1997 7g 8.3m³ 10d³ 12g³ 15.4m⁶
13.1s Oct 14] good-topped filly: fluent mover: fair handicapper: stays 1½m: acts on
fibresand and on good to firm and dead ground (well beaten on soft): often makes
running. *I. Campbell*

CLASSIC FORM (IRE)   4 b.f. Alzao (USA) 117 – Formulate 119 (Reform 132)   –
[1996 58: 7f² 10g⁴ 1997 8s a9.4g Oct 4] sturdy filly: lightly-raced maiden: tailed off
in 1997. *I. Campbell*

CLASSIC IMPACT (IRE)   2 ch.g. (Mar 29) Generous (IRE) 139 – Vaison La   73 p
Romaine 100 (Arctic Tern (USA) 126) [1997 8m⁵ 8s Oct 14] IR 65,000Y: tall,
unfurnished gelding: half-brother to 3-y-o Viva Verdi and several other winners,
including smart German middle-distance performer Vialli (by Niniski): dam,
runner-up in Britain at 2 yrs, later won over 7.5f in France: showed promise when
strong-finishing fifth of 13 behind Courteous in maiden at Salisbury: well held on
soft ground 2 weeks later: should prove suited by 1¼m+: should make a better 3-y-o.
P. W. Chapple-Hyam

CLASSIC JENNY (IRE)   4 b.f. Green Desert (USA) 127 – Eileen Jenny (IRE)   69
112 (Kris 135) [1996 NR 1997 a9.4g⁴ 10g⁵ 10s⁴ 8d Oct 28] 71,000Y: big filly: first
foal: third in Irish Oaks, half-sister to the dam of Irish Oaks winner Wemyss
Bight, out of disqualified Irish Oaks winner Sorbus: fair maiden: stays 1¼m: has
worn dropped noseband: has joined M. Channon. *I. Campbell*

215

CLASSIC LEADER   4 b.c. Thatching 131 – Tenderetta (Tender King 123) [1996   68
76: 6.9m⁶ 8m² 8d³ 8m⁵ 8m³ 1997 a7g a8.5g 8g 8.3s 6.1m² 6g⁵ 6d Jun 28]
good-bodied colt: fair maiden: finds 6f on sharp side, and stays 1m: acts on good to
firm and dead ground: often blinkered or visored: carries head high, and looks a hard
ride. *I. Campbell*

CLASSIC LINE   3 b.f. Last Tycoon 131 – Classic Beam (Cut Above 130) [1996   71
–p: 6.1f 6m 7f 1997 11.6s⁵ 14.1g* 16.2v³ 14m⁵ 17.5d⁴ 16s⁴ 14.1d⁴ Oct 30] leggy,
sparely-made filly: fair handicapper: won strongly-run contest at Redcar in June:
creditable efforts afterwards: suited by test of stamina: acted on good to firm and
heavy ground: blinkered last 4 starts: stud. *J. L. Dunlop*

CLASSIC MANOEUVRE (USA)   2 ch.c. (Feb 14) Sky Classic (CAN) – Maid   90
of Honor (USA) (Blushing Groom (FR) 131) [1997 6g⁴ 7g⁴ 7.1d² 7g Aug 13]
$110,000Y: good mover: second foal: dam, well beaten both starts here, later sprint
winner in USA: fairly useful form second and third starts, staying-on fourth in
Chesham Stakes at Royal Ascot and 9 lengths second of 4 to Muhtathir in minor
event at Sandown: again looked one-paced when below form final start (may benefit
from forcing tactics): should stay at least 1m. *R. Hannon*

CLASSIC MYSTERY (IRE)   3 ch.g. Classic Secret (USA) 91 – Mystery Bid   64
(Auction Ring (USA) 123) [1996 60: 5.2d 6m 6.1m⁴ a7g 7.3m 1997 12g³ 12.3g 11.6s
May 12] lengthy gelding: fluent mover: fair handicapper: pulled up due to respiratory
distress second start: should stay beyond 1½m: has taken keen hold: blinkered final
start at 2 yrs. *B. J. Meehan*

CLASSIC PARISIAN (IRE)   4 b.f. Persian Bold 123 – Gay France (FR) 91 (Sir   –
Gaylord) [1996 79: 10.5d³ 10m 10m² 10.2f³ 12m⁶ 10s² 12g³ 11.9v 1997 10s 13.1d⁵
10.2m Jul 17] plain filly: fair maiden: consistent as 3-y-o, well held in 1997: left I.
Campbell after second start. *R. J. O'Sullivan*

CLASSIC PARK   3 b.f. Robellino (USA) 127 – Wanton 106 (Kris 135) [1996   115
94: 5s* 5d³ 6g² 5m⁶ 5m⁴ 6g² 6g 6m 1997 7m* 8d* 8m⁴ 8m⁵ 8m⁵ 7d Oct 19]
       As officials who mistook him for a reveller at the Cheltenham Festival
will testify, trying to keep Aidan O'Brien out of the winner's enclosure these
days is well-nigh impossible. The twenty-eight-year-old has been the champion
trainer over jumps in Ireland in all four seasons since he took out a licence, and
in 1997 he swept all before him on the flat as well. Desert King was the
flagbearer, but, twenty-four hours before the first of that colt's two classics, he
was beaten to the honour of providing O'Brien's first classic win by the filly
Classic Park.
       At the end of the latest season, the current master of Ballydoyle was
trailing his great predecessor, Vincent O'Brien, by sixteen British classic
winners and twenty-four Irish classic winners. In this respect at least, it is early
days to be comparing the two men. We will however draw a parallel between
Classic Park and Vincent O'Brien's first classic winner, for, like the 1953 Irish
Derby victor Chamier, it looks as if Classic Park's place in the history books
will be as a curious footnote. There is her stud career to come, but on the
racecourse there is very little to remember her for besides that victory in the
Airlie/Coolmore Irish One Thousand Guineas. Before the race, Aidan O'Brien
seemed to have a reasonable chance of opening his classic account, but that was
chiefly with Generous' half-sister Strawberry Roan. She started the 4/1 second
favourite, in the midst of four British-trained challengers with Group 1 form in
Ryafan, Oh Nellie, Dazzle and Seebe. Classic Park had plenty of form, but none
of it was anywhere good enough to suggest she was overpriced at 20/1. A
one-win-from-eight-starts record in 1996 included sixth in the Queen Mary
and thirteenth in the Redcar Two-Year-Old Trophy to underwhelm British onlookers, but she had shown improvement in the Leopardstown One Thousand
Guineas Trial on her reappearance when she came from last entering the
straight to first on the post. With a short-priced stable companion in the line-up
that day, Classic Park started at 14/1. She again showed a good turn of foot to
pull off a similar surprise in the Guineas itself five weeks later. While Straw-

Airlie/Coolmore Irish One Thousand Guineas, the Curragh—
Classic Park provides Aidan O'Brien with his first classic success;
unlucky-in-running stable-companion Strawberry Roan is second

berry Roan encountered trouble in running, Classic Park made smooth headway to lead one furlong out and held on from her fast-finishing stable companion by a length.

Sympathy for Strawberry Roan was tempered by the knowledge that there would surely be a good middle-distance prize awaiting her, but neither filly managed to reach the first two in any race afterwards. Classic Park did not make the first three, but she continued to be highly tried, and fifth of nine (beaten about four lengths) in both the Sussex Stakes at Goodwood and Prix du Moulin de Longchamp were creditable efforts. Another 20/1 shock briefly looked a possibility at Goodwood when Classic Park nipped through on the rails to dispute the lead one and a half furlongs out, but she weakened quickly thereafter. She never threatened to land a blow in her two other races of 1997, the Coronation Stakes at Royal Ascot and the Prix de la Foret at Longchamp. Waiting tactics were the norm with the smallish, good-quartered Classic Park. Considered 'just' a sprinter by her owners as a two-year-old, she got a mile alright, won on soft going on her debut and on good to firm and dead as a three-year-old. She was tried in blinkers once at two years, performing well below her best.

		Roberto	Hail To Reason
	Robellino (USA)	(b 1969)	Bramalea
	(b 1978)	Isobelline	Pronto
Classic Park		(b 1971)	Isobella
(b.f. 1994)		Kris	Sharpen Up
	Wanton	(ch 1976)	Doubly Sure
	(ch 1983)	Brazen Faced	Bold And Free
		(ch 1975)	Maurine

In naming their filly, who had relations like Lovers Lane, Brazen Faced, Bimbo, Wanton and Rumpipumpy, Classic Park's owners did not exactly rise to the challenge, rather like Lord Howard de Walden when he named his champion hurdler Lanzarote instead of something suggested by close family members such as Coal Board, Shaft, Bunker, Seam, Smogland, Methane and (no relation of Classic Park) Slag. The aforementioned Rumpipumpy (by Shirley Heights) was a Grade 2 winner in the United States in 1997, and one of four winners from five foals produced before Classic Park by the mare Wanton. Another was the useful colt Wilde Rufo (by Sharrood), but the task of extending this good family record rests with the modest 1997 two-year-old Tom (by Petong). Wanton was a useful two-year-old five-furlong winner and is a half-sister to the smart sprinter Easy Option, in whose 1995 essay more details of this family can be found. Classic Park, a 30,000-guinea yearling, is a second Guineas winner for her sire Robellino, following Mister Baileys who, interestingly, is out of a mare by Sharpen Up, the sire of Classic Park's maternal grandsire Kris. *A. P. O'Brien, Ireland*

CLASSIC RIBBON (IRE)   4 b.f. Persian Bold 123 – House Tie (Be Friendly – 130) [1996 63p: 7g⁵ 1997 8.3s May 19] some promise only 3-y-o start, for R. Harris: pulled hard and well beaten only outing in 1997: should stay at least 1m: sent to Australia. *I. Campbell*

CLASSIC SILVER (IRE)   2 b.g. (Mar 2) Silver Kite (USA) 111 – Classic Ring – (IRE) 50 (Auction Ring (USA) 123) [1997 5m⁵ 5m 5f⁶ 7m Oct 7] 9,200 2-y-o: smallish, strong gelding: second foal: dam 2-y-o 7f seller winner: behind in maidens and claimer. *W. W. Haigh*

CLASSIC VICTORY   4 b.g. Puissance 110 – Seattle Mama (USA) (Seattle Song – (USA) 130) [1996 58, a–: a6g a7g a6g 8.3d² a7g a8.5g 8g 8m 1997 a8g 6.9g Apr 25] tall gelding: well beaten in 1997. *I. Campbell*

CLASSY CHIEF   4 b.g. Be My Chief (USA) 122 – Jalopy 71 (Jalmood (USA)   59 126) [1996 72§: 8.1g 8.3m⁵ 7f⁵ 10m 10m⁶ 11.5d 8g 8.2g² 7g 7g 1997 a13g* a13g⁶ a13g³ 9.7m 16m Sep 25] big gelding: modest performer: won weak maiden at Lingfield in January: left J. White only 980 gns after fourth start: pulled up only subsequent outing: stays 13f: acts on firm ground and equitrack. *J. E. Long*

CLASSY CLEO (IRE)   2 b.f. (Feb 26) Mujadil (USA) 119 – Sybaris 91   85 (Crowned Prince (USA) 128) [1997 5m² 5s³ 5m* 5g* 6g³ 5g 6d² 6m⁵ 6g 6d* 6g⁵ 6d³   a98 5s² 5.2f* 5m² 5d³ a6g* a5s* a7g² Dec 13] 9,800Y: neat filly: unimpressive mover: half-sister to 1988 Irish 2-y-o 7f winner Millennium Queen (by Mendez) and winners abroad by Tate Gallery and Red Sunset: dam 2-y-o 5f winner, later successful in USA: fairly useful on turf: won maiden at Beverley and minor event at Pontefract in April, claimer at Haydock (claimed out of R. Hannon's yard £12,000) in September and nursery at Yarmouth in October: useful on all-weather, winning nurseries at Southwell and Lingfield in November: best at 5f/6f: acts on firm and soft ground and on the all-weather: often sweats and gets on toes: tough. *P. D. Evans*

CLEAN SWOP (IRE)   3 b.g. Astronef 116 – Sauvignon (IRE) 63 (Alzao (USA) – 117) [1996 NR 1997 6g 10g Apr 26] 5,000Y: sturdy gelding: first foal: dam stayed 1m: no promise in maiden and seller. *T. D. Easterby*

CLEAR THE AIR   3 ch.f. Salse (USA) 128 – Belle Enfant 87 (Beldale Flutter – (USA) 130) [1996 58: 7m 8.1g 8f³ 1997 14.1d 10.8m⁶ May 24] tall, lightly-made filly: worthwhile form only on final 2-y-o start. *P. F. I. Cole*

CLEAR VIEW   2 b.g. (Mar 22) Beveled (USA) – Scenic Villa (Top Ville 129)   41 [1997 5m 6m 7m³ 6g 6m Aug 23] IR 7,000Y: half-brother to 4-y-o Globe Runner: dam poor maiden here and in France: only form when third in seller at Brighton in July: should stay beyond 7f: blinkered final start. *B. J. Meehan*

CLEF OF SILVER   2 b.c. (Mar 12) Indian Ridge 123 – Susquehanna Days   87 (USA) 68 (Chief's Crown (USA)) [1997 5g² 6s² 5.2m² 6g² 6g* Aug 15] 36,000Y: close-coupled colt: first foal: dam, 1m winner, from very good family: fairly useful form: won nursery at Catterick in August: should stay beyond 6f: below best on soft ground: has reared start: hung left last 2 outings. *W. Jarvis*

CLEMENCY (IRE)   5 ch.m. Kefaah (USA) 124 – Supreme Crown (USA) – (Chief's Crown (USA)) [1996 NR 1997 a8.5g 10.8d⁵ Aug 25] modest maiden: little encouragement in 1997, seeming reluctant on reappearance. *M. Tate*

CLERKENWELL (USA) 4 b.c. Sadler's Wells (USA) 132 – Forlene 108 (Forli 113
(ARG)) [1996 108+: 10g² 12m³ 12m² 16.2m 14g* 13.9m* 15d 1997 14g* 11g⁵ Sep
18] sturdy colt: good mover: smart performer: career-best effort when awarded
4-runner minor event at Salisbury in September, slightly impeded by narrow
first-past-post Samraan: inadequate trip 2 weeks later, only other start of 1997: best
form around 1¾m (stamina seemed stretched at 2m): acts on good to firm going.
M. R. Stoute

CLERMONT CITY (IRE) 2 b.c. (Apr 30) Royal Academy (USA) 130 – 57
Diamond Spring (USA) (Vaguely Noble 140) [1997 6g⁴ 7g⁵ 6.1m⁵ a7g* 8g 8m Oct a64
5] 20,000Y: compact colt: closely related to French middle-distance winner Didwana
(by Nijinsky) and half-brother to several winners in France (one listed winner by Far
North) and North America: dam, French 1m winner, from family of Lyphard and
Nobiliary: won nursery at Wolverhampton in August: not quite so good on turf and
tailed off last 2 starts (blinkered last one): should stay 1m: sold, to go to Norway.
P. W. Chapple-Hyam

CLEVER CAPTION (IRE) 3 b.c. Topanoora 118 – Fundraiser 113 (Welsh 104
Saint 126) [1996 5g⁵ 1997 5m³ May 3] IR 42,000Y: sparely-made colt: third foal:
half-brother to Italian 1m to 11f winner Prenom Carmen (by Persian Bold): dam
smart Irish sprinter: trained by A. Fabre at 2 yrs, winning 6-runner listed race at
Deauville on only start: did very well for one so inexperienced when ½-length third
of 12 to Deep Finesse in Palace House Stakes at Newmarket: should stay 6f: seemed
likely to improve further, but not seen out again. *Saeed bin Suroor*

CLIBURNEL NEWS (IRE) 7 b.m. Horage 124 – Dublin Millennium (Dalsaan 62
125) [1996 61, a–: 11.8d² 10g⁶ 14.1m⁵ 12m⁵ 11.8d⁶ 11.8m⁶ 14.1m⁶ 1997 11.8g 10.4s
16m* Sep 15] sparely-made mare: modest handicapper: only form in 1997 when
winning at Nottingham in September: stays 2m: acts on the all-weather and any turf:
usually held up. *D. Shaw*

CLIFTON BEAT (USA) 6 b.h. Danzatore (CAN) 120 – Amenity (FR) 76 –
(Luthier 126) [1996 NR 1997 10.3d 12d⁵ May 16] fair handicapper for Mrs J.
Ramsden in 1994: useful hurdler: well beaten on return to flat. *P. J. Hobbs*

CLIFTON GAME 7 b.g. Mummy's Game 120 – Brave Maiden 63 (Three Legs –
128) [1996 50: 11.5m* 16.4g⁴ 1997 11.9f⁴ Apr 11] tall gelding: lightly raced:
modest winner at 6 yrs before going novice chasing: well held only 7-y-o start.
M. R. Channon

CLIFTON WOOD (IRE) 2 b.c. (Mar 18) Paris House 123 – Millie's Lady –
(IRE) (Common Grounds 118) [1997 7g Aug 25] 19,000Y: workmanlike colt: first
foal: dam unraced: tailed off only start. *J. A. Glover*

CLINKING 6 b.g. Glint of Gold 128 – Kai (Kalamoun 129) [1996 NR 1997 14.1f –
Oct 29] third foal: half-brother to fairly useful 1¼m winner Kaytiggy (by Busted) and
fair 1¾m winner Fabillion (by Deploy): dam unraced: won NH Flat race at Kempton
(pulled very hard) in January: well beaten on flat debut. *Mrs A. J. Perrett*

CLOAK OF DARKNESS (IRE) 2 b.c. (Feb 8) Thatching 131 – Madame 73
Nureyev (USA) (Nureyev (USA) 131) [1997 7m⁶ 7.1m⁵ 8.2g⁶ Sep 28] IR 38,000Y;
fifth foal: half-brother to 5-y-o Bernard Seven, 7f winner Fen Dance (by Trojan Fen)
and Miss Universal (by Lycius, useful maiden at up to 1¼m here, now winner in
USA): dam French 2-y-o 6f winner: fair maiden: stays 1m. *R. Hannon*

CLODORA (FR) 3 b.f. Linamix (FR) 127 – Cloche d'Or 102 (Good Times 113
(ITY)) [1996 NR 1997 6g⁵ 8g* 8d² 7m² 8d* 8g⁵ 9.3f* Oct 5] second foal: half-sister
to Cloche du Roi (by Fairy King): dam, 2-y-o 6f winner who stayed 7f, out of 1¼m
winner: won minor event at Longchamp in April, listed race at Deauville in August
and very strongly-run 17-runner Prix de L'Opera at Longchamp (improved form, by
length from Squeak) in October: stays 9.3f: acts on dead ground but best effort on
firm. *A. Fabre, France*

CLONOE 3 b.g. Syrtos 106 – Anytime Anywhere 77 (Daring March 116) [1996 46
NR 1997 12g a7g a10g⁴ a8g³ a7g⁶ a7g Dec 18] strong, plain gelding: second foal:
half-brother to 4-y-o Flying Harold: dam best over sharp 5f: only worthwhile form
when third in maiden at Lingfield in December: tried blinkered. *R. Ingram*

CLO

CLOSE SHAVE 2 b.c. (Mar 20) Warning 136 – La Barberina (USA) (Nijinsky 79 p
(CAN) 138) [1997 7m⁴ 7m³ Oct 22] lengthy colt: first foal: dam, placed over 11f in
France, closely related to US Grade 1 8.5f winner Fantastic Look: eye-catching
fourth to Tamarisk in minor event at Kempton in September, hanging left but giving
impression he'd have finished second with more enterprising ride (run subject of
stewards' inquiry): only third of 13 to Jila when favourite for maiden at Yarmouth:
will stay 1m: still capable of better. *M. R. Stoute*

CLOSE UP (IRE) 2 ch.c. (Mar 8) Cadeaux Genereux 131 – Zoom Lens (IRE) 65 93 p
(Caerleon (USA) 132) [1997 7m⁵ 7g⁴ 7m² 8m* 8.1s* Oct 15] 60,000Y: unfurnished
colt: second foal: half-brother to 1996 2-y-o 5f winner Blue Movie (By Bluebird):
dam stoutly-bred maiden: won maiden at Pontefract and minor event at Haydock in
autumn, holding Giveaway by a head, pair clear, in latter: will stay at least 1¼m: acts
on good to firm and soft ground: useful colt in the making. *J. L. Dunlop*

CLOUDBERRY 2 b.f. (Jan 20) Night Shift (USA) – Chatterberry 67 (Aragon 88
118) [1997 5g 5.1m² 5.2m² 5m* 5.2m⁴ 6g 6d² 6g Oct 25] 13,000Y: smallish, sturdy
filly: has quick action: first foal: dam lightly-raced 2-y-o 5f winner, sister to smart
sprinter Argentum: fairly useful performer: made all in maiden at Sandown in July:
ran creditably in listed races next 3 starts (went down by short head to Karakorum at
the Curragh penultimate outing): speedy, but stays 6f: acts on good to firm and dead
ground: tailed off in blinkers final start: sold 28,000 gns in December. *B. J. Meehan*

CLOUD CASTLE 2 b.f. (Apr 6) In The Wings 128 – Lucayan Princess 111 (High 84 p
Line 125) [1997 7d³ Oct 17] rather unfurnished filly: seventh foal: half-sister to 5-y-o
Luso, 7-y-o Needle Gun and useful 6f winner Luana (by Shaadi): dam, 2-y-o 7f
winner, stayed 1½m: 6/1 from 3/1, shaped encouragingly when 1¼ lengths third of 6
to Lucayan Indian in steadily-run minor event at Newmarket, staying on well: sure to
do fair bit better, and win races over 1m+. *C. E. Brittain*

CLOUDINGS (IRE) 3 gr.c. Sadler's Wells (USA) 132 – Ispahan 85 (Rusticaro 112
(FR) 124) [1996 8s⁴ 8d* 1997 10.5m* 10.5d* 12g Jun 7] 1,000,000 francs Y: sturdy
colt: brother to French 10.5f winner Almuntasser and half-brother to 4 winners,
notably Lady Wishing Well (including 1m listed race, by Hero's Honor): dam, 6f (at
2 yrs) and 1m (in France) winner, from good family: lightly-raced French performer:
won fairly valuable auction event at Deauville at 2 yrs: successful at Longchamp in
spring in listed race and (took long time to wear down Zenith Rose and win by a
neck) weak 5-runner Prix Lupin: beaten 37 lengths when tenth in Derby at Epsom:
should stay 1½m: acts on good to firm and dead ground: has joined Godolphin.
A. Fabre, France

CLOUD INSPECTOR (IRE) 6 b.g. Persian Bold 123 – Timbale d'Argent 90
(Petingo 135) [1996 12g² 12s² 10d 10g 1997 15.8m² 16g² 14g² 16.1g³ 20m* 15g*
12.5g² 18g Oct 18] big, useful-looking gelding: from a family of many winners,
notably smart 1½m performer Hajade (half-brother, by Ile de Bourbon): dam showed
a little ability in France: ran in Ireland at 2 yrs: subsequently raced on the Continent,
winning over 11f and 15f (Swiss St Leger) in Switzerland at 3 yrs: fairly useful form
in 1997: won handicap at Goodwood in July and minor event in Switzerland in
August: stays 2½m: acts on good to firm and soft ground: tried blinkered earlier in
career: consistent. *M. Johnston*

CLOUDS HILL (FR) 4 b.g. Sarhoob (USA) 124 – Dana Dana (FR) (Pharly (FR) 61
130) [1996 70: 10g 9m⁵ 12d 11.5m⁴ 1997 12g 10g 10f⁴ 10s⁶ 8.3g⁵ 8m² 9m 8.1g 8g²
8g⁵ 8f² Sep 18] tall gelding: modest maiden handicapper: effective at 1m to easy
1¼m: acts on dead and firm going: effective with or without visor: sold 14,500 gns in
October. *R. Hannon*

CLOUDS OF GLORY 2 b.f. (Apr 28) Lycius (USA) 124 – Dance A Jig (Dance 61
In Time (CAN)) [1997 6m 7m 6g Oct 27] 5,500F, 15,000Y: sturdy, angular filly: sixth
foal: half-sister to 5f and 7f winner Tyrone Flyer (by Celestial Storm) and fairly
useful French sprinter Always Dancing (by Common Grounds): dam once-raced
granddaughter of smart sprinter Fluke: modest form final start in maidens, eighth of
22 at Leicester: headstrong and probably a sprinter. *R. Charlton*

CLUB ELITE 5 b.m. Salse (USA) 128 – Little Bittern (USA) 73 (Riva Ridge –
(USA)) [1996 26: a16g⁶ 17.2m 14.1f⁴ 14.1f⁶ 15.8m⁵ 1997 12g a16g a14g 14.1s Jul 5]
of little account nowadays. *Miss A. Stokell*

Sheikh Mohammed's "Cloudings"

CLUED UP 4 b.f. Beveled (USA) – Scharade 74 (Lombard (GER) 126) [1996 57: 10.8m a12g⁶ 7m⁵ 10m* 8.1m⁵ 10d⁶ 11.5m³ 10g 10.8f 1997 9.9m⁶ 8m² 10g⁵ 8.3s* 10m³ 8m⁶ 10.5m a8.5g 8.1s* 10m 10m⁶ 10g 10.1g⁴ 10m a12g Nov 21] tall, workmanlike filly: modest handicapper: won amateurs events at Hamilton in May and Chepstow in July: effective at 1m to 11.5f: acts on good to firm and soft ground, no form on all-weather: blinkered/visored nowadays: unreliable. *P. D. Evans* 57 § a– §

CLYTHA HILL LAD 6 b.g. Domitor (USA) 98 – Quae Supra 79 (On Your Mark 125) [1996 34: a8g a8g⁵ 8g 10m 8m 10.8m⁵ 1997 6.9m³ 8f² 8g⁴ 8.1m⁶ 8m* 7.1m* 7.6g² 7m* 8.1m* 7g⁴ 7.1g 8f Sep 17] big, lengthy gelding: modest handicapper: in good form for much of season, winning at Redcar (apprentices) and Chepstow in July and at Redcar (dead-heated) and Haydock in August: stays 1m: raced only on good ground or firmer on turf: usually bandaged: takes good hold and races prominently: game. *J. M. Bradley* 59

COALMINERSDAUGHTER (IRE) 2 b.f. (Apr 28) Dynaformer (USA) – Sportin' Notion (USA) (Sportin' Life (USA)) [1997 6g 6.9m 7m Oct 5] 14,500F, $45,000Y: angular filly: shows knee action: first foal: dam placed in USA, out of half-sister to Cacoethes: modest form in maidens: should stay at least 1m. *J. W. Hills* 60

COASTAL BLUFF 5 gr.g. Standaan (FR) 118 – Combattente (Reform 132) [1996 117p: 6f 5g* 6m* 6m* 1997 6g⁵ 5m* 6m 5d* 6d Sep 5] 118

The potential for mishap in the combination of man and horse is great. We see horses jumping fences without their jockeys and jockeys coming over fences without their horses, horses 'winning' races without their jockeys and even a jockey finishing a race on the wrong horse. The majority of these cases arise when horse and rider are at cross-purposes. A smaller number involve equipment failure. Here are a few of the painful results: riding over the last eight fences at Aintree without irons (John Thorne winning the 1978 Foxhunters on Spartan Missile, Tim Brookshaw finishing second in the 1959 Grand National on Wyndburgh); races lost by a head because of a broken stirrup (Dun

221

Gay Lass, 1991 Cheltenham Foxhunters); jockeys losing their whip and going down by a short head in a classic (Insan, 1988 Irish Derby); the reins coming apart when you are in a clear lead between the last two fences in the Grand National (Davy Jones, 1936); having to ride bareback as the saddle slips when you are challenging for the lead in the Oaks (Willie Carson on Dibidale, 1974).

The most famous such case remains the heroics of Fred Winter and Mandarin when they won the 1962 Grand Steeple-Chase de Paris, doing so in a desperately close finish after Winter had lost the use of his reins very early on when the bit broke. But there was a race almost to rival that for drama—even if it did not become fully apparent to most until the television replays—at York in 1997. The Nunthorpe Stakes saw Kevin Darley, on Coastal Bluff, ride more than four of the five furlongs without reins—and the race had its close finish, too! As with Mandarin, it was the bit which broke, and at an early stage, as Coastal Bluff and his fourteen opponents were just getting into their stride. There were no fences to be jumped and no turns to be negotiated, but, if another side of the coin were needed, remember the speed of the horses involved. The winning time was 59.58 seconds—making an average speed of nearly thirty-eight miles per hour. Darley had to hold on to the horse's mane, keep his balance, and, thanks to the ability and extreme willingness of his mount, he had to ride a finish. Perhaps things would have been a good deal more difficult for him if restraint and waiting tactics had been required, but the Nunthorpe is not that sort of race and Coastal Bluff not that sort of horse. In the front rank as soon as the stalls opened, Coastal Bluff had Mind Games and Evening-performance go past him at halfway, but he was in front again at the furlong marker and kept the lead until Ya Malak got to him with about thirty yards to go. A renewed effort kept Coastal Bluff upsides as they passed the post. With the whip in his right hand, Darley had given Coastal Bluff a reminder two furlongs out, and with the whip in his left hand he had driven out through the final furlong. The television replays, shown as twenty minutes passed before the judge announced a dead-heat, illustrated the full magnitude of this riding performance. Applying the brakes had not been required during the race and it proved possible afterwards only with the aid of Kieren Fallon (on third-placed Averti, who, by the way, had been beaten only a head) who got Coastal Bluff to slow down sufficiently for Darley to slide off. Coastal Bluff was caught quickly

*Nunthorpe Stakes, York—an astonishing contest as Kevin Darley and Coastal Bluff (No. 4),
without a bridle after the bit snapped early on, force a dead-heat with Ya Malak*

and, thankfully, this incredible event in racing history was not marred by any injury to horse or rider.

Had Coastal Bluff's bad luck stretched to the photo-finish as well, then he would not have had much to show for his season. It had taken him time to come to hand, and when he did return to action he could not be kept on the boil for long. He led the field in the July Cup before fading into fifth and followed that with a narrow victory in a £5,300 conditions stakes on the same course. A burden of 9-10 (19 lb higher than his 1996 mark) then proved too much in his bid to win a second Stewards' Cup at Goodwood. Coastal Bluff had looked every inch a pattern performer in registering that Stewards' Cup and Ayr Gold Cup double twelve months earlier, but he could prove it only in the Nunthorpe, as he ran poorly on his one subsequent appearance, in the Haydock Park Sprint.

Although he is well known for his achievements with sprinters, pattern-race performers are not the usual fare for Thirsk trainer David Barron. In fact, he began training as a permit holder in 1969 and did not have a runner on the flat until 1979. Initially planning to bring Coastal Bluff back in the King's Stand Stakes, he observed: 'I have a one-hundred percent record with my runners at Royal Ascot—they've all been stuffed.' His one previous pattern success had been with Sea Gazer in the 1993 Ballyogan Stakes. Losing the Nunthorpe because of that broken bit would have been cruel indeed.

		Zeddaan	Grey Sovereign
	Standaan (FR)	(gr 1965)	Vareta
	(gr 1976)	Castania	Orsini
Coastal Bluff		(b 1969)	Chios
(gr.g. 1992)		Reform	Pall Mall
	Combattente	(b 1964)	Country House
	(b 1978)	Tenzone	Aggressor
		(b 1966)	Tina II

Mrs D. E. Sharp's "Coastal Bluff"

While talking about a lack of the necessary equipment, Coastal Bluff will never have a career as a stallion. A tall, leggy, quite good-topped gelding, he is effective at five and six furlongs and acts on good to firm ground and good to soft. He has been heavily bandaged behind during the last two seasons. Perhaps he would not have appealed to breeders on pedigree anyway. The details were given in *Racehorses of 1996*, but, basically, although his third dam Tina II is the ancestress of many good flat horses (Guillotina, One Way Street, Grape Tree Road, Ever Genial, Mange Tout, Hecla, Rose Dubarry, and the 1997 Queen's Vase/Northumberland Plate winner Windsor Castle, to name some of them), none of them had previously cropped up in Coastal Bluff's branch of the family. That makes no difference now. Coastal Bluff has won his first pattern race and it should not be his last. *T. D. Barron*

COASTGUARDS HERO 4 ch.g. Chilibang 120 – Aldwick Colonnade 62 –
(Kind of Hush 118) [1996 57: a6g³ a6g* a6g⁵ a7g⁵ a6g⁵ 7m⁴ 5.1g 7m² 8m² 8.5g⁵
1997 6m 8d 7.1m 6s 8.1d 7f 7.1m 8.3m a7g a10g Dec 19] sturdy gelding: poor
performer: headstrong, and best up to 1m. *M. D. I. Usher*

COBLE 3 b.g. Slip Anchor 136 – Main Sail 104 (Blakeney 126) [1996 NR 1997 77 d
8g 8m 10s 14m⁴ 14.1m⁶ 8g 10.2d Aug 25] sixth foal: half-brother to 2 winners,
including fairly useful 13f winner Sailor Boy (by Main Reef): dam 7f to 8.2f winner
out of half-sister to Buoy and Bireme: disappointing maiden: tried blinkered: has
joined D. McCain and been gelded. *B. W. Hills*

COCHITI 3 b.f. Kris 135 – Sweet Jaffa 73§ (Never So Bold 135) [1996 NR 1997 35
8m 8g 10m 12f a12g 12m³ 12.4m⁴ 11.1d 13.8m⁶ Sep 20] unfurnished filly: first foal:
dam untrustworthy 7f winner: poor maiden: stays 1½m: acts on good to firm ground:
blinkered last 4 starts. *C. W. Thornton*

COCKSURE (IRE) 2 b.g. (Feb 13) Nomination 125 – Hens Grove (Alias Smith 72
(USA)) [1997 6f⁵ 6d⁶ Jun 23] 8,200F, 34,000Y: seventh foal: half-brother to 3
winners, including fairly useful Irish 1994 2-y-o 1m winner Distant Lover (later won
in Norway, by Distant Relative) and fair 7f winner Midnight Lover (by Beveled):
dam, maiden here, later won in Belgium: better effort in maidens when under 6
lengths sixth of 26 at Windsor: gelded after (presumably not quite so cocksure now).
J. M. P. Eustace

CODED MESSAGE (IRE) 2 b.g. (Apr 7) Deploy 131 – Princess Carmen (IRE) –
61 (Arokar (FR) 124) [1997 8g Oct 18] 2,000Y: first foal: dam, maiden who stayed
1m, ran only at 2 yrs: 25/1, never on terms in Redcar maiden. *J. A. Glover*

CODE RED 4 b.g. Warning 136 – For Action (USA) 83 (Assert 134) [1996 66: –
10g 10m⁶ 10.2g⁵ 12.5f³ 13.1m⁵ 14.1f⁵ 16.4g a14.8g³ a14g⁴ a14g³ a16g 1997 a16g⁶
a16g Jun 14] leggy gelding: fair maiden at 3 yrs: well held in 1997, leaving M. Muir
after reappearance. *J. Ffitch-Heyes*

COHIBA 4 b.g. Old Vic 136 – Circus Ring 122 (High Top 131) [1996 9m⁶ 12g 44
13g⁶ 12g⁵ 11d⁴ 10f⁶ 1997 a11g a9.4g 10.3m 14.1m 10g a14g 12g 10d 14.1m* Jul 19]
angular gelding: half-brother to several winners, including smart 7f (at 2 yrs) and
1¼m winner Lady Shipley (by Shirley Heights) and useful 1¼m winner Ellie
Ardensky (by Slip Anchor): dam unbeaten at 2 yrs but ran only once afterwards:
modest handicapper (rated 64) in Ireland in 1996: only form here when winning
selling handicap at Nottingham in July: stays 1¾m: acts on good to firm and dead
ground. *B. J. Curley*

COH SHO NO 4 b.f. Old Vic 136 – Castle Peak 90 (Darshaan 133) [1996 57: 9m⁵ 59
12.1g 10m 11.9g a13g³ a16g⁴ a16g³ a13g 1997 15.4m* 17.2d⁴ 14g³ 14.9d 17.2f⁴ 14g
16m⁵ 16.4g³ 16m² 15.4m³ 16.1g Oct 7] modest handicapper: won at Folkestone in
April: whipped round at start and unseated rider sixth outing: respectable efforts
after: stays 2m: acts on firm ground and equitrack. *S. Dow*

COINCIDENCE 3 ch.f. Niniski (USA) 125 – Baino Fit (USA) (Fit To Fight –
(USA)) [1996 NR 1997 10.2m Apr 29] fifth foal: half-sister to winners in Europe at
up to 11f by Diamond Shoal and Niniski: dam ran several times in France and USA:
tailed off in maiden at Bath. *M. R. Channon*

COINTOSSER (IRE)   4 b.f. Nordico (USA) – Sure Flyer (IRE) (Sure Blade   –
(USA) 130) [1996 66: a7g³ 6.9m² 8m² 7g* 8.2f* 8g* 8.1m⁴ 8m³ 8.1f* 1997 8m Jul
18] leggy filly: has screws in near-fore knee and has fractured a hind leg: fair winner
4 times in 1996: slowly away when mid-field in handicap only flat outing in 1997:
stays 1m well: acts on firm ground, yet to race on going softer than good: sometimes
hangs under pressure: consistent: won over hurdles in November for K. Morgan.
M. C. Pipe

COIS NA FARRAIGE (IRE)   4 b.g. Nashamaa 113 – Persian Sparkler (Persian   54 d
Bold 123) [1996 87: 6d 7v 9m⁶ 12m² 12m* 12f⁵ 12g² 12m² 14g⁶ 13.1m 11.9v 1997
12m 13d 11.1s 12d 12m⁶ 13m² 13g⁵ 12m⁴ 12.1m³ 16m 12.1g⁶ 13d 12.1m 12.1g 13.1s
Oct 13] tall gelding: fairly useful handicapper in Ireland in first half of 1996: very
disappointing here, including in blinkers and selling company: stays 1½m: acts on
firm ground. *Miss L. A. Perratt*

COLD FRONT   2 br.c. (Mar 27) Polar Falcon (USA) 126 – Chandni (IRE)   65 p
(Ahonoora 122) [1997 8d⁶ Oct 28] 17,000F, 50,000Y: second foal: dam (of no
account) out of sister to Kings Lake: 20/1, about 9 lengths sixth of 14 to Himself in
maiden at Leicester: should improve. *J. W. Hills*

COLD LAZARUS   3 br.g. Warning 136 – Indian Pink (USA) (Seattle Slew   –
(USA)) [1996 –p: 7f 1997 7.1g⁵ 8s 8s 7d⁵ 7g 10m Sep 22] leggy gelding: no worthwhile form: tried visored. *R. T. Phillips*

COLD STEEL   3 b.g. Warrshan (USA) 117 – Rengaine (FR) (Music Boy 124)   70 d
[1996 65: 7f⁵ 1997 a7g* a7g 7m 8g³ 10g 7m⁶ 7g Aug 22] disappointing after winning
maiden at Wolverhampton in January: stays 1m: acts on fibresand: tried blinkered,
no improvement: looks none too keen: gelded after final start. *W. Jarvis*

COLERIDGE   9 gr.g. Bellypha 130 – Quay Line 117 (High Line 125) [1996 57§,   47 §
a61§: a16g² a16g² a16g² a16g² 18s 17.2f* 16.4m 20f 14.9m³ 16f³ 20m 16.1f 16g⁶   a58 §
a16g² a16g² a16g⁶ 19f³ a16g a16g³ a16g* a16g² a16g³ a16.2g⁴ 16.4g⁵ 16g⁴
14.9m⁶ 16.4m⁵ 17.2m⁴ 17.2f⁶ Jul 23] tall gelding: unimpressive mover: modest
handicapper on the all-weather, poor on turf: put best foot forward when winning at
Lingfield in February: thorough stayer: best turf form on good ground or firmer: has
been visored, blinkered nowadays: tends to go in snatches: very slowly away/
reluctant to race on occasions. *J. J. Sheehan*

COLINS CHOICE   3 ch.f. Risk Me (FR) 127 – Give Me A Day (Lucky   59
Wednesday 124) [1996 59: a5g⁵ a5g a6g³ a7g² a7g³ 1997 8d a7g a8.5g* a8.5g⁴
a8.5g* a8g a9.4g* Dec 26] modest performer: won claimers at Wolverhampton in
July and September (apprentices) and handicap on same course in December: runs as
if will stay beyond 9.4f: well beaten only run on turf, raced on fibresand otherwise.
J. L. Spearing

COLLACAR   2 b.c. (May 11) Man Among Men (IRE) – Safety First (Wassl 125)   37
[1997 5m 5d⁶ 6m a5g a5g⁵ Jun 18] 2,300Y: third foal: half-brother to a 2-y-o 5f
winner by Statoblest: dam unraced from family of Celtic Swing: poor maiden.
D. Shaw

COLLEGE CLIPPER   2 b.c. (Feb 26) Sizzling Melody 117 – Mawaddah (USA)   –
(Topsider (USA)) [1997 5m a8g Dec 8] 2,000F: second foal: dam unraced: well
beaten in maiden and seller 6 months apart. *M. P. Bielby*

COLLEGE MOUNT   2 b.c. (Feb 28) Merdon Melody 98 – Young Whip (Bold   –
Owl 101) [1997 7.1g 8g Oct 18] big, strong colt: fifth foal: brother to a 2-y-o 6f
seller winner and 5-y-o Mountgate: dam unraced: well held in maidens at Haydock
(backward) and Redcar. *M. P. Bielby*

COLLEGE NIGHT (IRE)   5 b.m. Night Shift (USA) – Gertrude Lawrence   53
(Ballymore 123) [1996 54: 9.9d 8f² 8f² 7f³ 8g⁴ 8f 8m 7g⁵ 8m 8d⁵ 1997 7g⁵ 6.1m 6m*
7g⁵ 6f⁴ 5m⁶ 6m⁶ 6d⁵ Jul 17] angular mare: poor mover: modest handicapper: left
C. Dwyer after second start: won maiden event at Brighton in May: best recent efforts
at 6f to 1m: acts on firm and dead ground: visored (below form) once: often forces
pace. *S. C. Williams*

COLLEGE PRINCESS   3 b.f. Anshan 119 – Tinkers Fairy (Myjinski (USA))   53
[1996 –: 6f 5d a5g 1997 a5g³ a6g 5m 5.1f⁴ 5g² 5d³ 5m* 5.3m⁵ 5.2m³ 6.1m 5m Oct 2]
unfurnished filly: modest handicapper: trained first 3 starts by C. Dwyer: won selling

event at Redcar in July: should stay 6f: acts on firm and dead ground: sold only 700 gns after final start. *S. C. Williams*

COLLEGE ROSE   2 b.f. (Apr 22) Prince Sabo 123 – Tinkers Fairy (Myjinski –
(USA)) [1997 5m 5.1d Oct 8] second foal: half-sister to 3-y-o College Princess: dam
ran twice: signs of only a little ability in maidens at Windsor and Nottingham.
S. C. Williams

COLLEVILLE   2 gr.f. (Feb 4) Pharly (FR) 130 – Kibitka (FR) (Baby Turk 120)   78
[1997 7m 7g* 8.1s³ 8f³ Sep 18] sturdy filly: has a quick action: first foal: dam
unraced from family of very smart French stayer Shafaraz: fair form: won maiden at
Leicester in August: good third in Yarmouth nursery final start: should stay beyond
1m: acts on firm ground, possibly not soft: has been slowly away and swished tail.
M. A. Jarvis

COLLIER BAY   7 b.g. Green Desert (USA) 127 – Cockatoo Island 99 (High Top   99
131) [1996 NR 1997 16.2s⁴ Mar 29] well-made gelding: Champion Hurdler in 1996:
only second run on Flat since 1993 when 4 lengths fourth of 5 to Sweetness Herself
in minor event at Haydock in March, dictating pace: will stay well: has form on good
to firm, acts on soft (raced mostly on dead or softer over hurdles). *J. A. B. Old*

COLONEL CUSTER   2 ch.c. (Feb 17) Komaite (USA) – Mohican 75 (Great   63
Nephew 126) [1997 5v a6g* 7g Aug 19] tall, angular colt: half-brother to 2 NH Flat
race winners by Mandrake Major: dam 1½m winner at 5 yrs: won maiden at
Southwell in July: ran badly next time: should stay beyond 6f. *C. W. Thornton*

COLONEL'S PRIDE   3 ch.g. Superpower 113 – Yankeedoodledancer (Mashhor –
Dancer (USA)) [1996 59: 5m 5m 5m² 5.1m⁶ 1997 8g 6m 6g 6d 6m 5g 5m a8.5g
6g Sep 27] good-topped gelding: modest form at 2 yrs, none in 1997: tried visored.
R. M. Whitaker

COLOSSE   5 b.m. Reprimand 122 – French Cutie (USA) (Vaguely Noble 140)   56
[1996 55: a8g a12g* a12g³ a12g* 13d 12m⁵ 12g a12g a12g⁶ a12s² a12g 1997 a12g
a13g² a12g² Feb 20] useful-looking mare: has a round action: modest handicapper:
should stay beyond 13f: acts on good to firm ground (possibly not on dead) and
all-weather: no improvement blinkered/visored: normally held up. *J. L. Eyre*

COLOUR CODE   5 ch.g. Polish Precedent (USA) 131 – Reprocolor 114 (Jimmy   86
Reppin 131) [1996 NR 1997 12.1s² 10g² 10.3d³ 14.8m⁴ 13.9g 11.9s Oct 8] 26,000
4-y-o: tall, good-topped gelding: half-brother to several middle-distance winners,
notably Cezanne (by Ajdal), Colorspin (by High Top) and Bella Colora (by Bellypha), all smart or better: dam won Lingfield Oaks Trial and Lancashire Oaks: won
both starts in NH Flat races: fairly useful maiden on flat (should win races): stays
15f: acts on good to firm and soft ground: won over hurdles in December.
Mrs A. Swinbank

COLOUR COUNSELLOR   4 gr.g. Touch of Grey 90 – Bourton Downs 74   48
(Philip of Spain 126) [1996 47: a8g a10g 10m 11.9g* 14.1f 12f 15.4g⁴ 11.9f⁵ 11.9f⁵   a37
10f 11.9f* 12m 1997 a12g⁴ a16g 11.9f⁵ 11.9f² 11.5s³ 11.9m⁵ 11.5g³ 10g*
10m⁶ 10g³ 10f a12g⁵ a10g⁴ a12g a16g Dec 4] poor handicapper: won at Brighton
(third win there) in August: stays 1½m: acts on firm ground, soft and the all-weather:
usually blinkered: often front runner: inconsistent. *R. M. Flower*

COLOUR KEY (USA)   3 b.g. Red Ransom (USA) – Trend (USA) (Ray's Word –
(USA)) [1996 60p: 7.6d 1997 8g 10d Jun 20] close-coupled gelding: some promise
only 2-y-o start: well held in 1997. *D. R. C. Elsworth*

COLOURS TO GOLD (IRE)   2 ch.f. (May 11) Rainbows For Life (CAN) –   68
Brave Ivy 68 (Decoy Boy 129) [1997 5s*dis 6.3d Jun 27] IR 6,000Y: eighth foal:
half-sister to 2 2-y-o winners, including 1991 6f winner International Star (by Astronef), and a winner in Belgium by Bairn: dam, runner-up here at 5f at 2 yrs, later won
at up to 7.5f in Italy: first past post (disqualified after testing positive for procaine) in
maiden at Hamilton in May: well held in valuable sales race at the Curragh: should
stay further than 5f. *R. A. Fahey*

COLSTON-C   5 gr.g. Belfort (FR) 89 – Grand Occasion 63 (Great Nephew 126)   –
[1996 –, a54: a7g 5.7m 6.1m⁶ 5.1m 5.1f 5m 5g 6m a6g³ a5g 1997 a6g 5g a5g Nov 18]
angular gelding: on the downgrade, and well beaten in 1997. *P. D. Evans*

COLWAY RITZ 3 b.g. Rudimentary (USA) 118 – Million Heiress (Auction Ring 75
(USA) 123) [1996 NR 1997 6m⁵ 5m⁵ 5m² 7g 6g³ 7m 7m³ 6g⁶ 7d 7m³ 7g* 8.2d Oct
30] 22,000Y: big, strong gelding: good mover: third foal: half-brother to 1994 2-y-o
5f winner Stato One (by Statoblest), useful winner in Scandinavia up to 9f: dam poor
maiden: fair handicapper: won apprentice race at Doncaster in October: should stay
1m: acts on good to firm ground, ran poorly both starts on dead: no improvement in
blinkers. *J. W. Watts*

COMANCHE COMPANION 7 b.m. Commanche Run 133 – Constant 70
Companion 84 (Pas de Seul 133) [1996 73d, a–: 8s a8g⁶ 7g 8.1g 8m 8m 8.3d 8d a–
7g⁶ 7g 1997 8.1d 8.3m* 8.3m³ 7.6m² 8.5g⁵ 7g 9.8s³ 8m 8d² 10.5v Nov 29] plain,
close-coupled mare: has a quick action: fair handicapper: won at Windsor in July:
second of 30 at Newmarket penultimate start: far from disgraced when seventh of 11
in listed race at Saint-Cloud final outing: stays 10.5f: probably acts on any
all-weather/turf: has won for apprentice and when sweating. *T. J. Naughton*

COME DANCING 3 b.f. Suave Dancer (USA) 136 – Cominna (Dominion 123) –
[1996 48+: 6g⁶ 6m⁵ a5g 1997 a7g a6g⁴ 7m May 5] disappointing maiden: should stay
at least 7f. *M. Johnston*

COMEDY RIVER 10 br.g. Comedy Star (USA) 121 – Hopeful Waters 66 –
(Forlorn River 124) [1996 52: a10g 9m 8.5m³ 10m⁴ 9.2g⁶ 10m² a10g* 10.8f* 11.5m
a10s³ 1997 10d May 9] modest performer: badly hampered only 10-y-o start: stayed
1¼m: acted on firm ground and equitrack: dead. *N. E. Berry*

COMEOUTOFTHEFOG (IRE) 2 b.g. (May 20) Mujadil (USA) 119 – Local 53
Belle (Ballymore 123) [1997 5.8g⁶ 6.5s 8d⁵ 7m 7d 6g a6g² Dec 26] 4,800Y: sixth
foal: half-brother to 7f winner McKellar (by Lomond): dam Irish 1½m winner, sister
to Irish Derby runner-up Exdirectory: little worthwhile form in Ireland for M.
Halford first 6 starts (blinkered final one): second of 7 in claimer at Wolverhampton:
should stay beyond 6f. *D. J. S. ffrench Davis*

COME TOGETHER 3 b.f. Mtoto 134 – Pfalz 101 (Pharly (FR) 130) [1996 –: 68
5f 7.1v⁵ 6m 1997 8.2d 10.8s* 12d³ 10g 10.5s⁶ 10d Oct 28] small, sturdy filly: fair
handicapper: won at Warwick (maiden event) in July: stays 1½m: best efforts on
dead/soft going: takes keen hold: none too consistent. *D. W. P. Arbuthnot*

COME TOO MAMMA'S 3 ch.f. La Grange Music 111 – Purchased By Phone 53 d
(IRE) 48 (Wolverlife 115) [1996 53: a5g³ a5g² a5g* 5d⁴ a6g⁴ 5m³ a5g³ a5g* 5g⁶ a5g⁵
a6g 1997 a5g² a5g a5g⁵ 5.3f a5g May 24] leggy filly: modest performer: left Jack
Berry after third start: last in handicaps for new stable: stays 6f: acts on the
all-weather and good to firm ground, below form on dead. *G. C. Bravery*

COMIC'S FUTURE (USA) 4 b.c. Carnivalay (USA) – Destiny's Hour (USA) –
(Fit To Fight (USA)) [1996 –: 12.4g⁴ 10d 1997 12.1s 9.2m 16g Jul 7] big, lengthy
colt: little sign of ability: tried blinkered. *J. J. O'Neill*

COMMANDER CHARLIE 2 ch.g. (Feb 24) Alnasr Alwasheek 117 – Bentinck 86
Hotel 74 (Red God 128§) [1997 6g⁵ 6d² 7.1g* 7g⁶ Aug 1] 11,000Y: rangy gelding:
has a quick action: half-brother to numerous winners, including 3-y-o Lamarita,
8-y-o Bentico and useful 1989 2-y-o sprinter Shamshoon (by Shareef Dancer): dam
2-y-o 5f winner: fairly useful form: won maiden at Sandown in July: got poor run in
nursery at Ascot final start: should stay at least 1m: sent to Hong Kong. *I. A. Balding*

COMMIN' UP 4 b.f. Primo Dominie 121 – Ridalia 56 (Ridan (USA)) [1996 70d: 49
7.3d² 7m 8f⁵ 8.3m 9g a8s⁶ a10g 1997 a8g⁴ a8g a8g⁴ a7g⁴ 6m 8s a8g Jul 10] lengthy
filly: poor maiden: left J. W. Hills after second start, Miss J. Bower after fifth: stays
1m: acts on firm and dead ground and on fibresand. *Miss M. E. Rowland*

COMMON ROCK (IRE) 3 b.f. Common Grounds 118 – Quatre Femme 76 –
(Petorius 117) [1996 44: 6m a7g* a7g 1997 a8g Jan 27] tailed off both starts since
winning bad seller at Southwell at 2 yrs. *J. Norton*

COMMON VIEW (IRE) 2 b.g. (Apr 30) Scenic 128 – Stony Ground (Relko –
136) [1997 8.2m 8m 8m⁶ 8g Oct 18] IR 12,500Y: compact gelding: half-brother to
several winners, including useful French winner at up to 1¼m by Cyrano de Bergerac
and 1m winner/smart hurdler Bank View (by Crofter): dam Irish 1½m winner: little
worthwhile form in maidens. *N. Tinkler*

COM

COMPACT DISC (IRE)   3 b.f. Royal Academy (USA) 130 – Sharp Circle (IRE)   –
83 (Sure Blade (USA) 130) [1996 48: 5m⁵ 5.1m 6s⁵ 5m³ 5g 8f a7g* a8g⁴ a8g 1997
a8g Jan 2] angular filly: poor winner at 2 yrs: well beaten only start in 1997.
M. Johnston

COMPANYS GAMBLE   2 b.f. (Feb 7) Barrys Gamble 102 – Pleasant Company   –
(Alzao (USA) 117) [1997 5m 5g 5d a5g a7g Nov 29] 2,400Y: lengthy filly: first foal:
dam poor maiden: looks of little account. *B. P. J. Baugh*

COMPASSIONATE   2 b.g. (May 15) Seymour Hicks (FR) 125 – Snow Child 84   42
(Mandrake Major 122) [1997 8.2d 10d 8d Oct 28] workmanlike gelding: third
reported foal: dam won over 6f here at 2 yrs and later numerous times in Jersey: poor
maiden. *W. G. M. Turner*

COMPASS POINTER   4 gr.g. Mazilier (USA) 107 – Woodleys (Tyrnavos 129)   58
[1996 67: 10g 11.6m⁴ 11.8d² 13.3m 11.6g 11.8g 14m² 14d 13.9g 14.1s⁴ 12v² a14g*   a–
a16g 1997 a12g 13d 14d⁶ 11.6g 14.6d³ 14.1s* Jul 2] close-coupled gelding: modest
handicapper: won at Yarmouth in July: stays 1¾m: acts on good to firm and soft
ground and on fibresand: has had tongue tied: not an easy ride. *J. M. P. Eustace*

COMPATIBILITY (IRE)   3 b.c. Common Grounds 118 – Nikki's Groom (Shy   81
Groom (USA)) [1996 –: 6m 1997 7m⁵ 7g³ 7m⁵ 5.9m* 6g³ 6g⁵ 8.5d⁵ 7.1m 8m Oct 6]
sturdy, compact colt: has a roundish action: fairly useful performer: won maiden at
Carlisle in June: variable form in handicaps after: pulls hard, and best form up to 7f:
acts on good to firm ground: no improvement in blinkers or visor: looked none too
hearty seventh start: sold approx. £32,000 in Dubai in November. *J. H. M. Gosden*

COMPOSITION   2 ch.f. (Jan 26) Wolfhound (USA) 126 – Tricky Note 97 (Song   82
132) [1997 5g⁶ 5m³ 6g³ 6g* 6g 6d Oct 8] 52,000Y: useful-looking filly: fluent mover:
fifth foal: half-sister to Irish 1¼m winner Ros Castle (by Reference Point) and a
winner in Japan by Caerleon: dam sprinting sister to smart sprinter Jester: fairly
useful form: won nursery at Pontefract in July: ran poorly afterwards: likely to stay
7f: hung throughout on debut: has sweated. *M. A. Jarvis*

COMPRADORE   2 b.f. (Mar 3) Mujtahid (USA) 118 – Keswa 94 (Kings Lake   82
(USA) 133) [1997 5m² 5.2m* 5m 5m Aug 1] 14,000Y: angular, good-quartered filly:
fourth foal: dam 1m (at 2 yrs) and 1½m winner out of half-sister to Celestial Storm:
fairly useful form: won maiden at Newbury in May, making all: down the field in
Queen Mary Stakes at Royal Ascot and Molecomb Stakes at Goodwood: should be
suited by 6f. *M. Blanshard*

COMPROMISE (IRE)   3 b.c. Soviet Star (USA) 128 – Lower The Tone (USA)   81
(Master Willie 129) [1996 NR 1997 7.1s⁴ 7.1s⁵ 7m* 8.3m³ 8d Jun 29] good-topped
colt: fifth foal: half-brother to a winner in New Zealand by Sackford: dam unraced
half-sister to smart French 1m/1¼m performer Coup de Folie, herself dam of
Machiavellian and Exit To Nowhere: fairly useful performer: won maiden at
Warwick in May: stays 1m: acts on good to firm ground, below form on dead and soft
(though lost all chance by rearing stalls final start): sold approx. £27,500 in Dubai in
November. *B. W. Hills*

COMPTON PLACE   3 ch.c. Indian Ridge 123 – Nosey 96 (Nebbiolo 125)   125
[1996 108: 5.1m* 5m² 6g* 6m² 5m² 1997 5m² 5d 6g* 5d Aug 21]
'Our first and most striking observation on racegoers' body-language
was that complete strangers regularly make eye-contact and smile at each other
for no apparent reason. Eye-contact between racegoers is at least ten times
more frequent than in other public settings.' 'One astute male racegoer had
found that a day at the races was a far more effective seduction strategy than the
traditional first-date dinner or film.' Racing fans that we are, these and other
revelations contained within *The Racing Tribe*, a report by Kate Fox of The
Social Issues Research Centre, had to be among the season's biggest shock
results. Funding for the research was obtained from the BHB and the Tote. One
of *The Racing Tribe*'s less surprising observations was that the reactions of the
crowd are a very accurate guide as to which horse—favourite, outsider, etc—
has won the race. That is the strongest impression left by this year's July Cup.
A summer's day at the July Course could well play its part in what that 'one

228

astute male racegoer' had in mind, but after this year's renewal of the July Cup the smile ratio took a big dip and it was a stunned silence that greeted the race's 50/1-winner Compton Place.

This was a huge turn up, the biggest in the July Cup's history—and it was founded in 1876. Rambling Bear was also sent off at 50/1 in the nine-runner field, but no horse was at longer odds, and the favourite, Royal Applause, was at 11/10. We do not accept that the latter was a long way, if at all, below form. Without Compton Place, nobody would have questioned the result, but, with him, Royal Applause had to settle for second, going down by a length and three quarters, but finishing upwards of three lengths clear of the rest. Travelling strongly just behind the leaders, Compton Place quickened to the front over a furlong out and soon had the race won, keeping on in fine style up the hill. In the far-side group to start off with, he drifted left in the closing stages and ended up racing virtually on his own, all of which accentuated his superiority to bemused onlookers in the stands. Two who should have been among Compton Place's most dangerous rivals, the Cork And Orrery runner-up Blue Goblin and the 1996 July Cup second Lucayan Prince, finished in arrears, third and fourth spots being filled by the previous year's Mill Reef and Middle Park winners, Indian Rocket and Bahamian Bounty.

It was not a vintage renewal of the July Cup, but easily the best we have seen of Compton Place. None of his other form is in the same county, though in a previous era that would probably not have been said of a horse who had come within half a length of winning the Gimcrack. Second to Almaty, beaten two and a half lengths, in a listed race at Kempton on his 1997 debut at the end of May was an encouraging effort in the context of the balance of Compton Place's form, more encouraging certainly than his twelfth of eighteen under a forcing ride in the King's Stand at Royal Ascot. The dead ground was very probably a contributory factor at Royal Ascot, and the remainder of Compton Place's season was sadly taken up with a comedy of errors as his connections tried to avoid a repetition. In the Nunthorpe Stakes at York, they did not succeed and Compton Place finished fourteenth of fifteen; the false ground (after watering) might well have got him bad the heavy rain on raceday not done so anyway. At Haydock the following month, Compton Place was taken out at the final declaration stage when the ground turned soft again, and when conditions finally did turn in his favour, in the Diadem Stakes at Ascot, a cut on the inside of his leg meant that he was withdrawn on the day of the race. The injury was described as minor—it had resulted in some swelling—and Compton Place will stay in training. Indeed, his seventy-seven-year-old owner was reported to have said: 'My plan is to keep him in training for ever.' Hopefully, it will not take that long for Compton Place to turn up on raceday with ground conditions again

Darley July Cup, Newmarket—50/1-chance Compton Place shows a first-class turn of foot; the favourite Royal Applause finishes clear of the remainder

good or firmer. A degree of waiting tactics also seemed to benefit him in the July Cup, but it is still possible that he will prove as good at five furlongs as he is at six. Many remain to be convinced just how good that is. The July Cup (for which there was a poor timefigure) was Royal Applause's only defeat in Britain in 1997, and Compton Place's only win, but on the basis of that one performance we have rated Compton Place the higher. Of course, it would have been a good deal more satisfactory had Compton Place won two or three, repeating the form, but he had his excuses.

Compton Place (ch.c. 1994)	Indian Ridge (ch 1985)	Ahonoora (ch 1975)	Lorenzaccio
			Helen Nichols
		Hillbrow (ch 1975)	Swing Easy
			Golden City
	Nosey (b 1981)	Nebbiolo (ch 1974)	Yellow God
			Novara
		Little Cynthia (br 1974)	Wolver Hollow
			Fazilka

One group of onlookers that certainly were celebrating on July Cup day were the current owners of Indian Ridge, the stallion being represented not only by Compton Place, but also by Indian Rocket and the Bunbury Cup winner Tumbleweed Ridge. Indian Ridge's ability to sire the odd star had already been well established and many eyes will be on the 1998 batch of three-year-olds, the first since he was bombarded with mares on his switch to Ireland, and on future crops for which his mares featured obvious quality as well as quantity. Nosey could not have been placed in the former camp when she visited the December Sales carrying Compton Place in 1993. Having fetched 5,200 guineas five years earlier, Nosey had had only one winner, the fair hurdler Fierce (by Carwhite), from her first three foals. Indian Ridge was not then the height of fashion either, so the sum first spent to acquire the future July Cup winner was only 6,200 guineas. Nearly two years later, when the yearling

Duke of Devonshire's "Compton Place"

Compton Place went to Goffs, his half-sister Lloc (by Absalom) had shown fair form to win over five furlongs and half-brother Quakers Field (by Anshan) had embarked on the trail that took him to pattern races on the flat and a position among the top 1996/7 juveniles over hurdles. Compton Place made IR 92,000 guineas. Nosey had been sold again for 5,000 guineas in 1994, but she was bought back privately twelve months later and Compton Place's breeder has also now paid 14,500 guineas for Lloc. Nosey's 1995 foal, Mantles Star (by Beveled), won a maiden at Lingfield a few hours after Compton Place had won the July Cup and ended up winning a Grade 3 race over a mile in America in the latest season, and her 1998 two-year-old will be a colt by Rudimentary. Nosey herself was a fairly useful sprint winner at two years in Ireland, one of eight winners out of the one-mile winner Little Cynthia. Third dam Fazilka won over eleven furlongs in France. *J. A. R. Toller*

COMTEC'S LEGEND 7 ch.m. Legend of France (USA) 124 – Comtec 35 Princess 73 (Gulf Pearl 117) [1996 34, a43: a11g³ a12g⁶ a12g³ a14.8g² a12g⁵ 12.3g* a12g 16.2g 1997 a12g 10g⁶ 12g² 12m² Aug 20] small mare: poor handicapper: stays 15f: acts on good to firm and dead ground (possibly unsuited by soft) and the all-weather: sometimes hangs left: often bandaged near-fore. *J. Pearce*

CONCER ARALL 3 ch.g. Ron's Victory (USA) 129 – Drudwen (Sayf El Arab 54 (USA) 127) [1996 NR 1997 a6g⁴ a8g a8.5g³ a7g² a7g⁶ Dec 18] third foal: half-brother to 5-y-o Concer Un: dam won 13f NH Flat race: well backed, best effort when second in handicap at Wolverhampton penultimate start, keeping on: stays 8.5f: raced only on fibresand. *S. C. Williams*

CONCER UN 5 ch.g. Lord Bud 121 – Drudwen (Sayf El Arab (USA) 127) [1996 97 100: 8m 8m* 8m* 8.1g* 8m 7.9m* 7d* 8m 8g 1997 7g⁵ 8g 7.9g 8.1g a8.5f⁵ 7g 8.1g 6g⁶ 7.9d* 7d² 8m⁴ 7m 9g Oct 25] smallish, lengthy gelding: useful handicapper: won £23,600 Bradford & Bingley Rated Stakes at York in August (for second year running) by neck from Hawksley Hill: also ran well next start: needs good test at 7f, and stays 9.2f: acts on any going: sometimes bandaged: game and genuine: sold 9,500 gns in October. *S. C. Williams*

CONDITION RED 4 b.f. Sayf El Arab (USA) 127 – Forever Mary 81 (Red Alert – 127) [1996 –: 8f⁵ a8.5g 1997 a8.5g Mar 5] no sign of ability. *M. S. Saunders*

CONECTIS (IRE) 2 b.f. (Apr 26) River Falls 113 – Christle Mill (Pas de Seul 92 ? 133) [1997 5g² 5.1m⁵ 5m² 6m⁶ 5.1g² 6d* 6g⁵ 6g⁶ 6g Sep 19] IR 4,000Y: has a quick, fluent action: fifth reported foal: half-sister to a middle-distance winner in Italy by Mac's Imp: dam ran twice in Ireland at 2 yrs: fair performer on balance: won minor

Bradford & Bingley Rated Stakes (Handicap), York—
the game Concer Un (centre) wins this race for the second successive year;
Hawksley Hill (left) and Russian Music run him close

event at Goodwood in June: 50/1, appeared to excel herself when 3 lengths fifth to Asfurah in Cherry Hinton Stakes at Newmarket next time, but some way below that form in useful company subsequently: likely to stay 7f: acts on good to soft ground: sold 25,000 gns in October. *D. J. S. Cosgrove*

CONFIDANTE (USA)   2 b.f. (Apr 14) Dayjur (USA) 137 – Won't She Tell (USA) (Banner Sport (USA)) [1997 7d³ Oct 27] sixth foal: half-sister to 3 useful winners here, including 3-y-o Wind Cheetah, 1½m winner (best around 2m) Zuboon (by The Minstrel), and Grade 1-placed winner in USA, Dr Caton (by Seattle Slew): dam multiple winner in North America who stayed at least 9f, closely related to Affirmed: 3/1, slowly away and ran green until getting hang of things near end when around 4 lengths third of 10 to Housekeeper in maiden at Lingfield: should stay 1m: will improve. *M. R. Stoute*   83 p

CONFIRMATION   2 b.g. (Jan 31) Polar Falcon (USA) 126 – Blessed Event 117 (Kings Lake (USA) 133) [1997 6g a7g* 7d* 7.6g³ 8d⁵ Oct 20] lengthy, good-topped gelding: sixth foal: half-brother to 6-y-o Sacrament and 1991 2-y-o 7f winner Blessed Honour (by Ahonoora): dam, 1¼m winner out of a German Oaks winner: useful form: won maiden at Southwell and minor event at Ayr in September: probably asked to force too strong a pace final start: should stay at least 1m: acts on fibresand, raced only on good/dead going on turf: type to train on well. *Sir Mark Prescott*   96 p

CONFRONTER   8 ch.g. Bluebird (USA) 125 – Grace Darling (USA) (Vaguely Noble 140) [1996 84d: 8s 8v⁴ 8v⁴ 7.5v² 8s⁵ 8.1g 7.6m² 8.5m 8m⁴ 8f³ 8m⁶ 8d 8m 8g 8.2g 1997 8s² 8s 7.8d 8f 8g 8d 8f⁴ 8m* 8d 8f⁴ 8m⁶ 9g⁶ 8g a8s⁵ a10g* a9.4g⁵ a10g² Dec 22] tall gelding: modest handicapper: short-head winner at Bath in June and Lingfield in November: effective at 1m/1¼m: acts on equitrack and probably any turf: has run well in blinkers/visor, not tried since 5 yrs. *S. Dow*   64

CONICAL   2 b.f. (Apr 8) Zafonic (USA) 130 – De Stael (USA) 93 (Nijinsky (CAN) 138) [1997 8m Oct 1] roan unfurnished filly: eighth foal: half-sister to several winners over middle distances, including smart/very smart trio Turners Hill (by Top Ville), Wandesta (by Nashwan) and De Quest (by Nashwan): dam 2-y-o 6f winner, sister to Peacetime and Quiet Fling: 9/2, much too green to do herself justice when seventh of 13 in maiden at Salisbury: sure to improve. *R. Charlton*   – p

CONIC HILL (IRE)   6 ch.g. Lomond (USA) 128 – Krisalya 98 (Kris 135) [1996 51: a12g⁶ a12g 10m 10m⁶ 10.1m 9f² 9.7g 10f 10m 1997 10g 8d 9.2m 10f Oct 1] lengthy gelding: very much on the downgrade. *J. Pearce*   –

CONNEMARA (IRE)   3 b.f. Mujadil (USA) 119 – Beechwood (USA) (Blushing Groom (FR) 131) [1996 99+: 5g* 5.1g* 5m⁴ 6g 5m² 1997 7g 5m 5.7d⁴ 6d³ 6m² 6g 6g³ 5m 6m 5m⁵ 6f⁶ Sep 17] lengthy, good-quartered filly: useful performer: best effort when second to Blue Goblin in £22,500 handicap at Newmarket in May: stays 6f: acts on good to firm and dead ground: has run respectably when sweating: sometimes taken last and steadily to post: sold 40,000 gns in December. *C. A. Dwyer*   100

CONNOISSEUR BAY (USA)   2 b.c. (Apr 6) Nureyev (USA) 131 – Feminine Wiles (IRE) 110 (Ahonoora 122) [1997 7m² Oct 2] first reported foal: dam, 1m to 1¼m performer, out of half-sister to Legal Bid and Law Society: 12/1 from 9/2 and better for race, promising 1½ lengths second of 22 to Quiet Assurance in maiden at Newmarket, making most and keeping on well: will stay at least 1m: showed a markedly round action: sure to improve, and win races. *P. W. Chapple-Hyam*   91 p

CONON FALLS (IRE)   3 b.c. Sadler's Wells (USA) 132 – Cocotte 111 (Troy 137) [1996 86p: 7m 8.1g³ 1997 10.3d* 10d⁴ 12s³ 12g 10m³ 10d³ Sep 19] close-coupled, good-topped colt: half-brother to Pilsudski: useful performer: won maiden at Chester in May: in frame in listed race and 3 minor events afterwards, beaten 3½ lengths by Salmon Ladder at Windsor and 4¼ lengths by Clan Ben at Newbury last 2 starts: takes good hold and possibly better at 1¼m than 1½m: acts on good to firm and soft going. *J. H. M. Gosden*   106

CONSORT   4 b.c. Groom Dancer (USA) 128 – Darnelle 83 (Shirley Heights 130) [1996 91: 6.9m² 7m* 8.1g³ 7m⁵ 7m 8d⁴ 1997 7m⁴ 7m⁴ 8m² 8d³ 9g 8m* Nov 1] good-topped colt: has a quick action: fairly useful handicapper: best effort when winning valuable 28-runner race at Newmarket in November, leading close home: seems suited by 1m: acts on good to firm and dead ground: held up. *Mrs A. J. Perrett*   94

CONSPICUOUS (IRE) 7 b.g. Alzao (USA) 117 – Mystery Lady (USA) 97
(Vaguely Noble 140) [1996 88: 10.3g 10d 10.1m⁴ 10f³ 8m⁴ 8m 9d* 9g 9m 1997 8d
10.1g⁴ 10s² 10d 10m 8m* 9d 10m⁵ 10g* Oct 24] close-coupled gelding: has a quick
action: useful handicapper: better than ever in 1997, winning at Salisbury in August
and Newbury in October: effective at 1m to 1¼m: acts on any all-weather/turf:
visored (ran poorly) once as 6-y-o: takes good hold and is waited with. *L. G. Cottrell*

CONSPIRACY 3 b.f. Rudimentary (USA) 118 – Roussalka 123 (Habitat 134) 87
[1996 98p: 6d² 5f* 5m³ 5.1g² 5m* 1997 5.7d⁶ 6m⁶ 7g 6g² 6g Aug 23] small filly: has
a sharp action: useful at 2 yrs (won listed race): fairly useful at best in 1997: best
efforts at 5f: acted on firm going: stud. *J. L. Dunlop*

CONSTANT ATTENTION 2 ch.f. (Mar 29) Royal Academy (USA) 130 – 59
Impudent Miss 105 (Persian Bold 123) [1997 6.1s² 7g 7g⁶ 6g 8m² 9m² 7m⁴ Sep 30]
17,000Y: sparely-made filly: half-sister to several winners, including 3-y-o Enlisted
and miler Good Reference (by Reference Point): dam, Irish 2-y-o 5f winner,
half-sister to Sayyaf: modest maiden: has run in sellers (claimed out of P. Cole's
stable £6,000 penultimate start): ran creditably in nursery final start: probably stays
9f: looked leery in blinkers fourth start: sent to Saudi Arabia. *P. Mitchell*

CONTENTMENT (IRE) 3 b.c. Fairy King (USA) – Quality of Life (Auction 77
Ring (USA) 123) [1996 69+: 6g 6m 6g² 1997 9g 8g 10g⁵ 10g* 10.1s 10m⁴ 10m³ 9d
10m a10g Dec 10] small colt: fair handicapper: won at Windsor in June: well below
form last 3 starts, leaving J. W. Hills before final one: stays 1¼m: acts on good to
firm ground, well held on dead and soft: tail swisher, and possibly something of a
quirky character. *S. Dow*

CONTRACT BRIDGE (IRE) 4 b.f. Contract Law (USA) 108 – Mystery Bid –
(Auction Ring (USA) 123) [1996 51: a11g⁴ 8m⁶ 8g* 10m 11.1g³ 8.5m⁶ 8m⁵ 9.9f⁴
10d* 12.1g⁵ 1997 12.1g 12g 12.1m 14m 12.1d 10g Sep 3] smallish filly: modest
winner in 1996 for C. Thornton: no show in 1997, including in visor. *P. G. Murphy*

CONTRAFIRE (IRE) 5 b.g. Contract Law (USA) 108 – Fiery Song (Ballad –
Rock 122) [1996 76: 10.8g⁴ 12m⁴ 10m⁴ 10.1m² 12g² 12f⁴ 12g⁵ 1997 12g 12s⁶ May
11] angular gelding: fair handicapper as 4-y-o for W. Jarvis: well beaten in 1997.
Mrs A. Swinbank

CONTRARIE 4 b.f. Floose 99 – Chanita (Averof 123) [1996 37: 11.8d a12g 53
11.5m 12.1s⁴ 16.4v⁴ 1997 11.8m 16.2s² 13s 14.1m 14.1s⁵ 18d² 16s* 16s³ Oct 15]
modest handicapper: won at Nottingham in October: suited by a thorough test of
stamina: best efforts on ground softer than good. *M. J. Ryan*

CONTRARY MARY 2 b.f. (Feb 16) Mujadil (USA) 119 – Love Street 62 85
(Mummy's Pet 125) [1997 5.1d² 5m* 5g 5.2m⁵ 5m⁴ 6d Oct 16] 11,000Y: smallish,
lightly-made filly: third foal: half-sister to 5f winner La Belle Dominique (by
Dominion): dam sprint maiden out of smart sprinting 2-y-o Crime of Passion: fairly
useful performer: won minor event at Lingfield in May: good fourth in similar event
at Folkestone in September: highly tried in between: best form at 5f: yet to race on
extremes of going: has got upset in preliminaries, and often looked difficult ride.
G. Lewis

CONTRAVENE (IRE) 3 b.f. Contract Law (USA) 108 – Vieux Carre (Pas de –
Seul 133) [1996 54, a64: 5s⁴ a5g² 5m* 5m³ 6m³ a6g⁴ 6m⁵ 6f* 5m⁵ 6m² a7g* 7g⁵ 6m a42
1997 a6g⁵ 6g² a8.5g⁵ a7g⁴ a6g⁶ Mar 8] leggy filly: modest winner at 2 yrs: just poor
form in 1997: stays 7f: acts on firm ground and fibresand: tried blinkered. *J. Berry*

CONTROL FREAK 3 b.f. Inca Chief (USA) – Forest Nymph (Native Bazaar –
122) [1996 –: 6.9m 8.2m 8.2g⁵ 1997 7m 10m Apr 8] of little account. *A. G. Foster*

COOL AFFAIR (IRE) 2 ch.g. (May 19) Statoblest 120 – Ukraine's Affair –
(USA) (The Minstrel (CAN) 135) [1997 6d 7g Oct 27] IR 5,400Y: compact gelding:
fourth foal: half-brother to 3 winners, including 3-y-o Protocol and Irish 1994 2-y-o
5f winner Aliuska (by Fijar Tango): dam unraced from family of Poule d'Essai des
Pouliches winner Ukraine Girl: tailed off in maidens. *A. B. Mulholland*

COOL EDGE (IRE) 6 ch.g. Nashamaa 113 – Mochara (Last Fandango 125) 110
[1996 112: 8s* 8d² 7.1d* 8.1d⁴ 7.3m* 7g³ 7g² 8g⁶ 1997 7g* 7s² 8g⁴ 7d⁶ 7g⁵ Oct 25]
rangy gelding: smart performer: had run of race when winning 6-runner Gladness
Stakes at the Curragh in April by 2½ lengths from Desert King: creditable efforts

there in Ballycorus Stakes (went down by 4 lengths to Wizard King) and Desmond Stakes next 2 starts, but below form afterwards: effective at 7f/1m: probably acts on any going: visored (ran well) twice at 4 yrs: often early to post: keen sort. *M. H. Tompkins*

COOL GREY 3 gr.f. Absalom 128 – Crisp Air (Elegant Air 119) [1996 49: 8.1m – a7g⁶ a7g³ a7g⁴ 1997 13m Jul 11] workmanlike filly: poor maiden: well beaten over unsuitable trip only 3-y-o start: stays 7f: acts on fibresand. *J. J. O'Neill*

COOLIN RIVER (IRE) 2 b.g. (May 9) River Falls 113 – The Coolin (Don 128) 61 d [1997 6m⁵ 6d⁴ 6m 6g⁶ 7f Oct 3] IR 5,000Y: leggy gelding: second reported foal: dam placed over 5f (at 2 yrs) and 7f in Ireland: modest maiden: stays 6f. *K. R. Burke*

COOL LUKE (IRE) 8 b.g. Red Sunset 120 – Watet Khet (FR) 82 (Wittgenstein – (USA) 123) [1996 NR 1997 12g Apr 23] very lightly raced on flat nowadays, and well beaten only 8-y-o start. *F. Murphy*

COOL MYSTERY 2 ro.c. (Mar 15) Mystiko (USA) 124 – Romantic Saga 69 51 (Prince Tenderfoot (USA) 126) [1997 6g 5m⁴ 6d 6m 5m Sep 26] 1,600Y: big, work-manlike colt: fourth foal: half-brother to a 2-y-o 6f seller winner by Nomination: dam placed over 5f and 6f at 2 yrs: modest maiden: stays 6f. *A. B. Mulholland*

COOL PROSPECT 2 b.c. (Mar 24) Mon Tresor 113 – I Ran Lovely (Persian 70 Bold 123) [1997 6g⁵ 6m³ 5m² 5m 5d Nov 7] IR 8,200Y: neat colt: fluent mover: second foal: dam twice-raced daughter of smart 1978 2-y-o sprinter Sweet And Lovely: fair form when placed in maidens at Newcastle and Ripon: hung on latter course, and off 2 months before disappointing on return: unlikely to stay beyond 6f. *A. B. Mulholland*

COOL SECRET 2 gr.c. (Mar 4) Petong 126 – Cool Run 87 (Deep Run 119) 73 [1997 5g 5.9g⁶ 7m⁴ 6m⁵ 6m* 7g 6g⁴ 7v Oct 10] 6,600Y: strong, compact colt: shows knee action: second foal: dam 1m and 1¼m winner: fair performer: won nursery at Redcar in August: good fourth in similar event at Haydock in September: should stay beyond 6f: raced mainly on good/good to firm ground: tended to hang third start. *A. B. Mulholland*

COOL SPRAY (USA) 2 b.f. (Jan 14) Hansel (USA) – Kissogram Girl (USA) – p 100 (Danzig (USA)) [1997 8s Oct 14] lengthy, good-quartered filly: third foal: dam, 5f winner here at 2 yrs and at 8.5f in USA at 3 yrs, sister to Green Desert: 20/1 and in need of race, prominent 5f in maiden won by Mantusis at Leicester: likely to do better. *E. A. L. Dunlop*

COOL WATERS 2 b.f. (Apr 19) Puissance 110 – Keep Cool (FR) 42 (Northern – Treat (USA)) [1997 7g 7d Oct 27] 3,100 2-y-o: half-sister to a 2-y-o 5f winner by Governor General and a 6f seller winner by Lochnager: dam best at 1m/9f: tailed off in maidens. *J. R. Arnold*

COPENHAGEN 2 b.f. Midyan (USA) 124 – Crymlyn 68 (Welsh Pageant 132) – [1996 NR 1997 6g 5m 6.9d Oct 21] sixth reported foal: half-sister to 3 winners, including Rory (by Dowsing), quite useful at up to 1¼m: dam, maiden, stayed 7f: little sign of ability. *J. Akehurst*

COPERNICUS 2 b.c. (Mar 17) Polish Precedent (USA) 131 – Oxslip 106 (Owen 78 p Dudley 121) [1997 7m⁵ a8.5g² Sep 20] 36,000Y: leggy colt: half-brother to several winners, including 6-y-o Top Banana and 1¼m and 1¾m winner Sixslip (by Diesis): dam, 7f to 13f winner, half-sister to smart stayer Kambalda: better effort in maidens when neck second at Wolverhampton: will probably stay at least 1¼m: should improve again. *P. F. I. Cole*

COPPERBEECH (IRE) 3 ch.f. Common Grounds 118 – Caimanite 62 (Tap On – Wood 130) [1996 68: 5.2d² 6d⁶ 5m⁶ 6.1s 1997 a10g Nov 6] leggy filly: modest form at 2 yrs for P. Chapple-Hyam: tailed off on belated reappearance. *K. C. Comerford*

COPPER SHELL 3 ch.g. Beveled (USA) – Luly My Love (Hello Gorgeous – (USA) 128) [1996 –: 7.1m 1997 10.2m⁴ 10s 12.1g 14m 14.1g Oct 4] signs of ability but little worthwhile form. *A. P. Jones*

CORAL ISLAND 3 b.g. Charmer 123 – Misowni (Niniski (USA) 125) [1996 –: 59 6s 8.3d⁴ 7.9g 1997 8f* 10m 9g⁶ 12g 8g⁵ 8m Aug 7] leggy gelding: modest handi-capper: below form on flat after making winning reappearance at Carlisle in May:

should stay 1¼m: acts on firm ground: tried blinkered and visored: fair winning hurdler. *J. G. FitzGerald*

CORAL STRAND 3 ch.f. Indian Ridge 123 – Sea Venture (FR) 98 (Diatome 132) [1996 69?: 6m 7m⁴ 7m⁴ 1997 8m 8.5m⁴ Jun 4] compact filly: signs of ability at 2 yrs: tailed off in 1997: sent to Australia. *J. W. Watts* –

CORDATE (IRE) 3 b.f. Lahib (USA) 129 – La Romance (USA) (Lyphard (USA) 132) [1996 NR 1997 8g⁵ 8f⁴ 8m³ Jun 23] lengthy, good-bodied filly: seventh foal: half-sister to 4 winners, including useful Proposing (by Rainbow Quest), successful at up to 14.4f: dam French 1¼m winner out of half-sister to Green Dancer: fair form in maidens: third at Yarmouth: will stay 1¼m: sent to UAE. *J. H. M. Gosden* 74

CORETTA (IRE) 3 b.f. Caerleon (USA) 132 – Free At Last 115 (Shirley Heights 130) [1996 78p: 7g³ 1997 8.5m² 10.3d⁴ 10g* 10.1g³ 12g³ Sep 28] quite attractive filly: has rather a splayed action: useful performer: won handicap at Leicester in August: third in listed races at Newcastle (rated stakes) and Ascot (around ½ length behind stablemate Puce) final 2 starts: stays 1½m: yet to race on extremes of going: hung persistently second start: races prominently: sent to USA. *L. M. Cumani* 96

CORINCHILI 3 ch.f. Chilibang 120 – Corinthia (USA) (Empery (USA) 128) [1996 55: 5s⁵ 1997 5.1m⁴ 5.1m a6g⁴ a5g³ a5g⁵ 5m a6g⁵ Jun 27] sturdy filly: modest maiden handicapper: likely to prove best at 5f: acts on fibresand and good to firm ground, probably on soft. *G. G. Margarson* 60

CORNICHE (IRE) 2 b. or br.c. (Mar 16) Marju (IRE) 127 – Far But Near (USA) 88 (Far North (CAN) 120) [1997 8d² 10.2f² 8.2s* Oct 15] IR 29,000F, IR 170,000Y: second foal: half-brother to French 3-y-o 6.5f (at 2 yrs) to 1m winner Bon Eleve (by Mujtahid): dam 2-y-o 6f winner on only start, daughter of Coronation Stakes winner Kesar Queen: won maiden at Nottingham by short head from Edwardian but didn't look easy ride, rallying after hanging left for much of straight: will be suited by return to at least 1¼m. *P. F. I. Cole* 84

CORNICHE QUEST (IRE) 4 b.f. Salt Dome (USA) – Angel Divine (Ahonoora 122) [1996 61: 8g* 8m⁵ 7f 6m³ 7g*dis 6m⁶ 7g 7g 7d³ 7d⁴ 7f⁴ 6m* 7m 6.9d* a8g 1997 6.1d³ 5s² 5d* 6.1g* 7m 6m 6f⁵ 5g⁴ 6s⁶ 5.3f² 6m³ 6m⁴ 5g* 6m⁶ 5s⁶ 5g 5m 6.1g⁶ 6s 5d⁶ 6g⁶ a7g a7g a6g² a7g⁶ a6g Dec 26] leggy filly: fair on turf, modest on all-weather: won minor events at Carlisle and Nottingham in May and handicap at Pontefract in August: needs good test at 5f, stays 1m: acts on firm going, soft and fibresand: tends to carry head awkwardly: usually apprentice ridden: tough. *M. R. Channon* 74 a57

CORPORAL NYM (USA) 4 gr.g. Cozzene (USA) – Fiji Fan (USA) (Danzig (USA)) [1996 69: 7m 8m⁶ 6v 1997 6m 8.2d Oct 8] good-bodied gelding: lightly-raced maiden: no form in 1997. *M. R. Bosley* –

CORPORATE IMAGE 7 ch.g. Executive Man 119 – Robis 66 (Roan Rocket 128) [1996 NR 1997 14f⁶ 14.1s Oct 15] leggy gelding: second foal: brother to a winner in Italy: dam maiden at around 1m: poor hurdler: well beaten both starts on flat. *R. Simpson* –

CORPUS CHRISTI (IRE) 2 b.g. (Apr 2) Royal Academy (USA) 130 – Christi Dawn (USA) (Grey Dawn II 132) [1997 7m 7.1s 7m Nov 4] IR 7,500Y: tall gelding: has scope: has a long, round action: half-brother to several winners here and in USA, including fairly useful stayer Art Form (by Little Current): dam unraced: some promise in northern maidens (though not on soft going): should stay 1¼m+: looks type to do steadily better at 3 yrs. *M. Johnston* 63 p

CORRADINI 5 b.h. Rainbow Quest (USA) 134 – Cruising Height 112 (Shirley Heights 130) [1996 112: 16d³ 18.7g³ 16.5g⁴ 13.9m* 14.6g* 13.9m³ 14.6m* 16g 1997 14.1g⁴ 16.4g⁴ 12g* 16m 15.9g⁶ Aug 19] good-topped horse: poor mover: smart performer: good 2½ lengths fourth to Persian Punch in Henry II Stakes at Sandown in May: beat Pentad 1½ lengths in 5-runner minor event at Newmarket 2 months later: ran poorly in Goodwood Cup and Lonsdale Stakes at York (reportedly finished lame) afterwards: a stayer: acted on good to firm ground: sometimes flashed tail: to stand at Ganty Stud, Co. Galway, Ireland. *H. R. A. Cecil* 113

CORSECAN 2 ch.g. (Mar 31) Phountzi (USA) 104 – Sagareina (Sagaro 133) [1997 5m⁵ 5.7m 5d³ 5.3m⁶ 6d 5m 6d⁵ Oct 21] fourth reported foal: dam little worthwhile form: modest maiden at best. *S. Dow* 53

CORTACHY CASTLE (IRE) 2 ch.c. (Apr 20) Pips Pride 117 – Maricica 99
(Ahonoora 122) [1997 5.2m⁴ 5.1m* 5g² 5s² 6m⁶ 5d⁶ Oct 27] 16,000Y: well-made
colt: good walker: has a roundish action: sixth foal: dam Irish 1m winner: useful
form: won maiden at Nottingham in June: second in Windsor Castle Stakes at Royal
Ascot (went down by a neck to Asfurah) and Prix du Bois at Deauville (beaten 2
lengths by Zelding): disappointing in Richmond Stakes at Goodwood and on return
from 3 month-break in minor event at Lingfield final start: should stay 6f: acts on
good to firm and soft ground. *B. J. Meehan*

COSCOROBA (IRE) 3 ch.f. Shalford (IRE) 124§ – Tameeza (USA) (Shahra- 42
stani (USA) 135) [1996 47: 6m³ 1997 a6g³ 6.9d² May 9] poor maiden, lightly raced:
should stay 1m: upset in stalls and withdrawn on intended reappearance. *J. Berry*

COSMIC CASE 2 b.f. (Mar 30) Casteddu 111 – La Fontainova (IRE) (Lafontaine 46 +
(USA) 117) [1997 5m⁶ 7.1d⁶ 7.1m³ 6g⁶ 6g⁴ 6m 5m³ 6g³ 6g 6m Oct 28] 3,100Y:
first foal: dam unraced: poor maiden on balance: probably stays 7f: ran poorly in
visor once. *J. S. Goldie*

COSMIC COUNTESS (IRE) 2 b.f. (Apr 15) Lahib (USA) 129 – Windmill 74
Princess 55 (Gorytus (USA) 132) [1997 6g 6g⁵ 6d³ 7.6m⁴ 6f* Sep 28] sturdy filly:
third foal; half-sister to 3-y-o Cosmic Prince: dam placed at 1m and 11f, out of
half-sister to Blakeney and Morston: fair form: won maiden at Brighton by 1¼
lengths from The Boy John, making all: free-going sort, may prove best short of 1m:
acts on firm ground: swished tail second start. *M. A. Jarvis*

COSMIC PRINCE (IRE) 3 b.c. Teenoso (USA) 135 – Windmill Princess 55 95
(Gorytus (USA) 132) [1996 85p: 7m⁶ 7f³ 7g* 1997 8m³ 7m* 8.1g 7m 7m Sep 27] tall
colt: useful handicapper: won £25,000 event at Epsom in June: failed to get home
after setting furious pace next start, disappointing last 2: likely to prove best at 7f:
raced only on good ground or firmer: sometimes sweating and edgy: has bolted to
post, and taken early nowadays: free-going sort, possibly best allowed to stride on:
sent to USA. *M. A. Jarvis*

COSSACK COUNT 4 ch.c. Nashwan (USA) 135 – Russian Countess (USA) 90 +
104 (Nureyev (USA) 131) [1996 6d* 7s 6g* 5g⁵ 6m 1997 7m 7g a7g a7g* Dec 19]
ex-Irish colt: third foal: half-brother to 2-y-o Alboostan, 3-y-o Crown of Light and 2
other winners: dam French 2-y-o 1m winner: useful (rated 101) for M. Kauntze in
1996, won maiden and handicap: sold twice afterwards: subject of stewards inquiry
penultimate start, then impressive winner of handicap at Lingfield, always cruising:
stays 7f: acts on good to firm ground, dead and equitrack. *S. Dow*

COTTAGE PRINCE (IRE) 4 b.g. Classic Secret (USA) 91 – Susan's Blues 53
(Cure The Blues (USA)) [1996 42: 8m 11.1m 8.5m 8m³ 9.9g⁵ 11.1g³ 1997 9.9m
11f* 12s 12m* 12d 14.1g Jun 21] good-bodied gelding: modest handicapper: won at
Redcar in May and Catterick in June: stays 1½m: suited by good ground or firmer:
won over hurdles in October: game. *J. J. Quinn*

COTTEIR CHIEF (IRE) 6 b.g. Chief Singer 131 – Hasty Key (USA) (Key To 101
The Mint (USA)) [1996 NR 1997 a12g⁵ 9s May 18] close-coupled gelding: useful
performer: trained by M. Pipe at 4 yrs: much better effort in handicaps in 1997 at
Wolverhampton in April: stays 12.5f: acts on fibresand, ideally suited by good
ground or softer on turf: usually wears near-side pricker: held up. *R. Neville*

COUCHANT (IRE) 6 b.g. Petoski 135 – Be Easy 110 (Be Friendly 130) [1996 –
–: 10m 14.9g 1997 14.9m May 24] no form on flat since 1995: joined M. Pipe, and
won 4 hurdle races in the summer. *J. White*

COUNSEL 2 ch.g. (Feb 9) Most Welcome 131 – My Polished Corner (IRE) 53 56
(Tate Gallery (USA) 117) [1997 5m 6m⁵ 8.2m 6f² 7s 7m Oct 23] workmanlike
gelding: second foal: half-brother to 4-y-o Safecracker: dam stayed 11f: modest
maiden: should stay at least 1m: acts on firm ground: sold to join K. Burke.
C. E. Brittain

COUNT KENI 2 ch.g. (Feb 8) Formidable (USA) 125 – Flying Amy 40 (Norwick –
(USA) 125) [1997 7g 8.5g 7.9s Sep 3] 7,000 2-y-o: strong gelding: first foal: dam
poor maiden: well beaten in maidens. *J. M. Jefferson*

COUNTLESS TIMES 3 ch.g. Timeless Times (USA) 99 – Arroganza 62 –
(Crofthall 110) [1996 53: 5g 5g 6m 5m⁶ a7g a6g³ a5g² 1997 a5g a6g* a6g* a8g⁴ a7g⁵ a70

236

6m 7m a7g Oct 4] neat gelding: fair performer: came from well back to win maiden and handicap at Lingfield in January: gelded after fifth start, then off course for nearly 6 months and well beaten on return: best form at 6f: acts on equitrack: headstrong: flashes tail. *W. R. Muir*

COUNTRY GARDEN 2 b.f. (Jan 20) Selkirk (USA) 129 – Totham 84 100 (Shernazar 131) [1997 5.1d³ 5m³ 6g² 6.9m* 7g* 8g⁴ 8f² 8.5f1* 8g⁴ Nov 28] 7,500Y: third foal: half-sister to 3-y-o Cherokee Flight: dam, 1½m winner, granddaughter of 1000 Guineas winner Full Dress II: useful form: won maiden at Folkestone and nursery at Ascot for R. Hannon, then non-graded stakes at Hollywood Park (where also 2 lengths fourth in Grade 3 race) after transfer to USA: stays 8.5f: acts on firm ground: consistent: raced on medication in USA. *W. Greenman, USA*

COUNTRY THATCH 4 b.g. Thatching 131 – Alencon (Northfields (USA)) 49 [1996 –: 6g 7m 7g 8.1m 1997 9.7g 8d 10g 12f 9.7g³ 9.7m* 12m³ 8m 12v Oct 10] neat gelding: has had soft-palate operation: poor handicapper: narrowly won maiden event at Folkestone in August: stays 1½m: acts on good to firm ground. *C. A. Horgan*

COUNT TONY 3 ch.g. Keen 116 – Turtle Dove (Gyr (USA) 131) [1996 59: a7g⁴ 72 8g 8m 1997 10.8m* 12g⁵ 10.3d⁴ 11.9f a10g² 10g 10.1g* Aug 21] sparely-made gelding: fair performer: won handicap at Warwick in March and minor event at Yarmouth in August: should stay 1½m: acts on good to firm going and on all-weather: well beaten in visor: winning hurdler for M. Hammond. *S. P. C. Woods*

COURAGEOUS (IRE) 2 ch.c. (Apr 9) Generous (IRE) 139 – Legend of Arabia 79 p (Great Nephew 126) [1997 6v⁴ 8.2d³ Oct 30] 150,000Y: strong, good-bodied colt: sixth foal: half-brother to several winners, including French 2-y-o 13.5f winner by Kenmare and smart 1½m/1¾m winner Edbaysaan (by Slip Anchor): dam unraced daughter of Fair Salinia: fair form when in frame in autumn maidens at Ascot and Nottingham: likely to be suited by 1½m+: should do better. *P. F. I. Cole*

COURAGEOUS KNIGHT 8 gr.g. Midyan (USA) 124 – Little Mercy 90 (No 45 Mercy 126) [1996 –: 7.1m 1997 10d 10g 12f² 12d³ 12m⁵ 12.1m 14g³ 11.7m⁶ 14m Aug 21] good-topped gelding: poor handicapper: stays 1¾m: acts on firm and dead ground. *P. Hayward*

COURAGE UNDER FIRE 2 b.g. (Apr 24) Risk Me (FR) 127 – Dreamtime – Quest (Blakeney 126) [1997 6.9d⁶ a8g Nov 24] 1,600Y: second foal: half-brother to 3-y-o Interdream: dam, no form on flat or over hurdles, daughter of Fred Darling winner Rotisserie: only a little sign of ability in maidens. *D. W. P. Arbuthnot*

COURBARIL 5 b.g. Warrshan (USA) 117 – Free On Board 73 (Free State 125) 64 [1996 61§: a12g⁴ a12g 11.9f³ 15.4f² 17.2f³ 16d 11.5f 12m 11.9f² 11.6d² 1997 14g⁶ 14m⁶ 16.4s² Aug 29] neat gelding: useful hurdler: modest performer on flat: stays 17f: acts on equitrack and any turf going: usually blinkered/visored: not an easy ride, and refused to race (under inexperienced amateur) once in 1996. *M. C. Pipe*

COURSE FISHING 6 ch.g. Squill (USA) 122 – Migoletty 59 (Oats 126) [1996 43 49: 8f⁶ 10g 10f 12.3m* 12.3g⁵ 10.2g⁴ 14s 13.6m 1997 12m³ a12f 12m 12.3m⁴ 12d⁶ 16m 15.8g⁵ 16s² a14g² Dec 18] short-backed gelding: poor mover: poor handicapper: effective from 1½m to 2m: acts on firm ground, soft and fibresand. *B. A. McMahon*

COURTEOUS 2 b.c. (May 14) Generous (IRE) 139 – Dayanata (Shirley Heights 84 p 130) [1997 8.1d⁴ 8m* Oct 1] good-topped colt: fifth foal: half-brother to 3-y-o Carisbrooke, useful Irish 6f (at 2 yrs) to 1m winner Daryabad (by Thatching) and Irish 1¾m winner Dayadan (by Shernazar): dam unraced sister to Darshaan: won 13-runner maiden at Salisbury by ¾ length from Majestic Hills, soon prominent and running on strongly: will stay at least 1½m: should make a useful 3-y-o. *P. F. I. Cole*

COURT EXPRESS 3 b.g. Then Again 126 – Moon Risk 62 (Risk Me (FR) 127) 69 [1996 60: 7.1f⁵ 7g 6m⁵ 1997 7.5d 10m 5.9f* 5.9m* 5.9g² 8f 8m Oct 28] leggy gelding: fair performer: won maiden and handicap at Carlisle in June: best form at stiff 6f (should stay 7f): acts on firm ground. *T. J. Etherington*

COURT HOUSE 3 b.g. Reprimand 122 – Chalet Girl (Double Form 130) [1996 57 59: a5g a6g⁵ 5g 7m⁶ 1997 7m 8g* 10.1m 8m 6m⁴ 7g 7f a8g Nov 24] leggy, sparely-made gelding: modest performer: won seller at Pontefract (sold out of B. McMahon's stable 3,000 gns) in June: stays 1m: acts on good to firm going: has shown temperament. *M. C. Chapman*

COURTING DANGER 4 b.g. Tina's Pet 121 – Court Town 60 (Camden Town – 125) [1996 67: 8d³ 7m 1997 8m 8.3s May 12] workmanlike gelding: lightly raced and well beaten since 3-y-o reappearance, including in blinkers. *D. R. Gandolfo*

COURTING NEWMARKET 9 b.g. Final Straw 127 – Warm Wind 84 (Tumble – Wind (USA)) [1996 41: 8d 6f⁶ 7f 7m 1997 8m 6m May 5] leggy, good-topped gelding: on the downgrade, and no form in 1997. *Miss K. M. George*

COURT LANE (USA) 2 b.f. (Apr 22) Machiavellian (USA) 123 – Chicarica 81 (USA) 112 (The Minstrel (CAN) 135) [1997 6m³ 6s* 7.3g Oct 25] small, close-coupled filly: second foal: dam won Cherry Hinton Stakes: third in maiden at Newmarket in October then landed odds in weak similar race at Ayr by wide margin: well beaten in listed event at Newbury: should stay 7f. *D. R. Loder*

COURTLY TIMES 2 ch.f. (Apr 14) Machiavellian (USA) 123 – Dancing Moon 64 (IRE) (Dancing Brave (USA) 140) [1997 7.1m⁴ Jul 23] leggy, unfurnished filly: first foal: dam, ran once, from good family: 12/1 and better for race, under 7 lengths fourth of 9 to Trident in maiden at Sandown, short-lived effort after slow start: swished tail beforehand. *E. A. L. Dunlop*

COURT MINSTREL 8 br.g. Hadeer 118 – Sheer Bliss 76 (St Paddy 133) [1996 – NR 1997 6.9s Jul 2] modest handicapper at 6 yrs for L. J. Holt: well beaten on belated return. *R. Akehurst*

COURT NAP (IRE) 5 ch.g. Waajib 121 – Mirhar (FR) (Sharpen Up 127) [1996 58 NR 1997 a9.4g³ Jan 4] close-coupled gelding: modest maiden handicapper on flat, lightly raced these days: stays 9.4f: acts on fibresand and on firm and soft ground. *S. Mellor*

COURTNEY GYM (IRE) 2 ch.c. (May 9) Shalford (IRE) 124§ – Fair Or Foul 52 (Patch 129) [1997 5g 6m 6m² 6.1m² 6d Oct 21] 12,000 2-y-o: half-brother to a 2-y-o 6f seller winner by Runnett: dam Irish 2-y-o 1¼m winner: modest maiden: second in sellers at Windsor and Nottingham: should stay beyond 6f: disappointing on good to soft ground. *M. R. Channon*

COURT SHAREEF 2 b.c. (May 16) Shareef Dancer (USA) 135 – Fairfields – Cone (Celtic Cone 116) [1997 7g Jul 8] smallish colt: first foal: dam, lightly raced on flat, fairly useful over hurdles: sweating and burly, in rear in maiden at Newmarket. *R. Dickin*

COURTSHIP 3 b.c. Groom Dancer (USA) 128 – Dance Quest (FR) 117 (Green 88 Dancer (USA) 132) [1996 88p: 7m² 7m* 1997 8.2m⁵ 8m² 8s⁶ 8g Jul 10] rangy colt: brother to Pursuit of Love: fairly useful but lightly-raced handicapper: second at Pontefract in April, best effort of 1997: would have stayed 1¼m: best efforts on good to firm going: retired to Ballycrystal Stud, Co Offaly, Ireland. *H. R. A. Cecil*

COWTHAREE 3 ch.f. Arazi (USA) 135 – Hawait Al Barr 100 (Green Desert – (USA) 127) [1996 70p: 6.9m³ 1997 10.2m Apr 29] shaped quite well on debut: well beaten only 3-y-o start. *M. R. Stoute*

CRACKER 3 br.g. Lugana Beach 116 – Greta's Song (Faraway Times (USA) – 123) [1996 NR 1997 a7s⁶ Nov 10] third reported foal: dam of little account: last of 6 in Lingfield maiden. *G. Fierro*

CRACKERBOX 3 b.f. Lochnager 132 – Festival Flame (Blakeney 126) [1996 35 NR 1997 a6g⁴ a7g⁵ a8g⁴ 8.2g 8f⁵ 7f⁶ 7m a5g 6g Jul 7] 4,800 2-y-o: first foal: dam unraced half-sister to Grade 1 1½m winner Alex The Great: poor maiden at best: trained by H. Akbary first 2 starts. *C. A. Dwyer*

CRAFTY PET (IRE) 2 ch.f. (Mar 6) Petardia 113 – Frans Cap (Captain James 47 123) [1997 5g 5d³ 5g⁴ 5m 5d⁶ Aug 13] IR 2,200Y: well-grown filly: fifth foal: half-sister to a 1991 2-y-o 5f winner by Sarab: dam, Irish maiden, seemed to stay 1¾m: poor maiden: visored final start. *R. A. Fahey*

CRAIGARY 6 b.g. Dunbeath (USA) 127 – Velvet Pearl 52 (Record Token 128) 46 [1996 10g⁵ 11m⁵ 11d³ 12v 11d³ 1997 11.1s 13.8m 11.1s⁴ 10g⁴ 12.1g³ 11.1d² 12.1g* 12.1g 13.1s Oct 13] ex-Irish gelding: first foal: dam 1¼m winner: poor handicapper nowadays: won seller at Hamilton in September: stays 1½m: acts on dead going: effective blinkered/visored or not. *Mrs A. Swinbank*

CRAIGIE BOY 7 b.g. Crofthall 110 – Lady Carol 42 (Lord Gayle (USA) 124) 43 [1996 58d, a44: 7.5d 5g 6d⁶ 6s* 5s³ 7g 6g² 6g⁶ 6m 6d⁶ 6s 5g⁵ 6d 6m a7g⁶ a7g a6g² 1997 a7g³ a6g a7g a6g⁴ a6g 5m 7s 6m² a7g 6g 6s 5v Jul 5] leggy gelding: poor handicapper: seems to stay 7f: probably acts on any going: usually blinkered/visored nowadays: tends to wander. *N. Bycroft*

CRAIGIEVAR 3 b.c. Mujadil (USA) 119 – Sweet Home (Home Guard (USA) 100 129) [1996 94p: 6m⁴ 6f* 6.1s* 1997 8m³ 7.1s* 7m⁴ 7s 7d Sep 13] leggy colt: has a quick action: useful performer: won 5-runner rated stakes at Haydock in May (by 2½ lengths from Ramooz) despite drifting right under pressure: well held last 2 starts: probably best short of 1m: acts on firm and soft going. *J. R. Fanshawe*

CRAIGSTEEL 2 b.c. (Mar 9) Suave Dancer (USA) 136 – Applecross 117 (Glint 104 p of Gold 128) [1997 7.1g² 7g* 8g⁶ 8g⁴ Oct 25] close-coupled colt: good mover: fourth foal: half-brother to 3-y-o Invermark, useful Scandinavian performer Inchrory (1m winner here, stays at least 1½m, by Midyan) and 1m winner Pennycairn (by Last Tycoon): dam, 1¼m to 13.3f winner, second in Park Hill: useful form: favourite, won maiden at Newmarket in July: beaten just over a length in Royal Lodge Stakes at Ascot and not at all disgraced when 5 lengths fourth to Saratoga Springs in Racing Post Trophy at Doncaster: has raced only on good ground: open to progress when tried beyond 1m, and should stay at least 1½m. *H. R. A. Cecil*

CRAVEN HILL (IRE) 3 gr.g. Pursuit of Love 124 – Crodelle (IRE) (Formidable – § (USA) 125) [1996 –p: 7m 1997 8.2m 10s 8.2d Jun 23] lengthy gelding: well beaten all starts: tried blinkered: ungenuine. *N. A. Graham*

CRAZEE MENTAL 2 b.f. (Feb 21) Magic Ring (IRE) 115 – Corn Futures 78 107 (Nomination 125) [1997 5s² 6g* 5m² 6g² 6m² Sep 30] 8,500Y: sturdy filly: second foal: half-sister to 3-y-o Trading Aces: dam, 6f winner at 2 yrs, out of close relative to Wassl: useful performer: won maiden at Hamilton in June: excelled afterwards in Queen Mary Stakes at Royal Ascot (caught only final stride by Nadwah), Cherry Hinton Stakes at Newmarket (beaten length by Asfurah) and Cheveley Park Stakes, again at Newmarket: looking tremendously well, beaten 2½ lengths by Embassy in last named, switched and running on well: may stay 7f, probably not 1m: swishes tail in preliminaries: tends to veer left under pressure (did so markedly at Ascot), but is game. *D. Haydn Jones*

CRAZY CHIEF 4 b.c. Indian Ridge 123 – Bizarre Lady (Dalsaan 125) [1996 85: 83 7g⁵ 6.9m³ 8m⁴ 8.3m* 8.1d² 8.3m⁴ 10m² 10.3d 1997 9g⁴ Oct 25] lengthy, useful-looking colt: fairly useful handicapper: ran well only start at 4 yrs: stays 1¼m: acts on good to firm and dead ground: takes keen hold, and races prominently: consistent. *P. F. I. Cole*

CREDIT CALL (IRE) 9 br.g. Rhoman Rule (USA) – Maiacourt (Malacate – (USA) 131) [1996 NR 1997 a16g Jan 10] first living foal: dam never ran: no sign of ability. *R. G. Brazington*

CREDITE RISQUE 4 b.f. Risk Me (FR) 127 – Lompoa (Lomond (USA) 128) – [1996 –: 6.1d 1997 6.1g 10d Apr 29] leggy filly: little worthwhile form. *J. A. Glover*

CREDIT SQUEEZE 7 ch.g. Superlative 118 – Money Supply (Brigadier Gerard 64 144) [1996 NR 1997 12m 14.9d 12m* 11.7m Aug 12] good-topped gelding: good mover: modest handicapper: well ridden (dictated pace) when winning amateurs race at Salisbury in July: stays 1½m, possibly not 15f: acts on good to firm ground, dead and equitrack: often bandaged. *R. F. Johnson Houghton*

CREES SQAW 5 b.m. Cree Song 99 – Elsocko 76 (Swing Easy (USA) 126) [1996 – NR 1997 a5g 5f a7g Nov 14] lightly raced and no worthwhile form. *B. A. McMahon*

CRESCENT'S WHISPER (IRE) 3 gr.c. Shalford (IRE) 124§ – Checkers 56 (Habat 127) [1996 NR 1997 8.3s 8g 8f⁴ Jun 5] 15,000Y: eighth foal: half-brother to 4 winners, including Belfry Green (useful up to 1m, by Doulab): modest form in maidens: bandaged final start: dead. *B. Hanbury*

CREST WING (USA) 4 b.g. Storm Bird (CAN) 134 – Purify (USA) (Fappiano – (USA)) [1996 –: 10d 8g 10g⁴ 1997 11.6g Jun 2] tall gelding: tailed off in maidens and a handicap. *T. P. McGovern*

Phoenix Sprint Stakes, Leopardstown—
the high point of the blinkered six-year-old Cretan Gift's career as he finishes strongly to beat Azizzi

CRETAN GIFT   6 ch.g. Cadeaux Genereux 131 – Caro's Niece (USA) 86 (Caro   106
133) [1996 82, a94: a7g⁴ a6g³ a6g⁴ a7g² a7g² 6.1g² 7m a5g* a6g⁶ 6m² 6.1m a7g² 6m²
a6g* 6g⁴ 6m⁶ 6m³ 7.6m⁶ 6m⁶ 6.1d⁴ 5.1d 6f⁵ 5.1m* 6m* 6g 5g 6f* a7g⁵ 1997 a6g*
a5g² 6m 5m² 6g² 7m 6g⁶ 6g 6s* 7g⁵ 6f⁴ 7m⁴ 6m* 6g 6m 6d⁵ a7g³ 6s⁶ Nov 8] lengthy
gelding: useful performer: better than ever in 1997, successful in handicaps at
Southwell in February and Newcastle in June and in Phoenix Sprint Stakes (beat
Azizzi 2 lengths) at Leopardstown in August: effective at 5f to 7f: acts on firm and
soft ground and on fibresand (yet to race on equitrack): wears blinkers/visor: wears
crossed/dropped noseband: very tough and consistent: a credit to his trainer.
N. P. Littmoden

CRIMSON TIDE (IRE)   3 b.c. Sadler's Wells (USA) 132 – Sharata (IRE)   118
(Darshaan 133) [1996 95p: 7d² 7g* 1997 9m³ 10.4g 8.1g³ 8.5g³ 10d² 8f* 8.5s* 8d*
Nov 9] leggy colt: smart performer: really came to himself in the autumn, winning
minor event at Bath in September and Group 2 events at Dusseldorf (by 6 lengths
from Lagarto) in October and Rome (beat Gothenberg by ½ length) in November:
barely stays 1¼m: acts on firm and soft going: has found little (idled in front at
Rome) and goes well held up. *J. W. Hills*

CRISSEM (IRE)   4 b.f. Thatching 131 – Deer Emily (Alzao (USA) 117) [1996 –:   62
5d 1997 8g 6f 6.9m⁵ 6d⁵ 6d 8.1m 6d 7m⁴ 8d Oct 13] workmanlike filly: modest
handicapper: stays 7f: acts on firm ground and dead. *R. Hollinshead*

CRITICAL AIR   2 b.g. (Mar 14) Reprimand 122 – Area Girl 76 (Jareer (USA)   63
115) [1997 6m 5m a6g⁶ 6d⁴ a6g³ a7g² Nov 21] second foal: half-brother to 3-y-o

Dominant Air: dam 5f winner at 2 yrs: modest maiden: placed in nurseries at Southwell and Wolverhampton in November: shapes as though he'll stay 1m: best efforts on fibresand. *Sir Mark Prescott*

CROAGH PATRICK 5 b.g. Faustus (USA) 118 – Pink Pumpkin 52 (Tickled – Pink 114) [1996 –: 7m 7m 8.3m 7s a7s 1997 6m May 4] little sign of ability. *J. C. Fox*

CROCO ROUGE (IRE) 2 b.c. Rainbow Quest (USA) 134 – Alligatrix (USA) 108 p 111 (Alleged (USA) 138) [1997 9s* 10d⁴ Nov 1] brother to useful Tom Waller (should have stayed 1½m) and half-brother to several winners, including useful Alidiva (up to 1m, by Chief Singer), the dam of Taipan, Ali-Royal and Sleepytime: dam well-bred 2-y-o 7f winner, stayed 1m: won newcomers event at Longchamp in October: around ½-length fourth of 7 to Special Quest in Criterium de Saint-Cloud: stays 1¼m, should get 1½m: open to further progress. *P. C. Bary, France*

CROESO CYNNES 4 ch.f. Most Welcome 131 – Miss Taleca (Pharly (FR) 130) 59 [1996 70: 6g⁴ 6m² 5f⁴ 6g* 6m² 6m⁴ 5m* 6d⁴ 6m 6d 5.7g 6.1m a6g⁶ Oct 4] compact filly: fair sprint handicapper at best: disappointing in 1997: very best form on ground firmer than good. *B. Palling*

CROFTERS CEILIDH 5 ch.m. Scottish Reel 123 – Highland Rowena 59 101 (Royben 125) [1996 90: 5m 5.1f⁴ 5g 5m 5.2m 5.1d 5.2m⁴ 5.1g* 5s³ 5g⁶ 5g 1997 5m⁴ 5d² 6s⁵ 5g² 5m 5m 5.2m⁶ 5m² 5.1g² 5d⁴ 6.1d³ Oct 30] leggy mare: useful performer: in frame 7 times in 1997: best effort when fourth to The Puzzler in rated stakes at Newmarket penultimate start: ideally suited by 5f: acts on good to firm and dead ground: blinkered/visored sixth to final 4-y-o starts: usually races prominently: consistent. *B. A. McMahon*

CROFTERS EDGE 2 ch.c. (Apr 30) Beveled (USA) – Zamindara (Crofter – (USA) 124) [1997 6.1g 6d Nov 7] good-topped colt: seventh foal: brother to winning sprinters Secret Miss and Another Jade (latter fair) and half-brother to 5f winner Greetland Rock (by Ballacashtal): dam poor maiden who stayed 1m: well beaten in maidens. *A. P. Jarvis*

CROFT POOL 6 b.g. Crofthall 110 – Blackpool Belle 70 (The Brianstan 128) 113 [1996 111, a–: 5m 5m³ 5m² 5m³ 5m³ 6m 5f* 5m⁵ 5g³ 5m* 5d² 6s 1997 5g* 5d 6g 5m 5d 5m 5.2g⁴ 5m⁴ 5v 6d Oct 17] sturdy gelding: impresses in appearance: smart performer: won Temple Stakes at Sandown in May by ¾ length from Brave Edge: best efforts when fourth in listed races at Newbury and Newmarket (2 lengths behind Dashing Blue) in October: effective at 5f (best form) and 6f: acts on firm and dead going (no form on very soft), successful on the all-weather: visored (below form) once: tends to idle: tough and game: sent to USA. *J. A. Glover*

Temple Stakes, Sandown—
a muddling affair is won by Croft Pool from Brave Edge (rail) and Bolshoi (blinkers)

Sheikh Mohammed's "Crown of Light"

CROFT SANDS 4 ch.g. Crofthall 110 – Sannavally (Sagaro 133) [1996 NR 1997 – 7m 10f⁵ 8.2d Nov 3] sixth foal: brother to useful 6f to 8.5f winner Croft Valley, easily best relative: dam ran once: no sign of ability. *R. Akehurst*

CROMER PIER 2 b.g. (May 21) Reprimand 122 – Fleur du Val (Valiyar 129) – [1997 7m Oct 2] 5,500Y: fourth foal: half-brother to 3-y-o Peppiatt: dam unraced half-sister to Superpower: 50/1 and backward, never on terms in 22-runner maiden at Newmarket. *M. H. Tompkins*

CROMPTON LIGHTS 3 br.c. Sylvan Express 117 – Ela-Yianni-Mou 73 – (Anfield 117) [1996 NR 1997 8.2d 11.5s 10m Jul 14] third known foal: brother to 7f/1m winner Sylvan Princess and half-brother to 1½m winner Achilles Heel (by Superlative): dam sprinter: showed little in maidens. *D. J. S. Cosgrove*

CROSBY DON 2 b.g. (Apr 18) Alhijaz 122 – Evening Star 71 (Red Sunset 120) – [1997 7g⁶ 7.5v⁵ 7g⁵ Aug 23] 6,400Y: small gelding: third foal: dam 1m winner: soundly beaten in maidens: has sweated and been very reluctant to post: gelded after final start. *E. Weymes*

CROSBY NOD 3 b.g. Shalford (IRE) 124§ – Kirkby Belle 44 (Bay Express 132) 51 [1996 –: 6s 6m 6d 1997 6g⁵ 8g 8.2d Jun 23] sturdy gelding: form only when fifth in seller at Newcastle in March: should stay beyond 6f. *E. Weymes*

CROSS OF VALOUR 4 b.g. Never So Bold 135 – X-Data 93 (On Your Mark – 125) [1996 79: 7m 6f* 6f² 7m 6m 6m² 7.3m a6s 1997 a7g⁶ 7g 7d⁵ 8s Jul 3] sturdy gelding: fair form at 3 yrs: failed to beat a single horse in 1997. *P. Howling*

CROSS TALK (IRE) 5 b.g. Darshaan 133 – Liaison (USA) (Blushing Groom – (FR) 131) [1996 70, a62: a12g a16g a12g⁵ a12g⁴ a11g a11g⁵ a16g⁴ 13.8s* 12d a12g⁴

242

a16g⁶ 14.1g⁴ 12g⁵ 12s 12g a14.8g 12g² 14.1g* a14g⁴ a12g⁶ 1997 a12g a13g⁶ Feb 13] close-coupled gelding: fair handicapper at 4 yrs: well beaten in 1997. *R. M. Stronge*

CROSS THE BORDER   4 b.g. Statoblest 120 – Brave Advance (USA) 98 (Bold   85
Laddie (USA)) [1996 96d: 5g² 5d⁵ 5s 5f 5m 6v 5g 5s 1997 5g 6.1m 5g 5s⁶ 5g 5m²
5m* 5g* 5m⁶ 5g* 5g* 5d³ 5g* 5m³ 5.2m⁶ 5d Oct 20] strong gelding: fairly useful
handicapper: in fine form in the summer, winning at Doncaster, Catterick, Thirsk,
Beverley and Musselburgh, 3 of them apprentice races: best at 5f on good going or
firmer: died after suffering heart attack in his box in November. *D. Nicholls*

CROWDED AVENUE   5 b.g. Sizzling Melody 117 – Lady Bequick 81 (Sharpen   105
Up 127) [1996 105: 5.1g 5m³ 5f³ 5m 5m⁵ 5m 5m* 5g 1997 5.1m⁵ 6d³ 5m⁶ 5g² 5g 5m
5m 5m² 5g⁵ Oct 25] compact gelding: useful performer: best 5-y-o effort when close
eighth of 15 to Averti in King George Stakes at Goodwood on sixth start: best at 5f on
good ground or firmer: sometimes wears tongue strap: edgy sort, and tends to sweat.
P. J. Makin

CROWN COURT (USA)   4 b.c. Chief's Crown (USA) – Bold Courtesan (USA)   97
(Bold Bidder) [1996 91p: 8m⁶ 10d⁶ 8.5f³ 8g* 10m³ 9m 1997 7.6g² 8m² 7g Jul 10]
big, heavy-topped colt: impresses in appearance: has a round action: useful performer, lightly raced: runner-up in minor event at Lingfield and Royal Hunt Cup
(made most when ¾-length second to Red Robbo) at Royal Ascot: stays 1¼m: acts
on good to firm ground, did not look at ease on firm: normally bandaged: sold, to go
to Singapore. *L. M. Cumani*

CROWN OF LIGHT   3 b.f. Mtoto 134 – Russian Countess (USA) 104 (Nureyev   112
(USA) 131) [1996 77p: 7g* 1997 10m⁴ 11.5s* 12m³ 12g³ 11.9g³ 14.6m⁶ Sep 10]
lengthy filly: has a fluent action: smart performer: beat Book At Bedtime a length in
listed race at Lingfield in May: subsequently third in the Oaks at Epsom (beaten
around 2 lengths by Reams of Verse), Ribblesdale Stakes at Royal Ascot (very much
on toes, some way below form) and in Yorkshire Oaks (unseated rider and cantered
loose beforehand, 2½ lengths behind My Emma) at York: favourite, well held in Park
Hill Stakes at Doncaster final start, beaten too far out to blame longer trip: should
stay at least 1¾m: acts on good to firm and soft ground: takes keen hold and probably
not the easiest of rides: has joined Godolphin. *M. R. Stoute*

CROWN OF THORNS (USA)   3 b.g. Diesis 133 – Mystery Play (IRE) 104   89
(Sadler's Wells (USA) 132) [1996 NR 1997 8s⁵ 8.1m* Jul 24] smallish gelding: first
foal: dam, 7f (at 2 yrs) and 11.4f winner, out of half-sister to very good broodmare
Miss Manon: well-backed favourite, confirmed debut promise when beating Bright
Heritage a length in maiden at Sandown in July: should stay 1¼m: sold 12,000 gns in
December. *J. H. M. Gosden*

CRUINN A BHORD   2 b.f. (Jan 22) Inchinor 119 – Selection Board 75 (Welsh   82 p
Pageant 132) [1997 7m⁵ Nov 1] fifth foal: half-sister to 3 winners, including 6-y-o
Star Selection and 1m to 11f winner Officer Cadet (by Shernazar): dam twice-raced
sister to Teleprompter and half-sister to Chatoyant: 40/1, encouraging 3 lengths fifth
of 18 to Pontoon in maiden at Newmarket, going smoothly behind pace and not at
all knocked about final 1f: should stay 1m: sure to improve and should win races.
A. C. Stewart

CRUMPTON HILL (IRE)   5 b.g. Thatching 131 – Senane 86 (Vitiges (FR)   102
132) [1996 94: 8m³ 8m³ 7m* 7m³ 1997 7m 8.1g⁴ 8m 7g 8m² 7.9d⁵ 7m³ Sep 27]
workmanlike gelding: useful handicapper: better than ever in 1997, second of 20 to
Fly To The Stars in Schweppes Golden Mile at Goodwood and third of 25 to Jo Mell
in Tote Festival Handicap at Ascot: ran creditably only try at 9f, but races at 7f/1m
nowadays: acts on good to firm going, probably on dead: has a high head carriage:
has run well when sweating: takes keen hold, and usually held up. *N. A. Graham*

CRUZ SANTA   4 b.f. Lord Bud 121 – Linpac Mapleleaf 69 (Dominion 123) [1996   42
53: 7s² 7f⁶ 5g 6g 7g 1997 10g 8f⁴ a8g⁶ a11g a14g a11g Dec 8] poor maiden: left T. D.
Barron after third start: should stay beyond 1m. *M. C. Chapman*

CRYHAVOC   3 b.c. Polar Falcon (USA) 126 – Sarabah (IRE) 83 (Ela-Mana-Mou   96
132) [1996 90p: 5.7f 6f⁴ 5g³ 6m* 6m* 1997 6m² 6g⁴ 7m 7g⁵ 6d Sep 13] sturdy colt:
fairly useful performer: best effort when fourth in listed race at Baden-Baden in May:
stays 7f: raced mainly on good going or firmer: carries head awkwardly. *J. R. Arnold*

CRYSTAL CRAZE 2 b.f. (May 11) Warrshan (USA) 117 – Single Gal 97 –
(Mansingh (USA) 120) [1997 6d Oct 20] 1,650Y: sturdy filly: half-sister to several
winners, including 6-y-o Sally Slade and fairly useful 1¼m winner Age of Miracles
(by Simply Great): dam best at 6f: 33/1, beat only one in Pontefract maiden: moved
badly to post. *P. Byrne, USA*

CRYSTAL CROSSING (IRE) 3 b.f. Royal Academy (USA) 130 – Never So 99
Fair 65 (Never So Bold 135) [1996 99: 6m² 6f* 7g⁶ 1997 6m 8s⁵ 9f⁴ 8.5f² Oct 11] tall
sparely-made filly: useful form at 2 yrs: well held only 3-y-o start in Britain then left
P. Chapple-Hyam: gradually getting better in USA, beaten length in allowance race
at Keeneland last time: stays 8.5f: raced on medication in USA. *P. Byrne, USA*

CRYSTAL FALLS (IRE) 4 b.g. Alzao (USA) 117 – Honourable Sheba (USA) 79
(Roberto (USA) 131) [1996 –: 7g 1997 12g⁵ 12m Jun 26] fair handicapper, lightly
raced: stays 1½m: acts on good to firm and soft ground: gelded, and joined T.
Easterby. *J. J. O'Neill*

CRYSTAL GOLD 3 ch.g. Arazi (USA) 135 – Crystal Land (Kris 135) [1996 88
66p: 7f 7g 1997 8m² 8.5m² a9.4g* 10.5m² 10g Jun 21] strong gelding: fairly useful
handicapper: won at Wolverhampton in May: beaten short head at Haydock, much
better effort in June: stays 10.5f: acts on fibresand and good to firm ground, yet to
race on going softer than good: usually a front runner: sent to UAE. *M. R. Stoute*

CRYSTAL HEARTED 3 b.c. Broken Hearted 124 – Crystal Fountain (Great 116
Nephew 126) [1996 85p: 7.1m⁴ 7f* 1997 8g⁵ 8.2m² 10.3v* 12g 10m* 10g² 10g* Sep
21] rangy, good sort: impresses in appearance: smart performer: won 3-runner listed
race at Chester (by 13 lengths) in May, 3-runner Scottish Classic at Ayr (by neck from
Fahris) in July and Group 2 event at Frankfurt (gamely held Baleno by ¾ length) in
September: good second to Rajpoute in Group 2 race at Deauville penultimate start:
effective at 1¼m and worth another chance at 1½m (twelfth of 13 in the Derby): acts
on any ground: pulled too hard (when held up) on reappearance, more settled when
allowed to stride on: genuine. *H. Candy*

Tennent Caledonian Breweries Scottish Classic, Ayr—
a canny, front-running ride by Tony McGlone on Crystal Hearted, who beats Fahris (left) and Even Top

CRYSTAL HEIGHTS (FR)   9 ch.g. Crystal Glitters (USA) 127 – Fahrenheit 69   63 §
(Mount Hagen (FR) 127) [1996 73: a7g² a7g a7g³ a7g⁵ a7g* 7f⁶ 7f 7f 7g³ 7m 7f* 6f*
6f* 6g 1997 8m 6f⁶ 5.1m 6f 7f 7m² 7.1g 6m³ 7m⁵ a7g Oct 4] big gelding: modest
handicapper: mostly disappointing in 1997: effective at 6f and 7f: acts on firm ground
and all-weather, possibly not on soft: tried blinkered/visored: often bandaged: often
starts very slowly, and can't be relied upon. *R. J. O'Sullivan*

CRYSTAL HILLS (IRE)   3 b.g. Darshaan 133 – Lustre (USA) 90 (Halo (USA))   83 §
[1996 –p: 8d 1997 11.5s 14m² 14m 14m 14f* 15.8s⁵ Oct 16] strong, lengthy gelding:
fairly useful performer: found nothing third and fourth (blinkered, gelded after)
starts: won maiden at Lingfield in October: stays 1¾m: acts on firm ground:
blanketed for stalls entry: inconsistent and ungenuine: sold approx. £16,000 in Dubai
in November. *J. H. M. Gosden*

CRYSTAL LOUGH (IRE)   2 b.f. (May 8) Maelstrom Lake 118 – Holy Water   –
(Monseigneur (USA) 127) [1997 5g 5.1d 5m Oct 28] IR 2,000Y: half-sister to 1m (at
2 yrs) to 1½m winner Drinks Party (by Camden Town) and 7-y-o Broadstairs Beauty:
dam unraced daughter of sister to top-class sprinter Deep Diver: behind in maidens.
G. R. Oldroyd

CRYSTAL WATERS (IRE)   2 b.f. (Feb 4) River Falls 113 – Annie's Glen (IRE)   –
(Glenstal (USA) 118) [1997 5g 8.2d Oct 8] IR 400Y: second foal: dam unraced:
behind in maiden and seller. *G. R. Oldroyd*

CUBAN NIGHTS (USA)   5 b.g. Our Native (USA) – Havana Moon (USA)   53
(Cox's Ridge (USA)) [1996 –, a70: a11g⁶ a9.4g² a12g* a12g⁵ a12g* a12g⁵ 10.5d   a70 d
14f⁵ 1997 a12g² 16.2g² a16g³ a16g² Jun 18] sturdy gelding: fair
handicapper at best: effective at 1½m to 2m: acted on firm ground, better on
fibresand: blinkered 4 times: dead. *B. J. Llewellyn*

CUBAN REEF   5 b.m. Dowsing (USA) 124 – Cox's Pippin (USA) (Cox's Ridge   53
(USA)) [1996 52: 8m 8g 8m³ 8.3m 8.3g 8.2m² 8.1m⁵ 8.3d⁵ 10.4g⁴ 10m* 8.9g 10.1m   a–
1997 a10g⁶ a12g 9.9m 10.3d⁴ 10m* 10.5m² 9g² 10g⁴ 10.2m⁶ 10g⁶ 10m² Aug 7]
modest handicapper: won amateurs event at Lingfield in May: stayed 10.5f: acted on
firm and dead ground, no form on the all-weather: has run well when sweating: in
foal to First Trump. *W. J. Musson*

CUE MAN (IRE)   2 b.c. (Feb 19) Dancing Dissident (USA) 119 – Albona 76   –
(Neltino 97) [1997 5m May 28] 6,000 2-y-o: small colt: first foal: dam, 7f to 1½m
winner in Ireland, daughter of Cheveley Park winner Cry of Truth: in rear in maiden
at Ripon, tending to hang left. *J. L. Eyre*

CUESTA REY (USA)   3 ch.g. Lord At War (ARG) – Ms Hobby (USA) (Northern   –
Prospect (USA)) [1996 NR 1997 8m 8.5g⁵ 7m a7g 7g Oct 24] $12,200F, $37,000Y:
second foal: dam unraced half-sister to champion turf mare Just A Game: only a little
sign of ability: sold 500 gns in November. *J. W. Hills*

CUFF LINK (IRE)   7 ch.g. Caerleon (USA) 132 – Corinth Canal 77 (Troy 137)   99
[1996 –: 13.3d 1997 22.2d⁴ 13.9m³ 18.7m³ 16g³ 16g⁴ Sep 18] angular gelding: still
capable of useful form, and in frame all starts in 1997, including in listed event at
Baden-Baden on fourth start: thorough stayer, best with extreme test: acts on firm
and dead going: genuine. *Major W. R. Hern*

CUGINA   3 b.f. Distant Relative 128 – Indubitable 87 (Sharpo 132) [1996 68: 6m   99 p
7d⁶ 7.1s 1997 8.1g² 10.2s* 10s* 10.2g² 10v² Oct 11] sturdy filly: progressed into a
useful performer, winning handicaps at Chepstow and Sandown in the summer and
putting up best efforts when second to Bina Gardens in minor event at Chepstow and
to Alezal in rated stakes at Ascot last 2 starts: will stay 1½m: acts on heavy going:
likely to do better still. *G. B. Balding*

CUILLIN CAPER   5 b.m. Scottish Reel 123 – That Space (Space King 115)   –
[1996 NR 1997 17.2m Jun 25] winning hurdler: lightly raced and little form on flat.
T. R. Watson

CULCRAGGIE   2 b.c. (May 8) Weldnaas (USA) 112 – Strathrusdale (Blazing   71
Saddles (AUS)) [1997 7s⁴ 7.1s⁶ Nov 6] third foal: dam, signs of ability in NH Flat
races, from good family: around 1¾ lengths fourth at Ayr, much better effort in
maidens late in season. *J. L. Eyre*

CULRAIN 6 b.g. Hadeer 118 – La Vie En Primrose 104 (Henbit (USA) 130) [1996 –: a14.8g a12g 1997 a14g⁵ Feb 28] winning hurdler: of little account on flat nowadays. *T. H. Caldwell*

CULSYTH FLYER 6 b.g. Nomination 125 – Polly Worth 55 (Wolver Hollow – § 126) [1996 NR 1997 6f 6g Jun 16] modest sprinter at 3 yrs, well beaten in 1997: tried visored: sometimes takes little interest. *P. J. Bevan*

CULTURED KING (IRE) 2 b.g. (Apr 16) Imp Society (USA) – Regina St Cyr (IRE) (Doulab (USA) 115) [1997 7m 7.5f 7g Oct 27] 12,500Y: poor mover: second foal: half-brother to 3-y-o Cyrian: dam, Irish 9f winner, half-sister to very smart sprinter Cyrano de Bergerac: little worthwhile form in maidens. *J. G. Smyth-Osbourne*

CUMBRIAN CADET 2 br.g. (May 4) Handsome Sailor 125 – City Sound 63   71 (On Your Mark 125) [1997 5d 5m³ 5m⁵ 5g⁴ 5g² 5m² 5g⁶ 6g² 5m* 6g⁶ Sep 20] 7,000Y: half-brother to several winners, including fairly useful sprinter Ashley Rocket (by Roan Rocket) and 5-y-o Rymer's Rascal: dam 6f winner: fair performer: won maiden at Ripon in August: runner-up in valuable seller previous start: stays 6f: raced mainly on good ground or firmer: blinkered twice, running creditably first time: has been bandaged behind and unimpressive to post. *T. D. Easterby*

CUMBRIAN CARUSO 2 b.g. (Mar 27) Primo Dominie 121 – Conquista 87   86 p (Aragon 118) [1997 6f* 6m² 6s² Jun 30] 16,000Y: neat gelding: good walker: second foal: dam 1m winner: fairly useful form: won maiden at Redcar in June: good second in minor events at Ripon and Pontefract, worn down only near finish by The Rich Man on latter course: stays 6f: gelded after final start: type to train on and make a useful handicapper. *T. D. Easterby*

CURRER BELL 4 b.f. Belmez (USA) 131 – Hello Cuddles 99 (He Loves Me – 120) [1996 NR 1997 a10g Jan 28] half-sister to winners Samson-Agonistes (sprinter) and Inderaputeri (at up to 1m), both by Bold Fort: dam sprinter: no promise in Lingfield maiden. *C. Murray*

CURTELACE 7 ch.g. Nishapour (FR) 125 – Khandjar 77 (Kris 135) [1996 59§: – § 12g 10g² 10m⁵ 10f⁶ 8.9m 8.1f⁴ 1997 12.3m 8.5d⁶ 10d Sep 2] big, plain gelding: on the downgrade, and no form in 1997: irresolute. *M. P. Bielby*

CURZON STREET 3 b.f. Night Shift (USA) – Pine Ridge 80 (High Top 131)   70 [1996 64: 6m² 6m 7m 6g⁵ 1997 6m 7f² 6m 8d 12g⁴ 10s² 11.9g³ 10m a10g⁵ Nov 13] robust filly: fair maiden: left H. Candy after third start: stays 1½m: acts on firm ground, soft and equitrack: sometimes slowly away: has found little: not one to trust implicitly. *D. R. C. Elsworth*

CUT DIAMOND 2 ch.g. (Feb 27) Keen 116 – Diamond Princess 69 (Horage   60 124) [1997 6m⁶ 7g 6d Jun 23] 20,000Y: fourth foal: half-brother to 3-y-o Princess Topaz and 1¼m winner Prince of Spades (by Shavian): dam, 1½m winner, half-sister to smart sprinter Princess Seal: easily best effort in maidens at Goodwood on debut. *P. F. I. Cole*

CUTTHROAT KID (IRE) 7 b.g. Last Tycoon 131 – Get Ahead 58 (Silly Season – 127) [1996 67: 11.1d⁵ 13d 13s³ a16g³ 15.8s² 16f⁴ 15d 13.1g³ 1997 a14.8g⁴ Feb 12] sturdy gelding: fair staying handicapper: well beaten only 7-y-o start. *Mrs M. Reveley*

CUTTING ANSHAKE 2 gr.g. (Apr 5) Anshan 119 – Golden Scissors 76 (Kala- – glow 132) [1997 10s 8m a8g⁴ a8g* Dec 8] fourth foal: half-brother to 5-y-o Scissor   a51 Ridge: dam stayed 2m on flat, 3m over hurdles: won 16-runner seller at Southwell in December, hanging left: should stay 1¼m: well beaten on turf. *M. R. Channon*

CYBERTECHNOLOGY 3 b.c. Environment Friend 128 – Verchinina 99 (Star   87 Appeal 133) [1996 85: 7g 7.9g* 7m² 1997 10m⁴ 11.9d² 10.1g⁵ 10g 7m* 7f⁴ 8m 8d⁴ Oct 16] workmanlike colt: fairly useful handicapper: won at Newmarket in August: best form at 7f/1m: acts on firm and dead ground: blinkered (ran poorly) fourth start: sold 30,000 gns and joined Mrs J. Cecil. *B. W. Hills*

CYRANO'S LAD (IRE) 8 b. or br.g. Cyrano de Bergerac 120 – Patiala (Crocket   115 130) [1996 104: 6m⁶ 7g⁴ 5m⁶ 6m* 6.1m* 6m 6m⁴ 6m⁴ 6g² 5.6m 6g⁶ 6g 1997 7g⁶ 6m* 6g⁴ 6m* 6g 5d⁴ 5.2g 6m Sep 27] tall, good-topped gelding: unimpressive mover: smart performer, better than ever in 1997: won handicap at Newmarket and listed race at Lingfield (by head from My Best Valentine) in May: excellent fourth of 15 to dead-heaters Coastal Bluff and Ya Malak in Nunthorpe Stakes at York in August: best form at 5f/6f: acts on firm and dead going: suited by forcing tactics: game and genuine. *C. A. Dwyer*

CYRIAN (IRE) 3 b.g. Persian Bold 123 – Regina St Cyr (IRE) (Doulab (USA) 93 115) [1996 NR 1997 a8.5g* 10d² 12s* 11.9g 12m 13.9g⁶ Aug 19] 13,000F, 11,500Y: tall, good-topped gelding: first foal: dam, Irish 9f winner, half-sister to very smart sprinter Cyrano de Bergerac: fairly useful performer: won maiden at Wolverhampton in March and handicap at Newbury in May: badly hampered last 2 starts: should stay beyond 1½m: acts on fibresand, and on good to firm and soft ground: has a high head carriage: gelded after final start. *P. F. I. Cole*

CZARNA (IRE) 6 b.g. Polish Precedent (USA) 131 – Noble Dust (USA) (Dust 67 § Commander (USA)) [1996 84d: 8d 7g² 7m³ 8m 7.1d⁴ 7m 10m 10.1m⁴ 9g 10.4g 7g a44 § a8g a9.4g 1997 a12g⁴ a10g a8g 8f² 10g 8.2g May 17] big gelding: fair handicapper on turf, poor on the all-weather: probably stayed 1¼m: acted on firm going: sometimes tongue tied: unreliable: dead. *C. E. Brittain*

CZAR WARS 2 b.c. (May 19) Warrshan (USA) 117 – Dutch Czarina 45 (Prince 64 Sabo 123) [1997 7g⁵ 7m⁴ 7d* 7m 8g Oct 17] 18,000 2-y-o: first foal: dam 1¼m winner at 4 yrs, half-sister to useful stayer Double Dutch: made all in maiden at Warwick in August: well beaten both subsequent starts: should stay at least 1¼m. *P. T. Dalton*

CZECH MAITE 2 b.f. (Apr 4) Komaite (USA) – Miss Mint (Music Maestro 119) – [1997 6.1g Sep 28] 4,500Y: fourth foal: half-sister to a winner in Belgium by Tina's Pet: dam most disappointing maiden: showed nothing in maiden at Nottingham. *Mrs J. R. Ramsden*

D

DAANIERA (IRE) 7 gr.g. Standaan (FR) 118 – Right Cash (Right Tack 131) – [1996 –, a45d: a5g a5g⁴ a5g a5g a5g⁶ a5g a5g⁴ a5g⁵ a5g⁴ 1997 a5g³ a5g a5g Apr 8] a35 workmanlike gelding: poor mover: poor handicapper: has form at 7f, races at 5f nowadays: acts on any all-weather/turf: usually blinkered/visored: usually races prominently: none too consistent: sold and sent to Kuwait. *P. Howling*

DAAWE (USA) 6 b.h. Danzig (USA) – Capo di Monte 118 (Final Straw 127) 86 [1996 80: a7g⁶ a8g⁵ a6g* a7g² a6g a6g a6g* a6g 6.1g² 6m* 6g⁴ a5g* 6m* 6m 6f⁵ 6d⁴ 6g 5m³ 5d 5g 6g³ 6f³ 5s 1997 a6g⁵ 6m⁵ a5g* 6s 5d³ 6d³ 6g* 6s 6m⁵ 5m² 5g⁵ 5m⁶ 6g 5m 6g 5m⁶ Oct 1] big, robust horse: fairly useful handicapper: won at Southwell in April and Redcar (hung left) in June: left Mrs V. Aconley after thirteenth start: effective from 5f to 7f: acts on fibresand and on firm and dead ground, below form on soft: blinkered once, often used to be visored (only on last 3 starts at 6 yrs, when far from discredited): usually races prominently: tough and game. *J. A. Glover*

DA BOSS 2 ch.c. (Feb 19) Be My Chief (USA) 122 – Lady Kris (IRE) (Kris 135) 70 [1997 6d³ 7.1d⁶ 6g⁶ 7.1g⁶ 7g Sep 24] 34,000Y: lengthy colt: third foal: half-brother to Lima (by Distant Relative), fairly useful 6f winner at 2 yrs in 1996, and 4-y-o Al's Alibi (by Alzao): dam, Irish 1¼m winner, half-sister to Gimcrack winner Bel Bolide: fair form in maidens: disappointing third and final starts: should stay at least 1m. *W. R. Muir*

DAFFODIL EXPRESS (IRE) 4 b.f. Skyliner 117 – Miss Henry 78 (Blue – Cashmere 129) [1996 48d: 6g 6m⁴ 7m 6m 5m a7g a6g 1997 10d 11.1s a14g Dec 18] seems of little account nowadays. *M. J. Ryan*

DAGGERS DRAWN (USA) 2 ch.c. (Feb 18) Diesis 133 – Sun And Shade 114 93 (Ajdal (USA) 130) [1997 6g* 6m* 7m* 7g⁶ Oct 18]

When it came to the sharp end of what was expected to be his toughest battle, Daggers Drawn performed in a manner which suggested that the name Hasty Retreat would have been more appropriate. Unbeaten in three starts and considered the chief threat to the French challenger Xaar in the Dewhurst Stakes at Newmarket, Daggers Drawn was off the bit over two furlongs out and dropped right away going into the Dip, eased once his chance had gone and

Salomon Brothers Richmond Stakes, Goodwood—
Daggers Drawn justifies heavy support, landing the odds decisively from Lord Kintyre

beating only one of his six rivals home. Daggers Drawn had shown in the Laurent-Perrier Rose Champagne Stakes at Doncaster on his previous start that he was no quitter, and a reproduction of that form would have seen him finish second, albeit a remote second, to Xaar. By far the most likely explanation, therefore, is that all wasn't well with Daggers Drawn at Newmarket. He deserves another chance, though whether he'll be up to troubling the best is another matter. A compact colt with a none too impressive action in his slower paces, Daggers Drawn neither looks nor moves like a top-class racehorse, as well as still having a fair way to go in terms of form to be regarded as one.

The dogs had been barking Daggers Drawn for some time before he made his debut, in a minor event at Newmarket in July, and 11/4-on were the odds returned on him following a four-length win gained despite clear signs of inexperience. Daggers Drawn also started at odds on for his next two races, both of them Group 2 events. One of six runners in the Salomon Brothers

Laurent-Perrier Rose Champagne Stakes, Doncaster—
Daggers Drawn overcomes Docksider (left) and Saratoga Springs (visor)

Richmond Stakes, Daggers Drawn travelled better than he'd done first time up and was poised to challenge, though with nowhere to go, approaching the last two furlongs. Once clear he showed a good burst of speed to catch Lord Kintyre and go on to win by one and a half lengths. Daggers Drawn had just four opponents in the Champagne Stakes, one of whom, Stone of Destiny, looked well out of his depth. The Acomb Stakes winner Saratoga Springs, a 5/2-shot, was his chief market rival in receipt of 4 lb, with the Gimcrack winner Carrowkeel and Docksider, no match for Central Park in a Group 3 race at Goodwood on his previous outing, both going off at 9/1. Docksider took over after Stone of Destiny had set a sound pace for four and a half furlongs, followed closely by Daggers Drawn and Saratoga Springs, Carrowkeel now in trouble. Saratoga Springs couldn't quicken going into the final furlong but Daggers Drawn, still a length down at this point, responded willingly to strong pressure and caught Docksider around a hundred yards from home, beating him by half a length. It was no more than a workmanlike performance from the winner, one which made the 6/1 about him at the time for the Two Thousand Guineas look most unappealing.

		Sharpen Up	Atan
	Diesis	(ch 1969)	Rocchetta
	(ch 1980)	Doubly Sure	Reliance II
Daggers Drawn (USA)		(b 1971)	Soft Angels
(ch.c. Feb 18, 1995)		Ajdal	Northern Dancer
	Sun And Shade	(b 1984)	Native Partner
	(b 1989)	Shadywood	Habitat
		(ch 1982)	Milly Moss

Cliveden Stud's "Daggers Drawn"

Daggers Drawn was running on well at the end of the Champagne Stakes and an extra furlong shouldn't trouble him. Indeed, he may well stay a little further than a mile. Diesis has sired several horses who have won good races at middle distances, while Sun And Shade, whose first foal Daggers Drawn is, was successful over nine furlongs. Sun And Shade's win over that trip was one of three gained in two seasons' racing in the States, benefiting from being allowed to run on medication there after being found to be prone to breaking blood vessels after winning a six-furlong maiden at Ascot on her only outing as a two-year-old. There's plenty of stamina in the bottom line of Sun And Shade's pedigree. Her dam, Shadywood, showed fairly useful form at a mile and a quarter and a mile and a half and is a daughter of the Cheshire Oaks winner Milly Moss, a sister to the Nassau Stakes and Park Hill Stakes winner Mil's Bomb. There's another Park Hill winner in the family, too. Madame Dubois, Shadywood's first foal, won that race as well as the Prix de Royallieu in 1990. *H. R. A. Cecil*

DAHIYAH (USA) 6 b.g. Ogygian (USA) – Sticky Prospect (USA) (Mr Prospector (USA)) [1996 67, a62: a6g a7g² a6g* a6g³ a5g⁶ a6g⁵ 6f⁵ a6g 7f³ 6m* 5.1m 6f³ a7g 7g 1997 a7s* a7g⁵ a7g³ a6g 7m⁵ a6g May 8] rangy gelding: modest performer: won claimer at Southwell (first outing for present yard) in January: will prove best up to 7f: acts on firm ground and all-weather: usually visored: none too consistent. *B. Smart* — 49 a60

DAHLIDYA 2 b.f. (May 2) Midyan (USA) 124 – Dahlawise (IRE) 76 (Caerleon (USA) 132) [1997 6g 7g⁶ 6g⁴ Aug 22] 4,500Y: angular filly: third foal: half-sister to 3-y-o Denton Lad and 1995 2-y-o 7f winner Alfayza (by Danehill): dam, 2-y-o 6f winner, should have stayed 1¼m: glimmer of ability in sellers at Newmarket and Goodwood last 2 starts: should stay 1m+. *M. J. Polglase* — 32

DAHOMEY (USA) 2 b. or br.c. (May 8) Dayjur (USA) 137 – Dish Dash 118 (Bustino 136) [1997 6f Oct 3] $45,000Y: smallish colt: closely related to high-class miler Maroof (by Danzig) and half-brother to the dam of Desert King and several winners, including useful 1995 2-y-o 7f winner Mawwal (by Elmaamul): dam won Ribblesdale Stakes: 25/1, just over 7 lengths eighth of 14 to Daring Derek in maiden at Lingfield, good late headway from slow start without being given hard race: sure to do better. *C. E. Brittain* — 61 p

DAILY SPORT GIRL 8 b.m. Risk Me (FR) 127 – Net Call 108 (Song 132) [1996 43: 12.1d⁵ 11.8m² 13g³ a12g 1997 a16g a12g⁶ 13.1d⁴ 12.1g⁶ May 26] lengthy mare: unimpressive mover: poor handicapper: no form in 1997: tried blinkered. *B. J. Llewellyn* — –

DAINTREE (IRE) 3 b.f. Tirol 127 – Aunty Eileen (Ahonoora 122) [1996 66: 7m 6m⁵ 5v⁵ 1997 5m 5g 8.3g 8.2g⁴ 7g³ 7g³ 6.9m³ 7.1g³ 7g 6g⁴ a6g³ a7s² a8g⁶ Nov 17] leggy, angular filly: modest maiden: effective at 6f/7f: acts on good to firm going and the all-weather: visored last 6 starts. *H. J. Collingridge* — 50

DAINTY DAMSEL 4 b.f. Good Times (ITY) – Classy Lassy (Class Distinction) [1996 NR 1997 9m³ 8g⁵ Aug 17] second reported foal: dam ran twice at 3 yrs: little promise in maidens. *R. D. E. Woodhouse* — –

DAIRA 4 br.f. Daring March 116 – Ile de Reine 64 (Ile de Bourbon (USA) 133) [1996 72: 12d 9.9m² 12g* 12.3m 12f² 10.3d² 10m² 10m⁵ 10.4g 10m⁶ 1997 12g 12.3v 12f³ 12g³ 12g⁴ 12.4g³ 13.8g 12.1m 10.8g⁴ Oct 7] tall filly: modest handicapper: should stay beyond 1½m: acts on firm and dead ground (well beaten on heavy): blinkered penultimate start (ran poorly): sold 13,000 gns after final one. *J. D. Bethell* — 63

DALLAI (IRE) 6 b.g. Dance of Life (USA) – Wavetree (Realm 129) [1996 NR 1997 16d a16.2g Jul 25] won poor 2m maiden at Southwell in January, 1995: no form since. *G. P. Kelly* — –

DALLIANCE (IRE) 3 ch.g. Arazi (USA) 135 – Lastcomer (USA) 100 (Kris 135) [1996 NR 1997 8g 10g⁵ a9.4g* a9.4g² 9g³ 8.1d Jul 5] big, rangy gelding: fifth foal: half-brother to smart French miler Marble Maiden (by Lead On Time) and 2 other winners: dam 6f (at 2 yrs) and 1¼m winner out of half-sister to Gorytus: fairly useful form: won maiden at Wolverhampton in May: best efforts in handicaps next 2 — 94 starts, set too strong a pace final one: stays 9.4f: acts on fibresand, has raced only on good/dead ground on turf: visored final 2 starts: sold 44,000 gns and sent to Macau. *M. R. Stoute*

DALWHINNIE   4 b.f. Persian Bold 123 – Land Line (High Line 125) [1996 67:   65 d
10d⁶ 10m 13.3m³ 12g a11g 14d 12.1s⁶ 12g² 12v 1997 12g 12d³ 12d⁶ 11.9d⁵ 14.1m⁵
a14g Nov 17] poor mover: fair maiden handicapper at best: stays 13f: acts on good to
firm and dead ground, tailed off on heavy: blinkered (soundly beaten) last 2 starts:
inconsistent. *J. Wharton*

DAMANKA (IRE)   3 b.f. Slip Anchor 136 – Doumayna 79 (Kouban (FR)) [1996   –
–: 8g 7g 1997 7m 10f 10s Jun 23] workmanlike filly: well beaten in maidens and
handicaps: well bred, and sold 19,000 gns in December, to go to France. *M. Bell*

DAMARA   3 b.f. Damister (USA) 123 – Gem-May 71 (Mansingh (USA) 120)   –
[1996 NR 1997 7g⁶ 7m 10m 10.1g Oct 22] sixth foal: half-sister to 1989 2-y-o 5f
winner Susha (by Bay Express): dam, maiden plater, stayed 1½m: signs of ability but
no worthwhile form. *C. W. Fairhurst*

DAME LAURA (IRE)   3 b.f. Royal Academy (USA) 130 – Aunty (FR) 114   99
(Riverman (USA) 131) [1996 100: 5m² 5m* 5m² 5m² 6g 8m² 1997 7g 10.4g 6g* 6m
8v Oct 10] leggy filly: useful performer: made all in 3-runner minor event at
Newmarket in August: best effort as 3-y-o when eleventh of 14 to Elnadim in Diadem
Stakes at Ascot following month, never really in contention: stays 1m: acts on good
to firm ground (failed to impress in appearance on heavy). *H. Morrison*

DANCE DESIGN (IRE)   4 b.f. Sadler's Wells (USA) 132 – Elegance In   119
Design 105 (Habitat 134) [1996 119: 8d² 8m³ 10m* 12m* 10g² 1997 10m*
10g* 10d* 10d² 9.5g³ 10f 12f Nov 8]
    It has been said before that the only sure way to make a small fortune
out of owning racehorses is to start with a large one. Satish Sanan, described in
the racing Press as an 'Indian computer software tycoon', seems to have plenty
of the raw material so essential to compete with the leading international
racehorse owners—money. Mr Sanan's collection of prime bloodstock, put

Tattersalls Gold Cup, the Curragh—Dance Design dictates matters over Oscar Schindler and Taipan

together in the second half of the year, included the season's highest-priced yearling, a 2.3 million dollar colt by Mr Prospector purchased at Keeneland September Sale, and two record-breaking lots at Tattersalls December Sales. Mr Sanan paid 2.5 million guineas—a world record price for a foal—for a brother to the 1991 Horse of the Year, Generous, outbidding the Coolmore team, and then parted with the same amount to buy the four-year-old Sadler's Wells filly Dance Design, shattering the record auction price for a filly in training set twelve months earlier at the same sale by another daughter of Sadler's Wells, the Prix Saint-Alary winner Luna Wells.

The game and genuine Dance Design won the 1996 Kildangan Stud Irish Oaks and has a pedigree right out of the top drawer. It is planned to keep her in training for another year before retiring her to the paddocks. The decision of Dance Design's previous owners to continue racing her as a four-year-old paid off with successive victories on her first three starts, all at the Curragh, in a listed event and the Tattersalls Gold Cup (from Oscar Schindler and Taipan, both of whom were reappearing) in May and the Independent Newspapers Pretty Polly Stakes (for the second time) at the end of June. Dance Design's four remaining races were all in Group/Grade 1 events outside Ireland and she failed to add to her victories, finishing a good second to Oxalagu at Munich and a creditable third to Memories of Silver in the Beverly D Stakes at Arlington, both in August, before running well below form in the Yellow Ribbon Stakes at Santa Anita in November and, six days later, in the Breeders' Cup Turf at Hollywood Park.

		Northern Dancer	Nearctic
	Sadler's Wells (USA)	(b 1961)	Natalma
	(b 1981)	Fairy Bridge	Bold Reason
Dance Design (IRE)		(b 1975)	Special
(b.f. 1993)		Habitat	Sir Gaylord
	Elegance In Design	(b 1966)	Little Hut
	(ch 1986)	Areola	Kythnos
		(ch 1968)	Alive Alivo

The pedigree of the sturdy Dance Design was covered fully in *Race-horses of 1996*, though the record of her dam Elegance In Design (a winning sister to the Coronation Stakes winner Chalon) needs updating with the information that her third living foal, the two-year-old Hibernian Rhapsody (by Darshaan), became her second winning offspring when successful in a Galway maiden in September over an extended mile on his only start. Dance Design is effective at a mile and a quarter to a mile and a half, and acts on good to firm and dead ground, probably on soft. She is amenable to being held up or ridden in front and is altogether a likeable filly. *D. K. Weld, Ireland*

DANCE MELODY 3 b.f. Rambo Dancer (CAN) 107 – Cateryne (Ballymoss 136) [1996 –: 6m 6m⁶ 8.1m 7f⁶ a8.5g 1997 7g 8g⁶ a8g 11s 7m 8g Oct 22] no worthwhile form, including in sellers. *G. R. Oldroyd* –

DANCE PARADE (USA) 3 ch.f. Gone West (USA) – River Jig (USA) 98 (Irish River (FR) 131) [1996 102: 5m* 5m* 5m* 8d 1997 7.3g* 8m May 4] good-topped filly: good mover: useful performer: won Queen Mary Stakes at 2 yrs: won Fred Darling Stakes at Newbury, always well positioned in steadily-run race and leading inside last 1f to beat Seebe ¾ length: no danger from halfway in One Thousand Guineas at Newmarket following month (reported by trainer to have been very ill afterwards): should stay 1m: sent to N. Drysdale, USA. *P. F. I. Cole* 107

DANCE SO SUITE 5 b.g. Shareef Dancer (USA) 135 – Three Piece (Jaazeiro (USA) 127) [1996 94, a–: 12g* 12m* 12m 10m⁶ 10.4m³ 12g⁴ 12g³ 12s⁶ 1997 10.1m 10m⁴ 12s 12m⁵ 12d³ 12g* 12m³ 12d² Oct 16] close-coupled gelding: useful handicapper: won at Epsom in September: ran very well at Newmarket afterwards, head second of 20 to Ihtiyati final start: seems suited by around 1½m: acts on good to firm and soft ground, modest form on equitrack at 3 yrs: wears a dropped noseband: has been bandaged. *P. F. I. Cole* 101 a–

DANCES WITH DREAMS   3 b.f. Be My Chief (USA) 122 – Oh So Well (IRE)   109
(Sadler's Wells (USA) 132) [1996 98p: 6d* 8s² 1997 8d⁴ 10.5d 10.2m³ 8.1s Aug 30]
good-topped filly: useful performer: best effort when about length fourth of 7 behind
Always Loyal in Poule d'Essai des Pouliches in May: third to Fiji in listed race at
Chepstow in July, best subsequent run: should be suited by further than 1m: acts on
soft ground: has been bandaged behind. *P. W. Chapple-Hyam*

DANCES WITH HOOVES   5 b.g. Dancing Dissident (USA) 119 – Princesse   58 d
Legere (USA) (Alleged (USA) 138) [1996 82: 8s³ 7.5m² 8s 1997 a10g* a10g a8g 8s
9m 10m⁵ 8d 7.1m 8m 10m Oct 23] tall gelding: modest form at best in 1997: won
weak maiden at Lingfield in January: stays 1¼m: acts on good to firm and soft going
and on equitrack: tried blinkered, out of form. *D. J. S. ffrench Davis*

DANCETHENIGHTAWAY   3 gr.f. Efisio 120 – Dancing Diana 82 (Raga   100
Navarro (ITY) 119) [1996 82: 5.1f³ 5.1m* 5f² 6g² 5.2m⁴ 1997 6f⁴ a6g³ 5.1d* 6d⁶
5m⁶ 5g 5d 5.1m² 5m³ 5g 6m⁶ 5v* 5d Oct 16] leggy filly: useful handicapper: won at
Chester in May and at Ascot (best effort, led inside final 1f and held Ansellman a
neck) in October: stays 6f: acts on any going: active sort, often sweating and on toes:
tends to carry head high and edge right: inconsistent. *B. J. Meehan*

DANCE TO THE BEAT   2 b.f. (Mar 13) Batshoof 122 – Woodleys (Tyrnavos   58
129) [1997 5.1m 5.7g⁵ 7g 7m a8.5g² a8g⁶ a6g* a6g² Dec 22] 4,500Y: half-sister to   a52
4-y-o Compass Pointer and a winner in Germany by Local Suitor: dam unraced
daughter of Cheveley Park winner Cry of Truth: modest performer: won seller at
Wolverhampton in December by 5 lengths: best form at 6f, should stay further: stays
7f: acts on the all-weather: blinkered last 2 starts. *Martyn Meade*

DANCE TRICK (USA)   2 ch.f. (Apr 4) Diesis 133 – Performing Arts 104 (The   101
Minstrel (CAN) 135) [1997 6s* 6m* Jun 6] lengthy, unfurnished filly: fluent mover:
third foal: half-sister to 3-y-o Chorus Song and smart 1995 2-y-o 6f winner Wood-
borough (by Woodman): dam, 1990 sprint winner and third in Irish 1000 Guineas,
sister to The Noble Player: won maiden at Newbury in May and listed race at
Epsom in June, looking unbalanced on course for most part but beating Another
Fantasy by 1¾ lengths (rated value 3) in latter: should stay 1m: sold to Godolphin.
P. W. Chapple-Hyam

DANCING AL   2 br.c. (Apr 30) Alnasr Alwasheek 117 – Lyne Dancer (Be My   –
Native (USA) 122) [1997 6m 7s 7m 7g⁵ Aug 6] third foal: dam tailed off in a juvenile
hurdle: no worthwhile form. *J. S. Moore*

DANCING-ALONE   5 ch.g. Adbass (USA) 102 – Lady Alone 59 (Mr Fluoro-   50
carbon 126) [1996 NR 1997 a12g² Feb 10] first run since 1994 and first form when
second of 6 in minor event at Southwell, pulling hard. *R. J. R. Williams*

DANCING CAVALIER   4 b.g. Nalchik (USA) – Miss Admington 71 (Double   77
Jump 131) [1996 72§: a8g³ a8g* a11g* a11g² a11g² a12g⁴ 10.3d³ 12s³ a12g* 14.1g²
14.1m⁶ 14d³ 11.8g³ 16m⁴ 1997 a12g a12g⁵ a11g³ a12g a12g² 12m⁴ 13.8g* a14g⁴
14.1m* 16g⁵ 14.1g⁴ 14.1d⁶ 14d 14g⁶ 14.1g* 14.9d* 14.6d 15.9m⁶ 12m⁴ 13.8g³
16.2d⁶ 16.1d³ Aug 25] fair handicapper: won at Catterick in March, Nottingham in
April, and Nottingham (apprentices) and Warwick in June: effective at 1¾m to 2m:
acts on good to firm and soft ground and on fibresand: blinkered once (below form):
often gets behind. *R. Hollinshead*

DANCING CORMORANT   4 b.g. Shareef Dancer (USA) 135 – Cormorant   –
Creek 73 (Gorytus (USA) 132) [1996 NR 1997 11.1s⁵ Jul 1] well beaten at 2 yrs and
in claimer in July. *P. Monteith*

DANCING DERVISH   2 b.g. (Apr 30) Shareef Dancer (USA) 135 – Taj Victory   58 p
68 (Final Straw 127) [1997 6s⁶ 6.9d⁴ Oct 21] 26,000Y: good-bodied gelding: third
foal: dam, 1¼m to 13f winner, half-sister to Ascot Gold Cup winner Indian Queen:
better effort in maidens when front-running fourth of 9 at Folkestone: bred to be
suited by 1¼m+: will improve again. *I. A. Balding*

DANCING DESTINY   5 b.m. Dancing Brave (USA) 140 – Tender Loving Care   45
105 (Final Straw 127) [1996 48: 12.3m 10.1g 11f² 10.1g⁶ 1997 a8g 10.1g a8g³ a10g⁶
Dec 19] quite attractive mare: poor maiden: stays 11f: acts on firm ground, dead and
fibresand. *R. Bastiman*

DANCING DROP   3 b.f. Green Desert (USA) 127 – Moon Drop 103 (Dominion   103
123) [1996 92: 5g² 5m 5m³ 6g* 7m³ 6f* 7m³ 1997 7.1g³ 8d² 7g 8.1s 7d² 8v² 7g³
Oct 27] sturdy filly: useful performer: best efforts at 3 yrs when second in handicaps
at Ascot (to Brave Kris, in listed event) in June and Goodwood (to Law Commisson)
in September, and when beaten 1¼ lengths by Jafn in listed event at Ascot in October:
effective at 7f/1m: acts on any going. *R. Hannon*

DANCING EM   2 b.f. (Feb 16) Rambo Dancer (CAN) 107 – Militia Girl (Rarity   35
129) [1997 5g 6d 7g 7.5v³ 7m⁵ 8m Sep 25] tall, lengthy filly: closely related to 11f
winner Tasmim (by Be My Guest) and half-sister to 2 winners, including 4-y-o Jo
Mell: dam once-raced half-sister to Grade 1 middle-distance winner King's Island:
poor maiden: has run in seller. *T. D. Easterby*

DANCING FEATHER   3 ch.f. Suave Dancer (USA) 136 – English Spring   72 d
(USA) 116 (Grey Dawn II 132) [1996 NR 1997 10m⁵ 12.1m⁴ 12.3s³ 13.1g 11.1m
a10g⁶ a10g Nov 25] good-topped filly: seventh foal: half-sister to several winners,
including useful Fragrant Hill (up to 11f, by Shirley Heights): dam best at 1m/1¼m:
fair form in maidens first 2 starts: subsequently lost her way: stays 1½m: blinkered
final start. *B. W. Hills*

DANCING GREY   2 gr.g. (May 3) Petong 126 – Mountain Harvest (FR) 64§   –
(Shirley Heights 130) [1997 7m a7g⁶ Nov 15] third foal: half-brother to a winner in
Italy by Cyrano de Bergerac: dam (ran 4 times) probably stayed 1¾m: well held in
maidens. *P. W. Harris*

DANCING ICON (IRE)   2 b.f. (Feb 27) Mujtahid (USA) 118 – Babushka (IRE)   74
(Dance of Life (USA)) [1997 6d 5.2f 5m* 5s 5s Oct 15] IR 16,000Y: sturdy,
workmanlike filly: has a roundish action: first foal: dam Irish 2-y-o 1m winner out of
half-sister to high-class miler Then Again: won maiden at Haydock in August: well
beaten otherwise, including in nurseries: should stay at least 6f: probably unsuited
by soft ground: sweating and decidedly edgy second start: sold and sent to Czech
Republic. *R. Hannon*

DANCING IMAGE   4 ch.g. Salse (USA) 128 – Reflection 111 (Mill Reef (USA)   106
141) [1996 85: 8m² 8g³ 8g* 8m* 7.1m² 7m² 1997 7d² 8m⁴ 8.1g⁶ 7m* 7g³ 8.5g⁴ 7m
Sep 27] compact gelding: good mover: useful performer: won minor event (easily) at
Goodwood in August: best effort when 3½ lengths fourth to Intikhab in listed race at
Epsom following month: effective at 7f to 8.5f: acts on good to firm ground and dead:
ideally suited by waiting tactics in truly-run race: consistent: joined J. Sheppard in
USA but withdrawn from Grade 2 race Oct 18 after mistake in administration of
medication. *I. A. Balding*

DANCING JACK   4 ch.c. Clantime 101 – Sun Follower (Relkino 131) [1996   –
58d: a5g² a5g⁴ a5g² a6g⁵ a6g² 6f⁴ 5m 6g 5m 6f⁶ 5m a6g a10g a5g a5g 1997 a7g 5m
5.1m 8m 6m 5m Aug 18] of little account nowadays. *J. J. Bridger*

DANCING LAWYER   6 b.g. Thowra (FR) – Miss Lawsuit (Neltino 97) [1996 –,   53
a87d: a10g⁶ a8g* a8g 8f 7f 5.7m⁶ 6m a6g 8.5m a7g a7g a8g 1997 7f⁵ 7m⁵ 8g 7m
7.6g⁶ 8m 10g 8.1g³ 8m² Sep 24] sturdy gelding: modest performer nowadays: left B.
Meehan after fourth start: effective at 7f/1m: acts on firm and dead ground and on
equitrack: blinkered fourth start: takes keen hold. *K. R. Burke*

DANCING MYSTERY   3 b.g. Beveled (USA) – Batchworth Dancer 67   49
(Ballacashtal (CAN)) [1996 –: 5d 6g⁴ 1997 a6g 5.7d 5m 6d 5d⁵ 5m² 5g² 5g⁵ 5g 5.7g   a76
5m a6g* a5g* Nov 18] close-coupled gelding: fair on all-weather, poor on turf: won
maiden at Southwell in October and handicap (best effort) at Lingfield in November:
a sprinter: acts on good to firm going and the all-weather: pulls hard: sometimes
blinkered, including last 3 starts: has been unruly in stalls. *E. A. Wheeler*

DANCING PHANTOM   2 b.c. (Feb 2) Darshaan 133 – Dancing Prize (IRE)   91 p
99 (Sadler's Wells (USA) 132) [1997 7.6d² Aug 28] 120,000Y: third foal: dam,
lightly-raced maiden out of smart performer at up to 1m Aim For The Top, was third
in Lingfield Oaks Trial: 11/4, 1¼ lengths second of 11 to Mutamam in maiden at
Lingfield, staying on not knocked about: should stay at least 1¼m: should improve.
M. R. Stoute

DANCING QUEEN (IRE)   3 b.f. Sadler's Wells (USA) 132 – Bay Shade (USA)   64 d
90 (Sharpen Up 127) [1996 69+: 6m⁴ 7m³ 1997 10d⁵ 10m³ 12d 9.9v⁶ 10.1g⁴ a14.8g³

12g Sep 15] close-coupled filly: disappointing maiden: should stay 1½m: has hung badly left. *M. Bell*

DANCING RIO (IRE) 2 ch.g. (Mar 9) Roi Danzig (USA) – Tameen (FR) 63 (Pharly (FR) 130) [1997 5s⁵ 6m⁵ 6.1g⁵ a6g a7g a5g Dec 8] 20,000 2-y-o: strong gelding: half-brother to 1¼m winner Tambora (by Darshaan) and 3 winners abroad: dam French 1m and 1¼m winner: modest form in maidens and minor event on turf: well beaten on fibresand: should stay further than 6f. *P. C. Haslam*

DANCING SIOUX 5 b.g. Nabeel Dancer (USA) 120 – Sutosky 78 (Great Nephew 51 126) [1996 66d, a80d: a7g* a7g* a7g 7.1g⁵ a7g³ 7g a8.5g a7g 7g a7g⁴ a7g 7g a6g a65 1997 a7g a6g² a6g² 7.1d⁴ a8.5g³ a7g⁶ 6g³ Aug 2] angular gelding: modest handicapper: stays 8.5f: acts on any turf/all-weather: tried blinkered: none too consistent. *R. Guest*

DANCING WOLF (IRE) 2 b.f. (Apr 29) Wolfhound (USA) 126 – Aigue 96 76 (High Top 131) [1997 5m 6g⁴ 5m³ 6d Oct 16] 57,000 2-y-o: tall, unfurnished filly: fourth foal: half-sister to useful 7f (at 2 yrs) and 1¼m winner Mezzogiorno (by Unfuwain), also third in Oaks, and fairly useful 1¼m winner Rainbow Top (by Rainbow Quest): dam, stayed 1m, sister to smart Torchon from family of Mystiko: fair form in frame in minor event at Salisbury and maiden at Kempton: bandaged behind, disappointing in nursery at Newmarket: should stay beyond 6f. *Miss Gay Kelleway*

DANDE FLYER 4 b. or br.g. Clantime 101 – Lyndseylee 96 (Swing Easy (USA) 76 d 126) [1996 77: 5.1g 5.1g⁵ 5g³ 5.7m³ 5f⁴ 5m⁴ 5m⁴ 5m⁵ 5g 1997 a5g⁵ a6g⁵ a5g 5g² 5g 5g 5d 6f 5m 5m 5m⁵ 5m⁴ 5m⁴ 5.1g⁴ 5g⁶ 6m 5.3g³ Aug 27] neat gelding: fair handicapper: without a win since 2 yrs, and mostly disappointing in 1997: raced mainly at 5f: acts on fibresand, best on good ground or firmer on turf: no improvement in blinkers or visor: usually bandaged: sometimes slowly away: sometimes hangs left/finds little: gelded after final start. *D. W. P. Arbuthnot*

DANDE TIMES 2 ch.g. (May 7) Timeless Times (USA) 99 – Miss Merlin 79 54 (Manacle 123) [1997 5.1m⁵ 6f⁵ 6g³ 6m³ 6g⁶ 6d⁵ a5g⁴ a6g a5g⁴ Dec 19] 13,000Y: half-brother to several winners, including fairly useful 5f performer Lyndseylee (by Swing Easy): dam 6f winner, including at 2 yrs: modest maiden on turf, poor on all-weather: trained first 3 starts by D. Arbuthnot: stays 6f: blinkered fourth start. *K. T. Ivory*

DANDY REGENT 3 b.g. Green Desert (USA) 127 – Tahilla 112 (Moorestyle 69 137) [1996 –: 6m 1997 7m 6m 6m⁵ 7m⁴ 7m² Sep 25] angular gelding: fair maiden handicapper: off course over 4 months, best effort at Goodwood final start: will stay 1m: raced only on good to firm ground: sold 11,000 gns in October. *C. A. Cyzer*

DANEGOLD (IRE) 5 b.g. Danehill (USA) 126 – Cistus 123 (Sun Prince 128) 70 d [1996 81§, a–§: 10.1m 8m⁶ 10.5g² 10m⁵ 9f 10.2f 8m⁵ 10.5d³ 8d 8g 10s 1997 10m³ a–§ 10g 10s 11.7m 10s 10.2g⁶ 10d Oct 20] sturdy, close-coupled gelding: fairly useful handicapper at best: disappointing at 5 yrs: effective at 1m to 10.5f: acts on good to firm and soft ground, below form on all-weather: wears visor: has been reluctant to race: fairly useful hurdler: unreliable. *M. R. Channon*

DANEHILL DANCER (IRE) 4 b.c. Danehill (USA) 126 – Mira Adonde 107 (USA) (Sharpen Up 127) [1996 117: 7d* 8m⁶ 8g 6m⁵ 6.5d³ 6f 1997 6g May 15] big, lengthy colt: carries condition: one of the top 2-y-o's of 1995, winning 3 races, notably Heinz 57 Phoenix Stakes at Leopardstown and National Stakes at the Curragh: won Greenham Stakes at Newbury on reappearance at 3 yrs, but found it tough in good company afterwards: only seventh to Royal Applause in Duke of York Stakes in May: effective at 6f and 7f: acted on good to firm ground and dead: held up: retired to Kilsheelan Stud, Co Tipperary (fee Ir 4,000 gns, Oct 1st). *N. A. Callaghan*

DANEHILL PRINCESS (IRE) 3 b.f. Danehill (USA) 126 – Top Glad (USA) 51 § (I'm Glad (ARG)) [1996 62, a50: 5g⁴ 5.1g² 6.1m⁴ 6m⁴ 6m² 5.9f² 6d³ 7m⁵ 6m² 7m³ a– § 7g⁵ 6.1m⁵ 6f⁴ 6m a7g a7g³ 1997 a9.4f 7.1d 7g 8m⁴ 8f 6.1m Sep 15] stocky filly: modest maiden: stayed 7f: acted on firm and dead ground, and on fibresand: sometimes visored/blinkered: irresolute: in foal to King's Signet. *R. Hollinshead*

DANESKAYA 4 b.f. Danehill (USA) 126 – Boubskaia (Niniski (USA) 125) [1996 115 8g* 8g² 8g⁶ 1997 8g³ 8d³ 8d² 8g* 8m⁴ 7d⁵ Oct 19] 800,000 francs Y: first foal: dam,

French 1m winner, closely related to Gran Criterium winner Will Dancer and half-sister to useful sprinter Dancing Eagle: smart performer: won minor events in Provinces at 2 yrs and at Deauville at 3 yrs: off course over 2 months, improved to win Prix d'Astarte at Deauville in August by length from Rebecca Sharp: best effort when running-on 3¾ lengths fourth of 9 to Spinning World in Prix du Moulin de Longchamp: probably better at 1m than shorter: acts on good to firm ground, probably on soft: sent to USA. *A. Fabre, France*

DANESMAN (IRE)   4 b.g. Danehill (USA) 126 – Vernonhills (Hard Fought) 125)   – p
[1996 NR 1997 13.3d Sep 20] sturdy gelding: has a quick action: progressive form (rated 96p) at 2 yrs for J. Gosden: bought 18,000 gns and gelded shortly before reappearance: in need of race, ran much better than position suggests in handicap at Newbury, tiring under 2f out and eased: should stay at least 1¼m. *W. R. Muir*

DANETIME (IRE)   3 b.c. Danehill (USA) 126 – Allegheny River (USA)   119 p
(Lear Fan (USA) 130) [1996 96p: 5m⁴ 6m* 7g² 1997 8m 7m 6d 6g² 6g* 6m*
6d³ Sep 5]

If 'an old-fashioned gamble' ever really had gone out of fashion, then Michael Tabor is doing his best to bring about a revival. The former bookmaker clearly likes having a flutter himself. When he takes an interest, the prices tumble, and in the latest season he found a most promising vehicle for his investments in the three-year-old colt Danetime. Not once, but twice, those connected with Danetime went for a massive touch on him, and they did so in two of the most hotly-contested handicaps in the calendar, sending him off favourite in thirty-runner fields for both the Wokingham at Royal Ascot and the Stewards' Cup at Goodwood. The biggest gamble of the Royal meeting was the first indication that, in Danetime, Mr Tabor knew he had another pattern-class performer.

Unfortunately for his connections, Danetime did not actually win the Wokingham. The crucial moment probably occurred the previous morning when the draw was made and Danetime ended up in stall nineteen. Reportedly under strict instructions to switch to the stand rail, the American jockey Gary Stevens made a bold bid to complete the manoeuvre at the back of the field in

Vodafone Stewards' Cup (Handicap), Goodwood—
the most competitive sprint handicap of the season goes to the favourite Danetime (No. 7);
the angle is deceptive and he holds on from My Best Valentine, Dashing Blue (far rail) and Faraway Lass

the first furlong, but he was checked in the process and was so again when he then tried to look for a way forward. With only a handful of the runners behind him at the distance, Danetime made up the best part of ten lengths but went down by a head to Selhurstpark Flyer. That was off a BHB mark of 91. We rated him as a two-length winner, but subsequent events revealed that he was a much better horse even than that.

Danetime again looked a better horse than the bare result when winning a rated stakes at Newmarket in July from Elnadim, another horse on his way to the top. Next came the Stewards' Cup. No three-year-old had won the race since Autumn Sunset in 1983, and on this occasion when Danetime got a draw on the stand side it was widely thought to be a disadvantage. Off a BHB mark of 100, Danetime nevertheless came out on top in the most hotly-contested sprint handicap of the season. 'A bit more than £200,000' was won by his owner as Danetime went to the front on the stand side two furlongs out and held on, from My Best Valentine and Dashing Blue on the far side, by a neck and half a length. The second and third both went on to win listed races before the season was out. Danetime was pitched straight into into a Group 1. A high temperature ruled him out on the day of the Nunthorpe Stakes, so it was left to the Haydock Park Sprint Cup in September to demonstrate what virtually everyone was now certain of, that Danetime was a sprinter to be reckoned with at the highest level. Starting 3/1 second favourite, he could not get to grips with the one-and-a-quarter-length winner Royal Applause but finished in front of everything else; it required Portman Square's justified intervention to put Tomba ahead of him as well, after more manoeuvring early on had this time resulted in Danetime causing interference.

Two questions remain. What rank will Danetime take in 1998? To us, Danetime looks a serious candidate for champion sprinter. So how did he get to June on such a favourable mark in handicaps? His two-year-old campaign had shown he was a colt of potential, but on his first two starts in 1997 that potential was tested first over a mile and then over seven furlongs. He was very coltish on the latter occasion, but that sort of distance is too far for him anyway. A sturdy, good-quartered colt with a quick action, Danetime looks every inch a sprinter in physique, and his first performance in a sprint handicap, never placed to challenge one month before the Wokingham, hinted strongly that in his case appearances would not be deceptive. Unproven at five furlongs, he acts on good to firm and dead ground, but is unlikely to be risked on firm.

		Danzig	Northern Dancer
	Danehill (USA)	(b 1977)	Pas de Nom
	(b 1986)	Razyana	His Majesty
Danetime (IRE)		(b 1981)	Spring Adieu
(b.c. 1994)		Lear Fan	Roberto
	Allegheny River (USA)	(b 1981)	Wac
	(b 1987)	Allesheny	Be My Guest
		(ch 1982)	Bold Sands

Danetime is by the same sire, Danehill, as his owner's dual classic winner Desert King, and he's much more like Danehill in racing character. Sold for IR 13,000 guineas as a foal, and IR 36,000 guineas as a yearling, Danetime is the third foal of Allegheny River. The first two are both are by Tirol and both are winners, Ironic in Holland and Tirano over six and a half furlongs as a two-year-old in Ireland. The next foal is another by Danehill, called Dane River; he won a six-furlong maiden at the Curragh on his debut in July but was not seen out after finishing third of seven in a listed race later in the month. Dane River is trained by Jim Bolger, who also had charge of the dam and grandam. Grandam Allesheny was a highly-regarded two-year-old six-furlong winner who went backwards at three, while Allegheny River never appeared to be much good, tried in blinkers for the first time on the last of her nine starts when she got off the mark in November as a three-year-old in the aptly-named seven-furlong Getting Out Fillies Maiden at the Curragh. Allesheny is a close

relation to the smart stayer Dam Busters and a half-sister to the dam of Bolger's
1996 Heinz 57 Phoenix Stakes winner Mantovani. *N. A. Callaghan*

DANGERMAN (IRE)   2 ch.g. (Feb 2) Pips Pride 117 – Two Magpies (Doulab   70
(USA) 115) [1997 6d 5g² 5s⁴ Jun 30] 11,500Y: lengthy, well-grown gelding: has a
round action: first foal: dam Irish 7f and 1¼m winner: in frame in maidens at Redcar (best effort) and Pontefract: should stay at least 6f: moved poorly to post on debut.
M. W. Easterby

DANGEROUS DIVA (IRE)   3 ch.f. Royal Academy (USA) 130 – Loveliest   105
(USA) (Tibaldo) [1996 NR 1997 8g³ 8g* 7m* 8g² 8d³ 10g⁵ 7m⁴ 8d⁵ 7g Oct 18]
angular filly: good mover: half-sister to several winners, notably smart 6f (at 2 yrs)
to 10.5f winner Optimistic Lass (by Mr Prospector), later dam of high-class 6f
to 1m performer Golden Opinion: dam very useful up to 10.5f in France and USA:
useful form: won minor event and listed race at the Curragh in spring: ran well
when in frame in 3 Group 3 races after, notably when ¾-length second to Swift
Gulliver in Desmond Stakes at the Curragh in August: behind in Challenge Stakes at
Newmarket final start: should stay further than 1m: yet to race on extremes of going.
A. P. O'Brien, Ireland

DANGERUS PRECEDENT (IRE)   2 ch.c. (Mar 1) Polish Precedent (USA)   – p
131 – Circus Feathers 99 (Kris 135) [1997 6m⁶ 6g⁶ 6s⁵ Oct 16] 11,000F, 27,000Y:
lengthy colt: half-brother to 3-y-o Hen Harrier and a winner in Italy by
Soviet Star: dam 1m/9f winner out of Oaks winner Circus Plume: some promise,
green and never a threat after slow start, in maidens at Pontefract and Yarmouth in
August: seemed not to handle track at Catterick: bred to be suited by at least 1m:
should still do better. *C. R. Egerton*

DANIEL'S MASCOT   3 b.g. Sharpo 132 – Kirby's Princess (Indian King (USA)   –
128) [1996 NR 1997 10s Oct 8] fourth reported foal: half-sister to 2 winners,
including Saladar (up to 1½m in Germany, by Deploy): dam poor maiden: tailed off
both starts. *A. G. Newcombe*

DANISH RHAPSODY (IRE)   4 b.g. Danehill (USA) 126 – Ardmelody (Law   107
Society (USA) 130) [1996 81: 8g 10s² 1997 10s³ 9.7m* 11.9d 10m* 10m* 10.4g
10.1g² 9d* 10m* Sep 24] tall, good-topped gelding: had a fine season, improving
into a useful performer: won handicap at Folkestone in May, minor event at Lingfield
and handicap at Goodwood (£37,000 William Hill Cup) in July and 18-runner
handicap (under 10-0) and 5-runner listed race at Goodwood in September: allowed

*William Hill Cup (Handicap), Goodwood—Danish Rhapsody makes all for the third of his five wins;
Another Time (second left) comes next followed by Champagne Prince (No. 5)
and Zaralaska (broad white face)*

to dictate gallop in last-named, quickening 4f out and holding Proper Blue ½ length: suited by around 1¼m: acts on good to firm and soft ground: front runner: game, genuine and consistent. *Lady Herries*

DANJING (IRE) 5 b.g. Danehill (USA) 126 – Beijing (USA) 89 (Northjet 136) – § [1996 94: 16.4g³ 18.7m² 16.1m 18g 1997 18.7s May 7] well-made gelding: fairly useful staying handicapper on his day: downed tools in Chester Cup only outing on flat at 5 yrs (also most unreliable over hurdles nowadays): tried blinkered: one to leave alone. *M. C. Pipe*

DANKA 3 gr.g. Petong 126 – Angel Drummer 59 (Dance In Time (CAN)) [1996 58 61: 6m 7g⁶ 7.6d 7f⁴ 1997 10.3g a14.8g⁶ a12s⁴ a12g⁴ Dec 6] good-bodied gelding: modest maiden: barely stays 1½m: acts on firm going, dead and equitrack: sometimes visored, including last 3 starts: tail swisher. *P. T. Walwyn*

DANNISTAR 5 br.m. Puissance 110 – Loadplan Lass 63 (Nicholas Bill 125) 46 [1996 47: a8.5g a12g⁴ 10.8m² a12g 10f 1997 8m 10.8m⁶ 10g 10g⁵ 10.8g a12g Oct 18] poor handicapper: trained first 3 starts by P. D. Evans: stays 11f: acts on fibresand and on good to firm ground. *W. M. Brisbourne*

DANTESQUE (IRE) 4 b.c. Danehill (USA) 126 – I Want My Say (USA) (Tilt 100 p Up (USA)) [1996 69p: 8.3m⁵ 8d⁵ 1997 8f² 8g² 10g² 10.1g* 10.1m* 11.9g⁵ 12m* 12s Nov 8] lengthy colt: useful performer: won maiden at Newcastle in July, minor event at Yarmouth in August and handicap at Doncaster (travelled well to lead 2f out, idled before beating Elbaaha 1¼ lengths) in September: stays 1½m: best form on good going and firmer, probably unsuited by soft: likeable type, should do well again in 1998. *G. Wragg*

DANYROSS (IRE) 2 b.f. (Feb 9) Danehill (USA) 126 – Rosita 67 (Bold Lad 99 (IRE) 133) [1997 5m³ 5s* 5m⁴ 6d² 6g⁴ 6m⁶ 6d⁵ a6.5s⁴ a6f⁵ Nov 6] IR 28,000Y: small, sturdy ex-Irish filly: good walker: sixth foal: half-sister to 3 winners in Italy, including sprinters by Classic Music and Gorytus: dam 5f winner from good family: useful performer: won maiden at Navan in May: in frame in listed race at Sandown, 5-runner Railway Stakes at the Curragh (length second to King of Kings, best effort) and Cherry Hinton Stakes at Newmarket (under 3 lengths behind Asfurah) on next 3 starts: beaten around 8 lengths in Grade 2 event but tailed off in allowance race, both at Aqueduct: stays 6f: blinkered sixth start: trained until after next one by A. O. Brien. *G. Sciacca, USA.*

DANZAS 3 b.g. Polish Precedent (USA) 131 – Dancing Rocks 118 (Green Dancer 78 (USA) 132) [1996 NR 1997 8.1g⁵ 8.3s³ 10.2m³ 10.2f³ 10.3d 10g Oct 24] well-made, attractive gelding: half-brother to several winners, including smart Gai Bulga (up to 1¼m, by Kris) and useful 1993 2-y-o Glatisant (by Rainbow Quest): dam won Nassau Stakes: fair form in maidens second and third starts: poor efforts last 2, then sold (to join J. M. Bradley) 10,000 gns: stays 1¼m: has had tongue tied. *R. Charlton*

DANZIG FLYER (IRE) 2 b.c. (Mar 30) Roi Danzig (USA) – Fenland Express 67 (IRE) (Reasonable (FR) 119) [1997 7g⁴ a7g² 7g⁴ 7.5d³ 7s 10g 8d Oct 20] 6,200Y: a77 sturdy colt: first foal: dam unraced: fair maiden: stays 1m: acts on equitrack, yet to race on ground firmer than good on turf. *P. W. Harris*

DANZINO (IRE) 2 b.g. (Apr 19) Roi Danzig (USA) – Luvi Ullmann (Thatching – 131) [1997 6s 6g 5m 6m 7m Oct 23] IR 13,000Y: good-topped gelding: fifth foal: half-brother to useful 1996 2-y-o 5f winner Roman Imp (by Imp Society) and 3 winners in Italy: dam won 7 times in Italy at 5f/6f: well beaten in maidens. *A. P. Jarvis*

DARAPOUR (IRE) 3 b.g. Fairy King (USA) – Dawala (IRE) (Lashkari 128) 97 p [1996 NR 1997 10s 10.2m³ 10m 10m³ 11.9s³ 13.3d* Sep 20] neat gelding: has a quick action: first foal: dam, French 1½m winner, closely related to Prix du Jockey Club winner Darshaan, an outstanding family: most progressive sort: won maiden at Bath in July and Tote Autumn Cup (Handicap) at Newbury (beat Beauchamp Jade 1¼ lengths) in September: will stay 1¾m+: acts on good to firm and soft ground: sold 125,000 gns in October, and promising second over hurdles for A. P. O'Brien in December. *L. M. Cumani*

DARATOWN 4 b.g. Tragic Role (USA) – Darakah 78 (Doulab (USA) 115) [1996 – –: a8.5g a8.5g⁶ a8s 1997 a10g 8g 7g Aug 6] no worthwhile form: tried visored. *C. J. Hill*

DARAYDAN (IRE) 5 b.g. Kahyasi 130 – Delsy (FR) (Abdos 134) [1996 107: –
12s² 16.2m⁴ 18.7g² 16g 16.1m 16f⁴ 1997 22.2d³ 13.9g Aug 20] close-coupled
gelding: useful performer at best: ridden too forcefully in Queen Alexandra Stakes at
Royal Ascot then never going pace in Ebor at York in 1997: stays 18.7f: acts on firm
ground and soft: blinkered (below form) 3 times: has run well when sweating: smart
hurdler, won 3 times late in year. *M. C. Pipe*

DARAZARI (IRE) 4 b.c. Sadler's Wells (USA) 132 – Darara 129 (Top Ville 129) 117
[1996 123: 10g² 12d⁴ 12g* 12.5g* 12m² 12d 1997 12s⁴ 12d³ 12d⁴ Jun 29] strong,
well-made colt: very smart performer at 3 yrs: bit below that level in 1997, best effort
when length third of 5 to Steward in Grand Prix de Chantilly: stays 12.5f: acts on
good to firm ground, possibly on dead. *A. de Royer Dupre, France*

DARB ALOLA (USA) 3 b.c. Nureyev (USA) 131 – Kristana 96 (Kris 135) 85
[1996 96: 5.2s² 5m⁶ 5d² 1997 5m* 6m 5d 5.1m⁵ 5g⁶ Jul 26] good-quartered colt:
fairly useful performer: trotted up in weak maiden at Warwick in April: ran at least
respectably in face of stiff tasks in handicaps afterwards: should stay 6f: acts on good
to firm and soft ground: sent to UAE. *M. R. Stoute*

DARCY 3 ch.c. Miswaki (USA) 124 – Princess Accord (USA) 115 (D'Accord 97 ?
(USA)) [1996 NR 1997 8g 9d* 11.8d⁴ 10s³ 11.9g 11.9s Sep 4] 80,000Y: good-topped
colt: closely related to a winner in USA by Forty Niner: dam 6f (at 2 yrs)
to 9f winner: won maiden at Ripon in May: apparently useful form when in frame in
small fields in minor events at Leicester and Windsor but well beaten in handicaps
last 2 starts: probably stays 1½m: yet to race on going firmer than good: visored fifth
start: sold (to join N. Callaghan) 22,000 gns in October. *M. R. Stoute*

DARE 2 b.g. (May 14) Beveled (USA) – Run Amber Run (Run The Gantlet (USA)) –
[1997 6.1g⁶ Sep 28] 9,600Y: brother to useful 5f (at 2 yrs) and 7f winner Moon Over
Miami and a 1m winner, and half-brother to smart middle-distance stayer Quick
Ransom (by Hostage) and another winner: dam won up to 9f at 5 yrs in USA: never
dangerous in maiden at Nottingham: may do better. *C. James*

DARGO 3 b.c. Formidable (USA) 125 – Mountain Memory 109 (High Top 131) –
[1996 74p: 7m² 7d⁵ 1997 7.1s May 5] has a round action: better form in auction
events at 2 yrs (for M. Johnston) when fifth at Ayr: not given hard race only outing in
1997: will stay 1m. *C. W. Thornton*

DARIEN 3 b.c. Sadler's Wells (USA) 132 – Aryenne (FR) 125 (Green Dancer 72
(USA) 132) [1996 NR 1997 11g 12d³ 12m⁶ 16g 13.1g Sep 8] sturdy colt: ninth foal:
half-brother to several winners, including Derby winner Quest For Fame and smart
stayer Silver Rainbow (both by Rainbow Quest) and smart 1½m performer Yenda
(by Dancing Brave): dam, from fine family, won Criterium des Pouliches: fair
maiden: one paced, and should be suited by 2m+: unraced on extremes of ground:
has had tongue tied: visored final start: sold 26,000 gns in October and joined
R. Dickin. *R. Charlton*

DARING DEREK (USA) 2 ch.c. (Apr 4) Naevus (USA) – Gatap (USA) (Buck- 92 P
finder (USA)) [1997 6f* Oct 3] $75,000Y: compact colt: second foal: half-brother to
a winner in USA by Silver Hawk: dam, won up to 1m in USA, half-sister to Grade 1
2-y-o 8.5f winner Zoonaqua: sire (by Mr Prospector) smart at 1m/9f: short-priced
favourite, won 14-runner maiden at Lingfield impressively by 2 lengths from Jila,
soon travelling strongly from slow start and merely pushed along to settle issue:
should stay 1m, but doesn't look short of speed: held pattern race entries at 2 yrs, and
should go on to better things in 1998. *D. R. Loder*

DARING DESTINY 6 b.m. Daring March 116 – Raunchy Rita (Brigadier 95
Gerard 144) [1996 113: 6s 5.2d³ 7.1d⁶ 6m* 6g² 6f 6g* 6g* 6m 7m 1997 6m 6m 6d 6g
Oct 24] big mare: has a round action: smart performer at 5 yrs: useful form at best in
1997: has won at 7f, best as a sprinter: acts on firm and soft ground, below form on
heavy: effective blinkered/visored or not: has run well when sweating and edgy: sold
(barren to Salse) 27,000 gns in December. *K. R. Burke*

DARING FLIGHT (USA) 3 b.c. Danzig (USA) – Life At The Top 107 (Habitat 61
134) [1996 80: 5m⁴ 6g⁴ 5.7d 6m 1997 a8.5g⁴ 7g⁶ Jun 21] small colt: has a round
action: fair maiden at best: has twice run as though something amiss: stays 6f:
showed nothing on dead ground: inconsistent. *Lord Huntingdon*

DARING HEN (IRE)   7 b.m. Henbit (USA) 130 – Daring Glen (Furry Glen 121)   –
[1996 NR 1997 a16g Jan 10] NH Flat race winner but little hurdles form: visored,
well beaten in claimer only outing on flat. *R. T. Juckes*

DARING NEWS   2 b.g. (Mar 24) Risk Me (FR) 127 – Hot Sunday Sport 42 (Star   67
Appeal 133) [1997 7s⁵ 7m 7.1g 7.3d 8m Oct 5] 16,000Y: rangy gelding: third foal:
brother to temperamental 1994 2-y-o 5f winner Red Hot Risk: dam, plater, stayed
1½m: fair form in minor event and maiden at Salisbury first 2 starts: well held
afterwards: should stay 1m: joined O. O'Neill. *R. Hannon*

DARIO'S GIRL   4 b.f. Good Times (ITY) – Our Krystle 67 (Tender King 123)   –
[1996 NR 1997 10m 8d 9.2g 11.1s Jul 1] first reported foal: dam 2-y-o 6f winner: of
little account. *D. Moffatt*

DARK AGE (IRE)   4 b.c. Darshaan 133 – Sarela (USA) (Danzig (USA)) [1996   –
8g 8.5g³ 8g 8g 10g⁸ 8g 1997 a10g⁴ 11.6m⁶ 5g 9s 10d 12d 10m 10f 8s Nov 8]
ex-French colt: first foal: dam, ran once, close relation to smart 7f/1m filly Flamenco:
won minor event at Nancy as 3-y-o for J. Hammond: little worthwhile form in
Britain. *R. Akehurst*

DARK GREEN (USA)   3 ch.c. Green Dancer (USA) 132 – Ardisia (USA) 87   89
(Affirmed (USA)) [1996 89: 7.1g³ 8m³ 1997 12.4m² 12g² 11.7g⁵ Jun 28] has a fluent,
quick action: fairly useful maiden: second at Newcastle then Goodwood: disappointing in latter, and very much so final start: stays 1½m. *P. F. I. Cole*

DARK MENACE   5 br.g. Beveled (USA) – Sweet And Sure (Known Fact (USA)   52 §
135) [1996 51: 6m 6m 6f* 6m⁶ 6m 7m a7g a6g³ a7g² 1997 a7g a6g 6.9m⁶ 7f* 7m 7f
7m⁴ 7.1g 6m⁵ 6.9m⁶ 7f a6g⁴ a8g a7g Dec 18] workmanlike gelding: modest handicapper: won at Brighton (apprentices) in June: stays 7f: raced almost entirely on good
going or firmer, or equitrack: blinkered nowadays: unreliable. *E. A. Wheeler*

DARK MIDNIGHT (IRE)   8 br.g. Petorius 117 – Gaelic Jewel 89 (Scottish   –
Rifle 127) [1996 NR 1997 9f⁶ Jun 4] probably of little account. *D. A. Lamb*

DARK MILE (USA)   3 b.f. Woodman (USA) 126 – Fateful (USA) 90 (Topsider   87
(USA)) [1996 86p: 5m² 1997 5.7g⁵ 5f³ 6.1g* 6s³ 6m⁴ Nov 1] fairly useful performer:
made all in maiden at Nottingham in October: best effort when third of 22 in
handicap at Haydock 11 days later, first home on stand side: should stay beyond 6f:
acts on soft going and good to firm: has twice hung and carried head awkwardly: sold
54,000 gns in December, to go to France. *J. H. M. Gosden*

DARK MOONDANCER   2 b.c. (Mar 31) Anshan 119 – Oh So Well (IRE)   91
(Sadler's Wells (USA) 132) [1997 7f³ 7g² 7.1m² 7.1s* Oct 15] big, useful-looking
colt: has scope: third foal: half-brother to 3-y-o Dances With Dreams: dam unraced
daughter of Soba: fairly useful form: best effort second to Soviet Bureau in minor
event at Salisbury on second start: won maiden at Haydock by 1½ lengths from Pass
The Rest, under pressure halfway but staying on: should stay 1¼m: type to progress
physically, but possibly not an easy ride. *P. W. Chapple-Hyam*

DARK WATERS (IRE)   4 b.g. Darshaan 133 – Grecian Sea (FR) 107 (Homeric   65
133) [1996 –: 10m 1997 a14.8g⁴ 16s⁵ a16g⁶ 16.4d a16g² Aug 2] fair performer: won
apprentice maiden at Lingfield in June, dictating steady pace: well held afterwards
(possibly something amiss next time): stays 2m. *N. A. Graham*

DARLING CLOVER   5 ch.m. Minster Son 130 – Lady Clementine 68 (He   58
Loves Me 120) [1996 79: 9.9m* 9.9g² 10g 9.9m* 9.9f* 9.9f² 8.9g* 10.1m⁶ 9.2g⁶
8.9g 8m⁶ 8s 1997 8g 8.2m 10g 8.5f Sep 17] leggy mare: has a quick action: modest
handicapper: best form at 9f/1¼m but has won at 11.6f: acts on fibresand and firm
ground: held up. *R. Bastiman*

DARNAWAY   3 b.c. Green Desert (USA) 127 – Reuval 102 (Sharpen Up 127)   92 p
[1996 82p: 7g⁴ 1997 7g³ 8g² 7m* Sep 9] rangy colt: lightly-raced, but fairly useful
form: odds on, impressive 6-length winner of maiden at Lingfield: likely to prove
best up to 1m: raced only on good/good to firm going: open to further improvement
at 4 yrs. *H. R. A. Cecil*

DARU (USA)   8 gr.g. Caro 133 – Frau Daruma (ARG) (Frari (ARG)) [1996 NR   – §
1997 a16g Feb 3] one-time useful stayer: lightly raced of late: well beaten only start
at 8 yrs: often blinkered/visored: temperamental. *R. Hollinshead*

DARWELL'S FOLLY (USA)   2 ch.c. (Feb 2) Blushing John (USA) 120 –   73
Hispanolia (FR) (Kris 135) [1997 6g* 6m^6 6.1d Nov 3] 6,000 2-y-o: sturdy, good-
topped colt: has scope: fourth foal: dam, French 1m/9f winner, half-sister to Derby
winner Erhaab: won maiden at Newcastle in July by neck from Panama House: off
course 3 months, well held on return: should stay 1m. *M. Johnston*

DARYABAD (IRE)   5 b.g. Thatching 131 – Dayanata (Shirley Heights 130)   –
[1996 81: 9s 8.1d 10.1m 7m 8g 7m^5 7m* 7.1m 8g a8.5g 1997 a7g^5 a7g Feb 8] big,
strong gelding: formerly useful up to 1m: has lost his form: sometimes blinkered.
T. J. Naughton

DASHING BLUE   4 ch.g. Dashing Blade 117 – Blubella 86 (Balidar 133)   115
[1996 103: 5g* 6d^3 6m 6g^6 5m^4 6m 5m^3 5m^2 1997 5.2g 5.1m^2 6g 5m^5 5g^2 5g*
6m^3 5d^3 5.6m* 5.2g^2 5m* Oct 2]
   The big flat handicaps enjoy a significance to the racing follower that
bears little relation to the quality of the runners, as judged, for example, by the
ratings the winners of those races achieve. However, 1997 was a year in which
the quality of some of the winners was very high. The very smart sprinter
Danetime was an especially meritorious winner of the Stewards' Cup (having
been an unlucky second in the Wokingham), Zaralaska completed a Bess-
borough/Old Newton Cup double, Fly To The Stars bagged the Britannia and
Schweppes Golden Mile, Pasternak the Magnet Cup and Cambridgeshire,
while the likes of Centre Stalls, Ya Malak, My Best Valentine and Windsor
Castle put up very good efforts in handicaps, too. Not to be forgotten in this
crowd is Dashing Blue, who put up an excellent performance in defying top
weight of 9-12 in the Tote-Portland Handicap at Doncaster in September.
   A useful performer at two and three years, Dashing Blue had shown
himself to be even better than that by the time the Portland came round, despite

*Tote-Portland Handicap, Doncaster—top weight Dashing Blue shows himself better than ever;
Sharp Hat and My Best Valentine (far side) make it a close finish*

JRA Nakayama Rous Stakes, Newmarket—Dashing Blue gains another narrow victory; Bishops Court (centre) and Tipsy Creek (left) are his nearest rivals

having won only one of his eight races earlier in the season, humping 10-0 to victory at York in July. He'd also finished second to Ya Malak in the Vodac 'Dash' at Epsom and third to Danetime and My Best Valentine in that exceptionally hot Stewards' Cup. In a twenty-two runner field at Doncaster, Dashing Blue started fifth favourite at 10/1 behind the 13/2 shot My Best Valentine, to whom he was conceding 5 lb. Dashing Blue has won at both five furlongs and six, and the unusual trip of the Portland of five furlongs and one hundred and forty yards seemed very much his cup of tea. Waited with as usual, he improved to go third passing halfway, collared the long-time leader Lady Sheriff just inside the final furlong and battled on really gamely to reach the line half a length ahead of the 14/1 shot Sharp Hat, with My Best Valentine just a head away in third.

In a wide-open year for sprinters a race like the Prix de l'Abbaye could have seemed a good option for Dashing Blue. But it wasn't an option at all. The French authorities oddly choose to exclude geldings from the Abbaye but not, for example, from the Cadran, another Group 1. In Britain, geldings are allowed in all Group 1 races open to colts except those restricted to three-year-olds or two-year-olds (a ruling by the European Pattern Committee). It's a good job, too! The 1997 Nunthorpe, for instance, would have been half the race it turned out to be without the gelding dead-heaters Coastal Bluff and Ya Malak. The situation provides an anomaly that the European Pattern Committee could do with resolving, in our view in favour of greater opportunities for geldings, which could only increase competitiveness. Instead of the Abbaye, Dashing Blue took in two listed races, finishing a length second to Eveningperformance at Newbury and finishing strongly to beat Bishops Court by a length at New-market. Dashing Blue would only have had to have improved a bit further to have made the frame at Longchamp.

		Elegant Air	Shirley Heights
	Dashing Blade	(br 1981)	Elegant Tern
	(b 1987)	Sharp Castan	Sharpen Up
Dashing Blue		(ch 1977)	Sultry One
(ch.g. 1993)		Balidar	Will Somers
	Blubella	(br 1966)	Violet Bank
	(b 1982)	Blue Rag	Ragusa
		(b 1973)	Blue Butterfly

Discussion of Dashing Blue's pedigree is of somewhat academic interest where he is concerned, though tracing the provenance of horses who turn out to be good can be informative in itself. Dashing Blue's sire, Dashing Blade, won the Dewhurst and Gran Premio d'Italia and was exported to Germany shortly after his retirement in 1990. Dashing Blade has done well over there with numerous useful or better winners, including the champion German two-year-old of 1996, Eden Rock. In Britain he's also been responsible for the Royal Lodge runner-up Stiletto Blade and the useful sprinter Bowden Rose. Dashing Blue is the fourth living foal (and first of any real consequence) out of Blubella. Blubella won twice over sprint distances at Bath for Dashing Blue's trainer from just six runs. She was a big, well-made filly and her son is in a similar mould. Dashing Blue's best efforts have been on good going or firmer. For a while as a three-year-old he'd seemed to be becoming less than fully co-operative, but since being gelded at the end of that season he's proved himself notably game and consistent. Dashing Blue will be back in 1998 when a win in pattern company could be within his reach. *I. A. Balding*

DASHING CHIEF (IRE)   2 b.c. (Feb 20) Darshaan 133 – Calaloo Sioux (USA)   90
100 (Our Native (USA)) [1997 6m 7.6d⁴ 7m 10m* 10m⁵ Nov 1] compact colt:
half-brother to 3 winners, including useful Irish 1m winner/hurdler Master Tribe (by
Master Willie) and Helensville (won Norsk 1000 Guineas, second in Norsk St Leger,
by Horage): dam 7.6f winner out of half-sister to 3 speedy fillies: fairly useful
performer: won maiden at Pontefract in October by ½ length from Glory of
Grosvenor: good fifth in listed event won by Trigger Happy at Newmarket: rather
headstrong, but stays 1¼m: acts on good to firm ground. *M. A. Jarvis*

DASHING DANCER (IRE)   6 ch.g. Conquering Hero (USA) 116 – Santa   54
Maria (GER) (Literat) [1996 58: 6.1g 6f² 6f 6m⁵ 6m⁶ 6g⁴ a8.5g 1997 28g 6.1m   a–
6m² 6m a7g⁶ May 12] compact gelding: modest maiden: stays 6f: yet to race on
heavy going, acts on any other turf (well beaten on fibresand): tried blinkered: races
prominently. *D. Shaw*

DASHING INVADER (USA)   4 ch.g. Pirate Army (USA) 118 – Cherie's Hope   38
(USA) (Flying Paster (USA)) [1996 48: 10g 11.6m 11.8d 12g 14.9m 12m⁴ 12m³   a54
14.1d 1997 12.3m 12d⁵ 14.1m 12g 14.1g* a14g* a14g³ a16g² 14.1g⁵ a14g Sep 8]
heavy-topped gelding: has a powerful, round action: won at Southwell in July: stays
2m: acts on good to firm and dead ground: blinkered last 7 starts: front runner. *P. W. Harris*

DASHING KNIGHT (IRE)   2 b.c. (Mar 6) Night Shift (USA) – Hastening   61 p
(Shirley Heights 130) [1997 7m 7d Oct 14] smallish, good-bodied colt: sixth foal:
half-brother to several winners, including 4-y-o General Academy and 6-y-o General
Assembly (13.4f winner at 3 yrs): dam, unraced, from family of Kris and Diesis: still
green and carrying plenty of condition, better effort in Leicester maidens in October
when seventh of 13: should stay at least 1m: should do better: sold 17,500 gns after
final start. *D. R. Loder*

DAUGHTER IN LAW (IRE)   4 b.f. Law Society (USA) 130 – Colonial Line   –
(USA) 75 (Plenty Old (USA)) [1996 8g 9g³ 10m 8g⁶ 7f³ 13g 9s⁶ 9.5s 1997 9s 5m
a5g⁶ May 24] ex-Irish filly: half-sister to useful Secretary of State (winner up to

264

1¼m, by Alzao): dam, best at 2 yrs, 5f winner: poor performer (rated 34) at best: swerved left and unseated rider after 1f on second start, first in Britain. *P. R. Webber*

DAUNTING LADY (IRE) 2 b.f. (Mar 5) Mujadil (USA) 119 – Dauntess 94 (Formidable (USA) 125) [1997 5g* 5.1d* 5m³ 5d² 5.2f 6g³ Aug 30] IR 12,500Y: lengthy, angular filly: has scope: second foal: dam, 7f winner who stayed 1m, out of half-sister to dam of Mystiko: fairly useful performer: won maiden at Sandown in April and minor event at Chester in May: also placed in Queen Mary Stakes at Royal Ascot (second favourite), 3-runner listed event won by Bodyguard at Sandown and valuable sales race at the Curragh, below form in last-named: should stay 6f: disappointing on firm ground. *R. Hannon*

DAUNTLESS FORT 6 gr.m. Belfort (FR) 89 – Dauntless Flight (Golden Mal- – lard 103) [1996 –: a6g a6g a5g 1997 6g Jul 23] of little account. *Mrs V. A. Aconley*

DAUPHIN (IRE) 4 b. or br.g. Astronef 116 – Va Toujours 109 (Alzao (USA) 117) 57 [1996 48: a6g⁶ a7g⁵ 10.8g 10m 8m 10g 12m 12m² 11.9m* 12m 11.9g 9g⁴ 1997 9.7m² 10.8m* 11.8g 10g 12d³ 10m³ 11.6m⁴ 12m 12v* 12d Oct 21] workmanlike gelding: has a round action: modest handicapper: won at Warwick in May and at Ascot (amateurs) in October: effective from 1¼m to 1½m: acts on any ground: flashes tail and carries head high. *W. J. Musson*

DAVID JAMES' GIRL 5 b.m. Faustus (USA) 118 – Eagle's Quest 62 (Legal – Eagle 126) [1996 –, a57: a8g⁴ a8g⁵ a7g⁵ a8g* a8.5g³ a8g³ a8.5g a9.4g² a9.4g⁴ a9.4g⁶ a46 a7g³ a7g* a8g a7g³ 7.6m a8g⁶ 7d a12g⁵ 1997 a7g a9.4g³ a8g⁴ a8g⁵ 8m a8g³ a8g 8g 6.9m 8s 7.6m Jul 11] leggy mare: poor handicapper on all-weather: little worthwhile form on turf for long time: stays 9.4f: tried visored and blinkered. *A. Bailey*

DAVIDS REVENGE 3 b.g. Reprimand 122 – Tribal Lady 80 (Absalom 128) 70 [1996 70p: 6s 1997 7.3s 7g³ 6g 7m 8d Oct 13] big, useful-looking gelding: shows knee action: fair maiden: third at Newbury in June, making most: failed to repeat that form: barely stays 7f: sold, to go to Kuwait. *Major D. N. Chappell*

DAVIS ROCK 3 ch.f. Rock City 120 – Sunny Davis (USA) 71 (Alydar (USA)) 70 [1996 69: a7g² 5m² a7g² a6g* a8g⁵ a5g⁶ a7s 1997 6.1m⁶ 7m² 7v 6m³ 6.9m² 7g² 7g⁴ 6m a7g⁶ 7g² a6g³ a6g⁵ a8g³ Dec 18] fair performer: in frame on 10 of 14 starts at 3 yrs, winning seller at Folkestone in October: best form at 6f/7f: acts on fibresand and on good to firm and dead ground. *W. R. Muir*

DAVOSKI 3 b. or gr.c. Niniski (USA) 125 – Pamela Peach 81 (Habitat 134) [1996 80 77: 7m³ 8m⁶ 1997 a10g* 12.3s 12g 11.9f³ 10.5m* 10.5m⁵ 10m Sep 25] fairly useful performer: won maiden at Lingfield in April and falsely-run minor event at Haydock (given good ride) in August: stays 10.5f: acts on good to firm going: joined Miss V. Williams. *B. W. Hills*

DAWALIB (USA) 7 ch.g. Danzig Connection (USA) – Centavos (USA) (Scout – Leader (USA)) [1996 65, a–: 7d 6.9f 7m 7.6g 7s² 7.3s³ 7g 6m 7f⁴ 7m⁵ 6m 8f⁶ 7.1f² a65 7m 8d 1997 a7g a8g a7g⁵ a7g* a7g* a7g⁶ a7g³ a7g² a7g⁴ 7m a7g⁶ a7g² 7.5g 6.9s a7g⁵ a7g² 7.1g Sep 11] good-topped gelding: poor mover: fair handicapper: won at Southwell and Lingfield in February: pulled up distressed thirteenth start: stays 1m: acts on the all-weather and on any turf going (no form at 7 yrs): effective visored, blinkered (well beaten) final start: sold, to go to Italy. *D. Haydn Jones*

DAWAM ALLAIL (IRE) 3 b.g. Night Shift (USA) – Veronica (Persian Bold 75 123) [1996 71: 7g⁶ 7f³ 7f⁴ 6m⁵ 1997 7.5m 10d³ a9.4g² 10.8f² 10d³ 8s² 8m* a8g Aug 15] sturdy gelding: fair performer: 2/1 on, won 4-runner maiden at Ayr in July: ran poorly final start: stays 10.8f: acts on any turf going and on fibresand: front runner: sent to UAE. *M. A. Jarvis*

DAWN PATROL 2 ch.f. (Apr 9) Weldnaas (USA) 112 – Silverdale Rose (Nom- 65 d ination 125) [1997 5f 5.1m⁴ 5m⁴ 6m⁵ 6f 5f⁴ 6m⁶ 6m Aug 9] leggy filly: third foal: dam well beaten both starts at 2 yrs: fair maiden at best, but deteriorated: stays 6f. *K. W. Hogg, Isle of Man*

DAWN SUMMIT 3 ch.g. Salse (USA) 128 – Bereeka (Main Reef 126) [1996 –: 42 7d 6m 1997 12g⁶ a12g 12d⁶ 16f* 14.1m 14.1m 13.1m⁶ Jul 7] heavy-topped gelding: poor performer: won weak claimer at Yarmouth in May: stays 2m: acts on firm and dead ground: won over hurdles for P. Bradley in August. *B. Hanbury*

DAWN TREADER (USA)   2 gr.c. (May 16) El Prado (IRE) 119 – Marie de La   –
Ferte (Amber Rama (USA) 133) [1997 6g 6g a7g⁶ 8m 7g a8g⁶ Dec 10] IR 13,500Y:
half-brother to several winners in USA, including Grade 3 8.5f winner French Comic
(by Doonesbury): dam French maiden half-sister to Prix Jean Prat winner Dom
Racine: little sign of ability. *R. Hannon*

DAYBREAK   2 ch.f. (Feb 8) Komaite (USA) – Lady Day (FR) (Lightning (FR)   61
129) [1997 7g⁴ 7g⁶ 7d 6s* a6g⁴ Oct 20] fifth living foal: half-sister to 1995 2-y-o 1m
winner Ladykirk (by Slip Anchor), later stayed 1½m, and French middle-distance
winner Fair Child (by Crystal Glitters): dam won from 9f to 12.5f in France: modest
form: won nursery at Ayr in October: ran respectably in similar event at Southwell 6
days later: will stay at least 7f: sold, to go to Barbados. *J. W. Watts*

DAYDREAM ISLAND   4 ch.f. Never So Bold 135 – La Belle Vie 73 (Indian   –
King (USA) 128) [1996 –: 8g 6.1m 5.1m 1997 a6g Jan 28] unfurnished filly: no form.
R. J. Baker

DAYLAMI (IRE)   3 gr.c. Doyoun 124 – Daltawa (IRE) (Miswaki (USA) 124)   124
[1996 112p: 8d* 8g* 10s² 1997 8g* 8d* 8m³ 8m² 8m³ Sep 7]
   Big-money purchases by Sheikh Mohammed and other members of the
Maktoum family do not have much novelty value these days, and there was
hardly an eyelid batted in October when it was announced that Daylami had
been bought to race for the Godolphin team. But this was the acquisition of a
classic winner, not of some classic 'wannabe'—and one owned by the Aga
Khan at that. Daylami had lost three races, and presumably some of his value,
since his triumph in the Poule d'Essai des Poulains in May, but the sale of a
classic winner well before the end of its racing career is a rarity whatever the
circumstances. The Aga Khan's stud manager told us that this is the first time
that the Aga Khan has sold such a horse. With other owners, recent examples
among the colts are White Muzzle and Celtic Arms; among the fillies, Ravinella and User Friendly. Of Daylami, Godolphin racing manager Simon Crisford
reported: 'Sheikh Mohammed has a lot of faith in this horse both as a racehorse
in the immediate future and as a long-term stallion prospect.'
   Faith in Daylami the racehorse had been a good deal more widespread
after the Poulains, in which he came from last to first in the space of just over a
furlong to win by two lengths. That was not quite so impressive as it sounds,
given that there were just six runners, the smallest total for the race since Irish
River saw off three opponents in 1979, but the pace had been only fair and, after
producing the best turn of foot, Daylami was extending his advantage at the
finish. Second was Loup Sauvage, beaten an identical distance by Daylami in
the Prix de Fontainebleau the previous month, third was the Fabre-trained
Visionary, and the last three places were filled by the disappointing British
challenge comprising Yalaietanee, Fantastic Fellow and, Godolphin's most-
publicised purchase of 1996, Bahamian Bounty.

Dubai Poule d'Essai des Poulains, Longchamp—
Daylami produces a striking turn of foot to settle the issue with Loup Sauvage,
providing the Aga Khan with his sixth win in the race

A 16/10-chance, Daylami had been gaining his fourth win from five starts in the Poulains; the Fontainebleau followed two-year-old victories in a newcomers race at Longchamp and a listed race at Evry and a second to Shaka in the Criterium de Saint-Cloud. We had been impressed by that run in the Criterium, a lot more impressed possibly than Daylami's connections, because that race remains the only one in which Daylami has been tried at further than a mile. For a long time, admittedly, that was also his only defeat, but Daylami did not turn into a top-notch miler after the Poulains and we will be surprised and disappointed if he is not given another crack at longer distances in 1998. His effort in the St James's Palace Stakes was a bit disappointing strictly on the book, but he had two major bumps (and at least four in total) with Poteen on his outside early in the straight before staying on into third. There had also been an incident at the airport in which Daylami reportedly stumbled and grazed a leg. Kept thereafter to the top mile events in France, the Prix Jacques le Marois saw him improve to be beaten two lengths by the easy winner Spinning World, a margin that was increased to three and a quarter in the Moulin three weeks later, when the pair were also separated by Helissio, Daylami being driven along firmly from some way out. The idea that Daylami may benefit from a step up in trip could help to explain Sheikh Mohammed's interest in him, as may the hope that he will prove best on good going or softer—it is hard not to be confronted by this latter possibility when one sees Daylami's powerful, pronounced round action.

		Mill Reef	Never Bend
	Doyoun	(b 1968)	Milan Mill
	(b 1985)	Dumka	Kashmir II
Daylami (IRE)		(br 1971)	Faizebad
(gr.c. 1994)		Miswaki	Mr Prospector
	Daltawa (IRE)	(ch 1978)	Hopespringseternal
	(gr 1989)	Damana	Crystal Palace
		(gr 1981)	Denia

H. H. Aga Khan's "Daylami"

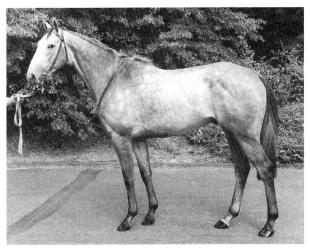

DAY

When Daylami—a well-made colt—does go to stud, the Aga Khan will still have a share in him, and if that, and being owned by Sheikh Mohammed, does not ensure him adequate patronage then nothing will. Doyoun is a good example of the Aga's support, as without his Adaiyka, Dalara, Manntari and now Daylami nothing much would have been heard of him. Although Doyoun is remembered chiefly for his Two Thousand Guineas triumph, third place in the Derby was as good as that in terms of form. The racing record of Daylami's dam, Daltawa, might also encourage another attempt beyond a mile with Daylami, because in a short career she won at ten furlongs as a two-year-old and at ten and a half (in a listed race) at three. Daylami is her first foal and her second is Daymarti (by Caerleon), who finished third in the Prix de Conde and Criterium de Saint-Cloud. Grandam Damana won three races in France, at up to a mile and three quarters, and the family's best days in Britain, in its more immediate branches, were provided by her dam's half-brother Raykour, who managed one place better than Daylami in the St James's Palace Stakes in 1988.
A. de Royer Dupre, France

DAYLIGHT DREAMS 3 b.f. Indian Ridge 123 – Singing Nelly 56 (Pharly (FR)   60
130) [1996 77: 5g* 6m 6d 6.5m 1997 12.5m⁴ 7.6m 7m 6.1m 8f⁴ 7f 5d a7g⁵ Oct 27]
workmanlike filly: generally disappointing since debut, only modest form at 3 yrs:
probably stays 1m: has taken keen hold. *C. A. Cyzer*

DAYMARTI (IRE) 2 b.c. (Jun 2) Caerleon (USA) 132 – Daltawa (IRE) (Mis-   108 p
waki (USA) 124) [1997 8d⁴ 9m³ 10d³ Nov 1] medium-sized colt: second foal: half-
brother to 3-y-o Daylami: dam French 1¼m (at 2 yrs) and 10.5f winner, second in
Prix Penelope: third of 7 to Thief of Hearts in Group 3 event at Longchamp and to
Special Quest in Criterium de Saint-Cloud (beaten around ½ length) last 2 starts:
stays at least 1¼m: probably a smart performer in the making, and sure to win races.
A. de Royer Dupre, France

DAYNABEE 2 b.f. (Feb 6) Common Grounds 118 – Don't Wary (FR) (Lomond   61
(USA) 128) [1997 5m 5g⁶ a5g³ a6g⁴ a5g² a5g² 5d* 6g* 5.1m* 6m³ 5m⁶ 5g 6m
Sep 22] 1,700Y: lengthy, angular filly: unimpressive mover: first foal: dam French
1m winner: modest performer: won sellers at Leicester and Newcastle and claimer at
Nottingham in the summer: good efforts in nurseries next 2 starts: stays 6f: acts on
fibresand, good to firm and dead ground: races prominently. *N. Tinkler*

DAYRELLA 3 ch.f. Beveled (USA) – Divissima 62 (Music Boy 124) [1996 –: 6m   57
6.1m 5m 6m 1997 a7g⁶ a7g³ a6g* a7g³ 6m* 6d 6g 6m⁵ 6m 6.1m Sep 23] lengthy,
unfurnished filly: modest handicapper: won at Lingfield in May and Windsor in
June: effective at 6f/7f: acts on good to firm going and equitrack, probably on fibresand. *W. R. Muir*

DAYS OF GRACE 2 gr.f. (Apr 25) Wolfhound (USA) 126 – Inshirah (USA) 90   68
(Caro 133) [1997 5m⁵ 5f⁴ 5g⁴ 5f* 6d⁶ 5.1m⁴ 5m³ 6g⁶ 5m³ Aug 9] 500F, 11,000Y:
lengthy filly: seventh foal: half-sister to French middle-distance winner Inchbracken
(by Mtoto) and a winner in Belgium by Bustino: dam 2-y-o 5f and 7f winner out of
Grand Criterium winner Femme Elite: fair performer: won maiden at Redcar in May:
generally ran creditably in minor events after: best form at 5f: acts on firm ground:
tends to carry head high. *Martyn Meade*

DAYVILLE (USA) 3 b.f. Dayjur (USA) 137 – Chain Fern (USA) (Blushing   86
Groom (FR) 131) [1996 79: 5.1m³ 6.9g³ a6g* 6d² 1997 6m* 5.7d⁵ 6m 6d 6.1m* 7m
6m 6d Sep 5] leggy, lengthy filly: fairly useful performer: won handicap at Pontefract
in April and minor event at Chepstow (dictated pace) in July: should prove as
effective at 5f as 6f (doesn't stay 7f): acts on fibresand, yet to race on extremes of
going on turf: has worn bandages. *J. Berry*

DAZILYN LADY (USA) 2 ch.f. (Feb 9) Zilzal (USA) 137 – Jetbeeah (IRE) 95   97
(Lomond (USA) 128) [1997 7d² 6.1m* 6g 6d* 7m⁵ Oct 4] 44,000Y: good-topped
filly: has a rounded action: first foal: dam 1m winner: useful performer: won maiden
at Nottingham in July and '50 Years of Timeform' Futurity at Pontefract (beat
Parisian Lady 3½ lengths) in September: not discredited in Lowther Stakes at York

in between and listed race at Newmarket final start: should stay 1m: yet to race on extremes of ground: on edge last 2 starts. *P. W. Harris*

DAZLA'S DOUBLE   3 b.f. Golden Heights 82 – Dazla (Dublin Taxi) [1996 NR   –
1997 9d 10.1s⁶ Jul 2] small filly: first foal: dam poor Irish 7f winner: in rear in maidens. *R. Rowe*

DAZZLE   3 b. or br.f. Gone West (USA) – Belle Et Deluree (USA) (The Minstrel   111
(CAN) 135) [1996 116d: 5f* 6g* 6m⁴ 7g² 1997 8m³ 8d 7m* 7.3m⁶ 7f² 6m⁵ 7g Oct
18] good-bodied filly: has an unimpressive, round action: smart performer, though not quite so good at 3 yrs as at 2: 4¾ lengths third to Sleepytime in One Thousand Guineas at Newmarket, every chance 1f out: won listed race (by ½ length from Unconditional Love) at Goodwood in July and most unlucky in similar event at Doncaster (finished fast but beaten head by Aunty Jane after suffering poor run) in September: looked past her best final start: best up to 1m: acts on firm ground, below form on dead: has pulled hard, and held up for a turn of foot: has been attended by 2 handlers in preliminaries. *M. R. Stoute*

DAZZLING   4 b.f. Rambo Dancer (CAN) 107 – Azaiyma 58 (Corvaro (USA)   –
124) [1996 74d: 8m⁴ 10m⁴ a9.4g⁵ a12g 1997 11.9m May 6] well beaten since debut.
D. C. O'Brien

DAZZLING STONE   3 b.g. Mujtahid (USA) 118 – Lady In Green (Shareef   –
Dancer (USA) 135) [1996 76p: 6f² 1997 10s 10.2m a8g 8m 10.4s 16s Oct 8] second in maiden for M. Stoute at 2 yrs: little sign of ability in 1997 and sold only 600 gns after final start. *Lady Herries*

DEAD AIM (IRE)   3 b.g. Sadler's Wells (USA) 132 – Dead Certain 123§ (Absa-   83
lom 128) [1996 78p: 7g⁶ 7f⁶ 6s⁶ 1997 9s³ 10.8m² 11.6m* 10.5d³ 15d⁵ Sep 18] strong, lengthy gelding: fairly useful handicapper: won at Windsor in August: stays 1½m: acts on good to firm and soft going. *I. A. Balding*

DEADLINE TIME (IRE)   4 b.g. Fayruz 116 – Cut It Fine (USA) (Big Spruce   48
(USA)) [1996 88: 10.3d² 12s² 12.3g 10d* 11.4d⁶ 10m² a9.4g⁴* 8.1g 10.3m 1997 8.9s⁶
9d⁶ 10.9s³ Oct 14] angular colt: has a round action: fairly useful at 3 yrs, but moved badly to post and reportedly finished lame final start: only poor form in claimers in 1997: stays 1½m: acts on good to firm ground and fibresand: has run well in visor (not tried in one in 1997). *Mrs M. Reveley*

DEADLY DUDLEY (IRE)   3 gr.c. Great Commotion (USA) 123 – Renzola   110
(Dragonara Palace (USA) 115) [1996 115: 5g* 5g* 6f³ 6g 6.5d* 1997 6 5d⁵ 7d³ 7g
Oct 18] leggy, unfurnished colt: smart performer: lightly raced at 3 yrs, best effort when 3 lengths fifth to Occupandiste in Prix Maurice de Gheest at Deauville in August: last of 12 in Challenge Stakes at Newmarket final start: stays 7f: acts on good to soft going: has looked headstrong: sent to France. *R. Hannon*

DEARDAW   5 b.m. Tina's Pet 121 – Faw (Absalom 128) [1996 39: 6m 5m 6m 5m   –
5.7m 6m 6m 5.1f² 5f 5.1m⁴ 5g a5g 5.1m 5m 1997 a5g 6g a5g⁶ 6m Apr 22] workmanlike mare: bad 5f maiden: tried visored. *Miss L. C. Siddall*

DEARIE ME   2 b.f. (May 6) Batshoof 122 – Cos I Do (IRE) (Double Schwartz   –
128) [1997 7m Oct 22] first foal: dam unraced half-sister to South African Grade 1 11f and 2m winner Devon Air: little promise in maiden at Yarmouth. *M. A. Jarvis*

DEAR JOHN (IRE)   4 b.g. Caerleon (USA) 132 – Alligatrix (USA) 111 (Alleged   –
(USA) 138) [1996 NR 1997 8.1g Sep 11] half-brother to several useful winners, including Alidiva (up to 1m, by Chief Singer) and Tom Waller (1¼m, by Rainbow Quest), former the dam of Ali-Royal, Sleepytime and Taipan: dam 2-y-o 7f winner (should have stayed much further): tailed off in seller on debut. *Miss A. Stokell*

DEBUTANTE DAYS   5 ch.m. Dominion 123 – Doogali 93 (Doon (124) [1996 70:   83
10.2m⁴ 11.9v⁶ 10s 14.1s 16.5s 1997 10m 11.9d* 12.4g* 11.8g* 13.3d 12g Oct 25] strong, lengthy mare: fairly useful handicapper: won at Haydock and Newcastle in July and Leicester (strong run to lead near finish) in August: below form last 2 starts: best form around 1½m, should stay further: acts on good to firm and soft ground: has flashed tail, but is game. *A. C. Stewart*

DECISION MAKER (IRE)   4 b.g. Taufan (USA) 119 – Vain Deb 66 (Gay   –
Fandango (USA) 132) [1996 78d: 8.2d⁴ 8d⁵ 10d⁵ 10m⁶ 10.2f 1997 a9.4g 12m a8g³

a10g^2 a8g^5 a8g 12f^2 a10s^4 Dec 21] good-bodied gelding: fairly useful at best in Britain, but lost his form: left K. Burke after second start: placed 3 times in Sweden: seems to stay 1½m: tried blinkered/visored. *M. Smith, Sweden*

DECISIVE ACTION (USA)   2 br.c. (Apr 19) Alleged (USA) 138 – Maria   91 p
Balastiere (USA) (Majestic Light (USA)) [1997 8.2s* Oct 15] second foal: dam won 4 times in USA, including 8.5f minor stakes: 12/1, won maiden at Nottingham by 4 lengths from Jaazim, left with bit to do when leaders quickened but running on to draw clear inside final 1f: will stay at least 1¼m: should make a useful 3-y-o. *P. F. I. Cole*

DECORATED HERO   5 b.g. Warning 136 – Bequeath (USA) (Lyphard   121
(USA) 132) [1996 119: 7g^3 8.1g 8m* 7m* 8d* 8d* 8v^2 a9.4g^2 1997 8d^6 7.1m* 7.3m* 7g^6 7.3m* 8f^2 7m* 8f* 7g^5 8f^3 7m^6 Dec 14]
    A leading role in a major production at Hollywood Park in November brought the talents of the five-year-old gelding Decorated Hero, already appreciated by those who had seen him perform in Britain and France, to a much wider audience. Decorated Hero, one of the outsiders in the twelve-runner field for the Breeders' Cup Mile, excelled himself in finishing just over two lengths third behind the favourite Spinning World. A bit slowly into his stride and with only two behind him going into the back straight, Decorated Hero made good headway to reach a challenging position on the home turn and kept on gamely without being able to trouble the winner, losing second only by a neck to the best of the home-trained runners, Geri. Another very long journey, to Hong Kong for the International Bowl, didn't pay off, though Decorated Hero's performance in finishing sixth of fourteen was by no means a bad one considering that he'd been unwell after travelling badly.
    Decorated Hero is a most genuine and consistent performer, who has won eleven of his twenty-six starts in three seasons' racing. Relieved of his duties as lead horse for Benny The Dip early in 1997, he thrived on racing and in a four-month spell from June to October won the John of Gaunt Stakes at Haydock, a minor event and the Grosvenor Casinos Hungerford Stakes, both at Newbury, the Charlton Hunt Supreme Stakes at Goodwood and the Eurostar Prix du Rond-Point at Longchamp, the last three all pattern races. Decorated Hero showed his ability to quicken off a slow pace when beating Bin Rosie by a length in the Hungerford Stakes, and showed the same virtue at the end of a strongly-run race when beating Restructure a length and a quarter in the

Charlton Hunt Supreme Stakes, Goodwood—the admirable Decorated Hero beats Restructure and Nwaamis

Eurostar Prix du Rond-Point, Longchamp—
Decorated Hero gains his fifth win of the year in this 4-runner contest;
Kaldou Star (No. 4), Marathon and Eden Rock follow him home

Supreme Stakes, on both occasions having something to spare. A good turn of foot is a highly desirable attribute in a racehorse, and when it is allied to the gameness Decorated Hero possesses then it makes for a formidable opponent, as the three horses who took on Decorated Hero in the Prix du Rond-Point discovered. Two of them were French-trained, Marathon and Kaldou Star, who had finished first and fourth respectively in the Prix Quincey at Deauville on their previous starts, with the smart German horse Eden Rock making up the field. Decorated Hero raced close up in second, as Marathon set a strong pace, before taking the lead one and a half furlongs out. Although tiring towards the finish, he held on tenaciously by three quarters of a length from Kaldou Star, who deprived Marathon of second place near the line. The Rond-Point wasn't so competitive as it might have been, but few could begrudge Decorated Hero his status as a Group 2 winner.

		Known Fact	In Reality
	Warning	(b 1977)	Tamerett
	(b 1985)	Slightly Dangerous	Roberto
Decorated Hero		(b 1979)	Where You Lead
(b.g. 1992)	Bequeath (USA)	Lyphard	Northern Dancer
	(b 1986)	(b 1969)	Goofed
		Bequa	Never Bend
		(gr 1976)	Hula Girl

Decorated Hero is the second foal of Bequeath, the winner of a nine-furlong maiden in the French Provinces and subsequently bought for 20,000 guineas at the 1990 December Sales. At the time of her sale Bequeath was carrying Beneficiary (by Jalmood), who went on to show fair form at up to seven furlongs, winning six races. Bequeath's third foal Give Warning, a full sister to Decorated Hero, won in Germany at two years, but her next two foals, both by Lahib, are still maidens. However, the two-year-old colt Mubrik, a stable companion of Decorated Hero, showed more than enough on the second of his two starts to suggest that he'll do better than that in 1998. Decorated Hero, a small, strong gelding who has been freeze fired on both forelegs, is known as 'Square Wheels' and 'Donkey Dec' in John Gosden's yard because he is such a poor mover in his slower paces, yet the majority of racehorses would look donkeys by comparison if they tried to match strides with him at racing pace over seven furlongs or a mile. The tough and genuine Decorated Hero, who acts on any going, should have plenty of opportunities in the next season or so to improve his already impressive record. *J. H. M. Gosden*

Dubai Racing Club Palace House Stakes, Newmarket—
blinkered for the first time, Deep Finesse comes out best in a bunched finish;
behind him (from right to left) are Hever Golf Rose, Clever Caption, To The Roof and Bolshoi

DEECEEBEE 2 b.g. (Feb 1) Rudimentary (USA) 118 – Do Run Run 75 (Commanche Run 133) [1997 5f 7.1d³ 6s* 6.1m⁶ 7.9s 6d 6s⁶ 7s 8m Nov 4] 15,500 2-y-o: angular gelding: has a powerful, rather rounded action: second foal: dam 1m winner: fair form at best: landed gamble in maiden at Newcastle in June: ran poorly 4 of last 5 starts (the exception being in a visor seventh outing): probably needs testing conditions at 6f, and should stay at least 1m: often a front runner. *W. Storey* 71

DEE PEE TEE CEE (IRE) 3 b.g. Tidaro (USA) – Silver Glimpse 108 (Petingo 135) [1996 57: 7m³ 6f⁶ 6g⁶ 7.9g⁵ 8m⁵ 8f 8g⁶ 8f⁶ 1997 7.5d 6m 7.5g* 7g 9g* 8m* 8.5v* 8g* 8m³ 8g⁴ 7.6s Aug 30] tall gelding: has a round action: fair performer, had good season: won handicaps at Beverley (2), Redcar and Musselburgh and minor event (on sixth start) at Carlisle, all in June/July: finds 1m a minimum, and will stay 1¼m: acts on good to firm and heavy ground: often front runner. *M. W. Easterby* 77

DEEP FINESSE 3 b.c. Reprimand 122 – Babycham Sparkle 80 (So Blessed 130) [1996 109: 5g* 5m³ 5.5m* 5d* 5m³ 6m⁵ 5d 1997 5s⁶ 5s* 5d 6g 5m⁶ 5.2g 5f Oct 5] sturdy, sprint type: useful performer: blinkered first time, made virtually all to win Palace House Stakes at Newmarket in May by ½ length from Hever Golf Rose: inconsistent afterwards (also blinkered next 2 starts), creditable effort in Prix de l'Abbaye de Longchamp final start: effective at 5f/6f: acts on dead ground, seems to go particularly well on good going or firmer: often sweating and edgy: races prominently: sold 60,000 gns after final start. *M. A. Jarvis* 109

DEEPLY VALE (IRE) 6 b.g. Pennine Walk 120 – Late Evening (USA) (Riverman (USA) 131) [1996 69, a76: a7g³ a6g⁴ a7g⁴ a6g* a7g 6m* a7g⁸ a6g⁵ a7g 1997 a7s⁵ a7g⁵ a7g⁴ a8g⁵ a6g⁶ 7s⁵ a7g* 7s⁶ 7s a7g Nov 14] strong, lengthy gelding: fair performer: trained first start by E. Wheeler, next 3 by P. Butler: won claimer at Southwell in August: effective at 6f/7f: acts on the all-weather and on good to firm and soft ground: sometimes gives trouble in stalls (withdrawn once). *G. L. Moore* 70 a66

DEEP MAGIC (USA) 2 b.f. (May 20) Gone West (USA) – Nimble Folly (USA) (Cyane) [1997 6g⁵ Aug 21] half-sister to numerous winners including smart 6f (at 2 yrs) to 10.5f (Grade 2 event in USA) winner Skimble (by Lyphard) and good 1984 American 2-y-o Contredance (by Danzig), successful up to 9f: dam unraced: 2/1 from 5/4, well-held fifth of 9 in maiden at Yarmouth, fading after disputing lead: sent to USA. *H. R. A. Cecil* –

DEEP SPACE (IRE) 2 br.c. (Feb 19) Green Desert (USA) 127 – Dream Season (USA) (Mr Prospector (USA)) [1997 6d⁴ 6d Sep 20] good-topped colt: first living 85 p foal: dam unraced sister to smart French/US performer around 1m Elizabeth Bay: better for race, considerably-handled fourth of 8 to La-Faah in newcomers event at Ascot, leading briefly 2f out: disappointing in maiden at Newbury (raced freely, found little) nearly 2 months later: promising at Ascot, and worth another chance. *E. A. L. Dunlop*

DEEP WATER (USA)   3 b.g. Diesis 133 – Water Course (USA) (Irish River (FR)   74
131) [1996 82p: 8f³ 1997 a8g³ 6f³ 8.1g 12d⁵ 12m² 10m⁵ 11.8d³ Oct 13] fair maiden:
stays 1½m: acts on dead going, probably firm (poor effort on fibresand): sold 20,000
gns and joined M. Hammond. *P. F. I. Cole*

DEERLY   4 b.f. Hadeer 118 – Grafitti Gal (USA) (Pronto) [1996 50: 6.1m 7g⁵ a6g⁶   53 §
7f 6d 6g 7.1f 6.1m 1997 5.7d⁵ 6.1g* 6m 6.1d a5g⁴ 6g 6.1m 6m a8.5g 8g a6g² a7g a6g
Dec 26] modest handicapper: made all at Chepstow in May: best at 6f/7f: acts on
good to firm ground and fibresand: visored once: inconsistent. *R. Dickin*

DEEVEE   8 b.h. Hallgate 127 – Lady Woodpecker 61 (Tap On Wood 130) [1996   46 d
69d: 8m 8m⁶ 8.5m 8g 8.3d 8d 8m 1997 10s 8d⁵ 8.3m 8m 10.8g 10m Oct 23] close-
coupled horse: poor mover: poor handicapper, on the downgrade: usually slowly
away. *C. J. Benstead*

DEFIANCE   2 b.c. (Apr 24) Warning 136 – Princess Athena 119 (Ahonoora 122)   76
[1997 5.7m⁶ 6m³ 6g³ Aug 10] fourth foal: half-brother to 4-y-o Waypoint: dam best
at 5f: fair form in summer maidens: will stay beyond 6f. *B. W. Hills*

DEFINED FEATURE (IRE)   4 ch.f. Nabeel Dancer (USA) 120 – Meissarah   91 d
(USA) (Silver Hawk (USA) 123) [1996 91: 7f⁴ 7m 6m⁴ 6m³ 1997 a7g² 8m 7g 9m
8.5d 7m 7g³ 8f 8g³ 8d Oct 16] fairly useful performer: generally disappointing after
reappearance at 4 yrs: should stay 1m: acts on firm ground and fibresand: blinkered
sixth and final outings: has been bandaged. *Dr J. D. Scargill*

Mr John E. Sims's "Deep Finesse"

DEG

DEGREE 4 b.f. Warning 136 – Krill (Kris 135) [1996 73: 8m³ 10g² 10g 1997   52
a9.4g⁴ a12g a8g 10m a8g² 8g* 9.7s Jul 2] modest performer: won weak maiden at
Musselburgh in June: stayed 1¼m: in foal to Sabrehill. *S. C. Williams*

DEKELSMARY 2 b.f. (Feb 12) Komaite (USA) – Final Call 79 (Town Crier 119)   61
[1997 6m 5m⁴ 5g⁵ 6.1m³ 6m² 6m Oct 6] 25,000Y: lengthy, good-topped filly: closely
related to 3-y-o Rude Awakening and half-sister to several winners, including 4-y-o
Anotheranniversary: dam 5f winner who ran only at 2 yrs, half-sister to good sprinter
On Stage: modest maiden: good efforts when placed in nurseries at Nottingham and
Leicester in September: shapes as though will be suited by further than 6f: yet to race
on ground softer than good. *J. Balding*

DEKI (USA) 2 b. or br.c. (Mar 24) Mujtahid (USA) 118 – Glamorous Bride (FR)   83
(Baillamont (USA) 124) [1997 6m* 6m³ 7g² 7.5d* Aug 14] first foal: dam, placed up
to 1¼m in Ireland, out of half-sister to Arc winner Gold River: fairly useful form:
won maiden at Lingfield in May and nursery at Beverley (made most) in August:
ridden with little enterprise penultimate start: will stay 1m: progressing well when
last seen out. *D. Morley*

DE LA HAYE 2 b.f. (Mar 8) Puissance 110 – Hibiscus Ivy (AUS) (Rancher   –
(AUS)) [1997 a6g Nov 21] 1,000Y: second reported foal: dam ran 3 times: 14/1,
always rear in seller at Wolverhampton. *R. Simpson*

DELAYED REACTION 2 b.g. (Mar 27) Theatrical Charmer 114 – Pingin   –
(Corvaro (USA) 124) [1997 6m 6d 8.2m Sep 15] 9,500Y, 36,000 2-y-o: shows knee
action: first living foal: dam ran once each on flat and over hurdles: well held in
maidens. *N. A. Callaghan*

DELCIANA (IRE) 2 b.f. (May 11) Danehill (USA) 126 – Delvecchia (Glint of   61
Gold 128) [1997 6g⁴ 6g³ 6g 7.3m⁶ 6.9g 6m³ Sep 22] 16,000Y: sturdy filly: second
foal: dam German 2-y-o 7f winner: modest form in maidens and nurseries: best
efforts at 6f. *P. W. Harris*

DELIGHT OF DAWN 5 b.m. Never So Bold 135 – Vogos Angel 54 (Song 132)   57
[1996 67: 7f 6m 8.3m* 10m 8.1f⁶ 7m⁶ 7.1m⁵ 8f⁴ 8m⁴ 10m 7g 10m 8g 1997 8g 7m 8d
7f³ 7m 8.3g⁴ 6.9m 8.3g² 7d⁶ 7.1m 7.6g⁴ 7d² 8.3m 7f 7m² 8.2d⁶ a8g 8.2d Nov 3]
angular mare: modest handicapper: stays 1m: acts on firm and dead ground: often
slowly away, and held up (needs a strongly-run race): blinkered third and last 4 starts.
E. A. Wheeler

DELILAH (IRE) 3 b.f. Bluebird (USA) 125 – Courtesane (USA) (Majestic Light   111
(USA)) [1996 75p: 7.1d³ 1997 7g² 8m³ 10.4g⁴ 10.1g² 10.4s* 12g⁴ 12v* 10d⁵ Nov 9]
tall good-topped filly: shows knee action: smart performer: off course 3½ months
after third start: hacked up in maiden at York in September: much improved form
when winning Princess Royal Stakes at Ascot in October by 3 lengths from Snow
Princess: not discredited when fifth to Taipan in Premio Roma final start: will stay
beyond 1½m: goes really well on soft/heavy going: visored last 5 starts: edgy sort
who tends to carry head high: has also flashed tail, and is not the easiest of rides: sold
165,000 gns in December. *M. R. Stoute*

DELLEN WALKER (IRE) 4 b.g. Pennine Walk 120 – Lady Ellen 67 (Horage   –
124) [1996 NR 1997 a7g Mar 17] 900 3-y-o: second foal: dam, placed over 5f at 2
yrs, half-sister to Indian Ridge: tailed off in claimer. *J. S. Wainwright*

DELLUA (IRE) 3 b.f. Suave Dancer (USA) 136 – Joma Kaanem (Double Form   69
130) [1996 NR 1997 7g 8g⁴ 8m 10.2d² 13.1g⁶ 9.7m* 9s⁴ Oct 13] 25,000Y: strong
filly: eighth foal: half-sister to several winners, including miler Fenjaan (by Trojan
Fen) and Irish 9f winner Genial Jenny (by Danehill): dam, ran once at 3 yrs in Ireland,
from family of Royal Palace: fair performer: reportedly bled from nose third start,
then off course nearly 3 months: won maiden (simple task) at Folkestone in
September: barely stays 13f: acts on good to firm and soft ground. *R. Guest*

DELPHIC WAY 2 b.f. (Feb 3) Warning 136 – Palace Street (USA) 103 (Secreto   59 p
(USA) 128) [1997 5.2m 5.1m⁶ Aug 12] leggy, angular filly: third foal: half-sister to
3-y-o Palaemon and 4-y-o Ca'd'Oro: dam won at 6f/7f: some promise, never
dangerous, in maidens at Newbury and Bath: should stay 1m: likely to do better at 3
yrs. *G. B. Balding*

Princess Royal Stakes, Ascot—Delilah revels in the mud and shows improved form;
Snow Princess (noseband) is second with Saafeya third

DELROB 6 b.m. Reprimand 122 – Stoneydale 83 (Tickled Pink 114) [1996 –, a57: a6g a5g⁵ a5g 5g 6m a6g⁴ a5g⁵ a6g a5g³ a5g³ a6g* a5g² 5g a6g* a6g a6g⁴ a6g⁶ a7g 1997 a6g a6g² a6g a6g⁵ a6g 6.1d⁵ a5g⁴ a6g⁶ a5g² 6m a5g 5.1m⁶ 5.1m⁶ 5m* 5.1m 5.7g Aug 7] sparely-made mare: modest handicapper on all-weather, poor on turf: won seller at Ayr in July: effective at 5f/6f: acts on good to firm ground and fibresand: usually blinkered/visored. *D. Haydn Jones*   43 a57

DELTA SOLEIL (USA) 5 b.h. Riverman (USA) 131 – Sunny Roberta (USA) (Robellino (USA) 127) [1996 94: 8s⁵ 7m 7g⁴ 7g 8g 1997 6m 7.6v 6g⁶ 6f² 6g⁵ 7m 6.1g⁴ 6m 7m² 8f⁶ a8s⁶ Nov 10] good-bodied horse: fairly useful handicapper: effective at 6f, barely stays 1m: acts on firm ground, shaped well on soft (well held only outing on all-weather): sometimes taken last and steadily to post: sold (to join V. Soane) 6,500 gns after final start. *P. W. Harris*   87

DEMOCRAT 3 b.g. Selkirk (USA) 129 – Land of Ivory (USA) 109 (The Minstrel (CAN) 135) [1996 NR 1997 6.1g 6m³ 7d⁶ a8g* a8g* a8g* a9.4g* a8.5g² Dec 26] 100,000Y: good-topped gelding: has been pin fired: sixth foal: half-brother to several winners, including 5-y-o Silently (won 3 times at 1¼m in 1995) and useful performer from 7f to 1¼m Heart of Darkness (by Glint of Gold): dam 5f (at 2 yrs) and 1m winner, half-sister to Gold And Ivory: progressed into a useful performer: impressive winner of minor event at Southwell and handicaps on same course and at Wolverhampton in November/December: good second to Lionize in handicap at Wolverhampton on final start: likely to stay 1¼m: acts on fibresand. *Sir Mark Prescott*   96

DEMOLITION JO 2 gr.f. (Mar 21) Petong 126 – Fire Sprite 83 (Mummy's Game 120) [1997 a5g⁴ 5.1v² 6g² 6m² 6g² 6.1g² 7.1m* 6.1d⁴ 7m² 7g⁴ 6g² 7v 6d* 6g 6.1d³ 7s a7g⁴ Nov 21] 4,200Y: small, sparely-made filly: fifth foal: sister to a poor maiden and half-sister to 3-y-o Always Alight and 6-y-o Six For Luck: dam 2-y-o 5f winner: fairly useful performer: won maiden at Musselburgh in August and well-contested nursery at Newmarket in October: respectable effort in nursery at Wolverhampton final start: stays 7f: acts on good to firm ground, dead and fibresand: visored sixth start onwards: tough and consistent. *P. D. Evans*   80

DENBRAE (IRE) 5 b.g. Sure Blade (USA) 130 – Fencing (Viking (USA)) [1996 75: 7s⁴ 6g 6m³ 6f³ 6d⁴ 6m² 6m⁴ 6m⁴ 6.1m* 6m 6f 6m⁵ 6m 1997 6m³ 6m 6s 6d³ 6d⁵ 6g⁴ 6m⁴ 7g*⁷ 7d Sep 19] lengthy gelding: fair performer: won minor event at Leicester in August: stays 7f well: acts on fibresand and on firm and dead ground: often soon off bridle: consistent. *D. J. G. Murray Smith*   75

DENSBEN 13 b.g. Silly Prices 110 – Eliza de Rich 57 (Spanish Gold 101) [1996 59: 6d 5.9d 5.9m 6g⁵ 6m⁵ 6m⁶ 6m³ 6.9f 6m² 7m⁴ 6m⁶ 6d* 8m 1997 6g 6g 7m⁴ 6.9f⁶ 6f³ 6d 8.2d 8m Oct 28] smallish, sparely-made gelding: modest handicapper nowadays, who has won or been placed in 52 of 181 career starts: suited by 6f/7f: acts on any going: below form when blinkered/visored: sometimes starts slowly, and is held up. *Denys Smith*   50

275

DENTARDIA (IRE) 2 br.c. (Apr 3) Petardia 113 – Modena (Sassafras (FR) 135) 65 ?
[1997 6d 7d 8m⁶ 8s Oct 13] IR 12,000Y: workmanlike colt: has scope: half-brother
to several winners, including 6f and 1m winner Mine's A Double and useful sprinting
2-y-o (later 7f and 1m winner) Crofter's Cline (both by Crofter): dam of no account:
possibly flattered when sixth in steadily-run maiden at Pontefract: poor form at best
otherwise. *J. M. P. Eustace*

DENTON LAD 3 b.g. Prince Sabo 123 – Dahlawise (IRE) 76 (Caerleon (USA) 70 d
132) [1996 61: 5m⁵ 6m⁶ 6m 6g 7g 1997 6g* 6g 6g 6g 8m 7.9s⁵ 8.3g⁴ 8m 18d 8s Nov
6] fair handicapper: won at Ripon in April: left J. W. Watts after fourth start: well
below form last 3 outings: stays 1m: best efforts on good going: blinkered seventh to
ninth starts. *W. T. Kemp*

DEPRECIATE 4 ch.c. Beveled (USA) – Shiny Penny 70 (Glint of Gold 128) 77
[1996 84: 6m⁴ 6m 1997 5.2g 6d⁴ 6g 5.7m a6f⁴ 6d 5m 6d³ 7s 6g a6g a5g Dec 18]
workmanlike colt: fair handicapper: left E. James before final start: stays 7f: acts
on good to firm ground, dead and fibresand: twice visored: none too consistent.
T. D. Barron

DERBY DARBAK (USA) 4 b.c. Lyphard (USA) 132 – Joy Returned (USA) 78
(Big Spruce (USA)) [1996 NR 1997 10m⁴ May 28] $160,000Y: heavy-bodied colt:
seventh foal: half-brother to Stalwars (by Stalwart), multiple winner in USA and
second in Grade 1 9f event, and useful French 7f/1m winner Joy Of Glory (by
General Holme): dam stakes winner up to 9f in USA: burly, green and moved poorly
to post when fourth in maiden at Ripon: sent to UAE. *J. H. M. Gosden*

DERI FACH 2 b.f. (Apr 21) Warrshan (USA) 117 – Cwm Deri (IRE) (Alzao 51
(USA) 117) [1997 5g² May 26] third foal: half-sister to 1995 2-y-o 6f winner
Kossolian (by Emarati): dam unraced: head second in claimer at Leicester: claimed
£7,000 and sent to Sweden. *B. Palling*

DERISBAY (IRE) 9 b.g. Gorytus (USA) 132 – Current Bay (Tyrant (USA)) –
[1996 NR 1997 a13g⁶ Jan 14] modest hurdler: no longer of much account on flat.
J. J. Bridger

DERNIER CROISE (FR) 2 ch.c. (Apr 23) Royal Academy (USA) 130 – 86
Guardian Spirit (USA) (Lyphard (USA) 132) [1997 5.1m 5.5s⁴ 5.1s⁶ 6g⁵ 5g⁴ 5m⁵ 6m
6f* 6m² 7m* Oct 28] 230,000 francs Y: leggy colt: second foal: dam unraced close
relative of Prix de la Salamandre winner Oczy Czarnie and half-sister to Criterium de
Saint-Cloud winner Glaieul: fairly useful performer: fourth in listed events at
Chantilly and Deauville prior to winning claimer at Lingfield and 4-runner minor
event at Redcar in October: stays 7f: acts on firm and soft going: seems effective with
or without blinkers: sent to USA. *B. J. Meehan*

DERRYQUIN 2 b.g. (Jan 28) Lion Cavern (USA) 117 – Top Berry 87 (High Top 97 p
131) [1997 6g 7d* 8d* Nov 7] lengthy, good-bodied gelding: fourth foal: half-
brother to 3-y-o Star Entry and 1994 2-y-o 7f winner Anna Bannana (by Prince
Sabo): dam, 1m winner, granddaughter of Cheveley Park runner-up Red Berry: most
progressive form in autumn, winning maiden at Lingfield and minor event at
Doncaster, quickening to score decisively on each occasion, by 1¾ lengths from
favourite Angstrom in latter: stays 1m (not bred to get very much further): yet to race
on ground firmer than good: gelded at end of season: likeable sort, and looks sure to
do well at 3 yrs. *R. Charlton*

DESERT ARROW (USA) 2 b.c. (Mar 3) Gone West (USA) – Afaff (USA) –
(Nijinsky (CAN) 138) [1997 7m Jul 12] fourth foal: half-brother to a winner in
Sweden by Shirley Heights: dam, placed over 1m from 2 starts, sister to Shadeed:
7/4, twelfth of 13 in Salisbury maiden: sent to France. *Saeed bin Suroor*

DESERT BEAUTY (IRE) 3 b.f. Green Desert (USA) 127 – Hellenic 125 103
(Darshaan 133) [1996 76p: 7g 1997 11.4s⁴ 10.2m² 8d* 8.1m² 7g* 8m³ Nov 1] good-
topped filly: progressed into a useful performer: won maiden at Salisbury in August
and 29-runner handicap at Newmarket (heavily backed, swept into lead inside final
1f and going away at finish) in October: improved again when 1½ lengths third of 5
to Samara in steadily-run listed race at Newmarket: needs a strong pace at 7f and
should stay beyond 1m: acts on good to firm and dead ground. *M. R. Stoute*

DESERT CALM (IRE) 8 br.g. Glow (USA) – Lancette (Double Jump 131) 51
[1996 58d: 7.5d 15.4m 7m³ 8s 8f⁶ 9m 8m⁵ 8.3g⁴ 10m⁶ 8f⁵ 7.1f 1997 a8g⁴ a10g⁵
Feb 25] tall gelding: modest handicapper: should stay 1¼m: acts on firm and soft
ground and on equitrack: normally blinkered (not in 1997): tends to get behind.
P. D. Evans

DESERT CAT (IRE) 4 b.g. Green Desert (USA) 127 – Mahabba (USA) 74 64 d
(Elocutionist (USA)) [1996 –: 7.6g 8g 1997 6.9g⁴ 7d 10m 9f³ 7.5g 10m 8m⁴ Aug 10]
big, strong gelding: carries condition: fair maiden at 2 yrs: form in 1997 only on
fourth start. *Martyn Wane*

DESERT DUNES 4 b.g. Unfuwain (USA) 131 – Palm Springs (Top Ville 129) 74
[1996 77: 10g 12m⁴ 14m⁴ 14m⁵ 16.1m 1997 14m² 14.8d⁴ Jun 11] lengthy gelding: has a quick action: fair maiden: should stay 2m: acts on good to firm going.
N. A. Graham

DESERT FIGHTER 6 b.g. Green Desert (USA) 127 – Jungle Rose 90 (Shirley 76
Heights 130) [1996 72: 13.8s 12g 10.3m 10f³ 1997 10.3m³ 12g* 12.4m* 12f⁴ Jun 2]
good-topped gelding: fair performer: won minor event at Thirsk (made all) in April
and 6-runner handicap at Newcastle in May: should stay 1¾m: acts on firm ground.
Mrs M. Reveley

DESERT GREEN (FR) 8 b.g. Green Desert (USA) 127 – Green Leaf (USA) 97 53
(Alydar (USA)) [1996 102: 8.1g⁴ 8m* 8.1d 8m 8m 7.9m 9s 1997 7g 8g² Sep 3] rangy
gelding: impresses in appearance: formerly useful handicapper: only modest form
when second in claimer at Brighton: stays 1m: acts on firm ground, well beaten on
soft and fibresand: has run well when sweating: goes well held up under tender
handling: joined R. Frost. *R. Hannon*

DESERT HORIZON 3 b.g. Danehill (USA) 126 – Sand Grouse (USA) (Arctic 101
Tern (USA) 126) [1996 91p: 8m⁴ 8.2s* 1997 10m⁴ 9d⁴ 8m⁴ 10m⁶ Aug 1] good-
topped gelding: good mover, with powerful action: has been fired: fourth in listed
race and minor races before sixth (bandaged, best effort) in £35,000 handicap at
Goodwood: better at 1¼m than 1m: acts on soft going and good to firm: sold 13,000
gns in October. *J. H. M. Gosden*

DESERT INVADER (IRE) 6 br.g. Lead On Time (USA) 123 – Aljood 111 –
(Kris 135) [1996 57, a78: a8.5g a7g⁴ a6g⁴ a7g* a6g³ a6g² a6g² 7m 6s³ 8.3s a7g² a8.5g a76
6m⁵ a6g⁴ a9.4g⁵ a7g² a8.5g a7g⁴ a9.4g⁶ a6g⁵ 6d¹² 7g a7g a6g² a7g⁴ a6g² a7g³ 1997
a8g² a7g⁴ a7f³ a6g³ a6g a7g⁶ a8g⁶ a6g³ a8g³ a6g⁴ a8g³ a7g² a6g* a7g* 6g a8.5g⁵
a7g 7g a6g* 6g a7g³ a7g⁶ a6g⁶ a8g Oct 20] strong, lengthy gelding: good mover:
fair performer on the all-weather: won at Wolverhampton (amateurs claimer) and
Southwell (claimer) in May and Wolverhampton (handicap) in June: best recent
efforts at 6f/7f: acts on all-weather, no form in 1997 on turf: occasionally blinkered,
not tried at 6 yrs. *D. W. Chapman*

DESERT KING (IRE) 3 b.c. Danehill (USA) 126 – Sabaah (USA) 65 129
(Nureyev (USA) 131) [1996 110+: 7g² 7m² 8d* 7g* 7g⁶ 1997 7g² 7m* 8g* 8m⁴
12d* 10.4g² 10g² Sep 13]
          The novelist George Eliot wrote that 'prophecy is the most gratuitous
form of error.' It is an occupational hazard of attempting to predict in horseracing that one will occasionally be made to look foolish (actually if this happens only 'occasionally' then it suggests you are probably doing rather well).
That said, some of our remarks on Desert King during his career suggest that
the horse was capable of running rings around us as well as many of his rivals
on the racecourse! *Racehorses of 1996* concluded that he would 'need to show
plenty of improvement to figure in any of the Guineas.' True enough. However,
that is not really the kind of tailpiece we can be proud of on a horse who not
only *did* show 'plenty of improvement' but also 'figured' very obviously in one
of the Guineas, winning the Irish version. Desert King then went on to prove
our subsequent reservations about his stamina—'he races as though he'll get
10f but isn't likely to stay 12f' (*Timeform Perspective*)—well wide of the mark
by winning a truly-run Budweiser Irish Derby on dead going.

Desert King's season started on a fairly low key, it's true, with defeat by
Cool Edge in the Gladness Stakes at the Curragh in April. But he gave an
indication that he could indeed make an impact at the top level when running
away with the Omni Racing Tetrarch Stakes on the same course at the
beginning of May, beating Rich Ground by five and a half lengths. As a result,
Desert King started second favourite at 3/1 for the Lexus Irish Two Thousand
Guineas behind the 11/10-chance Revoque in a field of twelve. Desert King
took full advantage of his main rival's poor showing. Soon close up, Desert
King was driven ahead over a furlong out and ran on well despite drifting left.
At the line he had three lengths and two lengths to spare over Verglas and
Romanov, with Revoque only sixth.

Desert King's connections' decision to go next for the St James's Palace
Stakes at Royal Ascot seemed to support doubts about the horse's stamina. His
running there—he was never moving well and came back a well-beaten fourth
to Starborough—was too bad to be true, but it hardly augured well for his
prospects in the Irish Derby just twelve days later. Starting at 11/2 third
favourite in a field of ten at the Curragh, Desert King again benefited from poor
efforts from his chief rivals, the Derby runner-up Silver Patriarch and the Irish
One Thousand Guineas second Strawberry Roan. Give Desert King his due,
though; he produced another high-class performance. Settled off the pace, and
racing with much more zest than at Ascot, he closed before the straight and ran
on strongly to lead inside the final furlong, holding on well to have a length to
spare over Dr Johnson and Loup Sauvage (who were separated by a short head),
with a further seven lengths and more back to the remainder. Silver Patriarch,
who dropped away to finish fifth after leading briefly early in the straight, and
Strawberry Roan (eighth) clearly weren't themselves. In the process Desert
King became the first horse to complete the Irish Two Thousand Guineas-Irish
Derby double since Grundy in 1975.

Lexus Irish Two Thousand Guineas, the Curragh—
Desert King completes an Irish Guineas double for trainer Aidan O'Brien;
the grey Verglas gives Ireland first and second

Budweiser Irish Derby, the Curragh—
Desert King becomes the first horse since Grundy to complete the Irish Two Thousand Guineas–Derby double;
Dr Johnson (rail) and Loup Sauvage chase him home

The original intention to run Desert King in the King George VI and Queen Elizabeth Diamond Stakes was shelved, but the horse did go on to be tried against the very best, confirming his standing as a high-class performer with seconds in the International at York and the Irish Champion at Leopardstown. In the former he was beaten one and a half lengths by Singspiel in a four-runner race, claiming the notable scalps of Benny The Dip and Bosra Sham. In the latter, a very strongly-run race in which he had a pacemaker, Desert King pulled fourteen lengths clear of the third but had no answer to the brilliant four-and-a-half length winner Pilsudski. A tilt at the Breeders' Cup Turf was planned, but it was announced shortly before the race that Desert King had a viral infection and was to be retired to Coolmore Stud at a fee of IR 17,500 guineas.

Desert King has plenty to recommend him as a potential stallion. He's a sturdy, good-quartered colt who generally took the eye, and he was a powerful mover with a round action into the bargain. He won a Group 1 race at two years as well as two of them at three, though his victory in the Aga Khan's Studs National Stakes as a juvenile was a long way removed from top-class. He's a well-bred individual, too, as to be expected of a horse who fetched 125,000 guineas as a yearling. Desert King's sire, the Cork And Orrery and Ladbroke Sprint Cup winner Danehill, continues to do very well at stud, both in Europe and in Australia. He's been a champion 'down under', and only narrowly failed to head the prize-money table (to no small degree due to Desert King himself) in Britain and Ireland in 1997. Danehill was also responsible during the latest season for the Vodafone Stewards' Cup winner and Haydock Park Sprint Cup runner-up Danetime. Desert King's dam, Sabaah, was just a modest maiden around seven furlongs and a mile, but her dam, Dish Dash, won the Ribblesdale Stakes and finished third in the Yorkshire Oaks and the Sun Chariot Stakes. At stud Dish Dash has produced several winners, notably the seemingly high-class miler Maroof (by Danehill's sire Danzig) and the useful two-year-old seven-furlong winners Arrasas and Mawwal. Maroof is now a sire in New Zealand. A year-younger half-brother to Desert King by Indian Ridge, called Wahj, fetched 330,000 Irish guineas as a yearling but has yet to race, while Dahomey, by Dayjur (a son of Danzig) out of Dish Dash, ran once as a two-year-old for Clive Brittain in 1997.

279

Mr M. Tabor & Mrs John Magnier's "Desert King"

		Danzig	Northern Dancer
	Danehill (USA)	(b 1977)	Pas de Nom
	(b 1986)	Razyana	His Majesty
Desert King (IRE)		(b 1981)	Spring Adieu
(b.c. 1994)		Nureyev	Northern Dancer
	Sabaah (USA)	(b 1977)	Special
	(ch 1988)	Dish Dash	Bustino
		(b 1979)	Loose Cover

Desert King's versatility also speaks in his favour—he showed high-class form at seven furlongs to a mile and a half in a period of less than two months—and he also acted on every type of going he was asked to race on, ranging from good to firm to good to soft. He sometimes wore a tongue strap. *A. P. O'Brien, Ireland*

DESERT LADY (IRE) 2 b.f. (Apr 28) Danehill (USA) 126 – Hooray Lady 92 90
(Ahonoora 122) [1997 5m* 5d² 5m* 5m² 5.2m⁶ Aug 16] 28,000F, 55,000Y: fourth
foal: half-sister to 3-y-o Carlton: dam won around 1m and seemed to stay 1½m: fairly
useful form: won minor events at Salisbury in June and July: very good second in
nursery at Goodwood, but not seen out after only sixth in listed race at Newbury:
should stay at least 6f: acts on good to firm ground. *R. Charlton*

DESERT LORE 6 b.g. Green Desert (USA) 127 – Chinese Justice (USA) (Diesis –
133) [1996 44: a8g⁴ a7g⁴ 7.1g 1997 a9.4g a8.5g Jan 8] small, strong gelding: very
much on the downgrade. *R. M. McKellar*

DESERT LYNX (IRE) 4 b.f. Green Desert (USA) 127 – Sweeping 104 (Indian 79
King (USA) 128) [1996 74: 6d* 6g 6s³ 6m⁶ 8g³ 8m 7.1d³ 7.1s³ 8f 10.3g 1997 8d 6d*
6m 6.1g Jul 30] small, plain filly: fair handicapper: won at Haydock in July: poorly
drawn and met trouble in running final start: has form at 1m, but better at 6f/7f: acts
on good to firm and soft ground. *T. R. Watson*

280

DESERT MIRAGE   2 b.c. (May 14) Green Desert (USA) 127 – Anodyne 100   67
(Dominion 123) [1997 7g a6g³ Dec 6] fifth foal: half-brother to 3 winners, including
fairly useful 1993 2-y-o 5f winner Stimulant (by Sharpo), later successful in USA,
and 6f (at 2 yrs) and 7f winner Pharmacy (by Mtoto): dam, 6f winner, sister to very
useful (at up to 1½m in USA) Domynsky: fair form in maidens at Warwick and
Wolverhampton, third of 13 to Wolfhunt in latter. *P. W. Chapple-Hyam*

DESERT MOUNTAIN (IRE)   4 b.g. Alzao (USA) 117 – Curie Point (USA)   –
(Sharpen Up 127) [1996 9s³ 12.5d³ 12d* 10d² 12m⁴ 1997 12m⁶ Mar 22] 52,000F,
IR 40,000Y: smallish, sturdy gelding: first foal: dam unraced half-sister to useful 7f
performer Mazilier: fairly useful winner (rated 90) in Ireland in 1996: soundly beaten
only outing at 4 yrs: stays 12.5f: acts on good to firm and soft ground: fairly useful
hurdler, successful in October. *N. A. Callaghan*

DESERT NATIVE   2 b.f. (Jan 24) Formidable (USA) 125 – Desert Nomad 56   42
(Green Desert (USA) 127) [1997 5m 5d⁴ 6d 5.7m 6.9g 6.1m a6g Nov 21] 13,000F, a?
25,000Y: first foal: dam 7f winner: poor maiden: trained first 3 starts by R. Hannon,
next 3 by C. Wall: stays 7f: visored in seller final start. *Mrs L. Stubbs*

DESERT PRINCE (IRE)   2 b.c. (Mar 14) Green Desert (USA) 127 – Flying   107
Fairy 79 (Bustino 136) [1997 6m* 6m² 6g⁵ 7g⁴ Oct 18] 62,000Y: tall, attractive colt:
has a fluent, round action: closely related to French 1994 2-y-o 1¼m winner Femme
Amoureuse (by Danehill): dam twice-raced daughter of 1000 Guineas winner Fairy
Footsteps: impressive winner of maiden at Doncaster in May: useful form afterwards
in Coventry Stakes at Royal Ascot (1½ lengths second to Harbour Master), Prix
Morny at Deauville and Dewhurst Stakes at Newmarket: beaten 9¾ lengths by
runaway winner Xaar in last-named, travelling strongly when produced 2f out, but
soon beaten: may well prove to be a sprinter: raced only on good/good to firm
ground. *D. R. Loder*

DESERT SAND   2 b.f. (Apr 15) Tragic Role (USA) – Miss Suntan (Bruni 132)   66
[1997 7g 6d* 6d⁶ Oct 8] 3,200Y: leggy filly: half-sister to useful 1990 2-y-o 7f
winner Miss The Point (by Sharpo), later successful in Italy, and 2 other winners
abroad: dam French 1½m winner from family of Wolver Hollow: fair form when
winning maiden at Ayr by 3 lengths from Ryefield, despite carrying head awkwardly
and drifting left: not discredited (given inexperience) in nursery at York following
month: should stay 1m+. *Miss S. E. Hall*

DESERT SPA (USA)   2 b.c. (Feb 22) Sheikh Albadou 128 – Healing Waters   65
(USA) (Temperence Hill (USA)) [1997 7.6d⁵ 8f⁴ 7d⁶ Oct 14] $25,000Y: round
actioned colt: fifth foal: half-brother to 3 minor winners in USA: dam, French 11f
winner, half-sister to St Leger second Minds Music and 1000 Guineas third Ajfan:
fair form in maidens. *P. W. Harris*

DESERT STORY (IRE)   3 b.c. Green Desert (USA) 127 – Aliysa 126 (Darshaan   115
133) [1996 110: 6d* 7m² 8g² 7.3s* 1997 8m* 8m⁶ 10.4g² 10d² 9.8m⁵ Oct 4] strong,
compact colt: has a fluent, round action: smart performer: won City Index Craven
Stakes at Newmarket by ¾ length from Grapeshot: ran with credit when about 8
lengths sixth to Entrepreneur in Two Thousand Guineas at Newmarket and 2½
lengths second to Benny The Dip in Dante Stakes at York: off course 4 months, better
effort in autumn when 6 lengths second of 5 to Fahris in Select Stakes at Goodwood:
effective at 1m/1¼m: acts on good to firm and soft ground: sent to UAE. *M. R. Stoute*

DESERT TIME   7 b. or br.g. Green Desert (USA) 127 – Supper Time 71   72 d
(Shantung 132) [1996 NR 1997 10g 8.1g² 8m 9m 8g 8d 10f Sep 28] sturdy gelding:
good mover: fair handicapper: only form at 7 yrs when second of 16 at Sandown in
June: stays 1m: acts on firm ground: sometimes bandaged behind: carries head high:
a tricky ride, who needs holding up: inconsistent. *C. A. Horgan*

DESERT TRACK   3 b.c. Green Desert (USA) 127 – Mill Path (Mill Reef (USA)   99
141) [1996 76p: 7f⁵ 1997 8s³ 8m* 8g* 8m Nov 1] angular colt: useful performer,
lightly-raced: won maiden at Newmarket in July and handicap at Redcar (still looked
green when beating Cee-N-K by 2½ lengths) in October: stays 1m: acts on good to
firm ground, ran poorly on soft: sold 40,000 gns in December. *J. H. M. Gosden*

DESERT VALENTINE   2 b.g. (Feb 21) Midyan (USA) 124 – Mo Ceri 63   – p
(Kampala 120) [1997 7.1g 6g Oct 24] 6,000Y: tall gelding: has high knee action:

third reported foal: half-brother to 5-y-o Mazilla: dam stayed 1¾m: signs of a little ability when not fully wound up in maidens at Chepstow (led to halfway) and Newbury: likely to do better. *L. G. Cottrell*

DESERT WARRIOR (IRE) 3 b.c. Fairy King (USA) – Highland Girl (USA) – (Sir Ivor 135) [1996 –: 6m 1997 8.2d⁶ 8s⁶ Jul 4] signs of ability but no worthwhile form in maidens. *K. Mahdi*

DESERT ZONE (USA) 8 ch.g. Affirmed (USA) – Deloram (CAN) (Lord – Durham (CAN)) [1996 57, a69: a7g 10.8m⁶ 8g 10.1m 8m⁵ 8m* a8g* 8.1s³ a8g² a8g³ a9.4g* 1997 a8g a9.4g Sep 30] rangy gelding: fair handicapper at 7 yrs: well beaten in 2 starts in September: stays 1¼m: acts on good to firm ground, soft and fibresand. *John A. Harris*

DESIGNER LINES 4 ch.g. Beveled (USA) – Parrot Fashion 86 (Pieces of Eight – 128) [1996 75: 6m⁶ 6g 7.6m* 8m 1997 10s Oct 14] close-coupled gelding: fair 7.5f winner in 1996 (visored last 2 starts): off course over a year and burly, well beaten in handicap only outing as 4-y-o. *C. James*

DESIGNER (USA) 2 b.c. (Feb 5) Danzig (USA) – Classy Women (USA) 105 (Relaunch (USA)) [1997 6m³ 6f³ 6m³ Oct 2] $550,000Y: robust, good sort: good mover: second foal: closely related to Irish 3-y-o Petite Princess (by Dayjur), 5f and 6f winner at 2 yrs: dam US Grade 3 8.5f winner from family of Grand Criterium winner Femme Elite: progressive form in newcomers event at Goodwood, minor event at Yarmouth and Middle Park Stakes at Newmarket, 25/1 when beaten a length by Hayil in last-named, setting pace and keeping on: probably a sprinter: withdrawn after breaking out of stalls second intended start: evidently well suited by being given his head: seems sure to win races. *J. H. M. Gosden*

DESIRE'S GOLD 2 br.g. (Apr 2) Grey Desire 115 – Glory Gold 59 (Hittite Glory – 125) [1997 5m 7m⁶ 6d Aug 30] 2,400 2-y-o: workmanlike gelding: brother to 7-y-o Gold Desire: dam 6f to 7.5f winner: well beaten in maidens. *M. Brittain*

DESPINA 3 ch.f. Waajib 121 – Staiconme (USA) (Pancho Villa (USA)) [1996 –: – 6m 1997 10s 8m 8m 8d Sep 19] big filly: little sign of ability: tried blinkered. *H. Candy*

DETERRENT 2 b.c. (Apr 14) Warning 136 – Delve (IRE) 102 (Shernazar 131) 98 [1997 6g 6s² 6g² 6.1m* 6m* 6g³ Oct 25] 160,000Y: strong, workmanlike colt: good mover: first foal: dam 1¼m winner, half-sister to smart sprinter Lugana Beach: useful performer: won maiden at Nottingham and minor event at Salisbury (overcoming some trouble in running) in autumn: ½-length third to Ikhteyaar in listed race at Doncaster: likely to prove best up to 1m: acts on good to firm going, probably on soft. *J. H. M. Gosden*

DETROIT CITY (IRE) 2 b.g. (Mar 19) Distinctly North (USA) 115 – Moyhora 64 ? (IRE) (Nashamaa 113) [1997 6m 5m 5f 6s Oct 16] 21,000Y: first foal: dam unraced: modest form first 2 starts: possibly flattered by draw third and well beaten final one. *J. Berry*

DEUX CARR (USA) 4 b.g. Carr de Naskra (USA) – Deux Chance (USA) – (Vaguely Noble 140) [1996 NR 1997 a12g Feb 5] second foal: dam unraced: sold out of D. Loder's stable 8,000 gns in 1996: no sign of ability in bad maiden on debut. *Bob Jones*

DEVA LADY 2 b.f. (Feb 26) Prince Sabo 123 – Known Line 100 (Known Fact 66 (USA) 135) [1997 5.7g⁶ 5.7m⁴ 6.1m³ 6g 6g³ 6m⁵ 7m Sep 16] 12,500Y: fifth foal: half-sister to 4-y-o Story Line, useful 2-y-o 7f winner, and 2 winners by Never So Bold, including 8.5f winner Party Line: dam, 1m winner at 2 yrs (better at 1½m), from family of Pure Grain and Quay Line: fair performer: third in valuable seller at York (claimed out of M. Channon's stable £10,000) in August: met trouble both subsequent outings, unseating rider final one: should stay beyond 6f: raced only on good/good to firm ground. *C. N. Allen*

DEVILISH CHARM (USA) 3 ch.g. Devil's Bag (USA) – Popularity (USA) 58 75 (Blushing Groom (FR) 131) [1996 NR 1997 10.2m⁵ 11.5m⁶ 11.7g⁵ 14g* 14.1g³ Oct 18] second foal: half-brother to a winner in USA by Cox's Ridge: dam twice-raced half-sister to top-class US middle-distance performer Vanlandingham: fair handicapper: won at Haydock in September: ran well at Redcar following month:

will stay 2m: raced only on good/good to firm going: sold 23,000 gns after final start. *Mrs A. J. Perrett*

DEVIL RIVER PEEK (USA)   5 b.h. Silver Hawk (USA) 123 – Black Tulip   117
(FR) (Fabulous Dancer (USA) 124) [1996 115: 8g² 8s³ 9m* 8g² 10d⁵ 10m² 8g³ 1997
10d 8d⁴ 8g² 8s 9g 10g* 10s* 8f* a9.5g* Dec 13] smart German horse: in good form
in second half of year, winning Group 3 events at Frankfurt (beat Shebar a length) in
July and Baden-Baden (beat Zero Problemo 1¾ lengths) in August, strongly-run
Premio Vittorio di Capua at Milan (by 1¼ lengths from Kierkegaard) in October and
minor event at Neuss in December: effective at 1m to 1¼m: acts on any going,
including, seemingly, sand. *B. Schutz, Germany*

DEWI SANT   3 ch.g. Nalchik (USA) – Secret Ingredient (Most Secret 119) [1996   –
NR 1997 11.7g 10.2m Jul 7] sixth reported foal: dam unraced: tailed off in maidens.
D. Burchell

DE-WOLF   2 gr.f. (Apr 6) Petong 126 – Doppio 62 (Dublin Taxi) [1997 6g⁵ Oct   74 p
27] leggy filly: eighth foal: sister to fair winning sprinters Garth (at 2 yrs, in 1990)
and Wandering Stranger and half-sister to 4-y-o Thordis: dam 2-y-o 5f winner: 33/1,
caught eye when just over 4 lengths fifth of 22 to Solo Spirit in maiden at Leicester,
held up going strongly and finishing well without being at all knocked about: sure to
be all the better for considerate introduction. *P. J. Makin*

DHES-C   4 b.f. Lochnager 132 – Keep Cool (FR) 42 (Northern Treat (USA)) [1996   –
55d: a6g⁶ a5g⁴ a6g³ a7g⁵ a6g³ a6g³ a8.5g⁶ a6g a5g a6g 7g⁵ a6g a6s 1997 a9.4g
a7g⁵ a6g 7m Mar 27] tall, workmanlike filly: modest all-weather sprint handicapper
at best: dead. *R. Hollinshead*

DIA GEORGY   6 b.g. Reesh 117 – Carpadia (Icecapade (USA)) [1996 –: a12g⁴   –
a8g a8g⁴ a10g a10g⁶ a7s 1997 a9.4g a7g a12g 10m 7f May 28] leggy gelding: little
worthwhile form since 1995. *C. A. Dwyer*

DIAMOND BEACH   4 b.g. Lugana Beach 116 – Cannon Boy (USA) (Canonero   – §
(USA)) [1996 74§: 7m³ 8f² 7f⁵ 7.6m² 7.1m⁴ 8m⁵ 8g 1997 8g Oct 18] tall colt:
fair maiden at best: soundly beaten only 4-y-o start on flat: probably ungenuine.
G. M. Moore

DIAMOND CROWN (IRE)   6 ch.g. Kris 135 – State Treasure (USA) (Secre-   45
tariat (USA)) [1996 50: 10m³ 12m 14.1f 11.1g⁴ 10m³ 10m⁵ 12g 6.9f³ 10f⁵ 10m³ 10f⁴
8m* 8m 8.1s⁶ 1997 8d² 10g 8m⁵ 10m³ 10g* 10g 10.9g⁵ 10m 8m⁶ 12g 12.1g⁵ 8g 11m⁵
10d⁵ Nov 3] leggy gelding: poor handicapper: won seller at Nottingham in June:
finds a minimum, and stays 1½m: acts on firm and soft ground, tailed off on
fibresand: held up, and often set plenty to do. *Martyn Wane*

DIAMOND DRILL (USA)   2 b.c. (Feb 14) Geiger Counter (USA) – Decollete   77
(USA) (Al Nasr (FR) 126) [1997 a8.5g³ 6.9d a7g* Dec 10] 17,000Y: third foal:
half-brother to a winner in USA by Bucksplasher: dam ran twice in France: best
effort when winning weak maiden at Lingfield by 8 lengths, clear final 2f and eased:
should stay 1m. *P. J. Makin*

DIAMOND EYRE   3 ch.f. Then Again 126 – Renira 60 (Relkino 131) [1996 45:   47
7f⁵ a7g⁵ a7g 1997 a8s² a8g³ a10g⁴ a7g* 8g⁵ 10g⁵ 8m⁴ Jun 26] modest per-   a57
former: landed gamble in seller at Wolverhampton in February: below that form in
handicaps on turf afterwards: probably stays 1¼m: acts on fibresand. *J. L. Eyre*

DIAMOND STEVE   2 b.g. (Apr 22) Rambo Dancer (CAN) 107 – Shoot To Kill   50 d
64 (Posse (USA) 130) [1997 5m 5g* a5g⁴ 5d 7f 5g⁴ 7.5v 7g Jul 23] 2,500Y:
leggy gelding: third foal: dam, maiden, stayed 1m: won claimer at Thirsk in April
for P. D. Evans: disappointing otherwise: usually visored/blinkered: sent to Macau.
N. Tinkler

DIAMOND WHITE   2 b.f. (Mar 13) Robellino (USA) 127 – Diamond Wedding   91
(USA) 65 (Diamond Shoal 130) [1997 6g² 6m 6m³ 6g³ 7m* 8g 7m Oct 4] workmanlike filly: second foal: dam (maiden) should have stayed beyond 1½m: fairly useful
performer: 25/1, won listed race at Newmarket in August by ¾ length from Stop Out:
behind in similar events at Deauville and Newmarket subsequently: stays 7f: raced
only on good/good to firm ground: has taken strong hold, including to post: has given
trouble at stalls and sweated. *G. C. Bravery*

DIBOLA 2 ch.g. (Feb 25) Dilum (USA) 115 – Bella Bambola (IRE) 42 (Tate – Gallery (USA) 117) [1997 5m 5m 5m 5m 6g 5s 5s a5g Nov 14] 8,700Y: first foal: dam sprint maiden: of little account. *J. S. Wainwright*

DICENTRA 4 b.f. Rambo Dancer (CAN) 107 – Be Noble (Vaguely Noble 140) – [1996 –: 10g 11.1g⁴ 1997 12.3m Aug 4] lightly raced and no worthwhile form. *C. W. Thornton*

DICK TURPIN (USA) 3 br.g. Red Ransom (USA) – Turn To Money (USA) 76 (Turn To Mars (USA)) [1996 71p: 7m⁶ 1997 7m 10d³ 10m⁴ 10.4d Oct 8] strong, lengthy gelding: has scope: fluent mover: fair maiden: should stay beyond 1¼m: held up: hung at York final start. *Lord Huntingdon*

DICTATION (USA) 5 b.g. Dayjur (USA) 137 – Mofida 115 (Right Tack 131) 58 [1996 63: 6s 5g 6m 6d 6g 6m 6m a7s 1997 a7s a6g³ a6g 7g⁴ 8m³ 8m² 7g² 8m³ 8m⁴ 7g 7d² Jun 21] good-quartered gelding: modest maiden handicapper: stays 1m: acts on good to firm and dead going: below form blinkered and visored. *J. J. O'Neill*

DIEGO 4 b.g. Belmez (USA) 131 – True Queen (USA) 79 (Silver Hawk (USA) 76 123) [1996 71: a10g* a10g⁵ 10.3d 9.9m 12.3g 10s³ 12g* 16.2f 12.3m 14m² 14m³ 14m² 11.8f⁴ 16g 1997 a11g⁴ 17.1m² 16.2s⁵ 14m* Jul 10] small gelding: fair handicapper: won at Lingfield in July: effective at 1¾m, and seems to stay 17f: acts on equitrack (probably on fibresand) and on firm and soft ground: fair winning hurdler. *C. E. Brittain*

DIET 11 b.g. Starch Reduced 112 – Highland Rossie 67 (Pablond 93) [1996 58d: 33 8.1g⁵ 6d 7.1g* 5s 6.9m² 5m⁴ 7.1g 6g 5.9f 6m 6m 8.1f² 7.1g 7.1m² 6m⁶ 1997 8s 8m 6.9g 6m⁶ 5g 7.1g⁶ 5g⁴ 5s³ 8d⁵ 6d⁶ 6m 6g 6g⁶ 5g Sep 1] sturdy, good-quartered gelding: carries condition: poor handicapper, on the downgrade: effective at 5f to 7f: acts on any going: blinkered earlier in career, visored nowadays: sometimes hangs under pressure: rarely races outside Scotland, and successful 8 times at Hamilton. *Miss L. A. Perratt*

DIFFIDENT (FR) 5 b.h. Nureyev (USA) 131 – Shy Princess (USA) 117 (Irish 110 River (FR) 131) [1996 122: a6g² 7m* 6f 7g 6m* 7g* 6s² 1997 6g⁵ 6f⁵ 7s⁶ 8m* Dec 4] small horse: has a short action: very smart performer in 1996: below that form in 1997, though fifth in Duke of York Stakes on reappearance and won listed race at Abu Dhabi (first race since leaving Saeed bin Suroor) by 1½ lengths from Intidab: best form at 6f/7f: acts on good to firm and soft ground and on sand: has won when sweating. *S. Seemar, UAE*

DIG FOR GOLD 4 ch.g. Digamist (USA) 110 – Formidable Task 61 (Formidable – (USA) 125) [1996 NR 1997 10d Sep 2] second foal: dam, out of sister to Highclere, stayed 6f: modest form in NH Flat races/over hurdles: showed little in seller on flat debut. *Miss S. E. Hall*

DIGITAL OPTION (IRE) 3 b.g. Alzao (USA) 117 – Elevated (Shirley Heights – 130) [1996 –: a8.5g 7m 1997 7f⁵ 11m 10m 12v² 10g 12m⁴ a14g Oct 20] robust gelding: little worthwhile form. *J. L. Spearing*

DIGPAST (IRE) 7 ch.g. Digamist (USA) 110 – Starlit Way 92 (Pall Mall 132) 42 § [1996 59, a77: a10g² a8g* a8g⁶ a10g⁶ 9.7m 10m 10m⁵ 9m 8.3g⁶ 1997 a10g⁶ a10g² a73 § a10g a10g 8m 8f 9g 7s⁶ 7m⁴ 8.3m 9g a7g⁶ a8g⁴ a10g Dec 22] lengthy, workmanlike gelding: fair handicapper on all-weather, poor on turf: none too consistent in 1997, trained by M. Madgwick first 4 starts: effective at stiff 7f to 1¼m: acts on any turf going, has gained all 4 British successes on equitrack: often blinkered, visored (below form) final outing: usually slowly away. *J. J. Bridger*

DIGWANA (IRE) 4 b.g. Digamist (USA) 110 – Siwana (IRE) (Dom Racine (FR) – 121) [1996 –: a8g⁶ 10d a8g 6f⁶ 1997 11.9f May 29] no worthwhile form. *T. M. Jones*

DIJON 3 ro.g. Chilibang 120 – Princess Fair (Crowned Prince (USA) 128) [1996 – –: 7g 1997 8g Jun 7] of no account. *Bob Jones*

DIKTAT 2 br.c. (Feb 25) Warning 136 – Arvola 75 (Sadler's Wells (USA) 132) 82 p [1997 7m Sep 9] angular colt: first foal: dam 1m winner out of Cheveley Park winner Park Appeal, herself half-sister to Desirable (dam of Shadayid) and Alydaress: 9/1, promising seventh of 18, beaten less than 7 lengths, in maiden won by Mudeer at

Leicester, looking and running as if race would do him good: sure to do better. *D. R. Loder*

DIL 2 b.g. (Apr 10) Primo Dominie 121 – Swellegant 84 (Midyan (USA) 124) 76
[1997 7g 6m² 5m⁶ 5d⁴ Sep 5] 38,000Y: lengthy, good-topped gelding: second foal: dam 2-y-o 5f winner, half-sister to speedy pair Millyant (by Primo Dominie) and Prince Sabo: fair maiden: in frame at Folkestone (flashed tail) and Haydock: unfavourably drawn in between: probably a sprinter: gelded after final start. *B. Hanbury*

DILIGENCE (IRE) 2 b.c. (Mar 9) Dilum (USA) 115 – Florinda (CAN) (Vice 99
Regent (CAN)) [1997 5.1s² 5d* 6m⁴ Jun 17] 36,000Y: smallish, strong colt: good walker and mover: third foal: half-brother to 3-y-o Canadian Fantasy: dam unraced half-sister to Irish Derby runner-up Insan: useful form: won maiden at Goodwood in May: 4½ lengths fourth of 15 to Harbour Master in Coventry Stakes at Royal Ascot: should stay at least 1m. *P. F. I. Cole*

DILKUSHA (IRE) 2 b.g. (Apr 15) Indian Ridge 123 – Crimson Glen 70 78 p
(Glenstal (USA) 118) [1997 6d⁶ 6d⁶ Oct 17] 29,000Y: rather leggy gelding: has a quick action: third foal: half-brother to 1½m winner Court Joker (by Fools Holme): dam Irish 7f and 9f winner: fair form in maidens at Goodwood then Newmarket, in latter beaten about 4 lengths by Atuf: should prove suited by further than 6f: should do better. *B. J. Meehan*

DILLY LANE (USA) 2 ch.f. (Feb 3) Personal Hope (USA) 118 – Trickily (USA) 50 +
(Trempolino (USA) 135) [1997 7m 7.1m 6.1g⁴ 7d Oct 16] 12,000 2-y-o: useful-looking filly: first reported foal: dam, placed in USA, half-sister to Prix Marcel Boussac winner Tropicaro: modest form in maidens and a Newmarket seller: should stay 1m. *P. R. Webber*

DI MATTEO (IRE) 2 ch.g. (Feb 12) Emarati (USA) 74 – Piney Lake 54 67
(Sassafras (FR) 135) [1997 7g³ 6g a7g² Sep 8] 14,000Y: good-topped gelding: has scope: shows knee action: half-brother to numerous winners, including 1994 2-y-o 6f seller winner by Forzando, 6f and 7f winner Cafe Solo (by Nomination) and 2m winner Lake Dominion (by Primo Dominie): dam placed at 1m and 1¼m: fair form when placed in maidens at Newcastle and Southwell: will probably stay 1m. *B. Hanbury*

DIMINUTIVE (USA) 4 b.g. Diesis 133 – Graceful Darby (USA) (Darby Creek 80
Road (USA)) [1996 86: 6.9m⁵ 8s⁶ 8f* 8f 10.3m⁵ 10.2f* 10.1m* 11.4d³ 10.1m⁵ 10m 10s 1997 10g 10.1m³ 10m 10.1f Sep 17] leggy colt: has a rather useful performer: only creditable 4-y-o effort on second start: stays 1¼m: acts on firm and dead ground: has run creditably when sweating and on toes. *J. W. Hills*

DIM OTS 2 b.f. (Apr 15) Alhijaz 122 – Placid Pet 65 (Mummy's Pet 125) [1997 79
5.1m* 5g² 5.1d* 5m² 5.1d³ 5d Nov 7] 3,800Y: leggy filly: has a fluent, round action: half-sister to several winners, including 3 fairly useful sprinters: dam, 1m winner, sister to Runnett: fair performer: won maiden at Nottingham and minor event at Bath in spring: ran creditably all subsequent starts (off for nearly 3 months before penultimate and final ones): speedy. *B. Palling*

DINA LINE (USA) 3 ch.f. Diesis 133 – Lajna 88 (Be My Guest (USA) 126) 49
[1996 NR 1997 10s⁶ 8g⁶ 8s⁴ Jun 28] workmanlike filly: sixth foal: half-sister to 4 winners, including Ninia (up to 1¼m, by Affirmed) and Gold Land (stayed 1m, by Gone West), both useful: dam twice-raced half-sister to very smart miler Soviet Line out of Oaks fourth Shore Line: poor maiden: easily best effort on second start: should stay 1¼m. *M. Bell*

DINO'S MISTRAL 4 b.g. Petong 126 – Marquessa d'Howfen 93 (Pitcairn 126) –
[1996 –: a12g 8.1g⁶ 11f⁴ 12g 1997 a7g⁴ a8.5g⁴ 12.3m a11g 10m a11g⁵ 10m 10.8g⁶ a35
11.5m Oct 22] leggy gelding: poor maiden: left F. Lee after seventh start: races freely, but seems to stay 1½m: best form on fibresand: blinkered (tailed off) fifth outing: inconsistent. *K. A. Morgan*

DIRAB 4 ch.g. Groom Dancer (USA) 128 – Double Celt 93 (Owen Dudley 121) 78 d
[1996 81: a7g⁵ a8g⁶ a11g* 11.1g 12f 12.3m⁶ 14.1m* 16f³ 16d* 15m 1997 a12g³
13.8g⁶ 16d⁴ 16.2s* 16g⁴ 15d⁵ 16.1s 16m 16s³ 16.1m³ 16.2d⁴ 16m³ 15.9d² 16g
17.1m⁶ Oct 6] sturdy gelding: fair handicapper: won at Beverley in May: in frame several times after, but not up to that form: thorough stayer: acts on good to firm

ground and fibresand, goes well on soft going: usually soon off bit (best form with strong handling): blinkered (out of form) once: sold 5,200 gns in November. *T. D. Barron*

DISALLOWED (IRE)   4 b.f. Distinctly North (USA) 115 – Miss Allowed – (USA) (Alleged (USA) 138) [1996 72: 12.4g² 9m a8g 9m³ 10.1g⁵ 9m* 8m⁶ 10d⁶ 8.3d 8.1m 8f³ 8f⁶ 1997 10g Sep 23] useful-looking filly: fair handicapper at 3 yrs, well held only flat outing in 1997: fairly useful hurdler, winner in October. *D. Nicholson*

DISCO TEX   2 b.g. (Apr 29) Rambo Dancer (CAN) 107 – Andbracket (Import   49 127) [1997 7.5v 7g⁵ 7m⁵ 8d 8m Oct 5] 10,000Y: workmanlike gelding: third foal: brother to 4-y-o Dispol Gem: dam unraced: poor maiden: stays 1m. *M. W. Easterby*

DISHY DIAMOND   4 b.f. Prince Daniel (USA) – My Diamond Ring 65 – (Sparkling Boy 110) [1996 NR 1997 a11s⁶ a8.5g 11.7g Sep 8] second foal: dam winning miler: well beaten in maidens. *W. R. Muir*

DISPOL CONQUEROR (IRE)   4 b.g. Conquering Hero (USA) 116 – Country Niece (Great Nephew 126) [1996 37: 10d 8g 10m 9f⁵ 10.3g 12s 1997 a8g Jan 6] workmanlike gelding: poor maiden handicapper: well beaten only 4-y-o start. *P. Calver*

DISPOL DANCER   6 ch.g. Salse (USA) 128 – High Quail (USA) (Blushing – Groom (FR) 131) [1996 –: 12m a16g a14g 13.8g 1997 a12g Jan 3] of little account. *Mrs V. A. Aconley*

DISPOL DIAMOND   4 b.f. Sharpo 132 – Fabulous Rina (FR) (Fabulous Dancer   53 (USA) 124) [1996 70d: 6g 7.1d 7.5m³ 7.5m³ 8m⁴ 8.5m 8f³ 8m 8s⁴ 8g 7g 1997 8m 7f* 7m² 7.5m⁴ 6g 7d 7g⁴ 7g 7m 8.2s³ 7g⁵ Oct 24] leggy filly: modest performer: won seller at Redcar in May: ran creditably most starts after: best at 7f/1m: acts on firm and soft ground. *G. R. Oldroyd*

DISPOL EMERALD   2 b.f. (May 6) Emarati (USA) 74 – Double Touch (FR) – (Nonoalco (USA) 131) [1997 5g⁵ 5s⁶ 5m⁵ Jul 18] 2,800Y: sister to a 2-y-o 6f winner and a disappointing maiden, and half-sister to 3 winners, including 15f winner Lady Madina (by Legend of France): dam unraced: little worthwhile form, including in a seller. *S. E. Kettlewell*

DISPOL GEM   4 b.f. Rambo Dancer (CAN) 107 – Andbracket (Import 127)   72 [1996 72d: 8g 8g⁵ 8.5m⁴ 8d⁴ 8d 8m³ 9m³ 9m⁵ 10d 8f 9m 8m³ 8s⁴ 1997 8m⁶ 8g² 8d 8.5s 9m* 9f² 8g⁴ 8g* 10m 8g 8m 8g 8.2g 8g⁴ 8s Nov 6] lengthy filly: shows a quick action: fair handicapper: won in big fields at Redcar in May and Ripon in July: stays 9f: acts on firm and soft ground: sold 4,200 gns after final start. *P. Calver*

DISPOL LASS   2 b.f. (Apr 20) Mazilier (USA) 107 – Hen Night (Mummy's – Game 120) [1997 a5g 6m⁴ 6g 5m⁴ 5m 6g 6g Aug 25] 1,200Y: second foal: dam unraced: no worthwhile form: tried blinkered. *P. Calver*

DISPOL PRINCE   4 b.g. Risk Me (FR) 127 – Gemma Kaye 91 (Cure The Blues – (USA)) [1996 NR 1997 7m 7m 10g 10g 14.1m Jul 19] 700Y: unfurnished gelding: sixth foal: brother to 4 animals, none better than fair: dam highly-tried maiden: well beaten, including in sellers. *G. R. Oldroyd*

DISSENTOR (IRE)   5 b.g. Dancing Dissident (USA) 119 – Helen's Dynasty   37 § (Habitat 134) [1996 44, a58: a5g⁶ a6g* a6g⁵ a6g a6g⁶ a6g² a7g² a6g³ 6.1g 6m a6g   a41 § 6m⁵ 6f⁴ 6m⁶ a5g a7g a6g 1997 a6g³ a6g a5g⁴ 5g 5m⁵ a7g⁵ May 12] compact gelding: poor handicapper: effective at 5f to 7f: acts on fibresand and firm going, yet to race on ground softer than good: usually visored/blinkered: unreliable. *J. A. Glover*

DISSINGTON TIMES   3 ch.g. Timeless Times (USA) 99 – Zam's Slave – (Zambrano) [1996 –: 5.9g a7g⁶ 1997 7m 10f 12d⁴ Jun 30] little worthwhile form on flat: won over hurdles in September and November. *W. McKeown*

DISTANT DYNASTY   7 br.g. Another Realm 118 – Jianna 60 (Godswalk (USA) – 130) [1996 –, a58d: a6g a5g² a5g a5g⁶ a5g a5g⁶ a7g 6m a5g a7g a6g a5g 1997 a5g a7g a6g 5m May 17] of no account nowadays. *B. A. Pearce*

DISTANT KING   4 b.g. Distant Relative 128 – Lindfield Belle (IRE) 78 (Fairy – King (USA)) [1996 NR 1997 5f 7m 10.1g 8m a8g Nov 17] of no account. *G. P. Kelly*

286

DISTANT MIRAGE (IRE)   2 b.c. (Feb 7) Caerleon (USA) 132 – Desert   101
Bluebell 83 (Kalaglow 132) [1997 7g² 8g* 10d⁵ Nov 1] 210,000Y: smallish, good-
quartered colt: has a quick action: fourth foal: half-brother to useful 1m winner
(probably stayed 1½m) Roses In The Snow (by Be My Guest) and a 6f to 9f winner
in Italy by Try My Best: dam, maiden who stayed 13.6f, sister to dam of Tenby:
odds on, made hard work of winning minor event at Newbury in October, edging
right in tight finish with Evander and Komistar: improved when 4½ lengths fifth of
7 to Special Quest in Criterium de Saint-Cloud: should be well suited by 1½m+.
P. W. Chapple-Hyam

DISTANT STORM   4 ch.g. Pharly (FR) 130 – Candle In The Wind 90 (Thatching   –
131) [1996 40: 11.9m⁵ 15.8m² 1997 a16g Mar 3] robust gelding: poor stayer on flat:
well beaten (all-weather debut) only 4-y-o start: won over hurdles in October and
November. *B. J. Llewellyn*

DISTINCTIVE DANCE (USA)   2 b.c. (Apr 1) Distinctive Pro (USA) –   88 p
Allison's Dance (USA) (Storm Bird (CAN) 134) [1997 7g² 7.9s⁴ Oct 8] $75,000Y:
strong, lengthy colt with scope: fifth foal: brother to Step To The Beat, sprint
winner and graded-stakes placed in USA at 2 yrs, and half-brother to a winner in
USA by Affirmed: dam, won up to 1m in USA, from very good family: sire (by Mr
Prospector) very smart at 6f/7f: shaped well under considerate ride when strong-
finishing second to Name of Love in maiden at Epsom: almost certainly unsuited by
gluepot conditions when only fourth in similar event at York following month:
should stay 1m: well worth another chance at 3 yrs. *Lord Huntingdon*

DISTINCTIVE DREAM (IRE)   3 b.g. Distinctly North (USA) 115 – Green   90
Side (USA) 37 (Green Dancer (USA) 132) [1996 –: 6g 7.9g 6m 6d 1997 6.1m⁴ 6.1m
a6g⁵ a8g 6f⁵ 8d⁴ 8d 7s² 6g* 6g* 6m* a5g* 5g* 6g² 5g⁶ 6d 6m* 6.1g² 5v⁶ 6g 6m²
Nov 1] strong, lengthy gelding: made into a fairly useful handicapper, winning at
Windsor (twice), Salisbury and Southwell in July, back at Windsor (hung right) in
August and at Kempton in September: best at 5f/6f: acts on any turf going and on
fibresand: usually blinkered: forfeited race by cocking jaw and hanging violently left
fourteenth start: sometimes slowly away: held up: quirky, but consistent. *K. T. Ivory*

DISTINCTLY LILLIE (IRE)   2 b. or br.f. (Apr 15) Distinctly North (USA) 115   47 §
– Richmond Lillie (Fairbairn) [1997 5.2g 6s 6f 7s 6.9m Jul 14] IR 4,000Y: tall filly:
fourth foal: half-sister to 2 winners in Italy, including 3-y-o Blue Staff (by Imp
Society), winner up to 11f: dam Irish maiden half-sister to Cheveley Park and Irish
1000 Guineas runner-up Millingdale Lillie: poor and untrustworthy maiden: often
slowly away, and refused to race third outing: sent to Czech Republic. *J. S. Moore*

DISTINCT VINTAGE (IRE)   2 b.c. (Apr 27) Distinctly North (USA) 115 –   88
Princess Raisa (Indian King (USA) 128) [1997 5m⁵ 6f* 5m 6g⁵ Sep 5] IR 7,500F,
62,000Y: sturdy colt: fourth foal: brother to a winner in Japan and half-brother to
1994 2-y-o sprint winner Prince Rudolf (by Cyrano de Bergerac): dam Irish maiden:
won maiden at Brighton in July by 8 lengths, making all: well held in pattern races at
Goodwood and Baden-Baden afterwards: probably better at 6f than 5f: sold 32,000
gns in October. *R. Hannon*

DITTY BOX   3 b.f. Northern State (USA) 91 – Upholder (Young Generation 129)   –
[1996 –: a6g a5g a6s 1997 a8g⁵ Jan 21] of no account. *M. D. I. Usher*

DIVIDE AND RULE   3 b.c. Puissance 110 – Indivisible 56 (Remainder Man   62 d
126§) [1996 76: 5g³ 6m⁵ 5m* 5g⁵ 5f 5m³ 1997 5m 6f⁶ 5g 5.1d³ 5.1d⁴ 5d 6m 5m 8d
5d a6g a5g a5g Dec 18] smallish colt: fair performer at best: largely well beaten at 3
yrs: stays 6f: acts on good to firm and dead going. *R. Hollinshead*

DIVINA LUNA   4 b.f. Dowsing (USA) 124 – Famosa (Dancing Brave (USA)   96
140) [1996 89: 8g* 7f² 8f³ 7.6m* 7f* 7m* 7d⁴ 8m⁵ 1997 7g⁵ 7s 7.6f⁵ 7m* 8m 7m³
7m⁵ 8m⁵ 6d⁶ 6.1d⁵ Oct 30] sturdy, workmanlike filly: useful performer: won minor
event at Warwick in July: best effort when sixth of 16 to My Best Valentine in listed
race at Newmarket penultimate start: effective at 6f to 1m: acts on firm and dead
ground. *J. W. Hills*

DIVINE MISS-P   4 ch.f. Safawan 118 – Faw (Absalom 128) [1996 68: 5m² 6g   63
1997 6g* 6.1d 6s 6g 5m 6d⁶ 7f 5.2m⁵ 5m 5d* 5d⁶ Sep 18] lengthy filly: modest
performer: won maiden at Thirsk in April and handicap at Yarmouth and claimer at

Warwick in August: a sprinter: acts on good to firm and soft ground: races prominently. *A. P. Jarvis*

DIVINITY 3 ch.f. Lycius (USA) 124 – Heavenly Abode (FR) (Habitat 134) [1996 – NR 1997 10g 14.1m³ 11.5s Jul 2] sturdy filly: fourth living foal: half-sister to modest 1½m winner Sacred Mirror (by Shaadi): dam never ran: signs of ability but no worthwhile form in maidens. *C. E. Brittain*

DIVVINAYSHAN (IRE) 2 b.c. (May 10) Darshaan 133 – Sharaniya (USA) 117 55 p (Alleged (USA) 138) [1997 7d⁵ Oct 27] 52,000Y: seventh foal: half-brother to several winners, including useful Sharazan (1½m to 2m in Ireland, by Akarad): dam, French 1¼m to 12.5f winner, half-sister to Prix Vermeille winner Sharaya: 9/2, ran green when about 8 lengths fifth of 9 to Khalas in steadily-run maiden at Lingfield, not given hard time: will improve over further, and should stay at least 1½m. *R. W. Armstrong*

DIXIE CROSSROADS 2 b.f. (Feb 1) Efisio 120 – Moments Joy 56 (Adonijah 46 126) [1997 5.2g 5d⁶ 6.1g⁵ 5g⁵ 6g⁴ 7g Aug 13] small filly: fifth foal: half-sister to 3-y-o Indian Rapture and Irish 1993 2-y-o 7f winner Oranedin (by Squill): dam (maiden) probably stayed 1½m: poor maiden: trained by R. Hannon first 4 starts: stays 6f. *S. Dow*

DIXIE D'OATS 2 b.f. (Apr 25) Alhijaz 122 – Helsanon (Hello Gorgeous (USA) 65 p 128) [1997 8.2g⁶ Sep 23] fourth foal: dam, poor maiden, out of half-sister to Oats: 16/1, staying-on sixth of 14 in maiden at Nottingham: should stay 1½m+: should do better. *E. A. L. Dunlop*

DIXIE EYES BLAZING (USA) 3 ch.f. Gone West (USA) – Mariakova (USA) 56 84 (The Minstrel (CAN) 135) [1996 –: a8.5g⁶ 1997 a7g⁴ Jan 23] modest form at best in all-weather maidens. *R. Charlton*

DIZZY TILLY 3 b.f. Anshan 119 – Nadema (Artaius (USA) 129) [1996 54?: 6g⁶ 68 7f⁴ a7g³ 6m 7m 1997 11.6s³ 11.6g* 11.4g⁵ 10s* 12g⁴ 12.3m² 10.1g 10.5s 12m⁵ 12v Nov 26] tall filly: fair performer: won handicap and minor event at Windsor in June: stays 1½m: acts on good to firm and soft going: often front runner: looked ill-at-ease at Epsom seventh start. *T. J. Naughton*

D J CAT 4 b.g. Ballad Rock 122 – Four-Legged Friend 101 (Aragon 118) [1996 –: 41 8.2d 8.2s 10s a8g a10g⁶ 1997 8m 8g⁴ a8.5g 8f 11.5m a12g Nov 6] rangy gelding: poor mover: poor maiden handicapper: stays 1m. *W. R. Muir*

D'MARTI 2 b.f. (Apr 16) Emarati (USA) 74 – Hellene (Dominion 123) [1997 5g² 70 5d³ 6s³ 5m⁶ Aug 9] 15,500Y: smallish, lengthy filly: half-sister to 6f winner Sideloader Special (by Song): dam unraced: fair maiden: stays 6f: best efforts on dead/soft ground (moved poorly to post final start). *C. B. B. Booth*

DOATING (IRE) 2 b.f. (Feb 26) Doyoun 124 – Hayat (IRE) (Sadler's Wells 72 (USA) 132) [1997 7g 8.1g⁵ Sep 27] IR 24,000Y: good-bodied filly: fourth foal: half-sister to 5-y-o Haya Ya Kefaah: dam unraced close relative of smart French colt (up to 11f) Lichine: still bit backward, better effort in maidens when keeping-on fifth of 7 to Muhaba at Haydock: will stay at least 1¼m. *J. W. Hills*

DOCKLAND EXECUTIVE 2 b.g. (Mar 5) Nomination 125 – Khadino – (Relkino 131) [1997 8.2m Sep 15] 8,200Y: fifth foal: half-brother to 3 winners by Komaite, including 4-y-o La Volta and 5-y-o Mr Teigh: dam no form: 33/1, behind in 17-runner maiden at Nottingham. *B. Smart*

DOCKLANDS CARRIAGE (IRE) 3 b.g. Anita's Prince 126 – Zestino 61 (Shack (USA) 118) [1996 67: 5g² 5.1m 5m⁶ 5.9g⁵ 6m* 6g* 6g³ 6f 6m 6g 1997 6.1m 7.5m⁵ 7g⁶ 6m 6m* 7m 6g 8.2g 8m 8.1m⁵ Aug 15] close-coupled, workmanlike gelding: has a round action: modest handicapper: mainly disappointing after winning at Catterick in May: best form at 6f, should stay further: acts on good to firm ground: often blinkered/visored: sent to Macau. *N. Tinkler*

DOCKLANDS COURIER 5 b.g. Dominion 123 – High Quail (USA) (Blush- – ing Groom (FR) 131) [1996 48, a52: 10m 10.1g⁴ a10g² 11f⁶ a9.4g 1997 a10g Jan 16] smallish, robust gelding: poor maiden handicapper: well beaten only 5-y-o start. *B. J. McMath*

DOCKLANDS DISPATCH (IRE) 2 b.g. (Mar 8) Distinctly North (USA) 115 49
– Frantesa (Red Sunset 120) [1997 5g 5g⁶ 5m⁵ 6g 7g⁶ a7g* 7g 8m 8g⁴ 7m 10d⁵ Oct a61
13] 4,000 2-y-o: compact gelding: first foal: dam Irish 1¼m to 1¾m (and jumps)
winner: modest form when winning seller at Southwell in July, only start on
all-weather: poor on turf: stays 1¼m: acts on fibresand: well beaten when visored
once. *N. Tinkler*

DOCKLANDS LIMO 4 b.c. Most Welcome 131 – Bugle Sound 96 (Bustino 91
136) [1996 78: a8g* 10.3d⁴ 10g* 9m⁶ 9m² 1997 10m 10g 10d³ 12m 10s³ 12.3m*
13.9g 12m Sep 12] leggy colt: has a round action: fairly useful performer: won listed
Ulster Harp Derby at Down Royal in July: seemed to find truly-run 1¾m just beyond
him when seventh to Far Ahead in Tote Ebor at York following month: found to have
viral infection final outing: stays 1½m: acts on equitrack, good to firm and soft
ground: bandaged last 5 starts. *B. J. McMath*

DOCKSIDER (USA) 2 ch.c. (May 2) Diesis 133 – Pump (USA) (Forli (ARG)) 109
[1997 6d⁵ 7m* 7m² 7m² Sep 12] useful-looking colt: fluent mover: eighth foal:
half-brother to several winners, including useful middle-distance performer Classic
Sport (by Nijinsky): dam (unraced) from family of Nureyev: useful performer: won
maiden at Salisbury in July: runner-up afterwards to 3-length winner Central Park in
Lanson Champagne Vintage Stakes at Goodwood, taking turn poorly, and ½-length
winner Daggers Drawn in Laurent-Perrier Rose Champagne Stakes at Doncaster,
running on well despite swishing tail in latter: should stay 1m: well beaten on dead
ground on debut: should win another race or two. *J. W. Hills*

DOC RYAN'S 3 b.c. Damister (USA) 123 – Jolimo 92 (Fortissimo 111) [1996 74
77?: 7f 7m⁶ 8.1s² 1997 7m 8d³ 9g 8s 8.3m 8d 10s³ 8.2s³ 8.2d³ 12s* Nov 6]
fair handicapper: in good form towards end of 1997, winning at Musselburgh in
November: stays 1½m well: suited by ground softer than good: blinkered last 4 starts.
M. J. Ryan

DOCTOR BRAVIOUS (IRE) 4 b.g. Priolo (USA) 127 – Sharp Slipper (Sharpo 68 d
132) [1996 69: a8.5g* 8d⁴ 10.5v 10f 1997 a9.4g 8f⁵ 8m⁴ 8.2g 8m a8.5f⁵ 8g 8m
Oct 28] rangy gelding: fair handicapper: well below best after third start: left M. Bell
after sixth one: should stay beyond 1m: acts on firm ground and fibresand: usually
visored: has found little, and sometimes hangs left and swishes tail. *B. Ellison*

DOCTOR'S REMEDY 11 br.g. Doc Marten 104 – Champagne Party (Amber –
Rama (USA) 133) [1996 –: 12.1d 15.8g 1997 a12g Feb 17] of no account nowadays.
Mrs J. Jordan

DODO (IRE) 2 b.f. (Mar 1) Alzao (USA) 117 – Dead Certain 123§ (Absalom 128) 82
[1997 5m⁵ 5d⁴ 6m² 6g² 6m⁴ Aug 9] fourth foal: half-sister to 3-y-o Dead Aim and
useful Irish 7f and 1¼m winner Hamad (both by Sadler's Wells): dam sprinter,
became temperamental: fairly useful maiden: second at Windsor and Ascot in the
summer: fractious start before disappointing final outing: should stay at least 1m.
D. R. C. Elsworth

DOG WATCH 2 ch.g. (Jan 25) Night Shift (USA) – Abet (USA) 64 (Alleged 83 p
(USA) 138) [1997 6.1g 7d* 7m² Nov 4] good-bodied gelding: first foal: dam,
thrice-raced half-sister to useful middle-distance filly Shemozzle, should have stayed
1¼m: easy winner of 3-runner private sweepstakes at Newmarket in October: 2
lengths second of 18 to Gypsy Passion in Redcar maiden: will stay at least 1m: should
do better. *J. H. M. Gosden*

DOKOS (USA) 3 b.c. Nureyev (USA) 131 – Pasadoble (USA) (Prove Out (USA)) 98
[1996 NR 1997 8g² 8d² May 5] strong, lengthy colt: fluent mover: brother to 3
winners, including outstanding miler Miesque and smart 1m winner (stayed 1¼m)
Siam: dam smart French miler out of half-sister to top-class 1½m filly Comtesse de
Loir: won 20-runner newcomers event at Newmarket in April: odds on, length
second of 6 to Peartree House in minor event at Doncaster following month: will stay
1¼m: edgy and attended by 2 handlers on debut. *H. R. A. Cecil*

DOLLIVER (USA) 5 b.g. Northern Baby (CAN) 127 – Mabira (Habitat 134) –
[1996 –: 10m 10m 11.7f a12g a9.4g 1997 a12g Jan 23] of little account nowadays.
C. A. Dwyer

DOMAPPEL 5 b.g. Domynsky 110 – Appelania 63 (Star Appeal 133) [1996 80: 76
10.8g⁵ 12m² 12m⁶ 11.9m 12f* 12.5f² 13.9g⁶ 12g 1997 12m 14.1m² May 26] lengthy
gelding: fair handicapper, lightly raced in 1997: stays 1¾m: acts on firm and dead
ground: has run well when sweating: joined M. Banks. *Mrs J. Cecil*

DOMINANT AIR 3 b.g. Primo Dominie 121 – Area Girl 76 (Jareer (USA) 115) 87
[1996 77+: 5m⁶ 5.7d 6g³ 5.2g* a5g a5g* 1997 a6g* a6g³ 5.1m* 7s² 7.1m⁵ 6m² 5m*
5d⁴ Oct 17] smallish, strong gelding: fairly useful performer: won claimer at
Southwell in January and handicaps at Bath (first start for nearly 6 months) in July
and Newmarket in October: effective at 5f to 7f: acts on good to firm and soft going
and on fibresand, ran poorly on equitrack. *Sir Mark Prescott*

DOMINANT DUCHESS 3 b.f. Old Vic 136 – Andy's Find (USA) (Buckfinder 86
(USA)) [1996 NR 1997 12.5m* 10g* 12.3s⁶ 11.6g² 14m² Aug 2] lengthy filly: sixth
foal: half-sister to 2 winners, including useful 1991 2-y-o 7f winner Artic Tracker
(later stayed 1¼m, by Eskimo): dam unraced: fairly useful form: won claimer at
Warwick in March and minor event at Nottingham in April: better efforts afterwards,
good second in competitive handicap at Goodwood final start, having been detached
(possibly reluctant) early: will stay 2m: acts on good to firm ground, ran poorly on
soft. *J. W. Hills*

DOMINELLE 5 b.m. Domynsky 110 – Gymcrak Lovebird 84 (Taufan (USA) 56
119) [1996 59: 5g 5.9m 5g 5g 5f* 5f² 5m³ 5m² 6f³ 6f³ 5m 5f² 5m⁴ 6.1m² 6d 5.1g²
1997 5g 5g⁵ 5f⁵ 5m⁶ 5g³ 5m 6g 6g 5d² 5g 5f 6d Sep 5] small mare: shows knee action:
modest handicapper: consistent at 4 yrs, not in 1997: stays 6f: acts on firm and soft
ground: blinkered once as 2-y-o: often sweating and edgy: tends to wander: flashes
tail. *T. D. Easterby*

DOMINO FLYER 4 b.g. Warrshan (USA) 117 – Great Dilemma 77 (Vaigly 71
Great 127) [1996 65, a71: a8g⁵ 8.3d³ a7g* 9.2s* a12g⁶ a9.4g a8g⁴ a9.4g a8.5g a8g²
a8g* a8g³ 1997 a8g* a8g³ a8g⁶ 10.1g* 11.1d a8g a8g 10.9d a12g⁴ 10d Nov 3] leggy,
angular gelding: fair handicapper: successful at Southwell (amateurs) in January and
Newcastle (made all) in March: mostly well below form afterwards: stays 1¼m well:
acts on fibresand and soft ground. *Mrs A. Swinbank*

DOMINO STYLE 3 b.f. Primo Dominie 121 – Corman-Style 52 (Ahonoora 122) –
[1996 54: 8g 7m⁴ 1997 8g⁵ Jul 7] modest maiden at 2 yrs: well beaten only 3-y-o
start: not certain to stay beyond 1m. *M. J. Camacho*

DOMULLA 7 br.h. Dominion 123 – Ulla Laing 107 (Mummy's Pet 125) [1996 –
105: 6s 6m⁴ 6f 1997 6g Jul 4] sparely-made horse: useful sprint handicapper, lightly
raced: ran as though something amiss only 7-y-o start. *R. Akehurst*

DONA FILIPA 4 ch.f. Precocious 126 – Quisissanno 76 (Be My Guest (USA) 51
126) [1996 6m 6m 6f⁶ 6g 7f⁶ 7m⁶ 1997 7d 10g 6.9f 5g⁴ 6d 5m³ 5m 6m⁵ 5g³ 5m
5m* 5g 5g 6.1m 5m 5s 5m Nov 4] good-topped filly: modest handicapper: won
maiden event at Musselburgh in August: best form at 5f: acts on good to firm and
heavy ground: none too consistent. *Miss L. C. Siddall*

DONEGAL SEAN 2 ch.c. (Jan 21) Alhijaz 122 – Malzeta (IRE) 49 (Alzao –
(USA) 117) [1997 6f⁵ 7d 6g 8m a6g Nov 13] 13,000Y: close-coupled colt: has a
round action: first foal: dam, maiden, stayed 1¼m: only a little sign of ability: trained
first 3 starts by K. McAuliffe. *N. A. Callaghan*

DONNA'S DANCER (IRE) 3 ch.g. Magical Wonder (USA) 125 – Ice On Fire 52 d
(Thatching 131) [1996 66: 5g 5m⁴ 6m 5m² 5f² 6m⁵ 5g² 1997 5m³ 5.9f³ 5g² 6s 5m
5g 7g Aug 9] tall gelding: modest maiden at best in 1997: stays 6f: acts on firm
ground, well beaten only start on soft: wears blinkers: very slowly away last 2 starts.
N. Tinkler

DONNA'S DOUBLE 2 ch.c. (Mar 21) Weldnaas (USA) 112 – Shadha 57 –
(Shirley Heights 130) [1997 5m 5m 7g 7.5v⁶ Jul 5] 12,000Y: brother to 4-y-o
Honestly and 1½m winner Last Corner and half-brother to 3 winners, including 5f (at
2 yrs) to 1½m winner Super Heights (by Superlative): dam ran twice at 2 yrs: no
worthwhile form in maidens and a seller. *N. Tinkler*

DON PEPE 6 br.g. Dowsing (USA) 124 – Unique Treasure (Young Generation 68
129) [1996 66: 7.1g 7f⁶ 7.1g 6m* 6f² 6m 7m 7m⁵ 7.1g² 7m 6m³ 6d² 5.7m 7m* 7m
6m³ 7g a7g 1997 5.7d 6m* 6s² 6m⁴ 7g⁴ 6m 6g 7f 6.9m 6m 6.1s Oct 15] leggy gelding:

has a round action: fair handicapper: won at Yarmouth in June: in-and-out form afterwards, blinkered final start: effective at 6f to 1m: acts on firm and soft ground, ran poorly only start on the all-weather: has joined D. Nicholls. *R. Boss*

DON SEBASTIAN   3 b.c. Indian Ridge 123 – Sunley Stars (Sallust 134) [1996   68
80: 5m⁶ 6f⁴ 5m⁵ 6.9d² 7s² 1997 a9.4g* a8.5g⁴ 9g 10g 8g⁴ 8.5s² 8g⁶ a8.5g a10f Dec   a79
19] close-coupled colt: fair performer: won maiden at Wolverhampton in February:
below form after next start, including in blinkers: last of 8 in Dubai final start: stays
9.4f: acts on fibresand, best turf efforts on good ground or softer. *W. J. Haggas*

DON'T CARE (IRE)   6 b.m. Nordico (USA) – Eyeliner (USA) (Raise A Native)   75 d
[1996 93: 6s 6d 5g* 5d* 5g² 6m⁴ 7m⁵ 6.3m² 5m⁵ 5m³ 6g* 6m 6v 6g 1997 7m⁵ 6s 7g
6g 6d 5m 6g² 6g 5g 6g Oct 22] ex-Irish mare: fair form at best in handicaps in Britain:
seems to stay 7f: acts on good to firm and dead ground: usually blinkered: inconsistent. *Miss L. A. Perratt*

DON'T DROP BOMBS (USA)   8 ch.g. Fighting Fit (USA) – Promised Star   41
(USA) (Star de Naskra (USA)) [1996 48, a45: a13g² a16g a12g³ a8g* a13g³ a8g²   a45
10.3d 8g 10.1m⁶ 9.7f² 10.1g* 10g⁴ 8m 12g² 10f* a10g⁶ a12g³ a10g³ 1997 a12g a10g⁶
a8g³ a13g⁴ a13g² a8g* 12g 11.5d⁵ 12g 8m⁴ 12g 10g a10g³ a12s³ a12g² a10g³ Dec 10]
angular gelding: poor handicapper: mainly runs in amateurs/ladies events: won at
Lingfield in March: left D. Thom after thirteenth start: effective at 1m to 13f: acts on
firm ground and the all-weather (not raced on fibresand since 6 yrs): usually visored:
mostly ridden by Miss J. Feilden: game. *R. McGhin*

DON'T FORGET MIKIE (IRE)   4 b.g. Don't Forget Me 127 – Sokolova 75   54
(Red Regent 123) [1996 6s² a7.5g* a7.5g⁴ 7.5f⁶ 8.5f³ 7h⁵ 7f² 8d 10d 9s 1997 8d 6m³
8s a6g⁶ a7.5g 9g⁵ 8g⁴ 7h 7g a7g 9.3g⁴ Oct 25] fair maiden for M. Heaton-Ellis at 2
yrs: won a minor contest in Belgium at 3 yrs: third of 16 in apprentice handicap at
Folkestone in April, but showed form only occasionally back in Belgium otherwise
in 1997: finds 6f a bare minimum, and stays 8.5f: acts on firm ground and equitrack:
ran poorly in visor. *Alex Vanderhaeghen, Belgium*

DON'T FORGET SHOKA (IRE)   3 gr.f. Don't Forget Me 127 – Shoka (FR)   25
86 (Kaldoun (FR) 122) [1996 45d: 5s⁵ 5g⁵ 5.3f⁵ a6g² 6.1d* 7f 7m⁴ 6g³ 6m 7.1m 1997
8.2m 6.9m⁵ 8.3m 6.9d Oct 21] workmanlike filly: poor performer: stays 7f: acts
on firm and dead ground: blinkered (raced too freely) final start: inconsistent.
J. S. Moore

DONT SHOOT FAIRIES   5 ch.h. Vague Shot 108 – Fairy Fans (Petingo 135)   –
[1996 73: 12m⁵ 12m⁵ 12g 13.3s⁴ 11.4m⁴ 1997 a11g⁶ Feb 10] neat horse: fair
handicapper in 1996: well beaten only 5-y-o start. *J. Pearce*

DON'T WORRY ME (IRE)   5 b.m. Dancing Dissident (USA) 119 – Diva   113
Encore 74 (Star Appeal 133) [1996 113: 10v 7.5v⁵ 6.5d* 6m* 6g* 5d⁵ 5m³ 6m³
5g⁴ 6g⁶ 6g² 5d 5d* 1997 5.5g⁵ 5d⁵ 5m⁴ 5d* 5m 5d 6g* 5f 7d 6s³ Nov 16]
     A total of forty-one runners contested Royal Ascot's two big sprints, the
King's Stand and the Cork And Orrery, the field of eighteen for the former
event being the largest since the Second World War and indicative of the fact
that the title of champion sprinter was up for grabs. The King's Stand did little
to make the hierarchy among the top sprinters any clearer, won as it was by
Don't Worry Me, a 33/1-shot trained in the French Provinces, ahead of the
other French-trained runner Titus Livius, who started as one of three 7/1 co-
favourites. Don't Worry Me had finished behind Titus Livius in all three of her
starts in the spring prior to Royal Ascot, and in her last two outings, the Prix de
Saint-Georges at Longchamp and the Prix du Gros-Chene at Chantilly she'd
finished behind one of the other co-favourites, Hever Golf Rose, as well. Only
one of the King's Stand field started at longer odds than Don't Worry Me, but
Olivier Peslier had already ridden a couple of big-priced winners in huge fields
earlier at the meeting (Fly To The Stars at 20/1 in the Britannia Handicap and
Red Robbo at 16/1 in the Royal Hunt Cup), and he gave Don't Worry Me a
confident ride, producing the mare to lead inside the final furlong, where she
held the even later challenge of the rather unlucky Titus Livius by a neck, with
Hever Golf Rose a length back in third. Much further down the field were Ya

King's Stand Stakes, Royal Ascot—
a French one–two as Don't Worry Me hangs on from the unlucky-in-running Titus Livius (rail);
Hever Golf Rose is a credible third

Malak and Compton Place, both set to win top sprints later in the season but neither at their best in the conditions, with heavy rain changing the going to good to soft during the afternoon.

Peslier has quickly made a name for himself in Britain and Don't Worry Me spent two full seasons racing here in her younger days, but the name of trainer Guy Henrot will be unfamiliar to most this side of the Channel. Remarkably, Don't Worry Me was Henrot's first runner in Britain, but neither he nor owner Jean-Francois Gribomont, a Belgian textile magnate, are exactly strangers to success. Henrot, from his base in western France, regularly makes the top five flat trainers in France by races won (he topped that list three times in the late 'eighties, once with 168 winners), while Monsieur Gribomont who owns around ninety horses (about a third of which he trains himself) announced after the King's Stand that this was his 1,122nd success as an owner!

Don't Worry Me returned to Britain for her next two starts, finishing a credible seventh under an 8-lb penalty to the King's Stand fourth Averti in the King George Stakes at Goodwood, then seemingly having no excuses for a below-form ninth in the Nunthorpe. She met with further success abroad, though, when beating another French runner, Dyhim Diamond, one and a half lengths in the six-furlong Jacobs Goldene Peitsche, a Group 2 event at Baden-Baden in September. Back on home turf she finished down the field in the Prix de l'Abbaye and the Prix de la Foret at Longchamp. But she ended the season with another good effort abroad, this time in Italy, when third in the Group 3 Premio Umbria in Rome.

As mentioned above Don't Worry Me was trained in Britain at two and three, when she showed useful form and bags of speed—best at the minimum trip with the ground firmer than good—for Francis Lee's stable. She was sold for 31,000 guineas at the Newmarket December Sales in 1995 and made her debut for her new connections the following month at Cagnes-sur-Mer—over a mile and a quarter in the mud! Don't Worry Me was soon returned to sprinting, and, after completing a hat-trick in a minor event in the Provinces and a couple of handicaps at Evry, she spent most of her four-year-old season competing in the top French sprints, reserving her best effort up to that point for her thirteenth and final outing of the year, a win in the Prix du Petit Couvert at Longchamp which prompted connections to aim for Royal Ascot in 1997.

		Nureyev	Northern Dancer
	Dancing Dissident (USA)	(b 1977)	Special
	(b 1986)	Absentia	Raise A Cup
Don't Worry Me (IRE)		(b 1979)	Cecelia
(b.m. 1992)		Star Appeal	Appiani II
	Diva Encore	(b 1970)	Sterna
	(br 1983)	Regal Twin	Majestic Prince
		(b 1972)	Times Two

Don't Worry Me is the product of extremes, by Temple Stakes winner Dancing Dissident out of Diva Encore, who won handicaps over a mile and three-quarters at Yarmouth and a mile and a half at Leicester and who stayed two miles. Diva Encore had already produced a fairly useful sprinter to Dancing Dissident in Encore M'Lady (also trained by Francis Lee), who won the valuable William Hill Trophy Handicap at York and was later successful at up to seven furlongs. Don't Worry Me also has a winning half-sister in France by Flash of Steel, the nine-furlong winner Eliade, and a winning half-brother in Italy by Magical Wonder, Golden Satin, who's won several races at up to a mile and a half. Grandam Regal Twin won at around a mile but appears in the pedigree of several above-average performers at shorter trips, including as the third dam of 1995 Prix Robert Papin winner Lucky Lionel and the latest European Free Handicap winner Hidden Meadow. Great grandam Times Two was placed in several stakes races in the USA, notably the Kentucky Oaks.

Don't Worry Me is a leggy, quick-actioned mare. Formerly a front-runner, she's ridden more patiently nowadays and is effective on soft ground as well as firm and at up to six and a half furlongs now, too. She again showed a tendency to sweat on occasions in the latest season, and she had her tongue tied at Goodwood. *G. Henrot, France*

DON'T WORRY MIKE   3 ch.g. Forzando 122 – Hat Hill (Roan Rocket 128)   49
[1996 52+: 7m 6m 8g⁶ 7m⁴ 8g 1997 a6g² a6g³ 7.5d 10s 8m 8.2m 6.9m² 7.1m² 7.1g a6g a7g⁴ 8g a8.5g² a10g Nov 18] leggy, workmanlike gelding: poor maiden: left F. Lee after ninth start: stays 8.5f: acts on good to firm going and fibresand: effective blinkered or not: none too consistent. *J. L. Spearing*

DOODLE   2 b.f. (Feb 3) Green Desert (USA) 127 – Quillotern (USA) (Arctic Tern   –
(USA) 126) [1997 5m 5f Sep 17] 40,000Y: fifth foal: half-sister to 3 winners, including 5-y-o Quilling and 4-y-o Harbour Dues: dam half-sister to Leap Lively, dam of Forest Flower: well held in maidens. *W. J. Haggas*

DOOMNA (IRE)   2 b.f. (Mar 4) Machiavellian (USA) 123 – Just A Mirage 76   93 p
(Green Desert (USA) 127) [1997 7m² Jul 31] close-coupled filly: second foal: sister to 3-y-o Kahal: dam maiden (stayed 1m) sister to smart 1m winner Distant Oasis and half-sister to very smart colts Reprimand and Wiorno: 6/1 and better for race, ½-length second of 11 to Midnight Line in maiden at Goodwood, leading most of final 1f after sluggish start: should stay 1m: has joined Godolphin: sure to improve, and win a race. *E. A. L. Dunlop*

DOOZE (IRE)   2 b. or br.f. (Apr 22) Marju (IRE) 127 – Angelus Chimes 80   –
(Northfields (USA)) [1997 6m 6d⁶ 6m Jul 14] IR 46,000Y: lengthy filly: half-sister to several winners, notably smart 6f (at 2 yrs) and 1¼m winner Revelation (by Thatching): dam Irish 4-y-o 1½m winner: well beaten in maidens: visored and gave impression something amiss final outing. *J. H. M. Gosden*

DORADO BEACH   3 b.f. Lugana Beach 116 – Cannon Boy (USA) (Canonero   47
(USA)) [1996 46: 6m 7f 1997 7m 6.9m 6.1m 6s 6.9m 6g⁴ 6m² 6m a7g* Oct 18] tall filly: poor performer: left B. Hills after reappearance: won maiden at Wolverhampton in October: stays 7f, not sure to get much further: acts on good to firm going and fibresand: visored (raced freely and below form) twice. *L. G. Cottrell*

DOR

DORAID (IRE)   2 b.c. (Feb 20) Danehill (USA) 126 – Quiche 83 (Formidable   81 p
(USA) 125) [1997 7.1g³ Sep 27] IR 95,000Y: robust colt: fourth living foal:
half-brother to useful Irish sprinter Symboli Kildare (by Kaldoun) and a winner in
Japan by Dancehall: dam 6f winner: 11/2 and green, encouraging 2 lengths third of
12 to Last Christmas in maiden at Haydock, looking big danger penultimate 1f:
showed a short, round action to post: likely to prove best up to 1m: sure to improve.
J. H. M. Gosden

DORMY THREE   7 b.g. Morston (FR) 125 – Dominant 86 (Behistoun 131)   –
[1996 67: 12m⁶ 12m 10.8g³ 10.8f⁴ 12g 10f⁵ 10.2m⁶ 11.7f⁴ 11.6d³ 12.1g⁵ 1997 10d
17.2d a11g May 19] compact gelding: fair handicapper at 6 yrs: well beaten in 1997.
R. J. Hodges

DORTON GRANGE   2 ch.f. (Apr 26) Absalom 128 – Stranger To Fear (Never   –
So Bold 135) [1997 5.1m 5s a5g 7g a8.5g Oct 18] 1,600Y: leggy filly: fourth foal:
dam, no form, out of half-sister to dam of Colonel Collins and Lit de Justice: little
sign of ability in maidens and a seller. *K. C. Comerford*

DOSSES DAN (IRE)   5 b.h. Danehill (USA) 126 – Flyaway Bride (USA) 104   –
(Blushing Groom (FR) 131) [1996 –: a8.5g 1997 a12g Dec 19] of little account
nowadays. *B. Preece*

DOT   2 b.f. (Jan 23) Reprimand 122 – Summer Eve 63 (Hotfoot 126) [1997 6f 7g   41
6m⁴ Jul 28] 4,000Y: half-sister to a 2-y-o winner in Holland by Chilibang: dam
(maiden) suited by 6f: poor maiden: should stay beyond 6f. *R. Hannon*

DOUBLE ACTION   3 br.g. Reprimand 122 – Final Shot 91 (Dalsaan 125) [1996   111
83+: 5m³ 5d⁴ 5m* 5f³ 1997 6m 5.1d⁵ 5d 6d² 6g* 6g⁴ 5g 6m 6m 6s* 6g² 6g⁴ Oct 24]
well-made gelding: has a quick action: smart handicapper: successful at Ripon in
June and York (£25,000 Lawrence Batley Handicap, by 8 lengths from Return of
Amin) in September: creditable ¾-length second of 29 to Wildwood Flower in Ayr
Gold Cup and fourth of 18 to My Best Valentine at Newbury: stays 7f: likely to stay 7f:
seems suited by good ground or softer: sometimes hangs left: should win more races
in 1998 when conditions are in his favour. *T. D. Easterby*

DOUBLE ALLEGED (USA)   3 b. or br.c. Alleged (USA) 138 – Danseuse   87
Etoile (USA) 102 (Buckpasser) [1996 70p: 7g⁶ 1997 10d² 12m² 10g³ 11.1g* 12v
12d⁶ 12g Oct 25] tall colt: fairly useful performer: landed the odds in 4-runner
maiden at Hamilton in September: stiff tasks in handicaps last 3 starts: stays 1½m:
acts on dead and good to firm ground: sold 20,000 gns, to go to Poland. *M. Johnston*

DOUBLE APPEAL (IRE)   2 b.f. (Apr 14) Waajib 121 – Leaping Salmon   –
(Salmon Leap (USA) 131) [1997 6g 6g a5g⁶ 6g⁴ 7m Oct 1] IR 2,700Y: leggy filly: a40
fifth foal: half-sister to a winner in Norway: dam well beaten in Ireland: poor maiden:
best effort in Southwell seller third start. *Capt. J. Wilson*

Lawrence Batley Rated Stakes (Handicap), York—
Double Action shows his rivals a muddy pair of heels, recording a smart performance

DOUBLE BLADE   2 b.c. (May 5) Kris 135 – Sesame 117 (Derrylin 115) [1997   81
8m⁵ 9m² Sep 26] 18,000Y: big, angular colt: third foal: half-brother to 3-y-o Hadidi
and 4-y-o Calendula: dam, middle-distance stayer, half-sister to Celeric: fair form in
maidens at Doncaster and Redcar, at latter course 2½ lengths second to stable-
companion Sinon in steadily-run event, pulling hard then wandering: should stay at
least 1½m: carried head awkwardly both starts. *M. Johnston*

DOUBLE BOUNCE   7 b.g. Interrex (CAN) – Double Gift 68 (Cragador 110)   91
[1996 94: 6g 6f³ 6m* 6m² 6m⁶ 6m 7m 1997 6d⁶ 6g 7g 6m 7m⁶ 6g 6.1g³ 6g⁵ 6m⁵
Nov 4] good-quartered gelding: fairly useful handicapper: failed to win in 1997, but
ran creditably last 3 starts: best form over 6f: acts on firm and dead ground: blinkered
(well held) sixth outing: successful when sweating: often early to
post: normally held up. *P. J. Makin*

DOUBLE BRANDY   2 ch.c. (Mar 13) Elmaamul (USA) 125 – Brand (Shareef   78 p
Dancer (USA) 135) [1997 6m⁵ 5d⁵ 6d² Oct 28] lengthy colt: second foal: dam
unraced half-sister to useful 1m and 1½m (in UAE) winner Clever Cliche, out of
sister to Height of Fashion, the dam of Unfuwain and Nashwan: fair form: ½-length
second of 21 to Bandbox in maiden at Leicester: should stay 1m+: probably capable
of better still. *I. A. Balding*

DOUBLE CLASSIC (USA)   2 br.c. (Mar 19) Riverman (USA) 131 – Adam's   78 p
Angel (USA) (Halo (USA)) [1997 8.2g⁵ 7f³ Oct 29] $190,000Y: half-brother to
several winners in USA, including one in minor stakes by Talc: dam won up to 9f in
USA: fair form in maidens at Nottingham and Yarmouth, readily outpaced closing
stages when 8½ lengths third to Asad in latter: will stay at least 1¼m: should do
better. *M. R. Stoute*

DOUBLE CREST (IRE)   3 b.f. Royal Academy (USA) 130 – Sweetbird (Ela-   57
Mana-Mou 132) [1996 69p: a7g⁵ a8.5g⁵ 1997 a8g⁴ a10g⁴ 10.8g a12f⁴ Dec 1]
lightly-raced maiden: form in Britain in 1997 only on first of 3 starts (reportedly lame
last of them) for M. Johnston. *M. Lindstrom, Sweden*

DOUBLE DASH (IRE)   4 gr.g. Darshaan 133 – Safka (USA) 104 (Irish River   –
(FR) 131) [1996 –: 13.1d⁴ 17.2f⁵ 16f 1997 16.1g Mar 25] good-topped gelding:
disappointing maiden: a hard ride and one to treat with caution. *D. Moffatt*

DOUBLE ECHO (IRE)   9 br.g. Glow (USA) – Piculet 69 (Morston (FR) 125)   –
[1996 55: 12g 12m⁶ 15.8s⁶ 14.8m² 14m 14.1d⁶ 12g 12m* 10m⁵ 11.9g a12g 1997
a14g a12s a14g Dec 18] sturdy, compact gelding: modest handicapper at 8 yrs: well
beaten late on in 1997: tried blinkered/visored. *J. D. Bethell*

DOUBLE ECLIPSE (IRE)   5 b.h. Ela-Mana-Mou 132 – Solac (FR) (Gay   120
Lussac (ITY) 116) [1996 122: 16.2g* 15m* 15.5d* 1997 20g⁶ 16m³ 15.9g*
15.5m² 16f² 15.5d⁵ Oct 26]
     'The engine is still there but he hasn't got the wheels.' The analogy used
by trainer Mark Johnston after Double Eclipse had finished fifth in the Prix
Royal-Oak at Longchamp in October was both appropriate and succinct. But
this smart stayer has done his connections proud in four seasons' racing, winning seven of his eighteen starts and earning nigh on £200,000 in win and place
prize money. A serious off-fore tendon problem had cut short Double Eclipse's
1996 campaign—he won all three of his starts that season but wasn't seen out
after May—and also made him difficult to train on his return. It was no surprise
that he could finish only a remote sixth in the Gold Cup at Royal Ascot following an absence from the course of thirteen months, but Double Eclipse did lead
from five furlongs out until tiring early in the straight, and the outing was just
what was needed to bring him back to near his best. Next time out he finished
third in the Goodwood Cup, two lengths behind Double Trigger, his full brother
who had beaten him a neck when the pair were first and second in the same
event two years earlier. Almost three weeks later Double Eclipse gained a
thoroughly deserved success in the Weatherbys Insurance Lonsdale Stakes
(upgraded from listed to Group 3 status before the latest running) at York, a
race he'd won in 1995. The 1996 winner Celeric was also in the field, but,
having won the Gold Cup in the meantime, he was set to concede 9 lb to Double

Weatherbys Insurance Lonsdale Stakes, York—
Double Eclipse repeats his 1995 win in the race, galloping his rivals into submission;
Samraan and Windsor Castle are in vain pursuit

Eclipse. Celeric was unable to trouble Double Eclipse, the latter well ridden by Michael Roberts who jumped him off in front and gradually increased the tempo. Double Eclipse, as game as ever, kept pulling out extra when pressed hard by Samraan in the straight and went on to beat that horse by two and a half lengths, with the three-year-old Windsor Castle staying on to take third. Double Trigger wasn't quite able to repeat this form in three subsequent outings, though he did finish second in both the Prix Gladiateur at Longchamp and the Jockey Club Cup at Newmarket. It's worth pointing out that he'd won over both courses earlier in his career, taking the Zetland Stakes at Newmarket as a two-year-old and the Prix de Barbeville and Prix Vicomtesse Vigier at four years. Trainer Mark Johnston has continued his excellent record in the Zetland Stakes, by the way, with his 1996 runner-up Eldorado and 1997 winner Trigger Happy being brother and sister, like 'the Doubles', by Ela-Mana-Mou.

		Pitcairn	Petingo
	Ela-Mana-Mou	(b 1971)	Border Bounty
	(b 1976)	Rose Bertin	High Hat
Double Eclipse (IRE)		(ch 1970)	Wide Awake
(b.h. 1992)		Gay Lussac	Faberge II
	Solac (FR)	(ch 1969)	Green As Grass
	(ch 1977)	Soragna	Orvieto II
		(b 1965)	Savigny

Solac has produced several winners besides the two brothers but none so good, although Farat (by Woodman) was a fairly useful stayer who finished third in the 1992 Cesarewitch. A half-sister to the Derby Italiano winner Sirlad

The Middleham Partnership's "Double Eclipse"

and the Derby Italiano runner-up Sortingo out of the 1968 Oaks d'Italia winner Soragna, Solac ran four times in Italy without success. Double Eclipse, a tall, well-made horse with a round action, acted on any going. It was a pity he didn't have an orthodox preparation for the Gold Cup, as it was the only time he tackled a distance beyond two miles and it should have suited him very well. There's no doubt that a fully-fit Double Eclipse wouldn't have been so easy to peg back in the home straight at Ascot. Double Eclipse, effective ridden from the front or held up, was thoroughly genuine. He is to stand at the Emral Stud, near Wrexham, at a fee of £1,250. *M. Johnston*

DOUBLE EDGED 2 ch.c. (Mar 18) Sabrehill (USA) 120 – Island Lake 97 (Kala-   85 p
glow 132) [1997 7.9s⁵ 8g⁴ 8s² a8g* Nov 24] strong, good-topped colt: has plenty of
scope: fifth foal: half-brother to Irish 7f and 12.5f winner Lowlack (by Niniski) and
German 7.5f winner Chester Barrie (by Indian Ridge): dam 1½m winner: fairly
useful form when ½-length second of 22 to Eco Friendly in maiden at Doncaster,
battling on well: odds on, workmanlike winner of similar event at Southwell later in
November: will stay at least 1¼m: likely to do better. *M. Johnston*

DOUBLE-E-I-B-A 3 br.g. Reprimand 122 – Doppio 62 (Dublin Taxi) [1996 –:   –
7.1m 8m 7m 1997 7s 8f Jul 16] of little account. *D. J. S. Cosgrove*

DOUBLE EIGHT (IRE) 3 b.f. Common Grounds 118 – Boldabsa 96 (Persian   77
Bold 123) [1996 –: 6m 7g a7g 1997 10f² 9.9v³ 11.9f* 12.3m* 11.9g 12m² a12g⁵   a–
Oct 6] fair performer: won minor event at Brighton and handicap at Chester in the
summer: stays 1½m: probably acts on any turf going, below form on fibresand: sold
21,000 gns in December. *B. W. Hills*

DOUBLE ESPRESSO (IRE) 3 b.f. Taufan (USA) 119 – Kilcoy (USA) (Sec-   78
reto (USA) 128) [1996 78: 6m 7.9g² a8.5g⁴ 8g* 8f² a8g* a8.5g³ 1997 a10g² a10g⁵
12g Sep 5] leggy filly: fair performer: below form in 1997 after reappearance,
something seemingly amiss on second start: stays 1¼m: acts on firm going and the
all-weather: front runner: sold, to go to Poland. *M. Johnston*

DOU

DOUBLE FLIGHT   3 b.f. Mtoto 134 – Sariah (Kris 135) [1996 71: 7f³ 7d 8m*   73
8g 1997 12.3d⁴ 10m 9.2g⁴ 8.5d⁵ 12.3m² 9.9d² 11.1m⁶ 10m⁵ Sep 15] big, angular
filly: fair handicapper: effective at 1¼m (granted decent test) to 1½m: acts on firm
and dead ground: sweating and edgy (gave impression something amiss) second start
at 2 yrs: joined Miss B. Sanders. *M. Johnston*

DOUBLE GOLD   3 b.f. Statoblest 120 – Adriya 94 (Vayrann 133) [1996 74: 6g   60
7m² 7f* 7.3m* 8m 6.5m 1997 7m 8m 9.9m² 10.8m* 10g* 10m 10g* 8g⁵ 7d 7m⁶ 10m
10f Oct 1] tall filly: modest performer: won claimers at Warwick in May and
Newbury and Sandown (then left B. Meehan) in June: well beaten last 4 starts, too
headstrong final 2: will prove best up to 11f: acts on firm going: blinkered second and
third starts: front runner: sold, to go to Saudi Arabia. *M. Bell*

DOUBLE INDEMNITY (IRE)   4 b.g. Doubletour (USA) – Splendid Pleasure   –
(Dunphy 124) [1996 8.5f³ 9g 1997 a9.4g a13g Jan 11] IR 3,000Y: ex-Irish gelding:
fourth reported foal: dam once-raced daughter of half-sister to Champion Stakes
winner Hurry Harriet: well beaten in maidens. *G. C. Bravery*

DOUBLE-J (IRE)   3 b.g. Fayruz 116 – Farriers Slipper (Prince Tenderfoot (USA)   81
126) [1996 82: 6s³ 5g⁵ 5f² 6.1m² 5m* 5f² 6m⁶ 6m 1997 6.1s² 7g 6f⁴ 6d 7.1g³ 7d 8d
Oct 16] close-coupled gelding: fairly useful handicapper: well held last 2 starts: stays
7f: acts on firm and soft ground: tried visored. *K. McAuliffe*

DOUBLE MARCH   4 b.g. Weldnaas (USA) 112 – Double Gift 68 (Cragador   57
110) [1996 84d: 7d² 7.1m 8.3g 7s 7g a8g a8.5s⁴ 1997 a10g⁵ a10g⁶ a8g⁵ 7.1g 8f 6m³
6g Oct 27] sturdy gelding: modest handicapper: trained by P. Webber until after third
start (off track 8 months subsequently): seems effective at 6f (in strongly-run race),
and may prove best up to 1m: acts on good to firm going and the all-weather.
K. T. Ivory

DOUBLE MATT (IRE)   5 b.g. Double Schwartz 128 – Kasarose (Owen Dudley   60
121) [1996 74: 6m⁴ 7f⁵ 7s 1997 6g 6d 6d³ 6g⁶ 6m Aug 9] strong gelding: modest
performer at best in 1997: stays 6f: acts on good to firm and dead ground. *Mrs P. Sly*

DOUBLE-O   3 b.g. Sharpo 132 – Ktolo 80 (Tolomeo 127) [1996 ?, a77: 6g 8g a6g³   a81
a6g* a7s⁵ 1997 a6g⁶ a6g* 6g 6.1s a6g a6g a6g a6g* Dec 26] leggy, lengthy gelding:
fairly useful handicapper: won at Southwell in March and Wolverhampton in December: no other form in 1997: stays 6f: form only on fibresand. *W. Jarvis*

DOUBLE OR BUST   4 ch.f. Presidium 124 – Defy Me 75 (Bustino 136) [1996
29: a5g 5.3f⁶ 5f 6.1m⁵ 6g 5m 1997 5m 5.3m a5g Aug 8] no longer of any account.
C. J. Hill

DOUBLE OSCAR (IRE)   4 ch.g. Royal Academy (USA) 130 – Broadway   87
Rosie 101 (Absalom 128) [1996 65§: 6m 6.1m⁴ 7f³ 7.1g² 7.1f³ 6.9f³ 8m 6f⁴ 6d⁶ 7m
1997 a6g⁶ a7g a5g² a6g a5g⁴ a6g⁴ a6g³ 5g 5.1g* 7f² 5s⁴ 6g 5f⁴ 6m³ 7.1g² 6m* 6m⁵
5m² 5g* 5m* 5d 6m 6g 5f* 6d⁶ 6g a6g³ 6m Nov 4] good-bodied gelding: fairly useful
performer: inconsistent at 3 yrs: in good form for most of 1997, and won claimer at
Nottingham and handicaps at Folkestone, Catterick, Pontefract and Carlisle by the
end of August, landing gambles on 3 occasions: has form at 7f, but best at 5f/6f: acts
on firm and dead going and the all-weather: visored once, usually blinkered
otherwise: has had tongue tied: held up: tough. *D. Nicholls*

DOUBLE POWER   2 ch.f. (Mar 19) Superpower 113 – Double Decree 69 (Sayf   56
El Arab (USA) 127) [1997 5.1g 5m³ 5m⁴ 5g⁶ Sep 15] 1,000Y: strong, close-coupled
filly: second foal: dam 6f winner: modest form in frame in maidens at Thirsk and
Ripon (hung right), showing speed: below form final start. *L. R. Lloyd-James*

DOUBLE RUSH (IRE)   5 b.g. Doulab (USA) 115 – Stanza Dancer (Stanford   44
121§) [1996 56, a70: 11.9f 10m 9.7m 9f⁶ a10g 12g 10f* 10f* 10g⁴ a10g* a10s* a10g   a66
1997 10d a10g⁴ 10g 10m 12d⁴ 10g 10g a10g Dec 10] rangy gelding: fair performer
on equitrack, poor at best on turf (acts on firm and soft ground) in 1997: probably
stays 1½m: blinkered (out of form) once. *T. G. Mills*

DOUBLE SPLENDOUR (IRE)   7 b.g. Double Schwartz 128 – Princess   101
Pamela 70 (Dragonara Palace (USA) 115) [1996 101: 6.1g* 6g⁴ 6m⁵ 6d² 6m² 6m*
6m² 6g³ 6m⁴ 6g² 1997 6g⁵ 6d⁴ 6s 7g 6s 6f³ 5d 6.1d 6m² Nov 4] good-topped gelding:
impresses in appearance: useful handicapper: best effort in 1997 when ¾-length

second of 25 to Primo Lara at Redcar on final start: stays 6f well: acts on firm and soft ground and on equitrack: held up. *P. S. Felgate*

DOUBLE STAR   6 b.g. Soviet Star (USA) 128 – Startino 111 (Bustino 136) [1996   –
NR 1997 10.1g⁴ 11.1g³ 14f⁵ Oct 3] tall gelding: third living foal: half-brother to fairly useful winner around 1¼m Stoney Valley (by Caerleon): dam, 1m and 1½m winner, also third in Park Hill Stakes: NH Flat race winner: little worthwhile form in 3 maidens on flat. *J. L. Harris*

DOUBLE TRIGGER (IRE)   6 ch.h. Ela-Mana-Mou 132 – Solac (FR) (Gay   123
Lussac (ITY) 116) [1996 123: 16.2m* 16.4d* 20m² 18m* 20d⁵ 1997 16.2m
20g 16m* 18f⁴ 20m⁵ Oct 4]
   With Double Trigger, it all seems to be a case of when push comes to shove. Nothing much has changed there, perhaps. But, whereas his jockeys could once be assured that their efforts would reap a rich reward, in 1997 they could not be certain of much more than their basic riding fee. Only twice did Double Trigger make the frame from five starts, and on one occasion that was when coming fourth of five. And yet, Double Trigger remains a favourite. If anyone wants to know why, then they should just take a look at a video of the 1997 Goodwood Cup. The race was a magnificent triumph for the horse and all those involved with him. They had been there before. In the 1995 running Double Trigger had got the better of a titanic struggle with his stable-companion and younger brother Double Eclipse. This time both were back, but with the five-year-old battling with his injured foreleg, the six-year-old struggling to find his form. Classic Cliche, whose encounter with Double Trigger in the Gold Cup had been one of the highlights of the 1996 season, was also in the line-up after his second in the latest Gold Cup, in which Trigger had been eighth and Eclipse sixth. Also ahead of them at Royal Ascot were Election Day (third) and Samraan (fifth), Election Day one of the seven horses who had had Double Trigger trailing in last place on his only other previous start of the season, the Sagaro Stakes at Ascot in April. With Grey Shot, Canon Can and Persian Punch also there, it was, in short, a competitive Goodwood Cup. Double Trigger, though, was never headed. The horse had to be in excellent form, of course, but much of the credit is down to Michael Roberts, taking the ride because Jason Weaver had chosen Double Eclipse. For many horses, the advantage in making the running lies in dictating and stealing an advantage

Crowson Goodwood Cup—
as in 1995 the brothers Double Trigger and Double Eclipse are involved in the finish,
but this time Classic Cliche (giving weight to both) splits the pair

when they quicken it, but Double Trigger is not a horse like this. He is at his best when turn of foot does not come into the equation but stamina does. Nowadays, he looks most effective when setting a good pace, even if that appears much faster than he would like to be going. At Goodwood, that meant Roberts ensuring first that he got ahead of Grey Shot from the stalls and then that he stayed there, and it was hard work. Challengers were queuing up entering the straight but at the furlong pole only two were left—Double Eclipse and Classic Cliche. This time Double Eclipse was booked for third place but, after hanging left close to the others and changing his legs, Double Trigger drew clear of Classic Cliche again to win by a length and a half.

His younger brother's injury problems are well known, and Double Trigger had given his trainer plenty to contend with as well, thanks to hoof problems in 1996 and, reportedly, an abscess on one foot before the Sagaro and on another after it. Sadly, he was not in top form in either of his races after Goodwood. A bid to join the nineteenth-century hero Beeswing in winning a hat-trick of Doncaster Cups saw him complete in only fourth of five, while fifth of seven, never getting to the front, was the best he could manage in the Prix du Cadran.

		Pitcairn	Petingo
	Ela-Mana-Mou	(b 1971)	Border Bounty
	(b 1976)	Rose Bertin	High Hat
Double Trigger (IRE)		(ch 1970)	Wide Awake
(ch.c. 1991)		Gay Lussac	Faberge II
	Solac (FR)	(ch 1969)	Green As Grass
	(ch 1977)	Soragna	Orvieto II
		(b 1965)	Savigny

A tall horse and an easy mover, Double Trigger remains in training. He acts on any going. The Goodwood Cup demonstrated that he is still capable of high-class form and willing to battle gamely, but consistency is now a worry. An irregular heartbeat helped shed some light on the Doncaster performance after, less persuasively, connections had first blamed the distracting presence of a television camera car. At Longchamp, Mark Johnston felt fate was conspiring against him again when the plane carrying Roberts (who had kept the ride after Goodwood) arrived late and the jockey had to be replaced by Jarnet, whom the trainer thought was not forceful enough. 'It was clear Thierry Jarnet understood his instructions,' said Johnston, 'but how can you prepare a French jockey for Double Trigger?'

Details of Double Trigger's breeding have been dealt with in past editions of *Racehorses* and can also be found in the latest essay on his brother Double Eclipse. *M. Johnston*

DOUBLE VINTAGE (IRE)   4 b.g. Double Schwartz 128 – Great Alexandra   –
(Runnett 125) [1996 NR 1997 a11g 12g May 16] of no account. *M. C. Chapman*

DOUBLING DICE   6 b.g. Jalmood (USA) 126 – Much Too Risky 87 (Bustino   –
136) [1996 NR 1997 12.1d Apr 2] poor maiden handicapper: well beaten only 6-y-o start. *R. Allan*

DOUBLY SHARP (USA)   3 ch.g. Diesis 133 – Nijana (USA) (Nijinsky (CAN)   60
138) [1996 NR 1997 12.3g 12d⁴ 10m² 13.8g⁵ Aug 5] $26,000Y resold IR 25,000Y: angular colt: half-brother to a winner in USA by Secretariat, also placed in Grade 2 1½m event: dam, won 10 times in USA, including Grade 3 6f event at 2 yrs, and graded-placed up to 1½m: modest maiden: blinkered, creditable effort in handicap final start: should stay 2m. *M. Johnston*

DOUGS DREAM (IRE)   2 ch.f. (May 7) Mac's Imp (USA) 116 – Lomond   –
Heights (IRE) (Lomond (USA) 128) [1997 5.9m 5.9g 7g⁶ 7m a7g Sep 8] IR 1,600Y: first living foal: dam, placed over 1m at 2 yrs in Ireland, out of May Hill winner Satinette: no worthwhile form. *Mrs A. Swinbank*

DOVEBRACE   4 b.g. Dowsing (USA) 124 – Naufrage (Main Reef 126) [1996 –:   65
6d⁵ 7.1d 7m 6g 7g 6d 1997 6m 6.1g 6s 6m a7g⁵ Dec 2] leggy gelding: useful at 2 yrs:

just fair form at best in handicaps in 1997: should stay beyond 7f: acts on good to firm ground, probably on soft and equitrack: blinkered/visored last 2 starts at 3 yrs. *T. D. Barron*

DOVEDON STAR 3 b.f. Unfuwain (USA) 131 – Whitstar 93 (Whitstead 125) 93
[1996 NR 1997 10d[4] 10.1s[3] 10g[4] 12m[3] 10s[3] 11.8d[2] 14d* 15v[5] Dec 1] lengthy, angular filly: has round action: fifth living foal: half-sister to useful 7f to 1¼m winner Two Left Feet and winning stayer Star Performer (both by Petorius): dam, 1¼m winner at 2 yrs, half-sister to smart 6f to 1¼m winner Homeboy: fairly useful performer: upped in trip, best effort to win strongly-run handicap at Newmarket in October (final win for trainer P. Kelleway before he retired) by 1½ lengths from Mithak, leading after 2f out: not disgraced in listed race at Maisons-Laffitte final start: will stay 2m+: has raced mainly on good ground or softer: has sweated. *A. Kelleway*

DOVER SOUL 2 ch.f. (Mar 26) Absalom 128 – Whirling Words 75 (Sparkler 63
130) [1997 5.7m[3] 5.1g[3] 6m[3] 5d a6g Nov 21] 5,500Y: half-sister to 3-y-o Chili a?
Concerto: dam 1m winner out of half-sister to smart sprinter Sound Barrier: modest form in maidens first 3 starts: poor efforts afterwards, in seller on all-weather debut final start: should stay further than 6f. *P. J. Makin*

DOWER HOUSE 2 ch.c. (Jan 26) Groom Dancer (USA) 128 – Rose Noble 96
(USA) 62 (Vaguely Noble 140) [1997 6d[5] 7m[2] 7.5g 8m* 8f* 8m4 Oct 19] has a fluent, round action: first foal: dam 11.5f winner, half-sister to Grand Lodge: useful colt: won maiden at Yarmouth in September: good efforts when fourth in listed event at Deauville and Gran Criterium at Milan, beaten about 9 lengths by Lend A Hand in latter: should be suited by 1¼m/1½m. *W. Jarvis*

DOWNCLOSE DUCHESS 2 ch.f. (Apr 1) King's Signet (USA) 110 – Lucky 49
Love 65 (Mummy's Pet 125) [1997 6.1m[4] 6.1d 7m[6] 5.7m 6.1m a6g Sep 30] half- a?
sister to 1994 2-y-o 7f winner Downclose (by Lugana Beach) and a winner abroad: dam won 6f seller: poor maiden: soundly beaten in seller final start. *M. Blanshard*

DOWN HEARTED (IRE) 3 b.g. Broken Hearted 124 – Italian Cashmere –
(Taufan (USA) 119) [1996 NR 1997 10.1g[3] 13.8m[5] 9.2g 8m Aug 20] second reported foal: dam lightly-raced maiden: of little account. *W. T. Kemp*

DOWN THE YARD 4 b.f. Batshoof 122 – Sequin Lady (Star Appeal 133) [1996 –
34, a42: a6g[6] a7g[3] a7g* a11g a8g a8g[3] a7g[2] 7.5g 13.9m[5] a8g[3] 7g a7g[5] 8m a6g[5] a8g a42
1997 a8g* a8g[6] a8g a8g[4] a11g a8g[5] a7g a8g 8f Jun 5] workmanlike filly: poor handicapper: below form on flat after winning weak apprentice event at Southwell in January, but won over hurdles in September and October: stays 1m: acts on good to firm ground and fibresand. *M. C. Chapman*

DOYELLA (IRE) 3 b.f. Doyoun 124 – Santella Bell (Ballad Rock 122) [1996 78
71p: 7g 7d[3] 9m[2] 9s* 10.2s[5] 9m 10d Aug 30] sparely-made filly: has a long stride: fair performer: won weak maiden at Goodwood in June: well held in handicaps last 2 starts: probably stays 1¼m: acts on good to firm and soft ground. *D. R. Loder*

DOYENNE 3 gr.f. Mystiko (USA) 124 – No Chili 86 (Glint of Gold 128) [1996 44
NR 1997 7g 8.2d[8] 8d 9.7s 12g 14m[4] 10.8g[5] 14.1f[3] a16g Nov 25] 17,000Y: lengthy filly: fourth foal: half-sister to a winner up to 1m in UAE by Imp Society: dam 1½m winner: poor maiden: stays 1¾m, at least in steadily-run race: acts on firm ground: blinkered last 4 outings. *G. Lewis*

DOZEN ROSES 3 b.f. Rambo Dancer (CAN) 107 – Andbracket (Import 127) –
[1996 47: 5s 5.1g a6g[5] 5f[4] 5.3f[4] 5f[3] 6f[4] 5d[2] 7f[5] 6.1m 5.3g a7g 1997 6.9m 8.3s 6m[6] 5m Sep 17] no form in 1997: blinkered second start, then left T. M. Jones. *J. E. Long*

DRAGONADA (USA) 3 b.f. Nureyev (USA) 131 – Don't Sulk (USA) 115 106
(Graustark) [1996 96+: 6.1m[2] 7f* 7.3s[4] 1997 8.5d* 8g[4] 8m[2] 10g[2] 8.1s[2] 8m[3] 9d Oct 23] angular filly: useful performer: won 3-runner minor event at Epsom in June: in frame in pattern, minor and listed company (5 lengths second to Dust Dancer at Salisbury on fourth outing) afterwards before leaving H. Cecil and below best final start: unlikely to stay much beyond 1¼m: acts on firm and soft going. *P. Bary, France*

DRAGON BOY 2 b.c. (Feb 19) Bustino 136 – Safe House 81§ (Lyphard (USA) –
132) [1997 7m[5] 7m[6] 6.1m 6.1d Nov 3] half-brother to several winners, including a

2-y-o 1m winner by Shirley Heights and 9.2f seller winner by Rainbow Quest: dam, temperamental, won at 10.8f: in rear in varied company. *I. P. Williams*

DRAGONJOY 4 b.g. Warrshan (USA) 117 – Nazakat 68 (Known Fact (USA) 135) [1996 –, a67: a7g³ a7g* a7g* a7g* a8g² 8.3d⁵ a8.5g* a9.4g a8.5g* a8.5g⁵ a7g⁵ a8g a9.4g a7g⁵ a8.5g⁶ a7g 8f a7g³ a6g³ a7g³ a8g a9.4g² a9.4g⁵ a8.5s 1997 a7g² a9.4g³ a9.4g a6g a8.5g* a7g⁴ 8g a8g⁶ a7g a8.5f³ a7g 8m Jul 19] good-topped gelding: modest performer on the all-weather: below form after winning minor event at Wolverhampton in April: lightly raced and little form on turf: stays 9.4f: usually blinkered/visored. *N. P. Littmoden* — a60

DRAGON'S BACK (IRE) 4 ch.g. Digamist (USA) 110 – Classic Choice (Patch 129) [1996 71: 10g³ 10m⁴ 10m 8.1d 1997 a10g 9.7m a8g⁴ 11.5f Oct 3] strong gelding: poor maiden at best in 1997: stays 1¼m: acts on good to firm ground and on fibresand. *D. C. O'Brien* — 49

DRAIN DOCTOR 2 b.g. (Mar 23) State Diplomacy (USA) – Stilvella (Camden Town 125) [1997 7g 7g 7m Oct 7] good-bodied gelding: third reported foal: half-brother to 4-y-o Pathaze, 5f winner at 2 yrs: dam twice-raced daughter of half-sister to top-class sprinter/broodmare Stilvi: no sign of ability in seller and claimers. *S. E. Kettlewell* — –

DRAMA KING 5 b.g. Tragic Role (USA) – Consistent Queen 55 (Queen's 42 Hussar 124) [1996 –, a46: a14g⁴ 12.3m a12g* a14.8g² a14g⁶ a12g a14g a14.8g⁵ 1997 15.9g 16.1g² 18d⁶ a14g⁵ Nov 17] sturdy gelding: poor handicapper: stays 2m well: acts on fibresand, yet to race on extremes of going on turf: often blinkered. *B. J. Llewellyn*

DRAMATIC MOMENT 4 b.f. Belmez (USA) 131 – Drama School 72 (Young 68 Generation 129) [1996 71: 9s³ 9.7m² 10m* 10f⁵ 12g 1997 10d 12f² 10s⁶ 11.4d⁶ 12m 11.1m Sep 22] leggy filly: has a quick action: fair handicapper: well beaten last 2 starts: stays 1½m well: best form on good ground or firmer: sold, to go to Qatar. *J. R. Arnold*

DRAMATIC PASS (IRE) 8 ch.g. Coquelin (USA) 121 – Miss Flirt (Welsh — Pageant 132) [1996 NR 1997 12s 14.1s⁵ Jul 5] no form in 1997 after long absence: clear when falling over fences in August: dead. *M. C. Chapman*

DR BONES (IRE) 4 b. or br.g. Durgam (USA) – Rose Deer (Whistling Deer 117) — [1996 16g³ 10g⁶ 9m³ 12m³ 10s 1997 12s⁴ 14g⁴ 18d Oct 20] ex-Irish gelding: brother to 3-y-o Stoned Imaculate: dam lightly-raced maiden: fair form (rated 77) in maidens at 3 yrs: no form in 1997, leaving M. J. P. O'Brien's stable after penultimate outing (blinkered) in August: should stay further than 1½m: acts on good to firm ground, well held on dead and soft: fairly useful hurdler, won in December. *F. Murphy*

DR CALIGARI (IRE) 5 b.g. My Generation 111 – Mallabee 92 (Pall Mall 132) — [1996 –: a7g a7g 1997 8.2d a7g a5g Dec 8] lightly raced and no form on flat since 1995. *S. Gollings*

DREAM CARRIER (IRE) 9 b.g. Doulab (USA) 115 – Dream Trader (Auction 45 Ring (USA) 123) [1996 –, a52: a8.5g a8g³ a8g⁴ a7g⁵ a8g³ 10.3d a8g 8g 1997 a8g a54 a8g⁵ a8g³ a7g³ a6g⁴ a8g² a8g⁴ a8.5g a7g* a8.5g³ 7.6m⁴ 7.1m⁴ a8.5g⁵ a8g³ a8g Dec 8] strong gelding: has a round action: modest handicapper, poor on turf: won amateurs event at Southwell in June: stays 1m: acts on firm ground and the all-weather: tried blinkered/visored, not in 1997: sometimes starts slowly. *R. E. Peacock*

DREAM OF NURMI 3 ch.g. Pursuit of Love 124 – Finlandaise (FR) (Arctic 100 Tern (USA) 126) [1996 78+: 7f⁴ 7.5m² a7g² 1997 9.9m⁴ 10.1g² 10.1m³ 11.9g* 12m² Jul 30] leggy gelding: useful handicapper: won at York in July: good third (promoted a place) to Maylane in Tote Gold Trophy at Goodwood later in month, leading over 2f out but wandering and worn down inside last: stays 1½m: has raced only on good ground or firmer on turf: visored final outing at 2 yrs: usually races prominently: reliable. *D. R. Loder*

DREAMS END 9 ch.h. Rainbow Quest (USA) 134 – Be Easy 110 (Be Friendly 88 130) [1996 83: 11.9m⁴ 10f 10.4m 13.9m 13.9g 11.9g² 8.9g* 12g⁴ 8g⁴ 1997 10m³ 9g⁶ 8.9d* 8m 11.9g⁵ 9f⁴ 13.9g 10.3m Sep 13] sparely-made horse: fairly useful handi-capper: came from well back to win at York in June: good fifth to Zaralaska in Old Newton Cup at Haydock following month: well held last 2 starts: effective at 9f to

1½m (won over 1¾m in 1993): acts on any going: sometimes bandaged: sometimes sweats: usually held up, and suited by strongly-run race: game. *P. Bowen*

DR EDGAR 5 b.g. Most Welcome 131 – African Dancer 116 (Nijinsky (CAN) 54 138) [1996 64: 10s 11.8g⁶ 9.9g 9g 8f³ 10m³ 10m⁴ 8.1g⁵ 10.3m 12g³ 11.1m⁵ 12g 1997 a10g a10g³ a12g² a12g⁵ a12g³ 12.3m Apr 9] strong gelding: modest handicapper: stays 1½m: acts on the all-weather, raced mainly on good going or firmer on turf: tried blinkered: takes good hold, and best efforts ridden prominently: has wandered under pressure: joined L. Eyre. *M. Dods*

DR FONG (USA) 2 ch.c. (Apr 6) Kris S (USA) – Spring Flight (USA) (Miswaki 102 p (USA) 124) [1997 7g* 8v* Oct 11] $425,000Y: quite good-topped, attractive colt: second foal: dam minor stakes-winning sprinter in USA: sire (by Roberto) minor stakes winner up to 9f: promising performer: won 17-runner maiden at Newbury in September in taking style, quickening well from modest position, and 4-runner listed race at Ascot in October, again quickening to beat Equity Princess ½ length, despite carrying head rather awkwardly and idling: may stay 1¼m, possibly not much further: sort to train on into a smart 3-y-o. *H. R. A. Cecil*

DRIFT 3 b.g. Slip Anchor 136 – Norgabie 94 (Northfields (USA)) [1996 59p: 6.1m 64 7f 7g 1997 12m⁵ a14g a8.5g 11.9f² 13.8s 12d³ Oct 21] good-topped gelding: modest a– maiden handicapper: likely to prove suited by test of stamina: acts on firm and dead ground, well beaten on fibresand and soft: none too consistent: sold 22,000 gns and joined Mrs A. E. Johnson. *Sir Mark Prescott*

DRIVE ASSURED 3 gr.g. Mystiko (USA) 124 – Black Ivor (USA) (Sir Ivor 135) 77 [1996 77: 6m⁶ 7m 7.1m⁶ 10.2d³ 8g⁵ 1997 10g³ 11.8d³ Apr 26] smallish gelding: fair maiden: creditable efforts both 3-y-o starts: stays 1½m: acts on good to firm and dead going. *C. E. Brittain*

DR JOHNSON (USA) 3 ch.c. Woodman (USA) 126 – Russian Ballet (USA) 122 (Nijinsky (CAN) 138) [1996 8d 9d⁴ 1997 10g² 12d* 10g* 12s* 12d² 14g* Aug 23]

It is fitting to see one of the most quoted men in the language now having his own name used in the context of a creature which his 1755 *Dictionary Of The English Language* defined as just a 'neighing quadruped, used in war and draught and carriage.' Asked why he had mistakenly defined 'pastern' as the knee of a horse, Samuel Johnson replied: 'Ignorance, madam, pure ignorance.' Anyway, the great man of letters had the extreme good fortune that, if his name had to be associated with a horse, the horse in question possesses a considerably greater virtuosity than the one he described in his dictionary. One of the more appropriate aspects is that the colt is trained in Ireland, the eighteenth-century Dr Johnson's title having been conferred upon him first by an Irish university, Trinity College, Dublin.

Dr Johnson the racehorse guaranteed some sort of place in the reference books for future generations with his effort in the Irish Derby in June. Sent into the lead just after the two-furlong marker, it looked briefly as if he was going to win. Dr Johnson swiftly opened up an advantage of about a length and a half, despite hanging to his right over to the rails, but Desert King was after him and had his measure a furlong later. The eventual distance between them was a length, with Dr Johnson holding on to second from Loup Sauvage by a short head. A 12/1-chance in the Irish Derby, Dr Johnson had never previously contested a pattern race. Fourth of nine in a listed event on his second start at two years had been promising, but he began 1997 in maiden races and was beaten four lengths by Irish Oaks winner Ebadiyla on his reappearance at the Curragh. Making amends at Leopardstown in May, further victories in a listed event at the Curragh (by two lengths from Sublime Beauty) and a minor event at Leopardstown (by a length from Zafarabad) had put him on course for the Irish Derby.

A second bid to enter the classic roll of honour was planned for the St Leger at Doncaster, a race in which Dr Johnson's owner, Vincent O'Brien, had forty years earlier gained the first of his sixteen British classic victories, with

Ballymoss. Dr Johnson was given his prep-race in a listed event at Leopardstown in late-August and, at 13/8-on, he did not have to be at his best to win easily by three lengths from Aliya. The outing demonstrated his well-being and that he could win over a mile and three quarters, but the former proved rather short-lived; Dr Johnson struck into himself on his near-fore ten days before Doncaster. It was a minor injury, but enough to rule him out for the rest of the season.

Dr Johnson's observation that 'when two Englishmen meet, their first talk is of the weather' seems to square with racing folk's preoccupation with meteorological matters and its implications for the state of going. A glance at Dr Johnson's form figures indicates cause for concern on that score as he has so far not been raced on ground firmer than good, but his trainer assures us that this is a coincidence and that he initially believed that Dr Johnson might not act on soft. Dr Johnson is a close-coupled colt with a rather round action. His form at a mile and a half is better than at a mile and a quarter, and he stays a mile and three quarters.

		Mr Prospector	Raise A Native
	Woodman (USA)	(b 1970)	Gold Digger
	(ch 1983)	Playmate	Buckpasser
Dr Johnson (USA)		(ch 1975)	Intriguing
(ch.c. 1994)		Nijinsky	Northern Dancer
	Russian Ballet (USA)	(b 1967)	Flaming Page
	(ch 1988)	Sex Appeal	Buckpasser
		(ch 1970)	Best In Show

He comes from a famous family, as his grandam is Sex Appeal, unraced herself but the dam of Try My Best and El Gran Senor (this is also the family of Xaar and Chief Contender). Those two colts were by Northern Dancer, which

Mr M. V. O'Brien's "Dr Johnson"

makes Dr Johnson's dam, Russian Ballet, a close relation. Russian Ballet's own racing record was limited to a couple of runs as a two-year-old, in both of which she made the frame. At stud, she has been kept to Woodman for her first five foals. Dr Johnson is the third, following the fairly useful Irish one-mile winner Marqueta, and another filly Matikanesasameyuki, whom commentators will be relieved to know is safely in Japan, where she has won two minor races at a mile and a quarter from eighteen starts. Next-in-line Golden Chimes ran in two maidens in 1997 and showed fair form. He is also with Charles O'Brien, who will again have Dr Johnson in training in 1998, when the top races at a mile and a quarter upwards will be on his agenda. Born in 1967, the trainer was assistant to his legendary father for six years before taking out his own licence in 1993, since when he has sent out the winners of four pattern races in Burden of Proof, Truth Or Dare and Ashley Park. Charles O'Brien once considered becoming an accountant, but perhaps he was not prepared to accept Dr Johnson's assertion that 'Human Life is everywhere a state in which much is to be endured, and little to be enjoyed.' *Charles O'Brien, Ireland*

DR MARTENS (IRE) 3 b.g. Mtoto 134 – Suyayeb (USA) (The Minstrel (CAN) 135) [1996 NR 1997 10g 8m² 8.3m* 8m⁶ Oct 3] IR 14,500F, IR 50,000Y: strong, compact gelding: has a quick action: first foal: dam unraced half-sister to 1¼m Hollywood Gold Cup winner Cutlass Reality: fairly useful form: sweating, justified favouritism in 17-runner maiden at Windsor in August: raced far too freely when last of 6 in minor event at Newmarket 2 months later: should stay beyond 1m if he settles: gelded after final start. *L. M. Cumani* 85

DR MASSINI (IRE) 4 b.c. Sadler's Wells (USA) 132 – Argon Laser 107 (Kris 135) [1996 115: 8m* 10.4f* 12m 1997 10m* 10g May 25] smart performer, lightly raced (missed 1996 Derby with lameness problems): looking in fine shape, made impressive return to win 5-runner listed race at Kempton in March by 2½ lengths from Germano, quickening in good style in slowly-run race: refused to race in Tattersalls Gold Cup at the Curragh on only subsequent start: should stay 1½m: raced only on good ground or firmer: held up and has good turn of foot. *M. R. Stoute* 117

DR WOODSTOCK 3 br.g. Rock City 120 – Go Tally-Ho 66 (Gorytus (USA) 132) [1996 –: 5.2d 1997 6.9m 5.1m⁶ 8m a8g 7s⁶ 8.1m² 7m³ 6.9m 8g⁶ Sep 8] tall gelding: poor maiden handicapper: stays 1m: acts on good to firm ground. *Martyn Meade* 47

DRYAD 2 ch.c. (Mar 18) Risk Me (FR) 127 – Lizzy Cantle 52 (Homing 130) [1997 a6g⁴ Dec 6] second reported foal: dam 7f winner: 33/1, about 9 lengths fourth of 13 to Wolfhunt in maiden at Wolverhampton, challenging over 1f out but no extra: should improve. *N. P. Littmoden* 63 p

DRY LIGHTNING 2 b.f. (Jan 28) Shareef Dancer (USA) 135 – Valkyrie 87 (Bold Lad (IRE) 133) [1997 6g⁶ 7d⁵ Jun 24] 12,000Y: sixth foal: half-sister to 3 winners, including 1m winner Clipping (by Kris) and 1987 2-y-o 6f to 1¼m winner Valentine (by Cure The Blues): dam 2-y-o 5f winner, half-sister to smart middle-distance performer Sabre Dance: modest form in maiden at Doncaster and minor event at Warwick: should stay at least 1¼m. *M. Bell* 56

DTOTO 5 b.g. Mtoto 134 – Deposit 73 (Thatch (USA) 136) [1996 –: 17.2m⁶ 10.2m 12.1m 13.1m 1997 10m Oct 1] no longer of any account. *R. J. Baker* –

DUBAI DOLLY (IRE) 4 b.f. Law Society (USA) 130 – Lola Sharp (Sharpen Up 127) [1996 8s 9d 11.9m 12d 9d 8m 1997 10.8g⁵ Jul 12] ex-Irish filly: half-sister to 4 minor winners, including Dawson City (up to 1½m, by Glint of Gold): dam won in Italy: no worthwhile form on flat: won selling hurdle (then joined N. Callaghan) in September. *J. W. Mullins* –

DUBELLE 7 b.m. Dubassoff (USA) – Flopsy Mopsy (Full of Hope 125) [1996 NR 1997 11.7g Sep 8] second foal: dam unraced half-sister to smart hurdler Sula Bula: winning chaser: well held in Bath maiden on belated flat debut. *J. S. King* –

DUBLIVIA 2 b.f. (Mar 20) Midyan (USA) 124 – Port Isaac (USA) 64 (Seattle Song (USA) 130) [1997 7m 6f⁵ 6m Oct 7] IR 5,200Y: tall filly: second foal: half-sister to a winner up to 1m in Italy by Reprimand: dam lightly-raced maiden from ?

very good American family: appeared to show a little ability in slowly-run race second start (could be rated 64), but last next time: saddle slipped on debut. *C. A. Dwyer*

DUCK ROW (USA) 2 ch.c. (Mar 30) Diesis 133 – Sunny Moment (USA) 104 p (Roberto (USA) 131) [1997 8d* 7.3g⁶ Oct 24] $82,000Y: sturdy, close-coupled colt: fourth foal: half-brother to 1994 French 2-y-o 9f winner Resolana (by Sovereign Dancer) and a winner in USA by Tejano: dam, won up to 9f in USA, half-sister to Grade 2 winner Tsarbaby: won 5-runner Haynes, Hanson and Clark Stakes at Newbury by 1½ lengths from Quiet Assurance: uneasy favourite, almost certainly not himself in Horris Hill Stakes there following month (stable reportedly under cloud), racing bit too freely and soon fading from 2f out: bred to stay at least 1¼m: looked a good prospect on debut and well worth another chance. *J. A. R. Toller*

DUDLEY ALLEN 2 ch.c. (Mar 26) Superlative 118 – Smooth Flight 78 (Sand- – hurst Prince 128) [1997 6.1m 7m Oct 5] second foal: dam miler: no promise in maidens. *T. T. Clement*

DUELLO 6 b.g. Sure Blade (USA) 130 – Royal Loft 105 (Homing 130) [1996 79: 73 7s² 8g 8s 7.3s* 7m³ 7.1m³ 8m² 8m⁶ 7.9g⁴ 8g⁴ 7.3m* 7m³ 7g 8g² 8g 1997 a8.5g⁴ 8m 7.6v 8s⁴ 7.3g⁵ 8m⁶ 8.5v⁴ 7m⁵ 7.1m² 8d⁴ 7g 7s 7.1m 8m 8.2d² 8d Oct 13] leggy gelding: has a round action: fair handicapper: failed to win in 1997, but ran creditably on several occasions: effective at 7f to 8.5f: acts on good to firm and heavy ground, shaped quite well on rare outing on fibresand on reappearance: blinkered once earlier in career. *M. Blanshard*

DUE SOUTH 2 b.f. (Apr 22) Darshaan 133 – Island Wedding (USA) 89 (Blushing 96 Groom (FR) 131) [1997 7.1d 7.5m⁴ 7.5d* 8g³ 8d³ Sep 12] leggy filly: fourth foal: half-sister to 4-y-o Winter Romance: dam, 7f and 8.5f winner, out of sister to Storm Bird: useful form: won maiden at Beverley in August: third in very valuable nursery at Newcastle and to Alboostan (beaten 1½ lengths) in 5-runner listed race at Goodwood: should be suited by 1¼m/1½m. *E. A. L. Dunlop*

DUFFERTOES 5 ch.g. High Kicker (USA) – Miss Poll Flinders (Swing Easy – (USA) 126) [1996 –: 7s 7m 8d⁶ 7g 1997 a8g a7g a12g⁶ 10.8m May 5] of no account nowdays. *M. J. Ryan*

DUKE VALENTINO 5 br.h. Machiavellian (USA) 123 – Aldhabyih 86 (General 61 Assembly (USA)) [1996 61, a86: a8g a7g a7g² a8g³ a7g² 8s 7.5m 8g a8g² 8.1d 8.1m² a86 8.1m³ 7m 7.1f 8.1d⁴ a8.5g* a6g³ 1997 a9.4g⁵ a8.5f a7g² a9.4g* a8.5g⁶ a7g⁴ a7g* a8g⁶ a8.5g 8m a8.5g⁶ 8m a8g 7.5g² 8.5v a8.5g² 7.5m 8.5m 8.1m Aug 8] strong horse: fairly useful performer on the all-weather, modest at best on turf: won handicap at Wolverhampton in January and claimer there in February: stays 9.4f: acts on good to firm and dead ground: often sweats: has had tongue tied: usually held up: none too reliable: sold 9,500 gns in November. *R. Hollinshead*

DUKHAN (USA) 3 b.c. Silver Hawk (USA) 123 – Azayim 111 (Be My Guest 75 (USA) 126) [1996 NR 1997 8f⁵ 10m⁶ 10m Sep 16] big, good-topped colt: fifth foal: half-brother to useful 1993 2-y-o 6f winner Watani and 7f winner Mufarej (both by Riverman): dam 8.5f and 1¼m winner: fair maiden: likely to stay 1½m: has raced only on ground firmer than good: sold 12,000 gns and joined E. Alston. *R. W. Armstrong*

DULAS BAY 3 b.g. Selkirk (USA) 129 – Ivory Gull (USA) 80 (Storm Bird (CAN) 53 134) [1996 –: 7.5m 7.5f 6m 1997 8d 12m⁵ a11g 12d 10m³ 14.1g² 15.8m 16.1m Oct 1] tall, plain gelding: modest maiden: better at 1¾m than shorter, but well held over 2m last 2 starts: yet to race on extremes of going. *M. W. Easterby*

DULCINEA 3 ch.f. Selkirk (USA) 129 – Ahohoney 118 (Ahonoora 122) [1996 73 –p: 7m 1997 8g 7m⁶ 7d* 8m² 7m 8g* 8m⁴ Oct 5] rangy, unfurnished filly: has a quick action: fair performer: won maiden in June and handicap in September, both at Salisbury: stays 1m: yet to race on extremes of going: takes good hold. *I. A. Balding*

DUMMER GOLF TIME 4 ch.c. Clantime 101 – Chablisse 69 (Radetzky 123) 73 [1996 70: a6g² a6g* 6g⁶ 6g⁴ 6m 6g³ 7.1m⁵ 7g² 7m* 7.1f² 8.1m⁵ 7g 1997 8m 8m 7s⁶ a63 7d⁴ 7g² 8g³ 7g* 7s² 7.1m 7m⁵ a7g⁵ a8g Nov 25] lengthy, workmanlike colt: fair handicapper: won at Kempton in August: effective at 7f to 1m: acts on firm ground, soft and the all-weather: usually visored: has been taken early to post: held up: consistent. *Lord Huntingdon*

DUNABRATTIN   4 b.c. Blakeney 126 – Relatively Smart 76 (Great Nephew   –
126) [1996 NR 1997 11.5m⁴ 10m⁵ 14.1s a12g 14.1d Nov 3] leggy, workmanlike colt:
half-brother to 7-y-o Ball Gown: dam, maiden, stayed 1½m: refused to enter stalls on
intended debut: little show in maidens and handicap. *D. T. Thom*

DUNCOMBE HALL   4 b.g. Salse (USA) 128 – Springs Welcome 86 (Blakeney   45
126) [1996 42: 9s 11.8m 10f⁴ 12m⁵ a10g 11.9f³ 16m³ 17.9g 1997 a10g³ 11.9f²
11.9m³ 16.4m³ a16g⁴ 12s 14m 16.4g* 16m 15.4m⁴ 14.1g Oct 18] small, sturdy
gelding: poor handicapper: gained first success at Folkestone in September: suited
by a test of stamina: acts on firm ground and equitrack, possibly unsuited by soft.
C. A. Cyzer

DUNDEL (IRE)   3 gr.f. Machiavellian (USA) 123 – Dunoof 92 (Shirley Heights   81
130) [1996 82p: 6m⁶ 7m⁶ 1997 11.4s⁵ 10d 10g⁴ 7d* 7m 8g⁴ 8g³ 9g³ 8m⁵ 8m Oct 23]
good-topped filly: fairly useful performer: won weak maiden at Ayr in June:
creditable efforts in handicaps most starts afterwards: stays 9f: acts on good to firm
and dead ground: tail flasher, and sometimes looks none too keen. *B. W. Hills*

DUNROWAN   4 b.f. Dunbeath (USA) 127 – Sun Lamp 76 (Pall Mall 132) [1996   –
54: 11.1g³ 11f* 12.1s 1997 12d 14g 12g⁶ Jul 7] only form when winning weak
maiden seller as 3-y-o. *Mrs M. Reveley*

DUNSTON BILL   3 b.g. Sizzling Melody 117 – Fardella (ITY) (Molvedo 137)   –
[1996 NR 1997 10g 10d Jul 17] 3,000Y: seventh foal: half-brother to fair 1¼m
winner Melancolia (by Legend of France): dam French 11f winner: little sign of
ability. *G. Barnett*

DUNSTON GOLD   3 ch.g. Risk Me (FR) 127 – Maria Whittaker (Cure The Blues   –
(USA)) [1996 –: 7.1v 7f a8g 1997 a9.4g Jul 11] of little account. *B. Preece*

DUNSTON STAR (IRE)   4 b.g. Poet's Dream (IRE) 95 – Cherry Glory 44 (Final   –
Straw 127) [1996 –: 8m a8.5g 1997 a12g⁵ Jul 11] tailed off in maiden and seller.
B. Preece

DURABLE GEORGE   3 ch.g. Durandal 114 – Sun Follower (Relkino 131)   48
[1996 NR 1997 7g 6m 6m 7d 5d a5g⁶ 7m 7g a6g³ a8g a6g a7g⁵ Dec 22] leggy
gelding: second foal: half-brother to modest 1995 2-y-o 5f winner Dancing Jack (by
Clantime): dam showed little: poor maiden: best effort final start: stays 7f: acts on
equitrack. *J. J. Bridger*

DURAID (IRE)   5 ch.g. Irish River (FR) 131 – Fateful Princess (USA) 95   89
(Vaguely Noble 140) [1996 NR 1997 12.4m⁴ 8m 10m⁵ 11.9g 10m⁴ 8g* 7.9g 8.5m²
9m⁴ 8g⁴ 7.9s 8m⁴ 8.1g* 8g Oct 18] 65,000Y, 7,000 3-y-o: workmanlike gelding: has
a round action: fourth foal: half-brother to useful 1m winner Masnad (by Mt Livermore): dam, in frame both starts at 1m in Britain, won in USA as 4-y-o: unbeaten in 4
NH Flat races: developed into a fairly useful handicapper: won at Newcastle in June
and Haydock in September: best at 1m/9f: acts on good to firm ground, soundly
beaten on soft: often apprentice ridden: has rather a high head carriage: probably
suited by waiting tactics. *Denys Smith*

DURAR   2 ch.c. (Mar 14) Wolfhound (USA) 126 – Mashair (USA) 100 (Diesis   68
133) [1997 6f⁵ 6g⁴ 7d⁴ 8s Oct 13] first foal: dam 1¼m winner out of high-class US 7f
to 9f winner Lucky Lucky Lucky: fair form when fourth in maidens at Salisbury and
Chester in August: ran poorly final start: should at least stay 1m: sold, to go to Czech
Republic. *J. L. Dunlop*

DURGAMS DELIGHT (IRE)   2 b.f. (Apr 10) Durgam (USA) – Miromaid   –
(Simply Great (FR) 122) [1997 6g 7g a7g 9m 8m Nov 4] second living foal: sister to
5-y-o Durgams First: dam placed at 1½m in Ireland: no worthwhile form: unseated
rider stalls on debut. *B. W. Murray*

DURGAMS FIRST (IRE)   5 ch.g. Durgam (USA) – Miromaid (Simply Great   60
(FR) 122) [1996 NR 1997 a12g 10g⁴ 12g⁶ 14.1f* 12g 12m⁴ 15.8s⁶ 12g² 12g² 14.1m²
12f* 12g⁶ 12m² 11m⁴ Oct 28] small gelding: has been fired: modest performer: won
handicap at Carlisle in May and claimer there (coaxed home) in August: stays 1¾m

DUR

Tripleprint Geoffrey Freer Stakes, Newbury—
Dushyantor (nearest camera) just gets the best of a three-way battle
with Panama City and Shantou (not in picture)

(pulled too hard over 2m): acts on firm and soft going and on fibresand: sometimes edgy: consistent but rather quirky. *Mrs M. Reveley*

DURHAM 6 ch.g. Caerleon (USA) 132 – Sanctuary (Welsh Pageant 132) [1996   73
73: a16g a14g⁴ a16g² 16g a16.2g³ 14m³ 17.2f⁵ 14.1m* a13g² 13.1f² 11.7m³ 12m⁴   a–
14m* 12f² 14.4g* 13.1m* 16.2m 13.9g³ 1997 12g 13.3g 14.1m 14s⁵ 14.9s⁶ 14m⁴
14.8m² 14g² 14.1m* 14.8m⁵ 14.4m² 16m a16s⁶ a16g⁵ Nov 25] sparely-made
gelding: fair handicapper: narrowly won at Yarmouth in August: best form around
1¾m: acts on firm ground, soft and equitrack: usually blinkered/visored. *G. L. Moore*

DURHAM FLYER 2 b.g. (Feb 9) Deploy 131 – Hyde Princess 75 (Touch Paper   70 ?
113) [1997 5m 5m⁶ 6f² 7.1d⁴ 7g⁴ 6m 8d Sep 19] 7,000Y: sturdy gelding: fifth
reported foal: half-brother to 7-y-o The Fed: dam sprinter: fair maiden at best: stays
7f (beaten long way out over 1m): acts on firm and dead ground: blinkered sixth
outing. *T. D. Easterby*

DUSHYANTOR (USA) 4 b.c. Sadler's Wells (USA) 132 – Slightly Dangerous   120
(USA) 122 (Roberto (USA) 131) [1996 123: 12m* 10.4m² 12m² 12m⁴ 11.9m*
14.6m² 12g 1997 12m² 12g⁶ 12g⁶ 13.3m* 12g² Sep 5] small colt: very smart
performer: runner-up in Derby and St Leger in 1996: won slowly-run 4-runner
Tripleprint Geoffrey Freer Stakes at Newbury in August, leading over 2f out and
holding Panama City by a neck: best other 4-y-o efforts when second in Coronation
Cup (5 lengths behind Singspiel) and September Stakes (1¾ lengths behind Maylane), both at Epsom: needs good test at 1½m and stays 14.6f: acts on good to firm
going, yet to race on softer than good: held up but lacks turn of foot: has joined
R. Frankel in USA. *H. R. A. Cecil*

DUST 3 b.f. Green Desert (USA) 127 – Storm Warning 117 (Tumble Wind (USA))   58
[1996 NR 1997 7g⁵ 7m⁴ 7m⁵ 6.1m a8g* Nov 17] seventh foal: sister to a lightly-raced
maiden and half-sister to 6-y-o Present Situation: dam sprinter: modest performer:
won minor event at Southwell in November: stays 1m: raced only on good/good to
firm ground and fibresand. *Lord Huntingdon*

Mr K. Abdulla's "Dushyantor"

DUST DANCER 3 ch.f. Suave Dancer (USA) 136 – Galaxic Dust (USA) 86   116
(Blushing Groom (FR) 131) [1996 74p: 7g⁵ 6m³ 1997 7m* 10d⁵ 10g⁵ 12d* 12m⁴
10g* 10g* 12m 10m Oct 4] close-coupled filly: has a quick action: smart performer:
won maiden at Leicester in March, minor event at Goodwood in June and listed

Prix de la Nonette, Deauville—
Dust Dancer (No. 2) and Pat Eddery gain a narrow victory over the Prix de Diane winner Vereva;
Gazelle Royale (stripes) and Proud Fillie make the frame

Hesmonds Stud's "Dust Dancer"

contest at Salisbury (beat Dragonada by 5 lengths) and Prix de la Nonette at Deau-ville (beat Vereva by a head), both in August: below form in Prix Vermeille at Longchamp and Sun Chariot Stakes at Newmarket (sweating and edgy) last 2 starts: effective at 1¼m to 1½m: best efforts on good going: keen type: game and reliable: stud. *J. L. Dunlop*

DUTCH 5 ch.g. Nicholas Bill 125 – Dutch Princess 70 (Royalty 130) [1996 NR 1997 11.5m 14.1s Oct 15] eighth foal: brother to useful stayer Double Dutch: dam staying maiden: tailed off in maidens. *G. P. Enright* —

DUTCH DYANE 4 b.f. Midyan (USA) 124 – Double Dutch 100 (Nicholas Bill 125) [1996 –: a10g a10g 1997 a13g⁶ a14g a16g⁶ 12s² Jun 27] lightly raced maiden: only form (previously raced on all-weather) in handicap at Folkestone on final start, hanging markedly left under 7-lb claimer: stays 1½m: acts on soft ground. *G. P. Enright* 39

DUTCH LAD 2 b.c. (May 13) Alnasr Alwasheek 117 – Double Dutch 100 (Nicholas Bill 125) [1997 6m 7m 7m 8d³ 8g² Oct 24] sturdy, angular colt: unimpressive mover: fourth foal: dam won Cesarewitch: fair form: easily best efforts in nurseries at Newmarket and Doncaster (½-length second of 14 to Panama House, pair clear) last 2 starts: will be suited by further than 1m, and may well stay beyond 1½m: should do better and win races at 3 yrs. *M. H. Tompkins* 72 p

DUTCH PATRIARCH 2 b.f. (May 16) Noble Patriarch 115 – Dunnington (Risk Me (FR) 127) [1997 6m⁵ 7.5v Jul 5] leggy filly: unimpressive mover: second foal: dam no worthwhile form: behind in sellers. *M. W. Easterby* —

DYCE 3 b.f. Green Ruby (USA) 104 – Miss Display 47 (Touch Paper 113) [1996 NR 1997 a6g 7d Oct 13] 1,400Y: big, strong filly: fifth foal: sister to 8-y-o Ned's Bonanza: dam (maiden) best at 5f: tailed off in maidens. *J. Balding* —

310

E

EAGER HERO 2 ch.c. (Mar 31) Keen 116 – Honour And Glory 46 (Hotfoot 126) –
[1997 6f 6g 7g Aug 22] 6,000Y: small colt: second foal: dam poor maiden half-sister
to smart sprinter Singing Steven: soundly beaten, including in sellers. *M. Brittain*

EAGER TO PLEASE 3 ch.g. Keen 116 – Ackcontent (USA) (Key To Content 55
(USA)) [1996 60, a67: 5.2d 5g⁶ 5.9g a6g* 6f² 6m⁴ a6g³ 6g⁶ a6g* 6m* 7m 6.1s a6g a72
a5g⁴ a6g³ 1997 a7g² a7g⁵ a6g* a7g² a5g* 5m a7g* 6.1m 7m⁶ 5.3f 7m* 7.1d Jun 23]
small gelding: fair on the all-weather, modest on turf: won seller, claimer and
handicap at Lingfield in February/March and claimer at Warwick in June: effective
at 5f to 7f: acts on firm ground, probably unsuited by going softer than good: usually
blinkered nowadays, though effective when not: tail flasher: sent to California.
Miss Gay Kelleway

EAGLE CANYON (IRE) 4 b. or br.g. Persian Bold 123 – Chrism (Baptism 74
119) [1996 85: a10g⁵ 10.3d 9g a8g* 8g² 9g² 10m⁴ 12.3m* 11.4g² 12m⁴ 12m⁴ 11.9g a–
11.9d 16.2d 1997 a12g a12g 10g⁴ 12.3v⁵ 12.4g² 12m³ 12s⁵ 12.3m 11.8d* Jul 17]
good-topped gelding: has a round action: fair performer: won claimer at Leicester
(claimed to join F. Jordan £10,000) in July: stays 1½m (unlikely to get 2m): acts on
fibresand, good to firm ground and dead, well beaten on soft/heavy: blinkered (ran
poorly) once: seems suited by waiting tactics. *B. Hanbury*

EAGLE DANCER 5 b.g. Persian Bold 123 – Stealthy 73 (Kind of Hush 118) 78
[1996 NR 1997 10s⁴ a9.4g⁵ May 24] compact gelding: first foal: dam 1m winner:
better effort in maidens on debut (sweating): slowly away and carried head
awkwardly next time: possibly temperamental. *Lady Herries*

EAGLE'S CROSS (USA) 2 b.c. (Jan 30) Trempolino (USA) 135 – Shining 83
Bright 98 (Rainbow Quest (USA) 134) [1997 7g⁴ 8d Oct 16] quite attractive colt: has
a fluent, rather round action: first foal: dam French 1¼m winner out of Oaks second
Bourbon Girl: fourth of 7 in useful minor event at Kempton, slowly away and
running on, not knocked about: raced freely when below that form in maiden at
Newmarket 2 months later. *R. Charlton*

EARLY PEACE (IRE) 5 b.g. Bluebird (USA) 125 – Everything Nice 107 49
(Sovereign Path 125) [1996 68d: 8.3m 8.1d* 12g 10m 12m 15.4g⁶ 17.1m⁶ 13.8g⁵
1997 14.1g³ 14d⁵ 16g⁴ a14g 12g³ Aug 17] strong gelding: poor handicapper: stays
2m: acts on good to soft going: blinkered last 3 starts. *M. Dods*

EASTBURY ROSE 3 ch.f. Beveled (USA) – Shapina 105 (Sharp Edge 123) –
[1996 NR 1997 12.1g May 26] half-sister to 3 winners (from 3 known foals to race),
including fairly useful pair Thorny Rose (up to 1½m, by Tap On Wood) and Rose
Elegance (up to 1¼m, by Bairn): dam won Fred Darling Stakes: 50/1, slowly away
and showed little in maiden at Chepstow. *A. P. Jones*

EASTERN EAGLE (IRE) 3 b.g. Polish Patriot (USA) 128 – Lady's Turn 53
(Rymer 121) [1996 58p: 6.9d⁵ 1997 6.9g⁵ 8d a9.4g Sep 30] good-topped gelding:
modest maiden at best: bred to stay beyond 7f, but is a keen type: sold only 500 gns
in November. *J. M. P. Eustace*

EASTERN FIREDRAGON (IRE) 3 b.f. Shalford (IRE) 124§ – Doobie Do –
106 (Derring-Do 131) [1996 48: 5f⁵ 5g⁶ 7g 6s 1997 7.5m Apr 11] small filly: poor
form at 2 yrs (blinkered final start) for T. Easterby: tailed off in handicap only outing
as 3-y-o: should be suited by further than 5f. *D. Nicholls*

EASTERN GLORY (USA) 2 ch.c. (Feb 18) Eastern Echo (USA) – Brattice –
Cloth (USA) (L'Enjoleur (CAN)) [1997 7.5m⁵ Jul 21] $57,000Y: third foal: half-
brother to fairly useful 1995 2-y-o 5f and 7f winner Evening Chime (by Night Shift),
later successful in Hong Kong: dam won 7 races in USA up to around 1m: sire (by
Damascus) Grade 1 7f winner, ran only at 2 yrs: 10/1, outpaced fifth of 8 in fairly
useful minor event at Beverley: sent to Macau. *Mrs J. R. Ramsden*

EASTERN LYRIC 2 gr.f. (Feb 27) Petong 126 – Songlines 78 (Night Shift 75
(USA)) [1997 5m* 5g⁵ 5g⁴ 5m 5m³ 6d⁴ 5.3g 5.2d⁴ 5m Oct 2] 14,000Y: lengthy, quite
good-topped filly: second foal: half-sister to 3-y-o Nightingale Song: dam (best at 5f)
out of half-sister to Town And Country: fair performer: won maiden at Warwick in

May: generally ran creditably afterwards, largely in nurseries: best form at 5f: yet to race on extremes of ground. *J. Berry*

EASTERN PROJECT (IRE)   3 b.c. Project Manager 111 – Diandra (Shardari   79
134) [1996 NR 1997 9d³ 8f⁵ 10d 9.6g⁴ 9g⁶ 8.5d⁴ 9.6g² 8m Oct 6] rather leggy colt: second foal: dam ran once: fair ex-Irish maiden: good second at Gowran Park in August: sold out of J. Bolger's stable IR 7,200 gns later in month: burly, tailed off in handicap on British debut: stays 9.6f: acts on good to soft ground. *M. D. Hammond*

EASTERN PROPHETS   4 b.g. Emarati (USA) 74 – Four Love (Pas de Seul   87 d
133) [1996 93d: 5g⁵ 5.5g³ 5.1g 7m 6m 5f 5m 5g⁵ 5g 5s⁵ 1997 6m* 5.2g³ 5g⁴ 6g
6g 5m 5g 6m 6g a6g² a5g⁶ a6g⁵ a6g² Dec 26] good-quartered gelding: fairly useful handicapper at best: won at Kempton in March: not so good in second half of year, but second twice at Wolverhampton: stays 6f: acts on firm going, dead and the all-weather: sometimes on toes and sweating: blinkered seventh start. *G. Lewis*

EASTERN PURPLE (IRE)   2 b.c. (Jan 22) Petorius 117 – Broadway Rosie 101   91
(Absalom 128) [1997 6m 6m* 6g⁵ 6m⁴ 5d⁴ Sep 18] 20,000Y: robust, strong-quartered colt: fourth foal: half-brother to 4-y-o Double Oscar and 1¼m winner in France, Mo's Main Man (by Taufan): dam, Irish 5f to 7f winner, out of half-sister to King's Stand winner African Song: fairly useful performer: won maiden at Newcastle in August: 5¼ lengths fifth of 7 to Carrowkeel in Gimcrack Stakes at York later in month and ran creditably in listed race at Ayr (blinkered) final start: stays 6f: yet to race on extremes of ground: has tended to hang. *R. A. Fahey*

EASTER OGIL (IRE)   2 ch.g. (Feb 25) Pips Pride 117 – Piney Pass (Persian   71 p
Bold 123) [1997 6f 6s² Oct 16] 23,000Y: half-brother to several winners, including 9-y-o Allinson's Mate: dam Irish 2-y-o 8.5f winner: 2½ lengths second of 8 to Robin Goodfellow in maiden at Catterick, still showing inexperience early on: should stay beyond 6f: burly on debut (moved short to post): should do better at 3 yrs. *I. A. Balding*

EASTLEIGH   8 b.g. Efisio 120 – Blue Jane 81 (Blue Cashmere 129) [1996 –, a48:   –
a8g a8.5g⁵ a11g⁵ a8g⁴ a8g⁴ a8g⁴ 7d 8.9g a7g⁴ a10g² a10g⁶ a10g a10g 1997   a48
a12g⁵ a11g⁴ a8g⁶ a10g a8g* a8g² a8g 8d a12g⁶ a9.4g² 10m a7g⁶ 8s a10g 10d a8.5g³
8.2s 10d Nov 3] lengthy, workmanlike gelding: poor handicapper on all-weather: won at Lingfield in February: no form on turf for long time: stays 1¼m: tried visored/blinkered: sometimes flashes tail. *R. Hollinshead*

EASTWELL HALL   2 b.c. (Apr 29) Saddlers' Hall (IRE) 126 – Kinchenjunga   –
67 (Darshaan 133) [1997 6m 6g 5m 8g 10g Sep 23] tall colt: first foal: dam, second over 1m on only 2-y-o start but showed nothing afterwards, closely related to useful middle-distance performer Konigsberg: little worthwhile form. *R. Curtis*

EASTWELL MINSTREL   2 ch.c. (Apr 11) Risk Me (FR) 127 – Ramz (IRE)   40
(The Minstrel (CAN) 135) [1997 5g 5s⁵ 7g Jul 23] tall colt: third foal: brother to a poor maiden: dam unraced from family of Poule d'Essai des Pouliches winner Ukraine Girl: won seller at Folkestone in July: tailed off other starts. *R. Curtis*

EASYCALL   3 b.c. Forzando 122 – Up And Going (FR) (Never So Bold 135)   109
[1996 115: 5g* 5m* 6m* 6m⁴ 5m* 6m⁶ 5d* 1997 5g 5d⁵ 6g⁶ 5m² 5d 5m⁵ 5.2g⁶
Sep 18] good-quartered colt: good walker: smart performer at 2 yrs, winning 5 times, including Cornwallis Stakes at Ascot: struggled in good company in 1997, best efforts when sixth to Compton Place in July Cup and narrowly beaten by Coastal Bluff in 5-runner minor event, both at Newmarket, on third and fourth starts: probably effective at 5f and 6f: unraced on extremes of going: blinkered (ran creditably) final start. *B. J. Meehan*

EASY DOLLAR   5 ch.g. Gabitat 119 – Burglars Girl 63 (Burglar 128) [1996 108:   108
6g² 6m⁴ 7g² 6f 6f³ 6f² 6.5d 6d 1997 6m² 6g² 6f³ 6g 7.3m⁶ Jul 18] tall, plain gelding: does not impress in appearance: useful performer: ran well first 4 starts at 5 yrs, including when second in listed races at Doncaster and Newmarket and third in Group 3 race at Baden-Baden (behind Monaassib): forced too strong pace final outing: effective at 6f, and stays 7.3f well: acts on firm going, seemingly unsuited by ground softer than good: wears blinkers/visor: consistent. *B. Gubby*

EASY LISTENING (USA)   5 b.g. Easy Goer (USA) – Queen of Song (USA)   –
(His Majesty (USA)) [1996 89: 10g 10.2f³ 10m² 12m⁶ 1997 13.3d Sep 20] rangy

312

gelding: lightly-raced handicapper, 1¼m winner at 3 yrs and fairly useful at 4 yrs for R. Charlton: well beaten only outing in 1997: stays 1½m: raced predominantly on good to firm/firm going: fairly useful hurdler. *N. J. Hawke*

EASY NOMI 7 b.g. Nomination 125 – Muna (Thatch (USA) 136) [1996 NR 1997 5v a7g Jul 10] no sign of ability in 3 races. *K. W. Hogg, Isle of Man* –

EASY RISK 2 ch.f. (Apr 25) Risk Me (FR) 127 – Egnoussa 76 (Swing Easy (USA) 126) [1997 6m Aug 18] 400Y: sister to 3 winning sprinters, and half-sister to 2 winners by Formidable: dam 7f winner, half-sister to Devon Ditty: tailed off in claimer. *Miss L. A. Perratt* –

EASY SONG (USA) 3 b.c. Easy Goer (USA) – Queen of Song (USA) (His Majesty (USA)) [1996 NR 1997 8d 8m³ 10g⁴ 8.5g² 10.1f³ 10f* a8.5f² Dec 28] rangy colt with plenty of scope: has a fluent, round action: brother to 5-y-o Easy Listening and half-brother to several winners, including Private Song (stays 1½m, by Private Account): dam, twice graded winner at 8.5f at 5 yrs, sister to smart 6f to 9f winner Cormorant: fairly useful performer: evens, looked a hard ride in first time visor when winning uncompetitive 5-runner maiden at Brighton in October: sold 32,000 gns from R. Charlton: distant second in allowance race at Santa Anita: should stay further than 1¼m: acts on firm ground. *Carla Gaines, USA* 81

EATON PARK (IRE) 3 ch.c. Mac's Imp (USA) 116 – Pepilin (Coquelin (USA) 121) [1996 62d: 5m² 6g⁴ 6g 7g 6m⁶ 1997 5.3f 5d Jun 23] leggy, rather unfurnished colt: modest form on debut: has deteriorated markedly: left R. Akehurst after reappearance. *Miss Gay Kelleway* –

EAT YOUR PEAR 3 ch.f. Dunbeath (USA) 127 – Track Angel 43 (Ardoon 124) [1996 NR 1997 8g⁶ a11g Nov 17] fourth foal: dam winning stayer on flat and at 2½m over hurdles: no encouragement in maiden and seller. *R. Bastiman* –

EAU BENITE 6 br.g. Monsanto (FR) 121 – Hopeful Waters 66 (Forlorn River 124) [1996 NR 1997 a12g Jun 27] brother to a winning hurdler and half-brother to another: dam 6f and 7f winner: no sign of ability. *N. E. Berry* –

EAU SECOURS (FR) 5 ch.m. Lesotho (USA) 118 – Nornina (USA) (Northjet 136) [1996 NR 1997 a11g Jun 13] 65,000 francs Y: ex-French mare: first foal: dam French maiden half-sister to 1000 Guineas winner Mrs McArdy: no form, including in blinkers. *R. Harris* –

EBADIYLA (IRE) 3 b.f. Sadler's Wells (USA) 132 – Ebaziya (IRE) 111 (Darshaan 133) [1996 NR 1997 10g* 10d³ 12m⁶ 12m* 12f 15.5d* Oct 26] 122
Should a newcomer win the next running of the Cill Dara Maiden at the Curragh it might be worth noting its name if you're a believer in coincidence. In the last two seasons Zagreb and Ebadiyla have made successful, belated debuts in this mile-and-a-quarter event and gone on to achieve classic success, Zagreb in the Irish Derby and Ebadiyla in the Kildangan Stud Irish Oaks and Prix Royal-Oak. Ebadiyla met with a couple of defeats before her return to the Curragh for the Irish Oaks, the second of them in the Oaks at Epsom where she was the Aga Khan's first runner in the race since Aliysa had been disqualified eight years earlier. Considering her inexperience and that she didn't get the clearest of runs, Ebadiyla acquitted herself well in finishing sixth behind Reams of Verse at Epsom, fading towards the finish after being rushed into the lead on the home turn. Just ahead of her came Yashmak and Etoile and both were in opposition again at the Curragh, the former a warm favourite following her runaway win in the Ribblesdale Stakes. Ebadiyla, aided by a pacemaker to ensure a truly-run race, and ridden with more restraint, not only turned the tables on this pair but ran out a most emphatic winner. Aliya, the pacemaker, was moved off the rail turning into the straight to allow Ebadiyla a clear run through, and the latter soon challenged the new leader, Yashmak, taking her measure just inside the final furlong and running on strongly to draw three lengths clear. The Prix de Diane third Brilliance again occupied that position, a head behind Yashmak.

Kildangan Stud Irish Oaks, the Curragh—Ebadiyla leaves her Epsom Oaks form behind;
Yashmak (light cap) and Brilliance battle for the minor honours

A slight set-back caused Ebadiyla to miss her intended next engagement in the Yorkshire Oaks, and it became a race against time to get her ready for the Prix de l'Arc de Triomphe. Ebadiyla's appearance in the paddock at Longchamp suggested that she was none the worse for a rushed preparation, but her performance showed otherwise, as she was unable to reach a challeng-

Prix Royal-Oak, Longchamp—Ebadiyla bounces back
after a below-form run again to register her second classic win of the year;
Snow Princess (No. 8) comes late for second with Oscar Schindler (No. 4) third

ing position and finished only twelfth of eighteen behind Peintre Celebre. All the sharper for that run, Ebadiyla came back to her best when returned to Longchamp for the Prix Royal-Oak three weeks later. With the Arc fourth Oscar Schindler and Jockey Club Cup winner Grey Shot among several who failed to give their running, the Royal-Oak took less winning than might have been expected but, that said, Ebadiyla couldn't have been much more impressive. Patiently ridden by Gerard Mosse, deputizing for the filly's usual partner John Murtagh, who was unable to do the weight, Ebadiyla began to make headway approaching the straight, took command over a furlong out and stormed clear to win by six lengths from Snow Princess, who came late to deprive Oscar Schindler of second. Ebadiyla, who acts on good to firm and good to soft ground, would definitely stay further given the chance and is just the type for Cup races. She reportedly remains in training in 1998.

		Northern Dancer	Nearctic
	Sadler's Wells (USA)	(b 1961)	Natalma
	(b 1981)	Fairy Bridge	Bold Reason
Ebadiyla (IRE)		(b 1975)	Special
(b.f. 1994)		Darshaan	Shirley Heights
	Ebaziya (IRE)	(br 1981)	Delsy
	(b 1989)	Ezana	Ela-Mana-Mou
		(ch 1983)	Evisa

Ebadiyla was the third classic winner in 1997 owned and bred by the Aga Khan, following Daylami (Poule d'Essai des Poulains) and Vereva (Prix de Diane). Her dam, Ebaziya, also trained by John Oxx, won three listed races and finished third in the Group 2 Blandford Stakes as a three-year-old. Ebaziya, who would have stayed beyond a mile and a half, is a daughter of Ezana, a

H. H. Aga Khan's "Ebadiyla"

winner over an extended eleven furlongs in France and half-sister to Demia, successful in a couple of Group 3 races over an extended ten furlongs there. Ezana, who was sold by the Aga Khan for IR 40,000 guineas in 1994, is out of Evisa, an unraced daughter of the Criterium de Maisons-Laffitte winner Albanilla. Ebadiyla is the first foal of Ebaziya. Her second, the two-year-old colt Enzeli (by Kahyasi), is in training with Oxx but has yet to race. *J. Oxx, Ireland*

EBEN ALBADOU (USA) 3 b.c. Sheikh Albadou 128 – Stealthy Lady (USA) (J – O Tobin (USA) 130) [1996 NR 1997 8g May 5] 38,000Y: sixth foal: half-brother to 1m winner Spanish Grandee (by El Gran Senor) and a minor winner in USA: dam unraced daughter of Stumped, dam also of Sonic Lady: tailed off in maiden at Kempton. *A. C. Stewart*

E B TREASURE 2 b.f. (May 9) Precocious 126 – Petite Elite 47 (Anfield 117) – [1997 a6g 5m 5s a7g6 5m 6.1m 6s6 a8g Nov 14] 500Y: fourth foal: half-sister to 3-y-o Effervescence and 4-y-o Efipetite and a 2-y-o 5f winner by Hallgate: dam, maiden, stayed 7f: of no account. *N. Bycroft*

ECCENTRIC DANCER 4 b.f. Rambo Dancer (CAN) 107 – Lady Eccentric – (IRE) (Magical Wonder (USA) 125) [1996 –, a47: 8.2g 6g 7.5g a8.5g3 10m 8m 8f a9.4g2 7f 8.2s a9.4g a7g 1997 a9.4g a8g a7g a8.5g Feb 21] lengthy filly: no worthwhile form at 4 yrs: sometimes blinkered. *M. P. Bielby*

ECO FRIENDLY 2 ch.c. (Mar 6) Sabrehill (USA) 120 – Flower Girl 108 (Pharly 101 (FR) 130) [1997 7g 8.1d2 8g2 8s* 8v* Nov 26] heavy-topped colt: second reported foal: half-brother to 3-y-o Water Flower: dam 6f winner: useful form: trained by J. Fanshawe first 2 starts: won maiden at Doncaster in November by ½ length from Double Edged and 6-runner Prix Saint-Roman at Saint-Cloud later in month by 8 lengths from Ten Bob: will be suited by 1¼m+: yet to race on going firmer than good, and goes well on heavy. *B. W. Hills*

EDAN HEIGHTS 5 b.g. Heights of Gold – Edna 92 (Shiny Tenth 120) [1996 81: 81 12g 12m 12m 11.4g* 10m 10m2 10m 10m4 12g 10s* 12s 1997 10g 10m 10g 10s2 10.3d 10.1d6 10g 10m3 10s5 10m* 10.3m 10d a12g3 a14g2 Nov 24] sturdy, plain gelding: fairly useful handicapper: won 18-runner apprentice event at Leicester in September: effective at 1¼m to 1¾m: acts on any turf/all-weather: none too consistent. *S. Dow*

EDDIE ROMBO 2 b.g. (May 18) Aragon 118 – Jolimo 92 (Fortissimo 111) [1997 – 6g 5s 7m 7g Aug 1] 9,000Y: tall gelding: has a round action: half-brother to several winners, including fairly useful performer up to 1½m/high-class hurdler Osric (by Radetzky): dam won from 1½m to 2¼m: little worthwhile form. *N. Tinkler*

EDEN DANCER 5 b.g. Shareef Dancer (USA) 135 – Dash (Connaught 130) 34 [1996 –: 10.3m 12.3m 12.1m5 1997 12m 12d4 12g Aug 23] sturdy gelding: poor performer nowadays: stays 1½m: acts on any going: fair hurdler. *Mrs M. Reveley*

EDEN ROCK (GER) 3 b.c. Dashing Blade 117 – Eriphyle (GER) (Surumu 113 (GER)) [1996 8s* 8s* 8d* 1997 8g* 8d5 11v 8g3 10d3 8g2 8f4 Oct 5] smallish colt: has rather a splayed action: brother to 1996 3-y-o listed 11f winner Eduardo (stays 1½m): smart performer: champion in Germany at 2 yrs, winning all 3 races, notably Preis des Winterfavoriten at Cologne: won Group 3 event at Hoppegarten in April by 2½ lengths from Happy Change: best effort when 3½ lengths third of 6 to Oxalagu in Bayerisches Zuchtrennen at Munich in August: stays 1¼m: acts on soft ground: consistent. *B. Schutz, Germany*

EDGAR KIRBY 6 ch.g. Caerleon (USA) 132 – Martha Stevens (USA) 102 – (Super Concorde (USA) 128) [1996 56: 8m4 7f 8g3 a8g 1997 7.5m Apr 5] sturdy gelding: lightly-raced maiden handicapper: below form only outing at 6 yrs. *P. W. Harris*

EDIPO RE 5 b.h. Slip Anchor 136 – Lady Barrister (Law Society (USA) 130) – [1996 94: 14m2 14d4 1997 11.8g4 16.5s Nov 8] rangy horse: fairly useful form on occasions, though probably flattered on 5-y-o return and tailed off in handicap at Doncaster 12 days later: stays 1¾m: often bandaged. *P. J. Hobbs*

EDNA'S GIFT (IRE) 2 b.f. (Apr 23) Cyrano de Bergerac 120 – Glenstal Priory 56 d
53 (Glenstal (USA) 118) [1997 6m* a6g² 6g 6.1s³ 7m a7g² a7g⁶ 7g⁶ a6g Sep 30] a50 d
small filly: first reported foal: dam stayed 2¼m: modest performer: won seller at
Thirsk in June: mostly disappointing afterwards: stays 6f. *J. Berry*

ED'S FOLLY (IRE) 4 b.g. Fayruz 116 – Tabriya 61 (Nishapour (FR) 125) [1996 59
59: 5d 6g 7f³ 7m⁶ 6f 1997 6m 6m³ 5.1g 6g² 6m 7d 6f³ 6m⁵ 7g² 7m⁴ a7g 7d³ a7g a45
a10g⁵ Dec 19] well-quartered gelding: modest maiden handicapper: effective at 6f,
probably 1¼m: acts on firm and soft ground, poor form on the all-weather. *S. Dow*

EDWARDIAN 2 ch.c. (Jan 20) Sanglamore (USA) 126 – Woodwardia (USA) 93 79 p
(El Gran Senor (USA) 136) [1997 8.2s² Oct 15] first foal: dam, 1m winner who
stayed 11.4f, out of unraced sister to Al Bahathri: 20/1, short-head second of 12 to
Corniche in maiden at Nottingham, leading inside final 2f, keeping on but caught
near line: should stay at least 1½m: should improve. *Mrs A. J. Perrett*

EDWARD SEYMOUR (USA) 10 b.g. Northern Baby (CAN) 127 – Regal
Leader (USA) (Mr Leader (USA)) [1996 NR 1997 a14.8g Jan 22] tailed off in seller
on first start on flat since 1991: untrustworthy winning selling hurdler. *W. Jenks*

EFFECTUAL 4 b.g. Efisio 120 – Moharabuiee 60 (Pas de Seul 133) [1996 72: 89
8m 10m³ 8.1d² 10m⁴ 1997 a10g* a8.5g³ a9.4g² 10d* 10g* 9.7m³ 10g⁶ Jun 13] sturdy
gelding: fairly useful performer: won maiden at Lingfield in February and handicaps
at Ripon and Kempton in May: creditable efforts afterwards: will prove best up to
1¼m: acts on good to firm and dead ground (unraced on extremes) and the all-
weather: swishes tail under pressure: sold 22,000 gns in August, and winner over
hurdles for Miss V. Williams. *Miss Gay Kelleway*

EFFERVESCENCE 3 ch.c. Efisio 120 – Petite Elite 47 (Anfield 117) [1996 86: 71
6m⁶ 5.7f⁴ 5.1m² 5m² 6m⁵ 5m 7d 7g² 7s a7g² a8.5g⁴ a7s² a7g* a7g⁸ 1997 a7g* 7m a86
7.6d a8g⁵ 7.1m² 8d 8.5s⁵ 7.1m a7g⁴ Oct 4] compact colt: has a short action: fair
on turf, fairly useful on all-weather: won handicap at Lingfield in January: ran
creditably in frame in claimers after: effective 7f to 8.5f: acts on all-weather and good
to firm ground, seemingly not on going softer than good: genuine. *R. Hannon*

EFFICACIOUS (IRE) 4 ch.f. Efisio 120 – Bushti Music 63 (Bustino 136) [1996 38
49d: 10.8g⁵ 9.7f² 8.3m 10.1f⁴ 12.5f⁶ 9.7g 10f³ 10f⁶ 11.9f² 11.9f a12g a8s⁵ a10g³ a12g
a12g⁵ a10g 1997 a13g a12g a14.8g a8.5g⁶ a9.4g⁵ a12g a10g³ 11.9f⁵ a10g⁵ 11.9f 8.1g
Aug 3] lengthy, plain filly: poor maiden handicapper: trained first 2 starts by
G. L. Moore: stays 1½m: acts on firm going and equitrack: has been blinkered.
P. Eccles

EFFICACY 6 b.m. Efisio 120 – Lady Killane 62 (Reform 132) [1996 39, a62: –
a6g⁵ a6g a7g² a7g³ a6g⁴ 6d⁴ 5.1g 6m⁶ 6m a6g² a6g 1997 a6g a6g³ a5g a5g Aug 8] a62
angular mare: bad mover: modest on the all-weather (though below form both
outings on equitrack): well below form last 2 starts (off course 4 months in between):
poor and lightly raced on turf: best up to 7f: often apprentice ridden: inconsistent.
A. P. Jarvis

EFIPETITE 4 ch.f. Efisio 120 – Petite Elite 47 (Anfield 117) [1996 –, a54d: a6g –
a7g⁴ a8g⁵ a8g³ a6g⁴ a8g³ a8g* a7g² a8g³ a8g⁴ a7g³ a7g³ a7g⁴ a8g⁶ a8g⁵ a8g 7s 8f 7d a41 d
10g 8m a8g a8g⁶ 1997 a8g³ a8g a8g⁵ a8g⁶ a8g³ a7g⁵ a8g⁶ 8m a8g⁴ a7g a7g a7g 8g 7d
a8g 8g 8.2m a7g Aug 15] close-coupled filly: poor and deteriorating handicapper
nowadays. *N. Bycroft*

EFODOS 2 ch.f. (Feb 5) Pursuit of Love 124 – Sariza 79 (Posse (USA) 130) [1997 –
6g Oct 27] angular filly: half-sister to fairly useful 8.5f winner Aratos (by Night
Shift): dam, best at 7f, out of 1000 Guineas second Tolmi, an excellent family: 20/1
and backward, last of 22 in Leicester maiden. *G. Wragg*

EFRA 8 b.g. Efisio 120 – Ra Ra (Lord Gayle (USA) 124) [1996 72: 6m² 6d⁶ 6d –
1997 6m 6f Apr 11] lengthy, good-topped gelding: has a round action: well held at 8
yrs: tried blinkered. *R. Hannon*

EGOLI (USA) 3 ch.f. Seeking The Gold (USA) – Krisalya 98 (Kris 135) [1996 93
NR 1997 7.1m* 8.1s 7d⁴ 8m² Oct 5] quite good-topped filly: third foal: half-sister to
1994 2-y-o 7f winner Crystal Cavern (stayed 1m by Be My Guest) and 1m and 1¼m
winner Conic Hill (by Lomond): dam, 10.4f winner, from good family: reportedly
had weak knees: fairly useful form: won 6-runner maiden at Sandown in August in

EGO

taking style: best effort when second in handicap at Leicester final start, slowly away, switched and running on strongly: should stay beyond 1m: acts on good to firm going, probably unsuited by ground softer than good (carried head high under such conditions): sent to USA. *G. Wragg*

EGO NIGHT (IRE) 2 b.c. (Apr 30) Night Shift (USA) – Sharp Ego (USA) (Sharpen Up 127) [1997 8.5m² Oct 31] IR 15,500F, IR 47,000Y: seventh foal: closely related to 1994 2-y-o 5f winner Sapiston Girl (by Nordico) and half-brother to 6-y-o El Bailador: dam Irish 5f winner: 1½ lengths second of 9 to Priwings in maiden at Milan. *M. Bell* ?

EIDER HILL 3 b.f. Alawir (FR) 97 – Matrah 77 (Northfields (USA)) [1996 NR 1997 8d⁶ 10m 8m Oct 22] unfurnished filly: third reported foal: dam 1¼m winner: only a little sign of ability. *D. Morris* –

EI EI 2 b.c. (May 6) North Briton 67 – Branitska (Mummy's Pet 125) [1997 6m 8.2m⁵ 8.2s³ Oct 15] seventh foal: brother to smart 1989 2-y-o 6f and 7.5f winner Call To Arms and half-brother to 1¼m winner Superluminal (by Unfuwain) and 1½m winner War Beat (by Wolver Heights): dam poor maiden from family of Dominion: trained by C. Brittain on debut: fair form in 2 maidens at Nottingham in autumn: stays 1m. *B. W. Hills* 75

EIFFEL TIGER (IRE) 2 b. or br.g. (May 2) Paris House 123 – Rosa Bengala (Balidar 133) [1997 6.1g 6d 6m Oct 31] 11,500 2-y-o: half-brother to Irish 9f winner Rupert The Great (by Prince Rupert) and several winners abroad, including Italian Group 2 1m winner Capo Nord (by Pitskelly): dam Italian 7f winner: no promise in maidens. *Bob Jones* –

EILEEN'S LADY 3 b.f. Mtoto 134 – Laughsome 76 (Be My Guest (USA) 126) [1996 NR 1997 a10g⁵ 8.2d Apr 29] leggy, unfurnished filly: first foal: dam, stayed 1¼m, half-sister to smart middle-distance fillies Braiswick and Percy's Lass out of Oaks fourth Laughing Girl, an excellent family: bought out of M. Stoute's stable 17,000 gns in 1996: little worthwhile form in maidens: well backed on debut. *G. G. Margarson* –

EJEER (IRE) 3 b.g. Jareer (USA) 115 – Precious Egg (Home Guard (USA) 129) [1996 –: 6g 1997 a8.5g⁴ a8g⁴ a5g⁵ 6g⁶ Mar 25] angular gelding: modest maiden: may prove suited by 6f/7f: raced only on good going/fibresand: sent to Germany. *M. R. Channon* 53

EKATERINI PARITSI 3 b.f. Timeless Times (USA) 99 – Wych Willow (Hard Fought 125) [1996 49, a52: 5.3f³ 5.1m³ 5s² 6m² a6g² 6f a7g⁵ a7g² a7g a6g³ a5g⁴ 1997 a5g³ a5g⁶ a5g⁶ a6g⁵ Feb 4] leggy filly: unimpressive mover: poor maiden: stays 7f: acts on any all-weather/turf: blinkered twice, visored nowadays. *W. G. M. Turner* – a49

ELA AGAPI MOU (USA) 4 b.g. Storm Bird (CAN) 134 – Vaguar (USA) (Vaguely Noble 140) [1996 53: 10.2g 10f 10s⁵ a13g⁶ 10m³ 11.9f² 11.5m a16g 1997 a12g 12m Apr 22] rather leggy gelding: has a round action: modest maiden: well beaten both starts in 1997: should stay beyond 1½m: acts on firm ground (no worthwhile form on all-weather): fairly useful hurdler. *G. L. Moore* –

ELA-ARISTOKRATI (IRE) 5 b.h. Danehill (USA) 126 – Dubai Lady 78 (Kris 135) [1996 117: 10g 10.1m* 10g⁴ 10.5m² 11.1m³ 1997 12g² 12m⁴ 12g⁵ 12g⁴ 12m³ Aug 3] sturdy horse: impresses in appearance: good mover: smart performer: trained at 4 yrs by L. Cumani: ran creditably all starts at 5 yrs, ½-length second to Whitewater Affair in John Porter Stakes at Newbury on reappearance and narrowly-beaten third to Harbour Dues in listed race at Klampenborg on final outing: stiffer tasks in between: stays 1½m: acts on firm going, not discredited only outing on good to soft: normally held up: sent to USA. *M. H. Tompkins* 113

ELABELLOU (IRE) 2 b.f. (Apr 30) Ela-Mana-Mou 132 – Salabella 64 (Sallust 134) [1997 10m a7g a8g⁶ Dec 8] 12,000Y: smallish, sturdy filly: half-sister to several winners up to 1m, including useful pair Dedicated Lady (by Pennine Walk) and Silk Petal (by Petorius): dam (stayed 11f) half-sister to Irish St Leger winner M-Lolshan: dropped in class, little worthwhile form in seller at Southwell final start. *M. Johnston* 41

ELAKIK 2 b.c. (Feb 6) Green Desert (USA) 127 – Narjis (USA) 87 (Blushing Groom (FR) 131) [1997 6g³ 6d³ 7m* 8g 8m³ 8m³ 8.5d* Dec 20] sturdy colt: sixth foal: half-brother to 3-y-o Shamikh and 1994 May Hill Stakes winner Mamlakah 82

318

(both by Unfuwain) and 1992 2-y-o 5f winner Tahasun (by Shareef Dancer): dam, 2-y-o 5f winner, out of smart 6f/7f stakes winner Mashteen: fairly useful performer in Britain: made heavy weather of winning maiden at Chester in August: sold out of J. Dunlop's stable 20,000 gns after penultimate start: won allowance race at Hollywood Park in December: should stay beyond 8.5f: unraced on extremes of going: looks a difficult ride: blinkered last 3 starts. *D. Vienna, USA*

ELA MAN HOWA   6 b.g. Mtoto 134 – Top Treat (USA) 101 (Topsider (USA)) [1996 50: 12.3g 12g⁴ 14.1f 13.1g⁶ 12m 16g⁴ 16.4g⁵ 13.1m⁶ 15.9g 1997 a16g⁴ a12g⁴ a13g a13g⁵ a16g⁴ Feb 13] lightly-made gelding: modest form on reappearance, ran badly last 3 outings: stays 2m: acts on good to firm and dead ground and equitrack: blinkered (ran too freely) last 2 starts at 5 yrs. *A. Bailey*   52 d

ELANAAKA   2 ch.f. (Feb 27) Lion Cavern (USA) 117 – Mousaiha (USA) (Shadeed (USA) 135) [1997 7.5g³ 7.5f² Sep 17] second foal: closely related to 3-y-o Hakkaniyah: dam (unraced) from family of good American horses Forty Niner and Swale: fair form when placed in maidens at Beverley in summer: may still do better. *D. Morley*   76

ELA-YIE-MOU (IRE)   4 ch.g. Kris 135 – Green Lucia 116 (Green Dancer (USA) 132) [1996 84: 12d 12m³ 14.1m* 14d² 12m⁴ 14f 14.6g 1997 9.8s 13d 12s 8d 16.1d⁵ 14.4m⁵ 14.4m³ 14.1g Oct 4] tall gelding: has a fluent, round action: generally disappointing handicapper, only fair form at best in 1997: stays 1¾m: acts on good to firm and dead going: has carried head awkwardly. *S. Dow*   67 d

ELAYSHA (USA)   3 ch.f. Gulch (USA) – Key Flyer (USA) (Nijinsky (CAN) 138) [1996 NR 1997 9m Jul 12] third foal: dam, won up to 11f (including minor stakes) in USA, from the family of Arazi and Ajdal: tailed-off last in maiden at Lingfield: sent to USA. *H. R. A. Cecil*   –

ELBAAHA   3 ch.f. Arazi (USA) 135 – Gesedeh 117 (Ela-Mana-Mou 132) [1996 78: 6m³ 8.1d² 8.2g³ 1997 9m⁴ 10.1s⁴ 11.5m⁴ 11.5m* 11.8g² 12m² 12g 14.6d² Nov 7] smallish, good-topped filly: useful performer: won maiden at Yarmouth in August by 7 lengths: best efforts when second at Doncaster in handicap 2 starts later and minor event (beaten 3 lengths by Sweetness Herself) final outing: sweating and swishing tail, helped force pace when well held seventh outing: stays 14.6f: acts on soft and good to firm ground: game and consistent. *M. A. Jarvis*   97

EL BAILADOR (IRE)   6 b.g. Dance of Life (USA) – Sharp Ego (USA) (Sharpen Up 127) [1996 68: a12g* a11g⁴ 1997 10s a12g Dec 6] lightly-raced handicapper: no show in 1997: tried blinkered. *J. D. Bethell*   –

ELBA MAGIC (IRE)   2 b.f. (Feb 13) Faustus (USA) 118 – Dependable (Formidable (USA) 125) [1997 6.9s 7m 7g⁶ 8g Oct 7] third foal: sister to 3-y-o Certain Magic: dam unraced daughter of half-sister to Chilibang: form only in maiden at Chester third start: trained by H. Collingridge on debut. *C. A. Dwyer*   53

EL BARDADOR (IRE)   4 b.g. Thatching 131 – Osmunda (Mill Reef (USA) 141) [1996 59: 8.1d 8.2m 7m 9.9g⁴ a11g 10.1m* 11.9g 11.5m 12s⁴ 1997 a8.5g 10.8m a11g May 19] lengthy gelding: modest winner: showed little in 1997: has been blinkered: possibly ungenuine. *R. J. Hodges*   –

ELBARREE (IRE)   2 b.g. (Mar 15) Green Desert (USA) 127 – Walimu (IRE) 82 (Top Ville 129) [1997 7d Nov 7] sturdy gelding: first foal: dam 1m to 1½m winner, granddaughter of Roussalka, herself half-sister to Oh So Sharp: 20/1 and burly, well held in maiden at Doncaster: should do better. *M. A. Jarvis*   – p

EL DON   5 b.g. High Kicker (USA) – Madam Gerard 50 (Brigadier Gerard 144) [1996 –: 8.2m⁶ 11.8d 10.1m 10.1m a11g 1997 a12g Jan 3] very tall gelding: disappointing maiden on flat: tried blinkered and visored: fair hurdler. *M. J. Ryan*   –

ELECTION DAY (IRE)   5 b.h. Sadler's Wells (USA) 132 – Hellenic 125 (Darshaan 133) [1996 116: 10g* 13.4g² 13.3d* 12f 12s⁴ 1997 12g⁵ 16.2m³ 13.4v⁶ 20g³ 16m⁴ 15.9g⁵ Aug 19] sturdy, attractive horse: smart performer on his day: reportedly injured near-fore penultimate start in 1996: good efforts in frame in Gold Cup at Royal Ascot (hung left when third behind Celeric, beaten 1¾ lengths) on fourth start and Goodwood Cup (stumbled halfway, kept on late when 4½ lengths fourth to Double Trigger): didn't impress with attitude final start, again hanging   119 badly left under pressure: suited by good test of stamina: acts on good to firm and dead ground: visored 4 times, including last 3 starts. *M. R. Stoute*

ELEGANT DANCE 3 ch.f. Statoblest 120 – Furry Dance (USA) (Nureyev   57
(USA) 131) [1996 57: 7m 1997 8g⁵ 8d May 19] rather leggy filly: modest maiden: took strong hold when well beaten final start. *J. J. Sheehan*

ELEGANT WARNING (IRE) 3 b.f. Warning 136 – Dance It (USA) (Believe   105
It (USA)) [1996 109: 6m² 6m³ 6m* 6g* 1997 7g³ 8m 6m² 6g⁶ 7g⁶ Oct 18] tall filly: has a quick action: useful performer: third (to Reunion) in Nell Gwyn Stakes and seventh (7½ lengths behind Sleepytime) in One Thousand Guineas, both at Newmarket: off course over 3 months, seemingly good sixth to Kahal in Group 2 event there final start, though probably flattered in coming off strong pace: should prove best at 6f/7f: raced only on good/good to firm going: held up: has shown signs of temperament, and tends to flash tail: sold 100,000 gns in December. *B. W. Hills*

ELEONORA D'ARBOREA 2 b.f. (Feb 28) Prince Sabo 123 – Kala Rosa 79   78
(Kalaglow 132) [1997 5m² 5m 6d⁵ 6.1m⁶ 6s* 6m⁶ 6d⁵ Sep 2] 20,000Y: workmanlike filly: fifth foal: sister to fairly useful 5f (at 2 yrs) to 7f winner Ortolan and half-sister to 2 winners, including 3-y-o Red Embers: dam, lightly-raced maiden, placed over 6f at 2 yrs: fair performer: won maiden at Redcar in July: below form final start: stays 6f: acts on good to firm and soft ground. *B. J. Meehan*

ELEVENTH DUKE (IRE) 2 b.c. (Feb 21) Imperial Frontier (USA) 112 –   90
Disregard That (IRE) (Don't Forget Me 127) [1997 5.1m⁴ 6m⁴ 6m 5g³ 5.7m* 5.1d* 5m² 5d 5m Oct 2] 29,000 2-y-o: useful-looking colt: first foal: dam unraced half-sister to useful Irish 1988 2-y-o Sedulous: fairly useful performer: won nurseries at Bath and Chepstow in August: stiff task penultimate start, bolted to post final one (bandaged behind): a sprinter: acts on good to firm and dead ground: has gone right leaving stalls: held up. *R. Hannon*

ELFLAND (IRE) 6 b.g. Fairy King (USA) – Ridge The Times (USA) 78 (Riva   93
Ridge (USA)) [1996 NR 1997 7m²ᵈⁱˢ 7d* 7g³ 6s⁵ 7f 6g Sep 20] has a very high knee action: lightly-raced handicapper: returned better than ever in 1997, winning at Newmarket in June: good efforts next 3 starts, never on terms in Ayr Gold Cup final one: effective at 6f and 7f: probably acts on any going. *Lady Herries*

ELHABUB 2 b.c. (Apr 28) Lion Cavern (USA) 117 – Million Heiress (Auction   86
Ring (USA) 123) [1997 6m² 6d² 6m² Oct 1] 55,000Y: well-made colt: fourth foal: half-brother to 1994 2-y-o 5f winner Stato One (by Statoblest), later successful (including in listed race in 1997) up to 9f in Scandinavia and 3-y-o Colway Ritz: dam poor maiden: fairly useful form when runner-up in newcomers event at Goodwood and maidens at York and Newcastle, finding little after making running at 9/4 on at last-named course: not sure to stay much further than 6f. *B. W. Hills*

ELHAFID (USA) 3 ch.c. Nureyev (USA) 131 – Shy Dame (USA) (Damascus   –
(USA)) [1996 66+: 7m 7m 8m 1997 11.5d Aug 28] modest form in maidens at 2 yrs: well beaten in handicap only outing in 1997: not certain to stay much beyond 1m: sold 4,500 gns in October, to go to Germany. *Major W. R. Hern*

ELHAYQ (IRE) 2 b.c. (Jan 19) Nashwan (USA) 135 – Mahasin (USA) 90   80 p
(Danzig (USA)) [1997 8m³ 8.2s⁴ Oct 15] lengthy, rather unfurnished colt with scope: second foal: half-brother to 3-y-o Musharak: dam 7f and 1m winner, closely related to William Hill Futurity winner Al Hareb and smart French 9f to 1¼m winner Dr Somerville: shaped well though green and slowly away when third in maiden at Salisbury: didn't get run of race at Nottingham later in month: should be suited by 1¼m+: remains capable of better, and sure to win races. *J. L. Dunlop*

ELISSA 11 ch.m. Tap On Wood 130 – Blakewood 75 (Blakeney 126) [1996 NR   –
1997 a14g Nov 14] of little account. *G. P. Kelly*

ELITE BLISS (IRE) 5 b.m. Tirol 127 – Krismas River (Kris 135) [1996 44: 12g³   –
10.2g³ 10m⁴ 10.3g 11f 11m⁵ a11g⁴ a14g³ 1997 a16s a16g 16.1g⁶ 12.3m Apr 9] big, workmanlike mare: no form at 5 yrs. *M. J. Camacho*

ELITE FORCE (IRE) 4 b.g. Fairy King (USA) – La Petruschka (Ballad Rock   –
122) [1996 80d: 8g³ 7d² 7.6g 6m⁶ 7.1m⁶ 8m 1997 a10g Feb 18] leggy, lengthy gelding: fairly useful maiden at best: has deteriorated. *M. Madgwick*

ELITE HOPE (USA) 5 ch.m. Moment of Hope (USA) – Chervil (USA) – (Greenough (USA)) [1996 71: 8.1g 7.6g 7.1m⁶ 7m 8.3d⁶ 8.1d 8.9g 10m a7g² a6g a7g* a7g a7g* 1997 a7g* a7f² a7g³ a7g⁴ 7.6v 7.1g a6g a6g* a6g³ Dec 26] small, sturdy mare: fair performer on fibresand: won handicap at Wolverhampton in January and claimer on same course in November: stays 7f: little form on equitrack and turf since 3 yrs: blinkered (well beaten) once: races prominently. *N. Tinkler*   a77

ELIZA 3 ch.f. Shavian 125 – One Degree 80 (Crooner 119) [1996 –p: 7.1s 1997 a6g⁶ 7m³ 6s 8.1m 8d a6g Oct 20] modest maiden: easily best effort third at Salisbury in June: sold 2,000 gns, to go to Saudi Arabia. *Lord Huntingdon*   66 d

ELIZA ACTON 2 b.f. (May 24) Shirley Heights 130 – Sing Softly 112 (Luthier 126) [1997 8.2s⁶ 8.2d* Oct 30] neat filly: sister to 7-y-o Top Cees and half-sister to 4-y-o Whispered Melody and 3-y-o Supreme Sound: dam, 6f winner at 2 yrs, won Lancashire Oaks: 13/2 from 12/1, won 12-runner maiden at Nottingham by head from Capri, staying on to lead inside last 1f: will stay at least 1½m: should improve again. *P. W. Harris*   70 p

ELJJANAH (USA) 2 b.c. (May 6) Riverman (USA) 131 – True Celebrity (USA) (Lyphard (USA) 132) [1997 7.1g 7d³ 7m² Jul 19] $250,000Y: well-made colt: has a quick action: second foal: dam, maiden in USA, closely related to smart 1985 2-y-o 7f winner Truely Nureyev: fair form when placed in maidens at Newmarket and Redcar: should stay at least 1m: looks rather headstrong: sent to UAE. *J. L. Dunlop*   76

ELLA FALLS (IRE) 2 ch.f. (Mar 10) Dancing Dissident (USA) 119 – Over Swing (FR) (Saint Cyrien (FR) 128) [1997 6m⁴ 6g 6g⁶ a7g Dec 18] 3,100Y: tall filly: third foal: half-sister to 4-y-o Caudillo: dam placed at 2 yrs in France: failed to repeat debut form, leaving T. D. Barron after penultimate start: should be suited by further than 6f. *D. Nicholls*   57

ELLA (IRE) 2 b.f. (Mar 20) Brief Truce (USA) 126 – The Queen of Soul 75 (Chief Singer 131) [1997 5d* 5.2f⁶ 6d* 5.5g⁵ 5v³ Oct 11] 12,000Y: fourth foal: half-sister to 1993 2-y-o 5f winner Domino Queen (by Primo Dominie) and a winner by High Estate: dam 5f and 6f winner: fairly useful performer: won minor event at Windsor in June and listed race at Cologne in August: good third to wide-margin winner Halmahera in Cornwallis Stakes at Ascot: stays 6f: acts on heavy ground, stiffish task on firm: sold 42,000 gns after final start. *Lord Huntingdon*   92

ELLA LAMEES 3 b.f. Statoblest 120 – Lamees (USA) (Lomond (USA) 128) [1996 –p: 6.9d 6d 1997 6m 8.2g 7d⁶ 6m² 6m* 7g 7m Nov 1] modest-looking filly: modest handicapper: led close home to win at Windsor in July: off course 3 months, well beaten last 2 starts: should stay 7f: best form on good to firm going. *W. J. Musson*   61

ELLAMINE 3 b.f. Warrshan (USA) 117 – Anhaar (Ela-Mana-Mou 132) [1996 NR 1997 a7g a8.5g a14.8g* Dec 13] 400Y, 1,300 2-y-o: third foal: dam half-sister to very speedy 1985 2-y-o Nashia: 25/1, first time when winning seller at Wolverhampton in December: evidently suited by test of stamina. *D. Haydn Jones*   49

ELLE MAC 4 b.f. Merdon Melody 98 – Tripolitaine (FR) (Nonoalco (USA) 131) [1996 –: 7f⁶ 10m a7g 1997 a12g Jan 3] seems of little account. *M. P. Bielby*   –

ELLENBER 2 ch.g. (Apr 4) Risk Me (FR) 127 – Brig of Ayr 90 (Brigadier Gerard 144) [1997 5s a5g 7g⁵ 6d³ 7g⁶ 6m a7g 8m Nov 4] 3,200Y: half-brother to several winners, including useful sprinter Brigg Fair (by Aragon): dam won at 1m to 11f at 4 yrs: poor maiden: best efforts at 6f/7f: looked none too keen in blinkers fourth and sixth starts. *W. McKeown*   43

ELLENBROOK (IRE) 2 b.f. (Feb 18) Petorius 117 – Short Stay (Be My Guest (USA) 126) [1997 5m⁵ 5g² 5m² a5g² a5g* a6g* 5g³ 5g* 5d* 5g² 5m³ 6g Sep 29] IR 5,500Y: easy mover: half-sister to winners abroad by Horage (up to 1¾m in Sweden) and Salt Dome: dam Irish middle-distance maiden: modest performer: won sellers at Southwell and Wolverhampton in May and claimers at Hamilton and Musselburgh in June: placed in nurseries after 3-month absence: stays 6f: acts on fibresand, yet to race on extremes of going on turf: blinkered last 8 starts: front runner: game and consistent. *J. Berry*   62

ELLENS LAD (IRE) 3 b.g. Polish Patriot (USA) 128 – Lady Ellen 67 (Horage 124) [1996 81p: 6m 5g 7m 5f³ 5m* 6s⁵ 5g* 1997 5m² 6m⁵ 5g⁶ 5g 5d⁴ 6g⁶ Jul 5] close-coupled, good-quartered gelding: fairly useful handicapper: ran well at Don-   87

caster on reappearance: didn't have things go his way most subsequent starts: best form at 5f: acts on firm and dead ground: consistent: gelded after final start. *R. Hannon*

ELLERBECK 2 b.f. (Feb 21) Priolo (USA) 127 – Cadisa 82 (Top Ville 129) – [1997 7g 7m Nov 4] sixth foal: half-sister to several winners, including 1¼m winner Calounia (by Pharly) and 1¾m winner Caliandak (by Darshaan), both Irish: dam 11f winner: well held in maidens. *J. M. Jefferson*

ELLE SHAPED (IRE) 7 b.g. Treasure Kay 114 – Mamie's Joy (Prince Tenderfoot (USA) 126) [1996 NR 1997 5m May 3] fairly useful handicapper in 1995 up to 7f on good going or firmer: reportedly lame only start of 1997. *D. Nicholls*

ELLEYSANTA 2 b.f. (May 3) Warrshan (USA) 117 – Sophisticated Baby 39 59 d (Bairn (USA) 126) [1997 a5g⁴ 6f⁴ 5.7g⁴ 6f 7d a5g⁶ 6g a8g⁶ Dec 10] 1,500Y: lengthy a39 filly: first foal: dam thrice-raced daughter of sister to Sigy: modest form second and third starts, but became disappointing. *A. G. Newcombe*

ELLWAY LADY (IRE) 3 br.f. Be My Native (USA) 122 – Scaravie (IRE) 60 (Drumalis 125) [1996 58: 5m 6f⁴ 6g 8m⁴ 1997 10s 10.2m 10m⁵ 11.9f³ Oct 1] modest maiden handicapper: should stay beyond 1¼m: acts on good to firm ground: sold 14,000 gns in October. *I. A. Balding*

ELLWAY PRINCE 2 b.g. (Apr 30) Prince Sabo 123 – Star Arrangement (Star 68 p Appeal 133) [1997 5g⁴ 7d⁴ Oct 27] 12,000Y: fifth foal: brother to a winner in Germany at 8.5f and half-brother to a sprint winner in Holland by Never So Bold: dam poor maiden half-sister to Bold Arrangement: fair form in maidens at Sandown and Lingfield 4 months apart: should stay 1m: will probably do better. *I. A. Balding*

ELLY FLEETFOOT (IRE) 5 b.m. Elmaamul (USA) 125 – Fleetwood Fancy 55 (Taufan (USA) 119) [1996 58, a–: a12g⁶ a12g⁶ a10g a10g⁴ 12.1d 9.7m 10.2m 11.6g² a– 11.6m³ 11.6g² 11.6m a10g 10m 1997 a12g 10d² 10g* 12.1g⁴ 11.6g Jun 2] sparely-made mare: modest performer: won seller at Nottingham in May: pulled up and dismounted final outing: stays 1½m: acts on good to firm ground and dead, little form on all-weather: effective blinkered, visored last 4 starts: inconsistent. *G. L. Moore*

ELNADIM (USA) 3 b. or br.c. Danzig (USA) – Elle Seule (USA) 122 126 p (Exclusive Native (USA)) [1996 83p: 6m⁴ 6g² 1997 6m* 6g² 6m* 6m* 6m* 7g⁴ Oct 18]

Man's preoccupation with travelling faster than ever before manifested itself in September with a successful British attempt on the land-speed record with the vehicle 'Thrust', a phenomenon that coincided with the emergence of something of a flying machine in the world of racing, too. Elnadim won't be breaking the sound barrier but it would come as little surprise if he broke a course record or two in the future; he's already come very close once and promises to get better.

Racal Diadem Stakes, Ascot—
Elnadim dominates from start to finish, putting up the best performance by a sprinter all year;
Monaassib, Averti and Russian Revival (rail) chase in vain

Elnadim's entrance into the big time came in the Racal Diadem Stakes at Ascot's Festival meeting, but he'd been threatening to make the breakthrough for a while. Elnadim was wintered in Dubai after two runs in maidens at two years when he had seemed very immature. He reportedly had a few problems on his return and his seasonal debut was delayed until June. His eight ordinary opponents in a maiden at Pontefract didn't really stand a chance; Elnadim easily landed odds of 2/1-on by four lengths. Next stop was a 0-100 handicap at Newmarket's July meeting. Elnadim was beaten, but this was no ordinary handicap; the winner, Danetime, had previously been a desperately unlucky loser of the Wokingham at Royal Ascot and went on to prove himself one of the best sprinters in training, while the third and fourth Soviet Leader and Double Action (later runner-up in the Ayr Gold Cup) both looked well ahead of the handicapper at the time. A win under top weight in a quite well-contested handicap at Yarmouth in July continued Elnadim's steady progress; the runner-up March Crusader is bordering on useful when in the mood and Elnadim conceded him 16 lb and beat him a head, the pair clear. It was time to raise the horse's sights. The Hopeful Stakes, a listed race at Newmarket in August, was the target, and it was a sign of the strength of Elnadim's form as well as his promise that he went off at 4/1 joint second-favourite in a field of eleven. Bollin Joanne, the favourite, is a reliable and decidedly useful performer who went on to win a listed event next time. That Elnadim could give her 5 lb more than weight-for-age and beat her by a length and a quarter was impressive. Looking in grand shape, Elnadim was ridden to lead two furlongs out and ran on strongly for a decisive success.

The Diadem, five weeks later, represented another considerable step up in class, but plenty were prepared to believe that Elnadim could overcome it. He was 4/1 second-favourite behind the recent impressive Newbury winner Russian Revival; the One Thousand Guineas third Dazzle, the King George Stakes winner Averti and the Prix de Ris-Orangis winner Monaassib were others at single-figure odds in a field of fourteen. Elnadim was a revelation. Soon bowling along at the head of affairs, he quickly got the better of Monaassib at the two-furlong pole, and, given just a few cracks with the whip, continued to put daylight between himself and his rivals. At the line he had three lengths (it looked to be getting on for four) to spare over Monaassib, who held the determined challenges of Averti and Russian Revival by a short head and half a length. The time of 1m 12.56sec was just three hundredths of a second outside the course record set by Shalford in 1992. 'Fast' times are often indicative of no more than that conditions are conducive to them. But this wasn't so in the Diadem. The timefigure, taking all of the relevant factors into account, comes out at a rating equivalent of an impressive 128—the best recorded by a sprinter in 1997. Just how good is the *form*, then? Well, Elnadim didn't have to face the likes of the shock July Cup winner Compton Place, the Haydock Park Sprint one-two Royal Applause and Danetime, or the Nunthorpe dead-heaters Coastal Bluff and Ya Malak. But Monaassib and Averti are not much behind those horses (Averti had finished fourth in the Haydock Park Sprint and had very nearly won the Nunthorpe) and Elnadim beat them pointless. 1997 wasn't a vintage year for sprinters, but on balance we regard Elnadim's win in the Diadem as the pick in that division in Europe during the year, marginally better than the best of Compton Place and Royal Applause.

Elnadim failed to repeat the form of his Ascot win in his one subsequent run but there were mitigating circumstances; Newmarket's Challenge Stakes was over seven furlongs, and after racing freely up with the strong pace he faded to finish fourth, beaten about two lengths by Kahal. In 1998 it's reasonable to assume that Elnadim's campaign will be built around the major sprints. He clearly goes well allowed to get on with things and should prove fully effective at five furlongs, at least on a relatively demanding track like Ascot. His ground? Elnadim, a powerful mover with a round action, has raced only on good and good to firm going, all of his wins coming on the latter.

To say that Elnadim is bred in the purple is an understatement. His sire Danzig is one of the best stallions of modern times and has shown the ability to produce not only a consistently high calibre of runner but many sons and daughters who have done very well at stud also. Elnadim's dam Elle Seule comes from one of the most illustrious families in the *Stud Book* and has done well herself in the short time that she's been in the paddocks. Elle Seule was a very smart runner into the bargain, winner of the Prix d'Astarte and in the frame in other pattern races in France from a mile to ten and a half furlongs. Elnadim is her sixth foal and he's closely related to the Irish One Thousand Guineas winner Mehthaaf (by Nureyev) as well as the fairly useful sprinter Jawlaat (by Dayjur) and the winning 1990 juvenile Only Seule (by Lyphard). The last-named is the dam of the easy 1997 Prix de la Foret winner Occupandiste. In addition, Elnadim's year-younger sister Ashraakat made a promising start to her career in the latest season.

		Northern Dancer	Nearctic
	Danzig (USA)	(b 1961)	Natalma
	(b 1977)	Pas de Nom	Admiral's Voyage
Elnadim (USA)		(b 1968)	Petitioner
(b. or br.c. 1994)		Exclusive Native	Raise A Native
	Elle Seule (USA)	(ch 1965)	Exclusive
	(ch 1983)	Fall Aspen	Pretense
		(ch 1976)	Chane Water

Elnadim's grandam Fall Aspen is one of the most successful dams of all time, responsible for the Group/Grade 1 winners Fort Wood, Hamas, Northern Aspen and Timber Country as well as the Group 2 winner Colorado Dancer and the Group 3 winner Mazzacano. What's more she's also the grandam of the Queen Anne winner Charnwood Forest and the Racing Post Trophy winner

Hamdan Al Maktoum's "Elnadim"

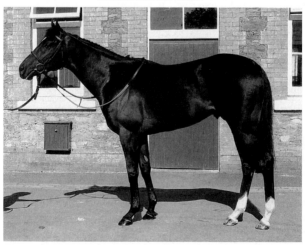

Medaaly, to name but two. A number of these are pretty closely related to Elnadim, notably the inconsistent 1993 July Cup winner Hamas, who is also by Danzig. Hamas has made a pretty good start to his career at stud, his first crop including the listed winner Regal Revolution as well as useful winners in Italy. Further details of this remarkable family can be found in past essays on Elnadim's relatives.

The big, good-topped, imposing Elnadim hasn't had much racing and seems likely to progress for a while yet. He and Danetime look the best prospects among the established sprinters for 1998. It'll take a good one to lower Elnadim's colours if he comes back in the kind of form he showed at Ascot. *J. L. Dunlop*

EL NIDO 9 ch.g. Adonijah 126 – Seleter (Hotfoot 126) [1996 –, a63: a16g³ a14.8g³ a12g⁴ a14g² a14g² 1997 a16g* a14.8g⁵ a12g⁴ a16g* a12g³ a12g⁴ a16g a14g⁴ a16g⁴ a12g⁶ 16.2s a14g 16m a14g 16.2d a14g a14g 14.1d a14g a14g Nov 17] good-topped gelding: has a round action: modest performer on all-weather (no recent form on turf): successful early in year at Southwell in claimer (trained by M. Camacho) and amateurs handicap, but lost his form completely later on: stays 2m: normally patiently ridden: blinkered final outing. *D. W. Chapman*   — a64 d

EL OPERA (IRE) 4 b.f. Sadler's Wells (USA) 132 – Ridge The Times (USA) 78 (Riva Ridge (USA)) [1996 100: 7f* 7m* 8g⁵ 10.1m⁶ 10.2f⁴ 1997 7d⁵ 7s 6m⁴ 7.1m⁴ Jun 7] robust filly: useful performer at 3 yrs: only fairly useful form over inadequate trips in 1997: stays 10.2f well: acts on firm ground, probably not soft. *P. F. I. Cole*   87

ELOQUENT 2 b.f. (Mar 1) Polar Falcon (USA) 126 – Lady Barrister (Law Society (USA) 130) [1997 5.9m* 7.1m² 7m Aug 9] lengthy, quite good-topped filly: has scope: fifth foal: half-sister to 3 winners, including 1995 2-y-o 7f winner Stately (by Be My Chief) and 5-y-o Edipo Re (1m winner at 2yrs): dam unraced from family of Kings Lake and Salmon Leap: won maiden at Carlisle in June: short-head second of 6 to Woodland Melody in listed race at Sandown month later, rallying despite swishing tail under pressure: appeared to gurgle in paddock when disappointing final start: will stay at least 1m. *Sir Mark Prescott*   94

EL PRESIDENTE 4 b.g. Presidium 124 – Spanish Princess (King of Spain 121) [1996 –: 10m 10.2f 8.5m 10d 9.7d 1997 10d a11g a16g a13g Dec 12] no worthwhile form. *G. P. Enright*   —

ELRAAS (USA) 5 b.g. Gulch (USA) – Full Card (USA) (Damascus (USA)) [1996 –: 8m 7g 5g 5.3m⁶ a6g a5g 1997 a7g⁶ Jan 29] stocky gelding: signs of ability but no worthwhile form: probably a sprinter: tried visored/blinkered. *R. J. O'Sullivan*   —

ELSAAYOURA (IRE) 2 b.f. (May 4) Indian Ridge 123 – Pursue 78 (Auction Ring (USA) 123) [1997 6.9m Aug 19] 32,000Y: seventh foal: half-sister to middle-distance winner Bold Pursuit (by Thatching), useful 1m winner at 2 yrs, and 3 winners abroad: dam 2-y-o 5f winner, half-sister to smart miler Alert: 33/1, signs of ability in maiden at Folkestone: sold 5,500 gns in October. *N. A. Graham*   —

ELSHAMMS 2 ch.f. (Feb 7) Zafonic (USA) 130 – Gharam (USA) 108 (Green Dancer (USA) 132) [1997 7g* 7g³ 7g⁵ Oct 18] good-topped, attractive filly: fourth foal: half-sister to 3-y-o Shaya and 10.5f winner Naazeq (both by Nashwan): dam, 6f winner at 2 yrs, third in Poule d'Essai des Pouliches and stayed 1½m: useful form: won maiden at Newmarket in striking style in July: close third in Prestige Stakes at Goodwood and fifth in Rockfel Stakes at Newmarket (one of 2 to exert most energy in false start): races freely and should prove as effective over 6f as 7f: flashed tail at start on debut, and carries head rather awkwardly. *A. C. Stewart*   95

ELSINORE (IRE) 2 b.f. (Apr 12) Danehill (USA) 126 – Park Heiress (IRE) (Sadler's Wells (USA) 132) [1997 6m 5.9m⁴ 6m 6m 7.5d 5g Sep 15] IR 17,000Y: leggy filly: first foal: dam unraced daughter of good-class Irish 1¼m/1½m filly Park Express: modest maiden: stays 6f (pulled very hard over 7.5f): not knocked about on occasions, but not yet living up to pedigree. *Mrs J. R. Ramsden*   57

ELSURUR (USA) 2 ch.f. (Mar 5) Storm Cat (USA) – Ajfan (USA) 112 (Woodman (USA) 126) [1997 6g⁴ 6m⁴ 7m* 7g Oct 18] useful-looking, rather unfurnished filly: has a quick action: first foal: dam, 7f (at 2 yrs) and 1m winner, third in   83

1000 Guineas: fairly useful form: won maiden at Kempton in September by 1¾ lengths from Inchtina: well held in Rockfel Stakes at Newmarket next time: should stay 1m: has had tongue tied. *Saeed bin Suroor*

ELTON LEDGER (IRE)   8 b.g. Cyrano de Bergerac 120 – Princess of Nashua (Crowned Prince (USA) 128) [1996 –, a77: a6g a6g a6g³ a6g a8g⁴ a6g* a7g* a6g⁴ a7g² a7g⁵ a5g⁴ a5g² a5g* a6g⁴ a7g³ a7g⁶ a5g* a6g² a8g² 1997 a7s² a7g² a6g* a6g a6g a6g* a6g² a6g⁶ a8g² Dec 18] good-topped gelding: fair performer: races almost exclusively at Southwell nowadays, and won handicap in January and seller (finished lame) in February there: off course over 7 months before final start: effective at 5f to 7f: has been blinkered, usually visored. *Mrs N. Macauley*   – a77

E-MAIL (IRE)   3 b.c. High Estate 127 – Water Pixie (IRE) (Dance of Life (USA)) [1996 63: 7g 6s 5v⁴ a6g² 1997 7m 7s Sep 4] smallish, sturdy colt: well beaten in handicaps as 3-y-o: bred to require further than 5f: acts on heavy ground and fibresand. *J. M. P. Eustace*   –

EMBASSY   2 b.f. (Mar 24) Cadeaux Genereux 131 – Pass The Peace 116 (Alzao (USA) 117) [1997 6g* 6d* 6g² 6m* Sep 30]   114
Sheikh Mohammed's stinging criticism of the level of prize money in British racing, outlined in a speech delivered on his behalf at the Gimcrack dinner in December, seems not to have affected his determination to recruit a strong team to represent his Godolphin operation in the 1998 classics. Central Park, winner of the Lanson Champagne Vintage Stakes at Goodwood, was acquired for a rumoured £1m from Paul Cole's yard later in December, joining an earlier purchase from Cole's string, Bintang, in Dubai for the winter. Also acquired by Godolphin and wintered in Dubai were four of Peter Chapple-Hyam's most promising two-year-olds, including a leading contender for the fillies' classics in Cape Verdi, who were purchased together for a reported £3m in September. As usual, Sheikh Mohammed has taken a number of his own horses from British trainers to join the Godolphin team, among them the winter favourite for the One Thousand Guineas Embassy.
Embassy and her stable-companion, the St James's Palace Stakes winner Starborough (who also joins Godolphin), represent a significant loss to the Loder stable which handled both in exemplary style in 1997. Embassy's trainer was said to have regarded her more highly than his leading two-year-old

Princess Margaret Stakes, Ascot—
Embassy takes this in pleasing style from Miss Zafonic (second left), Filey Brigg and Socket Set

Shadwell Stud Cheveley Park Stakes, Newmarket—
Embassy establishes herself as the leading two-year-old filly;
Crazee Mental (diamond on cap) runs another good race to be second,
with Royal Shyness, Cape Verdi (white cap, on left) and Heeremandi (visor) next

filly of 1995 Blue Duster. A lofty reputation preceded Embassy to the race-course and she started a heavily-backed odds-on shot against a well-bred bunch, most of whom held pattern entries, in a maiden at the Newmarket July meeting. Her trainer had clearly left something to work on but Embassy completed the task in workmanlike fashion, seeing her race out in good style up the hill and leaving the very clear impression that she would hold her own in better races. She came up against six previous winners next time in the Princess Margaret Stakes at Ascot on King George day and beat them decisively, idling in front and value for more than her two-length winning margin over the other joint-favourite Miss Zafonic. That pattern victory earned Embassy a 3-lb penalty for the Lowther Stakes at the York August meeting where she went down by a short head to the unpenalised Cape Verdi. Embassy was driven into the lead about a furlong and a half out in the Lowther but, after hanging quite markedly left under strong pressure, she stumbled slightly close home and, racing apart, was caught by Cape Verdi in the shadow of the post. Pat Eddery seemed to drop his hands on Embassy in the last few strides and said afterwards that he felt she had been an unlucky loser. 'She stumbled twice within a few strides of the line but for which she would definitely have won,' Eddery said. 'The ground is a lot slower than yesterday and she's definitely better on faster going than this.'

The going for Embassy's final race, the Shadwell Stud Cheveley Park Stakes, was good to firm and Embassy gained compensation for her York defeat in no uncertain manner. The first four in the Lowther were lined up again, along with the Newbury maiden winner Shmoose, regarded at one time as Godolphin's best two-year-old filly, and the Cherry Hinton runner-up Crazee Mental. A below-form effort from Cape Verdi, who had been bought by Godolphin shortly beforehand and was running her final race for Chapple-Hyam, left the way open for an impressive victory by Embassy. Clearly none the worse for her hard race at York, she was driven clear up the hill, after being held up, to beat Crazee Mental and another 16/1-shot Royal Shyness by two and a half lengths and one and a quarter, with Cape Verdi fourth and Shmoose seventh of eight.

The two-year-old fillies weren't an outstanding collection in the latest season and, in a normal year, Embassy would probably have to improve a little on her Cheveley Park form to win a Guineas. Judged on pedigree, it has to be open to some doubt whether Embassy, who has done all her racing so far at six furlongs, will actually improve for a step up to a mile, though we don't share the belief of some that she is unlikely to stay the Guineas trip. True, her sire Cadeaux Genereux was a champion sprinter, but he also won at seven furlongs and ran creditably when second to Polish Precedent in the Prix du Moulin. At stud, Cadeaux Genereux has proved, as expected, largely an influence for

Sheikh Mohammed's "Embassy"

speed, but some of his important winners, including Warning Shadows and Bijou d'Inde, have been effective at a mile and a quarter. Embassy emulated her dam Pass The Peace when she won the Cheveley Park, and Pass The Peace went on to run creditably in the One Thousand Guineas and its French equivalent the Poule d'Essai des Pouliches (in which she was beaten three quarters of a length by Pearl Bracelet). Pass The Peace, who probably stayed a mile and a quarter, didn't have a sprinting pedigree, her sire, Alzao, securing his only pattern-race victory at a mile and a half and her dam, Lover's Rose, winning four races at around nine furlongs at the minor tracks in Ireland. Pass The Peace's previous foals, including Take A Pew (by Reference Point), a winner in Belgium, and Puck's Castle (by Shirley Heights), successful over a mile at York as a two-year-old when she was also third in the Zetland Stakes over a mile and a quarter, offer few pointers to Embassy's stamina potential, as they were all by Derby winners.

		Young Generation (b 1976)	Balidar
	Cadeaux Genereux		Brig O'Doon
	(ch 1985)	Smarten Up	Sharpen Up
Embassy		(ch 1975)	L'Anguissola
(b.f. Mar 24, 1995)		Alzao	Lyphard
	Pass The Peace	(b 1980)	Lady Rebecca
	(b 1986)	Lover's Rose	King Emperor
		(br 1976)	Nonnie

The good-bodied, attractive Embassy, who has a quick action, is game and seems reliable. She has a good turn of foot and, generally speaking, horses of her type are always more likely to be favoured by conditions which place an emphasis on finishing speed. She may well prove a tough nut to crack on Guineas day, when good going or firmer would almost certainly enhance her prospects. *D. R. Loder*

EMBER　4 b.f. Nicholas (USA) 111 – Cinderwench 95 (Crooner 119) [1996 62d: 7m 6m 7m⁴ 10m 10d 8f 12g 1997 10m 10g Aug 13] modest maiden: little worthwhile form in 1997. *P. Hayward*　–

EMBROIDERED　4 br.f. Charmer 123 – Emblazon 91 (Wolver Hollow 126) [1996 –: 6f 7f 6.9g a10g 7f 8g 1997 a13g a12g 8f 5.7g³ 5d⁶ 6.1m Sep 15] poor maiden: left R. M. Flower after second start: headstrong and seems a sprinter: tried blinkered, not in 1997. *S. Dow*　46

EMBRYONIC (IRE)　5 b.g. Prince Rupert (FR) 121 – Belle Viking (FR) (Riverman (USA) 131) [1996 83: 14.1g³ 14d² 16g² 14d 16.1m⁴ 15m⁴ 18.7m³ 16.2f² 16.1m² 14.6m 16.2m⁶ 18g 1997 13.8g³ 14.9m² 17.1m⁵ 16g 16.5m* 16.1f* 18.7m⁵ Aug 3] leggy gelding: fairly useful handicapper: won at Doncaster in May and Newcastle in June: stays well: acts on firm and dead ground: consistent. *Martin Todhunter*　85

EMEI SHAN　4 br.f. Inca Chief (USA) – Tricata (Electric 126) [1996 –: 7g a6g a8g 1997 a11s⁴ a8.5g⁶ a10g a9.4g Mar 5] sparely-made filly: no worthwhile form. *W. G. M. Turner*　–

EMERALD HEIGHTS　2 b.c. (Feb 5) Shirley Heights 130 – Lady In Green (Shareef Dancer (USA) 135) [1997 8d⁵ Oct 28] fourth foal: half-brother to 1994 2-y-o 6f winner Green Seed (by Lead On Time) and a winner in USA by Mujtahid: dam unraced: 12/1, shaped well when about 8 lengths fifth of 14 to Himself in maiden at Leicester, not clear run before keeping on, not knocked about: should stay good deal further than 1m: sure to do better. *J. R. Fanshawe*　69 p

EMERGING MARKET　5 b.g. Emarati (USA) 74 – Flitterriss Park 62§ (Beldale Flutter (USA) 130) [1996 103: 7m⁴ 7m⁴ 7g⁶ 6f* 7m 6m 6m⁶ 7m 1997 7g³ 7m⁶ 6g 7g 6m² 6g 7m Sep 27] smallish, lengthy gelding: has a round action: useful handicapper: best 5-y-o effort when ¾-length second of 21 to Tadeo in Great St Wilfrid at Ripon in August: effective at 6f and 7f: acts on firm going, below form only run on ground softer than good: suited by waiting tactics. *J. L. Dunlop*　103

EMILY-JAYNE　3 b.f. Absalom 128 – Tearful Reunion (Pas de Seul 133) [1996 43: 5d 7f⁴ 7g 1997 8d 8g 10.9d 11s 12g⁴ Aug 28] poor maiden handicapper: no form in 1997, including in blinkers. *Mrs M. Reveley*　–

EMINENT　2 ch.c. (Mar 3) Alnasr Alwasheek 117 – Vague Lass 85 (Vaigly Great 127) [1997 6.1m⁵ 5.1d⁴ a6g² Nov 17] fourth living foal: half-brother to winning sprinters Bangles (by Chilibang) and 4-y-o Faraway Lass: dam sprinter: fair form in maidens at Nottingham (2) and Southwell, beaten a neck in 15 runner event (forced to race wide and ran on) final start: should stay 7f: capable of better still. *Lord Huntingdon*　68 p

EMMAJOUN　2 b.f. (Mar 6) Emarati (USA) 74 – Parijoun (Manado 130) [1997 6m 6m⁵ 5d Sep 18] strong, good-bodied filly: half-sister to 3-y-o Caspian Morn and 5f (at 2 yrs) and 7f winner Caspian Gold (by Clantime): dam of little account: fair form in maiden at Folkestone second start, travelling well long way: tailed off in listed race at Ayr (reportedly found to have mouth ulcers) next outing: still capable of better. *A. P. Jarvis*　69 p

EMMAS BREEZE　3 ch.f. Anshan 119 – Baby Flo 67 (Porto Bello 118) [1996 44: 5.1g⁶ 6g 7f⁵ 5.2f* 5m 6g 1997 6.1d 5m 5m 8m 7m Sep 16] leggy filly: won bad seller at 2 yrs: no other form: left J. King after second 3-y-o outing. *G. G. Margarson*　–

EMMA'S RISK　3 b.f. Risk Me (FR) 127 – Lana's Pet 70 (Tina's Pet 121) [1996 44, a–: a5g 6f³ 5g³ a5g a6g 1997 a5g⁶ a7g a7g Jun 13] no longer of any account. *R. Harris*　–

EMPEROR NAHEEM (IRE)　2 b.g. (Mar 18) Imperial Frontier (USA) 112 – Desert Gale (Taufan (USA) 119) [1997 5m⁵ 5d⁴ 5m⁵ 5m 5.2d² 5d⁴ Oct 21] 11,000Y: stocky gelding: fourth foal: brother to 3-y-o C-Harry: dam Irish 1½m winner: fair maiden: raced only at 5f: yet to race on extremes of ground: off course 3 months after second start (gelded) and over 2 after fourth: has hung. *B. J. Meehan*　71

EMPEROR'S GOLD　2 gr.g. (Apr 5) Petong 126 – Tarnside Rosal 68 (Mummy's Game 120) [1997 5m 6m³ 6d 8g⁵ a7g³ 8.2d⁵ 8.a5g* a8g² Nov 14] 13,000Y: first foal: dam, 5f/6f winner at 2 yrs, stayed 7.6f: modest performer: won selling nursery at　53 + a64

Wolverhampton in November: will stay beyond 8.5f: acts on fibresand: visored fourth start. *I. Campbell*

EMPIRE GOLD (USA) 2 ch.c. (Apr 1) Strike The Gold (USA) – Careless Halo 67 p
(USA) (Sunny's Halo (CAN)) [1997 7d⁵ Oct 14] $65,000Y: useful-looking colt: third foal: half-brother to a winner in USA by Cure The Blues: dam unraced half-sister to Grade 2 9f winner Moment of Hope: sire (by Alydar) won Kentucky Derby: 11/4 from 5/4 and very green, around 5 lengths fifth of 13 to Goodwood Cavalier in maiden at Leicester: will be suited by at least 1¼m: showed a quick action: should do fair bit better. *H. R. A. Cecil*

EMPIRE PARK 2 b.c. (Jan 31) Tragic Role (USA) – Millaine 69 (Formidable 73 ?
(USA) 125) [1997 5.9m³ 6m 7g³ Aug 9] 30,000Y: strong, lengthy colt: fifth foal: half-brother to several winners, including 4-y-o River Tern and fairly useful sprinter Amber Mill (by Doulab): dam stayed 1½m: third in maidens at Carlisle and Ayr, allowed to dictate pace when appearing to put up best effort in latter. *M. Johnston*

EMPIRE STATE (IRE) 2 b.g. (May 21) High Estate 127 – Palm Dove (USA) 69 p
(Storm Bird (CAN) 134) [1997 7m 6d 6d Nov 7] IR 12,500F, 31,000Y: strong, workmanlike gelding: seventh foal: brother to useful 1995 2-y-o 7f winner Parrot Jungle and half-brother to several winners, including French 9.5f winner Love Dove (by Last Tycoon): dam twice-raced close relative of very smart sprinter Nabeel Dancer: showed promise in large-field maidens at Newmarket and Doncaster, catching eye on latter course final start, finishing well but never placed to challenge: subsequently gelded: should stay 1m: type to make a better 3-y-o. *M. H. Tompkins*

EMPIRICAL (USA) 2 b.f. (Feb 23) Miswaki (USA) 124 – Louisville (FR) (Val 72 p
de L'Orne (FR) 133) [1997 6m⁶ 6g³ Oct 27] good-topped filly: has scope: sister to Le Belvedere, winner up to 9f in France and USA (including in Grade 2 event) and half-sister to several winners, including Concordial (by Nureyev), winner here and later smart around 1m in USA, and very smart French/US middle-distance performer Louis Le Grand (by Key To The Kingdom): dam French 1m winner: fair form in maidens at Goodwood and Leicester 3 months apart: should stay 1m: type to make a better 3-y-o. *J. H. M. Gosden*

ENAVIUS (IRE) 3 b.c. Lycius (USA) 124 – Enaya 99 (Caerleon (USA) 132) –
[1996 –: 7m 7f 1997 8.2d Jun 23] no form: sold, to go to Kuwait. *M. Bell*

ENCHANT 2 ch.f. (Mar 18) Lion Cavern (USA) 117 – Belle Et Deluree (USA) 65 p
(The Minstrel (CAN) 135) [1997 6m⁶ Oct 4] strong, deep-girthed filly: good walker: sixth foal: closely related to 3 winners, notably 3-y-o Dazzle, and half-sister to a winner in USA by Cozzene: dam, French 1m (at 2 yrs) and 1¼m winner, closely related to Cheveley Park second Dancing Tribute: 11/2, just over 9 lengths sixth of 10 to Qilin in maiden at Newmarket, never really going smoothly and not knocked about once held: unimpressive to post: has scope: and bred to do a fair bit better. *M. R. Stoute*

ENCHANTED GUEST (IRE) 4 ch.f. Be My Guest (USA) 126 – Last Blessing –
73 (Final Straw 127) [1996 74: 7d 6.9m 7g² 6g* 6m⁴ 6m a8.5g 1997 6d 7m May 3] angular filly: fair handicapper at best: tailed off in 1997. *V. Soane*

ENCHANTICA 3 ch.f. Timeless Times (USA) 99 – North Pine (Import 127) –
[1996 67d, a48: 5g⁴ 5g² 5.1f² 5g³ 5.1m⁴ 5g³ 5m³ 5s³ a5g⁵ a5g² a5g 1997 a5g⁶ a5f a56
a5g³ a5g² a5g⁶ Feb 26] workmanlike filly: modest 5f maiden: acted on firm and soft ground: tried visored: sold 3,000 gns in December, in foal to Mind Games. *J. Berry*

ENCHANTING EVE 3 ch.f. Risk Me (FR) 127 – Red Sails (Town And Country –
124) [1996 61?, a67: 5d* 5m⁶ 5d 6d⁴ a6g* a6g* 6.1f⁴ a6g a5g⁴ 1997 a6g³ a7g³ a8.5g⁶ a67
a7g⁵ a7g* a7g² a8g* a7g⁵ a7g² 6m a6g a10g² a10g³ 8.2g a8g³ a7g⁵ a8.5g Dec 26] leggy filly: fair performer: won claimers at Lingfield in February and March, making all in latter: barely stays 1¼m: goes well on equitrack, no form on turf in 1997. *C. N. Allen*

ENCORE 3 b.f. Be My Guest (USA) 126 – Lucia Tarditi (FR) (Crystal Glitters 52
(USA) 127) [1996 NR 1997 8.2m⁴ 8.1s 7m Sep 21] leggy, lengthy filly: first reported foal: dam Italian 2-y-o 7f listed winner: modest maiden: didn't manage an encore of her debut form. *J. H. M. Gosden*

ENERGY MAN 4 b.g. Hadeer 118 – Cataclysmic 78 (Ela-Mana-Mou 132) [1996 52 d
–: 10g 8g 7.5m 7m 1997 8m⁶ 9m 9.2m 8m 10.1g 8m Oct 28] strong gelding: has a
short action: modest maiden: well beaten last 4 starts, including in visor: stays 9f: yet
to race on extremes of going. *M. Dods*

ENGLISH INVADER 6 b.h. Rainbow Quest (USA) 134 – Modica 89 (Persian –
Bold 123) [1996 –: 14.9d 14s⁶ 11.9g 1997 a12g⁴ a13g* a12g² a16g⁴ a13g* a12g* a62
a12g⁴ 12g 11.9f⁴ a12g⁶ 11.8d⁵ 12g 11.6m a10g a12g* a14.8g a12g⁶ a12g a12g a12g
Nov 21] leggy horse: modest on the all-weather: won selling handicap at Lingfield in
February (for R. Akehurst), amateurs handicap there and claimer at Wolverhampton
in March and handicap at Wolverhampton in September: little form on turf nowadays: trained thirteenth start only by R. Spicer: effective at 1½m to 2m: well beaten
visored/blinkered: inconsistent. *C. A. Dwyer*

ENGLISH LADY (IRE) 2 b.f. (Apr 28) Fayruz 116 – Paradise Regained 41 64 ?
(North Stoke 130) [1997 5g⁴ 5m² 5d Oct 27] 9,000Y: half-sister to 5f (at 2 yrs) to
1½m winner Al Shany (by Burslem), 1m winner Cannizaro (by Gallic League) and a
winner in Italy by Soviet Lad: dam placed up to 15.4f: modest form first 2 starts: off
course 5 months, tailed off on return. *M. J. Haynes*

ENLISTED (IRE) 3 b.f. Sadler's Wells (USA) 132 – Impudent Miss 105 (Persian 83
Bold 123) [1996 81p: a8.5g² 1997 a8g³ 8.2d³ 10m* 10s² a12g a10g⁵ Dec 10] workmanlike filly: unimpressive mover: fairly useful handicapper: did well to win falsely-
run event at Newbury in July, having had plenty to do when tempo increased: best
effort when short-headed at Redcar next outing: stays 1¼m: acts on good to firm
ground, soft and fibresand. *Sir Mark Prescott*

ENTHRONE (USA) 3 b.f. Diesis 133 – Crowning Ambition (USA) 65 (Chief's –
Crown (USA)) [1996 NR 1997 8g 7m Sep 9] third foal: half-sister to 1m winner
Misrule (by Miswaki): dam, 7f winner, out of top-class USA 6f to 8.5f winner
Fabulous Notion: signs of just a little ability in maidens: sold 6,000 gns in December.
J. H. M. Gosden

ENTICE (FR) 3 b.f. Selkirk (USA) 129 – Loure (USA) 66 (Lyphard (USA) 132) 111
[1996 93p: 7m 7d* 8g* 1997 10.4g⁴ 10m² 11.9d 10.1m* 9.3f⁶ Oct 5] lengthy, quite
attractive filly: smart performer: best effort when 2½ lengths second of 7 to Ryafan
in Vodafone Nassau Stakes at Goodwood in August: won 8-runner listed race at
Yarmouth in September by ½ length from Meshhed, without rider using whip: stays
1¼m (too free at 1½m): acts on firm and dead ground. *Saeed bin Suroor*

ENTREPRENEUR 3 b.c. Sadler's Wells (USA) 132 – Exclusive Order 123
(USA) 120 (Exclusive Native (USA)) [1996 106p: 7m⁴ 7g* 7.6g* 1997 8m*
12g⁴ 8g Sep 27]
    An analysis of the form-book does scant justice to the phenomenon that
was Entrepreneur. Three entries in the 1997 edition reveal that Entrepreneur
won the Two Thousand Guineas, and that he then came fourth in the Derby
and seventh in the Queen Elizabeth II Stakes. Closer scrutiny of the result at
Newmarket reveals that Entrepreneur was no better than an average Guineas
winner, and examination of results later in the season indicates that a dozen or
so other three-year-olds went on to show superior form. Whether reviewing
the season in this manner would do justice to Entrepreneur and his ability is
something that can be argued at length, but there is no denying that it fails to tell
anything like the whole story of the horse's impact. To adapt words originally
penned for the 1870 Derby's 9/4-on loser Macgregor, everyone appeared at
some point or another to be seized with an impulse to 'get on' this new wonder
horse and speculators became Entrepreneur mad.
    A telling entry on Entrepreneur in the form-book is his starting price of
6/4-on in the Derby. That makes him a member of an elite club. Only thirty
horses in the two hundred and seventeen previous runnings of the race had
started at odds on, five (Tudor Minstrel, Sir Ivor, Shergar, El Gran Senor and
Tenby) in fifty-two runnings since the Second World War. A total of thirteen
had been sent off at shorter than 6/4-on, and thirteen is also the number of
previous odds-on losers, nine of which, like Entrepreneur, had been bidding to

add a Derby victory to one in the Two Thousand Guineas. Among those were the handful of colts who have been shorter-priced losers than Entrepreneur, the 13/8-on shots St Frusquin (1896) and Slieve Gallion (1907), Tudor Minstrel (1947) at 7/4-on, Macgregor, and Surefoot (1890) at 95/40-on. Classic success over a mile at Newmarket is usually the best proof available that a horse possesses the ability necessary to win the Derby, but is no proof that he has the necessary stamina. As far as Entrepreneur was concerned, his Guineas triumph was regarded as important chiefly as a proof of his class, because his stamina had been taken virtually for granted. As far as it was possible, his two-year-old career had not revealed any stamina limitations, but more convincing was his pedigree. His dam, the very smart French filly Exclusive Order, had been unproven beyond a mile and had registered her four wins over a furlong or two shorter. But Entrepreneur's sire, Sadler's Wells, is one of the most reliable sources of stamina there is. Evidence of this had already been provided by Entrepreneur's brother Sadler's Image, who had shown smart form over distances as far as an extended thirteen furlongs as a three-year-old in 1994, and by Entrepreneur's sister Dance A Dream, who had finished second in the Oaks in 1995. One possible interpretation of this pedigree was that Entrepreneur would not just stay the Derby distance, he would be suited by it.

For those who believed he would be effective at the Derby trip, Entrepreneur's performance in the Guineas was mightily impressive. While victory might have led some to wonder whether he might not be a miler after all, a much larger number were asking what on earth he would be capable of when stepped up to middle distances? This performance deserved enough praise in its own right, of course. Prix de la Salamandre and Grand Criterium hero Revoque was the only Group 1 winner in the line-up, but Zamindar, Poteen, Musical Pursuit and Muchea had all gone very close to winning a Group 1 as two-year-olds, and the last two of those were considered outsiders in a field that contained plenty of potential. Revoque had been beaten (narrowly) in his preparatory race, while Hidden Meadow, Desert Story, Poteen, Starborough and Green Card had won theirs. Zamindar, Putra, Musical Pursuit, and the Godolphin horses Shamikh (who had been well backed ante-post) and Tycoon Todd were among those who joined Entrepreneur in bidding to emphasize that today's trainers are fully capable of producing a Guineas winner first time out. That group met with widely-contrasting fates, Entrepreneur proving clearly the sharpest in a total field of sixteen. The 100/30-favourite Revoque finished just three quarters of a length behind him, but, whereas Revoque had been unable to improve his position after being slightly squeezed at the start, Entrepreneur was travelling with surprising ease just off the strong pace (set by Starborough) and went on himself over two furlongs out. Having to be switched to the outside, Revoque made up ground hand over fist in the final furlong but it was all too late; Entrepreneur kept on strongly and was always going to hold on. Poteen had put in his bid before the furlong marker, Starborough stuck to his guns gamely and Zamindar ran on from the rear, but there was a gap of five lengths back to the remainder. The winner returned an extremely good timefigure (the best of 1997), equivalent to a rating of 131. Standing at 14/1 co-favourite for the Derby at Christmas and as long as 33/1 co-seventeenth favourite for the Guineas at the same stage, Entrepreneur had fulfilled his first objective.

Pedigree and performance in the Guineas inevitably made Entrepreneur a short-priced favourite for Epsom, but what made this case different was his colossal reputation. Home reputation is a thing that some connections try hard to keep at home. An extreme example was the aforementioned Macgregor whose Two Thousand Guineas victory was his first appearance on a racecourse, as his owner 'wanted to keep the public in ignorance of the superlative merits of the champion of his stable.' Very few people seemed to be in ignorance of Entrepreneur. In three races as a juvenile, he was sent off at 9/4-on, 2/1-on and 6/1-on. The first of those races left connections stunned—they didn't even get

Pertemps Two Thousand Guineas Stakes, Newmarket—
Entrepreneur lives up to his reputation and repels a posse of challengers;
Revoque (far left) finishes best of all from Poteen (striped sleeves), Starborough (noseband) and Zamindar

a return each-way!—when Entrepreneur came fourth in a Newmarket maiden having apparently been unsettled in the stalls by the filly next door who was in season. So, although he had hardly been under wraps, when coughing prevented Entrepreneur running in the Dewhurst, form students were left to study just his wins in a Kempton maiden and a three-runner conditions stakes at Chester. Among similar 'talking horses' in recent years, the one that springs to mind is Nashwan, but while he was heavily backed for the Guineas— eventually starting favourite—odds of 40/1 had still been available one month before the race. The odds about Entrepreneur had been disappearing well before that. As with Nashwan, however, the final catalyst for stable confidence was a brilliant private gallop. Just how private proved galling when it transpired that Entrepreneur's startling work had taken place unnoticed at Sandown early on the morning of the Whitbread. Afterwards, with Entrepreneur now 4/1 favourite for the Guineas, his big-race jockey 'revealed': 'We went six and a half furlongs. It was the first time I'd sat on Entrepreneur and I was pleased with his work. It was fine.' After the Guineas had been landed, he said: 'I was so excited after last week's gallop at Sandown ... I left the track with butterflies.'

That jockey was Michael Kinane. John Reid had ridden the colt on his first two starts at two years, Walter Swinburn on the third, and the latter was due to take the ride in 1997 until he shocked the sport on April 21st by announcing that he was having to take 'a sabbatical from race-riding' because of 'a continuing weight problem.' At that stage, Entrepreneur was already a clear favourite for the Guineas and the Derby at around 9/2. Talking a few days later about him and about One Thousand hope Dazzle, Swinburn said: 'Millions in value could depend on Entrepreneur's performance in the Two Thousand, and I didn't want my failure to be one-hundred percent and firing to be the reason why they might not get their best chance. I couldn't have lived with myself. Unfortunately, the way things are, there's no way, short of a miracle, that I could have been one-hundred percent.' Happily, this outstanding jockey will return to race-riding, starting in Dubai over the winter.

During his charity walk in Ireland the previous winter, Swinburn had said that he believed Entrepreneur could provide him with his fourth Derby winner. Michael Stoute did little to discourage punters after the Guineas when

333

stating that Entrepreneur had more speed than Swinburn's first Derby winner, Shergar. The bookmakers' shade of odds against immediately after Newmarket proved short-lived, and 11/10 from one relatively minor firm on the morning of the Derby was the longest price that he had been for a month. Connections of other Derby runners said that they were running for the place money only. The front-page headline in *Racing Post* was 'Coronation Day' and in *The Sporting Life* it was 'Evens Entrepreneur!'. There was not a lot of the latter, as some £254,000 in recorded bets alone rained down on the favourite. 'Speculators became Entrepreneur mad.'

There have been many reasons given for the failures of Derby favourites, sometimes even that they weren't good enough. Of the shortest-priced loser ever in the Derby, Surefoot, it was said that 'he tried to savage more than one of his rivals while the race was being run. This procedure did not improve his chance, of course, but his failure was mainly due to lack of staying power.' Given that so many of the Derby's odds-on shots have been Guineas winners, it is not surprising that 'lack of staying power' figures prominently in the post-mortems. Most spectacularly, the step up in trip proved the undoing of a thoroughly intractable Tudor Minstrel, fifty years before Entrepreneur. For our money, though, it cannot be said that Entrepreneur's disappointing re-enactment of this jubilee occasion was solely or even chiefly due to insufficient stamina. There were those who did say it, of course, but if Entrepreneur did not look like much of a mile-and-a-half horse on Derby Day, he looked even less like a miler. Kinane was clearly unhappy with him almost from the stalls and was soon trying his utmost to get the favourite to take hold of his bit. Racegoers got a good view of Entrepreneur when Kinane brought him wide entering the straight, but what they saw, even at that stage, was very obviously not a Derby winner. Like Surefoot, Macgregor and Tudor Minstrel, the Derby's three shortest-priced losers, Entrepreneur could finish only fourth. Benny The Dip and Silver Patriarch were eight and a half lengths ahead of him.

It was odds on that some explanation of a physical nature would come to light for his defeat. None had been apparent in the parade ring, because Entrepreneur looked simply magnificent, easily the pick of the thirteen runners, though he was rather stirred up down at the start. The racing pundits had another two and a half weeks in which to air their opinions before it was announced by Michael Stoute that Entrepreneur had 'returned from Epsom with a right-side hamstring strain' and that all other tests had been negative. 'Intensive physiotherapy enabled him to resume cantering on June 17,' the trainer continued, 'but a weekend gallop determined that he would not be at peak fitness for the Curragh.' Neither, alas, was he at peak fitness for any other race over the next three months, and when Entrepreneur did finally return to action it turned out that the speculation about when this event might or might not take place had inspired far more column inches than the event itself. The Queen Elizabeth II Stakes at Ascot was his objective, and he confirmed his presence in the race with a satisfactory gallop on the course ten days before-hand. But in the event itself he finished only seventh of nine, quickly in trouble entering the straight and keeping on at only the one pace. For the record, he looked really well although just beginning to go in his coat. It was the last that was seen of him, as on October 10th it was announced that Entrepeneur had been retired. The following week's Champion Stakes was due to be his next engagement, but Entrepreneur missed out on Champions Day, as he did with the title 'champion' itself. He will be standing at Coolmore in 1998 at a fee of IR 17,500 guineas (October 1st).

Entrepreneur is an excellent example of why Michael Tabor believes in buying potential stallions at the yearling sales. Having Coolmore boss John Magnier as a business partner cannot do much harm. The top lots regularly fall to their bids or those of their representative, Irish vet Demi O'Byrne, and Entrepreneur was one of them, joint-top with Happy Valentine at 600,000 guineas at the Houghton in 1995. One name alongside just as many of those top

Mr M. Tabor & Mrs John Magnier's "Entrepreneur"

lots is that of Coolmore and European standard-bearer Sadler's Wells, and
when the sale of Entrepreneur's full brother at the latest Houghton proved
something of an anti-climax at 375,000 guineas, it was another Sadler's Wells
colt (out of Crystal Spray) who made the top price at 625,000 guineas—
knocked down to Demi O'Byrne. Many of the details of Entrepreneur's
pedigree have already been given in assessing his stamina potential. In such a
list of talent, it is easy to overlook Exclusive Order's five winners from six foals
before Sadler's Image; of those, Irish Order (by Irish River) and Mizaaya (by
Riverman) were both useful, with Exclusive Virtue (by Shadeed) not far behind
them. Exclusive Order's tenth foal, Exclusive (by Polar Falcon), won a maiden
at Kempton and was third in the Fillies' Mile at Ascot in the latest season. She
carries the colours of her breeders, the Cheveley Park Stud, who greeted
Exclusive Order's latest foal, a colt by Rainbow Quest, on the eve of the Two
Thousand Guineas. Ten years earlier, they had purchased Exclusive Order for
825,000 dollars at the Keeneland November Sale. In case her huge achievements force all trace of earlier generations from the sales catalogues, brother
Teddy's Courage was a smart performer in the USA, where their dam Bonavista
won three sprint races and was runner-up in two minor stakes.

		Northern Dancer	Nearctic
	Sadler's Wells (USA)	(b 1961)	Natalma
	(b 1981)	Fairy Bridge	Bold Reason
Entrepreneur		(b 1975)	Special
(b.c. 1994)		Exclusive Native	Raise A Native
	Exclusive Order (USA)	(ch 1965)	Exclusive
	(ch 1979)	Bonavista	Dead Ahead
		(b 1964)	Ribotina

In *Racehorses of 1981*, we described Exclusive Order as a 'most
attractive, strong, good-bodied filly.' The words we use to describe Entrepreneur are strong, deep-girthed, attractive and well balanced. He impressed a

EPI

great deal in appearance. Good ground or good to firm were all that he encountered in his six-race career. His best form was when winning the Guineas, but he should have stayed further—going into the Derby, we had few doubts that he would stay. Entrepreneur, the noun describing a risk-taking businessman, was a key word in the politics and economics of Conservative Britain; Michael Tabor has said that the horse is named after himself. All the evidence indicates that we will hear an awful lot more of Mr Tabor, but 1997 was not the Conservative Party's year, and neither did it turn out to be the year of Entrepreneur. *M. R. Stoute*

EPIC STAND 3 b.g. Presidium 124 – Surf Bird (Shareef Dancer (USA) 135) [1996 63: 5f⁵ 5.9f⁶ 5m 6g⁶ 7g 8f* 1997 10g² 8g² 10g³ 8g* 9m* 8m² 7g 8m* 9m 8g Oct 18] workmanlike gelding: fairly useful handicapper: had a good season, winning at Newcastle (gambled on, originally disqualified for causing interference but reinstated on appeal) in May, Ayr (amateurs) in July and Doncaster in September: has won at 9f, may prove best at 7f/1m: acts on firm ground, yet to race on going softer than good: takes keen hold, and usually held up: has carried head high: sold 30,000 gns, to go to USA. *Mrs J. R. Ramsden* — 88

EPONINE 3 ch.f. Sharpo 132 – Norska 67 (Northfields (USA)) [1996 65: 6d⁵ 6m⁶ 7d⁵ 8.1d³ 1997 10.2m 11.6s 9.9d³ 10g⁴ 13.8m* 14.1m³ 11.7m⁵ 12.1s³ 15.4s Jul 2] leggy filly: poor mover: fair maiden: landed odds in weak claimer at Catterick in June: gave impression something amiss last 3 starts, but joined E. Elliott and won juvenile hurdles in October and November: stays 1¾m: acts on good to firm and dead ground. *M. R. Channon* — 70

EPSILON 3 b.f. Environment Friend 128 – Girette (USA) (General Assembly (USA)) [1996 62: 6.9m⁶ 1997 8m Jun 23] twice-raced maiden: tailed off only 3-y-o start. *N. A. Graham* — –

EPSOM CYCLONE (USA) 2 ch.c. (Feb 2) Rahy (USA) 115 – Aneesati 85 (Kris 135) [1997 6d Sep 20] robust, good-bodied colt: first foal: dam 1m winner out of 1000 Guineas runner-up Dabaweyaa: 8/1 and bandaged behind, over 9 lengths eighth of 18 to Poly Blue in maiden at Newbury, showing up nearly 5f: should do better. *B. W. Hills* — – p

EPWORTH 3 b.f. Unfuwain (USA) 131 – Positive Attitude 82 (Red Sunset 120) [1996 66p: 8g 1997 8.2m⁴ 8.2d² 9d² 10.5m⁶ 10.1s² 11.6g³ 10s⁵ 10.2g⁶ 8.2s Oct 15] tall, useful-looking filly: fairly useful maiden: soundly beaten last 3 starts, slowly away and looking reluctant in blinkers on second of them: stays 1¼m, seemingly not 11.6f: best efforts on dead or soft ground: not one to trust: sold 2,000 gns in December. *J. A. Glover* — 81 d

EQUERRY 6 b.g. Midyan (USA) 124 – Supreme Kingdom 85 (Take A Reef 127) [1996 85, a–: 7m² 8.5m* 8m* a9.4g 7m* 8.1m 7m 8.9g³ 7m 8m* 1997 8g May 23] quite attractive gelding: fairly useful handicapper in 1996: well beaten only 6-y-o start. *M. Dods* — –

EQUITY PRINCESS 2 b.f. (Apr 21) Warning 136 – Hawait Al Barr 100 (Green Desert (USA) 127) [1997 6m⁶ 7g³ 7s² 8d* 8v² Oct 11] strong filly: second foal: dam, well bred, best at 2m: progressive form: won maiden at Ayr in September: easily best effort when ½-length second of 4 to cosy winner Dr Fong in listed race at Ascot: will stay at least 1¼m: acts on heavy ground. *M. Johnston* — 95

ERIC'S BETT 4 gr.g. Chilibang 120 – Mira Lady (Henbit (USA) 130) [1996 66: 9.9g 8g 8f⁶ 8.5m² 8g⁵ 8d 1997 8d 10g 10.2m 8g Jun 28] plain gelding: fair handicapper as 3-y-o: no form on flat in 1997, but won twice over hurdles in August. *P. G. Murphy* — –

ERIKA'S YOUNG MAN 2 b.c. (Apr 22) Unfuwain (USA) 131 – Tearful Reunion (Pas de Seul 133) [1997 6m 7.1d⁴ 7m 9m Sep 24] 7,000 2-y-o: third thoroughbred foal: dam poor maiden: looks of little account. *M. J. Haynes* — –

ERINRINCA (IRE) 3 ch.f. Waajib 121 – Rivulet (USA) (Irish River (FR) 131) [1996 NR 1997 8.3g⁶ 8.3m 8g⁴ 12g⁴ a10g Oct 27] 4,500F, 15,000 2-y-o: fourth foal: half-sister to 1¼m winner Irish Senor and a winner in Hungary (both by Al Hareb): dam lightly-raced maiden: little worthwhile form: tried visored. *J. E. Banks* — –

ERLKING (IRE) 7 b.g. Fairy King (USA) – Cape of Storms (Fordham (USA) 42
117) [1996 44: a12g* a13g⁵ 1997 12.1d³ 12.1g 10.8g Oct 7] fair hurdler, winner in
September: poor on flat these days: should stay beyond 1½m: acts on good to firm
and soft ground and the all-weather: often blinkered. *S. Mellor*

ERRANT 5 b.h. Last Tycoon 131 – Wayward Lass (USA) (Hail The Pirates (USA) –
126) [1996 56, a66: a10g⁴ a10g² a7g a12g⁵ a8g* a10g* a10g⁶ 10m⁶ 10d 11.6m 10f³
a10g a8g⁶ a8g³ 1997 10d 8m⁵ 9d a10g⁴ Dec 12] fair on equitrack and modest on turf
at 4 yrs: no worthwhile form in 1997. *D. J. S. Cosgrove*

ERRO CODIGO 2 b.g. (Feb 11) Formidable (USA) 125 – Home Wrecker (DEN) 60
(Affiliation Order (USA) 89) [1997 5g⁴ 5g⁵ 6g² 6g⁴ᵈⁱˢ 7g³ 6m² 5g² Aug 25] 11,000Y:
strong gelding: first foal: dam won twice in Denmark, including at 2 yrs: modest
maiden: second in sellers and claimer: stays 7f: raced mainly on good ground: joined
S. Kettlewell. *Mrs J. R. Ramsden*

ERTLON 7 b.g. Shareef Dancer (USA) 135 – Sharpina (Sharpen Up 127) [1996 73
83, a78: a8g a7g 7d 7f³ 7m a8g⁵ 7.1m 6.9f³ 7m 7.6m⁴ 7m 7m 7m*ᵈⁱˢ 8g 8m⁵ 7m⁶ a7g⁴ a82
a8g⁵ 1997 a7g² a8g² a8g⁴ a7g* 7f² 7f³ a8g² 7f³ 8.5m 7.1m 7g 6.9g⁶ 8f² 8f a7g⁶ Dec
2] close-coupled gelding: fairly useful performer at best: won claimer at Lingfield in
March: best efforts afterwards when placed: effective at 7f to 8.5f: probably acts on
any turf ground, best efforts on the all-weather: blinkered (ran creditably) once as
4-y-o: has been bandaged and had tongue tied. *C. E. Brittain*

ERUPT 4 b.g. Beveled (USA) – Sparklingsovereign 53 (Sparkler 130) [1996 74d: 68
6g⁴ 6f 6v 6m 1997 6m⁶ 7.6v⁵ 6d⁵ 6d⁵ 6m² 6.1d⁶ 6m⁶ 6m a6g Sep 20] plain, leggy
gelding: fair handicapper: should stay 7f: acts on good to firm and heavy ground:
used to be best in a visor, wore one only once in 1997: none too consistent: sold and
joined M. Brittain. *G. B. Balding*

ESCUDO (IRE) 2 ch.f. (Apr 4) Indian Ridge 123 – Eskaroon (Artaius (USA) 79
129) [1997 5.2m³ 5d* 5m* 6d 5d* Nov 7] 15,000F, 30,000G: smallish, sturdy filly:
has a quick action: ninth foal: half-sister to several winners here and abroad,
including 6-y-o Ashkernazy and useful Italian mare up to 1¼m Nenna (by Dancing
Dissident): dam unraced half-sister to Oaks runner-up Bourbon Girl: fair performer:
won maiden at Haydock in September and nursery at Doncaster in November, on
latter course always thereabouts and short-heading Rita's Rock Ape: best form at 5f:
acts on dead going: sent to France. *J. H. M. Gosden*

ES GO 4 ch.g. Dunbeath (USA) 127 – Track Angel 43 (Ardoon 124) [1996 NR –
1997 10.3d 8g 8g⁶ 11.9f⁴ a14g Nov 17] third foal: dam winning stayer on flat and at
2½m over hurdles: modest form in 2 NH Flat races: signs of a little ability but no
worthwhile form on flat. *R. Bastiman*

E SHARP (USA) 3 b.f. Diesis 133 – Elvia (USA) (Roberto (USA) 131) [1996 –: 49
5d⁵ 1997 6.9m² 8m Jun 23] poor maiden: second at Folkestone in April (reared
markedly stalls next time): sold 14,000 gns in December, in foal to Bishop of Cashel.
W. J. Haggas

ESHTIAAL (USA) 3 b. or br.c. Riverman (USA) 131 – Lady Cutlass (USA) 103
(Cutlass (USA)) [1996 79: 7d³ 8.2s⁵ 1997 10s² 10.1g³ 10m* 10.5m* 9.9d* 10m* Sep
25] tall, rangy colt: has a quick, fluent action: much improved in blinkers and with
forcing tactics, winning maiden at Ayr and handicaps at Haydock, Beverley and
Pontefract (by ¾ length from Pinchincha), all between July and September: stays
10.5f: acts on good to firm and dead ground: has been bandaged off-hind: sometimes looks difficult ride (tends to hang and carry head high), but game in a finish:
wintering in Dubai. *J. L. Dunlop*

ESKIMO NEL (IRE) 6 ch.m. Shy Groom (USA) – North Lady (Northfields 75
(USA)) [1996 69: 9.9d* 10d⁵ 10s* 9.9m² 11.9d* 10g⁶ 1997 11.9s² Mar 29] small
mare: useful hurdler on her day: lightly raced on flat, but mainly progressive, best
effort when second in handicap at Haydock only 6-y-o start: stayed 1½m: acted on
good to firm and soft ground: in foal to Imp Society. *J. L. Spearing*

ESPERTO 4 b.g. Risk Me (FR) 127 – Astrid Gilberto 75 (Runnett 125) [1996 45+: 55
10d* 1997 10g* 10g² 10.1f³ a12g² 9.7g⁴ a12g² a11g⁴ 10d³ Nov 3] good-topped
gelding: modest performer: won seller at Nottingham in May: in frame all subsequent

starts: stays 1½m: acts on firm and dead ground and on fibresand: pulls hard and carries head awkwardly. *J. Pearce*

ESPLA 6 b.g. Sure Blade (USA) 130 – Morica 88 (Moorestyle 137) [1996 NR – 1997 a6g May 1] fair handicapper at 3 yrs for Sir Mark Prescott: well held only start in 1997. *J. S. Moore*

ESPRESSO 2 br.g. (Apr 6) Faustus (USA) 118 – Shikabell (Kala Shikari 125) 49 [1997 6.1g 7m 7m⁴ 7g⁶ Aug 13] 5,400Y: first foal: dam, maiden on flat (stayed 1¾m), successful over hurdles: poor maiden on balance: should stay at least 1m: visored last 2 starts: looks far from easy ride: gelded after final start. *J. W. Hills*

ESSANDESS (IRE) 2 b.f. (Apr 30) Casteddu 111 – Ra Ra (Lord Gayle (USA) 49 124) [1997 5g⁵ 5d 6m 6m a5g⁴ a7g³ Dec 18] sparely-made filly: seventh foal: closely related to 6f winners Nakita and Efra (both by Efisio) and half-sister to 3 winners, including 3-y-o Broctune Line: dam unraced: poor maiden: good third in nursery final start: will stay 1m. *J. L. Eyre*

ESSAYEFFSEE 8 b.g. Precocious 126 – Floreal 68 (Formidable (USA) 125) 61 [1996 67: 10g³ 9.9f* 10m² 10.1m³ 11m⁵ 10f⁴ 10m* 10f⁶ 10f⁴ 9m⁵ 10g 10f 1997 10.3d 10d 9.9m³ 10g 12m⁴ 12.4m² 12g² 11g² 10d⁴ 10g⁵ 12m⁵ 10.1g² 10m² Nov 4] strong, workmanlike gelding: modest handicapper: best 8-y-o effort on final start: effective at 9f to 1½m: seems suited by good ground or firmer nowadays: blinkered at 3 yrs, not since: held up. *Mrs M. Reveley*

ESSE 2 ch.f. (Mar 22) Rudimentary (USA) 118 – School Concert 80 (Music Boy 49 124) [1997 6g 6d 8.1g 6s² 5s⁶ Nov 6] 12,000 2-y-o: good-topped filly: fourth foal: half-sister to 3-y-o The Gay Fox and 6f winner First Play (by Primo Dominie): dam 6f winner, sister to high-class French sprinter Kind Music: poor maiden: trained first 4 starts by E. Weymes. *J. Berry*

ESTA MARIA (IRE) 4 b.f. High Estate 127 – Maria Stuarda (Royal And Regal 30 (USA)) [1996 30: a10g⁵ a10g⁶ 12m a12g² a12g² 10f 10f³ 12f⁵ 11d 12.5d* 12d a13.5g² a13.5g a12g³ a12g 1997 13.5d a12g 12m a13.5g 11g³ 12.5g 13.5g 11g 11h 12.5g⁵ 11g a10.8g 11g² a12g³ 12d* a13.5g Nov 23] Belgian-trained filly: won handicap at Groenendaal in November: last of 10 in minor event at Folkestone on third start: stays 13.5f: acts on firm and good to soft ground and the all-weather: usually blinkered. *Paul Smith, Belgium*

ESTOPPED (IRE) 2 b.g. (Apr 24) Case Law 113 – Action Belle (Auction Ring 49 (USA) 123) [1997 5.1s⁴ 6g 6f 6s³ 7f Jul 15] 12,500Y: leggy gelding: half-brother to 3 winners, including 1988 2-y-o 5f and 6f winner Holster (by Gorytus) and 4-y-o Batoutoftheblue: dam sister to Meis El-Reem: poor form, including in a seller: joined M. Quinn. *M. R. Channon*

ETERNAL HOST (IRE) 3 b.g. Be My Guest (USA) 126 – To The Limit (Junius – (USA) 124) [1996 –: 8s a8.5g a8.5g 1997 a8g 10m 13.4v³ Jun 25] of no account. *R. Hollinshead*

ETERNALLY GRATEFUL 4 b.f. Picea 99 – Carpadia (Icecapade (USA)) – [1996 –: 8f 1997 6s 8.3m 10m⁶ 7g Aug 6] no form. *K. T. Ivory*

ETERNITY 3 b.f. Suave Dancer (USA) 136 – Chellita (Habitat 134) [1996 NR – 1997 8g 10m 12m⁴ 12m a16g Nov 25] 10,000Y: half-sister to several winners, including smart Tessla (7f and 1m at 2 yrs, stayed 10.5f, by Glint of Gold): dam ran once: signs of ability but little worthwhile form. *J. R. Fanshawe*

ETHBAAT (USA) 6 b. or br.g. Chief's Crown (USA) – Alchaasibiyeh (USA) 85 – (Seattle Slew (USA)) [1996 75: 8m 8m⁶ a8.5g³ a8.5g* a7g² a8.5g* a8.5g⁶ a9.4g a69 10.2f 10m 1997 a8g⁴ a9.4g³ a10g 8m 8d 8.2d a10g⁶ a10s⁵ a9.4g⁶ Dec 26] big gelding: fair performer on all-weather: best effort in 1997 on second start: stays 9.4f: no form for long time on turf: temperamental, refusing to enter stalls sixth intended start when visored. *M. J. Heaton-Ellis*

ETHEREAL 2 b.c. (Apr 13) Fairy King (USA) – Secret Seeker (USA) (Mr – p Prospector (USA)) [1997 7d Nov 7] tall, attractive colt: third living foal: half-brother to winners Hidden Oasis (7f at 2 yrs in 1995, by Green Desert), and 3-y-o Sekari: dam, 6f winner in USA, sister to Gone West and Lion Cavern, family of Known

Fact: uneasy favourite and bit backward, midfield in 18-runner maiden at Doncaster, fading final 2f: tended to carry head high: should do better. *D. R. Loder*

ETOILE DU NORD   5 b. or br.g. Tragic Role (USA) – Daisy Topper (Top Ville   26
129) [1996 –: 8m 12s a13g a16g 1997 a13g⁴ a12g a13g Jan 30] sparely-made
gelding: bad maiden. *H. J. Collingridge*

ETOILE (FR)   3 gr.f. Kris 135 – La Luna (USA) (Lyphard (USA) 132) [1996 99+:   111
6g 7m³ 7m* 7.3s³ 1997 10.4g³ 12m⁵ 12m⁶ 10m⁶ Aug 2] quite attractive filly: smart
performer: best effort when 3 lengths fifth to Reams of Verse in Vodafone Oaks at
Epsom (stayed on having been short of room): sixth in Irish Oaks at the Curragh and
in Vodafone Nassau Stakes at Goodwood (well below form) afterwards: stays 1½m:
acts on good to firm and soft ground: sent to Saudi Arabia. *P. W. Chapple-Hyam*

ETTERBY PARK (USA)   4 b.g. Silver Hawk (USA) 123 – Bonita Francita   83
(CAN) (Devil's Bag (USA)) [1996 79: 10g 10m 12f* 12.3m³ 12s* a12g* a14.8g*
12.3m² 16.2m 11.8m⁶ 12.3s³ 15m* 15.1m² 16.2m 14g³ 1997 a12g³ 14.9m³ 16.4g*
18.7s² a14g² 16.5m⁵ 20m 16.1s 18.7m⁶ 18.2f² 15.9g³ 18g 16g³ 16.5s Nov 8] small,
sturdy gelding: fairly useful handicapper: won at Sandown in April: ran well several
times afterwards, including in Chester Cup fourth start: needs at least 2m: acts on
firm and soft ground and on fibresand: genuine. *M. Johnston*

EULOGY (FR)   10 b. or br.g. Esprit du Nord (USA) 126 – Louange (Green   –
Dancer (USA) 132) [1996 –, a68: a16g* a16g⁴ a14.8g⁴ a14g* a11g² 16.1s a16g³
a16g⁴ a11g² 1997 a14.8f a11g⁵ Jan 31] good-topped gelding: fair stayer: well below
form in 1997. *K. R. Burke*

EUPHORIC ILLUSION   6 ch.g. Rainbow Quest (USA) 134 – High And Bright   43 d
95 (Shirley Heights 130) [1996 –: 16.2g⁵ 8.2m 1997 10m 18g⁴ 17.2m 15.9m 12m
18d³ Sep 2] tall, good-topped gelding: fair hurdler: poor staying maiden handicapper
at best on flat. *Mrs S. J. Smith*

EUROBOX BOY   4 ch.g. Savahra Sound 111 – Princess Poquito (Hard Fought   76
125) [1996 60: a9.4g⁵ 6.9f 8.3m 8g² 8.3m² 8m⁵ 7.1m⁶ 8m* 8g² 8m* 7.9g 7m² 9m   a63
1997 9.7g² 8.2m* 8g⁶ 7.3g 8g⁴ 8.9d² 10g⁵ a8.5g⁴ 8m* 8g* 8m 8.1g* 10m a10g⁴
Dec 2] fair handicapper: won apprentice races at Nottingham in April, Salisbury in
July and Sandown in August, all under accomplished rides from C. Carver: effective
at 1m to 1¼m: acts on good to firm and soft ground, probably on all-weather: tried
visored, better when not: consistent. *A. P. Jarvis*

EUROFEN   2 b↓.c. (Feb 2) Goldneyev (USA) 114 – Mineramare (IRE) (Kenmare   51 d
(FR) 125) [1997 5.1m 5m 5.2f² 5m a5g 5.2m⁶ 6.1m⁵ 7g 6d Sep 5] 2,800Y: close-
coupled colt: first foal: dam French 9f winner from good family: modest maiden:
deteriorated after third start: stays 6f: usually visored/blinkered: unreliable.
P. D. Evans

EURO FORUM   5 ch.g. Deploy 131 – Unique Treasure (Young Generation 129)   53
[1996 NR 1997 a14.8g² Oct 6] modest maiden handicapper: severed a tendon at end
of 3-y-o career: showed he retains plenty of ability only 5-y-o start: stays 2m: acts on
good to firm and soft ground and on fibresand: visored (well beaten) once: winning
hurdler with J. Gifford. *G. Lewis*

EUROLINK PROFILE   3 b.f. Prince Sabo 123 – Taiga 69 (Northfields (USA))   74
[1996 –p: 6m 1997 7f* 7s⁶ 7f⁴ 7g 5m Oct 2] tall filly: fair performer: won maiden at
Yarmouth in June: well below form last 2 starts: should stay 1m: best efforts on firm
ground: sold 7,500 gns in October. *L. M. Cumani*

EUROLINK SHADOW   5 b.g. Be My Chief (USA) 122 – Miss Top Ville (FR)   – §
(Top Ville 129) [1996 NR 1997 a16g Feb 3] lightly-raced maiden: ungenuine.
D. McCain

EUROLINK THE LAD   10 b.g. Burslem 123 – Shoshoni Princess (Prince   58
Tenderfoot (USA) 126) [1996 NR 1997 a12g² a7g² a8g a9.4g* Apr 26] useful
performer in 1991: not seen on flat again until 1997: came from last to win handicap
at Wolverhampton in April: ideally suited by further than 7f and seems to stay 1½m:
acts on fibresand, best turf efforts (in 1991) on good ground or softer. *D. Burchell*

EUROLINK WINDSONG (IRE)   3 ch.f. Polish Patriot (USA) 128 –   44
Delvecchia (Glint of Gold 128) [1996 –: 6m 1997 8.3d 12.1s 14.1m⁵ 14.1g² 15.8g⁶

14.1g[6] 16m 10m 13.1s[4] a14g Nov 17] sturdy filly: poor maiden handicapper: trained first 2 starts by R. McKellar: stays 1¾m (raced too freely at 2m). *Martyn Wane*

EUROQUEST   3 b.g. Ron's Victory (USA) 129 – Raaya 40 (Be My Guest (USA)   –
126) [1996 –: 6g[6] 1997 a8g[6] a6g* 7g 6m 8f[5] a8g[3] 7m[4] 5.9m[6] a7g Dec 18] lengthy,   a44
good-topped gelding: 20/1-winner of poor maiden at Southwell in February: stays
1m: seems best on all-weather: blinkered (looked hard ride) fourth start: reportedly
has hypersensitive skin: inconsistent. *D. Nicholls*

EURO SCEPTIC (IRE)   5 ch.g. Classic Secret (USA) 91 – Very Seldom (Rarity   61
129) [1996 61: 8.5m* 8g 9m 8.5m[4] 9.9f[4] 10.1m[4] 8m[6] 7.5m[2] 8.5m[6] 8f[2] 8g* 7.5f[4]
7.5g* 7g 8m 8.2g 8.2g 1997 7.5m 8g 8d 7.1d[6] 6.9f 7.5m[5] 7.5g[4] 8g[3] 6.9m[4] 8g[2] 7.5m[2]
8.5m 8m* 7.5d[4] 7.5g[2] 8.5f* 8m Oct 1] sturdy, close-coupled gelding: poor mover:
modest handicapper: won at Carlisle (apprentices) in August and Beverley in
September: effective at 7f to 8.5f: acts on firm ground: normally blinkered, but has
run well when not: consistent. *T. D. Easterby*

EURO SINGER   5 br.g. Chief Singer 131 – Crystal Gael 79 (Sparkler 130) [1996   –
–: a13g 1997 8f 12.1g Aug 3] fair winning jumper: lightly raced and no form on flat
last 2 seasons: dead. *T. Keddy*

EURO SUPERSTAR (FR)   3 b.g. Rock City 120 – Douceur (USA) (Shadeed   –
(USA) 135) [1996 –: 7.6d 8.1s 7d 1997 8d 11.6s 8f 10g[3] 8d[6] 9.7g 7d Jul 17] smallish
gelding: signs of some ability, but little worthwile form. *S. Dow*

EUROTWIST   8 b.g. Viking (USA) – Orange Bowl (General Assembly (USA))   –
[1996 42: 12.1d* 13d 15.1s 1997 12.1d 12.3m Apr 9] small gelding: poor handicapper: no form in 1997, including in blinkers. *S. E. Kettlewell*

EURO VENTURE   2 b.g. (Jan 26) Prince Sabo 123 – Brave Advance (USA) 98   70 p
(Bold Laddie (USA)) [1997 5g[3] 5d[5] 5g[6] 6g[4] Aug 22] 22,000Y: sturdy gelding:
half-brother to 4-y-o Cross The Border and 8-y-o Venture Capitalist: dam, 5f winner,
raced only at 2 yrs: fair form in maidens and a nursery, wandering and not seeming to
stride out closing stages in latter event at Thirsk (subsequently gelded): may well
prove best at 5f: should make a useful handicapper if all is well. *D. Nicholls*

EVA LUNA (USA)   5 b.m. Alleged (USA) 138 – Media Luna 119§ (Star Appeal   114
133) [1996 114: 11.4m* 11.9m* 14.6m* 16m[4] 12s[3] 12s[2] 1997 13.4v[5] 16.4g[3] 11.8d*
Jun 14] tall, quite good-topped mare: smart performer: followed third to Persian
Punch and Celeric, beaten ¾ length and length, in Henry II Stakes at Sandown with
runaway success in 5-runner listed race at Leicester: suited by good test at 1½m, and
stayed 16.4f: acted on good to firm and soft ground: was genuine and consistent:
sustained serious tendon injury at exercise in late-June and retired. *H. R. A. Cecil*

EVANDER (IRE)   2 ch.c. (Mar 20) Indian Ridge 123 – Heavenly Hope (Glenstal   90 p
(USA) 118) [1997 8g[2] Oct 25] 45,000Y: sturdy, close-coupled colt: second foal:
half-brother to 3-y-o Tyrolean Dream: dam winning Irish stayer/hurdler: 7/1
and quite backward, head second of 5 to odds-on Distant Mirage in minor event at
Newbury, staying on strongly again at finish: should stay 1¼m: looks sure to
improve. *P. F. I. Cole*

EVAN 'ELP US   5 ch.g. Executive Man 119 – Recent Events (Stanford 121§)   –
[1996 66: 7s[2] 7m 1997 a12g[6] 8g Apr 28] good-topped gelding: fair handicapper:
lightly raced and no form in 1997. *J. L. Eyre*

EVAPORATE   5 b.m. Insan (USA) 119 – Mona (Auction Ring (USA) 123)   37
[1996 NR 1997 a11g[3] a11g 11.8g* May 26] poor handicapper, lightly raced: won
apprentice event at Leicester in May, making all: stays 1½m: best efforts on good
ground. *M. J. Heaton-Ellis*

EVENING IN PARIS   4 ch.f. Be My Chief (USA) 122 – Photo Call 73 (Chief   –
Singer 131) [1996 –: 10.5d a7g[4] 1997 a8.5g[2] a12g a7g[2] 8s 9.9m Apr 24] smallish,   a48
sturdy filly: poor maiden: pulled up lame final start: bred to stay beyond 8.5f: acts on
fibresand, no form on turf. *M. Johnston*

EVENINGPERFORMANCE   6 b.m. Night Shift (USA) – Classic Design   113
(Busted 134) [1996 121: 5m[6] 5f 5m* 5m[6] 5m[2] 5m* 5d[6] 1997 5d 5m 5d[5] 5.2g* 5f Oct
5] strong, good-quartered mare: very smart performer in 1996, career-best effort
when second in Nunthorpe Stakes at York: best 6-y-o effort when winning 16-runner

EXB

listed race at Newbury in September by length from Dashing Blue, making all: ran poorly in Prix de l'Abbaye de Longchamp only subsequent outing: very speedy, and best over sharp 5f: acted on firm and soft ground: often sweating and edgy: front runner: said to have been retired. *H. Candy*

EVENING WORLD (FR) 2 ch.c. (May 22) Bering 136 – Pivoine (USA) 92 (Nureyev (USA) 131) [1997 7s³ 7.9s* 8d³ 8v⁴ Oct 11] 1,000Y, 50,000 2-y-o: tall, quite attractive colt: has badly scarred foreleg: second foal: dam unraced half-sister to smart French middle-distance performer Parme and graded stakes-placed dam of Peintre Celebre: fairly useful form: ran in France on debut: won maiden at York in September by wide margin: ran well when 5 lengths third of 5 to Duck Row in £9,400 event at Newbury: bred to stay well beyond 1m, but seems headstrong (pulled far too hard final start): raced only on good to soft ground or softer. *P. F. I. Cole*

EVEN TOP (IRE) 4 br.c. Topanoora 118 – Skevena 57 (Niniski (USA) 125) 115 [1996 127: 8m² 12m 11.9m⁵ 8.9g* 10g⁴ 1997 a10f 8d³ 10m⁴ 10m³ 10m² 8g Sep 20] robust, attractive colt: impresses in appearance: very good walker: has a roundish action: short-head second in 2000 Guineas in 1996: just a smart performer as 4-y-o, best efforts when third (6½ lengths behind First Island) in Lockinge Stakes at Newbury and Scottish Classic (length last of 3 to Crystal Hearted) at Ayr: should stay 1½m: acts on good to firm and dead ground: sent to UAE. *M. H. Tompkins*

EVERGLADES (IRE) 9 b.g. Green Desert (USA) 127 – Glowing With Pride – 114 (Ile de Bourbon (USA) 133) [1996 101: 6m² 6m 7m* 7m 7.3f² 7m 1997 7.1s⁵ 6d⁵ 7g Jun 12] sturdy gelding: still capable of useful form at 8 yrs, but well held in 1997. *R. Charlton*

EVERSET (FR) 9 b.g. Green Desert (USA) 127 – Eversince (USA) (Foolish – Pleasure (USA)) [1996 58, a79: a7g a7g³ a8g a7g⁵ a7g⁵ 7s a7g³ 8d⁶ 7.1g² 8.1f 7f 6m a68 7g 1997 8m a8.5g⁴ 7.1m a6f a8.5g⁴ 7g 6g a7g² a7g³ Nov 13] close-coupled gelding: unimpressive mover: fair handicapper on the all-weather, no form on turf in 1997: has form at 1m, best efforts at shorter: tried blinkered, no improvement: sometimes slowly away: none too consistent. *A. Bailey*

EVERY PENNY 2 b.f. (May 14) Interrex (CAN) – Shiny Penny 70 (Glint of Gold 42 128) [1997 7g⁵ 8m Sep 9] leggy filly: fourth reported foal: dam, maiden, probably stayed 1¾m: signs of ability in claimer on debut: tailed off in maiden month later. *A. P. Jones*

EVEZIO RUFO 5 b.g. Blakeney 126 – Empress Corina 74 (Free State 125) [1996 51 –: a9.4g 18s 16.2g⁵ 17.1g 18.7g 11.9v 10.3g⁴ 12v 1997 a14.8g⁶ a14.8g⁶ 18m 10 8m a11g* a11g³ 10.3m a14g⁴ a14g⁴ a12g a11g⁶ Nov 24] neat gelding: modest handicapper nowadays: won apprentice race at Southwell in May: stays 1¾m: acts on fibresand, best turf form on good going or softer: often blinkered/visored: has looked none too keen: inconsistent. *N. P. Littmoden*

EVIDENTLY (IRE) 3 b.f. Slip Anchor 136 – Evocatrice 91 (Persepolis (FR) – 127) [1996 NR 1997 8.3m 10m 8d 8.2d Nov 3] leggy filly: second foal: half-sister to French 9.5f to 11f winner Eccola (by Seattle Dancer): dam, French 2-y-o 7f winner (later stayed 1¼m), out of high-class French middle-distance performer Northern Trick: behind in 3 maidens and a handicap. *I. A. Balding*

EWAR BOLD 4 b.g. Bold Arrangement 127 – Monaneigue Lady (Julio Mariner – 127) [1996 6d: 10g⁵ 11d⁶ 12.1s³ 17.2g⁶ 11.6m⁶ 12g 16m⁶ 10d 10.8f 8g 15d 12s a12g 1997 15.4m⁵ Apr 10] probably of little account nowadays. *K. O. Cunningham-Brown*

EWAR SNOWFLAKE 3 b.f. Snow Chief (USA) – Petillante 101 (Petong 126) – [1996 NR 1997 9s⁵ 14m⁶ 8.3g 8m⁴ Aug 15] second foal: dam won Norfolk Stakes but did not train on: sire won 6 Grade 1 races at 2 yrs to 4 yrs, including Preakness: no form in maidens or claimer: tried visored and blinkered. *K. O. Cunningham-Brown*

EXACTLY (IRE) 4 b.f. Taufan (USA) 119 – Not Mistaken (USA) (Mill Reef 61 (USA) 141) [1996 73: a11g 10.3d⁶ 10g² 14.6m⁵ 12.3g* 12m⁶ 12.3m 12.4f* 12.3g⁴ 13.9g 1997 12g 12m⁵ 12g⁵ 12d⁴ 15.8m³ 12.1g⁶ 14.1m³ Oct 7] leggy filly: just a modest handicapper in 1997: stays 2m: acts on firm ground: has worn tongue strap. *J. L. Eyre*

EXBOURNE'S WISH (USA) 2 b.c. (Jan 28) Exbourne (USA) 125 – Social 82 ? Wish (USA) (Lyphard's Wish (FR) 124) [1997 6s⁴ 7g 6g³ 6g* 6.1s⁵ 5.2d 6m⁵ Oct 4]

341

big, lengthy, good sort: has plenty of scope: shows quick action: third foal: half-brother to 1996 2-y-o 5f winner Bold Catch (by Diesis) and a winner in USA by Known Fact: dam unraced half-sister to very smart 1¼m winner Two Timing out of half-sister to champion US filly Chris Evert: fairly useful form: won maiden at Thirsk (had favoured rail) in August: didn't progress as expected, though was not discredited on occasions: should stay beyond 6f: has given trouble at start: races freely: sold 16,000 gns in November. *B. W. Hills*

EXCELLED (IRE)   8 gr.m. Treasure Kay 114 – Excelling Miss (USA) (Exceller   31
(USA) 129) [1996 33: 10m 1997 17.2g⁵ 13.1m³ 12.5m³ 12.1g Aug 3] poor handicapper: stays 13f: acts on hard ground: tried blinkered, no improvement. *C. J. Drewe*

EXCLUSIVE   2 ch.f. (Apr 8) Polar Falcon (USA) 126 – Exclusive Order (USA)   103 p
120 (Exclusive Native (USA)) [1997 7m* 8g³ Sep 28] big, lengthy, attractive filly: has plenty of scope: fluent mover with a slightly round action: half-sister to several winners, notably Entrepreneur and smart middle-distance performers Dance A Dream and Sadler's Image (also by Sadler's Wells): dam French 6f to 7f winner: won minor event at Kempton in September in good style: very good 2¾ lengths third of 8, considering her inexperience, to Glorosia in Fillies' Mile at Ascot, still green and soon niggled along in rear, but improving to challenge briefly 1f out: should stay 1¼m: bandaged off-hind at Ascot: should make a smart 3-y-o. *M. R. Stoute*

EXECUTIVE DESIGN   5 b.g. Unfuwain (USA) 131 – Seven Seas (FR) 76   63
(Riverman (USA) 131) [1996 –: 14d 16.5s 1997 14s⁴ May 5] sturdy gelding: useful hurdler: lightly raced on flat nowadays, but still capable of modest form: will stay 2m: acts on good to firm and soft ground: refused to enter stalls second intended start. *Mrs M. Reveley*

EXECUTIVE OFFICER   4 b.g. Be My Chief (USA) 122 – Caro's Niece (USA)   31
86 (Caro 133) [1996 –: 10m 14m 10s a8g 1997 a12g 12m 11.8g 10m 10s a10g a10g² 9.7m⁶ 10g a10g a13g a13g Dec 22] tall gelding: poor maiden handicapper: stays 1¼m: acts on equitrack: usually blinkered. *R. M. Flower*

EXIT TO SOMEWHERE (IRE)   2 b.c. (May 4) Exit To Nowhere (USA) 122   83
– Zivania (IRE) 101 (Shernazar 131) [1997 7d⁶ 7.5m² Jul 29] IR 150,000Y: angular colt: third foal: half-brother to 3-y-o Ivan Luis and smart German 4-y-o (stays 1½m) Zero Problemo (by Priolo): dam, from good family, won at 1m to 9.5f at 2 yrs in Ireland and should have stayed 1½m: favourite both starts in maidens, better effort though still green when 2 lengths second of 13 to Alboostan at Beverley: should stay at least 1¼m. *H. R. A. Cecil*

EXPECTATION (IRE)   3 b.f. Night Shift (USA) – Phantom Row 37 (Adonijah   –
126) [1996 59: 6d⁴ 5.2f 5m 6.1s⁵ 5.2g⁶ 1997 6.1d May 9] leggy, good-topped filly: modest maiden: always behind only 3-y-o start. *P. R. Webber*

EXPECT TO SHINE   2 b.f. (Apr 10) Fairy King (USA) – Anjaab (USA) (Alydar   90
(USA)) [1997 6g² 6m* 6g 8g⁴ 7g⁶ Oct 18] leggy, quite attractive filly: lacks scope: fifth foal: dam unraced granddaughter of Moccasin, dam of Apalachee: fairly useful form: won maiden at Goodwood in July: good efforts when fourth in Fillies' Mile at Ascot and sixth in Rockfel Stakes at Newmarket (beaten 4 lengths), though faded after travelling strongly each time: will prove best up to 1m: raced only on good/good to firm ground: held up. *B. W. Hills*

EXPIALIODOOCIUS   3 b.c. Environment Friend 128 – Rainbow Ring (Rain-   62
bow Quest (USA) 134) [1996 NR 1997 10s 10m 10.8m² 10.8s 10.1g⁴ 8f Sep 18] angular colt: third foal: half-brother to 5-y-o Raindeer Quest: dam once-raced daughter of Lowther winner Circus Ring: modest maiden at best: stayed 11f: acted on good to firm going: dead. *J. R. Fanshawe*

EXPLOSIVE POWER   6 br.h. Prince Sabo 123 – Erwarton Seabreeze   58
(Dunbeath (USA) 127) [1996 64, a77: a10g* a10g³ a11g³ a9.4g* 9.7s 8f 10g 8.2g⁶   a–
10.1m² a8.5g⁴ a12g⁵ a9.4g 1997 a9.4g⁶ 8g 10g⁴ 10.8g a12g Nov 6] workmanlike horse: fair handicapper on the all-weather, modest on turf: below form in 1997, off course 8 months after reappearance: stays 1½m: blinkered once earlier in career: sometimes troublesome in preliminaries: inconsistent. *G. C. Bravery*

EXPRESS GIFT   8 br.g. Bay Express 132 – Annes Gift (Ballymoss 136) [1996 –:   56
8s 1997 11.1d⁶ 14g³ 14d* 12g⁴ 12.3m⁴ 14g⁵ Jul 4] angular gelding: useful hurdler

on his day: just a modest handicapper on flat nowadays, successful at Haydock in May: stays 1¾m well: goes well on ground softer than good: has joined M. Pitman. *Mrs M. Reveley*

EXPRESS GIRL   3 b.f. Sylvan Express 117 – Oh My Oh My (Ballacashtal   64 d (CAN)) [1996 75: 5d* 5d* 5m⁵ 5m⁵ 6.5m 5g³ 5d 1997 5g 6m 6g 5d³ 6f 6g 5.9m 8g Oct 22] tall, lengthy filly: just a modest handicapper in 1997: well beaten last 4 starts, leaving D. Moffatt before final one: stays 6f: goes well on dead ground, yet to race on anything softer. *Martin Todhunter*

EXPRESS ROUTING   5 b.g. Aragon 118 – San Marguerite 80 (Blakeney 126)   – [1996 –: 7.3s 7g⁶ 10m a9.4g 8g 1997 a6g 8g May 5] no longer of much account. *V. Soane*

EXTREMELY FRIENDLY   4 ch.g. Generous (IRE) 139 – Water Woo (USA)   – 102 (Tom Rolfe) [1996 –: 14m 1997 a12g Jan 16] neat gelding: modest form in maidens at 2 yrs for C. Brittain: none since. *Bob Jones*

F

FABLE   3 ch.f. Absalom 128 – Fiction 59 (Dominion 123) [1996 –: 7m 7m 1997   37 6m 8f² 8f⁶ 8m Aug 16] poor maiden: stays 1m. *J. A. R. Toller*

FABLED LIGHT (IRE)   3 b.c. Alzao (USA) 117 – Fabled Lifestyle (Kings Lake   92 p (USA) 133) [1996 60p: 7f⁶ 7g 1997 10g 10.3d⁵ 12.3d* May 18] strong, good-bodied colt: fourth foal: brother to useful Old Hickory (winner at 7.5f and 10.4f) and half-brother to a winner in Germany up to 1½m by Law Society: dam, Irish 9f winner, half-sister to Lyphard's Wish (by Lyphard): favourite, confirmed promise shown in maidens when winning 5-runner handicap at Ripon smoothly by 1¾ lengths: stays 1½m: acts on dead ground: reportedly had slight setback, but still in training, and should do better again in 1998. *G. Wragg*

FABRICE   2 b.g. (Feb 20) Pursuit of Love 124 – Parfum d'Automne (FR) (Sharpen   72 p Up 127) [1997 6d³ Nov 7] third foal: half-brother to 3-y-o Attitude: dam no form: 16/1 and green, shaped promisingly when keeping-on 2½ lengths third of 21 to Masha-Il in maiden at Doncaster: should stay 1m: sure to do better. *H. Candy*

FABULOUS MTOTO   7 b.h. Mtoto 134 – El Fabulous (FR) 111 (Fabulous   60 Dancer (USA) 124) [1996 58, a–: a16g 17.2f⁶ 14.9g⁴ 11.6m* 11.4m² 12m⁴ 10.2f⁴   a47 12m* 11.6g⁴ 11.9f³ 11.7m 11.5m⁶ 10f a12g 1997 a13g a10g* a12g⁵ a12g² a10g⁶ a12g² 12m 11.8m² 11.9f⁶ 10m⁵ 10.2m⁶ 12m 12m 12.1m⁴ 14g Aug 1] strong, rangy horse: modest handicapper: won at Lingfield in January: mostly ran respectably after: stays 1½m: acts on firm going, and the all-weather: has bled: takes good hold. *M. S. Saunders*

FACE-OFF   2 b.f. (Feb 26) Aragon 118 – Rock Face 77 (Ballad Rock 122) [1997   66 5.2g⁶ 6s⁵ 6d⁶ 6f⁴ 7f⁵ 7s⁴ Oct 16] 35,000Y: small, close-coupled filly: second foal: half-sister to 3-y-o Sheer Face: dam 1¼m to 1¾m winner: modest maiden: trained first 3 starts by R. Hannon: stays 7f: acts on firm and soft ground. *C. F. Wall*

FACILE TIGRE   2 gr.c. (Apr 30) Efisio 120 – Dancing Diana 82 (Raga Navarro   61 (ITY) 119) [1997 5d 6m 5.3m⁴ 5s 5.2d 6f⁴ Oct 1] 17,000Y: leggy, close-coupled colt: sixth foal: brother to 3-y-o Dancethenightaway and half-brother to several winners: dam 5f (at 2 yrs) to 1m winner: modest maiden: better form at 5f than 6f: sometimes slowly away: has carried head high: sold 2,000 gns in December. *S. Dow*

FACSIMILE   2 b.f. (Mar 27) Superlative 118 – Just Julia (Natroun (FR) 128)   59 [1997 5.1s² Jul 5] second foal: sister to fairly useful 1996 2-y-o sprint winner Just Visiting: dam no worthwhile form: 10/3, second of 7 in maiden at Nottingham (played up and unseated rider before start). *Capt. J. Wilson*

FA-EQ (IRE)   2 ch.c. (Mar 19) Indian Ridge 123 – Searching Star 63 (Rainbow   86 p Quest (USA) 134) [1997 6g² Oct 24] IR 450,000Y: sturdy, useful-looking colt: second foal: half-brother to fairly useful 1996 Irish 2-y-o 5f winner Hartstown House (by Primo Dominie): dam maiden half-sister to Beldale Star (smart around 1½m): heavily-backed favourite, neck second of 24 to Mister Rambo in maiden at Newbury, cruising most of way and leading over 1f out but cut down under less than hard driving close home: bred to stay 1m: sure to win races at 3 yrs. *Saeed bin Suroor*

FAHRIS (IRE)   3 ch.c. Generous (IRE) 139 – Janbiya (IRE) 89 (Kris 135)   119
[1996 97p: 7f* 8g² 1997 9m* 12g⁶ 10m² 10.5m³ 10m³ 10d* 12g⁴ 9d* Oct 17]
Fahris developed into a smart performer in the latest season, showing himself the best horse to have left Tom Jones on his retirement at the end of 1996. Joining Ben Hanbury, Fahris made a winning reappearance in the Greene King Feilden Stakes at Newmarket in April, scoring in good style by 3 lengths from Panama City—and in a good time—and earned a crack at the Vodafone Derby. However, after a training set-back and a small sinus operation, he ran below form at Epsom, briefly going a clear second two furlongs out before finishing a tired sixth of thirteen runners. Odds on in a field of three for his next outing, the Group 3 Tennent Caledonian Breweries Scottish Classic at Ayr, Fahris was undone by a far from true pace, front-running Crystal Hearted battling on to prevail by three quarters of a length.
Fahris had looked pattern-race material in the Feilden and, after running creditably in the Rose of Lancaster Stakes at Haydock (behind Romanov) and the Winter Hill Stakes at Windsor (behind Annus Mirabilis) in August, he finally confirmed that in the Group 3 Westminster Taxi Insurance Select Stakes at Goodwood. Fahris made all, quickening clear early in the straight, to give a six-length beating to the favourite Desert Story. Back up in trip for his next start in the Cumberland Lodge Stakes at Ascot later in September, Fahris seemed not to stay, racing freely and leading with over half a mile to run but then fading. Returned to Newmarket's nine furlongs, Fahris ended his season on a winning note in the listed Baring International Darley Stakes, making all and forging clear to beat Amid Albadu by three lengths. Shortly afterwards Fahris left Hanbury's yard to spend the winter in Dubai. He will race under the Godolphin banner in 1998.
Fahris is the second foal of Janbiya, who won at seven furlongs (as a juvenile) and a mile and a quarter for Tom Jones. Her first, A-Aasem (by Polish Precedent), was a fair maiden at up to ten furlongs before being sent to Dubai. Janbiya is a sister to the Irish Two Thousand Guineas winner Flash of Steel, the best offspring of Fahris's grandam Spark of Fire, who was unplaced. Spark of Fire's dam, Sparkalark, a Grade 1 winner in America, has produced several good performers, notably the Group/Grade 1 winners Spark of Life (Ladies Handicap), Musical Lark (Matron Stakes) and Fire of Life (Premio Roma).

Baring International Darley Stakes, Newmarket—the front-running Fahris gains his third win of the season, this time from Amid Albadu and Proper Blue

Mr Hamdan Al Maktoum's "Fahris"

		Caerleon	Nijinsky
	Generous (IRE)	(b 1980)	Foreseer
	(ch 1988)	Doff The Derby	Master Derby
Fahris (IRE)		(b 1981)	Margarethen
(ch.c. 1994)		Kris	Sharpen Up
	Janbiya (IRE)	(ch 1976)	Doubly Sure
	(ch 1988)	Spark of Fire	Run The Gantlet
		(br 1979)	Sparkalark

Fahris normally races prominently, acts on good to firm and dead ground and won on firm on his debut. He tends to sweat and get on edge, though this characteristic doesn't affect his performance. A big, good-topped colt, Fahris has occasionally been bandaged. *B. Hanbury*

FAHS (USA) 5 b. or br.g. Riverman (USA) 131 – Tanwi 101 (Vision (USA)) [1996   86 73: 12m⁴ 12.3g³ 13.3s⁶ 10m³ 10m² 10m 10f² 10m 10m 10.3m⁶ 10m³ 1997 8s 10g* 10.1g³ 10.4m 10m 10m⁶ 8.5d³ 10.3m⁶ 8m 10.1m* 12s Nov 8] strong, good sort: impresses in appearance: fairly useful handicapper: won at Sandown in May and at Yarmouth (held up, led near line) in October: has won at 1½m, possibly best around 1¼m: acts on firm ground and dead, probably not soft: usually races prominently. *R. Akehurst*

FAILED TO HIT 4 b.g. Warrshan (USA) 117 – Missed Again 84 (High Top 131)   – [1996 70: 5g² a9.4g⁴ 6m* 10.5s 8m a7g⁶ 1997 a7f a9.4g a7g⁶ a9.4g⁵ 10.8m 8.3s   a57 a8.5g² 7d a8.5g² a8.5g³ 8g a8g⁴ a9.4g³ a12g a9.4g Dec 26] strong, good-bodied gelding: modest handicapper on all-weather, no form on turf in 1997: stays 9.4f, probably not 1½m: blinkered or visored. *N. P. Littmoden*

FAIR AND FANCY (FR) 6 b.g. Always Fair (USA) 121 – Fancy Star (FR)   – (Bellypha 130) [1996 NR 1997 a14g Apr 1] 1¾m winner on fibresand in 1995: no promise only start at 6 yrs: won over hurdles twice later in 1997. *Miss M. K. Milligan*

FAIR DEAL (USA) 2 b.f. (Apr 18) Zilzal (USA) 137 – Fadetta (USA) (Fappiano 79
(USA)) [1997 6m³ 7.5d³ Aug 13] first foal: dam, winner in USA and placed in Grade
2 1m event, closely related to US Grade 1 1m and 9f winner King Glorious: fair form
when third in minor event at Windsor and maiden at Beverley: should stay 1¼m: sent
to UAE. *D. R. Loder*

FAIRELAINE 5 b.m. Zalazl (USA) 120 – Blue And White (Busted 134) [1996 –
54d: a7g⁶ 7f⁵ 8.3m 10m⁶ 8f 1997 10g Apr 18] smallish mare: disappointing maiden
handicapper: probably stays 1¼m: acts on firm ground, soft and equitrack: visored
once at 3 yrs. *K. C. Bailey*

FAIR ELLA (IRE) 5 ch.m. Simply Great (FR) 122 – Dance Or Burst (Try My –
Best (USA) 130) [1996 –: a10g 1997 a7g Jan 9] probably of little account nowadays.
G. L. Moore

FAIR GAME (IRE) 2 br.c. (Mar 2) Bluebird (USA) 125 – Blonde Goddess (IRE) –
(Godswalk (USA) 130) [1997 6g 7.1g a7g 10g 8m Oct 5] IR 41,000Y: smallish colt:
first foal: dam Irish 7f and 1m winner: only a little sign of ability in maidens and
nurseries: blinkered final start. *J. L. Dunlop*

FAIRLY SHARP (IRE) 4 b.f. Glenstal (USA) 118 – Bengala (FR) (Hard To –
Beat 132) [1996 12g* 12g² 12g* 12m 13d² 11f² 13g* 1997 17.2m Jun 14] IR 5,000Y:
half-sister to several winners including useful Badarbak (up to 15f, by Julio
Mariner): dam unraced half-sister to smart middle-distance performer Anazid: fair
(rated 74) for J. Coogan in Ireland in 1996, sold 10,000 gns at end of year: fairly
useful hurdler: tailed off only outing on flat at 4 yrs: stays 13f: acts on firm and dead
ground: front runner. *Graeme Roe*

FAIRLY SURE (IRE) 4 b.f. Red Sunset 120 – Mirabiliary (USA) 74 (Crow (FR) 37
134) [1996 50: 9f⁴ 8.5m⁴ 8f⁴ 7.6m* 8m⁵ 7m 7m 7g 1997 8g 8d 7m 7.6g⁵ 7f Sep 28]
poor form at best at 4 yrs: stays 1m: acts on firm going. *N. E. Berry*

FAIR SONIA 2 b.f. (Mar 24) Efisio 120 – Ausonia (Beldale Flutter (USA) 130) –
[1997 6.1m 7.1m 7m 7d 8d Oct 28] 5,000Y: small, leggy filly: fourth reported foal:
half-sister to a Italian 9f and 11f winner by Last Tycoon: dam, little sign of ability,
half-sister to Laurent Perrier Champagne Stakes winner Young Runaway: no form,
including in a seller: blinkered final start. *K. McAuliffe*

FAIRY DOMINO 2 ch.f. (Feb 26) Primo Dominie 121 – Fairy Fortune 78 66 d
(Rainbow Quest (USA) 134) [1997 5m³ 5s* 5.2f⁴ 5m³ a5g a7g Dec 18] 5,000Y: third
foal: half-sister to 3-y-o Italian 1¼m and 11f winner Quinolina (by Shareef Dancer):
dam, 7.6f winner, out of useful close relative of smart 1¼m colt Elegant Air: awarded
maiden at Hamilton in May on technicality: disappointing afterwards, leaving M.
Channon and off track 6 months before penultimate outing. *M. Quinn*

FAIRY FINGERS 3 b.f. Treasure Kay 114 – Nellie Moss (Le Moss 135) [1996 –
NR 1997 10s⁶ a10g⁵ Nov 18] half-sister to a winner in Norway at 1m to 11.5f by
Nordico: dam never ran: well beaten in maidens. *J. L. Eyre*

FAIRY KNIGHT 5 b.h. Fairy King (USA) – Vestal Flame 45 (Habitat 134) [1996 70
77: 10.3d 10.8g⁶ 10m 10.2f 12g 7f 9f⁴ 10g⁴ 12g² 12m 10m⁶ 12d* 10g* 12v⁴ 1997
a10g⁴ 12m 10.8m 12g² 11.9s* 10m⁵ 10g 12d⁶ 12d⁴ 12d Aug 25] sturdy, close-
coupled horse: fair handicapper: won 4-runner event at Haydock in May: creditable
efforts next 4 starts: effective at 1¼m/1½m: probably acts on any turf going (raced
only once each on equitrack and fibresand): tried blinkered/visored, no improvement: sometimes bandaged behind: best held up. *R. Hannon*

FAIRY PRINCE (IRE) 4 b.g. Fairy King (USA) – Danger Ahead (Mill Reef 79
(USA) 141) [1996 65: 6.1d 5.1g 5.9f³ 5.9f* 5m² 6m⁴ 5.1m⁶ 5.9f² 6m³ 1997 6.1m 5.9g
6m² 6g² 6m⁴ 6m* 5.1m* 6g* 5m 6g⁵ 5.7g 6d Sep 13] lengthy gelding: fair performer:
won minor events at Pontefract, Nottingham and Doncaster in July: effective at 5f/
6f: raced mainly on good going and firmer: consistent. *Mrs A. L. M. King*

FAIRY ROCK (IRE) 2 b.f. (Feb 16) Fairy King (USA) – Safe Home 94 (Home 73 p
Guard (USA) 129) [1997 6d 6g⁴ Oct 27] IR 30,000Y: workmanlike filly: half-sister
to 1m and 1¼m winner/useful hurdler Home Counties (by Ela-Mana-Mou) and a
prolific winner in Italy by Shardari: dam, best at 2 yrs when 5f winner in Ireland,
half-sister to smart sprinter Touch Paper: better effort in October maidens when
under 3 lengths fourth of 22 to Solo Spirit at Leicester, still green and keeping on not

knocked about: likely to prove best up to 1m: gone in coat at Leicester (also scratched to post): should do fair bit better again at 3 yrs. *B. W. Hills*

FAITH ALONE   4 b.f. Safawan 118 – Strapless 84 (Bustino 136) [1996 67: 6m   85
6m* 6f 6g a7g a8g 1997 6g⁴ 6d* 6d⁵ 6s* 5m* 6m³ 5.2m⁵ Aug 16] workmanlike filly:
fairly useful handicapper: in foal to Bin Ajwaad and much improved as 4-y-o,
winning at Leicester in June and Yarmouth and Sandown in July: best at 5f/6f: acted
on equitrack and on good to firm and soft ground: sold 11,000 gns in December.
C. F. Wall

FAITHFUL SON (USA)   3 b.g. Zilzal (USA) 137 – Carduel (USA) (Buck-   121
passer) [1996 NR 1997 8d* 7g* 8.5g² 8m⁵ 10.3m* 8g³ Sep 27]
    If those behind the naming of Faithful Son had been hoping he'd follow
in his father's footsteps they wouldn't have been too disappointed with his first
season. Like his sire Zilzal, Faithful Son put up his best performance in the
Queen Elizabeth II Stakes at Ascot, though he was able to finish only third,
eight years after Zilzal's outstanding win. There was nothing of Zilzal's ability
in a nine-runner field for the latest running but it nonetheless included six
Group 1 winners. Faithful Son belied his 16/1 starting price and ran a much
better race than his stable companion, the Two Thousand Guineas winner
Entrepreneur. Looking very well beforehand, Faithful Son tracked the less-
than-true pace, was unable to quicken immediately once in the straight, but kept
on well to hold third place narrowly ahead of Bahhare, about two lengths down
on the first two, Air Express and Rebecca Sharp.
    Like Zilzal, Faithful Son had been unraced at two and had evidently
inherited his sire's tendency to be something of a handful because he made his
debut at Newbury in May already a gelding. But, again like Zilzal, Faithful Son
quickly made up for lost time and proved a well-above-average performer.
After winning that mile maiden at Newbury when easy to back, he landed the
odds in impressive style in a seven-furlong minor event at Leicester eleven
days later, the same contest Zilzal had won on his debut. Zilzal's path to the
Queen Elizabeth II Stakes had then proceeded via wins in the Jersey Stakes

RJB Mining Conditions Stakes, Doncaster—Faithful Son puts a disappointing effort behind him;
he shows the best turn of foot against Alezal and Musalsal

at Royal Ascot, the Criterion Stakes at Newmarket and the Sussex Stakes at Goodwood. Faithful Son's route to Ascot in September took a more low-key approach. He was admittedly pitched into pattern company next time, when beaten half a length by the four-year-old Polar Prince in the Diomed Stakes at Epsom, but ran in minor events on his following starts at Goodwood and Doncaster. At Goodwood he ran disappointingly when an odds-on chance but reportedly returned with heat in a foot and a problem with one of his heels which meant his wearing stick-on shoes for his next start. At Doncaster he accounted for three rivals, quickening best in a race run at just a fair pace on his first attempt at a mile and a quarter and having Alezal a length and a quarter back in second at the line.

		Nureyev	Northern Dancer
	Zilzal (USA)	(b 1977)	Special
	(ch 1986)	French Charmer	Le Fabuleux
Faithful Son (USA)		(ch 1978)	Bold Example
(b.g. 1994)		Buckpasser	Tom Fool
	Carduel (USA)	(b 1963)	Busanda
	(b 1978)	Minstrelete	Round Table
		(b 1973)	Gay Violin

Faithful Son's dam, Carduel, ran only at two years, winning an eight and a half furlong maiden at Belmont. From nine foals prior to Faithful Son, she produced three other winners, including the fairly useful miler Asaasy (by Danzig) and a winner in Malaysia by Smarten. But easily the best was the very smart miler Always Fair (also by Danzig), who won the Coventry Stakes at two and the Prix Quincey at three and is now a successful stallion in France. The next two dams were also successful at around a mile in the United States, Minstrelete producing the smart Irish mile and mile-and-a-quarter performer Punctilio, and Gay Violin the top-class miler Gay Fandango, himself placed in the Queen Elizabeth II Stakes.

Faithful Son didn't run again after Ascot but will be back at four having been transferred to the Godolphin operation. A close-coupled, good-topped gelding with a fluent, round action, Faithful Son looks the sort to go on. As he's yet to win either a listed or pattern race he shouldn't be hard to place, though France's exclusion of geldings from the majority of their Group 1 races rules out the Prix Jacques le Marois and Prix du Moulin. He stays a mile and a quarter and is yet to race on extremes of going. *M. R. Stoute*

FAKHR (USA) 2 b. or br.c. (Jan 22) Riverman (USA) 131 – Roseate Tern 123   94 p
(Blakeney 126) [1997 7m* 8.1s⁴ Aug 30] good-topped, attractive colt: third foal: half-brother to 3-y-o Siyadah: dam, winner of Yorkshire Oaks and third in Oaks and St Leger, half-sister to Ibn Bey out of half-sister to Teleprompter and Chatoyant: made impressive debut when winning Salisbury maiden in July, slowly away and making deal of ground late in race without being hard ridden to beat Royal Bounty ¾ length: favourite, always in rear when well-beaten last of 4 in minor event won by Kilimanjaro at Sandown (walked poorly in paddock and unimpressive to post): should stay 1½m: remains a useful prospect: sent to UAE. *J. L. Dunlop*

FALAK (USA) 3 b.c. Diesis 133 – Tafrah (IRE) 71 (Sadler's Wells (USA) 132)   113
[1996 100: 7g² 7g* 7m³ 1997 10g² 10.3m* 12s* 12m Jul 29] well-made colt: has a powerful, round action: smart performer: ridden with more restraint when winning useful minor events at Doncaster (came from off strong pace to beat Stowaway ½ length) in May and Ascot (found extra to hold Monza by a head) in June: rare poor effort in Gordon Stakes at Goodwood final start: stays 1½m: acts on good to firm ground and soft: takes good hold, equipped with crossed noseband at 3 yrs: tongue tied: thoroughly genuine and likeable sort: sent to UAE. *Major W. R. Hern*

FALCON RIDGE 3 ch.g. Seven Hearts 98 – Glen Kella Manx 97 (Tickled Pink   –
114) [1996 –: 5v 1997 6m 7.6m 7d 8d a8g Dec 2] of little account. *J. C. Fox*

FALKENBERG (FR) 2 ch.g. (Mar 6) Polish Precedent (USA) 131 – Mithi Al   69 ?
Gamar (USA) 68 (Blushing Groom (FR) 131) [1997 5s 5m a7g³ 7g⁵ 8s 7g Oct 25] IR

10,500Y: smallish, sturdy gelding: first foal: dam 7f winner: some fair form, but well beaten in nurseries final 2 starts: stays 7f: best effort on fibresand. *M. Johnston*

FALLS O'MONESS (IRE) 3 b.f. River Falls 113 – Sevens Are Wild 40 (Petorius 117) [1996 62: 6g² 6m² 7s 6.9m³ 7m² 6g 7.5m 1997 7.1s 6m³ 6.9m⁴ 7.3s⁵ 6m 6d a6g⁵ 8m⁶ 8g⁶ 8f⁴ 7.1g³ 9d* 10g 10.5s⁴ 10.1g⁶ 10.3g Oct 25] unfurnished filly: fair performer: won claimer at Ayr in September: stays 10.5f: probably acts on any turf going: blinkered (out of depth) and visored (below form on all-weather) once each. *K. R. Burke* 65

FAME AGAIN 5 b.m. Then Again 126 – Starawak 68 (Star Appeal 133) [1996 86d: 8s 8g 8g 7.6g 6m⁴ 7g³ 6m⁶ 6m⁵ 6g⁶ 6f² 6m⁴ 7.5f⁵ 7m 7.1f 7m 7.1s 7g 7g 5s⁵ 1997 7g 6.1m 6.1d* 7d* 6m⁶ 6s² 6g 6g⁶ 7m⁶ 6g* Aug 17] compact mare: fair handicapper: won at Nottingham and Doncaster in the spring and Pontefract (ridden by 3-lb claimer) in August: was effective at 6f to 1m: had form on firm going, but was suited by good ground or softer: held up: dead. *Mrs J. R. Ramsden* 76

FAMILY MAN 4 ch.g. Indian Ridge 123 – Auntie Gladys 49 (Great Nephew 126) [1996 75: 8d⁶ 8.2m⁴ 8m⁴ 10.1m 1997 8m² 8.5d⁵ 8m* 8g 8d 8g Oct 18] angular, workmanlike gelding: fairly useful handicapper: well backed when winning at Newmarket in May: disappointing afterwards: should stay beyond 1m: yet to race on extremes of ground. *J. R. Fanshawe* 85

FANADIYR (IRE) 5 b.g. Kahyasi 130 – Fair Fight 84 (Fine Blade (USA) 121) [1996 –: 13d 13.1m⁴ 12.4m⁴ 1997 11.1s 12.1s⁵ 13.1g⁵ Jun 20] poor staying maiden: tried blinkered. *J. S. Goldie* –

FANCY A FORTUNE (IRE) 3 b.g. Fools Holme (USA) – Fancy's Girl (FR) (Nadjar (FR) 128) [1996 63§: 6m 7s³ 7m 7d 7f² 7f 8.1m⁴ 10f 8m 1997 8g³ 9m² 8g³ 7g* 8m³ 8.1m 10m a8g 7g⁴ Oct 24] lengthy gelding: modest handicapper: won apprentice event at Thirsk in August: effective at 7f to 9f: acts on any going: visored last 2 starts as 2-y-o: has carried head high: joined E. W. Tuer. *D. Nicholls* 64

*Rosehill Conditions Stakes, Doncaster—Falak gives a resolute performance
to get the better of Stowaway (left) in a notably good field for the type of race*

FANCY CLANCY   4 b.f. Clantime 101 – Bold Sophie (Bold Owl 101) [1996 –
43d: 5g⁴ 5f⁶ 5m 5g 5m 5g 5m 1997 a5g 5g 5m⁶ 5g 5d 5v 6m 5f 5g Oct 18] no longer
of any account. *Miss L. C. Siddall*

FANCY DESIGN (IRE)   4 b.f. Cyrano de Bergerac 120 – Crimson Robes 48   48
(Artaius (USA) 129) [1996 –: 6m 7m⁵ 7g a8g⁶ a8s⁶ a8g⁵ 1997 a5g a7g a7g⁴ a8g a6g⁵   a27
a8g 7m 7g 5m 6.9m 10g⁶ 8.3m² 8.3m² 7g 8.3m 8.1g 8.3m 8m⁶ 10.8g 10m Oct 23]
sturdy filly: poor maiden handicapper: stays 1m: acts on good to firm ground
(unraced on going softer than good) and on equitrack: tried visored (no form).
P. Mitchell

FAN OF VENT-AXIA   3 b.c. Puissance 110 – Miss Milton (Young Christopher   42
119) [1996 59: 5s⁴ 5g a5g³ 7f³ 7g⁴ 7f 8m 8g 1997 6.1m 6m⁶ 7f⁴ 8g 7f 8g Jul 25] small,
leggy colt: poor maiden: should stay 1m: tried blinkered/visored. *D. J. S. Cosgrove*

FANTAIL   3 b.c. Taufan (USA) 119 – Eleganza (IRE) 67 (Kings Lake (USA) 133)   89 p
[1996 71?: 7m 8m 8g⁶ 1997 10m 9g⁶ 11m* 11.1s* 10s* 11.9s⁵ 10m³ 10.1m 11m*
Nov 4] leggy, good-topped colt: has a fluent action: fairly useful handicapper,
generally progressive: won at Redcar (twice) and Hamilton from May to July:
improved again when winning 17-runner event back at Redcar in November by 3
lengths, always going well: will stay 1½m: acts on good to firm and soft ground:
should do better again at 4 yrs. *M. H. Tompkins*

FANTASTIC FELLOW (USA)   3 b.c. Lear Fan (USA) 130 – Chateaubaby   115
(USA) 62 (Nureyev (USA) 131) [1996 112p: 7g* 7g⁴ 6m⁴ 1997 7d⁵ 8d⁵ 8g⁵ 8.5g 8f*
8.5f* 9f⁴ 8f* 8f 9d Nov 30] sturdy, well-made colt: smart performer: made all in
listed event at Maisons-Laffitte in April: below best in Poule d'Essai des Poulains
and Irish 2000 Guineas, left C. Brittain after next start: won 3 of his first 4 starts in
USA, valuable non-graded race and Grade 3 events at Del Mar and Santa Anita (beat
Magellan a head): eighth in Breeders' Cup Mile (creditable effort) and Hollywood
Derby at Hollywood Park: stays 8.5f: acts on firm and dead ground: effective from
front, normally tracks pace: raced on medication in USA. *D. Wayne Lukas, USA*

FANTASTIC FLAME (IRE)   3 b.f. Generous (IRE) 139 – Gay Fantastic   79
(Ela-Mana-Mou 132) [1996 NR 1997 7g⁶ 8g⁶ 10.2d² 10g 10m⁵ 10g* 10.1g 10d⁴
10.3g Oct 24] strong, workmanlike filly: sister to 4-y-o Germano and half-sister to
several other winners, including Potentate (up 1¼m, smart hurdler, by Capote): dam
unraced sister to smart middle-distance filly Gay Hellene: fair performer: won
maiden at Windsor in August: ran well when staying-on fourth in handicap at Ayr
following month: will be suited by 1½m: yet to race on extremes of going. *P. J. Makin*

FANTASY FLIGHT   3 b.f. Forzando 122 – Ryewater Dream 72 (Touching Wood   –
(USA) 127) [1996 –p: 6g 1997 7m 9.2g⁵ 10m Oct 28] first foal: dam 1½m winner: no
worthwhile form. *M. A. Peill*

FANTASY GIRL (IRE)   3 br.f. Marju (IRE) 127 – Persian Fantasy 94 (Persian   55
Bold 123) [1996 –: 7g 7.6m 1997 10.2m⁵ 9.9d⁶ 11.1m 10s a12g⁶ 12m a10g Nov 25]
neat filly: modest maiden: stays 1½m: acts on fibresand, best turf efforts on good to
firm going. *J. L. Dunlop*

FANTASY ISLAND (IRE)   2 b.c. (Jan 24) Zafonic (USA) 130 – Um Lardaff   100 p
(Mill Reef (USA) 141) [1997 7m* Aug 22] strong colt: fourth foal: half-brother to
fairly useful 7f (at 2 yrs) and 1¼m winner Expensive Taste (by Cadeaux Genereux):
dam, French 11f and 1½m winner, sister to Shirley Heights: 9/4 on, won maiden at
Newmarket easily by 3½ lengths (rated value 5) from Air Attache, allowed to dictate
and quickening well, despite running green: entered in pattern races, but wasn't seen
out again (reportedly lame when due to run in Prix de la Salamandre): should stay at
least 1¼m: seems a smart performer in the making. *Saeed bin Suroor*

FANTASY NIGHT (IRE)   2 b.g. (Mar 1) Night Shift (USA) – Gay Fantasy   69 p
(Troy 137) [1997 7d 7m³ 8.2g Sep 28] compact, good-bodied gelding: closely related
to useful 1m/1¼m performer Lucky Guest (by Be My Guest) and half-brother to
several winners, including useful 1m to 1½m winner Son of Sharp Shot (by Sharp
Shot): dam unraced half-sister to smart middle-distance filly Miss Petard: shaped
promisingly all 3 starts, never placed to challenge in maiden at Nottingham final one
(subsequently gelded): will stay at least 1¼m: considerably handled to date, and sure
to make a better 3-y-o. *J. L. Dunlop*

Tote Ebor (Handicap), York—
at 33/1 Far Ahead (hooped sleeves) becomes the third longest-priced winner in the race's long history;
he gamely foils Media Star's attempt to make all,
with Puce (rail) and the grey Further Flight in close contention

FANTI DANCER (IRE) 2 b.f. (Feb 16) Anshan 119 – Maiden Way (Shareef 57
Dancer (USA) 135) [1997 7g 7g³ 7g² 7d³ 8m 7m 7d Oct 16] IR 6,500Y: rangy filly:
second foal: half-sister to 3-y-o Maremma: dam unraced: modest form at best: well
below it final 3 starts: should stay well beyond 7f: acts on dead going: blinkered fifth
outing: joined J. Pearce. *B. J. Meehan*

FAR AHEAD 5 b.g. Soviet Star (USA) 128 – Cut Ahead 85 (Kalaglow 132) [1996 94
87, a72: a11g⁴ a8g 9.9f⁶ 10m³ 11.1g² 12.3m³ 12f* 11.9m³ 12g* 13.1m³ 10.4g 12s a–
a12g 1997 a12g⁴ a12g⁶ 12m* 12m 11.9g 14m² 13.9g* Aug 20] angular gelding:
unimpressive mover: fairly useful handicapper: won at Beverley in June and Tote
Ebor at York in August: 33/1, always prominent and responded most generously to
pressure to lead near finish at York, beating Media Star a neck: better suited by 1¾m
than shorter and will stay 2m: acts on firm and dead ground and the all-weather:
usually held up: game. *J. L. Eyre*

FARASAN (IRE) 4 b.c. Fairy King (USA) – Gracieuse Majeste (FR) (Saint 104
Cyrien (FR) 128) [1996 115: 8m* 10.3g* 10m⁶ 12m⁶ 11.9m⁴ 10g³ 1997 9g Apr 16]
tall colt: fluent mover: smart performer in 1996: 5 lengths seventh of 11 behind
stable-companion Ali-Royal in Earl of Sefton Stakes at Newmarket, only outing at 4
yrs: needs further than 9f and stays 1½m: raced only on good or good to firm ground:
sent to France. *H. R. A. Cecil*

FAR ATLANTIC 4 b.f. Phardante (FR) 123 – Atlantic View (Crash Course 128) –
[1996 –: 11.5m 1997 8m³ Aug 7] leggy filly: well held in claimers. *C. A. Dwyer*

FARAWAY LASS 4 b.f. Distant Relative 128 – Vague Lass 85 (Vaigly Great 127) 92
[1996 80: 6.1m⁴ 6.1m* 6g² 6m* 6g³ 6m² 7f² 7.3m 6g* 1997 6m 6f⁴ 6m* 6m⁴ 6g⁵ 7m
5g³ Oct 25] rangy filly: fluent mover: fairly useful handicapper: improved again at 4
yrs, winning 21-runner race at York in July: less than a length fourth to Danetime in
Stewards' Cup at Goodwood next start, good third of 22 at Doncaster final one:
effective from 5f to 7f: acts on firm ground, unraced on softer than good. *Lord
Huntingdon*

FAREWELL MY LOVE (IRE) 3 b.f. Waajib 121 – So Long Boys (FR) 62 d
(Beldale Flutter (USA) 130) [1996 73: 5.1m² 5m* 6m⁶ 6g* 6.5m 7d⁶ 6s⁴ 1997 a6g⁶
6d 6.1m⁵ 6f⁶ 8.1s³ 6m 7g 7g Aug 11] smallish, sturdy filly: on the downgrade, and
modest form at best as 3-y-o: left P. Cole after fifth start: stays 6f: acts on good to
firm and soft ground: tried visored: sold 21,000 gns in December. *J. S. Wainwright*

351

FARFIELDS PRINCE 5 b.g. Weldnaas (USA) 112 – Coca (Levmoss 133) 46
[1996 NR 1997 9.9m 12m² 11.1d⁵ 9.9g² 10.9d³ 14.1g Oct 18] leggy gelding: poor
maiden handicapper: stays 1½m: acts on good to firm and dead ground: has looked
difficult ride. *D. Nicholls*

FARHANA 4 b.f. Fayruz 116 – Fahrenheit 69 (Mount Hagen (FR) 127) [1996 109: 109
6.1d* 6m* 6d* 6g² 1997 5.5g* 6g² 5g 6g Jun 19] rangy filly: useful performer: won
listed event at Maisons-Laffitte in April, and ran well when 1¼ lengths second to
Royal Applause, pair clear, in Duke of York Stakes (bandaged off-hind) following
month: below form in pattern events afterwards: will prove best up to 6f: yet to race
on extremes of going. *W. Jarvis*

FARHAN (USA) 3 b.g. Lear Fan (USA) 130 – Mafatin (IRE) 74 (Sadler's Wells 70
(USA) 132) [1996 81: 6m⁵ 7.1d² 7f² 1997 10s⁵ 10m Jun 3] big, lengthy gelding:
fairly useful performer at best: hasn't progressed since debut: tailed off in handicap
final start: should stay 1¼m: sold 15,500 gns in August, joined K. Morgan then
gelded. *P. T. Walwyn*

FARINGDON FUTURE 3 b.g. Distant Relative 128 – Lady Dowery (USA) 74
(Manila (USA)) [1996 74: 6m 6g² 6m⁴ 6.1s⁶ 1997 8g 8g⁶ 8.1m 8f² 8m³ Oct 6] robust,
good-bodied gelding: has a quick action: fair maiden: should be suited by 1¼m+:
acts on firm ground: sold 14,000 gns and sent to USA. *B. W. Hills*

FARLEY GREEN 3 b.f. Pharly (FR) 130 – Ring Cycle 64 (Auction Ring (USA) 70
123) [1996 NR 1997 6.1d³ 6.9m* 7g 6m² 7g⁶ Aug 20] first reported foal: dam 6f
winner from 2 starts at 2 yrs: fair form: won maiden at Folkestone in June: ran
creditably in handicaps final 2 outings: stays 7f well: unraced on extremes of going.
H. Candy

FARLEY MOUNT 3 b.g. Pharly (FR) 130 – Mossy Rose 78 (King of Spain 121) 67
[1996 NR 1997 a8g³ a10g⁴ 8g³ 11.7m⁴ 11.5m Jul 11] second foal: half-brother to
4-y-o Oscar Rose (by Aragon): dam stayed 1m: fair maiden: ran poorly on handicap
debut final start: should stay 1½m: possibly unsuited by going firmer than good:
carried head high on debut. *Lord Huntingdon*

FARMOST 4 ch.g. Pharly (FR) 130 – Dancing Meg (USA) 113 (Marshua's 106
Dancer (USA)) [1996 81: a6g* 8d⁵ 7.1d* 7g* 6.9m* a7g² 8f* 7.6f² a7g² a9.4g* 1997
a8g a8.5g 10.2f* 10m⁴ 12d⁶ 10f* a9.4g* a9.4g² a8.5g* a9.4g* Dec 6] big, good-

Wulfrun Stakes, Wolverhampton—
all-weather racing's most valuable event goes to the progressive Farmost who holds on from Running Stag

topped gelding: useful performer: improved again at 4 yrs, winning minor event at Bath in July, handicaps at Brighton and Wolverhampton (under 10-6) within 3 days in September and listed race at Wolverhampton (best effort, beat Running Stag by ½ length, pair clear) in December: ideally suited by around 1¼m (pulled too hard when tried at 1½m): acts on the all-weather and on firm and dead going: races up with pace: tough and genuine. *Sir Mark Prescott*

FARNDON PRINCESS 2 b.f. (Apr 6) Nomination 125 – Ankara's Princess 60
(USA) 81 (Ankara (USA) 106) [1997 5.1m³ 6m 6.1d⁵ Aug 29] lengthy, angular filly: third live foal: sister to 3-y-o Nominator Lad: dam, 2-y-o 5f winner, stayed 6f: modest form in maiden and minor event at Chester first and final starts. *R. Hollinshead*

FAR REMOVED (IRE) 2 b.c. (May 28) Distant Relative 128 – Cormorant 84 p
Creek 73 (Gorytus (USA) 132) [1997 5g 5m² 5g⁴ 5m² 6m* Sep 13] 35,000Y: tall, quite good-topped colt: third foal: half-brother to 3-y-o Spartan Royale: dam, 10.4f winner, half-sister to Cormorant Wood, dam of Rock Hopper: very eye-catching efforts second and fourth starts, before justifying favouritism in 16-runner nursery at Doncaster, going well long way but needing to be driven out to beat Blue Kite ½ length: should stay further than 6f: only just starting to show real capabilities, and should make at least a useful handicapper 3 yrs. *Mrs J. R. Ramsden*

FARRINGDON HILL 6 b.g. Minster Son 130 – Firgrove 73 (Relkino 131) 77
[1996 80: 12m⁶ 14m*¹ 14.6g 14m⁵ 14.1m² 12g⁴ 17.2d 1997 10s⁵ 10.5m³ 12d⁶ 11.6m* 11g* 10g Sep 23] rangy gelding: good mover: fair handicapper: easily best efforts at 6 yrs when winning amateur events at Windsor and Redcar (got first run in slowly-run race) in August: ridden with restraint final start: stays 1¾m: acts on firm and soft going: best in blinkers/visor and ridden up with pace. *J. H. M. Gosden*

FAR-SO-LA 2 b.g. (Apr 26) Absalom 128 – Fara 66 (Castle Keep 121) [1997 5m –
5.1m 6m 6g 9m Sep 24] 5,200Y: fourth foal: dam 1¼m seller winner: looks of little account. *T. M. Jones*

FASCINATING RHYTHM 3 b.f. Slip Anchor 136 – Pick of The Pops 109 –
(High Top 131) [1996 85p: 8.2g* 1997 12m⁵ 10.1m Sep 16] promising winner of maiden at Nottingham on only 2-y-o start: reportedly had reappearance delayed by a lung infection and disappointing both outings as 3-y-o: should stay at least 1¼m. *H. R. A. Cecil*

FASHION VICTIM 2 b.c. (Apr 20) High Estate 127 – Kirkby Belle 44 (Bay 76
Express 132) [1997 5.9g⁵ 5m* 6.1g 6m⁵ 6d⁴ 8d* 8s³ 8d 8.2d⁶ Oct 30] 17,000 2-y-o: close-coupled colt: second foal: dam, poor maiden, stayed 7f: fair performer: won maiden at Beverley in July and nursery at Ayr in September: below form final 2 starts: better at 1m than shorter: acts on good to firm and soft ground. *T. H. Caldwell*

FASIL (IRE) 4 ch.g. Polish Patriot (USA) 128 – Apple Peel 109 (Pall Mall 132) –
[1996 90: 8d 8g³ 10d⁶ 10m* 10m 12m* 12g 1997 12m⁶ Sep 22] lengthy gelding: has a round action: fairly useful at 3 yrs for C. J. Benstead: no encouragement only outing in 1997: suited by 1½m: acts on good to firm ground. *J. G. M. O'Shea*

FAST FRANC (IRE) 2 ch.g. (Apr 7) Paris House 123 – Elle Va Bon (Tanfirion 58
110) [1997 5g³ 5.2m³ 5s* 6d* 7m a6g 6d 7s 6g a6g⁵ Nov 13] 3,000Y: workmanlike a47
gelding: fifth reported foal: half-brother to 5-y-o Bon Luck: dam Irish 7f winner at 4 yrs: modest performer: trained by B. Meehan on debut: made all in sellers at Folkestone and Hamilton in the summer: below form afterwards: stays 6f: acts on soft ground: blinkered final start. *S. C. Williams*

FAST SPIN 3 b.g. Formidable (USA) 125 – Topwinder (USA) (Topsider (USA)) 60
[1996 60: 5g⁶ 7m a7g⁴ 7g⁶ a7g* 1997 a8s⁴ a8.5g⁵ a7g* a7g³ a7g³ Mar 17] sturdy, compact gelding: modest on all-weather: won seller at Southwell in January: best form up to 7f: acts on fibresand (poor form on turf): blinkered (below form) second start. *T. D. Barron*

FAST TEMPO (IRE) 2 b.f. (May 25) Statoblest 120 – Bellinzona (Northfields 74
(USA)) [1997 5g⁴ 5m² 5m* 5g³ 5d⁵ 5.1f² 5m 5s³ 5.2d 6.1d a5s Nov 28] 4,000Y: good-bodied filly: half-sister to several winners, including 5-y-o Maralinga and fairly useful 1m/1¼m performer Bellefan (by Taufan): dam French 9.5f winner: fair performer at best: won maiden at Lingfield in May: several creditable efforts after-

FAT

wards but well below form last 3 starts: will prove best at 5f: acts on good to firm and soft ground, looked ill-at-ease on firm: has flashed tail. *B. Palling*

FATAL BARAARI 3 b.g. Green Desert (USA) 127 – Possessive (Posse (USA) 78 §
130) [1996 81p: 7.1m³ 1997 8.1m⁴ 8g 8g³ Aug 17] good-topped gelding: fair maiden: visored penultimate start: temperamental, and best left alone: sent to UAE. *M. R. Stoute*

FATAL SAHRA (IRE) 3 ch.c. Caerleon (USA) 132 – Ploy 87 (Posse (USA) –
130) [1996 67p: 7m 1997 10d Apr 26] some promise in maiden on debut: always behind in similar event at Ripon only outing at 3 yrs: sent to UAE. *J. H. M. Gosden*

FATEFULLY (USA) 4 b.f. Private Account (USA) – Fateful (USA) 90 (Topsider 110
(USA)) [1996 110: 7m² 7d 7f* 8m² 8.1m* 8m* 8d* 8g³ 1997 a8f² a10f 8.5m⁴ 8d²
10m⁴ 9d Oct 17] rather leggy filly: good mover: smart performer: trained by Saeed bin Suroor first 3 starts: best subsequent effort when fourth to One So Wonderful in Sun Chariot Stakes at Newmarket: tailed off in listed race there final outing: probably stays 1¼m: acts on firm and dead ground, and on sand: often wears tongue strap. *E. A. L. Dunlop*

FATEHALKHAIR (IRE) 5 ch.g. Kris 135 – Midway Lady (USA) 126 (Alleged 37
(USA) 138) [1996 –, a42: 10g 8.1f a8g² a9.4g⁵ 7m a8g 1997 10.1g 8.3d⁵ 12g³
Aug 15] leggy, angular gelding: poor mover: poor maiden handicapper: will stay beyond 1½m: acts on fibresand and dead ground: visored (no improvement) second 4-y-o start: inconsistent: fairly useful novice hurdler. *B. Ellison*

FATHER DAN (IRE) 8 ch.g. Martin John – Sonia John (Main Reef 126) [1996 60
65: a12g a12g 10m 10m² 11.5m a10g³ a10s³ a10g² a10g* a10g³ 1997 a12g⁴ a12g
a8g³ 10.3m 9.7g⁶ 10m² 10d⁶ 10m⁶ 10g 10m² 10.2d⁵ a10g⁵ a12g 11.9f* a10s⁴ a10s³
Nov 28] plain gelding: poor mover: modest performer: won claimer at Brighton in September: effective at 1m to 1½m: acts on any turf going and the all-weather: visored (well beaten) once: held up. *Miss Gay Kelleway*

FATHER EDDIE 3 b.g. Aragon 118 – Lady Philippa (IRE) 77 (Taufan (USA) 56
119) [1996 49: 5m 6d⁶ 7d 1997 a8g a11g 8.3d⁵ a8g 9.9d* 12d⁶ 9.9m 10f Jun 10] a–
close-coupled gelding: modest performer: won seller at Beverley in May: no comparable form: stays 1¼m: acts on good to soft ground: visored final start. *J. J. O'Neill*

FATHER SKY 6 b.g. Dancing Brave (USA) 140 – Flamenco Wave (USA) 103 74
(Desert Wine (USA)) [1996 NR 1997 16m* Sep 25] fairly useful jumper (sometimes looks less than keen): still capable of fair form on flat: blinkered, won handicap (for NH jockeys) at Goodwood in September: stays 2m: acts on good to firm going. *O. Sherwood*

FAUGERON 8 ch.g. Niniski (USA) 125 – Miss Longchamp 94 (Northfields 46
(USA)) [1996 57: 12f⁵ 16m 14d 14.1m* 14m² 16.2f² 1997 12d 16g 14.1m 16m a16g²
a14g⁶ Jun 13] sparely-made gelding: only poor at best at 8 yrs: sold 500 gns after final start. *N. Tinkler*

FAUNA (IRE) 3 b.f. Taufan (USA) 119 – Labwa (USA) (Lyphard (USA) 132) 65
[1996 65: 7m 7g⁴ 1997 8g⁵ 8d⁴ 9.9d May 20] modest maiden: didn't look easy ride final start: stays 1m: acts on dead ground. *N. A. Graham*

FAWNING 2 b.f. (Mar 16) Alnasr Alwasheek 117 – Flattering (USA) (Nodouble 59
(USA)) [1997 6.9s³ 7m 6m⁶ 7.3d Sep 19] leggy filly: third foal: half-sister to fairly useful 1995 2-y-o 7f and 1m winner Opera (by Forzando) and a winner abroad by Doulab: dam Irish 2-y-o 6f winner: modest maiden on balance: should stay 1m. *M. Blanshard*

FAYEZ 2 ch.c. (May 7) Interrex (CAN) – Forest Nymph (Native Bazaar 122) [1997 56
7.1m a8.5g Dec 13] fifth foal: dam unraced: better effort in maidens when seventh at Wolverhampton on final start. *K. McAuliffe*

FAYIK 3 ch.c. Arazi (USA) 135 – Elfaslah (IRE) 107 (Green Desert (USA) 127) 76
[1996 76p: 7m⁵ 1997 8.1g³ 8g⁵ 6m⁴ 6d 7.1m 6s a6g³ a6g² a7g³ a8.5g⁴ Dec 26] stocky colt: type to carry condition: fair maiden: left M. Stoute after second start: effective at 6f to 1m: acts on good to firm going (not clear run on soft) and the all-weather: held up. *A. G. Newcombe*

354

FAYM (IRE)   3 b.f. Fayruz 116 – Lorme (Glenstal (USA) 118) [1996 65: a6s⁵ a6g²   56
1997 a7g³ a7g³ a9.4g⁴ a7g² a8g⁵ 8.2s⁶ 7g 8g⁵ Aug 11] fair maiden handicapper, better   a65
form on all-weather than turf: effective at 7f/1m: acts on fibresand (below form on
soft ground). *J. Wharton*

FAYRANA (IRE)   2 b.f. (Mar 29) Fayruz 116 – Paryiana (IRE) (Shernazar 131)   78
[1997 5.1m⁶ 5g 6m² 6f² 7g* 7m⁴ 6m⁵ 6g 7m⁶ Sep 30] IR 8,500Y: first foal: dam
(unraced) from good French family: fair performer: won maiden at Warwick in July:
not disgraced in nurseries and a valuable sales race at the Curragh (penultimate start)
afterwards: stays 7f: yet to race on ground softer than good. *J. W. Hills*

FEARLESS BRAVE   2 b.c. (Mar 17) Aragon 118 – Siouan 78 (So Blessed 130)   59
[1997 7d⁶ 7.9s a8g⁵ Nov 24] leggy colt: half-brother to several winners, including
very smart middle-distance colt Apache (by Great Nephew): dam, 1¼m winner,
half-sister to Warpath: shaped well on debut in maiden at Ayr but well held in similar
events on soft ground/fibresand afterwards: likely to stay at least 1¼m: may yet do
better. *C. W. Thornton*

FEARLESS CAVALIER   3 b.g. Bold Arrangement 127 – Gold Belt (IRE) 61   54
(Bellypha 130) [1996 60?: 7m³ 6m⁶ a6g⁴ a7g⁴ 5f⁴ 6m² 6.1m⁶ 6m³ 6d 6s⁴ 6g³ 5s*
1997 8.2g³ 7.1m³ 7m 8m 7d Oct 14] small gelding: has a round action: modest form:
clearly best effort at 3 yrs on reappearance: better at 1m than 7f: acts on fibresand,
probably on any turf ground. *R. Hollinshead*

FEARLESS SIOUX   3 b.f. Formidable (USA) 125 – Washita (Valiyar 129) [1996   –
48: 6g⁵ a6g⁴ a10g 1997 a8g² a8.5g² 8.3d⁶ 11m 12v⁶ Jun 30] workmanlike filly: has a   a48
round action: poor maiden: should be suited by at least 1¼m: acts on fibresand, little
form on turf. *C. W. Thornton*

FEAR NOT (IRE)   2 b.f. (Apr 30) Alzao (USA) 117 – Fear Naught 99 (Con-   56
naught 130) [1997 7s⁶ 8d⁴ Sep 20] IR 38,000Y: well-made filly: half-sister to 3-y-o
Howaida among several winners, including smart 7f winner Himiko (by Green
Desert): dam won Royal Hunt Cup: better effort in maidens when 13 lengths fourth
of 12 at Ayr, racing freely and keeping on: should stay 1¼m. *M. Bell*

FEATHER BED (IRE)   3 b.f. Fools Holme (USA) – Piffle 87 (Shirley Heights   –
130) [1996 71: 6g⁴ 5f² 7g⁵ 6g a8g* 1997 a10g Jan 7] ex-Irish filly: fair winner at 2
yrs: last only start of 1997: sold 22,000 gns in December, in foal to Charnwood
Forest. *M. A. Jarvis*

FEATHERSTONE LANE   6 b.g. Siberian Express (USA) 125 – Try Gloria   52
(Try My Best (USA) 130) [1996 52d, a77d: a5g³ a5g³ a5g³ a5g* a5g² a5g a5g⁵
5g⁶ 5g 5g³ 5g⁴ 5m⁶ 5.2m⁴ 5d⁴ 5g 6f 5.1m 5m⁵ a6g a5g⁶ 6m a5g³ a5g⁴ a5g a5g³ 5g⁵
1997 a6g a6g a5g³ a5g³ a6g⁶ a6g⁶ a5g² a5g a6g⁴ a5g² a5g 5.1g a5g² 5f⁴ 5f² 5f³ 5m⁵
5m a5g* 5g⁴ a5g² 5m³ a5g a5g a5g⁴ Dec 12] workmanlike gelding: modest
handicapper: won seller at Wolverhampton in August: effective at 5f and 6f: acts on
firm and dead ground and the all-weather: used to be visored, not after twelfth start in
1997: often slowly away. *Miss L. C. Siddall*

FEBRUARY   4 b.f. Full Extent (USA) 113 – Foligno (Crofter (USA) 124) [1996   –
–: 5m 8m⁵ 7f a7g 8.1f 8f 1997 6g 5m Aug 4] of little account. *N. P. Littmoden*

FEEL A LINE   3 b.g. Petong 126 – Cat's Claw (USA) (Sharpen Up 127) [1996   55
71: 6m 6m⁶ 5.3f² 6m 5g³ 6m 6s 1997 8.2m 9.7m 8g⁶ 8.3g 7m⁴ 7f* 8.2d³ 7s* 6.9m⁶
6.9m⁴ 7g⁴ 7.1g⁶ Aug 28] lengthy gelding: modest performer: won maiden handicap
at Brighton in June and sellers at Yarmouth in July and Ayr in August: probably stays
1m: yet to race on heavy going, acts on any other: blinkered nowadays: has carried
head high and looked difficult ride: joined M. Hammond. *B. J. Meehan*

FEEL FREE (IRE)   2 b.f. (May 17) Generous (IRE) 139 – As You Desire Me 112   – p
(Kalamoun 129) [1997 8.2g Sep 23] sister to 3-y-o Gentilesse, closely related to
useful 1m and 9f winner Reine d'Beaute (by Caerleon) and half-sister to several
winners, including untrustworthy but useful 6f to 1m winner Intimate Guest (by Be
My Guest): dam won 3 times at around 1m in France: 14/1, behind in maiden at
Nottingham, not knocked about: should do better in time. *Lord Huntingdon*

FEEL NO FEAR   4 b.f. Fearless Action (USA) 116 – Charm Bird 60 (Daring   –
March 116) [1996 NR 1997 7.1d³ 7.1m³ 7m a7g⁶ a7s a10g Dec 12] third foal:

FEL

half-sister to 6-y-o Sweet Magic (by Sweet Monday): dam sprinter: signs of just a little ability in maidens and handicaps. *W. R. Muir*

FELONY (IRE) 2 ch.c. (Mar 17) Pharly (FR) 130 – Scales of Justice 85 (Final Straw 127) [1997 7g Jul 23] 12,000 2-y-o: second foal: half-brother to 3-y-o Heart Full of Soul: dam untrustworthy 1m/9f winner: 33/1, in rear in maiden at Leicester. *D. J. G. Murray Smith* —

FENGARI 8 ch.g. Formidable (USA) 125 – Foreseen (Reform 132) [1996 NR 1997 8.1m a10g Aug 9] strong, lengthy gelding: first runs on flat since 3 yrs when behind in poor company in 1997. *M. Madgwick* —

FENIAN COURT (IRE) 6 b.m. John French 123 – Penny Maes (Welsh Saint 126) [1996 NR 1997 a11g a16g 12m May 31] ninth foal: half-sister to winning Irish hurdlers by Beau Charmeur and Strong Gale: dam ran once: no worthwhile form: tried blinkered: winning selling hurdler. *P. D. Evans* —

FEN WARRIOR 2 b.g. (Jan 19) Pursuit of Love 124 – Kennedys Prima 65 (Primo Dominie 121) [1997 6s⁵ Jul 2] 7,200Y: first foal: dam sprint maiden half-sister to high-class sprinter Mr Brooks: 14/1, fifth of 6 in maiden at Yarmouth, very green and jumping path soon after start. *W. J. Haggas* —

FERGHANA MA 2 br.f. (Apr 28) Mtoto 134 – Justine (GER) (Luciano) [1997 8d⁵ a8.5g Nov 29] half-sister to numerous winners, including fairly useful 1995 2-y-o sprint winner Just Ice (by Polar Falcon) and useful 1¼m winner Always On A Sunday (by Star Appeal): dam won 4 races in Germany: better effort in maidens when under 6 lengths fifth of 13 at Leicester on debut, not knocked about: will be suited by at least 1¼m. *S. C. Williams* 62

FERN'S GOVERNOR 5 b.m. Governor General 116 – Sharp Venita 84 (Sharp Edge 123) [1996 65: 10m 10d 10m⁴ 10m³ 11.6d* 12d 10m² 10m* 10.4g⁶ 12g 10f 1997 10m⁵ 10m³ 10s 10m 8d 8g⁵ 8.3m⁶ 10m³ 8.3m* 10g Sep 23] big, workmanlike mare: fair handicapper: won 16-runner event at Windsor in August: has won over 1½m, but best at 1m to 1¼m: acts on good to firm ground and dead (disappointing on soft): has found little and usually held up: sold 17,000 gns in October. *W. J. Musson* 65

FERNY HILL (IRE) 3 b.c. Danehill (USA) 126 – Miss Allowed (USA) (Alleged (USA) 138) [1996 76, a66: 6m⁴ a8.5g² 7g⁴ 1997 10m² 12.4m* 12m³ 12m* 14.1m* Sep 26] lengthy colt: progressive performer: won minor events at Newcastle in August and Kempton following month and 5-runner handicap at Redcar 4 days after latter, running on strongly to lead post and beat Wahiba Sands: will be suited by more strongly-run 1¾m, and will stay further: acts on good to firm going, yet to race on softer than good: open to further improvement at 4 yrs. *Sir Mark Prescott* 98 p

FESTIVAL FLYER 2 b.g. (Apr 27) Alhijaz 122 – Odilese 82 (Mummy's Pet 125) [1997 5m⁴ 6g 7g 8f⁴ 10m⁶ Oct 6] 13,500Y: tall, close-coupled gelding: fifth foal: half-brother to 6-y-o Tutu Sixtysix and 4-y-o Oriole: dam 6f winner: modest maiden: stays 1m: sweating and unimpressive in appearance final start. *R. Boss* 61

FEY ROUGE (IRE) 2 ch.f. (Apr 27) Fayruz 116 – Isa (Dance In Time (CAN)) [1997 5m 5.1d 6.1m Sep 23] IR 9,000Y: close-coupled filly: sister to 3 winners (including 2 sprinters) and half-sister to 3 others: dam never ran: soundly beaten in maidens and a minor event. *R. Hollinshead* —

FFESTINIOG (IRE) 2 b.f. (Feb 26) Efisio 120 – Penny Fan 58 (Nomination 125) [1997 5g 6m* 6d* 6m 7.3g* Oct 25] 24,000 2-y-o: leggy filly: first foal: dam, sprint maiden, closely related to a useful sprinter: won maiden at Folkestone and minor event at Ascot in June and listed race at Newbury in October, holding Amabel gamely by a length in last-named: will probably stay 1m: unraced on extremes of going: reportedly suffered from ringworm after fourth start: usually front runner. *P. F. I. Cole* 94

FIABA 9 b.m. Precocious 126 – Historia 71 (Northfields (USA)) [1996 44: a8g a8g⁶ a8g a8.5g a8.5g a6g* 6m a7g⁶ a8g⁶ a8g³ 1997 a6g³ a7g⁴ a8g⁶ a6g⁶ a8g Mar 14] close-coupled, sparely-made mare: poor performer: effective at 6f and has form over as far as 11.4f: acts on all-weather and firm ground: tried blinkered, visored nowadays: none too consistent. *Mrs N. Macauley* 44

FIAMETTA   3 ch.f. Primo Dominie 121 – Monaiya (Shareef Dancer (USA) 135)   92
[1996 NR 1997 6s* 6d 8v⁴ 10m Oct 31] 25,000Y: workmanlike filly: third foal:
half-sister to 2 winners, notably useful 7f (at 2 yrs) and 1¼m winner Musetta (by
Cadeaux Genereux): dam French 1m winner: won maiden at Folkestone in June:
easily best effort when fourth to Jafn in listed event at Ascot penultimate start,
keeping on: stays 1m: evidently acts well on soft/heavy going (ran poorly on good to
firm): twice slowly away. *C. E. Brittain*

FIAMMA (IRE)   2 b.f. (Mar 15) Irish River (FR) 131 – Florie (FR) (Gay Mecene   93 p
(USA) 128) [1997 7m* 7g Oct 18] big, rangy filly: has plenty of scope: sixth foal:
sister to 3-y-o Folgore and half-sister to Lancashire Oaks winner Fanjica (by Law
Society) and useful Italian performer up to 15f Almanor (by Akarad): dam placed up
to 1½m in France: won maiden at Milan in September by wide margin: still green,
got going only late on when eighth of 12 in Rockfel Stakes at Newmarket: should
stay at least 1¼m: sort to make a better 3-y-o. *J. L. Dunlop*

FIASCO   4 ch.f. Dunbeath (USA) 127 – Rainbow Trout 76 (Comedy Star (USA)   –
121) [1996 –: 10.1d⁵ 10.1g 8g 13g⁴ 1997 a11g a16g⁴ Feb 14] no worthwhile form.
M. J. Camacho

FIELD OF VISION (IRE)   7 b.g. Vision (USA) – Bold Meadows 80 (Persian   71
Bold 123) [1996 77: a7g a9.4g* a9.4g* a10g⁴ a9.4g⁶ a12g a10g⁵ 9.2d* 13s³ 10g⁴
a9.4g² a9.4g⁴ a9.4g 10f³ 12f² 13m³ 10g⁴ 1997 13.8g⁵ a8g Dec 8] neat gelding: has a
quick action: fair handicapper: consistent at 6 yrs, ran only twice in 1997: stays 1¾m:
acts on any turf/all-weather: effective blinkered or not. *Mrs A. Swinbank*

FIELDRIDGE   8 ch.g. Rousillon (USA) 133 – Final Thought (Final Straw 127)   –
[1996 77d: 10d⁴ 10.1m 10m⁶ 10g 15.9d 1997 17.2d⁵ 16g⁶ 16.1m⁴ Jun 9] tall, lengthy
gelding: formerly fairly useful: little recent form. *M. P. Muggeridge*

FIELDS OF OMAGH (USA)   2 b.g. (Mar 16) Pleasant Tap (USA) – Brave And   70 p
True (USA) (Fappiano (USA)) [1997 6g 7d⁶ Nov 7] big, good-topped gelding: has
scope: first reported foal: dam, sprint winner at 2 yrs in USA, out of half-sister to
Washington International winner Run The Gantlet: sire second in Breeders' Cup
Sprint and Classic, Grade 1 1¼m winner: better effort in large-field maidens in
autumn when about 5½ lengths sixth to High-Rise at Doncaster, staying on steadily:
should stay at least 1m: got upset stalls at Doncaster: type to improve with time.
I. A. Balding

FIERCELY GINGER   2 ch.c. (May 23) Interrex (CAN) – Broadway Stomp   –
(USA) 58 (Broadway Forli (USA)) [1997 7m 6f 7m Oct 23] fifth reported foal:
half-brother to 3-y-o Broadway Melody: dam poor maiden: no sign of ability.
E. A. Wheeler

FIERY FOOTSTEPS   5 ro.m. Chilibang 120 – Dancing Daughter 79 (Dance In   –
Time (CAN)) [1996 47d: a6g³ a6g a6g⁶ a6g a6g⁵ a5g⁶ a6g 5m 6m 8m a8g 1997 a10g
7m Mar 27] of no account nowadays. *C. L. Popham*

FIFE MAJOR (USA)   3 b.c. Gone West (USA) – Fife (IRE) 95 (Lomond (USA)   64
128) [1996 –p: 7d 1997 7g⁶ 8.3s a7g³ a9.4g 10.1g² 10g⁴ 10m 11.9f Oct 1] tall, good
sort: modest performer: stumbled and unseated rider fourth start: should be better at
1½m than shorter: acts on fibresand and good to firm going: sold approx. £13,000 in
Dubai in November. *B. W. Hills*

FIFTH EMERALD   2 b.f. (Mar 20) Formidable (USA) 125 – Glossary (Refer-   –
ence Point 139) [1997 6d a7g Dec 10] sturdy filly: first foal: dam unraced close
relative to smart middle-distance filly Valley of Gold: behind in maidens at Doncaster and Lingfield. *C. F. Wall*

FIGAWIN   2 b.g. (Feb 1) Rudimentary (USA) 118 – Dear Person (Rainbow Quest   54 d
(USA) 134) [1997 5.3m⁵ 6g⁴ a6g* 6g⁴ 7s⁴ 7s⁵ 5m³ 6g⁴ a8g a6g⁵ a6g⁴ Dec 12]   a43
16,000Y: second foal: dam twice-raced half-sister to Galtres Stakes winner Startino:
poor performer: won seller at Southwell in June: left G. Lewis after seventh start:
stays 6f: has hung: blinkered final start. *S. Dow*

FIGHTING TIMES   5 b.g. Good Times (ITY) – Duellist (Town Crier 119) [1996   57
70d: 10g⁴ 10g² 12m⁴ 12s⁵ 12m 12g 10m 10g 13.9g 1997 12m 12m⁶ 11.1d⁶ a11g²
10g* 10.8g* 10.1g⁴ 12s⁶ Nov 6] workmanlike gelding: modest handicapper: won at

Nottingham (seller) in September and Warwick in October: stays 1½m: acts on good to firm ground and fibresand, possibly not soft: visored last 5 starts. *C. A. Smith*

FIGLIA 3 b.f. Sizzling Melody 117 – Fiorini 54 (Formidable (USA) 125) [1996   57
62: 5f 5m⁵ 6g⁶ 6m 5d² a5g 1997 a6g² a5g* a5g a6g a6g Nov 24] strong, lengthy filly: modest performer: won seller at Wolverhampton in January: off course 8 months subsequently, and no form on return: best efforts at 5f: acts on dead going and fibresand: usually blinkered/visored: has had tongue tied. *J. L. Harris*

FIJI 3 b.f. Rainbow Quest (USA) 134 – Island Jamboree (USA) (Explodent (USA))   103 p
[1996 92p: 8.1m* 1997 10.2m* 9f² Dec 27] well-bred filly: won both her starts in Britain for H. Cecil, maiden at Sandown at 2 yrs and (having had reappearance delayed by lung infection) steadily-run listed event at Chepstow in July, latter by short head from Bint Baladee: beaten a nose in allowance race at Santa Anita: will stay beyond 1¼m: potentially smart. *N. Drysdale, USA*

FILEY BRIGG 2 b.f. (Feb 25) Weldnaas (USA) 112 – Dusty's Darling (Doyoun   80 +
124) [1997 5m 5d³ 5d³ 5d* 5g² 5.1d⁶ 5g⁴ 5m* 5m 6d³ 7g⁶ 6g 8g Sep 28] 1,000Y: sparely-made filly: first foal: dam no sign of ability: fairly useful performer on balance: won minor event at Hamilton in April and Hilary Needler Trophy at Beverley in June: highly tried afterwards, and appeared to excel when third in Princess Margaret Stakes at Ascot (could be rated 96) in July, but failed to confirm form, in Fillies' Mile at Ascot final start: should stay beyond 6f: has won on good to firm ground, seemingly best effort on dead: has run well when sweating. *W. T. Kemp*

FILFILAH 2 ch.f. (Mar 12) Cadeaux Genereux 131 – El Rabab (USA) 70 (Rob-   82
erto (USA) 131) [1997 6m² 6g* 6d⁵ 6.5m Sep 10] good-topped filly: good mover: second foal: half-sister to 3-y-o Marathon Maid: dam, 2-y-o 1m winner who stayed 11.6f, out of Breeders' Cup Juvenile Fillies winner Brave Raj: fairly useful form: won maiden at Goodwood in June: fair fifth in Princess Margaret Stakes at Ascot in July, but never going clear final start, 6 weeks later: should stay 1m. *P. T. Walwyn*

FILGRAVE (IRE) 2 b.c. (Mar 19) Petardia 113 – Party Guest (What A Guest   49
119) [1997 6.1g 5g 5m 7g³ 6.9m³ 7.5f 7m⁴ 7d a7g³ Oct 20] 16,000 2-y-o: leggy,   a43
close-coupled colt: first foal: dam, Irish middle-distance maiden, successful over hurdles: poor maiden: should stay beyond 7f: acts on fibresand and good to firm ground: probably effective visored or not. *C. A. Dwyer*

FILIAL (IRE) 4 b.g. Danehill (USA) 126 – Sephira (Luthier 126) [1996 84, a95:   65
8.1m³ 10m* 10m 12m 11.8f⁵ a10s⁶ a12g* 1997 12m 10.2m 12g 10s 8d 10m² 12m⁵   a82
a12g* a12g² a12g Nov 29] smallish gelding: fairly useful on the all-weather, fair on turf: won claimer at Wolverhampton (first start after leaving B. Meehan) in November: stays 1½m: acts on good to firm ground and the all-weather: blinkered (well beaten) once. *J. Pearce*

FILMORE WEST 4 b.g. In The Wings 128 – Sistabelle (Bellypha 130) [1996   –
89p: 10.4g² 10m* 1997 11.9s 12g Oct 25] smallish, good-topped gelding: fairly useful winner for P. Cole at 3 yrs: sold only 5,000 gns before reappearance: well held both outings at 4 yrs (subsequently gelded): should be suited by 1½m. *D. W. P. Arbuthnot*

FINAL CLAIM 2 b.g. (Apr 29) Absalom 128 – For Gold (Tina's Pet 121) [1997   51
6m² 6g Jun 17] 4,400Y: first foal: dam well beaten both starts: second in seller at Catterick in May: disappointing only subsequent start, then gelded. *J. G. FitzGerald*

FINAL GLORY 3 ch.f. Midyan (USA) 124 – Lady Habitat (Habitat 134) [1996   –
NR 1997 a8g⁶ Dec 2] half-sister to several winners, including useful Italian 9f winner Big Reef (by Mill Reef) and fairly useful middle-distance stayer The Gaelcharn (by Prince Bee): dam 5f (at 2 yrs) to 7.5f winner in Italy: always in rear after slow start when sixth of 8 in maiden at Lingfield. *Lord Huntingdon*

FINAL SETTLEMENT (IRE) 2 b.g. (May 12) Soviet Lad (USA) 94 – Tender   –
Time (Tender King 123) [1997 6m 8d 7g Oct 7] 14,000Y: angular gelding: good mover: fourth foal: half-brother to fairly useful 1994 2-y-o 6f winner Regal Fanfare (by Taufan): dam ran twice in Ireland: well held in maidens. *J. R. Jenkins*

FINAL STAB (IRE) 4 b.g. Kris 135 – Premier Rose 117 (Sharp Edge 123) [1996   79
–: 8m⁵ 8m 1997 8f 8g** 8.1g 7f 8d Oct 28] rangy, angular gelding: shows knee action: reportedly had stress fracture of hind leg in 1996: lightly raced since, easily best

effort when winning handicap at Bath in August: bred to stay beyond 1m: sold only 1,500 gns in October, and won selling hurdle in November for C. Dwyer. *P. W. Harris*

FINAL STAGE (IRE)   3 ch.g. Shalford (IRE) 124§ – Alpine Symphony (Northern Dancer) [1996 NR 1997 10g 10s⁴ 14d⁴ Jul 4] 28,000F, IR 43,000Y: workmanlike gelding: seventh foal: half-brother to 2 winners by High Estate, notably smart 1½m colt High Baroque: dam unraced half-sister to smart miler Captain James: fair form in maidens: shapes as if will stay well. *P. W. Chapple-Hyam*   67

FINAL TANGO   2 b.f. (Feb 20) Danehill (USA) 126 – Sombre Lady (Sharpen Up 127) [1997 6.1m² 6m² 7g* Oct 18] 30,000Y: second foal: dam French winner at around 9f: fairly useful form: runner-up in maidens at Nottingham and Redcar before justifying favouritism in similar event at latter course by a neck from Mondschein (pair clear): should stay at least 1m. *J. H. M. Gosden*   87

FINAL TRIAL (IRE)   3 b.c. Last Tycoon 131 – Perfect Alibi (Law Society (USA) 130) [1996 64: 7f⁴ 7d 1997 8m³ Mar 31] best effort in maidens when staying-on third at Newcastle, only start of 1997: will be suited by further than 1m. *G. Wragg*   78

FINAL WARNING   3 b.g. Warning 136 – Lovely Lagoon 68 (Mill Reef (USA) 141) [1996 NR 1997 8.2m⁶ 9m 8f 8.3m Aug 11] 9,600F: close-coupled gelding: fourth foal: half-brother to Lovely Prospect (by Lycius), 7f winner at 2 yrs, and very tough and prolific winner Vindaloo (stays 1¾m, by Indian Ridge): dam twice-raced 11f winner: signs of just a little ability in maidens: sold 600 gns in October. *J. E. Banks*   –

FINARTS BAY   3 b.f. Aragon 118 – Salinas 65 (Bay Express 132) [1996 59p: 6m 1997 7m⁴ 8f³ 7s 7f a7g⁵ a5g Nov 18] close-coupled filly: modest form when fourth at Kempton on reappearance (September): well beaten afterwards: tried blinkered. *Mrs J. Cecil*   54 d

FINE QUILL   3 ch.f. Unfuwain (USA) 131 – Quillotern (USA) (Arctic Tern (USA) 126) [1996 NR 1997 12m Jul 25] fourth foal: half-sister to 3 winners, including smart 4-y-o Harbour Dues: dam half-sister to Leap Lively, dam of Forest Flower: last of 11 in maiden at Newmarket. *J. H. M. Gosden*   –

FINESTATETOBEIN   4 ch.f. Northern State (USA) 91 – Haywain 58 (Thatching 131) [1996 –: 7s 12m 12g 1997 16s 12g 12m 14g⁵ a14g 14.1m⁴ 15.8g³ 14.1g⁴ 15.8m⁵ 15.8g 13.8s⁵ Oct 17] poor staying maiden handicapper: acts on good to firm and soft ground: visored 3 times. *F. Watson*   34

FINE TIMES   3 b.c. Timeless Times (USA) 99 – Marfen (Lochnager 132) [1996 68?: 5m⁶ 5m⁵ 5.9g⁶ 5.7m⁴ 5f 5s² 5.2g 5g 1997 a6g 5s 6m² a6g⁶ 6g 5.9m⁴ 6g 6d⁵ 6m 9s 8g Oct 22] compact colt: modest maiden handicapper at best: stays 6f: acts on good to firm and soft ground, well held on all-weather: usually visored: inconsistent. *C. W. Fairhurst*   58 d

FINISTERRE (IRE)   4 b.g. Salt Dome (USA) – Inisfail (Persian Bold 123) [1996 65, a61: 5s 7m⁶ 5s³ 5m³ 5m 6g* 6m 7m² 7m⁴ 6m² 6g⁵ 7g⁶ a6g a8.5s² 1997 6m³ 7s a7g Jun 6] leggy gelding: modest performer: third in seller on reappearance, only form at 4 yrs: stays 8.5f: acts on good to firm ground and fibresand, seemingly not soft: blinkered (well held) once as 2-y-o: usually held up. *J. J. O'Neill*   51 a–

FINSBURY FLYER (IRE)   4 ch.g. Al Hareb (USA) 123 – Jazirah (Main Reef 126) [1996 69: 7.1g* 7m⁴ 8.1m³ 10.2f³ 1997 10g 8.3s⁶ 8.3s* 8.1m⁵ 7.1m⁵ 8.3s⁶ 8.1m 8g Sep 8] workmanlike gelding: modest performer: won claimer at Windsor in May: below form last 4 starts: needs good test at 1m, stays 1¼m: probably acts on any going. *R. J. Hodges*   59 d

FIONN DE COOL (IRE)   6 b.g. Mazaad 106 – Pink Fondant (Northfields (USA)) [1996 72: 8m 7m 8m 8m⁴ 8m³ 8.1d⁵ 9g 8d² 8d³ 8g⁴ 1997 8s 8f⁶ 7d⁵ 8.1d⁶ 8m 8.5g* 8d Sep 12] small, sturdy gelding: poor mover: fair handicapper: dictated pace when winning (for only second time) at Epsom in August: stays 8.5f: acts on firm and dead ground. *R. Akehurst*   69

FIRE GODDESS   2 ch.f. (Apr 28) Magic Ring (IRE) 115 – Into The Fire 74 (Dominion 123) [1997 6m⁴ 5m⁴ 6f³ 6d³ 6m 6m⁶ 6.5m 6.9d³ 7.3g Oct 25] 2,600Y: leggy filly: half-sister to several winners, including sprinter Down The Middle (by   62

Swing Easy) and miler Cool Fire (by Colmore Row): dam, stayed 1¼m, winner in Guernsey: modest maiden: should stay 1m: acts on good to soft ground, probably on firm. *J. S. Moore*

FIRST BITE (IRE) 5 b.g. Be My Native (USA) 122 – Saga's Humour 61 – (Bustino 136) [1996 NR 1997 10v⁶ 8m 13.8g Aug 5] fair performer at 3 yrs: tailed off in 1997. *M. D. Hammond*

FIRST CHANCE (IRE) 3 b.f. Lahib (USA) 129 – Honagh Lee (Main Reef 126) 71 [1996 56p: 6g 6g⁴ 1997 a7g* a6g⁵ 8.2m³ 8f² 8.5m 8m 8f³ 8.3m⁴ 9g² 8.1m⁶ 8m⁵ 8d a8.5f³ Dec 20] good-topped filly: fair performer: won maiden at Lingfield in February: generally creditable efforts in handicaps afterwards: left D. Elsworth before final start: stays 9f: acts on equitrack and firm ground. *D. Vienna, USA*

FIRST CONSUL (USA) 2 ch.c. (Mar 6) Rubiano (USA) – Sunflower Fields 80 p (USA) (Fit To Fight (USA)) [1997 7g⁴ Aug 1] $170,000Y: useful-looking colt: second foal: dam, won up to 9f in USA, out of smart 2-y-o sprinter Tender Camilla: sire (by Fappiano) champion US sprinter: easy to back, shaped well under tender handling when just over 5 lengths fourth of 15 to Elshamms in maiden at Newmarket: should improve. *M. R. Stoute*

FIRST DANCE 2 b.f. (Mar 4) Primo Dominie 121 – Soviet Swan (USA) 65 (Nureyev (USA) 131) [1997 5m⁴ 6g⁴ 6m² 6d⁴ 5.2m 6g* Aug 22] leggy filly: first foal: dam unraced from family of high-class winners up to 1½m, On The Sly and Northern Trick: fair performer: in frame in maidens before winning seller at Goodwood (claimed to join Dr J. Scargill): stays 6f: acts on good to firm and dead ground. *R. Hannon*

FIRST FRAME 2 b.c. (Feb 9) Mukaddamah (USA) 125 – Point of Law (Law – Society (USA) 131) [1997 6s⁵ Jun 28] 13,500 2-y-o: first foal: dam unraced daughter of half-sister to Tirol: signs of a little ability in maiden at Newcastle. *J. L. Eyre*

FIRST GOLD 8 gr.g. Absalom 128 – Cindys Gold 69 (Sonnen Gold 121) [1996 46 57d, a62d: a8g⁴ a7g* a7g⁴ a8g a7g⁴ a8g³ 7d⁶ 7d⁵ 6.9m* 7m⁵ 8m a8g a8g 7f 8.2g 7g a7g² a8g⁵ 1997 a8g⁶ a7g⁵ a8g² 7m* a7g 6.9d³ 7g⁶ 8g⁶ 6.9m a7g 7.5v 8.2s a8g a8g Dec 18] lengthy gelding: carries condition: poor performer: won seller at Leicester in March: showed nil last 5 starts: effective at 6f to 1m: acts on fibresand and on any turf ground: tried blinkered/ visored: sometimes reluctant at stalls. *J. Wharton*

FIRST IDEA 2 b.f. (Apr 15) Primo Dominie 121 – Good Thinking (USA) (Raja 32 Baba (USA)) [1997 6m 6m⁵ 6m Aug 23] 5,000Y: half-sister to 7f and 1½m winner Thinking Twice (by Kris) and winners in USA by Fappiano and Northern Baby: dam Irish 2-y-o 7f winner: little form in sellers. *S. Dow*

FIRST ISLAND (IRE) 5 ch.h. Dominion 123 – Caymana (FR) (Bellypha 128 130) [1996 127: 8d* 9m³ 8.1g⁵ 7.9m* 10f* 8m* 10.4m² 8m³ 10g⁵ 9m* 1997 8.1g² 8d* May 16]

First Island's blossoming career ended prematurely after two runs as a five-year-old, which gave the clearest indication that he was at least as good as ever. He had progressed into a high-class and notably tough performer the previous year, ten starts yielding wins in the Sussex Stakes at Goodwood and the Hong Kong International Cup at Sha Tin, and good efforts in defeat in the Juddmonte International (second to Halling) and Queen Elizabeth II Stakes (third behind Mark of Esteem and Bosra Sham). With that record it was no surprise to see First Island at odds on for his reappearance in the Sandown Mile, despite looking as if the outing would bring him on. First Island just failed to concede 6 lb to Wixim, who had finished runner-up in the Earl of Sefton Stakes a fortnight earlier.

First Island clearly benefited from his reappearance and looked in great shape before the Juddmonte Lockinge Stakes at Newbury three weeks later. The late withdrawal of the two Godolphin runners, Alhaarth and Allied Forces, reduced the field to ten in what still looked a good renewal. French-trained Spinning World, winner of the Irish Two Thousand Guineas and Prix Jacques le Marois in 1996, headed the betting from First Island, the Earl of Sefton winner Ali-Royal and Even Top (having his first race over a mile since finish-

Juddmonte Lockinge Stakes, Newbury—
a fine display from First Island to beat Ali-Royal, Even Top and Spinning World (striped sleeves);
the rest of the season was the poorer for his absence

ing second in the 1996 Two Thousand Guineas). The race wasn't entirely satis-factory—a steady early pace favoured those who lay handy—but First Island and Ali-Royal, both racing prominently down the centre away from the main group, dominated the finish. First Island held the persistent Ali-Royal by one and a half lengths, with five lengths back to third-placed Even Top, and a further head to the waited-with Spinning World. It was a high-class perform-ance by First Island (and those behind by no means let the form down thereafter), one that suggested he would continue to give a good account in the top open-aged championship events at a mile to a mile and a quarter. Inter-estingly connections had reportedly planned to run him over a mile and a half at some stage.

		Derring-Do	Darius
	Dominion	(br 1961)	Sipsey Bridge
	(b 1972)	Picture Palace	Princely Gift
First Island (IRE)		(b 1961)	Palais Glide
(ch.c. 1992)		Bellypha	Lyphard
	Caymana (FR)	(gr 1976)	Belga
	(gr or ro 1985)	Antrona	Royal Palace
		(gr 1973)	Ileana

Unfortunately, First Island had to be put down after complications set in following an operation on a fracture to his off-fore cannon bone sustained on the Newmarket gallops in early-June, a reminder of how difficult it can be to save the life of even a highly-valuable horse, for whom presumably little expense would have been spared. A full account of First Island's pedigree can be found in *Racehorses of 1996*. He was the best offspring of his deceased sire who is not noted as an influence for stamina. First Island's dam Caymana was, however, successful at up to a mile and a half and it would certainly have been worth trying First Island over that trip, especially given the tractability he showed in his races. Despite the fact that he tended to wander off a true line in front, First Island was thoroughly genuine and reliable. He acted on firm and dead going (he never encountered softer), and had a good turn of foot.
G. Wragg

FIRST MAITE   4 b.g. Komaite (USA) – Marina Plata (Julio Mariner 127) [1996   84
83: a6g2 a6g5 a6g* a6g* a7g6 7s2 5d2 6g 6d5 6m4 7.1d 1997 a7g 5g5 a5g* 6m6 5d*
5d4 6m5 a6f6 5m a7g a6g6 6s2 5d Oct 20] tall, lengthy gelding: has a round action:
fairly useful performer: won claimer at Wolverhampton and handicap at Beverley
in the spring: particularly good effort when second of 22 in handicap at Haydock
penultimate start: best form at 5f (given test)/6f: acts on good to firm and soft ground
and on fibresand: usually blinkered: reliable. *S. R. Bowring*

FIRST MAN   3 b.g. Man Among Men (IRE) – Sharp Thistle 87 (Sharpo 132)   –
[1996 –: a7g a8g a6g 1997 10.2m 14.1d 17.2f 7.1m Jun 13] of little account.
B. J. Llewellyn

FIRST MASTER   2 ch.c. (Apr 22) Primo Dominie 121 – Bodham 88 (Bustino   68
136) [1997 7g 8m6 6.9d* Oct 21] 16,000Y: unfurnished colt: closely related to 5-y-o
Woodrising (modest 1¼m winner at 3 yrs) and half-brother to several winners,
including fairly useful 1½m winner Arabian Bold (by Persian Bold): dam, 1½m and
13.3f winner, out of half-sister to Blakeney and Morston: fair form: won maiden at
Folkestone by 1¾ lengths from Three Angels: should stay beyond 1m: bandaged in
front. *Miss Gay Kelleway*

FIRST OPTION   7 ch.g. Primo Dominie 121 – Merrywren (Julio Mariner 127)   –
[1996 –: a6g a5g a6g 5g 5f 5m 5.9f6 5f 5m 6g 5m 5m 5g 5.1g 1997 8m 6g Aug 2]
close-coupled gelding: tubed: little worthwhile form since 1994. *R. Bastiman*

FIRST PRINCIPLE   3 b.c. Rudimentary (USA) 118 – Revoke (USA) 70   91
(Riverman (USA) 131) [1996 NR 1997 a8f6 a8f a7f 6g2 5.7g* 5m5 a7f* a7f3 a8f4
Dec 19] 21,000Y: second foal: dam, maiden (effective at 7f/1m), half-sister to very
smart French/US 1½m performer Contested Bid: fairly useful performer: well beaten
in 3 starts in Dubai early in year: won maiden at Bath in September: left C. Wall after
next start and successful in handicap on return to Dubai: suited by 7f: acts on good to
firm ground and sand. *C. Rached, UAE*

FIRST VILLAGE (IRE)   2 b.f. (Apr 10) Danehill (USA) 126 – L-Way First   83
(IRE) (Vision (USA)) [1997 6m3 5v 5.2m 5.1m* 5.1d4 5m5 6s Oct 14] IR 19,000Y:
tall, useful-looking filly: first foal: dam Irish maiden who stayed 2m: fairly useful
performer: won maiden at Bath in August: ran creditably next 2 starts, tailed off final
one: should stay 6f: acts on good to firm and dead ground, no form on softer: well
held in blinkers once: has been bandaged behind. *J. Berry*

FISIOSTAR   4 b.g. Efisio 120 – Sweet Colleen 42 (Connaught 130) [1996 39: 8g   46 §
7.1f4 8.5m 7m4 7m3 7.1m3 7.1m 1997 6.9g 7f5 8g 6m 8g 5.9m3 7.1g4 6m2 6m 6m2
6m 7.1g Sep 15] workmanlike gelding: poor maiden: seems a sprinter: acts on firm
ground: visored/visored: unreliable. *M. Dods*

FIT FOR THE JOB (IRE)   3 ch.g. Mac's Imp (USA) 116 – Jolly Dale (IRE)   –
(Huntingdale 132) [1996 ?, a67: a5g5 5m4 a5g3 a5g a5g6 a5g3 a5g3 a6g* 1997 a6g4   a55 d
a5g4 a6g6 a6g4 a6g 6f 6.1g6 5.1g 5.1f 5.9m a6g a5g 6m Sep 22] unfurnished gelding:
modest form first 4 starts in 1997, little afterwards: stays 6f: acts on the all-weather:
tried blinkered. *T. Wall*

FIVE FAIRIES   2 ch.f. (Apr 29) Sabrehill (USA) 120 – Fivefive (IRE) 61 (Fairy   –
King (USA)) [1997 7g 7m 9m 7d a7g Oct 20] workmanlike filly: first foal: dam 5f (at
2 yrs) and 1m winner: little sign of ability: sold, to go to Trinidad. *N. A. Callaghan*

FIVE LIVE   3 b.f. Pharly (FR) 130 – Manageress 74 (Mandamus 120) [1996 57:   –
5f4 5g5 5m2 1997 9m Oct 7] workmanlike filly: tailed off in handicap only outing as
3-y-o: should be suited by further than 5f: sold 750 gns in October. *M. D. Hammond*

FIVEO'CLOCK SHADOW (IRE)   2 b. or br.g. (Mar 14) Magical Strike   74
(USA) 114 – U-Can Do It (Ballad Rock 122) [1997 5.3f3 5.3m2 6g5 7s 6s* 6g4 6f 6g
Aug 2] 6,400Y: good-topped gelding: first reported foal: dam unraced from family of
Prix Robert Papin winner Wakamba: fair performer on balance: won seller at Yarmouth in July: patchy form afterwards, sometimes highly tried: stays 6f: acts on firm
and soft ground: blinkered final start (well beaten): has found little: gelded and sent
to Macau. *B. J. Meehan*

FIVE-O-FIFTY   3 b. or br.g. Anshan 119 – Wyns Vision (Vision (USA)) [1996   –
51: 5.1m2 5s 6.1m 5g 1997 5m 8g 6m Oct 5] leggy, sparely-made gelding: has a
round action: no form as 3-y-o, leaving J. L. Eyre before final outing. *J. J. Birkett*

FIVE OF SPADES (IRE) 2 b.g. (Feb 21) Roi Danzig (USA) – Hellicroft (High 81
Line 125) [1997 5m 5m⁶ 5s² 6m 6g 6d* 6g 6.1d* 7s Nov 8] IR 6,000Y: sturdy
gelding: second foal: dam unraced: fairly useful performer: won nurseries at Pontefract in September and Nottingham in November, making all on latter course (well
beaten 5 days later): may prove best at 6f: easily best efforts on dead/soft going.
R. A. Fahey

FIZZED 2 ch.f. (Mar 13) Efisio 120 – Clicquot 101 (Bold Lad (IRE) 133) [1997 83
5g⁴ 5d* 6g Sep 19] 30,000Y: closely related to smart sprinter Premiere Cuvee (by
Formidable) and half-sister to winners abroad by Reprimand and Siberian Express:
dam 5f sprinter: won maiden at Beverley in August, wandering and rider (J. Weaver)
fined for using whip too forcefully: not discredited, short of room in rear halfway, in
listed race at Ayr following month: probably stays 6f: may still do better. *M. Johnston*

FIZZY BOY (IRE) 4 b.g. Contract Law (USA) 108 – Generation Gap (Young –
Generation 129) [1996 –: 10d 11.1g⁵ 1997 7d⁶ 14d 10.9g Jul 14] of little account.
P. Monteith

FLAG FEN (USA) 6 b. or br.g. Riverman (USA) 131 – Damascus Flag (USA) 61
(Damascus (USA)) [1996 63: 9.2d³ 9.9m 10g 9m⁴ 8f 7.3s 8m 6d⁵ 7f⁴ 8f² 7.6m² 8.1m
10m 8.1d 1997 a8g² a8g⁵ 10.1g 8d* 8m 8g⁶ Jul 7] rangy gelding: modest performer:
won seller at Ripon in May: has form at 11f, best recent efforts around 1m: acts on
firm and dead ground and fibresand: blinkered (inadequate trip) eighth 5-y-o outing:
often apprentice ridden: tends to hang right: inconsistent. *J. Parkes*

FLAGSHIP 3 ch.f. Rainbow Quest (USA) 134 – Bireme 127 (Grundy 137) [1996 84
77: 8d² 8.1s⁵ 1997 10m 10m* 11.9s⁴ Oct 8] small filly: off course 4 months, improved to win maiden at Sandown in September, settling better: not discredited in
minor event at York following month: probably stays 1½m. *Major W. R. Hern*

FLAGSTAFF (USA) 4 b.g. Personal Flag (USA) – Shuffle Up (USA) (Raja 39
Baba (USA)) [1996 55, a49: a6g⁴ a6g² 6f² 7f² 6f⁵ 7f⁵ 7f a7s a10g 1997 a9.4f⁶ a10g
a8.5g² a9.4g⁴ 8f 8d⁵ 8.2g⁵ 8g⁵ 10d⁴ 9.7s 8.1m 8m Aug 9] close-coupled gelding: poor
maiden: stays 1¼m, at least in steadily-run race: acts on fibresand, and firm and dead
ground: sometimes visored: has found little. *K. R. Burke*

FLAMBOYANCE (USA) 3 b.f. Zilzal (USA) 137 – Bridal Wreath (USA) (Stop 94
The Music (USA)) [1996 NR 1997 a7g* 8m² 10g⁶ 8d 8d³ 7m² 7f⁴ 7m⁶ Sep 27]
close-coupled filly: second foal: dam sprint winner at 2 yrs, half-sister to Grade 1 9f
winner Reluctant Guest: retained by trainer 7,000 gns Newmarket Autumn (1996)
Sales when catalogued as Floral Royal (USA): fairly useful performer: won maiden
at Wolverhampton in January: best efforts in frame in handicap at Newmarket and
listed race at Doncaster (beaten less than length by Aunty Jane) sixth and seventh
starts: probably best at 7f/1m: acts on firm going: tongue tied last 3 starts: sent to
USA. *J. R. Fanshawe*

FLAMBOYANT BELLE 2 b.f. (Feb 10) Lahib (USA) 129 – Mainmast 63 –
(Bustino 136) [1997 7g Oct 18] 13,000Y: sixth foal: half-sister to 7f (at 2 yrs) to 13f
winner Instantaneous (by Rock City) and fairly useful 1½m winner Progression (by
Reprimand): dam twice-raced granddaughter of smart sprinter Fluke: 20/1, behind in
Redcar maiden, slowly away and not knocked about. *Mrs A. J. Perrett*

FLAME TOWER (IRE) 2 ch.c. (Apr 6) Archway (IRE) 115 – Guantanamera 60
(USA) (El Gran Senor (USA) 136) [1997 5.5s 5.1m⁴ 5.1g a6g² 7m⁴ 7d 6d³ Oct 21]
10,500Y: strong, angular colt: first foal: dam unraced daughter of useful (up to 1½m)
Slow March: modest maiden: should stay beyond 6f: acts on fibresand. *R. Hannon*

FLAMING EMBER (IRE) 2 b.c. (Mar 15) Fayruz 116 – Embustera 73 88
(Sparkler 130) [1997 5f³ 5m* 6f² 6m³ 6m⁵ 6d 6m⁴ Oct 1] 14,000Y: sturdy colt:
half-brother to 2 winners, including useful but ungenuine 7f (at 2 yrs) and 1½m
winner Gorgeous Strike (by Hello Gorgeous): dam 10.4f winner: fairly useful
performer: won minor event at Warwick in May: good third in listed race at Epsom
(2½ lengths behind Dance Trick), and ran creditably next 2 starts: stays 6f: acts on
firm ground, probably on dead: below form in blinkers final outing: sold 21,000 gns,
and sent to Sweden. *B. J. Meehan*

FLASH D'OR (IRE) 2 b.f. (Feb 1) Shalford (IRE) 124§ – Gulf Craft (IRE) 48 §
(Petorius 117) [1997 5g* 5g⁶ 6g 6m 7g 5m a5g Jun 30] 3,500Y: good-topped filly:

third reported foal: dam unraced half-sister to smart sprinter Ginny Binny: looked tempermental after winning seller at Catterick in April: blinkered fifth start: sent to Holland. *M. W. Easterby*

FLASHFEET 7 b.g. Rousillon (USA) 133 – Miellita 98 (King Emperor (USA)) – [1996 –: a8g⁶ a7g a8.5g⁵ a7g⁶ 1997 7m May 31] little worthwhile form for some time. *K. Bishop*

FLASH IN THE PAN (IRE) 4 ch.f. Bluebird (USA) 125 – Tomona (Linacre – 133) [1996 49: 8.3s³ 9.2s⁴ a9.4g⁶ a14.8g⁶ 12d 1997 10.3m Mar 20] angular filly: poor maiden: well beaten only outing on flat as 4-y-o (had won over hurdles 6 days before). *J. S. Moore*

FLASH OF REALM (FR) 11 b.g. Super Moment (USA) – Light of Realm 116 – (Realm 129) [1996 NR 1997 16g 12.1m Jul 11] probably no longer of any account. *P. Monteith*

FLASHTALKIN' FLOOD 3 ch.g. Then Again 126 – Linguistic 95 (Porto 72 Bello 118) [1996 NR 1997 a10g⁶ 12g 8m 8f³ 10f⁵ 8.2d* 10g 8.2s a9.4g Dec 6] 7,000Y: tall gelding: half-brother to several winners, including fair stayers Castle Douglas (by Amboise) and Relatively Easy (by Relkino): dam won twice over 5f at 2 yrs: easily best effort when winning seller at Nottingham in June despite tending to wander: off course 3 months and well beaten in handicaps afterwards: should stay beyond 1m: acts on firm and dead going. *C. A. Dwyer*

FLAWLESS 2 b.f. (Feb 12) Warning 136 – Made of Pearl (USA) 107 (Nureyev 102 (USA) 131) [1997 7g* 8f² 7m² 7g⁴ Oct 18] lengthy, good-topped filly: has scope: half-sister to fairly useful 1¼m winner Seek The Pearl (by Rainbow Quest) and 1½m winner Cultured (by Saint Cyrien): dam French 7f and 1m winner: useful performer: won maiden at Salisbury in September: best effort when beaten ½ length by Midnight Line in May Hill Stakes at Doncaster, and not discredited in listed event and Rockfel Stakes at Newmarket last 2 starts (beaten over 2 lengths by Name of Love both times): should prove suited by at least 1¼m: has carried head awkwardly: sweated final outing. *Sir Mark Prescott*

FLAXEN PRIDE (IRE) 2 ch.f. (Apr 11) Pips Pride 117 – Fair Chance (Young 62 p Emperor 133) [1997 7m² 7g 7m Nov 4] IR 6,000Y: half-sister to several winners, including fairly useful 1990 2-y-o 5f winner Gold Futures (by Fayruz): dam Irish 2-y-o 5f and 7f winner: close second in maiden at Newcastle in October: never placed to challenge either subsequent start: will probably prove best up to 1m: should do better at 3 yrs. *Mrs M. Reveley*

FLEA IN YOUR EAR 2 b.f. (Apr 2) Young Senor (USA) 113 – Lowrianna – (IRE) 50 (Cyrano de Bergerac 120) [1997 5g Apr 19] small filly: first foal: dam 2-y-o 5f winner out of half-sister to Cheveley Park winner Pass The Peace: behind in claimer at Thirsk. *Martyn Meade*

FLEET CADET 6 ch.h. Bairn (USA) 126 – Pirogue 99 (Reliance II 137) [1996 – NR 1997 a8.5g Jan 8] fair hurdler, winner 6 times in 1997: first run on flat since mid-1995 when well held in Wolverhampton seller. *M. C. Pipe*

FLEETING FOOTSTEPS 5 b.h. Komaite (USA) – Hyperion Palace (Dragon- – ara Palace (USA) 115) [1996 –: 7g 6f 8.2m 1997 5.1g a6g May 19] no form. *D. Shaw*

FLEET LADY (IRE) 2 b.f. (Apr 21) Don't Forget Me 127 – Yavarro 44 (Raga – Navarro (ITY) 119) [1997 5m⁵ 5g 5m 6f 8.2m 8.2s Oct 15] IR 4,500Y: workmanlike filly: sixth foal: half-sister to 3-y-o Pelham: dam poor daughter of Cheshire Oaks winner Yelda: little sign of ability. *Mrs P. N. Dutfield*

FLEET RIVER (USA) 3 b.f. Riverman (USA) 131 – Nimble Feet (USA) 82 – (Danzig (USA)) [1996 93p: 7g* 1997 8.5g Sep 5] well-made filly: won maiden at Goodwood on only 2-y-o start: well held in Epsom listed event only outing in 1997: should have stayed at least 1m: stud. *H. R. A. Cecil*

FLEETWOOD (IRE) 2 ch.c. (Feb 10) Groom Dancer (USA) 128 – Up 107 P Anchor (IRE) 114 (Slip Anchor 136) [1997 7.1m* Sep 21]

Predicting great things for once-raced winners of maidens is one of the quickest routes to the poorhouse. But there are exceptions to the rule and Fleetwood could well be one of them. Fleetwood's claims do not rest solely on the good impression created by his victory. It is backed up by form that is decidedly useful, independently confirmed by analysis of the time of the performance. What's more, Fleetwood is a nicely-bred colt, in the care of an outstanding trainer and highly likely to go on. He's as short as 20/1 for the Derby already.

The race chosen for Fleetwood's debut was the Bulls Head Maiden at Haydock in September, a seemingly run-of-the-mill affair, though the previous year's winner Poteen had gone on to finish second in the Racing Post Trophy and third in the Two Thousand Guineas. Connections were clearly not entertaining an angel unawares as Fleetwood went off at odds on in a field of nine. He wiped the floor with his rivals, setting a sound gallop and powering clear from two furlongs out to win by eight lengths despite his jockey, Kieren Fallon, dropping his hands before the finish. So fresh was Fleetwood at the line that it took Fallon nearly another six furlongs to pull him up. The opposition was not outstanding, but the runner-up Mawsoof went down by just a short head in a Nottingham maiden next time and the eight-and-a-half length third Shart was beaten only a head and a neck in a similar event at Newmarket on his only subsequent start. The timefigure for Fleetwood on going probably a bit firmer than the official good is equivalent to a rating of 98.

Fallon described Fleetwood as 'in the same mould as Daggers Drawn' (the favourite for the Guineas at the time) and there was talk of his going for the Dewhurst, Royal Lodge or Horris Hill Stakes. In the end Fleetwood didn't reappear, amid rumours that he had suffered a minor set-back. But there's no reason to hold this softly-softly approach against him in the long run, even if it may count against him should connections decide to go for the Guineas.

		Blushing Groom	Red God
	Groom Dancer (USA)	(ch 1974)	Runaway Bride
	(b 1984)	Featherhill	Lyphard
Fleetwood (IRE)		(b 1978)	Lady Berry
(ch.c. Feb 10, 1995)		Slip Anchor	Shirley Heights
	Up Anchor (IRE)	(b 1982)	Sayonara
	(b 1989)	Pageantry	Welsh Pageant
		(b 1980)	Norfolk Light

Fleetwood's sire, Groom Dancer, hasn't been an outstanding success at stud (he was exported to Japan in 1994) following a racing career in which he established himself as high-class around a mile and a quarter. But he's sired several smart or better individuals, including Pursuit of Love (high-class up to a mile), Astair (winner of the Prix Daphnis over nine furlongs), the Chester Vase winner and Derby fifth Twist And Turn and the Prix de la Salamandre winner Lord of Men. As can possibly be detected, the stamina potential of Groom Dancer's offspring isn't always easy to predict. Interestingly, Lord of Men—out of a mare by Slip Anchor's sire, Shirley Heights—came back in the latest season to show himself effective at a mile and a quarter, possibly a mile and a half, and Fleetwood is a first foal of the St Simon Stakes winner Up Anchor, a filly who gave the strong impression she'd get beyond a mile and a half.

Fleetwood has some substance to him, too, being a good-bodied colt. Exactly what the future holds for him is difficult to say, but we'll be disappointed if he doesn't win listed/pattern races, probably at nine furlongs to a mile and a half. *H. R. A. Cecil*

FLEMENSFIRTH (USA) 5 b.h. Alleged (USA) 138 – Etheldreda (USA) 64 –
(Diesis 133) [1996 122: 9.8d* 10m* 1997 a10f Apr 3] rangy horse: very smart performer, very lightly raced: won Prix Dollar at Longchamp (for second time) and Premio Roma at 4 yrs: always struggling when last of 10 finishers in Dubai World Cup on only start in 1997: retired as NH stallion to The Beeches Stud, Co Waterford, Ireland. *J. H. M. Gosden*

FLETCHER 3 b.g. Salse (USA) 128 – Ballet Classique (USA) 84 (Sadler's Wells 96 d
(USA) 132) [1996 85§: 5m* 6f 6g⁴ 7f⁴ 6d 8m² 7.9g 1997 10g 12m³ 14m³ 16.2m⁶

14.8g[5] 14m 12m[6] 14.6m 16g 7g Oct 18] useful-looking gelding: easy mover: useful performer on his day: ran well facing stiff tasks when sixth of 11 to Windsor Castle in Queen's Vase at Royal Ascot and fifth of 9 to Three Cheers in listed race at Newmarket in the summer: well below that form all 5 subsequent starts, including in visor: stays 2m: acts on firm ground: carries head awkwardly and downed tools once. *H. Morrison*

FLEUR-DE-LYS 2 ch.f. (Apr 14) King's Signet (USA) 110 – Kind of Cute 52   37 (Prince Sabo 123) [1997 5d[4] 5g 5g 6g[5] Aug 11] 5,000Y: small filly: first foal: dam poor maiden sister to Mill Reef Stakes winner Princely Hush: poor maiden. *W. J. Musson*

FLEUVE D'OR (IRE) 3 gr.f. Last Tycoon 131 – Aldern Stream 102 (Godswalk   – (USA) 130) [1996 –: 6f 6.9d a7g[6] 1997 a7g Nov 29] workmanlike filly: little form. *D. Haydn Jones*

FLIBBERTIGIBBET 2 b.f. (Mar 22) Almoojid 69 – Stella Royale (Astronef   – 116) [1997 6.1g May 26] first reported foal: dam unraced: tailed off in seller only start. *C. J. Hill*

FLICKAN 2 ch.f. (Apr 15) Superpower 113 – Spark (IRE) 79 (Flash of Steel 120)   60 [1997 a5g[5] a5g[2] 6m[5] Jun 4] 4,200Y: first foal: dam 2-y-o 6f winner, later stayed 10.4f: modest form in maidens: stays 6f: acts on fibresand: sent to Denmark. *R. Guest*

FLICKER 2 b.f. (Apr 26) Unfuwain (USA) 131 – Lovers Light (Grundy 137)   65 [1997 7g 8.2s[5] a7g Dec 12] 7,000Y: closely related to 1993 2-y-o 6f winner Glimpse (by Night Shift) and a winner abroad by Mashhor Dancer and half-sister to 3 winners, including 1½m winner Eliki (by Nishapour): dam out of Oaks third Moonlight Night: best effort in maidens when about 12 lengths fifth of 13 at Nottingham in October: bred to be suited by 1¼m+. *Lord Huntingdon*

FLIGHT 2 ch.g. (Mar 4) Night Shift (USA) – Caspian Tern (USA) 89 (Arctic Tern   76 (USA) 126) [1997 7g 7g[5] 6g[3] 6g[3] a8g[2] Dec 19] 38,000Y: good-topped, attractive gelding: first foal: dam 1¼m winner who stayed 1½m, half-sister to American Grade 1 winners Al Mamoon and La Gueriere out of half-sister to Allez France: fair maiden: sold out of L. Cumani's stable 5,000 gns after third start: 3 lengths second to Hanuman Highway at Lingfield final one: stays 1m: carries head awkwardly. *S. Dow*

FLIGHT FOR FREEDOM 2 b.f. (Feb 17) Saddlers' Hall (IRE) 126 –   60 p Anatroccolo 47 (Ile de Bourbon (USA) 133) [1997 7.9s[4] Sep 3] IR 3,400Y: sparely-made filly: first foal: dam 7f (including at 2 yrs) and 1m winner: 10/1 and green, never dangerous behind wide-margin winner Evening World in maiden at York: should do better at 1¼m+. *J. R. Fanshawe*

FLINT AND STEEL 4 b.g. Rock City 120 – Brassy Nell 72 (Dunbeath (USA)   – 127) [1996 58: 6m[4] 8d 1997 a11g Jan 3] useful-looking gelding: modest maiden at best: well beaten in seller only 4-y-o start. *Bob Jones*

FLINT KNAPPER 3 ch.c. Kris 135 – Circe's Isle (Be My Guest (USA) 126)   89 p [1996 NR 1997 8m[3] 8.3m[6] 8d* 10.1f[2] 10m* Sep 30] second foal: half-brother to smart 7f (at 2 yrs) and 1¼m winner Don Micheletto (by Machiavellian): dam unraced close relative to 4-y-o Sasuru and half-sister to smart 7f performer Sally Rous: progressive form: won maiden at Warwick in August and 14-runner apprentice handicap at Newmarket (by short head, deserving extra credit for coming from well off steady pace) in September: stays 1¼m: acts on firm and dead ground: type to make a useful handicapper in 1998. *G. Wragg*

FLIRTATION 3 b.f. Pursuit of Love 124 – Eastern Shore (Sun Prince 128) [1996   – NR 1997 7.1s[5] Mar 29] lengthy filly: half-sister to several winners, including useful 1¼m winner Ruscino (by Rousillon): dam, granddaughter of very smart sprinter Lucasland, stayed 1½m: green and in need of race, signs of a little ability in maiden at Haydock on only start. *R. Charlton*

FLIRTINA 2 b.f. (May 13) Tina's Pet 121 – Immodest Miss 73 (Daring Display   – (USA) 129) [1997 5m 5g[6] 6m[6] 7m[6] Jun 11] 3,100Y: leggy filly: sister to 1996 2-yo 5f winner Bold Brief, closely related to fairly useful 5f (at 2 yrs) and 7f winner Itsagame (by Mummy's Pet) and half-sister to 2 winners: dam won 1¼m seller: no worthwhile form, including in sellers: blinkered third start. *P. D. Evans*

FLO

FLIRTING AROUND (USA)   3 b.c. Silver Hawk (USA) 123 – Dancing Grass   94
(USA) (Northern Dancer) [1996 82+: 7d² 8f 8.2s⁴ 1997 8m⁴ 12.3s² 13.9g* 16.2m
16.1s⁶ 14m Aug 2] sturdy, good sort: has a short, quick action: fairly useful performer: won minor event at York in May: better than positions suggest in Queen's
Vase at Royal Ascot and Northumberland Plate at Newcastle next 2 starts, not getting
home either time: well held in competitive handicap at Goodwood final start: should
prove ideally suited by 1½m/1¾m: acts on good to firm (possibly not firm) and soft
going: sold (to join R. Simpson) 25,000 gns in December. *M. R. Stoute*

FLOATING CHARGE   3 b.g. Sharpo 132 – Poyle Fizz (Damister (USA) 123)   73 p
[1996 NR 1997 8m 7m² Sep 9] 18,500F, 32,000Y: first foal: dam unraced daughter
of half-sister to Runnett: easily better effort in maidens when 6 lengths second of 15
to Darnaway at Lingfield, no chance with very easy winner but running on well: may
well be open to further progress. *J. R. Fanshawe*

FLOATING DEVON   3 br.g. Simply Great (FR) 122 – Devon Dancer 73   –
(Shareef Dancer (USA) 135) [1996 58: 6m⁴ a7g⁵ a6g 7m⁴ 7.5f⁶ 7.9g 1997 10m⁶ 12g
Apr 25] lengthy, angular gelding: modest maiden: should have stayed at least 7f:
dead. *T. D. Easterby*

FLOOD'S HOT STUFF   3 gr.f. Chilibang 120 – Tiszta Sharok 81 (Song 132)   43
[1996 –: 6m 6m⁶ 5g 8g 1997 a8.5g⁶ a5g a6g a6g 8.2m² 8.2g⁶ 8m* 10g 8g a8g
Dec 10] workmanlike filly: poor performer: made all in weak claimer at Brighton
in August: stays 1m, seemingly not 1¼m: acts on good to firm ground: visored/
blinkered last 4 starts. *N. P. Littmoden*

FLORAL PARK   2 b.f. (Apr 29) Northern Park (USA) 107 – Whitchurch Silk   –
(IRE) (Runnett 125) [1997 5d 7s⁴ 7m 7g Aug 13] first foal: dam no worthwhile form:
no worthwhile form in maidens and claimers. *G. B. Balding*

FLORAZI   2 b.c. (Jun 3) Arazi (USA) 135 – Flo Russell (USA) (Round Table)   94 p
[1997 7m⁵ 7.1m⁶ 7m* 7g* Oct 25] 45,000Y: tall, useful-looking colt: has a round
action: half-brother to several winners, including smart Irish sprinter Flowing (by El
Gran Senor) and useful Irish 1m winner Crockadore (by Nijinsky), later stayed 1½m:
dam placed in USA: progressive form, winning maiden at Leicester and nursery at
Doncaster in October, overcoming wide draw to beat Lido comfortably by neck in
latter: will stay 1m: raced only on good/good to firm ground: very much the type to
thrive in handicaps, and could well win a decent prize. *J. L. Dunlop*

FLORENCE ASHER   2 b.f. (Mar 1) Shardari 134 – Filicaia 79 (Sallust 134)   –
[1997 7m Nov 4] first foal: dam 5f and 6f winner: last of 18 in Redcar maiden. *Don
Enrico Incisa*

FLORENTINO (IRE)   4 b. or br.g. Machiavellian (USA) 123 – Helens   75
Dreamgirl 95 (Caerleon (USA) 132) [1996 73: 8d 7g 9.7m* 10.8f³ 10.2f* 11f⁶ 1997
12g 11.9f² 12m⁵ 10m³ 10g* 13.1g² 12s⁶ 10m⁴ 10.1m⁴ Oct 22] tall gelding: fair performer: won minor event at Pontefract in July: will prove best up to 13f: acts on
firm ground, below form on soft (subsequently gelded) seventh start: consistent: sold
32,000 gns and joined Mrs V. Ward. *B. W. Hills*

FLORISTAN (IRE)   3 b.c. Fairy King (USA) – Le Melody 102 (Levmoss 133)   75 p
[1996 NR 1997 8.3m 7.9s³ Sep 4] IR 30,000F, IR 71,000Y: lengthy, attractive colt:
closely related to smart 1¼m/1½m winner Larrocha (by Sadler's Wells) and
half-brother to several winners, notably Ardross (by Run The Gantlet): dam, won her
only starts at 7f (at 2 yrs) and 1¼m, half-sister to Irish 1000 Guineas winner Arctique
Royale: much better effort in maidens when never-nearer 7¾ lengths third of 8 to
Solar Storm at York: will improve at 1¼m+. *L. M. Cumani*

FLO'S CHOICE (IRE)   3 b.f. Dancing Dissident (USA) 119 – Miss Siddons   35
(Cure The Blues (USA)) [1996 –: 6g 5g⁵ 7g 6m 6m a6g 1997 5d⁴ 5m 5m⁵ 5m⁶ a6g
a7g Nov 14] leggy filly: poor sprint maiden. *J. O'Reilly*

FLOTILLA   3 b.g. Saddlers' Hall (IRE) 126 – Aim For The Top (USA) 111 (Irish   56
River (FR) 131) [1996 71: 5m⁶ a6g² 6.1g 7g² a7g 8f 1997 7m 9m 8.2g 8.2s 10m⁴ 12g
a9.4g Dec 6] good-topped gelding: poor mover: modest maiden: stays 1¼m (much
too keen when tried at 1½m): acts on firm going: visored (no improvement) fifth
start. *S. Mellor*

367

FLOURISHING WAY 3 b.f. Sadler's Wells (USA) 132 – Darayna (IRE) 67
(Shernazar 131) [1996 78: 6m 6m² 7.5m² 1997 7g⁴ 6m² 6s³ 6s Jul 4] smallish,
good-topped filly: fair maiden: disappointing on soft ground last 2 starts, too free in
blinkers on final one: keen sort, and will prove best up to 1m: races prominently.
R. Charlton

FLOW BACK 5 gr.g. Royal Academy (USA) 130 – Flo Russell (USA) (Round –
Table) [1996 62: 8f a10g⁶ 12m a12g* a12g⁶ a13g a11g 1997 a12g a12g⁵ Dec 19]
modest handicapper in 1996: well beaten both 5-y-o starts. *G. P. Enright*

FLOW BY 2 b.f. (Feb 16) Formidable (USA) 125 – Lobinda 80 (Shareef Dancer 75
(USA) 135) [1997 6g 6.9s² 7m* 7g⁴ 8d⁵ 8s³ Oct 13] sturdy filly: second foal:
half-sister to 3-y-o State Fair: dam 1m (at 2 yrs) and 1½m winner from family of
Highclere: fair performer: won maiden at Brighton in July: respectable efforts in
nurseries afterwards: may well stay beyond 1m: acts on good to firm and soft ground.
J. L. Dunlop

FLOWER MILLER 4 b.g. Formidable (USA) 125 – Sunflower Seed 70 –
(Mummy's Pet 125) [1996 NR 1997 8g 8m 9d Sep 19] of no account. *J. Hanson*

FLOWER O'CANNIE (IRE) 2 b.f. (Apr 24) Mujadil (USA) 119 – Baby's 82
Smile 68 (Shirley Heights 130) [1997 5g² 5m³ 5g⁶ 6m⁵ 6g 6s* 7.5v* 7g³ 7g³ 8g 8d³
8g Oct 24] 14,000Y: workmanlike filly: eighth foal: sister to 3-y-o Barba Papa and
half-sister to several winners, including 1m (at 2 yrs) and 1½m winner Smiles Ahead
(by Primo Dominie): dam suited by good test of stamina: fairly useful performer:
won maiden at Hamilton and minor event at Beverley in the summer: several good
efforts in nurseries afterwards: should stay at least 1¼m: acts on heavy ground,
lightly raced on good to firm: sweated final start. *M. W. Easterby*

FLOWING FORTUNE 3 b.g. Kenmare (FR) 125 – Green Flower (USA) 56 72
(Fappiano (USA)) [1996 67p: 7g² 1997 10g⁶ 10m⁴ 11.9s⁶ Oct 15] big, rangy gelding:
good mover: fair maiden: stays 1¼m: well beaten on soft ground: wandered second
start: sold 12,500 gns after final start. *E. A. L. Dunlop*

FLUSH (FR) 2 b. or br.f. (May 3) Warning 136 – Garden Pink (FR) (Bellypha 61 p
130) [1997 6g 7m 7f⁵ Oct 1] close-coupled filly: has a quick action: fourth foal:
half-sister to 3-y-o Spy Knoll: dam, French 1m and 10.5f winner, from family of
Green Dancer: progressive form in maidens at Ascot, Lingfield and Brighton: should
stay 1¼m: open to improvement. *J. W. Hills*

FLYAWAY BLUES 5 b.g. Bluebird (USA) 125 – Voltigeuse (USA) (Filiberto 42 §
(USA) 123) [1996 52§: 7g 10g 10d³ 7m 16m 8m³ 8.3g 8.5m 1997 9.9m⁵ 10g 13.1s³
11m Oct 28] tall, angular gelding: poor maiden: stays 1½m: acts on firm and soft
ground: often blinkered/visored: unreliable. *Mrs M. Reveley*

FLYAWAY HILL (FR) 3 b.f. Danehill (USA) 126 – Flyaway Bride (USA) 104 59
(Blushing Groom (FR) 131) [1996 70p: 7m⁵ 7d 1997 8f⁵ 8f 8m³ Jun 26] modest
maiden: should stay 1¼m: acts on firm ground. *P. W. Harris*

FLY BY NIGHT (IRE) 2 b. or br.c. (Mar 2) Night Shift (USA) – Fatah Flare 79
(USA) 121 (Alydar (USA)) [1997 7d 7m³ 8m³ 7g⁶ Oct 7] good-bodied colt: has a
fluent, round action: eighth foal: closely related to fairly useful 7f winner Mata Cara
(by Storm Bird) and half-brother to 2 winners, including fairly useful 1¼m winner
Refugio (by Reference Point): dam, 4f (at 2 yrs) and 10.5f winner, from excellent
family: fair form when third in maidens at Leicester and Pontefract in September:
stays 1m: sold approx. £26,000 in Dubai in November. *M. R. Stoute*

FLY BY NORTH (USA) 9 b.g. Northern Horizon (USA) – Lazy E (CAN) –
(Meadow Court 129) [1996 NR 1997 a11g Jan 10] no form: dead. *D. Nicholson*

FLY HIGH 3 b.f. Wing Park 104 – Nahawand 51 (High Top 131) [1996 NR 1997 40
8g⁶ 8g⁴ 7s⁶ 8g Jul 23] half-sister to 5f winner High Romance (by Today And
Tomorrow): dam, plater, stayed 7f: poor maiden: well beaten in sellers last 2 starts:
stays 1m. *D. Morris*

FLYING ANGEL 3 br.f. Almoojid 69 – Silvie 66 (Kind of Hush 118) [1996 NR –
1997 11.6m Jul 14] first reported foal: dam, 1½m winner, shaped like a stayer:
showed nothing in seller at Windsor. *A. Barrow*

FLYING BOLD (IRE) 2 ch.c. (Mar 23) Persian Bold 123 – Princess Reema   66 p
(USA) (Affirmed (USA)) [1997 a7g^2 a8.5g 7d 7.3g* Oct 25] 13,000F, 38,000Y:
eighth foal: half-brother to several winners, including useful 1994 2-y-o 6f to 7.3f
winner Lab Test (by Doulab) and useful Italian middle-distance stayer Pay Me Back
(by Master Willie): dam unraced: fair form: shaped well on debut on all-weather, and
won nursery at Newbury in October by 2 lengths from Acebo Lyons, strong late run:
will prove well suited by 1m+: reportedly had foot abcess when tailed off second
start: should improve further. *W. R. Muir*

FLYING CLOUDS 2 b.f. (Mar 11) Batshoof 122 – Fleeting Rainbow 65   –
(Rainbow Quest (USA) 134) [1997 8m 8.2s Oct 15] 9,600Y: second foal: half-sister
to smart Irish 3-y-o 5f (at 2 yrs) to 11f winner Quws (by Robellino): dam, should
have stayed 1½m, from good family: behind in maidens: burly and green on debut.
M. Blanshard

FLYING COLOURS (IRE) 3 b.f. Fairy King (USA) – Crazed Rainbow (USA)   61
(Graustark) [1996 –: 7d 1997 7g 7d 8f 10m 8d 8.2d a10s^5 a16g* a16g^2 Dec 4] big,
good-topped filly: modest performer: best efforts on the all-weather, and won
handicap at Lingfield in November: stays 2m: acts on equitrack. *C. J. Benstead*

FLYING ESPRIT 3 ch.g. High Kicker (USA) – Sport Lady (USA) (Sportin' Life   –
(USA)) [1996 NR 1997 a8g 10s 8g 15.4s Jul 2] first reported foal: dam seemingly
unraced: no sign of ability: tried blinkered. *G. G. Margarson*

FLYING FLIP 3 b.f. Rolfe (USA) 77 – Needwood Sprite 58 (Joshua 129) [1996   55
NR 1997 7g 8.1m a9.4g^4 10.5d 10s^4 10.1g 10d Nov 3] unfurnished filly: has a short,
round action: first reported foal: dam, 7f winner, also successful over hurdles: modest
maiden: should stay 1½m+. *B. C. Morgan*

FLYING HAROLD 4 b.g. Gildoran 123 – Anytime Anywhere 77 (Daring March   54
116) [1996 45: 7m 7m^6 7.1m 10m^5 8g^5 8f^2 8.3m^2 8m 8m 1997 6.9g^6 5.1m^2 6m^4 5.9d^4
5.7d^3 5m^2 6.1m* 6d^6 6s^4 5g 5.1g^5 5d 5m^2 6m 6m^6 5d Oct 17] close-coupled gelding:
modest handicapper: won at Chepstow (maiden event) in June: mostly creditable
efforts afterwards: stays 1m, but races mainly at sprint distances nowadays: acts on
firm and soft going (yet to race on heavy): no battler, tends to hang and goes well
covered up. *M. R. Channon*

FLYING HIGH (IRE) 2 b.c. (Feb 12) Fayruz 116 – Shayista (Tap On Wood 130)   –
[1997 5s^5 5f 5g Jun 20] 10,500Y: first foal: dam Irish NH Flat race/hurdles winner
out of useful French 2-y-o 5f winner Shayina: well beaten in maidens. *F. Murphy*

FLYING NORTH (IRE) 4 b.g. Distinctly North (USA) 115 – North Kildare   82
(USA) (Northjet 136) [1996 80: 8g^3 8m 8.2f^3 10.3m^6 8m^4 8g 8m 9.2g^2 8g 8g 1997
10d 9.9g* 10d^5 10.1g 10.3m Sep 13] leggy gelding: good mover: fairly useful
handicapper: came from off strong pace to win at Beverley in June: stays 1¼m: acts
on firm ground and dead: has taken keen hold: usually held up: carries head a bit
high: promising hurdler. *Mrs M. Reveley*

FLYING PENNANT (IRE) 4 gr.c. Waajib 121 – Flying Beckee (IRE) 60   61
(Godswalk (USA) 130) [1996 72: 8.2s 8d 7m* 7d^4 8g^2 8m^3 8.3g^2 7g 8.2g 1997 7g
7.6v 7m^4 7.1m^6 8.1d 7g 7f^5 8f Sep 28] strong, good-bodied colt: has a quick action:
modest handicapper, inconsistent in 1997: stays 1m: acts on good to firm ground and
dead: blinkered (not at best) last 2 starts. *J. M. Bradley*

FLYING SINGER 2 b.f. (Mar 4) Bluebird (USA) 125 – Singer On The Roof 62   54
(Chief Singer 131) [1997 5m 6d^5 6f^4 5.7m 6.9g 7m Sep 20] first foal: dam 1m winner,
half-sister to Prix Saint-Alary winner Air de Rien, from family of Blushing Groom:
modest maiden: probably stays 7f: tended to hang on firm ground: sold, to go to
Germany. *I. A. Balding*

FLY TO THE STARS 3 b.c. Bluebird (USA) 125 – Rise And Fall (Mill Reef   113
(USA) 141) [1996 83p: 6s^3 7f^2 1997 8m* 8m^2 7m^5 10.1m^4 8m* 8.1g 8m* 8g^2
8f^3 Sep 13]
The stars are among the few remaining places to which British-trained
racehorses haven't been flown. Smart performer Fly To The Stars, for example,
was raced in Ireland (twice), France and Turkey in the latest season, being
placed on three occasions. Although not yet successful on his travels, it was

FLY

appropriate that Fly To The Stars should be campaigned on a wider stage. Owner Peter Savill, president of the Racehorse Owners Association, in his various contributions to the debate about prize money in Britain has set great store by a league table compiled by the International Federation of Horseracing Authorities. The table has been used to show how badly owners fare in Britain compared to other countries, recovering less than a quarter of the keep and training costs. The only major racing country below Britain in the table is Ireland, where Savill also had several horses in training in 1997. It's surprising that Savill and others who bemoan the lack of prize money in Britain haven't acted more practically on the findings of this table and explored the benefits of racing in Korea, for example, a backwater where owners received a magnificent 252 percent return on their investment in 1996. Perhaps there's some Seoul searching to be done!

On the domestic scene Fly To The Stars did manage to make a significant contribution towards his training fees, landing the odds in good style in a maiden at Doncaster on his reappearance and then claiming a brace of valuable handicaps in the summer. In the Britannia Stakes at Royal Ascot—where he started at 20/1—he raced on the outside of the stand side bunch after being drawn in the middle of the twenty-eight runner field, before coming with a strong run to win by a length and a half from Komi and Rapier. Similar tactics were employed in the Schweppes Golden Mile at Goodwood where he again tracked the leaders (this time on the rail) before edging ahead inside the final furlong, coming home a length and a quarter in front of Crumpton Hill, Pride of Pendle and Strazo in a close finish for the places. His starting price of 14/1 reflected a disappointing run in between in the Hong Kong Jockey Club Trophy, his only poor run of the season.

Although Fly To The Stars was near the top of the handicap at Ascot and Goodwood he has so far proved unable to make a successful step up to better company. Earlier in the season he was second in the Leopardstown Two Thousand Guineas Trial and fifth in the Tetrarch Stakes at the Curragh. On his two starts after Goodwood he was beaten around a length and a half by Marathon in the Prix de Tourgeville at Deauville in August and by fellow British challengers Sandstone and Ramooz in the Topkapi Trophy at Veliefendi in Turkey in September, respectable efforts at best. The competing attractions of the international programme were brought sharply into focus when trainer

Britannia Stakes (Handicap), Royal Ascot—a decisive victory for Fly To The Stars and Olivier Peslier; Komi (left) and Rapier also finish in front of the group on the other side of the course

Schweppes Golden Mile (Handicap), Goodwood—
another very valuable contest falls to Fly To The Stars and France's champion jockey;
Crumpton Hill is second and the grey Pride of Pendle is about to deprive Strazo of third

Mark Johnston cancelled jockey Jason Weaver's retainer after the latter chose to ride Hever Golf Rose in Sweden rather than travel to Turkey. Ironically, Weaver had been passed over in favour of Olivier Peslier for the ride on Fly To The Stars at both Ascot and Goodwood.

		Storm Bird	Northern Dancer
	Bluebird (USA)	(b 1978)	South Ocean
	(b 1984)	Ivory Dawn	Sir Ivor
Fly To The Stars		(b 1978)	Dusky Evening
(b.c. 1994)		Mill Reef	Never Bend
	Rise And Fall	(b 1968)	Milan Mill
	(b 1984)	Light Duty	Queen's Hussar
		(b 1972)	Highlight

Although connections clearly feel Fly To The Stars is best at a mile, he ran creditably on his only start at a mile and a quarter and is worth another try at the trip; his half-brother Danseur Landais (by Damister) is a smart performer at a mile and a quarter to a mile and a half in France. Rise And Fall's two other foals before Fly To The Stars were also winners abroad. She herself was a lightly-raced daughter of the smart Light Duty and is a sister to the smart performers Paradise Bay and Special Leave, from the family of Highclere. A tall, angular colt and a powerful mover with a round action, Fly To The Stars acts on good to firm ground. Fly To The Stars was off on his travels again at the end of the year, this time being flown to the United Arab Emirates. It has still to be decided whether he will return to Britain. *M. Johnston*

FLYWAY (FR)   4 b.c. Priolo (USA) 127 – Flying Circus (Gay Mecene (USA) 128)   117
[1996 9.1g⁴ 8s⁴ 8d² 8g⁶ 10g³ 10g² 10d* 12g* 15d⁴ 12.5d⁴ 1997 12m* 12g⁴ 12s* 12d⁴
12f² Jul 20] smart ex-French colt: improved in 1997: won small-field listed race at
Longchamp in April by neck from Prussian Blue and Prix Jean de Chaudenay at
Saint-Cloud in May by 2 lengths from De Quest: good efforts afterwards, leaving E.
Lellouche before 1½ lengths second of 6 to Marlin in Grade 2 event at Hollywood
Park in July: effective at 1½m to 15f: acts on firm and soft ground: consistent.
B. Cecil, USA

FOIST   5 b.g. Efisio 120 – When The Saints (Bay Express 132) [1996 53+, a65+:   75 d
a6g* a6g* a6g* 5.9d⁵ 5g 6m⁵ 7g³ 8.5m³ 8.9g 1997 7g* 7m³ 6d* 7g² 6s* 6s⁴ 6m 6d

371

6d 6m 6g 6m 6d Sep 2] small, good-topped gelding: fair handicapper: won at Catterick in March and Hamilton in April and (by 7 lengths) May: out of sorts afterwards, reportedly finishing distressed penultimate start: needs good test at 6f, and should stay 1m: has form on good to firm going and fibresand, goes very well on ground softer than good: blinkered (raced too freely over 9f) final 4-y-o start: sometimes gives trouble at start. *M. W. Easterby*

FOLEYS QUEST (IRE) 3 b.f. River Falls 113 – Katie's Delight (Relko 136) 59 [1996 NR 1997 10g⁶ 14m⁵ 11.6m² 12g⁶ 12d Sep 19] sturdy filly: half-sister to several winners abroad: dam unraced: modest form at best in varied company, including selling. *J. S. Moore*

FOLGORE (USA) 3 ch.f. Irish River (FR) 131 – Florie (FR) (Gay Mecene – (USA) 128) [1996 83: 7d* 7.5d² 7.5s* 8s 1997 10.2g⁵ Sep 11] won twice at Milan at 2 yrs: tailed off in Chepstow minor event only start in 1997: stud. *J. L. Dunlop*

FOLKLORE 2 b.f. (Feb 5) Fairy King (USA) – Falsoola 84 (Kris 135) [1997 5g² 86 + 5m 5m 5d² 5m* 5.3g 5m Oct 2] angular filly: first foal: dam, 5f to 6.5f winner who ran only at 2 yrs, daughter of very smart filly at up to 1m Favoridge, an excellent family: best effort when winning nursery at Ripon in August, making all in probably favoured group: speedy, and almost certainly a 5f performer: acts on good to firm ground: has hung under pressure: sent to France. *D. R. Loder*

FOLLY FOOT FRED 3 b.g. Crisp 87 – Wessex Kingdom 68 (Vaigly Great 127) [1996 52: 5.1g* 5m⁴ 6g⁶ 5.1m⁶ 7m⁵ 1997 8.2m 7m 5.1f 7m 6g Jul 7] leggy gelding: won seller at 2 yrs: well below form in 1997. *B. R. Millman*

FOND EMBRACE 4 b.f. Emarati (USA) 74 – Detente 87 (Dominion 123) [1996 93 99: 5.1g* 5d* 5m 5d³ 5m 1997 5g⁵ 5.1s⁶ 5m Jul 25] leggy filly: fairly useful performer, lightly raced in 1997: wearing net muzzle and early to post, ran poorly final start: keen, and seems best at 5f: acts on good to firm and soft ground: sold 7,000 gns in December. *H. Candy*

FONTCAUDETTE (IRE) 3 b.f. River Falls 113 – Lune de Miel 80 (Kalamoun – 129) [1996 –: 7g⁵ 7f 6m 1997 a7g 8f 7s⁵ Jul 2] of little account. *J. E. Banks*

FONTEYN 3 b.f. Aragon 118 – Trull (Lomond (USA) 128) [1996 NR 1997 7g 74 7m² 6s² 6g³ 7m a7g² Oct 18] 10,000Y: third foal: closely related to 1994 2-y-o 7f winner Red Light (by Reprimand): dam ran once: fair maiden: clearly best efforts second and third starts: effective at stiff 6f/7f: acts on good to firm and soft going: has flashed tail and may be none too trustworthy. *A. C. Stewart*

FONZY 3 b.g. Phountzi (USA) 104 – Diavalezza (Connaught 130) [1996 64: a5g* 5m* 6g⁵ 5g³ 5m² 5f* 5g* 1997 6.9m a6g 6m 6d Sep 2] sparely-made gelding: won 4 times at 2 yrs: little encouragement in 1997. *Mrs S. J. Smith*

FOOLED YOU (USA) 3 br.g. Wild Again (USA) – Foolish Miz (USA) (Foolish 68 Pleasure (USA)) [1996 NR 1997 8m⁴ 10s May 17] $100,000Y: tall, quite attractive gelding: eighth foal: half-brother to 3 winners in USA: dam unraced: much better effort in maidens when fourth at Ripon: moved poorly to post over month later: subsequently gelded. *E. A. L. Dunlop*

FOOLISH FLUTTER (IRE) 3 b. or br.f. Fools Holme (USA) – Thornbeam 48 (Beldale Flutter (USA) 130) [1996 –: 5g 6g 7.5m 7.1m³ 7g 8f 10m 10g⁵ 1997 10m 9.9d⁶ 8s⁶ 10.8g² 12m* a12g² 11.9d³ 10s Oct 8] sparely-made filly: poor performer: won selling handicap at Beverley in July: stays 1½m: acts on good to firm and dead ground and on fibresand: often blinkered/visored (former when successful). *R. Bastiman*

FOOT BATTALION (IRE) 3 b.c. Batshoof 122 – Roxy Music (IRE) 63 (Song 80 132) [1996 85: 5s⁴ 5g* 5.1g² 6m⁶ 6g 5g² 6.1m³ 7m³ 6.1m² 7g⁵ 6m a7g² 1997 a7g* a91 a8.5g a7g³ a8.5g² a8.5g* 8m 9m⁶ 7.6d 7.9g 10.5m⁴ 8m 10.1s 10g 8g 8m⁶ 8.1m 8m³ 9s³ 10.3g Oct 24] close-coupled colt: fairly useful on the all-weather, successful in handicap at Wolverhampton in January and minor event there in March: fair on turf: stays 9f: acts on fibresand and on good to firm and soft ground: sold 17,000 gns in November. *R. Hollinshead*

FORCING BID 3 b.g. Forzando 122 – Cox's Pippin (USA) (Cox's Ridge (USA)) – [1996 68: 5g⁴ 6f³ 5d⁶ 7.1s⁵ 1997 a6g* a6g* 6m a7g 7m a6g³ a7g a6g 6d a6g* a7g a94

Dec 6] fairly useful handicapper: won at Wolverhampton (maiden event) and South-well within 3 days in April and again at Wolverhampton (best effort) in November: slowly away and soon tailed off final start: best form at 6f: goes well on fibresand, no turf form in 1997: blinkered last 2 starts: tends to go in snatches: inconsistent. *Sir Mark Prescott*

FORECAST   4 b.g. Formidable (USA) 125 – Princess Matilda 110 (Habitat 134)   –
[1996 61d, a–: a6g a7g 6.1m* 6d a6g 6f⁶ 7g 7d 10g 6m 1997 6g 5.9f⁵ 5.9m 6m Aug 9] won seller at 3 yrs: no other worthwhile form. *K. A. Morgan*

FOREIGN JUDGEMENT (USA)   4 b.g. El Gran Senor (USA) 136 – Numeral   –
(USA) (Alleged (USA) 138) [1996 –: 10m 10g 10m 12s 1997 10g 10.8s Jul 4] fair form as 2-y-o: none since. *W. J. Musson*

FOREIGN RULE (IRE)   3 b.g. Danehill (USA) 126 – Guida Centrale (Teenoso   80
(USA) 135) [1996 NR 1997 7m³ 8g⁶ 10.1m² 11.9f² 12.5m⁴ 14d* 14d Oct 17] IR 30,000Y: lengthy gelding: second foal: half-brother to 1996 Oaks d'Italia winner Germignaga (stays 11f, by Miswaki Tern): dam Italian 2-y-o 1m and 1¼m winner: fairly useful performer: granted stiffest test of stamina to date when winning handicap at Haydock (idled) in July: sold out of P. Chapple-Hyam's stable 26,000 gns in July: tailed off only subsequent outing: will stay 2m: acts on firm and dead ground, yet to race on softer. *J. R. Jenkins*

FOREST BOY   4 b.g. Komaite (USA) – Khadine 79 (Astec 128) [1996 73: 6s   79
8.3d* 7d⁴ 8.3s* 8d⁶ 10s 1997 a9.4g* a9.4g a9.4g⁵ Jan 29] sturdy, workmanlike gelding: fair handicapper: won at Wolverhampton in January: ran poorly later in month: stays 9.4f: acts on fibresand and soft ground: sometimes visored/blinkered (not in 1997), including when successful: has looked a difficult ride. *J. R. Bosley*

FOREST BUCK (USA)   4 ch.c. Green Forest (USA) 134 – Perlee (FR) 122   103
(Margouillat (FR) 133) [1996 111: 10.3f* 9g³ 1997 10m² May 3] close-coupled, angular colt: unimpressive mover: useful performer, lightly raced: 3½ lengths second of 6 to Germano in minor event at Newmarket (hung left) only 4-y-o start: better around 1¼m than shorter: yet to race on ground softer than good: sold only 7,500 gns in October, to go to Italy. *H. R. A. Cecil*

FOREST FANTASY   4 b.f. Rambo Dancer (CAN) 107 – Another Treat 92   61
(Derring-Do 131) [1996 61: 8g⁴ 10m⁶ 11m³ 12.3m 11f³ 9f* 8m² 10s⁴ 10f 1997 10g 10m³ 10d 8.2m* 8.1m 8m⁴ 9m Oct 7] workmanlike filly: modest handicapper: won at Nottingham in August: stays 1¼m: acts on firm going, seemingly not on dead/soft. *J. Wharton*

FOREST FIRE (SWE)   2 b.f. (Feb 22) Never So Bold 135 – Mango Sampaquita   55 p
(SWE) (Colombian Friend (USA)) [1997 7s⁵ Oct 16] second known foal: half-sister to a Swedish middle-distance winner by Mango Express, winner over hurdles here: dam 5f to 9f winner in Norway: 33/1, slowly away, kept on late when fifth of 13 to Shfoug in maiden at Catterick: should improve. *P. Mooney*

FOREST ROBIN   4 ch.g. Formidable (USA) 125 – Blush Rambler (IRE) (Blush-   68 d
ing Groom (FR) 131) [1996 87: 7g 8.1g² 9m³ 8f 10m³ 8.3d⁴ 8m² 10.4g 10s⁶ 11f 1997 10.3m 10m³ 8g 7m 7m 8m⁶ 8g³ 6d 8g 8m⁵ 10m 9m 8g 8d 8f³ 8m 8.2d 8s Nov 6] good-quartered gelding: fair handicapper at best in 1997, still a maiden: needs good test at 7f and stays 9f: acts on firm and dead ground: tried visored and blinkered. *Mrs J. R. Ramsden*

FORESTRY   3 b.g. Highest Honor (FR) 124 – Arboretum (IRE) 83 (Green Desert   –
(USA) 127) [1996 NR 1997 10g 7.6m 8m 10m Sep 16] first foal: dam, 6f and 7f winner, sister to listed 7f winner Himiko: well held all starts, though signs of a little ability. *J. G. Smyth-Osbourne*

FOREST SIGNAL   3 ch.c. Indian Forest (USA) 117 – Telegraph Callgirl 67   –
(Northern Tempest (USA) 120) [1996 NR 1997 9.9m 7.5m³ 7.5g 6d 8g Jul 7] 1,250Y: lengthy colt: third foal: dam 7f and 1m winner: signs of ability in maidens, but harshly treated and well held in handicaps. *M. Brittain*

FOREST TREASURE (IRE)   2 b.f. (Mar 14) Brief Truce (USA) 126 – In The   94
Clover (Meadow Mint (USA) 120) [1997 5d* 5m² 5m⁵ 6g³ 6d⁶ 8f⁵ 8.5f Nov 5] IR 17,000F, 64,000Y: tall, unfurnished filly: half-sister to several winners, including useful Santella Mac (up to 1m, by Gay Fandango), later successful in USA: dam won

over 7f at 2 yrs in Ireland: fairly useful performer: won minor event at Thirsk in May: 2½ lengths third to Asfurah in Cherry Hinton Stakes at Newmarket on penultimate start for J. Berry: unplaced both runs in USA (blinkered second time): should stay 1m: sometimes bandaged in Britain. *C. Whittingham, USA*

FORGET PARIS (IRE) 4 gr.f. Broken Hearted 124 – Miss Deauville (Sovereign Path 125) [1996 –: 8g 8g a11g⁶ 10f 10g 8.5f a8g 1997 a11g⁶ Jan 10] workmanlike filly: no worthwhile form: tried visored. *B. S. Rothwell*

FORGET TO REMINDME 3 b.f. Forzando 122 – Sandy Looks 69 (Music 51 d Boy 124) [1996 –: 6.9d⁴ 1997 7m* 7.1g 9.7m⁶ 8s a9.4g 8m Sep 24] 33/1, came from near last to win Salisbury claimer in May: well beaten otherwise, including when blinkered on all-weather debut: should stay 1m. *J. S. Moore*

FORGIE (IRE) 4 b.g. Don't Forget Me 127 – Damia (Vision (USA)) [1996 68: 81 10g 12d³ 14.1m* 14d 14.1f⁴ 16.1m² 17.1m² 16.1m² 14.1m 1997 14.1m⁵ 14.1d⁵ 12s³ 14g* 14d* 16m 16m⁴ 16g⁵ 13.9s* 15.9g* 14.6g⁵ 16.5s Nov 8] lengthy gelding: has a round action: fairly useful handicapper: had a good 1997, winning at Musselburgh (twice) in June and at York and Chester in September: suited by good test of stamina: acts on firm and soft going: consistent. *P. Calver*

FORGOTTEN DANCER (IRE) 6 ch.g. Don't Forget Me 127 – Dancing – Diana 82 (Raga Navarro (ITY) 119) [1996 –: 6m 8f 6.9m⁵ 7f 6m a8g a10g a10g 1997 a7g Jan 9] no longer of any account. *R. Ingram*

FORGOTTEN STAR (IRE) 2 b. or br.f. (Feb 11) Don't Forget Me 127 – Sterna 56 Star (Corvaro (USA) 124) [1997 7g 7d⁶ 7.9s³ 10g 8m Oct 5] IR 1,000Y: unfurnished filly: fourth foal: dam Irish 4-y-o 1½m winner out of half-sister to Star Appeal: modest form in maidens: well held in nurseries last 2 starts: should be suited by 1¼m+. *R. F. Johnson Houghton*

FORGOTTEN TIMES (USA) 3 ch.f. Nabeel Dancer (USA) 120 – Etoile 65 d'Amore (USA) 81 (The Minstrel (CAN) 135) [1996 70d: 6.1m⁶ 7f⁴ a6g⁴ a7g³ 1997 a68 a7g³ a6g² a6g* a6g² a6g² a6g* 6g 6.1m 6d 6g⁵ 6m 6m⁶ 7g Sep 3] good-quartered filly: fair performer: consistent on equitrack (yet to race on fibresand), and won maiden and handicap at Lingfield early in year: ran creditably only once on turf afterwards: best form at 6f. *T. M. Jones*

FORMAL GOLD (CAN) 4 b. or br.c. Black Tie Affair – Ingoldsby (USA) 132 (Screen King (USA)) [1996 a6f* a7f* a8f* a8.5f* a9f² a9f² a10f⁵ 1997 a9f* a10f⁶ a10f⁵ a9f² a9s* a10f³ a9f² a8.5f* a9f* Sep 20] $65,000Y: $75,000 2-y-o: fourth foal: half-brother to 2 winners: dam won 1 of 2 starts at 2 yrs: top-class American colt: unraced at 2 yrs: won maiden and 3 allowance events by wide margins at 3 yrs then ran well in graded stakes: improved in 1997: won Donn Handicap at Gulfstream Park in February by 1¼ lengths from Skip Away (who gave 10 lb): 6¾ lengths fifth of 10 finishers to Singspiel in Dubai World Cup: won Grade 2 handicaps at Belmont and Monmouth before putting up excellent performance to win 5-runner Woodwood Stakes at Belmont by 5½ lengths from Skip Away (at levels): best form at 9f: front runner on recent starts: proven on wet dirt: reportedly fractured right hind leg while being prepared for Breeders' Cup Classic. *W. Perry, USA*

FORMATION DANCER 2 ch.c. (Apr 6) Groom Dancer (USA) 128 – Golden – p Form (Formidable (USA) 125) [1997 8s Nov 8] angular colt: half-brother to 3 winners, including Rug (should have stayed 1¼m, by Persian Bold): dam 9f winner in Ireland: 20/1, far too free to post when in mid-division in 22-runner maiden at Doncaster: should do better. *P. W. Harris*

FORMER LOVE (USA) 2 b.f. (Feb 1) Dynaformer (USA) – Love And Legend 73 (USA) 84 (Lyphard's Wish (FR) 124) [1997 7g 7g⁵ 7.1m⁴ 7g⁴ Oct 27] well-made, good sort: has a round action: first foal: dam, second over 9f here at 3 yrs, won up to 9f at 4 yrs in USA: fair form in maidens and (best effort) a nursery: should stay at least 1m. *P. R. Webber*

FORMIDABLE FLAME 4 ch.g. Formidable (USA) 125 – Madiyla 73 (Darshaan 133) [1996 –p: 8d 10g 10d 10.5s 12.1s 1997 10s 12d 12s⁶ Jun 27] lengthy gelding: signs of ability at 3 yrs, well beaten in handicaps in 1997 (got loose before intended reappearance). *W. J. Musson*

FORMIDABLE LIZ 7 ch.m. Formidable (USA) 125 – Areej (Rusticaro (FR) –
124) [1996 66, a53: 6m 5m 6g² 6g⁴ a7g⁴ 6f 6m* 8g 6.1m³ 7g 1997 7m 6g 5m 6s⁴ 6g
7g Aug 5] sturdy, lengthy mare: still capable of fair form at 6 yrs, but well held in
1997. *M. D. Hammond*

FORMIDABLE SPIRIT 3 ch.g. Formidable (USA) 125 – Hicklam Millie 49 31
(Absalom 128) [1996 –: 5m⁶ a6g a7g⁶ 1997 a6g⁴ 5.3f⁶ 5m a8g 6g 6f Jul 16] bad sprint
maiden: tried visored. *M. J. Heaton-Ellis*

FOR THE PRESENT 7 b.g. Then Again 126 – Axe Valley 89 (Royben 125) 84
[1996 89: 5m 6m 5m 5m 6f* 5g 6m 5m³ 6m 6g 6.1d³ 5.6m⁶ 6m 1997 5g³ 5m 6g 6g
5g 5m 6g 6.1g³ 6g⁴ 6m 6m⁵ Sep 21] strong gelding: fairly useful handicapper, none
too consistent in 1997: stays 6f well: acts on firm and dead ground: usually comes
from off pace. *T. D. Barron*

FORT KNOX (IRE) 6 b.g. Treasure Kay 114 – Single Viking (Viking (USA)) 49
[1996 60, a63: a6g² a6g⁴ a6g² a7g³ a6g a8g* a7g* a8g⁶ 7f² a9g³ 6.9f⁵ 8g 8f² 6f⁵ a7g⁴ a63
8f² 8m⁵ 8m⁴ 7f a7g⁴ 1997 a7g² a7g² a7g⁶ a7g a8g⁴ 8f⁵ 7f 8f⁵ 7.6m 8m a7g a10g a10g
Dec 22] modest handicapper: little form in second half of 1997: stays 1m well: acts
on all-weather, best turf form on good ground or firmer: wears blinkers: edgy sort.
R. M. Flower

FORTUNE HOPPER 3 gr.g. Rock Hopper 124 – Lots of Luck 73 (Neltino 97) 48
[1996 NR 1997 12g³ 8g⁵ 16f³ 12v⁴ 13.1m⁵ 11.6m 14.1g³ Jul 30] close-coupled,
workmanlike gelding: first foal: dam 1m to 1½m winner: poor maiden handicapper:
should stay beyond 13f: got stirred up on second (visored) and fourth starts: won
selling hurdle in September. *J. Pearce*

FORTUNE HUNTER (IRE) 3 ch.g. Lycius (USA) 124 – Cardomine (Dom –
Racine (FR) 121) [1996 NR 1997 8d 7m 8m⁵ 10g Sep 23] 21,000F, 37,000Y: rangy,
angular gelding: third foal: half-brother to 1m winner (stays 1½m) Douce Maison
(by Fools Holme): dam, French maiden, is daughter of sister to Mtoto: no form:
trained first 3 starts by W. Jarvis, visored final one. *J. Norton*

FORTUNES COURSE (IRE) 8 b.m. Crash Course 128 – Night Rose (Sov- 55
ereign Gleam 127) [1996 54: 10m 12.1d 18m* 17.9g 1997 17.2d² 16.1g³ Oct 7]
smallish mare: fair jumper, successful over fences in November and December: still
capable of modest form on flat: out-and-out stayer: acts on good to firm and dead
going. *J. S. King*

FORTUNE'S WAY (IRE) 3 b.t. Distinctly North (USA) 115   Shanliss – p
(Blazing Saddles (AUS)) [1996 NR 1997 7g a5g a9.4g Aug 8] IR 2,000F, IR
15,500Y: second foal: dam unraced half-sister to useful German middle-distance colt
O'Connor: some promise in maiden at Thirsk but well beaten in similar events at
Wolverhampton afterwards: likely to prove best at 6f/7f: should still do better.
J. Wharton

FORTY LOVE (IRE) 2 b.g. (Mar 23) Second Set (IRE) 127 – Pharjoy (FR) 85 53
(Pharly (FR) 130) [1997 7g 6m 6g* 7.6m⁵ 6g a6g⁶ 7g⁶ Oct 27] 7,000 2-y-o: tall
gelding: half-brother to 3 winners, including fairly useful 7f to 1½m winner El
Volador (by Beldale Flutter): dam best at 2 yrs when 6f winner: modest performer:
won seller at Ripon in August: below form in nurseries after next start, including on
fibresand: should stay beyond 7.6f: tried blinkered/visored. *J. E. Banks*

FORUM 2 b.f. (Apr 23) Lion Cavern (USA) 117 – Top Society (High Top 131) 86
[1997 6d² 6g⁶ 7.1m³ 7.1m⁴ 7f* Oct 1] tall, good-topped filly: has plenty of scope:
easy mover: third foal: half-sister to useful 7f (at 2 yrs) and 1¼m winner Forthwith
(by Midyan): dam unraced: fairly useful performer: won maiden at Brighton in
October: ran well in Cherry Hinton Stakes at Newmarket and listed race at Sandown
second and third starts: will stay 1m: acts on firm ground: has high head carriage.
C. E. Brittain

FORWARD MISS 3 b.f. Bold Arrangement 127 – Maiden Bidder 66 (Shack –
(USA) 118) [1996 –: 6m 1997 6g 7.6g 8.1g 10m 10f 6.9d a7s⁵ Nov 10] of no account.
C. J. Benstead

FOR YOUR EYES ONLY 3 b.g. Pursuit of Love 124 – Rivers Rhapsody 104 95
(Dominion 123) [1996 90: 5g³ 6g* 5f* 5m 6m⁶ 6m⁶ 6d⁴ 8m 7s 1997 7g 6d

6s 7m³ 7.6m 8g⁶ 7g² 7.9s³ 8m 8m 8g² 8m² Nov 1] small gelding: unimpressive mover: useful handicapper: good second in big fields in handicaps won by Gulf Shaadi then Consort at Newmarket last 2 starts: stays 1m well: acts on firm and soft ground: blinkered 5 of last 6 starts: has wandered under pressure: bandaged at 2 yrs. *T. D. Easterby*

FORZA FIGLIO 4 b.c. Warning 136 – Wish You Well 78 (Sadler's Wells (USA) 132) [1996 86: 8d² 8m⁴ 8g* 10m³ 12.1m⁵ 1997 8g 10m² 9s⁵ 8m³ 8m 11.4g² 10m 12m⁴ 12d Oct 16] strong, angular colt: impresses in appearance: fairly useful handicapper: mostly good efforts in 1997: left Miss G. Kelleway after seventh start: effective from 1m to 1½m: acts on good to firm and dead ground: well below form only try in blinkers: usually bandaged behind. *R. Akehurst*   92

FORZAIR 5 b.g. Forzando 122 – Persian Air (Persian Bold 123) [1996 73d: a8g⁵ a12g* a12g⁶ 10.1s⁵ a12g* 12.3g⁵ 12m 12m² 13g⁴ 9.2g⁵ 10m 10m⁶ a9.4g 14s a12g a11g³ a12g³ a14.8g⁴ 1997 a11g² a11g² a12g⁴ a12g* a12g a16g⁴ a14g³ 12.3m⁵ 10g³ a12g⁶ a12g⁴ a14g⁶ a12g³ 10.5m 10.9d⁴ 11.9d² 12m 15.8g* 16.2d 12f² 10.9d 15.8g 12m³ 13.1s² 12s³ a14g Nov 17] sturdy gelding: modest performer: won weak sellers at Southwell in February and Catterick in August: stays 2m: acts on fibresand and on firm and soft ground: tried blinkered/visored, no improvement: winning hurdler. *J. J. O'Neill*   53

FORZARA 4 ch.f. Risk Me (FR) 127 – Valldemosa 81 (Music Boy 124) [1996 54: 5g⁶ 5f⁴ a5g 5m 5g* 5.1m 1997 5s 5g 5.1m 5.7g Aug 7] modest 5f handicapper: well beaten in 1997. *J. L. Spearing*   –

FOUNDRY LANE 6 b.g. Mtoto 134 – Eider 80 (Niniski (USA) 125) [1996 76+: 16.1m 13.9m 13.9g⁶ 1997 13.9g 13.9s⁵ 13.3d⁴ Sep 20] rangy gelding: usually looks well: has a fluent, round action: fair handicapper, lightly raced of late: shaped quite well when tenth in Ebor at York on reappearance, and again when fourth in Autumn Cup at Newbury on final start: stays 2m: acts on any going: promising novice hurdler. *Mrs M. Reveley*   77 +

FOURDANED (IRE) 4 b.g. Danehill (USA) 126 – Pro Patria 86 (Petingo 135) [1996 81d: 8g² 8m⁶ 8m⁵ 8d 10.5m 1997 10.3m⁵ a11g 10g 10s 12s⁴ 12m² 11.6m³ 12m 12v a16s a12g a12s Nov 28] small gelding: just a modest handicapper nowadays: left P. W. Harris after fourth start: stays 1½m: acts on good to firm and soft going: no form on the all-weather: well beaten in blinkers: carries head awkwardly, and hasn't impressed with attitude. *S. Dow*   60 a–

FOUR OF SPADES 6 ch.g. Faustus (USA) 118 – Fall To Pieces (USA) 101 (Forli (ARG)) [1996 58, a75: a7g a6g⁴ a7g a7g² a7g a8g² 8m⁶ a8g⁴ 8m³ a10g² a7g² a6g³ 8.3m⁴ a8g⁴ 7g² a7g 7m a7g 1997 a7g 10m 8.3g a7g Dec 10] tall, lengthy gelding: formerly fair performer: well beaten in 1997: left R. Hodges after third start. *K. R. Burke*   –

FOXES TAIL 3 gr.g. Batshoof 122 – Secret Gill 88 (Most Secret 119) [1996 74: 6d³ 7.1g* 7.5f⁵ 8m 8m* 8g 1997 8g 10g⁵ 10.1s⁶ 10.9s⁵ 10.3g Oct 24] tall gelding: fair handicapper: well below form last 3 starts: stays 1¼m: acts on good to firm and dead ground: usually bandaged. *Miss S. E. Hall*   69

FOXFORD LAD 3 b.g. Akid (USA) – Spring Rose (Blakeney 126) [1996 –: 7m a8g 1997 a10g a12g⁴ a12g⁵ 14.1m⁴ 17.2f⁶ 15.4s Jul 2] bad maiden: looked moody in blinkers final start. *T. M. Jones*   29

FOXIE LADY 2 ch.f. (Mar 15) Wolfhound (USA) 126 – Final Thought (Final Straw 127) [1997 7g Aug 25] 13,000Y: half-sister to 8-y-o Fieldridge (formerly fairly useful 1¼m/1½m winner) and a winner in Spain by Most Welcome: dam unraced half-sister to Middle Park and Greenham winner Creag-An-Sgor: 10/1 and green, mid-division in 17-runner maiden at Newcastle, not best of runs over 2f out and not knocked about: should improve. *E. A. L. Dunlop*   – p

FOX SPARROW 7 b.g. Sharpo 132 – Wryneck 89 (Niniski (USA) 125) [1996 NR 1997 13g 12g 14.1m⁶ Aug 9] fairly useful handicapper at best: lightly raced nowadays, and well beaten in blinkers in 1997. *N. Tinkler*   –

FRAGRANT MIX (IRE) 3 gr.c. Linamix (FR) 127 – Fragrant Hill 104 (Shirley Heights 130) [1996 8d⁴ 7.5v² 1997 10.5s* 10.5d* 11m* 12m⁴ Jun 1] angular colt: 115

first foal: dam smart performer 7f (at 2 yrs) to 11f winner: smart performer: won minor event in February and listed race in March, both at Saint-Cloud, and 6-runner Prix Noailles at Longchamp (by 3 lengths from Sendoro) in April: best form when 6½ lengths fourth of 14 to Peintre Celebre in Prix du Jockey-Club at Chantilly in June, left behind only in closing stages: stays 1½m: acts on good to firm ground, fairly useful form on soft/heavy. *A. Fabre, France*

FRANCESCA'S FOLLY   2 b.f. (Feb 12) Efisio 120 – Nashville Blues (IRE) 94   54
(Try My Best (USA) 130) [1997 5.7f 5d 7g⁴ 7.1s 8m* 9m⁶ 8d Oct 20] workmanlike filly: first foal: dam, 7f and 1m winner, was not one to trust implicitly: modest performer: won selling nursery at Leicester in September: stays 9f: sweating and edgy fourth start: has flashed tail. *J. W. Hills*

FRANDICKBOB   3 b.g. Statoblest 120 – Crimson Ring (Persian Bold 123) [1996   –
–: a5g 6g a5g a6s 1997 6.1g Apr 21] no form. *John A. Harris*

FRANKIE   3 b.g. Shalford (IRE) 124§ – Twilight Secret 70 (Vaigly Great 127)   –
[1996 –: 6d⁶ 1997 10.8m⁴ 10g 13m⁶ 12g Aug 2] little worthwhile form.
M. H. Tompkins

FRANKIE FAIR (IRE)   2 b.f. (Feb 18) Red Sunset 120 – Animate (IRE) (Tate   57
Gallery (USA) 117) [1997 5g⁴ 5g³ a6g³ 6.1m⁵ 7d⁵ 7g Oct 25] 10,000Y: sparely-made   a50
filly: first foal: dam Irish maiden out of half-sister to Providential and Play It Safe: modest maiden: ran creditably most starts, including on fibresand and in seller: stays 7f. *M. A. Jarvis*

FRANKIE FERRARI (IRE)   2 b.c. (Apr 14) Common Grounds 118 – Miss   – p
Kelly (Pitskelly 122) [1997 7g 7m 8s Oct 14] IR 90,000Y: good-bodied colt: has a round action: third foal: half-brother to 5-y-o Total Rach: dam Irish maiden: some promise in large fields of maidens at Newbury, Newmarket and Leicester, never placed to challenge on last 2 occasions: likely to do better. *D. R. Loder*

FRANKLIN LAKES   2 ch.c. (Feb 28) Sanglamore (USA) 126 – Eclipsing (IRE)   62
93 (Baillamont (USA) 124) [1997 8d 7d⁴ Oct 27] 37,000Y: second foal: brother to 3-y-o Vagabond Chanteuse: dam 1m winner from the family of Sanglamore: better effort in October maidens when about 5 lengths fourth of 9 to Khalas in steadily-run race at Lingfield: should be suited by 1¼m+. *C. A. Horgan*

FRANS LAD   5 ch.g. Music Boy 124 – Moberry 54 (Mossberry 97) [1996 NR   –
1997 a9.4g May 30] modest winner at 3 yrs: well beaten only start in 1997.
B. P. J. Baugh

FRECKLES   2 b.f. (Jun 7) High Kicker (USA) – Ship of Gold 78 (Glint of Gold   39
128) [1997 7g 6g 8.2g a7g⁵ Oct 20] third foal: dam, disappointing maiden, stayed 1½m: first form in seller at Southwell final start: tried blinkered, visored at Southwell. *M. J. Ryan*

FREDDIE MAC (IRE)   2 b.c. (Feb 18) River Falls 113 – Golden Thread (Glint   –
of Gold 128) [1997 8m May 30] 10,000Y: leggy, workmanlike colt: fourth foal: dam unraced half-sister to useful filly at up to 1¼m Golden Braid out of smart French miler Silk Slipper: 40/1, little promise in maiden at Newmarket. *G. C. Bravery*

FREDERICK JAMES   3 b.c. Efisio 120 – Rare Roberta (USA) 118 (Roberto   76 d
(USA) 131) [1996 –: 6g 1997 6.1d² 5g³ 7g⁶ 6d 7m 6.1g Oct 4] fair maiden: well below form last 3 starts: probably stays 7f: yet to race on extremes of going.
M. J. Heaton-Ellis

FREDRIK THE FIERCE (IRE)   3 b.g. Puissance 110 – Hollia 72 (Touch Boy   –
109) [1996 90: 5d⁴ 5.1g⁴ 5m² 5.1m* 5.2f 5m* 5m⁵ 5m 1997 5.1d 5d May 17] tall gelding: fairly useful form at 2 yrs: stiff tasks and well beaten in handicaps in 1997.
J. Berry

FRED'S DELIGHT (IRE)   6 b.g. Law Society (USA) 130 – Madame Nureyev   –
(USA) (Nureyev (USA) 131) [1996 –: a8g a8g a7g a7g 1997 a8g a12g⁵ a11g⁶ Feb 3] no longer of any account. *Mrs V. A. Aconley*

FRED'S IN THE KNOW   2 ch.g. (Apr 13) Interrex (CAN) – Lady Vynz   38
(Whitstead 125) [1997 5.3m⁶ 6m⁵ 6s Jul 3] 1,900Y: fifth foal: dam unraced half-sister to dam of Racing Post Trophy winner Beauchamp King: poor maiden. *C. Murray*

FREE 2 ch.c. (Apr 24) Gone West (USA) – Bemissed (USA) (Nijinsky (CAN) 138) ?
[1997 6g 8.2m a8g Dec 19] angular colt: good mover: half-brother to 1995 2-y-o 6f
winner (later useful over 1½m) Dismissed (by Dayjur), Oaks winner Jet Ski Lady (by
Vaguely Noble) and 2 winners in USA: dam graded winner at 9f at 2 yrs in USA:
probably flattered when seemingly showing fair form on debut: sold out of P. Cole's
stable 18,000 gns after next start (again seemed headstrong). *Mrs M. Reveley*

FREE AS A BIRD 3 b.f. Robellino (USA) 127 – Special Guest 67 (Be My Guest 62
(USA) 126) [1996 58: 7.1s⁵ 7g 1997 7f² 7.1g⁴ 7d 7g⁶ 8g⁵ Aug 1] modest maiden:
stays 7f, possibly not 1m: best efforts on good ground or firmer. *M. R. Channon*

FREE AS THE WIND (IRE) 2 b.c. (Apr 13) Brief Truce (USA) 126 – Skhiza 80 p
63 (Targowice (USA) 130) [1997 8m⁴ 8.2d² Oct 30] 80,000Y: strong, lengthy colt:
good walker: half-brother to several winners, including useful 1¼m winner La Vie
En Primrose (by Henbit) and Skevena (by Niniski), the dam of Even Top: dam 9.4f
and 1¼m winner: in frame in maidens at Newmarket and Nottingham, no match for
impressive 9-length winner Almandab on latter course: shapes as though will be
suited by further: should do better. *P. W. Chapple-Hyam*

FREEDOM CHANCE (IRE) 3 ch.g. Lahib (USA) 129 – Gentle Guest (IRE) 77
(Be My Guest (USA) 126) [1996 –: 7g 7m a8g⁵ 1997 8.2m* 10g a10g 8.5g³ 9g⁴
12.1m⁴ 11.9m² 11.9m² 12g 12m Sep 26] good-topped gelding: fair handicapper: won
at Nottingham in March: good second at Brighton twice in the summer: stays 1½m:
acts on good to firm going: visored last 4 starts: sold 15,000 gns and joined M.
Hammond. *J. W. Hills*

FREEDOM OF TROY 3 b.g. Puissance 110 – Wing of Freedom (Troy 137) –
[1996 –: 6m 6g 8.1s 1997 8.5m 7.1g 7m Oct 7] of little account. *J. L. Eyre*

FREEDOM QUEST (IRE) 2 b.c. (Apr 20) Polish Patriot (USA) 128 – 76
Rercherchee (Rainbow Quest (USA) 134) [1997 7g² 7f² a7g² Nov 15] IR 70,000Y:
third foal: brother to 3-y-o Recondite: dam unraced from family of Fair Salinia:
favourite, second in maidens at Chester, Brighton and Wolverhampton: will stay 1m.
Sir Mark Prescott

FREE OPTION (IRE) 2 ch.c. (Feb 17) Indian Ridge 123 – Saneena 80 (Kris 83
135) [1997 6g 8m² 8d 7d² 7m³ Nov 4] 25,000F, 46,000Y: strong, lengthy colt: fifth
foal: half-brother to 4-y-o Old Hush Wing and a winner (including at 11f) in
Germany by High Estate: dam 1½m winner out of close relative of Green Dancer:
fairly useful maiden: placed at Pontefract, Lingfield and Redcar: will probably stay
beyond 1m: yet to race on extremes of ground: has carried head awkwardly, and
raced freely. *B. Hanbury*

FREEQUENT 4 ch.c. Rainbow Quest (USA) 134 – Free Guest 125 (Be My Guest 114
(USA) 126) [1996 103: 7g³ 8.5m* 8d* 10.1m 10g⁶ 12m* 14g⁴ 12s⁴ 12s 1997 10.4g
10.1g⁵ 10f* Sep 21] good-bodied colt: smart performer: not seen out in 1997 until
August: improved form to win valuable event at Milan in September by a length from
Toto Le Moko, leading 100 yds out: effective at 1¼m to 1¾m: acts on firm and soft
ground: has wandered under pressure: sold (to go to Saudi Arabia) 140,000 gns in
October. *L. M. Cumani*

FRENCH CONNECTION 2 b.c. (Jan 29) Tirol 127 – Heaven-Liegh-Grey 90 72
(Grey Desire 115) [1997 7m 7.1m² 7.9s² Sep 3] 7,400Y: smallish, sturdy colt: second
foal: half-brother to 3-y-o Senate Swings: dam best around 5f: fair form in maidens
at Chester, Musselburgh and York: stays 1m. *J. Berry*

FRENCH GINGER 6 ch.m. Most Welcome 131 – French Plait (Thatching 131) 56
[1996 53d: a8g² a7g a10g 10.1m 10f 1997 8m⁴ a8g 7.1g* 8m 8g a7g a6g Nov 17]
lengthy mare: poor mover: modest handicapper: made all in maiden event at
Musselburgh in September: stays 1m: acts on good to firm and dead ground and on
equitrack: well beaten in visor. *L. R. Lloyd-James*

FRENCH GRIT (IRE) 5 b.g. Common Grounds 118 – Charbatte (FR) 93 (In 83
Fijar (USA) 121) [1996 78: 6g⁶ 5m² 6m 6m 6m 6m⁴ 5d⁶ 6f³ 6f² 6g² 5g³ 5m 6f⁵ 1997
6m* 6m 6s 6g 6m* 6g 6m 7g 6g 6m⁴ 6g Oct 22] workmanlike gelding: fairly useful
handicapper: won at Ripon in April and Pontefract in June: mostly well below form
in second half of year: has form at 7f, races mostly at 6f (on good ground or firmer)
nowadays: none too consistent. *M. Dods*

FRENCH HOLLY (USA)   6 b.g. Sir Ivor 135 – Sans Dot 92 (Busted 134) [1996 –
NR 1997 22.2d Jun 20] $2,000F: 20,000 4-y-o: big, rangy gelding: from family of
several winners, including stayers Sit Elnaas (full brother) and Deano's Beeno (by
Far North): dam, stayed at least 1¼m after 2 starts, out of Oaks winner Juliette
Marny: had 5 runs in NH Flat races, winning twice and running well in 3 Grade 1
events: tailed off in Queen Alexandra Stakes at Royal Ascot on flat debut: promising
novice hurdler. *F. Murphy*

FRENCH IVY (USA)   10 ch.g. Nodouble (USA) – Lierre (USA) (Gummo   66
(USA) 117) [1996 72: 16.2g 16.1g⁶ 16.2f³ 16.2m* 16.2m⁶ 16.1m⁴ 16d* 16g² 1997
16.2m 16.2s 16m⁴ 16.2s Jun 21] leggy gelding: fair handicapper: stays 2¼m: acts
on firm and soft ground: visored twice earlier in career: usually bandaged: held up.
F. Murphy

FRENCH KISS (IRE)   3 b.g. Petorius 117 – Cerosia (Pitskelly 122) [1996 –:   –
a7g⁴ 1997 a10g Jan 4] well beaten in maidens. *M. R. Channon*

FRENCH MIST   3 b.f. Mystiko (USA) 124 – Flambera (FR) (Akarad (FR) 130)   71
[1996 69: 6f 6g 7m⁵ 8.1d⁶ 8.1m⁵ 7m 1997 14.6d³ 10.4g 12m⁶ 14.1m² 14.1s⁶ 12m³
11.6g a13g Dec 12] tall filly: fluent mover: fair maiden handicapper: left C. Brittain
after fourth start: stays 14.6f: acts on good to firm and dead ground. *S. Dow*

FRENCH PRIDE (IRE)   2 b.f. (Mar 25) Pips Pride 117 – Reasonably French   –
(Reasonable (FR) 119) [1997 5g⁵ Aug 2] 7,000 2-y-o: third living foal: half-sister to
German 3-y-o 8.5f winner Red Facility (by Classic Secret): dam Irish 2-y-o 7f
winner: last of 5 in minor event at Hamilton. *A. R. Dicken*

FRENCH PROJECT (IRE)   5 b.m. Project Manager 111 – Malia 81 (Malacate   –
(USA) 131) [1996 NR 1997 12.1d 13s May 4] half-sister to 1½m winner in Ireland
by Nordico: dam 2-y-o 5f winner: winning hurdler and fairly useful maiden on flat
(for J. Bolger in 1995) in Ireland: no form in Britain. *Mrs S. C. Bradburne*

FRESH FRUIT DAILY   5 b.m. Reprimand 122 – Dalmally 89 (Sharpen Up 127)   73
[1996 70, a62: a10g³ a8g⁴ a8g³ 9m⁵ 7g 8.2m 6d³ a7g a8g 1997 a11s* a11g⁴ a11g   a47
a12g⁴ 9.7m* 10g⁵ a12g² 10m a12f⁴ 9.9m 10.1g a14.8g⁴ Sep 20] tall, angular mare:
fair on turf, poor on the all-weather: won apprentice maiden at Southwell in January,
amateurs handicap at Folkestone in April and novelty handicap (under peach of a ride
from local steward Diana Williams) at Wolverhampton in May: seems to stay easy
14.8f: acts on good to firm and dead ground and on all-weather: carries head
awkwardly: inconsistent. *P. A. Kelleway*

FRET (USA)   7 b.g. Storm Bird (CAN) 134 – Windy And Mild (USA) (Best Turn   –
(USA)) [1996 –: a16g 1997 16d⁶ Jun 23] no longer of any account. *J. S. Wainwright*

FRIAR'S OAK   5 b.g. Absalom 128 – Sunset Ray 74 (Hotfoot 126) [1996 NR   –
1997 9.7m 11.9f Apr 21] no longer of any account. *P. Butler*

FRIAR TUCK   2 ch.c. (Mar 31) Inchinor 119 – Jay Gee Ell 78 (Vaigly Great 127)   89
[1997 5d⁴ 6m* 6m³ 5d³ 6g⁴ 6g Oct 18] 20,000Y: leggy, lengthy colt: closely related
to winning sprinter We're Joken (by Statoblest) and half-brother to 1995 2-y-o 5f
winner Mystique Smile (by Music Boy): dam 2-y-o sprint winner later suited by
1¼m: fairly useful form: made all in maiden at Ayr in July: ran well when third to
Halmahera in listed race there and when fourth in nursery at Hamilton next start: stiff
task final outing: a sprinter: yet to race on extremes of ground: tends to swish tail.
Miss L. A. Perratt

FRIENDLY BRAVE (USA)   7 b.g. Well Decorated (USA) – Companionship   71
(USA) (Princely Native (USA)) [1996 78, a75: a6g⁴ a5g⁴ a6g a5g⁴ 5g 5m* 5.3f³
5.1g³ 5m⁴ 5d² 5m⁵ 5m⁵ 6m* 6m 5f* 5g³ 5m² 5m 5.1m* 5.1g⁵ 6v⁵ 6g 6.1s 5f² a5g⁵
a6g⁶ 1997 6m a6g⁴ 6f 5g⁵ 6d 5m⁵ 6s 5.7g² 5g 6m⁵ 5g⁶ 6m⁴ 5m a7g⁵ a5g⁶ a6g³ a5g*
Dec 22] good-quartered gelding: impresses in appearance: fair handicapper: won at
Lingfield in December: effective at 5f/6f (didn't stay 7f forcefully ridden): acts on
any turf/all-weather: effective blinkered or not: usually waited with: consistent. *Miss
Gay Kelleway*

FRIENDLY COAST   11 b.g. Blakeney 126 – Noreena (Nonoalco (USA) 131)   –
[1996 NR 1997 a11g Jan 31] very lightly raced and no form since 1990. *D. T. Thom*

FRI

FRIENDLY KNIGHT 7 b.g. Horage 124 – Be A Dancer (Be Friendly 130) –
[1996 –: 13d 1997 8.3s⁵ May 8] temperamental hurdler/chaser, bad maiden on flat.
J. S. Haldane

FRIENDLY WARNING 2 b.f. (Feb 16) Warning 136 – Dedara (Head For 82 +
Heights 125) [1997 6g² 7s* 7g⁴ 7.3g Oct 25] 180,000 francs Y: workmanlike filly:
has a quick action: third foal: dam, 1½m winner in France, half-sister to smart French
middle-distance colt Dastaan: showed fairly useful form in 2 outings in France,
winning minor event at Clairefontaine in August then fourth in similar race at
Maisons-Laffitte: well beaten in listed race at Newbury final start: likely to stay
1¼m: acts on soft ground. *J. E. Banks*

FRISKY LADY 2 b.f. (Jan 24) Magic Ring (IRE) 115 – Epithet 105 (Mill Reef 54
(USA) 141) [1997 5g⁶ 5m⁶ 6s³ a6g⁴ Jul 25] 6,200Y: eighth foal: half-sister to dam of
Shaamit and to several other winners here and abroad, including 7f winner A Chef
Too Far (by Be My Chief) and fairly useful 9f/1¼m winner Sugar Plum Fairy (by
Sadler's Wells): dam 2-y-o sprint winner who stayed 1½m: modest form: in frame
in maiden at Hamilton and nursery at Wolverhampton: will probably stay 1m.
T. D. Easterby

FRITTON (IRE) 2 br.g. (Apr 16) Petardia 113 – Calash (Indian King (USA) 128) –
[1997 6g⁶ 6g 6m Aug 23] IR 22,000Y: good-topped gelding: fifth reported foal:
half-brother to modest winners at up to 7f by River Falls, Salt Dome and by Prince
Rupert: dam half-sister to smart 1983 2-y-o 7f winner Knoxville: behind in maidens:
gelded. *M. H. Tompkins*

FROLICKING 2 b.f. (Apr 29) Mujtahid (USA) 118 – Perfect Desire (USA) 66
(Green Forest (USA) 134) [1997 5d 5.7m⁵ 6g⁴ 6.9g 7.3d⁴ 8m 6g⁵ a7g Nov 21]
angular, good-quartered filly: second foal: half-sister to German 3-y-o Irish Stainy
(by Robellino), 5f and 1m winner at 2 yrs: dam French maiden daughter of Poule
d'Essai des Pouliches runner-up Mysterieuse Etoile: fair form in maidens and
nurseries for J. Dunlop: well beaten on all-weather debut for new stable final start:
should stay 1m: acts on good to firm and good to soft ground. *N. P. Littmoden*

FROND 2 b.f. (Feb 5) Alzao (USA) 117 – Fern 100 (Shirley Heights 130) [1997 85 p
6f⁵ 7m⁵ 7m³ 7g* Oct 22] well-made filly: second foal: half-sister to 3-y-o German
1m and 9.5f winner Flying Heights (by Kris): dam 1½m winner, half-sister to Shamshir out of Free Guest: promising filly: won maiden at Newcastle more impressively
than bare result suggests, switched and quickening late on to beat Astrapi going away
by ½ length: will be well suited by 1m+: sure to do better over distances more in
keeping with her pedigree, and should make a useful filly at the least. *L. M. Cumani*

FRONT VIEW 3 b.g. Backchat (USA) 98 – Book Review (Balidar 133) [1996 –: –
a6g 1997 a9.4g Feb 12] tailed off in maidens at Wolverhampton. *B. J. Llewellyn*

FROST KING 3 gr.g. Northern State (USA) 91 – Celtic Image 51 (Welsh Saint –
126) [1996 –: 7.1m 7g 8g a8g 1997 11.5m 16m⁵ 16.4m⁵ Aug 19] little worthwhile
form. *Miss B. Sanders*

FROZEN SEA (USA) 6 ch.h. Diesis 133 – Ocean Ballad 104 (Grundy 137) 66
[1996 67: 14.1m* 14f⁴ 14.1m⁵ 1997 16g⁶ 12m 12m 12d 12m⁶ Sep 26] strong horse:
fair handicapper: well below form last 3 starts: probably stays 2m: raced mainly on
good ground or firmer. *G. P. Enright*

FRUGAL 4 b.g. Dunbeath (USA) 127 – Sum Music 56 (Music Boy 124) [1996 –
NR 1997 7g 7m 8g Jun 21] good-bodied gelding: third foal: dam poor sprint maiden:
well beaten in sellers and maiden. *B. W. Murray*

FRUITS OF LOVE (USA) 2 b.c. (Feb 15) Hansel (USA) – Vallee Secrete 102 p
(USA) (Secretariat (USA)) [1997 7m* 7m³ 7g² Aug 30] $70,000F, IR 75,000Y:
good-topped, attractive colt: easy mover: closely related to fairly useful 1991 2-y-o
6f winner (stayed 1¼m) Mutabahi (by Woodman) and half-brother to 3 winners,
including smart 1990 2-y-o sprinter Mujadil (by Storm Bird): dam French 1m winner
from excellent family: impressive winner of maiden at Newcastle in August: useful
form when 2 lengths third to Bahr in listed race at Newbury then strong-finishing
length second to Impressionist in Futurity Stakes at the Curragh: will be well suited
by at least 1m: has tended to edge right: should make a still better 3-y-o. *M. Johnston*

380

FRUNDIN 2 ch.f. (Mar 28) Anshan 119 – Freudenau (Wassl 125) [1997 5m⁶ a5g ?
a6g* 6v 6s³ 6.7g³ 6g³ 6v³ 6.7s⁴ a5.5g² Oct 2] 2,000 2-y-o: useful-looking filly: third
foal: half-sister to 2 winners in Italy by Executive Man: dam ran 3 times: no promise,
showing signs of temperament, in Britain first 2 starts: won maiden at Taby in June.
Mrs W. B. Allen, Norway

FULL MOON 2 b.g. (Apr 22) Almoojid 69 – High Time (FR) (Adonijah 126) –
[1997 5s 7.1m Jul 18] 4,600 2-y-o: close-coupled gelding: third reported foal: dam
unraced: well beaten, including in seller (blinkered). *P. D. Evans*

FULLOPEP 3 b.g. Dunbeath (USA) 127 – Suggia (Alzao (USA) 117) [1996 63: 69
7.1v 6g² 5m 1997 7m 8.5m 7g 12m* 14.1m 12g⁴ 15.8g⁴ 14.1g Oct 18] sturdy
gelding: fair performer: won weak maiden at Catterick in May: good efforts in
handicaps afterwards when fourth: should prove suited by good test of stamina: acts
on good to firm going. *Mrs M. Reveley*

FULL THROTTLE 4 br.g. Daring March 116 – Wheatley (Town Crier 119) –
[1996 73: 10m 12g 10m 10.8m³ 11.5m² 12.1m* 11.1g* 14m³ 11.8g² 1997 14g 10m
12v⁴ Jul 4] leggy gelding: fair handicapper at 3 yrs, no form in 1997. *M. H. Tompkins*

FULL TRACEABILITY (IRE) 3 b.f. Ron's Victory (USA) 129 – Miss Petella –
(Dunphy 124) [1996 53, a44: 5d² 5g* 5d 5m³ a5g⁵ 6f³ 5f² 6d 6s a6s 1997 a7g⁵ a12g
Feb 21] workmanlike filly: modest performer: well held in 1997: in foal to Cois Na
Tine. *J. J. O'Neill*

FULLY BOOKED 3 b.f. Midyan (USA) 124 – Vielle 123 (Ribero 126) [1996 –p: –
5.1m 6g 1997 10m 10g Jul 30] no worthwhile form. *J. W. Hills*

FUNCHAL WAY 5 b.g. One Man Band 71 – Dusky Nancy 65 (Red Sunset 120) –
[1996 –: 7.3f 1997 6m 12g a7g Nov 6] lengthy, sparely-made gelding: no sign of
ability: trained on reappearance by N. Babbage. *B. R. Millman*

FUNDANCE 2 b.g. (Apr 30) Rambo Dancer (CAN) 107 – Having Fun (Hard 70
Fought 125) [1997 6f⁴ 6g³ 6g 7m 6.1g³ a7g 5s Oct 15] 13,500Y: strong, good-bodied a?
gelding: brother to 3-y-o Mardrew and 2 winners around 1m in Italy: dam lightly-
raced half-sister to smart Hushang (best up to 1¼m): fair maiden: close third at
Nottingham (had favoured rail) fifth start: should stay at least 1m. *M. Dods*

FUN GALORE (USA) 3 b.c. Gone West (USA) – Ma Petite Jolie (USA) 80 84
(Northern Dancer) [1996 92: 6m* 7m* 7m 1997 7g 7s⁵ 7m 7g⁶ Oct 27] robust,
good-quartered colt: unimpressive mover: fairly useful performer: stiff tasks in 1997:
should stay 1m: sold 16,000 gns in October. *B. W. Hills*

FUNG SHUI (IRE) 2 b.c. (Mar 25) Night Shift (USA) – Isola (GER) (Konigs- –
stuhl (GER)) [1997 6g 7g a7g 7f Oct 3] 6,200Y: tall, workmanlike colt: third foal:
dam, German 2-y-o 6.5f winner, half-sister to German St Leger winner Index: no
worthwhile form. *R. Hannon*

FUNKY 4 ch.f. Classic Music (USA) – Foreno (Formidable (USA) 125) [1996 48: –
5m⁵ 8g⁶ 7g 8m² 8m 9g 1997 a7g 8s 8m⁶ Apr 14] no form in 1997. *D. Nicholls*

FUNNY HOWITHAPPENS 2 b.f. (May 27) Forzando 122 – Girl's Brigade –
(Brigadier Gerard 144) [1997 6g May 16] 2,100Y: half-sister to a fairly useful 2-y-o
by Absalom and a winner in Italy by Song: dam dead-heated over 7f at 2 yrs in
Ireland and stayed 1¼m: tailed off in maiden at Newmarket. *C. Murray*

FURNISH 3 b.f. Green Desert (USA) 127 – Eternal (Kris 135) [1996 87p: 7m³ 7g³ 87
1997 7.1d⁴ 5g* 5g² 6g Jul 5] strong, lengthy filly: has a quick action: fairly useful
performer: won weak maiden at Doncaster in June: best 3-y-o effort when second in
handicap at Ayr following outing: hard puller, likely to prove best at 5f: yet to race on
extremes of going. *B. W. Hills*

FURTHER FLIGHT 11 gr.g. Pharly (FR) 130 – Flying Nelly 107 (Nelcius 133) 115
[1996 107: 14.1g* 13.4g⁶ 14.6g³ 16m 14.6d³ 1997 13.4v² 13.3s² 13.9m⁴ 13.9g⁴
13.4s* 18f³ 16f³ 15.5d Oct 26] angular gelding: has a round action: usually relaxed
in preliminaries: a grand old campaigner, winner of Jockey Club Cup 5 years running
from 1991 (in which year had highest rating of 118) to 1995: below form in that race
at 11 yrs but was almost as good as ever, and won listed rated stakes at Chester in
August by 10 lengths from Kutta: also ran well when second in Ormonde Stakes on
same course (to Royal Court) first outing, fourth in Ebor at York (finished best of all)

Mr S. Wingfield Digby's "Further Flight"

fourth start and third in Doncaster Cup (to Canon Can) sixth appearance: needs a test of stamina when short of 2m these days, and stays 2¼m: acts on any going: wears small bandages: normally held up: outstandingly game and genuine. *B. W. Hills*

FURTHER OUTLOOK (USA)   3 gr.g. Zilzal (USA) 137 – Future Bright – (USA) (Lyphard's Wish (FR) 124) [1996 96: 7m² 7.5f* 8.1f³ 8.3g* 8s⁴ 1997 10d⁵ 10d⁶ 8m Jun 17] useful-looking gelding: fairly useful form at 2 yrs for M. Stoute: well held in 1997, wearing crossed noseband and sweating final outing: subsequently gelded. *Mrs A. J. Perrett*

FUR WILL FLY   3 br.f. Petong 126 – Bumpkin 108 (Free State 125) [1996 NR   66 1997 7g 6m² 7.3s⁶ 6m⁵ Jun 14] 24,000Y: good-topped filly: eighth foal: half-sister to modest 1¼m winner Pumpkin (by Top Ville): dam sprinter: fair maiden: raced too keenly both starts at 7f: hung left second start. *I. A. Balding*

FUTURE PERFECT   3 b.g. Efisio 120 – True Ring (High Top 131) [1996 73p: 99 p 7.1v* 1997 8m* 8m⁶ 8.1d² 8m 10m² 10m* 12s⁶ Nov 8] big, good-topped gelding: useful performer: won minor event at Pontefract in April and 18-runner £35,000

Volvo Contracts Globetrotter Handicap, Goodwood—Future Perfect springs a surprise

handicap at Goodwood in August, best effort when finishing strongly to beat Supply And Demand in latter, despite almost getting brought down early on: found stamina tested too much after looking sure to be involved in finish 3f out in November Handicap at Doncaster final start: may stay 1½m under less testing conditions: acts on good to firm and heavy ground: open to further progress. *P. F. I. Cole*

FUWALA   3 b.f. Unfuwain (USA) 131 – Lobela 77 (Lorenzaccio 130) [1996 NR   –
1997 10d⁶ 10m Sep 9] big, plain filly: half-sister to several winners, all up to 7f: dam won at 1m and 1¼m: no show in autumn maidens. *D. Shaw*

G

GABLESEA   3 b.g. Beveled (USA) – Me Spede (Valiyar 129) [1996 59: 7m 6.1m²   –
6f 6g 1997 7.1s⁶ 6g 7g⁵ 7v 7.6m 8.2m a8.5g* a8g 8.2d a7g* a7g⁶ a7g a7g⁴ a9.4g⁴   a59
Dec 26] tall gelding: modest handicapper: won at Wolverhampton (maiden event) in September and Southwell in November: effective at 7f to 8.5f: acts on good to firm going and on fibresand: inconsistent. *B. P. J. Baugh*

GADGE   6 br.g. Nomination 125 – Queenstyle 58 (Moorestyle 137) [1996 59, a–:   87
8g 8m⁶ 8m 8g⁵ 8.1m 8m 8.1s⁵ a9.4g⁶ a12g 1997 a7g⁶ a8g⁴ a10g a8g³ a8g* a8g³ a8g³   a60
8m* 8.3d² 10g 8g³ 8m* 8d* 7d* 6g* 7m⁵ 6.1s³ 6s⁵ 6m² 6m 6g 7d 6g a6g⁴ 6g a8g
Nov 25] sturdy, lengthy gelding: fairly useful handicapper on turf: had excellent first half of season, winning at Newcastle, Thirsk (Hunt Cup, by head from Gulf Shaadi), Bath, Goodwood and Ayr: only modest on the all-weather, winner at Lingfield in February: effective at 6f to 1m: acts on good to firm and soft going: tried visored/blinkered, not as 6-y-o: sometimes bandaged in front: usually races prominently: game. *A. Bailey*

GADROON   3 ch.g. Cadeaux Genereux 131 – Greensward Blaze 50 (Sagaro 133)   49
[1996 –: 8m 6d 1997 5s a9.4f⁵ 8.3s³ 9s² 10.1g Oct 22] good-topped gelding: poor maiden handicapper: stays 9f (pulled too hard over 1¼m): acts on soft ground. *P. C. Haslam*

GAD YAKOUN   4 ch.g. Cadeaux Genereux 131 – Summer Impressions (USA) 70   –
(Lyphard (USA) 132) [1996 65: 5m³ 6m⁶ 7g⁵ a7g* a6g a7g 1997 a7g⁵ a5f Jan 11] fair winner at 3 yrs: well below form both outings in 1997: stays 7f: acts on equitrack and on good to firm ground. *M. G. Meagher*

GAELIC QUINIE (IRE)   2 b.f. (Mar 29) River Falls 113 – Eliza Wooding 70   50 ?
(Faustus (USA) 118) [1997 5m⁵ 6g⁶ a6g 8g Oct 18] IR 500Y, 3,000 2-y-o: small, sparely-made filly: first foal: dam, 7f seller winner at 2 yrs, probably stayed 2m: signs of ability on debut, but well beaten afterwards, including in sellers (visored third start). *G. R. Oldroyd*

GAELIC STORM   3 b.c. Shavian 125 – Shannon Princess (Connaught 130)   95
[1996 77: 5m³ 5s⁴ 5f* 6g⁶ 5g³ 1997 6g⁶ 5m 5m* 5d* 6g⁵ 6g* 5d 5g 6m⁶ a7g Dec 6] small, sturdy colt: useful sprinter: won handicaps at Thirsk and Epsom in August and apprentice minor event at Catterick following month: acts on firm and dead ground, well beaten on fibresand when tried at 7f: tends to sweat, get on edge and start slowly: has been bandaged behind. *M. Johnston*

GAGAJULU   4 b.f. Al Hareb (USA) 123 – Rion River (IRE) (Taufan (USA) 119)   –
[1996 54: a5g a5g⁶ a5g³ a5g⁶ 5d 5g 5.1m⁶ 5m⁵ 5f⁶ 5m 5m 5.1m⁶ 6m 1997 5g 5m
May 2] close-coupled filly: has lost her form. *P. D. Evans*

GAILY MILL   2 b.f. (May 10) Keen 116 – Island Mill 79 (Mill Reef (USA) 141)   56
[1997 5d⁵ 5.7m 7m Oct 1] leggy, angular filly: has a round action: seventh foal: half-sister to 3-y-o Mara River, 1¾m winner Arrastra (by Bustino) and 2 middle-distance winners abroad: dam stayer: form in maidens only on debut: very upset stalls next time, then off 10 weeks. *I. A. Balding*

GAIN LINE (USA)   4 b.g. Dayjur (USA) 137 – Safe Play (USA) (Sham (USA))   60
[1996 64: 8m 9m⁵ 1997 7m 10d 7f⁴ 8d² 8d³ 6m 7g* 8f⁴ 7m 7f 7m⁶ Nov 1] big, strong gelding: modest handicapper: won at Yarmouth in July: generally good efforts afterwards (gelded at end of season): needs further than 6f, and stays 1m: acts on firm

and dead going (unraced on softer): ran badly in visor once: usually takes strong hold and races prominently. *Bob Jones*

GAJAN (IRE) 3 b.g. Ela-Mana-Mou 132 – Delightful Time (Manado 130) [1996 – NR 1997 7g 8.2d⁶ 10.2s⁶ Jul 1] 12,000 2-y-o: seventh foal: half-brother to fairly useful 1995 2-y-o 5f winner Beautiful Ballad (by Ballad Rock): dam maiden half-sister to Sassafras: no sign of ability in maidens. *J. Neville*

GALA MISS 2 b.f. (Mar 19) Sizzling Melody 117 – Luckifosome 45 (Smackover – 107) [1997 5g 6m 5m Jul 21] 1,000Y: leggy filly: first foal: dam, 5f winner, ran only at 2 yrs: showed nothing in poor company: visored first 2 starts. *P. D. Evans*

GALAPINO 4 b.g. Charmer 123 – Carousella 62 (Rousillon (USA) 133) [1996 81 86d: a8.5g⁴ a10g³ a10g* a9.4g* a8.5g² 10m 11.4d⁵ 9.9f⁵ 8g⁶ 10m 9.9f⁵ 8m⁶ 7.1f 10g⁴ 1997 a8.5g² a12g* a12g² 12m* 12.3m⁴ 12g² 12.3v 12m 12.5m* 14s² 14m² 16.2g 16.2v² 16g 16.5s² Nov 8] smallish gelding: fairly useful performer: won claimer at Wolverhampton in January (claimed out of G. Bravery's stable next start) and handicaps at Doncaster (apprentices) in March and Warwick in June: continued in good form afterwards, running particularly well in handicap at Doncaster final start: stays 2m: acts on good to firm going, heavy and the all-weather. *Miss Gay Kelleway*

GALAXY FLIGHT 3 ch.f. Superlative 118 – Glide Path 91 (Sovereign Path – 125) [1996 NR 1997 8.1m⁶ 7.6g⁵ Aug 2] 2,400F, 5,200Y: angular filly: half-sister to 1987 2-y-o 8.5f winner Stryder (by Jalmood) and useful 9f to 1½m winner Diamond Path (by Morston): dam, most genuine, won 7 times up to 13f: little worthwhile form in maidens: sold 500 gns in September. *Martyn Meade*

GALIBIS (FR) 3 b.g. Groom Dancer (USA) 128 – Damasquine (USA) (Damas- 76 d cus (USA)) [1996 75: 8m⁵ 8g 1997 a7g* 10g⁵ 7.1m 8m Oct 23] angular gelding: fair form: won maiden at Lingfield in January: last in minor events afterwards, leaving P. Kelleway after next start and sold only 1,400 gns in November: should stay 1¼m. *R. Hannon*

GALINE 4 b.f. Most Welcome 131 – Tarasova (USA) (Green Forest (USA) 134) 82 [1996 91: 6m⁵ 5g 6m² 6m⁴ 5m* 6g⁵ 5m⁴ 5f² 5m 6m⁵ 1997 6m 5d 6g⁶ Jul 18] strong, lengthy filly: fairly useful handicapper: lightly raced at 4 yrs, best effort on reappearance: effective at 5f and 6f: acts on fibresand and firm ground: has worn rope halter in preliminaries: held up. *W. A. O'Gorman*

GALLAASH (USA) 2 b.c. (Mar 27) Gulch (USA) – In View (USA) (In Reality) 55 [1997 7.1m⁶ 7g Aug 20] $280,000Y: lengthy, unfurnished colt: second foal: dam, won at up to 1¼m in USA, from family of Singspiel: modest form in maidens at Sandown (hung badly right) and Kempton. *J. H. M. Gosden*

GALLANT HEIGHTS 3 b.f. Anshan 119 – Marie Galante 73 (Shirley Heights 70 d 130) [1996 NR 1997 10g⁵ 12m⁵ 12m 16.4g 16m⁴ 10s 18d 12m Oct 31] leggy filly: sixth foal: half-sister to 7f to 1¼m winner Round By The River (by Superlative): dam staying maiden: fair maiden: well beaten last 3 starts: probably stays 2m: acts on good to firm going. *G. C. Bravery*

GAME BIRD 2 b.f. (Mar 12) Absalom 128 – Mistral's Dancer (Shareef Dancer 65 ? (USA) 135) [1997 5d 5m⁵ 5d 5d Nov 7] fourth foal: half-sister to 3-y-o Queen's Pageant and 5-y-o Kristal Breeze: dam, maiden, best at 7f: apparently fair form second start, but well below it on dead ground otherwise. *J. L. Spearing*

GAME PLOY (POL) 5 b.g. Deploy 131 – Guestimate (FR) (Be My Guest 100 (USA) 126) [1996 90: 10g 10.2g⁴ 10g* 10g* 10.3m* 9f³ 10m 10.2f² 10m* 9m 10s 12s 1997 10.3d⁵ 10.4g³ 10g² 10s⁵ 10.4m³ 10s² 10.4g⁴ 10d 9m Oct 4] tall gelding: has a round action: useful handicapper: very good efforts when third at York (Magnet Cup, won by Pasternak), second at Ascot and fourth at York on fifth to seventh outings: run best ignored last 2 starts, quite badly hampered first time then set a lot to do in Cambridgeshire: best form around 1¼m, should be effective at 1½m: probably acts on any going: held up: genuine and reliable. *D. Haydn Jones*

GANDOURA (USA) 2 b.f. (Apr 25) Sheikh Albadou 128 – Alqwani (USA) 83 70 p (Mr Prospector (USA)) [1997 6g 6m⁶ 6g Oct 27] stocky filly: fluent mover: third foal: half-sister to 3-y-o Kafaf and useful 7f/1m (in Dubai) winner Intidab (by Phone Trick): dam, 2-y-o 6f winner, out of half-sister to Bellotto: fair form in maiden at

Newbury second start: never dangerous at Leicester over 2 months later: likely to be well suited by 7f/1m: has scope and should do better. *J. H. M. Gosden*

GANGA (IRE) 3 ch.f. Generous (IRE) 139 – Congress Lady 93 (General 94 p Assembly (USA)) [1996 –: 7d 1997 8s* 8.5v 8g⁶ 10d* 10.5g 10g* Oct 18] smallish, sturdy filly: useful form: won maiden at Newcastle in June and handicaps at Ripon in August and Redcar (gamely, in 16-runner race) in October: should stay beyond 1¼m: raced only on good going or softer: held up, and suited by strongly-run race: lightly raced, and should progress further. *W. Jarvis*

GARLANDHAYES 5 b.m. Adbass (USA) 102 – Not Alone 84 (Pas de Seul 133) – [1996 –: 10f 1997 a14.8f Jan 11] second foal: dam disappointing maiden: tailed-off last in claimers. *Miss K. M. George*

GARNOCK VALLEY 7 b.g. Dowsing (USA) 124 – Sunley Sinner 93 (Try My 79 d Best (USA) 130) [1996 93, a73: 6d³ 5g* 5s⁶ 5g* 6d 5m* 6m⁵ 5m 6f 6m 7m 6v* 6g 6f a– a6g³ 1997 6m 5g 6s⁴ 6s² 6g⁴ 6g 5g⁴ 6s 6d 6g 7d a6g 6s⁶ 7m Oct 28] neat gelding: fairly useful handicapper at best: in-and-out form at 7 yrs: stays 6f: has won on firm going, goes particularly well on soft/heavy: usually blinkered nowadays. *J. Berry*

GAROLO (FR) 7 b.g. Garde Royale 120 – Valgoa (Valdingran (FR)) [1996 96 NR 1997 16.2m⁶ Apr 30] compact gelding: sixth foal: brother to 1¼m winner Valyroi and half-brother to 10.5f winner by Synefos: dam won at 9f/1¼m: 1½m winner on Flat in France as 3-y-o, when trained by F. Chevalier du Fau: useful hurdler/fairly useful chaser around 2m: 100/1, ran well when sixth of 8 to Orchestra Stall in Group 3 event at Ascot: may prove up to 2m. *C. P. E. Brooks*

GARUDA (IRE) 3 b.c. Danehill (USA) 126 – Ardmelody (Law Society (USA) 106 130) [1996 8g⁶ 1997 10g⁴ 10s* 10.3m⁵ 11.9g³ 11.9g⁵ Aug 19] big, strong colt: has plenty of scope: has a powerful, round action: fourth foal: half-brother to Memories (by Don't Forget Me), 6f (at 2 yrs) in USA) winner: dam unraced from family of Ardross: useful performer: trained at 2 yrs in France by L. Audon: won 15-runner maiden at Newbury in May: best effort when 2¼ lengths third of 6 to Ivan Luis in falsely-run listed event at Haydock in July: stays 1½m: acts on soft going: has taken strong hold (too free in Great Voltigeur Stakes at York final outing). *J. L. Dunlop*

GATES (USA) 4 ch.g. Jade Hunter (USA) – Royal Herat (USA) (Herat (USA)) 87 [1996 12g⁵ 8.5g* 11m³ 9d* 1997 8g 8m 9g 10m 9g⁴ 8d² 8s Oct 18] angular gelding: second start: closely related to a winning sprinter in North America by Allen's Prospect: dam unraced from good family: useful winner (rated 98) at 3 yrs: failed to reproduce best form in 1997: well beaten in Hunt Cup at Royal Ascot second start: creditable effort at 11f but probably better at 1m/9f: acts on good to soft ground, probably on good to firm: tried blinkered, no improvement. *D. K. Weld, Ireland*

GAY ABANDON 2 ch.f. (Mar 22) Risk Me (FR) 127 – School Dinners 74 – (Sharpo 132) [1997 7.1g 6.9s 7g⁴ 7g 10d Oct 13] leggy, close-coupled filly: second reported foal: dam, second at 7f, out of half-sister to smart stayer Petty Officer: no worthwhile form, including in sellers: blinkered final start. *K. McAuliffe*

GAY BREEZE 4 b.g. Dominion 123 – Judy's Dowry 80 (Dragonara Palace 54 p (USA) 115) [1996 –: 5m 7f 8g 1997 6.1m 6.1d³ 6m² 6d² 6m² 5g* 6f* 6g⁵ Oct 27] compact gelding: progressive and lightly-raced handicapper: won at Leicester in August and Yarmouth (18 ran) in September: stays 6f: acts on firm and dead going (yet to race on softer): races prominently: should go on again at 5 yrs. *P. S. Felgate*

GAY DA CHEEN (IRE) 2 b.f. (Mar 5) Tenby 125 – Gaychimes (Steel Heart – 128) [1997 6m 7.1m 7g Aug 22] 8,000Y: close-coupled filly: half-sister to several winners, including fairly useful 1996 2-y-o 6f winner Fanny's Choice (by Fairy King): dam unraced half-sister to Grade I 1¼m winner Gaily Gaily: well beaten in sellers. *J. M. Carr*

GAZELLE ROYALE (FR) 3 b.f. Garde Royale 120 – Beautywal (FR) 117 (Magwal (FR)) [1996 7g 8s⁴ 8g* 8d³ 1997 10d³ 12m² 10g³ 12m² 12f Oct 5]
Halfway up the home straight at Epsom it looked as though northern-based jockey Jimmy Fortune, having his first ride in a classic in Britain, might pull off a shock win in the Vodafone Oaks on the French-trained Gazelle

Royale. Fortune, an excellent jockey but more familiar to racegoers at the likes of Pontefract and Thirsk, rode most of the tricky Epsom course well, settling his mount towards the rear, pulling wide to avoid trouble three furlongs out and challenging soon after, a move which temporarily blocked the path of the favourite Reams of Verse. Gazelle Royale responded so well to her rider's urgings that she hit the front two furlongs out. But she had no answer to Reams of Verse once the latter obtained a clear run and was beaten one and a half lengths into second, drifting left under pressure and causing some interference, for which Fortune was given a two-day ban for failing to switch his whip. Gazelle Royale had not had a great deal to recommend her at Epsom, where she was sent off at 33/1, having won just one of her three starts at two years and been put firmly in her place by Brilliance in the Prix Saint-Alary at Longchamp on her reappearance. Her much-improved effort was no fluke, though, as her subsequent performances showed. Next time out, Gazelle Royale finished a close third behind Dust Dancer in the Prix de la Nonette at Deauville in August, and the following month she just managed to turn the tables on Brilliance only to find Queen Maud too good in the Prix Vermeille at Longchamp, going down by a length. Returned to Longchamp for the Prix de l'Arc de Triomphe, Gazelle Royale turned in a respectable effort, even though she beat only five of her seventeen rivals, racing prominently until early in the straight.

		Mill Reef	Never Bend
	Garde Royale	(b 1968)	Milan Mill
	(b 1980)	Royal Way	Sicambre
Gazelle Royale (FR)		(gr 1969)	Right Away
(b.f. 1994)		Magwal	Dictus
	Beautywal (FR)	(b 1979)	Val Gardena
	(ch 1989)	True Beauty	Sun Prince
		(ch 1979)	Be True

Mr K. Yoshida's "Gazelle Royale"

Gazelle Royale is by the well-bred Garde Royale (the sire of the Prix de Diane and Vermeille winner Carling), who showed very smart form over one and a half miles in France, out of Beautywal, a winner over a mile and a quarter at two years and placed at up to a mile and a half at three. Beautywal's sire, Magwal, won the Prix Jean Prat and Grand Prix d'Evry in 1984, the same year Garde Royale was successful in the Prix Jean de Chaudenay. Beautywal comes from a largely undistinguished family but she is a half-sister to several minor winners, including Chanson du Chenet (by Leading Counsel), successful over hurdles and fences in France in 1997.

Gazelle Royale isn't a prepossessing filly, being leggy and plain, but handsome is as handsome does and there weren't many three-year-old fillies around with better form over a mile and a quarter and a mile and a half. While her best performances were on good and good to firm ground, Gazelle Royale showed enough on her final start at two years and also on her reappearance to suggest that she's not inconvenienced by good to soft. *J. E. Hammond, France*

GEE BEE BOY 3 ch.g. Beveled (USA) – Blue And White (Busted 134) [1996 –p: 6m 1997 9m⁵ 12m⁵ 11g* 12.4g⁵ 10g⁵ 11.8g⁵ 10m⁴ 11m Nov 4] strong, close-coupled gelding: fair performer: won maiden at Redcar in June: respectable efforts next 4 starts: stays 11f: acts on good to firm ground: takes good hold (ran wide bend at Redcar). *A. P. Jarvis* 68

GEE BEE DREAM 3 ch.f. Beveled (USA) – Return To Tara (Homing 130) [1996 68: 6m 6m 6g² 6.5m 7m 1997 7m* 7m² 7s⁴ 7f⁵ 7m 8.1m 7m 7g Oct 24] big filly: shows quick action: fairly useful handicapper: won at Lingfield in May: ran well next 3 starts but subsequently lost her form: stays 7f: acts on soft going, probably on firm. *A. P. Jarvis* 81

GEIMHRIUIL (IRE) 3 b.c. Distinctly North (USA) 115 – Ventry (Stanford 121§) [1996 6m⁶ 6.5d² 6g³ 1997 7.1d² 7g* 8d 6m* Jul 25] neat ex-Irish colt: second foal: half-brother to an Italian juvenile 7f winner by Magical Wonder: dam unplaced: generally progressive form for current stable, winning maiden at Goodwood in June and handicap at Newmarket (readily) in July: likely to prove best at 6f/7f: yet to race on extremes of going: useful performer in making if all is well with him. *L. M. Cumani* 91 p

GEM 2 b.f. (Apr 20) Most Welcome 131 – Miss Top Ville (FR) (Top Ville 129) [1997 6.1g⁵ 6d Oct 28] 26,000Y: sixth foal: sister to 4-y-o Welville (6f winner at 2 yrs) and 6-y-o Wilcuma and half-sister to a winner in Germany by Petong: dam French middle-distance winner: some promise in maiden at Nottingham: well held at Leicester later in month. *P. J. Makin* 58

GEMOLLY (IRE) 4 b.f. Be My Native (USA) 122 – Hayhurst (Sandhurst Prince 128) [1996 NR 1997 8.1g Sep 11] second foal: dam, staying maiden on flat in Ireland, won over hurdles: no worthwhile form. *Martyn Meade* –

GENERAL ACADEMY (IRE) 4 b.g. Royal Academy (USA) 130 – Hastening (Shirley Heights 130) [1996 102: 10.5m⁵ 10g 7m⁶ 10g 7m³ 10g a9.4g 1997 7g 8.1g 8m 10.3d⁵ Jun 29] big, lengthy, good sort: useful form at best: well held in Royal Hunt Cup and handicap at Goodwood last 2 starts: stays 10.5f: acts on good to firm ground: visored (broke fast) final 3-y-o outing: joined J. W. Curtis. *P. A. Kelleway* 97

GENERAL ASSEMBLY (IRE) 5 b.g. Pharly (FR) 130 – Hastening (Shirley Heights 130) [1996 NR 1997 12m⁵ 14d 14g⁴ 22.2d Jun 20] rangy, good sort: poor mover: fairly useful performer, lightly raced: tailed off in Queen Alexandra Stakes at Royal Ascot final start: should be suited by at least 2m: acts on firm and dead ground: sold only 2,000 gns in October, then gelded and joined G. Margarson. *H. R. A. Cecil* 93

GENERAL EQUATION 4 b.g. Governor General 116 – Logarithm (King of Spain 121) [1996 63d: a5g³ a5g⁴ a5g* 5s³ 5d a5g a5g a6g a5g a5g⁶ 1997 a5g 5g a6g a5g Dec 8] modest 5f performer at best, no worthwhile form since March 1996. *J. Balding* –

GENERAL GLOW 4 b.g. Presidium 124 – Glow Again 78 (The Brianstan 128) [1996 64: 12s 14.1g 12d⁶ 13.1m 10f* 11.9f* 9.9f³ 10.5m* 10.5m³ 15m³ 11.8f⁶ 11f 1997 12m 14.1m 12d a12f⁶ 12m 11.6m⁵ 10.5m⁵ Aug 15] tall gelding: poor handi- 45

capper at 4 yrs: stays 1½m: form only on firm/good to firm going: blinkered last 2 starts. *P. D. Evans*

GENERAL HASTIE 3 b.g. Cadeaux Genereux 131 – Fast Car (FR) (Carwhite – 127) [1996 NR 1997 7g 7.1d 7g Jul 25] 18,000Y: plain gelding: sixth foal: half-brother to 5-y-o Squire Corrie: dam French 1m winner: well beaten in maidens: has been bandaged. *C. W. Thornton*

GENERAL HAVEN 4 ch.g. Hadeer 118 – Verchinina 99 (Star Appeal 133) 74 [1996 74: a6g³ a6g² a6g³ a7g* a6g³ 8.2m⁴ 8d³ a8g⁵ 8m⁵ 8.3g* a10g⁴ 10f⁴ 10g a12g² a81 a13g² 1997 a12g² a12g* a16g⁴ 12m 10.8m² a12g⁴ 10.8f 10g³ 10s 10m 10d⁶ 10m Aug 17] quite good-topped gelding: fairly useful handicapper on the all-weather, fair on turf: won at Lingfield in January: should stay beyond 13f: acts on firm ground and all-weather: joined M. Sowersby. *T. J. Naughton*

GENERAL JOEY 2 b.g. (Mar 6) Governor General 116 – Joie de Patina 34 (Forzando 122) [1997 5m 5g a5g⁵ 6g 5m⁴ 5s Jul 3] 3,000Y: small, good-bodied gelding: first foal: dam no sign of ability: poor maiden: blinkered 3 of last 4 starts. *M. Dods*

GENERAL KLAIRE 2 b. or br.f. (Apr 6) Presidium 124 – Klairover 50 52 (Smackover 107) [1997 6.1s⁶ 5.1m 7d⁵ 7.9s Sep 3] 9,000Y: second foal: dam, sprint winner who stayed 1m, half-sister to smart sprinter Bunty Boo: only form in maidens at Warwick third start: should stay 1m. *B. A. McMahon*

GENERAL MONCK 2 ch.g. (Feb 16) Formidable (USA) 125 – Merton Mill 68 75 ? (Dominion 123) [1997 8m 7.9s 8.2d³ Oct 30] tall gelding: poor mover: second reported foal: dam stayed 2¼m: easily best effort in maidens when third to Eliza Acton at Nottingham, keeping on despite edging left: likely to stay at least 1¼m. *D. Morley*

GENERAL MONTY 5 b.g. Vague Shot 108 – State Free (Free State 125) [1996 40 –: 10.3g 1997 8f 8f⁴ 8.3s 7.6m 8m⁶ 8m Aug 11] poor on balance of form: should stay beyond 1m. *T. D. Barron*

GENERAL MOUKTAR 7 ch.g. Hadeer 118 – Fly The Coop (Kris 135) [1996 59 d 62: 12m² 12m³ 12g 12m³ 11.9f² 12.5f³ 12g² 12g²dis 12m² 11.9f² 12.1m 12m 12g 1997 14d³ 20m 18s³ 15.9m 14m⁶ Jul 23] compact, good-quartered gelding: has a round action: modest handicapper: below form at 7 yrs after reappearance: stays 1¾m: probably acts on any going: effective blinkered/visored or not: tends to find little and usually held up: fair hurdler, won in August. *M. C. Pipe*

GENERAL SIR PETER (IRE) 5 br.g. Last Tycoon 131 – Nashya (Rousillon 61 (USA) 133) [1996 NR 1997 6m a5g* 5.1g² a5g 5g³ 5.1g 6g 6.1d 5g a5g 5g 5.1g* a75 5m⁴ 6g a5g Nov 6] tall gelding: fair on all-weather, modest on turf: won claimer at Wolverhampton in April and 19-runner handicap at Chepstow in September: unlucky not to follow up at Pontefract after latter: spoilt chance with slow start last 2 outings: should stay 6f: acts on firm and dead ground and on fibresand: effective blinkered or not. *N. A. Callaghan*

GENERAL SONG (IRE) 3 b.g. Fayruz 116 – Daybreaker (Thatching 131) – [1996 87: 7.5g* 6m 7.3s 1997 7.9g⁵ 7g Oct 18] strong, close-coupled gelding: fairly useful at 2 yrs: stiff tasks and well beaten in 1997 (off course 3 months after belated reappearance): stays 7.5f. *K. McAuliffe*

GENEREUX 4 ch.g. Generous (IRE) 139 – Flo Russell (USA) (Round Table) – [1996 NR 1997 14.1g⁵ Jun 20] no sign of ability. *S. Mellor*

GENEROSITY 2 ch.c. (Apr 4) Generous (IRE) 139 – Pageantry 83 (Welsh 75 p Pageant 132) [1997 7m⁶ 8.3g* 8d Oct 17] tall, rangy colt: rather weak at 2 yrs: sixth reported foal: half-brother to smart middle-distance winner Up Anchor (by Slip Anchor), dam of promising Fleetwood, and 2 winners by Dominion, including useful winner up to 9f Just Class: dam ran only at 2 yrs when placed over 5f and 6f: made heavy weather of landing odds in maiden at Hamilton in September, still looking green: midfield in 28-runner nursery at Newmarket following month: likely to stay 1½m+: should make a better 3-y-o. *P. F. I. Cole*

GENEROUS EMBRACE 2 b.f. (Feb 27) Cadeaux Genereux 131 – Hug Me 96 69 + (Shareef Dancer (USA) 135) [1997 5.1m⁵ 6d* 7.3d 8g Oct 7] 22,000Y: neat filly:

sixth foal: half-sister to 3 winners, including 1995 2-y-o 7f winner Villeggiatura (by Machiavellian), later stayed 1¾m, and 1½m/1¾m winner Embracing (by Reference Point): dam 7f (at 2 yrs) and 1½m winner: won claimer at Lingfield in August (claimed from D. Elsworth £20,000): well beaten in nurseries afterwards: should stay 1m: acts on dead ground: sold 11,000 gns in December. *M. Bell*

GENEROUS GIFT   3 ch.c. Generous (IRE) 139 – Barari (USA) (Blushing   96
Groom (FR) 131) [1996 82p: 6s 7g 8g² 1997 10m² 12.3d⁵ 12m* 12d 10m 10.4g 10.5m³ 10m³ Oct 5] smallish, well-made colt: useful performer: landed odds in maiden at Goodwood in June: faced mainly stiff tasks afterwards: creditable third in minor events at Haydock and Leicester last 2 starts: stays 1½m: acts on good to firm ground, probably good to soft: has sweated: sold 30,000 gns in October, to go to USA. *E. A. L. Dunlop*

GENEROUS LIBRA   3 b.g. Generous (IRE) 139 – Come On Rosi 77 (Valiyar   95
129) [1996 87p: 7g³ 1997 8d³ 7.5m* 8m 7.1g² 8m³ 8m 9m 12d Oct 16] rather leggy, unfurnished gelding: useful performer: long odds on, easy winner of maiden at Beverley in June: placed in handicaps at Haydock and Newmarket: gelded after sixth start: should stay 1¼m (didn't last home over 1½m): yet to race on extremes of going: carries head high, has hung right and doesn't seem easiest of rides. *D. R. Loder*

GENEROUS PRESENT   4 ch.g. Cadeaux Genereux 131 – Dance Move   –
(Shareef Dancer (USA) 135) [1996 60: 7.1g 8g 10m 8f* 8.3m* 8f³ 8m 8.1m 9.7d⁶ 1997 6.9g 8m 8m 10.1f 10.8g 8.2s Oct 15] tall gelding: has a round action: modest handicapper at 3 yrs: ran badly in 1997: should stay beyond 1m: acts on firm ground: tried blinkered. *J. W. Payne*

GENEROUS ROSI   2 b.c. (Mar 28) Generous (IRE) 139 – Come On Rosi 77   – p
(Valiyar 129) [1997 6m Oct 31] fourth foal: brother to 3-y-o Generous Libra and half-brother to useful sprinter Shanghai Girl and 5-y-o Bin Rosie (both by Distant Relative): dam 6f winner: 8/1, slowly away and never dangerous in maiden at Newmarket: should do better. *D. R. Loder*

GENEROUS TERMS   2 ch.c. (May 11) Generous (IRE) 139 – Time Charter 131   66 p
(Saritamer (USA) 130) [1997 8d Oct 16] close-coupled colt: seventh foal: half-brother to 3-y-o Illusion, 4-y-o Time Allowed and smart stayer Zinaad and useful 1988 2-y-o 7f winner By Charter (both by Shirley Heights): dam top class middle-distance performer: 20/1 and wearing dropped noseband, mid-division in 22-runner maiden won by Border Arrow at Newmarket, going on at finish: should do fair bit better over 1¼m+ at 3 yrs. *H. Candy*

GENIUS (IRE)   2 b.c. (Feb 3) Lycius (USA) 124 – Once In My Life (IRE) 114   57
(Lomond (USA) 128) [1997 6d⁶ 7.1g 7g 8d a8.5g⁴ Nov 29] 150,000Y: strong,   a65
good-bodied colt: second foal: dam French 6.5f (at 2 yrs) to 1m winner, half-sister to Poule d'Essai des Poulains winner No Pass No Sale: modest maiden: sold out of P. Cole's stable 10,000 gns after fourth start (when set too strong pace in blinkers): best effort when fourth of 10 at Lingfield final outing: stays 8.5f. *S. Dow*

GENOA   2 b.f. (May 2) Zafonic (USA) 130 – Yawl 112 (Rainbow Quest (USA)   73 p
134) [1997 7m⁶ Nov 1] first foal: dam, 7f (Rockfel) winner at 2 yrs but mostly disappointing afterwards, daughter of Oaks winner Bireme: 16/1, promising 7 lengths sixth of 18 to Pontoon in late-season maiden at Newmarket on only start, left behind from 2f out, not knocked about: should stay at least 1m: should improve. *B. W. Hills*

GENTILESSE   3 gr.f. Generous (IRE) 139 – As You Desire Me 112 (Kalamoun   81 p
129) [1996 NR 1997 10s* May 10] close-coupled, quite attractive filly: closely related to useful 1m and 9f winner Reine D'Beaute (by Caerleon) and half-sister to several winners, including untrustworthy Intimate Guest (up to 1¼m, by Be My Guest): dam won around 1m in France: last and steadily to post, won maiden at Lingfield in May by 3 lengths, leading over 1f out then edging left: should stay beyond 1¼m: seemed sure to improve: sent to USA. *H. R. A. Cecil*

GENTLEMAN SID   7 b.g. Brotherly (USA) 80 – Eugenes Chance (Flashback   –
102) [1996 –: a16g⁴ 18s 16.4g 17.2f 16.1f 16.2f 18f⁶ 16.2m 1997 15.4m⁵ 21.6g 17.2d May 11] strong gelding: very much on the downgrade at end of career: dead. *P. G. Murphy*

GENTLEMEN (ARG) 5 ch.h. Robin Des Bois (USA) 106 – Elegant Glance 124 +
(USA) (Loose Cannon (USA)) [1996 a8.5f⁶ 8.5f* 9f* 9f* a9s* 1997 a9f* a10f³ a136
a9.5f* a10f* a10f* 8g⁵ Sep 20] ex-Argentinian horse: went from strength to strength
in 1997: won Grade 2 event at Santa Anita in February, Pimlico Special (holding
Skip Away, who received 3 lb, by ½ length) in May, Hollywood Gold Cup (by 4
lengths and same from Siphon and Sandpit) in June, then 5-runner Pacific Classic at
Del Mar in August (by 2¾ lengths from Siphon): found to be suffering from throat
ulcer and well below form in Woodbine Mile back on turf: best form at 9f/1¼m,
Grade 1 winner in Argentina at 1½m: effective on turf, goes especially well on dirt:
often front runner (doesn't have to lead): thoroughly genuine and consistent: reportedly suffering from inflammation of a lung and missed Breeders' Cup Classic.
R. Mandella, USA

GENUINE JOHN (IRE) 4 b.g. High Estate 127 – Fiscal Folly (USA) (Foolish 74 d
Pleasure (USA)) [1996 77, a70: 7s³ 9d⁶ 8d 8d 7m² 6m 5g³ 9g³ 7g 9f⁶ 7g⁵ 8g 11.9f²
a8g³ a8.5s 1997 a11g a8g³ a8g⁵ a8g² a8g² a7g* 7g⁴ 7.5m³ 7g 8m 8.5d 7m³ 9f⁵ 7.1g
a9.4g 8d a8g 8s a7g a8g a7g⁵ a9.4g Dec 26] fair performer: won maiden handicap at
Southwell in March: mostly disappointing afterwards: has similar form from 7f to
1½m: acts on any turf ground and on fibresand: tried blinkered, at least as effective
when not: has looked none too keen. *J. Parkes*

GEORDIE LAD 3 ch.g. Tina's Pet 121 – Edraianthus 78 (Windjammer (USA)) –
[1996 –: 5.1m 5.7m 5f 1997 5.1m⁶ 6.9m 6f 8.2m 6g 6m⁶ 5.7g 8m a5g Dec 22] seems
of little account. *J. A. Bennett*

GEORGIA VENTURE 3 b.f. Shirley Heights 130 – Georgica (USA) (Raise A 98
Native) [1996 NR 1997 8g 10.5s² 12s⁴ 11.5d³ 14g* 14m³ 13.9g⁵ 14.6m² 16m* 16f⁶
Oct 4] smallish filly: has a short career: half-sister to several winners abroad: dam
won 3 races in USA and is from good family: progressed into a useful handicapper:
won at Sandown in July and Goodwood (4 ran) in September, in latter quickening to
lead well over 1f out and holding Media Star a length: out of depth in Jockey Club
Cup at Newmarket final start: will stay beyond 2m: acts on good to firm and soft
going: held up, and has turn of foot. *S. P. C. Woods*

GEORGINA (IRE) 3 b.f. Lycius (USA) 124 – Princess Nawaal (USA) 86 74
(Seattle Slew (USA)) [1996 67p: 7f⁵ 1997 10m³ 8.5g Sep 5] fair maiden: third at
Windsor in August: dead. *Major W. R. Hern*

GERMANO 4 b.c. Generous (IRE) 139 – Gay Fantastic (Ela-Mana-Mou 132) 116
[1996 103: 10.3g⁵ 12f⁴ 12v 1997 10m² 10m* 10d* 10f² 10.5m² 10s⁴ Aug 29] tall,
close-coupled colt: has a round action: smart performer: won steadily-run minor
event at Newmarket and strongly-contested listed race at Goodwood (led over 3f out
and held King Alex a head) in May: ran very well when second in listed race at
Newbury (neck behind Arabian Story) and in Rose of Lancaster Stakes at Haydock
(stayed on gamely, beaten ½ length by Romanov): below best in Group 3 at
Baden-Baden final outing: best efforts at 1¼m, should stay 1½m: acts on firm and
dead ground (possibly something amiss when tailed off on heavy). *G. Wragg*

GET A LIFE 4 gr.f. Old Vic 136 – Sandstream 72 (Sandford Lad 133) [1996 NR 48
1997 11.8f⁴ 14.1g⁶ 12.1s 10m 12g³ 12m 12m⁵ Aug 20] 5,800F, 2,500 3-y-o:
half-sister to several winners, including 1989 2-y-o Between The Sticks (5f, by
Pharly): dam, 2-y-o 6f winner, half-sister to Manado: poor form: left J. A. Harris after
third start: stays 1½m: often front runner. *J. O'Reilly*

GET THE POINT 3 b.c. Sadler's Wells (USA) 132 – Tolmi 122 (Great Nephew 73 d
126) [1996 85: 7m⁶ 7m 8g⁴ 1997 8m⁴ 10.5s⁶ 8.5m⁴ 8g⁴ 10d⁵ 10.3d 7.5d⁶ 8.5g² 8m⁶
10m⁶ 10.5m⁴ 8m² 7g⁵ 10m 7m⁵ Sep 26] sturdy, close-coupled colt: disappointing
maiden: probably best around 1m: acts on good to firm going, probably on dead:
wanders under pressure, and not the easiest of rides: sold 13,000 gns and joined S.
Gollings. *R. Hollinshead*

GHALIB (IRE) 3 ch.c. Soviet Star (USA) 128 – Nafhaat (USA) 91 (Roberto 109
(USA) 131) [1996 NR 1997 8d* 8v* 10m³ Oct 31] strong colt: third foal: half-brother
to fairly useful Hadeel (up to 1¼m, by Polish Precedent): dam 1½m winner: bandaged off hind and green, won maiden at Newbury in September and minor event at
Ascot (idled) following month: favourite, best effort when equal-third, 1¾ lengths
behind Saafeya, in steadily-run listed event at Newmarket, racing keenly and keeping

on: stays 1¼m: acts on good to firm and heavy going: has joined M. Tregoning.
Major W. R. Hern

GHALI (USA) 2 b.c. (Mar 27) Alleged (USA) 138 – Kareema (USA) (Coastal 89 p
(USA)) [1997 7m⁴ Sep 28] good-bodied colt: fourth foal: half-brother to a winner in
USA by L'Emigrant: dam won up to 1¼m in USA: 20/1, promising 8 lengths fourth
of 7 to Mudeer in useful minor event at Ascot, needing race and experience, held up
and not at all knocked about: should stay at least 1¼m: likely to do fair bit better.
J. L. Dunlop

GHARIB (USA) 3 b.c. Dixieland Band (USA) – The Way We Were (USA) 81
(Avatar (USA)) [1996 80p: 7g⁵ 1997 8.5m⁵ 7g⁴ 8.5v² 8.2m⁶ 5m² 5f* Sep 17]
smallish, sturdy colt: fairly useful performer: won 18-runner maiden at Beverley on
final start, leading inside final 1f: similar form from 5f to 8.5f: acts on any going: has
worn bandages behind: sent to UAE. *A. C. Stewart*

GHATAAS 3 b.c. Sadler's Wells (USA) 132 – Harmless Albatross 115 (Pas 111
de Seul 133) [1996 94p: 7.1v² 1997 11g* 12.3d⁴ 11.8d* 10f⁴ 10m⁴ 10.9d*
Sep 20]
    In a week in September that brought the Welsh the promise of a degree
of self-government, hopes were high in some quarters that the principality
might also be about to acquire a new racecourse. A proposal had been submit-
ted to the British Horseracing Board by the Pembrey Racecourse Company
Limited for racing at a site near Llanelli in south-west Wales, starting with
twenty fixtures in the year 2000. By all accounts the quality of the racing at
Pembrey would have been bread-and-butter stuff, at least to begin with. But
the arguments in favour of the enterprise (expounded by racehorse owner and
sponsor Mel Davies, the driving force behind it) included the fact that, as well
as being in a tourist area, Pembrey could draw on a sizeable catchment that is
not being catered for by existing racecourses. According to Mr Davies' figures,
Wales has eleven per cent of Britain's licensed betting offices. Yet it has only
two racecourses, at Chepstow and Bangor-on-Dee, both virtually on the border
and catering to a large degree for English-based racegoers (things have not
always been this way, as Chris Pitt's book *A Long Time Gone* eloquently test-
ifies). A racecourse at Pembrey would bring the opportunity to go racing to a
new audience. These arguments didn't impress the BHB, which was accused
by Mr Davies of being responsible for leaking its decision to the Press some
time before the official announcement that the application had been unsuccessful. Among the reasons given publicly for the decision were the 'low levels
of proposed investment in public facilities' and 'heavy dependence on Levy
Board funding.' Davies countered with the charge that Jockey Club members
on the panel considering the Pembrey application had a vested interest in
maintaining the status quo and had been hostile to the proposal from the outset.
The Jockey Club has a stake in twelve of Britain's fifty-nine courses. Davies
isn't the kind of man to take things lying down, and his pointed attacks on the
BHB/Jockey Club through the letters pages of the trade papers must have
caused those bodies some discomfort. With talk of lobbying the nascent Welsh
Assembly and seeking millennium funding, Davies has vowed to fight on.
    One of the final acts to gain publicity for the Pembrey venture before
the intended date of the BHB announcement was the sponsorship of a race at
Ayr's Gold Cup meeting. Unfortunately, the enterprise was effectively already
dead in the water by the time the first (and presumably last) Faucets for Pembrey in Wales Doonside Cup was won by the smart colt Ghataas.
    Ghataas lined up at 6/1 in a field of eight for the Doonside Cup, the
one-time leading Derby fancy Sacho and the tough and useful handicapper
Sandmoor Chambray being preferred to him in the betting. Ghataas had won
two of his six previous races, a competitive maiden at Newbury on his seasonal
return in April and a minor race at Leicester two months later. In addition, he'd
finished fourth in the Chester Vase (over a trip, of around a mile and a half, that
may be a bit beyond his best) and the Winter Hill Stakes (on going possibly

Faucets For Pembrey In Wales Doonside Cup, Ayr—Ghataas has it sewn up

firmer than ideal) at Windsor, both Group 3 races. Ghataas put up an improved effort at Ayr, keen in the early stages as usual and soon allowed to bowl along at the head of affairs, then quickening clear entering the straight. Two furlongs out he was still travelling strongly while the rest were being hard ridden; at the line he was fully three and a half lengths to the good over Sandmoor Chambray. Sacho disappointed, and Ghataas did get a good ride, but the time was fairly good and there's no reason to believe that Ghataas was anything other than the best horse in the race. Ghataas wasn't raced again in 1997, though Sandmoor Chambray went on to run very well on two of his three subsequent starts. It was later reported that Ghataas would continue his career in Dubai.

		Northern Dancer	Nearctic
	Sadler's Wells (USA)	(b 1961)	Natalma
	(b 1981)	Fairy Bridge	Bold Reason
Ghataas		(b 1975)	Special
(b.c. 1994)		Pas de Seul	Mill Reef
	Harmless Albatross	(b 1979)	Thereby
	(b 1985)	North Forland	Northfields
		(ch 1977)	Greenback II

Ghataas is a well-bred individual, by the top sire Sadler's Wells and the fifth foal of the smart French miler Harmless Albatross. His winning half-brothers are Volochine (by Soviet Star, very smart in France up to a mile and a quarter and also a winner in the USA), the fairly useful mile and a half winner Haniya (by Caerleon) and the 1997 four-year-old and two-year-old Mawared and Kahtan respectively (both by Nashwan). Harmless Albatross herself is a daughter of the Ribblesdale runner-up North Forland. *J. L. Dunlop*

GHAYAH (IRE) 3 ch.f. Night Shift (USA) – Blinding (IRE) (High Top 131) – [1996 NR 1997 8g May 5] 52,000F: second foal: half-sister to 4-y-o High Priority, fairly useful 5f winner at 2 yrs: dam (ran twice at 3 yrs), half-sister to smart 7f and 1m performer Hadeer, from a very successful family: tailed-off last in maiden at Kempton. *R. W. Armstrong*

GHAYYUR (USA) 3 ch.f. Riverman (USA) 131 – New Trends (USA) 106   59 (Lyphard (USA) 132) [1996 73: 6d² 7m⁵ 7.5g² 1997 8f³ 8d⁴ 8.1g⁴ May 26] tall filly:

reportedly broke blood vessel final outing at 2 yrs and only modest form in 1997: probably stays 1m: acts on good to firm and dead ground: well bred, and sold 86,000 gns in December. *J. L. Dunlop*

GHILLIES BALL   3 ch.g. Groom Dancer (USA) 128 – Highbrow 112§ (Shirley   91 p
Heights 130) [1996 NR 1997 10g³ 12d* Aug 1] lengthy gelding: fluent mover: fourth
foal: half-brother to fairly useful 1¼m/1½m winner Beyond Doubt (by Belmez):
dam, 2-y-o 1m winner later second in Ribblesdale Stakes, from family of Highclere
and Height of Fashion: better effort in maidens when winning in good style at Ascot,
travelling well to lead 1f out then idling: will stay beyond 1½m: useful performer in
making if all is well with him. *R. Charlton*

GHORAPANI (IRE)   2 b.f. (Mar 15) Fairy King (USA) – Kates Cabin 96   –
(Habitat 134) [1997 6g 7d 6m 5d 6d Aug 28] 24,000Y: fourth foal: half-sister to 1m
winner Dunloe (by Shaadi) and fair stayer Backwoods (by In The Wings): dam, 1m
winner, out of sister to very smart stayer Old Bill: little sign of ability: visored final 3
starts. *Mrs N. Macauley*

GHOSTLY APPARITION   4 gr.g. Gods Solution 70 – Tawny 81 (Grey Ghost   –
98) [1996 53: a5g³ a7g a6g⁴ a7g a7g a7g 1997 10g Jun 18] one-time modest maiden:
seems to have lost his way. *John R. Upson*

GIDDY   4 b. or br.f. Polar Falcon (USA) 126 – Spin Turn (Homing 130) [1996 60d: 45
7m 9m 8.3m 8m⁴ 10f⁴ 8m 8.3m 8d 8m 8g³ a8g* a9.4g a8g 1997 a8g⁴ a8g³ a8g a8g
Mar 17] close-coupled filly: poor handicapper: best form up to 9f: acts on good to
firm ground and fibresand. *J. Hetherton*

GIFTBOX (USA)   5 b.h. Halo (USA) – Arewehavingfunyet (USA) (Sham   33
(USA)) [1996 60, a55: a6g⁶ a7g a7g⁶ 9.2s* 10.9d⁴ 10.1f⁴ 12f³ 8.3g* 9.2m a9.4g²
8.3m⁶ a8g⁴ 12.1d 10f² 10.1m a11g 1997 10.1g 11.1d 8.3d 11f 8m 11.1m³ Aug 18]
workmanlike horse: poor form at best at 5 yrs: stays 11f: acts on fibresand and
probably any turf going. *N. Bycroft*

GIFTED BAIRN (IRE)   2 b.f. (Feb 24) Casteddu 111 – Latin Mass (Music Boy   47
124) [1997 5g⁶ a5g a5g⁴ a6g⁶ a5g² 5g Jul 7] IR 6,200Y: lengthy filly: first foal: dam
poor maiden half-sister to smart 7f performer All Systems Go: poor maiden: form
only on fibresand. *D. Nicholls*

GIFT OF GOLD   2 ch.c. (Feb 23) Statoblest 120 – Ellebanna 69 (Tina's Pet 121)   70
[1997 6m 6d 6m⁴ 8.3g² a8.5g⁵ a7g 8m⁶ 7.1s* Nov 6] 25,000Y: good-topped colt:
second foal: dam sprinter: fair performer: won maiden at Musselburgh in November
by 6 lengths, making all: will probably stay beyond 1m: acts on soft going, probably
on fibresand. *I. Campbell*

GIFT TOKEN   3 b.f. Batshoof 122 – Visible Form 99 (Formidable (USA) 125)   90
[1996 71: 7m³ 7m 7.1s⁴ 1997 8f* 8d 10m 10m 10m⁵ 10g⁵ 9m 10g Oct 24] tall filly:
fairly useful performer: won maiden at Salisbury in June: mostly good efforts in
handicaps afterwards: stays 1¼m: acts on any going: bandaged near-hind final start.
Major D. N. Chappell

GIKO   3 b.g. Arazi (USA) 135 – Gayane 125 (Nureyev (USA) 131) [1996 NR 1997   63
7g² 7m 7m 7d³ 6.1d³ 7m 7.1d* 7.1d³ a7g⁶ 8d 7g a8g⁴ a7g Dec 18] 4,500 2-y-o: leggy
gelding: has a round action: fifth foal: closely related to 6f winner Duel At Dawn (by
Nashwan): dam, 6f/7f winner, from family of Roussalka and Oh So Sharp: modest
performer: trained by Miss G. Kelleway on debut: won 5-runner maiden (set slow
pace) at Chepstow in August: faced stiffer tasks afterwards: stays 1m: acts on fibresand, best turf form on good/good to soft going. *Jamie Poulton*

GI LA HIGH   4 gr.f. Rich Charlie 117 – Gem of Gold 52 (Jellaby 124) [1996 60:   68
a5g³ a5g⁴ a5g* a5g a5g² 5s⁵ a5g a5g a5g a5g² 1997 a6s³ a6g⁵ a5g* a5g² a5g⁶ a5g*
a5g³ 5s² 5m³ 5.7m² a5g⁶ 5.2m 5m 6.1m⁴ 5.1g 5d a6g a7g a6g⁶ Dec 13] compact
filly: poor mover: fair handicapper: won at Wolverhampton in January and March:
effective at 5f and 6f: acts on the all-weather and probably any turf going: tried in
blinkers/visor at 2 yrs. *Martyn Meade*

GILDERSLEVE   2 ch.f. (May 15) Gildoran 123 – Fragrant Hackette 32 (Simply   64 d
Great (FR) 122) [1997 5m² 5m 6d 5d⁶ Sep 18] 500Y: second foal: dam poor maiden:
showed only poor form after debut, including in seller: has sweated on edge: sold, to
join N. Berry. *J. W. Watts*

GILDING THE LILY (IRE) 3 b.f. High Estate 127 – Millingdale Lillie 119 –
(Tumble Wind (USA)) [1996 58: 6g2 6g3 8g 1997 a8.5g 10g5 May 17] disappointing
maiden: should stay beyond 6f. *M. Johnston*

GILLING DANCER (IRE) 4 b.g. Dancing Dissident (USA) 119 – Rahwah 73 53
(Northern Baby (CAN) 127) [1996 60: 8.2m 8m 8.1f4 8f 8f* 8f 8.2m6 8m 1997 a8g
a8g 8g 8m5 8m 8m 10m 10m Aug 6] strong, angular gelding: modest handicapper:
stays 1m: acts on firm ground: blinkered (very slowly away) once at 3 yrs: often
sweating/on toes: inconsistent. *P. Calver*

GINAS GIRL 4 gr.f. Risk Me (FR) 127 – Grey Cree 64 (Creetown 123) [1996 –: –
a6g5 5m6 7d5 6m 7m 1997 a6g a5g Apr 1] of little account. *D. Shaw*

GINGER FLOWER 8 ch.m. Niniski (USA) 125 – Monterana 99 (Sallust 134) –
[1996 NR 1997 13.8s 10.1g 10m Oct 28] of no account nowadays. *G. P. Kelly*

GINGER ROGERS 3 ch.f. Gildoran 123 – Axe Valley 89 (Royben 125) [1996 71
–: 7.1s 8s a10g 1997 7.5d 10g5 14.1m2 14.1m* 16m* 17.2g* 16m3 16.1m4 Oct 1]
lengthy filly: fair handicapper: completed hat-trick at Yarmouth, Nottingham and
Bath in summer: good efforts last 2 starts: suited by good test of stamina: acts on
good to firm ground. *D. W. P. Arbuthnot*

GINGERSNAP 3 ch.f. Salse (USA) 128 – Humble Pie 92 (Known Fact (USA) 83 p
135) [1996 75p: 7g6 1997 7g6 6m2 Sep 16] strong, lengthy filly: lightly-raced
maiden: weak in betting on first run for 5 months, best effort when second of 5 at
Yarmouth, leading 2f out but edging left and headed near finish: probably a sprinter:
raced only on good/good to firm going: capable of better. *H. R. A. Cecil*

GINKA 6 b.m. Petoski 135 – Pine (Supreme Sovereign 119) [1996 30: 10f 12d6 35
16d3 14d3 17.9g4 16s 16.4v2 1997 15.4m3 17.2d 16.4m 16d4 14m 14g4 16m 16.1g
Oct 7] light-bodied mare: poor maiden handicapper: out-and-out stayer: probably
acts on any going: tried blinkered/visored. *J. W. Mullins*

GINNER MORRIS 2 b.g. (Apr 12) Emarati (USA) 74 – Just Run (IRE) 45 –
(Runnett 125) [1997 6d Sep 18] 11,000Y: third foal: brother to Italian 3-y-o 6f and
7.5f winner Toxie Triumphs and 1995 2-y-o 5f winner Just Lady: dam showed only a
little ability: behind in maiden at Ayr. *C. B. B. Booth*

GINNIESHOPE 2 ch.f. (Apr 20) Never So Bold 135 – Sweet Home (Home –
Guard (USA) 129) [1997 6.1d 5.7m 6g6 Aug 27] eighth foal: half-sister to several
winners, including 3-y-o Craigievar: dam 6f winner in USA: soundly beaten in
maidens. *S. G. Knight*

GINNY WOSSERNAME 3 br.f. Prince Sabo 123 – Leprechaun Lady 57 38
(Royal Blend 117) [1996 50, a36+: 5m5 6g2 a6g5 7m* 7g4 6.9m3 7f4 8f a7g3 a6g6 a–
1997 7m 7.1m4 8g 5.9m3 6g 6.9d a8g Nov 17] angular filly: poor handicapper: left
M. Meade after fifth start: stays 7f: acts on firm going: effective with or without
blinkers: usually races prominently. *W. G. M. Turner*

GINZBOURG 3 b.g. Ferdinand (USA) – Last Request 92 (Dancer's Image 86
(USA)) [1996 86p: 7f5 6.9d* 1997 8.2m 10m2 12d 10.1d 10.3g5 Jul 30] angular
gelding: fairly useful handicapper: shaped as though something amiss penultimate
start, back to form final one: should stay 1½m: acts on good to firm and dead ground:
upset in stalls and very slowly away on reappearance: sold 14,000 gns in October and
joined R. O'Sullivan. *J. L. Dunlop*

GIPSY MOTH 2 b.f. (Feb 15) Efisio 120 – Rock The Boat 52 (Slip Anchor 136) 83
[1997 6s 5g6 5d 6m 5.2m* 5m 5m* 5m6 Sep 16] 15,000Y: lengthy, rather unfurnished
filly: first foal: dam maiden half-sister to Kerrera and Rock City: fairly useful
performer: won maiden at Yarmouth in July and nursery at Haydock in August:
below form final start: best form at 5f: acts on good to firm ground. *B. J. Meehan*

GIPSY PRINCESS 3 b.f. Prince Daniel (USA) – Gypsy's Barn Rat 55 (Balliol 62
125) [1996 65: 5g 5m3 5g4 6g6 7g3 7g* 7.9g2 7g2 1997 6g 6m 8m 7d5 8.5m3 7.5m 7g5
7g4 6g4 6d6 7m 6m 7s 7g Oct 24] leggy filly: modest handicapper: effective at 6f to
8.5f: acts on good to firm and dead ground: effective with or without blinkers: often
forces pace. *M. W. Easterby*

GIRLIE SET (IRE) 2 b.f. (May 14) Second Set (IRE) 127 – Heavenward (USA) 47 p
(Conquistador Cielo (USA)) [1997 6.1g 7d a7g5 Nov 25] 25,000Y: big, close-

coupled filly: half-sister to 3-y-o Liquid Gold, fairly useful 1995 2-y-o 7f winner (stays 1¼m) Exalted (by High Estate) and 2 winners in Italy: dam ran once in USA: first form in maidens when never-nearer fifth of 11 at Lingfield: will stay at least 1m: open to further improvement. *Sir Mark Prescott*

GIRL OF MY DREAMS (IRE)   4 b.f. Marju (IRE) 127 – Stylish Girl (USA) 50 (Star de Naskra (USA)) [1996 51: 5g 7g 7m 7.1m⁶ 8f 1997 7d 8.2d a7g⁵ a7g* a9.4g Dec 26] good-topped filly: modest handicapper: won at Wolverhampton in November, easily best effort of 1997: stays 7f: acts on fibresand. *M. J. Heaton-Ellis*

GIVEAWAY   2 ch.c. (Mar 29) Generous (IRE) 139 – Radiant Bride (USA) (Blush- 93 p ing Groom (FR) 131) [1997 8.2g* 8.1s² Oct 15] good-topped colt: has scope: second foal: dam French 1m (at 2 yrs) to 1¼m winner, half-sister to top-class US middle-distance performer Vanlandingham: won maiden at Nottingham in September by short head from Mawsoof: head second of 4 to Close Up in steadily-run minor event at Haydock, rallying strongly: will prove suited by at least 1¼m: type to progress and should make a useful 3-y-o. *H. R. A. Cecil*

GIVE ME A RING (IRE)   4 b.g. Be My Guest (USA) 126 – Annsfield Lady 98 (Red Sunset 120) [1996 89p: 8.5d⁶ 8.3g⁴ a8g² 8.5m* 7.9g* 9m* 8m³ 9m 1997 8.1g² 10.4g* 12g⁶ Jun 7] useful-looking colt: useful handicapper: well ridden in falsely-run race when comfortable winner at York: ran poorly next time, reportedly injured soon after: effective at 1m to 1¼m: acts on good to firm ground: carried head awkwardly only start on all-weather: usually races up with pace. *C. W. Thornton*

GLADYS ALTHORPE (IRE)   4 b.f. Posen (USA) – Gortadoo (USA) (Sharpen 65 Up 127) [1996 75: 6g 8m* 8m⁶ 8m* 8m* 8.1d² 8g 8g 1997 8.5d 10m 8g 8m Sep 13] leggy filly: fair handicapper: only form at 4 yrs when seventh in apprentice race at Thirsk third start: stays 1m: acts on good to firm and dead ground: held up: sold 5,000 gns in December. *J. L. Eyre*

GLAMORGAN (IRE)   2 b.c. (May 6) Petardia 113 – Presentable 60 (Sharpen – Up 127) [1997 5g 7m 8.2d Oct 30] 12,000 2-y-o: tall colt: half-brother to several winners, including fairly useful 6f (at 2 yrs) to 1m winner in Italy Spaghetti Western (by Chilibang): dam, placed over 1½m, half-sister to Gimcrack winner Wishing Star: little sign of ability in maidens. *C. A. Dwyer*

GLASS RIVER   2 b.c. (May 19) Ardkinglass 114 – Rion River (IRE) (Taufan 50 + (USA) 119) [1997 a5g 5m⁴ 5f 6g⁶ 5.1m⁴ 5m 5.3f³ 5m⁵ 5s⁵ a5g Nov 14] 2,600Y: a– unfurnished mover: unimpressive mover: third foal: half-brother to 4-y-o Gagajulu (fairly useful 5f winner at 2 yrs): dam Irish 1¼m winner: modest maiden on balance: probably a 5f performer: acts on firm ground, well beaten on soft and fibresand. *P. D. Evans*

GLEAMING HILL (USA)   2 b.c. (May 2) Marquetry (USA) 121 – Mountain 70 p Sunshine (USA) (Vaguely Noble 140) [1997 7m³ Oct 1] $170,000Y: half-brother to 7-y-o Hatta Sunshine and several winners in North America, including Grade 2 1m winner Country Pine (by His Majesty): dam unraced half-sister to dam of Indian Skimmer: 6/1 from 3/1 and better for race, hampered and no extra final 1f when around 3 lengths third of 20 behind Lucky Double in maiden at Salisbury: should be suited by 1m+: should improve. *M. R. Stoute*

GLEN GARNOCK (IRE)   5 gr.g. Danehill (USA) 126 – Inanna 105 (Persian – Bold 123) [1996 52: 8m³ 5g⁶ 7.1m⁵ 8.9g 1997 a12g⁴ May 30] big, lengthy gelding: beaten long way in seller only outing as 5-y-o: probably stays 1m. *R. T. Juckes*

GLEN OGIL   3 b. or ch.g. Thatching 131 – Cormorant Bay 55 (Don't Forget Me 51 127) [1996 NR 1997 6g³ 8g⁶ 7m 6.9d 9m² 8s² Nov 6] 32,000Y: first foal: dam, maiden stayed 1¼m, half-sister to top-class Cormorant Wood (dam of Rock Hopper): modest maiden: claimed out of I. Balding's stable £6,000 on debut: best efforts in handicaps last 2 starts: will stay 1¼m: acts on good to firm and soft ground. *M. R. Channon*

GLEN PARKER (IRE)   4 ch.c. Bluebird (USA) 125 – Trina's Girl (Nonoalco 89 (USA) 131) [1996 83: 8g 8.3g⁶ 8m² 8m* 1997 8.3m³ 8m⁵ Sep 21] sturdy, good-bodied colt: good mover: fairly useful performer: better effort in handicaps at 4 yrs when third to Pomona at Windsor in August: should stay 1¼m: raced solely on good/good to firm going. *H. R. A. Cecil*

GLENSTAL LAD 2 b.c. (May 15) Nomination 125 – Glenstal Princess 71   35 +
(Glenstal (USA) 118) [1997 a5g⁴ a7g³ 5m 5s³ a8g Dec 8] second reported foal: half-
brother to 3-y-o Northern Princess (by Nomination), 9f winner in Holland: dam 6f
winner, including at 2 yrs: plater: probably stays 7f. *R. Hollinshead*

GLIDE PATH (USA) 8 ch.g. Stalwart (USA) – Jolly Polka (USA) (Nice Dancer
(CAN)) [1996 –: 10g 10.2f⁵ 12.3m⁶ 12m⁴ 12f⁶ 12m 11.9d 1997 a16g 12m a14g a12s
a12g Dec 4] close-coupled gelding: one-time useful handicapper, very much on the
downgrade. *J. R. Jenkins*

GLIDER (IRE) 2 b.f. (Mar 6) Silver Kite (USA) 111 – Song of The Glens   48 p
(Horage 124) [1997 a7g⁴ Dec 18] 5,000Y: fourth foal: half-sister to fairly useful 6f
winner Sepoy (by Common Grounds) and 1993 2-y-o 7f winner Syabas (by Northiam): dam maiden daughter of half-sister to 2000 Guineas winner Right Tack: nearest
finish after sluggish start when about 4 lengths fourth in seller at Southwell, not given
hard race: will do better. *C. W. Thornton*

GLIMMERING HOPE (IRE) 3 b.g. Petorius 117 – Angevin 61 (English   –
Prince 129) [1996 –: 7g 1997 a6g⁵ a6g 6.1m Mar 31] seems of little account. *D. Shaw*

GLITTERING (USA) 3 b.c. Local Talent (USA) 122 – Glitter (FR) 70 (Reliance   57
II 137) [1996 NR 1997 10v⁵ 9m⁵ 11.5m 7.6g³ 8.3m 8m⁵ 8m 10.5g 8g 11d 9d 8d²
Nov 9] rather leggy colt: half-brother to several winners, notably top-class French
1½m colt Village Star (by Moulin): dam, 1¼m winner, closely related to high-class
stayer Proverb: modest maiden: best form around 1m: has given trouble at start:
trained first 6 outings by C. Brittain. *S. Wattel, France*

GLITTER PRINCESS 2 ch.f. (Jan 25) Prince Sabo 123 – Maritime Lady (USA)   ?
61 (Polish Navy (USA)) [1997 6m⁴ 6m 7m 7d Oct 13] 11,500 2-y-o: good-topped
filly: second foal: dam (maiden) better at 1m than shorter, from good family:
appeared to show fair form in maiden at Ascot on debut, but disappointed afterwards:
sold, to join N. Berry. *Major D. N. Chappell*

GLOBAL RISK 2 b.g. (Mar 19) Risk Me (FR) 127 – Georgina Park 88 (Silly   –
Season 127) [1997 6m 6m 6.9m⁶ Aug 19] 5,800Y: half-brother to several winners,
including fairly useful miler Sandicliffe Star (by High Top) and useful sprinter Melody Park (by Music Boy): dam 2-y-o 7f winner: looks of little account. *C. Murray*

GLOBE RAIDER 2 b.g. (Apr 17) Safawan 118 – Polola 42 (Aragon 118) [1997   –
6g 5.9g Jul 5] 6,000 2-y-o: half-brother to Italian 4-y-o winner up to 13f Dino
Davidoff (by Sayf El Arab): dam third at 5f from 3 starts at 2 yrs: no promise.
J. J. O'Neill

GLOBE RUNNER 4 b.c. Adbass (USA) 102 – Scenic Villa (Top Ville 129)   68
[1996 50: 8g 8m 6g a6g⁶ a6g 5.9f⁶ 10f⁵ 8f* 6.9f 7d⁵ 8.3g⁵ a12s 1997 a8g 12.1d* 12m³
12.1m* 13.1d³ Sep 20] smallish colt: fair handicapper: improved at 4 yrs, winning at
Hamilton in April (off course 4 months afterwards) and August: stays 13f: acts on
firm and dead ground: blinkered (pulled hard) once at 3 yrs: reportedly suffers from
intermittent lameness: fairly useful hurdler, winner in November. *J. J. O'Neill*

GLOBETROTTER (IRE) 3 b.g. Polish Patriot (USA) 128 – Summer Dreams   –
(CAN) (Victoria Park) [1996 64: 6s 6m 7.5m³ 6m 7g 1997 a8.5g* a8g* a10g* a7g*   a85
a10g³ a9.4g² a8.5g* 8.5m 7m a9.4g* a8f* a9f⁵ a8.5f Oct 12] good-topped gelding:
fairly useful performer: enjoyed prolific spell on all-weather in first half of year,
winning minor events, handicaps and a claimer at Southwell, Lingfield (2) and
Wolverhampton (3) for M. Johnston: easily best effort in USA when winning claimer
at Del Mar in July: claimed to join M. Mitchell $40,000 final start: effective at 7f
to 1¼m: acts well on dirt/all-weather, well held both outings on turf at 3 yrs.
Kathy Walsh, USA

GLORIA IMPERATOR (IRE) 4 b.g. Imperial Frontier (USA) 112 – English   – §
Lily (Runnett 125) [1996 –: 5.1g 5m 7g a5g 1997 a7g a7g a6g a5g⁴ 6g Apr 18]
temperamental maiden. *A. B. Mulholland*

GLORIOUS DANCER 3 b.f. Past Glories 91 – Precious Ballerina 66 (Balla-   –
cashtal (CAN)) [1996 NR 1997 8.5m 8d 9d a8g 8.2g 9.9v 11m Nov 4] tall, lengthy
filly: first living foal: dam 1m winner at 6 yrs: soundly beaten in maidens and
handicaps. *J. Hetherton*

Fillies' Mile, Ascot—Glorosia holds Jibe's strong challenge; Exclusive is third

GLOROSIA (FR)   2 ch.f. (Mar 4) Bering 136 – Golden Sea (FR) (Saint   109 p
Cyrien (FR) 128) [1997 7g* 8f³ 8g* Sep 28]
    For the second year running, Ascot's short straight contributed to several of the principals in the Fillies' Mile meeting interference. Not for winner Glorosia though. It had been Dettori's intention to make the running on this free-running sort, but with a good pace he was content to settle Glorosia in mid-division of the eight-strong field. Coming wide on the home turn, Glorosia avoided a couple of incidents on her inside which left favourite Jibe short of room at an important stage and put second-favourite Midnight Line out of the reckoning completely. Glorosia quickened clear over a furlong out and, despite drifting right once in front, ran on well to account for Jibe, who had stayed on strongly once clear, by three quarters of a length. They were followed two lengths back by Entrepreneur's half-sister Exclusive, having just her second run, with the remainder five lengths and more behind, several having been eased once their chance had gone.
    Glorosia started at 10/1 at Ascot and showed a fair bit of improvement from her two previous outings, suggesting that even with a clear run Midnight Line would have struggled to confirm the superiority shown over her when they'd first met in the May Hill Stakes at Doncaster earlier in September. On that occasion Glorosia finished three and a half lengths third to Midnight Line in receipt of 5 lb, keeping on from mid-division as though more of a test of stamina would suit. Glorosia was second-favourite to Midnight Line at Doncaster but had been off the course for eight weeks beforehand, having 'gone flat' according to her trainer after making virtually all to win a seven-furlong maiden on her debut at Newmarket in July.
    Glorosia's sire, Bering, won the Prix du Jockey-Club and was second in the Arc but that hasn't stopped him getting winners in the top flight at two; indeed, Glorosia is the fourth of his five Group 1 winners to win at that level as juveniles, following Pennekamp in the Prix de la Salamandre and the Dewhurst, Peter Davies in the Racing Post Trophy and Steamer Duck in the Gran Criterium. Pennekamp went on to win the Two Thousand Guineas and a week later Matiara became Bering's second classic winner by taking the Poule d'Essai des Pouliches; she later added a Grade 1 handicap in America.
    Glorosia, the second foal and first runner of Golden Sea, cost 280,000 francs at the Deauville August Sales. The three mares on the bottom line of her pedigree have now all bred a pattern winner without being good enough to win such a race themselves. Golden Sea fell well short, with all her successes coming in the French Provinces; over seven furlongs on her only start at two

Mr Robert H. Smith's "Glorosia"

and three times at around a mile and a quarter at four. Next dam Green City went close when second in the Prix Fille de l'Air and was a useful winner at around a mile and a quarter in France. She bred the smart Prix Guillaume d'Ornano winner Glity. Third dam Gadfly was useful too, her win coming over a mile at two, and her pattern winner was Formidable Flight who took the Prix Chloe. The best performers from this family though are Gadfly's half-sister Aliocha, very smart at six and seven furlongs, and half-brother Bonhomie, successful in the Royal Lodge and King Edward VII Stakes and second in the Irish Derby.

		Arctic Tern	Sea Bird II
	Bering	(ch 1973)	Bubbling Beauty
	(ch 1983)	Beaune	Lyphard
Glorosia (FR)		(ch 1974)	Barbra
(ch.f. Mar 4, 1995)		Saint Cyrien	Luthier
	Golden Sea (FR)	(b 1980)	Sevres
	(ch 1987)	Green City	Green Dancer
		(ch 1981)	Gadfly

Luca Cumani won the Fillies' Mile in 1990 with Shamshir who was second in the Oaks but failed to add to her successes at three and didn't improve by as much as had seemed likely. It will be a big disappointment if the same is said of Glorosia in due course. She's a rangy, good-topped filly, a potential Oaks type who looks sure to make further progress at three when stepped up to a mile and a quarter or more, despite being rather a keen sort. She was on her toes and had two handlers in the preliminaries at Ascot. *L. M. Cumani*

GLORY OF GROSVENOR (IRE)   2 ch.c. (Feb 5) Caerleon (USA) 132 –   89 p
Abury (IRE) 104 (Law Society (USA) 130) [1997 8d⁴ 10m² Oct 6] strong, lengthy
colt: first foal: dam 7f (at 2 yrs) and 11.4f (Cheshire Oaks) winner, should
have stayed further: fairly useful form when 6 lengths fourth of 5 to Duck Row in
minor event at Newbury and ½-length second to Dashing Chief in maiden at
Pontefract, still showing inexperience in latter but rallying, despite swishing tail:
should stay at least 1½m: should improve and win races at 3 yrs. *P. W. Chapple-
Hyam*

GLORY OF LOVE   2 b.c. (Apr 27) Belmez (USA) 131 – Princess Lieven (Royal   61
Palace 131) [1997 8d⁵ 7m⁵ 8d Oct 16] 4,000Y: half-brother to several winners,
including 4-y-o Prince Kinsky: dam unraced daughter of sister to Brigadier Gerard:
modest form in maidens at Ayr, Newcastle and Newmarket (wore severe noseband):
should stay beyond 1m. *J. Hetherton*

GLOSSATOR (IRE)   5 b.g. Shardari 134 – Galandria 57 (Sharpo 132) [1996 8g   51
8v 1997 9m⁴ 7.5g⁵ 9m a9.3g⁴ a8g 7g⁴ 8.5g² 8m* 6g² 8g² 8s⁵ 9d a8g* Dec 2] Belgian-
trained gelding: modest performer: won minor event in Belgium in August and weak
seller at Lingfield in December: stays 9f: acts on good to firm ground and equitrack.
Alex Vanderhaeghen, Belgium

GLOW FORUM   6 b.m. Kalaglow 132 – Beau's Delight (USA) (Lypheor 118)   66
[1996 54, a77: 12d* 12m a12g* a12g* 11.5d² a12g* 11.9g⁵ a12g* 12g⁶ a12g 1997   a81
a12g³ a12g² a12g* a12g² a12g* 12d² 11.5s* 12s³ 12.1m* 12d⁵ 14s⁶ 11.1m a12g³
12d* 12m⁶ a12g⁶ Nov 29] leggy, angular mare: fairly useful handicapper on the
all-weather: won at Lingfield in January and Wolverhampton in May: not so good on
turf, but won at Lingfield and Chepstow (both apprentice races) in the summer and at
Folkestone in October: stays 13f: acts on any going: tough and reliable. *L. Montague
Hall*

GLOWING MANTLE (IRE)   9 ch.m. Glow (USA) – Dismantle 75 (Aureole   –
132) [1996 NR 1997 a14g May 12] of little account. *B. Preece*

GLOWING MOON   4 b.f. Kalaglow 132 – Julia Flyte 91 (Drone) [1996 NR   –
1997 10d 11.9f⁶ May 23] 3,000Y: rangy filly: sister to useful Alphard (should have
been suited by 1¾m+): dam 2-y-o 6f winner: well beaten in maidens. *Miss Gay
Kelleway*

GO BRITANNIA   4 b.g. Machiavellian (USA) 123 – Chief Celebrity (USA) 85   96
(Chief's Crown (USA)) [1996 90: 8m 7.1m² 8m* 8m⁵ 10m⁵ 1997 8g 16.5m³ 16 1s
20m⁴ 16.1g² 16g³ 18g Oct 18] tall gelding: has round action: useful handicapper:
stays 2½m: acts on good to firm going, below form on soft: visored (no improvement) once at 3 yrs: tends to carry head awkwardly, and not most straightforward of
rides: sold (to join F. Jordan) 20,000 gns. *D. R. Loder*

GOD KNOWS (IRE)   2 b.f. (May 1) Elbio 125 – Sweet Accord (Balidar 133)   –
[1997 5d 7g 7d 8m Sep 9] 5,000Y: half-sister to 3 winners, including useful 1¼m to
1½m winner Rock Chanteur (by Ballad Rock): dam Irish 1m and 1¼m winner:
probably of no account. *M. J. Fetherston-Godley*

GODMERSHAM PARK   5 b.g. Warrshan (USA) 117 – Brown Velvet 68   64
(Mansingh (USA) 120) [1996 72: 7g⁶ 7m³ 8d 7g 1997 7.5m 8g⁴ 9f² 8m 8.2g⁵
7f⁵ 7g 8f⁵ 8.2d a7g⁶ a8g* a7g* Dec 18] lengthy, good-topped gelding: modest
handicapper: won at Southwell in November and December: will prove best up to
9f: acts on firm ground and fibresand: well held only try in blinkers: inconsistent.
P. S. Felgate

GO FOR GREEN   3 br.f. Petong 126 – Guest List 85 (Be My Guest (USA) 126)   61
[1996 56: 6.1d 7f³ 7f 1997 7f⁵ a8g⁶ 8g² 8g 8m 8.2g 10s⁵ 8.2d Oct 30] leggy filly:
modest maiden: barely stays 1¼m: probably acts on any turf going, ran poorly on
equitrack. *Dr J. D. Scargill*

GO FOR SALT (USA)   3 b.f. Hawkster (USA) – Wall St Girl (USA) (Rich   79
Cream (USA)) [1996 75p: 7.6d² 1997 10g³ 11.5s⁴ 10.2m⁵ 10d* Jul 17] close-
coupled filly: fair performer: straightforward task when winning maiden at Leicester
(by 9 lengths): may stay 1½m: seems to act on good to firm and soft ground.
M. R. Stoute

GO GREEN FLAG   3 b.c. Salse (USA) 128 – One Last Glimpse 73 (Relko 136)   –
[1996 NR 1997 12m 12g⁶ May 16] 53,000Y: half-brother to several winners, notably
8-y-o Captain Horatius: dam effective from 1m to 11f: no promise in maidens.
Mrs J. Cecil

GO HENCE   3 b.c. Be My Chief (USA) 122 – Hence (USA) (Mr Prospector   67
(USA)) [1996 NR 1997 8g 8m 10m⁴ 12m⁵ 15.8g 11.5m³ 12m Oct 2] strong, lengthy
colt with scope: eighth foal: brother to a poor maiden and half-brother to 3 winners,
including Ruby Heights (1¼m, by Shirley Heights): dam 7f winner in USA: fair
maiden: reportedly choked fifth start and ran poorly afterwards: probably stays
1½m: has tongue tied: sold 6,000 gns in October, and has gone hence to Germany.
W. Jarvis

GOING FOR BROKE   3 b.g. Simply Great (FR) 122 – Empty Purse (Pennine   66
Walk 120) [1996 65, a63: 5m 6g² a7g 6f² a7g² 8d⁵ 7m² a7s 1997 a8s* a10g⁵ a11g³
9.9m* 9.2s* a8.5g* 10s² Jun 27] workmanlike gelding: fair performer: won handicap
at Southwell, and claimers at Beverley, Hamilton and Wolverhampton by end of
May: effective at 1m to 11f: acts on fibresand and probably any turf going: has given
trouble stalls and started slowly: joined C. Mann. *P. C. Haslam*

GOING GREEN   3 b.f. Environment Friend 128 – Pacific Gull (USA) 67 (Storm   59
Bird (CAN) 134) [1996 NR 1997 7g a8g³ 7m² 6.9m a8g⁴ a6.7f⁴ a6.7f a10g⁶ a10g
Nov 10] fourth foal: half-sister to a winner (including at 9f) in Belgium/Germany (by
Hadeer) and 7f to 1m winner Northern Chief (by Chief Singer): dam 8.5f winner:
disappointing maiden: sold 900 gns from J. Fanshawe after fourth start: stays 1m.
B. Nilsson, Sweden

GOING PLACES   2 b.f. (Mar 2) Risk Me (FR) 127 – Spring High 74 (Miami   72
Springs 121) [1997 5m⁵ 5g³ 5g³ 5m⁴ 5d* 5m 5s Aug 29] 2,000Y: rather leggy,
workmanlike filly: first foal: dam winning sprinter: fair form in first half of season:
won minor event at Windsor in May: well beaten both subsequent starts, 3 months
apart: raced only at 5f: best form on good ground or softer. *K. T. Ivory*

GOLBORNE LAD   4 ch.g. Jester 119 – Taskalady 47 (Touching Wood (USA)   –
127) [1996 –: a6g⁶ a6g 5m 1997 a6g Apr 26] no worthwhile form: tried visored.
J. Balding

GOLD BLADE   8 ch.g. Rousillon (USA) 133 – Sharp Girl (FR) 114 (Sharpman)   65
[1996 72: a12g² a12g* a13g⁶ 10g* 10.5d² 12.3m⁴ 11.1g³ 10g* 9.2m* 13.1g* 9.9m*
12g* 12m 10.1m a14g a14g⁶ a10g⁵ 1997 a13g⁴ 10.3m 10g 10.5m 11.5d⁴ 9.9v² 9m²
12d 11.5f Oct 3] big, good-topped gelding: poor mover: fair handicapper: inconsistent at 8 yrs: stays 13f: acts on any turf/all-weather: sometimes blinkered earlier in
career: held up: usually ridden by Mrs L. Pearce. *J. Pearce*

GOLD CLIPPER   3 b.c. High Kicker (USA) – Ship of Gold 78 (Glint of Gold   33
128) [1996 –: 8g 1997 8.2m 10d 8d⁴ 10m⁴ 10.8m a9.4f² 10s 10.8g 12s a10g² a10g³   a53
a9.4g a10g Dec 19] angular colt: modest maiden handicapper: stays 1¼m: best
efforts on equitrack: tried blinkered. *M. J. Ryan*

GOLD DESIRE   7 b.g. Grey Desire 115 – Glory Gold 59 (Hittite Glory 125)   68
[1996 52: 10.1s 12.1g² 12m⁴ 11.1g² 10g⁴ 11.1g⁴ 12m 12.1f⁶ 10m* 11.1m⁵ 11f³
10.4g* 10m⁵ 11.9g 8.9g 10.1m⁶ 1997 10.3d 9.9s³ 8.3s⁵ 10.9s* 10g* 10g 9.9g³ 10g³
10.1g⁴ 9.2m 12.3m² 10m⁴ 12d* 12m 12.3m² 12.3d³ 10.4s* 12m 13.1d² 12s⁵ 16s
Nov 6] sparely-made, plain gelding: poor mover: fair handicapper: won at Ayr in
May, Ascot in August and York in September (last 2 apprentice events): stays 13f:
acts on any going: sometimes bandaged: visored (ran poorly) once at 3 yrs: tough.
M. Brittain

GOLD EDGE   3 ch.f. Beveled (USA) – Golden October 62 (Young Generation   64
129) [1996 52: 5s⁵ 5.1m⁶ 5m² 5.3g³ 6d⁶ 1997 5g³ 5.3f² 5m² 5m³ 6d³ 5d⁵ 6.1d² 6f⁴
6.1d* 6m⁵ 6g⁵ 6d 6d 5d⁴ 5g⁵ 5s⁴ Oct 14] sturdy filly: modest handicapper: won at
Chepstow in August: acts on any going. *M. R. Channon*

GOLDEN ACE (IRE)   4 ch.c. Archway (IRE) 115 – Gobolino (Don 128) [1996   79 d
87: 8d* 7g⁵ 1997 10m⁶ 9s⁴ 10g 8d a7g 8.1m³ 8g* 7g 10.4s³ 8m 10m 8.2s Oct 15]
strong, lengthy colt: poor mover: formerly fairly useful: well below best after second
start: won seller at Newmarket in August (then left R. Hannon): stays 1¼m: acts on
good to firm and soft ground. *R. C. Spicer*

GOLDENACRES 2 b.g. (Apr 24) Desert Splendour 95 – Normanby Damsel 55 –
(High Line 125) [1997 6.1g^6 a6g^6 7s^5 7f 6m^6 Jul 28] third reported living foal of a
poor maiden: little worthwhile form in sellers and claimers: blinkered (pulled up)
fourth start. *J. Neville*

GOLDEN DICE (USA) 2 ch.c. (Jun 1) Diesis 133 – Fariedah (USA) 96 99 p
(Topsider (USA)) [1997 6g^4 7g* 7m^4 7.6g^2 Sep 24] small, quite attractive colt: has a
quick action: fifth foal: half-brother to fairly useful 7f winner (stayed 1m) Western
Fame (by Gone West): dam 2-y-o 6f winner, later successful in USA: progressive
form: won maiden at Newcastle in August: useful efforts in minor events afterwards when just under 2 lengths fourth of 6 to Teapot Row at Doncaster and 1¾
lengths second of 4 to Mutamam in steadily-run race at Chester: will stay 1m: should
continue improving. *H. R. A. Cecil*

GOLDEN FACT (USA) 3 b.g. Known Fact (USA) 135 – Cosmic Sea Queen 75 §
(USA) (Determined Cosmic (USA)) [1996 75§: 5m^2 5.2s^4 7f^4 7m^5 7.3m^4 6d 1997 8g
8m 7m^2 7.1g^3 Aug 3] angular, close-coupled gelding: fair maiden when in the mood:
stays 7f: acts on good to firm going: inconsistent. *R. Hannon*

GOLDEN FAWN 4 ch.f. Crowning Honors (CAN) – Hill of Fare (Brigadier –
Gerard 144) [1996 60: 10g 10.5m^2 10f^2 11.9g 12g 1997 a12g^6 10d May 9] modest
maiden: well beaten in 1997. *N. M. Babbage*

GOLDEN FISH 5 b.g. Efisio 120 – Fishpond 71 (Homing 130) [1996 NR 1997 –
8g 10.3m 8m 8.1m 8m 10d 10m^6 13.1s 11m Oct 28] of little account nowadays.
E. J. Alston

GOLDEN FORTUNE 2 ch.f. (Mar 20) Forzando 122 – Short And Sharp 88 84 p
(Sharpen Up 127) [1997 6m^6 5m 5m 6.1m* 7m* Sep 30] 19,000Y: strong, lengthy
filly: has plenty of scope: half-sister to 7f winner (stayed 1¼m) Step High (by
Dominion) and winners in Italy by Young Generation and Night Shift: dam placed
over 6f/7f at 2 yrs, only season to race: fairly useful form: much improved in
nurseries in September, justifying favouritism at Nottingham and Newmarket, beating Belle de Nuit decisively, pair clear, in valuable event on latter course: should stay
1m: raced only on good to firm ground: tends to carry head awkwardly: type to train
on and should make a useful handicapper. *D. R. Loder*

GOLDEN GLORY 4 b.g. Grey Desire 115 – Glory Gold 59 (Hittite Glory 125) –
[1996 NR 1997 12.3g 8g 8g Jul 7] brother to 7-y-o Gold Desire: dam 6f to 7.5f
winner. no sign of ability in maidens. *M. Brittain*

GOLDEN HADEER 6 ch.h. Hadeer 118 – Verchinina 99 (Star Appeal 133) 58
[1996 41, a50: 12m^6 12.1m^4 10m 11.6d 12d a14g^3 12v a14g* a12s^3 1997 a16s* a76
a14.8g* a16.2g* a12g^3 a16g^2 a16g* a13g^5 16s^2 13s* 16.2s^3 16g* 14.9m* 13.3g^2
13g^6 14.9d^3 16s 16s a14g^5 a14g^5 Dec 8] close-coupled horse: much improved
handicapper at 6 yrs, winning at Southwell and Wolverhampton twice each and at
Hamilton, Nottingham and Warwick before end of May: not in quite the same form
afterwards: effective at testing 13f to 2m: acts on soft and good to firm ground, goes
well on fibresand (seldom races on equitrack): usually races prominently and with
enthusiasm: tough, genuine and consistent. *M. J. Ryan*

GOLDEN HANOOF (USA) 5 ch.m. Slew O'Gold (USA) – Hanoof (USA) 79 –
(Northern Dancer) [1996 77: 10.8g^4 11g^2 8g 12g^6 a12g^4 1997 a12g^2 a12g^4 Feb 5]
one-time fair performer in France: showed little in 3 starts in Britain: seems to stay
1½m: sent to Australia. *Dr J. D. Scargill*

GOLDEN HAWK (USA) 2 ch.c. (Mar 15) Silver Hawk (USA) 123 – 81 p
Crockadore (USA) 102 (Nijinsky (CAN) 138) [1997 8m^3 Sep 22] 140,000Y: third
foal: half-brother to Irish 3-y-o Mynador (by Forty Niner), 6f winner at 2 yrs, and
Irish 6f winner Shunaire (by Woodman): dam 1m winner in Ireland, later smart
middle-distance winner in USA: 10/1, 4 lengths third of 17 to Taverner Society in
maiden at Kempton, prominent throughout but hanging markedly left and unable to
be ridden out properly: should stay at least 1¼m: should improve. *P. F. I. Cole*

GOLDEN HELLO 6 b.g. Glint of Gold 128 – Waltz 75 (Jimmy Reppin 131) –
[1996 NR 1997 12m 12m 14.1m^4 Oct 7] hobdayed: poor on flat nowadays: suited by
1½m+: acts on any going: visored (ran creditably) once: won chase in December.
T. D. Easterby

GOLDEN LYRIC (IRE) 2 ch.c. (Feb 23) Lycius (USA) 124 – Adjala 89 – p (Northfields (USA)) [1997 7m 7d Nov 7] IR 115,000Y: big, good-topped colt: half-brother to 7-y-o Law Commission and a winner in Germany (both by Ela-Mana-Mou): dam 2-y-o 5f winner, only season to race, from family of Blushing Groom: not knocked about in late-season maidens at Yarmouth and Doncaster (still burly): scopey sort, sure to do better at 3 yrs. *G. Wragg*

GOLDEN MELODY 3 b.f. Robellino (USA) 127 – Rose Chanelle (Welsh 55 Pageant 132) [1996 –: 6.9g 7g⁵ 7.1f 8g 1997 14.1m⁴ 14.1m⁶ 17.2m⁴ 16m⁶ a16g⁵ 14m⁵ 16s⁴ Oct 8] angular filly: modest maiden: suited by test of stamina: acts on good to firm and soft ground: no improvement visored: has run in snatches, and possibly not entirely hearty: won over hurdles in November. *M. J. Heaton-Ellis*

GOLDEN MIRAGE (IRE) 2 b.f. (Feb 14) Green Desert (USA) 127 – Please 94 Widd (IRE) (Thatching 131) [1997 5g⁵ 5s* 5d³ 5d* a6f⁴ 8f³ Sep 14] 17,000Y: first foal: dam, ran once in Ireland, out of half-sister to Greenland Park and Red Sunset: progressive form in first half of 1997 for M. Channon, winning maiden at Hamilton and listed race (beat Hopping Higgins ½ length) at the Curragh: in frame in stakes races in Canada, 4½ lengths third of 8 in Grade 1 event at Woodbine: seems to stay 1m: probably acts on any going: unraced on medication. *B. Girault, Canada*

GOLDEN POUND (USA) 5 b.g. Seeking The Gold (USA) – Coesse Express 85 (USA) (Dewan (USA)) [1996 89: a8g³ a8.5g² a8g² a7g² 8s⁴ 7d⁴ 6m* 7f⁶ 6d⁶ 6s³ 6m 5m³ 6g* 6f⁵ 6m² 6m³ 6m 6m 1997 6f⁶ 6d⁶ 5d⁶ 6s⁴ 6.1m⁴ 5m⁵ 6g* 6m⁵ 6d 7.3d a6g a6s Nov 28] lengthy gelding: good mover: fairly useful handicapper: mostly cred-itable efforts in 1997, well backed when winning at Brighton in August: best over 6f or stiff 5f: acts on the all-weather and on good to firm and soft going: no improve-ment in blinkers or visor: has worn tongue strap: has run well when sweating. *Miss Gay Kelleway*

GOLDEN REPRIMAND (IRE) 2 b.c. (Feb 8) Reprimand 122 – Elabella 85 p (Ela-Mana-Mou 132) [1997 6m 6d⁴ Oct 17] 34,000Y: quite good-topped colt: fourth foal: half-brother to useful sprinter Espartero (by Ballad Rock), later 1m winner in USA, and 1½m winner Typographer (by Never So Bold): dam never ran: showed plenty of promise on debut in August, and again when under 2 lengths fourth of 20 to Atuf in maiden at Newmarket, finishing well: should stay 1m: should improve again. *R. Hannon*

GOLDEN SADDLE (IRE) 3 b.f. Waajib 121 – Flying Beckee (IRE) 60 – (Godswalk (USA) 130) [1996 NR 1997 10s a7g a8g Dec 18] 7,000Y, 3,400 3-y-o: second foal: sister to 4-y-o Flying Pennant: dam lightly-raced sister to smart sprinter A Prayer For Wings: well beaten in maidens and a claimer. *Miss L. A. Perratt*

GOLDEN SADDLE (USA) 3 b. or br.g. Riverman (USA) 131 – Rossard (DEN) 61 (Glacial (DEN)) [1996 5m 1997 8g 6m⁶ 6m 11.4g 11g 10f⁴ 11.6m⁶ 10g⁵ Aug 20] IR 50,000Y: leggy ex-Irish gelding: eighth foal: half-brother to 2 winners, including useful Irish 1m and 9f winner Unusual Heat (by Nureyev): dam top 3-y-o filly in Scandinavia and Grade 1 1¼m winner at 4 yrs in USA: modest maiden: trained by D. Weld for debut: should stay beyond 1¼m: raced only on good ground or firmer: none too consistent. *P. F. I. Cole*

GOLDEN SILVER 4 b.f. Precious Metal 106 – Severals Princess 44 (Form- – idable (USA) 125) [1996 43: 6.1m 6g² 1997 a7g a7g Jan 9] narrow filly: poor maiden: tailed off in 1997. *J. S. Moore*

GOLDEN STRATEGY (IRE) 2 b.g. (Mar 27) Statoblest 120 – Lady Taufan 76 (IRE) (Taufan (USA) 119) [1997 6g 5m* 6m⁵ 5.3g² 5m³ 6d 6.1d Nov 3] 28,000Y: sturdy gelding: second foal: half-brother to 3-y-o Speedball: dam, Irish maiden, stayed 9f: fair performer: won maiden at Windsor in July: placed in nurseries at Brighton and Sandown: below form last 2 starts: should stay 6f: best form on good ground or firmer: heavily bandaged near hind penultimate outing. *R. Hannon*

GOLDEN THUNDERBOLT (FR) 4 b.g. Persian Bold 123 – Carmita 74 d (Caerleon (USA) 132) [1996 79: 8.3m⁶ 8m⁴ 9m³ 8m² 8m 8.5m⁴ 8g² 7f⁵ 1997 8g⁵ 9.9m 8.5d² 8.5d⁴ 8g* 8m 12m² 10m⁵ 12g³ 8.5d 12f³ 10.4d Oct 8] neat gelding: fair performer: not at best to win claimer at Pontefract in May, and mostly below even

402

that form afterwards: stays 1½m: acts on firm and dead ground: tried blinkered: has had tongue tied. *N. Tinkler*

GOLDEN TOUCH (USA) 5 ch.h. Elmaamul (USA) 125 – Tour d'Argent (USA) (Halo (USA)) [1996 67: a8g⁵ a8g a9.4g² a10g³ a8.5g* 9m* 10m* 10.3g⁵ 10d⁵ 8m 10f⁵ 10m⁶ 10m 8m 10g a9.4g² a10s⁵ a9.4g² a9.4g³ 1997 a9.4g² a9.4g 10.8m 10m 10.8m³ 10g³ 10g 10.1f⁵ 9.7s⁶ 10g 10.1g Aug 10] compact horse: modest handicapper: stays 10.8f: acts on dead ground, good to firm and the all-weather: usually held up: inconsistent. *D. J. S. Cosgrove* — 59 a52

GOLDEN TYKE (IRE) 4 b.g. Soviet Lad (USA) 94 – Golden Room (African Sky 124) [1996 49: a6g⁵ a6g⁴ 5s 1997 a8g Feb 14] close-coupled gelding: poor maiden handicapper: tailed off only 4-y-o start. *Miss M. K. Milligan* — –

GOLDFILL 2 b.f. (Jan 22) Marju (IRE) 127 – Briggsmaid 70 (Elegant Air 119) [1997 a7g³ 8f³ 9m⁴ a8g Nov 18] 16,500Y: first foal: dam won from 1½m to 2m: fair form in maidens on turf: much the better effort on all-weather on debut: should stay 1½m+. *W. A. O'Gorman* — 67 a59

GOLD HAWK 2 ch.c. (Mar 4) Weldnaas (USA) 112 – Bel Esprit (Sagaro 133) [1997 8s a7g Nov 25] sturdy, lengthy colt: brother to 3-y-o Madame Chinnery and 1¼m winner Double Up, and half-brother to several winners, including fairly useful 1¾m winner Wings Cove (by Elegant Air): dam no form on flat or over jumps: behind in maidens at Doncaster and Lingfield. *B. Smart* — –

GOLD LANCE (USA) 4 ch.g. Seeking The Gold (USA) – Lucky State (USA) (State Dinner (USA)) [1996 52+: 10d 10m a7g² 1997 a8.5g³ a8g a7g a8g⁴ 8m* 10d 8d⁴ 8f³ 8s 8.1m* 7.6g³ 8.3m* 8d* a10g Nov 25] angular gelding: fair handicapper: had a good season, winning sellers at Pontefract in April and Chepstow in July and non-sellers at Windsor in August and Goodwood in September: seems best around 1m: acts on good to firm and dead ground, only poor on all-weather: no improvement in blinkers. *R. J. O'Sullivan* — 70 a46

GOLD LINING (IRE) 4 ch.f. Magical Wonder (USA) 125 – Muntaz (ARG) (Search Tradition (USA)) [1996 –: 8.2m 8.3m 10.5d 14d⁵ 12.1m 8m 8.1m 7.1m 1997 a7g³ a7g³ a8.5g* a8g³ 8m 7g Oct 24] lengthy filly: poor handicapper: won apprentice maiden event at Wolverhampton in February: stayed 8.5f: acted on fibresand: tried visored: dead. *E. J. Alston* — 36

GOLDMASTER 2 b.g. (Apr 20) Most Welcome 131 – Miss Gorgeous (IRE) 76 (Damister (USA) 123) [1997 a7g 7f⁵ 6m 6d Oct 21] sparely-made gelding: poor mover: first foal: dam 6f (at 2 yrs) and 7f winner: well held in maidens, in blinkers final start. *W. A. O'Gorman* — –

GOLD MILLENIUM (IRE) 3 gr.g. Kenmare (FR) 125 – Gold Necklace 86 (Golden Fleece (USA) 133) [1996 NR 1997 8g May 24] tall gelding: fifth foal: half-brother to useful French 1¼m winner Melina Mou (by Persian Bold), now racing in USA: dam, Irish 2-y-o 7f winner, granddaughter of top broodmare Stilvi: 20/1, some late headway when seventh of 10 in maiden at Kempton. *C. A. Horgan* — 61

GOLD SPATS (USA) 4 b.c. Seeking The Gold (USA) – Foot Stone (USA) (Cyane) [1996 87: 8.1g² 8g² 7m* 7.9m 7m 1997 8g³ 8d* 8m 8.1g³ Jul 16] lengthy, attractive colt: useful handicapper: won at Goodwood in May: good third of 18 to Hawksley Hill in strongly-run Hong Kong Jockey Club Trophy at Sandown final start, just outstayed after leading briefly over 1f out: will prove best up to 1m: yet to race on extremes of going. *M. R. Stoute* — 100

GOLDTUNE 2 b.f. (Mar 10) Damister (USA) 123 – Tantalizing Song (CAN) (The Minstrel (CAN) 135) [1997 7m 7m⁴ 7.9s Oct 8] useful-looking filly: has a fluent, round action: ninth foal: sister to several winners, including 7f winner (including at 2 yrs) Victim of Love and 8.5f and 1¼m winner Miss Fascination and half-sister to a winner in USA: dam ran 5 times in North America: fair form when fourth of 8 to Exclusive in minor event at Kempton in September: all at sea in gluepot conditions next time: should stay at least 1m. *M. A. Jarvis* — 76

GOLLACCIA 3 gr.f. Mystiko (USA) 124 – Millie Grey 52 (Grey Ghost 98) [1996 –: 6f⁶ 6m 7m 1997 9f 14.1m May 27] little sign of ability. *G. M. Moore* — –

GONE FOR A BURTON (IRE) 7 ch.g. Bustino 136 – Crimbourne 83 84
(Mummy's Pet 125) [1996 88: 10m 10.4g 10s^2 12s 1997 10d 10.3g^5 12s Nov 8]
workmanlike gelding: fairly useful handicapper: lightly raced nowadays, and well
held last 2 starts: stays 1½m: acts on good to firm and soft ground: tried blinkered
earlier in career: held up. *P. J. Makin*

GONE SAVAGE 9 b.g. Nomination 125 – Trwyn Cilan 89 (Import 127) [1996 87
79: 5g^5 6m 5d^4 5m^3 6m 5g 5f^2 5m^4 5g* 5m^3 5g^2 5m^2 5d^2 5g* 5m 5s 1997 5g^2 5g* 5g
5m^3 5m^4 5d 5g* 5m^6 5v Oct 11] strong, good-bodied gelding: carries condition:
fairly useful handicapper: still in good heart at 9 yrs: won at Sandown (has a fine
record there) in April and at Newmarket in July: has won at 6f, races mostly at 5f
nowadays: acts on firm and soft ground and on equitrack: blinkered (below form)
twice: held up: tough and consistent. *W. J. Musson*

GONE TO PRESS 2 b.c. (Apr 6) Aragon 118 – Casamurrae 87 (Be My Guest –
(USA) 126) [1997 6m Sep 2] fourth foal: half-brother to an Italian 3-y-o 9f winner
and useful 1995 2-y-o 5f winner Take A Left (both by Formidable), latter also
successful at 1m in USA: dam, 1m and 1½m winner who stayed 16.5f, out of half-
sister to On The House: 33/1, pulled up lame in Folkestone maiden. *J. W. Payne*

GOODBYE GATEMEN (IRE) 3 gr.g. Soviet Lad (USA) 94 – Simple Love 67
(Simply Great (FR) 122) [1996 –: 5d 1997 a7g^2 6.9m^2 6f^2 6m 5s^2 5g* 5g 6m 6g a7g
a7g a5g a5g^5 a5g^2 Dec 22] fair performer: unimpressive in landing odds in maiden at
Leicester in July: disappointing after until second in handicap at Lingfield in
December: effective at 5f to easy 7f: acts on equitrack and on firm and soft going:
tends to hang left: not one to trust implicitly. *B. A. Pearce*

GOOD CATCH (IRE) 2 br.f. (Feb 11) Last Tycoon 131 – Good Reference (IRE) 71
84 (Reference Point 139) [1997 6m^3 7.1m^5 8.1d^5 8.1m^3 8m^6 Sep 25] 29,000Y: strong,
workmanlike filly: first foal: dam, 7f (at 2 yrs) and 1m winner who stayed 1¼m, out
of half-sister to very smart sprinter Sayyaf: fair form in maidens at Pontefract and
Sandown (2): well beaten on nursery debut final start: should stay beyond 1m:
disappointing on dead going. *P. R. Webber*

GOOD DAY 3 gr.g. Petong 126 – Courtesy Call (Northfields (USA)) [1996 56: 6d 53
6m a7g^4 6d^6 8g a7g 1997 a11g^5 a12g^5 a12g^2 a12g 10s* a12g 8.3g Sep 29] good-
topped gelding: fluent mover: modest performer: wide-margin winner of very weak
maiden claimer at Ayr in May: stays 1½m: acts on soft ground and fibresand:
blinkered last 3 starts: none too consistent. *C. W. Thornton*

GOOD FOR YOU 2 ch.c. (Apr 22) Ron's Victory (USA) 129 – To Oneiro 69 –
(Absalom 128) [1997 5d^6 5g^5 Aug 13] 6,400Y: half-brother to several winners,
including a 2-y-o plater by Chief Singer, later successful in Sweden, and 7-y-o The
Institute Boy and Athenian King (both sprinters by Fairy King): dam 5f and 6f
winner: no promise in maiden and claimer, then sold 800 gns. *S. E. Kettlewell*

GOOD HAND (USA) 11 ch.g. Northjet 136 – Ribonette (USA) (Ribot 142) 65
[1996 79: 16m* 16.2f 16.5m 15d^4 17.5m* 14.1f* 18g 1997 16f^2 14.1g* 14.1m^5
Sep 26] close-coupled, sparely-made gelding: fair performer: hacked up in 4-runner
seller at Redcar in August: dyed-in-the-wool stayer: acts on firm and soft ground:
below form when blinkered and visored earlier in career: sometimes bandaged: held
up: often hangs. *S. E. Kettlewell*

GOOD JUDGE (IRE) 3 b.g. Law Society (USA) 130 – Cuirie (Main Reef 126) –
[1996 49+: 7.9g 7.5m^5 7.9g 1997 10m 17.1m Oct 6] small, strong gelding: only sign
of ability on second 2-y-o start. *M. D. Hammond*

GOOD NEWS (IRE) 3 ch.f. Ajraas (USA) 88 – Blackeye (Busted 134) [1996 61
61: 5.3f^5 5m^5 6m 1997 7m* 8f^4 Jun 16] quite good-topped filly: modest performer:
blinkered, won claimer at Brighton in May: creditable fourth in handicap there
following month: stays 1m: acts on firm ground: often gives trouble at stalls.
M. Madgwick

GOOD ON YER 2 b.f. (Feb 27) Reprimand 122 – Princess Eurolink (Be My –
Guest (USA) 126) [1997 6g 7g^3 6m 6m 8m Nov 4] 4,800Y: second foal: half-sister to
a 2-y-o 7f winner by High Estate: dam no worthwhile form on flat or over hurdles:
little worthwhile form. *S. E. Kettlewell*

GOOD REPUTATION   3 ch.f. Bluebird (USA) 125 – Reputation (Tower Walk   66
130) [1996 NR 1997 8g 9d³ 9m² 11.7g⁶ 15.8m⁴ 13.8s a16s⁵ a16g³ Nov 25] lengthy
filly: fifth foal: half-sister to 3 winners, including Lost Reputation and New
Reputation, both fairly useful over 1½m+, by Law Society: dam maiden (stayed
1½m) from family of Nonoalco: modest maiden: demoted after passing post first in
weak race at Goodwood (jockey suspended for irresponsible riding) in May on
second start: stays 2m: acts on good to firm and dead ground and on equitrack: ran
creditably in blinkers final start: sold 8,000 gns in December. *B. W. Hills*

GOOD TO TALK   4 b.g. Weldnaas (USA) 112 – Kimble Blue 56 (Blue Refrain   44
121) [1996 46: 6g 5f⁴ 5g² 5f 7g 6f 5m² 5g⁴ 5g 5m 5.1g 1997 6m⁶ 5m 5d³ 5g 5g
5g 5m⁵ 5m⁶ Aug 16] well-made gelding: poor maiden: best form at 5f: acts on firm
and dead going: tried visored/blinkered: has had tongue tied. *T. D. Easterby*

GOODWOOD CAVALIER   2 b.g. (Jan 26) Efisio 120 – Brassy Nell 72   78
(Dunbeath (USA) 127) [1997 6m 7.1g 7d* Oct 14] 18,000Y: smallish, well-made
gelding: poor mover: fourth foal: half-brother to 7f winner Brass Tacks (by Prince
Sabo) and 1993 2-y-o 5f winner Dance Focus (by Aragon): dam 7.6f winner: 50/1-
winner of steadily-run maiden at Leicester, leading 2f out and beating Bombastic by
1¼ lengths: should stay 1m: showed little on good/good to firm going. *J. L. Dunlop*

GOODWOOD LASS (IRE)   3 b.f. Alzao (USA) 117 – Cutleaf 81 (Kris 135)   68
[1996 71: 6s⁶ 7g* 7.3m 8m 1997 10.2m 14.1g a12g* a12g Jun 30] smallish,
workmanlike filly: fair handicapper: won at Wolverhampton in June: well below
form otherwise in 1997: stays 1½m: acts on fibresand. *J. L. Dunlop*

GOPI   3 b.f. Marju (IRE) 127 – Chandni (IRE) (Ahonoora 122) [1996 64: 5.7g⁴ 5f²   64
5.2f⁵ 6g³ 5g⁴ 1997 a7g³ 6m⁴ 6d⁵ 6m⁶ 5d Aug 25] leggy, sparely-made filly: modest
maiden handicapper: below form in 1997 after reappearance: probably best up to 7f:
acts on firm ground and equitrack: has been bandaged: has pulled hard, and found
little. *R. Hannon*

GORDI (USA)   4 ch.g. Theatrical 128 – Royal Alydar (USA) (Alydar (USA))   107
[1996 109: 10s 10d⁴-10g³* 16.2m⁴ 14.6m 14m⁶ 1997 12s³ 14d⁴ 12g* 13.9g Aug 20]
tall individual: has a long stride: useful performer: won 4-runner listed race at
Leopardstown in July by length from Carnelly: stiff task, well beaten in Ebor at York
month later: well suited by test of stamina: acts on good to firm ground, probably on
dead: gelded after final start. *D. K. Weld, Ireland*

GORE HILL   3 b.f. Be My Chief (USA) 122 – Hollow Heart 89 (Wolver Hollow   –
126) [1996 –: 7d 7.1s 1997 8g 10.2d 11.6s Jun 23] good bodied filly: no worthwhile
form. *M. Blanshard*

GORETSKI (IRE)   4 b.g. Polish Patriot (USA) 128 – Celestial Path 101   88
(Godswalk (USA) 130) [1996 76: 6d² 6.1d 5d* 5.1g⁴ 5s² 5g² 5.3f² 5m⁶ 6d 5m 5m 5g
5s 1997 5s⁴ 6.1m 5g 5s* 5s² a5g* a5g* 5.1m* 5g* 5m² 5d* 5d 5m 5d 5d Nov 7] tall
gelding: unimpressive mover: fairly useful handicapper: started 1997 well in best
form, and won at Hamilton, Southwell (twice), Bath, Catterick and Beverley by
mid-August, including 2 apprentice events: soundly beaten last 2 starts: effective at
5f/6f: acts on good to firm and soft ground and on fibresand: tried in blinkers earlier
in career: usually a front runner: tough and genuine. *N. Tinkler*

GORGEOUS   2 b.f. (Mar 26) Prince Sabo 123 – Crackerjill 37 (Sparkler 130)   37
[1997 5.1m a5g a7g⁴ 6g Aug 11] 6,000 2-y-o: half-sister to 3 winners, including
useful sprinter Arabellajill (by Aragon) and fair 7f winner Petonellajill (by Petong):
dam, maiden on flat, winning hurdler: poor maiden. *N. P. Littmoden*

GORMIRE   4 ro.f. Superlative 118 – Lady of The Lodge 60 (Absalom 128) [1996   – §
52: 5m² 5m 6s⁴ 5g a6g 6d a6g 1997 a6g 7g 7.1m 7d 5m 5m Aug 4] of no account
nowadays. *J. Hetherton*

GOTHENBERG (IRE)   4 b.c. Polish Patriot (USA) 128 – Be Discreet (Junius   117
(USA) 124) [1996 113: 8g 7m⁴ 7d* 8g 7g³ 8m* 6m 8d 8g⁶ 8m⁵ 8d² 8m⁵ 1997 a8f⁴
a9g³ a10f⁴ a10f⁶ 8.1g⁴ 8d⁵ 8s* 8m 8d² 8g* 8m⁶ 8g 8g³ 8f⁵ 7d² 8d² Nov 9] tall, lengthy
colt: powerful mover with long stride: smart performer on his day: won Group 2
races at Milan (by 3¼ lengths from Zero Problemo) and Hoppegarten (beat La Blue
2½ lengths) in the summer: runner-up in Prix de la Foret at Longchamp (6 lengths
behind Occupandiste) and Premio Ribot at Rome (went down by ½ length to Crim-

405

Brian Yeardley Continental Ltd's "Gothenberg"

son Tide) last 2 starts: best at 7f/1m: acts on firm and soft ground, below form on sand: edgy type who often sweats: tends to carry head awkwardly: often a front runner, probably best when allowed to dominate. *M. Johnston*

GOT IT WRONG AGAIN   4 b.g. Reprimand 122 – Fine Asset (Hot Spark 126)   – [1996 NR 1997 8.3m Aug 11] 3,200F: seventh living foal: half-brother to 1991 2-y-o 6f winner Night Asset (by Night Shift) and 6f and 9f German winner Faultless Speech (by Good Times): dam poor half-sister to smart 7f performer Tudor Mill: well beaten in maiden at Windsor. *K. T. Ivory*

GO WITH THE WIND   4 b.c. Unfuwain (USA) 131 – Cominna (Dominion   63 § 123) [1996 69§: a7g⁴ 12d⁴ 12g³ 14.1f² 13.1m 12m² 16.2f² 12m⁶ 16.4m 13.1m⁴ 16m* 16.1m⁴ 1997 15d³ 14d⁴ Jun 30] lengthy colt: unimpressive mover: modest handicapper: stays 2m: acts on firm and dead ground: tried visored and blinkered: flashes tail under pressure: none too resolute and not one to trust. *J. S. Goldie*

GRACE   3 b. or br.f. Buzzards Bay 128§ – Bingo Bongo 60 (Petong 126) [1996 NR   55 1997 7.1m 8.1s⁵ 7.1d⁵ 6m 6g 6g⁴ 6.1m Sep 15] first foal: dam, maiden best up to 1m, became ungenuine: modest maiden: may prove best short of 7f: best effort on good ground: has shown signs of temperament. *J. M. Bradley*

GRACE BROWNING   2 b.f. (Apr 24) Forzando 122 – Queen Angel 88 (Anfield   84 p 117) [1997 6.1g³ 6g* Oct 7] 2,400Y: fourth foal: dam 11f winner, half-sister to Oaks third Pearl Angel: won maiden at Warwick by 1¾ lengths from Bandbox, still green, but quickening without being hard ridden: should stay 1m but not short of speed: could well develop into a useful handicapper. *H. Candy*

GRACEFUL LASS   3 b.f. Sadler's Wells (USA) 132 – Hi Lass 106 (Shirley   96 Heights 130) [1996 73p: 8.2g⁵ 1997 10m⁶ 10g² 11.5d* 12.1m* 11.9d⁶ 12g² 12v⁶

Oct 11] rather sparely-made filly: has a short, round action: useful performer: won handicaps at Lingfield and Chepstow in the summer: best effort when neck second of 6 to Puce in listed race at Ascot in September: ran poorly in Princess Royal Stakes there on final start: will stay 1¾m: acts on good to firm and dead ground, possibly not on heavy: sometimes bandaged near-hind: has had tongue tied. *D. R. Loder*

GRACIOUS IMP (USA)   4 ch.f. Imp Society (USA) – Lady Limbo (USA) – (Dance Spell (USA)) [1996 NR 1997 8.5m 8.3s 6m 12g a16g⁶ 12s 12.5m a10g Jul 26] sister to useful 1991 2-y-o 6f winner Governors Imp, and half-sister to several winners: dam minor 6f winner: no form: tried visored. *J. R. Jenkins*

GRALMANO (IRE)   2 b.c. (Feb 20) Scenic 128 – Llangollen (IRE) 87 (Caerleon   ? (USA) 132) [1997 a5g a6g³ 7d 7m a7g² 10g a8.5g² a8.5g* a7g* Dec 13] 7,000 2-y-o: a96 good-topped colt: third foal: half-brother to German 4-y-o 9f winner Welsh Thatcher (by Thatching): dam 1¼m/1½m winner who stayed 2m: made into a useful performer on fibresand at end of year, winning maiden and minor event at Wolverhampton: no worthwhile form on turf: should stay at least 1¼m. *N. P. Littmoden*

GRANBY BELL   6 b.g. Ballacashtal (CAN) – Betbellof 65 (Averof 123) [1996   – 55: 14.1g⁶ 14m⁵ 16s 13.3s* 16m⁶ 18g 14.1s 1997 12v⁶ Oct 10] tall, angular gelding: modest handicapper: well held only start in 1997. *P. Hayward*

GRAND APPLAUSE (IRE)   7 gr.g. Mazaad 106 – Standing Ovation (Gods-   39 walk (USA) 130) [1996 –: 11.6d 1997 11.5d³ 11.2g⁴ Jun 28] leggy, angular gelding: poor mover: poor maiden handicapper: stays 1¾m: acts on fibresand and on any turf ground: tried blinkered: held up. *M. Salaman*

GRAND CHAPEAU (IRE)   5 b.g. Ballad Rock 122 – All Hat (Double Form   75 130) [1996 63: 6d⁶ 6m 7m 6f 6g* 6m 5m 5g 6m 1997 5g 5m 6g a5g⁶ 5f 5g⁴ 6g² 6g* 6m* 5g⁵ 6d⁴ 6d³ 6m⁶ Sep 21] good-topped gelding: impresses in appearance: fair handicapper: won at Thirsk and Redcar (dead-heated) in August: good efforts last 2 starts (hung left final one): stays 6f when conditions aren't testing: acts on firm and dead ground: often a front runner. *D. Nicholls*

GRAND CRACK (IRE)   5 b.g. Runnett 125 – Foston Bridge 68 (Relkino 131)   – [1996 8d² 7.8d⁵ 7d 9f⁵ 7g 1997 a7g a10g Feb 4] ex-Irish gelding: fifth foal: half-brother to 4 winners, none better then fairly useful: dam third at 7f at 2 yrs: lightly-raced maiden (rated 48) in Ireland for J. Gorman: well beaten both starts in Britain: tried blinkered. *C. A. Dwyer*

GRAND CRU   6 ch.g. Kabour 80 – Hydrangea 73 (Warpath 113) [1996 NR 1997   72 a14g* a12g* a12g³ 16s* 16g³ 20m 16.4d⁶ 17.5d 18g Oct 18] angular gelding: fifth foal: brother to poor maiden on flat/winning pointer Hydropic: dam stayer: fair performer: won weak claimer (for Mrs M. Reveley) in February and apprentice seller in April, both at Southwell: claimed out of R. Craggs' stable £6,000 after third start: improved form when winning handicap at Newbury in May: well below form last 4 outings: suited by good test of stamina: acts on soft ground and fibresand. *J. Cullinan*

GRAND ESTATE   2 b.g. (Feb 10) Prince Sabo 123 – Ultimate Dream 74 (Kafu   72 p 120) [1997 6d 6m⁴ 6s⁴ 5m³ 6m⁴ 6g* 6d⁵ Oct 8] 10,000F: neat gelding: fourth reported foal: half-brother to 4-y-o Statoyork: dam 5f winner at 2 yrs: generally progressive form: shaped well before winning nursery at Thirsk in August, gambled on and making most: off 6 weeks before final start: seems a sprinter: slow-learner at 2 yrs, and should make at least fairly useful handicapper. *T. D. Easterby*

GRAND HOTEL (IRE)   3 ch.c. Be My Guest (USA) 126 – State Treasure   39 (USA) (Secretariat (USA)) [1996 NR 1997 8g 8d 8.3s 10m a9.4f* 9.7s a9.4g² 11.9d⁵ a52 Sep 5] IR 19,000Y: strong, lengthy colt: half-brother to fairly useful 7f (at 2 yrs) and 1m winner Double Diamond (by Last Tycoon), 6-y-o Diamond Crown and 2 winners in USA: modest handicapper at best: won at Wolverhampton in June: should stay at least 1¼m: acts on fibresand: blinkered last 2 outings: temperament under suspicion: joined R. McKellar. *P. W. Harris*

GRAND LAD (IRE)   3 ch.c. Mujtahid (USA) 118 – Supportive (IRE) (Nashamaa   104 113) [1996 104: 5m³ 5g* 5m⁵ 6m² 5d³ 1997 6f* Apr 3] lengthy colt: has a quick action: made all and not hard pressed to win 6-runner minor event at Leicester on only 3-y-o start by 2½ lengths from Indian Spark: speedy, but stays 6f: acts on firm and dead going. *R. W. Armstrong*

Mrs T. Von Halle & Mr M. Kerr-Dineen's "Grapeshot"

GRAND MUSICA 4 b.g. Puissance 110 – Vera Musica (USA) (Stop The Music 80 (USA)) [1996 97: 8.3m² 8.3d² 7g* 7g² 7.9g⁴ 1997 8m 8g 8.1m 8.1g 8d⁶ 8m 8s Nov 8] leggy gelding: just a fairly useful handicapper in 1997: stays 8.3f: acts on good to firm and dead ground: none too consistent. *I. A. Balding*

GRAND OVATION (IRE) 3 b.g. Green Desert (USA) 127 – Fitnah 125 (Kris 59 135) [1996 NR 1997 8g⁵ May 24] quite good-topped gelding: shows knee action: sixth foal: brother to 1990 2-y-o 5f winner Mayaasa and half-brother to 1m winner Fit On Time (by Lead On Time), later successful in Dubai: dam, French 1¼m winner, second in Prix de Diane, is out of good sprinter Greenland Park: bandaged and green, fifth of 12 in maiden at Kempton in May: sold 1,000 gns in October. *B. Hanbury*

GRAND SLAM (IRE) 2 b.c. (Apr 29) Second Set (IRE) 127 – Lady In The Park 77 p (IRE) (Last Tycoon 131) [1997 7g⁵ 8m⁴ Oct 1] IR 21,000Y: smallish, useful-looking colt: second foal: half-brother to fairly useful Irish 3-y-o 7f (at 2 yrs) and 9f winner Far Niente (by Don't Forget Me): dam Irish 2-y-o 1m winner from family of Ardross: promise both starts, still bit backward when keeping-on fourth to Courteous in maiden at Salisbury: likely to stay beyond 1m: should do better. *R. Hannon*

GRAND SPLENDOUR 4 b.f. Shirley Heights 130 – Mayaasa (FR) 82 (Green 78 Desert (USA) 127) [1996 79p: 12.1g⁴ 10m⁵ 10.5d² 10.4g² 1997 10g 12g 10s 9.9m⁴ 10s³ 9.9v⁴ 10.1g* 12d 10.5g Sep 27] lengthy filly: has a quick action: fair performer: won maiden at Yarmouth in August by 8 lengths: unsuited by muddling pace last 2 starts: stays 1½m: acts on good to firm and soft ground: edgy sort, sometimes taken down last and steadily: has had tongue tied: has pulled hard: held up and best with strong gallop. *Lady Herries*

GRANNY'S PET 3 ch.g. Selkirk (USA) 129 – Patsy Western 81 (Precocious 101 126) [1996 99: 5.2d² 5g² 5m* 5m 5m⁴ 7m³ 7d⁴ 1997 7g² 8g⁵ 7g³ 6d⁴ 6m 6g⁴ 7m Aug 1] angular, close-coupled gelding: has a quick action: useful performer: best efforts when second in European Free Handicap at Newmarket (beaten 5 lengths by Hidden Meadow) and fifth in Premio Parioli at Rome (5½ lengths behind Air Express) in April: blinkered in handicaps last 2 outings, not disgraced on first occasion: will prove best up to 1m: acts on good to firm and dead going: held up: gelded at end of season. *P. F. I. Cole*

GRAPESHOT (USA) 3 b.c. Hermitage (USA) – Ardy Arnie (USA) (Hold Your 114 Peace (USA)) [1996 108p: 6m³ 6m* 7m² 7m* 1997 8m² 10d* May 20] tall, rangy colt: fluent mover: progressive form: beaten ¾ length by Desert Story in Craven Stakes at Newmarket on reappearance: sweating and edgy, 2½-length winner from Running Stag of 6-runner listed race at Goodwood following month: reportedly strained a suspensory ligament in week before Derby, and not seen out again: should stay 1½m: yet to race on extremes of going. *L. M. Cumani*

GRAPEVINE (IRE) 3 b.f. Sadler's Wells (USA) 132 – Gossiping (USA) (Chati 88 (USA)) [1996 71p: 8.2g⁶ 1997 11g⁶ 11.4s² 11f* 13s³ 10f⁶ Sep 20] tall, rangy filly: fairly useful form: easily best effort in Britain when 11 lengths second of 5 to Kyle Rhea in listed event at Chester, final start for P. Chapple-Hyam: came from off pace to win maiden at Saratoga in August, easily best effort in New York: should stay 1½m: acts on firm and soft ground: raced on medication in USA. *P. Byrne, USA*

GRATE TIMES 3 b.g. Timeless Times (USA) 99 – Judys Girl (IRE) (Simply 59 Great (FR) 122) [1996 75: 5d⁴ 5g⁵ 5m³ 7m³ 7s* 7.5m² 7g 7m³ 7.5f³ 7d 7.9g⁴ 7g² 7d 7g 1997 a8g 7f⁴ 7g 7s 9.9m³ 9.9d 12g² 10m 10.9s² Oct 14] modest performer: stays easy 1½m: acts on firm and soft going (well beaten only start on fibresand): effective blinkered or not: inconsistent. *E. Weymes*

GRAZIA 2 b.f. (Apr 18) Sharpo 132 – Dance Machine 111 (Green Dancer 102 P (USA) 132) [1997 6m² 6g* Oct 18]

By the time the Two-Year-Old Trophy is run at Redcar at the end of October most of the contenders have had quite a bit of racing—for example the 1992 and 1994 winners, Pip's Pride and Maid For Walking, had had eight previous starts each—and the majority are exposed as useful performers at best. Framed to favour two-year-olds from less fashionable backgrounds, with each

Comcast Teesside Two-Year-Old Trophy, Redcar—Grazia lands a gamble

runner's weight determined by the previous year's median sale price of their sire's yearlings (the runners don't have to have been through the ring themselves), the winners of the first eight runnings have not generally been the sort of animals we could be especially enthusiastic about for the following season. We wouldn't say that about the latest winner Grazia, however.

There were all the signs that Grazia had been 'laid out' specially for the Two-Year-Old Trophy, worth just under £70,000 to the winner in its first year of sponsorship by Comcast Teesside. Unusually for one of her stable's debutants, she had come in for plenty of support in a Newmarket maiden earlier in October, starting the 15/8 favourite. She made a pleasing start, taking the lead under two furlongs out and running on well until headed well inside the last furlong and forced to check close home by the winner, Qilin. Pasternak landed a gamble that same afternoon in the Cambridgeshire, and Grazia went on to land another for the stable at Redcar a fortnight later, backed to 7/2 favourite from 6/1. Only four of her twenty-five opponents started at shorter than 10/1 and they included three who'd shown useful form in pattern races the time before—the Prix d'Arenberg runner-up Shudder, the Mill Reef fourth Mijana and, from Ireland, the Flying Five runner-up Hopping Higgins. Even allowing for Grazia's light weight of 8-2—only three carried less—she needed to show plenty of improvement. But she was helped by the strong pace set on her side of the track by Hopping Higgins and Chips. Grazia was soon going well behind the leaders and her rider was able to pick his moment before driving her clear inside the final furlong. Grazia's inexperience was evident as she idled in front but she still had a length to spare over Mijana (near the top of the weight range on 8-10) drawn on the other side of the track. Shudder was another half a length away in third.

		Sharpen Up	Atan
	Sharpo	(ch 1969)	Rocchetta
	(ch 1977)	Moiety Bird	Falcon
Grazia		(ch 1971)	Gaska
(b.f. Apr 18, 1995)		Green Dancer	Nijinsky
	Dance Machine	(b 1972)	Green Valley
	(b 1982)	Never A Lady	Pontifex
		(ch 1974)	Camogie

Grazia created a number of records at Redcar, being the first favourite, the first maiden, the most lightly raced and indeed the first not to be sold at auction among Two-Year-Old Trophy winners. Her dam did go through the ring but fortunately for owner-breeder Cyril Humphris he was able to buy her back for just 15,000 guineas at the Newmarket December Sales in 1993. 'Fortunately' because her then unraced two-year-old turned out to be the dual Eclipse and Juddmonte International winner Halling, a close relative of Grazia by Diesis. A third mating with a son of Sharpen Up resulted in the three-year-old Shaska (by Kris) who won one of her three starts at around a mile and a quarter in the latest season. Grazia is Dance Machine's seventh foal. Her first three were all winners in France, Brise de Mer and Bal de Mer (both by Bering) at a mile and Allez Wijins (by Alleged) over hurdles, the last-named a winning hurdler in Britain, too. Dance Machine, like Grazia, ended her two-year-old season with a 'large P', in her case after winning the Sweet Solera Stakes on her only outing that year, and then showed smart form when successful at a mile and a quarter at three. Further details of this family may be found in Halling's essays in *Racehorses of 1995* and *Racehorses of 1996*. Suffice to say that its successful members are many and varied, descendants of Grazia's fourth dam Mesopotamia including Haydock Park Sprint Cup winner Cherokee Rose, Prix du Cadran winner Molesnes and Champion Hurdler Alderbrook.

Grazia is a tall, good-topped filly with scope, and she looks open to plenty of improvement as a three-year-old when sure to be placed to advantage. The now-deceased Sharpo is much more of an influence for speed than Dance Machine's earlier mates and Grazia will almost certainly prove best at up to a mile. *Sir Mark Prescott*

GREAT BEAR 5 ch.g. Dominion 123 – Bay Bay 101 (Bay Express 132) [1996 –
51d: a8g⁶ a8g⁶ a8g a8g 7s 10g 8.1g 7m 8f² 8m* 7g⁴ 8m 8.3g 8f 8m 8m a9.4g a10g
a10g 1997 8m 10m 8.3g 8g a9.4g Dec 26] of no account nowadays. *D. W. Chapman*

GREAT CHIEF 4 ch.g. Be My Chief (USA) 122 – Padelia (Thatching 131) [1996 45
–: 8m 8.2m 8m 7g 1997 a6g 12.3m 8d 7g³ 8f 8.2d a7g⁴ a10g⁵ Dec 2] tall gelding:
poor maiden handicapper: stays 1m: acts on equitrack and firm going, below form on
dead: has had tongue tied and been bandaged behind. *Bob Jones*

GREAT CHILD 3 b.c. Danehill (USA) 126 – Charmina (FR) (Nonoalco (USA) 91
131) [1996 72+: 7d⁵ 7g⁴ 8.1s³ 1997 7g 7.6d* 7.9g² 7m 7m² 7.9d 8m³ 7.9s⁶ Oct 8]
strong, deep-girthed colt: fairly useful handicapper: in good form all year, and won at
Chester in May: stays 1m: acts on good to firm and soft going: visored final start:
usually races prominently: sent to UAE. *M. R. Stoute*

GREAT DANE (IRE) 2 b.c. (May 11) Danehill (USA) 126 – Itching (IRE) 89 p
(Thatching 131) [1997 7f² Oct 29] third reported foal: half-brother to 3-y-o Witching
Hour: dam unraced half-sister to useful Alidiva, dam of Ali-Royal, Taipan and
Sleepytime: 6/4 on, 1½ lengths second of 8 to Asad in steadily-run Yarmouth maiden,
free early and carrying head awkwardly when ridden, not striding out properly:
should stay at least 1m: looks sure to improve. *H. R. A. Cecil*

GREAT EASEBY (IRE) 7 ch.g. Caerleon (USA) 132 – Kasala (USA) 70
(Blushing Groom (USA) 131) [1996 66: 16g² 16g² 16.1g³ 20f 16.1g² 16f² 16.1m 16g*
1997 17.5d 18g Oct 18] sturdy, good-bodied gelding: useful hurdler: fair handicapper
on flat: suited by a thorough test of stamina: probably acts on any ground. *W. Storey*

GREATEST 6 b.g. Superlative 118 – Pillowing 69 (Good Times (ITY)) [1996 63, 58
a78: 8s 8.5m 8m² 8f⁵ 8m a8g² a8g⁶ a8g* a7g* a7g 1997 a7g a8g⁴ a7g* a7g* a7g² a75
6.9g 7d 7d 7g⁶ 7.1g* 8m⁴ a7g⁶ 7d⁵ Oct 14] leggy gelding: poor mover: fair on the
all-weather, modest on turf: won 2 claimers at Lingfield in February and seller at
Chepstow (hung left) in August: effective at 7f/1m: best turf form on good ground or
firmer: usually blinkered, has run well when not: races prominently: sold, to go to
Italy. *Miss Gay Kelleway*

GREAT HALL 8 gr.g. Hallgate 127 – Lily of France 81 (Monsanto (FR) 121) 39
[1996 50d: 7s 6m⁶ 6m 7m 6d⁵ 6m 8m a6g a7g 7m⁶ 6m 8f a7g 1997 6.1d⁴ 7m May 24]
compact gelding: unimpressive mover: poor handicapper nowadays: stays 7f: acts on
firm and soft going and the all-weather: best 6-y-o form in blinkers, visored once at 2
yrs: often bandaged behind. usually gets behind early on *P. D. Cundell*

GREAT LYTH LASS (IRE) 2 b.f. (Apr 11) Waajib 121 – Global Princess 67 d
(USA) (Transworld (USA) 121) [1997 5m³ 5.1m⁴ a6g 6.1m 7.1g⁵ 5d Sep 18]
10,000Y: half-sister to several winners abroad: dam placed in USA: fair maiden at
best, but deteriorated: visored/blinkered (in seller) final 2 starts. *P. D. Evans*

GREAT MELODY 2 ch.g. (Apr 17) Pips Pride 117 – Unbidden Melody 61
(USA) (Chieftain II) [1997 6m⁴ 5g⁶ 6.1g⁶ Oct 4] 24,000Y: eighth foal: half-brother
to several winners, including 4-y-o Muhandam: dam, ran twice in USA, half-sister to
Greenham winner Faustus: modest form in maidens: should stay beyond 6f: sold
4,300 gns, to join D. Cosgrove. *J. M. P. Eustace*

GREAT ORATION (IRE) 8 b. or br.g. Simply Great (FR) 122 – Spun Gold 106 68
(Thatch (USA) 136) [1996 58: 16.2m 17.1g⁴ 21.6m³ 16.2g 16.5g³ 18m* 15.8s³
15.9m* 16.2m⁵ 16.2f³ 17.5m³ 17.1m³ 1997 17.1m* 16g⁵ 16.1f³ 20m 15.9m³ 16m⁶
18.7m⁴ 17.1g* 15.9g Sep 24] rather leggy gelding: has round action: fair handicapper: won narrowly at Pontefract in April and (fourth win there) August: suited by
2m+: acts on any turf going and on fibresand: sometimes visored earlier in career:
usually held up: tough and consistent. *F. Watson*

GREAT TERN 5 b.m. Simply Great (FR) 122 – La Neva (FR) (Arctic Tern 58 +
(USA) 126) [1996 59p: a8.5g 11.7g⁶ 10d a14.8g⁴ 14m⁴ 14d* 14.6g* 1997 16d Sep
13] lengthy, workmanlike mare: modest handicapper, improved towards end of 1996:
reportedly broke pedal bone during winter: 11 lb out of handicap on first start for
nearly a year, pulled too hard but shaped as though retaining all her ability only 5-y-o
start (reportedly returned stiff): should stay 2m: possibly best on good ground or
softer: stays in training. *N. M. Babbage*

GRECIAN PRINCE   2 ch.c. (Mar 24) Risk Me (FR) 127 – Troyes 81 (Troy 137)   –
[1997 7m⁵ 8.1d 6d Oct 28] 20,000Y: good-bodied colt: sixth foal: brother to Italian
3-y-o 7f and 8.5f winner Ultima Chance and 4-y-o Trojan Risk, and half-brother
to 9f winner Tromond (by Lomond): dam, 1½m winner, half-sister to Yorkshire
Oaks winner Hellenic: only a little sign of ability in minor event and maidens.
J. G. Smyth-Osbourne

GREEBA   2 b.f. (Jan 16) Fairy King (USA) – Guanhumara (Caerleon (USA) 132)   63
[1997 6g 6m 5d⁵ 6.1m Sep 15] first foal: dam poor maiden half-sister to Cadeaux
Genereux and to dam of Ya Malak (by Fairy King): modest form in maidens and a
nursery: has gone poorly to post. *R. Hannon*

GREEK DANCE (IRE)   2 b.c. (Mar 21) Sadler's Wells (USA) 132 – Hellenic   88 p
125 (Darshaan 133) [1997 7m² Sep 10] strong, good sort: third foal: brother to 5-y-o
Election Day and half-brother to 3-y-o Desert Beauty: dam won Yorkshire Oaks and
second in St Leger: 11/4 from 7/4 and better for race, promising 6 lengths second of
11 to Tamarisk in minor event at Kempton, soon prominent and considerably
handled once winner quickened: will be suited by 1¼m+: didn't take eye to post:
looks sure to do fair bit better and win races once upped in trip. *M. R. Stoute*

GREEK PALACE (IRE)   3 b.c. Royal Academy (USA) 130 – Grecian Sea (FR)   96 p
107 (Homeric 133) [1996 NR 1997 8g³ 10.4g³ 10m* May 28] lengthy, useful-
looking colt: half-brother to several winners, including Yorkshire Oaks winner and
St Leger runner-up Hellenic (by Darshaan) and Golden Wave (useful up to 1½m, by
Glint of Gold): dam, won over 6f at 2 yrs in France, should have stayed 1¼m:
progressive form: coltish, won maiden at Ripon in May by neck, well clear, from
Taunt, always travelling best and needing only to be nudged along entering final 1f:
will stay 1½m: stays in training, and should do better. *M. R. Stoute*

GREENACRES GODDESS   3 ch.f. River God (USA) 121 – Greenacres Girl   –
(Tycoon II) [1996 NR 1997 10.8m⁵ 8g 6.9m⁶ a9.4g Aug 16] second foal to race here:
dam winning hurdler: of little account. *T. Wall*

GREENAWAY BAY (USA)   3 ch.g. Green Dancer (USA) 132 – Raise 'n Dance   81
(USA) (Raise A Native) [1996 NR 1997 7m* 8.1g⁶ 10.3m 8m 8g Jul 10] $110,000Y:
quite good-topped gelding: half-brother to 1m winner Full Cry (by The Minstrel) and
several winners in USA: dam 6f stakes winner: won maiden at Kempton in March:
rather disappointing afterwards: should stay 1m: sold 14,000 gns in October, then
gelded and joined W. Musson. *G. Wragg*

GREENBACK (BEL)   6 b.g. Absalom 128 – Batalya (BEL) (Boulou) [1996 NR   –
1997 16g May 24] angular gelding: fairly useful hurdler/chaser: well beaten only flat
outing in 1997. *P. J. Hobbs*

GREEN BOPPER (USA)   4 b.g. Green Dancer (USA) 132 – Wayage (USA)   –
(Mr Prospector (USA)) [1996 81d: 8s³ 8g* 8m 7f 8.3d 7m⁴ 7s 1997 10g 8.3s May 19]
close-coupled gelding: deteriorated at 3 yrs for M. Bell, and well beaten in 1997.
C. P. Morlock

GREEN BOULEVARD (USA)   3 ch.f. Green Forest (USA) 134 – Assez Cuite   57
(USA) 114 (Graustark) [1996 52+: 5m a6g⁵ a5g³ 1997 a5g* a5g⁶ Jan 23] modest
performer: won maiden at Lingfield in January: should stay 6f: acts on equitrack:
sent to USA. *J. Berry*

GREENBROOK   2 b.g. (May 3) Greensmith 121 – Comedy Lady 46 (Comedy   69
Star (USA) 121) [1997 6f a6g 7f³ 7g² 7.5v* a6g 7.1s⁴ 8g² 7m* a6g² Oct 18] 1,000
2-y-o: leggy, angular gelding: half-brother to fair 1987 2-y-o 5f winner Only In Gest
(by Aragon): dam won 1m seller at 4 yrs: fair performer: won seller at Beverley in
July and claimer at Redcar in October: barely stays 1m: has form on any turf going
and on fibresand: blinkered second start: usually a front runner: game and consistent.
W. G. M. Turner

GREEN CARD (USA)   3 b.c. Green Dancer (USA) 132 – Dunkellin (USA)   109
(Irish River (FR) 131) [1996 78p: 7m 1997 8m* 8m 8g³ 10g⁴ 10m² 10d³ 9d⁵ Oct 17]
quite attractive colt: useful performer: won maiden at Ripon in April: better efforts
all starts afterwards, ninth in 2000 Guineas at Newmarket and in frame in listed race
at Kempton, Meld Stakes at the Curragh, minor event at Windsor (1½ lengths second

to Salmon Ladder) and Select Stakes at Goodwood (third behind Fahris): barely stays 1¼m: yet to race on extremes of going. *S. P. C. Woods*

GREEN DOLPHIN 2 gr.f. (Mar 23) Greensmith 121 – Jane Herring (Nishapour –
(FR) 125) [1997 5.3f⁶ Jul 16] first foal: dam ran 3 times: tailed-off last in maiden.
W. G. M. Turner

GREEN GOLIGHTLY (USA) 6 b.g. Green Dancer (USA) 132 – Polly Daniels –
(USA) 110 (Clever Trick (USA)) [1996 –: 6m a6g a6g 1997 a7g⁵ a7g a8g 8d a5g Jul
11] one-time fair sprint handicapper: retains little ability. *R. M. Flower*

GREEN JACKET 2 b.g. (May 6) Green Desert (USA) 127 – Select Sale 72
(Auction Ring (USA) 123) [1997 7m 7g 7.1g³ 8g 7d² Oct 17] 35,000Y: sturdy,
workmanlike gelding: closely related to French 1½m winner Rachdane (by Polish
Precedent) and half-brother to several winners, including King Edward VII Stakes
winner Private Tender (by Shirley Heights): dam unraced half-sister to Ribblesdale
winner Queen Midas: fair form when placed in maiden at Chepstow and private
sweepstakes at Newmarket: well held in nursery in between: should stay 1¼m.
J. L. Dunlop

GREEN JEWEL 3 gr.f. Environment Friend 128 – Emeraude 84 (Kris 135) 108 ?
[1996 80: 6d³ 6g* 7m⁶ 6g² 7d² 1997 7m* 7d⁴ 8g⁶ 9g³ 9f⁵ 8f⁴ 9f³ Oct 18] tall,
unfurnished filly: easy mover: fairly useful handicapper: winner at
Newmarket in May: appeared to show much-improved form on first outing for new
trainer when fifth in Grade 1 Del Mar Oaks in August: in frame in non-graded stakes
afterwards: bred to stay beyond 9f, but races freely: acts on firm and dead ground:
raced on medication in USA. *C. Whittingham, USA*

GREENLANDER 2 b.c. (May 26) Green Desert (USA) 127 – Pripet (USA) 86 106
(Alleged (USA) 138) [1997 6s* 5.5d* 7g⁴ Sep 20] third foal: half-brother to 3-y-o
Priluki: dam staying sister to 1000 Guineas and Oaks winner Midway Lady: won
maiden at Yarmouth (impressively) and rather substandard Prix Robert Papin at
Maisons-Laffitte later in July, coming from off pace to beat Aurigny short neck: 9½
lengths fourth of 8 to Xaar in Prix de la Salamandre at Longchamp (reportedly
returned lame): should stay 1m. *C. E. Brittain*

Prix Robert Papin, Maisons-Laffitte—a short neck separates Greenlander (No. 1) and Aurigny

Michael Sobell Silver Tankard Handicap, York—
fourth of five wins during the season for the admirable Grey Kingdom

GREEN POWER 3 b.g. Green Desert (USA) 127 – Shaft of Sunlight 58   86
(Sparkler 130) [1996 78: 6m⁵ 6g³ 1997 8.2m⁵ 8.3s* 8m² 8.1s 8.1m³ 8d Oct 16]
strong, good-topped gelding: carries condition: fairly useful performer: won maiden
at Windsor in May: best effort in handicaps following start: will stay beyond 1m: acts
on good to firm and soft ground: has swished tail. *J. R. Fanshawe*

GREENSPAN (IRE) 5 b.g. Be My Guest (USA) 126 – Prima Ballerina (FR)   78
(Nonoalco (USA) 131) [1996 81: a12g* a12g⁴ a12g*, 11.9d⁵ a14.8g a11g² a12g*
a12g⁴ a9.4g* 1997 a11g a12g⁴ a12g* a12g* a12g* a12g³ a12g⁴ a12g² a16.2g³ a12g³
a11g² a14g⁴ a14g* Dec 8] useful-looking gelding: bad mover: fair performer: does
nearly all his racing on fibresand these days, and won claimers at Southwell in February (2, awarded race on second occasion), March and December: stays 2m:
blinkered (fell) third 3-y-o start. *W. R. Muir*

GREENSTEAD (USA) 4 b.c. Green Dancer (USA) 132 – Evening Air (USA) (J   91
O Tobin (USA) 130) [1996 99+: 10.3g⁵ 10g* 8m 10m* 11.9f 1997 12.3d³ 10v⁴ 12g
Oct 25] good-bodied, attractive colt: useful at 3 yrs: not so good in 1997, best effort
fourth in rated stakes at Ascot: should stay 1½m: best run on good to firm ground: has
sweated, including when successful: sold 45,000 gns in December. *J. H. M. Gosden*

GREENWICH FORE 3 b.g. Formidable (USA) 125 – What A Challenge 70   –
(Sallust 134) [1996 68: 6m 7.6d⁴ 8g 7.6m 7m⁴ 7.3s a8.5g³ a10g⁴ a8g³ 1997 a10g⁶
12g a16g⁵ Sep 8] small, compact gelding: fair performer: well below form in
1997. *T. G. Mills*

GRESATRE 3 gr.c. Absalom 128 – Mild Deception (IRE) (Glow (USA)) [1996   54
58+: 5s⁶ 5.1d 5m 6d³ 6m³ a7g⁴ 7.9g⁴ 7.6m⁶ 8m⁶ 8m 7m 8f⁵ 1997 a6g* a7g² a11g a6g   a64
7.5s 6g 6g⁵ 8d⁵ 8g⁵ 8m⁵ a6g⁴ 7g⁴ 7m 8m⁵ 8.2s⁶ 8g⁴ Oct 27] angular, good-bodied
colt: modest handicapper: better on the all-weather than turf, and won at Southwell
in March: effective at 6f to 1m: acts on good to firm and soft going and on fibresand:
tried visored: sent to Germany. *C. A. Dwyer*

GRESHAM FLYER 4 b.g. Clantime 101 – Eleanor Cross (Kala Shikari 125)   –
[1996 –: a7g a6g 8.2d⁶ 12m 1997 8g 14.1f Oct 29] small gelding: no worthwhile
form. *Mrs S. Lamyman*

GRETEL 3 ch.f. Hansel (USA) – Russian Royal (USA) 108 (Nureyev (USA) 131) 98
[1996 100: 7.1g* 7.1m⁶ 8m³ 8g 1997 10d⁴ 8d 8.5m⁶ 10.2m Jul 25] big, lengthy filly:
has a powerful, rounded action: useful performer: unplaced in listed events 1997,
best effort at Goodwood (behind Out West) on second start: best up to 1m: yet to race
on extremes of going: headstrong, and has been taken last and quietly to post: sent to
USA. *M. R. Stoute*

GREY AGAIN 5 gr.m. Unfuwain (USA) 131 – Grey Goddess 117 (Godswalk –
(USA) 130) [1996 –, a62: a7g⁵ a11g* a9.4g⁶ a12g² a8g⁵ a11g 7.5m 9.9m 1997 7m
8.2g a8.5g a12g⁶ Oct 20] leggy mare: modest performer at best: well beaten in 1997.
D. Shaw

GREY KINGDOM 6 gr.g. Grey Desire 115 – Miss Realm 86 (Realm 129) [1996 80
49: a11g 8.5m⁶ 10m 9m 7.5m² 7.5f* 8.1f³ 8.1g 7m* 8.3m⁴ 7.5g⁵ 8m⁵ a7g 1997 6.1m³
6.1g* 5.9g* 6g³ 7.1m* 7d 7g³ 6d* 7d³ 6s³ 7s* 7m⁴ 7m⁴ 6m² 6m³ 6g⁵ 7.6m⁶ 6g 7s⁴
8m 6g 6g Oct 22] angular, leggy gelding: had a splendid 1997, making into a fairly
useful handicapper and winning at Nottingham, Carlisle, Musselburgh, York and
Epsom by early-July: creditable efforts most starts afterwards: effective at 6f to
7.5f: acts on any turf (lightly raced on fibresand): often ridden by 7-lb claimer
D. Mernagh: races prominently: tough, genuine and consistent. *M. Brittain*

GREY LEGEND 4 gr.g. Touch of Grey 90 – Northwold Star (USA) 71 –
(Monteverdi 129) [1996 –: 6f 7m 1997 a7g⁶ a8g a10g 12m Apr 22] no longer of any
account. *R. M. Flower*

GREY PROSPECT 3 b.g. Grey Desire 115 – Nicky Mygirl 46 (Chief Singer –
131) [1996 NR 1997 7m 7m May 31] 700Y: first foal: dam 2-y-o 5f winner: showed
little in claimer and maiden. *M. Brittain*

GREY SHOT 5 gr.g. Sharrood (USA) 124 – Optaria 83 (Song 132) [1996 115: 117
16.2m² 13.9f⁴ 16g⁵ 16f* 15.9m⁴ 16m 1997 16.2m⁴ 15.5d² 20g 16m 13.4s³ 16g² 16f*
15.5d Oct 26] sparely-made gelding: fine, easy mover: good walker: smart stayer:

*Portland Place Properties Jockey Club Cup, Newmarket—Grey Shot makes all and sets a new course record.
Double Eclipse is his nearest pursuer*

short-head second of 7 to Stretarez in Prix Vicomtesse Vigier at Longchamp in May, caught post: below form next 3 starts: returned to best to win Jockey Club Cup at Newmarket in October, making all at strong gallop (smashed course record) and beating Double Eclipse by 2 lengths: tailed off in Prix Royal-Oak at Longchamp only subsequent outing: stays 2m, seemingly not 2½m: acts on firm and soft going: front runner: game: impressive winner on hurdling debut in December. *I. A. Balding*

GREY WAY (USA) 4 gr.f. Cozzene (USA) – Northern Naiad (FR) (Nureyev (USA) 131) [1996 105: 10g* 9m² 10d² 11d⁵ 11g* 10d* 10.5s 1997 10m* 10f⁵ 10m* 10m⁴ 10m⁶ 9f a12s³ Dec 27] tall, angular filly: useful ex-Italian performer: won minor event at Milan in March and listed race at Rome in June (final start for G. Botti): not discredited in Nassau Stakes at Goodwood on only start in Britain, best effort in North America (left J. Dunlop before penultimate run) when third in Grade 2 event at Calder: stays 1½m: acts on firm and dead ground. *P. Byrne, USA*   109

GRIEF (IRE) 4 ch.g. Broken Hearted 124 – Crecora (Royal Captive 116) [1996 9g² 10m² 10g* 11m² 10g⁶ 10d³ 11g⁶ 1997 10m⁵ 10m 12g* 10s² 10d 9g⁶ 12s⁵ Nov 8] rather leggy ex-Irish gelding: useful performer: won maiden at Roscommon at 3 yrs (sold out of J. Oxx's stable 17,000 gns at end of year): won handicap at Epsom in August: below form last 3 starts: effective at 1¼m and 1½m: acts on good to firm and soft ground: wears bandages. *D. R. C. Elsworth*   99

GRINKOV (IRE) 2 b. or br.g. (Apr 19) Soviet Lad (USA) 94 – Tallow Hill (Dunphy 124) [1997 6g Jun 12] 10,000Y: tall gelding: has scope: fifth living foal: half-brother to 2-y-o winners Talberno Boy (at 6f/7f in 1991) and Lowrianna (at 5f in 1992), both by Cyrano de Bergerac: dam unraced half-sister to Cheveley Park winner Pass The Peace: green, behind in maiden at Newbury. *H. Morrison*   –

GROG (IRE) 8 b.g. Auction Ring (USA) 123 – Any Price (Gunner B 126) [1996 NR 1997 12.1g 13.1s Oct 13] lightly raced and little worthwhile form on flat since 1992. *B. Mactaggart*   –

GROOMS GOLD (IRE) 5 ch.g. Groom Dancer (USA) 128 – Gortynia (FR) (My Swallow 134) [1996 –: 10.3d 1997 10m 8.2d³ a8g² a10g² Nov 25] lengthy gelding: lightly raced since 1995, but still capable of modest form: stays 1¼m: acts on firm and dead ground and the all-weather: forces pace. *P. W. Harris*   59

GROOM'S GORDON (FR) 3 b.g. Groom Dancer (USA) 128 – Sonoma (FR) 121 (Habitat 134) [1996 96: 6d⁴ 6.1m* 7.1g* 8g⁴ 7m 1997 8g² 7g⁵ 8d 7m 8m⁶ 7g² 8.2d⁴ Nov 3] well-made gelding: fairly useful performer: second in listed race at Kempton in March and minor event at Leicester in October: stays 1m: yet to race on extremes of going: lazy sort, blinkered fourth and fifth starts: consistent. *J. L. Dunlop*   94

GROSVENOR MISS (IRE) 2 b.f. (Apr 7) Tirol 127 – Somnifere (USA) 63 (Nijinsky (CAN) 138) [1997 5m 6m 7g Sep 5] second foal: closely related to 3-y-o Sea Mist: dam lightly-raced maiden, closely related to smart 1989 2-y-o Line of Thunder (dam of Thunder Gulch) and daughter of Irish Oaks winner and Gold Cup second Shoot A Line: behind in maidens and minor event: blinkered final start. *P. W. Chapple-Hyam*   –

GROSVENOR SPIRIT (IRE) 2 b. or br.f. (May 6) Fairy King (USA) – La Koumia (FR) 119 (Kaldoun (FR) 122) [1997 7g⁶ 7d Oct 27] closely related to 7f winner La Kermesse (by Storm Bird) and half-sister to 10.4f winner San Pietra (by Caerleon): dam 5.5f (at 2 yrs) to 1¼m winner in France, later Grade 1 winner in USA: showed a little promise in maiden at Warwick, but failed to confirm it next time. *P. W. Chapple-Hyam*   –

GROUCHO (USA) 3 b.c. Lyphard (USA) 132 – Alvernia (USA) (Alydar (USA)) [1996 NR 1997 10g Apr 15] strong, compact colt: first foal: dam 9f winner in USA: unimpressive to post (seeming green) and never a threat in Newmarket maiden on only day at the races: sold, to join N. Babbage, 6,500 gns in October. *R. Charlton*   –

GROUND GAME 4 b.f. Gildoran 123 – Running Game 81 (Run The Gantlet (USA)) [1996 95: 10.3m* 10g² 12m³ 10s* 10m⁴ 10s² 1997 a9.4g⁵ a12g² 12m Jun 18] rangy, workmanlike filly: has a long, round action: fairly useful performer: caught final stride in handicap at Wolverhampton in May: bred to stay beyond 1½m: acts on good to firm and soft ground and on fibresand: makes running/races prominently: has been bandaged behind: carries head rather high. *D. R. Loder*   92 ex text.

GROVEFAIR DANCER (IRE) 3 ch.f. Soviet Lad (USA) 94 – Naval Artiste –
(Captain's Gig (USA)) [1996 55: 6g⁵ 6f² a7g* a7g² 6f a8.5g⁵ a8.5g 1997 8.1g 13.8m⁵
Sep 20] won seller at 2 yrs: no form in 1997. *F. J. Yardley*

GROVEFAIR LAD (IRE) 3 b.g. Silver Kite (USA) 111 – Cienaga (Tarboosh   43
(USA)) [1996 49: 5m 6g 7f⁵ 6f³ 7g a7g² 6.9m⁴ 7.1m 10f⁴ 10g 1997 9f⁴ 10g 14.1m   a48
10f 8g⁴ 8.3s⁵ 10.8g 8m⁵ 11s⁶ 7g⁵ 10m⁴ 9.9g a9.4g a8g a12g⁵ a14g⁶ a12g² Dec 6]
close-coupled gelding: has a quick action: poor maiden handicapper: stays 1¾m:
acts on firm ground (probably soft), goes well on fibresand: tried blinkered/visored:
refused to race twelfth outing, and subsequently left Martyn Wane. *S. R. Bowring*

GROVEFAIR VENTURE 3 ch.c. Presidium 124 – Miramede (Norwick (USA)   –
125) [1996 –: 6m 6g 5g 7f 1997 8m⁶ 10g 8m⁶ 7g Sep 3] smallish, lengthy colt: little
worthwhile form: headstrong, and tail swisher. *K. Mahdi*

GUARANTEED 2 b.c. (May 30) Distant Relative 128 – Pay The Bank 81 (High   81
Top 131) [1997 6m 7m² a7g² 7d² 7g³ Oct 7] well-made colt: fluent mover: fourth foal   a76
(all by Distant Relative): brother to 4-y-o My Branch: dam 2-y-o 1m winner who
stayed 1¼m: fairly useful maiden: will be suited by further than 7f. *B. W. Hills*

GUARD A DREAM (IRE) 3 ch.g. Durgam (USA) – Adarenna (FR) (Mill Reef   –
(USA) 141) [1996 NR 1997 12g 9.9d 10s² 16g Sep 23] IR 5,000Y: plain gelding:
half-brother to French 1¼m and 12.5f winner by Shareef Dancer: dam unraced
half-sister to very smart French sprinter Adraan: poor maiden. *Mrs M. Reveley*

GUENIVITE (USA) 2 ch.f. (Feb 22) St Jovite (USA) 135 – Gueniviere (USA)   –
(Prince John) [1997 7g Aug 1] tall filly: half-sister to several winners in USA,
including Grade 1 9f winner Slew The Dragon and Grade 2 1m winner Slew The
Knight (both by Seattle Slew): dam won at up to 9f in USA: 16/1 and rather nervy in
paddock, behind in maiden at Newmarket, racing freely and fading: sent to Bond,
H.J. Bond, in USA. *D. R. Loder*

GUESSTIMATION (USA) 8 b.g. Known Fact (USA) 135 – Best Guess (USA)   67
(Apalachee (USA) 137) [1996 65, a–: 8g 9.7m 10m⁶ 10m⁵ 10m² 9.7m² 10m* 10.1g⁵   a56
10f⁵ 10.8m* 10g⁴ 10m 1997 10g 10g 8f⁶ 10g³ 10.8d* 10g² 10.9g* 10.1g⁵ 10g 10.8d*
10g* 10.1f² 10m 10.8g² a10g³ a10g² a11g² a10g⁴ a9.4g³ Dec 26] good-topped
gelding: fair performer on turf, modest on all-weather: successful in 1997 in sellers
at Warwick (2, awarded race on second occasion) and Ayr and claimer at Brighton in
the summer: stays 11f: acts on any turf/all-weather: visored once (respectable effort)
in 1997, not blinkered for long time; none the worse for heat: held up. *J. Pearce*

GUEST ALLIANCE (IRE) 5 ch.g. Zaffaran (USA) 117 – Alhargah (Be My   43
Guest (USA) 126) [1996 47, a66: a16g² a16g a12g² 11.9f⁶ 11.9f⁴ 14m a16g* a13g⁶   a66
a16g⁵ a16g² 1997 a16g³ a16g⁶ a16g² a16g⁵ 15.4m⁴ Apr 22] fair handicapper on the
all-weather, poor on turf: will stay beyond 2m: probably better on equitrack than
fibresand, acts on any turf going: has run well for amateur: won over hurdles in November. *G. L. Moore*

GUEST ENVOY (IRE) 2 b.f. (Apr 5) Paris House 123 – Peace Mission   –
(Dunbeath (USA) 127) [1997 7g Aug 11] IR 6,500Y: fourth foal: half-sister to 1994
2-y-o 7f winner Tara Colleen (by Petorius): dam Irish 1¼m winner: 33/1, showed
little in maiden at Leicester. *C. N. Allen*

GUILDHALL 2 b.c. (Apr 14) Saddlers' Hall (IRE) 126 – Queen's Visit (Top   79 p
Command (USA)) [1997 7g 7.9s³ Oct 8] 15,500 2-y-o: big, deep-bodied colt: eighth
foal: half-brother to 5f winner Bryan Robson (by Topsider): dam, maiden suited by
1¼m, half-sister to very smart 1984 staying 2-y-o Khozaam: looked to need both
starts in maidens, better effort when staying-on third of 15 to Chim Chiminey at
York: should stay at least 1½m: has plenty of scope, and should do better still.
B. J. Meehan

GUILSBOROUGH 2 br.c. (Mar 1) Northern Score (USA) – Super Sisters (AUS)   69
(Call Report) [1997 7g 7m⁵ Oct 5] close-coupled, workmanlike colt:
half-brother to 4-y-o Red Rusty, 1m winner at 2 yrs, and to a winner in USA (both by
The Carpenter): dam, won twice over 7f in Australia, half-sister to a Grade 2 winner
there: sire (by Northern Dancer) unraced half-brother to Rahy and Singspiel: better
effort in maidens when 7¼ lengths fifth of 11 to Florazi at Leicester in October,
tending to wander: should stay 1m+. *D. Morris*

The Mail On Sunday Mile Final (Handicap), Ascot—Gulf Shaadi continues to thrive on racing

GULF HARBOUR (IRE)   3 b.g. Caerleon (USA) 132 – Jackie Berry 97 (Connaught 130) [1996 NR 1997 10.3d⁶ May 6] rather leggy gelding: seventh foal: brother to smart Pencader (would have stayed beyond 1½m) and half-brother to 3 winners, including useful 7f (at 2 yrs) to 1½m winner Coneybury (by Last Tycoon): dam, Irish 7f and 8.5f winner is out of sister to smart 1¼m filly Cranberry Sauce: on toes, swishing tail and decidedly green, though favourite, around 10 lengths sixth of 10 to Conon Falls in maiden at Chester: sold 4,000 gns in October and gelded. *P. W. Chapple-Hyam*   87

GULF OF SIAM   4 ch.g. Prince Sabo 123 – Jussoli (Don 128) [1996 64§: 8g 8d 11m 9f² 8.5m² 9.2m³ 11.1m³ 5.5m 1997 a11g 10g 10d 7m 8m 10f Oct 1] ungenuine maiden, no longer worth a rating: left J. Mackie after third start. *E. A. Wheeler*   – §

Rothmans Royals North South Challenge Series Final (Handicap), Newmarket—
another valuable prize for Gulf Shaadi,
but he has to work much harder this time to get the better of For Your Eyes Only

GULF SHAADI　5 b.g. Shaadi (USA) 126 – Ela Meem (USA) (Kris 135) [1996 –,　100
a59: a9.4g a8g a7g a6g 8g a9.4g a7s³ a7g⁴ 1997 a7g⁴ a8g* a8g* a8g a9.4g⁴ a8g³ a7g⁴
a8g⁵ a7g⁶ 7g² 7.5m* 7g⁴ 8m² 7.6v⁴ 7m⁶ 8.1m 8m⁴ 7.6m 7.1m* 7.6s² 8m 8m* 9m⁴
8g* Oct 18] lengthy gelding: has a quick action: had a fine 1997, making into a useful
handicapper, winning at Southwell (twice) in January, Beverley in April, Sandown in
August, Ascot (Mail On Sunday Mile Final) in September and Newmarket (Rothmans Royals North South Challenge Series Final by ½ length from For Your Eyes
Only) in October: effective at 7f to 1¼m: acts on fibresand and on any turf going:
visored (below form) once at 4 yrs: often slowly away, and tends to come from
behind: has had tongue tied, but not last 4 starts: often early to post: outstandingly
tough, and a credit to his trainer. *E. J. Alston*

GULLAND　2 b.c. (Feb 6) Unfuwain (USA) 131 – Spin (High Top 131) [1997　106 p
7m⁴ 7m² 8d* Oct 20]
　　The famous chocolate and gold colours of the late Eric Moller which
were carried to victory in the 1983 Derby by Teenoso have since been
associated with several good horses running in the name of 'Mollers Racing'.
Ill luck has been a factor in none of them emulating Teenoso. Red Glow started
favourite for the 1988 Derby but didn't get the best of runs when fourth to
Kahyasi and since then neither trainer Geoff Wragg nor Mollers Racing have
been represented. Young Buster was shaping like a Derby contender in 1991
until back trouble caused him to miss the race, while the following year Young
Senor made it as far as the start but refused to enter the stalls. Pentire had
excellent credentials for the 1995 running—he'd won three of the recognised
Derby trials after all—but the small matter of not having an entry for the race
ruled him out. Perhaps they'll have better luck with Gulland.
　　Gulland had been plainly in need of both the race and the experience on
his debut when fourth in a maiden at Newmarket in August but was a different
proposition in the Queen's Own Yorkshire Dragoons Conditions Stakes, the
opening race of the St Leger meeting at Doncaster. He was one of the least
fancied in a field of six but ran a fine race despite still showing signs of greenness, edging ahead of the favourite Mahboob inside the last only to be collared
near the line by second favourite Teapot Row. By the time Gulland was turned
out again, for the listed Tote Silver Tankard Stakes at Pontefract at the end of
October, Teapot Row had won the Royal Lodge Stakes and there was plenty of
confidence in Gulland, who started at a shade of odds on against seven rivals. A
combination of a sound pace, good to soft ground and the stiff track made it a
true test. Gulland didn't look short of speed as he travelled strongly in touch
and readily quickened clear off the turn, looking at that stage likely to win
even more convincingly than he did. At the line he had two and a half lengths
to spare over the filly Rambling Rose, a Nottingham maiden winner, the pair
seven lengths clear of the Milan winner Clapham Common.
　　The Moller horses used to be home-bred at White Lodge Stud but
nowadays Mollers Racing, financed by a trust fund, derives its success from
astute purchases at the sales. Gulland was a 76,000 guineas buy at the Newmarket October Sales, the highest-priced yearling of 1996 by his sire Unfuwain. The now-retired Dick Hern won't be having any more runners in the
Derby but he's likely to be following Gulland's progress with interest as he
trained not only Unfuwain but Gulland's grandam Hurlingham. Gulland's dam,
Spin, never ran but she was bred by Mrs Hern. Dick Hern also trained Spin's
first foal—and best runner so far—Salchow (by Niniski) who won the Cheshire
Oaks and was second in the Park Hill Stakes. Five more winners preceded
Gulland, namely Girotondo (by Young Generation), a useful six-furlong win-
ner at two years successful at up to a mile and a quarter at three; Snowspin (by
Carwhite), a fair stayer; Top Spin, a full brother to Salchow who won on the flat
but is better known as a useful if unreliable staying hurdler; Three In One (by
Night Shift), a fairly useful miler; and Last Spin, a full sister to Gulland who
proved a disappointing maiden on the flat (she started at 200/1 in Moonshell's
Oaks) but won a juvenile hurdle at Fakenham. Had she raced herself, Spin

Tote Silver Tankard Stakes, Pontefract—Gulland looks very promising in beating Rambling Rose

would have stayed well judging by her half-brothers, Meadowbrook and Roark, who won the Ascot Stakes and Ladbroke Hurdle respectively. Their dam, Hurlingham, was a useful seven-furlong and mile-and-a-quarter winner, one of numerous winning offspring of the five-furlong winner (she ran only at two) No Slipper, among their number also the 100/1 winner of the Blandford Stakes Miss Therese.

		Northern Dancer	Nearctic
	Unfuwain (USA)	(b 1961)	Natalma
	(b 1985)	Height of Fashion	Bustino
Gulland		(b 1979)	Highclere
(b.c. Feb 6, 1995)		High Top	Derring-Do
	Spin	(b 1969)	Camenae
	(b 1979)	Hurlingham	Harken
		(ch 1972)	No Slipper

Gulland is a strong, lengthy colt, an easy mover, and a most likeable type who's sure to stay the Derby trip and probably further still if need be, though as we said he's not lacking in pace. He's potentially smart, and is sure to win more races. *G. Wragg*

GULLIVER 4 b.g. Rainbow Quest (USA) 134 – Minskip (USA) 64 (The Minstrel   78 d
(CAN) 135) [1996 79: 8m 10m 10m³ 10.4g⁴ 13.4g⁶ 1997 a12g³ 8f³ 6.9m⁵ 8f* 8g 8g⁵
8m⁶ 8m 8g 8d 8.5f Sep 17] good-topped gelding: has a fluent action: fair handicapper: left N. Walker after third start: got up close home to win at Thirsk in June:
finished lame next time, and well held afterwards: suited by 1m to 1¼m: has raced
mainly on good ground or firmer. *Mrs J. R. Ramsden*

GUMAIR (USA) 4 ch.g. Summer Squall (USA) – Finisterre (AUS) (Biscay   69
(AUS)) [1996 74: 11.4d 12m⁴ 12.1m⁴ 14f⁶ 12m⁶ 1997 12m 12m³ 14.1m⁴ 18s Jul 1]
good-bodied gelding: good mover: fair maiden: should stay 2m: acts on good to firm
ground, acts on soft: joined A. Dunn. *R. Hannon*

GUNBOAT DIPLOMACY 2 b. or br.g. (May 8) Mtoto 134 – Pepper Star (IRE)   –
(Salt Dome (USA)) [1997 6g 8d Oct 28] IR 18,500Y: second foal: dam unraced
half-sister to smart Irish 5f to 7f winner Cooliney Prince and useful middle-distance
performer/Champion Hurdler Kribensis: well beaten in maidens at Newbury (went
freely to post) and Leicester. *M. J. Fetherston-Godley*

GUNMAKER 8 ch.g. Gunner B 126 – Lucky Starkist 57 (Lucky Wednesday 124) – [1996 27, a45: a16g⁶ a16g² 18m³ 18m 1997 a16g⁶ a16g³ Feb 7] smallish gelding: poor stayer: well beaten on flat in 1997. *B. J. Llewellyn*

GUNNER B SPECIAL 4 ch.g. Gunner B 126 – Sola Mia 78 (Tolomeo 127) – [1996 37: 10d⁵ 14s 17.9g 1997 a7g⁶ 10g⁶ a11g 13.1m Jul 7] plain gelding: poor performer: well beaten in 1997, leaving S. R. Bowring after third start. *J. Neville*

GUNNERS GLORY 3 b.g. Aragon 118 – Massive Powder (Caerleon (USA) 59 d 132) [1996 69: 5m⁵ 5f³ 6d² 5.3f 1997 5m 6g 6.1g³ 6.1d⁶ 6g 5d⁶ 5m² 6g² 7g³ 8g 7m⁵ 10m 6.9d⁵ 7g Oct 24] rather leggy gelding: modest performer at best in 1997: trained by B. Meehan first 8 starts, by D. Marks (claimed £5,000) on ninth: stays 7f: acts on firm and dead ground: often blinkered/visored: inconsistent, and has looked none too genuine. *Mrs L. Stubbs*

GUNZELLS (USA) 2 ch.f. (Feb 8) Diesis 133 – High Sevens 90 (Master Willie 71 129) [1997 5.1m 5m³ 7m² 7g Oct 18] sparely-made filly: second foal: sister to 3-y-o Impulsif: dam, 6f winner at 2 yrs, half-sister to smart middle-distance performers Hateel and Munwar: fair form when placed in maidens at Windsor and Salisbury: well below form final start: should stay 1m. *H. Candy*

GURKHA 2 b.c. (Jan 30) Polish Precedent (USA) 131 – Glendera 81 (Glenstal 88 p (USA) 118) [1997 7m 6s* Sep 4] small, well-made colt: has a markedly round action: fifth foal: dam, 1¼m winner who stayed 1½m, half-sister to smart middle-distance winner Water Boatman out of half-sister to high-class stayer Sea Anchor: much fitter than for debut, won maiden at York by 9 lengths from Wolfhunt, soon going strongly and clear over 1f out: should stay further than 6f: clearly revelled in soft-ground conditions at York: should improve and make a useful 3-y-o. *R. Hannon*

GUY'S GAMBLE 4 ch.g. Mazilier (USA) 107 – Deep Blue Sea (Gulf Pearl 117) – [1996 –, a56: a7g* a8g³ a11g⁴ 8m 8.2s a7g 1997 7g⁴ a7g a6g a6g a9.4g 8g a7g⁶ a43 Aug 15] lengthy, workmanlike gelding: poor performer: well beaten most starts in 1997: stays 11f: acts on fibresand: tried blinkered. *J. Wharton*

GWESPYR 4 ch.g. Sharpo 132 – Boozy 111 (Absalom 128) [1996 69: 6.1d⁶ 6.1d 61 d 5s⁵ 5g 5g⁴ 5f³ 5m 5d* 5.1m³ 5.1m⁴ 5.1m⁶ 5m⁶ 5g 1997 6g⁶ 6f 7f³ 6d a7g 6m 7d 5f 5m a6g⁵ a6g⁶ a5g⁵ Dec 8] close-coupled gelding: modest performer: mostly well below form in 1997, leaving R. Hannon after seventh start: best form at 5f: acts on firm and dead ground: below form in visor. *Don Enrico Incisa*

GYMCRAK CYRANO (IRE) 8 b.m. Cyrano de Bergerac 120 – Sun Gift 33 (Guillaume Tell (USA) 121) [1996 NR 1997 16.2s 18g⁵ 14.1g 15.8s⁵ 16m Jul 18] sturdy mare: poor staying handicapper: acts on good to firm and soft ground. *N. Chamberlain*

GYMCRAK FLYER 6 b.m. Aragon 118 – Intellect (Frimley Park 109) [1996 73 71: 8m³ 8.5g⁴ 7g 6.9g 8f* 7m* 7f* 7m 7.1s 8f 7m 1997 7g 8g* 6m³ 7g* 7f 7.5m 8d 7m⁵ 8f* 8.2g⁶ 8g 7m Oct 28] small mare: fair performer: won minor event at Ponte-fract in April and handicaps at Redcar in May and Yarmouth in September: needs further than 6f, and stays 1m: acts on hard ground and dead, below form only run on fibresand: blinkered (bit below form) once: usually bandaged behind: usually held up: none too consistent. *G. Holmes*

GYMCRAK GORJOS 3 b. or br.f. Rock Hopper 124 – Bit O' May 71 47 (Mummy's Pet 125) [1996 –: 7.9g 1997 12s⁶ 8g⁴ 12g 11s² 10m² 10.1g Oct 22] close-coupled filly: poor maiden: stays 11f: acts on good to firm and soft ground: blinkered last 3 starts. *G. Holmes*

GYMCRAK MYSTERY 2 br.f. (Apr 13) Ballacashtal (CAN) – Little Unknown 51 + (Known Fact (USA) 135) [1997 5s⁶ a6g³ a5g⁵ Jun 30] second reported foal: dam unraced: modest maiden: third in seller at Southwell: possibly better at 6f than 5f. *G. Holmes*

GYMCRAK PREMIERE 9 ch.g. Primo Dominie 121 – Oraston 115 (Morston 76 (FR) 125) [1996 93d: 7m 8.5m³ 8m 7.9m 7.6d 8m 7.9g⁵ 7g 10.3g⁶ 1997 9.9m* 9.9s⁴ 10d 10m 10.1g⁵ 10.3m⁴ 10m⁴ 8m⁴ 7g⁴ 8.3g 7m* 9m⁶ 8m 10d⁴ Nov 3] lengthy, workmanlike gelding: fair performer: won handicap at Beverley in April and seller at Yarmouth (didn't have to be at best to justify good support) in September: effective from 7f to 1¼m: probably acts on any going: effective blinkered/visored or not:

usually bandaged behind: has worn near-side pricker: has hung markedly: held up, and well ridden by K. Fallon. *G. Holmes*

GYMCRAK TIGER (IRE)   7 b.g. Colmore Row 111 – Gossip (Sharp Edge   45
123) [1996 NR 1997 14.1g 16.2s 15.8s³ 16m⁵ Jul 18] tall gelding: poor performer, lightly raced on flat nowadays: stays 2m: acts on good to firm and soft going: blinkered (creditable efforts) last 2 starts. *G. Holmes*

GYMCRAK WATERMILL (IRE)   3 b. or br.f. River Falls 113 – Victorian   –
Pageant 95 (Welsh Pageant 132) [1996 –: 5f⁶ a5g 1997 a7g a6g 8.2d Jun 23] good-topped filly: no worthwhile form. *G. Holmes*

GYPSY HILL   2 ch.f. (Mar 14) Theatrical Charmer 114 – Mirkan Honey 83   74
(Ballymore 123) [1997 5m 5.1d* 6.1g³ 5.1m² 6d⁴ 7m⁶ Aug 2] 8,000Y: rather unfurnished filly: half-sister to several winners, including 1994 2-y-o 6f and 7f winner Fleet Hill (by Warrshan), later useful at up to 1¼m and successful in USA, and useful sprinter Lee Artiste (by Tate Gallery): dam Irish 4-y-o 2m winner: fair performer: won minor event at Bath in May: ran creditably in similar events next 3 starts: should stay at least 1m: yet to race on extremes of ground: often slowly away: has awkward head carriage. *D. Haydn Jones*

GYPSY PASSION (IRE)   2 ch.c. (Mar 9) Woodman (USA) 126 – Rua d'Oro   87 p
(USA) 103 (El Gran Senor (USA) 136) [1997 7d⁵ 7g 7m* Nov 4] IR 60,000Y: big, strong colt: third foal: brother to Irish 3-y-o 7f winner Buncrana: dam Irish 6f (at 2 yrs) and 1m winner out of smart French winner at up to 1½m Thorough: green first 2 starts, then improved markedly to win maiden at Redcar by 2 lengths from Dog Watch, leading over 2f out and staying on well: will stay at least 1m: sort to make a useful 3-y-o. *M. Johnston*

H

HAAMI (USA)   2 b.c. (Mar 2) Nashwan (USA) 135 – Oumaldaaya (USA)   106 p
111 (Nureyev (USA) 131) [1997 7g* 7g* 7.1s³ 7m* Oct 3]

    Haami, mooted as a Two Thousand Guineas prospect even before he'd set foot on a racecourse, ended the season with his classic credentials still intact and 20/1 the best price available about him for that race. He had been as short as 12/1, disputing favouritism, in the very early Guineas betting following quite impressive victories at Newmarket and Doncaster on his first two starts, only for his reputation to take a knock when he could finish only third in the Solario Stakes at Sandown. However, Haami went a long way to redeeming himself by winning the Somerville Tattersall Stakes at Newmarket, and he looks the type to make a better three-year-old, though it goes almost without saying that his form remains well short of classic-winning standard.

    A confidently-ridden Haami had shown plenty of speed when beating Tracking a neck in a minor event at Doncaster, and he was sent off favourite for

Somerville Tattersall Stakes, Newmarket—
Haami is back on song and pulls away from Bintang and Aix En Provence

the Solario despite meeting the latter on terms 7 lb worse. Haami didn't make the anticipated improvement, though, and finished two lengths behind Tracking who in turn was half a length behind the winner Little Indian. At the time it was thought Haami might have been unsuited by the soft ground, and that remains a possibility even though he was subsequently reported as having been off colour due to a throat infection. Five weeks later, fully recovered and racing on good to firm ground, Haami gave his best performance to date in the Somerville Tattersall, a race won in recent years by Grand Lodge and Even Top who both went on to finish second in the Guineas. Among his seven opponents, all of whom he met at level weights, were three horses who had won on their most recent appearance, Abreeze, Bintang and Iceband, while Tracking again renewed rivalry. Haami put them all firmly in their place. Taking a strong hold in fourth as Tracking forced the pace, Haami made his move running down the hill, at the same time as Bintang, and this pair had the race between them going into the final furlong, Haami staying on the stronger and drawing one and a half lengths clear.

		Blushing Groom	Red God
	Nashwan (USA)	(ch 1974)	Runaway Bride
	(ch 1986)	Height of Fashion	Bustino
Haami (USA)		(b 1979)	Highclere
(b.c. Mar 2, 1995)		Nureyev	Northern Dancer
	Oumaldaaya (USA)	(b 1977)	Special
	(b 1989)	Histoire	Riverman
		(b or br 1979)	Helvetie

Haami's dam, Oumaldaaya, was also a winner at seven furlongs as a two-year-old, and she did most of her racing at three at a mile and a quarter, winning the Lupe Stakes and the Group 2 Premio Lydia Tesio, the latter on softish ground. Her dam, Histoire, a winner at ten and a half furlongs in France, was carrying Oumaldaaya when purchased for a million dollars at the Keeneland Breeding Stock Sales in 1988, and three years later Histoire more than proved her worth by producing the Derby winner Erhaab. The next dam, Helvetie, won at a mile and bred numerous winners including the smart filly Hamanda, successful in the Prix de la Porte Maillot. Haami is the second foal of Oumaldaaya and has already proved better than her first, another Nashwan colt named Asas who has been well beaten in all four of his starts since winning a maiden at Newmarket at two years on his debut.

Haami, a well-made colt and a fluent mover, edged right under pressure on his second and third starts but did nothing wrong in the Somerville Tattersall. All four of Haami's races were over seven furlongs, and the speed he showed over that trip was highly encouraging. A mile will suit him better, and on breeding he should stay still further. *J. L. Dunlop*

HABETA (USA) 11 ch.h. Habitat 134 – Prise (Busted 134) [1996 53d: 8g 8.5m⁵ 9m³ 8m* 8f* 8m⁴ 8.3m⁵ 8.2d 8.3g 8f 8.9g 10.1m 1997 8d 9m³ 8m 8m 8.3m 8.3g Sep 29] quite good-topped horse: carries plenty of condition: poor handicapper: effective blinkered or not: held up and suited by strongly-run race: has looked temperamental. *J. W. Watts*   **40 d**

HACHIYAH (IRE) 3 b. or br.f. Generous (IRE) 139 – Himmah (USA) 85 (Habitat 134) [1996 69p: 7m 1997 10s² 10m³ 10d* 10.1d² 10.1m⁵ 10g 10.3d⁶ Nov 7] rather leggy filly: fairly useful performer: won maiden at Lingfield in June: good efforts in handicaps next and penultimate starts: suited by good test at 1¼m: best efforts on good/good to soft going: swished tail: visits Kayrawan. *D. Morley*   **91**

HADABET 5 b.g. Hadeer 118 – Betsy Bay (FR) 107 (Bellypha 130) [1996 NR 1997 12m Sep 10] sturdy, close-coupled gelding: fair performer at 3 yrs for Miss J. Doyle: only outing since: stays 1½m: acts on hard ground: races prominently. *R. T. Phillips*   **–**

HADADABBLE 4 ch.f. Hadeer 118 – Magnifica (Sandy Creek 123) [1996 43: 12s 8m a8g² 8.2m a8g⁴ a8g⁵ a8g⁵ 7.6m⁶ a7g⁶ 7.6m 9.7m⁵ 8m⁵ 9g⁵ 7.1m 9.7g⁶ 8f 9g   **36 a25**

a8g 1997 7g a8g 7f 8f⁴ 8d 10s a8g⁵ 8.1m 8m 10.1f 8.2s a8g⁵ Dec 2] angular filly: good mover: poor maiden: best efforts at 1m: acts on fibresand, best form on turf on good going or firmer: visored final start (raced freely): inconsistent. *Pat Mitchell*

HADAWAH (USA)   3 ch.f. Riverman (USA) 131 – Sajjaya (USA) 97 (Blushing   61
Groom (FR) 131) [1996 68: 6f 6g⁶ 6.9m⁵ 7f 1997 8.2m 8m⁶ 8f 10f Jul 16] small filly: modest maiden: stays 1m: raced only on good going or firmer: sold 25,000 gns in December. *J. L. Dunlop*

HADAYIK   2 b.f. (Apr 14) Unfuwain (USA) 131 – Almarai (USA) 73 (Vaguely   90
Noble 140) [1997 7m⁴ 7g* 8f⁶ Sep 11] lengthy filly: fourth foal: half-sister to Italian 7f winner Mutabassim (by Green Desert): dam, placed at 1m and 1¼m, half-sister to Washington D C International winner Buckhar: landed odds in 4-runner maiden at Goodwood in August: on toes, fairly useful form when just under 7 lengths sixth in May Hill Stakes at Doncaster following month: bred to stay at least 1¼m: races freely. *P. T. Walwyn*

HADIDI   3 b.g. Alzao (USA) 117 – Sesame 117 (Derrylin 115) [1996 –p: 7m 7.9g⁶   62
8g 1997 12d⁶ 14.1m⁵ 12g³ 16.2m Jul 21] good-topped gelding: fair maiden: stays 1¾m: unraced on extremes of going: sold to join C. Mann 24,000 gns after final start, and gelded. *D. Morley*

HADID (USA)   2 b.c. (Feb 10) Irish River (FR) 131 – Top Corsage (USA)   85
(Topsider (USA)) [1997 5.2m² 6m 7m⁴ 6.1m Sep 15] $120,000Y: well-made colt: fourth foal: half-brother to a winner in USA by Fappiano: dam won 15 races in USA including Grade 1 9f event: fairly useful form in frame in maidens at Newbury and Goodwood: stayed 7f: dead. *B. W. Hills*

HADITH   2 ch.c. (Feb 21) Nashwan (USA) 135 – Azyaa 101 (Kris 135) [1997   86
7.5d² 8.2m² 8m² Oct 23] good mover: sixth foal: closely related to 1995 2-y-o 6f winner Yarob (by Unfuwain), later used to up to 1¼m, and half-brother to 3 winners including useful 7f/1m performer Ihtiraz (by Soviet Star): dam, 7.5f winner, from good middle-distance family: fairly useful form in maidens at Beverley, Nottingham and Brighton: should stay at least 1¼m. *D. Morley*

HAJAT   3 ch.f. Mujtahid (USA) 118 – Nur (USA) 74 (Diesis 133) [1996 64: 5m⁴   48
5g³ 1997 6.9g 7.5d 7d⁵ 6.1d a5g* a5g 5g⁴ 5s Oct 14] lengthy, unfurnished filly: poor handicapper: left N. Graham after fourth start: won at Wolverhampton in July: a sprinter: acts on fibresand, and probably good to soft going. *J. Berry*

HAJR (IRE)   3 b.g. Rainbow Quest (USA) 134 – Dance By Night 84 (Northfields   91
(USA)) [1996 NR 1997 7g* 7d⁴ 8m 10m* 10m² 10d 12m Sep 30] 250,000Y: small, good-bodied gelding: unimpressive mover: half-brother to several winners (5 of them at least useful), including Poule d'Essai des Pouliches winner Danseuse du Soir (by Thatching) and Don Corleone (up to 1½m, by Caerleon): dam 2-y-o 7f winner: won maiden at Newbury in June and handicap at Newmarket in August: ran poorly last 2 starts: should stay beyond 1¼m: acts on good to firm and dead going: gelded after final start. *E. A. L. Dunlop*

HAKEEM (IRE)   2 ch.c. (May 14) Kefaah (USA) 124 – Masarrah 91   83 p
(Formidable (USA) 125) [1997 6g³ 6m* 6m⁴ Oct 4] sturdy, lengthy colt: fifth foal: brother to 7f winner Shefoog and half-brother to 1¼m winner Murheb (by Mtoto), both fairly useful: dam 6f winner: won maiden at Folkestone in September: creditable fourth in nursery at Newmarket, eased once held: should be well suited by further than 6f: good sort, and likely to do better yet. *R. W. Armstrong*

HAKKANIYAH   3 b.f. Machiavellian (USA) 123 – Mousaiha (USA) (Shadeed   –
(USA) 135) [1996 84+: 6.1m² 6m* 6f⁴ 1997 7s⁶ 7f Jul 12] tall, well-bred filly: has a quick action: progressive form at 2 yrs: well beaten in 2 starts in July: should stay 7f: sold 62,000 gns in December. *D. Morley*

HALAVADREAM   3 b.c. Mon Tresor 113 – Hala 57 (Persian Bold 123) [1996   –
NR 1997 9d 10.2m 11.8d Oct 14] leggy, short-backed colt: unimpressive mover: third foal: half-brother to 2 poor animals: dam should have been suited by further than 7f: no sign of ability. *M. J. Bolton*

HALBERT   8 b.g. Song 132 – Stoneydale 83 (Tickled Pink 114) [1996 59d, a48:
a6g² a6g⁴ a6g⁴ a5g³ 5s 6f 5g 5m⁶ 5d a5g⁵ 5m 5.2m 5.1f 5f a7g⁵ 6m a6g a6g* 1997 a6g a6g a6g 6f⁶ 7m 5m 6f May 29] sturdy, lengthy gelding: sprint handicapper: no

worthwhile form in 1997: left P. Burgoyne after third start: has been blinkered, usually visored nowadays. *M. D. I. Usher*

HALF A KNICKER 2 b.g. (May 4) Weldnaas (USA) 112 – Queen of The Quorn 62
53 (Governor General 116) [1997 5.9f⁵ a5g 5m³ 7g Aug 19] 5,800Y: sturdy gelding: first foal: dam 6f and 7f winner: modest maiden: best effort on debut: stiffish task in nursery final start: should stay 1m. *R. A. Fahey*

HALF AN INCH (IRE) 4 gr.g. Petoski 135 – Inch (English Prince 129) [1996 –
69d: 8.1g 7f 10m⁴ 11.6m⁶ 10s⁶ 8g³ 8.5g* a10g 8f⁵ 10g 8f a12g⁶ 1997 a10g Jan 25] sturdy gelding: formerly fair, seems to have lost his way completely: tried blinkered/visored. *T. M. Jones*

HALF-HITCH (USA) 2 b.f. (Apr 25) Diesis 133 – Marling (IRE) 124 (Lomond 88
(USA) 128) [1997 6g* 7g⁵ 6m³ Oct 22] second foal: half-sister to 3-y-o Moonshiner: dam won 7 of her 10 starts, including Cheveley Park and Sussex Stakes: 10/1 from 5/2, won maiden at Thirsk in July: put firmly in place in Group 3 Prestige Stakes at Goodwood, then fair third in minor event at Yarmouth: should stay 1m. *D. R. Loder*

HALF TONE 5 gr.h. Touch of Grey 90 – Demilinga (Nishapour (FR) 125) [1996 66
64, a74: a5g³ a5g⁴ a5g* 5m 5m³ 5m⁴ 6m 6m³ 5f³ 5g⁴ 5m² 5m² 5m* 1997 5g 5g 5d*
5m⁴ 6m 6s⁴ 5d³ 5d³ 5m⁴ 5m² 5m 6m 5g* 5s⁵ 5m⁵ a5g⁵ a6g⁶ Dec 19] leggy horse: fair handicapper: won at Goodwood (apprentices) in May and Sandown in August: effective at 5f and 6f: probably acts on any turf/all-weather: blinkered/visored: best coming off strong pace. *R. M. Flower*

HAL HOO YAROOM 4 b.c. Belmez (USA) 131 – Princess Nawaal (USA) 86 –
(Seattle Slew (USA)) [1996 84: 12.3m 14.1f* 15.4g* 15.9m 16.1m³ 1997 12g 14.4m
16.2v 14.6g Oct 24] angular colt: good mover: fairly useful performer at 3 yrs: well beaten in 1997: stays 2m: acts on firm going: front runner: won claiming hurdle in November, then joined J. Jenkins. *R. Akehurst*

HALMAHERA (IRE) 2 b.c. (Apr 2) Petardia 113 – Champagne Girl 67 109
(Robellino (USA) 127) [1997 5g⁴ 5d² 6.1d* 6m* 6m³ 6m² 5d* 5v* Oct 11]
      The peril of backing a two-year-old first time out, when its lack of experience often precludes it from reproducing form shown on the gallops, was illustrated by the remarks of Ian Balding, trainer of Halmahera, after the horse had spreadeagled the opposition in the Cornwallis Stakes at Ascot in October. 'We ran him at Kempton's Easter meeting, and he was the first two-year-old I have run in March for many years,' said Balding. 'We went for a gamble and

Timeform Harry Rosebery Trophy, Ayr—Halmahera and Its All Relative fight it out ahead of Friar Tuck

Willmott Dixon Cornwallis Stakes, Ascot—Halmahera revels in the mud

put Martin (Dwyer) up to get a better price. Halmahera had been working with older horses and had been going very well, but he only ran for three and a half furlongs and finished fourth.' The Kempton race was won by Wrekin Pilot, the only one of the six runners to have had an outing, and one who by the end of the season couldn't be regarded as within a stone of Halmahera.

Halmahera hardly stopped improving as he gained experience and won three races prior to Ascot, a maiden at Chepstow, a nursery at Goodwood and the Timeform Harry Rosebery Trophy at Ayr, the last-named a listed event in which he beat Its All Relative by three quarters of a length. The Cornwallis Stakes not only provided Halmahera with his stiffest test, but also the opportunity to race on heavy ground for the first time. Apart from on his debut Halmahera had encountered only good to firm and good to soft ground and shown himself equally effective on both. None of his twelve rivals had come across heavy going, either, but while most failed to cope with the extremely testing conditions Halmahera, who looked very well in the preliminaries, simply revelled in them, travelling well, taking the lead two out and bounding clear to win by four lengths and five from Lord Kintyre and Ella. The race provided the stable's good apprentice Dwyer with his first win in a pattern race. It would be unwise to get carried away by Halmahera's performance, the ground almost certainly having exaggerated his superiority, but he still deserves plenty of credit for it. We feel he won't *need* a similar set of circumstances to confirm himself a decidedly useful sprinter at three years.

		Petong	Mansingh
	Petardia	(gr 1980)	Iridium
	(b 1990)	What A Pet	Mummy's Pet
Halmahera (IRE)		(b 1981)	Moben
(b.c. Apr 2, 1995)		Robellino	Roberto
	Champagne Girl	(b 1978)	Isobelline
	(b 1991)	Babycham Sparkle	So Blessed
		(b 1980)	Effervescence II

Halmahera, a 17,000-guinea foal who fetched 36,000 guineas as a yearling, is from the first crop of Petardia. Winner of the Coventry Stakes and Laurent-Perrier Champagne Stakes as a two-year-old, Petardia gained his only success the following season in a seven-furlong minor event at Ascot. Petardia sometimes found little and was twice blinkered at three years, including when finishing a good fourth to Zafonic in the Two Thousand Guineas. Petardia had a sizeable crop to represent him in 1997 and finished second to Zafonic in win prize money for first season sires in Britain and Ireland. Halmahera is the first foal of Champagne Girl, who ran only at two years, winning a five-furlong maiden auction at Lingfield. Champagne Girl is a half-sister to several winners, easily the best of them the useful sprinter Deep Finesse, out of the two-year-old five- and six-furlong winner Babycham Sparkle. The next dam, Effervescence II, a half-sister to the top-class sprinter/miler Zeddaan, produced numerous winners apart from Babycham Sparkle, among them the smart El Famoso who won three times over middle distances in France before his export as a stallion to Scandinavia.

Halmahera, a leggy, quite attractive colt with a roundish action, is effective at five furlongs when the ground is testing and he stays six furlongs. A genuine and consistent sort, he should continue to do well. *I. A. Balding*

HALMANERROR   7 gr.g. Lochnager 132 – Counter Coup (Busted 134) [1996   63
71: 7g⁶ 6m 7g⁶ 6m 6m² 6.9f³ 6g⁴ 6g⁵ 6m* 6m⁵ 7m⁵ 6f 6f 7g 6m 6f 1997 6m 6.1g 6s*
7m 7g 6d 6d 6m 6m⁵ 6g⁶ 6d⁵ 6d² 7d⁶ Oct 14] lengthy, good-topped gelding: modest
handicapper: won at Doncaster in May: effective at 6f to 1m: acts on any ground:
sometimes gives trouble at stalls: suited by being covered up in truly-run race: joined
G. McCourt. *Mrs J. R. Ramsden*

HALOWING (USA)   3 b.f. Danzatore (CAN) 120 – Halo Ho (USA) (Halo   75
(USA)) [1996 86: 5g⁵ 6f² 6g⁵ 6f* 6m 6.5m⁴ 7m² 7m⁶ 1997 8m 8.1d⁶ 7g 7d³ 7g⁵ 7g
7m 7s² 6d⁵ Oct 21] good-topped filly: fair handicapper: should stay 1m: unraced on
heavy going, acts on any other turf: none too consistent: sold 16,000 gns in December. *J. G. Smyth-Osbourne*

HAL'S PAL   4 br.g. Caerleon (USA) 132 – Refinancing (USA) (Forli (ARG))   101
[1996 101: 8.2s² 8m a9.4g* a9.4g* 8m⁶ 8g² 7.9g² 8d 1997 a8.5g* 8.1g 8m⁵ 8.1d⁵   a106
8d⁵ 8f a7f* a6s⁴ Dec 6] rangy gelding: useful performer: won handicap at Wolverhampton in April: left D. Loder after fifth start: won optional claimer at Hollywood
Park in November but last of 4 in Grade 3 race there final start: effective at 7f to 9.4f:
acts on dirt/fibresand and on soft and good to firm going: seems effective blinkered/
visored or not: carries head high and hasn't always gone through with effort: raced
on medication in USA. *B. Cecil, USA*

HALTARRA (USA)   3 ch.c. Zilzal (USA) 137   Snow Bride (USA) 121 (Blush-   109
ing Groom (FR) 131) [1996 92+: 7g² 8m³ 1997 10m² 10g* 11.6m² 14.6m 10m² 12g⁶
Oct 25] smallish colt: half-brother to Lammtarra (by Nijinsky): useful performer: 5/1
on when winning maiden at Sandown in June: good second in minor events at
Windsor (head behind King Sound) and Kempton (beaten neck by Barnum Sands)
after: stays 1½m (failed to stay 1¾m in St Leger): yet to race on going softer than
good: often a front runner. *Saeed bin Suroor*

HAMERRA (IRE)   2 b.f. (Apr 17) Hamas (IRE) 125§ – Sound Performance   –
(IRE) (Ahonoora 122) [1997 5.2g 5d 5d⁵ 5g May 26] IR 3,400Y: small filly: first
foal: dam Irish 1½m winner out of half-sister to Stanerra: little sign of ability. *Martyn
Meade*

HAMILTON GOLD   4 ch.f. Safawan 118 – Golden Della (Glint of Gold 128)   –
[1996 49: 6m a8g 5m 5m³ 5.1m 6d 1997 5g 5m 5g Aug 5] shallow-girthed filly: poor
maiden. *M. G. Meagher*

HAMLEYS   3 ch.f. Superlative 118 – Child's Play (USA) 54 (Sharpen Up 127)   –
[1996 NR 1997 7m 7m 6.1g 6.1s Oct 15] first foal: dam, ran twice here then 10.5f
winner in France, from excellent family: little worthwhile form: visored final start.
D. Morris

HAMMERSTEIN   4 b.c. Kris 135 – Musical Bliss (USA) 117 (The Minstrel   103
(CAN) 135) [1996 110: 7g* 8m² 8.1d 8m* 8m* 7.3m⁵ 8g⁴ 8m⁵ 1997 a9f² a8f³ 7.9g
May 14] sturdy, good-topped colt: smart performer in 1996: below best at Nad Al
Sheba first 2 starts in 1997, tailed off (couldn't have looked any better) in listed rated
stakes at York final one: stays 1m well: acts on good to firm and dead going: edgy
sort. *Saeed bin Suroor*

HAN

HANAJIR (IRE)   3 b.f. Cadeaux Genereux 131 – Muhit (USA) 79 (El Gran Senor   –
(USA) 136) [1996 NR 1997 8g⁶ 8g⁴ 8m² a11g 10.1g Oct 22] first foal: dam 1m winner: signs of ability but little form: tailed off last 2 starts. *C. W. Thornton*

HANAN (USA)   3 b.f. Twilight Agenda (USA) 126 – Maikai (USA) (Never Bend)   –
[1996 83p: 6f⁵ 5.5g⁵ 1997 7d 6s⁶ 6m⁶ Aug 9] lengthy, good-topped filly: promising at 2 yrs, well beaten in 1997: should stay beyond 6f: blinkered final start.
P. A. Kelleway

HANBITOOH (USA)   4 b.g. Hansel (USA) – Bitooh 117 (Seattle Slew (USA))   –
[1996 64: 10s³ 12m⁴ 12m 9.9g³ 10g⁶ 17.2g 1997 15.4m Apr 10] tall, useful-looking
gelding: has a round action: modest maiden up to 1½m: last only start in 1997: tried
blinkered: not one to trust implicitly. *Mrs A. J. Perrett*

HANBY   5 b.g. Most Welcome 131 – My Princess (King Emperor (USA)) [1996   48
NR 1997 7g⁶ 9.2d⁵ 7m⁵ 8.3s May 17] half-brother to several winners, including smart
Moonlight Lady (best up to 1m, by Mummy's Pet): dam won at 2 yrs in Italy: poor
form in claiming/selling company first 3 starts: ran as if something amiss final one:
barely stays 9f. *J. S. Goldie*

HANCOCK   5 b.g. Jester 119 – Fresh Line 60 (High Line 125) [1996 –: a14g 1997   29
12g 18g 17.2m⁴ a14g⁴ Aug 15] modest hurdler: poor stayer on flat. *J. Hetherton*

HANDLEY CROSS (USA)   3 b. or br.g. Houston (USA) – Imaginary Lady   –
(USA) (Marfa (USA)) [1996 NR 1997 10.8m⁶ Jun 9] $100,000F: third foal: dam
won Grade 1 8.5f Santa Anita Oaks: well beaten in 7-runner maiden at Warwick.
I. A. Balding

HAND OF STRAW (IRE)   5 b.g. Thatching 131 – Call Me Miss (Hello Gorge-   46
ous (USA) 128) [1996 60d, a72d: a8.5g* a8g³ a10g a8g⁵ a9.4g² a9.4g 10.8g* 10.8f³
10.8g⁴ 10.8f 10.8f⁴ 10.2g 10.2f 13.1m⁵ a12g 11.8f a12g a9.4g⁵ a9.4g⁶ 1997 10g⁴ Apr
18] dipped-backed, lengthy gelding: has a round action: poor performer nowadays:
stays 11f: acts on firm and dead ground and the all-weather: tried blinkered/visored:
none too reliable. *Miss Z. A. Green*

HANDSOME RIDGE   3 ch.c. Indian Ridge 123 – Red Rose Garden 87 (Electric   115
126) [1996 87p: 7d⁴ 1997 8m² 9m² 8m 9d* 9d* 10g³ 10g³ 9.8m⁶ Oct 4] workmanlike colt: smart performer: won 4-runner minor event at Goodwood and
6-runner Prix Daphnis at Maisons-Laffitte (beat Aneysar a neck) in summer: best
efforts when third to Rajpoute in Prix Guillaume d'Ornano at Deauville (beaten a
length) and Loup Sauvage in slowly-run Prix du Prince d'Orange at Longchamp
(beaten 2 lengths): stays 1¼m: yet to race on extremes of going: consistent.
J. H. M. Gosden

HANDSON   5 ch.g. Out of Hand 84 – My Home 61 (Homing 130) [1996 NR 1997   32
12m⁶ Apr 22] modest hurdler: poor maiden on flat: dead. *B. R. Millman*

HANNAH'S USHER   5 b.g. Marching On 101 – La Pepper 63 (Workboy 123)   49
[1996 59, a76: a6g⁶ a6g⁴ a6g a5g⁵ a5g³ a5g³ a6g* a5g² 5m⁶ 6.1m 5g a6g⁶ 7.5m 7.1g   a65
1997 a6g⁵ a6g² a5g³ a6g 6m 7m 6d a6g³ 6f a6g⁴ a6g³ a6g² a6g² a6g⁴ Nov 21] leggy
gelding: fair performer on all-weather, modest on turf: best at 5f/6f: acts on all-
weather and any turf going: tried blinkered, not at 5 yrs. *C. Murray*

HANNALOU (FR)   4 b.f. Shareef Dancer (USA) 135 – Litani River (USA) (Irish   49
River (FR) 131) [1996 70: 7m 7.5m² 7.5f² 7.6m³ 6m⁶ 7g² 7m⁶ 7f² 7f⁶ a7g 1997 8f⁶
10f⁶ 7d 8m 8f⁴ Sep 29] small filly: poor maiden at 4 yrs: suited by around 7f: form
only on good going or firmer: visored final start: front runner. *T. G. Mills*

HANUMAN HIGHWAY (IRE)   2 b.g. (Mar 22) Alzao (USA) 117 – Cherry   85 p
Ridge 112 (Riva Ridge (USA)) [1997 a8.5g⁶ a8g* Dec 19] IR 12,500Y: seventh foal:
half-brother to 2 Irish winners, including useful 1¼m and 1½m winner Ayers Rock
(by In The Wings): dam, 1m winner, out of Cherry Hinton (dam also of Red Glow):
7/1, won 10-runner maiden at Lingfield comfortably by 3 lengths from Flight: will
stay 1¼m: should improve again. *M. H. Tompkins*

HAPPY BRAVE   5 b.g. Daring March 116 – Fille de Phaeton (Sun Prince 128)   38
[1996 NR 1997 a8.5g⁶ a7g⁴ a11g* a12g⁶ a11g May 12] leggy gelding: poor form:
won maiden handicap at Southwell in April: well held afterwards: better at 11f than

428

shorter: best efforts on soft ground or fibresand: blinkered (no improvement) once. *P. D. Cundell*

HAPPY DAYS 2 b.g. (Apr 23) Primitive Rising (USA) 113 – Miami Dolphin 85 79 d (Derrylin 115) [1997 5m² 5s⁴ 6g² 5m³ 6m 5g² 5m⁶ 6s Oct 14] workmanlike, gelding: fourth reported foal: dam sprinter: fair form when runner-up in maidens: well beaten in nurseries final 2 starts: stays 6f: inconsistent. *D. Moffatt*

HAPPY DAYS AGAIN (IRE) 2 b.f. (Apr 29) Elbio 125 – Tacheo 64 (Tachy- 83 pous 128) [1997 5m⁴ a5g² 5g* 6g⁵ 5m⁶ 5d² 5.2f⁴ 5m* a5s⁶ Nov 28] IR 6,200Y: a76 close-coupled filly: half-sister to Irish 1994 2-y-o 5f winner Double Risk and 7f winner Vilamar (both by Carmelite House): dam 2-y-o 5f winner, later successful over hurdles: fairly useful performer: won maiden at Ripon in July and nursery at Newmarket (set steady pace) in October: should prove best at 5f: acts on good to firm and good to soft ground, unable to dominate either start on all-weather: blinkered last 4 starts: possibly suited by front-running. *J. Wharton*

HAPPY GO LUCKY 3 ch.f. Teamster 114 – Meritus (IRE) 54 (Lyphard's 79 Special (USA) 122) [1996 81p: 5.7f 7m³ 8.1d* 8g 1997 10g⁴ 12d 10.8f* 10m⁵ 12m 10s 10g 12v⁴ 10g Oct 24] sparely-made filly: fair performer: made all in 4-runner minor event at Warwick in June: should stay 1½m: probably acts on any going. *R. J. O'Sullivan*

HAPPY MEDIUM (IRE) 4 b.g. Fairy King (USA) – Belle Origine (USA) 65 d (Exclusive Native (USA)) [1996 10g 10g 1997 a12g³ a11g⁴ 10.2d 12s a16s Nov 10] IR 200,000Y: strong ex-Irish gelding: half-brother to smart Lavinia Fontana (ran up to 7f, by Sharpo) and Irish 8.5f winner Ceide Dancer (by Alzao): dam French 9.5f winner: raced twice for C. O'Brien in 1996 (sold 6,000 gns at end of year): third in maiden at Lingfield, little other form. *G. P. Enright*

HAPPY MINSTRAL (USA) 3 b.g. Alleged (USA) 138 – Minstrelete (USA) 91 (Round Table) [1996 81p: 7m² 8.2m* 1997 12g² 11.8d 12m⁵ 12m 13.9g 12.1g 11.9s Oct 8] good-bodied gelding: fluent mover: fairly useful handicapper: easily best effort after reappearance when sixth (promoted a place) to Maylane in Tote Gold Trophy at Goodwood in July: should be suited by further than 1½m: acts on good to firm going: blinkered final start. *M. Johnston*

HAPPY WANDERER 2 ch.g. (Apr 17) Clantime 101 – Maha (Northfields 53 (USA)) [1997 6m a6g⁵ 5m Oct 28] 4,800Y: big gelding: has scope: half-brother to a a60 NH Flat race winner by Grey Desire: dam ran once in NH Flat race: modest form in maidens at Pontefract, Wolverhampton (best effort) and Redcar, slowly away last 2 starts. *P. C. Haslam*

HARBET HOUSE (FR) 4 b.g. Bikala 134 – Light of Hope (USA) 101 (Lyphard – (USA) 132) [1996 62: 10g a8g 12g 14.1m a14.8g³ a12g* a12g² a12g⁶ a16g a14g³ a14.8g 12s⁵ 1997 18d Oct 20] big, plain gelding: has a round action: modest performer for C. Cyzer at 3 yrs: well held only outing in 1997: shapes like a stayer: acts on soft ground and on fibresand (below form on equitrack): fair winning hurdler. *R. J. O'Sullivan*

HARBOUR DUES 4 b.c. Slip Anchor 136 – Quillotern (USA) (Arctic Tern 115 (USA) 126) [1996 103: 10d* 12m* 12m³ 13.9m⁴ 11.8m² 1997 12.3d* 13.3s⁴ 12g² 12d² 12m* 12s* 16m⁴ Nov 4] tall, good-topped colt: smart performer: won minor event at Ripon in April, very valuable listed race at Klampenborg in August (by 3 lengths from Arabian Story) and Group 3 Stockholm Cup at Taby in September: ran excellent race, finishing best of all, when length fourth of 22 to Might And Power in Melbourne Cup at Flemington final outing: stays 2m: acts on good to firm ground and soft: held up: genuine and consistent. *Lady Herries*

HARBOUR MASTER (FR) 2 b.c. (Jan 29) Bluebird (USA) 125 – Pharsala 108 (FR) (Hello Gorgeous (USA) 128) [1997 5g* 5d 6m* 6m³ 7g⁵ Sep 20] 750,000 francs Y: third foal: half-brother to French 1995 2-y-o 5.5f and 1m winner In Your Dreams (by Always Fair) and French 1¼m winner Phardoun (by Kaldoun): dam French 1m winner: useful colt: won maiden at the Curragh in April and Coventry Stakes (finished strongly to beat Desert Prince 1½ lengths) at Royal Ascot: good third in Phoenix Stakes at Leopardstown and not discredited when fifth to Xaar in

Coventry Stakes, Royal Ascot—Harbour Master is going away from Desert Prince close home

Prix de la Salamandre at Longchamp: should stay 1m: acts on good to firm ground: tends to race lazily early on, and easily best form in blinkers last 3 starts: sold to race in Hong Kong. *A. P. O'Brien, Ireland*

HARD LOVE   5 b.m. Rambo Dancer (CAN) 107 – Djimbaran Bay (Le Levanstell – 122) [1996 –, a55: a13g a11g³ a11g⁴ a16g² 18s⁶ 1997 a16g a16g 16.1g 13d Apr 10] leggy mare: soundly beaten in 1997. *J. L. Eyre*

HARD TO FIGURE   11 gr.g. Telsmoss 91 – Count On Me 77 (No Mercy 126)   93
[1996 113d: 6s⁴ 6g* 5.1g 6g³ 6f 6f 7.3f³ 6m 7g⁵ 6g 6m 6s a7g 1997 6d 6f⁵ 7d 6g 5.1m* 5.7f* 5.7g* 6g³ Sep 20] workmanlike gelding: one-time smart performer: still capable of fairly useful form and completed hat-trick at Bath (2 claimers and a handicap) in 3 weeks in summer: very good third of 28 to Perryston View in Ayr Silver Cup final start, first home on far side: stays 7f: acts on any going: usually held up: game and genuine. *R. J. Hodges*

HARDY DANCER   5 ch.g. Pharly (FR) 130 – Handy Dancer 87 (Green God 128)   75 d
[1996 92: a10g 10g³ 10m² 10.3g³ 10.1m⁶ 12m 10g 10m 10.1m 10m 8m⁶ 8g 1997 10m⁵ 10g 8g 10s 10g³ 10m³ Jul 21] close-coupled gelding: fair handicapper at 5 yrs, best effort on reappearance: stays 1¼m well: acts on firm going: visored penultimate start: has run well when sweating. *G. L. Moore*

HARLEQUIN WALK (IRE)   6 ch.m. Pennine Walk 120 – Taniokey (Grundy   52
137) [1996 42, a54: a12g* a16g⁴ 11.9g⁶ 9.7g* 10.2m² 10f⁴ a8g³ a10g⁶ a10g⁵ 1997 a8g a12g² a12g⁴ a12g⁴ a12g* a12g⁵ a10g⁴ 8f 9.7g 11.9m⁵ a10g⁴ a10g² 10g² a10g* 8m* 10f* a12g⁴ a13g³ a10g Dec 22] sturdy mare: modest handicapper: well placed to win 4 races as 6-y-o, at Lingfield in February and September (seller), Goodwood (claimer) later in September and Brighton in October: effective at 1m to easy 1½m: acts on firm ground and the all-weather: has won in blinkers, but wore them only once at 6 yrs. *R. J. O'Sullivan*

HARLESTONE HEATH   4 gr.f. Aragon 118 – Harlestone Lake 78 (Riboboy   –
(USA) 124) [1996 –: 10m⁶ 1997 a11g Jan 17] no sign of ability in maiden and seller. *M. Dods*

HARMONIC WAY   2 ch.c. (Feb 13) Lion Cavern (USA) 117 – Pineapple 77   89 p
(Superlative 118) [1997 6g* 6m⁴ 7d⁵ Oct 14] lengthy, angular colt: second reported foal: half-brother to 3-y-o Passiflora: dam 1½m winner, half-sister to In The Groove: won maiden at Salisbury in August: better efforts in minor events at Doncaster and Leicester: may prove best up to 1m: type to improve again at 3 yrs. *R. Charlton*

HARMONY HALL   3 ch.g. Music Boy 124 – Fleeting Affair 98 (Hotfoot 126)   70
[1996 70: 6m 7m⁶ 7m⁶ 7s 1997 10g 8g 8.2m⁴ 11.8g² 14m³ 13.1g 11.8d Oct 13] big,

lengthy gelding: fair maiden: barely stays 1¾m: acts on good to firm ground, well held on going softer than good: has been bandaged. *J. R. Fanshawe*

HARMONY IN RED 3 ch.g. Rock Hopper 124 – Lucky Song 91 (Lucky Wednesday 124) [1996 59: 5f⁴ 6m⁶ 6g⁵ a6g⁵ 1997 a5g² a6g⁴ a8g² a7g² Feb 6] compact gelding: fair maiden: barely stays 1m: acts on the all-weather: visored final start: sent to Macau. *C. A. Dwyer* — 65

HARNAGE (IRE) 2 b.g. (Apr 11) Mujadil (USA) 119 – Wilderness 88 (Martinmas 128) [1997 6g 6g 6g³ 6d⁴ 6m Jul 11] 10,000Y: close-coupled gelding: fluent mover: half-brother to several winners: dam 7f winner: poor form, including in sellers: stays 6f: well beaten on good to firm ground: has flashed tail. *M. R. Channon* — 47

HAROLDON (IRE) 8 ch.g. Heraldiste (USA) 121 – Cordon 89 (Morston (FR) 125) [1996 NR 1997 10m a12g 14m 12.5m 11.6s⁶ 10g* 10m⁴ 10m 10.2g 11.7m⁵ 10.8d² 12g⁵ a10g⁴ 10m a12g 10m a12g a10s Nov 28] good-bodied gelding: fair performer: first past post in handicap at Windsor in July and seller at Warwick (demoted, having hung right) in August: below form last 7 starts: effective at 1¼m to easy 1½m: acts on firm ground and dead: visored (below form) twice: not an easy ride. *B. Palling* — 71 d

HARPOON LOUIE (USA) 7 b.g. Eskimo (USA) – Twelfth Pleasure (USA) (Fappiano (USA)) [1996 a7.5g² a8.5g* a7.5g* 8g a9.3g* a9.3g* 1997 8s a9.3g³ a8g³ 9f³ 7g² 9g a9.3g* a9.3g² a9.3g⁵ a8g* a8g* Dec 2] big, lengthy, well-made gelding: one-time fair handicapper in Britain for M. H. Easterby: probably only modest nowadays: prolific winner of claimers in Belgium at 6 yrs and 7 yrs: also won weak seller at Lingfield in December: stays 9.3f: acts on good to firm ground (very likely on firm), soft and the all-weather. *Alex Vanderhaeghen, Belgium* — 52

HARRY'S TREAT 5 b.m. Lochnager 132 – Megara (USA) (Thatching 131) [1996 56?: a8g 7.1g 7m³ 8m 8g⁴ 10m 1997 a8g a7g⁴ 8s³ 8m 8g Jun 18] lengthy mare: poor maiden: should stay beyond 1m. *J. L. Eyre* — 46

HARRY WOLTON 3 b.c. Distant Relative 128 – Tashinsky (USA) (Nijinsky (CAN) 138) [1996 86p: 6g² 7m* 1997 8.1g² 8s⁴ 8.2m* 8.1g⁵ 10g³ 10.4g³ Aug 20] angular colt: useful performer: landed odds in minor event at Nottingham in June, despite edging right under pressure: very good efforts last 2 starts, soon off bridle in rear when third to Amyas in quite valuable handicap at York final one: likely to stay beyond 1¼m: acts on good to firm ground, seems unsuited by soft. *H. R. A. Cecil* — 107

HARVEST REAPER 5 gr.g. Bairn (USA) 126 – Real Silver 85 (Silly Season 127) [1996 45, a–: 8.2m 6m 7d 8m³ 8.1s a9.4g 1997 7f 8m Jun 2] leggy gelding: poor maiden: well beaten in 1997. *J. L. Harris* — –

HARVEY'S FUTURE 3 b.g. Never So Bold 135 – Orba Gold (USA) 67 (Gold Crest (USA) 120) [1996 56p: a5g⁶ 1997 5g⁶ 5g⁴ 5g 5f Sep 17] rather sparely-made gelding: maiden, no form since debut: left T. Clement after third start. *P. L. Gilligan* — –

HARVEY WHITE (IRE) 5 b. or br.g. Petorius 117 – Walkyria (Lord Gayle (USA) 124) [1996 69: 9.7s⁴ 10s⁵ 10m⁵ 10m² 10.8f* 10.8f³ 10.8f⁵ 10.1f³ 10m⁴ 9f³ 10d⁴ 10g 10m* 10m³ 8.9g 10f 10.1m³ 10g 12v 1997 10m 9m 10f 10m⁵ 9d* 9m 10m 10m 10f 10.8g² 10.1g a12g a11g Nov 17] rather leggy gelding: fair handicapper: won at Lingfield in June: stays 1½m: acts on firm going and soft, no form in 3 races on all-weather: usually held up: has hung under pressure: none too consistent. *J. Pearce* — 61 a–

HASTA LA VISTA 7 b.g. Superlative 118 – Falcon Berry (FR) (Bustino 136) [1996 54, a–: 12.3g⁴ 12d* 12.4d⁴ 13.9m⁶ 15.8g⁵ 15.8s⁴ 12.3m a14g 11.9g 1997 a12g⁴ 13.8g⁴ 12g² 12.4m³ a14g⁴ 16m² 16m* 14g² 13g* 16d² 15.8s* 16.2m⁵ 16s⁵ 13.8g* 16m³ 16g⁶ 12.3d* 17.5d 15.8g² 12m 12s 14.1d Oct 30] compact gelding: has round action: modest handicapper on turf, poor on all-weather: won 5 of 22 starts in 1997, at Musselburgh, Hamilton, Catterick (twice) and Ripon: well below form last 3 outings: effective at 1½m to 2m: acts on good to firm ground, soft and fibresand: blinkered nowadays: front runner/races prominently: tough, game and genuine. *M. W. Easterby* — 63 a39

HASTATE 2 b.g. (Feb 17) Persian Bold 123 – Gisarne (USA) 104 (Diesis 133) [1997 7g 7f⁶ 8.2s Oct 15] heavy-bodied gelding: first foal: dam 1¼m winner, stayed 1½m: towards rear in maidens. *W. Jarvis* — –

HATIMENA 3 b.f. Hatim (USA) 121 – Everingham Park 54 (Record Token 128) – [1996 NR 1997 8g 10g 8.5d Aug 13] fifth foal: half-sister to 2 winners, notably fairly useful 1994 2-y-o Super Park (by Superpower): dam 6f seller winner: well beaten in sellers and a claimer. *J. G. FitzGerald*

HATTAAFEH (IRE) 6 b.m. Mtoto 134 – Monongelia 98 (Welsh Pageant 132) 66 [1996 63: 15.4m² 16.4g⁵ 12m² 12m² 12m³ 16.2m⁴ 1997 a16g* a16g* a13g* a16g³ a79 a13g 16g⁴ 14m May 27] strong, workmanlike mare: fair handicapper: won 3 times at Lingfield (2 amateurs races) in January/February: effective at 1½m to 2m: acts on good to firm ground and all-weather: seems best held up. *Miss B. Sanders*

HATTAB (IRE) 3 b.c. Marju (IRE) 127 – Funun (USA) 84 (Fappiano (USA)) 107 [1996 91: 6m⁵ 6g⁴ 5m* 5m² 5d 1997 5d* 6d³ 5m 6m* 6f* 7d⁵ 7g Sep 18] good-topped colt: useful performer: won handicap at Sandown in April, minor event (4 ran) at Yarmouth in June and listed event (beat Soviet State 1¼ lengths) at Newbury in July: a sprinter: acts on firm and dead going (unraced on softer): effective from front or held up: sent to UAE. *P. T. Walwyn*

HATTA SUNSHINE (USA) 7 b.g. Dixieland Band (USA) – Mountain – Sunshine (USA) (Vaguely Noble 140) [1996 –, a57: a8g* a8g⁴ a8g³ a8g² a8g⁵ a10g a54 9m⁶ 12d a10s⁶ a10g a10g⁴ 1997 a8g* a8g⁶ a8g⁴ a8g⁶ a10g² a6g⁶ 8f 7f 9g 9.7g 8f 7.1g Aug 3] lengthy gelding: modest performer on all-weather: won claimer at Lingfield in January: stays 1¼m: acts on equitrack (had excuse only start on fibresand), no form on turf for some time: tried visored/blinkered. *G. L. Moore*

HAUNT THE ZOO 2 b.f. (May 4) Komaite (USA) – Merryhill Maid (IRE) 71 61 (M Double M (USA)) [1997 5.1m 6.1m⁴ 6.1g⁶ Sep 28] 3,000Y: second foal: dam sprinter: easily best effort in maidens at Nottingham on second start: raced widest of all next time. *J. L. Harris*

HAUTE CUISINE 4 b.g. Petong 126 – Nevis 61 (Connaught 130) [1996 44: 7.1g 44 a7g 7g⁵ 10f² 11.8f 11.5m 1997 a12g a8g³ a12g⁶ a8g³ Feb 22] strong, close-coupled

Hamdan Al Maktoum's "Hattab"

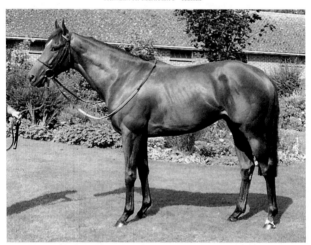

gelding: poor maiden: stays 1¼m: acts on firm ground and equitrack: blinkered final outing (stiff task): sold in March, to go to Denmark. *R. J. R. Williams*

HAVAGO 3 b.g. Risk Me (FR) 127 – Sporting Lass (Blakeney 126) [1996 70+: 6.1m⁶ 6s 6.9d* 6.9v⁴ 1997 7m 7.1g 7m 6.9s⁶ 7m 7m⁴ 6g⁴ Aug 27] strong, lengthy gelding: modest handicapper: stays 7f: acts on good to firm and soft ground: joined M. Salaman. *R. Hannon* — 61

HAVANA HEIGHTS (IRE) 4 ch.f. Persian Heights 129 – Havana Blade (USA) (Blade (USA)) [1996 52, a–: a8g⁶ a5g a11g⁶ a12g³ a14g 16.2g⁴ 13.8g* 14s 15.1s a14.8g⁵ a16g 1997 12.1m⁴ 12g⁴ 16m 12g 12.1g² a14g 10g⁶ 12m 13.8s 12s Nov 6] small, sparely-made filly: poor handicapper: stays 2m: probably acts on good to firm ground, no form on all-weather or going softer than good: none too consistent. *J. L. Eyre* — 40 a–

HAVANA MISS 5 b.m. Cigar 68 – Miss Patdonna 62 (Starch Reduced 112) [1996 39: 6m 6f a6g a8g a8g 1997 a7s⁴ a6g a7g a10g⁴ a10g Feb 4] leggy, sparely-made mare: poor performer: stays 1¼m: tried visored/blinkered: inconsistent. *B. Palling* — 38

HAVE A BREAK 2 b.c. (May 5) Most Welcome 131 – Miss Tealeaf (USA) (Lear Fan (USA) 130) [1997 5m 5g 6.1g Oct 4] third reported foal: dam once raced from good middle-distance family: well beaten in maidens. *C. R. Egerton* — –

HAWAII STORM (FR) 9 b.g. Plugged Nickle (USA) – Slewvindaloo (USA) (Seattle Slew (USA)) [1996 –, a71d: a7g⁶ a7g² a7g² a7g⁶ a7g⁶ 8d 7m a8g 8g a8g a7g³ a7g⁵ a8g⁵ 8g a8.5g⁶ a7s³ a8g⁴ a7g³ 1997 a7g³ a7g* a7g a7g² a8g* a7g⁵ a8g⁴ a7g⁵ a8g a8g 7f a8g⁵ 8g 6.9m 8f* 7.1m⁵ 8m 8g³ 8d 8f a8g⁵ a8g Dec 8] leggy gelding: poor mover: modest performer on all-weather: won seller and apprentice handicap at Lingfield in January/February: poor on turf, though won seller at Brighton in July: effective at 7f/1m: acts on firm and dead going, best form on all-weather: effective blinkered or not: often slowly away and brought wide: tough. *D. J. S. ffrench Davis* — 45 a56

HAWAIT (IRE) 3 gr.c. Green Desert (USA) 127 – Hayati 94 (Hotfoot 126) [1996 81: 5m⁴ 6f³ 6m* 7m 6m⁴ 1997 7.5m* 7.6d 8m 7.5m² 7m⁵ 8m⁵ 8m² 7m Oct 3] well-made colt: has a quick action: useful handicapper: won at Beverley in April: best effort when ½-length second to Russian Music at Doncaster in September: may prove best at 7f/1m: acts on good to firm going: blinkered last 2 starts: suited by strong galloping: sent to UAE. *B. W. Hills* — 98

HAWANAFA 4 b.f. Tirol 127 – Woodland View (Precipice Wood 123) [1996 48: 8g 7f⁶ 7g 6m 8.3g 10m³ 12g 8m 1997 10s May 12] tall filly: poor maiden: seems to stay 1¼m: winning selling hurdler. *Miss K. M. George* — –

HAWKER HUNTER (USA) 6 b. or br.g. Silver Hawk (USA) 123 – Glorious Natalie (USA) (Reflected Glory (USA)) [1996 NR 1997 12m² 11.4d⁵ 12g Aug 10] big gelding: powerful mover: fair form in handicaps first 2 starts as 6-y-o, tailed off final one: stays 1½m: acts on good to firm and dead going. *R. Akehurst* — 79

HAWKERS DEAL 4 b.g. K-Battery 108 – Boreen Geal (Boreen (FR) 123) [1996 NR 1997 8g⁶ Aug 17] first known foal: dam, winning chaser, stayed 2½m: tailed off in maiden at Pontefract. *A. R. Dicken* — –

HAWKISH (USA) 8 b.g. Silver Hawk (USA) 123 – Dive Royal (USA) (Inverness Drive (USA)) [1996 52: 10g³ 10d 10.3g² 11f⁴ 12.3m⁵ 10f² 1997 9.9m⁵ 12.3m Jun 19] sturdy gelding: poor mover: poor handicapper: ran creditably on first of 2 starts at 8 yrs: stays 1½m: acts on firm ground and dead: normally held up. *D. Morley* — 49

HAWKSBILL HENRY (USA) 3 ch.g. Known Fact (USA) 135 – Novel Approach (USA) (Codex (USA)) [1996 NR 1997 6g 6m 8m 8g 8.1m 7f⁴ Oct 3] $45,000Y, 7,500 2-y-o: useful-looking gelding: fourth foal: brother to 2 minor winners in USA at up to 9f: dam, modest form in maidens and handicaps: should stay 1m: unraced on going softer than good. *Mrs A. J. Perrett* — 51

HAWKSLEY HILL (IRE) 4 ch.g. Rahy (USA) 115 – Gaijin 97 (Caerleon (USA) 132) [1996 93: a7g* 11.1g* 10m* 10g² 8.2f* 8m* 8f² 8m² 8m⁶ 8m² 9m⁵ 8g* 8g 1997 8m² 8g* 8m 8.1g* 10m 7.9d² 8f⁶ 8f² Oct 18] big, workmanlike gelding: developed into a smart handicapper as 4-y-o: short-headed in the Lincoln at Doncaster on reappearance: awarded Spring Cup at Newbury following month (having — 110

Hong Kong Jockey Club Trophy, Sandown—
the visored Hawksley Hill takes this valuable handicap from 50/1-shot Supercal

been beaten 2 lengths by Hunters of Brora) then improved again to win £51,600 Hong Kong Jockey Club Trophy at Sandown in July by ½ length from Supercal: left Mrs J. Ramsden after seventh start: good second to Lucky Coin in Grade 2 handicap at Belmont final outing: effective at 1m to 1¼m: acts on fibresand and on firm and dead ground: visored last 4 starts in Britain: held up (tends to wander and idle), and suited by strongly-run race and strong handling: tough, genuine and consistent. *N. Drysdale, USA*

HAYA YA KEFAAH   5 b.g. Kefaah (USA) 124 – Hayat (IRE) (Sadler's Wells — (USA) 132) [1996 70: a12g² 12g* 11.8d 12m* 12g² 12m 11.9d* 1997 12d a11g Dec 8] angular gelding: fair handicapper at 4 yrs: well beaten in 1997: stays 1½m: acts on good to firm and dead going. *N. M. Babbage*

HAYBURNER   2 b.c. (Feb 26) Mujadil (USA) 119 – Kotsina 59 (Top Ville 129)   51 [1997 5m 5g 7g⁶ 6g 5s³ 6.1m⁴ 5m⁵ 5m² 5g⁴ Sep 15] 550Y: sparely-made colt: first foal: dam placed in France and Ireland: modest maiden: ran creditably in nurseries 2 of last 3 starts: best form at 5f: acts on good to firm ground: blinkered from sixth start. *M. W. Easterby*

HAY DANCE   6 b.g. Shareef Dancer (USA) 135 – Hay Reef 72 (Mill Reef (USA)   47 141) [1996 11f⁴ 1997 10.8m² Jun 9] close-coupled gelding: shows knee action: fairly useful 2m hurdler: lightly raced and poor form on flat: raced only on good to firm/firm going and fibresand: blinkered once. *P. J. Hobbs*

HAYDN JAMES (USA)   3 ch.c. Danzig Connection (USA) – Royal Fi Fi (USA)   66 94 (Conquistador Cielo (USA)) [1996 78: 7m⁴ 7.1m 1997 8g 8.3s 8.3g 10m⁵ 10.2d 8.2d a10g² a9.4g² a10g³ Dec 19] fair maiden: should stay beyond 1¼m: acts on good to firm ground and the all-weather: blinkered 6 of last 7 starts. *P. W. Harris*

HAYDOWN (IRE)   5 b. or br.g. Petorius 117 – Hay Knot (Main Reef 126) [1996   30 32: 12m 7.6f⁴ 11.6d⁵ 10m 1997 11.8g 8f a8.5g 10.2g⁴ 11.9m² 10.8d⁶ 11.9f Oct 1] poor maiden handicapper: probably stays 1½m. *M. R. Bosley*

HAYES WAY (IRE)   3 b.c. Lahib (USA) 129 – Edgeaway 70 (Ajdal (USA) 130)   94 [1996 79p: a8g* 1997 a8g* 8m⁴ 7g⁶ 8m 8m Jul 31] neat colt: fairly useful performer: won minor event at Lingfield in February: best effort in minor event at Doncaster next start: will stay beyond 1m: raced only on good/good to firm ground and equitrack. *T. G. Mills*

434

HAYIL (USA)   2 b.c. (Apr 18) Dayjur (USA) 137 – Futuh (USA) 95 (Diesis   108
133) [1997 6m² 6m⁵ 6m* 6m² 6m³ 6m* Oct 2]

Hayil was one of two Group 1 winners—the other was Celeric—
saddled in the latest season by popular Newmarket trainer David Morley, who
died suddenly in January, 1998. As he greeted Hayil after his Middle Park
Stakes victory, Morley laughed off the fact that he had had three separate heart
operations. 'I'm still here and it's wonderful to be able to train such good
horses.' Morley's end-of-term report on Hayil had also been typical of his sense
of humour: 'Would do better if he didn't look out of the window.' The Middle
Park was the first occasion Hayil had worn blinkers, as it had been for Fard
when he won the race for the same connections three years earlier, but the
motives for using the headgear were different this time according to the trainer.
'Fard was idle, really idle, but this one isn't idle; he just doesn't concentrate.'

Hayil started at 14/1 for the Middle Park, and his performance to win it
was several pounds better than anything he'd achieved previously. A good fifth
in the Coventry on his second outing ensured that he started odds on back in
maiden company at Newmarket in July. A narrow win was followed by two
beaten runs in minor company—both times behind Paul Cole-trained colts
(Jazz Club at Haydock and Bintang at Doncaster)—before the Middle Park.

The Middle Park has failed to attract a field worthy of its Group 1
status in recent years and the latest running, sponsored by the Thoroughbred
Corporation, was no exception. It was weakened further by the first two in the
betting, Arkadian Hero and Victory Note (also probably the best three-year-old
prospects in the line-up), failing to run up to their best. Few of the eight runners
got into the contest and Hayil held a prominent pitch throughout, travelling
easily in company with the maiden Designer, asserting with two furlongs to

*Thoroughbred Corporation Middle Park Stakes, Newmarket—blinkers bring out the best in Hayil.
Designer loses second place to Carrowkeel (partially obscured by winner)*

run and driven out up the hill to hold the late challenge of Gimcrack winner
Carrowkeel by three quarters of a length, with Designer a neck away third.

		Danzig	Northern Dancer
	Dayjur (USA)	(b 1977)	Pas de Nom
	(b 1987)	Gold Beauty	Mr Prospector
Hayil (USA)		(b 1979)	Stick To Beauty
(b.c. Apr 18, 1995)		Diesis	Sharpen Up
	Futuh (USA)	(ch 1980)	Doubly Sure
	(gr 1988)	Hardship	Drone
		(gr 1977)	Hard And Fast

Hayil is reportedly to be trained in France in 1998. He is a sprinter on
looks, a well-made colt and the sort to carry condition. He has a sprinter's
pedigree too, and the chances of him staying a mile are remote. In fact, he
should prove effective at five furlongs. He is the first Group/Grade 1 winner of
his American-based sire, Dayjur, who also had another useful two-year-old in
the Cherry Hinton winner Asfurah in the latest season. Hayil's dam, Futuh, was
a speedy and fairly useful two-year-old who broke the juvenile track record
when winning a Redcar maiden over six furlongs but she wasn't quite so good
at three, and was never tried beyond sprint distances. Hayil is her third foal and
second runner after Tamhid (by Gulch), who won at six furlongs in Britain as a
two-year-old and showed smart at a mile and a quarter in Dubai as a
four-year-old in 1997. Futuh's yearling of 1997 is a full brother to Hayil.
Grandam Hardship won at up to a mile in the USA (she was also third in the
Grade 1 Frizette Stakes as a two-year-old) and great-grandam Hard And Fast
was successful there at up to nine furlongs. They've produced plenty of winners
but the only one of any real note is Futuh's half-sister Rose Park, who won the
Selene Stakes over eight and a half furlongs in Canada and is herself dam of the

Hamdan Al Maktoum's "Hayil"

smart 1997 three-year-old Wild Rush, winner of the Grade 2 nine-furlong Illinois Derby. *D. Morley*

HAYLING-BILLY   4 ch.c. Captain Webster 69 – Mistress Royal 74 (Royalty 130) [1996 –: 14m 10g 1997 a13g Jan 11] of no account: dead. *P. R. Hedger*   –

HAZARD A GUESS (IRE)   7 ch.g. Digamist (USA) 110 – Guess Who 76 (Be My Guest (USA) 126) [1996 88: 10.3d² 10g* 9.9m³ 10g³ 10.1m 8.9m 10f² 10.3g⁶ 10g 10.4m⁵ 10.1f* 9.9f 10.4m 10.4g* 1997 8m 10m⁴ 12g³ 12m 10.3d⁵ 11.9g 11.9d 10m² 10m 9.9d² 11.9g 12d⁶ Aug 25] tall, leggy gelding: fairly useful handicapper: suited by 1¼m to 1½m: acts on any going: possibly unsuited by Epsom: usually held up, and suited by good gallop: won novice hurdle for B. Rothwell in December. *D. Nicholls*   88

HAZEL   5 ro.m. Risk Me (FR) 127 – Sir Tangs Gift (Runnett 125) [1996 57: 7m⁵ 6.9g a8.5g 1997 a10g³ a9.4f³ a12g a9.4g⁶ 7g 10f a16g³ 14m* Aug 17] good-topped mare: poor performer: won very weak seller at Lingfield in August: stays 2m: acts on good to firm ground and all-weather: effective blinkered/visored or not: sold 600 gns in October. *Miss Gay Kelleway*   32   a48

HEAD GARDENER (IRE)   3 b. or br.g. Be My Chief (USA) 122 – Silk Petal 105 (Petorius 117) [1996 73: 7.1m 7m⁴ 7f 1997 a11g* a12g⁵ a12g³ 10.3m 12g 10.3g a8g a12g⁵ Dec 26] good-bodied gelding: won maiden at Southwell in January: badly out of sorts afterwards: visored final start. *N. P. Littmoden*   64 d

HEAD GIRL (IRE)   3 ch.f. Masterclass (USA) 116 – Rebecca's Girl (IRE) (Nashamaa 113) [1996 63d, a48: 6m³ 6g² 6m⁴ 7g⁵ 6g⁵ a7g² a8g⁶ a8g* 1997 a8s³ a8g² a8g⁶ a8g* a8g⁴ Mar 14] leggy filly: poor performer: dead-heated in 4-runner seller at Southwell in February: will probably stay 1¼m: acts on fibresand: sometimes flashes tail: seems suited by forcing tactics. *C. W. Thornton*   –   a48

HEADHUNTER (IRE)   2 b.c. (May 4) Last Tycoon 131 – Erzsi 80 (Caerleon (USA) 132) [1997 6g* 6g³ 7m⁴ Sep 30] 62,000Y: fifth foal: half-brother to 3 winners,   95

Highclere Thoroughbred Racing Ltd's "Headhunter"

including fairly useful 1993 Irish 2-y-o 1m winner Broadmara (by Thatching) and 7f/ 1m winner Castan (by Persian Bold): dam, Irish 1¼m winner, half-sister to Salieri: useful colt: won maiden at Yarmouth in July: 3¾ lengths third to Carrowkeel in Gimcrack Stakes at York: lack-lustre fourth of 13 to Tamarisk in valuable sales race at Newmarket final start: should prove better at 7f/1m than 6f. *W. J. Haggas*

HEART FULL OF SOUL 3 ch.g. Primo Dominie 121 – Scales of Justice 85   54 (Final Straw 127) [1996 74+: 5m 5m 6m 7g² 8f* 8g 7.3s³ 1997 8.2g 8m 8.1s 8g³ 11.5m⁶ 10m⁴ 8f⁵ Oct 1] plain, good-topped gelding: disappointing at 3 yrs, modest form at best: stays 1m: acts on firm and soft going: usually blinkered: one to treat with caution: joined P. Shakespeare. *P. F. I. Cole*

HEART OF ARMOR 3 b.g. Tirol 127 – Hemline 77 (Sharpo 132) [1996 78: 7g³   85 8f³ 7m⁴ 1997 10.5s⁴ 10m 10.2m⁶ 11.6s* 12m² 12g 12d² 14m⁶ 11.9m² 11.9m Sep 21] tall gelding: fairly useful handicapper: won at Windsor in May: ran well afterwards until last outing (gelded after): stays 1¾m: acts on good to firm going and soft: races keenly: reliable. *P. F. I. Cole*

HEART OF GOLD (IRE) 3 ch.c. Broken Hearted 124 – Originality (Godswalk   98 (USA) 130) [1996 64p: 8.1m⁶ 7.9g 1997 8g⁴ 10.1m³ 10m* 12.3m* 12.4g² 11.9g⁴ 12m 15d* Sep 18] sparely-made colt: made into a useful performer: won maiden at Redcar in May and handicaps at Ripon in June and Ayr in September, best effort when beating Royal Crown 1¼ lengths in last-named: will stay 2m: acts on good to firm and dead going, yet to race on extremes: carries head high but is genuine: sold 90,000 gns, to go to Saudi Arabia. *Miss S. E. Hall*

HEATHYARD'S FLIGHT 3 b.c. Statoblest 120 – Jeanne Avril 99 (Music Boy   – 124) [1996 NR 1997 a7g a6g 6m a6g⁵ 6.1g Apr 21] 4,500Y, 10,500 2-y-o: sixth foal: half-brother to 3 winners, notably useful sprinter Mary Hinge (by Dowsing): dam 6f winner: seems of little account. *R. Hollinshead*

HEATHYARDS LADY (USA) 6 b.m. Mining (USA) – Dubiously (USA)   49 d (Jolie Jo Stakes (USA)) [1996 59, a72: 8m⁶ a7g⁵ a9.4g³ 7.5m⁵ 7.1m⁴ 8.2m a9.4g a9.4g³   a66 d a9.4g⁴ a9.4g⁴ 1997 7g 8f⁴ 8g a8g⁵ a9.4g⁶ 8f⁶ 8g⁵ 7.1d a7g a7g⁶ 7.5g⁶ a8.5g⁴ a7g² a7g⁴ a9.4g Dec 26] leggy mare: modest handicapper on all-weather, poor on turf: below best after fourth start: stays 9.4f: acts on any turf, goes well on fibresand. *R. Hollinshead*

HEATHYARDS PEARL (USA) 3 gr. or ro.f. Mining (USA) – Dance Dance   – Dance (IRE) (Dance of Life (USA)) [1996 65: 6m⁴ 6d⁴ 6m⁶ 7g a6g⁶ 1997 a7g a6g 8g 5.9f 5m 5.7g Sep 8] has lost her form: visored final start. *R. Hollinshead*

HEATHYARDS ROCK 5 br.g. Rock City 120 – Prudence 68 (Grundy 137)   63 [1996 82: a12g* a12g* a12g* a12g² a16g² 1997 12g* 13.1g² 12g⁵ 12.3m⁵ a12g⁶ Jun 27] tall gelding: suffered knee injury in 1996 and modest performer nowadays: won claimer for R. Hollinshead at Thirsk in May: stays 2m: acts on good to firm and dead ground and on fibresand: tried blinkered/visored: has refused to race over hurdles. *R. M. McKellar*

HEATHYARDS SHEIK 2 b.c. (Mar 4) Alnasr Alwasheek 117 – Wilsonic 78   68 (Damister (USA) 123) [1997 5m 6m 5m⁵ 6m⁵ 5m⁵ 6g 7m⁵ 8g³ 10s⁴ a8.5g³ Dec 13] 6,000Y: smallish colt: first foal: dam, maiden who stayed 13f, sometimes irresolute: fair maiden: will stay 1½m+: acts on good to firm and soft ground and fibresand. *R. Hollinshead*

HEAVENLY ABSTONE 2 b.f. (Feb 27) Interrex (CAN) – Heavenly Queen   79 (Scottish Reel 123) [1997 5d² 5m² 5m* 5.3f⁴ 5.1d² 5s* 5m⁶ 5m 5.9g³ 6.1m² 6.1m²   a? a6g³ 6.1d² 6d Sep 5] 6,500 2-y-o: sturdy filly: second foal: half-sister to 3-y-o Abstone Queen: dam little form: fair performer: won maiden at Musselburgh in April and minor event at Ayr in May: generally ran creditably afterwards, including in a nursery: will stay 7f: acts on good to firm and soft ground, ran poorly on firm and in one run on fibresand: visored except for debut: tough. *P. D. Evans*

HEAVENLY DANCER 3 b.f. Warrshan (USA) 117 – High Halo 64 (High Top   – 131) [1996 52?: 7g 6.9m² a7g⁶ 10f 1997 8.2m 6.1g Apr 21] tall, lengthy filly: maiden, has shown little since second start at 2 yrs: blinkered final outing. *Mrs N. Macauley*

HEAVENLY FALLS (IRE) 2 b.c. (Feb 9) River Falls 113 – Almost Heaven   57 (Corvaro (USA) 124) [1997 a5g 6m⁵ 6g 6g* 6g⁵ 7s⁵ 6.1m* 6g 6d 7m Sep 20] 2,400Y:

sparely-made colt: third foal: half-brother to winning sprinter Warwick Warrior (by Reasonable): dam Irish maiden: modest performer: won sellers at Lingfield in June and Nottingham in August: best form at 6f: acts on good to firm ground: has run well when sweating: sent to Macau. *C. A. Dwyer*

HEAVENLY HAND 3 ch.f. Out of Hand 84 – My Home 61 (Homing 130) [1996 –: a7g a8g 1997 a10g Apr 4] 525Y: fourth foal, all by Out of Hand: dam (2-y-o 5f winner) stayed 1m: no sign of ability, including in a seller. *G. L. Moore*

HEAVENLY MISS (IRE) 3 b.f. Anita's Prince 126 – Heavenly Blessed 69 d (Monseigneur (USA) 127) [1996 71, a68: 5g 6.1d² 6m⁶ a6g² 6m* 6m 6.1m* 6d⁴ 6s³ 6.1s⁵ a6g a5g* a6g⁵ a6g⁴ 1997 a5g² a8g⁴ a5g⁶ a7g³ 6g 5m⁶ 6g 6d² 5d 5.1f 6m⁵ 6g 6g 6m 5.7g 5g² 5g⁶ 6d 6.1s Oct 15] unfurnished filly: fair sprinter on her day: acts on good to firm ground, soft and equitrack: effective blinkered or not: unreliable. *J. J. Bridger*

HEAVENLY RAY (USA) 3 ch.f. Rahy (USA) 115 – Highest Truth (USA) (Aly- 81 + dar (USA)) [1996 –: 6m 1997 7m² 8f* 8v⁶ 8m⁴ Nov 1] unfurnished filly: fairly useful form: won maiden at Yarmouth in May: unable to challenge in listed races next 2 starts (probably flattered final one): may prove best up to 1m: seems to act on any going. *J. R. Fanshawe*

HEEREMANDI (IRE) 2 b.f. (Apr 18) Royal Academy (USA) 130 – La Dame 105 du Lac (USA) (Round Table) [1997 6d* 6g* 5m⁶ 6g³ 7d⁴ 6m⁵ Sep 30] IR 105,000Y: good-topped filly: has a quick action: closely related to several winners by Nijinsky, including useful Irish 1987 2-y-o 6f winner Lake Como (1m winner in France and dam of high-class US mare Flawlessly), and half-sister to several winners: dam, unraced, from very good family: useful performer: won maiden at Fairyhouse in May and listed race at Leopardstown in June: in frame in Prix Morny at Deauville (best effort, 1½ lengths third to Charge d'Affaires) and Moyglare Stud Stakes at the Curragh: ran in Queen Mary Stakes at Royal Ascot and Cheveley Park Stakes at Newmarket (visored, creditable fifth) other starts: needs further than 5f and should stay 1m: yet to race on extremes of ground. *A. P. O'Brien, Ireland*

HEIGHTH OF FAME 6 b.g. Shirley Heights 130 – Land of Ivory (USA) 109 45 (The Minstrel (CAN) 135) [1996 –, a76: a12g a14.8g⁶ a12g⁴ a13g* a16g² a12g² a16g a66 a12g³ a14.8g² a16.2g⁶ a12g² a13g* 1997 a14.8g² a13g³ a12g 13d⁵ 14.1g 14.1d a11g³ 9.9m a11g* 12m² a14g³ 12m a9.4g a9.4g⁵ a14g a12g⁶ Nov 21] good-topped gelding: fair performer on the all-weather, poor on turf: trained by D. Burchell reappearance: won seller at Southwell in June: seems best at 11f to 13f: acts on good to firm going and all-weather: races up with pace: game. *J. Hetherton*

HEIGHT OF HEIGHTS (IRE) 4 b.g. Shirley Heights 130 – Azallya (FR) 75 (Habitat 134) [1996 NR 1997 10s³ 10m 11.7g⁶ 14g* 17.2f⁶ 16s Oct 15] tall gelding: fifth foal: half-brother to fairly useful handicapper Serious (up to 10.5f, by Shadeed): dam, French 1m winner, half-sister to a smart French middle-distance winner out of another: fair form: won handicap at Salisbury in August: last both outings after (reportedly had breathing problems): stays 1¾m: acts on soft ground. *Lady Herries*

HEIRESS OF MEATH (IRE) 2 ch.f. (Apr 17) Imperial Frontier (USA) 112 – – Rich Heiress (IRE) 49 (Last Tycoon 131) [1997 5m 5.1g 7m Oct 1] leggy filly: first foal: dam, maiden, stayed 1m: no sign of ability. *M. D. I. Usher*

HE KNOWS THE RULES 5 b.g. Tirol 127 – Falls of Lora 107 (Scottish Rifle – 127) [1996 NR 1997 8m 16.2g Sep 27] close-coupled gelding: has had wind opera-tion: no worthwhile form on flat: fair winning hurdler. *R. H. Buckler*

HELENES HILL 2 b.f. (Mar 12) Sabrehill (USA) 120 – Sea of Clouds (Soviet – Star (USA) 128) [1997 5m 6g a5g Sep 30] 10,000 2-y-o: small filly: first foal: dam French 9.5f winner, half-sister to smart French middle-distance stayer Helen of Spain: signs of ability in seller, second and final start for C. Smith: well held in maiden at Wolverhampton on all-weather debut. *J. L. Harris*

HELICON (IRE) 4 b.c. Nashwan (USA) 135 – Hebba (USA) 80 (Nureyev 105 (USA) 131) [1996 NR 1997 10g² 10g⁵ Jul 16] angular colt: won maiden at Newmarket for H. Cecil at 2 yrs: reportedly suffered stress fracture of near-fore in spring 1996: better effort (and useful form) on return when ¾-length second to Cap

HEL

Juluca in minor event at Newbury in May: should be suited by at least 1¼m: yet to race on going firmer than good. *Saeed bin Suroor*

HELIOS 9 br.g. Blazing Saddles (AUS) – Mary Sunley 62 (Known Fact (USA) 60 135) [1996 68: a8g 7d 8f 8f 8g 8f* 8m* 8.2m⁴ 7.6m 8f* 8f³ 8.1f⁶ 8.5m 8d⁴ 1997 8d⁵ 8.1s³ 8m 7m Sep 9] angular gelding: unimpressive mover: modest handicapper: best form at 7f to 1m: probably acts on any going: blinkered (ran creditably) once as 5-y-o: often apprentice ridden. *D. J. G. Murray Smith*

HELISSIO (FR) 4 b.c. Fairy King (USA) – Helice (USA) (Slewpy (USA)) 133 [1996 136: 10d* 11f* 10.5g* 12m⁵ 12m* 12m* 12d* 12f³ 1997 10.5d* 12d* 12s³ 8m² 12f⁶ Oct 5]
So, the abiding memory of Helissio remained his brilliant victory in the 1996 Prix de l'Arc de Triomphe. For a pithy summary of Helissio's career afterwards, it is hard to beat that provided by his trainer, Elie Lellouche: 'After last year's Arc it was the Japan Cup, then Dubai. There was a quick preparation for the Ganay and then a virus before the Grand Prix de Saint-Cloud followed by the King George. It was very difficult, and then Helissio was raced in the Moulin de Longchamp against my wishes. He should have had the classic Arc prep in the Prix Foy. Last month I would not have been surprised to receive orders to enter him in the Abbaye!'
Helissio's four-year-old campaign was not a conventional one, it's true. Enrique Sarasola owned an outstanding racehorse, knew that he was unlikely to have another so talented, and was determined to enjoy the experience while he could, taking on all-comers and celebrating every new challenge. By the end of the latest season, even Mr Sarasola's own racing manager was criticising him, saying that: 'It wasn't that Helissio was any less than last season, it was just that he was asked too much.' One could never accuse Mr Sarasola of lacking the spirit of competition, though. It was he who had to foot the bills, and the cost should not be forgotten—soon after the 1996 Arc, he was offered a reported twenty-five million dollars for the horse.
Helissio's first target after that runaway Arc triumph was the Japan Cup just seven weeks later, in which he dead-heated for third on ground which subsequent evidence now suggests was too firm for him. Next stop was intended to be a race on going for which the form-book held few clues, the Dubai World Cup on sand in March, and this was an occasion when one might say that it was the trainer who failed to go through with his effort. 'Half-hearted' always seemed to overstate Elie Lellouche's enthusiasm for the venture. Helissio was prepared in Dubai for the race and was declared to run, but when the flood came and the event had to be postponed Helissio was put on the first plane home. With so much at stake during the conventional European season who could blame his trainer? For a significant number of European horses, the Dubai experience last year was a far less happy one than it was for the winner, Singspiel. Helissio's connections, though, had only the frustration of a wasted trip, and that cannot have seemed too overwhelming when his European season commenced in breathtaking style in the Prix Ganay at Longchamp at the end of April. Nearly seven months after the Arc, it was very much a case of Helissio starting where he had left off, as he administered a six-length thrashing to Le Destin, with Pilsudski another one and a half lengths back in third. The last horse to win the Ganay by so far had been Mill Reef. The latest winner now became the centre of that customary 'race of the year/decade/century' speculation when it appeared that he might take on the winner, Singspiel in the Coronation Cup. Sadly, the coughing Helissio could not meet that engagement, but the disappointment lasted less than two months as the French champion was sent over to take on even stronger opposition in the King George VI and Queen Elizabeth Diamond Stakes at Ascot, doing so four weeks after he had convinced most observers of his well-being with a five-length and three-length demolition of Magellano and Riyadian for his second success in the Grand Prix de Saint-Cloud. There were only four runners at Saint-Cloud

440

Prix Ganay, Longchamp—Helissio makes a stunning return

(last home was a disappointing Darazari) and Helissio was sent off a 10/1-on chance. But he produced a performance that, on a literal reading of the form, could be interpreted as only just behind his victory in the Arc.

It becomes important to remember that, because Helissio's remaining three races all ended in defeat. It always seemed to be raining at Ascot in the latest season and a downpour just before the opening race on King George day was widely thought likely to favour Helissio, who was sent off the 11/10 favourite. However, it was confirmed virtually from the off that Helissio and jockey Cash Asmussen (who had first taken the ride when Peslier was unavailable at Saint-Cloud) would have a fight on their hands. The pair set off at a good pace over the first furlong and a half, but when Kingfisher Mill set about going even faster Helissio was restrained and rather fought for his head. Back in the lead five and a half furlongs out, Asmussen still looked to be sitting pretty entering the straight, but Swain surged to the front before the Texan had started pushing, and when Helissio failed to respond immediately and Swain edged in front of him onto the rails there was no way back. Helissio went down by two and a quarter lengths to Swain and one and a quarter to Pilsudski, despite hanging right and carrying his head high. Not having things his own way may at least have been part of the reason for his defeat, but, at only a few pounds below his best, his performance was by no means a disgrace.

In hindsight, the King George might look like the beginning of the end, but that was not how it looked at the time. Helissio maintained his place at the head of the long-range Arc betting and actually strengthened that position (at around 3/1) with his next performance, despite running to a significantly lower level of form than he had in the King George. For this race, the Prix du Moulin de Longchamp, there was an obvious excuse. Helissio was a middle-distance

Grand Prix de Saint-Cloud—easy pickings for Helissio

horse, not a miler. Indeed, he had never run at a mile before, the closest being his win in a mile-and-a-quarter newcomers race at Evry in March as a three-year-old. Since then he had won the Lupin and Ganay over ten and a half furlongs, the Prix Noailles over eleven furlongs, and his seven other races had all been at a mile and a half. Helissio's emergence as a mile-and-a-half horse had been the cause of some surprise given his pedigree, so perhaps this was a betting opportunity for the breeding pundits? At any rate, Helissio did not lack for support, starting at even money against the best older miler still around, Spinning World, and seven others, including Poulains winner Daylami. We suspect that a study of Helissio's breeding was not the motivation for Mr Sarasola's opting for the Moulin, and, as it was his money at stake not ours, we applaud his sporting decision to give his star this new test. And he was rewarded with a bold show, Helissio beating all but Spinning World. Helissio did not make the running this time, but, having been boxed in approaching the final straight, he responded well to lead just inside the last two furlongs before Spinning World brushed him aside and beat him by three lengths. Being dropped from a mile and a half to a mile is usually the preserve of modest horses or failures at the longer distance, so the spectacle of Helissio taking on this new challenge was a treat for racegoers if not for his trainer.

A slightly longer-term view, however, is that going for the Moulin cost Helissio any remaining chance he had of being at his best for the 1997 Arc de Triomphe. No one can know for sure, but he could well have been shown up anyway—the ground in the Arc was firm and the other jockeys knew all about him. Helissio's pre-race demeanour didn't bode well; if anything he was looking a little sour. Asmussen by this stage might have been feeling a little

Mr E. Sarasola's "Helissio"

sour as well, because he had lost the ride, Lellouche stating that 'the horse doesn't run for him.' With Peslier (who had ridden him in the Moulin) now on Peintre Celebre, Helissio was reunited with Dominic Boeuf. This third partnership had been the one with which Helissio began his career, Boeuf being replaced after Helissio had fought strongly for his head in the Prix du Jockey-Club the previous June. There were no similar problems in the Arc as Helissio, the 5/2 second favourite, helped to set a strong early pace. He had a clear lead seven furlongs out and was still in front entering the straight, but this time that lead could not be extended. Peintre Celebre was the first to go past him, approaching the final furlong, and in the last hundred and fifty yards Helissio faded into sixth. Perhaps the real tragedy for him was not that he had lost, but that the brilliance of Peintre Celebre's success had made Helissio's own Arc triumph seem less special. We do just give Peintre Celebre the edge, but, rest assured, Helissio put up an exceptional performance to win twelve months earlier, the best in the race at that stage since Dancing Brave's in 1986.

		Northern Dancer (b 1961)	Nearctic
	Fairy King (USA) (b 1982)		Natalma
Helissio (FR) (b.c. 1993)		Fairy Bridge (b 1975)	Bold Reason
			Special
	Helice (USA) (b 1988)	Slewpy (b or br 1980)	Seattle Slew
			Rare Bouquet
		Hirondelle (b 1981)	Val de L'Orne
			Hermanville

On the day the news broke that television viewers would, from the end of the year, no longer be treated to the immaculate French pronunciations of long-serving BBC racing correspondent Julian Wilson, it was also made public that no race commentator would again have to call the name Helissio. As expected, retirement has taken Helissio, a tall, rangy colt, to stud in Japan, to Teruya Yoshida's Shadai Farm. Details of his pedigree were given in *Racehorses of 1996*—what details there are, that is, because there was not much to recommend the family until Helissio came along. He is the first foal of his dam, Helice, a two-year-old one-mile winner in France, but still came along too late to prevent the sale, for approximately £8,000 in 1993, which eventually led her from France to Saudi Arabia, where she died of colic in 1996. Helissio made about £39,700 at the same sale. Reports are still rather confused as to Helice's subsequent progeny, with a colt by Cricket Ball 'believed to be alive' in Kuwait and a 1996 colt in Saudi Arabia being positively identified by Weatherbys as being out of Helice and by one Power Lunch. The Power Lunch colt is unable to race outside Saudi Arabia because that country's stud book is not yet recognised internationally. *E. Lellouche, France*

HELLO DOLLY (IRE) 3 b.f. Mujadil (USA) 119 – Great Leighs 87 (Vaigly 61 Great 127) [1996 61, a69: 5s² 5g³ 5g⁶ 5f² a5g⁴ 6g* 6m⁴ 7f⁴ 7.1m² 8f³ 8g 8g⁶ a8.5g* a8.5g* a8g⁴ 1997 a10g³ a8.5g 12m² 8.5f³ Jun 20] sparely-made filly: modest handicapper: left K. Burke after third start: stays 1½m: acts on any going, including all-weather: often claimer ridden. *E. Truman, USA*

HELLO MISTER 6 b.h. Efisio 120 – Ginnies Petong (Petong 126) [1996 101: 102 5.1g⁶ 6m 6m⁵ 6g⁶ 6f 1997 5.2g 7d 6m 6m⁵ 6m⁵ 6g 7g⁴ 6f³ 6m 6m⁴ 7.3m 5.6m 7d 5m⁵ 5m 5d⁵ 6g Oct 24] sturdy, good-quartered horse: useful performer: generally in good form at 6 yrs, best effort when 1¾ lengths third to Hattab in listed race at Newbury in July: effective around 5f given a test, and probably stays 7f: probably acts on any going: often sweating and edgy: suited by waiting tactics: sold (to join N. Littmoden) 29,000 gns. *T. E. Powell*

HELLO THERE 3 b.g. Picea 99 – Estonia (Kings Lake (USA) 133) [1996 –: 7g – 6m 6m⁵ 1997 10m Apr 8] no sign of ability. *N. Tinkler*

HENBURY PRINCESS 4 ch.f. Teamster 114 – Record Flight (Record Token – 128) [1996 NR 1997 10g 11.7g Sep 8] first foal: dam, maiden on Flat, winning jumper: well beaten in maidens. *R. J. Hodges*

HEN HARRIER   3 ch.f. Polar Falcon (USA) 126 – Circus Feathers 99 (Kris 135)   94
[1996 78: 6m² 6.9g* 7f² 7m³ 8m⁵ 7m 1997 8g* 7.5m⁶ 10m⁴ 10g* 11.9g 10.1g 10.1m⁶
Sep 16] lengthy, unfurnished filly: has a quick action: fairly useful handicapper: won
at Ripon in April and Redcar in June: below form last 3 starts: stayed 1¼m: raced
only on good ground or firmer: suited by waiting tactics: stud. *J. L. Dunlop*

HENLEY (USA)   3 b.c. Salem Drive (USA) – Leap of The Heart (USA) (Nijinsky   86
(CAN) 138) [1996 83p: a6g a7s* 1997 11.8d⁵ 10m* 12d 10.1d 10.3g⁴ Jul 30]
smallish, well-made colt: fairly useful handicapper: won at Lingfield in May: good
fourth at Doncaster in July: may prove best up to 1¼m: easily best turf form on good/
good to firm going, also acts on equitrack: front runner: sent to USA. *D. R. Loder*

HENRY'S MOTHER   3 b.f. Rock City 120 – Sleepline Princess 86 (Royal   76
Palace 131) [1996 NR 1997 8g³ 8g* 10s³ Jun 20] 1,800 2-y-o: sister to useful 5-y-o
Rockforce and half-sister to several winners up to 9f: dam 2-y-o 6f winner: fair form:
won maiden at Leicester in May: ran well when third of 4 in handicap at Goodwood
following month: stays 1¼m: gave trouble stalls at Leicester. *M. R. Channon*

HENRY THE FIFTH   4 b.c. Village Star (FR) 131 – Microcosme 100 (Golden   83
Fleece (USA) 133) [1996 102: 8g⁴ 7d⁴ 10g³ 8f 12.5d 10s a8g 1997 10m⁵ 10m⁶ 10.1g
10s 7.6m⁶ 9d 8d 10d* 8.5m⁶ 9g 8s* 12d² 10.5s⁴ 10.5v Nov 23] leggy, workmanlike
ex-British colt: poor mover: was a useful 3-y-o, but no form in 1997 in 6 starts for
C. Brittain: had much more success in the vasty fields of France, winning minor
event at Le Lion d'Angers in August (trained by J. Pease) and claimer at Longchamp
in October: stays 1½m: acts on good to firm and soft ground: tried in blinkers.
C. Bauer, France

HENRY THE HAWK   6 b.g. Doulab (USA) 115 – Plum Blossom (USA) (Gal-   47
lant Romeo (USA)) [1996 53: 5.9d* 5s* 5m⁵ 6g⁶ 6g⁴ 5g⁵ 7m 6g⁴ 6m 5g² 6d a6g
1997 5m³ 5s⁴ 5s⁴ 6m* 6f⁴ 6g 6m 6g³ 6g⁶ 5m⁶ 6g⁵ a5g⁵ Sep 8] small gelding: poor
handicapper: won at Hamilton (apprentices) in June: generally creditable efforts
afterwards: stays 6f: probably acts on any turf/all-weather: effective visored/
blinkered or not: usually bandaged. *M. Dods*

HENRY THE PROUD (IRE)   2 ch.g. (May 14) Shalford (IRE) 124§ – June God-   61 ?
dess (Junius (USA) 124) [1997 5m⁶ 6m 6m a6g Oct 6] IR 25,000Y: good-quartered
gelding: seventh foal: half-brother to useful 1996 2-y-o sprint winner Miss Stamper
(by Distinctly North) and several winners abroad: dam Irish 7f winner: modest form
first 2 starts but ran poorly afterwards, in seller final outing: blinkered twice. *J. Berry*

HERBSHAN DANCER   3 b.g. Warrshan (USA) 117 – Herbary (USA) (Her-   59 §
bager 136) [1996 59?: 6m 7m⁶ 7f⁵ 7f⁶ 7m 1997 12g² 9.7m 11.6s³ 11.4g 11.6s³ 11.6s⁵
10m⁶ 12m⁵ a14.8g 12d Oct 21] modest maiden handicapper: stays 1½m: probably
acts on any ground: inconsistent, and not one to trust. *B. R. Millman*

HERE COMES A STAR   9 b.g. Night Shift (USA) – Rapidus (Sharpen Up 127)   52
[1996 80d: 5m³ 5g 5g³ 5m⁶ 6d³ 5m⁴ 5g⁶ 5m⁴ 6m 6f 6f⁴ 5g³ 5m 5g 5m³ 6m 1997 5g
5m 5.1g 5f 5f³ 5m⁵ 5.9m⁵ 5m 5m⁴ 6m Oct 5] sturdy, lengthy gelding: has a round
action: modest handicapper: effective at 5f and 6f: acts on hard and dead ground:
blinkered (well below form) earlier in career: best held up in strongly-run race.
J. M. Carr

HERE COMES HERBIE   5 ch.g. Golden Lahab (USA) – Megan's Move 36   76
(Move Off 112) [1996 42: 8g 7d⁶ 11.1g⁵ 11.1g² 12g* 11.9m⁴ 12f² 12.3m⁴ 12.1f⁶ 1997
16s* 12.1d² 16m⁴ 16d* 16g³ 15.9m² 16m³ 16s* 16.1g³ 18g 16s² Nov 6] lengthy
gelding: improved handicapper in 1997: won at Musselburgh in March, Ripon in
April and Redcar in July: excellent second of 17 at Musselburgh final start: stays 2m
well: probably acts on any going: held up. *W. Storey*

HERE'S TO HOWIE (USA)   3 b.c. Hermitage (USA) – Choice Comment   63
(USA) (Rich Cream (USA)) [1996 76: 7f³ 7.6m⁴ 8s⁶ 1997 a8g² 10f* 10.2m 11.4m
11.6s⁵ 11.8g⁶ 10m 10f⁶ 8.2d⁶ 9.7d⁵ Oct 21] tall colt: modest handicapper: won
maiden at Brighton in April: stays 1½m: acts on firm and dead ground: none too
consistent: joined M. Bosley. *R. Hannon*

HERITAGE   3 b.c. Danehill (USA) 126 – Misty Halo 93 (High Top 131) [1996   99
76p: 8m⁴ 1997 10.3m³ 10.5d* 12d* 11.9g 11.9s 12d⁴ 12s Nov 8] well-made colt:
useful performer: won maiden at Haydock and King George V Handicap at Royal

King George V Stakes (Handicap), Royal Ascot—
Heritage produces an astonishing burst to overhaul Taunt

Ascot (by length from Taunt, finishing well) in first half of season: best effort when close fourth in handicap at Newmarket in October, staying on strongly having been set plenty to do: will stay beyond 1½m: acts on dead ground, twice disappointing on soft: sold 120,000 gns in October. *J. H. M. Gosden*

HERMANUS 3 b.g. Lugana Beach 116 – Hitravelscene (Mansingh (USA) 120) – [1996 –: 6g⁵ 1997 7.1s a7g Apr 7] brother to 4-y-o Tropical Beach, and half-brother to winning sprinter B Grade (by Lucky Wednesday): no form: blinkered final start. *M. A. Jarvis*

HERMINIUS (IRE) 2 b.c. (Mar 8) Ballad Rock 122 – Scotia Rose (Tap On 84 p Wood 130) [1997 6m⁴ 7s⁴ 7f⁵ 8g* Oct 18] 29,000Y: half-brother to several winners, including 1989 2-y-o 6f winner Fanellan (by Try My Best) and 7-y-o Amiarge: dam, Irish middle-distance winner, half-sister to dam of Greenland Park and Red Sunset: promising colt: won maiden at Redcar by 2 lengths from Eco Friendly, left with bit to do when switched at halfway: shaped well first 2 starts, off 3 months after disappointing on third: shapes as though will be suited by at least 1¼m: should make a useful handicapper. *J. L. Dunlop*

HERNIECE 2 b.f. (Mar 17) Weldnaas (USA) 112 – Sizzling Sista (Sizzling – Melody 117) [1997 a6g a8.5g Dec 13] first reported foal: dam unraced: well held in maidens at Southwell (slowly away) and Wolverhampton. *J. L. Harris*

HERON ISLAND (IRE) 4 b.c. Shirley Heights 130 – Dalawara (IRE) (Top 116 Ville 129) [1996 114: 9m⁶ 10m* 11.5f² 12m 12m* 14.6m 12m⁴ 14v* 1997 15.5d³ 16.4g⁵ 20g⁴ Jun 19] leggy colt: smart performer: best efforts when 2½ lengths fifth to Persian Punch in Henry II Stakes at Sandown in May and 6¾ lengths fourth to Celeric in Gold Cup at Royal Ascot: stays 2½m: acts on any going. *P. W. Chapple-Hyam*

HERR TRIGGER 6 gr.g. Sharrood (USA) 124 – Four-Legged Friend 101 (Ara- 70 gon 118) [1996 82: a10g² 1997 10m 10g⁶ 10.5m³ 12g³ Aug 22] leggy gelding: fair a– handicapper: stays 1½m: acts on firm ground and on equitrack: blinkered nowadays: carries head high: has won when sweating and edgy: consistent. *Dr J. D. Scargill*

HERSHEBAR 7 ch.h. Stanford 121§ – Sugar Token 66 (Record Token 128) –
[1996 NR 1997 a6g a7g a7g a6g Mar 17] lightly raced since 4 yrs, and little sign of
ability nowadays. *Mrs V. A. Aconley*

HE'S GOT WINGS (IRE) 4 b.g. In The Wings 128 – Mariella 123 (Sir Gay- 57
lord) [1996 62: 8.2d 11.6m 14.1m a9.4g⁵ 10.8m² 10f⁵ 12.4m* 10.9m⁵ 16.1m* 17.1m
1997 12m 13d³ 14.1d 16.2s 17.1g Aug 17] smallish gelding: has a quick action:
modest handicapper: left Mrs J. Ramsden after fourth start: stays 2m well: acts on
good to firm and dead ground: sometimes visored/blinkered, only once in 1997: has
been bandaged near-hind. *M. A. Peill*

HETRA HEIGHTS (USA) 2 b.f. (Jan 28) Cox's Ridge (USA) – Top Hope 115 – p
(High Top 131) [1997 6d 6g Oct 27] 19,000Y: strong, lengthy filly: half-sister to
useful 1m winner Free Thinker (by Shadeed) and 1990 2-y-o 6f winner Moonflute
(by The Minstrel): dam, 7f winner at 2 yrs, later suited by 1½m: never placed to
challenge in big-field maidens at Newmarket and Leicester: has plenty of scope, and
should do better. *W. J. Musson*

HEUBACH BOY 3 b.g. Belmez (USA) 131 – North Pacific (USA) 81 (Hawaii) 42
[1996 NR 1997 7f⁶ 9d 7g 13d³ 15.4m a14g Nov 17] leggy, lengthy gelding: third
reported foal: dam 1m (at 2 yrs) and 1½m winner: poor maiden handicapper: left Mrs
A. Swinbank after fourth start: best effort at 13f: blinkered final start. *J. Pearce*

HEVER GOLF ANGEL (IRE) 3 b.f. Mujadil (USA) 119 – Doon Belle 36
(Ardoon 124) [1996 NR 1997 8g 5m 7.5s 7m⁶ 13.8m³ Sep 20] IR 1,000Y: lengthy,
unfurnished filly: closely related to a winner in Italy by Magical Wonder and
half-sister to 3 winners, including Astral Weeks (up to 1¼m), by Astronef): dam, Irish
5f and 7f winner, half-sister to smart Rocamadour: bad maiden. *P. C. Haslam*

HEVER GOLF CHARGER (IRE) 3 b.g. Silver Kite (USA) 111 – Peace 57
Carrier (IRE) (Doulab (USA) 115) [1996 60: 5g 6m 6g³ 7f⁵ 6m² 6m a5g⁶ 1997 a6g⁵
a6g² a6g² a7g* a8g² a7g⁶ a7g⁴ a7g³ a8g 7f⁶ 7m² a7g 6g Jul 7] close-coupled gelding:
modest performer: made all in claimer at Lingfield in February: generally not at best
afterwards: effective at 6f to 1m: raced only on good going or firmer on turf, acts on
the all-weather: tried blinkered: sold, to go to Macau. *T. J. Naughton*

HEVER GOLF CHARMER 3 b.g. Precocious 126 – Callas Star (Chief Singer 49
131) [1996 NR 1997 a6g 6m 8d a8g 8g³ 10.8s 12f Sep 17] first foal: dam unraced
half-sister to very smart (at up to 1¾m) Band: poor form at best: left T. J. Naughton
before final start: should stay beyond 1m. *B. S. Rothwell*

HEVER GOLF DANCER 3 b.g. Distant Relative 128 – Blue Rag 70 (Ragusa 51
137) [1996 64: 6m 6.1m⁴ 6m⁵ a6g⁴ 1997 a7g³ a8g a7g² 8.2d Apr 29] sturdy, angular
gelding: modest maiden: finished distressed second start: stays 7f: acts on fibresand
and good to firm ground. *T. J. Naughton*

HEVER GOLF EAGLE 4 b.g. Aragon 118 – Elkie Brooks 82 (Relkino 131) 47
[1996 –, a54: a6g a8g⁵ a7g³ a8g³ a10g² a8g⁶ 8.3s⁵ 8m 10g 10.1m a8g a8g³ 1997 a54
a11s² a12g a10g* a9.4g 8.3s 8s³ Jul 3] good-bodied gelding: modest performer on
all-weather: won (first time) minor event at Lingfield in February: poor on turf: stays
1¼m: acts on the all-weather and soft going: blinkered (ran poorly) once: inconsistent: joined G. L. Moore. *T. J. Naughton*

HEVER GOLF GLORY 3 b.c. Efisio 120 – Zaius 94 (Artaius (USA) 129) 99
[1996 NR 1997 8g⁴ 8g² 8d³ 8m* 8s⁶ 8m⁴ 9g Aug 24] sixth foal: half-brother to
French winner at up to 11f Fernando Cortez (by Darshaan): dam Irish 2-y-o 5f
winner: useful performer: placed in maiden at Warwick and listed race at Chantilly in
May: won equivalent of 2000 Guineas at Taby in Sweden in June: stays 1m: acts on
good to firm and dead ground: sold 14,000 gns in October. *T. J. Naughton*

HEVER GOLF LOVER (IRE) 3 b.f. Taufan (USA) 119 – Anagall (USA) 81 –
(Irish River (FR) 131) [1996 61: 5f 6f a6g a7g² a5g* 1997 a5g* a5g⁵ 7m 5.1g 6f Sep a57
18] angular filly: modest performer: landed odds in 4-runner minor event at Lingfield
in January: should prove effective over 6f: acts on equitrack, little form on turf: races
prominently. *T. J. Naughton*

HEVER GOLF MACHINE 2 ch.c. (Feb 18) Rudimentary (USA) 118 – Stop 61
Press (USA) 93 (Sharpen Up 127) [1997 5m³ 5g a5s Nov 10] 6,500F: workmanlike a?
colt: first foal: dam 1¼m winner, also successful at 1m and 11.5f in France at 4 yrs:

third at Sandown in July, easily best effort in maidens: will be suited by further than 5f. *T. J. Naughton*

HEVER GOLF MAGIC (IRE)   3 ch.f. Ballad Rock 122 – Track Twenty Nine   57
(IRE) (Standaan (FR) 118) [1996 –: 7d a7s 1997 6m⁴ 8g Sep 4] tall, leggy filly: modest maiden: form only when fourth at Folkestone. *T. J. Naughton*

HEVER GOLF MOVER   3 ch.f. Efisio 120 – Joyce's Best 58 (Tolomeo 127)   73
[1996 66: 5m⁴ 6m 5g a6g a8g³ a7g⁴ 1997 a7g⁶ 6f* 6m² a6g 6m⁴ 7.1d⁴ 7m 5.9m* 7m² 6g² 6.1m Sep 15] fair performer: won minor event at Brighton in April and handicap at Carlisle in August: best at 6f/7f: acts on firm going (probably on dead) and equitrack. *T. J. Naughton*

HEVER GOLF PASSION (IRE)   2 b.f. (Mar 22) Pips Pride 117 – Base Camp   66
80 (Derring-Do 131) [1997 7m 7d³ Oct 27] 4,200Y: half-sister to several winners, including stayer Revisit (by Busted) and useful performer at up to 1¼m Crampon (by Shirley Heights): dam won 3 times at up to 1¼m: better effort in maidens at Lingfield when running-on third to Madjamila: will stay at least 1m. *T. J. Naughton*

HEVERGOLF PRINCESS (IRE)   2 ch.f. (Jan 26) Petardia 113 – High Profile   –
(High Top 131) [1997 7m 8.2g a6g⁵ Dec 4] 4,200F: half-sister to 3 winners, including 7-y-o Panther and 7f/1m winner Kindergarten Boy (by Mon Tresor): dam unraced half-sister to Middle Park winner Mattaboy: well held in maidens. *T. J. Naughton*

HEVER GOLF RANGER   2 b.c. (May 9) Efisio 120 – Bold Green (FR) (Green   78 +
Dancer (USA) 132) [1997 7m 6f³ 7s² 8s⁶ Nov 16] close-coupled colt: half-brother to several winners, including 4-y-o Prima Verde and French 7f/1m winner Going Crazy (by Persepolis): dam French 5f and 1m winner: placed in October in maiden at Lingfield and minor event at Deauville: apparently best effort when close last of 6 in listed race at Bordeaux, final outing: stays 1m: moved poorly to post on debut. *T. J. Naughton*

HEVER GOLF ROCKET   3 b.g. Efisio 120 – Truly Bold 76 (Bold Lad (IRE)   78
133) [1996 NR 1997 6s⁴ 6g* 5m 6g³ 6m³ Aug 17] fourth foal: brother to 5-y-o Hever Golf Star and half-brother to 2 winners, including 11.5f winner Bold Buster (by Bustino): dam ran twice at 2 yrs: fair performer: won maiden at Folkestone in July: best efforts when third in handicaps last 2 starts: will stay beyond 6f. *T. J. Naughton*

HEVER GOLF ROSE   6 b.m. Efisio 120 – Sweet Rosina 61 (Sweet Revenge   112
129) [1996 118: 5m 6g² 6g² 5f⁴ 6v² 6m³ 5m² 5m³ 6g² 6f⁴ 5.2m² 5d³ 5s³ 1997 5.5g⁶ 5m² 5d* 5g 5m³ 6m* 5d³ 6d⁴ 6g 5d⁶ 6s⁵ 5.2g 5f 6d 5d* 6s⁵ Nov 16] small, strong mare: has a quick action: not quite so good as in her prime but still a smart performer: won Prix de Saint-Georges at Longchamp (by short neck from Titus Livius) in May, listed race at Taby in June and Prix du Petit Couvert at Longchamp (beat Kistena by

Prix de Saint-Georges, Longchamp—
Hever Golf Rose is all out to hold off Titus Livius (No. 2), Wardara (No. 4) and Hambye

447

1½ lengths) in October: effective at 5f and 6f: acts on any going: often bandaged behind: effective from front or held up: tough and game. *T. J. Naughton*

HEVER GOLF STAR   5 b.g. Efisio 120 – Truly Bold 76 (Bold Lad (IRE) 133)   63
[1996 78: a5g* a5g³ 1997 5m³ Apr 10] modest handicapper: barely stayed 5f: acted on firm ground, went well on the all-weather: dead. *T. J. Naughton*

HEVER GOLF STORMER (IRE)   3 b.c. Mujadil (USA) 119 – Clogher Head   49
(Sandford Lad 133) [1996 52, a42: 6m 5.1m 5g 5m² 5f⁵ 5.1m³ 5m³ 6m³ a5g⁶ a6g⁵   a38
a7g⁴ 1997 a6g⁵ a6g a5g 5m³ 6.1g 5m 6.9m a6g Nov 14] modest maiden on turf, poor at best on the all-weather: left T. J. Naughton after sixth start: probably stays 7f: yet to race on ground softer than good on turf: inconsistent. *B. A. Pearce*

HEY UP MATE (IRE)   2 b.g. (Apr 14) River Falls 113 – Damira (FR) (Pharly   –
(FR) 130) [1997 a5g 5.9f 6g 5g a6g 6m 6.1g⁵ Sep 28] 14,000 2-y-o: workmanlike gelding: half-brother to a winner abroad by Persian Bold: dam never ran: little worthwhile form: blinkered third start. *J. Berry*

HIBERNICA (IRE)   3 b. or br.f. Law Society (USA) 130 – Brave Ivy 68 (Decoy   69
Boy 129) [1996 – : 6m 1997 8d⁴ 7m⁶ 8.1s 7g Sep 4] leggy filly: fair maiden: easily best effort when fourth at Salisbury: should be suited by further than 1m. *G. B. Balding*

HIBLAZE (IRE)   3 b.c. Lahib (USA) 129 – Gezalle (Shareef Dancer (USA) 135)   –
[1996 NR 1997 10s Oct 8] IR 40,000Y: second foal: dam Irish 9f winner: tailed off in maiden. *K. McAuliffe*

HICKORY (IRE)   2 b.g. (May 6) Fayruz 116 – La Mortola (Bold Lad (IRE) 133)   74 ?
[1997 5m⁵ 6m 7.1m 7d Oct 27] 11,500Y: leggy, useful-looking gelding: brother to 4-y-o 7f winner More Risk and half-brother to 3-y-o Orange Jasmine (by Masterclass), fairly useful 7f winner at 2 yrs, and 1990 2-y-o 6f winner Luttrellstown (by Precocious), all in Ireland: dam unraced half-sister to Katies: appeared to show fair form in minor event and Coventry Stakes at Ascot first 2 starts: disappointed afterwards, off 3 months before final outing. *M. J. Haynes*

HIDDEN AGENDA (FR)   3 b.f. Machiavellian (USA) 123 – Ever Genial 117   55
(Brigadier Gerard 144) [1996 NR 1997 8f⁶ 10.3d 8.3m⁵ 12d 11.1m⁴ 9s⁶ Oct 13] sixth foal: half-sister to 3 winners at 1¼m+, including fairly useful Receptionist (by Reference Point): dam smart 7f/1m winner from good family: modest maiden handicapper: too free in blinkers final start: stays 11f: sold 22,000 gns in December. *R. Charlton*

HIDDEN MEADOW   3 b.c. Selkirk (USA) 129 – Spurned (USA) 91 (Robellino   114
(USA) 127) [1996 103p: 7m⁵ 7.9g* 7.3s³ 1997 7g* 8m 7g* 8m 7.3m⁴ 7d* 7g² 7m Oct 5] lengthy colt: good mover with a long stride: smart performer on his day: successful in European Free Handicap at Newmarket (by 5 lengths from Granny's

NGK Spark Plugs European Free Handicap, Newmarket—
Hidden Meadow shows much the best finishing speed in a steadily-run race

Pet) in April, valuable minor event at Epsom in June and listed race at York (beat Poteen ½ length) in August: ¾-length second to Russian Revival in listed race at Newbury in September: best efforts at 7f on good/dead ground. *I. A. Balding*

HIDING PLACE 2 b.f. (Mar 26) Saddlers' Hall (IRE) 126 – Sanctuary Cove 59
(Habitat 134) [1997 6.1g 6d⁵ 7g 8d⁴ 10d* 8m Nov 4] fourth foal: half-sister to 1m seller winner Amnesty Bay (by Thatching): dam half-sister to smart French stayer Cutting Reef: modest performer: won seller at Leicester in October (sold out of M. Bell's stable 10,000 gns): well held in nursery final start: should stay 1½m+: acts on dead going. *W. Storey*

HIGH AND LOW 2 b.f. (Mar 25) Rainbow Quest (USA) 134 – Cruising Height 78 p
112 (Shirley Heights 130) [1997 7d² Nov 5] well-made, attractive filly: fourth foal: sister to 5-y-o Corradini: dam, stayed 1½m, half-sister to Park Hill winner Trampship out of half-sister to Prix Vermeille winner Paulista: 7/1 from 9/2 and very green, shaped promisingly when 2½ lengths second of 19 to Scorned in maiden at Doncaster, soon niggled along then staying on well after being switched, clear of remainder: should be well suited by 1¼m+: sure to improve and win races. *B. W. Hills*

HIGH AND MIGHTY 2 b.g. (Apr 30) Shirley Heights 130 – Air Distingue – p
(USA) 120 (Sir Ivor 135) [1997 8d 7d Nov 7] sturdy, angular gelding: ninth foal: half-brother to several winners, including useful French middle-distance performer Stage Manner (by In The Wings) and Poule d'Essai des Poulains winner Vettori (by Machiavellian): dam, 6f to 8.5f winner, third in Prix de Diane: signs of ability in large-field maidens at Newmarket and Doncaster, then gelded: should stay at least 1½m: should do better at 3 yrs. *J. H. M. Gosden*

HIGHBORN (IRE) 8 b. or br.g. Double Schwartz 128 – High State 72 (Free 104
State 125) [1996 97: 6s 6g³ 7.6g* 7m⁴ 6.1m⁴ 7m² 6g 7d 7.1f 7m* 7g⁵ 1997 6m 7g 7.6v 7g 7m⁴ 8.1m 7d² 7g 7m 8g* 7d* 7m 8m Nov 1] sturdy gelding: useful handicapper: better than ever in 1997, carrying top weight to victory at Ripon (Ripon Rowels) and Chester (by head from Concer Un) within 5 days in August: effective at 7f (given a test) to 1m: acts on fibresand (yet to race on equitrack) and on firm and dead ground: has run well sweating and for apprentice: game and genuine. *P. S. Felgate*

HIGHBURY LEGEND 2 ch.g. (Apr 28) Mazilier (USA) 107 – Jans Contessa –
68 (Rabdan 129) [1997 5g 6d a7g⁴ a8g a10s⁵ a7g a6g Dec 22] 7,000Y, 6,200 2-y-o: fifth foal: brother to 1995 2-y-o 6f winner Don't Tell Vicki: dam sprint maiden out of sister to Runnett: little worthwhile form: visored last 2 starts. *Bob Jones*

HIGH CARRY 2 b.f. (Apr 5) Forzando 122 – Carn Maire 83 (Northern Prospect 84
(USA)) [1997 5m 6d 5m* 5d⁵ 6g³ 5s* 6g² 5m² 5m⁵ Oct 2] lengthy, good-topped filly: has scope: has rather round action: third foal: half-sister to fair 6f winner Maple Burl (by Dominion) and a winner in Holland by Robellino: dam 2-y-o 5f winner: fairly useful performer: won claimer (claimed out of J. Banks's stable £12,000) at Beverley in July and nursery at Sandown in August: stays 6f: acts on good to firm and soft ground: races prominently: consistent. *N. Tinkler*

HIGH DESIRE (IRE) 4 b.f. High Estate 127 – Sweet Adelaide (USA) 98 (The 47
Minstrel (CAN) 135) [1996 59: 12m³ 14.1m⁴ 11.8d 12g² 11.6m² 11.6g⁴ 12m 1997 12m 12m 12f⁶ 10g⁴ 10s⁵ 11.6m Jul 21] neat filly: poor maiden handicapper: stays 1½m: acts on good to firm ground, may be unsuited by soft. *J. R. Arnold*

HIGH DOMAIN (IRE) 6 b.g. Dominion Royale 112 – Recline 70 (Wollow 132) 71 d
[1996 77: 6f 5d* a6g 6d* 6g³ 6f 5m⁴ 6m 6f 6v 6.1s 5s* 1997 5g 5m³ 5m 5.7g⁵ 5v⁵ 6.1g 5m 5g 5.1g Sep 11] sturdy, strong-quartered gelding: good mover: fair handicapper: well below form in 1997 after second start: stays 6f: acts on good to firm and soft ground, below form on the all-weather: effective blinkered, rarely tried nowadays: edgy sort: usually races prominently. *J. L. Spearing*

HIGHFIELD FIZZ 5 b.m. Efisio 120 – Jendor 82 (Condorcet (FR)) [1996 50, 52
a–: 10.5d a11g 11m 10.5m⁵ 10s 10g⁶ 15.8g 14.1m* 16g 15.1s⁶ a14.8g 1997 12g a–
14.1s² 14.1m³ 14.1g⁴ 16.2m² 16m⁵ 16s² 16m⁵ 16g³ 12d⁵ 16g² 17.1m³ 14.1g²
18d² Oct 20] good-topped mare: has a round action: modest handicapper: formerly inconsistent, but in good form for most of 1997, runner-up 6 times: stays 2¼m: acts

449

on any turf ground: tends to carry head high: reportedly gurgled ninth start. *C. W. Fairhurst*

HIGHFIELD PET   4 b.g. Efisio 120 – Jendor 82 (Condorcet (FR)) [1996 –: 8g⁶   –
10m 1997 13.8g 16.1m 12g 10m Sep 26] of little account. *C. W. Fairhurst*

HIGH FIVE (IRE)   7 b.g. High Line 125 – Finger Lake (Kings Lake (USA) 133)   54
[1996 NR 1997 a12g a16g² a16g* 21.6g³ 17.2d* a14g² 16.2s Jun 21] leggy gelding: a39
modest handicapper: won at Lingfield in March and Bath in May: pulled up final
start: probably stays 21.6f: acts on dead ground and the all-weather. *R. Ingram*

HIGHFLYING   11 br.g. Shirley Heights 130 – Nomadic Pleasure 91 (Habitat 134)   76 d
[1996 84: 13.9m 16.5g⁵ 14d 11.9m 16.1m 12.3m* 14m⁶ 14.1m* 14.6m⁵ 14.1f³
13.9g 1997 16d 12.4m⁴ 16m 18g 16m Jul 19] strong gelding: usually impressed in
appearance: poor mover: won 15 of 62 races, notably Northumberland Plate in 1993:
mostly well below form in 1997: stayed 2m: acted on firm and dead going, not soft:
sometimes bandaged: went well with forcing tactics: genuine: retired. *G. M. Moore*

HIGH GAIN   2 b.f. (Feb 6) Puissance 110 – Femme Formidable (Formidable   69
(USA) 125) [1997 5.1d³ 5d² 6g 5.3f* 5.2g³ 5.3m³ 5.1g 5m⁴ Oct 31] 10,500Y: fifth
foal: sister to fair 1996 2-y-o 6f winner Shuwaikh and half-sister to 3 winners,
including 6f (at 2 yrs, fairly useful) and 9f winner Prima Volta (by Primo Dominie):
dam, poor maiden, stayed 1m: fair performer: won maiden at Brighton in July: in
frame in minor event and nurseries afterwards: should stay 6f: acts on firm and dead
ground: tends to flash tail: hung throughout penultimate start. *P. Howling*

HIGH INTRIGUE (IRE)   3 b. or br.c. Shirley Heights 130 – Mild Intrigue   91 p
(USA) 91 (Sir Ivor 135) [1996 68p: 8f⁶ 1997 12d⁴ 13.4v* 14m* 13.9g 16d* Sep
13] useful-looking colt: fairly useful form: unimpressive in landing odds in 3-runner
maiden at Chester in June: much better efforts to win handicaps at Sandown in July
and Goodwood (by head from Lady of the Lake) in September: will stay beyond 2m:
has won on heavy, much better form on good to firm and dead ground: capable of
better still. *H. R. A. Cecil*

HIGH JINKS   2 b.c. (Apr 8) High Estate 127 – Waffling 68 (Lomond (USA) 128)   –
[1997 6g⁵ 7g 8.2d Oct 30] 8,600Y: third foal: dam, maiden who probably stayed
1¼m, granddaughter of 1000 Guineas winner Night Off: well held in maidens and
minor event, off 2 months before final start. *B. Smart*

HIGHLAND LORD   2 b.c. (Mar 15) Primo Dominie 121 – Tarvie 101 (Swing   –
Easy (USA) 126) [1997 6d 6g a6g Dec 4] stocky colt: half-brother to several winners,
including sprinter Macfarlane and very speedy 1985 2-y-o Stalker (both by Kala
Shikari): dam sprinter: well beaten in maidens: blinkered final start. *M. J. Fetherston-Godley*

HIGHLAND PASS (IRE)   3 b.g. Petorius 117 – Whatawoman (Tumble Wind   –
(USA)) [1996 61: 5s 5g⁵ 5m⁶ 6.1s 8s 1997 a8g Mar 24] smallish, sturdy gelding:
modest maiden: tailed off only 3-y-o start. *G. Thorner*

HIGH LOW (USA)   9 b.g. Clever Trick (USA) – En Tiempo (USA) (Bold Hour)   43
[1996 NR 1997 a12g a7g 10g 8d 12.3m² 11.1d⁵ 9.9m Jul 29] strong gelding: poor
handicapper nowadays: left W. Jenks after second start: won twice over hurdles after
final one: stays 1½m: acts on firm and soft going. *M. D. Hammond*

HIGHLY PLEASED (USA)   2 b.c. (Feb 15) Hansel (USA) – Bint Alfalla   58
(USA) (Nureyev (USA) 131) [1997 7d³ 7f Oct 29] quite good-topped colt: has scope:
first reported foal: dam unraced daughter of a stakes-placed sprint winner at 2 yrs in
USA: modest form in 3-runner private sweepstakes at Newmarket (backward) and
Yarmouth maiden. *E. A. L. Dunlop*

HIGHLY PRIZED   3 b.g. Shirley Heights 130 – On The Tiles (Thatch (USA)   82
136) [1996 –p: 8m 1997 11g 12m² 12s 12g⁴ Jun 12] strong, deep-girthed gelding:
fairly useful maiden: will be suited by 1¾m+: well beaten on soft ground: sold (to
join J. King) 17,000 gns in October. *I. A. Balding*

HIGHLY RESPECTED (IRE)   3 b.f. High Estate 127 – Respectfully (USA)   57
(The Minstrel (CAN) 135) [1996 NR 1997 7m⁴ 10g 7g 7.6d 7s a7g 7m Oct 7] IR
5,000F, 14,500Y: close-coupled filly: sixth foal: sister to a maiden and half-sister to 3

winners, including Irish 1¼m and 2m winner Limbo Lady (by Theatrical): dam ran once in France: modest maiden: should be suited by 1m+: tailed off on soft going: tried blinkered. *A. Bailey*

HIGH MONEY 2 b.c. (Feb 13) Dilum (USA) 115 – Renira 60 (Relkino 131) 56
[1997 5g⁵ 6g⁵ 7g⁵ 6m 5.3m⁶ 5.3f² 8.2d a7g Oct 20] 16,000Y: rather leggy colt: eighth a?
foal: half-brother to several winners, including 3-y-o Diamond Eyre and 1990 2-y-o
Summer Sands (5f, by Mummy's Game): dam lightly-raced maiden: modest maiden
on balance: second in seller at Brighton in October: seems a sprinter: acts on firm
ground: blinkered fifth and final outings. *G. Lewis*

HIGH NOON 2 b.c. (Mar 31) Shirley Heights 130 – Hocus 88 (High Top 131) 67 p
[1997 7m Oct 2] 55,000Y: fifth foal: brother to fair 1¼m winner Trick and
half-brother to 1993 2-y-o 5f winner Hali (by Rousillon): dam, 7f winner, half-sister
to Middle Park winner Hittite Glory: 12/1 and green, mid-division in 22-runner
maiden at Newmarket won by Quiet Assurance, held up and not knocked about:
moved short to post: will do better. *L. M. Cumani*

HIGH ON LIFE 3 b.g. Mazilier (USA) 107 – Tina Rosa (Bustino 136) [1996 64: 67
8f 10g² 1997 10f² 12d² 14.1m 12m³ 11.9g³ 11.9d Sep 5] fair maiden: should stay
beyond 1½m: blinkered (took keen hold and saddle slipped) final start: sold 20,000
gns in October. *A. C. Stewart*

HIGH PREMIUM 9 b.g. Forzando 122 – High Halo 64 (High Top 131) [1996 88
85: a7g² a9.4g⁶ a9.4g⁴ a8g³ a8g* a7g* 7g⁴ 8g⁴ 8.1d⁴ a7g* 7.6d 8m⁵ 8m² 8.1d* 8d*
8g² 8g a9.4g³ 1997 a7s 8m⁵ 9.2d* 6.9g* 8m³ 8.5d* 8.5d³ 8.9d⁴ 8d⁴ 8.1m² 8m³ 8.9s²
Sep 3] sturdy gelding: fairly useful performer: won claimers at Hamilton and
Carlisle in April and handicap at Beverley in May: well below form last 3 starts:
ideally needs stiff test at 1m, and stays 1¼m: acts on firm and soft ground and on
fibresand: blinkered (ran creditably) once earlier in career: often bandaged: tough.
R. A. Fahey

HIGH PRIORITY (IRE) 4 b.c. Marju (IRE) 127 – Blinding (IRE) (High Top –
131) [1996 –: 6g⁵ 6d 5d 5.6m 1997 7g Oct 18] no form since fairly useful 2-y-o.
M. J. Haynes

HIGH PYRENEES 5 b.g. Shirley Heights 130 – Twyla 101 (Habitat 134) [1996 –
–: 16.5g 11.9m 1997 12.3m Jul 19] sturdy gelding: fair winner in 1995: well held last
2 seasons. *F. Murphy*

HIGH-RISE (IRE) 2 b.c. (May 3) High Estate 127 – High Tern 93 (High Line 84 p
125) [1997 7d* Nov 7] quite attractive colt: seventh foal: half-brother to 3-y-o Hi
Mujtahid, 10-y-o Sooty Tern and 2 winners abroad: dam winning staying half-sister
to very smart middle-distance stayer High Hawk (dam of In The Wings): 8/1, won
maiden at Doncaster more convincingly than result suggests, going well when short
of room over 1f out and quickening under pressure to catch Volontiers on post: should
stay at least 1¼m: should make at least a useful 3-y-o. *L. M. Cumani*

HIGH SHERIFF (IRE) 2 b.g. (Feb 17) High Estate 127 – Call Me Miss (Hello 92
Gorgeous (USA) 128) [1997 6s² 7m* Jul 19] IR 13,000Y: fourth foal: half-brother to
5-y-o Hand of Straw and a winner in Spain by Last Tycoon: dam Irish 1¼m winner:
landed odds comfortably in maiden at Warwick: had shown fairly useful form when
clear second to Toblersong in similar event at Epsom on debut: sent to Hong Kong.
W. J. Haggas

HIGH SHOT 7 b.g. Darshaan 133 – Nollet (High Top 131) [1996 –: 7g⁶ 11.7f³ –
1997 7d Apr 26] big ex-French gelding: last on all outings here. *G. Lewis*

HIGHSPEED (IRE) 5 ch.g. Double Schwartz 128 – High State 72 (Free State 59
125) [1996 63: a7g 7d* 8d* 8m² 10f⁶ 8d⁴ 8.3f 1997 8g 8f³ 8m 8.2m 8.1m 8g Aug 23]
small, lightly-made gelding: modest handicapper: ran as though something amiss
third start, and below form afterwards, including in blinkers: stays 1m: acts on firm
and dead ground: held up: joined P. Felgate. *S. E. Kettlewell*

HIGH SPIRITS (IRE) 3 b.g. Great Commotion (USA) 123 – Spoilt Again 91 80
(Mummy's Pet 125) [1996 63+: 5d⁶ 5d³ 5d 1997 8.5m⁵ 8g⁵ 6m⁶ 8s 6m³ 7m* 7g⁴
7.1d* 7s 8.5m* 7m² 8m* 9m* 8m 8m³ 8g Oct 18] big, close-coupled gelding: fairly
useful performer: progressed well in 1997, winning maiden at Catterick and handi-

caps at Musselburgh, Beverley, Newcastle and Ripon by mid-August, including 2 apprentice races: stays 9f: acts on good to firm and dead ground, well held on soft: best in blinkers: consistent. *T. D. Easterby*

HIGH SUMMER   7 b.g. Green Desert (USA) 127 – Beacon Hill 81 (Bustino 136)   –
[1996 –: 13.3m 16.2d 1997 a14g⁵ May 19] tall, workmanlike gelding: fair stayer at 4 yrs: no form since. *T. Thomson Jones*

HIGH TENSION (USA)   2 b.c. (Feb 23) Sadler's Wells (USA) 132 – Very   74 p
Confidential (USA) (Fappiano (USA)) [1997 8m⁴ 8m³ Oct 23] $625,000Y: first foal: dam US maiden half-sister to Grade 1 1¼m winner Awe Inspiring from family of Zilzal, Polish Precedent and Culture Vulture: fair form in maidens at Goodwood and Brighton: should be well suited by 1¼m+: should still do better. *P. F. I. Cole*

HIGHTIDE   5 b.m. Lugana Beach 116 – Moon Charter 45 (Runnymede 123)   –
[1996 –: a7g 1997 a10g Jan 16] no sign of ability. *J. R. Arnold*

HIGHWAYMAN (IRE)   2 b.c. (May 17) Danehill (USA) 126 – Millerette (Mill   82 p
Reef (USA) 141) [1997 7s⁵ 7f³ 8f⁴ Oct 29] IR 78,000Y: tall, attractive colt: on the weak side at 2 yrs: seventh foal: half-brother to several winners, including French 1996 2-y-o 7f winner Mille Flora (by Be My Guest) and fairly useful 7f (at 2 yrs) and 1¼m winner Baby Loves (by Sadler's Wells): dam 1¼m winner, half-sister to Irish St Leger winner Dark Lomond: progressive form in maidens: staying-on fourth to Publisher at Yarmouth: will be well suited by 1¼m, and may well stay further: type to make a better 3-y-o, and do well in handicaps. *M. R. Stoute*

HI HOH (IRE)   4 gr.f. Fayruz 116 – Late Date (Goldhill 125) [1996 NR 1997 a5g   –
a5g Jul 11] seems of little account. *N. P. Littmoden*

HILL FARM BLUES   4 b.f. Mon Tresor 113 – Loadplan Lass 63 (Nicholas Bill   69
125) [1996 –: a14.8g⁴ 12m⁴ 8s a11g 1997 10g* 10d² a12g 10.2m* 10.2m 10.1m 10g⁴ 10.9s⁵ 13.1s² 12g 14.1d Oct 30] fair handicapper: won at Nottingham (seller) in May and Bath in July: stays 13f: acts on good to firm and soft ground, poor efforts on fibresand: often stays away, and has looked reluctant: won novice hurdle in November. *W. M. Brisbourne*

HILL FARM DANCER   6 ch.m. Gunner B 126 – Loadplan Lass 63 (Nicholas   55
Bill 125) [1996 51, a72: a12g² a13g a12g* a12g* a12g² 12d 11.7g⁴ 12.3m³ 17.2m³   a82
11.9m⁵ 15.9d a14g 10.8f a12g⁴ a12g* a12g* a14.8g² a12g⁵ 1997 a12g* a9.4g³ a12g⁴
10m⁴ a12g⁶ 10.8m 11.7m³ a12g³ 10.8m⁵ Jun 9] sparely-made mare: fluent mover: fairly useful handicapper on the all-weather, modest on turf: won at Wolverhampton (sixth course success) in January: effective at 9.4f to 14.8f: better form on fibresand than equitrack: acts on firm ground, possibly not on going softer than good: normally held up: often ridden by apprentice. *W. M. Brisbourne*

HILL MAGIC   2 br.c. (Apr 15) Magic Ring (IRE) 115 – Stock Hill Lass 87 (Air   82
Trooper 115) [1997 6d² 5.7m* 6f⁵ 6m 6m 6g³ 7s Nov 8] close-coupled, useful-looking colt: fifth reported foal: dam won up to 1m: fairly useful form: won maiden at Bath in June: easily best of last 4 runs when third in nursery at Newbury in October, staying on despite meeting trouble: likely to stay beyond 6f (raced on disadvantageous side at 7f). *D. R. C. Elsworth*

HILLSWICK   6 ch.g. Norwick (USA) 125 – Quite Lucky 69 (Precipice Wood   46
123) [1996 27: 11.9g⁵ 12.5f 1997 11.9f² 14.9g² 14g⁴ 17.2m* 16.4s⁶ 16m⁵ 16m⁴ Sep 25] angular gelding: poor handicapper: won for first time at Bath (made most, well ridden by claimer A. Polli) in August: best at further than 1¾m: acts on good to firm and soft going: won over hurdles in October and November. *J. S. King*

HILLZAH (USA)   9 ch.g. Blushing Groom (FR) 131 – Glamour Girl (ARG)   –
(Mysolo 120) [1996 80, a74: a9.4g a12g* a12g 13.8s² 14.1g 16g⁵ a14.8g² 1997 10.2g 12s⁴ a14.8g a14.8g Nov 29] workmanlike gelding: fair handicapper up to 2m at 8 yrs: well held in 1997. *R. Bastiman*

HILTONS EXECUTIVE (IRE)   3 b.f. Petorius 117 – Theatral (Orchestra 118)   43
[1996 –: 5g 5s⁶ 7g 5m⁴ a5g⁵ 6g 1997 7.5d 6m 5d² 5m³ 5.9m 5m⁵ 5.7g 5s³ Oct 14] leggy filly: poor maiden handicapper: best form at 5f: acts on good to firm and soft ground: has pulled hard and hung off bridle: consistent. *E. J. Alston*

HIMSELF (USA)   2 b.c. (Apr 14) El Gran Senor (USA) 136 – Celtic Loot (USA)   88 p
(Irish River (FR) 131) [1997 8d* Oct 28] 84,000Y: fourth foal: brother to useful 7f
winner Don Bosio: dam minor winner around 1m in USA at 4 yrs: 7/2, won maiden
at Leicester by 3 lengths from Speaker's Chair, soon pushed along in rear but leading
over 1f out and drawing away without being hard ridden: should stay 1¼m: sure to
improve. *H. R. A. Cecil*

HI MUJTAHID (IRE)   3 ch.g. Mujtahid (USA) 118 – High Tern 93 (High Line   59
125) [1996 NR 1997 6.1g⁵ 5.1m 6g 6m 7.1d⁶ 6.9m⁶ 7s³ 7g² 7m* 7g² 6.9m³ 6g² 7.1g²
7m Sep 9] 600 2-y-o: lengthy, good-quartered gelding: sixth foal: half-brother to
10-y-o Sooty Tern (by Wassl) and 2 winners abroad: dam winning half-sister
to very smart middle-distance stayer High Hawk (dam of In The Wings): modest
handicapper: trained first 3 starts by J. M. Bradley: won at Ayr in July: effective at 6f
and 7f: acts on good to firm and soft going: effective blinkered or not. *S. E. Kettlewell*

HI NOD   7 b.h. Valiyar 129 – Vikris (Viking (USA)) [1996 106: 7g* 7m² 7.9g² 7m   96
7.9m 8m² 7m 7m⁴ 7g⁵ 1997 7.9g 7m 8m³ 8d⁴ 7m* 7.9d 7.9s Oct 8] strong horse:
impresses in appearance: useful performer: won 4-runner minor event at Chester in
August: ran poorly both subsequent starts: effective at 7f/1m: acts on any going: has
run well when sweating: usually tracks leaders: genuine. *M. J. Camacho*

HINT OF VICTORY   3 ch.g. Ron's Victory (USA) 129 – May Hinton 82 (Main   47
Reef 126) [1996 NR 1997 a7g⁴ a8g* a8g³ 8g⁵ 7m⁵ a7g⁶ Jun 28] third foal: half-   a66
brother to 5-y-o Hinton Rock: dam 2-y-o 6f winner: fair form on the all-weather,
successful in maiden at Lingfield in January: only poor on turf: may stay beyond 1m:
well held in blinkers final start. *M. Bell*

HINTON ROCK (IRE)   5 ch.g. Ballad Rock 122 – May Hinton 82 (Main Reef   39
126) [1996 78: 5.1g 5d 5.1m⁴ a6g 6.1m⁶ 6m³ 5m 1997 8s 5m 5g³ 7f⁵ 6h* 6g* a5g*
Oct 4] strong, compact gelding: fair handicapper in 1996 for A. Bailey: just poor
form at 5 yrs (ran at Folkestone second start): won claimers at Ostend in August and
September and handicap at Sterrebeek in October: stays 6f: acts on hard and dead
ground: often used to be blinkered/visored (not last 2 wins): often sweats:
inconsistent. *Alex Vanderhaeghen, Belgium*

HIO NOD   3 b.g. Precocious 126 – Vikris (Viking (USA)) [1996 –: a6g 1997 a8g   –
a8g 8g Jul 5] seems of little account. *M. J. Camacho*

HIPPIOS   3 b. or br.g. Formidable (USA) 125 – Miss Doody 63 (Gorytus (USA)   –
132) [1996 –: 6g 7d 1997 6.9g 9m 11.8g 12s 15.4s 16.2m⁵ a16g⁶ 16m 16g a12g³   a46
a14g³ a16g a14.8g⁵ a14g Dec 8] poor form: probably stays 15f: acts on fibresand:
tried blinkered. *S. Dow*

HIPPOCRACY   2 b.f. (Apr 20) Unfuwain (USA) 131 – Marielou (FR) (Carwhite   –
127) [1997 7m 8g Oct 24] closely related to 15.4f winner Dakota Girl (by Northern
State) and half-sister to a winner in Belgium by Petong: dam, winner in Belgium, is
sister to Criterium de Saint-Cloud winner Magistros: well held in maidens at
Lingfield and Doncaster: shapes like a stayer. *B. W. Hills*

HIPPY CHICK   3 b.f. Ron's Victory (USA) 129 – Enchanted Tale (USA) 59   –
(Told (USA)) [1996 –p: 6m⁶ 1997 6m 6.1d 8f⁶ May 28] signs of ability but no worthwhile form. *J. R. Jenkins*

HIRASAH (IRE)   3 b.f. Lahib (USA) 129 – Mayaasa (USA) 70 (Lyphard (USA)   103
132) [1996 76p: 6f* 1997 8.1g* 8.1s⁶ 7f Sep 11] lengthy filly: useful effort on first
start for over a year (reportedly had joint and knee problems) to beat Cape Cross,
who gave 13lb, a neck in 5-runner minor event at Sandown in August: well below
that form in listed races afterwards: stayed 1m: visits Marju. *R. W. Armstrong*

HIRST BRIDGE (IRE)   2 b.c. (Feb 21) Mujadil (USA) 119 – Mirabiliary (USA)   77
74 (Crow (FR) 134) [1997 5g² 5d* 5m⁵ 5m⁴ 6g² 7.9s⁴ Sep 4] 27,000Y: lengthy,
good-quartered colt: sixth foal: half-brother to several winners, including 4-y-o
Fairly Sure and 5-y-o Tribal Peace: dam 1¼m winner: fair performer: won maiden at
Carlisle in May: generally ran well afterwards, including in nurseries: stays 1m: acts
on good to firm and soft ground: blinkered fifth start: has got on edge: tends to hang
right: sent to Macau. *M. W. Easterby*

HI RUDOLF   2 b.g. (May 13) Ballet Royal (USA) – Hi Darlin' (Prince de Galles   –
125) [1997 6.1s Jul 1] fifth reported foal: dam poor selling jumper: sire still running
over jumps: tailed off in claimer only start. *A. J. Chamberlain*

HISAR (IRE) 4 br.g. Doyoun 124 – Himaya (IRE) (Mouktar 129) [1996 8g⁴ 10g²   78
10d* 1997 10.2g 7.1m 7.9s 10m² Sep 25] workmanlike ex-Irish gelding: first foal:
dam, second over 1½m from 2 starts in Ireland, daughter of Prix Vermeille winner
Highest Hopes: fairly useful (rated 85) when trained in 1996 by J. Oxx: clearly best
4-y-o effort when second in minor event at Pontefract: stays 1¼m: acts on good to
firm and dead ground: won over hurdles in October. *C. P. E. Brooks*

HIT THE SPOT (IRE) 2 b.f. (Apr 8) Night Shift (USA) – Winning Feature (Red   56
Alert 127) [1997 5d⁶ 6g a5s² Nov 10] 20,000Y: good-bodied filly: half-sister to 3
winners, including fairly useful 6f (at 2 yrs) to 1½m winner Braille (by Vision): dam
Irish 7f winner at 4 yrs: modest form in maidens: runner-up at Lingfield: has been
bandaged. *W. J. Haggas*

HOBART JUNCTION (IRE) 2 ch.c. (May 3) Classic Secret (USA) 91 – Art   65 p
Duo 86 (Artaius (USA) 129) [1997 8.5g⁴ 7.5f⁵ 6.9d⁵ Oct 21] 12,000 2-y-o: fourth
foal: half-brother to 3-y-o Amyas and a winner abroad by Law Society: dam fourth
in listed event at 2 yrs but failed to train on: fair form in maidens: never placed to
challenge when running-on fifth at Folkestone final start: will be suited by 1m+:
should do better. *S. C. Williams*

HOBBS CHOICE 4 b.f. Superpower 113 – Excavator Lady 65 (Most Secret 119)   –
[1996 51: 6s⁶ 6d* 6.1d⁵ 7d 6g 7f⁵ 8.3g² 10s 1997 10g a12g⁵ Aug 15] workmanlike
filly: modest handicapper in 1996: no sign of retaining ability. *G. M. Moore*

HOGAIF (IRE) 2 ch.c. (Apr 29) Persian Bold 123 – Camarat 69 (Ahonoora 122)   70
[1997 6m 7g² Jun 20] 85,000Y: lengthy, useful-looking colt: third foal: half-brother
to 1996 2-y-o 6f winner Colombia (by Mujtahid) and a winning sprinter in Austria by
Polish Patriot: dam 9f winner, half-sister to Park Hill winner Trampship: better effort
in maidens when second at Ayr: should be suited by further than 7f. *J. H. M. Gosden*

HOH CHI MIN 2 ch.f. (Apr 2) Efisio 120 – Special Guest 67 (Be My Guest   98 +
(USA) 126) [1997 5s* 5.2d³ 6d* 6g² 6g⁴ 7d³ 6m* Oct 19] 22,000Y: good-topped
filly: seventh foal: half-sister to several winners, including useful 7f winner
Cragganmore (by Faustus) and 1992 2-y-o 5f winner Special One (by Aragon): dam
2-y-o 7f winner who stayed 9f: useful performer: won maiden at Haydock in May,
minor event at Windsor in June and listed race (comfortably) at Milan in October:
good third in Group 3 event at the Curragh penultimate start: likely to stay 1m: acts
on good to firm and soft ground: consistent. *M. Bell*

HOH DANCER 3 ch.f. Indian Ridge 123 – Alteza Real 84 (Mansingh (USA)   –
120) [1996 66: 5m² 5m⁴ 6d 1997 5m³ 5m 7d Jun 25] sparely-made filly: disappointing maiden: tends to carry head high. *I. A. Balding*

HOH DOWN (IRE) 3 b.f. Fairy King (USA) – Tintomara (IRE) (Niniski (USA)   43
125) [1996 –: 7m a8.5g⁵ a7g⁵ 1997 a8g³ a8g⁴ a7g⁴ a14.8g 10.8g⁶ Jul 12] poor
maiden: best effort on reappearance: left K. McAuliffe after third start: stays 1m: acts
on fibresand: tried visored and blinkered. *R. T. Juckes*

HOH EXPLORER (IRE) 3 ch.g. Shahrastani (USA) 135 – Heart's Harmony   –
(Blushing Groom (FR) 131) [1996 NR 1997 11g 12m⁶ 12.3g 12.3g³ 13.8g⁶ a14g
17.5d Sep 19] IR 5,000Y, resold 58,000Y: seventh foal: dam French maiden: signs of
ability but no worthwhile form: left I. Balding after second start. *D. W. Barker*

HOH EXPRESS 5 b.g. Waajib 121 – Tissue Paper 95 (Touch Paper 113) [1996   94
99: 8s 8d 9s⁵ 8.1d⁶ 10.1m³ 10f 10m² 10.4m 10g³ 9g 10d⁴ 1997 10m 10.1m 10m
12d* 12g³ 12m 12d³ 14m⁶ 12g 12g⁶ 11.9s² 12s Nov 8] rangy gelding: fairly useful
performer: won handicap at Goodwood in May (tailed off in tongue strap time
before): left I. Balding after tenth start: stays 1¾m: acts on good to firm and heavy
ground: none too consistent. *Mrs J. R. Ramsden*

HOH FLYER (USA) 3 b.f. Northern Flagship (USA) 96 – Beautiful Bedouin   66
(USA) (His Majesty (USA)) [1996 66+: 6f 6g⁶ 6.5m 1997 9g 7g⁶ 8.5m a8g 11m⁵
May 26] good-topped filly: fair handicapper: below form last 3 starts: should stay
11f: has raced only on good ground or firmer on turf: sent to USA. *M. Bell*

HOH JUSTICE 2 b.c. (Apr 15) Petardia 113 – Cactus Road (FR) (Iron Duke (FR)   67
122) [1997 5d 5.1m² 7d³ 6f⁴ 7g⁴ 7d 5m⁵ Sep 17] 14,000Y: useful-looking colt:
seventh foal: dam French 1¼m to 13.5f winner: fair maiden: stays 7f: acts on firm

and dead ground: ran creditably in visor final start (disappointing previous 2): sold, to go to Austria. *I. A. Balding*

HOH MAJESTIC (IRE) 4 b.g. Soviet Lad (USA) 94 – Sevens Are Wild 40 – (Petorius 117) [1996 69d: 5d⁶ 6.1g⁶ 6g³ 6g 6g⁶ 8m⁶ 6f⁵ 6m⁵ 6g³ᵈⁱˢ a5g³ 6f² 5g 6d 6m a5g³ 1997 a6g² a6g² a5g⁵ a6g⁵ a6g² a6g* a5g⁵ a6g 7m a6g⁵ a6g* a6g a6g a6g a6g a7g Dec 18] modest handicapper: won at Southwell in March and Wolverhampton (apprentices) in June: ran poorly last 5 starts: seems suited by 6f: acts on firm ground and the all-weather: blinkered earlier in career, usually visored nowadays. *Ronald Thompson* — a60

HOH NAVIGATOR (IRE) 2 ch.c. (Apr 24) Common Grounds 118 – Flying Diva 100 (Chief Singer 131) [1997 5g³ Jun 16] IR 18,000Y: strong, lengthy colt: has scope: fourth foal: half-brother to 4-y-o White Plains: dam, 2-y-o 6f/7f winner, stayed 1m, out of sister to Flying Water: 6/1 and carrying condition, third of 5 in minor event at Windsor. *M. Bell* — 81

HOH RETURNS (IRE) 4 b.g. Fairy King (USA) – Cipriani 102 (Habitat 134) [1996 94: 6m⁶ 6m* 6m³ 6m 5f³ 1997 5.2g⁶ 6g 6d 6g 5m⁶ 6.1g 7m⁵ 6g 8g a6g Sep 20] good-topped gelding: unimpressive mover: fairly useful handicapper: disappointing in 1997 after reappearance, sold only 2,400 gns from M. Bell after ninth start: should stay 7f: raced mainly on good ground or firmer: ran poorly in visor. *B. Preece* — 90 d

HOLDERNESS GIRL 4 b.f. Lapierre 119 – Isobel's Choice 58 (Green God 128) [1996 NR 1997 a7g Dec 22] eighth live foal: half-sister to 2-y-o 6f seller winner Lean Streak (by Streak): dam won sellers from 5f to 1m: no form in 2 NH Flat races before showing a little ability when seventh of 15 in maiden at Lingfield. *Miss J. F. Craze* — 38

HOLDERS HILL (IRE) 5 b.g. Tirol 127 – Delightful Time (Manado 130) [1996 62: a8.5g² 1997 a9.4g² a9.4f 8g a8g⁵ Jun 19] modest maiden: should be suited by 1¼m+: acts on fibresand, best turf efforts on dead/soft: effective blinkered earlier in career, not tried last 2 seasons: shaped well over fences in November. *M. G. Meagher* — 59

HO LENG (IRE) 2 ch.g. (Apr 29) Statoblest 120 – Indigo Blue (IRE) 56 (Bluebird (USA) 125) [1997 6m* 7d² 6g⁵ Oct 18] 15,000Y: half-brother to 4-y-o Major Dundee: dam sprinting half-sister to Mistertopogigo: won maiden at Hamilton in August: ran well afterwards in minor event at Ayr and Two-Year-Old Trophy at Redcar, finishing strongly in latter: will probably stay 1m: has tended to start slowly and carry head high: should improve again. *Miss L. A. Perratt* — 92 p

HOLLOWAY MELODY 4 ch.f. Cree Song 99 – Holloway Wonder 93 (Swing Easy (USA) 126) [1996 55: a7g⁴ a6g³ 6.9m 7g³ 8.1m⁶ 8.2m⁵ 8f 8.2g* a8g a7g⁴ a7s a8g 1997 a8.5g 8g⁵ 8.2d a8g Nov 17] workmanlike filly: modest handicapper up to 1m as 3-y-o: well held in 1997. *B. A. McMahon* — –

HOLLOW HAZE (USA) 2 b. or br.f. (Feb 6) Woodman (USA) 126 – Libeccio (NZ) (Danzatore (CAN) 120) [1997 7d² 8g⁶ Sep 28] rangy, useful-looking filly: has plenty of scope: first known foal: dam out of American sprinting half-sister to Generous and Strawberry Roan: shaped well when second of 5 to Amabel in minor event at Newbury: gone in coat, well beaten in Fillies' Mile at Ascot, hanging markedly right early in straight, eased: should stay at least 1m: carried head awkwardly both starts. *P. W. Chapple-Hyam* — 90

HOLY SMOKE 2 b.f. (Feb 8) Statoblest 120 – Native Flair 87 (Be My Native (USA) 122) [1997 6m 8m 6m⁴ Oct 1] leggy filly: third foal: half-sister to 4-y-o Nosey Native: dam 1¼m/1½m winner: well held in maidens: probably needs much further than 6f. *J. L. Eyre* — –

HOLY WINE (USA) 2 ch.g. (Apr 26) Thorn Dance (USA) 107 – Gloria Mundi (FR) (Saint Cyrien (FR) 128) [1997 6m 6m 6m 7.6m* 8d Sep 19] first foal: dam, useful French middle-distance performer, won 4 listed races. justified favouritism readily in nursery at Lingfield in September: disappointing next time: should stay at least 1m: sent to Hong Kong. *D. R. Loder* — 74 +

HOMBRE 2 ch.g. (Apr 15) Shernazar 131 – Delray Jet (USA) (Northjet 136) [1997 7.5m⁵ 8.5g⁵ 7.5f Sep 17] 5,000Y: rather leggy gelding: fifth foal: dam unraced: fair form in maidens at Beverley first 2 outings (reportedly choked second time): well below form final start: should be suited by at least 1¼m. *J. W. Watts* — 68

HOME COUNTIES (IRE) 8 ch.g. Ela-Mana-Mou 132 – Safe Home 94 (Home   –
Guard (USA) 129) [1996 –: 10d⁶ 13.1s⁶ 10.5m⁵ 11.9m⁶ 1997 15.8g Sep 27]
lengthy gelding: smart hurdler at best: little form on flat since 1995. *D. Moffatt*

HO MEI SURPRISE 5 ch.h. Hadeer 118 – By Surprise 68 (Young Generation   –
129) [1996 37: a5g a6g⁵ a6g a5g⁵ a6g 5m 1997 a6g Jan 22] plain horse: poor maiden
handicapper: visored when tailed off only 5-y-o start. *B. Preece*

HOMESTEAD 3 ch.g. Indian Ridge 123 – Bertrade 75 (Homeboy 114) [1996   58
63?: 6m 7m 8.1g⁵ 7.3m 6m 7.3s 1997 8.2g 8f 6.1m 6g⁶ 7g* 8m* 8f³ a8.5g 9.7d² 8.2d
8.2d⁴ Nov 3] close-coupled gelding: unimpressive mover: modest performer: won
maiden handicap and minor event at Brighton in August: barely stays 9.7f: acts on
firm and dead ground, never placed to challenge on fibresand. *R. Hannon*

HONEST BORDERER 2 b.g. (Feb 10) Selkirk (USA) 129 – Tell No Lies 96   74 p
(High Line 125) [1997 7m⁵ 8.2s⁴ Oct 15] big, workmanlike gelding: first foal: dam
9f to 1½m winner: shaped with plenty of promise in maidens at Newmarket and
Nottingham in autumn, still green and not knocked about in latter: should stay at least
1¼m: very much the sort to do better at 3 yrs. *J. L. Dunlop*

HONESTLY 4 ch.f. Weldnaas (USA) 112 – Shadha 57 (Shirley Heights 130)   –
[1996 –, a71: a7g⁴ a7g⁶ 7f 8f a12g⁶ a9.4g* a9.4g³ 1997 a10g⁶ a10g³ a10g³ a10g³   a47
a12g² 10g Sep 28] leggy filly: poor all-weather performer nowadays: stays 1½m:
little form on turf: sold, to go to Saudi Arabia. *B. Smart*

HONEYHALL 4 b.f. Crofthall 110 – Attila The Honey 54 (Connaught 130)   –
[1996 –, a41: 5g 6g 7f 6m 6m a6g⁴ a6g* a6g 1997 a6s a5g⁴ a6g⁶ a6g⁵ Feb 25] sturdy   a32
filly: poor handicapper: stays 6f: acts on fibresand: twice visored, running well first
time: may not be one to trust implicitly. *N. Bycroft*

HONEYSHAN 5 b.m. Warrshan (USA) 117 – Divissima 62 (Music Boy 124)   –
[1996 –: 8.1m 10m 1997 8.5m Apr 23] of little account. *D. J. S. ffrench Davis*

HONEY STORM (IRE) 2 b.f. (Apr 25) Mujadil (USA) 119 – Milk And Honey   73
102 (So Blessed 130) [1997 6g³ 6g³ 6g 7m² 8.1g⁴ Sep 27] sparely-made filly:
half-sister to several winners, including 2-y-o sprint winners Hana Marie (by
Formidable) and Ideal Home (by Home Guard): dam sprint winner at 2 yrs but didn't
train on: fair form: in frame in maidens and in a valuable sales race at the Curragh:
probably stays 1m: raced only on good/good to firm ground. *M. R. Channon*

HONEY SUCKLE 2 br.f. (Apr 21) Petong 126 – May The Fourteenth 53   65 p
(Thatching 131) [1997 7m Oct 1] unfurnished filly: fourth foal: half-sister to 3-y-o
Phylida and 5-y-o Major Change: dam, stayed 1m, half-sister to good 1977 2-y-o
Aythorpe: 14/1, seventh of 20 in maiden at Salisbury won by Lucky Double, fading
only late on: should improve. *Miss Gay Kelleway*

HONG KONG EXPRESS (IRE) 3 b.f. Distinctly North (USA) 115 – North   –
Kildare (USA) (Northjet 136) [1996 55: 5g 7s⁴ 6m³ 6m 6f⁴ 6s 1997 7g⁵ 6m⁵ 7m⁵ 8g⁵
Jun 16] close-coupled filly: modest maiden: no form in 1997: tried blinkered/visored:
sent to Australia. *J. Berry*

HONIARA BAY 3 b.f. Welsh Captain 113 – Honiara 86 (Pitcairn 126) [1996 NR   –
1997 8g 7.1d⁵ 8.1m 5d 13.8m Sep 20] seventh foal: dam 2-y-o 5f winner: of little
account. *Miss A. Stokell*

HONOURABLE 3 gr.g. Old Vic 136 – Integrity 108 (Reform 132) [1996 NR   102
1997 7m³ a7g³ 7g⁶ 8g² 10g* 12.4g³ 10.3g² 11.9g* 11.9s² 12g Sep 28] small gelding:
half-brother to several winners, notably Radwell (smart up to 1m, by Dunbeath):
dam, ideally suited by 6f, is daughter of Cry of Truth: useful handicapper: first past
post at Pontefract in June and at York in August and September: beat Arctic Owl by
short head on final occasion, but hung left in dying strides and demoted: stays 1½m:
has raced mainly on good ground or softer: front runner: genuine: sold approx.
£61,000 in Dubai in November. *J. W. Watts*

HOOFPRINTS (IRE) 4 b.c. Distinctly North (USA) 115 – Sweet Reprieve   –
(Shirley Heights 130) [1996 64, a75: 10m 10m 13.1m⁶ 14m⁵ 15.4g⁵ 14.1m 13.6m⁴
a13g* a12g* a12s³ 1997 12m Aug 19] big, strong, rangy colt: fair performer: well
held only start in 1997. *Mrs A. J. Perrett*

HOPE CHEST 3 ch.f. Kris 135 – Hopeful Search (USA) 71 (Vaguely Noble 140) 65
[1996 70p: 7m³ 1997 11.9f³ 10.1s 10m⁵ Jul 19] sturdy filly: has a powerful, round
action: fair maiden: will prove best up to 1½m: well beaten on soft ground: sold 3,800
gns in December. *D. R. Loder*

HOPEFUL BID (IRE) 8 b.g. Auction Ring (USA) 123 – Irish Kick (Wind- –
jammer (USA)) [1996 NR 1997 8g 8.1g 8m 7m 7m Sep 16] close-coupled gelding:
modest 7f/1m handicapper in 1994: well beaten at 8 yrs. *P. Howling*

HOPEFULLY 2 b.f. (May 21) Salse (USA) 128 – Silver Maple (USA) 81 (Silver 47
Hawk (USA) 123) [1997 5m⁴ 5m² 5g² 5d² 6m³ 6g 5.2m⁴ Jun 23] small filly: first
foal: dam 1¼m winner from 2 starts: poor maiden: stays 6f: sold, to go to UAE.
M. R. Channon

HOPEFUL STAR (IRE) 2 ch.c. (Apr 22) Pips Pride 117 – Mijouter (IRE) 57
(Coquelin (USA) 121) [1997 6f⁶ 7d⁶ a5s³ a6g⁶ Dec 4] 6,400 2-y-o: first foal: dam a50
unraced half-sister to dam of very smart miler Pennine Walk: modest form at best in
maidens: stays 7f. *Miss Gay Kelleway*

HOPESAY 3 b.f. Warning 136 – Tatouma (USA) 79 (The Minstrel (CAN) 135) 67
[1996 84: 6g³ 6m³ 6m² 1997 7.6m⁵ 6m 6m⁵ 6m Sep 26] close-coupled filly: fair
maiden at best in 1997: stays 6f: raced only on good ground or firmer: visored
(creditable efforts) last 2 starts: sold 7,000 gns in December. *J. H. M. Gosden*

HOPE VALUE 2 b.g. (Mar 31) Rock City 120 – Folle Idee (USA) (Foolish 49
Pleasure (USA) 120) [1997 7g 6d³ a6g⁶ 7.5f Sep 17] workmanlike gelding: has a round
action: fifth reported foal: half-brother to 6f (at 2 yrs) to 1¼m winner Mhemeanles
(by Jalmood) and a winner abroad by Aragon: dam unraced: poor maiden: stays 6f:
blinkered second and fourth starts. *T. D. Easterby*

HOPPERETTA 3 b.f. Rock Hopper 124 – Can Can Girl 69 (Gay Fandango –
(USA) 132) [1996 45, a43: a7g³ a7g³ 6d⁵ 8f a7g 10f 10g a7g a7g⁴ a8g³ 1997 7d 10d
a11g a14.8g Dec 13] lengthy, workmanlike filly: poor maiden. *B. Palling*

HOPPING HIGGINS (IRE) 2 b.f. (Apr 3) Brief Truce (USA) 126 – Yellow 103
Creek (Sandy Creek 123) [1997 5d* 5d² 5g² 5d* 6m⁴ 5g² 6d⁵ 6g⁶ Oct 18] IR
10,000Y: sturdy, good-quartered filly: eighth foal: half-sister to fairly useful 1993
2-y-o 5f winner Wajiba Riva and Italian 3-y-o 1m winner Jever (both by Waajib) and
Irish 1989 2-y-o 7f winner Horrofic (by Kafu): dam Irish maiden: useful performer:
landed odds in maiden at Tipperary in May and listed race at Leopardstown in
August: short-headed in Norfolk Stakes at Royal Ascot third start, and reached frame
afterwards in Heinz 57 Phoenix Stakes (2 lengths fourth to Princely Heir) and Flying
Five (beaten ¾ length by Midnight Escape), both at Leopardstown: not discredited,
setting a strong pace, in Two-Year-Old Trophy at Redcar final start: barely stays 6f:
yet to race on extremes of ground: usually front runner: game. *A. P. O'Brien, Ireland*

HORNBEAM 3 b.c. Rich Charlie 117 – Thinkluckybelucky (Maystreak 118) 104
[1996 94?: 5f⁴ 6m⁵ 1997 7.3s* 7m³ 8.1g Jul 16] strong, workmanlike colt: useful
performer, lightly raced: won maiden at Newbury in May by 7 lengths despite
wandering: best effort when 3 lengths third of 20 to Among Men in Jersey Stakes at
Royal Ascot, staying on strongly: ran in snatches final start: should stay 1m: acts on
good to firm and soft ground. *J. R. Jenkins*

HORNPIPE 5 b.g. Handsome Sailor 125 – Snake Song 94 (Mansingh (USA) 120) 37
[1996 60: a8g a7g³ a9.4g² a8g a11g⁵ a8g a11g⁶ a12g³ 1997 a11g a12g³ a12g a7g²
a8.5g a7g⁵ a11g⁶ Apr 1] workmanlike gelding: poor maiden handicapper: stayed
9.4f: raced only on fibresand: blinkered from second start in 1997: dead. *J. Wharton*

HOSTILE NATIVE 4 b.g. Formidable (USA) 125 – Balatina 85 (Balidar 133) –
[1996 –: 6m 8d 6.1s 1997 7g 7.1g 5s Oct 14] strong, lengthy gelding: no form: tried
blinkered. *R. Guest*

HOTCAKE 4 b.g. Sizzling Melody 117 – Bold Cookie 75 (Never So Bold 135) 38
[1996 –: 6f 6g 1997 7m 7g⁶ 8m 9.2m Aug 18] poor maiden: best effort at 7f.
Miss S. E. Hall

HOT NEWS 3 b.c. Sizzling Melody 117 – In The Papers 87 (Aragon 118) [1996 –
NR 1997 6f⁶ 8d 6s⁵ 5m Jul 19] third foal: dam stayed 6f: seems of little account.
J. R. Jenkins

HOT SHOT 3 gr.g. Chilibang 120 – Free Rein (Sagaro 133) [1996 –: 7f 1997 10g –
8g a7g Jun 28] of little account. *G. L. Moore*

HOT SPOT 2 ch.g. (Apr 8) Bustino 136 – Royal Seal (Privy Seal 108) [1997 7d –
Nov 7] rangy, unfurnished gelding: fifth foal: dam unraced: 16/1, well held in 19-
runner maiden at Doncaster (had tongue tied): may do better in time. *I. A. Balding*

HOTSTEPPER 4 ch.f. Never So Bold 135 – Brilliant Timing (USA) (The Minstrel –
(CAN) 135) [1996 –: 8m 7f 1997 8d 8f Sep 29] of little account. *Mrs S. D. Williams*

HOT TOPIC (IRE) 2 ch.f. (Apr 27) Desse Zenny (USA) – Sajanjal (Dance In –
Time (CAN)) [1997 5m 7d a7s Nov 28] close-coupled filly: half-sister to several
winners here and in USA: dam unraced: little sign of ability. *A. Kelleway*

HOUSEKEEPER (IRE) 2 b.f. (Mar 3) Common Grounds 118 – Staff Approved 87 P
94 (Teenoso (USA) 135) [1997 7d* Oct 27] IR 28,000Y: third living foal: half-sister
to 4-y-o Polar Prince: dam, 1m winner at 2 yrs who should have stayed further out of
Klairtones, placed in Irish 1000 Guineas and Irish Oaks: 8/1 won 10-runner maiden
at Lingfield in very taking style by 3½ lengths from Red Rabbit, challenging full of
running over 1f out and merely nudged ahead, value much more: should stay
1m: open to considerable improvement and will go on to better things in 1998.
R. Charlton

HOUSE OF DREAMS 5 b.g. Darshaan 133 – Helens Dreamgirl 95 (Caerleon 61
(USA) 132) [1996 61: 13.8s6 12.1d6 12d2 1997 10m 9m5 12s3 Oct 16] small gelding:
very poor mover: modest maiden handicapper: stays 1½m: acts on firm and soft
ground: has been bandaged. *G. M. Moore*

HOUSE ON FIRE (IRE) 2 b.g. (May 13) Paris House 123 – La Fille de Feu 50
(Never So Bold 135) [1997 6m 6f 5d a5s a6g4 Dec 6] first foal: dam (unraced) from
family of Greenland Park and Red Sunset: modest form at best in maidens and seller:
has carried head high. *J. Berry*

HOWAIDA (IRE) 3 b.f. Night Shift (USA) – Fear Naught 99 (Connaught 130) 85
[1996 NR 1997 8m 8.3m* 7.1m3 8d2 Oct 28] 62,000Y: sister to fairly useful 5f to 7f
winner Raknah and half-sister to several winners, including useful pair Himiko (by
Green Desert) and Without Reserve (by Auction Ring), both best up to 1m: dam won
Royal Hunt Cup: fairly useful performer: won maiden at Windsor in July: creditable
efforts in minor race at Sandown and handicap at Leicester after: stays 1m well: acts
on good to firm and dead going: has swished tail. *M. R. Stoute*

HOW BIZARRE 3 b.g. Thatching 131 – Relatively Sharp 86 (Sharpen Up 127) –
[1996 NR 1997 7g 8d Oct 28] good-topped gelding: brother to fair 7f winner Phoenix
Venture and half-brother to several winners abroad: dam, winning sprinter, much
improved at 4 yrs, is half-sister to Tirol (by Thatching): tailed off both starts: trained
on debut by T. Hind: blinkered second outing. *R. Simpson*

HOWIES CHOICE (IRE) 2 b.g. (Apr 1) Petardia 113 – Better Goods (IRE) 66
(Glow (USA)) [1997 7d 6m4 5g4 7g Oct 7] 15,000Y: tall, leggy gelding: first foal:
dam Irish maiden: fair form when fourth in maidens at York and Catterick, off course
2½ months in between: should stay beyond 6f: has high head carriage. *W. McAuliffe*

HOW LONG 4 b.c. Alzao (USA) 117 – Fresh (High Top 131) [1996 98: 8s4 8.1d2 109
7.1m* 8m3 7m5 8m4 8m 7m 7.5s2 6g2 1997 7g4 6m2 7f2 6f3 7g2 7g2 Jul 26] good-
bodied, attractive colt: useful performer: in frame all 6 starts in 1997: 3 lengths
second of 20 to Tumbleweed Ridge in Bunbury Cup at Newmarket (under top
weight) on penultimate outing: 5 lengths second of 8 to Wizard King in Beeswing
Stakes at Newcastle on final one: effective at 6f to 1m: acts on firm and soft ground:
consistent: sent to USA. *L. M. Cumani*

HOYLAND COMMON (IRE) 2 ch.f. (Apr 28) Common Grounds 118 – Scoby –
Lass (Prominer 125) [1997 5v 5m 5m 6.1m a5g Aug 15] 5,200Y: close-coupled filly:
half-sister to several winners, notably useful sprinter Barrys Gamble (by Nishapour):
dam unraced: no worthwhile form: blinkered final start. *N. Tinkler*

HUGGER-MUGGER 2 br.g. (Feb 27) Prince Sabo 123 – Fair Eleanor –
(Saritamer (USA) 130) [1997 5.1d6 5g 5g 7f Jul 15] 21,000Y: workmanlike gelding:
seventh foal: half-brother to several winners, including 3-y-o Murron Wallace: dam
poor plater: no worthwhile form, including in seller: blinkered. *J. R. Arnold*

HUJOOM (IRE)   2 b.c. (May 7) Fairy King (USA) – Maellen (River Beauty 105)   89
[1997 6d³ 7m* 7g² 6m 6g* 6g Oct 25] 36,000Y: shows knee action: half-brother to
several winners, including useful 6f (at 2 yrs) to 1½m winner Lifewatch Vision (by
Vision): dam Irish 1½m winner: fairly useful performer: won minor event at
Salisbury in July and nursery at Ayr in September, in latter overcoming trouble: well
held in listed event final start: likely to prove best at up to 1m: yet to race on extremes
of ground: held up. *J. L. Dunlop*

HULAL   3 b.c. Arazi (USA) 135 – Almarai (USA) 73 (Vaguely Noble 140) [1996   65
–p: 7g 1997 8.2m 8m⁶ 9g³ 7s² 8.5g 9s 10d Nov 1] strong, compact colt: fair maiden
handicapper: short-headed at Catterick start before bought from A. Stewart in July:
well beaten in Ireland: may prove best up to 1m: acts on soft ground. *K. Prendergast,
Ireland*

HULLBANK   7 b.g. Uncle Pokey 116 – Dubavarna 72 (Dubassoff (USA)) [1996   71
65: a12g⁴ 13.8s 16.2m³ 14.1m 16.2g³ 14.1g² 14.1f⁵ 16.2m² 16.2m* 15.8g² 17.1m
1997 16.2s 16.2m* 18g² 16m² Jul 19] tall gelding: shows knee action: fair handicapper: better than ever at 7 yrs, winning at Beverley in June: stays 2¼m: acts on firm
going, below form both attempts on soft: often bandaged: blinkered (ran well) fifth
6-y-o start: held up. *W. W. Haigh*

HUMOURLESS   4 ch.c. Nashwan (USA) 135 – Sans Blague (USA) 108 (The   99
Minstrel (CAN) 135) [1996 95: 10g* 10.4m² 1997 12d³ 12m⁶ 10.4m 12m³ Aug 1]
good-topped, close-coupled colt: good mover: useful handicapper: off course over a
year before reappearance: creditable efforts on 3 of 4 starts in 1997: probably better
at 1½m than shorter: yet to race on extremes of going: often bandaged behind: sold
approx. £48,500 in Dubai in November. *L. M. Cumani*

HUNTERS OF BRORA (IRE)   7 b.m. Sharpo 132 – Nihad 76 (Alleged (USA)   102
138) [1996 –: 7.9m 10.1m 1997 8m 8g*ᵈⁱˢ 9m⁴ 8.1g 10.1g 10m 7.6s⁴ 8m 9m³ 8g Oct
18] sturdy, lengthy mare: useful handicapper, better than ever at 7 yrs: reportedly had
sinus operation before reappearance: disqualified for jockey's irresponsible riding
after passing post first in Spring Cup at Newbury in May: placed in Tote Cambridgeshire at Newmarket for third time on penultimate start, 1¾ lengths third to
Pasternak: effective at 1m to 1¼m: acts on firm and soft going: held up: tends to be
slowly away: genuine. *J. D. Bethell*

HUNT HILL (IRE)   2 b.c. (Feb 27) High Estate 127 – Royaltess (Royal And   – p
Regal (USA)) [1997 7m 7g 7d Oct 14] IR 38,000Y: well-made colt: sixth foal:
half-brother to useful 1989 ?-y-o 6f winner Makbul (by Fairy King) and a winner in
USA by Bluebird: dam unraced sister to useful Irish sprinter Regaltess: backward
and not given at all hard time when behind in maidens: will do better in 1998. *Sir
Mark Prescott*

HUNTING GROUND   9 b.g. Dancing Brave (USA) 140 – Ack's Secret (USA)   –
(Ack Ack (USA)) [1996 NR 1997 a16s a14.8g 16m⁶ 18g Jun 16] good-bodied
gelding: lightly raced nowadays, and no form in 1997. *B. P. J. Baugh*

HUNTSWOOD   2 b.c. (May 9) Warning 136 – Clarista (USA) 67 (Riva Ridge   84
(USA)) [1997 6g³ 5g⁴ 5.1m* 5m* 6g Sep 20] 33,000 2-y-o: small, quite attractive
colt: brother to useful 7f winner (including at 2 yrs) Indhar and half-brother to 3
winners, including 1¼m/1½m winner Formal Invitation (by Be My Guest): dam
(stayed 1¼m) half-sister to Topsy and Teenoso: fairly useful performer: won maiden
at Chester and minor event at Folkestone in the summer: off 6 weeks before
disappointing when well-backed favourite final start: a sprinter: raced only on good/
good to firm ground. *R. Hannon*

HURGILL DANCER   3 b.g. Rambo Dancer (CAN) 107 – Try Vickers (USA) 72   69
(Fuzzbuster (USA)) [1996 66: 6g a7g² 7m³ 8m⁶ 7.9g 8g³ 1997 10m 12.3g* 14d 11m
Nov 4] fair handicapper: best effort to win at Ripon in April: off course 6 months,
well held both subsequent starts: should stay 1¾m. *J. W. Watts*

HURGILL LADY   3 ch.f. Emarati (USA) 74 – Gitee (FR) (Carwhite 127) [1996   –
62: 6s² 6m⁶ 5g² 5g 1997 6m 7d Jun 11] modest maiden at 2 yrs: well held in 1997:
joined D. Nicholls. *J. W. Watts*

HURGILL TIMES   3 b.g. Timeless Times (USA) 99 – Crimson Dawn (Manado   –
130) [1996 64d: 6m⁴ 6m³ 7d 6g⁶ 8.3d⁵ 8m⁴ 1997 a5f⁶ a6g a8.5g a6g Nov 24] tall
gelding: disappointing maiden: tried blinkered/visored. *D. Shaw*

HURRICANE STATE (USA)   3 ch.c. Miswaki (USA) 124 – Regal State (USA)   99
122 (Affirmed (USA)) [1996 109: 7m² 6m* 6m 6.5g* 6.5d³ 1997 8g⁶ 8.5g Jun 7]
good-bodied colt: useful performer: much better effort in 1997 (below 2-y-o form)
when sixth of 12 to Air Express in Premio Parioli at Rome: stumbled start and never
going well in Diomed Stakes at Epsom: shapes as if will stay beyond 1m: yet to race
on extremes of going. *P. W. Chapple-Hyam*

HURTLEBERRY (IRE)   4 b.f. Tirol 127 – Allberry (Alzao (USA) 117) [1996   79
74: 7m 7s a8g² 1997 a7g* a8g³ 8d* 7m 9m 8m Nov 1] unfurnished filly: fair
performer, lightly raced: won minor event at Lingfield in January and handicap at
Goodwood in May: creditable efforts in valuable handicaps at Newmarket last 2
starts: stays 9f: acts on good to firm and dead ground and on equitrack, yet to race
on fibresand. *Lord Huntingdon*

HUSTLE AN BUSTLE (USA)   3 ch.f. Lomond (USA) 128 – City Crowds   59
(General Assembly (USA)) [1996 8.5m 8d 1997 7f 7g⁴ 6g 7v³ 12s a8s Nov 10] ex-
Irish filly: second foal: dam won in France and USA and placed in listed races at 9f/
1¼m: modest maiden: trained until after fourth start by J. Muldoon: sold 1,400 gns in
September and well held in Britain: stays 7f: seems to act on any going. *G. Fierro*

HUSUN (USA)   3 b.f. Sheikh Albadou 128 – Tadwin 109 (Never So Bold 135)   67
[1996 60p: 5m⁶ 1997 6m³ 6m⁴ 6s⁵ 6m 6.9g Sep 2] tall filly: fair maiden: below form
in 1997 after reappearance: stays 6f: acts on good to firm ground: ran poorly in visor:
sold 21,000 gns in December. *P. T. Walwyn*

HUTCHIES LADY   5 b.m. Efisio 120 – Keep Mum 63 (Mummy's Pet 125)   38
[1996 42: 8.3s* 8.3s⁴ 7.1g⁴ 8.1g² 9.2g⁴ 9.2g⁶ 8.1f a8.5g 9.2m⁴ 8d 10.9m 12.1s a11g
1997 11.1d 8.3d 8.3s⁴ 8.3s² 8.3s⁶ 10.5m 9.2g⁵ 9.2s 11.1d 9.2m 9m Jul 19] small,
sparely-made mare: poor handicapper: mostly well beaten in 1997: stays 9f: best
efforts on soft ground: tried blinkered. *R. M. McKellar*

HUXLEEN   2 ch.f. (Apr 17) Timeless Times (USA) 99 – Bergliot 51 (Governor   55 §
General 116) [1997 6.1g² 6m³ 7f* a6s Nov 1] first foal: dam poor sprint maiden:
modest performer: won at Redcar in June (wore near-side pricker after hanging left
time before) for W. G. M. Turner: gave deal of trouble stalls before withdrawn twice
in July, and subsequently banned from racing in Britain: well beaten only start in
USA. *D. Ruccio, USA*

HYPE ENERGY   3 b.f. Tina's Pet 121 – Stoneydale 83 (Tickled Pink 114) [1996   55
65: 6d 5.1m² 5f⁵ 1997 5m 6d 6g 5d⁴ 7m 5d⁴ 6d 5m² Sep 17] strong, compact filly:
modest maiden handicapper: best effort at 5f: acts on good to firm and dead ground:
effective blinkered or not: sold, to go to Germany. *G. Lewis*

HYPE SUPERIOR (IRE)   3 ch.g. Mac's Imp (USA) 116 – Katysue 98 (King's   55
Leap 111) [1996 NR 1997 6m 5m⁵ 10.3d 5s 6m 6g 5v² 6.1m a6g⁶ a7s⁴ Nov 10]
12,000Y: sturdy gelding: poor mover: half-brother to several winners, including
sprinter Maybank (by Contract Law): dam won 5 times over 5f at 2 yrs: modest
maiden: likely to prove best up to 1m: none too consistent. *A. Bailey*

I

IAMUS   4 ch.g. Most Welcome 131 – Icefern 88 (Moorestyle 137) [1996 87: 8.2d²   88
8g⁴ 7f⁶ 7g⁴ 7m 8.2m* 8m⁶ 10m 8d⁶ 1997 a8g⁶ a7g 8m⁴ 10.3d 8g³ 8g³ 8m 7.9g 8g*
8g³ Aug 2] tall gelding: fairly useful handicapper: best effort when winning at
Newcastle in July: suited by around 1m: acts on firm ground: visored (well beaten)
once at 3 yrs: usually ridden by Victoria Appleby: front runner/races prominently:
hurdling with D. Nicholson. *T. D. Barron*

IBIN ST JAMES   3 b.c. Salse (USA) 128 – St James's Antigua (IRE) 79 (Law   71
Society (USA) 130) [1996 70: 6m 7.5f⁴ 8f 8g 1997 10m* 12.3s⁴ 12m⁵ 10.1s³ 10m⁵
12g Aug 2] quite good-topped colt: fair handicapper: won at Ripon in April: poor
effort final start: stays 1½m: acts on good to firm ground and soft: has taken keen
hold, and sometimes gets on edge: blinkered last 4 starts: sold 11,000 gns in October.
J. D. Bethell

IBLIS (IRE)   5 b.g. Danehill (USA) 126 – In Unison (Bellypha 130) [1996 –: 8d⁶   87 d
1997 a7g⁴ 8g⁵ 7m 7s 7m⁴ 6g⁴ 6g a6g Oct 18] close-coupled, good-quartered gelding:
fairly useful handicapper at best: effective at 6f to 1m: acts on good to firm ground,
dead and fibresand: visored (ran poorly) final start: inconsistent. *G. Wragg*

IBN MASIRAH   3 b.g. Crowning Honors (CAN) – Masirah 62 (Dunphy 124)   –
[1996 51: 8g 8.1m³ 7m 8f 1997 12d⁶ 16.2m Jul 21] workmanlike gelding: well beaten
at 3 yrs: should stay beyond 1m. *Mrs M. Reveley*

I CAN'T REMEMBER   3 br. or g.g. Petong 126 – Glenfield Portion 86   76
(Mummy's Pet 125) [1996 78: 5.1g⁵ 5d 5s* 5m² 5g² 6m⁴ 6.1m* 5.7m⁵ 6m⁴ 7.1m⁵
7d* 6m 8m⁴ 8m² 8f⁵ 7d 8g* 7s⁴ 1997 a8.5g 7m⁶ 8m⁶ 8m 8g⁶ 7.6d⁴ 7.9g 7m 7v⁶ 8.2m
7.6s Aug 30] small, close-coupled gelding: fair handicapper: disappointing last 5
starts: stays 1m: probably acts on any going on turf (hampered only start on all-
weather): visored last 2 outings. *P. D. Evans*

ICE AGE   3 gr.c. Chilibang 120 – Mazarine Blue 65 (Bellypha 130) [1996 82: 5m*   62
5f⁶ 1997 6m 5.1d 5d 5m 5.1m⁵ 5g⁴ 5s⁴ 5.2s⁴ 5m⁶ 5g³ 5m 5m 5m a7g a6g² a5g⁵ Nov
29] workmanlike colt: modest performer: best at 5f/6f: acts on fibresand, suited by
good going or firmer on turf: effective with or without blinkers. *R. J. R. Williams*

ICEBAND (USA)   2 ch.c. (Mar 1) Dixieland Band (USA) – Zero Minus (USA)   95
(It's Freezing (USA) 122) [1997 6m² 6d* 7m⁶ Oct 3] $160,000F: strong, close-
coupled colt: sixth foal: closely related to a winner in USA by Herat and half-
brother to another by Mr Prospector: dam Grade 2 8.5f winner at 2 yrs: shaped well
on debut in July (suffered sore shin afterwards), and landed odds by 3 lengths from
Title Bid in maiden at Goodwood 2 months later: soon no impression in face of
stiffish task back on good to firm going in listed race at Newmarket: will probably
stay 1m. *J. H. M. Gosden*

I CRIED FOR YOU (IRE)   2 b.c. (Apr 14) Statoblest 120 – Fall of The Hammer   66
(IRE) (Auction Ring (USA) 123) [1997 5.7m 5m 6m 5.1g³ 7s³ Nov 8] 15,000F:
second foal: dam third over 7f at 2 yrs in Ireland: fair maiden: third in nurseries at
Nottingham and Doncaster: will probably stay 1m: acts on soft going. *R. Hannon*

ICY GUEST (USA)   3 b. or br.f. Clever Trick (USA) – Minstrel Guest 91 (Be My   71
Guest (USA) 126) [1996 68: 6.1f⁶ 1997 7.3s² a7g³ 6g⁵ 7s³ a7g* a8g Aug 15] tall filly: a81
fair handicapper: made all at Southwell in July, swishing tail under pressure: stays 7f:
acts on soft ground and fibresand: sold 7,000 gns in December. *P. J. Makin*

IDAHO (IRE)   2 ch.f. (Apr 3) Common Grounds 118 – Queen's Share (Main Reef   –
126) [1997 6g 8d Oct 28] IR 13,000Y: third living foal: half-sister to 1994 2-y-o 6f
winner Masruf (by Taufan): dam Irish sprinter: well held in maidens at Goodwood
and Leicester 4 months apart. *B. Gubby*

IDA LUPINO (IRE)   2 b.f. (Apr 18) Statoblest 120 – Alpine Symphony (North-   –
ern Dancer) [1997 7f⁶ 7g 7m 8m 7s Oct 16] IR 4,200F, 30,000Y: tall, good-topped
filly: eighth foal: half-sister to smart 1m to 1½m winner High Baroque and 1¼m
winner Dancing Heights (both by High Estate): dam unraced half-sister to smart
miler Captain James: soundly beaten: has looked headstrong: sold 13,000 gns in
December. *B. W. Hills*

I DON'T THINK SO   6 b.m. Mas Media – Misdevious (USA) (Alleged (USA)   –
138) [1996 NR 1997 a14g Feb 28] fifth reported foal: half-sister to 4-y-o Mogin and
3 winners abroad: dam unraced: no show on debut. *T. Hind*

IDRICA   3 b.f. Rainbow Quest (USA) 134 – Idraak (Kris 135) [1996 80: 8f* 7m 8g   88
1997 11.9m* 13.9s Sep 3] quite good-topped filly: has a quick action: fairly useful
form: best effort to win 5-runner handicap at Haydock in August: should be suited by
further than 1½m: acts on firm ground (raced too keenly on soft): seemingly not
easiest of rides: sent to Japan. *J. H. M. Gosden*

IECHYD-DA (IRE)   3 b.g. Sharp Victor (USA) 114 – Key Partner (Law Society   86
(USA) 130) [1996 82: 5s* 5d* 6g⁴ 7m² 7m 1997 10.5s³ 9m³ 12s⁶ 11.9d⁴ 10.3m Sep
10] lengthy, workmanlike gelding: fairly useful performer at best: well held after
second start at 3 yrs: stays 10.5f: acts on soft ground and good to firm: visored
(finished very tired) penultimate start: modest winning hurdler. *M. Bell*

IHTIMAAM (FR)   5 b.g. Polish Precedent (USA) 131 – Haebeh (USA) 88 (Aly-   – §
dar (USA)) [1996 –, a65: 11.1g 7m 10.2g 8f 11.1g a11g* a12g 10.1m a11g³ a11g*
a11g³ 1997 a11g a12g⁶ a12g 11.1s 15.8g⁶ Aug 5] compact gelding: fair form at 4 yrs:
has gone wrong way temperamentally: tried blinkered/visored. *Mrs A. Swinbank*

IHTIYATI (USA)   3 ch.c. Chief's Crown (USA) – Native Twine 114 (Be My   105
Native (USA) 122) [1996 86p: 6m⁶ 7f 7f* 1997 10m³ 12.3s³ 10m 10.3m² 10m 12d*
Oct 16] sturdy, lengthy colt: type to carry condition: useful handicapper: found
little penultimate start, then won 20-runner rated stakes by a head from Dance So
Suite: stays 1½m: acts on firm and dead ground: none too reliable: sent to UAE.
J. L. Dunlop

IJAB (CAN)   7 b.g. Ascot Knight (CAN) 130 – Renounce (USA) (Buckpasser)   34
[1996 –, a56: a16g* a14.8g⁴ 1997 14g 16g³ 14.1m a14g³ Oct 20] poor handicapper: a38
stays 2m: acts on good to firm going and fibresand: usually blinkered. *J. Parkes*

IJTINAB   3 b.c. Green Desert (USA) 127 – Nahilah 78 (Habitat 134) [1996 –: 6g   74 d
1997 7m³ 8.5m² 8g 7.1m⁵ 10m⁵ 7m 7m Sep 25] deep-girthed colt: poor mover: fair
maiden: prominent throughout when placed in slowly-run races at Kempton and
Epsom in the spring: well beaten after: may prove best short of 1m: raced only on
good/good to firm going: sold, and sent to Germany. *R. Akehurst*

IKATANIA   3 b.c. Highest Honor (FR) 124 – Lady Liska (USA) (Diesis 133)   83
[1996 74: 6s⁴ 7.1g⁴ 7m⁶ 8m³ 8g 1997 10m* 12.3g² 12g⁵ 12s Jul 2] close-coupled
colt: fairly useful handicapper: won at Nottingham in March: ran well next 2 starts,
poorly final one (sold later in July, and sent to Macau): should stay beyond 1½m: acts
on good to firm ground, probably soft. *J. L. Dunlop*

IKDAM (USA)   3 b. or br.f. Dayjur (USA) 137 – Orca (ARG) (Southern Halo   –
(USA)) [1996 92p: 6m³ 6.1f* 6d* 1997 6g May 5] useful-looking filly: looked
potentially useful sprinter at 2 yrs: found to be in season when running badly only
outing as 3-y-o. *Major W. R. Hern*

IKHTEYAAR (USA)   2 b. or br.f. (May 16) Mr Prospector (USA) – Linda's   103 p
Magic (USA) 114 (Far North (CAN) 120) [1997 6m² 6m² 6.1m* 6g* Oct 25] leggy,
close-coupled filly: sixth living foal: closely related to a 2-y-o 7f winner by Gulch
and 4-y-o Albaha, and half-sister to useful 7f/1m winner Mur Taasha (by Riverman)
and stayer Shujan (by Diesis): dam 6f/7f winner: progressive performer: won maiden
at Nottingham and listed race at Doncaster, having to be switched and running on
from rear to beat Special Treat ½ length in latter: bred to stay 1m: raced only on good/
good to firm ground: should continue to improve. *R. W. Armstrong*

Charles Sidney Mercedes Benz Doncaster Stakes—
Ikhteyaar catches Special Treat (blinkers) near the finish

IKHTISAR (USA)   3 b. or br.f. Slew O'Gold (USA) – Halholah (USA) 65   75
(Secreto (USA) 128) [1996 –: 7m⁶ 1997 10m⁵ 12.1m³ 14d³ 16.2m³ Jul 25] tall filly:
has a round action: fair handicapper: should stay at least 2m: unraced on extremes of
going: visored (pulled hard and well beaten) final start: sold 14,000 gns in December.
P. T. Walwyn

IKRAM BOY (USA)   3 b.g. Salem Drive (USA) – Vast Domain (CAN) (Vice   64
Regent (CAN)) [1996 NR 1997 7m 8m⁴ 7g a8.5g a8g⁴ Nov 25] closely related to
fairly useful 1m winner Grand du Lac (by Lac Ouimet) and half-brother to several
winners, including 9f stakes winner by Temperence Hill: dam won up to 1¼m: easily
best effort when fourth in maiden at Pontefract in October. *A. Bailey*

ILANDRA (IRE)   5 b.m. Roi Danzig (USA) – Island Goddess (Godswalk (USA)   –
130) [1996 –, a49: a13g a10g a10g⁵ a12g a10g 10.8g 12d a8g² a8g⁵ a10g⁴ 1997   a43 d
a10g⁴ a8g² a8g⁴ a13g 8f 8f a12g a8g a10g Nov 25] poor maiden handicapper on
all-weather: no form after third outing (left R. Akehurst next start): stays 1¼m.
G. L. Moore

IL DESTINO   2 b.c. (Mar 28) Casteddu 111 – At First Sight (He Loves Me 120)   70
[1997 6.1g 6d a7g* a8g² Dec 10] 4,200Y: sixth foal: dam unraced: fair form: won
maiden at Lingfield in November: good second in nursery there following month:
runs as if will stay beyond 1m. *P. J. Makin*

IL DORIA (IRE)   4 ch.f. Mac's Imp (USA) 116 – Pasadena Lady (Captain James   –
123) [1996 –: 6m³ 5m a5g a7g 1997 5m 7g 5m Sep 24] seems of little account
nowadays. *A. Hide*

ILE DE LIBRATE   3 b.g. Librate 91 – Little Missile (Ile de Bourbon (USA) 133)   –
[1996 NR 1997 10.3m 10m⁶ 10d Sep 13] unfurnished gelding: fifth foal: half-brother
to 6-y-o La Petite Fusee and 7-y-o Little Miss Ribot: dam (stoutly bred) of little
account: only sign of ability in maidens when sixth at Windsor in August.
R. J. O'Sullivan

ILE DISTINCT (IRE)   3 b.g. Dancing Dissident (USA) 119 – Golden Sunlight   81
(Ile de Bourbon (USA) 133) [1996 59: 6m 5.9f³ 7.9g 1997 9.9m⁵ 8m* 10m* 10m³
10.3g Oct 24] leggy gelding: fairly useful performer: won maiden at Musselburgh in
August and minor event at Nottingham (much improved form) in September: will
probably prove suited by 1½m: raced only on good going or firmer: sweating freely
(well beaten) final start. *Mrs A. Swinbank*

IL FALCO (FR)   3 ch.g. Polar Falcon (USA) 126 – Scimitarlia (USA) 84 (Diesis   51
133) [1996 NR 1997 7g⁶ 7m 6m⁵ 8.3g⁶ 10s Oct 8] 3,700F, IR 12,500Y: second foal.
dam, 1½m winner from 2 starts, daughter of Princess Royal winner Alia: modest
form in maidens and handicaps: should stay beyond 1m: sold, and joined R. Curtis.
Sir Mark Prescott

ILLEGALLY YOURS   4 br.f. Be My Chief (USA) 122 – Legal Precedent (Star   48 d
Appeal 133) [1996 44: a8g⁴ a10g⁶ 17.2g³ a16g² 16f⁵ a16g⁶ 1997 a13g³ a16g⁵
a12g a16g⁴ a13g² 11.6m a12g⁵ a16g⁶ Nov 25] leggy filly: poor maiden handicapper:
below best after second start: stays 2m: acts on equitrack, rarely races on turf: tried
blinkered/visored. *L. Montague Hall*

ILLUMINATE   4 b.g. Marju (IRE) 127 – Light Bee (USA) 86 (Majestic Light   63
(USA)) [1996 76: 10.2g³ 10m⁵ 12m 10.2m⁴ 9m⁵ 1997 a12g* a16g a11g 12m May
28] leggy, quite attractive gelding: modest form to win 5-runner maiden at Lingfield
in February: ran badly afterwards: should stay beyond 1½m. *D. C. O'Brien*

ILLUSION   3 b.c. Green Desert (USA) 127 – Time Charter 131 (Saritamer (USA)   103 p
130) [1996 NR 1997 8g² 7.9d* 8m² 10.4g Aug 20] well-made, attractive colt: sixth
foal: half-brother to 4-y-o Time Allowed, smart stayer Zinaad and useful 1988 2-y-o
7f winner By Charter (last 2 by Shirley Heights): dam top-class middle-distance
performer: easily landed odds in 4-runner maiden at York in June: useful form when
¾-length second to Intikhab in minor event at Doncaster following month: should
stay 1¼m (had too much use made of him when tried): capable of further progress at
4 yrs. *M. R. Stoute*

IL PRINCIPE (IRE)   3 b.g. Ela-Mana-Mou 132 – Seattle Siren (USA) 101   70
(Seattle Slew (USA)) [1996 –: 5m 6g a8g 1997 9g 10f⁵ 11.1d* 12.1m² 12m* a16g²
a14g* 16g* 15.8m* 15.4m Sep 26] fair handicapper: progressed well at 3 yrs,

winning at Hamilton (maiden), Musselburgh (twice), Southwell and Catterick (best effort), all in space of 5 weeks: stays 2m: acts on good to firm and dead ground, and all-weather: has given trouble stalls: races prominently. *John Berry*

IL TRASTEVERE (FR) 5 b.g. L'Emigrant (USA) 129 – Ideas At Work (Persepolis (FR) 127) [1996 –: 8.1g 8m 10g 8m a9.4g 1997 a12g³ a10g Jan 11] rather leggy gelding: little form since 3 yrs. *Miss Gay Kelleway* –

I'M A DREAMER (IRE) 7 b.g. Mister Majestic 122 – Lady Wise (Lord Gayle (USA) 124) [1996 NR 1997 a12g Mar 14] one-time fair handicapper: twice raced on flat since 1994, well beaten only outing at 7 yrs: stays 11f: acts on fibresand and on good to firm and soft ground: fair hurdler. *Miss M. E. Rowland* –

IMAGE MAKER (IRE) 4 gr.f. Nordico (USA) – Dream Trader (Auction Ring (USA) 123) [1996 –: a7g a12g⁵ a9.4g⁵ a14.8g 1997 a8g a8g Feb 7] probably no longer of any account. *P. D. Evans* –

I'M A NUT MAN 6 b.h. Shardari 134 – Zahiah 90 (So Blessed 130) [1996 41: 12.3g 10g³ 10.3m 11.1m² 10d² 10.2m⁵ 1997 8.3s 10g⁴ 9g 12.5m⁶ 9.9m⁶ Jul 29] workmanlike horse: poor maiden: seems to stay 1½m: acts on good to firm and dead ground. *C. A. Smith* 37

IMBACKAGAIN (IRE) 2 b.g. (May 19) Mujadil (USA) 119 – Ballinclogher (IRE) (Creative Plan (USA)) [1997 5g 6s a7g Aug 16] 15,000Y: strong, close-coupled gelding: second foal: dam unraced: modest form in maidens. *P. C. Haslam* 52

IMELDA (USA) 2 ch.f. (Apr 19) Manila (USA) – Rich And Riotous (USA) (Empery (USA) 128) [1997 7.5f Sep 17] $180,000Y: closely related to French/US winner Kraemer (by Lyphard), placed in Grade 2 9f event, and half-sister to several winners, notably very smart French miler Shaanxi (by Zilzal): dam French 1m winner: 7/2 and green, eighth of 9 in maiden at Beverley: sent to USA. *D. R. Loder* –

I'M NOT SURE 2 gr.f. (Mar 20) Petong 126 – Glenfield Portion 86 (Mummy's Pet 125) [1997 5m⁶ 5d 5m⁵ a5g³ a9.4g⁴ 5g³ a6g⁴ Oct 4] lengthy filly: sister to 4 winners, including 3-y-o I Can't Remember and 6-y-o Best Kept Secret: dam 2-y-o 5f winner: poor maiden: best efforts on fibresand: sold, to go to Austria. *J. Berry* 33 a48

IMPALA 3 ch.g. Interrex (CAN) – Raleigh Gazelle (Absalom 128) [1996 46: 6.1d⁴ a6g² 7.5m⁵ 6d 1997 7m⁶ 7m³ 7m² 8.5s* a9.4g 8d Aug 8] sparely-made gelding: modest performer: won claimer at Epsom in July: stiff tasks in handicaps after: stays 8.5f: acts on good to firm and soft ground and on fibresand. *W. G. M. Turner* 56

IMPENDING DANGER 4 ch.g. Fearless Action (USA) 116 – Crimson Sol (Crimson Beau 124) [1996 –: 8m 1997 a12g⁵ a12g 14.1d Nov 3] workmanlike gelding: little sign of ability. *K. S. Bridgwater* –

IMPERATOR (IRE) 2 b.c. (Apr 27) Mac's Imp (USA) 116 – Secret Hideaway (USA) (Key To The Mint (USA)) [1997 7s Jun 26] 17,000Y: sixth foal: half-brother to 3-y-o Chateauherault, fairly useful 5f (at 2 yrs) and 7f winner Muchtarak (by Try My Best) and a winner in Italy by Classic Secret: dam unraced: tailed-off last only start. *Lady Herries* –

IMPERIAL BID (FR) 9 b.g. No Pass No Sale 120 – Tzaritsa (USA) 113 (Young Emperor 133) [1996 57: a11g³ 1997 16m Apr 14] lightly raced nowadays and tailed off only outing at 9 yrs. *F. Murphy* –

IMPERIAL COURT (IRE) 2 b.c. (May 15) Imperial Frontier (USA) 112 – Fandikos (IRE) (Taufan (USA) 119) [1997 6g Aug 4] 7,200 2-y-o: fourth reported foal: dam unraced half-sister to useful sprinter Imperial Bailiwick (by Imperial Frontier): 33/1, soundly beaten in maiden at Windsor. *J. G. M. O'Shea* –

IMPERIAL GARDEN (IRE) 3 ch.g. Imperial Frontier (USA) 112 – Spindle Berry 92 (Dance In Time (CAN)) [1996 52+, a58: a5g 5f a5g* 6m 5f⁶ a6g 5s² 1997 a5g⁴ a5g² a5g³ a5g* a6g³ a5g² Mar 17] lengthy, plain gelding: modest performer: won 6-runner claimer at Lingfield in January: very best form at 5f: acts on all-weather, best turf run on soft: sold, to go to Macau. *P. C. Haslam* a62

IMPERIAL GLEN (IRE) 3 b.f. Imperial Frontier (USA) 112 – Tribute To Viqueen (Furry Glen 121) [1996 NR 1997 7m 10s⁵ 8.3g 6m 8m 16.4m³ Aug 19] first reported foal: dam pulled up lame only start over hurdles: poor maiden: seems a stayer. *M. D. I. Usher* 42

IMPERIAL HONEY (IRE)   2 b.f. (May 21) Imperial Frontier (USA) 112 –   60
Indian Honey (Indian King (USA) 128) [1997 5g⁵ 6m 5f⁵ 5m² 5m⁵ Aug 20] R
3,200Y: sixth foal: half-sister to several winners, including 3-y-o Jack The Lad and
Irish 1m winner Honeyschoice (by Distinctly North): dam unraced: modest maiden:
close second at Beverley in July: ran poorly final start: should stay beyond 5f.
Mrs A. Swinbank

IMPERIAL LINE (IRE)   3 ch.g. Mac's Imp (USA) 116 – Ellaline (Corvaro   39
(USA) 124) [1996 NR 1997 8f 7g 7g 6m 7m 7m a7g⁵ Nov 12] fifth foal: half-brother
to German 1m/9f winner Enkiou and Irish 13f winner Mobile Miss (both by Classic
Secret): dam Irish 7f winner: poor maiden: tried blinkered. *A. B. Mulholland*

IMPERIAL OR METRIC (IRE)   3 b.g. Prince Rupert (FR) 121 – Caroline's   65 d
Mark (On Your Mark 125) [1996 65: 5.9g 7m⁶ 7s⁶ 7.1g² 7g³ 6m 6g 8.1m* 7.9g 8g⁶
8g 1997 10g³ 8m 8s 9m 8g 8.2s 10.9s⁴ Oct 14] strong gelding: unimpressive mover:
fair form at best: seemed to have something go amiss third start, and well held
afterwards: left R. Fahey before final start and sold only 900 gns after it: stays 1¼m:
acts on good to firm ground, possibly not soft. *J. J. O'Neill*

IMPERIAL PRINCE   2 b.g. (Apr 12) Prince Sabo 123 – Joli's Girl 79 (Man-   62
singh (USA) 120) [1997 5.1d May 11] 17,500Y: sixth foal: brother to useful 6f (at 2
yrs) to 1m winner Joli's Princess and half-brother to 1¾m winner Side Bar (by
Mummy's Game): dam 9f winner who stayed 1½m: 12/1, seventh of 10 in minor
event at Bath. *K. McAuliffe*

IMPERIAL SCHOLAR (IRE)   3 b.f. Royal Academy (USA) 130 – Last Ball   94 d
(IRE) (Last Tycoon 131) [1996 75p: 6d² 1997 7g⁵ 8m⁵ 12m 10d² 10.2m⁶ Jul 7] tall,
lengthy filly: fairly useful form when fifth in Nell Gwyn Stakes at Newmarket on
reappearance: failed to repeat that form, finding little last start: refused to enter stalls
in August: should prove effective at 1¼m. *J. M. P. Eustace*

IMPETUOSITY (IRE)   3 ch.f. Imp Society (USA) – Catherine Clare 58 (Sallust   –
134) [1996 NR 1997 6g a7g⁶ a8g⁶ 11.1s May 17] 5,700F, 3,200Y: half-sister to 3
winners, including Irish 7f winner Black And Blaze (by Taufan): dam Irish miler:
poor maiden. *C. W. Thornton*

IMPETUOUS LADY (USA)   4 b.f. Imp Society (USA) – Urakawa (USA)   –
(Roberto (USA) 131) [1996 44: 6.1m⁴ 7.1m 8d 1997 10g 12.5d 8.3m 10.1g⁶ 12m⁶
16.2d Aug 14] leggy, good-topped filly: has a round action: poor maiden: best efforts
at 6f: won selling hurdle for R. Frost in September. *W. J. Musson*

IMPETUS   3 b.g. Puissance 110 – Cold Line 74 (Exdirectory 129) [1996 NR 1997   47
7m 9d 7.5g² Jun 11] leggy gelding: half-brother to fair staying hurdler Give Best (by
Dunbeath): dam 1½m winner: only form in maidens when second in weak event at
Beverley: should be suited by further than 1m. *J. Hetherton*

IMP EXPRESS (IRE)   4 b.g. Mac's Imp (USA) 116 – Fair Chance (Young Emp-   45
eror 133) [1996 50: 5d 5g 5d 6d 5g 5g 5g³ 5f⁵ 5m⁶ 5g 5m 1997 a7g a6g a6g⁶ a5g³
a5g⁶ a5g 5.9m 5g⁴ 5m⁴ 5g³ 5m² 5g⁶ 5g⁵ 5g⁴ 5g a6g a5g⁶ Dec 22] good-topped
gelding: poor handicapper: mostly ran well in 1997: trained by G. M. Moore first
15 starts: best at 5f: acts on all-weather, form on turf only on good going or firmer:
sometimes blinkered/visored (not after sixth start): often troublesome stalls.
P. S. Felgate

IMPISH (IRE)   3 ch.g. Imp Society (USA) – Halimah 56 (Be My Guest (USA)   57
126) [1996 –: 5m a5g 5m 6s 6g a8g 1997 a6g⁵ a6g⁶ a6g³ 6d³ 5m³ 5m⁵ 5s* 5g³ 6m 5g   a39
5g⁶ 5g⁶ a6g a5g a5g Dec 18] plain, stocky gelding: modest handicapper on turf, poor
on all-weather: won at Hamilton in May (dead-heated) at 5f/6f: goes well on
soft going: below form in blinkers at 2 yrs: none too consistent. *T. J. Etherington*

IMPISH LADY (IRE)   2 br.f. (May 7) Mac's Imp (USA) 116 – Wabarah 90   –
(Shirley Heights 130) [1997 6f a6f⁵ Jun 21] 6,400Y: fourth foal: sister to Italian 3-y-o
Chicco di Caffe, 5f winner at 2 yrs: dam 2-y-o 5f and 6f winner: tailed off in maiden
and seller. *Martyn Meade*

IMPLICITLY   2 ch.f. (Apr 25) Lion Cavern (USA) 117 – Pushkinia (FR) 95   65
(Pharly (FR) 130) [1997 6.1m 6s³ a7g a8g³ Dec 10] seventh foal: half-sister to seve-   a46
ral winners, including 1m winner Shift Again and 1¼m winner Legal Train (both by
Siberian Express): dam French 2-y-o 7f winner from good family: modest form in

465

maidens at Nottingham and Catterick: didn't repeat it on the all-weather: should stay at least 7f. *W. Jarvis*

IMPOSING TIME 6 b.g. Music Boy 124 – Jandell (NZ) (Shifnal) [1996 68, a77: 49
5s 5g³ 5g⁶ 5m² 5.3m² 5f 5.1f³ a6g² a6g* a6g² a6g 1997 6d 6d 5m⁵ 5.1m 6m 6d 5m a–
Sep 17] fair performer at 5 yrs: poor form at best in 1997: stays 6f: acts on good to
firm, soft ground and fibresand: often blinkered/visored: sold only 700 gns in
October. *Miss Gay Kelleway*

IMPRESSIONIST (IRE) 2 b.c. (Apr 28) Royal Academy (USA) 130 – Yash- 106 p
ville (Top Ville 129) [1997 7g² 7g* 7g* 7g³ Oct 18] 84,000Y: rangy, rather unfurnished colt: good mover: sixth foal: half-brother to 1992 2-y-o 7f/1m winner Boldville
Bash (by Bold Arrangement) and a winner in Belgium by Persian Heights: dam
unraced: useful form: won maiden at Cork in June and Futurity Stakes at the Curragh
in August, quickening clear 2f out then holding Fruits of Love by a length in latter:
just going in coat, beaten 9½ lengths behind wide-margin winner Xaar in Dewhurst
Stakes at Newmarket, not much room 2f out, running on again close home: should
stay 1m: should make a smart 3-y-o. *A. P. O'Brien, Ireland*

IMPULSE (IRE) 2 ch.g. (Feb 13) Imp Society (USA) – Kristar (Kris 135) 61
[1997 a5g² 6.1g⁴ 6m⁶ 5d⁶ 6g a7g⁵ 6g 7g* 7m⁴ 8d Oct 20] leggy gelding: ninth a54
foal: dam Italian 1m winner: modest performer: won seller at Thirsk (sold out of
A. Jarvis' stable 6,600 gns and gelded) in August: good fourth in nursery at
Catterick penultimate start: has shaped as though will stay 1m: acts on good to firm
ground: has run well when sweating and edgy: visored at Thirsk and previous start.
Mrs J. R. Ramsden

IMPULSIF (USA) 3 ch.c. Diesis 133 – High Sevens 90 (Master Willie 129) 73
[1996 73: 5m² 6m⁴ 6.1m³ 5.7f⁵ 7g* 7g 1997 9g 7d⁵ 7m 7f² 7.1m⁴ 6m⁴ 6m² 7m 7f 6m⁶
a8s² Nov 10] leggy colt: fair handicapper: effective at 6f to easy 1m: acts on firm
going and equitrack. *D. J. S. ffrench Davis*

IMPULSIVE AIR (IRE) 5 b.g. Try My Best (USA) 130 – Tracy's Sundown 69
(Red Sunset 120) [1996 69: 6.1m⁵ 7g 6.9f* 8.3m⁵ 8f* 8.3f³ 8m² 8.9g 8g⁴ 7g 1997
7m² 8m 7.6v⁶ 8g 8.1m⁵ 8g 8g⁴ 10m 10g² 8m² 8m* 7.1m* 8.3g⁶ 7d 8.2d⁴ 8g Oct 18]
strong gelding: carries condition: unimpressive mover: fair performer: won minor
events at Redcar and Musselburgh in August: stays 1¼m: acts on firm and dead
ground: tried visored. *E. Weymes*

IMPULSIVE DECISION (IRE) 2 gr.f. (Apr 2) Nomination 125 – Siva (FR) 60
(Bellypha 130) [1997 5m 5g⁴ 6m³ 6f³ 7d 6d* a7g⁴ Dec 13] IR 4,200Y: leggy filly: a71 ?
half-sister to 4-y-o May Queen Megan and winners abroad by Persian Bold and
Petorius: dam French 1m to 11f winner: modest performer: won maiden at Folkestone in October: appeared to run well in minor event on all-weather debut final start:
stays 6f: acts on firm and dead ground. *Martyn Meade*

IMPY FOX (IRE) 3 ch.f. Imp Society (USA) – Rusty Goddess (Hard Fought –
125) [1996 50, a53: 6m⁴ a6g* 6.1m⁴ 7g 1997 7.3s a6g Jun 27] close-coupled filly:
modest form at 2 yrs for C. Dwyer: tailed off in handicaps in 1997. *P. Mooney*

IMROZ (USA) 3 b.f. Nureyev (USA) 131 – All At Sea (USA) 124 (Riverman 99
(USA) 131) [1996 96: 6g* 6m⁵ 7f* 1997 6g² 7s² 7g* 7m⁴ 7d³ 6f² Sep 17] small-
ish, leggy filly: has a quick action: useful performer: won minor event at
Yarmouth in July, dictating pace: creditable efforts afterwards, 1½ lengths fourth (to
Dazzle) in listed race at Goodwood and ½ length second in minor event at Yarmouth:
stays 7f: acts on firm and soft going: tends to take good hold and carry head high:
has worn dropped noseband: consistent: to be trained by R. Frankel in USA.
H. R. A. Cecil

IMSHISHWAY (IRE) 2 b.c. (Mar 17) Royal Academy (USA) 130 – Mama 82 p
Lucia (Workboy 123) [1997 6d 6g 7m* 7.3g Oct 24] 16,500Y: tall colt: good mover:
fifth foal: dam unraced: won maiden at Goodwood comfortably by ½ length from
Titan, held up and quickening well: ran well when about 11 lengths seventh of 8 in
Horris Hill Stakes at Newbury following month: will stay 1m: should improve
further. *B. J. Meehan*

I'M STILL HERE 3 gr.g. Skyliner 117 – Miss Colenca (Petong 126) [1996 61d: 64
5s² 5d² 5s⁴ a5g⁶ 6f² 7.1m 6g⁶ 7.1s³ 1997 6d* 7g Apr 23] good-topped gelding:

modest handicapper: won at Hamilton in April, getting up near finish: bandaged front, ran poorly final start: effective at stiff 6f/7f: ran poorly only start on fibresand, acts on any turf going: joined J. K. M. Oliver. *J. Berry*

I'M TEF   2 b.g. (Mar 30) Noble Patriarch 115 – Who's That Lady 60 (Nordance (USA)) [1997 5s 6m 5m⁴ 7g 6m 6g 7m a6g² 5s⁴ a6g² a7g* Dec 18] compact gelding: second foal: dam 7f winner: modest performer: in good form in all-weather nurseries late in year, and won at Southwell in December: stays 7f well: tried blinkered, at least as effective without. *T. D. Easterby*   50 a61

IN A TIZZY   4 b.f. Sizzling Melody 117 – Tizzy 79 (Formidable (USA) 125) [1996 29, a–: 11.1m⁴ 9.9g 5g 1997 12s⁴ 10g 13d⁵ Jul 4] poor maiden handicapper: probably best up to 1½m: acts on soft going: visored once (soundly beaten) on all-weather. *A. B. Mulholland*   30 a–

IN CAHOOTS   4 gr.c. Kalaglow 132 – Royal Celerity (USA) (Riverman (USA) 131) [1996 46: 5.1g 9.9g a8.5g⁶ 10.2m 10d 11.9f 10f* 10.8f 1997 a10g⁴ a12g 10m May 17] leggy colt: poor performer: better at 1¼m than shorter: acts on firm ground: blinkered once (pulled too hard). *C. J. Hill*   40

INCANDESCENT   3 b.f. Inca Chief (USA) – Heavenly State (Enchantment 115) [1996 49?: 5.7g⁶ 6m a7g 1997 a8g Dec 4] poor maiden: tailed off only start at 3 yrs. *A. P. Jones*   –

INCANTRICE   4 ch.f. Faustus (USA) 118 – Dependable (Formidable (USA) 125) [1996 NR 1997 7g 9.2d 10g Apr 26] 1,000Y: first foal: dam unraced daughter of half-sister to Chilibang: tailed off in sellers and claimer (gurgled final start). *W. Storey*   –

INCATIME   3 b.g. Inca Chief (USA) – Parrot Fashion 86 (Pieces of Eight 128) [1996 63, a?: 5m³ 5m⁴ a6g a5g⁵ 1997 a5g⁵ 5g 7g³ 5.1g Sep 11] sturdy gelding: disappointing sprint maiden: blinkered twice. *A. G. Foster*   –

INCEPTA   2 b.c. (Apr 7) Selkirk (USA) 129 – Ringlet (USA) 58 (Secreto (USA) 128) [1997 7g Sep 18] 21,000Y: rangy, attractive colt: has scope: first foal: dam 1¼m and 13f winner, half-sister to Sure Blade and Sure Sharp: 33/1 and not fully wound up, never a factor after slow start in maiden at Newbury: withdrawn after breaking out of stall just over month later: looks sort to do better. *B. W. Hills*   – p

INCHAHOY   2 ch.f. (Apr 26) Inchinor 119 – Ackcontent (USA) (Key To Content (USA)) [1997 8.2d Oct 30] 6,000Y: smallish, sparely-made filly: fifth known foal: half-sister to 3-y-o Eager To Please and 5f (at 2 yrs) and 7f winner No Sympathy (by Ron's Victory): dam rare once at 2 yrs in North America: awkward stalls, slowly away and never a threat in maiden at Nottingham. *J. G. Smyth-Osbourne*   –

INCHALONG   2 b.f. (Mar 17) Inchinor 119 – Reshift 94 (Night Shift (USA)) [1997 5d⁵ 5m³ 5m⁵ 5m³ 5g² 6m⁶ 5g⁵ 6g² 6g* 5m² 6d⁵ 6m² 5d³ 6g⁶ 7.1g* 6m⁴ 7m³ 7g³ 7m³ 6d² 6d³ 7g³ 6.1d² 7s Nov 8] 4,500Y: small, leggy filly: unimpressive mover: first foal: dam 6f (including at 2 yrs) and 7f winner: extremely tough 2-y-o seen out from March to November: fair performer: won seller at Newcastle and nursery at Musselburgh in the summer: numerous good efforts in nurseries afterwards: suited by testing conditions at 6f and should stay 1m: acts on good to firm and dead ground, poorly drawn on soft: edged markedly right penultimate start: splendidly genuine and consistent. *M. Brittain*   74

IN CHARGE   2 ch.f. (Apr 20) Be My Chief (USA) 122 – Great Exception 84 (Grundy 137) [1997 7m Nov 1] sixth live foal: half-sister to 3 winners, including 1¼m winner Exemption and 1m and 1½m winner Exclusion (both by Ballad Rock): dam won at 1½m and 15f: 50/1, always behind in maiden at Newmarket. *H. Candy*   –

INCHCAILLOCH (IRE)   8 b.g. Lomond (USA) 128 – Glowing With Pride 114 (Ile de Bourbon (USA) 133) [1996 81: 16g 17.2d² 16.1f* 18g* 1997 18m⁶ 16g² 16g² 20m 22.2d⁶ 12m 18g Oct 18] big, strong, lengthy gelding: impresses in appearance: good mover: useful hurdler/chaser: fairly useful handicapper on flat: won Queen's Prize at Kempton in March: below form last 4 starts, in Cesarewitch final one (had won race in 1996): stays 2¼m well: stays very well: acts on firm going (won on soft at 3 yrs): held up: suitable mount for apprentice: genuine and versatile. *J. S. King*   89

INC

INCHELLA 4 b.f. Inca Chief (USA) – Sandy Cap 62 (Sandy Creek 123) [1996 –: 8.3g 1997 8f a12g 13.1m Jul 7] no sign of ability. *A. P. Jones* –

INCHTINA 2 b.f. (Feb 24) Inchinor 119 – Nikitina 106 (Nijinsky (CAN) 138) [1997 6g² 7m² Sep 22] 26,000Y: closely related to French 1m winner Eltecey (by Ahonoora) and half-sister to several winners, including useful Irish middle-distance stayer Excellenza (by Exceller): dam Irish 1¼m winner: second in steadily-run maidens at Salisbury and Kempton, beaten 1¾ lengths by Elsurur on latter course: will stay at least 1m: should improve again. *H. Candy* 78 p

INCLINATION 3 b.f. Beveled (USA) – Pallomere 85 (Blue Cashmere 129) [1996 64: 7g² 7.6d² 6m⁶ 1997 8d⁶ 7.3s 8f 7g³ 9.9v² 10m³ 10.1g³ 8g³ 7g³ 7g³ 6.1m 9.7d Oct 21] tall, lengthy filly: modest maiden handicapper: effective at 7f to 1¼m: acts on any ground: usually races up with pace: consistent. *M. Blanshard* 62

IN COMMAND (IRE) 3 b.c. Sadler's Wells (USA) 132 – Flying Melody (Auction Ring (USA) 123) [1996 114: 6m* 7m³ 7f² 6m³ 7g* 1997 7g⁴ 8m⁶ 8f Sep 11] sturdy, deep-girthed colt: has a quick action: smart 2-y-o, winner of Dewhurst Stakes: didn't go on at 3 yrs, fourth in Greenham Stakes at Newbury and down the field in St James's Palace Stakes at Royal Ascot and Group 3 at Doncaster: stays 7f: raced only on good going or firmer. *B. W. Hills* 104

INDIAN AFFAIR 3 b.f. Indian Ridge 123 – Steppey Lane 95 (Tachypous 128) [1996 NR 1997 8g Jun 18] first foal: dam 1¾m winner: soon tailed off in maiden at Ripon on debut. *W. W. Haigh* –

INDIANA PRINCESS 4 b.f. Warrshan (USA) 117 – Lovely Greek Lady (Ela-Mana-Mou 132) [1996 63: 10m⁵ 8m⁶ 9m⁶ 12m⁶ 14d⁵ 13.6m² 1997 12d 13.1g 14g Sep 27] workmanlike filly: modest maiden in 1996: no form at 4 yrs, hanging markedly left approaching straight and virtually pulled up (reportedly had problems with her mouth) on reappearance: shapes like a stayer: acts on good to firm going: won maiden hurdle in October. *Mrs M. Reveley* –

INDIAN BLAZE 3 ch.g. Indian Ridge 123 – Odile (Green Dancer (USA) 132) [1996 77: 7m 6g² 6m⁴ 7.1v⁵ 1997 8m 7.1s 7m 7d 6.9s 10m² Jul 24] workmanlike gelding: only worthwhile form at 3 yrs when second in falsely-run handicap at Brighton: stays 1¼m: acts on good to firm and heavy ground: blinkered fifth outing: has taken strong hold. *P. W. Harris* 58

INDIAN BRAVE 3 b.c. Indian Ridge 123 – Supreme Kingdom 85 (Take A Reef 127) [1996 82: 6m² 6g³ 1997 9m 8.1m⁴ Jun 7] lengthy colt: fair form in maidens at 2 yrs: well held in similar events in 1997, looking none too enthusiastic final start: may prove best up to 1m. *M. Johnston* –

INDIAN MISSILE 2 ch.c. (Apr 6) Indian Ridge 123 – Haitienne (FR) (Green Dancer (USA) 132) [1997 6d³ 6.1m* 7d² 7s⁴ 7v² Oct 10] 66,000Y: lengthy, useful-looking colt: seventh foal: half-brother to several winners, including 3-y-o Real Estate and useful Park Charger (1m/1¼m in Ireland, by Tirol): dam French 1m winner: fairly useful form: won minor event at Chepstow in June: good second in similar event at Epsom and nursery at Ascot, beaten 2½ lengths by Smart Squall in latter: should stay 1m: acts on good to firm and heavy ground: sold (to join Major D. Chappell) 30,000 gns in October. *J. L. Dunlop* 84

INDIAN NECTAR 4 b.f. Indian Ridge 123 – Sheer Nectar 72 (Piaffer (USA) 113) [1996 62: 8f⁴ 9m 10m⁴ 10g a11g 10d 1997 10m 10.8s 10.2m⁵ Jul 17] sparely-made filly: left G. B. Balding after reappearance (well beaten in visor): poor form at best afterwards: stays 1¼m well. *R. Brotherton* 47

INDIAN RAPTURE 3 ch.f. Be My Chief (USA) 122 – Moments Joy 56 (Adonijah 126) [1996 68: 8.1g⁶ 8.1m⁶ 8.2m⁶ 7.3s 1997 a8s a8g a11g a12g Feb 21] seems to retain little ability: tried visored: sold, to go to Denmark. *Ronald Thompson* –

INDIAN RELATIVE 4 b.f. Distant Relative 128 – Elegant Tern (USA) 102 (Sea Bird II 145) [1996 83: 8.2m 7.9f 7g³ 6f* 5.7m* 6m 6g² 6d⁵ 6m² 6m 5g 1997 6m 6d 6m⁴ 5.7g⁴ 6d 6.9m⁶ 6m 6f Sep 18] smallish, good-quartered filly: generally disappointing at 4 yrs, easily best effort on third outing: best form at sprint distances: possibly suited by going firmer than good: has been sweating and edgy: needs strong handling. *R. Guest* 74 d

468

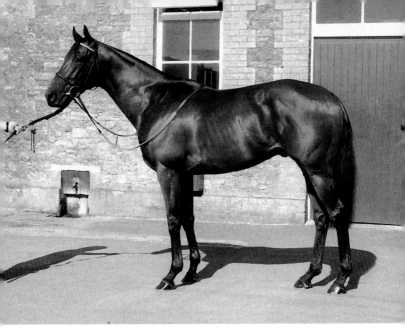

Khalil Alsayegh's "Indian Rocket"

INDIAN ROCKET 3 b.c. Indian Ridge 123 – Selvi (Mummy's Pet 125) [1996 115
113+: 6g² 6.1g* 6.1m² 6m* 6d* 6m* 6m 1997 6g⁵ 6g³ 5m³ 5d 6d Sep 5] attractive,
good-bodied colt: smart performer: best efforts at 3 yrs when 3½ lengths fifth of 23
to Royal Applause in Cork And Orrery Stakes at Royal Ascot and 4¾ lengths third to
Compton Place in July Cup at Newmarket first 2 starts: ran poorly in Haydock Park
Sprint Cup final outing: better form at 6f than 5f: unraced on extremes of going:
swerved right leaving stalls final 2-y-o start: has run well when sweating: often
bandaged: sent to UAE. *J. L. Dunlop*

INDIAN SERENADE 6 ch.g. Mansingh (USA) 120 – La Melodie 77 (Silly –
Season 127) [1996 –: 8g 8.1g a8g 6.9g 1997 6.9d 6m a8.5g⁵ 8.1m Jul 11] seems of
little account nowadays. *R. Simpson*

INDIAN SILVER 2 b.f. (Mar 11) Indian Ridge 123 – Ovideo 58 (Domynsky 110) 72
[1997 5g² 5g² 5m⁵ 6d⁵ Aug 25] 25,000Y: smallish, angular filly: first foal: dam, 2-y-o
7f winner, half-sister to smart middle-distance horse Captain Horatius: fair form
when second in maiden at Kempton and minor event at York (hung left): off course
nearly 3 months before final start: may prove best at 5f. *M. R. Channon*

INDIAN SPARK 3 ch.c. Indian Ridge 123 – Annes Gift (Ballymoss 136) [1996 102
94: 5d* 6m² 1997 8m 6f² 6m* 6g 6m⁶ 6g² 6m⁶ 5.6m 6g⁵ 5d 5g Oct 25] close-coupled
colt: poor mover: useful performer: off course 10 months before reappearance
(reportedly fractured joint in off-fore): won handicap at Salisbury in May: left
W. G. M. Turner after ninth start: respectable efforts last 2: effective at 5f and 6f: acts
on firm and dead going: usually races prominently. *J. S. Goldie*

INDIAN SPLENDOUR (IRE) 2 b.f. (Feb 17) Second Set (IRE) 127 – Clover 45
Honey (King of Clubs 124) [1997 a5s⁴ a6g Dec 6] IR 10,500Y: first foal: dam,

469

maiden, from family of Middle Park winner Balla Cove: poor form in maidens at Lingfield and Wolverhampton. *R. Guest*

INDIAN WOLF   4 ch.c. Indian Ridge 123 – Red Riding Hood (FR) 62 (Mummy's   –
Pet 125) [1996 –: 10.2g 8.3m 8.1d⁵ 7.1g 10m 8m 7g a7g 1997 a6g a6g 5m 5.1m 7.1m Jun 13] of little account. *B. J. Llewellyn*

INDIGO DAWN   3 b.f. Rainbow Quest (USA) 134 – Dame Ashfield 90 (Grundy   78
137) [1996 NR 1997 8g³ 12g³ 12s⁵ 12m³ 13.1g³ 13d* 14.9g* a14g* 16.1m² 16.4s 16g⁵ a12g² a14g a16s* a16g* Dec 10] tall, narrow filly: eighth foal: half-sister to several winners, including 4-y-o Shirley Sue: dam 1½m winner out of a Park Hill winner: fair handicapper: had good season, winning at Hamilton, Warwick and Southwell in July and Lingfield in November and December: very much a stayer: acts on good to firm and dead ground and the all-weather: blinkered last 4 starts: idles, flashes tail and has carried head awkwardly. *M. Johnston*

INDIMAAJ   2 b.c. (Mar 17) Mtoto 134 – Fairy Feet 78 (Sadler's Wells (USA) 132)   79 p
[1997 7g³ 7.5m³ 8.5g² Aug 23] 40,000Y: useful-looking colt: has a quick action: fifth foal: dam second over 11f on only start, half-sister to Fairy Footsteps and Light Cavalry: fair form when placed in maidens at Newmarket and Beverley (2), taking long time to find stride final start: will be well suited by 1¼m+: should make a better 3-y-o. *J. L. Dunlop*

INDISCREET (CAN)   3 b.c. St Jovite (USA) 135 – Imprudent Love (USA)   99
(Foolish Pleasure (USA)) [1996 105p: 6m* 1997 9.9s* 10d⁵ 7m Jun 18] quite attractive colt: fine mover: failed to live up to promise of only 2-y-o start: narrow winner of 3-runner minor event at Beverley in May: towards rear in listed race at Goodwood and Jersey Stakes at Royal Ascot (folded tamely) afterwards: bred to be very well suited by 1¼m+: sent to USA. *D. R. Loder*

INDIUM   3 b.g. Groom Dancer (USA) 128 – Gold Bracelet § (Golden Fleece   76
(USA) 133) [1996 80: 7.6m 8d³ 7m³ 1997 10.2m⁵ 10g⁵ Jun 6] fair maiden handicapper: may prove best up to 1¼m. *J. H. M. Gosden*

INDONESIAN (IRE)   5 b. or br.g. Alzao (USA) 117 – Miss Garuda 94 (Persian   46
Bold 123) [1996 –: 8d 10m 10g⁶ 12.3m 1997 12m² 12.3m 12g 12g Aug 23] sturdy gelding: fairly useful handicapper at best: just poor form in 1997, well beaten in seller final outing. *P. Calver*

INDRAPURA (IRE)   5 b.g. Gallic League 119 – Stella Ann (Ahonoora 122)   –
[1996 60: 8f 8.3m 7m 7.1m* 7m⁵ 7f⁶ 1997 10.2g 7.1m Sep 17] tall gelding: formerly fair 7f/1m winner: sold out of M. Pipe's stable 2,400 gns in February before reappearance: well beaten for new yard. *J. E. Long*

INDY KNIGHT (IRE)   2 ch.f. (Apr 15) Indian Ridge 123 – Bag Lady 86 (Be My   –
Guest (USA) 126) [1997 7g 7d Sep 18] 19,000F: unfurnished filly: half-sister to several winners, including Fresh Look (11f, by Alzao) and Bag of Tricks (1¼m/1½m, by Chief Singer): dam, ungenuine maiden who stayed 1m, from family of El Gran Senor: behind in maidens at Kempton and Ayr. *Martyn Meade*

INFAMOUS (USA)   4 ch.g. Diesis 133 – Name And Fame (USA) (Arts And   69
Letters (USA)) [1996 86: 11.8s* 12d² 14d 12m 8f 11.6g² 10.8f² 14f 10d 10.3m³ 1997 a12g³ a9.4g⁶ Jan 29] angular gelding: shows knee action: fairly useful at 3 yrs for P. Cole: only fair on the all-weather early in 1997: stays 1½m: acts on firm going and soft: well beaten only try in blinkers: won twice over hurdles in September. *R. J. O'Sullivan*

INFATUATION   4 b.g. Music Boy 124 – Fleeting Affair 98 (Hotfoot 126) [1996   93
79: 8.1m⁶ 10g⁴ 10.5d³ 1997 10s 10g 12g* 12.3m⁴ 12g² 10.3m* 10m³ 10g² Oct 18] tall, lengthy gelding: fairly useful handicapper: won at Beverley in June and at Doncaster in September: creditable placed efforts last 2 starts: stays 1½m: acts on good to firm and dead ground: often sweats: has flashed tail and carried head high: suited by waiting tactics. *Lady Herries*

INFLATION   3 b.f. Primo Dominie 121 – Fluctuate 87 (Sharpen Up 127) [1996   64
68: 6g³ 5f² 1997 6.1d⁵ May 9] modest sprint maiden: joined J. Leigh. *R. F. Johnson Houghton*

INFLUENCE PEDLER 4 b.g. Keen 116 – La Vie En Primrose 104 (Henbit (USA) 130) [1996 64: a11g 12s 14.1g³ 14.6m* 14.1m⁴ 16.4m² 14.1f* 15.4g² 16f² 16.4m⁴ 16m² 14.1g⁵ 1997 14.1d Oct 30] sturdy gelding: fairly useful hurdler: modest staying handicapper on flat: well held only 4-y-o start: sold 7,600 gns in December and joined Miss K. George. *J. A. B. Old* –

INGLEBOROUGH 3 b.g. Barrys Gamble 102 – Dreamy Desire 50 (Palm Track 122) [1996 NR 1997 8g 7.1d 10m³ 12s 10.1g Oct 22] big, workmanlike gelding: half-brother to ungenuine 1¼m seller winner Ghylldale (by Sweet Monday): dam free-going maiden: well held in maidens and a handicap. *D. Moffatt* –

INGLE BOY 2 b.g. (Mar 18) Barrys Gamble 102 – Maydrum 50 (Meldrum 112) [1997 7.1m 6m 8.3g Sep 1] seventh foal: half-brother to a 2-y-o 6f seller winner by Sylvan Express: dam third in 7f seller: no sign of ability, including in seller. *B. Mactaggart* –

IN GOOD FAITH 5 b.g. Beveled (USA) – Dulcidene 71 (Behistoun 131) [1996 66: 8d 10g 8.1s a8g³ 1997 a8g² 8.3s 10d 10m⁶ a8g 8.5m Jul 29] neat gelding: shows knee action: modest handicapper: barely stays 1¼m: acts on fibresand: best efforts on turf on good ground or softer: tried visored: inconsistent. *J. J. Quinn* a61

IN GOOD NICK 3 b.f. Nicholas (USA) 111 – Better Still (IRE) (Glenstal (USA) 118) [1996 61: 5m 5f³ 5f³ 6m 6g⁴ 6m³ 7m⁵ 1997 7.5m 7g³ 7.5d² 8g⁶ 7m⁴ 6d 6m 6g 7m 7m Oct 7] small, strong filly: modest maiden: well below form last 5 starts: stays 7.5f: acts on firm and dead ground: blinkered/visored: races prominently: sent to Holland. *M. W. Easterby* 61 d

INIMITABLE 3 b.f. Polish Precedent (USA) 131 – Saveur (Ardross 134) [1996 66p: 7f⁶ 8g 1997 10m⁶ 11.4g 10s* 12m⁴ Jul 16] big, lengthy filly: fair performer, lightly raced: won maiden handicap at Salisbury in June, making most: looked none too keen only subsequent start: takes strong hold, and barely stays 1½m: acts on soft and good to firm going: sold 20,000 gns in December. *J. L. Dunlop* 65

INJAZAAT (USA) 3 b. or br.f. Dayjur (USA) 137 – Basma (USA) 104 (Grey Dawn II 132) [1996 70: 6m⁶ 6m 6m² 1997 7m⁴ 7m Sep 21] quite attractive filly: modest maiden: much better effort in September when fourth: probably stays 7f: blinkered last 3 starts: sold 9,000 gns in December. *Major W. R. Hern* 60

INKWELL 3 b.g. Relief Pitcher 120 – Fragrant Hackette 32 (Simply Great (FR) 122) [1996 –: 6f 6.9d 1997 7m 8s⁴ 8g² 8m⁶ 9s 10m 8g³ 8d⁵ a12g a10g³ a10g Dec 19] smallish, robust gelding: poor maiden on balance of form: left A. Hide after ninth start: stays 1¼m: acts on good to firm ground, soft and equitrack: tried blinkered/visored. *G. L. Moore* 40

INNER KEY 2 b.g. (Apr 25) Interrex (CAN) – Key To Enchantment (Key To Content (USA)) [1997 6g⁶ 6m⁶ a7g Oct 20] fifth foal: dam ran twice: well beaten in sellers: trained by first 2 starts A. P. Jones. *P. D. Evans* –

INN ON THE PARK 2 b.g. (Feb 19) Northern Park (USA) 107 – Hotel California (IRE) 58 (Last Tycoon 131) [1997 6m⁶ 6m 8d Sep 13] 8,000F: leggy, unfurnished gelding: first foal: dam 2-y-o 7.5f winner from good family: well held in minor event and maidens: slowly away first 2 starts. *S. Dow* –

INOVAR 7 b.g. Midyan (USA) 124 – Princess Cinders 61 (King of Spain 121) [1996 –, a35: a12g a12g⁵ a12g* a11g 12.1g 12.1g a12g 1997 a12g Feb 28] big, workmanlike gelding: bad handicapper: well beaten only 7-y-o start. *C. B. B. Booth* –

IN QUESTION 3 br. or b.g. Deploy 131 – Questionable (Rainbow Quest (USA) 134) [1996 79p: 7m² 8.1m⁴ 1997 10m³ 10s³ 10.8m* 15d* 16.1g 16.1g Aug 25] big, workmanlike gelding: has scope: fairly useful performer: won maiden at Warwick and handicap (easily) at Ayr in June: tailed off in handicaps last 2 starts, looking none too keen final start (subsequently gelded): should stay beyond 15f: front runner last 3 starts: sold 13,000 gns in October. *B. W. Hills* 90

INSATIABLE (IRE) 4 b.c. Don't Forget Me 127 – Petit Eclair 94 (Major Portion 129) [1996 93: 8m³ 8f² 1997 7.9g³ 8.1g* May 26] workmanlike colt: progressive performer, very lightly raced: won strongly-run 17-runner Doubleprint Whitsun Cup (Handicap) at Sandown in May by 1¼ lengths from Bold Words, leading inside final 1f having been soon off bit and wide (tended to carry head to one side) on home turn: 109 p

Doubleprint Whitsun Cup Rated Stakes (Handicap), Sandown—
Insatiable shows himself still on the upgrade in beating Bold Words and Samara

will be at least as effective at 1¼m as 1m: acts on good to firm and dead ground: stays in training, and potentially smart if all is well with him. *M. R. Stoute*

INSHALLAH 2 ch.f. (Mar 29) Durgam (USA) – Kaliala (FR) (Pharly (FR) 130) 59 d [1997 5g 5f⁶ 6g⁴ 6.1m 6m³ 7.1g 6g 5s Nov 6] 10,000Y: sister to 1m seller winner Chauvelin and half-sister to 2 winners, including French winner up to 13.5f Kalaniya (by Kahyasi): dam French 1m winner: modest maiden: well beaten in selling nursery final start: stays 6f: gave trouble and withdrawn once: inconsistent. *Martin Todhunter*

INSIDER TRADER 6 b.g. Dowsing (USA) 124 – Careless Whisper 94 (Homing 70 d 130) [1996 82: 5g 5m 5g⁶ 5m 5g⁴ 5m³ 5f² 5m* 5g 5g 5m² 5m 5.1d³ 5m⁵ 5m 5m² 5g 5g 5m 5f⁵ 1997 5g 5g 5m 5d 5d 5m⁴ 5m³ 5.1m⁶ 5g³ 5m 5m 5g 5d 5m 5g Oct 22] lengthy, workmanlike gelding: poor walker and mover: fair 5f handicapper, disappointing in 1997: left Mrs J. Ramsden after thirteenth start: acts on firm and soft going, below form both starts on fibresand: often bandaged off-fore: effective in blinkers/visor or not. *B. S. Rothwell*

INSPIRATIONAL (IRE) 3 ch.f. Lahib (USA) 129 – Sun Breiz (FR) (Boran) – [1996 NR 1997 8m Oct 22] 8,500Y: half-sister to several winners abroad, including French 11f winner Gollestan (by Gay Mecene): dam French maiden half-sister to the dam of Sun Princess and Saddlers' Hall, a very good family: tailed off in maiden at Yarmouth. *C. A. Cyzer*

INTERACTION 3 ch.g. Interrex (CAN) – Kimbolton Katie 81 (Aragon 118) – [1996 NR 1997 6g 6m 7f 6m 12m 8g Jul 25] 3,000F, 1,500Y: first reported foal: dam 2-y-o 5f winner: poor maiden: seemed not to stay 1½m: dead. *R. Craggs*

INTERDREAM 3 b.g. Interrex (CAN) – Dreamtime Quest (Blakeney 126) [1996 80 66+: 7m 7f* 7.3m 8f 7m 1997 a10g 10m⁵ 8f³ 8.2d² 8m⁴ 8g³ 8.3g⁴ 8.1g 10f² 10m* 8.1m² 9g* 10.5d⁶ 8d Oct 16] close-coupled gelding: fairly useful handicapper: first past post at Brighton (twice, demoted on first occasion after causing interference) and Kempton (apprentices) in the summer: effective at 1m to 1¼m: acts on firm and dead ground: tends to hang, and not an easy ride: consistent. *R. Hannon*

INTERNAL AFFAIR (USA) 2 b.g. (Mar 11) Nicholas (USA) 111 – Gdynia 67 p (USA) (Sir Ivor 135) [1997 6d Oct 28] closely related to Belmont Stakes winner Danzig Connection and Grade 2 9f winner Roi Danzig (both by Danzig) and half-brother to Irish 1986 2-y-o 6f winner Rictorious (by Conquistador Cielo): dam won twice up to 1¼m: 5/1 from 8/1, shaped better than result suggests when seventh of 21 to Bandbox in maiden at Leicester, third home on disadvantageous stand side, held up and not given hard time: looks sure to improve. *W. J. Haggas*

INTERREGNUM 3 ch.f. Interrex (CAN) – Lillicara (FR) (Caracolero (USA) – 131) [1996 –: 7m 1997 8g 10d 14.1g Jul 30] of no account. *A. G. Foster*

IN THE BAND 4 b.f. Sharrood (USA) 124 – Upper Caen (High Top 131) [1996 64d: a10g² a8g³ a12g 11.9f⁵ 12m 10m⁴ 10m 1997 a12g⁴ a12g⁵ Mar 15] modest maiden: well below form in 1997: sent to Holland. *Lord Huntingdon*

IN THE GENES 3 b.g. Syrtos 106 – Ruby's Vision (Balinger 116) [1996 NR 64
1997 12d³ 10.3d⁶ 9m⁴ 12.3d 11.8d 10d³ 10m Nov 4] fourth foal: half-brother to
winning staying jumper Act of Faith (by Oats): dam tailed off both starts over
hurdles: modest maiden handicapper: trained by J. L. Eyre until after fourth start:
stays 1¼m well: yet to race on extremes of going. *I. P. Williams*

IN THE MONEY (IRE) 8 b.h. Top Ville 129 – Rensaler (USA) (Stop The Music 54
(USA)) [1996 62: a12g⁶ a12g² a12g* a12g* 12m a12g4 11.8m* a12g⁵ a12g³ 12.3m³ a62
11.8g³ 12m⁶ 11.8m 12m³ a12g 12m a11g⁴ a12g⁵ a12g⁴ a12g² 1997 a14.8g a14.8f³
a16g⁴ a12g* a12g* a12g³ a12g* a12g* 11.8m* a12g a12g a12g³ 14.1f³ 12g⁴ a12f
12g³ Jul 25] leggy horse: modest handicapper: successful at Lingfield (3 times),
Wolverhampton and Leicester early in year: below form last 2 starts: effective at
1½m to 2m: acts on good to firm and soft ground, best efforts on the all-weather:
usually held up: sold 4,500 gns in November. *R. Hollinshead*

IN THE SUN (USA) 2 b.f. (Feb 8) Alleged (USA) 138 – Pandysia (USA) (Storm 67 p
Bird (CAN) 134) [1997 7m 7d⁵ 8.2d⁵ Oct 30] $30,000F, 22,000Y: sturdy filly: first
foal: dam unraced half-sister to useful stayer Allegan (by Alleged): progressive
form in maidens, never placed to challenge under considerate ride final start: should
do better over further (will stay at least 1½m) at 3 yrs, particularly in handicaps.
J. L. Dunlop

INTIAASH (IRE) 5 br.m. Shaadi (USA) 126 – Funun (USA) 84 (Fappiano 81
(USA)) [1996 70, a79: a7g⁶ 6g a5g² a6g* 6d³ 6.1d⁴ a7g⁴ 6.1m⁵ 1997 a7g a5g⁶ a6g⁶ a74
a6g³ 5.1m* a5g 5.1d* a6f² 5.1s a7g² a5g* a7g⁴ 6m 5.1g 5g 5.7g 5m⁶ 6.1g 7g⁶ Oct 24]
tall, lengthy mare: fair performer: in good form for much of 1997, and won handicaps
at Bath in April and May and claimer at Lingfield in July: effective at 5f to 7f: acts on
any all-weather/turf: tried visored earlier in career: not the easiest of rides (tends to
hang left) and best held up. *D. Haydn Jones*

INTIKHAB (USA) 3 b.c. Red Ransom (USA) – Crafty Example (USA) (Crafty 113
Prospector (USA)) [1996 101p: 6m² 6m* 6m* 1997 8g² 7m² 8s² 8m* 8.5g* 8m*

Hamdan Al Maktoum's "Intikhab"

473

Oct 2] sturdy colt: has moved short to post: smart performer: won minor event at Doncaster in July and listed races at Epsom (by 1¾ lengths from Almushtarak) in September and Newmarket (by 2 lengths from Swiss Law) in October: stays 8.5f: acts on good to firm and soft going: reliable: joined Godolphin. *D. Morley*

INTISAB 4 b.f. Green Desert (USA) 127 – Ardassine (Ahonoora 122) [1996 NR 90
1997 6f* 8m⁵ 7.1g⁶ 7.1m⁶ 8d² 7g² Jul 16] strong, good-bodied filly: fairly useful performer: ran once at 2 yrs, withdrawn lame once in 1996: landed odds in maiden at Lingfield in April: good second in handicaps at Newmarket and Yarmouth last 2 starts: stayed 1m: acted on firm and dead going: visits Selkirk. *R. W. Armstrong*

INTO DEBT 4 b.f. Cigar 68 – Serious Affair (Valiyar 129) [1996 38: a7g 6m 7.1g 37
5.3f⁵ 6m² 6m 5m a6g a7g 1997 a6g a7g a7g* a8g a7g⁴ a7g³ a8g⁶ 6.1m 7m a8g 6d 6m
6m a7g⁶ a7s a8g a7g Dec 10] poor handicapper: won at Lingfield (apprentices) in January: inconsistent after: stays 7f: acts on equitrack, raced mainly on good going or firmer on turf: no improvement blinkered: sometimes slowly away. *Jamie Poulton*

INTREPID FORT 8 br.g. Belfort (FR) 89 – Dauntless Flight (Golden Mallard –
103) [1996 –: 7g 8m 8f 10.3g⁶ 9.9m⁶ 10g 9f⁵ 1997 a12g 8m 8g 8g 7g⁵ 9.9g Aug 23] workmanlike gelding: bad maiden: usually blinkered/visored. *B. W. Murray*

INTUITIVE 2 b.f. (Mar 19) Teenoso (USA) 135 – Hasland 40 (Aragon 118) [1997 –
6g 8.1d 6m⁵ Oct 1] unfurnished filly: fourth living foal: dam won 5f seller at 2 yrs: well beaten in maidens. *J. L. Eyre*

INVERMARK 3 b.g. Machiavellian (USA) 123 – Applecross 117 (Glint of Gold 94
128) [1996 87: 7m 8g⁵ 8g³ 1997 10m 11.5m* 10m⁵ 11.9m² 12s⁴ Nov 8] tall, workmanlike gelding: fairly useful performer: won maiden at Yarmouth in July: good efforts in handicaps afterwards, never-nearer fourth of 24 to Sabadilla in November Handicap at Doncaster on final start: will stay beyond 1½m: acts on good to firm and soft ground: flashes tail. *J. R. Fanshawe*

INVEST WISELY 5 ch.g. Dashing Blade 117 – Saniette (Crystal Palace (FR) –
132) [1996 85: 11.9m 16.5g 13.9m⁴ 16.1m 16.1g⁴ 16f⁶ 20m 16.1m 1997 18m⁵ 17.1m Apr 22] tall, narrow gelding: fairly useful staying handicapper at best: well beaten in 1997. *M. D. Hammond*

INVIGILATE 8 ch.g. Viking (USA) – Maria Da Gloria (St Chad 120) [1996 58d: –
6d 5g 5f⁵ 6m* 6m 5f⁵ 5m 6g⁶ 6f⁶ 6f 6d 5.1g 1997 6f 6m 6m Jun 11] workmanlike gelding: inconsistent sprint handicapper: no form in 1997. *M. R. Channon*

INVOCATION 10 ch.g. Kris 135 – Royal Saint (USA) (Crimson Satan) [1996 49
55, a71: a7g² a7g a6g² a7g⁶ a7g² a6g⁶ a6g⁴ a6g² 6f⁶ 6d 6m⁴ 6m³ 6m 5m⁴ 6f a7g⁴ a7g³ a68
a5g⁵ a7s⁵ a6g 1997 a6g* a6g a6g² a8g* a10g² a8g* a7g a8g⁵ a8g⁶ 6s 6d 8.3g a7g*
a7g 8m a9.4g a7g⁴ a7g³ a8g a10g⁶ Dec 12] big, strong gelding: bad mover: fair on the all-weather, modest on turf: won 2 handicaps and a claimer at Lingfield in January/February, and minor event there in July: effective at 6f to 1m: goes well on equitrack, and acts on good to firm and soft ground: often bandaged: tried blinkered/visored: sometimes slowly away. *G. L. Moore*

IOULIOS 3 ch.c. Shavian 125 – Touch of White 77 (Song 132) [1996 –: 6g 1997 –
5s 5m⁶ 5g a5g Sep 8] little sign of ability. *J. E. Banks*

IRISH ACCORD (USA) 3 b. or br.c. Cahill Road (USA) – Dimples (USA) 92
(Smile (USA)) [1996 90: 6m* 6g⁴ 1997 6f³ 8.1d 7.9g 8.1m⁴ 8m 7m⁵ 8m Jul 31] big, strong colt: has a fluent action: fairly useful performer: in frame in minor event at Leicester and handicap at Haydock: shaped quite well final 2 starts: may well prove best around 1m: acts on firm ground, below form on dead: hung right both 2-y-o starts, raced too freely third 3-y-o one: sent to Hong Kong. *Mrs J. R. Ramsden*

IRISH FICTION (IRE) 3 b.g. Classic Music (USA) – Wasmette (IRE) (Wassl –
125) [1996 66d: 5s² 5d² 5d³ 5.1m⁴ 5m² 7f* 7m² 7f 7m⁴ 6m² 6g 7f* 7g³ 8m⁶ a8g 1997 6.9g 8f 7m 10g 10.8d Jun 24] useful-looking gelding: fair at best: well beaten in 1997: stayed 1m: acted on any going: tried visored: dead. *D. J. S. Cosgrove*

IRISH GROOM 10 b.g. Shy Groom (USA) – Romany Pageant (Welsh Pageant –
132) [1996 –: 10.8f 1997 10.8d Aug 25] lightly raced and little recent form. *A. Streeter*

IRISH KINSMAN 4 b.g. Distant Relative 128 – Inesdela (Wolver Hollow 126) – [1996 –: 7g⁶ 7.1m⁵ 10d 8m 12m 1997 10.8m 10d 10g May 23] rangy gelding: no worthwhile form: tried blinkered. *G. H. Yardley*

IRISH LIGHT (USA) 3 ch.f. Irish River (FR) 131 – Solar Star (USA) 93 (Lear 91 Fan (USA) 130) [1996 NR 1997 8d* 8s 8.1m* 8m 8m Nov 1] smallish, good-bodied filly: first foal: dam, 6f winner at 2 yrs, granddaughter of Oaks fourth Shore Line, from the family of Soviet Line and Pure Grain: fairly useful performer: won maiden at Bath in May and handicap at Sandown in September: below form in valuable handicaps last 2 starts: should stay 1¼m: pulled muscle on soft going. *M. R. Stoute*

IRISH OASIS (IRE) 4 b.g. Mazaad 106 – Alpenwind (Tumble Wind (USA)) – [1996 49: 9.9g² 11m⁶ 13.8g 12g³ 10m² 7.5g 10g 11f 1997 12.3m 10g 8.5d Aug 13] big gelding: poor maiden: stayed 11f: visored once: dead. *B. S. Rothwell*

IRISH STAMP (IRE) 8 b.g. Niniski (USA) 125 – Bayazida (Bustino 136) [1996 – –: 16f 1997 16m Sep 15] fairly useful staying chaser: soundly beaten all starts on flat since 1993. *F. Murphy*

IRIS MAY 2 b.f. (May 1) Brief Truce (USA) 126 – Choire Mhor 100 (Dominion 68 123) [1997 5.1m² 6d² 6s² 5.1m⁶ 6g⁴ 6m³ 5f* 5s⁴ Oct 16] 17,000Y: good-topped filly: seventh foal: half-sister to 3-y-o Cathedral, a 2-y-o 1m winner by Last Tycoon and 11f winner by Sure Blade: dam ran only at 2 yrs when winner over 6f: fair performer: won maiden at Lingfield in October: stays 6f: acts on firm and soft ground: blinkered final 3 starts: usually front runner: consistent. *J. Berry*

IRON MOUNTAIN (IRE) 2 b.g. (Jan 24) Scenic 128 – Merlannah (IRE) (Shy 66 Groom (USA)) [1997 7.1g 5d⁵ 6s⁴ 7d³ 6g 10g² 8m⁵ 8d⁶ Oct 17] 34,000Y: lengthy gelding: second foal: half-brother to Italian 3-y-o Perla Nera (by Distinctly North), 5f and 7f winner at 2 yrs: dam Irish maiden half-sister to Anita's Prince: fair maiden: ran well in nurseries sixth and final starts: will stay 1¼m: best form on good ground or softer: blinkered second and final start: sold 16,000 gns after final one. *N. A. Callaghan*

IRSAL 3 ch.g. Nashwan (USA) 135 – Amwag (USA) 106 (El Gran Senor (USA) 82 136) [1996 70p: 7m⁵ 1997 8.2m⁶ 10.2m³ 12.1s³ 12g⁶ 10.2m³ 12m* 12m⁴ 14m⁶ Aug 14] quite attractive colt: has a round action: fairly useful performer: sold out of A. Stewart's stable 40,000 gns in July: won 4-runner handicap at Salisbury on first start for new stable and good fifth (promoted a place) to Maylane in Tote Gold Trophy (Handicap) at Goodwood later in month: unlikely to stay beyond 1½m: acts on soft ground and good to firm: won over hurdles in October. *M. C. Pipe*

IRTIFA 3 ch.f. Lahib (USA) 129 – Thaidah (CAN) 105 (Vice Regent (CAN)) 71 [1996 68: 5.7f² 6m* 6d⁵ 7.9g 1997 7m⁴ 7m⁴ 8.1s 8.1m³ 7m⁴ 8g Oct 7] quite attractive filly: fair handicapper: effective at 7f/1m: acts on good to firm going, well beaten on soft: visored last 3 starts: sold 42,000 gns in December. *P. T. Walwyn*

ISABELLA 2 ch.f. (Feb 22) Primo Dominie 121 – Scossa (USA) 52 (Shadeed – (USA) 135) [1997 5g 5m 7g Aug 5] strong, good-quartered filly: second foal: dam, maiden who stayed 1¼m, out of Grade 3 1½m winner Scythe: signs of just a little ability in maidens: mounted on track and last to post on debut: joined J. Noseda. *T. Keddy*

ISABELLA GONZAGA 3 b.f. Rock Hopper 124 – Lawful 76 (Law Society 60 (USA) 130) [1996 NR 1997 8.3s⁵ 8.3g⁶ 10s a10g⁴ Oct 27] 5,500Y: third foal: dam, second at 1¼m on both starts, is half-sister to smart French 1½m performer French Glory out of Prix de Diane winner Dunette: modest maiden: should stay 1½m: joined R. Cowell. *J. L. Dunlop*

ISCA MAIDEN 3 b.f. Full Extent (USA) 113 – Sharp N' Easy 62 (Swing Easy – (USA) 126) [1996 –: 6m 6f 7.1s 1997 8d 8d 10s⁵ 8m 8g⁶ Aug 1] no worthwhile form. *P. Hayward*

I SEE YOU SYDNEY (AUS) 3 ch.g. Al Hareb (USA) 123 – Sorrento (AUS) – (Best Western (AUS)) [1996 NR 1997 6g 7.9s 12m 11.9f a14.8g a10g a16g Dec 10] ex-Australian gelding: no form, including in visor. *M. J. Polglase*

ISHMAEL 4 b.g. Prionsaa 76 – Pert (Sayf El Arab (USA) 127) [1996 NR 1997 9s⁶ – Jun 20] first reported foal: dam plater: tailed off on belated debut. *G. L. Moore*

ISIS HONDA (IRE)   3 ch.f. Archway (IRE) 115 – Ceann-Na-Bann (Doulab   63
(USA) 115) [1996 NR 1997 a8g² a8.5g a8g⁴ a8g² 10.1f² 9.7m⁵ 9.7s³ 10.8s⁴ 10.1g⁵
Jul 28] IR 16,000Y: fourth foal: sister to useful 1995 French 2-y-o 5f to 6f winner
Ella Nico: dam ran twice at 2 yrs in Ireland: modest maiden handicapper: stays 1¼m:
acts on firm and soft ground and the all-weather: sold, and sent to Holland.
C. E. Brittain

ISIT IZZY   5 b.m. Crofthall 110 – Angie's Girl (Dubassoff (USA)) [1996 58:   –
8.5m⁴ 8m 1997 7g Oct 27] plain mare: modest maiden: stiff task, tailed off only 5-y-o
start. *B. A. McMahon*

ISITOFF   4 b.g. Vague Shot 108 – Plum Blossom (USA) (Gallant Romeo (USA))   84
[1996 72: a7g⁵ 10f³ a8g⁴ 11.6m* 11m² 14d⁵ 13.3m⁶ 11.5m³ 9.9f² 10m 1997 10.8m
11.9f⁴ᵈⁱˢ 12m* 10.8f⁶ 12s³ 11.6g² 10m* 10d³ Sep 20] lengthy gelding: fairly useful
performer: won minor event at Folkestone and handicap at Ripon (off bit some way
out) in August: stays 1½m: acts on firm and dead ground: game: sold 25,000 gns in
October. *S. C. Williams*

ISLAMABAD   2 gr.c. (Mar 14) Petong 126 – Kinlacey 74 (Aragon 118) [1997 5g²   98
5.1m* 6.1m* 5g⁴ Aug 20] 15,000Y: tall, useful-looking colt, rather unfurnished at 2
yrs: good mover: first foal: dam 7f winner: useful form: odds on, won minor events
at Bath (by 5 lengths) and Chester easily in the summer: only fourth of 7 in listed race
at York final start, tending to hang left: a sprinter: raced only on good/good to firm
ground: bandaged behind. *G. Lewis*

ISLAND GIRL (IRE)   2 br.f. (Apr 19) Elbio 125 – Miss Java 78 (Persian Bold   58 d
123) [1997 5m⁶ 6.1g* 7d⁴ 6f 7g 7.3d a6g⁵ a8.5g³ a7g a8g Nov 24] half-sister to
3-y-o Bold Oriental and 1994 2-y-o 5f winner Noosa (by Petorius): dam 1m winner
who stayed 1½m: modest performer: won seller at Chepstow in May: well beaten
last 2 starts: stays 8.5f: acts on firm and good to soft ground and fibresand.
D. W. P. Arbuthnot

ISLAND LORE (IRE)   3 ch.f. Polish Precedent (USA) 131 – Island Wedding   86
(USA) 89 (Blushing Groom (FR) 131) [1996 NR 1997 7g² Apr 18] lengthy filly:
third foal: half-sister to 4-y-o Winter Romance: dam, 7f and 8.5f winner, out of sister
to Storm Bird: promising length second of 19 to Kool Kat Katie in newcomers event
at Newbury: dead. *E. A. L. Dunlop*

ISLAND PRINCE   3 ch.g. Prince Sabo 123 – Island Mead 86 (Pharly (FR) 130)   –
[1996 47: 6m 7m 7m 8f a6g* a7g⁴ 1997 a7g a6g 8.2s a7g Nov 14] good-topped
gelding: winner at 2 yrs, but showed nothing in 1997 (for N. Callaghan first 2 starts):
tried blinkered. *N. M. Babbage*

ISLAND RACE   2 b.f. (Apr 20) Common Grounds 118 – Lake Isle (IRE)   –
(Caerleon (USA) 132) [1997 6m Sep 10] angular filly: third foal: half-sister to 3-y-o
Sherzetto and 4-y-o Krystal Max: dam, lightly-raced Irish 7f winner, from family of
Sadler's Wells: 20/1 and backward, never going pace in maiden at Kempton: moved
poorly to post. *J. R. Fanshawe*

ISLAND SANCTUARY (IRE)   3 ch.c. Fools Holme (USA) – Church Light 88   87
(Caerleon (USA) 132) [1996 NR 1997 8g⁶ a8g* 8.2g* 9s² 10d² 12g³ 11.9m⁶ 11.8d
Oct 13] IR 10,000Y: angular colt: fourth foal: half-brother to 3 winners, notably
fairly useful 1½m/1¾m winner and smart hurdler Shooting Light (by Shernazar):
dam stayed 1¼m: fairly useful performer: won maiden at Southwell in April and
handicap at Nottingham in May: ran well in handicaps next 3 starts: stays 1½m: acts
on soft going: sold (to join D. Nicholson) 36,000 gns in October. *P. J. Makin*

ISLE DE FRANCE (USA)   2 b.f. (Mar 30) Nureyev (USA) 131 – Stella Madrid   107 p
(USA) (Alydar (USA)) [1997 6g* 8d* 8f² Oct 5] $600,000Y: rangy, rather unfurn-
ished filly: has a quick action: third foal: half-sister to a winner by Deputy Minister:
dam won 3 Grade 1 races at 2 yrs (including at 6f) and another (at 1m) at 3 yrs:
progressive form: won newcomers event at Chantilly in July and listed race at Craon
(by ½ length from Frozen Groom) in September: bandaged behind, staying-on 1½
lengths second of 10 to Loving Claim in Prix Marcel Boussac at Longchamp: will be
suited by further than 1m: likely to improve further. *A. Fabre, France*

ISLE OF MAN (USA)   3 b.c. Manila (USA) – Princess of Man 104 (Green God   84
128) [1996 94p: 6m² 7.1m* 1997 10.3m⁶ 10.1m 12m³ 11.9s 12m³ Sep 22] tall,

good-topped colt: fluent mover: fairly useful performer: best efforts in 1997 when third in minor events at Newbury and Kempton: stays 1½m: acts on good to firm going, well beaten on soft: joined N. Drysdale in USA. *P. F. I. Cole*

ISMAROS   3 ch.c. Selkirk (USA) 129 – Trikymia 68 (Final Straw 127) [1996 NR   106 p
1997 10g* 10g⁴ Jul 16] rangy, good-topped colt: has scope: fifth foal: half-brother to 3 winners, including useful 6f/7f performer Epagris (by Zalzil) and 1¼m and 1½m winner Graegos (by Shareef Dancer): dam once-raced from good family: green and coltish, made up astonishing amount of ground to win 24-runner maiden at Windsor in June by a neck: found considerable improvement when around 3 lengths fourth of 6 to Lord of Men in useful minor event at Sandown month later, again slowly into stride, one-paced final 1f: may prove suited by around 1¼m: already useful, and capable of better still. *H. R. A. Cecil*

ITALIAN ROSE   2 ch.f. (May 12) Aragon 118 – Cayla (Tumble Wind (USA))   59
[1997 5.1g³ 5g 5m³ 5s⁵ 6m⁶ 6m⁵ a6s Nov 10] 7,500 2-y-o: good-bodied, close-   a?
coupled filly: half-sister to 3 winners, including sprinters Touch of White (by Song) and Factuelle (by Known Fact): dam, from good family, showed signs of ability: modest maiden: creditable efforts in nurseries on last 3 starts on turf: well below form on equitrack: stays 6f: acts on good to firm and soft ground. *W. J. Musson*

ITALIAN SYMPHONY (IRE)   3 b.g. Royal Academy (USA) 130 – Terracotta   40
Hut 99 (Habitat 134) [1996 70: 7f⁵ 6m⁴ 6m⁵ 7.1m⁶ 7g⁶ 7m³ 1997 a8g² 8s⁶ a8g⁶ 10s⁴   a74
8g 6.9g⁵ 8.2m⁵ 7g² 8.1m 6.9d⁶ a6g* a7g⁴ a7g a7g* a6g a6g⁶ Dec 26] close-coupled gelding: fair handicapper on all-weather, poor on turf nowadays: left M. Johnston after fourth start: won at Wolverhampton in November and Lingfield in December: effective at 6f to 1m: sometimes blinkered/usually visored: has seemed none too hearty. *P. D. Evans*

ITATINGA (USA)   3 b.f. Riverman (USA) 131 – Ivrea 109 (Sadler's Wells   66
(USA) 132) [1996 65?: 7.1v⁴ 7g 1997 10m 13.8s* 12g⁶ Jul 9] angular filly: fair performer: best effort to win 4-runner maiden at Catterick in July after threatening to run out passing unsaddling boxes: again ran wide on bends (at Folkestone) only subsequent start: stays 1¾m: best efforts on soft/heavy ground: sold 27,000 gns in December. *M. R. Stoute*

ITCH   2 b.c. (Mar 31) Puissance 110 – Panienka (POL) 70 (Dom Racine (FR) 121)   68 ?
[1997 a5g 6d* 7s Nov 8] 6,600 2-y-o: unfurnished colt: second foal: brother to 3-y-o Whizz Kid: dam stayer on flat, also won over hurdles: 40/1-winner of maiden at Pontefract in October: showed little other 2 starts, off stiffish mark in nursery on final one: shapes as though will stay beyond 6f. *R. Bastiman*

ITHAKI (IRE)   3 b.c. Sadler's Wells (USA) 132 – Idyllic (USA) (Foolish   115
Pleasure (USA)) [1996 7.5v³ 8v⁵ 1997 10m⁵ 12g* 11g³ 12m⁵ 10s² 10g⁶ 12m⁵ 8.5d³ Nov 30] sturdy colt: brother to several winners, notably Dewhurst dead-heater Scenic, and half-brother to 3 winners, including smart Silent Warrior (up to 10.5f in France, by Nashwan): dam (unraced) from family of Rainbow Quest, Warning and Commander In Chief: smart performer: won minor event at Maisons-Laffitte in April: 11½ lengths fifth of 14 to Peintre Celebre in Prix du Jockey-Club at Chantilly (never able to land a blow) then best effort when 2 lengths second of 7 to him in Grand Prix de Paris at Longchamp: well below form afterwards (reportedly having back trouble after next time), leaving J. Pease before final start: stays 1½m: best effort on soft ground. *R. McAnally, USA*

ITS ALL RELATIVE   2 gr.f. (Apr 8) Distant Relative 128 – Sharp Anne 74§   89
(Belfort (FR) 89) [1997 5m⁴ 5g* 5.1f* 5m 5.2m 5d² Sep 18] 6,200Y: leggy filly: fourth foal: half-sister to 6f seller and 7f Italian winner Sharp Monty (by Mon Tresor): dam unreliable sprinter: fairly useful performer: won maiden at Musselburgh in June and minor event at Bath in July: ran creditably next time and when ¾-length second to Halmahera in listed race at Ayr: speedy, and raced only around 5f: acts on firm and dead ground: often front runner. *J. Berry*

ITSINTHEPOST   4 b.f. Risk Me (FR) 127 – Where's The Money 87 (Lochnager   60
132) [1996 –, a66: 6.1d 6g a7g a6g³ a6g³ a6g 6d 1997 6m 5.7d a6g² a6g⁴ 6.9s* a7g*   a70
a7g Dec 19] leggy filly: has a very round action: fair performer: in good form in the summer, winning handicap at Folkestone (first form on turf since 2 yrs) and minor

477

event at Wolverhampton: off course 5 months before final start: stays 7f: acts on soft going and the all-weather: has been bandaged. *V. Soane*

ITS MY PLEASURE 3 b.f. Rock Hopper 124 – The Fink Sisters 75 (Tap On – p
Wood 130) [1996 NR 1997 9.2g³ Sep 29] second foal: dam, fair 2-y-o, won 2½m hurdle: signs of a little ability when around 9 lengths third to Tyrolean Dream in maiden at Hamilton, staying on: should do better over 1¼m+. *W. S. Cunningham*

ITSNOTYETNAMED 2 b.c. (Jun 5) Kasakov – Wych Willow (Hard Fought 45 ?
125) [1997 5v 7.5f⁶ 8.2d 6d⁴ Oct 20] 500Y: leggy, lengthy colt: second foal: dam unraced: appeared to show ability in maiden final start: well beaten in seller previous outing. *A. Smith*

IVAN LUIS (FR) 3 b.c. Lycius (USA) 124 – Zivania (IRE) 101 (Shernazar 131) 115
[1996 102: 7m⁵ 7f⁶ 8.5g² 8g* 8.3g³ 8s³ 1997 12g* 12.3d² 12f⁵ 11.9g* 12m³ 12m³ 12m⁶ Oct 19] lengthy, good-topped colt: smart performer: won minor event at Catterick in April and listed event at Haydock (by 1¾ lengths from Musical Dancer) in July: best efforts when third in Prix Niel at Longchamp (beaten neck and a length by Rajpoute and Peintre Celebre) and sixth in Gran Premio del Jockey Club at Milan (5½ lengths behind Caitano) last 2 starts: will stay 1¾m: acts on firm and soft ground: genuine. *M. Bell*

IVOR'S DEED 4 b.g. Shadeed (USA) 135 – Gena Ivor (USA) (Sir Ivor 135) 56
[1996 56: 10g 7.5g² 6g⁵ 7g* 7f² 7.1f³ 7f⁴ 7m 8m a7g³ 1997 6g³ 7.1m³ 6.9m* 8g 6.9m a69
a7g a7g* a7g³ Dec 19] sturdy gelding: impresses in appearance: fair on all-weather, modest on turf: won claimer at Folkestone (final start for C. Wall) in May and apprentice handicap at Lingfield in November: stays 7f, possibly not 1m: acts on firm ground and equitrack. *Miss Gay Kelleway*

IVOR'S FLUTTER 8 b.g. Beldale Flutter (USA) 130 – Rich Line (High Line 82
125) [1996 86: 16d⁶ 16m³ 22.2f⁶ 14m* 16g³ 16.2m⁴ 18g 1997 18g 16.5s Nov 8] workmanlike gelding: fairly useful handicapper: much better effort in autumn when eighth of 31 to Turnpole in Cesarewitch at Newmarket: suited by good test of stamina: acts on firm and soft ground: fairly useful hurdler: needs plenty of driving. *D. R. C. Elsworth*

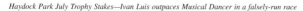

Haydock Park July Trophy Stakes—Ivan Luis outpaces Musical Dancer in a falsely-run race

IVORY CHARM 2 b.f. (Feb 9) Batshoof 122 – Amazing Journey (USA) – (Spectacular Bid (USA)) [1997 6g 7m 5m Sep 17] 6,200Y: third reported foal: sister to a poor animal: dam unraced: well behind in maidens. *K. T. Ivory*

IVORY CROWN (IRE) 2 b.f. (Apr 6) Chief's Crown (USA) – Royal Myth – p (USA) (Sir Ivor 135) [1997 7m Nov 1] 3,300F, IR 18,000Y: fourth foal: half-sister to 2 winners in USA by Fred Astaire: dam won at up to 9f in USA at 4 yrs: 25/1, green when eleventh of 18 in maiden at Newmarket, slowly away and outpaced in rear before leaving on: should improve. *E. A. L. Dunlop*

IVORY DAWN 3 b.f. Batshoof 122 – Cradle of Love (USA) 87 (Roberto (USA) 79 131) [1996 59: 6m 7f³ 7g⁶ 1997 7m 6g² 6m 7m 6d⁵ 6g 6g² 6g* 5d 5s² 7f³ 6m³ 7m 7m² 6m 7s 6d 6m Sep 22] leggy, workmanlike filly: fair handicapper: won at Goodwood in June: below form last 4 starts: stays 7f: acts on firm and soft ground: well beaten in visor: sometimes bandaged behind: has worn crossed noseband. *K. T. Ivory*

IVORY GIRL (IRE) 2 ch.f. (Apr 23) Sharp Victor (USA) 114 – Nordic Dance – (USA) (Graustark) [1997 a7g 8.2g Sep 28] 1,000 2-y-o: half-sister to 3 winners, including 1988 2-y-o 5f winner Celestial Heights (by Storm Bird): dam unraced on good family: well beaten in seller and a maiden. *K. G. Wingrove*

IVORY LEAGUE 2 b.f. (Apr 19) Last Tycoon 131 – Ivory Lane (USA) (Sir Ivor – p 135) [1997 7m 7m 7d Oct 13] tall, unfurnished filly: good mover: fourth foal: dam, lightly raced in USA, sister to Cherry Hinton winner Turkish Treasure: green and never dangerous to date, showing signs of ability on debut and running subject of inquiry final start: should do better, probably at further than 7f. *G. Lewis*

IVORY'S GRAB HIRE 4 b.g. Shavian 125 – Knees Up (USA) (Dancing 73 Champ (USA)) [1996 61§: 6.9s⁵ a7g⁴ 10.8g⁴ 9.7f⁶ a8g 8g³ 8.3m 7m³ 7f* 6m⁴ 6g⁵ 7f³ a60 7g 7m³ 7f² 7g⁶ 7d 7.1f³ 7m 6.1m³ 7m⁵ a7g 1997 a6g⁵ a6g² a5g* a6g⁵ a5g² a5g⁵ a5g* a6g⁴ a5g³ a6g 5m 5.7d 6f* 6f* 6g 6d⁵ 5g 7m⁴ 6m 6g² 5.2m⁴¹ 5.3g* 5.7g 5.2m 5.3f⁵ a7g Dec 19] lengthy, shallow-girthed gelding: fair handicapper: has looked of dubious temperament but in good form for most of 1997, winning at Lingfield (twice) and Brighton (3 times): best at 5f/6f: acts on firm ground and equitrack: wears blinkers: has run well when sweating profusely: sometimes slowly away: tough. *K. T. Ivory*

IVORY'S JOY 2 b.f. (Mar 31) Tina's Pet 121 – Jacqui Joy 63 (Music Boy 124) 70 [1997 5.1m a5g⁴ 5g⁶ 5g* 5.2m² 6d* 6f² 5m⁴ 5.2d* 5m³ 5s⁶ 5.2f⁵ 5d Nov 7] fifth foal: half-sister to 5f winner Miss Bigwig (by Distinctly North) and 7-y-o Rennyholme: dam best at 5f: fair performer: won 2 small-field sellers at Goodwood in June and a nursery at Newbury in September: not discredited afterwards: has won at 6f, better form at 5f: acts on firm and dead ground: has been bandaged in front: blinkered third to fifth starts: has wandered. *K. T. Ivory*

IVY BIRD (IRE) 2 b.f. (May 3) Contract Law (USA) 108 – Hollyberry (IRE) – (Runnett 125) [1997 7g a7g a8g Dec 8] third foal: half-sister to 4-y-o Amy Leigh: dam unraced: behind in maiden and sellers. *W. Jarvis*

J

JAATI (IRE) 2 b.g. (Mar 20) Alzao (USA) 117 – Majestic Amber (USA) (Majes- – p tic Light (USA)) [1997 7d Nov 7] 50,000Y: lengthy, useful-looking gelding: half-brother to Irish 1m and 9f winner Majestic Guest (by Be My Guest) and winners abroad by Plugged Nickle and Marju: dam won up to 7f in USA, including in minor stakes: 14/1 and burly, ran green when well behind in maiden at Doncaster: should do better. *J. H. M. Gosden*

JAAZIM 7 ch.g. Night Shift (USA) – Mesmerize (Mill Reef (USA) 141) [1996 56, – a60: a6g⁵ a7g⁴ a6g a5g a8g⁶ 8f 7m² 7m² 8g⁵ 7g² 7m² 6m⁵ 6m⁴ 8.3d⁵ 8f² 8f⁴ 8m 7s a7g 1997 7f 8d 6.9m 8d 6m Jul 14] strong gelding: modest handicapper at 6 yrs: well beaten in 1997, and sold 1,500 gns in August: stays 1m: acts on all-weather and on firm and dead going: tried blinkered. *M. Madgwick*

JAAZIM (USA) 2 b. or br.c. (Feb 13) Silver Hawk (USA) 123 – Alvear (USA) 83 p (Seattle Slew (USA)) [1997 7m 8m⁵ 8.2s² Oct 15] $410,000Y: good-topped, imposing colt: fluent mover: second foal: dam, winner up to 9f in USA, half-sister to Grade 2 1¼m winner Dynaformer out of Grade 1 9f winner Andover Way: progressive maiden: 4 lengths second to Decisive Action at Nottingham: will stay at least 1¼m: has given some trouble at stalls: sort to progress again at 3 yrs, and sure to win races. *M. R. Stoute*

JABAROOT (IRE) 6 b.g. Sadler's Wells (USA) 132 – Arctic Heroine (USA) – (Arctic Tern (USA) 126) [1996 –: 9.2d 14.1m 11.1g 12.1g 9.2g 11.1g 11.1m⁶ 13.1g 15d 12g⁵ 12.1f 16s 12.1m⁵ 10.1m 15.1m⁵ 1997 12.1d Apr 2] no longer of much account. *R. M. McKellar*

JACK DOYLE (IRE) 6 ch.g. Be My Native (USA) 122 – Sister Ida (Bustino 65 136) [1996 14g⁴ 1997 8g⁶ 10g⁵ May 30] ex-Irish gelding: fourth foal: brother to fair 15f winner Native Mission, better known as smart hurdler/useful chaser: dam never ran: fourth in maiden (rated 65) at Down Royal in 1996 for D. Weld: easily better effort in similar events in Britain when sixth at Thirsk: should stay at least 1¼m: fair jumper, joined N. Twiston-Davies. *J. J. O'Neill*

JACKERIN (IRE) 2 b.g. (Mar 17) Don't Forget Me 127 – Meanz Beanz (High 71 Top 131) [1997 5m* 5g* 6g³ 6d 7m 5m² 5m Aug 26] 4,200Y: strong, workmanlike gelding: half-brother to useful stayer Bean King (by Ardross) and 4-y-o Meg's Memory: dam unraced half-sister to very smart sprinter Chilibang: fair performer: won seller at Doncaster in March and minor event at same course in May: patchy form afterwards, though good second in nursery at Haydock: stays 6f: acts on good to firm ground: visored fourth outing: not well away last 3 starts, rearing in stalls final outing (subsequently gelded). *B. S. Rothwell*

JACK FLUSH (IRE) 3 b.g. Broken Hearted 124 – Clubhouse Turn (IRE) (King 67 of Clubs 124) [1996 64: 6g⁶ 7m⁴ 6.1m³ 6f² 6g 7f⁵ 8g 1997 7m 8g 10.3d⁶ 8g³ 8s* 8f² 8m⁴ 8g 8m 8.2s Oct 15] leggy gelding: fair handicapper: won 16-runner event at Thirsk in May: good efforts next 2 starts, ran poorly last 3: seems best around 1m: acts on any going: visored final outing: usually races prominently. *B. S. Rothwell*

JACKIES WEBB 2 b.f. (Mar 1) Selkirk (USA) 129 – Hawayah (IRE) 68 – (Shareef Dancer (USA) 135) [1997 5.7f 6f 5.1m Aug 12] 4,200Y: first foal: dam 2-y-o 7f winner out of Nell Gwyn winner Ghariba, herself half-sister to Braashee: signs of ability but no worthwhile form in maidens. *B. Smart*

JACKMANII 5 gr.g. Most Welcome 131 – Blue Flower (FR) (Carwhite 127) – [1996 NR 1997 12m⁶ Apr 5] modest handicapper at 3 yrs: first outing for 17 months, no encouragement in seller in April: stays 1½m: acts on firm ground: often blinkered as 3-y-o. *J. Berry*

JACK-N-JILLY (IRE) 2 b.f. (Apr 26) Anita's Prince 126 – Little Club (King of 43 Clubs 124) [1997 5g⁵ a5g⁶ a5g² a5g³ a6g² a6g³ a6f² 5s⁴ Jul 2] IR 2,100Y: fifth foal: sister to winning sprinter (including at 2 yrs) Who Told Vicky: dam unraced: poor maiden: best efforts when placed in sellers at Wolverhampton: stays 6f: acts on fibresand. *J. S. Moore*

JACK RUBY 2 b.c. (Apr 12) Risk Me (FR) 127 – Atisayin (USA) (Al Nasr (FR) 55 126) [1997 6m 6g⁵ 5d Sep 5] workmanlike colt: first reported live foal: dam poor maiden: modest form in maidens. *P. L. Gilligan*

JACK SAYS 3 b.g. Rambo Dancer (CAN) 107 – Madam Cody (Hot Spark 126) – [1996 53?, a59: 5m⁴ a5g³ a5g² 7s 7.9g 8m 7m 1997 a6g⁵ a6g⁴ a8g³ a7g³ a8g³ a59 d a6g⁴ 6.1m a5g a7g Dec 18] well-made gelding: modest maiden at best: off course 8 months before penultimate start: probably a sprinter: acts on fibresand: often blinkered. *D. Shaw*

JACKSON FALLS 3 gr.g. Dunbeath (USA) 127 – Hysteria (Prince Bee 128) – [1996 64: 6m² 7m⁴ 8m³ 1997 9.9m 8g 8f Jun 2] tall gelding: tailed off in handicaps at 3 yrs: blinkered final start: headstrong: dead. *T. D. Easterby*

JACKSON'S PANTHER (IRE) 5 ch.m. Jackson's Drift (USA) – Pitiless – Panther 97 (No Mercy 126) [1996 13g 10g 13g 12g⁴ 12v 1997 a8.5g Feb 21] ex-Irish mare: half-sister to 1¼m to 2m winner Lie In Wait (by Mill Reef): dam won over 6f at 2 yrs and stayed at least 7f: poor maiden handicapper (rated 43) for T. Carmody at 4 yrs (blinkered last 2 starts): showed little only outing in 1997: stays 13f. *C. A. Dwyer*

JACK THE LAD (IRE) 3 b.g. Shalford (IRE) 124§ – Indian Honey (Indian 81 King (USA) 128) [1996 64: 6m³ 6f 7f 6f³ 6d⁴ 7g⁴ a8.5g 1997 a7g⁶ a7g² a8g⁴ a8.5g 8.5m⁶ 12g⁴ 9f* 10.3d 8d* 10g* 8.5d* 10m² 10.5m 10.4d⁴ 10m 10.4d 10.3g a14.8g Nov 15] tall, close-coupled gelding: fairly useful handicapper: in good form in first half of year, winning at Redcar (twice), Carlisle and Beverley in May: ran badly all 4 starts in second half: best at 1m/1¼m: acts on fibresand, firm and dead ground. *J. Hetherton*

JACMAR (IRE) 2 br.c. (Jan 16) High Estate 127 – Inseyab 65 (Persian Bold 123) 91 [1997 5s² 6m* 7.1d² 7g² 6g* 6g⁴ 6g* 6g Oct 18] IR 1,600F, 11,500 2-y-o: second foal: dam 7f and 1m winner: fairly useful performer: won maiden at Hamilton in June and nurseries there in August and September: far from discredited in Two-Year-Old Trophy at Redcar final start: should stay 1m: genuine: sold 35,000 gns after final start. *Miss L. A. Perratt*

JACOBINA 2 b.f. (Feb 6) Magic Ring (IRE) 115 – Mistitled (USA) 54 (Miswaki 67 (USA) 124) [1997 5m 5f³ 5.1g 6g³ Jul 8] 8,000Y: workmanlike filly: first foal: dam 2-y-o 5f winner: fair form: third in maiden at Newcastle and nursery at Pontefract: will stay 7f. *T. D. Barron*

JADES SHADOW 4 gr.g. General Wade 93 – Gellifawr 80 (Saulingo 122) [1996 – –: 7m 6g 8.3d 5g 1997 6g Aug 1] of little account. *J. J. Bridger*

JAFN 3 ch.f. Sharpo 132 – Harold's Girl (FR) (Northfields (USA)) [1996 NR 1997 104 7g⁵ 7m* 8d⁵ 7g 8.1s⁴ 8v* Oct 10] 17,000F, 36,000Y: deep-girthed filly: has scope: half-sister to several winners abroad, including useful winner up to 1¼m in Germany by Pyjama Hunt: dam 2-y-o 6f winner in France, also won over jumps: useful performer: won maiden at Newmarket in May and listed event at Ascot in October, latter by 1¼ lengths from Dancing Drop: ran as if something amiss fourth start (moved poorly): looked likely to stay beyond 1m: won on good to firm going, best efforts on ground softer than good (acted on heavy): often bandaged off-hind: visits Red Ransom. *B. Hanbury*

JAGO 2 b.c. (Apr 6) Salse (USA) 128 – Wanda 74 (Taufan (USA) 119) [1997 7m – 7.5m 7g Aug 5] workmanlike colt: third reported foal (all by Salse): dam sprinter: never on terms in maidens, burly and green first 2 starts. *M. W. Easterby*

JALB (IRE) 3 b.g. Robellino (USA) 127 – Adjacent (IRE) 82 (Doulab (USA) 115) 67 [1996 69p: 6m⁶ 6d⁵ 7f 1997 10m 8m³ 8m⁶ 10s Jul 5] strong, well-made gelding: fluent mover: fair maiden handicapper: stays 1¼m: acts on good to firm ground and soft: joined P. G. Murphy. *A. C. Stewart*

JAMAICA BRIDGE 7 b.g. Doulab (USA) 115 – Mill Hill (USA) (Riva Ridge – (USA)) [1996 NR 1997 8.3g a8g Dec 18] modest on the all-weather in 1995: tailed off both outings as 7-y-o. *Mrs A. M. Naughton*

JAMAICAN FLIGHT (USA) 4 b.c. Sunshine Forever (USA) – Kalamona 75 (USA) (Hawaii) [1996 66: 7m⁴ 10.1m 11f⁵ 16.2f* 16.1m³ 16.4m² 1997 16.4g² 16.2s⁵ 16.1g⁵ 16.2d² 16m² 18d² 18.2f⁶ Sep 18] leggy colt: fair handicapper: trained first 2 starts by C. Smith: suited by good test of stamina: acts on firm and dead ground: front runner: upset at stalls third and fourth starts: consistent: fairly useful hurdler, winner 5 times in 1997. *Mrs S. Lamyman*

JAMEEL ASMAR 5 br.g. Rock City 120 – Barsham 94 (Be My Guest (USA) 76 + 126) [1996 NR 1997 8.9d 10.4m Jul 12] compact gelding: fairly useful handicapper in 1995: first runs since, better from position suggests both starts at 5 yrs, unable to get clear run in Magnet Cup at York on second occasion: stays 1½m: acts on good to firm and dead ground. *C. R. Egerton*

JAMORIN DANCER 2 b.c. (Apr 9) Charmer 123 – Geryea (USA) (Desert Wine 77 p (USA)) [1997 8m³ 10s² Oct 15] third foal: half-brother to 3-y-o Mythical: dam unraced from the family of Sure Blade: better effort in maidens when neck second to Wave Rock at Nottingham, making most and running on: should stay 1½m: should do better again. *M. A. Jarvis*

JAMRAT JUMAIRAH (IRE) 4 b.f. Polar Falcon (USA) 126 – Coryana 104   91
(Sassafras (FR) 135) [1996 88p: 8m* 1997 8g² 8g Aug 23] strong, lengthy filly:
carries condition: fairly useful performer, has had only 4 races: again bandaged,
beaten head by Beauchamp King in minor event at Doncaster, caught post: not
discredited when tenth of 16 in listed race at Deauville over 3 weeks later: stays 1m:
raced only on good going or firmer. *E. A. L. Dunlop*

JANARA 3 b.f. Aragon 118 – Aimee Jane (USA) 76 (Our Native (USA)) [1996   –
NR 1997 7m Sep 9] 5,500Y: third living foal: half-sister to a winner (up to 1½m) in
Germany by Niniski: dam 1½m winner: 14/1, midfield in maiden at Lingfield: sold
1,800 gns following month. *L. M. Cumani*

JANDAL 3 ch.c. Arazi (USA) 135 – Littlefield 100 (Bay Express 132) [1996 NR   –
1997 10g⁵ Jun 13] sixth foal: half-brother to 4 winners, including Hayaain (1½m, by
Shirley Heights) and useful 7f (at 2 yrs) and 1¼m winner Dahik (by Green Desert):
dam won from 6f (at 2 yrs) to 1m: 66/1, down the field in Sandown maiden,
wandering under pressure: sold 2,500 gns in October. *C. J. Benstead*

JANET LINDUP 2 b.f. (Jun 7) Sabrehill (USA) 120 – Tartan Pimpernel 109   –
(Blakeney 126) [1997 7d Nov 7] strong, lengthy filly: half-sister to several winners,
including Royal Hunt Cup winner Colour Sergeant (by Green Desert) and fairly
useful 1983 2-y-o 7f winner Elusive (by Little Current): dam, half-sister to
Dunfermline, won May Hill and Galtres Stakes: 8/1 and edgy, last of 18 in maiden at
Doncaster. *B. W. Hills*

JANGLYNYVE 3 ch.f. Sharpo 132 – Wollow Maid 73 (Wollow 132) [1996 48:   62
5s⁴ 6m 7g⁴ 7f³ 7.6m 1997 a7g⁵ a7g 8g* 8g* 8g² 10s* Jun 27] modest performer: won   a–
claimers at Newmarket and Leicester in May and Newmarket in June: stays 1¼m, at
least in a steadily-run race: acts on soft ground, poor efforts on fibresand: joined Mrs
Merrita Jones. *S. P. C. Woods*

JANIE'S BOY 3 b.c. Persian Bold 123 – Cornelian 78 (Great Nephew 126) [1996   71
69?: 5m⁵ 6m 6g³ 6m a6g 1997 8g* 10.8m 8d⁶ 7v Jun 25] leggy colt: fair form: won
maiden at Thirsk in May: barely stays 1m when conditions are testing: probably acts
on dead going, ran badly on heavy: blinkered final 2-y-o outing. *Mrs J. Cecil*

JAREER DO (IRE) 5 b.m. Jareer (USA) 115 – Shining Bright (USA) (Bold   –
Bidder) [1996 54, a–: 7f⁴ 7.1m² 6m a7g⁶ a7g a7g⁵ 1997 a7g Jan 10] lengthy mare:
modest performer in 1996: well in rear in seller only start at 5 yrs: should stay 1m:
acts on good to firm ground, no form on the all-weather. *B. Palling*

JARRAYAN 2 ch.f. (Apr 12) Machiavellian (USA) 123 – Badrah (USA) 69   64
(Private Account (USA)) [1997 6m⁶ 6m⁴ Aug 17] first foal: dam third once from 2
starts at 1m, half-sister to smart performer (best at 1¼m) Husyan: modest form in
maidens at Folkestone and Lingfield: bred to stay 1m+: sold 8,000 gns in December.
Major W. R. Hern

JARROW 6 ch.g. Jalmood (USA) 126 – Invite 79 (Be My Guest (USA) 126)   – §
[1996 –: a11g a11g⁶ 1997 13s 11.1s 13.8m⁵ May 30] lengthy gelding: bad maiden:
has been visored: probably temperamental. *Mrs A. M. Naughton*

JASEUR (USA) 4 b.g. Lear Fan (USA) 130 – Spur Wing (USA) (Storm Bird   98
(CAN) 134) [1996 79p: 10.5d⁴ 1997 11.5m⁵ 10g 11.5d⁵ 13.1g* 16.2g* 16.2v* 16g²
Oct 24] strong gelding: progressed into a useful handicapper: won at Bath and Ascot
(idled markedly) in September and Ascot (very easily) again in October: improved
again when second to Whitechapel at Newbury final start, wandering under pressure:
better at 2m than shorter: raced almost solely on good going or softer and acts on
heavy: visored last 5 outings. *J. H. M. Gosden*

JASMINE TEA 2 ch.f. (Apr 28) Alhijaz 122 – Come To Tea (IRE) (Be My Guest   –
(USA) 126) [1997 6g 7s⁶ Jun 26] 15,500Y: third reported foal: dam, Irish 2-y-o 7f
winner, half-sister to smart filly at up to 1¼m Danish: well beaten in maiden at
Doncaster and claimer at Salisbury. *Martyn Meade*

JATO DANCER (IRE) 2 b.f. (Apr 21) Mukaddamah (USA) 125 – Que Tran-   46
quila 65 (Dominion 123) [1997 7g 7m* 7.1s 7m 7f Oct 3] 9,000Y: leggy filly: half-
sister to temperamental 5f winner Katie-A (by Cyrano de Bergerac): dam, ran twice,
from the family of Pebbles: poor performer: won seller at Brighton in July: well held
in nurseries: should stay 1m: trained first 3 starts by M. Channon. *J. R. Arnold*

Allevamento Gialloblu's "Jaunty Jack"

JAUNTY JACK   3 b.c. Midyan (USA) 124 – Juliette Marny 123 (Blakeney 126)   110
[1996 90: 6g² 8m² 8.2s² 1997 10m² 10m* 10.1m* 10s* 12f³ Sep 21] rangy colt:
smart performer: won listed events at Milan in May and June and £18,000 handicap
at Epsom (by 2½ lengths from Supply and Demand) in between: creditable 1¼
lengths third to War Declaration in very valuable event at Milan final start: stays
1½m: acts on firm and soft ground: sold 100,000 gns in October, to A. Hyldmo in
Norway. *L. M. Cumani*

JAVA BAY   3 b.f. Statoblest 120 – Flopsy (Welsh Pageant 132) [1996 –: 6d 5.1m   –
6.9d⁵ 1997 8.2g 8.3g 7m 8.1s⁴ Jul 1] signs of only a little ability, including in a seller.
M. Blanshard

JAVA RED (IRE)   5 b.g. Red Sunset 120 – Coffee Bean (Doulab (USA) 115)   60
[1996 55: 10m 8m⁵ a8g 8.3g⁴ 1997 8m 6.9f⁵ 7.5m* 7g⁵ 7.5v⁴ 8m⁶ 8.1m³ 8.5d³ 10d*
8.5f³ 9m 10d 10m⁶ Nov 4] leggy gelding: modest performer: won handicap at
Beverley in June and seller at Pontefract in September: stays 1¼m: acts on fibresand
and probably any turf going: effective blinkered/visored or not: sometimes slowly
away. *J. G. FitzGerald*

JAVA SHRINE (USA)   6 b.g. Java Gold (USA) – Ivory Idol (USA) (Alydar   59
(USA)) [1996 NR 1997 12d 8.1m³ 11.7f⁶ 8.3g⁵ Aug 4] strong, lengthy gelding: fairly
useful form at 3 yrs for I. Balding: modest form in 1997, best effort second start:
should stay beyond 1m: form only on good/good to firm. *A. J. Chamberlain*

JAWAH (IRE)   3 br.g. In The Wings 128 – Saving Mercy 101 (Lord Gayle (USA)   91
124) [1996 8g 9s 7s 1997 9s 14d* 13d⁵ 14.1g² 14d⁵ 14.6g* 14.1d* 16.5s⁴ Nov 8]
30,000Y: lengthy gelding: eighth foal: half-brother to 7f/1m performer Arjuzah (by
Ahonoora) and Irish 1m/1¼m performer Ormsby (by Ela-Mana-Mou), both useful:
dam won Lincoln: fairly useful handicapper: won at Bellewstown in July (penul-

timate start for D. Weld) and Doncaster and Nottingham in October: effective at 1¾m to 2m: acts on soft going (unraced on firmer than good): has hung, and is suited by waiting tactics. *K. Mahdi*

JAWHARI 3 b.c. Lahib (USA) 129 – Lady of The Land 75 (Wollow 132) [1996 87 76: 6f² 6d⁴ 1997 7.6m* 7m 7m⁵ 7g Oct 18] small, sturdy colt: has a quick action: fairly useful performer: won maiden at Lingfield in July: off course nearly 2 months before final start (ran poorly), then sold (to D. Nicholls) 9,000 gns: should stay 1m: acts on good to firm ground. *J. L. Dunlop*

JAYANNPEE 6 ch.g. Doulab (USA) 115 – Amina 80 (Brigadier Gerard 144) 102 [1996 109: 5.2d 6m* 6m* 5m 6f 6f* 6m 6d⁴ 6m* 6m 1997 6d² 6m⁴ 6g 6g⁴ 6f 6m⁵ 6s 5m Sep 28] good-topped gelding: useful performer: none too consistent in 1997, best efforts when beaten a neck by Monaassib in 5-runner minor event at Goodwood in May and 5¾ lengths fifth to Elnadim in listed race at Newmarket in August: suited by 6f: acts on firm and dead ground, no form on soft: successful for apprentice: wears tongue strap. *I. A. Balding*

JAYBEE SILVER 2 gr.f. (Mar 16) Mystiko (USA) 124 – Pipistrelle 62 (Shareef 47 Dancer (USA) 135) [1997 5.1d 6s⁶ 6g² 7g⁴ 6m 6m 6m Sep 26] 5,500Y: second foal: dam 13f winner who stayed well: second in seller at Yarmouth, but mainly disappointing: should stay beyond 6f: often slowly away: visored final outing: sold to H. Howe in October. *M. H. Tompkins*

JAY-EM-BEE 4 b.g. Double Schwartz 128 – Kasarose (Owen Dudley 121) [1996 – NR 1997 8m 11.7g 5.1m Jul 17] brother to 6f winner Double Matt: dam, little sign of ability, and temperamental: seems of little account. *J. M. Bradley*

JAYESS ELLE 2 b.f. (Feb 5) Sabrehill (USA) 120 – Sorayah 89 (Persian Bold 55 p 123) [1997 6m⁶ 7g Oct 18] 16,000Y: sixth foal: half-sister to several winners, including 3-y-o Supercal: dam sprinter here, later won at up to 11f in USA: some promise in maidens at Redcar in October, not knocked about either time: should stay 1m: should do better. *J. G. FitzGerald*

JAY GEE (IRE) 2 b.f. (Mar 22) Second Set (IRE) 127 – Polynesian Goddess 93 (IRE) (Salmon Leap (USA) 131) [1997 5d⁵ 5g⁶ 5m 6m³ 6m* 6g* 7m 6.5m Sep 10] 12,000Y: sturdy filly: second foal: half-sister to 11f winner in Germany by Law Society: dam third at 7f in Ireland: fairly useful performer: won minor event at Windsor in July and valuable nursery at Newmarket in August: ran poorly final 2 starts: should stay 1m: acts on good to firm ground. *G. G. Margarson*

JAYIR (IRE) 2 b.g. (Jan 12) Mujtahid (USA) 118 – Arylh (USA) 87 (Lyphard 70 (USA) 132) [1997 7s⁴ 6f⁵ Sep 28] sturdy gelding: second foal: half-brother to Irish 1m winner Iftatah (by Cadeaux Genereux): dam 6f winner out of half-sister to smart French miler Lypheor: better effort in maidens when 4 lengths fifth at Brighton, tending to wander: burly on debut: should stay 1m: sold to D. Nicholls 9,500 gns in October. *A. C. Stewart*

JAY-OWE-TWO (IRE) 3 b.g. Distinctly North (USA) 115 – Fiery Song (Ballad 87 Rock 122) [1996 78: 6d a6g a6g² a6g* 1997 a6g 7m² 7.5m* 8g 7g 8m 8d 7.5m 7g⁴ 8m* 8d* 8m Nov 1] strong, lengthy gelding: fairly useful handicapper: won at Beverley in April and at Pontefract and Newmarket (30 ran) in October: stays 1m well: acts on fibresand, good to firm and dead ground: visored last 3 starts: game. *R. M. Whitaker*

JAZA 3 b.g. Pursuit of Love 124 – Nordica 99 (Northfields (USA)) [1996 NR 1997 – 7.1s 8g 8m Oct 6] 95,000Y: good-topped gelding: half-brother to 4 winners, including 5-y-o Secret Spring and useful Sueboog (at up to 1½m, by Darshaan): dam won 3 times at 1m in Britain then over 6f in Ireland: well beaten in maidens. *N. A. Graham*

JAZZ CLUB (USA) 2 b.c. (Feb 1) Dixieland Band (USA) – Hidden Garden 99 (USA) (Mr Prospector (USA)) [1997 6m* 7g⁶ 7v⁵ Oct 11] $260,000Y: smallish, heavy-bodied colt: has a quick, fluent action: second foal: closely related to a winner in USA by Danzig: dam, won up to 1m in USA, half-sister to dam of smart 1¼m performer Flagbird and dual Grade 1 winner Prospectors Delite: won useful minor event at Haydock in August by 1¾ lengths from Hayil (pair 8 lengths clear), quickening to lead under 2f out: failed to progress in Acomb Stakes at York (heavily bandaged off-fore), and tailed off on heavy going in minor event at Ascot: should stay 1m. *P. F. I. Cole*

JAZZ KING 4 br.g. Kalaglow 132 – Sabrine (Mount Hagen (FR) 127) [1996 83: 89 11.9f* 11.6g³ 14f⁴ 13.9m 1997 11.9g 11.6g* 13.3f* 14m⁴ 14.6m 13.3d Sep 20] big gelding: has a long, round stride: fairly useful performer: won minor event at Windsor and handicap at Newbury in July: rather disappointing afterwards: should stay beyond 1¾m: acts on firm ground. *Miss Gay Kelleway*

JAZZ SINGER 2 b.f. (Mar 2) Prince Sabo 123 – Blues Player 70 (Jaazeiro (USA) 54 127) [1997 6.9s⁶ 7g⁴ 7g³ Sep 3] 1,700F: lengthy filly: has a quick action: seventh foal: half-sister to 6-y-o Your Most Welcome and 3 winners abroad: dam 2m winner: some promise in maiden on debut, but poor efforts in sellers afterwards: sold, to go to Norway. *R. Hannon*

JAZZ TRACK (IRE) 3 b.c. Sadler's Wells (USA) 132 – Minnie Hauk (USA) 86 100 (Sir Ivor 135) [1996 NR 1997 12.3g 13.8g² 12m³ 12.3g³ 13.1d⁶ 15.8s* Oct 16] workmanlike colt: has a short action: has many winning siblings, notably 4-y-o brother Chief Contender and very useful close relative Aviance (best up to 1m, by Northfields), later dam of Chimes of Freedom and grandam of Spinning World: dam, winner at 7f and 1m, is from excellent family: fairly useful performer: placed in maidens before winning handicap at Catterick, staying on to lead close home: suited by good test of stamina: acts on good to firm and soft going: sold (joined M. Pipe) 28,000 gns in October. *P. W. Chapple-Hyam*

J B QUICK 3 b.c. Simply Great (FR) 122 – Quick J 61 (Jim J (USA)) [1996 NR 77 1997 10g Jul 8] half-brother to several winners (mostly abroad), including modest miler Every Effort (by Try My Best): dam Irish 6f winner: fair form when mid-division in maiden at Pontefract, unable to quicken final 2f. *P. W. Chapple-Hyam*

JEANNE CUTRONA 4 b.f. Risk Me (FR) 127 – Veuve Perrin (Legend of France – (USA) 124) [1996 –: 7m⁶ 1997 a11g Jan 3] 3,000Y: second foal: dam unraced: well beaten in maiden and seller. *K. G. Wingrove*

JEAN PIERRE 4 b.g. Anshan 119 – Astolat (Rusticaro (FR) 124) [1996 56: 10m 59 d 12.3m 10.8m² 10.2m² 9.7m 10.4g 9g 1997 9.9m² 10m³ 10m 10d³ 12m⁶ 12.1m² 12.5d 10s⁶ 10.2g⁵ Aug 7] modest and disappointing maiden handicapper: probably stays 1½m: acts on good to firm going, probably soft: has worn near-side pricker: none too genuine. *J. Pearce*

JEDI KNIGHT 3 b.g. Emarati (USA) 74 – Hannie Caulder (Workboy 123) [1996 82 66p: 6m⁴ 5f³ 5g⁴ 1997 5m 5g 8m⁵ 6g 7m² 7g* 8f* 8g² 8.3g⁴ 8g 7.5m 7m⁴ 8m* 7.6s 7.9s 8.1g² 8m⁶ 8g⁴ 8m² 10m* Nov 4] tall, good-topped gelding: fairly useful handicapper: won at Doncaster, Carlisle and Thirsk in the summer, and at Redcar on final start: keen sort, but stays 1¼m: acts on firm ground, probably unsuited by soft: has high head carriage: tough. *M. W. Easterby*

JEFFREY ANOTHERRED 3 b.g. Emarati (USA) 74 – First Pleasure 73 (Dom- 93 inion 123) [1996 93: 5.1m³ 5m* 6g³ 6g* 7.3m² 7s* a7g 1997 8m 7.6d² 7g 7m 7s⁶ 7m 6g³ 6s⁶ 6d 7m 7g⁵ 5d⁶ Nov 7] small gelding: fairly useful handicapper: mostly ran well in 1997 without winning, leaving K. McAuliffe before final start: likely to prove best at 6f to 1m: acts on good to firm ground and soft: visored (respectable effort) eighth start. *M. Dods*

JELALI (IRE) 4 b.g. Last Tycoon 131 – Lautreamont (Auction Ring (USA) 123) – [1996 65: 8m 10m 12.5f⁴ a11g 17.2d³ 16g 1997 17.1m 18d Oct 20] big gelding: winning hurdler: disappointing staying maiden on flat. *D. J. G. Murray Smith*

JENDALI PRINCESS 4 gr.f. Jendali (USA) 111 – Hyperion Princess (Dragon- – ara Palace (USA) 115) [1996 –: a7g a11g 1997 11.8d Jul 17] no sign of ability. *T. T. Bill*

JENNELLE 3 b.f. Nomination 125 – Its A Romp (Hotfoot 126) [1996 97: 5s* 85 5m* 5m 5m* 5m² 5g³ 5.5m⁴ 5v² 5d* 1997 5s 5.1m⁶ 5.1d 5m 6s⁴ 6g 5m 6g Aug 1] smallish, good-quartered filly: useful at 2 yrs, winning 4 times: not so good in 1997, fourth in minor event at Newmarket in June: barely stays 6f: acts on good to firm and heavy ground: sometimes slow to break: suitable mount for claimer: has been bandaged near-fore. *C. A. Dwyer*

JEN

JEN'S IN THE KNOW 2 br.f. (Feb 19) Presidium 124 – Lurking 69 (Formidable (USA) 125) [1997 a5g a5g a5g 5d Jul 17] 3,500Y: fourth foal: half-sister to 4-y-o Whittle Rock: dam 6f winner: no form, including in seller. *C. Murray*

JENZSOPH (IRE) 6 br.m. Glow (USA) – Taken By Force (Persian Bold 123) [1996 NR 1997 16.1m⁶ Jun 9] fourth foal: half-sister to 3 winners, including one up to 1½m by Valiyar: dam Irish middle-distance winner: poor maiden in Ireland at 3 yrs: very lightly raced and well beaten on flat since (blinkered only start in 1997): fair hurdler. *P. J. Hobbs*

JESTER MINUTE 3 gr.g. Jester 119 – Jealous Lover 56 (Alias Smith (USA)) [1996 NR 1997 10g Oct 24] 1,900 3-y-o: good-topped gelding: second foal: dam suited by 1½m: tailed off in maiden at Newbury. *B. A. Pearce*

JET SET SARAH (USA) 2 b.f. (Apr 2) Digression (USA) 116 – Little Jet Setter (USA) (Star de Naskra (USA)) [1997 7g⁵ 6.1m⁶ 7g 7g 8g Sep 15] tall, angular filly: sixth foal: half-sister to minor winners in USA by Broad Brush (2) and Our Native: dam won up to 9f in USA: no form in sellers and a claimer: visored/blinkered final 2 starts. *J. Berry*

JEWEL FIGHTER 3 br.f. Good Times (ITY) – Duellist (Town Crier 119) [1996 NR 1997 10d 8.1g Sep 11] sixth living foal: sister to Italian 11f to 15f winner Duel Times and modest 1¼m/11f winner Fighting Times: dam won twice around 9f in Italy: well beaten in maiden and seller. *C. A. Smith*

JEWEL (IRE) 2 b.f. (Apr 24) Cyrano de Bergerac 120 – Renzola (Dragonara Palace (USA) 115) [1997 5g⁵ 5.1v⁵ 5.1d 6g⁶ Oct 25] 15,500Y: sturdy filly: sister to 3 winning sprinters, including useful filly Miss Nosey Parker, and half-sister to 3-y-o Deadly Dudley: dam unraced half-sister to dam of very smart middle-distance colt Millkom: twice shaped promisingly in early-season maidens: absent 5 months afterwards, but showed signs of retaining ability in Newbury nursery final outing (missed break): should stay 6f. *R. Hannon* 64

JHAZI 3 b.c. Arazi (USA) 135 – Shoot Clear 111 (Bay Express 132) [1996 99p: 5m* 6m 6g⁴ 1997 6g 6g⁴ May 27] useful-looking colt: fluent mover: useful form at best at 2 yrs: disappointing in minor events in 1997: blinkered final start (raced freely): sent to UAE. *D. R. Loder*

JIBEREEN 5 b.g. Lugana Beach 116 – Fashion Lover 70 (Shiny Tenth 120) [1996 75: 7d⁶ 7g a6g* a6s⁴ 1997 a7g* a7g* a8g⁴ a7g⁵ a7g² a8g* 8.3s 7f⁶ 8.3g 7d* 8g 8m* a8g 7.9s 8d 7m⁴ 8s⁴ a7g Dec 6] strong gelding: fair performer: won claimers at Southwell and Wolverhampton in January and handicaps at Southwell in April and Newmarket in June (apprentices) and July: effective at 7f/1m: acts on good to firm ground, soft and goes well on fibresand: has been bandaged. *P. Howling* 65 a75

JIBE (USA) 2 b.f. (May 7) Danzig (USA) – Slightly Dangerous (USA) 122 (Roberto (USA) 131) [1997 7m⁴ 7m* 8g² Sep 28] 107 p

'The excellent band of broodmares Khalid Abdulla is building up suggests that the next few years ought to see his already familiar colours enjoying even greater success . . . Slightly Dangerous, acquired for an undisclosed sum after winning her first start at three, will not be out of place in this exalted company—she's a fine stud prospect whose second place in the Oaks showed her one of the best middle-distance fillies in Britain.'

So began the essay on Slightly Dangerous at the end of her racing career in *Racehorses of 1982*. Fifteen years on, and still going strongly, she's established an outstanding record at stud, earning her the Thoroughbred Breeders' Association's Award in 1997 for leading broodmare on the flat. With the exception of 1992 and 1996, when she hadn't been covered in the preceding year, she's produced a foal every year, her latest two-year-old Jibe being her eleventh. Of those, ten have run and nine have won. While most broodmares would do well to get one foal good enough to be rated at least 100 on Timeform's scale, remarkably all nine of the winners produced by Slightly Dangerous have shown useful form or better and have earned that supposedly all-important, though much more imprecise measure of merit, 'black type'.

The smart middle-distance colt Timefighter (rated 115, by Star Appeal) got things off to a good start and preceded her best runner, the champion miler Warning (136, by Known Fact). Then came the black sheep of the family Highly Dangerous (by Shirley Heights), the only runner who failed to win, to be followed by the Irish Derby runner-up Deploy (131, also by Shirley Heights) and, after the unraced Dancing Brave filly Stiletta, Deploy's useful sister Shirley Valentine (104). Further matings with Dancing Brave resulted in Derby and Irish Derby winner Commander In Chief (128) and Lancashire Oaks runner-up Totality (103). Dushyantor (123, by Sadler's Wells) went close to giving Slightly Dangerous another classic winner with second places in the Derby and St Leger, and her latest representatives on the racecourse are the Danzig fillies Yashmak (118), winner of the Ribblesdale, and Fillies' Mile runner-up Jibe. A filly foal by Sadler's Wells will have the task of keeping up the record in due course, and Slightly Dangerous visited Danzig again in 1997.

Second place in the Fillies' Mile is unlikely to be the highlight of Jibe's career. Just like the year before, Henry Cecil fielded two runners in the race, one the winner of the May Hill Stakes, the other the winner of a maiden. And just as the maiden winner Sleepytime had been preferred to Reams of Verse in 1996, so maiden winner Jibe was the 6/4 favourite and choice of stable-jockey Kieren Fallon ahead of Midnight Line for the latest running. Jibe had been green for her debut when fourth at Newmarket but had gone on to land the odds impressively at Lingfield in September by four lengths with plenty in hand from Bahri's sister Winsa. Jibe's demeanour beforehand at Ascot wasn't ideal —she was rather on edge despite her two handlers and was mounted early— though she proved better behaved at the stalls than her sister Yashmak. Like Sleepytime the year before, though to a lesser degree, Jibe's chances were spoiled when she met interference in the straight at Ascot. After tracking the leaders, she was left a little short of room when the rank outsider Filey Brigg began to weaken in front of her and just at the moment when Glorosia was beginning her winning run. As a result Jibe had too much ground to make up in the closing stages but rallied strongly late on to reduce Glorosia's advantage to three quarters of a length at the post.

		Northern Dancer	Nearctic
	Danzig (USA)	(b 1961)	Natalma
	(b 1977)	Pas de Nom	Admiral's Voyage
Jibe (USA)		(b or br 1968)	Petitioner
(b.f. May 7, 1995)	Slightly	Roberto	Hail To Reason
	Dangerous (USA)	(b 1969)	Bramalea
	(b 1979)	Where You Lead	Raise A Native
		(ch 1970)	Noblesse

In common with some other members of her family, Jibe is on the small side, but sturdy. She has a quick, fluent action. At the time of writing she's prominent in the One Thousand Guineas betting but seems more of an Oaks filly, a race which her great grandam Noblesse won and in which her grandam Where You Lead, as well as dam Slightly Dangerous, finished second. She looks sure to make her mark in 1998. *H. R. A. Cecil*

JIB JAB 3 br.g. Jendali (USA) 111 – No Rejection (Mummy's Pet 125) [1996 59p: 5m² 5d⁵ 7f⁶ 7m 6g 1997 6.1d 8.2g 10m Jun 2] sparely-made gelding: modest form at 2 yrs for D. Nicholls: well beaten in 1997: should stay at least 1m. *Mrs N. Macauley* —

JIGSAW BOY 8 ch.g. Homeboy 114 – Chiparia 82 (Song 132) [1996 60, a71: a6g⁶ a7g⁴ a7g* a7g³ 5.9d⁶ 6m⁵ 6f 7d a7g* a6g⁵ a6g a7g a7g* a6g a7s⁵ a7g 1997 a7g⁴ a7g² a7g³ a7g⁴ a7g a7g* 8m a7g a7g⁵ a8.5g a7g⁵ a7g⁶ Dec 18] good-topped gelding: modest performer: won claimer at Southwell in May: seems best at 7f: acts on fibresand and any turf going: has been visored (not at 8 yrs): usually held up. *P. G. Murphy* a59

JILA (IRE) 2 ch.c. (Mar 10) Kris 135 – Enaya 99 (Caerleon (USA) 132) [1997 6.1m³ 6f² 7m* Oct 22] compact colt: has a short, round action: second foal: dam 2-y-o 6f winner, later best at 1¼m, half-sister to very smart 7f/1m performer Gabr: 84 p

confirmed promise of first 2 starts when winning maiden at Yarmouth by short
head from Timbervati, leading going well 3f out and rallying when headed: should
stay 1m: raced only on good to firm/firm ground: should make a useful 3-y-o.
R. W. Armstrong

JILLY BEVELED 5 b.m. Beveled (USA) – Karens Valentine (Daring March 38
116) [1996 45: 8m⁵ 7d⁵ 8m⁴ 8d² a14.8g⁶ 1997 a7s a7g a7g⁶ a8.5g* a8g 8m a7g
a12g a8g a8g a7g³ 7.5v a7g a6g⁵ a7g Aug 15] leggy mare: poor handicapper: won
apprentice event at Wolverhampton in February: best up to 8.5f: acts on good to firm
ground, dead and fibresand. *Ronald Thompson*

JILLY WOO 3 gr.f. Environment Friend 128 – William's Bird (USA) 104 (Master 39
Willie 129) [1996 60d, a?: 5.7g³ 6g⁵ 6d⁵ 5f 6m 7m 6d³ a6g⁵ a7g 1997 8d 6.9m⁶ 8.1m⁴
10m⁵ a16g 8.5g⁴ Sep 5] lightly-made filly: poor maiden: trained until after fourth
start by D. Elsworth, next outing by B. Pearce: should stay beyond 8.5f: acts on good
to firm ground: blinkered last 4 starts at 2 yrs. *P. Hayward*

JILTED (IRE) 2 b.f. (May 5) Pursuit of Love 124 – What A Pity 97 (Blakeney 77
126) [1997 5d² 5g 6g² 7d 6m² 5.1m² 6.5m⁶ 6m⁴ 7g⁴ Oct 18] 130,000 francs Y:
sparely-made filly: half-sister to several winners, notably Italian miler Junk Bond (by
Last Tycoon), useful 6f and 7f winner here at 2 yrs: dam, lightly-raced 7f winner,
half-sister to College Chapel: fair maiden: below form last 3 starts, in blinkers
penultimate one: best form at 6f: acts on good to firm going: carries head awkwardly,
and has hung right: sold 32,000 gns in December. *R. Hannon*

JILVARRA 2 b.f. (Feb 27) Desert Splendour 95 – Charlotte Daughter (Brigadier –
Gerard 144) [1997 7f⁶ 7g a5g 6m Aug 23] fourth reported thoroughbred foal: dam
unraced: well beaten in claimer and sellers. *W. G. M. Turner*

JIM AND TONIC (FR) 3 ch.g. Double Bed (FR) 121 – Jimka (Jim French 115
(USA)) [1996 8g* 1997 12d 8d* 8m³ 8d² 8s⁵ 8s⁵ 8g* 8s* 8v⁵ Nov 21] brother to 2
winners in France (1 over jumps) and half-brother to 3 others (all including over
jumps): dam French 7f to 10.5f winner: began in relatively minor company, winning
twice in the Provinces (including only start at 2 yrs) then Saint-Cloud and Maisons-
Laffitte, but showed himself a smart gelding when winning Prix Perth at Saint-Cloud
in November by 2 lengths from Marathon: should stay beyond 1m: acts on soft
ground. *F. Doumen, France*

JIM DORE (IRE) 2 b. or br.g. (Mar 25) Mac's Imp (USA) 116 – Secret Assign- 67
ment 71 (Vitiges (FR) 132) [1997 5m⁴ Mar 22] IR 8,000Y: strong, useful-looking
gelding: half-brother to Irish 1995 2-y-o 1m winner Secret Magic (by Magical Strike)
and 2 winners abroad by Simply Great: dam, 1m winner from 3 starts, half-sister to
smart 7f to 1½m winner Sheer Grit: 10/1, green when fourth in maiden at Doncaster.
A. P. Jarvis

JIMJAREER (IRE) 4 br.g. Jareer (USA) 115 – Onthecomet (Chief Singer 131) 32
[1996 51: 6d 8m⁵ a8g a8g⁴ 8f³ 8f 8.2m 11m a8g 1997 10.5m 10.3d 8.3g 10.8g⁶ 12s⁵ a37
12s⁶ a11g⁵ Dec 8] good-bodied gelding: blind in off eye: poor handicapper: probably
stays 11f: acts on fibresand and firm ground. *Capt. J. Wilson*

JIMMY TOO 2 b. or br.c. (Feb 8) Nomination 125 – Cutlass Princess (USA) 41 103
(Cutlass (USA)) [1997 5.1m³ 5.1s* 6.1m³ 6.1s* 6d² Sep 20] lengthy, good-bodied
colt: third foal: half-brother to 4-y-o Princess Efisio: dam poor maiden: useful
performer: won minor events at Chester in June and August: easily best form when
neck second to Arkadian Hero in Mill Reef Stakes at Newbury, racing away from
winner initially but running on strongly, despite drifting left: will stay 7f: acts well
on good to soft/soft ground: genuine: type to win a useful early-season prize.
B. A. McMahon

JINGOIST (IRE) 3 b.f. Polish Patriot (USA) 128 – Hot Curry (USA) (Sharpen –
Up 127) [1996 52: a5g⁶ 5m a5g⁶ 5.2f² 5m⁵ a6g² 6g* 6f⁵ 8f² 7.5m² 6s a8.5g⁵ 1997 a6g
6.9m 7s Jul 2] leggy filly: modest form at 2 yrs: tailed off in 1997: usually blinkered:
swishes tail, and has looked less than keen. *J. L. Harris*

JIVE BOOGIE 3 b. or br.g. Nomination 125 – Jive Music 32 (Music Boy 124) –
[1996 –: 5m 1997 8g 8m⁶ Aug 7] no sign of ability, including in blinkers. *N. Bycroft*

JIYUSH 4 b.c. Generous (IRE) 139 – Urjwan (USA) 98 (Seattle Slew (USA)) 114
[1996 107: 10m³ 12.1d² 12m² 14m² 13.9g* 18.2m* 18g 16g 1997 16.2m 14d* 20g

15g^5 16g* 16f^4 Oct 4] big, good-topped colt: smart performer on his day: won rated stakes at Goodwood (made all) in May and valuable handicap at Newbury (beat Grey Shot 2½ lengths) in September: disappointing favourite (behind Grey Shot) in Jockey Club Cup at Newmarket final start: effective at 1¾m to 2¼m: acts on firm and dead going, yet to race on softer: tends to sweat: none too consistent: to be trained by Peter Hayes in Australia. *E. A. L. Dunlop*

JOBIE   7 b.g. Precocious 126 – Lingering 96 (Kind of Hush 118) [1996 63d: 6m^3 –
6m 5m 6f 6.9m 1997 a7g 6m Apr 10] no longer of much account. *R. T. Phillips*

JOB RAGE (IRE)   3 b. or br.g. Yashgan 126 – Snatchingly (Thatch (USA) 136)   –
[1996 NR 1997 8m^6 11.9s^5 a8.5g Nov 1] IR 3,500Y: leggy gelding: fourth foal: dam Irish 2-y-o 6f winner: well beaten in maidens. *A. Bailey*

JOCASTA   2 b.f. (Feb 19) Warning 136 – Breed Reference (Reference Point 139)   78 p
[1997 6d^5 Oct 17] 23,000Y: leggy, quite good-topped filly: first foal: dam placed in France from 1½m to 14.5f: 33/1, decidedly nervy and green, started slowly but ran on well under hands and heels after getting hampered when under 4 lengths fifth of 20 to Atuf in maiden at Newmarket: will stay at least 1m: sure to improve. *C. F. Wall*

JOCK'S DREAM   2 b.f. (Apr 27) Noble Patriarch 115 – Bold Sophie (Bold Owl   –
101) [1997 a7g Dec 18] 750F, 500Y: second foal: dam unraced: slowly away and always outpaced in seller at Southwell. *B. J. McMath*

JOCKWEILER (IRE)   2 b.g. (May 29) Night Shift (USA) – Johara (USA) 92   ?
(Exclusive Native (USA)) [1997 6s 5m 6g a5g a8g a7g^5 a8g Dec 8] 17,000Y: smal-   a34
lish, strong gelding: fifth foal: half-brother to 3 winners, notably Gold Cup winner Ashal (by Touching Wood): dam 2-y-o 6f winner: poor maiden: trained by Mrs J. R. Ramsden first 2 starts. *D. W. Chapman*

JOHAYRO   4 ch.g. Clantime 101 – Arroganza 62 (Crofthall 110) [1996 67d: a5g^4 69
a5g 5d 5d 5.1m 5.1f 5.1m^5 5m^2 5m 5.1g^6 5g 5s 1997 5s^6 5m* 5g* 6g^2* 5m^4 5g 5m^5 5g 5g^3 5m^6 5g^2 5g 6g^4 5g^3 6g^2 5g^5 5d 6m* 5m 6g 7m^2 6m Nov 4] close-coupled gelding: has a quick action: fair performer: in good form for most of 1997, and won minor events at Musselburgh and Catterick and handicap at Ripon in April and another handicap (apprentice) at Redcar in September: effective at 5f and 6f: best form on good ground or firmer: occasionally blinkered/visored: races up with pace. *J. S. Goldie*

JOHN BOWDLER MUSIC   2 b.c. (Apr 19) Soviet Star (USA) 128 – Arianna   –
Aldini (Habitat 134) [1997 6m Jun 2] 5,800Y: half-brother to 3 winners, including 5f to 1m winner Green's Bid (by Siberian Express), useful at 2 yrs, and fairly useful miler Langtry Lady (by Pas de Seul): dam unraced: 4/1, last in maiden at Hamilton, soon leading but dropping right out, possibly something amiss. *M. Johnston*

JOHN EMMS (IRE)   3 ch.g. Shalford (IRE) 124§ – Miss Lee Ann (Tumble Wind   77
(USA)) [1996 68p: 5m^5 6g 1997 6g^2 6m^3 6m^2 6.1s^6 6g^3 6m* 6g Aug 25] good-topped gelding: fair performer: won apprentice handicap at Salisbury in August: ran badly only subsequent start: stays 6f: acts on good to firm ground, below form (off course 3 months afterwards) on soft. *M. Bell*

JOHN FERNELEY   2 b.c. (Apr 6) Polar Falcon (USA) 126 – I'll Try 71 (Try My   57
Best (USA) 130) [1997 5.2m May 28] 36,000 2-y-o: eighth foal: half-brother to several winners, including fairly useful 1992 2-y-o 7f winner Anaxagoras (by Mtoto) and Irish middle-distance stayer Steel Mirror (by Slip Anchor): dam, 2-y-o 5f winner later successful in USA, out of half-sister to Katies: 9/4 favourite, seventh of 10 in maiden at Newbury, but hung markedly, looking virtually unrideable. *P. F. I. Cole*

JOHN LEE HOOKER   5 b.g. Superlative 118 – Aunt Jemima (Busted 134)   –
[1996 NR 1997 13.1g^6 16g^4 Jul 28] fair performer at 3 yrs: well beaten in 1997. *D. W. P. Arbuthnot*

JOHNNIE THE JOKER   6 gr.g. Absalom 128 – Magic Tower 76 (Tower Walk   53
130) [1996 51, a79: a6g a8g^5 7s^5 a8g^2 7g* 7.5m a6g^5 a7g* a9.4g^2 a9.4g a8.5g^5 a9.4g   a80
7m^3 8f 8m a8.5g 1997 a8g a12g a8g a7g^3 a7g a8g* a7g^2 a8g* a8.5g* a8.5g^3 a7g a8g^3 8.5f a12g^6 Oct 4] good-topped gelding: has a round action: fairly useful handicapper on the all-weather, modest on turf: won at Southwell (twice) and Wolverhampton in May/June: suited by 1m/9f: acts on firm and dead ground and on fibresand: usually visored/blinkered: usually races prominently. *J. P. Leigh*

Tote Festival Handicap, Ascot—the stand-side runners dominate,
Jo Mell proving much the best of them. Kayvee (grey) and Crumpton Hill give chase

JOHNNY STACCATO 3 b.g. Statoblest 120 – Frasquita (Song 132) [1996 91: 91 d
6d* 6m⁴ 7m⁶ 6g⁶ 1997 6d⁴ 6d 6m³ 5g* 5d 6f 5m 7.3m 6g³ a6s a6g a6g Dec 19] leggy
gelding: has a quick action: fairly useful performer: won minor event at Sandown in
June: lost his form afterwards, leaving J. Eustace for only 3,500 gns after ninth start:
needs good test at 5f, and probably stays 7f: acts on good to firm and dead ground:
sometimes slowly away. *R. J. O'Sullivan*

JOHN O'DREAMS 12 b.g. Indian King (USA) 128 – Mississipi Shuffle 78 50 d
(Steel Heart 128) [1996 54: 5g 5m³ 5.1g⁵ 5m⁵ 6f 5.2m* 5g 5f⁶ 5.1m³ 5m⁶ 5g⁶ 5.7m³
5m³ 1997 5g⁶ 5.1m³ 5g⁴ 5.7d 5m 5g⁶ 5m 5g 5g 5m Sep 17] good-topped gelding:
unimpressive mover: modest performer: below form in 1997 after third start: stays
5.7f: acts on any going: tried blinkered/visored earlier in career: often bandaged:
tends to start slowly and get behind. *Mrs A. L. M. King*

JOINT REGENT (USA) 2 br.c. (Apr 24) St Jovite (USA) 135 – Ice Fantasy 76
(USA) (It's Freezing (USA) 122) [1997 7m⁴ 7g⁶ Oct 24] $230,000Y: rangy colt: has
scope: half-brother to several winners, including fairly useful 1991 2-y-o 7f winner
Snow Forest (by Woodman) and US Grade 3 8.5f winner Fighting Fantasy (by
Fighting Fit): dam won up to 7f in USA: fair form in maidens at Newmarket and
Doncaster in October: should stay at least 1m. *B. W. Hills*

JOLI FILLE 2 b.f. (Apr 29) Merdon Melody 98 – Thabeh 57 (Shareef Dancer 40
(USA) 135) [1997 6s 6m 7.5f 7.9s a8g a8g a7g⁶ Dec 18] 1,500Y: lengthy filly: fourth
foal: dam poor maiden: poor maiden herself. *J. S. Wainwright*

JOLI FLYERS 3 gr.c. Joli Wasfi (USA) 48 – Hagen's Bargain 62§ (Mount Hagen –
(FR) 127) [1996 NR 1997 12m 10g a10g⁶ Nov 25] big colt: brother/half-brother to
several poor performers: dam ungenuine 2-y-o 5f seller winner: showed little in
maidens. *M. J. Haynes*

JOLI'S PRINCE 3 b.g. Superlative 118 – Joli's Girl 79 (Mansingh (USA) 120) –
[1996 –: 8m 8m 1997 6m 6m 7m 8f a11g Nov 24] poor maiden. *C. Murray*

JOLI'S SON 4 gr.c. Joli Wasfi (USA) 48 – Hagen's Bargain 62§ (Mount Hagen –
(FR) 127) [1996 NR 1997 10s 10m 10s⁴ 12g Aug 10] strong, workmanlike colt:
related to several poor performers: dam ungenuine 2-y-o 5f seller winner: little
worthwhile form. *M. J. Haynes*

JOLLYHACK 2 b.c. (Mar 29) Mon Tresor 113 – Spiritofaffection (Raga Navarro 57
(ITY) 119) [1997 6m 7.1g⁶ 7.9s Oct 8] big, rather unfurnished colt: fourth foal: dam
unraced: best effort in maidens when keeping-on sixth at Chepstow: not given hard
time in gruelling ground at York next time: slowly away first 2 starts. *J. G. M. O'Shea*

JOLLY HARBOUR 2 b.f. (Apr 22) Rudimentary (USA) 118 – Ask Mama 83 –
(Mummy's Pet 125) [1997 6f 6g a5g Nov 14] 7,800Y, 22,000 2-y-o: tall, workmanlike filly: good mover: seventh foal: half-sister to 3 winners, including 4-y-o Pleading: dam 1¼m winner: well beaten in maidens. *W. J. Haggas*

490

JOLLY JACKSON 3 br.c. Primo Dominie 121 – Pounelta 91 (Tachypous 128) 56
[1996 64: 7d a8g⁴ 1997 a8g² a8g⁵ a8.5g² 8d 7m 8.3g 8f⁵ 8s² 8.1m 7.6m 8m a8.5g³ a65
9.7d Oct 21] poor mover: modest maiden handicapper: stays 8.5f: acts on firm and
soft going and the all-weather. *R. Akehurst*

JO MAXIMUS 5 b.g. Prince Sabo 123 – Final Call 79 (Town Crier 119) [1996 78, 64
a–: 7f³ 7f² 7m 6m⁵ 7g 7f 7f* a8g⁶ a6g 1997 a7g³ a7g a7g⁶ 6f³ 7m 7g⁵ 6g Jun 16]
workmanlike gelding: just a modest handicapper in 1997: left S. Dow after fourth
start: stays 7f: acts on firm and soft ground and on equitrack: races prominently: has
gained all 3 wins at Brighton. *J. G. Smyth-Osbourne*

JO MELL 4 b.g. Efisio 120 – Militia Girl (Rarity 129) [1996 89: 8m 7g 7f 8.1d² 109
8g⁴ 7m³ 7m⁵ 7m³ 7.6d² 8.1v⁴ 7g³ 1997 6m 7m 6d 7m 6d 7s* 7.1g* 7.9g* 7.9d 8m⁶
7m* 7g* Oct 25] lengthy gelding: has a round action: useful performer, better than
ever in 1997 after a tie-back operation: won handicaps at Newcastle, Haydock and
York in the summer, and showed further improvement to win Tote Festival Handicap
at Ascot (led 3f out and beat Kayvee by 2½ lengths) in September: allowed to dictate
when easy winner by 1¾ lengths from Swiss Law of 6-runner minor event at
Doncaster on final start: effective at 7f/1m: acts on good to firm and heavy ground:
takes keen hold: usually races up with pace. *T. D. Easterby*

JONA HOLLEY 4 b.g. Sharpo 132 – Spurned (USA) 91 (Robellino (USA) 127) 59
[1996 41: 6.9m 7m 8.2m 10m⁵ 10m 1997 8g 8.3s⁵ 8.1m⁴ a8g² 8g² 9.7s* 10g² 10.2d
10.4s⁴ a8g* Oct 20] tall gelding: modest handicapper: left I. Balding after third start:
in good form for new yard, winning at Folkestone in July and Southwell (apprentice
race, landed gamble) in October: sold 12,000 gns later in October: stays 1¼m: acts
on good to firm and soft ground and on fibresand. *G. L. Moore*

JONAS NIGHTENGALE 2 b.g. (May 6) Deploy 131 – Springs Welcome 86 64
(Blakeney 126) [1997 7g³ 8.1d⁵ 8m⁶ 10g⁶ 8d Oct 20] 1,000Y: workmanlike gelding:
third foal: half-brother to 3-y-o Sipowitz and 4-y-o Duncombe Hall: dam stayed 2m:
modest maiden: ran creditably in nurseries last 2 starts: will be well suited by 1½m+.
C. A. Cyzer

JONATHAN'S GIRL 2 b.f. (Mar 30) Thowra (FR) – Sicilian Vespers 44 –
(Mummy's Game 120) [1997 5m a6f⁴ 6s 7m 8d a6g a7g Nov 18] small filly: fourth
live foal: sister to 3-y-o Alimerjam and 5-y-o Bellara: dam won 7f seller: little sign of
ability. *J. J. Bridger*

JONNY'S JOKER 3 b.g. Precocious 126 – Mardessa 74 (Ardross 134) [1996 –: –
5m 1997 8.2m 6.1m⁵ 8m⁶ Aug 20] no sign of ability. *F. H. Lee*

JORROCKS (USA) 3 b.g. Rubiano (USA) – Perla Fina (USA) (Gallant Man) 97 p
[1996 NR 1997 7g² 8.2d³ 7g² 7.1m* 7m* 7m⁶ 7.3d* 8f⁴ Sep 29] $47,000F: sturdy
gelding: has a short, round action: ninth foal: closely related to Grade 3 f winner
Electric Flash (by Fappiano) and half-brother to several winners in USA and France:
dam minor stakes-placed winner at around 1m: sire (by Fappiano) champion US
sprinter: useful performer: won handicaps at Sandown in July, Goodwood (£20,500

Seeboard Stakes (Handicap), Goodwood—
Jorrocks (near side) quickens past Great Child and Omaha City (hooped cap)

contest) in August and Newbury in September: far from discredited in minor event at Bath final start: likely to be as effective at 6f as 7f/1m: acts on good to firm (probably firm) and dead going: tends to carry head awkwardly when ridden, and suited by waiting tactics in truly-run race: should progress again in 1998. *I. A. Balding*

JOSEPH'S WINE (IRE) 8 b.g. Smile (USA) – Femme Gendarme (USA) (Policeman (FR) 124) [1996 –, a57+: a8g 1997 a8g* a11g a9.4g⁵ a10g* a8g a8g* Dec 18] lengthy gelding: fairly useful performer: trotted up in claimers at Southwell in January (made virtually all) and February: left D. Nicholls in March: returned from 10-month absence to win another claimer there (in good style by 5 lengths) in December: stays 11f: goes well on the all-weather, unraced on turf since 1995: best in blinkers: has run well when sweating: often held up. *J. Wharton* — a80

JOUST 3 b.g. Keen 116 – Tudorealm (USA) (Palace Music (USA) 129) [1996 NR 1997 8.1m⁵ 10.1g⁶ 11.5m Sep 9] big gelding: second foal: dam, bred to have been suited by further than 1m, granddaughter of Princess Royal winner Trillionaire: signs of ability on debut, but no worthwhile form. *C. E. Brittain* — –

JOVIAN 3 gr.f. Petong 126 – What A Pet (Mummy's Pet 125) [1996 –: 6m 1997 8d⁴ Aug 25] good-topped filly: signs of just a little ability in maidens: sold 12,500 gns in December. *R. Guest* — –

JOYFUL JOY 3 b.f. River God (USA) 121 – Joyfulness (FR) 78 (Cure The Blues (USA)) [1996 –: 6m 6d 5m a6s 1997 a6g⁶ a6g a6g 8.2m 7g 8d 6.1m 8.2d 8.2s 7g⁴ 8g 8.1m⁶ 6m a7g 8d Oct 28] plain filly: bad and deteriorating maiden. *B. P. J. Baugh* — 37 d

JOYRIDER 6 b.g. Risk Me (FR) 127 – Villajoyosa (FR) (Satingo 129) [1996 NR 1997 a16g Jan 10] winning hurdler: of little account on flat nowadays. *Miss M. K. Milligan* — –

JUBA 5 b.m. Dowsing (USA) 124 – Try The Duchess 99 (Try My Best (USA) 130) [1996 38: a6g⁴ 8.3m a8g a8.5g a8g a6g³ a7g a6g⁵ a6g 1997 a6s Jan 1] poor maiden: well beaten only 5-y-o start. *Dr J. D. Scargill* — –

JUBILEE SCHOLAR (IRE) 4 b.g. Royal Academy (USA) 130 – Jaljuli 107 (Jalmood (USA) 126) [1996 67: 8d 7m 7d⁶ a8g 1997 a9.4g a10g a7g a7g⁴ a6g⁵ a7g 6.9m 8f⁴ 7m 8.3g 7m 8m 8f 10m² 10d⁶ a10g* a9.4g⁵ a10g² Dec 19] modest handicapper: trained first 6 starts by K. McAuliffe: won at Lingfield in November: stays 1¼m: acts on all-weather, good to firm and soft ground: sometimes blinkered (was for win)/visored. *G. L. Moore* — 42 a54

JUBRAN (USA) 11 b.g. Vaguely Noble 140 – La Vue (USA) (Reviewer (USA)) [1996 NR 1997 16d⁵ 12d⁵ 12g 10.1g⁶ 12g⁶ 12g Aug 23] formerly fair handicapper: poor at best in 1997: stays 12.3f: probably acts on any ground: won over hurdles in September. *J. L. Eyre* — 42

JUCEA 8 b.m. Bluebird (USA) 125 – Appleby Park 98 (Bay Express 132) [1996 77: 5g 5.1g² 5.1f⁴ 5.7g* 5m* 6m 5.1f⁶ 5m³ 5m³ 5m 5f⁵ 5g³ 5.7m⁴ 5d 5g⁵ 5g 5m⁵ 1997 5.1g 5g 5s 5m² 5m 6m⁵ 5d Oct 20] sturdy mare: poor mover: just a modest handicapper in 1997: stays 5.7f: acts on firm ground and equitrack, seemingly not on going softer than good: no improvement in blinkers/visor. *J. L. Spearing* — 61

JUCINDA 3 gr.f. Midyan (USA) 124 – Catch The Sun (Kalaglow 132) [1996 –: 7f 7g 8s 1997 12m⁵ 14.1d² 14.1g² 14.1m⁵ 14.1m 16m⁵ 15.8g a16g Aug 28] leggy filly: modest maiden handicapper: best efforts when second twice at Nottingham in May: stays 1¾m: acts on good to firm and dead ground, tailed off on equitrack. *J. Pearce* — 58 d

JUDDY 3 ch.g. Clantime 101 – Two's Up (Double Jump 131) [1996 NR 1997 6.1g² 6g 6g Jul 16] half-brother to modest Burcroft (by Crofthall) and Bob-Double (by Import), both winners at up to 1½m: dam never ran: modest maiden: second in seller at Nottingham (would probably have won had he kept a straight course) on debut: left J. A. Harris after second start: raced only at 6f on good ground. *J. O'Reilly* — 55

JUDE 3 b.f. Darshaan 133 – Alruccaba 83 (Crystal Palace (FR) 132) [1996 NR 1997 10m 10m⁴ 12.1m⁵ 13.1g Sep 8] sister to useful Irish 1½m winner Alouette and Irish Oaks third Arrikala and half-sister to several winners, notably 4-y-o Last Second: dam 2-y-o 6f winner: modest maiden: should stay beyond 1½m: sold 92,000 gns in December. *P. F. I. Cole* — 53

JUDGE ADVOCATE (IRE) 5 b.g. Contract Law (USA) 108 – Brigadina – (Brigadier Gerard 144) [1996 NR 1997 12m 10.1g Oct 22] lightly raced and little form since 2-y-o days: pulled up lame final start. *J. J. O'Neill*

JUDICIAL SUPREMACY 3 b.c. Warning 136 – Song Test (USA) (The Minst- 77 rel (CAN) 135) [1996 82p: 7m² 1997 7g 8m⁶ 8d⁴ 10s⁶ Jun 27] sturdy, useful-looking colt: has a quick action: fair maiden: best effort of 1997 when fourth in handicap at Goodwood, despite being forced wide: likely to prove best around 1m: joined B. Hills. *J. R. Fanshawe*

JUGGLER 3 b.g. Soviet Star (USA) 128 – Wily Trick (USA) 83 (Clever Trick 80 ? (USA)) [1996 NR 1997 a7g³ 10g⁴ 10.2m 9m⁶ 10.3g Oct 25] second foal: dam, maiden stayed 1m, half-sister to very smart 7f to 1½m winner Height of Fashion (dam of Nashwan and Unfuwain) out of 1000 Guineas and Prix de Diane winner Highclere: fairly useful maiden: easily best effort fourth at Windsor in June: stays 1¼m: one to treat with caution. *Lord Huntingdon*

JUICY TING 3 ch.g. Hatim (USA) 121 – Floating Note 61 (Music Boy 124) – [1996 58: 5m 6m 6d³ 7g² 8.3d⁶ 1997 8g 10g 7g a9.4g⁴ Aug 16] workmanlike gelding: modest form at 2 yrs, none in 1997. *P. C. Haslam*

JUKEBOX JIVE 3 ch.f. Scottish Reel 123 – My Sweet Melody 62 (Music Boy 55 124) [1996 48: 7m 7.9g 1997 6g 5m⁴ 6f⁵ a7g 6.9m⁵ 8d² 8d* 10g Jul 8] lightly-made filly: modest performer: won claimer at Newmarket in June on final start for C. Dwyer: stays 1m well: goes well on dead ground, yet to race on softer: joined M. Hammond. *H. Akbary*

JULIA'S RELATIVE 3 b.f. Distant Relative 128 – Alkion (Fordham (USA) 51 117) [1996 –: 6g 1997 a6g³ a7g³ a7g² a6g⁶ a6g² a6g² a5g* a7g a7g a5g Sep 8] modest performer: won weak Southwell claimer (final outing for R. Guest) in April: well beaten afterwards: stays 7f: acts on the all-weather, unraced on turf in 1997: effective blinkered or not: not the easiest of rides. *Ronald Thompson*

JULIES JEWEL 2 ch.g. (May 14) Simply Great (FR) 122 – Melungeon 67 (Ardoon 124) [1997 6g 5.1g 7g 6g 6d⁶ 6.1g² 6d a5g⁶ a7g⁵ Dec 18] 3,200 2-y-o: compact gelding: has a short, round action: half-brother to useful French middle-distance performer Flanaghan Cocktail (by Tumble Wind): dam unraced: fair maiden: best effort when neck second at Nottingham in September, leading long way: best form at 6f: yet to race on ground firmer than good. *M. C. Chapman*

JULIETTA MIA (USA) 3 ch.f. Woodman (USA) 126 – Just Juliet (USA) (What – A Pleasure (USA)) [1996 72: 6g 6g⁴ 7g 7.6m² /m* 8g² 8g² 1997 8d 10m 10.5m⁵ Aug 8] close-coupled filly: progressive form at 2 yrs for B. Hills: well beaten in 1997. *W. R. Muir*

JUMP THE LIGHTS 4 b.g. Siberian Express (USA) 125 – Turtle Dove (Gyr – (USA) 131) [1996 58, a66: 12s⁶ a12g* 14.6m⁶ 12m⁴ 1997 11.8m 14.1g a12g³ a14g a63 11.8g a12g³ Jun 27] neat gelding: modest handicapper: should stay 2m: acts on fibresand and good to firm ground: joined P. Rodford. *S. P. C. Woods*

JUNCTION CITY (USA) 3 b.g. Forty Niner (USA) – Key Witness (USA) (Key – To The Mint (USA)) [1996 NR 1997 10g Jun 13] fifth foal: brother to Yale Twentyniner (Grade 2 runner-up at 1m in Argentina) and half-brother to 3 winners in USA, including Grade 1 winners at up to 1¼m You'd Be Surprised (by Blushing Groom) and Key Contender (by Fit To Fight): dam won 5 times in USA and placed in graded stakes at up to 11f: tailed off in Sandown maiden. *I. A. Balding*

JUNCTION TWENTYTWO 7 ch.g. Local Suitor (USA) 128 – Pollinella 108 – (Charlottown 127) [1996 –: a12g 1997 14.1s Jul 5] no longer of any account. *D. J. Wintle*

JUNE BOUNTY (USA) 2 b.f. (May 2) Red Ransom (USA) – June Bride (USA) – (Riverman (USA) 131) [1997 7m Nov 1] 15,000F: half-sister to several winners, including Kaher (around 1½m, by Our Native): dam, 1½m winner in USA, daughter of smart stakes winner at up to 9f Deesse du Val: 33/1, always behind and not knocked about in maiden at Newmarket: joined R. Cowell. *G. Wragg*

JUNGLE FRESH 4 b.g. Rambo Dancer (CAN) 107 – Report 'em (USA) 51 – (Staff Writer (USA)) [1996 –: 10g⁴ 7g⁶ 10.5d 1997 8d 12s 10g 16f⁴ Jun 10] no worthwhile form. *J. D. Bethell*

493

JUNGLE STORY (IRE)   2 b.f. (Mar 12) Alzao (USA) 117 – Jungle Jezebel 107   70
(Thatching 131) [1997 6m⁶ 7g⁴ 6m⁵ 7d² 7g* Sep 27] 13,000Y: angular filly:
unimpressive mover: fifth foal: half-sister to a winner over jumps in France by Ti
King: dam, 2-y-o 7f winner who stayed 1m, granddaughter of Irish 1000 Guineas
winner Lady Capulet: fair performer: won nursery at Catterick in September, needing
most of trip to get on top: will be at least as effective over 1m+. *P. T. Walwyn*

JUNIE (IRE)   3 ch.f. Astronef 116 – Numidia (Sallust 134) [1996 66: 6m 6m⁶ 6g   30
1997 6g 8f⁶ 8f a6g⁴ Nov 13] unfurnished filly: poor maiden: should stay beyond 6f.
T. G. Mills

JUNIKAY (IRE)   3 b.g. Treasure Kay 114 – Junijo (Junius (USA) 124) [1996 5d⁴   89 d
5d⁴ 5s² 7g 6g* 1997 7g⁵ 8m 6d 6d 7.1m 8.5d 8.1m 10g³ 11.8d⁵ 12d⁶ a12g
Nov 18] ex-Irish gelding: sixth foal: half-brother to fairly useful 6f winner Penka (by
Don't Forget Me): dam, unplaced, half-sister to smart middle-distance colt Project
Manager: fairly useful in Ireland (won maiden at Ballinrobe at 2 yrs) for J. Bolger,
sold after fourth start: modest at best in Britain: probably stays 1½m: ran poorly in
blinkers. *R. Ingram*

JUNIOR BEN (IRE)   5 b.g. Tirol 127 – Piney Pass (Persian Bold 123) [1996 51d: 35
12g⁴ 11.6m⁴ 12.5f 11.4g⁶ 14.1f⁴ 12g⁶ 12m 10.1m 14d 11.5m⁶ 14.1g 1997 12g² 12g⁵
16.2m⁶ 14.1g 10v² 16.2d⁶ 9.9g⁵ 10.1g Oct 22] quite attractive gelding: poor maiden:
stays 1¾m: acts on any going: tried blinkered. *M. E. Sowersby*

JUNIOR MUFFIN (IRE)   2 b.g. (Apr 20) Paris House 123 – Clodianus (Bay   67
Express 132) [1997 5s⁴ 5g⁵ 5m 5.1g* 5g* 5m³ 7g a6g Oct 18] IR 2,000F, 14,000Y: a?
half-brother to useful sprinter Terrhars (by Anita's Prince) and 1993 2-y-o 5f winner
Sporting Warrior (by Exhibitioner): dam unraced: fair performer: won seller at Bath
and claimer at Newcastle in August: well beaten final 2 starts, one on fibresand:
should stay 6f: acts on good to firm ground. *J. Berry*

JUPITER (IRE)   3 b.g. Astronef 116 – Native Flower (Tumble Wind (USA))   68 d
[1996 68: a5g* 6g 5f⁵ 5g⁶ 1997 6.1m⁵ 6.1m⁴ 7m⁶ 8.1g 6m 7.1m 7g Sep 3] tall
gelding: fair handicapper: ran poorly last 4 outings, too free in blinkers on final one:
stays 7f: acts on fibresand and good to firm ground: sometimes slowly away.
G. C. Bravery

JUS'CHILLIN' (IRE)   2 b.f. (May 9) Elbio 125 – Not Mistaken (USA) (Mill   60
Reef (USA) 141) [1997 6m² a7g⁶ 6g 7g 6g² 7m⁵ Oct 23] IR 900F: quite good-topped
filly: half-sister to several winners, including useful Irish 1m and 1½m winner Bay
Empress (by Empery): dam unraced: modest form when second in minor event at
Yarmouth and maiden at Brighton: well held otherwise, including on fibresand:
should stay 1m. *C. A. Dwyer*

JUST ALEX (IRE)   3 b.g. River Falls 113 – Picnic Basket (Pharly (FR) 130)   81
[1996 NR 1997 10m⁵ 12m⁵ Aug 9] IR 10,000F, 15,000Y: leggy gelding: fluent
mover: third foal: half-brother to German 1m to 11f winner Faber (by Mon Tresor):
dam unraced half-sister to Rakaposhi King: fifth in maidens at Ascot and Newmarket
(wore severe bridle), hanging markedly left and looking far from an easy ride: needs
to become more tractable. *T. G. Mills*

JUST ANOTHER TIME   2 ch.c. (Apr 11) Mazilier (USA) 107 – Entourage 75   62
(Posse (USA) 130) [1997 6m³ a6g⁴ 5.1m⁶ 5.1m² 6d² 6g 6m² 6g⁶ a6g* a5g* Dec 19]   a67
6,600 2-y-o: fourth foal: brother to a bad maiden: dam, fourth over 7f at 2 yrs, out of
half-sister to Forzando: modest on turf, fair on all-weather: won claimers at Lingfield
in November and December: stays 6f: acts on good to firm and dead ground and the
all-weather. *J. Berry*

JUST A STROLL   2 ch.g. (May 4) Clantime 101 – Willow Walk 74 (Farm Walk   43
111) [1997 5s² a6g 6.1m Aug 6] 5,000Y: half-brother to ungenuine 1½m winner
Willow Twig (by Bruni) and winning stayer Mischievous Miss (by Niniski): dam
1½m winner/winning jumper: second in seller at Folkestone on debut, but soundly
beaten subsequently. *J. S. Moore*

JUST BLINK (IRE)   4 b.f. Fairy King (USA) – Cooliney Princess 98 (Bruni 132)   –
[1996 NR 1997 5v 7m Aug 9] IR 11,000Y, 3,600 3-y-o: small, robust filly: closely
related to 4 winners, including fair 1988 2-y-o 6f winner Prince of The Glen (by
Glental), and half-sister to useful 1m and 11f winner Ridgepoint (by Gorytus): dam,

Irish 2-y-o 7f and 1½m winner, half-sister to Irish St Leger winner Conor Pass: well held in maiden and claimer, troublesome at start on debut. *S. C. Williams*

JUST BOB   8 b.g. Alleging (USA) 120 – Diami 81 (Swing Easy (USA) 126) [1996 75, a–: 5s⁶ 5g 5g³ 5g 5s* 5d* 5m* 5g² 1997 5g 5m 5s² 5s³ 6g³ 5g 6d 5g⁴ 5m 5m⁴ 5m 6g 6m 5m* 5d* 6m 5m* 5d 5d 5d 5m⁴ 5d Nov 7] smallish gelding: unimpressive mover: fairly useful handicapper: won in big fields at Doncaster and Ayr in September and at Newcastle in October: best form in strongly-run races at 5f: acts on any turf ground, no form in 4 tries on the all-weather: not blinkered since 1995: often slowly away and comes from behind: tough and game. *S. E. Kettlewell*   **81 a–**

JUST DESERTS   2 b.f. (May 10) Alhijaz 122 – What A Pet (Mummy's Pet 125) [1997 6g Oct 27] 20,000Y: half-sister to several winners, including smart performer up to 1m Petardia (by Petong) and French winner at up to 13f Bourrasque (by What A Guest): dam French 1m winner, sister to useful filly Teacher's Pet; 33/1, got upset in preliminaries when well beaten in Leicester maiden. *P. J. Makin*   **–**

JUST DICKENS   3 b.f. Robellino (USA) 127 – Lucy Manette 53 (Final Straw 127) [1996 NR 1997 8.3g 8.1m 8.1m Jul 30] 5,200Y: smallish filly: third foal: half-sister to Irish 1995 2-y-o 6f winner Zalzie (by Zilzal): dam should have stayed beyond 6f: well held in maidens: dead. *R. Ingram*   **–**

JUST DISSIDENT (IRE)   5 b.g. Dancing Dissident (USA) 119 – Betty Bun (St Chad 120) [1996 65: 6g 5m 6m⁵ 5g⁵ 6.9g 6m 6.1m 10g 5m² 5m³ 5m* 5m 5m⁵ 5f³ 5m⁴ 5m* 5m 5m 5m⁵ 1997 7m 6m⁵ 5g 5m 5m* 6.1g⁶ 5m 5d 5g 5f⁶ 5.7g 5.2m 5m 5m a5g³ a5g² a5g* Dec 22] good-topped gelding: has reportedly had back problems: fair handicapper: won at Pontefract (for second year running) in July and Lingfield in December: barely stays 6f: acts on firm ground and equitrack: effective visored, rarely tried: usually races prominently. *R. M. Whitaker*   **65**

JUST FLAMENCO   6 ch.g. Scorpio (FR) 127 – Suzannah's Song (Song 132) [1996 –: a12g 8g 9.2s 1997 a7g 10s 11.6m Jun 9] no longer of any account. *M. J. Ryan*   **–**

JUSTFORTHERECORD   5 br.m. Forzando 122 – Classical Vintage 80 (Stradavinsky 121) [1996 NR 1997 a7g a7g Feb 7] of no account. *B. R. Millman*   **–**

JUST FOR TINA   2 b.f. (Apr 14) Presidium 124 – Mushy Boff 65 (Tina's Pet 121) [1997 5g a5g a6g³ Dec 26] 3,200 2-y-o: first foal: dam 5f (at 2 yrs) and 7f winner: ran in seller for C. J. Hill on debut (tended to hang): first form when third of 7 in claimer at Wolverhampton. *W. G. M. Turner*   **–**

JUST GRAND (IRE)   3 b.g. Green Desert (USA) 127 – Aljood 111 (Kris 135) [1996 70: 7m⁴ 7d 1997 7m 8s³ 10g⁴ 12m* 12.1m⁵ Jul 11] leggy, useful-looking gelding: fairly useful handicapper: clearly best effort when winning at Carlisle in June: blanketed for stalls entry, ran poorly on final start, and subsequently gelded: should stay further than 1½m: acts on good to firm going, probably on soft: held up: joined Mrs Merrita Jones. *M. Johnston*   **87**

JUSTIN HOPE   2 b.g. (Jan 13) Prince Sabo 123 – Affirmation 75 (Tina's Pet 121) [1997 5.1m⁶ 6g Aug 20] third foal: half-brother to 3-y-o Arriving: dam 5f (at 2 yrs) and 1¼m winner: little promise in claimer (very slowly away) and seller: bandaged in front on debut. *C. E. Brittain*   **–**

JUSTINIANUS (IRE)   5 ch.h. Try My Best (USA) 130 – Justitia (Dunbeath (USA) 127) [1996 51d: a7g a6g a7g³ a8g³ a8g⁴ a8g a6g a6g a7g 6.9m³ 7f 6m 8.3g 7.1m 6g⁶ 7m.6m⁶ 5m a7g 7g a7g a6s a10g 1997 a7g⁴ a6g⁴ a6g* a8g⁵ a6g³ a6g 6f² 5.3f³ 7m² 6f³ 6f⁶ 7m⁴ 6s² 6d³ 6s⁵ 6g⁵ 6m³ 5g 6g⁵ 5.3g⁴ 5m 7f Sep 28] modest performer: won seller at Lingfield in February: mainly creditable efforts in handicaps afterwards: effective at 5f to easy 1m: acts on the all-weather and on firm and soft going: tried blinkered earlier in career: usually races up with pace: tough and consistent. *J. J. Bridger*   **51**

JUST IN TIME   2 b.c. (Apr 16) Night Shift (USA) – Future Past (USA) (Super Concorde (USA) 128) [1997 7m² Aug 1] 31,000F, 58,000Y: smallish, sturdy colt: fourth foal: half-brother to 3-y-o French 6f to 1m winner Fluorescence (by Alzao) and a winner in Spain by Mt Livermore: dam, won up to 9f in USA, from good French family: 25/1 and backward, ½-length second to Chester House in maiden at Goodwood, running on, not subjected to hard ride: should stay 1m. *T. G. Mills*   **89**

JUST LOUI   3 gr.g. Lugana Beach 116 – Absaloui 64 (Absalom 128) [1996 58, a83: a5g a5g* 6d⁶ 5f³ a5g a5g² 5.1g⁵ 5f⁶ a6g² a6g* a5g² a7g* a6g* 1997 a6g* a6g⁴ 6s⁴ a6g 5.7m⁴ 6f⁵ a7g² a5g⁵ 7m⁶ 6m 6g 7m a7g⁵ 6.1s Oct 15] sturdy gelding: fairly useful handicapper on the all-weather, fair at best on turf: won at Lingfield in January: claimed out of W. G. M. Turner's stable £10,000 seventh start: mostly well below form afterwards: effective at 6f/easy 7f: acts on good to firm and soft ground and the all-weather: usually races prominently: tried visored, no improvement. *K. R. Burke*   75 d a83 d

JUST NICK   3 b.g. Nicholas (USA) 111 – Just Never Know (USA) (Riverman (USA) 131) [1996 73: 5.1g³ 5.1m⁴ 5.7d³ 6s² 6v* 1997 7g² 7m³ 7g² 7d³ 8m⁵ 7m 7.3m⁴ 8.1s² 7m Sep 27] smallish, good-topped gelding: fairly useful handicapper: second at Newmarket, York and Sandown: stays 1m: acts on good to firm and heavy ground: usually races prominently: genuine and consistent. *W. R. Muir*   87

JUST NOBBY   2 b.g. (May 13) Totem (USA) 118 – Loving Doll 72 (Godswalk (USA) 130) [1997 5m 5m 6d 7.9s 8.3g⁴ Sep 29] 1,700Y: close-coupled, good-bodied gelding: brother to a maiden and half-brother to 8-y-o Nobby Barnes and 1¼m winner Ash Amour (by Hotfoot): dam stayed at least 7f: no worthwhile form, including in sellers: blinkered third start. *N. Tinkler*   –

JUST RACHEL   3 ch.f. Primitive Rising (USA) 113 – Glendyne 58 (Precipice Wood 123) [1996 –: a8.5g 1997 a7g a12g⁵ Feb 6] tailed off in maidens. *S. E. Kettlewell*   –

JUST SIDIUM   3 b.f. Nicholas (USA) 111 – Frimley Dancer 54 (Northern Tempest (USA) 120) [1996 NR 1997 7.1m a5g³ Jun 27] second foal: dam 6f winner: poor form: better effort at 5f on fibresand. *C. J. Hill*   46

JUST TESTING   2 br.f. (May 18) Sharpo 132 – Antoinette Jane 86 (Ile de Bourbon (USA) 133) [1997 6d⁵ a5g⁴ 6d⁶ Oct 20] 12,000 2-y-o: fourth foal: half-sister to 1995 2-y-o 1m winner Ancestral Jane (by Distant Relative): dam, 2-y-o 7f winner, granddaughter of July Cup winner Parsimony, also grandam of College Chapel: modest form in maidens, including at Wolverhampton: stays 6f. *J. L. Eyre*   52 +

JUST TYPICAL   3 ch.f. Timeless Times (USA) 99 – Mayor 86 (Laxton 105) [1996 –: 5g 1997 5s 5m a8g Jun 6] no worthwhile form. *N. Tinkler*   –

JUST VISITING   3 b.f. Superlative 118 – Just Julia (Natroun (FR) 128) [1996 85: a5g* 6m² 5g³ 6f² 6g* 6d³ 6.5m 1997 6g 6m 6m 6g 8.1g Sep 26] workmanlike filly: has a round action: fairly useful form at 2 yrs: fair at best in handicaps in 1997: stays 6f: acts on firm and dead ground and on fibresand. *Capt. J. Wilson*   68

JUST WHISTLE   5 gr.m. Absalom 128 – Aunt Blue 75 (Blue Refrain 121) [1996 NR 1997 9.2g⁴ Jun 11] poor maiden: well held in seller only 5-y-o start. *Miss M. K. Milligan*   –

JUVENILIA (IRE)   3 ch.f. Masterclass (USA) 116 – Amtico (Bairn (USA) 126) [1996 NR 1997 6.9m³ 7f³ Jun 5] IR 4,000F, 10,000Y: fourth foal: half-sister to 1993 2-y-o 6f winner Kingswell Prince (by Nashamaa): dam unraced: modest form when third in maidens at Folkestone and Yarmouth: will stay 1m. *J. A. R. Toller*   55

JUWWI   3 ch.c. Mujtahid (USA) 118 – Nouvelle Star (AUS) (Luskin Star (AUS)) [1996 96: 6.1m² 6m* 6g² 1997 7g 6g⁴ Jul 30] smallish, lengthy, robust colt: useful form at 2 yrs, beaten head in July Stakes at Newmarket: well beaten in Free Handicap at Newmarket and minor event at Doncaster in 1997: sold only 2,000 gns in October. *Major W. R. Hern*   –

K

KABCAST   12 b.g. Kabour 80 – Final Cast 50 (Saulingo 122) [1996 48: 5s⁵ 5m⁶ 5m 5m* 5m⁶ 5m 5m 5g⁵ 5g 1997 5g⁵ 5m 5g³ 5g 5m Sep 24] good-bodied gelding: poor handicapper: best at 5f: needs good going or firmer on turf, no form on the all-weather: wears blinkers: often sweats: races prominently. *D. W. Chapman*   40

KADASTROF (FR) 7 ch.h. Port Etienne (FR) – Kadastra (FR) (Stradavinsky –
121) [1996 81: 14.9d² 16d* 18.7g 16s 13.9m 13.9g 1997 16s 16s Oct 15] good-
topped horse: fairly useful handicapper: well beaten at 7 yrs: stays 2m: best form on
good going or softer: front runner: useful hurdler/chaser. *R. Dickin*

KADEENA 3 b.f. Never So Bold 135 – Alencon (Northfields (USA)) [1996 76: –
7g* 7m³ 1997 8f⁶ Jun 4] fair winner at 2 yrs: still green, stiff task in handicap only
outing as 3-y-o: should stay 1m. *M. Johnston*

KADIR 2 b. or br.c. (Jan 24) Unfuwain (USA) 131 – Rafif (USA) 68 (Riverman 70 p
(USA) 131) [1997 8.2d⁶ Oct 30] strong, angular colt: first foal: dam 1¼m winner
out of close relative of Ribblesdale winner Thawakib and half-sister to Celestial
Storm: 4/1 but gone in coat, sixth of 13 to wide-margin winner Almandab in maiden
at Nottingham, very green and never a threat: should stay at least 1½m: type to do
better: sent to France. *Saeed bin Suroor*

KAFAF (USA) 3 b. or br.f. Zilzal (USA) 137 – Alqwani (USA) 83 (Mr Prospector 78
(USA)) [1996 76: 7g 7g⁴ 8m² 1997 7g² 7g* 9g Aug 22] unfurnished filly: fair
performer: refused to enter stalls intended reappearance: landed odds in 4-runner
maiden at Thirsk in August: seemed to lose action final start: stays 1m: raced only
on good/good to firm going: has had tongue tied: sold 6,000 gns in December.
J. H. M. Gosden

KAFIL (USA) 3 b. or br.c. Housebuster (USA) – Alchaasibiyeh (USA) 85 (Seattle 74
Slew (USA)) [1996 75: 7d 6g 1997 8d 8.3m⁴ 8s³ 8.1g 8.1s 8f² a10g² a8g* a10g²
a10g⁶ Dec 22] leggy, useful-looking colt: fair performer: trained first 3 starts by
R. Hern: won maiden at Lingfield in November: ran creditably in handicaps on same
course after: stays 1¼m: acts on firm ground and equitrack, seems unsuited by going
softer than good. *G. L. Moore*

KAGSI 2 br.f. (May 8) King's Signet (USA) 110 – Azaiyma 58 (Corvaro (USA) –
124) [1997 a5g 5m May 31] 500Y: third reported foal: dam placed up to 1½m: well
beaten in maiden at Southwell and minor event at Lingfield. *D. C. O'Brien*

KAHAL 3 b.c. Machiavellian (USA) 123 – Just A Mirage 76 (Green Desert 118 p
(USA) 127) [1996 108p: 7f² 7g* 7g⁵ 1997 7m² 7.9g⁴ 6.5d⁴ 7d* 7g* Oct 18]
      Two horses from the third crop of Machiavellian, one of the leading
two-year-olds of 1989 and runner-up in the Two Thousand Guineas, fought out
the finish of the Challenge Stakes at Newmarket in October, with the colt Kahal
just getting the better of the filly Rebecca Sharp. Both came from behind in a
strongly-run race, making their moves approaching the final furlong, but,
whereas Rebecca Sharp kept to the inside and didn't enjoy the best of runs,

Challenge Stakes, Newmarket—the confidently-ridden Kahal (near side) holds Rebecca Sharp

Kahal, under a supremely confident ride from Frankie Dettori, was switched wide and avoided trouble. This manoeuvre enabled Kahal to gain the initiative and he always looked as if he'd maintain it despite seeming to idle once in front, having a neck to spare over Rebecca Sharp at the line. It was a smart performance from Kahal, one which he'd looked capable of producing from the time he'd won a two-year-old minor event at Ascot on only his second start and finished fifth in the Dewhurst Stakes. He left Ed Dunlop's stable after that to join the Godolphin operation.

Royal Ascot was the scene of Kahal's return to the racecourse, and it was almost a triumphant one. Well supported for the Jersey Stakes, partly on the strength of news of a gallop with Alhaarth and Allied Forces, Kahal took the lead a furlong and a half out but couldn't hold the renewed challenge of Among Men, who beat him by half a length. Kahal was tried over a mile at York and six and a half furlongs at Deauville on his next two starts. The trip couldn't be blamed for a disappointing run at York, where it was more than likely he hadn't recovered fully from his hard race at Ascot; Kahal acquitted himself quite well in the Prix Maurice de Gheest at Deauville, finishing fourth to Occupandiste. Prior to the Challenge Stakes, Kahal opened his account for the season with an easy success in a four-runner minor event at Goodwood.

		Mr Prospector	Raise A Native
	Machiavellian (USA)	(b 1970)	Gold Digger
	(b 1987)	Coup de Folie	Halo
Kahal		(b 1982)	Raise The Standard
(b.c. 1994)		Green Desert	Danzig
	Just A Mirage	(b 1983)	Foreign Courier
	(b 1989)	Just You Wait	Nonoalco
		(b 1980)	Sleat

Godolphin's "Kahal"

Kahal's dam, Just A Mirage, a lightly-raced maiden placed at up to a mile, is a sister to the smart miler Distant Oasis and closely related to the useful middle-distance performer Waiting, and is a half-sister to the very smart colts Reprimand and Wiorno, the former successful at up to nine furlongs, including in the Gimcrack Stakes and Sandown Mile, the latter up to an extended ten furlongs (he was also first past the post in the mile-and-a-half Rothmans International). The next dam, Just You Wait, is an unraced half-sister to the fairly useful mile-and-a-quarter winner Kristana (dam of Robert Papin winner Ozone Friendly) and a daughter of Sleat (a half-sister to the St Leger winner Athens Wood), who won the Sun Chariot Stakes. Kahal is the first foal of Just A Mirage. Her second, a full sister to Kahal named Doomna, has now also joined Godolphin and figures in the ante-post betting for the One Thousand Guineas, having finished a promising second in a Goodwood maiden for Ed Dunlop on her only start. Kahal, a good mover who acts on good to firm and good to soft going, seems best with waiting tactics.

Judged on his breeding, Kahal should stay a mile, though he's unlikely to get further and the fine turn of foot he showed at Newmarket may encourage connections to give him another chance at six furlongs. A strong, good-topped colt, the type to carry condition, Kahal looks the sort to improve with racing and there are more good races to be won with him. *Saeed bin Suroor*

KAHTAN   2 b.c. (Apr 3) Nashwan (USA) 135 – Harmless Albatross 115 (Pas de   92 p
Seul 133) [1997 8m⁴ 8m* Oct 1] good-topped colt: good walker: sixth foal: brother to 4-y-o Mawared, and half-brother to several winners, including 3-y-o Ghataas and very smart French performer at up to 1¼m Volochine (by Soviet Star): dam French miler: shaped well when very green in maiden at Doncaster in September, and landed odds in steadily-run similar event at Newcastle by neck from Bombastic, covered up into strong headwind and still showing inexperience when sent on: should stay at least 1¼m: should make at least a useful 3-y-o. *J. L. Dunlop*

KAILEY GODDESS (USA)   4 b.c. Nureyev (USA) 131 – Gay Senorita (USA)   67
(Raise A Native) [1996 NR 1997 8.2d 10g 7g*7.1m Jul 30] half-brother to 4 winners, notably smart 1989 2-y-o Cordoba (by El Gran Senor): dam, minor winner around 1m in USA, from good middle-distance family: only worthwhile form when fourth in maiden at Warwick in July: should stay 1m. *R. W. Armstrong*

KAILEY SENOR (USA)   4 ch.c. Woodman (USA) 126 – Sex Appeal (USA)   77
(Buckpasser) [1996 8g⁴ 8g² 10d 8s⁶ 1997 12.3d⁴ 11.7g⁴ 11.5m⁴ 8.1g 10.1m 8.1d³ 10.1m⁵ a8s a10g⁵ a14g* Dec 12] $200,000Y: sturdy ex-French colt: unimpressive mover: from an excellent family, half-brother to El Gran Senor and Try My Best: useful form at 3 yrs: fair handicapper in Britain: upped in trip, won at Lingfield in December: stays 13f: acts on equitrack, good to firm and dead ground: tends to carry head awkwardly. *R. W. Armstrong*

KAISER KACHE (IRE)   3 b.c. Treasure Kay 114 – Poka Poka (FR) (King of   84
Macedon 126) [1996 83: 6f 5.7m⁵ 7f² 6m² 6m* 6g 8m 6m 7.3s* 8d³ a8g³ 1997 9g⁵ 8.5m² 7m⁴ 7.9g 7m* 7.1m 8m 7m Jul 19] close-coupled colt: fairly useful handicapper: made all at Kempton in May: below form last 3 starts: effective at 7f to 8.5f: acts on equitrack, good to firm ground and soft: visored (poor effort) once. *K. McAuliffe*

KAITAK (IRE)   6 ch.g. Broken Hearted 124 – Klairelle (Klairon 131) [1996 69:   –
11.9g⁵ 11.9m 1997 12g⁶ Apr 19] workmanlike gelding: lightly raced on flat nowadays: well held only start at 6 yrs: stays 1½m: acts on good to firm and heavy ground: fairly useful hurdler: joined T. Easterby. *J. M. Carr*

KAJOSTAR   7 ch.m. Country Classic – Rasimareem (Golden Mallard 103) [1996   –
–: a6g a8g 1997 a7s⁶ a7g a7g a7g Jan 17] no worthwhile form. *S. W. Campion*

KALAKATE   12 gr.g. Kalaglow 132 – Old Kate 110 (Busted 134) [1996 NR 1997   –
a16g Feb 13] no longer of much account. *J. J. Bridger*

KALAMATA   5 ch.h. Kalaglow 132 – Good Try 92 (Good Bond 122) [1996 –:   –
a12g⁶ a12g 1997 a12g⁴ a12g* a12g⁵ 12m a16g* a16.2g³ 14.1d a14g* a14g* a14g*   a78
14.1g a14.8g a14g⁴ Dec 8] workmanlike horse: fair on fibresand: won minor event, 2

claimers and 2 handicaps at Southwell in first half of 1997: little worthwhile form on turf since 3 yrs: stays 2m. *J. A. Glover*

KALAR 8 b.g. Kabour 80 – Wind And Reign 55 (Tumble Wind (USA)) [1996 57, a79: a5g a5g⁶ a5g³ a5g⁵ a5g⁵ 5g 5g 5g³ 5g 5g⁵ a5g 5m² 5g² 5m⁶ 5g² 6f² 5m* 5g² 5m³ 5m 5g⁴ 5.1g a5g³ a5g* a5g a5g² a5g⁴ a6g² 1997 a6g² a5g* a5g* a5g⁴ 5g² 5m 5g⁵ a5g⁵ a6g⁶ 5d⁴ 5m 5m⁶ 5g 5g 6g a5g⁵ 5m a6g a5g Dec 8] good-bodied gelding: fair on the all-weather, modest on turf: won claimers at Wolverhampton in January and Lingfield in February: no form in second half of 1997: stays 6f: acts on any turf going/all-weather: usually blinkered, has been visored: suitable mount for 7-lb claimer. *D. W. Chapman*   57 d a79 d

KALA SUNRISE 4 ch.c. Kalaglow 132 – Belle of The Dawn (Bellypha 130) [1996 91: 7.5m⁶ 8.1d⁴ 10.5d 8f 8m⁶ 10m 11.9m 8.9g⁶ 8f⁴ 8m 7.9g* 1997 8m⁵ 8g 8.5d³ 8.5d² 8m 8d² 7.9g⁶ 7g 8.1m⁵ 8m³ 7.9s⁴ 8g 8.2d² Nov 3] tall, workmanlike colt: useful performer: ran well most starts in 1997, including second in minor event at Nottingham final start: best efforts up to 9f: probably acts on any going. *C. Smith*   95

KALIANA (IRE) 3 b.f. Slip Anchor 136 – Kadissya (USA) 107 (Blushing Groom (FR) 131) [1996 NR 1997 10.2s* 12m² 11.9d* 12m⁵ 12g* Oct 25]   118
  'The stable's on fire' is an expression usually used to illustrate how well a particular trainer's horses are running. Unfortunately for Luca Cumani it was also applicable in its literal sense on October 9th when part of his Bedford House yard, which had sent out no fewer than sixteen winners in the previous nineteen days, was badly damaged by fire. The good news was that it occurred in an area away from the racehorses and no injuries were suffered. Normal service was quickly resumed and, while the winners didn't flow so freely for what remained of the season, there were still plenty of victories for the stable to celebrate, none more so than that of Kaliana in the St Simon Stakes at Newbury. It was the first pattern-race winner trained by Cumani for the Aga Khan since the latter's return to British racing two years earlier, and the first for the stable's good apprentice Royston Ffrench.
  Ffrench, the season's leading apprentice with seventy-seven winners, had been going through a lean spell and was on a losing run of sixty-seven going into the St Simon Stakes, in which he was unable to claim his 3-lb allowance. He was also riding the relatively inexperienced Kaliana for the first time in public, but the confident manner in which he performed his task showed why he made such a name for himself in the latest season, producing the filly to lead approaching the final furlong having been content to bide his time as the

Galtres Stakes, York—the Cumani stable continues its great record in this event as Kaliana draws away from The Faraway Tree

favourite Busy Flight had taken the field along at a good pace. Kaliana, needing only to be kept up to her work once she'd hit the front, ran on strongly to draw three lengths clear of Kutta, who finished just over a length ahead of Busy Flight.

It was Kaliana's third win from five starts, following on from those gained in a maiden at Chepstow in July on her debut and in the Galtres Stakes at York the following month. Cumani's record in the Galtres is an outstanding one, 1996 being the only year in the 'nineties that he has failed to win it. Kaliana, the 7/4 favourite in a seven-runner field, had little difficulty in re-establishing her trainer's hold on the race, moving smoothly into the lead over two furlongs out and going on to beat The Faraway Tree by three lengths.

		Shirley Heights	Mill Reef
	Slip Anchor	(b 1975)	Hardiemma
	(b 1982)	Sayonara	Birkhahn
Kaliana (IRE)		(b 1965)	Suleika
(b.f. 1994)		Blushing Groom	Red God
	Kadissya (USA)	(ch 1974)	Runaway Bride
	(b 1979)	Kalkeen	Sheshoon
		(b 1974)	Gioia

Kaliana is closely related to the fair stayer Kadiri (by Darshaan) and half-sister to two other winners, the useful Kadamann (by Doyoun) who raced mainly around a mile and a half and a more illustrious performer at that distance, Kahyasi (by Ile de Bourbon). Also owned by the Aga Khan and trained by Cumani, Kahyasi won the Derby in England and Ireland in 1988. The dam Kadissya, successful over a mile and a quarter in France, comes from an old-

H. H. Aga Khan's "Kaliana"

established family, which has been producing winners for the Aga Khan's studs for many generations. Kadissya's fourth dam is Masaka, winner of the Oaks and Irish Oaks in 1948, and her third dam is the Park Hill winner Bara Biri, who is also the third dam of the Breeders' Cup Turf winner Lashkari. Gioia, the great grandam of Kaliana, was just a minor winner but her daughter, Kalkeen, won four races in France, including the listed Prix de la Seine.

Kaliana, a neat filly who already had her winter coat at Newbury, is a slow-maturing type according to her trainer, so it is quite possible there will be be a little more improvement from her in 1998, when more pattern races should come her way. She will stay beyond one and a half miles. The ground was good or softer when Kaliana gained her victories, and good to firm when she was defeated. While her fifth to Queen Maud, beaten three lengths, in the Prix Vermeille wasn't far below her best, she was being niggled at from an early stage and our impression is that less firm going does suit her ideally. *L. M. Cumani*

KALIMAT 3 b.f. Be My Guest (USA) 126 – Kantado 93 (Saulingo 122) [1996 74: 6g 6g² 7g² 1997 10f³ 10.3d⁶ a8g² a8g² 8m⁴ 6.9f² 7g⁴ 8.2g⁵ a8g* Dec 2] leggy filly: fair performer: easy winner of maiden at Lingfield: seems best around 1m: acts on firm ground and all-weather: ran well in blinkers fifth start. *W. Jarvis*   65   a72

KALININI (USA) 3 ch.c. Seattle Dancer (USA) 119 – Kaiserfahrt (GER) (Frontal 122) [1996 71p: 7g 8m³ 7.9g⁴ 1997 10m 10.8m 8s⁴ Jul 2] big, strong colt: has scope: fair maiden: easily best effort at 3 yrs when fourth in handicap at Yarmouth, given plenty to do: should stay 1¼m: acts on soft going: gave trouble in stalls on reappearance. *L. M. Cumani*   74

KALINKA (IRE) 3 b.f. Soviet Star (USA) 128 – Tralthee (USA) 111 (Tromos 134) [1996 83+: 6f³ 7m* 7m² 1997 8.1d⁴ 7.9g⁴ 8d⁴ 9m⁴ 10.1g⁶ 10g Sep 18] big, leggy filly: fairly useful handicapper: probably stays 1¼m: acts on firm and dead going: tends to carry head high and hang under pressure, but is consistent. *P. F. I. Cole*   88

KALISZ (IRE) 3 b.f. Polish Precedent (USA) 131 – Housefull 81 (Habitat 134) [1996 NR 1997 10g⁶ May 30] third living foal: closely related to 1992 2-y-o 5f winner Greenlet (by Green Desert) and half-sister to French 9f winner Dolforwyn (by Caerleon): dam, 1m winner, closely related to dam of Hot Touch out of 1000 Guineas winner Full Dress II: weak 6/1, tailed off in maiden at Ayr (subsequently found to be lame). *D. R. Loder*

KALMOOJID 3 b.g. Almoojid 69 – Skerryvore 66 (Kalaglow 132) [1996 NR 1997 10m 8g 7.6g Aug 2] 1,000Y: second foal: dam, half-sister to Italian St Leger winner Welsh Guide, stayed 1¼m: no promise in maidens and seller. *C. J. Hill*

KALOUSION 3 b.g. K-Battery 108 – Louise Moulton 90 (Moulton 128) [1996 –: 6m⁴ 7.1v 1997 7m⁶ 10f 8.3s 12g 8g⁶ 8.3d Aug 13] small gelding: no worthwhile form: tried blinkered. *T. J. Etherington*   –

KAMANEV (IRE) 3 b.c. Soviet Star (USA) 128 – Konigsrose (GER) (Cortez (GER)) [1996 NR 1997 10m³ 10m² 10g* 10.3d Aug 29] lengthy colt: fluent mover: fifth foal: half-brother to 3 winners in Germany: dam German winner up to 11f: fairly useful form: long odds on, won 3-runner maiden at Ayr in August on bridle: looked reluctant previous start, and weakened tamely in handicap final one: probably not one to trust implicitly: sold 5,200 gns in December. *M. R. Stoute*   85 §

KAMEEZ (IRE) 2 ch.f. (Apr 5) Arazi (USA) 135 – Kalikala (Darshaan 133) [1997 7g⁵ 8s³ Nov 6] fifth foal: half-sister to useful 1996 2-y-o 7.5f winner Mount Kamet (by Seattle Dancer), smart French 1¼m winner Kalajana (by Green Dancer) and smart winner up to 1½m Kalabo (by Trempolino): dam French 1½m winner, half-sister to dam of Kahyasi: showed ability whilst looking green and in need of stiffer test of stamina in autumn maidens at Newcastle and Musselburgh: likely to stay at least 1½m: should do fair bit better at 3 yrs. *M. Johnston*   69 p

KAMIN (USA) 3 b.c. Red Ransom (USA) – Sweet Rhapsody (USA) (Sea Bird II 145) [1996 67p: 7m 7m 1997 8.1m³ 7m⁴ 8.1m⁵ 10f⁶ 10.4d³ 10.1m² Oct 22] strong, close-coupled colt: fairly useful maiden handicapper: beaten short head by Fahs at

Yarmouth final start, best effort: stays 1¼m: acts on firm and dead ground: consistent: sent to UAE. *R. W. Armstrong*

KAMMTARRA (USA) 4 ch.c. Zilzal (USA) 137 – Snow Bride (USA) 121 –
(Blushing Groom (FR) 131) [1996 109+: 8m² 10.3g³ 8.3m* 8m³ 8f* 9m 1997 a8f* a118
a10f* a10f 8.5g⁶ a7.5s⁶ Oct 26] lengthy, attractive colt: half-brother to Lammtarra
(by Nijinsky): improved form when winning listed races at Nad Al Sheba in February
and March (beat Tamhid 1½ lengths, pair 7 lengths clear): failed to repeat that form,
sixth to Polar Prince in Diomed Stakes at Epsom in June (final outing for Saeed bin
Suroor): last in Grade 3 race in USA final start: effective at 1m to 1¼m: acts on firm
going (yet to race on going softer than good), best efforts on sand: effective from
front or held up. *K. McLaughlin, USA*

KANAWA 3 b.f. Beveled (USA) – Kiri Te (Liboi (USA) 76) [1996 –: 6.1m 1997 –
8d 6.9m⁶ 8f a8g 6f 5.3m 5.7g Aug 7] angular, unfurnished filly: little worthwhile
form. *A. P. Jones*

KANTONE (IRE) 2 ch.g. (Apr 18) Petardia 113 – Green Life (Green Desert –
(USA) 127) [1997 5.1d 7g⁶ 6g⁵ 5.1g⁶ 6d Oct 21] 32,000Y: sturdy, close-coupled
gelding: first foal: dam Irish maiden: little worthwhile form: blinkered/visored last 2
starts. *J. M. P. Eustace*

KARACHI 7 b.g. Nishapour (FR) 125 – Lady Dacre 86 (Queen's Hussar 124) –
[1996 NR 1997 11.5g⁶ 12m 8m Sep 24] fair handicapper at 4 yrs: off course 2½ years,
well held in 1997. *R. J. O'Sullivan*

KARAKIA (IRE) 3 b.f. Sadler's Wells (USA) 132 – Kissagram (USA) 79
(Alysheba (USA)) [1996 NR 1997 8.2d² 8.3g³ 8.3m² 9m* 10.5s Oct 15] rather leggy
filly: has a round action: first foal of an unraced daughter of an Irish 1000 Guineas
second: fair form, generally progressive: easy winner of maiden at Redcar in August:
stays 9f (didn't stay 10.5f on soft ground final start): acts on good to firm going: sold
62,000 gns in December. *J. H. M. Gosden*

KARA-LOVO 2 ch.f. (Feb 1) Rock City 120 – Lariston Gale 81 (Pas de Seul 133) –
[1997 5g 6m May 27] 3,300Y: fifth foal: sister to fairly useful 1995 2-y-o 6f winner Cyrillic (later stayed 1m) and half-sister to 3-y-o Nomore Mr Niceguy and a
winner in Germany by Formidable: dam quite stoutly bred 2-y-o 6f winner: behind in
claimer and a maiden. *J. Balding*

KARA QUEEN 3 ch.f. Silver Kite (USA) 111 Darakah 78 (Doulab (USA) 115) –
[1996 NR 1997 8d 8.1g⁶ May 26] second foal: dam suited by 7f/1m: tailed off in
maidens. *C. J. Hill*

KARAWAN 3 ch.f. Kris 135 – Sweetly (FR) 88 (Lyphard (USA) 132) [1996 55: 82
6m 6g⁴ 1997 7g* 7g² Aug 1] rather unfurnished filly: fairly useful performer: won
maiden at Thirsk (comfortably) in June: favourite, best effort when second in handicap at Salisbury: should have stayed 1m: raced only on good/good to firm going:
raced up with pace: stud. *J. H. M. Gosden*

KARAYLAR (IRE) 5 b.g. Kahyasi 130 – Karamana (Habitat 134) [1996 49: 10g –
8f⁶ 10m 12g⁶ 16.1m⁵ 15.8g⁶ 17.2m² 1997 15.8s 13.8g 16m⁶ Aug 26] small, good-
topped gelding: no form at 5 yrs: reportedly finished lame final outing: stays 17f: acts
on good to firm ground. *W. Storey*

KARENARAGON 2 b.f. (May 1) Aragon 118 – Rosy Sunset (IRE) (Red Sunset –
120) [1997 5m a5g³ a6g⁴ a7g⁴ a5g Jul 10] 550Y: second foal: dam, ran a few times,
half-sister to smart middle-distance horse Diaghilef: seems of little account. *Ronald
Thompson*

KARINSKA 7 b.m. Master Willie 129 – Kaiserchronik (GER) (Cortez (GER)) 67
[1996 63: a8g³ a8g⁶ a8g² a8g⁴ a8g a7g³ 7.5d 8g 8.5g⁵ 10m⁴ 8g⁵ 8g⁶ 10m 1997 a7g⁶
a8g 8m 8.2g 8s⁵ 7s* 7m⁵ 8g⁴ 10.1g* 7m² 10.1g³ 10d⁵ 7.9s 10.1m 7f 8.2g* Sep 28]
angular mare: has a quick action: fair handicapper: won at Yarmouth (twice) in July
and Nottingham in September: stayed 1¼m, in slowly-run race at least: acted on
fibresand, firm and soft ground: sometimes reluctant to post and slowly away: carried
head awkwardly and often flashed tail: usually claimer ridden and held up: in foal to
Rock City. *M. C. Chapman*

KARISMA (IRE)   4 b.g. Tirol 127 – Avra (FR) 65 (Mendez (FR) 128) [1996 70:   60
10g⁵ 12.4g⁶ 12.3m 12.3m⁴ 11.9g³ 14.6g³ 16.5s 1997 13.8g 13d² 10g 13s⁴ 10.4s 12g
14g⁶ 17.1m² 18d Oct 20] sturdy, angular gelding: modest maiden handicapper: stays
17f: acts on good to firm going, probably soft: has found little. *Denys Smith*

KARTTIKEYA (FR)   6 br.g. Darshaan 133 – Karosa (FR) (Caro 133) [1996 NR   –
1997 a14g Nov 14] formerly fair maiden: well beaten only start since 1995. *Mrs
N. Macauley*

KASHAN (IRE)   9 b.g. Darshaan 133 – Kamanika (FR) (Amber Rama (USA)   27
133) [1996 NR 1997 11.8m⁶ 17.2d May 11] close-coupled gelding: poor handicapper: should stay beyond 1½m: acts on good to firm ground: tried visored.
P. Hayward

KASS ALHAWA   4 b.g. Shirley Heights 130 – Silver Braid (USA) 101 (Miswaki   69
(USA) 124) [1996 76d: 10g² 12g⁵ a9.4g a9.4g a8.5g 7g 7f⁵ 12g 1997 a8g 7g 8m³   a–
a8g⁴ 8m⁴ 8m³ 8g* 6.9m 8g² 8m 7g* 8.3m⁴ 7.5g 8.2d² 7s⁴ 10d² 8s⁴ a10g Nov 25]
good-topped gelding: fair handicapper: won at Redcar (ladies maiden) and Catterick
(awarded race) in the summer: effective at 7f to 1¼m: acts on good to firm ground
and soft, no form on all-weather: tried blinkered once at 3 yrs: seems well suited by
waiting tactics: consistent. *D. W. Chapman*

KATAH   2 ch.f. (May 12) Arazi (USA) 135 – Kadwah (USA) 80 (Mr Prospector   67
(USA)) [1997 5.2m⁵ 5g³ 5m 7g² 7g⁵ Oct 27] angular filly: fourth foal: half-sister to
3-y-o Khassah and 7f (at 2 yrs) and 1m winner Awaamir, both useful fillies by Green
Desert: dam lightly-raced 1m and 1¼m winner out of high-class American turf
performer Castilla: fair maiden: best effort when second in nursery at Catterick in
September: should stay at least 1m: raced only on good/good to firm ground: sold
17,000 gns in December. *J. H. M. Gosden*

KATE LANE (IRE)   2 b.f. (Mar 22) Petardia 113 – Splendid Yankee (Yankee   72
Gold 115) [1997 6f 7m⁵ 7g 6g Aug 30] IR 6,600Y: half-sister to 2-y-o 5f winners
Racketeer (fairly useful in 1990, by Stalker) and Vail Star (Fayruz): dam Irish maiden
on flat and over hurdles: fair maiden: best effort in face of stiff task in valuable
sales race at the Curragh final start: stays 7f: hung markedly left second outing.
Mrs P. N. Dutfield

KATHERINE   3 ch.f. Chilibang 120 – Kaasiha (Kings Lake (USA) 133) [1996 –:   –
a7g 1997 a10g⁵ Feb 8] third reported foal: dam won NH Flat race: soundly beaten in
seller and maiden. *J. Ringer*

KATHIES PET   2 b.f. (Mar 12) Tina's Pet 121 – Unveiled 76 (Sayf El Arab   58
(USA) 127) [1997 5.1m 5.1g² 5m 5.3g 5.1g 6d² Oct 21] 800Y: first foal: dam 5f (at 2
yrs) to 7f winner: modest maiden: stays 6f: acts on good to firm and dead ground.
R. J. Hodges

KATHRYN'S PET   4 b.f. Blakeney 126 – Starky's Pet (Mummy's Pet 125) [1996   69
66: 11.8s⁴ 10g⁶ 10g³ 12.1s⁵ 10.5v 12g⁵ 12.1s 1997 12s* 10m⁴ 12.1s² 12d² 13.1g³
12.3s* 11.9d⁴ 12.1g 10d 12m Oct 31] sturdy filly: fair handicapper: won at Musselburgh (maiden) and Chester (enterprisingly ridden) in first half of season: well
below form last 3 starts: should stay beyond 1½m: acts on good to firm and soft
going: game. *Mrs M. Reveley*

KATIE KOMAITE   4 b.f. Komaite (USA) – City To City 55 (Windjammer   53
(USA)) [1996 48: a7g⁶ 8.2g 8.2m 7.5g 7g⁴ 5.9f 7g⁵ 8.1m 8.1m³ 7.1m 8m 1997 a6g
8.3s² 8s 8m⁴ 8.3d² 7.5g⁵ 7.1g⁴ 8.3g² 8.2d* 8d² 10.1g 10d⁶ 8.2d⁴ Nov 3] angular filly:
modest handicapper: finally broke duck at Nottingham in October: stays 1m: acts on
good to firm and soft ground: tried blinkered, visored nowadays: has been difficult at
stalls. *Capt. J. Wilson*

KATIE'S CRACKER   2 b.f. (Jan 31) Rambo Dancer (CAN) 107 – Tea-Pot 77   49
(Ragstone 128) [1997 6g a6g² 7.5v⁵ a7g² 7g³ 7g² 7g a8g² Dec 8] 2,600Y: angular
filly: sister to a fair but unreliable middle-distance maiden and half-sister to 11f to
13f winner One For The Pot (by Nicholas Bill) and Irish 1¼m winner Two Lumps
(by Nomination): dam out-and-out stayer on flat, also won over hurdles: poor maiden: trained prior to final start by M. Channon: creditable efforts when placed in
sellers: will stay at least 1¼m: acts on fibresand. *M. Quinn*

KATIE'S KID 7 br.g. Balidar 133 – Khahmens Delight (Come On Grey 96) [1996 NR 1997 10.1g⁵ Aug 10] poor handicapper: fifth in ladies contest at Epsom, only start since 5 yrs: stays 1½m: has worn bandages. *D. J. S. ffrench Davis* — 38

KATIES TREAT (IRE) 2 ch.f. (Apr 22) Superpower 113 – Fancied 62 (Dominion 123) [1997 5.3f a5g 6s 7g⁵ 6m 6.1g a6g Oct 6] 4,000Y: neat filly: second foal: dam 5f winner from 3 starts at 2 yrs: little worthwhile form, including in sellers: tried visored. *D. T. Thom* — –

KATY THOMAS 2 b.f. (Jan 8) Puissance 110 – Indian Summer 78 (Young Generation 129) [1997 5m* 5g⁴ 5d⁶ 6g Sep 20] 2,000F: half-sister to a 2-y-o 6f winner by Forzando and winners abroad by Forzando and Emarati: dam, won in Belgium, out of half-sister to Bustino: made all in minor event at Thirsk in May: tailed off last 2 starts, 3 months apart: probably suited by 5f. *J. Berry* — 58

KATYUSHKA (IRE) 2 b.f. (Apr 17) Soviet Star (USA) 128 – Welsh Note (USA) 111 (Sharpen Up 127) [1997 5g 6g 5.1g⁴ 5m Sep 26] 12,000Y: seventh foal: half-sister to 2 winners abroad, including French 1¼m winner by Lycius: dam 5f performer out of half-sister to Recitation: easily best effort when fourth in maiden at Bath: should stay at least 6f, has run freely. *Major D. N. Chappell* — 68

KAWAFIL (IRE) 2 b.f. (Jan 28) Warning 136 – Nur (USA) 74 (Diesis 133) [1997 5m⁴ 5d* 6g 5.7m⁴ 8g³ 7.6g⁴ 7d Oct 14] smallish, well-made filly: second foal: half-sister to 3-y-o Hajat: dam sprint winner at 2 yrs, sister to useful sprinter Ra'a: capable of fairly useful form on her day: made all in maiden at Salisbury in June: showed temperament afterwards, and well beaten final start: stays 1m: has hung markedly: needs treating with caution: sold 18,000 gns, and sent to Saudi Arabia. *P. T. Walwyn* — 85 §

KAWA-IB (IRE) 3 b.f. Nashwan (USA) 135 – Awayed (USA) 108 (Sir Ivor 135) [1996 78p: 7.1s³ 1997 9m³ 8f³ 7m² 7.1m 7.1g² 8m Oct 22] fair maiden: disappointing last 2 starts: effective at 7f to 9f: acts on firm and soft going: sold 5,800 gns in December. *P. T. Walwyn* — 78 d

KAYESAM 3 b. or br.g. Failiq (FR) 90 – Another-Kaye (Jimmy The Singer 113) [1996 NR 1997 10.1g 10m Sep 9] second reported foal: dam never ran: tailed off in maidens. *J. L. Harris* — –

KAYE'S SECRET 4 b.f. Failiq (FR) 90 – Another-Kaye (Jimmy The Singer 113) [1996 –: 16.2g⁶ 10f 12g 1997 a12g Jan 13] little show in varied company. *J. L. Harris* — –

KAYFIYAH (IRE) 3 b. or br.f. Marju (IRE) 127 – Princess Sucree (USA) (Roberto (USA) 131) [1996 NR 1997 10g 10m³ 12.3g³ 11.5s⁵ 11m³ 8m⁵ Aug 11] tall, lengthy filly: eighth foal: half-sister to several winners, notably smart Burooj (up to 13f, by Danzig): dam, placed over 6f and 8.5f at 4 yrs in USA, is half-sister to Kentucky Derby winner Cannonade: fair form when third in maidens at Ripon in May and June: disappointing afterwards: stays 1½m: sold 50,000 gns in December. *D. Morley* — 78 d

KAYF TARA 3 b.c. Sadler's Wells (USA) 132 – Colorspin (FR) 118 (High Top 131) [1996 NR 1997 10m² 10m* Jul 25] 210,000Y: well-made colt: has a quick action: brother to top-class 1¼m/1½m horse Opera House and closely related to smart 1¼m/1½m winner Highland Dress (by Lomond): dam, Irish Oaks winner, from excellent family: again weak in market, confirmed promise of highly encouraging debut when winning 8-runner maiden at Ascot by 3 lengths from Shaya, leading 1½f out and strong at finish: will stay at least 1½m: has rather a high head carriage: sent to UAE: capable of winning in better company at 4 yrs. *M. R. Stoute* — 103 p

KAY-JAY 3 b.f. Be My Chief (USA) 122 – Greenhil Jazz Time 70 (Music Boy 124) [1996 NR 1997 7m Mar 27] smallish, leggy filly: fifth foal: dam 5f winner: last in maiden on debut. *Miss S. J. Wilton* — –

KAYO 2 b.g. (May 1) Superpower 113 – Shiny Kay 65 (Star Appeal 133) [1997 6g⁴ 6m a7g⁴ 8g* a7g 8s* 8d Oct 20] 11,500Y: leggy colt: seventh foal: brother to 2 winners, including useful 1995 2-y-o sprinter Home Shopping (later stayed 1m), and half-brother to 3 winners, including 3-y-o Rambo Flyer (1¼m listed race winner in Norway, by Rambo Dancer): dam, 1½m winner, half-sister to K-Battery: fair performer: won claimer at Musselburgh in September and nursery at Ayr (hampered on — 69 a63 turn but got up inside last) in October: ran poorly final start: stays 1m well: acts on soft ground and fibresand. *T. J. Etherington*

KAYVEE 8 gr.g. Kaldoun (FR) 122 – Secret Life (USA) (Elocutionist (USA)) 95 [1996 101: 8s 7m 7m 7.9m 8m 8.1g⁴ 8m 7m² 7.3m⁴ 8.2d* 9g 7m² 9m 8g³ 1997 7m 8.1g 8m 8.1d 8d⁶ 7g 8.5g³ 7.3m³ 8.5d 7m² 7m 8m 8.2d³ Nov 3] big, close-coupled gelding: impresses in appearance: useful handicapper: generally ran creditably at 8 yrs, including when second of 25 to Jo Mell in Tote Festival Handicap at Ascot: effective at 7f (granted strong gallop) to 9f: acts on firm and dead ground: blinkered twice at 3 yrs: sometimes wears severe noseband: usually held up. *Mrs A. J. Perrett*

KAYZEE (IRE) 3 b.f. River Falls 113 – Northern Amber (Shack (USA) 118) 40 [1996 –: 6f 6g⁶ 1997 a8g³ a7g 7m a9.4g³ a10g a8.5g Sep 30] poor maiden: left S. Dow after third outing: stays 9f: acts on all-weather. *D. Burchell*

KAZIRANGA (USA) 3 b.f. Lear Fan (USA) 130 – Kazoo 108 (Shareef Dancer 69 (USA) 135) [1996 NR 1997 7g⁵ 7m⁴ 8.1m² 10m 10d⁶ Aug 30] compact filly: has roundish action: second foal: dam, won German 1000 Guineas, from good German family: fair maiden: stiff tasks in handicaps last 2 starts: should stay 1¼m: sent to Germany. *L. M. Cumani*

KEDWICK (IRE) 8 b.g. Be My Guest (USA) 126 – Lady Pavlova 111 67 (Ballymore 123) [1996 61: a10g a8g⁵ a10g* a10g 1997 a10g 9.7g* 10.8m 10s⁵ 9m Jul 31] workmanlike gelding: fair handicapper: won at Folkestone in March: best efforts around 1¼m: acts on equitrack and soft ground (both runs on good to firm best ignored): has been bandaged in front: has been visored, blinkered nowadays. *P. R. Hedger*

KEEN ALERT 3 b.g. Keen 116 – Miss Coco (Swing Easy (USA) 126) [1996 NR – 1997 6m a8g* 7m 8.3g Jun 16] first reported foal: dam never ran: ridden by 5-lb a77 claimer, fair form to win maiden at Southwell in April: well beaten in handicaps afterwards: should stay beyond 1m. *M. Bell*

KEEN COMPANION 4 b.f. Keen 116 – Constant Companion 84 (Pas de Seul 64 133) [1996 48: a10g³ 1997 7g 8.3s³ a8g 10s a10g⁶ Jul 26] modest maiden: staying-on third at Windsor, easily best run: should stay beyond 1m. *T. J. Naughton*

KEEN DANCER 3 ch.g. Keen 116 – Royal Shoe (Hotfoot 126) [1996 –: 8f 8.2g 66 1997 7g 8d⁴ 10m a8g⁴ 10s⁵ Jun 30] heavy-topped gelding: fair maiden: best effort at 1m on good to soft going: joined M. Pipe. *M. Bell*

KEENEST RELUCTANCE 3 gr.f. Environment Friend 128 – Baharlilys 67 – (Green Dancer (USA) 132) [1996 NR 1997 10g 10m May 6] tall, unfurnished filly: first foal: dam no worthwhile form at 3 yrs: last in maiden and seller (visored): sold in July, and sent to Saudi Arabia. *J. R. Fanshawe*

KEEN LADY 2 b.f. (Apr 19) Keen 116 – Bizarre Lady (Dalsaan 125) [1997 a6g⁵ – a7g 7g 6g⁵ 6g 7g Sep 3] 3,200 2-y-o: sixth foal: half-sister to fairly useful 1m winner (stays 1¼m) Crazy Chief (by Indian Ridge): dam ran once: seems of little account. *N. P. Littmoden*

KEEN SALLY 4 ch.f. Keen 116 – Super Sally 108 (Superlative 118) [1996 –: 7f – 1997 a6g a8g⁶ a7g Dec 22] well beaten, including in seller. *R. Guest*

KEEN TO PLEASE 3 ch.f. Keen 116 – Tasseled (USA) (Tate Gallery (USA) 45 d 117) [1996 60: 7.1g³ 5m³ 5m* 6m 5f³ 5g⁴ 5g² 1997 5g 6g⁴ 6g 5g 5d 5d a6g a5g Dec 8] sparely-made filly: poor form at best in 1997: trained first 5 starts by Denys Smith: barely stays 6f: acts on firm ground. *J. Parkes*

KEEN WATERS 3 b.f. Keen 116 – Miss Oasis 54 (Green Desert (USA) 127) 40 [1996 60: 6m 5m³ 5.1m⁴ 6f⁶ 5m² 5g 1997 5g 6.1m 7.3s 6.9m⁴ 7m 10f³ 10m 10m² 11.9m* a16g⁴ 16m⁴ 16.1g a12g⁶ Oct 27] workmanlike filly: poor handicapper: easy winner of seller at Brighton for J. R. Arnold in August: stays 2m: acts on firm ground and equitrack: blinkered twice, running well first time. *Mrs S. D. Williams*

KEEP BATTLING 7 b.g. Hard Fought 125 – Keep Mum 63 (Mummy's Pet 125) 56 § [1996 56: 12.1g³ 12.3g³ 10.9d² 11.1g³ 12.1f* 10m² 1997 11f⁵ 10d 10.9s⁴ 10g⁴ 12g⁵ 10.1g 10.3m² 10.1g² 10.5m⁵ 9m⁶ 8m 12s 10m Nov 4] angular gelding: modest handicapper: effective at 1¼m to 1½m: acts on firm and dead ground: visored (no form) twice at 3 yrs: held up: none too resolute (has refused to race over hurdles) and tends to find little. *J. S. Goldie*

KEEPSAKE (IRE)   3 b.f. Distinctly North (USA) 115 – Souveniers (Relko 136)   58
[1996 –: 5.7d 7.9g 7g 1997 8d 8m 11m⁶ 11.4g² 11.6s⁴ 12m⁵ 16m³ 12g² 12g* 14.1g⁴
14m⁴ 11.1m 16s⁵ 12m Oct 31] tall filly: modest handicapper: won at Salisbury in
August: needs good test at 1½m, and stays 2m: acts on soft and good to firm going:
usually ridden by R. Street: held up. *M. D. I. Usher*

KELANG   3 ch.f. Kris 135 – Ebbing Tide (USA) (His Majesty (USA)) [1997   –
7.5m Nov 1] closely related to 1¼m winner Surf (by Sharpen Up) and 12.2f winner
Tranquil Waters (by Diesis), both fairly useful, and half-sister to several winners:
dam thrice-raced half-sister to dam of Oh So Sharp (by Kris): last of 7 in maiden at
Milan. *Mrs J. Cecil*

KEMO SABO   5 b.g. Prince Sabo 123 – Canoodle 66 (Warpath 113) [1996 –: 8d⁴   64
1997 6.9g³ 7m² 6.9d⁴ May 19] lengthy gelding: good mover: modest performer: in
frame in claimers in 1997: stays 8.5f: acts on any going: has run well for amateur.
C. Parker

KENILWORTH DANCER   4 br.g. Shareef Dancer (USA) 135 – Reltop 72   –
(High Top 131) [1996 –: a12g⁵ a8g 1997 a12g a14g Nov 17] seems of little account
now. *B. R. Cambidge*

KENKAN (IRE)   2 b.f. (May 3) Kenmare (FR) 125 – Farewell Song (USA) 80   63
(The Minstrel (CAN) 135) [1997 5d³ 5.2m 7m Sep 9] close-coupled filly: sixth foal:
sister to 3-y-o Song Mist and half-sister to 6f winner Highland Rhapsody (by Kris)
and a winner in Austria by King of Clubs: dam, 1m winner, sister to Italian St Leger
winner Parting Moment: modest form in maiden at Salisbury on debut: raced too
freely afterwards. *P. F. I. Cole*

KENMIST   3 gr.f. Kenmare (FR) 125 – Mistral's Collette 87 (Simply Great (FR)   105
122) [1996 NR 1997 10s* 7g³ 8m³ 10g⁵ 8m* 8m³ Oct 19] approx. 19,000Y: leggy,
rather angular filly: first foal: dam 6f winner (at 2 yrs) in Ireland and up to 1¼m
in Italy: useful form: won maiden at Milan in June and listed handicap at Ascot in
September, latter by neck from Priena: creditable third in Group 3 event at Milan
final start: best efforts at 1m, should be as effective at 1¼m: acts on good to firm and
soft going: remains in training. *L. M. Cumani*

KENNEMARA STAR (IRE)   3 ch.g. Kenmare (FR) 125 – Dawn Star 94 (High   91 +
Line 125) [1996 66p: 7m 7.6d⁵ 7.1v⁶ 199/ 8d⁴ 7.9g 8m 8g² 8d* 8d Sep 20] tall,
angular gelding: fairly useful handicapper: won 19-runner events at Leicester in
April and Pontefract (made most) in September: favourite, weakened rapidly final 1f
last outing: stays 1m: probably needs good going or softer (ran no sort of race on
good to firm third start at 3 yrs): stays in training. *J. L. Dunlop*

KENNET   2 b.g. (May 3) Kylian (USA) – Marwell Mitzi 50 (Interrex (CAN))   73
[1997 5.2g² 5d⁶ 6m 6g a6g² 6g⁴ 7.3m 6m² a7g⁶ 6g a6g⁵ Nov 1] leggy, plain geld-   a64
ing: first foal: dam 6f winner at 4 yrs: fair maiden: better efforts on turf than
fibresand: should stay beyond 6f: acts on good to firm ground: none too consistent.
P. D. Cundell

KENTAVRUS WAY (IRE)   6 b.g. Thatching 131 – Phantom Row 37 (Adonijah   –
126) [1996 41: a12g a13g a10g a10g⁴ 1997 a10g Jan 11] good-bodied gelding: poor
form at best since 3 yrs: stays 1¼m: tried visored: ungenuine winning hurdler.
A. Moore

KENTUCKY DREAMS   7 b.g. Dreams To Reality (USA) 113 – Kentucky Tears   –
(USA) (Cougar (CHI)) [1996 NR 1997 7g 5f Aug 27] of little account. *Mrs
A. M. Naughton*

KENTUCKY FALL (FR)   4 b.f. Lead On Time (USA) 123 – Autumn Tint   76
(USA) (Roberto (USA) 131) [1996 69: 8g⁴ 8.1m⁴ 9.7g² 10.3g 1997 8s 8f² 7s⁵ 8.3m⁴
6g* 6.9g⁴ 7m 6m⁴ Oct 21] fair handicapper: won at Yarmouth in August: ran at
least respectably afterwards (raced on unfavoured side final start): effective at 6f/
easy 7f: best form on good going or firmer. *Lady Herries*

KERNOF (IRE)   4 b.g. Rambo Dancer (CAN) 107 – Empress Wu 62 (High Line   65
125) [1996 55: 8g 7.5g 8g 10m 11.1f² 10g* 9.9m⁵ 1997 10g 12g⁴ 12g 12d* 12m²

12m* 13d[6] Aug 13] leggy gelding: fair handicapper: won at Musselburgh in June and Beverley (gamely) in July: should stay beyond 1½m: acts on firm ground and dead: effective blinkered/visored or not. *M. D. Hammond*

KESTON POND (IRE) 7 b.g. Taufan (USA) 119 – Maria Renata (Jaazeiro (USA) 127) [1996 80: 6m 7g 6m[2] a6g[2] 8g 7m* 7g[2] 7m[2] 7m[4] 6m 7m[2] 7g 7m[5] 6f 1997 7g 7m 8m 10.3d 7g a6g 7g[6] 7m 7.1m[5] Aug 20] tall, good-topped gelding: very much on the downgrade and no worthwhile form at 7 yrs. *Mrs V. A. Aconley* –

KETTLESING (IRE) 2 b.f. (Apr 25) Mujadil (USA) 119 – Icefern 88 (Moorestyle 137) [1997 5s[5] 5v[5] 6s 6m 5g[4] 5d* 5.1g* 6s[2] 6m Oct 28] 15,500Y: lengthy filly: fifth foal: half-sister to 4-y-o Iamus, 5f winner Kensworth Lady (by Formidable) and a middle-distance winner abroad by Glint of Gold: dam sprinter: fair performer: won seller at Ayr in September and nursery at Nottingham in October: a sprinter: best form on good ground or softer: usually blinkered: lost chance when rearing stalls final start: tends to hang. *M. W. Easterby* 71

KEVASINGO 5 b.g. Superpower 113 – Katharina 105 (Frankincense 120) [1996 57: 9.7m 7d[6] 8f[3] 7.1g 9.7f 10f[5] 10m[4] 10f[3] 10.8f[4] 8m 1997 8.2m Apr 8] workmanlike gelding: modest handicapper: well beaten only outing at 5 yrs: stays 1¼m: acts on equitrack and firm ground: blinkered last 3 starts. *J. L. Spearing* –

KEWARRA 3 b.g. Distant Relative 128 – Shalati (FR) (High Line 125) [1996 71: 5m 6.1g[5] 6m[4] 5.1g[4] 1997 7m 7m 8.1g[2] 6.9m[3] 8g[5] 8.1m[3] 10m[3] 10.2g* 10m 10.2g* 10m* 10g 12s Nov 8] angular gelding: fairly useful handicapper: progressed well at 3 yrs: won at Chepstow in August and September and Newmarket in October: better at 1¼m than shorter: has raced mainly on good/good to firm going (tired dramatically over 1½m on soft): races keenly: game and consistent. *B. R. Millman* 91

KEYBOOGIE (USA) 3 b.f. Lyphard (USA) 132 – Key Dancer (USA) (Nijinsky (CAN) 138) [1996 NR 1997 7g 10d[3] 10g* 10d[4] 8.1g[4] 8d[2] Oct 14] strong, good-bodied filly: has a powerful, round action: sixth foal: half-sister to 3 winners, including Modest Hope (up to 1½m, by Blushing Groom) and Call Account (up to 8.5f, Grade 2 placed in USA, by Private Account): dam, stakes winner up to 11f, out of half-sister to Ajdal and Formidable: useful performer: simple task when winning Newmarket maiden in June: ran well when fourth to Dance Design in Pretty Polly Stakes at the Curragh following start and when second of 3 to Star Precision in minor event at Leicester: will stay 1½m: raced only on good/good to soft going. *R. Charlton* 97

KEY CHANGE (IRE) 4 b.f. Darshaan 133 – Kashka (USA) (The Minstrel (CAN) 135) [1996 117: 10s* 12g* 12m[2] 12m[3] 11.9m* 14m[2] 1997 12s[5] May 16] rangy, angular filly: smart performer: won Yorkshire Oaks in 1996 and also placed in Ribblesdale Stakes at Royal Ascot and Irish Oaks and Irish St Leger at the Curragh: reportedly finished distressed when tailed off in Prix Jean de Chaudenay at Saint-Cloud only 4-y-o outing: stayed 1¾m: acted on good to firm and soft ground: retired. *J. Oxx, Ireland* –

KEYSER SOZE 2 b.g. (Mar 4) Petong 126 – Lamees (USA) (Lomond (USA) 128) [1997 5f Apr 4] 22,000Y: fourth foal: half-brother to several winners, including 1994 2-y-o sprint winner Don Alvaro (by Forzando), 3-y-o Ella Lamees and 4-y-o Lomberto: dam unraced: tailed off in Lingfield maiden. *D. Haydn Jones* –

KEY TO 3 b.f. Interrex (CAN) – Key To Enchantment (Key To Content (USA)) [1996 NR 1997 10g[6] 11m Oct 28] fourth foal: dam, twice raced at 2 yrs, out of half-sister to a Park Hill winner: no show in claimers. *A. P. Jarvis* –

KEY TO MY HEART (IRE) 7 b.h. Broken Hearted 124 – Originality (Gods-walk (USA) 130) [1996 113: 10.4f* 12.3m[2] 11.9g* 10.5m[5] 13.3m[5] 10.9m* 12m[2] a9.4g 1997 14.1g[3] 13.9g[6] 11.8d[4] 10.4m 10.5m[5] 13.4s 12m[5] 12s Nov 8] good-topped horse: unimpressive mover: smart performer: won Yorkshire Cup at York in 1994: below form in 1997 after sixth in same race on second start, left Miss S. Hall after sixth: effective at 10.4f to 1¾m: acted on any going: usually bandaged: died undergoing surgery for twisted gut in November. *J. L. Eyre* 113

KHABAR 4 b.g. Forzando 122 – Ella Mon Amour 65 (Ela-Mana-Mou 132) [1996 63: 8.2s 6g 7.5g 8g 10f[2] 11.1g 9m 1997 9.9m 9.7s Jul 2] little worthwhile form since 2 yrs. *R. Bastiman* –

KHAFAAQ 3 b.c. Green Desert (USA) 127 – Ghanimah 98 (Caerleon (USA) 132) 91
[1996 –: 6s 1997 8g 8g⁵ 8d³ 7m² 7.1d² 7m* 7g³ 7f⁶ 7m* Sep 25] neat colt: fairly
useful performer: won minor event at Lingfield in August and handicap at
Goodwood in September: best form at 7f: acts on firm and dead ground: blinkered
last 4 starts: held up: consistent: sent to UAE. *Major W. R. Hern*

KHAIRUN NISAA 3 b.f. Never So Bold 135 – Sea Clover (IRE) 77 (Ela-Mana- –
Mou 132) [1996 64, a?: 6v² a7g a6g² 1997 6.1m Mar 31] failed by long way to repeat
debut form: dead. *M. J. Polglase*

KHALAS 2 b.c. (Mar 7) Wolfhound (USA) 126 – Absaar (USA) 76 (Alleged 91 p
(USA) 138) [1997 7m 7g² 7.1g² 7d* Oct 27] small, quite attractive colt: first live
foal: dam, 11f winner, half-sister to Grand Prix de Paris and Melbourne Cup winner
At Talaq: fairly useful form: close second in maidens at Newcastle and Chepstow
before landing odds in similar event at Lingfield, beating Storm Cry comfortably in
sprint finish: will stay at least 1m: acts on dead going (shaped well on good to firm):
open to improvement and should make a useful handicapper. *B. W. Hills*

KHALIK (IRE) 3 br.g. Lear Fan (USA) 130 – Silver Dollar 106 (Shirley Heights 73
130) [1996 NR 1997 8m 9d⁴ 7g² Jun 12] IR 44,000F: smallish, sturdy gelding:
unimpressive mover: sixth foal: half-brother to 1m winner Money Spinner (by
Teenoso): dam, 2-y-o 6f winner, should have stayed 1½m: fair form in maidens when
making running first and third starts: should stay beyond 1m: joined Mrs L. Stubbs.
E. A. L. Dunlop

KHAMSIN (IRE) 3 b.f. River Falls 113 – Burren Breeze (IRE) (Mazaad 106) –
[1996 NR 1997 8d 10.2f⁵ a11g Nov 17] IR 18,000Y: strong, lengthy filly: first foal:
dam unraced half-sister to smart 7f performer Braddells: little promise in maidens
and seller. *M. J. Heaton-Ellis*

KHASSAH 3 b.f. Green Desert (USA) 127 – Kadwah (USA) 80 (Mr Prospector 108
(USA)) [1996 105: 6f* 6g⁶ 8m* 8g² 1997 8m 8m⁵ 8g⁵ 8.1s Aug 30] massive filly:
has a powerful, round action: useful form: under 10 lengths eighth to Sleeptyme
in 1000 Guineas at Newmarket and 4½ lengths fifth of 6 to Rebecca Sharp in
Coronation Stakes at Royal Ascot on first 2 starts: didn't look at best and below
form afterwards: should stay beyond 1m: acts on firm ground: sent to USA.
J. H. M. Gosden

KHATIR (CAN) 6 gr.g. Alwasmi (USA) 115 – Perfect Poppy (USA) (Poppy Jay) –
[1996 NR 1997 a16g Jan 16] rangy gelding: poor and ungenuine hurdler: fair winner
on flat: blinkered, behind only start since 1994. *M. C. Pipe*

KHATTAFF (IRE) 2 ch.c. (Apr 5) Hamas (IRE) 125§ – Coven (Sassafras (FR) 69
135) [1997 6d 6d 7m⁵ 7.1g⁴ 7g Sep 24] smallish, strong colt: half-brother to 3-y-o
Khayali among several winners, 4 at least useful, notably Middle Park winner Balla
Cove (by Ballad Rock): dam won at 6f to 1¼m in Ireland: fair form in maidens at
Chester and Chepstow third and fourth starts: should stay 1m. *Major W. R. Hern*

KHAWAFI 3 b.f. Kris 135 – Tabdea (USA) 106 (Topsider (USA)) [1996 NR 1997 86
7m⁵ 7d⁶ 10g* 11.4g³ 12m 10s 11.9s Oct 8] quite attractive filly: third foal: dam 6f
and 1m winner: fairly useful performer: made all in maiden at Goodwood in June:
good efforts next 2 starts: stayed 1½m: acted on good to firm going, below form on
soft: raced freely: stud. *E. A. L. Dunlop*

KHAYALI (IRE) 3 b.c. Unfuwain (USA) 131 – Coven (Sassafras (FR) 135) 91
[1996 NR 1997 10d⁶ 10.1g⁴ 11.8m³ 10m* 10g³ 10.3m Sep 13] big, good-topped colt:
has scope: closely related to fair 1½m performer Dance Partout (by Glow) and
half-brother to 4 at least useful winners, notably Middle Park winner Balla Cove (by
Ballad Rock): dam won at 6f to 1¼m in Ireland: fairly useful form: won maiden at
Pontefract in July: should be suited by 1½m: yet to race on extremes of going: flashes
tail under pressure: front runner/races prominently: sent to UAE. *D. Morley*

KHAYAL (USA) 3 b.g. Green Dancer (USA) 132 – Look Who's Dancing (USA) 63
(Affirmed (USA)) [1996 NR 1997 8m 8g 8.3s⁴ 12g 10s Jun 30] $130,000Y: first
reported foal: dam, won 3 times at up to 9f in USA, from family of St Leger winner
Ragusa: worthwhile form only when fourth in maiden at Windsor in May: looked
ungenuine next time: hurdling with P. G. Murphy. *B. W. Hills*

KHAZINAT EL DAR (USA)   3 b. or br.f. Slew O'Gold (USA) – Alghuzaylah   78
90 (Habitat 134) [1996 NR 1997 8.3m³ 8.3g² 8.1s³ 10g Sep 18] leggy, quite good
topped filly: seventh foal: sister to very smart miler Zaahi and half-sister to 4
winners: dam, 2-y-o 5f winner stayed 1m, half-sister to very smart French 5.5f to
10.5f winner Pitasia: fair maiden: ran no sort of race final start: should have stayed
beyond 1m: stud. *Major W. R. Hern*

KHEYRAH (USA)   2 b. or br.f. (Jan 17) Dayjur (USA) 137 – Khwlah (USA) 99   86
(Best Turn (USA)) [1997 6g⁶ 6g* 6g* 6d⁶ Oct 16] good-topped filly: has a quick
action: seventh living foal: half-sister to several winners, including 1988 2-y-o 6f
winner Alkariyh (by Alydar) and 4-y-o Alsahib: dam, 6f winner at 2 yrs effective at
1¼m, half-sister to Saratoga Six and Dunbeath: fairly useful performer: won maiden
at Yarmouth in August and nursery at Haydock following month, latter by neck from
Branston Berry: below form final start: stays 6f: races prominently: sent to UAE.
E. A. L. Dunlop

KI CHI SAGA (USA)   5 ch.g. Miswaki (USA) 124 – Cedilla (USA) 111 (Caro   –
133) [1996 8m⁶ 10s⁶ 8m⁶ 8m 10v 9g 9.2g 1997 a7g a7g² a8g a8g* a8g⁴ a8g²   a67 d
8f a8g⁶ 8.1m 7m 8g 8.3s a7g a7g a10g Dec 19] stocky gelding: fair performer: won
minor event at Lingfield in March: lost form subsequently, leaving M. Madgwick
after twelfth start: stays 1m: recent form only on equitrack: blinkered once (tailed
off). *G. L. Moore*

KICKONSUN (IRE)   3 b.g. High Estate 127 – Damezao (Alzao (USA) 117)   31
[1996 –: 7f 7d⁶ 1997 7g 10m⁶ a12g 14.1m⁴ May 27] blinkered, first form when fourth
in maiden handicap at Redcar. *R. A. Fahey*

KID ORY   6 ch.g. Rich Charlie 117 – Woomargama 69 (Creetown 123) [1996 65d,   47
a–: 7s 7.5m 7m³ 7g³ 7g 7m³ 7s³ 8m³ 8.2m 7g⁶ 7m 7f⁶ a6g⁵ a7g⁶ 1997 a7g a7g⁵ 8m 7g   a41
5.9g⁴ 5.9d⁶ a6g³ 6.9f 6f² 6g⁴ 5s⁵ 6m 6m 7m Aug 10] close-coupled gelding: poor
handicapper: effective at 6f to 1m: acts on firm and dead ground (only respectable
efforts on soft): blinkered last 6 starts. *D. W. Chapman*

KIERANS BRIDGE (IRE)   2 ch.f. (May 21) Arcane (USA) – Rhein Valley   –
(IRE) (Kings Lake (USA) 133) [1997 8.2g 8.2g 8s Nov 8] third reported foal: dam
once-raced sister to Irish St Leger and Gold Cup runner-up Tyrone Bridge: signs of
ability in maiden at Nottingham second start: likely to need thorough test of stamina.
A. P. Jarvis

KIERANS MAIDEN   3 b.f. Inca Chief (USA) – Donosa (Posse (USA) 130)   –
[1996 NR 1997 6.9g 8.2m Apr 11] third foal: dam probably of little account: no form:
dead. *A. P. Jarvis*

KIERKEGAARD   4 ch.c. Indian Ridge 123 – Mists of Avalon (USA) 76   115
(Nureyev (USA) 131) [1997 8m² 8g⁵ 8g 8m* 8m* 8s⁴ 8d* 8m* 8f² 8d Nov 9]
28,000Y: sixth foal, previous 5 not nearly so good as himself: dam 1m (at 2 yrs)/7f
winner: smart Italian colt: successful on 5 occasions at 3 yrs (all at 1m/8.5f) and on
another 4 occasions in 1997: gained last 3 successes in listed race, valuable handicap
and listed race, all at Milan: best form when 1¼ lengths second of 9 to Devil River
Peek in Premio Vittorio di Capua at Milan, held up behind strong pace then running
on: best around 1m: acts on firm and soft ground: effective either making running or
held up. *D. Ducci, Italy*

KIKA   4 gr.f. Niniski (USA) 125 – Goeswell (Roan Rocket 128) [1996 NR 1997   46
11.7m³ 12g** 11.8g⁶ 16g 14m³ 11m Oct 28] tall, sparely-made filly: fifth foal: sister
to 2 fair staying maidens: dam maiden: poor performer: won handicap at Doncaster in
July: below form afterwards: should be suited by further than 1½m. *K. R. Burke*

KILCORA (IRE)   2 b.f. (Feb 25) Mujadil (USA) 119 – Miss Audimar (USA) (Mr   84
Leader (USA)) [1997 5g² 5.1d³ 5g* 5m⁵ 5m Jun 18] IR 36,000Y: lengthy, rather
unfurnished filly: half-sister to several winners, including smart Diaghilef (by Royal
Academy, won over 1¼m/1½m, best effort over 1¾m) and useful Irish 1990 2-y-o
sprint winner Noora Park (by Ahonoora): dam winner at up to 11f, graded-stakes
placed: won maiden at Sandown in May somewhat fortuitously after runner-up
faltered: ran creditably next time, but not seen again after finishing down field in
Queen Mary: will stay beyond 5f. *C. A. Dwyer*

KIL

KILCULLEN (IRE) 2 b. or br.g. (May 10) In The Wings 128 – Liffey Lass 81 p
(USA) 95 (Irish River (FR) 131) [1997 7g³ 8s⁴ Nov 6] good-topped gelding: ninth
foal: closely related to 3-y-o Liffre and French winner around 1m Colleen (both by
Sadler's Wells) and half-brother to several winners: dam, 2-y-o 7f winner, out of
half-sister to high-class colts Home Guard and Boone's Cabin: 3¼ lengths third to
Zaya in maiden at Doncaster, staying on once getting hang of things: uneasy joint
favourite, well below that form in similar event at Musselburgh (subsequently
gelded): should be well suited by 1¼m+: should still progress. *J. H. M. Gosden*

KILCULLEN LAD (IRE) 3 b.g. Fayruz 116 – Royal Home 69 (Royal Palace 86
131) [1996 74: 5m 6f* 6g 6f² 5f* 5g 5g² a5g² a5g* a6g* a6g⁵ 1997 5m² 6m* 5g⁴ 5d
5m 5m 5m² 6m 5.2m⁴ 6.1g Sep 28] smallish, workmanlike gelding: fairly useful
handicapper: won at Lingfield in May: best efforts afterwards when in frame:
effective at 5f and 6f: acts on firm ground and equitrack: takes good hold: tends to
hang/drift right: best form blinkered/visored: gelded after final start. *P. Mooney*

KILDEE BOY 3 b.g. Interrex (CAN) – National Time (USA) (Lord Avie (USA)) –
[1996 NR 1997 6.9m 7m 6s⁶ 5m Jul 14] closely related to 5-y-o Malibu Man and
half-brother to 7-y-o Kildee Lad and Meeson Times (by Enchantment), all sprinters:
dam ran twice at 2 yrs: gave trouble at start and withdrawn from intended debut:
tailed off in maidens and handicap: sold in October, and sent to Italy. *A. P. Jones*

KILDEE LAD 7 b.g. Presidium 124 – National Time (USA) (Lord Avie (USA)) 79 d
[1996 85: 5.7g 5g² 5m 5.7m⁴ 5.7m⁴ 6m* 5.7f* 5.1m⁴ 6.1d² 6m 1997 6m a6g 6d 5.1d²
6d 6m⁵ 5.7m⁶ 6d⁵ 5g⁶ 5.7f⁵ 6m 8m⁵ 8g Aug 27] leggy, close-coupled gelding: fair
handicapper at best in 1997: stays 6f: acts on fibresand and any turf going: below
form in visor/blinkers: usually held up. *A. P. Jones*

KILERNAN 6 ch.g. K-Battery 108 – Lekuti (Le Coq d'Or 101) [1996 51: 12.1g* 53
1997 12g* Aug 2] leggy gelding: unimpressive mover: modest handicapper: 16/1 on
first run for 16 months (reportedly sprained a ligament), won at Thirsk in August,
leading over 1f out: also won only race in 1996: stays 16.5f: acts on firm and soft
ground: used to front run: has run well when sweating. *T. D. Barron*

KILIMANJARO 2 b.c. (Feb 18) Shirley Heights 130 – Darara 129 (Top Ville 104 +
129) [1997 7m⁴ 8.1s* 8g⁴ 8g⁶ Oct 25] 500,000Y: quite attractive colt: has scope:
fluent mover: seventh foal: half-brother to several winners, including smart French
stayer Dariyoun (by Shahrastani) and very smart French middle-distance performer
Darazari (by Sadler's Wells): dam won Prix Vermeille and is half-sister to Darshaan:
won minor event at Sandown in August impressively, but didn't go on as expected in
better company: soon off bridle when 1¼ lengths fourth to Teapot Row in Royal
Lodge Stakes at Ascot, and dropped away tamely when well beaten in Racing Post
Trophy at Doncaster: will be suited by 1½m+: acts on soft ground. *M. R. Stoute*

KILLARNEY JAZZ 2 b.c. (May 3) Alhijaz 122 – Killarney Belle (USA) (Irish 58
Castle (USA)) [1997 a6g² 5d⁴ a6g Dec 6] half-brother to 2 winners, including fairly
useful Eire-Leath-Sceal (stayed 2m, by Legend of France): dam unraced: modest
form when in frame in seller at Wolverhampton and maiden at Catterick in October:
should stay at least 1m. *J. Wharton*

KILLERNAN KILMAINE (IRE) 2 b.c. (Apr 8) Sure Blade (USA) 130 – Rio –
Piedras 86 (Kala Shikari 125) [1997 5s Mar 29] 11,000Y: leggy colt: second living
foal: half-brother to 3-y-o Red Romance: dam suited by 1¼m: behind in maiden at
Haydock (unseated rider in paddock). *A. Bailey*

KILMA (USA) 3 b.f. Silver Hawk (USA) 123 – Nikishka (USA) (Nijinsky 97
(CAN) 138) [1996 NR 1997 10m⁴ 11.8m* 12.4g* 14m 14.6m 12m² 14d⁴ Oct 17]
$210,000Y: big, strong filly: third foal: dam, Grade 2 9f winner at 4 yrs and placed in
Grade 1 9f events as 5-y-o, is out of half-sister to Be My Guest: useful performer:
won maiden at Leicester and handicap at Newcastle in June: best efforts in handicaps
at Newmarket last 2 starts: barely stayed 1¾m: acted on good to firm and good to soft
going: tail swisher: stud. *L. M. Cumani*

KILMEENA LADY 3 b.f. Inca Chief (USA) – Kilmeena Glen (Beveled (USA)) –
[1996 –: 7.1s 1997 6m 6m 7m 6d a7g a6g a8g⁶ Dec 10] seems of little account.
J. C. Fox

KILNAMARTYRA GIRL 7 b.m. Arkan 78 – Star Cove 58 (Porto Bello 118) 43
[1996 –: 8.5m 8f 1997 a11g³ a11g³ a12g* a11g³ a16g a12g² a12g² 12m 9.9m a12g⁴ a46
a11g² 10g² 9.9m⁶ a12g⁴ 12g* a14g 13.8g Aug 5] lengthy mare: poor handicapper:
won at Southwell (amateurs) in January and Musselburgh in July: stays 1½m: acts on
firm ground and fibresand: tried blinkered/visored: often soon off bridle and suited
by strongly-run race. *J. Parkes*

KILSHANNY 3 b.f. Groom Dancer (USA) 128 – Kiliniski 119 (Niniski (USA) 70
125) [1996 70p: 6m 7d² 1997 8.2d⁴ 8g² 11.8m* 10g⁵ Jun 13] rangy filly: fair
performer: well ridden from front when making winning handicap debut at Leicester
in June: disappointing only subsequent start: stays 1½m: yet to race on extremes of
going: sold 43,000 gns in December. *L. M. Cumani*

KILVINE 4 b.g. Shaadi (USA) 126 – Kilavea (USA) 92 (Hawaii) [1996 86: 9g⁶ 71
8.1g⁶ 7g 7m⁴ 8m³ 7.5m² 7m⁶ 1997 5.2g 6.1m 7m 7.1m³ 7g³ 8g Aug 27] well-made,
attractive gelding: fair handicapper: stays 1m: has raced only on good ground or
firmer: hung right fifth 3-y-o start: sent to UAE. *W. J. Haggas*

KIMBERLEY 2 b.c. (Apr 6) Shareef Dancer (USA) 135 – Willowbank 66 (Gay – p
Fandango (USA) 132) [1997 7f⁵ Oct 29] fourth foal: closely related to 3-y-o Assured
Gamble: dam winning middle-distance stayer: 12/1, never dangerous when remote
fifth of 8 in steadily-run Yarmouth maiden: should do better over good deal further
than 7f. *G. Wragg*

KIMBERLEY BOY 7 b.g. Mtoto 134 – Diamond House (Habitat 134) [1996 –
NR 1997 12.3m Jun 19] modest performer at 5 yrs for M. Brittain: well beaten only
start in 1997. *Mrs M. Reveley*

KIM'S BRAVE 2 b.g. (Apr 10) Deploy 131 – Princess Dina 87 (Huntercombe 86
133) [1997 6s 6f* 7s⁴ 7m⁵ 8m⁵ 8g* 8f⁴ 7.3d⁵ 8d 10m Nov 1] 16,500Y: close-coupled
gelding: half-brother to several winners, including 1988 2-y-o 7f winner Labelon
Lady (by Touching Wood) and fairly useful 11f winner Family Line (by High Line):
dam in frame up to 9f: fairly useful performer: won seller at Brighton in June and
nursery at Bath in September: ran respectably in listed race at Newmarket final start:
probably stays 1¼m: acts on firm going, probably on soft: blinkered final 6 starts: not
an easy ride. *B. J. Meehan*

KIND OF LIGHT 4 b.f. Primo Dominie 121 – Kind Thoughts 71 (Kashmir II 74
125) [1996 83, a68: a5g a6g³ a6g³ 6g 6m* 6g* 6m³ 6.1d 6m⁴ 6m a7g 1997 6m 7d 6g a–
6m² 6g⁴ 5.2m⁵ 6g* 7g⁶ 6d Sep 13] fair handicapper: won at Newmarket (apprentices)
in August: creditable efforts both subsequent starts: best at 6f/7f: acts on good to firm
ground, dead and fibresand: visored (out of form) once: usually waited with: sold
12,500 gns in October. *R. Guest*

KINDRED GREETING 5 b.g. Most Welcome 131 – Red Berry 115 (Great 24
Nephew 126) [1996 38: a12g⁶ a16g 14.1f 16m 14.1m⁵ 14.1f² 14.1f² 12.3m 16m
17.1m⁵ 1997 14.1s 14.1m 16.2d 12g⁵ 14.1g³ Aug 23] stocky gelding: bad maiden:
stays 1¾m: acts on firm ground: tried visored, usually blinkered. *J. O'Reilly*

KING ALEX 4 b.c. Rainbow Quest (USA) 134 – Alexandrie (USA) 114 (Val de 112 p
L'Orne (FR) 133) [1996 111: 10g* 10.4f² 1997 11.7g* 10d² 12g 10g* Aug 16] tall,
rather unfurnished colt: has a round action: reportedly troubled by lameness after
making promising start to his career at 3 yrs: at least as good in 1997, easily landing
odds in minor event at Bath in May and winning Royal Whip Stakes at the Curragh
in August by short head from Rayouni after meeting trouble in running: ran well
when head second to Germano in listed race at Goodwood in between: should stay
1½m ridden with restraint: acts on dead ground, yet to race on softer: reportedly stays
in training, and probably capable of better still. *R. Charlton*

KING ATHELSTAN (USA) 9 b.g. Sovereign Dancer (USA) – Wimbledon Star 65
(USA) (Hoist The Flag (USA)) [1996 84d: 10m 10m⁴ 9.9f 10d 10m 10.3g 8s 1997
8m³ 8m 8g* 7m 8m 7m* 8m⁵ 7.5g Aug 23] lengthy gelding: fair handicapper: won
apprentice events at Warwick in May and July: stayed 10.4f: acted on good to firm
ground: none too consistent: dead. *B. A. McMahon*

KING CHESTNUT 6 ch.g. Efisio 120 – Sweet Colleen 42 (Connaught 130) [1996 –
NR 1997 7.1d 8g 8m 10d 8g 6m Jul 18] workmanlike gelding: fair in 1995, well
beaten in 1997. *M. Dods*

KINGCHIP BOY 8 b.g. Petong 126 – Silk St James (Pas de Seul 133) [1996 66, 69 d
a72: a8g a8g* a8g* a8g* a8g² a8g² a8g² 8d² 9.7m² a8g* 10m⁶ 7d 8g³ a8.5g 8f⁵ 7g   a82 d
8.2g³ 8.1s⁵ a8g² a7g a8g² 1997 a8g a7g* a8g* a8g* a8g a8g⁴ 8.5m⁵ 8m 8.3s⁴ 8m
8f⁵ 8.2g 7d 8s a8g a8g Dec 18] compact gelding: unimpressive mover: fairly useful
handicapper on the all-weather, fair on turf: gained hat-trick at Southwell (successful
there 7 times in all) in January/February: well below form last 7 starts: stays 9.7f:
acts on any going: effective with or without blinkers/visor: sometimes wanders under
pressure: usually ridden up with pace nowadays. *M. J. Ryan*

KING DARIUS (IRE) 2 ch.c. (Mar 10) Persian Bold 123 – Valiant Friend (USA)   78 p
(Shahrastani (USA) 135) [1997 5.2g 6m 5.7g 6.1s* 6d⁴ 7m³ 7g⁶ 8g⁴ Sep 8] 12,500Y:
strong colt: first foal: dam, ran twice in France, granddaughter of Oaks winner Val-
oris: fairly useful performer: won claimer at Chepstow in July: couldn't capitalize on
nursery mark afterwards, but gave impression needs stiffer test of stamina, and met
trouble under 7-lb claimer final start: acts on good to firm and soft ground: will make
a better 3-y-o at 1¼m+. *R. Hannon*

KINGDOM EMPEROR 3 b.g. Forzando 122 – Wrangbrook (Shirley Heights   50
130) [1996 37: 6m 6m 7.5m 1997 10m² 9f 10g 11s³ Jul 26] good-topped gelding: has
a round action: modest maiden: best effort on reappearance: stays 1¼m: acts on good
to firm ground: has shown temperament, pulling too hard only try in visor: won novic-
ice hurdle for W. Clay in October. *M. J. Camacho*

KINGDOM PEARL 3 ch.f. Statoblest 120 – Sunfleet 59 (Red Sunset 120) [1996   57
–: a6g 1997 a8g⁵ a7g 12g² 12m⁴ 12f³ a12g⁶ 12g² 12g⁵ 12g* 12m 12s⁴ Nov 6] modest
handicapper: won at Catterick in September: likely to stay beyond 1½m: acts on firm
and soft going, probably on fibresand: sold 10,000 gns in December. *M. J. Camacho*

KINGDOM PRINCESS 4 br.f. Forzando 122 – Song of Hope 103 (Chief Singer   –
131) [1996 69: a7g⁶ a8g* a7g* a8.5g⁶ 8.5d³ a8g 1997 a8g Jan 20] lengthy filly: fair
performer at 3 yrs: well beaten only start in 1997: sold 9,000 gns in December, in foal
to Piccolo. *M. J. Camacho*

KINGDOM QUEEN (IRE) 2 b.f. (Mar 30) Night Shift (USA) – Yashina (FR)   59
(Tennyson (FR) 124) [1997 7.5f³ 9m Sep 26] 16,000Y: half-sister to several winners,
including fairly useful 1¼m to 14.6f Yalanoura (by Lashkari): dam French 10.5f winner: showed some ability in maidens at Beverley and Redcar, better effort on debut:
should stay at least 1m. *M. J. Camacho*

KINGFISHER MILL (USA) 3 ch.c. Riverman (USA) 131 – Charming Life   120
(NZ) (Sir Tristram 115) [1996 70p: 7m 1997 10g* 10.4g⁴ 12d² 12s 11.9g³ 12g*
Sep 27]
Had Lord Howard de Walden been a more impetuous and less attentive
driver in his youth, the entire course of modern history could have been much
different. The story goes that, while on holiday in Germany in 1931, he nearly
ran over Adolf Hitler with his sports car but ended up shaking hands with him
instead. Still, his lordship is not the sort to dwell on missed opportunities, and
in his long time as a racehorse owner there must have been many. Arguably, his
Kingfisher Mill provided one or two of them in the latest season. A slow-
maturing colt, Kingfisher Mill wasn't entered for the Derby, yet at his best it's
reasonable to think he'd have run into a place. When he did get the chance to
compete in the very best company, in the King George VI and Queen Elizabeth
Diamond Stakes, he suffered a back injury and finished last, though he had his
work cut out that day anyway. That race was the only time Kingfisher Mill
finished out of the frame in six starts during the year, and he won three times.
Connections must have been regretting Kingfisher Mill's lack of a
classic engagement by the time he reappeared in an eighteen-runner maiden at
Newmarket in April. Despite having shown only a little promise on his sole
start at two, Kingfisher Mill went off favourite and ran out an impressive winner by five lengths from Purist. Kingfisher Mill's over three lengths fourth to
the subsequent Derby winner Benny The Dip in the Dante Stakes at York next
time didn't put him in the best light, though he did show plenty more improvement, racing keenly and never able to land a blow after being held up. The King

King Edward VII Stakes, Royal Ascot—Kingfisher Mill slams his four rivals

Edward VII Stakes at Royal Ascot was a different matter altogether. Marginally favourite in a disappointing field of five, Kingfisher Mill was strikingly impressive, soon sent into the lead, given a breather at halfway and quickening clear under pressure in the straight. He was eased a couple of lengths before the line but still reached it eight lengths ahead of the useful Palio Sky. This display was enough to ensure that Kingfisher Mill went off fourth favourite at 8/1 for the King George VI and Queen Elizabeth Diamond Stakes, ahead of such good horses as Shantou, Strategic Choice, Predappio and the winner, Swain. The back injury Kingfisher Mill suffered there proved not to be serious, and he was out less than a month later in the Great Voltigeur Stakes at York. Faced by the highly promising Stowaway and the short-head Derby runner-up Silver Patriarch, Kingfisher Mill was anything but disgraced in finishing two and a quarter lengths third to the former, racing in second and leading briefly under pressure two furlongs out.

Kingfisher Mill wound up his season in the Cumberland Lodge Stakes at Ascot in September. He faced no straightforward task under a bigger penalty than any of his rivals and went off at 7/2 in an eight-runner race, just behind the Derby third Romanov and level with the smart but enigmatic Maylane, a major rival who was out of the way almost at once after throwing his rider as the stalls opened. Salmon Ladder set a sound pace for a mile before Fahris went on. As the latter began to run out of stamina a furlong and a half out, Kingfisher Mill, who'd been close up taking a good hold, went on. He was soon challenged by Romanov, but, responding most gamely to strong pressure, had just enough left to hold on. The margin was a head, with Romanov, who was receiving 2 lb, just about in front soon after the line.

Kingfisher Mill is by the successful sire Riverman out of a dam whose family is well known in Australia. Charming Life won over seven furlongs

Cumberland Lodge Stakes, Ascot—
much harder for Kingfisher Mill this time, as Romanov finally warms to his task

there and is a sister to the Australian Guineas winner Zabeel and a half-sister to another winner of that race, Baryshnikov. Her dam, Lady Giselle, was unraced but from the family of Durtal, Detroit, Carnegie and Gildoran. Kingfisher Mill is a second foal, following the useful Lear Fan filly Dear Life, winner four times at around a mile and a half in 1996. The two-year-old of 1997, Rajati (by Chief's Crown), was tailed off on his only start.

		Never Bend	Nasrullah
	Riverman (USA)	(b 1960)	Lalun
	(b 1969)	River Lady	Prince John
Kingfisher Mill (USA)		(b 1963)	Nile Lily
(ch.c. 1994)		Sir Tristram	Sir Ivor
	Charming Life (NZ)	(b 1971)	Isolt
	(b 1987)	Lady Giselle	Nureyev
		(b 1982)	Valderna

Kingfisher Mill will have to improve a fair bit further to trouble the very best in 1998, but he's lightly raced and a tall individual with scope and that is certainly not out of the question. He often takes a good hold and wouldn't be sure to stay much beyond a mile and a half; indeed he could prove effective at a mile and a quarter given a good test. He's not been raced on going firmer than good since his debut. Lord Howard once referred to racehorse trainers as 'overpaid grooms'. Kingfisher Mill was turned out in fine shape for all of his starts and the overpaid groom who deserves plenty of credit in this instance is: *Mrs J. Cecil*

KING KATO 4 b.g. Unfuwain (USA) 131 – Sharmood (USA) (Sharpen Up 127) 91
[1996 93p: 10f³ 10.2d² 1997 10d³ 12m* 12s⁴ 12g Aug 20] big gelding: has a long stride: fairly useful performer: comfortably won apprentice maiden at Folkestone in July: good efforts starts either side: stays 1½m: successful on good to firm ground, but may prove suited by good or softer. *Mrs A. J. Perrett*

KING OF DANCE   2 ch.g. (Apr 12) King's Signet (USA) 110 – Times 55 (Junius   55
(USA) 124) [1997 5g⁴ 5m 5s 6g Aug 22] 17,000Y: smallish, sturdy gelding: sixth
reported foal: half-brother to winners around 1m by Forzando and by Superlative:
dam disappointing maiden: modest form first 3 starts, hampered final one: should
stay at least 6f. *B. S. Rothwell*

KING OF KINGS (IRE)   2 b.c. (Feb 27) Sadler's Wells (USA) 132 – Zum-   115
merudd (Habitat 134) [1997 6g* 6d* 6.3m² 7g* 8d* Sep 21]
    If column inches generated in the newspapers were always an accurate
indicator of success on the racecourse and in the breeding shed King of Kings
would already be a champion racehorse with an assured future as a sire of great
consequence. But they are not, and the fact is that, smart horse though he un-
doubtedly is, King of Kings hasn't yet fully matched his huge reputation where
it matters. The jury, as it were, is still out. But the good news is that there should
be further opportunities to assess King of Kings's merit on the course. An
operation on a bone chip in his off-fore knee after his final start of 1997
apparently went well and reports of probable retirement seem to have been
premature.
    Seldom can a debut win in an ordinary maiden have created such a stir
as King of Kings's racecourse bow at the Curragh (the venue for all of his races)
on Irish Two Thousand Guineas day in May. 'The next Nijinsky?' wondered
Michael Clower in *The Sporting Life* the next day, while jockey Christy Roche
claimed that the horse was better than the Derby winner Golden Fleece at
the same stage. Starting at 7/2 on, King of Kings treated his eight rivals like
platers, soon pulling double and striding almost effortlessly clear in the final
two furlongs to win by eight lengths. The drawback was that, though not
exactly platers, his rivals didn't strike us as a great bunch, judged on looks,
and first impressions were borne out when they managed just one win out of
twenty-three subsequent runs between them. Still, no-one could know that for
sure at the time, and, in any case, it was the horse's extraordinary homework
and the style of his victory more than its precise merit that presumably
prompted bookmakers to instal him as favourite for the Two Thousand Guineas
after it.
    It was a measure of the great expectations held for King of Kings that
his win in the Group 3 Arthur Guinness Railway Stakes on only his second start
came almost as an anticlimax. Only four were put up against him and he landed
odds of 9/2 by a length from his stable-companion, the useful Danyross, the
pair clear. King of Kings didn't have to be hard ridden to prevail but then again
he didn't seem to win with the proverbial ton in hand either. By now his odds
for the Two Thousand Guineas were amazingly around the 7/1 mark.
    King of Kings's fortunes ebbed and flowed in his three remaining races.
A shock short-head defeat by Lady Alexander in the Anglesey Stakes in July
was quickly explained away. King of Kings was found by the Turf Club vet
to be 'post-race abnormal' and he reportedly didn't eat up on returning home.
Christy Roche, who rode the horse in all of his races, claimed he'd wished he'd
withdrawn King of Kings at the start, and he was certainly at pains to give his
mount as easy a race as possible. The stewards accepted Roche's explanation
for not using his whip in view of the evidence.
    A win by one and a half lengths in a listed race in August revealed little
new about King of Kings; the Mark Johnston-trained runner-up Sharp Play is
of similar merit to Danyross. Neither was King of Kings's final win especially
informative. The Group 1 Aga Khan Studs National Stakes attracted nine runners in all, but none of the others had managed to win in pattern company (nor
did they subsequently) and the field finished in a bunch. That said, King of
Kings did well to overcome trouble in running, getting boxed in and quickening
nicely despite appearing to be struck over the head by a rival jockey's whip. At
the end of the mile on good to soft going King of Kings seemed not to have a
great deal in reserve in beating his stable-companion Celtic Cavalier by three

Aga Khan Studs National Stakes, the Curragh—King of Kings makes it four wins from five starts; his stable-companion Celtic Cavalier finishes second

quarters of a length, with the Sir Mark Prescott-trained Mountain Song just a short head further behind. In other respects his performance seemed fairly typical of him by now—he got rather warm in the preliminaries, took a bit of settling in the early stages and tended to carry his head high (understandable in the circumstances) in the closing stages.

What are King of Kings's prospects for 1998, assuming he has made a full recovery? Well, first off, it seems a good bet that a mile, a mile and a quarter at a push, will prove the limit of his stamina. Although by Sadler's Wells, a sire whose stamina index for older horses is around the twelve-furlong mark, King of Kings's distaff side boasts a lot of speed and his own racing characteristics seem to lean that way too. The dam, Zummerudd (who, at 240,000 guineas, cost only 10,000 guineas less as a yearling than King of Kings did as a foal), ran just twice but was a sister to the useful Irish two-year-old six-furlong winner Ancestral and the Italian seven-furlong and one-mile winner Steel Habit. Interestingly, when sent to Sadler's Wells, Steel Habit became the dam of the smart mile-and-a-quarter horse Batshoof, while to Be My Guest (like Sadler's Wells, a son of Northern Dancer) she produced the smart Sound Print, winner of the nine-furlong Hong Kong Derby but seemingly at least as effective at five furlongs. Zummerudd's dam, Ampulla, won the Cherry Hinton Stakes and was a half-sister to several speedy animals, including the Middle Park winner Steel Heart and the noted broodmare Chili Girl, dam of the King's Stand winner Chilibang. Zummerudd has had mixed fortunes at stud. Of her eight foals prior to King of Kings six were of little consequence but two (both by sons of Northern Dancer) were decidedly useful. Furajet (by The Minstrel) was best at the minimum trip, winning twice at two years, while General Monash didn't get a great deal further, gaining his biggest win in the five-and-a-half furlong Prix Robert Papin as a juvenile.

Mrs John Magnier's "King of Kings"

		Northern Dancer	Neartic
	Sadler's Wells (USA)	(b 1961)	Natalma
	(b 1981)	Fairy Bridge	Bold Reason
King of Kings (IRE)		(b 1975)	Special
(b.c. Feb 27, 1995)		Habitat	Sir Gaylord
	Zummerudd	(b 1966)	Little Hut
	(b 1981)	Ampulla	Crowned Prince
		(b 1974)	A.1.

Precocity as well as speed crops up time and again in the family, but at least King of Kings has the physical scope to go on from two to three years. He's a big, good-topped colt, and a good mover into the bargain. Apparently King of Kings may well go straight for the Two Thousand Guineas. At this stage we wouldn't put him in anything like the same league as Xaar, but connections reckon a strongly-run race (which also seems to suit the French colt) will bring the best out in their charge. If he does *need* a strongly-run race, then the likelihood of him staying beyond a mile will be lessened accordingly. It's to be hoped that King of Kings gets the chance to show his true colours in 1998. *A. P. O'Brien, Ireland*

KING OF PERU 4 br.c. Inca Chief (USA) – Julie's Star (IRE) 45 (Thatching 100 131) [1996 105d: 6g⁶ 6m³ 7f 7g* 7m 8m 6m 7g⁵ 6d² 7m⁵ 1997 6m³ 7m³ 7g 6m⁴ 6g 6g 6s⁴ 5.1m⁶ 6m⁶ 7g 6g Sep 20] tall colt: has a quick action: useful handicapper: left A. Jarvis after fifth outing: beaten less than 2 lengths when sixth in 30-runner Stewards' Cup at Goodwood on ninth start: effective at 6f to 7f: acts on firm and soft ground: blinkered (well held in Ayr Gold Cup) final outing: well below form when sweating and edgy once. *N. P. Littmoden*

KING OF SHOW (IRE) 6 b.g. Green Desert (USA) 127 – Don't Rush (USA) 42
93 (Alleged (USA) 138) [1996 62: 7.1m⁵ 5m* 5m* 6m² 5m 6m 6m 1997 5s 5s⁵ 5g
5.9m⁶ 8m 6m⁶ 8m Oct 1] leggy gelding: poor handicapper: effective at 6f to 1m: acts
on firm and soft ground: usually visored or blinkered nowadays. *R. Allan*

KING OF THE HORSE (IRE) 6 ch.g. Hatim (USA) 121 – Milly Whiteway –
112 (Great White Way (USA)) [1996 NR 1997 16m Apr 14] of little account nowadays. *W. Storey*

KING OF THE RIVER (USA) 2 b.c. (Feb 14) Kingmambo (USA) 125 – La 78
Favorita (FR) 115 (Nikos 124) [1997 7d³ 7m⁶ Oct 5] $140,000Y: first foal: dam
French 1m (including at 2 yrs) and 1¼m winner, later successful in USA: 4¼ lengths
third to Confirmation in minor event at Ayr: below that form in Leicester maiden
following month, soon beaten when asked, jockey not resorting to whip: will stay at
least 1m: flashed tail on debut. *P. W. Chapple-Hyam*

KING OF TUNES (FR) 5 b.h. Chief Singer 131 – Marcotte (Nebos (GER) 129) 92
[1996 79: a10g* a10g² 8m⁴ 10m² 1997 8m³ 8d⁶ 8g* 8m 9f⁶ 8m⁵ 10m⁶ 9d² 9m 10g
Oct 24] angular horse: fairly useful handicapper: won at Newmarket in June: left
J. Sheehan after slow start: creditable efforts on 3 of 4 outings for new trainer:
effective at 1m to 1¼m: acts on equitrack and on firm and soft ground: often early to
post: usually held up, and suited by strongly-run race. *M. J. Haynes*

KING PARROT (IRE) 9 br.g. King of Spain 121 – Red Lory 87 (Bay Express 58
132) [1996 59: a7g* a8g³ 7m* 7f* 7.1m* 8m⁴ 1997 8g 8m⁵ 7.6m⁴ 8g 8m Sep 24] big
gelding: modest handicapper: stays 1m: acts on the all-weather and firm ground: tried
visored, no improvement: used to go well fresh. *Lord Huntingdon*

KING PRIAM (IRE) 2 b.g. (Mar 2) Priolo (USA) 127 – Barinia (Corvaro (USA) –
124) [1997 7.1s Oct 15] 9,800F, 27,000Y: seventh foal: half-brother to 1½m/1¾m
winner Cuango (by Mtoto) and 3 winners abroad by Zino: dam French maiden:
backward and very green, behind in maiden at Haydock. *W. Jarvis*

KING PROTEA 3 b.c. Shareef Dancer (USA) 135 – Bright Crocus (USA) 119 –
(Clev Er Tell (USA)) [1996 NR 1997 10d Jul 17] sixth living foal: brother to Irish 13f
winner Saffron Crocus and half-brother to 2 winners abroad, including Colchis
Island (by Golden Fleece), maiden in Britain but stakes winner up to 1½m in USA:
dam 5f to 1m winner here at 2 yrs and Grade 3 8.5f winner in USA as 3-y-o: 5/2,
found little and tended to hang when tailed off in maiden at Leicester: sold approx.
£13,000 in Dubai in November. *J. H. M. Gosden*

KING RAT (IRE) 6 ch.g. King of Clubs 124 – Mrs Tittlemouse (Nonoalco –
(USA) 131) [1996 83: 7m 6.1m 6m 7m² 7.6d 7m 8m 7f a7g* 1997 a7g Feb 12] tall,
close-coupled gelding: still capable of fairly useful form at 5 yrs, but ran badly only
start in 1997. *J. G. M. O'Shea*

KINGS ARROW (IRE) 2 b.c. (Apr 24) Mujadil (USA) 119 – Great Leighs 87 71 p
(Vaigly Great 127) [1997 7d⁴ Oct 14] 24,000Y: leggy, useful-looking colt: sixth foal:
brother to 3-y-o Hello Dolly and half-brother to 2 winners, including miler Embank-
ment (by Tate Gallery): dam 1m winner: 5/1, seemed very green when just over 7
lengths fourth of 13 to Brave Reward in Leicester maiden, prominent for nearly 6f:
moved short to post: will improve. *M. Bell*

KINGS ASSEMBLY 5 b.h. Presidium 124 – To The Point 96 (Sharpen Up 127) –
[1996 81: 10g⁵ 10m* 10d³ 10m⁴ 10d 10.3m 10.4g 1997 10s 10.2g 10s Oct 14] tall
horse: fairly useful 1¼m handicapper at 4 yrs: well below form in 1997. *P. W. Harris*

KINGS CHECK 2 b.c. (Jan 30) Komaite (USA) – Ski Baby (Petoski 135) [1997 52
5m⁵ 6m⁶ a7g⁵ Sep 8] second foal: brother to fair 5f winner Queens Check: dam never a62
ran: modest maiden: well beaten in visor second start. *Miss J. F. Craze*

KINGSDOWN TRIX (IRE) 3 b.g. Contract Law (USA) 108 – Three of –
Trumps (Tyrnavos 129) [1996 50: 6g 7f⁶ 5f 7g a8g⁵ 1997 a8g⁴ a8g⁶ a10g* a12g⁴ a63
a12g* a11g⁶ a12g* 10m⁵ 12f a10g 10f 11.9m⁴ Aug 15] modest performer on the
all-weather: won handicaps at Lingfield in February and March (seller) and seller at
Wolverhampton in May: stays 1½m: no form on turf: joined R. Smith and won over
hurdles. *G. L. Moore*

Harefield Conditions Stakes, Windsor—King Sound (left) and Haltarra have it between them

KINGS HARMONY (IRE)   4 b.g. Nordico (USA) – Kingston Rose (Tudor   76
Music 131) [1996 71, a79: 6.1d⁶ 6f* 6.1m⁴ 5.1m 6g² 7.1m³ 7f* 7f⁶ a7g² a6g² a–
1997 7f⁴ 6g⁴ 7m* 6g⁴ 6g² 6.9g⁵ 6m a7g a6g Nov 21] lengthy gelding: fair performer:
made all in claimer at Brighton (successful 3 times there) in July: poor efforts final 3
starts: effective at 6f/7f: acts on firm ground and the all-weather: goes well with forcing tactics. *P. J. Makin*

KING'S HUSSAR   2 b.g. (Mar 22) Be My Chief (USA) 122 – Croire (IRE) 74   59
(Lomond (USA) 128) [1997 7.1g a7g⁶ 7g 8m Oct 5] 11,000Y: first foal: dam 1m
winner from good family: modest form, soon off bridle, in maidens and a nursery
(gelded after): should be suited by 1m+. *P. F. I. Cole*

KING SLAYER   2 b.c. (Mar 5) Batshoof 122 – Top Sovereign (High Top 131)   66 p
[1997 7d³ Oct 27] 10,000Y, 27,000 2-y-o: third living foal: dam French 1¼m winner
out of smart sprinter Sovereign Rose: 20/1, 4¼ lengths third to Khalas in steadily-run
maiden at Lingfield, not clear run then keeping on: should stay at least 1m: should
improve. *B. Smart*

KING'S MISTRESS   2 ch.f. (Apr 24) King's Signet (USA) 110 – Rectory Maid   –
74 (Tina's Pet 121) [1997 a7g Sep 8] 500Y: fourth reported foal: dam 2-y-o 6f
winner: well held in maiden at Southwell. *D. C. O'Brien*

KING SOUND   3 br.c. Caerleon (USA) 132 – Flood (USA) (Riverman (USA)   111
131) [1996 108p: 7g⁴ 8m* 8g³ 1997 10g³ 12m⁴ 11.6m* 12g³ Sep 27] smallish good-
bodied colt: has been fired: smart performer: won 4-runner minor event at Windsor
in August by a head from Haltarra, pair clear: best effort when 1¾ lengths third of 8
to Kingfisher Mill in Cumberland Lodge Stakes at Ascot final start, taking good hold
but staying on well: stays 1½m: yet to race on ground softer than good: sent to UAE.
J. H. M. Gosden

KING'S SHILLING (USA)   10 b.g. Fit To Fight (USA) – Pride's Crossing (USA)   –
(Riva Ridge (USA)) [1996 NR 1997 a11g Jan 10] no longer of any account. *H. Oliver*

KINGS VISION   5 gr.g. Absalom 128 – Eye Sight 67 (Roscoe Blake 120) [1996   –
NR 1997 8m Apr 12] no longer of any account. *W. Jenks*

KING UNO   3 b.g. Be My Chief (USA) 122 – The Kings Daughter 79 (Indian King   60
(USA) 128) [1996 54+: 5m a7g 6g⁵ 6m 7g 7m 1997 8.2m 8d 8g⁴ 6g* 6.9m² 6s³
5.9m⁵ 6g 6d* 7m³ 6g⁴ 7g³ Oct 24] strong, good-topped gelding: good mover: modest
handicapper: won at Pontefract in June and Haydock (22-runner seller, retained for
10,000 gns) in September: has form at 7f, but may prove ideally suited by strongly-
run 6f: acts on good to firm and dead ground, probably on soft: usually visored
nowadays: tends to hang, and sometimes looks none too keen. *Mrs J. R. Ramsden*

520

KINLOCHEWE   4 b.f. Old Vic 136 – Reuval 102 (Sharpen Up 127) [1996 102: – 10g* 10.4m² 10m 10m² 12m³ 1997 10g Aug 13] close-coupled filly: useful at 3 yrs for H. Cecil: tailed off only start in 1997: sold 120,000 gns in December, in foal to Cadeaux Genereux. *J. A. R. Toller*

KINNESCASH (IRE)   4 ch.g. Persian Heights 129 – Gayla Orchestra (Lord   72 Gayle (USA) 124) [1996 56: a8.5g 12d 10.2g 10.8g⁶ 8.3m 8.1g a12g² a12s 1997 a11g⁴ 10d* 11.6s* 10.5g³ 13.3f² Jul 19] small gelding: fair handicapper: won at Leicester in April and Windsor in June: effective at 1¼m/1½m: acts on hard and soft ground and on fibresand: fairly useful hurdler: genuine and consistent. *P. Bowen*

KINOKO   9 ch.g. Bairn (USA) 126 – Octavia (Sallust 134) [1996 NR 1997 16.1g*   47 16.2m* 16.2s 16g⁶ 16.2v⁵ 16m 15.8m Sep 20] sparely-made gelding: poor handicapper: won at Newcastle in March and Beverley in April: below form afterwards: stays 2m: acts on firm and dead going, unsuited by soft: tail swisher. *K. W. Hogg, Isle of Man*

KINTAVI   7 b.g. Efisio 120 – Princess Tavi (Sea Hawk II 131) [1996 NR 1997   58 14.1g³ 13s² 13s* 11.8g² 12m Jun 7] modest handicapper: in good form in first half of year, and won at Hamilton in May: effective at 1½m to 1¾m: acts on firm and soft ground: held up. *T. W. Donnelly*

KIPPILAW   3 ch.f. Selkirk (USA) 129 – Contralto 100 (Busted 134) [1996 63: 7m – 7m² 6d 1997 8g 7m⁴ 5.9f Jun 12] leggy, sparely-made filly: modest at best at 2 yrs: well below form in 1997: sold 10,500 gns in December. *M. Johnston*

KIRA   7 b.m. Starry Night (USA) – Irish Limerick 89 (Try My Best (USA) 130)   89 [1996 75: a6g² a6g* a5g* a6g² a6g⁴ a5g* a6g⁶ 5g* 5g⁵ 6.1m 6f² 5f* 5m* 5g³ 6g² 5m⁴   a76 5d 5g 1997 a7g⁵ a5g³ 6m* 6m² 5f* 5g⁵ a6g⁵ 6g² 5g 5g 5d⁴ 5d 5g 6m 5d Nov 7] leggy mare: fairly useful handicapper on turf, fair on all-weather: won at Doncaster in March and Redcar in May: good efforts afterwards when in frame: best efforts at 5f/6f: acts on firm going (probably on dead) and all-weather: effective from front or held up: usually bandaged: tough and genuine. *J. L. Eyre*

KIRBY OPPORTUNITY   9 ch.m. Mummy's Game 120 – Empress Catherine – 73 (Welsh Pageant 132) [1996 NR 1997 a14.8g⁶ Dec 13] modest winner around 1½m in 1992: twice raced and no form since: tried blinkered. *G. A. Ham*

KIRKHAM   3 ch.g. Golden Lahab (USA) – Topcliffe 66 (Top Ville 129) [1996 NR – 1997 10g a11g⁶ 12g⁵ Aug 5] first foal: dam, 1½m winner, stayed 17f: of little account. *Mrs V. A. Aconley*

KIRKWALL   3 ch.c. Selkirk (USA) 129 – Kamkova (USA) 62 (Northern Dancer)   118 [1996 8d⁶ 7.5s 1997 9d* 8d* 8m* 9.3s* 9m³ 10g* 10g⁵ Aug 15] sixth foal: half-

Prix Eugene Adam, Saint-Cloud—Kirkwall (No. 1) gets up to beat Rajpoute; Romanov is third

brother to 3 winners, notably fairly useful stayer Northern Fleet (by Slip Anchor):
dam, placed at 11.7f and 15.5f, from family of top-class middle-distance performers
Vanlandingham and Temperence Hill: smart French colt: won minor events at Compiegne and Saint-Cloud in March, listed race at Saint-Cloud in April, Prix de Guiche
at Longchamp (beat Aneysar a length) in May and Prix Eugene Adam at Saint-Cloud
(by short head from Rajpoute) in July: also ran well in defeat, staying on when 1½
lengths third of 5 to Starborough in Prix Jean Prat at Chantilly: likely to stay 1½m:
acts on good to firm and soft ground: to be trained by R. Frankel in USA. *A. Fabre,
France*

KIROV PROTEGE (IRE)   5 b.g. Dancing Dissident (USA) 119 – Still River   38
(Kings Lake (USA) 133) [1996 –: 10.8f 10d 12f⁴ 9.7g³ 7.6m 10d 10m a10g⁵ a10s⁶
a6g a8g a10g 1997 a12g⁵ a16g⁵ 15.4m⁶ 15.4m 10m⁵ 11.9f⁶ 16.4m 10.8m* 8d⁵ 10d³
9.7s 11.9m 11.5g 8g 11.9f³ 10.8g 10m Oct 23] smallish gelding: poor handicapper:
won apprentice event at Warwick in June: left Mrs L. Jewell after thirteenth outing:
stays 1½m, at least in steadily-run race: acts on firm and dead going: tried in blinkers
and visor, no improvement: inconsistent. *G. L. Moore*

KISSANDY   3 b.f. Batshoof 122 – Amazing Journey (USA) (Spectacular Bid   –
(USA)) [1996 NR 1997 a12g 12.4m⁵ 10m 14.1m 13.8g Aug 5] of little account.
Mrs V. A. Aconley

KISSAVOS   11 ch.g. Cure The Blues (USA) – Hairbrush (USA) (Sir Gaylord)   –
[1996 –: a10g a10g 1997 a8g⁶ a8g Jan 24] no longer of any account. *B. J. Meehan*

KISSEL   5 b.m. Warning 136 – Ice Chocolate (USA) 77 (Icecapade (USA)) [1996   52
–: 7.1d⁵ 9.2g⁵ 6m 10m⁶ 8g 1997 8g 7s³ a7g 8m 10d Aug 30] modest performer: stays
1m: acts on good to firm and heavy ground, seemingly on fibresand. *S. E. Kettlewell*

KISTENA (FR)   4 gr.f. Miswaki (USA) 124 – Mabrova 108 (Prince Mab (FR)   116
124) [1996 123: 6.5g⁵ 5.5m* 5.5g² 5m* 6m² 6g* 6g* 5d* 1997 6g³ 5f⁴ 5d² 6f Dec
14] sturdy French filly: reportedly suffered chip in left knee when winning 1996 Prix
de l'Abbaye de Longchamp, and off course nearly a year (also reportedly had a back
problem) before reappearance: easily best of 4 runs in 1997 when never-nearer
¾-length fourth of 12 to Carmine Lake in Abbaye again: stays 6f: acts on dead
ground, probably on firm. *Mme C. Head, France*

KITE   2 ch.f. (Mar 25) Thatching 131 – Melaka (Kris 135) [1997 6s 7g⁵ 7m³ 7m⁴   44
8m⁶ 6m⁴ a6g³ Sep 30] 2,800Y: workmanlike filly: shows knee action: first foal: dam,
placed over 1½m in France, from good family: poor maiden: stays 7f: below form on
fibresand: sold, and sent to Holland. *M. Bell*

KITOPH (IRE)   2 b.f. (May 22) Night Shift (USA) – Soxoph 67 (Hotfoot 126)   – p
[1997 7m Oct 1] IR 10,000Y: eighth foal: half-sister to useful 6f (at 2 yrs) to 1½m
winner Bearall (by Al Hareb) and French 5.5f (at 2 yrs) and 7f winner Improvement
(by Try My Best): dam, 1m winner, closely related to Domynsky: 14/1 and burly,
better than bare result when eleventh of 20 in at Salisbury, slowly away and not
knocked about: should do better. *E. A. L. Dunlop*

KITTY KITTY CANCAN   4 b.f. Warrshan (USA) 117 – Kittycatoo Katango   –
(USA) (Verbatim (USA)) [1996 73: 10m² 12m 9m 11.6m⁵ 12m 11.8g⁴ a10g³ 1997
a10g Jan 9] fair maiden handicapper: well beaten only 4-y-o start: in foal to Gold-
mark. *Lady Herries*

KLIPSPINGER   4 ch.f. Formidable (USA) 125 – Distant Relation (Great   –
Nephew 126) [1996 –, a68d: a6g* a8g a6g² a6g² a6g³ 5m a5g⁵ a6g a6g a6g 1997 a6s²   a58
a6g⁵ a6g a6g⁵ a6g 5.1g 7.5v Jul 4] strong, lengthy filly: modest performer at best on
fibresand, no form on turf: stays 6f: usually blinkered/visored: has had tongue tied.
B. S. Rothwell

KLONDIKE CHARGER (USA)   3 b.g. Crafty Prospector (USA) – Forever   75
Waving (USA) (Hoist The Flag (USA)) [1996 68: 7m 6m 7d 1997 8d 8g³ 10m²
12.3m² 16.5g³ 16m² 16m Aug 26] useful-looking gelding: fair maiden: barely stays
2m: acts on good to firm ground, well below form on dead: ran badly in visor final
start: sold 13,000 gns in October, to join J. Old, then gelded. *B. W. Hills*

KNAVE   4 b.g. Prince Sabo 123 – Royal Agnes 71 (Royal Palace 131) [1996 57d: 38 d
7s⁵ 8.2g 8.1g 11.1g 9.2g⁴ 1997 8s⁴ 8m 10g 7.1g⁵ 10.9g 11.1g⁶ 9.2d Aug 13]
disappointing maiden: tried visored. *P. Monteith*

KNAVE'S ASH (USA)   6 ch.g. Miswaki (USA) 124 – Quiet Rendezvous (USA)   79
(Nureyev (USA) 131) [1996 a9.9g⁵ a10g⁶ a8g a10g⁶ 1997 a9f a8f 6g 6m⁶ 7g⁵ 7.6s
8m 8g⁶ 7m Oct 28] compact, attractive gelding: useful performer for M. Stoute at 4
yrs: unplaced on all 6 starts in Dubai, and sold 12,500 gns in July: fair at best in 7
runs in handicaps for new trainer: stays 1¼m: acts on firm going: blinkered (on sand)
once. *D. Nicholls*

KNIFE EDGE (USA)   2 b. or br.c. (Apr 15) Kris S (USA) – My Turbulent Miss   – p
(USA) (My Dad George (USA)) [1997 7m Oct 22] $250,000F: brother to 3 winners
in USA/Japan, notably Breeders' Cup Turf winner Prized and half-brother to several
winners in USA: dam unraced: sire (by Roberto) minor stakes winner at up to 9f:
14/1 and green, never-dangerous seventh of 13 to Misbah in maiden at Yarmouth:
seems sure to do fair bit better over 1m+. *M. R. Stoute*

KNIGHTCRACKER   2 b.f. (Mar 30) Cadeaux Genereux 131 – Top Treat (USA)   –
101 (Topsider (USA)) [1997 7d a7g a7g Dec 12] 1,000Y: sixth foal: half-sister to
4-y-o Rehaab and 6-y-o Ela Man Howa: dam 6f winner who probably stayed 1m: no
sign of ability. *R. E. Peacock*

KNOBBLEENEEZE   7 ch.g. Aragon 118 – Proud Miss (USA) (Semi-Pro) [1996   80
80: 8s 7s 7g 7s⁶ 7.3s² 7m* 8m⁴ 8f⁵ 8d³ 7.3m⁵ 7.6d 7.1f 7.3m⁴ 7m 7g 7g 7s 7g 1997
8m 8d* 7.6v² 8d 7d³ 7.3g 7m 7.1m 7.6m 7m 7g 7s⁵ 8d⁵ 7d* 7m 8s Nov 6] sturdy
gelding: fairly useful handicapper: won at Ripon (ladies race) in April and Ayr in
September: effective at 7f/1m: has form on firm going, but best recent efforts on
good ground or softer: successful on equitrack earlier in career: usually visored, but
effective when not: good mount for inexperienced rider: tough. *M. R. Channon*

KNOTTY HILL   5 b.g. Green Ruby (USA) 104 – Esilam 62 (Frimley Park 109)   77
[1996 77: 8g⁵ 8f² 8s⁶ 7m³ 8f 8d 7m³ 8s 1997 a7g* a8g a7g² 7m 6d² 5m 6g³ 7s 6g 6g   a87
8s Nov 8] tall, workmanlike gelding: fairly useful performer: won maiden at Southwell in February: creditable efforts when placed in handicaps afterwards: well beaten
last 4 starts: probably best at 6f/7f: acts on firm and dead ground and on fibresand:
usually races prominently. *R. Craggs*

KOATHARY (USA)   6 b.g. Capote (USA) – Jeffo (USA) (Ridan (USA)) [1996   83 d
86: 10g⁴ 10.8f⁴ 10d³ 11.4m 10g 9f* 8.1d* 9m* 1997 8s 8.3m⁶ 8s² 8.1d³ 8d 9d 8d 10g
Oct 24] big, lengthy gelding: fairly useful handicapper: well below form last 5 starts:
best form at 1m/9f: acts on firm and soft ground: usually held up: sold 20,000 gns in
November. *L. G. Cottrell*

KOLBY   2 b.g. (Mar 25) Superpower 113 – Abrasive 53 (Absalom 128) [1997 5g²   58
6d⁴ Jul 3] 12,500Y: robust gelding: half-brother to winning 2-y-o sprinters Oyston's
World (in 1989, by Reesh) and Mary From Dunlow (in 1990, by Nicholas Bill): dam,
stayed 6f, ran only at 2 yrs: close second in seller at Windsor: odds on, disappointing in similar event under a month later (subsequently gelded): blinkered both starts.
A. Bailey

KOMASEPH   5 b.g. Komaite (USA) – Starkist 81 (So Blessed 130) [1996 NR   48
1997 a6g a7g² 6m⁶ a6g a6g 7g Aug 20] workmanlike gelding: half-brother to several
winners, notably fairly useful miler Star of A Gunner (by Gunner B): dam 2-y-o 5f
winner: poor maiden on balance of form: stays 7f. *R. F. Marvin*

KOMASTA   3 b.g. Komaite (USA) – Sky Fighter 43 (Hard Fought 125) [1996 64:   64
a5g³ 5.9g 5m⁴ a5g³ a6g a6g a7g* 1997 a8.5g² a7g a7g² 6.1m a6g a8.5g Aug 8] rather
leggy gelding: modest handicapper: stays 8.5f: acts on good to firm ground, goes
well on fibresand: sometimes sweats: best form without visor. *Capt. J. Wilson*

KOMI   3 b.g. Soviet Star (USA) 128 – Home Address 83 (Habitat 134) [1996 NR   96
1997 7g² 8.1g³ 8g* 8m² 10.4m Jul 12] deep-bodied gelding: seventh foal: half-
brother to useful 1¼m winner Howard's End (by Shaadi) and a winner in Italy by
Persian Bold: dam, 10.8f winner, out of 1000 Guineas winner Full Dress II: useful
performer: won maiden at Thirsk in May: best effort when 1½ lengths second of 28
to Fly To The Stars in Britannia Handicap at Royal Ascot, staying on well: never
placed to challenge only subsequent outing: should stay at least 9f: sold approx.
£74,000 in Dubai in November. *M. R. Stoute*

KOMISTAR   2 ch.c. (Mar 25) Komaite (USA) – Rosie's Gold 57 (Glint of Gold   95
128) [1997 6g 7g* 8g³ Oct 25] 6,000Y: workmanlike colt: first foal: dam 1½m win-

KOM

ner: 33/1, easy 5-length winner of maiden at Warwick in October: improved again when close third of 5 to Distant Image in minor event at Newbury, making running and rallying: will stay 1¼m: useful. *P. W. Harris*

KOMLUCKY 5 b.m. Komaite (USA) – Sweet And Lucky (Lucky Wednesday 53
124) [1996 53: a7g³ a8g 7.1g 6g⁵ a7g² 6m² 6m a6g 8m a7g² 6.9f⁴ 7f² 7d² 7g* 7g a7g⁴ a7g⁶ 1997 a6g a7g 7g 7f³ 7g* 7m³ 7d 6s⁵ 7g 7g 7m 7m Oct 28] leggy mare: modest performer: won seller at Thirsk in May: stays 7f: acts on fibresand and on firm and dead ground: usually blinkered/visored: takes keen hold: none too consistent. *A. B. Mulholland*

KOMODO (USA) 5 ch.g. Ferdinand (USA) – Platonic Interest (USA) (Drone) –
[1996 42: a10g 8m 10m 8.3m 6.9m⁵ 8.1g a10g³ a8g a10g a10g 1997 a13g a10g a10g a10g 6.9m⁶ 6.9m Jul 14] no longer of much account. *J. E. Long*

KOMPLETELY 3 b.f. Komaite (USA) – Lucky Councillor (Lucky Wednesday –
124) [1996 NR 1997 a7g a8g Dec 18] third reported foal: dam never ran: no sign of ability. *J. Neville*

KOMREYEV DANCER 5 b.g. Komaite (USA) – L'Ancressaan 67 (Dalsaan –
125) [1996 80, a84: a9.4g⁴ a9.4g a9.4g² a8g⁵ a10g⁴ 9.9m* 10.3g 10g* 9.9f³ 10f 10m³ 10g⁶ 10m² 10.1m⁶ 1997 a8.5g a10g⁵ a9.4g Dec 13] leggy gelding: has a round action: fairly useful winner at 1¼m as 4-y-o: showed nothing in 3 starts late in 1997. *A. Bailey*

KONKER 2 ch.g. (Mar 6) Selkirk (USA) 129 – Helens Dreamgirl 95 (Caerleon 65 ?
(USA) 132) [1997 6m⁶ 8m 10m⁵ Oct 6] 22,000Y: unfurnished gelding: half-brother to 4-y-o Florentino and 5-y-o House of Dreams: dam 1¼m winner: modest form first 2 starts in maidens: edgy and sweating final outing: should stay 1¼m. *W. J. Haggas*

KOOL KAT KATIE (IRE) 3 gr.f. Fairy King (USA) – Miss Toot 72 (Ardross 120
134) [1996 NR 1997 7g* 8g* 10m² 10m* Oct 19] tall filly: has scope: has a quick action: third living foal: closely related to NH winner by Scenic: dam 1¼m and 15f winner on only starts: won newcomers event at Newbury in April (reportedly lame) and listed race at Deauville in August before neck second of 8 to One So Wonderful in Sun Chariot Stakes at Newmarket (strong challenge final 2f) on final start in Europe: won 9-runner E P Taylor Stakes at Woodbine in October, having to wait for a run before beating Mousse Glacee 1¼ lengths, reportedly bleeding after race despite having been given medication beforehand: stays 1¼m well: raced only on good and good to firm ground: due to stay in USA (reportedly with J. Sheppard): sure to win more good races provided all is well with her. *D. R. Loder*

KOORDINAITE 3 b.f. Komaite (USA) – Fair Dino 48 (Thatch (USA) 136) –
[1996 –: 6g 6d 6m 1997 a8g Jun 6] of little account. *W. J. Musson*

KORALOONA (IRE) 4 b.g. Archway (IRE) 115 – Polynesian Charm (USA) 66
(What A Pleasure (USA)) [1996 –: 8m 8.3g⁶ 8.3m 10m 9.7d 1997 10s 10g² 9g⁴ 10s* 12d* 10m⁵ 11.6g* 12g⁴ 12v Oct 10] tall gelding: fair handicapper: in good form in the summer, winning at Goodwood (twice, second an amateurs event) and Windsor: stays 1½m: acts on good to firm and soft ground. *G. B. Balding*

KOSEVO (IRE) 3 b.g. Shareef Dancer (USA) 135 – Kallista (Zeddaan 130) 49
[1996 –: 9f⁵ 1997 10m 8s a8.5g⁵ 7m⁴ 7f⁵ a7g⁵ Nov 13] poor maiden handicapper: stays 7f: acts on firm ground: reluctant to race in visor on debut, hung right final start. *M. G. Meagher*

KOTA 4 b.g. Kris 135 – Lady Be Mine (USA) 76 (Sir Ivor 135) [1996 NR 1997 71
11.8f* 10s 10g May 27] half-brother to several winners, including leading 1989 2-y-o (successful at 6f to 1m) Be My Chief and 9f to 14.6f winner Chief Bee (both by Chief's Crown): dam 1m winner out of half-sister to dam of Marwell: won slowly-run 6-runner maiden at Leicester in April: disappointing in minor event at Windsor and handicap at Leicester afterwards, and subsequently gelded: should prove as effective at 1¼m as 1½m. *J. Wharton*

KRABLOONIK (FR) 3 b.g. Bering 136 – Key Role (Be My Guest (USA) 126) 55
[1996 NR 1997 8.3s a9.4g a7g⁶ a9.4g⁴ 10s Jul 5] 40,000Y: half-brother to 3 winners, including Italian 1994 2-y-o 7.5f winner Kafkaienne and French 1¼m winner Kellerman (both by Groom Dancer): dam French maiden: modest maiden: should stay 1¼m: joined W. G. M. Turner. *Sir Mark Prescott*

KRAM 3 ch.g. Kris 135 – Balenare (Pharly (FR) 130) [1996 7d⁴ 8.5m 8d 8g⁵ 9s   60
1997 6g 8d 8d⁶ 8.5g² 7s⁶ 5g* 5m² 5d⁴ 7g⁵ Oct 24] leggy ex-Irish gelding: third foal:
half-brother to 2 winners in France, including useful 7f (at 2 yrs) to 9f winner Contare
(by Shirley Heights): dam half-sister to a Park Hill runner-up: modest handicapper:
won at Tralee in August on final start for P. J. Prendergast: creditable efforts all
3 starts in Britain: effective at 5f to 8.5f: acts on good to firm and dead ground.
Mrs P. N. Dutfield

KRAYYAN DAWN 7 ch.g. Krayyan 117 – Tana Mist 71 (Homeboy 114) [1996   44
NR 1997 11.6g 12m 12d 10.8g³ a12g³ a12g⁶ Nov 6] stocky gelding: just a poor
handicapper nowadays: stays 1½m when conditions aren't testing: acts on good to
firm and dead ground and on equitrack. *J. Akehurst*

KRISAMBA 2 ch.c. (Feb 25) Kris 135 – Lia's Dance (Lead On Time (USA) 123)   80
[1997 6.1m 7d³ 7m⁵ Nov 4] 31,000Y: angular colt: first foal: dam French 2-y-o 1m
winner from family of Irish River and champion US sprinter Cardmania: easily best
effort in maidens when running-on third to Brave Reward at Leicester, despite having
virtually bolted to post: should stay 1m. *B. J. Meehan*

KRISCLIFFE 4 ch.c. Kris 135 – Lady Norcliffe (USA) (Norcliffe (CAN)) [1996   –
83: 9m² 8.1d⁶ a7g 10m⁴ 12m 10m 10.5s 1997 a10g⁵ 10m 8m 10s 9.7m 8g Oct 22]
good-topped colt: fairly useful at best, but no form in 1997. *G. Lewis*

KRIS GREEN (IRE) 3 ch.c. Kris 135 – Green Lucia 116 (Green Dancer (USA)   92
132) [1996 8g 7g* 1997 10f³ 12g⁶ 14g⁴ 10f⁴ 12m Sep 12] good-topped ex-Irish colt:
brother to 2 winners, notably useful Korambi (stayed 1½m), and half-brother to
several winners, notably smart 1½m winner Luchiroverte (by Slip Anchor): dam
placed in Irish and Yorkshire Oaks: fairly useful performer: trained first 4 starts by
D. Weld, on third of them: fourth of 8 in listed race at Leopardstown in May: tailed
off only outing in Britain: stays 1¾m: yet to race on ground softer than good:
blinkered (well beaten) fourth start: sold 15,000 gns and joined L. Lungo. *R. Hannon*

KRISPY KNIGHT 2 ch.c. (Mar 22) Kris 135 – Top Table 65 (Shirley Heights   91
130) [1997 6g³ 6m* 7g³ 7g⁵ Aug 30] heavy-topped colt: second foal: dam, maiden,
stayed 1½m, from family of On The House and Rebecca Sharp: fairly useful form:
won minor event at Newmarket in July: ran creditably afterwards in similar event at
Salisbury and Futurity Stakes at the Curragh: should stay 1m. *J. W. Hills*

KRISTAL BREEZE 5 ch.m. Risk Me (FR) 127 – Mistral's Dancer (Shareef   60
Dancer (USA) 135) [1996 62: 10.1s 10g⁴ 12d² 10d* 11.1m⁶ 11.6m* 12.3m⁵ 12g*
10g* 11.9g 10g⁴ 12g 1997 9.7g 10d 10g 10g³ 10m⁶ 10d³ 11.6s 12g* Jul 9] lengthy
mare: modest handicapper: won at Folkestone in July: effective at 1¼m and 1½m:
acts on good to firm and dead ground, well held in visor both starts on fibresand:
genuine. *W. R. Muir*

KRISTAL BRIDGE 3 ch.f. Kris 135 – Connaught Bridge 124 (Connaught 130)   75 d
[1996 NR 1997 9m⁶ 10m⁶ 10m⁶ 8d⁶ 8.3m a11g³ 11.1m a9.4g Oct 4] tall filly: shows
plenty of knee action: half-sister to several winners, notably smart 1986 French 2-y-o
Conmaiche (later won at 11f, by King's Lake) and useful 1½m to 1¾m winner Wassl
Reef (by Wassl): dam won Nassau Stakes and Yorkshire Oaks: fair maiden at best:
below form last 6 starts, well beaten in blinkers on final 2. *P. W. Harris*

KRISTOPHER 3 ch.c. Kris 135 – Derniere Danse (Gay Mecene (USA) 128)   60
[1996 –: 7g³ 8.2s 1997 8.2m a7g⁶ 8.3g a8g³ 7.1d⁴ 8d 8d Oct 28] strong colt: modest
maiden: stays 1m: acts on good to firm ground and on equitrack: none too consistent.
J. W. Hills

KROSNO 3 ch.g. Kris 135 – Pastorale 91 (Nureyev (USA) 131) [1996 NR 1997   73
a8g⁵ a9.4g a8.5g⁵ 8s² 8m* 10.2m² 11.6s² 11m⁴ 14.1m⁶ 11.5m* 11.5g⁴ 12m 12m
Sep 26] 5,000 2-y-o: lengthy gelding: has a markedly round action: first foal: dam,
7f winner from 3 starts, from very good family: fair performer: won maiden at
Musselburgh in April and handicap at Lingfield in July: stays 11.5f, possibly not
1¾m: acts on good to firm and soft ground: usually makes running, set too strong
pace last 2 starts: sold 12,500 gns in October, and went to Ireland. *S. C. Williams*

KRYSTAL DAVEY (IRE) 3 b.g. Classic Music (USA) – Robin Red Breast 74   57
(Red Alert 127) [1996 57: 5m⁶ a5g a6g 1997 a5g* a6g⁵ a5g⁶ a5g Dec 8] modest
handicapper: won at Lingfield in January: sold out of T. D. Barron's stable 1,100 gns

before final start (first for 9 months): best form at 5f: acts on good to firm ground and equitrack. *S. R. Bowring*

KRYSTAL MAX (IRE) 4 b.g. Classic Music (USA) – Lake Isle (IRE) (Caerleon (USA) 132) [1996 72, a88: a5g* a7g* 5d⁶ 6.1g 6m⁵ 7s a6g a7g 1997 a5g² a6g³ a5g* a6g⁵ a7g a6g a6g 6g 6f Jun 4] smallish, good-topped gelding: fair at best on all-weather in 1997: claimed out of T. D. Barron's stable £7,000 after winning claimer at Lingfield in January: little form for new stable: stays 7f: acts on firm and dead ground and on all-weather. *J. Cullinan* — a77 d

K S SUNSHINE (USA) 3 b.f. Sunshine Forever (USA) – Lake Worth (USA) (Cure The Blues (USA)) [1996 NR 1997 a6g⁴ a6g³ Apr 8] first foal: dam minor winning sprinter in USA: poor form in fibresand maidens: will stay 7f. *W. J. Haggas* — 43

KUALA LIPIS (USA) 4 b.c. Lear Fan (USA) 130 – Caerna (USA) (Caerleon (USA) 132) [1996 91: 8d⁵ 10m⁴ 7.9m* 10m⁶ 1997 a8.5g⁴ 8m* 8g 10.3d² 8.1g 12m 10.4m 10s⁴ 10.4g⁵ 10.3m 10.5m⁵ 10m⁴ Oct 5] strong, angular colt: reportedly had sinus operation before reappearance: useful handicapper: won Lincoln Handicap at Doncaster in March by short head from Hawksley Hill: best efforts afterwards at Chester and Sandown on fourth and fifth starts: effective at 1m (given strong gallop) to 1¼m, probably not 1½m: acts on fibresand and on good to firm and soft going: tried blinkered, better form when not: sometimes wanders under pressure. *P. F. I. Cole* — 95

KULEPOPSIE (IRE) 4 b.f. Contract Law (USA) 108 – Flight Fantasy (USA) 54 (Air Forbes Won (USA)) [1996 –: a9.4g⁶ 1997 a9.4f a7g⁴ 12.4m³ 16.2d 10.4s 15.8m Sep 20] poor maiden: should stay 1¾m: acts on good to firm ground: well beaten in blinkers. *A. B. Mulholland* — 41

KUMAIT (USA) 3 b. or br.g. Danzig (USA) – Colour Chart (USA) 122 (Mr Prospector (USA)) [1996 86: 6f 6m³ 7d⁶ 6m² 6m³ 6g³ 6g* 1997 5g 8g³ 7.9d 8m³ Sep 12] strong-quartered gelding: fluent mover: fairly useful performer: best effort (first run after leaving Saeed bin Suroor) when close third of 7 to Beauchamp King in minor event at Doncaster in July, though did have run of race: soundly beaten both subsequent outings: probably stays 1m: acts on good to firm and dead ground: sometimes wears tongue strap: joined E. Dunlop and gelded. *D. R. Loder* — 94

KUMATOUR 3 b.c. Batshoof 122 – Runelia (Runnett 125) [1997 8s² Nov 14] 28,000Y: fifth foal: half-brother to 3-y-o Rock Fantasy, 1995 2-y-o 5f seller winner Sporting Fantasy (by Primo Dominie) and 7f (at 2 yrs) and 8.3f winner Rock Foundation (by Rock City): dam half-sister to smart sprinter Touch Paper: runner-up in minor event at Milan in November. *L. M. Cumani* — 83 p

Worthington Lincoln Handicap, Doncaster—
the winner Kuala Lipis is almost hidden by runner-up Hawksley Hill
as the pair go past the blinkered Tumbleweed Ridge

KUSTOM KIT KATE 2 b.f. (Apr 28) Tragic Role (USA) – Wing of Freedom 55
(Troy 137) [1997 a7g^4 a6g 5m^3 6.1m Sep 15] 3,800 2-y-o: unfurnished filly: has a
fluent, round action: fifth foal: half-sister to 1995 2-y-o 5f winner Montrestar (by
Mon Tresor): dam staying maiden in Ireland: modest form in maiden and nursery last
2 starts: ran on fibresand first 2. *S. R. Bowring*

KUSTOM KIT KLASSIC 3 b.c. Chilibang 120 – Norvi (Viking (USA)) [1996 47
–: a6g a8.5g^4 1997 a7g^3 11.8g a8g^6 a12g^3 10.8s a9.4g^4 Jul 11] poor handicapper, raced mainly on fibresand: stays 1½m: blinkered (well beaten) final start.
S. R. Bowring

KUSTOM KIT XPRES 3 gr.f. Absalom 128 – Miss Serlby 65 (Runnett 125) –
[1996 69, a?: 5m^2 5f^4 6m^5 6g a5g 1997 a8g a6g 6.1m 8.2g a14.8g^6 8.2g 8.2d Jun 23]
angular filly: poor maiden: no form in 1997: tried blinkered. *S. R. Bowring*

KUTTA 5 b.h. Old Vic 136 – Ardassine (Ahonoora 122) [1996 115: 10.4m 13.3m* 115
12s^2 12s^2 1997 12g^3 12m 13.9g^5 16.4g^6 12d* 12.5g^2 13.4s^2 12g^2 Oct 25] compact
horse: good mover: smart performer: won listed event at Newmarket in June by 4
lengths from Harbour Dues: runner-up afterwards in Prix Maurice de Nieuil at
Maisons-Laffitte (beaten head by Surgeon), listed rated stakes at Chester and St
Simon Stakes at Newbury (for second year running, beaten 3 lengths by Kaliana):
effective at 1½m, probably at 2m: has won on good to firm ground, very best efforts
on good or softer: travels well through his races, but doesn't always find much:
consistent: to be trained by Peter Hayes in Australia. *R. W. Armstrong*

KWEILO 3 b.g. Mtoto 134 – Hug Me 96 (Shareef Dancer (USA) 135) [1996 –p: 64
6.1m^6 6g 8g 1997 8g^5 11m 10f^4 11g^4 Jun 20] workmanlike gelding: modest maiden:
stays 1¼m: raced only on good ground or firmer: weak finisher, and may not be one
to trust. *J. W. Payne*

Hamdan Al Maktoum's "Kutta"

KWI

KWIKPOINT 3 ch.g. Never So Bold 135 – Try The Duchess 99 (Try My Best 54 +
(USA) 130) [1996 NR 1997 8f⁴ 8g⁵ 7m⁵ Sep 20] 11,000Y: fifth foal: half-brother to 3
winners, including fair (up to 1½m) performer Uncharted Waters (by Celestial
Storm): dam 2-y-o 6f winner: modest form in maidens on first and final starts: late
progress in latter, and trainer fined £1,500, jockey suspended for 8 days, and horse
banned for 30 days under 'non-trier' rule: may do better. *Martin Todhunter*

KYLE RHEA 3 b.f. In The Wings 128 – Rynechra 102 (Blakeney 126) [1996 76p: 104
8g² 1997 10m* 11.4s* 12m⁶ May 31] rather leggy filly: useful performer: won
maiden at Pontefract in April and listed Cheshire Oaks at Chester (spreadeagled her
4 rivals by 11 lengths and more) in May: creditable sixth of 8 in Prix de Royaumont at
Chantilly only subsequent outing, beaten just over 3 lengths: will stay beyond 1½m.
H. R. A. Cecil

L

LAA JADEED (IRE) 2 b.c. (Jan 27) Petorius 117 – Sea Mistress (Habitat 134) 64
[1997 7m a8.5g⁶ Dec 13] y2,000Y: sixth foal: brother to smart Irish colt Nautical Pet,
1m winner at 2 yrs but better at 6f/7f, and half-brother to 3 winners: dam, unraced,
from family of Irish 2000 Guineas winner Pampapaul: modest form in maidens at
Yarmouth (sold out of A. Stewart's stable 11,000 gns later in October) and Wolverhampton. *J. A. Glover*

LAAZIM AFOOZ 4 b.g. Mtoto 134 – Balwa (USA) 101 (Danzig (USA)) [1996 –
63: 11.5m⁶ 12m³ 12g* 11.8g 1997 10.8m Jun 9] small gelding: modest performer:
stiff task only outing at 4 yrs: stays 1½m: raced only on good going or firmer.
R. T. Phillips

LA BELLE OTERO (USA) 3 ch.f. Nureyev (USA) 131 – Part Time Lover 60
(USA) (Proud Clarion) [1996 NR 1997 8.1s⁵ Aug 30] $180,000Y, $400,000 2-y-o:
leggy, quite good-topped filly: half-sister to several winners in North America, including Grade 3 9f winner Summer Matinee (by Summing): dam won at up to 9f:
swished tail and edgy prior to fifth in maiden at Sandown: moved well to post.
H. R. A. Cecil

LABEQ (IRE) 3 b.c. Lycius (USA) 124 – Ahbab (IRE) 81 (Ajdal (USA) 130) 94 p
[1996 81: 6d 7g² 1997 9m* 10m 10m* Aug 23] strong, good-topped colt: has a round
action: fairly useful form: won maiden at Lingfield (easily) in July and strongly-run
handicap (best effort) at Newmarket in August: likely to stay 1½m: acts on good to
firm going: injured elbow penultimate start, reported in October to be suffering from
a muscular problem: has scope, and should go on again at 4 yrs. *P. T. Walwyn*

LA BRIEF 5 b.m. Law Society (USA) 130 – Lady Warninglid (Ela-Mana-Mou 62
132) [1996 –: 14s 1997 16.1g² 16d Apr 26] compact, workmanlike mare: progressive
staying handicapper at 3 yrs: had just 3 races afterwards: acted on soft ground and the
all-weather: dead. *M. J. Ryan*

LAB TEST (IRE) 5 ch.g. Doulab (USA) 115 – Princess Reema (USA) (Affirmed –
(USA)) [1996 –: 5.5f 5.5f a7.5f 7g 1997 8m Jul 19] well beaten since useful at 2 yrs:
pulled up after breaking blood vessel only outing as 5-y-o. *J. L. Eyre*

LABUDD (USA) 7 ch.h. Deputy Minister (CAN) – Delightful Vie (USA) (Barbs –
Delight) [1996 49, a59: a8g* a8g³ a10g⁶ a8g a7g⁴ a8g a8g 10g 10.8f 8.3m 8g⁶ a58
9f 11.6g² 10g 12g⁵ a16g⁶ 1997 a12g² Jan 16] good-topped horse: modest handicapper: good second in seller at Lingfield only outing in 1997: stays 1½m: acts on
equitrack: tried blinkered: inconsistent (has reportedly suffered from fibrillating
heart). *R. Ingram*

LA CHATELAINE 3 b.f. Then Again 126 – La Domaine 89 (Dominion 123) 54
[1996 –p: 7d 1997 5m⁴ 8g 7f⁴ 7d² 8d² 7d⁵ 7.1m 7m* 8.3m 8m Sep 24] modest
handicapper: led close home when winning at Brighton in August: well beaten afterwards: stays 1m: acts on good to firm and dead going. *G. Lewis*

LACHESIS 4 ch.f. Lycius (USA) 124 – Chance All (FR) 88 (Glenstal (USA) 118) 50
[1996 64d: 8g³ 7.5f⁴ 6g 7.6m³ 8.2m⁵ 7g 7f⁶ a6g a8g 1997 a8g⁴ a7g⁵ a8g⁵ a8g 7.5m⁶ a46

8g 6.1d[4] a8g 6.1d a8g 6d* a6g 5g 6d 7f a6g Nov 14] compact filly: modest handicapper: had 4 different trainers at 4 yrs: won at Leicester in July (for D. Shaw): effective at 6f to 1m: acts on firm and dead going and on fibresand: tried in blinkers: none too consistent. *Mrs S. Lamyman*

LA CURAMALAL (IRE)   3 b.f. Rainbow Quest (USA) 134 – North Telstar 104   76
(Sallust 134) [1996 –p: 7g 1997 10g[6] 10g[3] 12m[2] Jul 14] leggy filly: fair maiden: stays 1½m: raced only on good/good to firm ground. *G. Wragg*

LA DOLCE VITA   3 b.f. Mazilier (USA) 107 – Actress 73 (Known Fact (USA)   70
135) [1996 70: 5m 5m 5g* 1997 a6g[5] a7g[3] a6g a7g* 7m 6m[5] 7g 6m[4] 7g[2] 7.1d 6.1g[6]   a76
6g 7g[4] 7d[6] 7g* 7g[6] 7m[5] 7g* 7m Sep 9] rangy, angular filly: fair performer: won seller at Southwell in March, handicap at Leicester in July and claimer at Newmarket (left T. D. Barron's stable) in August: suited by 7f: best turf form on good going or firmer, also acts on fibresand: successful for 7-lb claimer: consistent. *N. M. Lampard*

LA DOYENNE (IRE)   3 ch.f. Masterclass (USA) 116 – Sainthill (St Alphage   49
119) [1996 –: 5m 1997 5m 5s 5m[5] 5d[5] 6.1m[3] 8.1m[3] 7g* 7g[6] 7m 7g a6g a5g* a5g[4]   a55
Dec 18] small, good-topped filly: modest performer: won maiden at Brighton in August and handicap at Southwell in December: ran well from long way out of handicap final start: effective at 5f (best form) to 7f: acts on fibresand: has carried head awkwardly: usually races prominently. *C. B. B. Booth*

LADY ALEXANDER (IRE)   2 ch.f. (Apr 17) Night Shift (USA) – Sandhurst   102 +
Goddess 103 (Sandhurst Prince 128) [1997 5m[3] 5s[2] 5d* 6.3m* 5m* 7d 5v[6] Oct 11] compact filly: third foal: closely related to 3-y-o Star Profile and half-sister to 1994 2-y-o 5f winner Lady Davenport (by Contract Law): dam Irish 5f to 7f winner: useful performer: won maiden at Naas in June, Anglesey Stakes at the Curragh (by short head from tenderly-ridden King of Kings) in July and Jockey Club of Kenya Molecomb Stakes at Goodwood (beat Mugello ½ length) in August: stays 6f: has won on dead ground, best form on good to firm. *C. Collins, Ireland*

LADY ALMITRA   2 b. or br.f. (Apr 1) Presidium 124 – Armaiti (Sayf El Arab   50
(USA) 127) [1997 5g[6] 6m[3] a6g Oct 4] 5,200 2-y-o: close-coupled filly: first foal: a?
dam 7f winner, half-sister to useful Italian winner at up to 11f Dancer Mitral: strong-finishing third in claimer at Folkestone in September, only form: last at Wolverhampton on all-weather debut. *C. J. Hill*

LADY ANNA   2 b.f. (Feb 11) Anshan 119 – Minteen (Teenoso (USA) 135) [1997   –
5.1d May 9] first foal: dam no sign of ability: last of 9 in minor event at Nottingham. *J. R. Jenkins*

LADYBOWER (IRE)   5 b.m. Pennine Walk 120 – Eimkar (Junius (USA) 124)   33
[1996 –, a49: a8g* a8g[2] a8g[2] 8f a7g 8.3g 1997 a7g 6.9m[2] 8f[5] 6.9s 6.9m 8m a10g 8g a7g a8g[5] a8g Dec 10] small mare: poor handicapper: trained first 2 starts by Lord Huntingdon: stays 1m: acts on firm ground and the all-weather: visored (hampered and unseated rider) final start. *Jamie Poulton*

LADY CARLA   4 b.f. Caerleon (USA) 132 – Shirley Superstar 94 (Shirley   –
Heights 130) [1996 122: 11.5f* 12m* 12m[4] 1997 12g 12g Jul 8] sturdy filly: reportedly had minor back problems: very smart performer at best, most impressive

Jockey Club of Kenya Molecomb Stakes, Goodwood—
Lady Alexander (noseband) and Mugello are both very game under pressure

winner of 1996 Vodafone Oaks at Epsom: very disappointing by comparison subsequently, making little show in Hardwicke Stakes at Royal Ascot and Princess of Wales's Stakes at Newmarket at 4 yrs: stayed 1½m well: acted on firm ground: retired, and visits Gone West in 1998. *H. R. A. Cecil*

LADY CAROLINE LAMB (IRE)   4 b.f. Contract Law (USA) 108 – Tuft Hill   68
92 (Grundy 137) [1996 68: 5d² 5s* 5d³ 5m* 5.2m⁶ 5m 5m 1997 5g² 5g 5.1s Aug 30]
small filly: fair handicapper: second of 19 at Catterick, easily best of 3 runs in
August: best at sharp 5f: probably acts on any going: races prominently: has missed
break. *R. Bastiman*

LADY CHARLOTTE   2 b.f. (May 6) Night Shift (USA) – Circulate (High Top   70
131) [1997 5m⁵ 5m 5.7f* 6d Oct 16] 30,000Y: robust filly: closely related
to fairly useful 9f/1¼m winner Ecliptic (by Lomond) and half-sister to 3 winners,
including 1993 2-y-o 7f winner Highly Fashionable (by Polish Precedent): dam Irish
1¼m winner from family of Nashwan: won maiden at Bath in September: stiffer task,
well held in nursery at Newmarket over 2 weeks later: should be suited by 6f+: acts
on firm ground: sold 14,500 gns in December. *D. R. C. Elsworth*

LADY D'ABO   2 b.f. (Mar 23) Ron's Victory (USA) 129 – Lady Sabo 69 (Prince   – §
Sabo 123) [1997 a5g 5d 5m Sep 21] first foal: dam 5f (at 2 yrs) to 6f winner who
stayed 1m: tailed off first 2 starts, refused to race final one. *R. C. Spicer*

LADY DIESIS (USA)   3 b.f. Diesis 133 – Sedulous 107 (Tap On Wood 130)   75
[1996 83: 6m⁶ 6g* 5d⁵ 1997 8g 6m 6s³ 6m 6.1g 6m 6d Sep 13] fair handicapper:
respectable efforts last 5 starts: bred to stay 1m, pulled hard when tried: seems to act
on good to firm and soft ground: sold 17,000 gns in December. *B. W. Hills*

LADY ECLAT   4 b.f. Nomination 125 – Romantic Saga 69 (Prince Tenderfoot   –
(USA) 126) [1996 –: a6g a5g a6g a6g a9.4g 1997 a8g a8g Jan 17] good-topped filly:
no form since 2 yrs. *K. G. Wingrove*

LADY EIL   2 ch.f. (Apr 10) Elmaamul (USA) 125 – Oakbrook Tern (USA) (Arctic   48
Tern (USA) 126) [1997 7g a7g 10d⁴ a8.5g² a8g* a8g⁴ a7g Dec 18] small filly: fourth
foal: half-sister to French 1m winner Highest Oak (by Highest Honor): dam French
2-y-o 1m winner: poor performer: won 16-runner seller at Southwell in November:
should stay beyond 8.5f: acts on fibresand. *B. Smart*

LADY EMRAL   2 br.f. (May 21) Handsome Sailor 125 – Precious Jay (Hotfoot   –
126) [1997 5g⁵ 5g Sep 27] first reported foal: dam unraced: no promise in claimer or
maiden. *Miss J. F. Craze*

LADY FELIX   2 br.f. (Jan 30) Batshoof 122 – Volcalmeh 67 (Lidhame 109) [1997   –
6g 7.6d 7.1g 8s Nov 8] 4,800Y: good-topped filly: second foal: dam, 7f winner,
stayed 1¼m: behind in maidens. *S. Mellor*

LADY FROM LIMERICK (IRE)   2 ch.f. (Apr 21) Rainbows For Life (CAN)   61
– Coshlea 63 (Red Alert 127) [1997 6f² 6m 5d³ 6.5m 6m⁶ 6s⁵ Oct 3] closely related
to 5f (at 2 yrs) to 1½m winner No Hard Feelings (by Alzao) and half-sister to several
winners, including 5f (at 2 yrs) to 13f winner Dale Park (by Kampala): dam placed
from 11f to 15f: modest form first 3 starts: well held in 2 nurseries, and disappointing
in blinkers final outing: should stay beyond 6f. *J. Berry*

LADY GODIVA   3 b.f. Keen 116 – Festival Fanfare (Ile de Bourbon (USA) 133)   59
[1996 69: 7.1m 7m² 7g³ 8d² 7.9g* 7m⁴ 1997 10.3m 8g 12d 9s 8.3g⁶ 7.5m⁶ 7g 7m⁶
a8g⁴ a9.4g⁵ Dec 13] tall filly: modest handicapper: form in 1997 only on fifth start:
barely stays 1m: acts on good to firm and dead ground: blinkered eighth outing.
M. J. Polglase

LADY IMZA   2 b.f. (May 11) Polar Falcon (USA) 126 – Blade of Grass 78 (Kris   55
135) [1997 a7g 6f Oct 3] 19,500Y: rather unfurnished filly: fifth foal: sister to useful
French 1m winner Brindle and half-sister to useful sprinter Warning Star (by Warning) and 1¼m to 1½m winner Lawn Lothario (by Pursuit of Love): dam 7f winner:
better effort in maidens when ninth of 14 at Lingfield (bandaged behind) second start:
should stay at least 1m. *W. J. Haggas*

LADY IN WAITING   2 b.f. (Mar 17) Kylian (USA) – High Savannah 77 (Rousil-   103
lon (USA) 133) [1997 6s⁵ 5m* 6d² 6d* Jun 28] workmanlike filly: has scope: good
mover, with a long stride: second foal: half-sister to 3-y-o Sabina: dam, maiden

stayed 1½m, half-sister to 2 useful 2-y-o sprinters: sire (by Sadler's Wells) unraced: useful form: won maiden at Leicester and listed race at Newmarket in June, strong run to beat Land of Dreams by 1¾ lengths in latter: should stay 1m: held up. *P. F. I. Cole*

LADY KOMAITE   4 b.f. Komaite (USA) – Hyperion Girl 59 (Royal Palm 131)   –
[1996 NR 1997 a7g 7m Mar 27] third known foal: dam second at 6f at 2 yrs: no promise in maiden and seller. *T. T. Bill*

LADY LAPHROAIG (FR)   2 ch.f. (Mar 11) Elmaamul (USA) 125 – Venerate   56
(IRE) (Ahonoora 122) [1997 6m⁶ 6g⁴ a6g a7g³ a7g² Dec 18] 6,000Y: first foal: dam French 11f winner out of sister to dam of Mt Livermore and Magical Wonder: modest maiden: bred to stay beyond 1m: acts on fibresand. *W. R. Muir*

LADY MAGICIAN   3 ch.f. Lord Bud 121 – Miss Merlin 79 (Manacle 123) [1996
NR 1997 11s⁵ 12.4m 10g Aug 20] 1,300Y: half-sister to several winners, including useful 5f performer Lyndseylee (by Swing Easy): dam 6f winner: little sign of ability, including in seller. *C. W. Fairhurst*

LADY MOLL   2 b.f. (May 3) King's Signet (USA) 110 – Simply Style (Bairn   81 d
(USA) 126) [1997 5g* 5g* 5m⁴ 5g 5.2f 5.3m³ 5m Aug 26] 5,200Y: small filly: third foal: half-sister to 3-y-o Weet And See and 4-y-o Loch Style: dam unraced: won maiden at Folkestone and minor event at Ripon in spring: fair form at best after, twice highly tried: should stay 6f: raced only on good ground or firmer: has gone early to post: sold 11,000 gns in December. *R. Boss*

LADYOFDISTINCTION (IRE)   2 b.f. (Apr 29) Distinctly North (USA) 115 –   –
Lady Anna Livia (Ahonoora 122) [1997 6s 7m⁵ 7.5f 7m Oct 1] IR 4,600Y: half-brother to 1990 2-y-o 7f winner Plan of Action (by Krayyan), later successful in Italy, Irish 9f winner Karoi (by Kafu) and a winner in Italy by Nabeel Dancer: dam won in Holland: little worthwhile form in maidens. *J. S. Wainwright*

LADY OF GLENDOWAN   4 b.f. Teenoso (USA) 135 – Mearlin (Giolla Mear   –
113) [1996 NR 1997 8d 10m 9.7m Sep 26] lengthy filly: second known foal: dam winning 2½m chaser: no sign of ability. *Mrs Barbara Waring*

LADY OF THE DANCE   2 b.f. (Feb 23) Tragic Role (USA) – Waltz 75 (Jimmy   –
Reppin 131) [1997 8g 8s Nov 8] lengthy, good-topped filly: half-sister to 7f/1m winner Dancing Domino (by Primo Dominie) and fairly useful 1½m winner Golden Hello (by Glint of Gold): dam 1m winner: well beaten in autumn maidens at Doncaster. *M. A. Jarvis*

LADY OF THE LAKE   3 b.f. Caerleon (USA) 132 – Llyn Gwynant 115 (Persian   104
Bold 123) [1996 68+: 7f³ 8.2m⁴ 7f 7m⁷ 10g² 12d 12f⁵ 17.2m* 16.2m* 16.2d* 16d² 16m⁴ 16m* Oct 31] tall filly: improved into a useful handicapper: won at Bath (maiden), Chepstow and Beverley in the summer: best effort when winning 4-runner listed rated stakes at Newmarket by ½ length from Mawared final start, leading 3f out and rallying when pressed: very much a stayer: acted on firm and dead ground: raced prominently: genuine: stud. *J. L. Dunlop*

LADY RACHEL (IRE)   2 b.f. (Apr 5) Priolo (USA) 127 – Alpine Spring 95   59
(Head For Heights 125) [1997 8d³ 8m 8g Oct 24] IR 16,000Y: sturdy filly: fourth foal: half-sister to 1m to 1¼m winner Pennine Pink (by Pennine Walk): dam Irish 2-y-o 7f winner, seemed best at up to 1¼m: modest form in maidens at Ayr, Newcastle and Doncaster: should stay 1¼m. *J. L. Eyre*

LADY RALPHINA   2 b.f. (May 27) General Wade 93 – Lady Regent (Wolver   –
Hollow 126) [1997 5g⁵ 6m⁶ 5m 5.1m 6g⁶ 6m 5m 6f Oct 3] sparely-made filly: half-sister to 6f/7f winner Trojan General (by Trojan Fen) and a German 10.5f winner by Deploy: dam, Irish 7f winner, half-sister to very smart middle-distance filly Infamy: little worthwhile form, including in sellers. *J. J. Bridger*

LADY ROCHELLE   2 b.f. (Mar 17) Noble Patriarch 115 – Panic Button (IRE)   –
48 (Simply Great (FR) 122) [1997 7m 7g⁵ 6m 7.5f Sep 17] first foal: dam, poor maiden who stayed 1m, half-sister to German 1000 Guineas winner Kazoo: no worthwhile form, including in sellers. *T. D. Easterby*

LADY ROCKSTAR   2 b.f. (Apr 14) Rock Hopper 124 – Silk St James (Pas de   –
Seul 133) [1997 7g 7m 8.2d Oct 30] fair sort: sixth reported foal: half-sister to several

LAD

winners, including 3-y-o Silk St John and 8-y-o Kingchip Boy: dam unraced: well beaten in maidens, in blinkers second start. *M. J. Ryan*

LADY SALOME 3 gr.f. Absalom 128 – Lady River (FR) (Sir Gaylord) [1996 –: 5m 6m 7g 1997 12d 10f Jun 10] compact filly: no worthwhile form. *J. G. FitzGerald* —

LADY SHERIFF 6 b.m. Taufan (USA) 119 – Midaan (Sallust 134) [1996 90d, a68: a6g² 5m³ a5g* 5.1g⁴ 5m⁵ 5m⁶ 5.1m² 5m 6.1m⁶ 5g⁴ 6m 5m a6g⁶ a6g 5.6m 5d 5g 5f⁴ 5s 1997 5g 5f² a5g* 5d² 5g* 5m² 5d³ 5g⁴ 5v² 5g⁴ 5g² 5m* 5d⁴ 5.6m⁶ 5d 5.1g³ 5m 5d Oct 17] workmanlike mare: has a markedly round action: fairly useful handicapper on turf, fair on all-weather: held her form really well at 6 yrs, winning at Southwell and Newcastle in May and Goodwood in July: best around 5f: acts on any turf going and on fibresand: wears blinkers: successful for claimer: front runner/races prominently: splendidly tough and consistent. *M. W. Easterby* 90 a74

LADY SILK 6 ch.m. Prince Sabo 123 – Adduce (USA) (Alleged (USA) 138) [1996 46§, a52§: a8g 7.5d 8.1g⁶ 9.2g⁶ a8g a6g* a6g⁵ a7g⁶ 7g a7g 6.1m 7g⁵ 8f 7g a8g³ a8g 1997 a7g a6g* a6g a6g³ a7g⁶ 5.9g 8m a7g a6g 7.1g³ 7d 7.1g⁶ 12g⁵ a12g⁶ 6.1m a8.5g³ 8g a12g⁵ 10d a8g⁵ Nov 17] leggy mare: modest performer at best: won handicap at Southwell in January: stays 8.5f: acts on good to firm ground, soft and fibresand: effective blinkered/visored or not: temperamental, and often soon off bridle. *Miss J. F. Craze* 39 d a52 d

LADY SO BOLD 2 ch.f. (Apr 13) Bold Arrangement 127 – Lady Blues Singer (Chief Singer 131) [1997 7g 7.5v 7g Sep 3] 400Y: unfurnished filly: third foal: dam, maiden, seemed to stay 7f: soundly beaten in sellers. *Mrs L. Stubbs* —

LADY SWIFT 6 ch.m. Jalmood (USA) 126 – Appealing 49 (Star Appeal 133) [1996 –: 8g 14.1g 1997 14.1s May 9] of little account. *K. W. Hogg, Isle of Man* —

LADY WESTBURY (IRE) 6 b.m. Superpower 113 – Fleur-De-Luce (Tumble Wind (USA)) [1996 NR 1997 a8g a7g⁵ a6g 6f 6.1g May 23] poor maiden at 2 yrs: no form in 1997. *P. C. Ritchens* —

LADY YAVANNA 2 ch.f. (Feb 28) Lycius (USA) 124 – Isotonic 74 (Absalom 128) [1997 5m⁶ 7.1g 6m⁴ 6d 8f Sep 11] 20,000Y: good-bodied filly: has a round action: second foal: dam won 3 times at 5f as 2-y-o, only season to race: fair form in maidens: not well drawn in nurseries final 2 starts: probably stays 7f: visored fourth start: has gone early to post. *K. McAuliffe* 65

LA-FAAH (IRE) 2 ch.c. (May 10) Lahib (USA) 129 – Rawaabe (USA) 87 (Nureyev (USA) 131) [1997 6d* 7g 7v* 7.3g* Oct 24] sturdy, lengthy colt: third foal: half-brother to 4-y-o Afaan: dam 5f winner, closely related to smart sprinter Doulab: useful performer: won newcomers event at Ascot in July and minor event at York and 8-runner Group 3 Horris Hill Stakes (showed good turn of foot once getting in the clear to beat Sensory by 1¾ lengths) at Newbury in October: should stay 1m: yet to race on ground firmer than good: has scope and may do better still in 1998. *B. W. Hills* 107

Vodafone Horris Hill Stakes, Newbury—
La-Faah is kept up to his work ahead of stable-companion Sensory (rails) and Victory Note

LAFFAH (USA)   2 b.c. (Feb 17) Silver Hawk (USA) 123 – Sakiyah (USA) (Silver   67 p
Hawk (USA) 123) [1997 7d 7m Jul 12] heavy-topped colt: first foal: dam US 1m
winner from family of Storm Bird: never dangerous in maidens at Newmarket (very
much in need of race) and Salisbury: should do better over 1m+. *J. H. M. Gosden*

LA GALLERIA   2 ch.f. (Feb 6) Royal Academy (USA) 130 – Two And Sixpence   –
(USA) 74 (Chief's Crown (USA)) [1997 6d 8.2g Oct 4] 8,000Y: tall, workmanlike
filly: has a round action: second foal: dam 17f winner: well beaten in maidens at
Newbury and Nottingham. *J. S. Moore*

LAGAN   4 b.g. Shareef Dancer (USA) 135 – Lagta 75 (Kris 135) [1996 –: a8g 8.5m   39
7g 9f 10.8m 14.1m 16m 16m 10g a16g 1997 13m² Jul 11] good-bodied gelding: poor
maiden handicapper: probably stays 1¾m: tried blinkered: tail swisher: fair hurdler.
K. A. Morgan

LAGO DI VARANO   5 b.g. Clantime 101 – On The Record 72 (Record Token   92
128) [1996 92: 7g 5m* 5.1g² 5m 6m 6f⁴ 5g* 5g⁵ 5m² 6m 5m⁵ 5.2m⁴ 5m⁴ 6g⁴ 5.6m³
6m 5d 5g² 5g³ 1997 6m 6s⁵ 5g² 5m 5d 5d 5g 5m 5g* 5m 6g 5.6m⁵ 5d 5g 6m Nov 4]
strong gelding: good walker: fairly useful handicapper: made most when winning at
Newcastle in July: none too consistent otherwise in 1997: effective at 5f/6f: acts on
firm and soft ground: usually visored/blinkered. *R. M. Whitaker*

LAGUNA BAY (IRE)   3 b.f. Arcane (USA) – Meg Daughter (IRE) (Doulab   58
(USA) 115) [1996 65?: 7m 7m⁴ 7g 1997 8.5m⁶ 9.2s² 12d 11.4g⁴ 12g⁵ 10.1m* 10g⁴
11.5m² 11.1m⁵ 12m Oct 31] close-coupled filly: modest performer: won claimer at
Yarmouth in August: rather unlucky second in similar event there following month:
stays 11f: acts on good to firm going and soft. *A. P. Jarvis*

LAHAB NASHWAN   3 ch.g. Nashwan (USA) 135 – Shadha (USA) 77 (Devil's   –
Bag (USA)) [1996 67p: 8.2g⁵ 1997 12m⁵ 10s May 17] showed promise on debut,
none since. *M. R. Channon*

LAHIK (IRE)   4 b.g. Lycius (USA) 124 – Sangala (FR) (Jim French (USA)) [1996   –
–: 8.2d 9.7f 12.5f 8.3m 8g 12m 16f⁵ a13g⁵ 9.7g 7g 8f a8s⁴ a10g a8g a10g 1997   a43
a8g⁴ a10g⁵ a7g⁵ a10g³ a10g⁴ a12g⁶ a12g⁴ Mar 27] poor maiden: stays 1¼m: acts on
equitrack. *K. T. Ivory*

LAKE ARIA   4 b.f. Rambo Dancer (CAN) 107 – Hinge (Import 127) [1996 NR   –
1997 8f 10m 7d a5g⁶ a6g Nov 14] first foal: dam never ran: seems of no account.
J. O'Reilly

LAKE DOMINION   8 b.g. Primo Dominie 121 – Piney Lake 54 (Sassafras (FR)   –
135) [1996 NR 1997 a16.2g* 16m a14.8g⁵ a14.8g⁶ Oct 6] poor handicapper, lightly   a45
raced: 50/1, won strongly-run amateurs event at Wolverhampton in July: stays 2m:
acts on firm going, dead and fibresand: no improvement in blinkers at 3 yrs.
K. C. Comerford

LAKELAND PRIDE (IRE)   2 gr.c. (Feb 28) Pips Pride 117 – Divine Apsara   71 d
(Godswalk (USA) 130) [1997 5d⁵ 6g⁵ 5.9f³ 6d³ 7g³ 6d 7g 7s⁴ 7.9s⁵ Sep 4] 15,000Y:
good-bodied colt: half-brother to 3 winners, including 4-y-o Veni Vidi Vici and 1989
2-y-o Burslem Beau (5f, by Burslem): dam Irish 5f to 1m winner: fair form in
maidens first 5 starts, but deteriorated: should stay beyond 7f: acts on firm and dead
ground: blinkered last 2 starts. *P. D. Evans*

LAKE TAAL   2 ch.f. (May 11) Prince Sabo 123 – Calachuchi 74 (Martinmas 128)   59 p
[1997 5f⁶ 6g⁶ Oct 22] second foal: half-sister to 3-y-o Quezon City: dam prolific
winner from 7.5f to 12.4f: promising sixth in maidens at Beverley and Newcastle
(carried head awkwardly and not knocked about) a month apart: should stay at least
1m: should do better. *M. J. Camacho*

LAKE WOBEGONE (IRE)   2 ch.g. (May 4) Inchinor 119 – Westerlake (Blake-   –
ney 126) [1997 6f⁵ 5d Jul 17] 2,800 2-y-o: half-brother to 3 winners, including 7f/1m
performer Legend Dulac (by Legend of France) and 1¾m and 2m winner College
Don (by Kalaglow): dam, ran twice, from good family: well beaten in sellers. *John
Berry*

LAKOTA BRAVE   3 ch.c. Anshan 119 – Pushkinia (FR) 95 (Pharly (FR) 130)   –
[1996 NR 1997 8g May 26] sixth foal: half-brother to several winners, including fair
Shift Again (1m) and modest Legal Train (1¼m), both by Siberian Express: dam,

French 2-y-o 7f winner, from good family: pulled hard when down the field in maiden at Leicester. *C. N. Allen*

LALINDI (IRE) 6 b.m. Cadeaux Genereux 131 – Soemba 86 (General Assembly 71 (USA)) [1996 79: 18s 16g 14.9d⁶ 14m² 17.2f² 13.1g² 12g⁴ 11.5f* 11.9d* 16.1g 13.3f 13.3m 14m² 12s 16.5s 1997 9.7m⁵ 14.1d 10m 12v* Jul 4] big mare: fair handicapper: best effort at 6 yrs when making all in 4-runner amateurs event at Beverley: stays 17f: acts on fibresand and any turf going: usually blinkered in 1996 and at Beverley: lazy sort who takes plenty of driving. *A. C. Stewart*

LA LINEA 3 gr.f. Rock City 120 – Altaia (FR) 90 (Sicyos (USA) 126) [1996 NR – 1997 a10s Nov 28] 1,350 2-y-o: second foal: half-sister to Silver Tzar (by Dominion), 7f winner at 2 yrs: dam 6f to 7f winner: no promise in seller at Lingfield. *M. C. Pipe*

LALLANS (IRE) 4 b.c. Old Vic 136 – Laluche (USA) 100 (Alleged (USA) 138) 88 [1996 104: 12d* 12m² 13.9m³ 16.2m 1997 16.1s 14m 12m Aug 16] smallish, good-topped colt: good mover: useful form at 3 yrs, not seen out after June: just fairly useful form in handicaps first 2 starts as 4-y-o: should be suited by 2m: acts on good to firm and dead ground: sold only 6,000 gns in October. *M. Johnston*

LA LYONESSE 2 b.f. (Mar 28) Lion Cavern (USA) 117 – Princess Sioux 69 57 (Commanche Run 133) [1997 7m 7g 7m⁵ Oct 1] angular filly: first foal: dam, maiden who stayed 1¼m, out of half-sister to very smart middle-distance performer Defensive Play: first form in maidens when about 6 lengths fifth at Salisbury (tended to carry head high): should stay 1m. *J. W. Hills*

LAMARITA 3 b.f. Emarati (USA) 74 – Bentinck Hotel 74 (Red God 128§) [1996 81 71: 5f⁴ 6m² 6d⁶ 1997 6g⁴ 5.1m² 5g* 5.1d 5d³ 5.1m* 5s³ Jun 27] good-topped filly: has a quick action: fairly useful performer: won minor event at Thirsk in April and handicap at Nottingham in June: best form at 5f: acts on good to firm going and soft: sometimes hangs left. *J. M. P. Eustace*

LAMBRINI LAD (IRE) 2 b.g. (Apr 27) Shalford (IRE) 124§ – Swift Reply (He – Loves Me 120) [1997 7g Jul 11] 9,400Y: good-topped gelding: brother to useful Irish 3-y-o 7f and 1m winner Ministerial Model and half-brother to 2 winners, including fairly useful 1994 2-y-o 8.5f winner That Old Feeling (by Waajib): dam 1½m winner: tailed off in maiden at York: unseated rider before start. *A. Bailey*

LAMBS LANE 2 b.c. (Apr 10) Petoski 135 – Collison Lane 80 (Reesh 117) [1997 56 5g 5m⁵ 6m 6m 8m Oct 5] smallish, sturdy colt: second foal: dam 2-y-o 5f winner: modest form in maidens first 3 starts: soundly beaten in nurseries, blinkered penultimate outing: should stay beyond 6f. *T. D. Easterby*

LA MENORQUINA (USA) 7 b.m. Woodman (USA) 126 – Hail The Lady – (USA) (Hail The Pirates (USA) 126) [1996 31, a–: a16g 14.9m 16m⁴ 1997 a16g² a56 a16g³ a16.2g* 16.4g a14g² a14.8g² a14g⁵ a14g² Nov 17] quite good-topped mare: modest on all-weather, poor on turf: won handicap at Wolverhampton in April: good second 3 times after: stays 2m: best form on fibresand: often comes from long way off pace. *D. Marks*

LA MODISTE 4 b.f. Most Welcome 131 – Dismiss 95 (Daring March 116) [1996 90 –: 7g 10.1m 8m³ 7f 8f⁶ 1997 a8g⁴ a10g a7g³ 8.5m* 8g 8.1m* 8.5m 8d a10g* 10m² 8.5d² 7g* 8d³ 8g Oct 18] angular filly: fairly useful performer: claimed out of S. Dow's stable 5,000 gns after third start: improved for new stable, winning minor event at Epsom in April, claimer at Sandown in May and handicaps at Lingfield in July and Salisbury in September: effective from 7f to 1¼m: acts on hard and dead ground and on equitrack: game: sold 20,000 gns in October. *Miss Gay Kelleway*

LAMORNA 3 ch.f. Shavian 125 – Malibasta 83 (Auction Ring (USA) 123) [1996 57 73: 6f⁵ 5f 7m³ 7f⁵ 5.7m 6m* 7d⁵ 5.2m³ 6m 6m 7.3s 1997 7m 7.3s 6m⁶ 6g⁵ 6g 5.9m² 6g³ 6.1m 7m* 7f 6.9d² Oct 21] lengthy filly: has quick action: modest handicapper: won 17-runner event at Catterick in September: stays 7f: acts on firm and dead ground. *M. R. Channon*

LAMOURA 2 ch.f. (May 5) Executive Man 119 – Armalou 54 (Ardoon 124) – [1997 a5g 5.7f 5g 6m Jul 28] 2,600 2-y-o: sister to 2 winners in Italy and half-sister to a 2-y-o 6f seller winner by Derrylin: dam 1¼m seller winner: no worthwhile form, including in sellers. *R. Brotherton*

LAMSAAT (IRE) 2 b.f. (Mar 5) Thatching 131 – Fair Shirley (IRE) 75 (Shirley   – p
Heights 130) [1997 7m Sep 22] first foal: dam, 1¼m winner from 2 starts, daughter
of close relative to Sadler's Wells: 33/1, behind in maiden at Kempton, green and not
knocked about: likely to do better. *M. A. Jarvis*

LANARA 2 b.f. (Mar 3) Formidable (USA) 125 – Alnasr Jewel (USA) (Al Nasr   –
(FR) 126) [1997 6.1s 7g 6.1m Aug 6] 2,600Y: second foal: dam unraced: no sign of
ability: tried visored. *Mrs N. Macauley*

LANCASHIRE KNIGHT 3 b.g. High Estate 127 – Just A Treat (IRE) 47   –
(Glenstal (USA) 118) [1996 –: 6g 6g 1997 10d⁶ 10g Jul 7] smallish gelding: no
worthwhile form in maidens and handicap: raced freely final outing. *S. Dow*

LANCASHIRE LEGEND 4 gr.g. Belfort (FR) 89 – Peters Pet Girl (Norwick   53 §
(USA) 125) [1996 –, a70: a8g² a8g³ a8g³ 6s 8f⁵ 7f 8g 8.3m a7g* a7g⁴ a8g 1997 a7g   a70 §
a7g³ a7g⁵ a7g³ a7g⁴ a7g² 6f⁵ 7f 6.9m² 7g 7.1m 6m a7g⁵ a7g a7g⁵ a7s a7g Dec 2] fair
on the all-weather, modest on turf: barely stays 1m: acts on firm ground and
equitrack: visored (pulled too hard) once: carries head high: reluctant to race twelfth
start: inconsistent, and not one to trust implicitly. *S. Dow*

LANCE'S PET 3 b.f. Warning 136 – Snub (Steel Heart 128) [1996 NR 1997   –
a8.5g Nov 1] half-sister to several winners, including sprint plater Whittingham Girl
(by Primo Dominie) and stayer Pavonis (by Kalaglow): dam, Irish 7f and 9f winner,
later successful in USA: slowly away and always behind in maiden. *D. C. O'Brien*

LANDLER 4 b.g. Shareef Dancer (USA) 135 – Les Dancelles (Pas de Seul 133)   –
[1996 NR 1997 14.1g⁶ Jun 20] 3,000 3-y-o: second foal: half-brother to Emirates
Express (by Shaadi), fairly useful 7f winner: dam Irish stayer: fair
NH Flat winner: tailed-off last in maiden at Redcar. *J. Norton*

LANDLORD 5 b.g. Be My Chief (USA) 122 – Pubby 73 (Doctor Wall 107) [1996   54
–: a10g a10g a16g 11.7f⁶ 1997 10.8m 14.9m⁴ 16.4m* 17.2f Jul 23] modest
handicapper: won at Folkestone in June: poor effort final outing: stays 2m: acts on
good to firm going and the all-weather: usually blinkered: front runner. *P. Bowen*

LAND OF DREAMS 2 b.f. (Feb 11) Cadeaux Genereux 131 – Sahara Star 95   105 +
(Green Desert (USA) 127) [1997 6m* 6d² 6g 6g² 5m* 5v⁴ Oct 11] robust filly:
second foal: dam, won Molecomb Stakes, daughter of smart sprinter Vaigly Star:

Polypipe plc Flying Childers Stakes, Doncaster—Land of Dreams sprints clear of Tippitt Boy

won maiden at Pontefract in June and Polypipe plc Flying Childers Stakes at Doncaster in September, quickening to beat Tippitt Boy by 2½ lengths most readily under confident ride in latter: creditable second in listed races at Newmarket and Ripon, but well held in Cherry Hinton Stakes at Newmarket and Cornwallis Stakes at Ascot: speedy, and best effort at 5f: acts on good to firm ground (drawn wide on heavy): has flashed tail and faltered when ridden: held up. *M. Johnston*

LANDRFUN 2 b.c. (Mar 21) Lugana Beach 116 – Basic Fun (Teenoso (USA) – 135) [1997 a6g a6g Dec 4] small, sparely-made colt: second reported foal: dam maiden who probably stayed 1¾m: well beaten in maidens. *H. J. Collingridge* –

LANGARA HEIGHTS 3 br.c. Golden Heights 82 – Cushina 61 (Sparkler 130) [1996 NR 1997 8g 8.3m 10m a11g 16m Sep 15] second reported foal: dam ran twice: no form. *B. J. Llewellyn* –

L'ANNEE FOLLE (FR) 4 b.f. Double Bed (FR) 121 – Gai Lizza (FR) (Gairloch 122) [1996 108: 10g* 10d5 10g4 10m2 12m* 1997 10d 10d2 10d2 12g4 10m3 10d Nov 15] useful French filly at 3 yrs (off course 9 months after final start) and no better in 1997 with notable exception of 1¼ lengths third of 9 to Kool Kat Katie in E P Taylor Stakes at Woodbine in October: should prove better at 1½m than shorter: acts on good to firm and dead ground. *F. Doumen, France* 118

LA NUIT ROSE (FR) 2 b.f. (Jan 26) Rainbow Quest (USA) 134 – Caerlina (IRE) 120 (Caerleon (USA) 132) [1997 7d* Oct 13] leggy, sparely-made filly: second foal: dam, winner from 5.5f (at 2 yrs, when second in Prix Marcel Boussac) to 10.5f (including in Prix de Diane), from a good middle-distance family: 7/4, won maiden at Leicester, cruising through under 2f out and merely nudged clear to beat Yanabi 4 lengths, value much more: didn't walk well and showed quick action to post: should stay 1m+: rather lacking in scope (so was dam), but should make her mark in better company. *Saeed bin Suroor* 93 p

LA PERDOMA 3 b.f. Sylvan Express 117 – Oratava Valley (Mansingh (USA) 120) [1996 NR 1997 5.9m5 7g5 6.9m5 10m 12f Aug 27] 2,200Y: leggy filly: third foal: half-sister to 1994 2-y-o 6f winner Eighth Heaven (by Skyliner) and a winner in Sweden by Marching On: dam, poor maiden, form only at 7f: no worthwhile form: refused to race final start. *Miss M. K. Milligan* – §

LA PERRUCHE (IRE) 4 b.f. Cyrano de Bergerac 120 – Red Lory 87 (Bay Express 132) [1996 49: a7g3 a7g4 a7g5 1997 a8g Mar 4] poor maiden: stiff task on first run for over 10 months, only outing in 1997: probably stays 7f: raced only on the all-weather. *Lord Huntingdon* –

LA PETITE FUSEE 6 br.m. Cigar 68 – Little Missile (Ile de Bourbon (USA) 133) [1996 84: 6m3 6d3 5m2 6m3 6.1m* 6m* 6g 6m3 6.1s 1997 8m 6d 6s2 6.1g 6m 6m3 7m3 6d 6m a6s a7g4 a7g Dec 19] rangy, workmanlike mare: fairly useful handicapper: effective at 6f/7f: acts on firm going, soft and fibresand: usually bandaged: usually front runner (unable to dominate last 4 starts): often mounted on course and early to post: has bled. *R. J. O'Sullivan* 82

LAPIMI 2 b.f. (May 18) Lapierre 119 – Miami Pride 48 (Miami Springs 121) [1997 a6g Jul 26] second reported foal: dam maiden sprint plater: behind in claimer at Southwell. *Mrs N. Macauley* –

LAPU-LAPU 4 b.f. Prince Sabo 123 – Seleter (Hotfoot 126) [1996 62: 5m5 a6g4 6d 6g 6m 8m* 8m4 8g5 8.9g4 10.1m* a11g 1997 9.9m 10.3d 10g3 10g2 12m5 8.3d* 9.9m5 10m 9m 10.1g3 a11g Nov 24] lengthy filly: modest performer: won 4-runner minor event at Hamilton in July: stays 1¼m: acts on fibresand, good to firm and dead ground. *M. J. Camacho* 59

LARAMANIA 2 ch.g. (Apr 4) Safawan 118 – Lara's Baby (IRE) 78 (Valiyar 129) [1997 6m 7d 7.1g 7s 7g 8m a8g a7g3 Nov 29] close-coupled gelding: first reported foal: dam 1½m winner: visored, first worthwhile form when third in seller at Wolverhampton: should stay 1m. *P. D. Evans* – a49

LARGESSE 3 b.c. Cadeaux Genereux 131 – Vilanika (FR) 81 (Top Ville 129) [1996 80: 6m2 5g* 6.1m6 5f4 7.3m 1997 5s 9m4 8g 10.5d* 10.1f5 11.9m* a12g6 Nov 13] tall colt: has a long, round action: fairly useful handicapper: won twice at Haydock in September: suited by testing conditions at 1¼m and stays 1½m well: acts on firm and dead ground, below form on equitrack. *John Berry* 85

LARK'S RISE 3 b.f. Niniski (USA) 125 – Line of Cards 83 (High Line 125) – [1996 NR 1997 10d⁶ 12m⁵ 14.1s Oct 15] half-sister to a middle-distance winner in France by Jalmood and a 2-y-o 7.5f winner in Italy by Lion Cavern: dam lightly-raced 1½m winner: no worthwhile form in maidens. *H. Candy*

LA ROCHELLE (IRE) 2 b.f. (May 6) Salse (USA) 128 – Lagta 75 (Kris 135) 72 p [1997 8d⁶ Oct 16] rangy filly: has plenty of scope: seventh foal: half-sister to useful middle-distance performer Rudagi (by Persian Bold): dam 1½m and 1¾m winner: 50/1, promising 12 lengths sixth of 22 to Border Arrow in maiden at Newmarket, going smoothly behind pace and not knocked about as principals asserted: will be well suited by further than 1m: sure to do better at 3 yrs. *C. E. Brittain*

LASCENSA (USA) 2 ch.f. (Apr 27) Lord At War (ARG) – Trattoria (USA) 62 – (Alphabatim (USA) 126) [1997 a8.5g 10d Oct 13] second foal: dam, 5f winner at 2 yrs: behind in maiden and seller: sent to Germany. *P. A. Kelleway*

LASHAM 2 ch.g. (May 13) Presidium 124 – Travel Myth 66§ (Bairn (USA) 126) 55 [1997 5m⁴ 5g⁴ 7m² 6g 6m² 7.1g⁴ 6g 6f⁵ a6g³ Oct 20] small, close-coupled gelding: second reported foal: dam, ungenuine maiden, stayed 1¼m: modest performer: won seller at Folkestone in April: mostly creditable efforts afterwards: stays 7f: acts on firm ground and fibresand, yet to race on softer than good on turf: sold, and sent to Kuwait. *N. A. Callaghan*

LA SPAGNA 6 ch.m. Aragon 118 – Ringed Aureole 77 (Aureole 132) [1996 NR – 1997 5d a7g 9.7s 14.1s 11.6m Jul 21] probably no longer of any account. *M. D. I. Usher*

LAST AMBITION (IRE) 5 b.m. Cadeaux Genereux 131 – Fabulous Rina (FR) – (Fabulous Dancer (USA) 124) [1996 29: 12m⁵ 11.6m 5.1m⁴ 1997 6f Sep 18] poor maiden: seems a sprinter. *R. Champion*

LAST CHANCE 3 b.c. River Falls 113 – Little Red Hut (Habitat 134) [1996 73d: 64 d 6m⁴ 5.1m* 6f² 6g² 5f⁵ 5m 5g a6g 1997 7m² 8m 8m 7m³ 7s⁴ a5g 7g 6g⁶ 7g Aug 11] leggy colt: modest handicapper: below form after reappearance: stays 7f: acts on good to firm ground, well beaten on soft and on equitrack: has had tongue tied: visored/blinkered last 3 starts. *D. J. S. Cosgrove*

LAST CHRISTMAS 2 b.c. (May 18) Salse (USA) 128 – State Ball 61 (Dance In 91 p Time (CAN)) [1997 7m³ 7.1g* Sep 27] IR 20,000Y: lengthy, useful-looking colt: rather weak at 2 yrs, but has plenty of scope: half-brother to 3 winners abroad, including a sprinter in Italy by Last Tycoon: dam, placed around 1½m, half-sister to dam of Fairy Footsteps and Light Cavalry: promising third in maiden at Leicester in September, and landed odds in similar event at Haydock, by ½ length from The Gene Genie: will be well suited by 1m+: should make a better 3-y-o. *B. W. Hills*

LAST KNIGHT (IRE) 2 b.g. (Mar 1) Distinctly North (USA) 115 – Standing 61 Ovation (Godswalk (USA) 130) [1997 5g⁴ 5m 5d⁶ May 20] 19,000Y: neat, good-bodied gelding: half-brother to several winners, 3 by Mazaad, including Irish 1¼m winner Crowded House: dam Irish 1½m winner: easily best effort in maidens on debut. *M. R. Channon*

LAST LAP 2 b.f. (Mar 9) Noble Patriarch 115 – Warning Bell 88 (Bustino 136) 40 [1997 7f⁴ 7g 7.5v⁴ 7g⁶ a7g³ Jul 25] 500Y: leggy, angular filly: sixth foal: half-sister to 1994 2-y-o 5f winner Warning Shot (by Dowsing) and 6-y-o Virtual Reality: dam, 1¼m winner, from family of Circus Ring: poor maiden: will stay at least 1m: ran creditably in blinkers on fibresand final start. *T. D. Easterby*

LAST LAUGH (IRE) 5 b.m. Last Tycoon 131 – Little Me (Connaught 130) 61 [1996 NR 1997 11.7m* Apr 29] modest handicapper: 25/1, won at Bath in April, only start of 1997: will stay beyond 1½m: acts on firm ground, no form on going softer than good. *N. M. Babbage*

LAST SECOND (IRE) 4 gr.f. Alzao (USA) 117 – Alruccaba 83 (Crystal Palace – (FR) 132) [1996 121p: 8m² 10m* 10m* 1997 10.5d 10m* Aug 2] good-topped filly: reported by trainer to be a fragile individual: very smart performer at 3 yrs, winning Vodafone Nassau Stakes at Goodwood and Sun Chariot Stakes at Newmarket: disappointing in Prix Ganay at Longchamp and Nassau Stakes as 4-y-o: stayed 1¼m well: acted on good to firm and dead ground: held up and had fine turn of foot: reportedly retired. *Sir Mark Prescott*

LAS VISTAS 3 b.f. Tina's Pet 121 – Maravista (Swing Easy (USA) 126) [1996   54 d
NR 1997 7m 6f³ 7g 7g³ 7g⁵ 7g⁴ 8m a7g a8g Nov 24] third foal to race: dam in rear
in NH Flat race: modest maiden: below form after fourth start: should stay 1m.
H. J. Collingridge

LATALOMNE (USA) 3 ch.g. Zilzal (USA) 137 – Sanctuary (Welsh Pageant   97
132) [1996 NR 1997 8.2m* 8.1g⁵ 7d² 8f² Sep 29] close-coupled gelding: half-brother
to 4 winners, notably Sheikh Albadou (by Green Desert) and 7-y-o Captain Jack:
dam unraced half-sister to Little Wolf: useful performer: won maiden at Nottingham
in April: off course 5 months after next start (reportedly sustained stress fracture):
runner-up in minor events at Goodwood and Bath last 2 starts: keen sort, but needs
further than 7f and should stay 1¼m: has hung and looked difficult ride: front runner:
gelded after final start. *E. A. L. Dunlop*

LATE NIGHT OUT 2 b.c. (Feb 14) Lahib (USA) 129 – Chain Dance 88 (Shareef   91
Dancer (USA) 135) [1997 6v³ 6.1d* 6v⁵ Nov 24] compact colt: first foal: dam 6f
winner at 2 yrs, stayed 1¼m but refused to race final 2 outings: fairly useful form:
won minor event at Nottingham in October by 1½ lengths from Ring Dancer: creditable fifth of 7 in listed race at Maisons-Laffitte: should stay 1m. *W. Jarvis*

LATIN BAY 2 b.c. (Mar 10) Superlative 118 – Hugging 78 (Beveled (USA))   50 ?
[1997 5s 5d 7d 6.9m⁵ 7d 7.6m Sep 9] 4,800Y: small, leggy colt: first foal: dam 1m
winner: only a little sign of ability: withdrawn after bolting to post once. *P. W. Harris*

LATIN NEXUS (USA) 2 b.f. (Feb 16) Roman Diplomat (USA) – Miami Game   67
(USA) (Crozier) [1997 6g³ 6.9s⁵ 7g Aug 11] $7,000F, $50,000Y: half-sister to
numerous winners in USA, including 3 minor stakes winners: dam won 9 times at
up to 9f in USA and placed in Grade 3 event: best effort in maidens on debut at
Leicester: should be suited by further than 6f. *P. F. I. Cole*

LA TIZIANA 2 b.f. (Jan 21) Rudimentary (USA) 118 – Tizona (Pharly (FR) 130)   72
[1997 7m⁴ 7s³ Oct 16] second foal: half-sister to fair 7f (at 2 yrs) and 9f winner
Striffolino (by Robellino): dam unraced: fair form in maidens at Leicester and Catterick, carrying head rather high on latter course: should stay at least 1m. *W. Jarvis*

L A TOUCH 4 b.f. Tina's Pet 121 – Silvers Era 72 (Balidar 133) [1996 58: 5f²   45
5m² 6m⁴ 6m² 6.1m 1997 5d 5m 5f 6d 5m 6g² 6m Aug 9] strong, lengthy filly: poor
handicapper: effective at 5f and 6f: best form on good going or firmer. *J. J. Quinn*

LATVIAN 10 gr.g. Rousillon (USA) 133 – Lorelene (FR) 97 (Lorenzaccio 130)   57 §
[1996 70§: 12.4d* 12g 12.1g³ 12.1f 12f⁶ 11.1m² 15.8g² 16.1m 13.1g² 12m* 15.1m
11.1d⁵ 15.1s 1997 12m* 12g⁴ 12d³ 12.1m² 12.4m⁶ Aug 6] lengthy gelding: modest
performer: won claimer at Musselburgh (fifth course success) in June: effective at
11f to 15f: acts on hard ground and dead: effective blinkered/visored or not: carried
head high, and none too resolute: goes well fresh. *R. Allan*

LAUREL DELIGHT 7 ch.m. Presidium 124 – Foudroyer (Artaius (USA) 129)   81
[1996 90: 5m 5.1g⁵ 5m 5m 5g³ 5g³ 5m* 5m 1997 5g 5g Jun 20] lengthy mare: good
mover: produced Laurel Pleasure (see below) in 1995: formerly useful handicapper,
only fairly useful form in 2 runs in 1997: best at 5f: acts on firm and dead ground: has
run well when sweating: often a front runner: bandaged nowadays: game. *J. Berry*

LAUREL PLEASURE 2 ch.f. (Feb 2) Selkirk (USA) 129 – Laurel Delight 104   74
(Presidium 124) [1997 5m 5g* May 17] unfurnished filly: first foal: dam (see above)
half-sister to Paris House: made all in claimer (claimed £15,000) at Thirsk in May:
sold only 1,500 gns in October, to M. Smith in Sweden. *J. Berry*

LAUREL SEEKER (USA) 3 b.g. Mining (USA) – L'On Vite (USA) (Secret-   66
ariat (USA)) [1996 NR 1997 12m⁵ 10.2m 11.9f⁴ 11.5f³ 14.1d⁵ a12g* Dec 19]
$42,000Y, 10,000 2-y-o: leggy gelding: fourth foal: half-brother to Heart of Oak
(by Woodman), listed winner at up to 1m abroad: dam unraced from top Canadian
family: fair performer: won amateurs minor event at Lingfield in December: stays
1½m: acts on firm going and equitrack. *Mrs A. J. Perrett*

LAUREN'S LAD 2 ch.c. (Apr 21) Tachyon Park 87 – Glory Isle 60 (Hittite Glory   60
125) [1997 7s 7g 7g 7m⁵ 7f* 7m⁶ a8g⁵ Dec 10] 5,200Y: seventh foal: half-brother to
7f (at 2 yrs) to 1¼m winner Rio Piedras (by Kala Shikari) and 2 winners abroad: dam
9f winner: modest performer: comfortably won 16-runner nursery at Lingfield in

October: ran creditably in similar event there final start: stays 1m: acts on firm ground and equitrack: blinkered last 4 starts. *G. Lewis*

LA VASO VERDI   2 b.f. (Mar 18) Ardkinglass 114 – Emerald Gulf (IRE) (Wassl – 125) [1997 5m 7.1m 6g 7m Oct 7] leggy, unfurnished filly: third foal: dam, bred to stay 1¼m, ran once: probably of little account. *R. M. Whitaker*

LAVENDER DELLA (IRE)   4 gr.f. Shernazar 131 – All In White (FR) (Car- 64 white 127) [1996 66, a–: 10.2g² 10m 10f² 10s a10g⁴ a12g 1997 10m 12.5d³ 13.3f Jul a– 19] neat filly: modest maiden handicapper: easily best effort at 4 yrs when third at Warwick in June: should stay further than 1½m: acts on firm and dead ground, no form on all-weather. *M. J. Fetherston-Godley*

LAVERNOCK LADY   2 b.f. (Feb 11) Don't Forget Me 127 – Danissa (Dancing – Brave (USA) 140) [1997 7g 6g 8.3g Sep 29] IR 5,200Y: workmanlike filly: first foal: dam French 2-y-o 9f winner: no show in maidens. *J. J. Quinn*

LA VIZELLE (IRE)   2 b.f. (Apr 4) Distinctly North (USA) 115 – Queen of Erin – (IRE) (King of Clubs 124) [1997 7d 6s 7g 6g Aug 4] IR 4,500Y: second foal: dam unraced: no worthwhile form, including in sellers: tried blinkered. *R. Guest*

LA VOLTA   4 b.f. Komaite (USA) – Khadino (Relkino 131) [1996 –: 9s 8m⁶ 8.1m 52 1997 8m 7.5m 8g a7g 5f 5.9f⁴ a6g 5m⁴ 5g 6.1m* 7m Sep 20] strong, lengthy filly: modest performer: trained by J. FitzGerald first 6 starts: 20/1, won 20-runner handicap at Nottingham in September: stays 1m: acts on firm ground: blinkered last 4 starts. *Miss J. F. Craze*

LAWAHIK   3 b.c. Lahib (USA) 129 – Lightning Legacy (USA) 78 (Super Concorde 94 (USA) 128) [1996 NR 1997 12.4m³ 10d* 10.3m⁴ 10.4d³ 11.9g⁶ Jul 11] 34,000F, IR 46,000Y: rather leggy colt: half-brother to 2 winning stayers and useful Black Monday (up to 1½m, by Busted): dam (maiden) stayed 1m: fairly useful performer: won maiden at Ripon in April: in frame minor event at Doncaster and handicap at York next 2 starts, failing to quicken after travelling well: should stay 1½m: unraced on extremes of going: not easiest of rides. *D. Morley*

LAW COMMISSION   7 ch.g. Ela-Mana-Mou 132 – Adjala 89 (Northfields 99 (USA)) [1996 98: 5.1f 7.3s⁴ 6m* 6f 6m* 6f⁴ 7m* 7g² 7m⁵ 7g 1997 8d⁶ 8d 8m 8s 7g 6m⁶ 6m⁶ 7g² 7.3m² 7d* 8m 7g 8m⁵ Nov 1] small, sturdy gelding: useful handicapper: generally in good form at 7 yrs, and won at Goodwood in September: flattered when seventh in Challenge Stakes at Newmarket penultimate start: effective at 6f to 1m: acts on any going: sometimes hangs under pressure: held up: has broken out of stalls and been withdrawn twice. *D. R. C. Elsworth*

LAW DANCER (IRE)   4 b.g. Alzao (USA) 117 – Judicial (USA) (Law Society 53 (USA) 130) [1996 74, a78: a8.5g⁴ a9.4g* 10g⁶ a9.4g* 10g⁶ 8.1d a8.5g² a9.4g⁴ 8f³ a69 10m⁴ 10g⁶ 10v 10m 1997 a10g a9.4g⁴ a10g⁵ a10g 8.5m 10m² 10.1f⁵ 9d a8g² a10g⁶ 10m² 10f Oct 1] small gelding: fair handicapper on all-weather, modest on turf: stays 1¼m: acts on all-weather and firm ground, well beaten on heavy: visored (not discredited) once. *T. G. Mills*

LAWFUL CONTRACT (IRE)   2 br.g. (Apr 29) Contract Law (USA) 108 – – Lucciola (FR) (Auction Ring (USA) 123) [1997 a5g 6d a6g 5g Sep 27] IR 1,500Y: leggy gelding: fourth foal: half-brother to a winner in Germany at up to 1m by Nashamaa: dam unraced: soundly beaten in maidens. *R. Hollinshead*

LAWFULL BLUE (IRE)   3 b.f. Bluebird (USA) 125 – Maraquiba (FR) (Ken- – mare (FR) 125) [1996 NR 1997 10m⁶ 8m a8.5g a8g Nov 25] IR 6,500Y: sister to 2-y-o Blueridge Dancer and half-sister to ungenuine 1m to 1½m winner by Hard Fought: dam won at 7.5f at 2 yrs in France: no form in maidens. *C. A. Dwyer*

LAWFUL LOVE (IRE)   7 b.g. Law Society (USA) 130 – Amata (USA) (No- 34 double (USA)) [1996 28: 11.8m 12.1g² 1997 14.1m⁴ 16.2s May 10] leggy gelding: shows knee action: bad performer. *T. W. Donnelly*

LAWLESS BRIDGET   2 b.f. (May 16) Alnasr Alwasheek 117 – Geoffrey's – Sister (Sparkler 130) [1997 a5g⁵ Apr 26] half-sister to several winners, including smart 6f/7f performer Mac's Fighter (by Hard Fought): dam miler: always behind in seller at Wolverhampton. *Martyn Meade*

LAW

LAWN LOTHARIO 3 ch.g. Pursuit of Love 124 – Blade of Grass 78 (Kris 135)   88
[1996 64: 8g 8m² 8.2g 7.1s⁴ 1997 a10g³ a10g* a10g* a11g* a12g* Mar 1] strong,
angular gelding: much improved handicapper on all-weather early in year, winning
at Lingfield (twice), Southwell and Wolverhampton within space of 5 weeks: stayed
1½m: dead. *M. Johnston*

LAWSIMINA 4 b.f. Silly Prices 110 – Star of The Sea (Absalom 128) [1996 47:   –
a5g⁶ 6m 7g a6g⁵ a6g⁶ a5g⁵ a6g⁵ a6g 1997 a5g May 24] poor sprinter: sometimes
slowly away: has refused to enter stalls. *D. Shaw*

LAWZ (IRE) 3 br.c. Lahib (USA) 129 – Sea Port (Averof 123) [1996 NR 1997   80 d
8.3s² 7.6m⁶ 8.5g³ 8d 10g Oct 24] IR 19,000Y: tall colt: half-brother to several
winners, including useful Irish 1m (at 2 yrs) to 11f winner Qualtron (by Marju) and
thorough stayer Old Red (by Ela-Mana-Mou): dam, fourth on only start, is half-sister
to high-class stayer Sea Anchor: disappointing maiden: bred to stay at least 1¼m
(much too free over trip): sold 18,000 gns after final start. *C. J. Benstead*

LAY THE BLAME 4 b.c. Reprimand 122 – Rose And The Ring (Welsh Pageant   75
132) [1996 77: 8.1d 8f 7m⁵ 7m 7d 1997 8m³ 8g 10g² 8m 10m⁶ 10.1g³ 12g Aug 2]
good-bodied colt: fair handicapper: stays 1¼m: acts on good to firm ground: inconsistent. *M. D. Hammond*

LEADING NOTE (USA) 3 ch.f. Blushing John (USA) 120 – Beat (USA)   79
(Nijinsky (CAN) 138) [1996 74p: 8g³ 8s³ 1997 10g⁵ 11.5g³ 12d⁴ 10.5s Oct 15] big,
workmanlike filly: fair maiden: stays 11.5f: raced only on good going or softer: sold
23,000 gns in December. *L. M. Cumani*

LEADING PRINCESS (IRE) 6 gr.m. Double Schwartz 128 – Jenny Diver   53
(USA) (Hatchet Man (USA)) [1996 54: 5g 6d 5g 6s 5d⁶ 5s 5m 5f* 5m² 6m 5m 5m²
5g 6m* 6f³ 5m⁶ 5m 6d⁵ 6m* a6g 1997 5s 5m⁵ 5s* 5s 5s 5g 5g³ 5g 6s³ 6d³ 6m³ 5m 6g
5d 5s Oct 14] leggy mare: modest performer: won minor event at Hamilton in May:
effective at 5f/6f: probably acts on any turf (below form on fibresand): has been
visored, blinkered nowadays: sometimes carries head high, and has drifted markedly
left: usually races prominently. *Miss L. A. Perratt*

LEADING SPIRIT (IRE) 5 b.g. Fairy King (USA) – Shopping (FR) (Sheshoon   84
132) [1996 88: 10s 12.3g² 12m* 12.3m⁴ 12m³ 12g³ 12m* 1997 a12g* a12g⁴ Mar 17]
well-made gelding: fairly useful handicapper: very well treated on turf form, easily
landed gamble at Wolverhampton in February: very disappointing next time: should
stay 1¾m: acts on good to firm ground, dead and fibresand (yet to race on equitrack):
front runner/races prominently. *C. F. Wall*

LEAD SINGER 2 b.g. (Feb 22) Ballad Rock 122 – Parisana (FR) (Gift Card (FR)   –
124) [1997 6m Oct 22] seventh foal: half-brother to 3 winners, including Swift Cert
(11f and 13f in Ireland, by Robellino): dam, unraced, from family of Chief Singer:
soon behind in minor event at Yarmouth. *J. M. P. Eustace*

LEA GRANDE 2 ch.f. (Feb 20) Highest Honor (FR) 124 – Lovely Rita (USA)   89 p
(Topsider (USA)) [1997 7.5f³ 7m⁴ Nov 1] first foal: dam, French 11f to 13.5f winner,
half-sister to Japan Cup winner Marvellous Crown and US Grade 1 1½m winner
Grand Flotilla: fairly useful form in minor event at Milan in September and maiden
won by Pontoon at Newmarket, hanging left and caught close home in latter: should
stay at least 1m: should improve further. *L. M. Cumani*

LEAR JET (USA) 4 b.g. Lear Fan (USA) 130 – Lajna 88 (Be My Guest (USA)   73
126) [1996 90d: 10.2g* 12m³ 10m² 10.5d 10m⁵ 10m³ 1997 12m⁵ 14.4m⁶ Sep 10]
strong, rangy gelding: fair form in handicaps at 4 yrs: stays 1¾m: acts on good to
firm ground: strong galloping front-runner. *Bob Jones*

LEAR SPEAR (USA) 2 b.c. (Apr 11) Lear Fan (USA) 130 – Golden Gorse   81
(USA) (His Majesty (USA)) [1997 7g⁶ 7m³ 8m³ Sep 24] $25,000Y: tall, work-
manlike colt: has scope: has a long, round action: fifth foal: half-brother to Irish 2m
winner Gleaming Heather (by Irish River): dam, winning sprinter in USA, half-sister
to smart performers at up to 1¼m Lotus Pool and Golden Larch: fairly useful form
when third to Tamarisk in minor event at Kempton and Mutawwaj in maiden at
Goodwood: should stay beyond 1m. *D. R. C. Elsworth*

LEATHER AND SCRIM (IRE) 2 b.f. (Apr 12) Imperial Frontier (USA) 112 –   47
Yola (IRE) (Last Tycoon 131) [1997 5g⁶ 5g⁵ 5g 6g Aug 20] IR 1,000Y: lengthy filly:

540

second foal: dam unraced: poor maiden: didn't look easiest of rides final start: stays 6f: claimer ridden. *D. Nicholls*

LEATHERNECK (IRE) 4 b.g. Sadler's Wells (USA) 132 – Louveciennes (USA) (Super Concorde (USA) 128) [1996 NR 1997 12m⁶ 10d 10s 11.8g 11.6g Jun 2] sturdy gelding: fifth foal: closely related to French 1m and 11f winner Liberty Song (by Lomond) and half-brother to 2 winners in France: dam unraced daughter of Oaks winner Lupe: no worthwhile form: often slowly away: visored (looked very difficult ride) final start. *P. Mooney*

LE BAM BAM 5 ch.h. Emarati (USA) 74 – Lady Lustre 70 (On Your Mark 125) [1996 –: 5m 7m⁶ 8.3m a7g a8g⁶ 7m 1997 a7g 7g Sep 5] smallish, lengthy horse: little worthwhile form for long time. *C. N. Allen*

LEBEDINSKI (IRE) 4 ch.f. Soviet Lad (USA) 94 – Excavate (Nishapour (FR) – 125) [1996 38: 9.9g⁴ 10.8g 10m⁵ 10m 10g 1997 a11g a11g⁵ Jan 17] workmanlike filly: poor form. *Mrs P. Sly*

LE DESTIN (FR) 4 b.c. Zayyani 119 – My Darling (Ela-Mana-Mou 132) [1996   119 § 117: 8s⁵ 10g* 10.5g² 12g³ 10.5m⁴ 12.5g⁵ 10d⁵ 12m 12d⁶ 12.5d 1997 10d² 10.5d² 12m³ 12m³ 12f 12d⁴ Oct 19] angular colt: smart performer, though has won only once, a minor event at Saint-Cloud early in 1996: ran best races in 1997 when second in Prix Ganay (6 lengths behind Helissio) at Longchamp on second start and third in Coronation Cup (beaten 5½ lengths by Singspiel) at Epsom: effective at 10.5f in testing conditions, stays 1½m well: acts on good to firm and dead ground: tends to get behind: unreliable. *P. H. Demercastel, France*

LEDGENDRY LINE 4 b.g. Mtoto 134 – Eider 80 (Niniski (USA) 125) [1996   79 73p: 10.3s³ 10g 10.1d⁴ 12.4g⁴ 14d⁴ 10.5s 1997 11.9s³ 12m² 12m 13.1g* 12.4g⁴ 16m 12.3d⁶ 13.1d⁴ 13.1s³ Oct 14] good-topped gelding: fair handicapper: won maiden event at Ayr in June: likely to prove suited by 1½m/1¾m: acts on good to firm going, probably on dead: held up, and suited by truly-run race: promising novice hurdler. *Mrs M. Reveley*

LEGAL BRIEF 5 b.g. Law Society (USA) 130 – Ahonita 90 (Ahonoora 122) – [1996 –: 8.5m⁶ 8.5m 8g 10m 8f 1997 7g Aug 1] of little account. *J. S. Wainwright*

LEGAL ISSUE (IRE) 5 b.h. Contract Law (USA) 108 – Natuschka (Authi 123)   65 [1996 71, a66: a7g⁴ a8g² a8g 7.5d⁴ 8m 8.5g 7g³ 7g* 7s* 7m 7g 7g a6g⁵ a8g⁵ a7g⁴ a7g⁵ 1997 7d 8.2g⁶ a7g⁵ 7.5m² 7g 7s² 8m⁵ 7g⁶ a8.5g* 8d² a9.4g⁴ a8.5g⁶ 10d⁴ a8g² a8g² a10g* Dec 19] sturdy horse: poor mover: fair handicapper: won at Wolverhampton in August and Lingfield in December: effective at 7f to 1¼m: acts on any all-weather/turf: tried visored: consistent. *W. W. Haigh*

LEGAL LARK (IRE) 2 ro.g. (Apr 16) Case Law 113 – Park Silver (Beldale   64 Flutter (USA) 130) [1997 5g 6m 5m⁵ 6m* 6f⁶ a6g 5d a6g⁶ Nov 13] 10,500Y: workmanlike gelding: has knee action: closely related to a winner abroad by Nashamaa: dam unraced: modest on turf, poor on all-weather: won claimer at Folkestone in September: well beaten afterwards: stays 6f: acts on good to firm ground. *P. Howling*

LEGAL LUNCH (USA) 2 b.c. (May 5) Alleged (USA) 138 – Dinner Surprise   84 p (USA) (Lyphard (USA) 132) [1997 7g² Oct 24] 300,000 francs Y: well-made colt: half-brother to several winners, including 3-y-o Mr Sponge and US Grade 3 9f winner Freewheel (by Arctic Tern): dam, placed in USA, from family of Legal Case: 16/1, shaped well when beaten 2 lengths by Zaya in maiden at Doncaster, no match for winner, but taking second without being hard ridden: will be well suited by 1m+: good sort, sure to improve and win races. *P. W. Harris*

LEGAL RIGHT (USA) 4 b.g. Alleged (USA) 138 – Rose Red (USA) 92 – (Northern Dancer) [1996 101: 10.3g* 10g⁴ 12f 12.5g⁵ 12m 1997 10m 12.3d⁵ Apr 26] angular gelding: fluent mover: useful performer at best: no worthwhile form in 1997: blinkered (too free) final start: hurdling with J. J. O'Neill. *P. W. Chapple-Hyam*

LEG BEFORUM (IRE) 3 b.g. Distinctly North (USA) 115 – Paulines Girl   48 (Hello Gorgeous (USA) 128) [1996 –: 5g 1997 a10g a8g⁴ a8g⁴ a10g² a12g⁴ a10g³   a56 12g⁶ a9.4g⁴ 10m⁴ 10f a8g Jun 21] modest maiden: should stay beyond 1¼m: tried blinkered/visored. *L. Montague Hall*

LEGENDARY LOVER (IRE)   3 b.c. Fairy King (USA) – Broken Romance   79
(IRE) (Ela-Mana-Mou 132) [1996 NR 1997 8g 10.2d³ 10d⁶ 12g⁴ 10.5d Sep 5]
46,000Y: strong, rangy colt: second foal: dam unraced half-sister to very smart
performer up to 1¼m Guns of Navarone: fair maiden: quite keen sort, best up to
1¼m: yet to race on going firmer than good: sold 21,000 gns in October. *R. Charlton*

LEGEND OF ARAGON   3 b.f. Aragon 118 – Legendary Dancer 90 (Shareef   51
Dancer (USA) 135) [1996 67: 5.1d⁴ 5g⁴ 5d* 5g⁵ 1997 8.2m 8g 6.1d 7.5d⁵ a7g a7g⁶
6g 5.9m⁴ 7.5v a6g⁴ a7g³ 7g² 8.2d⁵ a7g² a7g a8g⁶ Nov 24] close-coupled filly: modest
handicapper: effective at 6f to 1m: acts on fibresand and dead going: tried blinkered/
visored. *J. A. Glover*

LEGEND OF LOVE   2 b.g. (Mar 17) Pursuit of Love 124 – Legendary Dancer   74
90 (Shareef Dancer (USA) 135) [1997 6s³ 6m 6m⁴ 8d 7s Nov 8] 12,500Y: workmanlike gelding: has a round action: fifth foal: half-brother to 3-y-o Legend of
Aragon and 4-y-o Riccarton: dam 1½m winner from family of Wassl: fair form when
in frame in minor event at Pontefract and maiden at Haydock: well below that form
in nurseries last 2 starts: should stay at least 1m. *J. A. Glover*

LE GENEREUX   2 ch.g. (Apr 15) Cadeaux Genereux 131 – Casbah Girl 79   –
(Native Bazaar 122) [1997 a7g a8g Nov 24] 10,000Y: half-brother to 3 winners,
including useful sprinter Sabre Rattler (by Beveled) and 5f to 7f winner Mister Bloy
(by Dowsing): dam 6f and 7f winner: tailed off in sellers. *M. R. Channon*

LEGGERA (IRE)   2 b.f. (Feb 15) Sadler's Wells (USA) 132 – Lady Ambassador   98 p
(General Assembly (USA)) [1997 7.1m* 7m³ 7.3g³ 8s* Nov 12] rangy, quite
attractive filly: takes the eye: has scope: has a round action: third reported foal:
closely related to German 7f winner Lovely Louisa (by Be Me Guest) and half-sister
to a winner in Germany by Persian Bold: dam 6f winner out of sister to Seymour
Hicks: progressive form: won maiden at Sandown in August and listed race at
Maisons-Laffitte (beat Queen Catherine ½ length) in November: will stay at least
1¼m: best form on good ground or softer: should improve further. *J. L. Dunlop*

LE GRAND GOUSIER (USA)   3 ch.c. Strawberry Road (AUS) 128 – Sandy   60
Baby (USA) (Al Hattab (USA)) [1996 60: a7g 7.6d 10g⁴ 1997 14.1d 11.6s 12m⁴
11.6m⁵ a16g² 17.2m 11.6m² 12.5m⁴ 12g⁵ 11.5m⁴ a12g⁶ a14.8g⁵ Dec 13] modest
performer: made all in selling handicap at Warwick in July: effective at 1½m to easy
2m: acts on good to firm going and equitrack: blinkered final 3 starts, leaving
R. Williams after first of them. *R. J. Price*

LEGS BE FRENDLY (IRE)   2 b.c. (Mar 28) Fayruz 116 – Thalssa (Rusticaro   82
(FR) 124) [1997 5m² 6s³ a5g² 7s² 6g² 6m⁴ 6g² 6m² 5v 5d* Oct 27] 13,000Y:
good-bodied colt: has scope: fifth reported foal: dam unraced from family of Bold-
boy: fairly useful performer: won minor event at Lingfield by ½ length from Rare
Indigo: generally ran well earlier, including in nurseries: effective at 5f to 7f: acts on
good to firm and soft ground, probably on fibresand (stiff task on heavy): visored
seventh start, blinkered at Lingfield: consistent. *K. McAuliffe*

LEGUARD EXPRESS (IRE)   9 b.g. Double Schwartz 128 – All Moss 66   –
(Prince Tenderfoot (USA) 126) [1996 39: 8f³ 8g²* 8m² 8f 1997 7m 8g Aug 7]
good-topped gelding: carries condition: poor handicapper: in rear both starts at 9 yrs:
blinkered. *O. O'Neill*

LEIF THE LUCKY (USA)   8 ch.g. Lemhi Gold (USA) 123 – Corvine (USA)   60
(Crow (FR) 134) [1996 64: a9.4g a8g 8.5m 8.9m 10.5g³ 10.1m⁵ 12.3s 10.4g³ 10f⁶
a9.4g³ 1997 9.2d⁴ 10m⁶ 9m⁵ 9.2g³ 10.3d² 10.5g⁴ 10m⁴ 10.4s Sep 4] short-backed
gelding: modest handicapper: on a long losing run: effective at 1m to 1¼m: acts on
any ground, but has gained all 5 successes on good ground or softer: usually held up,
and tends to find little. *Miss S. E. Hall*

LEIGH CROFTER   8 ch.g. Son of Shaka 119 – Ganadora (Good Times (ITY))   –
[1996 58, a78d: a6g a6g a6g³ a5g³ a5g a6g⁴ 5s 6.1g 6g a6g⁶ 7d 6d³ 6s⁴ a6g a6g a6g   a70 d
7s a8g a7g* a7g* a6g⁴ a7s* a7g⁴ 1997 a7g* a6g⁴ a7g a8.5g⁵ a7g a7g² a6g a8g a6g
a7g 6.1d a6g a6g 7g a7g a7g Nov 21] workmanlike gelding: fair handicapper: won at
Wolverhampton in January: lost his form after sixth start: seems best at 7f on fibresand: has been visored, usually blinkered. *P. D. Cundell*

LEMON BRIDGE (IRE) 2 b.c. (Apr 14) Shalford (IRE) 124§ – Sharply – p
(Sharpman) [1997 8d Oct 16] 19,000Y: well-made colt: sixth foal: half-brother to a
2-y-o 6f seller winner by King of Clubs and a winner in Italy by Celestial Storm: dam
1¼m winner: 33/1, signs of ability when thirteenth of 22 to Border Arrow in maiden
at Newmarket: will do better. *J. W. Hills*

LENA'S PRIDE 4 b.f. Precious Metal 106 – Lucky Lena (Leander 119) [1996 –
NR 1997 10g a12g a6g Nov 21] first known foal: dam of little account: showed
nothing in seller and claimers. *W. Clay*

LEND A HAND 2 b.c. (Apr 4) Great Commotion (USA) 123 – Janaat 74 114 p
(Kris 135) [1997 6g² 6d* 7g* 7.5m* 8f* 8m* Oct 19]

A return trip to Italy in the spring is on the cards for Lend A Hand. His
visit to Milan in October resulted in such an impressive win in Italy's premier
event for two-year-olds, the Gran Criterium, that connections are understandably keen to take him to Rome for the Italian equivalent of the Two Thousand
Guineas, the Premio Parioli. The form Lend A Hand showed at Milan is well
up to that required to win a Premio Parioli, and the race looks likely to provide
him with a good chance of classic success.

Lend A Hand won't need to win a classic to fare better in his second
season than the last two British-trained winners of the Gran Criterium. Torrismondo, who was successful in 1993, ran just once at three years, finishing
tailed off in the Craven Stakes; and while the 1996 winner Hello did manage to
win a Grade 3 event in the USA, he sadly broke a leg in July and was put down.
Whereas Torrismondo did all his racing at two years in Italy, Lend A Hand's

Ralph Raper Memorial Prince of Wales Cup (Nursery), Doncaster—
Lend A Hand defies top weight

Gran Criterium, Milan—Lend A Hand turns Italy's top two-year-old race into a one-sided affair.
Overseas challengers fill the first four places

appearance at Milan was his only one outside Britain, where he was unbeaten in four starts after finishing a promising second on his debut. Those four victories were gained at Epsom, Catterick, Beverley and Doncaster, the pick of them his performance under top weight in a twenty-one runner nursery at Doncaster. Lend A Hand, stepping up to a mile, led the favoured far-side group from the start and ran on well to beat Rabah by one and a half lengths. Two runners from Britain and two from Ireland were among Lend A Hand's nine opponents in the Gran Criterium, the best of whom looked to be Mowbray, trained, like Torrismondo, by Paul Cole and sent off at odds on. Lend A Hand, second favourite at 5/2, gave Mowbray and the others short shrift. In a race run at a sound pace, he travelled easily in second and quickened right away when shaken up two furlongs out. Mowbray, off the bridle for much of the race, stayed on well to snatch second, but was still seven and a half lengths behind Lend A Hand at the line.

		Nureyev	Northern Dancer
	Great Commotion (USA)	(b 1977)	Special
	(b 1986)	Alathea	Lorenzaccio
Lend A Hand		(b 1975)	Vive La Reine
(b.c. Apr 4, 1995)		Kris	Sharpen Up
	Janaat	(ch 1976)	Doubly Sure
	(b 1989)	Triple First	High Top
		(b 1974)	Field Mouse

Lend A Hand stays a mile well and should get further. His sire, Great Commotion, was a very smart sprinter, winner of the Cork And Orrery, but he also had plenty of form at a mile, including when second in the Irish Two Thousand Guineas. Lend A Hand is a first foal of Janaat, who showed fair form in four races around a mile and a half, winning a maiden at Salisbury, and would have been suited by further. Janaat is a sister to the smart French filly Trefoil, who stayed one and a half miles, and half-sister to three good performers at up to that distance, Richard of York, Maysoon and Three Tails. Richard of York won the Prix Foy, while both fillies were placed in the Oaks. Another half-sister, Third Watch, won the Ribblesdale Stakes. Their dam Triple First finished fourth in the Oaks but was better at a mile and a quarter, over which distance she won the Musidora, the Nassau and the Sun Chariot. The next dam Field Mouse was a useful sprinter.

Lend A Hand, a good-bodied colt, has raced only on good going or firmer since winning on good to soft at Epsom (where he didn't seem entirely at ease on the track), showing at Doncaster that he acts on firm. *M. Johnston*

LENNOX LEWIS 5 b.g. Superpower 113 – Song's Best (Never So Bold 135) [1996 88d: 6g 5.2d 5g 6d⁵ 6m 6f 6m 6g 6m 5f⁴ a7g⁵ 1997 6m 6m 5g 6g a5g⁶ 5d 6m 5d a5g Dec 18] good-quartered gelding: has a quick action: useful handicapper at 3 yrs: disappointing since, and left A. Jarvis after second 5-y-o start: ridden by inexperienced apprentice last 5 starts: stays 6f: acts on dead ground, best efforts on good to firm: visored once. *D. Nicholls* –

LEOFRIC 2 b.c. (Apr 24) Alhijaz 122 – Wandering Stranger 69 (Petong 126) [1997 5m³ 5g⁴ 5m³ 6g 7g 5m 6m³ 6m³ 7f³ 8d a7g Nov 14] 10,000Y: leggy colt: first foal: dam 6f winner: fair maiden: generally ran creditably, though often soon off bridle: should stay 1m: acts on firm going, well beaten on dead and fibresand: often blinkered/visored. *M. J. Polglase* 65 a?

LEONATO (FR) 5 b.g. Law Society (USA) 130 – Gala Parade 78 (Alydar (USA)) [1996 103: 8.2m⁶ 10m⁵ 10m⁶ 13.4d² 11.9f 12g 16g² 1997 12g Mar 5] tall gelding: has knee action: useful form at 4 yrs: tailed off on all-weather debut at Wolverhampton in March: suited by test of stamina: acts on dead ground. *P. D. Evans* –

LER CRU (IRE) 8 b.g. Lafontaine (USA) 117 – Kirsova (Absalom 128) [1996 NR 1997 a12g Dec 19] no longer of any account. *G. P. Enright* –

LE SHUTTLE 3 b.f. Presidium 124 – Petitesse 55 (Petong 126) [1996 49: 5f 5f⁴ 6m 6g³ 6m² 5d⁴ 5m³ 5.3g² 6d 5s⁶ a5g⁶ 1997 a5g⁵ a6g a8g³ 7m 6.9m May 28] poor maiden: no form in 1997: stays 6f: best form on good going or firmer: visored final outing. *M. H. Tompkins* –

LESLEY'S ADVENTURE (IRE) 2 b. or br.f. (Feb 14) Petardia 113 – Island Adventure (Touching Wood (USA) 127) [1997 6g 6m 7.1m Aug 20] IR 4,400Y: third foal: dam successful in Denmark: well beaten in maidens. *Capt. J. Wilson* –

LE SPORT 4 b.g. Dowsing (USA) 124 – Tendency 77 (Ballad Rock 122) [1996 –, a90d: a8.5g a10g⁵ a6g* a8.5g* a8.5g² 7s 7.6g⁶ 7m a8.5g⁶ a9.4g⁶ 7.6m a8.5g a9.4g a9.4g 7g 10g 10.3g 1997 a8g⁴ a8g⁴ a8g² a8g² a7g⁵ a8.7g* a8g³ a12g³ a8s* a8s* a10s² Nov 3] sturdy gelding: fair performer for D. Nicholls, but left him after sixth start, in February: did very well after transfer to Sweden, winning at Jagersro (quite valuable event) and twice at Taby: stays 1¼m, probably 1½m: goes well on dirt: tried blinkered. *M. Smith, Sweden* a90

LETS BE FAIR 2 b.f. (Mar 29) Efisio 120 – Play The Game 70 (Mummy's Game 120) [1997 5g⁴ 5m* 5g* Aug 2] 8,200Y: fourth foal: half-sister to 4-y-o Power Game: dam 2-y-o 5f winner: won maiden at Beverley in July by wide margin and easily landed odds in minor event at Hamilton: speedy: fairly useful, and looked sure to improve further, but reportedly chipped bones in knee. *J. Hanson* 94

LETTYFAK (FR) 3 br.c. Akarad (FR) 130 – Lettyfana (USA) (Fappiano (USA)) [1996 9g⁴ 9d⁴ 1997 12d* 12m 14s² 14.8g Jul 10] lengthy colt: second foal: dam, French 2-y-o 1m winner, out of half-sister to champion 1987 US 3-y-o filly Saca-huista: won sales race at Compiegne in March on third of 4 starts for A. Fabre: well beaten in minor event and listed race (sweating, set strong pace 6f) in Britain: stays 1½m: acts on good to soft going. *I. P. Williams* 81 ?

LEVELLED 3 b.g. Beveled (USA) – Baino Charm (USA) (Diesis 133) [1996 72: 5g³ 5m* 6g 6s 1997 7m 5m* 6g 6m³ 6f* 5g⁵ 5g 5.1m⁴ 6m² 6g 5.2m⁵ 6m³ 5.3f* 6.1g³ 5v Oct 11] angular gelding: fairly useful performer: won claimer at Folkestone in April and handicaps at Brighton in June and September: effective at 5f and 6f: acts on firm going, well beaten on soft/heavy: often apprentice ridden, including successful. *M. R. Channon* 82

LEVITICUS (IRE) 3 b.g. Law Society (USA) 130 – Rubbiera (IRE) (Pitskelly 122) [1996 72?: 7g⁴ 7m⁵ 7d⁴ 7.9g 8.3d³ 8g 1997 10d² 11.9d⁶ 9.9v³ 12.3m³ 12m⁴ 16g* Aug 22] leggy, unfurnished gelding: fairly useful handicapper: improved form in making all at Thirsk in August: better at 2m than shorter: acts on good to firm and 83 dead ground (disappointing on heavy): tends to wander, and sometimes looks none too keen: fairly useful hurdler. *T. P. Tate*

LIA FAIL (IRE) 4 b.f. Soviet Lad (USA) 94 – Sympathy 77 (Precocious 126) [1996 53: a6g⁴ a6g² a6g* a9.4g 8f a6g a7g a7s⁴ a9.4g⁵ 1997 a7g³ Jan 4] leggy, angular filly: modest handicapper: below form only outing at 4 yrs: stays 7f: acts on fibresand, raced only on firm/good to firm going on turf: sold 1,600 gns, and sent to Holland. *R. Hollinshead*

LIATHACH 6 b.g. Shirley Heights 130 – Reuval 102 (Sharpen Up 127) [1996 NR 1997 a14g 16d 14.1s² 16.2d⁴ 12g Sep 2] poor handicapper, lightly raced: gave impression something amiss last 2 starts: stays 1¾m: acts on soft ground. *J. R. Fanshawe*   35

LIBERALIS 2 ch.f. (May 16) Interrex (CAN) – Hello Lady (Wolverlife 115) [1997 5d 5m 5g Jun 16] sparely-made filly: first foal: dam of little account over hurdles: tailed off, including in a seller. *G. F. H. Charles-Jones*   –

LIBERTE BELL (IRE) 2 b.f. (Jan 30) Petorius 117 – Ransomed (IRE) (Ballad Rock 122) [1997 a5g a5g 5d 6s³ Oct 14] 15,500Y: first foal: dam Irish 1¼m winner from good family: off course 3 months, easily best effort when staying-on third in well-run nursery at Ayr: should stay 1m: likely to do better. *Sir Mark Prescott*   56 p

LICKETYSPLIT 2 b.f. (Apr 5) Rock City 120 – Constant Companion 84 (Pas de Seul 133) [1997 a5g Nov 14] 900F, 3,200Y: sixth foal: half-sister to 1993 2-y-o 7f winner Hobart (by Reprimand), later successful in Hong Kong, and fairly useful 7f/1m performer Comanche Companion (by Commanche Run): dam 1m winner who stayed 1¼m: 14/1, always well behind in maiden at Southwell. *N. Bycroft*   –

LIDO (IRE) 2 ch.c. (May 15) Waajib 121 – Licimda (GER) (Konigsstuhl (GER)) [1997 6f³ 6g² 5.7m* 6g⁴ 6m 6d 7g² Oct 25] IR 8,000Y: tall, close-coupled colt: poor walker: has a quick action: first foal: dam winner at 2 yrs in Germany (later 9f listed placed) from good German family: fairly useful performer: landed odds in maiden at Bath in July: rather disappointing subsequently until very good neck second to Florazi in nursery at Doncaster: should stay at least 1m: type to do better at 3 yrs. *B. W. Hills*   86 p

LIFE OF RILEY 3 ch.c. Caerleon (USA) 132 – Catina 102 (Nureyev (USA) 131) [1996 NR 1997 10s³ 10m* 12d⁴ 12g 13.3d Sep 20] 62,000Y: big, good-topped colt: fifth foal: half-brother to 2 winners, including useful 1½m winner Tinashaan (by Darshaan): dam Irish 2-y-o 6f winner suited by 1m: fairly useful performer: won maiden at Pontefract in June: best effort when fourth in handicap at Newmarket next start, ran badly last 2: should stay 1¾m. *G. Lewis*   88

LIFE ON THE STREET 3 b.f. Statoblest 120 – Brave Advance (USA) 98 (Bold Laddie (USA)) [1996 62: 5.2d⁵ 5s³ 5f³ 5g 6g 5.1g³ 7f³ 1997 7.1g 5.1g 6.1m Sep 23] sturdy filly: modest maiden at 2 yrs for R. Hannon: well held in 1997. *D. Nicholls*   –

LIFE SENTENCE 2 ch.c. (Apr 9) Timeless Times (USA) 99 – Marfen (Lochnager 132) [1997 a5g 5m⁴ 5m 7g⁵ 6d⁵ 6m 6d⁶ Oct 21] 6,200Y: small, good-quartered colt: third foal: brother to 4-y-o Ramsey Hope: dam unraced: disappointing maiden: visored/blinkered final 3 starts: jinked and unseated rider third outing: sold 600 gns, and sent to Germany. *J. G. Smyth-Osbourne*   42

LIFFRE (IRE) 3 b.f. Sadler's Wells (USA) 132 – Liffey Lass (USA) 95 (Irish River (FR) 131) [1996 74p: 8.2g⁴ 1997 12d³ 11.5s² 14m* 13.9g³ 15d Sep 18] well-made filly: good mover with a long stride: fairly useful handicapper: upped in trip, improved to win at Goodwood in August: ran well at York next time: raced too freely in blinkers final start: should stay 2m: sold 100,000 gns in December. *J. H. M. Gosden*   92

LIFT BOY (USA) 8 b.g. Fighting Fit (USA) – Pressure Seat (USA) (Ginistrelli (USA) 117) [1996 52, a69: a5g* a6g⁶ a6g³ a5g* a5g⁵ a6g* a5g⁶ 5m⁶ 5m² 5m⁴ 5m* 7f 5.3m⁴ 5f a5g⁴ a6g 1997 a6g⁴ a5g³ a6g a7g³ a7g* a7g² a6g⁶ 6f a5g a6g a7g Dec 19] small, sturdy gelding: modest performer on the all-weather, poor (and lightly raced) on turf: won apprentice handicap at Lingfield in February: below form last 5 starts: effective at 5f to 7f: tried visored. *G. L. Moore*   – a66

LIFT THE OFFER (IRE)   2 ch.c. (Apr 4) Ballad Rock 122 – Timissara (USA)   72
(Shahrastani (USA) 135) [1997 7m⁶ 7g² 7d³ 8d 8g a8g* a7s* Nov 28] IR 15,000Y: a85
close-coupled, workmanlike colt: third foal: half-brother to 3-y-o Timissa and fairly
useful Irish 1½m winner Timidjar (by Doyoun): dam Irish 1m and 1½m winner:
fairly useful on all-weather, fair on turf: won nursery (best effort) and minor event
(odds on) at Lingfield in November: stays 1m: acts on equitrack. *R. Hannon*

LIGHTEN UP   3 b.f. Nashwan (USA) 135 – Lagta 75 (Kris 135) [1996 NR 1997   67
8g 10g⁴ 10.4s 11.1m 16.1m³ 14.1g Oct 18] rangy filly: has plenty of scope: sixth foal:
half-sister to useful 1¼m and 1½m winner Rudagi (by Persian Bold): dam 1½m
and 1¾m winner: fair maiden: off course over 4 months after debut: close third in
handicap at Newcastle in October: badly hampered only subsequent outing: likely to
prove suited by a test of stamina: sold 17,000 gns in December. *C. E. Brittain*

LIGHTNING REBEL   3 b.g. Rambo Dancer (CAN) 107 – Ozra 63 (Red Alert   –
127) [1996 67: 6.1d⁵ 8.3d² 8.1s⁵ 1997 a8g⁶ 10m 9.2d 12g⁶ Aug 28] unfurnished
gelding: fair at 2 yrs, disappointing in 1997. *C. W. Thornton*

LIGHT PROGRAMME   3 b.c. El Gran Senor (USA) 136 – Nashmeel (USA)   89 p
121 (Blushing Groom (FR) 131) [1996 NR 1997 10d² 10g* Jul 9] well-made,
attractive colt: fifth foal: closely related to 2 winners, including useful French miler
Light Music (by Nijinsky), and half-brother to 2 winners, including smart French
miler Battle Dore (by Sanglamore): dam, French 1m winner, stayed 1¼m: evens,
confirmed debut promise when winning maiden at Newmarket in July by head from
Marilaya, driven ahead over 1f out and keeping on gamely: showed a relaxed attitude
in paddock: underwent knee operation afterwards but stays in training and should be
capable of further improvement if recovering. *H. R. A. Cecil*

LIGHT REFLECTIONS   4 b.g. Rainbow Quest (USA) 134 – Tajfah (USA)   –
(Shadeed (USA) 135) [1996 NR 1997 11.7g⁵ 10.2d 12.5d Jun 24] no worthwhile
form. *P. G. Murphy*

LIGHTS OF HOME   3 b.g. Deploy 131 – Dream Chaser 92 (Record Token 128)   –
[1996 –: 6v⁶ a7s 1997 a6g a6g a8g⁴ Feb 17] no worthwhile form, including in sellers.
Miss C. Johnsey

LIGHT STEP (USA)   2 b.f. (Mar 1) Nureyev (USA) 131 – Nimble Feet (USA)   74
82 (Danzig (USA)) [1997 7d³ 6m³ 6g Oct 27] smallish, quite attractive filly: sixth
foal: half-sister to several winners, including 3-y-o Fleet River, smart sprinter Forest
Gazelle (by Green Forest) and very smart performer up to 1¼m Eltish (by Cox's
Ridge): dam, 2-y-o 5f winner, sister to good US 1994 2-y-o Contredance: fair form
when third in maidens at Doncaster and Redcar: off 4 months after latter and
disappointing final start: should stay 1m. *H. R. A. Cecil*

LIKELY STORY (IRE)   2 b.f. (Apr 22) Night Shift (USA) – Perfect Alibi (Law   86
Society (USA) 130) [1997 6g³ 6g² 6g² 5.2m 6d* 6m⁵ 6g⁵ Sep 19] good-bodied filly:
fluent mover: third foal: half-sister to 3-y-o Final Trial and 5-y-o Acquittal (11f
winner at 3 yrs): dam (unraced) from good family: fairly useful performer: won
maiden at Epsom in August: ran creditably in listed races at Kempton and Ayr
following month: should stay 1m: yet to race on extremes of going. *J. L. Dunlop*

LILANITA   2 b.f. (Apr 22) Anita's Prince 126 – Jimlil 99 (Nicholas Bill 125)   –
[1997 6d⁵ 6.1m Jul 19] first foal: dam 6f (at 2 yrs) and 1m winner: only a little sign of
ability in maidens. *B. Palling*

LILA PEDIGO (IRE)   4 b.f. Classic Secret (USA) 91 – Miss Goldie Locks (Dara   –
Monarch 128) [1996 62: a6g a6g 6d 8g⁵ 8.2m² 8m⁵ 8f² 10m⁵ 10g* 10d³ 10m⁶ 10m
1997 a10g 9.9m 8g 10d 10g 10g Jul 8] leggy filly: modest handicapper at 3 yrs, little
show in 1997. *Miss J. F. Craze*

LILIAN MARKS (IRE)   2 gr.f. (Apr 9) Astronef 116 – Alicia Markova 64   –
(Habat 127) [1997 6g 5.7g 7g 7m Jul 22] IR 6,000Y: leggy filly: half-sister to several
winners, including 5-y-o Sharp Consul: dam ran 3 times at 2 yrs: no worthwhile
form, including in sellers: sent to Czech Republic. *B. J. Meehan*

LILLIBELLA   4 b.f. Reprimand 122 – Clarandal 80 (Young Generation 129)   60
[1996 64: 5d⁵ 5f³ 7f³ 6m⁴ 6.1m² 5.3f³ 6m⁶ 6.1m 1997 8g⁶ 7.1m⁶ 7m 6f* 5g* 5g 5g
6.1m 5m⁵ 5m 5d⁴ Oct 20] tall filly: good walker: modest handicapper: won at Redcar
and Musselburgh in the summer: in and out afterwards: effective at 5f and 6f: acts on

firm and dead ground: blinkered (out of form) once: not an easy ride, often spoiling chance by hanging left. *Mrs J. R. Ramsden*

LILLI CLAIRE   4 ch.f. Beveled (USA) – Lillicara (FR) (Caracolero (USA) 131)   104
[1996 91: 8g 8m* 8s 8.5m 8m² 7g* 7m 8m 7g⁶ 1997 7.6g* 8d² May 22] sparely-made filly: useful performer: won minor event at Lingfield in May, by 4 lengths from Crown Court, quickening impressively: very good ¾-length second to Out West in listed race at Goodwood only subsequent outing: stays 1m: acts on good to firm and dead ground: held up: reportedly fractured near-fore knee in late-July. *A. G. Foster*

LILY JAQUES   3 b.f. Petong 126 – Scossa (USA) 52 (Shadeed (USA)) [1996   50
50: 6d⁵ 6.1m⁶ 6g⁶ a6s a7g² 1997 a8g³ a7g² a8g a10g⁵ 10m May 17] modest maiden: well held last 3 starts: stays 1m: acts on equitrack, no form on fibresand. *R. Guest*

LIMELIGHT   3 b.f. Old Vic 136 – Nellie Dean 59 (Song 132) [1996 NR 1997 8g   56
10.2f⁴ 10g 10s 10g³ a11g 10m Sep 25] first foal: dam, 7f winner, stayed 1m: modest maiden: better at 1¼m than shorter: acts on firm going, well beaten on fibresand: no improvement blinkered. *J. A. R. Toller*

LIME STREET BLUES (IRE)   6 b.g. Digamist (USA) 110 – Royal Daughter   63
(High Top 131) [1996 NR 1997 8m 14.9d⁶ 16.1g 14m³ 13.8g² 14.4m 14m 14.1g Oct 4] smallish gelding: modest handicapper: stays 1¾m: acts on any ground: untrustworthy over hurdles. *T. Keddy*

LIMNI (USA)   3 ch.c. Gone West (USA) – Lightning Fire 105 (Kris 135) [1996   78
NR 1997 10m³ 8d⁴ 10.5g⁴ Sep 26] strong colt: unimpressive mover: fourth foal: closely related to 2 winners, notably dam's 1¼m winner Flame Valley (by Gulch), and half-brother to useful French 1m winner Beyrouth (by Alleged): dam, sister to Common Grounds, 7f and 1m winner: in frame in maidens, best effort at Haydock on final outing: stays 10.5f: bandaged each start: looked difficult ride on debut. *Mrs J. Cecil*

LINCOLNSHIRE (USA)   2 b.g. (May 1) Shadeed (USA) 135 – Linkit (USA)   73
(Linkage (USA)) [1997 5m⁵ 7.1g⁵ 7d⁴ 7g² Aug 9] $30,000Y: third foal: dam won 4 times at up to 1m in USA: fair maiden: didn't handle turn well when second at Ayr final start: should stay 1m: has pulled hard: sent to Hong Kong. *P. F. I. Cole*

LINDA   2 b.f. (Mar 6) Risk Me (FR) 127 – Farrh Nouriya (IRE) (Lomond (USA)   –
128) [1997 6m a7g a7g a6g Sep 30] 1,600Y: third foal: dam unraced from family of Shirley Heights: little sign of ability: blinkered in seller final start. *N. A. Callaghan*

LINDEN HEIGHTS   2 b.c. (Feb 28) Distinctly North (USA) 115 – Enaam 65§   103
(Shirley Heights 130) [1997 6d² 6s* 6g² 6m⁴ Jul 31] 5,400F, 19,000Y: robust colt: third foal: half-brother to ungenuine 1m winner Linda's Joy (by Classic Secret): dam ungenerous maiden, out of half-sister to Give Thanks: useful performer: landed odds in maiden at Newmarket in June: 2 lengths second to Bold Fact in July Stakes (best effort) and over 6 lengths fourth to Daggers Drawn in Richmond Stakes at Goodwood after: stays 6f: tends to flash tail: sent to Hong Kong. *L. M. Cumani*

LINDEN'S LAD (IRE)   3 b.c. Distinctly North (USA) 115 – Make Or Mar 84   51
(Daring March 116) [1996 –: 6m 6m⁵ 6m⁶ 8m 1997 9g 7g 7.1g 8.3g 7f⁵ 8.2s² 9m Oct 31] workmanlike colt: modest maiden handicapper: good second at Nottingham: not sure to stay beyond 1m: acts on firm and soft ground: visored last 2 starts. *J. R. Jenkins*

LINDESBERG   2 b.f. (May 20) Doyoun 124 – Be Discreet (Junius (USA) 124)   71
[1997 6m³ 6g⁶ 6d² Nov 7] 22,000Y: leggy, workmanlike filly: seventh foal: half-sister to several winners, including 3-y-o Omaha City and 4-y-o Gothenberg: dam won at up to 7f in France: best effort in maidens when length second to Masha-Il at Doncaster, keeping on despite wandering: should stay at least 1m. *M. Johnston*

LINDRICK LADY (IRE)   3 b.f. Broken Hearted 124 – Fiodoir (Weavers' Hall   70
122) [1996 NR 1997 12g² 7.5s* 12d* 10g 10g 9.9v* 9.9m⁴ 12g⁵ 16.2d 10.4s 12f Sep 17] IR 2,000Y: unfurnished filly: half-sister to Irish 1½m winner Motility (by Yashgan): dam Irish 1½m winner: fair performer: won claimer and handicap at Beverley in May and handicap there in July: well below form last 4 starts: should stay beyond 1½m: goes well on dead ground or softer: front runner. *B. S. Rothwell*

LIT

LINEA-G   3 ch.f. Keen 116 – Horton Line 89 (High Line 125) [1996 NR 1997   –
10.1m⁵ 12d⁵ 8f Jun 2] half-sister to 2 winners, notably 5-y-o Angus-G: dam 1½m
winner: tenderly handled in maidens at Newcastle and Musselburgh in May: very
awkward leaving stalls and always tailed off only subsequent outing. *Mrs M. Reveley*

LINEAGE   2 b.f. (Mar 12) Distant Relative 128 – Hymne d'Amour (USA) 58   –
(Dixieland Band (USA)) [1997 7d Oct 13] stocky filly: first foal: dam lightly raced
on flat, winning hurdler, out of half-sister to Alzao: 10/1, burly and green, behind in
maiden at Leicester, some late headway, not knocked about. *N. A. Graham*

LINGUISTIC DANCER   2 ch.f. (Mar 15) Aragon 118 – Linguistic 95 (Porto   –
Bello 118) [1997 7d Oct 13] leggy filly: half-sister to several winners, including fair
stayers Castle Douglas (by Amboise) and Relatively Easy (by Relkino) and 3-y-o
Flashtalkin' Flood: dam won twice over 5f at 2 yrs: 50/1 and very green, behind in
maiden at Leicester, starting slowly: moved poorly to post. *A. G. Newcombe*

LINNETSONG   2 b.f. (Feb 20) Rambo Dancer (CAN) 107 – Blue Linnet 96   53
(Habitat 134) [1997 5g 5s 7g* 7.5v⁴ 7m 7.9s a7g Dec 18] leggy filly: half-sister to
several winners abroad: dam 5f winner: won seller at Redcar in June: little show
afterwards: reportedly struck into when tailed off penultimate start, and subsequently
left G. Oldroyd: stays 7f: visored after second start. *D. W. Chapman*

LIONELS LUCKY LADY   2 ch.f. (Apr 19) Emarati (USA) 74 – Gaynor   –
Goodman (IRE) 43 (Fayruz 116) [1997 5g 5d 5.3f Oct 1] small filly: first foal: dam
poor sprint maiden: well beaten in sellers. *J. S. Moore*

LIONIZE (USA)   4 ch.c. Storm Cat (USA) – Pedestal (High Line 125) [1996 83+:   105
7m* 9g 8g 1997 8g 10.3d 10m⁶ 8d* a8.5g⁴ a8g* a8.5g* Dec 26] quite attractive colt:
useful performer: left P. Chapple-Hyam after second start: won handicap at Leicester
in October and minor event at Lingfield then handicap at Wolverhampton in December, making all to beat Democrat by 1¾ lengths in last-named: stays 8.5f: acts on
good to firm, dead going and all-weather: has had tongue tied: blinkered last 4 starts.
Mrs J. Cecil

LIQUID GOLD (IRE)   3 b. or br.c. Fairy King (USA) – Heavenward (USA)   73
(Conquistador Cielo (USA)) [1996 NR 1997 9d⁶ 8.2d* 8m⁶ 8g⁶ a8g* 10m⁴ Aug 26]   a92
54,000Y: big, strong colt: third foal: half-brother to fairly useful 1995 2-y-o 7f
winner Exalted (by High Estate) and winners in Italy: dam ran once in USA: won
maiden at Nottingham in June and handicap at Southwell (by 6 lengths, easily best
run) in August: probably stays 1¼m: goes very well on firebsand: decidedly coltish 3
times: hung right final start: sent to B. Jackson, USA. *W. A. O'Gorman*

LISA'S PRIDE (IRE)   2 ch.f. (Apr 24) Pips Pride 117 – Brazilian Princess 66   68
(Absalom 128) [1997 5g 5g 6f* 6d 5g 7f⁵ Sep 28] 7,000Y: compact, workmanlike
filly: fifth living foal: half-sister to several winners, including fair sprinter Soba
Guest (by Be My Guest) and Irish 9f winner Wolfies Rascal (by Northiam): dam,
maiden who stayed 1m, is half-sister to Soba: won maiden at Salisbury in June: well
below that form otherwise, off nearly 3 months before final start: should stay 7f: acts
on firm ground. *Miss Gay Kelleway*

LISTED ACCOUNT (USA)   3 b.f. Private Account (USA) – Sypharina (FR)   80
(Lyphard (USA) 132) [1996 77p: 8.1m³ 8.1s 1997 8d⁶ 10m⁴ 7s² 6g² 6m³ 5.3f² 6m²
Oct 7] close-coupled filly: has a rather round action: fairly useful maiden: may prove
best short of 1m: acts on firm and soft going: looked none too keen final start, and not
one to place much faith in: sent to USA. *L. M. Cumani*

LITERARY   3 b.f. Woodman (USA) 126 – Book Collector (USA) 80 (Irish River   79
(FR) 131) [1996 76: 6g⁶ 6f² 7m 7997 7f³ 7d² 7s⁴ 8g 9.7m⁵ 8.3m³ 10m 7f⁴ 8d*
8d⁶ Oct 28] leggy filly: fair handicapper: mostly disappointing before winning at Leicester in October: best coming from off a strong gallop at 1m: acts on firm and soft
going: sometimes a weak finisher: sold 94,000 gns in December. *J. H. M. Gosden*

LITERARY SOCIETY (USA)   4 ch.c. Runaway Groom (CAN) – Dancing   88
Gull (USA) (Northern Dancer) [1996 73: 6m 6m 5.2m³ 5.3f* 5m² 5g* 5m 5m 5m²
5g⁴ 1997 5g² 5.1d⁵ 5m* 6g 6g³ 6m* 6g 5.2m² Sep 16] small, sturdy colt: has a quick
action: fairly useful handicapper: won at Newmarket in May and Newbury in July:
effective at 5f and 6f: has form on dead ground, best efforts on good or firmer: usually

549

races prominently: sweating and edgy (rare poor effort) seventh start: game and reliable. *J. A. R. Toller*

LITTLE ACORN   3 b.g. Unfuwain (USA) 131 – Plaything 69 (High Top 131)   91
[1996 53: 8.2g a7g⁵ 1997 a8.5g² 12g⁸* 12g* 12m² 12g³ 12s² 14m² 15d Sep 18] fairly useful handicapper: won at Catterick in March and Carlisle in April: good efforts next 4 starts: stays 1¾m: acts on good to firm and soft ground: sometimes wanders and flashes tail: consistent: sold 20,000 gns in October. *S. C. Williams*

LITTLE ANNIE   3 b.f. Syrtos 106 – Anne's Bank (IRE) 77 (Burslem 123) [1996   –
NR 1997 6f⁶ 6m 7g May 9] first foal: dam, Irish 7f winner, should have stayed 1½m: well held in maidens. *G. L. Moore*

LITTLE BRAVE   2 b.g. (Feb 16) Kahyasi 130 – Littlemisstrouble (USA) (My   70
Gallant (USA)) [1997 9m⁵ 8g Oct 18] 26,000Y: fourth foal: half-brother to 4-y-o Polar Prospect: dam won up to 9f in USA: better effort in maidens at Redcar on debut: likely to need 1¼m+. *J. M. P. Eustace*

LITTLE CHARMER   2 b.f. (Apr 1) Theatrical Charmer 114 – Saysana 63 (Sayf   –
El Arab (USA) 127) [1997 8m a8g Nov 13] first reported foal: dam 5f (at 2 yrs) to 9.7f winner: well beaten in maidens. *R. Rowe*

LITTLE CRACKER   2 ch.f. (Jan 25) Tina's Pet 121 – All That Crack (Stanford   44
121§) [1997 6m a7g 8.2d³ a7g⁶ Nov 14] 400Y: leggy filly: third reported foal: dam, modest Irish maiden, stayed 1m: best effort when third in seller at Redcar in October. *A. G. Newcombe*

LITTLE EMILY   2 gr.f. (Mar 28) Zafonic (USA) 130 – Petillante 101 (Petong   48
126) [1997 6.9s a7s⁴ a6g Dec 6] third foal: dam won Norfolk Stakes but did not train on: form only when fourth in minor event at Lingfield in November. *C. E. Brittain*

LITTLE FIZZ   2 b.f. (May 15) Efisio 120 – Apprila (Bustino 136) [1997 5g³ 6f⁵   63
5.1g⁵ a5g⁵ a6s⁴ a5s Nov 28] 2,100Y: half-sister to 1m winner Blasted (by Statoblest):   a52 +
dam ran 4 times: modest maiden: failed to repeat debut form: best at 5f. *B. J. Meehan*

LITTLE HOOLIGAN   6 b. or br.g. Rabdan 129 – Nutwood Emma (Henbit   –
(USA) 130) [1996 NR 1997 a16g Nov 25] poor handicapper: lightly raced and no form on flat since 1994: usually visored. *S. G. Knight*

LITTLE IBNR   6 b.g. Formidable (USA) 125 – Zalatia 97 (Music Boy 124) [1996   –
62, a77: a7g a6g a7g a5g a5g a6g⁵ a6g* 6.1g a6g⁵ 7.6g 5.1m a6g 6m⁶ 6m⁵ 7.6m 5g⁶   a73 d
a6s 1997 a7s⁶ a7g³ a6g⁵ a7f⁸* a6g³ a6g⁴ a7g⁶ a6g a5g* a6g a6g³ a5g³ a6g a5g a6g²
a6g a6g a7g a6g a5g Dec 8] workmanlike gelding: fair performer: won minor event in January and seller at Wolverhampton: left P. D. Evans after fifteenth start and lost his form: stays 7f: best on all-weather: sometimes blinkered/visored. *P. D. Cundell*

LITTLE INDIAN   2 ch.c. (Apr 16) Little Missouri (USA) – Both Sides Now   105
(USA) (Topsider (USA)) [1997 6d³ 6g* 7m³ 7.1s* 8g Oct 25] 10,000F, 21,000Y: smallish, sparely-made colt: lacks scope: fluent mover: eighth foal: half-brother to several winners here and in USA, including 3-y-o Mukaddar and 7f (at 2 yrs) and 1½m winner Seckar Vale (both by Elmaamul): dam showed a little ability in USA: sire (by Cox's Ridge) very smart 9f and 1½m winner in USA: useful performer: won maiden at Haydock in July and Solario Stakes at Sandown in August, leading near finish to beat Tracking ½ length in latter: never threatened to play part in Racing Post Trophy at Doncaster final start: should stay well beyond 7f: acts on good to firm and soft ground. *S. P. C. Woods*

LITTLE LUKE (IRE)   6 b.h. Somethingfabulous (USA) – Yours Sincerely   –
(USA) (Stalwart (USA)) [1996 –: 8g 11.6m 10.8m 11.6d 1997 a16g Jan 11] no longer of any account. *P. Butler*

LITTLE MISS HUFF (IRE)   2 b.f. (Mar 11) Anita's Prince 126 – Regal   70
Charmer (Royal And Regal (USA)) [1997 7g⁵ 7d* Aug 25] IR 5,000Y: sister to several winners, including Irish 1994 2-y-o 6.5f winner Anita's Galaxy and 1¼m winner Galaxy High: dam Irish 1½m winner: justified favouritism in maiden at Warwick by 3½ lengths from Thelonius, running on strongly: will stay 1m. *R. Guest*

LITTLE MISS LUCY   3 b.f. Petoski 135 – Puki Puki (Roselier (FR)) [1996 NR   52
1997 10g⁴ 10g⁴ 11.7g Sep 8] first reported foal: dam winning hurdler/pointer: modest maiden: pulled up lame final start: should stay beyond 1¼m. *M. J. Heaton-Ellis*

LITTLE MISS RIBOT   7 b.m. Lighter 111 – Little Missile (Ile de Bourbon (USA) 133) [1996 NR 1997 a10g a10g⁵ Dec 19] poor winner at 1¼m on equitrack in 1995: well held both starts since. *R. J. O'Sullivan*   –

LITTLE MISS ROCKER   3 b.f. Rock Hopper 124 – Drama School 72 (Young Generation 129) [1996 59: 7m 8m⁵ 1997 10.2f³ 11.9f² 10.8s 11.8d⁴ 11.9g* 12g Sep 15] fair performer: won 3-runner maiden at Brighton in August on final start for I. Balding: stays 1½m: acts on firm ground, below form on dead and soft: won juvenile hurdle in October. *A. R. Dicken*   65

LITTLE MURRAY   4 b.g. Mon Tresor 113 – Highland Daisy (He Loves Me 120) [1996 –: 8.3m 8m 1997 a8.5g Jan 15] of little account. *F. Murphy*   –

LITTLE PAPOOSE   4 b.f. Cree Song 99 – Little Tich (Great Nephew 126) [1996 NR 1997 a5g a5g a7g a5g 5.9m Jun 25] third reported foal: half-sister to poor 6f winner Swinging Tich (by Swing Easy): dam unraced twin: no form. *B. A. McMahon*   –

LITTLE PILGRIM   4 b.g. Precocious 126 – Bonny Bright Eyes 58 (Rarity 129) [1996 –: 8.2d 6m 5m a8g a8g⁶ 1997 a10g a10g a7g⁶ 8s 6.9m² 8.1m 7.6g 8m 10.8g a– 10d a7g Dec 19] tall, lengthy gelding: poor maiden: lost his form: stays 7f: acts on good to firm ground. *T. M. Jones*   50 d

LITTLE PROGRESS   3 b.g. Rock City 120 – Petite Hester 85 (Wollow 132) [1996 –: 6g 6g 6m 5d a6g 1997 5m a8g 8.3s a8g Dec 2] of no account. *T. M. Jones*   –

LITTLE RISK   2 b.f. (Apr 17) Risk Me (FR) 127 – Little Preston (IRE) 53 (Pennine Walk 120) [1997 8.1d a6g⁵ 10d a7g Oct 20] lengthy filly: second reported foal: dam, maiden, stayed 1¼m: signs of a little ability on debut, but well held in sellers afterwards. *K. McAuliffe*   –

LITTLESTONE ROCKET   3 ch.c. Safawan 118 – Miss Hocroft (Dominion 123) [1996 –: 6m a6g 5m 1997 6g⁶ 5m 5.1m 5m⁶ 5.1f 5m* 5m⁴ 5m⁵ 5g³ 5m a5g 5.1g 5m Sep 17] modest performer: won seller at Folkestone in June: creditable efforts next 3 starts, well beaten last 3: raced mainly at 5f: yet to race on ground softer than good: visored/blinkered since fourth start. *W. R. Muir*   55

LITTLE TOLERANCE   2 ch.f. (Feb 16) Weldnaas (USA) 112 – Beau Dada (IRE) 66 (Pine Circle (USA)) [1997 6m Aug 9] first reported foal: dam 6f (at 2 yrs) and 1m winner who stayed 1¼m: tailed off in minor event at Lingfield. *J. Cullinan*   –

LITTLE TUCKER   3 ch.g. Hadeer 118 – Fly The Coop (Kris 135) [1996 NR 1997 a9.4g Feb 12] fifth foal: brother to 7-y-o General Mouktar, fairly useful 10.5f to 1½m winner at best: dam Irish 11f winner: well beaten in fibresand maiden. *B. Preece*   –

LITTLE TUMBLER (IRE)   2 b.f. (Mar 2) Cyrano de Bergerac 120 – Glass Minnow (IRE) 59 (Alzao (USA) 117) [1997 6m² 7m² 6m⁴ 7d⁵ 8m 7m Oct 23] IR 1,500Y: neat filly: second foal: sister to 3-y-o Mike's Double: dam, placed up to 9f in Ireland, out of sister to high-class sprinter Abergwaun: poor maiden: in frame in sellers first 3 starts: stays 7f. *S. Woodman*   46

LIVE PROJECT (IRE)   5 b.g. Project Manager 111 – Saturday Live (Junius (USA) 124) [1996 67: a8.5g² a7g 1997 a7g⁴ a8.5f a6g⁶ a7g* a8g a8g² a8g* a8g³ 8m a61 8.3d a8g a8.5g 10.1g 12s a7g* Dec 18] modest handicapper: won at Southwell in February, Lingfield in March and, after series of poor efforts (left M. Johnston after tenth start), Southwell again in December: stays 8.5f: acts on good to firm ground, heavy and the all-weather. *R. Craggs*

LIVINGSTONE   2 b.c. (Apr 9) Dilum (USA) 115 – Batra (USA) 60 (Green Dancer (USA) 132) [1997 5m 5m⁶ May 3] 10,000F, 6,200Y: big, lengthy colt: has scope: third foal: half-brother to 1995 2-y-o 6f winner Double Point (by Alzao): dam 2-y-o 5f winner: only a little sign of ability in maidens at Doncaster and Newmarket. *C. A. Dwyer*   –

LIVIUS (IRE)   3 b.g. Alzao (USA) 117 – Marie de Beaujeu (FR) 108 (Kenmare (FR) 125) [1996 NR 1997 10.2m² Jul 7] fifth foal: half-brother to German Derby winner All My Dreams (by Assert) and winners in France by Deep Roots and Synefos: dam, French 2-y-o 5.5f and 6.5f winner, did not train on: 20/1, staying-on ½-length second to Meteor Strike in maiden at Bath: gelded and not seen out again. *Major D. N. Chappell*   79

LIZIUM 5 b.m. Ilium 121 – Lizaway (Casino Boy 114) [1996 –: 10m 7m 10m 12g – 10g 1997 12g 10.1g 12.1d a8g a16g Dec 10] of little account. *J. C. Fox*

LLANASA 2 br.f. (Jan 23) Petong 126 – Chasing Moonbeams 99 (Final Straw 60 § 127) [1997 5s³ 5d³ 6g 6s 6m Aug 18] 16,000Y: sparely-made filly: easy mover: seventh foal: half-sister to 3-y-o Tinkerbell, fair 5f winner Desert Dagger (by Green Desert) and a winner in UAE by Salse: dam 2-y-o 5f winner who deteriorated: third in maidens first 2 starts, but became temperamental: reluctant to race and unseated rider in blinkers in claimer final start. *J. Berry*

LOBKOV 5 ch.m. Dunbeath (USA) 127 – Lucy Manette 53 (Final Straw 127) – [1996 NR 1997 6m May 17] of no account. *R. Simpson*

LOBUCHE (IRE) 2 b.c. (Apr 20) Petardia 113 – Lhotse (IRE) (Shernazar 131) 58 d [1997 5d 5.3m⁴ 6f² 7.3m 6.9g 7.6m⁶ 7f⁶ 8m⁶ Oct 5] 10,000Y: neat colt: first foal: dam Irish maiden: demoted after first past post in seller at Brighton in May: off course nearly 3 months and below best afterwards: should stay beyond 6f: raced mainly on good to firm/firm ground. *R. Hannon*

LOCHANGEL 3 ch.f. Night Shift (USA) – Peckitts Well 96 (Lochnager 132) 104 p [1996 94p: 6m² 6m* 1997 7s³ 6d⁴ 6m 6m Oct 3] big, rangy filly: has scope: good walker: has a quick action: useful performer: in frame in listed race and handicap first 2 starts (4 months apart): best effort when 6 lengths ninth of 14 to Elnadim in Diadem Stakes at Ascot on penultimate outing: may prove best around 6f: acts on good to firm and dead going, probably on soft: lightly raced, and should progress again in 1998. *I. A. Balding*

LOCH BERING (USA) 5 ch.h. Bering 136 – Passerine (USA) (Dr Fager) [1996 100 103: 9g⁵ a12g² 12d⁵ 14g⁵ a10g² 9d³ a8g³ 8g² a10g* a9.4g⁶ 1997 9g³ 8g³ 9.8m a8g⁶ 11.5f² 9g⁶ a8g⁴ a12g* a10s* a10s* a9.4g⁵ Dec 6] useful performer: had a good autumn in Sweden, winning listed event then 2 other races at Taby: below-form fifth of 7 to Farmost in listed race at Wolverhampton final start: stays 1¾m: effective on turf and dirt and in blinkers. *A. Lund, Norway*

LOCHDENE (IRE) 2 b.c. (Mar 19) Robellino (USA) 127 – Cat's Claw (USA) 69 (Sharpen Up 127) [1997 5s⁵ 5.9f⁴ May 29] 15,500Y: fourth foal: half-brother to 3-y-o Feel A Line: dam unraced granddaughter of US Grade 1 placed filly Funny Cat: better effort in maidens in May when fourth at Carlisle. *M. Johnston*

LOCH-HURN LADY 3 b.f. Lochnager 132 – Knocksharry 58 (Palm Track 122) 53 [1996 62: 5g 5d 6m⁵ 6m 5m⁴ 5m² 7g 6g⁴ 8g 1997 5g* 5m 6.1s 5d 5.1g 6g 8.5m 7g Oct 24] small, sturdy filly: unimpressive mover: modest performer: won minor event at Catterick in March: harshly treated in handicaps after until final start (respectable run): best efforts at 5f: acts on good to firm ground: often a front runner. *K. W. Hogg, Isle of Man*

LOCH LAIRD 2 b.g. (Mar 30) Beveled (USA) – Daisy Loch (Lochnager 132) 73 [1997 5f² 5g² 5g³ Aug 13] lengthy gelding: sixth reported foal: brother to 7-y-o Loch Patrick: dam poor plater: fair form when placed in maidens at Lingfield and Windsor and minor event at Sandown: off track 3 months after debut (reportedly with sore shins). *M. Madgwick*

LOCHLASS (IRE) 3 b.f. Distinctly North (USA) 115 – Littleton Song 73 (Song 48 132) [1996 59: a6g⁶ 6m a8g³ a10g⁵ a8g³ 1997 a10g³ 9.9v 10m 10g⁶ 8m⁶ a7g 8f⁶ a– 10m³ 10m⁶ a10g Oct 27] angular filly: poor maiden: stays 1¼m: acts on equitrack and firm going, well beaten on heavy: effective blinkered or not: none too consistent. *S. P. C. Woods*

LOCHON 6 br.g. Lochnager 132 – Sky Mariner 59 (Julio Mariner 127) [1996 –, – a60: a5g a6g* a6g³ a6g⁴ a6g⁴ 6d⁶ 5g 6g 5g a5g 1997 a6g a7g a6g³ a6g a5g a5g⁶ 6g a53 d 6.1d⁶ a6g 6m a5g a7g⁵ a6g Jun 27] compact, workmanlike gelding: modest handicapper, all-weather/turf: disappointing in 1997: seems best at 6f: acts on any all-weather/turf going: tried blinkered/visored. *Mrs N. Macauley*

LOCH PATRICK 7 b.g. Beveled (USA) – Daisy Loch (Lochnager 132) [1996 93 106: 6m³ 6g* 6f⁵ 5f 5m⁴ 6m 7m³ 6m⁵ 5g 1997 6m⁴ 6m⁶ 6m 7.3m 5s 6d Sep 13] well-made gelding: just a fairly useful performer in 1997: effective at 5f to 7f: acts on firm and dead going: no improvement in blinkers: usually waited with. *M. Madgwick*

LOCH STYLE   4 b.g. Lochnager 132 – Simply Style (Bairn (USA) 126) [1996   57 d
57, a62: a12g a7g⁵ a7g⁵ a8.5g⁶ a9.4g³ a7g³ 10.3g 8m* 9g a7g⁵ a8g⁶ 1997 a8.5g* a8g   a62 d
a8g a7g a9.4g⁵ 7g² 8m a7g a7g⁶ 6g⁵ 6.9m⁶ a8.5g a8.5g⁵ a8g a8g⁶ Dec 18] plain
gelding: unimpressive mover: modest performer: well backed, won seller at Wolverhampton in January: mostly below form afterwards: effective at 7f, probably 9.4f:
acts on fibresand and good to firm ground: often starts slowly, and has hung right:
inconsistent. *R. Hollinshead*

LOCKSILL   3 b.c. Silly Prices 110 – Steelock 68 (Lochnager 132) [1996 NR 1997   –
5s 6g 7m 5f a8g Nov 17] 750Y: heavy-topped colt: fifth foal: dam sprinter: behind in
maidens/minor event. *A. Smith*

LOGANLEA (IRE)   3 gr.f. Petong 126 – White's Pet (Mummy's Pet 125) [1996   54
–p: 5v⁶ 1997 8g⁶ 7m 8d 5g 5m Oct 2] close-coupled filly: modest maiden: effective
at 5f, probably 1m: acts on good to firm ground: none too easy a ride. *W. J. Musson*

LOGIE PERT LAD   5 b.g. Green Ruby (USA) 104 – Rhazya (Rousillon (USA)   29
133) [1996 29: 5m 5.3m 5.1f a6g a10g a6g⁴ a7g a6s a7g 1997 a5g a6g⁵ a6g⁶ a5g⁵
a5g⁵ a5g 5m a12g a6g⁵ a7s a8g Dec 2] leggy gelding: bad sprint maiden: tried
blinkered/visored. *J. J. Bridger*

LOKI (IRE)   9 ch.g. Thatching 131 – Sigym (Lord Gayle (USA) 124) [1996 69d:
8m² 10d 12g⁶ 12g 12m⁴ 12m⁴ 11.8f² 11m² a12g² 1997 a13g a12g⁴ Mar 13] strong
gelding: on the downgrade, and well held in 1997. *G. Lewis*

LOMBARDIC (USA)   6 b.h. Private Account (USA) – If Winter Comes (USA)   –
(Dancing Champ (USA)) [1996 95: 11.9g* 12m 12s 12m 11.9m 11.9f⁴ 1997 12g
Jun 7] good-topped horse: useful handicapper at 1½m at 5 yrs: tailed off only start in
1997: won over hurdles in October. *J. A. B. Old*

LOMBERTO   4 b.c. Robellino (USA) 127 – Lamees (USA) (Lomond (USA) 128)   95
[1996 –: 7d 10m⁴ 10m⁵ 11.1m 10d 1997 8.1g 10m* 10s² 11.9g 10m 10s 10d² 10v³
Oct 11] good-topped colt: useful performer: won minor event at Salisbury in June:
good efforts in competitive handicaps last 2 starts: should stay 1½m: acts on good to
firm and heavy ground: tried blinkered earlier in career: usually held up, and suited
by truly-run race: sent to USA. *V. Soane*

LOMOND LASSIE (USA)   4 b.f. Lomond (USA) 128 – Herbivorous (USA)   –
(Nashua) [1996 –: 12.3m 10.3g 12g 15.8g 8m 10m 11f 8.2s 1997 a8g 8m 7g Oct 24]
of little account. *T. Kersey*

LONDON LIGHTS   3 b.c. Slip Anchor 136 – Pageantry 83 (Welsh Pageant 132)   79
[1996 NR 1997 11.1m³ 10m⁵ Sep 9] 125,000Y: useful-looking colt: fifth reported
foal: brother to St Simon Stakes winner Up Anchor (dam of promising 2-y-o
Fleetwood) and half-brother to 2 winners by Dominion, including useful miler Just
Class: dam ran only at 2 yrs when placed over 5f and 6f: fair form in maidens at
Kempton and Leicester (fifth of 19 to Sacho) 5½ months apart: has taken keen hold,
but should be suited by 1½m+: sold 8,000 gns in October. *P. F. I. Cole*

LONDON NEWS (SAF)   5 ch.h. Bush Telegraph (SAF) – Soho Secret (SAF)   120
(Regent Street (ARG)) [1996 8g² 10g³ 9g* 8g³ 10g* 11g* 10g⁶ 8g³ 6g⁶ 1997 8g*
10g* 10m* 10m³ 8d⁵ 8g 6g² Dec 6] 140,000 rand Y: big, good-topped horse: brother
to a sprint winner and half-brother to numerous winners in South Africa: dam won 10
races at up to 9f and Grade 1 placed in South Africa: sire, champion at 2 and 3 yrs in
South Africa, won up to 11f: compiled a fine record in South Africa (won 9 and
placed in 5 of 17 starts, including 2 important races early in 1997): went to Hong
Kong and beat Privilege and Annus Mirabilis ½ length and same in Queen Elizabeth
II Cup at Sha Tin: well held in Group 2 races won by Bosra Sham at Royal Ascot and
Alhaarth at the Curragh in brief stay in Europe with B. Hills: returned to South
Africa, and beaten ½ length in Grade 2 event final start: stays 11f, seems at least
as effective at 1m: probably acts on good to firm and dead ground: normally races
prominently. *Alec Laird, South Africa*

LONDON'S HEART (USA)   3 b.f. Woodman (USA) 126 – Seattle Belle (USA)   64
(Seattle Slew (USA)) [1996 NR 1997 10f³ 10m 10d 7.3s⁶ May 17] 45,000Y:
unfurnished filly: third foal: dam unraced half-sister to top-class French miler
Bellypha: modest maiden: best effort on debut. *P. F. I. Cole*

LONELY HEART 3 b.f. Midyan (USA) 124 – Take Heart 84 (Electric 126) 79 [1996 67: 6m 7f⁶ 7.1s⁴ 1997 8g² 10m² 9m⁵ 12f³ 10.2d⁴ 10m⁴ 8d 10g* 10m⁵ 12v Oct 10] sparely-made filly: fair performer: won maiden at Goodwood in August, making all (often held up in the past): flattered in listed race there penultimate start: stays 1½m: best form on good ground or firmer: has worn eyecover near side: twice hung badly right at Salisbury, and said to need a rail to her right. *D. R. C. Elsworth*

LONELY LEADER (IRE) 4 ch.c. Royal Academy (USA) 130 – Queen To 106 Conquer (USA) 112 (King's Bishop (USA)) [1996 100: 7.1m* 7m⁴ 7g⁴ 9m⁶ 1997 8m⁶ 8g² 8g² 10d 8m⁶ 8.1g 8d 8m a8f⁴ Dec 28] useful-looking colt: easy mover: useful handicapper: ran well when placed at Newbury (promoted to second in Ladbrokes Spring Cup) and Kempton and when sixth of 32 (second home on far side) in Hunt Cup at Royal Ascot: may prove best around 1m: acts on good to firm ground, probably on dead: trained by R. Hannon before final start. *W. D. Mather, UAE*

LONE PIPER 2 b.c. (Feb 16) Warning 136 – Shamisen 86 (Diesis 133) [1997 7s³ 91 ? 7m⁶ 7g Aug 19] smallish, sturdy colt: first foal: dam, 2-y-o 7f winner, sister to smart miler Enharmonic: length third of 5 in muddling minor event at Yarmouth in July: appeared to run best race, though last of 6, in Lanson Champagne Vintage Stakes at Goodwood later in month: possibly something amiss in Acomb Stakes at York: difficult to assess. *C. E. Brittain*

LONESOME DUDE (CAN) 2 b.c. (Feb 13) With Approval (CAN) – Local 91 p Lass 106 (Local Suitor (USA) 128) [1997 7g² Oct 27] $60,000F, 68,000Y: angular colt: first foal; dam, 7f winner here at 3 yrs, later successful at 5/6 yrs in USA: sire high-class middle-distance performer: 7/1, promising 2 lengths second of 13 to odds-on Altibr in Leicester maiden, taking a while to warm up then running on strongly after winner had gone clear: should stay at least 1m: looked lethargic and didn't stretch out to post: sure to do a fair bit better and win races at 3 yrs. *M. R. Stoute*

LONG BOND (IRE) 2 ch.c. (May 19) Kris 135 – Compton Lady (USA) 100 74 p (Sovereign Dancer (USA)) [1997 7.5f² 7g² Sep 28] 10,000Y: sixth foal: half-brother to a winner in Norway by Slip Anchor: dam 7f (at 2 yrs) and 1½m winner: runner-up in maiden at Beverley and minor event at Dielsdorf (in Switzerland) in September: should stay at least 1¼m: should do better. *M. Johnston*

LONGBOWMAN 2 ch.g. (Apr 27) Prince Sabo 123 – Nuit de Lune (FR) (Crystal – Palace (FR) 132) [1997 7d a7g Nov 18] 11,000Y, 2,700 2-y-o: plain, lengthy gelding: poor walker: eighth foal: half-brother to fairly useful French 3-y-o Periode Bleue (by Pistolet Bleu), 1m winner at 2 yrs, and useful French 1¼m winner Night Watch (by Soviet Star): dam, 1½m winner in France, half-sister to 15f Grand Prix de Paris winner Soleil Noir: well beaten in maiden and seller. *Mrs L. Stubbs*

LONGCROFT 5 ch.m. Weldnaas (USA) 112 – Najariya (Northfields (USA)) 38 [1996 42: 12m 16.5g⁶ 16m⁴ 16.2m⁴ 15.8g 1997 16s 16f³ 18g 16d⁵ 17.2f Jul 23] sparely-made mare: poor stayer: left S. Kettlewell after fourth start: acts on firm going: won selling hurdle in August. *C. L. Popham*

LONG ISLAND 2 ch.g. (May 9) Elmaamul (USA) 125 – Ginny Binny 113 65 (Ahonoora 122) [1997 5m 7m 5d 6d a6g³ a8g⁶ Nov 13] 17,000F: fifth foal: half-brother to 1m/9f winner My Gina (by Be My Chief): dam Italian sprinter: modest maiden: stays 6f: acts on fibresand and dead ground. *R. Hannon*

LONG SIEGE (IRE) 2 ch.c. (Mar 19) Brief Truce (USA) 126 – Sugarbird 82 78 p (Star Appeal 133) [1997 6g⁵ Jul 9] IR 50,000Y: strong, good-topped colt: seventh foal: half-brother to 3 winners, including smart 1990 2-y-o 7f (Horris Hill) winner Sapieha (both by Petorius) and smart French stayer Dajraan (by Shirley Heights): dam 2-y-o 5f winner: 33/1 and better for race, about 8 lengths fifth of 9 to Daggers Drawn in minor event at Newmarket, fading over 1f out: moved fluently to post: should improve. *D. R. Loder*

LONGWICK LAD 4 ro.c. Chilibang 120 – Bells of St Martin 89 (Martinmas 80 128) [1996 80p: 5g² 6g⁵ 6m 5m² 5g 5g⁴ 5.7m* 5.2m² 5m⁶ 1997 6m 5g 5m* 6g 5m 5m 5.1g⁶ 5.2m Aug 16] workmanlike colt: fairly useful handicapper: won at Thirsk in May: below form after: effective at 5f and 6f: has raced only on good ground or firmer. *W. R. Muir*

554

LOOKINGFORARAINBOW (IRE) 9 ch.g. Godswalk (USA) 130 – Bridget 64 d
Folly (Crofter (USA) 124) [1996 78: 10d² 10s⁴ 8g⁵ 10m⁵ 11.9m 12m² 12m² 10.4m
9f⁶ 13.9g 1997 10m 12g³ 12s⁵ 12d⁵ 11.9f³ 10m⁶ 12m 11.9m Oct 23] close-coupled
gelding: modest handicapper, on the downgrade: stays 14.6f: acts on firm and dead
ground: visored once: takes good hold, and normally held up: has hung and found
little, and well ridden by M. Wigham. *Bob Jones*

LOOKINGFORLOVE DEL (IRE) 2 b.f. (Apr 28) Be My Guest (USA) 126 –
– Debenham (Formidable (USA) 125) [1997 7g 7m 8m a7g Nov 18] 2,000Y: second
foal: dam unraced granddaughter of a Park Hill winner: seems of little account.
N. A. Callaghan

LOOKOUT 3 b.f. Salse (USA) 128 – Sea Pageant (Welsh Pageant 132) [1996 77
70p: 8f⁵ 1997 10g⁶ 10.3d⁵ 12.3m⁶ 11.8g* 11.8g⁵ 14.4m* 14m³ 14.6g Oct 24]
smallish, sturdy filly: has a short action: fair performer: won minor event at Leicester
in August and handicap at Kempton in September: good front-running third in
handicap at Sandown week after latter: stays 14.4f: acts on firm and dead ground.
B. W. Hills

LOOK WHO'S CALLING (IRE) 4 b.g. Al Hareb (USA) 123 – House Call 67 d
(Artaius (USA) 129) [1996 79: 8.2s⁶ 7d⁶ 7.1d⁵ 6g³ 1997 6g⁶ 7f² 7.1d³ 7g 8m 7.5d⁶ 6d
7m Sep 26] big, good-topped gelding: fair maiden: well held in 1997 after third start:
likely to prove best up to 7f: acts on firm and dead going: cocked jaw and hung badly
right final 3-y-o start. *B. A. McMahon*

LORD ADVOCATE 9 br.g. Law Society (USA) 130 – Kereolle (Riverman 55
(USA) 131) [1996 54: 12.1d 12.1g⁶ 13d⁵ 13s* 14.1m⁶ 13m³ 11.1g* 13g* 12.1f²
11.1g⁵ 13.1s³ 11.1g⁵ 11.1m⁴ 12.4m² 11.1m³ 12f³ 13m⁶ 12.1f² 12.1m 8.3g 13.1m
12.1d⁵ 10.1m 15.1s⁵ 1997 16s⁴ 11.1d² 16m 11.1s⁶ 13s⁵ 13s² 12d 13m*ᵈⁱˢ 13g* 13g⁵
11.1d 12m⁵ 13d 11.1m² 14g⁵ 8.3g 10.9d 13.1d 12.1g² 13.1s 12s Nov 6] workmanlike
gelding: bad mover: modest handicapper: successful in 2 weak events at Hamilton in
June (disqualified on first occasion after testing positive for prohibited substance):
effective at 11f to 2m: acts on firm and soft ground and the all-weather: visored
earlier in career, blinkered nowadays: often forces pace: tough. *D. A. Nolan*

LORDAN VELVET (IRE) 5 br.g. Lord Americo – Danny's Miracle (Superlative –
118) [1996 9.5s* 8.8g⁴ 10g 8.8g 11m 1997 a8g⁶ a16g 8m a12g Apr 28] workmanlike
gelding: ran in Britain in 1995: has also run elsewhere in Europe, winning over 11.5f
in Norway later in 1995 and over 9.5f in Germany in 1996: well held in 4 claimers in
Britain in 1997. *Mrs W. B. Allen, Norway*

LORD CORNELIOUS 4 b.c. Lochnager 132 – Title (Brigadier Gerard 144) –
[1996 –: 12.1s⁶ 12.1m⁶ 5g 5f 5m⁵ 5m 5.9f 5m 1997 5s 5m 5g 5m 5m Jul 21] of little
account. *D. A. Nolan*

LORD CROMBY (IRE) 3 ch.c. Risen Star (USA) – Havinia (Habitat 134) 116
[1996 8.5m⁴ 8d⁶ 9s 7g 1997 8g² 8g* 8m² 10g* 10d² 10g⁴ 11s² 9.8m² 9d⁵ Nov 30] tall,
close-coupled colt: first foal: dam, unraced, from family of Cherry Hinton winner
Wild Wings: modest form (rated 63) at 2 yrs in Ireland for J. Coogan: vastly
improved in 1997, winner of minor events at Longchamp in April and Deauville in
July: looking very well, best effort when running-on length second of 8 to Alhaarth
in Prix Dollar at Longchamp: sold for 4 million francs from R. Collet's stable:
mid-division in Hollywood Derby: stays 11f: blinkered once (well beaten) at 2 yrs.
R. Frankel, USA

LORD DISCORD 3 b.g. Primo Dominie 121 – Busted Harmony (Busted 134) 61
[1996 58: 6f⁵ 7.5m⁴ 7g 7g³ 8.3d⁴ 1997 8.5v⁶ 10s⁴ 10m² 10g⁵ 11.9d Sep 5] lengthy,
angular gelding: modest maiden handicapper: reportedly distressed final start:
should stay beyond 1¼m: acts on good to firm and soft ground: visored (found little)
third start: won over hurdles in November. *T. D. Easterby*

LORD ELLANGOWAN (IRE) 4 ch.g. Astronef 116 – Gossip (Sharp Edge –
123) [1996 –, a47: a8g a10g² a10g a10g⁴ a12g² a10g 12f 12m 10m 9g 1997 a10g
a12g Feb 18] small gelding: poor maiden: ran badly in 1997. *R. Ingram*

LORD EUROLINK (IRE) 3 b.c. Danehill (USA) 126 – Lady Eurolink 55 91
(Kala Shikari 125) [1996 NR 1997 8g³ 8d* 10.3m 8s³ 10m Aug 1] sturdy, good sort:
fourth foal: half-brother to 1½m performers, notably useful Duke of Eurolink (by

LOR

Jupiter Island): dam 1m winner: fairly useful performer: won maiden at Doncaster in May: best efforts in minor event at Ascot and handicap at Goodwood last 2 starts: stays 1¼m well: acts on good to firm and soft ground: held up. *J. L. Dunlop*

LORD HASTIE (USA) 9 b.g. Affirmed (USA) – Sheika (USA) (Minnesota 49 d Mac) [1996 70: 9.9d⁵ 13d* 13s² 11.9m⁴ 12g⁶ 13g⁵ 11.9m⁶ 12g 11.9d⁶ 13.9g 1997 11.1d 13d⁶ 13s⁵ 14.1s⁶ 12.4g³ 14.1m⁵ 10.3d 12g Jul 5] tall gelding: has been fired: poor handicapper at best in 1997: stays 2m: acts on any turf going and on fibresand: blinkered (winner) once in 1992 and last 2 starts: tends to hang left and sometimes wears near-side pricker: joined N. Tinkler. *C. W. Thornton*

LORD HIGH ADMIRAL (CAN) 9 b.g. Bering 136 – Baltic Sea (CAN) 90 (Danzig (USA)) [1996 95: 6s 5.2d 5d 5f* 5m³ 5m* 5m 5m 5.2m 5f² 5d* 1997 6m 5g 5g² 5d⁶ 5g 5m 5m⁵ 5g* 5m 5g⁶ 5g Oct 25] tall gelding: impresses in appearance: fairly useful handicapper: had plummeted in weights prior to bolting up at Salisbury in September: best at 5f: acts on good to firm and soft ground: effective with or without blinkers/visor: has run creditably sweating: taken down early/alone: front runner: none too consistent. *M. J. Heaton-Ellis*

LORD HIGH EMPEROR 3 b.g. High Estate 127 – The Last Empress (IRE) 73 – (Last Tycoon 131) [1996 NR 1997 a8g a7g⁵ a11g Jan 31] 1,400 2-y-o: first foal: dam best around 2m: well beaten, including in sellers. *D. Shaw*

LORD JIM (IRE) 5 b.g. Kahyasi 130 – Sarah Georgina 79 (Persian Bold 123) 106 [1996 107: 13.9m⁵ 14m* 14g* 16g² 14.5d² 20s³ 1997 12g 16.2m⁵ 16g³ 16s 12g Oct 25] good-bodied gelding: useful performer: best effort in 1997 when 2 lengths third to Camp David in Oleander-Rennen at Baden-Baden: needs at least 1¾m and stays 2½m: acts on good to firm and soft ground, probably on fibresand: visored nowadays: promising novice hurdler for J. Old. *Lord Huntingdon*

LORD KINTYRE 2 b.c. (Feb 23) Makbul 104 – Highland Rowena 59 105 (Royben 125) [1997 5.1d⁴ 6m* 5g⁴ 5.2f* 6m² 6g⁴ 5v² Oct 11]
Having a close relative of celebrity status can have its pleasant spin offs, particularly in the closely-knit world of racing, where whole careers have seemingly been sustained on the back of the individual concerned happening to be related to someone or something of note. The latest season provided an interesting equine instance of this phenomenon, though the horse concerned in this case, the sire Makbul, is arguably making his name on his own behalf now.
Makbul was a useful winner of a couple of races as a juvenile but became injured and was nothing like the same force in three subsequent runs. Retired in 1991, he combined his post as a part-time (*very* part-time) sire with being the family pet. His first 'crop' in 1993 numbered two thoroughbreds, his second the same, and his third three. Reportedly only two mares visited him in 1995, and he was transferred to Longdon Stud in Staffordshire. Spotting an opportunity, the proprietors of that stud went about vigorously advertising their sire's credentials, notably that he was a well-bred son of the by-then very fashionable sire Fairy King. A full brother to Sadler's Wells and bred on similar lines to Nureyev, the once-raced Fairy King has continued to prosper, with the Arc winner Helissio and Grand Criterium winner Revoque to his name in 1996. The upshot for Makbul was that nineteen mares visited him in 1997 at £450 a time and his role as a family pet is presumably now behind him. Makbul has sired only two runners in Britain to date, one the decidedly undistinguished Mustang Scally, the other the useful two-year-old Lord Kintyre. The efforts of Lord Kintyre should ensure that more breeders give Makbul a chance. There were better two-year-olds around in 1997 but few tougher or gamer and very few who earned more than he did in his seven races.
The vast bulk of the £100,000 or so win and place prize money Lord Kintyre earned came in the Weatherbys Super Sprint at Newbury in July, a race restricted to horses sold for under 30,000 guineas at specified public auctions. Lord Kintyre fetched 9,200 guineas at the Doncaster October Yearling Sales, a half-brother to the fairly useful Crofters Ceilidh (by Scottish Reel) and the ordinary seller winner Highland Fawn (by Safawan) out of the modest (and

556

modestly-bred) handicapper Highland Rowena, all of them best at five furlongs. Lord Kintyre had won a maiden at Windsor in good style and finished about two lengths fourth to Asfurah in the Windsor Castle Stakes at Royal Ascot and went off at fourth favourite at 7/1 in a field of twenty-three at Newbury. It was clear some way out that Lord Kintyre was going to take a hand in the finish, as he was held up going notably well on the stand side. He swept through to lead a furlong out and despite drifting left always looked like holding the challenge of Pure Coincidence, which he did by three quarters of a length; Banningham Blade (a filly in a similar mould to Lord Kintyre) was two lengths back in third in a race run in juvenile course record time. Lord Kintyre thereafter took in some of the top two-year-old races. While he didn't win, he acquitted himself with considerable credit when runner-up in the Richmond Stakes (beaten one and a half lengths by Daggers Drawn) at Goodwood and the Cornwallis Stakes (four lengths behind Halmahera) at Ascot and was only a little below his best when four and a half lengths fourth to Carrowkeel in the Gimcrack Stakes at York.

		Fairy King	Northern Dancer
	Makbul	(b 1982)	Fairy Bridge
	(b 1987)	Royaltess	Royal And Regal
Lord Kintyre		(br 1982)	Devil's Drink
(b.c. Feb 23, 1995)		Royben	Takawalk II
	Highland Rowena	(ch 1968)	Pochette
	(ch 1985)	Highland Lassie	Highland Melody
		(b 1971)	Atair

The good-topped Lord Kintyre will have his work cut out to have anything like so successful a time of it in 1998. In his favour though is his splendid attitude and the fact that, as the stable star, the *Programme Book* is sure to be scoured on his behalf. Trainer Rod Millman does very well with the limited resources at his disposal. In 1997 the stable had just three two-year-old runners and all of them (Shalad' Or and Tempus Fugit were the others) were winners. It would be a surprise if Lord Kintyre stayed much beyond six furlongs, and, like a number of his relatives, he may even prove best at five. He acts on any going. *B. R. Millman*

LORD LIEUTENANT 2 b.g. (Feb 1) Primo Dominie 121 – Danzig Harbour 81 p (USA) (Private Account (USA)) [1997 5d 5f* 6g Oct 18] 36,000Y: strong, useful-looking gelding: fourth foal: brother to 4-y-o Allstars Dancer and half-brother to 1994 2-y-o 6f winner Puppet Master (by Prince Sabo): dam Irish 7f winner: won maiden at Beverley in September by 1½ lengths from Sarah Stokes, making most on favoured rail: stiff task in Two-Year-Old Trophy at Redcar, fading when short of room and eased (gelded subsequently): has scope, and should make useful sprint handicapper. *M. Bell*

LORD NASKRA (USA) 8 b.g. Naskra (USA) – Corvallis (USA) (Sir Ivor 135) – [1996 NR 1997 a7g 10d Sep 2] no longer of any account. *G. Woodward*

LORD OBERON (IRE) 9 b.g. Fairy King (USA) – Vaguely Jade (Corvaro 55 (USA) 124) [1996 NR 1997 8d⁵ 7g 10m 8m⁴ 8.2d 7d Oct 14] good-topped gelding: modest handicapper: effective at 1m to 1¼m: acts on firm and soft ground, twice below form on heavy: visored earlier in career. *J. Akehurst*

LORD OF LOVE 2 b.g. (May 16) Noble Patriarch 115 – Gymcrak Lovebird 84 61 (Taufan (USA) 119) [1997 5.9f 6g 7.1d⁵ 5.9g⁴ 7m³ 7s 7.1g³ 7.9s⁶ 10g 8g⁴ Oct 24] 6,000Y: leggy gelding: has a round action: fourth foal: half-brother to 5-y-o Dominelle and a 6f winner in Sweden by Mazilier: dam 5f (at 2 yrs) to 1¼m winner: modest maiden: third in nurseries at Chester and Musselburgh: stays 1m: acts on good to firm and soft going. *T. D. Easterby*

LORD OF MEN 4 ch.c. Groom Dancer (USA) 128 – Upper Strata 109 (Shirley 115 Heights 130) [1996 NR 1997 8d* 10g* 10g* 12.5s³ 10d³ Nov 9] robust colt: not the best of walkers: smart 2-y-o: fractured pelvis in spring of 1996: right back to form in 1997, winning minor events at Doncaster and Sandown (by 2½ lengths from Silence

Prix Gontaut-Biron, Deauville—not much to choose between the five runners.
Lord of Men (No. 4) comes out on top

Reigns) and Prix Gontaut-Biron at Deauville (favoured by weights) in the summer: third to Taipan in Grand Prix de Deauville (beaten 3½ lengths) and Premio Roma (beaten 5½ lengths) last 2 starts: stays 12.5f: successful on good to firm ground, best efforts on good or softer: has worn crossed noseband and had blanket for stalls entry: flashes tail under pressure, but game. *J. H. M. Gosden*

LORD OLIVIER (IRE)   7 b.g. The Noble Player (USA) 126 – Burkina (African   82
Sky 124) [1996 82: 5.2d 6m 6d 6.1m 6g* 6m* 6m⁵ 6m³ 6g 1997 6m* 6m 6s 6g 6m
6.1g 6m² 6g 7f* 7f² Oct 29] strong gelding: usually looks well: bad mover: fairly
useful performer: won handicap at Epsom in April and minor event at Brighton in
September: stays 7f: acts on firm and dead going, unsuited by soft: tried blinkered
earlier in career. *W. Jarvis*

LORD SKY   6 b.g. Emarati (USA) 74 – Summer Sky 75 (Skyliner 117) [1996 –,   54
a72: a5g⁶ a5g a7g a7g³ a5g⁴ a6g² a6g² a5g⁴ 5d 5.7g a5g 6g⁵ a6g a6g⁴ a6g 1997 a5g   a75
a6g* a5g² a6g a5g⁶ a6g³ a5g² a6g a5g* a5g 5s³ 5s 5d 5.7m⁵ Jun 14] leggy gelding:
fair on the all-weather, modest on turf: won claimer at Lingfield in January and
handicap there in March: best up to 7f: acts on good to firm and soft ground: tried in
blinkers/visor: often claimer ridden: usually races prominently: tail swisher: none too
consistent. *A. Bailey*

LORD SMITH   2 ch.g. (Apr 17) Greensmith 121 – Lady Longmead (Crimson   92
Beau 124) [1997 5m² 5.1m* 5g⁵ 6g* 7s* 7s* 7m* 7m* 8f* 8.5f⁵ Nov 6] rather plain
gelding: third reported foal: dam winning selling hurdler: fairly useful performer:
won seller at Nottingham, claimers at Newcastle, Salisbury (claimed out of W. G. M.
Turner's stable £9,000) and Warwick, and nurseries at Chester and Newmarket, then
left M. Pipe: won restricted stakes at Santa Anita then badly hampered at Hollywood
Park in the autumn: stays 1m: acts on firm and soft ground: raced prominently here,
came from off pace in USA: hung right on left-handed tracks in Britain: tough and
consistent. *B. Jackson, USA*

LORD WARFORD   2 b.g. (Apr 23) Bustino 136 – Jupiter's Message (Jupiter   64
Island 126) [1997 7.1g 8.1d⁶ 7.1g⁵ 8d Oct 17] 17,000Y: smallish, sturdy gelding:
third foal: half-brother to 1¾m winner Bellator (by Simply Great): dam unraced:
modest maiden: stiff task and never placed to challenge in nursery final start: bred for
stamina. *G. B. Balding*

LORINS GOLD   7 ch.g. Rich Charlie 117 – Woolcana 71 (Some Hand 119) [1996   50
43: 6m 6f* 6g² 7.1g⁴ 6m² 6m⁵ 6f⁵ 5m⁶ 8m⁵ 1997 6.1d 6f 8f* 9.7s⁴ 7d² 7.6g* Aug 2]
well-made gelding: tends to look dull in coat: modest handicapper: in good form in

the summer, winning amateurs event at Warwick and apprentice contest at Lingfield: stays 1m: acts on firm and dead going, probably on soft: effective blinkered, not tried in 1997: usually races prominently. *Andrew Turnell*

LOST IN THE POST (IRE)   4 ch.g. Don't Forget Me 127 – Postie (Sharpo 132) [1996 NR 1997 a7g a7g⁶ a8g 12.3m Apr 9] good-topped gelding: fourth foal: half-brother to 2 winners by Cyrano de Bergerac, including fair 1993 2-y-o 5f winner Post Mistress: dam unraced: no worthwhile form. *C. W. Thornton*   –

LOST LAGOON (USA)   5 ch.h. Riverman (USA) 131 – Lost Virtue (USA) (Cloudy Dawn (USA)) [1996 83: 8g² 8.2m³ 1997 11.6m Jun 9] close-coupled horse: fairly useful maiden at 4 yrs for H. Cecil: sold cheaply, and well held only start for new yard. *P. Eccles*   –

LOSTRIS (IRE)   6 b.m. Pennine Walk 120 – Herila (FR) (Bold Lad (USA)) [1996 40: 12.3g⁶ 13s⁶ 14.1m² 14.1m⁶ 18m² 18m³ 17.1m² 18g 1997 16.1g Mar 25] big, good-bodied mare: poor maiden handicapper: tongue tied, well beaten only 6-y-o start. *M. Dods*   –

LOUBIN LANE   2 b.f. (Feb 19) Deploy 131 – Another Lane 73 (Tina's Pet 121) [1997 6m 7g 8.2g 8d⁵ Oct 20] second foal: half-sister to 5f (at 2 yrs) and 1m winner Poly Lane (by Mazilier): dam 2-y-o 5f winner: modest maiden: best effort fifth in Pontefract nursery: will stay beyond 1m. *A. G. Newcombe*   50

LOUGH ERNE   5 b.m. Never So Bold 135 – Laugharne (Known Fact (USA) 135) [1996 83: 6d 6g² 6f* 6.1d* 7m³ 6v³ 7g 1997 5g 7g 6m Nov 4] tall mare: fairly useful handicapper at 4 yrs: always behind in 1997. *C. F. Wall*   –

LOUIS PHILIPPE (USA)   2 b.c. (Mar 2) El Gran Senor 136 – Naqiyah (USA) (In Reality) [1997 7d⁵ 7m² Oct 28] $60,000Y: smallish, sturdy colt: sixth foal: half-brother to Irish 1993 2-y-o 5f winner Mahaseal (by Ferdinand): dam, unraced half-sister to smart 7f/1m winner Magical Strike, from good US family: fairly useful form in steadily-run minor events at Newmarket and Redcar in October, beaten ½ length by Dernier Croise on latter course: will stay 1m: should progress. *J. H. M. Gosden*   82 p

LOUP SAUVAGE (USA)   3 ch.c. Riverman (USA) 131 – Louveterie (USA) 123 (Nureyev (USA) 131) [1996 8d* 1997 8g² 8d² 12d³ 10g* 10g² Oct 18]   122

    When asked to nominate a horse for Timeform's *Fifty To Follow* publication in 1997 the top French jockey Olivier Peslier chose the Andre Fabre-trained and Daniel Wildenstein-owned three-year-old Loup Sauvage. Whilst Loup Sauvage turned out some way behind Peintre Celebre, who raced for the same connections, he proved a very smart performer in his own right and deserved more reward for his efforts than a single win in a Group 3 at Long-

Prix du Prince d'Orange, Longchamp—
Loup Sauvage doesn't need to be at his best to land the odds

champ. He was placed on his four other starts and was beaten at most two lengths each time, including in the Poule d'Essai des Poulains, the Irish Derby and the Champion Stakes.

Loup Sauvage's racecourse experience amounted to a win in a new-comers event at Longchamp as a two-year-old at the time he was pitched in against colts already proven in pattern company on his reappearance in the Prix de Fontainebleau at the same course. The race was to prove a significant pointer for the Poule d'Essai des Poulains three weeks later, with Loup Sauvage beaten two lengths into second by Daylami. Peslier expected to turn the tables from that first meeting but Loup Sauvage had no response to Daylami's striking turn of foot and he went under by the same margin in the Poulains itself. With Peintre Celebre doing duty in the Prix du Jockey-Club and the Grand Prix de Paris, Loup Sauvage was next seen out in the Irish Derby. Given that it was still only his fourth race, Loup Sauvage was almost certainly improving anyway, regardless of the step up in trip, but he looked well suited by the truly-run mile and a half at the Curragh. After racing in rear, he took closer order entering the straight and stayed on strongly to be beaten about a length behind Desert King in third, failing by just a short head to take second from Dr Johnson.

Loup Sauvage returned for an autumn campaign of just two races. The Prix du Prince d'Orange at Longchamp in September was much the easiest task he faced all year and he didn't need to show anything like his best form to account for the maiden Bonapartiste, the John Gosden-trained Handsome Ridge and two others. Firm ground at the Arc meeting ruled out a clash with Alhaarth in the Prix Dollar and the Indian summer was still in evidence at Newmarket two weeks later, when, on good ground, Loup Sauvage took his chance in the Champion Stakes. He was noticeably cooler in the preliminaries than many of his rivals but proved easy to back after opening as second favourite. Nonetheless, he was the one who fared best of the five three-year-

Mr Daniel Wildenstein's "Loup Sauvage"

olds in the field against Pilsudski, easing to the front well over a furlong out but having no answer once that rival found a clear run on his inside.

Loup Sauvage has had just six races to date but that's one more than his year-older half-brother Loup Solitaire (by Lear Fan) managed in a career curtailed by back trouble—his 'only' win came in the Grand Criterium. Loup Sauvage's two-year-old full brother, Loudeac (his dam's fourth foal), made a promising start by winning on his debut at Maisons-Laffitte in November, and there's a yearling filly by Riverman's son Irish River called Louve coming along too. The dam, Louveterie, didn't have much racing either, her four starts comprising wins on her only outing at two and then in the Prix Vanteaux, followed by second places in the Prix Saint-Alary and the Prix de Diane. Her half-sisters, Louve Bleue and Louve Romaine, were placed in the Prix Saint-Alary as well (the latter in the Diane too). The pattern winners Leonardo da Vinci (White Rose Stakes), L'Ile du Reve (Cheshire Oaks), Legend of France (Earl of Sefton Stakes) and Lascaux (Prix Jean de Chaudenay) are the other notable winners out of the Oaks and Coronation Cup winner Lupe.

		Never Bend	Nasrullah
	Riverman (USA)	(b 1960)	Lalun
	(b 1969)	River Lady	Prince John
Loup Sauvage (USA)		(b 1963)	Nile Lily
(ch.c. 1994)		Nureyev	Northern Dancer
	Louveterie (USA)	(b 1977)	Special
	(ch 1986)	Lupe	Primera
		(b 1967)	Alcoa

The good-topped Loup Sauvage looks the sort to train on at four and win more pattern races. Often bandaged behind, he's a poor mover and has been kept away from going firmer than good so far. He'll be kept away from Peintre Celebre too, of course, but in terms of distance there seem to be plenty of options open to him from around a mile and a quarter up to a mile and a half. *A. Fabre, France*

LOVE ACADEMY 2 b.c. (Feb 26) Royal Academy (USA) 130 – Quiet Week-End 99 (Town And Country 124) [1997 7g⁴ 6s² 6g* Oct 22] 50,000Y: leggy, good-topped colt: fourth foal: half-brother to fairly useful 1996 2-y-o 1m winner Home Alone (by Groom Dancer), useful 7.5f (at 2 yrs) and 10.5f winner Pleasant Surprise (by Cadeaux Genereux) and 1m winner Tranquillity (by Night Shift): dam, 2-y-o 6f and 7f winner later successful in USA, half-sister to Lemon Souffle: landed odds in maiden at Newcastle by 1¾ lengths from Ryefield, making all, despite edging left and carrying head bit high: should stay at least 1m: reportedly split hoof on debut, and absent 4 months afterwards: should progress. *M. Johnston* 79 p

LOVE AGAIN 2 br.f. (Apr 10) Reprimand 122 – Town Lady 93 (Town Crier 119) [1997 5f² 5g² a5g² 6d Oct 16] 9,000Y: lengthy, unfurnished filly: half-sister to several winners, including useful 1996 2-y-o 6f winner Demolition Man (by Primo Dominie) and 1¼m and 1½m winner The Freshes (by Good Times): dam 2-y-o 5f winner: fair maiden: best effort when second at Wolverhampton: should stay at least 6f: acts on fibresand: sent to USA. *M. Bell* 63 + a75

LOVE HAS NO PRIDE (USA) 3 gr.g. El Prado (IRE) 119 – Chili Lee (USA) 87 d (Belted Earl (USA) 122) [1996 83: 7.1g⁶ 7m⁶ 6f* 6g 8m² 7.9g* 8g 1997 10.3m² 10m 9g⁴ 10.4g 9.7m⁴ 10m⁴ 11.6g⁵ Jul 7] rather leggy gelding: has a fluent, round action: fairly useful handicapper: below form in 1997 after third start: should stay beyond 1¼m: raced only on good ground or firmer: sent to USA. *R. Hannon*

LOVE KISS (IRE) 2 b.c. (Apr 29) Brief Truce (USA) 126 – Pendulina 102 81 (Prince Tenderfoot (USA) 126) [1997 7.1s 7g⁴ 8d³ Nov 7] IR 36,000Y: tall, useful-looking colt: has scope: half-brother to several winners, including 6-y-o Pendolino and useful Irish 1988 2-y-o Sedulous (up to 1m, by Tap On Wood), later successful in USA: dam won 3 times around 1m in Ireland: fairly useful form when in frame in maiden and minor event at Doncaster, keeping-on third of 5 to Derryquin in latter: should stay beyond 1m. *M. Johnston*

LOVE LEGEND   12 ch.g. Glint of Gold 128 – Sweet Emma 108 (Welsh Saint   –
126) [1996 50, a45: a8g a8g⁴ a8g a7g² a8g³ a8g 7f⁶ 8g 7.1g 8f a10g 1997 a8g³ 7m⁶   a37
7.1m Jun 13] smallish, sparely-made gelding: often dull in coat: has a quick action:
one-time useful handicapper, only poor nowadays: stays 8.5f: acts on firm and dead
ground and the all-weather: tried visored/blinkered. *D. W. P. Arbuthnot*

LOVELY MORNING   4 b.f. Thowra (FR) – Sweet Pleasure 88 (Sweet Revenge   –
129) [1996 –: a9.4g 8m³ 10f⁶ 8d 1997 a8g⁶ Feb 22] workmanlike filly: little
worthwhile form. *D. J. G. Murray Smith*

LOVE ME DO (USA)   3 b.g. Minshaanshu Amad (USA) 91§ – I Assume (USA)   72
(Young Emperor 133) [1996 69: 7g³ 8m⁴ 7.9g 8g 1997 a10g⁵ a8g³ a11g² a12g³ a12g*
12g⁶ 14d³ 11.1d⁶ 16.2m⁴ 17.1g⁶ 14.1g* Aug 23] sturdy, useful-looking gelding: fair
performer: won maiden at Southwell in February and handicap at Redcar in August:
should stay beyond 1¾m: yet to race on extremes of going on turf, acts on fibresand.
M. Johnston

LOVE OVER GOLD   3 ch.f. Primo Dominie 121 – Salacious (Sallust 134)   –
[1996 NR 1997 a8g a7g⁶ a7g 5s 7m a11g⁵ 5m 10m Sep 22] seventh living foal: sister
to 4-y-o Playmaker, 5f winner at 2 yrs, and half-sister to 2 minor winners: dam Irish
7f and 9f winner: of little account. *M. C. Chapman*

LOVERS KNOT   2 b.f. (Mar 9) Groom Dancer (USA) 128 – Nemea (USA) 97   89 p
(The Minstrel (CAN) 135) [1997 7m² Nov 1] 60,000Y: first foal: dam 1¼m winner
who probably stayed 2m: 5/4 favourite in large field of well-bred fillies, short-head
second to Pontoon in maiden at Newmarket, travelling well up with the pace and
keeping on strongly without being hit with whip: hampered and took heavy fall after
line: should stay at least 1¼m: should improve and win races. *D. R. Loder*

LOVE VENTURE   3 b.f. Pursuit of Love 124 – Our Shirley 84 (Shirley Heights   68 d
130) [1996 NR 1997 8d⁴ 10m 8m⁴ 8.2g² 10.1g³ 8.5g 8f⁶ 8d Oct 28] rather leggy filly:
half-sister to several winners, including 5-y-o Pearl Venture and ungenuine miler
Soviet Express (by Siberian Express): dam 1¼m winner: fair maiden: below form
after fourth start: should stay 1¼m: has been bandaged: has carried head awkwardly:
joined Miss M. Rowland. *S. P. C. Woods*

LOVEYOUMILLIONS (IRE)   5 b.g. Law Society (USA) 130 – Warning   –
Sound (Red Alert 127) [1996 88d: a6g² a7g 7s⁶ 12d⁵ 9.2s⁴ 12g² 8.1d² 8m⁴ a9.4g 1997
a9.4g a8g 10.3m⁶ 12m Apr 5] strong gelding: fairly useful handicapper at best at 4
yrs: no form in 1997, reportedly breaking blood vessel final start. *N. Tinkler*

LOVING AND GIVING   3 b.f. Sharpo 132 – Pretty Poppy 67 (Song 132) [1996   83 d
84p: 5.1m* 5v⁴ 1997 6g 5g 6m⁴ 6g⁵ 5g 6m 6.1g Oct 4] lengthy filly: promising juvenile: mostly disappointing in handicaps in 1997, including in blinkers: a
sprinter: acts on good to firm and heavy ground: sold 3,000 gns in December.
H. Candy

LOVING CLAIM (USA)   2 b.f. (Jan 20) Hansel (USA) – Ville d'Amore   110 p
(USA) (Irish River (FR) 131) [1997 8m* 8f* Oct 5]
    Criquette Head's stable can normally be relied upon to contain a leading
two-year-old filly and the latest season was no exception. Loving Claim, her
trainer's third winner of the Prix Marcel Boussac in the last six runnings, ended
her first season with an identical record to that of the stable's 1994 winner
Macoumba, both fillies having made a winning debut in the Prix de la Cascade,
a newcomers race over the Marcel Boussac course and distance in September.
    The latest running of the Marcel Boussac had a field of ten and was a
stronger contest than in Macoumba's year, although there was just the one
pattern winner in the line-up, the favourite Anna Palariva, who'd won the Prix
d'Aumale at Chantilly. Second-favourite Ashraakat represented another trainer
with a good record in the race, John Dunlop, and she was accompanied from
Britain by the recent Milan listed-race winner Silent Tribute. Third choice in
the betting, Loving Claim impressed as the most imposing member of the field
beforehand—she's a well-made, attractive filly—and she dominated her rivals
in the race too, making all and keeping on determinedly under firm handling to
maintain her advantage in the closing stages. Isle de France, the least-fancied

Prix Marcel Boussac (Criterium des Pouliches), Longchamp—Loving Claim makes all from Isle de France (No. 10) and Plaisir des Yeux (No. 5)

of three runners from the Fabre stable, which included the favourite, stayed on from the rear to be beaten one and a half lengths, as did the third, outsider Plaisir des Yeux, who was beaten a further three quarters of a length. Silent Tribute and Ashraakat finished sixth and seventh respectively, neither beaten very far, while Anna Palariva was never going well in rear after a slow start. Of the principals, only the fifth home Desert Drama was turned out again but did little for the form in three subsequent starts.

Loving Claim is from the third crop of Hansel, who won the Preakness Stakes and the Belmont Stakes. She is his most notable winner to date and he

Maktoum Al Maktoum's "Loving Claim"

has also had a couple of smart colts in Kentucky Derby third Prince of Thieves and the seven-furlong to mile-and-a-quarter performer Magellan, though a halving of his fee suggests he hasn't lived up to early expectations at stud. Dam Ville d'Amore ran only at three years, winning once over seven furlongs at Maisons-Laffitte and twice in listed races over a mile at Longchamp. Loving Claim is her third foal and second to race after the French 1996 two-year-old mile winner Diplomatic Count (by Shadeed). Ville d'Amore was bred to stay further than a mile. Her dam, Hanoof, has recouped little of the two million dollars she cost as a yearling, either on the racecourse, where her only success was in an eleven-furlong maiden at Ayr, or at stud where Ville d'Amore is the only winner she's bred to date. Hanoof's close relative is the useful stayer Le Corsaire and they are out of the high-class middle-distance filly Little Bonny, who was second in the Irish Oaks and the Prix Vermeille and won the Grade 2 Pan American Handicap over a mile and a half at four. Little Bonny had a smart brother over middle distances in Noelino.

		Woodman	Mr Prospector
	Hansel (USA)	(ch 1983)	Playmate
	(b 1988)	Count On Bonnie	Dancing Count
Loving Claim (USA)		(b 1981)	Buena Notte
(b.f. Jan 20, 1995)		Irish River	Riverman
	Ville d'Amore (USA)	(ch 1976)	Irish Star
	(ch 1988)	Hanoof	Northern Dancer
		(b 1983)	Little Bonny

Loving Claim is entitled to plenty of respect on her trainer's record alone if she's sent over for the Guineas and on form she's not far behind the best of her age and sex in Europe, Embassy. However, the chances are that Loving Claim will ultimately prove best at distances beyond a mile. She's open to improvement after just two starts, both of which were on ground firmer than good. *Mme C. Head, France*

LOXLEY'S GIRL (IRE) 3 b.f. Lahib (USA) 129 – Samnaun (USA) (Stop The Music (USA)) [1996 –: 5m 5g 6f 1997 a7g⁶ a8.5g⁴ a8g a10g 7f³ Oct 3] sturdy, lengthy filly: poor maiden handicapper: stays 1m: acts on firm going and fibresand: blinkered once at 2 yrs. *H. Akbary*   **39**

LUCAYAN BEACH 3 gr.g. Cyrano de Bergerac 120 – Mrs Gray 61 (Red Sunset 120) [1996 68: 5.2d⁴ 5g² 6f⁵ 1997 7d 6g 6m Nov 1] angular gelding: fair form in early-season maidens at 2 yrs: behind after 17-month absence on return. *B. Gubby*   **–**

LUCAYAN INDIAN (IRE) 2 ch.c. (Mar 27) Indian Ridge 123 – Eleanor Antoinette (IRE) (Double Schwartz 128) [1997 6d 6m* 7d* Oct 17] 40,000Y: angular colt: second foal: dam unraced half-sister to useful performer up to 1½m Lifewatch Vision: won maiden at Newcastle and Houghton Stakes at Newmarket in October, leading inside last 1f to beat Astrologer a length in steadily-run race for latter: should stay at least 1m: moved short to post at Newmarket: should progress further. *D. R. Loder*   **96 p**

LUCAYAN PRINCE (USA) 4 br.c. Fast Play (USA) – Now That's Funny (USA) (Saratoga Six (USA)) [1996 123: 7d⁶ 8m³ 7g² 7m* 6m² 6f⁵ 6m² 7m⁵ 1997 6d³ 7.1m² 6g 6g 7g a6f* a8f² Nov 29] close-coupled colt: reportedly had testicular operation before reappearance: very smart performer when in mood: creditable efforts first 2 starts in 1997, in Greenlands Stakes at the Curragh and listed race at Haydock (length behind Decorated Hero): most disappointing next 3 starts and left D. Loder: won allowance race then beaten a neck in Grade 1 Cigar Mile, both at Aqueduct in the autumn: effective at 6f to 1m: acts on firm going, dead and dirt: often blinkered in Europe, not in USA: covered up for late run: raced on medication in USA: seemed to have become unreliable before leaving Britain. *W. Mott, USA*   **118 §**

LUCKY ARCHER 4 b.g. North Briton 67 – Preobrajenska 93 (Double Form 130) [1996 85: 8d⁶ 8d⁵ 7m³ 7m⁵ 7.1m⁶ 6g 7m 6m³ 7d⁵ 8.5m² 7.1m³ 8.5m 7m 7f²   **–**

1997 8m 8g[5] 8g Oct 27] smallish, well-made gelding: fairly useful maiden at 3 yrs: well below form in 1997. *J. M. Bradley*

LUCKY BEA   4 b.g. Lochnager 132 – Knocksharry 58 (Palm Track 122) [1996 –
61: 6s[3] 6d[3] 8g[5] 8d* 10m[5] 12.3g 8g[2] 8m[3] 10m 8m[3] 8.5m 8g a8g 8f 8m 1997 9.9m[5]
Apr 11] robust, close-coupled gelding: modest handicapper at 3 yrs: well held (over
possibly too far) only start in 1997. *M. W. Easterby*

LUCKY BEGONIA (IRE)   4 br.f. Simply Great (FR) 122 – Hostess 81 (Be My   54
Guest (USA) 126) [1996 65: 8m 8d[5] 8m[6] 10g 1997 8s 10g 8.2g[5] 9m[2] 10.1g[2] 11.5m[2]
8.2d a12g[2] Nov 21] sturdy, workmanlike filly: modest maiden handicapper: stays
1½m: acts on good to firm ground and fibresand, below form on dead and soft.
W. J. Musson

LUCKY BLUE   10 b.g. Blue Cashmere 129 – Cooling 89 (Tycoon II) [1996 NR   –
1997 11.8m Mar 27] poor handicapper: well beaten only 10-y-o start. *Simon Earle*

LUCKY DIP   3 b.f. Tirol 127 – Miss Loving 89 (Northfields (USA)) [1996 65: 6d   68
7m[4] 7m 1997 6.9m[6] 6m[4] 5.1f* 5m[2] 5.7g[6] a5g[4] 5.1m[4] a5g Nov 6] fair performer: a52
dropped to 5f, clearly best efforts on third and fourth starts, winning claimer at Bath
in May: acts on firm ground, below best on equitrack: tried blinkered: has shown
signs of temperament (gave trouble at stalls second start). *D. R. C. Elsworth*

LUCKY DOUBLE   2 b.c. (May 7) Green Desert (USA) 127 – Lady Bentley 109   82 p
(Bellypha 130) [1997 6s 8m[6] 7m* Oct 1] leggy, close-coupled colt: fourth living foal:
brother to fair maiden (best at 7f at 2 yrs) Green Bentley and half-brother to Irish 7.5f
(at 2 yrs) and 1½m winner Lord Bentley (by Rousillon): dam Italian Oaks winner,
out of half-sister to smart stayer Yawa: progressive form: won maiden at Salisbury
by neck from Gunzells, coming from off pace: should stay at least 1m: should improve further. *R. Hannon*

LUCKY HOOF   4 b.f. Batshoof 122 – Lucky Omen 99 (Queen's Hussar 124)   –
[1996 69: 10.1g 11.5m[2] 11.5m 14d 1997 16.2m 14.1f[5] Jun 5] sparely-made filly:
form only when second of 4 in maiden at Yarmouth at 3 yrs: visored in 1997: sold
7,000 gns in December, in foal to Alhijaz. *K. A. Morgan*

LUCKY MYST   2 b.c. (Feb 21) Mystiko (USA) 124 – Lucky Omen 99 (Queen's   62
Hussar 124) [1997 7m[3] Jul 19] 4,800Y: half-brother to several winners, including
smart 6f and 9.2f winner Lapierre (by Lafontaine) and useful sprinter Lucky Hunter
(by Huntercombe): dam 2-y-o sprint winner: 5½ lengths third in Warwick maiden,
keeping on. *C. E. Brittain*

LUCKY REVENGE   4 b.f. Komaite (USA) – Sweet And Lucky (Lucky   55
Wednesday 124) [1996 66: 7m[2] 7m 6m 6m[4] 6m[2] 6f[4] 7m* 6m[4] 6d[6] 8g[2] 7m[3] 7m 8f
1997 a5g a6g[5] a6g[6] a5g 6m[6] 7m May 5] leggy, angular filly: modest handicapper:
probably best at 7f/1m: acts on firm going (probably on fibresand), poor efforts on
dead ground and equitrack: well beaten in blinkers. *D. Nicholls*

LUCY GLITTERS (USA)   2 b.f. (Mar 7) Cryptoclearance (USA) – Way of The   60 p
World (USA) (Dance of Life (USA)) [1997 6g[6] Oct 24] sparely-made filly: first
known foal: dam, 1m stakes winner in USA, half-sister to smart performer up to 9f
Hoy, from family of smart 1¼m performer Elegant Tern: sire high class at up to 1½m:
20/1, about 7 lengths sixth of 24 to Mister Rambo in maiden at Newbury, outpaced
final 2f and not knocked about: should do better. *I. A. Balding*

LUCY IN THE SKY (IRE)   3 b.f. Lycius (USA) 124 – Nazwa 105 (Tarboosh   59
(USA)) [1996 7.5d 8g 1997 9g 9g 6.5m 7d 7.8m 9f 13f 5m[3] 5s a5g a5g* a6g* Dec 4]
ex-Irish filly: half-sister to 3 winners, including fairly useful Irish 1987 2-y-o 5f
winner Saintly Lass (by Halo): dam useful winner up to 7f in Ireland: modest
handicapper: left A. J. Martin after seventh start: blinkered, won twice at Lingfield in
December, getting up near finish: stays 6f: acts on equitrack, only turf form on good
to firm going. *B. J. Meehan*

LUCY OF ARABIA (IRE)   3 b.f. Mujadil (USA) 119 – Fleur-De-Luce (Tumble   45
Wind (USA)) [1996 48: 5m 6m 6g 1997 a5g[5] a6g[5] a5g a6g[4] a7g[4] a6g[6] 8f May 23]
poor maiden: probably stays 7f: blinkered last 3 starts: has carried head awkwardly.
J. J. Sheehan

LUCY TUFTY 6 b.m. Vin St Benet 109 – Manor Farm Toots 70 (Royalty 130) [1996 42: 10m⁴ 11.9g 14.1g⁴ 12s* a14.8g 1997 a13g 11.9f a16g³ a13g⁴ 14.1s⁶ Jul 5] poor handicapper: stays 2m. *J. Pearce* — a29

LUDERE (IRE) 2 ch.g. (Apr 27) Desse Zenny (USA) – White Jasmin 53 (Jalmood (USA) 126) [1997 6f 7.5v 7.1m⁵ 7g a7g Dec 18] 5,800 2-y-o: good-bodied gelding: fourth foal: brother to 3-y-o The Deejay: dam 2m winner, also successful over hurdles: no worthwhile form, including in sellers. *W. W. Haigh* —

LUDO 3 br. or gr.c. Petong 126 – Teacher's Game 64 (Mummy's Game 120) [1996 69?: 6f 6f⁴ 7g 1997 6.1m 6m 8.3s² 10g² 10m* 10g 11.7m² 10s⁶ 11.5m 11.8g 12.1d Aug 25] useful-looking colt: modest handicapper: won at Leicester in June: mostly below form afterwards, blinkered last 2 starts: stays 1½m: acts on good to firm ground, probably on soft. *R. Hannon* 62

LUNAR MIST 4 b.f. Komaite (USA) – Sugar Token 66 (Record Token 128) [1996 –: 5g⁶ 5m 7d 1997 5g² 6m 5.1d³ 6g³ 6g⁵ 5.1s³ 5g Jul 8] smallish filly: fair handicapper: good efforts in 1997 when placed: effective at 5f and 6f: acts on good to firm and soft going. *Martyn Meade* 77

LUNAR MUSIC 3 b.f. Komaite (USA) – Lucky Candy 61 (Lucky Wednesday 124) [1996 67: 5d 5m³ 5f* 6m⁴ 5m⁵ 6m⁵ 5m* 6m 5f 1997 a5g² a6g⁴ a5g⁴ a5g³ 5m⁶ 6.1g 8.2d 5d 5f 5m⁴ 5g 5m⁵ 5g Jul 30] angular filly: modest performer: left Martyn Meade after fifth start: below form afterwards: effective at 5f and 6f, not 1m: acts on firm ground and the all-weather: tried blinkered. *Ronald Thompson* 47 a56

LUNCH PARTY 5 b.g. Beveled (USA) – Crystal Sprite 74 (Crystal Glitters (USA) 127) [1996 59: 7g* 7g² 9g 7g 6d 1997 5s 6d 6g 7g 7f* 6.9m 7f⁴ 8s* Nov 6] modest handicapper: won at Yarmouth (gambled on in apprentice race) in September and Musselburgh in November, checked a couple of times but quickening well in latter: stays 1m: acts on firm and soft ground. *D. Nicholls* 51 +

LUNCHTIME GIRL 2 ch.f. (Jan 1) Cadeaux Genereux 131 – Thewaari (USA) 68 (Eskimo (USA)) [1997 5g 5v a7g⁵ 6m Oct 6] angular filly: second foal: dam 7f winner: well beaten in maidens and a nursery. *J. D. Bethell* —

LUSO 5 b.h. Salse (USA) 128 – Lucayan Princess 111 (High Line 125) [1996 124: 9m* 10.5m² 12m* 12m² 12m⁶ 12g* 12g⁴ 12m* 1997 a10f 12m⁵ 12f* 12f² 12g* 12m² 12g² 12g² 12m² 12m* Dec 14] 124

Targeting races abroad has become part and parcel of the weekly routine at virtually all the top stables. Among the regular globetrotters from British stables over the last few seasons have been Hever Golf Rose (twenty-eight out of her sixty-one starts have been overseas), Needle Gun (twenty out of thirty-six), Captain Horatius (twenty out of forty-three), Luso (eighteen out of twenty-eight), Mongol Warrior (sixteen out of nineteen) and Strategic Choice (thirteen out of twenty-four). Such enterprise unfortunately deprives British racegoers of seeing some of the top horses in action as often as they might like, but the rewards for connections can be enormous. Of the twenty-eight British-trained older horses rated 120 or more by Timeform in 1997 only four weren't raced abroad; First Island's season was tragically cut short and, interestingly, the three others, Bosra Sham, Ali-Royal and Dushyantor, were all trained by Henry Cecil. Luso's trainer, Clive Brittain, has always been keen to travel his horses. Over the last two seasons, Luso and his stable-companion and half-brother Needle Gun have between them had twenty-eight of their last thirty-three starts abroad. Needle Gun has won only once in that time, but Luso has been much more successful and in 1997 repeated his wins in the Premio Ellington at Rome and the Hong Kong International Vase at Sha Tin, and again picked up a Group 1 race in Germany. Luso finished either first or second in each of his last eight races, six of them Group 1, reflecting great credit on his shrewd trainer.

At Rome, Luso returned to winning ways after below-form efforts in the Dubai World Cup and the Jockey Club Stakes (his only outing in Britain), making just about all the running and having three quarters of a length to spare over Toto Le Moko. Luso was twice returned to Italy, both times to Milan,

Hong Kong International Vase, Sha Tin—
with six countries represented, the two British runners Luso and Posidonas fight out the finish

where he finished second to Shantou in the Gran Premio di Milano in June and, on his penultimate outing in October, when he found only Caitano too good for him in the Gran Premio del Jockey Club. Luso's efforts at Milan were handsomely rewarded; on the first occasion he earned far more than the winner of Royal Ascot's Hardwicke Stakes five days later, and on the second he earned a similar amount to that won by the third in the Arc. Luso's four races in between were all in Germany, though prize money for these events was not so lucrative as for those in Italy. Luso won the first of the four, the WGZ Bank Deutschlandpreis at Dusseldorf in July, an alternative to Ascot's King George VI and Queen Elizabeth Stakes, in which he'd finished a well-beaten sixth the previous year. Recording his third Group 1 win, Luso made all to beat Wurftaube by three lengths, still picking up more than Helissio did for finishing third at Ascot. Luso was unable to repeat his 1996 win in the Aral-Pokal at Gelsenkirchen in August, this time beaten a length and three quarters by Caitano, putting up a performance to rank with his very best. Luso's second in the Grosser Preis von Baden to Borgia, just ahead of Predappio, was another fine effort, particularly considering how well first and third ran in the Arc a month later. A defeat by Taipan in the Europa Preis at Cologne later in September was avenged when that horse could finish only fourth behind Caitano and Luso in the Gran Premio del Jockey Club. Luso's final outing, in the Hong Kong International Vase at Sha Tin in December, when he just pipped Posidonas after meeting considerable trouble in running, took his career win and place earnings to over one and a half million pounds, not bad for a horse around 10 lb behind the best of his generation.

Luso's pedigree has been dealt with in detail in the last two editions of *Racehorses*. Lucayan Princess's seventh foal, the two-year-old filly Cloud Castle (by In The Wings), also trained by Brittain, shaped encouragingly when

Mr Saeed Manana's "Luso"

third in her only race. Lucayan Princess was barren to Green Desert in 1996, produced a filly by Sadler's Wells in 1997 and was then covered by Caerleon.

	Salse (USA)	Topsider	Northern Dancer
	(b 1985)	(b 1974)	Drumtop
Luso		Carnival Princess	Prince John
(b.c. 1992)		(ch 1974)	Carnival Queen
	Lucayan Princess	High Line	High Hat
	(b 1983)	(ch 1966)	Time Call
		Gay France	Sir Gaylord
		(b 1976)	Sweet And Lovely II

Luso, a big, strong, rangy horse, is effective at nine furlongs but is raced mainly at a mile and a half nowadays. He acts on firm and dead ground and has never raced on soft. He wore blinkers once, when a surprise pacemaker for Lammtarra in the 1995 Arc. The good news is that Luso stays in training; the bad news, of course, is that the British racing public is unlikely to see much of this tough, genuine and consistent performer. *C. E. Brittain*

LUTINE BELL   2 b.g. (Feb 3) Fairy King (USA) – Bell Toll 87 (High Line 125)   – [1997 7d Nov 7] unfurnished gelding: fourth reported foal: brother to 6-y-o Prince Babar, closely related to useful 1m (at 2 yrs) to 11f (in France in 1997) winner Warning Order (by Warrshan) and half-brother to 4-y-o Angel Chimes: dam 2-y-o 7f and 1m winner: behind in maiden at Doncaster, slowly away and tending to hang. *J. E. Banks*

LYCIAN (IRE)   2 b.c. (Mar 9) Lycius (USA) 124 – Perfect Time (IRE) (Dance of   47 p Life (USA)) [1997 7.1g 7f 8m 7m⁴ Oct 23] 62,000Y: tall, lengthy colt: has scope:

second foal: dam, French 1m winner, half-sister to Prix Marcel Boussac winner Play
It Safe and Washington International winner Providential: poor form: staying-on
fourth in nursery at Brighton: should stay at least 1m: sold 15,000 gns in October. *Sir
Mark Prescott*

LYCILITY (IRE)   3 b.f. Lycius (USA) 124 – She's The Tops 83 (Shernazar 131)   92
[1996 86: 6m* 5m 6g 7.1m³ 8m 7m 1997 8g² 8g 11.5s⁵ 10d⁶ 11.9s 10m Sep 25] small
filly: fairly useful on her day: best effort when second in listed race at Kempton in
March: went in snatches and found little final outing: may prove best around 1m:
suited by good ground or firmer: blinkered (well held) once: sold 30,000 gns in
December. *C. E. Brittain*

LYCIUS TOUCH   3 b.f. Lycius (USA) 124 – Homely Touch 84 (Touching Wood   –
(USA) 127) [1996 50: 5g⁶ 5s* 5m⁶ 5f a6g⁴ 6f³ 7.1m 7.5m⁵ 8.1m⁵ a8.5g³ 1997 a7g⁶
a8g 10.1f a8g Jun 6] smallish, leggy filly: modest at 2 yrs: well beaten in 1997.
A. G. Newcombe

LYNTON LAD   5 b.g. Superpower 113 – House Maid 95 (Habitat 134) [1996 79d: 74
8s² 10.8d 8m 7.3s 1997 7.6g⁴ 7g⁴ 8.1m 8.2g² 7s⁴ 7m Jul 18] good-topped gelding:
fair performer: suited by around 1m: acts on soft ground (below form last 3 starts on
good to firm): occasionally blinkered: none too consistent. *C. P. E. Brooks*

LYPHIELO (USA)   3 b.f. Lyphard (USA) 132 – Miss Concielo (USA) (Conquist-   –
ador Cielo (USA)) [1996 NR 1997 8m 8g 9.7m⁵ Sep 26] fourth foal: half-sister to
a minor winner in USA by Sovereign Dancer: dam won up to 9f in USA: showed
nothing in maidens. *L. M. Cumani*

LYSANDROS (IRE)   3 b.c. Lycius (USA) 124 – Trojan Relation (Trojan Fen   72
118) [1996 NR 1997 8.3m 10m⁵ 10s² 14.6g Oct 24] IR 13,000F, 72,000Y: fourth foal:
half-brother to fairly useful 6f winner Darren Boy (by Ballad Rock): dam unraced:
fair form in maidens: should stay 1¾m: acts on good to firm and soft ground: sold
21,000 gns, and sent to France. *J. H. M. Gosden*

M

MAAS (IRE)   2 br.c. (Mar 16) Elbio 125 – Payne's Grey (Godswalk (USA) 130)   –
[1997 6d Oct 28] 6,800Y: second reported foal: dam unraced. 20/1, well beaten in
maiden at Leicester. *P. J. Makin*

MAAZOOM (IRE)   2 b. or br.g. (Apr 21) Be My Guest (USA) 126 – Lancette   – p
(Double Jump 131) [1997 7g Jul 8] IR 20,000F, IR 67,000Y: good-bodied gelding:
closely related to 2 winners by Glow, including 8-y-o Desert Calm (formerly fairly
useful Irish winner up to 9f), and half-brother to several winners, including Darcy's
Thatcher (by Thatching) and Rasa Penang (by Gay Fandango), both smart performers up to around 1m: dam placed up to 1½m in France: 20/1, very much in need of
experience when seventh of 9 in maiden at Newmarket, missing break completely
and not given a hard time: should do better. *J. H. M. Gosden*

MABLI   2 b.f. (Mar 6) Dilum (USA) 115 – Eastwood Heiress (Known Fact (USA)   –
135) [1997 5g May 17] 950F: second foal: dam out of half-sister to
2000 Guineas winner Mon Fils: reportedly finished lame when last in claimer.
M. W. Easterby

MACARI   3 gr.g. Arzanni 115 – View Halloa (Al Sirat (USA)) [1996 –: 8.2g a8g⁵   45
a8g⁵ 1997 8g⁴ 8.2d a9.4g⁶ 10m³ 10m⁵ 12.1g 10m Sep 26] tall gelding: poor maiden:
takes keen hold and may prove best at 1m to 1¼m: acts on good to firm going.
B. P. J. Baugh

MACARIBO   3 ch.c. Machiavellian (USA) 123 – Sweet Mover (USA) 95   77
(Nijinsky (CAN) 138) [1996 NR 1997 8m³ 7.9s⁵ 8m² Oct 6] good-topped colt: sixth
foal: half-brother to 4-y-o Mattawan and useful French sprinter Wedding of The Sea
(by Blushing Groom): dam 1¼m winner: best effort in maidens when staying-on
second at Pontefract: hung fire/carried head awkwardly first 2 starts: sent to UAE.
J. H. M. Gosden

MAC

MACCA LUNA (IRE) 2 b.f. (Mar 26) Kahyasi 130 – Medicosma (USA) 80 (The 62 p
Minstrel (CAN) 135) [1997 8m⁶ 8.3g* Sep 29] 5,200F, 32,000Y: smallish, sturdy
filly: third foal: dam, 1½m and 2m winner, half-sister to smart middle-distance stayer
Eva Luna out of Oaks second Media Luna: odds on, won weak maiden at Hamilton
by 11 lengths: will stay 1½m+: open to further improvement. *M. H. Tompkins*

MACGILLYCUDDY (IRE) 8 b. or br.g. Petorius 117 – My Bonnie 61 (High- 58
land Melody 112) [1996 6g⁶ 6d³ 5d² 6g 5d⁴ 6g 6g 5g 6f 5s 1997 6g 5m⁶ 5d 6d⁶ 7.1g
6.1s Oct 15] sturdy, close-coupled ex-Irish gelding: modest form at best in Britain:
a sprinter: acts on good to firm and soft ground: normally blinkered nowadays.
Mrs P. N. Dutfield

MACHIAVELLI 3 b.c. Machiavellian (USA) 123 – Forest Blossom (USA) 56 85
(Green Forest (USA) 134) [1996 NR 1997 10d³ 10m⁴ 12.3g⁴ 12g* 12m⁴ 14.6m
Sep 10] 37,000F, IR 80,000Y: strong, good-bodied colt: half-brother to 2 winners,
including fairly useful Forest Heights (up to 11f, by Slip Anchor): dam, winner in
Holland, is half-sister to Yorkshire Oaks winner Magnificent Star: fairly useful
performer: won maiden at Pontefract in July: good fourth in minor event at Newbury
next time, but well held in face of stiff task final start: stays 1½m: unraced on
extremes of going: genuine: sold 18,000 gns in October. *H. R. A. Cecil*

MACH ONE (FR) 2 b.g. (Mar 30) Sanglamore (USA) 126 – Douceur (USA) –
(Shadeed (USA) 135) [1997 6f Oct 3] 17,000Y: strong, lengthy gelding: has scope:
fourth foal: half-brother to 1¼m winner It'sthebusiness (by Most Welcome): dam
French 9.5f winner from good family: 33/1, last of 14 in maiden at Lingfield, soon
tailed off after very slow start: moved poorly to post. *Sir Mark Prescott*

MAC OATES 4 b.g. Bairn (USA) 126 – Bit of A Lass 59 (Wassl 125) [1996 51: 57
8.3m 10m 7.1m 5.3f² 7m⁶ 5f 1997 8g 8m* 10f a7s a7g⁵ Dec 18] lengthy gelding: a49
modest handicapper: won 22-runner claiming event at Goodwood in September,
easily best effort at 4 yrs: stays 1m: acts on firm going, poor form on all-weather.
P. R. Hedger

MAC'S BACK (USA) 2 br.c. (May 1) Momsfurrari (USA) – Peace Sister (USA) 57
(Hold Your Peace (USA)) [1997 6m⁵ a7g³ Dec 10] $8,000Y: fourth reported foal:
closely related to a winner in USA by Elocutionist and half-brother to winners there
by Jungle Savage and Hilal: dam won up to 1m in USA: off course 5 months, much
better effort when staying-on third in weak maiden at Lingfield. *W. A. O'Gorman*

MAC'S DELIGHT 3 b.g. Machiavellian (USA) 123 – Bashoosh (USA) (Danzig –
(USA)) [1996 62?: 6g 7g³ 1997 11.1m⁶ 10g 10m 8d Oct 13] small gelding: little
worthwhile form. *H. Akbary*

MAC'S TYPE (IRE) 2 b.f. (Apr 25) Mac's Imp (USA) 116 – Pass No Problem –
(Pas de Seul 133) [1997 6g 7.1s Nov 6] 2,400 2-y-o: half-sister to several winners
abroad: dam unraced: tailed off in maidens. *W. Storey*

MAD ALEX 4 b.g. Risk Me (FR) 127 – Princess Mona 56 (Prince Regent (FR) 47
129) [1996 –: a10g a8g 1997 a10g a7g⁵ a8g 8.3s³ 9.7s⁵ 8.1m Jul 23] leggy gelding: a–
poor maiden: best effort when third in claimer at Windsor in May: stays 1m: acts on
soft going, no form on all-weather. *M. J. Haynes*

MADAME CHINNERY 3 b.f. Weldnaas (USA) 112 – Bel Esprit (Sagaro 133) 80
[1996 76: 5m⁵ 6g² 7f² 7m* 7m⁵ 8g⁴ 1997 11.4m² 12d 11.9d⁶ Jul 3] lengthy, unfurnished filly: fairly useful handicapper: runner-up at Sandown on reappearance: ran as
if something amiss afterwards: should stay at least 1½m: has carried head high but is
genuine: has run well when sweating and edgy. *J. M. P. Eustace*

MADAME CLAUDE (IRE) 2 b.f. (Mar 27) Paris House 123 – Six Penny 70
Express (Bay Express 132) [1997 5.2m 5m² 5m⁶ 6f* 7m Sep 30] IR 28,000Y: seventh
foal: half-sister to several winners, including useful Irish/German sprinter Nashcash
(by Nashamaa): dam Irish maiden: fair form: landed gamble in maiden at Yarmouth
in September: tailed off in valuable nursery at Newmarket fortnight later: stays 6f:
raced only on good to firm/firm ground. *J. A. R. Toller*

MADAME JONES (IRE) 2 ch.f. (Mar 24) Lycius (USA) 124 – Gold Braisim 62
(IRE) (Jareer (USA) 115) [1997 6m 6d³ 7m³ 7d Oct 16] IR 6,000Y: first foal: dam
Irish 6f winner: modest maiden: third in claimer at Haydock and minor event at
Goodwood: stays 7f. *B. J. Meehan*

570

MADAME MAXI   3 ch.f. Ron's Victory (USA) 129 – New Pastures (Formidable – (USA) 125) [1996 NR 1997 7m⁶ 6.9d 8d Oct 28] fourth foal: dam unraced: no worthwhile form, including in a seller. *P. R. Hedger*

MADAM LUCY   3 ch.f. Efisio 120 – Our Aisling 82 (Blakeney 126) [1996 –: 5f   49 7f 7.5m⁶ 1997 a11g 12g⁶ a8g³ a8.5g² a8g⁴ 10g⁴ a9.4g* a8.5g⁵ 10.1g³ 12g a8.5g⁵ a12g⁴ a12g Nov 1] poor performer: won apprentice claimer at Wolverhampton for W. Haigh in July: trained next start only by P. Howling: effective from 9f to 1½m: acts on fibresand, raced mostly on good going on turf. *J. L. Spearing*

MADAM ZANDO   4 ch.f. Forzando 122 – Madam Trilby (Grundy 137) [1996   27 51d, a37: a6g⁵ a6g a7g⁵ 6d² 6d 6g² 5g⁵ 5.9f⁵ 6m⁴ 6f⁴ 6m 6d⁶ 7g 6.1m 1997 5g 6m 6d 6m⁴ 6g 6m 6g 7m Sep 26] good-topped filly: poor maiden handicapper: acts on firm ground, probably on dead: tried blinkered/visored: inconsistent. *J. Balding*

MADDIE   5 b.m. Primitive Rising (USA) 113 – Dubavarna 72 (Dubassoff (USA))   37 [1996 NR 1997 a16g 10.1g⁴ 14.1m³ 17.2f Aug 27] third foal: half-sister to 7-y-o Hullbank: dam poor 1½m maiden: poor form: tailed off in handicap final outing. *W. W. Haigh*

MADE BOLD   3 b.f. Never So Bold 135 – Classical Vintage 80 (Stradavinsky   61 121) [1996 80p: 6.1m³ 1997 7.1d³ 7g 11.1m 10s Oct 8] smallish filly: modest maiden: form in 1997 only when third at Chepstow: stays 7f. *H. Candy*

MADGE'S PET   3 b.f. Precious Metal 106 – Lucky Lena (Leander 119) [1996 NR   – 1997 7.1d 7g Jul 12] second known foal: dam of little account: behind in maidens. *G. Barnett*

MADISON MIST   3 gr.f. Mystiko (USA) 124 – Hi-Li (High Top 131) [1996 NR   65 1997 8.2m⁴ 7f⁴ 8g 10m⁶ 8f Jun 10] 17,000Y: angular filly: has a quick action: third foal: dam unraced daughter of useful miler Leipzig: modest maiden: best efforts first 2 starts: lost a shoe final one: stays 1m: has been reluctant at stalls. *Mrs J. R. Ramsden*

MADISON'S TOUCH   4 b.f. Touch of Grey 90 – Cabinet Shuffle (Thatching   – 131) [1996 –: 6.9d a7g a7g⁵ a10g 1997 8f Jun 5] of no account. *R. M. Flower*

MADISON WELCOME (IRE)   3 b.g. Be My Guest (USA) 126 – Subtle Change   65 § (IRE) 102 (Law Society (USA) 130) [1996 56: 6d 6m⁴ 6g 6g⁵ 7g⁵ 1997 10.3m 10m³ 14.6d⁵ 11m³ 10.3d⁴ 11.1d² 12g 11g⁴ 11.9d⁶ 16g 16s Oct 8] regular gelding: fair maiden handicapper: stays 11f: acts on good to firm and dead ground: visored 3 of last 4 starts: temperamental: sold, and sent to Germany. *Mrs J. R. Ramsden*

MADJAMILA (IRE)   2 b.f. (Feb 11) Doyoun 124 – Madaniyya (USA) (Shah-   89 p rastani (USA) 135) [1997 7d* Oct 27] first foal: dam Irish 9f and 1¼m winner from family of Slip Anchor: 9/2, won maiden at Lingfield in good style by 3½ lengths from Pursuit Venture, running green but not having to come under strong pressure to draw away: should be well suited by 1¼m+: sure to improve and win more races. *L. M. Cumani*

MADLY SHARP   6 ch.g. Sharpo 132 – Madison Girl 68 (Last Fandango 125)   93 [1996 106: 6m* 6m² 6f 6m 6f 7m² 6s⁶ 1997 7g 6d 6.1s 7m 6g 6g 7m² 7g Oct 18] big, workmanlike gelding: has a round action: useful handicapper: didn't always have things go his way in 1997: effective at 6f/7f: acts on good to firm ground, not at best on going softer than good: sometimes sweating/on toes/flashes tail: normally races just off pace: tried blinkered: sold 30,000 gns, and joined D. Vienna in USA. *J. W. Watts*

MADMAN'S MIRAGE (FR)   2 b.g. (Jan 28) Green Desert (USA) 127 –   51 Layaali (USA) (Diesis 133) [1997 6m 6m 8d Sep 20] IR 21,000Y: workmanlike gelding: second foal: brother to 3-y-o March Crusader: dam Irish 1m winner out of useful French 1986 2-y-o Touching Love: modest form at best in maidens: shapes as if will stay beyond 1m. *M. Johnston*

MAD MILITANT (IRE)   8 b.g. Vision (USA) – Ullapool (Dominion 123) [1996   68 55, a71: 12g⁴ 11.9g⁴ 12g⁶ a12g³ a12g³ a12g³ 1997 a11g³ 10.8m* 10.8m⁵ 10.8f* 12g 10.3m³ 11.6m³ 10.3d 12m³ 11m³ Oct 28] compact gelding: unimpressive mover: fair handicapper: won at Warwick in March and June: stays 1½m, probably not 2m: acts on any turf going, and on fibresand (only once raced on equitrack): held up. *A. Streeter*

MADONNA DA ROSSI   4 b.f. Mtoto 134 – Granny's Bank 88 (Music Boy 124)   25
[1996 43: a7g 8.2d⁴ 8m 7.1g 6f 7g³ 7d² 7.1m 1997 a7g⁵ a7g³ a8g a7g a8g Feb 22]
lengthy filly: poor maiden: headstrong, but stayed easy 8.5f: acted on firm and dead
ground and all-weather: stud. *M. Dods*

MADRINA   4 b.f. Waajib 121 – Mainly Sunset (Red Sunset 120) [1996 67, a70:   –
5.1d⁶ 5m 5g⁵ 5f⁵ 7m³ 8.1g⁵ 8.1g⁴ 6m³ a6g³ a6g* a6g⁴ a6g a5g 1997 a5g² a5g⁴ a5g²   a70
a5g⁶ Mar 5] lengthy, workmanlike filly: fair performer: badly hampered leaving
stalls final start: barely stays 6f: acts on firm ground and on all-weather: usually races
prominently. *J. Berry*

MAEDALEY   2 b.f. (Apr 26) Charmer 123 – Carousella 62 (Rousillon (USA)   45
133) [1997 5g³ a5g 5g 6g³ 7.5f² 7g a6g⁵ a6g Nov 1] 2,100 2-y-o: third foal: sister to
4-y-o Galapino: dam 1m winner out of Cheshire Oaks winner Salchow: poor maiden:
trained before final start by P. Haslam: placed in sellers/selling nurseries: should stay
1m+. *Ronald Thompson*

MAENAD   6 gr.m. Sharrood (USA) 124 – Now In Session (USA) (Diesis 133)   –
[1996 NR 1997 10g⁴ Aug 13] lengthy mare: modest placed form in NH Flat races:
probably flattered by fourth of 6 in maiden at Sandown on flat debut. *D. J. S. ffrench
Davis*

MAFTOOL   3 ch.c. Machiavellian (USA) 123 – Majmu (USA) 105 (Al Nasr (FR)   86
126) [1996 78: 6m 7m⁵ 7g⁴ 1997 8g* 8g 8s⁴ 10.1s Jun 28] strong, close-coupled
colt: has a round action: fairly useful performer: easy winner of maiden at Newcastle
in March: easily best susequent effort when staying-on fourth to Right Wing in
strongly-run minor event at Ascot: should stay 1¼m: acts on good to firm and soft
ground. *J. H. M. Gosden*

MAFTUN (USA)   5 ch.g. Elmaamul (USA) 125 – Allesheny 85 (Be My Guest   55
(USA) 126) [1996 60: 12d 9.9g⁶ 10m 10m⁵ 13g² 12.4m* 12f⁵ 12.3s 13.6m 1997   a62
a11g³ a11g² a11g² a11g² a12g³ a12g* a12g 12.3m³ a11g Dec 8] workmanlike
gelding: unimpressive mover: modest handicapper: won at Southwell in February:
off course 8 months before poor run final start: stays 13f: acts on fibresand and on
good to firm ground, possibly softer than good: has had tongue tied: forces pace/
races prominently. *G. M. Moore*

MAGAONA (FR)   3 b.f. Slip Anchor 136 – Movieland (USA) 109 (Nureyev   –
(USA) 131) [1996 NR 1997 10.5s⁵ 10m 8f Jun 10] 180,000 francs Y: workmanlike
filly: half-sister to a French 10.5f winner by Kris: dam, Group 3 2-y-o 1m winner,
sister to smart miler Only Star: no promise in maidens. *R. Hannon*

MAGAZINE GAP   4 ch.g. Weldnaas (USA) 112 – Divissima 62 (Music Boy   –
124) [1996 51p: a7g³ 1997 a7g⁵ a7g⁴ 6.1m 6.1g 5m 6m a8g⁴ 10s 11.9f⁵ a8g⁶ 8m   a50 d
a10g² 8m a10g a10g a10s a8g³ a10g Dec 19] leggy gelding: poor maiden on
equitrack: well beaten last 5 starts: best effort at 1¼m. *Pat Mitchell*

MAGELLANO (USA)   3 b. or br.c. Miswaki (USA) 124 – Mount Holyoke 93   123
(Golden Fleece (USA) 133) [1996 NR 1997 10g³ 12g* 12s* 12d² Jun 29] sixth foal:
closely related to smart Wootton Rivers (stayed 1½m, by Woodman), and half-
brother to fairly useful 7.5f winner Marigliano (by Riverman): dam, 1m winner, is
daughter of smart sprinter Amaranda: very smart French colt: won useful minor
event in April and Prix la Force (beat Six Zero 1½ lengths) in May, both at Longchamp: kept on without posing a threat to Helissio when 5 lengths second of 4 in
Grand Prix de Saint-Cloud, best effort: stays 1½m: acts on soft ground, yet to race on
firmer than good. *A. Fabre, France*

MAGGICE   2 b.f. (Apr 13) Magic Ring (IRE) 115 – Ice Chocolate (USA) 77   –
(Icecapade (USA)) [1997 6g⁵ 6m 6m 7.1g 6m a6g a8g a6g a6g⁴ Dec 26] IR 1,600Y:
leggy filly: sixth foal: half-sister to 3 winners, including 5-y-o Kissel, fairly useful
1m winner in France in 1995: dam, 1m winner at 4 yrs, from family of Oh So Sharp:
little worthwhile form. *R. Hollinshead*

MAGICAL   2 b.c. (May 11) Magic Ring (IRE) 115 – Cal Norma's Lady (IRE) 87   84
(Lyphard's Special (USA) 122) [1997 6.1m* 6g⁵ Aug 25] 16,000Y: leggy, angular
colt: second foal: half-brother to 1996 2-y-o 5f winner Under Pressure (by Keen):
dam, 6f and 7f winner at 2 yrs, stayed 1¼m: won maiden at Chepstow in July: good

fifth, beaten 5½ lengths, to Arkadian Hero in listed race at Ripon: should stay beyond 6f: joined K. Webster in USA. *W. R. Muir*

MAGICAL COLOURS (IRE) 2 b.f. (May 4) Rainbows For Life (CAN) – Immediate Impact (Caerleon (USA) 132) [1997 6g⁶ 7m Sep 9] IR 11,500Y: sixth foal: half-sister to 5-y-o River Keen and 3 winners abroad: dam Irish 1¼m winner: sire (by Lyphard) champion in Canada, winner from 6f to 1¼m: signs of ability in maidens at Salisbury and Lingfield (met trouble): likely to do better. *J. L. Dunlop* – p

MAGICAL DANCER (IRE) 2 b.f. (May 14) Magical Wonder (USA) 125 – Diva Encore 74 (Star Appeal 133) [1997 5.1m⁵ 5.2g 5.1d 5m 5.1m⁶ 7m 5m⁶ 5.3g⁶ 6.1m Sep 15] IR 10,500Y: leggy, unfurnished filly: seventh foal: sister to a winner in Italy and half-sister to 3 winners, including 5-y-o Don't Worry Me and fairly useful performer up to 7f Encore M'Lady (both by Dancing Dissident): dam 1½m and 1¾m winner: poor maiden: not disgraced over 7f, though pulled hard. *Mrs P. N. Dutfield* 48

MAGICATION 7 b.m. Nomination 125 – Gundreda 93 (Gunner B 126) [1996 –: a11g 1997 a8g a11g Jan 10] probably no longer of any account. *K. G. Wingrove* –

MAGIC COMBINATION (IRE) 4 b.g. Scenic 128 – Etage (Ile de Bourbon (USA) 133) [1996 12m² 9g* 12m⁵ 14g*¹ 12g³ 12g* 12m⁴ 16g 16d² 1997 18m 16g 12m 14g 12d⁵ 11.4d* 16.2m³ 14m 12m 12v 10.1m 16.5s Nov 8] IR 4,200Y: leggy gelding: fifth foal: half-brother to unreliable 1¼m/1½m winner Tirolette (by Tirol): dam winner in Germany: formerly useful (rated 96) Irish performer: won at 2 yrs (1m) and 3 times at 3 yrs for K. Prendergast: won handicap at Sandown (making nearly all) in July: below form last 4 starts: effective at 11f to 2m: acts on good to firm ground and dead. *B. J. Curley* 79

MAGIC FALLS (IRE) 2 b.c. (Apr 9) River Falls 113 – Simply Inch (Simply Great (FR) 122) [1997 a7g 10s Oct 15] 9,000 2-y-o: third foal: half-brother to 5-y-o Water Hazard (formerly fair winner up to 1½m): dam unraced: behind in maidens. *M. J. Polglase* –

MAGIC FIZZ 3 gr.c. Efisio 120 – Strawberry Pink 87 (Absalom 128) [1996 55: a6g a5g⁵ a6g³ 1997 a6g⁶ a6g³ a6g² 5s 5m³ a5g a6g 7g 6f a6g⁵ Oct 20] sturdy colt: modest maiden handicapper: stays 6f: acts on good to firm ground and fibresand: blinkered last 2 starts. *T. J. Etherington* 55

MAGIC HILL 3 b.f. Danehill (USA) 126 – Magic Flute (USA) (The Minstrel (CAN) 135) [1996 NR 1997 7g 8g⁴ Jun 18] second foal: dam unraced sister to Free Handicap winner Noble Minstrel: better effort in maidens when fourth at Ripon: sold 9,500 gns in December. *J. H. M. Gosden* 59

MAGIC LAHR (GER) 4 ch.g. Dashing Blade 117 – Miraflores (GER) (Esclavo (FR)) [1996 NR 1997 10g 10.3d 8s 8m 8m⁴ 10.2d³ Aug 25] 16,000Y: second foal: half-brother to German 6f winner My Inspiration (by Alkalde): dam placed in Germany as 2-y-o: modest maiden: stays 1¼m: acts on good to firm going and dead. *I. A. Balding* 61

MAGIC LAKE 4 b.f. Primo Dominie 121 – Magic Kingdom 76 (Kings Lake (USA) 133) [1996 47: 8m 7g 7.1d a6g⁴ 7m* 7m 7g² 7.1m⁶ 7g 6d³ 8g 1997 5g a5g 7g⁶ 7.6m 7.5m³ 6d⁶ 8g 6.1m² 6m* 7m Nov 1] lengthy, good-topped filly: modest handicapper: back to form last 3 starts, winning 21-runner race at Leicester in October: effective at 6f to 1m: acts on firm and dead ground: has worn visor, including last 3 starts: sold 8,500 gns in November. *E. J. Alston* 52

MAGIC MELODY 4 b.f. Petong 126 – Miss Rossi (Artaius (USA) 129) [1996 –: 10.2m 10m⁶ 6m 6m 1997 6.1m 8.3s a7g a8g Jun 30] leggy filly: no form since 2 yrs: blinkered final outing. *J. L. Spearing* –

MAGIC MILL (IRE) 4 b.c. Simply Great (FR) 122 – Rosy O'Leary (Majetta 115) [1996 NR 1997 7m 7.5m⁶ 7m³ 6s 7g⁵ 8g⁵ 8m⁶ a10g² a7g Dec 2] sparely-made colt: fairly useful handicapper: reportedly choked fifth start: second in amateurs race at Lingfield in November, best effort of 1997: barely stays 1¼m: acts on firm ground and equitrack: tried visored. *J. L. Eyre* 82

MAGIC MORNING 2 ch.g. (Apr 25) Magic Ring (IRE) 115 – Incarnadine 67 (Hot Spark) [1997 6d 6m Oct 31] 9,000Y: smallish, stocky gelding: half-brother to several winners, including 9-y-o Rise Up Singing and middle-distance performer –

Sunderland Echo (by Daring March), both fairly useful at best: dam 7f (at 2 yrs) and 1m winner: well beaten in 2 maidens at Newmarket. *W. J. Musson*

MAGIC OF ALOHA (IRE)   2 ch.f. (May 18) Diesis 133 – Satz (USA) 50 (The   79 p
Minstrel (CAN) 135) [1997 7m⁵ Sep 30] 57,000Y: second foal: half-sister to a winner
in USA by Quiet American: dam, lightly raced here and in USA, half-sister to smart
7f/1m performer Satin Flower and US Grade 1 1¼m winner Martial Law: 25/1, about
10 lengths fifth of 13 to Tamarisk in valuable sales race at Newmarket, pulling hard
and prominent 5f: should improve if learning to settle. *B. W. Hills*

MAGIC POWERS   2 ch.g. (Apr 16) Magical Wonder (USA) 125 – Kissin'   67 p
Cousin 74 (Be Friendly 130) [1997 5m 7m⁴ 5.1d⁶ Oct 8] 9,000Y: half-brother to 3
winners, including smart sprinter Coquito's Friend (by Owen Dudley): dam twice-
raced sister to smart sprinter As Friendly: best effort in maidens when fourth at
Salisbury in October: found 5f too short next time: should do better. *G. B. Balding*

MAGIC RAINBOW   2 b.c. (Apr 30) Magic Ring (IRE) 115 – Blues Indigo 103   75 +
(Music Boy 124) [1997 5m⁴ 5d* 6f⁵ Jul 12] 16,000Y: leggy colt: third living foal:
half-brother to 5f winner Blue Sioux (by Indian Ridge): dam sprinter: fair form: won
minor event at Leicester in June: promised better, but didn't look to be striding out
when only fifth on firm going in nursery at Lingfield: should stay 6f: awkward
leaving stalls first 2 starts. *M. Bell*

MAGIC SPRING (IRE)   2 ch.f. (Feb 12) Persian Bold 123 – Oasis (Valiyar 129)   59
[1997 6g 7d⁵ 7d Nov 7] smallish filly: third foal: half-sister to 4-y-o White Settler:
dam, winner twice over hurdles, half-sister to Magic Ring: only worthwhile form in
maidens when fifth at Lingfield in October: sweated final start. *K. McAuliffe*

MAGINOT (USA)   2 gr.c. (May 22) St Jovite (USA) 135 – Gardien du Jour   56 +
(USA) 59 (Grey Dawn II 132) [1997 6m Jul 14] fourth foal: dam maiden who should
have stayed 1m: easy to back, just over 8 lengths eighth in maiden at Folkestone,
eased near line: will be suited by further than 6f. *D. R. Loder*

MAGNI MOMENTI   2 b.f. (Mar 31) King's Signet (USA) 110 – Halka (Daring   –
March 116) [1997 5.7g Jun 28] 6,000Y: seventh live foal: half-sister to 3-y-o Raivue
and 2 winning sprinters both by Martinmas: dam unraced: tailed off in maiden at
Bath. *R. Hannon*

MAGYAR TITOK (IRE)   3 br.c. Treasure Kay 114 – Aliyna (FR) (Vayrann 133)   –
[1996 47, a42: 5.2f⁴ 7d 5s a5g³ 6g a6g⁶ 1997 a6g Jan 21] leggy colt: poor form: stays
6f: tends to sweat and get on edge. *Bob Jones*

MAHAB (USA)   2 b.f. (Mar 1) Nureyev (USA) 131 – Personal Business (USA)   70 p
(Private Account (USA)) [1997 6.1m⁴ Sep 23] fourth foal: half-sister to US Grade 3
7f winner In Conference (by Dayjur): dam US Grade 1 1¼m winner: 9/2 and green,
just under 8 lengths fourth to Ikhteyaar in 18-runner maiden at Nottingham, slowly
away then staying on under hands and heels: sure to improve. *Saeed bin Suroor*

MAHBOOB (IRE)   2 b. or br.c. (Apr 24) Marju (IRE) 127 – Miss Gris (USA)   102 p
120 (Hail The Pirates (USA) 126) [1997 7f² 7m* 7m³ Sep 10] rangy colt: fifth foal:
half-brother to 4-y-o Nabhaan, 1¾m winner Elflaa (by Sure Blade) and a winner in
Italy by Wassl: dam won Italian 1000 Guineas and Italian Oaks: useful form: won
19-runner maiden at Newbury in August by length from Prolix: favourite, close third
of 6 to Teapot Row in well-contested minor event at Doncaster, cruising much of way
but unable to quicken, still bit green: will be well suited by further than 7f, and should
stays 1½m: raced only on good to firm/firm ground: should do better again at 3 yrs.
D. Morley

MAIDEN CASTLE   4 b.g. Darshaan 133 – Noble Destiny 89 (Dancing Brave   –
(USA) 140) [1996 94: 10s* 11d⁵ 10.3f⁵ 12m⁵ 1997 10.4g May 15] angular gelding:
has a quick action: fairly useful performer, lightly raced: not given hard race when
down the field in handicap at York only outing at 4 yrs: should stay 1½m: acts on soft
ground: wears bandages: sold approx. £8,000 in Dubai in November. *J. H. M. Gosden*

MAID OF CAMELOT   3 br.f. Caerleon (USA) 132 – Waterfowl Creek (IRE) 88   102
(Be My Guest (USA) 126) [1996 NR 1997 10g⁶ 10.2m* 10d* 12g 11.9g⁶ 10m 10.1g⁴
10.1m⁵ Sep 16] sturdy filly: first foal: dam, 1m winner, from family of smart
performers Guest Artiste, Inchmurrin and Welney: useful performer: won maiden at
Bath in April and listed race at Goodwood (set slow pace, beat Priena 1¼ lengths in

May: best efforts when sixth in Lancashire Oaks at Haydock and fourth in listed handicap at Newcastle: stays 1½m: yet to race on extremes of going: effective blinkered/visored: hung right fourth start: sent to USA. *R. Charlton*

MAIELLA   2 ch.f. (Apr 4) Salse (USA) 128 – Forelino (USA) 62§ (Trempolino – p (USA) 135) [1997 6m 7.9s Sep 3] 5,500Y: unfurnished, useful-looking filly: second foal: half-sister to 3-y-o Tough Act: dam 10.6f winner, should have been effective over further: signs of ability in big fields of maidens at Newbury (burly and green) and York. *R. Hannon*

MAIL SHOT (IRE)   2 b.g. (Mar 3) Maledetto (IRE) 103 – Pallachine (FR) – (Lichine (USA) 117) [1997 6g 7m 6g Sep 25] 6,600Y: half-brother to a winner abroad by Midyan: dam unraced: well held in maidens. *S. Dow*

MAIN STREET   2 b.g. (Feb 23) Emarati (USA) 74 – I'm Yours 65 (Forzando 66 122) [1997 6m⁴ 7m a6g² a7g³ Nov 14] 50,000Y: first foal: dam, third at 6f at 2 yrs, but no form afterwards, half-sister to smart pair up to 1m Osario and Only Yours: fair form: best efforts when placed in maiden at Wolverhampton and nursery at Southwell in November: stays 7f: acts on fibresand. *W. J. Haggas*

MAI TAI (IRE)   2 b.f. (Apr 18) Scenic 128 – Oystons Propweekly (Swing Easy 67 (USA) 126) [1997 5m³ 5.1d⁵ May 11] IR 4,000Y: good-topped filly: half-sister to 2-y-o winners by Pennine Walk and Taufan: dam 2-y-o 5f winner: fair form in early-season minor events at Warwick and Bath. *Mrs P. N. Dutfield*

MAITEAMIA   4 ch.g. Komaite (USA) – Mia Scintilla 54 (Blazing Saddles 76 d (AUS)) [1996 76: a6g* a7g² 6.1d a6g* 5s* 6d² 5g* 5.1m² 6m² 6m 1997 5m³ 6m³ 6d 6d 6g a7g 5g Aug 23] robust gelding: fair handicapper: well below form last 5 starts: suited by 5f/6f: acts on good to firm and soft ground and on fibresand: visored once, now blinkered: races prominently: often apprentice ridden. *S. R. Bowring*

MAJAARI   2 b. or br.c. (Feb 25) Marju (IRE) 127 – Ahbab (IRE) 81 (Ajdal (USA) 95 130) [1997 6g² 6m* 6m⁴ Sep 10] strong, good-topped colt: second foal: half-brother to 3-y-o Labeq: dam 7f winner out of half-sister to Fairy Footsteps and Light Cavalry: landed odds easily in maiden at Ripon in August by 2 lengths from Requestor, making all: good fourth to Mijana in listed race at Kempton: should stay 1m. *P. T. Walwyn*

MAJAL (IRE)   8 b.g. Caerleon (USA) 132 – Park Special (Relkino 131) [1996 –: 52 d 12d 12m 1997 9m⁶ 12m² 12d⁵ 10.9g 10g 8g Oct 22] good-bodied gelding: unimpressive mover: modest handicapper: ran poorly final 3 starts: stays 1½m: probably acts on any turf ground and on equitrack. *J. S. Wainwright*

MAJALIS   2 b. or br.f. (Mar 23) Mujadil (USA) 119 – Rose Barton (Pas de Seul 68 133) [1997 5.1g³ 5m⁶ 6g⁴ Oct 7] 13,500Y: fifth foal: half-sister to 1992 2-y-o 7f winner Peaceful Air and 8-y-o My Abbey (both by Hadeer) and a winner in Germany by Formidable: dam unraced: fair form in maidens when in frame at Bath and Warwick: reportedly gurgled in between. *R. Guest*

MAJESTIC HILLS   2 b.c. (Mar 1) Shirley Heights 130 – Regent Miss (CAN) 83 p (Vice Regent (CAN)) [1997 8m² 8s Oct 14] 35,000Y: strong, lengthy colt: has plenty of scope: seventh foal: half-brother to 2 winners by Master Willie, notably very smart performer here and in USA at up to 1¼m Deputy Governor: dam won Canadian Oaks: well-backed favourite despite looking backward, promising ¾-length second to Courteous, pair clear, in maiden at Salisbury, quickening past most of field from slow start: may have found race coming too soon 2 weeks later: should be well suited by 1¼m+: fine type, sure to progress and win races at 3 yrs. *J. L. Dunlop*

MAJESTY (IRE)   3 b.g. Sadler's Wells (USA) 132 – Princesse Timide (USA) 107 72 (Blushing Groom (FR) 131) [1996 NR 1997 8m³ 10g³ 10.4s⁶ Sep 3] IR 310,000Y: close-coupled colt: from family of winners, including smart Psychobabble (up to 1m, by Caerleon) and Louis Cyphre (stayed 1½m well, by Nijinsky): dam French 7.5f and 1¼m winner: fair form when third in maiden at Leicester and Goodwood: bandaged behind, tailed off on soft ground final start: should be suited by 1¼m+: sold 12,000 gns and joined S. Dow. *P. F. I. Cole*

MAJOR BALLABY (IRE)   2 b.c. (Mar 28) Balla Cove 119 – Surreal 69 (Bus- 66 tino 136) [1997 8g 7.9s 7.5f 8m⁵ 8d 7d Oct 30] IR 1,200Y: tall colt: second known foal: dam sprinter: fair form when fifth in steadily-run maiden at Pontefract and seventh in similar event at Navan in the autumn: stays 1m: acts on good to firm and dead going. *Mrs S. A. Bramall, Ireland*

MAJOR CHANGE   5 gr.g. Sharrood (USA) 124 – May The Fourteenth 53   95
(Thatching 131) [1996 95: 10m³ 9s² 10m* 12m 10g 10d 10.1m⁶ 1997 13g a12g²
12m³ 11.9s 10.1m* 10.4g² 8.1g⁶ 10.1g⁵ 10.4m 10g⁶ 10.1m³ 10.4g Aug 20] close-
coupled gelding: useful handicapper: ridden more patiently than usual when narrow
winner at Epsom in April: effective over strongly-run 1m, barely stays 1½m: probably acts on any turf going and fibresand: gelded since final start. *Miss Gay Kelleway*

MAJOR DUNDEE (IRE)   4 b.g. Distinctly North (USA) 115 – Indigo Blue   –
(IRE) 56 (Bluebird (USA) 125) [1996 77: 10g 8f² 7m³ 9m* 10m⁶ 10.2m⁵ 11.9m²
14d³ 12m³ 1997 20m Jun 17] useful-looking gelding: impresses in appearance: good
mover: fair handicapper: progressive hurdler in early in 1997: tailed off in Ascot
Stakes at Royal Ascot, only outing on flat as 4-y-o: stays 1¾m: acts on firm ground.
M. C. Pipe

MAJORIEN   4 ch.c. Machiavellian (USA) 123 – Green Rosy (USA) (Green   114
Dancer (USA) 132) [1996 116: 7g* 7g⁴ 8m² 8g² 1997 8g⁴ 8d⁵ 10.5m* 11m* 12d*
12f Nov 8] smart colt: one of the best 2-y-o's in France in 1996, runner-up in Grand
Criterium at Longchamp: disappointing first 2 starts on return, then won minor event,
listed race and Prix du Conseil de Paris (by length from Tamure), all at Longchamp,
in September/October: behind in Breeders' Cup Turf final start: stays 1½m: acts on
good to firm and dead ground. *Mme C. Head, France*

MAJOR MOUSE   9 ch.g. All Systems Go 119 – Tzu-Hsi (Songedor 116) [1996   48
NR 1997 a7g a8g a8g a8g⁶ a8g⁵ a8g² a8g 8m 9m 10g⁵ 10g a8g⁴ a9.4g Aug 16] mod-   a56
est performer: seems best around 1m: acts on fibresand and good to firm ground:
none too consistent. *W. W. Haigh*

MAJOR QUALITY   4 b.g. Sizzling Melody 117 – Bonne de Berry (Habitat 134)   –
[1996 99: 5m* 5d² 6m 1997 5.2g Apr 18] sturdy gelding: takes the eye: has a quick
action: useful performer at 3 yrs: off course 10 months, soon outpaced in handicap
only outing in 1997: best at 5f: unraced on extremes of going. *J. R. Fanshawe*

MAJOR TWIST (IRE)   3 b.g. Dancing Dissident (USA) 119 – Kafsa (IRE)   –
(Vayrann 133) [1996 –: 6d 6m 1997 a8g² 8.2m 7m May 6] only form when short-   a68
headed in claimer at Lingfield in March: should stay beyond 1m. *R. Hannon*

MAKAHU DON   2 ch.g. (May 2) Derrylin 115 – Rockalong 35 (Native Bazaar   56 d
122) [1997 5s⁶ 5m* 5m² 5d² 6g⁴ 7g 7.1m⁴ 6g⁵ 6m 5m a5g 6g 5s Oct 16] 1,000 2-y-o:
smallish gelding: fourth reported foal: dam stayed 1¼m: won seller at Musselburgh
in May but lost form completely: stays 6f: tried blinkered. *W. T. Kemp*

MAKATI   3 b.g. Efisio 120 – Seleter (Hotfoot 126) [1996 NR 1997 7f 5s 6m 8g   –
Jul 5] strong, compact gelding: half-brother to several winners, including fair 1¼m
performer Alabang (by Valiyar) and 9-y-o El Nido: dam no form: probably of little
account. *M. J. Camacho*

*Prix du Conseil de Paris, Longchamp—Majorien, one of the leading two-year-olds of 1996,
gains his first pattern success at the chief expense of Tamure*

MAKE BELIEVE 2 ch.f. (Apr 28) Caerleon (USA) 132 – Sleeping Beauty 87   58
(Mill Reef (USA) 141) [1997 5.7f 6.1g³ a8.5g⁵ Dec 13] sixth foal: closely related   a50
to 5-y-o Twilight Sleep and half-sister to 4-y-o Threadneedle and 8.5f to 1½m winner
Magic Junction (both by Danzig Connection): dam, 1m winner, half-sister to 2
Galtres Stakes winners: modest form last 2 starts in minor event at Nottingham (off
course 6 months afterwards, and sold out of R. Charlton's stable 12,000 gns) and
maiden at Wolverhampton: will stay further than 8.5f. *M. J. Polglase*

MAKE IT SO 2 ch.f. (Apr 4) Henbit (USA) 130 – H And K Gambler (Rheingold   –
137) [1997 6m Jun 4] 400Y: half-sister to a winner in Italy by Oats: dam won over
hurdles: tailed off in maiden at Folkestone. *J. S. Moore*

MAKE READY 3 b.f. Beveled (USA) – Prepare (IRE) 58 (Millfontaine 114)   61
[1996 61: a5g² a5g⁶ a5g* a5g³ a5g* 1997 a6g a5g 6.1g³ 6d 6d⁴ 5.1m⁵ 5.1m 5g 5g⁵ 6d
6m Sep 22] tall filly: modest handicapper: tailed off last 2 starts: a sprinter: acts on
fibresand, yet to race on extremes of going on turf: visored penultimate start.
J. Neville

MAKIDARTI 2 ch.f. (May 25) Akid (USA) – Middletown Girl (Steel City 93)   –
[1997 6g Aug 25] fourth reported foal: dam unraced: behind in seller at Ripon.
C. W. Fairhurst

MALABI (USA) 3 b.c. Danzig (USA) – Gmaasha (IRE) (Kris 135) [1996 NR   70
1997 6f² 6m³ 7g Jul 12] first foal: dam unraced sister to smart 7f/1m winner Hasbah
out of Al Bahathri: fair form in maidens first 2 starts: failed to handle bend at
Warwick when well beaten final one. *J. L. Dunlop*

MALADERIE (IRE) 3 b.g. Thatching 131 – Native Melody (Tudor Music 131)   66
[1996 83: 6m⁴ 6m² 6m* 7.1g³ 7m⁴ 8.1g⁴ 1997 8g 7m 7m 9g 8g 7.1m 6g² 5.7g 7.1g⁶
6f³ 6.1m² 7f 7m² 6.1s⁵ 7g Oct 24] close-coupled gelding: fair handicapper: ran
consistently well after sixth start at 3 yrs: effective at 6f to 1m: acts on firm going,
probably on soft: has had tongue tied. *M. R. Channon*

MALE-ANA-MOU (IRE) 4 ch.g. Ela-Mana-Mou 132 – Glasson Lady (GER)   88
108 (Priamos (GER) 123) [1996 90+: 8m³ 8.3m³ 10m* 12m 10g 12m 13.9m 1997
11.7g³ 14d 10g 12g⁵ 16d⁵ 16m³ Sep 25] rather leggy gelding: fairly useful handicapper: stays 2m: acts on good to firm and dead ground (yet to race on extremes).
D. R. C. Elsworth

MALIBU MAN 5 ch.g. Ballacashtal (CAN) – National Time (USA) (Lord Avie   80
(USA)) [1996 72: 5s² 5g 5.1g 6s⁶ 5m² a5g⁴ 5.1m² 5.1f* 5m 5g 1997 5g* 5g³   a86
a5g³ 5g⁶ 5m a5g* 5d⁴ 5m³ 5m 5.1g* 5m 5.1s 5m⁵ a6g² Sep 30] quite good-topped
gelding: has a round action: fairly useful handicapper: won at Folkestone in March,
Wolverhampton in June and Bath in August: best at 5f/sharp 6f, on good ground or
firmer/fibresand (yet to race on equitrack): blinkered (unsuited by ground) once: has
run well when sweating: often spoils chance by starting slowly, but speedy front
runner when getting away on terms. *E. A. Wheeler*

MALLIA 4 b.g. Statoblest 120 – Pronetta (USA) (Mr Prospector (USA)) [1996 86:   71
6g⁵ 6g² 6m* 6m 1997 6m 6s 6m 5d 6s 6m 6m 5g 6d² 6d 6m 6.1g² 6m a6g* a6g* Dec   a86
13] lengthy, dipped-backed gelding: fairly useful handicapper on all-weather, fair on
turf: won at Southwell in November and Wolverhampton (best effort) in December:
stays 6f well: acts on good to firm going, dead and fibresand (possibly unsuited by
soft): sometimes blinkered, including last 2 starts: none too consistent. *T. D. Barron*

MALOZZA 2 b.f. (May 4) Michelozzo (USA) 127 – Lis Na Mon (Gleason   58 d
(USA)) [1997 a5g* 6f 6d⁵ a7g a6g* a6g³ a6g³ 6m a7g a6g Nov 21] 4,300 2-y-o:
leggy filly: first known foal: dam showed nothing in Irish points: modest performer
on all-weather: won maiden at Southwell in May and seller at Wolverhampton in
September: stays 6f: acts on fibresand, no form on turf: blinkered fourth start: tends
to sweat. *P. D. Evans*

MALSISIO 5 b.m. Efisio 120 – Moonlight Fling (Imperial Fling (USA) 116)   –
[1996 NR 1997 a5g⁵ 8.2s Oct 15] seems of little account. *N. P. Littmoden*

MAMALIK (USA) 3 b.c. Diesis 133 – Have It Out (USA) (Roberto (USA) 131)   115
[1996 NR 1997 8g* 9m² 8m 7d³ Sep 12] sturdy, lengthy colt: first reported foal: dam,
won up to 9f in USA, half-sister to Grade 2 9f winner Suivi (by Diesis), from good
family: won maiden at Newbury (very easily) in April: smart form when 1½ lengths

second of 5 to Starborough in Prix Jean Prat at Chantilly 6 weeks later, tending to wander under pressure: reportedly struck into when last behind same horse in St James's Palace Stakes at Royal Ascot, and only third of 4 when odds on for minor event at Goodwood final start: stays 9f: sent to UAE. *J. H. M. Gosden*

MAMBLE'S PENSION (IRE) 2 ch.f. (Mar 24) Elmaamul (USA) 125 – Chance 27
All (FR) 88 (Glenstal (USA) 118) [1997 a6g a5g a7g⁶ Nov 29] 3,600Y: third foal: half-sister to 4-y-o Lachesis: dam 2-y-o 5f winner out of half-sister to Young Generation: signs of a little ability on third start at Wolverhampton in seller. *A. Bailey*

MAMBO MUSIC (FR) 3 gr.f. Rusticaro (FR) 124 – Musical Soul (USA) (Youth –
(USA) 135) [1996 NR 1997 a10g⁶ Feb 8] 70,000 francs Y, 5,000 3-y-o: sister to a prolific winner in Italy and half-sister to 2 winners abroad, including Wedge Musical (up to 1m, by What A Guest), later dam of Queen's Vase winner/smart hurdler Silver Wedge: dam French 11f and 1½m winner: showed nothing in maiden at Lingfield. *D. J. S. Cosgrove*

MAMMA LUIGI (IRE) 3 b.f. Classic Music (USA) – Second Movement (Music –
Boy 124) [1996 NR 1997 7g 8g 7d May 21] 11,000Y: angular filly: half-sister to 4 winners, notably Italian Group 2 6f winner Piero Gardino (by Faraway Times) and Italian multiple listed 1m winner Gigi Scaglia (by Alzao): dam unraced from good sprint family: no promise in maidens. *G. Lewis*

MAMMA'S BOY 2 b.g. (Jan 28) Rock City 120 – Henpot (IRE) 68 (Alzao (USA) 68
117) [1997 5d² 5m³ 5g³ 5s⁴ 6g³ 6m⁵ 7.1g 6d³ Sep 18] 10,000Y: sturdy gelding: second foal: half-brother to 4-y-o Sweet Wilhelmina: dam 1¼m winner at 2 yrs: fair maiden: stays 6f: acts on good to firm and dead ground: consistent. *J. Berry*

MAMORA BAY (IRE) 2 b.c. (Mar 21) High Estate 127 – Amenaide 79 (Known 71 d
Fact (USA) 135) [1997 5m³ 5g⁶ 6d 6f³ 7s² 6g 7.9s 8f a8.5g⁴ 7d Oct 16] 10,500Y: sturdy colt: fourth foal: half-brother to 6f winner P G Tips (by Don't Forget Me): dam 2-y-o 5f winner (stayed 7f) out of half-sister to Irish Oaks winner Swiftfoot: disappointing maiden: well beaten in seller final outing: stays 8.5f: tried visored/blinkered: temperament under suspicion: sold, and sent to Holland. *M. H. Tompkins*

MANABAR 5 b.g. Reprimand 122 – Ring of Pearl (Auction Ring (USA) 123) – §
[1996 66§, a69§: a10g a8g a9.4g a7g⁴ a8g³ a8g a7g 7d³ 9.7m³ 10g 10m⁴ 7g⁶ 9g⁵ 13g a55 d
10m 11.6d 7.9g 8.1f a8g² a10g⁶ a10g³ 1997 a10g⁶ a7f⁴ a7g⁶ a8g a8g a8g 8m a8g 7m
Aug 9] lengthy gelding: modest form at best at 5 yrs: stays 1¼m: acts on firm and dead ground and the all-weather: tried visored/blinkered: unreliable: sold 600 gns and joined M. McCausland in Ireland. *M. J. Polglase*

MANALOJ (USA) 4 ch.c. Gone West (USA) – Deviltante (USA) (Devil's Bag –
(USA)) [1996 87: 8m 8m* 10.3g 8f 8.1v 197 10m 7.3s⁴ 8f 10m Jul 30] good-topped colt: well beaten in 1997: sold, and sent to New Zealand. *R. Hannon*

MANAZIL (IRE) 3 ch.f. Generous (IRE) 139 – Stay Sharpe (USA) (Sharpen Up 98
127) [1996 NR 1997 8.2d* 7g⁵ 9g 12.3s² 10g⁶ 10g* 10m* 10g Aug 13] sparely-made filly: had a round action: fourth foal: half-sister to fair winners Ishtiyak (sprinter) and Fawz (up to 1¼m, both by Green Desert): dam unraced: useful performer: won maiden at Nottingham in April and handicaps at Newmarket and Ascot (best effort, leading inside final 1f) in July: effective at 1¼m and 1½m: acted on soft going and good to firm: game: visits Indian Ridge. *R. W. Armstrong*

MANDHAR (IRE) 2 b.c. (Apr 25) Scenic 128 – Clonross Lady (Red Alert 127) –
[1997 7g 8m Sep 22] IR 4,800Y resold 20,000Y: half-brother to 3 winners, including 1993 2-y-o sprint winner Phoneaholic (by Heraldiste): dam lightly raced: well held in maidens at Epsom and Kempton. *G. Lewis*

MANDILAK (USA) 3 b.c. El Gran Senor (USA) 136 – Madiriya 119 (Diesis 104
133) [1996 96P: 7g 8g* 1997 8.2m² 10s² 11.9g⁴ 12m⁶ Jul 30] well-made colt: has round action: highly promising winner at 2 yrs: proved to be just useful in 1997: runner-up in small-field minor events at Nottingham and Windsor: best efforts when fourth in listed race at Haydock (3½ lengths behind Ivan Luis) and when seventh (promoted a place) behind Maylane in Tote Gold Trophy (Handicap) at Goodwood: stays 1½m: acts on good to firm and soft ground. *L. M. Cumani*

MANFUL 5 b.g. Efisio 120 – Mandrian 103 (Mandamus 120) [1996 76: a11g 79
a12g⁵ a11g⁵ 10.3d* 11.1d³ 10g 10.9d* 11.1g⁴ 12.1f 10.1m² 10.1m 12.3s 12m 11.1d* a–

578

10.4g⁴ a12g* a11g* a12g² 1997 a11g⁴ a12g 10.3m⁴ 11.1d* 12g 11.1s* 10.9s² 12g³ 10.1g 11.9g 12.1g 10.9s 10.3g⁶ a12s Nov 28] fairly useful handicapper: trained first 2 starts by J. Hetherton: won at Hamilton in April and May: below best last 6 outings: stays 1½m: acts on any going, goes very well on softer than good: tried visored, blinkered nowadays: tough. *Miss L. A. Perratt*

MANGUS (IRE) 3 b.c. Mac's Imp (USA) 116 – Holly Bird (Runnett 125) [1996 73 62: 5m⁵ 5f⁵ a6g⁴ 5m⁴ 5m³ 1997 a6g² a5g² 5m* 5.1d² 5d 5d⁵ 5.1s 5.1m⁶ Jul 17] workmanlike colt: fair handicapper: won at Warwick in April: stays 6f: acts on good to firm going, dead and fibresand: inconsistent. *K. O. Cunningham-Brown*

MANHATTAN DIAMOND 3 ch.f. Primo Dominie 121 – June Fayre (Sagaro 47 133) [1996 54d: 5.1g⁶ 5d² 5.1m⁵ 6d 5.2g 7s a6g a7g 1997 a8.5g⁵ 8s⁴ 8d 6m⁵ 6.9m Jun 26] good-topped filly: has a quick action: poor maiden handicapper: effective at 6f to 8.5f: acts on dead ground and fibresand: tried blinkered: tends to start slowly. *A. Bailey*

MAN HOWA (IRE) 3 ch.c. Lycius (USA) 124 – Almuhtarama (IRE) 84 (Rain- 97 bow Quest (USA) 134) [1996 94p: 6m² 6m* 1997 6s³ 6d² 7m Jun 18] useful-looking colt: useful performer: placed in minor event (behind Tomba) and handicap (heavily-backed favourite) at Haydock in May: below form in Jersey Stakes at Royal Ascot final outing: bred to stay at least 7f: acts on good to firm and soft going: sent to UAE. *L. M. Cumani*

MANIKATO (USA) 3 b.c. Clever Trick (USA) – Pasampsi (USA) (Crow (FR) 68 d 134) [1996 68: 5g⁴ 6m 5.3f⁴ 6m⁴ 6m² 5f⁴ 7m 7d² 7g 1997 9g 6.9m² 8g⁴ 7f⁴ 10s 9.7m⁶ 10.1m⁵ 8d a7g⁴ a8g² Nov 25] close-coupled colt: fair maiden: below best after third start: stays 1m: acts on firm ground, good to soft and equitrack: tried visored. *D. J. S. Cosgrove*

MANILA MOON (USA) 2 b.c. (May 25) Manila (USA) – Sign Language – (USA) (Silent Screen (USA)) [1997 8g 8s Nov 8] $19,000Y, 26,000 2-y-o: big colt: half-brother to 3 minor winners in USA: dam, won up to 9f at 4 yrs in USA, sister to Preakness Stakes third Screen King: well held in maidens: refused to enter stalls on intended debut. *J. J. O'Neill*

MANILENO 3 ch.g. K-Battery 108 – Andalucia 57 (Rheingold 137) [1996 –: 8m⁴ 65 8.3d⁵ 1997 10.3m 8.3d³ 9.9m³ 11.9f* 11.5d* 14.9s* 17.2f³ Jul 23] small, light-framed gelding: has a round action: fair performer: claimed from J. Hetherton for £4,000 third outing: won next 3 starts, handicaps at Brighton (selling), Lingfield (amateurs) and Warwick: seems to stay 17f: acts on any ground: blinkered final 2-y-o outing: front runner: fairly useful winning hurdler. *M. C. Pipe*

MANNEQUIN (IRE) 2 b.f. (Mar 29) In The Wings 128 – Pretty Lady 98 (High 79 Top 131) [1997 7.5d⁴ Aug 13] sixth foal: half-sister to useful Irish 6f (at 2 yrs) to 11f winner Lacinia (by Groom Dancer): dam, 2-y-o sprint winner, half-sister to smart middle-distance performer Mack The Knife out of Oaks third The Dancer: 10/1, 4 lengths fourths of 12 in maiden at Beverley, not given hard time: should be suited by 1¼m+. *B. W. Hills*

MANOLO (FR) 4 b.g. Cricket Ball (USA) 124 – Malouna (FR) (General Holme 70 (USA) 128) [1996 66: 5m 6d 5m⁴ 5m 5g² 5m* 5m⁴ 1997 5m⁴ 5m* 5m 5m a5g² 5s⁵ 5g² 5m⁴ 5m⁴ 5m⁵ 5f⁴ 5d 5g a6g² Dec 2] small, lengthy gelding: fair handicapper: won apprentice race at Pontefract in April: generally creditable efforts afterwards: stays 6f: acts on firm ground and equitrack, well beaten on ground softer than good: usually blinkered nowadays: twice ruined chance by starting very slowly at 4 yrs: joined D. Loder. *J. Berry*

MANSAB (USA) 4 b.g. Housebuster (USA) – Epitome (USA) (Summing (USA)) – [1996 76d: 7s² 6.9f³ 8.1d 7g 6.1m⁵ 5.1g 6m³ 1997 a6g* a6g* a7g* 6m 6d 7.1m 7g a88 a8f* a6f* Dec 18] neat gelding: unimpressive mover: fairly useful on fibresand/sand: won minor event and handicap at Southwell and handicap at Wolverhampton in January/February: trained first 7 starts by P. Murphy: won handicaps at Nad Al Sheba in November (reinstated on appeal) and December: stays 1m: no form on turf in 1997. *C. Rached, UAE*

MANSA MUSA (IRE) 2 br.c. (Apr 10) Hamas (IRE) 125§ – Marton Maid 74 71 p (Silly Season 127) [1997 6f⁴ Sep 28] IR 13,000Y: half-brother to several winners,

MAN

including 3-y-o Penlop and 6f to 1½m winner Mr Devious (by Superpower): dam inconsistent maiden half-sister to very smart sprinter Haveroid: 12/1, keeping-on fourth of 8 in maiden at Brighton: should improve. *M. R. Channon*

MANTELLO 2 ch.c. (Mar 15) Mon Tresor 113 – Laena 72 (Roman Warrior 132) – p [1997 6m 6d 6g Oct 24] 5,000F, 17,000Y: big, good-topped colt: third reported foal: half-brother to winning sprinters Calamango and Cape Merino (both by Clantime), latter useful: dam third over 7f at 2 yrs, and over hurdles: bit backward and never dangerous in maidens, signs of ability in big fields at Newbury final 2 starts: should do better in modest handicaps. *Major D. N. Chappell*

MANTLES PRIDE 2 b.c. (Feb 22) Petong 126 – State Romance 67 (Free State 79 125) [1997 5g⁵ 6g² 6d 5m* 6m⁵ 5d⁵ Oct 27] 16,500F, 61,000Y: sparely-made colt: fluent mover: brother to 1995 2-y-o 5f winner What Fun, later successful in Scand-inavia up to 1¼m, and half-brother to 3 winners by Chukaroo, including Stewards' Cup winner Very Adjacent: dam 7f/1m winner: fair performer: won nursery at Folke-stone in September: ran creditably afterwards: stays 6f: acts on good to firm and dead ground: has been bandaged: sold 15,000 gns in November, and joined P. Calver. *G. Lewis*

MANTLES PRINCE 3 ch.g. Emarati (USA) 74 – Miami Mouse (Miami Springs 84 121) [1996 79p: 5m³ 6g² 6m⁵ 6m⁶ 6m² 1997 9g⁴ 10m⁶ 8m⁴ 8.2g² 8.5m⁵ 9m⁶ 9g⁴ 9s⁴ 8.1m⁴ 12v² Oct 10] tall, good-topped gelding: fairly useful maiden handicapper: held up when very good second to Taunt (pair clear) at Ascot final start (sold 30,000 gns later in October): effective at 1m to 1½m: acts on good to firm and heavy going: effective blinkered or not: usually races prominently: has been edgy: consistent. *G. Lewis*

MANTLES STAR 2 ch.c. (May 11) Beveled (USA) – Nosey 96 (Nebbiolo 125) 106 [1997 6s⁵ a7g* 7m² 7g³ 6g 8g* Nov 29] 8,000F, 46,000Y: rangy, rather unfurnished colt: has plenty of scope: good mover: seventh foal: half-brother to 3 winners, notably 3-y-o Compton Place and smart middle-distance performer Quakers Field (by Anshan), 6f and 7f winner at 2 yrs: dam Irish 2-y-o sprint winner: won maiden at Lingfield in July: left G. Lewis after mid-division Two-Year-Old Trophy at Redcar on fifth start: racing on medication, won Grade 3 event at Hollywood Park in November by a length, coming from off pace, showing useful form: stays 1m: acts on equitrack and good to firm ground (shaped well on soft). *Kathy Walsh, USA*

MANTUSIS (IRE) 2 ch.c. (Feb 27) Pursuit of Love 124 – Mana (GER) (Wind- 86 p wurf (GER)) [1997 8m² 8s* Oct 14] 24,000F, IR 37,000Y: rangy colt with scope: half-brother to several winners, including 1996 2-y-o 6f and 7f winner Jay-Gee-Em (by Aragon) and 1¼m winner Spray of Orchids (by Pennine Walk): dam listed winner at 2 yrs in Germany: well backed, won 17-runner maiden at Leicester by 1½ lengths from Ta Aruf, leading well inside final 1f: shapes as though will stay beyond 1m: slowly away both starts: sure to improve further. *P. W. Harris*

MANUETTI (IRE) 3 b.f. Sadler's Wells (USA) 132 – Rosefinch (USA) 117 86 (Blushing Groom (FR) 131) [1996 68p: 7m 1997 10.5s³ 10.1s² Jul 2] rangy, attractive filly: fluent mover: fairly useful form: trained by Saeed bin Suroor on reappearance: easily best effort when second in maiden at Epsom, setting steady gallop: will be suited by 1½m: acts on soft going. *E. A. L. Dunlop*

MANUFAN 2 b.c. (Mar 4) Sabrehill (USA) 120 – The Last Empress (IRE) 73 (Last Tycoon 131) [1997 7.9s Oct 8] IR 10,000Y: second foal: dam best around 2m: 20/1 and very green, slowly away and tailed off in York maiden. *R. F. Johnson Houghton*

MAPENGO 6 b.g. Salse (USA) 128 – Premiere Cuvee 109 (Formidable (USA) – 125) [1996 –: 8f a14.8g 10d a10g a7g a14.8g² a16g⁶ 1997 a13g a16g³ a14.8g a16g³ 13s a14g⁴ 14.1m 11.9m 12.1d Aug 25] little worthwhile form in 1997. *J. Cullinan*

MAPLE BAY (IRE) 8 b.g. Bold Arrangement 127 – Cannon Boy (USA) (Can- – onero (USA)) [1996 84, a87: a9.4g* a8.5g* a8g* a12g² a9.4g² a8g² a9.4g* a8g⁶ 8.2d* 8.3d 12.3g⁶ 8g* a8.5g 8.1g* 8.1m⁴ 8f³ 8m⁴ 8f⁵ 8m⁴ a9.4g⁵ 8m³ 8.2d* 7.6d⁴ 8g* 7.1f 8m 8.1d⁶ 8d⁶ 8g 8s a8.5g 1997 8m 8m Oct 1] tall, workmanlike gelding: genuine and versatile handicapper at his best: well beaten both outings at 8 yrs: effective at 7.6f to 1½m: acts on firm and dead ground, and on fibresand: tried blinkered, not when successful. *B. Ellison*

MARADATA (IRE)   5 ch.m. Shardari 134 – Maridana (USA) 86 (Nijinsky   65
(CAN) 138) [1996 68: a12g a12g⁶ a12g³ a9.4g a9.4g⁶ 10.1s⁴ 10d⁴ 9.9m³ 10.3m²
10g* 9m 10.3m* 8.9m 10.3m 10g⁶ 10.2f 8.5m² 8f 10.4g 10g* a10s² a9.4g³ a10g
1997 a9.4g² a12g⁴ 10g 10.5m Aug 15] rather sparely-made mare: fair handicapper:
form at 5 yrs only on reappearance: effective at 8.5f to 11f: acted on good to firm
ground, soft and the all-weather: sold 20,000 gns in December, in foal to Sri Pekan.
R. Hollinshead

MARADI (IRE)   3 b.g. Marju (IRE) 127 – Tigora (Ahonoora 122) [1996 73: 7g   75
7g⁶ 7.5f³ 7.5f³ 7.9g³ 8m³ 7.9g 1997 a12g* 10m 12.5m² a12g 10m³ 12d 12.3g⁴ 10m
10.1f 10s 10m Nov 4] leggy gelding: fair performer: landed odds (very easily) in
maiden at Southwell in February: below form last 4 starts, leaving M. Bell for 13,000
gns before final one (not knocked about): stays 1½m: acts on fibresand, best turf form
on good going or firmer: races freely. *B. J. Curley*

MARAEINCA   4 b.f. Inca Chief (USA) – Countess Mariga (Amboise 113) [1996   –
NR 1997 6f 6m May 4] fifth live foal to thoroughbred stallion: dam never ran: no
promise. *P. R. Hedger*

MARAHILL LAD   2 b.c. (Mar 27) Mazilier (USA) 107 – Harmonious Sound   –
(Auction Ring (USA) 123) [1997 5g⁶ 6s⁶ 5.2m 7f Sep 17] 5,600F, 16,500Y: half-
brother to 3 winners, including 1½m to 2m winner Puff Puff (by All Systems Go) and
7f and 1m winner Nellie's Gamble (by Mummy's Game): dam unraced: well held in
maidens. *P. Howling*

MARALINGA (IRE)   5 ch.g. Simply Great (FR) 122 – Bellinzona (Northfields   103
(USA)) [1996 106: 10g 10.1m 9m³ 10g 10g 10m* 8.9g⁴ 8m 8d⁴ a9.4g 1997 12.3m*
10.3m² 10s 10m⁶ Aug 18] workmanlike gelding: useful performer: won 2-runner
minor event at Chester in June then 2 lengths second to Bright Water in similar race
on same course following month: ran poorly last 2 starts: effective at 9f to 1½m: acts
on any going: front runner: has tongue tied nowadays: fairly useful form to win
novice hurdle in November. *Lady Herries*

MARA RIVER   3 b.f. Efisio 120 – Island Mill 79 (Mill Reef (USA) 141) [1996   86
62p: 6m⁴ 7.1f⁵ 1997 6m* 6s³ 7.1m* 8g* 8m⁵ 9m⁵ 8.1s 8m⁶ Sep 27] angular filly:
fairly useful performer: won maiden at Salisbury in May and handicaps at Sandown
and Bath in June: better at 1m than shorter, and will stay 1¼m: yet to race on heavy
going, probably acts on any other: held up. *I. A. Balding*

MARATHON MAID   3 gr.f. Kalaglow 132 – El Rabab (USA) 70 (Roberto   82
(USA) 131) [1996 82: 5g* 6m³ 6g* 7m 6m⁶ 6m 1997 10.4g 8d 13.9g⁴ 11.9s⁶ 15d⁶
Sep 18] leggy filly: fluent mover: fairly useful handicapper: easily best effort at 3 yrs
when fourth in Melrose Handicap (to Sausalito Bay) at York in August: will prove
best at 1½m+: best form on good going or firmer: blinkered second start. *R. A. Fahey*

MARAUD   3 ch.g. Midyan (USA) 124 – Peak Squaw (USA) 75 (Icecapade (USA))   – §
[1996 69: 5m⁶ 6m³ 7.1m 7m³ 7d² 7.1m² 8f 7m* 1997 8m 8.1m 8g 10.1g Oct 22]
sparely-made gelding: showed nothing at 3 yrs, seeming to go wrong way
temperamentally: left J. Spearing's stable after third start: tried blinkered: won
juvenile hurdle in December. *L. R. Lloyd-James*

MARCH CRUSADER   3 b.c. Green Desert (USA) 127 – Layaali (USA) (Diesis   92 §
133) [1996 NR 1997 8.2m 7g⁴ 7m⁴ 6f² 6m* 6s 5m⁵ 6m² 6g 6m 6g* 6d⁵ 5d Oct 16]
good-bodied colt: first foal: dam Irish 1m winner: fairly useful on his day: won
maiden at Lingfield in June and handicap at Hamilton in September: good fifth of 29
to Wildwood Flower in valuable event at Goodwood penultimate start: should be as
effective at 5f as 6f: acts on firm and dead going: has been unruly in stalls, and
unseated rider leaving them final outing: can't be trusted: sent to UAE. *B. Hanbury*

MARCH FOURTEENTH (USA)   2 b.f. (Jun 4) Tricky Creek (USA) – Ruby   61
Tuesday (USA) (T V Lark) [1997 6m 6g⁵ 7g⁶ Sep 5] $22,000Y: good-topped filly:
half-sister to several winners, including useful stayer Zero Watt (by Little Current),
Stewards' Cup winner Green Ruby (by Shecky Greene) and the dam of Poule d'Essai
des Pouliches winner Ta Rib: dam, half-sister to very smart Cresta Rider, placed
once from 5 starts: sire (by Clever Trick) Grade 2 8.5f winner as 2-y-o: modest form
in summer maidens: should be suited by 1m+: sold 22,000 gns in December.
J. H. M. Gosden

MARCHMAN 12 b.g. Daring March 116 – Saltation 111 (Sallust 134) [1996 53: 53 10m* 10m⁵ 12g⁵ 12.5f² 10d 1997 10f² Jun 3] big, strong gelding: modest performer: first past post in claimer at Brighton, only start in 1997, demoted for giving runner-up slight bump: has form at 1¾m, effective from 1m to 1½m in recent years: best form on good going or firmer: goes well fresh: usually held up. *J. S. King*

MARCH STAR (IRE) 3 b.f. Mac's Imp (USA) 116 – Grade A Star (IRE) (Alzao 95 (USA) 117) [1996 89+: 5.2d³ 5m³ 6d* 5g⁴ 5m⁵ 1997 6g² 6m 6f* Sep 17] quite good-topped filly: easy mover: useful performer: off course nearly a year before reappearance: won minor event at Yarmouth (by ½ length from Imroz), best effort: should stay 7f: acts on firm and dead ground. *J. A. R. Toller*

MARDI GRAS (IRE) 3 b.c. Danehill (USA) 126 – Gracieuse Majeste (FR) 74 (Saint Cyrien (FR) 128) [1996 77+: 7m⁵ 8g² 8d⁵ 1997 10.5s⁵ 12m² 12.1g⁵ 12s Jun 27] rather leggy colt: fluent mover: fair maiden: stays 1½m: acts on good to firm going: blinkered final outing (too free): sold, and sent to South Africa. *J. L. Dunlop*

MARDREW 3 b.c. Rambo Dancer (CAN) 107 – Having Fun (Hard Fought 125) 69 [1996 NR 1997 a8g* a7g³ a9.4g⁶ a8g³ 8.2m³ 8d 8.2d³ 7.5d³ 8.2g⁴ 10g² 10.1f⁴ 11.6s² 11.5m⁶ 11m² 10g 11.6m⁴ 10g⁴ 11.9m⁵ 10m⁵ Sep 30] 14,000 2-y-o: neat colt: poor mover: brother to 2 winners around 1m in Italy: dam, ran a few times, half-sister to smart Hushang (best up to 1¼m): fair performer: has had 4 different trainers: landed gamble in seller (for D. ffrench Davis) at Southwell in January: generally ran well in handicaps after: stays 1½m: acts on fibresand, and on dead and good to firm going (looked ill-at-ease on firm): has hung under pressure: tough. *John Berry*

MAREEBA 2 b.f. (Mar 5) Last Tycoon 131 – Albufeira (IRE) (Be My Guest (USA) 75 126) [1997 7g⁴ 8.3g⁴ 8.2g³ 8m⁵ a8.5g² a8g* Dec 10] second foal: dam unraced close relative of useful Italian middle-distance stayer Tarvisio: fair performer: best effort when winning nursery at Lingfield: will stay 1¼m+: acts on equitrack: has edged left. *M. Johnston*

MAREMMA 3 b.f. Robellino (USA) 127 – Maiden Way (Shareef Dancer (USA) 48 135) [1996 –: 7m⁵ 7f 7g 7m⁶ 7m 8m 1997 a8g 14.1m³ a11g 9.9m⁵ 14.1d 12d 14.1m 12f⁵ 12.1s⁴ 13m⁴ 16.2m 11s* 9.9d⁶ 14.1g 16g 16g 16.1m Oct 1] quite good-topped filly: poor performer: won maiden seller at Redcar in July: effective at 11f under testing conditions, and should stay beyond 1¾m: acts on good to firm and soft ground. *Don Enrico Incisa*

MARENGO 3 b.c. Never So Bold 135 – Born To Dance 76 (Dancing Brave 71 d (USA) 140) [1996 77d: 6m³ 6g 6m 1997 6m² 6f 6f³ 6d² 6s⁶ 5m 5.1m⁵ 7d 5g 6.1m 6.1s Oct 15] small, well-made colt: fair maiden handicapper: well beaten last 4 starts: possibly best at 6f (pulled hard over 7f): acts on firm going, probably soft: tried visored: has looked temperamental: none too consistent. *J. Akehurst*

MARGARETROSE ANNA 5 b.m. Handsome Sailor 125 – Be Bold (Bustino – 136) [1996 –, a58d: a5g a5g a7g² a7g a7g⁶ 5g a5g 5.1g a6g⁶ a6g⁴ 1997 a6g⁵ a6g⁴ a6g⁶ a6g 6.1m a6g a6g May 19] workmanlike mare: poor maiden: recent form only on fibresand: stays 7f: tried blinkered. *B. P. J. Baugh*

MARGARET'S DANCER 2 b.g. (Apr 25) Rambo Dancer (CAN) 107 – Cate- – ryne (Ballymoss 136) [1997 5m a5g 6g⁴ a6g 7.5v 7g a5g 8m Sep 9] 1,200Y: sturdy gelding: half-brother to 3 modest winners at up to around 1m: dam ran once: little worthwhile form, mainly in sellers: usually blinkered. *C. Smith*

MARGONE (USA) 3 b. or br.f. (Jan 25) Dayjur (USA) 137 – Whispered Secret – p (CAN) (Secretariat (USA)) [1997 6g Oct 27] $240,000Y: small filly: first foal: dam unraced half-sister to Breeders' Cup Distaff winner Dance Smartly (by Danzig) from excellent Canadian family: 14/1, never dangerous in maiden at Leicester: moved well to post: should do better. *G. Wragg*

MARIANA 2 ch.f. (Mar 30) Anshan 119 – Maria Cappuccini 70 (Siberian Express 65 d (USA) 125) [1997 5g³ 5g 6m⁵ 5.1g 6m 5.1g Oct 4] rather leggy filly: third foal: sister to 4-y-o Agent: dam 5f winner effective up to 7f, half-sister to smart performer up to 7f Marina Park: fair maiden: well below best last 2 starts, visored final outing: yet to prove effective beyond 5f: refused to enter stalls once. *R. M. Whitaker*

MARIE DORA (FR) 3 gr.f. Kendor (FR) 122 – Marie de Vez (FR) (Crystal 86 Palace (FR) 132) [1996 NR 1997 7g 8g* 8.5m 8d⁵ 7g⁵ 10m⁴ 10.1g 10g Sep 18]

450,000 francs Y: big, good-topped filly: sister to 2 winners, including smart Marie de Ken (up to 10.5f) and half-sister to French middle-distance winners by Bikala, Assert and Zino: dam, French 9f winner, half-sister to high-class Dom Alari: fairly useful performer: won maiden at Kempton in May by 5 lengths: good fourth in handicap at Newbury in August: stays 1¼m: unraced on extremes of going: visored (poor effort) final start. *I. A. Balding*

MARI-ELA (IRE)   2 ch.f. (Apr 2) River Falls 113 – Best Swinger (IRE) (Ela-   60
Mana-Mou 132) [1997 5d⁴ 5m⁶ 5m⁵ 6g⁴ 6.9m 7.6m 7d* 7.3g⁵ Oct 25] 5,000Y:
unfurnished filly: second foal: dam Irish 7f winner: modest performer: won 29-
runner seller at Newmarket in October: not discredited in 2 of 3 nurseries: should
stay 1m: best efforts on good/good to soft ground. *J. R. Arnold*

MARIE LOUP (FR)   2 ch.f. (Mar 15) Wolfhound (USA) 126 – Marie de   80 p
Fontenoy (FR) (Lightning (FR) 129) [1997 6f³ 6m⁴ Sep 27] 450,000 francs Y:
quite attractive filly: half-sister to several winners in France, including (up to 7f)
Kentucky Coffee (by Kenmare): dam French 1¼m winner, half-sister to very smart
French winner up to 1m Sakura Reiko: fairly useful form in frame in maiden at
Yarmouth and minor event at Ascot, favourite though still backward in latter: should
stay 1m: should do better. *L. M. Cumani*

MARIE RAMBERT (IRE)   3 b.f. Common Grounds 118 – Ninette de Valois   68
(FR) (Gay Mecene (USA) 128) [1996 6s 1997 6d⁶ 5g a10g Nov 18] IR 5,500Y: ex-
Irish filly: half-sister to useful One False Move (should have stayed 1¼m, by Don't
Forget Me) and 2 winners up to 9f in Italy by Classic Music: dam once-raced
daughter of very useful 5f to 7f winner Martinova, half-sister to Lucky Wednesday:
only form in maidens when sixth at the Curragh on reappearance: left E. Lynam
before final start. *C. A. Dwyer*

MARIGLIANO (USA)   4 b.g. Riverman (USA) 131 – Mount Holyoke 93   –
(Golden Fleece (USA) 133) [1996 90: 8m³ 7.5m* 8g³ 1997 10m Oct 5] tall gelding:
has a round action: fairly useful (for M. Stoute) as 3-y-o: tailed off in Leicester minor
event only outing at 4 yrs: should stay 1¼m: has been bandaged. *K. A. Morgan*

MARILAYA (IRE)   3 b.f. Shernazar 131 – Mariyada (USA) (Diesis 133) [1996   96
NR 1997 10g² 9m* 9m 10.5m* 8v Oct 10] rather unfurnished filly: first foal: dam
French 10.5f winner: useful form: won maiden (despite slipped saddle) at Ripon in
July and minor event (bandaged near-hind) at Haydock in September, in latter
settling in front and increasing steady pace from 3f out: stays 10.5f: acts on good to
firm ground: too headstrong third and final starts. *L. M. Cumani*

MARIMBO (IRE)   2 b. or br.g. (Apr 10) Elbio 125 – Nikara (FR) (Emerson)   –
[1997 6g 6g Aug 20] 2,300Y: half-brother to 3 winners, including useful sprinter Gilt
Throne (by Thatching): dam won at 6f and 7.5f at 2 yrs in France: no promise,
including in seller. *C. Murray*

MARINO STREET   4 b.f. Totem (USA) 118 – Demerger 61 (Dominion 123)   60 d
[1996 60, a55: a6g² a7g³ a5g² a6g⁵ a7g² a5g² a6g⁵ a6g³ a8.5g⁵ a7g 5.9f³ 7s⁵ 5.1m³   a42
5g* 6f⁶ 5.9f⁵ 5m⁴ 5.1f 6.1m⁵ 7g a6g⁶ a6g a6g 1997 6m a6g³ 5f² 5.9m a6g⁶ 5.1m a5g⁴
7g 5g 6d Sep 5] small, leggy filly: modest handicapper on turf, poor on the all-
weather: well below form last 4 starts: effective at 5f to 7f: acts on firm ground and
the all-weather: effective visored/blinkered or not: inconsistent. *P. D. Evans*

MARION'S PET   2 ch.f. (Mar 2) Tina's Pet 121 – Fay Eden (IRE) 60 (Fayruz   –
116) [1997 5.1g 6m 6.1m Sep 15] second foal: dam 6f winner: well beaten in sellers
and a maiden. *R. J. Hodges*

MARISA'S PET   3 gr.f. Petong 126 – Always On A Sunday 101 (Star Appeal   –
133) [1996 NR 1997 7d a7g Dec 22] 11,000Y, 2,800 3-y-o: fourth foal: half-sister to
4-y-o No Cliches: dam 1¼m winner: little promise in maidens. *T. E. Powell*

MARJAANA (IRE)   4 b.f. Shaadi (USA) 126 – Funun (USA) 84 (Fappiano   82
(USA)) [1996 71: 7.5m⁵ 7g⁵ 7f⁴ 7m² 7g 8.1m 8m 7g 1997 8d² 8m* 7m² 6.9m* 10.1s⁶
8s⁶ 7.5d* 5m 7g² 7.3d² 7m Oct 4] lengthy filly: fairly useful performer: won handicaps at Warwick in May and Beverley in August and minor race at Folkestone in
between, all amateurs events ridden by Miss S. Samworth: suited by 7f/1m: acts on
firm and dead ground: visored last 2 starts at 3 yrs: consistent: sold 13,000 gns in
December. *P. T. Walwyn*

MARJORIE ROSE (IRE) 4 b.f. Magical Strike (USA) 114 – Arrapata (Thatch-   59
ing 131) [1996 64, a67: 5d 5.1d⁴ 7g 6d 5f 5g⁴ 6f⁵ 5m a5g* a5g⁴ 5g* a6g⁴ a6g a6s*   a65
a7g² 1997 a7g⁶ a6g⁵ a6g⁴ a6g 5s⁴ a5g³ 5m a5g² a6g⁶ Aug 15] workmanlike filly: fair
handicapper on all-weather, modest on turf: stays easy 7f: acts on good to firm
ground, soft and fibresand: tried blinkered: sometimes looks none too keen. *A. Bailey*

MARKAPEN (IRE) 3 b.f. Classic Music (USA) – Dahsala (Top Ville 129) [1996   –
NR 1997 12g⁴ Apr 18] 2,500Y: neat filly: fourth reported foal: half-sister to a French
1¼m winner by Lashkari and a winner up to 1½m in UAE by Alzao: dam, French
11.5f winner, half-sister to very smart 1½m winner Dazari: 20/1 and in need of race,
last of 4 in maiden at Thirsk. *C. N. Allen*

MARK OF PROPHET (IRE) 2 b.c. (Apr 21) Scenic 128 – Sure Flyer (IRE)   71
(Sure Blade (USA) 130) [1997 7.1m 7g⁵ 7m Oct 22] 4,000F, 13,500Y: third living
foal: half-brother to Irish 3-y-o 5f winner Sandomierz and 4-y-o Cointosser: dam
placed at 5f and 7f in Ireland at 2 yrs: best effort in maidens when keeping-on fifth at
Warwick: should stay at least 1m. *J. E. Banks*

MARKSMAN (IRE) 2 b.c. (Feb 5) Marju (IRE) 127 – Warg (Dancing Brave   99
(USA) 140) [1997 6d* Jun 20] IR 38,000Y: first foal: dam unraced daughter of
sister to Shirley Heights: 5/2, beat some fairly useful opposition in emphatic style in
maiden at Newmarket, travelling comfortably and not hard ridden to draw 3 lengths
clear: should stay 1m+: looked likely to go on to better things, but wasn't seen out
again. *L. M. Cumani*

MARL 4 ch.f. Lycius (USA) 124 – Pamela Peach 81 (Habitat 134) [1996 94: 6d²   89
7m 6g⁵ 5m⁴ 5m⁶ 5m 6m³ 6m² 8m⁶ 8d⁶ 1997 7m⁵ 6d⁵ 6g 6m Jul 18] sparely-made
filly: fluent mover: fairly useful handicapper: easily best effort at 4 yrs on second
start, lack-lustre efforts final 2: best form at 6f: acted on good to firm and dead going:
often on toes/edgy: none too consistent: sold 45,000 gns in December, in foal to Polar
Falcon. *R. Akehurst*

MARNIES WOLF 6 ch.g. Little Wolf 127 – Marnie's Girl (Crooner 119) [1996   –
NR 1997 a14g Dec 8] fourth foal: dam placed in selling hurdles: no promise in 2 NH
Flat races: pulled up in claimer at Southwell on flat debut. *T. T. Bill*

MAROULLA (IRE) 3 ch.f. Caerleon (USA) 132 – Mamaluna (USA) 114   83
(Roberto (USA) 131) [1996 67p: 7g 1997 9m* 10g Jun 12] lengthy filly: impressive
winner of maiden at Kempton: beat only one in steadily-run listed race at Newbury
12 days later: should be well suited by 1¼m+: sold 75,000 gns in December.
M. R. Stoute

MAROZIA (USA) 3 ch.f. Storm Bird (CAN) 134 – Make Change (USA)   76 +
(Roberto (USA) 131) [1996 –p: 7g 1997 8m² a7g³ Nov 6] fair maiden: off course
almost a year, head second to stable-companion Mount Holly at Yarmouth, leaving
impression would have won ridden with more enterprise: uneasy favourite, again
given rather unenterprising ride and would believe that form when third at Lingfield 2
weeks later: stays 1m: may do better still. *J. H. M. Gosden*

MARRAN (IRE) 2 br.c. (Apr 28) Caerleon (USA) 132 – Tanouma (USA) 114   82
(Miswaki (USA) 124) [1997 7.1d³ 7m² 8d⁴ 7f* 8.5d⁵ Dec 20] neat colt: seventh foal:
half-brother to several winners, including 3-y-o Nawasib, smart stayer Khamaseen
(by Slip Anchor) and Geoffrey Freer Stakes winner Azzilfi (by Ardross): dam, 6f (at
2 yrs) and 7f winner who stayed 1m, out of very speedy French 2-y-o Diffusion:
fairly useful form: won nursery at Brighton in September by a neck from Night Flyer,
clear over 1f out: sold out of J. Dunlop's stable 24,000 gns in October: fifth in
allowance race at Hollywood: should stay at least 1m: acts on firm ground: has gone
freely to post and shown tendency to hang. *D. Vienna, USA*

MARSAD (IRE) 3 ch.c. Fayruz 116 – Broad Haven (IRE) (Be My Guest (USA)   71
126) [1996 76: 6m⁶ 6m³ 6m³ 6g² 6g⁴ 6m 5d² 1997 6m 6d⁶ 6m Jul 12] good-topped
colt: fair maiden handicapper: better at 6f than 5f: unraced on extremes of going.
R. Akehurst

MARSAYAS (IRE) 4 ch.g. Classic Music (USA) – Babiana (CAN) 90 (Sharpen   60
Up 127) [1996 59: 10g 12d 12f² 15.1f⁴ 14.1m⁴ 16f² 16m² 15.8g* 15.8g⁴ 15.8g⁵ 1997
15.8m³ 18g 16m³ 15.8g² Aug 5] workmanlike gelding: modest performer: stays 2m:
acts on firm going and dead: races prominently. *M. J. Camacho*

MARSH MARIGOLD   3 br.f. Tina's Pet 121 – Pulga (Blakeney 126) [1996 58+:   65
$5g^3$ $6m^3$ $6g^5$ $5m^4$ $7g^2$ $7.1m^5$ $7.5m^6$ $7m^2$ $6s^*$ $7m^6$ 7.3s 1997 $a8s^6$ $a8g^4$ 8g $10.3d^5$ 10g
$10d^6$ 10m* $10g^4$ $9g^2$ $10v^3$ 9.9v⁴ $12g^5$ 9.9m Jul 21] sparely-made filly: fair handicapper: left M. Meade after second start: won apprentice race at Pontefract in June by
5 lengths: creditable efforts 3 times afterwards: probably stays 1½m: acts on good to
firm and heavy ground, ran poorly on all-weather: has hung left: tends to get behind
and is suited by strongly-run race. *J. Hetherton*

MARSH'S LAW   10 br.g. Kala Shikari 125 – My Music 68 (Sole Mio (USA))   –
[1996 –: 8f 1997 13s May 4] very lightly raced, no form on flat for long time.
G. P. Kelly

MARSKE MACHINE   2 ch.f. (Mar 9) Prince Daniel (USA) – Ciboure 74   64
(Norwick (USA) 125) [1997 $5s^6$ $5f^6$ $5s^3$ $6m^5$ $6s^4$ $7g^4$ 7s $6g^*$ $6g^4$ 7.1s* $7g^4$ $7s^6$ $8d^2$ $8m^4$
Nov 4] strong, workmanlike filly: has round action: third foal: dam 6f (at 2 yrs) and
1m winner: modest performer: won selling nurseries at Leicester and Sandown
(bought in 13,200 gns) in August: will stay at least 1¼m: acts on good to firm and
soft ground: blinkered final 7 starts: tough and reliable. *N. Tinkler*

MARSUL (USA)   3 b. or br.c. Cozzene (USA) – Beside (USA) (Sportin' Life   92
(USA)) [1996 –p: 8m 1997 $10.2m^4$ $11.5m^3$ $12d^3$ 12m* 14.6m 11.9g* Sep 26] tall,
lengthy colt: fairly useful performer: made most to win maiden at Newmarket in
August and handicap at Haydock in September, allowed to dictate steady pace in
latter: stays 1½m (stiff task over 14.6f): unraced on extremes of going: visored last 3
starts: sold 53,000 gns in October. *J. H. M. Gosden*

MARTINDALE (IRE)   4 b.g. Fairy King (USA) – Whist Awhile (Caerleon   38
(USA) 132) [1996 –: 7g 7f 1997 8.5m 7s 7.5m 6.1d $6g^4$ Jul 23] poor sprint maiden.
J. Hanson

MARTINE   3 ch.f. Clantime 101 – Marcroft 91 (Crofthall 110) [1996 68?: $5m^3$ 5g   –
$5m^3$ $6.1d^4$ 6m 1997 $5g^6$ 6g 7g 8m 7.1g $a6g$ Nov 17] small, sparely-made filly: poor
mover: fair maiden at 2 yrs: little worthwhile form in 1997: sprint bred. *A. Bailey*

MARTON MOSS (SWE)   2 b.g. (Feb 25) Polish Patriot (USA) 128 – Arrastra   82 +
59 (Bustino 136) [1997 $6d$ 5m $5s^*$ $6.1m^5$ $6m^*$ $6g^4$ 5s Oct 15] 16,500Y: tall gelding:
first foal: dam 1¾m winner: fairly useful performer: won maiden at Pontefract in
June and minor event at Ripon in August: moved poorly down penultimate start, then
off 7 weeks and well beaten: should stay 1m: acts on good to firm and soft ground.
T. D. Easterby

MARX MISTRESS   3 b.f. Batshoof 122 – No Jazz 55 (Jaazeiro (USA) 127)   –
[1996 NR 1997 10s May 12] 1,400Y: fifth foal: dam, miler, half-sister to dam of
smart sprinter Al Sylah: showed nothing in Windsor maiden. *I. Campbell*

MARY CORNWALLIS   3 ch.f. Primo Dominie 121 – Infanta Real 108 (Formid-   82
able (USA) 125) [1996 NR 1997 $6g^4$ $6m^2$ $5d^4$ $6m^3$ $a6g$ $a6s^4$ $a5g$ Dec 18] fourth foal:
half-sister to 3 winners, including Empty Quarter (useful up to 1m, by Night Shift):
dam, 5f and 6f winner from 3 starts, out of half-sister to Forzando: fairly useful sprint
maiden: trained first 4 starts by G. Wragg: ran well only once for new stable: acts on
equitrack, unraced on extremes of going on turf. *R. M. H. Cowell*

MARY CULI   3 gr.f. Liboi (USA) 76 – Copper Trader 53 (Faustus (USA) 118)   59
[1996 –: 7m $7.1s^6$ 1997 $7m^5$ 8f $8m^6$ 7.6g 10m 11.9f $10g^3$ Oct 24] smallish, lengthy
filly: unimpressive mover: modest maiden: stays 1¼m: acts on good to firm going:
inconsistent. *H. Candy*

MARY JANE   2 b.f. (Apr 23) Tina's Pet 121 – Fair Attempt (IRE) (Try My Best   63
(USA) 130) [1997 5f $a5g^3$ 5m* $a6s^6$ Nov 10] 4,400Y: first foal: dam unraced granddaughter of top 1975 2-y-o filly Pasty: modest form: won maiden at Redcar in
October, making all: ran well on fibresand previous start, and for a long way on
equitrack final start: likely to prove best at 5f. *J. Berry*

MARYJO (IRE)   8 b.m. Tale Quale 113 – Down The Aisle (Godswalk (USA)   –
130) [1996 NR 1997 $a14.8g$ $12d$ Oct 21] ex-Irish mare: poor form to win handicap at
Clonmel at 6 yrs: well held in handicaps in Britain: should stay 2m: refused to race
once. *G. L. Moore*

MARYLEBONE (IRE) 3 ch.g. River Falls 113 – Pasadena Lady (Captain James   63
123) [1996 67: 5m² 6g⁴ 5m² 5g 1997 6g² 5m² 5m⁶ 6g⁴ 5.7g 7m⁶ 6.1s Oct 15] tall,
shallow-girthed gelding: modest sprint maiden: raced almost solely on good/good to
firm going: blinkered once (but below best). *J. Berry*

MARY LOU (IRE) 2 b.f. (Mar 31) Tirol 127 – Kilcsem Eile (IRE) (Commanche   43
Run 133) [1997 6g 6s⁵ 8.1d⁶ 7g 8m 10g a8.5g 10d⁵ a8.5g⁴ a8g³ a8g⁴ Nov 24] IR
7,000Y: leggy filly: first foal: dam Irish maiden out of half-sister to Oaks second
Game Plan: poor maiden: probably stays 1¼m: acts on fibresand and dead ground:
has run creditably visored. *M. R. Channon*

MARY MAGDALENE 3 b.f. Night Shift (USA) – Indian Jubilee 81 (Indian   78
King (USA) 128) [1996 –p: 6s 1997 5v* 6g³ 6g² 5g 6m 6s Oct 15] big, robust filly:
has plenty of scope: fair form: won maiden at Beverley (by 6 lengths) in July:
generally ran creditably in handicaps, until disappointing final start: will prove suited
by stiff 5f or 6f: acts on heavy going and good to firm. *M. Bell*

MARYS PATH 3 b.f. Rock Hopper 124 – Jasmin Path (Warpath 113) [1996 NR   –
1997 10m 12g 9.9d 14.1m 14.1g⁶ Jul 30] first foal: dam, of little account on flat,
irresolute winning plater over hurdles: of little account. *S. Gollings*

MARYTAVY 3 b.f. Lycius (USA) 124 – Rose Parade (Thatching 131) [1996 –p: 76
6g 6g⁶ 6m 1997 9.7m² 9.9m² 9.2g⁶ a11g* Sep 8] good-topped filly: shows knee
action: fair form: best effort to win maiden handicap at Southwell by 8 lengths, sent
on over 4f out: will stay 1½m: acts on fibresand, yet to race on going softer than good
on turf: joined P. Webber. *Sir Mark Prescott*

MARZOCCO 9 ch.g. Formidable (USA) 125 – Top Heights (High Top 131)   28
[1996 NR 1997 13s 8f⁶ 6.9m³ 9m⁴ Jul 19] very lightly raced since 1992 and poor
nowadays. *T. A. K. Cuthbert*

MASAMADAS 2 ch.c. (Mar 31) Elmaamul (USA) 125 – Beau's Delight (USA)   69 p
(Lypheor 118) [1997 7d a8g² Nov 24] 15,000Y: tall, useful-looking colt: fifth foal:
half-brother to several winners, including Italian 3-y-o 9f winner La Bella Di Roma
(by Shavian) and 4-y-o Zaforum: dam should have stayed at least 1m: better effort in
maidens when length second of 8 to Double Edged at Southwell, prominent
throughout: should stay at least 1¼m: open to further improvement. *C. F. Wall*

MASHAB 2 b.c. (Feb 17) Pursuit of Love 124 – Kukri (Kris 135) [1997 7g 7d⁵ Oct   69 p
14] 28,000Y: good-bodied colt: fourth foal: half-brother to 4-y-o Blessed Spirit and
6-y-o Sharp Rebuff: dam never ran: still in need of for race, much better effort in
maidens when 8 lengths fifth of 13 to Brave Reward at Leicester: pulled hard to post
on debut 2 months earlier: should stay 1m: should do better again. *N. A. Graham*

MASHA-IL (IRE) 2 b.c. (Mar 18) Danehill (USA) 126 – Valley Lights (IRE)   83 p
(Dance of Life (USA)) [1997 6d 6s³ 6d* Nov 7] IR 190,000Y: good-topped colt: sort
to carry condition: second foal: dam, lightly-raced Irish maiden, half-sister to Then
Again, also family of Sun Princess and Saddlers' Hall: progressive colt: won
21-runner maiden at Doncaster, meeting some trouble before quickening to beat
Lindesberg by a length: should stay 1m: raced on good to soft/soft going: sure to do
better still. *J. H. M. Gosden*

MASHARIK (IRE) 3 b.f. Caerleon (USA) 132 – Rosia Bay 102 (High Top 131)   93
[1996 NR 1997 10.2s² 10m* 11.9d⁵ Aug 21] rangy filly: half-sister to several
winners, including high-class pair Ibn Bey (up to 1¾m, by Mill Reef) and Roseate
Tern (1½m, by Blakeney): dam, miler, is half-sister to Teleprompter and Chatoyant:
favourite, won 16-runner maiden at Windsor in July: not disgraced when well-held
fifth of 7 in listed race at York, floundering under pressure from 3f out: should have
been suited by 1½m+: visits Barathea. *Major W. R. Hern*

MASHHAER (USA) 3 b. or br.c. Nureyev (USA) 131 – Life's Magic (USA)   91
(Cox's Ridge (USA)) [1996 94p: 7m* 1997 7m² 8m³ 9d Sep 12] angular colt: has
a quick action: won maiden at Newmarket for Saeed bin Suroor at 2 yrs: fairly useful
form when placed in minor events at Goodwood and Salisbury (odds on): stays 1m:
acts on good to firm going, not discredited on good to soft. *M. R. Stoute*

MASHKORAH (USA) 3 ch.f. Miswaki (USA) 124 – Tom's Lassie (USA) (Tom   –
Rolfe) [1996 –: 7.1s 1997 9d 8f 8f Jun 16] unfurnished filly: no form in maidens and
a handicap. *R. Hannon*

MASRRAH (IRE)   3 b.g. Old Vic 136 – Masarrah 91 (Formidable (USA) 125)   –
[1996 NR 1997 a11g a10g⁴ a12g³ 11.6s 14.1g May 23] fourth foal: half-brother to   a61
fairly useful pair Murheb (1¼m, by Mtoto) and Shefoog (7f, by Kefaah): dam 6f
winner: best effort when third in 1½m maiden at Wolverhampton in April: acts on
fibresand, no form on turf: blinkered final start: sent to UAE. *R. W. Armstrong*

MASRUF (IRE)   5 b.g. Taufan (USA) 119 – Queen's Share (Main Reef 126)   –
[1996 –: 6m 7m 6m 6m 1997 a7g a7g Feb 15] good-bodied gelding: no form since 2
yrs. *K. C. Bailey*

MASSYAR SEVENTEEN   3 b.g. Chilibang 120 – Westminster Waltz (Dance In   70
Time (CAN)) [1996 NR 1997 8g⁴ 8s 8.1m⁵ 10g⁴ 10s 11.8d⁵ a10g* a10g³ a10g Dec   a75
22] close-coupled gelding: fifth foal: half-brother to 2 winners, notably fairly useful
Seventeens Lucky (stayed 1½m, by Touch of Grey): dam twice-raced daughter of
half-sister to Busted: fair performer: won maiden at Lingfield in November: ran well
next start: stays 1¼m: acts on equitrack, ran poorly on soft. *H. J. Collingridge*

MASTER BEVELED   7 b.g. Beveled (USA) – Miss Anniversary §§ (Tachypous   77
128) [1996 77, a71: a8g² a8g⁶ 10.8d⁴ 9m⁵ 10m 8d⁶ 7.9g 10.3m 8g 10.5v* 8f* 8.9g 8g   a72
a10g⁵ 1997 a10g³ 10.8m⁴ 10m⁴ 8s² 10g⁵ 8.1m 8.9d⁵ 10s 8.1g 10.4d² 8d⁵ 10g⁵ 10g⁵
a10g³ a10g⁴ a12g⁶ Nov 18] lengthy gelding: fair handicapper: generally creditable
efforts at 7 yrs: stays 11f: acts on any going: effective blinkered/visored or not: sometimes bandaged near-fore: useful hurdler: tough and consistent. *P. D. Evans*

MASTER BOBBY   3 b.g. Touch of Grey 99 – Young Lady (Young Generation   –
129) [1996 –: a6g 1997 a8.5g a8g⁴ 10f 10m a10g a10g Nov 18] no sign of ability.
R. M. Flower

MASTER BOOTS   4 br.c. Warning 136 – Arpero 107 (Persian Bold 123) [1996   96
105: 8m 7d* 7.1d* 7.1d 8d⁶ 1997 7.9g a6g 7g a7g* 7m 7g Oct 18] good-topped colt: a99
poor mover: useful handicapper: eighth in Bunbury Cup (Handicap) at Newmarket
start before winning at Southwell in July: should stay 1m: acts on dead ground and
fibresand, unsuited by going firmer than good: held up: sold 25,000 gns in October.
D. R. Loder

MASTER CASTER (IRE)   2 b.g. (Apr 28) Night Shift (USA) – Honourable   – p
Sheba (USA) (Roberto (USA) 131) [1997 7m 7d Oct 14] 30,000Y: close-coupled,
heavy-bodied gelding: fourth foal: half-brother to 3-y-o Olivo and 4-y-o Crystal Falls
(fairly useful 1m winner at 2 yrs): dam (unraced) from family of Lear Fan: well held
but not knocked about in Leicester maidens: should do better in due course.
D. R. Loder

MASTER CHARTER   5 ch.g. Master Willie 129 – Irene's Charter 72 (Persian   85
Bold 123) [1996 87: 7g* 8g* 7m² 8m² 10m⁵ 10m* 8m² 8m⁵ 8m 9m 1997 7m 8g³ Jun
27] lengthy, workmanlike gelding: poor mover: reportedly had knee operation after
final 4-y-o start: fairly useful handicapper: much better effort at 5 yrs when third at
Newcastle, not knocked about when cannoned into by winner (Duraid) 1f out:
effective at 7f to 1¼m: acts on good to firm ground, yet to race on softer than good:
held up. *Mrs J. R. Ramsden*

MASTER FOLEY   3 ch.c. Cigar 68 – Sultans Gift 47 (Homing 130) [1996 61:   55
a5g 5g a6g a5g⁴ a5g⁵ a6s* 1997 a6g⁴ a6g⁶ a6g² a5g⁵ a6g² 5g⁵ 6.1m² 6.1m³ a6g⁶ a5g²   a61
a5g 6g Aug 25] leggy colt: modest handicapper: stays 6f: acts on fibresand (yet to
race on equitrack) and on good to firm ground. *N. P. Littmoden*

MASTER FOODBROKER (IRE)   9 br.g. Simply Great (FR) 122 – Silver   55
Mantle 70 (Bustino 136) [1996 –: 10.3g 16.4v 1997 a16s³ a16g² a16g² a16g* 18m³
Mar 21] heavy-topped gelding: modest handicapper: won at Southwell in February,
leading post: out-and-out stayer: acts on fibresand, good to firm and dead ground:
usually blinkered: tends to get well behind, and suited by strong pace. *W. J. Musson*

MASTER MAC (USA)   2 br.c. (Apr 15) Exbourne (USA) 125 – Kentucky Blonde   79
(USA) (General Assembly (USA)) [1997 6m⁴ 7.1g 7d* 6f* 6m 7d² 7.3d 8d Oct 17]
$11,000Y: small colt: fluent mover: first foal: dam won up to 7f in USA: fair form at
best: won maiden at Goodwood in June and nursery at Lingfield in July: good second
in nursery at Epsom, but well beaten last 2 starts: should stay 1m: acts on firm and
dead ground. *R. Akehurst*

MASTER M-E-N (IRE) 5 ch.g. My Generation 111 – Secret Lightning (USA) 64
78 (Secretariat (USA)) [1996 61: 10.3m³ 10m² 10.2g⁵ 10m 10m 8f* 8f⁶ 1997 7f⁴
8.5m³ 8d⁵ 8g 7f 8g Sep 4] close-coupled gelding: modest performer: ran poorly last 3
outings, off course 3 months before final one: effective at 7f to 1¼m: acts on firm and
dead ground (well beaten on soft and fibresand): has been blinkered, normally
visored nowadays. *N. M. Babbage*

MASTER MILLFIELD (IRE) 5 b.g. Prince Rupert (FR) 121 – Calash (Indian 55
King (USA) 128) [1996 72: a6g a7g⁵ a7g⁵ a8g 5.7m 5.7m³ 8.1m 8m⁵ 6m 5.7m a–
10m³ 8.1s³ a9.4g² a12s² 1997 10g 10.8m 8d 8d 7.6g 10g⁵ 6.9m* a12g⁴ Oct 4] tall
gelding: modest handicapper: dead-heated in apprentice event at Folkestone in
September: effective at 7f to sharp 1½m: acts on any going: visored (below form)
once. *C. J. Hill*

MASTER OF PASSION 8 b.g. Primo Dominie 121 – Crime of Passion 115 67
(Dragonara Palace (USA) 115) [1996 89d: 5g⁴ 6m 5m 6f 5m 5g 6m 5m 6m 5s a5g⁴ a73
a5g* 1997 a5g⁶ a6g 5g 5d⁵ 5m a5g⁴ 6m 5g⁶ Oct 18] lengthy, angular gelding:
has a quick action: fair handicapper nowadays: best at 5f/6f: acts on firm and dead
ground and the all-weather: tried blinkered/visored: usually races prominently.
J. M. P. Eustace

MASTERPIECE 3 br.g. Primo Dominie 121 – Swift Return 79 (Double Form 68
130) [1996 NR 1997 6.9g² 6m⁵ 8g 8.2g 7.1m 6.9g 7f Oct 3] 8,000Y: big,
rangy colt: half-brother to fairly useful sprinter Abom Swift (by Absalom) and 2
winners abroad: dam, 2-y-o 6f winner, half-sister to smart Skyliner: fair form in
maidens first 3 starts: well beaten in handicaps afterwards: probably stays 1m:
unraced on going softer than good. *R. Hannon*

MASTER PLANNER 8 b.g. Night Shift (USA) – Shaky Puddin (Ragstone 128) –
[1996 –: 6m⁶ 1997 6m 6d May 21] strong, close-coupled gelding: one-time useful 6f
handicapper (suited by good going or firmer): reportedly injured a leg after only start
in 1996: soundly beaten in large fields as 8-y-o. *C. A. Cyzer*

MASTER SHOWMAN (IRE) 6 b.g. Alzao (USA) 117 – Arctic Winter (CAN) –
(Briartic (CAN)) [1996 NR 1997 a12g Apr 28] has shown nothing since 3 yrs.
D. J. Wintle

MASTERSTROKE 3 b.g. Timeless Times (USA) 99 – Fauve 71 (Dominion 61 d
123) [1996 65: 5g³ 5.3f* 5d⁶ 6m* 7m⁴ 6m 6m⁵ 6m⁴ a6g a6g³ a8g⁵ 1997 a7g⁴ a7g*
6f a7g 6m 7g⁵ 8g Sep 8] leggy, unfurnished gelding: won seller (by 8 lengths) at
Lingfield in January: subsequently off course 5 months, and no form afterwards:
stays 7f: acts on firm ground and equitrack. *B. J. Meehan*

MATATA (IRE) 2 b.f. (Feb 25) In The Wings 128 – Ville Sainte (FR) (Saint 73
Estephe (FR) 123) [1997 7d² 7g⁴ 6.9m² 7.9s Sep 4] workmanlike filly: third reported
foal: half-sister to 3-y-o Chairmans Daughter: dam French 1¼m winner out of
half-sister to To-Agori-Mou: in frame in maidens at Newmarket (2) and
Folkestone: tailed off in testing conditions final start: should be suited by 1¼m+.
N. A. Callaghan

MATOAKA 3 b.f. Be My Chief (USA) 122 – Echoing 93 (Formidable (USA) 125) 72
[1996 66: 6m⁴ 1997 7m 8f² 8g⁴ 8d⁵ 7g² 8m⁶ 8f* a7g a7g⁴ Dec 19] fair performer:
won minor event at Brighton in October, best effort: seems better at 1m than 7f: acts
on firm going, below form on good to soft and equitrack. *V. Soane*

MATTAWAN 4 ch.c. Nashwan (USA) 135 – Sweet Mover (USA) 95 (Nijinsky –
(CAN) 138) [1996 92: 12.1m* 11.8g² 14.8m⁵ 11.9f³ 12.3g* 1997 13.9m Jul 12] tall,
good-topped colt: has a markedly round action: fairly useful performer at 3 yrs: stiff
task, last in listed handicap at York only outing as 4-y-o: should be suited by further
than 1½m: yet to race on going softer than good. *M. Johnston*

MATTHIAS MYSTIQUE 4 gr.f. Sharrood (USA) 124 – Sheznice (IRE) 58 62
(Try My Best (USA) 130) [1996 59, a66: 10m 12m² 11.9g⁶ a13g² a16g³ a16g* a16g³
a13g⁶ 1997 a16g⁶ a16g* a16g³ a16g⁶ 16.4m² 17.2m² 14m Jul 10] leggy filly: fair
handicapper: won selling event at Lingfield in February: fell there final start: suited
by good test of stamina: acted on good to firm ground and equitrack: dead.
Miss B. Sanders

MATTIMEO (IRE)   4 b.g. Prince Rupert (FR) 121 – Herila (FR) (Bold Lad   89
(USA)) [1996 74: a10g² a8g² 10m* 11.9m 12m 12m² 12d 10.1g* 9f 10d*
11.9g 10.3m 10m² 12v³ 12s Nov 8] heavy-topped gelding: fairly useful handicapper:
won at Newcastle and Ascot in the summer: set too much to do penultimate start,
disappointing final one: probably stays 1½m: acts on equitrack and good to firm and
heavy ground (looked ill-at-ease on firm). *A. P. Jarvis*

MAURANGI   6 b.g. Warning 136 – Spin Dry (High Top 131) [1996 –: 7.1d 8f   34
10.1f⁶ 10.5m 8f 8m 1997 8g⁵ 8g a7g 8g⁴ 8s⁴ 10g⁵ 9m 11m 12s a14g Nov 17] tall,
leggy gelding: poor handicapper: stays 1¼m: acts on good to firm ground and probably soft, well beaten on fibresand: tried blinkered: usually held up. *B. W. Murray*

MA VIELLE POUQUE (IRE)   3 ch.f. Fayruz 116 – Aussie Aisle (IRE) (Gods-   52
walk (USA) 130) [1996 52p: 5.1m⁵ 1997 a5g⁴ a5g³ a5g³ a5g⁵ a5g a5g* a6g³ a5g⁴ 5m
a5g Nov 29] modest performer: won seller at Southwell in March: best form at 5f:
acts on the all-weather. *W. G. M. Turner*

MAWARED (IRE)   4 ch.c. Nashwan (USA) 135 – Harmless Albatross 115 (Pas   102
de Seul 133) [1996 75: 8d 8m 9g³ 11.8f³ 12.1s 1997 10g 12m⁴ 14m* 14m* 16m*
14.8m* 18g³ 16m² Oct 31] tall, good-topped colt: progressed really well at 4 yrs,
improving into a useful handicapper: won at Sandown (twice), Newbury and Newmarket in summer: excellent third to Turnpole in Tote Cesarewitch at Newmarket
penultimate start, and creditable second of 4 to Lady of The Lake in listed event there
final one: stays 2¼m: easily best form on good going or firmer: has been bandaged:
held up: stays in training. *J. L. Dunlop*

MAWINGO (IRE)   4 b.c. Taufan (USA) 119 – Tappen Zee (Sandhurst Prince   95
128) [1996 84: 6.9m⁶ 7f* 7.9f⁵ 8m* 8g* 10m⁵ 10m⁶ 1997 7m³ 8m 7.6m² 8m 8g³
7.9s² Oct 8] leggy colt: useful performer: second in minor event at Lingfield in July
and handicap (beaten 1¼ lengths by Solar Storm, best effort) at York in October: goes
well with test at 1m, and probably stays 1¼m: acts on any ground: often apprentice
ridden: ran creditably only try in blinkers. *G. Wragg*

MAWSOOF   2 b.c. (Jan 31) Alzao (USA) 117 – Guilty Secret (IRE) 109 (Kris 135)   90 p
[1997 7.1m² 8.2g² Sep 28] small, attractive colt: first reported foal: dam, 1½m
winner who stayed 1¾m, out of very smart performer up to 1½m Miss Toshiba:
runner-up in maidens at Haydock (beaten 8 lengths by most impressive Fleetwood)
and Nottingham (caught on line by Giveaway, pair clear), both in September:
will stay at least 1¼m: should improve and is clearly capable of winning races.
M. R. Stoute

MAX'S MAGIC (USA)   4 b.g. Chief's Crown (USA) – Pattyville (USA)   –
(Crozier) [1996 NR 1997 9m⁶ 8.3m 8m Aug 23] $40,000F, $60,000Y, only 600 gns
3-y-o: half-brother to several winners in USA, including a Grade 2 placed winner by
Well Decorated: dam won 3 times in USA: well beaten in maidens. *G. L. Moore*

MAYDORO   4 b.f. Dominion Royale 112 – Bamdoro 54 (Cavo Doro 124) [1996   45
NR 1997 5m 5g 5.1g 6m 7g 5g 5g⁵ 6m 6g⁵ Aug 2] half-sister to modest winners at up
to 7f by Hard Fought and Lochnager: dam 1m to 1½m winner: poor maiden
handicapper: best efforts at 5f: inconsistent. *M. Dods*

MAYFAIR   3 b.f. Green Desert (USA) 127 – Emaline (FR) 105 (Empery (USA)   –
128) [1996 82: 6m* 7d⁵ 7g⁴ 1997 6m 8s 7m Aug 23] smallish, angular filly: easy
mover: won maiden at Ascot on debut: disappointing since: should stay beyond 6f:
sold 23,000 gns in December. *P. F. I. Cole*

MAYFLOWER   3 b.f. Midyan (USA) 124 – Chesnut Tree (USA) 97 (Shadeed   52
(USA) 135) [1996 73: 5.2f² 6g⁵ 6.1m³ 7f⁵ 1997 8g 7m 7m 12d 8m 8d³ a8g a8g⁶ Dec
4] leggy filly: modest maiden: trained first 3 starts by I. Balding: only form of 1997
when third in handicap at Leicester in October: stays 1m: acts on firm and dead
going: tried blinkered/visored: races freely: tail flasher. *M. H. Tompkins*

MAY KING MAYHEM   4 ch.g. Great Commotion (USA) 123 – Queen Ranava-   54
lona (Sure Blade (USA) 130) [1996 45: 7f 8g⁴ 9f 10d 12m⁶ 13.8g 1997 a12g 11.8m⁵
a14g 10m 11.9m⁶ 12g 11.8g³ 12g 10s² 12s⁵ 12g* 14.9g³ 12m⁶ 12m⁵ Aug 4] close-
coupled gelding: has a round action: modest handicapper: won (for first time, by 10
lengths) at Carlisle in July: stays 15f: acts on good to firm and soft going: has gone in
snatches and seemed unco-operative. *Mrs A. L. M. King*

MAY

MAYLANE   3 b.g. Mtoto 134 – Possessive Dancer 118 (Shareef Dancer   118 §
(USA) 135) [1996 85p: 7.1d⁵ 7f² 7d* 1997 8g 8m⁵ 9g* 10g² 12m* 12g* 12g
Sep 27]

Maylane completed an unusual and undesirable double in the latest
season, ducking left and unseating his rider as the stalls opened on both his first
and final starts. His behaviour was far from exemplary in between as well. Yet,
despite that, his undoubted ability did manage to shine through. Gelded after
his second start, Maylane made remarkable progress and won three of his four
subsequent completed starts, notably the Group 3 September Stakes. He should
have won all four, as he failed by just a head to peg back Memorise in a valuable
handicap at Newmarket after forfeiting at least a dozen lengths at the start.

Maylane evokes memories of Knockroe, an equally talented yet wayward middle-distance performer of the early-'seventies, who progressed into a
very smart performer capable of winning good races outside handicap company. Knockroe, also a gelding, was sometimes reluctant to race and didn't take
kindly to being hustled along in the early stages, but on his day he could
produce an impressive turn of finishing speed. In terms of number of races won
Knockroe's three-year-old season was his most successful, but he went on to
show better form at four and five. There's a chance that Maylane, still relatively
unexposed, will improve again and be a force to be reckoned with in all but the
best company in 1998, provided, of course, that he consents to put his best
foot forward. It's possible a change of scene—he has joined the Godolphin
operation—will benefit Maylane, though, equally, it would come as no surprise
if it had the opposite effect. Trainer Alec Stewart and jockey Michael Roberts
deserve praise for the manner in which they handled this quirky performer in
the latest season.

Roberts was seen to particularly good effect when winning on Maylane
at Goodwood, twice, and Epsom. The second of Maylane's wins at Goodwood
came in the highly-competitive Tote Gold Trophy Handicap, run over a mile
and a half in July, a race in which he was set to concede weight to all but one of
his fourteen rivals, including Memorise, with whom he had a 1 lb pull in the
weights compared to Newmarket. Maylane got away on level terms this time,
but Roberts settled him in the rear and the horse was in last place turning for
home. Switched to the outside soon after, Maylane was asked to make up his
ground steadily and delivered his challenge approaching the final furlong, at
the same time as Memorise, who was unable to obtain a clear run. With Roberts
merely waving the whip at him, Maylane responded willingly to take the lead

Tote Gold Trophy Stakes (Handicap), Goodwood—Maylane (No. 2) on one of his good days;
Memorise (partially hidden) is about to burst through to gain second place
but he is subsequently disqualified and placed last;
Dream of Nurmi (left) and Real Estate (dark colours) take the minor honours

September Stakes, Epsom—Maylane (left) is too good for Dushyantor (centre) and Posidonas

and then needed only to be pushed along to hold the challenge of the subsequently-disqualified Memorise by half a length.

Maylane took on older horses for the first time at Epsom, in the Group 3 September Stakes, a race transferred from Kempton, where rebuilding was taking place, and increased in distance by a furlong to a mile and a half. A couple of very smart older horses, Dushyantor and Posidonas, also took part, the pair meeting Maylane on terms 5 lb worse than weight for age. Dushyantor, winner of the Geoffrey Freer Stakes on his previous start, was sent off favourite at a shade of odds on, but there was plenty of confidence behind Maylane, who was next in the betting at 3/1. Maylane's supporters must have feared the worst when the horse put the brakes on after taking one stride. But he then consented to race and, with the gallop just a steady one, was able to make up the lost ground quickly. Allowed to lob along at the back of the field, Maylane had plenty to do when the race began in earnest early in the straight, but once again showed a good turn of foot to cut down his rivals, Roberts coaxing him along while at the same time preventing him from hanging too much to the left. Dushyantor had just taken the measure of Posidonas when Maylane swept by entering the final furlong, and at the line he was a length and three quarters up and still going away. Prospects of another Group 3 win were thwarted when Maylane unshipped Roberts leaving the stalls in the Cumberland Lodge Stakes at Ascot, a race, incidentally, which Knockroe won twice.

Maylane is the second foal of Possessive Dancer, a mare purchased by his owner shortly before she won the Oaks d'Italia and went on to take the Irish Oaks. Possessive Dancer cut little ice in two further runs at three years, and she was retired after finishing last of nine in the Jockey Club Stakes on her only outing the following season. Possessive Dancer was bred by Walter Swinburn Ltd, the jockey having purchased her dam, Possessive, for 45,000 guineas in foal to Dara Monarch. That foal, named Possessive Lady, is one of several other winners out of Possessive, the best of them the twice-raced Desert Courier, who won over six furlongs as a two-year-old. Maylane's great grandam, Front Row, won the Irish One Thousand Guineas and bred ten winners, notably the smart miler Long Row and the Norfolk Stakes winner Colmore Row.

Sheikh Ahmed Al Maktoum's "Maylane"

		Busted	Crepello
	Mtoto	(b 1963)	Sans Le Sou
	(b 1983)	Amazer	Mincio
Maylane		(b 1967)	Alzara
(b.g. 1994)		Shareef Dancer	Northern Dancer
	Possessive Dancer	(b 1980)	Sweet Alliance
	(b 1988)	Possessive	Posse
		(b 1982)	Front Row

Maylane, a smallish, leggy gelding, who may well stay a mile and three quarters, acts on firm and good to soft going. It will be interesting to see how he fares on his return. *A. C. Stewart*

MAYLAN (IRE) 2 br.f. (Feb 1) Lashkari 128 – Miysam 60 (Supreme Sovereign 119) [1997 6v 7.3g a6g a10s⁴ Nov 28] 1,000Y: angular filly: half-sister to a 2-y-o 5f winner by On Your Mark, later successful abroad: dam 5f winner at 2 yrs: first form when fourth in maiden at Lingfield. *D. M. Hyde* 47

MAYPOLE (IRE) 3 ch.g. Mujtahid (USA) 118 – Dance Festival 101 (Nureyev 68 (USA) 131) [1996 66p: 6s 1997 7.1g³ Sep 26] dipped-backed gelding: twice-raced maiden: third at Haydock on only start in 1997, seeming unbalanced and carrying head high: sold approx. £13,000 in Dubai in November. *D. R. Loder* 68

MAY QUEEN MEGAN 4 gr.f. Petorius 117 – Siva (FR) (Bellypha 130) [1996 47 56: 6.9s⁶ 6.1d 6g⁴ 6f⁶ 6.1d 7f⁶ 6f² 6m* 6m 6m⁴ 1997 6m 6m 6m 6d 7.6m⁶ 6.9m⁴ 8.1m⁴ 8f² 7f⁶ 8.2g³ 8g² 7f Oct 29] leggy filly: poor handicapper: stays 1m: acts on firm ground: blinkered once: consistent at 4 yrs. *Mrs A. L. M. King* 47

MAYSIMP (IRE) 4 ch.f. Mac's Imp (USA) 116 – Splendid Yankee (Yankee Gold –
115) [1996 –: 6.1m 6d³ 6m 5d 6f 6m⁶ 8.1m 1997 a6s a7g a6g a6g a5g 6.1m 6g 6m 5g
Aug 22] leggy filly: little worthwhile form. *B. P. J. Baugh*

MAYTONG 2 gr.f. (Mar 24) Petong 126 – Bit O' May 71 (Mummy's Pet 125) 54
[1997 6g⁶ 5g⁶ 5g Sep 27] 10,500Y: sister to a winner in Germany and half-sister to
6f winner Summer Express (by Bay Express): dam daughter of half-sister to Oaks
runner-up Mabel: best effort in maidens second start: unruly in stalls on debut.
J. Berry

MAZAMET (USA) 4 b.g. Elmaamul (USA) 125 – Miss Mazepah (USA) (Nijin- –
sky (CAN) 138) [1996 10m⁵ 12g* 14d 14g³ 16g 1997 18.7s May 7] big, workmanlike ex-Irish gelding: half-brother to several winners, notably dual Gold Cup winner
Sadeem (by Forli): dam, won up to 9f, out of Oaks winner Monade: fairly useful form
(rated 89) for J. Oxx at 3 yrs, winning Galway maiden and sold for 25,000 gns at end
of year: tailed off in Chester Cup (bandaged near-hind) only outing as 4-y-o: stays
1¾m. *O. O'Neill*

MAZARA (IRE) 3 b.f. High Estate 127 – Shy Jinks (Shy Groom (USA)) [1996 –: –
8.1d 1997 12.5m⁵ 11g 14.1d 17.2f⁴ May 30] no worthwhile form: dead. *A. G. Foster*

MAZBOON (USA) 2 ch.c. (Mar 12) Diesis 133 – Secretaire (USA) 61 (Secre- 100
tariat (USA)) [1997 6g* 7s* Jul 3] $72,000F, $130,000Y: lengthy, useful-looking
colt: has scope: fourth foal: dam, ran 4 times (looked reluctant final start) at 2 yrs,
from family of Danzig: won 18-runner maiden at Newbury by 1½ lengths from
Starmaker: odds on, had to work hard in 5-runner minor event at Yarmouth 3 weeks
later, setting slow pace, headed 1f out but gradually getting on top again to beat
Behold ½ length, still seeming green: sent to UAE. *E. A. L. Dunlop*

MAZEED (IRE) 4 ch.g. Lycius (USA) 107 – Maraatib (IRE) 93 (Green Desert 74
(USA) 127) [1996 –: 6m 7g⁶ 6f³ 7d 1997 a8f⁶ a8s 5.1s 7f 6.1s 7f 8s⁵ a7g a9.4g*
a9.4g* Dec 26] neat gelding: fair handicapper: behind in Dubai first 2 starts: sold
2,200 gns in July: easy winner by 9 lengths then 6 lengths at Wolverhampton in
December: stays 9.4f: acts on firm going and fibresand, probably soft: tried
blinkered, visored final 4 starts. *P. D. Evans*

MAZILLA 5 b.m. Mazilier (USA) 107 – Mo Ceri 63 (Kampala 120) [1996 59: a8g 51
a8g a11g a11g* a11g* a12g a12g⁶ 10.8f a11g 10m 10d⁵ 8m⁵ 10.8f 10m* 10g⁴
10.8m* 10f* 10.1g* 10m³ 8.5m⁵ 10m 10d 1997 10d 10g 10.8m³ 10d⁵ a10g⁵ 10m⁶
10.3d Aug 29] leggy mare: modest performer: best around 1¼m: acts on good to
firm ground, soft and the all-weather: effective visored or not: usually waited with.
A. Streeter

MAZIRAH 6 b.g. Mazilier (USA) 107 – Barbary Court (Grundy 137) [1996 –: 7d 38
7.1g 10m a12g 8g 1997 10s 12s⁴ Jun 27] tall gelding: poor performer: stays 1½m:
acts on any turf ground and fibresand: blinkered (ran respectably) once. *R. Curtis*

MAZUREK 4 b.c. Sadler's Wells (USA) 132 – Maria Waleska (Filiberto (USA) 80
123) [1996 74: 10m 10s a7g² a8g* 1997 a8g a8g a12g 11.9m* 12m* 12m⁴ 11.9g 14g
Jul 16] smallish colt: fairly useful handicapper: trained by M. Meagher first 3 starts:
improved afterwards, winning at Brighton (made all) and Salisbury in May, and good
fourth in Bessborough Stakes at Royal Ascot: helped force too strong a pace final
start: should stay 1¾m: acts on equitrack and good to firm ground. *M. C. Pipe*

MAZZARELLO (IRE) 7 ch.g. Hatim (USA) 121 – Royal Demon (Tarboosh –
(USA)) [1996 49d, a–: 5s 5g 6m³ 5.1g 5m² 5m 5m 6m 5m 5m 1997 6m 5g Jun 21]
probably of little account nowadays. *R. Ingram*

MBULWA 11 ch.g. Be My Guest (USA) 126 – Bundu (FR) 88 (Habitat 134) [1996 62
66, a–: 8m 7m³ 8.5m* 10f 8g² 7.9g⁴ 7.9g 8m 1997 8d 8.9d 8g 8m 7m 8m² 9m² 8.5d⁴ a–
10m 8.5f² 8m⁵ Sep 24] smallish, sturdy gelding: modest handicapper: close second 3
times as 11-y-o: effective at 7f to 1¼m: all 8 wins on good going or firmer, below
form in 3 runs on the all-weather: effective blinkered (not tried for long time): often
early to post and mulish at stalls, but game in a finish: usually races prominently.
R. A. Fahey

MCGILLYCUDDY REEKS (IRE) 6 b.m. Kefaah (USA) 124 – Kilvarnet 78 76
(Furry Glen 121) [1996 46: 11.1m 11.1g⁶ 12m 8g⁶ 10.1m⁴ 10f⁶ 11.8f³ 11.5m³ 11m³
a12g⁴ 1997 9.9m⁶ 11f⁴ 8.5s⁵ 10g⁶ 9.9m² 8f³ 10.9d 8g* 9.9m* 9.9m* 10m* 10.5m²

10d² 10.3m 10m 10.4d* 10g 12g⁶ 10.3d⁴ Nov 7] smallish mare: fair handicapper: had a splendid season, winning at Pontefract, Beverley (twice) and Nottingham in July/August, and at York in October: probably stays 1½m: acts on any turf going and fibresand: often slowly away: tongue tied: tough. *Don Enrico Incisa*

MEADGATE'S DREAMER (IRE)   2 br.f. (Apr 19) Petardia 113 – Avidal Park 68 (Horage 124) [1997 6.1g⁵ 6m 7.1g a7g Jun 30] 6,000Y: tall, close-coupled filly: fifth living foal: half-sister to 3 winners, including 3-y-o Projectvision and 1½m winner Real Popcorn (by Jareer): dam 2-y-o 5f winner: no worthwhile form. *B. Palling*

MEADOW BLUE   4 b.f. Northern State (USA) 91 – Cornflower (USA) (Damascus (USA)) [1996 –: 10g⁶ 10m 8f⁶ 8.1m 12.1m⁶ 1997 12g 16m 10g a12g⁶ 6.9f Aug 27] of little account. *Miss L. C. Siddall*   –

MEANS BUSINESS (IRE)   2 ch.g. (Apr 5) Imp Society (USA) – Fantasise (FR) (General Assembly (USA)) [1997 5.1m 5.1d⁴ 5d² 5m* 5m⁵ 5m³ 5s 6d Oct 16] IR 4,500F: 15,000Y: leggy gelding: fifth foal: half-brother to 3-y-o Papita, 4-y-o Mullagh Hill Lad (fair 5f winner at 2 yrs) and 2 winners abroad: dam second at 7f at 2 yrs in Ireland: modest performer: made all in seller at Lingfield in July: good efforts next 2 starts but well beaten final 2: raced mainly at 5f: acts on good to firm and dead ground: blinkered final 5 starts: sold, joined J. Hetherton and gelded. *B. J. Meehan*   62

MECCA PRINCESS   2 ch.f. (May 8) Weldnaas (USA) 112 – Parfait Amour 73 (Clantime 101) [1997 7g Jul 16] 600Y: first foal: dam 6f (at 2 yrs) to 1m winner: tailed off in minor event at Catterick. *R. M. Whitaker*   –

MECHILIE   3 b.f. Belmez (USA) 131 – Tundra Goose 101 (Habitat 134) [1996 –: 6g 8g a7g 1997 10m 12g 14.1m 14.1g⁵ 16m³ 14g⁵ Sep 27] workmanlike filly: poor handicapper: will stay beyond 2m. *J. W. Payne*   47

MEDAALY   3 gr.c. Highest Honor (FR) 124 – Dance of Leaves (Sadler's Wells (USA) 132) [1996 114: 7.1g² 7m* 8.1g* 8g⁵ 8g* 1997 10.4g May 14] good-bodied, useful-looking colt: has a fluent, round action: smart 2-y-o, winning Racing Post Trophy at Doncaster final start (reportedly chipped a bone in his knee): bitter disappointment in Dante Stakes at York only outing at 3 yrs: should stay at least 1¼m. *Saeed bin Suroor*

MEDAILLE MILITAIRE   5 gr.h. Highest Honor (FR) 124 – Lovely Noor (USA) (Fappiano (USA)) [1996 112: 10g 10g 10.4f² 10d 10.1g* 12s* 1997 10d³ 11.8d⁵ 12m 11.9s³ Oct 15] tall horse: smart performer in 1996: 3½ lengths third to Germano in listed race at Goodwood on return, but most disappointing afterwards, leaving J. Dunlop before final start (when reportedly distressed): stays 1½m: acts on any going: normally held up: one to treat with caution. *M. C. Pipe*   109 d

MEDIA EXPRESS   5 b.g. Sayf El Arab (USA) 127 – Far Claim (USA) 35 (Far North (CAN) 120) [1996 57d: a8g⁴ a8g 10g 10g 7d 7f 8f 11.5m 1997 a10g⁴ a13g⁵ a8g⁵ a10g Feb 25] small, leggy gelding: poor performer at best: seems to stay 1¼m: acts on any turf going, and equitrack: blinkered in 1997. *Mrs L. Stubbs*   47 d

MEDIA STAR (USA)   4 b.c. Lear Fan (USA) 130 – Media Luna 119§ (Star Appeal 133) [1996 NR 1997 10d 12.1s⁶ 14.1g* 18s* 16.1g* 14m* 13.9g² 16m² 18g Oct 18] big, lengthy colt: has a round action: half-brother to several winners, including 5-y-o Eva Luna: dam unreliable winner at 1¼m and second in Oaks: unraced at 2/3 yrs: progressed really well, winning maiden at Redcar and handicaps at Chepstow, Newmarket and Goodwood in the summer: ran very well when second in Tote Ebor at York (beaten neck by Far Ahead) and in rated stakes at Goodwood (length behind Georgia Venture): well held in Cesarewitch final start: stays 2¼m: acts on good to firm and soft ground: bandaged first 2 starts and showed little: visored thereafter: useful. *J. H. M. Gosden*   103

MEDIATE (IRE)   5 b.g. Thatching 131 – Unheard Melody (Lomond (USA) 128) [1996 –§, a64§: a8g a8g⁵ 8f 8m 8.3m 10g 8m⁴ 7m a8g⁴ a10g² 1997 a10g⁵ a8g³ a10g⁶ a10g 8d 8.3g 8m Sep 24] compact gelding: has a quick action: modest form at best at 5 yrs: stays 1¼m: acts on equitrack, no form on turf since 3 yrs: blinkered/visored nowadays: irresolute. *A. Hide*   – §   a50 §

MEDIEVAL LADY   4 ch.f. Efisio 120 – Ritsurin 79 (Mount Hagen (FR) 127) [1996 89: 7m* 8f³ 8d 1997 8g 9m³ 9s 10m Jun 11] sturdy filly: carries condition: 92

fairly useful performer: best effort at 4 yrs when third to Balalaika in listed race at Newmarket in May: upset in stalls and slowly away when tailed off final start: stays 9f: acts on firm ground, not discredited on dead: sold 18,000 gns in December. *I. A. Balding*

MEDINA MISS 2 b.f. (Apr 23) Rudimentary (USA) 118 – Podrida 48 (Persepolis (FR) 127) [1997 a5g⁴ a5g² 6f² a6f³ 7m⁴ 7m⁶ a5g 6m Sep 26] first foal: dam, thorough stayer on flat, also successful over hurdles: poor maiden: well beaten after leaving W. G. M. Turner's stable sixth start, in visor final one: stays 6f: acts on fibresand: front runner/races prominently. *G. M. McCourt* — 42

MEDLAND (IRE) 7 ch.g. Imperial Frontier (USA) 112 – Miami Dancer 55 (Miami Springs 121) [1996 –, a49: a8.5g² a10g a8g a8g⁴ a8g a10g 1997 a8g a7g⁴ a9.4g a11g⁵ a8.5g⁶ a5g a8g Dec 18] no worthwhile form at 7 yrs. *B. J. McMath* — –

MEGAN CAREW 3 ch.f. Gunner B 126 – Molly Carew (Jimmy Reppin 131) [1996 –: 5.9f 8.1m 7f 1997 11.1d 17.2f Aug 27] unfurnished filly: little sign of ability. *D. Moffatt* — –

MEGA TID 5 b.g. Old Vic 136 – Dunoof 92 (Shirley Heights 130) [1996 –: a12g a11g 12m 11.5f a10g 1997 a12g 12m 12g 11.5d a16g Dec 10] leggy gelding: no form since 3 yrs. *Jamie Poulton* — –

MEGRED 2 b.f. (Apr 15) Soviet Star (USA) 128 – Dancing Meg (USA) 113 (Marshua's Dancer (USA)) [1997 7m² Oct 1] 7,800Y: sister to useful 1993 2-y-o 7f winner Mytilene and half-sister to several winners, including 4-y-o Farmost and useful 6f performer Flower Girl (both by Pharly): dam won at 6f and 1m at 2 yrs and stayed 1½m: 5/1, 2½ lengths second of 11 to Misalliance in maiden at Newcastle, slowly into stride and staying on: should stay at least 1m: will improve. *J. H. M. Gosden* — 72 p

MEG'S MEMORY (IRE) 4 b.f. Superlative 118 – Meanz Beanz (High Top 131) [1996 59: 10.2g* 11.6m 10.1f⁵ 8m 10.2f⁵ 10.2m⁶ 17.2m³ 16.4m a16g 1997 12.1m⁵ 12m 12.3m³ Aug 3] rather leggy filly: modest handicapper: suited by good test at 1½m and stays 17f: has raced only on good going or firmer on turf: tried blinkered: inconsistent. *A. Streeter* — 57

MEILLEUR (IRE) 3 b.g. Nordico (USA) – Lucy Limelight 98 (Hot Spark 126) [1996 NR 1997 7m⁵ 7.6m 8.3m 10g 11.7g³ 14.1g⁶ 12d⁴ a16g² Dec 10] IR 24,000Y, 6,500 2-y-o: brother to a winning sprinter (including listed race at 2 yrs) in Italy and half-brother to 3 winners, including useful sprinter Lucedeo (by Godswalk): dam 2-y-o 5f winner: fair maiden: stays 2m: acts on equitrack, unraced on extremes of going on turf. *Lady Herries* — 65

MELBOURNE PRINCESS 3 ch.f. Primo Dominie 121 – Lurking 69 (Formidable (USA) 125) [1996 56, a52: 5g 5g³ 5m 5f⁶ 5m⁴ 5m² 5m a5g³ a5g a5g² 1997 5g 5m⁴ 5d 5m⁴ 5m 6.1g 6m a6g a6g a5g⁵ Dec 22] smallish filly: poor maiden: probably best at 5f: acts on firm going and equitrack, well beaten on dead: visored (creditable effort) once. *R. M. Whitaker* — 45

Grosvenor Casinos Cup (Handicap), Goodwood—
a new race at the 'Glorious Goodwood' meeting sees Media Star promoted to Ebor favourite;
he makes all to beat Puce, the grey Benatom and Jazz King

MELIKSAH (IRE) 3 ch.c. Thatching 131 – Lady of Shalott 61 (Kings Lake 92
(USA) 133) [1996 97: 5m* 5f 6g⁵ 5s⁵ 5.2m* 5m* 5d 1997 6m⁴ 5d³ 5m⁵ 5m 5g 5.2m
Sep 16] robust, lengthy colt: unimpressive mover: fairly useful handicapper: poor
efforts last 2 starts: speedy, and best form at 5f: acts on good to firm and dead ground:
races prominently. *M. Bell*

MELLORS (IRE) 4 b.c. Common Grounds 118 – Simply Beautiful (IRE) 67 d
(Simply Great (FR) 122) [1996 67: 8.2g 7m⁴ 7.5g³ 6g* 6f a6g 6f² 6f² 5.3f² 7.1s⁶ 1997
a7g⁵ a6g* a6g² a7g⁶ a7g⁵ a6g² a6g 6f 6.1d 6m 6g 6m 6f 6m a6g Nov 1] well-made
colt: fair handicapper: won at Lingfield in January: probably best at 5f/6f: acts on
equitrack (no form on fibresand), ran poorly on turf at 4 yrs: blinkered/visored once
each. *M. J. Heaton-Ellis*

MELLWOOD (IRE) 3 b.g. Maledetto (IRE) 103 – Traminer (Status Seeker) –
[1996 –: 6g 6m a7g 8g 1997 14.1d⁶ 14.1m May 27] good-bodied gelding: little sign
of ability: sold, and sent to Holland. *M. H. Tompkins*

MELODIAN 2 b.c. (Apr 19) Grey Desire 115 – Mere Melody 88 (Dunphy 124) –
[1997 6g 5f Sep 17] first living foal: dam, sprinter who was fairly useful at 2 yrs but
became unreliable, half-sister to Lyric Fantasy, Royal Applause and In Command:
well held in maidens. *M. Brittain*

MELODICA 3 b.f. Machiavellian (USA) 123 – Melodist (USA) 118 (The Mins- 84
trel (CAN) 135) [1996 67p: 7d³ 1997 10m² 12.1m² 14m* 14m⁵ 14m Aug 9] sparely-
made filly: fairly useful performer: won maiden at Lingfield in July: best effort when
fifth in handicap at Sandown (dropped away tamely 2f out final start, jockey
reporting that filly made a noise): stays 1¾m: yet to race on extremes of going: sold
80,000 gns in December. *M. R. Stoute*

MELODIC DRIVE 7 b. or br.g. Sizzling Melody 117 – Gleneagle 91 (Swing –
Easy (USA) 126) [1996 NR 1997 6g 7f May 28] fair winning handicapper at
5 yrs never on terms in large fields as 7-y-o: best efforts over 6f: acts on firm and
dead ground: tried blinkered, including last 5 outings: usually starts slowly.
J. A. Glover

MELODIC SQUAW 3 b.f. Merdon Melody 98 – Young Whip (Bold Owl 101) –
[1996 NR 1997 a11g a12g a11g 16g Sep 23] fourth foal: sister to 4-y-o Welsh
Melody, and 5-y-o Mountgate: dam unraced: no form. *M. P. Bielby*

MELOMANIA (USA) 5 b.g. Shadeed (USA) 135 – Medley of Song (USA) (Sec- –
retariat (USA)) [1996 –: 8.1d⁴ 10m 14g 10m a8.5g 1997 a11g Apr 1] of little account.
S. R. Bowring

MELOS 4 b.f. Emarati (USA) 74 – Double Stretch (Double-U-Jay 120) [1996 –: –
8.2g 1997 11.7m⁵ 7d Aug 8] of no account. *G. Thorner*

MELS BABY (IRE) 4 br.g. Contract Law (USA) 108 – Launch The Raft (Home 77
Guard (USA) 129) [1996 73, a54: a7g² 8.1g⁶ 6.1g⁴ a7g 7g² 7g² 5.9f⁶ 8f² 7s² 8.5m² a45
9f³ 10.4g⁵ 8f* 8m* 8s* a9.4g⁶ 1997 a7g⁴ 10.3m² 8.3d³ 9.9s* 10d⁵ 8.9d 10g Jun 21]
tall, light-bodied gelding: fair handicapper: won at Beverley in May: rare poor efforts
last 2 starts: needs a thorough test at 7f nowadays and stays 10.4f: acts on any turf
ground, only poor form on fibresand: tried blinkered/visored, at least as effective
when not: good mount for amateur/apprentice. *J. L. Eyre*

MELTEMISON 4 b.g. Charmer 123 – Salchow 116 (Niniski (USA) 125) [1996 –
72: a10g² a12g³ a11g⁵ 10g 10m³ 11m 11.5f* 11.8f 1997 12.3m Apr 9] neat gelding:
fair handicapper: sweating, well beaten only outing in 1997: stays 1½m: acts on
all-weather and firm ground: signs of temperament over hurdles. *M. D. Hammond*

MEMBERS WELCOME (IRE) 4 b.g. Eve's Error 113 – Manuale Del Utente –
(Montekin 125) [1996 54: 6.1g² 5.1g⁴ 6g⁴ 7.1g⁴ 6g 5f⁵ 5m 5.7m⁴ 6f 6m 6m 6m 1997
a7g a6g Mar 13] lengthy, angular gelding: well beaten in 1997: best form at 5f/6f:
acts on firm ground: effective visored or not. *W. G. M. Turner*

MEMORABLE 6 b.g. Don't Forget Me 127 – Jhansi Ki Rani (USA) 94 (Far 30
North (CAN) 120) [1996 NR 1997 16.2v² 16m Sep 15] workmanlike gelding: poor
and lightly-raced staying handicapper nowadays: acts on any ground: often visored/
blinkered: a hard ride, and not one to trust implicitly. *K. W. Hogg, Isle of Man*

MEMORIAL (IRE) 2 b.c. (Apr 26) Imperial Frontier (USA) 112 – Alitos Choice 51 +
(Baptism 119) [1997 5g⁴ 6.1g 6g 6m 7f a6g⁵ Oct 18] IR 6,000F, 17,000Y: good-
bodied colt: shows knee action: half-brother to fairly useful 1994 2-y-o 7f winner
Winners Choice (by Conquering Hero) and a winner abroad by Millfontaine: dam
unraced: modest maiden: stays 6f: probably acts on good to firm ground and
fibresand: blinkered penultimate start. *R. Hannon*

MEMORISE (USA) 3 b.c. Lyphard (USA) 132 – Shirley Valentine 104 (Shirley 112
Heights 130) [1996 64p: 7m⁶ 1997 8g⁴ 10.3d⁴ 10.1g* 12d⁴ 10g* 12m²ᵈⁱˢ 12m² 12f²
Oct 3] rather leggy, angular colt: smart performer: won maiden at Newcastle in May
and £19,800 handicap (by head from Maylane) at Newmarket in July: good efforts
afterwards in Tote Gold Trophy (Handicap) at Goodwood (to Maylane, disqualified
having had poor run) and small-field listed events at Doncaster (beaten 3 lengths by
Busy Flight) and Newmarket (went down by 1½ lengths to Mons): will stay beyond
1½m: acts on firm and dead ground: game and consistent. *H. R. A. Cecil*

MEMORY'S MUSIC 5 b.g. Dance of Life (USA) – Sheer Luck 72 (Shergar –
140) [1996 –: 12s 12s 1997 a12g a10g 8m 10m a10g⁶ Dec 19] sturdy gelding: no
form since 3 yrs: visored once: won selling hurdle in November. *M. Madgwick*

MEMPHIS DANCER 2 b.f. (May 6) Shareef Dancer (USA) 135 – Wollow 60 p
Maid 73 (Wollow 132) [1997 7g 7g Sep 4] 11,000Y: half-sister to several winners,
including 3-y-o Janglynyve and 7f and 1m winner Reverand Thickness (by Prince
Sabo): dam 1¼m winner, refused to race once: some promise when never dangerous
in maidens at Leicester (difficult to settle) and Salisbury: should stay at least 1¼m:
should do better. *J. W. Hills*

MENDOZA 3 b.g. Rambo Dancer (CAN) 107 – Red Poppy (IRE) 58 (Coquelin 54
(USA) 121) [1996 –: 6m 7f 8.5m⁵ 8f 1997 a7g a8g* a10g4 a10g² a10g⁴ a8g² 8f⁴ 8.5m a60
8g a8g Dec 12] modest handicapper: won at Lingfield in January: raced infrequently
and below form last 3 starts: seems not quite to stay 1¼m: acts on firm ground, goes
well on equitrack. *D. J. G. Murray Smith*

MENGAAB (USA) 3 b.c. Silver Hawk (USA) 123 – Cherie's Hope (USA) 88
(Flying Paster (USA)) [1996 90p: 7g³ 1997 10g⁴ 10d⁵ 10.2s³ 10m⁴ 10.3g⁶ 12g* 14s
Aug 30] smallish, good-bodied colt: fairly useful performer: won handicap at
Goodwood by short head: favourite, tailed off 8 days later: should stay beyond 1½m:
acts on good to firm and soft going: has been bandaged behind: blinkered/visored last
4 starts: sent to UAE. *J. H. M. Gosden*

MENIATARRA (USA) 2 ch.f. (Feb 3) Zilzal (USA) 137 – Snow Bride (USA) 68 p
121 (Blushing Groom (FR) 131) [1997 7m Nov 1] fifth foal: sister to 3-y-o Haltarra
and 4-y-o Kammtarra and half-sister to Lammtarra (by Nijinsky): dam, awarded
Oaks, out of Yorkshire Oaks winner and Arc third Awaasif: 11/1 from 5/1, 9 lengths
seventh of 18 to Pontoon in maiden at Newmarket, dropping away from 2f out:
should do better. *Saeed bin Suroor*

MEN OF WICKENBY 3 b.c. Shirley Heights 130 – Radiant Bride (USA) –
(Blushing Groom (FR) 131) [1996 NR 1997 9.2d a12g⁶ 12g⁵ 10g May 12]
6,000 2-y-o: first foal: dam, French 1m (at 2 yrs) to 1¼m winner, half-sister to
top-class US middle-distance performer Vanlandingham: little sign of ability.
R. M. McKellar

MENTALASANYTHIN 8 b.g. Ballacashtal (CAN) – Lafrowda 71 (Crimson 69
Beau 124) [1996 73, a81: a12g² a11g⁶ a12g* a12g² a12g 12g 13.8s 12.1d² 10m 13m²
13m² 12.1f* 10.3m⁴ 10.9m 13.1m⁴ 12.1d 11.9v 10m⁴ 10f 1997 a9.4g 12s* 13s³
11.1g² 11.9g 8.3g⁴ 10.9d 13.1d 12.1g Sep 29] sturdy gelding: fair handicapper: won
at Beverley in May: well beaten last 3 starts: suited by 1¼m to 13f: acts on any going:
has won for amateur/apprentice. *D. Haydn Jones*

MERANTI 4 b.g. Puissance 110 – Sorrowful (Moorestyle 137) [1996 59: 6.1d⁵ 64
6m² 6m⁴ 7m 6f⁴ 6g 7g 6f 1997 5g 6.1m* 5g⁴ 7g* 6.1d 6g⁶ 5.7m 6g² 6m* 6d 5.7f 6g
7g 7f Sep 17] leggy gelding: modest handicapper: won at Nottingham and Thirsk in
April and Salisbury in July: finished last final 3 starts, reportedly suffering back
problem after penultimate one: suited by 6f/7f: probably best on good going or
firmer: has hung left, and suited by strong handling. *J. M. Bradley*

MERCH RHYD-Y-GRUG 2 b.f. (Jun 7) Sabrehill (USA) 120 – Al Washl – (USA) 79 (The Minstrel (CAN) 135) [1997 5m 6.1m a5g a8g Dec 19] 1,100Y: eighth foal: half-sister to several winners, including fairly useful sprinter Hufoof (by Known Fact): dam placed at 5f/6f at 2 yrs: no promise in maidens. *D. L. Williams*

MERCILESS 2 gr.f. (Apr 4) Last Tycoon 131 – Galava (CAN) (Graustark) [1997 94 p 8g* Oct 24] big, long-backed filly: fourth foal: half-sister to 1¾m winner Grey Galava (by Generous): dam placed at 7f and 1m in France: 11/2 from 7/2, made taking debut in 18-runner maiden at Doncaster, soon going strongly in front and holding on well despite idling and edging persistently right to beat Silver Rhapsody by 1½ lengths, pair clear: will be well suited by further than 1m: has potential to hold her own in stronger company. *Saeed bin Suroor*

MERCILESS COP 3 ch.g. Efisio 120 – Naturally Bold (Bold Lad (IRE) 133) 73 [1996 68: 6s 5g³ 6g 7f 7.3m⁵ 8m⁴ 7m* 7d³ 7.3s⁴ a7g⁴ a6g⁵ 1997 8m 10.5m⁶ 8g* a9.4g* 8s⁶ 10s 8.2m* 8g 9g⁶ 9s³ Aug 29] heavy-topped gelding: fair performer: won claimer at Goodwood and handicaps at Wolverhampton in June and Nottingham in July: stays 9f: acts on good to firm ground, soft and the all-weather: effective blinkered or not. *B. J. Meehan*

MERCI MONSIEUR 4 ch.g. Cadeaux Genereux 131 – Night Encounter (Right – Tack 131) [1996 8g 10g 11.5g 1997 7.1d⁴ 11.5m 8d⁵ Sep 20] good-topped gelding: half-brother to several winners, notably smart French performer North Col (up to 15f, by Head For Heights): dam, French 1m and 1½m winner, sister to high-class Take A Reef: ex-French gelding: runner-up in 9f maiden on only 2-y-o start: well beaten since, including in blinkers. *J. A. B. Old*

MERCURY FALLING 2 ch.f. (Mar 27) Magic Ring (IRE) 115 – Try The 54 ? Duchess 99 (Try My Best (USA) 130) [1997 6f 5m⁴ 5.1m 5.1g 6d a5g Nov 6] 4,200Y: leggy, unfurnished filly: half-sister to 1¼m and 1½m winner Uncharted Waters (by Celestial Storm) and 2 winners abroad: dam 2-y-o 6f winner: showed some ability in maidens second and third starts, but disappointing otherwise: has been bandaged behind: blinkered final start. *D. W. P. Arbuthnot*

MERCURY (IRE) 4 b.g. Contract Law (USA) 108 – Monrovia (FR) (Dancer's 44 Image (USA)) [1996 –, a72: 7g a8g* 8.5m a9.4g 1997 7m a6g⁴ a7g 9.9s⁵ a8g⁵ 10g⁶ a62 a8g⁴ 12m 10g 10.5m⁶ a12g⁴ a12g² a12g a9.4g Dec 26] strong, lengthy gelding: modest handicapper: stays 1½m: best form on fibresand: blinkered twice (found nothing first occasion): none too consistent. *B. P. J. Baugh*

MERIT (IRE) 5 b.h. Rainbow Quest (USA) 134 – Fur Hat (Habitat 134) [1996 83 88: 18.7g* 20f⁶ 1997 11.9s⁵ 18g 16.5s⁶ Nov 8] rangy horse: fairly useful but lightly-raced handicapper: not seen out until autumn at 5 yrs, and seemed not so good as he was (hung badly left on reappearance): suited by a test of stamina: acts on equitrack and any turf going. *P. F. I. Cole*

MERLIN'S RING 2 br.c. (Mar 28) Magic Ring (IRE) 115 – Dramatic Mood 107 (Jalmood (USA) 126) [1997 6d² 6m* 7m* 7g⁵ 6m³ 6g* 6.5s* Oct 17] 26,000Y: leggy, quite good-topped colt: third foal: has a fluent, round action: half-brother to 4-y-o Absolutelystunning and fair Irish 3-y-o 1½m winner Lifesforliving (both by Aragon): dam unraced: progressed extremely well: won maiden at York and nursery at Goodwood in the summer and listed event at Maisons-Laffitte and Prix Eclipse at Saint-Cloud in autumn: beat subsequent pattern-race winners Roi Gironde and Gold Away by 3 lengths and 4 lengths in last named, putting up decidedly useful effort: should stay 1m: has won on good to firm ground, best form on good or softer: genuine, and a credit to his trainer. *I. A. Balding*

MERRILY 4 gr.f. Sharrood (USA) 124 – Babycham Sparkle 80 (So Blessed 130) 51 [1996 73d: 6m⁵ 6m³ 6f³ 6m 5g² 6d 6m 1997 6g³ 6g⁶ 6g⁶ 6m Aug 9] sparely-made filly: fluent mover: disappointing sprint maiden: often sweating/edgy. *Miss S. E. Hall*

MERRYHILL MARINER 3 ch.g. Superlative 118 – Merryhill Maid (IRE) 71 – (M Double M (USA)) [1996 –: 5m 6d a7g 1997 a7g⁵ Feb 7] plain gelding: no worthwhile form. *J. L. Harris*

MERSEY BEAT   3 ch.c. Rock Hopper 124 – Handy Dancer 87 (Green God 128)   96
[1996 76p: a10g* 1997 a10g² 10g 10g³ 12m Jul 30] well-made colt: good mover:
useful performer: easily best effort when staying-on third of 16 to Memorise in
£19,800 handicap at Newmarket in July: should stay 1½m: refused to enter stalls in
August and temporarily banned from racing after failing 2 subsequent stalls tests.
G. L. Moore

MESHHED (USA)   3 ch.f. Gulch (USA) – Umniyatee 104 (Green Desert (USA)   102
127) [1996 96p: 6m² 7m* 1997 10d⁴ 7m* 7m 7g⁴ 7.3m 10.1m² 9.3f 7g* Oct 27]
big, good-topped filly: useful performer: made all in minor events at Leicester in
June and October: good ½-length second to Entice in listed race at Yarmouth in
September: effective at 7f to 1¼m: acted on good to firm and dead going, stiff task on
firm: tended to sweat: mounted in saddling boxes: visits Halling. *B. Hanbury*

MESSINA (IRE)   3 b.f. Sadler's Wells (USA) 132 – Magic of Life (USA) 118   77
(Seattle Slew (USA)) [1996 NR 1997 10m³ 11.9s⁴ Oct 15] lengthy, good sort: has a
round action: fifth foal: half-sister to 3 winners at 1¼m+, notably useful From
Beyond (by Kris): dam, Mill Reef and Coronation Stakes winner, from excellent
family: much better effort in maidens when staying-on third at Sandown in September, despite
seeming very green: should stay beyond 1¼m: sold 75,000 gns in December.
R. Charlton

METEOR STRIKE (USA)   3 ch.g. Lomond (USA) 128 – Meteoric 102 (High   87
Line 125) [1996 NR 1997 10.2m* 10.1m² 10.3m 11.9g Sep 26] rather leggy,
workmanlike gelding: seventh foal: half-brother to French 1¼m winner From Afar
(by Riverman) and winners by Topsider in USA and Denmark: dam, sprinter, from
good family: made all in maiden at Bath in July: best effort when second of 5 to
Dantesque in minor event at Yarmouth: never held last 2 starts: stays 1¼m: none too
easy a ride (drifts left): sold 12,000 gns in October. *Mrs A. J. Perrett*

METHMOON (IRE)   2 b.c. (Mar 4) Darshaan 133 – Truly Special 116 (Caerleon   65 p
(USA) 132) [1997 8m Sep 22] sixth foal: brother to smart French middle-distance
filly Truly A Dream and half-brother to French 11f winner Solo de Lune (by Law
Society): dam, won 10.5f Prix de Royaumont, from good family: 7/2 from 6/4, 13
lengths eighth of 17 to Taverner Society in maiden at Kempton, keeping on well not
at all knocked about from slow start: will be well suited by 1¼m+: sure to do fair bit
better. *Saeed bin Suroor*

MEZZORAMIO   5 ch.g. Cadeaux Genereux 131 – Hopeful Search (USA) 71   59
(Vaguely Noble 140) [1996 54: a8g³ a7g⁴ a8g* a8g a8g⁶ 8f 10m⁵ a8g 7m* 8m² 8m*
9g 10m 1997 8.2m 10g 8g² 7f² 8d 7m* 8m² 7g⁵ 7f³ 6f² 8m 8.2d 7f Oct 29]
workmanlike gelding: modest handicapper: won at Yarmouth in July: best at 6f to
1m: acts on fibresand, suited by good going or firmer on turf: has been blinkered,
usually visored nowadays: good mount for inexperienced rider: often a front runner:
game. *K. A. Morgan*

MIAMI MOON   3 ch.f. Keen 116 – Two Moons (Bold Lad (IRE) 133) [1996 46:   41
a6g a6g³ 1997 8g a8g⁶ 8g⁶ 11.1s² 13m⁵ 11.8d 14.1d a10s³ a11g³ Nov 17] stocky filly: a48
poor maiden: left C. Thornton after fifth start: stays 11f well: acts on soft ground and
the all-weather, ran poorly on good to firm. *G. F. Johnson Houghton*

MICHAEL VENTURE   3 b.c. Shirley Heights 130 – Ski Michaela (USA)   – §
(Devil's Bag (USA)) [1996 84: 8m 8f² 8g 1997 12.3g 11.5s⁵ 10.8f⁴ 10.1m 10g⁶ a10g*   a65 §
8m⁵ Aug 10] strong, good-bodied colt: only form at 3 yrs when making all in appren-
tice maiden handicap at Lingfield in July: blinkered second start: most unreliable: sent to Macau. *S. P. C. Woods*

MICHELEE   2 b.f. (Feb 21) Merdon Melody 98 – Hsian (Shantung 132) [1997   ?
5m a6g* a6f* 7s³ Jul 4] 2,900Y: sister to a winner in Italy at up to 1m and half-sister   a58
to 2 winners, including a miler by Night Shift: dam lightly-raced half-sister to 2 smart
performers: won 2 sellers at Wolverhampton in June decisively: well held in claimers
on turf: should stay further than 6f: acts on fibresand. *P. D. Evans*

MICK'S TYCOON (IRE)   9 b.g. Last Tycoon 131 – Ladytown (English Prince   –
129) [1996 NR 1997 12g 17.2m Jun 25] probably of no account nowadays.
T. R. Watson

MIDAS MAN 6 ch.g. Gold Claim 90 – Golden Starfish (Porto Bello 118) [1996 –: – 8s 10m 11.1d 1997 5m 5g 5g⁶ 5s⁴ 9.2d⁵ Jul 4] of no account. *D. A. Nolan*

MIDDAY COWBOY (USA) 4 b.g. Houston (USA) – Perfect Isn't Easy (USA) – (Saratoga Six (USA)) [1996 75: 7m³ 8m 7m² 9m⁴ 8m⁶ 7m 8g 1997 7g 10g 8.2g 8m 8g 10g 8m Jul 18] good-topped gelding: fair form at 3 yrs for G. Harwood: showed nothing in 1997. *M. D. Hammond*

MIDDLE EAST 4 b.g. Beveled (USA) – Godara (Bustino 136) [1996 74: 5d 6m² 77 6f* 6m⁶ 6d³ 6m 6m³ 5m⁶ 1997 5m 6g 6g 5g 5g 5f 6d³ 6f⁵ 6.1m* 6m⁴ 6.1s* a6g* Nov 24] tall gelding: fair performer: won large-field minor events at Nottingham in September and October and handicap at Southwell in November: stays 6f: acts on fibresand, and any turf going: goes well blinkered (was last 4 starts). *T. D. Barron*

MIDDLE TEMPLE 2 b.c. (Feb 15) Midyan (USA) 124 – Temple Fortune 78 (USA) 74 (Ziggy's Boy (USA)) [1997 6m⁵ 6.1d⁵ 7.1g⁴ 8m² Oct 22] 22,000Y: first foal: dam 5f/6f winner out of half-sister to Our Native: fair maiden: best effort close second in nursery at Yarmouth, first start for 3 months: stays 1m: sold 22,000 gns, and sent to Czech Republic. *E. A. L. Dunlop*

MIDNIGHT ESCAPE 4 b.g. Aragon 118 – Executive Lady 59 (Night Shift 111 (USA)) [1996 99: 5m* 5f* 5m 5.6m 5g 5g* 1997 5.2g 5m 5m⁵ 5m² 5g* 5.2g 5d³ Oct 26] close-coupled gelding: improved into a smart performer: won Flying Five at Leopardstown (rallied to beat Hopping Higgins ¾ length) in September: good 1¾ lengths third to Hever Golf Rose in Prix du Petit Couvert at Longchamp final start: best form at 5f: acts on firm going, yet to race on softer than dead. *C. F. Wall*

MIDNIGHT LINE (USA) 2 ch.f. (May 2) Kris S (USA) – Midnight Air 108 + (USA) 111 (Green Dancer (USA) 132) [1997 6g⁵ 7m* 7g* 8f* 8g⁵ Sep 28]

The day after declaring a dead-heat for first place in the Nunthorpe Stakes at York, racecourse judge Jane Stickels might well have arrived at the same conclusion in the seven-furlong Prestige Stakes at Goodwood, a race which saw a desperately close finish between Midnight Line and Alignment. Yet, following much deliberation, Mrs Stickels awarded the race to Midnight Line, admitting that it was only the filly's flared nostril which made the difference. While judges are under instruction to declare an outright winner whenever possible, surely few would have quibbled had a dead-heat been given in this instance. 'That is as close to a dead-heat as I have seen in twenty-four years of riding, and I find it hard to believe the Nunthorpe could have been closer' was the verdict of the runner-up's rider John Reid. Alignment's trainer Michael Stoute was also adamant that the wrong decision had been made, but was instructed by the filly's owner not to appeal against the judgement. 'I'm very reluctant to challenge the referee's decision, it's just not the British thing to do that. Added to that, the owner of Midnight Line is a good friend of mine' said Lord Weinstock.

As when getting off the mark in a maiden over the same course and distance three weeks earlier, Midnight Line stuck gamely to her task at Goodwood after coming off the bridle a long way from home. Her battling qualities were once again in evidence when she completed her hat-trick, in the May Hill Stakes at Doncaster in September, conceding 5 lb all round. Midnight Line's trainer, Henry Cecil, has virtually monopolised the May Hill, which attracted nine runners, six of them, apart from Midnight Line, having won on their previous starts. Once again Midnight Line took a long time to warm to her task, and at halfway in a truly-run contest was still in last place. It wasn't long before she began to improve her position, though, and when Flawless took up the running two furlongs out Midnight Line had just over a length to make up on her. For a while it looked as though the leader might be able to hang on to her advantage but Midnight Line, proving well suited by the step up to a mile, gradually wore her down and led close home to win by half a length, with Glorosia a further three lengths back in third.

May Hill Stakes, Doncaster—a second Group 3 win for Midnight Line (left);
Flawless runs a good race to be beaten only half a length

The winner and the third met at level weights later in the month, in the Fillies' Mile at Ascot, where Midnight Line was passed over by stable-jockey Kieren Fallon in favour of Cecil's other runner, Jibe. Whereas both Glorosia and Jibe showed improved form to finish first and second respectively, Midnight Line came a well-beaten fifth after losing her chance when badly hampered twice as she was attempting to deliver her challenge early in the straight. She should confirm herself better than that in 1998, though it's unlikely that she will be a major contender for the top prizes.

Midnight Line, who acts on firm going and has yet to race on ground softer than good, will stay a mile and a quarter, probably a mile and a half. Her sire, Kris S, won three races at up to nine furlongs from five outings, including a minor stakes, and his leading produce, which include the Breeders' Cup Distaff winner Hollywood Wildcat, the Breeders' Cup Turf winner Prized and the Belmont Stakes runner-up Kissin Kris, all stayed at least that distance. Midnight Line's dam, Midnight Air, the eighth of Cecil's eleven May Hill winners, was disqualified after passing the post first in the Fillies' Mile on her next start and failed to live up to expectations at three, running her best races when placed in listed events at a mile and a mile and a quarter. Midnight Air was sold for 270,000 guineas at the end of 1992 and two years later produced her first foal, Midnight Watch (by Capote). The latter showed fair form at up to a mile and a quarter for Cecil in the latest season, but he was still a maiden

HRH Prince Fahd Salman's "Midnight Line"

		Roberto	Hail To Reason
	Kris S (USA)	(b 1969)	Bramalea
	(b or br 1977)	Sharp Queen	Princequillo
Midnight Line (USA)		(br 1965)	Bridgework
(ch.f. May 2, 1995)		Green Dancer	Nijinsky
	Midnight Air (USA)	(b 1972)	Green Valley
	(br 1989)	Evening Air	J O Tobin
		(br 1982)	Nellie Forbes

when sold at the Newmarket Autumn Sales. Evening Air, the unraced grandam of Midnight Line, is a daughter of Nellie Forbes, who won at a mile in Ireland on her only start at two, and granddaughter of Comely Nell, dam of the Kentucky Derby and Belmont Stakes winner Bold Forbes. *H. R. A. Cecil*

MIDNIGHT ROMANCE 3 b.f. Inca Chief (USA) – Run Amber Run (Run The –
Gantlet (USA)) [1996 –: 7m 1997 8.5m⁶ 8.2d 9g a8g Jul 10] smallish, leggy filly: no form in maidens or handicaps. *A. P. Jarvis*

MIDNIGHT SHIFT (IRE) 3 b.f. Night Shift (USA) – Old Domesday Book 93 73
(High Top 131) [1996 69: 7m 6g 6m⁴ 1997 6m 6d 6m³ 5m⁴ 6g* 6m 6m 7g² 7m 7m 6g* 6m Nov 4] good-topped filly: fair performer: won maiden at Redcar in June and 22-runner handicap at Leicester in October: stays 7f: acts on good to firm ground, poor effort on dead. *R. Guest*

MIDNIGHT STING 2 gr.f. (Feb 11) Inchinor 119 – Halvoya 64 (Bay Express 60 +
132) [1997 6g⁶ 6m 7d Oct 13] 3,000Y: angular filly: third reported foal: dam best at 5f: modest maiden: off 6 weeks before bandaged final start. *M. A. Jarvis*

MIDNIGHT TIMES 3 b.f. Timeless Times (USA) 99 – Midnight Lass 59   52
(Today And Tomorrow 78) [1996 –: a5g 5f 5.1f⁵ 5.3f 1997 5m a5g³ a5g a5g⁴ a5g a5g
Dec 22] modest maiden: form only when in frame in handicaps at Wolverhampton
and Lingfield: raced only at 5f on all-weather or firm/good to firm going on turf.
D. C. O'Brien

MIDNIGHT WATCH (USA) 3 b.c. Capote (USA) – Midnight Air (USA) 111   81
(Green Dancer (USA) 132) [1996 77p: 8.2g² 1997 10g⁶ 10.4s⁴ 13.4g⁶ 8d³ Oct 28]
leggy colt: fairly useful maiden: good third in handicap at Leicester final start,
staying on well: stays 1¼m (seemingly not 13.4f): yet to race on going firmer than
good: sold 16,000 gns and joined P. Winkworth. *H. R. A. Cecil*

MIDSUMMER NIGHT (IRE) 2 b.f. (Mar 4) Fairy King (USA) – Villota (Top   69
Ville 129) [1997 5m³ 5g² 6m 5m⁴ 5m⁵ Oct 31] lengthy, unfurnished filly: second
foal: half-sister to a winning sprinter abroad by Lycius: dam, ran once in Ireland,
daughter of high-class sprinter/miler Vilikaia: fair maiden: good fourth in nursery at
Newmarket penultimate start: should stay 6f (off 3 months before only try): raced
only on good/good to firm ground. *R. Hannon*

MIDSUMMER ROMANCE (IRE) 2 b.f. (May 6) Fairy King (USA) –   – p
Jealous One (USA) (Raise A Native) [1997 7.3g Oct 25] IR 20,000Y: tall, angular
filly: has scope: eighth foal: closely related to a winner in Italy by The Minstrel and
half-sister to 3 winners abroad: dam won up to 9f in USA: never-dangerous
tenth of 13 in listed race at Newbury: should do better. *B. J. Meehan*

MIDYAN BLUE (IRE) 7 ch.g. Midyan (USA) 124 – Jarretiere 78 (Star Appeal   75 d
133) [1996 81: 11.8g³ 13.9m⁴ 14d⁶ 14m³ 14d⁴ 15m⁶ 13.9g² 13.3m⁶ 13.9g² 14.6g
12s 1997 12m 11.9s³ 14.1g 13.9g³ 14m 20m 14g⁴ 14m⁵ 13.9s⁴ 14.1g⁵ 12g⁵ Oct 25]
sparely-made gelding: shows plenty of knee action: fair handicapper at best
nowadays: best at 1½m/1¾m: acts on good to firm and heavy ground: has run well
when sweating: used to go well at York: inconsistent. *J. M. P. Eustace*

MIDYAN CALL 3 b.c. Midyan (USA) 124 – Early Call 102 (Kind of Hush 118)   92
[1996 NR 1997 7.1s 6m² 7m⁵ 6m* 6g 8m² 7g Oct 18] 9,000F, IR 21,000Y: big, sturdy
colt: has scope: fourth foal: brother to 5-y-o Sarasi and half-brother to 6f (at 2 yrs) to
13f winner Global Dancer (by Night Shift): dam won up to 11.5f: fairly useful form:
off course over 3 months, won maiden at Newmarket in August: easily best effort
after when second of 6 in minor event at Newmarket in October, wandering and no
extra near finish: stays 1m: acts on good to firm ground. *M. Bell*

MIDYAN QUEEN 3 b.f. Midyan (USA) 124 – Queen of Aragon 76 (Aragon 118)   64
[1996 60+: 6d 5.1m³ 5s³ 5g⁶ 1997 7s 6m⁴ 6g 7g* 8g 6.9f⁴ 7s Sep 4] leggy filly:
modest handicapper: won at Warwick in July, easily best effort of 1997: should stay
1m: probably acts on any going: bled from nose final 2-y-o start. *R. Hollinshead*

MIGHT AND POWER (NZ) 4 b. or br.g. Zabeel – Benediction 99 (Day Is   127
Done 115) [1996 6.5s⁴ 6.5g⁵ 7g* 7.5g² 1997 6.8g 9v² 9.5g* 9.5d* 9g² 10g 12g⁴ 10g*
6g* 7v² 7.5d² 8f 12g* 16m* Nov 4] $40,000Y in Australia: third foal: half-brother to
2 winners, including Elite (up to 11f in Hong Kong, by Star Way): dam, Irish 7f
winner, stayed 1m: sire showed fairly useful form in Britain then won Australian
Guineas: high-class Australian gelding: won minor handicap at Randwick on
penultimate start for A. Cummings in 1996: has won 6 times for current stable, really
coming to himself on last 2 outings: won 18-runner Caulfield Cup in course-record
time by 7½ lengths from Doriemus in October: followed up in 22-runner Melbourne
Cup at Flemington in November by short head from same rival, with Harbour Dues
(effectively received 10 lb, taking weight-for-age into account) a length back in
fourth, increasing pace 6f out, running on gamely in straight and just lasting home:
stays 2m: has form on heavy ground, best efforts on good/good to firm: blinkered
nowadays: looked a resolute galloper at Flemington, one best allowed to stride on.
Jack Denham, Australia

MIGHTY FLOW 3 b.f. Nicholas (USA) 111 – Mighty Flash 81 (Rolfe (USA)   – §
77) [1996 NR 1997 11g 12m 10s 8.3m Jul 14] leggy, workmanlike filly: half-sister to
1993 2-y-o 7f winner Mighty Forum (by Presidium), later smart up to 8.5f in USA:
dam staying sister to Derby third Mighty Flutter: no worthwhile form: seems to have
plenty of temperament. *Mrs P. N. Dutfield*

MIGHTY MAGIC 2 b.f. (Feb 28) Magic Ring (IRE) 115 – Mighty Flash 81   57
(Rolfe (USA) 77) [1997 5m³ 5.7f⁴ 6d⁵ 6m 5.1g 7.3d Sep 19] 9,500Y: leggy filly: fifth
foal: half-sister to 1993 2-y-o 7f winner Mighty Forum (by Presidium), later smart up
to 8.5f in USA: dam staying sister to Derby third Mighty Flutter: modest maiden on
balance: stays 6f. *Mrs P. N. Dutfield*

MIGHTY PHANTOM (USA) 4 b.f. Lear Fan (USA) 130 – Migiyas 87 (Kings   68
Lake (USA) 133) [1996 78: 6.9f⁶ 10m⁵ a16g⁴ 15.4g³ 12m* 14f⁵ a16g² 13.9g⁴ 14.1f²
1997 11.7m 13.1d⁶ 16g³ 14m² 14m 11.6g⁵ 14.1g³ Aug 21] sturdy filly: fair
handicapper: effective at 1½m to 2m: acts on firm ground and equitrack, well below
best on dead: joined R. T. Phillips. *J. W. Hills*

MIGHTY SURE (IRE) 2 b.f. (Apr 25) Treasure Kay 114 – Mighty Special (IRE)   64
(Head For Heights 125) [1997 5d* 5g³ 6g⁶ 6g² 5d⁴ 5m⁴ 5m* 5m⁶ Oct 2] IR 500Y:
tall, sparely-made filly: second foal: dam poor Irish maiden: modest performer: won
seller at Doncaster (for P. Calver) in May and nursery at Redcar (for M. W. Easterby)
in September: ran well from out of handicap final start: stays 6f: blinkered sixth start:
sent to Saudi Arabia. *C. R. Egerton*

MIGRATE (USA) 2 ch.f. (Mar 10) Storm Bird (CAN) 134 – Home Leave (USA)   69
(Alydar (USA)) [1997 6g⁵ 7d⁴ 8.2g⁵ Oct 4] $400,000Y: fourth foal: half-sister to a
winner in USA by Polish Navy: dam, winner at 4/5 yrs in USA, half-sister to Breeders' Cup Sprint winner Dancing Spree and the dam of high-class American mare
Heavenly Prize: fair form in maiden at Newmarket on debut, but didn't repeat it, off
over 3 months before final start (missed break after playing up). *J. H. M. Gosden*

MIGWAR 4 b.g. Unfuwain (USA) 131 – Pick of The Pops 109 (High Top 131)   – p
[1996 99: 10g² 12d² 10.3m* 10m* 12m 1997 10d Sep 20] deep-girthed, attractive
gelding: carries condition: useful handicapper: sustained injury at Royal Ascot final
outing at 3 yrs: midfield in £16,200 event at Newbury only outing in 1997, given
nothing like a hard time once tiring: should stay beyond 1¼m: acts on good to firm
ground: tends to sweat and get on edge. *L. M. Cumani*

MIHNAH (IRE) 2 br.f. (Feb 3) Lahib (USA) 129 – Nafhaat (USA) 91 (Roberto   84
(USA) 131) [1997 7g⁴ 6m² 6s* 7.3g Oct 25] big, useful-looking filly, rather unfurnished at 2 yrs: fluent mover: fourth foal: half-sister to 7.6f and 1¼m winner Hadeel
(by Polish Precedent) and 3-y-o Ghalib: dam 1½m winner who stayed 15f: won
maiden at York in October by 5 lengths, making all: well beaten in listed event at
Newbury final outing: should stay at least 1m. *D. Morley*

MIHRIZ (IRE) 5 b.g. Machiavellian (USA) 123 – Ghzaalh (USA) 87 (Northern   77
Dancer) [1996 –: 8s 8.3m⁶ 6.9f⁴ 8m 6f 8d 8g 1997 7m³ 7.9g 8d* 9d 9m 8v⁶ Oct 11]
sturdy gelding: fluent mover: fair handicapper: best effort since 3 yrs when winning
at Salisbury (by 5 lengths) in August: needs further than 7f, and stays 9f: acts on good
to firm ground and dead: inconsistent. *R. Akehurst*

MIJANA (IRE) 2 b.c. (Mar 26) Tenby 125 – Fabled Lifestyle (Kings Lake (USA)   107
133) [1997 5.2g* 7g² 6m* 6g³ 6m* 6d⁴ 6g² Oct 18] 56,000F, IR 50,000Y: small,
compact colt: impresses in appearance: fourth living foal: half-brother to useful 7.5f
and 10.4f winner Old Hickory (by Alzao) and a winner in Germany at up to 1½m by
Law Society: dam, Irish 9f winner, half-sister to Dante winner Lyphard's Wish:
useful performer: won minor events at Newbury (had sore shins afterwards) in April
and Windsor in August and listed race at Kempton (by 1¼ lengths from Tadwiga) in
September: in frame afterwards in Mill Reef Stakes at Newbury and Two-Year-Old
Trophy at Redcar, good length second of 26 to Grazia in latter: effective at 6f, bred to
stay 1m+: best efforts on good/good to firm ground: genuine: sent to Hong Kong.
J. H. M. Gosden

MIJAS 4 ch.f. Risk Me (FR) 127 – Out of Harmony 79 (Song 132) [1996 80: 6m*   –
6m⁶ a6g 7f 5m⁵ 6m⁵ 5m a5g⁶ a6g a5g* a6g 1997 a5g*ᵈⁱˢ a5g a5g a5g⁴ a5g² 6m 5g⁶   a80 d
5m 5m a5g a7g a5g a5g⁴ a7g Dec 10] fairly useful handicapper on all-weather:
disqualified after passing post first at Lingfield in January: generally disappointing
last 9 starts: stays easy 6f: acts on equitrack (below form only outing on fibresand),
no recent form on turf: ran badly in blinkers third 4-y-o start (free to post): best racing
up with pace. *L. Montague Hall*

MIKE'S DOUBLE (IRE) 3 br.g. Cyrano de Bergerac 120 – Glass Minnow   64
(IRE) 59 (Alzao (USA) 117) [1996 47: 5g⁶ 5.3f⁴ 6d 5f 6.1s³ 6m² 1997 6.1m³ 6.1m⁵   a73

6.1m³ 7d² 6.1d a6g* a8.5g⁴ 7g⁵ a6g² 6.1s⁴ 6.9d³ a7g a6g⁴ a6g³ Dec 26] sturdy gelding: fair on all-weather, modest on turf: trained first 2 starts by G. Lewis: won maiden at Wolverhampton in July: generally ran at least respectably after: effective at 6f/7f: acts on good to firm ground, soft and all-weather: sometimes blinkered (was last 6 starts). *Miss Gay Kelleway*

MILE HIGH   3 b.g. Puissance 110 – Jobiska (Dunbeath (USA) 127) [1996 88:   87
6.1m⁴ 6m² 1997 6m² 5.1m* 6m⁶ 5m Aug 9] good-topped gelding: fairly useful performer: won maiden at Nottingham in March, making most: good effort next start, off course over 3 months and stiff task final one: a sprinter: raced solely on good to firm ground: gave trouble at stalls on reappearance: sent to UAE. *M. R. Channon*

MILETRIAN CITY   4 gr.g. Petong 126 – Blueit (FR) 101 (Bold Lad (IRE) 133)   49
[1996 60: 7s 7d 8m 10d⁴ 8.1f⁶ 8.1f⁴ 8m⁴ 7g² 6.9f* 7d⁴ 8.3m³ 7.1m² 7.1m⁶ 1997 a7g⁶ 7g 8m⁵ 7f 8g 7.1g⁴ 8g² 6.9m 10.9g 8m² 8m 9.2d 9.2m 8.3g 8m Oct 1] smallish, strong gelding: has a quick action: poor handicapper: left J. Berry after eighth start: effective at 7f/1m: acts on firm and dead ground: blinkered/visored. *Miss L. A. Perratt*

MILETRIAN REFURB (IRE)   4 b. or br.g. Anita's Prince 126 – Lady of Man   61
85 (So Blessed 130) [1996 63: 6s* 6.1d⁴ 5.1g² 6d 5.1g² a5g 1997 a6g a6g 5g⁴ 5d a7g   a–
Nov 14] compact gelding: unimpressive mover: modest handicapper: only form at 4 yrs when fourth at Folkestone in March: off course 7 months before next start: stays 6f: acts on good to firm and soft ground, no form on all-weather. *M. R. Channon*

MILITARY (USA)   3 b.c. Danzig (USA) – Wavering Girl (USA) (Wavering   92
Monarch (USA)) [1996 NR 1997 8.1g⁴ 8d³ 10.3d* 10g⁴ 10g² Aug 2] $250,000Y: big, good-topped colt: has scope: second foal: dam, listed winning sprinter in North America at 2 and 3 yrs, from good family: fairly useful performer: got an excellent ride from the front when winning 18-runner maiden at Doncaster in June: good efforts in handicaps at Newmarket afterwards: likely to prove best up to 1¼m: raced only on good/good to soft going: sent to D. Wayne Lukas, in USA. *H. R. A. Cecil*

MILKY WAY   3 b.f. Statoblest 120 – Evening Star 71 (Red Sunset 120) [1996 NR   –
1997 8m a8.5g a8g⁶ a11g Dec 8] 4,200Y: second foal: dam, 1m winner, half-sister to useful performer at up to 1½m Mac's Reef: well beaten in maidens and a handicap. *S. P. C. Woods*

MILL DANCER (IRE)   5 b.m. Broken Hearted 124 – Theatral (Orchestra 118)   –
[1996 –: a11g⁵ a11g a8g⁴ 8.3d 9.9m 8g⁶ 8.1g⁵ 10m 7f⁵ 8.1m 9.2f 8g a11g 1997 a8.5f a13g Jun 28] leggy mare: little form since 3 yrs. *J. G. M. O'Shea*

MILL END BOY   3 ch.g. Clantime 101 – Annaceramic 83 (Horage 124) [1996   53
60: 5d 5g³ 5m 7s⁴ 7g 6f⁵ 6g⁴ 6m 1997 6m 5m 5m⁵ 5.9f³ 7.1d 6m 7g 7m Oct 7] small, lengthy gelding: modest maiden handicapper: stays 7f: probably acts on any going: tried visored: sent to Holland. *M. W. Easterby*

MILL END QUEST   2 b.f. (Apr 26) King's Signet (USA) 110 – Milva 56   65 d
(Jellaby 124) [1997 5g⁵ a5g 5g* 5g⁶ 6g⁶ 6d 6m 5m⁵ 6m Oct 28] 8,400Y: small filly: half-sister to several winners, including fairly useful 6f winner Milagro (by King of Spain) and 1¾m winner Serious Time (by Good Times): dam 6f winner: won maiden at Musselburgh in July: largely disappointing afterwards, including in seller: best form at 5f. *M. W. Easterby*

MILLESIME (IRE)   5 ch.g. Glow (USA) – Persian Myth (Persian Bold 123)   54
[1996 –: 5m 5g 5.1m⁵ 5f 1997 6g² 5s⁵ 6.1d 6m 6f⁶ Jun 10] unfurnished gelding: modest performer nowadays: effective at 5f and 6f: acts on firm ground, below form on softer than good: has had tongue tied: races prominently. *Martyn Wane*

MILLING (IRE)   2 b.f. (Jan 19) In The Wings 128 – Princess Pati 124 (Top Ville   –
129) [1997 7m Nov 1] 13,000Y: ninth foal: closely related to smart 1¼m/1½m winner and Yorkshire Cup second Parthian Springs (by Sadler's Wells) and half-sister to several winners, including 4-y-o Pasternak: dam won Irish Oaks: 50/1, always behind in 18-runner maiden at Newmarket. *R. Guest*

MILLITRIX   2 br.f. (Apr 8) Doyoun 124 – Galatrix 72 (Be My Guest (USA) 126)   82
[1997 7g² 7d⁴ Sep 19] rather sparely-made filly: fourth foal: half-sister to a 6f winner in Sweden by Persian Bold: dam, 1m winner, half-sister to dam of Sleepytime, Ali-Royal and Taipan: fair form when in frame in maiden at Salisbury (beaten length

by Flawless) and 5-runner minor event at Newbury in September: should stay 1m. *M. R. Stoute*

MILL ORCHID 3 b.f. Henbit (USA) 130 – Milinetta (Milford 119) [1996 NR – 1997 8g 10m 9.2g Sep 29] third live foal: half-sister to 1993 2-y-o 1m winner Mill Force (by Forzando) and hurdles winner Mill Thyme (by Thowra): dam won over hurdles: well beaten in maidens. *J. Berry*

MILLPET 3 br.f. Petong 126 – Pattis Pet (Mummy's Pet 125) [1996 NR 1997 7m 51 6m 5m² 5m⁵ 8d⁶ 7.1d³ 7g a6g Oct 20] 9,200Y resold 12,000Y: compact filly: sister to 1990 2-y-o 7f winner Black Armorial, later successful in Italy, and half-sister to 2 winners, including fairly useful 1994 2-y-o sprinter Sylvandra (by Mazilier): dam lightly raced: modest maiden at best: probably a sprinter: acts on good to firm ground: none too consistent: blinkered final start. *R. Guest*

MILLROY (USA) 3 ch.g. Carnivalay (USA) – Royal Millinery (USA) (Regal – And Royal (USA)) [1996 82: 6m³ 7m⁶ 5m³ 6m⁶ 8m 6m a7s² a7g* a7s³ a7g² 1997 a90 a9.4f* a8.5g² a8g² a10g⁶ a11g² a8.5g³ 8m 9m 8m 7m a8.5f³ 6.5f Dec 27] strong, lengthy gelding: fairly useful and consistent handicapper on all-weather, winning at Wolverhampton in January: little form on turf in 1997: effective at 1m, barely stays 11f: has been blinkered, usually visored at 3 yrs: trained first 10 starts by P. Kelleway. *D. R. Peterson, USA*

MILLY OF THE VALLY 3 b.f. Caerleon (USA) 132 – Mill On The Floss 117 93 (Mill Reef (USA) 141) [1996 NR 1997 11g 12s* 14s² 14m 16.1g² Aug 25] compact filly: half-sister to several winners, including useful pair Yeltsin (up to 1½m, by Soviet Star) and Milly Ha Ha (should have stayed 1¾m, by Dancing Brave): dam 7f (at 2 yrs) and 1½m winner from very good family: fairly useful performer: won maiden at Thirsk in May: good second in handicaps at Goodwood and Newcastle: will stay beyond 2m: acts on soft ground, probably on good to firm. *H. R. A. Cecil*

MILOS 6 b.g. Efisio 120 – Elkie Brooks 82 (Relkino 131) [1996 64, a74: a6g⁶ a7g⁵ – a6g* a6g³ a7g* a7g a7g³ a7g⁵ a7g² a6g⁴ 6f³ 6.9m⁴ 6f 8.1m 8.1d² 8f 7.1f 6d 7.1s³ a7g⁵ a67 a7g 1997 a7g* a8g² a7g² a8g⁵ Feb 11] big, strong gelding: shows knee action: fair performer on the all-weather: made hard work of landing odds in seller at Lingfield in January, penultimate start for T. J. Naughton: effective at 6f to 1m. *G. L. Moore*

MILS MIJ 12 br.g. Slim Jim 112 – Katie Grey 60 (Pongee 106) [1996 NR 1997 28 15g³ 17.1g Aug 17] poor stayer on flat nowadays: acts on good to firm and heavy going. *T. A. K. Cuthbert*

MILTON ABBOT 4 b.g. Full Extent (USA) 113 – Auto Connection 68 (Blushing – Scribe (USA) 107) [1996 NR 1997 8s 7g a12g a7s Nov 28] second foal: dam 1¼m winner: no sign of ability. *M. S. Saunders*

MILTONFIELD 8 ch.g. Little Wolf 127 – Kingsfold Flash 50 (Warpath 113) 93 [1996 16s³ 14g³ 14g* 16g² 16g² 14d² 16g* 16s* 16d⁴ 1997 11d 14g⁵ 20m Jun 17] tall, angular gelding: half-brother to top-class chaser Flashing Steel (by Broadsword): dam plater: fairly useful hurdler: also fairly useful on flat (won 3 times in 1996, ran only once previously): fifth in listed event at Leopardstown before midfield in Ascot Stakes at Royal Ascot: very much a stayer: probably suited by good ground or softer. *J. E. Mulhern, Ireland*

MIMOSA 4 ch.f. Midyan (USA) 124 – Figini 74 (Glint of Gold 128) [1996 67, 61 a63: 7d 10g 7d 8m 8f 9m 8m* 8m 9f⁵ 10g⁵ 8m 8d⁴ 9.7d² 10g a8g⁶ a10s⁴ a10g 1997 a10g⁴ a10g³ 9.7g 8f² 8m⁶ a10g⁴ 9g 9s⁶ 8.3m⁶ 8.1g 8m³ Sep 24] strong, close-coupled filly: modest handicapper: stays 1¼m: acts on firm ground, dead and equitrack: tried visored: tends to get behind: none too reliable. *S. Dow*

MIND GAMES 5 b.h. Puissance 110 – Aryaf (CAN) (Vice Regent (CAN)) [1996 108 121: 5g* 5f² 6m 5m⁴ 6f⁶ 1997 5d Aug 21] leggy, lengthy stallion: very smart sprinter at 4 yrs: had a season at stud before showing he retains plenty of ability (narrow lead from halfway until over 1f out) when midfield behind dead-heaters Coastal Bluff and Ya Malak in Nunthorpe Stakes at York: best at 5f: acts on firm and dead ground: has worn small bandage near hind: best forcing pace. *J. Berry*

MINDRACE 4 b.g. Tina's Pet 121 – High Velocity 53 (Frimley Park 109) [1996 64 70: 6s 5g⁶ 6m 6m 7f⁴ 5m⁴ 5g⁴ 5.1m* 5m² 5.1m⁴ 5m 5m 5m⁴ 1997 6m 5m 5g 5g 5m 5m² 5.7m 5m⁴ 5m* 5m 5g 5.7g⁶ 6f 5m 6m Oct 5] plain, leggy gelding: modest handicapper: made most when winning at Sandown in July: best at 5f: acts on firm ground: occasionally visored: has had tongue tied: none too consistent. *K. T. Ivory*

MINERSVILLE (USA) 3 b.g. Forty Niner (USA) – Angel Fever (USA) (Danzig (USA)) [1996 83P: 7g³ 1997 8m* 10g⁶ 9g⁶ 10m⁶ 10m Aug 26] big, strong gelding: has plenty of scope: has been fired: very much caught the eye only outing at 2 yrs: had to work hard to land odds in maiden at Newcastle in March: most disappointing afterwards, markedly reluctant in visor penultimate start: should stay beyond 1m: sold approx. £35,500 in Dubai in November. *J. H. M. Gosden*   83 d

MINETTA 2 ch.f. (Mar 27) Mujtahid (USA) 118 – Minwah (USA) (Diesis 133) [1997 a5g³ 5.9f* 5g 6g 8m⁴ 8d Oct 17] 6,200Y: lengthy filly: second living foal: dam unraced daughter of smart middle-distance stayer Ivory Fields: fair performer: won maiden at Carlisle in May: good fourth in nursery at Newmarket in August: likely to stay beyond 1m: acts on firm ground, showed promise on fibresand. *M. Bell*   75

MINIVET 2 b.g. (Apr 9) Midyan (USA) 124 – Bronzewing 103 (Beldale Flutter (USA) 130) [1997 7m³ Oct 2] leggy, plain gelding: sixth foal: half-brother to 3-y-o Redwing and 2m winner Sun Grebe (by Arctic Tern): dam 6f and 1m winner: 50/1 and very green, 6½ lengths third of 22 to Quiet Assurance in maiden at Newmarket, keeping on well: will stay at least 1m: sure to improve. *M. Bell*   78 p

MINJARA 2 b.c. (May 10) Beveled (USA) – Honey Mill 67 (Milford 119) [1997 7m 6d Oct 28] second foal: dam, maiden, should have stayed 1m: well beaten in maidens 3 months apart. *A. P. Jones*   –

MINSTER MOORGATE 2 ch.f. (Mar 12) Minster Son 130 – Find The Sun 81 (Galivanter 131) [1997 7.1s a8g Nov 14] half-sister to 11f winner Carlton Colleen (stayed 2m well, by Sagaro): dam, 2-y-o 7f winner, stayed well: soundly beaten in maiden and seller. *M. W. Easterby*   –

MINSTER STAR 3 ch.f. Minster Son 130 – Star of The Sea (Absalom 128) [1996 NR 1997 8s 10d³ 10g 10m a12g 10d Oct 28] 1,000Y: unfurnished filly: second foal: dam of little account: only worthwhile form when third in maiden at Leicester in July. *J. L. Spearing*   63 d

MINT CONDITION 3 ch.g. Superlative 118 – Penny Mint 79 (Mummy's Game 120) [1996 –: 5f 5.1m⁴ 7g 1997 a11g Dec 8] leggy, workmanlike gelding: no sign of ability. *Don Enrico Incisa*   –

MIQUELON 2 b.c. (Apr 15) Primo Dominie 121 – Miquette (FR) (Fabulous Dancer (USA) 124) [1997 5m 5g* 5m³ 5m⁴ 5m³ 6m² 6g 8s⁴ 8m⁴ Oct 22] 5,000F, IR 20,000Y: good-bodied colt: half-brother to 1993 2-y-o sprint winner Floating Trial (by Dowsing), 4-y-o Oops Pettie and a winner in France by Shernazar: dam French 1½m and 13.5f winner: fairly useful performer: won maiden at Newcastle in March: in frame most subsequent starts, including in nurseries: will stay at least 1¼m: acts on good to firm and soft ground: well beaten only try in blinkers: sold 20,000 gns, and sent to Switzerland. *R. Hollinshead*   83

MIRACLE KID (USA) 3 b.c. Red Ransom (USA) – Fan Mail (USA) (Zen (USA)) [1996 75p: 8g a8g* 1997 10.3m* 9d 9m 10g Oct 18] good-bodied colt: fairly useful handicapper at best: impressive winner of 16-runner race at Doncaster in March: off course nearly 6 months and well held afterwards: stays 1¼m: acts on good to firm ground and equitrack: visored (raced freely) final start. *J. H. M. Gosden*   83

MIRROR FOUR LIFE (IRE) 3 b.f. Treasure Kay 114 – Gazettalong 80 (Taufan (USA) 119) [1996 73: 5.1m* 5.1m⁴ 6g⁴ 5m⁵ 7g* 7g 7m 1997 7m 7.1g 7m Jul 24] sparely-made filly: fair performer at 2 yrs: tailed off in 1997: visored last start. *M. H. Tompkins*   –

MIRROR FOUR SPORT 3 ch.f. Risk Me (FR) 127 – Madison Girl 68 (Last Fandango 125) [1996 50?: 5g⁴ a6g⁵ a7g⁶ 6.1m 6m a7g 1997 a8g⁶ a6g³ a6g² a8g* a7g⁴ a12g⁶ a7g⁵ a8g* a12g³ a8.5g⁵ 10m a9.4g* a7g⁵ 11.1s² 8f a11g* a12g 12g Aug 1] unfurnished filly: modest performer: successful at Southwell (2 selling handicaps and an apprentice claimer) and Wolverhampton (seller) in first half of year: left M. Johnston's stable £3,000 after last win: needs further than 7f and stays 11f: seems to act on both all-weather, best effort on turf on soft going. *S. R. Bowring*   47 a59

MISALLIANCE 2 ch.f. (Feb 21) Elmaamul (USA) 125 – Cabaret Artiste 74
(Shareef Dancer (USA) 135) [1997 7d 7.5f⁴ 7m* 7s Oct 17] 4,500Y: first foal: dam
unraced: shaped promisingly before winning maiden at Newcastle in October by 2½
lengths from Megred: not knocked about and never dangerous in nursery later in
month: should be suited by 1m+: may do better. *C. F. Wall*

MISBAH (USA) 2 b.c. (Jan 28) Gilded Time (USA) 118 – For Dixie (USA) 92 p
(Dixieland Band (USA)) [1997 7g⁴ 7m² 7m* Oct 22] $175,000Y: good-topped colt:
first foal: dam won up to 7f in USA: sire (by Timeless Moment) champion US 2-y-o
colt in 1992: progressive colt: won maiden at Yarmouth by 1½ lengths from Chattan,
dictating pace and holding on well: should stay 1m: sent to UAE: has scope to
continue improving. *B. Hanbury*

MISCHIEVOUS TIME 3 ch.g. Clantime 101 – Mischievous Tyke 50 (Flying –
Tyke 90) [1996 NR 1997 5g⁵ 5v⁶ 7.5m⁴ 5g 6m⁵ 8d a6g Nov 14] second foal: half-
brother to 1995 2-y-o Lugana Boy (by Lugana Beach), who was banned from racing
on flat after refusing to race all 3 starts: dam stayed 7.5f: signs of ability but no
worthwhile form. *A. Smith*

MISCONDUCT 3 gr.f. Risk Me (FR) 127 – Grey Cree 64 (Creetown 123) [1996 46
NR 1997 7g a5g 6s a7g a7s³ a8g² a7g³ Dec 22] 3,800Y: lengthy filly: fifth reported
live foal: sister to 2 poor animals: dam 2-y-o 5f and 6f winner: poor maiden: placed
at Lingfield late in year: stays 1m: acts on equitrack. *G. L. Moore*

MISELLINA (FR) 3 b.f. Polish Precedent (USA) 131 – Misallah (IRE) (Shirley – §
Heights 130) [1996 57p: 8.1s⁵ 1997 8d 10m 11.8m 10.8s 8f Sep 29] no form in
1997, for J. S. Moore first 4 starts: refused to race first appearance for new stable.
R. Akehurst

MISHRAAK (IRE) 2 ch.c. (Mar 3) Mujtahid (USA) 118 – Dora Da Caserta 88
(IRE) (Caerleon (USA) 132) [1997 5.1m⁶ 6f² 6d⁴ 5g* 5g⁴ 5m⁶ 5.3m* 5m³ Sep 2]
40,000Y: strong colt: second foal: half-brother to Italian 5f and 6f winner Gyroscope
(by Primo Dominie): dam Italian 9f and 11.5f winner: fairly useful performer: won
nurseries at Folkestone in July and Brighton in August: good third in minor event at
Folkestone final start: likely to prove best at 5f/easy 6f: acts on good to firm ground,
probably on dead: has got on edge and tended to wander: ran creditably when
blinkered once: sold 28,000 gns in October. *R. W. Armstrong*

MISKIN HEIGHTS (IRE) 3 ch.f. Sharp Victor (USA) 114 – Nurse Jo (USA) 35
(J O Tobin (USA) 130) [1996 –: 5g 6m a7g 1997 9s 10.8g⁴ 10m a10g⁶ a8g Dec 2]
only form when fourth of 19 in handicap at Warwick in October. *K. R. Burke*

MISKY BAY 4 b.g. Shareef Dancer (USA) 135 – Rain Date (Rainbow Quest 46 §
(USA) 134) [1996 71§, a60§: 8g 8.5m³ 12.3g 10.5d 8.5m 10g⁴ 10.1g a7g⁴ a7g 1997
a10g⁶ a8g² a8g a7g⁶ Mar 14] small, stocky gelding: fair maiden at best, but has
become thoroughly temperamental, refusing to race when blinkered penultimate
outing and starting very slowly on final one. *D. J. S. Cosgrove*

MISLEAD (IRE) 2 b.f. (Feb 10) Distinctly North (USA) 115 – Chez Nous 77
(Habitat 134) [1997 5g 5g* 7s 5g² 5g* 5m* 5d Aug 13] 3,800 2-y-o: good-quartered
filly: half-sister to a winner over jumps in France by Be My Guest: dam, lightly raced
in France, from good family: fair performer: won seller at Windsor in June and
nurseries at Leicester and Goodwood in July, easily best effort when beating Desert
Lady ½ length on last-named course: tailed off final start: probably a 5f performer:
acts on good to firm ground. *J. S. Moore*

MISLEMANI (IRE) 7 b.g. Kris 135 – Meis El-Reem 124 (Auction Ring (USA) 55 d
123) [1996 53: a8g² a8g a8g³ a9.4g³ 8m 8.5m 7.1m³ 7f 7g 1997 a8g⁶ a8g 8g* 10.2m
7.1g 8f 8.2d a8g a10g Dec 19] sturdy, close-coupled gelding: modest handicapper: off course 5 months, clearly best 7-y-o effort when winning at Bath in
June: stays 9.4f: acts on firm going, dead and fibresand, well beaten on equitrack.
A. G. Newcombe

MISMEWMEW 2 b.f. (Feb 15) Weldnaas (USA) 112 – Joan's Gift (Doulab –
(USA) 115) [1997 6g 6m Sep 2] first foal: dam no form: no promise in maidens,
flashing tail persistently. *C. J. Benstead*

MISS ALICE 3 b.f. Komaite (USA) – Needle Sharp 64 (Kris 135) [1996 –: 5f⁶ –
a7g⁴ 6.1d 7.5m 6s 1997 8g⁶ 10s 16.2m 14.1g⁴ Jul 30] sparely-made filly: little
worthwhile form. *C. Smith*

MISS ALL ALONE   2 ch.f. (Apr 4) Crofthall 110 – Uninvited 73 (Be My Guest – (USA) 126) [1997 5.1m Apr 8] unfurnished filly: second foal: dam, maiden on flat, winning selling hurdler: tailed off in maiden at Nottingham. *J. A. Glover*

MISS ARAGON   9 b.m. Aragon 118 – Lavenham Blue (Streetfighter 120) [1996 50 ? 42: 5.9m 6g 6g⁵ 6f 6.1m 6f 6d⁶ 6m 6m a6g⁴ a6g⁶ a6g³ a6g⁵ a5g³ 1997 6d a6g 6g 6m 6g⁶ 6g⁵ Sep 27] rangy mare: good mover: just a poor handicapper nowadays: only form in 1997 when 20 lb out of handicap on penultimate outing: effective at 5f and 6f: possibly unsuited by very firm ground, acts on any other. *Miss L. C. Siddall*

MISS BANANAS   2 b.f. (Apr 30) Risk Me (FR) 127 – Astrid Gilberto 75 (Runnett 49 125) [1997 a6g⁵ a7g 6g a5g² a5g⁴ a5g³ Dec 19] 400Y: workmanlike filly: fourth foal: sister to 4-y-o Esperto: dam 2-y-o 5f/6f winner: poor maiden on the all-weather: best effort third in claimer at Lingfield: best at 5f. *T. T. Bill*

MISS BARCELONA (IRE)   3 b.f. Mac's Imp (USA) 116 – National Ballet 53 d (Shareef Dancer (USA) 135) [1996 53: 5m 6g² 6m 6g⁵ a5g⁵ 5f² 6m³ 5.7m² 5m⁴ 7m⁴ 6g⁴ 6g 5m⁴ 7m 1997 a7g⁴ a6g 10m⁵ 10f⁴ 12.3g⁶ 10.2m 14.1m 10f⁵ 8g⁴ 7f⁶ 8d³ 8.5s⁴ 8.5m 8g 8m Aug 9] small, workmanlike filly: has a quick action: modest maiden: well beaten last 4 starts: probably stays 1½m: acts on firm ground, probably on dead: often forces pace: none too consistent: sold 14,000 gns in December. *M. J. Polglase*

MISS BEVELED   2 b.f. (Apr 29) Beveled (USA) – Reach Forward 41 (Reach 44 d 122) [1997 5m 5d³ 5d³ a6g⁶ 5m⁶ 5g 5d⁴ 5g a6g a7g Oct 20] 700Y: sparely-made a– filly: first foal: dam (maiden) best at 5f: third in early-season sellers: showed little afterwards: tried visored/blinkered. *M. Brittain*

MISS BUSSELL   2 ch.f. (Mar 2) Sabrehill (USA) 120 – Reel Foyle (USA) 77 65 p (Irish River (FR) 131) [1997 7m Nov 1] third foal: half-sister to 3-y-o Unshaken: dam 5f winner: 50/1, about 10 lengths eighth of 18 to Pontoon in maiden at Newmarket, never dangerous: should do better. *B. W. Hills*

MISS CAROTTENE   4 b.f. Siberian Express (USA) 125 – Silk St James (Pas de – Seul 133) [1996 49d: a7g⁴ a6g* a6g 8f 6.9d a7g a6g 1997 6.1m Apr 8] good-topped filly: well beaten since winning at Lingfield early in 1996. *M. J. Ryan*

MISS CHARLIE   7 ch.m. Pharly (FR) 130 – Close To You 44 (Nebbiolo 125) – [1996 46: a7g 6.9m* 8m⁵ 8f⁴ 8f a6s 1997 a8.5g⁴ a7g a7g a8g a7g⁵ Feb 26] leggy, angular mare: poor performer: well held in 1997: headstrong. *A. Bailey*

MISS CHIEF MAKER   2 ch.f. (Feb 14) Be My Chief (USA) 122 – Waitingfor- – margaret 78 (Kris 135) [1997 6s 6.9m 7g 6f Sep 28] 13,000Y: fourth foal: half-sister to 3 winners, including 3-y-o Brandon Jack and 4-y-o Tarry: dam, 2-y-o 5f winner, out of useful sprinter Princess Seal: no promise in maidens: sold, and sent to Germany. *W. R. Muir*

MISS DANGEROUS   2 b.f. (Apr 29) Komaite (USA) – Khadine 79 (Astec 128) 66 d [1997 5d² 6m 6f 6g⁶ a6g⁴ Oct 6] 6,000Y: rather dipped-backed filly: sister to 4-y-o Forest Boy and half-sister to winner abroad by Night Shift: dam stayer: fair maiden: didn't progress, and ran in seller final start: joined M. Quinn. *M. R. Channon*

MISS DILLETANTE   2 b.f. (Apr 10) Primo Dominie 121 – Misguided 106 – (Homing 130) [1997 7g 7g 6d Sep 20] strong, good-bodied filly: half-sister to several winners, including 3-y-o Scoss and useful winner up to 1¾m Misbelief (by Shirley Heights): dam sprinting half-sister to smart 6f and 1m winner Missed Blessing: only a little sign of ability in maidens. *R. F. Johnson Houghton*

MISSED DOMINO   2 ch.f. (Apr 22) Ron's Victory (USA) 129 – Far Claim 46 (USA) 35 (Far North (CAN) 120) [1997 6m 7.5f 7m Oct 1] 2,100Y: fourth foal: half-sister 5-y-o Media Express (formerly fair winner up to 1m): dam sprint plater: poor form in maidens, though hinted may be capable of better. *Mrs A. Swinbank*

MISSED MAY   3 br.f. Petong 126 – Altara (GER) (Tarim) [1996 NR 1997 a7g⁶ a7g a8g⁵ 12.5m⁶ 12m⁶ 12g 9.9d May 10] half-sister to 3 winners abroad: dam lightly-raced daughter of top German filly Alaria: of little account. *B. P. J. Baugh*

MISSED THE BOAT (IRE)   7 b.g. Cyrano de Bergerac 120 – Lady Portobello – (Porto Bello 118) [1996 42: a12g a16g 12.1m⁶ 12g⁴ 1997 a12g Feb 21] poor handicapper: well beaten only 7-y-o start. *A. G. Newcombe*

MISSED THE CUT (IRE) 2 b.f. (Apr 24) Classic Secret (USA) 91 – Missish 67
(Mummy's Pet 125) [1997 5m² 5f² Oct 3] small, close-coupled filly: has a quick
action: fifth foal: half-sister to 4 winners at up to 7f by Presidium, including 3-y-o
Andreyev: dam unraced: second in autumn maidens at Folkestone and Lingfield: will
stay further than 5f. *R. Hannon*

MISS ELIMINATOR 2 b.f. (Apr 11) Komaite (USA) – Northern Line 92 57 +
(Camden Town 125) [1997 5g 5m³ 5m⁶ 5m* 6m 5m Aug 26] 2,100Y: has been fired:
fourth foal: dam 2-y-o 5f winner: modest performer: won maiden at Beverley in July:
stiff tasks in nurseries afterwards: best form at 5f (too free at 6f): has been bandaged
off-hind: blinkered final 3 starts. *M. W. Easterby*

MISS EQUAL 2 ch.f. (Feb 24) Presidium 124 – Dissolution 73 (Henbit (USA) – §
130) [1997 5.1d 5g a6g Jun 7] 2,100Y: sister to a fairly useful hurdler: dam 2-y-o 7.5f
winner: no form and temperamental. *M. C. Pipe*

MISSFORTUNA 3 b.f. Priolo (USA) 127 – Lucky Round 82 (Auction Ring 71
(USA) 123) [1996 66p: 6m 6.1m 7d 1997 10m* 11.7f² 9m⁴ 10.2g 11.1m³ 10m Oct 1]
sturdy filly: fair performer: won maiden at Nottingham in July: best subsequent
efforts when placed: stays 1½m: acts on firm going: sold 17,000 gns in October. *Sir
Mark Prescott*

MISS FUGIT PENANCE 3 br.f. Puissance 110 – Figment 75 (Posse (USA) –
130) [1996 –: 5m⁶ 5m 5m 1997 5.1g a6g May 1] no form. *P. D. Evans*

MISS GOLDEN SANDS 3 ch.f. Kris 135 – Miss Kuta Beach 91 (Bold Lad 80
(IRE) 133) [1996 71: 6g 6m⁶ 1997 8g⁵ Mar 29] strong filly: fluent mover: fairly
useful performer: best effort on only start of 1997, fifth of 8 to Calypso Grant in listed
race at Kempton, setting good pace: stays 1m. *G. Wragg*

MISS HIT 2 b.f. (Mar 1) Efisio 120 – Jennies' Gem (Sayf El Arab (USA) 127) –
[1997 5g Apr 25] 6,000Y: third foal: half-sister to 1996 2-y-o 5f seller winner Hit Or
Miss (by Be My Chief): dam won 3 times at 5f at 2 yrs: burly and green, behind in
maiden at Sandown: joined Miss G. Kelleway. *M. R. Channon*

MISSILE TOE (IRE) 4 b.g. Exactly Sharp (USA) 121 – Debach Dust 64 (Indian 60
King (USA) 128) [1996 68: 6g 7m 6m⁶ 6f⁵ 6f 5m 7m⁵ 8m⁴ 8m² 8f² 8m 8g³ 1997
8m 8.1g⁶ 10.1m² 10m a10g a10g Dec 2] good-topped colt: poor walker: modest
handicapper: off course over 4 months, well beaten last 3 starts: stays 1¼m well: acts
on firm ground and fibresand: below form in blinkers and visor: takes good hold.
D. Morris

MISS IMP (IRE) 3 b.f. Mac's Imp (USA) 116 – Be Nimble (Wattlefield 117) –
[1996 NR 1997 7g 8g 7g 10.8g a10g a10g Dec 19] 6,200Y: fourth foal: half-sister to
fair 5f and 6f winner Trentesimo (by Imperial Frontier): dam Irish 7f winner: of no
account. *P. Mitchell*

MISS KALAGLOW 3 b.f. Kalaglow 132 – Dame du Moulin 81 (Shiny Tenth 55
120) [1996 –: 8.2m 7.9g 1997 7.6g² 10g a11g Sep 8] lightly-made filly: only form
when neck second in maiden at Lingfield on reappearance: should be suited by
further than 1m. *C. F. Wall*

MISS KEMBLE 3 b.f. Warning 136 – Sarah Siddons (FR) 122 (Le Levanstell –
122) [1996 NR 1997 10.2m Jul 7] sister to useful 1m winner Side Note (now in USA)
and half-sister to high-class 1¼m to 1½m performers Seymour Hicks (by Ballymore)
and Princess Pati (by Top Ville), the dam of Pasternak, among other winners: dam
won Irish 1000 Guineas and Yorkshire Oaks: green, well beaten in maiden at Bath:
sold 27,000 gns in December. *B. W. Hills*

MISS LADY LYDIA 2 ch.f. (Apr 5) Tina's Pet 121 – Kinfauns Dancer (Celtic –
Cone 116) [1997 5m 6g a6g Nov 13] 400F: first foal: dam lightly-raced maiden
hurdler: no sign of ability. *Jamie Poulton*

MISS MAIN STREET (IRE) 2 b.f. (Feb 27) Shalford (IRE) 124§ – Bonvin 57
(Taufan (USA) 119) [1997 5g 6g⁵ 7g⁴ 7m* 7.5d⁴ 7.9s 8m Sep 25] IR 4,000Y: sturdy
filly: has a round action: half-sister to 1992 2-y-o 1m winner Bonarme (by Vacarme):
dam Irish 5f (at 2 yrs) and 1m winner: modest performer: won nursery at Newcastle
in August: well below form final 2 outings: stays 7.5f: acts on good to firm and dead
ground. *J. J. Quinn*

MISS MEZZANINE   3 b.f. Norton Challenger 111 – Forest Fawn (FR) 51 (Top   –
Ville 129) [1996 –: 8.1s 1997 10m 9m 10.2m 14.1g 11.6m Aug 11] of no account.
E. A. Wheeler

MISS MIGHTY   4 b.f. Bigivor – Fancy Blue (Fine Blue 103) [1996 NR 1997   –
a8.5g Jul 25] non-thoroughbred filly: second foal: dam never ran: tailed off only flat
outing. *J. H. Peacock*

MISS MONEY SPIDER (IRE)   2 b.f. (Apr 8) Statoblest 120 – Dream of Jenny   65 p
73 (Caerleon (USA) 132) [1997 6v⁵ a5s⁵ Nov 10] leggy filly: second reported foal:
dam, maiden who ran only at 2 yrs (suited by 7f+), from good family: some promise
when fifth in maidens at Ascot and Lingfield: joined N. Callaghan: should improve.
R. Hannon

MISS MUFFETT (IRE)   2 b.f. (Apr 14) Hero's Honor (USA) – Grain de Folie   48
(FR) (Top Ville 129) [1997 6s 6g 6d⁶ 7m⁶ 7f⁴ 7m a8g Dec 10] 2,000F: first foal: dam
unraced close relative of Gravieres, Grade 1 9f winner in USA: poor maiden: should
stay 1m: acts on firm ground, probably on dead. *P. Mooney*

MISS OFFSET   4 ch.f. Timeless Times (USA) 99 – Farinara (Dragonara Palace   –
(USA) 115) [1996 40, a73: a8g a10g⁵ a6g* a6g⁵ a6g⁴ a7g* a7g⁴ 7.1g³ a7g² a7g* a6g³
7.5g 8.1g 6d⁵ 7.1f a7g a6g* a7s⁶ 1997 a7f Jan 11] leggy filly: fair handicapper on the
all-weather, poor on turf: ran as if something amiss only 4-y-o start. *M. Johnston*

MISS PEREGRINE   3 b.f. Polar Falcon (USA) 126 – Good Thinking (USA)   51
(Raja Baba (USA)) [1996 NR 1997 6.1d⁴ 7m 5m⁵ 6d³ Jun 28] 13,000Y: small,
deep-girthed filly: half-sister to fair 7f and 1½m winner Thinking Twice (by Kris)
and winners in USA by Fappiano and Northern Baby: dam Irish 2-y-o 7f winner:
modest maiden: needs further than 5f: joined N. Babbage. *R. Guest*

MISS PICKPOCKET (IRE)   4 b.f. Petorius 117 – Fingers (Lord Gayle (USA)   46
124) [1996 58d: a6g³ a5g² a6g⁵ 7.1m a7g 1997 a6g⁶ a6g³ Jan 18] leggy filly: only
poor form in 1997: stayed 7f: acted on dead ground and the all-weather: sold IR
17,500 gns in November, in foal to Lake Coniston. *Miss Gay Kelleway*

MISS PIGALLE   6 b.m. Good Times (ITY) – Panayr (Faraway Times (USA)   44
123) [1996 44: 7d³ 7.1g³ 6.9g 8.1f² 7.1g 8.1m⁴ 7m³ 7g³ 6m 7m 8m 8.1s 1997 10.1*
8m 7d 8d⁴ 7g² 7m 7g⁵ 8.3g Sep 29] leggy mare: poor handicapper: won at Musselburgh in May: effective at 7f/1m: acts on firm and dead ground: effective blinkered
or not: inconsistent. *Miss L. A. Perratt*

MISS PRAVDA   4 ch.f. Soviet Star (USA) 128 – Miss Paige (AUS) (Luskin Star   –
(AUS)) [1996 52d: 8g 8m* 8f 9.7m⁴ 10f⁵ 10f⁶ 12.1m 14.1m⁴ a12g⁴ a11g a14.8g⁵
a12g a14.8g 1997 11.9f 13.1d May 19] plain filly: modest form at best: well beaten
in 1997: in foal to Son Pardo. *B. J. Llewellyn*

MISS PRISM   4 b.f. Niniski (USA) 125 – Reflected Glory (SWE) (Relko 136)   53
[1996 60: 8g 12m 12.5f⁴ 16m³ 16m a16g² 13.1m² 15.4g² 17.9g 13.8g² 12.1s a14.8g²
a16g² 1997 a12g a12g⁶ Jan 25] angular filly: modest maiden handicapper: lacks a
turn of foot, and runner-up on 6 occasions: stays 2m: acts on the all-weather and on
firm ground: blinkered in 1997. *J. L. Dunlop*

MISS PUCI   2 b.f. (Feb 15) Puissance 110 – Kind of Shy 61 (Kind of Hush 118)   66
[1997 5g³ a5g⁶ 5d³ 5m³ 6m⁴ 5f* 6.1m Sep 15] 5,400Y: leggy filly: third foal: sister to
a 2-y-o 5f winner and half-sister to a 2-y-o 6f seller winner by Mon Tresor: dam,
plater, stayed 1m: fair performer: won maiden at Carlisle in August: stiffish task
when well held in nursery subsequently: stays 6f: acts on firm ground, well beaten in
one run on fibresand. *J. Berry*

MISS PUGH   2 b.f. (May 12) Puissance 110 – Crymlyn 68 (Welsh Pageant 132)   –
[1997 6s 6m Aug 6] big, leggy filly: seventh reported foal: half-sister to 3 winners,
including 1992 2-y-o 7f winner Cropton (by Flash of Steel), later successful in USA,
and fairly useful 1m to 1¼m winner Rory (by Dowsing): dam, maiden, stayed 7f:
never a factor in maidens at Newcastle. *C. W. Fairhurst*

MISS RIVIERA   4 b.f. Kris 135 – Miss Beaulieu 106 (Northfields (USA)) [1996   103
103: 9.9m² 8m⁴ 10.4m⁶ 8f² 7g² 7m³ 8g³ 8g³ 8f² 1997 7d⁶ 8d³ 7m³ 7.3m 7f³ 7g⁴ Sep
20] compact filly: useful performer: hasn't won since 2 yrs, but creditable efforts
when in frame in listed races at Goodwood (2), Doncaster (beaten narrowly by Aunty

Jane and Dazzle) and Longchamp in 1997: best at 7f/1m: acts on firm and dead going: races keenly. *G. Wragg*

MISS RIVIERA ROSE   3 ch.f. Niniski (USA) 125 – Miss Beaulieu 106 (North-   78 d
fields (USA)) [1996 61: 6m⁵ 6m 1997 10m⁴ 10s 10.2f² 10m⁵ 10.2d⁶ 8g 10.1m⁴ a7g
8f³ 8f 10.3g Oct 25] lengthy, dipped-backed filly: capable of fair form up to 1¼m,
but is still a maiden, and has gone the wrong way temperamentally: sold, and sent to
Germany. *G. Wragg*

MISS SALSA DANCER   2 ch.f. (Apr 30) Salse (USA) 128 – Thakhayr (Sadler's   59
Wells (USA) 132) [1997 6m⁵ 6g³ 6m⁴ 8d⁶ 7s Oct 17] 5,200Y, 28,000 2-y-o: small,
close-coupled filly: fifth foal: half-sister to a winner up to 1m in USA by Kris: dam
once-raced: modest maiden: stays 1m: well beaten on soft going. *Denys Smith*

MISS SANCERRE   3 b.f. Last Tycoon 131 – Miss Bergerac (Bold Lad (IRE)   95
133) [1996 86p: 6g² 7d* 1997 7g⁴ Apr 15] tall, lengthy filly: has a quick action:
useful performer: best effort when 5½ lengths fourth of 10 to Reunion in Nell Gwyn
Stakes at Newmarket on only start in 1997: should stay 1m. *G. Wragg*

MISS SCOOTER   2 ch.f. (May 1) Beveled (USA) – Donosa (Posse (USA) 130)   53 ?
[1997 5m 5m² a5g⁶ 5.3f⁵ Jul 16] fourth foal: sister to a poor sprint plater: dam
probably of little account: poor form, including in sellers: has given trouble at stalls.
A. P. Jones

MISS SKYE (IRE)   2 b.f. (Mar 31) Common Grounds 118 – Swift Chorus (Music   52
Boy 124) [1997 5g 6s 7m⁶ 7d⁵ 7.6m 6d a8g³ a7g⁶ a7g Dec 18] 6,500Y: third foal:
sister to Italian 3-y-o 7f (at 2 yrs) and 8.5f winner Anegada Passage and half-sister to
a 2-y-o 5f winner by Taufan: dam, Irish 2-y-o 6f winner, from good middle-distance
family: modest maiden: ran badly in seller at Southwell final start: will probably
prove best around 1m: acts on equitrack. *T. J. Naughton*

MISS SLENDER   2 gr.f. (Mar 29) Inchinor 119 – Tulapet (Mansingh (USA) 120)   –
[1997 6m 6.1g 7m Oct 5] 13,500Y: close-coupled filly: second foal: dam, poor
maiden (stayed 7f), sister to Petong: well beaten in maidens. *R. Hannon*

MISS ST KITTS   3 ch.f. Risk Me (FR) 127 – So Beguiling (USA) 49 (Woodman   – §
(USA) 126) [1996 –§: 5f⁶ 5f⁶ 5f 1997 5g 7.1d 5d 5m Jul 21] unsatisfactory maiden:
tried visored. *J. S. Goldie*

MISS THE BEAT   5 b.m. Music Boy 124 – Bad Start (USA) (Bold Bidder) [1996   –
NR 1997 a12g Jan 15] soundly beaten in claimers. *S. Mellor*

MISS VITA (USA)   3 b.f. Alleged (USA) 138 – Torrid Tango (USA) (Green   57
Dancer (USA) 132) [1996 NR 1997 8m⁵ 12.3s⁴ 10m 9.7m³ 12m Oct 31] 360,000
francs Y: sparely-made filly: third foal: half-sister to a winner in USA by North
Prospect: dam lightly-raced half-sister to Suavite (by Alleged), the dam of Suave
Dancer: modest maiden: best efforts at 1¼m. *R. J. R. Williams*

MISS VIVIEN   2 b.f. (Feb 24) Puissance 110 – Madam Bold (Never So Bold 135)   73
[1997 6m⁶ 6m⁴ 7d⁴ 6m* 6s Oct 14] 11,500Y: leggy filly: fourth foal: half-sister to a
6f winner in Sweden by Midyan, and 1994 2-y-o 5f winner Rigsby (by Fools Holme):
dam (unraced) from family of Sigy and Sonoma: fair performer: well ridden to win
nursery at Pontefract in October, racing wide and poaching clear lead off turn: faded
final 1f in testing conditions next time: likely to prove best at short of 1m: acts on
good to firm ground. *Miss L. A. Perratt*

MISS WATERLINE   4 br.f. Rock City 120 – Final Shot 91 (Dalsaan 125) [1996   –
77: 6g 6m 6m² 7m⁶ 6g 5m 6m⁶ 7.1s 6g 6f 1997 6m Mar 21] neat filly: fair handicapper at 3 yrs: well held only start in 1997. *P. D. Evans*

MISS ZAFONIC (FR)   2 b.f. (Mar 20) Zafonic (USA) 130 – Miss Silca Key 102   98
(Welsh Saint 126) [1997 6m* 6d² 6g⁴ 6m Sep 30] rather leggy, unfurnished filly:
half-sister to several winners, including smart Central City (by Midyan), best at up to
7f, and useful 6f winner Silca Supreme (by Chief Singer): dam won Jersey Stakes:
useful form: won maiden at Windsor in July in good style: in frame in Princess
Margaret Stakes at Ascot (2 lengths second to Embassy) and Lowther Stakes at York
(4½ lengths fourth behind Cape Verdi): last of 8 in Cheveley Park Stakes at Newmarket: headstrong sort (has had 2 handlers in paddock) and may prove effective at
5f: sent to UAE. *R. Hannon*

MISTER ASPECTO (IRE)   4 b.g. Caerleon (USA) 132 – Gironde (USA) (Raise   60
A Native) [1996 78: a8.5g⁴ a12g² a12g* a10g* a11g* 9g 9.9m⁵ 12.5f⁵ 12m⁵ 12f³   a84
15.1f² 15.1g³ 12m* 13m* 14.1m⁴ 12m 16.1m³ 15.8g⁶ 1997 a12g³ 13.8g 13d 21.6g
a12g² 13.1g a14g³ a16.2g³ a12g² 12m² a16g* a16g* 12.1m⁵ 14g³ a12g² 14.1g
14.1d Oct 30] quite good-topped gelding: fairly useful on the all-weather, modest
on turf: won minor event and handicap at Lingfield in August: effective at 1½m to
2m: acts on firm ground, well held on dead: usually blinkered/visored: sometimes
goes in snatches/flashes tail/carries head awkwardly: usually races prominently.
M. Johnston

MISTER BANKES   2 ch.g. (Mar 24) Risk Me (FR) 127 – Eternal Triangle (USA)   82 d
76 (Barachois (CAN)) [1997 5m² 5d* 5.3f⁵ 5m⁶ 6g⁴ 5g⁶ 5.1m⁴ 5d Jun 30] 1,800F,
6,800Y: good-topped gelding: second reported foal: dam 2-y-o sprint winner who
stayed 1m: fair performer: won maiden at Hamilton in April: probably best at 5f: acts
on good to firm and dead ground, didn't seem at ease on firm: blinkered (well below
form) sixth start: usually a front runner: sent to Macau. *W. G. M. Turner*

MISTER BENJAMIN (IRE)   2 b.g. (Apr 17) Polish Patriot (USA) 128 – Frau   74 +
Ahuyentante (ARG) (Frari (ARG)) [1997 7g⁶ a7g* 8d Oct 17] IR 15,000Y: quite
good-topped gelding: half-brother to Irish 11f winner Miss Roberto (by Don
Roberto) and several winners abroad: dam unraced: won maiden at Southwell in
September, making all and eased: in rear in Newmarket nursery following month:
should stay beyond 7f. *S. P. C. Woods*

MISTER BUNCH   2 b.g. (Mar 12) Efisio 120 – Mellow Gold (Meldrum 112)   –
[1997 7.5d 7g 8.2m Sep 15] deep-girthed gelding: first foal: dam second in novice
hurdle: well beaten in maidens. *E. Weymes*

Maktoum Al Maktoum's "Miss Zafonic"

MIS

MISTER DAMASK   2 b.c. (Mar 27) Damister (USA) 123 – Smelter 111 (Prominer 125) [1997 5.1m Jun 4] 6,600Y: brother to 2 winners abroad and half-brother to 2 winners in Ireland, including 1m (at 2 yrs) and 9f winner Northern Vision (by Vision): dam won twice at 7f from 3 starts in Ireland: tailed off in maiden at Chester. *E. J. Alston*   –

MISTER GLUM   3 ch.g. Ron's Victory (USA) 129 – Australia Fair (AUS) (Without Fear (FR) 128) [1996 NR 1997 6m Apr 22] ninth living foal: half-brother to useful sprinter Double Blue (by Town And Country) and a winner abroad: dam once-raced daughter of a useful Australian middle-distance stayer: last of 10 in maiden at Folkestone, carrying head high. *I. A. Balding*   –

MISTER JAY   3 b.g. Batshoof 122 – Portvasco 90 (Sharpo 132) [1996 47: 6m 7.6d⁶ 8d 1997 8f 9f 11.6s a14g 10m Aug 16] dipped-backed gelding: little form, including in a seller and a visor: left P. Walwyn after third start. *K. A. Morgan*   –

MISTER JOLSON   8 br.g. Latest Model 115 – Impromptu 88 (My Swanee 122) [1996 81: 6s 6g⁴ 5g* 6m 5.1f 6m² 6g 5m* 6f³ 5m 6m 6.1d 1997 6d³ 6s⁵ 6g⁶ 6f 5d⁵ 5.1s 5m³ 5.1g³ 6g 6g 6d² Oct 21] workmanlike gelding: impresses in appearance: fairly useful handicapper: won at Kempton in May: tried in blinkers for only second time, good effort final start: effective at 5f/6f: acts on good to firm and soft ground and on equitrack: held up. *R. J. Hodges*   81

MISTER PINK   3 gr.g. Absalom 128 – Blush Rambler (IRE) (Blushing Groom (FR) 131) [1996 84: 6s⁵ 6m³ 6f² 7m³ 7m* 7.3m³ 8m 10f³ 10g⁶ 1997 10.5s* 10m 12m³ 12.3s⁵ 12d 16.1g 12m 11.9s³ 14d Oct 17] leggy, lengthy gelding: had a round action: fairly useful handicapper: won at Haydock in March: mostly disappointing afterwards: stayed 1½m well: acted on firm and soft going: ran well in visor/blinkers at 2 yrs: dead. *R. F. Johnson Houghton*   90

MISTER RAIDER   5 ch.g. Ballacashtal (CAN) – Martian Melody 62 (Enchantment 115) [1996 52, a58: a6g a7g a6g* a7g⁵ a7g 5.1m⁵ 5m³ 6f a5g* a5g a5g a5g* 1997 a6g⁶ a5g 5m⁵ 6m 5.3f² 5m 6m* 6s a5g³ 5.3m 5m⁴ 6f⁶ 6m a5g² a5g a6g⁴ a5g³ Dec 22] fair handicapper on all-weather, modest on turf: won seller at Leicester in June: generally ran creditably after: effective at 5f/6f: acts on firm ground, dead and equitrack: wears blinkers. *E. A. Wheeler*   52 a65

MISTER RAMBO   2 b.g. (Apr 20) Rambo Dancer (CAN) 107 – Ozra 63 (Red Alert 127) [1997 6g* Oct 24] 8,400Y: brother to 3-y-o Lightning Rebel and a poor maiden and half-brother to useful 6f (at 2 yrs) to 1m winner Jimlil (by Nicholas Bill): dam 6f/7f winner: 20/1, won 24-runner maiden at Newbury, strong run to catch Fa-Eq close home: should stay 1m: should improve. *B. J. Meehan*   87 p

MISTER SEAN (IRE)   4 b.g. Mac's Imp (USA) 116 – Maid of Mourne (Fairy King (USA)) [1996 –: 5m 5m 5g 5.1g 1997 5g 5.1g 5.1m 7f 6f 5.1m 5m 5g Sep 1] of little account. *J. M. Bradley*   –

MISTERTON   3 ch.g. Mystiko (USA) 124 – South Shore 102 (Caerleon (USA) 132) [1996 NR 1997 8.2m 9.9m 7.5s 8f 8.2d⁶ 12v 10m⁶ 10.8g* 10.1g a11g a8g Dec 18] sturdy gelding: third foal: half-brother to useful 6f/7f performer South Rock (by Rock City) and 4-y-o Stonecutter: dam (stayed 1½m) out of Oaks fourth Shore Line: poor performer: best effort when winning claiming handicap at Warwick in October: stays 11f: best efforts on good ground or firmer: tried blinkered. *J. A. Glover*   42

MISTER TRICKY   2 ch.c. (Apr 5) Magic Ring (IRE) 115 – Splintering 80 (Sharpo 132) [1997 7d a10s⁶ Nov 28] 2,800 2-y-o: fifth foal: half-brother to 3 winners, including sprinter Midnight Break (by Night Shift) and 7f winner Smithereens (by Primo Dominie), later successful in USA: dam sprinter: signs of just a little ability in maidens. *P. Mitchell*   –

MISTER WESTSOUND   5 b.g. Cyrano de Bergerac 120 – Captivate 79 (Mansingh (USA) 120) [1996 73d: 6d² 6m³ 5.9m⁵ 6d³ 6g⁴ 6m³ 7m⁵ 7m⁶ 6m 6d⁵ 6m⁶ 6f 6m 6f 7g 6m⁴ 8.1s 1997 6d 5.9g 8.3s 7s 8g 5g⁴ 6g* 7d* 6d² 6m 7m 6g³ 7m Oct 28] workmanlike gelding: modest handicapper: had plummeted in weights prior to winning at Hamilton and Ayr in June: stays 7f: acts on firm and dead ground: has been visored, blinkered nowadays: tends to start slowly and get well behind: sometimes hangs. *Miss L. A. Perratt*   54

MISTER WOODSTICK (IRE)   4 b.g. Distinctly North (USA) 115 – Crannog –
(Habitat 134) [1996 60: 6s 8.3d 8m* 7m³ 8m* 8m⁶ 8f 8g³ 7f⁶ 8.1d 1997 8.3g Sep 1]
robust gelding: modest handicapper at 3 yrs for M. Jarvis: well held only 4-y-o start,
but won selling hurdle in November. *C. Parker*

MISTRAL LORD (IRE)   3 br.g. Fairy King (USA) – Walkyria (Lord Gayle –
(USA) 124) [1996 NR 1997 8g 7m 10m Aug 18] 13,500F, 800 (from L. Cumani)
2-y-o: half-brother to 3 winners, including 5-y-o Harvey White and useful 5f to 7.6f
winner Corals Dream (both by Petorius): dam Irish middle-distance winner from
family of Slip Anchor: well beaten in maidens and claimer. *M. Madgwick*

MISTY CAY (IRE)   3 b.f. Mujadil (USA) 119 – Quai Des Brumes (USA) (Little   62
Current (USA)) [1996 65d: 5.3f³ 6g⁴ 6f* 6m² 7m³ 7g* 7g⁵ 8m⁶ 7m⁵ 7g a6g⁴ 1997   a57
a8g* a7g* a8g⁵ a7g³ a8g⁴ a7g³ 8.1m 8g 8m² 8g* Sep 3] leggy filly: modest performer: won 2 claimers at Lingfield in January and another at Brighton in September:
stays 1m: acts on firm ground and equitrack: sometimes gets behind early: fair
winning hurdler for Mrs V. Ward. *S. Dow*

MISTY MOOR   2 b.f. (Mar 8) Wolfhound (USA) 126 – Corley Moor 97 (Habitat   60
134) [1997 5g² 6d Aug 25] half-sister to several winners, including useful 1m and 9f
winner (stays 1¼m) Alkateb (by Rock City) and middle-distance performer Shirley
Rose (by Shirley Heights): dam 2-y-o 5f winner: 6 lengths second to Bay Prince in
maiden at Pontefract, but slowly away and green: well beaten at Epsom 8 days later:
should stay 6f. *M. Johnston*

MISTY POINT   3 ch.f. Sharpo 132 – Clouded Vision 74 (So Blessed 130) [1996   67
NR 1997 8g⁴ 8f 7.1d 6g³ 7g⁵ 7g⁵ 6g² 8d Oct 13] half-sister to several winners,
including fairly useful pair Clouded Elegance (up to 1¼m, by Elegant Air) and
Voltage (1½m, by Electric): dam 6f winner: fair maiden: well below form last 2
starts: stays 1m: best efforts on good ground. *I. A. Balding*

MISTY RAIN   3 br.f. Polar Falcon (USA) 126 – Ballerine (USA) (Lyphard's Wish   61
(FR) 124) [1996 –p: 6m 1997 7g a8.5g⁴ 8f 10s³ 9m⁵ 9.9d⁴ 10g³ 7g 9m 10m Oct 23]
leggy filly: modest maiden handicapper: needs further than 7f, and stays 1¼m: acts
on firm and soft ground: tends to hang left: sold and joined J. Spearing. *B. W. Hills*

MITCH PASSI (IRE)   2 ch.g. (Apr 9) Exit To Nowhere (USA) 122 – Stormed   78 p
(USA) (Storm Bird (CAN) 134) [1997 7m 6s² a5s⁴ Nov 10] 15,500F, 28,000Y:
second foal: dam, French maiden, closely related to smart sprinter Dancing Dissident: best effort in maidens when short-head second at Catterick in October: should
still do better, particularly in handicaps. *Sir Mark Prescott*

MITHAK (USA)   3 b.g. Silver Hawk (USA) 123 – Kapalua Butterfly (USA)   99
(Stage Door Johnny) [1996 81p: 7g³ 7m³ 1997 10.3m* 12g³ 11.9g⁵ 14m⁴ 12m⁶
13.9g² 13.9s 14d² Oct 17] rather unfurnished gelding: useful performer: won maiden
at Doncaster in March: good second in handicaps at York (rated stakes) and
Newmarket: will stay 2m: acts on good to firm and dead ground: effective blinkered/
visored (wore neither at Newmarket, where took long time to respond): sold 35,000
gns in October, then gelded and joined Mrs J. Ramsden. *B. W. Hills*

MITHALI   4 b.c. Unfuwain (USA) 131 – Al Bahathri (USA) 123 (Blushing   102
Groom (FR) 131) [1996 NR 1997 a8f⁶ 7m 8.2d* 7.3m 10m⁵ 10.3m* 10m* 9g Oct
25] tall, useful-looking colt: good mover: sixth foal: closely related to 1m winners
Goalwah (useful) and Alyakkh (both by Sadler's Wells) and half-brother to very
useful 7f/1m performer Hasbah (by Kris): dam won Lowther Stakes and Irish 1000
Guineas: behind in 2 races in Dubai in the spring: useful form here, winning maiden
at Nottingham in June and minor events at Doncaster in September and Leicester in
October (by ½ length from Zerpour): stays 1¼m: yet to race on extremes of going:
races prominently: stays in training. *B. W. Hills*

MIZOG   2 b.f. (Apr 9) Selkirk (USA) 129 – Embroideress 80 (Stanford 121§)   –
[1997 7m Sep 28] 3,000 2-y-o: leggy filly: eighth foal: half-sister to 3 winners,
including fairly useful sprinter Sacque (by Elegant Air) and 1m and 1¼m seller
winner Tom Clapton (by Daring March): dam 5f to 7f winner: tailed off in £12,000
event at Ascot. *J. E. Long*

MIZYAN (IRE)   9 b.g. Melyno 130 – Maid of Erin (USA) (Irish River (FR) 131)   –
[1996 60, a65: a14.8g⁵ a16g⁴ a16g³ 15.4f⁵ 14.1m³ 14.9f⁵ 14.9m² 16m³ 16.1m⁶ 16m⁶   a58

17.1m 18g 1997 a16.2g⁶ 13.8g Aug 5] tall gelding: has a round action: fairly useful hurdler: modest handicapper on flat: stays 2m: acts on good to firm and dead ground, and the all-weather: blinkered (no improvement) twice at 5 yrs. *J. E. Banks*

MO-ADDAB (IRE) 7 b.g. Waajib 121 – Tissue Paper 95 (Touch Paper 113) [1996 82: 8m 8s⁴ 8m 8m 8g 8m 8m² 8g 1997 8.1g* 8d³ 8d³ 8g 8g 8g 8d 8m 8g 8d Oct 28] useful-looking gelding: fair performer: won minor event at Chepstow in May: well beaten in handicaps last 2 starts: best efforts at 1m: acts on firm and soft going: sometimes flashes tail: has run well when sweating. *A. C. Stewart* — 78

MOCKERY 2 b.f. (Apr 22) Nashwan (USA) 135 – Laughsome 76 (Be My Guest (USA) 126) [1997 7m Nov 1] second foal: dam, 9f winner, half-sister to smart middle-distance fillies Braiswick and Percy's Lass out of Oaks fourth Laughing Girl, an excellent family: 20/1, slowly away and always behind in maiden at Newmarket: should do better: sent to France. *M. R. Stoute* — – p

MOCK TRIAL (IRE) 4 b.g. Old Vic 136 – Test Case 90 (Busted 134) [1996 67: 7s 7g 8.5m 8m⁶ 10d² 12m* 12m² 17.1m 12g² 15m⁵ 10.3g 1997 10d 12.4m⁶ May 5] tall, strong gelding: fair handicapper: well beaten in 1997. *Mrs J. R. Ramsden* — –

MODESTO (USA) 9 b.g. Al Nasr (FR) 126 – Modena (USA) (Roberto (USA) 131) [1996 NR 1997 a11g Jul 21] very lightly raced these days, and tailed off only start in 1997. *K. O. Cunningham-Brown* — –

MOET (IRE) 2 b.f. (Mar 22) Mac's Imp (USA) 116 – Comfrey Glen 63 (Glenstal (USA) 118) [1997 7.5g⁶ Aug 23] 4,900 2-y-o: fifth foal: half-sister to a winner in Austria by Legend of France: dam (maiden) stayed 1m: 20/1, never-dangerous sixth of 8 in maiden at Beverley. *J. L. Eyre* — 53

MOGIN 4 ch.f. Komaite (USA) – Misdevious (USA) (Alleged (USA) 138) [1996 56, a46: a6g a8g⁶ a6g⁴ a7g⁴ a6g a6g³ 8.3g⁴ 7g 7m* a8g 8g a8g a8g² 1997 a8g a10g 7m 8f a8g³ a7g⁶ Dec 19] big, plain filly: poor performer: stays 1m: acts on good to firm going and the all-weather: has given trouble at stalls. *T. J. Naughton* — – a46

MOGUL 3 b.g. Formidable (USA) 125 – Madiyla 73 (Darshaan 133) [1996 –p: 8s a7g⁵ 1997 a10g² a10g² 10.3m 10g 14.1g a9.4f⁶ a10g Jul 26] tall, workmanlike gelding: fair maiden at best: first past the post in weak race at Lingfield in February on second start, but edged right and demoted: well held in handicaps and minor event afterwards, including in blinkers: should stay 1½m: acts on equitrack. *N. A. Graham* — 66

MOHAWK (IRE) 2 b.c. (Feb 1) Indian Ridge 123 – Dazzling Fire (IRE) 78 (Bluebird (USA) 125) [1997 6m³ 6g⁴ a7g⁵ 7m 7f³ 6g Oct 25] 18,000Y: sturdy, lengthy filly: first foal: dam 1½m winner: fair form when in frame in maidens and a nursery: well beaten otherwise, including on fibresand: should stay beyond 7f. *J. L. Dunlop* — 66

MOHAWK RIVER (IRE) 4 b.c. Polish Precedent (USA) 131 – High Hawk 124 (Shirley Heights 130) [1996 92: 11d⁴ 10.4g* 11.8m⁴ 1997 10g* 13.9g⁵ 13.4s Aug 30] lengthy, good sort: useful handicapper: readily won at Newmarket in August: ran well considering inexperience (only fifth race) when fifth to Far Ahead in Tote Ebor at York later in month: may prove best around 1½m: seemed unsuited by soft going final start: sold approx. £71,000 in Dubai in November. *M. R. Stoute* — 101 p

MOI CANARD 4 ch.c. Bold Owl 101 – Royal Scots Greys 38 (Blazing Saddles (AUS)) [1996 61, a73: a7g⁶ a6g² a7g* a7g² a7g³ a7g* 6f⁵ 7m 7f⁴ 7m a8.5g 6.9g 7m a7g 1997 8d 10m 9d 5.3m⁴ 6m⁶ 7m a7g a6g Sep 20] compact colt: just a poor handicapper in 1997: should stay 1m: acts on firm ground and all-weather surfaces, below form on soft: tried blinkered: held up. *B. A. Pearce* — 42 a–

MOLE CREEK 2 gr.f. (Apr 30) Unfuwain (USA) 131 – Nicholas Grey 100 (Track Spare 125) [1997 7d Nov 7] 52,000Y: rather leggy, useful-looking filly: closely related to a listed winner in Italy by Dance In Time and half-sister to several winners, notably very smart 9f to 1½m performer Terimon (by Bustino): dam 2-y-o 5f to 7f winner, second in Oaks d'Italia: 20/1 and on toes, about 8 lengths seventh of 18 to High-Rise in maiden at Doncaster, held up and not given hard time: sure to do better over 1¼m+. *J. R. Fanshawe* — 62 p

MOLLY MUSIC 3 b.f. Music Boy 124 – Carlton Glory (Blakeney 126) [1996 48: 5s⁴ 5d³ 5d³ 5.1g⁶ a5g⁴ 6d⁶ 5m² a5g⁴ a5g 1997 5g⁶ a7g³ a7g² a8g* 7d a7g⁵ a8.5g⁶ — – a62

MON

8g a7g³ a8.5g³ a7g⁴ a8g² a7g⁵ Nov 29] sturdy filly: modest handicapper on all-weather: won at Southwell in June: stays 8.5f: acts on fibresand, little recent form on turf: has been blinkered/visored (only on reappearance in 1997). *G. G. Margarson*

MOMENTARILY (USA) 2 b.f. (Feb 27) Gilded Time (USA) 118 – Saratoga 58 +
Dame (USA) (Saratoga Six (USA)) [1997 6.1m⁵ Jul 19] $32,000F, $16,000Y: first foal: dam minor stakes winner up to 9f in USA: sire (by Timeless Moment) champion US 2-y-o colt in 1992: 11/1, 9¼ lengths fifth in maiden at Nottingham, hampered inside last 2f and unable to recover. *E. A. L. Dunlop*

MONAASSIB 6 ch.g. Cadeaux Genereux 131 – Pluvial 90 (Habat 127) [1996 117
106: 7m² 7.9m⁵ 7.6f⁶ 6f 7g² 7m 6m* 6.5d² 7m² 1997 6m* 6g* 6d* 6f* 6g⁴ 6g*
6.5d² 6d 6m² Sep 27]

The Ed Dunlop stable lost its best horse, the very smart sprinter Iktamal, to the Godolphin operation before the latest season began but found an immediate replacement to contest the top sprints in Monaassib. It would have been asking a lot for Monaassib to make as much progress as Iktamal had managed in the previous season, particularly as Monaassib began 1997 with twenty races and three seasons' racing already under his belt. But he went a long way towards it, rattling up an early-season four-timer and figuring prominently in good company thereafter.

A winning reappearance in a minor event at Kempton in March was followed by the Abernant Stakes at Newmarket in April, another minor event at Goodwood in May and, at the end of the same month, the Group 3 Benazet-Rennen in course-record time at Baden-Baden, where he had Easy Dollar two lengths behind in third. Fourth place under a penalty in a fiercely competitive Cork And Orrery Stakes at Royal Ascot behind Royal Applause was another fine effort and only a temporary halt in his winning spree which resumed in the Prix de Ris-Orangis at Deauville in July. That defeat of the favourite Zamindar by three quarters of a length made Monaassib a warm order himself in the Group 1 Prix Maurice de Gheest at the same course a month later, and although he showed further improvement it wasn't enough to avoid a half-length defeat by another progressive sort, the French four-year-old filly Occupandiste. A

Prix de Ris-Orangis, Deauville—the last of Monaassib's wins in a very successful season; behind him are Zamindar (far side), Nombre Premier (No. 7) and Brave Edge (stars)

617

poor effort next time, even allowing for the better opposition in the Haydock
Park Sprint Cup, can be overlooked because Monaassib bounced back to his
best form in the Diadem Stakes at Ascot on his final outing of the season,
although no match for the impressive three-length winner Elnadim. That result
suggests that if Monaassib is to add to his pattern-race wins in 1998, he may
have to be sent abroad again.

		Young Generation	Balidar
	Cadeaux Genereux	(b 1976)	Brig O'Doon
	(ch 1985)	Smarten Up	Sharpen Up
Monaassib		(ch 1975)	L'Anguissola
(ch.g. 1991)		Habat	Habitat
	Pluvial	(gr 1971)	Atrevida
	(ch 1976)	Pelting	Vilmorin
		(ro 1958)	Firmament

Monaassib cost 550,000 francs at Deauville, making him Cadeaux
Genereux's most expensive first-crop yearling. He's belatedly added to an
already lengthy list of pattern winners descending from grandam Pelting,
among them Bassenthwaite, Braashee, Hadeer, Keen Hunter and, another from
the latest season, Central Park. We needn't elaborate much further on gelding
Monaassib's breeding, except to say that his dam Pluvial, a fairly useful
sprinter, has bred three other winners to date, notably smart miler Rain Burst
(by Tolomeo) and useful mile-and-a-quarter and mile-and-a-half performer
Plymouth Hoe (by Busted). Pluvial's latest foal to race, Rainswept (by Selkirk)
showed a fair amount of ability in a couple of two-year-old maidens at the
Curragh for Charles O'Brien.

The smallish, stocky Monaassib, an unimpressive mover, is built like a
sprinter and six furlongs or thereabouts seems to be his ideal trip. He has,

Maktoum Al Maktoum's "Monaassib"

though, been tried over a range of distances from five furlongs to a mile, showing useful form on his only attempt at the latter trip. Earlier victories came over six/seven furlongs in a maiden at Salisbury (on his racecourse debut when beating Lake Coniston) and minor events at Haydock, Doncaster and Yarmouth. As for ground, Monaassib acts on firm and good to soft going and hasn't been raced on anything softer. A summary of his six-year-old season wouldn't be complete without reference to Daragh O'Donohoe who partnered Monaassib in all his races, even when ineligible to claim his allowance in listed and pattern events when still an apprentice. He has a tough, genuine and consistent partner in Monaassib who usually races prominently. *E. A. L. Dunlop*

MONACLE 3 b.g. Saddlers' Hall (IRE) 126 – Endless Joy 90 (Law Society (USA) 130) [1996 NR 1997 8m 10.1m⁶ 11.5m⁵ 12m 14.1s 11.5m 14.1f⁵ Oct 29] big gelding: third foal: dam 2-y-o 6f and 1m winner: no worthwhile form: blinkered last 2 starts. *D. Morris* –

MONACO GOLD (IRE) 5 b.g. Durgam (USA) – Monaco Ville (Rheingold 137) [1996 46: 14.1m⁵ 13.1m* 14.1f⁴ 13m* 12.1m 15.8g⁶ 1997 13g 12.1s* 11.1s* 12.1g² 12.1m Aug 18] sparely-made gelding: poor performer: won claimers at Hamilton in June and July: should stay 2m: acts on good to firm and soft ground: won over hurdles in September. *Mrs M. Reveley* 48

MONACO (IRE) 3 b.g. Classic Music (USA) – Larosterna (Busted 134) [1996 NR 1997 7g⁴ 10m⁴ 9s³ 8g⁴ 8g 12s 6g 8s Nov 6] IR 19,000Y: tall gelding: half-brother to 2 winners by Shy Groom, notably 1988 Lowther Stakes winner Miss Demure (dam of 2-y-o Royal Shyness): dam once-raced daughter of Molecomb winner Lowna: disappointing maiden (fair form at best): left L. Cumani after fifth start. *R. Allan* 71 d

MONARCH'S PURSUIT 3 b.g. Pursuit of Love 124 – Last Detail 73 (Dara Monarch 128) [1996 52: 6d⁵ 6m⁶ 1997 8m 10g⁶ 14.1m³ 12.3m⁵ 12.3m⁶ 12g* 16.1m⁵ Oct 1] good-topped gelding: fair performer: won claimer at Musselburgh in August: best effort on final start: stays 2m: acts on dead and good to firm ground: well beaten in visor: fairly useful hurdler. *T. D. Easterby* 65

MON BRUCE 3 ch.c. Beveled (USA) – Pendona 72 (Blue Cashmere 129) [1996 67, a74: 6g⁶ 6m⁵ a6g² 6.1s a6g² a7s⁵ 1997 a6g* 6g 6d 6m⁵ 6g⁴ 5.1m³ 5m 5.1m a5g* 5m* 5m² 5d 5g³ 5d Nov 7] unfurnished colt: fair performer: won maiden at Wolverhampton in April and claimer at Southwell (final start for W. Muir) and handicap at Pontefract in September: best at 5f/sharp 6f: acts on the all-weather and on good to firm going, seemingly not on dead. *M. Dods* 71

MONDRAGON 7 b.g. Niniski (USA) 125 – La Lutine 95 (My Swallow 134) [1996 70: 18s 16.2m⁴ 16g⁶ 16m³ 16.1g⁴ 15.8g⁴ 17.1m⁴ 1997 a14g⁵ Dec 18] smallish, leggy gelding: good mover: fair handicapper: late headway after slow start on only outing in 1997: suited by at least 2m: probably acts on any turf ground: tends to edge right: held up. *Mrs M. Reveley* – p

MONDSCHEIN 2 b.f. (Mar 18) Rainbow Quest (USA) 134 – River Spey 96 (Mill Reef (USA) 141) [1997 7m 7g² Oct 18] 80,000Y: sister to smart middle-distance stayer Jahafil and French 11f winner Merrow and half-sister to 2 winners, including useful 7f/1m winner Dune River (by Green Desert): dam 2-y-o 7f winner who later stayed 1½m: neck second to Final Tango in maiden at Redcar, still looking to need experience, wandering a little: should be well suited by 1¼m+: should do better again. *J. L. Dunlop* 86 p

MONEGHETTI 6 ch.g. Faustus (USA) 118 – The Victor Girls (Crofthall 110) [1996 –, a43: a7g³ a8g⁵ a8.5g 7m 1997 8g⁴ a7g 8g 8m⁵ 10g 8s² 8.1m a8.5g⁶ 10m Aug 7] good-topped gelding: poor performer: stays 8.5f: acts on the all-weather and good to firm going: visored final start. *J. L. Harris* 40

MONGOL WARRIOR (USA) 4 b.c. Deputy Minister (CAN) – Surely Geor-gie's (USA) (Alleged (USA) 138) [1996 114: 8s* 10s² 10g² 11s* 12g* 12g⁶ 12v² 12m* 1997 12g 12g³ 15.5d 12g 11s³ 12g⁵ 12g⁶ 12d⁶ 12d² 12v* Dec 7] strong, good-quartered colt: smart performer: mostly campaigned overseas: placed in Group 2 events at Cologne (2 lengths third to Wurftaube) and Hamburg (length third to Oxalagu) and Group 3 race at Dusseldorf (beaten ¾ length by Saugerties) prior to 114 winning listed event at Toulouse: stays 1½m, probably not 15.5f: acts on heavy going and good to firm: has been bandaged: inconsistent. *Lord Huntingdon*

MONIS (IRE) 6 ch.g. Waajib 121 – Gratify 65 (Grundy 137) [1996 49, a59: a7g³ a6g⁵ a6g² a7g³ a6g⁵ 7m 7m⁶ a7g⁵ a6g⁴ a5g³ a6g⁴ 7m a6g⁶ a6g³ a7s² a8g⁵ 1997 a6g a7g a7g a6g 8m⁴ 12s 10m⁵ 18g 12.5m 10m⁵ 9.2m⁴ 12f⁴ 8g* Oct 22] neat gelding: poor handicapper: left J. Balding after fourth start, Ronald Thompson after twelfth: made winning start for current yard at Newcastle in October: effective at 1m to 1½m: acts on firm and dead ground and the all-weather: effective blinkered/visored or not: none too consistent. *B. Ellison* — 39

MONITOR 3 ch.g. Machiavellian (USA) 123 – Instant Desire (USA) 86 (Northern Dancer) [1996 NR 1997 10g³ 10d⁵ 10d³ 10m² 10m* Aug 4] big, strong gelding: second foal: half-brother to 5-y-o Speed To Lead: dam, stayed 1¼m, half-sister to Poule d'Essai des Poulains and Prix Lupin winner Fast Topaze: fairly useful form in maidens, accomplishing simple task at Ripon in August: will stay at least 1½m. *H. R. A. Cecil* — 88

MONKEY FACE 6 gr.m. Clantime 101 – Charming View 62 (Workboy 123) [1996 32: 6m⁶ 7g⁴ 1997 6g May 12] leggy, lengthy mare: poor maiden: well beaten only 6-y-o start. *W. W. Haigh* — –

MONO LADY (IRE) 4 b.f. Polish Patriot (USA) 128 – Phylella (Persian Bold 123) [1996 59: 8.3m 10m⁴ 8m 11.1g⁶ 9.7d* 8.2s⁶ a8g⁴ a8.5s⁶ 1997 a9.4g* a8g* a8g³ a12g² a12g 10.8m³ 10d⁵ a10g* 9.7m³ 12g² 10.2m 12.1g² 11.9g* Sep 3] leggy, unfurnished filly: fair handicapper: had a good season, winning at Wolverhampton and Southwell in January, Lingfield in May and Brighton in September: effective at 1m to 1½m: acts on good to firm and dead going and the all-weather: usually blinkered. *D. Haydn Jones* — 73

MONOPOLY (IRE) 2 ch.c. (Apr 23) Sharp Victor (USA) 114 – Faye 79 (Monsanto (FR) 121) [1997 5d a5g⁵ 7g a8.5g Nov 1] 10,000Y: well-grown colt: sixth foal: brother to useful Irish 1m to 9f winner Wray and Irish 1993 2-y-o 5f winner Sharp Phase: dam 2-y-o 6f winner later successful in USA: modest form at best in maidens and a selling nursery: has flashed tail: sold 1,600 gns in December. *M. Johnston* — 54

MONS 4 b.c. Deploy 131 – Morina (USA) (Lyphard (USA) 132) [1996 119: 10g³ 12m⁴ 11.9m² 14.6m⁴ 12s⁵ 1997 12m³ 13.9g² 12f* 12m³ 12m Nov 23] neat colt: fluent mover: unimpressive walker: reportedly suffered from sore shins after first — 120

Racing Post Godolphin Stakes, Newmarket—
Mons, having his first run for four and a half months, benefits from a fine ride by Frankie Dettori;
battling it out for minor honours are Memorise, The Fly (right) and Shaya (striped cap)

3-y-o start: very smart performer: placed in Jockey Club Stakes at Newmarket (1½ lengths behind Time Allowed) and Yorkshire Cup at York (beaten short head by Celeric but reportedly fractured a tibia) in May: first subsequent race when winning 4-runner listed event at Newmarket in October, making all and beating Memorise by 1½ lengths: good 2¼ lengths third of 9 to Caitano in Gran Premio del Jockey Club at Milan before below-par effort in Japan Cup final start: effective at 1½m and should stay 2m: acts on firm ground and dead (held up only outing on soft): resolute galloper who goes well with forcing tactics: often sweating/edgy, and has been fractious at stalls. *L. M. Cumani*

MONSAJEM (USA) 2 ch.c. (Mar 6) Woodman (USA) 126 – Fairy Dancer 84 (USA) 94 (Nijinsky (CAN) 138) [1997 6g⁴ 7.1g⁴ 8.1d* 8f⁵ 8d⁵ Oct 17] 290,000Y: rangy, rather unfurnished colt: has plenty of scope: eighth foal: brother to fairly useful 1m winner Lothlorien and a 2-y-o winner in USA and half-brother to several winners, including 1¾m winner Wand (by Reference Point): dam twice-raced Irish 6f winner at 2 yrs, closely related to Sadler's Wells: fairly useful performer: won maiden at Chepstow in August: creditable fifth in large-field nurseries at Doncaster and Newmarket: will prove suited by further than 1m: joined E. Dunlop: may yet do better. *Saeed bin Suroor*

MONTANO (USA) 2 b.c. (Feb 1) Manila (USA) – Leery Baba (USA) (Well 75 Decorated (USA)) [1997 6d³ 5d⁵ 7m 7g² a7g⁴ 7m³ a6s* Nov 10] $28,000Y: un- a81 furnished colt: third foal: half-brother to a 2-y-o winner in USA by Conquistador Cielo: dam minor stakes-winning sprinter in USA: fair performer: won nursery at Lingfield by 3½ lengths from Phantom Ring: twice placed in similar events on turf: free-going sort, seems best at 6f: acts on good to firm ground and equitrack, probably on fibresand. *P. F. I. Cole*

MONTE CAVO 6 b.g. Bustino 136 – Dance Festival 101 (Nureyev (USA) 131) 64 [1996 34: 7.1g 8.3s 8m 8.1m 12.3m 10.5m² 9.9g³ 14s 1997 a11g² 12.3m⁵ a8g² 7s a7g⁵ 8d* a8g* 9.2m³ 8m³ 8.5m 10g* 10m³ 9.9d³ 7.9s 8.5f 8d Oct 16] lengthy gelding: modest handicapper: won at Newmarket (apprentices) and Southwell in June and back at Newmarket in August: below form last 3 starts: best at 1m (given good test) to 11f: acts on good to firm and dead ground and on fibresand: no improvement in visor or blinkers: tough. *M. Brittain*

MONTECRISTO 4 br.g. Warning 136 – Sutosky 78 (Great Nephew 126) [1996 80 79: a10g⁴ a10g* a10g² a12g* a12g⁶ 12s³ 10g³ 9.9m* 12.3g*dis 12m⁶ 1997 a9.4g⁴ a12g a12g⁵ a16.2g⁶ 11.9f⁵ 10.1f 9.9m⁴¹ 11 1m* 12d* a12g* 14.1d* a12g* a12g³ Nov 21] leggy, sparely-made gelding: fairly useful performer: in good form in second half of year, winning apprentice handicap at Hamilton, ladies handicap at Newbury and minor events at Southwell, Nottingham (amateurs) and Wolverhampton: stays 1¾m: acts on good to firm and dead going (probably soft) and the all-weather: usually held up. *R. Guest*

MONTE LEMOS (IRE) 2 b.g. (Mar 27) Mukaddamah (USA) 125 – Crim- 96 bourne 83 (Mummy's Pet 125) [1997 5.1m³ 5m* 5m* 5.2d³ 6m* 6g⁶ Oct 25] IR 9,500F, IR 30,000Y: tall, lengthy gelding: has scope: fluent mover: seventh foal: closely related to 3-y-o winner Secret Combe and half-brother to 3 winners, including 7-y-o Gone For A Burton (winner around 1¼m): dam, maiden best at 7f, daughter of smart 1m to 1½m winner Lucent: useful performer: won maiden at Windsor in July and nurseries at Sandown in August and Newmarket in October: not discredited in listed race at Doncaster final start: stays 6f: unraced on extremes of going: hung for first 2 wins: gelded at end of season. *R. Charlton*

MONTENDRE 10 b.g. Longleat (USA) 109 – La Lutine 95 (My Swallow 134) 84 [1996 102: 6s⁵ 6m 6g² 6m 6d² 6f 7.1g³ 6d 6s⁴ 6.1s³ 1997 6m 6s⁵ 6d 6f² 5m² 6d³ 5.1m² 6.1d² 6m³ 5.7g* 6m 6s Oct 15] leggy gelding: shows traces of stringhalt: fluent mover: one-time smart performer, fairly useful nowadays: left R. Hodges after seventh start: gained first win for over 2 years in handicap at Bath in September: stays 7f: acts on any going: often has tongue tied: held up. *M. J. Heaton-Ellis*

MONTFORT (USA) 3 b.g. Manila (USA) – Sable Coated (Caerleon (USA) 132) 96 p [1996 60p: 8.1s 1997 10.3d³ 11.9f* 11.9d* 14s* Jun 26] angular gelding: useful performer: won maiden at Brighton in May and minor events at York (gave trouble stalls, bit slipped through mouth, flashed tail under pressure) and Salisbury in June, all in small fields: stays 1¾m: acts on firm and soft ground: tends to go in snatches, and has hung: gelded after final start: probably still capable of better. *P. F. I. Cole*

MONTONE (IRE)   7 b.g. Pennine Walk 120 – Aztec Princess (Indian King   –
(USA) 128) [1996 69, a67: a12g⁴ a8g⁴ᵈⁱˢ a8g⁵ a13g a10g³ a8g⁵ a8g² 9.7m⁴ a8g² 10m²   a69 d
8g* 8f* a7g* a8g² 9.7f* 11m³ 10g 10m⁴ 9g⁶ a8g⁴ 10m 8m* 12d a10g⁴ a8g* a10g²
1997 a8g⁴ a12g⁵ a8g* a8g 9.7m a8g² 8m 8f a7g 11.5d 8m 7.5d a8g 10g a10g a10g
Dec 10] good-topped gelding: fair handicapper: usually runs in amateur events, and
won one at Lingfield in February: mostly disappointing afterwards: effective at 7f to
1½m: probably acts on any going: often blinkered/visored: sometimes early to post.
J. R. Jenkins

MONTRESTAR   4 ch.g. Mon Tresor 113 – Wing of Freedom (Troy 137) [1996   74
68: a5g⁶ 5s² 5d² 5m⁴ 6g² 5g 6.1g 6d 6f 1997 6m² 5m⁴ 5g⁶ Sep 1] strong gelding: fair
handicapper: clearly best effort in 1997 when fourth in ladies race at Newmarket:
stays 6f: acts on firm and soft ground: effective blinkered/visored or not: sold only
500 gns in November. *A. Bailey*

MONUMENT   5 ch.g. Cadeaux Genereux 131 – In Perpetuity 90 (Great Nephew   70
126) [1996 71: 8.1d⁴ 8m* 10.2m 10m* 11.6m⁵ 10g 10.2f⁶ 12.1d 1997 10g⁴ 10.2m³
11.6s 10g* 10m⁶ 10.2g³ 10m Oct 1] quite good-topped gelding: fair performer: won
minor event at Nottingham in July: effective at 1¼m, and stays 11.6f when conditions
aren't testing: acts on good to firm and dead ground: usually races prominently:
game. *J. S. King*

MONZA (USA)   3 b.c. Woodman (USA) 126 – Star Pastures 124 (Northfields   104
(USA)) [1996 107p: 7m³ 7m* 9d² 1997 8m 10.4g⁵ 12s² 11.9g⁵ 10.9m 12m Dec 14]
smallish, quite attractive colt: useful performer: beaten head by Falak in 5-runner
minor event at Ascot penultimate outing for P. Chapple-Hyam: well beaten in Hong
Kong: stays 1½m: best efforts on good ground or softer: has reportedly suffered eye
problems, and has a high head carriage. *L. Ho, Hong Kong*

MOONAX (IRE)   6 ch.h. Caerleon (USA) 132 – Moonsilk (Solinus 130) [1996   103 §
120§: 12d³ 14d* 20d² 15.5d² 1997 13.4v³ 20g Jun 19] tall, lengthy, attractive horse:
carried condition: had a quick, unimpressive action: very smart performer on his day,
winner of St Leger and Prix Royal Oak in 1994 and Yorkshire Cup following year:
thoroughly mulish before finishing third of 7 to Royal Court in Ormonde Stakes at
Chester in May: sweating, ran poorly in Gold Cup at Royal Ascot 6 weeks later:
effective from 1¾m to 2½m: successful on good to firm ground, best form on good
or softer: sometimes hung under pressure: tail flasher: gave trouble in preliminaries:
sometimes took plenty of driving and wasn't one to trust: retired to stand at Clongeel
Stud, Co Cork (fee Ir £700). *B. W. Hills*

MOON BLAST   3 gr.g. Reprimand 122 – Castle Moon 79 (Kalamoun 129) [1996   89
67p: 7.1m³ 7g⁵ 1997 8f* 9g⁵ 10.8m⁴ 8.3m* 10g² 8.2m 8m 12g⁴ 12m² Sep 22] useful-
looking gelding: fluent mover: fairly useful performer: won maiden at Brighton in
April and minor event at Windsor in June: good effort in minor event at Kempton
final start: effective at 1m to 1½m: acts on good to firm going, yet to race on softer
than good: tried visored: pulls hard, tends to wander under pressure, and no easy ride.
Lady Herries

MOONCLARET   2 b.f. (Mar 28) Beveled (USA) – Miss Monte Carlo 75   –
(Reform 132) [1997 6m Sep 26] sister to a winner in Hong Kong and half-sister to
several winners: dam, sprinting 2-y-o later successful in Italy, half-sister to Lupe
winner Miss Beaulieu: tailed off in claimer at Folkestone. *C. James*

MOON COLONY   4 b.g. Top Ville 129 – Honeymooning (USA) (Blushing   84
Groom (FR) 131) [1996 12m³ 10.8g³ 10.8g⁵ 12d 1997 12m 10.2d⁶ 10m 14m² 12m²
13.1g² 14.1s* 14.6g⁶ 16.5s³ Nov 8] quite attractive ex-French gelding: second foal:
half-brother to Montanelli (by Dowsing), successful at 7f and 1m: dam, French 1½m
winner, daughter of Island Charm, one of leading sprinters in USA in 1981: placed in
minor events at Longchamp and in Provinces at 3 yrs for A. Fabre and M. Zilber:
fairly useful form here: won Nottingham maiden in October: very good third in
handicap at Doncaster final start: stays 2m well: acts on soft ground, probably on
good to firm: possibly suited by waiting tactics. *Lady Herries*

MOON FAIRY   3 ch.f. Interrex (CAN) – Zamoon (Zambrano) [1996 NR 1997   61
7m² 7g² 6.1m* 7g a8g Dec 4] first reported foal: dam unraced: modest form: landed

odds in weak maiden at Nottingham in August: raced too freely next start, in need of run final one: may prove best at 6f: flashed tail at Nottingham, and may be rather temperamental. *J. G. Smyth-Osbourne*

MOON GORGE 2 b.f. (Feb 4) Pursuit of Love 124 – Highland Light 105 (Home Guard (USA) 129) [1997 6g⁵ Oct 24] small, good-topped filly: half-sister to several winners, including fairly useful miler Gravette (by Kris) and very smart middle-distance stayer in Italy, Welsh Guide (by Caerleon): dam sprinter: 20/1 and very green, promising fifth of 24, beaten about 7 lengths by Mister Rambo, in maiden at Newbury, well there until over 1f out: sure to improve. *W. Jarvis* 61 p

MOONLIGHTANDROSES 2 b.f. (Apr 14) Aragon 118 – Lively (IRE) 53 (Digamist (USA) 110) [1997 7g 6.1m Sep 23] first foal: dam 1¼m winner: tailed off throughout both outings, seeming reluctant to race first time. *N. P. Littmoden* –

MOONLIGHT FLIT 2 b.f. (Feb 25) Presidium 124 – Moonwalker (Night Shift (USA)) [1997 6m⁵ 6g⁵ 6d 7.5f* 8m⁵ Sep 25] small, sturdy filly: third foal: dam unraced: modest form: best effort to win selling nursery at Beverley in September: stays 7.5f: acts on firm ground: blinkered last 2 starts. *J. G. FitzGerald* 54

MOONLIGHT INVADER (IRE) 3 br.g. Darshaan 133 – Mashmoon (USA) 80 (Habitat 134) [1996 63+: 8m⁶ 7.1v 1997 10s 12d 13d⁴ Jul 4] big, good-bodied gelding: disappointing maiden: looked none too resolute final outing, then gelded. *E. A. L. Dunlop* –

MOONLIGHT PARADISE (USA) 3 b.f. Irish River (FR) 131 – Ottomwa (USA) (Strawberry Road (AUS) 128) [1996 111p: 6m* 6g* 6m² 6m² 7g* 1997 8m 8m⁶ 6f⁵ Sep 17] strong, rangy filly: impresses in appearance: good walker and powerful mover: smart juvenile, winner of Rockfel Stakes at Newmarket: disappointing in 1997 in 1000 Guineas at Newmarket (second favourite, but only tenth), Coronation Stakes at Royal Ascot (finished last) and minor event at Yarmouth: should stay 1m: raced only on good ground or firmer. *Saeed bin Suroor* –

MOONRAKING 4 g.r.g. Rusticaro (FR) 124 – Lunaire (Try My Best (USA) 130) [1996 54: 7g a8g² 7.1d a12g² a12g⁶ 1997 a12g³ a12g* 11.1d³ 14.1g⁵ 11.1s³ 14.1m 14g⁶ a14g 12s³ a11g* a12g² Dec 13] leggy, close-coupled gelding: modest handicapper: won at Southwell in March (apprentices) and November: unlucky final start, challenging strongly when rider seemed to become unbalanced close home (unseated after line): effective at 11f granted good gallop and should stay 2m: acts on soft going and fibresand: has carried head high, usually soon off bridle and is a tricky ride. *T. J. Etherington* 50 a62

MOONSHADOW (IRE) 2 b.f. (Feb 28) Be My Guest (USA) 126 – Ballet Shoes (IRE) 75 (Ela-Mana-Mou 132) [1997 7g⁵ Oct 7] 84,000Y: first foal: dam, half-sister to Spectrum, from family of Sun Princess and Saddlers' Hall, won only over 5f: favourite, fifth in maiden at Warwick: dead. *H. R. A. Cecil* –

MOONSHIFT 3 b.g. Cadeaux Genereux 131 – Thewaari (USA) 68 (Eskimo (USA)) [1996 NR 1997 8g 10s 8.2g⁵ a12g Nov 18] lengthy, quite good-topped gelding: first foal: dam 7f winner: well beaten in maidens and a handicap: left M. Stoute for 2,600gns after second start. *H. J. Collingridge* –

MOONSHINE GIRL (USA) 3 ch.f. Shadeed (USA) 135 – Fly To The Moon (USA) 90 (Blushing Groom (FR) 131) [1996 97+: 5g* 5m³ 6m⁵ 6m⁵ 1997 7g³ 6g 7.6f Jul 12] leggy, close-coupled filly: easy mover: useful at 2 yrs: not so good in 1997: barely stays 7f: raced only on good ground or firmer: twice attended by 2 handlers in paddock: edgy (below form) final 2-y-o start: sent to USA. *M. R. Stoute* 83

MOONSHINER (USA) 3 b.c. Irish River (FR) 131 – Marling (IRE) 124 (Lomond (USA) 128) [1996 83: 6m 6m² 6g² 1997 8m⁵ 7g⁶ 6.1s 6m 8.3g 7.1g* 8m Oct 6] small, sturdy colt: has a quick action: fairly useful performer: mostly disappointing in 1997, but benefited from change of tactics when making all in maiden at Haydock in September: stays 7f, possibly not 1m: tried blinkered, visored last 2 starts: often takes strong hold: sold 6,500 gns in October. *G. Wragg* 85

MOON SONG 3 b.f. Presidium 124 – Martian Melody 62 (Enchantment 115) [1996 NR 1997 6g³ 6.9m⁴ 7f⁴ 8g 6g⁶ 7g⁶ 5g 6m⁶ a6g⁵ Nov 17] sparely-made filly: third foal: half-sister to 5-y-o Mister Raider and a winning sprinter by Beveled: dam 55

suited by 6f: modest maiden: probably a sprinter: raced only on good going or firmer or fibresand: visored 3 of last 4 starts. *A. P. Jarvis*

MOONSPELL 3 b.f. Batshoof 122 – Shimmer 55 (Bustino 136) [1996 64: 7.1m – 8.1g³ 8d 1997 11.6s⁶ 12.1g May 26] strong, lengthy filly: modest maiden: well beaten both outings in 1997. *R. Charlton*

MOONSTONE (IRE) 2 b.f. (Feb 12) Statoblest 120 – Opening Day (Day Is 69 Done 115) [1997 7g⁶ 7m⁶ 6g 6.1m 6m² 6g 7s Nov 8] IR 7,000Y: lengthy filly: half-sister to fairly useful Irish sprinter (6f winner here at 2 yrs) Norwegian Blue (by Mac's Imp), 6f winner Evanro (by Common Grounds) and a winner in Italy by Fayruz: dam Irish 1m winner: fair maiden: running-on second in nursery at Pontefract in October: running well when brought down next time: should stay beyond 6f: ran poorly on soft ground. *A. P. Jarvis*

MOON STRIKE (FR) 7 b. or br.g. Strike Gold (USA) – Lady Lamia (USA) 104 (Secreto (USA) 128) [1996 85: 7f⁵ 6.9m* 7g 7.1f² 5d* 5f⁶ 6m⁵ 1997 5m² 5g* 5m³ 5m* 5s⁴ 5.2g 5m Sep 28] lengthy gelding: usually looks very well: useful handicapper, better than ever in 1997: won Gosforth Park Cup at Newcastle (final outing for H. Akbary) in June and Coral Handicap at Haydock (by neck from Midnight Escape) in August: ran creditably in listed race at Newbury penultimate start but reportedly lame when running poorly final one: has form over as far as 1m, but best efforts at 5f: acts on equitrack and on firm and dead ground (tailed off on heavy): tried in blinkers earlier in career: idles in front, and best held up in strongly-run race: consistent. *P. Howling*

MOONTABEH 2 b.c. (Jan 28) Mujtahid (USA) 118 – Desert Girl (Green Desert 82 (USA) 127) [1997 5.1m² 5d³ 6m* 6m* 5g⁵ 6m 7v Oct 10] 21,000F, 42,000Y: well-made colt: unimpressive mover: first foal: dam thriced-raced daughter of smart middle-distance filly Upend, herself half-sister to dam of Royal Gait: fairly useful performer: won maiden at Folkestone in July and nursery at Yarmouth in August: well held afterwards: should stay beyond 6f: acts on good to firm and dead ground, possibly not heavy: visored final start: sold 26,000 gns after it. *P. T. Walwyn*

MOONTALK 3 b.f. Emarati (USA) 74 – Pearl Pet 56 (Mummy's Pet 125) [1996 – NR 1997 8.5s 7.6g⁶ Aug 2] 2,100Y: half-sister to 6f seller winner Easy Does It (by Swing Easy) and several winners abroad, including 1996 3-y-o Pearl Pet (by Faustus), winner of Czech Oaks: dam, maiden, stayed 11f: little show in claimer and maiden. *M. J. Haynes*

MOORBIRD (IRE) 3 b.g. Law Society (USA) 130 – Heather Lark (Red Alert 32 127) [1996 53: 7.5m 8.3d³ 8g 1997 a11g a12g⁵ 14.1d 16f⁴ a14.8g⁵ 17.2m Jun 25] good-bodied gelding: modest staying maiden: well below form in 1997, trained until after reappearance by M. Johnston: tried visored and blinkered. *J. L. Harris*

MOOR HALL PRINCESS 3 gr.f. Chilibang 120 – Forgiving (Jellaby 124) – [1996 –: 6g⁵ a6g⁶ 7m⁶ 6m a6g 1997 a9.4f 5.1m a6g⁵ a6g Nov 21] of little account. *A. W. Carroll*

MOOTHYEB (USA) 2 b. or br.c. (Mar 16) Dayjur (USA) 137 – Orca (ARG) 67 (Southern Halo (USA)) [1997 6f³ 6.1d 6m³ 6.9g 8d Oct 17] useful-looking colt: second foal: brother to 3-y-o Ikdam: dam, won Argentinian 1000 Guineas, from good South American family: fair maiden: trained by Saeed bin Suroor first 2 starts: well held in nurseries last 2 (blinkered final one): stays 6f: sold 8,000 gns, and sent to Poland. *N. A. Graham*

MORAN 3 b.c. Bustino 136 – Ower (IRE) 71 (Lomond (USA) 128) [1996 NR – 1997 10m 10m 10.4s 8m Sep 22] strong colt: second foal: dam, 7f winner who stayed 1m, half-sister to smart middle-distance colts Weigh Anchor and Dr Massini: signs of ability but little worthwhile form. *R. F. Johnson Houghton*

MORATORIUM (USA) 2 b.c. (Mar 17) El Gran Senor (USA) 136 – Substance 68 p (USA) (Diesis 133) [1997 8.2d Oct 30] good-bodied colt: first foal: dam unraced half-sister to several good winners, including Ribblesdale winner Ballinderry (dam of Sanglamore): 7/2 from 6/4, burly and green, about 15 lengths seventh to Almandab in maiden at Nottingham, losing place home turn then keeping on: will improve. *H. R. A. Cecil*

MORE BILLS (IRE)   5 b.g. Gallic League 119 – Lady Portobello (Porto Bello   –
118) [1996 –: a13g 1997 a12g May 11] of little account nowadays. *J. Neville*

MOREDUN (IRE)   3 b.g. Waajib 121 – Izba (Thatching 131) [1996 NR 1997   –
7.1m 8.1m 6g Aug 1] 19,000Y: lengthy gelding: tubed: seventh foal: half-brother to
a winner in UAE by Rousillon: dam Irish 7f winner: little show in claimers.
I. A. Balding

MORE THAN YOU KNOW (IRE)   4 ch.f. Kefaah (USA) 124 – Foston   70
Bridge 68 (Relkino 131) [1996 84d: 8m⁶ 7f⁵ 7m⁵ 10.4m 12g a12g³ a9.4g a13g³ 1997
a12g³ a12g³ 12g² a12g⁶ 12d Aug 25] leggy, angular filly: fair handicapper: below
form after reappearance: stayed 13f: acted on good to firm and dead ground and on
equitrack: sometimes found little: blinkered final start: won over hurdles: dead.
K. R. Burke

MORNING SIR   4 b.g. Southern Music 104 – Morning Miss 59 (Golden Dipper   –
119) [1996 –: 8m⁶ 10m 10d 10.2g 10.8m 8g 1997 12.3m Apr 9] of little account.
A. Streeter

MORNING STAR   3 b.f. Statoblest 120 – Moushka (Song 132) [1996 58: 6m   –
5m* 1997 6m 5s a5g 5d 6g 6g Aug 2] modest for M. Johnston at 2 yrs: little form in
1997. *W. McKeown*

MOROCCO (IRE)   8 b.g. Cyrano de Bergerac 120 – Lightning Laser 68   63
(Monseigneur (USA) 127) [1996 63: 7d 7m* 7d⁵ 7g 7m 8m⁵ 7g⁵ 6.9m⁵ 7f 7m* 6.9g³
8.2g⁴ 7f³ 8m 1997 7m⁴ 7m³ 8g⁶ 7s² 8g 7m 7.1m⁶ Jul 25] small, workmanlike gelding:
unimpressive mover: modest handicapper: below form last 3 starts: effective at 7f/
1m: acts on any going: blinkered/visored 4 times earlier in career: sometimes finds
little (usually held up) but often runs well for inexperienced rider: none too
consistent. *M. R. Channon*

MOSCOW MIST (IRE)   6 b.g. Soviet Star (USA) 128 – Ivory Dawn (USA) (Sir   80
Ivor 135) [1996 83: 8s 8.1d 8g⁴ 8m* 8m 8g 1997 8m⁶ 7.6s 8d 8m a8s Nov 10]
lengthy, good-topped gelding: fairly useful handicapper, lightly raced: ran creditably
on reappearance: should stay beyond 1m: best efforts on good going and firmer: has
run well when sweating. *B. Palling*

MOSS SIDE MONKEY   2 b.g. (Apr 21) Presidium 124 – Lady of Leisure 75   43 §
(Record Run 127) [1997 5m² a5g⁶ 6g 6m⁴ 7f⁵ 6d⁵ 7.5f Sep 17] 4,600Y: seventh foal:
dam 5f winner, including at 2 yrs: poor maiden: stays 7f: sometimes blinkered/
visored: sometimes slowly away: ungenuine. *J. Berry*

MOST RESPECTFUL   4 ch.g. Respect 95 – Active Movement 36§ (Music Boy   –
124) [1996 NR 1997 12.4m 8m 6.9g⁵ 5.9d 7.1d May 19] plain gelding: signs of
ability but no worthwhile form. *Denys Smith*

MOST WANTED (IRE)   4 ch.f. Priolo (USA) 127 – Dewan's Niece (USA)   –
(Dewan (USA)) [1996 38: 10.5d 10m 8g⁶ 7f⁴ 10.4g 7g 12.1g 1997 14g 8g Oct 22]
tall, lengthy filly: poor maiden: won novice hurdle in November. *W. McKeown*

MOST WELCOME NEWS   5 b.g. Most Welcome 131 – In The Papers 87   –
(Aragon 118) [1996 –: a8g a8g 6m 1997 11.9f⁶ a14g⁵ Nov 17] well-made gelding:
lightly raced and no form on flat since 1995. *G. L. Moore*

MOTCOMBS CLUB   3 ch.c. Deploy 131 – Unique Treasure (Young Generation   41
129) [1996 58: 7.1m 6g 8.1m 8g⁵ a8g⁶ a8g 1997 11.4m 11.4g 15.4s⁴ 16m⁴ Jul 26]
small, lengthy colt: has a round action: modest at 2 yrs: well below form in 1997,
including in blinkers. *N. A. Callaghan*

MOTET   3 b.c. Mtoto 134 – Guest Artiste 110 (Be My Guest (USA) 126) [1996   102
74p: 7m³ 1997 a10g* 10m³ 12d⁴ 12m³ 16.1g² 16.1g* 18.2f* 18g Oct 18] good-
bodied colt: made into a useful performer, winning maiden at Lingfield in March and
handicaps at Newcastle in August and Yarmouth (by 1½ lengths from Etterby Park)
in September: well held in Cesarewitch at Newmarket final start: stays 2¼m: acts on
firm and dead going: ran poorly when blinkered fourth start. *G. Wragg*

MOTHERS HELP   2 b.f. (Feb 11) Relief Pitcher 120 – Laundry Maid 89   –
(Forzando 122) [1997 7d Oct 27] 500F: second foal: dam 7f winner: very green when
well beaten in maiden at Lingfield, slowly away. *H. Candy*

MOUCHE   3 b. or br.f. Warning 136 – Case For The Crown (USA) 70 (Bates Motel   80
(USA)) [1996 NR 1997 5.1m* 6d⁵ 8m 7s 7m 6m 5m⁵ 6g⁵ 6.1m* 6.1g 6.1g⁴ 6g² 6m
Nov 4] 12,000Y: lengthy, unfurnished filly: first foal: dam 9.7f winner at 6 yrs: fairly
useful performer: won maiden at Nottingham in April and handicap there in
September: best at 5f/6f: acts on good to firm going: effective visored or not.
Mrs J. R. Ramsden

MOULTAZIM (USA)   7 b.g. Diesis 133 – Maysoon 121 (Shergar 140) [1996 NR   –
1997 8.1s 8m Jul 18] unreliable maiden. *Mrs S. D. Williams*

MOUNTAINEER (IRE)   3 b.c. Tirol 127 – Icecapped 91 (Caerleon (USA) 132)   65
[1996 NR 1997 a11g⁵ 12s² a12g⁴ 14.1d³ 17.2f⁵ 14.1g 12s⁴ Oct 16] 21,000 2-y-o:
good-topped, workmanlike colt: brother to a winner at up to 1¼m in Sweden and
German 1¼m winner Enamorata, and half-brother to 2 other winners: dam 1½m and
16.5f winner: fair maiden: very much a stayer: best efforts on dead/soft ground:
blinkered (well below form) third start. *M. Bell*

MOUNTAIN MAGIC   2 b.f. (May 15) Magic Ring (IRE) 115 – Nevis 61   54
(Connaught 130) [1997 5.1s⁵ 5.1g⁵ 6m⁴ 6.1m 7f⁶ 6d Oct 21] close-coupled filly: third
foal: half-sister to 3-y-o Naivasha: dam lightly-raced half-sister to Paris House:
modest maiden: best form at 6f: well beaten on dead ground. *D. J. S. ffrench Davis*

MOUNTAIN SONG   2 b.c. (May 11) Tirol 127 – Persian Song 45 (Persian Bold   103
123) [1997 6f³ 7g* 7s* 8d³ 8g Oct 25] 7,000Y: second foal: brother to 3-y-o Raindancing: dam thrice-raced sister to high-class performer up to 1¼m Bold Arrangement: useful performer: won maiden at Thirsk and auction event at Salisbury in June,
latter most decisively: off nearly 3 months, ¾-length third to King of Kings in
National Stakes at the Curragh: edgy and free to post, far too free in race itself when
well-beaten last of 8 in Racing Post Trophy at Doncaster: should stay beyond 1m:
acts on soft ground: races prominently. *Sir Mark Prescott*

MOUNTGATE   5 b.g. Merdon Melody 98 – Young Whip (Bold Owl 101) [1996   70 §
79§: 8.5g 8g⁵ 8m⁶ 7m² 7m 8f* 7m⁴ 8d 7.9g 8m 7m 7m⁶ 7g 1997 7g² 7m⁴ 7.5m⁶ 7d
8g² 8m 8g 8m 8.1g 7m 10d Nov 3] robust, good-quartered gelding: fair handicapper:
well beaten last 3 starts: best at 7f/1m: acts on firm and dead ground: no improvement
in blinkers: has given trouble in preliminaries, and sometimes mounted on track:
sometimes very slowly away: unreliable. *M. P. Bielby*

MOUNT GENIUS (USA)   4 b. or br.g. Beau Genius (CAN) – Mount Jackie   –
(USA) (Mount Hagen (FR) 127) [1996 NR 1997 10d 8f⁵ 14.6d Nov 7] $6,500Y: neat
gelding: fourth foal: half-brother to minor winners in USA by Advocator and High
Brite (2): dam unraced: signs of ability but no worthwhile form: trained by D.
Cosgrove on debut. *Bob Jones*

MOUNT HOLLY (USA)   3 b.c. Woodman (USA) 126 – Mount Helena 82   81
(Danzig (USA)) [1996 69p: 7m⁵ 1997 8g² 8d³ 8d 8m* 8s³ Nov 8] good-bodied colt:
has short, round action: fairly useful performer: tongue tied, made all in maiden at
Yarmouth in October: good third of 23 in ladies handicap at Doncaster final start:
should be suited by 1¼m+: acts on good to firm and soft ground: sold 30,000 gns in
December and joined K. Mahdi. *J. H. M. Gosden*

MOUSEHOLE   5 b.g. Statoblest 120 – Alo Ez 100 (Alzao (USA) 117) [1996 78:   78
6.1g 6g 5.7g⁵ 5m² 5m* 6f² 6m³ 6m⁶ 5m 5d⁵ 5f² 1997 6g 6g 6m⁴ 5m² 5d 5g² 5m* 5m²
5g³ 5.1m* 5m Aug 23] strong gelding: fair performer: won minor events at Warwick
and Bath in the summer: lost all chance by starting slowly in ladies race final start:
effective at 5f/easy 6f: best on good ground or firmer: successful in blinkers, not tried
in 1997: consistent. *R. Guest*

MOUSSE GLACEE (FR)   3 b.f. Mtoto 134 – Madame Est Sortie (FR)   118
(Longleat (USA) 109) [1996 112p: 8d* 8d* 1997 8g² 8d⁶ 10.5d² 12m⁴ 10m² Oct 19]
quite attractive filly: smart performer: in frame on 4 of 5 starts in 1997, including 1½
lengths second of 12 to Vereva in Prix de Diane at Chantilly, around a length fourth
of 9 to Queen Maud in very strongly-run Prix Vermeille at Longchamp and 1¼
lengths second of 9 to Kool Kat Katie in E P Taylor Stakes at Woodbine: stays 1½m:
acts on good to firm and dead going, unraced on firm or soft. *J. Lesbordes, France*

MOVE SMARTLY (IRE)   7 b.g. Smarten (USA) – Key Maneuver (USA) (Key   47
To Content (USA)) [1996 58: 8g 7g⁶ 7m² 8m⁵ 1997 7f⁴ 6.1m 8m⁶ 7.1g³ 6.9m 8.1g 7m

Sep 16] sturdy gelding: doesn't move smartly: poor performer: effective at 7f to 9f: acts on firm and dead ground: often blinkered/visored: none too consistent. *Mrs L. Stubbs*

MOVE THE CLOUDS   3 gr.f. Environment Friend 128 – Che Gambe (USA)   50 §
(Lyphard (USA) 132) [1996 63+: 8g a8.5g³ 1997 a9.4f⁵ a8g 6g⁴ 8.5m 6.1g 6m a11g Sep 8] big, strong, lengthy filly: modest maiden: sold out of J. Fanshawe's stable after second start and out of D. Nicholls' after sixth: stays 8.5f: tailed off when blinkered: tail flasher: not to be relied on. *B. Ellison*

MOVE WITH EDES   5 b.g. Tragic Role (USA) – Good Time Girl 65 (Good   56
Times (ITY)) [1996 71: 8.3m² 7d 7g⁶ 6.9f* 8f⁴ a7g* 1997 7.6g⁶ 7m 6.9g⁴ 8.3g a7g Oct 4] leggy gelding: modest performer: form in 1997 only when fourth in claimer at Carlisle: stays 1m: acts on firm ground and fibresand. *W. G. M. Turner*

MOVING ARROW   6 ch.g. Indian Ridge 123 – Another Move 69 (Farm Walk   92 d
111) [1996 99: 8s 8.1d² 8m 8.1g 10m* 10.4m 8d⁵ 1997 a9.4g 10m 8.1m⁶ 10.3d⁶ 7.9g 8g 8m⁵ 8d Sep 20] lengthy gelding: still a fairly useful handicapper on his day, but mostly below form in 1997: effective at 1m to 1¼m: probably acts on any ground: visored twice at 4 yrs: effective from front/held up: inconsistent. *Miss S. E. Hall*

MOVING OUT   9 b.g. Slip Anchor 136 – New Generation 91 (Young Generation   53
129) [1996 NR 1997 16m⁶ 16.1g⁶ Oct 7] fair hurdler: lightly raced but still capable of modest form on the flat: stays well. *Miss H. C. Knight*

MOVING PRINCESS   2 b.f. (Apr 1) Prince Sabo 123 – Another Move 69 (Farm   61 +
Walk 111) [1997 6m³ 6m⁵ 5f⁵ 6m Sep 20] 5,500F: smallish, strong filly: half-sister to several winners, including 5-y-o Another Time and 6-y-o Moving Arrow: dam, 1½m winner, sister to useful middle-distance stayer Move Off: modest form first 3 starts: second run in 4 days when well beaten final outing: should stay beyond 6f: raced only on good to firm/firm ground: has been bandaged off-hind. *Miss S. E. Hall*

MOVING UP (IRE)   4 ch.f. Don't Forget Me 127 – Our Pet 64 (Mummy's Pet   42
125) [1996 51d: a8g a8g 10g³ 8.1g 10m 9.7g 11.9f⁴ 11.9f 10g 12s a13g 1997 5.1m⁴ 5.3m⁶ 7.6g Aug 2] sparely-made filly: poor performer: seems to stay 1½m, raced over much shorter trips in 1997: acts on good to firm ground: ran poorly only try in visor. *T. E. Powell*

MOWBRAY (USA)   2 b. or br.c. (Mar 7) Opening Verse (USA) 126 – Peppy Raja   101
(USA) (Raja Baba (USA)) [1997 7g² 7g* 7g* 8d⁴ 8m² Oct 19] good-bodied colt: good mover: fourth foal: half-brother to winners in USA by Broad Brush and Miswaki: dam, won up to 9f at 4 yrs in USA, from family of Slewpy: useful form: won maiden at Catterick and minor event at Kempton in August: good efforts in frame subsequently in National Stakes at the Curragh (1½ lengths fourth to King of Kings) and Gran Criterium at Milan (beaten 7½ lengths by Lend A Hand): should be suited by at least 1¼m: yet to race on extremes of ground: tends to run in snatches, and looks difficult ride. *P. F. I. Cole*

MOWELGA   3 ch.c. Most Welcome 131 – Galactic Miss 78 (Damister (USA)   79 p
123) [1996 NR 1997 8g 10.5g³ 10g* Oct 24] short-backed colt: first foal: dam, 1m and 1¼m winner, sister to very smart middle-distance performer Zimzalabim: fair performer, lightly raced: best effort on second start: won maiden at Newbury following month by short head from Ricardo: quite keen sort, but should stay 1½m: will do better. *Lady Herries*

MOWJOOD (USA)   3 b.c. Mr Prospector (USA) – Bineyah (IRE) 109 (Sadler's   72
Wells (USA) 132) [1996 –p: 6m 7m 1997 7g⁵ 10.8s³ 10m² 9.9d³ 8g Aug 27] tall, attractive colt: fair maiden handicapper: easily best effort on third start: will stay 1½m: acts on good to firm ground: visored last 3 outings: sent to UAE. *M. R. Stoute*

MOWLAIE   6 ch.g. Nashwan (USA) 135 – Durrah (USA) 93 (Nijinsky (CAN)   55 d
138) [1996 –, a55: a11g 1997 12m⁴ a11g 8m 10.5m* 12.3m a11g⁶ 12.3m³ 12.1g 12g 10.9d 10g Sep 28] modest handicapper: virtually only form in 1997 when winning amateurs event at Haydock in June: stays 1½m: acts on good to firm and dead ground and on fibresand: inconsistent. *D. W. Chapman*

MOY (IRE)   2 ch.f. (Mar 2) Beveled (USA) – Exceptional Beauty 94 (Sallust 134)   49
[1997 5g⁶ 5m 6.1s⁵ 5m⁵ 6d 6d⁵ Oct 20] 4,000Y: small filly: seventh foal: half-sister

to 2 fair 2-y-o 5f winners by Siberian Express: dam 1½m winner: poor maiden: patchy form: should stay beyond 6f: well beaten in blinkers once. *M. Brittain*

MOZAMBIQUE (IRE) 3 b.c. Fayruz 116 – Lightning Laser 68 (Monseigneur (USA) 127) [1996 NR 1997 7m³ 6.1g⁵ a6g² a7s* a7s⁴ a7g² Dec 10] 9,000F, 14,000Y: fourth foal: brother to fairly useful Irish 1995 2-y-o 5f/6f winner Kingsandvaga-bonds, subsequently successful over 7f in Hong Kong (under different name), and half-brother to 2 winners by Cyrano de Bergerac, including 8-y-o Morocco: dam, 7f winner, ran only at 2 yrs: fair performer: won weak maiden at Lingfield in November: stays 7f: acts on the all-weather, unraced on going softer than good on turf. *Mrs J. Cecil*   65

MR BEAN 7 b.g. Salse (USA) 128 – Goody Blake 103 (Blakeney 126) [1996 –: a12g⁵ a12g⁶ a14g 1997 a13g⁶ 12.1g Sep 1] one-time fair handicapper: no form last 2 seasons. *K. R. Burke*   –

MR BERGERAC (IRE) 6 b.g. Cyrano de Bergerac 120 – Makalu 79 (Godswalk (USA) 130) [1996 92: 6g 6f 5.1f⁵ 6f² 6f* 6m² 6m² 6g 5g 6f a7g 1997 5.2g 5g 6m 6g* 6g 6s 6.1m³ 6.1g⁵ 6g² 6g* 6g 7d⁵ 7f 6g⁵ 7m a6g 7g⁴ a7g 6m a6g³ a7g⁵ Dec 6] sparely-made gelding: fairly useful handicapper: won at Leicester in May and Newmarket in August: best at 6f/7f: acts on firm going, soft and the all-weather: successful when sweating. *B. Palling*   92 a80

MR BOMBASTIQUE (IRE) 3 b.g. Classic Music (USA) – Duende 75 (High Top 131) [1996 83: 6m⁵ 6.1m* 7m⁴ 7.9g⁵ 8g² 1997 10.5s² 10.4g 10g³ May 28] sturdy gelding: unimpressive mover: fairly useful performer: placed in handicap then claimer (below form) early in 1997: likely to prove best up to 10.5f: acts on good to firm and soft ground: sweating (tailed off) once at 2 yrs: joined Mrs J. Brown. *B. W. Hills*   84

MR BROWNING (USA) 6 br.g. Al Nasr (FR) 126 – Crinoline 72 (Blakeney 126) [1996 73: 11.4g 12m² 11.5d 12m 12g⁴ 16.2d 16g 1997 12m 11.9f* 12d 11.9f⁴ 12g⁶ 12m Sep 10] well-made gelding: fair handicapper: allowed uncontested lead when winning at Brighton in June: little other form in 1997: probably stays 2m: acts on firm and dead ground: usually blinkered: unreliable, and seems to need things his own way: joined Miss G. Kelleway. *R. Akehurst*   67 §

MR CAHILL (USA) 2 b.c. (Feb 17) Cahill Road (USA) – Sympathetic Miss (USA) (Proudest Roman (USA)) [1997 7m* 7g Aug 19] $130,000Y: tall, close-coupled colt: has scope: half-brother to several winners in USA, including minor stakes winners by Providential and Superbity: dam won up to 1m in USA: sire (brother to champion 1990 US 3-y-o Unbridled) Grade 1 9f winner: won minor event at Yarmouth in August by 1¼ lengths from Dower House: looked in fine shape but soundly beaten in Acomb Stakes at York, presumably not himself: will stay at least 1m. *M. R. Stoute*   94 +

MR CUBE (IRE) 7 ch.h. Tate Gallery (USA) 117 – Truly Thankful (CAN) (Grau-stark) [1996 61, a–: 7m 7f⁴ 7f 7g 7.1g 8.3m² 8f³ 6.9g⁵ 7f⁵ 8f⁵ 7.6m⁵ 8.2d 8f³ 7m 6.9g* 8d a7g 1997 8g 8g³ 8m² 8f⁴ 7f 7g² 6.9m² 7d* 7f 8m² 6.9g 8f⁶ 8.2s⁶ Oct 15] sturdy horse: modest handicapper: won at Epsom in July: effective at 7f and 1m: acts on firm and soft ground and the all-weather: blinkered/visored: tends to wander and carry head awkwardly (comes from behind and suited by strong pace) but has won for apprentice: tough. *J. M. Bradley*   61 a–

MR FORTYWINKS (IRE) 3 ch.g. Fools Holme (USA) – Dream On 54 (Absalom 128) [1996 58: 5d⁵ 5m 5m³ 5m 1997 5.9m 6m⁶ 9.2d* 10d² 10.9d² 12m² 9m⁴ a12g* a12g³ Dec 4] sparely-made gelding: fair performer on all-weather, modest on turf: won seller at Hamilton in August and handicap at Wolverhampton (by 9 lengths) in November: best efforts at 1½m: acts on good to firm ground, dead and the all-weather. *J. L. Eyre*   54 a66

MR FROSTY 5 b.g. Absalom 128 – Chadensh 94 (Taufan (USA) 119) [1996 –, a86: a8g⁵ a7g 8s a6g* a6g* a6s* 1997 a6g⁶ a7g⁵ a6g a6g 6s³ 7d a6g a7g Dec 10] lengthy gelding: fair handicapper: right out of sorts final 3 outings: effective at 6f, given good test, to 1m: goes well on the all-weather, best turf efforts on good ground or softer. *W. Jarvis*   66 d a73 d

MR FUND SWITCH 2 ch.g. (Mar 5) Chilibang 120 – Purple Fan (Dalsaan 125) [1997 5m 5d⁶ 5m 5d 7g 6m⁶ a5g⁵ 5m⁶ 6m⁴ a6g Oct 20] 2,100Y: compact gelding: 39

fifth foal: half-brother to 5-y-o Cats Bottom and 6f winner (stays 1¼m) Bold Mick (by Never So Bold): dam ran twice: poor maiden: probably stays 7f: blinkered seventh/eighth starts. *D. Nicholls*

MR HACKER   4 b.g. Shannon Cottage (USA) 86 – Aosta (Shack (USA) 118)   –
[1996 –: 7d 7.1m 10g 8.3d 8m 1997 a8g Jan 28] no form: tried blinkered. *G. Thorner*

MR LOWRY   5 b.g. Rambo Dancer (CAN) 107 – Be Royal 97 (Royal Palm 131)   –
[1996 NR 1997 a12g Mar 29] modest maiden on flat, tailed off only 5-y-o start: won maiden hurdle in May. *L. J. Barratt*

MR MAJICA   3 b.c. Rudimentary (USA) 118 – Pellinora (USA) (King Pellinore   86
(USA) 127) [1996 –p: 6m 1997 7m² 7.1s⁶ 5.7g³ 6m* 7g a7g a8g Dec 12] big, robust colt: fairly useful performer: clearly best effort when winning maiden at Yarmouth in September, unable to go strong pace but responding to pressure to get up near finish: likely to prove best at 6f/7f: acts on good to firm ground: blinkered last 2 starts. *B. J. Meehan*

MR MIYAGI   2 b.g. (Apr 23) Full Extent (USA) 113 – All The Girls (IRE) 49   ?
(Alzao (USA) 117) [1997 7d 8.1d⁶ 6d 7d⁶ 7d Oct 16] 4,200Y: small gelding: first foal: dam poor maiden who stayed 1m: form only in maiden at Haydock on second start: blinkered in seller final outing. *A. Bailey*

MR MONTAGUE (IRE)   5 b.g. Pennine Walk 120 – Ballyewry (Prince Tender-   –
foot (USA) 126) [1996 NR 1997 10m⁶ 10d 8g 10m⁶ 8.1g Aug 3] workmanlike gelding: half-brother to fairly useful sprinter Balandra Bay (by Jareer): dam Irish 2-y-o 6f winner who stayed 9f: little worthwhile form on flat. *T. W. Donnelly*

MR MORIARTY (IRE)   6 ch.g. Tate Gallery (USA) 117 – Bernica (FR) 114   –
(Caro 133) [1996 –, a46: a12g* a11g² a12g² a12g* a16g⁶ a12g² a12g⁵ 9.2s   a31
a11g a7g⁶ 8.2d a9.4g⁵ 18g a14g 1997 a12g³ a12g Feb 28] neat gelding: poor handicapper: stays 1½m: acts on fibresand and on firm and dead going: tried blinkered, no improvement: often bandaged: usually races prominently: fairly useful hurdler, winner 5 times in 1997. *S. R. Bowring*

MR MUSIC   3 ch.g. La Grange Music 111 – Golden 69 (Don 128) [1996 –: 7d 8s   –
1997 a8.5g⁶ a8g 11.7m Jun 14] no form: tried visored. *K. McAuliffe*

MR NEVERMIND (IRE)   7 b.g. The Noble Player (USA) 126 – Salacia 93   –
(Seaepic (USA) 100) [1996 67, a82: a8g² a8g³ a8g³ a7g² a7g* a10g⁶ 8f⁴ 8f⁵ 8.3m 7g²   a90
7.1g 8m 8f* 8.5m³ a7g* a8g* 1997 a8g* a7g* a8g³ a7g* 7m Jun 11] useful-looking gelding: has a quick action: fairly useful on all-weather: in fine form early in year, and won handicaps at Lingfield in January and February and Wolverhampton (fibre-sand debut, career-best effort) later in February: stays 8.5f: only fair on turf, but has form on any ground: effective with blinkers at 2 and 3 yrs: genuine. *G. L. Moore*

MR OSCAR   5 b.g. Belfort (FR) 89 – Moushka (Song 132) [1996 96: 5.1g 5m 5m   – §
5m 1997 6m 6s 6g May 30] formerly useful 5f performer: well held in 1997, all but refusing to race final start: one to avoid. *W. McKeown*

MR PARADISE (IRE)   3 b.g. Salt Dome (USA) – Glowlamp (IRE) 93 (Glow   77
(USA)) [1996 71+: 6m 6.9d⁶ 6g² 6v² 7v² 1997 a7g² a8g³ 8d³ 8g² 8.5m* 10.1m 7g*   a66
a7g 8.5d 8.1m² 8d⁶ 8m 8g a8s a10g a7g² Dec 18] leggy gelding: fair performer: won maiden at Beverley and minor event at Lingfield in June: left T. J. Naughton after thirteenth start: effective at 7f to 8.5f: acts on good to firm ground, heavy and fibresand: usually races prominently. *R. M. H. Cowell*

MR ROUGH   6 b.g. Fayruz 116 – Rheinbloom 66 (Rheingold 137) [1996 64: 8f⁶   59
10.3m 10m⁶ 10.3m⁴ 8m 8m³ 8g² 8m³ 9f 8.3d 8m³ 8g⁶ a8g⁵ a8g⁶ 1997 10.3d 8d 8f*   a–
8g⁵ 8s 8m 8.1m a10g 10.1f⁶ 8m 7d a8g Nov 17] sturdy gelding: modest handicapper: won seller at Yarmouth in June: stays 1¼m: goes well on good going or firmer: blinkered once at 5 yrs: below best in blinkers/visor: none too consistent. *D. Morris*

MRS DRUMMOND (IRE)   4 br.f. Dromod Hill – Dear France (USA) (Affirmed   33
(USA)) [1996 –: 10m⁶ a9.4g⁴ 10.1m 11f 1997 a12g a16g⁵ 16m⁶ a14g³ Aug 15] poor maiden handicapper: left A. Jarvis after second start: stays 2m. *G. M. McCourt*

MRS KEEN   4 b.f. Beveled (USA) – Haiti Mill 68 (Free State 125) [1996 –: 8.1f⁵   –
11.9f⁶ 8f 1997 a7g Jun 19] of little account. *P. Butler*

MRS MALAPROP 2 b.f. (Feb 25) Night Shift (USA) – Lightning Legacy (USA) 83 +
78 (Super Concorde (USA) 128) [1997 6m 5m2 5g* 5v 5.2f Oct 29] IR 28,000Y:
sturdy, lengthy filly: has scope: half-sister to several winners, including 3-y-o
Lawahik, fairly useful Cabochon (up to 2½m, by Jalmood) and useful Black Monday
(up to 11f, by Busted): dam (maiden) stayed 1m: fairly useful form when 5-length
winner of maiden at Catterick in September: stiff task next start and possibly hadn't
recovered from that race final outing: should stay much further than 5f: may still do
better at 3 yrs. *M. R. Channon*

MRS MCBADGER 4 ch.f. Weldnaas (USA) 112 – Scottish Lady (Dunbeath –
(USA) 127) [1996 –: 6s5 6.1d5 6m a6g6 7m a6g 1997 a6g Jan 8] fair maiden as 2-y-o:
little form since. *B. Smart*

MRS MIDDLE 2 b.f. (Apr 14) Puissance 110 – Ibadiyya 120 (Tap On Wood 130) 60
[1997 6g6 6m4 6f6 5.3m4 6d* 6.9g 7m Sep 16] 4,200F: half-sister to several winners
abroad, including Italian 3-y-o 5f (at 2 yrs) and 6f winner Magic Surprise (by Bluebird): dam, awarded Prix Chloe, stayed 1¼m: modest performer: won nursery at
Warwick in August: well beaten after: should stay 1m: acts on good to firm and dead
ground. *N. A. Callaghan*

MRS MINIVER (USA) 3 b.f. Septieme Ciel (USA) 123 – Becomes A Rose 93
(CAN) (Deputy Minister (CAN)) [1996 92: 7g4 7m3 8m 8g6 1997 10m5 11.9d4 10m6
10m5 Oct 4] angular filly: has a quick action: fairly useful maiden: highly tried on
several occasions and well held in 1997 (flattered when 9 lengths fifth of 8 in Sun
Chariot Stakes at Newmarket on final start): appears to stay 1½m: unraced on
extremes of going: sold 36,000 gns, and sent to USA. *P. A. Kelleway*

MR SPEAKER (IRE) 4 ch.g. Statoblest 120 – Casting Vote (USA) 54 (Monte- 65
verdi 129) [1996 62: 8g 8m 8.3m 6.1m* 6m 7m4 7d 1997 6s2 6g 6d 6m 7g2 7.1g 6m
8.2s 7f6 Oct 29] close-coupled, workmanlike gelding: fair handicapper: effective at
6f/7f: acts on firm and soft ground: inconsistent: joined G. Bravery. *C. F. Wall*

MR SPECULATOR 4 ch.g. Kefaah (USA) 124 – Humanity (Ahonoora 122) –
[1996 63, a56: 8m 9m 10.1m 12.5f5 14.9m* 14.9m a12g6 16g 15.1s a14g3 a12g* a58
1997 a14.8g2 a11g3 a12g* a12g a12g3 12m 14s a12g3 14.1g 12d Oct 21] strong,
lengthy gelding: modest handicapper: made all at Wolverhampton in February: finds
11f bare minimum, and should stay 2m: acts on fibresand, no form on turf in 1997:
usually visored/blinkered nowadays. *J. E. Banks*

MRS PICKLES 2 gr.f. (Mar 21) Northern Park (USA) 107 – Able Mabel 77 –
(Absalom 128) [1997 5m 7g a6g Oct 4] 4,500 2-y-o: third foal: dam 6f mudlark: no
promise in maidens. *M. D. I. Usher*

MRS POLLOCK 4 b.f. Precocious 126 – Power And Red (Skyliner 117) [1996 –
NR 1997 a8.5g Jul 25] third foal: half-sister to modest 5f (at 2 yrs) and 6f winner
Abbey House (by Efisio): dam Irish 5f winner: well beaten in claimer. *J. L. Harris*

MR SPONGE (USA) 3 ch.c. Summer Squall (USA) – Dinner Surprise (USA) 91
(Lyphard (USA) 132) [1996 NR 1997 7m3 7m* 7d3 7.3m5 7.6s3 8d 7m3 a7g Nov 1]
$130,000F: good-topped colt: not a good walker: ninth foal: half-brother to several
winners, including American Grade 3 9f winner Freewheel (by Arctic Tern): dam
from family of Legal Case: sire won Preakness Stakes: fairly useful performer:
landed odds in maiden at Salisbury in June: good efforts in handicaps most starts
afterwards: should stay 1m: acts on good to firm and soft ground, below form on
fibresand. *I. A. Balding*

MR TEIGH 5 b.g. Komaite (USA) – Khadino (Relkino 131) [1996 72, a81: a8g* 80
a8g6 8.1d3 a9.4g* a9.4g* 10.3m3 8.1f4 8m2 10f 1997 9.9s 10d 8m5 9.9m* 9.9g5 8d4
8m5 7.6m* 6m 6g6 7f3 6g 7m6 Oct 4] sturdy gelding: fairly useful handicapper:
successful at Beverley in June and Chester in August: effective at 7f to 1¼m: acts on
firm and dead ground and the all-weather: below form in blinkers/visor at 3 yrs: has
been early to post. *Mrs J. R. Ramsden*

MR TITCH 4 b.g. Totem (USA) 118 – Empress Nicki (Nicholas Bill 125) [1996 –
–: 8.1g 13.8g6 8m 8f 1997 a8.5g Feb 21] no worthwhile form. *W. McKeown*

MR WILD (USA) 4 b.g. Wild Again (USA) – Minstress (USA) (The Minstrel 81
(CAN) 135) [1996 73: 10m4 10g4 14.1g6 1997 12g* 12d5 May 22] good sort: fairly
useful handicapper, lightly raced on flat: won at Kempton in May, and ran well only

subsequent start: should stay beyond 1½m: acts on good to firm and dead ground. *R. Akehurst*

M T VESSEL   3 b.g. Risk Me (FR) 127 – Brown Taw 66 (Whistlefield 118) [1996 – –: 5d 5m³ 5.1m 5m⁶ 5f 5f 1997 6g 5s⁶ 5d 5m 8m⁵ Aug 15] no worthwhile form: blinkered third and fourth starts. *J. R. Jenkins*

MUARA BAY   3 gr.c. Absalom 128 – Inca Girl (Tribal Chief 125) [1996 –: 6v   55 1997 6g 6.9m⁵ a6g a8g² a7g³ 7g³ 8g* 10f² 10.1g⁵ a9.4g² Dec 26] modest handicapper: won at Brighton in August: good second on same course and at Wolverhampton after: stays 1¼m: acts on firm ground and fibresand. *G. Lewis*

MU-ARRIK   9 b. or br.h. Aragon 118 – Maravilla 73 (Mandrake Major 122) [1996   35 46d, a–: 6d 5.9d² 6s 5.9m⁴ 7g 6m 6.1m 5m 6m 5m 6m a8g a7g⁶ a6g 1997 a7g a7g 5s   a– 7g 7s 7m 6m⁵ 5f 6s 6g⁵ 6g 6m⁴ a8g a6g⁶ a7g Dec 10] sparely-made horse: poor handicapper: effective at 6f and 7f: probably acts on any going: has been blinkered, usually visored. *R. Oldroyd*

MUBARIZ (IRE)   5 b.g. Royal Academy (USA) 130 – Ringtail 102 (Auction   44 d Ring (USA) 123) [1996 84d: 7.5m² 8.2m² 8s⁴ 8m 7f⁴ 8d⁶ 8.1f 8m 1997 7m⁴ 8m 7f 8.2g 8f 10.3d 6.9m 10g Jul 30] well-made gelding: fairly useful maiden at best: has been hobdayed and tubed, and poor at best in 1997. *C. Smith*

MUBRIK (IRE)   2 b.c. (Mar 8) Lahib (USA) 129 – Bequeath (USA) (Lyphard   86 p (USA) 132) [1997 7.6d⁴ 7g³ Sep 18] 65,000Y: well-made colt: fluent mover: fifth foal: brother to 3-y-o Santa Rosa and half-brother to 3 winners, notably 5-y-o Decorated Hero: dam lightly-raced 9f winner in France: in frame in maidens at Lingfield then Newbury, much better effort when length third of 17 to Dr Fong, making most: should stay at least 1m: should go on again, and win a race. *J. H. M. Gosden*

MUCH COMMENDED   4 b.f. Most Welcome 131 – Glowing With Pride 114   100 (Ile de Bourbon (USA) 133) [1996 90p: 6.1m* 6m³ 1997 8g³ 8v³ May 11] tall, lengthy filly: useful performer: third in Premio Regina Elena at Rome (less than 3 lengths behind Nicole Pharly) and Henkel Rennen at Dusseldorf (beaten 5 lengths by Que Belle): bred to stay beyond 1m: acts on good to firm and heavy ground. *G. Wragg*

MUCHEA   3 ch.c. Shalford (IRE) 124§ – Bargouzine 67 (Hotfoot 126) [1996 115:   113 5d³ 5s* 5m* 5m³ 6g² 6g* 6m² 1997 7g³ 8m 6d⁶ 7g 6m⁶ 7g³ Oct 18] quite attractive colt: good mover: smart performer: reportedly pulled a muscle in 2000 Guineas at Newmarket on second start, and subsequently off course 4 months: back to form last 2 starts, sixth to Elnadim in Diadem Stakes at Ascot then 2 lengths third of 12 to Kahal in Challenge Stakes at Newmarket: best form at 6f and 7f: acts on good to firm and soft going. *M. R. Channon*

MUDALAL (USA)   2 b.c. (Apr 27) Dixieland Band (USA) – Barakat 93 (Bustino   76 p 136) [1997 7d⁴ 7g³ Oct 27] fourth foal: half-brother to 3 winners, including 3-y-o Mumaris and useful 1¼m winner Ta Awun (by Housebuster): dam, stayed 1¾m, is half-sister to Ibn Bey and Roseate Tern out of half-sister to Teleprompter: similar form in Leicester maidens won by Goodwood Cavalier and Altibr: will be well suited by 1m+: should do better. *D. Morley*

MUDEER   2 b.c. (Apr 22) Warning 136 – Colorvista (Shirley Heights 130)   113 [1997 7m* 7m* 8g² Oct 25]

Defeat in the Racing Post Trophy (or its predecessors) isn't necessarily a bar to success in the Derby, as 1980 runner-up Shergar and 1996 third Benny The Dip illustrated. Mudeer finished a good deal closer than either of that pair, beaten a short head by Saratoga Springs, but at 33/1 at the time of writing doesn't seem especially overpriced for the Epsom classic. The 1997 Racing Post Trophy seemed by no means a strong edition, though confirmation is still required since none of the runners ran later in the year. Mudeer, who had gone in his coat, had every chance but could never quite get past the winner (who seemed to be idling in front) and might have been fortunate to keep second as Mutamam, a length behind, was hampered by him over two furlongs out as he hung left. Still, Mudeer had put up a smart performance, better than his win in a maiden at Leicester on his debut and probably better than his two-length defeat

Sunday Conditions Stakes, Ascot—Mudeer steps up in class and wins from newcomer Pegnitz

of the tenderly-handled Pegnitz in the Sunday Conditions Stakes at Ascot later in September.

There are other reasons to be cautious about Mudeer's Derby prospects, however. He runs as if he'll stay beyond a mile but is no certainty to get a mile and a half. While there's a reasonable amount of stamina on the dam's side, Warning is much more an influence for speed, largely known for siring sprinters and milers and responsible for very few horses fully effective at a mile and a half. Mudeer's dam, Colorvista, is an unraced half-sister to the One Thousand Guineas third Bella Colora (who seemed best short of a mile and a quarter), the Irish Oaks winner Colorspin and the Irish Champion Stakes winner Cezanne. Bella Colora went on to become the dam of the high-class mile-and-a-quarter horse Stagecraft, while Colorspin produced the top-class Opera House, whose very best form was over a mile and a half. Mudeer is the fifth foal of Colorvista, following the fairly useful winner over thirteen and an extended fourteen furlongs, Durable (by Caerleon), and a winner in Japan by Cadeaux Genereux.

		Known Fact	In Reality
	Warning	(b 1977)	Tamerett
	(b 1985)	Slightly Dangerous	Roberto
Mudeer		(b 1979)	Where You Lead
(b.c. Apr 22, 1995)		Shirley Heights	Mill Reef
	Colorvista	(b 1975)	Hardiemma
	(b 1986)	Reprocolor	Jimmy Reppin
		(ch 1976)	Blue Queen

Also to be considered is the manner in which Mudeer races. He had an ungainly action at two and his tendency to hang left, evident at Doncaster, will have to be corrected if he's to adapt to the unique nature of the course at Epsom. He also flashed his tail when hit with the whip on his first two starts. A strong, lengthy, angular colt who cost 350,000 guineas as a yearling, Mudeer has raced only on good going and good to firm. *Saeed bin Suroor*

MUDFLAP 3 b.f. Slip Anchor 136 – River's Rising (FR) 88 (Mendez (FR) 128) – [1996 82: 6.9g⁵ a6g² a7g* 8m⁵ 7.9g 1997 8s⁵ May 21] angular filly: fairly useful winner at 2 yrs: tailed off only start in 1997: sold 2,700 gns in December. *Sir Mark Prescott*

MUDLARK 5 b.g. Salse (USA) 128 – Mortal Sin (USA) 65 (Green Forest (USA) 134) [1996 –: a12g a16g⁵ a14g⁵ 1997 14g⁵ 16.2s May 10] good-bodied gelding: poor maiden: no form on flat since 3 yrs. *J. Norton*

MUFTUFFENUF 2 ch.f. (Apr 14) Elmaamul (USA) 125 – Tower Glades 90 62 (Tower Walk 130) [1997 6.1g² 6m³ 5g⁴ 7m 6m³ 6m³ 6m Sep 9] 9,200Y: third foal:

632

half-sister to French 3-y-o 1m winner Jack Sharp (by Sharpo) and 7-y-o Tee-Emm: dam 2-y-o 5f winner: modest maiden: creditable third twice in nurseries: should stay beyond 6f: raced only on good ground or firmer: gave trouble at stalls first 2 starts, slowly away third. *P. R. Webber*

MUGELLO   2 b.f. (Mar 18) Emarati (USA) 74 – Fleur de Foret (USA) 61§ (Green   96
Forest (USA) 134) [1997 5m2 5m* 5m 5.1m2 6f2 5m2 5.2m 5m6 Sep 13] smallish, quite attractive filly: has a quick action: fifth foal: half-sister to a 2-y-o 5f seller winner by Tragic Role and 7f and 1m winner Proud Image (by Zalazl): dam, sprint maiden, became ungenuine at 3 yrs: useful performer: won maiden at Warwick in June and minor event at Chepstow in July: close second in listed race at Newbury (beaten 1½ lengths by Victory Note) and Molecomb Stakes at Goodwood (went down by ½ length to Lady Alexander): not discredited in Flying Childers Stakes at Doncaster final outing: speedy, but stays 6f: raced only on good to firm/firm ground: front runner/races prominently. *A. P. Jarvis*

MUHABA (USA)   2 ch.f. (Feb 12) Mr Prospector (USA) – Salsabil 130 (Sadler's   96 p
Wells (USA) 132) [1997 7m5 8.1g* 8s4 Oct 21] fourth foal: sister to smart 1996 2-y-o 6f and 7f winner Sahm, and half-sister to smart 6f (at 2 yrs) to 1¼m winner Bint Salsabil (by Nashwan): dam won 1000 Guineas, Oaks and Irish Derby and is half-sister to Marju: made all when 6-length winner of maiden at Haydock in September: better form when 4¾ lengths fourth of 7 to Zalaiyka in Prix des Reservoirs at Deauville: should be suited by 1¼m+: likely to do better. *Saeed bin Suroor*

MUHANDAM (IRE)   4 b.g. Common Grounds 118 – Unbidden Melody (USA)   76 d
(Chieftain II) [1996 –§: 7m a5g6 1997 6d* 6m a8g 8.2s4 7g Oct 24] compact gelding: fair performer, lightly raced: has had several trainers: won 22-runner handicap at Doncaster in June on only start for Bob Jones: well below that form afterwards, including in visor: probably stays 1m: acts on soft ground: sometimes looks none too keen: sold, and sent to Germany. *P. A. Kelleway*

MUHANDIS   4 b.c. Persian Bold 123 – Night At Sea 107 (Night Shift (USA))   73
[1996 82: 7f* 7.1d5 1997 a7f3 8m a7f a7f 6.9g 8m a8s a10g a7s a10g* Dec 19] good-bodied colt: fairly useful winner at 3 yrs for J. Gosden: trained in Dubai by S. Seemar first 4 starts in 1997: best effort on return to Britain (but not up to Dubai form) when winning handicap at Lingfield, finishing lame: will prove best at up to 1¼m: acts on equitrack: tried blinkered (was at Lingfield)/visored. *G. L. Moore*

MUHASSIL (IRE)   4 ch.g. Persian Bold 123 – Nouvelle Star (AUS) (Luskin Star   –
(AUS) [1996 69: 8m4 1997 7m 10m 10m5 10s Oct 14] rangy gelding: fair maiden, lightly raced: no form in 1997: sold out of R. Hern's stable after reappearance. *K. A. Morgan*

MUHAWWIL   3 b.c. Green Desert (USA) 127 – Ardassine (Ahonoora 122) [1996   –
NR 1997 8.2m Apr 8] smallish, rather angular colt: eighth foal: brother to very smart miler Gabr and 4-y-o Intisab, and half-brother to 2 winners, notably 5-y-o Kutta: dam 1½m winner from family of Slip Anchor: green, only a little sign of ability in maiden at Nottingham: showed a round action. *R. W. Armstrong*

MUHIB (USA)   2 b.c. (Apr 30) Red Ransom (USA) – Sensorious (CAN) (Vice   76 p
Regent (CAN)) [1997 7.6d3 8s4 Oct 14] $57,000F, $150,000Y: well-made colt: fifth foal: dam won up to 9f in USA: fair form, shaping pretty well, when in frame in maidens at Lingfield then Leicester, fading after going best long way in latter: should do better. *M. R. Stoute*

MUHTADI (IRE)   4 br.g. Marju (IRE) 127 – Moon Parade 73 (Welsh Pageant   – §
132) [1996 76d: 10g* 12d 14.1m 12m 10.2m5 1997 12.3m Jun 19] big, good-topped gelding: fair handicapper at best at 3 yrs for J. Dunlop: well beaten only flat outing in 1997: ungenuine. *Lady Herries*

MUHTAFEL   3 b.c. Nashwan (USA) 135 – The Perfect Life (IRE) 106 (Try My   90
Best (USA)) [1996 NR 1997 8f2 8g* 8.2m2 8d5 Aug 8] second foal: brother to useful 1995 2-y-o 6f winner Najiya: dam, winner at 5f (at 2 yrs) and 7f in France, sister to Last Tycoon: fairly useful form: won maiden at Redcar in June: ran well on handicap debut following month, but never going fluently (on dead ground) only subsequent outing: raced only at 1m: sold 7,500 gns in October and joined M. Quinn. *J. L. Dunlop*

MUHTATHIR 2 ch.c. (Feb 25) Elmaamul (USA) 125 – Majmu (USA) 105   117
(Al Nasr (FR) 126) [1997 6m⁶ 7.1g* 7.1d* 8m² 8g Sep 28]

Forget about Muhtathir's performance on his final outing, when he
trailed home last of eight in the Royal Lodge Stakes at Ascot. It's more than
likely that his hard race in the Prix des Chenes at Longchamp just two weeks
earlier had left its mark. We're confident that the likeable Muhtathir, a tall,
rangy, good sort with a relaxed demeanour, will recapture the smart form he
showed in France (about as good as any shown by a British-trained juvenile in
1997) and pick up a good prize at three years.

Muhtathir made the running at Ascot before fading with over a furlong
to run, unlike at Longchamp where he took the lead early in the straight and ran
on gamely even after Second Empire had taken his measure a furlong out,
pulling well clear of his other rivals in the process. Second Empire, who went
on to win the Grand Criterium, beat Muhtathir by two and a half lengths. This
represented further improvement from Muhtathir, who had followed up a
promising run at Newmarket on his debut with two victories over seven
furlongs at Sandown. The first was in the maiden in which his stable-
companion Benny The Dip had finished runner-up twelve months earlier,
Muhtathir holding on by half a length from Craigsteel after quickening clear
well over one furlong out. The second was a four-runner minor event which
had seemed a virtual match between Muhtathir and the Chesham Stakes fourth
Classic Manoeuvre. In the event it proved a very one-sided contest. Muhtathir,
despite being decidedly lethargic in the paddock, was soon in front, travelling
well, and drew right away in the last two furlongs to win by nine lengths.

	Elmaamul (USA) (ch 1987)	Diesis (ch 1980)	Sharpen Up Doubly Sure
Muhtathir (ch.c. Feb 25, 1995)		Modena (b 1983)	Roberto Mofida
	Majmu (USA) (b 1988)	Al Nasr (b 1978)	Lyphard Caretta
		Affirmative Fable (ch 1981)	Affirmed Fairway Fable

John Gosden also trained Muhtathir's dam, Majmu, a game winner of
the May Hill Stakes, who failed to win in three subsequent starts, although she
did run well when third in a mile-and-a-quarter listed event on her first outing
as a three-year-old. Majmu's first foal, Maftool (by Machiavellian), has done
most of his racing at up to a mile, showing quite useful form on occasions and
winning a maiden in the latest season. The next dam, Affirmative Fable, was a
minor winner around a mile in the States and is one of several winners produced
by Fairway Fable (who was placed in graded company at around a mile), the
best of them Northern Fable, who was successful in a Grade 3 event over a
mile and produced the 1987 Fillies' Mile runner-up Haiati. Fairway Fable's
stakes-winning dam, Fairway Fun, was a half-sister to the 1972 Prix Morny
winner Filiberto and the triple US Grade 1 winner White Star Line. The
last-named has produced the smart French filly Whitehaven and, in the latest
season, the useful two-year-old Titanic. Muhtathir is by the Derby third
Elmaamul, who went on to show better form when returned to a mile and a
quarter, winning the Eclipse Stakes and Phoenix Champion Stakes.

A mile and a quarter will be within Muhtathir's compass, and he may
stay a mile and a half. A tall, rangy colt with a round action, he acts on good to
firm and good to soft ground and has yet to race on extremes. *J. H. M. Gosden*

MUJA'S MAGIC (IRE) 2 b.f. (Apr 6) Mujadil (USA) 119 – Grave Error   43 +
(Northern Treat (USA)) [1997 6m 5.1m⁴ 6d 5g⁵ 6d 7m⁶ 6g³ 7g a5g 9m 8.2d a6g² a7g³   a53
a6g³ a6g* a6g Dec 22] 3,000 2-y-o: half-sister to 2 winners abroad by Anita's Prince:
dam Irish 1½m winner: modest on all-weather: won nursery at Lingfield in December: should stay 7f: acts on equitrack, poor form on turf: has run creditably blinkered.
K. T. Ivory

MUJI   2 b.f. (Feb 25) Safawan 118 – Tame Duchess 71 (Saritamer (USA) 130)   53 ?
[1997 5.1g 6d⁶ 6m Oct 31] 6,800Y: seventh foal: half-sister to several winners,
including one at 7f by Efisio: dam, maiden who stayed 1¼m, half-sister to smart
sprinter Son of Shaka: modest form at best in maidens. *A. P. Jarvis*

MUJOVA (IRE)   3 b.c. Mujadil (USA) 119 – Kirsova (Absalom 128) [1996 80:   84
5d⁶ 5.1d³ 5.1g³ 5.1m³ 5g² 5.1m⁵ 5m⁴ 6m* 6g² 6g⁶ 7m⁵ 7.6g⁴ 6m 6.1s 1997 7m 7f³
7.5m⁴ 8m a8.5g 7d⁶ 7.1m* 7.1g⁶ 7m⁴ 8g 7g⁵ Oct 27] lengthy colt: has a quick action:
fairly useful performer: won minor event at Sandown in September despite not
getting best of runs: none too consistent otherwise in 1997: stays 7f: acts on firm and
dead going. *R. Hollinshead*

MUKADDAR (USA)   3 ch.c. Elmaamul (USA) 125 – Both Sides Now (USA)   98
(Topsider (USA)) [1996 99: 6g* 7g³ 7m² 1997 7g 6d 7g⁶ 8.1d³ 10s 8m 7.9s Oct 8]
leggy colt: has a quick action: useful performer: easily best 3-y-o effort when third
in handicap at Sandown in July: likely to prove best around 1m: acts on good to
firm ground and dead, well beaten on soft: none too consistent: sent to UAE.
C. J. Benstead

MUKARRAB (USA)   3 b. or br.g. Dayjur (USA) 137 – Mahassin (NZ) (Biscay   76 d
(AUS)) [1996 8g⁴ 1997 8s⁴ 8m 6.5s⁶ 9m 9g a6g a6g Nov 21] second foal: dam Grade
1 winning sprinter in Australia: fair maiden (blinkered last 4 starts) in Ireland for
D. Weld, sold 5,200 gns in August and gelded: off track 4 months, well held in 2
claimers on fibresand in Britain. *D. W. Chapman*

MUKDAR (USA)   3 b. or br.c. Gulch (USA) – Give Thanks 123 (Relko 136)   –
[1996 NR 1997 10g 10.3d Jun 28] sturdy, good-bodied colt: has a round action:
half-brother to 3 winners, including 1½m winner Saffaanh (by Shareef Dancer, later
the dam of Harayir): dam won from 9f to 1½m, including Irish Oaks: well held in
maidens at Windsor (upset in stalls) and Doncaster. *Major W. R. Hern*

MUKHATAB   5 b.h. Soviet Star (USA) 128 – Azyaa 101 (Kris 135) [1996 a7g   78
a6g⁵ 1997 8f 11m* 11g² a10f 9m 8d 9m³ Oct 7] fairly useful in 3 starts for H. Thomson
Jones: won handicap at Abu Dhabi in February for K. McLaughlin: sold 12,000 gns
after fourth start: best effort on return to Britain (bit below Dubai form) when third of
16 in handicap at Redcar: stayed 11f: acted on good to firm ground: dead. *J. J. Quinn*

MUKHLLES (USA)   4 b.c. Diesis 133 – Serenely (USA) (Alydar (USA)) [1996   71
82: 8d³ 1997 10f⁴ 12g 10d 8f⁴ 7m 8m³ 8d 6.9m³ 7s a10g⁵ Dec 12] small colt: fair
maiden handicapper: clearly best efforts in 1997 when in frame: best at 7f/1m: acts
on firm going and dead: has run well when sweating: has had tongue tied: none too
consistent. *Bob Jones*

MULAHEN   2 b.g. (Mar 22) Robellino (USA) 127 – Moon Watch 64 (Night Shift   83
(USA)) [1997 7.1g³ 7.1d⁴ 7d³ 8d³ Oct 28] 24,000F, IR 85,000Y: good-topped
gelding: has scope: first foal: dam, second over 6f at 2 yrs, half-sister to smart
middle-distance stayer Lemhill: fairly useful maiden: best efforts when third at
Sandown and Leicester minor event) first and third starts: should stay 1m: raced only
on good/good to soft ground. *D. Morley*

MULLAGH HILL LAD (IRE)   4 b.g. Cyrano de Bergerac 120 – Fantasise   56
(FR) (General Assembly (USA)) [1996 48, a–: 6.1d 6.1d 7.5g 6g⁴ 5.9f⁶ 6g⁶ 6s 6.1m   a68
6m⁶ 1997 a5g⁴ 5.7g³ 5g a6g a6g⁵ Dec 26] dipped-backed gelding: fair on all-weather,
modest on turf: good efforts first 2 starts: left B. McMahon after breaking down next
time and off course 5 months: stays 6f: acts on good to firm and soft ground, goes
well on fibresand: twice blinkered: tends to hang. *N. P. Littmoden*

MULLITOVER   7 ch.g. Interrex (CAN) – Atlantic Air (Air Trooper 115) [1996   84 d
92: 7m³ 8m⁶ 7.3m 7m 1997 7g⁶ 7.1m 7f 7m 7g Oct 18] close-coupled, workmanlike
gelding: fairly useful handicapper: disappointing in 1997 after reappearance: suited
by 7f/1m: acts on firm and soft going and the all-weather: usually races prominently.
M. J. Heaton-Ellis

MULTAN   5 b.g. Indian Ridge 123 – Patchinia 77 (Patch 129) [1996 52: 7g 5g 6d   37
7.1m⁴ 7g 10g 1997 a7g⁵ Jan 9] tall gelding: poor maiden: stays 7f: acts on good to
firm ground and on equitrack: headstrong. *G. L. Moore*

MULTICOLOURED (IRE)   4 b.c. Rainbow Quest (USA) 134 – Greektown   111
(Ela-Mana-Mou 132) [1996 111p: 10m² 12.3d² 10.4g* 10g² 1997 10d² 12m⁴ Sep 12]

good-bodied, attractive colt: fluent mover: smart performer: good 2½ lengths second of 7 to Sasuru in Gordon Richards Stakes at Sandown in April, making much of running: long way below that form in listed race at Doncaster (on faster ground) 4½ months later: should prove better around 1½m than 1¼m: best efforts on good or dead ground, unraced on extremes. *M. R. Stoute*

MULTI FRANCHISE   4 ch.g. Gabitat 119 – Gabibti (IRE) 82 (Dara Monarch   51
128) [1996 56, a60: a8g⁴ a8g² a10g* 10f² 10.2m⁴ 9.7g 8f* 8f a10g 1997 a10g a8g
a8g 8f 8.1g 8.3g⁴ 7f⁴ 7.6g 8.3m³ 10g 8m 8f⁴ 10m⁵ a10g* a10g⁶ a10g a10g⁴ Dec 22]
leggy gelding: modest handicapper: trained by B. Gubby first 3 starts: won at
Lingfield in November: stays easy 1¼m: acts on firm ground and the all-weather: no
improvement in visor/blinkers: tough. *R. M. Flower*

MUMARIS (USA)   3 b. or br.c. Capote (USA) – Barakat 93 (Bustino 136) [1996   89
NR 1997 8.2m⁵ 10d² 10g² 12.3g* 12d⁴ Jun 29] tall, lengthy colt: third foal:
half-brother to useful 1¼m winner Ta Awun (by Housebuster) and 7f winner Fakih
(by Zilzal): dam, stayed 1¾m, is half-sister to Ibn Bey and Roseate Tern out of
half-sister to Teleprompter: fairly useful performer: justified favouritism in maiden
at Ripon in June: last of 4 in minor event at Goodwood later in month: should stay
beyond 1½m: acts on dead going: sold 10,000 gns in October. *A. C. Stewart*

MUMKIN   3 b.c. Reprimand 122 – Soon To Be 84 (Hot Spark 126) [1996 76+: 6g*   –
6g³ 6m 1997 6.1m 6.1g 6g 6m 7g a8g³ Dec 2] tall, leggy colt: fair winner at 2 yrs:
little form in 1997, in seller final start: sold 2,800 gns out of T. Thomson Jones's
stable after second start. *Mrs L. Stubbs*

MUMTAAZ   2 b.c. (Mar 9) Warning 136 – Jameelaty (USA) 96 (Nureyev (USA)   83
131) [1997 6m⁵ 7g 8g 7d² 6d* Nov 13] close-coupled, useful-looking colt: third
foal: dam, 2-y-o 6f winner who stayed 1m, out of sister to versatile graded stakes
performer (stayed 1½m) Bounding Basque: fairly useful form, not knocked about, in
maiden at Newmarket in May: well beaten in similar event at York next time (final
outing for Saeed bin Suroor): won minor event at Le Croise-Laroche in November:
should stay 1m: acts on dead going: attended by 2 handlers and swished tail
throughout preliminaries on debut. *N. Clement, France*

MUNGO PARK   3 b.g. Selkirk (USA) 129 – River Dove (USA) 86 (Riverman   73 §
(USA) 131) [1996 68p: 6.1m 5s 5g⁴ 5d 1997 7m 8.5m 8.2d 7.5d 5f* 6g³ 5g³ 5m 5m
8m 5g* 5d³ Nov 7] big, strong gelding: has a round action: fair performer: won minor
event at Carlisle in May and handicap at Newcastle in October: best at 5f/6f: acts on
firm and dead ground: well beaten in visor: sometimes unruly in stalls: tends to flash
tail and find little under pressure: appeared to try to bite a rival on ninth start:
unreliable. *Mrs J. R. Ramsden*

MUNICIPAL GIRL (IRE)   3 b.f. Mac's Imp (USA) 116 – Morning Welcome   53 d
(IRE) (Be My Guest (USA) 126) [1996 40: 5.1m⁵ a5g⁶ 6d⁴ 7m 6g a6g a5g a8g⁵ 1997
6.1g* 6.1d 5m 6m² 6.1m⁴ 6.1d 5m 7.1g⁵ 6g⁶ 6m 6m a6g a7g Nov 29] angular filly:
modest performer: won seller at Nottingham in April: generally disappointing afterwards: best form at 6f: acts on good to firm going. *B. Palling*

MURCHAN TYNE (IRE)   4 ch.f. Good Thyne (USA) 98 – Ardnamurchan (Ard-   60
ross 134) [1996 NR 1997 10.3d 10.3m⁶ 13.8g⁵ 17.2f⁴ 13.1g⁵ Sep 8] first foal: dam
second in 2m maiden hurdle in Ireland: NH Flat race winner: modest maiden on flat:
best effort in 17f handicap at Carlisle. *E. J. Alston*

MURMOON   2 b.c. (Apr 27) Danehill (USA) 126 – Reflection 111 (Mill Reef   71
(USA) 141) [1997 7f³ 7.5m⁶ 6s⁶ Sep 4] 16,000F, IR 34,000Y: strong colt: half-
brother to several winners, including 4-y-o Dancing Image and 5-y-o Shaft of Light:
dam, 2-y-o 5f to 7f winner, became disappointing: fair form: best effort third in minor
event at Lingfield in July: possibly unsuited by soft going final start: sent to UAE.
B. Hanbury

MURPHY'S GOLD (IRE)   6 ch.g. Salt Dome (USA) – Winter Harvest (Grundy   57
137) [1996 58: 7.5d 8m⁶ 8m 8.5m 7.5m⁴ 7.5f² 7.5m⁴ 8.5m 8.5m⁴ 8m 1997 8g⁴ 8m³
8.5m* 8m 6.9m 7.5d 8m⁵ 8.2d 8g Oct 18] tall gelding: modest handicapper: won at
Beverley (third course success) in June: stays 8.5f well: acts on firm ground, below
form on going softer than good: blinkered (well beaten) twice as 3-y-o: successful for
apprentice and amateur. *R. A. Fahey*

MURRAY GREY   3 gr.f. Be My Chief (USA) 122 – Couleur de Rose (Kalaglow   53
132) [1996 –: 7.5m 7.1v 7m⁶ 1997 6d⁴ 8m² 8m* May 2] strong, lengthy filly: modest
performer: won minor event at Musselburgh in May: subsequently found to have
hair-line fracture of cannon-bone: bred to stay further than 1m. *E. Weymes*

MURRAY'S MAZDA (IRE)   8 ch.g. M Double M (USA) – Lamya 73 (Hittite   –
Glory 125) [1996 56: 7.1g* 7.5m⁵ 7m* 7m³ 6g² 6m 7m 7f⁴ 8m a7g* 1997 a7g Jan
17] leggy gelding: modest handicapper: ran as though something amiss only 8-y-o
start. *J. L. Eyre*

MURRON WALLACE   3 gr.f. Reprimand 122 – Fair Eleanor (Saritamer (USA)   54
130) [1996 53: 5g⁶ 6m⁵ 7m⁵ 8g⁵ 1997 8.3d⁵ 8m⁵ 9.2g⁵ 7m³ 7.1g² 8.3d* 8g* 8.3g
Sep 29] modest handicapper: left R. Whitaker after second start: won at Hamilton
(maiden event) in August and Bath (seller) in September: stays 1m: acts on good to
firm and dead going. *D. Haydn Jones*

MUSAFI (USA)   3 b.g. Dayjur (USA) 137 – Ra'a (USA) 106 (Diesis 133) [1996   66
NR 1997 6m³ May 17] third foal: half-brother to fairly useful 6f winner Awayil
(by Woodman): dam sprinter: keeping-on 4¼ lengths third of 17 to Blue Goblin
in Lingfield maiden: sold to join K. Morgan 10,000 gns in October and gelded.
Major W. R. Hern

MUSALSAL (IRE)   3 b.c. Sadler's Wells (USA) 132 – Ozone Friendly (USA)   110
107 (Green Forest (USA) 134) [1996 89p: 6m⁵ 8g* 1997 8m* 10.4g³ 12g 10.3m³ 10g
9d⁴ Oct 17] quite good-topped colt: smart performer: won minor event at Doncaster
in March: 3¼ lengths third of 9 to Benny The Dip in Dante Stakes at York, but   20
lengths behind him when eighth of 13 in the Derby at Epsom, bumped numerous
times: creditable 1½ lengths third of 4 to Faithful Son in minor event at Doncaster in
September but below best last 2 starts: keen type, but stays 10.4f: yet to race on
extremes of going: tends to go freely to post. *B. W. Hills*

MUSALSE   2 b.g. (May 11) Salse (USA) 128 – Musical Sally (USA) (The Minstrel   –
(CAN) 135) [1997 7d a6g a8.5g Dec 13] 18,000Y: sturdy, workmanlike gelding:
half-brother to 5-y-o Always Grace, a 2-y-o 7f winner by Primo Dominie and 2
winners in USA by Summing: dam unraced: well beaten in maidens. *P. C. Haslam*

MUSCATANA   3 b.f. Distant Relative 128 – Sauhatz (GER) (Alpenkonig (GER))   63
[1996 47+: 5.7f 5.1m 6g⁶ 7.5m 1997 7g* a7g 6.9m⁴ 7v² 7s 6.9g 8.1m⁵ 7m⁶ Oct
17] small, angular filly: modest handicapper: won at Catterick in April: keen sort, but
stays 1m: acts on good to firm and heavy ground (reportedly resented kickback on
fibresand): inconsistent. *B. W. Hills*

MUSHARAK   3 b.c. Mujtahid (USA) 118 – Mahasin (USA) 90 (Danzig (USA))   82
[1996 69p: 6d⁴ 6m 1997 7.1s² 7g 7m* 8s⁵ Oct 13] strong, lengthy colt: unimpressive
mover: fairly useful form: finished lame second start and off course over 4 months:
favourite, 6-length winner of maiden at Kempton on return in September: ran badly
only subsequent outing: should stay 1m: acts on good to firm and soft going: sold
7,000 gns, and sent to Italy. *J. L. Dunlop*

MUSHRAAF   2 b. or br.c. (Feb 9) Zafonic (USA) 130 – Vice Vixen (CAN) (Vice   94
Regent (CAN)) [1997 6s⁴ 6g* 7m⁵ Sep 10] 40,000F, $325,000Y: big, rangy colt: has
scope: fifth foal: half-brother to smart middle-distance filly Cunning (by Bustino)
and fair Irish 1½m winner Samira (by Rainbow Quest): dam unraced: won steadily-
run 4-runner minor event at Salisbury in August: stiff task, not at all discredited,
though no impression from rear, when fifth of 6 to Teapot Row in minor event at
Doncaster: bred to stay at least 1m: edged left last 2 starts. *J. L. Dunlop*

MUSICAL DANCER (USA)   3 ch.c. Dixieland Band (USA) – Parrish Empress   114
(USA) (His Majesty (USA)) [1996 102: 7g⁵ 7.5m* 7g² 6g⁶ 7f² 7m² 1997 10m³ 12f
12d³ 11.9g² Jul 5] close-coupled colt: good walker and fluent mover: smart
performer: best effort when 1½ lengths fifth of 16 (demoted) to Single Empire in
Derby Italiano at Rome in May, hanging markedly left under strong pressure: placed
otherwise in listed events at Newmarket and Haydock and King Edward VII Stakes
(9½ lengths third to Kingfisher Mill) at Royal Ascot: stayed 1½m: died of colic in
late-July. *E. A. L. Dunlop*

MUSICAL PET (IRE)   2 ch.f. (Apr 1) Petardia 113 – Musical Gem (USA) (The   –
Minstrel (CAN) 135) [1997 5m 7.5v 7g Aug 1] 3,200 2-y-o: lightly-made filly:

second foal: half-sister to a winning plater by Mac's Imp: dam Irish 2-y-o 7f winner: no worthwhile form, including in a seller. *J. L. Eyre*

MUSICAL PURSUIT 3 b.c. Pursuit of Love 124 – Gay Music (FR) (Gay   97
Mecene (USA) 128) [1996 113p: 6m⁵ 6m* 7g² 1997 8m 8g 7d 8d³ Sep 20] tall colt:
good walker: second in Dewhurst Stakes at 2 yrs, disappointing in 1997: well held in
2000 Guineas (saddle slipped) and Irish 2000 Guineas (reportedly wrong in blood) in
the spring: only useful form when third in minor event at Newbury on final start:
takes good hold, but should prove well suited by further than 7f: yet to race on
extremes of going: joined J. Noseda. *M. H. Tompkins*

MUSICAL TWIST (USA) 2 ch.f. (Jan 19) Woodman (USA) 126 – Musicale   97
(USA) 109 (The Minstrel (CAN) 135) [1997 6m² Aug 15] quite attractive filly: has a
fluent, round action: second reported foal: dam unbeaten in 5 starts at 2 yrs and won
Fred Darling Stakes, should have been well suited by 1m: 16/1 from 8/1, 1½ lengths
second of 16 to Shmoose in maiden at Newbury, running on very strongly once
getting hang of things: looked promising, but not seen again. *P. W. Chapple-Hyam*

MUSIC EXPRESS (IRE) 3 b.f. Classic Music (USA) – Hetty Green (Bay   51
Express 132) [1996 56: 6m⁵ 7.1g⁴ a6g 1997 8m³ 8m 8g⁵ May 22] modest maiden
handicapper: stays 1m: below form in visor. *J. L. Eyre*

MUSIC GOLD (IRE) 4 b. or br.g. Taufan (USA) 119 – Nonnita 71 (Welsh Saint   93
126) [1996 91: 5g⁴ 5m⁴ 5m⁵ 1997 5d³ 5m⁵ 6g 5m Sep 9] close-coupled gelding: fairly
useful performer, lightly raced: best effort staying-on third in handicap at Sandown
on reappearance: should stay 6f: acts on good to firm and soft ground: usually
blinkered: has been equipped with rope halter: sold 10,000 gns, and sent to Italy.
W. A. O'Gorman

MUSICK HOUSE (IRE) 4 b.c. Sadler's Wells (USA) 132 – Hot Princess 101   93 d
(Hot Spark 126) [1996 92: 8d³ 7.1d* 8d 7m 10m 1997 7.1s³ 7.9g⁶ 10s 7.9d 7f 8v 7g
Oct 18] smallish, angular colt: fairly useful handicapper: good efforts first 2 starts:
well held afterwards, leaving P. Chapple-Hyam after third outing and sold 21,000 gns
after final one: stays 1m: acts on good to firm and soft going: no improvement
blinkered. *Miss Gay Kelleway*

MUSTANG 4 ch.g. Thatching 131 – Lassoo 87 (Caerleon (USA) 132) [1996 –:   43
7.1g a8.5g⁶ 1997 a12g⁵ a12g⁴ a12g⁴ a13g⁴ a11g a8.5g a7g* a6g⁶ a6g⁴ a7g² 6.1d⁶   a56
a8g⁴ a7g² a7s* a7g Dec 18] strong, lengthy gelding: modest handicapper: won at
Wolverhampton (maiden event) in March and Lingfield (improved effort) in
November: ridden too forcefully final outing: best at 7f: acts on dead going, raced
mainly on the all-weather: best in blinkers: game: races prominently: game and
consistent. *C. W. Thornton*

MUSTARD 4 ch.f. Keen 116 – Tommys Dream (Le Bavard (FR) 125) [1996 –:   –
8.2m 8m 8m 1997 8f 10m 10g Jun 20] of little account: keen sort. *A. B. Mulholland*

MUSTIQUE DREAM 2 b.f. (Apr 16) Don't Forget Me 127 – Jamaican Punch   75
(IRE) (Shareef Dancer (USA) 135) [1997 5.7m² a7g² 7g² Aug 11] third foal: half-
sister to fairly useful 1996 2-y-o 6f winner Close Relative and 1½m winner
Oversman (by Keen): dam ran twice: fair form: second in maidens at Bath, Southwell
and Leicester: should stay at least 1m. *R. Charlton*

MUTABARI (USA) 3 ch.c. Seeking The Gold (USA) – Cagey Exuberance   73
(USA) (Exuberant (USA)) [1996 70: 6.1m⁵ 7.1v³ 8.2g 1997 12.3g³ 11.8d 10m 10s⁴
8d 8m⁵ 8.2d⁴ a8s Nov 10] rangy colt: fluent mover: fair maiden at best: left D. Morley
after second start: barely stays 1½m: acts on good to firm and heavy going, well
beaten on equitrack: none too consistent. *K. Mahdi*

MUTABASSIR (IRE) 3 ch.g. Soviet Star (USA) 128 – Anghaam (USA) 80   –
(Diesis 133) [1996 NR 1997 8d⁵ Aug 25] first foal: dam, 1¼m winner, stayed 1½m:
very green when 15 lengths fifth of 9 in maiden at Warwick: sold in October and
joined G. L. Moore. *A. C. Stewart*

MUTADARRA (IRE) 4 ch.g. Mujtahid (USA) 118 – Silver Echo (Caerleon   73
(USA) 132) [1996 81§: 7m² 7g³ 6g* 7.1m 6.1m 1997 a10g 8.3s 9m⁵ 10s 10g² 10m*
12g⁴ 12m 10m 10g Oct 24] tall, angular gelding: fair handicapper: landed gamble at
Newmarket in July under fine ride from Pat Eddery: ran at least respectably after:
effective at 1¼m to 1½m: acts on good to firm going, below form on soft: no

improvement in blinkers: quirky, and probably suited by sound pace and strong handling. *W. J. Musson*

MU-TADIL 5 gr.g. Be My Chief (USA) 122 – Inveraven 53 (Alias Smith (USA)) – [1996 –: 11.7m⁵ 17.2d 1997 14m Oct 1] sturdy gelding: no worthwhile form on Flat since 3 yrs: has looked thoroughly unco-operative over hurdles. *R. J. Baker*

MUTAFARIJ (USA) 2 ch.c. (Jan 27) Diesis 133 – Madame Secretary (USA) 70 p (Secretariat (USA)) [1997 7.1g⁵ 8.2s Oct 15] lengthy colt: has a round action: half-brother to several winners, including Poule d'Essai des Pouliches winner Ta Rib (by Mr Prospector) and useful sprinter/miler Tabdea (by Topsider): dam 1m winner in USA, half-sister to useful stayer Zero Watt: fair form in maidens at Chepstow (backward and started slowly) and Nottingham: sent to UAE: should do better. *E. A. L. Dunlop*

MUTAHADETH 3 ch.g. Rudimentary (USA) 118 – Music In My Life (IRE) 59 54 (Law Society (USA) 130) [1996 56: 7m 7.5f 8f⁵ 8m⁶ 1997 a9.4f⁵ a8g* a11g² a8.5g⁵ a65 a8.5g² 8.5m 8m a8g³ 10s⁵ 8g³ 8m 8m³ 8g a8g Sep 8] angular gelding: modest handicapper: won at Southwell in February: in and out afterwards: effective at 1m to 11f: acts on good to firm ground, best efforts on fibresand: has worn bandages: no improvement blinkered/visored. *D. Shaw*

MUTAMAM 2 b.c. (Apr 28) Darshaan 133 – Petal Girl 96 (Caerleon (USA) 111 p 132) [1997 7.6d* 7.6g* 8g³ Oct 25]

By the Prix du Jockey-Club winner Darshaan, out of a useful half-sister to the late-developing King George and dual Eclipse Stakes winner Mtoto, is a pedigree that takes some living up to. Mutamam hasn't made a bad start, showing himself smart already in just three runs at two. It is no surprise to see him fairly prominent in the ante-post lists for the Derby.

Mutamam lined up for the Racing Post Trophy at Doncaster in late-October pretty much an unknown, for all that he'd won both his previous starts. They'd done ordinary affairs—a maiden at Lingfield in August and a four-runner minor event at Chester in September. Given his breeding, it was impressive that he'd won those races over about seven and a half furlongs at all, the first of them by a length and a quarter from Dancing Phantom, the second, quickening well in a tactical contest, by a length and three quarters from Golden Dice. But the form was useful at best, and he seemed to have more improving to do than most of the seven other runners in the Racing Post field to reach the standard usually required to win the race. At 13/2, he was preferred in the betting to only two. Mutamam put up a very bold showing, held up going well and staying on steadily after being hampered over two furlongs out to finish a short head and a length behind Saratoga Springs and Mudeer. Mutamam's jockey, Richard Hills, objected to the first two for taking his ground but the result was allowed to stand—on the day, he wouldn't definitely have beaten the runner-up, whose fault it seemed to be. It's quite possible, though, that Mutamam will come out best of the trio with more experience behind him and over a longer trip.

		Darshaan	Shirley Heights	Mill Reef
		(br 1981)	(b 1975)	Hardiemma
	Darshaan		Delsy	Abdos
Mutamam	(br 1981)		(br 1972)	Kelty
(b.c. Apr 28, 1995)			Caerleon	Nijinsky
	Petal Girl		(b 1980)	Foreseer
	(ch 1989)		Amazer	Mincio
			(b 1967)	Alzara

Darshaan's progeny generally possess plenty of stamina, the average winning distance of his offspring at three years and over being around the mile and a half mark. Mutamam's dam, Petal Girl, won twice at a mile as a three-year-old but could have been expected to stay further (she was tried only once). Besides being a half-sister to Mtoto, she is a sister to the smart winner around a mile and a quarter (stayed an extended mile and a half) Savoureuse Lady and a half-sister to numerous other winners, including the smart middle-distance performers Astonished and Button Up and to the dams of the smart sprinter Lugana Beach and the useful middle-distance filly Berenice. Mutamam, a medium-sized individual and a good mover, is Petal Girl's second foal and cost 185,000 guineas as a yearling. He's a good prospect for 1998. *A. C. Stewart*

MUTASAWWAR 3 ch.g. Clantime 101 – Keen Melody (USA) 60 (Sharpen Up 66 127) [1996 –: 6m 6g 1997 6m⁴ 5.1d² 5.1m⁴ 5s 5g a7g⁶ a7g² a7s⁵ Nov 28] fair maiden: left E. Dunlop after third start: stays easy 7f: acts on good to firm ground, dead and the all-weather: tail flasher: usually bandaged. *M. S. Saunders*

MUTAWWAJ (IRE) 2 b.c. (Mar 26) Caerleon (USA) 132 – Himmah (USA) 85 102 (Habitat 134) [1997 6d³ 7g² 8m³ 8m* Sep 24] smallish, good-topped colt: fourth foal: closely related to 3-y-o Hachiyah and half-brother to useful 6f to 1m winner Hiwaya (by Doyoun): dam 6f and 7f winner from good family: useful form: landed odds in maiden at Goodwood: placed earlier behind La-Faah in newcomers event at Ascot, Saratoga Springs in Acomb Stakes at York (beaten 5 lengths) and City Honours in maiden at Doncaster: should stay 1¼m: has carried head awkwardly and tended to wander. *Saeed bin Suroor*

MUYASSIR (IRE) 2 b.c. (Mar 25) Brief Truce (USA) 126 – Twine (Thatching 71 131) [1997 6m 6d 6f⁴ 6d Oct 16] 58,000F: compact, deep-bodied colt: ninth foal: half-brother to several winners, including 5-y-o Restructure and very smart 1¼m performer/Champion Hurdler Alderbrook (by Ardross): dam unraced: only form when fourth in maiden at Lingfield: tailed off final start, burly first 2: should stay 1m: sold 20,000 gns after final start. *C. J. Benstead*

MY ABBEY 8 b.m. Hadeer 118 – Rose Barton (Pas de Seul 133) [1996 NR 1997 52 5g⁴ 5f Aug 27] rather close-coupled mare: formerly fair handicapper: just modest form in 2 runs in 1997: best form at 5f, should stay 6f: acts on firm ground, possibly not on dead or softer: visored (ran creditably) earlier in career: often early to post: inconsistent. *A. Bailey*

MY ACHATES 4 b.f. Prince Sabo 123 – Persian Air (Persian Bold 123) [1996 – NR 1997 7f May 1] fifth foal: half-sister to 5-y-o Forzair and 3-y-o Italian 1m winner Setmatt (by Rudimentary): dam well beaten: reluctant at stalls, tailed off in seller. *M. Brittain*

MYASHA (USA) 8 b.g. Imp Society (USA) – Mauna Loa (USA) (Hawaii) [1996 58 44: a7.5g⁴ 7s 5m² 5f 5f⁶ 5h³ 5f 6g⁵ 5d³ 6s 1997 5m⁶ 6g⁶ 5d⁵ 6g⁶ 5f 5g⁴ 5g³ 4d² 6d* 6v a5g Dec 2] neat gelding: modest performer: raced mainly in France and Belgium, winning claimer in the Provinces in the autumn: below form both times in Britain in 1997: effective at 5f to 7f: acts on hard ground, dead and equitrack: tried blinkered: often bandaged behind. *Alex Vanderhaeghen, Belgium*

MY BELOVED (IRE) 3 b.f. Polish Patriot (USA) 128 – Arbour (USA) 76 61 (Graustark) [1996 69: 5m⁵ 6d⁴ 5.7m* 7f³ 1997 8m 8m 7m² 8.3g 8g³ 10s⁴ 8g² 8m² 8d Sep 12] leggy filly: modest performer: stays 1m well: acts on firm and dead ground, soundly beaten on soft: none too consistent: sold, and sent to Norway. *R. Hannon*

MY BEST VALENTINE 7 b.h. Try My Best (USA) 130 – Pas de Calais (Pas de 118 Seul 133) [1996 96: 7f* 6m 7s⁵ 6m² 7g² 6m⁶ 6g 7d² 7g⁵ 8.5m 7m⁵ 7g 1997 7m⁴ 6m⁴ 7.6v 7d⁵ 6m² 6g⁵ 5d* 6m² 6m 5.6m³ 6m 6d* 6g* 6s² Nov 8] strong horse: carries condition: impresses in appearance: improved markedly at 7 yrs, making into a smart performer: won handicap at Sandown (first start since leaving J. White) in July and listed race at Newmarket (by neck from Bollin Joanne) and handicap at Newbury in October: also placed in Stewards' Cup at Goodwood, Portland Handicap at Doncaster and listed races at Lingfield and Doncaster, on last-named course on final start unlucky neck second to Snow Kid, finishing strongly: best at 5f (given test)/6f: acts on any turf going, except possibly heavy: below form in blinkers: tough: a credit to his trainer. *V. Soane*

MY BET 2 b.f. (May 21) Noble Patriarch 115 – Estefan 58 (Taufan (USA) 119) 49 d [1997 5s 5m⁴ 5g³ a5g* 5.1d⁵ a5g⁴ 6g⁶ 6m⁶ 7s⁶ 6m 7g⁵ 7.5f⁵ Sep 17] 700Y: close-coupled filly: fourth foal: half-sister to 1996 2-y-o 5f winner Mill End Girl (by Superpower): dam stayed 6f: poor performer: won seller at Southwell in April: in and out afterwards, though ran well only other start on fibresand: stays 7f. *M. W. Easterby*

Bedford Lodge Hotel Bentinck Stakes, Newmarket—
the much improved seven-year-old My Best Valentine gains his most valuable win;
the reliable Bollin Joanne is second ahead of Snow Kid

MY BETSY 3 gr.f. Absalom 128 – Formidable Task 61 (Formidable (USA) 125) –
[1996 54: 6m⁵ 6d 1997 a8g May 8] strong, lengthy filly: modest maiden, lightly
raced: well beaten only 3-y-o start. *Miss S. E. Hall*

MYBOTYE 4 br.g. Rambo Dancer (CAN) 107 – Sigh 75 (Highland Melody 112) 67
[1996 79: 6.1d³ 7.5m³ 7.9f 6m⁵ 7f* 7.5m⁶ 7.1d 7m 8s 1997 10.3m 7.5m 10g 8.2g 6.9s
7g*ᵈⁱˢ 7m² 7s³ 7.1g* 6.1s⁶ 7f³ 8s⁵ a7g⁴ Nov 21] sturdy gelding: has a round action:
fair handicapper: first past post at Catterick (disqualified for causing interference) in
August and Chepstow in September: seems best around 7f: acts on firm ground and
soft, probably on fibresand: blinkered (below form) fifth start: often hangs left, and
wears near-side pricker. *R. Bastiman*

MY BRANCH 4 b.f. Distant Relative 128 – Pay The Bank 81 (High Top 131) 103
[1996 111: 8m⁴ 8d³ 7m 7m 7m* 7m⁴ 7m³ 8g⁵ 1997 7g⁴ 7.1m³ 7d⁴ 7.3m³ 7m⁵ Jul 31]
leggy, attractive filly: smart at best: in frame in Cheveley Park Stakes at 2 yrs and
1000 Guineas and Irish 1000 Guineas at 3 yrs: just a useful performer in 1997, best
efforts when in frame in listed race at Haydock and Van Geest Criterion Stakes at
Newmarket (length fourth to Ramooz) second and third starts: stayed 1m: acted on
good to firm and dead going: held up: in foal to Polar Falcon. *B. W. Hills*

MY BROTHER 3 b.g. Lugana Beach 116 – Lucky Love 65 (Mummy's Pet 125) –
[1996 NR 1997 7m Sep 21] brother to useful 1994 2-y-o 7f winner Downclose and
half-brother to a winner abroad: dam won 6f seller: showed little in maiden at
Kempton. *Simon Earle*

MY CADEAUX 5 ch.m. Cadeaux Genereux 131 – Jubilee Song 71 (Song 132) 84
[1996 93: 6m* 6g 6d 6s² 6s 1997 5g⁶ Apr 20] angular mare: poor mover: fairly useful
performer: not disgraced when sixth of 9 in listed race at Dusseldorf on only outing
at 5 yrs: stays 6f: acts on good to firm ground, best run on soft. *R. Guest*

MY EMMA 4 b.f. Marju (IRE) 127 – Pato 90 (High Top 131) [1996 115: 118
11.9g⁵ 12f* 10g³ 12m* 1997 12.5g³ 11.9g* 12f Oct 5]

In October it was reported that jockey Darryll Holland had just been
filmed 'winning' twenty-five times in one day at Lingfield for the benefit of a
television commercial. If it had been his own accomplishments and not those of
a cigarette manufacturer that had needed the advertising, we would have
heartily recommended a film of Holland's ride on My Emma in the Yorkshire
Oaks. Sitting well out of your ground before bringing your mount with a

Aston Upthorpe Yorkshire Oaks, York—two older fillies, My Emma and Whitewater Affair, lead the way as the Epsom Oaks winner Reams of Verse fails to run up to her best

flamboyant late flourish is seldom a recommended tactic, but it was de rigueur for My Emma, and in Holland she found a cool practitioner who was able to bring out the best in her. A strong pace up front is an important part of the plot, and My Emma got it in the Yorkshire Oaks thanks to another four-year-old, Whitewater Affair. My Emma was still last of the eight runners and had six lengths to make up approaching the three-furlong marker, but those ahead of her were beginning to tire, while My Emma was going so strongly that Holland's chief task now was to point her in the right direction. 'She stays well but has one run' said My Emma's trainer Rae Guest. 'If she can use it, it is a good weapon.' With Holland having overcome any temptation to use her too soon, My Emma moved through the field on the inside before being switched outside Whitewater Affair, then went on to win by three quarters of a length.

Another contributory factor to that Yorkshire Oaks victory, of course, was the disappointing showing of 7/4-on Reams of Verse who finished fourth. The only other previous Group 1 winner in the field, My Emma was a 7/1 chance. Perhaps she was overpriced, but she was not a filly with a high profile in Britain despite being trained here. Her Group 1 win as a three-year-old, in a blanket finish to the Prix Vermeille, had been at Longchamp, one of just six career starts before York, half of which had been in France. With her training in 1997 geared solely around the Group 1 prizes on offer in the second half of the season, My Emma had her Yorkshire Oaks warm-up at Maisons-Laffitte, where she was a good third of five to Surgeon and Kutta, giving them weight, in the Prix Maurice de Nieuil. Her next race after York was to be the Prix de l'Arc. The risks in waiting for a late-season target, however, were graphically illustrated when My Emma took a fall on her way back from exercise two weeks before the race. Her health was affected and her training interrupted by a haematoma on her near-side quarter, and My Emma was declared a doubtful runner. In the end, she did take her place in the Arc field but completed in only eleventh of eighteen. She would have had to have improved a good deal to figure in the shake-up, but was still clearly below her best. It was also the final race of her career, so connections will be doubly thankful that Holland had brought part one of the grand plan to fruition in the Yorkshire Oaks. She is reportedly likely to be covered by Machiavellian.

		Last Tycoon	Try My Best
	Marju (IRE)	(b 1983)	Mill Princess
	(br 1988)	Flame of Tara	Artaius
My Emma		(b 1980)	Welsh Flame
(b.f. 1993)		High Top	Derring-Do
	Pato	(br 1969)	Camenae
	(b 1982)	Patosky	Skymaster
		(b 1969)	Los Patos

My Emma's pedigree has been described in the last two Annuals under her entry and also those on her half-brother Classic Cliche, while Pato's 1994 filly by Pursuit of Love has given little cause for an update—Lust, alas, never saw action on the racecourse and, appropriately, beat My Emma to the paddocks. A workmanlike filly, My Emma stayed at least twelve and a half furlongs and never raced on going softer than good. She had a good turn of foot. *R. Guest*

MY FIREBIRD 3 b.f. Rudimentary (USA) 118 – Miss Rossi (Artaius (USA) 129) [1996 NR 1997 7.1s 10m May 28] 7,400Y: long-backed filly: sixth live foal: half-sister to several winners, notably useful sprinters Dancing Music (by Music Boy) and Heather Bank (by Nordance): dam unraced: burly, never placed to challenge in northern maidens. *J. J. O'Neill* –

MY FLOOSIE 2 b.f. (May 9) Unfuwain (USA) 131 – My Chiara 95 (Ardross 134) [1997 8g Oct 24] small filly: first foal: dam winning stayer on flat and over hurdles: tailed off in maiden at Doncaster. *P. J. Bevan* –

MYFONTAINE 10 b.h. Persepolis (FR) 127 – Mortefontaine (FR) (Polic 126) [1996 74, a58: 10.8d³ 10g 10.8f 10.8g* 10.8f⁵ 10m⁴ 10g 10m 10g⁵ 10g 8.9g⁵ 10.1m 8.2g² 10g a10s⁴ a13g 1997 a11g³ a8g a9.4g 10s May 12] leggy horse: fair handicapper at best, winner of 11 races, 8 of them at Warwick: only poor form in 1997: effective at 1m to 11f: used to act on any going, but possibly not at his best on ground firmer than good in later years: held up: retired to stud at Little Paddock, Buckinghamshire *K. T. Ivory* a49

MY GIRL 3 b.f. Mon Tresor 113 – Lady of Itatiba (BEL) (King of Macedon 126) [1996 33, a39: 5f³ 5m 5f⁶ 5m⁵ 6m a5g³ a5g 6s 1997 a5g³ a6g a6g Mar 8] close-coupled filly: poor maiden: should stay 6f: tried blinkered at 2 yrs. *R. Hollinshead* a39

MY GIRL LUCY 3 b.f. Picea 99 – English Mint 66 (Jalmood (USA) 126) [1996 –: 6.9g⁶ 1997 7g 8f 7s⁴ 7g 8g a9.4g a9.4g Aug 16] angular filly: little worthwhile form: tried blinkered. *P. Mitchell* –

MY GODSON 7 br.g. Valiyar 129 – Blessit 79 (So Blessed 130) [1996 60, a–: a7g⁶ 5g 6s 7d* 7g² 7m 7.5m* 6g³ 6f⁴ 7m* 7.5g³ 7.9g 8.5m 7g 1997 7.5m 7g 8m a5g a7g 7d 8g Oct 22] sturdy gelding: formerly modest handicapper: gave impression something amiss most starts in 1997. *M. Dods* –

MY HANDSOME PRINCE 5 b.g. Handsome Sailor 125 – My Serenade (USA) 45 (Sensitive Prince (USA)) [1996 43: 8g² 8f⁵ 10m 8.1g a8.5g⁵ a8.5g 8m⁵ 8.1m 10d a8.5g a9.4g⁴ 1997 6.9d⁶ 8d⁴ 10g a9.4g 8s³ 8m² 6.9m 8m Aug 12] sturdy gelding: poor maiden: stays 1m: acts on firm and soft ground: tried blinkered/visored. *P. J. Bevan* 35

MY HERO (IRE) 3 b.f. Bluebird (USA) 125 – Risacca (ITY) (Sir Gaylord) [1996 71: 6m⁵ 7m⁴ 8d 1997 14.4m a14.8g⁴ Dec 13] well-made filly: fair form at 2 yrs: well beaten in 1997. *T. G. Mills* –

MY JESS 3 b.f. Jester 119 – Miss Levantine (Levanter 121) [1996 NR 1997 8d 10.2f⁶ 7.1d Jul 5] fourth reported foal: dam winning pointer: soundly beaten in maidens. *S. G. Knight* –

MY LEARNED FRIEND   6 b. or br.g. Broken Hearted 124 – Circe 73 (Main   83
Reef 126) [1996 86: 10m 12g 12m² 11.9g³ 13.9m 12m⁶ 12g 12g 1997 12m⁶ 12d 12d²
11.9g² 13.3f⁴ 14g⁶ 11.9g 12m 11.9g Sep 26] workmanlike gelding: still a fairly useful
handicapper, though again went without a win in 1997: second at Newmarket and in
Old Newton Cup at Haydock: well below form last 3 outings, blinkered on final one:
stays 1¾m: acts on firm and dead ground: held up. *A. Hide*

MY LEGAL EAGLE (IRE)   3 b.g. Law Society (USA) 130 – Majestic Nurse   –
80 (On Your Mark 125) [1996 5d 8d⁵ 8g 9s 1997 a10g⁴ Jan 4] ex-Irish gelding:
half-brother to several winners, including 11-y-o Awesome Power: dam won Irish
Cambridgeshire: modest maiden (rated 64) for M. Cunningham: below form only
start here: should stay 1¼m: best effort on good ground: blinkered final start at 2 yrs.
J. W. Hills

MY LEWICIA (IRE)   4 b.f. Taufan (USA) 119 – Christine Daae 74 (Sadler's   97
Wells (USA) 132) [1996 100: 8m² 8d* 8m² 8m⁶ 1997 10g⁵ 8.2m⁴ 8s⁴ 8.1g 10.1m²
11.9g 10.3m Sep 13] angular, workmanlike filly: useful handicapper: good second to
Sandmoor Chambray at Newcastle in August: well beaten last 2 starts: stays 1¼m:
acts on good to firm and soft ground: none too consistent. *P. W. Harris*

MY LOST LOVE   2 b.g. (Feb 2) Green Desert (USA) 127 – Love of Silver (USA)   54
110 (Arctic Tern (USA) 126) [1997 6g⁶ 6m 6s⁴ Oct 16] tall gelding: first foal: dam,
6f and 7f winner at 2 yrs and third in Prix Marcel Boussac, should have been well
suited by 1½m: modest form in maidens: off course 3½ months after debut: bred to
be suited by further than 6f. *M. Johnston*

MY MELODY PARKES   4 b.f. Teenoso (USA) 135 – Summerhill Spruce 70   102
(Windjammer (USA)) [1996 102: 7m⁴ 8m 6m² 6m 6d⁴ 5g³ 1997 6g 6.1s 7m² 6m²
6m⁴ 5d* 6g 5.1g⁴ Sep 28] strong, lengthy filly: useful performer: best 4-y-o effort
when winning minor event at Lingfield in August by ½ length from Cathedral: best
up to 7f: acts on good to firm and dead going: usually races prominently: genuine.
J. Berry

MY MILLIE   4 ch.f. Midyan (USA) 124 – Madam Millie 99 (Milford 119) [1996   49
52: 8m 7f 6g 6g 7g 11f² 12m 10.1m 1997 8g 9.9m 11f² 10g² 10g⁵ 12g* 12.4g⁴ 16m
15.8g⁶ 12m Oct 6] tall, lightly-made filly: poor performer: won claimer at Catterick
for D. Barker in July: stayed 1½m: acted on firm going: visored (well beaten) once:
tail flasher: dead. *W. Storey*

MYOSOTIS   3 ch.g. Don't Forget Me 127 – Ella Mon Amour 65 (Ela-Mana-Mou   38
132) [1996 60?: 6g 7m 7f⁶ 6g⁶ a7s 1997 8m 8.3g 8f⁶ 10s 16.4s a14g Nov 24] angular
gelding: disappointing maiden: may prove suited by test of stamina: often blinkered:
possibly temperamental. *P. W. Hiatt*

MY PLEDGE (IRE)   2 b.c. (Apr 13) Waajib 121 – Pollys Glow (IRE) (Glow   61 p
(USA)) [1997 7m Oct 1] IR 32,000Y: second foal: dam Irish 1m (at 2 yrs) and 1½m
winner, half-sister to Irish 1000 Guineas winner Prince's Polly: 33/1, some promise
when ninth of 20 in maiden at Salisbury, slowly away and not knocked about: moved
well to post: should improve. *C. A. Horgan*

MYRMIDON   3 b.g. Midyan (USA) 124 – Moorish Idol 90 (Aragon 118) [1996   92
88: 6s² 6m⁶ 6d² 5g⁴ 5m 5d* 1997 5s² 5d 5d⁵ 6d⁶ 5d 5.1s a6s Nov 28] rather sparely-
made gelding: good walker: fairly useful performer: best effort when second in listed
race at Haydock on reappearance: off course 5 months, reportedly finished lame final
start: best at 5f on good ground or softer: blinkered penultimate start: normally led to
post early. *Mrs L. Stubbs*

MY ROLAND (IRE)   3 ch.c. Topanoora 118 – Value Voucher (IRE) (Kings Lake   –
(USA) 133) [1996 NR 1997 10s⁶ 10m 12m 12d Oct 21] IR 3,500Y: first foal: dam
unraced: well beaten in maidens and handicap. *J. Ffitch-Heyes*

MY ROSSINI   8 b.g. Ardross 134 – My Tootsie 88 (Tap On Wood 130) [1996 –:   –
14.1m 1997 14.1g Jun 18] modest staying handicapper: dead. *P. J. Bevan*

MYRTLEBANK   3 ch.f. Salse (USA) 128 – Magical Veil 73 (Majestic Light   83
(USA)) [1996 81: 8.1d* 8s⁶ 1997 10m³ 12g⁵ 12g Sep 5] close-coupled filly: fairly
useful performer: ran well first 2 starts: stays 1½m: acts on good to firm and dead
going. *H. R. A. Cecil*

MYRTLE QUEST 5 b.g. Rainbow Quest (USA) 134 – Wryneck 89 (Niniski 82 (USA) 125) [1996 NR 1997 11.9s⁶ 10g 8m* 8v 8m Nov 1] lengthy, good-topped gelding: unimpressive mover: fairly useful handicapper, lightly raced: clearly best 5-y-o effort when winning 17-runner event at Kempton in September: stays 1¼m: best efforts on good/good to firm going. *R. Charlton*

MY SALTARELLO (IRE) 3 b.g. Salt Dome (USA) – Daidis 66 (Welsh Pageant 35 132) [1996 48: 5m⁴ 6m 7f 1997 8.3d 10g 5m⁴ 5g⁵ 7g Jul 28] poor maiden: best efforts at sprint distances: sometimes blinkered. *A. B. Mulholland*

MYSTAGOGUE 2 ch.c. (May 14) Mystiko (USA) 124 – Malibasta 83 (Auction 59 Ring (USA) 123) [1997 6.1d 7m⁵ 6m 6d⁶ 8d 8g⁶ 8m⁶ a7g² a10s* Nov 28] 11,000Y: angular colt: third foal: half-brother to 3-y-o Lamorna: dam 6f (at 2 yrs) and 1m winner: modest performer: second in seller at Lingfield before winning maiden there: stays 1¼m: acts on equitrack and good to firm ground: has shown signs of temperament. *R. Hannon*

MYSTERIOUS ECOLOGY 2 gr.f. (May 26) Mystiko (USA) 124 – Ecologic- 72 p ally Kind (Alleged (USA) 138) [1997 7g 8m⁴ Sep 22] first foal: dam unraced: better effort in maidens (trained by C. Brittain on debut) when staying-on fourth at Kempton, still green: should stay beyond 1m: open to further progress. *B. W. Hills*

MYSTERIUM 3 gr.c. Mystiko (USA) 124 – Way To Go 69 (Troy 137) [1996 –: – 6m a7g⁶ 1997 a7g* a8.5g⁵ 8g 7d a11g² a9.4g³ a12g Dec 13] tall, leggy colt: modest a58 performer: won maiden at Wolverhampton in February: placed in apprentice claimers at Southwell and Wolverhampton in the summer: stays 11f: acts on fibresand, no form on turf. *N. P. Littmoden*

MYSTERY 3 b.f. Mystiko (USA) 124 – Dismiss 95 (Daring March 116) [1996 55 68d: 5g⁴ 6m² 6m 6m 7d 6d a6g a7s a6g⁴ 1997 a7g* Jan 11] sturdy filly: modest performer: won handicap at Lingfield by 6 lengths, only start in 1997. *S. Dow*

MYSTERY GUEST (IRE) 2 b.g. (May 22) Alzao (USA) 117 – Lora's Guest 99 62 p (Be My Guest (USA) 126) [1997 5d 6s⁵ 6f² 6g Aug 2] IR 72,000Y: fifth foal: half-brother to 4-y-o Centre Stalls and 1¾m winner Nawahil (by Shirley Heights): dam, 7f winner who stayed 1m, sister to 1000 Guineas winner On The House: modest form in maidens at Epsom and Brighton second and third starts: ran poorly when favourite on nursery debut: should be better suited by at least 1m: has given trouble stalls (gelded at end of season): type to do fair bit better as 3-y-o. *Sir Mark Prescott*

MYSTERY HILL (USA) 3 b.f. Danehill (USA) 126 – Tendermark (Prince 72 Tenderfoot (USA) 126) [1996 NR 1997 7g 7s 8f⁵ 8.3s⁶ 8m⁶ 7d⁶ Aug 25] IR 24,000Y: well-made filly: half-sister to Irish 7f and 1¼m winner Monica's Choice (by Shaadi) and Italian 6f and 7.5f winner Rainbow Velvet (by Royal Academy): dam, Irish 7f winner, stayed 1m: fair maiden: clearly best effort on third start: stays 1m: acts on firm ground: tried visored: sent to UAE. *J. H. M. Gosden*

MYSTERY MAN 2 gr.g. (Apr 1) Mystiko (USA) 124 – Baileys By Name 66 – (Nomination 125) [1997 5m 5m Jul 21] 6,700 2-y-o: sturdy gelding: third foal: half-brother to 4-y-o Prime Partner: dam 2-y-o 6f winner: no show, including in claimer. *P. C. Haslam*

MYSTERY MATTHIAS 4 b.f. Nicholas (USA) 111 – Devils Dirge 68 (Song 44 132) [1996 54: a7g⁶ a6g³ a7g⁴ 6m³ 6m⁴ 5m⁶ 6m⁶ 7g⁶ 7f 6.9g⁵ a5g a6g⁴ a6g² 1997 a6g⁴ a7g³ a6g² a7g⁶ a6g² Feb 25] workmanlike filly: poor maiden handicapper: stays 7f: acts on firm ground and equitrack: blinkered/visored: usually races prominently. *Miss B. Sanders*

MYSTICAL 3 gr.f. Mystiko (USA) 124 – Midnight Imperial (Night Shift (USA)) 71 [1996 NR 1997 6.1d² 5s 5.1f⁵ 5m³ 5g 5d⁴ 5d* 5.7g² 5m 6g* 5.1g 6m² 6d a5g a5g a6g* Dec 2] 9,000Y: lengthy filly: fourth foal: half-sister to 3 winners, including Harveys Point (useful up to 7f, by Keen) and White Sorrel (fairly useful up to 7f, by Chilibang): dam poor maiden: fair performer: won selling handicap at Musselburgh and handicap Brighton in the summer and claimer at Lingfield in December: effective at 5f (given test) to 6f: acts on firm ground, dead and equitrack: usually visored. *Mrs L. Stubbs*

MYSTICAL ISLAND 3 b.f. Deploy 131 – Do Run Run 75 (Commanche Run — 133) [1996 –: 6g 1997 12m a11g Jun 19] no worthwhile form. *C. A. Cyzer*

MYSTICAL RODGE 2 b.g. (Mar 31) Mystiko (USA) 124 – Deux Etoiles 86 — (Bay Express 132) [1997 6g 5m Oct 28] 4,500Y, 20,000 2-y-o: close-coupled gelding: half-brother to several winners, including 1991 2-y-o Gemini Bay (6f, by Petong) and Five Star Affair (1¼m seller, by Mummy's Game): dam 2-y-o 5f winner: never going pace in maidens 2 months apart. *M. Dods*

MYSTICAL SONG 2 ch.f. (Apr 5) Mystiko (USA) 124 – Jubilee Song 71 (Song 68 p 132) [1997 5d Oct 21] half-sister to several winners, notably 5f peformers Prince Sabo (very smart, by Young Generation) and Millyant (smart, by Primo Dominie): dam 5f winner: 16/1 and green, not knocked about when keeping-on eighth in maiden at Folkestone: sure to improve. *R. Guest*

MYSTIC FLIGHT (USA) 2 b.f. (Feb 20) Silver Hawk (USA) 123 – Wand 70 p (IRE) 69 (Reference Point 139) [1997 7d Nov 7] close-coupled filly: second foal: half-sister to 3-y-o Vanishing Trick: dam, 1¾m winner, is out of close relative of Sadler's Wells: 10/1, on toes and green, shaped quite bit better than bare result (rated accordingly) when tenth to High-Rise in maiden at Doncaster, short of room as race began in earnest and not knocked about: bred to be well suited by 1¼m+: sure to do better and worth noting for a maiden. *R. Charlton*

MYSTICISM 2 ch.f. (May 4) Mystiko (USA) 124 – Abuzz 101 (Absalom 128) 79 [1997 5g⁴ 6g⁵ 5s² 5m² 5.2f⁵ 5m 6m⁴ 5.1g⁶ 6g Oct 18] 4,500Y: sturdy filly: fifth foal: sister to 3-y-o Puzzlement and half-sister to 4-y-o World Premier: dam won at 5f (at 2 yrs) and 7f and is half-sister to dam of Revoque: fair maiden: second in nursery at York fourth start: stiff tasks and ran creditably next 2 starts: poor efforts final 3: should stay 6f: acts on firm ground. *C. E. Brittain*

MYSTIC MAID (IRE) 4 b.f. Mujtahid (USA) 118 – Dandizette (Danzig (USA)) — [1996 62: 6g 5m³ 1997 8d 6m May 27] smallish, good-topped filly: modest maiden: well beaten in 1997. *J. L. Harris*

MYSTIC QUEST (IRE) 3 b.g. Arcane (USA) – Tales of Wisdom 70 (Rousillon 66 (USA) 133) [1996 65, a69: a6g³ 7s 6.9m⁴ 7f² 7m⁴ 7.6m a8.5g* 7g 7.3s 1997 10.8m³ a80 10.3d² 11.8g² 14.1g 14.1g a12g* a10g Nov 6] quite attractive colt: fairly useful handicapper on all-weather, fair on turf: easily best effort when winning at Lingfield in October: stays 1½m, seemingly not 1¾m: acts on firm and dead ground (showed little on soft) and the all-weather: has gained both wins in visor. *K. McAuliffe*

MYSTIC RIDGE 3 ch.g. Mystiko (USA) 124 – Vallauris 94 (Faustus (USA) 84 118) [1996 –: 5.2s⁶ 1997 8g³ 10s 10g² 10g³ 11m Nov 4] good-bodied gelding: fairly useful maiden: sold out of D. Elsworth's stable 32,000 gns before final start (reluctant stalls and well held): stays 1¼m. *B. J. Curley*

MYSTIC STRAND 4 b.f. Lugana Beach 116 – Tantra 72 (Song 132) [1996 NR 49 1997 8f² 10.2d 11.9f⁶ 9.7s a12g* a12g³ a12g Nov 1] rather leggy filly: half-sister to 3 minor winners: dam won 3 sprint races at 2 yrs: poor performer: won seller at Wolverhampton in July: off course 3 months, slowly away and tailed off final start: stays 1½m: acts on fibresand and firm ground. *W. G. M. Turner*

MYSTIC TIMES 4 b.f. Timeless Times (USA) 99 – Chikala 81 (Pitskelly 122) 28 [1996 40: 6.1m 6g 5g 6.1m 7.5m 7d 9.2f* 8m⁵ 11.1g⁴ 8.3g 1997 8m 11.1s 12d 8g 8g⁴ 10.9g⁴ 8m 9.2d⁴ 9.2m Aug 18] small, sparely-made filly: poor handicapper: stays 1¼m: acts on firm and dead ground: below form in visor/blinkers. *B. Mactaggart*

MYSTIQUE AIR (IRE) 3 b.f. Mujadil (USA) 119 – Romany Pageant (Welsh 65 Pageant 132) [1996 66?: 7m³ 7.9g⁵ 1997 7s⁵ 7m³ 9g⁵ 5.9m² 7g* 6.9f⁵ 7s 7.1g 7m 7s Oct 17] tall, rather plain filly: fair performer: won weak maiden at Catterick in July: well below form last 3 starts: stays 7f: acts on good to firm and soft ground. *E. Weymes*

MYSTIQUE SMILE 4 ch.f. Music Boy 124 – Jay Gee Ell 78 (Vaigly Great 127) 36 [1996 45: 5d 6g 5.3f³ 5f⁶ 5f 1997 5g 6m 5g 5g 6.1m Sep 15] leggy filly: poor sprint handicapper: acts on good to firm ground: blinkered (well beaten) once. *J. S. Goldie*

MYTHICAL 3 gr.f. Mystiko (USA) 124 – Geryea (USA) (Desert Wine (USA)) 75
[1996 55p: 6m a6g⁴ 1997 8m* a8.5g² 6.1g a7g² a8g* a9.4g⁶ a8g* Sep 8] big, rangy
filly: fair performer: won 2-runner Newmarket Challenge Whip in May, minor event
at Southwell in July and handicap (amateurs) there in September: best form at 1m:
acts on fibresand, raced only on good going or firmer on turf: best with waiting
tactics: sold 18,000 gns, and sent to Saudi Arabia. *Sir Mark Prescott*

MYTTONS MISTAKE 4 b.g. Rambo Dancer (CAN) 107 – Hi-Hunsley 82 83
(Swing Easy (USA) 126) [1996 74, a71: a7g³ a6g³ a7g² a5g³ a7g³ 6.1g² 5.1m 6m a70
7m⁵ 5.1m⁴ 6m³ 5g 5d 5.1d 5m 6d 7g³ a6g a7g³ 1997 a7f⁶ a6g² a6g² a6g⁴ a5g³
6.9f 7m 7d⁴ 7.6m⁴ 6m⁴ 7.6m⁴ 7g⁴ 7g² 7.5g* 7.6s 7s 7.1m* 7d 7m 8g* 10d⁶ a8g⁵
a7g Dec 10] leggy, workmanlike gelding: fairly useful handicapper on turf, fair on
all-weather: in good form for most of year, winning at Chester (apprentices) in July,
Beverley in August, Sandown in September and Leicester (apprentice claimer, by 8
lengths) in October: left A. Bailey after final win: stays 1m: acts on the all-weather,
best turf form on good ground or firmer: below form in blinkers: tough and
consistent. *R. J. Hodges*

MY TYSON (IRE) 2 b.c. (Apr 30) Don't Forget Me 127 – Shuckran Habibi 59
(Thatching 131) [1997 6g 7m 6d 7g 6m a5s* Nov 10] 800Y: lengthy, good-bodied a66
colt: half-brother to winners abroad by Cyrano de Bergerac (2) and Al Hareb: dam
ran once: fair form when winning maiden at Lingfield, making most: only modest on
turf: probably a sprinter: acts on equitrack. *K. Mahdi*

MY VALENTINA 3 b.f. Royal Academy (USA) 130 – Imperial Jade 105 (Loch- 77
nager 132) [1996 84p: 7m² 7.1s* 10g 1997 7.3s⁵ 7.1g 9f 10.3d² 10g⁶ 10.5g 10m Oct
3] rangy filly: fair handicapper: stays 1¼m: acts on good to firm and soft ground:
headstrong early in year. *B. W. Hills*

N

NAAYEL (IRE) 2 b.c. (Feb 3) Brief Truce (USA) 126 – Diamond Lake (Kings –
Lake (USA) 133) [1997 6m 5.2m⁵ 6g 7f Oct 3] 50,000Y: sturdy colt: fifth foal: half-
brother to 3-y-o Smart Kid, 1½m seller winner Bunker (by Scenic) and a winner in
Austria by Last Tycoon: dam Irish 2-y-o 7f winner from good family: only a little
sign of ability in maidens and nursery: has hung and carried head awkwardly: blinkered third outing. *C. J. Benstead*

NABHAAN (IRE) 4 b.c. In The Wings 128 – Miss Gris (USA) 120 (Hail The 109
Pirates (USA) 126) [1996 102: 10g² 12.3m* 12d³ 12m⁶ 11.9g³ 14.8d⁴ 10s³ 12s³
1997 11.4g* 12m² 13.3s⁶ 11.5m² 12m² 11.9g⁴ 12g⁴ 14g³ Sep 26] big, strong,
close-coupled colt: useful performer: won minor event at Nottingham in April:
ran well in similar race at Lingfield (neck second to Taufan's Melody), behind
Zaralaska in Bessborough Handicap at Royal Ascot and Old Newton Cup at Haydock
fifth and sixth starts and in September Stakes at Epsom (5¾ lengths fourth to
Maylane) penultimate outing: effective at 1½m to 1¾m: acts on good to firm and soft
ground: visored (finished last) once: tricky ride (has gone in snatches, and hangs off
bridle) and best held up in truly-run race: not one to trust implicitly: sent to UAE.
D. Morley

NABJELSEDR 7 b.g. Never So Bold 135 – Klewraye (Lord Gayle (USA) 124) 40 §
[1996 43: 7m 10d 8.1m³ 8.1m 8f⁴ 1997 8f³ 9g 8.1m Jul 11] leggy gelding: unimpressive mover: poor handicapper: refused to race final start: stays 1m: acts on firm
ground: one to treat with caution. *A. G. Newcombe*

NABURN LOCH 7 b.m. Lochnager 132 – Balgownie 43 (Prince Tenderfoot –
(USA) 126) [1996 NR 1997 8f 10.2m⁶ 10.8d Jun 24] seems of little account.
D. M. Hyde

NADWAH (USA) 2 b.f. (Jan 23) Shadeed (USA) 135 – Tadwin 109 (Never So 107
Bold 135) [1997 5.2d* 5m³ 5m* 6g³ 6m⁶ Sep 30] strong, good-quartered filly: fourth
foal: half-sister to 3-y-o Husun, 1995 2-y-o 5f winner Tarf (by Diesis) and fairly useful sprinter Iltimas (by Dayjur): dam sprinting half-sister to smart sprinter Reesh:
useful form: won minor event at Newbury and Queen Mary Stakes at Royal Ascot,

missing break in latter but getting up to short-head Crazee Mental, pair clear: good
1½ lengths third to Cape Verdi in Lowther Stakes at York: raced too freely when
below best in Cheveley Park Stakes: stays 6f: acts on good to firm ground, has won
on dead: has been taken early to post. *P. T. Walwyn*

NAGOBELIA   9 b. or br.g. Enchantment 115 – Lost Valley 60 (Perdu 121) [1996   –
NR 1997 a12g 14m⁵ Aug 17] second foal: dam winning selling hurdler: well beaten
in sellers. *J. Pearce*

NA HUIBHEACHU (IRE)   6 ch.g. Nostrum (USA) – Royal Slip (Royal Match   36
117) [1996 9d² 9g² 12g⁴ 12.3m² 8.5g⁴ 9g⁴ 12m 1997 9s⁶ 9f⁵ 10m⁴ 11.9m⁶ a8g⁴ a10g
Dec 19] ex-Irish gelding: half-brother to smart and very tough American mare Irish
Linnet (by Seattle Song): dam Irish 6f/7f winner at 5 yrs: poor maiden handicapper
(rated 48 at 5 yrs): trained first 2 starts in 1997 by D. Hughes: stays 1½m: acts on
good to firm and good to soft ground, best run in Britain on equitrack: tried blinkered.
J. S. Moore

NAILS TAILS   4 b.g. Efisio 120 – Northern Dynasty 65 (Breeders Dream 116)   40
[1996 –: 10m 1997 a10g⁶ a10g⁴ a12g⁴ a8g⁵ 9.7m³ 12m⁵ 11.5d⁵ 11.5s⁴ 12d⁵ Jun 29]
poor maiden handicapper: effective from 1m to 1½m: acts on good to firm and soft
going and on equitrack: swishes tail. *S. Dow*

NAISSANT   4 b.f. Shaadi (USA) 126 – Nophe (USA) 95 (Super Concorde (USA)   63 d
128) [1996 71: 7.6g 7.5m⁵ 10m 6m³ 6d 6m⁵ 6f² 6d* 6.9m* 7g 6m 7.1d 6d⁵ 6g
6g⁶ a6g 1997 a6g 6d 8g 6s² 5.9d 5s 6d 6.1m⁵ 7m 5s Oct 14] sparely-made filly: has
roundish action: modest handicapper: below form after fourth start, leaving
R. McKellar after sixth: effective at 6f to 7f: probably acts on any turf ground,
seemingly not on all-weather: not to be trusted. *Martyn Wane*

NAIVASHA   3 gr.f. Petong 126 – Nevis 61 (Connaught 130) [1996 62: 5f⁴ 6f³ 5f⁵   53
6d* 6m 1997 a6g a6g⁴ a8g² a7g a8g 8.3g* 8g³ 7g⁶ 7m⁵ Jul 21] lengthy filly: modest
performer: enterprisingly ridden, won 5-runner minor event at Hamilton in June:
creditable efforts most other starts: barely stays 1m: acts on firm ground, dead and
fibresand. *J. Berry*

NAJJAR (USA)   2 gr.c. (Apr 7) El Prado (IRE) 119 – With Strawberries (USA)   71
(Maudlin (USA)) [1997 6d⁶ 8.5g³ 8.2m Sep 15] $50,000Y: workmanlike colt: has a
round action: first foal: dam stakes-placed winner at up to 7f in USA: fair form in
newcomers event at Ascot and steadily-run maiden at Beverley: well beaten final
start: not sure to stay beyond 8.5f: sold 20,000 gns in October. *P. T. Walwyn*

Hamdan Al Maktoum's "Nadwah"

NAJM MUBEEN (IRE) 4 b.g. Last Tycoon 131 – Ah Ya Zein (Artaius (USA) 99
129) [1996 96: 10m* 9s² 1997 10m³ 10m 8m 10.4m² 10m 10.4g Aug 20] good-
topped gelding: useful handicapper: best effort when ½-length second of 21 to
Pasternak in steadily-run Magnet Cup at York in June, settled rear then (despite
hanging violently left from 3f out) finishing very strongly: best form at 9f/1¼m: acts
on good to firm and soft ground: not an easy ride (sweating profusely, pulled even
harder than usual final start): gelded after final start: sent to UAE. *A. C. Stewart*

NAKAMI 5 b.g. Dashing Blade 117 – Dara's Bird 57 (Dara Monarch 128) [1996 –
51: 6g⁴ 5g 6d 1997 5m Mar 31] one-time modest performer: very much on the downgrade. *A. J. Chamberlain*

NAKED OAT 2 b.g. (Feb 20) Imp Society (USA) – Bajina (Dancing Brave (USA) 65
140) [1997 6d⁶ 7d⁵ 7m 8g⁶ 10g 8g⁵ 8d a8g³ a7g⁵ a7g⁴ Dec 18] smallish, strong a69
gelding: first foal: dam unraced daughter of useful 1987 2-y-o sprinter Babita: fair
form at best in maidens/nurseries: stays 1m: acts on dead ground and fibresand, well
below form on equitrack. *B. Smart*

NAKHAL 4 b.g. Puissance 110 – Rambadale 68 (Vaigly Great 127) [1996 57: 57
6.9s³ 7m⁵ 7m 9.7g 8m⁴ a10g³ 8g⁴ 8g a8.5g 1997 a10g² a10g a10g² a10g⁵ a12g²
a12g⁴ Feb 13] workmanlike gelding: unimpressive mover: modest maiden: virtually
pulled up final start: stays 1½m: acts on good to firm ground, soft and equitrack: has
pulled hard: tried blinkered/visored. *D. J. G. Murray Smith*

NAMBUCCA 3 b.f. Shirley Heights 130 – Cephira (FR) (Abdos 134) [1996 NR 69
1997 10.3m² Mar 21] leggy filly: unimpressive mover: closely related to 1¼m
winner Set Adrift (by Slip Anchor) and half-brother to several winners, including

649

useful 1987 French 2-y-o 5f winner Shaindy (by American Stress), later winner up to 7f: dam fourth over 6f at 2 yrs: tongue tied, 4 lengths second to Mithak in maiden at Doncaster. *Mrs J. Cecil*

NAME OF LOVE (IRE) 2 b.f. (Feb 22) Petardia 113 – National Ballet (Shareef Dancer (USA) 135) [1997 6s² 7g* 7m* 7g* Oct 18] 27,000Y: rather leggy, quite attractive filly: second foal: dam unraced close relative of useful middle-distance stayer Saxon Maid out of Oaks third Britannia's Rule: progressed into useful filly in autumn: won maiden at Epsom, and listed race and Owen Brown Rockfel Stakes (both at Newmarket), finishing strongly from off pace for last 2 successes, beating Flawless by 2 lengths on first occasion, Tadwiga by 1¼ lengths on second: shapes as though will be suited by 1m+. *D. R. Loder*   105

NAME OF OUR FATHER (USA) 4 b.g. Northern Baby (CAN) 127 – Ten Hail Marys (USA) (Halo (USA)) [1996 74: 10g 10g 10g a8.5g⁵ 1997 a9.4f 16.4s Aug 29] close-coupled gelding: has a markedly round action: one-time fair performer: well beaten at 4 yrs: stays 1¼m: useful staying hurdler. *P. Bowen*   –

NAMPARA BAY 3 b.f. Emarati 74 – Dewberry 68 (Bay Express 132) [1996 –: a5g⁶ 6m 1997 6g 6f³ 5m a6g² 5.3f a5g 5g 6.1m Sep 15] modest sprint maiden: acts on equitrack and firm going: blinkered final start: inconsistent: sold 500 gns in November. *G. C. Bravery*   44 a50

NANCYS GEM 3 b.f. Most Welcome 131 – Nancy Chere (USA) (Gallant Man) [1996 NR 1997 9.7m⁶ Sep 26] closely related to 3 winners by Be My Guest, including fair 1½m to 2¼m winner Eightandahalf and useful 1¼m and 1½m winner Cameo Performance: dam stakes-placed winner up to 1m from good family: well held in maiden at Folkestone. *D. C. O'Brien*   –

NANOUCHE 3 b.f. Dayjur (USA) 137 – Habibti 136 (Habitat 134) [1996 NR 1997 7g Apr 18] seventh living foal: closely related to 1994 Irish 2-y-o 5f winner Desert Lily (by Green Desert): dam outstanding sprinter, also third in 1000 Guineas: never going pace in newcomers event at Newbury: stud. *J. L. Dunlop*   –

NANOUSHKA (IRE) 2 b.f. (May 7) Taufan (USA) 119 – West Chazy (USA) (Gone West (USA)) [1997 6g* 6g³ 7m⁴ Oct 4] IR 6,000F, IR 30,000Y: close-coupled, leggy filly: second foal: half-sister to Irish 3-y-o Gunfire (by Great Commotion), 7f winner at 2 yrs: dam Irish 1m winner, half-sister to smart French middle-distance stayer Robertet from family of Solford: won maiden at Ascot in August in good style: didn't go on quite as expected, though in frame in minor event at Salisbury and in listed race at Newmarket (5½ lengths fourth to Name of Love): should stay at least 1m. *R. Hannon*   91

Owen Brown Rockfel Stakes, Newmarket—Name of Love makes it three wins in a row, defeating Tadwiga (black cap), Statua (left), Flawless and Elshamms (striped cap)

NANTGARW 4 b.f. Teamster 114 – Dikay (IRE) 44 (Anita's Prince 126) [1996 –: – 10.3g 1997 a8g a6g Feb 3] small filly: first foal: dam lightly-raced maiden: no sign of ability. *D. Burchell*

NANTON POINT (USA) 5 b.g. Darshaan 133 – Migiyas 87 (Kings Lake (USA) 79 133) [1996 75+: 16s⁶ 1997 16g 14g² 16g⁵ 20m 16.4d⁴ 16m⁴ 16d⁴ 16g⁵ Oct 24] lengthy, robust gelding: fair handicapper: suited by good test of stamina: acts in front and dead ground, probably soft: visored penultimate start: genuine. *Lady Herries*

NANT Y GAMER (FR) 3 b.c. Warning 136 – Norfolk Lily 63 (Blakeney 126) 78 [1996 77: 5.9f⁵ a6g 6m* 6g² 6m³ 8m 1997 6f⁵ 6.1s⁵ 7.9g 7m² a7g⁶ 7f 6.9m* 7g⁶ 6m* 7g* a7g⁵ Nov 18] strong colt: fair performer: won claimers at Carlisle in August and Pontefract and Doncaster in October: effective at 6f (on a testing course) to 7f: acts on fibresand, raced mainly on good going or firmer on turf: races prominently. *J. Berry*

NAPHTALI 4 b.f. Nicholas Bill 125 – My Concordia 58 (Belfort (FR) 89) [1996 – –: a8g 1997 a10g Jan 2] first foal: dam 1m winner: tailed off in minor event and maiden. *J. R. Arnold*

NAPIER STAR 4 b.f. Inca Chief (USA) – America Star (Norwick (USA) 125) 43 [1996 –, a68: a7g a7g⁴ a8g⁵ a6g 5.1d a6g* a6g⁵ a5g³ a5g* a5g* a5g⁵ a5g² a5g² a71 a6g⁴ a6g² a6g a6g⁴ a5g⁴ a5g³ a5g² a5g* a5g³ a5g² 1997 a6s a5g² a5g³ a5g a6g a5g² a5g* a5g⁶ a5g³ a6f³ 5m a7g² a5g⁶ 5.2m a7g 6.1m a6g³ a5g⁶ a7g a6g⁶ a5g³ a5g a6g Dec 26] leggy filly: fair handicapper on the all-weather: won at Wolverhampton in May: lightly raced and poor form on turf: effective at 5f to 7f: usually visored, blinkered once at 4 yrs: hangs left: none too consistent. *Mrs N. Macauley*

NAPOLEON'S RETURN 4 gr.g. Daring March 116 – Miss Colenca (Petong 42 126) [1996 49: 8g 6d 6m 8.1g³ 6g 8.1f 8m* 8f² 7s² 7m 7g a6g 7g a8g⁴ a7g⁵ 1997 a8g 8m 8m 6g 9m 7g* 7.6g Aug 2] close-coupled gelding: poor handicapper: won apprentice event at Catterick in July, only worthwhile form at 4 yrs: stays 1m: acts on fibresand and probably any turf going: effective blinkered/visored or not: usually apprentice ridden. *J. L. Eyre*

NAPOLEON STAR (IRE) 6 ch.g. Mulhollande (USA) 107 – Lady Portobello 55 (Porto Bello 118) [1996 –: a6g a8.5g 7f 8g 8g 7g 1997 a7g a6g a7g a8g⁴ a6g a6g* a51 a6g⁵ 6m* 6.1g⁵ 7d⁶ 5.1g 6m³ 6m* 6g⁵ 6d 5v⁴ 5m 6d 7g 6m a7g a6g a5g⁴ a5g⁶ Dec 22] sparely-made gelding: modest handicapper: won at Southwell (seller), War-wick and Catterick in first half of 1997: below form after leaving S. R. Bowring twentieth start: effective at 5f to 7f: acts on the all-weather and good to firm and dead ground, probably on heavy: usually blinkered/visored: has had tongue tied: comes from behind. *Miss J. F. Craze*

NARBONNE 6 b.m. Rousillon (USA) 133 – Historical Fact 78 (Reform 132) – [1996 –: 8.3d 8g 1997 10m a8s a10g Nov 25] workmanlike mare: lightly raced and soundly beaten since 4 yrs. *B. J. McMath*

NARROGIN (USA) 2 ch.g. (Feb 19) Strike The Gold (USA) – Best Regalia 71 (Sharpen Up 127) [1997 5m⁴ 6s⁶ 6m 7m⁵ 7m⁶ 8m³ 8f 10g³ 8m² 8d⁴ 8.2d⁵ Oct 30] $30,000Y: tall, good-topped gelding: half-brother to several winners in USA, including Grade 2 9f winner Wait For The Lady (by Believe The Queen): dam won up to 9f in USA: fair maiden: stays 1¼m: acts on good to firm and dead ground: visored 3 times but best form when not: got worked up in stalls once: gelded at end of season. *M. R. Channon*

NASHAAT (USA) 9 b.g. El Gran Senor (USA) 136 – Absentia (USA) 108 (Raise – A Cup (USA)) [1996 80: a11g a6g a8g⁴ a7g³ a7g* a8g 7s⁶ 7m³ 7g 8.5g⁶ 8m 7g² 7m² a63 7f* 7g* 7g* 7m 7m² 1997 a8.5f a8g² a8g⁶ a7g⁴ Jan 31] stocky, good-topped gelding: modest form at best on all-weather at 9 yrs: effective at 7f to 8.5f: acts on any going: tried blinkered: sometimes gives trouble at stalls, refusing to enter them final intended: has run well when sweating. *K. R. Burke*

NASHALONG (IRE) 4 ch.g. Nashamaa 113 – Rousalong (Rousillon (USA) 47 133) [1996 7v 10d 9m 7g⁴ 8m⁴ 7m⁵ 8.5g 12g⁶ 6.5d 7.5g 1997 a7g 9f 8d 7s⁴ 7.8m⁶ Aug 15] second foal: dam unraced daughter of smart Ski Sailing: poor maiden: well beaten at Southwell (for J. Quinn) only start in Britain: stays 1½m: acts on good to firm and soft ground: blinkered (creditable effort) once at 3 yrs. *G. M. Lyons, Ireland*

NASKHI 2 b.f. (Mar 28) Nashwan (USA) 135 – Calpella 81 (Ajdal (USA) 130) [1997 6g⁴ 6g³ 7m⁵ 8m* 8s Oct 13] tall, rather angular filly: second foal: dam 1m winner out of smart Irish 1m and 1¼m winner Calandra, herself half-sister to Oaks winner Intrepidity: fairly useful form: progressed well first 4 starts, winning nursery at Pontefract in September should stay at least 1¼m: acts on good to firm ground, disappointing favourite on soft: has been bandaged behind: should still do better. *M. Johnston* 82 p

NATALIA BAY (IRE) 3 b.f. Dancing Dissident (USA) 119 – Bayazida (Bustino 136) [1996 83: 5m* 6s² 6g⁴ 1997 8g⁶ 7m² 8.5d² 10.2m⁶ Jul 25] lengthy filly: useful performer: good sixth of 8 to Fiji in steadily-run listed event at Chepstow final start: stays 1¼m: acts on good to firm and dead ground: sold 30,000 gns in October, and sent to USA. *P. F. I. Cole* 96

NATALIE'S PET 2 b.f. (Apr 12) Merdon Melody 98 – Tripolitaine (FR) (Nono-alco (USA) 131) [1997 5m 6.9m Aug 19] 6,000Y: sturdy, good-quartered filly: sister to a poor maiden and half-sister to several winners, including fairly useful sprinter Walk In The Park (by Valiyar): dam won twice at around 11f in France: behind in maidens. *G. Lewis* –

NATAL RIDGE 4 b.g. Indian Ridge 123 – Song Grove 61 (Song 132) [1996 54: 5d 7m 6.1m 6.1m 1997 a7g a6g⁴ a7g a8g Mar 14] quite attractive gelding: poor performer: probably a sprinter: blinkered once (finished last). *D. Haydn Jones* 46

NATAYIG 2 b.f. (Feb 8) Fairy King (USA) – Cunning 118 (Bustino 136) [1997 7m Nov 1] first foal: dam won Princess Royal Stakes and second in Prix Vermeille: 25/1, little promise in maiden at Newmarket. *J. L. Dunlop* –

NATIONAL WISH (USA) 2 ch.c. (May 19) Forty Niner (USA) – Regent's Walk (CAN) (Vice Regent (CAN)) [1997 7.1m⁵ Sep 21] $200,000Y: heavy-bodied colt: eighth foal: brother to useful French 1994 2-y-o 6.5f winner Queens Gallery, closely related to US Grade 1 9f and 1¼m winner Marquetry (by Conquistador Cielo), 7f winner here at 2 yrs, and smart French sprinter Spain Lane (by Seeking The Gold) and half-brother to a winner in USA: dam won up to 7f in North America: 14/1 and decidedly burly, remote fifth of 9 to impressive Fleetwood in maiden at Haydock, staying on steadily: likely to do fair bit better in due course. *E. A. L. Dunlop* 70 p

NATIVE PRINCESS (IRE) 3 ch.f. Shalford (IRE) 124§ – Jealous One (USA) (Raise A Native) [1996 62?: 6m⁶ 7.5m⁵ 7g 1997 10.3m 14.1m 9.9d⁵ 10f⁴ 8.2g 8.2d Jun 23] plain filly: poor performer: probably stays 1¼m: unraced on going softer than dead: blinkered final outing (raced too freely). *B. W. Hills* 45

NATIVE RHYTHM (IRE) 3 ch.f. Lycius (USA) 124 – Perfect Time (IRE) (Dance of Life (USA)) [1996 71: 6m² 1997 7d³ 7.1d⁶ a7g⁴ 7.1g Sep 11] quite attractive filly: modest maiden: third at Ayr in June, best effort of 1997: should stay at least 1m: blinkered penultimate outing: sold 15,000 gns in December. *P. W. Chapple-Hyam* 60

NATIVE THATCH (IRE) 3 b. or br.f. Thatching 131 – Native Guile 91 (Lomond (USA) 128) [1996 NR 1997 a7g⁶ a7g⁶ a7g⁵ 6.9g 6d² 6m⁶ Apr 16] 7,000F: third foal: dam, 2-y-o 7f winner, daughter of Jersey Stakes winner Merlins Charm: poor maiden handicapper: possibly a sprinter: best effort on good to soft going. *W. G. M. Turner* 47

NATTIE 3 b.g. Almoojid 69 – Defy Me 75 (Bustino 136) [1996 47: 5s 5.1g⁴ 5m⁵ 6.1d³ 1997 a8g a8g 8m Sep 24] leggy gelding: tailed off in 1997. *C. J. Hill* –

NATURAL EIGHT (IRE) 3 b.c. In The Wings 128 – Fenny Rough 114 (Home Guard (USA) 129) [1996 81p: 8m³ 1997 10g⁵ 10.2m² 10.2d³ 10g Oct 24] un-furnished colt: fairly useful maiden: best effort when second at Bath in April: left B. Hills after next start then off course 5 months: will stay 1½m: yet to race on extremes of going. *R. W. Armstrong* 83

NATURAL KEY 4 ch.f. Safawan 118 – No Sharps Or Flats (USA) 67 (Sharpen Up 127) [1996 74: 6d 6.1g 5g 5m³ 5g 6m* 6m* 5m⁴ 6m³ 6g* 5m⁵ 7m 5g* 1997 7f⁵ 6g⁴ 5g² 6g² 6m 6m 6g³ 6g* 5g 6g⁶ 6s Oct 15] smallish filly: fair handicapper: does 74

most of her racing at Hamilton and gained fifth win there in August: barely stays 7f: acts on firm ground: tried blinkered at 2 yrs. *D. Haydn Jones*

NATURE DANCER 3 ch.f. Environment Friend 128 – Preobrajenska 93 63 ? (Double Form 130) [1996 NR 1997 10m² 12.3g⁶ Aug 25] half-sister to winners abroad by North Briton and Blakeney: dam won at 5f and 6f at 2 yrs then seemed to go wrong way temperamentally: 8 lengths second of 3 to Monitor in maiden at Ripon: tailed off in similar event there 3 weeks later. *B. W. Hills*

NAUGHTY BLUE (USA) 2 b.c. (Apr 4) Danehill (USA) 126 – Blue Note (FR) 97 122 (Habitat 134) [1997 6d 7f* 7.3g⁴ Oct 24] well-made colt: sixth foal: closely related to 3 winners, notably smart 6f/7f performers Zieten and 4-y-o Blue Duster (both by Danzig), winners of Middle Park and Cheveley Park respectively at 2 yrs: dam French 5f (at 2 yrs) to 7f winner: useful form: won maiden at Yarmouth in September by 5 lengths from Brimming, having appeared to show little on debut: 4¼ lengths fourth to La-Faah in Horris Hill Stakes at Newbury, short of room but no impression once clear: should stay 1m. *Saeed bin Suroor*

NAUGHTY PISTOL (USA) 5 ch.m. Big Pistol (USA) – Naughty Nile (USA) 58 d (Upper Nile (USA)) [1996 57, a66: 6m 8g⁵ 6f⁶ 6.9f⁶ a5g⁴ a6g 6m⁵ 6m 6f* 6d 7g⁴ a69 d a6g* a6g* 1997 a6g³ a7g² a7g⁵ a6g 7g 7g³ 5.9g 7.1d a7g⁶ 8g³ 8g⁴ a7g⁵ 8g 10m 8.1m Aug 15] leggy mare: poor mover: fair handicapper on the all-weather, modest on turf: below form last 9 starts: probably stays 1m: acts on firm and dead ground: visored/blinkered. *P. D. Evans*

NAUTICAL JEWEL 5 b.g. Handsome Sailor 125 – Kopjes (Bay Express 132) – § [1996 –§, a58d: a8g² a12g⁶ a9.4g⁴ a11g⁶ 10m 12s⁵ a8g a12s Jan 3] plain, good-topped gelding: modest maiden handicapper at best (not an easy ride): has lost his form. *M. D. I. Usher*

NAUTICAL STAR 2 b.c. (Mar 3) Slip Anchor 136 – Comic Talent 105 (Pharly 80 (FR) 130) [1997 7.1d⁵ 7g* 8d Oct 17] 15,000Y: workmanlike, good-topped colt: fifth foal: dam 7f to 9f winner: landed odds in maiden at Ayr: well held facing much stiffer task in Newmarket nursery over 2 months later: should be well suited by 1¼m/1½m. *J. W. Hills*

NAUTICAL WARNING 2 b.c. (Feb 7) Warning 136 – Night At Sea 107 (Night 62 p Shift (USA)) [1997 6m⁶ 7d 6d 6.1d Nov 3] 34,000Y: sturdy colt: fourth foal: half-brother to 4-y-o Muhandis and 1¼m winner South Sea Bubble (by Bustino): dam sprinter: signs of ability in maidens and a nursery: should be suited by further than 6f: joined J. Noseda: likely to do better. *M. H. Tompkins*

NAVAL GAMES 4 b.g. Slip Anchor 136 – Plaything 69 (High Top 131) [1996 57 NR 1997 10g⁵ 12m⁴ 11.8d² a14g⁶ a12g⁵ a14.8g a14g Dec 8] workmanlike gelding: second foal: dam lightly-raced 1m winner: modest maiden: left S. Williams after second start, M. Pipe after third: below form for new yard: stays 1½m. *J. M. Bradley*

NAVIASKY (IRE) 2 b. or br.g. (Feb 18) Scenic 128 – Black Molly (IRE) (High 74 p Top 131) [1997 5s⁶ 6m⁶ 5m* 8g⁶ 8f 8d 7g⁵ 7s Nov 8] 12,000Y: sturdy, lengthy gelding: third foal: dam ran twice: fair form: won maiden at Thirsk in August: twice caught eye in competitive nurseries subsequently, and seemed to find ground against him on 2 other occasions: stays 1m: form only on good going or firmer: has scope, and sort to fare much better in handicaps at 3 yrs. *Mrs J. R. Ramsden*

NAWAJI (USA) 4 b.f. Trempolino (USA) 135 – Nobile Decretum (USA) (Noble 43 Decree (USA) 127) [1996 45: 10g 8g 8.3d 10d 9.7d⁴ a11g a10g 1997 a10g⁵ a13g² a12g⁴ a16g⁵ a12g³ 11.9m⁵ a12g⁵ 11.8g⁶ 14.1g Jun 21] smallish, plain filly: poor maiden: stays 13f: acts on equitrack and good to firm ground, probably on dead: blinkered once. *W. R. Muir*

NAWASIB (IRE) 3 b.f. Warning 136 – Tanouma (USA) 114 (Miswaki (USA) 94 124) [1996 82: 6m⁵ 7g⁶ 7m² 1997 8m 10s* 10d⁴ 10g 10s⁵ Nov 9] smallish, leggy filly: fairly useful performer: won maiden at Goodwood in June: left J. Dunlop (70,000 gns) in July: equal-fourth to Red Affair in listed event at the Curragh, best effort: stays 1¼m: acts on good to firm going and soft. *M. J. P. O'Brien, Ireland*

NAZMI (IRE) 5 b.g. Doyoun 124 – Nawazish (Run The Gantlet (USA)) [1996 63
16m 13g⁴ 16g³ 12.5m 1997 16m³ 22.2d Jun 20] IR 5,400 3-y-o: leggy gelding:
half-brother to 4 winners, including useful stayer Nafzaawa (by Green Dancer) and
Nangarar (listed winner in Sweden, by Topsider): dam, useful French 6f to 1½m
winner, from family of Shergar: modest Irish maiden handicapper: stays 2m, very
stiff task and soon tailed off at Royal Ascot over 2¾m. *Patrick O'Leary, Ireland*

NEBL 2 ch.f. (Feb 4) Persian Bold 123 – Maraatib (IRE) 93 (Green Desert (USA) 80
127) [1997 7g³ 8.1m* 8d Oct 17] sturdy filly: second foal: half-sister to 4-y-o
Mazeed: dam sprinter: won steadily-run maiden at Sandown in September by 2½
lengths from Sahara: edgy when running poorly final start: stays 1m. *Major
W. R. Hern*

NEBUCHADNEZZAR 2 gr.g. (Apr 15) Absalom 128 – Golden Decoy 73 –
(Decoy Boy 129) [1997 5d 8d 8.3g Sep 29] 7,000Y: brother to 1993 2-y-o sprint
winner Dangerous Shadow and half-brother to winning sprinter For Real (by Tina's
Pet): dam 7f winner: behind in Scottish maidens. *J. J. O'Neill*

NED'S BONANZA 8 b.g. Green Ruby (USA) 104 – Miss Display 47 (Touch 56
Paper 113) [1996 66: 5g 6g 5g 5f⁶ 6m 5m 6m⁴ 5f³ 5m* 5f 6f 5m² 5f⁶ 5m³ 5m⁵ 5f³
5.7m² 5m³ 5m⁵ 5g 1997 5g 6g 5d 5f³ 5m 5.7m³ 5g 5m⁵ 5m 5g 5m 8.2d 5g Oct 22]
workmanlike, good-topped gelding: modest handicapper: 8 career successes all came
in June/July: came to hand same time in 1997, but failed to win: effective at 5f/easy
6f: probably best on good ground or firmer: probably effective blinkered/visored:
held up, and suited by strongly-run race: dead. *M. Dods*

NEEDLE GUN (IRE) 7 b. or br.h. Sure Blade (USA) 130 – Lucayan Princess 117
111 (High Line 125) [1996 119: a10g 10d² 10g* 10f 10d 10f 10g 10m³ 9m 1997
a10f² 10d⁶ 10f² 11f³ 12f⁶ 10d⁶ Aug 3] tall horse: showed knee action: smart performer: won only 3 times, including Meld Stakes in 1995 and Gallinule Stakes in
1996 (both at the Curragh), but was in frame on numerous other occasions: best
efforts at 7 yrs when length second to Tamayaz in extremely valuable race in Dubai
in April and 1¾ lengths third to Oxalagu in Group 2 race at Baden-Baden in June:
stayed 1½m: acted on any going, including sand: genuine: retired to Park House
Stud, Co Carlow, Ireland. *C. E. Brittain*

NEEDLE KNOT (IRE) 4 b.g. Don't Forget Me 127 – Needlewoman 73 –
(Moorestyle 137) [1996 NR 1997 a14g 6m Aug 3] lengthy gelding: poor mover:
modest at 2 yrs for M. Johnston: no promise in claimer and seller as 4-y-o. *F. Murphy*

NEEDLE MATCH 4 ch.c. Royal Academy (USA) 130 – Miss Tatting (USA) 89 66
(Miswaki (USA) 124) [1996 59: 8.2d⁵ 10g 8m 7m⁵ 8.2m 6m 6m 1997 a6g* a5g³ a72
a6g* 6d⁶ 5.9g 5s 5.9d 5.9m² 6s 8m³ 7.5g³ 8.1m² 7.5g³ 6.9f* 7.9s 8m⁶ 8.2d⁵ 8m 8s⁶
Nov 6] big, good-topped colt: fair performer: successful in handicaps at Wolverhampton and Southwell early in year and minor event at Carlisle in August: effective
at 6f, unlikely to stay beyond 1m: acts on firm ground and fibresand, yet to run well
on soft: tried blinkered: suited by strong pace and exaggerated waiting tactics.
J. J. O'Neill

NEEDWOOD EPIC 4 b.f. Midyan (USA) 124 – Epure (Bellypha 130) [1996 –: 49
10m 10.8m a12g 13.6m 12g 1997 14.1g² 16m 16m⁴ a14g² 12g³ a14g³ a14.8g⁵ a14g* a61
a14g² Nov 17] big, good-topped filly: modest handicapper on the all-weather, best
effort when winning at Southwell (by 7 lengths) in October: poor on turf: seems to
stay 2m: acts on good to firm ground and fibresand: often blinkered/visored: front
runner. *B. C. Morgan*

NEEDWOOD LEGEND 4 b. or br.c. Rolfe (USA) 77 – Enchanting Kate –
(Enchantment 115) [1996 –: 10g 1997 10m 10d 10d 10d⁵ a11g Dec 8] close-coupled
colt: little worthwhile form. *B. C. Morgan*

NEEDWOOD NUTKIN 4 b.f. Rolfe (USA) 77 – Needwood Nut 70 (Royben 28
125) [1996 –: 10g 1997 a7g a7g a8.5g 9.9m⁴ 11.1s⁵ 12m³ a12g³ 12g Jul 5] close-
coupled filly: bad mover: poor maiden handicapper: stays 1½m: acts on good to firm
and soft ground. *B. C. Morgan*

NEEDWOOD POPPY 9 b.m. Rolfe (USA) 77 – Needwood Nap (Some Hand –
119) [1996 NR 1997 13s⁶ a16g⁴ Jun 6] modest staying hurdler: poor on flat.
B. C. Morgan

NEEDWOOD SPIRIT   2 b.c. (Feb 8) Rolfe (USA) 77 – Needwood Nymph 45   71
(Bold Owl 101) [1997 8.2s⁵ 8d⁴ Oct 28] fifth foal: brother to a bad maiden: dam,
1½m winner, probably stayed 2m: fair form in maidens at Nottingham and Leicester:
will be suited by 1½m+. *B. C. Morgan*

NEEDWOOD SPITFIRE   2 b.f. (Mar 15) Rolfe (USA) 77 – Lime Brook 56   –
(Rapid River 127) [1997 6g 7d Nov 7] leggy filly: third foal: sister to a poor maiden:
dam sprinter: well beaten in maidens at Leicester and Doncaster. *B. C. Morgan*

NEFERTITI   3 b.f. Superpower 113 – Vico Equense (Absalom 128) [1996 –: a5g⁶   –
a5g 5.2f⁴ 1997 a5g a5g 5m May 30] of little account. *R. F. Marvin*

NEGATIVE   3 gr.f. Deploy 131 – Rashah 67 (Blakeney 126) [1996 NR 1997   –
10.2m 11.7g Sep 8] 2,000Y: sixth foal: half-sister to a winner in Hungary by Kalaglow: dam probably stayed 1½m: tailed off in maidens at Bath. *M. Salaman*

NELLIE NORTH   4 b.f. Northern State (USA) 91 – Kimble Princess (Kala   54 §
Shikari 125) [1996 68d: 6m³ 5.1g⁴ 6m 5f⁵ 8.3g 6g³ 6.1d⁵ 5f 6.1m 1997 6m 10d 6.1d²
6.1d 6s⁶ 5m³ 6g² 6m 6d⁴ 6m 6.1m Sep 15] lengthy filly: modest handicapper:
effective at 5f and 6f: acts on good to firm and dead ground: effective visored/
blinkered or not: unreliable. *G. M. McCourt*

NEON DEION (IRE)   3 b.g. Alzao (USA) 117 – Sharnazad (IRE) (Track Barron   36
(USA)) [1996 38: 5g⁴ 5m a6g 8d 7f⁶ a8.5g a8g 1997 a8g³ a8g⁵ a11g⁵ a12g³ Feb 27]
good-topped gelding: poor maiden: probably stays 1½m: usually blinkered/visored.
S. C. Williams

NERONIAN (IRE)   3 ch.g. Mujtahid (USA) 118 – Nimieza (USA) 70 (Nijinsky   73
(CAN) 138) [1996 NR 1997 7m⁶ 8.5m 8m⁴ 8.5m² 8.5g* 9g³ Jun 20] tall, lengthy
gelding: first live foal: dam, maiden who probably stayed 1¾m, half-sister to
smart 1¼m performer Placerville: fair performer: won 5-runner minor event at
Beverley in June: should be suited by 9f+: raced only on good/good to firm ground.
B. W. Hills

NERVOUS REX   3 b.g. Reprimand 122 – Spinner 59 (Blue Cashmere 129) [1996   57
69d: 5s⁶ 5.1d² 5g⁴ 5m⁴ 5m 5.1g⁶ 6m⁴ 1997 6.9g⁴ 8f⁵ 6f⁴ a6g 6f⁴ 5.9f² 5.9m* 6g⁴
6m 6.1d⁴ 6d 6m³ 7g Oct 24] useful-looking gelding: modest performer: won seller at
Carlisle in June: mainly creditable efforts afterwards: best at 6f/7f: acts on firm and
dead going: below form in blinkers/visor, including only run on fibresand. *W. R. Muir*

NESALA   2 gr.f. (Feb 16) Neshad (USA) 108 – Waadi Hatta (USA) (Upper Nile   –
(USA)) [1997 6m Aug 23] 6,200Y: half-sister to fairly useful 5f (at 2 yrs) to 1¼m
winner Gymcrak Lovebird (by Taufan) and a winner in Germany by Al Hareb: dam
4-y-o 1½m winner: 25/1, towards rear in maiden at Windsor. *Martyn Meade*

NESBET   3 b.g. Nicholas (USA) 111 – Brera (IRE) 45 (Tate Gallery (USA) 117)   –
[1996 –: 7d⁶ a6g 1997 a5g⁵ a6g⁶ a6g⁴ Jul 25] workmanlike colt: little worthwhile
form in maidens: sold, and sent to Denmark. *B. R. Cambidge*

NEUILLY (USA)   3 ch.c. Trempolino (USA) 135 – Haleallah (USA) (Hawaii   116
[1996 NR 1997 8s* 8s⁴ 8g* 8m³ 8m⁶ 9d Nov 30] brother to a winner in USA and
half-brother to 7 winners in France/USA, including Grade 1 7f winner Engine One
(by Our Michael): dam unraced: smart colt: won newcomers event at Saint-Cloud
and Prix Messidor at Deauville (by short head from Simon du Desert): 8 lengths third
of 6 to Spinning World in Prix Jacques Le Marois at Deauville and bit better form
when closer to him in steadily-run affair for Prix du Moulin at Longchamp, one paced
in straight and beaten 5 lengths (last outing for A. Fabre): behind in Hollywood
Derby final start: stays 1m: acts on good to firm and soft ground. *R. Ellis, USA*

NEUWEST (USA)   5 b.h. Gone West (USA) – White Mischief 103 (Dance In   106
Time (CAN)) [1996 86: a7g⁶ a8g⁴ 8s 7f⁴ 8m 7f* 6m³ 7.1m² 6.9f* 7m 7m² 7f* 7.3m
1997 8m 7f² 7m 7g* 7g 7m* 7g⁶ 7m Sep 27] robust horse: usually looks well: poor
walker: has a round action: useful performer: improved for new stable (trained first 3
starts by N. Walker), winning handicaps at Newbury in June and Newmarket (sweating, by 2½ lengths from Philistar) in August: creditable sixth to Russian Revival in
listed event at Newbury: effective at 6f to 1m: acts on equitrack and probably any turf
going: held up, and has good turn of foot: none too consistent. *R. Akehurst*

NEVER CEASE 2 ch.c. (Apr 26) Nomadic Way (USA) 104 – Cease To Be – (Sharpo 132) [1997 8.1d Sep 5] angular colt: first foal: dam unraced: showed nothing in maiden at Haydock. *A. Streeter*

NEVEROLD (IRE) 7 b.g. Never So Bold 135 – Fraulein Tobin (USA) 71 (J O Tobin (USA) 130) [1996 NR 1997 10g 12.1d Aug 25] ex-Irish gelding: half-brother to several winners, including smart German 1¼m performer Fabriano (by Shardari): dam 1m winner out of smart Fruhlingstag: lightly raced and little recent sign of ability on flat. *P. C. Ritchens*

NEVER THINK TWICE 4 b.g. Never So Bold 135 – Hope And Glory (USA) 87 (Well Decorated (USA)) [1996 70, a59: 5d 6f⁶ 8g 6m 7g³ 6m⁴ 6m* 6g³ 6m⁵ 6m* 6d² 6f 7m 6m a6g a7s a6g a6g² a7g² 1997 a7g² 6g⁵ 6d² 6d² 6s⁴ 6m 7.6g a6g 6m⁵ 6d⁴ 5m 6m⁴ Sep 22] quite attractive gelding: fair on turf, useful 1¼m winner on all-weather: best form at 6f/7f: acts on good to firm ground, dead and equitrack: blinkered/visored: has been bandaged: has shown signs of temperament. *K. T. Ivory* — 70 a63

NEVILLE THE DEVIL 3 gr.g. Thethingaboutitis (USA) 106 – Sovereign Love – 75 (He Loves Me 120) [1996 NR 1997 a12g Apr 12] fifth foal: half-brother to sprint winners Paradise Forum (by Prince Sabo) and Kerb Crawler (in Ireland, by Tina's Pet): dam 1m winner: tailed off in maiden at Wolverhampton. *N. P. Littmoden*

NEWALA 2 b.f. (Feb 9) Royal Academy (USA) 130 – African Dance (USA) (El – Gran Senor (USA) 136) [1997 5f⁶ 5.1d a5s⁶ Nov 10] dipped-backed filly: fourth foal: half-sister to 3-y-o Telemania and fairly useful 1¼m winner Congo Man (by Rainbow Quest): dam maiden daughter of Irish Oaks second Fleur Royale: only a little sign of ability in maidens: bred to need much further than 5f. *W. J. Haggas*

NEWBRIDGE BOY 4 b.g. Bustino 136 – Martyrdom (USA) (Exceller (USA) 56 129) [1996 58: 8m 10.5d a8g² 12.1m² a12g* a12g⁴ a12g 10.5s⁵ 10.1m⁴ 10.3g⁵ 1997 10.1g 10.3d a9.4g 12s 10m⁴ a10g³ Nov 13] tall gelding: modest handicapper: stays 1½m: acts on good to firm ground (possibly soft) and the all-weather: front runner/ races prominently. *M. G. Meagher*

NEW CENTURY (USA) 5 gr.g. Manila (USA) – Casessa (USA) (Caro 133) 86 [1996 95: 8s⁶ 8g 8g* 7m² 8m 8g* 8m 7.9m 1997 a9.4g* a8.5g² 8m a8.5g² 7g 7.9g a8.5f³ a8.5f a8f⁴ a8f³ a8.5f² a9f Dec 21] big, good-bodied gelding: useful handicapper here: won at Wolverhampton in February: good second there in March and April (beaten beaten by Hal's Pal): trained by D. Nicholls until after sixth start: placed in Grade 3 handicap at Del Mar in July and valuable events at Santa Anita and Golden Gates in October/November: stays 9.4f: acts on firm going, dirt and fibresand: tends to sweat and get on toes. *D. Vienna, USA* — 86 a107

NEWGATE NOBLESSE 2 b.f. (May 7) Noble Patriarch 115 – Mummys – Colleen 75 (Mummy's Pet 125) [1997 5m 7f 7g Jul 23] half-sister to fair winning sprinter Jesters Pet (by Cawston's Clown) and a winner abroad: dam won twice over 5f: looks of little account. *B. W. Murray*

NEWHARGEN (IRE) 2 b.g. (Apr 30) Astronef 116 – Brandywell (Skyliner 48 117) [1997 5g 5m⁵ 5.1s⁵ 5g⁴ 5m² 6g⁵ 6s⁵ 5m⁴ 6.1m Aug 3] 4,100Y: leggy gelding: sixth foal: brother to 3-y-o Parijazz: dam poor Irish maiden: barely stays 6f: tried blinkered: weak finisher. *P. D. Evans*

NEWINGTON BUTTS (IRE) 7 br.m. Dowsing (USA) 124 – Cloud Nine 97 – (Skymaster 126) [1996 –, a58: a5g⁴ a6g³ a6g⁵ a6g⁴ a6g⁶ a6g 5g a6g* a6g 1997 a6g a6g² a6g 7m Aug 15] small, close-coupled mare: poor handicapper: tailed off last 2 starts: stays easy 7f: acts on all-weather, rarely raced on turf nowadays: effective blinkered or not: often a front runner: inconsistent. *K. McAuliffe* — a43

NEW INN 6 b.g. Petoski 135 – Pitroyal 74 (Pitskelly 122) [1996 56: a12g a12g⁴ 56 1997 15.9g⁶ 14.1g 12v² 18d Oct 20] workmanlike gelding: modest handicapper: best effort at 6 yrs when second in amateurs race at Ascot in October: probably best up to 2m: acts on good to firm ground, heavy and fibresand: well beaten in visor: races prominently: useful hurdler, winner twice in December. *S. Gollings*

NEWLANDS CORNER 4 b.f. Forzando 122 – Nice Lady 65 (Connaught 130) 61 [1996 63: 8f 6m 8.3m 6m 6m 6m² 6f² 5.9f* 6m* 6m* 1997 6m 7m⁶ 6.1g² 7f⁵ 6d⁴ 7d⁴ 7g⁴ a6g* 6.1m⁵ 6g a6g³ a6g Nov 24] stocky filly: fair handicapper: in good form for — 61 a65 most of 1997, and won at Southwell in August: best form at 6f: acts on firm ground, dead and fibresand: usually comes from behind: blinkered. *J. Akehurst*

NEWPORT KNIGHT 6 ch.g. Bairn (USA) 126 – Clara Barton (Youth (USA) 67
135) [1996 77: 10d 11.4m 11.6g* 11.6g* 11.7m² 12d 1997 12m a12g 10.8m
10m 11.6s 11.7f⁴ 11.6g³ 11.5d⁴ 11.5f⁴ 11.9m Oct 23] lengthy, dipped-backed
gelding: fair handicapper: stays 1½m: probably acts on any ground: carries head
high. *R. Akehurst*

NEW REGIME (IRE) 4 b.f. Glenstal (USA) 118 – Gay Refrain (Furry Glen –
121) [1996 –: 7.5m 8g 14.1g 1997 a11g 7m Mar 27] quite good-topped filly: no sign
of ability. *P. T. Dalton*

NEW TECHNIQUE (FR) 4 br.f. Formidable (USA) 125 – Dolly Bea Sweet –
(USA) (Super Concorde (USA) 128) [1996 –: a8g⁶ a7g a7g a5g 7f 10.3g 1997 a10g
Jan 2] small filly: no form. *K. McAuliffe*

NEWTONS CORNER (IRE) 3 ch.g. Masterclass (USA) 116 – Princess –
Galicia 82 (Welsh Pageant 132) [1996 NR 1997 7.5m⁶ 6g⁶ 7g Jul 25] 10,000 2-y-o:
half-brother to 3 winners, including Broughton Blues (up to 1m, by Tender King):
dam, maiden, stayed 1m: no form. *D. Nicholls*

NEXT ROUND (IRE) 2 b.f. (Feb 24) Common Grounds 118 – Debbie's Next 83
(USA) 82 (Arctic Tern (USA) 126) [1997 6d⁴ 6.9s* 7.1m⁵ 7s 7m Sep 30] small,
angular filly: fourth foal: half-sister to 5-y-o Nordinex and French middle-distance
winner Debbie's Law (by Law Society): dam, maiden, stayed 1m: won maiden at
Folkestone in July: ran well in listed race at Sandown next time, poorly in 2 nurseries:
should stay 1m. *M. Bell*

NGAERE PRINCESS 2 br.f. (May 5) Terimon 124 – Zippy Zoe 46 (Rousillon –
(USA) 133) [1997 5g 5m 5g 5g 6g 5g⁵ 5g 5m⁶ 5g³ 5g⁵ a5g 8g 8.3g³ 7s 5s Nov 6]
3,500 2-y-o: sturdy filly: first foal: dam once-raced half-sister to useful 1m/9f winner
Eton Lad: no worthwhile form, including in sellers: tried blinkered. *W. T. Kemp*

NICHOL FIFTY 3 b.g. Old Vic 136 – Jawaher (IRE) 60 (Dancing Brave (USA) 83
140) [1996 52p: 6.9d 1997 10g 10d 8s⁵ 10g² 12.3m* 14s⁵ 11.8d⁴ 11.8d* 16s³ Nov 6]
workmanlike gelding: fairly useful performer: won minor events at Chester in July
and Leicester in October: good third in handicap at Musselburgh final start, wandering under pressure: stays 2m, at least as effective around 1½m: acts on good to firm
and soft going: consistent. *M. H. Tompkins*

NICKER 3 b.g. Nicholas (USA) 111 – Glimmer 58 (Hot Spark 126) [1996 NR 67 d
1997 6m 8f³ 8d 6f² 7m 6m 8g⁵ Sep 3] 7,000Y, 1,800 2-y-o: half-brother to 12-y-o
Royal Acclaim: dam second at 5f at 3 yrs: best effort when runner-up in maiden
handicap at Brighton in July: ran badly last 3 starts: should stay 7f: acts on firm
ground. *W. Jarvis*

NICK OF TIME 3 b.f. Mtoto 134 – Nikitina 106 (Nijinsky (CAN) 138) [1996 68
–: 7m 7.1s 1997 10d 11.8g 15.4s² 16m⁴ 16.4s⁴ 16.1g⁴ 16g Oct 24] quite attractive
filly: fair handicapper: suited by good test of stamina: best efforts on good going or
softer: sold 14,000 gns, and sent to Poland. *J. L. Dunlop*

NICOLA'S PRINCESS 4 b.f. Handsome Sailor 125 – Barachois Princess 47
(USA) 62 (Barachois (CAN)) [1996 56: 5.1d⁵ 6g⁶ 7g 7f a6g a8.5g⁵ a8.5g² a9.4g⁶
a8.5g* 8f a8g 1997 a8g a9.4g³ 10d⁴ 16m⁶ 10m a12g² 10.3s² 12.3m a11g² 12g⁴
a12g³ 10.3d⁴ 10m Sep 16] big, lengthy filly: poor handicapper: stays 11f: acts on
fibresand, best on good going or softer on turf. *B. A. McMahon*

NICOLE PHARLY 3 b.f. Pharly (FR) 130 – Debbie Harry (USA) 70 (Alleged 107 p
(USA) 138) [1996 8g² 9d* 9s* 1997 10m* 8g* 11m* May 18] 4,500Y: ex-Italian
filly: third foal: dam, stayer, out of a sister to Irish Derby winner Law Society:
progressive form: won maiden and minor event at Rome at 2 yrs: unbeaten in
1997, landing minor event (by 6 lengths) and Premio Regina Elena (beat Orange
Jasmine by 2¼ lengths) at Rome and Oaks d'Italia (found extra inside final 1f to
beat Attitre a length) at Milan: will stay 1½m: acts on good to firm and soft ground:
joined M. Stoute but did not reappear: may well be capable of better still. *A. Verdesi,
Italy*

NIFTY NORMAN   3 b.g. Rock City 120 – Nifty Fifty (IRE) 97 (Runnett 125)   77
[1996 62: 5m 5m² 5m² 5m 5s³ 1997 5s* 6f 5g* 5.1m 5m⁶ 5m Sep 12] leggy, angular
gelding: fair performer: won maiden at Beverley in May and handicap at Ayr in June:
should stay 6f: easily best form on good going or softer. *J. Berry*

NIGELS CHOICE   5 gr.g. Teenoso (USA) 135 – Warm Winter 65 (Kalaglow   –
132) [1996 53: 11.9f³ 1997 10.2d 12.1g May 26] strong, lengthy gelding: soundly
beaten in maidens at 5 yrs. *C. J. Hill*

NIGEL'S LAD (IRE)   5 b.g. Dominion Royale 112 – Back To Earth (FR)   86
(Vayrann 133) [1996 81, a–: a9.4g a10g 8s 9.9m⁵ 9.2s⁶ 8.5m⁶ 10f 12.4m³ 12.3s² 12g   a–
10.3m 9m a12g 1997 10m 11.1s⁴ 16m* 15.8m* 17.1m* 20m 12m⁵ a14.8g⁶ 18g Oct
18] sturdy gelding: fairly useful handicapper: completed hat-trick within space of a
week at Ripon, Catterick (despite probably unsuited by tight track) and Pontefract in
May/June: off course 3 months after next start and subsequently below form: suited
by a good test of stamina: acts on soft ground, good to firm and all-weather: useful
hurdler, winner in December. *P. C. Haslam*

NIGHT AUCTION (IRE)   2 b.f. (Jan 30) Night Shift (USA) – Maria Stuarda   53 +
(Royal And Regal (USA)) [1997 5.1m 6.1m 6.1m⁵ 5.1g 8.2d a6g⁶ a6g⁵ Dec 26]
sturdy filly: half-sister to 3 winners abroad: dam winner in Italy, including Group 2
1m event at 2 yrs: modest maiden: apparently best effort (could be rated 67) third
start: should stay further than 6f. *B. Palling*

NIGHTBIRD (IRE)   3 b.f. Night Shift (USA) – Pippas Song 75 (Reference Point   108
139) [1996 95p: 5f* 5.2g⁴ 6.5m* 7m* 6g* 1997 8d⁵ 6m* 7m⁵ 6g⁴ Jul 11] lengthy,
good-quartered filly: good mover: useful performer: made all and beat Elegant
Warning 3½ lengths in listed race at Newmarket in May, getting run of race: fading
fifth of 20 to Among Men in Jersey Stakes at Royal Ascot penultimate start, disappointing in listed race at York final one: best forcing pace at 6f: has form on dead
ground, probably suited by good to firm/firm. *Saeed bin Suroor*

NIGHT CHORUS   3 b.g. Most Welcome 131 – Choral Sundown 81 (Night Shift   70
(USA)) [1996 62?, a?: 6g 5m 6g² a7g 1997 8.2d* 8.2g³ 8g 8.1m 8.5m* 8.2m⁴ 9.2g²   a–
8.1m⁶ 8m⁴ 8m Oct 28] strong, lengthy gelding: fair handicapper: won at Nottingham
in April: stays 9f: acts on good to firm and dead ground, possibly unsuited by
fibresand: visored (ridden too forcefully) once: tends to edge left. *B. S. Rothwell*

NIGHT CITY   6 b.g. Kris 135 – Night Secret 86 (Nijinsky (CAN) 138) [1996 107:   98 d
9s* 10s 8m⁴ 9m 8.1s⁴ 1997 8.1g 10.1d⁴ 8.5g 9d⁴ 10.9d a12g 12s² 8d a12g* a14g   a81
a13g* Dec 22] useful-looking gelding: useful performer at best: trained by Lady
Herries for reappearance, easily best effort of year in minor event at Epsom next start:
won claimer at Lingfield in November and apprentice handicap there in December:
stays 13f: acts on soft ground and equitrack: best with forcing tactics nowadays: edgy
sort: inconsistent. *K. R. Burke*

NIGHT DANCE   5 ch.h. Weldnaas (USA) 112 – Shift Over (USA) 62 (Night   73
Shift (USA)) [1996 –: 8s 8d 8m 8g 8d 1997 8m⁶ 7.5m* 8.1g 8f 7m 7g Oct 24]
good-topped horse: fair performer nowadays: made all in minor event at Beverley in
April: below form in handicaps afterwards: effective at 7f to 1m: acts on soft ground
and good to firm (possibly not firm): has worn tongue strap. *K. A. Morgan*

NIGHT EXPRESS   3 ch.g. Night Shift (USA) – New Edition 72 (Great Nephew   62 §
126) [1996 NR 1997 8.5m⁶ 7g³ 6g⁴ a7g² 7g⁴ 6.1d⁵ 5g 7g 6g³ 6m⁵ 5m³ a5g⁶ 5m Sep   a76 §
25] good-topped gelding: seventh foal: half-brother to fair 7.5f winner Arabian King
(by Sayf El Arab): dam, 2-y-o 5f winner, appeared to stay 7f: disappointing maiden:
stays 7f: best effort on fibresand: has worn bandages and tongue strap: has hung:
sometimes finds little: not to be trusted. *B. Hanbury*

NIGHT FLIGHT   3 gr.g. Night Shift (USA) – Ancestry (Persepolis (FR) 127)   80
[1996 70: 5g² 5m³ 7f⁵ 5g² 6m 1997 6g* 6.1s 7g 6f³ 5g³ 6s 6g 7d 6g Sep 20]
good-bodied gelding: fair handicapper: won strongly-run race at Pontefract in April:
well below form last 4 starts: probably suited by 6f: acts on firm going, seems unsuited by soft. *J. J. O'Neill*

NIGHT FLYER   2 b.c. (Feb 1) Midyan (USA) 124 – Scandalette (Niniski (USA)   80
125) [1997 6m³ 5.7m 6m⁵ 6m⁶ 7d* 8f 7f² Sep 28] IR 60,000Y: angular, good-
quartered colt: first foal: dam unraced half-sister to high-class sprinter Polish Patriot:

fairly useful performer: won nursery at Epsom in August: hung left there and when good running-on second in similar event at Brighton: should stay 1m: acts on good to soft and firm ground: sweating and flashed tail fourth start. *J. W. Hills*

NIGHT HARMONY (IRE)   4 ch.c. Digamist (USA) 110 – Quaver 86 (Song 132) [1996 57, a61: 6.1d³ 5f⁶ 6.1m 6d 5.1g⁴ a5g² a6g⁵ a7g³ a6g⁴ 1997 a5g a6g 5m⁶ 5.1g⁵ 5.7d* 6m 5.7g⁶ 6d 5d⁵ 6.1d a6g⁴ a6g⁶ a6g Dec 13] leggy colt: modest handicapper: won at Bath in May: effective at 5f to 7f: acts on firm ground, dead and fibresand: tried visored: has been bandaged. *Miss S. J. Wilton*   58

NIGHTINGALE SONG   3 b.f. Tina's Pet 121 – Songlines 78 (Night Shift (USA)) [1996 64: 5.3f³ 5m⁵ 5d 5.1m² 5.7m⁴ 5m⁴ 6g* 6m³ 5m³ 1997 a5g⁵ a5g³ a5g⁶ a6g 5m 5d⁵ 5.7g 5d 8d Oct 13] sparely-made filly: fair handicapper: effective at 5f/6f (not 1m): acts on firm ground and all-weather: suitable mount for apprentice: inconsistent: sold 3,200 gns in October. *Martyn Meade*   66

NIGHTLARK (IRE)   3 b.f. Night Shift (USA) – Overcall (Bustino 136) [1996 77p: 8.2m² 1997 12m² 12s³ 12g² 12g² 12d² 12.3s* 10g 13.1s⁴ Oct 14] leggy filly: easy mover: fairly useful performer: won weak maiden at Chester in August by a distance: well beaten in handicaps last 2 starts: stays 1½m: acts on good to firm and soft ground. *D. R. Loder*   85

NIGHT MIRAGE (USA)   3 b.f. Silver Hawk (USA) 123 – Colony Club (USA) (Tom Rolfe) [1996 70p: 8.1s 8d⁵ 1997 11.8f² 12g² 13.1d³ 10.5m⁵ 10g 10s² 9m* 9.2g* 9m² 10.5m² 10.5d⁴ 8m 10.3g³ 11m² a9.4g Dec 13] strong, workmanlike filly: fairly useful performer: won minor event at Redcar and handicap at Hamilton in the summer: finds 9f a minimum, and stays 13f: acts on firm and soft going: blinkered (raced too freely) once: consistent. *M. Johnston*   80

NIGHT OF GLASS   4 b.g. Mazilier (USA) 107 – Donna Elvira 80 (Chief Singer 131) [1996 64: 8.2m 8m 7f⁵ a8g 8g² 7g³ 8m* 8f 9g 1997 9.9m³ 10g⁶ 8m 8.5v² 7.5m⁵ 8.5m³ 7.5g 7.9s² 8.1g³ 7s* 7m 8s Nov 8] small gelding: fair handicapper: won at Catterick in October: suited by 7f/1m: acts on good to firm going and heavy: usually blinkered/visored. *J. L. Eyre*   69

NIGHT OWL   2 b.f. (Apr 9) Night Shift (USA) – Sarah Georgina 79 (Persian Bold 123) [1997 6m³ 6g⁶ 6m⁵ 7m Sep 30] 100,000Y: neat filly: fourth foal: half-sister to 5-y-o Lord Jim and useful French 1m winner Intellectuelle (by Caerleon): dam 2-y-o 6f winner: fair form in minor event at Newbury and maiden at Kempton first and third starts: stiffish task final outing: headstrong (has virtually bolted to post) and needs to learn to settle. *R. Charlton*   73

NIGHT PEOPLE   2 ch.c. (Feb 22) Night Shift (USA) – Front Line Romance 89 (Caerleon (USA) 132) [1997 5d 5d 5.1m⁴ 6m Aug 23] close-coupled, good-bodied colt: good mover: fourth foal: half-brother to 3-y-o Signs And Wonders and 1995 2-y-o 6f winner Fog City (by Damister): dam stayed 1¼m: fair form: best effort when fourth in maiden at Nottingham in July: raced freely in nursery final outing: should stay at least 6f. *W. Jarvis*   69

NIGHT RULE   2 b.f. (Apr 26) Shirley Heights 130 – Hafwah (Gorytus (USA) 132) [1997 8.2g³ 10m² Nov 1] fifth foal: half-sister to 6f/7f winner Courageous Dancer (by Cadeaux Genereux), 9f winner Rupan (by Taufan) and 4-y-o What A Fuss: dam unraced half-sister to dam of Sure Blade: shaped promisingly when placed in maiden at Nottingham and listed race at Newmarket, finishing well once switched when beaten 1¾ lengths by Trigger Happy in latter: should stay at least 1½m: should improve further and win races. *B. Hanbury*   89 p

NIGHT SHOT   2 br.g. (May 10) Night Shift (USA) – Optaria 83 (Song 132) [1997 7m² 7m⁵ 6d² 6m³ Sep 13] good-quartered gelding: third reported foal: half-brother to 5-y-o Grey Shot and 13f winner Sight'N Sound (by Chief Singer): dam sprinter: fairly useful form in maidens, and when strong-finishing third to Far Removed in nursery at Doncaster: stays 7f: should still do better. *I. A. Balding*   85 p

NIGHT VIGIL (IRE)   2 b.c. (Apr 22) Night Shift (USA) – Game Plan 118 (Darshaan 133) [1997 6s 7.1g a7g⁴ 7.3g a8g* a8g³ Nov 18] strong, good sort: fourth foal: half-brother to fairly useful Irish 1¼m and 1½m winner Power Play (by Nashwan): dam, 1¼m winner and second in Oaks, daughter of top 1978 staying 2-y-o filly Formulate: fair form: made all in maiden at Lingfield in November and ran creditably   76 in nursery there 5 days later: should stay beyond 1m: best efforts on equitrack: has been bandaged behind. *B. W. Hills*

NIGHT WATCH (USA) 4 b.g. Night Shift (USA) – Christchurch (FR) 88 (So 98 Blessed 130) [1996 NR 1997 12.3m² 10d³ 10s Jul 26] strong, compact gelding: useful performer: easily best effort of 1997 when close third in handicap at Sandown in July: stays 1¼m: acts on firm and dead ground: heavily bandaged last 2 starts, returning sore on near-fore on final one: needs treating with caution. *I. A. Balding*

NIGHT WINK (USA) 5 ch.g. Rahy (USA) 115 – Lady In White 94 (Shareef 79 Dancer (USA) 135) [1996 90: 8s 7g⁵ 8d⁵ 8.5m⁴ 7g 7g 8f* 8m 8m⁵ 9g* 9g² 8.5m⁵ 8d 9s a10s² a8g² 1997 a10g⁴ a10g⁵ 8m 8.1g 8m 8.5m 8m⁴ 8.5d⁵ 8f⁶ 8f⁵ 10m* 8.5g 10m⁵ 10g² 8g* Sep 3] sturdy, lengthy gelding: good mover: fair performer: won claimers at Brighton in July and September: stays 1¼m: acts on firm and dead ground and on equitrack: below form when visored: sometimes tongue tied: tends to pull hard, wander and is usually a weak finisher: has joined Mrs V. Ward. *G. L. Moore*

NIGRASINE 3 b.c. Mon Tresor 113 – Early Gales (Precocious 126) [1996 100: 103 6m* 6g* 6m⁵ 6g² 6m⁴ 6m² 1997 7g 8g⁵ 8m 6g* 6m 5.6m 6g 7g³ Oct 25] close-coupled colt: has a quick, fluent action: useful handicapper: won at Haydock in July: ran at least respectably after: best at 6f/7f: raced only on good or good to firm ground: visored last 3 starts: usually races prominently: consistent. *J. L. Eyre*

NIJMEGEN 9 b.g. Niniski (USA) 125 – Petty Purse 115 (Petingo 135) [1996 57: a12g⁴ 16s 16g⁵ 1997 a11g Jan 13] good-bodied gelding: fairly useful hurdler: very lightly raced on flat nowadays, and well beaten only 9-y-o start. *J. G. FitzGerald*

NIKI (IRE) 2 b.f. (Feb 11) Fairy King (USA) – Nicola Wynn 83 (Nicholas Bill 79 p 125) [1997 7.5f² 6m⁶ 8g⁴ Oct 24] IR 15,000F, 60,000Y: fourth foal: half-sister to 1m winner Bold Acre (by Never So Bold): dam 1½m winner, half-sister to grandam of Baratheia: progressive maiden: fourth of 18 to Merciless at Doncaster, keeping on under considerate handling: should stay 1¼m: swished tail and had 2 handlers second start: open to further improvement. *J. H. M. Gosden*

NIKITA'S STAR (IRE) 4 ch.g. Soviet Lad (USA) 94 – Sally Chase 101 (Sallust – 134) [1996 69, a80: a9.4g* a9.4g² a12g² 12s 11.6m 12m a11g* 12m* 14m⁵ 12m² a78 11.9f⁵ 11.4m⁴ 11.5m a12g* 1997 a12g⁵ a12g⁴ a12g² a12g² a12g a12g6 12m 12m 11.8d⁶ 12f a12g⁵ a14.8g² Nov 29] sturdy gelding: unimpressive mover: fair handicapper, inconsistent in 1997: stays 1½m: best form on fibresand, not as good on equitrack: best turf form on good ground or firmer: tried visored/blinkered, no improvement. *D. J. G. Murray Smith*

NIKKI STAR 3 b.f. Presidium 124 – Nikki Noo Noo 58 (Precocious 126) [1996 – NR 1997 7.1m 5.1m 5g⁵ Jul 23] first foal: dam 5.3f to 1m winner: no promise in modest company: has flashed tail. *C. J. Hill*

NILE VALLEY (IRE) 3 b.f. Royal Academy (USA) 130 – Sphinx (GER) 67 (Alpenkonig (GER)) [1996 68: 8.1g² 8.1d⁴ 7f 1997 10.8m⁵ 12g⁵ 17.2f² 16.1m² 15.4s a– 16.2m⁴ a14.8g a16s Nov 10] angular filly: fair maiden: very much a stayer: acts on firm ground and dead, possibly not soft: well beaten in blinkers. *P. W. Chapple-Hyam*

NINEACRES 6 b.g. Sayf El Arab (USA) 127 – Mayor 86 (Laxton 105) [1996 69: 69 5m 5.1f 6.1m⁶ 8f 7g² 5s³ 1997 a6g³ 6s⁴ 6.1d 5g³ 6s a6g⁶ Nov 1] angular, a60 workmanlike gelding: fair handicapper on turf, modest on all-weather: effective at 5f to 7f: has won on firm going and the all-weather, but seems to go particularly well on good ground or softer: has run well in blinkers, visored nowadays. *N. M. Babbage*

NINTH CHORD 3 gr.g. Alzao (USA) 117 – Jazz 76 (Sharrood (USA) 124) [1996 – 85p: 7d² 1997 9m⁴ Jul 12] strong gelding: shaped well only 2-y-o start: ran as though needing race when well below that form on return: subsequently gelded and sold: should prove suited by further than 7f. *J. H. M. Gosden*

NINTH SYMPHONY 3 ch.g. Midyan (USA) 124 – Good As Gold (IRE) 50 – (Glint of Gold 128) [1996 73: 6g 6g⁶ 6d² 6g⁵ 7f* 7m⁵ 7m³ 8m 8m 7m a7g⁶ a7s⁶ 1997 8s 8m⁴ 8.3g 11.1s⁵ Jun 25] good-bodied gelding: fair winner at 2 yrs: no form in 1997. *P. C. Haslam*

NIRVANA PRINCE 8 ch.g. Celestial Storm (USA) 132 – Princess Sunshine – (Busted 134) [1996 –: 10m⁶ 16.2g⁴ 1997 10.3m Mar 20] rangy gelding: fairly useful hurdler: lightly raced and little form on flat. *B. Preece*

NISABA (IRE) 2 b.f. (Mar 24) Belmez (USA) 131 – Nibabu (FR) 101§ (Nish- 60
apour (FR) 125) [1997 6s⁵ 7g 8.2g 8g⁶ a7s a8g³ Dec 10] half-sister to French 3-y-o
7.5f winner Zazca (by Nashwan) and smart if quirky 7f/1m performer Nijo (by Top
Ville): dam mainly disappointing, best at 7f/1m: little worthwhile form on turf for M.
Johnston first 4 starts: better effort for new stable when third in nursery at Lingfield:
should stay 1¼m. *J. S. Moore*

NISHAMIRA (IRE) 5 gr.m. Lashkari 128 – Nishila (USA) 90 (Green Dancer 52 +
(USA) 132) [1996 NR 1997 a12g* 12.1d⁴ Apr 10] IR 6,200 3-y-o: third foal:
half-sister to Irish 1993 2-y-o 7f winner Nicea (by Dominion): dam, 1m winner, is
daughter of smart 5f to 1m winner Nasseem: fairly useful form in bumpers: landed
odds in weak maiden at Southwell in January by 24 lengths: fourth in minor event at
Hamilton only subsequent outing: may do better: joined D. Nicholson, and won 3
times over hurdles late in 1997. *T. D. Barron*

NITE BITES 3 b.g. Thatching 131 – Buraida 64 (Balidar 133) [1996 NR 1997 a7g –
May 14] 13,000Y: second foal: half-brother to fairly useful 7f and (in USA) 9f winner
Oleana (by Alzao): dam, 6f winner, sister to smart sprinter Carol's Treasure: always
behind in maiden at Lingfield (reported by vet to be lame). *C. A. Cyzer*

NITE OWLER 3 b.g. Saddlers' Hall (IRE) 126 – Lorne Lady (Local Suitor –
(USA) 128) [1996 NR 1997 7m 7m 8.2g Sep 23] 7,500Y: second foal: half-brother to
Italian winner Laura's Show (up to 1m, by Polar Falcon): dam French maiden: well
beaten in maidens. *J. O'Reilly*

NITEOWL RAIDER (IRE) 4 ch.g. Standaan (FR) 118 – Havana Moon –
(Ela-Mana-Mou 132) [1996 –, a64d: a7g a8g³ a6g* 5s a6g* a5g a6g 6m a6g 6.1m 5m
5.1m 6m a6g 7g a6g 1997 a6g a6g 6m a8g Dec 18] angular gelding: very much on
the downgrade, and no form in 1997. *M. Waring*

NITE WONDER 3 br.g. Magical Wonder (USA) 125 – Black Fighter (USA) 79 –
(Secretariat (USA)) [1996 NR 1997 7m 7f⁵ Jun 3] 880 3-y-o: third foal: half-brother
to a minor American sprint winner by Siberian Express: dam, disqualified 1m
winner, stayed 1¼m: well beaten in maidens. *G. L. Moore*

NKAPEN ROCKS (SPA) 4 b.g. Risk Me (FR) 127 – Debutina Park 87 (Averof 57 §
123) [1996 63d, a–: 7.1g³ 7d 8g a7g⁵ 7.1f² 8.1g² 7m 7.1f 8.1d a7g a6g 1997 7d⁴ a– §
7.1d 7d⁶ 7.1d⁵ 8g² 8m 8.2d⁵ 8.2d 8s³ Nov 6] tall, leggy gelding: modest maiden
handicapper: stays 1m: acts on firm and soft ground, well beaten on fibresand: races
freely: hung markedly left fourth start: inconsistent. *Capt. J. Wilson*

NOBALINO 3 ch.c. Sharpo 132 – Zipperti Do 70 (Precocious 126) [1996 NR 75
1997 a6g² 5.7g⁶ 5f⁴ 6.1g² a6g⁴ 5m² a5g³ a5g⁴ a5g* a5g² Dec 18] fourth foal:
half-brother to fair 1¼m winner Wonderful Day (by Niniski): dam 1m winner: fair
performer: gained deserved success in handicap at Southwell in December: effective
at 5f and 6f: acts on the all-weather, has raced only on good ground or firmer on turf:
consistent. *Mrs N. Macauley*

NOBBY BARNES 8 b.g. Nordance (USA) – Loving Doll 72 (Godswalk (USA) 46
130) [1996 45: a8g 8g² 9.2s² 8.3s⁶ 8g 9.2g a8g 8f⁴ 8.2m⁶ 10m⁶ 9g 8.3g 7.9g⁶ 10.4g⁶
1997 a7g 10.1g 10m 8.3s³ 8.3s² 9m² 9.2m⁴ 8.9d 9.2s⁴ 8g⁵ 9.2m² 8.2m 8m⁴ 9m 8.3m⁵
8.9s³ 8.3g Sep 29] neat gelding: has a round action: poor handicapper, mostly in good
form in 1997: stays 1¼m: acts on firm ground, soft and the all-weather: tends to get
behind and find trouble, and suited by strong pace. *Don Enrico Incisa*

NOBBY BEACH 3 ch.g. Sharpo 132 – Sunshine Coast 86 (Posse (USA) 130) –
[1996 NR 1997 a8g 7.6m 7m Aug 21] 7,000Y, 5,400 3-y-o: fifth foal: half-brother to
2 winners abroad: dam suited by 7f: no promise in maidens. *W. R. Muir*

NOBEL LAD 3 b.g. Highest Honor (FR) 124 – Aldbourne 113 (Alzao (USA) 117) 74 d
[1996 NR 1997 8.2m 8.5m³ 9d⁵ 10g 11m⁶ 12m³ 10d Oct 28] 30,000Y: close-coupled
gelding: third foal: half-brother to Italian 11.5f winner Mushtari (by Rainbow Quest):
dam third in 1000 Guineas: fair maiden: clearly best effort on second start, left
J. Dunlop after fifth: may prove best short of 1½m: yet to race on extremes of going.
M. C. Pipe

NOBLE CANONIRE 5 b.m. Gunner B 126 – Lucky Candy 61 (Lucky Wednes- –
day 124) [1996 44, a58: a12g* a11g* a11g² a12g⁴ 9.9d⁴ 12.3g a9.4g² a8g⁵ a11g⁴ 1997 a38

a11g a11g a12g a12g a8g⁴ 9.9m 8g a8.5g a8g Jun 30] sturdy, plain mare: bad walker: poor handicapper on all-weather: stays 11f: often blinkered. *D. Shaw*

NOBLE DANE (IRE)   3 b.f. Danehill (USA) 126 – Noble Dust (USA) (Dust   74
Commander (USA)) [1996 79p: 7g³ 8.1s* 1997 8g⁴ 10.4g 8g 8g 8d⁶ 9m 10.1m²
11.8g³ 12g 10g 10s Oct 8] rangy, angular filly: fair handicapper: stays 1½m, at least
in steadily-run race: acts on good to firm and soft going: raced too freely in blinkers
fifth start: none too consistent: sold 28,000 gns after final start. *P. W. Harris*

NOBLE DEMAND (USA)   2 b.g. (Jun 7) Red Ransom (USA) – Noble Nordic   86 p
(USA) (Vaguely Noble 140) [1997 5m 6m⁴ 6m 7.9s* 8d² Oct 17] $60,000Y: strong
gelding: good mover, with a long stride: third foal: dam maiden from 10 starts in
USA: showed promise over inadequate trips first 3 starts, then won nursery at York
in September decisively: excellent neck second of 28 to The Glow-Worm in similar
event at Newmarket, plenty to do 3f out: gelded subsequently: will stay at least 1¼m:
progressive, and should make a useful handicapper. *Mrs J. R. Ramsden*

NOBLE HERO   3 b.g. Houston (USA) – Noble Devorcee (USA) (Vaguely Noble   58 d
140) [1996 60, a70: 7m⁵ 6m⁴ 8m 8f a8g² a10g³ 1997 a7g⁴ a10g 10.8m 10m 10g⁴
11.9f⁵ a12g⁶ Dec 19] tall gelding: disappointing maiden: stays 1¼m: acts on equitrack, raced only on good ground or firmer on turf: tried blinkered: left J. Sheehan
before final start. *K. A. Morgan*

NOBLE INVESTMENT   3 b.g. Shirley Heights 130 – Noble Destiny 89   – §
(Dancing Brave (USA) 140) [1996 70+: 7m 7m⁴ 7m⁵ 7m 1997 12.3g 9s⁵ a7g⁴ 6g Jun
24] heavy-topped gelding: disappointing maiden: tried blinkered and over variety of
trips: not one to trust: sold, and sent to Germany. *J. M. P. Eustace*

NOBLE LORD   4 ch.g. Lord Bud 121 – Chasers' Bar (Oats 126) [1996 70: 12m³
10m 8.3m 11.6m 10d 1997 14g⁵ May 16] workmanlike gelding: fairly useful hurdler:
maiden on flat, and well beaten only 4-y-o start. *R. H. Buckler*

NOBLE PATRIOT   2 b.c. (May 17) Polish Patriot (USA) 128 – Noble Form
(Double Form 130) [1997 7m 6f a6g Oct 18] 9,500Y: quite good-topped colt:
unimpressive mover: fifth foal: dam French 1m and 10.5f winner, half-sister to smart
French middle-distance mare Darine: signs of just a little ability in maiden and
claimers, including on fibresand. *R. Hollinshead*

NOBLE SAJA   2 b.g. (Apr 11) Noble Patriarch 115 – Saja (USA) 56 (Ferdinand   –
(USA)) [1997 5m Mar 22] 2,800Y: workmanlike gelding: first foal: dam thrice-
raced granddaughter of sister to Mill Reef: well beaten in maiden at Doncaster.
T. D. Easterby

NOBLE STORY   3 br.f. Last Tycoon 131 – Certain Story (Known Fact (USA)
135) [1996 61p: 5m⁴ 1997 6g Jul 18] showed ability only start at 2 yrs: tailed off only
outing in 1997. *R. Akehurst*

NOCATCHIM   8 b.g. Shardari 134 – Solar 120 (Hotfoot 126) [1996 NR 1997
11.8d Oct 14] rangy gelding: fairly useful jumper: visored on first flat outing since
1993 when well beaten in Leicester claimer. *K. A. Morgan*

NO CLASS   3 ch.f. Keen 116 – Plie 75 (Superlative 118) [1996 48: 6m 5.1m 6f⁵
7m a6g 1997 6.9m May 28] poor maiden: well beaten only 3-y-o start. *I. Campbell*

NO CLICHES   4 ch.g. Risk Me (FR) 127 – Always On A Sunday 101 (Star   73 d
Appeal 133) [1996 78: 10g 8.1g 8s 10.1m⁶ 8.1m² 10m² 8m² 8m 1997 7g 6d 8.5d 10g
8m² 10m² 10.3g 8.5d 8m 9m 10d Oct 20] lengthy, workmanlike gelding: has a quick
action: fair handicapper: second at Pontefract and Newmarket in July: most disappointing otherwise in 1997, reluctant to start once: stays 1¼m: best form on good
ground or firmer: tried blinkered and visored: not to be trusted. *D. Nicholls*

NOCTURNE (IRE)   2 b.f. (Mar 8) Tenby 125 – Phylella (Persian Bold 123)   – p
[1997 7g Sep 4] IR 5,800F, 13,000Y: fifth foal: half-sister to 3-y-o Reunion, 4-y-o
Mono Lady and 1994 Irish 2-y-o 6f winner Foravella (by Cadeaux Genereux): dam
won in France (at 1¼m) and USA: 20/1, raced on unfavoured stand side when
eleventh of 14 in Salisbury maiden, showing signs of ability: should do better.
J. W. Hills

NOEPROB (USA)   7 b.m. Majestic Shore (USA) – Heat Haze (USA) (Jungle   57
Savage (USA)) [1996 57: 9.7s 7d² 8g 8g³ 8.3m* 7.1g³ 8.3g³ 8.3g 8.1m 1997 8d² 10g

8m 8.3g[6] 8g[4] 8.3g 8.3g[6] 8m[3] 8.3m 8.1g Sep 11] rather shallow-girthed mare: modest performer: probably best around 1m: acts on firm and dead ground: often sweating: none too consistent. *R. J. Hodges*

NOETIC   3 ch.f. Nomadic Way (USA) 104 – Pretty Soon 75 (Tina's Pet 121) [1996 –: a8g 1997 a8g Jan 6] soundly beaten in sellers: tried blinkered. *G. Holmes*   –

NO EXTRAS (IRE)   7 b.g. Efisio 120 – Parkland Rose (Sweet Candy (VEN)) [1996 –: 6f 6g 5.2m 6g 6m 7g 1997 6.9m 7d[4] 7.1m 8d* 8.1d[2] 8m* 6m 6g[2] 6d[2] 7m 6g Oct 24] quite good-topped gelding: useful handicapper: suffered leg injury early in 1996: back almost to best at 7 yrs, winning at Goodwood in June and July and good second in competitive events there afterwards: effective at 6f to 1m: acts on good to firm and soft going: visored once earlier in career: held up: consistent. *G. L. Moore*   95

NO GROUSING (IRE)   3 b.g. Robellino (USA) 127 – Amenaide 79 (Known Fact (USA) 135) [1996 NR 1997 8g[2] 8.3s[2] 8g[2] 8g a7g* Nov 21] 16,000Y: third foal: half-brother to fair but temperamental 6f winner P G Tips (by Don't Forget Me): dam 2-y-o 5f winner (stayed 7f) out of half-sister to Irish Oaks winner Swiftfoot: fair performer: won maiden at Wolverhampton: likely to prove best up to 1m: acts on fibresand, well below form on soft ground. *P. C. Haslam*   76

NOIRIE   3 br.c. Warning 136 – Callipoli (USA) 81 (Green Dancer (USA) 132) [1996 67p: 7.1d[6] 7.9g[4] 1997 8g[4] 10m 10g 6m 7.5d 7g 12.3g[5] 16.2m Jul 21] disappointing maiden handicapper: tried blinkered. *M. Brittain*   –

NOISETTE   3 ch.f. Nashwan (USA) 135 – Nadma (USA) 82 (Northern Dancer) [1996 66p: 8.1d 1997 8m* 10.4g 7g* 7m 7f 8m[3] 8.5f[4] 8.5f[2] Dec 11] good-topped filly: good mover: useful performer: won minor event at Ascot in April and rated stakes at Newmarket in July: in frame in listed handicap at Ascot (length third to Kenmist) and valuable handicap (final start for J. Gosden) and allowance race, last 2 at Hollywood Park: best form up to 8.5f: acts on firm going, unraced on softer than good since debut. *R. Mandella, USA*   106

NOMINATOR LAD   3 b.c. Nomination 125 – Ankara's Princess (USA) 81 (Ankara (USA) 106) [1996 72: 6.1m 7d[2] 6m 8.2g[3] 8.2s 1997 7v[4] 8.2m[5] 8.2m* a8g[5] 7s 8.1m 7.1g* 8m Oct 5] sturdy colt: fair performer: won maiden at Nottingham in July and handicap at Haydock in September: unlikely to stay much beyond 1m: yet to race on firm going, seems to act on any other. *B. A. McMahon*   75

NOMORE MR NICEGUY   3 b.c. Rambo Dancer (CAN) 107 – Lariston Gale 81 (Pas de Seul 133) [1996 87: 5.1g 5m[2] 5.1m[4] 5g* 6.1m[4] 6m 5m[6] 7g 5d[5] a7g[3] a7g[3] a7s* 1997 7g[4] a8.5g[3] a6g[2] 7m[3] a7g* 7.5m[2] 7.6d[5] 7g[3] 7m[2] 8m[6] 8m /d 7f 6m[4] 7g Oct 18] big, good-bodied colt: fairly useful handicapper: won at Wolverhampton in March: generally ran at least respectably after: effective from 6f to 1m: acts on good to firm and dead ground and on fibresand: consistent. *E. J. Alston*   91

NO MORE PRESSURE (IRE)   3 ch.g. Thatching 131 – High Pressure 105 (Kings Lake (USA) 133) [1996 86p: a8.5g* 1997 7.5m[2] 8.1d[3] 7.6d 8f 8d 8d 8s Nov 8] strong, lengthy gelding: fairly useful performer: left N. Walker after third start: well below form 3 of 4 starts for new yard: stays 8.5f: acts on fibresand and dead going. *Mrs J. R. Ramsden*   82

NOMOTHETIS (IRE)   3 b.f. Law Society (USA) 130 – Tamassos 67 (Dance In Time (CAN)) [1996 NR 1997 8.3m Aug 11] sixth foal: half-sister to several winners, notably 5-y-o Posidonas: dam, 1¼m winner, half-sister to Ile de Chypre: tailed off in maiden at Windsor: sold 18,500 gns in October. *P. F. I. Cole*   –

NONONITO (FR)   6 b.h. Nikos 124 – Feuille d'Automne (FR) (Crystal Palace (FR) 132) [1996 121: 15s[4] 15.5g[4] 15m 15.5d[2] 20m[3] 15g[2] 15.5m[4] 20d* 15.5d[4] 1997 15.5d[6] 20g Jun 19] good-topped horse: good walker: very smart performer at 5 yrs, winner of Prix du Cadran at Longchamp: below form in Prix Vicomtesse Vigier there and Gold Cup at Royal Ascot (found to have been off colour) in 1997: suited by good test of stamina: acts on good to firm and heavy going: won over hurdles in November. *J. Lesbordes, France*   111

NON VINTAGE (IRE)   6 ch.g. Shy Groom (USA) – Great Alexandra (Runnett 125) [1996 54: a12g 14.6g 12m 16.1m[2] 16s 13.9g 18.2m 18g 1997 12g[4] 12d Sep 2] lengthy, sparely-made gelding: fairly useful hurdler, poor on flat nowadays: seems to stay 2¼m: probably acts on any ground on turf, not at best on fibresand: often   43

blinkered in 1994, rarely since: has an awkward head carriage and often hangs left.
M. C. Chapman

NOPALEA   3 b.f. Warrshan (USA) 117 – Nophe (USA) 95 (Super Concorde   72
(USA) 128) [1996 75: 6g⁴ 6m² 6m³ 6.1m⁴ 5m³ 5.2g³ 1997 a5g⁴ a5g⁴ a6g⁴ 5.1m² 5.3f³
5.1f² 5m* 5g³ 5d³ 6d Oct 21] lengthy, good-quartered filly: fair sprint handicapper:
won at Warwick in June: best form on good ground or firmer (poor efforts on equitrack). *T. J. Naughton*

NO PATTERN   5 ch.g. Rock City 120 – Sunfleet 59 (Red Sunset 120) [1996   –
78d: a10g⁶ a12g 12d³ 12m 12m 13.3m 12g³ 11.5m⁵ 10g a12g⁴ a10g⁴ 1997 a10g
Jan 21] leggy gelding: fair handicapper at best in 1996: well held only 5-y-o start.
G. L. Moore

NO PROBLEM JAC   4 b.f. Safawan 118 – Out On A Flyer 55 (Comedy Star   –
(USA) 121) [1996 NR 1997 6.9g 10m⁵ 10.1g⁵ Jul 28] leggy filly: second living foal:
dam sprinter: poor form in 2 NH Flat races: no promise on flat. *J. J. O'Neill*

NORCROFT JOY   2 b.f. (Mar 1) Rock Hopper 124 – Greenhills Joy 90   47
(Radetzky 123) [1997 8.2s 7m 8.2d Oct 30] angular filly: third live foal: half-sister to
fair 1½-mile winner Meghdoot (by Celestial Storm): dam beat around 1½m: poor form
in maidens at Nottingham (twice) and Yarmouth in October: bred to be suited by
1½m+. *M. J. Ryan*

NORDANSK   8 ch.g. Nordance (USA) – Free On Board 73 (Free State 125) [1996   57
55: 12m² 11.8m⁴ 12m* 16d 14.4g⁴ 1997 10g² 10m 10s 14m⁴ 12g 16m Sep 25]
workmanlike gelding: modest handicapper: effective at 1¼m to 1¾m: acts on any
going: tends to hang. *M. Madgwick*

NORDIC BREEZE (IRE)   5 b. or br.g. Nordico (USA) – Baby Clair 79 (Gulf   76
Pearl 117) [1996 72: 10.3g 9.9g⁴ 8m 8.5m² 8.1d⁶ 9g 8.3f 1997 a8g² 8.1s⁴ Jul 1] leggy
gelding: fairly useful hurdler: fair handicapper on flat: stays 1¼m: acts on firm
ground and fibresand, below form on soft: tried blinkered/visored: has run creditably
when sweating. *M. C. Pipe*

NORDIC CREST (IRE)   3 b.g. Danehill (USA) 126 – Feather Glen (Glenstal   77
(USA) 118) [1996 76: 8d² 8.2g⁶ 1997 10m⁴ 12m³ 12d 14.1m³ 10m⁵ 11.5d Aug 28]
good-bodied gelding: fair maiden: ran poorly last 4 starts, attacked by another horse
(Badge of Fame) at start on first of them: stays 1½m well: yet to race on extremes of
going: sold 15,500 gns in October, then gelded. *P. W. Harris*

NORDIC GIFT (DEN)   4 ch.g. Bold Arrangement 127 – Nordic Rose (DEN)   –
(Drumhead 122) [1996 –: 8g 7g 7m⁴ 8s 8.1m 1997 12s 8.3s May 4] of little account.
Mrs D. Thomson

NORDICO MELODY (IRE)   3 b.g. Nordico (USA) – Musical Essence 65   –
(Song 132) [1996 –: 7m 1997 7g⁶ a7g 8g 10m 10d Sep 2] signs of ability but little
worthwhile form. *Mrs S. J. Smith*

NORDIC PIRJO   2 b.f. (Feb 13) Nordico (USA) – Victoria Mill 59 (Free State   – p
125) [1997 7.5f 6.1g 6d Oct 20] 4,000Y: fifth foal: half-sister to French 1¼m and
12.5f winner Victory Mill (by Ron's Victory): dam suited by 1¼m: signs of a little
ability in maidens, steadied early and never dangerous final start: capable of better
back over 7f+. *Mrs J. R. Ramsden*

NORDINEX (IRE)   5 b.g. Nordico (USA) – Debbie's Next (USA) 82 (Arctic   –
Tern (USA) 126) [1996 79, a75: a10g a8g* a8g 8m 8g⁵ 8m⁴ 8m 8.1d³ a9.4g 9m 1997
a8g a7g⁶ 7.1m 7g a8s Nov 10] well-made gelding: fair handicapper in 1996 for R.
Armstrong: no rateable form at 5 yrs. *D. R. C. Elsworth*

NORDISK LEGEND   5 b.g. Colmore Row 111 – Nordic Rose (DEN) (Drum-   –
head 122) [1996 –: 8g 10g 7.1g 5g 5d 5m 1997 16s 13s May 4] of no account.
Mrs D. Thomson

NORD LYS (IRE)   6 b.g. Nordico (USA) – Beach Light 89 (Bustino 136) [1996   –
–: a8.5g 10.5d⁶ 10.2m 9.9m 8f 7m 1997 a11g Jan 10] small gelding: no worthwhile
form on flat. *B. J. Llewellyn*

NOR-DO-I   3 ch.g. Primo Dominie 121 – True Nora 99 (Ahonoora 122) [1996   74
79+: 6g 6d² a5g⁴ 1997 6s 5m 5s⁵ 6g a7g⁵ a8.5g* a8g 7.1g³ 8g Oct 18] big, lengthy   a86
gelding: fairly useful handicapper on all-weather, fair on turf: made all at Wolver-

hampton in August: stays 8.5f: acts on dead ground and goes well on fibresand: effective blinkered or not: inconsistent: sold 23,000 gns, and sent to USA. *J. M. P. Eustace*

NOREASTERN (IRE) 2 ch.c. (Apr 24) Zafonic (USA) 130 – Hayati 94 – (Hotfoot 126) [1997 7.1g Sep 11] 65,000Y: tall, unfurnished colt: seventh foal: half-brother to several winners, including 3-y-o Hawait and very smart performer at around 1¼m Ruby Tiger (by Ahonoora): dam 7f and 1¼m winner: withdrawn after giving trouble stalls on intended debut: slowly away and well held in maiden at Chepstow: sold 5,000 gns in October. *P. F. I. Cole*

NORLING (IRE) 7 ch.g. Nashamaa 113 – Now Then (Sandford Lad 133) [1996 – – : 6m 5.7m 6m⁶ 6m 1997 a6g⁴ a6g⁴ a6g⁵ a7g a6g⁴ a6g⁴ 6f⁶ a6g 6g Jun 16] sturdy a51 gelding: modest performer: best form at 6f to 7f: acts on the all-weather, little recent form on turf. *K. O. Cunningham-Brown*

NORMAN CONQUEST (USA) 3 ch.c. Miswaki (USA) 124 – Grand Luxe 67 d (USA) (Sir Ivor 135) [1996 71p: 7m⁵ 7g 8d⁴ 1997 9.9m⁵ 12g⁶ 10.3d 8f⁶ 10d⁶ 8m Sep 24] strong, heavy-bodied colt: disappointing maiden: stays 1¼m: acts on good to firm and dead going: tried visored: sold, and joined M.Hammond. *I. A. Balding*

NORNAX LAD (USA) 9 b.g. Northern Baby (CAN) 127 – Naxos (USA) (Big 49 d Spruce (USA)) [1996 NR 1997 11f 12m⁵ 11.8g 13m* 12f 17.2g³ 13.1m⁴ 12.1g⁶ a16g³ 17.2m⁴ 12g⁴ 16m 14m 18d⁵ Oct 20] leggy gelding: poor handicapper: awarded race at Hamilton in June: well below form last 3 starts: effective at 13f to 17f: best turf form on good ground or firmer, also acts on equitrack: effective blinkered or not: usually races prominently: none too consistent. *Martyn Meade*

NORSKI LAD 2 b.c. (Feb 25) Niniski (USA) 125 – Lady Norcliffe (USA) 58 p (Norcliffe (CAN)) [1997 7m 8g 7g 8m Nov 4] tall, lengthy colt: shows knee action: closely related to 1989 Irish 2-y-o 5f and 7f winner Shagudine (by Shadeed) and half-brother to 3 winners, including 1½m winner Lady St Lawrence (by Bering): dam good winner up to 11f in USA: clear signs of ability in maidens and a nursery (off course 5 months after debut): will be suited by further than 1m, and should stay at least 1½m: likely to do better at 3 yrs. *Sir Mark Prescott*

NORSONG 5 b.g. Northern State (USA) 91 – Winsong Melody (Music Maestro 53 § 119) [1996 56: 7f 9.7m⁴ 10.1m 9.7f⁵ 11.9f³ 12g² 14m* 14m 14.4g 14m 1997 14.1m⁶ 14.1d 14.9m 12g 12f* 12m* 12d Sep 19] rangy gelding: modest handicapper: won at Salisbury (final start for R. Akehurst) in June and Folkestone in August: stays 1¾m: acts on firm and soft ground: races prominently: broke blood vessel over hurdles in November: unreliable. *J. Akehurst*

NORTH ARDAR 7 b.g. Ardar 87 – Langwaite (Seaepic (USA) 100) [1996 65d: 10.2g* 10m* 10f* 10m* 10m² 8.3m* 12f³ 8.9g⁶ a8g* 8m⁴ 11.1d⁴ a8.5g 10g a8g⁶ a8g⁶ a12s 1997 a11g⁶ a12g a9.4g⁶ a9.4g⁵ Dec 26] close-coupled, angular gelding: fair performer at best: soundly beaten in 1997, including in visor. *N. P. Littmoden*

NORTH BEAR 5 b.g. North Briton 67 – Sarah Bear (Mansingh (USA) 120) – [1996 61: 11.1m³ 12f² 12m³ 12f* 13.8g 1997 10g 10d May 9] sturdy gelding: modest performer at 4 yrs for Mrs S. Smith: well beaten in handicaps in 1997. *G. M. McCourt*

NORTHERN ACCORD 3 b.g. Akarad (FR) 130 – Sioux City (Simply Great – (FR) 122) [1996 NR 1997 7m 8m a8.5g⁵ Nov 1] 20,000Y: second foal: half-brother to 1996 French 3-y-o 1¼m and 11.5f winner Dorsoduro (by Highest Honor): dam Group 3 placed French 1¼m and 1½m winner: signs of just a little ability in maidens: bred to need further than 1m. *Mrs J. R. Ramsden*

NORTHERN ANGEL (IRE) 3 b.c. Waajib 121 – Angel Divine (Ahonoora 83 122) [1996 –: 7g 1997 8.3s 7.6m² 8.3m⁴ 8.3g³ 7m* 7m a7g³ a8.5g² a8g Dec 12] fairly useful performer: won maiden at Salisbury in August: left Mrs J. Cecil after sixth start: should stay 1m: acts on good to firm ground and the all-weather: reportedly lame when pulled up final outing. *P. W. Harris*

NORTHERN BLESSING 3 b.f. Waajib 121 – Last Blessing 73 (Final Straw 86 p 127) [1996 NR 1997 8.2g* 8v⁵ Oct 10] lengthy filly: fluent mover: third foal: half-sister to 4-y-o Enchanted Guest and Prime Match (by Primo Dominie), both sprint winners: dam 7f and 1m winner: easy winner of maiden at Nottingham in September: good fifth of 10 to Jafn in listed race at Ascot on only subsequent outing, weakening having raced up with strong pace in testing conditions: looks a useful performer in the making. *P. W. Harris*

NORTHERN CHARMER   5 br.g. Charmer 123 – Trading 74 (Forlorn River – 124) [1996 NR 1997 a12g⁶ Mar 14] no worthwhile form on flat. *E. J. Alston*

NORTHERN CLAN   4 b.g. Clantime 101 – Northern Line 92 (Camden Town – 125) [1996 39d: 6.1d 9.9m⁵ 12m⁶ 8g 6m⁴ 12.1m a12g 11.6m 7f 6m a9.4g 1997 8.3g 8m Aug 12] of no account. *A. J. Chamberlain*

NORTHERN DIAMOND (IRE)   4 b.g. Distinctly North (USA) 115 – Mit- – subishi Diamond (Tender King 123) [1996 9d 8g 5g 7m 5g 5m 1997 a9.4g Jan 4] ex-Irish gelding: half-brother to useful Irish 7f/1m performer Mister Chippy (by Conquering Hero): dam won in Belgium at 3 yrs: no form in Ireland for A. Mullins, and well beaten only flat outing here. *Miss M. E. Rowland*

NORTHERN DRUMS   4 b.g. Sadler's Wells (USA) 132 – Repercutionist (USA)   52 111 (Beaudelaire (USA) 125) [1996 10s 10g⁶ 7d 12m 13d 12s 1997 12m⁴ 14.1d 17.2m⁶ 11.6m³ 13.1g Sep 8] 52,000Y, 5,000 3-y-o: workmanlike ex-Irish gelding: has reportedly been tubed: second foal: dam French 2-y-o 5f and 7f winner (and fourth in Cheveley Park Stakes): modest maiden: trained at 3 yrs (rated 61) by A. O'Brien: well held most starts in 1997: stays 1½m: acts on good to firm and soft ground: visored last 2 starts: successful 4 times over hurdles in October, joining M. Pipe after first win. *N. M. Babbage*

NORTHERN FAN (IRE)   5 b.g. Lear Fan (USA) 130 – Easy Romance (USA)   59 d (Northern Jove (CAN)) [1996 –, a90: a8.5g* a8.5g* 7m 10.4g 8s 1997 a9.4g a8.5g a7g⁵ a8g³ a8g* a9.4g² a8g⁵ a7g 7m² a7g⁵ 10g⁵ 8m⁵ 10.3d³ 8.3s 10.3m 10d a8g a11g a9.4g a8g Dec 18] good-topped gelding: modest performer: won seller at Southwell in February: well below form last 7 starts: effective at 7f, barely stays 1¼m: acts on fibresand and on good to firm and dead ground: sometimes bandaged. *N. Tinkler*

NORTHERN FLASH   3 b.g. Rambo Dancer (CAN) 107 – Spinster 75 (Grundy   68 137) [1996 NR 1997 10m⁶ 10m³ 8s² 10s⁶ 10.5d 13.1s⁶ Oct 13] 1,100Y: quite good-topped gelding: half-brother to fair 1993 2-y-o 7f winner Mheanmetoo (by Roi Danzig): dam 1½m winner: fair maiden: ran poorly last 3 starts, in blinkers final one: stays 1¼m: acts on good to firm and soft ground: joined J. Haynes. *F. Murphy*

NORTHERN FLEET   4 b.c. Slip Anchor 136 – Kamkova (USA) 62 (Northern   76 Dancer) [1996 87: 12m² 12m³ 11.6g⁴ 16.2g* 16.2m² 16.2d⁵ 1997 16.4g⁴ 16g 20m 16.1g Jul 9] quite good-topped colt: fair handicapper: very much a stayer: acts on good to firm going: blinkered and wore off-side brush pricker (well held) final start: won novice hurdle in August. *Mrs A. J. Perrett*

NORTHERN GREY   5 gr.g. Puissance 110 – Sharp Anne 74§ (Belfort (FR) 89) [1996 52, a48: a8.5g⁶ a7g a7g² a6g a6g⁵ 8s 8m² 7f⁶ 8m 8m 8m³ 8f a8g 1997 10g⁶ 10.8g Oct 7] close-coupled gelding: modest maiden handicapper: well held in 1997, leaving Dr J. Scargill for only 500 gns after reappearance. *A. W. Carroll*

NORTHERN JUDGE   4 ch.g. Highest Honor (FR) 124 – Nordica 99 (North-   42 § fields (USA)) [1996 65d: 7.1d 10m 7f² 6.9f 8m 10m⁶ 7m² a7g⁶ 7d* 7m 8.2g 8m 1997 6m 6.9f a7g 7s⁴ 7.1d 7m 8.1m Aug 15] strong gelding: poor handicapper: stays 7f: acts on soft ground: often blinkered: seems none too resolute. *A. P. James*

NORTHERN LASS (IRE)   2 br.f. (Mar 19) Rainbows For Life (CAN) – – Intrepid (Rousillon (USA) 133) [1997 7m 7m 7m Oct 22] 8,800Y: third foal: dam unraced sister to French 1m listed winner Silly Bold: well beaten in maidens. *M. H. Tompkins*

NORTHERN MAESTRO   3 ch.g. Rock Hopper 124 – Thimbalina 63 (Salmon – Leap (USA) 131) [1996 NR 1997 10g 10.5d⁵ 11.9d⁴ 8.3s⁶ 8.3d Aug 13] 9,000Y: first foal: dam 1¼m to 1½m winner: of little account. *Mrs M. Reveley*

NORTHERN MOTTO   4 b.g. Mtoto 134 – Soulful (FR) (Zino 127) [1996 60:   56 10.3d 10g⁴ 10g 11.1g 12m 10m⁴ 13.1s² 11.1m 16.1m 15.1s* a12g⁴ 1997 a12g* a12g 13.8g 13d⁴ 13s⁴ 16m³ 12m* 20m 12.4g⁶ 15.9m 16s Nov 6] leggy gelding: modest handicapper: won at Wolverhampton in February and Doncaster in June: effective at 1½m to 2½m: acts on fibresand and on good to firm and soft ground. *J. S. Goldie*

NORTHERN SAGA (IRE)   4 b.g. Distinctly North (USA) 115 – Saga's Hum-   –
our 61 (Bustino 136) [1996 43: 8.3g 10.8m 8m³ 10g 8d 11.8f 1997 10.2m⁴ 8.1m
11.6m 10.8g a10g a16g Nov 25] poor maiden: tried blinkered. *C. J. Drewe*

NORTHERN SAL   3 ch.f. Aragon 118 – Sister Sal 74 (Bairn (USA) 126) [1996   57 d
59: 5d* 5m⁴ 5.1g 5f 5f 1997 6d⁵ 5m² 5m⁵ 5g 5m 6g 5g 5g Sep 1] modest performer:
well held after third start: should stay 6f: acts on firm and dead ground: nervy sort,
and sometimes starts slowly. *Miss L. A. Perratt*

NORTHERN SPRUCE (IRE)   5 ch.g. Astronef 116 – Perle's Fashion (Sallust   –
134) [1996 –: 8d 12f 10s⁶ a9.4g 1997 a12g Jan 20] of little account. *A. G. Foster*

NORTHERN SUN   3 b.g. Charmer 123 – Princess Dancer (Alzao (USA) 117)   83
[1996 82: 7f* 6m⁵ 7f* 7g³ 7d⁶ 8m³ 7.9g 8g 1997 9g* 12m 10m⁴ 12d 10.1d Jul 9]
small, close-coupled gelding: fairly useful handicapper: won at Kempton in March:
creditable efforts next 2 starts: probably stays 1½m: very best form on good ground
or firmer: has drifted under pressure. *T. G. Mills*

NORTHERN TOUCH   3 b.f. Warrshan (USA) 117 – Shirley's Touch (Touching   54
Wood (USA) 127) [1996 –: 8g 1997 10f⁶ 10s⁴ 10g 10s 10.1g³ 12m² Jul 29] angular
filly: modest maiden: placed in sellers last 2 starts: stays 1½m: acts on soft and good
to firm going. *S. C. Williams*

NORTH OFTHE BORDER   2 b.c. (Apr 5) Primo Dominie 121 – Valika 75   75 p
(Valiyar 129) [1997 7s³ 7g⁴ 7d⁴ Nov 7] 60,000Y: big, good-bodied colt: sixth
foal: brother to 1993 Middle Park winner First Trump and 6f and 7f winner
First Veil and half-brother to 2 winners by Prince Sabo, including useful 1995 2-y-o
5f winner Prancing: dam, maiden placed up to 1½m, half-sister to high-class sprinter
Mr Brooks: fair form in autumn maidens at Ayr, Leicester and Doncaster: likely to
prove best short of 1m: has plenty of scope, and should do better still at 3 yrs.
M. Johnston

NORTH REEF (IRE)   6 b.h. Danehill (USA) 126 – Loreef (Main Reef 126)   77
[1996 79: 10m² 10.5m³ 10v 8.5m⁵ 8f⁶ 10g³ 12v a8.5g⁶ a9.4g² 1997 10.8m* 10.1m⁶dis
10d³ 12g 12m 12m⁴ 10s³ 10d Oct 28] tall, lengthy horse: fair handicapper: won at
Warwick in May: below form after third start (lost shoe and suffered overreach final
onc): stays 11f: acts on good to firm (probably soft) ground and the all-weather:
usually races prominently: has bolted before start and looked temperamental.
J. Pearce

NORTH WHITE PLAINS   3 b.c. Shareef Dancer (USA) 135 – Clare Court 89   – §
(Glint of Gold 128) [1996 NR 1997 10f⁵ 10.2m 10s 14m May 31] 10,000R, 9,000Y:
quite attractive colt: second foal: brother to smart Italian 9f and 1¼m winner Snake
Snap: dam, 1m (at 2 yrs) to 1¾m winner, half-sister to smart French sprinter Wessam
Prince: fifth in maiden at Milan in April: refused to race or virtually so afterwards:
one to leave alone: sent to Italy. *C. E. Brittain*

NOSEY NATIVE   4 b.g. Cyrano de Bergerac 120 – Native Flair 87 (Be My   66 d
Native (USA) 122) [1996 73: 12d⁵ 12d 12m⁵ 10m 10.8f⁶ 12s³ 12m 12.1m⁶ 16.5m⁶
15d² 14.1m⁴ 12m 10.5s* 10f 8.2g⁵ 1997 12m 10.8m 10g 10.8m³ 11.9d 12.3m* 11.1d
12m 12.1m 12g⁴ 15g⁶ 14.1g⁴ a14.8g a14g³ a14g⁶ a12g⁶ Dec 4] leggy gelding: fair
handicapper: awarded ladies event at Ripon in June: below best afterwards: stays
1¾m: acts on the all-weather and probably on any turf going: tried visored: tends to
get behind: none too consistent. *J. Pearce*

NO SHAME   2 b.f. (Apr 19) Formidable (USA) 125 – Jalopy 71 (Jalmood (USA)   56 d
126) [1997 6s 6g 6g⁶ 7g⁵ 8g 8f 8m 8m Oct 22] 12,000Y: good-topped filly: fifth foal:
half-sister to 4-y-o Classy Chief and 2 winners in France by Warrshan: dam, 5f winner, half-sister to useful sprinter Point of Light: modest form at best, but became
disappointing, reluctant to race when visored penultimate start: stays 7f: sold 600 gns
in October. *J. G. Smyth-Osbourne*

NO SPEECHES (IRE)   6 b.g. Last Tycoon 131 – Wood Violet (USA) (Riverman   –
(USA) 131) [1996 –, a67: a10g a12g* a10g³ 1997 a12g⁴ 9.8s⁶ 9.8s 11d a10g² Mar   a68
24] fair handicapper: no form in 3 runs at Cagnes before good second at Lingfield:
stays 1½m: acts on firm ground, dead and equitrack. *S. Dow*

NO SUBMISSION (USA)   11 b.h. Melyno 130 – Creeping Kate (USA) (Stop   –
The Music (USA)) [1996 40, a62: a8g³ a8.5g a8g² a11g* a8g⁵ a12g³ a12g a8g²   a42

a9.4g* a8.5g² 10.1s a10g 8.1g⁶ 8g² a8g⁶ a8g 11.1m 10m 10d a8g a8g a8g a11g* a10g a8g a12g a11g 1997 a11g⁶ a12g 12.1d a12g Apr 7] tall horse: winner of 23 races, 15 of them at Southwell, and rated 87 at his best: poor form in 1997: reportedly to stand at stud. *D. W. Chapman*

NOT A LOT 3 ch.g. Emarati (USA) 74 – Spanish Chestnut (Philip of Spain 126) [1996 50: 6m 5g² 6m 7g 5f⁴ 5m⁴ 7.5m 8m⁶ 8g 1997 10m 7m 6g⁶ May 12] leggy, close-coupled gelding: poor maiden: no form in 1997. *M. W. Easterby*

NOTARY 3 b.g. Mtoto 134 – Nadina 116 (Shirley Heights 130) [1996 NR 1997 10m 12.3g Jun 18] small gelding: fourth foal: dam French 10.5f winner: behind in maidens: sold, and sent to Germany. *J. W. Watts*

NOTATION (IRE) 3 b.c. Arazi (USA) 135 – Grace Note (FR) 99 (Top Ville 129) 54 [1996 NR 1997 10.5g 12d 10d 10m 7m a14g 12s a14g a14g* a16g a14g* Dec 18] eighth foal: half-brother to 3 winners, including top-class 1½m performer Belmez (by El Gran Senor): dam 1¼m winner (stayed 1½m) from good family: left A. Fabre for only 3,500 gns after second start: modest form in Britain, winning handicaps at Southwell in November and December, coming from long way off pace on second occasion: should stay 2m: acts on fibresand, little form on turf or equitrack: well beaten in blinkers. *D. W. Chapman*

NOT FORGOTTEN (USA) 3 b.g. St Jovite (USA) 135 – Past Remembered 78 d (USA) (Solford (USA) 127) [1996 –: 8.5v⁵ 10v 1997 a10g⁶ 12g⁴ 12g⁴ 14.6d⁴ 12g⁴ 10.1s 10m 16m a14g⁶ 16.4s 16m⁶ Sep 15] smallish gelding: disappointing maiden: seems very much a stayer: often blinkered/visored: joined R. Hoad. *P. A. Kelleway*

NOTHING DOING (IRE) 8 b.g. Sarab 123 – Spoons (Orchestra 118) [1996 43: 49 12g a12g⁶ 11.6m² 11.6g³ 12.1f⁵ 14d* 12d 12s² a13g³ a16g⁴ 1997 a13g² a12g⁶ a38 11.6g² 12s³ 12s 11.6m* 11.6g Aug 4] sturdy gelding: has a round action: poor handicapper: won seller at Windsor in July: stays easy 2m: acts on any all-weather/turf: tried blinkered (tailed off): sometimes looks rather temperamental. *W. J. Musson*

NOT OUT LAD 3 b.c. Governor General 116 – Sorcha (IRE) (Shernazar 131) – [1996 –: 6g 1997 a5g 7m 8d Oct 28] no form. *P. Butler*

NOUFARI (FR) 6 b.g. Kahyasi 130 – Noufiyla 68 (Top Ville 129) [1996 82: 75 16.2g³ a14.8g³ 18.7g 16.5g³ 20f 16.1m⁵ 16.1g 16.1m⁴ 15.9g 16.5s a12g⁵ 1997 a14.8g³ a16.2g² a16.2g² 18m² a14.8g³ 14s a16.2g² 16g⁵ 16.1f² 16.1s 13.1g* 14m³ 16.1g 13.1d a12g³ 14.6g a14.8g³ Nov 15] quite good-topped gelding: fair performer: won minor event at Ayr in July: stays 2½m: acts on firm ground (unsuited by soft) and fibresand: not an easy ride and sometimes gets behind. *R. Hollinshead*

NUBILE 3 b.f. Pursuit of Love 124 – Trojan Lady (USA) (Irish River (FR) 131) 53 [1996 71p: 7g 1997 8g³ 8f⁴ 10.2s⁶ 11.6m* a12g 12m a12g Nov 18] modest performer: not at best to win seller at Windsor in July on final start for B. Hills: subsequently off course over 3 months, and well beaten on return: shapes as if should stay beyond 11.6f. *W. J. Musson*

NUCLEAR DEBATE (USA) 2 b.g. (Feb 8) Geiger Counter (USA) – I'm An 90 Issue (USA) (Cox's Ridge (USA)) [1997 5v⁶ 5m² 6m² 6m³ 5m 6d⁵ Oct 16] $57,000Y: big, strong gelding: has scope: first foal: dam winning sprinter in USA: fairly useful maiden: ran creditably in competitive nurseries last 3 starts, though produced little final start: may prove best at 5f/easy 6f: acts on good to firm and dead ground: sweating freely and decidedly edgy fourth start (subsequently gelded): has ability to win races. *Mrs J. R. Ramsden*

NUIT D'OR (IRE) 2 ch.g. (Apr 10) Night Shift (USA) – Sister Golden Hair 61 (IRE) (Glint of Gold 128) [1997 a7g⁶ 7.1g a8.5g⁶ a6g Oct 20] 15,500 2-y-o: small gelding: first foal: dam German 2-y-o 1m winner: modest form in maidens: well beaten in nursery final outing: probably needs at least 7f. *M. Johnston*

NUKUD (USA) 5 b.g. Topsider (USA) – Summer Silence (USA) (Stop The Music 22 (USA)) [1996 –: 7s 8m⁶ 7m 10g 1997 a6g⁶ a8g⁵ a8.5g² 8m 9f 10s³ 8g 8g 9.9m⁶ 8m⁶ a39 9.9g⁴ Aug 23] small, robust gelding: poor maiden: stays 1¼m: usually blinkered/visored. *G. R. Oldroyd*

NUNTHORPE   2 ch.f. (Mar 22) Mystiko (USA) 124 – Enchanting Melody 71   71 p
(Chief Singer 131) [1997 6s⁶ 6m² 7.9s Oct 8] big, workmanlike filly: has scope: third
reported foal: half-sister to a winner in Italy by Petoski: dam maiden who stayed 1m:
easily best effort in maidens when neck second to Prompt Delivery at Pontefract in
September: should stay 1m: possibly not at best on soft going: type to make a better
3-y-o. *J. A. Glover*

NUVELLINO   2 b.c. (Apr 26) Robellino (USA) 127 – Furry Dance (USA)   –
(Nureyev (USA) 131) [1997 6d Aug 28] third foal: dam once-raced close relative of
smart 1¼m/1½m winner Florid: showed nothing in claimer at Lingfield. *S. G. Knight*

NWAAMIS (USA)   5 b.h. Dayjur (USA) 137 – Lady Cutlass (USA) (Cutlass   114
(USA)) [1996 114: 8d³ 8.1g⁴ 8d⁶ 1997 8m* 7.6m* 8m⁴ 8f⁵ 7m³ Sep 25] tall, rangy,
good sort: shows a powerful, rather round action: smart performer: reportedly injured
pelvis in 1995, and missed much of 1996 with rare bacterial infection: back to near
best in 1997, winning minor events at Ascot in April and Lingfield in May and fourth,
beaten 3 lengths by Allied Forces, in Queen Anne Stakes at Royal Ascot: below form
last 2 starts, finishing lame on final one: stays 1m: acts on good to firm ground,
impressive winner on debut on first of 3 runs on dead: tends to carry head awkwardly/
high, and usually held up. *J. L. Dunlop*

O

OAKBROOK ROSE   3 b.f. Forzando 122 – Oakbrook Tern (USA) (Arctic Tern   –
(USA) 126) [1996 52: 6.1m⁴ 6g 6.9d 1997 8.2d 6m 9s Aug 29] leggy filly: modest
form at 2 yrs: tailed off in 1997: blinkered final start. *M. P. Muggeridge*

OAKBURY (IRE)   5 ch.g. Common Grounds 118 – Doon Belle (Ardoon 124)   –
[1996 40: 12g 12.3g 10g 14.1m 10.3m 8m 10m 10.5m⁶ 10d² 11.8f 10.1m 1997 10g
12s Oct 17] angular gelding: poor maiden on flat nowadays: tried blinkered.
Miss L. C. Siddall

OARE KITE   2 b.f. (Apr 26) Batshoof 122 – Portvasco 90 (Sharpo 132) [1997 5d⁶   65
6.1m⁶ 7g³ Oct 7] sixth foal: sister to a poor maiden and half-sister to 5f (at 2 yrs) and
6f winner (stays 1m) Midwich Cuckoo (by Mydian) and 6f/7f winner Oare Sparrow
(by Night Shift): dam 6f winner: modest form in maidens: third at Warwick final
start: should stay 1m: off course 2½ months after debut. *P. T. Walwyn*

OATEY   4 ch.f. Master Willie 129 – Oatfield 69 (Great Nephew 126) [1996 68:   61
a7g⁵ 6d 8g 5m* 5.9f³ 5g³ 5m² 5g* 5m 6m 1997 5f 5g 6g³ 5g 5g Jun 16] workmanlike
filly: fluent mover: modest handicapper: best effort at 4 yrs when third at Doncaster
in June: brought down previous start: best at 5f/6f: acts on firm ground: held up.
Mrs J. R. Ramsden

OBELOS (USA)   6 ch.g. Diesis 133 – Fair Sousanne 75 (Busted 134) [1996 77,   72 §
a71: 10s³ 10m⁴ 10.3m 10.5d² 10.4g² a9.4g³ a12g⁶ a12g⁶ a9.4g² 1997 a8g a12g a9.4g   a– §
10m* 9.9m⁶ 10.5m⁶ 12g⁴ 10m 10m 10m⁶ Sep 25] workmanlike gelding: has a round
action: fair handicapper: easily best effort at 6 yrs when winning at Leicester in
March: stays 1½m: acts on good to firm and soft ground, well beaten on fibresand in
1997: tried visored: not one to trust. *Miss S. J. Wilton*

OBERONS BOY (IRE)   4 b.g. Fairy King (USA) – Bold Starlet (Precocious   63 §
126) [1996 71§: 8f 8.1g 7.5m⁴ 10m³ 10m⁴ 11.6m⁶ a9.4g a7g⁶ 1997 a8g² a8g⁶ 6.9g
a8g 10s 10.8m² 11.9f⁶ 10f³ 12d⁵ 14g⁴ 12m 10.2g Sep 11] useful-looking gelding:
modest handicapper: effective at 1m, probably at 1½m: acts on equitrack (well
beaten only start on fibresand) and any turf going: has been blinkered, not at 4 yrs:
inconsistent, and none too genuine: sold 1,400 gns, and sent to Italy. *S. Dow*

OBERON'S DART (IRE)   4 b.g. Fairy King (USA) – Key Maneuver (USA)   62
(Key To Content (USA)) [1996 77: 7.1d⁶ a7g* a7g² 6g⁵ a6g³ 7.1d² 7g 1997   a71
7.6v 8d a6f 6s⁵ a7g a7g* 7s a7g³ 7g Oct 24] workmanlike gelding: fair performer: won claimer at Southwell in August by 8 lengths, best effort as 4-y-o: stays

7f: acts on fibresand, raced only on good going or softer on turf: none too consistent. *P. J. Makin*

OBERON'S MISTRAL   2 b.f. (Mar 12) Fairy King (USA) – La Venta (USA)   79
(Drone) [1997 7m 7g² 8m³ Sep 9] good-topped, attractive filly: second reported foal: dam, 6.5f winner in France, sister to dam of Dancing Brave: fair form in maidens: placed behind Hadayik at Goodwood and Bristol Channel at Leicester: not sure to stay beyond 1m: taken last to post final start. *H. R. A. Cecil*

OBSESSED   2 b.f. (Feb 20) Storm Bird (CAN) 134 – Secret Obsession (USA) 89   80
(Secretariat (USA)) [1997 6g 7.1m⁴ 6m³ 6s* Oct 16] lengthy, good-topped filly: sister to 7f winner Storm Nymph and half-sister to 1995 2-y-o 6f winner Obsessive (by Seeking The Gold), useful at 1¼m, and a winner in USA by Woodman: dam 1¼m winner out of half-sister to Chris Evert: fairly useful form: won maiden at Catterick in October, leading post: ran well in listed event at Sandown second outing: should stay 1m: has looked rather headstrong, and sweated third outing (off course 8 weeks afterwards). *M. R. Stoute*

OCCAM (IRE)   3 ch.g. Sharp Victor (USA) 114 – Monterana 99 (Sallust 134)   66 ?
[1996 58p: 6g⁴ 1997 8.2m 8g⁴ 8.2g⁴ 8.2d Oct 8] leggy gelding: fluent mover: fair maiden: should stay further than 1m: well beaten on good to soft going: sold 1,300 gns in December, gelded and joined L. J. Barratt. *G. Wragg*

OCCHI VERDI (IRE)   2 ch.f. (Feb 25) Mujtahid (USA) 118 – Mali (USA)   77
(Storm Bird (CAN) 134) [1997 5g* 5m⁶ 5g² 6.3d⁴ 5.2f 8g 6.5m⁴ 7m⁵ 6g Oct 18] IR 15,000Y: workmanlike filly: first foal: dam French 1m winner out of 1000 Guineas fourth Ala Mahlik, herself sister to Rockfel winner/1000 Guineas third Negligent: fair performer: won maiden at Ripon in April: ran creditably most subsequent starts: should stay beyond 6.5f: seems highly strung, and has been reluctant stalls and early to post: has tended to hang: sent to USA. *M. Johnston*

OCCUPANDISTE (IRE)   4 b.f. Kaldoun (FR) 122 – Only Seule (Lyphard   123
(USA) 132) [1996 106: 8m⁴ 8d³ 9d² 1997 8d* 7s* 6g⁵ 6.5d* 7d* Oct 19]
    'Who?' That might well be the response if you mentioned the name Occupandiste to the average British racing enthusiast. The answer to the question is: a very well-bred filly, with a top trainer, who won all but one of her starts in 1997, the last of them a seven-furlong Group 1 event by no less than six lengths. 'Oh, *that* Occupandiste!' Yes, well, a degree of ignorance would be understandable—Occupandiste has yet to race outside France and, until well into the second half of the season, seemed just a useful performer. If she's kept

Prix Maurice de Gheest, Deauville—
Occupandiste reverses previous form with Monaassib;
Titus Livius takes third place

Prix de la Foret, Longchamp—a runaway success for Occupandiste,
who has six lengths to spare over British challengers Gothenberg (left) and Tomba

in training, as her trainer would like, it's a good bet that she'll be making a big impact outside her own backyard.

Occupandiste had been a promising enough two-year-old, the winner of two of her four races, including the Group 3 Prix des Reservoirs at Longchamp. But things seemed to go wrong the following year. She was last of four on her reappearance and off the course for nearly six months subsequently. Significantly, that run was her last on going firmer than good. She returned in the autumn to finish placed in a couple of listed events, still a far cry from what might have been expected of her at the season's outset.

She started off 1997 at lowly Compiegne in a fillies conditions race, which she took by half a length from Daneskaya, another filly destined for better things. Then it was the Group 3 Prix de la Porte Maillot at Longchamp, won again by half a length, this time from Vernoy. Her one defeat of the year followed in the Prix de Ris-Orangis at Deauville over a shorter trip and on less testing ground; Occupandiste was beaten little more than a length into fifth by Monaassib. The Ed Dunlop-trained gelding, coupled at 6/5 favourite with Kahal, was among her main rivals in the Prix Maurice de Gheest over six and a half furlongs at Deauville in August; the King's Stand runner-up Titus Livius was 6/4 and Occupandiste at over 8/1. Occupandiste was soon in the lead as usual and galloped on determinedly to hold off Monaassib by half a length, with Titus Livius finishing well into third, three quarters of a length further behind. This couldn't be described as an outstanding Group 1, though, and didn't really hint at what Occupandiste would prove capable of two months later. The ten-runner Prix de la Foret at Longchamp was again not strong by Group 1 standards (Occupandiste was a warm favourite at 7/5), though Gothenberg and Tomba are no slouches. Occupandiste trounced them, making all and going clear before the final furlong to win by six lengths from Gothenberg, with Tomba three quarters of a length behind in third. Occupandiste was an intended runner for the Breeders' Cup Mile, but ground conditions at Hollywood Park ended up firm and she was pulled out.

As we said, Occupandiste, a daughter of the good French sire Kaldoun, is a very well-bred filly, and she's a good-looking one, too, as the accompanying portrait shows. Occupandiste is the first foal of the French two-year-old seven-and-a-half furlong winner Only Seule. The second foal, the Last Tycoon colt Lonely Tycoon, was a useful two-year-old winner himself in 1996 over the same trip. Further details of Occupandiste's terrifically successful family can be found in the essay on Only Seule's half-brother Elnadim.

Wertheimer et Frere's "Occupandiste"

		Caro	Fortino II
	Kaldoun (FR)	(gr 1967)	Chambord
	(gr 1975)	Katana	Le Haar
Occupandiste (IRE)		(b 1970)	Embellie
(b.f. 1993)		Lyphard	Northern Dancer
	Only Seule	(b 1969)	Goofed
	(ch 1988)	Elle Seule	Exclusive Native
		(ch 1983)	Fall Aspen

Under certain conditions—seven furlongs and ground softer than good —there were few horses we'd have put up against Occupandiste in Europe by the end of 1997. If indeed she does stay in training, it remains to be seen if front-running tactics are important to her and how versatile she actually is with regard to her trip; she is a winner twice at a mile. Occupandiste seems unlikely to be risked on going firmer than good in the future. *Mme C. Head, France*

OCEAN BREEZE 3 ch.g. Most Welcome 131 – Sea Power 88 (Welsh Pageant 132) [1996 –: 6m 9f⁴ 1997 7.5s 14.1m 17.2m⁵ 12v³ 16.2m 15.8g³ 17.2f⁶ Aug 27] big, good-topped gelding: poor staying maiden handicapper: blinkered/visored last 4 starts. *J. S. Wainwright*   39

OCEAN LIGHT 3 ch.f. Anshan 119 – Waveguide 76 (Double Form 130) [1996 –: 7.1d 6m 1997 a8.5g⁶ Feb 26] close-coupled filly: no worthwhile form in maidens: should stay beyond 1m. *A. Bailey*   –

OCEAN LINE (IRE) 2 b.c. (Mar 16) Kefaah (USA) 124 – Tropic Sea (IRE) (Sure Blade (USA) 130) [1997 7.1m 7m 7.1g 8m³ Nov 4] IR 7,500Y: sturdy colt: first foal: dam unraced from middle-distance staying family: easily best effort when third of 27 to Bawsian in nursery at Redcar: should be at least as effective over 1¼m+: twice slowly away: should do better. *A. P. Jarvis*   59 p

OCEAN PARK 6 b.g. Dominion 123 – Chiming Melody 71 (Cure The Blues (USA)) [1996 78, a91: a8.5g* a9.4g⁵ a10g* a10g* 10d* 8m 10m 12g* 10.4g 1997   72 a–

a10g 10.8m⁶ 10s⁴ 12m⁴ 12m⁴ 10m² 12g² Sep 2] good-bodied gelding: good mover: fairly useful handicapper at best on the all-weather, fair on turf: unlucky in seller at Folkestone final start: stays 1½m: goes well on all-weather, probably acts on any turf going: blinkered (raced too freely) once as 3-y-o: best held up in strongly-run race. *Lady Herries*

OCEAN RIDGE (USA)   3 b.f. Storm Bird (CAN) 134 – Polar Bird 111 (Thatch-   115
ing 131) [1996 108: 6m* 6g² 5.5g* 6g⁴ 6m³ 1997 8m⁵ 8m² 8g² 8g⁶ Aug 3] quite attractive filly: has a sharp action: smart performer: 5½ lengths fifth to Sleepytime in 1000 Guineas at Newmarket: best efforts when ¾-length second to Rebecca Sharp in steadily-run Coronation Stakes at Royal Ascot and to Ryafan in Falmouth Stakes at Newmarket (unable to hold on last 100 yds): disappointing in Prix d'Astarte at Deauville final start: barely stays 1m: raced only on good/good to firm ground: rather headstrong at 2 yrs, more settled in 1997: made much of running last 3 starts: genuine and reliable: sent to USA. *Saeed bin Suroor*

OCEAN STREAM (IRE)   4 b.g. Waajib 121 – Kilboy Concorde (African Sky   –
124) [1996 –: a6g⁴ 7s 8g 1997 a7g a8g 8d 6f 12s Oct 16] formerly fair maiden: no form in 1997: tried visored: dead. *J. L. Eyre*

OCHOS RIOS (IRE)   6 br.g. Horage 124 – Morgiana (Godswalk (USA) 130)   63 §
[1996 64, a–: 7.5d 7.5m⁶ 7m² 7g² 7g 6m 8m³ 7m³ 7m⁴ 8m 9g 7g* 7m 7g 7g⁶ 1997   a– §
7d³ 8.2g 7g 6g⁵ 7m³ 8.1m 8.5f 8.2d 7d 7m Nov 1] small gelding: good mover: modest handicapper on his day: stays 1m: acts on good to firm going, heavy and fibresand: poor efforts in blinkers: inconsistent: sold only 700 gns in November. *B. S. Rothwell*

OCKER (IRE)   3 br.g. Astronef 116 – Violet Somers (Will Somers 114§) [1996   59
77+: 5m 5.9g 6g² 6m 6d² 1997 6m⁵ 6.1d⁶ 7d⁴ 7g 7g⁵ 8g⁴ 6f 7d⁴ a7g a7g Nov 21] leggy gelding: modest maiden: should stay 1m: acts on dead ground: no improvement visored. *M. H. Tompkins*

OCTAVIA HILL   4 ch.f. Prince Sabo 123 – Clara Barton (Youth (USA) 135)   59
[1996 60: 6g 6m 7g⁶ 7m 1997 a7g 7m² 7d⁴ 7f³ 7g³ 8m⁶ 7g* Sep 5] useful-looking filly: modest handicapper: won 16-runner maiden event at Epsom in September: should stay 1m: acts on firm and dead going: effective blinkered or not: has found little, and possibly not entirely genuine: sold 2,500 gns in October. *P. W. Harris*

ODETTE   2 b.f. (Jan 31) Pursuit of Love 124 – On Tiptoes 107 (Shareef Dancer   72
(USA) 135) [1997 5.1m² 5f³ 5.1d³ 5d² Oct 17] second foal: dam, best at 5f, won Queen Mary Stakes: fair form when placed in maidens: will be suited by 6f. *Sir Mark Prescott*

OFF AND RUNNING   2 gr.g. (May 31) Paris House 123 – I Don't Mind 97   –
(Swing Easy (USA) 126) [1997 a5g⁴ a5g⁵ Jul 10] 6,000Y: half-brother to several winners, including useful middle-distance stayer/high-class hurdler Swingit Gunner (by Gunner B) and sprinter Dokkha Oyston (by Prince Sabo): dam won 10 races at 5f/6f: well held in sellers at Southwell 10 weeks apart. *J. Berry*

OFFICE HOURS   5 b.g. Danehill (USA) 126 – Charmina (FR) (Nonoalco (USA)   –
131) [1996 68d, a–: a10g a7g⁶ a6g a9.4g 6.9f³ 7f 7g⁵ 7g 10f 7f² 6m 8f⁴ 8m 8m 1997 8m Apr 14] formerly fair maiden: has lost his form: tried blinkered. *W. G. M. Turner*

OFF THE RAILS   3 b.f. Saddlers' Hall (IRE) 126 – Sliprail (USA) 86 (Our   57
Native (USA)) [1996 –p: 7f⁶ 1997 10m³ 10g 10.2m 8g 12m⁵ Sep 26] modest maiden: probably stays 1½m: raced only on good going or firmer. *H. Candy*

OGGI   6 gr.g. Efisio 120 – Dolly Bevan 53 (Another Realm 118) [1996 78: 6.1g 6m   98
6d 6m 6f* 6m³ 7m 6m* 1997 6d* 6m 6d* 6g⁴ 6m⁴ 6m⁵ 6g³ 6g Sep 20] angular gelding: useful handicapper: better than ever at 6 yrs, winning at Leicester in April and Goodwood in May: good efforts in highly-competitive events afterwards, fourth in Wokingham at Royal Ascot next time and much the best of those drawn low when third of 20 at Goodwood penultimate start: stays 6f: acts on firm ground, dead and fibresand: successful in blinkers earlier in career: used to have tongue tied: game and reliable. *P. J. Makin*

OH DEARIE ME   5 b.m. Puissance 110 – Tyrian Princess 73 (Comedy Star   –
(USA) 121) [1996 NR 1997 8f⁴ Sep 29] of no account. *J. G. M. O'Shea*

OHH

OH HEBE (IRE) 2 b.f. (Mar 29) Night Shift (USA) – Why So Silent (Mill Reef 74
(USA) 141) [1997 6g⁴ 5.1m³ Aug 12] lengthy filly: fifth foal: half-sister to 3-y-o
Calypso Grant and useful 7f (at 2 yrs) to 1½m winner Poppy Carew (both by
Danehill): dam unraced daughter of Pretty Polly Stakes and Lancashire Oaks winner
Sing Softly: better effort in maidens when third of 17 at Bath, helping force pace:
bred to stay at least 6f: pulled hard on debut, when also bandaged behind. *P. W. Harris*

O' HIGGINS (IRE) 2 b.g. (Feb 14) Magical Wonder (USA) 125 – Lightning 77 §
Laser 68 (Monseigneur (USA) 127) [1997 5m³ 5f 5.1d 6d⁶ 7.5d⁵ 10.2f⁴ 8g³ Oct 18]
12,500Y: close-coupled gelding: fifth foal: half-brother to 4 winners, including 3-y-o
Mozambique and 8-y-o Morocco: dam, 7f winner, ran only at 2 yrs: some fair form,
but inconsistent and looks difficult ride: probably suited by 1m+: tends to hang: not
to be trusted. *R. Boss*

OHIO ROYALE 3 ch.g. Shalford (IRE) 124§ – Jupiter's Message (Jupiter Island –
126) [1996 –: 6m 5f a8.5g 1997 7m⁵ 5.9f 6m Oct 6] workmanlike gelding: little
worthwhile form. *Mrs A. Swinbank*

OH NELLIE (USA) 3 b. or br.f. Tilt The Stars (CAN) – Miss Enjoleur (USA) 113 d
(L'Enjoleur (CAN)) [1996 a5.5f* a6f* 7f* a8g⁴ 1997 6m² 7g² 8m² 8d⁵ 7m⁶ 7m⁵ 10d
Oct 16] $3,000Y, $14,000 2-y-o: tall, lengthy filly: third foal: dam maiden: won
maiden and 2 allowance races at Woodbine at 2 yrs: runner-up in minor event at
Kempton, Nell Gwyn Stakes and 1000 Guineas at Newmarket, best effort when
beaten 4 lengths by Sleepytime in last-named: rather disappointing in Irish 1000
Guineas next time, even more so last 3 outings (tailed off final one): effective at 6f to
1m: acts on firm going and dirt: wore blinkers all 4 starts in North America: usually a
front runner: returned to USA. *N. A. Callaghan*

Mr M. Tabor's "Oh Nellie"

674

OH NEVER AGAIN (IRE) 2 br.g. (Feb 7) Ballad Rock 122 – Play The Queen 69
(IRE) (King of Clubs 124) [1997 5g³ 5m² a6g* 6f⁶ 7g⁶ Jul 23] IR 7,500Y: third foal:
brother to a winner in Sweden and half-brother to 3-y-o Salty Jack: dam Irish 7f
winner out of Coronation Stakes winner Orchestration: fair performer: won maiden
at Wolverhampton in May: ran creditably in nursery next start: stays 6f: sent to
Macau. *M. Johnston*

OHNONOTAGAIN 5 b.m. Kind of Hush 118 – Dear Glenda 66 (Gold Song 112) 42
[1996 –: a7g 5m 6.9d⁴ 7g a7g 8f 8g⁵ 1997 8m 6m⁵ a6g 5g 5f 6m² 5g 7s 6d 6m⁶ 6g³ 6g a–
a7g 7m⁶ 6g⁴ 5g a6g Nov 13] small mare: poor maiden: trained until after eleventh
start by L. Lloyd-James, next 2 by Mrs N. Macauley: stays 6f: acts on good to firm
ground, dead and fibresand: tried blinkered/visored. *N. Tinkler*

OH SO EASY 2 ch.c. (Apr 18) Forzando 122 – Hat Hill (Roan Rocket 128) [1997 67
5m 5g⁶ 6g⁴ 5m⁴ 6m³ 7d⁴ 7m Oct 23] IR 8,600Y: rather leggy, useful-looking colt:
brother to 3-y-o Don't Worry Mike and half-brother to 3 winners: dam ran 4 times:
fair form: in frame in maidens, nursery and a seller: likely to prove best up to 7f: acts
on good to firm and dead ground: ran much too freely when blinkered final start: has
given trouble stalls. *B. J. Meehan*

OH SO MISTY 4 b.f. Teenoso (USA) 135 – Miss Bali Beach 88 (Nonoalco –
(USA) 131) [1996 NR 1997 10s 10g⁵ 8m⁶ Jun 2] lengthy, workmanlike filly: sister to
useful maiden Tetradonna (placed up to 1½m) and half-sister to 2 winners by Taufan:
dam, from good family, 2-y-o 7f winner: little sign of ability. *S. Dow*

OH WHATAKNIGHT 4 b.f. Primo Dominie 121 – Carolside 108 (Music –
Maestro 119) [1996 –: 6m 8.3d 7.1d 6m 1997 5m 5g a6g 6d Aug 30] workmanlike
filly: fairly useful winner as 2-y-o: has shown nothing since. *R. M. Whitaker*

OISIN (IRE) 2 b.c. (Feb 25) Maledetto (IRE) 103 – Morgiana (Godswalk (USA) 53 +
130) [1997 5d 5m 6m 7d 6m⁴ 6g 8g 10s 8g Oct 24] IR 4,800Y: sturdy, lengthy colt:
half-brother to 3 winners, including 3-y-o Scottish Mist (by Digamist), 6f and 1m
winner in Sweden, and 6-y-o Ochos Rios: dam poor maiden: modest maiden: stiff
tasks final 4 starts: should stay beyond 6f: acts on good to firm going: sold, and sent
to Germany. *Mrs P. N. Dutfield*

OKAY BABY (IRE) 5 b.m. Treasure Kay 114 – Miss Tuko (Good Times (ITY)) 35
[1996 –: 8m 8m 1997 8.2m 7f 6.9m 7f² 8g 6.9m⁴ 7m⁶ 6g 7g 6.1m⁶ Sep 15]
sparely-made mare: poor performer: stays 1m: acts on firm going: tried blinkered/
visored (well beaten). *J. M. Bradley*

OK BABE 2 b.f. (Mar 13) Bold Arrangement 127 – Celtic Bird 77 (Celtic Cone 64
116) [1997 6g⁵ 5d⁶ a6g³ a6g* a6g⁵ Dec 22] 1,300Y: fifth foal: dam sprinter: modest a58 +
form: best effort in maiden at Folkestone second start: won seller at Wolverhampton
in November: effective at 5f/6f. *J. Akehurst*

O'KELLY (DEN) 2 b.f. (Mar 10) Last Tycoon 131 – Laser Show (IRE) (Wassl 82
125) [1997 6.1d 7g 7d* 7g³ 8s³ Nov 1] leggy filly: second foal: half-sister to fair Irish
3-y-o 9f winner Blue Jazz (by Bluebird): dam, ran twice, from family of Marju
and Salsabil: much improved effort to win maiden at Chester in August: third in
Denmark's top 2-y-o races at Klampenborg last 2 starts, leaving R. Guest before final
one: probably stays 1m. *S. Jensen, Denmark*

OK JOHN (IRE) 2 b.c. (Feb 7) Mac's Imp (USA) 116 – Ching A Ling (Pampa- 58
paul 121) [1997 6d 5m² 5.1g⁴ a5g² 5.3g³ 5m³ Sep 26] 6,000Y: half-brother to 1993
2-y-o 5f winner As Such (by Ajraas): dam Irish 4-y-o 5f winner: modest maiden:
creditable third in nurseries: seems a 5f performer: acts on fibresand: has carried head
awkwardly. *J. Akehurst*

OKRA 3 ch.f. Chilibang 120 – Mollified 67 (Lombard (GER) 126) [1996 NR 1997 –
5v 8m⁴ 7.1g⁵ Sep 26] lengthy filly: half-sister to 4 winners (3 over middle distances):
dam stayed 1¼m: little promise in maidens. *J. D. Bethell*

OLD COLONY 3 b.f. Pleasant Colony (USA) – Annoconnor (USA) (Nureyev 54
(USA) 131) [1996 –: 8.1d⁵ 8.2g a8g⁴ 1997 17.2f³ May 30] big, leggy filly: modest
maiden: third in handicap at Bath on only outing at 3 yrs: seems a stayer: sent to
Australia. *P. F. I. Cole*

OLD

OLD HOOK (IRE) 6 b. or br.h. Digamist (USA) 110 – Day Dress (Ashmore 40
(FR) 125) [1996 56: a7g a8g a8g* 8g⁵ 8g⁵ 7f³ 8f⁴ 7d 1997 9m⁶ 7.5g⁶ 7.5g² 6.9m 7f³
8.5g⁴ 8g⁵ 7h 8h⁶ 6g Sep 14] neat Belgian-trained horse: poor performer: seventh
in claimer at Folkestone fourth start: stays 8.5f: acts on firm going and equitrack:
unreliable. *Paul Smith, Belgium*

OLD HUSH WING (IRE) 4 b.g. Tirol 127 – Saneena 80 (Kris 135) [1996 52: 46
5m 5m 8.3s³ 8g a8.5g⁶ a12g³ 1997 a12g a12g⁶ a12g a16g² 17.2m⁶ 13m* a14g⁴ Nov
17] good-topped gelding: poor performer: won maiden handicap at Hamilton in July:
stays 2m: acts on good to firm going: tried visored: fair winning hurdler. *P. C. Haslam*

OLD RED (IRE) 7 ch.g. Ela-Mana-Mou 132 – Sea Port (Averof 123) [1996 NR –
1997 16.1g 13.9s Sep 3] rated 74 when winning Tote Cesarewitch at Newmarket in
1995: tailed off at 7 yrs: stays very well: acts on fibresand and any turf going: tends
to pull hard and hang: has gone early to post. *Mrs M. Reveley*

OLD ROMA (IRE) 4 b.f. Old Vic 136 – Romantic Past (USA) 82 (Miswaki –
(USA) 124) [1996 76d: 6g² 8.1d 8m⁶ 10g 1997 8m 10d 7m Sep 16] workmanlike
filly: soundly beaten in sellers at 4 yrs. *John Berry*

OLD ROUVEL (USA) 6 b.g. Riverman (USA) 131 – Marie de Russy (FR) 104
(Sassafras (FR) 135) [1996 104: 16.2g² 16.2m⁵ 16g⁴ 22.2f³ 16g⁶ 18m⁵ 16m⁵ 16g⁵
1997 16.2s² 18.7s⁵ 22.2d² 16.1s 18d* 18f⁵ 16f Oct 4] tall gelding: shows knee action:
useful performer: ran well when beaten a neck by Canon Can in Queen Alexandra
Stakes at Royal Ascot in June: didn't have to be anywhere near best to land odds in
Phil Bull Trophy at Pontefract in September: stiff tasks last 2 starts: suited by 2m+:
probably acts on any going: visored (below best) third to fifth 5-y-o starts: sometimes races lazily, hangs right under pressure and carries head a little awkwardly.
D. J. G. Murray Smith

OLIFANTSFONTEIN 9 b.g. Thatching 131 – Taplow (Tap On Wood 130) [1996 –
–: 6f 6.9f 1997 6f 7.5v Jul 4] probably no longer of much account. *J. S. Wainwright*

OLIVER (IRE) 3 b.g. Priolo (USA) 127 – Daniella Drive (USA) (Shelter Half 45
(USA)) [1996 –: 7m 7d a8g 1997 12g⁴ 14.1m Mar 31] third reported foal: poor
maiden handicapper: should stay beyond 1½m. *R. W. Armstrong*

OLIVE THE TWIST (USA) 2 ch.f. (Apr 18) Theatrical 128 – Lady of The 70 p
Light (USA) (The Minstrel (CAN) 135) [1997 7d⁵ Nov 7] sister to smart Irish 6f (at 2
yrs) to 1m winner Asema and half-sister to Irish 7f and 1¼m winner Katie McLain
(by Java Gold) and 2 winners in USA: dam unraced close relative of top-class filly
Sabin and half-sister to Musidora winner Fatah Flare: 14/1 and bandaged behind,
about 3½ lengths fifth to High-Rise in maiden at Doncaster, swerving badly left at
start but soon in touch with main group and keeping on strongly, not given at all hard
time: will stay 1m, probably more: should do fair bit better. *J. H. M. Gosden*

OLIVO (IRE) 3 ch.g. Priolo (USA) 127 – Honourable Sheba (USA) (Roberto 71
(USA) 131) [1996 79: 6f³ 6m³ 7d⁶ 1997 10m 7g³ 8m 8m* 8m² 9g 8.1m 12m Sep 24]
strong, close-coupled gelding: fair handicapper: won at Brighton in July: stays 1m:
acts on firm going: has gone in snatches and looked untrustworthy. *C. A. Horgan*

OLLIE'S CHUCKLE (IRE) 2 b.c. (Mar 13) Mac's Imp (USA) 116 – Chenya 73 ?
(Beldale Flutter (USA) 130) [1997 5m⁴ 5m⁶ Aug 11] IR 3,800F, 8,500Y: useful-
looking colt: third foal: half-brother to a winner in Italy by Classic Secret: dam won
over hurdles in Ireland: appeared to show fair form in minor event at Doncaster: 6/5,
ran poorly in maiden at Thirsk about 4 weeks later. *J. A. Glover*

OMAHA CITY (IRE) 3 b.g. Night Shift (USA) – Be Discreet (Junius (USA) 104
124) [1996 99: 5.1m* 6f² 5m⁴ 6d² 6g² 6m⁶ 5d⁴ 6g³ 1997 7g 6d⁵ 7m 5d 6f⁶ 7m³ 8m⁶
7g* 8.5g⁶ 7g 7m 6d Oct 17] useful-looking gelding: useful performer: best effort
when beaten neck by Swiss Law in handicap at Goodwood, finishing strongly after
being hampered by winner and awarded race: well held in listed races and handicap
after: seems suited by 7f: acts on firm and dead ground: edgy sort, sometimes has 2
handlers and early to post. *B. Gubby*

OMAR'S ODYSSEY (IRE) 2 ch.c. (May 7) Sharifabad (IRE) 96 – Tales of –
Homer (Home Guard (USA) 129) [1997 7g 7d a7g a7g⁶ Dec 18] 5,000 2-y-o:
half-brother to Irish 1987 2-y-o 5f winner Taree Gold (by Tumble Wind) and winners
in Ireland and Italy by Glenstal: dam unraced: little worthwhile form. *P. Mitchell*

676

OMBRA DI NUBE (FR)   2 gr. or ro.f. (Apr 23) Bakharoff (USA) 130 – Shamsha   –
(FR) (Bold Lad (USA)) [1997 6m 7m 6.9d Oct 21] 620Y: half-sister to 1987 2-y-o 5f
winner Fair Port (by Belfort): dam unraced half-sister to good French stayer Shafaraz
and the dam of Ashkalani: only a little sign of ability in maidens. *C. James*

ON CALL   2 gr.f. (Mar 9) Alleged (USA) 138 – Doctor Bid (USA) (Spectacular   –
Bid (USA)) [1997 8.2g 8.2g 7g Oct 18] fourth foal: half-sister to 1996 2-y-o 7.5f
winner Lyrical Bid (by Lyphard) and fairly useful 5f/6f winner Doctor's Glory (by
Elmaamul): dam unraced half-sister to smart 1986 2-y-o 7f winner Glory Forever,
later third in Poule d'Essai des Poulains: behind in maidens. *Sir Mark Prescott*

ONCE MORE FOR LUCK (IRE)   6 b.g. Petorius 117 – Mrs Lucky (Royal   70
Match 117) [1996 70: 10f³ 12g⁴ 12g⁶ 12m² 11m* 1997 12g*ᵈⁱˢ 12m 13.1s* 12g⁴
Oct 25] sturdy gelding: fair performer: won claimer at Southwell in February
(reportedly returned with fractured pedal bone and subsequently disqualified for
testing positive to procaine) and weak seller at Ayr in October: stays 13f: acts on
fibresand and probably any turf going: sometimes finds little: won 3 times over
hurdles in December. *Mrs M. Reveley*

ONE DINAR (FR)   2 b.c. (Mar 5) Generous (IRE) 139 – Lypharitissima (FR)   –
(Lightning (FR) 129) [1997 7m 8d Sep 13] tall colt: has a markedly round action:
fourth reported foal: dam unraced sister to Prix de Diane winner Lypharita: behind in
maidens at Newbury and Goodwood, sweating and burly on debut. *J. H. M. Gosden*

ONE DREAM   4 b.g. Weldnaas (USA) 112 – Superb Lady 106 (Marcus Superbus   –
100) [1996 –: 6g 6m⁴ a7g⁴ 1997 a9.4g Jan 4] no worthwhile form. *B. Smart*

ONE FOR BAILEYS   3 b.g. Unfuwain (USA) 131 – Three Stars 93 (Star Appeal   85
133) [1996 66p: 8.1s⁴ 1997 10.3m⁴ 12.1s* 14.8g 13.9s 13.1s⁵ Oct 14] tall, unfurnished gelding: has a long stride: won maiden at Hamilton in May, making virtually
all: soundly beaten in listed race and handicaps afterwards: suited by a good test
at 1½m, and should stay further: acts on any going: edgy sort, often sweating.
M. Johnston

ONEFORTHEDITCH (USA)   4 gr.f. With Approval (CAN) – Wee Dram   63
(USA) (Nostrum (USA)) [1996 69: 6m⁵ 7g³ 7m⁶ 9m⁴ 8f⁵ 1997 a9.4g* a9.4g* 9.9s   a79
10m 10g* 10.1m a9.4g² Dec 13] leggy filly: fair on all-weather, modest on turf: won
maiden and handicap at Wolverhampton in January and minor event at Nottingham
in October: stays 1¼m: acts on fibresand and firm going. *J. R. Fanshawe*

ONEFOURSEVEN   4 b.g. Jumbo Hirt (USA) 90§ – Dominance (Dominion 123)   80
[1996 59: a8g a11g⁶ a11g⁵ a9.4g³ 10d⁶ 17.2m⁴ 15.8g* 16.1m⁵ 18g² a14g* a16g*
1997 a14.8g⁴ 18m* 17.1m³ 16g* 16.1s³ 20m 14.6m a14.8g* 18g Oct 18] angular
gelding: shows knee action: fairly useful handicapper, much improved at 4 yrs: won
at Doncaster and Thirsk in spring and Wolverhampton in September: best effort when
staying-on third to Windsor Castle in Northumberland Plate in June: stays 2¼m: acts
on fibresand and good to firm going, goes very well on soft: used to be blinkered:
tends to idle in front, but is game and consistent. *J. L. Eyre*

ONE IN THE EYE   4 br.g. Arrasas (USA) 100 – Mingalles 65 (Prince de Galles   34 §
125) [1996 62d: 7m³ 7m 10m 10m⁶ a10g⁵ 8d⁴ 9g a10g 1997 a12g a8g 9.7g 8.2m⁶
10g 12g 10m 10s³ 10.2g³ 8.1g 10g 8f³ 8g Oct 27] leggy gelding: poor maiden
handicapper: probably stays 1½m: acts on good to firm going and soft: blinkered
twice: ungenuine. *Jamie Poulton*

ONEKNIGHT WITH YOU   3 gr.f. Rudimentary (USA) 118 – Inshirah (USA)   –
90 (Caro 133) [1996 73: 5m⁴ 6m 5.7f³ 5m⁵ 5.1m⁴ 6.5m³ 7d 7.3s 1997 6m 7m 8f 6.9g
7m 7d Oct 14] workmanlike filly: disappointing maiden handicapper: tried blinkered: tends to hang. *M. J. Fetherston-Godley*

ONE LIFE TO LIVE (IRE)   4 gr.c. Classic Music (USA) – Fine Flame (Le   54
Prince 98) [1996 50: 10g⁴ 8g⁶ 10m 1997 8.3s⁴ 9.2g² 10.3d⁵ 9.2m a14g Jul 21]   a–
close-coupled colt: modest maiden handicapper: easily best effort at 4 yrs when
second in blinkers at Hamilton: visored next time: stays 1¼m: best efforts on good
ground and fibresand. *S. E. Kettlewell*

ONEMORETIME   3 b.f. Timeless Times (USA) 99 – Dear Glenda 66 (Gold   –
Song 112) [1996 –: 6g 5m 5g⁴ 1997 6m⁶ 6d 8g 5.9m 8.2g a6g Nov 14] of little
account. *B. W. Murray*

ONE

ONE OFF THE RAIL (USA) 7 b.h. Rampage (USA) – Catty Queen (USA) –
(Tom Cat) [1996 –, a76: a12g⁶ a12g* a12g³ a12g* 10f 1997 a12g⁶ a12g² a12g³ a12g² a68
a16g² May 14] good-bodied horse: has a round action: fair performer who has gained
all but one of his 10 wins on the all-weather at Lingfield (has also run well at
Wolverhampton): effective at 1½m to 2m. *G. L. Moore*

ONEOFTHEOLDONES 5 b.g. Deploy 131 – Waveguide 76 (Double Form 42
130) [1996 –: 10d 8m a8g 12.3s 1997 a8g a8g⁵ a11g⁵ a8g a11g a8g 10.3d 7m⁶ 8m 8d
10m Jul 19] good-topped gelding: has a round action: poor handicapper: best form
up to 1m: acts on good to firm going, soft and fibresand. *J. Norton*

ONE SHOT (IRE) 4 b.g. Fayruz 116 – La Gravotte (FR) (Habitat 134) [1996 39: –
8.2g 7m⁵ 8g⁶ 7m⁵ 7.1g 1997 a8g Nov 24] lengthy gelding: disappointing maiden:
well beaten on belated reappearance: tried blinkered: headstrong. *W. R. Muir*

ONE SINGER 2 ch.c. (Apr 27) Anshan 119 – Moushka (Song 132) [1997 a5g* 83
5g* 5s² 5g⁶ 5m³ 5g² 5m 6g⁵ a7g² 6g a7g³ Dec 13] 5,000Y: leggy, quite good-topped
colt: third live foal: half-brother to 3-y-o Morning Star and 5-y-o Mr Oscar (formerly
useful 5f winner): dam unraced: fairly useful performer: won maiden at Wolverhampton and minor event at Redcar in May: generally ran well afterwards: left
M. Johnston prior to final start: effective at 5f to 7f: acts on good to firm ground and
fibresand, probably on soft. *N. P. Littmoden*

ONE SO WONDERFUL 3 b.f. Nashwan (USA) 135 – Someone Special 121 p
105 (Habitat 134) [1996 93p: 7g* 1997 8.1s* 10m* Oct 4]
The Equity Financial Collections Sun Chariot Stakes at Newmarket
saw the arrival of a new order as One So Wonderful and Kool Kat Katie drew
clear from Reams of Verse. It was the Oaks winner's last race, but Kool Kat
Katie went on to a Grade 2 victory shortly afterwards at the commencement of
her North American career, while One So Wonderful should be lining up in the
highest company in Europe in 1998. Both look assured of further success, but
perhaps nothing should be taken for granted given their limited appearances so
far. One So Wonderful's season did not begin until August 30th. She had had
her only previous race nearly a year earlier in a minor event at Kempton and

Equity Financial Collections Sun Chariot Stakes, Newmarket—
two lightly-raced but very smart fillies in One So Wonderful and Kool Kat Katie

won it by three and a half lengths. Even her trainer did not see that much of her in the summer because, after taking until May to get her coat, One So Wonderful was sent back to her owner's stud for a month.

Luca Cumani had her right enough in the autumn, though. That reappearance took place in a listed race at Sandown, where thirteen opponents presented a strong numerical threat, but, it turned out, none at all on the score of ability. Co-favourite at 11/2, One So Wonderful came from the rear and stretched eight lengths clear in the final furlong and a half for a most impressive success. In the Sun Chariot five weeks later, she made most of the running and once again moved clear of the pack, but this time one horse was able to stick with her. Kool Kat Katie looked just as unwilling to relinquish her own unbeaten record, but it was One So Wonderful's head that was always just in front. The winning margin was a neck, with another three and a half lengths back to Reams of Verse.

		Blushing Groom	Red God
	Nashwan (USA)	(ch 1974)	Runaway Bride
	(ch 1986)	Height of Fashion	Bustino
One So Wonderful		(b 1979)	Highclere
(b.f. 1994)		Habitat	Sir Gaylord
	Someone Special	(b 1966)	Little Hut
	(b 1983)	One In A Million	Rarity
		(b 1976)	Singe

One So Wonderful's arrival as a very smart performer may have surprised in its speed and timing, but it is no surprise to see a horse of this calibre carrying the black and white colours of Helena Springfield Ltd. One So Wonderful is related to two of their most famous representatives, as her grandam is One Thousand Guineas winner One In A Million and her dam is a half-sister to the top-class miler Milligram. Twelve months before Milligram

Helena Springfield Ltd's "One So Wonderful"

trotted up at 5/4 on in the Coronation Stakes, her half-sister Someone Special had had a crack at the same race, at 33/1 finishing two and a half lengths third to Sonic Lady. Someone Special ended her career after five races with one win, in a maiden at Goodwood. One So Wonderful is her fifth runner and the fourth to contest a pattern race, following the 1992 Craven and Dante Stakes winner Alnasr Alwasheek (by Sadler's Wells), the 1993 Rockfel winner Relatively Special (by Alzao) and the useful but disappointing All Time Great (by Night Shift). Between them, that trio ran in five classics. They did not find them a happy hunting ground, however, comfortably their best collectively being Relatively Special's third in the Irish One Thousand Guineas. One So Wonderful missed the classics, but has already shown better form than those predecessors, and that after just the three starts. Further improvement is more than a possibility.

A lengthy, good-topped filly, One So Wonderful acts on good to firm and soft ground. She is probably suited by a good test when at a mile, and stays a mile and a quarter well. There is little on the dam's side of One So Wonderful's pedigree, however, to suggest that she will stay a mile and a half; Alnasr Alwasheek's failure in the Derby was due to lack of stamina as well as ability. The progeny of One So Wonderful's sire Nashwan do not have so high an average winning distance as one might have expected either, for all that the best known of them so far is probably Swain. *L. M. Cumani*

ONE TO GO (IRE) 2 b.g. (Apr 20) Petorius 117 – Caroline's Mark (On Your Mark 125) [1997 6g 7d⁶ 7.5f 7m 6m⁴ 7.1s² Nov 6] IR 6,800Y: close-coupled gelding: half-brother to several winners, including 3-y-o Imperial Or Metric and Irish 1¼m winner Bothsidesnow (by Exhibitioner): dam Irish 2-y-o 5f winner: modest maiden: should stay 1m: acts on firm and soft ground. *J. Berry* — 60

ONLY FOR GOLD 2 b.c. (Feb 9) Presidium 124 – Calvanne Miss 48 (Martinmas 128) [1997 5.1s* 5m* a6g⁴ Aug 16] 21,000 2-y-o: close-coupled, good sort: third foal: dam sprinter: looked promising when making all in maiden at Chester in May and £8,700 event at Beverley in June: not seen out again until well below form at odds-on in valuable sales race at Wolverhampton: should stay 6f: has presumably had problems, but may yet do better. *J. Berry* — 96

ONLY IN DREAMS 2 b.f. (Jan 31) Polar Falcon (USA) 126 – Dream Baby (Master Willie 129) [1997 6.1m 6.1g³ 7d* Oct 13] first foal: dam once-raced daughter of half-sister to very smart colt Noir Et Or: improved effort in maidens when winning at Leicester by 1½ lengths from Astrapi, leading 1f out and driven out: should stay 1m. *B. J. Meehan* — 78

ONLY JOSH (IRE) 3 gr.g. Waajib 121 – Carlyle Suite (USA) (Icecapade (USA)) [1996 NR 1997 a7g⁴ a8.5g a8.5g³ 8.2m 7g 6m 6m a8g Jun 30] IR 8,200Y: tall gelding: fourth reported foal: half-brother to 1991 Irish 2-y-o 6f winner Suite Applause (by Magical Wonder): dam winning sprinter in North America: modest form in frame in maidens on all-weather early in year: well held in handicaps afterwards: left Mrs J. Ramsden after seventh outing: stays 8.5f. *Mrs V. A. Aconley* — 52 d

ON MERIT 3 b.g. Terimon 124 – Onika 54 (Great Nephew 126) [1996 NR 1997 11.5m⁶ Aug 6] 4,800Y: fourth live foal: dam 1m winner: showed nothing in maiden at Yarmouth: refused to enter stalls following month. *S. Gollings* — –

ON THE GREEN 4 br.f. Pharly (FR) 130 – Regal Wonder 74 (Stupendous) [1996 –: 10g⁶ 1997 a10g⁶ 10m 7f 7m⁵ 7d⁴ 8.3m 7g² 7m³ 7g 7f 8g* a9.4g Dec 6] poor handicapper: won at Newcastle in October on final start for A. Hide: stays 1m: acts on good to firm and dead ground: usually blinkered or visored: none too consistent. *B. Preece* — 47

ON THE MAT 2 b.g. (Apr 24) Reprimand 122 – Secret Freedom (USA) 87 (Secreto (USA) 128) [1997 6m 7g⁶ 6g 7g² 7m 7.1g Aug 28] 12,000 2-y-o: third foal: dam, 6f winner at 2 yrs, half-sister to Gimcrack winner Full Extent: modest maiden: well held in nurseries last 2 starts, wandered in blinkers final time (then gelded): should stay 1m. *J. J. O'Neill* — 51

ON THE PISTE   4 gr.f. Shirley Heights 130 – Snowing (USA) (Icecapade (USA)) – [1996 68: 12.1g⁵ 1997 a10g⁵ Jan 28] twice-raced maiden: dead. *R. A. Fahey*

ON THE RIGHT SIDE   2 b.g. (Apr 17) Pursuit of Love 124 – La Masse (High 72 p Top 131) [1997 8.2s 8d⁴ Oct 28] 15,000Y: half-brother to 4 winners abroad, including useful German 3-y-o 1m to 10.5f winner Turbo Drive (by Be My Chief): dam French middle-distance winner: better effort in autumn maidens when about 3 lengths fourth to Baffin Bay at Leicester: will stay beyond 1m: should improve again. *J. W. Hills*

ON THE WILDSIDE   4 ch.f. Charmer 123 – No Control 82 (Bustino 136) [1996 – 57: 8.3m 8.1f² 10f 1997 11.8m 9.9m 11.7m 10.8m 11.1s 11.6m Jun 9] modest maiden: well beaten in 1997: sold, and sent to Spain. *M. R. Channon*

OOPS PETTIE   4 ch.f. Machiavellian (USA) 123 – Miquette (FR) (Fabulous 93 Dancer (USA) 124) [1996 89: 10d⁵ 12g 10.2f* 10m⁵ 10m⁵ 10.3m* 10m² 1997 12m 10g 11.9g⁴ 10.3m 12g⁴ 10.3d* Nov 7] tall, lengthy filly: fairly useful performer: won minor event at Doncaster by 5 lengths from Unconditional Love: stayed 1½m: acted on firm and dead going: ran well when sweating: stud. *Mrs J. Cecil*

OOZLEM (IRE)   8 b.g. Burslem 123 – Fingers (Lord Gayle (USA) 124) [1996 38 43, a47: a10g⁵ a8g a8g* a8g a8g⁵ 8m a10g 8.3m² 8.1m a10g a10g⁴ 1997 a12g³ a13g a42 a13g⁴ 8.1m 8.3g³ 10g³ 10.8g³ a10g a10g⁶ a13g⁶ Dec 12] workmanlike gelding: poor handicapper: stays 1½m: acts on equitrack and any turf going: usually blinkered/visored: tends to start slowly and get behind. *L. Montague Hall*

OPALETTE   4 b.f. Sharrood (USA) 124 – Height of Folly 81 (Shirley Heights 75 130) [1996 74: 10m⁴ 10g² 10.5s 1997 10g 10.8m 10g* 9.7m* 10g* 9.9m² 9m⁶ 10f Sep 28] big, workmanlike filly: fair handicapper: won at Pontefract in May and at Folkestone and Ripon in June: stays 1¼m: acts on good to firm ground, well beaten on soft: best waited with. *Lady Herries*

OPAQUE   5 b.g. Shirley Heights 130 – Opale 117 (Busted 134) [1996 73: 12m 82 14.1m² 14g* 16g⁶ 14.1m 1997 16.1g 12.4m² 13.9g² 16.1f⁵ 16.1s 12g 13.9s³ 17.5d² 16s⁶ 16.5s* Nov 8] tall, lengthy gelding: has a quick action: fairly useful handicapper: good efforts in 1997 when placed, and improved form to win at Doncaster in November: needs further than 1½m, and stays 17.5f: acts on good to firm and heavy ground: usually held up. *W. Storey*

OPEN AFFAIR   4 ch.f. Bold Arrangement 127 – Key To Enchantment (Key To 52 Content (USA)) [1996 55: 8m³ 10m⁴ 8m³ 10g 10.4g 8m 1997 a16g 10.3m 12.3m⁴ 11.9f 12g⁶ Jun 7] tall, sparely-made filly: modest maiden: should stay beyond 1½m: acts on good to firm ground. *H. Akbary*

OPEN CREDIT   3 ch.f. Magical Wonder (USA) 125 – Forest Treasure (USA) 89 (Green Forest (USA) 134) [1996 96+: 5f² 6g* 6g² 1997 7g 7.1d² 7f 6g² 6g Oct 24] deep-girthed, attractive filly: fluent mover: fairly useful performer, lightly raced: may prove best up to 7f: acts on dead ground: sold 42,000 gns, and sent to Saudi Arabia. *H. R. A. Cecil*

OPENING MEET   2 ch.f. (Apr 30) Wolfhound (USA) 126 – Carnival Spirit 92 74 p (Kris 135) [1997 6f² Sep 17] fourth foal: half-sister to useful French 9f (at 2 yrs) to 1½m winner Carniola (by Rainbow Quest) and French 11f winner Robber's Dance (by Groom Dancer): dam, 1m winner, half-sister to Arc winner Saumarez: long odds on, beaten head by Madame Claude in maiden at Yarmouth: should improve. *D. R. Loder*

OPENING NIGHT   2 b.g. (Apr 22) Theatrical Charmer 114 – First Time Over 50 (Derrylin 115) [1997 7d 6d a6g Nov 13] fifth reported foal: half-brother to 1991 a– 2-y-o 6f winner Gabes (by Aragon): dam second at 1m, half-sister to smart but temperamental middle-distance performer Out of Shot: showed ability in seller at Newmarket on debut but well held (stiffer tasks) afterwards. *R. Simpson*

OPENING RANGE   6 b.m. Nordico (USA) – Waveguide 76 (Double Form 130) 48 [1996 –: a8g a8g a8g 10m 8.2m 7f 1997 a7g a6g⁵ a6g² a5g* 5m* 6d⁴ 6f⁴ a5g² a5g³ Dec 12] workmanlike mare: poor handicapper: in good form in second half of year, winning at Wolverhampton in July and Windsor (apprentices) in August: best at 5f/6f: acts on firm and dead going and the all-weather: tried blinkered, not in 1997: front runner: sometimes hangs right. *N. E. Berry*

681

OPERA BUFF (IRE) 6 br.g. Rousillon (USA) 133 – Obertura (USA) 100   81
(Roberto (USA) 131) [1996 74, a98: a12g² a12g³ 12m³ 18.7g 12s⁴ 13.3s³ 14m a12g⁵   a93
a10s a12g³ 1997 a12g* 12m a12g a14.8g 12m 11.9f* 12m⁶ 12g 12.1m³ 12d⁴ 11.9m*
12d 12d⁶ 12m* a12g⁵ 11.9m³ Oct 23] big, good-topped gelding: fairly useful
performer: won handicap at Wolverhampton in January, minor event in May and
handicap in August, both at Brighton, and another minor event at Folkestone in
September: stays 15f: acts on firm and soft going and the all-weather: below form in
visor (reluctant) and blinkers at 4 yrs: tends to hang left: held up, and suited by strong
pace. *Miss Gay Kelleway*

OPERA FAN (IRE) 5 b.g. Taufan (USA) 119 – Shannon Lady 67 (Monsanto   39
(FR) 121) [1996 NR 1997 12m 10g⁵ 10.8g Jul 12] modest maiden handicapper at 3
yrs: poor at best in 1997: stays 1¼m: acts on hard and dead going: won 3 selling
hurdles (including in visor) in second half of 1997. *K. A. Morgan*

OPERA KING (USA) 2 ch.c. (Jan 29) Storm Bird (CAN) 134 – Jewel In My   95 p
Crown (CAN) (Secretariat (USA)) [1997 7g² 7g* Jul 30] $550,000Y: sturdy, angular
colt: first foal: dam, won up to 1¼m in North America, sister to Canadian Oaks winner Tiffany's Secret: runner-up to Haami in maiden at Newmarket, and landed odds
in 16-runner similar event at Doncaster later in month by ¾ length from Quintus,
confidently ridden: should stay 1¼m: became very upset start on debut: should still
be open to improvement. *Saeed bin Suroor*

OPERATIC 2 b.f. (Feb 15) Goofalik (USA) 118 – Choir Mistress (Chief Singer   52
131) [1997 7g a7g* 7g² Aug 1] first foal: dam unraced half-sister to smart
middle-distance horse Sacrament: won seller at Wolverhampton in July: good second
in claimer at Thirsk week later: will be suited by further than 7f: slowly away first 2
starts: joined P. D. Evans. *M. Bell*

OPERATIC DANCER 6 b.g. Germont – Indian Dancer (Streak 119) [1996 NR   –
1997 9.2g 13m 16m Jul 18] no worthwhile form. *R. M. McKellar*

OPOPMIL (IRE) 2 b.f. (Jan 19) Pips Pride 117 – Limpopo 49 (Green Desert   68
(USA) 127) [1997 a5g³ 5v² 5d⁵ Aug 14] 6,500Y: workmanlike filly: third foal:
half-sister to a winner in USA by Common Grounds: dam poor maiden daughter of
smart Irish miler Grey Goddess: placed in maidens at Southwell and Beverley: not
knocked about final outing: probably a sprinter. *T. D. Easterby*

OPPORTUNE (GER) 2 br.c. (Apr 12) Shirley Heights 130 – On The Tiles   53 +
(Thatch (USA) 136) [1997 7.1m 7m 8.1d 8d 9m⁵ 8m 8m Nov 1] deep-bodied colt:
seventh foal: closely related to Prix Saint-Alary winner Air de Rien (by Elegant Air),
and half-brother to 2 winners, including smart but temperamental Stiletto Blade (by
Dashing Blade): dam, from family of Blushing Groom, Irish 1¼m winner: modest
maiden on balance: left D. Elsworth after fifth start: will stay beyond 9f. *C. A. Smith*

OPPOSITION LEADER 2 b.g. (May 6) Be My Chief (USA) 122 – Seek The   75
Pearl 91 (Rainbow Quest (USA) 134) [1997 5m⁴ 6.1g³ 7d* 7f 7s⁵ 8g² 8g Oct 24]
17,000Y: unfurnished gelding: first foal: dam 1¼m winner: fair performer: won
minor event at Warwick in June: good second in nursery there penultimate start, and
ran respectably final outing: should stay beyond 1m: below form on extremes of
ground: sold 15,500 gns in November. *B. W. Hills*

OPTIMISTIC 2 b.f. (Feb 13) Reprimand 122 – Arminda (Blakeney 126) [1997   85 p
6g 7g* 7g* 8f Sep 11] 16,000Y: unfurnished filly: fifth foal: half-sister to several
winners, including 3-y-o Woodbeck and 4-y-o Carburton: dam unraced half-sister to
Madam Gay: fairly useful and progressive form: won maiden at Yarmouth in July
and nursery at York in August, latter by 3 lengths from Alconleigh: ran well when
under 10 lengths seventh of 9 in May Hill Stakes at Doncaster: stays 1m: probably
still open to improvement. *M. H. Tompkins*

OPULENT 6 b.g. Robellino (USA) 127 – One Half Silver (CAN) (Plugged Nickle   81
(USA)) [1996 77: 8d 10.1m³ 10m 1997 11.1s 10.9s⁵ 10.1g² 8.5v* 7s⁶ Jul 26] sturdy
gelding: fairly useful handicapper: won at Beverley in July despite wandering markedly: ran badly only subsequent outing: effective at 1m/1¼m: acts on good to firm
and heavy ground: often tongue tied: tends to carry head high, and not the easiest of
rides. *Mrs M. Reveley*

ORANGE AND BLUE   4 br.f. Prince Sabo 123 – Mazarine Blue 65 (Bellypha   –
130) [1996 39: 8.1g a7g⁵ a6g³ 5f⁴ a5g 5m⁶ 5g 5g 6m 1997 a7g a6g a6g Feb 24] leggy
filly: poor performer: well held in 1997. *Miss J. F. Craze*

ORANGE BUSH (IRE)   2 ch.g. (Feb 10) Pips Pride 117 – Kew Gift (Faraway   54
Son (USA) 130) [1997 6s⁵ a5g⁴ a8g Dec 8] 9,000Y: half-brother to winners abroad
by Digamist and Sandhurst Prince: dam lightly-raced Irish maiden: best effort
never-dangerous fifth of 8 in maiden at Catterick, not knocked about. *P. C. Haslam*

ORANGE ORDER (IRE)   4 ch.g. Generous (IRE) 139 – Fleur d'Oranger 110   –
(Northfields (USA)) [1996 75: 9f⁵ 10m* 1997 8.3s May 12] fair form at 3 yrs for
G. Harwood: well beaten only run on flat in 1997: should stay beyond 1¼m: joined
M. Hourigan and has won over hurdles. *J. White*

ORANGE PLACE (IRE)   6 ch.g. Nordance (USA) – Little Red Hut (Habitat   82
134) [1996 78: a10g⁶ a7g⁴ 7s³ 7f⁶ 7f⁵ 8.3m³ 7s* 7m 7.1m 1997 6m 7.6v³ 8d² 8.5m 8s   a56
8m² a8g 7.1m³ 8.1g a7g a7g⁴ a9.4g⁴ Dec 26] lengthy gelding: reportedly hobdayed:
fairly useful handicapper on turf, modest on all-weather: trained by T. J. Naughton
first 5 starts: best form at 7f/1m: acts on good to firm and heavy going, and the
all-weather: respectable efforts in blinkers/visor final 2 starts: often a front runner.
B. J. Llewellyn

ORCHESTRA STALL   5 b.g. Old Vic 136 – Blue Brocade 91 (Reform 132)   121
[1996 107p: 10s² 16g* 16s⁴ 16.1m* 18g 16g* 16.5s² 1997 16.2s³ 16.2m* 16.4g
14d* 15g² 15.5m* Sep 7]
    The fortunes of Old Vic, winner of the Prix du Jockey-Club and Irish
Derby in 1989, have taken a downturn since he began stud duties at Dalham
Hall in 1991 at a fee of £25,000. Nowadays he stands at Sunnyhill Stud, Co
Kildare, where the mares available to him suggest that his success as a sire may
well rest on the performances of his offspring that race over jumps rather than
on the flat. Ironically, Old Vic enjoyed his best season as a sire in 1997, due
mainly to the exploits on the flat of one of his first crop, Orchestra Stall, who
developed into a very smart stayer and won three races, including the Prix
Gladiateur at Longchamp on his final start.
    Orchestra Stall, a slow-maturing type, has been brought along steadily.
Restricted to just one race in each of his first two seasons due to problems
related to chipped bones in his knees, he didn't open his account until April,
1996, on only his tourth outing, narrowly winning a handicap at Ripon off a
mark of 75. By the end of that year he'd gained two more victories, and on

*Prix Gladiateur, Longchamp—a good performance from Orchestra Stall,
who beats Double Eclipse (rail), Chief Contender and Always Earnest*

his final start had shown further improvement in finishing a close second at Doncaster off a mark of 98. Handicaps didn't figure on Orchestra Stall's agenda in 1997, and it wasn't long before he showed that he was capable of winning outside them. Second time up, Orchestra Stall gave an impressive performance in the Insulpak Sagaro Stakes at Ascot, quickening clear two furlongs out to beat Wilawander by three and a half lengths. Orchestra Stall's good turn of foot was in evidence again in the Waterford Crystal World Sports Curragh Cup and the Prix Gladiateur, both of which he won by five lengths, the former from the useful Irish three-year-old Zafarabad, the latter from the other British challengers in the seven-runner field, Double Eclipse and Chief Contender. In between his last two wins Orchestra Stall acquitted himself well in the Prix Kergorlay at Deauville, finishing two lengths second to Classic Cliche.

		Sadler's Wells	Northern Dancer
	Old Vic	(b 1981)	Fairy Bridge
	(b 1986)	Cockade	Derring-Do
Orchestra Stall		(b 1973)	Camenae
(b.g. 1992)		Reform	Pall Mall
	Blue Brocade	(b 1964)	Country House
	(b 1981)	Bridestones	Jan Ekels
		(b 1975)	Lucky Stream

Orchestra Stall, whose win at the Curragh was gained over a mile and three quarters, does the majority of his racing at two miles and isn't certain to be so effective over further. On the only occasion he was tried beyond two miles he finished seventh in the 1996 Cesarewitch, appearing not quite to get home. Significantly he wasn't even entered for the latest Gold Cup at Royal Ascot, which is run over two and a half miles. Orchestra Stall's dam Blue Brocade had

Mr D. Sieff's "Orchestra Stall"

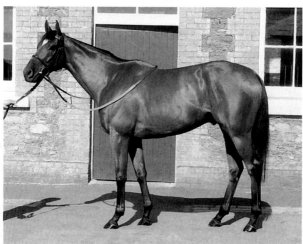

stamina limitations, her sole victory coming over an extended mile and a quarter, but there are plenty of stayers in the bottom half of her pedigree, notably the Doncaster Cup winner Crash Course, also a leading sire of jumpers. Crash Course is a half-brother to Blue Brocade's dam Bridestones, a fairly useful winner of four races at up to one and a half miles. Bridestones has produced several winners apart from Blue Brocade, the best of them Lockton, a smart performer at up to a mile and a quarter. Orchestra Stall himself is a half-brother to a couple of winners, including Berlin Blue (by Belmez) who has shown fairly useful form at up to fifteen furlongs.

Orchestra Stall, a good-topped gelding with a splayed, round action, has shown his form on ground ranging from good to firm through to soft. However, he's usually bandaged nowadays and reportedly finished lame at Longchamp, so it's possible that he won't stand much more racing on a firm surface. If he remains free of injury in 1998 then this genuine and consistent gelding should win more good races. *J. L. Dunlop*

ORDAINED 4 b.f. Mtoto 134 – In The Habit (USA) 88 (Lyphard (USA) 132) 63 [1996 61: a8g⁵ a10g³ 10g⁶ 12d 8.3s 10m² 10m⁵ 10m* 9f³ 10.1m 10f³ 12m⁶ 11f* a– 12.3g⁶ 10g² 11.1g 10f 10.5s 1997 10.9s³ 11.8m² 12m³ 12.3m⁶ 12g⁴ 14m⁴ 11.8g⁴ 10m 10.5g⁴ 14.1m² 10.3g² 12m* 12s a12g a12g Dec 13] dipped-backed filly: modest handicapper: in good form all year, gaining deserved success in 29-runner event at Newmarket in October: best at 1¼m/1½m on good ground or firmer: consistent. *E. J. Alston*

ORIEL GIRL 2 b.f. (Apr 20) Beveled (USA) – St Helena (Monsanto (FR) 121) 65 [1997 5m⁵ 5d⁴ 5d² 5m a5g⁵ 5g³ 5d³ 5s* 5m* 5g⁵ 5g² 5m⁴ 5m* 5g² 5m 5.3f⁶ Oct 1] 3,200Y: small, leggy filly: good walker: unimpressive mover: sister to a winner in Italy and half-sister to 3 others, plus 3-y-o Swino: dam, won 7 sprints in Italy, half-sister to useful sprinter Up And At 'Em: modest performer: won seller at Catterick and claimer and nursery at Musselburgh in the summer: sold out of P. D. Evans' stable after fourteenth start: poor efforts afterwards: raced only at 5f: acts on good to firm and soft ground, not well drawn on firesand: often visored, including when successful, blinkered final outing: joined G. L. Moore. *B. J. Meehan*

ORIEL LAD 4 b.g. Colmore Row 111 – Consistent Queen 55 (Queen's Hussar 41 124) [1996 69d: a9.4g⁶ a8g a7g 6.1g 7f² 7s 6m 7f⁴ 6f 7m⁴ 6f 6m⁵ 7g a8g 1997 7f 6g a8g 7m 7.5m³ 7.5g⁶ 6.9m 7.5v⁶ 7.5m⁶ 9.2d² 9.2m⁶ 8m Aug 26] sparely-made gelding: poor handicapper nowadays: stays 9.2f: acts on firm and dead ground, probably on heavy: best in visor or blinkers: held up (often starts slowly), and suited by strong pace: joined Miss K. Milligan. *Don Enrico Incisa*

ORIOLE 4 b.g. Mazilier (USA) 107 – Odilese 82 (Mummy's Pet 125) [1996 48d: 55 7s 6d 8g 6g 8m³ 7f⁴ 7s* 7m⁶ 7m 8g 7f 7m 8.2s 1997 a7g 8g 7d 8g* 8g 7g 8g² 7g³ 7m* 8g³ 7m 8g³ 8m Oct 28] leggy gelding: modest handicapper: won at Redcar in May (lady riders) and August (dead-heat): stays 1m: acts on firm and soft ground: tried in blinkers, has won in visor: usually ridden by Kim Tinkler. *Don Enrico Incisa*

ORLEANS (IRE) 2 b.g. (Feb 11) Scenic 128 – Guest House (What A Guest 119) – [1997 7g 8.1d 7.1m Sep 21] IR 9,500Y: big, workmanlike: fourth living foal: half-brother to a winner in Scandinavia by Runnett: dam Irish 1½m winner: behind in maidens at Doncaster and Haydock (2). *T. P. Tate*

ORNAMENTAL 2 b.f. (Jan 28) Saddlers' Hall (IRE) 126 – Hope And Glory – (USA) 87 (Well Decorated (USA)) [1997 8s a7g Nov 25] smallish, plain filly: sixth foal: sister to 3-y-o Saddlers' Hope and half-sister to 4-y-o Never Think Twice and 2 winners abroad: dam, 2-y-o 6f winner, only season to race, is from family of Law Society: towards rear in maidens at Doncaster and Lingfield: sold 2,600 gns in December. *J. R. Fanshawe*

ORONTES (USA) 3 b.g. Lomond (USA) 128 – Chateau Princess (USA) 64 (Majestic Prince (USA)) [1996 80?: 6m³ 7g* 8.1g⁶ 7d 1997 9s⁶ 7.1g 8.1d⁵ 9s 8.2s Oct 15] strong, useful-looking gelding: fluent mover: fair winner at 2 yrs: modest form at best in 1997: probably best up to 1m. *R. Hannon*

Mr Wafic Said's "Oscar"

ORSAY 5 gr.g. Royal Academy (USA) 130 – Bellifontaine (FR) (Bellypha 130) 85 [1996 81: 8m² 8.3d³ 9g⁶ 7m 1997 8d³ 8m² 10g* 10d⁴ 10.4m 10m³ 10m 9d Sep 12] big, lengthy horse: fairly useful handicapper: won at Sandown in June: good efforts afterwards when in frame: finds 1m on sharp side, and stays 1¼m: acts on good to firm and dead ground: usually races prominently: has run well sweating. *W. R. Muir*

ORSINO 2 b.g. (Apr 21) Theatrical Charmer 114 – Sonoco 61 (Song 132) [1997 77 6g⁵ 6d⁵ 6g⁵ Sep 25] compact gelding: unimpressive mover: second reported foal: dam sprint maiden: best effort in maidens at Goodwood penultimate start, squeezed out after 1f and stumbling halfway but finishing strongly: should stay 7f. *S. Dow*

ORTELIUS 3 b.g. Rudimentary (USA) 118 – Third Movement 75 (Music Boy 68 124) [1996 71p: 7.1m 8.1s 7m* 1997 8.1d 8d 10m 10g 8m³ 8.5d 10m 8f³ 10g Oct 4] strong gelding: fair handicapper: stays 1m: acts on good to firm ground, probably not on dead or softer: visored (out of form) fourth start: inconsistent: sold 17,000 gns after final start. *R. Hannon*

OSCAR (IRE) 3 b.c. Sadler's Wells (USA) 132 – Snow Day (FR) 123 (Reliance 122 II 137) [1996 9d² 1997 12m* 11g² 12m² Jun 1] has a short, quick action: brother to Derby second Blue Stag, closely related to 1½m winner Snowkist (by The Minstrel), and half-brother to French 11.5f (listed race) and 1½m winner Ionian Sea (by Slip Anchor) and winning French stayer Snow Bank (by Law Society): dam 10.5f winner in France, stayed 1½m: progressed significantly with each race: won minor event at Saint-Cloud in April: runner-up at Chantilly in Prix Hocquart (to Shaka) and Prix du Jockey-Club (stayed on resolutely when beaten 2 lengths by Peintre Celebre), but not seen out again: suited by a good test at 1½m and would have stayed further: retired to Grange Stud, Co Cork, Ireland, as NH stallion. *P. Bary, France*

OSCAR ROSE 4 b.g. Aragon 118 – Mossy Rose 78 (King of Spain 121) [1996 31 53d: 8.2m⁴ 10m 8f 8m 10g 1997 10.8m 11.6g 12f 17.2g 17.2m³ 14g Aug 1] small, lightly-made gelding: poor maiden handicapper: stays well: raced only on good going or firmer: visored (well beaten) final 3-y-o start. *M. J. Bolton*

OSCAR SCHINDLER (IRE)   5 ch.h. Royal Academy (USA) 130 – Saraday   127
(Northfields (USA)) [1996 127: 12s² 13.4g* 12f* 12m⁴ 14m* 12d³ 16m 1997
10g² 12m⁵ 10g³ 14d* 12f⁴ 15.5d³ 12m Nov 23]

    By winning his second successive Jefferson Smurfit Memorial Irish St
Leger in September, Oscar Schindler emulated Vintage Crop who achieved the
same feat in 1993 and 1994. The Irish St Leger's claims to classic status can
be questioned nowadays—only three of the seven who lined up for the 1997
renewal were three-year-olds—but Oscar Schindler's connections won't have
any complaints. Sent off the 2/1 joint favourite at the Curragh, he travelled
smoothly throughout, cruising to the front inside the final two furlongs to beat
the four-year-old Persian Punch by two lengths despite idling near the line. The
big disappointment of the race was Oscar Schindler's rival at the head of the
market, Classic Cliche, who trailed in last and was promptly retired.

    The Irish St Leger was the only success for Oscar Schindler in a rather
in-and-out campaign which had begun in May with a satisfactory second to
Dance Design in the Tattersalls Gold Cup at the Curragh. From there Oscar
Schindler made an unrewarding trip across the Irish Sea for the Coronation
Cup, producing a lack-lustre effort and finishing last of the five runners. Afterwards his trainer announced that Oscar Schindler had met with a set-back and
would be forced to miss the King George VI and Queen Elizabeth Diamond
Stakes. He resumed in August with an encouraging third to King Alex over an
inadequate ten furlongs in the Royal Whip Stakes at the Curragh. The race put
Oscar Schindler spot on for a second St Leger victory, after which connections
followed the same path as the previous year by heading to Longchamp for
the Prix de l'Arc de Triomphe. Oscar Schindler's regular partner in Ireland,
Stephen Craine, was once again passed over for the Arc ride in favour of Cash
Asmussen, who'd been criticised for giving the horse too much to do in the race
twelve months earlier. Oscar Schindler produced another fine performance,
hampered early on but staying on gamely to finish fourth, seven and a half
lengths (we made it nearer six) behind Peintre Celebre. Having run as well as
ever, Oscar Schindler was below form on his last two starts, possibly feeling

*Jefferson Smurfit Memorial Irish St Leger, the Curragh—
a second successive win in the race for Oscar Schindler;
Persian Punch gets the better of Whitewater Affair for second*

Mr Oliver Lehane's "Oscar Schindler"

the effects of his Arc exertions when only third as a short-priced favourite for the Prix Royal-Oak later in the month. He managed only eighth of fourteen in the Japan Cup in November.

		Nijinsky	Northern Dancer
	Royal Academy (USA)	(b 1967)	Flaming Page
	(b 1987)	Crimson Saint	Crimson Satan
Oscar Schindler (IRE)		(ch 1969)	Bolero Rose
(ch.h. 1992)		Northfields	Northern Dancer
	Saraday	(ch 1968)	Little Hut
	(ch 1980)	Etoile Grise	Sea Hawk II
		(gr 1972)	Place d'Etoile

The big, rangy Oscar Schindler's pedigree was discussed at length in *Racehorses of 1996*, though we should add that his year-younger full-brother, Johann Strauss, also trained by Kevin Prendergast, made a successful race-course debut in a Tipperary bumper and won a two-mile maiden at Clonmel in the latest year. Effective at a mile and a half to a mile and three quarters, Oscar Schindler acts on any going, usually comes from behind and is game and genuine. *K. Prendergast, Ireland*

OSCILIGHTS GIFT   5 b.m. Chauve Souris 108 – Oscilight 112 (Swing Easy   – (USA) 126) [1996 41?: 7f 8f 6m 5g³ 5.1m³ 5m⁵ 5f a5g 1997 a6g⁶ a6g Jan 22] light-framed mare: poor maiden handicapper: well beaten both starts early in 1997. *Mark Campion*

OSOMENTAL   3 gr.g. Petong 126 – Proper Madam 93 (Mummy's Pet 125) [1996   – 88+: 5d⁴ 5d⁴ 5m⁵ 6g² 5m* 5g* 6d 6.1d⁴ 6m⁶ 5m 6m 1997 6g 5d 6d 7m 6g⁵ Sep 1] strong gelding: fairly useful 2-y-o: well beaten in handicaps in 1997: sent to Macau. *D. Haydn Jones*

OSO RICH   2 b.g. (May 20) Teenoso (USA) 135 – Weareagrandmother (Prince Tenderfoot (USA) 126) [1997 8.1d 6d Sep 5] second reported foal: dam 1m (at 2 yrs) and 12.5f winner, also successful over hurdles: always behind in maiden and claimer. *P. M. Rich*   –

OTHER CLUB   3 ch.g. Kris 135 – Tura (Northfields (USA)) [1996 74p: 8d⁶ 7g⁶ 1997 a8g³ a8.5g² Dec 26] lengthy, good-bodied gelding: fluent mover: modest maiden, lightly raced: second of 6 at Wolverhampton: stays 8.5f. *J. A. R. Toller*   57

OTTO E MEZZO   5 b.g. Persian Bold 123 – Carolside 108 (Music Maestro 119) [1996 –: 10s⁶ 9.2g³ 10m 10m 8m⁵ 7m 12f 11.9d 12g⁶ 1997 16g³ Apr 18] compact gelding: rated 94 at 2 yrs for J. Dunlop: no form in 1996, but fared better for step up to 2m when third in handicap at Newbury only 5-y-o start, finishing well: used to act on any going. *M. J. Polglase*   78

OUAISNE   2 b.c. (Apr 20) Warning 136 – Noirmant (Dominion 123) [1997 5g* 5s⁴ 5m 6m⁴ Aug 20] close-coupled colt: fourth foal: half-brother to 3-y-o Soviet Leader and fairly useful sprinter Portelet (by Night Shift): dam half-sister to very smart middle-distance stayer Braashee: won maiden at Redcar in June by 5 lengths: fourth in Prix du Bois at Deauville then possibly not at best on good to firm going in Molecomb Stakes at Goodwood (never going smoothly) and listed race at La Teste: should stay 6f. *R. Guest*   90

OUR DAD'S LAD   2 ch.g. (Feb 11) Inchinor 119 – Depeche (FR) (Kings Lake (USA) 133) [1997 7g Jul 9] 13,500Y: second foal: closely related to Italian 3-y-o Miss Statoblest (by Statoblest), winner at 5f to 8.5f: dam French maiden: behind in seller at Newmarket. *S. C. Williams*   –

OUR DROWSY MAGGIE   3 b.f. Puissance 110 – Loadplan Lass 63 (Nicholas Bill 125) [1996 NR 1997 a9.4g 5.1m 8d Oct 28] fourth foal: sister to 5-y-o Dannistar (modest 9.4f winner at 3 yrs), and half-sister to 2 winners, including 6-y-o Hill Farm Dancer: dam maiden, bred to stay middle distances: no form, including in sellers. *W. M. Brisbourne*   –

OUR EDDIE   8 ch.g. Gabitat 119 – Ragusa Girl (Morston (FR) 125) [1996 –, a65d: a10g⁶ a10g⁴ a10g* 9g a12g a12g⁴ a10g⁶ a10g⁴ 1997 a10g a10g⁵ a10g⁴ a10g⁵ Feb 4] sparely-made gelding: just a poor performer in 1997: probably stays 1½m: easily best efforts on equitrack: tried blinkered, usually visored: none too reliable. *B. Gubby*   a46

OUR EMMA   8 b.m. Precocious 126 – Miller's Daughter (Mill Reef (USA) 141) [1996 NR 1997 a8g Mar 27] of little account. *R. J. O'Sullivan*   –

OUR FUTURE (IRE)   3 b.g. Imp Society (USA) – Petite Realm 95 (Realm 129) [1996 64: 5d⁴ 5g 6d 6g³ 7g² 8g 1997 a9.4g a8g 9m⁵ Jul 19] big, good-topped gelding: modest 2-y-o for M. Johnston: no form in 1997 and sold only 700 gns in November. *Ronald Thompson*   –

OUR KEVIN   3 gr.g. Chilibang 120 – Anse Chastanet (Cavo Doro 124) [1996 63: 5.3f⁴ 5s³ a5g⁴ 6g⁴ 6g* 7f² a6g² 6.1f⁶ 7g² a7g* 7f 7m⁶ 6m³ 6m a6g⁶ a8.5g⁶ a7g 1997 a8g² a8g⁴ a7g⁶ a8g⁵ 6.9g a7g 9.7m Apr 22] strong, lengthy gelding: poor handicapper: left K. McAuliffe after second start, and soundly beaten afterwards: stays 1m: acts on firm ground and fibresand, probably on equitrack: usually blinkered/visored. *B. A. Pearce*   41

OUR KRIS   5 b.g. Kris 135 – Our Reverie (USA) (J O Tobin (USA) 130) [1996 63: 20f 14.9m⁴ 14g³ 1997 16.2m Apr 11] strong gelding: lightly-raced handicapper on flat nowadays: well held only 5-y-o start. *M. E. Sowersby*   –

OUR MAIN MAN   7 ch.g. Superlative 118 – Ophrys 90 (Nonoalco (USA) 131) [1996 –, a53: 10g 8.9g 10g a10g⁵ a12g³ a14g² a14g² a13g⁶ 1997 14.1g a12g* 12m 12.3m⁵ a12g a14g a13g⁵ Dec 22] good-topped gelding: hobdayed: modest all-weather handicapper: clearly best effort in 1997 when winning at Southwell in June: stays 1¾m well: no form on turf since 1995: tried visored: best with waiting tactics: inconsistent. *R. M. Whitaker*   a58

OUR

OUR MOLLY MALONE   2 ch.f. (Mar 1) Deploy 131 – Lady Clementine 68 –
(He Loves Me 120) [1997 7.6d 6.1m 7d 7g Oct 27] sturdy, angular filly: half-sister to
3 winners, including 5-y-o Darling Clover and fairly useful middle-distance stayer
Much Sought After (by Adonijah): dam 5f winner: signs of just a little ability in
maidens. *D. Morley*

OUR PEOPLE   3 ch.g. Indian Ridge 123 – Fair And Wise 75 (High Line 125)   83
[1996 90: 8m³ 8f* 8g³ 1997 9s⁴ 12s 10m⁶ 8g a8g⁴ 8d 7.1g Sep 27] leggy,
useful-looking gelding: fairly useful handicapper: best effort of 1997 in blinkers on
third start: stays 1¼m: acts on firm ground: carried head awkwardly final start as
2-y-o: inconsistent. *M. Johnston*

OUR ROBERT   5 b.g. Faustus (USA) 118 – Duck Soup 55 (Decoy Boy 129)   –
[1996 59: a7g³ a8g⁴ a11g 1997 a7g⁵ Jan 17] modest maiden: tailed off only flat outing
in 1997, but won over hurdles in March: joined A. Streeter. *J. G. FitzGerald*

OUR SHADEE (USA)   7 b.g. Shadeed (USA) 135 – Nuppence 79 (Reform 132)   –
[1996 54d, a73d: a8g a7g a6g⁵ a6g² a6g³ a6g* a6g² a6g* a6g³ a6g³ a6g³   a49
5.7g⁴ 6f³ 6f⁴ 6f⁶ 7m⁴ 7g 7.6m* 8.3d⁶ 7.6m⁶ a7g 7g⁵ 7f 7m⁵ 8m a7g 7g a7s a10g³
a8g⁵ a7g 1997 a6g a7g⁶ a8g³ a8g² a8g⁵ a8g⁵ a7g a10g Dec 19] lengthy gelding: poor
handicapper nowadays: successful only up to 7.6f, but stays easy 1¼m: acts on firm
and soft ground, raced mainly on the all-weather: nearly always visored/blinkered
nowadays: usually held up. *K. T. Ivory*

OUR TOM   5 br.g. Petong 126 – Boa (Mandrake Major 122) [1996 –, a72d: a11g*   –
a12g a11g⁵ a9.4g⁶ 9.7s 10m 8.2m a9.4g a9.4g 1997 a8g 8g 10g 8g Jun 18] no longer
of any account. *J. Wharton*

OUR WAY   3 ch.f. Forzando 122 – Hanglands (Bustino 136) [1996 70?: 6f² 6m   72
6m² 7m 1997 8g 7g 8f* 9g⁴ 8d 8g⁶ 9m Jul 30] lengthy, good-quartered filly:
unimpressive mover: fair handicapper: got up near finish to win at Yarmouth in May:
ran creditably next 2 starts: finds 1m a minimum, and should stay 1¼m: acts on firm
and dead going. *C. E. Brittain*

OUT LIKE MAGIC   2 ch.f. (Apr 3) Magic Ring (IRE) 115 – Thevetia 65   82 d
(Mummy's Pet 125) [1997 5m⁴ 5m* 5g² 5g² 6g² 6m 6s⁴ 7m² 7.5m⁴ 7s 7s a7g   a65
a7s² a8g Dec 10] 4,600F: small filly: fifth reported foal: half-sister to 3 winners,
including useful 1993 2-y-o 7f/1m winner In Like Flynn (by Handsome Sailor) and
6f (at 2 yrs) and 1m winner Mac Kelty (by Wattlefield): dam should have stayed 7f:
fairly useful at best: won maiden at Ripon in April: runner-up 5 of next 7 starts but
mostly well below form subsequently: stays 7.5f: acts on good to firm going: has
been bandaged behind: visored once. *P. D. Evans*

OUT LINE   5 gr.m. Beveled (USA) – Free Range 78 (Birdbrook 110) [1996 72:   72
6m 8.3m 6f⁴ 6m² 6m³ 7.1d³ 7g 5m⁶ 1997 7m⁶ 6m 7m 7.1g* 7s⁴ 6m* 6m⁵ 7m 7g 6m²
6d Oct 21] good-topped mare: has a round action: fair handicapper: won at Sandown
(first time) in May and Lingfield in July: effective at 6f/7f: acts on good to firm and
dead ground, probably on soft: usually soon off bridle, and seems best in strongly-run
race. *M. Madgwick*

OUT OF SIGHT (IRE)   3 ch.c. Salse (USA) 128 – Starr Danias (USA) (Sens-   82
itive Prince (USA)) [1996 81: 5d⁵ 6m⁵ 7m⁵ 6g⁶ 6m 7s 1997 10g 10d⁴ 7.9g* 8.1d⁴
May 24] deep-girthed colt: fairly useful performer: 33/1, gained first win in 19-
runner handicap at York in May: bit below that form in smaller field later in month:
should stay 1¼m: best efforts on good ground or firmer. *B. A. McMahon*

OUT ON A PROMISE (IRE)   5 b.g. Night Shift (USA) – Lovers' Parlour 83   66
(Beldale Flutter (USA) 130) [1996 –: 11.9g 12m 10m 10.8g 1997 a12g a12g 9.2g
12g³ Jul 5] compact gelding: fair handicapper nowadays: only form in 1997 when
third at Carlisle: stays 1½m: acts on good to firm and soft ground, and successful on
fibresand at 2 yrs: blinkered (pulled too hard) sixth 3-y-o start: fairly useful 2m
hurdler. *L. Lungo*

OUT ON THE STREET (USA)   2 br.c. (Mar 3) Known Fact (USA) 135 – Fat   –
To Fit (USA) (Fit To Fight (USA)) [1997 8.2g Sep 28] $115,000Y: first foal: dam,
won up to 9f in USA, half-sister to Breeders' Cup Juvenile runner-up It'sali'l-
knownfact (by Known Fact): 10/1 from 16/1, slowly away and well behind in maiden
at Nottingham. *T. D. Barron*

OUTSET (IRE)   7 ch.g. Persian Bold 123 – It's Now Or Never 78 (High Line 125)   76
[1996 –: 16.5s 1997 14.1g* 16s* Nov 6] leggy gelding: best known as a fairly useful
hurdler these days, but still capable of fair form on flat, and won handicaps at Redcar
(33/1) and Musselburgh in the autumn: stays 2m: probably acts on any going: makes
running/races prominently: game. *M. D. Hammond*

OUTSOURCING (USA)   2 ch.c. (Jan 28) Alwuhush (USA) 121 – Nice Dancing   81
(USA) (Bering 136) [1997 6m 6g² 7g⁴ 7.1g² 7m² 8m* Aug 22] $55,000F, $70,000Y:
close-coupled colt: first foal: dam, half-sister to dam of triple Grade 1 Australian
winner Flying Spur, twice-raced granddaughter of Canadian champion filly Fanfre-
luche: fairly useful performer: ran consistently before making all in nursery at Newmarket: should stay beyond 1m: raced only on good/good to firm ground: races
prominently: sold 30,000 gns, and sent to USA. *P. F. I. Cole*

OUTSTAYED WELCOME   5 b.g. Be My Guest (USA) 126 – Between Time   49
75 (Elegant Air 119) [1996 65d: a16g 12g² 12.3g² 12m² 12.5f⁵ 12.3m³ 14.9m
12.1m³ 12.3m 14.4g 12m⁶ 11.5m⁶ 1997 a12g a16g² 12m Apr 23] leggy gelding:
poor handicapper nowadays: dictated pace when second at Lingfield, best 5-y-o
effort: seems to stay 2m: acts on any going: blinkered twice at 2 yrs: front runner.
M. J. Haynes

OUT WEST (USA)   3 br.f. Gone West (USA) – Chellingoua (USA) (Sharpen   103
Up 127) [1996 90p: 7.5g* 7m⁴ 1997 8d* 8.5m³ 8d⁴ Jun 29] leggy, good-topped
filly: useful performer: won listed race at Goodwood in May by ¾ length from Lilli
Claire, despite hanging markedly left: badly squeezed out at start when creditable
fourth to Samara in similar event at Epsom following month: ran as though
something amiss final start: likely to stay 1¼m: yet to race on extremes of going.
H. R. A. Cecil

OVER THE MOON   3 ch.f. Beveled (USA) – Beyond The Moon (IRE) 58   –
(Ballad Rock 122) [1996 –: a7s⁶ 1997 7m 7m 6m 7.6g 8m Aug 12] signs of ability
but no worthwhile form: tried visored. *M. J. Fetherston-Godley*

OVER TO YOU (USA)   3 ch.c. Rubiano (USA) – Overnight (USA) (Mr Leader   85
(USA)) [1996 77p: 8.2m³ 8.2g* 1997 8m 10m⁴ 7.9g³ 8m 10g 8.1m 8.1m Sep 21]
close-coupled colt: fairly useful handicapper: disappointed after third start, including
in visor: needs good test at 1m, and stays 1¼m well: has raced only on good/good to
firm ground: sold 16,500 gns in October. *E. A. L. Dunlop*

OVERTURE (IRE)   2 gr.c. (Mar 15) Fairy King (USA) – Everything Nice 107   81
(Sovereign Path 125) [1997 5g* 7d³ 6m 5.3m² Aug 15] 38,000Y: compact colt: fluent
mover: closely related to 7f winner My Everything (by Be My Guest) and half-
brother to numerous winners, notably Irish 1000 Guineas winner Nicer (by Pennine
Walk): dam won from 5f (at 2 yrs) to 10.5f: fairly useful form: won maiden at
Sandown in June: strong-finishing second in nursery at Brighton final start: pulled
hard in between: should stay at least 6f. *R. Hannon*

OWDY   3 ch.g. Country Classic – Miami Pride 48 (Miami Springs 121) [1996 NR   –
1997 11.8f⁶ a8g 10g 7m Jun 9] first foal to race: dam sprint plater: well beaten in
varied events. *Mrs N. Macauley*

OXALAGU (GER)   5 br.h. Lagunas – Oxalis 64 (Ashmore (FR) 125) [1996 118:   123
10g* 12g⁴ 11d² 11d⁵ 10g* 10m⁴ 1997 10d* 11f* 11s* 10d* 10d² 12m Dec 14] very
smart German horse: won Group 3 event (for second year running) at Gelsenkirchen
in April, Group 2 races at Baden-Baden (by ½ length and 1¼ lengths from Wurftaube
and Needle Gun) and Hamburg (beat Surako ¾ length) and 6-runner Group 1 Bayerisches Zuchtrennen at Munich (wore Dance Design down close home, by ½ length)
between April and August: respectable 3 lengths second to Taipan in Premio Roma
but below best in Hong Kong International Vase: effective at 1¼m to 1¾m: acts on
any going. *B. Schutz, Germany*

OXBANE   3 b.f. Soviet Star (USA) 128 – Oxslip 106 (Owen Dudley 121) [1996 –:   57
6m 1997 8.2d⁶ 7.3s⁵ 6.1d 7f 8.2m⁶ 7g³ 7g 6f² 8m 8d⁶ 7g⁶ 7m a7g a7s⁴ a8g Dec 4]   a51
deep-girthed, angular filly: modest maiden handicapper: left H. Candy after sixth
start: stays 1m: acts on firm and soft going, and on equitrack: hard puller: none too
consistent. *C. A. Dwyer*

691

P

PAARL ROCK 2 ch.c. (Jan 21) Common Grounds 118 – Markievicz (IRE) (Doy-   69 p
oun 124) [1997 6g 6m 8.2g Sep 28] 23,000F, 45,000Y: sturdy, close-coupled colt:
first foal: dam Irish 6.5f winner: 25/1, first form when never-dangerous seventh in
maiden at Nottingham final start, held up and considerably handled: shapes as
though will stay at least 1¼m: should do better at 3 yrs. *D. R. Loder*

PABELLA BLUEBIRD (IRE)   2 b.f. (Apr 24) Mac's Imp (USA) 116 – Blue
Diana (IRE) (Bluebird (USA) 125) [1997 5g 5g 5.1d 5m Oct 28] IR 400Y: first foal:
dam Irish 1½m winner: no worthwhile form, visored final start. *G. R. Oldroyd*

PACIFICA   2 b.f. (Jan 19) Robellino (USA) 127 – Pooh Wee 71 (Music Boy 124)   90 d
[1997 5s² 5g* 5.2d² 5m 6d⁴ 6.5m 7m 6g Oct 18] 4,000Y: strong, lengthy filly: third
foal: dam 6f (at 2 yrs) and 1m winner out of half-sister to Irish 1000 Guineas winner
Favoletta and dam of Teenoso: fairly useful performer at best: won maiden at Newmarket in April: good second in minor event at Newbury following month: off course
10 weeks after next start, and only fair form afterwards: probably stays 7f: acts on
dead ground, probably on good to firm. *R. Boss*

PADAUK   3 b.c. Warrshan (USA) 117 – Free On Board 73 (Free State 125) [1996   68
76?: 7g 7g⁶ 8m⁵ 7d⁵ 1997 10g 9g 11.6s 12m³ 11.4g³ 14d³ 16m³ 14m 15.4m² a16s⁴   a65
a16g Nov 25] lengthy colt: has a round action: fair maiden handicap: effective at
1½m to 2m: acts on equitrack and on good to firm on firm and dead. *M. J. Haynes*

PADDY DEUX   2 b.c. (Mar 30) Perpendicular 119 – Plie 75 (Superlative 118)   –
[1997 7.1s 7d Oct 27] 7,000Y: smallish colt: fourth foal: half-brother to 2 winners in
Sweden, including 1995 2-y-o 7f winner Red Simba (by Absalom): dam, 2-y-o 6f
winner, stayed 1m: behind in maidens at Haydock and Lingfield. *V. Soane*

PADDY HURRY   3 b.g. Silver Kite (USA) 111 – Little Preston (IRE) 53 (Pennine   –
Walk 120) [1996 –: 6m 8g 6g 7.8f⁴ 7m 1997 9.7m 10g 8f a7g⁵ a10g⁴ a10g 14f⁴ Oct 3]   a37
workmanlike gelding: poor performer: best effort at 7f (flattered at 1¾m): sometimes
blinkered. *N. A. Callaghan*

PADDY LAD (IRE)   3 b. or br.g. Anita's Prince 126 – Lady of Man 85 (So   89 d
Blessed 130) [1996 91: a6g⁶ 6m⁵ 5m* 6g² 6m³ 1997 5d⁶ 6m⁵ 6m 6m³ 7f 6g⁴ Jul 23]
sturdy gelding: fairly useful performer: good fifth in handicap at Salisbury in May:
well below form after: should stay 7f: acts on good to firm ground: sent to Macau.
R. Guest

PADDY MCGOON (USA)   2 ch.g. (Mar 17) Irish River (FR) 131 – Flame   69 ?
McGoon (USA) (Staff Writer (USA)) [1997 6d 7.6d Aug 28] $30,000Y: fourth foal:
half-brother to winners in USA by Tank's Prospect and Ruhlmann: dam won 5 times
in USA, including 1m minor stakes at 2 yrs: 20/1 and very green, appeared to show
some ability in steadily-run newcomers event at Ascot: well beaten in maiden at
Lingfield month later. *D. R. C. Elsworth*

PADDY'S RICE   6 ch.g. Hadeer 118 – Requiem (Song 132) [1996 65: 7f* 7g 7m   59
7m⁵ 7f³ 7.6m⁴ 7g² 7.1f 7m 1997 6.1g 8d 8f* 8f 8.3g 8f⁴ Jul 23] sparely-made gelding:
modest handicapper: best effort at 6 yrs when winning 15-runner event at Brighton in
May: stays 1m: goes well on good to firm/firm going: usually held up: none too consistent. *M. Blanshard*

PAGEBOY   8 b.g. Tina's Pet 121 – Edwins' Princess 75 (Owen Dudley 121)   63
[1996 72, a75: a6g* a6g² a6g⁶ a6g⁵ 5g⁵ 5m 6f 6m* 6m² 6d⁴ 6g a6g* 5m² 5m   a80
5g⁶ 1997 a6g* a6g⁶ a6f 5g 6.1g 6g 5g 6f a6g Sep 30] small, sturdy gelding:
unimpressive mover: fairly useful handicapper on all-weather, just modest on
turf: well below form after winning at Lingfield in January (third year running he's
won on reappearance at course): best form at 5f/6f: acts on all-weather and firm
ground: often a front runner: effective with blinkers/visor (wore neither at 8 yrs).
P. C. Haslam

PAINT IT BLACK   4 ch.g. Double Schwartz 128 – Tableaux (FR) (Welsh   56
Pageant 132) [1996 78§: 7m 7f 8f 8g 8.1m² 8f⁵ 6m 7d⁴ 8f 8.2g⁶ 1997 a7s⁴ a7g

a6g[4] a6g[5] 7g 8g* 8d 7m[5] 8f[6] 8m 8.9d 6.9m 8m a8g Dec 18] sturdy gelding: modest handicapper: won 17-runner event (easily) at Thirsk in April: best form at 7f/1m: suited by good going or firmer: tried blinkered: none too consistent. *D. Nicholls*

PAIR OF JACKS (IRE)   7 ch.g. Music Boy 124 – Lobbino 72 (Bustino 136)   25
[1996 28: a7g a8g 6m 6.9g[4] 1997 a12g[3] Jan 2] strong, lengthy gelding: poor handicapper: stays 1½m: best efforts on equitrack or good going or firmer on turf: tried blinkered/visored, not for some time. *G. L. Moore*

PAIRUMANI STAR (IRE)   2 ch.c. (Apr 30) Caerleon (USA) 132 – Dawn Star   68 p
94 (High Line 125) [1997 7.6d 8.2m[6] 9m[6] Sep 26] half-brother to several winners, including 3-y-o Kennemara Star, Dawning Street (up to 1m, by Thatching) and Special Dawn (up to 1¼m, by Be My Guest), last 2 late-maturing but useful: dam 1¼m and 11f winner: showed promise in maidens, particularly when staying-on sixth at Nottingham penultimate start: turned out quite quickly when rather disappointing joint favourite at Redcar: should prove well suited by further than 1m: should make a fair bit better 3-y-o. *J. L. Dunlop*

PALACEGATE CHIEF   4 b.g. Inca Chief (USA) – Sports Post Lady (IRE) 72   –
(M Double M (USA)) [1996 –: 6.1m a8.5g 1997 a6g Jan 22] seems of little account. *N. P. Littmoden*

PALACEGATE JACK (IRE)   6 gr.g. Neshad (USA) 108 – Pasadena Lady   71
(Captain James 123) [1996 82, a85: 5.1g 5.1g 5.1m[3] 5m[3] 5m a5g* 5f[3] 5f[2] 6v 5g   a78
5f* a5g[2] a6s[6] 1997 a5g[4] a5g[5] a5g[6] a5g[3] 5g[4] 5s 5m[6] 5f* 5g* 5m 5m* a5g[3] 5d
a5g* 5.1g 5g[4] a5g[2] a5g* a5g Dec 18] lengthy, workmanlike gelding: fair performer, had a fine season: trained by C. Dwyer first 3 starts: won sellers at Newcastle and Hamilton in June, handicap at Musselburgh in July, claimer at Southwell in September and handicap at Lingfield in November: best at 5f: acts on any going: effective blinkered/visored or not: often hangs left: has been bandaged off-fore: front runner. *J. Berry*

PALACEGATE JO (IRE)   6 b.m. Drumalis 125 – Welsh Rhyme (Welsh Term   –
126) [1996 36: a8g[6] a8g[6] a9.4g a11g a11g[2] 11.5f[5] a12g[2] 1997 a8g[6] a8g a11g a8g a12g Jul 26] leggy mare: little worthwhile form at 6 yrs. *D. W. Chapman*

PALACEGATE TOUCH   7 gr.g. Petong 126 – Dancing Chimes (London Bells   86
(CAN) 109) [1996 85: 6g 6.9d* a6g[2] 6.9m[5] a7g[4] a7g[3] a6g 6d[4] a5g* 5f* 6g[3] 5g* 5m[2]
a5g[3] 5f* 5m 5d[6] 5g* 5g 1997 6m 5g[4] 6.9g[6] 5g* 5g 5m[3] 5m[3] 5d[5] 6d* 6m 6g[2] 6m[3] 6m*
5g[6] 5.1s 5m 6m 5d[5] a7g[2] a7g* a6g[2] Dec 19] tall, good-topped gelding: fairly useful performer, had another fine season: won claimers at Doncaster and Catterick (dead-heated) in the spring, handicap at Hamilton and claimer at Haydock in the summer, and apprentice handicap at Lingfield in November: effective at 5f to easy 7f: acts on the all-weather, firm and dead going: usually blinkered/visored: tends to hang left and race with head high: tough. *J. Berry*

PALACE RIVER (IRE)   9 b.m. Dragon Palace (USA) 96 – Rosebrook (Brother   –
Birdbrook 74) [1996 NR 1997 9.2g 17.2m Jun 25] plain mare: modest winning hurdler: broke pelvis final start on flat: dead. *D. Moffatt*

PALAEMON   3 b.g. Slip Anchor 136 – Palace Street (USA) 103 (Secreto (USA)   64
128) [1996 64: 6d[5] 7m 7g 7.6m[3] 8m[5] 7.3s[6] 1997 8m 11.4m[6] 12g[5] 12d[2] 11.5d[3] 16m[3]
16s[3] Oct 8] workmanlike gelding: modest maiden handicapper: stays 2m: acts on good to firm and soft ground: effective visored or not. *G. B. Balding*

PALAMON (USA)   4 ch.c. Sanglamore (USA) 126 – Gantlette (Run The Gantlet   79
(USA)) [1996 82: 10d[3] 10m[2] 12m[5] 10m* 1997 14.9m[6] 12m 10d[6] 16.2s 11.6s[2] 11.9m[4]
Aug 15] strong, lengthy colt: fair handicapper: bought out of J. White's stable after third start (blinkered): bred to stay beyond 1½m: acts on good to firm and soft ground: fairly useful hurdler. *P. Eccles*

PALATIAL STYLE   10 b.g. Kampala 120 – Stylish Princess (Prince Tender-   82
foot (USA) 126) [1996 NR 1997 10.3m 10d 9m 10.1m[6] Oct 22] lengthy gelding: smart performer at 4 yrs: lightly raced since, showing fairly useful form in minor event and handicaps in 1997: stays 1¼m: best form on good going or firmer. *P. J. Makin*

PAL

Mr R. E. Sangster's "Panama City"

PALDOST 3 b.c. Efisio 120 – Fishki 36 (Niniski (USA) 125) [1996 –: 7s⁵ 6m 6g 45
1997 8.3s⁴ 8g 6g 7.1d⁵ 6m* 7m 6g 6g Aug 13] workmanlike colt: had a round action:
poor handicapper: won seller at Hamilton in July: should have stayed beyond 6f:
acted on good to firm ground: dead. *M. D. Hammond*

PALIO SKY 3 b.c. Niniski (USA) 125 – Live Ammo 94 (Home Guard (USA) 110
129) [1996 87p: 7d³ 8.1m* 1997 10g* 12m* 12d² 12m⁵ 14g² 15d* 14m⁴ Oct 5]
leggy, good-topped colt: smart performer: won small-field minor events at Kempton
and Epsom (didn't handle descent particularly well) in the spring and 4-runner listed
race at Chantilly in September: good second to Kingfisher Mill (beaten 8 lengths) in
King Edward VII Stakes at Royal Ascot and Pentad (beaten ½ length) in steadily-run
listed race at Goodwood in between: stays 15f: yet to race on extremes of going: races
rather lazily: consistent: stays in training. *J. L. Dunlop*

PALISADE (USA) 3 b.f. Gone West (USA) – Peplum (USA) 108 (Nijinsky 87
(CAN) 138) [1996 85p: 7g* 1997 6f⁴ 8v Oct 10] leggy filly: won maiden at Newmarket on only start at 2 yrs: fourth in useful minor event at Yarmouth and down the
field in listed race at Ascot (probably unsuited by heavy going) nearly a year later:
should be suited by 1m+: sent to USA. *H. R. A. Cecil*

PALISANDER (IRE) 3 ch.g. Conquering Hero (USA) 116 – Classic Choice –
(Patch 129) [1996 62, a?: 6d⁶ 6m 6m⁵ 7m a8g 1997 8.5d 8.5g a7g a10g⁴ a10g* a10g a68
Dec 2] fair performer: won handicap at Lingfield in November: stays 1¼m: acts on
equitrack. *S. Dow*

PALLIUM (IRE) 9 b.g. Try My Best (USA) 130 – Jungle Gardenia (Nonoalco 56
(USA) 131) [1996 58d: 5g 5f⁵ 6m 5g 5f⁴ 5m 5m³ 6f² 5m 5g 5m 6f 1997 5m⁴
6m³ 5g⁶ 6g 5g⁶ 5s² 5g² 5m* 5m⁴ 6m 6g 5f 5g² 5g⁵ 5d 5s⁵ 5d⁶ 5d Nov 7] good-bodied
gelding: unimpressive mover: modest handicapper: ran consistently well in 1997,

694

PAP

winning at Hamilton (amateurs) in July: effective at 5f and 6f: acts on any going: blinkered since sixth 9-y-o start: has hung: sometimes has tongue tied: tough. *D. A. Nolan*

PALMETTO BAY (IRE)   2 b.c. (May 11) Royal Academy (USA) 130 – Surmise (USA) 75 (Alleged (USA) 138) [1997 6m⁴ 7g³ 7f³ 6s⁶ Oct 16] fourth foal: half-brother to a winning sprinter in Italy by Be My Guest: dam 7f winner: fair form at best in minor events and maidens: stays 7f: well beaten on soft ground: has tended to wander: sold 15,000 gns after final start. *M. R. Stoute*   74

PALO BLANCO   6 b.m. Precocious 126 – Linpac Mapleleaf 69 (Dominion 123) [1996 82: 5g 5g⁶ 6d* 6g² 6g³ 6m 6m 6g⁵ 6f⁶ 1997 6s⁵ 6g² 6.1g 5.1m² 7s² 6.9s³ a7g⁶ 8.3m a8g 7g 5m* 6.1g 5d⁵ 5d² a6g³ Nov 24] rangy, workmanlike mare: fair performer: left T. D. Barron after second start: won claimer at Sandown (made all, nowhere near best) in September: effective at 5f to 7f: acts on fibresand and soft going, probably on firm: usually edgy. *G. L. Moore*   78 a68

PAMELA'S BOY   3 ch.c. Clantime 101 – Allez-Oops 65 (Moulin 103) [1996 –: 7g 1997 a8s a8g⁶ a8g Jan 13] of little account. *A. Smith*   –

PAMPASA (FR)   3 br.f. Pampabird 124 – Dounasa (FR) (Kaldoun (FR) 122) [1996 –: 6g 1997 8d Jun 25] first foal: dam unraced: little sign of ability. *C. James*   –

PANAMA CITY (USA)   3 b.c. El Gran Senor (USA) 136 – Obeah 112 (Cure The Blues (USA)) [1996 102p: 8.1g² 8m* 8s² 1997 9m² 12.3d* 12f³ 12d⁴ 13.3m² 14.6m⁶ 12f⁵ 12f* Dec 20] good-topped, attractive colt: has a long, round action: smart performer: won 5-runner Chester Vase by head from Ivan Luis and length third of 16 to stable-companion Single Empire in Derby Italiano at Rome, both in May: ran very well when neck second of 4 to Dushyantor in slowly-run Geoffrey Freer Stakes at Newbury, making most and rallying: respectable sixth of 10 to Silver Patriarch in St Leger at Doncaster (never a threat on final outing for P. Chapple-Hyam): won Grade 2 handicap at Calder on final start: probably stays 14.6f: acts on firm and soft ground. *P. Byrne, USA*   115

PANAMA HOUSE   2 ch.g. (Mar 25) Rudimentary (USA) 118 – Lustrous 73 (Golden Act (USA)) [1997 6m² 5.9m² 6m² 6g² 7m* 8g 8f 8g* Oct 24] 11,000Y: lengthy, useful-looking gelding: has scope: half-brother to several winners, including 8.5f winner Budby (by Rock City) and 8-y-o Vanborough Lad: dam 1½m winner: won maiden at Thirsk in August and nursery at Doncaster in October, improved form to beat Dutch Lad ½ length, pair well clear, in latter: should stay 1¼m: raced mainly on good/good to firm ground: has had tongue tied, not at Doncaster: usually races prominently: gelded at end of season: should progress again and make a useful handicapper. *T. D. Easterby*   78 p

PANORAMA   3 b.f. Shirley Heights 130 – Lycia (USA) (Lyphard (USA) 132) [1996 NR 1997 12m 10.1g⁵ 10m Sep 25] compact filly: second foal: dam French winner at around 1¼m: little worthwhile form in maidens. *L. M. Cumani*   –

PANTAR (IRE)   2 b.c. (Mar 21) Shirley Heights 130 – Spring Daffodil 97 (Pharly (FR) 130) [1997 7g 7m Sep 30] 60,000Y: third foal: half-brother to Irish 1m winner Lower The Tone (by Phone Trick): dam Irish 7f and 1m winner, later successful in USA: backward on debut: fair form when 11½ lengths seventh to Tamarisk in valuable sales race at Newmarket next time, keeping on: should stay at least 1¼m: swishes tail: has plenty of scope, and type to do better at 3 yrs. *I. A. Balding*   81 p

PANTHER (IRE)   7 ch.g. Primo Dominie 121 – High Profile (High Top 131) [1996 75, a50: a6g a7g⁶ a7g 6d⁴ 6d* 6s² 6m* a7g³ 6g³ 6f* 6m⁶ 6m² a7g⁴ 5.1d* 5m⁶ 5m 5.1g 1997 a7g a6g 5g 6d 6g 5g 6m³ 7.1m⁴ 6d 6d⁶ 5m 5g a6g Nov 21] leggy gelding: modest handicapper: best form at 5f: acts on firm ground and soft: usually blinkered/visored: tends to hang: sometimes starts very slowly. *P. D. Evans*   57 a–

PANTO QUEEN   6 b.m. Lepanto (GER) – Tyqueen (Tycoon II) [1996 –: 11.6m 10m 10.8f 1997 a9.4g Mar 1] no sign of ability. *C. R. Barwell*   –

PAPERING (IRE)   4 b.f. Shaadi (USA) 126 – Wrapping 108§ (Kris 135) [1996 114: 8m 10s³ 10.2m* 10m² 10m² 11.9m² 12m² 12d⁴ 1997 10.4g* 12f² 10m³ 11.9g⁵ 11m* 10m* Sep 28] tall filly: smart performer: won listed event at York in May, Premio Federico Tesio at Milan in September (made all and beat Salmon Ladder by 3   111

695

Sheikh Mohammed's "Papering"

lengths) and Premio Lydia Tesio at Rome (by ½ length from Bedside Story): stayed 1½m: went well on firm/good to firm going: genuine: stud. *L. M. Cumani*

PAPERWORK PETE (IRE)   5 b.g. Kahyasi 130 – Palitana (Nonoalco (USA) – 131) [1996 NR 1997 13.8m 10m 10g⁶ 13.1m 8m Jul 19] seventh foal: half-brother to Irish 7f winner Ardlea House (by Precocious): dam, French 6f and 1m winner, half-sister to 2 good winners: seems of little account. *W. Storey*   –

PAPITA (IRE)   3 b.f. Law Society (USA) 130 – Fantasise (FR) (General Assembly (USA)) [1996 77?: 6g⁵ 6m* 7m 6m 7m⁶ 7d 1997 6g⁶ 6m 6d 6d 7s 8.3m⁶ 9.9m³ 11.9m a12g Dec 19] sturdy filly: fair handicapper, on downgrade: left S. Dow before final start: stays 1¼m: seems suited by good going or firmer. *N. M. Lampard*   72 d

PAPUA   3 ch.g. Green Dancer (USA) 132 – Fairy Tern 109 (Mill Reef (USA) 141) [1996 104: 6m⁴ 7f* 7m* 7g² 7m* 8g⁵ 1997 8g³ 12m² 11.5s⁴ 12g 10g³ 10m 13.9g 12m⁶ 12d⁵ Oct 16] tall gelding: useful form when placed in minor events at Epsom (1¾ lengths second to Palio Sky) in April and Sandown (3 lengths third to Lord of Men) in July: below that form last 4 starts: stays 1½m: acts on firm and dead ground: tried visored: sometimes gets on edge: not one to trust implicitly. *I. A. Balding*   102 d

PARADISE NAVY   8 b.g. Slip Anchor 136 – Ivory Waltz (USA) (Sir Ivor 135) [1996 75§: 16.4g 16d 16.1f³ 20f 16.2f⁴ 16.4g 14m⁴ 17.2f* 20m⁴ a16g* a16g³ 16d⁶ 18.2m 15.4g³ 16.1f⁴ 18g 16g³ 14.1s³ 16.5s⁴ a14g⁴ 1997 a16.2g⁴ 15.4m* 17.2d⁶ 14.9m³ 16.2m³ 17.2m³ 14.9d 14.9g⁶ 16.2m 16.5g* a16g⁵ 14.1g* 14s 13.9s a14.8g⁶ a14.8g⁴ 11.8d⁴ 14.1f* a14g⁵ Nov 14] close-coupled gelding: poor walker: fair performer: given good rides when winning handicaps at Folkestone in April, Doncaster (amateurs) in July and Yarmouth (ladies) in August, as well as in claimer at   77 §

Yarmouth in October: effective at 1¾m to 2½m: acts on any turf going and equitrack: usually blinkered: tends to find little and usually waited with, though not for last 3 wins: not one to trust. *C. R. Egerton*

PARADISE SOUL (USA)   2 b.f. (Feb 28) Dynaformer (USA) – River Valley   77
(FR) (Riverman (USA) 131) [1997 7g 9m³ 10m³ Oct 6] $37,000Y: close-coupled filly: half-sister to several winners, notably useful French stayer River Test (by Riverman): dam, French 10.5f winner, half-sister to dams of Lypharita and Belmez: fair form when third in maidens at Redcar and Pontefract, making most on latter course: should stay 1½m+. *D. R. Loder*

PARDAN   3 b.g. Pharly (FR) 130 – Silent Pool 68 (Relkino 131) [1996 NR 1997   48
10s 10m 10.8m⁵ 9.7m 7g a7g 8g 6g³ a6g Oct 20] 2,700Y: sturdy gelding: half-brother to several winners, including modest Water God (up to 1¼m, by Dominion): dam slow daughter of Park Hill winner Idle Waters: poor maiden: despite breeding, shapes as if will prove best short of 1m: well beaten on fibresand: blinkered seventh start (too free). *B. Palling*

PARELLIE   4 b.f. Inca Chief (USA) – Parklands Belle 73 (Stanford 121§) [1996   –
–: a9.4g 1997 a7s 6.1m Jun 13] seems of little account. *C. J. Hill*

PARIJAZZ (IRE)   3 b.f. Astronef 116 – Brandywell (Skyliner 117) [1996 68:   –
6.1m⁵ 6d² 5.1m 6m² 6g* 1997 6.1m a6g 7m 6g⁶ 7.1g 5m Aug 18] sparely-made filly: little worthwhile form at 3 yrs. *Martyn Meade*

PARIS BABE   5 b.m. Teenoso (USA) 135 – Kala's Image 55 (Kala Shikari 125)   84
[1996 –: 7f⁶ 6s 1997 6g⁴ 6g 6d* Jul 9] smallish, workmanlike mare: fairly useful performer: didn't have to be near best to win claimer at Epsom in July: a sprinter: acts on good to firm and dead ground: usually held up. *D. Morris*

PARISH WALK (IRE)   6 ch.g. Pennine Walk 120 – Baby Caroline (Martin John)   –
[1996 NR 1997 11.6m Aug 11] poor winning handicapper at 4 yrs: well beaten only outing in 1997. *K. J. Drewry, Isle of Man*

PARISIAN LADY (IRE)   2 b.f. (Apr 7) Paris House 123 – Mia Gigi (Hard   91
Fought 125) [1997 6f* 6m* 7m⁴ 6d² 7m Oct 4] 2,000Y: tall, rather shallow-girthed filly: fourth reported foal: half-sister to a winner in Denmark by Common Grounds and an Irish bumper winner by Mister Majestic: dam Irish maiden: fairly useful performer: won maiden in June and minor event in July, both at Salisbury: creditable fourth in listed race at Newmarket next time, but below form afterwards: free-going sort and may prove ideally suited by 6f. *A. G. Newcombe*

PARKLIFE (IRE)   5 ch.g. Double Schwartz 128 – Silk Trade (Auction Ring   a48
(USA) 123) [1996 44: a12g⁴ a12g² a12g a8g³ a11g 16.1f² 1997 a12g* a16.2g⁶ a16g⁶
a16g⁵ Feb 14] compact gelding: poor handicapper: improved to win maiden event at Southwell in January by 6 lengths: well beaten afterwards: stays 2m: acts on fibresand and firm ground: tried visored: a difficult ride, and not one to trust implicitly. *P. C. Haslam*

PARLEZ MOI D'AMOUR (IRE)   2 gr.f. (Apr 9) Precocious 126 – Normanby   –
Lass 100 (Bustino 136) [1997 6g a7g⁵ Jul 26] 2,600Y: seventh foal: half-sister to 3-y-o Bonnie Lassie and fair middle-distance stayer Keep Your Distance (by Elegant Air): dam 2-y-o 7f winner: well held in maidens. *C. W. Thornton*

PARONOMASIA   5 b.g. Precocious 126 – The Crying Game 55 (Manor Farm   –
Boy 114) [1996 –, a37: a8g³ a6g a7g a8g⁵ a8g 8.2d a11g 10.3m⁶ 11.1g 10m 14.1m   a43
14.1f 15.1g⁵ 14.9m 10f 8m a10g² a10s² a8g a10g 1997 a10g a8g⁵ a10g² 10.1f a11g a14g Dec 18] workmanlike gelding: poor maiden handicapper: stays 1¼m: acts on equitrack, little worthwhile form on turf: tried visored/blinkered: inconsistent, and looked none too keen final start. *J. L. Harris*

PARROT'S HILL (IRE)   4 b.g. Nashamaa 113 – Cryptic Gold (Glint of Gold   –
128) [1996 55: 10g 8f 10m 13.8s² 11.6m⁴ 12m 11.5m⁵ 12m 1997 12m⁶ 14.1g Oct 18] compact gelding: has a long stride: modest maiden handicapper: below form at 4 yrs: probably stayed further than 1½m: probably acts on soft and good to firm ground. *M. H. Tompkins*

PARSA (USA)   4 b.f. Risen Star (USA) – Pallanza (USA) (Lyphard (USA) 132)   –
[1996 66: 10m 10m* 10.1f² 9.9m² 10.1g³ 11.8g⁵ 10d⁶ 8f⁴ 8.2s³ 1997 8g 8.5s a9.4g⁵

8g 8.2s 8.2d Nov 3] big, good-topped filly: fair handicapper at 3 yrs: disappointing in 1997: visored final start: sold 28,000 gns in December. *J. L. Dunlop*

PARTICULAR FRIEND   2 ch.f. (Mar 16) Cadeaux Genereux 131 – Pamela   88
Peach 81 (Habitat 134) [1997 7g² 7m⁵ Aug 9] 160,000Y: tall, good-topped filly: fourth foal: half-sister to 3 winners, including 3-y-o Davoski and 4-y-o Marl: dam maiden here (effective at 6f/7f) who later won in USA: neck second to Glorosia in maiden at Newmarket: never-dangerous fifth of 8 in listed race there 22 days later (moved scratchily to post): should stay at least 1m: slowly away both starts. *E. A. L. Dunlop*

PARTY ROMANCE (USA)   3 gr.c. Black Tie Affair – Tia Juanita (USA) (My   91
Gallant (USA)) [1996 87: 7m⁴ 7g⁴ 7.1m³ 7.9g² 7.1v⁴ 1997 10g 7.6d 10g* 10g² 12d 10g 10.1g* 10m 10.3m⁴ Sep 10] close-coupled, good-bodied colt: fairly useful performer: won maiden at Ayr in May and handicap at Newcastle in July: very good fourth to Mithali in minor event at Doncaster final start: keen sort, probably best around 1¼m: acts on good to firm ground: steadily to post last 4 starts, tongue tied last 3: usually races prominently. *B. Hanbury*

PAS DE MEMOIRES (IRE)   2 b.c. (Mar 15) Don't Forget Me 127 – Bally   87 p
Pourri (IRE) (Law Society (USA) 130) [1997 6d 7.9s 6.9d⁶ 8m² a7g* a7g* Nov 21] 10,000Y: second foal: half-brother to 3-y-o Treasure Touch: dam Irish 1¼m winner: progressive form: impressive winner of nurseries at Southwell and Wolverhampton in November, eased to win by 4 lengths in latter: should stay 1¼m: useful performer in making. *M. H. Tompkins*

PAS DE REPONSE (USA)   3 b.f. Danzig (USA) – Soundings (USA) (Mr   118
Prospector (USA)) [1996 113p: 6g* 6g³ 5.5m* 6m* 1997 7d* 8m⁴ 6s* 5f² a6f Nov 8]
  The One Thousand Guineas favourite failed to stay. She made the frame, but something better than fourth place had looked on the cards for the French filly Pas de Reponse when she was poised within half a length of the lead just over two furlongs out. However, Freddie Head, on his final ride in Britain, had probably already suspected that he was not going to have a fourth

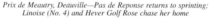

Prix de Meautry, Deauville—Pas de Reponse returns to sprinting;
Linoise (No. 4) and Hever Golf Rose chase her home

British classic winner, to join Zino, Ma Biche and Miesque, when Pas de Reponse failed to settle over the first quarter mile. A 12/1-shot for the Guineas over the winter after her win in the Cheveley Park, Pas de Reponse had had a 10/3-on stroll against two rivals in the Prix Imprudence as a warm-up for her return to Newmarket. After Newmarket it was clear that Criquette Head had a second candidate in the Wertheimer colours for the top sprints, to go with the 1996 Prix de l'Abbaye winner Kistena.

The pair turned up at Longchamp for the 1997 running of the Abbaye coupled as favourite at 9/5. There is no doubt which of the two was more fancied. Pas de Reponse had been off the course virtually throughout the summer following a bad bout of flu and had had only one race in the five months since Newmarket, while Kistena had likewise had just one recent outing. Pas de Reponse had been easily the more impressive as she came with a late run to beat her six opponents (Hever Golf Rose third, Brave Edge fifth) in the Prix de Meautry at Deauville on the last day of August. That was over six furlongs. The Abbaye demonstrated clearly that she had no problems with five either. Eveningperformance, as usual, was not hanging about, but Pas de Reponse was able to keep with her and go past by halfway. Royal Applause mounted a strong

		Northern Dancer	Nearctic
	Danzig (USA)	(b 1961)	Natalma
	(b 1977)	Pas de Nom	Admiral's Voyage
Pas de Reponse (USA)		(b or br 1968)	Petitioner
(b.f. 1994)		Mr Prospector	Raise A Native
	Soundings (USA)	(b 1970)	Gold Digger
	(b 1983)	Ocean's Answer	Northern Answer
		(b 1976)	South Ocean

Wertheimer et Frere's "Pas de Reponse"

bid through the last furlong and a half, but, between horses, Carmine Lake finished best of all and got up to win by half a length. Changing smoothly from classic challenger to leading European sprinter is one thing, adapting to conditions in the Breeders' Cup Sprint quite another, and Pas de Reponse was well beaten at Hollywood Park five weeks later.

Soundings, the dam of Pas de Reponse, was already the sister of one smart sprinter and the dam of a classic winner. The sprinter was Al Zawbaah, who led the field for four furlongs when he finished in mid-division in the 1985 Abbaye. The classic winner is the 1994 Poule d'Essai des Poulains hero Green Tune (by Green Dancer), who went on to take the Prix d'Ispahan over an extended nine furlongs. Soundings won two races at up to a mile as a four-year-old in the United States. Her dam, Ocean's Answer, is a close relation to Storm Bird and the Canadian Oaks winner Northernette. The latter proved as good at stud, producing the Beresford Stakes winner Gold Crest and the Grade 1 Flower Bowl Handicap winner Scoot (both by Mr Prospector). Other daughters of South Ocean include South Sea Dancer, who produced a double Grade 3 winner in Signal Tap, and Stormette, who produced the Musidora Stakes winner Marillette and the Feilden Stakes winner Storm Trooper (both to Diesis). Pas de Reponse, then, is a most valuable broodmare prospect. An angular, good-quartered filly with a short, round action, she acts on firm and soft ground. *Mme C. Head, France*

PASSAGE CREEPING (IRE) 4 b.f. Persian Bold 123 – Tiptoe (Dance In Time (CAN)) [1996 75: 7m 8d⁵ 7g² 8g⁶ 8f² 10.1g⁴ 8.3d a8s² a8g² 1997 a10g³ a10g² a10g 8f³ 9.7m² 10m 10m³ 10.1g 10m Oct 23] lengthy filly: fair maiden handicapper on turf, modest on all-weather: ran poorly last 4 starts: stays 1¼m: acts on firm ground and equitrack, seems unsuited by going softer than good: sold 1,000 gns in December. *S. Dow* **70 d a50 d**

PASSI D'ORLANDO (IRE) 3 ch.c. Persian Bold 123 – When Lit (Northfields (USA)) [1996 91+: 7d⁵ 7f³ 8s* 9s² 8g³ 1997 10.3m⁵ 10f² 10s⁵ 11g⁶ Sep 7] tall colt: half-brother to smart Guado d'Annibale (stayed 1½m, by Glint of Gold): fairly useful form: beaten neck by Barba Papa in minor event at Milan in June: left J. Dunlop after next start: should stay beyond 1¼m: acts on firm and soft ground. *V. Caruso, Italy* **93**

PASSIFLORA 3 ch.f. Night Shift (USA) – Pineapple 77 (Superlative 118) [1996 75: 6m* 6g² 7s 1997 7g 8m 7.1g 10g⁴ Jun 13] workmanlike filly: easy mover: reportedly suffers from bouts of lameness: fair winner at 2 yrs: little worthwhile form in handicaps in 1997: former only at 6f: stud. *J. L. Dunlop* **–**

PASSING STRANGERS (USA) 4 b.g. Lyphard (USA) 132 – The Way We Were (USA) (Avatar (USA)) [1996 60: 7m 10m 11.5m³ 1997 12.1d⁶ 12g⁶ 12.5d² 12m* 12d² 11.7m 11.9g⁵ 10g² 10d⁵ Oct 20] workmanlike gelding: fair handicapper: won at Pontefract in July: largely creditable efforts afterwards: stays 1½m: yet to race on extremes of going: sold 13,000 gns after final start. *P. W. Harris* **68**

PASSION 3 ch.f. Risk Me (FR) 127 – Gotcher 74 (Jalmood (USA) 126) [1996 61p: 6m⁵ 1997 7g⁵ a7g a10g Oct 27] showed ability only start at 2 yrs: well beaten in 1997: visored penultimate start. *T. G. Mills* **–**

PASSIONATTI 3 b.f. Emarati (USA) 74 – Ration of Passion 71 (Camden Town 125) [1996 NR 1997 5m a5g 5f⁶ 6g* 5m³ 5d³ a5g⁵ Nov 6] 500Y: rather dipped-backed filly: second reported live foal: dam sprint maiden: fair performer: won maiden at Catterick in September: better efforts in frame in handicaps afterwards: likely to prove best at 5f: acts on firm and dead ground: has run well when edgy. *S. Gollings* **66**

PASSIONELLE 3 b.f. Nashwan (USA) 135 – Height of Passion (Shirley Heights 130) [1996 NR 1997 10v⁴ 12g⁶ Jul 8] angular, unfurnished filly: closely related to useful Rainbow Heights (should have stayed 1½m, by Rainbow Quest), and half-sister to several winners, including smart Precede (stayed 1½m, by Polish Precedent): dam ran 3 times: better effort in maidens on debut. *B. W. Hills* **56**

PASSION FOR LIFE 4 br.g. Charmer 123 – Party Game 70 (Red Alert 127) [1996 116: 5d³ 6g* 6m* 6f⁶ 6g* 7g⁶ 6v 6g² 1997 6m⁶ 5.5g 5m 5g 5m 5m⁴ 6g 5.1g⁵ **100**

Sep 28] good-topped gelding: unimpressive mover: smart performer at 3 yrs: disappointing and only useful form in 1997: sold 23,000 gns in October: stays 6f: acts on good to firm ground and soft: blinkered third and final starts as 4-y-o: usually early to post. *G. Lewis*

PASS THE REST (IRE)   2 b.c. (Apr 21) Shalford (IRE) 124§ – Brown Foam   76
(Horage 124) [1997 7.1s² 7m³ 7d⁴ Nov 7] IR 13,000Y: close-coupled colt: third reported foal: dam ran twice: fair form in maidens and minor event: likely to prove best up to 1m. *J. L. Eyre*

PASTERNAK   4 b.c. Soviet Star (USA) 128 – Princess Pati 124 (Top Ville   109 p
129) [1996 93p: 8.3s⁵ 8.2f² 9f 10g³ 10.2d* 10.4g* 1997 10.4m* 9m* Oct 4]
What captures the imagination of racing's general public so effectively as a big gamble? One of the few definites would be to be part of the gamble and to see it landed. Add a touch of secrecy and plotting, and the betting coup has a central role in the sport's mystique. Elements of all this help explain the success of the 1990 book *The Druid's Lodge Confederacy*, subtitled *The Gamblers Who Made Racing Pay*. A leading player in this work of non-fiction was the filly Hackler's Pride, whom the Druid's Lodge team sent out to land a massive gamble in the Cambridgeshire in 1903, reputed to have netted them the equivalent at 1990 values of £10.5 million. With today's bookmakers, betting coups on that scale are not possible for one set of connections, but wholesale gambles continue to become part of racing folklore as will surely be the case with the one landed on the 1997 Cambridgeshire winner Pasternak.
A best-priced 11/1 in the morning and 10/1 with the 'Big Three', Pasternak opened at 9/2 on the course and was sent off at 4/1, taking the bookmakers for what Sunday's papers estimated was £5 million. Although this public gamble was partly media-driven—'Why you must back Pasternak' was plastered over the front page of the *Racing Post*, for example—there was more than a whiff of 'the coup' and a careful plan brought to fruition about Pasternak's success as well. One of the aforementioned chapters covering the Hackler's Pride story was titled 'Superhuman Cleverness', which is what many racing fans credit Sir Mark Prescott, Pasternak's trainer, with. Unlike Hackler's

John Smith's Magnet Cup (Handicap), York—
Pasternak (right) lands some sizeable ante-post bets on his seasonal reappearance;
Najm Mubeen and Game Ploy (blaze) finish to some effect to take second and third places

Pride, though, there was no question of Pasternak getting a favourable handicap
mark through not being run on its merits. The colt had made six appearances in
1996 and won the last two of them (thanks in part to settling much better than
he had previously) in a style that stamped him as an individual of great
potential. In 1997, the public were indeed kept in the dark about just how
talented this horse was, but that was because they saw virtually nothing of him;
Pasternak was let loose on the racecourse only twice and, under assured rides
from veteran George Duffield, he took home two of the biggest handicap prizes
in the Calendar. 'Pasternak is a marvellous horse for the big handicaps,' said
his trainer after the Cambridgeshire. 'He's not an easy horse, so I thought he
ought to run in the big ones—if you win the small ones you still go up.'

The first of these 'big ones' was the John Smith's Magnet Cup at York
in July, for which Pasternak was priced up at 8/1 earlier in the week, 3/1 when
betting opened on the course, and 13/2 at the off. Close up in a steadily-run race
but waiting impatiently for a clear run in the straight, Pasternak was pulled out
to go on at the furlong pole and held off Najm Mubeen by half a length. Part-
owner Graham Rock, the journalist and BBC betting expert, blamed the
winner's dramatic swings in the market on bookmaker 'hype' followed by
connections' publicly-waning confidence as the ground dried out. Nearly three
months later, similar doubts about the ground were expressed just before the
Cambridgeshire—Pasternak even having an alternative entry on the same day
in a £5,500 handicap on the all-weather at Wolverhampton—but this time the
public were having none of it. It was the usual huge field, but as the cameras
panned back through the thirty-six runners at halfway they did not have to go
far before spotting Pasternak swinging on the bridle. Pushed along to challenge
for the lead two furlongs out, Pasternak then faced his biggest threat from
stablemate Rudimental (whose rider earned a whip ban) but had three quarters
of a length to spare at the line.

A good-topped colt with scope, Pasternak has always looked the part,
and a glance at his breeding—sire the high-class sprinter/miler Soviet Star,
dam the Irish Oaks winner Princess Pati—makes a pretty good impression too.
Princess Pati is herself a daughter of the Irish One Thousand Guineas and York-

*Tote Cambridgeshire Handicap, Newmarket—more of the same from Pasternak as he justifies 4/1 favouritism,
with Rudimental making it a Sir Mark Prescott-trained one—two;
Hunters of Brora is placed in the race for the third time*

Mr Graham Rock's "Pasternak"

		Nureyev	Northern Dancer
	Soviet Star (USA)	(b 1977)	Special
	(b 1984)	Veruschka	Venture VII
Pasternak		(b 1967)	Marie d'Anjou
(b.c. 1993)		Top Ville	High Top
	Princess Pati	(b 1976)	Sega Ville
	(b 1981)	Sarah Siddons	Le Levanstell
		(b 1974)	Mariel

shire Oaks winner Sarah Siddons and a half-sister to the high-class middle-distance colt Seymour Hicks. Many readers will remember Princess Pati's all-the-way victory in the Irish Oaks under Pat Shanahan, because it was one of the few occasions when one could say that Lester Piggott (on runner-up Circus Plume) had been outwitted. Pasternak, a 30,000-guinea yearling, is the seventh foal out of Princess Pati. The 1996 two-year-old six-furlong winner Arapi (by Arazi) did not appear in 1997, while Milling (by In The Wings) has so far run just the once. All of the dam's first three winners, Srivijaya (by Kris), Maxwelton Braes (by Lomond) and the Yorkshire Cup runner-up Parthian Springs (by Sadler's Wells), won over at least a mile and a half. Connections have seriously considered running Pasternak at that trip, a bout of coughing reportedly preventing him from reappearing in the latest season in the Bessborough, and on occasions (notably his final start in 1996) it has looked as if he would get it. But it could be a risk that is not worth taking given that he has so much speed and remains somewhat headstrong. Having won the Magnet Cup off 85 and the Cambridgeshire off 91, further tilts at the big handicaps are an entirely viable option, but Pasternak is a pattern-race performer in the making surely. A winner on dead ground, good, and twice on good to firm on his last four starts, Pasternak is unlikely to be risked again on firm. He looks certain to win another good race or two, just like Hackler's Pride, who landed another gamble in the Cambridgeshire of 1904. *Sir Mark Prescott*

PASTICHE   3 b.f. Kylian (USA) – Titian Beauty (Auction Ring (USA) 123) [1996 61p: a8g⁴ 1997 a8g* a8g⁴ 8.3s⁵ 8g 8f Sep 28] modest performer on all-weather: won weak maiden at Lingfield in January: poor form on turf: takes good hold and not sure to stay beyond 1m. *T. G. Mills*   38 a58

PAST MASTER (USA)   9 b.g. Chief's Crown (USA) – Passing Look (USA) (Buckpasser) [1996 NR 1997 a12g Feb 7] half-brother to several winners, including a Grade 1 winner at 2 yrs by Vice Regent: dam won 4 races in USA: formerly a smart performer at around 1m in Europe: also successful in Dubai, but seems to retain little ability (poor hurdler in 1995/6). *S. Gollings*   –

PATER NOSTER (USA)   8 b.h. Stately Don (USA) 122 – Sainera (USA) 89 (Stop The Music (USA)) [1996 94: 10g 8.2d⁴ 1997 a8.5f⁶ a9.4g³ a8.5g⁴ a9.4g² a8.5g³ 8m 8.1g 10.3d⁴ 8.5d 8.1m⁶ May 27] leggy horse: has a round action: has had a history of leg trouble: fairly useful form at Wolverhampton early in year, not so good last 5 starts and well beaten in claimer final one: probably stays 1¼m: acts on fibresand, probably needs going softer than good on turf: usually races prominently: sold only 3,500 gns in October, and sent to Italy. *John A. Harris*   91 d

PATHAZE   4 b.f. Totem (USA) 118 – Stilvella (Camden Town 125) [1996 51: 6.1g 6d³ 6d 6m³ 5m² 5.9f² 6m⁴ 6f⁶ 7m³ 6m² 5m³ 6m² 7g 6g⁵ 1997 5f a5g 5g 6m 5g² 7g 6g 5g 5g⁶ 5g 6.1m² 5s a6g Nov 17] workmanlike filly: poor handicapper: stays 6f: acts on firm and dead ground: inconsistent at 4 yrs. *N. Bycroft*   45

PATIALA (IRE)   4 b.f. Nashwan (USA) 135 – Catherine Parr (USA) 109 (Riverman (USA) 131) [1996 –: 10s 14.6d⁵ a12g a14.8g⁶ 1997 a12g Jan 2] lengthy filly: no sign of ability. *R. W. Armstrong*   –

PATINA   3 ch.f. Rudimentary (USA) 118 – Appledorn 99 (Doulab (USA) 115) [1996 51: 7m a7g³ a6g³ 1997 a7g² a8g a7g³ a7g⁵ a7g⁴ 5g6 6d⁶ 7d 6g 6.9m³ 7g 8g⁴ a6g⁶ a9.4g a8.5g³ Dec 26] workmanlike filly: modest maiden: stays 8.5f: acts on dead ground and fibresand. *R. Hollinshead*   51

PATRICIA OLIVE (IRE)   2 ch.f. (Mar 31) Case Law 113 – My Special Guest (IRE) (Be My Guest (USA) 126) [1997 5m⁵ 5m⁴ 6f⁶ 5g² 7g 6d 6m³ 6g³ 8m⁵ 7d 7m⁵ Oct 23] IR 5,000Y: good-bodied filly: first foal: dam lightly-raced Irish maiden: modest maiden: deteriorated after fourth start: probably stays 7f: tried visored: sold, and sent to Holland. *M. H. Tompkins*   58 d

PATRICIUS   2 b.f. (Apr 16) Noble Patriarch 115 – Bad Payer 72 (Tanfirion 110) [1997 6m May 27] fifth reported live foal: half-sister to winning sprinters Penny Hasset (by Lochnager) and Pocket Edition (at 2 yrs in 1994, by Domynsky): dam 2-y-o 5f winner: last in maiden at Redcar: dead. *T. D. Easterby*   –

PATRICK   3 b.g. Backchat (USA) 98 – Girton Degree 41 (Balliol 125) [1996 NR 1997 a8g a7g a8g 7m⁶ 10m 8.2m⁴ 8g 11.5m a8g Dec 2] plain gelding: first foal: dam (maiden, stayed 1m) sister to smart sprinter Singing Steven: form only when fourth in seller at Nottingham in April: subsequently off course 5 months. *D. Burchell*   51 ?

PATRIOT GAMES (IRE)   3 b.c. Polish Patriot (USA) 128 – It's Now Or Never 78 (High Line 125) [1996 NR 1997 8g⁶ 8g⁶ 9m* 10d² 10m 10s³ 12m⁴ 11.9s⁶ Oct 8] 12,000F, 27,000Y: smallish, sturdy colt: fluent mover: sixth foal: brother to French 4-y-o Emperor Davis, 6f winner at 2 yrs, and half-brother to 2 winners, including 7-y-o Outset: dam 1¼m winner: fairly useful performer: won maiden at Lingfield in May: best efforts when placed in handicaps at Sandown: stays 1¼m (seemingly not 1½m): acts on good to firm and soft ground: sold 50,000 gns. *M. R. Stoute*   88

PATRITA PARK   3 br.f. Flying Tyke 90 – Bellinote (FR) 71 (Noir Et Or 125) [1996 42: 5m 5s 7m⁵ a7g a7g⁵ 1997 6.1d 7.5s 6g 10g 11.5f Oct 3] small filly: poor maiden. *W. G. M. Turner*   –

PAT SAID NO (IRE)   3 b.f. Last Tycoon 131 – Fiddle-Faddle 85 (Silly Season 127) [1996 59: 5f² 6.1m⁵ 1997 6m 10.1m 7g Jul 23] smallish filly: well beaten at 3 yrs: bred to stay at least 1¼m: blinkered final start. *D. J. S. Cosgrove*   –

PATSY CULSYTH   2 b.f. (Mar 17) Tragic Role (USA) – Regal Salute 68 (Dara   70
Monarch 128) [1997 5g⁶ 5s⁶ a5g⁵ 5m² 5f² 5m⁵ 6g² 5.1g⁴ 5d* 5g³ 6d Oct 18]
6,400Y: useful-looking filly: fourth foal: half-sister to 1995 2-y-o 5f winner Monsieur Culsyth (by Mon Tresor) and a winner in Denmark by Puissance: dam maiden
suited by 1¼m: fair performer: trained by M. Johnston first 7 starts: won claimer at
Beverley in August for Mrs L. Stubbs: ran well in seller at Ayr final start: best form
at 5f: acts on firm and dead ground, poorly drawn on fibresand: visored 4 of final 5
starts. *N. Tinkler*

PATSY GRIMES   7 b.m. Beveled (USA) – Blue Angel (Lord Gayle (USA) 124)   95
[1996 94: a7g³ a7g a6g² a7g⁴ a6g⁴ 6m* 6m 6.1d* 6g⁵ 7g* 7m 7m 6m* 6m 7m 1997
6m⁴ 6m⁶ 7.9g 6g 7d 7g⁶ 6m⁵ 5m² 5s² 5.6m 5.2g 5g* 6m 5v³ 6g 6.1d Oct 30] leggy
mare: useful handicapper: gained deserved success at Haydock in September: effective at 5f to 7f: acts on any going: effective blinkered/visored, though not tried for
long time: often apprentice ridden: usually comes from behind: tough and consistent.
J. S. Moore

PAYASO   3 b.g. Midyan (USA) 124 – Sugar Plum Fairy 91 (Sadler's Wells (USA)   –
132) [1996 NR 1997 10m 10g Aug 27] 13,000Y: fourth foal: half-brother to fairly
useful 1¼m winner (also useful hurdler) Country Star (by Persian Bold): dam winner
at up to 11f: no sign of ability. *R. M. Stronge*

PAY HOMAGE   9 ch.g. Primo Dominie 121 – Embraceable Slew (USA) (Seattle   72
Slew (USA)) [1996 81: 8m 8g⁴ 8.5m⁶ 8.9m 8m⁵ 10.2m³ 9f 9g² 10.2f⁵ 9m³ 1997 12m
10.8m³ 10g 10.8m⁵ 10s 9m⁶ 12.5m² 12v³ 12m⁶ 11.7f* 12.1g⁵ 11.7m⁴ 10.2g 10m
Oct 1] workmanlike gelding: fair performer: won minor event at Bath in July: seems
best around 1½m nowadays: best form on good going or firmer: blinkered/visored
earlier in career: held up: often ridden by inexperienced apprentice, best efforts with
stronger handling. *I. A. Balding*

PAY ON RED (USA)   2 br.c. (Feb 18) Red Ransom (USA) – Mo Jo Kate (USA)   74
(Mr Leader (USA)) [1997 7d 7g⁵ 6m³ 8g⁵ 7v³ Oct 10] $55,000Y: tall, close-coupled
colt: first foal: dam won up to 9f in USA: fair form in maidens and nurseries: should
stay at least 1m: acts on good to firm and heavy going. *P. F. I. Cole*

PC'S CRUISER (IRE)   5 b.g. Homo Sapien 121 – Ivy Holme (Silly Season 127)   40
[1996 51: a8g³ a8g a8g⁵ a10g a8g⁴ 7.1g² 8m² 6.9g 7g² a7g⁴ a8g³ 8m a7g a8g* 8.3g
a8g⁶ 8m⁴ a8g⁴ a8g 1997 a11g a8g⁵ 10.3d a11g⁴ a9.4g⁵ a7g a7g⁴ a7g⁵ a8.5g 8.3g⁴ Aug
4] sturdy gelding: poor performer: left J. L. Eyre after reappearance: stays 1m: acts
on fibresand (below form only run on equitrack) and good to firm ground: effective
blinkered/visored or not: tends to start slowly. *N. P. Littmoden*

PEACE AND QUIET   3 ch.f. Niniski (USA) 125 – Quiet Harbour (Mill Reef   56
(USA) 141) [1996 NR 1997 8.3g⁵ Jul 7] half-sister to several winners, including
fairly useful Count Basie (1¼m, by Batshoof) and useful Irish performer Jazz Ballet
(up to 11f, by Jaazeiro): dam lightly-raced half-sister to good middle-distance horses
Peacetime and Quiet Fling: fifth in steadily-run maiden at Windsor: bred to be suited
by at least 1¼m: sold 40,000 gns in December. *I. A. Balding*

PEACEFULL REPLY (USA)   7 b.h. Hold Your Peace (USA) – Drone Answer   –
(USA) (Drone) [1996 54d: a8.5g a11g a7g² a8g a7g 7g 8m a7g 7.1g 8f 8m a8g a6s⁵
a6g⁵ 1997 a7g 6g 6.9m Aug 4] no form at 7 yrs. *F. H. Lee*

PEACEFUL REIGN   2 ch.g. (Apr 4) King's Signet (USA) 110 – Consistent   –
Queen 55 (Queen's Hussar 124) [1997 6g Jun 27] 4,800F, 10,000Y: half-brother to
several winners, including 1995 2-y-o 6f and 7f winner Oriel Lad (by Colmore Row)
and 1½m winner Lifetimes Ambition (by Hotfoot): dam 1m seller winner: burly,
behind in seller at Newcastle: sold 500 gns in August. *Mrs J. R. Ramsden*

PEACEFUL SARAH   2 b.f. (Feb 22) Sharpo 132 – Red Gloves 83 (Red God   55 ?
128§) [1997 6f 6s⁴ 6m Oct 31] 18,000Y: leggy, angular filly: sister to fairly useful
winners Red Nymph (at 6f at 2 yrs in 1995) and Takdeer (at 6f and 1m) and half-sister
to 2 winners: dam, placed here at 2 yrs, later successful in Norway: apparently best
effort in maidens in steadily-run race at Newmarket final start. *P. Mooney*

PEAK PATH (IRE)   2 b.c. (Apr 6) Polish Precedent (USA) 131 – Road To The   84 p
Top 84 (Shirley Heights 130) [1997 7.1m³ Sep 16] eighth foal: closely related to
1½m winner Green Lane (by Green Desert) and half-brother to 3 winners, including

PEA

smart 7f/1m winner Painter's Row (by Royal Academy): dam 1¼m winner, from
good family: 9/1 from 7/2, promising 7 lengths third of 13 to emphatic winner
Abreeze in maiden at Sandown, starting slowly but running on strongly: will be
suited by further than 7f: sure to improve a fair bit, and should win races. *M. R. Stoute*

PEARL ANNIVERSARY (IRE) 4 ch.g. Priolo (USA) 127 – Tony Award –
(USA) (Kirtling 129) [1996 –, a59: 10g⁶ a12g* 11.1m a16g⁴ a12g* a14.8g² 14.1f⁵ a50
a13g⁴ 14.1m⁵ a12g² a16g³ a12g² a14.8g⁵ 1997 a14.8g a14.8g² a12g* Dec 26] leggy,
lengthy gelding: modest performer: easily best of 3 runs at Wolverhampton very late
in 1997 when second in seller: stays 2m: best efforts on fibresand. *Miss S. J. Wilton*

PEARL DAWN (IRE) 7 b.m. Jareer (USA) 115 – Spy Girl (Tanfirion 110) [1996 59
73d, a–: a6g a6g a6g 6f² 6m 5.7m⁵ 6g⁴ 7f⁵ 8f* 7f⁵ 7g 6f⁴ 6.9g 8f⁴ 7f 7.1s 1997 6f⁵ 8f a–
7m a10g 5m² 8f 5m⁵ 5m 7m⁶ 6.9m³ 7f⁶ 7m⁵ 6m 7m³ 10g³ Aug 27] sparely-made
mare: modest performer at best: effective at 5f to 1m: acts on hard and dead ground,
well below form on the all-weather: none too consistent. *P. C. Clarke*

PEARL SILK 4 br.f. Cigar 68 – Purrlea Atoll (Gulf Pearl 117) [1996 NR 1997 –
10d 8m⁵ a9.4g Aug 16] third foal: dam no form: seems of little account. *T. T. Bill*

PEARL VENTURE 5 b.m. Salse (USA) 128 – Our Shirley 84 (Shirley Heights –
130) [1996 80: 8s 8.1g 10.3m⁶ 8.5m 14.4g² 14.9f² 16.4g* 18.7m 14m⁵ 18.2m⁴ 16.2m
16s 16g 1997 12g⁴ Apr 19] lengthy, angular mare: fair handicapper: below form only
outing at 5 yrs: best form at 1¾m to 2¼m: probably acts on any going: blinkered/
visored (ran poorly) once each: best with waiting tactics. *S. P. C. Woods*

PEARLY QUEEN 2 ch.f. (Apr 14) Superlative 118 – Miss Kimmy (Tower Walk 51
130) [1997 6m a5g⁵ a6g⁴ a5g³ Dec 22] 2,200Y: half-sister to 1985 2-y-o 6f winner
Mischievous Lad (by Riboboy), later successful in Hong Kong, and 2 other winners
abroad: dam unraced: modest form: best effort when fourth in maiden at Lingfield in
December: should stay 7f: slowly away all starts. *G. C. Bravery*

PEARTREE HOUSE (IRE) 3 b.c. Simply Majestic (USA) – Fashion Front 100
(Habitat 134) [1996 87: 6m⁴ 6m* 6g⁴ 7m* 8m⁶ 1997 8g² 8d* 8g 7m⁶ 8m⁵ 8m 8g³ 8d⁴
Sep 20] rangy, workmanlike colt: useful performer: won minor event at Doncaster in
May by a length from Dokos: stiff tasks afterwards, creditable sixth in Jersey Stakes
at Royal Ascot: stays 1m: acts on dead ground and good to firm: has been bandaged
behind: sometimes carries head high, and gives impression ideally suited by waiting
tactics. *W. R. Muir*

PECAN PRINCESS (IRE) 4 b.f. Prince Rupert (FR) 121 – Route Royale (Roi –
Soleil 125) [1996 NR 1997 7f May 1] half-sister to several winners, including stayer
Little Big (by Indian King): dam never ran: no promise in seller. *C. A. Smith*

PEDALTOTHEMETAL (IRE) 5 b.m. Nordico (USA) – Full Choke 77 50
(Shirley Heights 130) [1996 50: a12g² a11g⁶ 12m 16.4m 17.2m⁴ 17.2f² 15.1m⁵ 14m
1997 a16g² a16g Jan 27] angular mare: modest maiden handicapper: stays 17f: acts
on firm ground and the all-weather: tried blinkered: held up. *P. Mitchell*

PEDRO (IRE) 2 b.c. (Mar 7) Brief Truce (USA) 126 – Mrs Fisher (IRE) 94 79 p
(Salmon Leap (USA) 131) [1997 7m a8.5g* a7g⁵ Oct 6] good-topped colt: second
foal: dam 7f winner, including at 2 yrs: won maiden at Wolverhampton in September:
not discredited in nursery there 16 days later (had also shown promise on turf on
debut): stays 8.5f: should do better. *Sir Mark Prescott*

PEEP O DAY 6 b.m. Domynsky 110 – Betrothed (Aglojo 119) [1996 45: a16g –
15.1m² 10.1m 12.1s* a14g 1997 12m 12.1g 12s⁶ 12s⁵ Nov 6] poor handicapper:
soundly beaten at 6 yrs. *J. L. Eyre*

PEGASUS BAY 6 b.g. Tina's Pet 121 – Mossberry Fair 28 (Mossberry 97) [1996 69
NR 1997 8m² 10.8d³ 8.1g⁵ 10.1f* 10g² a7g* a10g⁵ Nov 6] 5,200 5-y-o: second foal:
dam won over hurdles: modest winning hurdler in 1996/7: fair performer: won seller
at Yarmouth in September and strongly-run minor event at Lingfield in October:
better than position suggests final start: effective at 7f to 1¼m: acts on firm going and
equitrack. *Mrs A. Johnson*

PEGNITZ (USA) 2 b.c. (Apr 17) Lear Fan (USA) 130 – Likely Split (USA) 100 p
(Little Current (USA)) [1997 7m² 7g⁵ Oct 18] 46,000Y: tall, unfurnished colt: looked
weak at 2 yrs: half-brother to 3 winners abroad, including a 2-y-o in USA by Leo

Castelli: dam French maiden half-sister to very smart French sprinters Cricket Ball and Ancient Regime: 2 lengths second to Mudeer in £12,000 event at Ascot, considerately handled against more experienced rival: 50/1, again shaped well when 11¾ lengths fifth of 7 to Xaar in Dewhurst Stakes at Newmarket, travelling strongly to past halfway and not knocked about as faded: should stay 1m: very much the type to do well from 2 yrs to 3 yrs, and looks sure to win races. *C. E. Brittain*

PEINTRE CELEBRE (USA)   3 ch.c. Nureyev (USA) 131 – Peinture Bleue   137
(USA) (Alydar (USA)) [1996 8g* 8m³ 1997 10.5g* 12m* 10s* 12m² 12f*
Oct 5]

For the second year in succession, the winner of the Prix de l'Arc de Triomphe drew comparisons with Sea Bird II, whose crushing victory over the 1965 Arc field remains, by common consent, one of the greatest performances in racing history. The recently-published *Favourite Racehorses*, which contains a selection of the best reading from fifty years of the Timeform Annuals, leaves no doubt about the impression Sea Bird made at the time. Sea Bird's achievements—he won all five of his races in 1965, including the Derby without coming off the bit—begin a chapter on 'The Greats'. 'The greatest performance by any horse in my time' and 'something quite out of this world' were the views of the respected journalists reporting the Arc for the *Sporting Chronicle* and *The Sporting Life* respectively. Sea Bird's jockey summed him up as 'by far the best horse I have ever seen—let alone ridden'. These views were echoed the racing world over and Sea Bird earned a Timeform rating of 145, the benchmark by which great horses, when they have come along, have been judged ever since. Five of the twenty runners in Sea Bird's Arc were Derby winners, including Reliance, who had won the Prix du Jockey-Club, Meadow Court the Irish Derby and Tom Rolfe the American, and there wasn't an older horse in Europe whose absence could be said to diminish the field significantly. Sea Bird made the opposition look ordinary, coming away in the straight to win by six lengths from Reliance, suffering the only defeat of his career. Reliance's superiority over the remainder was as overwhelming as that of Sea Bird over him; he had five lengths to spare over the Prix du Jockey-Club runner-up Diatome, who went on to defeat representatives of America, Canada, Argentina and England in the Washington International on his next start, and to win further good races at four.

The performances of Sea Bird, Reliance and Diatome underlined the superlative excellence of the 1965 French classic crop. The 1997 crop—with the notable exception of Peintre Celebre—was anything but vintage and there

United Arab Emirates Prix du Jockey-Club, Chantilly—
Peintre Celebre, giving his owner and trainer their first triumph in the race, is an emphatic winner;
Oscar is about to overhaul Astarabad for second place

Grand Prix de Paris, Longchamp—
Peintre Celebre completes the Prix du Jockey-Club–Grand Prix de Paris double
last achieved in 1971; Ithaki and Shaka finish closer to the winner than in the Jockey-Club

were only three French-trained three-year-olds in the Arc line-up. They were the first and second in the Prix Vermeille, Queen Maud and Gazelle Royale, and Peintre Celebre, the only three-year-old colt in the field. There were three others of the age group among the eighteen runners, Germany's leading fillies Borgia and Que Belle being joined by the Irish Oaks winner Ebadiyla. All the evidence pointed to Peintre Celebre being by some way the best of the three-year-olds in the Arc. He had won both the Prix du Jockey-Club and the Grand Prix de Paris (a rare double also completed by Reliance when the Grand Prix was run over one mile and seven furlongs and a more important race than it is now) before suffering his first defeat of the season in unfortunate circumstances in the Prix Niel.

After winning a minor event and finishing third in the Prix des Chenes at two, Peintre Celebre had come into serious reckoning for the Prix du Jockey-Club with a two-length success over Astarabad in the Prix Greffulhe at Longchamp on his reappearance. There was a similar distance between the pair when they were split by the Prix Hocquart runner-up Oscar in the United Arab Emirates Prix du Jockey-Club, the first three pulling clear of the rest. Peintre Celebre started favourite at Chantilly and produced a late burst under strong pressure to gain an emphatic two-length win. Peintre Celebre was the first Prix du Jockey-Club winner for both his owner and trainer. Andre Fabre at first announced that the King George VI and Queen Elizabeth Stakes was on the agenda. Plans were changed in favour of a traditional French preparation for the Arc after Peintre Celebre's straightforward victory in the Grand Prix de Paris, in which he didn't have to reproduce his best to win from the Jockey-Club fifth and sixth Ithaki and Shaka. What looked a simple task for Peintre Celebre in his Arc trial, the Prix Niel at Longchamp in September, turned into something of a nightmare for his rider Olivier Peslier, who couldn't secure a clear passage in the five-runner field until too late. Once extricated, Peintre Celebre showed a tremendous turn of speed which all but got him home. Tempers flared as Peslier accused Cash Asmussen of deliberately keeping him in—but connections accepted the result with a Gallic shrug of the shoulders. 'This is the Prix Niel, not the Arc,' was Fabre's response.

The supposed acrimony between Peslier and Asmussen was said by Peslier to have stemmed from Asmussen's losing the ride on Helissio, on whom Peslier had won the Arc twelve months earlier. Peslier was bound by contract to ride for Peintre Celebre's owners in the latest season and, after Peslier had partnered Helissio to victory in the Prix Ganay on his reappearance, Asmussen rode him to an effortless victory in the Grand Prix de Saint-Cloud and a third in the King George VI and Queen Elizabeth Stakes. With Asmussen on Spinning World, Peslier rode Helissio in his tune-up race for the Arc, the one-mile Prix du Moulin, after which, despite being beaten three lengths by Spinning World, Helissio retained ante-post favouritism for the Arc. Helissio's position as favourite came under threat on the weekend of the Prix Niel, Peintre Celebre displacing him in Hill's book and Pilsudski, impressive in the Irish Champion Stakes at Leopardstown, becoming favourite with Ladbroke (most other main bookmakers stuck with Helissio). Peintre Celebre and Helissio started first and second favourite respectively on the pari mutuel as the French public backed them to keep the Arc at home. The leading British-trained challengers Swain and Pilsudski, first and second in the King George, had both finished in the frame behind Helissio in the 1996 Arc, along with the dual Irish St Leger winner Oscar Schindler. The overseas fillies' challenge was made up to four by the British-trained Yorkshire Oaks winner My Emma, whose preparation had been interrupted by a fall on the gallops.

Helissio, who'd made all the running for his most impressive victory the previous year, was soon vying for the lead with the British outsider Busy Flight in a very strongly-run race. After going a couple of lengths clear in the middle part of the race, he looked, for a time at least, as if he might stage a repeat. Peintre Celebre was niggled along from early on and had more in front of him than behind as the field turned for home. Switched from the rails after looking short of room at one point, Peintre Celebre began to make striking progress and reached the leading group with a furlong and a half to run. Bursting past Helissio and the always-handy Swain, Peintre Celebre quickly drew clear and, kept firmly up to the mark under hands and heels, won by an official margin of five lengths (we made it four). Pilsudski kept on very well for second again, decisively beating the remainder; there were two and a half lengths (again we made it slightly less) back to a blanket finish for third, Borgia coming from well back to snatch it from another strong finisher, Oscar Schindler, with Predappio, up there all the way, Helissio and Swain also involved in the photo. Peintre Celebre's dramatic victory was achieved in a record time for the race, 2m 24.6sec, over a second and a half inside the previous best, set in 1987 under similar circumstances—a cracking gallop from the start and firm conditions underfoot—by another Fabre-trained winner, Trempolino.

Peintre Celebre gave Andre Fabre his fourth Prix de l'Arc winner, following Trempolino, Subotica and Carnegie, and, at first, the trainer was reluctant to place him ahead of Trempolino ('such a great horse on the day he won his Arc'). Not surprisingly, however, Fabre's considered view is that

Prix de l'Arc de Triomphe, Longchamp—
a magnificent performance from Peintre Celebre, who shatters the course record;
Pilsudski takes the runner-up spot for the second successive year, officially five lengths behind the winner

Peintre Celebre is the best middle-distance horse he has trained (when discussing Xaar, he said he was better than Zafonic but not so good as Peintre Celebre!). In our view, Peintre Celebre's supreme performance in the Arc was clearly the best by a horse trained in Europe in 1997 and one of the best at middle distances in recent times. We cannot recall, since Sea Bird, a three-year-old ending the season rated so far in front of the rest of the classic generation (Desert King, 8 lb behind Peintre Celebre, was Timeform's second highest three-year-old of 1997). The form of the Arc looks rock-solid. Pilsudski was successful afterwards in the Champion Stakes and the Japan Cup and Borgia was a good second in the Breeders' Cup Turf. Peintre Celebre wasn't seen out again but he remains in training and his future looks bright indeed.

The close-coupled, quite attractive Peintre Celebre, who was bandaged behind on all his starts during the latest season, is a product of the Wildenstein racing empire. He became the fourth Arc winner—following Allez France, All Along and Sagace—to carry the colours of French art dealer and collector Daniel Wildenstein, whose private stud book in 1997 listed one hundred and nineteen horses in training, thirty-eight yearlings and sixty-five mares at stud. Peintre Celebre is a product of the American branch of the breeding operation, though, before being sent into training in France, he was partly reared at a stud in Yorkshire where some of the Wildenstein foals and yearlings from America are sent. According to Alec Wildenstein, whose functions in the family's racing set-up include planning the matings, 'Yorkshire is an extremely cold place and we think the horses need that to toughen them up, it's good for their bones' (some at Timeform wouldn't disagree with that first bit!).

Daniel Wildenstein's "Peintre Celebre"

Peintre Celebre's dam, Peinture Bleue, is one of three minor pattern winners produced by Petroleuse, a half-sister to the Wildensteins' Oaks, Prix de Diane and King George winner Pawneese (who, incidentally, died in March, having produced not a single 'black-type' performer in a lengthy career at stud). Petroleuse showed more speed than stamina, winning the Blue Seal Stakes at Ascot as a two-year-old and the Princess Elizabeth Stakes over an extended mile at Epsom at three before being sent to the United States. Stamina was the long suit, though, of her daughter Peinture Bleue, who gained her most important wins in the Prix Charles Laffitte over a mile and a quarter at Long-champ and a division of the Long Island Handicap over a mile and a half at Belmont Park. Peinture Bleue remained in America after her racing days were over and Peintre Celebre is her second foal. Her first, a colt by Steinlen called Pareo Bleu, has failed to win in just two runs in France, but Peintre Celebre's owner-breeders have a year-younger full sister to Peintre Celebre, called Pine Chip, in training. Peinture Bleue also has a yearling filly, Peace Signal (by Time For A Change), and a filly foal, Pyramid Lake (by Broad Brush), and visited Kingmambo in 1997, underlining the fact that repeat matings for the Wilden-stein mares are not usual. The mating of Peinture Bleue with Nureyev is, however, surely one that will be repeated again. Peintre Celebre's Arc victory provided Nureyev with his hundreth European pattern-race victory as a sire; Sadler's Wells, Habitat and Northern Dancer are the only other members of 'the hundred club'. Habitat, the sire of Peintre Celebre's grandam Petroleuse, also has an outstanding record as a sire of broodmares, no fewer than sixty of his daughters having now produced a pattern-race winner in Europe.

	Nureyev (USA) (b 1977)	Northern Dancer (b 1961)	Nearctic Natalma
Peintre Celebre (USA) (ch.c. 1994)		Special (b 1969)	Forli Thong
	Peinture Bleue (USA) (ch 1987)	Alydar (ch 1975)	Raise A Native Sweet Tooth
		Petroleuse (b 1978)	Habitat Plencia

Peintre Celebre will eventually stand at one of the studs run by Coolmore, who bought a fifty percent stake in him before the Arc. Before that, however, he will have the chance to enhance his claims to be regarded as one of 'the greats'. He is suited by a mile and a half and acts on firm and soft going. If Peintre Celebre has a fault it is that he tends to race lazily in the early part of his races—'he's a little cold and needs warming up', says his jockey—but, once opened out, he can produce an outstanding turn of foot. *A. Fabre, France*

PEKAY 4 b.g. Puissance 110 – K-Sera 95 (Lord Gayle (USA) 124) [1996 11g⁵ 9.5g⁴ 11d² 10d⁴ 11g 1997 a9.4g 8.2g³ 10g⁵ 9.2m* 8.5m³ 8f² 9.2m⁶ 10g² 8.3m² 8.3g 8.5f 10.4d⁴ 10.9s* 10g⁴ 12g³ Oct 25] leggy gelding: ran in Britain as 2-y-o: fairly useful in Germany for B. Schutz in 1996: fair handicapper in Britain: won at Hamilton in June and Ayr in October: stays 1½m: acts on good to firm and soft ground: usually held up: sold 32,000 gns, and winning hurdler with M. Pipe. *M. Johnston* 78

PELAGOS (FR) 2 gr.c. (Feb 20) Exit To Nowhere (USA) 122 – Southern Maid (USA) (Northern Dancer) [1997 7g⁶ 8s⁶ Oct 14] close-coupled, angular colt: half-brother to numerous winners, including French listed winner Scarlet Flutter (by Beldale Flutter): dam unraced daughter of useful French 7f and 1m performer Midou: sixth of 17 to Dr Fong in steadily-run maiden at Newbury: well below that form on softer ground at Leicester 4 weeks later, off bridle long way out: should stay at least 1m. *R. Charlton* 76

PELHAM (IRE) 3 b.c. Archway (IRE) 115 – Yavarro 44 (Raga Navarro (ITY) 119) [1996 92: 5.2d 5.1g* 5.1g² 6m⁴ 6f* 6f⁵ 6m² 6g³ 7m³ 6m 1997 8m⁶ 8g* 8m⁶ 5m 7g 9m 7m 8.2m Dec 3] useful-looking colt: useful performer: won listed race (by 4 lengths from Groom's Gordon) at Kempton in March: creditable 3 lengths sixth behind Desert Story in Craven Stakes at Newmarket: raced in Hong Kong thereafter 104 under the name Winning Scene, showing just fair form: stays 1m: acts on firm ground. *P. C. Kan, Hong Kong*

PEMBERLEY (IRE) 3 b.g. Taufan (USA) 119 – Miss Darcy (IRE) (Glow (USA)) [1996 NR 1997 10m⁶ 8.5s⁶ 7.6m 12g 10m Aug 16] IR 13,000F, IR 20,000Y: first foal: dam Irish 2m winner, half-sister to Jersey Stakes winner Rasa Penang: no worthwhile form, including in a seller: sold, and sent to Kuwait. *W. J. Haggas* —

PENDOLINO (IRE) 6 b.g. Thatching 131 – Pendulina 102 (Prince Tenderfoot (USA) 126) [1996 43: 11.9m 10m⁴ 10m⁶ 11.1g⁴ 12m⁴ 1997 10.1g³ 12.3m* 10m* 10d Apr 26] lengthy gelding: has a markedly round action: modest handicapper: won at Ripon (20-runner seller) and Pontefract in April: effective at 1¼m to 1½m: acts on good to firm going: used often to be blinkered, not in 1997. *M. Brittain* 50

PEN FRIEND 3 b.g. Robellino (USA) 127 – Nibbs Point (IRE) 107 (Sure Blade (USA) 130) [1996 NR 1997 8m⁶ 8.2m a8g⁶ 11.5m⁴ 16.2m* 16g³ 16m* 16m⁴ 16.1m² Oct 1] 19,000Y: workmanlike gelding: fluent mover: first foal: dam, 1¼m and 1½m winner, stayed 2m: modest handicapper: won at Beverley (maiden event) in July and Thirsk (made most) in August: also first past the post at Newcastle final start, but demoted for causing minor interference: will stay beyond 2m: yet to race on going softer than good: game and consistent: should go on again at 4 yrs. *W. J. Haggas* 62 p

PENGAMON 5 b.h. Efisio 120 – Dolly Bevan 53 (Another Realm 118) [1996 88: a7g³ a7g a8g* 8s 7g² 8.1g⁵ 7.6g⁶ 7g² 8m 1997 a7g a8.5g 7g a8g* a8g³ 7.1m 7d 7s⁶ 7m Jul 22] smallish well-made horse: carries condition: fairly useful handicapper: won at Lingfield in May: creditable efforts next 2 starts: effective at 7f to 1m: acts on firm going and the all-weather: usually held up. *H. J. Collingridge* 80

PENLOP 3 b.g. Mac's Imp (USA) 116 – Marton Maid 74 (Silly Season 127) [1996 64: 7g 6g⁵ 7.6m 1997 5g 6.1m 7f⁵ a6g³ a8g* 8g⁴ 8d a9.4g 8d⁴ Oct 13] leggy gelding: fair performer: won claimer (easily) at Southwell in May: left B. Meehan after next start: better at 1m than shorter: acts on fibresand and good to firm and dead ground: effective blinkered or not: has looked none too keen. *A. C. Stewart* 62 a66

PENNILESS (IRE) 2 b.f. (Apr 27) Common Grounds 118 – Tizzy 79 (Formidable (USA) 125) [1997 5m⁴ 5g* 5.1d 5g³ 5g* 5m⁶ 5m⁵ 7g 6.1d a6g a5g Dec 8] IR 11,000Y: close-coupled filly: has a round action: half-sister to 3 winners, including fairly useful 1989 2-y-o 5f winner La Galerie (by Glenstal) and 3-y-o Banana (by Primo Dominie), successful at 6f in Denmark: dam 9f and 1¼m winner: won minor event at Thirsk in April (easily best effort) and claimer at Beverley in June: speedy: best efforts on good/good to soft ground. *N. Tinkler* 74 d

PENNY PEPPERMINT 5 b. or br.m. Move Off 112 – Cheeky Pigeon (Brave Invader (USA)) [1996 –: 12f⁶ 12m 12m⁶ 15.8g 1997 11f⁶ 15.8m⁶ 14g 17.2m³ 16m⁶ 15.8g⁴ 17.2f² 18d⁴ Sep 2] leggy mare: poor maiden handicapper: out-and-out stayer. *R. E. Barr* 31

PENNYS FROM HEAVEN 3 gr.c. Generous (IRE) 139 – Heavenly Cause (USA) (Grey Dawn II 132) [1996 84p: 7m 8m³ 1997 11.1m⁴ 11.6s⁴ 12g³ 10.2s⁵ 10.8m³ 14m 11.7m* 12d² 12m⁶ 11.8d Oct 13] tall colt: fairly useful handicapper: won at Bath (idled) in August: carried across course in straight when second in falsely-run minor event at Goodwood, easily best of last 3 starts: best around 1½m: acts on good to firm and soft ground: blinkered fifth start: often used to make running, held up latterly: sold 36,000 gns after final start. *H. Candy* 81

PENNYWELL 3 b.f. Nicholas (USA) 111 – Fee 111 (Mandamus 120) [1996 NR 1997 a9.4g² a8.5g* 10.3m 8.2m² 8.2d⁶ a8g* a7g³ 8f* 8f⁶ a10s⁴ 9f Dec 27] angular filly: half-sister to several winners, including Tart (by Tragic Role), fairly useful winner at 8.5f (2 yrs) and 11.4f: dam, French 1¼m winner (stayed 1½m), from good family: fair performer: won maiden at Wolverhampton in February, minor event at Lingfield (penultimate start for R. F. Johnson Houghton) in June and claimer at Del Mar in September: effective at 7f to 9.4f: acts on firm ground and all-weather. *T. Pinfield, USA* 65

PENNY WHISTLE 2 b.f. (Apr 2) Clantime 101 – Penny Hasset 73 (Lochnager 132) [1997 5g 5d 5d Sep 18] compact filly: first foal: dam winning sprinter: appeared to show modest form in slowly-run race on debut, but well beaten afterwards, in seller final start. *T. D. Easterby* ?

PENROSE (IRE)   2 ch.f. (May 16) Wolfhound (USA) 126 – Mill Path (Mill Reef   75 p
(USA) 141) [1997 7m⁵ Sep 9] half-sister to useful 6f (at 2 yrs) and 7f winner Queen's
View (by Lomond) and 3-y-o Desert Track: dam once-raced half-sister to Irish Oaks
winner Give Thanks, an excellent family; 25/1 from 10/1, 6½ lengths fifth of 15 to
Jibe in maiden at Lingfield, free and not knocked about: will improve. *B. W. Hills*

PENSION FUND   3 b.g. Emperor Fountain 112 – Navarino Bay 102 (Averof 123)   84
[1996 78: 5m 5g⁵ 5m 5m* 5f³ 7m* 8m⁶ 1997 8g 8d 9.9s 8s 9m 7g² 8m² 8d 7g 11m²
9.9d* 11.9g² Aug 21] tall, leggy gelding: fairly useful handicapper: won at Beverley
in August: best effort when second at York 8 days later: stays 1½m: acts on firm and
dead ground (not in much form when well beaten on soft): none too easy a ride
(pulled hard in blinkers ninth start), goes well held up. *M. W. Easterby*

PENTAD (USA)   3 b.c. Quest For Fame 127 – Nifty Fifty (USA) (Honey Jay   111
(USA)) [1996 NR 1997 11g⁴ 11.7g* 12g² 14g* 15m⁶ 12g⁵ Oct 25] strong, angular
colt: third foal: half-brother to stakes-winning 2-y-o sprinters in USA by Silver Ghost
and Country Pine: dam, won 3 times in USA, half-sister to several stakes winners:
smart performer: won maiden at Bath in June and listed race at Goodwood (set steady
gallop when beating Palio Sky ½ length) in August: better of last 2 runs when fifth to
Kaliana in St Simon Stakes at Newbury: stays 1¾m (weakened near end of 15f):
raced only on good/good to firm ground: stays in training. *R. Charlton*

PENYGARN GUV'NOR   4 b.g. Governor General 116 – Alumia (Great Nephew   –
126) [1996 –: 8g 9.9m⁵ a8.5g⁴ 1997 7g Aug 1] of little account. *J. M. Bradley*

PEOPLE DIRECT   4 ch.f. Ron's Victory (USA) 129 – Ayr Classic (Local Suitor   –
(USA) 128) [1996 –, a63: a8g* a8g³ a8g* a8g² a8g* a8.5g⁶ a7g* a7g³ a8g² a8g⁶   a64
a8g 8.5g⁶ a8.5g* a7g³ a8.5g⁴ a8g 1997 a8.5g a9.4g a8g a7g a8.5f* a8g² a8.5g* a7g
7.6m a8.5g Aug 16] sparely-made filly: modest performer, campaigned almost
exclusively on the all-weather: won claimer at Wolverhampton in June (final start for
K. McAuliffe) and handicap there in July: stays 8.5f: best form on fibresand, well
beaten on equitrack: usually front runner. *N. P. Littmoden*

PEPPERS (IRE)   4 b.f. Bluebird (USA) 125 – Pepilin (Coquelin (USA) 121)   70
[1996 71: 10d 10.3g 9g² a9.4g⁶ 1997 10m³ 10d² 10s⁴ 10m⁶ 10d⁵ 11.9d² 11.7f³ 12m⁴
6.9f 10d⁵ Sep 19] angular filly: fair maiden handicapper: generally good efforts at 4
yrs: stays 1½m: acts on firm and dead ground, probably soft: visored penultimate
start: may prove best with waiting tactics. *K. R. Burke*

PEPPIATT   3 ch.c. Efisio 120 – Fleur du Val (Valiyar 129) [1996 NR 1997 6m*   88
7d² 7f* Jul 12] 15,000Y: third foal: dam unraced half-sister to Superpower: fairly
useful form: won maiden at Folkestone in April and handicap at Lingfield (flashed
tail) in July: runner-up to Snow Kid in minor event at Salisbury in between: stays 7f:
sold 18,000 gns in October. *R. Akehurst*

PERANG POLLY   5 br.m. Green Ruby (USA) 104 – Perang Peggy (Bay Express   63 d
132) [1996 60: 7g⁴ a8g 1997 a7g² a7g³ 8g 8.2g May 23] lightly-raced maiden: easily
best effort when second at Lingfield in February: likely to prove best up to 1m:
visored last 2 outings: broke blood vessel final start at 4 yrs. *Lord Huntingdon*

PERCHANCE TO DREAM (IRE)   3 b.f. Bluebird (USA) 125 – Foliage   –
(Thatching 131) [1996 54: 6f 6m 5.7d 1997 5.7d 5m 7d 8.3g 8.3m 8.3m⁶ Jul 28]
heavy-topped filly: modest form around 6f at 2 yrs: disappointing in 1997: blinkered
final start. *B. R. Millman*

PERCY   2 ch.g. (May 25) Precocious 126 – Manna Green (Bustino 136) [1997 6f   49
5v 6m a6g³ a7g 7m⁶ a7g² Oct 20] leggy gelding: half-brother to several winners,   a56
including at around 1½m by Belfort and Bairn: dam ran twice: modest maiden:
trained first 5 starts by J. Bottomley: placed in claimer and seller at Southwell: stays
7f: acts on fibresand. *J. Hetherton*

PERCY ISLE (IRE)   3 br.c. Doyoun 124 – Percy's Girl (IRE) 103 (Blakeney   86
126) [1996 79: 8m 8.1s³ 8s³ 1997 12g² 12m* 12s³ 15d² 14g⁵ 12m³ 14g⁵ Aug 13]
small colt: fairly useful performer: made all and idled in maiden at Salisbury in May:
ran creditably in handicaps after: will stay 2m+: acts on good to firm and dead
ground, probably soft: possibly none too easy a ride: sold approx. £26,000 in Dubai
in November. *M. R. Stoute*

PERCY-P 2 ch.c. (Feb 21) Superpower 113 – Song's Best (Never So Bold 135) 78
[1997 5s⁵ 5m³ May 15] 12,000Y: useful-looking colt: fourth foal: brother to 5-y-o
Lennox Lewis (formerly useful): dam unraced half-sister to smart sprinter Reesh:
fair form when third in maiden at Salisbury. *W. R. Muir*

PERECAPA (IRE) 2 b.f. (Mar 9) Archway (IRE) 115 – Cupid Miss (Anita's –
Prince 126) [1997 a7g⁶ 7g Aug 11] second reported foal: half-sister to a 5f winner in
Italy by Fayruz: dam Irish 6f (at 2 yrs) and 1m winner: soundly beaten in maidens at
Southwell and Leicester. *B. Palling*

PERFECT ANGEL (IRE) 3 b.f. Maledetto (IRE) 103 – Blue Infanta (Chief –
Singer 131) [1996 –: 7m 7m 6m 8f 1997 a11g 10g 10.1f May 28] seems of little
account. *M. H. Tompkins*

PERFECT BEAR 3 b.g. Wing Park 104 – Sarah Bear (Mansingh (USA) 120) –
[1996 –: 6g⁵ 1997 7.1d 7g 10m Aug 16] good-topped gelding: well beaten in varied
company, including selling. *Mrs S. J. Smith*

PERFECT BERTIE (IRE) 5 b.g. Cyrano de Bergerac 120 – Perfect Chance 83 33
(Petorius 117) [1996 NR 1997 13.1m 12.1m⁵ 12g Sep 2] poor maiden handicapper:
stays 1½m: acts on firm and soft ground: twice visored: tends to hang left and carry
head high: none too consistent. *N. M. Babbage*

PERFECT BRAVE 6 b.g. Indian Ridge 123 – Perfect Timing 107 (Comedy Star 56
(USA) 121) [1996 59, a75: a6g a6g² a5g² 5g⁶ a5g² 5g 5s a5g 1997 a5g⁵ a5g² a5g a5g⁵ a66
a5g a6g 5g⁵ a5g Jul 26] workmanlike gelding: fair handicapper on all-weather,
modest on turf: effective at 5f and 6f: acts on good to firm ground, heavy and
fibresand: has given trouble at stalls, and almost unseated rider leaving them final
start: usually races prominently. *J. Balding*

PERFECT HARMONY (IRE) 2 b.f. (Mar 3) Pips Pride 117 – Harmer (IRE) 64
72 (Alzao (USA) 117) [1997 5d² 5s³ 5.1g 6s 6g Oct 25] strong, lengthy filly:
third foal: half-sister to fairly useful 1995 2-y-o 5f winner Amaretto Bay (by Common Grounds), later winning sprinter abroad, and a 1m winner in Germany by Silver
Kite: dam stayed 7f: modest form in maidens and a nursery: running well when
brought down final start: sold 6,800 gns in December. *B. J. Meehan*

PERFECT LADY 2 gr.f. (Mar 11) Petong 126 – Petit Peu (IRE) (Kings Lake –
(USA) 133) [1997 6.1m 8.2g Oct 4] 12,500Y: second foal: sister to 3-y-o Silvery:
dam, ran once over hurdles in Ireland, half-sister to smart performer up to 1m
Petardia (by Petong): well beaten in maidens at Nottingham. *J. M. P. Eustace*

PERFECT PAL (IRE) 6 ch.g. Mulhollande (USA) 107 – Gone (Whistling Wind 73
123) [1996 NR 1997 a13g 7g² 6m⁴ 7.3g 7.1m⁵ 7g⁵ Aug 10] half-brother to 2 winning
jumpers by Green Shoon: dam maiden hurdler: won 2 NH Flat races in 1994/5: fair
maiden: should stay 1m: raced only on equitrack and good/good to firm going. *Miss
Gay Kelleway*

PERFECT PARADIGM (IRE) 3 b.c. Alzao (USA) 117 – Brilleaux 73 103 +
(Manado 130) [1996 79: 8m 10m² 8.1s² 1997 12.4m* 12.3s* 12m Jun 1] attractive
colt: has a round action: useful form: won maiden at Newcastle in March and handicap at Chester in May, in latter making all impressively: well beaten behind Peintre
Celebre in Prix du Jockey-Club at Chantilly in June, eased after disputing lead for
around 1¼m: will stay beyond 1½m: acts on good to firm and soft ground: stays in
training. *J. H. M. Gosden*

PERFECT PEACH 2 b.f. (Apr 1) Lycius (USA) 124 – Perfect Timing 107 78
(Comedy Star (USA) 121) [1997 5s⁶ 5m² 5g* 5d* 5m⁵ Aug 26] 20,000Y: quite
good-topped filly: half-sister to 6-y-o Perfect Brave and a winner abroad by Belfort:
dam sprinter: fair performer: won maiden at Thirsk and nursery at Beverley in
August: ran creditably final outing: speedy. *J. Berry*

PERFECT POPPY 3 b.f. Shareef Dancer (USA) 135 – Benazir 91 (High Top 57
131) [1996 73: 7.5m³ 8s⁴ 1997 a8.5g⁶ 8g 7m⁶ 7g³ 7f 7d 8m⁵ 7g⁶ 6.9m Sep 26]
deep-girthed filly: only modest at 3 yrs and left J. Fanshawe after sixth start: stays
1m: acts on good to firm and soft ground. *S. Dow*

PERFECT WAY 2 b.c. (May 25) Norton Challenger 111 – Russet Way 34 –
(Blushing Scribe (USA) 107) [1997 7m 8.2d Oct 8] second reported foal: dam third
in 5f seller from 2 starts at 2 yrs: no promise, including in a seller. *Mrs N. Macauley*

PERICLES 3 b.g. Primo Dominie 121 – Egalite (FR) (Luthier 126) [1996 71: 6m^2 80
6f^3 7m^2 a6g* 7g^6 7m^4 1997 6d 7g 7d* 7g^2 a7g* 7m a7g 7m^4 8g^2 7g 7s 7d^3 a6g^5 a7g* a87
8d a7g Nov 1] sturdy, close-coupled gelding: fairly useful performer: won handicaps
at Leicester and Wolverhampton in June and claimer at Wolverhampton (by 8
lengths, final start for M. Johnston) in October: best at 7f/easy 1m: acts on fibresand
and probably any turf going: often makes running: tail swisher. *Miss Gay Kelleway*

PERIDOT 2 b.f. (Mar 4) Green Desert (USA) 127 – Alinova (USA) 89 (Alleged –
(USA) 138) [1997 7d Oct 27] first foal: dam middle-distance stayer out of half-sister
to Zilzal, family also of Polish Precedent and Culture Vulture: 7/1 and very green,
last in maiden at Lingfield. *J. H. M. Gosden*

PERILOUS PLIGHT 6 ch.g. Siberian Express (USA) 125 – Loveskate (USA) 54 d
78 (Overskate (CAN)) [1996 66, a71: a7g^2 a8g^4 a7g^3 a10g^6 a8g* a7g^4 7f* 8g 7g^4 8f^4 a59 d
a8g^2 8.1f* 8g^3 7f 8m^2 7f* 7m^3 6.9m^3 7f^5 8.2g a7g^3 a7g^6 a7g 1997 a7g^6 a7g^4 a8g^3 6.9g
7.5m 6.9g 8m 7.5g 7g a10g Sep 9] lengthy, angular gelding: modest form early in
year but lost his way: left Mrs L. Stubbs after eighth start: stays 1m: acts on equitrack
(probably on fibresand), best efforts on turf on good going or firmer: visored final
outing. *A. Streeter*

PERLETHORPE 3 b.f. Anshan 119 – Naturally Fresh 91 (Thatching 131) [1996 57
NR 1997 7m^4 7g 6m 10s 12m^4 a12g^2 12g^4 16.4m^2 17.2f^3 14m Oct 1] 15,000Y: leggy, a60
close-coupled filly: seventh foal: half-sister to winners abroad by Valiyar and Petoski: dam 2-y-o 5f winner: modest maiden handicapper: stays 17f: acts on firm ground
and fibresand: sold 11,500 gns in October. *M. Bell*

PERPETUAL LIGHT 4 b.f. Petoski 135 – Butosky 71 (Busted 134) [1996 56, 45
a67: 8g^6 a8g* a11g a8g* 9.9m 10d 8g 9g 1997 a8g^6 a11g^4 8.2m 10.9d a9.4g* 8d a70
8.2d^6 a9.4g^3 Dec 6] quite good-topped filly: has a round action: fair handicapper on
the all-weather, poor on turf: won at Wolverhampton in October: stays 9.4f: goes well
on fibresand. *J. J. Quinn*

PERRYSTON VIEW 5 b.h. Primo Dominie 121 – Eastern Ember 85 (Indian 97
King (USA) 128) [1996 90: 6m^3 6m 5g 6m^4 6g 5.6m 5m 1997 6m* 6g 6m 6g 6g* 5g^2
Oct 25] lengthy, angular horse: has reportedly been hobdayed: useful handicapper:

Ladbroke (Ayr) Silver Cup (Handicap)—
with the visor back on, Perryston View makes virtually all;
Almasi is second with Hard To Figure and Kira (No. 12) leading home the far-side group

won valuable races at Newmarket in May and Ayr (Silver Cup) in September, making all to beat Almasi 1¼ lengths in latter: hampered start when good second at Doncaster final outing: effective at 5f and 6f: probably acts on any going: often visored, only last 2 starts at 5 yrs: used to hang under pressure: usually races prominently. *P. Calver*

PERSEPHONE 4 ch.f. Lycius (USA) 124 – Elarrih (USA) (Sharpen Up 127) – [1996 44?: 8.2m 9m 10.1m 8f 8m² 7g a7g 8.5g⁶ 8g 1997 7d 8.5s 7f 10m 8d 7d 8m 7g 7m 11.5m Oct 22] seems of little account. *C. N. Allen*

PERSEVERE 3 b.f. Pursuit of Love 124 – Seastream (USA) (Alleged (USA) 138) [1996 NR 1997 8d³ a7g⁴ 5.7g⁴ 7d 8.2d Oct 30] 8,000Y: leggy filly: first foal: dam placed up to 9f in France: modest maiden: well held last 2 starts: yet to race on going firmer than good. *Lord Huntingdon* 64

PERSIAN BLUE 3 b.f. Persian Bold 123 – Swift Pursuit 57 (Posse (USA) 130) [1996 –: 7m 1997 8.2d 10m 11.8g³ 11.4g 12g 12g³ 11.9g 12d Oct 21] close-coupled filly: modest maiden handicapper: stays 1½m well: unraced on extremes of going: may need waiting tactics. *R. Hannon* 64

PERSIAN BUD (IRE) 9 b. or br.g. Persian Bold 123 – Awakening Rose (Le Levanstell 122) [1996 –: 12s 1997 a13g⁴ a16g⁵ a14.8g a16g⁵ Feb 13] well-made gelding: poor handicapper: probably stays 2m: acts on good to firm and soft ground, probably on equitrack: tried visored. *M. R. Bosley* 28

PERSIAN BUTTERFLY 5 b.m. Dancing Dissident (USA) 119 – Butterfly Kiss 69 (Beldale Flutter (USA) 130) [1996 67d: 5d⁴ 6d 6m⁵ 6g 7.1m 6g 6g 10.2g 8g 1997 a10g 11.6m 12.5d⁶ Jun 24] good-bodied mare: formerly fair maiden: has lost her form. *R. M. Stronge* –

PERSIAN CONQUEST (IRE) 5 b.g. Don't Forget Me 127 – Alaroos (IRE) (Persian Bold 123) [1996 –, a67: 10m 12m 10d 10g 12d a12g* a12g⁶ a10g* a13g a12g³ 1997 a13g* a12g* a12g² a12g* Feb 20] smallish gelding: poor mover: fair performer on all-weather: justified favouritism in claimers at Lingfield in January (2) and February: stays 13f: no form on turf since 3 yrs: blinkered: usually races prominently. *R. Ingram* a70

PERSIAN DAWN 4 br.f. Anshan 119 – Visible Form 99 (Formidable (USA) 125) [1996 –: 8g 10m 8g 6f 8d 1997 10g a7g 8d³ 8.1m 8.1m Jul 23] tall filly: poor maiden. *R. T. Phillips* 35

PERSIAN FANTASIA 2 b.f. (Mar 1) Alzao (USA) 117 – Persian Fantasy 94 (Persian Bold 123) [1997 6g Jun 13] second foal: half-sister to 3-y-o Fantasy Girl: dam 1½m winner who stayed 2m: 25/1 and very green, slowly away and always outpaced in maiden at Goodwood: likely to do better at 1m+. *J. L. Dunlop* – p

PERSIAN FAYRE 5 b.g. Persian Heights 129 – Dominion Fayre 49 (Dominion 123) [1996 90: 8g⁶ 7.6g² 7.1g² 8d² 7m 8f³ 7m* 7.1f⁵ 7m 7g* 7g* 1997 a8.5g 7m 7m 7m² 7g⁴ 7s 7m² 8g² 6g 7g 8m⁶ Nov 1] sturdy gelding: fairly useful handicapper: good second 3 times, also ran well final start: stays 1m: acts on firm and dead ground: front runner/races prominently: genuine and reliable. *J. Berry* 90

PERSIAN FORTUNE 2 b.f. (May 10) Forzando 122 – Persian Air (Persian Bold 123) [1997 5m a5g* 6f⁴ 5.1m⁵ 6.1s² 7f³ a6g² a7g 6.9g³ 8g Sep 8] seventh foal: sister to 5-y-o Forzair and half-sister to 2 winners abroad, including 3-y-o Italian 7f (at 2 yrs) and 1m winner Setmatt (by Rudimentary): dam well beaten: modest performer: won seller at Southwell in May: good efforts when placed in claimers and a nursery afterwards: stays 7f, possibly not 1m: acts on good to firm and soft going and fibresand: claimer ridden. *W. G. M. Turner* 53

PERSIANO 2 ch.c. (Apr 3) Efisio 120 – Persiandale (Persian Bold 123) [1997 6s⁵ 6.1m 6.1g⁴ 6d⁴ Oct 16] 47,000Y: big, lengthy colt: has plenty of scope: fifth foal: half-brother to 3 winners, including useful performer up to 7f Margaret's Gift (by Beveled): dam unraced: brought along considerably in maidens then gambled on when fourth of 17 to Demolition Jo in nursery at Newmarket, running on well from mid-division, though edging left near finish: should stay 7f, probably 1m: very much the type to progress physically, and sure to win a race or two. *J. R. Fanshawe* 73 p

*Bonusprint Henry II Stakes, Sandown—Persian Punch is given an enterprising ride;
Celeric, conceding weight all round, emerges with great credit in second place*

PERSIAN PUNCH (IRE)   4 ch.g. Persian Heights 129 – Rum Cay (USA) 75   118
(Our Native (USA)) [1996 112p: 10m* 14g* 16.2m³ 14.8m* 16f³ 16m³ 1997 12m
13.3s* 16.4g* 20g 16m⁵ 15g⁵ 18f² 14d² 20m³ Oct 4] tall, useful-looking gelding:
impresses good deal in appearance: shows plenty of knee action: smart performer:
won listed race at Newbury and Henry II Stakes at Sandown in May, latter by ¾
length from Celeric: ran well last 3 starts, second in Doncaster Cup (went down by
1¾ lengths to Canon Can) and Irish St Leger (beaten 2 lengths by Oscar Schindler) at
the Curragh and third in Prix du Cadran (made running when length behind Chief
Contender) at Longchamp: effective at testing 13.3f, and stays 2½m: acts on firm and
soft ground: game and genuine. *D. R. C. Elsworth*

PERSIAN SABRE   2 b.f. (May 21) Sabrehill (USA) 120 – Wassl's Sister (Troy   62
137) [1997 5m⁵ 5.2f 5m⁶ 6m⁶ 6.9d Oct 21] 3,800Y: half-sister to 3 winners, including
7f and 1m winner Waseela (by Ahonoora) and 1¼m winner (stays 2m) Prague Spring
(by Salse): dam 1½m maiden, half-sister to Wassl: modest maiden: ran poorly final
start: should stay beyond 6f: has given trouble stalls and flashed tail. *V. Soane*

PERSIAN SUNSET (IRE)   5 b.m. Persian Mews 116 – Fifth Gear (Red Sunset   39
120) [1996 NR 1997 a7g 8g⁶ a9.4g⁶ 10g⁴ 11.8g 9.9m 10m⁶ a8g 8m 12g⁴ Jul 30]
sturdy mare: second foal: dam lightly-raced maiden: poor maiden: stays 1½m: best
efforts on good going. *G. Woodward*

PERSIAN VENTURE   2 b.c. (May 11) Midyan (USA) 124 – Scharade 74   62
(Lombard (GER) 126) [1997 6m 7d⁶ 7f⁴ 7m 7.1s² 7.6m Sep 9] 13,000Y: neat colt:
half-brother to 4-y-o Clued Up and several winners abroad: dam 1¼m winner from
good German family: modest maiden: head second in selling nursery at Sandown in
August: should stay at least 1¼m: acts on soft ground. *B. J. Meehan*

PERSICA   4 b.f. Persian Bold 123 – Nadina 116 (Shirley Heights 130) [1996 10g   –
10s² 9.5s⁴ 1997 8g Jul 8] 4,000 3-y-o: useful-looking ex-Irish filly: third foal: dam
French 10.5f winner: fair form (rated 74) in frame in maidens for D. Weld at 3 yrs
(blinkered final outing): very slowly away and always well in rear in handicap only
outing in 1997: stays 1¼m: yet to race on going firmer than good. *K. Mahdi*

717

PERSUASION   4 b.f. Batshoof 122 – Primetta (Precocious 126) [1996 72p: 10s   79
a10g* 1997 a12g* a12g⁴ Feb 15] unfurnished filly: fair form, has had only 5 races:
won handicap at Lingfield in January: disappointing there next time: stays 1½m.
Lord Huntingdon

PERTEMPS MISSION   3 b.c. Safawan 118 – Heresheis 69 (Free State 125)   –
[1996 69?: 7.9g 8f⁶ 10m 1997 12g 12d 16.2m Jul 21] workmanlike colt: has a very
round action: seemed to show fair form in maidens at 2 yrs: well beaten in 1997:
should stay beyond 1¼m. *J. Pearce*

PETALING (IRE)   2 b.f. (Feb 23) Petardia 113 – Lyphards Goddess (IRE)   53
(Lyphard's Special (USA) 122) [1997 5m 6f 7s² 7g⁶ 6m 6d³ 6d Oct 21] 7,000Y:
second foal: dam lightly-raced Irish maiden half-sister to a useful 2-y-o 5f winner:
modest maiden: placed in claimers: stays 7f: acts on good to firm and soft ground:
blinkered last 2 starts. *B. J. Meehan*

PETANE (IRE)   2 b.g. (Mar 4) Petardia 113 – Senane 86 (Vitiges (FR) 132) [1997   59
6.1d 6g 6g 8d Oct 17] 14,000Y: good-bodied gelding: has a quick action: half-brother
to 3-y-o Zoom Up, 5-y-o Crumpton Hill and several other winners: dam 1m winner
who stayed 1½m and was possibly ungenuine, half-sister to Oaks second Game Plan:
modest form in maidens and a nursery (still looked bit backward): shapes as though
will stay beyond 1m. *J. R. Arnold*

PETARA (IRE)   2 ch.c. (Feb 19) Petardia 113 – Romangoddess (IRE) (Rhoman   63
Rule (USA)) [1997 5d⁶ 6d⁴ 6g 7g³ 7.5v 7g⁵ 7g³ 7.5d 7m⁴ 6m³ 7s⁵ 8m Nov 4] 7,800
2-y-o: close-coupled colt: second foal: dam Irish 2-y-o 7f winner: modest performer:
won nursery at Catterick in September: effective at 7f/stiff 6f: best efforts on good/
good to firm going: visored final 6 starts. *J. S. Wainwright*

PETARGA   2 b.f. (Jan 25) Petong 126 – One Half Silver (CAN) (Plugged Nickle   78
(USA)) [1997 6g⁴ 5.7f² 5.1m* 5.2f 6m Aug 23] 11,000Y: close-coupled filly: fifth
foal: half-sister to 3 winners, including 7f winner Silver Standard (by Jupiter Island)
and French 1½m winner Garboesque (by Priolo): dam unraced half-sister to smart
French middle-distance filly Gamberta: fair performer: won maiden at Bath in June:
ran well in Super Sprint at Newbury next start: asked to force too strong a pace final
outing: should stay 6f: raced only on good ground or firmer. *J. A. R. Toller*

PETAZ   3 b. or br.f. Petong 126 – Tasmim 63 (Be My Guest (USA) 126) [1996 NR   –
1997 5f 8g 8g Jun 21] second foal: dam 11f winner at 4 yrs: well beaten, including in
seller. *M. W. Easterby*

PETER PERFECT   3 gr.g. Chilibang 120 – Misdevious (USA) (Alleged (USA)   54
138) [1996 54: 7.1m 7g 5d a6g³ 1997 6m 6.9m 6m² 6g⁶ 6d² 7.1m² 11.5d 8.5f Sep 17]
modest maiden: trained by G. Lewis until after sixth start (usually blinkered up to
then): stays 7f: acts on good to firm ground, dead and equitrack. *R. Curtis*

PETER'S IMP (IRE)   2 b.g. (Feb 12) Imp Society (USA) – Catherine Clare 58   77
(Sallust 134) [1997 5s³ 6g³ a5g⁴ 6m* 6g 6g³ 6g Oct 18] 9,000F, 36,000Y: good-
bodied gelding: half-brother to 3 winners, including fair 1995 sprinting 2-y-o
Bozeman (by Cyrano de Bergerac), later winner in Belgium: dam Irish miler: fair
performer: won nursery at Newcastle in August on first run since being gelded: good
third penultimate start, very stiff task final one: will stay 7f. *J. Berry*

PET EXPRESS   3 b.g. Petoski 135 – Hush It Up (Tina's Pet 121) [1996 –: a5g a6g   63
a6s 1997 a7g* a6g* a6g* a7g³ a6g² a6g⁶ 8s 7d² 7g⁵ 8g a6g Dec 18] quite good-
topped gelding: modest handicapper: won 3 races at Southwell in January: off course
5 months before final start: effective at 6f and 7f: acts on dead ground (unraced on
firmer than good) and fibresand (below form on equitrack). *P. C. Haslam*

PETITE DANSEUSE   3 b.f. Aragon 118 – Let Her Dance (USA) (Sovereign   66
Dancer (USA)) [1996 79: 5g⁵ 5.1f* 5m* 5m⁴ 5m 5g⁶ 5m 6m³ 6m² 6m³ 6m² 6m⁴   a72
7.3s² 6.1s a6g 1997 a6g³ 8g a5g 7.5m⁵ 6g⁵ 7g* 7g² 7g² 7m⁴ 6m* 7m a6g⁵ a7s⁵
Nov 28] small filly: fair performer: won claimers at Leicester in August and (final
start for C. Dwyer) September: effective at 6f and 7f: acts on good to firm ground,
soft and equitrack. *D. W. Chapman*

PETITE LADY   2 b.f. (Mar 25) Noble Patriarch 115 – Rough Guess (IRE) 52   –
(Believe It (USA)) [1997 5g⁴ 5f May 1] 3,000Y: first foal: dam, second at 5f at 2 yrs,

daughter of smart winner up to 7f Fenny Rough: signs of ability on debut: tailed off only subsequent start. *P. D. Evans*

PETITE RISK 3 ch.f. Risk Me (FR) 127 – Technology (FR) 82 (Top Ville 129) 58
[1996 –: 5f 5f 6m 1997 7m⁶ 8d³ 7.5s² 8.2g⁵ 8.5v⁵ 8.5m 7.5m 5.9m 8.5d* Aug 13] sparely-made filly: modest performer: won claimer at Beverley in August, leading inside final 1f: will probably stay beyond 8.5f: acts on soft going: joined M. Pipe. *K. W. Hogg, Isle of Man*

PETITE TACHE 2 b.f. (Mar 10) Minster Son 130 – Perioscope (Legend of –
France (USA) 124) [1997 5.9g 7.1m 7g 8.3g Sep 29] 900Y: third reported foal: half-sister to fairly useful Irish 1995 2-y-o 7f winner Chuffed (by Batshoof) and a 6f winner by Nishapour: dam second at 6f in Scandinavia: seems of no account. *N. Chamberlain*

PETIT FLORA 5 b.m. Lord Bud 121 – Pretty Soon 75 (Tina's Pet 121) [1996 –: 40 d
8.5m⁶ 8m 10m 15.8g 1997 9.9m³ 10g 8g 12g⁶ 9.2m Aug 18] leggy mare: poor maiden handicapper: worthwhile form only when third at Beverley in April: should stay beyond 1¼m. *G. Holmes*

PETOSKIN 5 b.g. Petoski 135 – Farcical (Pharly (FR) 130) [1996 57, a71: a8g 8s 55
10.8d 12m 12m 11.5f⁴ 12m⁵ 12g 11.5m* 12s a11g a14.8g* a14.8g* 1997 a14.8g³ a73
a16g a14.8g* a16g² a14.8g⁶ 12m 16s 12.3m³ 11.9f* a16g* 13.8m⁶ a16.2g* 11.7m* 16g⁶ a14.8g⁴ a14g Dec 8] close-coupled gelding: fair on the all-weather, modest on turf: won claimers at Wolverhampton (2), Lingfield and Brighton in first half of year, and seller (odds on) at Bath in July: effective at 1½m to 2m: probably acts on any going: visored (inadequate trip) once: inconsistent. *J. Pearce*

PETRACO (IRE) 9 b.g. Petorius 117 – Merrie Moira (Bold Lad (IRE) 133) 60 d
[1996 68: 5g³ 5m³ 5g⁴ 5.9d 5.7g 6.1m 5m⁴ 5m 6m⁵ 5g⁶ 6m 6m³ 5m⁵ 6m* 5f 6.1m 6m 1997 5m⁴ 6.1g 6m⁴ 5d⁵ 6g 6m⁶ 6.1d 6g 5g⁶ 6d Sep 5] workmanlike gelding: has a quick action: modest sprint handicapper: below form after reappearance at 9 yrs: acts on any going: tried blinkered (not since 5 yrs): sometimes hangs: often apprentice ridden. *N. A. Smith*

PETRICO 5 b.g. Petong 126 – Balearica 90 (Bustino 136) [1996 NR 1997 12.4m –
9.2m 8m Oct 1] signs of ability but no worthwhile form. *P. Beaumont*

PETROS PRIDE 4 b.f. Safawan 118 – Hala 57 (Persian Bold 123) [1996 –: 10.2g –
8.5m 12m⁵ 10.8f 16.4v⁵ 1997 a12g Feb 18] compact filly: no worthwhile form. *M. J. Bolton*

PETRUCHIO (IRE) 2 b.g. (May 25) Petardia 113 – Rising Lady (Alzao (USA) –
117) [1997 7.1d 7g 7.1m 8.2s Oct 15] 13,000Y: fifth foal: half-brother to 2 winners abroad: dam placed up to 1m in Ireland: little form in maidens, and showed signs of temperament (gelded at end of season). *Major D. N. Chappell*

PETSONG 3 b. or br.c. Petong 126 – Petriece 64 (Mummy's Pet 125) [1996 –: 7d –
1997 6g 8.3s 7g 6m Jul 19] no worthwhile form: sent to USA. *V. Soane*

PETULA BOY 3 gr.g. Nicholas (USA) 111 – Tulapet (Mansingh (USA) 120) –
[1996 –: 5.2d⁶ 5m a6g a7g 7g 1997 a8g⁵ a11g 10m⁵ a8g 8g a9.4f³ a11g⁴ 10s 7g⁶ a7g a36
9.9g Aug 23] small gelding: poor maiden: stays 9.4f: best efforts on all-weather: tried blinkered/visored. *S. R. Bowring*

PETUNTSE 3 b.g. Phountzi (USA) 104 – Alipampa (IRE) (Glenstal (USA) 118) 33
[1996 NR 1997 a8.5g 8g⁶ 8g³ 10m 6m Oct 6] tall gelding: second foal: dam unraced granddaughter of Irish Oaks winner Pampalina: poor maiden: headstrong, and likely to prove best up to 1m: bandaged behind and tongue tied last 3 starts. *J. G. Smyth-Osbourne*

PHANAN 11 ch.g. Pharly (FR) 130 – L'Ecossaise (Dancer's Image (USA)) [1996 –
–: a11g⁵ a12g a13g 16.5m 10m a12g a12g 1997 a11g⁵ a12g 10.5m 12.3m 12.1m Jul 25] no worthwhile form since 4 yrs. *R. E. Peacock*

PHANTOM RING 2 ch.f. (Mar 26) Magic Ring (IRE) 115 – Follow The Stars 62
86 (Sparkler 130) [1997 5.1s⁴ 6g 6m 5.2f⁶ a6s² a6g⁵ a5g² Dec 8] 14,000Y: half-sister to several winners, including sprinter Montserrat (by Aragon): dam 8.5f and 1¼m winner: modest maiden: second in nurseries at Lingfield and Southwell late in year: stays 6f: acts on the all-weather. *A. Bailey*

PHA

PHANTOM WATERS 2 b.f. (Mar 28) Pharly (FR) 130 – Idle Waters 116 (Mill   59
Reef (USA) 141) [1997 5.7f 6g⁶ 7m 7m 7.5g⁵ 8f⁶ Sep 18] sister to useful 1½m/1¾m
winner Secret Waters and half-sister to several winners, including smart stayer
Shining Water (by Kalaglow), dam of Tenby: dam 1½m to 14.6f winner: modest
maiden: should stay 1¼m+: raced only on good ground or firmer. *R. F. Johnson
Houghton*

PHARAOH'S JOY 4 b.f. Robellino (USA) 127 – Joyce's Best 58 (Tolomeo 127)   61
[1996 65: 6.1d 6g 6m 5f* 6m⁵ 5m³ 5.2m* 5f⁴ 5m 5.1g 1997 6m 5f⁶ 5m³ 5g⁴ 6m⁵   a–
5.1m³ 5.2m² 6f 5.3f³ a6g a7g a6g Nov 24] lengthy filly: modest handicapper: trained
by J. W. Payne until after seventh start: has won at 6f, ideally suited to 5f: best efforts
on firm/good to firm going, no form on the all-weather: usually races prominently:
tried blinkered. *A. G. Newcombe*

PHARLY DANCER 8 b.g. Pharly (FR) 130 – Martin-Lavell Mail (Dominion   –
123) [1996 65, a77: a12g³ a12g³ a12g² a12g³ 12.1g² 12g³ a14g* 12s* 11.9d* 12m³   a63
12.1d 14.1m⁵ 12g⁶ a12g* a14.8g³ a14g* 1997 a12g⁶ a12g² a12g⁴ a14g 13.8m⁴ a16g⁶
a14g* a14g³ a14g⁴ Dec 18] angular gelding: has had knee problems: has a round
action: modest performer: off course 5 months, won handicap at Southwell (eighth
course win) in November: stays 1¾m: acts well on fibresand: often has tongue tied
and tends to carry head awkwardly. *W. W. Haigh*

PHARLY REEF 5 b.g. Pharly (FR) 130 – Hay Reef 72 (Mill Reef (USA) 141)   –
[1996 –: a9.4g⁵ a12g⁵ 1997 a11g Jan 13] rather unfurnished gelding: lightly raced on
flat nowadays, and retains little ability. *D. Burchell*

PHARLY STAR 3 ch.g. Pharly (FR) 130 – Norapa 91 (Ahonoora 122) [1996 NR   –
1997 9d⁶ a7g 7.1d Jul 3] heavy-topped gelding: fourth foal: half-brother to winners
Durano (1¼m, by Dunbeath) and 1992 2-y-o Norstano (5f, by Stanford): dam 2-y-o
6f winner: no form in maidens. *D. Shaw*

PHILANTHROP (FR) 5 br.h. Machiavellian (USA) 123 – Schezerade (USA)   116
(Tom Rolfe) [1996 10m 10d⁶ 12.5s⁵ 13.5s⁵ 12.5s* 1997 9.8s* 13d⁴ 13g² 10.5s² 10s*
15.5g² 12m⁵ 15.5d² 15.5d³ 12g* 15d* 15g* Jul 11] third foal: dam, winner in France
at 10.5f and 1½m, is closely related to April Run: won minor event at Saint-Cloud
and listed race at Deauville at 3 yrs and 2 minor events in the provinces late on at 4
yrs: had a very good first 7 months in 1997, winning minor races at Cagnes and
Maisons-Laffitte and listed races at Lyon, Maisons-Laffitte and Chantilly (by 5
lengths from Yokohama): good placed efforts behind Stretarez in Prix de Barbeville
and Prix Vicomtesse Vigier (beaten a length) at Longchamp on eighth and ninth
starts: stays 15.5f: acts on soft ground: tough and consistent. *J-P. Gallorini, France*

PHILGEM 4 b.f. Precocious 126 – Andalucia 57 (Rheingold 137) [1996 25: 10g   35
10d⁶ 8.1g⁵ 7.5m⁵ 7d 10g⁵ 11.1m⁶ 10.9m 13.8g⁶ 12.1g 12g a13g 1997 12m 10g⁶ 8.5s⁴
11.1s* 12m⁴ a11g⁶ 10.9d³ 11.1s³ 12g⁴ 11.1s³ 8.5d⁵ 12.1g Sep 1] small filly: poor
handicapper: gained first win in seller at Hamilton in May: probably stays 1¾m: acts
on good to firm and soft going: blinkered/visored last 4 starts. *C. W. Fairhurst*

PHILISTAR 4 ch.c. Bairn (USA) 126 – Philgwyn 66 (Milford 119) [1996 72: 7m   82
8g⁵ 10m a8g⁵ a10g* a9.4g³ a9.4g a10g³ a12g⁶ a10g⁴ 1997 9.9m² 12g⁶ 10s⁶ 8.3s³
8.1m² 9f* 8.5m* 8.3g* 10f* 10d 9f 8m 7m² 8d⁵ 7m 9m 8m Nov 1] good-topped colt:
fairly useful performer: left J. Eustace after fourth start: in excellent form for new
stable, winning minor event at Newcastle, handicaps at Epsom (£18,000 race) and
Hamilton and minor event at Brighton, all in June: effective at 7f to 1¼m: acts on
firm ground, dead and the all-weather: blinkered (ran well first time, pulled hard
otherwise) first 3 4-y-o starts: has run well when sweating: held up. *K. R. Burke*

PHILMIST 5 b.m. Hard Fought 125 – Andalucia 57 (Rheingold 137) [1996 50,   58
a55: a12g³ a12g² a14.8g 12.1d⁵ 13d⁴ 13s² a11g* 13g² 12.3m⁵ 12.1m² 13.1g⁴ 17.5m
a13g⁵ 1997 a14.8g⁴ a12g a14.8g³ 12.1d³ 13d 10g 13s⁴ 13s⁶ 13g⁴ 11.1d* 11.1g* 13d²
11.1m⁵ 10.9d* 10.9s⁴ 16s a12s⁵ Nov 28] leggy mare: modest handicapper: trained
first 3 starts by J. Hetherton: won lady amateurs event in July and apprentice race in
August, both at Hamilton, and amateurs event at Ayr in September: best form at 11f
to 13f: acts on good to firm ground, soft and fibresand, probably on equitrack:
blinkered: best patiently ridden. *Miss L. A. Perratt*

PHILOSOPHIC 3 b.g. Be My Chief (USA) 122 – Metaphysique (FR) (Law   61
Society (USA) 130) [1996 52p: 6.1m⁵ 6f⁵ 7m 7.6m 1997 9.7m³ a12g² 16.2m² 16s

720

15.8s[6] Oct 16] big, workmanlike gelding: has scope: progressive form in handicaps first 3 starts at 3 yrs: ran as though something amiss final one: stays 2m: acts on good to firm ground and fibresand: sold 23,000 gns after final start. *Sir Mark Prescott*

PHOENIX PRINCESS 3 b.f. Nomination 125 – Princess Poquito (Hard Fought 125) [1996 NR 1997 8.2d a8g[4] a8.5g[4] a8g[3] 8.2g[3] 8d[6] a8g* a8g[3] a8.5g a8.5g[2] a6g* a7g a7g Nov 29] 3,200Y: workmanlike filly: third foal: half-sister to 4-y-o Eurobox Boy and Miss Poquito (7f winner in Germany, by Dunbeath): dam unraced half-sister to smart 1¼m to 1¾m filly Senorita Poquito: fair handicapper on the all-weather, lightly raced on turf: won at Southwell in July and November: keen sort, best up to 1m. *B. A. McMahon*
45 + a65

PHONE ALEX (IRE) 2 b.f. (Apr 30) Tirol 127 – Parkeen Princess (He Loves Me 120) [1997 5.2g 5g[2] 6f[2] 5g* 5.2f 6g[6] 6m* 6.5m 7m Sep 30] 10,000Y: tall, shallow-girthed filly: ninth foal: half-sister to several winners, including 1991 2-y-o 6f winner Strange Knight (by Gorytus), later successful in Italy, and 1m/9f winner Transitional (by Dalsaan): dam unraced: fair performer: won maiden in June and minor event in August, both at Lingfield: well below form last 2 starts: stays 6f: raced only on good ground or firmer: sold 20,000 gns in October. *R. Hannon*
72

PHONETIC 4 b.g. Shavian 125 – So True 116 (So Blessed 130) [1996 78: 8m 8d[3] 10.2f[5] 8m[4] 8m 10s[5] 1997 8m 8s* 8.9d 8.1d[2] 7.9s 8v 8d Oct 28] tall, workmanlike gelding: fair handicapper: 25/1, easily best effort at 4 yrs when winning 17-runner event at Newbury in May: should be suited by further than 1m: acts on good to firm and soft ground. *G. B. Balding*
78

PHOTOGENIC 2 b.f. (May 9) Midyan (USA) 124 – Colorsnap (Shirley Heights 130) [1997 6s[4] 5g[2] 6d* 7g[3] 7g* 7m[6] Sep 30] 54,000Y: second living foal: half-sister to 1996 2-y-o 1m winner General's Star (by Night Shift): dam unraced half-sister to Bella Colora (dam of Stagecraft), Colorspin (dam of Opera House) and Cezanne: fairly useful performer: won maiden and listed race at Leopardstown in August: below form in valuable sales race at Newmarket final start: will stay at least 1m: acts on dead ground. *A. P. O'Brien, Ireland*
93

PHYLIDA 3 b.f. Mazilier (USA) 107 – May The Fourteenth 53 (Thatching 131) [1996 64+, a?: 5m 6m[4] 7d[6] 6g[2] a7g[6] a7g[3] 1997 7m[6] 8g* 10g* 8d Oct 13] small, angular filly: has a round action: modest performer: won claimers at Newmarket in July and Leicester in August: stiff task final start: stays 1¼m: best efforts on good going: has run well when sweating. *P. J. Makin*
56

PIANIST (IRE) 2 ch.c. (May 11) Balla Cove 119 – Hit For Six (Tap On Wood 130) [1997 6m 5g[5] 6d[6] 6.9m[2] 7.1s[5] 10g[5] 10d[2] Oct 13] IR 11,000Y: leggy, close-coupled colt: sixth foal: half-brother to winners in Italy by Cyrano de Bergerac and Soviet Lad: dam, Irish 2-y-o 5f winner, from family of this colt's sire: modest maiden: ran well when blinkered in seller final start: stays 1¼m well: acts on dead ground: joined Miss K. George. *G. Lewis*
58

PICARD (IRE) 4 b.g. Durgam (USA) – Miners Society (Miner's Lamp 114) [1996 7s 9d[4] 11.9m[2] 11d[4] 12m 13d[4] 10g 1997 a11g[6] 10.1g 12s[4] 12.3m Apr 9] smallish gelding: first foal: dam, jumps bred, placed in a bumper: modest maiden (rated 59) up to 1½m in Ireland at 3 yrs (blinkered final start): no form in Britain. *F. Murphy*
–

PICCADILLY 2 ch.f. (Mar 20) Belmez (USA) 131 – Polly's Pear (USA) (Sassafras (FR) 135) [1997 7.5g[4] 7.5f[6] 8.2s[6] Oct 15] 13,000Y: sister to useful 1¾m winner Pedraza and half-sister to several winners, including fairly useful miler Themaam (by Night Shift): dam unraced: modest form in maidens at Beverley (2) and Nottingham: bred to be suited by 1¼m+: should still do better. *T. J. Etherington*
62 p

PICCOLO CATIVO 2 b.f. (Mar 4) Komaite (USA) – Malcesine (IRE) 46 (Auction Ring (USA) 123) [1997 a5g* 6g[6] a6g[5] a5g Dec 8] 1,000Y: first foal: dam 1m seller winner, should have stayed 1½m: won maiden at Southwell in May: just poor form afterwards in minor event and nurseries: claimer ridden. *Capt. J. Wilson*
63

PICHON BARON (USA) 2 ch.c. (Feb 27) Zilzal (USA) 137 – Flora Lady (USA) (Track Barron (USA)) [1997 5.5d[3] 5.5m[4] 6s[3] 7d[3] 8d* 8g* 8d[5] 8.1m[4] 6m[6] Oct 1] $3,000Y: leggy, sparely-made colt: fourth foal: half-brother to a winner in USA by Seattle Dancer: dam, won around 1m in USA, half-sister to Grade 2 9f winner
67 ?

Exclusive Partner: won claimers at Clairefontaine (claimed out of J. C. Rouget's stable 123,000 francs) and Deauville (claimed out of R. Collet's stable 210,117 francs) in August: well held in listed race and minor events in Britain. *B. J. Meehan*

PICKENS (USA) 5 b.g. Theatrical 128 – Alchi (USA) 112 (Alleged (USA) 138) 54 [1996 59: 12m 16g 12m 14d⁴ 12f* 12m⁵ a16g 1997 12g 10m⁵ 10d 10.3g 11m* 10m a11g⁴ a11g⁵ a14g³ Dec 8] stocky gelding: modest performer: gamely won claimer at Redcar in October: stays 1¾m: acts on fibresand and firm ground, possibly not on softer than good: tried blinkered: has had tongue tied. *Don Enrico Incisa*

PIERPOINT (IRE) 2 ch.g. (Mar 19) Archway (IRE) 115 – Lavinia (Habitat 134) 72 [1997 5m⁵ 5d² 5m* 6m³ 6g⁴ 5m² 6g³ 6d⁴ Oct 8] 10,000Y: smallish gelding: poor mover: half-brother to winners in Italy (2) and USA: dam third at 5f in Ireland: fair performer: won claimer at Hamilton in June and nursery there in July: in frame afterwards, running creditably, including in seller and claimer: should stay at least 7f: acts on good to firm going and dead: visored sixth start. *R. A. Fahey*

PIETRO BEMBO (IRE) 3 b.g. Midyan (USA) 124 – Cut No Ice 97 (Great 75 Nephew 126) [1996 71p: 7.6m⁶ 6m⁵ 6m 8m* 1997 12g³ 12m 12m 12s² Oct 16] workmanlike colt: fair handicapper: stays 1½m: acts on good to firm and soft ground: tried blinkered: hung badly left on reappearance, found nothing third outing: sold 23,000 gns, and joined N. Henderson. *Sir Mark Prescott*

PIGEON 2 b.f. (Apr 9) Casteddu 111 – Wigeon 80 (Divine Gift 127) [1997 6m* 63 ? 5.9g 6m³ 6g² Aug 15] 2,000Y: half-sister to several winners, including fairly useful 6f winner Premier Lad (by Tower Walk) and 5f to 1¼m winner Ma Pierrette (by Cawston's Clown): dam won up to 1¼m: won seller at Catterick in May: placed in minor event (possibly flattered) and nursery afterwards: likely to prove best short of 1m: has given trouble stalls. *D. W. Barker*

PIKE CREEK (USA) 4 b.f. Alwasmi (USA) 115 – Regal Heights (USA) (Forli 77 (ARG)) [1996 86: 11.9f* 11.9m 12m⁴ 16.2m 16.2d 1997 12m⁴ 11.7m² 13.9g 14.8d² 14.8m⁶ 12m 16.2g Sep 27] lengthy filly: fair handicapper: stays 15f: acts on firm and dead going: ran poorly when sweating: none too reliable. *I. A. Balding*

PILIB (IRE) 6 b.g. Salt Dome (USA) – Princess Elinor (Captain James 123) [1996 – NR 1997 a12s Nov 28] lightly raced, disappointing maiden. *J. Pearce*

PILSUDSKI (IRE) 5 b.h. Polish Precedent (USA) 131 – Cocotte 111 (Troy 134 137) [1996 129: 10g² 10d* 10f 10m* 12m* 12d² 12g* 1997 10.5d³ 12g² 10d* 12s² 10g* 12f² 10g* 12m* Nov 23]
'Leave them wanting more,' goes the old showbiz adage. It may seem odd to apply the saying to a five-year-old who has run in top company as often as Pilsudski, but he improved every season and a string of magnificent performances in 1997, again climaxing in the autumn, left the impression that there might have been even better to come had he remained in training at six. Alas, Pilsudski's future is at stud in Japan (secured for a reported twenty million dollars), where he achieved the last, and most valuable, victory of his career in the Japan Cup at Tokyo in late-November. A hard-fought success there came at the end of a tough campaign that had begun at Longchamp in April and seen Pilsudski successful in three of the major open-aged championship races of the European season, the Coral-Eclipse Stakes at Sandown, the Esat Digifone Champion Stakes at Leopardstown and the Dubai Champion Stakes at Newmarket, as well as finishing second in the King George VI and Queen Elizabeth Stakes and the Prix de l'Arc de Triomphe. Pilsudski also won the Racehorse of the Year award—confined to horses which have run in Britain—by a very wide margin, polling twenty-one of the twenty-three votes cast by the Press panel.
    Pilsudski's victories in the Eclipse Stakes and the two Champion Stakes were among fifteen gained by older horses in the twenty Group 1 races open to three-year-olds and upwards in Britain, Ireland and France. The three-year-olds collectively were well and truly overshadowed in these races by a fine collection of older horses, only Compton Place (July Cup), Air Express (Queen Elizabeth II Stakes), Peintre Celebre (Prix de l'Arc), Ebadiyla (Prix Royal-Oak) and Carmine Lake (Prix de l'Abbaye) winning for the younger brigade.

Coral-Eclipse Stakes, Sandown—Pilsudski wins with a little in hand;
Bosra Sham (right) suffers a nightmare passage and is finally unable to take second place off Benny The Dip

The Prix du Jockey-Club winner Peintre Celebre was the only one of the three major European Derby winners to get the better of Pilsudski during the season, beating him in clear-cut fashion in a strongly-contested Arc. Neither the Epsom Derby winner Benny The Dip nor the Irish Derby winner Desert King had the slightest excuse when second to Pilsudski in the Eclipse and the Irish Champion Stakes respectively. Pilsudski's Eclipse win came as something of a surprise at the time in that the four-year-old filly Bosra Sham started odds on after a particularly eye-catching victory at Royal Ascot. Pilsudski had been the beaten favourite in the Hardwicke Stakes, unable to hold the renewed challenge of Predappio. The magnificent-looking Pilsudski appeared fitter at Sandown than he had at Royal Ascot (he had definitely needed the outing when third in the Prix Ganay on his seasonal debut) and won with a little in hand, appearing to idle in front as Benny The Dip and Bosra Sham, who had met trouble in running, fought a close battle for second. Pilsudski was sent next to Ascot for the King George VI, a race dominated by older horses. Pilsudski, just about the paddock pick in a fine-looking field, ran another good race to finish a game second, beaten a length by Swain, with Helissio and Singspiel third and fourth, after torrential rain on the morning of the race put the emphasis firmly on stamina.

Pilsudski's performances at Sandown and Ascot put him very much back in the Prix de l'Arc picture and after his next victory, in the Irish Champion in September, Pilsudski replaced that horse as ante-post favourite. Pilsudski shaded favouritism over Desert King at Leopardstown, with Alhaarth the only other runner in the seven-strong line-up at shorter than 10/1. In the race itself there was only one horse in it! Pilsudski beat Desert King pointless, the pair finishing a street ahead of third-placed Alhaarth. Desert King was provided with a pacemaker to ensure a truly-run race, but Pilsudski, always travelling strongly, moved up easily on the home turn and, though Desert King improved in his wake, Pilsudski forged ahead to beat him by four and a half lengths, eased near the finish. Pilsudski's performance showed him better than ever and he looked sure to give a very good account of himself in the Arc. But for the

723

second year running he caught a tartar in the shape of a three-year-old who produced a tip-top performance on the day. As usual, the Arc field was thoroughly representative of the season's top European middle-distance form, though the classic crop mustered only six representatives, five of them fillies. The field included five of the first six home the previous year, and, for the second year running, Pilsudski finished ahead of Swain, Oscar Schindler and Le Destin, while also turning the tables on the front-running Helissio. But Pilsudski couldn't hold a candle to Peintre Celebre, who ran out a brilliant five-length winner (we made it four), with Pilsudski, probably not quite at his best, keeping on to finish two and a half lengths ahead of the strong-finishing pair Borgia and Oscar Schindler, with Predappio, Helissio and Swain also involved in a five-way photo for the minor placings.

Thirteen days after the Arc, Pilsudski was in action again, taking in the Champion Stakes at Newmarket having satisfied his trainer in his homework that he had recovered fully from his exertions at Longchamp. Pilsudski overcame trouble in running, in a muddling race, losing his place at one point and then having to be extricated from an awkward position. He produced a fine turn of foot in the final furlong that saw him home a clear-cut two-length winner from Loup Sauvage, with Bahhare, Stowaway, Revoque, Benny The Dip and Bijou d'Inde the others in a seven-horse field. Pilsudski's victory may have handed a compliment to Peintre Celebre but it also reflected enormous credit on Pilsudski himself and those who handled him at Freemason Lodge, a point emphasised again by his subsequent win at Tokyo. The bare form of the Japan Cup is not even as good as the Champion Stakes, but the race will live long in the memory of those that saw it for the supremely game performance of the winner. Under a very strong ride, Pilsudski really stuck his neck out to edge past Air Groove in the straight then hold the Japanese filly's late rally. In under

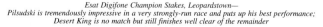

Esat Digifone Champion Stakes, Leopardstown—
Pilsudski is tremendously impressive in a very strongly-run race and puts up his best performance;
Desert King is no match but still finishes well clear of the remainder

Dubai Champion Stakes, Newmarket—
the ultra-tough Pilsudski shows no ill effects from his Arc run thirteen days earlier;
Loup Sauvage is a good second with Bahhare third

fifteen months, Pilsudski had won at the highest level in Germany, Canada, Britain, Ireland and Japan—some record!

Pilsudski's trainer Michael Stoute topped the trainers' prize-money table in Britain for the fifth time, having taken the title in 1994 and three times in the 'eighties. Entrepreneur provided him with his eighth British classic winner (and his first since the 'eighties) but the five-year-olds Pilsudski and Singspiel were the stars of the show. Singspiel contributed to Stoute's domestic trainers' championship with victories in the Coronation Cup and the Juddmonte International, while his Dubai World Cup win provided the springboard for another highly successful year for Stoute-trained horses overseas. According to figures provided by the International Racing Bureau, Stoute's overseas earnings were £2,670,791, following £2,948,136 in 1996, when Singspiel and Pilsudski also contributed the lion's share.

We paid tribute in the essay on Pilsudski in *Racehorses of 1996* to Stoute's skill with late-developing types, citing Opera House, Saddlers' Hall, Rock Hopper and Ezzoud as other examples of horses that needed—and were given—time to develop. Californian trainer Richard Mandella, another who seems to excel with older horses, was asked to explain his success in an interview in the latest season. 'It's because it takes me a long time to figure out how to train them', was his reply. Stoute cites the autumn of their four-year-old days as the time when Singspiel and Pilsudski both 'made enormous improvement', while pointing to differences in physique between the pair, Pilsudski—'one of the best-looking horses you'll see ..... with an iron constitution'—needing more work to get him fully fit than the 'beautifully made, medium-sized' Singspiel. 'They have both been wonderful horses and are so close that you cannot separate them,' is Stoute's diplomatic conclusion. For the record, Pilsudski and Singspiel met three times in racecourse competition. Singspiel finished in front in their first encounter, when they filled the first two places in the Gordon Richards Stakes at Sandown on their reappearance as four-year-olds. Singspiel, who had been campaigned in pattern races at three, had much better form at the time than Pilsudski, whose lines had been cast in calmer waters. Pilsudski had progressed steadily as a three-year-old, running his last four races in handicap company, including victories in the Duke of Cambridge at Newmarket and the Tote Gold Trophy at Goodwood. Pilsudski's second meeting with Singspiel

725

Japan Cup, Tokyo—Pilsudski goes out in a blaze of glory,
winning from the home-trained pair Air Groove and Bubble Gum Fellow (left)

came in the Breeders' Cup Turf on his final outing at four, by which time Pilsudski had firmly established himself in the top class with his second in the Arc. Pilsudski beat Singspiel into second at Woodbine, winning fairly and squarely by a length and a quarter. Their third meeting came when they were both in the frame in the latest King George VI and Queen Elizabeth Stakes, in which the margin between them was three and three quarter lengths, the unusually testing conditions for the race probably inconveniencing Singspiel more than Pilsudski.

		Danzig	Northern Dancer
	Polish Precedent (USA)	(b 1977)	Pas de Nom
	(b 1986)	Past Example	Buckpasser
Pilsudski (IRE)		(ch 1976)	Bold Example
(b.h. 1992)		Troy	Petingo
	Cocotte	(b 1976)	La Milo
	(b 1983)	Gay Milly	Mill Reef
		(b 1977)	Gaily

    Pilsudski's improvement from three to four, and again from four to five, went hand in hand with his physical development. He matured into a big, good-topped, attractive individual who stood out in the paddock, taking the eye with both his physique and well-being. Pilsudski, a son of Polish Precedent (he takes his name from the Polish military and political leader Joseph Pilsudski) is a product of the Weinstocks' Ballymacoll Stud, which must regret selling his dam Cocotte (who showed smart form at a mile and a quarter) at the 1992 December Sales, even though she made 120,000 guineas. The stud also sold the first four fillies that Cocotte produced, including the fairly useful Glowing Ardour (by Dancing Brave). Since Pilsudski, the last of Cocotte's foals produced at Ballymacoll, Cocotte has produced Purbeck, an unraced sister to Pilsudski, whom she was carrying at the time of her sale, and three offspring to Sadler's Wells, the first of them the useful three-year-old Conon Falls and the third a yearling filly who passed through the ring at the latest Houghton Sales for 480,000 guineas, reportedly retained by her consignors Barronstown Stud. Pilsudski's grandam, the fair winning miler Gay Milly, a daughter of the Irish One Thousand Guineas winner Gaily, is still at Ballymacoll, as is another of

Lord Weinstock's "Pilsudski"

Gaily's winning daughters Gay Hellene. The last-named showed smart form when trained, like many Weinstock and Sobell horses down the years, including Gay Milly and Cocotte's sire Troy, by Dick Hern. The Weinstock family's ambition to win the Arc has been well documented. Pilsudski's two second places followed placed efforts with Homeric, Troy, Ela-Mana-Mou and Sun Princess, all trained by Hern.

The game and genuine Pilsudski was effective at a mile and a quarter to a mile and a half. His round action was often cited to support a theory that he wasn't so effective in top-of-the-ground conditions as on good ground or softer—connections delayed a decision about his participation in the King George because of the possibility of firm ground—but he confirmed in the latest Arc that he was effective enough on firm. Another theory—that Pilsudski was better on a left-handed track—is also hard to sustain.True, he never put up a better or more impressive performance than when winning the Irish Champion Stakes at Leopardstown, but he recorded plenty of good efforts on right-handed tracks such as Sandown, Ascot and Longchamp. All in all, he was a grand racehorse. *M. R. Stoute*

PINCHINCHA (FR) 3 b.g. Priolo (USA) 127 – Western Heights (Shirley Heights 130) [1996 62p: 8s a8g* 1997 a8s² a10g² a9.4g³ 9g⁶ 9.7m* 10.3d* 12s⁴ 10m* 10.3d³ 10m⁴ 10.1m⁴ 12m 10m² 12g 12s Nov 8] workmanlike gelding: fairly useful performer: won handicap at Folkestone in April, minor event at Doncaster (despite wandering) in May and handicap at Pontefract in June: should stay 1½m: acts on all-weather and good to firm and dead ground: consistent. *D. Morris* 89

PINE CREEK 3 ch.f. Bold Arrangement 127 – Sweet Enough 79 (Caerleon –
(USA) 132) [1996 NR 1997 a8g Nov 25] fourth foal: dam stayer: little sign of ability
on debut. *L. G. Cottrell*

PINE RIDGE LAD (IRE) 7 gr.g. Taufan (USA) 119 – Rosserk (Roan Rocket   62
128) [1996 69, a89: a9.4g³ a7g² a8g* a7g² a7g* 7.5d* 8m 7.6m* 7g² 8f⁵ 8m³ 7g 7g   a76
10g 1997 7g 8m 8g 8.3g* 6g 8m 8s⁴ a8g³ a8g Dec 18] good-topped gelding: fair
handicapper on the all-weather, modest on turf: won at Hamilton in September:
needs further than 6f nowadays, and stays 9.4f: acts on any going: tried visored/
blinkered: front runner/races prominently: has won for apprentice: tough and game.
J. L. Eyre

PINK TICKET 2 b.f. (Apr 20) Emarati (USA) 74 – Foreign Mistress (Darshaan   47
133) [1997 5m³ 5.1m³ a5g⁴ 5m⁶ a5g³ 7g³ 7g⁴ a7g² 8m a8.5g* a8.5g a7g Nov 14]   a51
3,000Y: sparely-made filly: third foal: half-sister to a winner in Italy by Sharpo: dam
placed several times in Italy: modest performer: won seller at Wolverhampton in
October: ran poorly afterwards: stays 8.5f: acts on fibresand, raced only on good/
good to firm on turf: races prominently. *P. D. Evans*

PINMIX (FR) 2 gr.c. (Mar 21) Linamix (FR) 127 – Pinaflore (FR) (Formidable   108 p
(USA) 125) [1997 5.5g² 7g² 8d* 8g* Sep 23] fourth foal: brother to French
1m winner Pinaflorix and half-brother to useful French 1m winner Pinfloron (by
Caerleon), later successful in USA: dam French 7.5f and (including at 2 yrs) 1m
winner: won 7-runner minor event at Saint-Cloud in September and 4-runner Prix La
Rochette (by neck from Trans Island) at Chantilly later in month: stays 1m: should
improve further. *A. Fabre, France*

PINOCHET (USA) 2 ch.f. (Apr 12) Storm Cat (USA) – Pink Turtle (USA) 120   65 p
(Blushing Groom (FR) 131) [1997 5m⁶ Sep 21] second foal: dam French 7.5f and
10.5f winner (stayed 1½m), half-sister to Canadian Grade 1 middle-distance
winner Great Neck: 6/1 from 5/2, around 6 lengths sixth to Refined in maiden at
Kempton, some late headway: should improve: sold 28,000 gns in December.
J. H. M. Gosden

PINSHARP (IRE) 2 b.c. (Apr 21) Sharp Victor (USA) 114 – Binnissima (USA)   –
(Tilt Up (USA)) [1997 8m 7g 7d Nov 7] 12,000Y: good-bodied colt: has a round
action: fifth foal: brother to Irish 1993 2-y-o 6f winner Viva Victor, later successful
in USA: dam minor winner in USA: well beaten in maidens: has been bandaged in
front. *P. Howling*

PINUP 2 gr.f. (Feb 17) Risk Me (FR) 127 – Princess Tara 85 (Prince Sabo 123)   44
[1997 6m 6m⁵ a7g 6m⁵ 6f⁴ a6g a8g a6g Dec 6] 20,000Y: angular filly: second foal: a–
sister to 3-y-o Bilko: dam 6f (at 2 yrs) and 1m winner, half-sister to high-class French
sprinter Kind Music: poor maiden on turf (trained first 5 starts by G. Lewis): no form
on the all-weather: stays 6f. *C. A. Dwyer*

PIPED ABOARD (IRE) 2 b.g. (Apr 4) Pips Pride 117 – Last Gunboat 50   69
(Dominion 123) [1997 6d⁵ 6.1d⁶ 7d⁶ Nov 7] 33,000Y: strong, good-bodied gelding:
poor walker: half-brother to several winners, including 3-y-o Battle Ground and
Italian Group 3 11f winner Bateau Rouge (by Red Sunset): dam maiden half-sister to
Oaks-placed Suni and Media Luna: fair form in minor event at Goodwood (off course
4 months after) and maiden at Doncaster first and third starts: should stay 1m.
J. L. Dunlop

PIPE MUSIC (IRE) 2 b.g. (Apr 15) Mujadil (USA) 119 – Sunset Cafe (IRE)   54
(Red Sunset 120) [1997 6g 6d a6g⁵ Nov 17] 40,000Y: compact gelding: first foal:
dam Irish 1½m winner, sister to smart middle-distance performer Beeshi: modest
form in autumn maidens. *P. C. Haslam*

PIPPAS PRIDE (IRE) 2 ch.c. (Apr 17) Pips Pride 117 – Al Shany 92 (Burslem   –
123) [1997 5g 5m 6g Aug 4] 8,500Y: second foal: dam effective at 1¼m to 1½m:
well held in maidens. *M. J. Fetherston-Godley*

PIP'S ADDITION (IRE) 2 ch.f. (Apr 24) Pips Pride 117 – Mint Addition 50   55
(Tate Gallery (USA) 117) [1997 5d 5m 5.1g³ a5g³ a6g² a7g* Dec 18] 3,200 2-y-o:
useful-looking filly: second foal: dam maiden bred to stay 1m+: modest performer:
won seller at Southwell, best effort: will stay 1m. *J. A. Glover*

PIPS SONG (IRE)   2 ch.g. (Mar 8) Pips Pride 117 – Friendly Song 48 (Song 132)   73
[1997 6m⁶ Jul 18] 36,000Y: lengthy gelding: third foal: half-brother to 1995 2-y-o 5f
winner Kustom Kit (by Timeless Times): dam poor maiden sister to smart sprinter
Fayruz: 16/1, just over 3 lengths sixth in steadily-run minor event at Newbury:
unimpressive to post: sold 9,000 gns in October. *I. A. Balding*

PIQUANT   10 b. or br.g. Sharpo 132 – Asnoura (MOR) (Asandre (FR)) [1996 NR   65 d
1997 a7g⁴ a8g⁴ 7m 9m³ a10g 10g 10g 9g 8d 10m⁴ Oct 23] small, stocky gelding:
carries lot of condition: fair handicapper: below form after fourth start: probably best
at 7f to 9f: acts on equitrack and any turf going: visored (below form) 3 times:
sometimes swishes tail. *Lord Huntingdon*

PIRONGIA   3 b.f. Wing Park 104 – Gangawayhame 91 (Lochnager 132) [1996 –:   –
7m 7f 7m 1997 8f 5m Jun 4] seems of little account. *P. Howling*

PISTOL (IRE)   7 ch.g. Glenstal (USA) 118 – First Wind (Windjammer (USA))   75
[1996 80: 9.7s 8m 12m⁶ 8s 10f² 9.7g* 9.7m* 11.7f* 10m² 11.7m* 12m⁵ 1997 10g
12g⁵ 10g⁶ 9f 10d⁵ 10g⁴ 12m⁴ 12m² Sep 26] workmanlike gelding: fair performer:
generally creditable efforts at 7 yrs: stays 1½m: acts on firm and dead ground:
blinkered (ran poorly on equitrack) once as 2-y-o: has found little, and best held up.
C. A. Horgan

PISTOLS AT DAWN (USA)   7 b.g. Al Nasr (FR) 126 – Cannon Run (USA)   –
(Cannonade (USA)) [1996 61: a13g a11g a12g⁴ a12g⁴ 1997 a11g a12g a12g Jan 24]
lengthy gelding: poor mover: no form at 7 yrs. *B. J. Meehan*

PISUM SATIVUM   3 ch.f. Ron's Victory (USA) 129 – Trojan Desert 97 (Troy   –
137) [1996 NR 1997 7f 7g Jul 16] third foal: half-sister to winners abroad by
Kalaglow and Local Suitor: dam 7f winner, later won in USA: tailed off in maidens.
J. L. Harris

PITCHMARK (IRE)   2 ch.f. (Apr 28) Mac's Imp (USA) 116 – Sassalin   –
(Sassafras (FR) 135) [1997 5m 8d Sep 20] 2,800 2-y-o: sparely-made filly: half-sister
to several winners: dam Irish 2-y-o 7.5f winner: last in maidens. *E. Weymes*

PIXIELATED (IRE)   2 b.f. (Feb 8) Fairy King (USA) – Last Embrace (IRE) 86   64
(Shernazar 131) [1997 7m 7d 6g Oct 24] close-coupled filly: first foal: dam, 1¼m
and 1½m winner, half-sister to smart miler Crown Witness and to useful Overplay,
the dam of Vintage Crop: some promise in maidens first 2 starts: well in rear final
outing: will prove suited by at least 1m. *D. R. Loder*

PIZZICATO   3 b.f. Statoblest 120 – Musianica 92 (Music Boy 124) [1996 NR   64
1997 a5g* 5.3f* 5g⁴ 5g⁵ 5g Aug 28] 15,000F, 17,000Y: workmanlike filly: third foal:
half-sister to 5-y-o Barrel of Hope and Dime Time (fairly useful 7f winner, by
Midyan): dam 2-y-o 6f winner: modest form: won maiden at Wolverhampton in June
and minor event at Brighton in July: creditable efforts in handicaps afterwards: raced
only around 5f. *R. J. R. Williams*

PLAISIR D'AMOUR (IRE)   3 b.f. Danehill (USA) 126 – Mira Adonde (USA)   99 p
(Sharpen Up 127) [1996 65: 6m⁴ 6m² 6g⁴ 1997 7m* 7f* 6m⁴ 7.1g 6m⁴ 5d³ 6s* 7g²
6g* 6g 6m² 6d Oct 17] sturdy filly: most progressive on the whole, and made into a
useful handicapper: won at Leicester in March and April, Epsom in July and York
(£14,600 event, led close home to beat Tiler by ½ length) in August: excellent second
at Newmarket penultimate start, too free for own good in listed race there final one:
seems best at 6f/7f: yet to race on heavy going, acts on any other: sometimes hangs:
tough and consistent: should do well again in 1998. *N. A. Callaghan*

PLAN-B   2 b.c. (Feb 22) Polish Precedent (USA) 131 – Draft Board 78 (Rainbow   83 p
Quest (USA) 134) [1997 7m⁵ 8f² Sep 18] 310,000Y: useful-looking colt: second foal:
half-brother to useful French 3-y-o 1¼m winner Theatre King (by Old Vic): dam 6f
winner out of sister to Teleprompter: improved on debut effort when second to easy
winner Dower House in maiden at Yarmouth: stays 1m: should do better again.
J. H. M. Gosden

PLAN FOR PROFIT (IRE)   3 b.g. Polish Patriot (USA) 128 – Wild Sable   86
(IRE) 88 (Kris 135) [1996 74: 5m⁵ 5d⁴ 5.9g 5m² 5m* 5m³ 5m⁶ 6d⁵ 6m⁴ 7f² 1997
a8.5g⁵ a7g² a7g² a6g⁴ 7g 7.1g* 7m 8m³ 8g 7.1g 9m⁴ 8g⁶ 9m⁵ 8v 7g⁴ a7g⁶ a8s*
Nov 10] tall, good-topped gelding: fairly useful handicapper: won at Sandown in

May and Lingfield in November: effective at strongly-run 7f to 9f: acts on firm ground, dead and the all-weather: has flashed tail and edged left: best held up. *M. Johnston*

PLASTERED IN PARIS (IRE) 2 b.c. (Apr 29) Paris House 123 – Sarah-Clare 67 (Reach 122) [1997 6g 6m 8m Sep 22] workmanlike colt: first foal: dam 1m to 1¼m winner: no worthwhile form in maidens. *B. J. Meehan* —

PLAYGROUP 2 ch.f. (Mar 30) Rudimentary (USA) 118 – Miss Paige (AUS) 60 p (Luskin Star (AUS)) [1997 7m Nov 1] third foal: closely related to 4-y-o Miss Pravda: dam won over 5.5f in Australia: 25/1, gave trouble at start and began slowly when mid-division in maiden at Newmarket, soon chasing leaders and not knocked about: should do better. *Mrs J. Cecil*

PLAYMAKER 4 b.g. Primo Dominie 121 – Salacious (Sallust 134) [1996 74d: 7.1d⁶ 6m⁵ 5m 6f⁶ 6f 6s 7g 5m 5m a5g² a6g 1997 a6g a5g⁶ 5m 5m 5d 7s May 21] workmanlike gelding: one-time fair performer: has lost his form. *D. Nicholls* —

PLAY SAFE 2 b.c. (Apr 25) Sanglamore (USA) 126 – Livry (USA) (Lyphard 58 (USA) 132) [1997 7g⁶ Oct 27] IR 8,000Y: sixth foal: brother to 3-y-o Sophomore and half-brother to 6f winner Deliver (by Rousillon): dam, French 11f winner, half-sister to very smart middle-distance performer Defensive Play, from family of 1000 Guineas winner Musical Bliss: 16/1 and bandaged behind, needed race and experience when never-dangerous sixth to Altibr in Leicester maiden: should stay 1¼m+: sold 14,500 gns, and sent to Poland. *B. W. Hills*

PLAY THE TUNE 4 b.g. Music Boy 124 – Stepping Gaily 79 (Gay Fandango — (USA) 132) [1996 –: 5d 7m 7m 6s 1997 6d 5g 10d a6g Nov 21] lightly raced and no worthwhile form. *A. W. Carroll*

PLEADING 4 b.g. Never So Bold 135 – Ask Mama 83 (Mummy's Pet 125) [1996 87 94+: 6m* 6d* 6m² 6g 1997 7m⁶ 7.1g 7g 7m 7m⁴ 6.1g 7g 5d Nov 7] smallish, good-topped gelding: fairly useful handicapper: best efforts at 4 yrs on first 2 starts: left H. Candy after seventh: stays 7f: unraced on extremes of going. *W. J. Musson*

PLEASANT DREAMS 2 ch.f. (May 6) Sabrehill (USA) 120 – Tafila 101 52 (Adonijah 126) [1997 6g⁵ 6m 8d⁶ Sep 20] 6,400Y: fourth foal: half-sister to French 1½m winner Udina (by Unfuwain): dam 1m and 1¼m winner: modest form at best in maidens: got upset in stalls on debut. *Denys Smith*

PLEASURE 2 ch.f. (Feb 7) Most Welcome 131 – Peak Squaw (USA) 75 — (Icecapade (USA)) [1997 7m Nov 1] fifth reported foal: half-sister to 3-y-o Maraud: dam Irish 2-y-o 6f winner: 50/1, in rear in maiden at Newmarket. *R. W. Armstrong*

PLEASURE BOAT 3 ch.c. Suave Dancer (USA) 136 – Pilot 117 (Kris 135) — [1996 NR 1997 10s 12m 10s Oct 8] second reported foal: dam, 7f winner and second in Musidora Stakes from 3 starts, from excellent family, including Bireme and Buoy: well beaten in maidens: sold, and sent to Switzerland. *N. A. Graham*

PLEASUREDANCER (USA) 2 gr.g. (Apr 7) Thorn Dance (USA) 107 – Istiara 77 p (FR) (Crystal Palace (FR) 132) [1997 7m³ a8g³ Dec 19] $6,000Y: half-brother to fairly useful 1987 2-y-o 7f and 1m winner Ilishpour (by Kris) and a winner in France by Darshaan: dam, French 9f and 1¼m winner, from good French family: about 4 lengths third in maidens won by Benin at Leicester and Hanuman Highway at Lingfield (got boxed in): will stay 1¼m: should improve. *W. A. O'Gorman*

PLEASURELAND (IRE) 4 ch.g. Don't Forget Me 127 – Elminya (IRE) (Sure 68 Blade (USA) 130) [1996 61: 8.2g 10m a12g³ a16g³ a16g⁵ 14d 1997 16.4m⁶ 20m⁶ 18d Jul 5] sturdy gelding: fair handicapper: best effort when close sixth of 25 in Ascot Stakes at Royal Ascot on second start: suited by test of stamina: acts on equitrack and on good to firm and dead ground: tried blinkered. *R. Curtis*

PLEASURE SHARED (IRE) 9 ch.g. Kemal (FR) 120 – Love-In-A-Mist — (Paddy's Stream 80) [1996 NR 1997 22.2d Jun 20] 10,000 7-y-o: big, deep-girthed gelding: half-brother to a useful jumper by Deep Run: dam won NH Flat race and over hurdles: good-class staying hurdler: saddle reportedly slipped when tailed off in Queen Alexandra Stakes at Royal Ascot. *P. J. Hobbs*

PLEASURE TIME 4 ch.g. Clantime 101 – First Experience 58 (Le Johnstan 69 123) [1996 66: 5d³ 5.1g 5m⁵ 6g⁵ 5g⁴ 5.1m³ 5m⁵ 5m 5.1m⁵ 5m 1997 5.1g* a5g 5g³ 5g

5g² 5m 5m⁵ 5d³ 5d Oct 17] leggy, good-topped gelding: fair 5f handicapper: made all at Nottingham in May: respectable efforts at least most starts afterwards: acts on firm and dead ground, ran poorly only all-weather outing: effective with or without blinkers/visor. *C. Smith*

PLEASURE TRICK (USA)   6 br.g. Clever Trick (USA) – Pleasure Garden   49
(USA) (Foolish Pleasure (USA)) [1996 46: 7.5f 8m 8m⁶ 8.5m 7g 8g⁵ 8m a8g⁴ a8g   a57
a7g* a8g 1997 a7g* a7g³ a8g⁶ a7g² a8g a8g* a8g⁵ a8g⁵ a8g 7m 8g 6.9f 8f³ 8m² 7d a8g
8m* 8.5m⁶ 8.1m 8d 7m 8.2d a8g Nov 24] good-quartered gelding: modest
handicapper: won at Southwell in January and February and at Pontefract in July:
stays 1m: best turf form on good ground or firmer, goes well on fibresand: effective
blinkered or not: usually held up, and suited by strong pace. *Don Enrico Incisa*

PLEIN GAZ (FR)   4 b.g. Lesotho (USA) 118 – Gazzara (USA) (Irish River (FR)   53
131) [1996 72: a5g⁵ a7g⁴ 6s 6g 8d⁵ 8d 6m⁶ 6d² 7g⁵ 7g² 7g⁵ 7g 7d⁵ 6s 7d 6g² 1997 6m⁴
6g 5g 5g⁴ a7g 5g³ 5g 6d a6g Dec 19] ex-Belgian gelding: fair form at best at 3 yrs:
ran in France/Belgium for A. Hermans first 8 starts in 1997: well beaten on first run
for new trainer here: stays 7f: acts on soft ground and equitrack: has been blinkered:
front runner. *J. J. Bridger*

PLENTY OF SUNSHINE   4 ch.f. Pharly (FR) 130 – Zipperti Do 70 (Precocious   –
126) [1996 NR 1997 a10g a7g Feb 19] third foal: half-sister to 1¼m winner
Wonderful Day (by Niniski): dam 1m winner: well beaten in maidens. *I. Campbell*

PLUM FIRST   7 b.g. Nomination 125 – Plum Bold 83 (Be My Guest (USA) 126)   56
[1996 68, a52: 5d² 5g² 5g⁴ 6m 6g³ 5g 6g³ 6m⁴ 6m 6m 5m 6.1m 5m a6g⁶ a6g a6g³   a53
1997 a7g² a7g 5g 6d 6d² 7f 6m 5g⁵ 7m⁶ 5m a8g⁴ a8g Nov 24] lengthy, workmanlike
gelding: has round action: modest handicapper: left J. L. Eyre after sixth start: plum
last tenth one: stays 7f: acts on any turf ground and on fibresand: effective visored/
blinkered or not: has started slowly: tends to hang left. *M. A. Peill*

PODDINGTON   6 b.g. Crofthall 110 – Bold Gift 61 (Persian Bold 123) [1996   –
105: 9f* 10.1g⁴ 1997 10.3m⁶ Jun 7] has had only 4 races: showed useful form on
second 5-y-o start, but well held only outing in 1997: stays 1¼m: raced only on good
going or firmer: clearly difficult to train. *R. Akehurst*

POETRY IN MOTION (IRE)   2 gr.f. (Mar 24) Ballad Rock 122 – Nasseem   62 p
(FR) 118 (Zeddaan 130) [1997 6m 6g 6m⁵ Oct 7] tall, good-topped filly: has plenty
of scope: half-sister to several winners, including useful miler Sharpen Up (by Sharpen
Up) and fairly useful 6f (at 2 yrs) to 1¼m winner Percy Braithwaite (by Kahyasi):
dam won Cherry Hinton Stakes and third in Coronation Stakes: showed ability in
maidens at Haydock and Redcar, promising better to come when never-dangerous
fifth to Sense of Wonder on latter course: stiff task in between: type to do much better
at 3 yrs. *E. J. Alston*

POETTO   2 ch.c. (Apr 21) Casteddu 111 – Steamy Windows § (Dominion 123)   60
[1997 5g³ 5d⁴ 5g 6m 5.7m⁶ 6g² 6m a5g² a6g⁶ a5g⁵ Dec 8] 4,200F, 18,000Y: sturdy   a57
colt: second foal: dam, maiden, sister to smart 1986 2-y-o sprinter Dominion Royale:
modest maiden: runner-up in sellers at Goodwood and Wolverhampton (visored on
final start for B. Meehan): below best in nurseries for new stable last 2 starts: stays
6f: best efforts on good going and fibresand: blinkered (ran poorly) third start: shows
signs of reluctance. *J. Hetherton*

POINTE FINE (FR)   3 b.f. Homme de Loi (IRE) 120 – Pointe Argentee (Pas de   61
Seul 133) [1996 58: 7f 7d⁵ 1997 6.9m² a8.5g³ 10m 11g² 16.2m⁴ 11.9g² a12g³ a14.8g
14g Sep 27] modest maiden: stays 2m: acts on good to firm going and on fibresand.
J. W. Hills

POINTELLE   3 b.f. Sharpo 132 – Clymene 86 (Vitiges (FR) 132) [1996 –: 7g   –
1997 7m 8m 6g 9m a10s Nov 10] signs of ability but no worthwhile form. *A. Hide*

POINTER   5 b.g. Reference Point 139 – Greenhill Lass (Upper Case (USA)) [1996   61
61: a8.5g⁵ 9.9d 6m⁴ 6m⁶ 7d* 7f 7g³ 6m* 6m* 5.7f⁴ 6m² 7g⁶ 7g 1997 6m⁵ 6.1m⁴ 5g⁵
7m 7m⁶ 5d² 6m 5.7g 5.1g³ 6.1m 6m⁵ 5d 5d Oct 20] tall gelding: modest handicapper:
failed to win at 5 yrs, but ran creditably most starts: effective at 5f to 7f: acts on firm
and dead ground: successful for amateur: usually races prominently: consistent: sold,
and sent to Saudi Arabia. *Mrs P. N. Dutfield*

*Vodafone Diomed Stakes, Epsom—Polar Prince springs a surprise;
Faithful Son (left) is second and Cap Juluca (rail) third*

POKER PRINCESS   3 br.f. Waajib 121 – Mory Kante (USA) (Icecapade (USA))   54
[1996 47+: 5.7m⁶ 6g 5m 5f 1997 8.2m a7g² a7g⁵ 8f³ 10.1f⁶ 10.1m³ a9.4f⁴ 8d² 10s³ 8g
9.9g⁶ 8f Sep 18] modest maiden handicapper: stays 1¼m: acts on firm and soft
ground and on fibresand: sold, and sent to Germany. *M. Bell*

POKER SCHOOL (IRE)   3 b.g. Night Shift (USA) – Mosaique Bleue (Shirley   88 d
Heights 130) [1996 8d³ 1997 8g⁴ 8d² 8s² 9g* 8g 10m 7m 10s Aug 30] smallish,
sturdy ex-Irish gelding: second foal: dam unraced half-sister to Prix Royal-Oak
winner Mersey and Prix Saint-Alary winner Muncie: fairly useful performer in
Ireland for C. O'Brien, winning maiden at Dundalk in May on final start for him: no
worthwhile form here: stays 9f: acts on soft going. *N. A. Callaghan*

POLAR CHAMP   4 b.g. Polar Falcon (USA) 126 – Ceramic (USA) (Raja Baba   84
(USA)) [1996 77, a80: 8m⁵ 8f² 10f⁴ 10g a9.4g² 10.1m² 10f* 12m a12g² 1997 9.9m
10.3d* 10g 10.1m³ 10m⁴ 10.2f⁵ 10.5m³ 12m a12g* Oct 4] leggy gelding: has a round
action: fairly useful handicapper: won at Doncaster (made most) in May and Wolverhampton (led last strides) in October: effective at 1¼m to 1½m: acts on the
all-weather and on firm and dead ground: effective blinkered/visored or not: often
soon off bridle: none too consistent. *S. P. C. Woods*

POLAR ECLIPSE   4 ch.g. Polar Falcon (USA) 126 – Princess Zepoli 61   –
(Persepolis (FR) 127) [1996 95d: 7g⁴ 10d⁵ 8g² 8m 8m 10m⁶ 7.9g 10s⁶ 1997 a8.5g⁵
10.3d 8v 8d 7m Nov 1] rangy gelding: fairly useful performer at best: long way below
form in 1997, leaving M. Johnston after second start. *B. J. Meehan*

POLAR FLIGHT   3 br.c. Polar Falcon (USA) 126 – Fine Honey (USA) 90   92
(Drone) [1996 92p: 8.2m 6m² 7f⁴ 8m² 8s* 1997 8m 10m 8s³ 8g* 10.4g⁶ 9g⁵ Oct 25]
tall, angular colt: has a round action: fairly useful performer: in good form in spring,
following third in Swiss equivalent of 2000 Guineas at Dielsdorf by winning minor
event at Cologne: off course over 5 months before well held final start (sold 23,000
gns shortly after): stays 10.4f: acts on good to firm ground, better efforts on good and
soft: tends to edge/hang left. *M. Johnston*

POLARIZE   3 ch.g. Polar Falcon (USA) 126 – Comhail (USA) (Nodouble (USA))   60
[1996 –: 7.9g 7f 1997 a7g⁴ 8s* 10g 8d³ 9g⁵ a8g 8g* 8g Aug 1] modest handicapper:
won at Musselburgh in March and Thirsk (seller) in July: should have stayed beyond
1m: acted on soft going: effective blinkered or not: dead. *T. D. Barron*

POLAR MIST   2 b.g. (Feb 13) Polar Falcon (USA) 126 – Post Mistress (IRE) 79   70 p
(Cyrano de Bergerac 120) [1997 a6g² Dec 6] first foal: dam 5f winner at 2 yrs, her
only season to race, out of half-sister to useful sprinter Case Law: 6/1, 6 lengths

second of 13 to Wolfhunt in maiden at Wolverhampton, headed over 1f out and keeping on (not given too hard a time): will improve. *Sir Mark Prescott*

POLAR PRINCE (IRE) 4 b.c. Distinctly North (USA) 115 – Staff Approved 94   115
(Teenoso (USA) 135) [1996 108: 8d² 8m³ 8.1d⁵ 7m* 7m 7m* 7m⁶ 7g* 7m 7m⁶ 1997
7d² 7f* 8.5g* 8d³ 8g³ 8g² 8.5g⁵ Sep 5] robust, lengthy colt: impresses in appearance:
good mover: smart performer: won listed race at Rome in May and strongly-run Diomed Stakes at Epsom (by ½ length from Faithful Son) in June: placed afterwards
in Budweiser American Bowl International at the Curragh (1½ lengths third to
Alhaarth), Prix Messidor at Deauville (2 lengths third to Neuilly) and Tripleprint
Celebration Mile at Goodwood (promoted to second on disqualification of Cape
Cross): effective at 7f to 8.5f: acts on firm and dead going, yet to race on soft: held up
and has good turn of foot: consistent. *M. A. Jarvis*

POLAR PROSPECT 4 b.g. Polar Falcon (USA) 126 – Littlemisstrouble (USA)   64
(My Gallant (USA)) [1996 76: 7.3s² 8d 7.5f* 7.1m⁴ 8m 10m⁴ 8.5g 7.9g 8.1v⁶ 1997
7m 7g 8.3g² 8.5f⁴ 10m³ 9m* Oct 7] good-topped gelding: modest handicapper: won
at Redcar: stays 1¼m: acts on firm ground, well held on heavy: has been bandaged:
joined P. Hobbs, and won over hurdles in December. *B. Hanbury*

POLAR REFRAIN 4 ch.f. Polar Falcon (USA) 126 – Cut No Ice 97 (Great   –
Nephew 126) [1996 59, a–: 6s² 5m 7m 6m³ 6m³ 7m 7g⁴ a6g a6g⁶ a8g⁶ a7g⁶ 1997 8g
10d 8.5s 10g 8g Jun 18] workmanlike filly: modest maiden handicapper: no form in
1997. *J. Norton*

POLEAXE 3 b.f. Selkirk (USA) 129 – Sarmatia (USA) (Danzig (USA)) [1996 NR   –
1997 8.3s 7.1d⁵ Jul 3] sparely-made filly: first foal: dam unraced half-sister to Kris,
Diesis and Keen (all by Sharpen Up, also sire of Selkirk): well held in maidens at
Windsor (missed break) and Haydock. *Mrs J. Cecil*

POLENISTA 3 b.f. Polish Precedent (USA) 131 – Princess Genista 108 (Ile de   68 d
Bourbon (USA) 133) [1996 NR 1997 10g⁵ 10g 10g 12d³ 14.1g Oct 18] angular filly:
fifth foal: half-sister to 4-y-o Tsarnista and useful pair Sovinista (best up to 1m, also
by Soviet Star) and Tomos (1m and 1½m winner, by Sure Blade): dam 1m winner
who stayed 15f: fair maiden: easily best effort on debut: stud. *J. L. Dunlop*

Mrs Christine Stevenson's "Polar Prince"

POLENKA (IRE)   3 ch.f. Polish Precedent (USA) 131 – Amana River (USA) 77   55
(Raise A Cup (USA)) [1996 NR 1997 8.5m³ 8m³ 10d 7m⁶ 7m Oct 7] has round
action: third foal: half-sister to 2-y-o 6f winners Amanita (by Lead On Time) and
Bridge of Fire (by Mtoto): dam, 5f and 1m winner, out of half-sister to high-class US
2-y-o filly Althea (stayed 9f) and the dam of Green Desert: modest maiden: probably
needs at least 1m. *J. W. Watts*

POLGWYNNE   3 ch.f. Forzando 122 – Trelissick (Electric 126) [1996 NR 1997   48
a8g⁶ a7g* 6.1d 7m⁵ 6.1d 7m 6.1m 6m⁵ a7g a7g a8g Dec 18] 2,000Y: fifth foal: dam
little sign of ability: poor performer: won maiden at Lingfield in March: should prove
at least as effective over 6f as 7f: acts on equitrack and good to firm ground, seems
unsuited by dead: inconsistent. *B. Smart*

POLISHED STEEL (IRE)   3 ch.g. Polish Precedent (USA) 131 – Galava   58
(CAN) (Graustark) [1996 NR 1997 8g 8g 8g a10g* a10g Dec 22] workmanlike
gelding: third foal: half-brother to 1¾m winner Grey Galava (by Generous): dam
placed at 7f/1m in France: form only when making all in apprentice minor event at
Lingfield in December: pulled up final start: blinkered last 3 starts: had been tongue
tied: dead. *Lady Herries*

POLISH PILOT (IRE)   2 b.c. (Apr 4) Polish Patriot (USA) 128 – Va Toujours   61
109 (Alzao (USA) 117) [1997 6g 5m 6s³ a6s Nov 10] leggy, workmanlike colt:
second reported foal: half-brother to 4-y-o Dauphin: dam 6f (at 2 yrs) to 9f winner:
modest maiden: third at Catterick in October: never dangerous on all-weather debut
at Lingfield: bred to stay beyond 6f. *W. R. Muir*

POLISH RHYTHM (IRE)   4 b.f. Polish Patriot (USA) 128 – Clanjingle   77
(Tumble Wind (USA)) [1996 69: 8.3m⁶ 6m 8.1m⁵ 7m 10.1m 1997 10d 8s* 8g⁴ 8.1s
8m² 8m³ 8v⁵ 8m Nov 1] workmanlike filly: poor mover: fair performer: won
handicap at Yarmouth in July: flattered in listed events fourth and sixth starts: probably best around 1m: acts on good to firm and soft ground, probably on heavy:
usually races up with pace. *G. A. Hubbard*

POLISH ROMANCE (USA)   3 b.f. Danzig (USA) – Some Romance (USA)   77
(Fappiano (USA)) [1996 83: 6m⁴ 6g⁵ 1997 6g³ 5g² 6g³ 7g² 7g² 7d* 7m Sep 9] lengthy
filly: fluent mover: fair performer: made all in maiden at Epsom in August: stays 7f:
yet to race on extremes of going: very slowly away fourth start: not one to trust
implicitly. *M. R. Stoute*

POLISH SWINGER (IRE)   4 b.g. Polish Patriot (USA) 128 – Girl On A Swing   –
79 (High Top 131) [1996 NR 1997 8f⁴ Apr 21] IR 62,000Y, 8,500 (from J. Toller)
3-y-o: half-brother to several winners, including 1¾m winner Dame Elusive (by
Blakeney): dam, placed twice at around 7f, is out of half-sister to Irish Oaks winner
Pampalina: easy to back, well held in maiden at Brighton. *Miss Gay Kelleway*

POLISH WARRIOR (IRE)   3 ch.g. Polish Patriot (USA) 128 – Opuntia   88
(Rousillon (USA) 133) [1996 88: 6g⁴ 6g² 6g³ 5f* 1997 5d⁶ 6m⁵ 5d⁴ 5d³ 5.1m² 5g
Aug 20] big, strong gelding: fairly useful handicapper: creditable efforts first 5 starts,
swished tail before poor run final one: at least as effective at 5f as 6f: acts on firm
ground and dead: has awkward head carriage and possibly temperamental: blinkered
last 4 starts: sent to Macau. *T. D. Barron*

POLLYDUU   2 ch.f. (May 3) Casteddu 111 – Polly Packer 81 (Reform 132) [1997   –
a8g a8g a6g⁶ Dec 26] half-sister to several winners, notably useful stayer Regal
Reform (by Prince Tenderfoot): dam, second over 7f and 1m, out of smart miler Vital
Match: slowly away and well beaten in sellers and claimer. *N. P. Littmoden*

POLLY GOLIGHTLY   4 ch.f. Weldnaas (USA) 112 – Polly's Teahouse 68   69
(Shack (USA) 118) [1996 77d: 5d 5.1g⁴ 5.1f 6m⁵ 5.1m 7m⁴ 7m³ 6g⁴ 5m 5m³ 6m³ 6f
5.1m 8f 1997 5m 5m⁵ a7g 5g³ 5.1g² 5m* 5m* 5m⁵ 5g² 5d 5m 5.2m⁴ 5.2m 5d 5m
5.1g⁵ 5d² 5d* 5d⁴ Nov 7] smallish filly: fair handicapper: successful at Lingfield in
May, Goodwood in June and Catterick in October: best at 5f: acts on firm and dead
ground: effective blinkered (usually is)/visored or not: has swished tail: tends to edge
left. *M. Blanshard*

POLLY IN PARIS (IRE)   2 b.f. (Feb 24) Paris House 123 – Persian Tapestry 70   –
(Tap On Wood 130) [1997 5.1m 5m⁵ 5d Sep 18] IR 5,000Y: sixth foal: half-sister to
5f winner Need You Badly (by Robellino): dam 1¼m winner: well beaten, including
in sellers. *Martyn Meade*

POLLY PECULIAR 6 b.m. Squill (USA) 122 – Pretty Pollyanna (General –
Assembly (USA)) [1996 69, a49: a10g³ 10g 8m⁶ 7.5f* 7g* 8f⁶ 8.2g* 8s³ a8g⁴ 1997
10g 8m May 24] leggy mare: formerly fair handicapper up to 1¼m: well beaten in
1997: acted on firm ground, soft and equitrack: dead. *B. Smart*

POLLYTEKNICK 2 gr.f. (Feb 26) Terimon 124 – Flute Royale 74 (Horage 124) –
[1997 7g a5g⁶ 5m Jul 21] third reported foal: half-sister to 5-y-o Silk Cottage: dam
2-y-o 5f winner: soundly beaten, including in seller. *N. P. Littmoden*

POLONAISE PRINCE (USA) 4 b.g. Alleged (USA) 138 – La Polonaise –
(USA) (Danzig (USA)) [1996 –: 10g 10s 1997 11.7g a12g 10g Oct 4] strong gelding:
little worthwhile form. *V. Soane*

POLO VENTURE 2 ch.g. (Mar 9) Polar Falcon (USA) 126 – Ceramic (USA) 67
(Raja Baba (USA)) [1997 6g 6m⁵ a7g³ 8m 8d³ Oct 20] seventh foal: brother to 4-y-o
Polar Champ and half-brother to 3 winners, including 1993 2-y-o 6f winner Little
Beaut (by Prince Sabo): dam ran once in Ireland: fair maiden: third at Southwell and
Pontefract (nursery): shapes as though will stay 1¼m+. *S. P. C. Woods*

POLSKA MODELLE (FR) 2 ch.c. (Apr 6) Polish Precedent (USA) 131 – – p
Model Village 101 (Habitat 134) [1997 7.1s Oct 15] rather unfurnished, useful-
looking colt: fourth foal: dam 7f and 1m winner: 5/1 and green, well-held seventh of
13 to Dark Moondancer in maiden at Haydock, missing break completely then not
knocked about: unimpressive to post: will do better. *J. H. M. Gosden*

POLSKA PRINCESS (GER) 3 br.f. Polish Precedent (USA) 131 – Pikante 74
(GER) (Surumu (GER)) [1996 NR 1997 8g 9m 10.2s⁴ 10g⁴ 10g Oct 24]
sparely-made filly: half-sister to several winners, including 4-y-o Power Flame and
1992 German Derby winner Pik Konig (by Konigsstuhl): dam German 11.5f and
jumps winner: fair maiden: stays 1¼m: well beaten on soft ground. *Lord Huntingdon*

POLTARF (USA) 6 b.h. Alleged (USA) 138 – La Polonaise (USA) (Danzig 106
(USA)) [1996 107: 12m⁶ 13.4d 14d³ 16m⁶ 14.6d² 14v 1997 15d³ 14g² 11.9s⁵ 16m⁴
Oct 31] big, strong horse: carries condition: shows knee action: useful performer:
placed in listed race at Maisons-Laffitte in June and minor event at Haydock (short-
headed by The Faraway Tree) in September: well beaten afterwards: acts on 2m well:
acts on firm and dead ground, seems unsuited by soft: below form when sweating
first 2 starts at 5 yrs. *J. H. M. Gosden*

POLY BLUE (IRE) 2 ch.f. (Feb 27) Thatching 131 – Mazarine Blue (USA) 74
(Chief's Crown (USA)) [1997 7g 6d* 6m 6g Oct 25] IR 15,000Y: quite good-topped
filly: first foal: dam, ran twice in France, half-sister to dual Gold Cup winner Sadeem
(mostly a speedy family otherwise): won maiden at Newbury in September: eased
when beaten next outing and persistently short of room final one: should stay 7f. *Miss
Gay Kelleway*

POLYPHONY (USA) 3 b.c. Cox's Ridge (USA) – Populi (USA) (Star Envoy 72
(USA)) [1996 NR 1997 a12g² 12g* 14.1g⁴ 14.8d³ Jun 11] brother to 2 winners,
notably top-class American middle-distance performer Vanlandingham, and half-
brother to several winners in France and USA: dam, 7f winner at 2 yrs in USA,
half-sister to champion middle-distance 3-y-o Temperence Hill: fair performer: won
maiden at Carlisle in April: creditable efforts from starts afterwards, though free in
blinkers on second occasion: stays 15f: sold 21,000 gns in October. *R. Charlton*

POMONA 4 b.f. Puissance 110 – Plum Bold 83 (Be My Guest (USA) 126) [1996 93
89: 7d 8f 7d² 7g 8.3d² 8.1d³ 8g* 1997 8.1g 7.3s³ 8.1m³ 8m 7.9g⁵ 8.3m* 8m⁵ 8m⁴ 8m
Nov 1] leggy filly: fairly useful handicapper: won strongly-run race at Windsor in
August: creditable efforts afterwards: stays 1m: acts on good to firm and dead
ground: held up. *P. J. Makin*

PONTOON 2 br.f. (Feb 17) Zafonic (USA) 130 – Dockage (CAN) (Riverman 89 p
(USA) 131) [1997 7m* Nov 1] seventh foal: half-sister to several winners, including
1993 2-y-o 1m winner Colza (by Alleged) and smart 6f (at 2 yrs) to 9f (in USA)
winner Wharf (by Storm Bird): dam, useful 1m/9f winner in France, from family of
Dahlia: 3/1 from 6/4, won maiden at Newmarket by short head from Lovers Knot,
niggled along from halfway but running on well for pressure despite hanging slightly
left (more markedly so just after post): will stay at least 1m: sure to improve and win
more races. *H. R. A. Cecil*

*Doubleprint Arc Trial, Newbury—the first running of this event
goes to Posidonas (centre) from the grey Arabian Story and odds-on Swain*

POOL MUSIC 2 ch.c. (Apr 14) Forzando 122 – Sunfleet 59 (Red Sunset 120) 101
[1997 5m* 5m* 5g⁵ 6g³ 6m 6d³ 6g Oct 18] 11,000F, 60,000Y: tall, quite attractive
colt: impresses in appearance: sixth foal: brother to 4-y-o Russian Music and half-
brother to 3 winners, including 5-y-o No Pattern: dam maiden: useful performer: won
maiden at Salisbury and listed race at Sandown (by 1¼ lengths from Banningham
Blade) in May: best efforts in pattern events when third to Bold Fact in July Stakes at
Newmarket and Arkadian Hero in Mill Reef Stakes at Newbury: should stay 7f,
probably 1m: yet to encounter extremes of ground. *R. Hannon*

POPPY MY LOVE 4 ch.f. Clantime 101 – Yankeedoodledancer (Mashhor Dan- –
cer (USA)) [1996 41: 5g⁵ 1997 5m 5m May 28] workmanlike filly: poor sprint
maiden: well beaten in 1997. *I. Campbell*

PORTHILLY BUOY 2 ch.g. (Mar 18) Keen 116 – Hissma 84 (Midyan (USA)) –
124) [1997 7.1g 6g 7g a10s Nov 28] IR 1,400Y: second foal: dam 2-y-o 6f winner
who stayed 1m: no worthwhile form. *M. J. Haynes*

PORTITE SOPHIE 6 b.m. Doulab (USA) 115 – Impropriety (Law Society (USA) 47
130) [1996 31, a37: 12.3g⁶ 11.1m 11.1f 11.1m⁴ a8.5g* a7g 1997 12m³ 8.3d⁴ 9.9m² a50
11.7m⁴ 8.5s⁶ 11.1s⁴ 10g 12g² a11g* a12g⁴ 12.3m⁴ 10.5m⁴ 12g² 10.3d⁵ 12f a8.5g²
a12g² 10.1g Oct 22] small, wiry mare: modest performer: won claimer at Southwell
in July: needs strong pace at 8.5f, and stays 1½m: acts on firm and soft going and on
fibresand: tried blinkered (well below form): tough and consistent. *M. Brittain*

PORTO FORICOS (USA) 2 b.c. (May 6) Mr Prospector (USA) – Gallanta (FR) – p
(Nureyev (USA) 131) [1997 6m⁶ 6d⁴ Aug 21] attractive colt: closely related to 1994
Queen Mary and Cheveley Park winner Gay Gallanta (by Woodman) and half-
brother to 3 winners, including very smart Irish 7f and 1¼m winner Sportsworld (by
Alleged): dam, 5.5f to 1m winner in France, is half-sister to Gay Mecene: green,
promised better in maidens at Goodwood then York (valuable event won by Bintang)
less than a month apart, rearing and banging head stalls on latter course and tiring
badly. *H. R. A. Cecil*

PORTUGUESE LIL 4 ch.f. Master Willie 129 – Sabonis (USA) 68 (The 56
Minstrel (CAN) 135) [1996 69: 8m 9.9m⁵ 12m 7f³ 8m 8.5g 1997 8.5m⁵ Jun 5] sturdy
filly: fair maiden at 3 yrs: blinkered, modest form only 4-y-o start: should be suited
by 1m+: acts on firm going: edgy type. *J. L. Eyre*

POSATIVE   3 ch.f. Charmer 123 – Suprette 64 (Superlative 118) [1996 NR 1997   –
7g Jun 12] 1,400Y: workmanlike filly: third foal: dam (maiden) stayed 7f: burly, well
held in maiden at Newbury. *M. Salaman*

POSEIDON   3 b.c. Polar Falcon (USA) 126 – Nastassia (FR) (Noble Decree   110
(USA) 127) [1996 ?: 6g* 1997 8m⁵ 8g 10.3m* 12s⁴ 12g² 12m² 14.6m 12g⁵ 12d⁵ Oct
26] lengthy colt: smart performer: won minor event at Doncaster in June: good
second in July in listed race at Hamburg and Gordon Stakes at Goodwood (beaten 3
lengths by Stowaway): bit below best in St Leger at Doncaster, Cumberland Lodge
Stakes at Ascot and Group 3 race at Dusseldorf afterwards: probably stays 14.6f: acts
on good to firm ground, looked all at sea on soft. *M. R. Channon*

POSIDONAS   5 b.h. Slip Anchor 136 – Tamassos 67 (Dance In Time (CAN))   119
[1996 123: 13.3d³ 12f³ 12g* 12m² 13.3m² 14m⁴ 12f 1997 10m⁵ 12g³ 11g* 12f 12m²
Dec 14] good-topped horse: shows knee action: usually impresses in appearance:
very smart performer in 1996: retained most of his ability at 5 yrs: won listed race at
Newbury in September by short head from Arabian Story: blinkered, good ninth to
Peintre Celebre in the Arc at Longchamp: ran well when head second to
Luso in Hong Kong International Vase in December: needs further than 1¼m, but
finds 1¾m stretching his stamina: acts on firm and dead going: had 2 handlers and
was keen to post at Longchamp: tends to carry head shade high, but is genuine and
consistent. *P. F. I. Cole*

POSITIVE AIR   2 b.f. (Mar 11) Puissance 110 – Breezy Day 85 (Day Is Done   72
115) [1997 5g⁵ 5d 5.1d² 7d⁶ 6g 5d³ 6.1m² 7g 7s⁶ 6g² Oct 27] 5,200F: tall filly: first
foal: dam sprinter: fair maiden: in-and-out form: stays 6f: acts on good to firm and
dead ground. *B. A. McMahon*

POSITIVE RESULT (IRE)   5 ch.m. Doulab (USA) 115 – Second Service (Red   –
Regent 123) [1996 NR 1997 a5g 5.7d May 19] no sign of ability. *R. J. Price*

POTEEN (USA)   3 b.c. Irish River (FR) 131 – Chaleur (CAN) (Rouge Sang   118
(USA)) [1996 113p: 7.1v* 8g² 1997 7g* 8m³ 8m⁵ 7d² 8f⁴ Sep 11] good-bodied,

Lord Vestey's "Poteen"

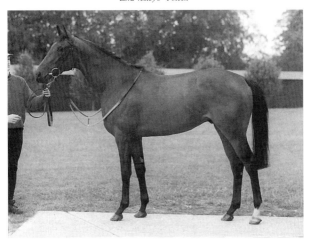

attractive colt: easy mover: smart performer: won minor event (at 1/3) at Newmarket in April: best effort when 2¼ lengths third to Entrepeneur in 2000 Guineas there following month: disappointing afterwards in St James's Palace Stakes at Royal Ascot (fifth to Starborough), listed race at York (beaten ½ length by Hidden Meadow) and Park Stakes at Doncaster (didn't look altogether genuine in first-time blinkers behind Almushtarak): will prove best up to 1m: acts on good to firm and heavy ground: not one to trust implicitly. *L. M. Cumani*

POT OF TEA 3 b.f. Tina's Pet 121 – Ebony Park (Local Suitor (USA) 128) [1996 NR 1997 8g May 26] 800F: third foal: dam unraced: tailed off in Leicester maiden. *A. Streeter* –

POWER FLAME (GER) 4 ch.g. Dashing Blade 117 – Pikante (GER) (Surumu (GER)) [1996 8g² 9.5g* 11g 9g* 8.8g* 9g* 8d³ 1997 8g 8g* 8s* 8d* 8g⁴ 8g* Sep 27] half-brother to several winners, notably German Derby winner Pik Konig (by Konigsstuhl): dam German 11.5f and jumps winner: useful (rated 106) at 3 yrs: made into smart performer in 1997: won minor event at Baden-Baden and national listed race at Hamburg before landing Group 3 event by 3½ lengths from Kalatos and Group 2 race by head (well clear) from Accento, both at Cologne: stays 9.5f: acts on soft going. *A. Wohler, Germany* 116

POWERFUL SPIRIT 5 b.g. Presidium 124 – Spiritofaffection (Raga Navarro (ITY) 119) [1996 NR 1997 13.8g Jul 23] second foal: dam unraced half-brother to smart juvenile hurdler The Grey Bomber: no promise in maiden at Catterick: won novice hurdle in August. *J. G. M. O'Shea* –

POWER GAME 4 b.g. Puissance 110 – Play The Game 70 (Mummy's Game 120) [1996 69: 6m 6g² 8.1d³ 6m 6.9f² 8.1m⁴ 8m 8.1m² 7d³ a8.5g 8g* 8m 8.3g* 7m³ 8.2g 8g* 1997 7.5m⁴ 8m⁵ 8g⁵ 8d³ 8d* 8m* 8m 8.2g 8m⁵ 8.3d³ 8m Jul 18] leggy gelding: modest performer: won seller and handicap at Musselburgh in May: stays 1m: acts on firm and dead ground, ran poorly only all-weather outing: has been visored, usually blinkered nowadays: joined D. Nolan. *J. Berry* 60

POW WOW 3 b.c. Efisio 120 – Mill Hill (USA) (Riva Ridge (USA)) [1996 60?: 5.1m⁴ 5g 5m 1997 10.8m 8.1g Sep 11] modest maiden at 2 yrs: tailed off in 1997. *P. Eccles* –

PRADESH 3 ch.f. Generous (IRE) 139 – Bareilly (USA) (Lyphard (USA) 132) [1996 NR 1997 10g 10m 10m⁵ 12s⁵ 11m⁴ Nov 4] close-coupled filly: first living foal: dam, unraced, closely related to Prix de Diane second Baya: fair maiden: should be suited by 1½m+: below form on soft ground: visored (ran creditably) final start: sold 38,000 gns in December. *J. H. M. Gosden* 67

PRAEDITUS 3 b.g. Cadeaux Genereux 131 – Round Midnight 64 (Star Appeal 133) [1996 75p: 6d⁶ 6s⁴ 1997 8g⁵ 7g* 7m³ 8m 7f 7.9s 8.1m 10s 10.3g⁶ Oct 24] big, strong gelding: fair performer: won maiden at Lingfield in May: well below form after next outing: stays 7f: acts on good to firm and soft ground: pulled hard and well beaten only start in blinkers: has carried head high, and doesn't look an easy ride. *R. Hannon* 76 d

PRAETORIAN GOLD 2 ch.c. (Apr 22) Presidium 124 – Chinese Princess (Sunny Way 120) [1997 5.1m 7m⁶ 7.6d 8f 6.1g* 7m 8.2d³ Oct 30] 14,500 2-y-o: rather leggy, useful-looking colt: half-brother to several winners, including 7f winner Cunning Plan (by Belfort): dam unraced: fair performer: won maiden at Nottingham in September: good third in nursery there final start: stays 1m: acts on good to firm and dead going. *R. Hannon* 73

PRAIRIE FALCON (IRE) 3 b.c. Alzao (USA) 117 – Sea Harrier (Grundy 137) [1996 69p: 7m³ 7g⁵ 1997 11.1m² 12g⁵ 12.1g* 12d⁵ 12m 13.9g 10g Oct 24] attractive colt: good mover: fairly useful performer: won maiden at Chepstow in May: creditable efforts in competitive handicaps next 3 starts: free-going sort (often held up), but probably stays 1¾m: acts on good to firm and dead going. *B. W. Hills* 88

PRAIRIE MINSTREL (USA) 3 b.g. Regal Intention (CAN) – Prairie Sky (USA) (Gone West (USA)) [1996 55?: 6s⁶ 7m⁶ 6.1d⁶ 10m 1997 11.7m 10s 8m⁵ 8g Aug 20] sturdy, deep-girthed gelding: modest maiden handicapper: effective at 1m and 1¼m: acts on soft and good to firm ground: below form in blinkers: has had tongue tied. *R. Dickin* 52

PRAISE BE (FR)   7 b.g. Baillamont (USA) 124 – Louange (Green Dancer (USA)   –
132) [1996 NR 1997 a10s a8g Dec 18] third reported foal: half-brother to 1¼m to 2m
winner Eulogy (by Esprit du Nord): dam French 13f winner: appears to be winner of
2 maidens, at Moulins in 1993 when trained in France by J. Hammond and at Nad Al
Sheba in 1995 when trained in Dubai by K. McLaughlin: sold 17,000 gns in 1996,
but for only 750 gns in August: well beaten both starts in Britain: stays 1½m: usually
visored in Dubai. *D. W. Chapman*

PRE CATELAN   2 ch.f. (Jan 28) Polar Falcon (USA) 126 – Anneli Rose 56 (Super-   –
lative 118) [1997 6g 5m 5f Sep 17] 30,000Y: angular filly: third foal: half-sister to
1994 Middle Park winner Fard (by Reprimand) and 7f winner Double-O-Seven (by
Tirol): dam, 6f winner, half-sister to Gallic League: signs of a little ability but no
form. *M. Bell*

PRECEDENCY   5 b.g. Polish Precedent (USA) 131 – Allegedly Blue (USA) 106   41
(Alleged (USA) 138) [1996 –, a67: 14.1f⁶ 11.9d⁶ 9.7m a11g² a14g² a14.8g⁶ a11g
12m 1997 a12g⁵ a14g 11.6m 10g 10.8d⁶ Jun 24] lengthy gelding: poor performer at
best in 1997: stays 1¾m: acts on fibresand: well beaten in visor. *K. McAuliffe*

PRECIOUS GIRL   4 ch.f. Precious Metal 106 – Oh My Oh My (Ballacashtal   –
(CAN)) [1996 76: 5d⁴ 6g⁶ 5m* 5f⁵ 6m 5g 5m 1997 6d Apr 10] workmanlike filly:
fair handicapper at 3 yrs: long way below form on only start in 1997. *D. Moffatt*

PRECIOUS ISLAND   4 b.f. Jupiter Island 126 – Burmese Ruby (Good Times   –
(ITY)) [1996 –: 11.8m 8.1f⁶ 11.8f 11.8g⁵ 1997 21.6g Apr 28] plain filly: little
worthwhile form. *P. T. Dalton*

PRECIOUS PRINCESS   2 br.f. (Feb 1) Precocious 126 – Magyar Princess   58
(Beldale Flutter (USA) 130) [1997 a5g⁵ a6g² a5g⁵ Dec 22] 6,400Y, 600 2-y-o:
workmanlike filly: first living foal: dam, lightly raced abroad, half-sister to high-
class sprinter Elbio (by Precocious): modest form on first 2 starts in maidens: shaped
as if needing further than 5f final start. *R. Guest*

PRECISELY (IRE)   2 b.g. (Apr 8) Petorius 117 – Indigent (IRE) (Superlative   –
118) [1997 a5g a6g a5g a6g Nov 21] IR 5,800Y: first foal: dam thrice-raced close
relative of useful Irish middle-distance colt Sondrio, later good winner in North
America and over hurdles: no worthwhile form. *J. Wharton*

PRECISION FINISH   2 ch.f. (Mar 20) Safawan 118 – Tricky Tracey (Form-   –
idable (USA) 125) [1997 7d Oct 13] stocky filly: half-sister to 1990 2-y-o 5f winner
Domino Trick (by Primo Dominie) and a French 1m winner (by Try My Best): dam
unraced: backward, showed nothing in maiden at Leicester. *J. Cullinan*

PREDAPPIO   4 b.c. Polish Precedent (USA) 131 – Khalafiya 104 (Darshaan   127
133) [1996 117: 8g* 10m² 10m³ 12m* 11s* 1997 10m² 12g* 12s 12g³ 12f⁵
Oct 5]

Polish Precedent was represented by two high-class sons in 1997, one
the four-times Group 1 winner Pilsudski, the other the rather lesser-known
Predappio. The pair met on three occasions and the score went in favour of Pilsudski overall. But Predappio did get the better of Pilsudski in the Hardwicke
Stakes at Royal Ascot.

Like the year-older Pilsudski, Predappio improved with time. At two he
won his only start, a twenty-two runner maiden at Fairyhouse at odds on. At
three he won three of his five races—a minor event at Gowran Park, a listed
contest at Galway and the Group 2 Blandford Stakes (by a length from Sanoo-
sea) at the Curragh before being transferred from John Oxx to Godolphin and
Saeed bin Suroor at the end of 1996. His British debut, in the Brigadier Gerard
Stakes at Sandown in May, suggested strongly that he'd progressed further.
Predappio was beaten only half a length by Bosra Sham, the pair five lengths
clear. The winner hadn't looked fully wound up, however, and Predappio had
perhaps benefited from an enterprising ride.

It was the Hardwicke which showed the true extent of Predappio's
improvement. Lining up at 6/1 joint second-favourite behind Pilsudski in a
field of ten, Predappio was settled in mid-field alongside Pilsudski before

Hardwicke Stakes, Royal Ascot—
Predappio (rail) rallies gamely to beat Pilsudski; Whitewater Affair is third

moving into second at halfway as the runners made their way over to the outside rail on the rained-on ground. Predappio slipped through on the inside to lead halfway round the home turn, pursued immediately by Pilsudski. Two furlongs out Predappio came under strong pressure and shortly afterwards was headed by Pilsudski, but, with the rest beaten off, Predappio refused to go down without a fight against a rival possibly not quite so fit as he was, managing to force his head in front again fifty yards out and hold on by half a length; Whitewater Affair was next home, a further two and a half lengths back. The race showed top American jockey Gary Stevens to good effect and provided him with his first win in Britain. 'This definitely rates right up there with my three Kentucky Derby wins,' he said afterwards, intimating that he would like a spell in Europe—'the racing is much more challenging than back in the States'—at some stage of his career.

Predappio ran three more times. His next start resulted in a disappointing seventh of eight in the King George VI and Queen Elizabeth Diamond Stakes back at Ascot, where he was, in contrast, held up by Stevens and never on terms; Pilsudski finished second. After missing the Geoffrey Freer Stakes in August when getting cast in his box, Predappio finished a respectable third to the top German filly Borgia and fellow British raider Luso in the Grosser Preis von Baden, beaten two lengths by the winner at the end of a steadily-run race. His final run proved to be just about his best. In a strongly-contested race, even by its usual high standards, Predappio battled on well to finish fifth of eighteen in the Prix de l'Arc de Triomphe at Longchamp, beaten under eight lengths by the impressive winner Peintre Celebre, and only about two and a half lengths by the runner-up Pilsudski. Among those just behind Predappio were the King George winner Swain and the previous year's Arc winner Helissio.

Connections have kept Predappio in training for 1998 and will, doubtless, be hoping to 'do a Pilsudski' with him. He's relatively lightly raced (eleven starts to date) and has had few opportunities in a strongly-run race at a mile and a half, and none over further. Further pattern races should come his way and would enhance his value as a stallion. Predappio's sire was a top-class miler and his dam won the Group 3 Meld Stakes over a mile and a half. Predappio's grandam, Khalisiyn, was useful also, winning over seven furlongs and a mile, and is a half-sister to the very smart 1983 two-year-old Kalim and to Kadial, who was in the frame in the King Edward VII Stakes and the Scottish Derby at three in 1986 and won a Grade 2 event at thirteen furlongs in America

Godolphin's "Predappio"

two years later. This is perhaps a less well-known branch of a famous family, as Khadaeen's half-sister, Kalkeen, produced Kadissya, the dam of the Derby and Irish Derby winner Kahyasi.

		Danzig	Northern Dancer
	Polish Precedent (USA)	(b 1977)	Pas de Nom
	(b 1986)	First Example	Buckpasser
Predappio		(ch 1976)	Bold Example
(b.c. 1993)		Darshaan	Shirley Heights
	Khalafiya	(br 1981)	Delsy
	(b 1987)	Khalisiyn	Shakapour
		(gr 1982)	Khadaeen

Predappio's going requirements are difficult to pinpoint. A strong, attractive colt, with a fluent, round action, he's won on soft going but has put up his very best performances on good going or firmer. That said, the going at Royal Ascot was bordering on good to soft (we called it such after the next race), and its probably best to regard him as being pretty versatile in this respect for now. He's been blinkered once, finishing third (to Pilsudski) in the Royal Whip at the Curragh as a three-year-old, a creditable effort at the time. *Saeed bin Suroor*

PREMIER 3 b.g. Rainbow Quest (USA) 134 – Formosanta (USA) (Believe It (USA)) [1996 76: 10m⁵ a8g² a8.5g* 1997 a8g³ 12g 8m 8.2s Oct 15] smallish, leggy gelding: fair winner at 2 yrs: no form in 1997, leaving M. Johnston after second start and sold 3,000 gns after final one. *K. T. Ivory*

PREMIER BAY 3 b.c. Primo Dominie 121 – Lydia Maria 70 (Dancing Brave (USA) 140) [1996 95: 6s* 6m² 6g² 1997 8d⁴ 8s³ 10.3m⁴ 10.4d* 10.3m³ 10s 10m 8m 10m⁴ 10v⁶ Oct 11] well-made colt: type to carry condition: useful performer: won handicap at York in June: mainly creditable efforts afterwards: should stay beyond 10.4f: acts on good to firm and soft ground: effective blinkered or not: races prominently: sold 28,000 gns, and joined P. Hobbs. *P. W. Harris*

PREMIER DANCE 10 ch.g. Bairn (USA) 126 – Gigiolina (King Emperor 47
(USA)) [1996 49, a75: a12g⁶ a12g* a12g* 12g 13d a14.8g⁵ a12g* 12.1m³ 11.6g a12g a70
1997 a11g a12g⁵ a12g⁴ a12g³ a12g⁴ a14.8g* a12g² a14.8g⁶ a12g* a12g⁴ 12s⁶
a14.8g a12g³ Nov 29] compact gelding: has quick action: fair handicapper on the
all-weather, poor on turf: races mainly at Wolverhampton, and won there in March
and May: stays 15f: successful on equitrack, best form on fibresand: effective with
blinkers/visor earlier in career: sometimes carries head high, and tends to edge left:
usually held up. *D. Haydn Jones*

PREMIER ECLIPSE 3 b.g. Primo Dominie 121 – Remany 66 (Bellypha 130) –
[1996 NR 1997 8m 8g 8g May 5] 6,000F, 8,000Y: rangy gelding: first foal: dam 1¼m
and 11.4f winner: signs of ability but no worthwhile form. *P. W. Harris*

PREMIER GENERATION (IRE) 4 b.g. Cadeaux Genereux 131 – Bristle 96 74
(Thatch (USA) 136) [1996 65: 8m 8m⁶ 8m 10g 10.5m⁵ 8d⁵ 1997 a8.5g⁴ 10d² 9.9s²
10s* 10g³ 10.2m⁵ 11.4d² 11.5g⁵ 12v 10g a11g³ Dec 8] leggy, quite good-topped
gelding: has a long stride: fair handicapper: won at Newbury in May: mostly
respectable efforts afterwards: effective at 1¼m, barely stays 11.5f: acts on fibresand,
seems to need good ground or softer on turf. *D. W. P. Arbuthnot*

PREMIER JET 2 br.f. (Apr 18) Dilum (USA) 115 – Lady Shikari (Kala Shikari –
125) [1997 6m Jul 14] third reported foal: dam unraced: tailed off in maiden at
Folkestone. *M. Madgwick*

PREMIER LEAGUE (IRE) 7 gr.g. Don't Forget Me 127 – Kilmara (USA) 78 –
(Caro 133) [1996 63d: a10g 9.7m 10m⁶ 11.6m³ 10f 10g² 10g⁴ 10m 10g⁵ 10m⁵ 8m a37
a10g⁶ a8g a10g⁵ 1997 a12g² a13g⁴ a12g a16g Apr 1] strong, round-barrelled gelding:
poor performer at best in 1997: stays 1½m: acts on firm and soft ground and on
equitrack. *J. E. Long*

PREMIER NIGHT 4 b.f. Old Vic 136 – Warm Welcome 89 (General Assembly 88
(USA)) [1996 74: 8m⁴ 9s⁵ 8g² 9f³ 12.1s 1997 12m* 11.9s⁴ 13.3g* 22.2d 16m² 14m
13.9g 14.6m⁴ 16g⁶ Sep 18] lengthy filly: has a short action: fairly useful performer:
won maiden at Folkestone in April and handicap at Newbury in May: only creditable
efforts afterwards only when in frame: stays 2m: acts on firm going, well beaten all
starts on dead or softer: sold 24,000 gns in December. *S. Dow*

PREMIER STAR 7 ch.g. Precocious 126 – Grove Star (Upper Case (USA)) –
[1996 –: a10g 1997 12g Jun 7] of no account. *K. G. Wingrove*

PREMIUM GIFT 5 ch.m. Most Welcome 131 – Emerald Eagle 78 (Sandy Creek 59
123) [1996 63: 6.1m 6m 6g³ 5g² 5g 5.1m⁶ 5f⁴ 5.2m⁴ 5.1g 1997 5g⁵ 5d Jun 29]
good-topped mare: modest handicapper: ran only twice in 1997, bleeding from nose
on final start: best form at 5f: raced mainly on good going or firmer: probably best
held up. *C. B. B. Booth*

PREMIUM PRINCESS 2 b.f. (Apr 30) Distant Relative 128 – Solemn 68
Occasion (USA) (Secreto (USA) 128) [1997 5g 5m 5m² 5m 6.1m⁶ 6.1g² 6d² 6m³ Oct
28] 8,000 2-y-o: good-bodied filly: fourth foal: dam twice-raced half-sister to smart
miler Soprano: fair maiden: will be suited by further than 6f: yet to race on extremes
of going. *J. J. Quinn*

PREMIUM PURSUIT 2 b.g. (Apr 17) Pursuit of Love 124 – Music In My Life 80
(IRE) 59 (Law Society (USA) 130) [1997 5s 5g⁵ 6g* 5g² 6m³ 6m 6g² 6d Oct 16]
15,500Y: sturdy, good-bodied gelding: second foal: half-brother to 3-y-o Mutahadeth: dam (maiden) stayed 1m: fairly useful performer: won maiden at Doncaster
in June: ran well afterwards when placed in minor events and nursery: will stay 7f,
probably 1m: acts on good to firm ground: raced much too freely when blinkered
once. *R. A. Fahey*

PREMIUM QUEST 2 b.g. (May 16) Forzando 122 – Sabonis (USA) 68 (The 69
Minstrel (CAN) 135) [1997 7.5m 7.5f 7m³ 8d* 8m Nov 4] 8,500Y: strong, useful-
looking gelding: unimpressive mover: fourth foal: dam 2-y-o 6f winner: fair
performer: easily best effort when winning 19-runner nursery at Pontefract in
October, all out having come from off pace: shapes as though will stay further than
1m. *R. A. Fahey*

PREMIUM RATE (USA) 2 ch.c. (Apr 14) Phone Trick (USA) – Excitable Gal 89
(USA) (Secretariat (USA)) [1997 6m³ May 24] $50,000F, $90,000Y: rather leggy

colt: half-brother to several winners in USA, one in stakes by Deputy Minister: dam, won up to 9f in USA, half-sister to Nell Gwyn winner Martha Stevens: 9/1, 3 lengths third to ready winner Desert Prince in maiden at Doncaster, soon going strongly in behind and not given hard time. *E. A. L. Dunlop*

PRENDS CA (IRE)   4 b.f. Reprimand 122 – Cri de Coeur (USA) 82 (Lyphard   98
(USA) 132) [1996 95: 8d 7.6g* 7.1d³ 7m⁴ 8f⁵ 7g⁴ 7m 7d⁶ 6m⁶ 6m* 1997 7g 7s⁵ 6g⁶
7m 6g² 6g 6d² 6m* 6m⁴ 6d⁴ 6g³ 6s⁵ Nov 8] smallish filly: useful performer: won
handicap at Haydock in September: in frame on 3 of 4 subsequent starts, including
in listed company: effective at 6f to 7.6f: acts on good to firm and soft ground: no
improvement in blinkers: usually held up. *W. R. Muir*

PRENONAMOSS   9 b.g. Precocious 126 – Nonabella 82 (Nonoalco (USA) 131)   59
[1996 NR 1997 8g⁴ 8m 8v Oct 11] lengthy gelding: formerly fairly useful handicapper: modest in 1997, and form only on reappearance: stays 1¼m: has form on any
going, though well beaten last 3 tries on firm: tried blinkered/visored: often
bandaged: held up. *D. W. P. Arbuthnot*

PREROGATIVE   7 ch.g. Dominion 123 – Nettle 106 (Kris 135) [1996 58d: –
11.9f⁴ 12m 16m 17.2f 11.9f 1997 14m 11.9m Jul 28] fair jumper: disappointing
maiden on flat. *G. L. Moore*

PRESENT ARMS (USA)   4 b.c. Affirmed (USA) – Au Printemps (USA)   105
(Dancing Champ (USA)) [1996 89: 10.8f² 12m² 10.1m* 11.6m* 11.8f* 12s 1997
10.3d* 11.9g 10s* 10.4g 10.1g⁶ 12d Oct 16] workmanlike colt: unimpressive mover:
useful handicapper on his day: won at Doncaster in June and Ascot (by 2½ lengths
from Game Ploy) in July: disappointing otherwise in 1997: effective at 1¼m (given
good test), and should stay 1¾m: best form on good ground or softer: tried blinkered,
not in 1997: has been bandaged behind. *P. F. I. Cole*

PRESENT CHANCE   3 ch.c. Cadeaux Genereux 131 – Chance All (FR) 88   80 d
(Glenstal (USA) 118) [1996 61: 7f⁴ 7g 1997 6g² 6m² 7.9d² a7g 5v⁵ 7m³ 8d 8g³ 7.9s⁴
7m³ 7.1g⁴ 8m Oct 5] strong, good-bodied colt: fair maiden: well below form last 4
starts: effective at 6f to 1m: acts on good to firm and dead ground, below form on soft
and fibresand. *B. A. McMahon*

PRESENT GENERATION   4 ch.g. Cadeaux Genereux 131 – Penny Mint 79   81
(Mummy's Game 120) [1996 81: 8g 8d² 7.1m² 6m² 1997 7d 8d 8g 7m² 7g² 6m² 7g*
6g 7m 7m Sep 27] good-topped gelding: fairly useful performer: second in 3 handicaps before winning maiden at Epsom in August: below form afterwards: effective at
6f to 1m: yet to race on extremes of going: well held when sweating. *R. Guest*

PRESENTIMENT   3 b.g. Puissance 110 – Octavia (Sallust 134) [1996 54: a6g   52
6d 6m⁶ 8.1m 7.5m 8.3d² 8g 1997 8m⁶ 5.9f 6d⁵ 6.1d⁴ 6m³ 7g⁵ 7g a8.5g⁴ a7g a7g⁴ Nov   a45
21] leggy gelding: modest maiden handicapper: left M. Wane after seventh outing:
effective at 6f to 1m: acts on good to firm and dead ground, poor form on fibresand.
S. R. Bowring

PRESENT 'N CORRECT   4 ch.g. Cadeaux Genereux 131 – Emerald Eagle 78   53
(Sandy Creek 123) [1996 57, a–: 6g 8m 6g³ a6g 5g* 6m a7g a6s 1997 5g⁵ 5s 5g 5m   a–
Jul 15] workmanlike gelding: modest handicapper: well held after reappearance: best
at 5f/6f: best efforts on good ground, soundly beaten all 3 all-weather outings.
C. B. B. Booth

PRESENT SITUATION   6 ch.g. Cadeaux Genereux 131 – Storm Warning 117   74
(Tumble Wind (USA)) [1996 66, a74: a7g* a7g² a7g⁴ 7m⁴ 8m⁵ 8d² 8g 8f* a8g 1997
a8g* 8m 8.5g⁴ 8.5d* 9d⁶ 8d 8m 8g Oct 18] sparely-made gelding: unimpressive
mover: fair handicapper: won at Lingfield in February and Epsom in August: ran
as if something amiss sixth start and below form afterwards: stays 8.5f: acts on the
all-weather (better form on equitrack than fibresand), firm ground and dead: genuine.
Lord Huntingdon

PRESS AGAIN   5 ch.m. Then Again 126 – Silver Empress 63 (Octavo (USA)   43 ?
115) [1996 –: 8.3d 8.3d 10m a6g a8g 1997 6d 7m⁵ 7.6g 7g Sep 5] unfurnished mare:
poor maiden handicapper: should prove best up to 1m. *P. Hayward*

PRESS AHEAD   2 b.c. (May 20) Precocious 126 – By Line 64 (High Line 125)   55
[1997 a6g⁵ 6m 7m a6g Oct 4] 14,000 2-y-o: leggy colt: second foal: dam, maiden on

flat who stayed 1¼m, winning hurdler: first form in maidens when seventh of 13 at Wolverhampton final start. *B. A. McMahon*

PRESS ON NICKY   4 b.f. Nicholas (USA) 111 – Northern Empress 80   72 d
(Northfields (USA)) [1996 75: 7d³ 8g 7m* 7d⁶ 8m 7.3m² 7m 7s 1997 6.9m 8d⁴ 9m 8d 7m 8m Sep 28] sturdy filly: fair handicapper at best: well below form last 4 starts: stays 1m: acts on good to firm and dead ground. *W. R. Muir*

PRESSURISE   2 ch.g. (Mar 19) Sanglamore (USA) 126 – Employ Force (USA)   – p
(Alleged (USA) 138) [1997 7m 7g 7d Oct 14] 4,600F, 14,000Y: big, good-bodied gelding: has plenty of scope: sixth foal: closely related to a winner in Italy by Kris and half-brother to another there by Big Reef: dam, placed over 1½m in Italy, from family of Oh So Sharp: not knocked about when down the field in maidens at Salisbury, Warwick (a little reluctant at stalls) and Leicester (still in need of race): should do better over further than 7f. *Sir Mark Prescott*

PRESTIGE LASS   4 ch.f. Weldnaas (USA) 112 – Monalda (FR) (Claude) [1996   –
–: 10m 10m 9m 12d 1997 10m Jul 28] little worthwhile form. *Miss K. M. George*

PRESUMING ED (IRE)   4 b.g. Nordico (USA) – Top Knot (High Top 131)   –
[1996 NR 1997 a12g⁴ Feb 17] no worthwhile form. *N. J. H. Walker*

PRETTY SALLY (IRE)   3 b.f. Polish Patriot (USA) 128 – Sally Chase 101   –
(Sallust 134) [1996 –, a47: 6g a6g⁶ a6g⁶ 6d a6g 1997 a6g² a6g³ a7g a6g Mar 8] sturdy   a51
filly: modest sprint maiden: placed in sellers at Wolverhampton: raced mainly on fibresand: tried blinkered: has flashed tail and carried head high. *D. J. G. Murray Smith*

PRETTY SHARP   3 ch.f. Interrex (CAN) – To The Point 96 (Sharpen Up 127)   – §
[1996 64?: 8.1d⁵ 7m⁴ 7f² 8g 1997 7m⁵ 10d a7g Dec 22] sparely-made filly: modest maiden at 2 yrs: well held in 1997, looking temperamental second start (final one for N. Babbage). *J. Berry*

PRICELESS   2 b.g. (Feb 13) Rock City 120 – Good As Gold (IRE) 50 (Glint of   90 ?
Gold 128) [1997 6m* 7g⁵ 8d⁴ 7m⁶ Sep 24] 5,800Y: quite good-topped gelding: second foal: half-brother to 3-y-o Ninth Symphony: dam maiden: fairly useful form: won maiden at Pontefract in August: stiffish tasks next 2 starts, and seemed unlucky in auction event at Goodwood final outing, meeting considerable trouble: stays 7f: sold 26,000 gns in October. *W. J. Haggas*

PRIDDY GREEN   2 b.f. (Apr 26) Formidable (USA) 125 – No Can Tell (USA)   –
(Clev Er Tell (USA)) [1997 6.1g 7s Oct 16] seventh foal: half-sister to 1990 2-y-o 5f winner Anonoalto (by Noalto) and a winner in Hungary: dam maiden: behind in maidens at Nottingham and Catterick: sold to join J. Hetherton. *H. Candy*

PRIDE OF BRIXTON   4 b.g. Dominion 123 – Caviar Blini 80 (What A Guest   –
119) [1996 91: 6s³ 5.1g² 5m 5.1g* 5m 5m 5m⁵ 5m 5.1g 5g² 1997 5.1v 5d 5d a6g 5d 5d a6g a6g Dec 13] lengthy gelding: fairly useful sprint handicapper at 3 yrs for G. Lewis: long way below form in 1997. *C. W. Thornton*

PRIDE OF BRYN   2 br.f. (Mar 29) Efisio 120 – Alpine Sunset (Auction Ring   49
(USA) 123) [1997 a5g 5m⁴ 6g⁴ 5m 6m⁵ 5d 7m² Oct 7] 1,000Y: big filly: fifth foal: half-sister to 5f to 1m winner Alpine Johnny (by Salse) and useful sprinter Afif (by Midyan): dam unraced half-sister to Cyrano de Bergerac: poor maiden: second in claimer at Redcar: stays 7f: acts on good to firm going. *Denys Smith*

PRIDE OF FASHION   2 gr.g. (Apr 6) Triune – Fashion Princess (Van Der Lin-   –
den (FR)) [1997 9m 8.2d Oct 8] first reported foal: dam, lightly raced and no form on flat, successful over hurdles: well beaten in sellers. *S. G. Knight*

PRIDE OF HAYLING (IRE)   6 ch.m. Bold Arrangement 127 – Malham Tarn   62
(Riverman (USA) 131) [1996 67: 5g⁶ 5m³ 6m³ 6m* 6f³ 5.3f* 7f⁶ 6m 5m² 5.1g 6d 1997 6f 6g⁶ 6m 5.1m³ 6m³ 5.7g 5m Sep 24] compact mare: modest sprinter: acted on firm ground (broke leg) final start: dead. *P. R. Hedger*

PRIDE OF MY HEART   2 b.f. (Feb 28) Lion Cavern (USA) 117 – Hearten   74
(Hittite Glory 125) [1997 6m⁴ 7.1m⁶ 7m⁶ Sep 9] leggy, useful-looking filly: half-sister to several winners, including 3-y-o Racing Heart and smart sprinter Northern Goddess (by Night Shift): dam unraced: fair form in minor event at Windsor and maidens at Sandown and Lingfield: should stay at least 1m. *I. A. Balding*

PRIDE OF NARVIK   3 b.c. Pharly (FR) 130 – Ulla Laing 107 (Mummy's Pet   –
125) [1996 NR 1997 8d 8m 7d Oct 13] sparely-made colt: half-brother to useful
sprinter Domulla (by Dominion) and 1½m winner (stayed 2m) Belafonte (by Derrylin): dam 2-y-o 5f winner who stayed at least 7f: behind in maidens. *M. R. Channon*

PRIDE OF PENDLE   8 gr.m. Grey Desire 115 – Pendle's Secret 73 (Le Johnstan   80
123) [1996 NR 1997 7g⁵ 8.5g 8g⁶ 7g 8.5m 7g⁵ 9f 8f⁶ 7.9g 8g² 8m³ 8m* 8g 8.9g 8g 1997 7g
9m 8.5m 8m 8d* 8g 7.9g³ 8g⁴ 8m³ 9m* 9m 8g² 7.9s 8m 8d 8m 9m 8g Oct 18] leggy,
angular mare: fairly useful performer, as good as ever: won handicap at Doncaster in
June and minor event at Newcastle in August: stays 9f well: acts on any going: held
up, and best in strongly-run race: splendidly tough and genuine. *Martyn Wane*

PRIDE OF PLACE (IRE)   2 b.f. (Mar 31) Caerleon (USA) 132 – Pro Patria 86   71
(Petingo 135) [1997 7m³ 7f⁶ Oct 1] half-sister to several winners, notably Oaks and
Irish Oaks winner Unite (by Kris): dam, won over 5f and 6f at 2 yrs from 4 starts,
sister to smart miler Patris: better effort in maidens about a month apart when third at
Lingfield: should stay at least 1m. *D. R. Loder*

PRIDEWOOD PICKER   10 b.g. Joshua 129 – Guinea Feather (Over The River   –
(FR)) [1996 NR 1997 a9.4f Jan 11] first foal: dam lightly raced: modest winning
hurdler: tailed off on belated flat debut. *R. J. Price*

PRIENA (IRE)   3 ch.f. Priolo (USA) 127 – Isabena (Star Appeal 133) [1996 86p: 95
7f* 1997 10d² 10g² 10g 10m 10.2g⁴ 8m² 8v 8d³ Oct 14] lengthy filly: useful
performer: runner-up in 1997 in listed races at Goodwood, Newbury and Ascot (rated
stakes, beaten neck by Kenmist): effective at 1m/1¼m: acts on firm and dead going,
well beaten on heavy: visored/blinkered last 3 starts: has high head carriage.
D. R. Loder

PRILUKI   3 b.f. Lycius (USA) 124 – Pripet (USA) 86 (Alleged (USA) 138) [1996   65
NR 1997 8m⁶ 10m 9.7m² 13.8s* 12m Oct 31] 3,000 2-y-o: second foal: half-sister to
2-y-o Greenlander: dam staying sister to 1000 Guineas and Oaks winner Midway
Lady: fair performer: best effort to win minor event at Catterick in October: should
stay 2m: acts on good to firm and soft going. *C. E. Brittain*

PRIMA FACIE   2 b.f. (Feb 22) Primo Dominie 121 – Soluce 98 (Junius (USA)   64
124) [1997 6d Nov 7] small filly: sixth living foal: half-sister to several winners,
including useful sprinter Splice (by Sharpo) and fairly useful miler Alfujairah (by
Diesis): dam Irish 7f winner: 6/1 from 3/1, mid-division in maiden at Doncaster: may
do better. *D. R. Loder*

PRIMARY COLOURS   2 b.f. (Feb 7) Saddlers' Hall (IRE) 126 – Go For Red   78
(IRE) (Thatching 131) [1997 7d 8m³ 8m³ a8g* a8g² a7g² Dec 18] tall, lengthy filly: has
plenty of scope: first foal: dam unraced granddaughter of smart French/US 5.5f to
11f winner Warfever: fair performer: won at Southwell in November (by 15
lengths, bought out of W. Haggas' stable 10,200 gns): ran well both starts afterwards:
should be suited by further than 1m: acts on both all-weather, showed promise on
turf. *J. Pearce*

PRIMA SILK   6 b.m. Primo Dominie 121 – Silk St James (Pas de Seul 133) [1996   77
74, a80: a7g⁶ a8g 6f 6.1m⁶ 6f* 5.7g⁶ 6f² 6m⁴ 6g 5.7m² 6g 6g 5.7m² a7g² 6.1d 7f⁵ 7m   a82
6d² 6d⁶ 6f a6g* a6g a6g⁵ 1997 a6g a6g* a7g a6g⁴ 6m² 6d² a6f 6g 6m 7m a7g² 7g Aug
15] angular mare: seldom impresses in appearance: fairly useful handicapper on her
day: won at Southwell in January: effective at 5f to 7f: acts on firm and dead ground,
very best efforts on firesand: tried in blinkers and visor, not in 1997: sometimes
wanders markedly: inconsistent. *M. J. Ryan*

PRIMATICCIO (IRE)   2 b.g. (Feb 20) Priolo (USA) 127 – Martinova 111 (Mar-   – p
tinmas 128) [1997 6f Oct 3] very tall, sturdy gelding: has considerable scope:
half-brother to several winners, including smart French sprinter Export Price (by
Habitat) and 1m winner Salda (by Bustino): dam, third in Irish 1000 Guineas,
half-sister to high-class 1¼m performer Lucky Wednesday: 25/1 and very much in
need of race, behind in maiden at Lingfield, missing break completely: sure to do
better, particularly in the longer term. *Sir Mark Prescott*

PRIMAVERA   2 b.f. (Feb 8) Anshan 119 – Fair Maid of Kent (USA) 68 (Diesis   65
133) [1997 6s 7.1d 7m² Jul 19] 3,000F: workmanlike filly: has a round action: first
foal: dam 1m winner from 2 starts at 2 yrs, half-sister to Grade 1 1¼m winner Clear

Choice: first worthwhile form in maidens when second to of 13 at Warwick: should stay at least 1m. *M. J. Haynes*

PRIMA VERDE 4 b.f. Leading Counsel (USA) 122 – Bold Green (FR) (Green 81 Dancer (USA) 132) [1996 –p: 8.1m 1997 7.5m* 8d* 8g³ Jul 16] smallish, sturdy filly: fairly useful performer, very lightly raced: won maiden at Beverley and handicap at Newmarket in June: stays 1m: yet to race on extremes of going. *L. M. Cumani*

PRIME HAND 2 ch.f. (Apr 29) Primo Dominie 121 – Rechanit (IRE) (Local 86 Suitor (USA) 128) [1997 5g² Jul 7] 9,000Y: third foal: half-sister to 3-y-o Rechullin and fairly useful 1¼m winner Simply Katie (by Most Welcome): dam, ran once here then won 4 times in Italy up to 7f, half-sister to Sapience: 5/1, would have made winning debut in maiden at Ripon but for running green, failing by head. *W. J. Haggas*

PRIME LIGHT 4 ch.g. Primo Dominie 121 – Flopsy (Welsh Pageant 132) [1996 73 75: 7m³ 7d³ 7m⁵ 1997 a8g⁵ 8.3g⁵ 8s 8m⁴ 7m 8g⁴ Oct 7] strong, lengthy gelding: fair maiden: stays 1m: acts on good to firm ground, possibly unsuited by soft: blinkered last 3 starts, running well only first time. *G. Wragg*

PRIMELTA 4 b.f. Primo Dominie 121 – Pounelta 91 (Tachypous 128) [1996 –: 6g 49 6f 7s 1997 a6g 6s 6m 6.9m* 8.3m 6.9m 8d Oct 13] good-topped filly: poor handicapper: won at Folkestone in August, leading near finish: well below form afterwards: stays 7f, pulled too hard at 1m: acts on good to firm going: none too consistent. *R. Akehurst*

PRIME MINISTER 3 ch.c. Be My Chief (USA) 122 – Classic Design (Busted – 134) [1996 NR 1997 10g⁶ Jun 13] 46,000Y: fifth foal: half-brother to 4-y-o Well Drawn and 6-y-o Eveningperformance: dam unraced half-sister to Tirol: well held in Sandown maiden: sold cheaply to join G. Jones. *R. Charlton*

PRIME PARTNER 4 b.g. Formidable (USA) 125 – Baileys By Name 66 (Nom- 40 ination 125) [1996 –, a49: 6m 6g a8g a7g³ 7.1m a6g⁶ 1997 7g 8.2g⁶ 9.9m 8g* 6.9m⁴ 7.1d³ 7.5v³ 8m⁵ 8m³ 8g 8m 8.1m 8m a8.5g⁴ Sep 30] strong gelding: poor handicapper: won apprentice seller at Ripon in June: likely to prove best up to 1m: acts on good to firm and heavy ground and on all-weather: no improvement in blinkers. *T. D. Easterby*

PRIMERO (IRE) 3 b.g. Lycius (USA) 124 – Pipitina 91 (Bustino 136) [1996 NR – 1997 10m 11.8g⁵ a12g a11g Nov 24] 7,200 3-y-o: big, lengthy gelding: second foal: half-brother to German 1m winner Larissa (by Soviet Star): dam 2m winner: tailed off in maiden and minor events. *A. Barrow*

PRIME TIME GIRL 2 b.f. (Mar 12) Primo Dominie 121 – Timely Raise (USA) 73 p (Raise A Man (USA)) [1997 6m Sep 10] strong filly: sixth known foal: half-sister to 3 winners, including fairly useful 9f and 1¼m winner Double Bluff (by Sharrood) and useful sprinter Poker Chip (by Bluebird): dam, miler successful 6 times in North America, sister to smart middle-distance stayer Primitive Singer: 20/1, mid-division in maiden at Kempton won by Royal Shyness, missing break completely but making considerable ground (rated much closer): unimpressive to post: sure to do better. *I. A. Balding*

PRIMEVAL 3 b.g. Primo Dominie 121 – Class Adorns (Sadler's Wells (USA) 70 132) [1996 NR 1997 10m⁵ 10d³ Aug 30] third foal: dam well-beaten daughter of high-class 1¼m and 1½m performer Connaught Bridge: fair form in maidens at Windsor and Ripon: will stay 1½m. *P. W. Harris*

PRIMFAHEIGHTS 2 b.f. (Feb 15) Reprimand 122 – Hafhafah (Shirley Heights – 130) [1997 5m⁵ 6f 6m Aug 23] 3,000Y: second foal: half-sister to an Italian 1¼m and 1¾m winner by Taufan: dam 1m winner: well beaten in sellers. *T. M. Jones*

PRIMO LARA 5 ch.h. Primo Dominie 121 – Clara Barton (Youth (USA) 135) 97 [1996 89: 7.5d³ 7.5m* 7m* 8g 7m⁴ 7m² 6m 7.1f* 7m 7g³ 6f 1997 7.3d⁵ 7m³ 7g 6m* a7g³ Dec 6] big, strong, lengthy horse: poor mover: useful handicapper: not seen out until mid-September, but returned better than ever, winning 25-runner race at Redcar in November: good third to Chewit in competitive event at Wolverhampton next time: best at 6f/7f: acts on firm and dead going and on fibresand: races up with pace. *P. W. Harris*

PRIMORDIAL (FR) 2 b.g. (Mar 25) Lesotho (USA) 118 – Prilly (FR) (Saint –
Cyrien (FR) 128) [1997 6g Oct 24] 110,000 francs 2-y-o: close-coupled gelding:
second foal: dam French 2-y-o 7f winner: 33/1 and bandaged behind, slowly away
and always behind in maiden at Newbury. *S. Dow*

PRIMULA BAIRN 7 b.m. Bairn (USA) 126 – Miss Primula 81 (Dominion 123) –
[1996 –, a68: a5g a6g a6g⁵ a5g* a5g⁵ a5g* a5g³ a5g² 5.2m a5g a6g² a6s⁴ 1997 a5g⁶
a5g Jan 22] workmanlike mare: fair performer at 6 yrs, well held in 1997. *D. Nicholls*

PRINCE ALEX (IRE) 3 b.c. Night Shift (USA) – Finalist 78 (Star Appeal 133) 73 p
[1996 NR 1997 12d 10.3d 10m 12g* 12m³ Sep 24] 89,000Y: sturdy colt: carries a
deal of condition: has a quick action: fourth foal: closely related to 7f winner Cubist
(by Tate Gallery) and half-brother to winners around 1m by Thatching and 1½m by
Bluebird: dam twice-raced daughter of Galtres winner Deadly Serious: refused to
enter stalls on intended debut: stepped up on form in maidens to win handicap at
Newmarket in August despite tending to hang: ran creditably only subsequent outing
despite not getting run of race: will stay beyond 1½m: probably capable of better:
sold 22,000 gns in November. *A. C. Stewart*

PRINCE ASHLEIGH 2 b.g. (Apr 6) Anshan 119 – Fen Princess (IRE) 72 (Tro- 71
jan Fen 118) [1997 5m⁶ 6m⁶ 7g⁴ 8s² 7s² 8g a7g⁵ Nov 14] second foal: half-brother to
1996 2-y-o 7f winner Ben's Ridge (by Indian Ridge), later useful in USA: dam 15f
winner at 4 yrs: fair maiden: second in nurseries at Ayr and Catterick in October:
below form in similar events last 2 starts: should stay beyond 1m: goes well on soft
ground. *P. C. Haslam*

PRINCE BABAR 6 b.g. Fairy King (USA) – Bell Toll 87 (High Line 125) [1996 104
103: 7g⁶ 7m³ 6f² 8m³ 7m² 6m³ 7m 8d* 8g² 1997 9g 7.9g² 6g 7g⁶ Jul 10] sparely-made
gelding: has a round action: useful handicapper: best effort when second to Centre
Stalls in listed rated stakes at York in May: stays 9f: below form on heavy ground at
3 yrs, acts on firm and dead: often apprentice ridden: game and consistent: fractured
off-hind cannon bone in July. *J. E. Banks*

PRINCE BALTASAR 8 ch.g. Claude Monet (USA) 121 – Farababy (FR) (Far- –
away Son (USA) 130) [1996 NR 1997 12g⁵ Aug 17] poor maiden jumper: tailed off
in seller on belated flat debut. *N. Bycroft*

PRINCE BATSHOOF 2 b.c. (May 5) Batshoof 122 – Sipsi Fach 100 (Prince 59
Sabo 123) [1997 7d 6.1g 6.9d³ Oct 21] 10,000Y, 24,000 2-y-o: third foal: half-brother
to 3-y-o Supply And Demand: dam 6f (at 2 yrs) to 1¼m winner: modest maiden: third
at Folkestone: should stay 1m+. *M. Bell*

PRINCE CONFEY (IRE) 3 b.c. Tirol 127 – Filet Mignon (USA) (Topsider –
(USA)) [1996 NR 1997 8s 9g 6.5m 9f 8d 7.8m 7.5g 9g 6d a7g a8g Dec 21] third foal:
dam once-raced sister to Doulab: little worthwhile form in Ireland for G. Creaner or
in 2 outings in Britain: tried blinkered. *D. J. Wintle*

PRINCE DANZIG (IRE) 6 ch.g. Roi Danzig (USA) – Veldt (High Top 131) 64
[1996 67, a88: a12g³ a12g⁴ a12g* a10g⁴ a12g a12g⁵ 11.9f* 11.9f³ 14m⁵ 12g 11.9f⁴ a88
11.9m² 11.9f⁴ 11.5d⁴ a12g* 1997 a12g⁵ a12g⁵ a10g³ a10g² 11.8m³ 12g⁵ 11.9m²
11.9f⁵ 14m⁵ 11.9m⁶ a12g⁵ a12g Nov 29] close-coupled gelding: good mover: fairly
useful handicapper on the all-weather, fair on turf: well below form last 5 starts:
effective at 1¼m to 1½m: acts on any going: has worn blinkers and visor (not since
1994), better form without. *D. J. G. Murray Smith*

PRINCE DE LOIR 3 b.c. Be My Chief (USA) 122 – Princesse Vali (FR) (Val de 75
L'Orne (FR) 133) [1996 –: 7m 1997 10g 8g⁴ 10m² Aug 14] big, strong colt: fair
maiden: off 11 months prior to reappearance: best effort on final start: will stay 1½m:
may do better still. *D. J. S. Cosgrove*

PRINCE DOME (IRE) 3 ch.g. Salt Dome (USA) – Blazing Glory (IRE) (Glow 91
(USA)) [1996 69: 5f 6g⁶ 5g² 1997 5m⁵ 5d 6f⁶ 6d⁶ 5d* 6g 5m⁵ 5g³ 6s³ 5.6m Sep 10]
leggy, lengthy gelding: has a round action: fairly useful performer: won maiden at
Beverley in April and handicaps at Newcastle and Ascot (beat Bishops Court a neck
in quite valuable event) in June: ran creditably in handicaps most starts after: stays
6f: acts on firm ground and soft ground: game. *Martyn Wane*

PRINCE EMAR 3 b.g. Emarati (USA) 74 – Selaginella 49 (Pharly (FR) 130) –
[1996 NR 1997 a7g a6g a7g Feb 21] 5,200Y: first foal: dam stayed 1¼m: behind in
maiden and sellers. *T. D. Easterby*

PRINCE FOLEY 2 ch.c. (Apr 27) Greensmith 121 – Jadebelle 66 (Beldale 100
Flutter (USA) 130) [1997 5f* 5.3f² 5.1d³ 5g* 5g* 5m4 5g* 6m* 5.2g² 8g⁶
Nov 29] good-bodied colt: second reported foal: dam 2-y-o 6f winner who stayed
1½m: useful performer: progressed very well, winning maiden at Leicester and
minor events at Lingfield, Newcastle, Windsor and Doncaster by mid-July for
W. G. M. Turner: beaten around 9 lengths in Grade 3 race at Hollywood Park after
4-month break: stays 6f: acts on firm and dead ground: tough and reliable.
R. C. Mettee, USA

PRINCE JORDAN 3 ch.g. Keen 116 – Diami 81 (Swing Easy (USA) 126) –
[1996 –: 7f 7m 8g 1997 a8.5g⁴ Sep 20] big, strong gelding: no form. *I. Campbell*

PRINCE KINSKY 4 ch.c. Master Willie 129 – Princess Lieven (Royal Palace 82
131) [1996 79: a10g* 10.5d⁶ 12.1m³ 14g⁶ 14.1s a12g⁴ 1997 12m* 12d 12m³ 14.6m
Sep 10] angular colt: fairly useful handicapper: won 19-runner event at Epsom in
April: well below form on 2 of 3 subsequent starts: stays 1½m: acts on equitrack and
good to firm going, below form on dead and soft: carries head high: won over hurdles
in October. *J. A. B. Old*

PRINCELY AFFAIR 4 b.g. Prince Sabo 123 – Shillay (Lomond (USA) 128) –
[1996 54: 10.8g 12m a8g³ 10.1m* 10m² a12g³ 11.5f² 10.1g⁶ 10m 10g 10.1m 1997
a9.4g⁵ a11g a8g 10.8m 10m 10.5m 12.1g Sep 1] good-bodied gelding: modest
winner at 3 yrs, but little form in 1997. *J. M. Bradley*

PRINCELY HEIR (IRE) 2 b.c. (Apr 20) Fairy King (USA) – Meis El-Reem 111
124 (Auction Ring (USA) 123) [1997 5m* 5v* 6.3m³ 6m* Aug 10]

Although Double Eclipse and Double Trigger continued to do their
stuff, it was the two-year-olds Lend A Hand and Princely Heir who provided
trainer Mark Johnston with his Group 1 victories in 1997, the former in the
Gran Criterium at Milan, the latter in the Heinz 57 Phoenix Stakes at Leopardstown. Princely Heir's win came on the last of his four starts, in early-August,
just two and a half months after he'd justified favouritism in a maiden at Ripon
on his debut.

On edge and very coltish in the paddock at Ripon, Princely Heir was
much more settled when reappearing in a four-runner minor event at Beverley
and won so easily that it was decided to pitch him in against the much vaunted
King of Kings in the Omni Racing Anglesey Stakes at the Curragh. King of
Kings lost his unbeaten record in this event, but not to Princely Heir, who was
five lengths back in third as Lady Alexander and King of Kings fought out

Heinz 57 Phoenix Stakes, Leopardstown—Princely Heir (No. 3) lands this valuable prize from Asfurah

the finish. Princely Heir, who apparently coughed after the race, put this disappointing run well behind him when returned to Ireland four weeks later for the Phoenix Stakes, one of three British challengers in a nine-runner field. The pick of the trio looked to be the Windsor Castle and Cherry Hinton Stakes winner Asfurah, while Harbour Master, who had won the Coventry Stakes on his previous start, led the home-trained challenge, the pair dominating the betting with Princely Heir one of the outsiders at 12/1. Harbour Master's stable-companion Hopping Higgins made the running, pressed by Princely Heir who hung in behind the leader when asked for his effort approaching the two-furlong marker. Once straightened, Princely Heir responded gamely to very strong pressure—his rider Jason Weaver incurred a four-day ban for misuse of the whip—mastered Hopping Higgins going into the final furlong, and held Asfurah's challenge by a head; Harbour Master finished well to take third. Princely Heir showed plenty of speed, and while his pedigree suggests he should stay beyond six furlongs we think he'll turn out to be a sprinter.

		Northern Dancer (b 1961)	Nearctic Natalma
	Fairy King (USA) (b 1982)	Fairy Bridge (b 1975)	Bold Reason Special
Princely Heir (IRE) (b.c. Apr 20, 1995)		Auction Ring (b 1972)	Bold Bidder Hooplah
	Meis El-Reem (b 1981)	Tavella (b 1972)	Petingo Tintoretta

Princely Heir's sire, Fairy King, is more of an influence for speed than his brother Sadler's Wells, though he is responsible for the Prix de l'Arc de Triomphe winner Helissio and the Two Thousand Guineas runner-up Revoque.

Maktoum Al Maktoum's "Princely Heir"

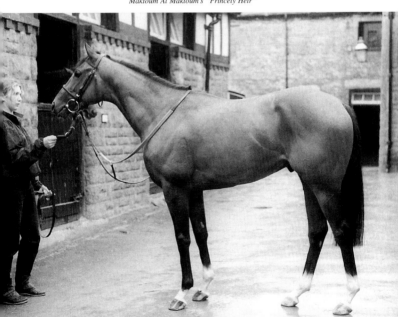

The dam, Meis El-Reem, who gained both her wins at two years over five furlongs, finished second in the One Thousand Guineas and then went on to win two races at a mile, the Child Stakes and the Prix d'Astarte. Meis El-Reem is a daughter of the two-year-old six-furlong winner Tavella, who is out of a half-sister to the 1958 Prix du Jockey-Club winner Tamanar. Apart from Princely Heir, her seventh foal, Meis El-Reem hasn't achieved much success at stud, her only other winning produce being the fair milers Cartel and Mislemani, both of whom are by Kris. Princely Heir, a good-quartered colt who cost IR 40,000 guineas a yearling, has shown himself effective on good to firm and heavy ground. *M. Johnston*

PRINCELY SOUND 4 b.g. Prince Sabo 123 – Sound of The Sea 91 (Windjammer (USA)) [1996 69§, a75§: a6g* a6g⁴ a5g* 5d 6m⁶ 6.1g* 5m 6g⁵ 5.1m⁵ 6f⁴ 6d 5.7m 1997 a6g* a6g a5g 5.3f⁶ 7d 6g³ 5m 5.1g 6m Oct 5] good-topped gelding: fairly useful handicapper on all-weather, fair on turf, on his day: well backed, made all at Lingfield in February: left M. Bell after fifth start: effective at 5f and 6f: acts on good to firm ground and equitrack, probably on fibresand: no improvement in visor: seems to need to dominate: unreliable. *J. E. Banks*   67 § a86 §

PRINCE NICHOLAS 2 ch.g. (Mar 1) Midyan (USA) 124 – Its My Turn 80 (Palm Track 122) [1997 5m 5m 7.5v⁶ 7m Jul 19] sparely-made gelding: seventh foal: half-brother to 3 run-of-the-mill winners, 2 by Nomination: dam miler: no form in maiden and minor events. *K. W. Hogg, Isle of Man*   –

PRINCE OF ANDROS (USA) 7 b.h. Al Nasr (FR) 126 – Her Radiance (USA) (Halo (USA)) [1996 114: 10g⁶ 10d 10g² 10m⁴ 10.3m* 10m⁴ 10f a9.4g* 1997 10m⁴ 10d⁴ May 22] tall, lengthy horse: forrmerly smart performer: useful form in 1997 when fourh to Germano in minor event at Newmarket and listed race at Goodwood (better effort, beaten 3½ lengths): stays 1½m: acts on good to firm and soft ground and on fibresand: effective blinkered/visored, not tried in 1997: held up: suffered hairline fracture of a foreleg after final start. *C. F. Wall*   109

PRINCE OF BHUTAN (IRE) 3 ch.g. Night Shift (USA) – Lassalia (Sallust 134) [1996 NR 1997 8g 8d 10.3g 10d a11g Nov 17] 20,000Y: smallish, stocky gelding: closely related to 2 winners by Fairy King, including Italian 4-y-o Enhorabuena (up to 1m), and half-brother to several winners, notably smart 1¼m performer Free Flyer (by Bluebird): dam placed from 6f to 9.5f in Ireland: signs of ability but no worthwhile form: left R. Hannon after second start. *R. Akehurst*   –

PRINCE OF DENIAL 3 b.c. Soviet Star (USA) 128 – Gleaming Water 81 (Kalaglow 132) [1996 70: 7d 7f⁴ 7m² 1997 9g* 10m 10m³ 8d* 9m 8g⁶ 9g* 8m a9.4g⁶ Dec 6] rather leggy colt: made into a useful handicapper: won at Kempton in May and at Newbury in September and October (beat Strazo ½ length): well held in listed race at Wolverhampton (all-weather debut) final start: stays 1¼m: acts on good to firm and dead ground: reportedly injured right fetlock second start and sometimes bandaged afterwards. *D. W. P. Arbuthnot*   105

PRINCE OF FORTUNE 3 b.g. Prince Sabo 123 – Beautiful Orchid (Hays 120) [1996 –: 6m 1997 a8g 7m⁴ 8f 7.1m³ 8.2d⁴ 6.9m⁴ 7m 6g Aug 1] poor maiden: stays 1m: acts on good to firm and dead going. *M. Blanshard*   49

PRINCE OF INDIA 5 b.g. Night Shift (USA) – Indian Queen 115 (Electric 126) [1996 102: 8f 7g 8f⁵ 1997 8.1d 7m 7g⁴ 8m Nov 1] deep-bodied gelding: one-time useful performer: well below form in 1997. *Lord Huntingdon*   –

PRINCE OF MY HEART 4 ch.c. Prince Daniel (USA) – Blue Room 70 (Gorytus (USA) 132) [1996 104: 10g² 12d* 12.3g³ 12m 10d⁴ 10.3f³ 9m 10m⁵ 1997 10d 10m⁵ 9s* 8.5g 10.4m 10m⁵ 10.4g⁶ Aug 20] tall colt: impresses in appearance: good mover: useful handicapper: easy winner at Newbury (raced alone far side) in May, and also ran well when fifth of 18 to Danish Rhapsody in William Hill Cup at Goodwood in July: stays 1½m: acts on firm and soft ground: joined D. Haydn Jones. *B. W. Hills*   107

PRINCE OF PARKES 3 b.g. Full Extent (USA) 113 – Summerhill Spruce 70 (Windjammer (USA)) [1996 –: 5g 6d 1997 6g³ 6m³ 6m⁵ 6g 5d² 6s⁶ 5m Aug 16]   58 sturdy, lengthy gelding: modest maiden: should stay 7f: acts on good to firm ground: blinkered last 4 starts. *J. Berry*

PRINCE OF SALSA 2 b.g. (Mar 2) Emarati (USA) 74 – Salinas 65 (Bay – Express 132) [1997 7d Oct 27] 6,400Y: sixth foal: dam sprint maiden: 33/1, behind in maiden at Lingfield. *K. McAuliffe*

PRINCE OXLEY 2 ch.c. (Apr 2) King's Signet (USA) 110 – Precious Air (IRE) 50 82 (Precocious 126) [1997 5g 7d 6g a7g⁴ Nov 18] strong colt: first foal: dam 5f (at 2 yrs) to 1m winner out of half-sister to very smart sprinter Ballad Rock: first worthwhile form when fourth in seller at Lingfield. *G. L. Moore*

PRINCE RUDOLF (IRE) 5 b.g. Cyrano de Bergerac 120 – Princess Raisa – (Indian King (USA) 128) [1996 39: a6g a6g⁶ a6g⁶ a8g 8g 7.1f⁵ 8m 8m 8f⁴ 10m⁴ 8m a10g 1997 a7g Feb 6] workmanlike gelding: poor performer: well beaten only 5-y-o start. *W. G. M. Turner*

PRINCESS BELFORT 4 b.f. Belfort (FR) 89 – Domino Rose 67 (Dominion – 123) [1996 –: 5.1g a6g 1997 12g⁶ Jul 30] no worthwhile form. *G. Barnett*

PRINCESS DANIELLE 5 b.m. Prince Daniel (USA) – Bells of St Martin 89 70 (Martinmas 128) [1996 63: 10.3d³ 10s² 8m 10m 10g⁵ 10m³ 10g² 10d³ 10s² 10.1m 10d³ 10g 1997 10s³ 10g* 10m* 10g³ 10m⁴ᵈⁱˢ 11.6g⁶ 10m³ 10m 10.4d⁶ Oct 8] leggy, plain mare: easy mover: fair handicapper: won in big fields at Leicester in May and Windsor in June: probably ideally suited by 1¼m: acts on good to firm and soft ground: genuine and consistent. *W. R. Muir*

PRINCESS DEYA 2 b.f. (Jan 13) Be My Guest (USA) 126 – Sumoto 101 (Mtoto – 134) [1997 6m 7g Aug 13] 10,000Y: first foal: dam 6f (at 2 yrs) and 7f winner from good family: tailed off both starts, seeming reluctant to race. *Dr J. D. Scargill*

PRINCESS EFISIO 4 b.f. Efisio 120 – Cutlass Princess (USA) 41 (Cutlass 67 (USA)) [1996 67: 5.1g⁶ 5m a5g⁵ 6.1m 5f⁴ a5g* a6g* a7g² a8.5g 7.1s² a7g⁵ 1997 a8.5g a7g⁵ a7g* 8.2g³ 8f Sep 10] smallish, rather dipped-backed filly: fair handicapper: won at Southwell in June on penultimate start for B. McMahon: effective at 7f/1m: acts on fibresand, possibly needs good ground or softer on turf: blinkered (on firm going) once at 3 yrs. *E. Truman, USA*

PRINCESSE LYPHARD 4 gr.f. Keen 116 – Bercheba (Bellypha 130) [1996 – 36: 8m 10m 7f 8f⁶ 7f³ a10g 1997 a7g⁵ Jan 4] lengthy, plain filly: poor maiden: well beaten only 4-y-o start. *M. J. Polglase*

PRINCESS LONDIS 2 ch.f. (Feb 20) Interrex (CAN) – Princess Lucianne 59 (Stanford 121§) [1997 5.2g⁴ 5m⁵ 6s⁶ May 17] close-coupled filly: fourth foal: half-sister to 1994 2-y-o 5f winner Satisfied Prince (by Full Extent) later successful in Germany: dam of little account: modest form in maidens and minor event: bandaged in front on debut. *A. G. Foster*

PRINCESS NATALIE 2 b.f. (May 2) Rudimentary (USA) 118 – X-Data 93 (On 78 Your Mark 125) [1997 5d* 5m 6g 6m 7s 7g 8m Nov 4] 15,000 2-y-o: sturdy filly: has scope: half-sister to several winners, including fairly useful sprinter Dry Point (by Sharpo) and Irish 6f and 1m winner Omar Mukhtar (by Faraway Times): dam winning sprinter: won minor event at Doncaster in June: well held afterwards (left T. D. Barron after next start), but often gave impression of retaining plenty of ability over trips too far: may well prove best at 5f: acts on dead ground: starts 3-y-o season potentially very well treated. *M. W. Easterby*

PRINCESS OF HEARTS 3 b.f. Prince Sabo 123 – Constant Delight 80 (Never 61 § So Bold 135) [1996 61: 6m 5.1m 6g⁴ 6.9m* 8m⁴ 8.1m³ 10m 8f 7m² a8.5g² 7m 8g⁴ a6g³ 1997 8.2m* 8.2d 8g² 8.3g³ 10.1m⁵ 10f⁵ 8.2g 8.2d Oct 8] ngthy filly: modest performer: won seller at Nottingham in April on final start for B. Meehan: well below form last 3 outings: stays 1¼m: acts on good to firm ground and fibresand: blinkered: ungenuine: joined G. L. Moore. *M. C. Pipe*

PRINCESS OLIVIA 2 b.f. (Mar 15) Prince Sabo 123 – Les Amis 70 (Alzao – (USA) 117) [1997 6g⁴ 5.2m Jul 22] third foal: half-sister to Italian 3-y-o Dancing Ilary (by Never So Bold), 1m winner at 2 yrs: dam 6f (at 2 yrs) and 1m winner who stayed 1¼m: only a little sign of ability in maidens at Yarmouth, bandaged on second occasion. *M. J. Ryan*

PRINCESS RENATA (IRE)   4 ch.f. Maelstrom Lake 118 – Sajanjal (Dance In   –
Time (CAN)) [1996 –: a6g 1997 6.9m 6g⁴ 6.1m 6f Sep 18] little worthwhile form.
Pat Mitchell

PRINCESS SARARA (USA)   3 ch.f. Trempolino (USA) 135 – Name And   –
Fame (USA) (Arts And Letters) [1996 –: a8.5g a8g 1997 a7g Jan 23] soundly beaten
in all-weather maidens. *Sir Mark Prescott*

PRINCESS SENORITA   2 gr.f. (May 7) Timeless Times (USA) 99 – Misty   –
Rocket 75 (Roan Rocket 128) [1997 6f Jun 10] 2,500Y: seventh foal: sister to a poor
maiden: dam won sellers at 1¼m and 1½m, also successful over hurdles: 50/1,
slowly away when behind in maiden at Salisbury. *P. Eccles*

PRINCESS TOPAZ   3 b.f. Midyan (USA) 124 – Diamond Princess 69 (Horage   82
124) [1996 70: 6g² 6f² 6g 8m³ 7.9g⁴ 1997 10m 10d 11.9f 10.1m 9.7m³ 10m³ 12g*
14m* 14g⁵ 16.2g² 14d Oct 17] leggy, angular filly: fairly useful handicapper: won at
Newmarket (ladies event) and Sandown in August: stays 2m: acts on good to firm
ground, soundly beaten on dead: held up. *C. A. Cyzer*

PRINCE ZANDO   3 b.g. Forzando 122 – Paradise Forum 78 (Prince Sabo 123)   63
[1996 NR 1997 6g⁵ 6m³ 7g⁶ 6g³ 7d⁶ Jun 25] first foal: dam, 2-y-o 5f winner: fair
maiden: likely to prove best at 5f/6f: yet to race on extremes of going. *C. A. Horgan*

PRINCE ZIZIM   4 b.g. Shareef Dancer (USA) 135 – Possessive Lady 62 (Dara   36
Monarch 128) [1996 –: 8m 8.2m 8.3m 10f 12m 8g⁶ 9.9g 10f 1997 a13g a11g 6.9s⁵
8.2m 8m 6.9m 8g Oct 27] small gelding: poor maiden: should stay beyond 1m: acts
on soft going: tried blinkered/visored. *R. C. Spicer*

PRINCIPAL BOY (IRE)   4 br.g. Cyrano de Bergerac 120 – Shenley Lass   50
(Prince Tenderfoot (USA) 126) [1996 –, a55: a6g² a7g* a9.4g⁵ a6g² a7g a6g⁵ a6g³   a43
a7g* a8g a7g⁴ 6m a8g⁴ a7g a8g⁴ 1997 a8g a6g a6g 8.3s* 9.2m² 8.3g² 9.2g* 9.2s³
9.2s⁵ 9.2m 8.3g⁶ 8s a7g⁶ a8g⁶ Nov 24] compact gelding: has a round action: modest
handicapper: won at Hamilton in May and June: stays 9f: acts on fibresand and good
to firm and soft ground: no improvement in blinkers/visor: takes good hold: genuine.
T. J. Etherington

PRINIA   3 b.f. Priolo (USA) 127 – Calandra (USA) 114 (Sir Ivor 135) [1996 NR   –
1997 7g 8g May 24] half-sister to several winners, including useful Irish miler
Golden Temple (by Golden Fleece): dam, Irish 1m and 1¼m winner, fourth in Irish
Oaks: well beaten in newcomers event at Newbury and (sweating and edgy) maiden
at Kempton. *G. Lewis*

PRINTERS QUILL   5 b.g. Squill (USA) 122 – On Impulse 63 (Jellaby 124)   44
[1996 56: 10m 12m 17.2f 10.2m* 10.2g 10m³ 10m 13.6m 1997 10m 10.8m⁶ 11.5g
Aug 2] leggy gelding: poor handicapper: stays 1¼m: acts on good to firm ground.
Major D. N. Chappell

PRIOLETTE (IRE)   2 b.f. (May 14) Priolo (USA) 127 – Celestial Path 101   59
(Godswalk (USA) 130) [1997 7m 5d⁶ 6s⁴ 7.5f⁴ 8m Nov 4] compact filly: half-sister
to several winners, including 4-y-o Goretski and fairly useful performer at up to 1¼m
Karazan (by Nishapour): dam Irish 5f to 7f winner: modest maiden: ran poorly in
nursery final start: stays 7.5f: acts on firm and soft going. *J. G. FitzGerald*

PRIOLO PRIMA   4 b.c. Priolo (USA) 127 – Jungle Rose 90 (Shirley Heights   78
130) [1996 NR 1997 a8.5g* a8g 8m³ 8.2m⁵ 10m 9m² 10s* Oct 14] good-topped
gelding: fractured pastern after only start in 1995: fair performer: won maiden at
Wolverhampton in January and handicap at Leicester (got up on line) in October:
should stay beyond 1¼m: acts on good to firm and soft ground and on fibresand: sold
30,000 gns, and sent to USA. *Sir Mark Prescott*

PRIORS MOOR   2 br.c. (Feb 5) Petong 126 – Jaziyah (IRE) (Lead On Time   48 +
(USA) 123) [1997 6g 8d 7f 7.3g a8g⁴ Dec 10] 25,000Y: sparely-made colt: first foal:
dam unraced: poor form in maidens/nurseries: stays 1m. *R. W. Armstrong*

PRIORY GARDENS (IRE)   3 b.g. Broken Hearted 124 – Rosy O'Leary   46
(Majetta 115) [1996 –: 6.1m 6.1d 7m 6.1s 1997 6m⁴ 6.1m⁴ 6g* 5.9m⁶ 6m⁶ 6.1d 6f
Sep 18] poor handicapper: well drawn, best effort when winning ladies race at Thirsk
in June: stays 6f: acts on good to firm going. *J. M. Bradley*

PRIVATE AUDIENCE (USA) 4 b.c. Private Account (USA) – Monroe (USA) 79
102 (Sir Ivor 135) [1996 –: 12g⁵ 1997 8g 9s⁵ 10m 8.5m 8.5m a12g⁴ a12s⁶ a12g a13g⁵
Dec 12] close-coupled, good-topped colt: has a quick action: fair performer: bought
out of J. Hammond's yard 17,500 gns after second start: stays 1½m: acts on
equitrack. *W. R. Muir*

PRIVATE FIXTURE (IRE) 6 ch.g. The Noble Player (USA) 126 – Pennyala 53
(Skyliner 117) [1996 –: 8d a7g a8g 1997 a7g⁶ a8g⁴ a10g⁶ a7g³ a7g⁶ a7g² a8g a8g a71
11.9f³ a11g* 13.1m² a12g* 16.4s³ a14.8g³ a14g⁶ Dec 8] quite good-topped gelding:
fair performer on the all-weather, modest on turf: won claimer and seller at Southwell
in the summer: stays 2m: acts on firm and soft going: twice blinkered, running
creditably first time. *D. Marks*

PRIVATE SEAL 2 b.g. (May 1) King's Signet (USA) 110 – Slender 79 (Aragon 64
118) [1997 6f³ 5d⁶ 7f² 6m 5.3m⁵ 5.3f* 5d⁶ a5s³ a6g³ a5g² Dec 19] workmanlike gelding: second foal: dam, 11f winner, half-sister to smart 1m to 1½m winner Karinga
Bay: modest performer: won seller at Brighton in October: placed in nurseries/
claimer at Lingfield last 3 starts: stays 7f: acts on firm ground and equitrack, probably
on dead: has carried head awkwardly. *G. L. Moore*

PRIX DE CLERMONT (IRE) 3 b.g. Petorius 117 – Sandra's Choice 57 (Sandy 52
Creek 123) [1996 –: 7f 6v a5g 1997 a7g⁵ 6m a7g⁶ a10g⁴ a12g* a13g⁶ Dec 22] sturdy
gelding: modest handicapper: won at Wolverhampton in December: stays 1½m: acts
on the all-weather, little form on turf. *G. Lewis*

PRIX STAR 2 ch.c. (Mar 8) Superpower 113 – Celestine 62 (Skyliner 117) [1997 79
5g² 5d² 5g⁴ 6g² 5d* 5m⁴ 6m⁶ Aug 16] first foal: dam won from 5f (at 2 yrs) to 7f:
fair performer: won maiden at Hamilton in July: ran well in nursery at Goodwood
penultimate start, but poorly final outing: stays 6f: acts on good to firm and dead
ground: visored final 3 starts. *C. W. Fairhurst*

PRIZEFIGHTER 6 b.g. Rambo Dancer (CAN) 107 – Jaisalmer 97 (Castle Keep –
121) [1996 70: a8g⁶ a8g* 7g 8f* 8.1m⁵ 1997 a10g Mar 4] neat gelding: fairly useful
hurdler: fair handicapper on flat, tailed off only 6-y-o start. *J. L. Eyre*

PRODIGAL SON (IRE) 2 b.c. (Mar 20) Waajib 121 – Nouveau Lady (IRE) 61
(Taufan (USA) 119) [1997 7.1g 7g a7g⁵ 8f Sep 18] IR 7,800F, 20,000Y: rangy colt:
has scope: second foal: half-brother to a winner abroad by Al Hareb: dam unraced:
modest form in maidens, including on fibresand: stiffish task in nursery final start:
should stay 1m. *R. J. R. Williams*

PROFESSION 6 b.g. Shareef Dancer (USA) 135 – Mrs Warren (USA) (Hail To –
Reason) [1996 NR 1997 a14g a12g a12g Dec 19] very lightly raced and little form
since 1994. *G. P. Enright*

PROJECTVISION (IRE) 3 b.g. Roi Danzig (USA) – Avidal Park 68 (Horage 72
124) [1996 NR 1997 a8g* 7f 7m 7m 7m 9m Dec 17] 9,500F, 15,500Y: fourth living
foal: half-brother to 2 winners (up to 1½m by Jareer): dam 2-y-o 5f winner: clear-cut
winner of maiden at Southwell in January for W. Muir: behind in Hong Kong late in
year (blinkered final start): stays 1m: acts on fibresand. *D. A. Hayes, Hong Kong*

PROLIX 2 ch.c. (Apr 22) Kris 135 – Ajuga (USA) 102 (The Minstrel (CAN) 135) 105
[1997 7m² 8m² 8g² Sep 28] big, strong, good-topped colt: has plenty of scope: has a
quick action: fifth living foal: half-brother to 1992 2-y-o 1m winner Ajanta (by Rousillon) and smart German middle-distance colt Bad Bertrich Again (by Dowsing):
dam 6f and 7f winner out of Irish 1000 Guineas and Champion Stakes winner Cairn
Rouge: useful form: second in maidens at Newbury and Doncaster (short-headed by
City Honours) and Royal Lodge Stakes at Ascot, held up, checked slightly and
edging right before going down by ¾ length to Teapot Row in last-named: free-going
sort, but may stay bit further than 1m: sure to win a race. *B. W. Hills*

PROMINENT 3 b.g. Primo Dominie 121 – Mary Bankes (USA) (Northern Baby 55 d
(CAN) 127) [1996 NR 1997 6m 6g³ 8g⁶ 7m⁶ 6.1d 6s⁴ 7.5m 6g 6g 8m⁵ Aug 20]
46,000Y: close-coupled gelding: fourth foal: half-brother to 4-y-o Santella Katie
and 1993 2-y-o 5f winner Mild Rebuke (by Reprimand): dam out of half-sister to
high-class filly Treizieme and Gold Cup second Eastern Mystic: disappointing
maiden: trained first 2 starts by Mrs J. Ramsden: tried blinkered and visored.
Mrs V. A. Aconley

PROMPT DELIVERY (USA)   2 b.c. (Mar 28) Zilzal (USA) 137 – Bold 'n   77 p
Determined (USA) (Bold And Brave) [1997 6m⁴ 7m² a7g³ 6m* 6d Oct 8] smallish,
attractive colt: half-brother to several winners abroad, including Argentinian graded
stakes winner Happy Holiday (by Turkoman): dam won 16 times in USA, including
6 Grade 1 events from 1m to 1½m at 3 yrs: fair form: won maiden at Pontefract in
September, making most: ran poorly on dead going on nursery debut: should stay
1m: acts on good to firm ground and fibresand: early to post final 2 starts: sent to
UAE: type to improve, and do well in handicaps. *M. R. Stoute*

PROPELLANT   3 b.g. Formidable (USA) 125 – Kirsheda 73 (Busted 134) [1996   –
–: 6m 7.1v 6m 1997 a11g 12d a14.8g 16d Jun 23] smallish, sturdy gelding: no
worthwhile form. *C. W. Thornton*

PROPER BLUE (USA)   4 b.c. Proper Reality (USA) – Blinking (USA) (Tom   109
Rolfe) [1996 112p: 9m⁵ 10d* 10g* 1997 10m³ 12g⁶ 10d⁶ 10d⁴ 10m² 9d³ 10m³ Oct
31] small, stocky colt: useful performer: best efforts in 1997 in listed races at
Kempton (to Dr Massini) and Newmarket (beaten 1¾ lengths by Saayefa) first and
last starts: ran at least respectably most starts in between: best form at 9f/1¼m: acts
on firm and dead going: has worn crossed noseband: usually held up. *T. G. Mills*

PROPHETS HONOUR   5 ch.g. Deploy 131 – Cat's Claw (USA) (Sharpen Up   56
127) [1996 NR 1997 a11s⁵ a9.4f² a12g Jan 15] workmanlike gelding: fairly useful in
1995: only modest form early at 5 yrs, best effort on second start. *P. C. Haslam*

PROPHITS PRIDE (IRE)   5 ch.g. Carmelite House (USA) 118 – Asinara (Julio   –
Mariner 127) [1996 NR 1997 12.1g 13.1s Oct 13] IR 1,500Y: third reported foal:
dam Irish stayer: fair winning hurdler for A. O'Brien in Ireland but only a modest
maiden on flat: well beaten here. *P. Monteith*

PROSE (IRE)   2 gr.c. (Apr 8) Priolo (USA) 127 – Nicea (IRE) 90 (Dominion 123)   96
[1997 5g³ 5d³ 6d² a7g* 7m² a8f⁴ Nov 6] IR 13,500F, IR 30,000Y: small, workmanlike colt: first foal: dam Irish 2-y-o 7f winner from 2 starts, granddaughter of smart 5f
to 1m winner Nasseem: useful form: won maiden at Southwell in June by 7 lengths
on penultimate start for R. Hannon: well beaten in allowance race on US debut:
should stay at least 1m: acts on fibresand. *D. Vienna, USA*

PROSPECTOR'S COVE   4 b.g. Dowsing (USA) 124 – Pearl Cove 63 (Town   75 d
And Country 124) [1996 96: 10g* 9m 10.3g 1997 11.9s 11.9g 9.7m 11.5m³ 9.9g⁶
10.1m⁵ 10g 11.5g 14.8m 16m³ Aug 6] workmanlike gelding: useful performer at 3
yrs: disappointing in 1997, including in visor: probably stays 2m: acts on good to
firm and soft ground. *J. Pearce*

PROSPECTRESS (USA)   2 ch.f. (Feb 18) Mining (USA) – Seductive Smile   82 p
(USA) (Silver Hawk (USA) 123) [1997 7m³ Oct 5] 39,000Y: second foal: dam
unraced close relative of smart American middle-distance performer Don Roberto
and half-sister to very smart French middle-distance stayer Nizon: sire (by Mr
Prospector) high class at up to 7f: 33/1, 2½ lengths third to Florazi in Leicester
maiden, quickening to dispute lead 2f out then running green and not knocked about:
should improve and win a race. *Lord Huntingdon*

PROSPERING   3 b.f. Prince Sabo 123 – Flourishing (IRE) 85 (Trojan Fen 118)   50
[1996 NR 1997 6.1d 7.1m* 7g 6m Jul 28] first foal: dam, 2-y-o 7f winner, stayed 1m:
modest performer: 20/1, won steadily-run claimer at Chepstow (for J. Smyth-
Osbourne) in June: last in handicaps for new yard: should stay 1m. *R. J. Hodges*

PROSPERO   4 b.g. Petong 126 – Pennies To Pounds 80 (Ile de Bourbon (USA)   75
133) [1996 77p: 10m⁶ 10g⁵ 12g² 11.8g* 1997 12m 11.7m 11.5d² 12g 12d⁵ 17.2f²
16g⁶ Oct 24] big, strong, lengthy gelding: fair handicapper: easily best efforts in 1997
when second: stays 17f: acts on firm and dead ground. *Mrs A. J. Perrett*

PROTARAS BAY   3 b.c. Superpower 113 – Vivid Impression (Cure The Blues   42
(USA)) [1996 –: 5m 6g 6m 1997 8.3m 9.9g 11.9d² 9m³ 12s⁵ a10g⁴ a10g² Dec 19]
angular colt: poor maiden handicapper: stays 1½m: acts on equitrack and good to
firm and dead ground, below form on soft. *P. L. Gilligan*

PROTEKTOR (GER)   8 b.h. Acatenango (GER) 127 – Prioritat (GER) (Frontal   114
122) [1996 120: 12g² 11d* 12m³ 12m⁶ 12g² 12v* 12m⁴ 1997 12g⁵ 11s⁴ 12g³ 12m⁴
12g³ 12d³ 12m Dec 14] grand campaigner in Germany, winner of over 1 million
marks and 4 pattern races (more career details in last year's essay): only smart form

in 1997, in frame in Group 1 races at Dusseldorf (third to Luso), Gelsenkirchen (fourth to Caitano) and Cologne (third to Taipan) before under length third to Saugerties in Group 3 race (he'd won twice before) at Gelsenkirchen: best form around 1½m: acted on good to firm and heavy ground: consistent and tough: retired to stud. *A. Lowe, Germany*

PROTOCOL (IRE) 3 ch.c. Taufan (USA) 119 – Ukraine's Affair (USA) (The Minstrel (CAN) 135) [1996 72: 8f 8g⁴ a8g² 1997 a10g² 10.2m⁴ 11.4m* 12g⁴ 12d 14m 11.6m⁵ 12g² 11.8d⁴ Oct 28] useful-looking colt: has had soft palate operation: fair handicapper: won at Sandown in May: creditable efforts last 2 starts: should stay beyond 1½m: acts on good to firm going and equitrack: has had tongue tied. *J. W. Hills* 77

PROUD BRIGADIER (IRE) 9 b.g. Auction Ring (USA) 123 – Naughty One Gerard (Brigadier Gerard 144) [1996 55d: 8.3g⁵ 8.3d⁴ 8m 8d 8m 1997 9.7g⁵ 10g⁶ 8d⁶ 10g 10.5m 9g 8.1s⁵ 9.7g 11.6m Jul 21] lengthy, sparely-made gelding: steadily on the downgrade, and just a poor handicapper in 1997: stays 9.4f: probably acts on any going. *M. R. Bosley* 41 d

PROUD MONK 4 gr.g. Aragon 118 – Silent Sister 78 (Kind of Hush 118) [1996 78: 7d² 8d² 7.6g 8.5m⁴ 8f 9d³ 8m 7.1m⁵ 7s⁴ 8s 1997 8m 8.5m 8s⁴ 10s 7g a7g Dec 18] strong, lengthy gelding: fair handicapper at 3 yrs: no form in 1997. *M. R. Bosley* –

PROUD NATIVE (IRE) 3 b.g. Imp Society (USA) – Karamana (Habitat 134) [1996 106: 5g* 6m* 6m* 6m⁴ 6m 6m² 6m* 6.5d⁵ 1997 7g 5d⁴ 6f 5m⁵ 6m* 6m 6g Sep 20] sturdy gelding: poor walker/mover: useful performer: returned to best when close fifth of 15 in King George Stakes at Goodwood in July: made all in minor event at Yarmouth (wandered markedly but beat My Melody Parkes a neck) following month: effective at 5f/6f: acts on good to firm and dead ground: edgy before running poorly fifth 2-y-o start: sold (to D. Nicholls) 40,000 gns in October. *A. P. Jarvis* 106

PROVENCE 10 ch.g. Rousillon (USA) 133 – Premier Rose 117 (Sharp Edge 123) [1996 NR 1997 a16.2g Jul 25] fairly useful handicapper at 7 yrs: lightly raced and well below form on flat since. *A. W. Carroll* –

PROVE THE POINT (IRE) 4 b.f. Maelstrom Lake 118 – In Review (Ela-Mana-Mou 132) [1996 –: 7g 8.5m 1997 8m 12f 10.8d Jun 24] of little account nowadays. *Mrs P. N. Dutfield* –

PRUDENT PRINCESS 5 b.m. Puissance 110 – Princess Story 64 (Prince de Galles 125) [1996 5⁷d: a7g a8g⁴ 8g a8g a7g 6s a6g⁵ 6m a6g 1997 a6g¹ a6g a7g 8s Jul 3] angular mare: poor maiden handicapper: on the downgrade, and no form in 1997. *A. Hide* –

PSICOSSIS 4 b.c. Slip Anchor 136 – Precious Jade 72 (Northfields (USA)) [1996 64p: 12g⁶ 1997 12m⁴ 12.1g⁴ 14g⁵ 13.5g² 12g³ 13d⁶ 13.5g* Sep 21] well-made colt: brother to smart Italian/American middle-distance performer Slicious: fair form in maidens and a handicap for H. Cecil first 3 starts: won minor event at Lyon Villeurbanne in September: will stay 2m. *C. Laffon-Parias, France* 78

PUBLIC PURSE (USA) 3 b.c. Private Account (USA) – Prodigious (FR) (Pharly (FR) 130) [1996 NR 1997 10.5g* 16.2m⁵ 12d* Oct 8] tall colt: has a powerful, round action: half-brother to several winners in USA, notably Grade 1 1¼m winner Super Staff (by Secretariat): dam French 1m and 1¼m winner: smart form: won newcomers event in May and listed race (by 2½ lengths from Niederhoff) in October, both at Saint-Cloud: better form at 1½m than 2m (took fierce hold in Queen's Vase): acts on good to soft ground: should improve again. *A. Fabre, France* 110 p

PUBLISHER (USA) 2 b.c. (Mar 8) Kris S (USA) – Andover Way (USA) (His Majesty (USA)) [1997 8f* Oct 29] closely related to smart USA winner up to 1½m Dynaformer (by Roberto) and half-brother to several winners in USA, including a minor 2-y-o stakes winner by Seattle Slew: dam, won 9 times in USA (including Grade 1 9f event at 4 yrs), half-sister to Belmont Stakes third Darby Creek Road: sire (by Roberto) minor stakes winner at up to 9f: 12/1 from 8/1 and green, won maiden at Yarmouth in much more taking style than bare result suggests, held up going strongly and making up several lengths to beat Star Crystal a neck without being at all hard ridden: should stay at least 1¼m: backward sort (reportedly over 17 hands at 2 yrs), and looks sure to go on to much better things as he matures. *J. R. Fanshawe* 92 P

Fittocks Stud's "Puce"

PUCE   4 b.f. Darshaan 133 – Souk (IRE) 98 (Ahonoora 122) [1996 88p: 8g 9m² 112
10g* 12m³ 11.9g* 1997 10g⁵ 11.9f² 14m² 13.9g³ 14.6m³ 12g* 12m² Nov 1] small,
sparely-made filly: often failed to impress in appearance: made into a smart
performer, third to Far Ahead in Tote Ebor at York (not clear run) and to Book At
Bedtime in Park Hill Stakes (clearly best effort, beaten a length) at Doncaster: won
6-runner listed race at Ascot in October by neck from Graceful Lass: stayed 14.6f
well: raced only on good going or firmer: reliable: stud. *L. M. Cumani*

PUIWEE   2 b.f. (Apr 1) Puissance 110 – Glow Again 78 (The Brianstan 128) [1997   –
7d Nov 7] workmanlike filly: has a round action: sixth foal; half-sister to 4-y-o
General Glow and 1994 2-y-o 5f winner Double Glow (both by Presidium): dam
2-y-o 5f and 6f winner: behind in maiden at Doncaster. *P. T. Dalton*

PUNKAH (USA)   4 b.g. Lear Fan (USA) 130 – Gentle Persuasion 95 (Bustino   70
136) [1996 78: a10g* 12d⁴ 10m⁵ 10m* 1997 a8.5f³ a8.5g a10g* a10g 10m 10g⁴ 8m   a80
12d 10s Oct 14] well-made gelding: carries condition: fairly useful handicapper on
all-weather, fair on turf: won at Lingfield in February: stays 1¼m: none too
consistent: fairly useful hurdler. *G. M. McCourt*

PUPIL MASTER (IRE)   3 b.g. Masterclass (USA) 116 – Lamya 73 (Hittite Glory   –
125) [1996 –: 5m 7m a8g⁶ 1997 12g⁵ 12g Apr 25] no form. *Denys Smith*

PURCHASING POWER (IRE)   3 b.c. Danehill (USA) 126 – Purchasepaper-   78
chase 104 (Young Generation 129) [1996 –: 7g 6s a8g⁶ 1997 8.3d* 8.5m² 10m 7g*
7.1g⁵ 8g⁴ 7d* 7d³ Jun 28] robust colt: fair performer: won maiden at Hamilton in
April, minor event at Newmarket in May and handicap at Epsom in June: stays 1m
(too free at 1¼m): acts on good to firm and dead ground: front runner: hurdling in
Ireland. *N. A. Callaghan*

PURE COINCIDENCE   2 b.c. (Mar 12) Lugana Beach 116 – Esilam 62   95
(Frimley Park 109) [1997 5d⁵ a5g* 5.1s³ 5.2f² 5m⁶ 5g* 5m² 5v Oct 11] 10,500Y:

rather leggy colt: has a short action: sixth foal: half-brother to 5-y-o Knotty Hill and a winner in Hungary by Bold Arrangement: dam, 2-y-o 5f winner here, won up to 1m in Italy: useful performer: won maiden at Southwell in June and minor event at Redcar in August: better efforts when second in Super Sprint at Newbury and minor event at Haydock, and when sixth in Molecomb Stakes at Goodwood: speedy: acts on firm ground and fibresand, well below form on softer than good. *G. Lewis*

PURE NOBILITY (IRE) 2 br.c. (May 2) Darshaan 133 – Ma Pavlova (USA) 102 (Irish River (FR) 131) [1997 7m 7g* 7g³ Oct 27] strong, rangy colt: sixth foal: half-brother to 3 winners, including useful Irish 9f and 1½m winner and winning hurdler L'Opera (by Old Vic): dam French 2-y-o 6.5f winner: won maiden at Chester in September: good third in nursery at Leicester, rallying: will be well suited by further than 7f: good sort, and should make a useful handicapper. *B. W. Hills* **81 p**

PURIST 3 b.c. Polish Precedent (USA) 131 – Mill Line 71 (Mill Reef (USA) 141) [1996 71p: 7d 1997 10g² 11.8m² 11.5s* 13.9g Aug 20] rather finely-made colt: useful performer: comfortably made all in maiden at Yarmouth in July: ran poorly in the Ebor at York only subsequent outing: should stay beyond 1½m: acts on good to firm and soft ground: sold 12,000 gns, and sent to Poland. *M. R. Stoute* **96**

PURPLE FLING 6 ch.g. Music Boy 124 – Divine Fling (Imperial Fling (USA) 116) [1996 76: 6d² 6g⁶ 6.1m³ 6m⁴ 5g⁵ 5f⁵ 6v 6d* a6g⁴ 1997 a7g⁴ a6g⁶ 6d 6f* 7s* 6g 6d³ 5m 6g Sep 20] strong gelding: fairly useful performer: won handicap at Salisbury in June (final start for L. G. Cottrell) and minor event at Redcar in July: best effort when third in handicap at Ripon in August: stays 7f: acts on any ground: consistent. *D. W. Chapman* **83**

PURPLE MAIZE 3 b.g. Mazilier (USA) 107 – Hen Night (Mummy's Game 120) [1996 NR 1997 6.9m⁶ 10d a8g⁵ 10m⁶ a8g 6d a11g Nov 17] 4,000Y: angular gelding: first foal: dam unraced: poor maiden: trained first 6 starts by J. Akehurst: form only at 1m on fibresand: tried blinkered. *S. Dow* **– a47**

PURPLE SPLASH 7 b.g. Ahonoora 122 – Quay Line 117 (High Line 125) [1996 95: 14.9d* 14d* 14s³ 16g 14.6d⁴ 1997 a14.8g 13.9g 13.9d* 16.1g⁶ 16d⁶ Sep 13] smallish, good-topped gelding: has a scratchy action: fairly useful handicapper: won at York in June: ran creditably both subsequent starts: stays 2m: has run respectably on good to firm ground, but goes particularly well on good or softer: visored/blinkered. *P. J. Makin* **93**

PURSUIT VENTURE 2 b.f. (Mar 3) Pursuit of Love 124 – Our Shirley 84 (Shirley Heights 130) [1997 7d³ 7d² Oct 27] tall, useful-looking filly: half-sister to several winners, including 5-y-o Pearl Venture and 6f (at 2 yrs) to 1m winner Soviet Express (by Siberian Express): dam 1¼m winner: fair form when placed in maidens at Leicester and Lingfield: should stay at least 1¼m: should improve. *S. P. C. Woods* **72 p**

PUSEY STREET GIRL 4 ch.f. Gildoran 123 – Pusey Street 96 (Native Bazaar 122) [1996 87: 7m 8f 7g* 6m³ 1997 8m 7g 6d Apr 26] rangy filly: fairly useful form at 3 yrs: well beaten in handicaps in 1997. *M. R. Bosley* **–**

PUSH A VENTURE 3 b.f. Shirley Heights 130 – Push A Button (Bold Lad (IRE) 133) [1996 58: 6m 8.1m 7d⁴ 1997 a11g 8.2d 8.2g 7d³ a8g 7m Jul 22] angular filly: modest maiden: should stay at least 1m: well beaten both starts on the all-weather. *S. P. C. Woods* **51**

PUTERI WENTWORTH 3 b.f. Sadler's Wells (USA) 132 – Sweeping 104 (Indian King (USA) 128) [1996 NR 1997 10m 12.1g 10g 12d⁴ 14.1s 12s* Nov 6] 90,000Y: fourth foal: half-sister to 4-y-o Desert Lynx: dam, 2-y-o 6f winner, is out of half-sister to Bassenthwaite, a good family: fair handicapper: best effort when coming from rear to win at Musselburgh by 6 lengths: should stay at least 1¾m: acts on soft ground. *Miss Gay Kelleway* **73**

PUTRA (USA) 3 ch.c. Dixie Brass (USA) – Olatha (USA) (Miswaki (USA) 124) [1996 113p: 7.1m* 7m* 1997 8m May 3] tall, leggy colt: has a long stride: smart at 2 yrs, winner of Champagne Stakes at Goodwood: much too free to post (almost out of control) and ran no sort of race in 2000 Guineas at Newmarket only start in 1997: should stay 1m: has reportedly had an operation on his palate, and stays in training. *P. F. I. Cole* **–**

PUTUNA   2 b.f. (Feb 14) Generous (IRE) 139 – Ivoronica 89 (Targowice (USA)   84
130) [1997 7m³ 8g³ Oct 24] 70,000Y: good-topped filly: half-sister to several
winners, including useful sprinter Lochonica (by Lochnager) and 7-y-o Tykeyvor:
dam 2-y-o 5f winner: fairly useful form in valuable sales race won by Tamarisk at
Newmarket and maiden won by Merciless (beaten 5 lengths) at Doncaster, having to
be switched and running on in latter: should be suited by at least 1¼m. *I. A. Balding*

PUZZLEMENT   3 gr.g. Mystiko (USA) 124 – Abuzz 101 (Absalom 128) [1996   65
60: 5m⁶ 6s⁵ 7m 8m 8m⁵ 6m 6.1s 1997 a7g⁵ a8g* a9.4g* a11g⁵ 9g² 8m 8d 7m 10m⁶   a93
a8s* a8g* a9.4g³ Dec 6] big, good-bodied gelding: fairly useful on the all-weather,
fair on turf: won handicaps at Lingfield and Wolverhampton in February and at
Lingfield (2) in November: easily best effort when third to Farmost in listed race at
Wolverhampton: stays 9.4f: best turf form on good ground or firmer. *C. E. Brittain*

PWLLGLAS   3 br.g. Puissance 110 – Glas Y Dorlan 80 (Sexton Blake 126) [1996   –
NR 1997 a9.4g Aug 16] half-brother to winners abroad by Red Sunset and Mister
Majestic: dam 1½m winner: well beaten in seller. *S. C. Williams*

PYRRHIC DANCE   7 b.g. Sovereign Dancer (USA) – Cherubim (USA) (Stev-   –
ward) [1996 NR 1997 a12g a16g a12g⁵ Feb 20] very lightly raced on flat nowadays,
and no form in 1997. *M. J. Haynes*

Q

Q FACTOR   5 br.m. Tragic Role (USA) – Dominiana (Dominion 123) [1996 84,   90
a69: a6g a8g⁴ a8g⁵ a8g³ a8g⁴ 8d³ 8.1d 8.2m* 8.1m⁵ 8.3m* 8.3d 8.3d* 7.1s* 6.1s⁶   a–
1997 8m 8s 8g 8.1m 8d³ 6.9s* 7.1g 7m⁶ 7g* 8.1m⁴ 7d³ 7f 8v² Oct 11] leggy mare:
has quick action: fairly useful handicapper: won at Folkestone in June and Salisbury
in August: stays 1m well: has won on good to firm going, goes well on good or softer:
visored once at 2 yrs: often bandaged behind: tough. *D. Haydn Jones*

QILIN (IRE)   2 b.f. (Mar 30) Second Set (IRE) 127 – Usance (GER) (Kronen-   92 p
kranich (GER) 118) [1997 6m 6m* 7g Oct 18] 8,000F, 22,000Y: robust, good-bodied
filly: seventh foal: half-sister to several winners, including Irish 9f/1¼m winner
Magical Lady (by Magical Strike): dam German 1m winner: well backed, won
maiden at Newmarket by 1¼ lengths from Grazia, drifting left: pulled hard when
over 5 lengths ninth to Name of Love in Rockfel Stakes at Newmarket later in
October: should stay 1m: has scope, and should still do better. *M. H. Tompkins*

QISMAT   2 b.f. (Apr 20) Selkirk (USA) 129 – Plaything 69 (High Top 131) [1997   64
7m a8.5g² Dec 13] 3,800Y: fourth foal: half-sister to 3-y-o Little Acorn: dam
lightly-raced 1m winner: better effort in maidens when ¾-length second of 13 at
Wolverhampton, making most: should stay further than 8.5f. *H. Akbary*

QUAINT DESIRE   4 br.g. Grey Desire 115 – Aquainted 63 (Known Fact (USA)   –
135) [1996 NR 1997 7.5g⁵ 12.3g 8g⁵ 10m Jul 19] second reported foal: dam,
disqualified 2-y-o 7f winner, half-sister to useful sprinter Nusantara: no worthwhile
form. *M. Brittain*

QUAKERESS (IRE)   2 b.f. (Jan 28) Brief Truce (USA) 126 – Deer Emily (Alzao   65
(USA) 117) [1997 5.1m³ 5m² 5g³ Aug 23] 14,000Y: fourth foal: half-sister to 4-y-o
Crissem (5f winner at 2 yrs) and fairly useful Irish 7f and 9f winner Damani (by
Persian Bold): dam, Irish 6f (at 2 yrs) and 1½m winner, half-sister to a useful stayer:
modest form in maidens and a minor event: looks a 5f performer. *John Berry*

QUALITAIR BEAUTY   4 b.f. Damister (USA) 123 – Mac's Princess (USA) 67   40
(Sovereign Dancer (USA)) [1996 –: a8g 1997 10g 11.8d 10m⁶ a9.4g² 10d a11g
Dec 8] only form when staying-on second in seller at Wolverhampton in August.
Miss L. C. Siddall

QUALITAIR PRIDE   5 b.m. Siberian Express (USA) 125 – Qualitairess 49   43 d
(Kampala 120) [1996 NR 1997 a12g² a12g* a12g⁵ a13g a16g 12.1d a12g Aug 15]
poor handicapper: won amateurs race at Southwell in January by 9 lengths, making
all: below form afterwards, giving impression all was not well final start: stays 1½m:

has form on good to firm ground, best efforts on fibresand or going softer than good: has worn blinkers, not at 5 yrs. *J. F. Bottomley*

QUALITAIR SILVER 3 gr.f. Absalom 128 – Irish Limerick 89 (Try My Best (USA) 130) [1996 NR 1997 a7g³ a7g⁶ a6g³ 6.1m a7g a6g³ a6g a8g a7g Jul 21] 5,000Y: half-sister to 7-y-o Kira and Matching Lines (by Thatching), both sprinters: dam 2-y-o 6f winner: poor maiden: likely to prove best up to 7f: raced almost exclusively on fibresand: blinkered final start: inconsistent. *J. F. Bottomley* — 46

QUARTERSTAFF 3 b.g. Charmer 123 – Quaranta 83 (Hotfoot 126) [1996 –p: 8s 1997 7g a7g 8.3g 12d⁵ 10.1f³ Sep 17] good-bodied gelding: modest performer: best effort at 1¼m: acts on firm going. *C. F. Wall* — 59

QUE BELLE (CAN) 3 b.f. Seattle Dancer (USA) 119 – Qui Bid (USA) (Spectacular Bid (USA)) [1996 8v* 1997 8g* 8v* 11s* 12m³ 12f Oct 5] $62,000Y: resold IR 70,000Y: tall, good-topped filly: sixth foal: half-sister to minor winners in USA by Timeless Native (3) and Falcon Bid and another in Japan by Storm Cat: dam, unraced, from fine family, notably Bakharoff and Emperor Jones: very smart German filly: won maiden at Dusseldorf late on at 2 yrs, listed race at Cologne in April, Henkel Rennen at Dusseldorf in May and Preis der Diana at Mulheim (beat Borgia 1½ lengths, pair clear) in June: reportedly injured herself after creditable third to Caitano in Aral-Pokal at Gelsenkirchen in August: ran well to finish eighth to Peintre Celebre in the Arc at Longchamp final one, particularly as not clearest of runs: stays 1½m: acts on any going: stays in training. *H. Remmert, Germany* — 120

QUEENFISHER 5 b. or br.m. Scottish Reel 123 – Mavahra 93 (Mummy's Pet 125) [1996 –: 6m 7.6f⁶ 7m 8g a6g 1997 a8g Jan 18] leggy mare: one-time fairly useful performer: little encouragement since 3 yrs. *G. L. Moore* — –

QUEEN MAUD (IRE) 3 b.f. Akarad (FR) 130 – Modiyna (Nishapour (FR) 125) [1996 6g⁴ 7g* 7s³ 8s 8d² 1997 10m* 9.3d* 10.5d 9g³ 12m* 12f Oct 5] — 119

The three pattern races run over a mile and a half at Longchamp in mid-September—the Prix Vermeille, Prix Niel and Prix Foy—known collectively as the 'Arc trials' can serve their intended purpose but are just as likely to be tactical affairs with little relevance as form-guides to the Arc itself. There must have been more than one set of connections considering themselves victims of a miscarriage of justice after the latest running. The Prix Niel saw the controversial defeat of Peintre Celebre at 10/1 on, the steadily-run Prix Foy went to the outsider of eight in a blanket finish and the Prix Vermeille went to another long-shot in Queen Maud.

As a Group 1 event, the Prix Vermeille is an important contest in its own right and until recently was often the most competitive of the Arc trials, frequently deciding the title of Europe's top middle-distance three-year-old

Prix Vermeille, Longchamp—Queen Maud comes out on top from Gazelle Royale (stripes); Brilliance (No. 3) just gets the better of Mousse Glacee for third

filly. The latest running had the look of a consolation prize, though, in the absence of the various Oaks winners Reams of Verse, Ebadiyla and Vereva and the top German filly Borgia. Apart from Queen Maud, those who did make the line-up in the Vermeille included Gazelle Royale and Mousse Glacee, runners-up to Reams of Verse in the Oaks and Vereva in the Prix de Diane respectively; Brilliance, who'd been third at Chantilly and to Ebadiyla in the Irish Oaks; Galtres winner Kaliana (accompanied by pacemaker Ridaiyma); and Dust Dancer, who'd beaten a below-form Vereva in the Prix de la Nonette.

Queen Maud couldn't claim such good form beforehand. Her only win at two had come in a minor event at Vichy but she'd ended her first season with a second to Mousse Glacee in the Prix des Reservoirs. She'd won a minor event and the Prix Vanteaux (by three quarters of a length from Tashiriya), both at Longchamp, on her return at three, but ninth place in the Prix de Diane didn't do her justice; Queen Maud was shut in for much of the straight and she might well have made the frame with a clear run. On her final start before the Vermeille, Queen Maud had been fourth past the post, promoted to third, in the nine-furlong Prix Chloe at Maisons-Laffitte.

Trying a mile and a half for the first time in the Prix Vermeille, Queen Maud showed a good deal of improvement. Ridaiyma ensured a very strong pace and was a spent force when Queen Maud took over halfway up the straight. Running on bravely, Queen Maud held Gazelle Royale by a length, with a nose and the same back to Brilliance and the favourite Mousse Glacee. Peintre Celebre apart (his Niel conqueror Rajpoute didn't even run in the Arc), the Arc trials' contribution to the big race itself consisted of supplying the last six home with Queen Maud (a workmanlike filly who didn't take the eye

Mr Gary A. Tanaka's "Queen Maud"

beforehand) fifteenth of the eighteen runners. Late in the year it was reported
that she had joined Ben Cecil in the USA.

		Labus	Busted
	Akarad (FR)	(b or br 1971)	Cordovilla
	(b or br 1978)	Licata	Abdos
Queen Maud (IRE)		(b 1969)	Gaia
(b.f. 1994)		Nishapour	Zeddaan
		(gr 1975)	Alama
	Modiyna	Monique	Tanerko
	(b or br 1982)	(b 1960)	Matina

A look at the names on both sides of Queen Maud's pedigree reveals
origins with the Aga Khan. Queen Maud's dam Modiyna was sold in foal to the
Aga's Prix du Jockey-Club runner-up Akarad in 1993 and just over a year later
that foal—Queen Maud—went for just 6,500 guineas at the December Sales.
Modiyna, an eleven-and-a-half furlong winner at Maisons-Laffitte, had served
the Aga well at stud, with five winners from five previous foals. There were
useful Irish performers among them, including the National Stakes runner-up
Manashar (by Doyoun) and the two-year-old seven-furlong winner Marwazi
(by Darshaan). Both continued their careers under different names in Hong
Kong, Manashar without much distinction but Marwazi, alias Wonderful
World, taking the prestigious Queen Mother's Cup. Modiyna was the tenth and
final winner out of Monique, who won the Prix de Royallieu. Monique's earlier
foals included the Prix d'Aumale winner Ortanique and the smart stayer
Marasali. The family stems from Germany where great grandam Matina was
successful; her other descendants include the high-class filly Leandra who was
second in the Prix Vermeille. *J. de Roualle, France*

QUEEN OF ALL BIRDS (IRE) 6 b.m. Bluebird (USA) 125 – Blue Bouquet 64
(Cure The Blues (USA)) [1996 75, a86: a8g⁵ a8g* a8g² a8g² 8s⁶ 7.6m³ 8m⁵ 8.2m⁶ a69
9m 7.1s a8g* 1997 a9.4g⁵ a8g 7d a8g* 9s² 8g³ 5h⁶ 8m³ 8d² 8.5d Oct 23] workmanlike
mare: fair on all-weather, modest on turf: trained first 2 starts by R. Boss: won minor
event at Sterrebeek in June: best form at 1m: acts on heavy and good to firm going,
and the all-weather: tried visored. *J. Arnou, France*

QUEEN OF SHANNON (IRE) 9 b.m. Nordico (USA) – Raj Kumari (Vitiges 59 §
(FR) 132) [1996 53: 8.1g² 8.1m 10.8m a8.5g 8.3m* 8f³ 8m 7f 8m⁶ 1997 8.3s⁴ 8s*
8.3g 8.3m 7.1g⁵ 7d 8g⁵ 8.2d a8g Nov 24] angular mare: has reportedly had 3 wind
operations: modest handicapper: won seller at Warwick in July: looked reluctant
final 2 starts: seems best around 1m: acts on any going: occasionally blinkered or
visored: inconsistent. *A. W. Carroll*

QUEEN OF TIDES (IRE) 2 b.f. (Apr 19) Soviet Star (USA) 128 – Tidesong 62
(Top Ville 129) [1997 7m 8.1g⁶ Sep 27] leggy, sparely-made filly: first foal: dam
unraced: better effort in maidens on debut at Lingfield: bandaged behind and carried
head high at Haydock later in September: sent to France. *M. R. Stoute*

QUEEN SALOTE 2 b.f. (Mar 28) Mujtahid (USA) 118 – Island Ruler 79 (Ile de 67 +
Bourbon (USA) 133) [1997 6m 7m 6m⁴ 6.5m Sep 10] 94,000Y: good-topped filly:
third foal: half-sister to useful German 3-y-o Abou Lahab (by Kenmare), 7f winner
at 2 yrs, and 1995 2-y-o 7f winner Cebwob (by Rock City): dam 1½m winner in
France at 4 yrs, out of half-sister to Dominion: fair form: considerably handled in
maidens: heavily bandaged, never dangerous in valuable nursery at Doncaster final
start: should be suited by at least 1m: raced only on good to firm going (moved poorly
to post third start): may do better. *D. R. Loder*

QUEENS CHECK 4 b.f. Komaite (USA) – Ski Baby (Petoski 135) [1996 –, a69: –
5s⁶ a5g* 5m a5g* 5g a6g a5g³ a6g² a6g 1997 5s⁵ a5g Apr 1] fair sprint handicapper
on the all-weather, modest at best on turf: well below form in 1997. *Miss J. F. Craze*

QUEENS CONSUL (IRE) 7 gr.m. Kalaglow 132 – Queens Connection (Bay 94
Express 132) [1996 87, a–: 8s⁵ 7.5m⁵ 8m² 8.5m⁵ 7g* 8.1d³ 8.9m⁶ 8g 8.5m 7.9g² 7.6m a–
8.1m 8d* 7d 8m 8m 10.4g 8g 8s 1997 7g a8.5g⁵ 8m 8.5d 8f² 9m² 8g 8.5m* 9m³
8.1m* 8g 7.6s* 8m² 8m 7.9s⁵ 8g 8m Nov 1] tall mare: fairly useful handicapper: in

fine form in the summer, winning at Beverley, Haydock and Chester: stays 9f: acts on firm and soft going, below form on fibresand: usually races prominently: game. *B. S. Rothwell*

QUEEN'S HAT 2 b.f. (Feb 8) Cadeaux Genereux 131 – Greenlet (IRE) 79 (Green Desert (USA) 127) [1997 6g Jul 10] 35,000F, 64,000Y: robust, lengthy filly: has plenty of scope: first foal: dam 2-y-o 5f winner, granddaughter of 1000 Guineas winner Full Dress II: 33/1 and in need of race, well beaten in maiden at Newmarket. *B. Hanbury* –

QUEEN SIGI (IRE) 2 b.f. (Mar 16) Fairy King (USA) – Quinsigimond 71 (Formidable (USA) 125) [1997 5s May 17] IR 16,000Y: first foal: dam 6f and 7f winner out of half-sister to Leap Lively, dam of Forest Flower: last in maiden at Hamilton, very slowly away. *Sir Mark Prescott* –

QUEEN'S INSIGNIA (USA) 4 b.f. Gold Crest (USA) 120 – Years (USA) (Secretariat (USA)) [1996 –: 7.3d 8.2s a8g^5 a10s 1997 8g^5 8f^2 9.7m^4 8f^3 8.3s* 8.3m^5 8m 8.3m^2 8.3m^4 8d Oct 13] tall filly: modest handicapper: won at Windsor in June: stays 1m: acts on firm and soft going: no improvement in blinkers. *P. F. I. Cole* 63

QUEEN'S PAGEANT 3 ch.f. Risk Me (FR) 127 – Mistral's Dancer (Shareef Dancer (USA) 135) [1996 78: 5g^3 6g^5 5s* 6m 1997 7d 6g 6s 8v^5 a8.5g^3 Dec 26] workmanlike filly: fairly useful performer: quite highly tried in 1997 before best effort when third in handicap at Wolverhampton: stays 8.5f: acts on fibresand, probably on heavy. *J. L. Spearing* 88

QUEENS STROLLER (IRE) 6 b.m. Pennine Walk 120 – Mount Isa (Miami Springs 121) [1996 –: a10g a11g a12g 10m a8.5g a12g a9.4g^4 a10g^6 1997 a8g^2 a8g^5 a10g^3 a8g^2 8.2m^4 a8g* 10.3m^4 9d 10.2d^5 8.1g a7g^2 a9.4g Dec 26] lightly-made mare: poor handicapper: won at Southwell in May: in-and-out form after: effective at 7f to 1¼m: acts on any turf/all-weather: well beaten in blinkers/visor. *R. E. Peacock* 48

QUEST FOR BEST (USA) 3 b. or br.f. Quest For Fame 127 – Chic Monique (USA) (Halo (USA)) [1996 64p: 7.6d^3 1997 10g 9m^6 10m^4 11g^3 13.8s^2 12s 12m Aug 18] modest maiden: trained by J. Gosden until after fifth start: soundly beaten for new stable: probably stays 13.8f: tried visored/blinkered, no improvement: carries head high: seems a weak finisher. *Michael Halford, Ireland* 57

QUEZON CITY 3 ch.c. Keen 116 – Calachuchi 74 (Martinmas 128) [1996 –: 6m 1997 8m a8g^6 10g 11m^2 12.1m* 12.1s^3 11m^5 Jul 19] tall, close-coupled colt: modest performer: best effort second in handicap at Redcar: week later won 3-runner minor event at Hamilton in June, dictating pace: stays 1½m: acts on good to firm ground, probably on soft. *M. J. Camacho* 58

QUIBBLING 3 b.f. Salse (USA) 128 – Great Exception 84 (Grundy 137) [1996 63p: 5m 7.1s^6 1997 7.1d^2 8g 10g^5 8d 8m 10s^3 12m Oct 31] rather leggy filly: modest maiden: placed at Chepstow and Nottingham: stays 1¼m: acts on soft ground: below form when blinkered: joined Miss H. Knight. *H. Candy* 62

QUIET ARCH (IRE) 4 b.g. Archway (IRE) 115 – My Natalie 64 (Rheingold 137) [1996 69, a66: 8d 6m 10.2g a8g^4 a8g* a8g^3 a10g^5 a8g 9g^4 12m^5 12m^3 10.4g^2 9.7d^3 a11g^5 1997 a10g* a10g^2 a10g* a10g^3 a10g^3 a10g a10g^4 10g^2 10.3m^2 10g 10m 10g^6 a10g Dec 22] good-topped gelding: has a round action: fair performer: won minor event and handicap at Lingfield in January: best efforts when second: stays 1½m: acts on good to firm and dead ground and on equitrack (not at best on fibresand): ran poorly in visor: held up. *W. R. Muir* 71 a68

QUIET ASSURANCE (USA) 2 ch.c. (Feb 10) St Jovite (USA) 135 – Silent Turn (USA) (Silent Cal (USA)) [1997 7m^3 7m^2 8d^2 7m* 8g^5 Oct 25] $180,000Y: strong colt: has a round action: fourth foal: closely related to useful stayer Candle Smile (by Pleasant Colony) and half-brother to a winner in USA by Spend A Buck: dam won 10 races in USA, including Grade 3 8.5f event at 2 yrs: useful form: won 22-runner maiden at Newmarket in October: runner-up previously at Newbury to Bahr in listed race and Duck Row in minor event, and not discredited when 7½ lengths behind Saratoga Springs in Racing Post Trophy at Doncaster final start: free-running sort, bred to stay beyond 1m: bandaged in front all starts: races prominently. *E. A. L. Dunlop* 103

QUIET VENTURE   3 b.c. Rainbow Quest (USA) 134 – Jameelaty (USA) 96   76
(Nureyev (USA) 131) [1996 NR 1997 10d 10m⁴ 10m³ 11.8d Oct 13] unfurnished
colt: second foal: dam 2-y-o 6f winner who stayed 1m: fair maiden: should stay 1½m:
acts on good to firm going, well held on dead: joined I. Semple. *E. A. L. Dunlop*

QUILLING   5 ch.g. Thatching 131 – Quillotern (USA) (Arctic Tern (USA) 126)   77
[1996 77: 8g 7g 7m⁵ 7g⁶ 7m² 7m³ 7m 7g³ 8.5m³ 7g⁴ 9g⁵ 8m⁴ 7.9g³ 7m* 8m 7f* 7g
8m 7m³ 7g 1997 8g² 8.5d 7m² 8m⁶ Jun 25] rangy gelding: fair handicapper: effective
at 7f to 9f: acted on firm ground, probably not on dead: effective visored or not:
sometimes gave trouble in preliminaries: consistent: broke shoulder after collapsing
past post at Carlisle in June: dead. *M. Dods*

QUINTUS (USA)   2 ch.c. (Jan 27) Sky Classic (CAN) – Superbe Dawn (USA)   81
(Grey Dawn II 132) [1997 7f⁴ 7g² 7g Aug 13] $85,000Y: big, lengthy colt: has scope:
easy mover: seventh foal: half-brother to several minor winners in USA: dam won at
up to 9f in USA: easily best effort when beaten ¾ length by comfortable winner
Opera King in maiden at Doncaster in July: should stay 1m. *P. F. I. Cole*

QUINZII MARTIN   9 b.g. Song 132 – Quaranta 83 (Hotfoot 126) [1996 –, a59:   –
a7g a7g a7g³ a7g³ a7g³ a8.5g² a7g³ a8.5g a7g² a7g⁴ a8g³ a8.5g⁶ a7g⁴ a7g a8.5g³   a46
a7s* a7g 1997 a8g a8g⁶ a7g a7g⁴ a7g a7g⁵ a8g 8.3g a7g⁴ 8g Sep 3] strong, good-
bodied gelding: poor handicapper: yet to win on turf, but successful 9 times on the
all-weather: races mainly at 7f/1m nowadays, probably stays 11f: often blinkered/
visored: inconsistent. *D. Haydn Jones*

QUITE HAPPY (IRE)   2 b.f. (Mar 28) Statoblest 120 – Four-Legged Friend 101   62
(Aragon 118) [1997 5.1d 5m² Oct 28] fifth foal: half-sister to fairly useful 1m and
1¼m winner Herr Trigger (by Sharrood): dam sprinter: much better effort in October
when ½-length second to Mary Jane at Redcar: may improve again. *Dr J. D. Scargill*

QUIVER TREE   2 b.f. (Jan 31) Lion Cavern (USA) 117 – Quaver (USA) 74 (The   68
Minstrel (CAN) 135) [1997 6m⁵ 7g 7m Aug 22] strong, lengthy filly: first foal:
dam 7f winner out of useful performer up to 1m Que Sympatica: easily best effort in
maidens at Newmarket on debut: seemed rather headstrong subsequently.
D. R. Loder

QUIZ MASTER   2 ch.g. (Mar 6) Superpower 113 – Ask Away (Midyan (USA)   67
124) [1997 5m³ 5d² 5s² 5.9f⁶ 6g⁵ 5v⁴ 5m⁴ 5m² 5m⁶ 5f 6g 5s³ 5m³ Oct 28] 7,200Y:
workmanlike gelding: first foal: dam unraced: fair maiden: best form at 5f: acts on
good to firm and soft ground: blinkered/visored 5 of last 6 starts: has carried head
awkwardly and hung (gelded after final start): consistent. *E. Weymes*

QUIZ SHOW   2 b.f. (Apr 22) Primo Dominie 121 – Aryaf (CAN) (Vice Regent   71 +
(CAN)) [1997 5g 5.2m⁴ 7g⁵ 6.1m⁴ 6m Sep 22] sturdy, good-quartered filly: fifth foal:
half-sister to 5-y-o Mind Games and 1993 2-y-o 1m winner Able Fun (by Double
Schwartz): dam thrice-raced granddaughter of Irish 1000 Guineas winner and
excellent broodmare Front Row: fair form in maidens and a nursery: reportedly in
season final start: may prove best at 5f. *R. Hannon*

QUWS   3 b.c. Robellino (USA) 127 – Fleeting Rainbow 65 (Rainbow Quest (USA)   112 p
134) [1996 5s* 6g* 6m³ 6.3g³ 8s³ 1997 8d⁵ 9d 8d* 9d* 11s* Oct 18] first foal: dam,
should have stayed 1½m, from good family: smart performer: won listed handicap
by 1½ lengths from Wray, listed race by 2½ lengths from Mr Lightfoot and 6-runner
Blandford Stakes by 1½ lengths from Spirit of Tara, all at the Curragh in the autumn:
will stay 1½m: acts on good to firm and soft ground: should progress again in 1998.
K. Prendergast, Ireland

R

RAAHA   3 b.f. Polar Falcon (USA) 126 – Ostora (USA) 83 (Blushing Groom (FR)   87
131) [1996 76p: 6m 1997 7.5d* 7d 8g* 8g* 8g⁵ 7m* 7f 7m Oct 4] lengthy, unfurnished
filly: fairly useful performer: won maiden at Beverley in May and handicaps at Yarmouth in July and Lingfield in August: effective at 7f/easy 1m: acts on good to firm

and dead ground: inconsistent, and has shown tendency to wander and carry head high (not hard ridden for wins): sold 12,500 gns in December. *R. W. Armstrong*

RAASED 5 b.g. Unfuwain (USA) 131 – Sajjaya (USA) 97 (Blushing Groom (FR) 131) [1996 43: 8g 9.2g³ 8.3m 8.3f⁶ 1997 12g 10m 12s 11m⁶ 12s Nov 6] tall gelding: has been hobdayed: no worthwhile form at 5 yrs. *F. Watson*

RAAZI 2 ch.f. (Mar 24) My Generation 111 – Botvyle Flame (IRE) (Reprimand 122) [1997 a5g⁶ 5g 6g⁵ Jun 12] first known foal: dam unraced: soundly beaten, including in all-weather seller. *R. M. Stronge*

RABAH 2 b.c. (Jan 25) Nashwan (USA) 135 – The Perfect Life (IRE) 106 (Try My   97
Best (USA) 130) [1997 7g 7g² 7g* 8f² 8v³ 8m* Oct 31] well-made, attractive colt: good mover: third foal: brother to 3-y-o Muhtafel and 1995 2-y-o 6f winner (stayed 7f) Najiya: dam, winner at 5f (at 2 yrs) and 7f in France, sister to Last Tycoon: useful form: won minor events at Redcar in August and Newmarket in October, rallying to beat Albarahin a neck in steadily-run race on latter course: likely to stay 1¼m: acts on firm ground, seemed unsuited by heavy: genuine. *J. L. Dunlop*

RABEA (USA) 2 b.f. (Apr 8) Devil's Bag (USA) – Racing Blue (Reference Point   –
139) [1997 8.2g 8g Oct 24] leggy filly: first reported foal: dam, German 1½m winner, also third in German St Leger: well held in maidens at Nottingham and Doncaster. *J. L. Dunlop*

RABI (IRE) 2 b.c. (Mar 7) Alzao (USA) 117 – Sharakawa (IRE) (Darshaan 133)   105 p
[1997 7g* 7m* Sep 22] IR 52,000F: strong, angular, good sort: first foal: dam un-raced daughter of Prix Vermeille winner Sharaya: thought immature at 2 yrs, and not highly tried, but made most favourable impression when winning maiden at New-market in August (beat The Gene Genie easily by 4 lengths) and 3-runner minor event at Leicester when long odds on: will be well suited by 1m+: joined Godolphin: a smart colt in the making, sure to win a decent prize. *E. A. L. Dunlop*

RACHAELS NORTH (IRE) 2 gr.c. (Mar 10) Night Shift (USA) – Anne de   73 p
Beaujeu (Ahonoora 122) [1997 6d⁶ Nov 7] IR 42,000Y: robust colt: third foal: half-brother to a winner in Italy by Alzao: dam, useful Irish 6f and 7f winner, sister to smart French filly at around 1¼m (useful in Britain) Ahohoney: 33/1 burly and green, sixth of 21 in maiden won by Masha-Il at Doncaster, chasing pace and not given hard time: sure to improve. *R. W. Armstrong*

RACHEL'S ROCK 4 b.f. Rock City 120 – Rachel's Dancer (IRE) 75 (Lomond (USA) 128) [1996 NR 1997 a8g⁶ a8g⁵ Feb 1] first foal: dam 2-y-o 7f winner: well held in claimer and maiden: sent to Saudi Arabia. *G. L. Moore*

RACING BRENDA 6 b.m. Faustus (USA) 118 – Icecapped 91 (Caerleon (USA) 132) [1996 49, a–: 8.2m 8g 8.2m⁴ 8.2m³ 8.2d⁵ 8.3g² 10.8f a9.4g 1997 a8g 8g Jul 5] sturdy mare: poor handicapper at 5 yrs: well beaten in 1997. *B. C. Morgan*

RACING CARR 3 ch.f. Anshan 119 – Bamian (USA) (Topsider (USA)) [1996 –:   –
6m 6g 7m a7g⁴ a7g a8g⁴ 1997 a8g a11g Feb 14] close-coupled filly: little worthwhile form. *T. J. Naughton*

RACING HAWK (USA) 5 ch.g. Silver Hawk (USA) 123 – Lorn Lady (Lorenz-   39
accio 130) [1996 55: a12g 11.9f 12d 8.3m⁴ 10m³ 10f* 10f⁶ 10g 8f 1997 a10g 8g 10g 12f 10.2m³ 10g 17.2g Jun 28] rather leggy gelding: poor performer: effective at 1¼m/1½m: acts on firm ground and fibresand, well beaten on soft: visored third start: winning selling hurdler (has broken blood vessels). *M. S. Saunders*

RACING HEART 3 b.f. Pursuit of Love 124 – Hearten (Hittite Glory 125) [1996   59
–: 6m 7f 7.1f 7m 1997 8m 8f⁴ a8g 8.2m* 8g² 8g⁶ 8d Oct 13] tall filly: modest performer: won claimer at Nottingham in July: hampered and possibly unlucky in handicap at Salisbury next outing: stays 1m: well beaten only try on all-weather, raced mainly on good going or firmer on turf. *P. J. Makin*

RACING SURVEYOR 2 b.f. (Apr 6) Mazilier (USA) 107 – Ruthenia (IRE) (Taufan (USA) 119) [1997 5m 5m Apr 11] small filly: fourth foal: dam unraced: last in sellers. *M. W. Easterby*

RACING TELEGRAPH 7 b.g. Claude Monet (USA) 121 – Near Enough   39
(English Prince 129) [1996 43, a32: a8g⁴ a8g 7g⁴ 7g³ 8g⁵ 7m 10g³ a10g⁵ a8g a12g   a–
1997 8g⁵ 7f 8m 11.8d Oct 14] tall, angular gelding: has had wind operation: poor

handicapper: probably stays 1¼m: acts on firm and dead ground and on equitrack: blinkered (too free) penultimate outing. *C. N. Allen*

RADAR (IRE)   2 b.c. (Mar 6) Petardia 113 – Soignee (Night Shift (USA)) [1997   77
7d⁵ 7.1g 8m 7m² 8.2d* Oct 30] IR 31,000Y: good-topped colt: second foal: dam
unraced half-sister to Italian Group 1 winners Stone (1½m) and Stouci (1m at 2 yrs):
fair form: comfortable winner of nursery at Nottingham: will stay further than 1m:
acts on good to firm and dead going. *M. A. Jarvis*

RADAR O'REILLY   3 b.g. Almoojid 69 – Travel Bye 62 (Miller's Mate 116)   62
[1996 –: 5.1d 1997 8g a8g³ 9s² 7f* a7g³ Jul 26] leggy, good-topped gelding:
fair form: very easy winner of 2-finisher maiden at Brighton in July: stays 9f.
R. J. R. Williams

RADIANCY (IRE)   3 ch.f. Mujtahid (USA) 118 – Bright Landing 78 (Sun Prince   77
128) [1996 NR 1997 7s² 7.9d⁴ Jun 14] sturdy filly: half-sister to 4 winners, including
useful stayer Upper Strata (by Shirley Heights), dam of 4-y-o Lord of Men: dam
second at 5f at 2 yrs: 33/1 and in need of race, much better effort in maidens when
neck second at Chester, looking sure to win 2f out but tiring and caught near finish:
bandaged, last at York over 5 weeks later. *J. P. Leigh*

RAED   4 b.c. Nashwan (USA) 135 – Awayed (USA) 108 (Sir Ivor 135) [1996 74:   69
10m⁴ 10.8f⁴ 9m 7.9g⁴ 10m 8f² 8m⁵ 1997 7f³ 9m 8.5g⁵ 8m 7g⁵ 7g 7s 8g⁶ a11g² a11g*
Dec 8] sturdy colt: fair handicapper: generally ran creditably before winning at
Southwell: stays 11f: acts on fibresand and firm going, well beaten on dead/soft:
twice hung badly at 3 yrs: usually races up with pace. *Mrs A. Swinbank*

RAE UN SOLEIL   3 b.f. Rushmere 92 – Double Shuffle 103 (Tachypous 128)   –
[1996 NR 1997 a7g Jun 28] 625F: sixth reported foal: dam 1½m winner: 50/1, last in
claimer at Lingfield. *J. Ffitch-Heyes*

RAFFAELLO (IRE)   2 b.c. (May 13) Fairy King (USA) – Silver Dollar 106   69 p
(Shirley Heights 130) [1997 7f⁴ Oct 29] IR 20,000F, IR 65,000Y: seventh foal:
half-brother to 1m winner Money Spinner (by Teenoso): dam 2-y-o 6f winner out of
half-sister to Highclere: 14/1, left behind from 2f out when around 10 lengths fourth
to Asad in steadily-run Yarmouth maiden: should do better. *M. R. Channon*

RAFFLES ROOSTER   5 ch.g. Galetto (FR) 118 – Singapore Girl (FR) 117   83
(Lyphard (USA) 132) [1996 64: a10g⁶ 7g 10g 12g⁴ 14d³ 16.2d 1997 a12g² a12g*
a11g* 12m² a14g² a12g* 12.3v² 13.9g⁵ 11.9d* 11.9g³ 18.7m² 13.9g 16g Sep 18]
workmanlike gelding: has a round action: fairly useful handicapper: in very good
form at 5 yrs, winning at Southwell (twice), Wolverhampton and York (lady amateurs) in first half of year: best efforts when placed in valuable events at Haydock and
Chester next 2 starts: effective at 1½m to 19f: acts on good to firm ground, heavy and
the all-weather: blinkered (well beaten) once in France: often claimer ridden: has
worn crossed noseband: usually produced with a late run. *A. G. Newcombe*

Queen Mother's Cup (Ladies) Handicap, York—
Raffles Rooster (Miss Emma Ramsden up) is a clear-cut winner of Europe's most valuable ladies race

RAFTER-J 6 b. or br.g. Petoski 135 – Coming Out (Fair Season 120) [1996 –: 34
a11g a8g a7g a7g⁶ 1997 7m⁵ 8.2m 8m⁵ 8g Apr 28] lengthy gelding: poor performer:
stays 1m: acts on firm and dead going: tried blinkered. *John A. Harris*

RAGAMUFFIN ROMEO 8 b.g. Niniski (USA) 125 – Interviewme (USA) –
(Olden Times) [1996 NR 1997 a14g a16g⁵ Dec 4] modest winning hurdler: maiden
stayer on flat: well held both starts of 1997. *H. J. Collingridge*

RAGAZZO (IRE) 7 b.g. Runnett 125 – Redecorate (USA) (Hatchet Man (USA)) –
[1996 28, a51?: 5.9d 7m 11.1g 8f 6m⁶ 5m⁵ 5g³ 6f a6g a7g a7g⁴ 1997 a7g a6g⁵ a7g⁶
a6g 6g 5.9f 6g 8.5d Aug 13] angular gelding: has a round action: little worthwhile
form at 7 yrs. *J. S. Wainwright*

RAGFORD (IRE) 2 b.g. (Feb 28) Shalford (IRE) 124§ – Raggy (Smoggy 115) –
[1997 6d a6g Jun 18] IR 6,000Y: close-coupled gelding: third living foal: dam French
9f winner: soundly beaten in maidens, blinkered second time: unseated rider start and
ran loose on intended debut: sold, and sent to Holland. *J. M. P. Eustace*

RAGTIME COWGIRL 4 ch.f. Aragon 118 – Echo Chamber 89 (Music Boy 35
124) [1996 44: 6s a6g 6.1g a9.4g³ 12g* 12.1m³ 12m³ 12.4m³ 10g³ 10d³ 11.1m*
10.9m 12.1g 12.1s 1997 8m 8.3s 5s³ 6m 9.2g 8g 5s* 12g⁵ 6m 6g 9.2d Aug 13]
light-framed filly: poor handicapper: made all at Hamilton (only runner not to exert
herself after false start) in June: effective at 5f to 1½m: acts on good to firm ground,
soft and fibresand: versatile. *D. A. Nolan*

RAHEEN (USA) 4 b.c. Danzig (USA) – Belle de Jour (USA) (Speak John) [1996 91
79+: 8g⁴ a8.5g* 1997 a9.4g⁶ 8m⁵ 7m³ 7.6m⁴ 7.3m Jul 18] rather leggy colt: fairly
useful performer: good efforts in frame in handicap at Thirsk and minor event at
Lingfield in May: stays 8.5f: acts on firm ground and fibresand: blinkered/visored
final 3-y-o start onwards: races keenly, too much so final start. *W. G. M. Turner*

RAINBOW HIGH 2 b.c. (Mar 2) Rainbow Quest (USA) 134 – Imaginary (IRE) 76 +
94 (Dancing Brave (USA) 140) [1997 7g⁴ 7m⁴ 7.1s⁴ Oct 15] sturdy colt: first foal:
dam 1¼m winner, half-sister to Lowther winner Kingscote, the dam of smart miler
Rainbow Corner (by Rainbow Quest): fair form when fourth in maidens at Newmarket, Ascot and Haydock, helping force pace on last 2 courses: should stay at least
1¼m. *B. W. Hills*

RAINBOW RAIN (USA) 3 b.g. Capote (USA) – Grana (USA) (Miswaki (USA) 76
124) [1996 78: 5.1g⁴ 6g³ 7g 6m⁵ 6m² 1997 7m 5s⁶ 6g⁴ 8m* 8g 7.5m⁵ 8m a8.5g Nov
15] well-made gelding: has a long stride: fair handicapper: won at Carlisle in June:
below form after, leaving M. Johnston sixth start: stays 1m: form only on good to
firm/good ground: edgy sort, gelded after final start. *S. Dow*

RAINBOW WAYS 2 b.c. (Apr 3) Rainbow Quest (USA) 134 – Siwaayib 97 85
(Green Desert (USA) 127) [1997 7m² 8d⁴ Oct 16] first foal: dam 6f winner (including
at 2 yrs): fairly useful form in maidens at Leicester (second to Benin, pair clear) and
Newmarket (7 lengths fourth of 22 to Border Arrow) in October: showed a quick
action and went freely to post in latter: should win a race. *B. W. Hills*

RAINDANCING (IRE) 3 b.f. Tirol 127 – Persian Song 45 (Persian Bold 123) 84 §
[1996 94: 6d⁴ 6m² 6m* 6m³ 8m⁵ 7m 1997 8g³ 10g 10m 9m 10m Aug 15] tall filly:
has a quick action: fairly useful form at best: well below form after reappearance at 3
yrs: stays 1m: yet to race on extremes of going: tried blinkered: not one to trust.
R. Hannon

RAINDEER QUEST 5 ch.m. Hadeer 118 – Rainbow Ring (Rainbow Quest 53
(USA) 134) [1996 48: 8.1g⁴ 8g* 8g³ 9.2s⁴ 8.1g 8m⁴ 10g² 10m³ 10.5m⁴ 10f 8.1s a8g⁵ a45
a10g⁴ a11g* 1997 a11g² a12g² a12g⁶ a12g 8f* 10.4s 10m⁴ 8.3g⁴ 10d⁶ 10.1g⁵ 10m
a11g Dec 8] sturdy mare: has knee action: modest handicapper: off course 6 months,
won at Carlisle in August: mostly ran creditably after: effective at 1m (on stiff track)
to 11f: acts on fibresand, best turf form on good ground or firmer. *J. L. Eyre*

RAINMAKER 2 b.c. (Feb 9) Last Tycoon 131 – Starr Danias (USA) (Sensitive –
Prince (USA)) [1997 7g 8s 8d a7g Dec 18] 21,000Y: lengthy colt: fifth foal:
half-brother to 3-y-o Out Of Sight, fairly useful 7f winner Yaa Wale (by Persian
Bold) and 6f (at 2 yrs) and 1½m winner Potsclose (by Miswaki): dam lightly raced in
USA, half-sister to smart 7f winner Zahdam: well held in maidens/nursery: burly on
first 2 starts. *M. A. Jarvis*

RAINWATCH 3 b.c. Rainbow Quest (USA) 134 – Third Watch 114 (Slip Anchor 107 136) [1996 83p: 8m^5 1997 8g^2 10.4g^5 12g* 12d* 14.8g 13.4s^6 13.3d^5 11.9s* Oct 15] tall colt: useful performer: won handicaps at Newbury and Salisbury (by 7 lengths) in June and minor event at Haydock in October (by 20 lengths but probably the only one of the 7 to give running): best around 1½m on good to soft going or softer: front runner: sold 60,000 gns, and promising hurdler for M. Pipe. *J. L. Dunlop*

RAISE A KING 2 b.g. (May 2) Ardkinglass 114 – Bias 108 (Royal Prerogative 98 + 119) [1997 5m^3 5g* 6f* 6m^2 Oct 4] 24,000Y: tall, leggy gelding: has a powerful, round action: half-brother to several winners, including smart 6f and 7f winner Casteddu and useful 1993 2-y-o 7f and 1m winner Barbaroja (both by Efisio): dam won from 7f to 10.4f: useful form: won minor events at Sandown in August and Yarmouth in September: heavily backed and looking in tremendous shape, good running-on second in nursery at Newmarket: should stay at least 7f. *J. W. Payne*

RAISE A PRINCE (FR) 4 b.g. Machiavellian (USA) 123 – Enfant d'Amour 90 (USA) (Lyphard (USA) 132) [1996 76: 8d^4 8m 10m^2 10.3d^5 10.5d^4 10g^2 10.3g^4 1997 10m a9.4g^3 12d 10s* 12g* a12g* a12g^4 Nov 29] rather leggy gelding: unimpressive mover: fairly useful performer: won handicap at Nottingham in July (maiden event, for J. W. Hills), claimer at Newbury in October and minor event (best effort) at Lingfield in November: stays 1½m: acts on good to firm, soft going and equitrack: has had tongue tied: visored at Nottingham. *S. P. C. Woods*

RAIVUE 3 ch.g. Beveled (USA) – Halka (Daring March 116) [1996 –: 7.1v 1997 86 8f^2 10m* 10m^3 10.3m^6 8m 10g Oct 18] tall, good-topped gelding: has markedly round action: fairly useful performer: won maiden at Ripon in June: best efforts in minor events at Ayr and Doncaster next 2 starts, ran poorly final 2: stays 1¼m: acts on good to firm going: tends to sweat. *E. Weymes*

RAJAH 4 b. or br.g. Be My Chief (USA) 122 – Pretty Thing 83 (Star Appeal 133) – [1996 53: a7g^6 a7g a6g^4 a8.5g* 11.1g^3 a8g 1997 a9.4g^6 a11g Dec 8] modest winner on firesand at 3 yrs: showed little both starts in 1997. *C. W. Thornton*

RAJATI (USA) 2 b.c. (May 9) Chief's Crown (USA) – Charming Life (NZ) (Sir – Tristram 115) [1997 8d Oct 16] strong, angular colt: third foal: half-brother to 3-y-o Kingfisher Mill and useful 1½m winner Dear Life (by Lear Fan): dam, 7f winner in Australia, sister to Australian Grade 1 1m winner Zabeel: 33/1 and burly, tailed off in maiden at Newmarket. *Mrs J. Cecil*

RAJPOUTE (FR) 3 b.c. Double Bed (FR) 121 – Gai Lizza (FR) (Gairloch 122) 118 [1996 NR 1997 12d^2 10.5s^4 13.5d^5 12d$^+$ 10g^2 10g* 12m* 12f^6 Nov 8] tall, lengthy colt: fourth foal: brother to 4-y-o L'Annee Folle: dam, 1¼m (at 3 yrs) to 16.5f winner

Prix Niel, Longchamp—
Rajpoute wins a controversial affair from unlucky-in-running Peintre Celebre;
British-trained Ivan Luis is third

in France, also listed placed: won minor event at Chantilly in June, Prix Guillaume
d'Ornano at Deauville (narrowly from Crystal Hearted and Handsome Ridge) in
August and Prix Niel at Longchamp (held most unlucky Peintre Celebre by neck) in
September: left F. Doumen for $ 1.25m afterwards: not discredited when sixth in
Breeders' Cup Turf: stays 1½m well: acts on good to firm and dead ground, probably
on firm. *R. McAnally, USA*

RAKIS (IRE)   7 b. or br.g. Alzao (USA) 117 – Bristle 96 (Thatch (USA) 136)   84
[1996 80, a92: a7g* a7g* a7g* a7g* 7f⁵ 7g⁶ 8s 8m³ 7.1m* 7m 7g⁴ 7m 7m³ 7.1m*   a97
8.1d⁵ 7g a7g⁴ 1997 a7g* a8g⁵ a7g 7f³ 8.1g⁶ 7m² 7.3s² 7.3g 7.1m² 7d⁴ 7.6m³ 7.1m 7g
7.1m Sep 16] good-topped gelding: useful handicapper on the all-weather, fairly
useful on turf: won at Wolverhampton in February: well below form last 3 starts: best
form around 7f: probably acts on any all-weather/turf: effective blinkered in 1993:
usually held up: tough. *Mrs L. Stubbs*

RALITSA (IRE)   5 b.g. Nordico (USA) – Bold-E-Be (Persian Bold 123) [1996 –:   – §
14.1m 1997 12m 12g 16g Sep 15] compact gelding: well held since 3 yrs, and has
become one to avoid. *R. M. Whitaker*

RAMBLING BEAR   4 ch.c. Sharrood (USA) 124 – Supreme Rose 95 (Frimley   110
Park 109) [1996 112: 6m⁶ 6g* 6f* 6m 6f⁵ 5m* 6d³ 6f 5d 1997 6g⁶ 5m⁶ 5m³ 5d 6s³ 6g
5m 5m³ 5.2g⁵ 6m 7m² Oct 7] leggy, workmanlike colt: smart performer: generally
ran creditably at 4 yrs, often in face of stiffish tasks: best efforts when third in listed
race at Kempton (to Almaty) and when seventh in July Cup at Newmarket and
Diadem Stakes at Ascot on sixth and penultimate starts: probably best at 5f/6f:
unraced on heavy going, acts on any other: takes keen hold, and is usually held up:
often taken alone to post: genuine. *M. Blanshard*

RAMBLING ROSE   2 ch.f. (Apr 3) Cadeaux Genereux 131 – Blush Rambler   96 p
(IRE) (Blushing Groom (FR) 131) [1997 7g³ 8m² 8.2g* 8d² Oct 20] angular filly:
third foal: half-sister to 3-y-o Mister Pink: dam, Irish 1½m winner, half-sister to
useful Irish stayer Excellenza: progressive form: won maiden at Nottingham in September: 2½ lengths second of 8 to impressive Gulland in listed event at Pontefract
following month, no match for winner but going on strongly, clear of remainder:
likely to be well suited by 1¼m+: should improve again. *M. R. Stoute*

RAMBOLD   6 b.m. Rambo Dancer (CAN) 107 – Boldie 81 (Bold Lad (IRE) 133)   56
[1996 66: 6.1d³ 6g* 6g 6.1m² 6m 5.7f³ 6g* 6f³ 6m³ 6m⁴ 5.7m 6.1m 6m⁵ 1997 6.1g
6m⁵ 6g 6m Jul 28] angular mare: modest handicapper: stays 6f: acts on firm and dead
ground: sometimes sweats: usually races prominently. *N. E. Berry*

RAMBO'S RUMTIME   5 b.m. Rambo Dancer (CAN) 107 – Errol Emerald 60   –
(Dom Racine (FR) 121) [1996 –: 6.9f 11.1m⁶ 1997 8d May 18] of little account.
F. Watson

RAMBO TANGO   3 b.g. Rambo Dancer (CAN) 107 – Jumra (Thatch (USA)   –
136) [1996 –: a7g 1997 7m 8.2d⁵ 8.5m 8m 10.8g Oct 7] no form. *B. R. Cambidge*

RAMBO WALTZER   5 b.g. Rambo Dancer (CAN) 107 – Vindictive Lady   72
(USA) (Foolish Pleasure (USA)) [1996 69, a85: a8g* a9.4g⁵ a8g⁶ a7g* a8g⁶ 7.5d²   a90
8.3d* 8m* 8g* 8g 8.5g 9g 7.6d 8g 8m 8.1d 8.9g 8g a9.4g 1997 a7s⁵ a8g* a8g² a7g*
a7g² a8g² a8g² a8g* a8.5g* 7g³ 7.5m² 8.3d* 7g⁵ 8m⁶ 8g⁵ a9.4g³ a9.4g⁵ a8g⁵
Dec 18] smallish, sturdy gelding: fairly useful performer on fibresand: won 2
apprentice claimers at Southwell in January and handicaps there in February and
Wolverhampton (£14,100 contest) in March: fair on turf: won handicap at Hamilton
(apprentices) in April: reportedly finished lame penultimate outing, and off course
over 6 months before well below form on final one: effective at 7f to 1¼m: acts on
good to firm going and dead (no form on very soft): visored (below form) once as
3-y-o: good mount for inexperienced rider. *D. Nicholls*

RAMIKE (IRE)   3 b.g. Caerleon (USA) 132 – Marie Noelle (FR) 114 (Brigadier   81
Gerard 144) [1996 –: 8.1s 8.2s 1997 a12g* 14.1m* 14.6d* 16.4d² 15.9m⁵ 16s⁴ 14m
17.2f⁴ Sep 29] sturdy gelding: fairly useful performer: won maiden at Lingfield and
handicaps at Nottingham and Doncaster in the spring: will stay beyond 2m: acts on
good to firm ground, dead and equitrack: flashes tail. *M. Johnston*

RAMOOZ (USA)   4 b.c. Rambo Dancer (CAN) 107 – My Shafy 92 (Rousillon   109
(USA) 133) [1996 109: 8m* 10m³ 7m* 7m² 7g⁵ 8g⁶ 7g² 7m⁴ 7g⁴ 1997 7d³ 7.1s² 8m

Mr Hilal Salem's "Ramooz"

7d* 8m* 7g⁴ 7d⁶ 8f² 8m⁴ 7m⁴ Nov 1] rangy colt: impresses in appearance: useful performer: won Van Geest Criterion Stakes at Newmarket (by head from Almushtarak) in June and 5-runner Ragusa Stud Minstrel Stakes at the Curragh (beat below-par Burden of Proof 3 lengths) in July: ran several other fine races in defeat, including when neck second to Sandstone in valuable event in Turkey: best at 7f/1m: probably acts on any going: often bandaged: blinkered once at 2 yrs: has a turn of foot and suited by waiting tactics: reliable. *B. Hanbury*

RAMSEY HOPE   4 b.c. Timeless Times (USA) 99 – Marfen (Lochnager 132)   66 §
[1996 78: 5d 5g 6g 6g 6g² 6m 6m 5f² 6s 6f⁵ 5m 5m 5m⁵ a6g² 5m 6.1m a5g* a5g*   a82 §
a5g² 1997 a5g³ a5g⁴ a5g a5g* a5g 5g 5.9g 5d a6g 5f* 5g 5g 7g 5d 5f⁵ 5g a6g 6g a6g*
a6s⁶ a6g a6g³ a6g² Dec 26] compact colt: fairly useful on all-weather, fair on turf:
won handicaps at Lingfield in February and Carlisle (apprentices) in June and
claimer at Southwell in November: best at 5f/6f: acts on all-weather, best turf efforts
on good going or firmer: visored: sometimes hangs left: unreliable. *C. W. Fairhurst*

RANDOM KINDNESS   4 b.g. Alzao (USA) 117 – Lady Tippins (USA) 83 (Star   73
de Naskra (USA)) [1996 76: 10.2g 10.2g³ 10m³ 12.3m² 12m 1997 a13g⁵ a16g² a13g²   a87
a12g² a16.2g* 16g a14.8g* a16.2g⁴ 13.3d 11.5f* 11.9m² 14.1d a12g* Nov 29]
angular gelding: fairly useful on all-weather, fair on turf: won minor event and 2
handicaps at Wolverhampton and an amateurs minor event on turf at Lingfield:
effective at 1½m to 2m: acts on firm going and the all-weather, below form on good
to soft. *R. Ingram*

RANGER SLOANE   5 ch.g. Gunner B 126 – Lucky Amy (Lucky Wednesday   50
124) [1996 –: a16.2g a14.8g 8f 10m 1997 15.8m² 15.8g* 17.1m⁵ a16s Nov 10] leggy   a–
gelding: modest handicapper: won at Catterick in September: stays 2m: acts on good

RAN

to firm ground and fibresand, tailed off on equitrack final outing: tried blinkered at 3 yrs: fair hurdler, winner twice in December. *G. Fierro*

RANNA   2 b.f. (Mar 2) Warning 136 – Jasoorah (IRE) 98 (Sadler's Wells (USA) 132) [1997 7g³ Oct 18] second foal: dam, 1m (at 2 yrs) to 1½m winner, granddaughter of Irish 1000 Guineas and St Leger winner Pidget: 11/1, green when 4¼ lengths third to Final Tango in Redcar maiden, not at all knocked about once held: should be suited by 1m+: sure to improve. *A. C. Stewart*   80 p

RAPID LINER   4 b.g. Skyliner 117 – Stellaris (Star Appeal 133) [1996 –: 6.1d a6g 7f 8g 1997 a8g⁶ 12f 17.2g Jun 28] of little account. *R. J. Baker*   –

RAPID MOVER   10 ch.g. Final Straw 127 – Larive 80 (Blakeney 126) [1996 36: 11.1d 12.1g 8.3d⁶ 8.3s³ 11.1g⁶ 8.1g 9.2g 8.3g 8.1f 11.1g⁶ 11.1m⁴ 11.1m 8.3f⁵ 12.1m 1997 16s 11.1d⁵ 11.1s 8.3s 9.2m⁵ 8.3g 10.9d 9.2s 11.1d 9.2m 11.1g³ 6g⁴ 11.1m⁴ Aug 18] workmanlike gelding: poor handicapper: stays 1½m: acts on good to firm and soft ground: wears blinkers: inconsistent. *D. A. Nolan*   36

RAPID RELIANCE   2 b.f. (Apr 21) Emarati (USA) 74 – Chiquitita 44 (Reliance II 137) [1997 5m⁵ 6m 5.1g 5m* 5m⁶ a5g⁵ a6s a7g Nov 18] 6,800 2-y-o: unfurnished filly: half-sister to 1992 2-y-o 6f and 7f winner Another Kingdom (by Another Realm), later middle-distance winner in Germany, and 1986 2-y-o 5f winner Quite So (by Mansingh), later ungenuine: dam won 1¼m seller: modest performer: won claimer at Sandown in September (claimed out of D. Elsworth's stable £6,000): well beaten in seller (blinkered) final start: should stay 6f: acts on good to firm going and equitrack. *R. Ingram*   57 a52

RAPIER   3 b.g. Sharpo 132 – Sahara Breeze 85 (Ela-Mana-Mou 132) [1996 79: 6d³ 8f* 7.6g³ 1997 8m² 8.1d⁵ 10m 8m³ 8g 8d² 8m⁴ 9g Oct 25] leggy, unfurnished colt: has a fluent, round action: fairly useful performer: third in Britannia Handicap at Royal Ascot: stays 1m: acts on firm and dead ground: hung very badly (at Lingfield) third start. *R. Hannon*   87

RAPIER POINT (IRE)   6 gr.g. Cyrano de Bergerac 120 – Renzola (Dragonara Palace (USA) 115) [1996 –: 6m 6m 7g a7g 1997 a6g a7g a8g Jan 16] strong, compact gelding: no form since 4 yrs. *C. Murray*   –

RAPTURE   2 b.f. (Mar 5) Primo Dominie 121 – Hello Cuddles 99 (He Loves Me 120) [1997 6m Aug 9] 12,500Y: rather unfurnished filly: half-sister to 7f/1m winner Inderaputeri and winning sprinter Samson-Agonistes (both by Bold Fort): dam sprinter: always rear after slow start in maiden at Haydock: moved poorly to post. *R. Hannon*   –

RA RA RASPUTIN   2 b.c. (Mar 14) Petong 126 – Ra Ra Girl 77 (Shack (USA) 118) [1997 5m 5.1m⁶ a6g⁶ 6.1g a6g* 7s 6m Sep 13] 7,000 2-y-o: workmanlike colt: has a quick action: fourth reported foal: half-brother to 6-y-o Sing With The Band: dam 6f winner: 50/1-winner of valuable Weatherbys Dash at Wolverhampton in August, beating Blue Kite 3 lengths: no comparable form: stays 6f: often slowly away. *B. A. McMahon*   63 a80

RARE INDIGO   2 b.f. (Apr 29) Timeless Times (USA) 99 – Miss Ritz 65 (Robellino (USA) 127) [1997 5g⁵ 5m 5g⁴ a5g* 5d* 5d² 5d⁵ Nov 7] 5,200Y: smallish filly: first foal: dam 7f winner: fairly useful performer: won seller at Wolverhampton and minor event at Catterick in October: ran creditably after: speedy, and raced only at 5f: acts on fibresand and dead ground. *J. Berry*   80 +

RARE TALENT   3 b.c. Mtoto 134 – Bold As Love (Lomond (USA) 128) [1996 NR 1997 10.3m⁶ 12m³ 12g² 12.1s⁴ 11.1s⁴ 11.5m⁵ 12g 10m* 10g 10.5d 10m* 10s 10d 10.3g Oct 24] leggy, angular colt: unimpressive mover: first foal: dam unraced, from quite speedy family: fair performer: won sellers at Ripon in August and Leicester (final start for M. Channon) in September: well below form last 3 starts: effective at 1¼m to 1½m: acts on good to firm and soft ground: inconsistent. *S. Gollings*   69 d

RASAYEL (USA)   7 b.m. Bering 67 – Reham 67 (Mill Reef (USA) 141) [1996 68, a55: a9.4g 10.3m* 13.1g³ a11g⁶ 10.5d³ 10.3g⁴ 10.2m³ 12.3m* 12g² 10.3d⁵ 10.4g 15.9g 12g³ 12g 12.1s² a14.8g³ a11g⁴ a10g a12s* a12g⁶ a13g* 1997 a13g² a12g² a12g⁵ 10g* 10d⁶ 12.3v³ 13.1d² 10.3m 11.9d a12g 12.3s³ 10.2m³ 12.3m⁶ 18.7m 10.3d* 10.4s 10.5g 12v a12g 14.1d³ a12s Nov 28] big mare: has round action: fair handicapper on turf, modest on all-weather: won at Nottingham (ladies) in April and   79 § a55 §

770

Chester (apprentices) in August: effective at 1¼m (in strongly-run race) to 1¾m: best turf form on good going or softer: blinkered once: unreliable. *P. D. Evans*

RASH GIFT   4 ch.f. Cadeaux Genereux 131 – Nettle 106 (Kris 135) [1996 73: 7f³   58
8m 1997 a8g⁵ 10d² Jun 24] lightly-raced maiden: only form at 4 yrs when second in steadily-run apprentice handicap at Lingfield: probably stays 1¼m: acts on firm and dead ground. *Lord Huntingdon*

RASHIK   3 ch.c. Cadeaux Genereux 131 – Ghzaalh (USA) 87 (Northern Dancer)   97
[1996 NR 1997 8g* Apr 19] useful-looking colt: third foal: half-brother to 4-y-o Zuhair and 5-y-o Mihriz: dam, second at 1¼m from 2 starts, out of Irish Oaks winner Give Thanks and is closely related to dam of Harayir: won 15-runner maiden at Newbury, travelling smoothly off pace and leading over 1f out: lethargic in paddock: will stay 1¼m: to be trained by M. Tregoning. *Major W. R. Hern*

RASPBERRY SAUCE   3 b.f. Niniski (USA) 125 – Sobranie 86 (High Top 131)   40
[1996 NR 1997 7g⁶ a8g a8g⁴ Dec 2] 3,300Y: second foal: dam 1¼m winner on only start: fourth at Lingfield, only form in maidens. *C. A. Cyzer*

RATB   3 ch.g. Be My Guest (USA) 126 – Al Shaqrah (USA) 76 (Sir Ivor 135) [1996   –
NR 1997 8g 10d Apr 26] compact gelding: second foal: dam, staying maiden: no sign of ability in maidens: dead. *S. Dow*

RATIYYA (IRE)   2 ch.f. (May 18) Mujtahid (USA) 118 – Sharayif (IRE) (Green   67
Desert (USA) 127) [1997 5g⁵ 6g⁵ 6.9m³ 7m⁴ 8.2g⁶ a7s⁶ Nov 28] good-topped   a?
filly: second foal: dam unraced sister to useful 7f/1m winner Umniyatee out of 1000 Guineas and Oaks winner Midway Lady: fair maiden: trained first 5 starts by B. Hanbury: well beaten on all-weather debut final outing: should stay 1m. *P. Howling*

RATTLE   4 b.g. Mazilier (USA) 107 – Snake Song 94 (Mansingh (USA) 120)   –
[1996 52: 6s⁵ 8.3d³ 8.3d⁵ 12m 10d² 11.1m⁴ 10d³ a14.8g 13g⁵ 11.1m⁵ 1997 8s 8.3d 8m 8.3s 7.1d 6.9f 13.1g 9.2d³ 9.2m Jul 11] small gelding: no form at 4 yrs. *D. A. Nolan*

RAVE-ON-HADLEY (IRE)   7 b.g. Commanche Run 133 – Fleet Fact §§   –
(Known Fact (USA) 135) [1996 NR 1997 17.1m 18d Oct 20] lightly-raced maiden: no form since 1994. *N. Bycroft*

RAW DEAL   4 ch.f. Domynsky 110 – Close The Deal 51 (Nicholas Bill 125) [1996   –
–: a8g 1997 a12g⁴ Jul 11] no sign of ability in claimer and seller. *B. Preece*

RAWI   4 ch.g. Forzando 122 – Finally (Final Straw 127) [1996 64: a8g² a7g² a7g³   56
a8g³ a7g² 6m⁵ a8g⁶ 7.1m 5.3f⁴ 6m⁶ 7f³ a8.5g a6g³ a7g* 1997 a8g⁵ a7g* a8g⁵ a8g⁴ a7g 6.9m 7f a8g 6.9m* 7m³ 6m³ a7g 8m² 7g Oct 24] workmanlike gelding: modest performer: won apprentice handicap at Lingfield in January and claimer at Folkestone in July: very best efforts at 7f/easy 1m: acts on firm ground and the all-weather, unraced on going softer than good: sometimes blinkered/visored (former on last 6 starts): winning hurdler for J. Charlton. *Miss Gay Kelleway*

RAYIK   2 br.c. (Jan 26) Marju (IRE) 127 – Matila (IRE) 98 (Persian Bold 123)   84 p
[1997 7g⁵ Oct 24] sturdy colt: first foal: dam 6f winner: 9/1, backward and green, shaped well when 3½ lengths fifth to Zaya in maiden at Doncaster, keeping on under considerate handling from slow start (shade upset stalls): should stay at least 1m: sent to UAE: sure to do better. *R. W. Armstrong*

RAY OF SUNSHINE (IRE)   2 ch.g. (Apr 10) Rainbows For Life (CAN) –   70
Maura's Guest (IRE) (Be My Guest (USA) 126) [1997 5g 7m² 6.1g 7s* 7s Nov 8] 13,000Y: big, strong gelding: has scope: has a quick action: third foal: half-brother to a winner abroad: dam unraced half-sister to 2 smart French sprinters: fair form: won nursery at Catterick in October: looked past best for season next time (heavily bandaged off-fore): should stay 1m: acts on good to firm and soft ground. *Mrs J. R. Ramsden*

RAY RIVER   5 b.g. Waki River (FR) 120 – Mrs Feathers 57 (Pyjama Hunt 126)   –
[1996 NR 1997 a13g Mar 4] 3,300F, IR 15,500Y: eighth foal: half-brother to 4-y-o Two Socks and fairly useful 1988 2-y-o 5f to 8.5f winner Nightstalker (by Night Shift), later won in USA: dam maiden: modest maiden up to 1½m in Ireland at 3 yrs: tailed off in handicap first outing since. *K. G. Wingrove*

RAY

RAY'S FOLLY (IRE) 2 b.g. (Feb 28) Scenic 128 – Avec L'Amour 75 (Realm 80
129) [1997 7.1d² 7g 7g Sep 5] IR 17,000F, IR 55,000Y: good-bodied gelding: half-
brother to 3 winners, including smart sprinter Duck And Dive (by Lomond) and 6f to
9.4f winner Gallery Artist (by Tate Gallery): dam largely disappointing: easily best
effort in maidens when neck second to Almutawakel at Sandown: carried head high
final start: should stay 1m: sent to Hong Kong. *M. A. Jarvis*

RAZOR 2 b.c. (Mar 18) Warning 136 – Smarten Up 119 (Sharpen Up 127) [1997 81 p
7m Sep 30] 58,000Y: half-brother to several winners, including top-class sprinter
Cadeaux Genereux (by Young Generation) and useful middle-distance stayer Bright-
ner (by Sparkler): dam sprinter: 33/1, slowly into stride and nearest finish when
around 12 lengths eighth to Tamarisk in valuable sales race at Newmarket: sure to
improve. *S. C. Williams*

REACH FOR A STAR 2 b.g. (Mar 20) Midyan (USA) 124 – Hard Task 82 –
(Formidable (USA) 125) [1997 5m 6s 6g⁶ 8d 10d Oct 13] 17,000Y: small colt: first
foal: dam 1½m winner, half-sister to smart 1½m/1¾m performer Midnight Legend:
little worthwhile form. *C. W. Thornton*

READY FONTAINE 2 b.c. (May 8) Dilum (USA) 115 – Prepare (IRE) 58 –
(Millfontaine 114) [1997 5d 6d 6d Jul 9] 9,200Y: second foal: half-brother to 3-y-o
Make Ready: dam, 7f winner, half-sister to high-class sprinter Anita's Prince: well
beaten in maidens. *J. Neville*

READY TEDDY (IRE) 4 b.f. Fayruz 116 – Racey Naskra (USA) 75 (Star de 49 d
Naskra (USA)) [1996 51: 6d 5s⁶ 5g² 5f 5f² 5g³ 5m³ 5f 1997 5m³ 5s 5s⁴ 5m 5g 5m⁵
5m Aug 20] poor maiden handicapper, seems on downgrade: reportedly hobdayed
and tubed before final start: best efforts at 5f: acts on firm going, probably on soft:
visored final 2 outings. *Miss L. A. Perratt*

REAGANESQUE (USA) 5 b.g. Nijinsky (CAN) 138 – Basoof (USA) 83 54
(Believe It (USA)) [1996 57: 14.1s 16.4g 12m⁴ 12.5f⁴ 12.5f* 12.1m* 14m 12m²
11.9m* 1997 11.8m⁴ 14.1g⁶ 12d⁶ 13.3g³ 12.5m³ 14m³ 14m 12.1g⁴ Aug 3] tall,
lengthy gelding: has a round action: good efforts at 5 yrs when in frame: effective at
1½m to 1¾m: acts on firm going, below form on ground softer than good: often a front
runner: game. *P. G. Murphy*

REAL ESTATE 3 b.c. High Estate 127 – Haitienne (FR) (Green Dancer (USA) 92
132) [1996 68: 6m⁶ 8m 1997 8f⁶ 10g² 11.6s* 12.3g* 12m³ Jul 30] strong colt:
impresses in appearance: made into fairly useful handicapper: won at Windsor in
June and Ripon (easily) in July: best effort when running-on fourth (promoted a
place) to Maylane in Tote Gold Trophy (Handicap) at Goodwood: likely to stay beyond 1½m: acts on good to firm and soft going: winning hurdler with D. Nicholson.
C. F. Wall

REAL FIRE (IRE) 3 b.g. Astronef 116 – Golden Arum 67 (Home Guard (USA) –
129) [1996 47, a?: 5m⁶ 5m a6g 8.1m 8m 6s 6g a8.5g 1997 10.8d 12v⁵ Jun 30] leggy
gelding: unimpressive mover: poor maiden: well beaten in 1997: tried blinkered.
M. G. Meagher

REALLY DONE IT NOW (IRE) 2 b.f. (Mar 29) Distinctly North (USA) 115 64 d
– Judy Loe (Red Alert 127) [1997 5g 5g⁴ 5m³ 5g⁵ 5m 6m 6d 6d a6g a5g Nov 15]
leggy, quite good-topped filly: sixth foal: half-sister to fairly useful Irish 1m winner
Lenni Lenape (by Be My Native) and a winner in Germany by Broken Hearted: dam,
unplaced, out of half-sister to very smart sprinter Noble Mark: modest maiden at
best, but became disappointing: possibly best at 5f: blinkered/visored fifth and sixth
starts. *K. R. Burke*

REAL MADRID 6 b.g. Dreams To Reality (USA) 113 – Spanish Princess (King –
of Spain 121) [1996 –, a50: a10g² a8g a10g* a10g a12g² a12g⁵ a10g 10.1f⁶ 10f 1997 a37
a12g a12g⁶ a10g⁵ Feb 25] good-bodied gelding: poor handicapper: stays 1½m: acts
on equitrack (well beaten only outing on fibresand), little turf form in Britain (though
successful on heavy ground in Belgium): has been blinkered, visored nowadays.
G. P. Enright

REALMS OF GLORY (IRE) 4 b.g. Reprimand 122 – Wasaif (IRE) 79 (Lomond –
(USA) 128) [1996 –, a51: 6s 8m a8g⁵ a8g 10f 8m 10.4g 1997 a10g Feb 25] lengthy
gelding: tailed off only outing as 4-y-o. *P. Mitchell*

REAMS OF VERSE (USA)   3 ch.f. Nureyev (USA) 131 – Modena (USA)   121
(Roberto (USA) 131) [1996 108p: 7m² 7d* 8m* 8g* 1997 8m⁶ 10.4g* 12m*
11.9g⁴ 10m³ Oct 4]

Reams of copy was written on whether Reams of Verse would stay the
trip in the Oaks. Even after she'd won the race there were still doubts lingering
in some quarters about her effectiveness at a mile and a half. On breeding she
had certainly looked a doubtful stayer—by Nureyev (whose three-year-olds'
average winning distance is around a mile) out of an unraced daughter of Mofida, a smart performer at up to seven furlongs. At two she stayed a mile well,
as wins in the May Hill Stakes and the Fillies' Mile testified. However, a mile
looked like being on the short side for her at three and that view was borne
out by her performance on her reappearance in the One Thousand Guineas.
Reams of Verse started the 11/1 fourth favourite at Newmarket to her stable-
companion Sleepytime, whom she'd beaten in the Fillies' Mile when Sleepytime had met trouble in running. This time Reams of Verse came off the worse
of the pair, beaten about seven lengths behind Sleepytime in sixth place,
chasing the leaders and staying on. The five fillies who finished ahead of her all
proved to be sprinters or milers.

Breeding counts for little once a horse has shown clear indications of its
potential to stay a given trip with a performance on the racecourse, and Reams
of Verse gave just such a display nine days later in the Tattersalls Musidora
Stakes at York. The Musidora is run over a mile, two furlongs and eighty-five
yards, and the manner of Reams of Verse's win suggested strongly that the Oaks
trip would not prove beyond her. Indeed, she seemed to be ridden at York with
the purpose of testing to the full her potential to see out the longer trip at Epsom.
A fair early pace increased noticeably from the home turn and Reams of Verse
was soon in front after joining issue on the bridle three out. From then on she
stretched further and further clear, still ridden along once she'd put the issue
beyond any doubt and running on strongly at the line, by which time she'd put
eleven lengths between herself and her nearest pursuer, Vagabond Chanteuse.

It had been a most impressive trial, and although those she beat at York
were largely second-raters, it was sufficient to see her sent off at 6/5-on at
Epsom, attempting to become the first odds-on winner of the Oaks since Noblesse in 1963. Khalid Abdulla had already owned three Oaks runner-ups, most
recently the non-staying All At Sea in 1992, and he strengthened his hand for
the latest running by fielding second favourite Yashmak (coincidentally a great

Tattersalls Musidora Stakes, York—Reams of Verse wins her Oaks trial by eleven lengths

granddaughter of Noblesse, and also a daughter of her owner's first Oaks runner-up Slightly Dangerous) who'd won her Oaks trial at Newbury by a wide margin as well. The twice-raced Irish hope Ebadiyla was the Aga Khan's first runner in the race since his 1989 winner Aliysa was disqualified and was a well-backed third favourite, whilst the Lingfield Oaks Trial winner Crown of Light and the Pretty Polly Stakes winner Siyadah started 11/1, the remainder of the twelve-strong field at 25/1 or longer. If anyone wanted a precedent for Nureyev siring a mile-and-a-half classic winner they didn't have to look too far back to find one—just five days earlier Peintre Celebre had won the Prix du Jockey-Club.

Stamina proved no problem to Reams of Verse but trouble in running did. Kieren Fallon settled her towards the rear in a strongly-run race early on but had moved her into a challenging position by Tattenham Corner, with Yashmak on her outside. Once into the straight, Reams of Verse's run was blocked initially by Yashmak drifting across the camber in front of her, a move which eventually took Yashmak to the rails, squeezing out Ebadiyla. Meanwhile she'd been replaced on Reams of Verse's outer by the French outsider Gazelle Royale, which meant the favourite had to check a second time before getting a clear run. Once switched, Reams of Verse responded well to lead inside the final furlong and, despite idling in front, was well on top at the finish. Gazelle Royale was one and a half lengths back in second with three quarters of a length to the staying-on Crown of Light and another half length to Yashmak. The outsider Etoile was a close fifth and Ebadiyla sixth, neither of them having had the smoothest of runs. The rest were beaten a long way, with the three pace-setters (including the visored Siyadah) paying for their efforts and finishing tailed off. Reams of Verse thus became Henry Cecil's fifth Oaks winner after Lady Carla the year before and Oh So Sharp, Diminuendo and Snow Bride in the 'eighties. It was the second year running that he'd trained the winner of both fillies' classics. Fallon had also ridden the stable's One Thousand Guineas winner Sleepytime, but he'd only been able to ride at all in the Oaks once the Italian stewards had deferred a ten-day ban he'd incurred for a riding offence in the Italian Derby.

For our part, the strongly-run Oaks proved not only that Reams of Verse stays a mile and a half but that she stays it well. However, on her very next outing, in the Yorkshire Oaks, her stamina was called into question again, this time by her trainer. There was every reason to think Reams of Verse would progress further after the Oaks and her trainer considered her much stronger after Epsom. Against seven rivals, Reams of Verse started the favourite at York at 7/4-on, carrying £200,000 in major on-course bets alone. But the Ebor meeting proved one the Cecil stable would prefer to forget, with the defeats

Vodafone Oaks, Epsom—much closer this time for Reams of Verse, as she overcomes trouble in running to beat Gazelle Royale

of favourites Bosra Sham, Chester House and Bold Fact, as well as Reams of Verse. The last-named's pre-race demeanour hadn't given cause for concern before (she'd looked in fine shape at Newmarket and Epsom, just a little on her toes before the Oaks) but she became edgy when mounted at York and was taken down earlier than scheduled to prevent her boiling over. Although Reams of Verse settled well enough in the race, her response once brought to challenge the pace-setting Whitewater Affair was disappointing and she was run out of a place by the Oaks third Crown of Light, clearly running below her Epsom form. 'She was travelling well but found nothing' Henry Cecil said afterwards. 'It was a truly-run race here and the good gallop found her out...she's not bred to get a mile and a half, and she didn't stay the trip today.'

Reams of Verse therefore made what turned out to be her final appearance back at a mile and a quarter in the Sun Chariot Stakes at Newmarket in October. The task of giving 6 lb (her Group 1 penalty) to the lightly-raced One So Wonderful and Kool Kat Katie proved beyond her. Although she ran creditably at the weights to be beaten just under four lengths. Reams of Verse again got above herself in the preliminaries and was taken early to post, starting an uneasy favourite. Strictly speaking, the Musidora and the Sun Chariot were Reams of Verse's best efforts, with the *bare* form of the Oaks falling a little short, but that doesn't allow for the trouble she met in running, nor her idling in front; whatever, she stayed a mile and a half perfectly well but gave the impression that her hard race at Epsom left its mark in subsequent starts.

It's interesting to note that very similar comments concerning stamina were made on Reams of Verse's half-brother, Elmaamul (by Diesis). He too showed his *best* form at a mile and a quarter, but, despite an apparently good

Mr K. Abdulla's "Reams of Verse"

effort when third in Quest For Fame's Derby, connections were adamant that he hadn't stayed and he was subsequently campaigned at around a mile and a quarter. Reams of Verse's other relatives to race were detailed in *Racehorses of 1996*. She has an unraced year-younger sister called Post Modern. Her dam's yearling colt by Diesis died but she was in foal to El Gran Senor in the latest season.

		Northern Dancer	Nearctic
	Nureyev (USA)	(b 1961)	Natalma
	(b 1977)	Special	Forli
Reams of Verse (USA)		(b 1969)	Thong
(ch.f. 1994)		Roberto	Hail To Reason
	Modena (USA)	(b 1969)	Bramalea
	(b 1983)	Mofida	Right Tack
		(ch 1974)	Wold Lass

Reams of Verse, a tall, leggy filly and a fluent mover, has been retired to Juddmonte Farms in the USA. She was genuine and raced with plenty of enthusiasm. Khalid Abdulla enjoyed an excellent season with his three-year-old fillies Reams of Verse, Ryafan and Yashmak, who between them also won the Musidora, the Falmouth, the Nassau and the Ribblesdale (and in the United States) the Flower Bowl Invitational, the Queen Elizabeth II Challenge Cup, the Yellow Ribbon and the Matriarch. *H. R. A. Cecil*

REAP REWARDS 2 gr.c. (Mar 26) Barrys Gamble 102 – Bo' Babbity 75 (Strong Gale 116) [1997 5s⁴ 6g* 5m³ Jun 5] 12,000F: fifth live foal: brother to 3-y-o Barresbo and half-brother to 4-y-o Blue Iris and a winner in Jersey (both by Petong): dam, 2-y-o 5f winner, half-sister to high-class sprinter Anita's Prince: progressive form: won maiden at Ayr in May: good third to Only For Gold in £8,700 event at Beverley 6 days later: stays 6f. *J. G. FitzGerald* — 87

REAR WINDOW 3 b.c. Night Shift (USA) – Last Clear Chance (USA) (Alleged (USA) 138) [1996 NR 1997 11g 10s⁵ 12g a16g³ 16s Oct 8] compact colt: half-brother to 3 winners, including 1992 2-y-o 6f winner Diskette (later stayed 1½m, by Local Suitor): dam ran once: only worthwhile form when third in handicap at Lingfield in August: will stay beyond 2m: visored last 2 outings: sold 12,000 gns after final one. *Lord Huntingdon* — 57

REBALZA (IRE) 2 b.c. (Jan 27) Alzao (USA) 117 – Rebecca's Song (Artaius (USA) 129) [1997 6m 6f⁴ 7g 7m² 8g 8f² Sep 18] 10,000F, IR 28,000Y: workmanlike colt: half-brother to 3 winners abroad: dam French 1m to 9f winner: modest form: second in nurseries at Newcastle and Yarmouth: stays 1m: acts on firm ground, yet to race on softer than good. *J. M. P. Eustace* — 63

REBECCA SHARP 3 b.f. Machiavellian (USA) 123 – Nuryana 107 (Nureyev (USA) 131) [1996 82p: 7g² 1997 7g* 8m 8m* 8g⁶ 8g² 8m 8g² 7g² Oct 18] — 122

In Thackeray's novel *Vanity Fair* the heroine Rebecca Sharp overcomes the obstacles of her lowly birth and upbringing to scheme her way into high society. Some one hundred and fifty years on her equine namesake caused a stir of her own when bursting into the upper echelons of the racing world with victory in Royal Ascot's Coronation Stakes, a performance she bettered in the autumn when she was unluckily defeated in another Group 1 race, the Queen Elizabeth II Stakes.

Not that the latter-day Rebecca Sharp had anything like so many disadvantages to overcome in the first place. In fact, it was far from a long-shot that this result of a mating between the blue-blooded Machiavellian (hence the name, we imagine) and a useful mile winner from a good family, in the care of one of the leading trainers, would be rubbing shoulders with the best of her generation sooner rather than later. Rebecca Sharp's only appearance as a two-year-old—a considerately-handled second in a big field of maidens at Newmarket—had promised plenty, and a striking victory in a similar race on the same course when decidedly backward on her return saw her pitched straight in against the best in the One Thousand Guineas. It was asking a lot

Coronation Stakes, Royal Ascot—Rebecca Sharp (noseband) holds on from Ocean Ridge; Sleepytime (black cap) is only third

of Rebecca Sharp at this stage of her career for her to win in such exalted company, but it came as a major disappointment that she managed to beat only two in a field of fifteen; it was later reported that she'd been off colour. Over six weeks later, Rebecca Sharp took on the winner of the Guineas, Sleepytime, as well as that of the Irish equivalent, Classic Park, in a six-runner race for the Coronation Stakes at Royal Ascot. It was no surprise that she started at a good deal longer odds than her two main rivals, but 25/1 outsider of the lot looked generous given her earlier promise. In a falsely-run race, Rebecca Sharp tracked the leaders Khassah and Ocean Ridge until quickening best of all to lead over a furlong out, thereafter holding on well under pressure despite still seeming green. Ocean Ridge kept on for second, three quarters of a length down, with Sleepytime (who wasn't raced again) two lengths further away and Classic Park a never-dangerous fourth.

Even allowing for excuses for her rivals, the Coronation Stakes represented a smart performance by Rebecca Sharp and she seemed back on course for big things. But it took her a while to confirm that impression fully. Easily the best of her next three runs was in the Prix d'Astarte at Deauville, in which she only just held second from some inferior rivals, a length behind Daneskaya. As a consequence it was as an outsider again that she lined up for the Queen Elizabeth II Stakes, the highlight of Ascot's September Festival. Rebecca Sharp ought to have won. Tracking the leaders going well, she became boxed in soon after reaching the straight, her rider (Michael Hills, as for all her races) having to sit and suffer through the penultimate furlong, and finished strongly once extricated at the distance. At the line Rebecca Sharp was a short head behind Air Express, who had got first run on her. A stride or two after the line and Rebecca Sharp was in front. Trouble in running came Rebecca Sharp's way on her final start, too, but her neck second to Kahal in the Challenge Stakes at Newmarket wasn't necessarily an unlucky defeat as the winner came from a similarly unpromising position. Shortly afterwards it was announced that Rebecca Sharp had been retired, her owner citing lack of opportunities for older milers to meet rivals on level terms after they've won a Group 1 as a major reason for it.

As we've said, the equine Rebecca Sharp is a well-bred individual. Her sire, the champion two-year-old and Two Thousand Guineas runner-up Machiavellian, is proving a good stallion, with an excellent ratio of winners to runners and a fine overall standard of offspring. Rebecca Sharp is just about his best performer, though he was also represented in 1997 by her conqueror in the Challenge Stakes, Kahal. Rebecca Sharp is the fifth foal and fifth winner out of Nuryana, the others being Mystic Park (a two-year-old mile winner by Rainbow Quest), Nuryandra (a two-year-old six-furlong winner by Reference Point), Mystic Hill (by Shirley Heights, and a winner from around ten to thirteen furlongs) and the Caerleon colt Mystic Knight. The first three were fairly useful, no better, but Mystic Knight was smart, winning the Lingfield Derby Trial and finishing sixth to Shaamit in the Derby in 1996. Nuryana's dam, Loralane, was an ordinary seven-furlong winner but a half-sister to the 1982 One Thousand Guineas winner On The House. The leggy, angular Rebecca Sharp bears some similarities to On The House, who was also an unprepossessing individual and not renowned for her consistency (her classic win came at 33/1 and a victory in the Sussex Stakes was at 14/1). Loralane's and On The House's dam, Lora, was closely related to the high-class sprinter D'Urberville and to Klairessa, the dam of the outstanding sprinter Habibti. The family has also achieved considerable success in Australia with descendants of Klairessa and her relative No Relation, including the 1997 Golden Slipper winner Guineas.

Rebecca Sharp (b.f. 1994)	Machiavellian (USA) (b 1987)	Mr Prospector (b 1970)	Raise A Native
			Gold Digger
		Coup de Folie (b 1982)	Halo
			Raise The Standard
	Nuryana (b 1984)	Nureyev (b 1977)	Northern Dancer
			Special
		Loralane (b 1977)	Habitat
			Lora

Rebecca Sharp raced only at seven furlongs and a mile and on good and good to firm going. She might not have been the best of lookers but she was the most superb mover and she had plenty of other fine qualities, including a good turn of foot. It will be interesting to see if she passes any of these virtues on to her offspring. *G. Wragg*

REBEL COUNTY (IRE) 4 b.f. Maelstrom Lake 118 – Haven Bridge 88 76 (Connaught 130) [1996 97: 7s 7m⁶ 7m⁵ 8g* 8g* 8f³ 10m² 10.3m* 10.5g⁶ 10.3m 10.3m 8.1m⁴ 8f² 8.5g* 7.6d³ 7f³ 8m 10m* 8g⁵ 8.1v* 8g 9s a9.4g 1997 a9.4g 8.9d 8d 7.6m 8g 10m⁶ 8.3g 10.3m 10d² 8d⁴ 8m 8s Nov 8] good-topped filly: tough and useful handicapper in 1996: only fair at best as 4-y-o, well beaten most starts: seems suited by 1m to 1¼m: acts on any turf going: effective visored or not: tends to carry head awkwardly: has had tongue tied. *A. Bailey*

RECESSIONS OVER 6 b.g. Komaite (USA) – Lucky Councillor (Lucky 37 Wednesday 124) [1996 –: a8g 1997 a7g a8.5g⁴ a7g² a7g Jun 13] poor maiden handicapper: probably stays 1m: raced only on fibresand. *N. P. Littmoden*

RECHULLIN 3 ch.f. Niniski (USA) 125 – Rechanit (IRE) (Local Suitor (USA) 86 128) [1996 82p: 6.9d³ a7g* 1997 8m⁵ 7.6d 7m* a7g⁴ 7g⁴ Jul 8] good sort: fairly useful handicapper: won at Catterick in May: best effort when fourth to Noisette in strongly-run contest at Newmarket final start, tending to carry head rather high: stoutly bred, but best form at 7f: acts on good to firm going and fibresand. *D. R. Loder*

RECKLESS 3 gr.f. Mystiko (USA) 124 – Swift And Sure (USA) 98 (Valdez – (USA)) [1996 NR 1997 8.2m Apr 8] lengthy filly: half-sister to fairly useful 6f to 1m performer Sooty Swift (by Akarad) and a minor 1m winner abroad by Hadeer: tailed off in maiden at Nottingham. *J. E. Banks*

RECLUSE 6 b.g. Last Tycoon 131 – Nomadic Pleasure 91 (Habitat 134) [1996 –§: 27 § 13d 11.1m 15.1f 1997 12m³ 14.1s 16m⁴ 14g⁶ 16d⁶ Jun 30] well-made gelding: poor handicapper: probably stays 2m: usually blinkered: not one to trust. *W. T. Kemp*

RECOGNITION 2 b.c. (May 10) Rock City 120 – Star Face (African Sky 124) 68 [1997 6d 6m 6m² 6.1g⁴ 6d³ Oct 20] 8,500Y: half-brother to several winners, including smart 7f to 11f winner Lord of The Field (by Jalmood) and a stayer by Be

My Chief: dam French 10.5f winner: second in maiden at Folkestone in September, easily best effort: should stay 1m: sold and joined M. Polglase. *W. Jarvis*

RECONDITE (IRE) 3 b.c. Polish Patriot (USA) 128 – Recherchee (Rainbow Quest (USA) 134) [1996 99: 5d² 5m* 6g³ 7m* 8g² 8g 1997 9m Apr 17] tall, useful-looking colt: has a short, round action: useful at 2 yrs: stiff task, raced too freely and tailed off in listed race at Newmarket only outing as 3-y-o: stays 1m: yet to race on extremes of going. *M. R. Channon* —

RECORD LOVER (IRE) 7 b.g. Alzao (USA) 117 – Spun Gold 106 (Thatch (USA) 136) [1996 33, a43: a12g³ a12g³ a16g* a16g a14g⁴ a12g a16g⁴ a16g⁴ 18m⁶ 12m² 12g⁶ 11.5m⁵ a14g 1997 a16s² a16g a16g a16g Mar 3] close-coupled gelding: no worthwhile form at 7 yrs. *M. C. Chapman* —

RECOURSE (USA) 3 b.c. Alleged (USA) 138 – Queens Only (USA) (Marshua's Dancer (USA)) [1996 78: 8f⁴ 8m⁵ 1997 10g 11.8d² 10m* Oct 5] tall, good-topped colt: fairly useful form: off course 6 months, readily landed odds in maiden at Leicester, making all and drawing clear final 2f: will prove suited by 1½m+: acts on good to firm going and dead: lightly raced, and probably capable of better. *H. R. A. Cecil* 88 p

RED ADMIRAL 7 ch.g. Formidable (USA) 125 – Dancing Meg (USA) 113 (Marshua's Dancer (USA)) [1996 64, a69: 6f⁴ 5f⁴ 6g² 7f³ 6m² 6g⁶ 6f⁶ a6g⁶ a6g* a6g 1997 7m 6m a7g Aug 28] heavy-topped gelding: fair sprint handicapper at 6 yrs: well held in 1997. *C. Murray* —

REDBRIDGE (USA) 3 b.c. Alleged (USA) 138 – Red Slippers (USA) 111 (Nureyev (USA) 131) [1996 NR 1997 11g³ Apr 18] lengthy, good-topped colt: first foal: dam, 7f (at 2 yrs) and 1¼m winner, closely related to Balanchine: well-backed 4/1, though very green, third of 18 behind Ghataas in maiden at Newbury, not unduly knocked about: subsequently underwent an operation. *J. H. M. Gosden* 98

RED BROOK LAD 2 ch.g. (Apr 15) Nomadic Way (USA) 104 – Silently Yours (USA) 53 (Silent Screen (USA)) [1997 8m 8.2s Oct 15] half-brother to 8-y-o Tommy Tempest: dam 5f winner: soundly beaten in autumn maidens at Kempton and Nottingham. *S. Dow* —

RED CAMELLIA 3 b.f. Polar Falcon (USA) 126 – Cerise Bouquet 75 (Mummy's Pet 125) [1996 116: 5.9f* 7.1m* 7d* 8g⁴ 1997 8d³ 7m⁴ Sep 25] lengthy filly: had a short action: smart performer: found to have fractured a bone in her off fore after final start at 2 yrs: tired closing stages when under a length third of 7 to Always Loyal in Poule d'Essai des Pouliches at Longchamp in May: below form in Supreme Stakes at Goodwood (carried head awkwardly) only subsequent run: stayed 1m: acted on firm and dead ground: game and genuine front runner: reportedly to visit Selkirk. *Sir Mark Prescott* 110

RED CASCADE (IRE) 2 b.f. (May 12) Danehill (USA) 126 – Fair Flutter (Beldale Flutter (USA) 130) [1997 7g Jul 11] 30,000Y: useful-looking filly: has scope: seventh foal: half-sister to fairly useful 7f to 9f winner Hand Craft (by Dancing Dissident) and 6-y-o Silence In Court: dam (unraced) out of sister to Master Willie: 14/1, green and better for race, ninth of 10 in maiden at York. *B. W. Hills* —

RED EMBERS 3 gr.f. Saddlers' Hall (IRE) 126 – Kala Rosa 79 (Kalaglow 132) [1996 64: 5.7g* 6g⁵ 1997 a7g⁴ a7g³ a8.5g³ a11g⁵ 9.9m⁶ 7g 10m 11.9d a8.5g 12m Oct 31] tall, sparely-made filly: modest handicapper at best: had 4 different trainers as 3-y-o and no form after third start: should stay beyond 8.5f: acts on fibresand: often on toes and has bolted to post. *R. C. Spicer* a52

RED GUARD 3 ch.g. Soviet Star (USA) 128 – Zinzara (USA) 119 (Stage Door Johnny) [1996 86: 7m 7m³ 8g⁴ 1997 8g 10m³ 7.6m⁵ 8m³ 10m⁶ 8g² Aug 25] big, useful-looking gelding: fluent mover: fairly useful maiden: second at Newcastle: stays 1¼m: has raced only on good/good to firm ground: consistent: sold (to J. Gifford) 26,000 gns in October. *G. Wragg* 81

RED HEAD AND DOTTY 2 ch.f. (Feb 25) Risk Me (FR) 127 – Sharper Still (Sharpen Up 127) [1997 6d Jun 23] half-sister to several winners, including smart 5f to 7f performer Jimmy Barnie (by Local Suitor) and fairly useful 1m to 1¼m performer Samba Sharply (by Rambo Dancer): dam never ran: well beaten in maiden at Windsor. *B. J. McMath* —

Royal Hunt Cup (Handicap), Royal Ascot—
Red Robbo (white cap) lands a gamble and is trainer Reg Akehurst's last major flat winner;
Crown Court (near side) follows him home

RED LEGGINGS   2 b.f. (Jan 25) Shareef Dancer (USA) 135 – Anchorage (IRE)   84
86 (Slip Anchor 136) [1997 7m⁵ 7g⁵ 7.3g⁵ Oct 25] small filly: first foal: dam, 1½m
winner, half-sister to smart dual-purpose performer Brunico: fairly useful form: won
maiden at Warwick by 3 lengths: 8½ lengths fifth to Ffestiniog in listed race at
Newbury later in October: bred to be suited by 1¼m+. *J. W. Hills*

RED LIGHT   5 b.g. Reprimand 122 – Trull (Lomond (USA) 128) [1996 –: 14.1m⁵   –
1997 a12g Apr 28] sparely-made gelding: fairly useful winner as 3-y-o: no promise
since: tried blinkered/visored: poor and irresolute winning hurdler. *J. R. Jenkins*

RED MAPLE (USA)   2 br.c. (Feb 11) With Approval (CAN) – Sheer Gold (USA)   57
(Cutlass (USA)) [1997 6s⁵ 6m 6d⁴ 7m 7m 6.9g⁵ 7.6m 10g⁴ 10d³ Oct 13] $37,000F,
$70,000Y: smallish, leggy colt: first foal: dam stakes-placed winner up to 1¼m in
USA: modest maiden: third in Leicester seller final start: will stay beyond 1¼m: best
form on good ground or softer: seems effective with or without blinkers: often soon
off bridle. *P. F. I. Cole*

REDOUBTABLE (USA)   6 b.h. Grey Dawn II 132 – Seattle Rockette (USA)   72 +
(Seattle Slew (USA)) [1996 a7g² a6s* a6g⁵ 1997 5g 7d a7g a6g* Dec 26] smart at 3
yrs for R. Hannon, then raced in Dubai, winning twice: sold only 5,500 gns before
reappearance and showed just fair form in 1997: won handicap at Wolverhampton:
effective at 6f to 1m: acts on firm ground, sand and fibresand, probably on soft: takes
keen hold: has reportedly had back problems. *D. W. Chapman*

RED PEPPER (IRE)   2 br.g. (Feb 27) Chilibang 120 – Magic Flame 70 (Sayf El   62
Arab (USA) 127) [1997 a5g⁶ 6.1d 6m 5m⁵ 5.3m⁵ 5m 5m³ 6g a5g a5g a5s a7g² Dec
10] 7,500Y: second foal: dam, 6f winner here, also successful in Scandinavia: modest
maiden: stays 7f: acts on good to firm ground and equitrack. *P. Howling*

RED PHANTOM (IRE)   5 ch.g. Kefaah (USA) 124 – Highland Culture (Lomond   53
(USA) 128) [1996 66: a12g a12g³ a14g³ a11g³ a12g⁵ 12d a12g³ 1997 a14.8g a14.8g
a9.4g* a14g a12g a12g² Dec 26] modest performer: won seller at Wolverhampton
in August: only other form in 1997 when blinkered final start (visored on 3 other
occasions): stays 1½m: acts on fibresand (unraced on equitrack). *S. Mellor*

RED RABBIT   2 b.f. (Feb 18) Suave Dancer (USA) 136 – Turban 80 (Glint of   86
Gold 128) [1997 7g² 8.1m⁵ 7d² Oct 27] fifth foal: half-sister to several winners,
including useful 8.5f winner Papaha (by Green Desert) and 1m and 11.8f winner
Lovely Lyca (by Night Shift): dam, 1¼m winner, half-sister to Old Vic: fairly useful

780

maiden: second at Salisbury in September and Lingfield in October: got worked up in stalls when last of 5 in between: bred to be suited by much further than 7f, but is headstrong. *B. W. Hills*

RED RAJA 4 b.g. Persian Heights 129 – Jenny Splendid 101 (John Splendid 116) 64
[1996 –: 12m 16.1f⁶ 12.1s 1997 a14.8g 16.4g² 16m⁶ Sep 25] workmanlike gelding: modest maiden: best effort when second in a handicap at Folkestone in September: stays 2m: ran poorly only outing on fibresand: useful hurdler. *P. Mitchell*

RED RISK 2 ch.g. (Feb 19) Risk Me (FR) 127 – Red Sails (Town And Country –
124) [1997 5.1m a6g 7g 6.1d a8g a8g⁶ Dec 19] 8,000Y: second foal: brother to 3-y-o Enchanting Eve: dam poor novice hurdler from the family of Bireme and Buoy: soundly beaten in maidens. *P. W. Harris*

RED ROBBO (CAN) 4 b.c. Red Ransom (USA) – Aunt Jobiska (USA) (What 98 §
Luck (USA)) [1996 93: 8.1g³ 10.3g 197m⁶ 10.4g 8m* 8.1g 7.9d 8m Sep 21] strong, good-topped colt: carries condition: useful handicapper: lightly raced for H. Cecil at 3 yrs: supported at long odds, won Royal Hunt Cup at Royal Ascot by ¾ length from Crown Court, responding well to get up last 75 yds: soundly beaten all other starts as 4-y-o: stays 1m: acts on good to firm ground: has twice given trouble at stalls: blinkered final outing (dropped himself out): untrustworthy. *R. Akehurst*

RED ROMANCE 3 b.g. Prince Daniel (USA) – Rio Piedras 86 (Kala Shikari 53
125) [1996 60: 5m³ 5g² 6g 5m² 5g³ 5f² 5m⁴ 7.1s⁶ 1997 5s 5g 5d 5.9f⁴ 5d 5m⁶ Jun 26] leggy gelding: modest maiden: stays 6f: best form on good to firm/firm going: sold, and sent to Macau. *Denys Smith*

RED RUSTY (USA) 4 ch.g. The Carpenter (USA) – Super Sisters (AUS) (Call –
Report (USA)) [1996 –, a56d: 7m a9.4g a8g³ 8.2f⁵ a10g⁶ a8g⁶ 11.4m a8.5g 8g a10g 1997 a8g Jan 7] strong, workmanlike gelding: formerly fair 1m winner: has lost his form. *P. R. Hedger*

RED SHIFT (IRE) 2 b.g. (Mar 23) Night Shift (USA) – Histoire Douce (USA) –
(Chief's Crown (USA)) [1997 7d Oct 27] 21,000Y: fourth foal: closely related to a French 7.5f winner by Fairy King and half-brother to French 11.5f winners by Salse and Don't Forget Me: dam French 9f and 11f winner: 10/1, last in maiden at Lingfield, eased from halfway (reportedly lame near-fore). *R. Hannon*

RED SKY CHARLIE 2 b.c. (Apr 27) Warning 136 – Shameem (USA) 65 (Nur- 74
eyev (USA) 131) [1997 6m⁵ 7g Sep 18] 31,000Y: rather leggy colt: second foal: dam thrice-raced half-sister to Kentucky Oaks winner Lucky Lucky Lucky: better effort in steadily-run maidens when around 5½ lengths seventh to Dr Fong at Newbury, in touch throughout: very green on debut: sent to USA. *Lord Huntingdon*

REDSPET 3 ch.f. Tina's Pet 121 – Manabel 73 (Manado 130) [1996 –: 5m 1997 –
a5g a8g 6m 8.2s a8g a5g⁴ a5g 7m a7g a6g Nov 14] of no account. *S. R. Bowring*

REDSWAN 2 ch.g. (Mar 21) Risk Me (FR) 127 – Bocas Rose 106 (Jalmood 61
(USA) 126) [1997 6.1m 5m Oct 28] 5,500Y: fourth foal: brother to 1994 2-y-o 6f winner Moody and a winner in Norway: dam sprinter: better effort in maidens on debut at Nottingham: slowly away both starts. *S. C. Williams*

RED TEL (IRE) 5 b.g. Alzao (USA) 117 – Arbour (USA) 76 (Graustark) [1996 –
NR 1997 a12g⁶ Jul 26] 15,000Y: second foal: half-brother to 4-y-o Alpine Hideaway: dam twice-raced 1½m winner: modest NH Flat winner/hurdler, probably none too genuine: well beaten in seller at Southwell on flat debut. *M. C. Pipe*

RED TIE AFFAIR (USA) 4 b.c. Miswaki (USA) 124 – Quiet Rendezvous –
(USA) (Nureyev (USA) 131) [1996 54: a8g⁴ 7f 7m 7m⁵ 10.8m⁶ a12g 10m³ 12m 10m⁶ 12.1g⁶ 1997 a9.4g⁶ a12g Jan 13] good-bodied colt: modest maiden handicapper at 3 yrs: stays 1¼m: raced only on good going or firmer on turf, no form on all-weather: has run well visored. *J. M. Bradley*

RED TIME 4 br.g. Timeless Times (USA) 99 – Crimson Dawn (Manado 130) –
[1996 56: a8.5g 5.1g⁵ 7f³ 6s³ 8g 6g 5.1m⁶ 6m⁶ 7m⁵ 5f 5m 1997 a7g 6m 6m 5m a7g a8g Nov 17] modest maiden handicapper at up to 7f as 3-y-o: showed little, including in visor, in 1997. *M. S. Saunders*

RED WHIRLWIND 7 b.g. Shadeed (USA) 135 – Red Red Rose (USA) 90 –
(Blushing Groom (FR) 131) [1996 NR 1997 a16g⁵ 16g a14g a12g⁵ Jul 26] tall gelding: modest up to 2m as 5-y-o: well beaten in 1997. *R. Simpson*

REDWING   3 b.g. Reprimand 122 – Bronzewing 103 (Beldale Flutter (USA) 130)   89
[1996 83+: 7m³ 7m* 8.3g⁶ 1997 7g 8m 7f⁶ 7g³ 7g Aug 25] big, workmanlike gelding:
fairly useful handicapper: best effort when close third to Chewit at Ascot in August,
dictating steady pace: should stay 1m: raced only on good going or firmer: sent to
Hong Kong. *J. L. Dunlop*

REEDS   3 b.g. Thatching 131 – Bayadere (USA) 61 (Green Dancer (USA) 132)   53
[1996 NR 1997 a7g⁵ a7g⁵ 7g⁴ 8g 8g 9s 10.1f⁵ 11.5m Oct 22] first foal: dam, staying
maiden: modest maiden: probably stays 1¼m: has had tongue tied: visored (ran
creditably) penultimate start 1m: sold, and joined G. M. Moore. *J. R. Fanshawe*

REFERENDUM (IRE)   3 b.c. Common Grounds 118 – Final Decision (Tap On   101
Wood 130) [1996 107: 5.2d³ 6f² 6g* 7g² 8g⁴ 1997 7g⁶ 6d² 6m May 31] good-topped
colt: has a fluent, round action: useful performer: not discredited in Free Handicap at
Newmarket (refused to settle) and minor event at Newbury (forced strong pace and
collared only inside last 1f by Tomba) in spring: reportedly sore final start: stays 1m:
usually front runner. *G. Lewis*

REFINED (IRE)   2 b.f. (Apr 30) Statoblest 120 – Annsfield Lady (Red Sunset   95 p
120) [1997 6d 5m* 5s* Oct 16] 38,000Y: leggy filly: sixth foal: half-sister to several
winners, including 4-y-o Give Me A Ring and smart 6f (at 2 yrs) to 1m winner Pipe
Major (by Tirol): dam Irish 9f/1¼m performer: promising performer: easy winner of
maiden at Kempton and nursery at Catterick a month apart, in latter impressive in
beating Carol Singer 3 lengths: speedy, but should stay 6f: likeable sort, and
potentially useful. *L. M. Cumani*

REFUSE TO LOSE   3 ch.c. Emarati (USA) 74 – Petrol 73 (Troy 137) [1996 74p: 81
6m⁵ 6g* 1997 6g⁴ 6m² 6m 7.1m² 7m⁶ 8d Oct 16] big, lengthy colt: fairly useful
performer: second in handicap at Newmarket and minor event at Sandown: seemed
not to stay 1m in testing conditions: usually races prominently. *J. M. P. Eustace*

REGAIT   3 b.c. In The Wings 128 – Rowa 83 (Great Nephew 126) [1996 –p: 8m   87
8.2s 1997 12g* 16.1g 14m Aug 9] quite attractive colt: has a round action: fairly
useful form: won 4-runner maiden at Thirsk in April: subsequently off course nearly
3 months and below that form in handicaps: should stay further than 1½m: looked
difficult ride final start: sent to UAE. *M. A. Jarvis*

REGAL ARROW   2 br.g. (Jan 28) Superlative 118 – A Little Hot (Petong 126)   –
[1997 6d 6d Nov 7] second reported foal: dam sprint maiden: well beaten in maidens.
A. G. Foster

REGAL EAGLE   4 b.g. Shirley Heights 130 – On The Tiles (Thatch (USA) 136)   65
[1996 72: 10d 10.5d 12m⁵ 13.3m 11.6d 1997 16.2m⁵ 16.2m 12.4g Jun 27] angular,
good-bodied gelding: fair maiden handicapper: well held after reappearance: stays
2m: acts on good to firm going: joined Mrs J. Harrington in Ireland. *M. D. Hammond*

REGAL EQUITY   3 b.c. Keen 116 – Nazmiah 73 (Free State 125) [1996 64: 6f   –
7f⁶ 5m³ 6g 5f 5.2g⁴ 5d 1997 a8g 8.2g May 23] strong, sturdy colt: fair form at 5f at 2
yrs for B. Meehan: well beaten in 1997: blinkered (ran poorly) once. *M. C. Pipe*

REGALO   2 b.c. (Apr 22) Nalchik (USA) – Stardrop (Starch Reduced 112) [1997   54 +
5.1d 5m 5.1m 5.7m⁴ 5.1m 6m 5s⁵ 5d³ Oct 27] 400Y: tall colt: third foal: dam unraced:
modest maiden on balance: probably stays at 5f: front runner. *D. M. Hyde*

REGAL PATRIARCH (IRE)   2 br.c. (Apr 28) Marju (IRE) 127 – Early Rising   70 p
(USA) (Grey Dawn II 132) [1997 7m 8d 8.2d⁵ Oct 30] big, good-topped colt: has
plenty of scope: not best of walkers: half-brother to several winners, notably 3-y-o
Silver Patriarch, smart stayer My Patriarch (by Be My Guest) and fairly useful sprinter Silver Singing (by Topsider): dam minor winner in USA at around 1m, is out of
half-sister to top-class Key To The Mint: backward sort, showed plenty of promise in
maidens in October at Newmarket (2), and Nottingham: likely to stay 1½m+: very
much type to make a better 3-y-o, and should win races. *J. L. Dunlop*

REGAL PATROL   3 b.g. Red Ransom (USA) – River Patrol 96 (Rousillon   80
(USA) 133) [1996 72: 6m⁴ 7.1m⁴ 1997 7m⁵ 9.9m* 9s³ 10m² 11m⁴ Aug 10] well-
made gelding: has a quick action: fairly useful handicapper: won at Beverley in
April: best effort when second at Lingfield following month: stays 1¼m: acts on
good to firm ground and soft: visored final start: tends to hang and carry head
awkwardly: sent to UAE. *M. R. Stoute*

Shadwell Stud Firth of Clyde Stakes, Ayr—Regal Revolution holds the challenge of Sapphire Ring

REGAL REPRIMAND 3 b.g. Reprimand 122 – Queen Caroline (USA) 67 74
(Chief's Crown (USA)) [1996 –p: 7f 8.1s 1997 6.9g 9.9m³ 10g² 11.6s² 10g³ 8.3g
9.7m* 9.9m* 10d⁴ 10.2g⁴ Sep 11] sturdy gelding: powerful mover: fair performer:
won steadily-run minor events at Folkestone and Beverley in July: probably stays
1½m: acts on good to firm going and soft: has been bandaged behind: consistent: sold
31,000 gns in October. *G. Lewis*

REGAL REVOLUTION 2 br.f. (Apr 5) Hamas (IRE) 125§ – True Queen 105
(USA) 79 (Silver Hawk (USA) 123) [1997 5.7g² 6g* 6m* 6m* 7g⁴ 6g* 6g* Sep 19]
3,000Y: fourth foal: half-sister to 4-y-o Diego: dam 1¼m winner: progressed very
well, winning maiden at Folkestone, nurseries at Ayr and Windsor, minor event at
Salisbury and listed race at Ayr between July and September: 16/1, made virtually all
to beat Sapphire Ring gamely by a neck in last-named: should stay 7f: raced only on
good/good to firm ground: useful. *P. T. Walwyn*

REGAL SPLENDOUR (CAN) 4 ch.g. Vice Regent (CAN) – Seattle Princess – §
(USA) (Seattle Slew (USA)) [1996 71: 8d 7m² 8.2m 7f² 7s 1997 a10g⁵ a8g* a8g a66 §
7f⁶ 8d a7g Dec 19] good-topped gelding: fair performer: won amateurs handicap at
Lingfield in February, only worthwhile form at 4 yrs: stays 1m well: acts on firm
ground and equitrack, possibly unsuited by soft: unreliable. *J. J. Bridger*

REGAL THUNDER (USA) 3 b.c. Chief's Crown (USA) – Summertime 73
Showers (USA) (Raise A Native) [1996 76p: 7m⁵ 1997 7g 7g³ 10g 10m 8d⁵ 7d 8d
8m³ Oct 22] good-topped colt: fair maiden handicapper: stays 1¼m: visored
(below form) twice: sold 25,000 gns, and sent to USA. *M. R. Stoute*

REGGIE BUCK (USA) 3 b. or br.c. Alleged (USA) 138 – Hello Memphis 87 d
(USA) (Super Concorde (USA) 128) [1996 NR 1997 8g² 11.9s³ 10g⁶ Oct 24]
$40,000F, IR 30,000Y: smallish, workmanlike colt: fourth foal: half-brother to
French 10.5f winner Magic Memphis (by Secreto) and a winner in USA by Mining:
dam once-raced half-sister to smart 1988 2-y-o Classic Fame: best effort when second in newcomers event at Newmarket in April, only start for L. Cumani (off course
6 months after): should stay 1½m. *R. J. O'Sullivan*

REHAAB 4 b.f. Mtoto 134 – Top Treat (USA) 101 (Topsider (USA)) [1996 72: 59
8m² 10m* 10.1m 11.9f⁵ 1997 a12g⁵ a11g a10g⁶ a10g⁵ 10m 10g⁶ 11.8m⁵ 12g 9.7g
10m 8m² 10g² 10g⁵ 10m 12d a12g² a10s* a10g a16g³ a13g² a13g⁴ Dec 22]
workmanlike filly: modest performer: left D. Morris after thirteenth start: won minor
event at Lingfield in November, also runner-up 4 times in handicaps: stays 13f: acts
on good to firm going and equitrack: visored from eleventh start. *Miss B. Sanders*

REHEARSAL (IRE) 3 b.g. Royal Academy (USA) 130 – Yashville (Top Ville – 129) [1996 73: 6m³ 7g 7g³ 1997 9m Apr 9] useful-looking gelding: fair form on last of 3 starts as 2-y-o: broke leg on reappearance: should have stayed beyond 7f. *C. A. Cyzer*

REIMEI 8 b.g. Top Ville 129 – Brilliant Reay 74 (Ribero 126) [1996 74: 12g⁵ – 12m* 13.3f 16.2m 12g 1997 12g 12.1m 14m 10m 12d Oct 21] tall, angular gelding: one-time fair handicapper: little form at 8 yrs, leaving R. Akehurst after reappearance: blinkered last 3 starts. *K. C. Comerford*

REINE WELLS (IRE) 4 b.f. Sadler's Wells (USA) 132 – Rivoltade (USA) (Sir 104 Ivor 135) [1996 107: 10m⁴ 12g² 12m 12d³ 12v* 1997 10g⁶ 11s³ 12f⁴ 13.5g⁵ 12v⁴ 10.5s⁵ Nov 11] good-topped filly: useful performer: generally ran creditably in pattern/listed races in 1997, but disappointing in Princess Royal Stakes at Ascot (tended to carry head high) in October: probably stays 13.5f: acts on good to firm and heavy ground. *P. Bary, France*

REINHARDT (IRE) 4 b.g. Bluebird (USA) 125 – Rhein Bridge 107 (Rheingold 46 137) [1996 81d: 8d³ 12d³ 8f⁵ 8m⁴ 8g 12f⁴ 10.1f 8.3m 9.9g 11f⁶ 1997 5m* 7.5g³ 6g 8g⁶ 7.6m⁶ 5m⁶ 6g 6m 9.2m 7.5g⁴ 10.4s Sep 4] angular gelding: good mover: poor handicapper: won at Beverley in June on debut for current stable: mainly creditable efforts subsequently: had form over 1¼m as 2-y-o, but clearly effective at strongly-run 5f: acts on good to firm and dead going: tried blinkered and visored: formerly reluctant. *D. Nicholls*

REJECTED 2 b.c. (Apr 11) Puissance 110 – Dalby Dancer 71 (Bustiki) [1997 5f⁴ 79 5m* 5g⁵ 5.2f 6m⁴ 6d³ 6g Oct 18] 3,600F, 21,000Y: tall colt: has scope: good mover: third foal: half-brother to 3-y-o Yabint El Sultan: dam stayed well: fair performer: won maiden at Haydock in June: often faced stiffish tasks afterwards, but ran well in nursery penultimate start: stays 6f: acts on good to firm and dead ground, possibly not on firm. *R. Hannon*

RELATE 2 b.f. (Apr 2) Distant Relative 128 – Pulga (Blakeney 126) [1997 5g⁵ 69 5.2f 5.1g² 5m⁵ 6d⁴ 8.2g² 7d Oct 13] 11,000Y: sturdy filly: third foal: half-sister to 3-y-o Marsh Marigold: dam unraced: fair maiden: second at Chepstow and Nottingham: should stay beyond 1m. *Martyn Meade*

REMAADI SUN 5 gr.g. Cadeaux Genereux 131 – Catch The Sun (Kalaglow 132) 87 [1996 89: 6s 10d³ 10s⁶ 10m* 11.9m* 12g⁵ 12m⁶ 16.1m 11.9g⁴ 18.7m 13.9m⁵ 11.9f⁵ 13.3m⁴ 12g 1997 10m 12g 10.3d² 11.9g² 10m 10s 11.9g 11.9g² 13.3f³ 12s⁵ 12m⁵ 11.9g³ 12g⁶ 12m⁶ 12g Sep 28] workmanlike, quite good-topped gelding: carries condition: has a round action: fairly useful handicapper: creditable efforts when placed at 5 yrs: effective at 1¼m to 1¾m: acts on firm and dead going: effective blinkered/visored or not: has run well when edgy: usually set plenty to do and suited by strongly-run race. *M. D. I. Usher*

REMEMBER FRIMLEY 2 b.f. (Apr 3) Presidium 124 – Frimley Dancer 54 – (Northern Tempest (USA) 120) [1997 a7g⁶ 5m a5g Oct 4] 2,700 2-y-o: third foal: dam sprinter: no promise, including in sellers. *C. J. Hill*

RENATA'S PRINCE (IRE) 4 b.g. Prince Rupert (FR) 121 – Maria Renata 68 (Jaazeiro (USA) 127) [1996 77d: 12.5d⁶ 9m⁵ 9m* 10g⁴ 9g 8d 10f a10g a9.4g 1997 10g 10g⁵ 10m² 9d³ 8.1d* 8.5d² 9m Jul 31] quite attractive gelding: fair handicapper: won at Sandown in July: something possibly amiss final start: effective at 1m to 1¼m: acts on good to firm and dead ground: blinkered (out of form) once. *K. R. Burke*

RENNYHOLME 6 ch.g. Rich Charlie 117 – Jacqui Joy 63 (Music Boy 124) 54 [1996 –, a60d: a5g⁴ a6g a5g² a5g³ a5g³ 5g a5g a5g³ a5g³ a5g a7g a5g a5g 1997 a47 a5g a5g a5g⁵ a5g⁵ a5g a5g⁴ a5g 5m⁵ 5f⁶ 5f⁶ 5g 5m² 5g 6m 5g a5g⁴ a5g⁴ a6g Dec 26] close-coupled gelding: modest handicapper: trained by J. Hetherton first 8 starts: best effort at 6 yrs when unlucky second at Beverley in July: best form at 5f: acts on firm ground and the all-weather: effective blinkered/visored or not: inconsistent. *A. B. Mulholland*

RENO'S TREASURE (USA) 4 ch.f. Beau Genius (CAN) – Ligia M (USA) – (Noholme Jr (USA)) [1996 –: 7g 8.2f⁵ 10m⁵ 10.1m⁵ 10d 1997 a12g⁵ Feb 5] tall filly: little sign of ability. *John A. Harris*

RENOWN 5 b.g. Soviet Star (USA) 128 – Starlet 119 (Teenoso (USA) 135) [1996 65
75, a80: a10g a10g* 10m 11.9f* 9g 10g² a12g 1997 a10g² a10g⁵ 10m 11.9f³ May 23] a77
small, angular gelding: fair handicapper: effective at 1¼m to 1½m: acts on firm
ground and the all-weather: usually races prominently. *Lord Huntingdon*

RENZO (IRE) 4 b.g. Alzao (USA) 117 – Watership (USA) (Foolish Pleasure 89
(USA)) [1996 84§: 10g⁴ 10.2f² 12m³ 10m² 14m³ 11f* 1997 12g 14m⁵ 14g⁴ 14m
12m² 14.4m* 16.2g³ Sep 27] strong gelding: fairly useful handicapper: won (for first
time) at Kempton in September: stays 2m: acts on firm going, yet to race on softer
than good: sometimes slowly away: tried blinkered: hasn't always looked genuine:
sold 26,000 gns in October. *Mrs A. J. Perrett*

REPERTORY 4 b.g. Anshan 119 – Susie's Baby (Balidar 133) [1996 89: 5g² 5g 92
6m 5g 6s 1997 5.2g* 5.1m⁴ 5g 5g 6g 5.1s 5s³ 5.6m 5v⁴ 5d⁶ 5g⁴ Oct 25] tall, angular
gelding: fairly useful handicapper: won at Newbury in April: very good efforts last 2
starts: best form at 5f: acts on good to firm and heavy going. *M. S. Saunders*

REPOSE (IRE) 2 gr.f. (May 14) Posen (USA) – Dream Trader (Auction Ring –
(USA) 123) [1997 6m 7.9s Sep 3] IR 850Y: smallish, angular filly: half-sister to
several winners, including Irish 3-y-o 1m to 9f winner Lady Oranswell (by Nordico)
and 9-y-o Dream Carrier: dam unraced: well beaten in maidens. *G. R. Oldroyd*

REPTON 2 ch.g. (Feb 6) Rock City 120 – Hasty Key (USA) (Key To The Mint –
(USA)) [1997 7d 6s⁶ 5m Oct 28] 11,500Y: closely related to 6-y-o Cotteir Chief
(winner at 6f, at 2 yrs, to 1½m) and half-brother to several winners, including useful
1989 2-y-o 7f winner Cutting Note (by Diesis): dam won up to 9f in USA: slowly
away and no form in maidens. *Mrs A. Swinbank*

REQUESTED 10 b.g. Rainbow Quest (USA) 134 – Melody Hour 105 (Sing Sing –
134) [1996 55: 14d⁵ 16.2f² 16.2m 14.1d⁴ 14.4g 16m² 1997 14.1m 16.2s Jun 21]
sparely-made gelding: poor mover: formerly fairly useful staying handicapper:
last both starts at 10 yrs, trained on reappearance by R. Ingram: tried blinkered.
M. D. I. Usher

REQUESTOR 2 br.c. (Mar 26) Distinctly North (USA) 115 – Bebe Altesse 82
(GER) (Alpenkonig (GER)) [1997 5v³ 6m² 6m² 6m² 7d³ 6g Oct 18] 12,500F: strong,
good-bodied colt: has scope: has fluent action: half-brother to several winners,
including 1m and 9f winner Akura (by Vision): dam won in Germany: fairly useful
maiden: ran well in face of stiff task in Two-Year-Old Trophy at Redcar final start:
should stay 7f: sure to win a race. *J. G. FitzGerald*

RESERVATION ROCK (IRE) 6 ch.g. Ballad Rock 122 – Crazyfoot 76 –
(Luthier 126) [1996 NR 1997 12m a9.4g Dec 6] tall gelding: modest form around 1m
at 3 yrs: showed nothing in handicaps in 1997. *R. Simpson*

RESIST THE FORCE (USA) 7 br.g. Shadeed (USA) 135 – Countess Tully 71
112 (Hotfoot 126) [1996 NR 1997 a8g⁴ a8g* 7d 8m⁴ a8g⁴ 6m² 6m* 6m* 6g³ 6m⁴ 6g
a7s³ a7g⁵ Dec 10] big, lengthy gelding: winning hurdler in 1996: fair performer: won
handicap at Lingfield in May and minor event and handicap at Brighton in July:
effective at 6f to easy 1m: acts on good to firm going and equitrack: best held up.
C. A. Cyzer

RESOUNDER (USA) 4 b.g. Explodent (USA) – Rub Al Khali (USA) (Mr 90
Prospector (USA)) [1996 –: 6m⁴ 6m⁶ 7.1g⁴ 7g 7m 1997 7m 7.9g 8m⁴ Aug 21]
useful-looking gelding: useful performer at 2 yrs: best effort since when eighth of 25
to Tregaron in Victoria Cup at Ascot on reappearance: ran as if something amiss next
time: stays 7f, probably not 1m: has raced mainly on good going or firmer: visored
final start at 4 yrs. *J. H. M. Gosden*

RESPECTABLE JONES 11 ch.g. Tina's Pet 121 – Jonesee 64 (Dublin Taxi) –
[1996 –, a54d: a7g⁴ a6g³ a6g³ a6g 5f 5.9f 6d⁶ 7f a7g 1997 a7g a6g 6m Apr 22] a light
of other days. *R. Hollinshead*

RESPOND 2 b.f. (Feb 24) Reprimand 122 – Kina (USA) (Bering 136) [1997 6s 5g 67
7d³ a7g³ 7g 7s 7.3g⁶ a8g* Dec 10] well-grown filly: third reported foal: half-sister to a75
a winner in Denmark by Prince Daniel: dam never ran: fair performer: improved
effort to win nursery at Lingfield: should stay beyond 1m: acts on equitrack and good
to soft ground. *G. L. Moore*

RES

RESTLESS SPIRIT (USA) 3 b.c. Sheikh Albadou 128 – Wayward Lass (USA) 89
(Hail The Pirates (USA) 126) [1996 83p: 6.1m⁴ 6m² 6.1s* 1997 6s 7m⁴ 6d 7s 6g²
Jul 5] robust colt: fairly useful handicapper: best effort when second at Haydock,
keeping on despite hanging right: effective at 6f/7f: acts on good to firm and soft
going: sold 26,000 gns, and sent to Macau. *M. Johnston*

RESTRUCTURE (IRE) 5 b.h. Danehill (USA) 126 – Twine (Thatching 131) 114
[1996 118: 9m⁵ 8.2m* 8f² 8m* 8m⁵ 8g⁴ 8m³ 8g 8m² 1997 9g 10d 8m 7.9g³ 7.3m² 7g⁴
8m 7m² 7m* Oct 7] big, deep-bodied horse: impresses in appearance: poor mover in
slower paces: smart performer: not quite so good in 1997 as he was, but ran creditably
when second to Decorated Hero in minor event at Newbury in July and Supreme
Stakes at Goodwood (beaten 1¼ lengths) in September, then won 4-runner minor
event at Redcar: effective at 7f to 9f: goes well on good to firm/firm going: has won
when sweating: game. *Mrs J. Cecil*

RESURRECTION (IRE) 2 b.f. (Apr 22) Midyan (USA) 124 – Tolstoya (North- 51
fields (USA)) [1997 7g 7m 5m 7d Oct 16] 13,000 2-y-o: leggy filly: half-sister to
several winners, including 3-y-o Zaretski and 4-y-o Wildwood Flower: dam Irish
2-y-o 5f winner: well beaten after debut in claimer: has tended to hang. *R. Hannon*

RETENDER (USA) 8 br.g. Storm Bird (CAN) 134 – Dandy Bury (FR) (Exbury –
138) [1996 –: a16g a12g 1997 a10g Dec 10] useful-looking gelding: one-time fair
handicapper: lightly raced and no form since 1995. *J. Pearce*

RET FREM (IRE) 4 b.g. Posen (USA) – New Light 78 (Reform 132) [1996 70: –
8.2g 11.6m³ 8.3m* 8g² 8f⁴ 8m* 8m 1997 8.3g Sep 1] well-made gelding: fair
handicapper up to 1½m at 3 yrs for M. Jarvis: off course nearly a year, tailed off only
outing in 1997: won maiden hurdle later in month. *C. Parker*

RETOTO 3 ch.f. Totem (USA) 118 – Responder 70 (Vitiges (FR) 132) [1996 49?: –
6m² 6g* 7f 6m 1997 a7g a9.4g Dec 6] won 6f seller in July, 1996: no form since.
B. J. McMath

RETURN OF AMIN 3 ch.c. Salse (USA) 128 – Ghassanah 73 (Pas de Seul 133) 92
[1996 82: 5g⁶ 6m a7g³ 6m 7m³ 6.9v* a7g* 1997 7m⁴ 6d² 6g⁴ 7.6d⁶ 7m⁵ 6d* 6s² 6g⁶
6s² 6g 7m 7g² Oct 18] angular, good-bodied colt: has a quick action: fairly useful

William Hill Trophy (Handicap), York—
Return of Amin (near side) wins the feature race on Timeform Charity Day
(which raised £145,158) from Double Action and Bishops Court

handicapper: won 19-runner William Hill Trophy at York in June by neck from Double Action: better form when second afterwards at Newcastle, York (rated stakes won by Double Action) and Newmarket: effective at 6f/7f: acts on good to firm going and fibresand, best efforts on good ground or softer: reliable. *J. D. Bethell*

RETURN TO BRIGHTON 5 b.m. Then Again 126 – Regency Brighton (Royal   37
Palace 131) [1996 51, a–: 8m² 8m* 8m⁴ 8f⁵ 8.1m 8.3m⁵ 9.2f a8g a10s 1997 a8g 8m⁶   a–
8.2m³ 8d 8g 10g 8f 8g Jun 28] rather leggy mare: poor handicapper: stays 1m: acts on good to firm ground, well beaten on all-weather. *J. M. Bradley*

REUNION (IRE) 3 br.f. Be My Guest (USA) 126 – Phylella (Persian Bold 123)   108
[1996 88?: 6m* 7f³ 1997 7g* 8m May 4] tall filly: greatly improved form to win Nell Gwyn Stakes at Newmarket in April, bursting through from rear to lead entering last 1f and beat Oh Nellie a length: failed to impress to post when tailed-off last in 1000 Guineas there 19 days later (subsequently reported to have been suffering from a bacterial infection): missed Falmouth Stakes in July with reported muscle injury: should prove effective at 1m: reportedly stays in training. *J. W. Hills*

REVENGE IS SWEET 2 b.c. (Mar 31) Absalom 128 – Welsh Secret 85 (Welsh   –
Captain 113) [1997 a5g 5.1m Jul 25] 3,000Y: second foal: half-brother to 5f winner (including at 2 yrs) Secret Voucher (by Vouchsafe): dam sprinter: behind in maidens. *B. A. McMahon*

REVERSE CHARGE 5 b.g. Teenoso (USA) 135 – Ebb And Flo 82 (Forlorn   –
River 124) [1996 NR 1997 a8g Feb 7] no worthwhile form. *D. Nicholls*

REVOQUE (IRE) 3 b.c. Fairy King (USA) – La Bella Fontana (Lafontaine   121
(USA) 117) [1996 122p: 6m* 7m* 7m* 8g* 1997 7g² 8m² 8g⁶ 8m* 8g 10g⁵ Oct 18]

The showdown between Revoque and Bahhare turned out to be more long-awaited than eagerly-anticipated and not so much a showdown as a polite shaking of hands. What had been scheduled for the Two Thousand Guineas on May 3rd took place instead at Doncaster on September 12th in the final race on the card, a class C conditions stakes. Bahhare had been absent for 364 days, Revoque for 110, and if the only other runner, Kumait, had been able to take advantage then the two top two-year-olds of 1996 would have gone through 1997 without a win between them. As it was, Revoque took home the £4,950 by beating Bahhare one and a quarter lengths. A good deal more was at stake when the two met again in the Queen Elizabeth II Stakes and Champion Stakes, but neither was able to regain their former pre-eminence. Revoque came off worse on each occasion, completing in eighth of nine and fifth of seven, well below his best. It was a disappointing end to his career and to a three-year-old season which, at its best, had been a case of nearly but not quite.

On Two Thousand Guineas day Revoque was in the line-up and the 100/30 favourite. He had been beaten favourite in the Greenham Stakes at

Sun Princess IJF Challenge Trophy, Doncaster—
the two top two-year-olds of 1996 meet at last, Revoque beating Bahhare in this minor contest

Newbury on his reappearance, going down by a head to Yalaietanee. But on the same day that Entrepreneur was galloping unnoticed at Sandown, Revoque, contrastingly, had become the subject of bullish reports after a 'brilliant' work-out at Newbury. Little went right for him in the Guineas itself. Slightly squeezed just after the stalls, Revoque started towards the back of the field. It was always going to be difficult for him from there, and from halfway until approaching the furlong marker Revoque made it look hard work. Coming seven horses wide, however, he ate up the ground late on, still closing but three quarters of a length down on Entrepreneur at the line. Disappointed enough at the time, how would connections have felt then if learning that this was to be easily the highlight of Revoque's season? The Derby (for which he was hardly the ideal type) was a possible target until a thoroughly dispirited display, both in the preliminaries and the race, in the Irish Two Thousand Guineas saw him embark on that summer break. Revoque was sick on his return from Ireland and had other problems, including a pulled muscle behind which ruled him out of the Sussex Stakes, before the return to action with Bahhare at Doncaster.

Revoque will be standing at the Morristown Lattin Stud, County Kildare, in 1998 at a fee of IR £7,500. A lengthy, good-topped colt, particularly striking among his contemporaries as a two-year-old, Revoque impressed in his physical appearance. As already mentioned, though, we were far less taken with his pre-race demeanour at the Curragh, where he had his ears flat back in the parade and was sweating and repeatedly flashing his tail at the start, and he looked similarly ill-at-ease before the Queen Elizabeth. On both of those occas-

Mr R. E. Sangster's "Revoque"

ions, he went on to run poorly. His best form in 1997 was very smart, shown in a strongly-run race over a mile in the Guineas, and he raced on only good ground or good to firm. Peter Chapple-Hyam's view in the autumn was that he was 'really a mile-and-a-quarter horse' and Revoque shaped on a number of occasions as if that might well have been the case, but he failed to prove it when given the one opportunity.

		Northern Dancer	Nearctic
	Fairy King (USA)	(b 1961)	Natalma
	(b 1982)	Fairy Bridge	Bold Reason
Revoque (IRE)		(b 1975)	Special
(b.c. 1994)		Lafontaine	Sham
	La Bella Fontana	(b 1977)	Valya
	(b 1985)	Sorebelle	Prince Tenderfoot
		(b 1974)	La Belle

Revoque's pedigree, as detailed in last year's Annual, is far from stamina-laden. It was also fairly unremarkable until Revoque came along, as illustrated by sales prices of IR 1,100 guineas as a foal and IR 54,000 guineas as a yearling for his year-younger half-sister by Distinctly North. Called North-umbrian Belle, that filly was in training with Jonjo O'Neill in the latest season but did not run. The dam, La Bella Fontana, a half-sister to the useful five-furlong to seven-furlong winner Abuzz, ran only once, as a three-year-old in a maiden race (over a mile) at Newcastle in which she finished fourth of five. *P. W. Chapple-Hyam*

REWARD 3 br.g. Highest Honor (FR) 124 – Intimate Guest 110§ (Be My Guest (USA) 126) [1996 NR 1997 8g³ 10g 7g⁶ Jun 12] 26,000Y: tall, angular gelding: fourth foal: half-brother to 3 winners, including 4-y-o French 1½m winner Guest of Anchor (by Slip Anchor): dam, May Hill winner, later untrustworthy, out of smart 1m/1¼m performer As You Desire Me: third in maiden at Kempton on debut: well beaten in similar events subsequently: should be suited by further than 1m: sold 14,000 gns in October, and joined C. Mann. *P. F. I. Cole* — 70

REWARDIA (IRE) 2 b.f. (Apr 16) Petardia 113 – Riwaya (IRE) (Nishapour (FR) 125) [1997 6g⁵ 7m³ 7m⁴ 7d⁵ 7g³ a6g Oct 4] IR 2,000F: light-framed filly: first foal: dam won in Germany and Scandinavia: fair maiden: best efforts when third at Chester in August and September: long way below form at Wolverhampton on fibresand debut: should stay 1m: visored fourth outing. *P. D. Evans* — 66 a?

REX MUNDI 5 b.g. Gunner B 126 – Rose Standish 71 (Gulf Pearl 117) [1996 68: 10g 10m 10f² 10m³ 15.8g⁴ 10.9m* 11.9d⁴ 12d⁵ 10g³ 10f³ a13g³ 1997 10.5m 12m³ 12v² 15.9m* 11.8g² 12m 10.9d⁶ 15.9g a12g* 13.8s a12g⁴ a14g a12g a12g³ a12g* Dec 26] tall, angular gelding: fair performer: won handicap at Chester in July and minor event then seller at Wolverhampton in October and December: effective at 1½m to 2m: acts on any turf/all-weather: races prominently: visored final 2 starts: game. *P. D. Evans* — 71

RHAPSODY IN BLUE (IRE) 2 b.c. (Apr 25) Magical Strike (USA) 114 – Palace Blue (IRE) (Dara Monarch 128) [1997 6g 7m 6d Oct 28] 9,000 2-y-o: close-coupled colt: second foal: half-brother to German 3-y-o 9f winner Pinella (by Diga-mist): dam unraced: no promise in maidens: has been bandaged. *Andrew Turnell* — –

RHAPSODY IN WHITE (IRE) 3 b.g. Contract Law (USA) 108 – Lux Aeterna (Sandhurst Prince 128) [1996 70?, a?: 6m 7f² a8g⁴ 1997 8g³ 8f* 10g³ 12s⁶ 10m 12m 10m 8.2s Oct 15] smallish gelding: fair performer: landed odds in 4-runner maiden at Brighton in May, carrying head high under pressure: best effort in handicap at Goodwood next time, showed nothing thereafter: stays 1¼m: blinkered last 3 outings. *M. A. Jarvis* — 77 d

RHEINBOLD 3 br.g. Never So Bold 135 – Rheinbloom 66 (Rheingold 137) [1996 –p: 7g 1997 a8g² 12d* 12m 12g² 14d 11m Nov 4] strong gelding: shows knee action: won weak maiden at Musselburgh in May: easily best effort when second in handicap at Thirsk in August: stays 1½m. *T. J. Etherington* — 80

RHEIN HILL (IRE) 2 b.c. (May 20) Danehill (USA) 126 – Rhein Bridge 107   71
(Rheingold 137) [1997 7.1g 7g⁴ Oct 7] 10,000Y: small colt: half-brother to several
winners, easily best of them Gold Cup and Irish St Leger second Tyrone Bridge (by
Kings Lake): dam won Lancashire Oaks: improved on debut effort when keeping-on
fourth in maiden at Warwick: should be well suited by 1¼m+. *P. W. Harris*

RHEIN LADY 3 b.f. Gildoran 123 – Houston Belle 59 (Milford 119) [1996 NR   –
1997 9.7m⁴ Sep 26] sixth foal: dam, maiden on flat, winning hurdler: stayed on into
remote fourth in 7-runner maiden at Folkestone. *R. Rowe*

RHINEFIELD BEAUTY (IRE) 2 ch.f. (May 2) Shalford (IRE) 124§ –   52
Humble Mission (Shack (USA) 118) [1997 5f⁴ 5g⁵ 5g⁶ 5.2f 5g 5m⁴ 6s⁵ Oct 14]
10,500Y: fifth foal: half-sister to 3-y-o Young Bigwig, best of 3 winners:
dam placed over 7f and 1m in Ireland: modest maiden: stays 6f. *J. S. Goldie*

RIBBLE ASSEMBLY 2 ch.g. (Apr 26) Presidium 124 – Spring Sparkle 95   49
(Lord Gayle (USA) 124) [1997 6d² 7g² 7g 6m 8m Nov 4] 3,800Y: smallish gelding:
fifth foal: half-brother to a winner abroad by Robellino: dam, disappointing maiden
best at 6f/7f, out of half-sister to Annie Edge, dam of Selkirk: poor maiden: second in
sellers: stays 1m: slowly away last 3 starts. *R. A. Fahey*

RIBBLESDALE 2 b.f. (Jan 23) Northern Park (USA) 107 – Tarib 108 (Habitat   73 p
134) [1997 6d 6d⁶ 8s⁴ Nov 8] IR 17,000Y: rangy filly: eighth foal: half-sister to 7f
winner Tajdid (by Caerleon): dam sprinter: progressive maiden: races as though she'll stay beyond 1m: should
improve further. *J. L. Dunlop*

RIBBONLETTA 3 b.f. Goldsmiths' Hall 100 – Ribbon Lady (Kinglet 98) [1996   –
NR 1997 9.2d⁴ 12.1m⁶ Jul 11] first foal: dam tailed off over hurdles: has shown
nothing in claimers. *Miss L. A. Perratt*

RICARDO 3 b.g. Sanglamore (USA) 126 – Nurica (USA) (Nureyev (USA) 131)   83
[1996 NR 1997 10g³ 10g² 10s² 10g² Oct 24] big, deep-girthed gelding: first foal:
dam, thrice-raced French maiden, half-sister to smart French colt The Scout (at up to
1½m) out of Prix Marcel Boussac winner Tropicaro: fairly useful maiden: should
stay beyond 1¼m: unraced on going firmer than good: sold (to join Mrs Pitman)
46,000 gns in October. *R. Charlton*

RICCARTON 4 b.g. Nomination 125 – Legendary Dancer 90 (Shareef Dancer   59
(USA) 135) [1996 52: 8g 8g 8g 8.1d⁵ 7s³ 8.1m³ 6.9f² 8.3g³ 8m⁶ 1997 8g³ 10.3d³ 10g⁴
8g⁵ 8.1m⁶ 9.9g* 10g² 12s⁴ Oct 16] big gelding: modest handicapper: won 18-runner
apprentice maiden at Beverley in August: seemed not quite to stay 1½m in testing
conditions final start: acts on firm and soft ground: blinkered (pulled hard) fifth start:
often raced hung left: consistent. *P. Calver*

RICHARD HOUSE LAD 4 b.c. Warrshan (USA) 117 – Sirenivo (USA) 113   36
(Sir Ivor 135) [1996 49, a–: 8.2d a12g⁶ 8g⁴ 8m 8.2m⁴ 8.2m⁵ 8m⁶ 8m 10g⁶ 8m* 8.2g   a–
a8g a9.4g 1997 8.2m⁵ 8g 8f 8m Aug 11] smallish colt: poor handicapper: stays 1m:
acts on good to firm ground. *R. Hollinshead*

RICH CHOICE 2 gr.f. (Apr 12) Presidium 124 – Gratclo 65 (Belfort (FR) 89)   69
[1997 5f⁴ 5s³ 5m⁴ 6.5m 6m² Oct 28] 12,000Y: leggy filly: good mover: fourth foal:
half-sister to 3-y-o Rich Ground: dam seemed suited by 7f: fair maiden: good second
in nursery at Redcar final start: probably a sprinter. *J. D. Bethell*

RICH GLOW 6 b.g. Rich Charlie 117 – Mayglow (Sparkling Boy 110) [1996 67:   62
5s 6g 5.9d 6m 6m 6d 6m 5m³ 5d* 5g⁶ 5g 6m⁴ 5m⁵ 5m* 5f 5m⁶ 6f 5m⁶ 5.1g 5m 1997
6m 5g 5m 5d 5s* 6m 5f 5g³ 5g² 5g 5m³ 5m⁶ a5g 6g⁵ 5m⁶ 6g 5d 5m 5m 5s 5g Oct 22]
leggy, angular gelding: modest handicapper: gained fifth course win at Ayr in May:
in-and-out form after: effective at 5f and 6f: acts on firm and soft ground, well beaten
on fibresand: effective blinkered or not: has worn tongue strap: held up, and suited by
strongly-run race. *N. Bycroft*

RICH GROUND 3 gr.c. Common Grounds 118 – Gratclo 65 (Belfort (FR) 89)   106
[1996 96: 6g 6m* 6g* 6g⁴ 6m 1997 7g³ 7m² May 3] close-coupled colt: has a fluent
action: useful performer: third to Hidden Meadow in Free Handicap at Newmarket
(kept on strongly) and 5½ lengths second of 6 to Desert King in Tetrarch Stakes at the
Curragh in spring: should stay 1m: raced only on good/good to firm going: reportedly
sold to race in USA. *J. D. Bethell*

RICH IN LOVE (IRE)   3 b.f. Alzao (USA) 117 – Chief's Quest (USA) (Chief's   81
Crown (USA)) [1996 95: 6g² 6m* 6g⁵ 7.1m⁵ 7m² 8m⁴ 7m 1997 8.1d 10m 10m⁶ 9g⁵
11.6g⁴ 10m 7m* 7g 7m 7f Sep 11] fairly useful handicapper: best effort at 3 yrs when
5-length winner at Yarmouth in August: best form at 7f/1m: acts on good to firm
ground: blinkered sixth start: inconsistent. *C. A. Cyzer*

RICHMOND HILL   2 b.c. (Apr 22) Sabrehill (USA) 120 – Mrs Warren (USA)   –
(Hail To Reason) [1997 7m Oct 2] half-brother to Irish 7f winner No Dreaming (by
In Reality) and a winner in USA: dam high-class winner from 5.5f (at 2 yrs) to 9f in
USA: 50/1 and backward, towards rear in maiden at Newmarket. *B. W. Hills*

RICKENBACKER (IRE)   3 b.c. Bluebird (USA) 125 – Sodium's Niece   99
(Northfields (USA)) [1996 NR 1997 7.1s* 9.2g³ 10g⁴ 10.3d Aug 29] IR 120,000Y:
brother to Italian 9f and 1¼m winner Shariba and half-brother to 6f (at 2 yrs) and 9f
winner Danzarin (by Kings Lake): dam, lightly raced, third at 8.5f at 2 yrs in Ireland:
won maiden at Haydock in May: useful form in minor events at Hamilton and
Newmarket (behind Annus Mirabilis) next 2 starts, ran poorly final one: stays 1¼m:
sold only 4,000 gns in October. *P. W. Chapple-Hyam*

RICKY TICKY TAVIE (USA)   3 b.c. Dixieland Band (USA) – Save The Doe   90
(USA) (Spend A Buck (USA)) [1996 97p: 7g² 1997 7m* 8s³ Oct 13] smallish colt:
second to Kahal in minor event at Ascot only outing at 2 yrs: reportedly suffered from
serious sinus problem in the spring: workmanlike in landing odds in Redcar maiden
in September: better form when third of 5 to Right Wing in minor event at Ayr 2½
weeks later: likely to prove best up to 1m: sent to UAE. *D. R. Loder*

RICO SUAVE (IRE)   2 b.g. (Feb 7) Persian Bold 123 – Ballet Review (IRE)   87 p
(Sadler's Wells (USA) 132) [1997 6.1d⁴ a7g² 7m* 8g 8m* Sep 25] 20,000Y:
good-topped gelding: has scope: third foal: dam twice-raced (in Ireland) granddaughter of Irish 1000 Guineas runner-up Bold Fantasy, herself dam of Lowther
winner Kingscote: fairly useful performer: won maiden at Ayr in July and nursery at
Goodwood in September: will probably stay 1¼m: sold 45,000 gns in October: type
to progress further at 3 yrs. *Sir Mark Prescott*

RIDAIYMA (IRE)   3 b.f. Kahyasi 130 – Riyda 101 (Be My Guest (USA) 126)   107 p
[1996 9m³ 12.1m* 12g* 12m⁶ 12g* 12s Nov 8] rangy, unfurnished filly:
fifth foal: half-sister to 3 winners in Ireland, including Riyama (1¼m, by Doyoun):
dam, 1m and 1¼m winner, half-sister to smart Irish performer at up to 1¾m Rayseka:
useful performer: won maiden at Chepstow in June, handicap at Kempton in August
and Tote Sunday Special Handicap (awarded race after being squeezed on turn when
¾-length second to Taufan's Melody) at Ascot in September: acted as pacemaker in
Prix Vermeille on fourth outing and did well to be beaten only 8 lengths by Queen
Maud: well below best in November Handicap at Doncaster final start: needs test
at 1½m and will be suited by further: acts on good to firm going: may well prove
capable of better still at 4 yrs. *L. M. Cumani*

Tote Sunday Special Handicap, Ascot—
Ridaiyma (dark colours) gets the race after Taufan's Melody (noseband) is demoted

RIDGEWAY (IRE)   2 b.c. (Mar 26) Indian Ridge 123 – Regal Promise (Pitskelly   71 p
122) [1997 7m 7m Sep 30] IR 45,000F, 100,000Y: tall, useful-looking colt: ninth
foal: brother to a winner in Hong Kong and half-brother to several winners, including
fairly useful 1987 2-y-o 6f winner Butlers Wharf (by Burslem), later an ungenuine
middle-distance performer: dam Irish 11f winner: fair form in maiden at Leicester
and valuable sales race at Newmarket: looked weak at 2 yrs, and likely to do better in
due course. *G. Wragg*

RIFIFI   4 ch.g. Aragon 118 – Bundled Up (USA) (Sharpen Up 127) [1996 60: 6.9f   84 +
6m⁵ 6g⁴ 6m 1997 a5g* a5g* a6g⁵ 5g 5g⁵ 7m 6m³ 6g* 6d 6g* 6g* 6d 6.1g⁵ 6d 6.1d
Oct 30] small, sturdy gelding: poor mover: reportedly had operation on knee after
3-y-o career: fairly useful performer, much improved in 1997: won maiden at Lingfield and handicaps on same course and at Windsor, Newmarket and Goodwood
between February and August: stiff tasks and probably flattered last 2 starts: stays 6f
well: acts on equitrack, raced mainly between good to firm and dead ground on turf:
has worn bandages. *R. Ingram*

RIGHT CROSS JONNY (USA)   2 ch.c. (Feb 19) Regal Classic (CAN) –   –
Bounteous (USA) (Master Derby (USA)) [1997 8.5g 8m Sep 24] $25,000Y: half-
brother to several winners in North America, including Canadian sprint stakes
winner Dargai (by It's Freezing): dam unraced half-sister to smart French 1975 2-y-o
Wood Green: tailed off in maidens. *P. W. Chapple-Hyam*

RIGHT MAN   3 gr.c. Robellino (USA) 127 – High Matinee (Shirley Heights 130)   86 p
[1996 –p: 6g⁵ 6m 6m 1997 10.8m⁶ 9.7m⁴ 11.6s* 14.1g* 16.2s² 16.4d* 14m⁶ Aug 2]
sturdy, close-coupled colt: most progressive handicapper: won at Windsor and Nottingham in May and Sandown in July (by 10 lengths): unlucky sixth at Goodwood
final start: will stay beyond 2m: acts on soft and good to firm ground: reported to
have had a set-back whilst being prepared for the Cesarewitch but can continue on
upgrade at 4 yrs. *G. Lewis*

RIGHT TUNE   3 b.f. Green Desert (USA) 127 – Triste Oeil (USA) 103 (Raise A   92
Cup (USA)) [1996 81p: 6g 7m* 8d⁴ 7g² 1997 8g 8s³ 8d 8g² 8.1d⁶ 9m* 8g* Jul 30]
big, good-bodied filly: has a fluent, round action: fairly useful handicapper: won at
Lingfield and Doncaster in July: stays 9f: possibly best on good going or firmer: goes
well with forcing tactics: sent to Australia. *B. Hanbury*

RIGHT WING (IRE)   3 b.c. In The Wings 128 – Nekhbet 74 (Artaius (USA)   98
129) [1996 67p: 7.1v³ 1997 11g 8m³ 8s* 8.1g 8f³ 8s* 9g Oct 25] smallish,
useful-looking colt: useful performer: won minor events at Ascot in June and Ayr in
October: rare modest effort in handicap final start: should stay 1¼m: acts on any
going: has rather high head carriage: consistent: joined J. Dunlop. *Major W. R. Hern*

RIGHTY HO   3 b.g. Reprimand 122 – Challanging 95 (Mill Reef (USA) 141)   76
[1996 60: 6d 7.9g 7.5m⁴ 8f 1997 8.5m 7m⁵ 8g⁴ 8.3g⁶ 8s* 9m³ 8.1g⁶ 10.1g* 10g²
10.9d 10f a10g Nov 13] tall, leggy gelding: fair handicapper: won at Salisbury
(amateurs) in June and Epsom (ladies) in August: needs good test at 1m and stays
1¼m: probably acts on any turf, ran poorly on equitrack: visored last 6 starts: joined
W. H. Tinning. *P. T. Walwyn*

RILEY   2 b.c. (Mar 2) Komaite (USA) – Miss Calculate 67 (Mummy's Game 120)   69
[1997 6.1d 7m³ 7.5d 8g 7f⁴ Sep 28] 100,000Y: first foal: dam 6f and 7f winner: fair
maiden: ran creditably in blinkers in nursery final start: may prove best short of 1m.
R. Charlton

RIMOUSKI   9 b.h. Sure Blade (USA) 130 – Rimosa's Pet 109 (Petingo 135) [1996   – §
NR 1997 a11g Jan 10] poor staying handicapper on flat in 1994: reluctant to race at
Southwell (amateurs) on only flat outing since: tried visored. *B. R. Cambidge*

RING DANCER   2 b.c. (Mar 22) Polar Falcon (USA) 126 – Ring Cycle 64   92 p
(Auction Ring (USA) 123) [1997 6d* 6.1d² Oct 30] 11,000Y: useful-looking colt:
good walker: second foal: half-brother to 3-y-o Farley Green: dam 6f winner from 2
starts at 2 yrs: made taking debut in Ripon maiden, beating Cease Fire by 3 lengths:
ran well when 1½ lengths second of 6 to Late Night Out in minor event at Nottingham 2 months later, disputing lead and battling on: type do better again at 3 yrs.
P. J. Makin

RINGLEADER   2 b.g. (Jan 30) Magic Ring (IRE) 115 – Kinlet Vision (IRE) 56   69
(Vision (USA)) [1997 a6g⁴ 6d⁵ 6d 7g³ 7.3m 6m 8m⁵ 7d 8m* Nov 1] 20,000Y: leggy
gelding: first foal: dam 2-y-o sprint winner, also successful over hurdles: fair form:
won large-field seller at Newmarket by head from Blue Zola, rallying: may stay
beyond 1m: unraced on extremes of going: has run creditably in blinkers: joined
N. Tinkler. *P. F. I. Cole*

RING THE CHIEF   5 b.g. Chief Singer 131 – Lomond Ring (Lomond (USA)   44
128) [1996 43: a7g a8.5g⁵ a8.5g a7g⁶ a7g² a7g⁵ a8.5g³ 10g³ 1997 a8g a8g a7g⁵ a8g³
a8.5g³ a7g* a6g³ a6g⁴ 7s 10g⁶ 9g⁶ a7g* a6g 10m³ 7d* 8.3m⁵ 10m⁴ 8m⁴ a6g Nov 24]
poor handicapper: won amateur/apprentice events at Southwell in February and June
(seller) and Salisbury in August: effective at 7f to 1¼m: acts on fibresand, firm and
dead ground, possibly not soft. *M. D. I. Usher*

RING THE RAFTERS   2 b.f. (May 14) Batshoof 122 – Soprano 112 (Kris 135)   –
[1997 5.2g⁵ Apr 19] useful-looking filly: eighth foal: half-sister to 3 winners,
including fairly useful 1992 2-y-o 1m winner Zenith (by Shirley Heights) and 1½m
winner Trumpet (by Dominion): dam, 1m winner, closely related to smart 1m/1¼m
performer Enharmonic: joint favourite but green, slow-starting fifth in maiden at
Newbury (attended by 2 handlers): joined W.Haggas. *I. A. Balding*

RINUS MAGIC   4 ch.g. Timeless Times (USA) 99 – Callace 51 (Royal Palace   –
131) [1996 NR 1997 a8.5g a9.4g⁵ 10m 8g May 12] no worthwhile form. *E. J. Alston*

RIO (IRE)   2 b.g. (Apr 19) Superpower 113 – Apocalypse (Auction Ring (USA)   67 d
123) [1997 5m⁶ 5m³ a6g 6d a8.5g 6d Oct 20] 14,000 2-y-o: workmanlike gelding:
half-brother to irresolute 5f (at 2 yrs) and 1m winner Lars Porsena (by Trojan Fen)
and 5f winner Cellito (by Flash of Steel): dam French 1m winner from good family:
fair form second start, but largely disappointing. *J. Berry*

RIOJA   2 ch.c. (Feb 5) Anshan 119 – Executive Flare (Executive Man 119) [1997   72
7g² 7m³ 6m⁴ 6d 7s⁵ Nov 8] 1,700F: tall, useful-looking colt: first foal: dam placed in
Italy: fair maiden: ran creditably in nursery at Doncaster final start: will stay 1m: acts
on good to firm and soft ground. *T. P. Tate*

RIOT   2 b.c. (Feb 25) Fairy King (USA) – Lucia Tarditi (FR) (Crystal Glitters   61 p
(USA) 127) [1997 6g Oct 24] sturdy, good-bodied colt: second reported foal: dam
Italian 2-y-o 7f listed winner: 10/1, considerably handled when over 8 lengths eighth
to Mister Rambo in maiden at Newbury, starting slowly and running on near finish:
type to do better at 3 yrs. *J. H. M. Gosden*

RISADA (IRE)   2 b.f. (Mar 1) Lahib (USA) 129 – Sparkish (IRE) (Persian Bold   68 ?
123) [1997 6m 6.9m 7.6d³ 7m 8d Oct 20] IR 6,000F, 26,000Y: first foal: dam
unraced: form only when third in maiden at Lingfield in August: virtually pulled up
final start: sold only 3,800 gns in October. *D. R. Loder*

RISCATTO (USA)   3 b.g. Red Ransom (USA) – Ultima Cena (USA) (Leonardo   47
Da Vinci (FR)) [1996 –, a54?: 6g⁶ a7g² a7g⁴ 7.3m 7.1m 1997 a8.5g³ 10m* 9.7m   a57
13.1m 11.6m a10g 12m Oct 6] tall, plain gelding: modest performer at best: well
beaten after winning weak selling handicap at Nottingham in April: stays 1¼m: acts
on good to firm ground and the all-weather: tried blinkered: carries head high.
W. R. Muir

RISE ABOVE (IRE)   3 b.f. Simply Great (FR) 122 – La Tanque (USA) (Last   –
Raise (USA)) [1996 NR 1997 8.2d Jun 23] IR 1,000F: fifth foal: half-sister to 4-y-o
The Barnsley Belle: dam Irish 5f winner: no promise in Nottingham maiden. *T. Hind*

RISE 'N SHINE   3 ch.f. Night Shift (USA) – Clunk Click 72 (Star Appeal 133)   –
[1996 67: 6m⁶ 5f² 5m³ 6g² 5m² 5f³ 5m 1997 6s 5.3f⁵ 6g 5.1m 5.3f⁵ 5.3m 5m 6f Sep
18] workmanlike filly: fair maiden at 2 yrs: well held in 1997. *C. A. Cyzer*

RISE UP SINGING   9 ch.g. Noalto 120 – Incarnadine 67 (Hot Spark 126) [1996   –
49: 6m 7g 8g 7g² 8m 7.6f³ 7.6m 1997 7d 7g 7m 7m Oct 4] formerly fairly useful, and
a standing dish at Newmarket: on the downgrade, and no form in 1997. *W. J. Musson*

RISING DOUGH (IRE)   5 br.g. Dowsing (USA) 124 – Shortning Bread 83   72 §
(Blakeney 126) [1996 74: 9.7m 12m 10.1m* 12g⁴ 11.9f² 10.1g³ 10m⁴ 12m 1997
10.3m 11.9m⁴ a10g⁶ 11.5s² 10.1d* 11.9f⁵ Jul 16] workmanlike gelding: fair handi-

capper: won at Epsom in July: probably stayed 1½m: acted on firm ground and soft: visored once: tended to edge left: inconsistent: dead. *G. L. Moore*

RISING MANE   2 b.c. (Feb 12) Reprimand 122 – Petastra 62 (Petoski 135) [1997   –
7d⁶ Oct 27] 6,500Y: second foal: dam lightly-raced maiden half-sister to smart middle-distance performer Lord of The Field: 25/1 and green, remote sixth of 9 in maiden at Lingfield, slowly away and not given hard time: joined Miss Gay Kelleway. *D. R. C. Elsworth*

RISING OF THE MOON (IRE)   2 gr.f. (Feb 1) Warning 136 – Dazzlingly   82
Radiant 81 (Try My Best (USA) 130) [1997 5m* 5m* 6g Jul 8] IR 4,100F, 18,000Y: close-coupled filly: has a quick action: fourth foal: sister to fairly useful Irish 3-y-o 6f winner Alarme Bell: dam 6f winner from family of Poule d'Essai des Pouliches winner Danseuse du Soir: won maiden at Doncaster and minor event at Warwick in spring: absent 3 months, behind in Cherry Hinton Stakes at Newmarket, tending to hang left: should stay at least 6f. *R. Hannon*

RISING SPRAY   6 ch.g. Waajib 121 – Rose Bouquet 78 (General Assembly   75
(USA)) [1996 66: 11.4m⁵ 10.8m 14f³ 16.2m 12m⁶ 12m* 12m* 10.2g² 12m² 1997 12m* 14m* 13.3g 12m³ 11.7m³ 16d 14.4m⁴ Sep 21] quite good-topped gelding: has a quick action: fair handicapper: better than ever in 1997, winning at Folkestone (third course-and-distance success) in April and Salisbury in May: effective at 1½m/ 1¾m: acts on good to firm and dead going: sometimes slowly away, and usually held up. *C. A. Horgan*

RISKING   4 b.f. Risk Me (FR) 127 – Dark Kristal (IRE) 66 (Gorytus (USA) 132)   –
[1996 48: 7d 6f³ 5f a5g a5g a7s 1997 8f 8g 10.8g Oct 7] good-topped filly: poor maiden: well beaten in 1997, trained on reappearance by M. Channon. *R. J. Price*

RISK ME TOO   3 b.c. Risk Me (FR) 127 – Mandrake Madam 88 (Mandrake   –
Major 122) [1996 NR 1997 a6g⁵ Mar 14] 4,400F, 8,000Y: third reported foal: dam barely stayed 6f: no real promise in maiden at Southwell. *P. W. Harris*

RISKNOWT GETNOWT   2 b.g. (May 9) Ron's Victory (USA) 129 – Scottish   –
Tina (Scottish Reel 123) [1997 a5g a6f⁶ 7m 7d 8m 6.1g Sep 28] 5,200 2-y-o: close-coupled gelding: first foal: dam, no worthwhile form, out of half-sister to Middle Park winner and 2000 Guineas second Mattaboy: little sign of ability, including in sellers: tried blinkered. *T. Wall*

RISKY FLIGHT   3 ch.g. Risk Me (FR) 127 – Stairway To Heaven (IRE) 74   –
(Godswalk (USA) 130) [1996 –: 5s 5m⁶ 5f a5g 5m 1997 6g 5m 7g 5m 10m 10m Sep 22] plain, angular gelding: no worthwhile form: tried blinkered. *A. Smith*

RISKY GIRL   2 ro.f. (Apr 12) Risk Me (FR) 127 – Jove's Voodoo (USA) 74   62 +
(Northern Jove (CAN)) [1997 6g* 5.9g Jul 5] 8,600 2-y-o: half-sister to several winners, including 7.5f winner Brightness (by Elegant Air) and 1½m winner Spirit Away (by Dominion): dam 6f winner: won maiden at Pontefract in June: ran poorly after becoming upset in stalls only subsequent start. *M. J. Heaton-Ellis*

RISKY LOVER   4 b.f. Risk Me (FR) 127 – Dawn Love 73 (He Loves Me 120)   –
[1996 NR 1997 a7g 6g a5g⁵ a6g a8g Nov 24] second foal: dam, 1½m winner, also successful over hurdles: little sign of ability: tried blinkered. *T. T. Bill*

RISKY MISSILE   3 b.f. Risk Me (FR) 127 – Veuve Perrin (Legend of France   –
(USA) 124) [1996 64+: 6f⁴ 5d³ 1997 7g Oct 24] lengthy filly: in frame in maidens at 2 yrs for J. Banks: off course a year, well beaten in Doncaster claimer. *D. Morris*

RISKY ROSE   5 b.m. Risk Me (FR) 127 – Moharabuiee 60 (Pas de Seul 133)   41
[1996 49: 10m 10m 10.8f² 14.1f* 14.1f⁴ 12.1m 15.8m³ 10f 1997 12m⁴ 13.8m² 10.8d 12g³ 12.5m Jul 19] neat mare: poor performer: stays 1¾m: acts on firm ground and the all-weather. *R. Hollinshead*

RISKY TU   6 ch.m. Risk Me (FR) 127 – Sarah Gillian (USA) (Zen (USA)) [1996   46
46: a10g⁴ a10g⁵ 11.9f⁵ 9.9m⁵ 11.9f³ 14.1g⁴ 12m 10f⁵ 11.9f⁶ a11g³ 1997 a11g⁴ Jan 20] tall mare: poor handicapper: stays 2m: acts on any all-weather/turf. *P. A. Kelleway*

RISKY WHISKY   2 b.g. (Mar 19) Risk Me (FR) 127 – Desert Gem 87 (Green   67
Desert (USA) 127) [1997 5s* 5d² 5m⁶ a6g a5g* 5m* 5m⁵ a6g⁵ 5m⁴ 5s a5g*   a61
a5g a5g⁵ Dec 19] 5,000Y: workmanlike gelding: has a round action: third foal: dam (maiden) stayed 1m: fair performer: won maiden at Haydock in March, sellers at

Wolverhampton and Carlisle in June, and nursery at Lingfield in November: likely to prove best at 5f: acts on good to firm and soft ground and the all-weather: blinkered after fourth start: none too consistent. *J. Berry*

RISQUE 2 ch.g. (Apr 27) Risk Me (FR) 127 – Sweet And Sour 96 (Sharpen Up 127) [1997 6g 6g 7d 8m Sep 9] 5,000 2-y-o; half-brother to several winners, including 7f/1m performer Hackforth and 1¼m winner C U Coral (both by Hard Fought): dam 2-y-o 5f winner: looks of little account. *Mrs A. J. Bowlby* –

RISQUE LADY 2 ch.f. (May 9) Kenmare (FR) 125 – Christine Daae 74 (Sadler's Wells (USA) 132) [1997 5m* 6m 5m* 6m⁶ Oct 4] smallish, good-quartered filly: fourth foal: half-sister to 4-y-o My Lewicia and 5-y-o To The Roof: dam, stayed 1¼m, from good family: fairly useful form: won maiden at Windsor in August and minor event at Haydock in September, driven out to beat Pure Coincidence a neck in latter: swerved badly right stalls final start: may prove best at 5f: has gone freely to post, and taken down early last 2 starts: has been bandaged near-hind. *P. W. Harris* 94

RITA'S ROCK APE 2 b.f. (Apr 28) Mon Tresor 113 – Failand 36 (Kala Shikari 125) [1997 6.1m 6m 5m⁴ 5.1g² 5d² Nov 7] first reported foal: dam 7f/1m winner: fair maiden, generally progressive: caught post by Escudo in nursery at Doncaster on final start: speedy. *R. Brotherton* 69

RITUAL 2 ch.g. (Apr 1) Selkirk (USA) 129 – Pure Formality 84 (Forzando 122) [1997 7d⁶ Oct 14] tall, rather unfurnished gelding: second foal: half-brother to 1996 2-y-o 7f winner Avinalarf (by Fools Holme): dam 2-y-o 6f winner, from good family: 20/1, took strong hold to post and in race when sixth of 13 to Brave Reward in Leicester maiden, running on late without being knocked about at all: should improve, particularly if settling better. *H. Candy* 63 p

RIVAL BID (USA) 9 b.g. Cannonade (USA) – Love Triangle (USA) (Nodouble (USA)) [1996 74, a62: a10g* a10g³ a12g⁵ a12g⁶ 10d 9m 10.8f* 10m a12g⁵ a10g 10m 10g⁴ 8.2d 10f³ 10m⁴ 12g⁵ 10f* 10g⁵ 1997 a10g a9.4g⁴ a9.4g 10.8m 10m 10m 10m 14.1g 10.8g a12g Oct 20] workmanlike gelding: formerly fair handicapper: no form after second outing in 1997, finishing lame final start. *Mrs N. Macauley* 56 d

RIVER BAY (USA) 4 ch.c. Irish River (FR) 131 – Buckeye Gal (USA) (Good Counsel (USA)) [1996 121: 10.5m³ 8s* 8d⁵ 10d* 8v* 1997 10m* 10.5d⁴ 11f 12f* Dec 14] good-topped colt: smart performer: won Prix d'Harcourt at Longchamp in March by 2½ lengths from Nero Zilzal: 9½ lengths fourth of 8 to easy winner Helissio in Prix Ganay there in April: below form in Man o'War Stakes at Belmont on last outing for J. Hammond (France): best effort to win Hollywood Turf Cup by 1¼ lengths from Awad: stays 1½m: acts on any going: held up: raced on medication in USA. *R. Frankel, USA* 123

RIVER BEAT (IRE) 2 b.g. (Apr 18) River Falls 113 – Aughamore Beauty (IRE) (Dara Monarch 128) [1997 7g 7g 7g Aug 20] 15,500Y: leggy, good-topped gelding: third foal: dam unraced daughter of sister to high-class French middle-distance filly Saraca: only a little sign of ability in maidens at Newmarket (2) and Kempton. *M. H. Tompkins* –

RIVER CAPTAIN (USA) 4 ch.g. Riverman (USA) 131 – Katsura (USA) (Northern Dancer) [1996 –: 10g 1997 a13g⁴ a11g* a12g a12f Jun 21] close-coupled gelding: only form when winning weak maiden at Southwell in March: tailed off in handicaps afterwards. *D. J. G. Murray Smith* 62

RIVER ENSIGN 4 br.f. River God (USA) 121 – Ensigns Kit (Saucy Kit 76) [1996 NR 1997 7m 8m a6g⁴ 5m a5g³ a6g⁴ a5g⁵ 6g* 6m 6m a6g³ a7g³ a6g⁵ a6g⁴ Dec 26] smallish, plain filly: dam, winning jumper, well beaten on flat: poor handicapper: won at Thirsk in August: stays 7f: acts on fibresand, raced only on good/good to firm on turf. *W. M. Brisbourne* 43

RIVER FRONTIER (IRE) 2 b.f. (Mar 22) Imperial Frontier (USA) 112 – River Low (IRE) (Lafontaine (USA) 117) [1997 6d⁴ 5m 5.1g a5g 7.1s 5m a6g a6g³ a7g Dec 18] workmanlike filly: second reported foal: dam unraced half-sister to useful sprinter Imperial Bailiwick (by Imperial Frontier): poor maiden: stays 6f. *M. D. I. Usher* 39

RIVER KEEN (IRE) 5 ch.h. Keen 116 – Immediate Impact (Caerleon (USA) 132) [1996 84+, a102: a12g* 16g 12g⁵ 12g⁶ 1997 a12g* 11.9s a9f* a10f⁵ Aug 9] tall a117

sparely-made horse: unimpressive mover: progressive handicapper in Britain on the all-weather, winning at Southwell in March by 8 lengths on penultimate start for R. Armstrong: won Grade 2 event at Hollywood Park in June by length from subsequent Breeders' Cup Sprint runner-up Hesabull: tailed off in Pacific Classic at Del Mar: stays 1½m: possibly needs good or softer ground on turf: effective blinkered, not tried since 1995. *R. Hess jnr, USA*

RIVER NORTH (IRE)   7 ch.g. Lomond (USA) 128 – Petillante (USA) (Riverman (USA) 131) [1996 109: 10d⁵ 11d³ 10m³ 12m 12m⁵ 1997 10g⁴ 11.8d² 12d⁴ 14d* 16g⁴ Sep 3] sturdy gelding: impresses in appearance: has a quick action: very smart in 1994: has reportedly had sinus operation and leg problems since, and useful form at best nowadays: best 7-y-o effort when winning listed race at Vichy in July by 6 lengths: stays 1¾m: best on good ground or softer: wears bandages: held up and sometimes hangs under pressure: has had tongue tied. *Lady Herries*   107

RIVER OF FORTUNE (IRE)   3 b.f. Lahib (USA) 129 – Debach Delight 97 (Great Nephew 126) [1996 68: 6g⁶ 7f³ 6m² 7g² 7g² 7g² 7.5m² 7g 7m² 7m* 7.3s⁵ 1997 7m 8f 10s⁴ 9.9v⁵ 10.1m² 10g³ 12g³ Aug 28] leggy, lengthy filly: modest performer: stays 1¼m, not 1½m: acts on good to firm and soft ground. *M. H. Tompkins*   55

RIVER PILOT   3 b.c. Unfuwain (USA) 131 – Cut Ahead 85 (Kalaglow 132) [1996 NR 1997 8g 10.2d* 11.8d⁵ 10g Jul 9] leggy, useful-looking colt: good mover: fourth foal: half-brother to useful 5-y-o Far Ahead: dam 1¼m winner from good family: won maiden at Bath in May: well beaten on handicap debut at Newmarket (too free) final start: stays 1½m: keen sort, often edgy in preliminaries: sold 18,500 gns in October. *R. Charlton*   91

RIVER RUN (IRE)   5 b.h. Nordico (USA) – Irish Call (USA) (Irish River (FR) 131) [1996 64d: 10m* 7.8d⁴ 10d* 12g 10g⁶ 9g⁵ a9.4g a11g a9.4g 1997 a9.4g a10g 10g³ 10g 10g⁵ 10m⁴ 10g Jun 18] workmanlike ex-Irish horse: only poor form in Britain: stays 1¼m: acts on firm and dead ground, little show on the all-weather: usually blinkered in Ireland, tried only once here. *R. Hollinshead*   43

RIVER SEINE (FR)   5 b.m. Shining Steel – River Sans Retour (FR) (Vacarme (USA) 121) [1996 50: a7g a6g³ a8g⁴ a7g* 1997 a6g a7g³ a8g a7g² a7g⁴ a8g 6m 6.9s 8m 7d³ Aug 8] poor handicapper: should stay 1m: probably acts on any going: has had tongue tied and worn bandages. *S. G. Knight*   44   a49

RIVERSIDE GIRL (IRE)   3 b.f. River Falls 113 – Ballywhat (IRE) (Be My Native (USA) 122) [1996 –: 8.2g⁶ 7m 1997 8g⁵ 8.3g 9.9g Aug 23] poor performer: stays 1m. *J. S. Moore*   38

RIVERS MAGIC   4 b.g. Dominion 123 – Rivers Maid 83 (Rarity 129) [1996 78: 7m 7.1d* 8d 6.1s 1997 6g a8.5f⁶ 8d⁴ 7s 11.6m⁶ a10g Dec 22] sturdy gelding: poor form at best since winning 7f maiden at Haydock at 3 yrs. *J. J. Bridger*   47

RIVER'S SOURCE (USA)   3 b.g. Irish River (FR) 131 – Singing (USA) 91 (The Minstrel (CAN) 135) [1996 81: 7d⁴ 7f² 1997 8m² 10m* 10.1m 10.3d 10m 10.3g³ Jul 30] sturdy gelding: fairly useful handicapper: won at Newmarket in April: best subsequent effort on final start: should stay 1½m: acts on good to firm ground: blinkered fourth start: sold 9,000 gns in October. *B. W. Hills*   83

RIVER TERN   4 b.g. Puissance 110 – Millaine 69 (Formidable (USA) 125) [1996 71§: a7g⁵ 6f² 5m 6m³ 5g³ 6g* 6f 6m 5m 1997 5g² 5.1m 6g* 6.1g⁴ 7m 5g³ 5g* 6m⁵ 5.1m⁶ 5g⁴ 5g* 5d⁶ 5g 5m Sep 22] tall gelding: has a high knee action: fair performer: more reliable in 1997 than in the past, and won claimer at Redcar in May, handicap at Warwick in July and claimer at Catterick in August: spoilt chance with slow start last 3 outings: effective at 5f/6f: acts on firm and dead ground: often visored/blinkered at 3 yrs: carries head high: not one to trust implicitly. *J. M. Bradley*   72

RIVER TWEED   3 ch.f. Selkirk (USA) 129 – Twixt (Kings Lake (USA) 133) [1996 NR 1997 8f 8g³ 7.1d 6g 6g⁶ Aug 21] sixth foal: closely related to 1¼m winner Dagger Point (by Kris) and half-sister to 2 winners abroad, notably smart 1m to 1¼m winner Bon Point (by Soviet Star): dam, French 7f winner, daughter of Cambridgeshire winner Intermission, herself dam of Interval and Interim: modest maiden: well beaten last 3 starts: stays 1m: headstrong (upset in stalls final outing): sold 23,000 gns in December. *J. H. M. Gosden*   61

RIVER USK   3 b.c. Caerleon (USA) 132 – Shining Water 111 (Kalaglow 132)   103
[1996 98p: 7.1d* 7f⁴ 8g* 1997 10.1g³ 10.9d Sep 20] smallish, well-made colt: useful
performer, lightly raced: best effort when 5 lengths third to Sandmoor Chambray in
rated stakes at Epsom in September: well held in listed race at Ayr final start: should
stay 1½m: acts on dead ground: sold 58,000 gns, and sent to UAE. *H. R. A. Cecil*

RIYADIAN   5 ch.h. Polish Precedent (USA) 131 – Knight's Baroness 116   119
(Rainbow Quest (USA) 134) [1996 120: 12m* 1997 9.2g* 12d³ Jun 29] lengthy
horse: has a short action: smart performer, lightly raced: odds on, easily won 3-runner
minor event at Hamilton on return in June: creditable 8 lengths third of 4 to Helissio
in Grand Prix de Saint-Cloud only subsequent start, left behind in straight: stays 1½m
well: acts on good to firm and dead ground. *P. F. I. Cole*

ROAD RACER (IRE)   4 br.g. Scenic 128 – Rally 88 (Relko 136) [1996 56: 8.2m   64
8m 8f⁴ 8g⁴ 10.4g 12m³ 12.1g⁴ 12m 1997 a11g⁵ a16g* 16.1g⁴ 14.1m² 14.1g 10g*
12d 12g* 10.3m³ 12g² 10.1g 12m 9.9m⁴ Jul 29] tall gelding: easy mover: modest
handicapper: won at Southwell in March and Pontefract in April and May: winner at
2m, better form over 1¼m/1½m: acts on fibresand and good to firm going (below
form on dead): carries head high: best with waiting tactics and strong handling:
consistent: very promising hurdler for P. Webber. *Mrs J. R. Ramsden*

ROAR ON TOUR   8 b.g. Dunbeath (USA) 127 – Tickled Trout 70 (Red Alert   26 §
127) [1996 –§, a62§: a8g a8g a8g 8.2d 8.3s⁶ 8m 8m a8g* a8g a8g a8g 1997 a8g a8g   a– §
8.3s³ May 8] good-bodied gelding: modest all-weather handicapper at 7 yrs: poor on
turf in 1997: unreliable. *Mrs M. Reveley*

ROBANNA   2 b.f. (Feb 22) Robellino (USA) 127 – Pounelta 91 (Tachypous 128)   60
[1997 6.9m 7m 7d Oct 13] tall, leggy filly: eighth foal: half-sister to several winners,
including 4-y-o Primetta and 5-y-o Anistop (1m winner at 3 yrs): dam, 2-y-o 7f
winner who probably stayed 1½m, half-sister to Dead Certain: modest form in
maidens at Kempton and Leicester final 2 starts: should stay 1m+. *R. Akehurst*

ROBBAN HENDI (USA)   3 b. or br.c. A P Indy (USA) – Real Jenny (USA)   82
(Valid Appeal (USA)) [1996 NR 1997 9d 10m² 10g Jul 9] $150,000Y: smallish,
useful-looking colt: half-brother to several winners in North America, 3 of them
stakes winners: dam won up to 9f: fairly useful maiden: clearly best effort at
Pontefract on second start, dictating steady pace, caught post: sweating next time:
sent to UAE. *M. A. Jarvis*

ROBBO   3 b.g. Robellino (USA) 127 – Basha (USA) (Chief's Crown (USA)) [1996   65
NR 1997 a8g⁵ a8.5g⁵ a9.4g⁶ a8g 8.3g² 8m³ 10s⁵ a14g* a16g a14g⁶ a14.8g* a14.8g*   a76
15.8s³ a14.8g² Nov 15] 5,600Y: first foal: dam twice-raced daughter of high-class
(up to 9f) My Darling One: fair performer: won amateurs maiden handicap at
Southwell in August and minor event and amateurs handicap at Wolverhampton in
September/October: stays 2m: acts on fibresand and soft ground: blinkered sixth start
onwards: sold (to join Mrs M. Reveley) 21,000 gns in November. *C. W. Thornton*

ROBEC GIRL (IRE)   3 ch.f. Masterclass (USA) 116 – Resiusa (ITY) (Niniski   50
(USA) 125) [1996 66, a69: 5s³ 5g* 5m² 5m³ 5g⁴ 5m 5m³ 5m⁴ a5g* a6g³ a6g* 1997
6.1d 6m⁵ 6m Jun 10] leggy filly: only modest in handicaps in 1997, looking difficult
ride in visor last 2 starts: stays 6f: acts on good to firm ground and on fibresand.
K. McAuliffe

ROBEENA   2 b.f. (Apr 8) Robellino (USA) 127 – Raheena (USA) 69 (Lyphard   64
(USA) 132) [1997 6g³ 6m³ 7.1m⁶ 6g⁴ 6g 7g Sep 24] 7,200 2-y-o: small filly: first
foal: dam, second at 1½m, from family of Mark of Esteem: modest maiden on
balance: well held in nurseries last 2 starts. *C. N. Allen*

ROBELLION   6 b.g. Robellino (USA) 127 – Tickled Trout 70 (Red Alert 127)   59
[1996 74: a8g⁴ a8g* a7g³ a10g* a10g³ a10g a10g³ a10g⁵ 8g 6.9f 6m² 5.1m* 6m* 5m⁴   a72
6g 6.1d 6g⁴ 5.7m⁶ 6m⁵ 7f⁵ 5.1g 1997 a8g² a10g a8g² a8g² a8g³ a8g³ a10g a10g 6f 5d
6m⁶ 6g⁶ 5.1m⁴ 6m 5.1g 5m⁵ 6m* 6m 5d³ a8s⁴ a8g⁶ a8g² Dec 10] sturdy gelding:
carries plenty of condition: fair performer on the all-weather, modest on turf: won
apprentice handicap at Salisbury in October, coming from last: effective at 5f to
1¼m: acts on equitrack, firm and dead ground: wears bandages behind: effective
visored or not: usually held up: tough and versatile. *D. W. P. Arbuthnot*

ROB

ROBERT'S DAUGHTER 2 b.f. (Mar 22) Robellino (USA) 127 – Cache –
(Bustino 136) [1997 a5g 7m a6g Oct 18] 4,200 2-y-o: second foal: half-sister to 4-y-o
Swan Hunter: dam, maiden, closely related to useful 1¼m to 1½m winner Black
Monday: no promise in maiden and claimers. *J. Balding*

ROBERT THE BRUCE 2 ch.g. (Apr 17) Distinct Native 89 – Kawarau Queen –
(Taufan (USA) 119) [1997 6m 7g Aug 22] third reported foal: dam 1m winner: well
beaten in sellers. *R. A. Fahey*

ROBERTY BOB (IRE) 2 ch.g. (Feb 18) Bob Back (USA) 124 – Inesdela –
(Wolver Hollow 126) [1997 6g 8.1d 8.2g Sep 28] good-bodied gelding: sixth foal:
half-brother to fairly useful Irish 1990 2-y-o sprint winner Seneca Reef (by Simply
Great): dam unraced: signs of ability in maidens. *P. T. Walwyn*

ROBIN GOODFELLOW 2 b.c. (Feb 21) Fairy King (USA) – La Tuerta 96 77
(Hot Spark 126) [1997 6d 6s* 6g Oct 25] 42,000Y: stocky, sprint type: brother to
6-y-o Ya Malak, closely related to fairly useful 1992 2-y-o 5f winner Kamaatera (by
Night Shift) and half-brother to several winners: dam sprinting half-sister to Cadeaux
Genereux: made all in maiden at Catterick in October, beating Easter Ogil by 2½
lengths: slowly away when well beaten in nursery at Newbury. *P. T. Walwyn*

ROBIN LANE 2 b.f. (Jan 21) Tenby 125 – Hiawatha's Song (USA) (Chief's 67
Crown (USA)) [1997 5m⁶ 7d⁵ 5.1m 6.5m⁵ 7s Oct 16] 9,500F, IR 50,000Y: first foal:
dam French 1½m winner out of Criterium des Pouliches winner Hippodamia: fifth in
nursery at Doncaster in September: no comparable efforts, particularly disappointing
on good to soft/soft ground: should stay at least 1m. *I. A. Balding*

ROBO MAGIC (USA) 5 b.g. Tejano (USA) – Bubble Magic (USA) (Clever 38
Trick (USA)) [1996 52, a86: a6g³ a7g⁴ a6g* a6g* a6g⁵ 5d 6f 6m 6m⁶ 6m⁴ 5m 6f a6g a85
1997 a6g⁶ a6g* a6g² a6g⁶ a5g³ a5g⁵ a6g² 6.1g⁴ a5g* a6g³ a6f⁵ 5m a7g a6g a6g a7g²
a6s⁵ a6g Dec 19] neat gelding: fairly useful on the all-weather, poor on turf: won
claimer at Lingfield in January and handicap at Wolverhampton in May: effective at
5f to 7f: acts on good to firm and dead ground, below form on soft: effective
blinkered, not tried in 1997. *L. Montague Hall*

ROBORANT 2 b.g. (Mar 4) Robellino (USA) 127 – Sunny Davis (USA) 71 73
(Alydar (USA)) [1997 6m 6d 7g³ 8m⁶ 8d Oct 17] 13,000Y: useful-looking gelding:
third foal: half-brother to 3-y-o Davis Rock and 1995 2-y-o 6f and 7f winner
Warming Trends (by Warning), latter useful miler in Sweden: dam, 2-y-o 7f winner,
out of sister to Larida (dam of Magic of Life) and Miss Oceana: fair maiden: off 8
weeks before running poorly final start: stays 1m. *J. L. Dunlop*

ROBSART (IRE) 2 b.f. (Mar 20) Robellino (USA) 127 – Sharp Girl (FR) 114 70
(Sharpman) [1997 6m⁵ 6g² Aug 22] leggy filly: half-sister to several winners,
including 4-y-o Tart and 8-y-o Gold Blade: dam French 1¼m winner who stayed
1½m, from good family: fair form in maidens at Windsor and Thirsk (3½ lengths
second to Exbourne's Wish): will be suited by further than 6f. *J. R. Fanshawe*

ROCHEA 3 br.f. Rock City 120 – Pervenche (Latest Model 115) [1996 67, a?: 6m⁶ 51 §
6m⁴ a6g⁴ 1997 a8g³ a8g⁴ a8g³ a6g a8g⁵ 8.2m 10m³ 12g⁵ 9.9d⁵ 10g³ 10g 8m² 8.2g⁵
8.5m 8g² 8.2m 7g 8g 8d³ Oct 28] big, leggy filly: modest maiden: trained first 3 starts
by W. Haggas: stays 1¼m: best efforts on good going or firmer: tried in blinkers/
visor: tends to carry head high: ungenuine. *Mrs N. Macauley*

ROCKAROUNDTHECLOCK 3 b.g. Rock City 120 – Times 55 (Junius 55 d
(USA) 124) [1996 65d, a?: 5d³ 5m 6d⁵ 6f³ a6g 6.1s 1997 6.1m a6g⁶ 6.1g³ 6.1d⁵ 6m³ a–
5.9f⁵ 8m 6d 8f Sep 29] close-coupled gelding: disappointing maiden: sold out of P.
D. Evans' stable before seventh start: should stay 7f: acts on firm and dead going:
often visored/blinkered: sometimes slowly away. *T. R. Watson*

ROCKCRACKER (IRE) 5 ch.g. Ballad Rock 122 – Forest Blaze (USA) 82 59
(Green Forest (USA) 134) [1996 67, a56: a6g³ a6g a6g 5s⁵ 6f⁴ 5.1g 6f* 5m² 5.7g 6f a–
7f⁵ 6m* 6g⁵ 5m 6.1d 5.7m 6.1m 6m 1997 5m 6d⁶ 5.7d⁶ 6m* 6g 6m 6m 6m⁶ 6f 6m³
6g a6g Nov 24] strong, neat gelding: modest handicapper: won at Folkestone in June:
stays 6f: acts on firm and soft ground and the all-weather: usually blinkered/visored:
none too consistent. *G. G. Margarson*

ROCKETTE 2 ch.f. (Mar 24) Rock Hopper 124 – Primulette 82 (Mummy's Pet –
125) [1997 7g 7.5m 7.5d 7.9s 7.5f Sep 17] sparely-made filly: sixth foal: half-sister

798

to several winners (all successful at 2 yrs), including Makhbar (by Rudimentary), 6f winner in 1996, and fairly useful Bring On The Choir (by Chief Singer), 5f winner in 1994: dam 5f (at 2 yrs) and 1m winner: little worthwhile form, in seller final start: blinkered penultimate outing. *J. W. Watts*

ROCK FALCON (IRE)   4 ch.g. Polar Falcon (USA) 126 – Rockfest (USA) 104   93 §
(Stage Door Johnny) [1996 NR 1997 7g* 7.6m⁵ 8s 7s 8.1g* 7m⁵ 8v* Oct 11] 8,500 2-y-o: half-brother to several winners, including smart 1½m performer Rainbow Lake (by Rainbow Quest) and useful 1½m winner Vertex (by Shirley Heights): dam, 2-y-o 7f and 1m winner, stayed 1½m: won maiden at Lingfield in May, seller at Chepstow in September and handicap at Ascot (clearly best effort) in October: refused to race third and fourth starts: stays 1m: acts on heavy ground: visored fourth start, blinkered thereafter: remains one to treat with caution. *Lady Herries*

ROCK FANTASY   3 b.f. Keen 116 – Runelia (Runnett 125) [1996 57d: 6m⁵ 6m⁴   –
7m 7m 6g 8m 1997 a8g a8g a11g⁴ a12g 6f a8g May 8] leggy, angular filly: disappointing maiden: tried blinkered. *C. Murray*

ROCKFORCE   5 ch.g. Rock City 120 – Sleepline Princess 86 (Royal Palace 131)   97
[1996 NR 1997 8m 10g* 10.3d⁴ 10.1g 12m 10.3d² 11.9g Jul 5] sturdy gelding: useful handicapper: won 22-runner event at Newbury in April: good efforts in frame afterwards, and had excuses other starts: suited by around 1¼m: acts on firm and dead ground: has run well when sweating. *M. R. Channon*

ROCK FROM THE SUN   2 b.f. (Feb 18) Rock City 120 – Amathus Glory 76   46
(Mummy's Pet 125) [1997 5m³ a5g a6g⁴ a7g* a7g³ 6g⁶ a7g⁵ a5g⁴ a6g⁶ a8.5g Oct 18] 3,800Y: third foal: dam 2-y-o 5f winner: poor performer: won seller at Wolverhampton in June: stays 7f: raced mainly on fibresand: blinkered last 4 starts. *W. G. M. Turner*

ROCKIE THE JESTER   3 b.g. Rock Hopper 124 – Magic Steps 74 (Nomin-   –
ation 125) [1996 NR 1997 8.2d 8s 10m a14g Aug 15] first foal: dam, 5f winner at 2 yrs, should have stayed 1m: no worthwhile form. *J. P. Leigh*

ROCK ISLAND LINE (IRE)   3 b.g. New Express 95 – Gail's Crystal (Crofter   74
(USA) 124) [1996 NR 1997 8.3d* 7m* 8g² 7g³ 7v³ 6g 7.6m 8.1g a7g² 8.2s Oct 15] IR 1,000Y, 5,000 2-y-o: fourth foal: brother to 5f winner The Real Whizzbang and half-brother to a winner in Italy by Don't Forget Me: dam poor maiden: reportedly had bad joints and was unraced at 2 yrs: fair performer: won seller at Hamilton in April and claimer at Newcastle in May: below form last 4 starts: likely to prove best up to 1m: acts on good to firm and heavy going, probably on fibresand. *J. Berry*

ROCK IT ROSIE   3 ch.f. Rock Hopper 124 – Rockin' Rosie 59 (Song 132) [1996   42
NR 1997 10f 12g 9.9d³ May 10] 6,200Y: plain filly: second foal: dam 5f winner: tongue tied, first sign of ability when third in seller at Beverley: should stay 1½m. *Dr J. D. Scargill*

ROCK RIVER   3 ch.f. Rock Hopper 124 – Emmer Green 64 (Music Boy 124)   –
[1996 NR 1997 8.1m Jul 24] 4,000Y: plain, lengthy filly: third foal: dam best at 5f: always behind in Sandown maiden. *D. C. O'Brien*

ROCK SCENE (IRE)   5 b.g. Scenic 128 – Rockeater 94 (Roan Rocket 128)   –
[1996 NR 1997 10m Sep 9] modest maiden at 3 yrs: tailed off only start in 1997. *A. Streeter*

ROCK SOUNDS   2 br.g. (Apr 20) Rock City 120 – Shernborne (Kalaglow 132)   –
[1997 7f 7m 7d Oct 16] 5,200Y: tall gelding: third foal: dam out of half-sister to Blakeney and Morston: no form, including in seller. *N. A. Callaghan*

ROCKSWAIN (IRE)   2 ch.g. (Apr 4) Ballad Rock 122 – Uninvited Guest 57 (Be   57
My Guest (USA) 126) [1997 6g a5g* Nov 15] 10,000Y, 4,000 2-y-o: half-brother to 3-y-o Bon Guest and a winner abroad by Simply Great: dam placed up to 7f in Ireland: off course over 4 months, 40/1 and ridden by 7-lb claimer, made all in seller at Wolverhampton. *P. C. Haslam*

ROCK SYMPHONY   7 ch.g. Ballad Rock 122 – Shamasiya (FR) (Vayrann 133)   –
[1996 88d: 5g⁶ 6m 6m 6m⁴ 6.1m 6g 6m⁴ 6m 6g 1997 6g 6d 7m 7g⁶ 6d Aug 30] useful sprinter at one time, but a light of former days. *W. J. Haggas*

ROCK THE BARNEY (IRE)   8 ch.h. Coquelin (USA) 121 – Lady Loire 94   50
(Wolverlife 115) [1996 53d: 11.8d⁵ 11.6m⁶ 11.4m 12m 10m² 14d 11.9g 11.5m² a12g⁴
a13g 1997 10g 11.6g⁶ 12f³ 11.4d⁴ 14m 12d 10g 12g⁵ 10m* 10g 12m 10d² Oct 28]
smallish horse: poor mover: modest handicapper: won strongly-run apprentice event
at Sandown in September, coming from well off pace: needs strong pace at 1¼m, and
stays 1½m: acts on any going: blinkered last 4 starts, tried visored earlier in career:
sometimes slowly away and looks none too keen: inconsistent. *M. D. I. Usher*

ROCK THE CASBAH   3 ch.g. Rock City 120 – Romantic Saga 69 (Prince   –
Tenderfoot (USA) 126) [1996 59d: 6m⁴ 6m 7d a5g a7g a8g⁶ 1997 11m⁴ 12m⁵ Jul 29]
modest maiden: dead. *J. Hetherton*

ROCK TO THE TOP (IRE)   3 b.c. Rudimentary (USA) 118 – Well Bought   69
(IRE) 35 (Auction Ring (USA) 123) [1996 66: 6m 7g 6.9d a5g⁴ a5g a6g² 1997 a6g³
Jan 16] fair performer: better at 6f than 5f: acts on equitrack. *J. J. Sheehan*

ROCKY DANCE (FR)   3 b.f. Rock Hopper 124 – Open Date (IRE) (Thatching   70
131) [1996 NR 1997 9d² 10.1s 10m 8g* 8g² 8g⁵ Aug 20] IR 4,600Y: lengthy,
useful-looking filly: first foal: dam unraced half-sister to useful sprinter Peace Girl:
fair handicapper: won at Salisbury in August: creditable efforts both subsequent
starts: should stay beyond 1m: joined A. Severinsen in USA. *A. P. Jarvis*

ROCKY OASIS (USA)   4 b.c. Gulch (USA) – Knoosh (USA) 113 (Storm Bird   93
(CAN) 134) [1996 93: 10d² 1997 9g 10d* 10.4g 10m⁴ 12g 10d⁵ Oct 16] tall, rangy
colt: impresses in appearance: has had a wind operation: good mover: fairly useful
on balance of form: narrowly landed odds in maiden at Leicester in April: flattered in
Brigadier Gerard Stakes at Sandown on fourth start: not sure to stay beyond 1¼m:
yet to race on extremes of going: sent to UAE. *M. R. Stoute*

ROCKY'S PROFILES (IRE)   4 b.g. Roi Danzig (USA) – Viceroy Princess 65   –
(Godswalk (USA) 130) [1996 NR 1997 12g Sep 2] half-brother to several winners,
notably useful 1987 2-y-o 5f performer Classic Ruler (by Dominion): dam won 7f
seller as 2-y-o: last in seller at Folkestone. *Miss K. M. George*

ROCKY WATERS (USA)   8 b. or br.g. Rocky Marriage (USA) 95 – Running   39
Melody 86 (Rheingold 137) [1996 59: 6g 6.1g 7f² 8g² 8g a8.5g⁴ 8f² 8.1m⁵ 7f⁴ a7g³
8g 8m 1997 a8g⁶ 8f 7m⁴ a7g 8.3s 8.3g² 8g⁴ 10f a7g⁶ a8g² Dec 2] leggy, lightly-made
gelding: poor handicapper: stays easy 8.5f: acts on all-weather and firm ground,
probably on soft: usually blinkered/visored: tends to sweat. *M. D. I. Usher*

RODINIA (USA)   2 ch.c. (Feb 28) Diesis 133 – Rangoon Ruby 110 (Sallust 134)   70 +
[1997 5m⁴ 7.1g 8.5d Dec 1] sixth foal: brother to useful 6f (at 2 yrs) to 1m winner
Gneiss and half-brother to 2 winners in USA: dam Irish 6f to 1m winner later successful in USA, half-sister to Sun Chariot winner Duboff: signs of ability in maidens,
first 2 starts for G. Lewis in Britain. *C. L. Baker, USA*

ROFFEY SPINNEY (IRE)   3 ch.c. Masterclass (USA) 116 – Crossed Line   75
(Thatching 131) [1996 65: 6v³ a8g 1997 a7g³ a6g* a5g* a6g³ a6g 7m 6.1g⁵ 6d³ 6g
a7g Nov 6] fair performer: won maiden and handicap at Lingfield in February: creditable efforts most starts afterwards: best at 5f/6f: acts on dead ground and equitrack
(ran poorly on fibresand). *R. Hannon*

ROGER ROSS   2 b.c. (Mar 2) Touch of Grey 90 – Foggy Dew 45 (Smoggy 115)   –
[1997 a5s Nov 10] third foal: brother to a bad maiden: dam 1¼m winner: always
behind in maiden at Lingfield. *R. M. Flower*

ROI BRISBANE   2 b.c. (Apr 9) Roi Danzig (USA) – Crystal Cup (USA)   76
(Nijinsky (CAN) 138) [1997 6m³ 6g a6g* Nov 1] 34,000Y: sturdy, good-topped colt:
has scope: closely related to very smart 6f/7f performer Iktamal (by Danzig Connection) and half-brother to 3 winners, including fairly useful 1½m/1¾m winner Crystal
Cross (by Roberto): dam twice-raced daughter of top-class Rose Bowl: favourite,
confirmed debut promise when winning maiden at Wolverhampton by 4 lengths from
Main Street: should stay at least 7f: didn't walk well beforehand and disappointed
second start. *M. Johnston*

ROI DE DANSE   2 ch.c. (Mar 4) Komaite (USA) – Princess Lucy 42 (Local   77
Suitor (USA) 128) [1997 5.7g 6m 6g⁵ 6g* 7d 6g Oct 18] 10,500Y: lengthy, workmanlike colt: fourth foal: half-brother to 5-y-o Royal Philosopher: dam poor daughter of

smart French mare (at around 1¼m) Jalapa: fair performer: won maiden at Kempton in August: stiff task final start: stays 6f. *J. W. Hills*

ROI DU NORD (FR)   5 b.g. Top Ville 129 – Ridja (FR) (Djakao (FR) 124) [1996   –
72d: 8m⁶ 10.1m³ 10s 10.1m 10m⁶ 1997 10m 10m Sep 15] workmanlike gelding: fair
form at best at 4 yrs, none in 1997. *N. Bycroft*

ROISIN CLOVER   6 ch.m. Faustus (USA) 118 – Valiyen (Valiyar 129) [1996   71
73d: 12m* 12m 12m 12m⁵ 12g 12m 14m³ 11.5m² 12g 1997 12m* 12s Jul 2] lengthy
mare: fair handicapper: goes well fresh, and made winning reappearance at Kempton
(fourth course success) in May: always behind only subsequent outing: probably
stays 1¾m: acts on firm and dead going: normally held up. *R. Rowe*

ROISIN SPLENDOUR (IRE)   2 ch.f. (Apr 29) Inchinor 119 – Oriental   50
Splendour 85 (Runnett 125) [1997 6g³ 6.1m Jul 19] 9,000Y: fourth foal: half-sister to
Irish 3-y-o 7f (at 2 yrs) and 1½m winner Really Chuffed (by Shavian) and winning
sprinter Sizzling (by Sizzling Melody): dam best at 7f: modest form in maidens at
Folkestone and Nottingham 10 days apart. *S. Dow*

ROKEBY BOWL   5 b.g. Salse (USA) 128 – Rose Bowl (USA) 131 (Habitat 134)   93
[1996 95: 10g³ 10m⁴ 12m⁵ 1997 10m³ 12m³ 14d⁶ 12m 11.9g⁶ 11.4g* 12m* 12d
Oct 16] small gelding: has had leg trouble: fairly useful performer: justified favouritism in minor events at Sandown in July and Newbury in August: stays 1½m well:
acts on firm ground, below form on softer than good: has run well when sweating:
held up: genuine and consistent. *I. A. Balding*

ROLLING HIGH (IRE)   2 ch.c. (Apr 2) Roi Danzig (USA) – Sally Chase 101   –
(Sallust 134) [1997 8s Oct 14] good-bodied colt: brother to 1994 2-y-o 7f and 1m
winner Unanimous Vote, later smart in USA, and half-brother to several winners, including 4-y-o Nikita's Star: dam, sprinter, ran only at 2 yrs: burly, tailed off in maiden
at Leicester. *D. J. G. Murray Smith*

ROLLING STONE   3 b.c. Northern Amethyst 99 – First Sapphire (Simply Great   65
(FR) 122) [1996 NR 1997 10g³ Jun 13] first foal: dam of no account: sire became
ungenuine: 9 lengths third of 8 in maiden at Sandown, slowly away (upset in stalls,
jockey reportedly injured) and running on. *Lady Herries*

ROMALITO   7 b.g. Robellino (USA) 127 – Princess Zita 90 (Manado 130) [1996   45
–: a16g 17.2f 1997 16.1g⁵ 16.2m³ 16.2s⁴ 14.9m² 16.2m² 16.1m³ 14.9d 14.9g 17.1g⁵   a–
a16g Nov 25] good-topped gelding: has a markedly round action: poor handicapper:
stays 17f: best efforts on good ground or firmer: blinkered/visored (below form) once
each. *M. Blanshard*

ROMANOV (IRE)   3 b.c. Nureyev (USA) 131 – Morning Devotion (USA) 102   117
(Affirmed (USA)) [1996 NR 1997 7.1s* 8.1g* 8g³ 12g³ 10g³ 10.5m* 12g² 12m³
Oct 19] tall, rangy colt: usually impresses in appearance: fluent mover: reportedly
fractured a pastern at 2 yrs and has 5 pins in his leg: brother to smart 7f and 1¼m
winner Red Slippers and closely related to 2 winners by Storm Bird, notably Irish
Derby winner Balanchine: dam, 2-y-o 6f winner, stayed 1½m: quickly developed
into a smart performer: won maiden at Haydock in March, minor event at Sandown
in April and Rose of Lancaster Stakes at Haydock in August, last-named by ½ length
from Germano: placed on all other starts, Irish 2000 Guineas at the Curragh (5
lengths third to Desert King but reportedly returned home with a runny nose), Derby
at Epsom (5 lengths third to Benny The Dip), Prix Eugene Adam at Saint-Cloud,
Cumberland Lodge Stakes at Ascot and Canadian International at Woodbine (5½
lengths third to Chief Bearhart): should stay 1¾m: acts on good to firm and soft
ground: genuine and consistent: stays in training, and seems ideal sort for Ormonde
Stakes at Chester in May. *P. W. Chapple-Hyam*

ROMAN REEL (USA)   6 ch.g. Sword Dance – Our Mimi (USA) (Believe It   61
(USA)) [1996 69, a60: a8g² a8g² a8g² a8g⁴ 8g 10f* 10f* 8.1m² 10.1g 10f⁶ 10m² 10f³   a65
10f 1997 a8g a8g* a10g⁶ 9.7m⁶ 11.9f³ a8g⁶ 10m³ 8m 10f* 9d 10d 10m⁵ 10g* 10f⁴
10f³ a10g Nov 6] lengthy, good-quartered gelding: good mover: fair performer: won
amateurs handicaps at Lingfield in March and Brighton in September: awarded
claimer at Brighton (successful 5 times over course and distance in all) in June:
effective at 1m and 1¼m: better form on equitrack than fibresand, suited by good
ground or firmer on turf. *G. L. Moore*

ROMANTIC SECRET 2 ch.f. (Apr 9) Executive Man 119 – Tria Romantica – (Another Realm 118) [1997 a6g 5d Jul 17] 2,200 2-y-o: sixth foal: sister to 2 winners in Italy: dam Italian maiden: well beaten in sellers. *R. T. Juckes*

ROMANTIC WARRIOR 4 b.g. Welsh Captain 113 – Romantic Melody 56 – (Battle Hymn 103) [1996 –: 8.2m 10g⁶ 1997 a11g 11.8m Mar 27] of no account. *K. S. Bridgwater*

ROMIOS (IRE) 5 ch.h. Common Grounds 118 – Domino's Nurse 104 (Dom 92 Racine (FR) 121) [1996 90§: 10g 8d 10.3g 10d 11.9m³ 11.9g² 10m³ 12g⁶ 11.9f² 12g 12m³ 12s 1997 10m* 10m⁴ 10m⁴ 12g⁵ 10s⁴ 12d² Jun 29] sturdy horse: fairly useful performer: won Rosebery Handicap at Kempton in March: mostly creditable efforts afterwards: effective at 1¼m to 1½m: acts on any going: successful in blinkers at 2 yrs, not tried since: tends to pull hard, and goes well in strongly-run races: sometimes looks none too keen. *P. F. I. Cole*

RONQUISTA D'OR 3 b.c. Ron's Victory (USA) 129 – Gild The Lily 83 (Ile de 45 Bourbon (USA) 133) [1996 –: a7g 8.1s 1997 12.5m³ a12g 10.8m² 12f a12g⁵ 18d⁶ a52 13.8m² 14m a14g⁶ Dec 18] sturdy colt: modest maiden handicapper: stays 1¾m: acts on good to firm ground and fibresand. *G. A. Ham*

RON'S PET 2 ch.g. (Apr 15) Ron's Victory (USA) 129 – Penny Mint 79 81 (Mummy's Game 120) [1997 5d² 5s² 5m³ 6d 6m² 7g* 8m² 8d Oct 17] 16,500Y: tall gelding: third foal: half-brother to 4-y-o Present Generation: dam 2-y-o 6f winner out of sister to Saher: fairly useful performer: won maiden at Brighton in August: good second in nurseries at Goodwood and Newmarket: off 8 weeks before final outing: stays 1m, not sure to get further: acts on good to firm ground and dead. *R. Hannon*

RON'S ROUND 3 ch.c. Ron's Victory (USA) 129 – Magical Spirit 70 (Top Ville 47 129) [1996 –: 6m 1997 a7g a8.5g 6g a9.4g⁴ a10g³ 8g⁵ 10m² 8f² 9.7d⁴ Oct 21] rather leggy colt: poor maiden handicapper: left K. Cunningham-Brown after second start: stays 1¼m: acts on firm and dead ground and on equitrack. *C. A. Dwyer*

ROOD MUSIC 6 ro.g. Sharrood (USA) 124 – Rose Music 86 (Luthier 126) [1996 – –: 8.3m 8.1m⁵ 10.1m a9.4g 1997 a14.8g² a16.2g Jan 15] lengthy, workmanlike a73 gelding: disappointing handicapper, only form since 1995 when second at Wolverhampton: stays 15f: acts on fibresand. *M. G. Meagher*

ROSALEE ROYALE 5 ch.m. Out of Hand 84 – Miss Ark Royal (Broadsword – (USA) 104) [1996 NR 1997 a10g⁵ a12g⁶ 10.8d 8f⁵ 8g⁶ 9.7m Aug 5] first foal: dam maiden: little sign of ability: trained first 2 starts by J. Long. *John Berry*

ROSA ROYALE 3 b.f. Arazi (USA) 135 – Gussy Marlowe 118 (Final Straw 127) 61 [1996 NR 1997 10m⁶ 8d⁶ 10m 8m⁶ Sep 22] 54,000F: first foal: dam won Falmouth and Musidora Stakes: modest maiden: best efforts at 1m. *Mrs J. Cecil*

ROSEATE LODGE 11 b.g. Habitat 134 – Elegant Tern (USA) 102 (Sea Bird II 48 145) [1996 47: 10.3d 8g 8.5g 8g 7.1g 8m 8.1m⁶ 6m* 7m² 8m³ 6f⁶ 8.3g⁶ 8g³ 8m 1997 a7g a7g 8s 8m⁶ 8f 7.5g 6.9m* 7d³ 7g³ 8g* 6g⁵ 7.5d 7g⁶ Aug 15] compact gelding: poor handicapper: in good form most of 1997, and won at Carlisle (ladies) and Thirsk (apprentices) in the summer: effective at 7f/1m: acts on any going: blinkered once earlier in career: usually held up. *S. E. Kettlewell*

ROSE BURTON 3 b.f. Lucky Wednesday 124 – Holly Burton 73 (King Emperor 42 (USA)) [1996 NR 1997 a7g a6g⁵ a8g* a10g⁶ Mar 1] half-sister to a winner in Hong Kong by Skyliner: dam, second at 5f at 2 yrs, half-sister to smart sprinter Tackerton: only worthwhile form when dead-heating with Head Girl in 4-runner seller at Southwell in February. *T. D. Barron*

ROSE CARNIVAL 3 b.f. Salse (USA) 128 – Jungle Rose 90 (Shirley Heights – 130) [1996 74: 6m 7g* 7m 1997 10.5d Sep 5] rangy filly: fair winner at 2 yrs: well held only start in 1997: sold 3,800 gns in December. *D. R. Loder*

ROSE FLYER (IRE) 7 b.m. Nordico (USA) – String of Straw (Thatching 131) – [1996 NR 1997 6g⁵ 6d 6f Sep 18] robust mare: triple 7f winner in 1993: produced Rosies Miracle (see below) in 1995: retains little ability. *M. C. Chapman*

ROSENKAVALIER (IRE) 3 b.g. Classic Music (USA) – Top Bloom (Thatch 51 (USA) 136) [1996 –: 5.1f 6g 6m 8f 1997 7m 7f 8.3g 8.1m Jul 11] smallish gelding:

modest maiden: form only on reappearance: stays 7f: raced only on good ground or firmer: blinkered final start. *L. G. Cottrell*

ROSE OF GLENN 6 b.m. Crofthall 110 – May Kells (Artaius (USA) 129) [1996   51
45: a16g⁴ a16g a13g a16g 14.1d a14g 15.4g 14d² 11.8f⁵ a12g a14.8g² a14.8g a14.8g⁵ a42
1997 a13g⁵ 17.2d 13.8m* 14.1g⁵ 16d³ 13.1m 14.1m⁴ 13.8g 17.1g² 16.4g⁶ 16m 15.8g
14m⁶ 14.1f⁴ a16s² a16g⁴ a16g⁴ Dec 4] sparely-made mare: modest performer: won
seller at Catterick (fourth success there) in May: creditable efforts in frame after:
stays 17f: acts on any turf/all-weather: visored (below form) once: usually races
prominently: has unseated rider in preliminaries. *B. Palling*

ROSEWOOD LADY (IRE) 2 b.f. (Mar 14) Maledetto (IRE) 103 – Thrill   50
Seeker (IRE) (Treasure Kay 114) [1997 a5g² a5g 5g⁴ 6g² 6d² 6m* 7.6m a6g⁴ a8.5g a46
Oct 18] 3,600 2-y-o: first foal: dam (maiden) stayed 1¼m: modest performer: won
seller at Windsor in August: no form beyond 6f: acts on good to firm and dead
ground: visored 3 starts prior to final one. *K. R. Burke*

ROSIES MIRACLE 2 b.g. (Apr 20) Rambo Dancer (CAN) 107 – Rose Flyer   –
(IRE) 63 (Nordico (USA)) [1997 a6g Nov 17] 9,000Y: first foal: dam (see above)
stayed 1m: 33/1, showed little in maiden at Southwell. *M. C. Chapman*

ROSSEL (USA) 4 b.g. Blushing John (USA) 120 – Northern Aspen (USA) 120   58
(Northern Dancer) [1996 67: 6.9m 8.2m 11f³ 12.1g* 15m⁵ 12.4f⁴ 13m 12.1f 1997
12.1d 13d 13s³ 13s May 8] rangy gelding: modest handicapper: form in 1997 only on
third start: probably stays 15f: acts on firm and soft ground: visored (wandered and
looked none too keen) third 3-y-o start: inconsistent. *P. Monteith*

ROSY OUTLOOK (USA) 3 b. or br.f. Trempolino (USA) 135 – Rosyphard   79
(USA) (Lyphard 132) [1996 6s: 6m⁶ 7g 1997 6m* 6m 6g³ 7.5g⁵ Jul 7] rather
leggy filly: fair performer: won maiden at Pontefract in April, flashing tail: best effort
when third in handicap at Newmarket: bred to stay beyond 6f: yet to race on ground
softer than good: carries head awkwardly and tends to hang. *I. A. Balding*

ROTHERFIELD PARK (IRE) 5 b.m. High Estate 127 – Alriyaah 73 (Shareef   36
Dancer (USA) 135) [1996 40: 5g 5g⁶ 6m⁵ 5f² 6.1m⁵ 5m⁴ 5m⁴ 5f 1997 6.1d 5g 6g³
5m⁶ 6m Aug 8] neat mare: poor sprint handicapper: acts on firm ground and the all-
weather. *C. Smith*

ROTOR MAN (IRE) 3 b.g. River Falls 113 – Need For Cash (USA) (Raise A   62
Native) [1996 67?: 6m 6g 6g 1997 7m⁵ 8g 7.1g³ 7g⁶ 6d 7.1m⁶ 7.1g Sep 15] leggy,
useful-looking gelding: modest maiden handicapper: below form last 3 starts: best
form at 7f: tried blinkered and visored. *J. D. Bethell*

ROUFONTAINE 6 gr.m. Rousillon (USA) 133 – Bellifontaine (FR) (Bellypha   83
130) [1996 85: a12g* a12g 12.1d* 10.2g* 10.2m* 9f⁴ 10m⁶ 10m* 10.2f⁴ 10m⁵ 12d a67
1997 11.7m⁶ 10s* 12.1g² 10.2m² 12.3s⁵ 10g³ 10.2g³ 10.2g a12g⁵ Dec 4] workmanlike mare: fairly useful on turf, fair on all-weather: won minor event at Windsor in
May: good efforts afterwards when placed in handicaps: effective at 1¼m to easy
1½m: acts on firm and soft ground: blinkered once: usually waited with. *W. R. Muir*

ROUND ROBIN (IRE) 3 ch.g. Royal Academy (USA) 130 – Flying Fantasy   72
(Habitat 134) [1996 NR 1997 7.1s⁴ 7.5d³ 7.5g⁶ 9m⁵ 10g² a9.4g Dec 6] 6,400Y:
smallish gelding: half-brother to useful 6f/7f winner Flying Diva (by Chief Singer)
and a winner abroad by Persian Bold: dam sister to 1000 Guineas and Champion
Stakes winner Flying Water: fair maiden: placed at Beverley and Ayr (blinkered):
stays 1¼m: acts on dead ground: tends to carry head awkwardly. *C. W. Thornton*

ROUSSI (USA) 5 b.g. Nureyev (USA) 131 – Iva Reputation (USA) (Sir Ivor 135)   44
[1996 –: 10.1s 8g 9.9g a8g a9.4g 1997 a9.4g⁴ a8g*ᵈⁱˢ a8g² 10.3m 10.1g Mar 25]
good-bodied gelding: poor performer: landed gamble in handicap at Southwell in
January, subsequently disqualified for testing positive to prohibited substance: stays
1m: acts on fibresand, stiff tasks on turf in 1997: finished lame final start. *D. Nicholls*

ROVING MINSTREL 6 ch.h. Cree Song 99 – Klairove 74 (Averof 123) [1996   90
95: 8s² 7m³ 7m 7.1d 1997 8m Mar 22] good-topped horse: often looks very well:
fairly useful handicapper: creditable eighth in Lincoln at Doncaster (a race he won
in 1995) on only 6-y-o start: effective at 7f to 1m: twice below form on very firm
ground, acts on any other, including fibresand: races close up: game. *B. A. McMahon*

ROWLANDSONS CHARM (IRE) 4 b.f. Fayruz 116 – Magic Gold (Sallust –
134) [1996 –, a62: a8g* a7g² a8g* a10g² a10g⁴ a8g* a8g³ a7g² 8.3m 9.7d a10g²
a13g⁵ a13g 1997 a10g⁶ a10g Nov 25] sturdy, workmanlike filly: modest performer at
7f to 1¼m at 3 yrs: well beaten both starts in 1997: usually visored. *Miss B. Sanders*

ROWLANDSONS STUD (IRE) 4 b. or br.g. Distinctly North (USA) 115 – Be 46
My Million (Taufan (USA) 119) [1996 52, a63: a6g² a6g³ a6g³ a5g³ a6g² a6g⁶ a6g* a53
6f³ 5.1g 5g 6m 5.1f a6g⁴ 7m 6m a6g 1997 5.1m⁵ 5.3m³ a5g 5d 5.3g 6f a5g³ Dec 22]
modest handicapper on all-weather, poor on turf: stays 6f: acts on equitrack and firm
ground: tried blinkered: inconsistent. *K. C. Comerford*

ROY 2 ch.g. (May 9) Keen 116 – Billante (USA) (Graustark) [1997 8m Sep 22] –
7,000 2-y-o: half-brother to several winners, including 1¾m winner Ela Billante (by
Ela-Mana-Mou): dam unraced from family of Environment Friend: 33/1, never a
factor in maiden at Kempton. *H. Morrison*

ROYAL ACCLAIM 12 ch.g. Tender King 123 – Glimmer 58 (Hot Spark 126) 28 §
[1996 –§, a33§: a8g a11g a9.4g⁵ 10g a8g³ 10.5d 9.7f⁶ 8.1f 1997 a8g⁵ a8g² a11g* a37 §
a10g a16g a7g⁴ a12g⁶ a8g 12m 8m⁴ 8s 8g⁴ 8.1g 10m⁴ 10.8d 10g⁵ 11.5f⁶ Oct 3]
sturdy gelding: poor handicapper: won amateurs event at Southwell in January: left
R. Dickin after fifth start, C. Jackson after eighth: effective at 1m to 1½m: best
all-weather form on fibresand, probably acts on any turf going: tried blinkered,
nearly always visored: often gets behind and is none too resolute. *K. R. Burke*

ROYAL ACTION 4 b.g. Royal Academy (USA) 130 – Ivor's Honey 91 (Sir Ivor –
135) [1996 75, a83: 8.2s⁵ 10g 8m³ 8.3m⁵ 11.5f² 10.1m⁴ 12m 11.9g 8m³ a8s* 1997 a96
a9.4g* a8.5g* a10g* a8.5g 10.1m Apr 23] good-topped gelding: good mover: much
improved on the all-weather early in year, winning well-contested handicaps at
Wolverhampton in January and February and minor event at Lingfield in March:
effective at 8.5f to 11.5f: tried blinkered (ran badly): often forces pace: won over
hurdles for O. Sherwood in November. *J. E. Banks*

ROYAL AMARETTO (IRE) 3 b.c. Fairy King (USA) – Melbourne Miss 112
(Chaparral (FR) 128) [1996 103: 7g³ 7.1m⁴ 7.1f* 7.3s² 1997 10g* 8g 10s⁵ 10f³ Jul
19] big, strong colt: smart performer: clearly best 3-y-o effort when trouncing 9
rivals, led home by Falak, in minor event at Newbury in April: well beaten in Irish
2000 Guineas at the Curragh next time: not entirely disgraced in Grand Prix de Paris
(10½ lengths fifth of 7 to Peintre Celebre) at Longchamp and listed race at Newbury
afterwards: takes good hold but should stay beyond 1¼m: has won on firm ground,
but easily best efforts on good or softer. *B. J. Meehan*

ROYAL APPLAUSE 4 b.c. Waajib 121 – Flying Melody (Auction Ring 124
(USA) 123) [1996 109: 8m 5f⁶ 6m* 6f 1997 6m* 6g* 6g* 6g² 6d* 5f³ a6f
Nov 8]
  The three-year-old careers of the two best juveniles of 1995, Alhaarth
and Royal Applause, didn't turn out quite as predicted. Both won five out of
five as two-year-olds (Royal Applause the Coventry, the Gimcrack and the
Middle Park) and both seemed to possess the physical scope to train on. The
parallels continued when they managed just a single win as three-year-olds,
though Royal Applause appeared to lose his way much more than Alhaarth,

Duke of York International Factors Stakes, York—Royal Applause is too good for Farhana

Cork And Orrery Stakes, Royal Ascot—Royal Applause justifies favouritism again; the grey Blue Goblin is second and Catch The Blues (No. 5) third

who at least performed to a consistently high level without being able to keep up with the very best. Alhaarth won the Prix du Rond-Point at Longchamp on Arc day but Royal Applause failed to come close to his juvenile form, tenth in the Guineas before unimpressively landing the odds in a five-runner minor event at Doncaster in July. Both Alhaarth and Royal Applause enjoyed much more success as four-year-olds, Alhaarth winning pattern races at the Curragh and Longchamp and Royal Applause belatedly fulfilling his potential by showing himself one of the best sprinters around.

Royal Applause was never tried beyond six furlongs in the latest season. He looked potential championship material almost from the outset, a smooth win in a useful listed event at Doncaster's opening turf fixture being followed by a most decisive one in the Duke of York International Factors Stakes at the York May meeting. Royal Applause made all in the Duke of York to win by a length and a quarter from Farhana, the only one to mount a serious challenge from two furlongs out. With the lack of good sprinters already in evidence, the prospects for Royal Applause were looking rosy and he made it three out of three for the season in the Cork And Orrery Stakes at Royal Ascot, starting favourite in a field of twenty-three and running out a length and a half winner from Blue Goblin after being in command most of the way. The form of the Cork And Orrery looked significantly better than that of the much more valuable five-furlong pattern race at the Royal meeting, the King's Stand Stakes, which attracted an unusually large field of eighteen.

The re-emergence of Royal Applause and the dearth of top sprinters was evidenced by the composition of the field for the July Cup at Newmarket, and by the betting on it. Royal Applause started 11/10 favourite in a field of nine, in which the three-year-old Bahamian Bounty, a Middle Park winner reverting to sprinting after failing to get the trip in the Poule d'Essai des Poulains, was second favourite. Blue Goblin and the Cork And Orrery fifth Indian Rocket were the only others shorter than 10/1; the three who had contested the King's Stand, Easycall, Rambling Bear and Compton Place (fifth, seventh and twelfth respectively), started the rank outsiders. Channel 4 viewers, incidentally, experienced an unusual diversion as John McCririck, in camera providing a betting show, was pounced upon (was it a waste of a good cream cake or not?). Royal Applause suffered a metaphorical slap in the face in the race itself as 50/1-shot Compton Place brought his winning sequence to an end. It goes almost without saying that Compton Place produced a performance that few, outside his connections, had thought him capable of. Royal Applause travelled strongly as usual but couldn't quicken with the patiently-ridden winner when he took the lead over a furlong out. A length and three quarters down at the line, Royal Applause beat the rest decisively, having three lengths to spare over third-placed Indian Rocket.

*Haydock Park Sprint Cup—jockey Michael Hills glances round for dangers;
Danetime (virtually hidden behind Royal Applause), Tomba and Averti (far right) fight it out for the placings*

Royal Applause seemed to run at least as well in the July Cup as he had in the Cork And Orrery and he was again favourite when sent next for the Haydock Park Sprint Cup. British racing was cancelled on Saturday September 6th, the day of the funeral of the Princess of Wales, the Sprint Cup being brought forward a day. Royal Applause made the most of his draw right against the stand rail and, soon in front, missed the scrimmaging which took place early on as Danetime crossed from an outside draw. Royal Applause had the race sewn up approaching the distance and won comfortably by a length and a quarter from Danetime, with Tomba third and the close Nunthorpe third Averti back in fourth. Tomba and Averti both suffered in the interference caused by Danetime and the placings of second and third were reversed after a Jockey Club inquiry. Royal Applause effectively completed his racing career with a close third, raced at the minimum trip for the first time during the year and never quite in front, to Carmine Lake and Pas de Reponse in the Prix de l'Abbaye on Arc day. Plans were announced for Royal Applause to take the place of the deceased Shirley Heights at the Sandringham Stud in Norfolk (fee for 1998, £6,500 with the October 1st concession), but, as an afterthought, he was sent for the Breeders' Cup Sprint, in which he came back last of fourteen.

The medium-sized Royal Applause, a good mover, is a very different type of racehorse to the one he has replaced at the Royal studs. Derby winner Shirley Heights was a strong influence for stamina, noted mostly for the achievements of his three-year-olds and upwards. Royal Applause, whose sire Waajib was a miler, can be expected to sire mainly precocious and speedy sorts, types that abound on the distaff side of his pedigree. The dam Flying Melody was a useful racemare who spent most of her time in sprints; the grandam Whispering Star was a sprinter, as was the great grandam Peggy West, a half-sister to the top-class sprinter of the 'fifties Pappa Fourway. The majority

806

		Try My Best	Northern Dancer
	Waajih	(b 1975)	Sex Appeal
	(b 1983)	Coryana	Sassafras
Royal Applause		(b 1976)	Rosolini
(b.c. 1993)		Auction Ring	Bold Bidder
	Flying Melody	(b 1972)	Hooplah
	(b 1979)	Whispering Star	Sound Track
		(ch 1963)	Peggy West

of Flying Melody's six winning offspring have turned out to be sprinters, including Lyric Fantasy (by Tate Gallery), the only two-year-old to win the Nunthorpe Stakes in the past forty years. Lyric Fantasy's three-year-old career proved an anti-climax and the same can be said of Flying Melody's third Group 1 winner, the Dewhurst victor In Command (by Sadler's Wells), who failed to reach a place in three races in his second season. Royal Applause was ideally suited by six furlongs and showed his best form on good and dead going. *B. W. Hills*

ROYAL ATY (IRE)   3 b.c. Royal Academy (USA) 130 – Atyaaf (USA) 48 (Irish   96
River (FR) 131) [1996 90p: 8d² 1997 a8g* 8g⁶ 8g 7g² 7g³ 6g a7s Nov 16] useful
performer, lightly raced: very easy winner of maiden at Lingfield in January: placed
in listed event at Newmarket (second to Andreyev) and minor contest at Leicester
(penultimate start for P. Kelleway) in the spring: off course 5 months, well beaten in
allowance race at Aqueduct: stays 1m. *A. Penna, jnr, USA*

ROYAL AXMINSTER   2 b.c. (Feb 24) Alzao (USA) 117 – Number One Spot   –
71 (Reference Point 139) [1997 6s May 18] 14,000Y: useful-looking colt: first foal:
dam 7f winner, from top-class family: 'double carpet', in rear in maiden at Newbury.
Mrs P. N. Dutfield

ROYAL BLACKBIRD 3 br.f. Most Welcome 131 – Thulium (Mansingh (USA) 120) [1996 64: 6m 5.3g* 5.2g² 5d³ 1997 7g 6.1g 6g Jul 7] modest winner as 2-y-o: well beaten in 1997: sold, and sent to Zimbabwe. *J. E. Banks* –

ROYAL BLUE 2 ch.g. (May 4) Ron's Victory (USA) 129 – Angels Are Blue 73 (Stanford 121§) [1997 5m 5.1d⁵ 5d Oct 21] fifth foal: half-brother to 1991 French 2-y-o 7f winner Valiant Miss (by Valiyar): dam, 5.8f winner, half-sister to smart sprinter Polykratis: modest form at Nottingham, second start in maidens. *M. D. I. Usher* 63

ROYAL BOUNTY (IRE) 2 b.f. (May 24) Generous (IRE) 139 – Queen Helen 112 (Troy 137) [1997 7.1g⁶ 7m² 7.5g* 8f Sep 11] leggy, close-coupled filly: fifth live foal: half-sister to 3-y-o Boss Lady, 11f winner Helen's Bower (by Bellypha) and a winner in Denmark: dam 7f (at 2 yrs) and 1¾m winner but best at 1¼m/1½m: fairly useful form: won maiden at Beverley in August: not discredited in unfavoured group in nursery at Doncaster following month: should prove suited by at least 1¼m: raced only on good ground or firmer. *Major W. R. Hern* 80

ROYAL CARLTON (IRE) 5 b.g. Mulhollande (USA) 107 – Saintly Angel 87 (So Blessed 130) [1996 58+: 6f 6m a8g³ a8g* 1997 a7g* a7g⁴ a8g* a7g⁵ a8g⁶ a8g² 6.9g a7g a7s a7g Dec 19] fair handicapper on the all-weather, modest on turf: won twice at Lingfield in January: well below form last 4 starts: stays 1m: acts on dead going, better all-weather form on equitrack than fibresand: tends to idle. *G. L. Moore* a74

ROYAL CASCADE (IRE) 3 b.g. River Falls 113 – Relative Stranger (Cragador 110) [1996 56: a6s⁶ a7g² 1997 a6g* 6g 6f⁶ 5.9m⁵ a5g a6g⁵ a6g⁶ a7g Nov 21] made all in seller at Wolverhampton in February: just poor form afterwards: should stay beyond 6f. *B. A. McMahon* a59 d

ROYAL CASTLE (IRE) 3 b.c. Caerleon (USA) 132 – Sun Princess 130 (English Prince 129) [1996 65p: 7d 1997 11g 10.2d⁵ 12m* 14s 12m⁴ 14.1m* 14d³ Oct 17] sturdy, lengthy colt: good mover: progressive handicapper: won at Pontefract in June and Redcar (easily) in October: will stay at least 2m: acts on good to firm and dead going: sent to France: should make useful stayer. *Major W. R. Hern* 90 p

ROYAL CEILIDH (IRE) 4 b.f. Prince Rupert (FR) 121 – Isa (Dance In Time (CAN)) [1996 82: 6g³ 6g⁶ 8m* 7f³ 8m⁶ 8g² 8d³ 7.9g² 8m 8g 7m 8s 1997 8m⁴ 8.5d⁶ 7m⁵ 7s 7m⁵ 10.1g⁴ 8g⁴ 8g⁵ 8d 9m Oct 7] big, strong filly: has a quick action: fair handicapper: best 4-y-o effort on reappearance: effective at 7f to 1¼m: acts on firm ground and dead, poor efforts on soft: no improvement in visor. *Denys Smith* 79 d

ROYAL CIRCUS 8 b.g. Kris 135 – Circus Ring 122 (High Top 131) [1996 42, a47: a13g⁴ a16g⁴ a12g* a12g⁵ a12g⁵ a16g 16.1f² 14.1m² 12f³ 14.9m⁶ 16.2m 1997 a12g a13g³ 13.1m* 14.9g⁵ 17.2f⁵ 13.8g a16s a14g Nov 17] workmanlike gelding: poor handicapper: trained first 2 starts by P. Webber, next 4 by I. Williams: won selling event at Bath in July: below form last 4 starts: effective at 1½m and 2m: acts on firm and dead ground and equitrack: front runner. *P. W. Hiatt* 45

ROYAL CITIZEN (IRE) 8 b.g. Caerleon (USA) 132 – Taking Steps 100 (Gay Fandango (USA) 132) [1996 NR 1997 a14.8f² 16.1g a16.2g a14.8g Apr 26] close-coupled gelding: modest performer: stays 15f: acts on fibresand, suited by good ground or firmer on turf: often blinkered/visored earlier in career: reluctant to race second start. *J. F. Bottomley* a54

ROYAL COURT (IRE) 4 b.c. Sadler's Wells (USA) 132 – Rose of Jericho (USA) (Alleged (USA) 138) [1996 116: 12.1d* 11.9g* 11.9m³ 12m⁴ 1997 13.4v* 12d⁵ 12g⁴ 12g⁴ Jul 27] good-topped colt: has a long stride: smart performer: gained most important success when beating Further Flight by ¾ length after splendid tussle in Ormonde Stakes at Chester in May: fourth in Hardwicke Stakes at Royal Ascot (behind Predappio) and Group 1 event at Dusseldorf (to Luso) last 2 starts: needs really good test at 1½m and will stay 1¾m+: may well prove best on good ground or softer: sometimes bandaged near-fore: sold only 21,000 gns in December. *P. W. Chapple-Hyam* 116

ROYAL CROWN (IRE) 3 b.g. Sadler's Wells (USA) 132 – Rose of Jericho (USA) (Alleged (USA) 138) [1996 74p: 8m 1997 12m⁴ 11.7g² 12g³ 15d² 14.1s² 16g⁴ Oct 24] smallish, well-made colt: fairly useful maiden: best efforts in handicaps at 94

Ayr and Newbury on fourth and final starts: will stay beyond 2m: sold 57,000 gns after final start. *P. W. Chapple-Hyam*

ROYAL CRUSADE (USA)   3 b.c. Diesis 133 – Sainte Croix (USA) (Nijinsky – (CAN) 138) [1996 89P: 8m* 1997 10m⁶ 8.1g⁵ 10.3m 11.9s 8g Oct 18] tall, lengthy, good sort: very impressive winner of only race at 2 yrs: virtually bolted to post before finishing tailed off on reappearance: soundly beaten afterwards: sold 11,000 gns in October, and sent to Sweden: none too tractable. *W. J. Haggas*

ROYAL DIVERSION (IRE)   4 b.f. Marju (IRE) 127 – Royal Recreation (USA)   63 (His Majesty (USA)) [1996 82: 7d³ 9m 10d³ 10m 9m⁶ 10m³ 11.4m³ 11.9g³ 12s* 1997 12m³ 12v Oct 10] leggy filly: fairly useful at 3 yrs for J. Dunlop: just modest form in 2 starts in 1997: stays 1½m: goes well on soft ground. *M. C. Pipe*

ROYAL DOME (IRE)   5 b.g. Salt Dome (USA) – Brook's Dilemma 80 (Known   78 Fact (USA) 135) [1996 78: 5m² 5m 5g 5m⁴ 5g 5m² 5m* 6m² 5m* 6m 5m 5m 5d³ 5g 5d 1997 5g 5m 5m 5g* 5g⁵ 5m⁵ 5m⁵ 5m* 6g² 5m 6g 5g 5.2m 5m 5d 5g² 6g 6m Nov 4] good-quartered gelding: fair performer: won minor events at Pontefract and Beverley in the summer: generally not in same sort of form afterwards: stays an easy 6f: acts on good to firm and dead ground: visored (ran creditably) once at 3 yrs: sometimes hangs left under pressure. *Martyn Wane*

ROYAL DREAM   2 b.f. (Jan 25) Ardkinglass 114 – Faraway Grey 99 (Absalom   74 128) [1997 a5g⁵ 5d* 6m* 6g 6.1m³ 6m⁶ 6d Sep 5] 5,000Y: half-sister to 1m winner Mrs Dawson (by Sharrood): dam 2-y-o 5f winner who stayed 1m: fair performer: won seller at Beverley in May and minor event at Ripon in June: gave impression something amiss in claimer final start: stays 6f: inconsistent. *J. Berry*

ROYALE FIGURINE (IRE)   6 ch.m. Dominion Royale 112 – Cree's Figurine   106 63 (Creetown 123) [1996 107: 6f³ 5f⁵ 6m⁶ 6m* 6m⁶ 5d 6g⁶ 6s 1997 5.7d* 5g⁴ 6g⁶ 5d 7s³ Jul 3] quite attractive mare: useful sprinter: won listed race at Bath in May by 3½ lengths from Arethusa: good efforts when fourth of 10 to Croft Pool in Temple Stakes at Sandown and sixth of 23 to Royal Applause in Cork And Orrery Stakes at Royal Ascot: effective at 5f and 6f: acted on firm and soft ground: usually held up: genuine: in foal to Most Welcome. *M. J. Fetherston-Godley*

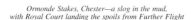

Ormonde Stakes, Chester—a slog in the mud,
with Royal Court landing the spoils from Further Flight

ROYALE FINALE (IRE) 3 ch.g. Royal Academy (USA) 130 – Final Farewell 76 (USA) (Proud Truth (USA)) [1996 65p: 7d³ 1997 8g⁵ 8m May 4] lengthy gelding: fair maiden: best effort at Newbury on reappearance: likely to prove short of 1m: sold only 3,500 gns in October, and joined R. Marvin. *H. R. A. Cecil*

ROYAL EMBLEM 3 gr.f. Presidium 124 – Lily of France 81 (Monsanto (FR) – 121) [1996 56: 5.3f² 5g³ 6.1m⁵ 5.3f² 6g a6g 1997 5m⁶ a7g 6.1d 6m 6s 6f 8m a5g a7g Dec 22] close-coupled filly: modest maiden at 2 yrs: no form in 1997: tried blinkered. *E. A. Wheeler*

ROYAL ROSE (FR) 3 ch.f. Bering 136 – Rose Blanche (USA) (Nureyev 75 (USA) 131) [1996 8s 8.3s⁵ 1997 8g² 10g 8s 8g² 8g⁵ 8.3m 8m* 10.5d 8.1m² 8.1m 8m Oct 6] tall, sparely-made filly: first reported foal: dam French 8.5f winner: trained by C. Laffon-Parias in France until after fourth start: first form here when winning maiden at Newmarket in August: should stay beyond 1m: acts on good to firm going: blinkered fourth start, visored 3 of last 4: inconsistent. *A. Bailey*

ROYAL EXPRESSION 5 b.g. Sylvan Express 117 – Edwins' Princess 75 77 (Owen Dudley 121) [1996 76: a12g³ 16.2g* 16.1g² 14.1g* 16.5g² 1997 13.8g 17.1m⁴ 16g² 17.1m³ 16f* 12.1s² 16.4d⁵ Jul 5] tall gelding: has a round action: fair performer: nowhere near best when winning claimer at Redcar in June: left Mrs M. Reveley after next start: effective at 1¾m to 17f: acts on firm ground and on equitrack: blinkered (ran well) final 2-y-o start: fairly useful hurdler, successful in July and August. *F. Jordan*

ROYAL GROUND (IRE) 2 b.c. (Mar 2) Common Grounds 118 – Miss 59 Goodbody (Castle Keep 121) [1997 7g 7d⁶ 8d⁶ 9m³ 8.2d² 10d 8g Oct 24] 20,000Y: compact colt: has a round action: half-brother to Irish 1990 2-y-o 5f winner Jambo Jambo (by Kafu) and 3 winners abroad: dam lightly raced: modest maiden on balance: beaten in sellers 3 of last 4 starts: stays 9f: has hung: sold, and sent to Austria. *M. R. Channon*

ROYAL INTERVIEW (IRE) 2 b.g. (Apr 14) Mukaddamah (USA) 125 – 55 Empress Wu 62 (High Line 125) [1997 5g⁶ 5.2g⁶ 5f⁵ 7s 7m Oct 23] 18,000Y: sturdy, lengthy gelding: fourth foal: half-brother to 4-y-o Kernof: dam ran twice: only modest form at best: off course over 5 months after second start: has seemed reluctant. *M. R. Channon*

ROYAL INTRUSION 4 ch.g. Roman Warrior 132 – Image of War 70 (Warpath – 113) [1996 –: 10m 6g⁶ 7g 8f 1997 6.1m Jun 13] no worthwhile form. *R. J. Hodges*

ROYAL LEGEND 5 b.g. Fairy King (USA) – Legend of Arabia (Great Nephew 57 126) [1996 56: a13g³ 10.1m 8g 12.1m³ a12g² 1997 a13g a11g* a12g⁶ a11g³ a11g⁵ a11g³ Dec 8] leggy gelding: modest performer: won claimer at Southwell in May: third in seller and handicap on same course after: stays 1½m: acts on fibresand and good to firm going: visored/blinkered second to fifth starts (left J. Pearce after latter): none too consistent. *R. M. Flower*

ROYAL MARK (IRE) 4 b.g. Fairy King (USA) – Take Your Mark (USA) 96 (Round Table) [1996 88: 8m⁵ 7f² 8f 6g³ 7m 7d 7g 1997 7m⁶ 6d⁵ 7m 7m* 7m 7d⁴ Aug 29] good-topped gelding: useful handicapper: won at Newcastle in August: races mostly at 7f, but used to be at least as effective at 1m: acts on firm and dead ground: tried blinkered: joined T. Easterby. *T. D. Barron*

ROYAL ORCHID (IRE) 3 ch.f. Shalford (IRE) 124§ – Indigo Blue (IRE) 56 – (Bluebird (USA) 125) [1996 74: 5m² 5m⁶ 6m⁴ 6m⁵ 7f⁴ 7.1s a6g 1997 5d 7f Jul 15] neat filly: fair maiden at 2 yrs: well beaten in 1997, lame final start. *R. Hannon*

ROYAL PHILOSOPHER 5 b.h. Faustus (USA) 118 – Princess Lucy 42 (Local – Suitor (USA) 128) [1996 111: 8d* 7.1d 8.1d² 8g* 8g³ 8g⁴ 8m 8v⁴ a9.4g⁵ 1997 8.1g 9s 10m⁴ 8v⁴ Oct 10] big, strong horse: smart performer at 1m/9f at best: well beaten in 1997: joined K. Bailey. *J. W. Hills*

ROYAL RESULT (USA) 4 b. or br.g. Gone West (USA) – Norette (Northfields 81 (USA)) [1996 85: 7g 8g⁵ 8.1m² 8f* 9g 9.2g⁴ 8m³ 1997 8m 10m 8g⁶ 8m 8.5d⁶ 8g⁵ 7s 7d⁴ 7m* 7m⁵ Oct 28] good-bodied, attractive gelding: fairly useful performer: left T. D. Barron after seventh start: finally took advantage of good mark when winning handicap at Newmarket in October: probably better at 7f than 1m: acts on firm and dead ground, probably not on soft. *M. W. Easterby*

ROYAL RIGHTS 2 ch.c. (Mar 11) Lion Cavern (USA) 117 – Noble Destiny 89   79
(Dancing Brave (USA) 140) [1997 6g³ 6m⁵ 7s⁵ Oct 14] 250,000Y: lengthy, useful-
looking colt: third foal: half-brother to 4-y-o Maiden Castle: dam, 2-y-o 7f winner
but disappointing at 3 yrs, out of useful mare Tender Loving Care: easily best effort
in maidens when third at Yarmouth: reportedly lost action at Goodwood next time:
sold approx. £22,500 in Dubai in November. *D. R. Loder*

ROYAL ROULETTE 3 ch.f. Risk Me (FR) 127 – Princess Lily 65 (Blakeney   54
126) [1996 45+: 6g a8.5g⁵ 8.2g a8.5g³ 8g a7g⁵ a8g² a7g 1997 a8s* a8.5g³ a9.4g³   a69
a12g² a12g 11.8d 9.7d³ a12g* a12s a16g⁴ Dec 10] fair on all-weather, modest on turf:
trained by S. Woods first 7 starts: won seller at Southwell in January and handicap
at Lingfield in November: stays 1½m: acts on dead ground and both all-weather:
usually visored/blinkered before final 3 starts. *Miss B. Sanders*

ROYAL SCIMITAR (USA) 5 ch.g. Diesis 133 – Princess of Man 104 (Green   –
God 128) [1996 100: 11.7f* 12s³ 13.9m³ 11.9g² 12m 13.4d* 1997 12m 14d May 21]
close-coupled gelding: useful handicapper at 4 yrs for P. Cole: well held in 1997:
joined M. Tompkins. *Mrs A. J. Perrett*

ROYAL SEATON 8 b.g. Blakeney 126 – Aldbury Girl 79 (Galivanter 131) [1996   –
NR 1997 10m 10g⁶ 14m⁶ 12d⁴ 11.4d 12g 16.2v 14.6g Oct 24] sturdy gelding:
formerly fairly useful: missed 1995 and 1996 seasons, and signs of retaining only a
little ability at 8 yrs. *Mrs P. N. Dutfield*

ROYAL SHOCK (IRE) 2 b.c. (Feb 21) Brief Truce (USA) 126 – Rince Deas   73
(IRE) 53 (Alzao (USA) 117) [1997 7m⁶ a8.5g⁶ 8m³ Oct 1] 21,000F: 62,000Y: neat
colt: third foal: half-brother to 3-y-o Shock Value and fairly useful 7f to 9f winner
Panata (by Tirol): dam, placed at 5f at 2 yrs, sister to smart miler Mirror Black: fair
form in maidens, running on belatedly to snatch third at Newcastle: shapes as though
will be suited by further than 1m: sent to UAE. *D. R. Loder*

ROYAL SHYNESS 2 b.f. (Mar 22) Royal Academy (USA) 130 – Miss Demure   104
106 (Shy Groom (USA)) [1997 6m³ 5m² 6m* 6m³ Sep 30] fourth foal: half-sister to
4-y-o Steamroller Stanly and useful 1994 2-y-o 6f winner Missel (by Storm Bird):
dam won Lowther Stakes: progressive form: won maiden at Kempton in September
by ½ length from Ikhteyaar: 16/1, very good third of 8 to Embassy in Cheveley Park
Stakes at Newmarket, beaten 3¾ lengths, held up and no extra final 1f: will probably
stay 7f: raced only on good to firm ground. *G. Lewis*

ROYAL SOUTH (IRE) 4 b.c. Common Grounds 118 – Arkadina's Million   –
(King of Clubs 124) [1996 6s³ 5s 6g 6.3m 9g² 7m 9d 8.5m 7d⁶ 1997 7m⁶ 7.5m 7m 6g
8.2g 8d 8g 8.2m 7.5g Aug 23] close-coupled colt: second foal: dam, placed in Ireland
up to 1½m, from family of Ezzoud: fairly useful (rated 85) but inconsistent handicapper in Ireland at 3 yrs: little worthwhile form for current stable. *P. S. Felgate*

ROYAL SQUARE (CAN) 11 ch.g. Gregorian (USA) 124 – Dance Crazy (USA)   64
(Foolish Pleasure (USA)) [1996 NR 1997 a12g² Jul 26] big, strong gelding: first run
on flat since 1991 when second of 9 in Southwell seller: won over fences month later.
N. P. Littmoden

ROYAL VELVET 2 b.f. (May 2) Perpendicular 119 – Stellaris (Star Appeal 133)   –
[1997 6m⁵ 7.5d 7g Aug 25] half-sister to several winners, including 3-y-o Time Can
Tell and fairly useful 6f/1m performer Ashdren (by Lochnager): dam lightly raced:
well beaten in minor event and maidens. *C. W. Fairhurst*

ROY BOY 5 b.g. Emarati (USA) 74 – Starky's Pet (Mummy's Pet 125) [1996 –:   63
10m⁶ 12g⁶ 1997 7m 7m³ Jun 14] rangy, good-topped gelding: good mover: modest
maiden handicapper, lightly raced these days: stays 7f: acts on good to firm and dead
ground: below form only try in blinkers: sometimes carries head awkwardly and
looks temperamental. *C. A. Horgan*

ROYRACE 5 b.g. Wace (USA) 82 – Royal Tycoon (Tycoon II) [1996 –: 11.8d⁶   –
12m 14.1m 14.9g⁵ 17.9g 18g 1997 a12g Feb 28] tall gelding: no worthwhile form.
W. M. Brisbourne

RUBAMMA 2 b.c. (Apr 23) Kris 135 – Idle Gossip (USA) (Lyphard (USA) 132)   74
[1997 6m 8.1d 7f⁴ 7s³ a8g³ a8.5g³ a7g Dec 18] smallish, robust colt: sixth foal: a68
closely related to Idle Son (by Sharpen Up), winning miler in France/Italy (listed
race) later successful in USA: dam, won from 6f to 9f in USA, from excellent family:

fair maiden: probably stays 1m: probably acts on both all-weather, best turf run on soft going. *P. T. Walwyn*

RUBY ANGEL 4 ch.f. Superlative 118 – Queen Angel 88 (Anfield 117) [1996 47: 7.1d⁶ a8.5g⁵ a8g³ 1997 a8g 10s May 17] compact filly: poor maiden: left H. Candy after reappearance. *Miss B. Sanders* –

RUBY BEAR 2 gr.f. (Apr 7) Thethingaboutitis (USA) 106 – Hitravelscene (Mansingh (USA) 120) [1997 7g a7g a8.5g⁶ Oct 18] 3,500 2-y-o: half-sister to winning sprinters by Lugana Beach and Lucky Wednesday: dam poor plater: no promise in maidens and seller. *W. M. Brisbourne* –

RUBY ESTATE (IRE) 6 b.m. High Estate 127 – Tuesday Morning (Sadler's Wells (USA) 132) [1996 NR 1997 a10g Dec 19] modest performer at 3 yrs, lightly raced and well beaten since. *N. A. Graham* –

RUDE AWAKENING 3 b.g. Rudimentary (USA) 118 – Final Call 79 (Town Crier 119) [1996 79: 5g² 5m² 5g* 6g⁶ 5m⁴ 7m 1997 7m 6m 6g 7.5d⁴ 8s 8f⁴ 8m 7g 7.1g 8.5f 6.1m Sep 23] sturdy gelding: fair 2-y-o for G. Lewis: mostly well below form in handicaps in 1997: stays 7.5f: acts on firm and dead ground: no improvement in blinkers: carries head high under pressure and possibly ungenuine. *C. W. Fairhurst* 69 d

RUDE SHOCK 2 gr.g. (Feb 6) Rudimentary (USA) 118 – Frighten The Life (Kings Lake (USA) 133) [1997 7g 7m⁶ 8.2m 8m Oct 22] 13,500Y: lengthy gelding: third foal: dam unraced daughter of sister to Ballad Rock: no worthwhile form. *M. H. Tompkins* –

RUDIMENTAL 3 b.g. Rudimentary (USA) 118 – Full Orchestra 83 (Shirley Heights 130) [1996 74: a7g³ a6g* 1997 9g* 10s² 8g 10m² 10.3m³ 9m² Oct 4] big, good-bodied gelding: useful handicapper: won at Sandown in June: unimpressive in appearance, clearly best effort when ¾-length second of 36 to stable-companion Pasternak in Cambridgeshire at Newmarket on final start, keeping on gamely under strong ride: stays 1¼m: acts on good to firm going and fibresand, possibly unsuited by soft: should progress again in 1998. *Sir Mark Prescott* 101 p

RUDI'S PET (IRE) 3 ch.c. Don't Forget Me 127 – Pink Fondant (Northfields (USA)) [1996 92: 5m⁴ 6m⁶ 5g* 5m⁵ 5m⁴ 5m³ 5g* 5d⁶ 6.5g⁵ 1997 5s³ 5.1d 7d 7m 5d⁶ 6d² 5d 5m⁵ 5s* 6g 5v 5g* Oct 25] strong, close-coupled colt: useful handicapper: won at Sandown (made all) in August and Doncaster (hampered start, came from well off pace to beat Perryston View by 2½ lengths) in October: stays 6f: has form on good to firm going, best efforts on good or softer: blinkered fifth start onwards: sold 42,000 gns in October, and joined Mrs J. Ramsden. *R. Hannon* 104

RUDOLPHINE (IRE) 6 ch.g. Persian Bold 123 – Ruffling Point (Gorytus (USA) 132) [1996 NR 1997 a8g⁴ a10s Nov 28] 36,000Y, 500 4-y-o: second foal: half-brother to 7f/1m winner Certain Way (by Sure Blade): dam unraced half-sister to Gordon Stakes winner John French: well beaten in maiden and seller. *Bob Jones* –

RUFALDA (IRE) 3 b.f. Sadler's Wells (USA) 132 – Smageta (High Top 131) [1996 NR 1997 8.5d 10g 10g 12g⁵ 11.8g 11.9g⁴ 14g³ Sep 27] good-topped filly: half-sister to several winners including 1996 3-y-o 7f winner Robamaset (by Caerleon) and 10.6f winner Regordes (by Commanche Run), both fairly useful: dam Group 3 1m winner in Italy at 2 yrs and third in Italian 1000 Guineas and Oaks: fair maiden: best effort in handicap at Haydock final start: will stay 2m: ran creditably in blinkers: takes good hold and may prove best with strong handling. *L. M. Cumani* 72

RUMBUSTIOUS 3 b.f. Rambo Dancer (CAN) 107 – Persian Alexandra (Persian Bold 123) [1996 65: 6g 7m² 6m* 7f* 7.6m 7m⁵ 6.1s⁶ 1997 8.5m 7.3s 8f 8g* 8.2g 8g 6.9m⁴ 8g⁴ 8d a10s Nov 28] leggy filly: modest performer: won seller at Newmarket in June: stays 1m: acts on firm ground, possibly unsuited by softer than good: tried blinkered: joined J. S. Moore. *R. Hannon* 57

RUM LAD 3 gr.g. Efisio 120 – She's Smart 88 (Absalom 128) [1996 65: 5m³ 5g⁶ 5m⁴ 6g² 6d 6m⁶ 1997 7m 8.5m 7g⁵ 8m 6g⁴ 6m⁴ 6m* 6f⁵ 6g⁴ 5m* 6s* 6m 6d 6.1g 6s Oct 15] sturdy gelding: fair performer: won maiden at Catterick (made all) in May and handicaps at Carlisle in June and Catterick in July: ran creditably penultimate start: best at 5f/6f: has form on firm ground, very best effort on soft. *J. J. Quinn* 71

RUMPELSTILTSKIN 5 ch.g. Sharpo 132 – Ouija 104 (Silly Season 127) [1996 –
–: a7g 1997 a11g a10g Jan 23] good-topped gelding: signs of ability but no worthwhile form. *H. S. Howe*

RUMUZ (IRE) 3 b. or br.f. Marju (IRE) 127 – Balqis (USA) 93 (Advocator) 64
[1996 NR 1997 9m^2 10m^4 8.1s Aug 30] angular filly: eighth foal: half-sister to
several winners, including useful 1½m performer Libk (by Kalaglow): dam 2-y-o 5f
winner: modest form in maidens first 2 starts. *E. A. L. Dunlop*

RUNADRUM 2 b.g. (May 7) Prince Daniel (USA) – Runabay (Run The Gantlet –
(USA)) [1997 6s 7m Nov 4] sixth reported foal: half-brother to a winning jumper in
France: dam French maiden: no promise in maidens. *W. W. Haigh*

RUNAROUND 2 b.f. (Apr 21) Northern Park (USA) 107 – Party Game 70 (Red –
Alert 127) [1997 6m 6m 6m^6 Aug 9] good-bodied filly: closely related to 6f winner
Belle Soiree (by Night Shift) and half-sister to several winners, including 4-y-o
Passion For Life: dam 6f winner: no worthwhile form. *S. Dow*

RUNIC SYMBOL 6 b.g. Warning 136 – Pagan Deity 88 (Brigadier Gerard 144) 37
[1996 43: 8f^2 8g^4 10d^3 10m* 10g^2 10m^5 10g^3 10m 10g 9m a9.4g^5 1997 10g^5 9m 9.9m
10.8d^3 9.7s^6 10.8g^3 10g^2 8m^6 10g^4 8.1g^6 10.1f 10.8g a10g a14g Dec 18] leggy,
angular gelding: poor performer: effective at 1m to 11f: acts on any turf ground: ran
poorly in blinkers. *M. Blanshard*

RUN LUCY RUN 3 b.f. Risk Me (FR) 127 – Pat Or Else 72 (Alzao (USA) 117) –
[1996 55: 5f^5 a5g^2 a5g^2 a6g* 7g^4 7g^3 8g^4 7.1m* a7g^6 7g 6.9v^5 a7g^5 1997 a7g^5 Jan 11]
sparely-made filly: modest winner at 2 yrs: blinkered, well beaten only 3-y-o start:
sold 9,500 gns in December, in foal to Namaqualand. *Miss Gay Kelleway*

RUNNING BEAR 3 ch.g. Sylvan Express 117 – Royal Girl 67 (Kafu 120) [1996 –
NR 1997 6m 5.9m^4 6g Jul 23] tall gelding: first foal: dam 6f and 7f winner: signs of
ability but no form, giving impression something amiss when well backed on final
start. *Miss S. E. Hall*

RUNNING FREE (IRE) 3 b.g. Waajib 121 – Selchis (Main Reef 126) [1996 55: 56
6m 7g 7g^4 8m 7m a8.5g^4 1997 10.2m 11.6s^5 11.4g 10.8s 11.6m^3 11.6m^5 11.9m^3
14.1g* 12d* 11.9m^4 12v^5 Oct 10] workmanlike gelding: modest handicapper: won at
Nottingham and Salisbury (dictated steady gallop) in the summer: stays 1¾m: acts
on good to firm and dead ground and on fibresand: tried blinkered/visored, no
improvement: sold 13,000 gns after final start. *M. J. Fetherston-Godley*

RUNNING GREEN 6 b.g. Green Desert (USA) 127 – Smeralda (GER) 67
(Dschingis Khan) [1996 63: 11m a8g^4 a8g* a7s 1997 a8g 8s^2 8.3d 8m^4 7s^5 8g^2 8g*
8m^3 8.1m 8.3g^5 8d 9m 8m 8s Nov 6] fair handicapper: won apprentice seller at Ayr in
June: mostly creditable efforts afterwards: best form around 1m: acts on soft and
good to firm ground and on fibresand: usually visored. *D. Moffatt*

RUNNING STAG (USA) 3 b.c. Cozzene (USA) – Fruhlingstag (FR) 112 105
(Orsini 124) [1996 8g^6 8g 7.5g^2 1997 a10g* 10g^2 8m^5 10d^2 8m 8m^4 8d^4 11m^2 10m^4
a10g^2 a9.4g^2 Dec 6] well-made colt: half-brother to several winners, including smart
French 1996 3-y-o 1m winner Blackwater (by Irish River): dam second in Poule
d'Essai des Pouliches: trained at 2 yrs by M. Zilber in France: useful performer: won
weak maiden at Lingfield in February: creditable efforts most starts afterwards,
including in several listed and pattern races: ½-length second to Farmost in Wulfrun
Stakes at Wolverhampton final start: effective at 1m to 11f: acts on good to firm and
dead ground and the all-weather: tried blinkered at 2 yrs: has run creditably sweating:
consistent. *P. Mitchell*

RUN OR BUST (IRE) 4 b.f. Commanche Run 133 – Busteds Fancy (Busted –
134) [1996 NR 1997 8m May 5] first reported foal: dam seemingly unraced: well
held in Warwick maiden. *R. Ingram*

RUNS IN THE FAMILY 5 b.m. Distant Relative 128 – Stoneydale 83 (Tickled 69
Pink 114) [1996 55, a52: 5g^5 a5g^3 5m^3 5m^4 6g 6s^6 5m 1997 a6g^6 a5g 6.1d^2 a5g^5 5g* a38
5.1g^6 5.7d^2 5m^3 5m^3 5g* 5.1s^2 5m 5m 5.1m 5s 5.1g Sep 11] sturdy, useful-looking
mare: fair handicapper on turf, poor on all-weather: won at Lingfield in May and
Warwick in June: below form last 5 starts: speedy front runner, barely stays 6f: acts
on fibresand, goes well on good ground or softer: tried visored, usually blinkered
nowadays. *G. M. McCourt*

RUP

RUPERT MANNERS   4 b.g. Mazilier (USA) 107 – Entourage 75 (Posse (USA)   –
130) [1996 –: 7f⁶ 8m 6g 1997 a9.4g Jan 4] tailed off: dead. *E. J. Alston*

RUSHCUTTER BAY   4 br.g. Mon Tresor 113 – Llwy Bren (Lidhame 109) [1996   93
92: 5m⁶ 6m 5.1m* 5f 5m² 5.1m⁵ 6m³ 5m⁴ 5m⁴ 6g 5.6m 1997 5d 6g 5m⁴ 5m 5.2m
5.2m 6.1g⁴ Sep 28] close-coupled gelding: impresses in appearance: fairly useful
handicapper: good fourth at Ascot (final outing for T. Clement) on third start: mostly
disappointing afterwards, though shaped as if on way back final start: effective at
5f to easy 6f: acts on good to firm going, below form only start on softer than good:
effective visored or not. *P. L. Gilligan*

RUSHEN RAIDER   5 br.g. Reprimand 122 – Travel Storm 77 (Lord Gayle
(USA) 124) [1996 77: 10m 10.3m 9.9g⁵ 11.8m* 12m* 12m* 16.2f* 14.6m⁴ 17.5m⁴
1997 14s⁶ 16.2s 16g 16.2m Jul 15] leggy, shallow-girthed gelding: fair performer in
1996: no form on flat in 1997. *K. W. Hogg, Isle of Man*

RUSH ME NOT (IRE)   4 b.g. Treasure Kay 114 – Elegant Act (USA) (Shecky   –
Greene (USA)) [1996 NR 1997 8g 12m 7.5g Jun 11] small gelding: fourth foal: dam
won 5 races in USA: no form. *M. P. Bielby*

RUSH OFF   2 b.c. (Mar 7) Robellino (USA) 127 – Arusha (IRE) 84 (Dance of Life   65 p
(USA)) [1997 6d Oct 17] first foal: dam 2-y-o 1m winner, half-sister to Don't Forget
Me: 33/1, slow-starting ninth of 20 to Atuf in maiden at Newmarket, green most of
way but keeping on not knocked about: sure to do fair bit better. *R. Akehurst*

RUSK   4 b.g. Pharly (FR) 130 – Springwell 73 (Miami Springs 121) [1996 79: 10m⁶   84
10m² 11.9m 12.3s⁴ 11.9d³ 11.9v⁵ 11f⁵ 1997 12s² 12.3m⁵ 16.2m* 16.1g 14.6g Oct 24]
smallish, good-topped gelding: has a round action: farley useful handicapper: best
effort when winning narrowly at Ascot in July: subsequently gelded, and soundly
beaten: stays 2m: acts on good to firm and soft ground: keen sort, usually held up:
joined T. Easterby. *J. Pearce*

RUSSIAN ABOUT (IRE)   2 b.f. (Apr 24) Polish Patriot (USA) 128 – Molly   51
Carter (IRE) (Dr Carter (USA)) [1997 5.2m 5m 6m² 6m 7d a5g 6m Sep 22] 5,600Y:
leggy filly: first foal: dam, Irish 2-y-o 5f winner, half-sister to useful Irish 5f to 1m
winner The Bower: modest maiden: probably stays 7f: has been awkward at stalls.
M. R. Channon

RUSSIAN ASPECT   3 br.g. Al Nasr (FR) 126 – Bourbon Topsy 108 (Ile de   –
Bourbon (USA) 133) [1996 –: 7.1d 7.9g 1997 10m 7s Jul 3] tall gelding: well beaten
in maidens and handicap: bred for stamina. *M. W. Easterby*

RUSSIAN DELIGHT (IRE)   2 b.f. (Mar 23) Soviet Lad (USA) 94 – Geraldville   46
(Lord Gayle (USA) 124) [1997 6v⁶ 6.9d⁵ Oct 21] IR 7,200Y: workmanlike filly: half-
sister to several winners: dam Irish middle-distance winner: poor form in maidens at
Ascot and Folkestone. *R. Hannon*

RUSSIAN MUSIC   4 b.g. Forzando 122 – Sunfleet 59 (Red Sunset 120) [1996   108
105: 7m* 7g² 8f³ 8m³ 8m² 7m² 7.1g² 7g² 7m³ 8d² 6s 1997 8m 7m* 9g 7d⁴ 7.9g⁵
7.6m³ 6g 7.6f⁴ 10s³ 7.9d³ 8m* 7m⁴ 9m a9.4g⁴ Dec 6] smallish, good-quartered
gelding: impresses in appearance: useful performer: won minor event at Warwick
(made all) in March and handicap at Doncaster (beat Hawait ½ length) in September:
effective at 7f to 1¼m: acts on firm and soft ground, below best on fibresand: effective blinkered or not: tends to hang left: consistent. *Miss Gay Kelleway*

RUSSIAN OLIVE   3 b.f. Primo Dominie 121 – Cottonwood 80 (Teenoso (USA)   –
135) [1996 70p: 7g 8s⁴ 1997 8.3s 8g⁶ 11.7f Jul 23] fair form in maidens at 2 yrs:
disappointing in 1997: sent to Czech Republic. *L. M. Cumani*

RUSSIAN PARTY (IRE)   2 ch.c. (Mar 16) Lycius (USA) 124 – Sherkova (USA)   69 p
(State Dinner (USA)) [1997 7d³ 8.2d Oct 30] 40,000Y: rangy colt: has scope: good
mover: third foal: half-brother to 2m winner Norma's Lady (by Unfuwain): dam unraced half-sister to Prix de Diane winner Lady In Silver: shaped well when considerately-handled third to Goodwood Cavalier in maiden at Leicester: held up and
never on terms in similar race at Nottingham later in month: likely to make a better
3-y-o. *A. C. Stewart*

RUSSIAN REVIVAL (USA)   4 ch.c. Nureyev (USA) 131 – Memories (USA)   117
(Hail The Pirates (USA) 126) [1996 116: 8d 7m 6m² 6d 6m* 6g* 7g² 6s³ 1997 a6f

814

6m³ 7g* 6m⁴ 7d⁶ 7m² Dec 14] angular colt: fine mover: smart performer: left Saeed bin Suroor after second start: right back to form to win valuable listed race at Newbury in September, quickening in good style to beat Hidden Meadow ¾ length: good efforts when 3½ lengths fourth of 14 to Elnadim in Diadem Stakes at Ascot and 1¼ lengths second of 14 to Catalan Opening in Hong Kong International Bowl: stays 7f: acts on good to firm and soft going: tongue tied in 1996. *J. H. M. Gosden*

RUSSIAN ROMEO (IRE)   2 b.c. (Mar 28) Soviet Lad (USA) 94 – Aotearoa (IRE) (Flash of Steel 120) [1997 a5g a5g⁶ 5.9f 5m 5.7g 5.1s⁴ a5g⁴ 7g⁵ 7g 6g* 6d a5g⁵ a6g* a7g a6g² Nov 17] 5,500 2-y-o: leggy colt: first foal: dam unraced from family of Cyrano de Bergerac and Arcadian Heights: modest performer: won seller at Leicester in August and claimer at Wolverhampton in October: best form at 6f: acts on fibresand, below form on ground firmer than good: often visored/blinkered: often looks less than genuine. *B. A. McMahon*   60 §   a65 §

RUSSIAN ROSE (IRE)   4 b.f. Soviet Lad (USA) 94 – Thornbeam (Beldale Flutter (USA) 130) [1996 74: 10m 10d 10m* 10s 1997 12m⁴ 12m² 17.2m* 16.1g² 16m⁵ 13.3d⁶ Sep 20] smallish filly: fairly useful handicapper: won at Bath in June: best effort when second at Newmarket following month: seems suited by 2m+: acts on good to firm ground, probably on dead. *J. A. R. Toller*   82

RUSSIAN RULER (IRE)   3 b.g. Bering 136 – Whitecairn (Sure Blade (USA) 130) [1996 78p: 7g⁵ 7f³ 1997 10g² 10g 10m 11.5m⁴ Aug 6] quite attractive gelding: fair maiden: stays 1¼m (took keen hold over 11.5f): has raced only on good ground or firmer: may be best held up. *A. P. Jarvis*   75

RUSTIC SONG (IRE)   4 b.f. Fayruz 116 – Red Note (Rusticaro (FR) 124) [1996 –: 6.1d 6.1d 8.2m a7g⁴ a8.5g a6g 1997 6m a8g a7g Jun 19] no longer of any account. *J. Wharton*   –

RUSTY BABE (IRE)   2 ch.g. (Jan 30) Red Sunset 120 – Derring Dee 85 (Derrylin 115) [1997 5f 5.1d* 5g² 6g* 5m² 6m Jun 17] IR 9,000Y: useful-looking gelding: half-brother to an Irish 2-y-o 1m winner by Bob Back, later successful at middle distances in Italy: dam 2-y-o sprint winner: fairly useful form: won early-season minor events at Nottingham and Pontefract: good second in £8,700 event at Beverley penultimate start: only tenth in Coventry Stakes at Royal Ascot: stays 6f: acts on good to firm and dead ground: sent to Hong Kong. *J. J. Quinn*   92

Porcelanosa Rated Stakes (Handicap), Doncaster—
Russian Music (spotted cap) finishes strongly to beat the blinkered Hawait and Al Azhar

RUTHS GEM (IRE) 2 ch.f. (Apr 18) Imperial Frontier (USA) 112 – Hossvend –
(Malinowski (USA) 123) [1997 a5g a5g 6s Jul 3] 1,000Y: third foal: dam once-raced
half-sister to To-Agori-Mou: has shown nothing, including in a seller. *D. T. Thom*

RUTLAND CHANTRY (USA) 3 b.g. Dixieland Band (USA) – Christchurch 72 p
(FR) 88 (So Blessed 130) [1996 NR 1997 8.3m⁵ a9.4g² 12.3g⁴ a9.4g² 10d* Oct 20]
robust gelding: closely related to 2 winners and half-brother to numerous winners,
including smart 6f to 10.5f winner Church Parade (by Queen's Hussar) and smart
middle-distance stayer Castle Rising (by Blakeney): dam, 1½m winner, half-sister to
Highclere: lightly-raced handicapper: won 19-runner race at Pontefract, battling on
gamely: stays 1¼m: acts on good to firm and dead ground and on fibresand: open to
progress. *Lord Huntingdon*

RUZEN (IRE) 2 b.c. (May 5) Fayruz 116 – Stifen (Burslem 123) [1997 5d* 6g⁴ 76
5d³ 5m² Jul 18] IR 11,500Y: good-quartered colt: half-brother to 3 winners abroad,
including Italian 3-y-o Keeps Ground (by Common Grounds), sprint winner at 2 yrs:
dam unraced: fair form: won maiden at Leicester in April: in frame in minor events
subsequently: best efforts at 5f: acts on good to firm and dead ground. *B. Palling*

RYAFAN (USA) 3 b.f. Lear Fan (USA) 130 – Carya (USA) (Northern 121
Dancer) [1996 110: 7g* 7g² 8d* 1997 8d⁴ 10.5d⁴ 8g* 10m* 9f* 10f* 10d*
Nov 30]
  Our summary of Ryafan at the end of her two-year-old season concluded by stating the likelihood that she'd end her career in the United States.
She was, after all, from a good American family, she would have plenty of
opportunities in America over what was likely to prove her optimum trip—ten
furlongs—and her owner Khalid Abdulla had already successfully transferred
a number of his horses to race in the States once opportunities had become
limited for them in Europe. What couldn't have been predicted though was just
how successful Ryafan would prove once switched across the Atlantic. Her
three Grade 1 wins from three starts there in the autumn took her earnings well
past the million-dollar mark and secured her the Eclipse Award for best turf
filly or mare.
  Ryafan had rounded off her two-year-old season with a narrow defeat
of another of Khalid Abdulla's fillies, Yashmak, in the Prix Marcel Boussac at
Longchamp. That hadn't looked a particularly strong renewal at the time but
exactly a year later both fillies won Grade 1 events on their American debuts on
the same day, Ryafan taking the Queen Elizabeth II Challenge Cup at Keeneland by one and a half lengths from the smart filly Auntie Mame, and Yashmak
the Flower Bowl Invitational Handicap at Belmont. Moving on to Santa Anita

Vodafone Nassau Stakes, Goodwood—Ryafan pulls clear of Entice and Papering (rail)

at the beginning of November, Ryafan faced older fillies and mares in the Yellow Ribbon Stakes. Her rivals included stable-companion Squeak, the ex-British mare Fanjica, Irish four-year-old Dance Design and favourite Memories of Silver, who'd won the Queen Elizabeth II Challenge Cup in 1996 and the Beverly D Stakes in the latest season. Memories of Silver and Dance Design were involved in an incident in the home straight which necessitated a fifteen-minute stewards' inquiry—an eternity by American standards. 'I've waited longer in England' Ryafan's trainer told the media, 'because they can never wrestle up all the stewards. Some of them get lost in the bar.' Ryafan, who passed the post a length and a quarter ahead of Fanjica, with Memories of Silver in third, kept the race.

Four weeks later, at Hollywood Park, Ryafan had passed into the care of Khalid Abdulla's American trainer, Bobby Frankel—at least, officially—but John Gosden was present to help saddle Ryafan and jointly accept the prize after she'd won the Matriarch Stakes. The only three-year-old in the field this time, Ryafan had the placed horses from the Yellow Ribbon well beaten. Her biggest threat came instead from Maxzene, who'd finished second in the Beverly D and to Yashmak in the Flower Bowl. Ryafan held on by a head to complete her American hat-trick (a five-timer in all) and clinch her Eclipse Award. Gosden hailed Ryafan as 'the best [filly] I've had since Royal Heroine,' his 1984 Eclipse Award winner who won the inaugural Breeders' Cup Mile when he was training in California.

Ryafan's success in the autumn more than compensated for a classic campaign which had been a little disappointing. Her first two starts saw her finish fourth in the Irish One Thousand Guineas (for which she started favourite) and the Prix de Diane. She'd apparently taken a while to come to hand, but by midsummer Ryafan was in fine form. On only her second start in Britain she put up a typically game effort to win the Amcor Falmouth Stakes at Newmarket

Queen Elizabeth II Challenge Cup, Keeneland—
the first of three successive Grade 1 victories in the States for Ryafan

by three quarters of a length from the Coronation Stakes runner-up Ocean Ridge, having looked held over a furlong out. Ryafan's final start in Britain was in the Vodafone Nassau Stakes at Goodwood over her ideal trip of a mile and a quarter, in which she put up her best effort in Europe. After replacing the previous year's winner Last Second as favourite and looking the paddock pick beforehand, Ryafan ran out the two and a half length winner from Entice, having taken it up over two furlongs out.

		Roberto	Hail To Reason
	Lear Fan (USA)	(b 1969)	Bramalea
	(b 1981)	Wac	Lt Stevens
Ryafan (USA)		(b 1969)	Belthazar
(b.f. 1994)		Northern Dancer	Nearctic
	Carya (USA)	(b 1961)	Natalma
	(ch 1986)	Autumn Glory	Graustark
		(br 1978)	Golden Trail

A well-made, attractive filly, Ryafan is due to begin her stud career with a visit to Zafonic. Ryafan's pedigree was discussed in detail in *Racehorses of 1996*. She's the second foal and much the better winner out of the French maiden Carya; her dam's latest produce are a yearling filly (also by Lear Fan) and a colt foal by Theatrical. Ryafan is the latest successful cross between sons of Roberto (or Roberto himself) and descendants of Ryafan's great grandam Golden Trail, an approach which has produced numerous stakes winners, including Memories of Silver (by Roberto's son Silver Hawk), mentioned earlier as one of Ryafan's opponents in the Yellow Ribbon and the Matriarch. Ryafan was ideally suited by a mile and a quarter and acted on firm and dead ground. She retired the winner of seven of her ten starts and was a tough, game and likeable filly. *R. Frankel, USA*

RYEFIELD   2 b.c. (Mar 26) Petong 126 – Octavia (Sallust 134) [1997 6d² 6g² Oct 22] 9,400F, 17,000 2-y-o: half-brother to numerous winners, including a 2-y-o 7.5f winner by King of Spain and 9-y-o Kinoko: dam showed a little ability: second in maidens at Ayr and Newcastle a month apart, keeping on when beaten 1¾ lengths by Love Academy on latter course: should improve. *Miss L. A. Perratt*   73 p

RYEFIELD STAR   2 b.g. (Mar 22) Marju (IRE) 127 – Awayed (USA) 108 (Sir Ivor 135) [1997 7d 7m a7g⁴ Nov 15] IR 5,200Y, 19,000Y 2-y-o: compact gelding: fourth foal: half-brother to 4-y-o Raed: dam Irish 1m/9f winner from good family: first form in maidens when fourth of 10 at Wolverhampton: upset in stalls and withdrawn second intended start: gelded after final one. *J. Berry*   63

RYMER'S RASCAL   5 b.g. Rymer 121 – City Sound 63 (On Your Mark 125) [1996 –: 7g 1997 a6g 6d a6g⁵ 8g 7.1m² 5.9d³ 7.1d³ 6.9f³ 7.5g 6.9m⁶ 7.5m* 8m⁶ 7g* 7s* 7d⁶ 7m⁴ 7s Oct 17] sturdy gelding: fair handicapper: in good form most of year, and won at Beverley in July, Catterick in August and York in September: stays 7.5f: acts on firm and soft ground. *E. J. Alston*   73

S

SAAFEYA (IRE)   3 b.f. Sadler's Wells (USA) 132 – Safa 109 (Shirley Heights 130) [1996 74p: 7.9g³ 1997 10g⁵ 10m³ 8g* 10.3m² 10.5g* 12v³ 10m* Oct 31] attractive filly: has a quick action: progressed into a useful performer: won maiden at Pontefract in August, handicap at Haydock in September, and listed event at Newmarket (by length from Sandmoor Chambray) in October: didn't quite get home when over 3 lengths third to Delilah in Princess Royal Stakes at Ascot over very testing 1½m: acts on good to firm and heavy ground: consistent. *J. H. M. Gosden*   107

SABADILLA (USA)   3 b.c. Sadler's Wells (USA) 132 – Jasmina (USA) (Forli (ARG)) [1996 NR 1997 10m⁴ 10.4s⁵ 12m² 11.9s* 12s* Nov 8] $250,000Y: workmanlike colt: has a short, round action: fourth foal: brother to French 1¼m winner   107 p

Tote Credit November Handicap, Doncaster—
Sabadilla is an easy winner of the big race on the final day of the flat season on turf

Bold Bold: dam, stakes winner around 1m, half-sister to Polish Precedent out of half-sister to dam of Zilzal: most progressive colt: won maiden at Haydock and 24-runner November Handicap at Doncaster (smooth headway from midfield, led 2f out and forged clear to beat Taunt 8 lengths) in autumn: will stay beyond 1½m: clearly goes extremely well on soft ground: should make a smart performer in 1998. *J. H. M. Gosden*

SABHAAN 2 b.c. (Mar 22) Green Desert (USA) 127 – Al Theraab (USA) 81 (Roberto (USA) 131) [1997 6m² 6m³ 6d³ Sep 12] strong, lengthy colt: has a quick action: third foal: dam, 1m winner, best at 1½m: fair form in minor event at Newbury and when third in maidens at Goodwood: shapes as though will be suited by further than 6f: coltish on debut, and has carried head bit high. *Major W. R. Hern*   **81**

SABINA 3 b.f. Prince Sabo 123 – High Savannah 77 (Rousillon (USA) 133) [1996 87p: 6m³ 5.7d* 5d 1997 5d² 5.1d⁴ 5d 5.1m⁴ 5m 5d 5.7g Sep 8] lengthy filly: fairly useful handicapper: generally disappointing after reappearance: effective at 5f and 6f: yet to race on extremes of going: has started slowly. *I. A. Balding*   **86**

SABLE CLOAK 2 b.f. (Feb 2) Prince Sabo 123 – Edge of Darkness 62 (Vaigly Great 127) [1997 5d Oct 17] 3,200Y: first foal: dam won over 2m but best up to 1½m: behind in Catterick maiden. *J. L. Harris*   **–**

SABO'S JOY 2 b.f. (Apr 10) Prince Sabo 123 – Port Na Blath (On Your Mark 125) [1997 5m Sep 17] 4,500Y: seventh foal: half-sister to 2-y-o 6f winners by Then Again and by Primo Dominie, latter fairly useful: dam Irish 6f winner: 25/1, not knocked about in mid-division in maiden at Sandown. *C. N. Allen*   **–**

SABOT 4 b.c. Polar Falcon (USA) 126 – Power Take Off 109 (Aragon 118) [1996 86: 7m² 7m* 7.9g⁴ 7m⁴ 7m 1997 a8.5f² a8.5g² a8.5g² 8m 7g² May 16] tall, good-topped colt: useful performer on all-weather, fairly useful on turf: second in handicaps and minor event at Wolverhampton and handicap (swished tail) at Newmarket: reportedly injured on gallops in June: stays 8.5f: acts on good to firm and dead ground and on fibresand. *C. W. Thornton*   **92**
  a98

SABRE BUTT 2 gr.g. (Feb 2) Sabrehill (USA) 120 – Butsova 93 (Formidable –
(USA) 125) [1997 6m 8s 8.2d Oct 30] 40,000Y: strong, sturdy gelding: sixth foal:
half-brother to 11f winner (stayed 2m) Bustinetta (by Bustino): dam 6f winner, half-
sister to Terimon: burly and green, soundly beaten in maidens: off course nearly 5
months after debut: joined J. Noseda. *M. H. Tompkins*

SABRE DANCER 3 b.g. Rambo Dancer (CAN) 107 – My Candy 81 (Loren- 69
zaccio 130) [1996 NR 1997 10m⁴ 12d 10g⁵ 12d² 10.1g³ Jul 28] 8,200Y: half-brother
to several winners, including Amelianne (up to 1¾m by Bustino) and Summer
Fashion (up to 1¼m, by Moorestyle), the dam of Definite Article: dam second at 7f
at 2 yrs: trained by T. Stack in Ireland first 4 starts, best effort on debut: third of 6 in
maiden at Newcastle on first outing in Britain: stays 1¼m: yet to race on extremes of
going. *R. Allan*

SABRE GIRL 2 b.f. (Feb 22) Sabrehill (USA) 120 – Yasmeen Valley (USA) 76 47
(Danzig Connection (USA)) [1997 5m 7g 6m 5m Sep 16] 12,000F: first foal: dam 6f
winner: form only in claimer at Sandown final start. *R. Hannon*

SABU 5 gr.g. Jumbo Hirt (USA) 90§ – Shankhouse Girl (General Ironside 121) –
[1996 NR 1997 8f⁵ 12.3g 8g 12g 9m Jul 19] second foal: dam maiden jumper: little
worthwhile form in maidens and handicaps. *J. I. A. Charlton*

SACCHETTI (IRE) 2 b.c. (Apr 5) Alzao (USA) 117 – Merriment (USA) (Go 67
Marching (USA)) [1997 5f⁵ 6d 5f³ 5s Oct 16] IR 41,000Y: small, quite attractive colt:
brother to Irish 3-y-o 9f winner Alzaro and high-class miler Second Set and half-
brother to 3 minor winners abroad: dam lightly-raced maiden sister to high-class
French miler Brinkmanship: fair maiden: third at Lingfield in October: well beaten
in nursery final start: withdrawn after getting upset at start once: bred to stay beyond
5f, but rather headstrong. *M. R. Channon*

SACHO (IRE) 4 b.c. Sadler's Wells (USA) 132 – Oh So Sharp 131 (Kris 135) 95
[1996 89p: 10m² 1997 10m* 10.9d⁶ Sep 20] lengthy, good sort: has a fluent, round
action: highly promising colt at 2 yrs but suffered hock injury on sole run in 1996:
won 19-runner maiden at Leicester in September, despite being sent plenty to do and
carrying head awkwardly: heavily backed, useful form when sixth of 8 to Ghataas in
listed event at Ayr next time, unable to challenge: will stay at least 1½m: sold only
7,000 gns in December. *J. H. M. Gosden*

SACRAMENT 6 b.h. Shirley Heights 130 – Blessed Event 117 (Kings Lake 106
(USA) 133) [1996 118: 9m 12m³ 12.5g* 11.1m* 14m³ 12s² 12m 1997 12g 12m 13.9g
12s* 12v³ Dec 7] tall horse: smart performer at best: still capable of useful form: well
held first 3 starts (trained by M Stoute): first race for 5½ months and favourably
treated by weights, won listed race at Nantes in November by a nose: 3½ lengths
third to Mongol Warrior in similar event at Toulouse: stays 1¾m: acts on good to firm
and heavy ground. *J. E. Hammond, France*

SACRED SPIRIT 5 b.g. Totem (USA) 118 – Dream Again 88 (Blue Cashmere –
129) [1996 NR 1997 7g 5m⁶ Jun 13] fifth foal: dam 2-y-o 5f winner: behind in seller
and claimer. *A. P. Jarvis*

SADA 2 b. or br.f. (Mar 24) Mujtahid (USA) 118 – Peace Girl 98 (Dominion 123) 74
[1997 5g³ 5m 6d³ 6m⁴ 5m⁵ 5.7m³ 5.3g 6m⁴ a5s³ a6g Dec 6] smallish, lengthy filly:
fifth foal: half-sister to 3-y-o Sharkiyah and 3 winners, including useful 6f/7f performer Matila (by Persian Bold): dam Irish sprinter: fair maiden: trained first 8 starts
by R. Hern: stays 6f: acts on equitrack, yet to race on extremes of ground on turf: has
been slowly away. *C. A. Dwyer*

SADDLERS' HOPE 3 b.f. Saddlers' Hall (IRE) 126 – Hope And Glory (USA) 84
87 (Well Decorated (USA)) [1996 75: 7m³ 8.1d⁴ 1997 8m² 9.9d⁴ 12g 10.2m* 10m³
10.1m* 10.1g⁵ Aug 25] fairly useful handicapper: won at Bath in July and Yarmouth
in August: should stay beyond 1¼m: acts on good to firm and dead ground, unraced
on extremes: has run well when sweating: races prominently: sold 38,000 gns, and
sent to Saudi Arabia. *J. R. Fanshawe*

SADDLERS' ROE (IRE) 2 b.g. (Mar 7) Saddlers' Hall (IRE) 126 – Ladyfish 79 72 +
(Pampapaul 121) [1997 6m⁵ 7s⁶ 6g³ 8f Sep 11] 3,900F, 14,000Y: rangy, unfurnished
gelding: half-brother to several winners, including 1992 2-y-o 6f winner Colyan (by
Midyan), later successful in USA, and fairly useful winner at up to 1½m Tony's Fen

SAF

(by Trojan Fen): dam, 1m winner, half-sister to Carroll House: fair form in maidens at Doncaster and Kempton first and third starts: raced on unfavoured side in nursery final outing: should be suited by at least 1m: has sweated and got on toes: gelded after final start. *B. W. Hills*

SADEEBAH 2 b.g. (Mar 5) Prince Sabo 123 – Adeebah (USA) 94 (Damascus (USA)) [1997 a7g 5m 6.1g Sep 28] 6,200Y: half-brother to 3 winners, including 7f winner Junuh (by Jalmood) and 1½m winner Jeewan (by Touching Wood): dam 2-y-o 5f winner: no sign of ability. *M. Johnston* –

SADIAN 2 b.c. (Feb 24) Shirley Heights 130 – Rafha 123 (Kris 135) [1997 7.6d* Aug 28] third live foal: closely related to useful 1m (at 2 yrs) and 1½m winner Al Widyan (by Slip Anchor): dam won Prix de Diane and also over 1½m: 3/1, won maiden at Lingfield by neck from Zydeco, soon close up and leading from over 1f out: sustained cut on hind-joint: should be well suited by 1¼m+: sure to improve. *H. R. A. Cecil* 91 p

SADIR 2 ch.c. (May 3) Zafonic (USA) 130 – Ghanimah 98 (Caerleon (USA) 132) [1997 6g 7g 7m Sep 9] compact colt: sixth foal: half-brother to 3-y-o Khafaaq and 1992 2-y-o 7f winner Faez (by Mtoto): dam, ran only at 2 yrs, winning at 6f, half-sister to Marwell: towards rear in large-field maidens: has tongue tied and wears crossed noseband: sold 2,500 gns in October. *Major W. R. Hern* –

SADLER'S BLAZE (IRE) 3 b.c. Alzao (USA) 117 – Christine Daae 74 (Sadler's Wells (USA) 132) [1996 –p: 7.1f 1997 10d 10.2d 11.6g 10g³ 12s Jul 2] big, close-coupled colt: only form when third in strongly-run handicap at Pontefract: stays 1¼m: blinkered/visored last 2 starts: has carried head high and looked way-ward. *P. W. Harris* 54

SAD MAD BAD (USA) 3 b.g. Sunny's Halo (CAN) – Quite Attractive (USA) (Well Decorated (USA)) [1996 71: 6g³ 7.6d* 8m 1997 10m 12.3g⁵ 14.6d² 14.1g 14.9d 13.1g³ 16m⁶ 17.1g a16g 15.8s² 18d⁴ Oct 20] strong, workmanlike gelding: fair handicapper: left M. Johnston after fifth start: stays 2m: best efforts on good ground or softer: winning hurdler. *Mrs M. Reveley* 67

SAEEDAH 2 ch.f. (May 6) Bustino 136 – Galaxie Dust (USA) 86 (Blushing Groom (FR) 131) [1997 7.1g³ 7g³ Aug 11] 160,000Y: fluent mover: sister to smart 7f (at 2 yrs) to 1¼m winner Bulaxie and half-sister to several winners, including 3-y-o Dust Dancer and very smart winner up to 1½m Zimzalabim (by Damister): dam 2-y-o 6f winner: fair form when third in large fields of maidens at Sandown and Leicester: should be suited by at least 1¼m. *J. H. M. Gosden* 75

SAFABEE 2 ch.f. (Feb 27) Safawan 118 – Bewails (IRE) 53 (Caerleon (USA) 132) [1997 6m 7.1m 7.6d 5m a6g a5.8g Nov 1] workmanlike filly: first foal: dam twice-raced maiden from family of Yorkshire Oaks/Park Hill winner Attica Meli: little sign of ability. *J. Cullinan* –

SAFA DANCER 4 b.f. Safawan 118 – Dalby Dancer 71 (Bustiki) [1996 –, a41: a8g³ 8.2m a8.5g⁶ 8g 10g 8.1f 1997 10g a11g a9.4g 8f a11g⁶ 8g⁶ 8s Jul 4] poor maiden: stays 1m: acts on soft ground and fibresand: inconsistent. *B. A. McMahon* 26

SAFARI SAM (IRE) 2 b.g. (Feb 1) Cyrano de Bergerac 120 – Light Hand 80 (Star Appeal 133) [1997 6g 6d 6m Sep 2] good-topped gelding: first foal: dam 1¼m winner: little promise, including in seller. *M. H. Tompkins* –

SAFECRACKER 4 ch.g. Sayf El Arab (USA) 127 – My Polished Corner (IRE) 53 (Tate Gallery (USA) 117) [1996 67: a8g² 9.7f* 10m 11.6m 10g 1997 a12g⁴ 10m a12g⁵ Nov 6] lengthy gelding: good mover: fair 1¼m winner in 1996: no form at 4 yrs: tried blinkered/visored. *C. P. Morlock* –

SAFEY ANA (USA) 6 b.g. Dixieland Band (USA) – Whatsoraire (USA) (Mr Prospector (USA)) [1996 63: 7m 7m 7m⁶ 6m 7m² 7m⁴ 7g⁴ 7.3m 8.2g 1997 7f⁶ 8f* 8m 7g 7f* 8m 7.6m* 7.6m⁵ 8m⁴ 7m* 8f⁵ Sep 17] good-bodied gelding: poor mover: fair handicapper: had good season, winning at Brighton in April, Yarmouth in May and Lingfield in July and September: has form at 1¼m, races at 7f/1m nowadays: acts on firm and dead ground: effective blinkered, not tried for long time: wears band-ages: sometimes rears stalls. *B. Hanbury* 76

821

SAFFRON LANE (IRE) 2 b.f. (Feb 18) Hamas (IRE) 125§ – Saffron (FR)   87
(Fabulous Dancer (USA) 124) [1997 6g³ 6.1g* 6d⁴ 7.3m* 8.1m² 7m Sep 30]
10,000Y: workmanlike filly: has a fluent, round action: fourth foal: half-sister to
fairly useful 1m (at 2 yrs) and 10.5f winner Roman Gold (by Petorius): dam French
12.5f winner: fairly useful form: won minor event at Nottingham in May and nursery
at Newbury in August: second to easy winner Setteen in minor event at Sandown in
September: ran poorly final start: probably stays 1m: yet to race on extremes of
ground: reluctant at stalls first 2 starts. *R. Hannon*

SAFFRON ROSE 3 b.f. Polar Falcon (USA) 126 – Tweedling (USA) (Sir Ivor   74
135) [1996 66: 6m 7m⁵ 7.1f⁴ 7g 7m 1997 8.2d⁴ 8m 10g⁶ 8.2g* 8.2s* 8.2g⁵ 8g 8.1s
Aug 29] tall, unfurnished filly: has a round action: fair handicapper: won at Nottingham in June and July: best efforts around 1m: probably acts on any going: races up
with pace: sometimes flashes tail, but is game. *M. Blanshard*

SAFIO 4 ch.g. Efisio 120 – Marcroft 91 (Crofthall 110) [1996 –: 6g 7g⁴ 7f⁶ 7.1m   84
7.5m⁵ 6d 1997 a7g a5g⁶ 6m² 6d 6d⁵ 6g 6d⁴ 7g* 6g* 7g* 7f* 8d³ 7m 7g⁵ 7m³
Nov 1] workmanlike gelding: fairly useful handicapper: had a fine season, winning
at Newcastle (twice), Ayr and Doncaster: good efforts at Newmarket last 2 starts,
finishing best of all when third of 25 to Wild Sky on final one: barely stays 1m in
testing conditions: acts on firm and dead ground: held up, and has idled. *A. Bailey*

SAGE 2 ch.c. (Apr 13) Greensmith 121 – Bluebell Copse (Formidable (USA) 125)   52
[1997 a5g* Apr 8] 5,000 2-y-o: second foal: half-brother to Italian 7f winner Rechan
(by Faustus): dam, winner in Jersey, half-sister to Sapience: won seller (sold 4,600
gns) at Wolverhampton in April: sent to Sweden. *W. G. M. Turner*

SAGEBRUSH ROLLER 9 br.g. Sharpo 132 – Sunita (Owen Dudley 121)   57
[1996 81d: 7g³ 6.9d³ 7d⁴ 7m⁵ 7m⁴ 7g² 7.6m⁵ 7g⁴ 7s a6g a7g 1997 7m⁵ 7d 7s 10.3d³
9m⁵ 9.9m³ 9.2m 10.3d³ 10.9d Sep 18] rangy gelding: modest handicapper nowadays (last won in 1994): stays 1¼m: probably acts on any going: visored once at 4
yrs, blinkered last 2 starts: sometimes hangs under pressure, and best held up: joined
J. J. O'Neill. *J. W. Watts*

SAGUARO 3 b.g. Green Desert (USA) 127 – Badawi (USA) 103 (Diesis 133)   73 p
[1996 NR 1997 7d² Oct 13] quite attractive gelding: has a quick action: has been
fired: first foal: dam 1m/9f winner: in need of race, second to Shalaal in apprentice
maiden at Leicester, going like winner long way but flashing tail and edging left
under pressure: should improve. *J. H. M. Gosden*

SAHARA 2 b.f. (Feb 11) Green Desert (USA) 127 – Marie d'Argonne (FR) 104   75
(Jefferson 129) [1997 7g⁵ 8.1m² 8g Oct 24] smallish, sturdy filly: sixth foal: sister to
1m and 1¼m winner Mokuti and half-sister to 2 winners, notably high-class French
6f to 1m performer Polar Falcon (by Nureyev): dam won up to 1¼m in France/USA:
fair form in maidens, edging right when second at Sandown in September: may prove
best up to 1m. *P. F. I. Cole*

SAHARA RIVER (USA) 3 b.f. Riverman (USA) 131 – Sahara Forest (Green   54
Desert (USA) 127) [1996 80p: 6m⁴ 1997 7m 8s⁴ 10.5d Sep 5] smallish, well-made
filly: failed to fulfil debut promise: should stay 1¼m. *R. Charlton*

SAIFAN 8 ch.g. Beveled (USA) – Superfrost 49 (Tickled Pink 114) [1996 89: 8.1g   93 §
8m 8s³ 8m* 8m⁴ 7m⁶ 8g 8f* 8m² 8m 8m⁶ 8g 8g 8g* 1997 8g³ 7g⁴ 8g 8m 8.1g 8d
8m* 8d⁴ 8g 8m a8.5g Nov 15] tall, angular gelding: has a round action: fairly useful
handicapper: won at Redcar in August: effective at 7f/1m: probably acts on any
going: wears blinkers/visor: sometimes slowly away: held up: reportedly bled from
nose penultimate start: unpredictable. *D. Morris*

SAILORMAITE 6 ch.g. Komaite (USA) – Marina Plata (Julio Mariner 127)   – §
[1996 87§, a80§: a7g⁵ 5.2d⁴ 6g 6d 5d* 5m 5m⁶ 6g 6.1d 5d⁶ 6v⁶ 7g 5g² a7g⁶ 1997 a6g   a78 §
6d 6m a8g 7g 6g a7g a6g⁴ Nov 15] tall gelding: fairly useful handicapper up to 7f on
his day, but refused to race first, second and sixth outings: trained by Miss J. Craze
third to fifth starts: occasionally blinkered, not at 6 yrs: best left alone. *S. R. Bowring*

SAINT ALBERT 2 ch.g. (Mar 25) Keen 116 – Thimbalina 63 (Salmon Leap   54
(USA) 131) [1997 5.9g 7m 7.1m⁴ 7.6m Sep 9] 6,000Y: second foal: dam 1¼m to
1½m winner from 4 to 6 yrs: modest form at best in maidens and a nursery: stays 7f:
visored second start. *P. T. Walwyn*

SAINT AMIGO   5 gr.g. Presidium 124 – Little Token (Shack (USA) 118) [1996   –
–: 6m 5m a7g 1997 7g 12g⁵ 8.5d a9.4g⁶ Aug 16] of little account. *B. P. J. Baugh*

SAINT ANN (USA)   2 b.f. (Feb 4) Geiger Counter (USA) – Swan Princess 106   66
(So Blessed 130) [1997 5m⁴ 6g⁶ 5m⁶ 6g Aug 2] 29,000Y: sturdy filly: ninth foal:
half-sister to a 2-y-o winner in USA by Seattle Dancer: dam speedy half-sister to
very smart sprinter Primo Dominie: fair form on debut, but failed to repeat it, looking
somewhat temperamental. *M. Johnston*

SAINT CIEL (USA)   9 b.h. Skywalker (USA) – Holy Tobin (USA) (J O Tobin   42
(USA) 130) [1996 NR 1997 12d³ Sep 19] strong horse: modest handicapper on flat in
1994: third of 21 in ladies handicap at Newbury in September: stays 1½m: acts on
any going: below form in blinkers: sometimes runs tongue tied: held up: won twice
over hurdles in November. *F. Jordan*

SAINTES   2 b.g. (Apr 4) Be My Chief (USA) 122 – Latakia 80 (Morston (FR) 125)   –
[1997 7m⁵ 7.9s 7d 7m Oct 1] 6,600Y: strong gelding: half-brother to several winners,
including 9.4f winner Penmar (by Reprimand) and fairly useful 1¼m winner Sobranie (by High Top): dam 1½m winner: well held in maidens. *W. McKeown*

SAINT EXPRESS   7 ch.g. Clantime 101 – Redgrave Design 77 (Nebbiolo 125)   86
[1996 83: 5m 5g 5m 5m 6m 6m 5.6m 5m³ 6g 5m 7m⁴ 6f⁴ 1997 6g² 5g⁵ 6m 5d⁵ 5f³
5.7g⁵ 6m³ 6m² 5m 6g 7m* Oct 28] lengthy, workmanlike gelding: has quick action:
fairly useful handicapper: generally in good form at 7 yrs, winning at Redcar: effective at 5f to 7f: best efforts on good going or firmer: effective blinkered (not tried in
1997). *Mrs M. Reveley*

SAINT KEYNE   7 b.h. Sadler's Wells (USA) 132 – Sancta 106 (So Blessed 130)   –
[1996 NR 1997 a16g⁶ Apr 1] seems of little account nowadays. *D. L. Williams*

SAINTLY MANNER (USA)   3 b.f. St Jovite (USA) 135 – Azzurrina (Knightly   –
Manner (USA)) [1996 NR 1997 10.5s⁴ May 5] compact filly: closely related to useful
South Salem (should have stayed beyond 1¼m, by Salem Drive), and half-sister to
several winners, including useful Irish performer Too Phar (up to 2m, by Pharly):
dam raced winner in Italy from 7f (at 2 yrs) to 1¼m: weak 6/1, distant fourth of 6 in
maiden at Haydock: showed a fluent, round action to post: sent to USA. *D. R. Loder*

SAINT MALO (USA)   2 b. or br.c. (Apr 27) Nureyev (USA) 131 – Jeany's Halo   62
(CAN) (Sunny's Halo (CAN)) [1997 6m⁵ 7g Aug 25] $300,000F: smallish, sturdy
colt: fourth foal: half-brother to winners in USA by Afleet and With Approval: dam
unraced from family of Sky Classic: better effort in maidens when fifth at Folkestone: sold approx. £10,500 in Dubai in November. *D. R. Loder*

SAINTS BE PRAISED (USA)   2 ch.c. (Apr 29) St Jovite (USA) 135 –   87
Cincinnati Pops (USA) (Dixieland Band (USA)) [1997 7g⁵ 7g⁵ Jul 8] $12,000Y: tall,
close-coupled colt: second foal: half-brother to a winner in Mexico by Cozzene: dam
unraced: 7¼ lengths fifth to Central Park in listed Chesham Stakes at Royal Ascot:
below that form in maiden at Newmarket 19 days later: should stay at least 1m: sent
to USA. *D. R. Loder*

SAKBAH (USA)   8 b.m. Al Nasr (FR) 126 – Delray Dancer (USA) (Chateaugay)   –
[1996 NR 1997 a16g Jan 10] very lightly raced, and no form. *J. A. Pickering*

SAKHAROV   8 b.g. Bay Express 132 – Supreme Kingdom 85 (Take A Reef 127)   54 d
[1996 59: 7m* 8.1g 5.9f² 7.5m³ 8m⁵ 1997 8.3g a8g⁶ a7g a8.5g 8.3g 8m a8g Dec 10]
leggy gelding: modest performer: mostly disappointing in 1997: stays 1m: acts on
firm ground, dead and fibresand: tried blinkered. *P. Eccles*

SALAMAH   3 b.g. Sadler's Wells (USA) 132 – Ala Mahlik 116 (Ahonoora 122)   88
[1996 NR 1997 12g² 10s* 10.3m 12d Jun 19] well-made, attractive gelding: has a
powerful, round action: fifth foal: closely related to 12.5f winner Storm Crossing
and French 1m winner Mali (both by Storm Bird) and half-brother to 1½m winner
Sherpas (by Shirley Heights): dam, 2-y-o 6f winner and second in 10.5f Musidora
Stakes, is sister to Negligent and half-sister to Ala Hounak: fairly useful form: won
maiden at Lingfield in May: disappointing afterwards, soon needing reminders final
outing (gelded after it): should be better at 1½m than shorter: acts on soft ground.
R. Charlton

SALAMANCA 2 gr.f. (Mar 16) Paris House 123 – Amber Mill 96 (Doulab (USA) 88 +
115) [1997 5d* 5m² 5.1d⁴ 5.2f 5m³ 5m* 5d Aug 30] 4,000Y: tall filly: second foal:
dam sprinter: fairly useful performer: made all in maiden at Musselburgh in March
and minor event at Lingfield in August: barely stays 5f and ideally suited by sharp
track and conditions. *J. Berry*

SALEELA (USA) 2 b.f. (Feb 7) Nureyev (USA) 131 – Allegretta 101 (Lombard 64 p
(GER) 126) [1997 7m⁶ Oct 5] $600,000F: half-sister to several winners, notably Arc
winner Urban Sea (by Miswaki) and smart French 1m and 10.5f winner Allez Les
Trois (by Riverman): dam, sister to German St Leger winner Anno, won over 1m and
9f at 2 yrs: 5/1, promising sixth of 12 to Benin in Leicester maiden, improving 2f out
away from principals and not knocked about: should stay 1¼m+: wintered in Dubai:
sure to do better. *J. L. Dunlop*

SALFORD 2 ch.g. (May 7) Salse (USA) 128 – Bustellina 81 (Busted 134) [1997 – p
7m 8m 8s Oct 14] 30,000Y: strong, useful-looking gelding: half-brother to 1¼m to
1¾m winner Cumbrian Rhapsody (by Sharrood), winning sprinter Emmer Green (by
Music Boy) and a winner in Hong Kong by Scottish Reel: dam 1m winner: not fully
wound up and well held in maidens at Newmarket, Kempton and Leicester: type to
do better. *L. M. Cumani*

SALFORD LAD 3 b.c. Don't Forget Me 127 – Adjusting (IRE) (Busted 134) –
[1996 –: 7g 8s 1997 8m Oct 6] well beaten in maidens. *G. Wragg*

SALIGO (IRE) 2 b.f. (Mar 24) Elbio 125 – Doppio Filo (Vision (USA)) [1997 61
5m 5.7g 7g 7g³ 6d⁴ 6.1m⁵ Sep 15] IR 3,200Y: third foal: half-sister to 7f (at 2 yrs) and
1m winner Iron Man (by Conquering Hero): dam unraced: modest maiden: got bit
better with each start: should stay 7f: blinkered fourth and fifth starts. *H. Morrison*

SALINGER 9 b.g. Rousillon (USA) 133 – Scholastika (GER) (Alpenkonig (GER)) –
[1996 NR 1997 12s 14.1d Nov 3] poor winning handicapper up to 1½m as 7-y-o: no
form in 1997. *J. Parkes*

SALLY ARMSTRONG 4 b.f. Batshoof 122 – Salinity (NZ) (Standaan (FR) –
118) [1996 –: a6s 1997 a7s a9.4g⁵ a10g a6g Mar 5] signs of ability but no form in
varied company. *C. W. Thornton*

SALLY GREEN (IRE) 3 b.f. Common Grounds 118 – Redwood Hut (Habitat 79
134) [1996 ?, a65: 6g 5.1m 6d a6g* a7g⁵ 1997 a6g⁵ 6d³ 6m² 5d* 5m³ 5m 5d Oct 20]
angular filly: fairly useful handicapper: won at Sandown in July: ran well next 2
starts: effective at 5f/6f: acts on good to firm ground, dead and fibresand: has sweated
and had 2 handlers in preliminaries. *C. F. Wall*

SALLY SLADE 5 b.m. Dowsing (USA) 124 – Single Gal 97 (Mansingh (USA) 77
120) [1996 80: 6g 5g 5g⁵ 6.1d⁶ 5m* 5m⁵ 5m⁵ 6g 5g 5g 5.2m⁵ 5g 5g⁶ 5f a5g² 1997
a6g⁶ a5g* a5g* a5g⁶ a5g² a5g⁶ 6g 5m⁵ 5g⁴ 5s³ 5d 5g⁵ 5m 5.2m⁶ 6g² 8.1s⁵ Aug 30]
leggy mare: fair handicapper: in good form on the all-weather early in year, winning
twice at Lingfield in January: in-and-out form after: flattered in listed race at
Sandown final start: a sprinter: acts on good to firm ground, soft and equitrack: well
beaten only try in blinkers. *C. A. Cyzer*

SALLY'S TWINS 4 b.f. Dowsing (USA) 124 – Bird of Love 82 (Ela-Mana-Mou –
132) [1996 60: 12m⁶ 11.6g 9.7d 12s³ 1997 a16.2g Apr 12] good-topped filly: modest
maiden: well beaten only start at 4 yrs: stays 1½m: acts on soft going. *J. S. Moore*

SALMON LADDER (USA) 5 b.h. Bering 136 – Ballerina Princess (USA) (Mr 110
Prospector (USA)) [1996 117: 9.2g* 10f* 10g 10f² 12m* 10d² 11.1m² 12m² 12s*
1997 12g⁴ 13.4v 10m* 11m² 12g 12g Oct 25] good-topped horse: impresses good
deal in appearance: had wind operation as 3-y-o: smart performer at best: landed
odds in minor event at Windsor in August by 1½ lengths from Green Card: in frame
in John Porter Stakes at Newbury and Group 3 race at Milan, but tailed-off last on his
other 3 starts in 1997: effective at 1¼m to 1½m: seems unsuited by heavy going, acts
on any other: front runner/races prominently: often sweating. *P. F. I. Cole*

SALSEE LAD 3 b.g. Salse (USA) 128 – Jamarj 113 (Tyrnavos 129) [1996 –: 7m 63
1997 10g⁴ 10.3d 10m⁴ 14m⁵ 16.4g a14.8g³ 16s Oct 8] strong, lengthy gelding: modest maiden: shapes like a stayer: acts on good to firm ground and probably fibresand:
poor efforts on good to soft/soft going: sold, and joined I. Semple. *J. R. Fanshawe*

SAM

SALSETTE 2 b.f. (Feb 19) Salse (USA) 128 – Amber Fizz (USA) (Effervescing (USA)) [1997 6g^5 6m^5 6.1d^3 7m Sep 30] big, lengthy, strong-quartered filly: ninth foal: half-sister to several winners, including smart 5f to 7f performer Cool Jazz (by Lead On Time) and 5-y-o Ambidextrous: dam ran once: fair form in maiden at Goodwood and minor event at Chester second and third starts: missed break in valuable nursery at Newmarket final start: should be suited by further than 6f: has plenty of scope and should still do better at 3 yrs. *C. E. Brittain*   73 p

SALSKA 6 b.m. Salse (USA) 128 – Anzeige (GER) (Soderini 123) [1996 58: 10.5d^5 14.1m^2 14.1f 14.6g^3 14.9m* 14.1f* 1997 14d 12m 14.1m* 14.9d^5 14.9g 16m* 16.2m^5 16.5g^5 14.1g^5 18g 14.1d^2 16s Nov 6] strong, lengthy mare: fair handicapper: generally in good form at 6 yrs, winning at Nottingham in June and Redcar in July: stays 2m: acts on firm and dead ground: tried visored. *A. Streeter*   69

SALTANDO (IRE) 6 b.g. Salt Dome (USA) – Ange de Feu (Double Form 130) [1996 62: 12m 8m^6 10d^2 11.8m 12m 8.1m^6 a8g 10m 8m 10m 8d 8m* 8g 1997 7f^6 10d 7g^5 8m 8d 10d 8m 10g 8.9s^5 8.1g 10.1f 8m^5 8g 8.2s 10d Nov 3] angular gelding: modest handicapper: stays 1¼m: acts on good to firm going, soft and fibresand: tried visored: most unreliable. *Pat Mitchell*   56 §

SALTIMBANCO 3 ch.c. Green Forest (USA) 134 – Tea And Scandals (USA) (Key To The Kingdom (USA)) [1996 68: 6m^6 6g 6m^3 6m 1997 6m 6m 7.1g 7f 11.5m 12d^6 14m^3 14m Oct 1] workmanlike colt: disappointing maiden. *R. Akehurst*   28

SALTY BEHAVIOUR (IRE) 3 ch.c. Salt Dome (USA) – Good Behaviour (Artaius (USA) 129) [1996 83: 5d^3 6m* 5d^6 5d 5v* 1997 6m 6g* 6m^2 7g^6 a6g a8g* Dec 10] rangy colt: fair performer: won claimers at Salisbury in August and Lingfield in December: stays 1m: acts on good to firm going, heavy and equitrack. *R. Hannon*   75

SALTY GIRL (IRE) 4 b.f. Scenic 128 – Sodium's Niece (Northfields (USA)) [1996 64: 10g 10m^3 11f^6 12g^5 1997 16g Mar 29] sturdy filly: disappointing maiden: possibly temperamental. *J. S. Moore*   –

SALTY JACK (IRE) 3 b.c. Salt Dome (USA) – Play The Queen (IRE) (King of Clubs 124) [1996 81: 5m 6g^3 6m^3 6m* 7g^3 7.3m^3 1997 7m 7g 6m^5 7g^4 a7g* a7g^2 Dec 10] small colt: has a roundish action: fairly useful handicapper: won at Lingfield in December: stays 7f: acts on equitrack, raced only on good/good to firm going on turf. *V. Soane*   83

SALTZ (IRE) 5 b.g. Salt Dome (USA) – Heather Hut (Shack (USA) 118) [1996 NR 1997 a9.4g Dec 6] modest winning mile handicapper at 3 yrs: well beaten on return. *P. T. Dalton*   –

SAMARA (IRE) 4 ch.f. Polish Patriot (USA) 128 – Smeralda (GER) (Dschingis Khan) [1996 96: 8.2m* 8g* 8f^4 1997 8.1g 8.1g^3 8.5m* 8f^3 9.3f^5 8m* Nov 1] rangy, good-topped filly: reportedly cracked a sesamoid at end of 3-y-o season: useful performer, better than ever at 4 yrs: won listed events at Epsom in June and Newmarket in November, in latter beating Balalaika ¾ length: ran well in Park Stakes at Doncaster (third to Almushtarak) and Prix de l'Opera at Longchamp in between: stayed 9f: raced only on good going or firmer after early in career: genuine and reliable: stud. *J. L. Dunlop*   108

SAMARA SONG 4 ch.g. Savahra Sound 111 – Hosting (Thatching 131) [1996 61: a9.4g 8.3m^6 7f^5 a7g^4 8g^5 6f^5 8m^2 8d 10.8f a7g^6 1997 a7g 8f^2 8.3g^2 8m^3 8f^2 9.7m^4 8m^2 8g^3 7m* 7.1g^2 8m^3 Sep 22] lengthy gelding: fair handicapper: out of frame only once in 11 starts at 4 yrs: gained first success in 20-runner race at Leicester in September: best at 7f/1m: acts on good to firm ground and equitrack, probably on fibresand: used to be effective in blinkers (didn't wear them in 1997), visored once: suited by waiting tactics: tough and consistent. *I. P. Williams*   66

SAMATA ONE (IRE) 2 b.c. (Apr 26) River Falls 113 – Abadila (IRE) (Shernazar 131) [1997 6d 6d Oct 28] 5,200Y: unfurnished colt: first foal: dam, ran twice in Ireland, daughter of smart French 9f and 10.5f winner Abalvina: always behind in maidens at Pontefract and Leicester. *W. J. Haggas*   –

SAMBAC (USA) 3 b.f. Mr Prospector (USA) – Kingscote 118 (Kings Lake (USA) 133) [1996 96: 6m^3 6g* 6m* 6.1d^6 6m^5 7g^4 1997 7m^6 7s^6 May 10] neat filly: has a short, round action: useful at 2 yrs: long way below form in minor event   –

(sweating and edgy) and listed race in 1997: stays 7f: acts on good to firm and dead ground: sent to USA. *H. R. A. Cecil*

SAMIM (USA)   4 b.c. Nureyev (USA) 131 – Histoire (FR) (Riverman (USA) 131)   –
[1996 78d: 10.3d 10.5g⁵ 12.3m⁴ 12.3g⁴ 10.3m 10.5d⁵ 10.5s⁶ 10.4g⁵ 1997 13.9g 10g
12m Jul 29] small, attractive colt: disappointing, and no form at 4 yrs: blinkered
nowadays. *S. Gollings*

SAMMY'S SHUFFLE   2 b.c. (Apr 28) Touch of Grey 90 – Cabinet Shuffle   –
(Thatching 131) [1997 a8g a7s a8g Dec 19] sixth foal: brother to a bad maiden: dam
unraced: well beaten in maidens and minor event. *R. M. Flower*

SAM PEEB   3 b.g. Keen 116 – Lutine Royal 46 (Formidable (USA) 125) [1996 –:   40
6m 6s 7.5m 1997 a11g⁴ 12m³ a12g⁴ 12d⁵ a14.8g³ 10g Jul 8] long-backed gelding: a48
unimpressive mover: poor handicapper: 20/1, best effort when winning at Southwell
in May: stays 1½m: acts on fibresand and dead ground. *R. A. Fahey*

SAMPOWER LADY   2 ch.f. (May 14) Rock City 120 – Travel On 111 (Tachy-   55
pous 128) [1997 5g⁵ 5m a6g⁵ 6m⁶ 7.3g Oct 25] 12,000 2-y-o: half-sister to winners
abroad by Formidable and Final Straw: dam won Cherry Hinton Stakes: modest
maiden: well held in nurseries final 2 starts: should stay 7f. *W. J. Musson*

SAMRAAN (USA)   4 br.c. Green Dancer (USA) 132 – Sedra 116 (Nebbiolo 125)   116
[1996 117: 10g* 12m³ 12d* 12m* 11.9g⁴ 12m⁶ 13.3m⁴ 14f* 14.6m³ 14d⁵ 1997 12g
12m⁶ 13.9g⁴ 20g⁵ 16m⁶ 15.9g² 14g² 14d⁶ 15f* Oct 4] useful-looking colt: smart
performer: demoted after first past post in minor event (for second successive year)
at Salisbury in September on seventh start, beating Clerkenwell a short head, hanging
under pressure: didn't have to be at best to win listed race at Milan: also ran well
when fourth in Yorkshire Cup (2¼ lengths behind Celeric) and second in Lonsdale
Stakes at York (beaten 2½ lengths by Double Eclipse): stays 2m: acts on firm and
dead going: reliable: stays in training. *J. L. Dunlop*

SAM ROCKETT   4 b.g. Petong 126 – Art Deco (Artaius (USA) 129) [1996 43:   48
7g 8d 8m 10m 10g 11.9f 14d⁴ 12d⁶ a16g a12g² 1997 a13g a12g 12d⁴ 12g³ 10.8f³   a–
10m² 12.5d a10g⁵ 12.1d⁵ Aug 25] leggy gelding: poor maiden handicapper: trained
by P. Mooney first 2 starts at 4 yrs: effective at 1¼m/1½m: acts on firm going, dead
and equitrack: genuine: fair hurdler for M. Pipe. *Miss Gay
Kelleway*

SAMSOLOM   9 b.g. Absalom 128 – Norfolk Serenade 83 (Blakeney 126) [1996   –
64: a6g⁶ a6g 6s 6g 6m⁵ 6f⁶ 6m 6.1m 6f⁵ 6f³ 6m 6m 6m³ 7m² 7g⁵ 6.9m 7m³ 7g 7m 7m
6m a7g⁶ a6g⁴ a7g 1997 a6g a6g a7g⁵ 7m May 31] modest handicapper up to 7f in
1996: no form at 9 yrs: left P. Howling cheaply after reappearance. *M. E. Sowersby*

SAMSPET   3 ch.g. Pharly (FR) 130 – Almond Blossom 69 (Grundy 137) [1996   43
43d: 5m 7m⁴ 7f a7g⁵ 6m⁵ 8.1m 6s 1997 a8g⁵ 8d⁵ 8d² 8m a8g 7.5v² 8.5m⁶ 8m 8.3g 8g
Oct 22] small, compact gelding: poor handicapper: best up to 1m on going softer than
good: blinkered/visored last 3 starts at 2 yrs: headstrong. *R. A. Fahey*

SAMSTOTRY   7 b.g. Starch Reduced 112 – Karousa Girl (Rouser 118) [1996 NR   –
1997 9.2d 8m 6.9g Apr 25] sturdy gelding: brother to 2 run-of-the-mill winners: dam
unraced: no sign of ability. *Miss L. A. Perratt*

SAMSUNG SPIRIT   3 b.f. Statoblest 120 – Sarong 97 (Taj Dewan 128) [1996   79
71: 6d* 6m³ 7m² 7m⁵ 6g⁵ 1997 6.1s³ 6s⁶ 8m 8g 6g* 6g⁶ 6s Oct 15] lengthy, good-
topped filly: has a quick action: fair handicapper: well drawn when winning at Ripon
in August, making most: well beaten afterwards: best efforts at 6f on good going or
softer: inconsistent. *E. Weymes*

SAM'S YER MAN   3 b.g. Full Extent (USA) 113 – Falls of Lora 107 (Scottish   –
Rifle 127) [1996 –: 6m 7m 8g 1997 10g Aug 20] little sign of ability, including in
sellers. *T. T. Clement*

SAMUEL SCOTT   4 b.g. Shareef Dancer (USA) 135 – Revisit 86 (Busted 134)   84
[1996 62: 8m 7m 11.8d⁶ 14d 1997 14.1g² 16s³ 14g* 16.2s Jun 21] tall, workmanlike
gelding: fairly useful handicapper: made all at Haydock in June: broke down next
time: stayed 2m: acted on soft going: dead. *M. C. Pipe*

SAMWAR   5 b.g. Warning 136 – Samaza (USA) 90 (Arctic Tern (USA) 126) [1996   77
98: 7m⁶ 7.6g 6m⁴ 6g* 6g² 5g² 5d 6s 1997 5.2g 7m 6g 6m 5.1s⁵ 6d 6g 5d 6s

Oct 15] small gelding: unimpressive mover: only fair handicapper at 5 yrs: left Miss G. Kelleway after third start: best at 5f/6f: has won on equitrack, best efforts on good going on turf: often bandaged: usually held up: inconsistent: sold 8,000 gns, and to return to Miss G. Kelleway. *M. R. Channon*

SANDABAR 4 b.g. Green Desert (USA) 127 – Children's Corner (FR) 106 (Top Ville 129) [1996 76+: 6.9m* 1997 6m 7d 8.5m 7d Jun 20] strong gelding: won maiden early in 1996: stiffish tasks in handicaps and no form at 4 yrs: should be suited by further than 7f. *M. R. Stoute* –

SANDAR 2 ch.f. (Mar 3) Sanglamore (USA) 126 – Darnelle 83 (Shirley Heights 130) [1997 7.1m 7.5f³ Sep 17] fifth foal: half-sister to 3 winners, including 3-y-o Caerfilly Dancer and 4-y-o Consort: dam, 7.6f (at 2 yrs) and 9f winner, half-sister to Oaks and Irish Oaks second Bourbon Girl: fair form in maidens at Sandown and Beverley, keeping-on third to Alborada on latter course: will be suited by 1m+: sold 16,000 gns in December. *B. W. Hills* 73

SANDBAGGEDAGAIN 3 b.g. Prince Daniel (USA) – Paircullis (Tower Walk 130) [1996 74: 5g 7s⁵ 5f³ 7m² 7.9g³ 8m² 8m³ 7.9g³ 1997 7m⁵ 8.5m³ 11.9d* 12g 10.1s 9.9d⁵ 7.9s Sep 3] leggy, shallow-girthed gelding: fairly useful performer: won 4-runner maiden at York in June: disappointing in handicaps afterwards: stays 1½m: acts on good to firm and dead ground: sometimes hangs. *M. W. Easterby* 80

SANDBLASTER 4 ch.f. Most Welcome 131 – Honeychurch (USA) 93 (Bering 136) [1996 55: 7d⁶ 8m² 8g³ 8g² 9f⁶ 8f⁶ 9.9f⁵ 9.9m⁵ 8.9g 1997 9.9m 8m⁵ 8.5s³ a7g 7.5g⁵ 8d* 8g 8m Aug 11] sparely-made filly: poor handicapper: won at Musselburgh in June: very slowly away next start, too stirred up final one: stays 1m: acts on firm and dead ground, probably on soft: has been early to post. *J. L. Eyre* 48

SAND CAY (USA) 3 ch.c. Geiger Counter (USA) – Lily Lily Rose (USA) (Lyphear 118) [1996 –: 8g 7.1v 8g 1997 11.6s 8f⁶ 8f² 7d⁵ 8m⁵ 8g Sep 4] rangy colt: modest maiden handicapper: stays 1m: best run on firm going: has been early to post. *R. Hannon* 64

SANDICLIFFE (USA) 4 b.f. Imp Society (USA) – Sad Song (USA) (Roberto (USA) 131) [1996 –: 7s 9m 10m⁵ 10.8m 16m⁴ 16m 14.1d 1997 a10g 6.9m* 8.3m⁵ 8m* 7f⁴ 7m Oct 4] tall, lengthy filly: fair performer: won claimer at Folkestone (left B. Hills) in May and ladies handicap at Newmarket (by 5 lengths) in August: did very well from poor draw when narrowly beaten in apprentice handicap at Yarmouth penultimate start: effective at 7f/1m: acts on firm ground. *J. A. R. Toller* 66 +

SANDMOOR CHAMBRAY 6 ch.g. Most Welcome 131 – Valadon 72 (High Line 125) [1996 88: 8g² 8.5m 8g² 8.5m³ 8.9m* 8m² 8.5m² 10.1m 9g² 10v⁵ 8m 8g 8g⁶ 8g 8s² 1997 8m⁴ 8m 8.1m 8.9d³ 10g⁴ 10.3d⁴ 7.9g⁶ 10m* 10.1m* 10.4g² 10m² 10.1g* 10.9d² 9m⁵ 10d³ 10m² Oct 31] lengthy gelding: poor mover: much improved at 6 yrs, and is a smart performer: won handicaps at Ripon in July, Newcastle in August and Epsom (by 2½ lengths from Danish Rhapsody) in September: good efforts afterwards when second to Ghataas in listed event at Ayr, fifth to Pasternak in Cambridgeshire at Newmarket and second to Saafeya in listed race at Newmarket: suited by around 1¼m: acts on good to firm and soft ground: has been blinkered, only twice in 1997: usually races prominently: game and consistent: a credit to his trainer. *T. D. Easterby* 110

SANDMOOR DENIM 10 b.g. Red Sunset 120 – Holernzaye 93 (Sallust 134) [1996 –, a69d: a8g⁴ 8.3s a9.4g³ 8g a9.4g* a8.5g a8.5g³ a9.4g a11g⁶ a8g a8.5g a8g a9.4g³ a8g a11g 1997 a8g³ a8g² a7g³ a8g² a8g⁴ a8g⁶ 8m² a7g a8g 8d² 10g² 10m 10g a8g⁵ 8s a8.5g² 10.4s Sep 4] close-coupled gelding: carries condition: modest handicapper: stays 1¼m: probably acts on any going: blinkered (below form) earlier in career: usually bandaged. *S. R. Bowring* 53 a50

SANDMOOR TARTAN 2 b.c. (Mar 16) Komaite (USA) – Sky Fighter 43 (Hard Fought 125) [1997 5m⁴ 5g 6g 6.1m* 6g³ 5m 6d⁶ 7s⁴ 7g Oct 25] 12,000Y: third foal: brother to 3-y-o Komasta: dam, poor maiden, stayed 1½m: modest performer: won nursery at Chester in August: generally ran creditably in similar races afterwards: stays 7f: acts on good to firm and soft ground. *T. D. Easterby* 58

SANDOWN SUE 3 b.f. Norton Challenger 111 – Tino Reppin 46 (Neltino 97) [1996 NR 1997 a11g Jun 13] fourth reported foal: dam suited by 7f: no promise in seller. *T. R. Watson* –

SANDSIDE 2 b.g. (Jan 2) Mazaad 106 – Deverells Walk (IRE) (Godswalk (USA) 85 d 130) [1997 5m⁴ 5d* 5m* 6f² 5.1s² 5v⁴ 6m⁴ 5g³ 5g* 6g 6d⁵ 5d⁵ Sep 18] 5,000Y: angular gelding: second foal: dam well beaten all 3 starts in Ireland at 2 yrs: fairly useful performer at best: won maiden at Musselburgh and minor event at Redcar in May and claimer at Hamilton in August: beaten in sellers 2 of last 3 starts: stays sharp 6f: acts on firm and soft ground, seemingly not heavy: makes running/races prominently. *J. Berry*

SAND STAR 5 b.m. Lugana Beach 116 – Overseas 48 (Sea Hawk II 131) [1996 – 73d: a8g³ 7g 7m³ 7.1d 7.1m 7m 7f 6.9g² 8.2g 1997 a8g a7g 8.2g 6d 7.1m Jul 25] sturdy, close-coupled mare: modest handicapper at 4 yrs: well beaten in 1997: visored last 2 starts. *D. Haydn Jones*

SANDSTONE (IRE) 3 b.c. Green Desert (USA) 127 – Rose de Thai (USA) 99 107 (Lear Fan (USA) 130) [1996 100: 7m* 7g⁵ 8.1f² 7m⁵ 8g 1997 8.2m³ 10m* 10m² 10.5m⁴ 8f* Sep 24] leggy, quite good-topped colt: useful performer: won listed race at Newmarket (by head from Haltarra) in May and valuable event in Turkey (by neck from Ramooz) in September: ½-length third to Danish Rhapsody in another listed race at Goodwood on final start: stays 1¼m: acts on firm ground, yet to race on softer than good: consistent: sold 105,000 gns, and sent to Saudi Arabia. *J. L. Dunlop*

SANDWELD 3 b.c. Weldnaas (USA) 112 – Scottish Lady (Dunbeath (USA) 127) 37 [1996 –: 5m a5g⁴ 7.1v 1997 7m 8g⁵ 6d 6.9m a6g Jul 21] angular colt: has reportedly had chipped knee and respiratory problems: poor form at best: blinkered final start (finished last). *C. A. Dwyer*

SANDY FLOSS (IRE) 4 b.g. Green Desert (USA) 127 – Mill On The Floss 117 72 (Mill Reef (USA) 141) [1996 80: 8.2s³ 7m⁴ 10d² 10.5d³ 1997 8d 10.8f⁴ 16.2s 18s⁶ 13.3f⁶ 11.6m² 13.1g 16m⁵ Sep 25] good-topped gelding: good walker and easy mover: fair maiden handicapper: left R. Buckler after sixth start: stays 2m (at least when conditions aren't testing): probably acts on any going: has been mulish at stalls and gone in snatches. *J. S. King*

SANDY SADDLER 3 ch.g. Most Welcome 131 – Beryl's Jewel 86 (Siliconn 60 121) [1996 NR 1997 6m 7g⁴ 7m⁵ a10g Dec 2] half-brother to several winners, best being useful sprinter Lingering (by Kind of Hush): dam best at 5f: modest maiden: best efforts at 7f. *S. Dow*

SANDY SHORE 2 b.f. (Apr 10) Lugana Beach 116 – City Link Lass 92 (Double 71 Jump 131) [1997 5.1m⁴ 5g³ 5g² 6.1d² 6m⁴ 7.5d 6.1m Sep 15] half-sister to several winners, including useful 1m winner John Rose (by Tina's Pet) and 4-y-o Anak-Ku: dam 2-y-o 6f and 7f winner: fair maiden: stays 6f: acts on good to firm and dead ground. *J. Wharton*

SANDYSTONES 3 b.f. Selkirk (USA) 129 – Sharanella (Shareef Dancer (USA) 60 135) [1996 –p: 7m 1997 8g 9d⁴ 11g⁵ Jun 20] leggy filly: has a round action: only worthwhile form in maidens when fourth in steadily-run event at Goodwood in May. *N. A. Graham*

SAN FRANCISCO 3 b.g. Aragon 118 – Sirene Bleu Marine (USA) (Secreto – (USA) 128) [1996 NR 1997 7.9s⁶ 9.2g⁶ 10s Oct 14] sturdy, close coupled gelding: has markedly round action: third foal: half-brother to 6f (at 2 yrs) to 1¼m winner Society Girl (by Shavian): dam never ran: well beaten in maidens. *C. W. Thornton*

SANG D'ANTIBES (FR) 3 ch.f. Sanglamore (USA) 126 – Baratoga (USA) 41 (Bering 136) [1996 58: 6g⁴ 6g 1997 7m 8g 5.2s² 6f⁶ 5.3m 7g Aug 11] lengthy filly: poor maiden: should stay 7f: none too tractable. *D. J. S. Cosgrove*

SAN GLAMORE MELODY (FR) 3 b.g. Sanglamore (USA) 126 – Lypharitis- 56 sima (FR) (Lightning (FR) 129) [1996 NR 1997 10g 10.5d⁴ 12g³ 14.1g² 18d a16g Aug 28] sturdy gelding: has a round action: third reported foal: dam unraced sister to Prix de Diane winner Lypharita: form only when second in maiden at Redcar: sold out of J. Gosden's stable after next start: tried visored. *R. Ingram*

SANS PERE 4 b.g. Shadow Minister (USA) 93§ – Creetown Sally 44 (Creetown – 123) [1996 NR 1997 10.2m a12g 11.6m⁵ Aug 11] second foal: dam poor maiden sprinter: seems of little account. *N. M. Babbage*

SANS RIVALE 2 ch.f. (Feb 16) Elmaamul (USA) 125 – Strawberry Song 87 57
(Final Straw 127) [1997 5.2f³ 6m² 5.1g 5.3f⁴ 5g* 5g⁶ Sep 15] 5,800Y: sixth foal: dam
1¼m winner: modest performer: won seller at Musselburgh (sold out of B. Meehan's
stable 5,200 gns) in August: ran respectably next time: should prove effective over
6f. *J. L. Eyre*

SANTA COURT 2 b.g. (Apr 23) Be My Native (USA) 122 – Christmas Show 60
(Petorius 117) [1997 6.1m⁵ 6.1d⁵ 7g 6d² 7.3d Sep 19] 1,800F: leggy gelding: third
foal: brother to a winner in Belgium: dam Irish 1½m winner: modest maiden: best
effort when second in nursery at Pontefract in September: should stay at least 7f.
R. Dickin

SANTA FAYE (IRE) 2 b.f. (Jan 28) Fayruz 116 – Florissa (FR) (Persepolis (FR) 74 +
127) [1997 5.1d⁴ 5.1g* 6d a7g³ a6g* a6s⁵ Nov 10] workmanlike filly: fourth foal: a77
half-sister to a winner in Belgium by Common Grounds: dam French 2-y-o 7f winner: fair form: won maiden at Chepstow in August and nursery at Southwell in October: will probably prove best up to 7f: easily best turf effort on good going, also acts
on fibresand, not discredited on equitrack. *B. Palling*

SANTARENE (IRE) 2 b.f. (Mar 10) Scenic 128 – Rising Spirits 77 (Cure The –
Blues (USA)) [1997 8m 8g Oct 24] leggy, unfurnished filly: fifth foal: half-sister to
1½m winner Nine Barrow Down (by Danehill) and a winner in Germany by Shaadi:
dam, winner at 7f at 2 yrs in Ireland and later in USA, is out of 1000 Guineas winner
Mrs McArdy: well held in maidens at Goodwood and Doncaster (bandaged behind).
P. Howling

SANTA ROSA (IRE) 3 b.f. Lahib (USA) 129 – Bequeath (USA) (Lyphard –
(USA) 132) [1996 64+: 7d⁴ 6m⁴ 7m³ 1997 8.2d 10m Jul 18] tall sparely-made filly:
fluent mover: half-sister to 5-y-o Decorated Hero: modest form in maidens at 2 yrs:
well held in handicaps in 1997: should be suited by further than 7f: sold 19,000 gns
in December. *J. L. Dunlop*

SANTELLA KATIE 4 ch.f. Anshan 119 – Mary Bankes (USA) (Northern Baby –
(CAN) 127) [1996 71: 7m⁶ 7.1m² 8.1m⁴ 10.2m⁵ 1997 a7s a7g 7g 10g May 23] leggy,
lightly-made filly: fair form up to 1m in maidens at 3 yrs: showed nothing in 1997.
Mrs L. Stubbs

SANTILLANA (USA) 4 ch.c. El Gran Senor (USA) 136 – Galway (FR) (Irish 110
River (FR) 131) [1996 116: 9g* 10g* 1997 10d* 10d⁴ Nov 9] rangy, attractive colt:
smart in the spring of 1996, winning Thresher Classic Trial at Sandown on second
start: reportedly damaged a hock and absent for 18 months, won muddling minor
event at Newmarket, needing to be at best: much better form when 7 lengths
fourth to Taipan in Premio Roma following month: not bred to stay much beyond
1¼m: acts on dead ground, yet to race on firmer than good. *J. H. M. Gosden*

SANTONE (IRE) 2 b.c. (Jan 12) Fairy King (USA) – Olivia Jane (IRE) (Ela- 77 p
Mana-Mou 132) [1997 5.2m 7m⁴ 7g⁵ Aug 13] second foal: half-brother to 3-y-o
Ziggy's Viola: dam unraced daughter of smart Irish middle-distance filly Green
Lucia, herself half-sister to Old Vic: fair form in maidens and a minor event, not
knocked about at Salisbury in latter: will be well suited by further than 7f: should do
better. *R. Hannon*

SAPPHIRE RING 2 b.f. (Mar 19) Marju (IRE) 127 – Mazarine Blue 65 (Belly- 99
pha 130) [1997 6g* 6d* 6d⁴ 6g² 7m² Sep 30] 80,000Y: strong, well-made filly: third
foal: half-sister to 3-y-o Ice Age and 4-y-o Orange And Blue (5f winner at 2 yrs): dam
sprinting half-sister to smart sprinter Rich Charlie: useful performer: won maiden at
Leicester in May and minor event at York in June: off course nearly 3 months after
third start, but ran well on return behind Regal Revolution in listed race at Ayr and
Tamarisk in valuable sales race at Newmarket: will probably stay 1m: yet to race on
extremes of ground: usually held up. *R. Charlton*

SAPPHIRE SON (IRE) 5 ch.g. Maelstrom Lake 118 – Gluhwein (Ballymoss 57
136) [1996 54, a52: 6.9m² 8m⁵ a8g⁴ 6.9g² 7m 6.9m⁴ 7d 6.9g⁴ a7g a8g a8g a10g² a41
1997 a12g⁵ a13g⁵ a12g a12g³ a13g⁴ 11.9f³ 12m⁴ 11.6g⁴ 9.7g 11.6m² 11.9m² 11.5g*
11.9m² 11.9m⁵ Oct 23] sparely-made gelding: modest handicapper on turf, poor on
all-weather: won at Lingfield in August: best up to 1½m: acts on firm ground and the
all-weather: effective with or without visor. *P. C. Clarke*

SARABI 3 b.f. Alzao (USA) 117 – Sure Enough (IRE) (Diesis 133) [1996 64: 5g – 5.1m⁵ 5.1m 6m 5g* 5.2g 5d 1997 5s 5m 7g 6m 5g Jun 11] small, sturdy filly: has lost her form. *J. Pearce*

SARAH STOKES (IRE) 2 b.f. (May 2) Brief Truce (USA) 126 – Almaaseh 76 (IRE) 63 (Dancing Brave (USA) 140) [1997 5.1m⁴ 5d² 5f² 6.1d⁴ Oct 30] 62,000F, 49,000Y: close-coupled filly: fluent mover: third foal: half-sister to 4-y-o Almaty: dam twice-raced daughter of Al Bahathri: fair maiden: best effort when fourth in minor event at Nottingham final start: stays 6f. *R. Guest*

SARAMAH (USA) 3 ch.f. Forty Niner (USA) – Cheval Volant (USA) (Kris S – (USA)) [1996 NR 1997 8.3m 10d Aug 30] third foal: closely related to 1m winners Amanah and Alrayyih (both by Mr Prospector): dam won up to 8.5f in USA, twice in Grade 1 events: well beaten in maidens: sold 35,000 gns in December. *J. H. M. Gosden*

SARA MOON CLASSIC (IRE) 2 b.c. (Mar 15) Fayruz 116 – Irish Affaire 64 (IRE) (Fairy King (USA)) [1997 6m⁴ 6m⁶ 6d a6g⁶ a6g³ Nov 17] IR 16,000Y: leggy colt: first foal: dam Belgian 2-y-o 7f winner: modest maiden: probably a sprinter: hung badly second outing: well beaten in visor fourth. *K. McAuliffe*

SARASI 5 ch.g. Midyan (USA) 124 – Early Call 102 (Kind of Hush 118) [1996 72: 59 a11g³ a8.5g³ a11g² a8g* a8.5g a9.4g 1997 a11g* a8g* a8g a9.4g a8g a11g⁶ Dec 8] angular gelding: modest performer: won seller in January and claimer in February, both at Southwell: disappointing afterwards, off course 9 months before final start: successful at 11f, best form up to 8.5f: acts on the all-weather, raced only once on turf since 2 yrs: tried visored/blinkered. *M. J. Camacho*

SARASOTA STORM 5 b.g. Petoski 135 – Challanging 95 (Mill Reef (USA) – 141) [1996 59: 10s 10.3m 10.8g 15.1f* 16.2m⁶ 15.1m* 16.2m 14.1m⁴ 14.4g 15.1m* 1997 16d⁴ 14.9g 16m 16g Sep 15] workmanlike gelding: modest staying handicapper at 4 yrs, winning 3 times at Musselburgh: no form in 1997. *M. Bell*

SARATOGA RED (USA) 3 ch.c. Saratoga Six (USA) – Wajibird (USA) (Storm 61 Bird (CAN) 134) [1996 71: a6g³ 6m³ 6f 7d 1997 a6g 7g a8g 10g a8g³ 8.1m² 8m 8d a73 8d² a7g* a8g³ a10g Dec 22] strong colt: has a round action: fair performer: won maiden at Lingfield in November: never going well final start: effective at 7f/1m: acts on good to firm ground, dead and all-weather: blinkered/visored last 8 starts. *W. A. O'Gorman*

SARATOGA SPRINGS (CAN) 2 ch.c. (Jan 21) El Gran Senor (USA) 136 113 – Population (General Assembly (USA)) [1997 7d³ 7g* 7g² 7g* 7m³ 8s* 8g* Oct 25]

There seemed hardly enough races at times in the Irish calendar for the Aidan O'Brien stable. Take the weekend of October 11th/12th for example. The stable had thirty runners declared in the fifteen races at Cork and Naas (five in the nursery at Naas alone) from an original total entry of eighty-three! The result was a double at Cork and a four-timer at Naas. The stable's two-year-olds in particular were queuing up to take each other on all season, even in the best races. Another consequence of the stable's numerical strength was that many of its best runners were sent overseas, and in Saratoga Springs's case he was seen almost as much in Yorkshire as he was in Ireland. His third outing in Britain, in the Racing Post Trophy at Doncaster, was his seventh start of the year, but Saratoga Springs was improving with his racing and needed to be kept busy because, according to his trainer, 'he just eats and sleeps' at home. In fact, Saratoga Springs had had a run just a week before the Racing Post Trophy when gaining a clear-cut win against just fairly useful opposition in the Juddmonte Beresford Stakes at the Curragh as an alternative to a last piece of work on the gallops.

Saratoga Springs began his career with a sizable reputation to match the 825,000 dollars he cost his connections, and started odds on for his first three starts. He narrowly failed to overcome considerable greenness at the Curragh on his debut, but made amends at Gowran Park in July, before being beaten half a length by Tarascon (giving 10 lb to that horse, the future Moyglare Stud

Stakes winner) in a minor event back at the Curragh. A sound enough start, but Saratoga Springs left his previous form well behind on his first outing in Britain in the Acomb Stakes at York. The Goodwood maiden winner Chester House, himself highly regarded, started favourite in a field which included five other last-time-out winners, but Saratoga Springs, sharpened by the first-time visor, ran out an impressive winner once quickening into the lead two furlongs out. He had five lengths to spare over Chester House, who dead-heated with Mutawwaj for second, putting up a performance which entitled him to a clash with the Richmond winner Daggers Drawn in the Laurent-Perrier Rose Champagne Stakes at Doncaster just over three weeks later. Visored again, Saratoga Springs failed to make the same impression and couldn't raise the pace when it mattered, finishing two and a quarter lengths behind Daggers Drawn in third, in receipt of 4 lb from the winner.

The visor was left off for the Beresford Stakes and again when Saratoga Springs returned to Doncaster for the Racing Post Trophy. It was an open-looking renewal of the latter contest, with Kilimanjaro, in the same ownership as Saratoga Springs, 7/2 favourite after finishing fourth in the Royal Lodge. Although Michael Kinane had chosen him ahead of the favourite, Saratoga Springs was a 9/2 chance with only two in the field of eight starting at longer than 13/2. Kinane made the right choice, but it took some firm driving to keep Saratoga Springs's head in front once they'd taken up the running around two furlongs out. Saratoga Springs edged left to the far rail and raced lazily in front, having only a short head to spare over Mudeer at the line, with Mutamam a length back in third. Both placed horses finished strongly and Mutamam's rider lodged an objection to the first two after having to switch under three furlongs out. Mudeer had hung left at that point but Saratoga Springs seemed to have little part in the incident and no action was taken. Kilimanjaro finished a well-beaten sixth.

For all that he won the Irish Derby, El Gran Senor's very best performance came in the Guineas, and, with the average winning distance of his three-year-old and upwards British runners at just over a mile, he can't be considered a strong influence for stamina. Saratoga Springs's dam, Population, was untried at beyond a mile and a quarter and proved disappointing in Ireland; she was placed on both her starts at two and on her reappearance at three but refused to enter the stalls on her next intended outing and ran poorly in two

Racing Post Trophy, Doncaster—Saratoga Springs (rail) just holds off Mudeer; Mutamam is third

subsequent starts, in blinkers on the last of them. She has now bred four diverse winners from as many foals, the first three being a Miswaki colt in Japan, the juvenile hurdler Melt The Clouds (by Diesis) and the mile-and-a-half Catterick maiden winner from the latest season, Alakdar (by Green Dancer). Population was all the more disappointing considering the achievements of some of the other foals out of the fairly useful mile-and-a-quarter winner Prudent Girl. Population's full sister, Popularity, had useful winning form at a mile and a quarter in Ireland (she stayed eleven furlongs), while half-brother Providential won the Washington D. C. International and half-sister Play It Safe the Prix Marcel Boussac. Prudent Girl was herself the daughter of the Queen Mary winner and outstanding broodmare Bride Elect, whose best offspring was Hethersett, the colt brought down in a pile-up when favourite for the 1962 Derby but who gained compensation in the St Leger.

		Northern Dancer	Nearctic
	El Gran	(b 1961)	Natalma
	Senor (USA)	Sex Appeal	Buckpasser
Saratoga Springs (CAN)	(b 1981)	(ch 1970)	Best In Show
(ch.c. Jan 21, 1995)		General Assembly	Secretariat
	Population	(ch 1976)	Exclusive Dancer
	(b 1986)	Prudent Girl	Primera
		(b 1968)	Bride Elect

The O'Brien-Tabor-Magnier combination thus completed a hat-trick in Group 1 mile events for two-year-old colts, following King of Kings in the National Stakes and Second Empire in the Grand Criterium, both of whom have shown better form than Saratoga Springs so far (particularly Second Empire). Saratoga Springs is bred to stay a mile and a quarter and he may progress further over such a trip as a three-year-old. It looks as though he'll be campaigned outside Ireland again in 1998, perhaps outside Europe altogether. His partici-

Mr M. Tabor and Mrs John Magnier's "Saratoga Springs"

pation in the Kentucky Derby (and probably a prep race in America before-hand) was described by Aidan O' Brien as a 'distinct possibility . . . He looks the right type of horse . . . If we're going to have a runner in the race, he's more likely than any of the others.' Saratoga Springs is a well-made, attractive colt, with a quick, fluent action. He acts on good to firm and soft ground. He'd already proved a good investment for at least one party before he ever ran, having been bought for 220,000 dollars as a yearling at Keeneland in January before being sold for nearly four times that amount there six months later. *A. P. O'Brien, Ireland*

SARAWAT 9 b.g. Slip Anchor 136 – Eljazzi 92 (Artaius (USA) 129) [1996 72: 12g 13.8s⁵ 13d² 13s* 13.9m⁵ 1997 a11g a11g² a12g⁵ Feb 7] smallish gelding: hobdayed: formerly fairly useful winner, including of Ebor in 1993: second in a seller at South-well in January: dead. *D. Nicholls* – a53

SARAYIR (USA) 3 b.f. Mr Prospector (USA) – Height of Fashion (FR) 124 (Bustino 136) [1996 100p: 7f* 7m* 1997 8m 12g 10.2m⁴ 10g² 10.1g* 10m Oct 4] tall, rangy, unfurnished filly: useful performer: best effort when winning listed rated stakes at Newcastle in August, just holding on from Delilah: looked and ran as though past her best in Sun Chariot Stakes final start: stayed 1¼m: acted on firm going: sweated freely (ran creditably) fourth 3-y-o start: visits Fairy King. *Major W. R. Hern* – 104

SARBARON (IRE) 3 b.c. Danehill (USA) 126 – Salette 110 (Sallust 134) [1996 NR 1997 10d⁶ 10s 11.8m⁶ a12g⁴ a12g⁴ 11.5g⁴ 12g a12g⁵ Aug 16] IR 34,000Y: big, good-topped colt: half-brother to 3 minor winners, and to dam of smart sprinter Late Parade: dam won at 5f (at 2 yrs) and 1m: modest maiden handicapper: stays 1½m: acts on fibresand, ran badly only run on going firmer than good. *P. W. Harris* – 64

SARMATIAN (USA) 6 br.g. Northern Flagship (USA) 96 – Tracy L (USA) (Bold Favorite (USA)) [1996 77: 9.2s⁵ 10g² 10d* 10f 10.3g⁵ 8.5m 1997 9.2s³ 9.2m Jul 11] leggy gelding: fair handicapper: stays 1¼m: acts on any going: ran poorly in blinkers final 5-y-o start: fairly useful hurdler. *M. D. Hammond* – 74

SARUM 11 b.g. Tina's Pet 121 – Contessa (HUN) (Peleid 125) [1996 56d: a8g⁵ a9.4g⁴ a8g* a8g⁵ a8g⁶ a10g a8g a8g 7d 6.9m 9m 9.7f a8g 7g a10g a8g⁶ a8g 1997 a12g a8g⁴ a8.5g 6.9m⁶ 8.1s 7d a8.5g 10g Sep 3] tall gelding: poor mover: very much on the downgrade. *J. E. Long* –

SASEEDO (USA) 7 ch.g. Afleet (CAN) – Barbara's Moment (USA) (Super Moment (USA)) [1996 99, a–: 7m 6m⁶ 7g* 6f 6g* 7.1d* 7m 7m⁵ 7g 7m³ 7g 1997 7g 6m 7g 7m Oct 4] close-coupled gelding: poor mover: useful 6f/7f handicapper in 1996: never a factor in 1997: blinkered penultimate start: highly-strung, and often slowly away, badly so last 3 outings: sold only 3,500 gns in October. *W. A. O'Gorman* –

SASSIVER (USA) 7 b.g. Riverman (USA) 131 – Sassabunda 108 (Sassafras (FR) 135) [1996 40: a16g⁶ a12g³ a13g⁵ 1997 a13g³ a16g⁵ Jan 16] strong gelding: poor handicapper: stays 2m: acts on soft going and the all-weather: blinkered in 1996. *P. A. Kelleway* – 35

SASSY (IRE) 2 b.f. (Mar 27) Imp Society (USA) – Merrie Moment (IRE) (Taufan (USA) 119) [1997 6d⁶ 6m 6.1m 6m* 6m² 6m⁴ 6.9g⁶ 7m⁵ 7m Oct 23] IR 1,800F: tall filly: third foal: dam unraced half-sister to Stewards' Cup winner Autumn Sunset: modest performer: won seller at Windsor in July: well below form last 2 starts: shapes as if will stay 1m: acts on good to firm ground. *A. P. Jarvis* – 57

SASSY LADY (IRE) 2 b.f. (May 7) Brief Truce (USA) 126 – Taken By Force (Persian Bold 123) [1997 6g⁴ 6m 8d Oct 16] IR 10,000Y: sparely-made filly: half-sister to several winners, including 7f (at 2 yrs) to 1½m winner Hunter Valley (by Valiyar): dam Irish 1¼m to 1½m winner: modest form first 2 starts in maidens: should stay 1m. *C. A. Dwyer* – 63

SASSY STREET (IRE) 4 b.g. Danehill (USA) 126 – Sassy Lane (Sassafras (FR) 135) [1996 NR 1997 10d 10.2d 7d 12.1m 16.4g Sep 2] tall gelding: half-brother to winners abroad by Silent Cal and Persian Heights: dam French 1¼m and 1½m winner: no form. *R. F. Johnson Houghton* –

Prix d'Ispahan, Longchamp—No. 6 Sasuru just gets the better of fellow British raider Wixim

SASURU   4 b.c. Most Welcome 131 – Sassalya (Sassafras (FR) 135) [1996   121
113p: 12m² 12.3g⁴ 10.1g* 10.4m* 10d* 1997 10d* 9.3d* 10d⁵ Jul 5]
      Stable-companions Sasuru and First Island both had curtailed cam-
paigns in 1997 after winning Group 1 events early in the season. Unlike the ill-
fated First Island, Sasuru will be back in 1998 having been reported in the
autumn as making a recovery from a slight problem which had caused him to
miss the Juddmonte International at York in August. Sasuru's three-year-old
season had ended fairly abruptly, too, on a hat-trick in a maiden at Newcastle, a
rated stakes at York and the Group 2 Prix Guillaume d'Ornano at Deauville.
But his progress resumed where it had left off when he returned from an eight-
month absence to win the David Lloyd Leisure Gordon Richards Stakes at
Sandown in April. Giving weight to all bar one of his six rivals in the Group 3
event, Sasuru put up a very smart performance, cruising up to the leaders halfway up the straight and merely coaxed clear to beat Multicoloured by two and a
half lengths.
      It didn't require any further improvement from Sasuru for him to take
his winning sequence to five in a substandard Prix d'Ispahan over an extended
nine furlongs at Longchamp a month later. Sasuru was joined from Britain by
the Sandown Mile winner Wixim (who had beaten First Island by a head in that
event) and the Dubai Duty Free winner Tamayaz, the latter from the out-of-
sorts Godolphin stable. The French opposition was by no means out of the top
drawer, consisting of the colts Simon du Desert, Baroud d'Honneur and Nero
Zilzal. Tamayaz set the early pace, but it was the other British raiders who
fought out the finish, with Sasuru asserting only near the post to win by a short-
neck, having been carried left by Wixim in the closing stages. Simon du Desert
was beaten three lengths in third. Sasuru's absence from Royal Ascot was a
deliberate ploy to keep him fresh for the Eclipse back at Sandown. Allowing
for the likes of Pilsudski, Bosra Sham and Benny The Dip making it a Group 1
much more worthy of the name, Sasuru was rather disappointing, tapped for
foot when the pace quickened and fading to finish last of the five runners.
      Sasuru's win in the Prix d'Ispahan came not long after the death of his
dam, Sassalya, at the age of twenty-four; she suffered complications giving
birth to what would have been a full brother or sister to Sasuru. Sassalya had
been a marvellous broodmare for the Oppenheimers' Hascombe Stud, produc-

ing sixteen foals in all (the last was a colt by Inchinor born in 1996) of which a dozen have now won. Sasuru is the best, but the smart fillies Sally Rous (a seven-furlong performer by Rousillon) and The Faraway Tree (by Suave Dancer), second in the latest Park Hill Stakes, weren't far behind. Ebor runner-up Chauve Souris (by Beldale Flutter) was one of several more who were useful. Sassalya herself won at seven furlongs and a mile and a quarter in Ireland and as a four-year-old finished fourth in the Princess Royal Stakes.

		Be My Guest	Northern Dancer
	Most Welcome	(ch 1974)	What A Treat
	(ch 1984)	Topsy	Habitat
Sasuru		(ch 1976)	Furioso
(b.c. 1993)		Sassafras	Sheshoon
	Sassalya	(b 1967)	Ruta
	(b 1973)	Valya	Vandale II
		(b 1965)	Lilya

Sasuru is due to be tried again at a mile and a half in 1998. He was raced at that trip at the start of his three-year-old campaign, beaten a head in a Newmarket maiden and finishing fourth in the Chester Vase, when evidently considered something of a stayer. He's subsequently shown better form at around a mile and a quarter, but that's not to say he'll necessarily find the longer trip beyond him. A fluent mover with a good turn of foot, Sasuru has yet to race on extremes of going and is usually bandaged. He reportedly gave his jockey some anxious moments going to post at Longchamp but has shown no quirks once racing. *G. Wragg*

SATIN STONE (USA) 3 b.c. Mr Prospector (USA) – Satin Flower (USA) 115 78 (Shadeed (USA) 135) [1996 NR 1997 7g 7m² 7m Jun 18] quite attractive colt: first foal: dam won Jersey Stakes and stayed 9f: form only when second of 17 in maiden at Kempton: reportedly swallowed tongue on debut: very stiff task (wore crossed noseband) final start: should stay 1m. *J. H. M. Gosden*

SATIS (IRE) 2 b.f. (Apr 20) Last Tycoon 131 – Nazwa 105 (Tarboosh (USA)) 49 [1997 5m 6.1s⁴ 6g⁶ 5s a6g² a5g 5s² a5g Nov 15] IR 15,500Y: leggy filly: half-sister to 3 winners, including fairly useful Irish 1987 2-y-o 5f winner Saintly Lass (by Halo): dam useful winner up to 7f in Ireland: poor maiden: second in sellers at Wolverhampton and Musselburgh: stays 6f: acts on fibresand and soft ground. *M. R. Channon*

SATURIBA (USA) 4 b.g. Fighting Fit (USA) – My Popsicle (USA) (Raja Baba – (USA)) [1996 NR 1997 8m 7d 6m May 27] tall, angular gelding: modest maiden at 2 yrs: tailed off in 1997: dead. *John A. Harris*

SAUDI 2 b.c. (Mar 25) Green Desert (USA) 127 – Emaline (FR) 105 (Empery 68 (USA) 128) [1997 7g⁵ 7m 7d Oct 14] small, close-coupled, robust colt: has a round action: ninth foal: brother to 3-y-o Mayfair and smart 1991 2-y-o sprinter Magic Ring and half-brother to several winners, including middle-distance stayer Monarda (by Pharly): dam French 2-y-o 7f winner: fair form in large fields of maidens at Newcastle and Leicester on first 2 starts: well held final one: should stay 1m. *P. F. I. Cole*

SAUGERTIES (USA) 3 ch.c. Trempolino (USA) 135 – Stalwart Moment (USA) 114 (Stalwart (USA)) [1996 7g* 7g² 1997 8g⁶ 10.5g⁴ 11v³ 12g 12s* 11g 12d* Oct 26] third foal: half-brother to fair 1m winner Dawawin (by Dixieland Band): dam won both her starts up to 1m at 3 yrs in USA: won maiden at Hanover and close second in national listed event at Krefeld at 2 yrs: 5 lengths third of 12 to Caitano in Group 2 event at Cologne in June: won valuable national listed race at Hanover in August and improved to win Group 3 race at Dusseldorf (beat Mongol Warrior ¾ length) in October: stays 1½m: acts on heavy ground. *H. Jentzsch, Germany*

SAUNDERS WREN 3 b.f. Handsome Sailor 125 – Saunders Lass 68 (Hillandale – 125) [1996 65d: 5m* 5m 6g³ 5m 5f* 5f 1997 5d May 10] long-backed filly: won maiden and claimer at 2 yrs: soundly beaten in handicap only outing in 1997: stays 6f: acts on firm ground. *Mrs L. Stubbs*

Mr J. C. Smith's "Sausalito Bay"

SAUSALITO BAY   3 b.c. Salse (USA) 128 – Cantico 58 (Green Dancer (USA)   111
132) [1996 81p: 8d⁵ 8.1s* 1997 10m⁴ 10m³ 16.2m 12.1m² 14m 13.9g* 14.6m* 15m⁴
Oct 4] tall, useful-looking colt: has scope: smart performer: much improved last 3
starts, winning Melrose Handicap at York (by 6 lengths) in August and Mallard Handicap at Doncaster (beat Georgia Venture a head) in September: good 2½ lengths
fourth to Three Cheers in Prix de Lutece at Longchamp final start: possibly unsuited
by undulations at Goodwood fifth outing: needs further than 1½m and will stay 2m:
acts on good to firm and soft going. *I. A. Balding*

SAVONA (IRE)   3 b.f. Cyrano de Bergerac 120 – Shannon Lady 67 (Monsanto   57
(FR) 121) [1996 70: 5s⁴ 6.1s³ 6d⁵ 1997 6d 6s³ 6d Aug 8] smallish, sturdy filly:
unimpressive mover: modest maiden: should stay 7f: raced only on dead and soft
going. *P. J. Makin*

SAVOURY   2 b.f. (Apr 13) Salse (USA) 128 – Metaphysique (FR) (Law Society   67
(USA) 130) [1997 7g⁴ 7m 7g Oct 7] third foal: half-sister to 3-y-o Philosophic: dam,
French 1¼m winner, out of sister to Try My Best and El Gran Senor: fair form in
maiden on debut, but well beaten both subsequent starts (seemed ill-at-ease on good
to firm going first of them): should be suited by 1¼m+. *J. L. Dunlop*

SAVU SEA (IRE)   3 b.f. Slip Anchor 136 – Soemba 86 (General Assembly   –
(USA)) [1996 NR 1997 10d⁶ 12s 12m⁴ 12g 12s Oct 16] tall, lengthy filly: shows knee
action: seventh foal: half-sister to 4 winners, including useful Sumonda (up to 1m, by
Lomond) and 6-y-o Lalindi: dam, 9f winner, from good family: remote fourth in
maiden at Newmarket in July, only sign of ability: visored final start (found nothing):
temperament under suspicion. *C. F. Wall*

SAWLAJAN (USA)   6 ch.g. Woodman (USA) 126 – Crafty Satin (USA) (Crimson Satan) [1996 10.9g 10.9g 1997 7g Oct 24] useful 1m winner for J. Dunlop at 3 yrs: ran twice at Abu Dhabi early in 1996: no encouragement in handicap only outing in 1997. *T. R. Watson*   –

SAXON BAY   5 ch.g. Cadeaux Genereux 131 – Princess Athena 119 (Ahonoora 122) [1996 57: 8.2m a8g⁵ 1997 8.5m⁴ a7g 8.3s⁶ 6.1m⁶ 6s⁶ 6g a6g 8g a5g 8f 10.8g Oct 7] workmanlike gelding: unimpressive mover: modest maiden handicapper: well beaten last 6 starts: probably a sprinter: acts on good to firm going: tried blinkered. *K. O. Cunningham-Brown*   59 d

SAXONBURY   3 b.g. Shirley Heights 130 – Dancing Vaguely (USA) (Vaguely Noble 140) [1996 –: 8d 1997 a10g⁴ a12g⁶ Feb 27] seventh foal: half-brother to 2 winners in France, including Vagamo (up to 10.5f, by Nashwan): dam French 1½m winner: no form: visored final start (pulled hard and saddle slipped). *G. L. Moore*   –

SAXON VICTORY (USA)   2 b.g. (Apr 1) Nicholas (USA) 111 – Saxon Shore (USA) (Halo (USA)) [1997 5m 5f 6m 8m³ Oct 5] leggy, close-coupled gelding: second foal: brother to fairly useful Irish 3-y-o 1m winner Mac Nicholas: dam twice-raced daughter of a mare placed in Grade 1 6f event: poor maiden: easily best effort when third in nursery at Leicester: stays 1m. *W. J. Haggas*   49

SAYYARAMIX (FR)   4 br.c. Linamix (FR) 127 – Sayyara 81 (Kris 135) [1996 8s⁶ 6d² 6m³ 5.5m³ 6m⁵ 5.5m a7g* 1997 6m 5.5g 6g 7d² 8m a8g² 8s 7g 7g³ a6g⁶ 8v Dec 1] tall, angular colt: second foal: half-brother to a winner in France at 7f/1m by Lashkari: dam, 1m winner, out of smart (up to 1¼m) Safita: useful form (rated 98) when placed 3 times at Evry for A. Fabre at 3 yrs, then on final start won minor event in Belgium: behind in minor event at Kempton on reappearance: second in France and Belgium after: stays 1m: acts on good to firm and dead ground, and on sand. *J. Van Landschoot, Belgium*   72

SCAPESTRATA (USA)   2 b.f. (Mar 17) Distinctive Pro (USA) – Southern Tradition (USA) (Family Doctor (USA)) [1997 7g Oct 7] second foal: half-sister to a winner in USA by Unbridled: dam won 3 Grade 3 races at 8.5f/9f: little promise in maiden at Warwick: sold 1,200 gns in November. *P. F. I. Cole*   –

SCARABEN   9 b.g. Dunbeath (USA) 127 – Varushka 74 (Sharpen Up 127) [1996 79: 7g 8g 8g 8m 8g³ 8.3g³ 8m⁴ 8m² 8m* 8m³ 8f⁴ 8m 8m 8g 8.1s* 1997 8g⁴ 8m³ 8.3g⁴ 9.2s* 9.2d² 9d⁵ 8.2s² Oct 15] big, lengthy gelding: has a quick action: fair handicapper: won 3-runner event at Hamilton in June: stays 1¼m: acts on any going: has had tongue tied: has run well for amateur: usually held up: genuine: sold 2,000 gns in November. *S. E. Kettlewell*   76

SCARLET CRESCENT   3 b.f. Midyan (USA) 124 – Scarlet Veil 75 (Tyrnavos 129) [1996 66+: 6.1m³ 6m³ 7m* 7m 1997 8f⁴ 10d³ a10g⁴ 8.2m* 8d 8m³ 8.3m 8m 10.1m Oct 22] close-coupled, angular filly: fair handicapper: won at Nottingham in June: well held afterwards: best form at 1m: acts on firm and dead ground, ran poorly only start on equitrack: visored final start: sold 7,500 gns in December. *P. T. Walwyn*   67

SCARROTS   3 b.c. Mazilier (USA) 107 – Bath 76 (Runnett 125) [1996 59: 5.1d 6.9m⁵ 7m 7g⁶ 7.5m* 8f⁴ 1997 a8.5g⁶ 9.7m⁶ 10g⁴ 11.8g* 12f⁶ 12.3m⁶ 12g⁶ 11m³ 14.1g 12f² 11.8d Oct 13] good-bodied colt: fair handicapper: won at Leicester in May and Carlisle in June: stays 1½m well: acts on firm ground, below form on dead: front runner: game: sold 25,000 gns, and joined N. Henderson. *S. C. Williams*   74

SCATHEBURY   4 b.g. Aragon 118 – Lady Bequick 81 (Sharpen Up 127) [1996 62§: a8.5g³ 8f⁴ a8.5g⁴ 6.9m² a7g 6g⁴ a5g 7.6m 7g² 6m⁴ 7.1m* 7g 8.1m 6.9g 6m 6.9d² a7g a7g a6g⁶ 1997 6.9g³ 6m² 8m* 8.3s* 9.7m 8g 7.1g² 8.3s 6m⁵ 6.9g 7.1g 8m 7d* 8g³ 8s³ Nov 6] compact gelding: modest handicapper: won seller at Musselburgh in April, claimer at Windsor in May and another seller at Leicester in October: effective at 6f to 1m: acts on fibresand and any turf going: effective blinkered/visored, not tried at 4 yrs: has run poorly when sweating: carries head awkwardly. *K. R. Burke*   62

SCATTERGUN   3 ch.c. Rainbow Quest (USA) 134 – Cattermole (USA) (Roberto (USA) 131) [1996 NR 1997 10s² May 17] close-coupled colt: has been fired: first foal: dam, French 8.5f winner, half-sister to good 7f performer Condrillac: ¾-length second of 15 to Garuda, pair well clear, in maiden at Newbury, flashing tail under pressure: lame afterwards but stays in training. *J. H. M. Gosden*   91

SCBOO   8 b.g. Full Extent (USA) 113 – Maygo 57 (Maystreak 118) [1996 –: a6g   –
a7g⁵ a12g 1997 a7g Feb 4] no sign of ability. *R. E. Peacock*

SCENE (IRE)   2 b.f. (Apr 4) Scenic 128 – Avebury Ring (Auction Ring (USA)   68
123) [1997 5.1m⁴ 5.1d 6m⁶ 6g 5.7m 6g 6g³ 7d⁶ 6d³ 7s* Nov 8] IR 2,400Y: good-
topped filly: half-sister to several winners, including 7f (at 2 yrs) and 1½m winner Te
Amo (by Waajib): dam Irish 5f winner: improved form to win nursery at Doncaster
by ¾ length from Alconleigh: beaten in sellers previously: will stay at least 1m:
clearly goes well on soft ground. *Martyn Meade*

SCENICRIS (IRE)   4 b.f. Scenic 128 – Princesse Smile 99 (Balidar 133) [1996   59
73, a54: a8.5g³ a8.5g⁶ a8g⁵ a8g a7g 7m³ 9.9m 7f 7m³ 7.6m 7m 8.1m⁴ 8m³ 8m⁵ 8m³   a39
8.2s* a8g⁴ 1997 a8g⁴ a8g a12g⁶ 10m 7.5m⁵ 10m a8g 10.3m⁶ 8.2g 8g 10m² 8.2m² 8d⁴
8.3g 8.2d⁴ 10.1g 8.2d² Nov 3] smallish, workmanlike filly: modest handicapper on
turf, poor on all-weather: best form around 1m: has form on firm ground, ideally
suited by good to soft/soft: held up. *R. Hollinshead*

SCENT OF SUCCESS (USA)   2 b.f. (Mar 12) Quiet American (USA) – Mous-   79 +
quet (USA) (Shadeed (USA) 135) [1997 7m³ 7.5g² 7.5f* 7v⁴ Oct 10] first foal: dam
unraced close relative of Lammtarra, out of Snow Bride (awarded Oaks), herself
daughter of Yorkshire Oaks winner and Arc third Awaasif: sire (by Fappiano) ran 3
times in Britain, then Grade 1 1m winner in USA: fair form: won maiden at Beverley
in September: creditable fourth to Smart Squall in Ascot nursery, sent clear briefly in
very testing ground: should stay at least 1m: seems to act on any ground: visored second and final starts: seems to idle in front, and may prove suited by more exaggerated waiting tactics. *M. R. Stoute*

SCEPTRE LADY (IRE)   3 ch.f. Common Grounds 118 – The Saltings (FR)   76
(Morston (FR) 125) [1996 NR 1997 7g⁴ 7s³ 7d 7.6m³ 8.2m⁵ 8.1s* Aug 30]
IR 42,000Y: unfurnished filly: sister to smart American performer Earl of Barking
(stayed 1½m) and Italian 2-y-o 7f winner Kathy Grounds, and half-sister to 2
winners: dam twice-raced from good sprinting family: fair performer: variable form
prior to winning maiden at Sandown: stays 1m: acts on good to firm and soft going:
sold 28,000 gns in December. *B. W. Hills*

SCHARNHORST   5 b.g. Tacheron 52 – Stardyn (Star Appeal 133) [1996 80: a8g   –
7s* 7d 6.9f* 7.6g⁵ 6d* 7.1m 7m 6m 6m⁶ 1997 6d 6g 6g 7s Oct 17] sturdy,
useful-looking gelding: fairly useful short of 1m as 4-y-o for S. Dow: off course
nearly a year and last all starts in 1997. *A. R. Dicken*

SCHISANDRA   3 b.f. Petong 126 – Volcalmeh 67 (Lidhame 109) [1996 –: 6f 7g   –
6m 7m 1997 8.3s 8.2g Jun 18] no form. *M. J. Fetherston-Godley*

SCHNOZZLE (IRE)   6 b.g. Cyrano de Bergerac 120 – Sun Gift (Guillaume Tell   55
(USA) 121) [1996 NR 1997 11.8g⁴ 12.5d* 14.9g⁴ Jul 12] modest handicapper: won
maiden event at Warwick in June, always going well: unlikely to stay beyond 15f:
acts on any going: sometimes carries head awkwardly. *K. S. Bridgwater*

SCHOOL OF SCIENCE   7 b.g. Then Again 126 – Girl's Brigade (Brigadier   28
Gerard 144) [1996 –: 12.1g 12.1g⁶ 13g 8.1g³ 8.3m³ 10d 11.1m⁵ 1997 12.1m⁵ 9m
12.1g⁵ 11.1d⁴ 9.2m⁵ 8m³ Aug 20] workmanlike gelding: bad handicapper: stays
1½m: acts on good to firm and soft ground: tried blinkered. *D. A. Nolan*

SCISSOR RIDGE   5 ch.g. Indian Ridge 123 – Golden Scissors 76 (Kalaglow   65
132) [1996 70, a76: a6g⁵ 6m² 7m a7g⁶ 7m 6m² 6m⁵ 6m* 7m⁴ 6m³ 6m² 6m 6f² 6m²   a77
6m² 6m⁴ 5m* 5d 6m⁶ a5g a6g* a5g* a6g⁴ 1997 a6g² a7g⁴ a5g³ a6g⁴ a6g⁵ 5m 6g 5d
6m 6m 7.6m³ 6m⁵ 6m² 6g⁶ 6d 5m 6m⁴ 7g⁴ 7m a6s³ a7g² a6g⁴ Dec 19] sparely-made
gelding: fair handicapper: stays easy 7f: acts on firm going, dead and the all-weather:
tried blinkered (not at 5 yrs): takes keen hold, and usually races prominently: tough
and consistent. *J. J. Bridger*

SCOLDING   2 b.f. Reprimand 122 – Tinkerbird 76 (Music Boy 124)   –
[1997 5.1d⁶ 5m 5.1g 5m 6d Aug 30] 3,600Y: third foal: half-sister to 4-y-o Batelour:
dam sprinter: little worthwhile form: swerved and unseated rider shortly after start
second outing. *K. A. Morgan*

SCONCED (USA)   2 ch.c. (Apr 17) Affirmed (USA) – Quaff (USA) 115 (Raise A   71 p
Cup (USA)) [1997 6m 7f⁴ 7m⁵ Oct 22] $40,000Y: leggy, unfurnished colt: fourth
foal: dam French 1m winner at 2/3 yrs, later 9f winner in USA: progressed in

maidens: keeping-on fifth to Jila at Yarmouth final start: will be well suited by 1m+: type to make a better 3-y-o. *G. Wragg*

SCORNED (GER) 2 b.c. (Apr 8) Selkirk (USA) 129 – Spurned (USA) 91   **89 p** (Robellino (USA) 127) [1997 8d 7d* Nov 7] tall, useful-looking colt: has plenty of scope: fourth foal: brother to 3-y-o Hidden Meadow and half-brother to fairly useful sprinter Overbrook (by Storm Cat) and 4-y-o Jona Holley: dam stayed 1¼m: won maiden at Doncaster in good style by 2½ lengths from High And Low, leading over 2f out and running on strongly: started slowly and considerately handled on debut: should stay at least 1m: looks sure to make a useful 3-y-o at the least. *I. A. Balding*

SCOSS 3 b.c. Batshoof 122 – Misguided 106 (Homing 130) [1996 NR 1997 7.5m⁶   **82** 10s² 10.2f* 10m² 10s 10m 10m* Sep 28] 42,000Y: lengthy, angular colt: has knee action: half-brother to several winners, including useful Misbelief (up to 15f, by Shirley Heights): dam sprinting half-sister to smart 6f and 1m winner Missed Blessing: fairly useful performer: won maiden at Bath in May and minor event at Milan in September: should stay beyond 1¼m: probably acts on any going: winning hurdler for T. Walsh in Ireland. *L. M. Cumani*

SCOTCH TIME 2 ch.g. (Feb 11) Timeless Times (USA) 99 – Scotch Imp 83   **52 ?** (Imperial Fling (USA) 116) [1997 5d 6m⁴ 5m 5g⁴ Aug 13] 900Y: lengthy, good-quartered gelding: second living foal: half-brother to 3-y-o Why O Six: dam best at 6f/7f: form only in maiden at Hamilton on second outing: blinkered subsequently, swerving stalls on next start. *R. A. Fahey*

SCOTLAND BAY 2 b.f. (Apr 11) Then Again 126 – Down The Valley 73   **51** (Kampala 120) [1997 6g a7g⁴ a8g⁴ Dec 19] good-topped filly: fourth foal: sister to fairly useful 7f/1m winner (including at 2 yrs) Down D Islands: dam, 2-y-o 5f winner who stayed 11f, out of sister to high-class sprinter Abergwaun: modest form when fourth in maidens at Lingfield. *R. Hannon*

SCOTTISH BAMBI 9 ch.g. Scottish Reel 123 – Bambolona 108 (Bustino 136)   **60** [1996 66: 9.7m* 10g 10m⁴ 10m⁵ 1997 10m⁶ Sep 9] rangy, workmanlike gelding: has a round action: modest handicapper: creditable effort only outing as 9-y-o: stays 1¼m: acts on firm and dead ground: normally held up: fair hurdler/fairly useful chaser. *P. R. Webber*

SCOTTISH HERO 4 b.c. North Briton 67 – Tartan Pimpernel 109 (Blakeney   **–** 126) [1996 –: 10m 10m 14.1f⁴ 12m 1997 9.7g 8.2g 8m Jun 2] compact colt: no form: blinkered last 2 starts. *Lady Herries*

SCOTTISH PARK 8 ch.m. Scottish Reel 123 – Moss Agate (Alias Smith   **30** (USA)) [1996 47: a8.5g a10g³ a10g 7d⁴ 8g³ 10m⁶ 8m* 8.1f³ 10.8m⁴ 11.7m⁶ 1997 a9.4g 10.2m 8d 8s 12.5m⁴ Jul 19] sturdy, lengthy mare: poor performer: probably stays 12.5f: acts on good to firm ground, soft and the all-weather: effective visored/blinkered or not: difficult ride. *M. C. Pipe*

SCOTTISH WEDDING 7 b.m. Scottish Reel 123 – Pearl Wedding 86 (Gulf   **–** Pearl 117) [1996 NR 1997 a14.8g Jan 8] has shown little on flat since 1993. *T. Wall*

SCOTT'S RISK 7 b.g. Risk Me (FR) 127 – Madam de Seul 104 (Pas de Seul 133)   **–** [1996 –: 7g 5g 6.1m 1997 a7g⁶ Feb 26] of little account. *L. J. Barratt*

SCURRILOUS 2 ch.f. (Jan 14) Sharpo 132 – Tea And Scandals (USA) (Key To   **–** The Kingdom (USA)) [1997 5.1d 5d Oct 17] eighth reported foal: half-sister to high-class French sprinter Ron's Victory (by General Holme): dam French 6f winner: slowly away and behind in maidens at Nottingham and Catterick. *M. Bell*

SEA BUCK 11 b.g. Simply Great (FR) 122 – Heatherside 80 (Hethersett 134)   **–** [1996 –: 16m 1997 16m Sep 15] no form on flat since modest maiden at 3 yrs. *H. Candy*

SEA DANE 4 b.c. Danehill (USA) 126 – Shimmering Sea 89 (Slip Anchor 136)   **–** [1996 107: 7d 6m* 6f 6d 6g 5.6m 5g⁵ 6g 1997 6m 6g 6g 6f Jul 19] sturdy, close-coupled colt: has a powerful, round action: useful 6f performer on his day at 3 yrs: showed nothing in 1997, and sold only 1,000 gns in October, to go to Sweden: usually bandaged: sometimes slowly away. *P. W. Harris*

SEA DANZIG 4 ch.g. Roi Danzig (USA) – Tosara 84 (Main Reef 126) [1996 68:   **60** 6.1d² 6m 8.2m 8g⁵ 8.1m 8.2m 6g⁶ 6g 6m² 7m⁵ 5g 7g⁵ 7m⁴ 7m 7m* 7s 7g⁶ a8g⁴ a7s³   **a76**

1997 a7g a6g³ a7g* a7g² a8g⁴ 6s 6m⁴ 5m⁶ 8.1g⁵ 7s³ 7d² 7m 7.1m 7.6g 10.2d⁶ 10.2g⁵ 8m 10m² 12d⁵ a10g* a10g⁴ a10g³ a10g Dec 10] big, plain gelding: fair handicapper on all-weather, modest on turf: won at Lingfield in January and November, and generally ran well otherwise: stays 1¼m: acts on good to firm ground and soft, goes well on all-weather: front runner/races prominently: reliable. *J. J. Bridger*

SEA-DEER   8 ch.g. Hadeer 118 – Hi-Tech Girl 98 (Homeboy 114) [1996 94: a6g⁴   94
a5g³ a5g⁵ a6g⁴ a6g³ a6g² 5m³ 6g² 5m² 6m⁴ 5g* 5g* 6f* 6f* 6m² 5g⁶ 5m³ 5f* 6m 5m³   a85
5.2m² a6g* 5.6m 6m 6v 5g 1997 6m³ 6m² 5.2g⁵ 6m⁵ 6d³ 6d² 6g 6m* 5g 6m 5g 6m a6g² a7g Dec 6] strong, deep-girthed gelding: fairly useful performer: ran consistently well in defeat in competitive handicaps then won 4-runner minor event at Yarmouth in June: not at best afterwards: effective at 5f/6f: acts on fibresand, firm and dead ground: held up: tough. *C. A. Dwyer*

SEA DEVIL   11 gr.g. Absalom 128 – Miss Poinciana 78 (Averof 123) [1996 –,   a63
a66: a7g a6g² a6g* a6g² 7s 6g a6g² a7g 1997 a7s³ a7g³ a7g⁴ a6g³ a7g* a7g⁴ a6g² a7g Mar 17] lengthy, heavy-topped gelding: unimpressive mover: grand old campaigner, successful at least once a year in the 'nineties: won claimer at Southwell in February: stays 7f: acts on fibresand and any turf going: visored (well below form) once: usually held up. *M. J. Camacho*

SEA DREAMS (IRE)   6 b.g. Midyan (USA) 124 – Davill 83 (Record Token 128)   –
[1996 NR 1997 a6g⁵ 8.3s a7g Jun 7] IR 1,700Y, 4,000 2-y-o: second reported foal: dam sprinter: won newcomers race at Milan at 2 yrs: no sign of retaining ability. *D. M. Hyde*

SEA FIG   2 gr.f. (Mar 28) Robellino (USA) 127 – Aimee Jane (USA) 76 (Our   –
Native (USA)) [1997 6g Aug 22] 7,200Y: workmanlike filly: fourth living foal: half-sister to a German middle-distance winner by Niniski: dam 1½m winner: in need of race, not knocked about in mid-division in maiden at Thirsk. *T. D. Barron*

SEA FREEDOM   6 b.h. Slip Anchor 136 – Rostova 91 (Blakeney 126) [1996   73
66§: 18s⁵ 16g 14.9d³ 14m⁶ 16d² 14d² 20f 18m⁵ 14g² 15d³ 16d² 16.4g⁶ 17.2d⁴ 16.2d² 16s⁵ 1997 16g⁵ 13d* 14.1d* 14g² 16g⁴ 14g³ 20m* 12m 14.8m⁵ 20m Jul 30] strong, workmanlike horse: has a quick action: fair handicapper: won at Hamilton (first success) and Nottingham in April and 25-runner Ascot Stakes at Royal Ascot (stayed on from off pace to edge ahead inside last) in June: effective at 13f to 2½m: probably acts on any ground: visored nowadays: consistent. *G. B. Balding*

SEA GOD   6 ch.g. Rainbow Quest (USA) 134 – Sea Pageant (Welsh Pageant 132)   a53
[1996 44, a52: a8g⁴ a7g⁵ a8g² a8g⁴ a11g* a11g⁵ a11g⁵ 9.9d 10.1f⁶ 10.3g³ 10f⁴ 12g 1997 a11g⁵ a11g² a12g a12g² a12g³ a16g⁶ a11g⁵ a12g⁶ a12g a11g Dec 8] tall, angular gelding: modest handicapper: ran poorly after fifth start, pulled up lame final 2: stays 1½m: acts well on fibresand. *M. C. Chapman*

SEA IMP (IRE)   2 b.f. (Mar 21) Mac's Imp (USA) 116 – Sea Glen (IRE) (Glenstal   60
(USA) 118) [1997 5f³ 5.1m³ 5m 5s Jul 3] IR 4,000Y: first foal: dam unraced half-sister to several winners, including useful 2-y-o sprinter (later stayed 1m) Crofter's Cline: modest form in maidens first 2 starts: well beaten in sellers final 2, off over 2 months before last one. *Martyn Meade*

SEALED BY FATE (IRE)   2 b.c. (Mar 31) Mac's Imp (USA) 116 – Fairy Don   54
(Don 128) [1997 5s 6.1g⁶ 5m⁶ 6f 6m⁶ 7g a7g Dec 18] 12,000 2-y-o: big, workmanlike colt: third foal: dam won from 7f to 9f in Ireland: some modest form: well beaten last 4 outings, including when visored: stays 6f. *J. S. Wainwright*

SEA MAGIC (IRE)   2 br.f. (Apr 3) Distinctly North (USA) 115 – Danger Ahead   85
(Mill Reef (USA) 141) [1997 5d* 6d³ 6g⁴ 6m² 7g⁴ 7.3m³ 7g⁴ Oct 25] IR 6,500F, 26,000Y: tall, lengthy filly: has scope: half-sister to winning sprinters Fajjoura (by Fairy King, at 2 yrs in 1994) and 4-y-o Fairy Prince: dam unraced half-sister to a smart 2-y-o 5f winner: fairly useful performer: won maiden at Haydock in May: good efforts in nurseries last 4 starts: stays 7.3f: yet to race on extremes of ground: has run well when edgy and sweating. *B. W. Hills*

SEA MIST (IRE)   3 ch.f. Shalford (IRE) 124§ – Somnifere (USA) 63 (Nijinsky   –
(CAN) 138) [1996 53: 5g 5.1m 7m 7g⁶ 7g a8.5g 1997 8f Jun 10] good-topped filly: modest maiden at 2 yrs for P. Chapple-Hyam: tailed off only outing in 1997. *P. G. Murphy*

Ascot Stakes (Handicap), Royal Ascot—the visored Sea Freedom wins from Shirley Sue (second right)

SEAMUS 3 ch.c. Almoojid 69 – Royal Celerity (USA) (Riverman (USA) 131) –
[1996 –: 5s 1997 6f 6.1g 8d 8.2d 8f⁶ 6m 7g 8m Aug 16] sturdy colt: no form. *C. J. Hill*

SEANCHAI (IRE) 4 b.g. Treasure Kay 114 – Blue Infanta (Chief Singer 131) –
[1996 –: a6g a6s 1997 a7s a7g a6g 5v 6g Aug 2] tall gelding: no sign of ability.
P. S. Felgate

SEA PENNANT 3 br.f. Adbass (USA) 102 – Doubtfire 71 (Jalmood (USA) 126) 36
[1996 NR 1997 a6g a8g² a8g⁶ Dec 18] first reported foal: dam, 2-y-o 6f seller winner,
probably stayed 1¼m: poor form when second in seller at Lingfield: flattered later in
December. *Mrs H. L. Walton*

SEA SPOUSE 6 ch.g. Jalmood (USA) 126 – Bambolona 108 (Bustino 136) [1996 41
46, a67: a11g⁵ a8g³ a8g* a8g³ a8.5g³ 6.9s* 7m a7g a7g³ a7g* 7.1d 8.3d a7g² a7g⁵ a67
a7s⁴ 1997 a8g² a8g* a8g⁴ a8g³ a7g⁶ a8g a7g 8g 8.3g 6.9s² 7g a8g⁶ a9.4g⁴ a8g⁴ a9.4g⁴
Dec 6] workmanlike gelding: fair handicapper on fibresand, poor on turf: successful
twice at Southwell (awarded race on first occasion) in January: back to form later in
year: effective at 7f/1m: acts on fibresand, best recent turf efforts on soft going: goes
well with forcing tactics. *M. Blanshard*

SEATTLE ALLEY (USA) 4 b.g. Seattle Dancer (USA) 119 – Alyanaabi (USA) 69
74 (Roberto (USA) 131) [1996 68: 7s 8d 8g 10.3m⁴ 10m¹* 10m* 1997 a12g³ a10g⁵ a63
10g⁶ 10m⁴ 10m⁵ Oct 1] good-topped gelding: easy mover: fair handicapper: effective
at 1¼m, probably 1½m: acts on good to firm ground and equitrack. *P. R. Webber*

SEATTLE ART (USA) 3 b.c. Seattle Slew (USA) – Artiste 95 (Artaius (USA) 82
129) [1996 –p: 8g 1997 12d² 14.1m² 14m³ 14m Aug 14] big, close-coupled colt:
fairly useful form when neck second in maiden at Newmarket in June: disappointing afterwards: best form at 1½m on dead ground: sold 36,000 gns in October.
H. R. A. Cecil

SEATTLE SWING 3 b.f. Saddlers' Hall (IRE) 126 – Sweet Slew (USA) 96 83
(Seattle Slew (USA)) [1996 68p: 8.2m⁵ 1997 11.1m⁵ 8.5m³ 10s* 10.2s⁴ 10m 10m*
9g 10.2g 12m² Sep 24] angular filly: fairly useful handicapper: won at Windsor in
June (left J. Gosden after next start) and August (apprentices): effective at 1¼m to
easy 1½m: acts on soft and good to firm ground: sold 15,000 gns in December, to
M. Nygard in Norway. *A. J. Perrett*

SEA VICTOR 5 b.g. Slip Anchor 136 – Victoriana (USA) (Storm Bird (CAN) 77
134) [1996 84: 11.8g 18.7g 16g³ 16g a16g* 14.4g* 20f⁴ 16.1m 15.9m⁴ 20m² 18.7m*
16.2f⁶ 16.1m 16.2m 14.1m⁴ 18g⁵ 16g² 16.5s a12g² 1997 a11g⁴ 15.9d⁶ 14.6m⁵ 18.2f⁵
14.4m² 16.2g⁶ 16.2v 18g 16s Nov 6] sturdy, good-topped gelding: fair handicapper:
effective at 1½m to 2½m: acts on the all-weather, seems to need good going or firmer
on turf: effective visored or not. *J. L. Harris*

SEA WAVE (IRE) 2 b.c. (Feb 12) Sadler's Wells (USA) 132 – Three Tails 121 73 p
(Blakeney 126) [1997 8.2d⁴ Oct 30] strong, angular colt: sixth foal: brother to 4-y-o
Triple Leap and 5-y-o Tamure and half-brother to 3-y-o Three Cheers: dam, 1½m
winner, half-sister to Maysoon (placed in 1000 Guineas and Oaks) out of smart Triple
First: 5/2, around 1½ lengths staying-on fourth to Eliza Acton in maiden at

SEA

Nottingham: will be well suited by 1¼m+: should do a fair bit better. *Saeed bin Suroor*

SEA YA MAITE 3 b.g. Komaite (USA) – Marina Plata (Julio Mariner 127) [1996 53
–: 7g 1997 a8g 6.1d a5g⁴ a5g³ 6d a6g* a6g³ a5g a8.5g³ 8g² a8.5g* 7g 8.2d Oct 30] a74
fair handicapper on the all-weather, modest on turf: won at Southwell in July and
Wolverhampton in October: stays 8.5f: acts on fibresand (yet to race on equitrack),
below form all starts on good to soft ground. *S. R. Bowring*

SEBASTIAN DUKE (FR) 5 br.g. Iron Duke (FR) 122 – Abimaba (Vayrann –
133) [1996 11g 1997 a7g a12g Feb 5] no worthwhile form. *J. Cullinan*

SECOND CHORUS (IRE) 2 b.f. (Feb 26) Scenic 128 – Never So Fair 65 –
(Never So Bold 135) [1997 6m Aug 15] angular filly: fourth foal: half-sister to 3-y-o
Crystal Crossing and 1¼m winner Lady Bankes (by Alzao): dam thrice-raced from
family of Amaranda and Favoridge: 7/1 from 4/1, well-held tenth in maiden at Newbury, never travelling fluently: moved poorly to post. *P. W. Chapple-Hyam*

SECOND COLOURS (USA) 7 b. or br.g. Timeless Moment (USA) – Ruffled –
Silk (USA) (Our Hero (USA)) [1996 69, a81: a9.4g a8g* a8g* a8g³ 10.3m² 8.5m³ a85
8m 8f 10.3d⁴ 1997 a9.4g* a8g a9.4g² a12g³ a9.4g⁵ a12g⁶ Mar 5] strong, compact
gelding: carries condition: unimpressive mover: fairly useful handicapper on all-
weather: won at Wolverhampton in January: stays 1½m: visored (ran well) once:
successful when sweating: held up, and best in strongly-run race. *M. C. Pipe*

SECOND EMPIRE (IRE) 2 b.c. (Apr 29) Fairy King (USA) – Welsh Love 122 p
(Ela-Mana-Mou 132) [1997 8m* 8m* 8s* Oct 12]
    Michael Tabor was behind the three most expensive yearling purchases
at public auction in the British Isles in 1996: a Woodman colt (now named
Twickenham) who cost IR 1,125,000 guineas, a son of Kingmambo (called
Singer Sargent) who went for 880,000 guineas and Second Empire who made
IR 640,000 guineas. Twickenham's predecessors as the highest or joint-highest
priced yearlings of their respective crops, Entrepreneur in 1995 and Bosra
Sham in 1994, went on to win a classic. He'll do well to emulate them as, like
Singer Sargent, he was unraced at two (comments on both appear on
p. 1071)—but the unbeaten Second Empire has made an excellent start as a
classic prospect.
    The Prix des Chenes, a Group 3 event run over a mile at Longchamp
four weeks before the Grand Criterium over the same course and distance, isn't
normally a race that makes many headlines. But the latest running was one of
the most competitive two-year-old races run in France all year and produced a
winning performance worthy of the Grand Criterium itself. All ten runners
were winners and the field had an international look to it, with seven home-
trained runners (including Swain's half-brother Thief of Hearts from the Fabre
stable) opposed by Tenbyssimo, the winner of his last three starts in Italy,
Muhtathir, who'd won his last two outings at Sandown, and Second Empire
from Ireland. A supplementary entry, Second Empire started the 6/4 favourite
having won his only start, a maiden at Leopardstown five weeks earlier, in
impressive style, needing only to be shaken up to land the odds by five lengths.
A rangy, good-topped colt, Second Empire looked a cut above his rivals in the
paddock at Longchamp and more than confirmed that impression in the race
itself. The headstrong outsider Zarco set a fast pace but his efforts took their toll
soon after the home turn, where Muhtathir, who'd raced in a clear second for
much of the way, went on. But Second Empire was soon sent in pursuit, took
Muhtathir's measure about a furlong out and ran on strongly to beat him by two
and a half lengths. There was a further gap of five lengths to Tenbyssimo in
third and another three to Thief of Hearts. Second Empire immediately earned
short quotes for the Guineas and the Derby, but a week later Xaar put up at least
as good a performance in the Prix de la Salamandre. With Xaar headed for the
Dewhurst, Second Empire had little left to fear in the Grand Criterium,
normally France's most prestigious event for two-year-olds, though circumstances made the latest running something of a damp squib.

842

*Grand Criterium, Longchamp—it's late in the day by the time the race finally gets under way;
a forlorn spectator braves the rain to watch Second Empire win from Charge d'Affaires*

For a start, the Grand Criterium, worth about five times as much as the Prix des Chenes, was actually a less competitive affair. Second Empire's chief rival was Charge d'Affaires who had beaten Xaar in the Morny but been put firmly in his place by the same colt in the Salamandre. The Middle Park runner-up Carrowkeel was joined from Britain by the Goodwood listed race winner Alboostan, with French outsider Worms completing the field. Judging from the photograph, the field of five was in danger of outnumbering the spectators present. That was because the Grand Criterium was run in rain and fading light at just before six in the evening and had been one of only two races (it had to take second place to the day's tierce handicap) salvaged from a card hit by a stable lads' blockade of the premises of the firm used to transport horses from the training centre at Chantilly to Longchamp. Most of the intended runners declared for the meeting (though none from the Grand Criterium itself) couldn't reach the track. By the time the big race was run the ground was even softer than the official penetrometer reading (of 4.1) taken earlier in the day. Fears about Second Empire's handling the conditions (his first two starts had been on good to firm going) proved largely unfounded and he went on over a furlong out to beat Charge d'Affaires by a length and a half, with Alboostan a further three lengths away third. Second Empire's jockey, however, reported he was hating the ground.

Second Empire is Fairy King's second consecutive Grand Criterium winner after Revoque. He's from a much better family than the 1996 winner, though, and one which virtually guarantees he'll stay beyond a mile. His dam, Welsh Love, gained her only win in a four-runner minor event at Dundalk over a mile and a half but showed fairly useful form when second in a listed race over a mile and a quarter at Phoenix Park. Her half-sister, Flame of Tara, was a very smart filly at up to a mile and a half but she's better known nowadays as a top-class broodmare thanks to Salsabil and Marju, who are among several good performers she's produced. Another of Welsh Love's half-sisters, Fruition, is the dam of Breeders' Cup Turf winner Northern Spur and the high-class but short-lived stayer Kneller. Welsh Love herself already had a good winner to her

Mr M. Tabor's "Second Empire"

name before Second Empire (her fifth foal) came along, in the smart seven-furlong to mile-and-a-quarter winner Ihtiram (by Royal Academy), as well as the useful Irish mile-and-a-quarter winner Catalyst (by Sadler's Wells) and Ihtiram's brother Shi-Ar, who won over nine furlongs at Fairyhouse in the latest season. All three stayed, or probably stayed, a mile and a half. Further back, grandam Welsh Flame was a useful miler and third dam Electric Flash was a half-sister to Derby winner Parthia.

		Northern Dancer	Nearctic
	Fairy King (USA)	(b 1961)	Natalma
	(b 1982)	Fairy Bridge	Bold Reason
Second Empire (IRE)		(b 1975)	Special
(b.c. Apr 29, 1995)		Ela-Mana-Mou	Pitcairn
	Welsh Love	(b 1976)	Rose Bertin
	(b 1986)	Welsh Flame	Welsh Pageant
		(b 1973)	Electric Flash

Not surprisingly, members of this family invariably attract a great deal of interest when sent to the sales. Second Empire's yearling half-sister by Barathea went for IR 950,000 guineas at Goffs a few days before he won the Grand Criterium. The struggle to secure the filly, in which Second Empire's owner had to give best to Godolphin, made her the most expensive yearling filly worldwide in 1997. Twickenham, mentioned in the opening lines, is from the same family (he's a son of one of Flame of Tara's daughters, Danse Royale), as is Happy Valentine, the joint-highest priced yearling in the British Isles with Entrepreneur in 1995. Quite apart from his breeding Second Empire has plenty going for him as a three-year-old. His form is second only to Xaar's, he's with a top-class stable and he looks the part physically with lots of scope to progress. He seems sure to win more good races. *A. P. O'Brien, Ireland*

SECONDS AWAY 6 b.g. Hard Fought 125 – Keep Mum 63 (Mummy's Pet 125) [1996 31: a7g 5d² 5m 7.1g⁵ 5g 6g 6m⁶ 7.1g³ 8.1m² 6m⁴ 8.3m 8.3m³ 9.2f⁴ 12.1m 8m 8m⁶ 1997 a8.5g⁵ 8m³ 7.1m 7.1d⁵ 6m⁴ 8g⁵ 8m* 5m³ 6g 8m³ 9.2m² 8.3g² 5s 8g Oct 22] small gelding: poor handicapper: won at Musselburgh in July: finds 5f on sharp side, and stays 9f: acts on good to firm and dead ground: effective blinkered/visored or not. *J. S. Goldie* 43 a–

SECOND SUN 2 ch.g. (May 3) Clantime 101 – Sun Follower (Relkino 131) [1997 5.7m 5m 5m⁴ 5.1d⁶ 6d Sep 12] third foal: brother to 4-y-o Dancing Jack (5f winner at 2 yrs): dam showed little over hurdles: little form, including in blinkers. *J. J. Bridger* –

SECOND TERM (IRE) 2 b.f. (Apr 20) Second Set (IRE) 127 – Trinida (Jaazeiro (USA) 127) [1997 7g 7m⁴ 7m Nov 4] 2,500Y: half-sister to several winners abroad, including a Grade 1 winner in Brazil by Gorytus: dam Irish middle-distance winner: soundly beaten all starts. *W. Storey* –

SECOND WIND 2 ch.c. (Mar 15) Kris 135 – Rimosa's Pet 109 (Petingo 135) [1997 5m* Apr 17] 26,000Y: workmanlike colt: has a round action: closely related to smart sprinter Kerrera (by Diesis) and 9-y-o Rimouski (winner at 1½m) and half-brother to several winners, including very smart sprinter/miler Rock City (by Ballad Rock): dam 6f to 10.5f (Musidora) winner: won minor event at Newmarket by short head from Arpeggio in April on only start. *P. F. I. Cole* 82

SECRECY 2 b.c. (Mar 6) Polish Precedent (USA) 131 – Blonde Prospect (USA) (Mr Prospector (USA)) [1997 8s 8d a8.5g Nov 29] 170,000Y: well-made colt: fourth foal: closely related to a winner in France and Spain by Polish Navy and half-brother to fairly useful 1m winner White Palace (by Shirley Heights): dam, lightly raced in USA, from family of Ajdal, Formidable and Arazi: modest form at best in maidens. *P. F. I. Cole* 58

SECRET ALY (CAN) 7 b.g. Secreto (USA) 128 – Bouffant (USA) (Alydar (USA)) [1996 87: a10g a8g 10g 12m⁵ 10.3g⁴ 8.9m 10m² 10.4m 10m 10.1m* 10.5d⁶ 10s 1997 a10g² a9.4g⁶ a10g* 10m² 8g 10s 10.4m⁵ 10m⁶ 10.1m⁵ 10m 10.1f⁴ 9m Oct 4] good-bodied gelding: usually impresses in appearance: fairly useful handicapper: won at Lingfield in March: best around 1¼m: acts on the all-weather and goes well on good to firm/firm going on turf: none too consistent. *C. E. Brittain* 87

SECRET ARCHIVE 2 b.c. (Feb 12) Salse (USA) 128 – Lycia (USA) (Lyphard (USA) 132) [1997 7m³ 7g* Aug 20] 72,000Y: has scope: third foal: dam French 1¼m winner: odds on, won maiden at Kempton in August, driven right out to beat Taverner Society ½ length: will be suited by further than 7f. *R. Hannon* 88

SECRET BALLOT (IRE) 3 b.c. Taufan (USA) 119 – Ballet Society (FR) (Sadler's Wells (USA) 132) [1996 55: 6m 6g 8.2g 1997 8d⁶ 7d² 10s* 9.7m⁴ 10m³ 10m 10g⁶ 10s* 11.8d* 10.3g² 11.8g³ 12s Nov 8] tall colt: has a round action: fairly useful performer: won minor event at Nottingham in July and handicaps in large fields at Nottingham and Leicester in October: stiff tasks last 2 starts: stays 1½m: acts on good to firm and soft ground. *K. Mahdi* 83

SECRET BOURNE (USA) 2 b.f. (May 8) Exbourne (USA) 125 – Secret Angel (Halo (USA)) [1997 7d Oct 27] second foal: half-sister to a 2-y-o 5f winner in USA by Known Fact: dam US 1m winner out of high-class American mare Ack's Secret: pulled hard when well beaten in maiden at Lingfield. *B. W. Hills* –

SECRET COMBE (IRE) 3 b.f. Mujadil (USA) 119 – Crimbourne 83 (Mummy's Pet 125) [1996 74: 5.7m² 6m* 5.2f⁶ 6d⁴ 6m 6.1s⁵ a6g⁵ 1997 7m⁵ 7d 7g² 6m 7g⁴ Aug 11] small filly: fairly useful handicapper: stays 7f: acts on firm ground, soft and fibresand: inconsistent: sold only 2,500 gns in October. *P. J. Makin* 81

SECRET MISS 5 ch.m. Beveled (USA) – Zamindara (Crofter (USA) 124) [1996 55, a–: a6g 5s 5g⁴ 5m⁵ 5.1g 5m⁴ 5f⁶ 5.1f 1997 5m 5.1g⁵ a5g 5m 5d Jun 28] sparely-made mare: poor sprint handicapper: acts on good to firm and dead ground, well beaten on fibresand: tried blinkered/visored: sometimes hangs: inconsistent. *A. P. Jones* 41 a–

SECRET SERVICE (IRE) 5 b.g. Classic Secret (USA) 91 – Mystery Bid (Auction Ring (USA) 123) [1996 78: a12g⁵ 12.4d³ 14d³ 13.3s 14.4g³ 16.1m³ 15m 13.9g⁵ 11.9d 18g 1997 a16.2g³ 14d⁴ 15d⁴ 13.1g⁴ 11.9m³ Aug 15] compact gelding: fair handicapper: stays 2m: acts on good to firm ground, dead (possibly not soft) and 73 fibresand: blinkered last 2 starts (well below best): won over hurdles later in August: sold (joined C. Barwell) 11,500 gns in November. *C. W. Thornton*

SECRET SPRING (FR) 5 b.g. Dowsing (USA) 124 – Nordica 99 (Northfields 91 (USA)) [1996 93: a10g² a8g* a8g* a8g⁵ 7.3m⁶ 9m 9s 1997 8m³ 9m⁶ 8m* a8g⁵ Dec 4] leggy gelding: fairly useful performer: good sixth (set plenty to do) in Cambridgeshire: won minor event at Brighton later in October, getting up near finish in steadily-run race: lost chance with very slow start final outing: effective at 1m to 1¼m: acts on good to firm ground and equitrack: held up. *P. R. Hedger*

SECRET STRENGTH 3 ch.g. Formidable (USA) 125 – Lovers Tryst 91 (Castle 45 Keep 121) [1996 NR 1997 7g 8g 6s 6g 8m⁵ 7.1g⁶ Sep 15] second reported foal: dam 1¼m winner: poor maiden: stays 1m: sold, and sent to Italy. *Lady Herries*

SECRET TANGO 2 ch.f. (Mar 11) Interrex (CAN) – Seymour Ann (Krayyan – 117) [1997 5d 6m 6m⁶ 6g⁵ Aug 27] fifth foal: sister to a winner in Jersey, closely related to 5-y-o Captain's Day and half-sister to 3-y-o Silver Lining: dam unraced: soundly beaten in maidens and a seller. *A. P. Jones*

SEDBERGH (USA) 4 b.g. Northern Flagship (USA) 96 – Crumbaugh Pike 72 (USA) (Within Hail (USA)) [1996 71p: 10.3d 11.1g³ a12g² 12.1s⁴ 11.8d 13.8g* 16f* a77 14.1m⁵ 1997 a14g* a12g² a14.8g 16g⁵ 14.1m⁴ a16g* a14g² 16d⁶ Jun 23] goodtopped gelding: fair performer: won apprentice handicap in April and claimer in June, both at Southwell: helped force too strong a pace final outing (claimed to join Mrs V. Ward): resolute galloper, will stay beyond 2m: acts on fibresand and probably any turf going. *Mrs M. Reveley*

SEEBE (USA) 3 b.f. Danzig (USA) – Annie Edge 118 (Nebbiolo 125) [1996 103: 112 5f* 6m* 6m³ 6m³ 1997 7.3g² 8d² 8d⁶ May 24] rangy filly: good walker: has a fluent, round action: smart performer: runner-up in Fred Darling Stakes at Newbury (beaten ¾ length by Dance Parade) in April and strongly-run Poule d'Essai des Pouliches at Longchamp (stayed on well when head second to Always Loyal) in May: reportedly injured knee in Irish 1000 Guineas at the Curragh: stays 1m well: acts on firm and dead ground: genuine: joined J. Sheppard in USA. *I. A. Balding*

SEE YOU SOON 3 b.g. Distant Relative 128 – Our Resolution (Caerleon (USA) – 132) [1996 –: 6m 1997 a7g 9.2d 8d May 19] unfurnished gelding: no form: sold, and sent to Germany. *C. W. Thornton*

SEFTON BLAKE 3 b.g. Roscoe Blake 120 – Rainbow Lady 65 (Jaazeiro (USA) 55 127) [1996 NR 1997 12.3g 10g 10m 10.5d 13.8s 11m⁵ a14.8g⁵ a12g Dec 6] lengthy, a– workmanlike gelding: fourth reported living foal: half-brother to a winning hurdler by Handsome Sailor: dam, stayer, winning hurdler: modest form: should stay beyond 11f: acts on good to firm ground, well beaten on fibresand. *M. G. Meagher*

SEJAAL (IRE) 5 b.g. Persian Heights 129 – Cremets 94 (Mummy's Pet 125) 50 [1996 –: 8.1g 8.3d 7m 8.5m 1997 8m 8f 8g 8g² a7g a10g Dec 19] rangy gelding: modest at best nowadays: second in claimer at Brighton in September, final outing for R. Akehurst and only form of 1997: stays 1m: acts on hard ground, poor efforts on good to soft: takes strong hold. *R. M. Flower*

SEKARI 3 b.c. Polish Precedent (USA) 131 – Secret Seeker (USA) (Mr Prospector 103 + (USA)) [1996 88p: 7m* 1997 8.2m* Apr 11] good-topped colt: won only start as 103 + 2-y-o and only one of 1997, coming from poorish position when pace quickened to beat Crystal Hearted ½ length in minor event at Nottingham in latter: will stay beyond 1m: raced only on good to firm ground: fractured a fetlock joint before start of Premio Parioli later in April. *D. R. Loder*

SELBERRY 3 b.g. Selkirk (USA) 129 – Choke Cherry (Connaught 130) [1996 82 76p: 6g⁴ a8.5g² 1997 a7g² a8.5g* 10.3m⁴ 10g a8.5g Nov 15] good-topped gelding: fairly useful handicapper: won at Wolverhampton in January: off course 7 months, well beaten last 2 starts: stays 1¼m: raced only on good/good to firm ground and fibresand. *P. C. Haslam*

SELECT CHOICE (IRE) 3 b.g. Waajib 121 – Stella Ann (Ahonoora 122) 79 d [1996 77: 6g⁵ 6m 6m 6m³ 6m³ 6.9d² 1997 8.2m 7g² 6d 6g⁵ 7g⁵ Jul 16] tall gelding: has a quick action: fair maiden: form at 3 yrs only when second at Catterick in April: seems suited by 7f: yet to race on extremes of going: swerved leaving stalls penultimate outing: inconsistent, and best treated with caution. *A. P. Jarvis*

Wokingham Stakes (Handicap), Royal Ascot—
Selhurstpark Flyer holds the late challenge of the unlucky Danetime (rail);
Bollin Joanne is third and Oggi fourth

SELECT STAR (IRE) 3 b.g. Arcane (USA) – Chevrefeuille 87 (Ile de Bourbon 62 d
(USA) 133) [1996 65§: 7m² 7g 8.1g³ 7.9g 8m² 8m³ 8f 1997 11.6s 10.1f 10s³
12.1m 16m a14.8g⁵ 10.8d⁴ 10m Oct 23] good-bodied gelding: modest performer at
best: stays 1¼m: acts on soft going and good to firm: visored last 2 starts: unreliable,
and has shown unsatisfactory temperament. *A. P. Jarvis*

SELFISH 3 ch.f. Bluebird (USA) 125 – Sariza 79 (Posse (USA) 130) [1996 NR 77
1997 7g³ 8g² 8d² 8d 7.6m³ Jul 10] workmanlike filly: easy mover: half-sister to fairly
useful 8.5f winner Aratos (by Night Shift): dam, best form at 7f, out of 1000 Guineas second Tolmi, an excellent family: fair maiden: barely stays 1m: unraced on
extremes of going. *H. R. A. Cecil*

SELHURSTPARK FLYER (IRE) 6 b.g. Northiam (USA) – Wisdom To Know 105
(Bay Express 132) [1996 93: 7m⁴ 5.9m* 6m³ 6m* 6f 6.1m² 6m 5.2m⁵ 6m* 6m 6d
1997 6m² 5.1v² 6g³ 6g* 6.1s⁵ 6m 6g Sep 20] leggy, workmanlike gelding: useful
handicapper: placed in competitive events prior to winning Wokingham at Royal
Ascot by a head from Danetime, forcing pace and rallying splendidly: poor efforts
afterwards: effective at 5f (given test) to 7f: acts on any ground: below form in
blinkers/visor in 1994: usually races prominently (goes well for claimer P. Roberts):
usually bandaged in front: game. *J. Berry*

SELKIRK ROSE (IRE) 2 b.f. (Feb 15) Pips Pride 117 – Red Note (Rusticaro 74
(FR) 124) [1997 5s⁴ 6m² 5m* 5m 6g 6s⁴ Oct 14] 11,000Y: fifth foal: half-sister to 2
winners, one a 2-y-o 5f winner by Fayruz, the other in Hungary: dam unraced: fair
performer: won maiden at Carlisle in August: stiff tasks afterwards: stays 6f: acts on
good to firm and soft ground: tail flasher. *Miss L. A. Perratt*

SELLETTE (IRE) 3 ch.f. Selkirk (USA) 129 – Near The End (Shirley Heights 88
130) [1996 74: 7.1f 8.2m³ 8d³ 1997 8.2d² 8d² 10.5m³ 8.3s* 10m⁶ 10.3d⁶ 10.5d² 10g
Sep 18] rangy filly: fairly useful performer: won maiden at Windsor in June: best
effort in handicaps after when second of 18 at Haydock: stays 1¼m: acts on good to
firm and soft ground. *D. Haydn Jones*

SELMESTON (IRE) 5 b.g. Double Schwartz 128 – Baracuda (FR) (Zeddaan 55
130) [1996 45: a8g⁵ a12g a12g³ a12g⁵ a16g* 16.1s 16.2m a16g a16g 1997 17.2g* a–
16g⁶ 16.2d* 17.5d* 16s⁵ 16s a16g Nov 25] leggy gelding: modest handicapper:

returned from 13-month absence to win at Bath in June, Beverley in August and Ayr (given another enterprising ride): acts on fibresand and dead ground, probably on soft: usually front runner. *S. C. Williams*

SEMI CIRCLE   2 b.f. (Mar 9) Noble Patriarch 115 – True Ring (High Top 131)   49
[1997 7g^6 5.9g 7g* 7m 7m Sep 20] 3,000Y: fourth reported foal: half-sister to 3-y-o Future Perfect: dam, well beaten both starts at 2 yrs, out of 6f-winning half-sister to Circus Ring: form only when winning seller at 50/1 at Catterick in July: will stay 1m: blinkered when successful and on final start. *T. D. Easterby*

SENATE SWINGS   3 gr.c. Timeless Times (USA) 99 – Heaven-Liegh-Grey 90   –
(Grey Desire 115) [1996 48, a56: 5g^6 5m^3 6g^3 a5g^5 6d^3 a6g^4 6s a8g^2 a7g^3 a7g^5 1997   a51
a8.5g^3 a8g^4 a8g Jan 27] lengthy, good-quartered colt: modest maiden: best form at 6f/7f: acts on fibresand: blinkered final start: sold, and sent to Denmark. *W. R. Muir*

SENOR HURST   2 b.c. (May 21) Young Senor (USA) 113 – Broadhurst 68   –
(Workboy 123) [1997 7m Jul 22] fifth foal: dam 7f and 1m winner: tailed off in seller at Yarmouth. *Mrs P. Sly*

SENORITA MATILDA (USA)   3 b.f. El Gran Senor (USA) 136 – Copperama   76
(AUS) (Comeram (FR) 127) [1996 73p: 6m^6 6g^5 1997 7d 6d 6m^2 6f* 6m Sep 22] small, sturdy filly: fair performer: won maiden handicap at Brighton in July: not clear run next start: should stay 7f: acts on firm going, possibly unsuited by good to soft: sold 30,000 gns in December. *R. Hannon*

SENSATION   4 b.f. Soviet Star (USA) 128 – Outstandingly (USA) (Exclusive   –
Native (USA)) [1996 114: 8g* 8d* 8m* 8g* 8d 9f 1997 8s 9.3f Oct 5] close-coupled filly: smart form for Mme C. Head as 3-y-o: well below form in Group 2 events at Milan (for Saeed bin Suroor) then Longchamp in 1997: should stay beyond 1m: has won on dead going, best efforts on good/good to firm going: effective as front runner or tracking pace. *J. H. M. Gosden*

SENSE OF PRIORITY   8 ch.g. Primo Dominie 121 – Sense of Pride (Welsh   58
Pageant 132) [1996 66, a70: a6g* a7g^3 a7g a6g^2 a7g^4 a6g* a6g* a6g^6 6m 5g^5 6m   a77
5.9f* 6d^2 5g 6m^5 6f^6 6f^6 a6g^3 1997 a7g a7g* a6g* a6g* a6g^3 a6g* a7g* 6m 7g^6 a7g^4 5.9f^2 5g 6g^6 6g^6 5g Aug 17] leggy, workmanlike gelding: fair performer: has won 14 times in sellers and claimers since 2 yrs, mainly on the all-weather: successful at Southwell (4) and Wolverhampton in January/February: never placed to challenge last 4 starts: best at 6f/7f: goes well on the all-weather, and acts on hard and dead ground on turf: visored twice at 4 yrs: usually held up. *D. Nicholls*

SENSE OF WONDER   2 br.f. (Mar 30) Inchinor 119 – Downshire (IRE) (Dar-   80
shaan 133) [1997 6m 6m* 7g 6.1d^6 Nov 3] 13,500Y: tall, sparely-made filly: second living foal: half-sister to 4-y-o 7f (Dubai) winner Music Theatre (by Dancing Spree): dam ran once: fairly useful form when winning maiden at Redcar in October: bit disappointing in nurseries, flashing tail and wandering on first occasion: should stay 7f/1m: carries head awkwardly. *B. J. Meehan*

SENSORY   2 b.c. (Apr 21) Selkirk (USA) 129 – Illusory 81 (Kings Lake (USA)   103
133) [1997 7g^5 7m* 7.3g^2 Oct 24] strong, rangy, good sort: has short, round action: fourth foal: half-brother to 3-y-o Tarski, 1994 2-y-o 5.7f winner Painted Desert (by Green Desert) and useful 1m and 9f winner Phantom Quest (by Rainbow Quest): dam 6f winner, daughter of Irish 1000 Guineas second Bold Fantasy: won maiden at Leicester in September: much better form when 1¾ lengths second to stable-companion La-Faah in Horris Hill Stakes at Newbury, leading 2f out but soon cut down: should stay at least 1m: has scope and may do better still in 1998. *D. R. Loder*

SENTINELLA KEY (IRE)   2 b.f. (May 16) Statoblest 120 – Key Tothe Mins-   –
trel (USA) 108 (The Minstrel (CAN) 135) [1997 5m Jun 2] IR 20,000Y: sturdy filly: half-sister to several winners, including 3-y-o Bandore and Irish 8.5f winner Best Academy (by Roberto): dam 2-y-o 6f winner and fourth in Fillies' Mile, is out of unraced half-sister to top-class animals Fort Marcy and Key To The Mint: 20/1, eighth in maiden at Leicester: sent to Denmark. *M. J. Heaton-Ellis*

SEQUOIA PRINCE (CAN)   3 ch.g. Woodman (USA) 126 – Loren's Baby   –
(USA) (Czaravich (USA)) [1996 NR 1997 8g 8g 6m 11.6s 8m Aug 7] $75,000Y: workmanlike gelding: seventh foal: half-brother to 3 winners in North America,

including Vid Kid (by Pleasant Colony) one of leading 2-y-o's in Canada in 1991: dam ran once in USA: no sign of ability. *M. Bell*

SERAPE   4 b.f. Primo Dominie 121 – Absaloute Service 96 (Absalom 128) [1996   47
59: 7g 7m 6g⁶ 6f 1997 a6g a10g⁴ 7.5m 7g² 8m 7g 7m 7m² 7.1d⁵ 6.9m Jul 14] plain
filly: poor maiden: best form at 7f: acts on good to firm going. *Mrs L. Stubbs*

SERENADE (IRE)   3 gr.g. Classic Music (USA) – Friendly Thoughts (USA) (Al   49
Hattab (USA)) [1996 61?, a49: 7.1m 7g⁶ 8s a8g⁴ a10g 1997 a8g² a8g⁵ a10g⁴ Jan 18]
close-coupled gelding: poor maiden: should stay 1¼m. *M. J. Haynes*

SERENDIPITY (FR)   4 b.g. Mtoto 134 – Bint Damascus (USA) (Damascus   68 +
(USA)) [1996 86: 8g 9.9m* 10m⁴ 12m 10m 8m³ 8d 10.3m⁵ 8g 8m³ 1997 10m 10g
10m 8.1d 8m 7.1m 8g³ 8d 10m³ 10d⁴ Oct 20] good-quartered gelding: fair
handicapper: takes strong hold but stays 1¼m: best form on good going or firmer:
blinkered once (well beaten): sometimes starts slowly, and often given plenty to do:
sold (joined M. Pipe) 22,000 gns in October. *B. R. Millman*

SERENGETTI   2 ch.f. (May 8) Lion Cavern (USA) 117 – Melanoura (Imperial   54
Fling (USA) 116) [1997 6.1m Sep 15] 6,200F: seventh foal: closely related to fairly
useful 1995 2-y-o 6f winner Meldorf (by Lycius) and half-brother to several winners,
including 3-y-o Space Race: dam ran twice: 20/1, just under 8 lengths eighth in
maiden at Nottingham, slowly away. *J. Berry*

SERENITY   3 b.f. Selkirk (USA) 129 – Mystery Ship 105 (Decoy Boy 129) [1996   98
98: 6m⁵ 6m* 6m* 7g³ 1997 7g⁶ 7g² 7m⁶ 8.5f⁴ Dec 11] leggy, shallow-girthed filly:
useful performer: best efforts at 3 yrs on last 2 starts (left J. Fanshawe after first of
them): probably stays 8.5f: raced only on good going or firmer. *Kathy Walsh, USA*

SERETSE'S NEPHEW   3 b.g. Chilibang 120 – Bunnyloch 49§ (Lochnager   47
132) [1996 43, a55: 7m⁵ 5.3g⁶ 7m a6g* a5g³ a6g 1997 a5g³ a6g a6g a5g⁴ a6g⁵ 6d⁶
6g² 6m² 5g 7.1g⁵ 6f Sep 18] poor handicapper: seems suited by 6f: acts on good to
firm ground and the all-weather: blinkered (went too fast) once at 3 yrs: usually front
runner. *M. J. Polglase*

SERGEANT IMP (IRE)   2 b.g. (Apr 27) Mac's Imp (USA) 116 – Genzyme   57
Gene 38 (Riboboy (USA) 124) [1997 5g⁶ 5g 5g 6g 6.9g 7d 5m⁴ 6f 7m Oct 23] 7,800
2-y-o: small, well-made gelding: half-brother to several winners, including 1995
2-y-o Veshca Lady (5f and 7f, by Contract Law), later stayed 1½m: dam, plater,
stayed 1¼m: modest maiden: best efforts at 5f: acts on good to firm ground: ran well
in blinkers seventh start. *P. Mitchell*

SERGEYEV (IRE)   5 ch.h. Mulhollande (USA) 107 – Escape Path (Wolver   –
Hollow 126) [1996 102: 6m 6m³ 7m⁵ 8g 6m² 7m⁶ 7g⁶ 1997 7d Apr 26] useful-
looking horse: has had a wind operation: smart performer at 3 yrs, winner of Jersey
Stakes: useful form at best since, carrying head high when disappointing only start in
1997: pulls hard, but stays 7f: joined O. Sherwood. *R. Hannon*

SERIOUS ACCOUNT (USA)   4 b.c. Danzig (USA) – Topicount (USA) (Priv-   –
ate Account (USA)) [1996 –: 8m 1997 8g³ 13.8g 7.1g Sep 15] second foal: half-
brother to Laguna Seca (by Seattle Slew), 6.5f listed winner in USA: dam minor
stakes winner up to 9f: no worthwhile form, including when well-backed favourite
final start. *J. L. Eyre*

SERIOUS HURRY   9 ch.g. Forzando 122 – Lady Bequick 81 (Sharpen Up 127)   –
[1996 51d: a5g 5g 5g 5g⁵ 5g² 5f⁴ 5f 5g⁴ 5m⁶ 5d 5m 5.1m 1997 5g 5g Jul 23]
heavy-topped gelding: has a quick action: formerly fairly useful at 5f: has lost his
form. *R. M. McKellar*

SERIOUS TRUST   4 b.c. Alzao (USA) 117 – Mill Line 71 (Mill Reef (USA)   64
141) [1996 60: 12m* 11.1f⁴ 14.1m³ 16f³ a16g 1997 12m² 14m 12.5m 12s 14m 14g⁵
12m 14m* 16.4s Aug 29] good-topped colt: modest handicapper: second start within
3 days, made all at Salisbury in August: stays 2m: acts on firm ground, seemingly not
soft. *Mrs L. C. Jewell*

SERPENTARA   3 ch.f. Kris 135 – Sardegna 111 (Pharly (FR) 130) [1996 NR   75
1997 12m 10g³ 10m³ 11m Nov 4] big, good-topped filly: has scope: second foal:
sister to useful 1996 3-y-o 1¼m winner Sardonic: dam, 7f (at 2 yrs) and 1¼m winner
who stayed 13f, daughter of Lancashire Oaks winner Sandy Island from family of

Slip Anchor: third in maidens at Sandown and Leicester: off course nearly 2 months and tailed off final outing: should stay 1½m+: sold 42,000 gns in December. *H. R. A. Cecil*

SETTEEN 2 b.c. (Apr 25) Robellino (USA) 127 – Agama (USA) 44 (Nureyev (USA) 131) [1997 6s³ 7m* 8.1m* Sep 17] 20,000F, 62,000Y: tall, attractive colt: has scope: second foal: half-brother to 3-y-o Can Can Lady: dam poor form in 2 starts here at 2 yrs, then won over 13.5f in France as 3-y-o: useful form when most decisive winner of maiden at Ascot in July and 4-runner minor event at Sandown in September: made all to beat Saffron Lane most readily by 3 lengths in latter: will stay at least 1¼m: joined Godolphin: looks sure to improve further and hold his own in stronger company. *M. A. Jarvis*   107 p

SET THE FASHION 8 br.g. Green Desert (USA) 127 – Prelude 89 (Troy 137) [1996 61§: 8m⁵ 11.5f⁵ 10.2m⁴ 9.9m² 8.2m* 9f 8.2d⁶ 8f 16m 14.5g* a12g 1997 a12g a7f⁵ Jan 11] good-topped gelding: had a round action: modest and unreliable handicapper: seemed to stay 14.5f: probably acted on any going: best in visor (tried blinkered): dead. *D. L. Williams*   57 §

SET TRAIL (IRE) 2 b.f. (May 16) Second Set (IRE) 127 – Trail (Thatch (USA) 136) [1997 6m 6g 7d² 7s* Oct 14] IR 24,000Y: lengthy, quite attractive filly: half-sister to several winners abroad, including Japanese 9f listed winner by Waajib: dam unraced: considerately handled first 2 starts, then fair form in maidens at Ayr, making most and rallying to short-head Chocolate on final occasion: will stay at least 1m: has been bandaged behind. *J. Hanson*   76

SEVEN 2 ch.g. (Feb 26) Weldnaas (USA) 112 – Polly's Teahouse 68 (Shack (USA) 118) [1997 6d 6.1g 6d Nov 7] big, lengthy gelding: sixth live foal: brother to 4-y-o Polly Golightly and a winner in Hong Kong: dam sprint maiden: best effort in maidens when blinkered at Doncaster final start. *B. Smart*   68

SEVENTH EDITION 4 b.g. Classic Music (USA) – Funny-Do (Derring-Do 131) [1996 –: 10g 10f 10d⁵ 10m 14.1m 10m⁴ 12.1m a9.4g 1997 a9.4g⁵ a11g 11.6g 12f Jun 10] seems of little account. *P. G. Murphy*   –

SEVENTH HEAVEN 2 ch.g. (Feb 8) Clantime 101 – Portvally (Import 127) [1997 5f 5d⁴ 6d⁶ 5m⁶ 5g 6m⁶ 5g⁶ 7.5f Sep 17] 10,000Y: close-coupled gelding: brother to fairly useful sprinter No Monkey Nuts and half-brother to a 2-y-o 6f seller winner by Crofthall: dam unraced: modest maiden: deteriorated after second start (trained first 4 by J. Berry): stays 6f: blinkered seventh outing. *D. Nicholls*   62 d

SEVERITY 3 b.c. Reprimand 122 – Neenah 107 (Bold Lad (IRE) 133) [1996 NR 1997 6g 7g³ 8.2m³ Jul 25] half-brother to several winners, notably smart N C Owen (up to 1½m, by Bustino): dam, half-sister to Irish Oaks winner Swiftfoot, won over 6f at 2 yrs and stayed 1½m: easily best effort in maidens when third at Yarmouth in July: stays 7f. *W. J. Haggas*   74

SEVERN MILL 6 ch.g. Librate 91 – Staryllis Girl 67 (Star Moss 122) [1996 –: 7g 10m 8.2m⁵ 7.1m 10.2m⁶ 8f 8m 1997 10.8m 9f 6m 7m 6.1m⁵ 6m 7.1m 7g Aug 1] poor maiden handicapper: bred to be suited by much further than 6f. *J. M. Bradley*   31

SHAANXI ROMANCE (IRE) 2 b.g. (Apr 25) Darshaan 133 – Easy Romance (USA) (Northern Jove (CAN)) [1997 7g⁵ 8.3g³ Sep 1] IR 62,000Y: good-topped colt: fourth foal: half-brother to 5-y-o Northern Fan and a winner in USA by Rare Performer: dam won up to 7f in USA: fair form in maidens at Newmarket and Hamilton (third to Generosity): should stay beyond 1m. *M. Bell*   69

SHABANAZ 12 b.g. Imperial Fling (USA) 116 – Claironcita 97 (Don Carlos) [1996 69: 12m² 10m⁶ 11.9d³ 11.6g* 10m* 11.6d* 12.1g² 10g² 10.1m⁶ 12m 11.8f⁶ 1997 10g² 10f 11.6m⁴ 11.9d³ 11.7m² 11.6m 12.4m⁵ 12.1d⁶ Aug 25] rangy, angular gelding: veteran who mainly contests sellers or claimers nowadays: poor form at best in 1997: stays 13f: acts on fibresand and probably any turf going: visored once: has run well in blinkers, not tried for long time: suitable mount for a claimer. *W. R. Muir*   48

SHADDAD (USA) 3 b.c. Shadeed (USA) 135 – Desirable 119 (Lord Gayle (USA) 124) [1996 75p: 6m 6m⁵ 1997 8g 10s⁴ Jun 20] big, lengthy colt: well bred, but showed nothing at 3 yrs: sold 6,800 gns Newmarket July Sales. *J. L. Dunlop*   –

SHADED (IRE)   3 b.g. Night Shift (USA) – Sarsaparilla (FR) 60 (Shirley Heights   57 d
130) [1996 60p: 7m a7g⁵ 6g 1997 8.2m⁵ 9.9m⁶ a12g³ 8d⁵ a8g⁵ 10g 11.5d 8f a10g
Oct 27] good-topped gelding: modest maiden handicapper: well beaten last 4 starts:
barely stays 1½m: acts on good to firm ground and fibresand. *S. Dow*

SHADES OF LOVE   3 b.c. Pursuit of Love 124 – Shadiliya 90 (Red Alert 127)   64
[1996 –: 7d 1997 7m⁶ 8.2d⁴ 6m² 6m⁴ 7m 6.1m a7g³ Dec 18] good-topped colt:
modest maiden: effective at 6f, seemingly 1m: acts on fibresand, yet to race on
extremes of going on turf. *V. Soane*

SHADIANN (IRE)   3 b.c. Darshaan 133 – Shakanda (IRE) (Shernazar 131) [1996   83
NR 1997 10g 11.7g³ 10.4s² 11.9s² 10g⁴ Oct 24] smallish, sturdy colt: unimpressive
mover: first foal: dam Irish 1½m winner, half-sister to dam of Prix Vermeille winner
Sharaya: fairly useful maiden: runner-up at York and Haydock: should stay beyond
1½m: raced only on good going and soft: sold 32,000 gns, and joined P. Murphy.
L. M. Cumani

SHADIRWAN (IRE)   6 b.h. Kahyasi 130 – Shademah 88 (Thatch (USA) 136)   77
[1996 82: 18s* 16d 16d 20f 16.4g 18.7m⁶ 1997 16.4g⁶ 16s 20m 17.2f² 20m² 16.4s
18g 16.5s Nov 8] small horse: fair handicapper: second at Bath and Goodwood
(Goodwood Stakes) and very good seventh on penultimate start to Turnpole in
Cesarewitch at Newmarket: needs in excess of 2m: acts on any going: blinkered (out
of form) once as 4-y-o: has twice run poorly when sweating: inconsistent and
possibly none too enthusiastic. *R. Akehurst*

SHADOOF   3 b.c. Green Desert (USA) 127 – Bermuda Classic 98 (Double Form   83
130) [1996 NR 1997 6m³ 7m³ 7.3s³ 7.1g⁶ 10.5m* 10.1m⁵ 10m⁶ 10.3m⁴ 11.9m
Sep 21] 200,000 francs Y: lengthy colt: fifth foal: brother to very smart sprinter
Tropical and half-brother to very smart miler Shake The Yoke (by Caerleon): dam,
Irish 2-y-o 5f/6f winner, stayed 1m: fairly useful handicapper: won at Haydock in
June: should stay 1½m: acts on good to firm and soft ground: usually held up:
consistent. *W. R. Muir*

SHADOW JURY   7 ch.g. Doulab (USA) 115 – Texita 65 (Young Generation 129)   68
[1996 70, a81: a5g* a5g⁴ 5s 5g 5m 6g 5m⁴ 5f³ 5m 5g⁵ 5m² 5g* 5g 5.7f² 5m
5.1m² 5m 5d 5m 5g 5m² 5s a5g a6g⁶ 1997 a5g⁴ a6g a6g³ a5g a5g 5m³ 5m⁶ 6m* 5d⁴
5m* a5g² a5g⁵ 5v a5g⁵ 5m 5f 5m a6g 6m 5d 5g a6g a5g³ a5g⁵ Dec 18] fair performer:
won minor event at Warwick and handicap at Musselburgh in May: effective at 5f
and 6f: acts on the all-weather, best recent turf form on good going or firmer:
blinkered/visored nowadays: usually races prominently: tough. *D. W. Chapman*

SHADOW OF DOUBT (IRE)   2 b.c. (Jan 25) Pips Pride 117 – Sarah Siddons   95
(Reform 132) [1997 6d* 6m⁶ Jun 17] IR 65,000Y: smallish, sturdy colt: half-brother
to several winners, including 6f/7f winner Maggie Siddons and 1991 2-y-o 5f winner
Night Duty (both fairly useful by Night Shift): dam French 8.5f winner: odds on, won
maiden at Goodwood in May: better effort on form, though never going with same
fluency, when 6½ lengths sixth to Harbour Master in Coventry Stakes at Royal
Ascot: sent to Hong Kong. *P. W. Chapple-Hyam*

SHAFFISHAYES   5 ch.g. Clantime 101 – Mischievous Miss 73 (Niniski (USA)   77
125) [1996 70: 8m* 8g³ 9m⁴ 8.9g 10g⁶ 10f² a12g² a11g 1997 a8.5g³ 10g² 12d³
12.4g* 11.9d² 12s* 11.9g⁶ 13.1d⁵ 10.9s² 10m Nov 4] lengthy gelding: fractured
cannon bone as 3-y-o: fair handicapper: won at Newcastle in May and Newmarket
in June: ran really well when short-head second at Ayr penultimate start: effective at
1¼m to 13f: acts on fibresand and probably any turf going: suited by waiting tactics
and a truly-run race: usually early to post: consistent. *Mrs M. Reveley*

SHAFT OF LIGHT   5 gr.g. Sharrood (USA) 124 – Reflection 111 (Mill Reef   103
(USA) 141) [1996 –: 12m 1997 10g 16.2s³ 11.9g³ 18.7m* 12d* 14.6m³ 16g⁵ 12s³
Nov 8] tall gelding: has a round action: useful handicapper: won £15,000 event at
Chester and £10,400 amateurs race at Epsom in August: good third to Sabadilla in
November Handicap at Doncaster final start: effective at 1½m to 19f: yet to race on
heavy going, acts on any other: sometimes blinkered/visored (latter last 4 starts):
resolute galloper, suited by forcing tactics: genuine and reliable. *Lord Huntingdon*

SHAHBOOR (USA)   3 b.g. Zilzal (USA) 137 – Iva Reputation (USA) (Sir Ivor   75
135) [1996 –p: 7g 1997 8m 10d⁴ 10m 14.1m² 14.4m Sep 21] tall gelding: fair form:

best effort when second in handicap at Yarmouth in August: pulled too hard last outing (gelded subsequently): stays 1¾m. *M. R. Stoute*

SHAHEEN (USA) 3 b.c. Danzig (USA) – Hidden Light (USA) (Majestic Light 96 (USA)) [1996 NR 1997 8.2m³ 8g² 8d² 7m* 7m 7m Aug 1] $385,000 2-y-o: compact colt: fourth foal: closely related to a winner in USA by Nijinsky and half-brother to another by Ferdinand: dam won Grade 1 8.5f and 9f events: useful performer: won maiden at Kempton in May, making most: well held in Jersey Stakes at Royal Ascot and £20,500 handicap at Goodwood (poorly drawn and never on terms) afterwards: effective at 7f and 1m: acts on good to firm and dead ground: last and steadily to post last 2 starts: visored final outing: joined W. Dollase in USA. *H. R. A. Cecil*

SHAHIK (USA) 7 b.g. Spectacular Bid (USA) – Sham Street (USA) (Sham 71 (USA)) [1996 71: a12g a7g a7g³ a9.4g² 12g 10d* a12g a9.4g* a9.4g a9.4g⁴ a12g⁴ 1997 a11g⁶ a11g 10m² 8.1m⁵ 11.5d a10g a12s a12g Dec 19] good-bodied gelding: fair handicapper at best: left D. Haydn Jones after fifth start: stays 1¼m: acts on fibresand, good to firm ground and dead: no form in a visor. *K. C. Comerford*

SHAHRUR (USA) 4 b. or br.g. Riverman (USA) 131 – Give Thanks 123 (Relko 77 136) [1996 –: 8m 1997 14d* 16g⁴ a10g² 16.2g Sep 27] strong, good sort: trained at 3 yrs by A. Stewart: won maiden at Down Royal in May by 12 lengths: left D. K. Weld 2 starts later and gelded: ran as though something amiss on return to Britain: stays 1¾m: acts on good to soft going: winning hurdler (reluctant to start when successful in December). *G. L. Moore*

SHAILENDRA (IRE) 3 ch.f. Persian Bold 123 – Good Policy (IRE) 80 – (Thatching 131) [1996 NR 1997 10m 10m⁶ 10.1g 10m Sep 15] IR 40,000Y: big plain filly: second foal: half-sister to useful Honest Guest (up to 1¼m, by Be My Guest): dam 1m winner at 2 yrs: little promise in maidens and minor event: sent to UAE. *J. H. M. Gosden*

SHAJI (IRE) 2 ch.c. (Feb 27) Mukaddamah (USA) 125 – Alkariyh (USA) 79 71 p (Alydar (USA)) [1997 6d⁴ Nov 7] lengthy, good-topped colt: third foal: half-brother to 1994 2-y-o 6f winner Kabil (by Doyoun), 7f winner in UAE in 1997, and 6f winner Al Wujud (by Polish Precedent): dam 2-y-o 6f winner out of half-sister to Saratoga Six and Dunbeath: 33/1 and very green, around 3 lengths fourth to Masha-Il in maiden at Doncaster, going strongly in rear after slow start and making good late headway, despite wandering: sure to improve. *C. J. Benstead*

SHAKA 3 b.c. Exit To Nowhere (USA) 122 – Serafica (No Pass No Sale 120) 114 [1996 113p: 6g² 6g* 8d* 8g* 10s* 1997 11m³ 11g* 12m⁶ 10s³ 9.5f⁵ Jul 20] smart French colt: won Prix Hocquart at Chantilly in May by a length from Oscar: never-dangerous sixth of 14 to Peintre Celebre in Prix du Jockey-Club at Chantilly: creditable 3 lengths third of 7 to Peintre Celebre in Grand Prix de Paris at Long-champ: below-form fifth in Grade 2 race at Arlington final start: should stay 1½m: acts on soft ground and possibly not at best on firmer than good. *J-C. Rouget, France*

SHAKIYR (FR) 6 gr.g. Lashkari 128 – Shakamiyn (Nishapour (FR) 125) [1996 – 54, a72: a14.8g³ a14.8g² a16.2g* a12g⁶ 18s 16.2m⁶ 17.1g⁶ 14d⁵ a14.8g⁶ 15.9m³ a64 15.8g⁴ 15.9d⁴ 14s 14.6g⁶ 14.1s 15.1s³ a16g⁶ 1997 a16g³ a14.8g* a14.8g⁵ a14.8g² 16.1g a16g³ a16.2g a14.8g 14.1g a14g a14.8g⁶ a14g² Dec 8] workmanlike gelding: modest performer: won seller at Wolverhampton in January: stays 2m: goes well on fibresand, no form on turf in 1997: blinkered second to seventh and penultimate starts: comes from behind, and often soon off bridle: inconsistent. *R. Hollinshead*

SHALAAL (USA) 3 b.g. Sheikh Albadou 128 – One Fine Day (USA) (Quadratic 78 (USA)) [1996 76p: 7g⁶ 7.1m⁵ 7m 1997 7g 6m⁴ 8m 7d* 7g a6g a8g Dec 8] big, useful-looking gelding: has a rather round action: fair performer: sold out of E. Dunlop's stable after reappearance: won apprentice maiden at Leicester in October, best effort: should stay beyond 7f: acts on dead going, well held on fibresand last 2 starts. *M. C. Chapman*

SHALABELLA (IRE) 2 br.f. (Feb 25) Shalford (IRE) 124§ – Perfect Swinger 45 (Shernazar 131) [1997 5g 7m 7g³ 9m Sep 24] IR 16,500Y: third foal: dam poor Irish maiden half-sister to smart sprinter Showbrook: only form when third in seller at Brighton: raced too freely next time: joined J. W. Mullins. *M. R. Channon*

SHALAD'OR 2 b.f. (Apr 10) Golden Heights 82 – Shalati (FR) (High Line 125) 70
[1997 5m 6f⁵ 7g⁶ 7g* 6m² 8g² Sep 8] 1,800Y: sixth reported foal: half-sister to
several winners, including 4-y-o Shalateeno and 3-y-o Kewarra: dam French 1m
winner: fair performer: won maiden at Leicester in July: good second in nurseries at
Windsor and Bath: races freely but stays 1m: raced only on good ground or firmer.
B. R. Millman

SHALATEENO 4 b.f. Teenoso (USA) 135 – Shalati (FR) (High Line 125) [1996 75
70: 7d 10.2g⁴ 10m 12.1d⁶ 17.2g⁴ 12.5f² 10g⁶ 12.1m 8g⁶ 10g³ 10.2g* 10.5m² 12m
1997 10m² 10.8m⁴ 10.8m⁴ 12.1g³ 12f* 10.2d² 12g² 13.3d³ Sep 20] sturdy filly: fair
handicapper: won at Salisbury in June: good third to Darapour in £14,300 event at
Newbury final start: stays 13f: acts on firm and dead going: has worn severe bridle
and gone early to post: front runner: game and consistent. *B. R. Millman*

SHALFORD'S HONOUR (IRE) 2 ch.c. (Feb 3) Shalford (IRE) 124§ – Petite 89
Epaulette 70 (Night Shift (USA)) [1997 5.2m³ 5m⁴ 5.1d* 6g Oct 18] IR 29,000F,
42,000Y: small, deep-bodied colt: first foal: dam, 5f winner, ran only at 2 yrs, granddaughter of Irish 1000 Guineas winner Front Row: fairly useful form: won maiden at
Nottingham in October in good style: took strong hold and eased once held in face of
much stiffer task final start: sold 38,000 gns in October, to go to USA. *W. Jarvis*

SHALSTAYHOLY (IRE) 3 ch.f. Shalford (IRE) 124§ – Saintly Guest (What 84
A Guest 119) [1996 60: 5.1m 6.9d² 7g 6v⁴ 1997 a7g* a6g² 7.3s⁴ 7m³ 6g* 7m⁴ 6g³
6g⁴ 5m* 5g² 5m² 5m⁴ 5v Oct 11] plain, good-topped filly: fairly useful performer:
won maiden at Lingfield in February and handicaps at Newmarket in June and
Sandown in July: effective at 5f to 7f: acts on good to firm ground, heavy and
the all-weather: visored fourth to seventh starts: tough and consistent: joined
T. E. Powell. *G. L. Moore*

SHALVERTON (IRE) 3 b.f. Shalford (IRE) 124§ – Kilfenora (Tribal Chief 125) –
[1996 NR 1997 8.3g 8.3m 7.1m⁴ Aug 14] half-sister to several winners, notably
4-y-o Kahir Almaydan: dam Irish 2-y-o 5f winner: little form in maidens. *W. R. Muir*

SHALYAH (IRE) 2 ch.f. (Feb 27) Shalford (IRE) 124§ – Baheejah (Northfields 65
(USA)) [1997 6m 6g⁵ 6m⁴ 5g² 7g³ 8m 6.5m Sep 10] IR 4,200F, 8,200Y: strong,
lengthy filly: half-sister to several winners, including 1½m winner Talish (by Persian
Bold): dam lightly-raced half-sister to Irish Oaks winner Olwyn: fair maiden: placed
in nurseries at Thirsk and Newmarket in August: should stay 1m: raced only on good
ground or firmer. *Mrs J. R. Ramsden*

SHAMANIC 5 b.g. Fairy King (USA) – Annie Albright (USA) (Verbatim (USA)) 79
[1996 89: 6m 6m 6m⁴ 7g³ 6f 6m 7.3m⁶ 6m 6m 1997 6m² 6.1m⁶ 6m⁵ 6g 7.1m 7m²
8m⁶ Oct 23] smallish, useful-looking gelding: fair performer: second in small fields
in minor events at Yarmouth in June and Newcastle in October: stays 7f (pulled too
hard at 1m): raced only on good going or firmer: none too consistent. *S. P. C. Woods*

SHAMBLES 2 ch.f. (Feb 19) Elmaamul (USA) 125 – Rambadale 68 (Vaigly –
Great 127) [1997 7d 6d Oct 28] 1,000Y: leggy filly: fourth foal: dam 2-y-o 6f winner
who stayed 1m: little sign of ability in maidens at Leicester. *G. G. Margarson*

SHAMIKH 3 b.c. Unfuwain (USA) 131 – Narjis (USA) 87 (Blushing Groom (FR) –
131) [1996 96+: 7m* 1997 8m May 3] well-made colt: freeze fired on forelegs after
winning Chesham Stakes at Royal Ascot on debut: subject of sustained ante-post
support and in fine shape, refused to settle in 2000 Guineas at Newmarket, beaten
long way into fourteenth of 16: reportedly lame on off-fore following morning. *Saeed
bin Suroor*

SHAMOKIN 5 b.g. Green Desert (USA) 127 – Shajan (Kris 135) [1996 –: 8m⁶ 38
8m⁵ 8.3m⁵ 12g 10.1m a8g 1997 10.1g⁵ 10m 11.1s 10.9d 10.9g⁶ 8m³ 9.2m Aug 18]
workmanlike gelding: poor maiden handicapper: probably stays 1¼m: possibly unsuited by soft going. *F. Watson*

SHAMWARI SONG 2 b.g. (May 20) Sizzling Melody 117 – Spark Out 63
(Sparkler 130) [1997 5m⁴ 5s 5.1m⁵ 6m⁵ 7m⁵ 7m* 7g Oct 27] 3,600Y: tall gelding:
half-brother to sprint winners by Smackover (at 2 yrs) and Street Kafu: dam probably
of little account: modest performer: won maiden at Newcastle in October: stays 7f:
has carried head awkwardly. *J. A. Glover*

SHANGHAI LIL 5 b.m. Petong 126 – Toccata (USA) 64 (Mr Leader (USA)) 24
[1996 32, a49: a8g⁵ a6g⁶ a8.5g² 8.2m 8m⁶ 8.1f 8.2g a8g* a10g³ 1997 a8g* a8g² a56
a10g² a10g³ a9.4g a10g 8d 8g 8s a8g⁵ a10g⁵ Dec 22] smallish mare: modest
handicapper on all-weather, poor on turf: won at Lingfield in January: back to form
final start: stays 1¼m: acts on good to firm and dead ground: below form when
blinkered. *M. J. Fetherston-Godley*

SHANILLO 2 gr.g. (Feb 28) Anshan 119 – Sea Fret 96 (Habat 127) [1997 7g Sep 72 p
18] 24,000Y: tall gelding: has scope: half-brother to 3-y-o Cauda Equina and several
other winners, including useful 1995 sprint 2-y-o Flying Squaw (by Be My Chief)
and Top Wave (1m winner, by High Top): dam, 2-y-o 6f winner, out of smart Fluke,
a half-sister to Buoy and Bireme: 33/1 and in need of race, around 6½ lengths eighth to
Dr Fong in steadily-run maiden at Newbury, not knocked about: should improve.
M. R. Channon

SHANNON (IRE) 2 b.f. (Apr 7) Mujadil (USA) 119 – Eimkar (Junius (USA) 50 §
124) [1997 5g 5.3f 5m 6g² 7m 6m* 6m 7g⁶ 6.1m 6m⁴ a6g⁶ Oct 18] IR 5,400Y: sixth
foal: half-sister to 5-y-o Ladybower: dam unraced half-sister to high-class French
miler Daring Display: capable of modest form on her day: won seller at Folkestone
in August: probably stays 7f: raced only on good ground or firmer on turf: looks a
difficult ride (best held up) and not one to trust. *C. A. Dwyer*

SHANNON'S SECRET (IRE) 2 b.c. (Mar 12) Shalford (IRE) 124§ – Shenley ?
Lass (Prince Tenderfoot (USA) 126) [1997 6g 6d 7.1g⁵ 7.5m 6m 7g 7.3g Oct 25]
25,000Y: half-brother to a 2-y-o 1¼m seller winner and 4-y-o Principal Boy (both by
Cyrano de Bergerac): disappointing maiden: stays 7f: has had tongue tied and worn
dropped noseband: blinkered final 2 starts: sold, and sent to Holland. *B. J. Meehan*

SHANONS SHINANIGAN (IRE) 3 ch.g. Salt Dome – Insight (Ballad –
Rock 122) [1996 NR 1997 10m Oct 5] IR 4,000Y, IR 3,100Y: third foal: dam
unraced: soon behind in maiden at Leicester. *M. H. Tompkins*

SHANOORA (IRE) 4 gr.f. Don't Forget Me 127 – Shalara (Dancer's Image 36
(USA)) [1996 –: a7g a8g⁵ a12g⁵ a6g⁶ a7g a7g 1997 a8g⁴ a11g a8g a7g Feb 3] lengthy
filly: poor performer: stays 1m: acts on all-weather: sometimes blinkered/visored.
Mrs N. Macauley

SHANTARSKIE (IRE) 3 b.c. Mujadil (USA) 119 – Bay Supreme (Martinmas 74
128) [1996 65p: 6m⁴ 1997 a7f³ a7f a7f² 7m 5f⁵ Sep 17] fair performer: ran in UAE
for Ali Mohsen Khair Al Dine first 3 starts at 3 yrs: better effort back in Britain when
fifth in maiden at Beverley: may prove best up to 7f: returned to UAE. *C. F. Wall*

SHANTHI 2 b.f. (Apr 5) Reprimand 122 – Scarlett Holly 81 (Red Sunset 120) 49
[1997 5g³ 6d³ 5.3f³ 6m³ 7g² 7g a6g⁶ a7g Oct 20] 4,500Y: third foal: half-sister to a?
3-y-o Siouxrouge and 1m winner Little Scarlett (by Mazilier): dam 6f and 7f winner:
poor maiden: below form last 3 starts (blinkered first 2 of them): stays 7f. *P. J. Makin*

SHANTOU (USA) 4 b.c. Alleged (USA) 138 – Shaima (USA) 110 (Shareef 125
Dancer (USA) 135) [1996 124: 8m³ 10.3g² 10d* 12m³ 12f³ 11.9g² 11.6d*
14.6m* 12s* 12g⁴ 1997 12f* 12g* 12s⁵ 13.3m³ Aug 16]
    Those who made the decision to inflate the prize money for the Gran
Premio di Milano in June must have been disappointed with the turn-out for

Princess of Wales's Stakes, Newmarket—Shantou (star on cap) rallies to beat Swain; Taipan is back in third

Gran Premio di Milano—
a 1,2,3,4 for British challengers as Shantou leads home Luso, Taipan and Strategic Choice (white face)

Italy's richest race, even though there were half as many runners again as in 1996, when Strategic Choice and Luso had finished first and second. Those two were involved again, two of five British-trained challengers in a six-runner field, with the Italian colt Toto Le Moko making up the numbers. It would have been reasonable to expect a more competitive race for an event with a first prize of around a quarter of a million pounds and place money, for all that there were no good Italian-trained horses around to speak of. The race did manage to attract one other established high-class performer, however, in Shantou, who was making his seasonal reappearance. Eight months earlier Shantou had won the Gran Premio del Jockey-Club over the course and distance, after winning the St Leger at Doncaster in a thrilling finish with Dushyantor.

Shantou has his quirks and is no easy ride, but he does go particularly well for Frankie Dettori, who once again got the best out of him at Milan. Dettori brought Shantou wide to challenge early in the straight, kept him on an even keel when he began to hang right after taking up the running over a furlong out and drove him out to win by a length and a quarter from Luso, with Taipan showing improved form to deprive Strategic Choice of third place. Shantou and Taipan met again in the Princess of Wales's Stakes at Newmarket the following month, a Group 2 event—worth £32,908 to the winner—which attracted Dushyantor, the 1996 Coronation Cup winner Swain (making his reappearance), the 1996 Oaks winner Lady Carla, the smart Ela-Aristokrati and Celeric, winner of the Gold Cup on his previous start. Dushyantor made the running at a fair pace from Swain, who was tracked by Shantou. This was the order until approaching the two-furlong marker, where Swain struck the front and Shantou was switched outside to challenge him. The pair were involved in a tremendous duel up the hill with both horses giving their all, Shantou gaining the upper hand close home to win by a head. Taipan again finished third, four lengths behind the principals.

This represented high-class form again from Shantou, but he was unable to reproduce it in his two subsequent races. With Dettori choosing to ride Singspiel, Gary Hind was on board Shantou when the horse, starting slowly and hampered around halfway, finished fifth to Swain in the King George VI and Queen Elizabeth Diamond Stakes at Ascot. Shantou was reunited with Dettori in the Geoffrey Freer Stakes at Newbury but came off third best in a desperately close finish with Dushyantor and Panama City, his chance not helped by a slow early pace.

	Alleged (USA) (b 1974)	Hoist The Flag (b 1968)
		Tom Rolfe
		Wavy Navy
		Princess Pout (b 1966)
		Prince John
Shantou (USA) (b.c. 1993)		Determined Lady
	Shaima (USA) (b 1988)	Shareef Dancer (b 1980)
		Northern Dancer
		Sweet Alliance
		Oh So Sharp (ch 1982)
		Kris
		Oh So Fair

Sheikh Mohammed's "Shantou"

Shantou is the first foal of Shaima, winner of the Radley Stakes at New-bury as a two-year-old and of a nine-furlong listed race at York and the Grade 2 Long Island Handicap over a mile and a half at Belmont Park at three. Her second foal, the three-year-old filly Shimna (by Mr Prospector), wore blinkers when finishing fourth in a maiden at Roscommon in August, her only outing to date. Shaima is out of Oh So Sharp, winner of the One Thousand Guineas, Oaks and St Leger in 1985.

Shantou, a small, quite attractive colt with a powerful, round action, is still sometimes rather edgy in the preliminaries but it doesn't affect his performance, and his record since we doubted his willingness halfway through 1996 has been hard to fault. Shantou stays in training in 1998, when hopefully he'll get to run more often than the four times he managed in the latest season. He is effective at a mile and a half and stays a mile and three quarters well and he acts on any going. *J. H. M. Gosden*

SHANTUNG (IRE) 2 ch.f. (Apr 6) Anshan 119 – Bamian (USA) (Topsider (USA)) [1997 8m 7d⁴ 6d Nov 7] IR 9,000Y: leggy, useful-looking filly: second foal: sister to a bad maiden: dam, French 10.5f winner, closely related to Breeders' Cup Juvenile third Slavic: fourth at Lingfield in October, easily best effort in maidens: should stay at least 1m. *K. McAuliffe*   65

SHAPE SHIFTER (IRE) 2 ch.c. (Jan 20) Night Shift (USA) – Zabeta (Diesis 133) [1997 7g Aug 8] 36,000F, IR 100,000Y: small colt: has a quick action: first foal: dam French 1m winner out of half-sister to Prix de Diane winner Harbour: 6/1 from 10/1, over 9 lengths seventh behind wide-margin winner Rabi in maiden at New-market, green and pulling hard, not knocked about: likely to improve. *R. Hannon*   69 p

SHARAF (IRE) 4 b.g. Sadler's Wells (USA) 132 – Marie de Flandre (FR) 109 (Crystal Palace (FR) 132) [1996 87d: 11.8s² 12m* 14d³ 16.4g⁴ 14f 11.9m⁴ 13.3m 14m⁴ 16.2d 16s 1997 12.1d⁵ 16.4g 14s⁵ a12g⁵ 14g Jun 14] lengthy gelding: fairly useful up to 2m at best in 1996: disappointing at 4 yrs: tried blinkered and visored: has unsavoury attitude, and best left alone. *W. R. Muir*   – §

SHARAF KABEER 4 ch.c. Machiavellian (USA) 123 – Sheroog (USA) 77 (Shareef Dancer (USA) 135) [1996 110: 10d² 12g* 12m 14g* 14.6m 12m³ 1997 11.8d³ Jun 14] tall colt: impresses in appearance: fluent mover: useful performer: not discredited when over 9 lengths third of 5 to Eva Luna in listed race at Leicester, only outing at 4 yrs: stays 1¾m: yet to race on extremes of going. *Saeed bin Suroor*   102

SHARAZAMATAZ 3 b.f. Shareef Dancer (USA) 135 – Phylae (Habitat 134) [1996 49?: 5.1m 6g⁵ 6.9m⁶ 7f² 6d 1997 a6g a6g a10g Dec 19] small, compact filly: poor form at 2 yrs: well beaten late in 1997: should be suited by 1m+. *K. T. Ivory*   –

SHARBADARID (IRE) 3 b.g. Night Shift (USA) – Sharenara (USA) (Vaguely Noble 140) [1996 NR 1997 8d 8f³ 7.9d³ 10m⁵ 10g² 10.4s Sep 4] deep-bodied gelding: fourth foal: closely related to French (1m) and US winner Sharekann (by Be My Guest) and half-brother to 2 winners, including French 1¼m winner Sharepar (by Darshaan): dam twice-raced maiden half-sister to Shahrastani: fair maiden handi-capper: stays 1¼m well: acts on good to firm and dead ground: joined S. Dow. *L. M. Cumani*   78

SHARE DELIGHT (IRE) 3 b.c. Common Grounds 118 – Dorado Llave (USA) (Well Decorated (USA)) [1996 68: 6m 6d⁶ a6g² a6g⁶ 1997 7m* 7g 8m 7.9g⁶ 8g⁵ 10m⁵ 8.1m Aug 9] sparely-made colt: fair handicapper: won at Doncaster in March: stays 1m: acts on good to firm ground: reportedly swallowed tongue final 2-y-o start, tongue tied most starts since: has hung and carried head awkwardly: inconsistent, and not one to trust: sold 5,000 gns (to D. Nicholls) in October. *B. W. Hills*   81 §

SHARERA (IRE) 2 b.f. (Mar 29) Kahyasi 130 – Sharenara (USA) (Vaguely Noble 140) [1997 7d⁴ Oct 27] fifth foal: half-sister to 3 winners, including French (1m) and US winner Sharekann (by Be My Guest) and French 1¼m winner Sharepar (by Darshaan): dam twice-raced maiden half-sister to Shahrastani: some promise when around 5½ lengths fourth to easy winner Housekeeper in maiden at Lingfield, leading nearly 6f: should be well suited by 1¼m+: will do better. *L. M. Cumani*   65 p

SHARK (IRE)   4 b.g. Tirol 127 – Gay Appeal 76 (Star Appeal 133) [1996 –: 8d   53
1997 a9.4g 5.9m 8m³ 8m³ 8f* 7d Oct 14] modest performer: won 19-runner maiden
handicap at Yarmouth in September, making most: should stay beyond 1m: acts on
firm ground, possibly not on good to soft. *K. A. Morgan*

SHARKIYAH (IRE)   3 ch.f. Polish Precedent (USA) 131 – Peace Girl 98   72 d
(Dominion 123) [1996 75p: 7g 1997 7g⁴ 8.2d 8m⁴ 7m 10.5s Oct 15] rather
sparely-made filly: unimpressive mover: fair form on reappearance: has regressed:
reportedly returned lame final start: sold 7,000 gns in December. *R. W. Armstrong*

SHARP COMMAND   4 ch.g. Sharpo 132 – Bluish (USA) (Alleged (USA) 138)
[1996 61: 8.2d⁶ 6.9m 12g 10m a8g⁴ 10.5m a8.5g⁵ 12d⁵ a14g⁴ a12g² a14.8g* a16g
1997 a16s a16.2g⁵ a12g⁶ 13d Apr 10] good-topped gelding: modest handicapper at
up to 15f on fibresand as 3-y-o: ran badly in 1997: fairly useful hurdler. *P. Eccles*

SHARP CONSUL (IRE)   5 br.g. Exactly Sharp (USA) 121 – Alicia Markova 64   94
(Habat 127) [1996 80: 9m⁶ 10g 10d* 8g³ 10.2m² 9f 10d* 10v⁶ 1997 10m² 12d²
10.4m 12s³ 10.2g⁵ 10d* 10g³ Oct 24] tall gelding: poor mover: fairly useful handicapper: won £16,200 event at Newbury in September: creditable third there following month: barely stays 1½m: acts on good to firm going and soft: travels strongly
and is held up: has won for 7-lb claimer. *H. Candy*

SHARP CRACKER (IRE)   2 b.f. (Apr 26) Hamas (IRE) 125§ – Ascensiontide   77
(Ela-Mana-Mou 132) [1997 5f² 5s³ 6m³ 5m² 7g⁴ 5m⁴ 7m³ 6g 7s² 6d* Oct 20] 2,200F,
8,400Y: leggy, filly: easy mover: seventh foal: half-sister to fairly useful 1m winner
Elmi Elmak (by Fairy King) and 2 winners abroad: dam Irish 1½m winner out of
Child Stakes winner Rose Above: fair performer: gained deserved first win when
making all to land odds in maiden at Pontefract: best at 7f/stiff 6f: acts on firm and
soft ground. *M. Johnston*

SHARP DEED (IRE)   3 ch.g. Sharp Victor (USA) 114 – Fabulous Deed (USA)   59
77 (Shadeed (USA) 135) [1996 60: 7f 6g 1997 7g 10m⁵ 8.5m² 10g⁴ 8m 8f 10.8g
11.5m⁴ 14.1d Nov 3] strong, close-coupled gelding: modest maiden handicapper:
probably stays 11.5f: acts on good to firm ground: visored last 4 outings: joined
M. Madgwick. *P. J. Makin*

SHARP FELLOW   2 ch.g. (Mar 22) Keen 116 – Clarandal 80 (Young Generation   50
129) [1997 5m⁶ a6g a6g Nov 17] 5,800Y: leggy gelding: half-brother to 7f winner   a?
Akabusi (by Absalom), 4-y-o Lillibella and 2 winners in Norway by Jalmood: dam
1m winner: poor form in maidens. *I. A. Balding*

SHARP GAZELLE   7 ch.m. Beveled (USA) – Shadha 57 (Shirley Heights 130)   –
[1996 46, a49: a11g⁴ a11g* a11g⁴ a14g⁵ 10f⁵ 10d* 10f 1997 a12g³ Feb 14] leggy   a37
mare: has a round action: poor performer: probably stays 1½m: acts on dead going
and fibresand: has broken blood vessel over hurdles. *B. Smart*

SHARP HAT   3 ch.c. Shavian 125 – Madam Trilby (Grundy 137) [1996 81: 7m   99
7f² 6g 6m* 6m* 6m² 6m 1997 7g⁵ 6m⁴ 6s* 6m 7.3m⁶ 5.6m² 6g 5m Sep
28] leggy, angular colt: useful handicapper: won at Newbury in May: good efforts
afterwards in frame in £22,500 event at Newmarket, William Hill Trophy at York and
Tote-Portland at Doncaster (½-length second of 22 to Dashing Blue): races keenly
and seems best around 6f: acts on good to firm and soft ground: has run well when
sweating: sometimes free to post: reliable. *R. Hannon*

SHARP HOLLY (IRE)   5 b.m. Exactly Sharp (USA) 121 – Children's Hour   –
(Mummy's Pet 125) [1996 –: 5f a5g a7g 7f⁶ 8f⁵ 8m 1997 a5g³ a6g⁶ a6g 7f 6.1m Jun
13] shallow-girthed mare: no form since 3 yrs. *J. A. Bennett*

SHARP IMP   7 b.g. Sharpo 132 – Implore 71 (Ile de Bourbon (USA) 133) [1996   70
62: a6g* a7g a6g² a6g² a6g² a6g⁴ 6f 6g 6m 6f³ 6f* 6.9g 7f⁶ 6m³ 7f* 6f³ 5.3f⁴ a7g 7f³   a65
7m 7m a6g³ 1997 a6g² a6g* a6g a6g⁴ a6g⁵ 6f⁴ 6f² 6f² 7m² 7f⁵ 6m² 6m⁴ a7g
7m a7g⁴ a6g³ a7g Dec 19] workmanlike gelding: fair performer: won handicap at
Lingfield in January and minor event at Folkestone in August: effective at 6f and 7f:
acts on the all-weather, raced mainly on good going or firmer on turf: usually
blinkered: tends to edge left: sometimes slowly away and usually held up: tough and
reliable. *R. M. Flower*

SHARP LABEL   2 ch.f. (Feb 10) Sharpo 132 – Labelon Lady 87 (Touching Wood   –
(USA) 127) [1997 8.1d 8.2g a8g Dec 8] fourth foal: half-sister to a 2-y-o 6f winner
by Prince Sabo: dam 2-y-o 7f winner: behind in maidens and seller. *J. L. Harris*

SHARP MONKEY   2 b.c. (Apr 1) Man Among Men (IRE) – Sharp Thistle 87   43
(Sharpo 132) [1997 a7g⁴ 8.2d⁶ 10s a8.5g⁶ a8g⁵ a8g² a7g² a8g Dec 8] third reported   a49
living foal: half-brother to a winner abroad by Kalaglow: dam 7f winner at 2 yrs who
stayed 1½m: poor maiden: second in sellers at Southwell and Wolverhampton: stays
1m: visored last 5 starts. *Mrs N. Macauley*

SHARP MOVE   5 ch.m. Night Shift (USA) – Judeah 69 (Great Nephew 126)   –
[1996 –: 7g 7m 5m 6m a7g 1997 a6g Nov 13] lightly raced and little form since poor
at 2 yrs. *B. A. Pearce*

SHARP 'N SHADY   4 b.f. Sharpo 132 – Shadiliya 90 (Red Alert 127) [1996 59:   64
6.9s 7d³ 7.3d 8m 7g⁵ 7g³ 1997 6.1d 6.1g⁴ 7d* 7d³ 7s* 8.3m Jul 14] heavy-topped
filly: modest performer: won handicap at Newmarket in June and minor event at
Catterick (led close home) following month in July: should stay 1m: suited by good
going or softer: game. *C. F. Wall*

SHARP 'N SMART   5 ch.g. Weldnaas (USA) 112 – Scottish Lady (Dunbeath   70 d
(USA) 127) [1996 75d: a7g* a6g⁶ 7d 6f 7.3s 6m⁶ 7m 6d² a7g a7g³ 1997 a7g² a8g⁵
a7g 6.9g* 6.9m⁶ 7d 7m 6m 6d Oct 21] workmanlike gelding: fair handicapper: won
at Folkestone in March: disappointing afterwards: stays 7.6f: probably acts on any
ground: races prominently: tried blinkered: sold 1,400 gns in October. *B. Smart*

SHARPO WASSL   3 ch.g. Sharpo 132 – Wasslaweyeh (USA) 66 (Damascus   72
(USA)) [1996 NR 1997 a7g² 6.9g* 7.5m⁶ 7g³ 8m* 7.1g 7m Oct 7] close-coupled
gelding: seventh foal: brother to 3 winners, including (fair up to 1½m) Slmaat:
dam stayed 1¼m: fair performer: won maiden at Folkestone in March and
handicap (despite seeming ill-at-ease on track) at Brighton in August: had excuses
final 2 starts: will prove best up to 1m: yet to race on going softer than good: likely to
prove best with waiting tactics: sold approx. £32,000 in Dubai in November.
W. J. Haggas

SHARP PEARL   4 ch.g. Sharpo 132 – Silent Pearl (USA) (Silent Screen (USA))   88
[1996 77: 6m 5.1g² 5.3f* 5f 6g 5.1m³ 5m 5.3m⁵ 5f⁴ 5m a5g³ a6g 1997 a5g a6g⁴ 6f⁴
5.3f* 5.1d 6g⁶ 6d⁴ 5m 5.7f² 6g³ 5.2m² 5m* 6d 5.1g⁴ Sep 24] good-topped gelding:
fairly useful handicapper: won at Brighton in April: left J. White after sixth start:
better than ever for new yard, winning ladies race at Newmarket in August: effective
at 5f/easy 6f: acts on firm ground, dead and equitrack: blinkered: has had tongue tied:
held up: consistent. *P. R. Webber*

SHARP PET   2 b.f. (Apr 26) Petong 126 – Harmony Park 55 (Music Boy 124)   –
[1997 5g a5g 5s Jul 3] 5,000Y: fifth foal: sister to 1994 2-y-o 6f winner Vocalize:
dam, 7f winner at 4 yrs, sister to useful sprinter Melody Park: no promise, including
in sellers: blinkered final start. *D. McCain*

SHARP PLAY   2 b.c. (Jan 21) Robellino (USA) 127 – Child's Play (USA)   102
(Sharpen Up 127) [1997 7g* 7g² 7.1s⁴ 8g Sep 28] 26,000Y: smallish, good-topped
colt: second foal: dam ran twice here, then 10.5f winner in France, from family of
Precocious, Jupiter Island and Pushy: useful form: won maiden at York in July: in
frame in listed race at the Curragh (1½ lengths second to King of Kings) and Solario
Stakes at Sandown, then creditable seventh of 8 to Teapot Row in Royal Lodge
Stakes at Ascot, beaten less than 3 lengths: will stay beyond 1m. *M. Johnston*

SHARP PROGRESS   4 b.g. Inca Chief (USA) – Sharp Venita 84 (Sharp Edge   –
123) [1996 –: 8g 12m⁵ 10m 12m 1997 a12g Nov 21] signs of ability but no worthwhile form. *A. P. Jones*

SHARP REBUFF   6 b.h. Reprimand 122 – Kukri (Kris 135) [1996 84: 7m⁵ 7s⁴   91
8m⁵ 7m² 8m* 1997 7m 7.3g³ 8d* 8.1d⁶ 7.9s³ 8m Nov 1] lengthy horse: poor mover:
fairly useful handicapper: won at Warwick in June: good third to Solar Storm at York
penultimate start, rare poor effort final one: stays 1m: acts on good to firm and soft
ground, below form only start on fibresand: held up. *P. J. Makin*

SHARP RETURN   3 b.c. Sharpo 132 – Langtry Lady 91 (Pas de Seul 133) [1996   53
59: 5m⁴ 6m 6g 5m 6m⁶ 7.6m 6s³ 6d* 6.1s² a7g³ a6g⁴ 1997 a6g⁵ a6g⁶ 6m 6s⁶ 6d 6m
6s a6g 8.2d 7d 6.9d⁴ Oct 21] rather leggy colt: modest performer: stays 7f: acts on
soft ground and the all-weather: blinkered (below form) twice: inconsistent: sent to
Sweden. *M. J. Ryan*

SHA

SHARP SHOOTER (IRE)   2 b.g. (May 12) Sabrehill (USA) 120 – Kermesse   –
(IRE) (Reference Point 139) [1997 5m 6g 6m 6m⁵ 8d Oct 20] 9,000Y: workmanlike
gelding: third foal: dam unraced: signs of only a little ability in maidens and nurseries. *Mrs J. R. Ramsden*

SHARP SHUFFLE (IRE)   4 ch.g. Exactly Sharp (USA) 121 – Style (Homing   83
130) [1996 76: 8m 7.1m³ 8m² 8.5g² 8m² 8m 7g* 8m⁵ 7g³ 1997 8m³ 8f* 10.1m⁶ 8d²   a76
8.1g³ 8m* 9m⁵ 8.1m³ 7.6s 8d 9m 8g a10g a8s⁵ Nov 10] smallish gelding: unimpressive mover: fairly useful performer: won minor event at Brighton in April and
handicap at Goodwood in June: best at 7f to 9f: acts on firm and dead ground,
probably on equitrack: sometimes bandaged: has run well sweating: suited by
waiting tactics. *R. Hannon*

SHARP STEEL   2 ch.g. (Jun 5) Beveled (USA) – Shift Over (USA) 62 (Night   –
Shift (USA)) [1997 5m⁶ 6g 6d Aug 28] 4,400F: leggy gelding: fourth foal: half-
brother to 5-y-o Night Dance: dam, third at 6f at 2 yrs, from family of April Run:
signs of only a little ability in maidens and a claimer: tends to sweat and get on edge.
G. L. Moore

SHARP STOCK   4 b.g. Tina's Pet 121 – Mrewa (Runnymede 123) [1996 –: 6s 6m   65 d
1997 5.1m 5d⁴ 5m 5m 5g⁶ 5g³ 5.1m⁵ 5m 5g 5g 6m Oct 5] sturdy gelding: fair maiden
handicapper: well beaten last 4 starts: probably best at 5f: acts on dead and good to
firm going: visored once: has hung and shown signs of temperament. *R. J. Hodges*

SHARP TEMPER   3 ch.c. Sharpo 132 – Kerali 88 (High Line 125) [1996 NR   84
1997 6.9g³ 7g* 8d⁵ 7m³ 8m 8.1m 9m Oct 4] compact colt: unimpressive mover: sixth
foal: half-brother to 3 winners, including 6f and 1m winner Zerali (by Alzao): dam 7f
winner, half-sister to very smart sprinter So Factual: fairly useful performer: won
maiden at Catterick in April: best effort when third of 17 to Cosmic Prince in £25,000
handicap at Epsom: should stay 1m: acts on good to firm going: sold 20,000 gns in
October, and joined N. Twiston Davies. *B. W. Hills*

SHARP THRILL   6 ch.g. Squill (USA) 122 – Brightelmstone 105 (Prince Regent   32
(FR) 129) [1996 –: a13g⁶ a12g⁶ a12g⁶ 1997 a13g⁵ a13g³ Feb 8] poor maiden: stays
13f: mostly races on all-weather: tried visored/blinkered: inconsistent. *B. Smart*

SHARP TO OBLIGE   10 ch.g. Dublin Taxi – Please Oblige (Le Levanstell 122)   –
[1996 NR 1997 16.2s May 10] of no account. *R. M. Whitaker*

SHARPWITTED   3 b.f. Sadler's Wells (USA) 132 – Oh So Sharp 131 (Kris 135)   58
[1996 NR 1997 7m⁴ 8m⁶ 8.5g⁶ Sep 5] eighth foal: sister to 4-y-o Sacho, closely
related to smart winner at up to 1½m Shaima (by Shareef Dancer), now dam of
Shantou, and half-sister to several winners, including smart 1¼m filly Rosefinch (by
Blushing Groom): dam won 1000 Guineas, Oaks and St Leger: modest form in
maidens: should be suited by 1¼m+. *J. H. M. Gosden*

SHART (IRE)   2 b.c. (Mar 8) Last Tycoon 131 – Simaat (USA) 72 (Mr Prospector   90
(USA)) [1997 7m² 7.1m³ 6d³ Oct 17] unfurnished colt: good mover: first foal: dam
1m winner: fairly useful form in maidens at Leicester, Haydock and Newmarket,
needing to be switched but beaten only narrowly behind Atuf on last-named course:
not short of speed, but bred to stay 1m: sure to win a race. *J. H. M. Gosden*

SHARWAY LADY   2 b.f. (Apr 2) Shareef Dancer (USA) 135 – Eladale (IRE)   44
(Ela-Mana-Mou 132) [1997 a7g a6g a7g Dec 18] 1,000Y, 800 2-y-o: second foal:
dam unraced: well beaten in maidens and seller. *B. A. McMahon*

SHASHI (IRE)   5 br.m. Shaadi (USA) 126 – Homely Touch 84 (Touching Wood   58
(USA) 127) [1996 67: 5m 6m 7g 6g⁴ 6f⁶ 5.9f* 5.1m² 5m⁵ 6.1m 7f 7.1s 6m a6g* a6g⁶
a6s² 1997 a6g⁶ a6g⁵ a6g a6g⁴ 7g⁵ a7g⁴ a6g 7m 6.1d³ 6s 6.9m* 6.9m⁵ 7m⁵ 6m³ 6m
6.9f 7m³ 6.1m⁶ 7d Oct 14] smallish mare: modest handicapper: won claimer (not at
best) at Folkestone in July: effective at 5f to 7f: acts on firm ground, dead (possibly
not soft) and the all-weather: effective in blinkers (not worn them for some time), ran
poorly in visor. *Pat Mitchell*

SHASKA   3 ch.f. Kris 135 – Dance Machine 111 (Green Dancer (USA) 132) [1996   90 p
NR 1997 10g⁶ 10s* 10g² Sep 18] rangy, rather unfurnished filly: sixth foal: closely
related to Halling (by Diesis) and 2-y-o Grazia and half-sister to 2 winners in France
at 1m by Bering: dam 7f and 1¼m winner: progressive form: landed odds in slowly-

run maiden at Sandown in August: very good second of 17 in handicap at Newbury following month: will stay 1½m: open to further improvement. *J. H. M. Gosden*

SHAVELING 2 ch.c. (Apr 1) Sharpo 132 – Sancta 106 (So Blessed 130) [1997 73 p 7m⁶ Nov 4] closely related to smart 7f (at 2 yrs) and 1¼m winner Carmelite House (by Diesis) and 1¼m winner Khrisma (by Kris) and half-brother to 3 winners, including 7-y-o Saint Keyne (formerly useful stayer): dam 1m and 1¼m winner: 7/1, keeping-on sixth to Gypsy Passion in Redcar maiden, slightly hampered at start, not knocked out: will do better. *Mrs J. Cecil*

SHAVINSKY 4 b.c. Shavian 125 – Alteza Real 84 (Mansingh (USA) 120) [1996 – 69: 8m 8m⁶ 8.1d a8g 6m² 6m 6m² 6g⁶ 5.2m⁵ 1997 5g 6.1g 6m 6s a5g a6g Aug 15] lengthy, good-topped colt: fair 6f maiden: no show in handicaps in 1997. *P. Howling*

SHAWAF (USA) 3 b.c. Mr Prospector (USA) – Shadayid (USA) 122 (Shadeed 98 (USA) 135) [1996 80p: 6m³ 1997 7g* 7g⁵ 8.2m³ a7f* a6f² a6f Oct 19] rather leggy colt: won maiden (idled) at Newmarket in April and (first start after leaving J. Dunlop) allowance race at Saratoga in August, latter by 10 lengths: seems to stay 1m: raced only on good/good to firm going on turf, acts on dirt: raced on medication in USA. *K. McLaughlin, USA*

SHAWDON 2 b.c. (Feb 6) Inchinor 119 – Play With Me (IRE) 73 (Alzao (USA) 96 117) [1997 5s 6.1g* 6m* 5g* 6d⁶ 7m⁵ 6g* 6f² 5m² 6g Oct 25] smallish, well-made colt: first foal: dam 1¼m winner, half-sister to Italian Oaks winner Lady Bentley out of half-sister to smart stayer Yawa: useful performer: won maiden at Nottingham in May, minor events at Yarmouth and Ripon in June, and nursery at Epsom in September: rare poor effort final start (sold 18,000 gns shortly after it): effective at 5f and 6f: acts on firm ground, well beaten both starts on softer than good: often front runner. *Sir Mark Prescott*

SHAWM 3 b.c. Alzao (USA) 117 – Flute (USA) 87 (Woodman (USA) 126) [1996 104 84p: 7g³ 1997 8.2m² 7.5d⁴ 7m⁶ 7.1g² 8g* 8m 8.1s* 8.1m* 7.9s Oct 8] lengthy colt: useful performer: won maiden (simple task) at Ripon in July and handicaps at Sandown in August and Haydock (held Desert Beauty by ¾ length, pair clear) in September: something possibly amiss final start: stays 1m: acts on good to firm and soft going: has had tongue tied and shown tendency to hang: fitted with crossed noseband last 3 starts: sold approx. £178,000 in Dubai in November. *D. R. Loder*

SHAYA 3 ch.c. Nashwan (USA) 135 – Gharam (USA) 108 (Green Dancer (USA) 111 132) [1996 86P: 8f² 1997 10.4g² 10m² 10m² 10g* 14.6ᵢ₁₁ 12f¹ Oct 3] big, lengthy colt: has scope: fluent mover: smart performer: won maiden at Sandown in August: much better form when about 11 lengths seventh of 10 to Silver Patriarch in St Leger at Doncaster and 2 lengths last of 4 to Mons in falsely-run listed race at Newmarket: may prove suited by around 1½m: raced only on good going or firmer: has carried head high. *Major W. R. Hern*

SHAYNES DOMAIN 6 b.g. Dominion 123 – Glen Na Smole 86 (Ballymore – 123) [1996 45: a7g a8g a6g⁵ a6g 6m 10m 7d³ 6m 7g 1997 a7g a7g⁶ a8g 8f Apr 21] lengthy gelding: poor handicapper: well held in 1997: usually blinkered. *R. M. Flower*

SHEATH KEFAAH 4 ch.c. Kefaah (USA) 124 – Wasslaweyeh (USA) 66 – (Damascus (USA)) [1996 NR 1997 8.3m Aug 11] signs of only a little ability in 3 runs on flat: winning hurdler. *J. R. Jenkins*

SHECANDO (IRE) 2 ch.f. (Mar 23) Second Set (IRE) 127 – Carado 82 (Manado 53 130) [1997 6m 5.7g 6g 7.6m 6m⁶ Sep 26] 9,000Y: fifth foal: half-sister to 4-y-o Siege Perilous and 6f winner In The Game (by Mummy's Game): dam 1m winner later successful over hurdles: modest form first 2 starts, but showed little after: visored in claimer final start. *C. James*

SHEDANSAR (IRE) 5 b.g. In The Wings 128 – Evening Kiss (Kris 135) [1996 – –: a12g a13g a13g a13g a16g⁶ 11.5m a11g a8g a8g 1997 a12g Jan 24] no form. *R. C. Spicer*

SHEEFIN (IRE) 3 b.f. Danehill (USA) 126 – Starlust 79 (Sallust 134) [1996 7g⁵ 63 d 1997 8m 12s 8.5g⁴ 12s 9s a14g Dec 18] IR 2,800F, IR 50,000Y: ex-Irish filly: half-sister to several winners, including useful Bronzewing (up to 1m, by Beldale

Flutter) and fair Travel Storm (1¼m, by Lord Gayle): dam 2-y-o 5f winner: modest maiden at best: trained by N. Meade until before final start: stays 1½m. *J. Parkes*

SHEEMORE (IRE) 4 b.g. Don't Forget Me 127 – Curie Abu (Crofter (USA) 35 124) [1996 46: a8.5g 10g⁵ 1997 a12g⁵ a16g 13d 10g Apr 28] big gelding: has a round action: poor maiden: seems to stay 1½m: tail swisher. *M. D. Hammond*

SHEEP STEALER 9 gr.g. Absalom 128 – Kilroe's Calin (Be Friendly 130) – [1996 NR 1997 12.1g a14g⁵ 10g⁶ 12d 11.5f⁵ a10g a12g Nov 15] workmanlike gelding: second foal: dam winning hurdler/chaser: modest hurdler/chaser: signs of ability but no worthwhile form. *R. E. Peacock*

SHEER DANZIG (IRE) 5 b.h. Roi Danzig (USA) – Sheer Audacity (Troy 137) 108 [1996 105: 10g 9s 10m³ 10g⁴ 10m³ 11.9m² 11.1m⁵ 12g² 12s 1997 12m* 12m⁴ 14.1g² 10m⁵ 12s Nov 8] tall, rangy horse: impresses in appearance: useful performer: won minor event (easily) at Doncaster in March: good second to Nabhaan in similar race at Nottingham following month: reportedly had bone chip removed from near-fore in May: best subsequent effort when fifth to Saafeya in steadily-run listed event at Newmarket: stays 1¾m: best on good going or firmer, also acts on fibresand: usually held up. *R. W. Armstrong*

SHEER FACE 3 b.c. Midyan (USA) 124 – Rock Face 77 (Ballad Rock 122) 84 [1996 85: 7.1m⁶ 7m⁵ 7f* 7.3m² 8m* 7m⁴ 8d³ 1997 10m 8.1d 9s² 10m 10m 9m³ 10m⁴ 8g² 10.3m 8.1m³ 8.1g⁵ 8m Oct 5] close-coupled colt: fairly useful handicapper: seems best at 1m/9f: yet to race on heavy going, acts on any other: consistent. *W. R. Muir*

SHEER FOLLY (USA) 3 ch.c. Woodman (USA) 126 – Why So Much (USA) – (Northern Baby (CAN) 127) [1996 88: 7m* 1997 11.8d⁶ 8g 8.3m Aug 23] tall colt: fairly useful form when winning maiden at Kempton (carried head high) at 2 yrs: showed little in 1997, and sold only 1,800 gns in October. *P. F. I. Cole*

SHEGARDI 2 b.c. (Apr 18) Primo Dominie 121 – Party Doll 108 (Be My Guest 89 (USA) 126) [1997 5d² 5f² 5g a5s* Nov 10] 200,000Y: smallish, lightly-made colt: fourth foal: half-brother to 4-y-o Titus Livius: dam French 5f (at 2 yrs) to 1m winner: fairly useful form: blinkered, won maiden at Lingfield on first start for nearly 5 months: best turf effort on debut: speedy: sent to USA. *D. R. Loder*

SHEILA-B 2 ch.f. (Mar 27) Formidable (USA) 125 – Good Woman 60 (Good 54 p Times (ITY)) [1997 6g Oct 24] 2,000F: sixth foal: half-sister to 3 winners, including 2-y-o 6f winners Gangleader and Lady Thiang (both by Petong), latter successful at 1m in France in 1997: dam, maiden who probably stayed 6f, half-sister to smart 1985 2-y-o 5f and 7f winner Moorgate Man: 33/1 and in need of run, around 9 lengths ninth to Mister Rambo in maiden at Newbury, good speed 4f: sure to do better. *P. J. Makin*

SHEILAS DREAM 4 b.f. Inca Chief (USA) – Windlass (Persian Bold 123) 41 [1996 53: a7g⁶ a9.4g² a7g 8.5f² 1997 10m 10m⁶ a8g 11.6m⁵ 11.6m⁶ a10g⁶ Aug 9] poor maiden handicapper: stays 1¼m: acts on firm going and fibresand: below form in visor/blinkers. *G. L. Moore*

SHELTEEZ (USA) 3 b. or br.f. St Jovite (USA) 135 – Dictina (FR) (Dictus (FR) 55 + 126) [1996 NR 1997 10g 10g 8.2d 16m² 16m² 17.1g³ Aug 17] IR 34,000Y: tall, lengthy filly: seventh foal: half-sister to several winners, including fairly useful pair Dilazar (1m, by Zilzal) and Legal View (9f, by Riverman): dam Grade 3 9f winner: modest handicapper: ridden by 5-lb claimer last 3 starts, unlucky at Pontefract on final one: thorough stayer: unraced on extremes of going. *M. Bell*

SHELTERING SKY (IRE) 3 b.c. Selkirk (USA) 129 – Shimmering Sea 89 90 p (Slip Anchor 136) [1996 NR 1997 8m⁶ 7.1d* 7m² 7d⁵ 7g³ Oct 18] IR 12,000Y: angular colt: second foal: half-brother to 4-y-o Sea Dane: dam, 2-y-o 5f and 7f winner who stayed 1m, half-sister to Petoski: fairly useful form: won maiden at Haydock in July: good efforts in handicaps after, best of stand-side group when third of 29 to Desert Beauty at Newmarket final start: will stay 1m: has been bandaged: type to progress, and should do well in handicaps in 1998. *J. L. Dunlop*

SHEPHERDS REST (IRE) 5 b.g. Accordion – Mandy's Last (Krayyan 117) – [1996 27: a12g³ 1997 a12g³ Jan 3] poor maiden: pulls hard, and is worth another try over short of 1½m: fair hurdler. *S. Mellor*

SHERATON GIRL 3 b.f. Mon Tresor 113 – Sara Sprint (Formidable (USA) –
125) [1996 49d: 5g⁵ 5m³ 5m 6m⁴ 5m⁵ a5g⁵ 8f⁵ 7.5m⁴ 8.1m 1997 a8.5g a9.4g⁶ a7g* a41
7.5d a8.5g⁵ 7.1g 7m Aug 15] sturdy filly: poor performer: won handicap at Southwell
in April, only form at 3 yrs: probably best around 7f: acts on fibresand and good to
firm going, soundly beaten on dead: blinkered (ran poorly) twice at 2 yrs: tends to
hang right: inconsistent. *N. P. Littmoden*

SHERAZ (IRE) 5 b.g. Persian Bold 123 – Miss Siddons (Cure The Blues (USA)) 50
[1996 61d, a68d: 8s⁶ 12m⁵ 10.3g 12g 7.1d a8g* a8g⁶ 7.1d⁵ 10.5g a8g a7g⁶ a8g a10g⁴
a12g⁴ a11g⁶ 1997 a10g⁴ a10g² a10g² a12g⁵ a10g⁴ 8m⁴ 8m 8d⁵ 7m⁴ 8d⁶ 8m 7g Oct
24] strong gelding: carries condition: fluent mover: modest handicapper: very best
form at 7f to 1¼m: acts on the all-weather and on good to firm and dead ground: often
tongue tied: blinkered nowadays. *N. Tinkler*

SHERGANZAR 2 b.c. (Mar 10) Shernazar 131 – Victory Kingdom (CAN) 76
(Viceregal (CAN)) [1997 8.1d³ 7m⁶ 8d⁵ 6d⁵ 8s⁶ Nov 8] 30,000 2-y-o: lengthy,
good-topped colt: half-brother to numerous winners, including sprinters Tharwa (by
Last Tycoon) and Prince Azzaan (by Rousillon) and the dams of 5-y-o Bin Rosie and
useful 1993 2-y-o The Deep (by Shernazar): dam won 5 times in USA: similar form
all starts: stays 1m. *M. Salaman*

SHERIFF 6 b.g. Midyan (USA) 124 – Daisy Warwick (USA) 91 (Ribot 142) –
[1996 60: a16g* 14.9g² 16m⁵ a16g⁴ 1997 14.1d 14.1g 17.2m⁵ Aug 12] small, close-
coupled gelding: bad mover: modest staying handicapper at 5 yrs: below form in
blinkers: fairly useful hurdler. *J. W. Hills*

SHERMOOD 4 b.f. Shere Khan – Jalebird Blues (Jalmood (USA) 126) [1996 42, 31
a–: a7g⁵ 10m 8m 6f⁶ 7g⁴ 8m 7g⁵ 8m³ a10g⁶ 7d³ 8m 7m 7m a6g a8g⁵ a7g 1997 a7g a–
a5g⁶ 7m 8.3s 6f⁶ 6.9m 6.9s 6.9m⁵ 7m 8m a7g Aug 15] leggy, lightly-made filly: poor
maiden: stays 1m: acts on firm and dead ground (no form on all-weather). *K. T. Ivory*

SHERPA (IRE) 2 ch.g. (Mar 22) Shernazar 131 – Ezana (Ela-Mana-Mou 132) –
[1997 7g Aug 13] seventh foal: half-brother to 2 Irish middle-distance winners,
notably Ebaziya (smart, also 7f winner at 2 yrs, by Darshaan), dam of 3-y-o Ebadiyla:
dam, French 11.5f winner, half-sister to French Group 3 winner Demia: 50/1, behind
in minor event at Salisbury, never near leaders after sluggish start: sold 7,000 gns in
October, and sent to Germany. *D. R. C. Elsworth*

SHEROY (IRE) 5 br.g. Persian Bold 123 – Turkish Treasure (USA) 111 (Sir Ivor 65
135) [1996 NR 1997 a8g a10g 10.1g 12.3m² 12g⁴ 13.1g⁴ 13g² 11.9d 12m* 12g⁵ 12m³
9.9m⁵ 12.4m* 12v⁶ a12g³ a12s a12s² Dec 21] close-coupled gelding: has been
hobdayed: fair performer: won amateurs minor event at Carlisle and seller at Newcastle in the summer for S. Kettlewell: placed twice in Sweden: stays 13f: acts on
firm and dead ground, seemingly on dirt. *C. Bjorling, Sweden*

SHERZETTO 3 b.f. Classic Music (USA) – Lake Isle (IRE) (Caerleon (USA) –
132) [1996 68: 6m 6f* 6d⁴ a6g 1997 a7g a6g 8.2g 6f May 29] smallish, sturdy filly:
fair form when winning maiden as 2-y-o: no encouragement in 1997: sold 7,500 gns
in December, in foal to Efisio. *R. T. Phillips*

SHE'S A CRACKER 3 b.f. Deploy 131 – Red Secret (IRE) 49 (Valiyar 129) –
[1996 –: 8m 1997 8.2d⁴ 8.3g a9.4g a7g a9.4g⁶ Dec 26] only a little sign of ability in
maidens/handicaps. *Mrs N. Macauley*

SHE'S A GEM 2 b.f. (Mar 22) Robellino (USA) 127 – Rose Gem (IRE) 62 58
(Taufan (USA) 119) [1997 8s a8.5g⁵ a7g³ Dec 18] 1,400 2-y-o: smallish filly: first
foal: dam probably best at 7f: modest form: hung left when favourite for seller final
start. *Mrs N. Macauley*

SHE'S A MADAM 6 b.m. Kabour 80 – Mrs Buzby 71 (Abwah 118) [1996 –: a5g –
5m a6g a5g 1997 a6g a6g Jan 10] of little account. *L. R. Lloyd-James*

SHE'S A WINNER (IRE) 4 ch.f. Classic Music (USA) – Eyre Square (IRE) –
(Flash of Steel 120) [1996 49: 8.3d* 8.3s⁵ 9g⁶ 9.2g 8m 1997 8d³ 12m 14g Jun 16]
leggy filly: no sign of retaining ability at 4 yrs. *P. Monteith*

SHE'S DAWAN (IRE) 3 b.f. Taufan (USA) 119 – Bellinzona (Northfields 52
(USA)) [1996 –p: 7f 1997 a6g³ a7g² 6.9g Mar 26] modest form when placed in
maidens at Lingfield in January/February: will be suited by 1m+. *P. Mitchell*

863

SHE'S ELECTRIC 3 ch.f. Superlative 118 – What A Looker (USA) (Raise A – Native) [1996 –: a6g a6g a7g a5g⁶ 1997 a7g⁶ 10m 7.6g 6m Aug 19] of no account. *J. J. Bridger*

SHE'S SIMPLY GREAT (IRE) 4 b.f. Simply Great (FR) 122 – Petrine (IRE) – (Petorius 117) [1996 54: 11.1g² 11.1g⁴ 10m 8f 8g² 8.1m 10g² 10s⁶ 1997 10g 10m⁵ 8g 8m 8m a9.4g⁶ Aug 16] smallish filly: modest maiden handicapper at up to 11f in 1996: no form at 4 yrs. *J. J. O'Neill*

SHFOUG (USA) 2 b.f. (Jan 31) Sheikh Albadou 128 – Pure Misk 55 (Rainbow 85 p Quest (USA) 134) [1997 6m³ 7s* Oct 16] first foal: dam twice-raced half-sister to useful 1993 2-y-o 6f winner Fast Eddy and useful 1¼m performer Stone Mill: shaped well in minor event at Ascot (very free to post) on debut, and won maiden at Catterick by short head from Sharp Cracker, held up and ridden to lead near finish: should stay 1m: should do better yet. *B. W. Hills*

SHIFT AGAIN (IRE) 5 b.m. Siberian Express (USA) 125 – Pushkinia (FR) 95 – (Pharly (FR) 130) [1996 63+: 10g 12.1d 12g⁵ 1997 14.1g 16s Oct 15] tall mare: formerly fair performer: well beaten in 1997: blinkered last 3 starts: tends to carry head high. *O. Sherwood*

SHIFTING 2 ch.f. (Mar 3) Night Shift (USA) – Preening 62 (Persian Bold 123) 68 [1997 6d³ 6m⁵ 7.1m a7g Nov 21] workmanlike filly: third reported foal: half-sister to a winner in Switzerland by Alzao: dam 1½m winner from good family: fair form: best effort in minor event at Doncaster on debut: should stay at least 7f. *C. W. Thornton*

SHIFTING MOON 5 b.g. Night Shift (USA) – Moonscape 87 (Ribero 126) – [1996 –: 10s 1997 10.2f⁶ Jul 23] stocky gelding: poor mover: fairly useful handi-capper at 3 yrs: lightly raced and well beaten since: tried visored/blinkered: modest winning hurdler. *F. Jordan*

SHIFTING TIME 3 b.f. Night Shift (USA) – Timely Raise (USA) (Raise A Man 58 (USA)) [1996 70: 6m⁴ 6m 6m² 1997 6d 5m⁴ 6m 5g 7f Jul 15] attractive filly: modest maiden: should stay further than 6f: acts on good to firm going: sold 11,500 gns in December, and joined Lord Huntingdon. *I. A. Balding*

SHIFTY MOUSE 2 b.f. (May 10) Night Shift (USA) – Top Mouse (High Top 44 131) [1997 6m 6g Aug 20] useful-looking filly: half-sister to several winners, including 5f winner Idrak (by Young Generation) and 4-y-o Chief Mouse: dam twice-raced from good family: signs of ability first start, well beaten in seller second. *D. Morley*

SHII-TAKE 3 b.c. Deploy 131 – Super Sally 108 (Superlative 118) [1996 91: 6m² 103 7m² 7m* 7d³ 1997 8m 8m 10d³ 16.2m Jun 18] compact colt: has a round action: useful performer: similar form first 3 starts when seventh at Newmarket in Craven Stakes and 2000 Guineas (beaten 9½ lengths) and third to Grapeshot in listed race at Goodwood (beaten 3½ lengths): beat only one in Queen's Vase at Royal Ascot: will stay beyond 1¼m, but not sure to get 2m: yet to race on extremes of going: usually a front runner. *R. Akehurst*

SHILLING (IRE) 3 b.f. Bob Back (USA) 124 – Quiche 83 (Formidable (USA) 64 125) [1996 NR 1997 10m 11.9f³ 10d⁴ 12g² 14.1g 12f⁴ a12g Oct 18] IR 4,000Y: plain filly: third foal: half-sister to useful Irish sprinter Symboli Kildare (by Kaldoun) and a winner in Japan by Dancehall: dam 6f winner: modest maiden: suited by 1½m: acts on firm going, below best on fibresand: sold 20,000 gns after final start. *A. C. Stewart*

SHIMAAL 2 b.f. (Mar 19) Sadler's Wells (USA) 132 – Grace Note (FR) 99 (Top 95 Ville 129) [1997 7m² 8.2g⁴ Sep 23] useful-looking, unfurnished filly: ninth foal: closely related to Belmez (by El Gran Senor) and useful Irish middle-distance per-former Dowland (by Sovereign Dancer) and half-sister to 1½m winner Dvorak (by Darshaan): dam 1¼m winner (stayed 1½m) from good family: 10/1 from 6/1, 1¾ lengths second to Ashraakat in maiden at Newmarket (had tongue tied, and didn't impress to post): uneasy favourite, well below that form in similar event at Not-tingham month later, not taking turn well and dropping away quickly: bred to be suited by 1¼m/1½m. *Saeed bin Suroor*

SHINDIUM 2 b.f. (Feb 9) Presidium 124 – Shining Wood 65 (Touching Wood 37 (USA) 127) [1997 5m⁵ 7d Oct 16] 3,000 2-y-o: lengthy filly: second foal: dam, maiden, stayed 1¾m: better effort in sellers 6 months apart on debut. *C. A. Dwyer*

SHINEROLLA 5 b.g. Thatching 131 – Primrolla 64 (Relko 136) [1996 88: a7g³ 82
8s⁴ 8d 8.1d 1997 a8.5g⁵ 8m² 8.5d 8.3g 8m 8g Oct 18] tall gelding: fairly useful a92
handicapper on all-weather, fair on turf: best efforts of 1997 on first 2 starts: stays
1¼m: acts on fibresand and probably any turf going: held up: effective blinkered.
C. Parker

SHINING CLOUD 4 ch.f. Indian Ridge 123 – Hardiheroine 76 (Sandhurst 73 d
Prince 128) [1996 71: 6g 7.1d 6.1m* 5m³ 1997 6m 6g 6g 5.2s³ 6g⁵ 6.1m⁵ 7f Oct 29]
lengthy filly: fair handicapper: easily best effort at 4 yrs on reappearance: probably
best at 6f: acts on good to firm ground: blinkered final start: front runner. *M. Bell*

SHINING DANCER 5 b.m. Rainbow Quest (USA) 134 – Strike Home 82 (Be 71
My Guest (USA) 126) [1996 66: 10m⁶ 10m* 10m 12g³ 12g³ 11.5d³ 12m² 16s
1997 16g³ 12m 16g* 20m⁵ 14g³ 16.2m 20m 14g 16.2g⁵ 14.6g Oct 24] angular mare:
has a markedly round action: fair handicapper: well ridden by J. Egan to win at
Kempton in May: better than position suggests last 2 starts: effective at 1¾m to 2½m:
acts on good to firm and dead ground, well beaten both outings on soft: takes good
hold and suited by strong handling. *S. Dow*

SHINING EXAMPLE 5 ch.g. Hadeer 118 – Kick The Habit 94 (Habitat 134) 75
[1996 75: 10m⁶ 10m* 12m⁵ 10m⁶ 8.9g⁶ 10s 1997 10g 10s 10g⁵ 9g* 8.1s 10m 9g² 10s
Oct 14] strong, workmanlike gelding: fair handicapper: won amateurs event (comfortably) at Goodwood in June: badly hampered final start: stays 1¼m: acts on good
to firm ground, soft and fibresand: sometimes sweats: sold (to join J. J. O'Neill)
14,000 gns in November. *P. J. Makin*

SHIPLEY GLEN 2 b.c. (Feb 9) Green Desert (USA) 127 – Lady Shipley 111 – p
(Shirley Heights 130) [1997 6s 6g 6d Nov 7] 46,000Y: sturdy colt: fourth foal:
half-brother to a winner in Spain by Rousillon: dam, 7f (at 2 yrs) and 1¼m winner
who stayed 1½m, daughter of Lowther winner Circus Ring: signs of ability though in
rear in maidens, pulling hard and knocked about final start: should do better at 3 yrs.
Sir Mark Prescott

SHIP'S DANCER 4 b.f. Shareef Dancer (USA) 135 – Sunderland (Dancer's 30
Image (USA)) [1996 56d: 10.8g 12m⁴ 14.1m⁵ 14.1f³ 14.1f⁶ 16.2f⁴ 12f⁶ 15.8g 11.1g
13.8g 16.1m⁶ 1997 a16g a14g 16.1g 12m 12.3m 14.1m 16.2m 16f⁵ 17.2m 16.2m
14.1m³ 15.8g⁴ 16m⁴ 16.2d³ Aug 14] poor handicapper: a stayer: acts on good to firm
and dead ground: usually blinkered/visored. *Don Enrico Incisa*

SHIRAZAN (IRE) 3 b.g. Doyoun 124 – Sharaniya (USA) 117 (Alleged (USA) –
138) [1996 NR 1997 10g 10g Jun 16] sixth foal: half-brother to 4 winners, including
useful Irish 4-y-o Sharazan (1½m to 2m, by Akarad): dam, smart French performer
up to 1½m, half-sister to Prix Vermeille winner Sharaya: signs of ability though well
held in maidens at Windsor: joined J. Glover and gelded. *L. M. Cumani*

SHIRLATY 4 b.f. Shirley Heights 130 – Jameelaty (USA) 96 (Nureyev (USA) –
131) [1996 –: 10.5d 8.2s 1997 13g a12g Jul 26] quite well bred, but of little account
on the course: in foal to Selkirk. *C. W. Thornton*

SHIRLEYS GIRL (IRE) 2 br.f. (Apr 22) Contract Law (USA) 108 – Maiden's –
Dance 65 (Hotfoot 126) [1997 6g 5s 5g 6g 5g Aug 28] 3,800Y: angular, quite
good-topped filly: fifth foal: half-sister to 3 winners, including fairly useful 1m and
9f winner Dancing Monarch (by Dara Monarch): dam, maiden who stayed 1m, possibly temperamental: no promise, mainly in sellers: visored final start. *W. Storey*

SHIRLEY SUE 4 b.f. Shirley Heights 130 – Dame Ashfield 90 (Grundy 137) 79
[1996 76: 8.1g 12.5f 13g* 14.1m⁶ a14g* a12g² 16.1m* 16g* 16m⁴ 16s² 15.9d 16g⁶
17.5m² 17.1m⁴ 16.5s⁵ 1997 16.2m² 17.1m² 14s 16.5m⁶ 20m² 20m³ 16.1g⁴ 16.1g⁵
17.5d⁶ 18g 16.5s Nov 8] sturdy filly: fair handicapper: suited by thorough test of
stamina: acts on fibresand, good to firm and soft ground: flashes tail: usually races
prominently: genuine and consistent: sold 32,000 gns in December. *M. Johnston*

SHIRLEY VENTURE 4 b.f. Be My Chief (USA) 122 – Our Shirley 84 (Shirley 71
Heights 130) [1996 74: 12g² 12m³ 12m 14g⁵ 14.1m³ 16.2g³ 14m⁵ a13g⁴ 1997 15.4m²
Apr 22] unfurnished filly: fair maiden: may well stay beyond 2m: raced only on
good/good to firm going on turf (poor effort on equitrack): sold (to join Miss
V. Williams) 12,000 gns in July. *S. P. C. Woods*

SHIRTY 3 b.g. Shirley Heights 130 – Sassy Lassy (IRE) 70 (Taufan (USA) 119) [1996 NR 1997 11.5m⁵ Aug 6] second reported foal: half-brother to French 9f and 1¼m winner Sandalo (by Royal Academy): dam 7f winner, granddaughter of Poule d'Essai des Pouliches winner Pampered Miss: tailed off in maiden at Yarmouth: sold 700 gns in September. *D. Morley* –

SHMOOSE (IRE) 2 b.f. (Jan 26) Caerleon (USA) 132 – Kerrera 115 (Diesis 133) [1997 6m* 6m Sep 30] well-made filly: has a quick, fluent action: fourth foal: half-sister to fairly useful winner 7f winner Kerry Ring (by Sadler's Wells) and a 1m/1¼m winner abroad by Nashwan: dam, half-sister to Rock City, runner-up in 1000 Guineas but headstrong and as effective sprinting: came with big reputation when landing odds of 3/1 on in maiden at Newbury in August by 1½ lengths from Musical Twist, making all and clear when veering sharply left final 1f: very easy to back (had reportedly had bruised foot) when beating only one in Cheveley Park Stakes at Newmarket 6 weeks later, dropping away tamely. *Saeed bin Suroor* 101 +

SHMOOZY 8 b.m. Nomination 125 – Myricagale 68 (Wollow 132) [1996 NR 1997 9.2d 5g Apr 17] signs of ability only start in 1991, none in claimers as 8-y-o. *J. S. Goldie* –

SHOCKER (IRE) 2 b.f. (May 10) Sabrehill (USA) 120 – Fenjaan 77 (Trojan Fen 118) [1997 5d a6g a6g⁶ Nov 17] fourth foal: half-sister to 1¼m winner Shehab (by Persian Bold) and a winner in Dubai by Doyoun: dam miler from family of Royal Palace: signs of ability in maidens, on final start (at Southwell) considerably handled and banned for 30 days under non-triers' rule: should do better. *W. J. Haggas* 47 p

SHOCK VALUE (IRE) 3 b.c. Danehill (USA) 126 – Rince Deas (IRE) 53 (Alzao (USA) 117) [1996 98p: 6m* 6f⁶ 7m⁴ 1997 9m⁶ 7s⁴ 7g⁶ 6g Oct 24] sturdy colt: good mover: useful performer: fourth in minor event at Yarmouth in July: very free to post when running poorly final start (sold 20,000 gns shortly after it): should stay at least 1m: acts on good to firm and soft going. *M. R. Stoute* 95

SHOHRA WA JAAH 2 b.g. (Apr 3) Mtoto 134 – Pipina (USA) 81 (Sir Gaylord) [1997 8f 8.2d⁶ Oct 30] good-topped gelding: brother to fairly useful middle-distance maiden Pipers Pool, closely related to winning stayer Pipitina (by Bustino) and smart 1¼m to 1½m winner Pipsted (by Busted) and half-brother to several winners: dam, 10.5f winner, half-sister to Amaranda and Favoridge: burly and green still, 6½ lengths sixth to Eliza Acton in maiden at Nottingham, not knocked about: likely to do better over further than 1m. *M. A. Jarvis* 61 p

SHOJA 4 ch.g. Persian Bold 123 – Dancing Berry (Sadler's Wells (USA) 132) [1996 –: 11f 12g 1997 a8g Jan 3] no sign of ability. *Mrs V. A. Aconley* –

SHONARA'S WAY 6 b.m. Slip Anchor 136 – Favorable Exchange (USA) (Exceller (USA) 129) [1996 –: 13.1m 1997 16s Nov 6] leggy mare: useful handicapper at 4 yrs: tailed off both starts since: modest staying hurdler, won in December. *P. Monteith* –

SHONTAINE 4 b.g. Pharly (FR) 130 – Hinari Televideo 97 (Caerleon (USA) 132) [1996 65: a6g⁴ a7g⁶ 6g 6m 7f³ 7s⁶ 7.1g² 7g* 7m³ 7m 6d 7g⁵ a6g³ 6.9d³ 7s 8.1s a7g³ a7g* a8g⁶ a7g⁶ 1997 a7g⁴ a7g a7g a6g* a6g 7m⁶ 8.2m 5.9g 7.1m⁴ a7g² 6.9f* 7.5g 6g⁶ 8g³ a6g⁶ 7.5v 6m⁴ 6g⁵ 8m* 6d 6d 7m² 8.3g* a8g⁶ 8m 8s⁵ a8s³ a7g³ a8g⁵ a7g⁴ Dec 10] small gelding: fair performer: won claimer at Lingfield in March and handicaps at Carlisle in May, Thirsk (seller) in August and Hamilton in September: suited by good test at 6f and stays 1m: acts on firm and soft going and all-weather: tough. *M. Johnston* 65 a61

SHOOTING LIGHT (IRE) 4 b.g. Shernazar 131 – Church Light 88 (Caerleon (USA) 132) [1996 79: 10g² 12.1s* 14.1m³ 14g³ 14d⁴ 14m 16.2m 1997 14s* Aug 30] rangy gelding: fairly useful handicapper: won at Sandown in August, on only start of 1997: should stay 2m: acts on good to firm and soft ground: smart hurdler. *P. G. Murphy* 82

SHOOTING STAR (IRE) 3 b.c. Polish Precedent (USA) 131 – Outstandingly (USA) (Exclusive Native (USA)) [1996 NR 1997 10g⁵ 10d⁴ 10d a12g Oct 6] workmanlike colt: half-brother to, amongst others, smart French miler Sensation (by Soviet Star): dam won from 5.5f (at 2 yrs) to 9f, including Breeders' Cup Juvenile 69

Fillies: form only when fourth in maiden at Ripon in August, dictating pace: visored last 3 starts: sold approx. £21,000 in Dubai in November. *J. H. M. Gosden*

SHORELEAVE 3 ch.c. Superlative 118 – Lunagraphe (USA) (Time For A Change (USA)) [1996 NR 1997 16f⁶ May 28] first foal: dam, little worthwhile form in Britain, out of half-sister to high-class 7f to 9f winner in USA Polish Navy: tailed-off last in claimer at Yarmouth. *Bob Jones* –

SHORT ROMANCE (IRE) 2 b.f. (Apr 9) Brief Truce (USA) 126 – Lady's Turn (Rymer 121) [1997 6.1m⁴ 7m³ 7d 7.6m³ 8m⁴ Sep 25] 8,800Y: fair sort: half-sister to Irish 9f and 1½m winner Myella Prince and Irish 11f and 2m winner From The Hip (both by Coquelin): dam ran once: modest maiden: in frame in nurseries at Lingfield and Goodwood last 2 starts: will stay beyond 1m. *J. W. Hills* 63

SHOSHALOZA (USA) 3 ch.f. Diesis 133 – Martha Sophia (USA) (Drone) [1996 NR 1997 7g⁴ 7.1d⁴ 7g⁵ 8g 8.1m⁶ 8.2d Oct 30] sparely-made filly: first foal: dam, won 4 minor races in USA, half-sister to Lancashire Oaks winner Pharian and useful sprinter Raah Algharb: modest maiden: stiff tasks in handicaps last 3 starts: should stay at least 1m: acts on dead going, probably on good to firm. *P. R. Webber* 59

SHOTLEY MARIE (IRE) 2 b.f. (Apr 8) Scenic 128 – Hana Marie 101§ (Formidable (USA) 125) [1997 6.1m 7s 6g Oct 22] 5,000Y: third foal: dam 2-y-o sprint winner, became untrustworthy: behind in maidens, blinkered final start. *N. Bycroft* –

SHOTLEY PRINCESS 3 ch.f. Risk Me (FR) 127 – Miss Camellia 70 (Sonnen Gold 121) [1996 –: 5d⁶ a5g⁴ a5g 6m a5g 5m 5f 1997 a8g 12.1s⁶ 9.9v 8g Jul 8] of little account. *N. Bycroft* –

SHOUK 3 b.f. Shirley Heights 130 – Souk (IRE) 98 (Ahonoora 122) [1996 81p: 7m 7m² 1997 10g 10.5s* May 5] rangy filly: second foal: closely related to 4-y-o Puce: favourite, won maiden at Haydock by 1½ lengths from Georgia Venture: will stay 1½m: acts on soft going: open to further progress if all is well with her. *L. M. Cumani* 81 p

SHOULDBEGREY 4 ch.g. Siberian Express (USA) 125 – Miss Magnetism (Baptism 119) [1996 50: 8d 6.9m 7.3s⁴ 8g 8.2m³ a9.4g⁴ 10f 10m⁵ 8g 8m³ 8d* 9g⁵ 1997 8.2m 8d 8d⁵ 8f 8.3s⁴ 8.3g 8.1m Jul 11] tall gelding: poor handicapper: stays 9f: acts on good to firm and soft ground: visored third to fifth starts. *W. R. Muir* 39

SHOUMATARA (USA) 3 ch.c. Seeking The Gold (USA) – Crown Quest (USA) (Chief's Crown (USA)) [1996 84: 7g⁵ 7.1m² 7f² 7m 1997 8g 10d 7f* Jun 3] rangy colt: fairly useful form at 2 yrs: ran as if amiss first 2 starts in 1997: visored, won 5-runner maiden at Brighton in June by short head: sold twice after, for only 2,000 gns in October: has had tongue tied. *M. R. Stoute* 72

SHOWBOAT 3 b.c. Warning 136 – Boathouse 116 (Habitat 134) [1996 92p: 7f* 7.3s 1997 7m³ 8g 8m* 7d⁶ Sep 13] close-coupled, useful-looking colt: has a short, unimpressive action: fairly useful performer: won 4-runner minor event at Salisbury (by head from Tarski) in August, leading near finish: ran well considering false pace and shorter trip in handicap at Goodwood final start: should stay beyond 1m: acts on firm going and dead. *B. W. Hills* 94

SHOWCASE 3 b.f. Shareef Dancer (USA) 135 – Perfolia (USA) 104 (Nodouble (USA)) [1996 68: 7g⁵ 7g 1997 a7g 12m 10s 17.2m⁵ 10m Jul 19] modest form in maidens for M. Stoute at 2 yrs: showed nothing in 1997: blinkered final start. *J. W. Hills* –

SHOW FAITH (IRE) 7 ch.g. Exhibitioner 111 – Keep The Faith 86 (Furry Glen 121) [1996 –: 8s 8g 9m 8d 8g a8g 1997 8m 8.3m 9g* Aug 23] good-topped gelding: fair handicapper nowadays: won amateurs event at Goodwood in August: effective from 1m to 1¼m: acts on good to firm and soft ground: tried blinkered: usually held up: has looked temperamental. *R. Hannon* 67

SHOWGIRL 3 ch.f. Handsome Sailor 125 – Early Doors (Ballad Rock 122) [1996 59: a7g⁶ a6g* 1997 a7g⁶ 6m 6g 7m a7g a7g Nov 29] lengthy filly: has lost her form (reportedly bled from nose fourth start). *Capt. J. Wilson* –

SHOWSTOPPER 3 b.g. Today And Tomorrow 78 – Alexzena (Upper Case (USA)) [1996 NR 1997 10m 10m a7g 12g⁵ 13.1s Oct 13] tall, sparely-made gelding: eighth living foal: dam no worthwhile form: well beaten in varied events. *T. J. Etherington*

SHUDDER 2 b.c. (Feb 19) Distant Relative 128 – Oublier L'Ennui (FR) 79 95 (Bellman (FR) 123) [1997 6g* 5.5g² 6g³ 6m³ Nov 1] 32,000Y: first living foal: dam, probably stayed 1½m on flat, winner over hurdles/fences: won maiden at Goodwood in August: useful form in 5-runner Prix d'Arenberg at Chantilly (beaten a nose) and Two-Year-Old Trophy at Redcar, 1½ lengths third behind Grazia in latter: bit below form in mixed-aged event at Newmarket last start: bred to be well suited by further than 6f. *W. J. Haggas*

SHUHRAH (USA) 2 b. or br.f. (Mar 15) Danzig (USA) – Sajjaya (USA) 97 101 (Blushing Groom (FR) 131) [1997 6m* 6g 7m³ Oct 4] well-made filly: has scope: third foal: closely related to 5-y-o Raased (formerly fairly useful 1¼m winner) and half-sister to 3-y-o Hadawah: dam, 7f and 1m winner, half-sister to Lahib: won newcomers event at Ascot in July by 1½ lengths from Ashraakat: 2½ lengths third to Name of Love in listed race at Newmarket, faring best of front runners: ran poorly in Lowther Stakes in between: will prove best short of 1m. *Saeed bin Suroor*

SHUTTLECOCK 6 ch.g. Pharly (FR) 130 – Upper Sister (Upper Case (USA)) – [1996 39, a47: a8g⁶ a8g a8g⁵ a8g 10d 8m 10m³ 10m a8g⁶ 10f a8g 10d 11.8f a12g⁶ a45 1997 a16g⁴ a14.8g⁶ a12g² a12g² a11g⁴ a12g a11g⁵ a12g a11g⁴ a9.4g⁵ Dec 26] angular gelding: poor all-weather performer: left Mrs N. Macauley after third start: stays 1½m: acts on good to firm ground, dead and the all-weather: tried visored/blinkered: often front runner. *D. W. Chapman*

SHY PADDY (IRE) 5 b.g. Shy Groom (USA) – Griqualand (Connaught 130) 44 [1996 –: 11.8d 12m 1997 12f 18s⁴ a14g² a14g² Jul 21] workmanlike gelding: poor handicapper: stays 1¾m well: acts on fibresand and any turf going: blinkered (tailed off) once as 3-y-o. *K. O. Cunningham-Brown*

SIBERIAN MYSTIC 4 gr.f. Siberian Express (USA) 125 – Mystic Crystal (IRE) 47 85 (Caerleon (USA) 132) [1996 39: 9.7f 8m 9.9g* 1997 12g² 11.9g 12d 12m* 12m Oct 31] lengthy filly: poor handicapper: won apprentice race at Pontefract in October: stays 1½m: raced mainly on good going or firmer: good mount for inexperienced rider: none too consistent: won over hurdles in December. *P. G. Murphy*

SIBOR STAR 3 b.g. Man Among Men (IRE) – My Ratbag 56 (Main Reef 126) – [1996 39: a7g⁵ 1997 a8g 8m a12g⁴ a12g⁶ Dec 26] angular gelding: little sign of ability, including in sellers. *D. Burchell*

SICK AS A PARROT 2 ch.c. (Mar 24) Casteddu 111 – Sianiski (Niniski (USA) 79 125) [1997 7m* 7g² 7m³ 7g² 7g 8f* 8m* Oct 22] 750F, 3,200Y: angular colt: first foal: dam ran 3 times: fair performer: won seller at Yarmouth in June, and nurseries there in September and October, rallying well when beating Middle Temple by head for final win: better at 1m than shorter: raced only on good going or firmer: has ungainly head carriage: showed more resolution once visored final 2 outings: front runner. *C. A. Dwyer*

SIDE BAR 7 b.g. Mummy's Game 120 – Joli's Girl 79 (Mansingh (USA) 120) 29 § [1996 NR 1997 a16g² 14.1m Jul 19] poor handicapper: second in seller at Lingfield (for P. Mooney) in May: stays 2m: usually blinkered/visored: none too keen: unreliable jumper. *K. C. Comerford*

SIDEMAN (IRE) 2 b.c. (May 3) Brief Truce (USA) 126 – Millie Musique 95 (Miller's Mate 116) [1997 5d* 6d* 7g 7g 8d 6d³ Oct 4] IR 21,000F, 62,000Y: rangy, good-topped colt: third foal: half-brother to 3-y-o Alpine Time and a 7f and 9f winner in UAE by Persian Heights: dam once-raced daughter of top-class French filly Luth Enchantee: useful performer: odds on, won small-field minor events at Leopardstown in May and the Curragh in June: behind in Chesham Stakes at Royal Ascot next start: best effort when very close third of 6 to Karakorum in listed race at the Curragh final start: should stay beyond 6f: sold 55,000 gns in October, and sent to USA. *A. P. O'Brien, Ireland*

SIDNEY THE KIDNEY 3 b.f. Mystiko (USA) 124 – Martin-Lavell Mail 50 (Dominion 123) [1996 53, a?: 6.9d³ a7g a7g⁴ 1997 10m² 10g 7s 9.7d 10d a8g a11g⁴ a36 a12g³ Dec 26] modest maiden on turf, poor on all-weather: probably stays 1½m: acts on good to firm going and fibresand. *M. J. Ryan*

SIEGE PERILOUS (IRE)   4 b.g. Taufan (USA) 119 – Carado 82 (Manado 130)   81
[1996 74: 12s* a11g³ 14.1g* 12d² 14.6m³ 11.9m⁶ 15.8g⁴ 14.1s² 12v³ 1997 16g² 16d³
13.9g⁴ 14g* 16.1s⁴ 14g² 16.4s* 18g⁶ 16.5s Nov 8] rangy gelding: fairly useful
handicapper: won at Sandown in June and August: good sixth of 31 to Turnpole in
Cesarewitch at Newmarket penultimate outing: stays 2¼m well: has form on good to
firm ground, goes well on good or softer: genuine and consistent. *S. C. Williams*

SIENA (GER)   2 ch.f. (Apr 27) Platini (GER) 126 – Smeralda (GER) (Nebos   55
(GER) 129) [1997 6g 6.9s 8m 9m* 8m Oct 22] approx 10,300Y: close-coupled filly:
first foal: dam German 1m winner: only worthwhile form when winning seller at
Goodwood in September: should stay at least 1¼m. *M. R. Channon*

SIFWA   3 ch.f. Safawan 118 – Wigeon 80 (Divine Gift 127) [1996 NR 1997 a7g   –
6.9m⁵ 7f² 10m a10g a8g⁵ Dec 2] 4,000F, 3,200Y: half-sister to several winners,
including Premier Lad (6f, by Tower Walk) and Ma Pierrette (5f to 1¼m, by Cawston's Clown): came from up to 1¼m: signs of ability but little form. *D. C. O'Brien*

SIGGIEWI   3 ro.f. Mystiko (USA) 124 – Shadiyama 58 (Nishapour (FR) 125)   –
[1996 NR 1997 8.1m⁴ 11.7g Sep 8] 8,500Y, 1,300 2-y-o: leggy, lengthy filly: third
reported foal: half-sister to a winner in Germany by Never So Bold: dam second over
6f at 2 yrs: only a little sign of ability in seller and maiden. *N. M. Babbage*

SIGNATORY   2 ch.c. (May 4) King's Signet (USA) 110 – Pearl Pet 56 (Mummy's   81 +
Pet 125) [1997 6f⁴ 7d² a7g⁵ 7m⁶ 7d³ 6m⁴ 7v 7m* Oct 23] 8,600Y: workmanlike colt: a?
half-brother to 6f seller winner Easy Does It (by Swing Easy) and 3 winners abroad:
dam maiden: much improved form to win maiden at Brighton by 5 lengths: will
probably stay 1m: acts on good to firm ground and probably on dead: sold 10,000
gns, and sent to Switzerland. *R. Hannon*

SIGNED AND SEALED (USA)   3 b.g. Rahy (USA) 115 – Heaven's Mine   61
(USA) (Graustark) [1996 NR 1997 10g 12m 12m a14g⁴ a14.8g a14g a16s a16g²
a16g* a16g³ Dec 10] $42,000Y: workmanlike gelding: half-brother to smart 1m/
1¼m performer Andromaque (by Woodman) and a winner in USA by Little Current:
dam unraced sister to a Grade 3 8.5f winner in USA: modest performer: won minor
event at Lingfield in December, making most and rallying: suited by test of stamina:
acts on equitrack: blinkered last 3 starts. *C. A. Cyzer*

SIGNS AND WONDERS   3 b.f. Danehill (USA) 126 – Front Line Romance 89   71 §
(Caerleon (USA) 132) [1996 67: 6g⁴ 6m² 6m⁶ 5f 1997 6m a6g³ 5d⁵ 7.1g² 8.5m³ 7m⁶   a65 §
8g⁵ 8m⁴ a7g² a10g² 7m a7g⁴ Aug 28] lengthy, angular filly: fair maiden handicapper:
barely stays 1¼m: acts on equitrack and good to firm going, probably also on dead:
edgy sort: not an easy ride, and probably not to be trusted. *C. A. Cyzer*

SIHAFI (USA)   4 ch.g. Elmaamul (USA) 125 – Kit's Double (USA) (Spring   51
Double) [1996 72d: 6s⁴ 6d⁵ 5m² 7g⁴ 6f² 6d 5g 7m a6g a7s a6g* a5g² 1997 a5g⁵ a6g*   a66
7g 6d 5.9g 6g⁵ 7.5m 6d 5m 6m a5g Dec 18] tall gelding: fair handicapper on the
all-weather: won at Lingfield in February: modest form on turf afterwards: left
J. Carr before final start: stays 6f: acts on firm and dead ground, goes well on
equitrack: takes keen hold: usually held up and suited by strong pace. *D. Nicholls*

SILANKKA   3 b.f. Slip Anchor 136 – Mary Sunley 62 (Known Fact (USA) 135)   70
[1996 NR 1997 10g 10.2m⁴ Jul 7] 27,000Y: rangy filly: sixth foal: closely related to
a winner in Denmark by Shirley Heights and half-sister to 3 winners, including 9-y-o
Helios and Storm Dust (1½m, by Celestial Storm): dam, maiden suited by 1¼m,
half-sister to Roseate Tern and Ibn Bey: reportedly split a pastern at 2 yrs: much
better effort in maidens when fourth behind Darapour at Bath: will be suited by 1½m.
M. R. Channon

SILCA KEY SERVICE   2 b.f. (Mar 29) Bering 136 – Aquaglow 84 (Caerleon   73
(USA) 132) [1997 6m⁵ 6.9m Aug 19] 11,500F, IR 23,000Y: good-topped filly: fifth
foal: half-sister to 3 winners, including 3-y-o Attitre and useful 6f/7f winner Please
Suzanne (by Cadeaux Genereux): dam 7f/1m winner: in need of run, fair form in
newcomers event at Goodwood: favourite, slowly away and never a threat in maiden
at Folkestone 17 days later: bred to stay much further than 6f. *M. R. Channon*

SILCA KEY SILCA   3 ch.f. Polar Falcon (USA) 126 – Night Transaction 59   84
(Tina's Pet 121) [1996 77: 5m³ 5g⁵ 6g* 5.2m⁵ 5m² 1997 7d⁶ 6g* 6d 6g⁵ 6m⁴ 6g 7g⁴
6g a7g² Oct 6] sparely-made filly: fairly useful handicapper: won at Lingfield in June

(by 6 lengths, raced against favoured rail): generally creditable efforts afterwards: effective at 6f/7f: acts on good to firm going and fibresand: sold 12,000 gns, and sent to Saudi Arabia. *M. R. Channon*

SILENCE IN COURT (IRE)   6 b.g. Law Society (USA) 130 – Fair Flutter   96 +
(Beldale Flutter (USA) 130) [1996 NR 1997 14.6g² Oct 24] useful performer (rated 108 in 1995): bandaged after 2½ years off, encouraging return when ¾-length second of 22 to Jawah in handicap at Doncaster, running on strongly after winner had gone clear: should stay 2½m: acts on firm and dead ground, never travelling well on heavy: often reluctant at stalls: genuine. *A. Bailey*

SILENCE REIGNS   3 b.g. Saddlers' Hall (IRE) 126 – Rensaler (USA) (Stop The   107
Music (USA)) [1996 NR 1997 10g² 10v* 10g² 12m⁶ Jul 29] 75,000Y: close-coupled, unfurnished gelding: has a short, round action: closely related to useful Opera Lover (1½m/1¾m, by Sadler's Wells), and half-brother to several winners, including Jovial (by Northern Jove), very smart graded winner up to 1¼m in USA: quickly developed into a useful performer: landed odds in maiden at Pontefract in June: much better form when 2½ lengths second to Lord of Men in minor event at Sandown and 5 lengths fourth (demoted to sixth, having been switched 2f out) behind Stowaway in Gordon Stakes at Goodwood: stays 1½m. *M. R. Stoute*

SILENTLY   5 b.g. Slip Anchor 136 – Land of Ivory (USA) 109 (The Minstrel   86 §
(CAN) 135) [1996 83§: 10.8d⁶ 10.2f⁶ 10d² 10.8f² 10m⁶ 12g² 16f⁵ 12m 12m² 12g 16.2m 11.9g³ 1997 12m⁴ 14.9d² 14g² 14m² Jul 23] good-topped gelding: fairly useful handicapper: probably stays 2m: acts on dead and hard ground: blinkered (ran poorly) once: tends to hang, and is none too genuine (twice threw away winning opportunities at 5 yrs). *J. S. King*

SILENT MIRACLE (IRE)   3 b.f. Night Shift (USA) – Curie Point (USA)   77
(Sharpen Up 127) [1996 61p: 6m 1997 6m³ 5.1m³ 6m² a6g* 7g⁶ 6d 5g³ 5g⁶ 5m 5m³   a80
5m⁵ 5g⁵ 6m⁵ 5d Oct 8] stocky, round-barrelled filly: fair handicapper: made all at Wolverhampton in May (only all-weather outing): mostly respectable efforts after: effective at 5f/easy 6f: yet to race on extremes of going or equitrack: sent to UAE. *M. Bell*

SILENT PRIDE (IRE)   2 ch.f. (Feb 21) Pips Pride 117 – Suppression (Kind of   63 d
Hush 118) [1997 5g³ 5.1d 5d⁴ 6f 5g⁴ a5g⁶ a7g² a7g⁶ 6g 5m⁴ 6m² 5s⁶ 6m 7f 6d Oct 21] 2,000Y: leggy filly: poor mover: first foal: dam ran once: modest maiden: deteriorated: stays 6f. *M. D. I. Usher*

SILENT SYMPHONY   5 ch.m. Music Boy 124 – City Link Rose (Lochnager   –
132) [1996 NR 1997 a6g a7g 6s 5.1m 7d⁵ Aug 8] half-sister to 2 winners up to 7f by Tina's Pet and fairly useful sprinter Bodari (by Prince Sabo): dam ran 3 times: seems of little account. *Mrs S. D. Williams*

SILENT SYSTEM (IRE)   4 gr.g. Petong 126 – Light Thatch (Thatch (USA)   23
136) [1996 –: a5g 7m 1997 a8g 8m 5.9g 6m 8f 8g 8.3s⁴ 10v⁵ 8g⁶ 10g 9.9g 12.1g Sep 1] bad maiden: stays 1m: acts on soft ground: tried blinkered. *D. W. Chapman*

SILENT TRIBUTE (IRE)   2 b.f. (Feb 4) Lion Cavern (USA) 117 – Tribal Rite   104
95 (Be My Native (USA) 122) [1997 6g* 6d³ 7g² 7m³ 8f* 8f⁶ Oct 5] IR 100,000Y: smallish, quite attractive filly: sixth foal: half-sister to 1½m winner Danesrath (by Danehill) and Irish 6f and 7f winner Scalp (by Thatching): dam Irish 6f (at 2 yrs) to 1¼m winner, half-sister to Middle Park winner Balla Cove: useful performer: won maiden at Newmarket in May and listed race at Milan in September: placed in listed races all other outings in Britain, and best effort when around 2½ lengths sixth in Prix Marcel Boussac at Longchamp final start: stays 1m: acts on firm ground and dead: has been unimpressive to post. *M. Bell*

SILENT VALLEY   3 b.f. Forzando 122 – Tremmin 67 (Horage 124) [1996 47: 7g   59 §
a6g 7f² 6.1m 7g 7m⁶ 7g a6g⁴ a6g² a8g⁶ 1997 a9.4f³ a8g a8g 8g³ 8g 8.5m 8.2m⁴ 10g*   a48 §
8m³ 9m 10.3m 10m 10.1g Oct 22] sparely-made filly: modest performer: trained by D. Nicholls first 3 starts: won maiden at Nottingham in July, best effort: started slowly when below form afterwards (virtually refusing to race once) though did win twice over hurdles in December: stays 1¼m: acts on firm going and the all-weather: usually blinkered/visored: not to be trusted. *Miss L. C. Siddall*

SILENT WARNING 2 b.c. (Apr 4) Ela-Mana-Mou 132 – Buzzbomb 98 – p
(Bustino 136) [1997 7d 7m Oct 22] 54,000Y: fourth foal: half-brother to Irish 1¾m
winner Bourdonner (by Pharly): dam middle-distance performer, half-sister to smart
6f and 1¼m winner Missed Blessing: easy to back and not given hard time in maidens
at Leicester and Yarmouth in October: sure to do better once tried at 1¼m+. *Sir Mark
Prescott*

SILENT WEAPON 3 ch.g. Primo Dominie 121 – On Request (IRE) 53 (Be My 44
Guest (USA) 126) [1996 5m⁶ 6g 7g⁶ 1997 a7g⁴ a6g Jan 21] 30,000Y: first foal:
dam lightly raced at 2 yrs (shaped like a stayer), sister to smart 6f to 1¼m winner
Invited Guest: modest form (rated 50) in maidens in Ireland at 2 yrs: only poor form
in Britain in 1997: stays 7f: acts on fibresand: tried blinkered/visored. *K. McAuliffe*

SILENT WELLS 3 b.f. Saddlers' Hall (IRE) 126 – Silent Plea 43 (Star Appeal –
133) [1996 –: a7g 7f 6.1m⁴ 6f 1997 a12g⁵ May 1] no form. *L. R. Lloyd-James*

SILK COTTAGE 5 b.g. Superpower 113 – Flute Royale 74 (Horage 124) [1996 55
66: 5g 6g 5g³ 5m⁵ a5g² 5d² 5m* 5m³ 5g⁵ 5m⁵ 5.1m² 5m 5m 5.1d 5.1m 5g 5g⁴ a60
a5g a5g a5g 1997 a5g* a5g² 5g a5g⁶ 5s⁶ a6g² a5g a5g⁴ a6g⁴ 6g⁴ 5m³ a6g a5g a5g³
a6g⁴ a6g⁴ a6g a5g⁶ Nov 29] sturdy, good-quartered gelding: modest performer: won
seller at Wolverhampton in March: generally creditable efforts afterwards: stays 6f:
acts on good to firm ground, soft and the all-weather: effective blinkered/visored or
not: sometimes hangs markedly left: usually races prominently. *R. M. Whitaker*

SILKEN DALLIANCE 2 b.f. (Apr 26) Rambo Dancer (CAN) 107 – A Sharp 67 p
(Sharpo 132) [1997 6.1m a6g² 6d⁴ Oct 28] second living foal: dam unraced: fair form
in frame in maidens at Wolverhampton and Leicester, doing comfortably best of
those to race stand side on latter course: will stay beyond 6f: should do better yet.
Lord Huntingdon

SILK ST JOHN 3 b.g. Damister (USA) 123 – Silk St James (Pas de Seul 133) 87
[1996 72: 6g⁶ 7m⁵ 7m 7m² 6.9v² 1997 8s³ 8g* 7m³ 8.1s⁴ 8m² 9m 8d 8m a8g³ a8.5g a80
Dec 26] close-coupled gelding: fairly useful handicapper: won at Newmarket in
August: mostly good efforts after until final start: should stay 1¼m: acts on good to
firm going, heavy and fibresand: held up. *M. J. Ryan*

SILVAZINE 2 gr.f. (Feb 20) Silver Kite (USA) 111 – Dorazine 77 (Kalaglow 132) –
[1997 5.7f 5s⁴ Jun 27] 3,500F: first foal: dam 7f to 10.5f winner out of half-sister to
St Leger winner Bruni: tailed off in maiden and a seller. *D. J. S. ffrench Davis*

SILVERANI (IRE) 3 b.c. High Estate 127 – Rose Society (Caerleon (USA) 132) 105
[1996 91: 7g² 8s² 1997 8g* 10.4g² 10m² 10d⁶ 10.1f* Oct 29] smallish, sturdy colt:
useful performer: won maiden (easily) at Ripon in April and minor event (beat
Unconditional Love ¾ length in 3-runner contest) at Yarmouth in October: good
second in handicaps at York and Newmarket (wandered) in between: should stay
beyond 1¼m: best efforts on good going or firmer: sent to USA. *L. M. Cumani*

SILVER BUTTON 3 b.g. Silver Kite (USA) 111 – Klairover 50 (Smackover –
107) [1996 53+: 6m 6s 7d 1997 8s⁵ 10m 13.8m³ a14.8g⁴ a9.4g Aug 16] lengthy,
good-quartered gelding: well beaten since debut. *S. R. Bowring*

SILVER FUN (FR) 3 b.f. Saumarez 132 – Riviere d'Argent (USA) (Nijinsky 115
(CAN) 138) [1996 9s* 1997 10.5d² 12s* 12m 15.5d⁴ Oct 26] sixth foal:
half-sister to winners in France by Shirley Heights (12.5f), Wassl (1¼m) and Nashwan (would have stayed 1¼m), the last 2 listed placed: dam, French 1½m winner,
closely related to 3 good winners in France out of Arc winner Gold River: won minor
event at Evry at 2 yrs: beaten a nose by Allurement in slowly-run Prix Cleopatre at
Saint-Cloud on return: best effort when winning Prix de Malleret at Longchamp in
June by 2½ lengths from Tenuous: creditable fourth of 11 to Ebadiyla in Prix Royal-
Oak at Longchamp final start: stays 15.5f: acts on soft ground, twice well beaten on
good to firm. *Mme C. Head, France*

SILVER GROOM (IRE) 7 gr.g. Shy Groom (USA) – Rustic Lawn (Rusticaro 84
(FR) 124) [1996 85: 10m⁵ 10g⁴ 10m² 10d 9m 1997 10m⁶ 10.1m⁵ 10m² 10m 10d Sep
20] smallish, angular gelding: fairly useful handicapper: best effort at 7 yrs when
second at Newmarket in August: ridden closer to pace than usual and well beaten last
2 starts: stays 1¼m well: successful on soft ground at 3 yrs and over hurdles, goes

very well on firm/good to firm: held up, and has turn of foot: joined M. Channon. *R. Akehurst*

SILVER HARROW 4 gr.g. Belmez (USA) 131 – Dancing Diana 82 (Raga   63
Navarro (ITY) 119) [1996 63, a50: 7d 5.1g³ 7m² 7m⁵ 6.1m⁴ 8m³ 8f⁴ 8.5g³ a8.5g⁵   a–
8.1f⁴ 7f* 7g⁵ a7g a8.5s⁵ a8g⁶ 1997 a10g⁵ a8g 10f⁶ 7m² 7.6m² 7.6m 8g² 7f 8g² a10g
Dec 19] workmanlike gelding: modest handicapper: stays 1m, pulled too hard over
1¼m: acts on firm ground, below form on the all-weather: tried blinkered at 2 yrs.
A. G. Newcombe

SILVER HOPE (IRE) 2 ch.c. (Apr 28) Silver Kite (USA) 111 – Cloven Dancer   –
(USA) 86 (Hurok (USA)) [1997 6f 7g⁶ 7m 8m 10d Oct 13] IR 2,000F, IR 4,500Y:
big, good-bodied colt: fluent mover: half-brother to several winners, including 6f and
7f winner Boursin (by Taufan) and 7-y-o Texas Cowgirl: dam Irish 1m winner: little
worthwhile form, including in seller. *R. Hollinshead*

SILVERING (FR) 5 b.h. Polish Precedent (USA) 131 – Silvermine (FR) 124   109
(Bellypha 130) [1996 110: 8.5g* 8g³ 10g⁴ 10g⁶ 8d* 9.8d 1997 8d³ 8s⁶ 7d Aug 21]
lengthy horse: smart at 4 yrs for Mme C. Head in France: best effort in listed events
in 1997 when third at Saint-Cloud in March: trained until after next start by J.
Hammond: eased right off when last at York on final outing: very best form at 1m:
acts on soft going, yet to race on ground firmer than good: returned to France.
Mrs J. R. Ramsden

SILVER JOY 2 b.f. (Apr 29) Silver Kite (USA) 111 – Oh My Joy 57 (Grundy   –
137) [1997 5d 7g a7g Dec 10] third reported living foal: dam suited by 1¼m: no
promise in maidens and minor event. *K. McAuliffe*

SILVER JUBILEE 3 b.f. Sylvan Express 117 – Addison's Jubilee 73 (Sparkler   –
130) [1996 –: a5g⁵ 1997 8.2m 8.2d 6d 8.1s Jul 1] leggy filly: no sign of ability.
B. Palling

SILVER KRISTAL 3 gr.f. Kris 135 – Reine d'Beaute 97 (Caerleon (USA) 132)   76
[1996 77p: 6m³ 7g⁴ 1997 7.6m⁴ 7m⁵ 7d² 7m² 6.1g⁴ Oct 4] good-bodied filly: unimpressive mover: fair maiden: should stay beyond 7f: unraced on extremes of going.
R. Akehurst

SILVER LINING 3 b.g. Beveled (USA) – Seymour Ann (Krayyan 117) [1996   66
64?: 5m* 6f⁵ 5d 6m 1997 6.1g⁴ 5.1m³ 6d 5.1f 7m* 8.3g 7d* 7.1m⁴ Jul 30] fair
handicapper: won amateurs events at Salisbury in June and Leicester (best effort,
well ridden by Mr J. Goldstein) in July: seems suited by 7f: acts on good to firm
ground and dead. *A. P. Jones*

SILVER MARBLE (IRE) 3 b.f. Silver Kite (USA) 111 – Friendly Song 48   –
(Song 132) [1996 NR 1997 7g⁶ 10f⁴ Oct 1] 14,000Y, 2,100 3-y-o: second foal:
half-sister to 1995 2-y-o 5f winner Kustom Kit (by Timeless Times): dam poor
maiden sister to speedy Fayruz: tailed off in maidens. *R. Hannon*

SILVER MOON 3 gr.f. Environment Friend 128 – High And Bright 95 (Shirley   –
Heights 130) [1996 –: a7g⁵ 6.1m a6g⁶ 6s 1997 8.5m a8g 6m Jun 2] leggy filly: no
worthwhile form: quite stoutly bred. *B. A. McMahon*

SILVER PATRIARCH (IRE) 3 gr.c. Saddlers' Hall (IRE) 126 – Early   125
Rising (USA) (Grey Dawn II 132) [1996 98p: 7g 8.2m⁴ 10m* 10g* 1997 10d³
11.5s* 12g² 12d⁵ 11.9g² 14.6m* Sep 13]

His head was in front just before the line, it was in front just after
it—Epsom have erected marker posts to show where nearly all the post-war
Derby winners have hit the front, but there will not be one bearing the name
Silver Patriarch. For him, the 1997 Derby meant a place alongside Trafalgar
(1806), Raphael (1815), Louviers (1909), Rheingold (1972) and El Gran Senor
(1984) as one of the Derby's short-head losers. It has been said that only winners are remembered, but we cannot believe that Silver Patriarch's performance
in the Derby will be forgotten in a hurry. First and second passed the post
simultaneously, or as near as damn it, but the way in which they got there could
hardly have been more different, for while Benny The Dip adapted perfectly to
the course and moved smoothly into the lead coming down Tattenham Hill,
Silver Patriarch was plumb last and being ridden along. Coming from last place

to win the Derby is virtually unheard of, though on this occasion there were only twelve rivals to be passed instead of the twenty-seven that lay ahead of Psidium in 1961. Santa Claus came from among the backmarkers to win in 1964, as did Troy in 1979 and Golden Fleece in 1982, the last-named ridden with astonishing confidence by Pat Eddery. Eddery was the man on top again in 1997 but this time there was no question of his coming from behind by design. He bounced Silver Patriarch out of the stalls and tried to push him up into a prominent position, but the grey was unable to hold his place and paid the price by getting squeezed. Last before halfway, Silver Patriarch became detached by a couple of lengths as the field went downhill and had passed only the rank outsider Papua turning for home, where he was on the inside and at least ten lengths adrift of the leader. With a clear passage up the straight, Silver Patriarch went second one and a half furlongs out, still about six lengths adrift of Benny The Dip, and then mounted that colossal and almost irresistible effort, which treated spectators to one of the very best Derby finishes.

Silver Patriarch was sent off the 6/1 second favourite in the Derby. If there had been long-term ante-post betting for the St Leger, he would probably have been at the head of it for seven months already, since the mile-and-a-quarter Zetland Stakes at Newmarket had provided him with his second win from four starts as a two-year-old. Stamina was never going to be in any doubt with him, as was illustrated again by his two races before Epsom. In the Thresher Classic Trial at Sandown on his reappearance, he seemed to find his stride only at the death, going down by a head to Benny The Dip as the pair of them chased home Voyagers Quest. Two weeks later, Silver Patriarch justified favouritism in the Tripleprint Derby Trial at Lingfield and did it impressively, pulling seven lengths clear of Tanaasa in testing conditions without Eddery having to ask for everything by any means.

Silver Patriarch did indeed start favourite for the St Leger, and at 5/4, though he had been beaten on his two starts between Epsom and Doncaster. The first of these was when also sent off at 5/4 favourite in the Irish Derby, the only disappointing performance of Silver Patriarch's career so far. Eddery was

Pertemps St Leger, Doncaster—Silver Patriarch begins to draw clear; close behind him, from left to right, are The Fly, Book At Bedtime, Vertical Speed and Windsor Castle

understandably keen to keep him up with the pace from the off, only to have Silver Patriarch tamely beaten off two furlongs out and finish a well-beaten fifth of ten. It emerged afterwards that he was slightly lame on his off-fore and had 'a significant amount of mucus in his lungs.' If the King George had ever been an option, it wasn't now, and Silver Patriarch was put away for an orthodox preparation for the St Leger with his next appearance in the Great Voltigeur Stakes at York. Defeat in this race was by only half a length and afterwards saw him disputing the St Leger favouritism with Stowaway, the horse who had just battled back to beat him after he had led two furlongs out. Edging left and losing out in the last fifty yards, Silver Patriarch may well have needed the race to put him right.

The pair were still inseparable in most betting lists on the morning of the St Leger, but racegoers were robbed of a fascinating rematch when Stowaway was found to be lame in his box. With him out of the way, second favourite in a ten-horse race was the Fabre challenger Vertical Speed at 7/2, followed on 10/1 by the Cecil-trained Beseige, Derby fifth The Fly, and the Queen's Vase and Northumberland Plate winner Windsor Castle. The Voltigeur aside, all the evidence was that Silver Patriarch could be relied upon to be running on at the finish, and the St Leger fitted this pattern exactly. Silver Patriarch was nudged along disputing fifth place on the turn, but when the muddling pace was set aside in the straight he was the one who worked his way to the front. Vertical Speed attempted to go head to head with him from two and a half furlongs out, but the favourite began to stretch clear at the furlong pole and was three lengths in front at the post. The Fly, who had made smooth headway from the rear early in the straight, was beaten a further neck in third.

The St Leger was a milestone victory for his jockey Pat Eddery. Coincidentally, Frankie Dettori had recorded the 1,000th winner of his career on Classic Cliche in the race two years earlier, and Silver Patriarch's triumph was Eddery's 4,000th in Britain. Only Sir Gordon Richards (4,870) and Lester Piggott (4,493) have notched up more, and only Willie Carson (3,828) and Doug Smith (3,111) have also had more than 3,000. It was Eddery's fourth St Leger win, his fourteenth in all in a British classic. The word professional could have been made to describe him. Praise for his longevity and resilience, and confident predictions that he would move past Lester's win total, looked a little mistimed when Eddery had to end his 1997 season five days after the St Leger because of a chronic back problem, but the eleven-times champion has had an operation and was fully confident that he would return as good as new in 1998.

Silver Patriarch was ridden and trained by men who are no strangers to the big time, but the background of his owner-breeder, Peter Winfield, is rather different. Winfield's racing operation is on a small-scale—with seven horses in training according to *The Turf Directory 1997*—but big enough for him to have made the 160,000-dollar outlay for Silver Patriarch's dam, Early Rising, at the Keeneland November Sales in 1988. The dam of four foals before her sale (three of whom won), Early Rising produced another three winners from four foals before Silver Patriarch; the two who did not win both died young. The best of all those winners were the useful sprinter Silver Singing (by Topsider) and the smart stayer My Patriarch (by Be My Guest). The two-year-old Regal Patriarch (by Marju) showed promise in the latest season and Early Rising is now carrying a brother or sister to Silver Patriarch. Early Rising's former owner was Paul Mellon. Early Rising won only one small race at about a mile as a three-year-old in the United States, but she is from one of his most successful families as her grandam is Key Bridge, the dam of Fort Marcy, Key To The Mint, Key To The Kingdom and Key To Content. Fort Marcy was champion turf horse in the US in 1967 and 1970, while, to help with any confusion, Key To The Mint was their champion three-year-old in 1972, Key To The Kingdom the sire of Ma Biche and Key To Content the very smart winner of over 350,000 dollars. Another of Key Bridge's offspring, Silver Patriarch's grandam Gliding By, was reportedly a twin who had just one race, which she won.

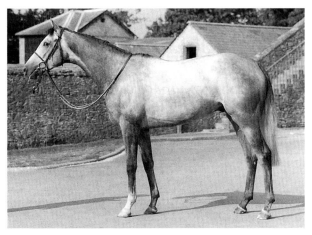

Mr Peter S. Winfield's "Silver Patriarch"

One omission in the spiralling success story of Sadler's Wells is a Derby winner, and his son Saddlers' Hall so nearly beat him to it at the first attempt! The good-looking, regally-bred Saddlers' Hall was a late foal who bypassed the Derby, but he hit the headlines shortly afterwards with a win in the King Edward VII Stakes and was runner-up in the St Leger to the Eddery-ridden Toulon. Marginally better, but not quite in the top bracket, over a mile and a half as a four-year-old, Saddlers' Hall produced Silver Patriarch for a fee of £7,500, the same charge that will be made for his services in 1998.

		Sadler's Wells	Northern Dancer
	Saddlers' Hall (IRE)	(b 1981)	Fairy Bridge
	(b 1988)	Sunny Valley	Val de Loir
Silver Patriarch (IRE)		(b 1972)	Sunland
(gr.c. 1994)		Grey Dawn II	Herbager
	Early Rising (USA)	(gr 1962)	Polamia
	(gr 1980)	Gliding By	Tom Rolfe
		(b 1975)	Key Bridge

Silver Patriarch is a tall, leggy colt, who acts on good to firm and soft going, never having raced on firm. He remains in training. At the close of his sire's three-year-old campaign, *Racehorses* predicted that Saddlers' Hall would be chasing shadows in top-class company over a mile and a half as a four-year-old, and it is tempting to say the same now about his son. Silver Patriarch clearly has stamina in abundance, which is part, but not all, of the reason why his style of running means that a strong pace and/or testing ground conditions will be necessary if he is to be seen at his best over a mile and a half. Except for Peintre Celebre, the 1997 three-year-olds are not a group that can be rated highly, but, that said, Silver Patriarch came within a short head of winning the Derby. He is most unlikely to prove a true top-notcher at the distance, but to say that there are not still good races to be won with him at a mile and a half would be going much too far. *J. L. Dunlop*

SILVER PEARL   6 gr.g. Insan (USA) 119 – Vanishing Trick 83 (Silly Season   43 d
127) [1996 NR 1997 13s* 13g⁶ 10.9d 12g 13.1s Oct 13] poor handicapper: 33/1 on
first run on flat since 3 yrs, won at Hamilton in May: tailed off afterwards: will stay
beyond 13f: acts well on soft going: visored final start. *Mrs A. M. Naughton*

SILVER PURSE   3 ch.f. Interrex (CAN) – Money Supply (Brigadier Gerard 144)   62
[1996 67: 5.7f* 6m³ 5.2m 1997 6g 6d 5.1d³ 6.1g⁶ 6g 8m 6m 6d 6m⁵ 7m Aug 15]
sturdy filly: modest handicapper: stays 6f: acts on firm going and dead: has flashed
tail: effective blinkered/visored (was last 3 starts): none too consistent. *A. P. Jones*

SILVER RHAPSODY (USA)   2 b.f. (Feb 6) Silver Hawk (USA) 123 – Sister   91 P
Chrys (USA) (Fit To Fight (USA)) [1997 8g² Oct 24] $195,000Y: big, rangy filly:
third foal: dam, winning sprinter in USA, is from fairly stoutly bred and very successful American/Japanese family: 2/1-favourite but green, promising 1½ lengths
second of 18 to Merciless in maiden at Doncaster, keeping on strongly to pull clear of
remainder without being unduly hard ridden: likely to be well suited by 1¼m/1½m:
rather nervy in preliminaries at Doncaster: will do very much better and win races.
H. R. A. Cecil

SILVER SEA (USA)   2 gr.f. (Mar 5) Java Gold (USA) – Gray And Red (USA)   –
(Wolf Power (SAF)) [1997 5.1g Aug 3] second known foal: dam won up to 7f in
USA: green and always behind in maiden at Chepstow. *I. A. Balding*

SILVER SECRET   3 gr.c. Absalom 128 – Secret Dance (Sadler's Wells (USA)   67
132) [1996 62: 6g 6g 7f³ 7m⁵ 1997 8f 8.3s 8.1m⁴ 8g 6m* 7m 6.1m Sep 23] fair
performer: won maiden at Folkestone in August: ran poorly afterwards: stays 1m:
acts on firm ground: visored final start. *M. J. Heaton-Ellis*

SILVERSMITH (FR)   2 b.c. (Jan 22) Always Fair (USA) 121 – Phargette (FR)   75
(Lyphard (USA) 132) [1997 6m 6m² 7m² Oct 23] 230,000 francs 2-y-o: sturdy,
close-coupled colt: second foal: dam, ran once, from family of Suave Dancer: fair
form: second in maidens at Lingfield in August (best effort) and Brighton in October:
should stay at least 7f. *S. Dow*

SILVER STRAND (IRE)   2 b.f. (Jan 6) Waajib 121 – Jendeal (Troy 137) [1997   75
6g 6.1s* 6m² Jul 12] IR 4,500Y: good-bodied filly: fifth foal: half-sister to fairly
useful 1¾m winner Farmin (by Rousillon): dam unraced: progressive form: won
maiden at Nottingham in July: staying-on second behind impressive Parisian Lady in
minor event at Salisbury week later: should be suited by 7f+. *B. W. Hills*

SILVER SUN   2 gr.f. (Feb 18) Green Desert (USA) 127 – Catch The Sun (Kala-   64 p
glow 132) [1997 8d Oct 16] 28,000Y: rather leggy, useful-looking filly: sixth foal:
half-sister to several winners, notably smart stayer Tioman Island (by Midyan) and
5-y-o Remaadi Sun: dam unraced: 50/1, about 15 lengths tenth of 22 to Border
Arrow in maiden at Newmarket, held up and running on: should do better.
D. R. C. Elsworth

SILVERTOWN   2 b.c. (Apr 18) Danehill (USA) 126 – Docklands (USA)   80
(Theatrical 128) [1997 7.1m² 7m Aug 16] lengthy, attractive colt: first foal: dam, ran
once here at 2 yrs and winner at 1m and 1¼m in France at 4 yrs, half-sister to smart
performer at up to 9f Wharf from family of Dahlia: promising staying-on second to
Trident in maiden at Sandown: favourite, something possibly amiss in similar event
at Newbury (moved short to post) month later: blanketed for stalls both starts.
J. H. M. Gosden

SILVER WHIRL (USA)   3 b.f. Silver Hawk (USA) 123 – With A Twist (USA)   70
(Fappiano (USA)) [1996 NR 1997 10m³ 11.8m⁵ 8.1m⁴ 10g⁴ 12g³ 12m Oct 31]
$125,000Y: rangy filly: good mover: fourth foal: half-sister to a winner in Spain by
Topsider and a minor winner in USA by Pleasant Colony: dam won Grade 3 9f event
at 5 yrs in USA: fair maiden: well beaten last 2 starts: best form at 1m/1¼m: raced
only on good/good to firm going. *R. Charlton*

SILVER WONDER (USA)   3 ch.g. Silver Hawk (USA) 123 – Upper Class   82
Lady (USA) (Upper Nile (USA)) [1996 NR 1997 12g² 14m⁶ May 31] $42,000F,
$310,000Y: good-topped gelding: first foal: dam, ran 5 times in USA, half-sister to
Prix de Diane winner Lady In Silver (by Silver Hawk): second of 6 in maiden at
Newmarket, running on and not knocked about: disappointing favourite in similar
event there 2 weeks later: joined N. Henderson and gelded. *L. M. Cumani*

SILVERY 3 gr.f. Petong 126 – Petit Peu (IRE) (Kings Lake (USA) 133) [1996 NR 67 1997 8d 10g 10g 10s² 10.8m⁴ 10d* 10.5s Oct 15] 14,000Y: unfurnished filly: first foal: dam maiden half-sister to smart Petardia (up to 1m, by Petong): 16/1, won maiden at Goodwood, easily best effort: not sure to stay beyond 1¼m: sold 13,000 gns after final start. *J. A. R. Toller*

SILVRETTA (IRE) 4 br.f. Tirol 127 – Lepoushka 97 (Salmon Leap (USA) 131) [1996 73: 8m⁴ 8d 10g 12.1g³ 13.8g³ 12g* 1997 11.6g 11.8g 16.4g 16s 12m Oct 31] leggy filly: has a round action: fair 1½m winner at 3 yrs: no form in 1997: has refused to race over hurdles. *R. C. Spicer*

SIMAFAR (IRE) 6 b.g. Kahyasi 130 – Sidama (FR) (Top Ville 129) [1996 –: a16g⁵ 16.2m 1997 16s Mar 27] sparely-made gelding: fair handicapper (up to 2½m) at 4 yrs: soundly beaten since. *R. Allan*

SIMLET 2 b.g. (Jan 30) Forzando 122 – Besito 79 (Wassl 125) [1997 6.1d⁶ 7.1g⁶ 65 7m 6.9g² 7.6m² Sep 9] 17,000Y: second foal: half-brother to 3-y-o Italian 5f winner Catnil (by Statoblest): dam 2m winner: fair maiden: second in large-field nurseries at Folkestone and Lingfield, flashing tail slightly both times (gelded at end of season): stays 7.6f. *W. Jarvis*

SIMON DU DESERT (FR) 4 gr.c. Kaldoun (FR) 122 – Canaletto (FR) (Iron 116 Duke (FR) 122) [1996 8d* 8g² 9m² 1997 8s* 8d* 8m* 8d² 9.3d³ 8g² Jul 13] 640,000 francs Y: fifth foal: half-brother to 3 winners, notably useful pair Collecta (1m, by Caerleon) and Fay Wray (up to 11f, by Primo Dominie): dam French 1m to 11f winner, including in listed race: smart French colt: won 2 of 6 starts, in minor races, prior to 1997: successful in the spring in apprentice event, listed race and Prix Edmond Blanc (by ¾ length from Precious Ring) all at Saint-Cloud: head second of 7 to Spinning World (gave 6 lb) in Prix du Muguet there, 3¼ lengths third of 6 to Sasuru in Prix d'Ispahan at Longchamp and short-head second of 7 to Neuilly in Prix Messidor at Deauville: stayed 9.3f: acted on good to firm and soft ground: most consistent: retired to Berlais Stud, France (fee 12,000 francs). *R. Collet, France*

SIMPLE LOGIC 3 ch.f. Aragon 118 – Dancing Chimes (London Bells (CAN) 70 109) [1996 73: 6d³ 6g* 7m³ 7m 7m⁵ 7g Aug 20] leggy filly: fair performer: last final start: stays 7f: acts on good to firm and dead ground. *A. G. Foster*

SIMPLY GIFTED 2 b.c. (May 4) Simply Great (FR) 122 – Souveniers (Relko 76 p 136) [1997 7g³ 7g* 7g⁴ 7.9s³ Sep 4] 8,400Y: big, strong colt: has plenty of scope: half-brother to several winners, including 1994 2-y-o 5f winner Nazute (by Cyrano de Bergerac), 8-y-o Whatever's Right and 3-y-o Keepsake: dam Irish maiden daughter of Princess Royal winner Aloft: won maiden at Newcastle in July, despite being very awkward leaving stalls: good efforts in nurseries at York subsequently: will be very well suited by 1¼m+: raced only on good ground or softer: fine type, and looks sure to progress at 3 yrs. *T. D. Easterby*

SIMPLY SUPER 2 ch.f. (Apr 19) Superlative 118 – Real Princess 78 (Aragon 72 118) [1997 6g* 7m⁶ Sep 10] strong, close-coupled filly: fifth foal: half-sister to a winner in USA by Petong: dam 7f winner out of very speedy 2-y-o Mange Tout: won maiden at Brighton in August: better effort when just under 8 lengths sixth to Exclusive in minor event at Kempton: bred to be best up to 1m. *C. E. Brittain*

SINAN (USA) 2 ch.c. (Feb 26) Mr Prospector (USA) – Gmaasha (IRE) (Kris 135) 70 [1997 7m 8d Oct 28] rangy, angular colt: second foal: dam unraced sister to smart 7f/ 1m winner Hasbah out of Irish 1000 Guineas winner Al Bahathri: midfield in maidens at Newmarket and Leicester, in latter disputing lead but finding little. *Saeed bin Suroor*

SINCH 2 ch.f. (Mar 9) Inchinor 119 – Swinging Gold 80 (Swing Easy (USA) 126) – [1997 6m 7g⁴ Aug 23] 3,400Y: lengthy, workmanlike filly: sixth living foal: half-sister to fairly useful 6f (at 2 yrs) to 1m winner So So (by Then Again) and 1990 2-y-o 5f winner Spinechiller (by Grey Ghost): dam sprinter: showed only glimmer of ability in maiden at Pontefract and minor event at Redcar. *T. D. Barron*

SINGAAR 2 ch.c. (Mar 9) Risk Me (FR) 127 – Don't Smile 76 (Sizzling Melody – 117) [1997 a8.5g Dec 13] first reported foal: dam 6f (at 2 yrs) and 9f winner: last in maiden at Wolverhampton: dead. *M. Kettle*

*Derby Italiano, Rome—The Chapple-Hyam pair Single Empire (nearside)
and Panama City (No. 6) are split by German challenger Ungaro*

SING AND DANCE 4 b.f. Rambo Dancer (CAN) 107 – Musical Princess 66 48
(Cavo Doro 124) [1996 50: 10m 8m² 9.9m³ 10.5m 10m 8m 12g 12.1s⁵ 1997 10.1g²
11.1d 10g 9f³ 10.9s⁶ 10g⁴ 10.1g³ 8g⁵ 9.9m⁶ 10m* 10d⁴ 12g⁴ 8.3g 10.9s 10.1g Oct 22]
big, workmanlike filly: poor handicapper: won maiden at Redcar in August: stays
1½m: best efforts on good going or firmer: reportedly had heart irregularity when
tailed off fifth start. *E. Weymes*

SING FOR ME (IRE) 2 b. or br.f. (Feb 4) Songlines (FR) 121 – Running For 50
You (FR) (Pampabird 124) [1997 5m 6g 7g³ 6.1g⁴ 7.5d 7d⁴ 7g⁵ 6m⁶ 6.1d a7g⁴ a6g⁶ a37
a7g Dec 18] 3,000 2-y-o: first foal: dam French 1m winner: poor maiden: should stay
further than 7f: acts on dead ground and fibresand. *R. Hollinshead*

SINGFORYOURSUPPER 3 ch.f. Superlative 118 – Suzannah's Song (Song 47
132) [1996 47: 5.3f⁶ 5g⁴ 6g 6.9g 5.3f⁴ 6m⁴ 5d* 6m a5g⁴ 7m⁶ 1997 8f a8g 5d² 5m
5.3m Jul 28] workmanlike filly: poor handicapper: best efforts at stiff 5f on dead
going: has run well when edgy. *G. G. Margarson*

SINGLE EMPIRE (IRE) 3 ch.c. Kris 135 – Captive Island 116 (Northfields 116
(USA)) [1996 NR 1997 11.1m* 10g⁵ 12m* 12f* 12g Jun 7] angular, good-topped
colt: has round action: sixth foal: half-brother to 3 winners, notably smart Court of
Honour (by Law Society) and useful Rubhahunish (by Darshaan), both staying types:
dam French 6f and 1m winner: smart performer: won maiden at Kempton in March,
steadily-run minor event at Newmarket in May and 16-runner Derby Italiano at
Rome later in May, settling better and producing strong late burst to short-head
Ungaro in last-named: 33/1 and on toes, tailed off in the Derby at Epsom 13 days
later (suffered slight knock in race): stays 1½m: acts on firm ground, yet to race on
softer than good: stays in training. *P. W. Chapple-Hyam*

878

SINGLE MAN (IRE)   4 b.g. Mansooj 118 – Sniggy 46 (Belfort (FR) 89) [1996   –
NR 1997 11.9d⁴ 12g 13.4g 14.1d a14g Nov 14] third foal: dam poor and ungenuine
maiden: little sign of ability. *B. P. J. Baugh*

SINGSPIEL (IRE)   5 b.h. In The Wings 128 – Glorious Song (CAN) (Halo   133
(USA)) [1996 127: 10g* 12m² 12g² 10g* 12s* 12g² 12f* 1997 a10f* 12m*
12s⁴ 10.4g* Aug 19]

Late-season performances tend to make the biggest impression on the
Press panel which determines the Racehorse of the Year award. Pilsudski ran
away with the 1997 award, with Silver Patriarch and Xaar the only others to
receive a vote. It was nonetheless surprising that Singspiel didn't figure at all.
His spectacular achievements, including wins in the Dubai World Cup, the
Coronation Cup and the Juddmonte International, would have made him a front
runner for the award itself had a poll been taken at almost any time up to the
end of September. But Singspiel wasn't seen out after the York August meeting,
his eleventh-hour withdrawal from the Breeders' Cup Turf in November, after
fracturing his off-fore cannon-bone, denying him a good opportunity of ending
his season, as he had started it, in a blaze of glory.

One of the major benefits of the richly-endowed Dubai World Cup in
the Arabian Gulf has been to provide a most welcome target early in the season
for the best of the middle-distance older horses that have remained in training.
Singspiel, who ended his four-year-old career with a second in the Breeders'
Cup Turf and a win in the Japan Cup, was one of six British-trained runners in
the twelve-strong line-up at Nad Al Sheba. The rescheduled Dubai World Cup
(the race was put back five days after a downpour flooded the track) coincided
with the opening of Aintree's Grand National meeting, enabling the BBC to
provide television coverage in Britain. Singspiel had been prepared in Dubai
for two months, but, despite reportedly working well on the sand-based surface
(he had previously been raced only on turf), it was widely felt that the crack
American challenge would prove too strong under the conditions. Cigar had
led home an American one-two-three in the inaugural running, with top-class
European turf performers Pentire and Halling among those down the field. The

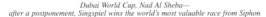

Dubai World Cup, Nad Al Sheba—
after a postponement, Singspiel wins the world's most valuable race from Siphon

three American challengers in the latest Dubai World Cup, Siphon, Sandpit and Formal Gold, had finished first, second and sixth respectively in the prestigious Santa Anita Handicap on dirt in early-March. Siphon (tactics: 'jump from the bell and go like hell') ensured a strongly-run race, but Singspiel, never far away, wore him down under very strong pressure inside the final furlong to win by a length and a quarter, with Sandpit a length and a half away third. A five-year-old winning from a six-year-old and an eight-year-old! The form of Singspiel's victory looked, if anything, even better than that of his Breeders' Cup or Japan Cup performances. The mantle 'world champion' was even bandied about, his rider Jerry Bailey comparing him favourably with Cigar, whom he had ridden the previous year. 'When it comes to looking for the best horse in the world at the moment, Singspiel heads the list,' he said. Singspiel's owner, Sheikh Mohammed, the driving force behind the Dubai World Cup, must have been pleased to read in more than one paper that 'the Dubai World Cup justified its claim to be racing's world championship.'

The Dubai World Cup, which will have official Group 1 status in 1998, takes place a month or so before the first of the Group 1 races open to four-year-olds and upwards in Britain or France, the Prix Ganay at Longchamp at the end of April. Thirteen of the twenty-five Group 1 races in Britain are open to four-year-olds and upwards but only three of them, the recently-upgraded Lockinge Stakes over a mile at Newbury in mid-May, the Coronation Cup at Epsom and the Gold Cup at Royal Ascot, take place before July. The older horses fare slightly worse overall in France where they are eligible for only eleven of the twenty-five Group 1s, though the spread is a little more even, with the Prix d'Ispahan in May and the Grand Prix de Saint-Cloud in June following the Prix Ganay. Of Ireland's nine Group 1s, only the Irish Champion and the Irish St Leger are open to four-year-olds and upwards. The older-horse challenge in the top races was particularly strong in the latest season—the extent of the domination is outlined in the essay on Pilsudski—and bears out a trend that has been emerging for some time. The number of older horses running on the flat in Britain has been rising steadily. Taking the number of older horses with a rating in the *Racehorses* annuals, there has been a year-on-year rise each year since 1988 (when there were fewer than a thousand) and in 1996 they outnumbered the three-year-olds for the first time in Timeform's records since 1947, a position repeated in 1997. At the top end, four-year-olds and upwards with a Timeform rating of 115 or higher have significantly outnumbered the three-year-olds in each of the past two years. All of which begs the question: should the racing programme in Europe continue to be framed to offer the lion's share of the rewards to horses bred and trained to be successful at two and three?

Vodafone Coronation Cup, Epsom—it's easy for Singspiel; Dushyantor is his nearest pursuer

Juddmonte International Stakes, York—a brilliant performance that turns out to be the last in a fine career; Singspiel accounts for Desert King, Benny The Dip and Bosra Sham

More good-class older horses are staying in training nowadays because the commercial pressure to retire the top three-year-olds to stud is no longer irresistible. The collapse of the stallion market from its dizziest heights in the late-'eighties fortuitously coincided with a signficant growth in the worldwide opportunities for top older horses, with the advent of events such as the Breeders' Cup series and the Japan Cup, which are being added to all the time (most recently by the upgraded International series in Hong Kong in December). A group chaired by Michael Osborne, organiser of the Dubai World Cup, is now trying to set up a new, worldwide series of races for older horses, 'with some sort of final', the aim being to 'establish the best horse in the world.'

Singspiel's next appearance after the Dubai World Cup came in the Coronation Cup at Epsom, his first race in Britain since winning the Select Stakes at Goodwood the previous September. Singspiel won in scintillating style by five lengths from the previous year's Derby runner-up Dushyantor, with the Prix Ganay runner-up Le Destin half a length further behind in third. Singspiel had the race sewn up as soon as he quickened clear early in the straight, Dettori allowing him to coast home in the final furlong. Singspiel then suffered his only defeat as a five-year-old when fourth in the King George VI and Queen Elizabeth Diamond Stakes at Ascot in July, run, after torrential rain, in conditions as testing as any Singspiel encountered. Singspiel didn't cope so well as the first three, Swain, Pilsudski and Helissio, fading and finishing tired after reaching the firing line two furlongs out. York provided good ground for the Juddmonte International, in which Singspiel and the four-year-old filly Bosra Sham (who started odds on) met the Derby winners Benny The Dip and Desert King. Singspiel's trainer, Michael Stoute, reportedly harboured doubts at one time about whether the horse would make the line-up at York after his hard race at Ascot—'he was very quiet and tired for a week'—and Singspiel drifted in the betting from 9/4 to 4/1 on the day. The market proved a misleading guide on this occasion as Singspiel's performance belied his gruelling experience at Ascot less than four weeks earlier. He recorded a most decisive victory, ridden in similar style to Epsom and dominating in the last three furlongs. Singspiel never really looked likely to be caught after quickening into the lead and passed the post a length and a half ahead of Desert King, with Benny The Dip the same distance away third and Bosra Sham, who lost a shoe during the race, last of the quartet.

Singspiel's victory at York led to more extravagant talk about his being the 'world champion'. His rider, Frankie Dettori, hailed Singspiel as 'the undisputed heavyweight champion of the world. Halling and Lammtarra were both very special horses, but on all-round performance and guts, this fellow must be number-one.' Singspiel's victory took his total earnings over the £3.5m mark; £3,671,039 will be quoted in most record books, though such an exact figure is clearly open to question as it depends on which conversion rates were used for overseas prize-money. The German-trained Lando, winner of the 1995 Japan Cup, was the previous holder of the prize-money record for a European-trained horse, while Singspiel had already replaced Snurge at the top of the list of British-trained money-earners when winning the 1996 Japan Cup. The thoroughly game, genuine and iron-constitutioned Singspiel was successfully operated on after the accident at exercise at Hollywood Park, two days before he was due to contest the Breeders' Cup Turf. He will stand his first season as a stallion at Dalham Hall Stud, Newmarket, at a fee of £25,000, with the October 1st concession. He retires as the winner of Group 1 races in four countries—Canada, Japan, Dubai and Britain—and showed himself effective at a mile and a quarter to a mile and a half, and on turf (firm and soft) and sand, such manifested adaptability to different surfaces being very unusual in a top horse. The achievements of Singspiel and the rest of his outstanding older-horse contemporaries contributed greatly to the racing year. We are fortunate to have had them around.

		Sadler's Wells	Northern Dancer
	In The Wings	(b 1981)	Fairy Bridge
	(b 1986)	High Hawk	Shirley Heights
Singspiel (IRE)		(b 1980)	Sunbittern
(b.h. 1992)		Halo	Hail To Reason
	Glorious Song (CAN)	(b or br 1969)	Cosmah
	(b 1976)	Ballade	Herbager
		(b 1972)	Miss Swapsco

Sheikh Mohammed's "Singspiel"

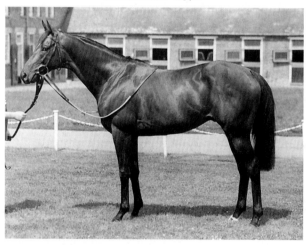

The cleverly-named Singspiel (which is a type of opera consisting of songs and dialogue) is by In The Wings, who likewise won Group 1 races in different countries, taking the Coronation Cup, Grand Prix de Saint-Cloud and Breeders' Cup Turf. Singspiel's dam, Glorious Song, was also a top performer, winning seventeen races and achieving the distinction of being Canadian Horse of the Year, and Champion Older Mare in both Canada and the States. At least five of Glorious Song's previous foals—the useful three-year-old Song of Freedom (by Arazi)—is her latest winner—are reportedly at stud around the world, including the Middle Park runner-up Rahy (by Blushing Groom), who went on to win in graded company in the States. Rahy has done well at stud and his fee rose to 65,000 dollars in 1997 after the successes of such as the high-class American filly Serena's Song and European pattern winners Applaud and Raphane. Meanwhile, another son of Glorious Song, Rakeen (bred along similar lines to Singspiel, as he is a son of Northern Dancer, and a Grade 2 and Grade 3 winner around a mile and a quarter in South Africa) looks a promising sire judged on his first two crops, which include the Grade 1 winner North By Northwest and Jet Master. Rakeen has recently been transferred from South Africa to America. Glorious Song is one of eight winners out of Ballade, including Devil's Bag, the top American two-year-old of his year, and Saint Ballado, who won the Arlington Classic and is the sire of Captain Bodgit, narrowly beaten in the latest Kentucky Derby and Preakness Stakes. The strong, lengthy, quite attractive Singspiel, who is a good walker, should further enhance the record of his famous family at stud. *M. R. Stoute*

SING WITH THE BAND 6 b.m. Chief Singer 131 – Ra Ra Girl 77 (Shack (USA) 118) [1996 73, a80: 5g 6.1g 5g² 5d² 5.1m 6g⁶ a6g³ 5f* 5d⁶ 5m⁶ 5m² a6g² 5m 5d 5m⁵ 5s 1997 a5g³ a5g⁵ 5m 6.1m 5g 6.1d a5g 5d 5d 5f 6g⁶ 7d 6d² 7g² 7g 6.1m Sep 15] strong, compact mare: fairly useful handicapper at best on the all-weather, only poor on turf in 1997: barely stays 7f: acts on firm ground, dead and fibresand: blinkered (below form) once: joined R. Hollinshead. *B. A. McMahon*   49 a80 d

SINON (IRE) 2 ch.c. (Mar 7) Ela-Mana-Mou 132 – Come In (Be My Guest (USA) 126) [1997 9m* 10m⁶ Nov 1] 14,000Y: sixth foal: half-brother to a winner abroad by Salt Dome: dam maiden in Ireland and USA: won maiden at Redcar in October: rallying well at finish when beaten about 2½ lengths behind stable-companion Trigger Happy in listed event at Newmarket: will be very well suited by 1½m+: should do better still. *M. Johnston*   92 p

SIOUX 3 ch.f. Kris 135 – Lassoo 87 (Caerleon (USA) 132) [1996 76p: 7g 8.2s³ 1997 8m⁵ 10.1s⁵ 11.9m 12.1g 13.1s Oct 14] leggy, unfurnished filly: fair maiden: should be suited by further than 1m: acts on good to firm and soft going: none too reliable. *C. W. Thornton*   65

SIOUXROUGE 3 b.g. Indian Ridge 123 – Scarlett Holly 81 (Red Sunset 120) [1996 73p: 5g 6m³ a7g³ a6g³ 1997 a6g² a7g³ a6g* a6g⁵ a5g⁶ 7m³ 6.1m a8f a8.5s 8g² Dec 22] leggy gelding: fair performer: easy winner of maiden at Wolverhampton in January: left P. Haslam after seventh start (hung right, found little): second in claimer final one: stays 1m: acts on good to firm ground, fibresand and dirt. *C. Whittingham, USA*   75

SIPHON (BRZ) 6 b.h. Itajara (BRZ) – Ebrea (BRZ) (Kublai Khan (ARG)) [1996 a6f² a6f* a8.5f* a8.5f* a10f* a10f³ 1997 a8.5g* a10f* a10f² a10f² a10f⁴ Oct 18] lengthy, good-quartered horse: won 10 of 19 races prior to 1997, on last occasion Hollywood Gold Cup: off course 5½ months, won allowance race in January then Santa Anita Handicap (by 3 lengths from stablemates Sandpit and Gentlemen) early in 1997: good 1¼ lengths second to Singspiel in Dubai World Cup (had good battle until held in last 100 yds) in April then second to Gentlemen in Hollywood Gold Cup (beaten 4 lengths) in June and Pacific Classic at Del Mar (beaten 2¾ lengths) in August: reportedly suffered ankle injury when well below form final start: stayed 1¼m: front runner, at his best when able to dominate: game and genuine: retired to Airdrie Stud, Kentucky (fee $15,000). *R. Mandella, USA*   130

SIPOWITZ 3 b.g. Warrshan (USA) 117 – Springs Welcome 86 (Blakeney 126) [1996 –: 8m 1997 8.5m 12m a14.8g* a12g⁵ 15.4s 16m* 17.2g³ a16g⁴ a16g* 16m⁵   68

16g² 17.1m* 18d* a16s Nov 10] fair handicapper: had good season, winning at Wolverhampton in June, Lingfield in July and August and Pontefract (2) in October: beaten long way out final start: suited by thorough test of stamina: acts on good to firm ground, dead and the all-weather. *C. A. Cyzer*

SIPPING SODA 2 b.f. (Apr 29) Silver Kite (USA) 111 – Red Magic (Red God – 128§) [1997 5m a5g⁶ 7g 6.9m⁵ 6m Aug 23] 1,000Y: half-sister to a 2-y-o 6f winner by Dalsaan and 2m winner As Always (by Hatim): dam lightly raced: of little account. *K. T. Ivory*

SIR ALIDAF 3 b.g. Broadsword (USA) 104 – Bolton Flyer (Aragon 118) [1996 – –: 5.1g⁴ 1997 a9.4g a12g⁶ a11g Apr 1] no sign of ability. *O. O'Neill*

SIR ARTHUR HOBBS 10 b.g. Lyphard's Special (USA) 122 – Song Grove 61 61 (Song 132) [1996 58: 9.2g² 8m* 9.2g* 8f* 8m³ 8m⁴ 1997 7g⁵ 8f² Jun 2] strong gelding: unimpressive mover (has reportedly broken down twice): modest performer: stays 9.2f: acts on firm ground, dead and fibresand: tried blinkered (refused to enter stalls) and visored, not for long time: genuine. *J. L. Eyre*

SIR JOEY (USA) 8 ch.g. Honest Pleasure (USA) – Sougoli (Realm 129) [1996 90 92: 6s 6g 5g² 6m² 5.1f⁵ 6d 6g* 6f⁵ 5.1f³ 6m³ 6g⁵ 5.6m 6m 5d³ 5g 1997 6m 6m 5.2g 6m² 6d² 6f³ 6d⁴ 6m² 6m 6g 6d⁴ a6g⁴ a7g² a6g Nov 15] lengthy, workmanlike gelding: has been hobdayed: fairly useful handicapper: ran creditably most starts in 1997 without winning: effective at 5f to 7f: acts on any turf going and fibresand: held up, and suited by strongly-run race: has had tongue tied: tough. *P. G. Murphy*

SIR PAGEANT 8 b.g. Pharly (FR) 130 – National Dress 64 (Welsh Pageant 132) – [1996 NR 1997 16s Oct 8] very lightly raced and no form on flat since 1992. *K. S. Bridgwater*

SIR RICKY (USA) 3 b.g. Woodman (USA) 126 – Opera Queen (IRE) (Sadler's 84 Wells (USA) 132) [1996 –p: 7m 1997 11.7g⁴ 12m² 12m² 11.7g² Sep 8] useful-looking gelding: has a round action: fairly useful maiden: runner-up twice at Newmarket and once at Bath: stays 1½m: raced only on good/good to firm going: has run well sweating: hung left penultimate start: sold 27,000 gns in October. *R. Charlton*

SIR SILVER SOX (USA) 5 gr.g. Corwyn Bay 115 – Sox In The Box (USA) 53 (Cresta Rider (USA) 124) [1996 104d: 7s 6g⁴ 6d⁶ 6f 6m 6.3m 7d⁶ 7g 6s 1997 7g⁵ 6m Apr 9] leggy ex-Irish gelding: useful handicapper at best: modest in 1997: best efforts at 6f: dead. *N. Tinkler*

SIR TALBOT 3 b.g. Ardross 134 – Bermuda Lily 78 (Dunbeath (USA) 127) 96 [1996 73: 7d⁴ 7.9g⁵ 1997 8m* 10m 9g² 10m* 10m 11g Aug 31] close-coupled gelding: fairly useful performer: won maiden at Leicester in March and handicap at Windsor in July: far from disgraced when eighth in Group 3 race at Baden-Baden final start: should stay 1½m: acts on good to firm ground: often a front runner: game: sold 56,000 gns in October, and joined J. Old. *R. Hannon*

SIR TASKER 9 b.h. Lidhame 109 – Susie's Baby (Balidar 133) [1996 54d, a66d: 51 a6g² a6g³ a5g⁴ a6g⁴ a6g³ a6g⁵ a6g⁴ a6g a6g³ 5.1g⁴ a5g⁵ 6g 6d 6m a5g a6g a6s⁵ 1997 a6g⁴ a5f⁵ a6g* a6g a6g² a5g³ a6g 6m⁵ 6.1g a6g 6m 6g² 6m⁵ 7m 6f a6g a5g Dec 8] compact horse: modest sprinter: won minor event at Lingfield in February: acts on firm and dead ground and the all-weather: effective blinkered/visored or not: usually races prominently: inconsistent. *J. L. Harris*

SI SENORITA 2 b.f. (Apr 27) Young Senor (USA) 113 – Raunchy Rita (Brigadier – Gerard 144) [1997 6m⁶ Jul 19] half-sister to 6-y-o Daring Destiny: dam ran 3 times: in rear in maiden at Ayr. *B. Mactaggart*

SIS GARDEN 4 b.f. Damister (USA) 123 – Miss Nanna 56§ (Vayrann 133) [1996 64 49, a65: 7m 8m 12g a11g³ a9.4g² a8g a8.5g² 8m² 8f 7m 7d⁵ 8m a7g* 7g³ a7g* a8g a7g³ a7g 1997 6.9g⁵ a7g² a8g⁶ 8f* 8f³ 7s 8.3m 8.1g* 8.2m⁵ 8.3m² 8g⁶ 8m⁴ 8.2d 8s Nov 8] modest handicapper: won at Brighton in May and Chepstow (ladies) in August: good efforts when in frame afterwards: best form at 7f/1m: acts on fibresand and on firm and dead ground, seemingly not soft: effective blinkered/visored, or not: best ridden up with pace. *J. Cullinan*

SIX CLERKS (IRE) 4 b.g. Shadeed (USA) 135 – Skidmore Girl (USA) (Vagu- 57 ely Noble 140) [1996 58, a69: a8g² 10.3d⁵ 12d 10m 8g⁵ 1997 12.1s³ 12m² 12m 10g a–

Jul 30] tall, strong gelding: modest maiden: acts on good to firm and soft ground, best form in 1996 on the all-weather: no improvement blinkered. *J. G. FitzGerald*

SIX FOR LUCK   5 b.g. Handsome Sailor 125 – Fire Sprite 83 (Mummy's Game 120) [1996 61§: 5g 5g⁵ 5m 5g⁶ 5g 5g⁵ 5m⁵ 5m⁵ 6m³ 6m³ 6d² 5m 5m 5g 5m 1997 6d 6s 5g⁴ 5m⁵ 5m⁵ 6m 6g 5g 5d 5s 8s Nov 6] leggy, lengthy gelding: good mover: poor sprint handicapper: acts on good to firm and dead ground: tried blinkered: usually bandaged: has had tongue tied: carries head high: not one to trust. *D. A. Nolan*   45 §

SIXPENCE   2 b.f. (Apr 20) Saddlers' Hall (IRE) 126 – Half A Dozen (USA) 57 (Saratoga Six (USA)) [1997 6m 6m⁵ 6g Oct 27] leggy, useful-looking filly: second foal: half-sister to Italian 3-y-o 1m (at 2 yrs) and 11f winner Mont Royal (by Polar Falcon): dam, third at 7f at 2 yrs, from good family: some promise in maidens, best effort at Newmarket second start: will be well suited by further than 6f: should do better. *G. Wragg*   67 p

SIX SHOOTER   3 b.f. Damister (USA) 123 – Ten To Six 66 (Night Shift (USA)) [1996 –: 7f 1997 7m 10s Oct 8] soundly beaten in maidens. *E. Weymes*   –

SIXTH AVENUE (IRE)   2 b.f. (Feb 28) Common Grounds 118 – Tarativa (USA) (Sensitive Prince (USA)) [1997 5d⁶ 5g 6g a7g⁴ a7g 9m a7g Oct 20] 5,500 2-y-o: angular filly: half-sister to 3 winners in minor company: dam won up to 11f in France: little form, mainly in sellers: visored final start: sold, and sent to Trinidad. *R. M. Whitaker*   –

SIXTIES MELODY   3 b.g. Merdon Melody 98 – Balidilemma 77 (Balidar 133) [1996 –: 7f 1997 a10g³ 10g 14.1m 17.2g² a16g 16m Sep 15] modest maiden at best: seems a stayer. *R. Boss*   52 a–

SIYADAH (USA)   3 ch.f. Mr Prospector (USA) – Roseate Tern 123 (Blakeney 126) [1996 79p: 7g³ 7m⁵ 1997 10m* 12m 12g a7f 10f³ 10f Oct 10] lengthy, unfurnished filly: easy mover: easily best effort when winning listed event at Newmarket in May by ¾ length from Attire: well beaten, showing clear signs of temperament, in Oaks at Epsom (visored) and Ribblesdale Stakes at Royal Ascot before leaving Saeed bin Suroor: no better than third in allowance company in New York: should have stayed at least 1½m: raced only on good and good to firm going: visits Danzig. *K. McLaughlin, USA*   106

SIZZLING   5 b.g. Sizzling Melody 117 – Oriental Splendour 85 (Runnett 125) [1996 64: 6.1g 6m 6f 6m² 6m⁵ 6m⁴ 5m⁵ 1997 6f* 7m 6f⁵ 6d³ 6m 6m⁶ 6m⁶ 6f a7g² a7s⁶ a7g⁵ Dec 19] smallish, sturdy gelding: modest performer: won claimer at Brighton in April: stays 7f: acts on firm ground, dead and equitrack: well beaten only try in blinkers: inconsistent. *R. Hannon*   62

SKELTON COUNTESS (IRE)   4 ch.f. Imperial Frontier (USA) 112 – Running Brook (Run The Gantlet (USA)) [1996 59, a–: 8.2m⁶ a8g a7g a7g 1997 6m 8g 5m 6g⁴ 5f 8g Oct 27] leggy filly: poor maiden handicapper: stays 1m: no form on fibresand. *R. Hollinshead*   38 a–

SKELTON SOVEREIGN (IRE)   3 b.c. Contract Law (USA) 108 – Mrs Lucky (Royal Match 117) [1996 63, a59: a5g⁵ a6g 5f⁶ 7f⁴ 7g⁴ 7.5f² 8m 7d 8m 8f 10f* 8g a8.5g² a8.5g⁵ 1997 a8s³ a8.5g⁴ a9.4f⁴ a11g³ a12g³ a8.5g³ a8g³ 10.8m⁴ a11g 12g⁴ a12g³ 9.9d² 12d a12g* 12f⁴ a12g² 14d⁴ 14.1g⁵ 13.8m⁴ 16.1m a12g³ a12g Dec 26] smallish colt: fair on all-weather, modest on turf: won seller at Wolverhampton in May: stays 1¾m: acts on firm ground, dead and fibresand: no improvement in blinkers: sometimes slowly away (very much so final start). *R. Hollinshead*   56 a66

SKIDDAW SAMBA   8 b.m. Viking (USA) – Gavea (African Sky 124) [1996 NR 1997 12m⁶ 12.1g Sep 1] winning hurdler: little form in 4 runs on flat. *Mrs M. Reveley*   –

SKIP AWAY (USA)   4 gr. or ro.c. Skip Trial (USA) – Ingot Way (USA) (Diplomat Way (USA)) [1996 a8.5f a8.5f* a9f³ a9s* a10f a9.5f² a12f² a9f* a9f* a10f³ a9f* a10f* 1997 a9f² a10f² a8f³ a9.5f² a9f* a10f* a9f³ a8.5f² a9f² a10f* a10f* Nov 8] top-class American colt: champion 3-y-o in 1996: won very valuable Grade 3 event at Suffolk Downs by a head from Formal Gold (rec 5 lb) in May and Grade 2 event at Belmont by 1½ lengths from Will's Way (rec 6 lb) in July: below form next 3 starts (twice beaten over 5 lengths by Formal Gold) and did not have to be at best to win weak renewal of Jockey Club Gold Cup at Belmont (for second year running, easily) in October: back to absolute peak when winning Breeders' Cup Classic at Hollywood   131

SKI

Park by 6 lengths from Deputy Commander, dominating race in last 4f: needs further than 1m, and stays 1½m: effective on a wet track: wears blinkers: tough, game and genuine: stays in training. *H. Hine, USA*

SKIPPOOL CREEK (IRE)   2 b. or br.f. (Apr 23) Petardia 113 – Tambora 75   36
(Darshaan 133) [1997 5m 5g⁵ 6g 6m⁵ May 31] 5,800Y: close-coupled filly: second foal: half-sister to a 6f winner in Sweden by Mac's Imp: dam 1¼m winner: poor maiden: blinkered third start. *T. D. Easterby*

SKIPPY WAS A KIWI (IRE)   3 b.f. River Falls 113 – Hit For Six (Tap On   –
Wood 130) [1996 47: 5m⁴ 6m² 6m⁵ 1997 a8.5g 6g 7m 6.9m May 28] leggy, lightly-made filly: no form in 1997, including in visor. *A. P. Jarvis*

SKRAM   4 b.g. Rambo Dancer (CAN) 107 – Skarberg (FR) (Noir Et Or 125) [1996   –
–: 12m 10g 1997 a16g Mar 3] lengthy gelding: winning hurdler: no form on flat since poor 2-y-o. *R. Dickin*

SKY COMMANDER (USA)   3 b. or br.c. Storm Bird (CAN) 134 – Fairy   92
Footsteps 123 (Mill Reef (USA) 141) [1996 91p: 6m² 1997 7.1s² a7g* 8.1d⁵ 10s*
10g⁵ 10.5m⁴ Sep 21] close-coupled colt: fairly useful performer: won maiden at Lingfield in May and rated stakes at Newmarket in June: better around 1¼m than shorter: acts on good to firm and soft ground and on equitrack: has been bandaged: keen sort, often taken steadily to post: consistent: sent to UAE. *M. R. Stoute*

SKY DOME (IRE)   4 ch.g. Bluebird (USA) 125 – God Speed Her (Pas de Seul   86
133) [1996 92: 7m* 7m⁶ 7.9f 8m 8m* 8d* 8g 9m 8g⁵ 1997 8m 8g⁵ 8m 7g 8d
Oct 16] lengthy, leggy gelding: fairly useful handicapper: ran creditably in Lincoln at Doncaster and Spring Cup at Newbury first 2 starts, but well below best afterwards: probably stays 9f: acts on good to firm ground and dead: often makes running. *M. H. Tompkins*

SKYERS A KITE   2 b.f. (Feb 28) Deploy 131 – Milady Jade (IRE) (Drumalis   –
125) [1997 7.5f a8g Nov 14] 400Y: second foal: dam unraced: no promise in maiden and seller. *Ronald Thompson*

SKYERS FLYER (IRE)   3 b. or br.f. Magical Wonder (USA) 125 – Siwana   68
(IRE) (Dom Racine (FR) 121) [1996 77, a?: 5s⁶ 5d⁴ 5m* 6g³ 5m³ 5m⁴ 6m² 5g⁴ 6f³
5.3f* 5f⁵ 6.5m 6m 7f⁵ a6g 1997 6g² 6.1g 6.1d* 6m 5d³ 8m² 6m² 5.9f⁶ 7.5m³ 6m* Aug
3] rangy, angular filly: has a round action: fair performer: won sellers at Nottingham (flashed tail) in April and Newcastle (sold to join Martyn Wane 7,800 gns) in August: effective at 5f, probably 1m: acts on firm and dead going, well beaten on fibresand: races keenly: tends to carry head high: quirky, and not one to trust implicitly. *Ronald Thompson*

SKYERS TRYER   3 b.f. Lugana Beach 116 – Saltina (Bustino 136) [1996 54, a–:   –
5f 5f⁵ 6d⁶ 5m* a5g a8.5g⁶ a6g 1997 6.9f 6m a5g Dec 8] lengthy filly: modest winner at 2 yrs: well beaten in 1997. *Ronald Thompson*

SKY MOUNTAIN (IRE)   2 b.c. (Jan 11) Danehill (USA) 126 – Molvina (ITY)   60
(Final Straw 127) [1997 6m 5g 5d 6f³ Jul 15] 18,000Y: first foal: dam ran once in Italy at 2 yrs: modest form in maidens second and final starts: stays 6f: has started slowly: sold, and joined S. R. Bowring. *G. Lewis*

SKY RED   2 gr.f. (Jan 29) Night Shift (USA) – Noble Haven 74 (Indian King   61
(USA) 128) [1997 5.1v⁴ 6m 6g Oct 27] 37,000F, IR 70,000Y: sturdy, sprint type: fourth foal: sister to useful 1993 French 2-y-o 5f winner Shoalhaven, later successful up to 1m in Dubai, and half-sister to a winner in Italy by Faustus: dam, 2-y-o 6f winner, half-sister to useful sprinter Night At Sea: off 5 months after debut: modest form in maidens at Newmarket and Leicester on return. *M. Bell*

SKY ROCKET   2 ch.c. (May 17) Storm Cat (USA) – Oriental Mystique 97 (Kris   95 p
135) [1997 6m² 6.1g* Oct 4] 250,000Y: strong, lengthy colt: third foal: half-brother to useful 7f winner (probably stayed 1¼m) Mandarina (by El Gran Senor): dam 7f/1m winner, daughter of very smart Miss Toshiba: shaped most promisingly against more experienced rivals in useful minor event at Doncaster, beaten 1¼ lengths by Bintang, and landed odds in maiden at Nottingham following month with plenty to spare: bred to stay further than 6f: a useful prospect. *M. R. Stoute*

SLAPY DAM   5 b.g. Deploy 131 – Key To The River (USA) (Irish River (FR) 131) [1996 53: a12g⁶ 11.8g 12g 11.8m 14.6g 12m⁶ 10m⁴ 11.8m⁵ 10.4g 10f 1997 12.3m 11.1s 12g 12d⁴ 14.9s⁵ 12g Aug 23] close-coupled gelding: poor handicapper: stays 1½m: acts on good to firm and soft ground: sometimes visored: unreliable. *C. A. Smith*   48 §

SLASHER JACK (IRE)   6 b.g. Alzao (USA) 117 – Sherkraine 98 (Shergar 140) [1996 NR 1997 12m 12.3m 12g 12.1g 10s⁵ 12s² Nov 6] rather leggy gelding: just a fair handicapper at 6 yrs: left D. Nicholls after third start, best effort at Musselburgh on final one: stays 1¾m: acts on firm and soft ground: blinkered (ran well) last 2 starts at 4 yrs. *R. A. Fahey*   70

SLEDMERE (IRE)   2 ch.g. (Apr 16) Shalford (IRE) 124§ – Jazirah (Main Reef 126) [1997 8m 8m 7d Oct 16] 12,500 2-y-o: big, plain gelding: fifth foal: half-brother to 4-y-o Finsbury Flyer: dam unraced from family of Halling: no form, including in seller. *N. Tinkler*   –

SLEEPLESS   3 b.f. Night Shift (USA) – Late Evening (USA) (Riverman (USA) 131) [1996 81: 6m² 5f³ 7m⁴ 1997 7g⁴ 7.3s* 7m 8d³ 8g 7g Sep 4] smallish, good-topped filly: fairly useful handicapper: won at Newbury in May: good third at Newmarket following month: met trouble in running last 2 starts: stays 1m: acts on soft going. *N. A. Graham*   85

SLEEPYTIME (IRE)   3 b.f. Royal Academy (USA) 130 – Alidiva 105 (Chief Singer 131) [1996 108P: 7.1m* 8g³ 1997 7.3g⁴ 8m* 8m³ Jun 18]   121

Sleepytime came good when it really mattered. Unlucky in running in her big test at two and again in her trial for the One Thousand Guineas on her return, she got a good gallop and room to manoeuvre in the big one itself and duly ran out the race's most clear-cut winner of recent times.

Sleepytime's claims for the One Thousand Guineas were being spoken of even before she had made her debut. Odds of 40/1 before she'd set foot on the course, became 6/1 after she'd strolled home in front in an ordinary maiden at Sandown on her debut. It then became 9/2 after Sleepytime endured a nightmare run when third in the Fillies' Mile at Ascot on her only other two-year-old start, giving the strong impression she'd prove to be the best filly in the race. *Racehorses of 1996* went on record as saying that she 'clearly has the makings of a filly who should prove well up to normal Guineas-winning standard.' By the time of her reappearance in the Dubai Duty Free Fred Darling Stakes at Newbury she was down to 5/2 favourite. Confidence in her took a bit of a knock when she managed only fourth, beaten two and three quarter lengths by Dance Parade. But there were extenuating circumstances. Sleepytime got into a muddling race over a trip short of her best and, after having to wait for a run, could make only a limited impression on the trio ahead of her.

Come One Thousand Guineas day, Sleepytime at 5/1 had been deposed as favourite by the French-trained Cheveley Park winner Pas de Reponse (5/2), successful in the Prix Imprudence on her return, and was also headed in the betting by the Cheveley Park runner-up Moonlight Paradise (7/2), making her reappearance and reported to have been going well. Others in the field of fifteen included the Cheveley Park third and Robert Papin winner Ocean Ridge, the Nell Gwyn first three, Reunion, Oh Nellie and Elegant Warning, the first two in the Fillies' Mile, Reams of Verse and Khassah, Dance Parade and the joint-best two-year-old filly of 1996, Dazzle. All in all it looked a strong field, with few notable absentees. The ex-North American Oh Nellie ensured the good gallop, but Sleepytime couldn't lie up and by halfway was in an unpromising position, several lengths off the lead. Most of the others were beginning to cry enough by two furlongs out, where Oh Nellie looked in danger of being swamped by Pas de Reponse and Dazzle and Sleepytime still had as many in front of her as behind. A furlong later the picture had changed dramatically. Pas de Reponse and Dazzle were challenging Oh Nellie but couldn't get past, while Sleepytime had found her stride with a vengeance and swept through to dispute the lead. Sleepytime sustained her run, while Oh Nellie could keep on at just one pace

Pertemps One Thousand Guineas Stakes, Newmarket—Sleepytime bursts clear;
Oh Nellie comes off best in the fight for second with Dazzle (rail) and Pas de Reponse (blaze)

and Dazzle and Pas de Reponse could do no more. Drawing away under pressure in the final furlong, Sleepytime reached the line four lengths to the good over Oh Nellie, with Dazzle and Pas de Reponse, separated by a head, three quarters of a length away in third and fourth respectively. Excuses could be forwarded for a number of the beaten horses—Dance Parade and Reunion clearly didn't give their running, the lightly-raced Rebecca Sharp wasn't the horse she later became, Reams of Verse (never better than sixth) and Yashmak proved better over further, while Pas de Reponse (and possibly Dazzle) found the trip a bit too far. But that shouldn't be used to take much away from Sleepytime, who provided a first classic win for Kieren Fallon. Her winning margin was the longest in the race since Humble Duty won by seven lengths in 1970 and her form, for all the limitations of some of those behind, compares favourably with that put up by other recent winners in the race itself, marginally the best on Timeform ratings since Salsabil ran to 122 in 1990.

Of course, one of the winners of the One Thousand in the interim was Bosra Sham, like Sleepytime trained by Henry Cecil, who went on to prove herself a very good filly indeed. Similar hopes were held for Sleepytime, naturally. But in fact she ran only once more and was beaten again in a race that didn't go her way. The Coronation Stakes at Royal Ascot attracted just five other runners, among them the Irish One Thousand winner Classic Park. Sleepytime went off at a shade of odds on, but, in a steadily-run affair, was settled just off the pace. When things hotted up Sleepytime couldn't respond immediately (pretty much what could have been expected given the way she'd gone at Newmarket) and merely plugged on into third, two and three quarter lengths behind the 25/1-winner Rebecca Sharp and two lengths behind Ocean Ridge, only fifth in the One Thousand. It was decided to give Sleepytime a mid-season break at her owners' stud with a view to pursuing an autumn campaign but that campaign never materialised. Despite encouraging noises about her well-being it was announced at the end of September that she would miss the Sun Chariot and the rest of the season. The welcome, if somewhat surprising, news is that she will remain in training in 1998.

Sleepytime is the third foal out of Alidiva, and all have won Group 1 races, unique for a mare with her first three foals, though as described in the essay on Elnadim there is at least one other dam around with a similarly remarkable record. Interestingly, those Group 1 wins came in 'reverse' order, with the three-year-old Sleepytime in May being followed in July by the four-year-old Ali-Royal and in September by the five-year-old Taipan. Sleepytime's year-younger half-brother by Fairy King, named Anytime, is also held in high regard but reportedly underwent an operation on a sesamoid early in 1997. The 1996 product of Alidiva is a full sister to Sleepytime and Ali-Royal, the 1997 one is a foal by Fairy King, and at the time of writing Alidiva is reportedly in foal to Sadler's Wells. Alidiva was a useful filly at up to a mile, winning her only start at two years and two of her four—the Masaka Stakes and the listed Oak Tree Stakes—at three. Her dam, Alligatrix, became disappointing after winning over seven furlongs and finishing third in the Fillies' Mile at two. At stud she's produced several winners besides Alidiva, including the useful brothers Tom Waller and Croco Rouge, the latter a close fourth in the Criterium de Saint-Cloud in the latest season. Alligatrix's dam, Shore, was smart in America herself and a sister to even better performers in Cabildo and Canal as well as to the dam of the 1987 Prix de l'Abbaye winner Polonia. With relatives like this Sleepytime will be quite a prospect when indeed she does go to stud.

	Royal Academy (USA) (b 1987)	Nijinsky (b 1967)	Northern Dancer Flaming Page
Sleepytime (IRE) (b.f. 1994)		Crimson Saint (ch 1969)	Crimson Satan Bolero Rose
	Alidiva (b 1987)	Chief Singer (b 1981)	Ballad Rock Principia
		Alligatrix (br 1980)	Alleged Shore

Greenbay Stables' "Sleepytime"

A tall, close-coupled filly, with a quick, fluent action, Sleepytime is suited by a strong gallop at a mile and may well benefit from being tried over further, though a hefty penalty for her Group 1 success may rule her out of many such races early in the season. She's sometimes attended by two handlers in the preliminaries and has raced only on good and good to firm going. *H. R. A. Cecil*

SLEW MAGIC (IRE) 2 b.f. (Feb 12) Don't Forget Me 127 – Sound Pet (Runnett   49
125) [1997 5m³ a7g 7g* 7g 7g Aug 22] 1,100Y: fourth foal: half-sister to unreliable
5f to 7f winner Rockville Pike (by Glenstal): dam placed in Germany: won seller at
Brighton in August: only other form on debut: stays 7f. *W. G. M. Turner*

SLIEMA CREEK 3 gr.g. Beveled (USA) – Sea Farer Lake 74 (Gairloch 122)   65
[1996 –p: a6g⁵ 1997 a7g² a8g² a7g³ a8g Apr 28] fair maiden on flat: stays 1m: acts
on fibresand: sold 4,400 gns, and won juvenile hurdle in October for P. Hobbs.
T. D. Barron

SLIEU WHALLIAN 3 b.f. In The Wings 128 – Ladyfish 79 (Pampapaul 121)   54
[1996 NR 1997 8.1s 8m⁵ 10g⁵ 11m Nov 4] 25,000Y: sturdy filly: half-sister to several
winners, including fairly useful 1¼m and 1½m winner Tony's Fen (by Trojan Fen):
dam, 1m winner, is half-sister to Carroll House: modest form in maidens: well held
in handicap final start: stays 1¼m. *R. Hannon*

SLIEVENAMON 4 br.g. Warning 136 – Twice A Fool (USA) (Foolish Pleasure   –
(USA)) [1996 59+: 8m 8f 8.3m a8.5g⁵ a9.4g* a8g* 1997 a8g 8m a10g⁶ a8.5g a8g   a53
a7g³ a7g Dec 10] close-coupled gelding: modest handicapper: left J. Banks after
fourth start: easily best effort in 1997 when third at Lingfield in December: effective
from 7f to 9.4f: best on the all-weather: blinkered/visored 4 of last 5 starts.
R. Simpson

SLIGHTLY OLIVER (IRE) 3 b.g. Silver Kite (USA) 111 – Red Note (Rusti-   §§
caro (FR) 124) [1996 §§: 8.5m⁶ 8.2g⁴ a7g² a7g³ a8g 1997 a14.8g Dec 13] modest
maiden: most temperamental and best avoided. *D. L. Williams*

SLIGHTLY SPECIAL (IRE) 5 ch.g. Digamist (USA) 110 – Tunguska 76   –
(Busted 134) [1996 NR 1997 a12g⁵ 10s a14g Aug 15] 5,200Y: eighth foal:
half-brother to 1m winner Trooping (by Auction Ring): dam 1¼m winner: poor
maiden in Ireland at 2/3 yrs for J. Gorman: winning hurdler here, but no form on flat.
D. T. Thom

SLIM PRIOR 2 gr.g. (May 5) Norton Challenger 111 – Hopeful Katie 67 (Full of   57
Hope 125) [1997 5d a5g 6g⁵ 6d⁵ 6f a7g⁴ a7g* a8g⁴ Dec 10] sturdy gelding: half-
brother to fairly useful 1991 2-y-o sprint winner Fort Hope (by Belfort), later most
ungenuine: dam 6f/7f winner: modest performer: won seller at Lingfield in November, best effort: stays 7f: visored second start. *K. R. Burke*

SLIP JIG (IRE) 4 b.g. Marju (IRE) 127 – Taking Steps 100 (Gay Fandango   73
(USA) 132) [1996 84, a71: 8g 7d* 7m³ 8m 10m⁶ 8.5g³ 8m 8g a7g a8g³ a10g² a10g²   a71
1997 a12g* a9.4g² a12g 12.3v⁴ 12d 10g⁶ 12.3m² 12.3m⁵ 14m a16g⁴ Aug 2] sturdy
gelding: fair performer: won apprentice claimer at Lingfield in January on final start
for R. Hannon: creditable efforts most starts afterwards: stays 1¾m: acts on good to
firm and heavy ground and the all-weather. *K. R. Burke*

SLIPPER 2 b.f. (Mar 10) Suave Dancer (USA) 136 – Horseshoe Reef 88 (Mill   74 p
Reef (USA) 141) [1997 7.5f⁵ 8g⁶ Oct 24] leggy filly: fourth foal: half-sister to 4-y-o
Warning Reef and 1m winner (probably stayed 1¾m) Pumice (by Salse): dam 1¼m
winner, daughter of smart miler Miss Toshiba: fair form in maidens at Beverley and
Doncaster, on latter course (sixth to Merciless) held up and starting to stay on very
strongly as race was all but over, not knocked about: will be well suited by 1¼m+:
sure to do better as stamina comes into play. *L. M. Cumani*

SLIPPERY FIN 5 b.m. Slip Anchor 136 – Finyska (FR) (Niniski (USA) 125)   –
[1996 51: a12g³ a16g a12g² 1997 a13g Jan 11] modest maiden: well beaten only start
in 1997. *W. G. M. Turner*

SLIPSTREAM 3 b.g. Slip Anchor 136 – Butosky 71 (Busted 134) [1996 NR   –
1997 10g 8m May 4] big, lengthy gelding: half-brother to several winners, including
Ebor runner-up Bush Hill (by Beldale Flutter): dam 1½m winning half-sister to very

smart sprinter Crews Hill and the dam of Classic Cliche and My Emma: signs of ability but no form in Newmarket maidens. *R. Guest*

SLIPSTREAM STAR 3 b.f. Slip Anchor 136 – Alsiba 68 (Northfields (USA)) 71 [1996 –p: 7d 1997 10s 8.3g² 8m³ 8.3m³ 8.1m 9.2g² 10d Nov 3] angular filly: fair maiden: stays 9f: acts on good to firm ground: often makes running: tends to edge left. *I. A. Balding*

SLIP VENTURE 2 b.c. (Jan 22) Slip Anchor 136 – Sherkraine 98 (Shergar 140) 69 [1997 8.2s 8f 8s Nov 8] sparely-made colt: sixth foal: brother to 3-y-o Ukraine Venture and half-brother to 2 winners, including 6-y-o Slasher Jack: dam, Irish 2-y-o 6f winner, out of Poule d'Essai des Pouliches winner Ukraine Girl: showed ability in maidens at Nottingham, Yarmouth and Doncaster in autumn: will be suited by 1½m+. *S. P. C. Woods*

SMALL RISK 3 b.f. Risk Me (FR) 127 – Small Double (IRE) 55 (Double – Schwartz 128) [1996 48: 5d³ 5m² a5g 1997 8g 6s Jun 26] angular filly: poor maiden: well held in 1997, too keen in visor final start. *T. T. Clement*

SMART BEAU (USA) 2 ch.c. (Mar 8) Beau Genius (CAN) – Brittney Erin 55 (USA) (Restless Restless (USA)) [1997 6d⁵ 7m⁴ 7g 6m⁶ 6.9g Sep 2] $110,000Y: good-topped colt: first foal: dam won 11 times in USA at up to 9f from 2 to 5 yrs: modest form on balance: well held final outing: stays 7f. *R. Charlton*

SMART BOY (IRE) 3 ch.c. Polish Patriot (USA) 128 – Bouffant (High Top a73 131) [1996 77: 5m* 6f³ 7f 1997 7g 8d a10g* a10g* 11m a10g⁶ Dec 10] small, leggy colt: fair performer: won 2 minor events at Lingfield in May: little other form in 1997: stays 1¼m: acts on equitrack, winner on good to firm ground at 2 yrs. *P. F. I. Cole*

SMART DOMINION 3 b.c. Sharpo 132 – Anodyne 100 (Dominion 123) [1996 – 74p: 6s 1997 7.3s May 18] lengthy, good topped colt: shaped well only start at 2 yrs, but ran as if something amiss on return. *Lord Huntingdon*

SMARTER CHARTER 4 br.g. Master Willie 129 – Irene's Charter 72 (Persian 72 Bold 123) [1996 81: 5d 8m⁴ 7.5g* 8m² 8g² 8m⁶ 8.5m³ 10g⁶ 8m⁶ 8.5m* 8m⁵ 9m⁴ 1997 8m 7m 7.5m³ 8g³ 8.5d 8.5d 9m 8.5d 10g 8g⁴ 8m² a10s Nov 10] leggy gelding: fair handicapper at best in 1997: should stay 1¼m: acts on good to firm ground, possibly not on softer than good: held up, and suited by strongly-run race and firm handling. *Mrs L. Stubbs*

SMART GUEST 5 ch.g. Be My Guest (USA) 126 – Konbola 91 (Superlative 49 118) [1996 60: a8g⁵ 8s 6g* 7.6g 1997 a6g a5g 6.1g 5g a7g⁶ a7g a8.5g 7.5v⁵ 7d⁵ 7g⁵ Jul 28] sturdy, lengthy gelding: unimpressive mover: poor handicapper: stays 1m: acts on firm and dead ground: tried blinkered, no improvement. *D. Shaw*

SMART KID (IRE) 3 b.g. Lahib (USA) 129 – Diamond Lake (Kings Lake 76 § (USA) 133) [1996 NR 1997 8g 6m* 6m a7g Oct 6] 17,000F, 35,000Y: workmanlike gelding: fourth foal: half-brother to 1½m seller winner Bunker (by Scenic) and a winner in Austria by Last Tycoon: dam, Irish 2-y-o 7f winner, from good family: fair form: landed odds in maiden (carried head awkwardly) at Salisbury in May: off course nearly 5 months and well held in handicaps afterwards, looking unenthusiastic final start: joined Miss G. Kelleway and gelded. *P. F. I. Cole*

SMART PLAY (USA) 4 gr.c. Sovereign Dancer (USA) – Casessa (USA) (Caro – 133) [1996 101: 11d⁵ 12g* 10.3g⁴ 12f⁶ 12m 1997 14s³ 11.4g⁴ 14m Jul 30] good-topped colt: useful in 1996: showed little in 1997. *Lord Huntingdon*

SMART PRINCE 2 b.g. (May 2) Prince Sabo 123 – She's Smart 88 (Absalom 57 128) [1997 5g⁶ 5v 5m⁵ 5g⁵ 6g⁶ Aug 22] smallish gelding: has a round action: second foal: half-brother to 3-y-o Rum Lad: dam sprinter: modest maiden on balance: looks a sprinter. *J. J. Quinn*

SMART PROSPECT 3 b.g. Superpower 113 – Bustily 65 (Busted 134) [1996 – –: 7g 7m a7g 1997 12g Apr 28] no sign of living up to his name. *B. J. Meehan*

SMART SPIRIT (IRE) 3 b.f. Persian Bold 123 – Sharp Ego (USA) (Sharpen Up 71 d 127) [1996 66p: 7.9g 8.1d 8.1s³ 8f 1997 8m² 7.9g 8d⁴ 10g⁴ 9m³ 10g 8d 9m⁵ Oct 31] tall, good-topped filly: fair maiden handicapper: below form in 1997 after reappearance: unlikely to stay beyond 9f: acts on good to firm ground and soft: takes strong hold (too stirred up before second start). *Mrs M. Reveley*

SMART SQUALL (USA) 2 b.c. (Feb 6) Summer Squall (USA) – Greek Wedding (USA) (Blushing Groom (FR) 131) [1997 5m 7.1g* 7v* 7.3g⁵ 8v* Dec 7] $82,000Y: smallish, good-bodied colt: first foal: dam French 9f (including at 2 yrs) to 11.5f winner out of Washington International runner-up Persian Tiara: sire, leading 2-y-o, won Preakness Stakes: progressive form: won maiden at Chepstow in September, nursery at Ascot in October and (after staying-on fifth of 8 to La-Faah in Horris Hill Stakes at Newbury) listed race at Toulouse in December, last-named by short neck from Bouccaneer: will stay at least 1¼m: acts on heavy ground: has likeable attitude and should improve further. *Lord Huntingdon* — 97 p

SMART VENTURE 2 b.g. (Feb 12) Sabrehill (USA) 120 – Water Well 96 (Sadler's Wells (USA) 132) [1997 5.1s⁶ a7g Aug 16] 4,000Y: rather leggy gelding: third foal: half-brother to 4-y-o Soaked: dam, stayed 1m, daughter of Soba: well beaten in maidens at Chester and Wolverhampton. *R. Hollinshead* — –

SMILE FOREVER (USA) 4 b.f. Sunshine Forever (USA) – Awenita (Rarity 129) [1996 –: a7g 8m 9.7g⁵ 11.9g a10g⁴ a12s 1997 12.3m Apr 9] sturdy filly: no form since modest 2-y-o. *Miss Gay Kelleway* — –

SMILING BESS 4 b.f. Salse (USA) 128 – Wanda 74 (Taufan (USA) 119) [1996 –: 10m⁴ 6.1m a8.5g 1997 6f 8g 6.9m 6.1m 5m Sep 24] angular filly: poor maiden: best effort at 7f. *J. S. King* — 41

SMILING VOTER (IRE) 2 b.c. (Mar 20) Balla Cove 119 – Ravensdale Rose (IRE) (Henbit (USA) 130) [1997 6m a7g 8.2m⁴ 10m⁴ 10s⁶ Oct 15] IR 4,800Y: second foal: dam ran twice at 2 yrs in Ireland: fair maiden: easily best efforts when fourth at Nottingham and Pontefract: stays 1¼m: well held on soft ground. *R. Hannon* — 77

SMOKE'N'JO (IRE) 3 ch.c. Masterclass (USA) 116 – Alpine Dance (USA) 62§ (Apalachee (USA) 137) [1996 44+: 6m 5m⁶ 7.5f⁵ 7g 8.5g⁶ 1997 9.9g a11g Sep 8] plain colt: poor maiden: well beaten in 1997. *M. W. Easterby* — –

SMOKEY FROM CAPLAW 3 b.g. Sizzling Melody 117 – Mary From Dunlow 49 (Nicholas Bill 125) [1996 63: 5g 6m* 7g 5m² 7.1m 1997 6d 7g 6m* 6g* 6g⁶ 7m⁶ 6g⁶ 6g⁴ 7g 8.1m 8.1g 7m* 7s 8m Oct 28] strong, compact gelding: has a round action: fair handicapper: won at Newcastle and Thirsk in May and at Redcar in October: likely to prove best from 6f to 1m: acts on good to firm ground, well beaten on soft: has carried head awkwardly. *J. J. O'Neill* — 76

SMOOTH PRINCESS (IRE) 2 gr.f. (Feb 21) Roi Danzig (USA) – Sashi Woo (Rusticaro (FR) 124) [1997 6m 5m 7.5f 7g a7g* a7g² a7g Dec 18] IR 7,000Y: good-topped, useful-looking filly: half-sister to winners Grey Charmer (sprinter, by Alzao) and 6-y-o Sushi Bar: dam lightly-raced Irish maiden: poor form on turf before trotting up in seller at Southwell in October: second in nursery on same course following month: stays 7f. *J. G. FitzGerald* — ? a61

SMOOTH SAILING 2 gr.g. (Feb 2) Beveled (USA) – Sea Farer Lake 74 (Gairloch 122) [1997 5f⁵ 5d* 5g² 6g² 6m⁵ 7.9s 8.1m³ 7v⁴ 6g 5d⁶ a6g Nov 17] tall gelding: sixth foal: brother to a winning hurdler and half-brother to a 2-y-o 6f winner by Enchantment: dam 1m and 1¼m winner: fair performer: won maiden at Sandown in April: placed in minor events afterwards, but became rather disappointing: probably stays 1m: acts on dead ground (hampered on fibresand): has been visored/blinkered. *K. McAuliffe* — 86 d a?

SNAP CRACKLE POP (IRE) 3 b.f. Statoblest 120 – Spinelle 88§ (Great Nephew 126) [1996 87: 5.2f 5m² 5m* 5.2m⁴ 5m³ 6m 6m 1997 5d 6g³ 6m 6m⁴ 7g Jul 8] leggy, workmanlike filly: fairly useful performer: clearly best 3-y-o effort when close third in minor event at Kempton in May: stays 6f: acts on good to firm going: blinkered third start: sold 17,000 gns in December. *R. F. Johnson Houghton* — 87

SNAPPY TIMES 2 ch.g. (Mar 6) Timeless Times (USA) 99 – Hill of Fare (Brigadier Gerard 144) [1997 5m⁵ 5m 6m 5m³ 6g 5m 6g³ 6m⁴ 7g² 7g⁴ a5g³ a6g* Oct 6] 8,800Y: leggy, sparely-made gelding: half-brother to 6f winner Thorny Bishop (by Belfort) and a winner in Belgium: dam lightly raced: modest performer: won seller at Wolverhampton in October: possibly best at 6f: acts on fibresand: twice blinkered: carries head high. *M. Dods* — 50 a59

SNOWBALLS 2 gr.c. (Mar 4) Chilibang 120 – Golden Panda 77 (Music Boy 124) 64
[1997 5f³ 6d 6g⁵ Oct 22] 5,000F, 11,000Y: fourth foal: half-brother to 1996 2-y-o 6f
winner Pandiculation (by Statoblest) and 2 winners abroad: dam 1m winner: modest
maiden: best effort at Newcastle final start, though under pressure before halfway:
stays 6f. *Miss L. A. Perratt*

SNOWCAP (IRE) 3 b.f. Snow Chief (USA) – Very Subtle (USA) (Hoist The
Silver (USA)) [1996 NR 1997 12m 12m 10s⁵ Aug 29] workmanlike filly: fourth foal:
half-sister to a minor winner in USA by Alydar: dam won Breeders' Cup Sprint: no
form in maidens: sold 18,000 gns in December. *G. Wragg*

SNOW CARNIVAL 4 ch.g. Belmez (USA) 131 – Winter Queen 60 (Welsh
Pageant 132) [1996 NR 1997 8.5m 10g 9s⁴ 12m 8.5f Sep 17] 18,000 3-y-o:
good-bodied gelding: eighth living foal: half-brother to 3-y-o Winter Garden and 3
other winners, notably smart stayer Safety In Numbers (by Slip Anchor): dam Irish
13f winner: well beaten in maidens and handicaps: sold 2,000 gns, and sent to
Germany. *Lady Herries*

SNOW CLOUD 3 b.f. Today And Tomorrow 78 – Fancy Pages 67 (Touch Paper
113) [1996 NR 1997 a6g Oct 20] 2,500Y: fifth foal: sister to modest 1990 2-y-o 5f
winner Today's Fancy: dam 2-y-o 5f seller winner: no promise in weak maiden at
Southwell. *D. C. O'Brien*

SNOW DOMINO (IRE) 4 ch.g. Habyom – Magic Picture (Deep Diver 134) –
[1996 38: a8g⁵ 1997 12m May 31] poor maiden, lightly raced. *J. M. Jefferson*

SNOW KID 3 b.c. Indian Ridge 123 – Sarcita 111 (Primo Dominie 121) [1996 NR 113 p
1997 a7g* 7d* 7s* 8g 7d² 6d³ 6s* Nov 8] 100,000Y: good-topped, handsome colt:
first living foal: dam won Ayr Gold Cup: quickly made into a smart performer at 3
yrs, winning maiden at Wolverhampton and minor events at Salisbury and Yarmouth
in midsummer and listed race at Doncaster (by neck, clear, from My Best Valentine,
forging ahead 2f out and just holding on) in November: likely to prove best at 6f/7f:
acts on fibresand, raced only on good ground or softer on turf: has the scope to go on
again in 1998, and well up to winning a pattern race. *D. R. Loder*

SNOW PARTRIDGE (USA) 3 ch.c. Arctic Tern (USA) 126 – Lady Sharp (FR) 85
(Sharpman) [1996 84+: 7m² 7.9g³ 1997 8d⁶ 12.1m³ 14m⁵ 10m² 11.5m³ 12m Sep 24]
useful-looking colt: fairly useful maiden: stays 1¾m: acts on good to firm ground:
blinkered (well beaten) final start. *P. F. I. Cole*

SNOW PRINCESS (IRE) 5 b.m. Ela-Mana-Mou 132 – Karelia (USA) 111 (Sir 111
Ivor 135) [1996 104: 16.5g* 16.1m² 13.9m 13.4d³ 15d* 15s⁴ 1997 18.7s 14d⁴ 13.9m⁵
14.6m⁴ 12v² 15.5d² Oct 26] leggy mare: smart performer: second in Princess Royal
Stakes at Ascot (beaten 3 lengths by Delilah) and Prix Royal Oak at Longchamp
(career-best effort, beaten 6 lengths by Ebadiyla): stays 16.5f well: has form on good
to firm ground, goes well on dead or softer: normally held up. *Lord Huntingdon*

SNOWY MANTLE 4 gr.f. Siberian Express (USA) 125 – Mollified 67 (Lom- 54
bard (GER) 126) [1996 –: a8g⁴ 10m³ 10f⁵ 8f 1997 9.9m 8.5s² 10g⁴ 10.9d 8g³ 8.2m*
10g³ 8g 8d 8.2d Nov 3] tall, lengthy filly: modest handicapper: won at Nottingham
in July by 5 lengths: well held last 3 starts: will prove best around 1m: has form
on soft ground, best run on good to firm: reportedly broke blood vessel fifth start.
J. D. Bethell

SOAKED 4 b.g. Dowsing (USA) 124 – Water Well 96 (Sadler's Wells (USA) 132) 39
[1996 66: 7m 8d⁶ 10m 8g⁴ 8.3g 1997 a7g⁶ a7g² a7g a7g⁵ a6g⁶ 5f a6g⁴ 5m 5m 5g³ 5g
5s⁶ a5g⁵ Dec 8] poor maiden handicapper: effective at 5f, and has form at 1m:
blinkered last 7 starts, also tried visored earlier in career: often slowly away.
D. W. Chapman

SOAKING 7 b.g. Dowsing (USA) 124 – Moaning Low 85 (Burglar 128) [1996 54, 51 d
a80: a7g* a7g⁴ a7g⁵ 6.9s 8f 7m⁵ 8g 7g 7m* 7m 7.1f 8m⁶ 7g a7g² a8g* 1997 a8g* a76 d
a8g³ a7g⁵ a8g 8m 8.1g⁴ 10d 8.1g 8m 8.2d a8s a8g Nov 25] strong, useful-looking
gelding: fair performer on equitrack, modest on turf, at best: won claimer at Lingfield
in January on penultimate start for P. Burgoyne: trained third outing only by N. Berry:
well held last 6 starts: stays 1m, not 1¼m: acts on firm and soft ground: sometimes
swishes tail: inconsistent. *M. D. I. Usher*

SO AMAZING   5 b.m. Hallgate 127 – Jussoli (Don 128) [1996 55, a84d: a7g* –
a7g* a8g* a7g* 7.5m 6g 8g⁴ 7g a8.5g a7g⁵ 1997 a8g Jan 10] fairly useful performer,
best up to around 1m on the all-weather: collapsed fatally at Southwell only 5-y-o
start. *J. L. Eyre*

SOAP STONE   2 b.f. (Apr 4) Gunner B 126 – Tzarina (USA) (Gallant Romeo –
(USA)) [1997 7d a8g a8.5g Nov 29] 640Y: half-sister to 3 winners, including fairly
useful sprinter Mandub (by Topsider): dam placed 3 times in USA: no promise in
maidens. *A. Bailey*

SOCIAL CHARTER (USA)   2 b.c. (Feb 17) Nureyev (USA) 131 – Aunt Pearl   90
(USA) (Seattle Slew (USA)) [1997 6d² 6g* 6g⁶ 6m⁵ 7d* 6v⁶ Nov 24] smallish,
compact colt: has a powerful action: first reported foal: dam, won up to 7f at 4 yrs in
USA, out of sister to dam of Dowsing: fairly useful performer: made all in maiden at
Salisbury in August and minor event at Leicester in October, holding Swing Sister
gamely by ½ length in latter: not disgraced in Gimcrack Stakes at York third start but
well held in listed race at Maisons-Laffitte final start: should stay 1m: acts on good to
soft going: goes well with forcing tactics. *P. W. Chapple-Hyam*

SOCIETY KING (IRE)   2 b.c. (Mar 28) Fairy King (USA) – Volga (USA)   –
(Riverman (USA) 131) [1997 6d Oct 17] 13,000Y: lengthy colt: has scope: second
foal: dam, won up to 1¼m in USA, out of Argentinian Grade 1 winner: 20/1, poorly
to post and no promise in maiden at Newmarket. *J. E. Banks*

SOCIETY ROSE   3 b.f. Saddlers' Hall (IRE) 126 – Ruthless Rose (USA)   88
(Conquistador Cielo (USA)) [1996 79p: 7m* 1997 10.4g⁵ May 13] rather leggy,
lengthy filly: winner of only 2-y-o start: fifth of 10 behind 11-length winner Reams
of Verse in Musidora Stakes at York only outing in 1997: stud. *M. R. Stoute*

SOCIETY TIMES (USA)   4 b.g. Imp Society (USA) – Mauna Loa (USA)   –
(Hawaii) [1996 NR 1997 10.1m⁶ 12.1s 8f⁶ May 29] brother to 8-y-o Myasha
(formerly fair sprint winner) dam 7f winning half-sister to top-class middle-distance
stayer Exceller: won poor NH Flat race for M. Pipe in February: no form in 3
northern maidens in May, reluctant to post on final start. *D. A. Nolan*

SOCKET SET   2 b.f. (Mar 2) Tragic Role (USA) – Elsocko 76 (Swing Easy   91
(USA) 126) [1997 a5g* 6d 5m* 6d⁴ 5.2m³ 6.1d* Aug 29] 7,500 2-y-o: close-coupled
filly: fifth foal: half-sister to 1993 2-y-o 5f winner Dominion King (by Dominion
Royale), later successful in Hong Kong, and a useful 6f winner in Hong Kong by The
Noble Player: dam maiden who stayed 7f: fairly useful performer: won maiden at
Southwell, nursery at York and minor event at Chester in the summer: ran well in
frame in Princess Margaret Stakes at Ascot and listed race at Newbury: effective
at 5f/6f: yet to race on extremes of ground: races prominently: sent to USA.
B. A. McMahon

SODA   3 gr.g. Belfort (FR) 89 – Bella Seville 71 (King of Spain 121) [1996 58d: 48
5m³ 5m³ 5m 6m⁶ a6g⁴ a5g 1997 a6g³ 5g² 6.1m 5g⁴ 7m⁶ 6.1m a6g 6.1d 5.1m
Jul 7] leggy gelding: poor maiden: left T. D. Barron after fifth start: stays 6f: acts on
good to firm going and the all-weather: usually blinkered: has started slowly.
J. L. Spearing

SODA POP (IRE)   3 b.c. River Falls 113 – Riviere Salee (FR) (Luthier 126)   67 d
[1996 64?: 6m⁵ 7.1f 1997 a7g 10m² 11.4g 8g⁴ 10.1g² 11.9m* 11.5g 10m 12g⁶ 10m
Oct 23] leggy colt: fair handicapper: won seller at Brighton in July for C. Brittain:
well below form afterwards, including in visor: stays 1½m: acts on good to firm
going. *G. L. Moore*

SODELK   3 ch.f. Interrex (CAN) – Summoned By Bells 55 (Stanford 121§) [1996   –
–: 7g⁶ a7g 1997 a6g a7g Feb 21] no form. *J. Hetherton*

SODEN (IRE)   3 b.f. Mujadil (USA) 119 – Elminya (IRE) (Sure Blade (USA)   65
130) [1996 68: 6.9g 6.1f³ 7m 7m* 7.3m 7.9g 8m 1997 9g 10m³ 10g a10g* 10.1g⁵   a73
10m a9.4g³ a10g⁵ a12g a10g a13g³ Dec 22] smallish, good-topped filly: fair handicapper: won at Lingfield in August: best form on the all-weather, raced
only on good going or firmer on turf. *T. G. Mills*

SOFT TOUCH (IRE)   2 b.f. (Apr 14) Petorius 117 – Fingers (Lord Gayle (USA)   78 ?
124) [1997 5.3f³ 5.3f² 6m 6.3d² 6.1m² 7m⁴ a6g Oct 4] IR 4,000Y: sister to 4-y-o   a?

Miss Pickpocket (5f winner at 2 yrs) and useful 5f (at 2 yrs) and 1m winner Premier Touch and half-sister to several winners, including useful Hollow Hand (by Wolver Hollow), successful over 1¼m: dam Irish 1½m winner: fair maiden: seemingly best effort in valuable sales race at the Curragh fourth start: stays 7f: acts on good to firm and dead ground, slowly away on fibresand debut. *Miss Gay Kelleway*

SOFYAAN (USA) 4 b.g. Silver Hawk (USA) 123 – Tanwi 101 (Vision (USA)) [1996 8s² 9s 10d⁶ 9d* 10g² 1997 10m 12m 10g⁵ 12d³ 12.3m⁴ 10m Jul 24] rangy gelding: second foal: half-brother to 5-y-o Fahs: dam, Irish 5f to 1m winner, out of half-sister to dam of Flame of Tara, herself the dam of Salsabil: fairly useful (rated 91) at 3 yrs: won maiden at Dundalk for K. Prendergast in 1996 (sold 33,000 gns after final start): best effort in handicaps here when third at Newmarket: stays 1½m: acts on soft ground, not at best on good to firm: bolted to post and withdrawn fifth intended start: winner twice over hurdles in October. *Lady Herries*   86

SO INTREPID (IRE) 7 ch.h. Never So Bold 135 – Double River (USA) (Irish River (FR) 131) [1996 84: a6g³ a7g³ 6g 6g* 6f⁴ 5g³ 6d³ 6d⁵ 6m* 6m* 6m 5m⁶ 6m 6m⁶ 6m 6.1s⁵ 6f 1997 a5g 6m⁴ 6m 6m 6m 6m* 6g 6m³ 6m³ 6d 6d³ 5.1s* 6m* 6m* 6m 6g 6g Sep 20] tall horse: fairly useful performer, who won 13 races in all: better than ever in 1997, won handicaps at Thirsk in May and Chepstow in July, apprentice minor event at Goodwood in August and handicap at Ripon in August: suffered fatal heart attack at Ayr in September: stayed 6f: acted on firm ground, soft and fibresand: had run well when sweating: usually held up. *J. M. Bradley*   87

SO KEEN 4 ch.g. Keen 116 – Diana's Bow (Great Nephew 126) [1996 –: 10.5d 8.1d 10m⁶ 13.4m⁵ 17.2m 14d 1997 14d 16.2m 12m⁶ 10.8s⁶ a11g 14.1f Oct 29] rather leggy gelding: little worthwhile form. *A. Bailey*   –

SOLAR DAWN 3 ch.f. Soviet Star (USA) 128 – Haebeh (USA) 88 (Alydar (USA)) [1996 NR 1997 a7g a10g³ a8.5g⁶ a8g a12g May 8] second known foal: half-sister to 5-y-o Ihtimaam: dam 1¼m winner: poor maiden at best: well held apart from second start. *M. Johnston*   46

SOLAR STORM 3 ch.c. Polar Falcon (USA) 126 – Sister Sophie (USA) (Effervescing (USA)) [1996 NR 1997 8m 7g⁴ 7.9s* 8d* 7.9s* Oct 8] 62,000Y: lengthy, rather unfurnished colt: poor mover: seventh foal: half-brother to 3 winners, notably smart 1m and 1¼m performer Port Lucaya (by Sharpo): dam, 1¼m winner in USA, is half-sister to Diminuendo: progressive form: off course approaching 5 months before winning maiden at York and handicaps at Ayr and York in the autumn: clearly best effort when beating Mawingo by 1¼ lengths on final start, idling having been shaken up to lead over 1f out: will prove best up to 1m: best efforts on going softer than good: a smart colt in the making, sure to win more races. *M. Bell*   104 p

SOLDIER COVE (USA) 7 ch.g. Manila (USA) – Secret Form 120 (Formidable (USA) 125) [1996 50: 8f⁶ 8.5m 8f 14s a10g² 1997 a12g² a14.8f⁶ a11g⁴ a6g⁶ a8g* a9.4g* a8g* 8s* 9.7m⁴ a8g 10.2d a10s⁴ a9.4g Dec 26] sparely-made gelding: modest performer: won seller, claimer and 2 selling handicaps in February/March, at Lingfield, Wolverhampton, Southwell and Musselburgh: left M. Meade before penultimate start: seems to stay 1½m: acts on soft ground and the all-weather. *D. Burchell*   51 a60

SOLDIER MAK 4 ch.g. Infantry 122 – Truly Blest 75 (So Blessed 130) [1996 66: 7m² 8m 11.4d³ 11.7m³ 14.1f³ 11.5m² 11.9m⁴ 11.9g² 12g⁴ 1997 a12g³ 11.8g⁶ 10g Aug 11] workmanlike gelding: maiden handicapper: no worthwhile form in 1997, leaving A. Hide after reappearance. *J. Mackie*   –

SOLFEGIETTO 3 b.f. Music Boy 124 – Maria Isabella (FR) (Young Generation 129) [1996 76: 6g³ 5f² 5g* 6m⁶ 1997 8m 8.2m⁴ 7s⁵ Jul 26] tall, angular filly: good mover: fair performer: not at best in 1997, and reportedly broke blood vessel final start: probably stays 7f: has raced mainly on good ground or firmer: sold 15,000 gns in December. *M. Bell*   66

SOLO MIO (IRE) 3 b.c. Sadler's Wells (USA) 132 – Marie de Flandre (FR) 109 (Crystal Palace (FR) 132) [1996 92p: 7g 8m² 8g 1997 10.3d² 10.2d* 12d⁵ 12m 13.9g 12m 12m* 12d³ Oct 16] rangy, good-bodied colt: impresses in appearance: fine mover: useful performer: won maiden at Bath in May: best efforts in rated stakes at Newmarket last 2 starts, winning by 2½ lengths from Kilma then finishing ½ length   106

895

Timeform Silver Tankard Maiden Stakes, Bath—Solo Mio wins in good style

third to Ihtiyati: seems best at 1½m: acts on good to firm and dead ground: used to race keenly, but more settled last 2 starts: sold 120,000 gns, and sent to France. *D. A. Nolan*

SOLO SONG 2 ch.f. (Feb 20) Executive Man 119 – Aosta (Shack (USA) 118) –
[1997 5s 5s⁵ 6m Jul 19] second foal: dam unraced: signs of ability second outing, but tailed off otherwise. *D. A. Nolan*

SOLO SPIRIT 2 b.f. (Mar 7) Northern Park (USA) 107 – Brown Taw 66 77
(Whistlefield 118) [1997 6g⁴ 7m 6m⁴ 5m 6g* Oct 27] close-coupled filly: easy mover: fourth reported foal: half-sister to 5f winner Stormy Heights (by Golden Heights): dam won 5f seller: fair performer: won maiden at Leicester by 2 lengths from Positive Air, leading 2f out: free-going sort, likely to prove best at 5f/6f. *J. R. Jenkins*

SOLWAY LASS (IRE) 2 b.f. (Apr 29) Anita's Prince 126 – Northern Amber –
(Shack (USA) 118) [1997 5g⁴ 5d⁵ 5.1m 5g a7g Jul 10] 5,400Y: sister to a winning sprinter and half-sister to another by Mon Tresor: dam ran several times: showed glimmer of ability on debut, none afterwards. *P. Eccles*

SOMAYDA (IRE) 2 b.c. (Apr 13) Last Tycoon 131 – Flame of Tara 124 (Artaius 83 p
(USA) 129) [1997 7m⁵ 7m⁵ Aug 16] IR 550,000Y: unfurnished colt: brother to high-class 1m to 1½m performer Marju and unreliable 1½m and 14.6f winner Rajai, and half-brother to several winners, notably Salsabil (by Sadler's Wells): dam best at 3 yrs, winning Pretty Polly Stakes and Coronation Stakes: fifth in maidens won by Setteen at Ascot and Mahboob at Newbury, keeping on from midfield despite tending to edge left (bandaged in front and unimpressive to post) on latter course: will be well suited by further than 7f: wintering in Dubai: should do better. *J. L. Dunlop*

SOME HORSE (IRE) 4 ch.g. Astronef 116 – Daniela Lepida (ITY) (El-Muleta) –
[1996 –: 8.1d 7.1d 9f 8m 1997 10m Jun 19] tall gelding: fairly useful form at 2 yrs: appears to retain little ability: sent to Sweden. *M. G. Meagher*

SOMERTON BOY (IRE) 7 b.h. Thatching 131 – Bonnie Bess 95 (Ardoon 124) 77
[1996 75: 7g 7g 7g 7m* 7m⁶ 7m³ 8f³ 7.6d⁶ 8m 7g⁶ 1997 7m 7g 7d² 8g* 8g 8m³ 8m⁶
8d² 8g 8m Oct 28] good-topped horse: fair handicapper: won at Ayr (has gained 4 of his 5 wins British there) in May: stays 1m: acts on any going: blinkered twice early in career: held up: inconsistent. *P. Calver*

SOMMERSBY (IRE) 6 b.g. Vision (USA) – Echoing 93 (Formidable (USA) –
125) [1996 –, a50: a12g a12g a12g a14.8g⁶ a9.4g⁴ a12g³ a14.8g 1997 a12f⁵ a12g
a10g a14g 10m Jul 28] sturdy gelding: reportedly finished lame final 5-y-o start, and no form in 1997. *Mrs N. Macauley*

SOMOSIERRA (IRE)   2 b.g. (Mar 27) Paris House 123 – Island Heather (IRE)   56 +
69 (Salmon Leap (USA) 131) [1997 5m 5g⁵ 6.1m⁴ 6m 5.7m 5g Sep 15] 15,500Y: tall,
unfurnished gelding: first foal: dam, Irish 6f winner who stayed 9f, out of half-sister
to top-class sprinter Bay Express: modest maiden on balance of form: well held last
2 starts: may well prove best at 5f. *J. Berry*

SO NATURAL (IRE)   5 ch.m. Sharpo 132 – Sympathy 77 (Precocious 126)   –
[1996 –, a49: a5g a7g⁶ a7g⁴ a7g³ a7g a6g⁶ 6s 6g a6g 1997 a7g a7g a7g⁶ Feb 17]
workmanlike mare: poor maiden: well held at Southwell in 1997. *W. Storey*

SONDERISE   8 br.g. Mummy's Game 120 – Demderise 80 (Vaigly Great 127)   44
[1996 57: 5s⁴ 5g⁴ 5.9d³ 5.9m³ 5g⁵ 6g* 6m³ 6.1m⁶ 6m³ 5m⁴ 5m³ᵈⁱˢ 6f 1997 6g 5d 6m⁶
Jun 6] lengthy, rather dipped-backed gelding: carries condition: poor handicapper:
stays 6f: acts on good to firm and heavy going: tried in blinkers/visor, better without:
usually held up: sometimes wanders under pressure. *N. Tinkler*

SONG FOR JESS (IRE)   4 b.f. Accordion – Ritual Girl (Ballad Rock 122) [1996   –
–: 11.7m⁶ 11.8m⁵ 1997 a12g⁵ Feb 14] well beaten on flat. *F. Jordan*

SONG MIST (IRE)   3 gr.f. Kenmare (FR) 125 – Farewell Song (USA) 80 (The   72
Minstrel (CAN) 135) [1996 74: 5m⁴ 6.9g² 6f* 6m⁵ 6.5m⁶ 7m⁶ 1997 6m² 6.1s⁴ 6s⁵ 6f³
7d⁴ 7g 6g⁶ 5.3g⁶ 7f⁵ Sep 28] leggy filly: fair handicapper: below form after fourth
start: stays 7f: acts on firm and soft going: tried blinkered: has run well when sweating: races prominently: sold 12,000 gns in October. *P. F. I. Cole*

SONG OF FREEDOM   3 ch.c. Arazi (USA) 135 – Glorious Song (CAN) (Halo   95
(USA)) [1996 78p: 7f⁴ 1997 10g² 10g* 10m⁵ 10m* 10s 10.3m⁵ 12g⁶ Sep 28] rangy
colt: useful performer: won maiden at Pontefract and handicap at Newbury in
the summer: creditable efforts last 2 starts: seems best around 1¼m: acts on good
to firm ground, well beaten on soft: held up: has swished tail in preliminaries.
J. H. M. Gosden

SONG OF SKYE   3 b.f. Warning 136 – Song of Hope 103 (Chief Singer 131)   84
[1996 82: 5.2f* 5.2g² 6m⁵ 6m 6s 1997 6m 7.1g⁵ 7m 7s³ 7.1m² 7.1m 7g⁴ 7m Aug 17]
leggy, close-coupled filly: fairly useful handicapper: best 3-y-o efforts when in
frame: stays 7f: acts on firm and soft ground: has hung left. *T. J. Naughton*

SONG OF THE SWORD   4 b.g. Kris 135 – Melodist (USA) 118 (The Minstrel   –
(CAN) 135) [1996 12g³ 12m* 12m* 12.3m⁴ 12m 12g³ 10d 1997 11.9s⁵ 12g 12d
Oct 16] tall, rangy gelding: fourth foal: half-brother to winning hurdler Melnik (by
Nashwan): dam Italian Oaks winner and Irish Oaks dead-heater: useful (rated 97)
in Ireland at 3 yrs, winning 1½m minor events at Roscommon and Gowran Park
before sold out of M. Kauntze's stable 35,000 gns: well held in handicaps in 1997.
J. A. B. Old

SONGSHEET   4 b.f. Dominion 123 – Songstead 92 (Song 132) [1996 69: 5.1g*   73
5m⁵ 5.7m⁵ 5.2g² a5g² 5.7m³ 5m⁵ 5m⁴ 5.1f a5g⁶ 1997 a5g 5m² 5.3f⁵ 6.1g 5m* 5m*   a55
5g⁵ 5.7g 5.2s* 5g 5.1m³ 5m 5.1g⁵ 5g⁶ 5s 5g² 5.1g² 5m⁴ 5d⁶ 5g⁵ a5g⁴ a6g⁴ Nov 17]
lengthy filly: fair on turf, modest on all-weather: won handicap at Folkestone in May
and minor events at Windsor in June and Yarmouth in July: best around 5f: acts on
the all-weather and on good to firm and soft going: often claimer ridden: tough and
consistent. *M. S. Saunders*

SON OF GOOD TIMES   2 ch.g. (May 8) Good Times (ITY) – Pullandese   –
(Kinglet 98) [1997 7.1g 5.7f⁴ 10d Oct 13] sturdy gelding: eighth foal: dam of no
account: has shown little, including in seller. *P. G. Murphy*

SON OF SKELTON   2 ch.g. (Feb 24) Minster Son 130 – Skelton 70 (Derrylin   56
115) [1997 6g 7.5v² Jul 5] fifth foal: half-brother to 1¼m winner Charm Dancer (by
Rambo Dancer) and 5f (at 2 yrs) and 6f winner Caress (by Godswalk): dam 2-y-o 7f
seller winner: strong-finishing head second in seller at Beverley: will stay at least
1¼m. *J. Wharton*

SONYA MARIE   4 b.f. Green Ruby (USA) 104 – Susie Hall (Gold Rod 129)   –
[1996 NR 1997 a7g a8g⁶ a13g Jan 30] no form: dead. *J. G. FitzGerald*

SOOJAMA (IRE)   7 b.g. Mansooj 118 – Pyjama Game 56 (Cavo Doro 124)   60 §
[1996 54, a–: 15.4m 12m 12m* 16.4g 16.2m 12m² a16g⁵ 1997 a12g³ a12g a12g*
a12g² a16g* 15.4m² 16.4g³ 14g* 14.9m 10g a16g Aug 9] rather leggy gelding:
modest handicapper: won at at Lingfield (twice) in February and Newmarket in May:

897

refused to race last 2 starts: effective at 1½m to 2m: acts on good to firm and soft ground and on equitrack: blinkered nowadays: has won for amateur: one to treat with caution. *R. M. Flower*

SOOTY TERN 10 br.h. Wassl 125 – High Tern 93 (High Line 125) [1996 72, a59: a8.5g⁴ a8g⁴ a8.5g⁴ 9m² 8g⁶ a8g* 8g 8f⁵ 8m 8.5m⁵ 8m 8.3f* 8m² 8m 8.1d a8g⁴ a8g² a8g⁵ a7g² 1997 a7g² a8g³ a8g³ a8g³ 8.5m⁴ 7.6v a7g⁴ 8f* 8m³ 8d 8.5d* 8f* 8f³ 8m⁵ a8.5g⁶ 8.5d 8.3g 8f Sep 17] compact horse: grand old campaigner, winner of 19 of his 117 starts, on a wide variety of tracks, and still capable of fair form on turf (modest on all-weather): successful in 1997 in handicaps at Brighton in June and Epsom and Brighton in July: effective at 7f to 9f: acts on firm and soft going: usually races prominently: often ridden by apprentice: tough and game. *J. M. Bradley* — 79 a56

SOPHIE LOCKETT 4 b.f. Mon Tresor 113 – Silverdale Rose (Nomination 125) [1996 –: 11.8m⁶ 10m⁶ 10.5m 1997 16.2v⁶ a14g 16m Sep 15] of little account. *K. W. Hogg, Isle of Man* — –

SOPHOMORE 3 b.c. Sanglamore (USA) 126 – Livry (USA) (Lyphard (USA) 132) [1996 83p: 7g* 1997 10g 10.4g⁴ 9g⁴ 10g⁶ Oct 24] strong, rangy colt: fairly useful performer, lightly raced: best effort when sixth of 21 in handicap at Newbury on final start: stays 1¼m: raced only on good going: sold 20,000 gns in October, and joined N. Henderson. *B. W. Hills* — 88

SORRIDAR 2 b.f. (May 20) Puissance 110 – Sorrowful (Moorestyle 137) [1997 5d 5g⁵ 6m⁴ 5s Oct 15] 2,000Y: leggy, unfurnished filly: sister to 4-y-o Meranti and half-sister to a winner in Norway by Grey Desire: dam ran twice: modest form in maidens: well held on nursery debut: sprint bred: wandered and carried head high second start. *J. L. Eyre* — 55

SOSTENUTO 4 b.f. Northern State (USA) 91 – Pride of Ayr (Recoil) [1996 NR 1997 12.3s⁵ 13.4g 11.9s Oct 15] good-bodied filly: third foal: dam ran once: well beaten in maidens. *R. Hollinshead* — –

SOTONIAN (HOL) 4 br.g. Statoblest 120 – Visage 75 (Vision (USA)) [1996 36: 5g a7g 10m 6f 5.1m 5.1g a5g a5g³ 1997 a5g* a5f* a5g a5g a5g a5g⁵ 5m² a5g⁵ 5m 5.1g³ 5m⁴ a5g³ a5g⁵ 5g 5g⁴ 5g⁵ 6d 5m Sep 22] rather sparely-made gelding: poor handicapper: won twice at Wolverhampton in January: mostly creditable efforts afterwards: best at 5f: acts on firm ground and fibresand: blinkered twice earlier in career: often a front runner. *P. S. Felgate* — 47

SOTTVUS (IRE) 2 ch.c. (Apr 13) Royal Academy (USA) 130 – Lorne Lady (Local Suitor (USA) 128) [1997 7m* Sep 27] third foal: half-brother to a winner in Italy by Polar Falcon: dam French maiden daughter of half-sister to Awaasif, an excellent family: won maiden at Milan by 1¾ lengths from Sikesting: will stay 1m: difficult to assess. *L. M. Cumani* — ?

SOUND APPEAL 3 b.f. Robellino (USA) 127 – Son Et Lumiere (Rainbow Quest (USA) 134) [1996 69: 7m 7.9g⁵ 7.1s 7d⁴ 1997 8g 7.3s 8f 10s⁴ 10f⁶ 8m Sep 22] leggy, unfurnished filly: modest maiden on flat: will stay beyond 1¼m: acts on firm and soft going: often blinkered or visored: useful juvenile hurdler. *A. G. Foster* — 60

SOUNDS LEGAL 4 b.f. Rich Charlie 117 – Legal Sound 85 (Legal Eagle 126) [1996 68: a8.5g² a8.5g⁵ 1997 a9.4g a10g³ a9.4g⁴ 8s⁶ 7f May 1] lightly-raced maiden: no worthwhile form in 1997: blinkered last 2 starts. *P. D. Evans* — –

SOUND THE TRUMPET (IRE) 5 b.g. Fayruz 116 – Red Note (Rusticaro (FR) 124) [1996 56: a6g⁵ a5g² a6g 6.1g⁵ 6f a6g⁵ 6m² 6m⁴ 5m a6g⁶ 1997 a6g a6g a7g a8g⁶ 6.9g⁴ 6.1m⁶ 5d⁵ 6m⁴ 5m⁶ 5g² 5g 6d 5g Oct 22] rangy gelding: modest handicapper: has form at 7f, but at least as good at 5f/6f: acts on fibresand, suited by good going or firmer on turf: often blinkered or visored earlier in career: has had tongue tied. *R. C. Spicer* — 56 a–

SOUPERFICIAL 6 gr.g. Petong 126 – Duck Soup 55 (Decoy Boy 129) [1996 63: 7.5m 7m 7g a6g 6m 5d a7g³ a8g a5g⁴ 5.1m* 6m a5g⁵ 5.1m⁶ 5f* 5.1g 5g 6m² a6g⁴ a6g a7s 1997 6.1g⁶ 6g 5d 6g 6f 6.1d⁴ 6s* 6g⁶ 6d⁴ 6g 5g 7.5g 6.1m 6m a7g a6g Nov 24] sturdy gelding: modest performer: won minor event at Hamilton in July: well beaten last 7 starts, leaving N. Tinkler before penultimate one: needs good test at 6f, and stays 7f: acts on firm ground, soft and fibresand: visored nowadays: often slowly away. *Don Enrico Incisa* — 57 d

SOURA (USA)   3 ch.f. Beau Genius (CAN) – First Division (CHI) (Domineau   49
(USA)) [1996 49?: 7m 6m a8g⁶ a7g³ 1997 7g a6g⁴ 8g² 8g³ 7m³ Jun 9] tall, lengthy
filly: poor maiden: stays 1m: acts on good to firm ground and the all-weather:
sometimes looks none too keen. *P. A. Kelleway*

SOUTH CHINA SEA   3 b.f. Robellino (USA) 127 – Danzig Harbour (USA)   –
(Private Account (USA)) [1996 NR 1997 8.3m 7g 8.9s⁴ 8m Sep 24] 16,500Y: third
foal: half-sister to fair 1994 2-y-o 6f winner Puppet Master (by Prince Sabo): dam
Irish 7f winner: reportedly had debut delayed by pelvic injury: signs of ability but no
form. *P. F. I. Cole*

SOUTHDOWN CYRANO (IRE)   2 b.c. (May 2) Cyrano de Bergerac 120 –   –
Value Voucher (IRE) (Kings Lake (USA)) 133) [1997 6g 5g 7.1m Sep 16] 4,500
2-y-o: sturdy colt: second foal: dam unraced: soundly beaten in maidens and a minor
event. *P. Butler*

SOUTH EASTERN FRED   6 b.h. Primo Dominie 121 – Soheir 74 (Track Spare   52
125) [1996 52, a89: a9.4g² a10g⁵ a9.4g³ a12g³ a9.4g⁵ a12g⁶ a10g 9.7m⁵ 10m 9.7g²   a96
10m a9.4g⁴ a9.4g* 8.5m a10s³ a9.4g* 1997 a9.4g³ a9.4g* a8.5g³ a9.4g a10g 9.7g³
10d a9.4g May 11] tall, workmanlike horse: poor mover: has had leg problems:
useful handicapper on the all-weather, modest at best on turf: better than ever when
winning easily at Wolverhampton in January: ran badly there final start: stays 9.4f.
H. J. Collingridge

SOUTHERLY WIND   3 b.g. Slip Anchor 136 – Karavina (Karabas 132) [1996   92
79p: 5g 6m* 8m⁵ 8m² 8m* 8g³ 1997 8g* 10m² 12d 10.4m⁶ 10m 8g⁴ 9m Oct 4] big,
rangy gelding: has scope: impresses in appearance: fairly useful handicapper: won at
Pontefract (third course win) in May: mostly creditable efforts afterwards, but never
dangerous in Cambridgeshire at Newmarket final start: will prove best at 1m to 1¼m:
form on good going or firmer: joined O. Sherwood. *Mrs J. R. Ramsden*

SOUTHERN-BE-GEORGE   2 b.c. (Feb 18) Be My Chief (USA) 122 –   –
Southern Sky 89 (Comedy Star (USA) 121) [1997 8m Sep 25] 3,500F: big colt:
fourth live foal: half-brother to fairly useful 1993 2-y-o 6f winner Southern Ridge
(by Indian Ridge) and 5-y-o Southern Dominion: dam 7f and 1m winner: 50/1 and
backward, prominent to turn when well beaten in maiden at Pontefract: has plenty of
scope, and may do better in due course. *W. G. M. Turner*

SOUTHERN DOMINION   5 ch.g. Dominion 123 – Southern Sky 89 (Comedy   63
Star (USA) 121) [1996   , a62d: a5g⁴ a6g⁵ a5g² a6g a6g a6g 5g 6f 7g⁵ 6.9g 7f 1997
a6g a6g³ a6g a6g⁵ a5g 5.1g 5m* 5s 5m 5m⁴ 6.1d⁵ 5g³ 5m² 5g 5g⁴ 6f⁴ 6m² 5s* 5g⁴
5d* a6g³ a5g Dec 8] small gelding: modest handicapper: in good form in 1997,
and made all at Musselburgh (amateurs) in May, Ayr in October and Doncaster in
November: poorly drawn final start: effective at 5f and 6f: acts on any going: usually
visored/blinkered: tough, game and consistent. *Miss J. F. Craze*

SOUTHERN MEMORIES (IRE)   7 b.g. Don't Forget Me 127 – Our Pet 64   41
(Mummy's Pet 125) [1996 NR 1997 7m 8m 8g² a10g Nov 25] poor handicapper: best
at up to 1m: acts on good to firm and dead ground: blinkered (below form) once at 3
yrs: races prominently. *W. J. Musson*

SOUTHERN RULE   10 b.g. Law Society (USA) 130 – Isobelline (USA)   –
(Pronto) [1996 41d: 5s 5d⁶ 5m 5m 5s⁶ a6g⁶ a6g⁶ a6s 1997 a9.4g⁵ a8g⁵ 7m 5s Jul 1]
bad sprinter for several trainers here: usually blinkered. *P. Mooney*

SOVEREIGN   3 b.f. Interrex (CAN) – Shiny Penny 70 (Glint of Gold 128) [1996   –
NR 1997 5m⁶ 7m 8.3s 5.1f May 30] third reported live foal: dam, maiden, probably
stayed 1¾m: of little account on flat. *M. P. Muggeridge*

SOVEREIGN CREST (IRE)   4 gr.g. Priolo (USA) 127 – Abergwrle (Absalom   54
128) [1996 –: 8.3m 8.3d 10g 10m 1997 12m⁶ 8f 10m³ 9d⁶ 11.9m⁴ 11.9m* 11.9m³
14m⁴ 14m 14m Oct 1] workmanlike gelding: modest handicapper: won at Brighton
in July: probably stays 1¾m: acts on good to firm going: visored or blinkered last 5
starts: often slowly away, and comes from off pace: has tended to hang. *C. A. Horgan*

SOVEREIGN PAGE (USA)   8 ch.g. Caro 133 – Tashinsky (USA) (Nijinsky   76
(CAN) 138) [1996 83: 10m⁵ 10g 10.8f* 8.9m⁵ 10.1f* 10.2m 1997 10g 10.8f⁵ Jun 4]
tall gelding: good mover: fairly useful handicapper: would probably have been second with a clear run at Warwick on final start: best around 1¼m: goes very well on

good to firm/firm ground: blinkered (no improvement) twice at 3 yrs: usually bandaged: held up. *B. Hanbury*

SOVEREIGNS COURT   4 ch.g. Statoblest 120 – Clare Celeste 73 (Coquelin   81 p
(USA) 121) [1996 71p: 7m 7m 7m⁵ 7g 8d³ 7g 7s² 1997 7m 7.3g 6g 7d⁶ 8m 8d 8d⁴
8.2s* 10d* Nov 3] tall, angular gelding: fairly useful handicapper: better than ever at
4 yrs, winning by 5 lengths at Nottingham in October (carried head awkwardly) and
November: stays 1¼m well: best efforts on ground softer than good: usually held up:
may well be capable of better still. *L. G. Cottrell*

SOVIET BRIDE (IRE)   5 b.m. Soviet Star (USA) 128 – Nihad 76 (Alleged   65 +
(USA) 138) [1996 77: 11.7g² 12m³ 12m 10m² 10.1g* 10m⁶ 10f⁴ 10.2f* 1997 a10g⁴
10m⁶ 10.1m 8f 11f 8f⁶ 9f⁴ 9f 8g⁵ a8f Dec 31] lengthy mare: fair performer: below
form first 3 starts (trained by S. Dow in Britain): fourth in claimer, best effort in USA:
stays 1½m: acts on firm ground, well beaten only run on soft. *J. Orman, USA*

SOVIET BUREAU (IRE)   2 ch.c. (Apr 5) Soviet Lad (USA) – Redwood Hut   99 p
(Habitat 134) [1997 7g* Aug 13] IR 8,700F, IR 22,000Y: fifth foal: half-brother to
3-y-o Sally Green and 1m winner Jackatack (by Astronef): dam unraced from fair
family, mainly at 1m+: 14/1, won minor event at Salisbury in taking style by 1¼
lengths from Dark Moondancer, behind and green to halfway but improving strongly
without being hard ridden: will stay at least 1m: not seen out again (reportedly
considered immature), but could well make a better than useful 3-y-o. *Miss Gay
Kelleway*

SOVIET KING (IRE)   4 b.g. Soviet Lad (USA) – Finessing (Indian King (USA)   –
128) [1996 56: 8.3d⁴ 8m⁵ 10f³ 12m⁴ 1997 a9.4g⁶ a13g³ a12g* a12g⁶ a12g⁴ a16g⁴   a45
Feb 27] angular gelding: has a round action: poor performer: won weak Southwell
maiden in January: not seen out after following month: stays 13f: acts on firm ground
and the all-weather. *P. Mitchell*

SOVIET LADY (IRE)   3 b.f. Soviet Lad (USA) – La Vosgienne (Ashmore (FR)   44
125) [1996 54+: 5d 6m³ 7g⁶ a7g³ 7m⁵ 6m⁵ 7d⁴ 7.5m³ 1997 7g³ 6m 7f 7.5s⁴ a7g 7m
8g⁵ 7f Sep 28] sparely-made filly: poor handicapper: left J. L. Eyre after fifth start:
should stay 1m: acts on good to firm and dead going and on fibresand: visored (raced
freely but ran creditably) fourth outing. *J. E. Long*

SOVIET LEADER   3 b.g. Soviet Star (USA) 128 – Noirmant (Dominion 123)   89
[1996 NR 1997 6m 6.1d* 6g³ 6g⁴ 5d 6g³ 5s⁶ 6d 6g Sep 20] sturdy, lengthy gelding:
third foal: half-brother to fairly useful sprinter Portelet (by Night Shift): dam half-
sister to very smart 1¼m to 2m winner Braashee: fairly useful performer: won maiden at Nottingham in May: respectable efforts at least in handicaps last 4 starts:
probably a sprinter: raced mainly on good ground or softer: dead. *R. Guest*

SOVIET STATE (USA)   3 b.c. Nureyev (USA) 131 – Absentia (USA) 108   103
(Raise A Cup (USA)) [1996 88: 6s² 6d* 6s⁵ 1997 6g* 6g 6f² 5m 6m⁵ 7g⁵ 6.1d⁶ Oct
30] leggy, attractive colt: has a short action: useful performer: won minor event at
Thirsk in April: best subsequent efforts in listed races at Newbury in July (1¼ lengths
second to Hattab) and September (5 lengths fifth to Russian Revival, on penultimate
start): effective at 6f/7f: acts on firm and soft going: has run well when sweating.
P. W. Chapple-Hyam

SPACE RACE   3 b.g. Rock Hopper 124 – Melanoura (Imperial Fling (USA) 116)   82
[1996 NR 1997 7g⁴ 8m 8d* 10.2f² 7.1m⁶ 9g⁵ Aug 22] 10,000F, 16,000Y: workmanlike gelding: sixth foal: half-brother to fairly useful 1995 2-y-o 6f winner Meldorf (by Lycius) and 3 other sprint winners: dam ran twice: fairly useful performer:
won maiden at Bath in May: ran well (caught near finish) in minor event there 2
months later, but disappointing in handicaps afterwards: probably stays 1¼m: acts on
firm and dead ground. *C. A. Cyzer*

SPA LANE   4 ch.g. Presidium 124 – Sleekit 78 (Blakeney 126) [1996 63: 8.2m²   58 d
10m* 10f⁴ 10.8f³ 14.1d* 1997 a12g 12m 12m⁴ 14.1g 14.6d² 16.1g 16m a14g 16m
16s 14.1g⁶ Oct 18] leggy gelding: modest handicapper on his day: well beaten last
4 starts: stays 14.6f, possibly not 2m: acts on firm and dead ground: inconsistent.
M. Bielby

SPANIARDS CLOSE   9 b.g. King of Spain 121 – Avon Belle 75 (Balidar 133)   67
[1996 77: 5f² 6m² 1997 5.7g⁵ a5g² a6g 6s Oct 15] lengthy, workmanlike gelding:

lightly raced and just a fair performer nowadays: stays 6f: acts on fibresand, best turf efforts on good and dead ground (possibly unsuited by extremes): visored (tailed off) once at 5 yrs: held up. *P. J. Makin*

SPANIARD'S MOUNT 3 b.c. Distant Relative 128 – Confection (Formidable (USA) 125) [1996 67, a?: 6f⁵ 6m 7f 8g 7g⁶ 7.1s* 6.9v³ a7g⁵ 1997 a10g² a7g* 8d 8s* Jul 5] small, sturdy colt: poor mover: fair on all-weather, modest on turf: won handicap at Lingfield in February and claimer at Yarmouth in July: stays 1m, pulled too hard over 1¼m: acts on heavy ground and equitrack: best form in visor, but has won without: sold, and sent to Macau. *M. H. Tompkins*   58 a73

SPANISH EYES 2 b.f. (Mar 25) Belmez (USA) 131 – Night Transaction 59 (Tina's Pet 121) [1997 8d Oct 28] 5,000Y: third foal: half-sister to 3-y-o Silca Key Silca: dam 1m winner at 4/5 yrs: 33/1, well held in maiden at Leicester, slowly away and soon driven along. *J. A. R. Toller*   –

SPANISH FERN (USA) 2 b. or br.f. (Jan 22) El Gran Senor (USA) 136 – Chain Fern (USA) (Blushing Groom (FR) 131) [1997 7m³ Nov 1] fifth foal: sister to fairly useful 1m winner (stayed 11.4f) Woodwardia and half-sister to 3-y-o Dayville: dam unraced sister to Al Bahathri: 12/1, very close third of 18 to Pontoon in maiden at Newmarket, chasing pace and running on well despite being carried slightly left: blanketed for stalls: sure to improve and win a race. *R. Charlton*   89 p

SPANISH KNOT (USA) 3 b.f. El Gran Senor (USA) 136 – Ingenuity 68 (Clever Trick (USA)) [1996 75: 6m⁵ 7g² 8f⁵ 1997 7f² 7m Sep 21] fair maiden: ½-length second in minor event at Thirsk in June: helped force too strong a pace next time: should stay 1m: raced only on good ground or firmer. *Lord Huntingdon*   72

SPANISH SERENADE 3 b.f. Nashwan (USA) 135 – Fair Rosamunda (Try My Best (USA) 130) [1996 9g³ 10g⁴ 1997 11m² 11m 7.5d⁴ 11.5d⁵ 7.6m* 11d* 8m Aug 26] fourth foal: half-sister to French 1m winner Mille Roses (by Cadeaux Genereux): dam French middle-distance winner: trained by J. C. Rouget when winning twice within 9 days in French Provinces in June, showing fair form: sold 12,000 gns in July: well held in claimer at Ripon on only start here: stays 11.5f: acts on good to firm and dead ground. *M. J. Camacho*   76

SPANISH STRIPPER (USA) 6 b.g. El Gran Senor (USA) 136 – Gourmet Dinner (USA) (Raise A Cup (USA)) [1996 57, a–: a7g 7f a6g 6g 8m² 7g 7m 6m 7f 9m 11.5m a8g a11g 1997 a8g a8g⁵ a8g³ a11g a6g⁴ a7g⁶ a7g⁴ a7g a6g a7g⁶ 5m⁶ 7f a7g 7f 8f 6m⁴ a7g² 8s⁵ 10g⁴ 7g 8.9s 10.1f Sep 17] good-topped gelding: poor performer: effective at 7f to 1¼m: acts on good to firm ground and fibresand: tried blinkered: inconsistent. *M. C. Chapman*   34

SPANISH VERDICT 10 b.g. King of Spain 121 – Counsel's Verdict (Firestreak 125) [1996 72: 7s 8d 8g 8g 6.9g 8f* 8f² 8f² 8m 8f⁴ 9g 8d³ 8g 8m 10f⁶ 9m² 8m⁶ 10m 10f 1997 10.1g 8g⁵ 8g 8g⁶ 9m⁴ 8f 8f⁵ 8m 8g 8m² 8g 8m 8.1m³ 8g 8.5f 8.3g³ 8g Oct 18] sturdy, good-quartered gelding: impresses in appearance: has a round action: modest handicapper: effective at 7f, probably at 1¼m: has some form on soft going, but goes particularly well (all but one of 13 wins) on ground firmer than good: sometimes visored early in career, soundly beaten only try in blinkers: often claimer ridden: genuine: won novice hurdle in October. *Denys Smith*   59

SPANISH WARRIOR 3 b.g. Warrshan (USA) 117 – Spanish Heart 86 (King of Spain 121) [1996 –: 6g 1997 8.2m a8g⁵ 8.2g a9.4f 8.1s⁶ Jul 1] angular gelding: poor mover: modest maiden, form only on fibresand on second start. *J. W. Hills*   – a58

SPARE MY BLUSHES 3 b.f. Puissance 110 – Juris Prudence (IRE) 61 (Law Society (USA) 130) [1996 NR 1997 8f a8g 12g 10m⁴ 8.2m Aug 6] 500Y: first foal: dam staying maiden: no form, and temperamental to boot. *B. A. McMahon*   – §

SPARKLING EDGE 3 b.f. Beveled (USA) – Sparkalot (USA) (Duel) [1996 54: 6m* 6d⁵ 5f 7d 5.2g⁵ a5g⁶ a5g* a5g 1997 a6g³ a5g* a5g⁴ a5g⁴ a5g³ 5.1f a6g Jun 27] modest handicapper: won at Lingfield in January, and ran creditably next 3 starts: stays 6f: acts on good to firm ground and the all-weather: sold, and sent to UAE. *C. A. Dwyer*   56

SPARKLING HARRY 3 ch.g. Tina's Pet 121 – Sparkling Hock (Hot Spark 126) [1996 60: 5m⁶ 5.1m 5m⁶ 5s 5m 5s⁶ 6g³ 6.1s 1997 6m 5s 6g⁶ 6m 5.9f⁶ 6d⁶ 7g⁶ 6m a6g 8g Oct 27] quite good-topped gelding: modest maiden handicapper: probably stays   50

7f: acts on good to firm and soft ground: often blinkered/visored: none too consistent. *Miss L. C. Siddall*

SPARKLING SECRET 2 ch.g. (Mar 23) Tina's Pet 121 – Sparkling Hock (Hot — Spark 126) [1997 7m Jun 11] 1,000 2-y-o: sixth foal: brother to 3-y-o Sparkling Harry: dam ran once: always rear in seller at Yarmouth. *C. Murray*

SPARKY 3 b.g. Warrshan (USA) 117 – Pebble Creek (IRE) (Reference Point 139) 75 [1996 56: 5m⁶ 6m⁴ 7f 7g 6f* 7.5f* 7.9g 8m 6m³ 1997 8m⁶ 8s 8f³ a8g* 10f² 10g⁶ a81 a9.4g² 8m² a8g² 8.3g³ 10.5d 12g 9m Oct 7] workmanlike gelding: has a round action: fairly useful handicapper on all-weather, fair on turf: won at Southwell in June: mostly creditable efforts afterwards: has form at 1¼m, possibly best in strongly-run races over 1m: acts on firm ground and fibresand: best in blinkers, visored once: held up. *M. W. Easterby*

SPARTAN GIRL (IRE) 3 ch.f. Ela-Mana-Mou 132 – Well Head (IRE) (Sadler's 91 Wells (USA) 132) [1996 62p: 7.1v⁴ 1997 10.1s* 10d Oct 25] lengthy filly: fairly useful form at best: clearly best effort when winning maiden at Epsom in July by 2 lengths from Manuetti: last of 12 in listed race at Gelsenkirchen nearly 4 months later: will stay 1½m: has raced only on dead ground or softer. *Lord Huntingdon*

SPARTAN HEARTBEAT 4 b.g. Shareef Dancer (USA) 135 – Helen's Dream 80 § (Troy 137) [1996 106: 10g³ 10f³ 12.4g³ 12m 12m⁶ 16f⁵ 1997 13.4g² 14f² 14.6g 14.1d⁶ 12s Nov 8] good-bodied gelding: useful form in exalted company as 3-y-o: nowhere near best in 1997, and remains a maiden: stays 2m: acts on firm and dead ground: tried blinkered: has tended to sweat and be edgy/coltish (gelded at end of year): sometimes finds little, and not one to trust: sold (to join J. O'Shea) 10,000 gns in November. *C. E. Brittain*

SPARTAN ROYALE 3 b.c. Shareef Dancer (USA) 135 – Cormorant Creek 73 85 d (Gorytus (USA) 132) [1996 NR 1997 10d² 10m⁵ 13.9g⁴ 12g 12m Oct 2] IR 34,000Y: sturdy, close-coupled colt: second foal: dam, 10.4f winner, half-sister to Cormorant Wood, dam of Rock Hopper (by Shareef Dancer): disappointing maiden: tailed off last 2 starts: should stay beyond 1¼m: sold, and joined S. Dow. *C. E. Brittain*

SPAZACA (USA) 2 b.f. (Jan 18) Sheikh Albadou 128 – Diary Date (USA) (Aly- 86 ? sheba (USA)) [1997 7m⁵ 7.5m* Nov 1] first reported foal: dam unraced half-sister to very smart 1¼m winner Two Timing from the family of champion US filly Chris Evert: has raced only in Italy, winning a minor event at Milan in November by length, clear, from British newcomer Totom: difficult to assess. *L. M. Cumani*

SPEAKER'S CHAIR 2 b.c. (Mar 14) Shirley Heights 130 – Lead Note (USA) 81 62 (Nijinsky (CAN) 138) [1997 7g³ 7m⁵ 8d² Oct 28] sturdy, lengthy colt: first foal: dam 2-y-o 1m winner (her only start), half-sister to Rainbow Quest: fairly useful form: placed in maidens at Newmarket in August and Leicester in October, beaten 3 lengths by Himself in latter: not discredited in listed event at Newbury in between: should be suited by 1¼m+. *R. Charlton*

SPECIAL·K 5 br.m. Treasure Kay 114 – Lissi Gori (FR) (Bolkonski 134) [1996 64 ? 65: 7m⁴ 8g 7.5m 7.5f⁴ 7.9g 10.3m⁵ 8m 9g⁶ 6.9m² 8g 8.5m 7g 1997 8m 8g⁶ 7.5v* 8m* 8.5m⁴ 8m 8.5d⁴ 8m² 8.2s 8g Oct 22] leggy mare: modest performer: won sellers at Beverley (handicap) and Ripon in July: seemingly back to best in claimer at Ripon on eighth start: stays 8.5f: acts on any ground: usually races prominently: visored (respectable effort) final 4-y-o start: often apprentice ridden: inconsistent. *E. Weymes*

SPECIAL PERSON (IRE) 2 ch.f. (Mar 4) Ballad Rock 122 – Hada Rani 65 p (Jaazeiro (USA) 127) [1997 a8g² Nov 13] IR 1,400F 4,800 2-y-o: sister to 3-y-o Begorrat, closely related to a winner in Belgium by Bold Lad and half-sister to a winner in Germany by Salt Dome: dam ran twice: 16/1, staying-on 3 lengths second of 11 to Night Vigil in maiden at Lingfield: should improve. *P. Mitchell*

SPECIAL QUEST (FR) 2 b.c. Rainbow Quest (USA) 134 – Mona Stella (USA) 109 p 117 (Nureyev (USA) 131) [1997 7.5g* 9m² 10d* Nov 1] lengthy colt: fifth foal: closely related to French 1½m winner Fashionman (by Nashwan) and half-brother to 2 winners in France: dam, smart French 9f/1¼m winner, closely related to high-class filly Dancing Maid: won newcomers sales race at Deauville in August: length second of 7 to Thief of Hearts in Group 3 event at Longchamp: won 7-runner Criterium

Criterium de Saint-Cloud—
Special Quest comes out best in a close finish with Asakir, Daymarti and Croco Rouge

de Saint-Cloud by neck from Asakir, making virtually all: will be suited by 1½m+: blinkered: probably capable of further improvement. *Mme C. Head, France*

SPECIAL TREAT 2 b.f. (Mar 17) Wolfhound (USA) 126 – Just A Treat (IRE) 95
47 (Glenstal (USA) 118) [1997 6m 7g⁴ 6m* 6d* 6g² Oct 25] 44,000Y: lengthy, rather sparely-made filly: third foal: dam 2-y-o 5f winner from family of Golden Fleece and Be My Guest: progressive form: won maiden at Redcar in September and nursery at York in October: good ½-length second to Ikhteyaar in listed race at Doncaster: should stay 7f, probably 1m: acts on good to firm and dead ground: blinkered last 3 starts: carries head high/awkwardly, and usually soon off bridle (well handled by K. Fallon). *D. R. Loder*

SPECTACLE JIM 8 b.g. Mummy's Game 120 – Welsh Blossom 100 (Welsh 37
Saint 126) [1996 48: 6g⁶ 6m 6f 8g 6.9m⁵ 6m 6g a7g 1997 a8g⁴ a8g⁵ a8g a8g 6m⁶ 7m 6.9m⁵ 11.5d a13g⁶ Jun 28] leggy gelding: poor handicapper: acts on equitrack and on firm and dead ground: often blinkered/visored. *B. A. Pearce*

SPECULATIVE 3 b.c. Suave Dancer (USA) 136 – Gull Nook 120 (Mill Reef –
(USA) 141) [1996 NR 1997 13.1s⁵ 12s 11m Oct 28] 10,000 2-y-o: sixth foal: half-brother to several winners, notably top-class 1¼m to 1½m winner Pentire (by Be My Guest): dam, lightly-raced 10.5f and 1½m winner, out of half-sister to Shirley Heights: well held in seller and claimers. *W. Storey*

SPECULATOR (IRE) 3 b.c. Last Tycoon 131 – Abbeydale 110 (Huntercombe 90
133) [1996 NR 1997 7m 8.2m³ 8s* 8m² 8.5g² 8m Sep 28] IR 28,000Y: good-topped colt: fluent mover: half-brother to leading 1985 2-y-o Huntingdale (by Double Form), later third in 2000 Guineas, and 2 winners by Habitat: dam second in 1000 Guineas: fairly useful performer: won maiden at Warwick in July: good second in handicaps at Newmarket and Epsom (looked unsuited by track) next 2 outings: ran poorly in blinkers final start: should stay 1¼m: acts on good to firm and soft ground: has pulled hard in steadily-run races: sent to Hong Kong. *W. J. Haggas*

SPEEDBALL (IRE) 3 b.c. Waajib 121 – Lady Taufan (IRE) (Taufan (USA) 119) 99
[1996 96: 6g³ 6m* 6d² 6m 1997 8.2m⁶ 7m² 7g⁴ 7d⁵ 7m 7.9s Oct 8] quite good-topped colt: a fluent action: useful handicapper: respectable efforts at least second to fifth starts despite twice being poorly drawn: should stay 1m: acts on good to firm and dead ground, ran poorly on soft: sold 70,000 gns, and sent to USA. *I. A. Balding*

SPEEDBOAT (USA) 3 ch.c. Diesis 133 – Ocean Ballad 104 (Grundy 137) [1996 61
80p: 7g³ 1997 10g⁶ 7.5m⁴ 7m⁴ 6s 10m⁶ Oct 28] modest maiden: stays 7f: seems rather headstrong: sold 2,000 gns in November. *J. L. Eyre*

SPEEDFIT TOO (IRE) 2 b.c. (Mar 31) Scenic 128 – Safka (USA) 104 (Irish   106
River (FR) 131) [1997 6m³ 6m 7m⁶ 6g* 6m² 6m* 7g³ Sep 20] 11,000F, 17,000Y: tall,
quite attractive colt: has a quick action: sixth foal: half-brother to several winners,
including 1994 2-y-o 1m winner Sannkayya (by Soviet Star) and 9f winner Safkana
(by Doyoun), both Irish: dam 2-y-o 5f winner out of smart French mare Safita, dam
also of smart miler Safawan: useful performer: won maiden at Windsor and valuable
nursery under top-weight at Newmarket in August, beating Halmahera decisively in
well-contested event for latter: good third, beaten 3 lengths and 5 behind Xaar, in
Prix de la Salamandre at Longchamp: should stay 1m: raced only on good ground or
firmer: carries head high, and has flashed tail. *G. G. Margarson*

SPEED ON 4 b.g. Sharpo 132 – Pretty Poppy 67 (Song 132) [1996 103: 5d² 5m*   100
5f² 6m³ 5m⁶ 5g 1997 5.1v⁵ 5m 5g⁶ 5d 5m³ 5.1g³ Sep 28] compact gelding: reportedly
chipped knee as 2-y-o: useful performer: none too consistent in 1997, best efforts
when seventh of 9 in listed race at Almaty in May and close third of 5 to Tadeo
in minor event (on final start) at Nottingham: best efforts at 5f: acts on firm and dead
ground. *H. Candy*

SPEED TO LEAD (IRE) 5 b.m. Darshaan 133 – Instant Desire (USA) 86
(Northern Dancer) [1996 90: 12m² 16.4g³ 16m* 22.2f² 16.1m⁶ 1997 22.2d Jun 20]
leggy, workmanlike mare: fairly useful staying handicapper at 4 yrs for H. Cecil:
tailed off in Queen Alexandra Stakes at Royal Ascot only start in 1997: sold only
3,200 gns in December. *Miss Gay Kelleway*

SPEEDY CLASSIC (USA) 8 br.g. Storm Cat (USA) – Shadows Lengthen 73   67
(Star Appeal 133) [1996 63, a85: a6g⁴ a6g a7g* a6g³ 6f² 6f 5m 6g 6m⁵ 6f a7g* 7.1f*   a92
6.1m⁴ 7m⁶ a7g⁵ a7g* 1997 a7g a7g³ a6g* 7f⁴ 6g 7.1m² 6.1d⁵ 7g 7.1g 6.9m⁵ 7f* a6g⁵
a6s² Nov 28] workmanlike gelding: has round action: fairly useful handicapper on
the all-weather, fair on turf: successful at Lingfield (seventh course win) in March
and Yarmouth in October: effective at 6f to 7f: probably needs good ground or firmer
or turf: has won in blinkers, not tried in 1997: has given trouble at stalls and often
taken down early. *M. J. Heaton-Ellis*

SPEEDY SNAPS PRIDE 5 gr.g. Hallgate 127 – Pineapple's Pride 60 (John de   –
Coombe 122) [1996 53, a36: a6g a7g⁶ a7g a7g⁶ 6.9s 9.7m⁶ 10m 10d⁴ a8g³ 7m³
8.1m 7m³ 7d* 6m 7f 8m 1997 a6g 10g May 26] plain, sparely-made gelding: poor
handicapper: well beaten in 1997. *P. D. Cundell*

SPENCER'S REVENGE 8 ch.g. Bay Express 132 – Armour of Light (Hot   –
Spark 126) [1996 81d: a8g* a7g³ a8g² a8g² a7g³ 7s⁶ 8d⁵ a8g* a9.4g⁵ a8g⁶ a8g⁴ 1997   a62
a8g² a8.5g a11g a8g² a8g a8g⁴ a10g* a8g⁴ a7g³ a7g³ 7.6g 8.1g Aug 13] sturdy
gelding: poor mover: just a modest performer nowadays: left N. Tinkler after fourth
start: won claimer at Lingfield in February: effective at 7f to 1¼m: acts on the all-
weather, no form on turf in 1997: tried visored/blinkered, no improvement: sometimes slowly away, and often soon off bridle. *P. Butler*

SPENCER STALLONE 4 b.g. Rambo Dancer (CAN) 107 – Armour of Light   –
(Hot Spark 126) [1996 –: a8g⁵ 8d⁴ 8.3g 8g⁵ 1997 16.1g Oct 7] no form. *Graeme Roe*

SPENDER 8 b. or br.g. Last Tycoon 131 – Lady Hester (Native Prince) [1996 80,   86
a91: a6g a5g² a6g a6g³ a5g* a5g⁶ 6g 5f² 5g² 5m 5.1m³ 5f 5.2m⁶ 5g³ 5s⁴ 1997 a5g⁴   a89
6f* 6m⁶ 5.1d 5m⁵ 5.7m* 5.2m 6g 5g 5.2m* 5.3f 5g Oct 25] small, well-made gelding:
fairly useful handicapper: successful at Brighton (idled) in April, Bath in June and
Yarmouth in September: effective at 5f and 6f: acts on any going: game. *P. W. Harris*

SPICE GIRL 2 ch.f. (May 7) Alhijaz 122 – Imagery (Vision (USA)) [1997 6m 6g   –
7g Aug 11] 12,500Y: sparely-made filly: lacks scope: first foal: dam, no worthwhile
form, daughter of smart 5f to 7f winner Petty Purse: well beaten in maidens.
P. D. Evans

SPICETRESS 3 gr.f. Chilibang 120 – Foreign Mistress (Darshaan 133) [1996 52:   –
6f 6g⁴ 8s 1997 7.1g a7g Nov 14] lengthy filly: modest maiden: soundly beaten in
handicaps at 3 yrs, leaving J. Spearing after reappearance. *I. P. Williams*

SPICK AND SPAN 3 b.g. Anshan 119 – Pretty Thing 83 (Star Appeal 133) [1996   58
NR 1997 10m 11.9d³ 10.3d 12g⁵ 10.9d 14.1g⁴ a14g² a14g Nov 17] 11,000Y: unfurnished gelding: fourth foal: half-brother to 4-y-o Rajah: dam, suited by 1½m, out of
half-sister to Oaks second Maina: modest maiden handicapper: stays 1¾m: acts on

fibresand, yet to race on extremes of going on turf: sold 33,000 gns in November, and joined P. Hedger. *C. W. Thornton*

SPINNING WORLD (USA)   4 ch.c. Nureyev (USA) 131 – Imperfect Circle   130 (USA) 111 (Riverman (USA) 131) [1996 125: 8m³ 8g² 8d* 8f⁶ 8d* 8m² 8g² 1997 8d* 8d⁴ 8m* 8m* 8f* Nov 8]

      Spinning World was denied the title of France's top miler at three but made amends at four when his dominance extended to being the best at that trip in Europe. A win in the Breeders' Cup Mile arguably gave him claims to being the best miler on turf on either side of the Atlantic, too. The best of his contemporaries, notably Ashkalani in France and Mark of Esteem in Britain, had been retired to stud, the year-older First Island had his season cut tragically short, and the three-year-old crop failed to produce a top-class miler. But Spinning World didn't earn his position by default—far from it. He improved again from three to four, put up a top-class effort to win a second Prix Jacques le Marois, followed up in France's other top mile race the Prix du Moulin and went one better than the year before at the Breeders' Cup.

      Spinning World returned to action in the Prix du Muguet at Saint-Cloud in May and ran right up to his three-year-old best to defeat the in-form Simon du Desert by a short neck, giving 6 lb. It was a performance that entitled Spinning World to start a short-priced favourite for the Lockinge Stakes fifteen days later. Spinning World had run well below form on his only previous start in Britain—on firm ground in the St James's Palace Stakes at three—and, despite having good to soft going at Newbury, British racegoers were again denied the opportunity of seeing him anywhere near his best. Allowing for the tactical nature of the race, Spinning World ran disappointingly and was never able to land a blow as First Island and Ali-Royal drew clear, eventually losing third place on the line to Even Top. He was subsequently found to be suffering from a virus and given a three-month break before returning at Deauville in August.

      The Prix Jacques le Marois, sponsored by his owners' stud the Haras de Fresnay-Le-Buffard, has more often than not seen the Niarchos family win back their own money in the last ten years thanks to Miesque in 1987 and 1988, Hector Protector in 1991, Exit To Nowhere in 1992, East of The Moon in 1994 and Spinning World himself in 1996. The field of six in the latest season was the smallest since Miesque completed her double but in a strongly-run race it saw Spinning World put up the best effort of his career. He had five three-year-old colts as rivals, headed by the Jean Prat and St James's Palace winner Starborough and the Poule d'Essai des Poulains winner Daylami. The Fabre

Prix du Haras de Fresnay-Le-Buffard Jacques le Marois, Deauville—
Spinning World wins for the second year running (lowering the race record time); Daylami chases him home

stable fielded the Two Thousand Guineas fifth Zamindar and the progressive Neuilly, while Spinning World was provided with a pacemaker, Piperi. The last-named fulfilled his role perfectly by contesting the lead with the front-running favourite Starborough, with the result that the latter was a spent force from under two furlongs out. At that point Daylami challenged but Spinning World went with him travelling the better and asserted to win by two lengths. Daylami had six lengths to spare over Neuilly who kept on for third, with the rest well beaten.

There is only three weeks between the Jacques le Marois and the Prix du Moulin de Longchamp but winning both races—one run on a straight course, the other on a round one—has proved surprisingly difficult in recent seasons. Miesque managed it in 1987 and Polish Precedent two years later but Spinning World was the first to do the double in the 'nineties; he'd found Ashkalani too good at Longchamp twelve months earlier. Despite Spinning World's decisive win at Deauville, Daylami and Neuilly took him on again. The fillies Classic Park, winner of the Irish One Thousand Guineas, and the first two in the Prix d'Astarte, Daneskaya and Rebecca Sharp (the latter the winner of the Coronation Stakes), joined them, along with Bijou d'Inde who was returning from injury sustained when brought down in the Dubai World Cup. But the most interesting rival to Spinning World was Helissio, trying a mile for the first time as part of an unorthodox preparation for the Arc. Remarkably, against specialist milers, Helissio started evens favourite with Spinning World at 6/4. Once again Spinning World was able to use his turn of foot to good effect after Piperi had again ensured a sound gallop. Although Helissio briefly looked a danger after being pocketed, Spinning World soon settled the issue in the home straight and went away to win by two lengths, with Daylami half a length back in third. Daneskaya and Classic Park finished close behind, their proximity holding down the form of the principals somewhat.

Hollywood Park hosted the Breeders' Cup for the third time but by the meeting's usual standards stars were in short supply. Injuries had taken their toll on a number of leading contenders, notably top American horses Gentlemen and Formal Gold, who missed the Classic, and, at a very late date, Europe's main hope Singspiel, who was ruled out of the Turf. The European challenge was just seven, the smallest transatlantic raiding party on the meeting so far. On form, Spinning World was entitled to start favourite but there were several factors to consider which hadn't come into play when he was second to Da Hoss at Woodbine the year before. One was the heat, and to help him cope with the Californian climate he'd reportedly been allowed to enjoy 'lie-ins' at

Emirates Prix du Moulin de Longchamp—
Spinning World uses his finishing speed to good effect in accounting for Helissio and Daylami

Breeders' Cup Mile, Hollywood Park—Spinning World crowns a fine season; Geri (second left), Decorated Hero and Lucky Coin (rail) follow him home

his Chantilly stable so that he'd miss the chilly early mornings and therefore not begin to grow his winter coat before being shipped out. That still left the tight turns, the firm conditions and the possibility of meeting trouble on the very short run to the first bend to be overcome. As for his opponents, the progressive front-runner Lucky Coin and the Woodbine Mile winner Geri were the biggest local dangers. Decorated Hero, a 40/1 chance, was the only other European-trained runner but there were some ex-patriate names among the outsiders, including the former Clive Brittain-trained pair Fantastic Fellow (the only three-year-old) and Magellan, and the dual Lockinge winner Soviet Line.

The Breeders' Cup Mile couldn't have gone more smoothly for Cash Asmussen and Spinning World, who occupied a place in the first four throughout after a remarkably trouble-free run into, and around, the first bend. 'I rode him like he was the best today and he didn't let me down. I followed the speed horse [Lucky Coin], had a perfect trip, and just made sure I had some room at the final bend. We went fast fractions, but he's a horse that stays every yard of the mile.' Spinning World didn't need to show his best form to beat Geri easily by two lengths, with Decorated Hero an excellent third just a neck further back. While Asmussen's first Breeders' Cup win was overdue—he'd had twenty-two unsuccessful rides in the series—Spinning World's other connections had been successful at previous meetings; his owners twice with Miesque in the Mile, and his trainer with Tikkanen in the 1994 Turf. Spinning World's win was the seventh by European horses in the Mile, following Last Tycoon and Miesque's two wins for France, Royal Academy and Ridgewood Pearl for Ireland, and Barathea for Britain.

Spinning World had little time to rest on his laurels. The morning after the Breeders' Cup he was flown to Kentucky where he starts his stallion career at Coolmore's Ashford Stud at a fee of 50,000 dollars. There's little to add to the notes on Spinning World's immediate family which appeared in *Racehorses of 1996*. His two-year-old sister Ring of Fire has yet to race and his dam's third foal is a yearling filly by Kingmambo. But in his wider family it was an outstanding year for descendants of his fourth dam Best In Show; as well as Spinning World, they included champion two-year-old Xaar, Prix du Cadran winner Chief Contender and Irish Derby runner-up Dr Johnson. The rather leggy, good-topped Spinning World did all his racing at a mile with the excep-

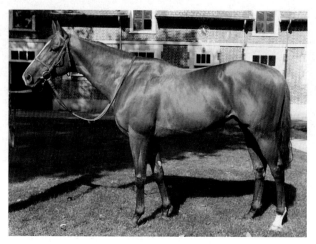

Niarchos Family's "Spinning World"

		Northern Dancer	Nearctic
	Nureyev (USA)	(b 1961)	Natalma
	(b 1977)	Special	Forli
Spinning World (USA)		(b 1969)	Thong
(ch.c. 1993)		Riverman	Never Bend
	Imperfect Circle (USA)	(b 1969)	River Lady
	(b 1988)	Aviance	Northfields
		(ch 1982)	Minnie Hauk

tion of a win in the nine-furlong Prix Saint-Roman on his final outing, at two and he'd almost certainly have stayed a mile and a quarter. He acted on soft ground and, as he proved at Hollywood Park, firm too. A top-class miler, Spinning World was genuine and consistent, finishing out of the frame just once in fourteen starts. In Asmussen he had an ideal partner for a horse that needs to be ridden for a turn of foot. *J. E. Pease, France*

SPIRAL FLYER (IRE) 4 b. or br.f. Contract Law (USA) 108 – Souveniers 36 (Relko 136) [1996 41: a7g⁶ 9.7f 8m 8g 8m 10g⁶ 8m 1997 8.2g 11.8g⁵ 11.5d 17.2g² 18d³ a16.2g 14m Aug 21] good-topped filly: poor maiden handicapper: stays 17f: inconsistent. *M. D. I. Usher*

SPIRIT LADY 3 b.f. Salse (USA) 128 – Wanda 74 (Taufan (USA) 119) [1996 NR – 1997 7.1d 8d 10s⁴ 11.1m Sep 22] workmanlike, angular filly: second reported foal: dam sprinter: signs of ability but no worthwhile form. *J. S. King*

SPIRITO 2 b.c. (May 17) Mystiko (USA) 124 – Classic Beam (Cut Above 130) – [1997 10s Oct 15] 7,500Y: sixth foal: half-brother to 3-y-o Classic Line and a winner in Germany by Bluebird: dam, in frame in Irish 2m maiden and NH Flat races, from family of Salsabil: 12/1, slowly away and always behind in maiden at Nottingham. *Lord Huntingdon*

SPIRIT OF LOVE (USA) 2 ch.c. (May 8) Trempolino (USA) 135 – Dream – p Mary (USA) (Marfa (USA)) [1997 8d a8.5g Nov 29] IR 1,000Y: first foal: dam, won up to 1¼m in USA and placed in Grade 3 event, out of half-sister to US Grade 1 winner Imaginary Lady: behind in maidens at Leicester and Wolverhampton: should do better at 1¼m+. *M. Johnston*

SPIRIT OF SPORT   4 b.f. Forzando 122 – What's The Matter 57 (High Top 131)   –
[1996 –: a8g⁶ a8.5g 1997 8.1m 8s Jul 4] no form: dead. *A. G. Newcombe*

SPIRIT OF THE NILE (FR)   2 b.f. (Mar 1) Generous (IRE) 139 – Egyptale   69
(Crystal Glitters (USA) 127) [1997 7.1m 8.1d⁴ 7g Sep 4] tall, leggy filly: first
reported foal: dam French 10.5f winner, half-sister to smart French performers Sand
Reef and Egyptown: fair form first 2 starts in maidens: should prove suited by 1¼m+.
P. F. I. Cole

SPIRITO LIBRO (USA)   4 b.f. Lear Fan (USA) 130 – Teeming Shore (USA)   –
110 (L'Emigrant (USA) 129) [1996 89: 8.1g² 7.1g⁴ 8m* 7.9f³ 10.1m* 9m⁴ 10g³
10.4m² 1997 10.4g⁵ 10.1g Jun 7] smallish, sparely-made filly: fairly useful handicapper at 3 yrs for C. Allen: well held both starts in 1997. *D. J. S. Cosgrove*

SPITFIRE BRIDGE (IRE)   5 b.g. Cyrano de Bergerac 120 – Maria Renata   –
(Jaazeiro (USA) 127) [1996 –: a10g⁵ 10g 10m 10.2m⁶ 1997 a11g Jan 10] compact
gelding: no form on flat since 1995: won selling hurdle in March. *G. M. McCourt*

SPLASHED   3 gr.f. Absalom 128 – Riverain 65 (Bustino 136) [1996 61: 6g⁴ 6m³   53
a5g³ 1997 a6g⁴ a7g⁴ 6g⁴ 6g 6m 6m May 27] modest maiden: well below form last 4
starts: stays 7f: acts on fibresand. *T. D. Barron*

SPLENDID (IRE)   2 ch.f. (Feb 16) Mujtahid (USA) 118 – Braneakins (Sallust   – p
134) [1997 6s³ 7g 6d Nov 7] 65,000F: leggy, lengthy filly: half-sister to Irish 1¼m to
1¾m winner Bryn Clovis and smart but temperamental 1m (at 2 yrs) and 1½m
winner Peking Opera (both by Sadler's Wells): dam Irish 1½m winner, half-sister to
Park Appeal, Desirable and Alydaress: showed a little promise in autumn maidens
first and third starts: ran as though something amiss in between: likely to be well
suited by 1m+: should do better. *Sir Mark Prescott*

SPLENDID ISOLATION (USA)   2 b.c. (Mar 14) Hermitage (USA) – Hord   80 p
(USA) (Private Account (USA)) [1997 6d 6m³ Oct 31] $7,700Y: first foal: dam un-
raced: sire (by Storm Bird) unraced close relative of Sadler's Wells: showed promise
in maidens at Newmarket in autumn, considerably handled on debut, then 2¾
lengths third to Tussle in steadily-run race, pulling hard to fore but keeping on: bred
to stay further than 6f: should do better again. *L. M. Cumani*

SPLICING   4 ch.f. Sharpo 132 – Soluce 98 (Junius (USA) 124) [1996 82: 5.1d*   –
6g* 6g² 7g a6g 6d² a6g³ 6m 5m 6v 6.1s⁴ 5f³ 5s 1997 5g 6s May 4] lengthy filly: fair
sprint handicapper: soundly beaten in 1997. *W. J. Haggas*

SPONDULICKS (IRE)   3 b.g. Silver Kite (USA) 111 – Greek Music (Tachy-   49 §
pous 128) [1996 55§: 5s³ 5g² 5m⁴ 6d⁵ 7m⁴ 7g⁶ 7f² 7g⁵ 6.9m⁵ 7.1m⁴ 8f³ 10m a8.5g⁶
1997 10.8m 10m⁴ a9.4g³ a12g² a12g⁶ 14.1d⁵ 14.1m 13.4v² 12.3m Jul 11] workmanlike gelding: poor maiden: barely stays 1¾m: acts on any going: visored twice:
unreliable. *B. P. J. Baugh*

SPORTY SPICE (IRE)   2 b.f. (Apr 8) Indian Ridge 123 – Intrinsic (Troy 137)   –
[1997 6.1m 7m 8.1d Aug 25] IR 21,000Y: sixth foal: half-sister to 3 winners,
including Irish 9f winner Bizana (by Kings Lake): dam showed signs of ability but
headstrong: see Baby Spice. *J. L. Harris*

SPOTTED EAGLE   4 ch.g. Risk Me (FR) 127 – Egnoussa 76 (Swing Easy   66
(USA) 126) [1996 81: 6s 6f* 6m 6m 6d 6.1s 1997 6s 6g³ 7m⁵ 6m 6g 6g* 6g 7g a5g
Sep 8] close-coupled gelding: has a quick action: fair performer: didn't have to be at
best to win seller at Catterick (sold out of M. Wane's stable 6,800 gns) in July: below
form for new stable: best efforts at 6f: acts on firm going, no form on ground softer
than good. *D. Nicholls*

SPREE ROSE   2 ch.f. (Mar 31) Dancing Spree (USA) – Pinkie Rose (FR)   66 ?
(Kenmare (FR) 125) [1997 6m 7g² 7g a7g a7s⁵ Nov 28] unfurnished filly: first foal:
dam, French 1½m winner, out of French 13f winning half-sister to 3 French Group 1
winners: easily best effort when front-running 3 lengths second to Red Leggings in
maiden at Warwick in October: too free next 2 starts. *K. O. Cunningham-Brown*

Mr Gary A. Tanaka's "Squeak"

SPRING CAMPAIGN (IRE)   4 b.g. Sayaarr (USA) – March The Second (Mill-   47
fontaine 114) [1996 –: 10m 10.2f⁶ 12m⁶ 8.2g 8.2s 1997 10s 11.8g 10g³ Jun 18] big,
angular gelding: just a poor maiden nowadays: should be suited by further than 1¼m:
acts on firm ground: tried blinkered and visored. *M. C. Pipe*

SPRING FEVER   2 b.c. (Apr 3) Indian Ridge 123 – Tender Moment (IRE) 78   69 +
(Caerleon (USA) 132) [1997 6m⁶ 6m 6m⁶ Oct 31] good-bodied, attractive colt: first
foal: dam 7f winner who stayed 1m: rated on final start, in maiden at Newmarket,
hampered and eased (flattered in minor event on debut): will probably stay beyond
6f. *B. W. Hills*

SPRING MARATHON (USA)   7 b.g. Topsider (USA) – April Run 131 (Run   –
The Gantlet (USA)) [1996 NR 1997 16s 16.4m 20m 18s⁵ Jul 1] good-topped gelding:
fairly useful hurdler: no form on flat in 1997: very much a stayer. *Mrs P. N. Dutfield*

SPY KNOLL   3 b.c. Shirley Heights 130 – Garden Pink (FR) (Bellypha 130)   81
[1996 79p: 7m⁶ 8f⁴ 1997 8.2m 10m³ 12.3d³ 12d³ 14.1s² 16.2m⁴ 13.9s 13.4g* Sep 24]
very tall, rangy colt: fairly useful performer: in frame 5 times in 1997 before making
all in maiden at Chester: stays 2m: acts on firm and soft going: ran poorly in visor
seventh start: sold (to join P. Hedger) 30,000 gns in October. *M. R. Stoute*

SQUABBLE   2 b.f. (Apr 25) Reprimand 122 – Hability (Habitat 134) [1997 6g Oct   56 p
24] 15,000Y: tall filly: eighth foal: half-sister to 1989 2-y-o 7f winner Antoinette
Jane (by Ile de Bourbon) and 2 winners abroad by Sharrood, including Chadleigh
House, also 5f winner here at 2 yrs in 1992: dam unraced from excellent sprinting
family: 12/1, over 8 lengths seventh of 24 to Mister Rambo in maiden at Newbury,
keeping on under hand riding: has scope to do better at 3 yrs. *R. F. Johnson Houghton*

SQUARED AWAY   5 b.h. Blakeney 126 – Maureen Mhor 70 (Taj Dewan 128)   52
[1996 55: 8g 8.5m 8m 10m 12m 8f* 10.1g² 8m 8f 8f⁵ 9m 1997 10.3m 10g³ 8d 8m⁴
10.5m 9g 10.1s² 8s⁵ 10.1g⁶ 7.5d⁵ Aug 13] good-topped horse: modest handicapper:

should stay beyond 1¼m: acts on firm and soft ground: usually blinkered (gained sole win wearing them for first time): often contests amateurs events. *J. W. Payne*

SQUARE DEAL (FR)   6 b.g. Sharpo 132 – River Dove (USA) 86 (Riverman (USA) 131) [1996 71d: a7g² a7g* a8g² a8g a8g⁴ a7g⁵ a8.5g⁶ 6.1g a5g a6g⁵ a6g a7g a11g 1997 a8g* a8g⁵ a8.5g² a7g⁶ a7g 8.3s Jun 30] modest performer on his day: won claimer at Southwell in March: tailed off last 2 starts: stays 8.5f: acts on fibresand: blinkered (well beaten) once: tends to hang markedly left: none too consistent. *S. R. Bowring*   – a60

SQUARE MILE MISS (IRE)   4 b.f. Last Tycoon 131 – Call Me Miss (Hello Gorgeous (USA) 128) [1996 42: 8f⁶ 10g 7f 8g 7d⁶ 7m 8m 8g a7g⁶ 1997 a10g⁶ a8g⁴ 8m² 8.2g 8f 9m³ 10m a11g⁶ a8g² Dec 4] poor handicapper: left P. Howling after seventh start: stays 9f: acts on firm ground and equitrack: carries head high: inconsistent. *N. E. Berry*   43

SQUEAK   3 ch.f. Selkirk (USA) 129 – Santa Linda (USA) (Sir Ivor 135) [1996 83p: 7g* 7m* 1997 10g* 11.9g* 11.9g* 10f⁴ Nov 2] lengthy filly: smart performer: won steadily-run listed race at Newbury and Lancashire Oaks at Haydock (held up last in a race not run at a strong gallop, edged left and beat Tulipa a short head) in the summer: ran very well to be length second of 17 to Clodora in Prix de l'Opera at Longchamp then 4 lengths fourth to Ryafan in Yellow Ribbon at Santa Anita: effective at 9f to 1½m: acts on firm ground, unraced on softer than good: joined B. Cecil in USA. *J. H. M. Gosden*   111

SQUIRE CORRIE   5 b.g. Distant Relative 128 – Fast Car (FR) (Carwhite 127) [1996 70, a64: a6g a6g 6.1g 5m 5m 5f 7g 7m 5f⁵ 5m* 5m⁵ 5m² 5d³ 5g* 5f* 6m 5m⁴ 5g³ a5g a6g a5g³ 1997 a5g a5g* a6g⁵ a6g² a6g* a6g² a6g 5g⁴ 5m⁴ 5d⁴ 5g* 5m⁶ 5g* 5d⁵ 5g* 5d² 5g⁵ 5m 6m 5m 5m³ 5.1s² 5d 5.1g 5g³ 5m³ 5d² 5g Oct 25] tall, workmanlike gelding: unimpressive mover: fairly useful handicapper on turf, fair on all-weather: had an excellent year, winning at Wolverhampton, Lingfield, Thirsk, Hamilton, York and Ayr in first half and holding his form well in second: stays an easy 6f: acts on firm and soft going and the all-weather: often blinkered/visored in the past, better form when not: tends to sweat: successful for apprentice: races prominently: splendidly tough and consistent. *D. W. Chapman*   90

SQUIRE'S OCCASION (CAN)   4 b.g. Black Tie Affair – Tayana (USA) (Wajima (USA)) [1996 72: 12.5d 7m³ 8d⁵ 6.5m⁴ 6m 7g 7g⁵ 8m 1997 a10g a12g* a12g³ 12d 14.4m a13g Dec 22] smallish gelding: fair performer: won amateurs handicap at Lingfield in January on third of 4 starts for R. Akehurst: well held on flat for new yard, but did win over hurdles in October: stays 1½m: acts on equitrack, yet to race on extremes of going on turf: no improvement in blinkers. *R. Curtis*   – a66

STACKATTACK (IRE)   4 b.g. Salt Dome (USA) – Must Hurry (Kampala 120) [1996 65, a73: 8.3g a6g³ 7m⁶ 7.9g 8.1f⁵ 10d 7g² 7g 8s⁶ 1997 10d 6.9f² 7m* 7.1m* 7s 7m* 7m 8g 7.5d² 7m⁵ Oct 4] tall, useful-looking gelding: fairly useful performer: won minor event at Catterick in May and handicaps at Chepstow (amateurs) and York in the summer: best efforts in handicaps last 2 starts: will prove best up to 1m: acts on firm and dead ground (seemingly not on soft) and on fibresand: has carried head high and hung left: sold 20,000 gns in October. *Mrs J. R. Ramsden*   80

STAGE WHISPER   2 b.c. (May 6) Alzao (USA) 117 – Starlet 119 (Teenoso (USA) 135) [1997 8m⁴ a8.5g* Dec 13] fourth foal: half-brother to 5-y-o Renown and 1¼m winner Success Story (by Sharrood): dam best at 1¼m/1½m as 4-y-o: favourite, still green when winning maiden at Wolverhampton by ¾ length from Qismat: should improve, particularly over 1¼m+. *Lord Huntingdon*   70 p

STAHR   3 b.g. Liboi (USA) 76 – Celia Brady 62 (Last Tycoon 131) [1996 –: 8g 7d 1997 10.2d 11.7m³ 12s* 12m* 14s 11.9g⁶ Sep 26] fair handicapper: won twice at Folkestone in July, making most each time: should stay beyond 1½m: acts on good to firm and soft ground: blinkered last 4 starts. *H. Candy*   73

STAKIS CASINOS BOY (IRE)   3 ch.g. Magical Wonder (USA) 125 – Hardiona (FR) (Hard To Beat 132) [1996 NR 1997 10m 10.1m* 12m² 12.3m⁴ 12m⁶ 13.1d 12g Oct 25] 20,000Y: half-brother to several winners, notably high-class French 1¼m and 1½m performer Saint Andrews (by Kenmare): dam French 10.5f winner: fairly useful performer: won maiden at Newcastle in May: well below form   83 in handicaps last 4 outings: stays 1½m: yet to race on extremes of going: sold 13,500 gns in October, and joined B. Ellison. *M. Johnston*

STAKIS CASINOS LAD (IRE)   3 ch.c. Red Sunset 120 – Stradey Lynn 57   –
(Derrylin 115) [1996 50: 5m 6g a7g* 1997 a7g⁴ a8g Jan 27] modest winner at 2 yrs: well held in sellers in 1997: sold, and sent to Macau. *M. Johnston*

STALLED (IRE)   7 b.g. Glenstal (USA) 118 – Chauffeuse 76 (Gay Fandango   51 §
(USA) 132) [1996 57, a61: a13g³ a16g⁵ 10.3d 16g⁵ 15.4m³ 14d³ 16s 12m 14.4g 12m³   a54 §
14s⁵ 12d⁴ a14g² a12g⁵ a14g⁵ a12g² 1997 a16g a16g⁴ a16g a13g⁶ a14g³ 14.9m 12.3m³
11.1d³ a16.2g² 15g 12d a14.8g a14.8g a14g Nov 14] sturdy gelding: modest handicapper: ran badly last 5 starts: stays 2m: acts on good to firm going, soft and the all-
weather: visored (well below form) once at 3 yrs: sometimes weighs: usually contests
amateurs events: often set plenty to do and suited by a good pace: inconsistent, and
not one to trust. *P. T. Walwyn*

STALWART LEGION (IRE)   2 b.f. (Mar 26) Distinctly North (USA) 115 – La   –
Posada 48 (Procida (USA) 129) [1997 7m 7g 7d 8m Oct 5] IR 8,200Y: first foal: dam
ran 3 times: signs of just a little ability in maidens and a nursery. *J. W. Hills*

STAMP (IRE)   3 ch.c. Sharpo 132 – Likeness 101 (Young Generation 129) [1996   –
71+: 7d² 6d 1997 8.2d a7g⁶ Nov 21] fair form on debut: well held since: sold 1,250
gns in December. *B. Smart*

STANDOWN   4 b.g. Reprimand 122 – Ashdown (Pharly (FR) 130) [1996 72, a75:   57
a5g* 6g 5.1g⁵ 6.1m* 6m⁶ 6f³ a6g⁵ 5m⁴ 6g⁵ 6d 6d 6m² 5.1g a7g⁵ a6g 1997 a7s
6m* 6g⁵ 6f* Jun 4] compact gelding: modest performer: won seller at Pontefract in
April and claimer at Warwick (made all) in June: stays 6f: acts on fibresand and firm
ground: often apprentice ridden: visored (well beaten) once: sold 1,600 gns in August, to go to Sweden. *J. Berry*

STAND TALL   5 b.g. Unfuwain (USA) 131 – Antilla 87 (Averof 123) [1996 63,   84
a84: a6g³ a6g* a6g² a6g* a6g* a5g² 5g⁴ 6m³ 6d⁴ 6g² 6d⁴ a6g⁵ 6g* 7g 1997 a6g⁴ a7g³
7f* 6s³ 7s 7f² 6m* 7g 6d* 6m² 6.1g* Sep 28] tall gelding: fairly useful performer:
won minor event at Brighton in May and handicaps at Folkestone in August and
Pontefract and Nottingham in September: stays easy 7f: acts on firm and soft ground
and the all-weather: genuine and consistent. *Lady Herries*

STANOTT (IRE)   2 b.c. (Mar 13) Mukaddamah (USA) 125 – Seme de Lys (USA)   –
61 (Slew O'Gold (USA)) [1997 7m Jul 26] 12,000F, 34,000Y: third foal: dam maiden
(stayed 1m) daughter of half-sister to Exceller: tailed off in 8-runner minor event at
Merano. *L. M. Cumani*

STANTON HARCOURT (USA)   3 b.c. Sovereign Dancer (USA) – Island   101
Style (USA) (Manila (USA)) [1996 90: 7m³ 7g⁶ 8m² 1997 10f* 10m* 12f 10g⁵ 8m*
8m 9m 8m Nov 1] lengthy, useful-looking colt: useful performer: won maiden at
Leicester and minor event at Pontefract in the spring: better form in handicaps,
winning competitive event at Newmarket in July and running well behind Consort
there on final start: races keenly and likely to prove best at 1m/1¼m: raced only on
good ground or firmer. *J. L. Dunlop*

STAR   2 b.f. (Jan 27) Most Welcome 131 – Marista (Mansingh (USA) 120) [1997   83
5.1d* 5m³ 6g Oct 18] 16,000Y: useful-looking filly: has a quick action: half-sister
to several winners, including useful 1988 2-y-o 5f winner Four-Legged Friend (by
Aragon) and 1991 2-y-o 6f winner Super Strike (by Superlative), later Grade 3 7f
winner in USA: dam lightly raced and showed temperamental: fairly useful form:
won minor event at Nottingham in May by 6 lengths: good third in similar contest at
Haydock over 4 months later, but well below form final start, carrying head high:
should stay at least 6f. *M. A. Jarvis*

STARBOROUGH   3 ch.c. Soviet Star (USA) 128 – Flamenco Wave (USA)   126
103 (Desert Wine (USA)) [1996 102: 6g* 6m³ 7.3s⁴ 1997 8g* 8m⁴ 9m* 8m*
8m² 8m⁴ Aug 17]
          Flamenco Wave's first three foals achieved nothing to suggest that
Starborough would turn out to be a high-class miler. But, after a relatively quiet
beginning to his career, he's done just that. He started off in run-of-the-mill
company, a maiden at Thirsk, a race he won easily. His two other starts as a juv-

Prix d'Abu Dhabi Airport Duty Free–Prix Jean Prat, Chantilly—
Starborough stays on strongly to account for Mamalik and Kirkwall (No. 1)

enile seemed to indicate that he was no better than a useful performer, however;
he finished a close third in the Sirenia Stakes at Kempton then about a length
fourth in the Horris Hill Stakes at Newbury, putting in his best work at the finish
both times. Starborough's three-year-old reappearance resulted in a win in the
three-runner Thirsk Classic Trial. The form of the Horris Hill was beginning to
look a good deal better than it had at the time, but Starborough still only dis-
posed of the useful Intikhab (from whom he was receiving 5 lb) in workmanlike
fashion by two lengths. Starborough took his chance in the Two Thousand
Guineas, at 33/1 presumably more in hope than expectation, and ran surprisingly well. The front-running tactics employed at Thirsk were tried again, this
time at a much stronger pace. Starborough had several of his better-fancied
rivals in trouble some way out and found only Entrepreneur, Revoque and
Poteen too good for him in the closing stages, beaten just over two lengths by
the first-named.

Starborough was no outsider when he lined up for the Prix d'Abu Dhabi
Airport Duty Free-Prix Jean Prat at Chantilly, though the locally-trained Kirk-

St James's Palace Stakes, Royal Ascot—Starborough (noseband) battles on well to defeat Air Express

wall was preferred to him in the betting. This was a Group 1 race in name only, however, and Starborough probably had to do no more than reproduce his Guineas form to prevail. He gradually stepped up the pace in the straight and ran on with plenty of zest to beat the John Gosden-trained colt Mamalik by one and a half lengths, with Kirkwall a short head behind in third. A much stronger field showed up for the St James's Palace Stakes at Royal Ascot later in the month and it was no surprise that, smart performer though Starborough now was, the winners of the French and Irish equivalents of the Guineas (Daylami and Desert King respectively), as well as Poteen, figured ahead of him in the betting in a field of eight. Also present was the British-trained Italian and German Guineas winner Air Express. Starborough put up a most tenacious display, setting a searching gallop and seeing off all his challengers except Air Express by the two-furlong marker. Starborough came under strong pressure but showed no signs of stopping, if anything pulling away again at the line, which he reached a length to the good. There were some disappointing performances behind (Daylami four lengths back in third and Desert King another half a length back in fourth were clearly below form) but Starborough had turned in a high-class effort, as independently confirmed by time analysis of the performance.

Starborough went off favourite for his next race, the Sussex Stakes at Goodwood, and made a bold bid, going down by three quarters of a length to Ali-Royal. Starborough again bowled along in front, but on the sharper track he couldn't get clear and was collared at the furlong pole. His final race of the season came in the Prix Jacques le Marois at Deauville. He ran poorly, having been taken on by the pacemaker for the winner Spinning World. Starborough dropped right away in the closing stages to finish eleven lengths behind in fourth. In October it was announced that he'd been transferred to Godolphin and that he would be wintered in Dubai before returning in 1998.

Sheikh Mohammed's "Starborough"

Starborough is the fifth foal out of the useful two-year-old winner Flamenco Wave, who flopped in her only two starts at three. Two of them were the ordinary winners Father Sky (by Dancing Brave) and Cante Chico (by Reference Point), though Father Sky has won a Grade 2 novice hurdle and shown himself to be useful over fences too. Flamenco Wave's fourth foal (the one before Starborough) fared better, however, the Belmez filly Spanish Falls winning the Prix de Royaumont over a mile and a half at Saint-Cloud in 1996. Flamenco Wave produced a filly by Wolfhound in 1995 called Sanchez (as yet unraced), failed to get into foal that year by Green Desert, then visited Sadler's Wells. Her dam, Armada Way, was one of the leading two-year-old fillies in Canada in 1978, but she's produced just three minor winners besides Flamenco Wave. Starborough's sire, Soviet Star, was a high-class sprinter/miler whose best offspring in Europe have also included the Arc and Breeders' Cup Turf runner-up Freedom Cry, the Poule d'Essai des Poulains winner Ashkalani, the dual Lockinge winner Soviet Line and the very smart Volochine (the last two now racing in the USA). Soviet Star was exported to Japan in 1994.

		Nureyev	Northern Dancer
	Soviet Star (USA)	(b 1977)	Special
	(b 1984)	Veruschka	Venture VII
Starborough		(b 1967)	Marie d'Anjou
(ch.c. 1994)		Desert Wine	Damascus
	Flamenco Wave (USA)	(b 1980)	Anne Campbell
	(ch 1986)	Armada Way	Sadair
		(ch 1976)	Hurry Call

Starborough's win at Royal Ascot was just about the best performance by a three-year-old miler in 1997. Although it wasn't a strong year, in his favour he seems likely to get a mile and a quarter (indeed, the stiffer the track and the sounder the pace at a mile the better, it seems) and is a thoroughly genuine sort. An angular, good-bodied colt, Starborough has produced his best efforts on good to firm going, the Horris Hill being the only time he's run on softer than good. *D. R. Loder*

STAR CRYSTAL (IRE)   2 b.f. (Jan 25) Brief Truce (USA) 126 – Crystal Spray 75 (Beldale Flutter (USA) 130) [1997 8f² Oct 29] third living foal: half-sister to smart 1995 2-y-o 6f and 1m winner Solar Crystal (by Alzao) and smart 7f (at 2 yrs) and 1½m winner State Crystal (by High Estate): dam, daughter of half-sister to Royal Palace, won over 1¾m at 4 yrs in Ireland: 5/2 and green, neck second to ready winner Publisher in maiden at Yarmouth, ridden along in front from halfway and edging a bit right, not appearing to stride out fully: will stay at least 1¼m: should improve. *H. R. A. Cecil*   80 p

STAR ENTRY   3 b.f. In The Wings 128 – Top Berry 87 (High Top 131) [1996 50+, a45: 6m⁵ a7g⁴ a8g⁵ 1997 10.2d 11.7g⁴ 14m⁶ 9.7d* 12m Oct 31] fair handicapper: best effort when winning at Folkestone in October by 4 lengths: best around 1¼m: acts on good to firm and dead ground, below form on fibresand. *Major D. N. Chappell*   67 a–

STAR GAMBIT (USA)   3 b.f. Defensive Play (USA) 118 – Etoile Eternelle (USA) (Timeless Moment (USA)) [1996 NR 1997 8.1s² 8d⁵ Sep 19] $57,000Y: leggy, quite good topped filly: second foal: half-sister to Lago (by Lac Ouimet), second in Grade 2 9f event: dam won up to 9f in USA: neck second of 11 to Sceptre Lady in maiden at Sandown in August, leading 2f out but wandering and carrying head awkwardly: well below that form only subsequent outing. *R. Akehurst*   75

STAR INVADER   3 b.c. Nashwan (USA) 135 – Sahara Star 95 (Green Desert (USA) 127) [1996 NR 1997 8d³ 7m⁵ 7d⁴ Oct 13] strong, well-made colt: first foal: dam, won Molecomb Stakes, half-sister to 3-y-o Yalaietanee out of smart sprinter Vaigly Star: fair form at best: reportedly finished lame on debut (seemingly best effort) and subsequently off course for 4 months. *M. R. Stoute*   72 ?

STARLIGHT WALTZER   4 b.g. Arzanni 115 – Marchiness Drake (Marechal Drake 101) [1996 –: 10g 1997 14.1s Oct 15] soundly beaten in maidens. *K. S. Bridgwater*   –

STARLINER (IRE) 2 ch.f. (Mar 2) Statoblest 120 – Dancing Line (High Line   57
125) [1997 6g³ 5g 6m 7m 6.1m 7m⁶ Oct 1] 8,400Y: third foal: half-sister to winners
abroad by Jareer and Absalom: dam ran twice at 2 yrs in Ireland: third in maiden at
Doncaster, but largely disappointing afterwards. *M. Brittain*

STARMAKER (IRE) 2 b.g. (Mar 6) Fairy King (USA) – Miss Toshiba (USA)   86
113 (Sir Ivor 135) [1997 6g² 7.5v² Jul 5] lengthy, useful-looking gelding: has a quick
action: closely related to useful French 9f (at 2 yrs) and 1½m winner Youm Jadeed
and fairly useful 1¼m winner Ikebana (both by Sadler's Wells) and half-brother to
several winners: dam won from 7f to 1½m: favourite, promising second to Mazboon
in maiden at Newbury: odds on, below that form in minor event at Beverley following month: should stay at least 1m: sent to Hong Kong. *P. W. Chapple-Hyam*

STAR MANAGER (USA) 7 b.g. Lyphard (USA) 132 – Angel Clare (FR) (Mill   91
Reef (USA) 141) [1996 89: 8.1g* 8m⁴ 9s⁴ 8m⁵ 7.9m⁰ 10.1m 9m 9s³ 1997 8.1g³ 8g
10.4g⁶ 10.1g² 10s⁶ 10.4m⁴ 10m 12g⁵ 10d⁴ 10g Oct 24] close-coupled gelding: fluent
mover: fairly useful handicapper: creditable efforts most starts in 1997, fourth in
Magnet Cup at York in July: effective at 1m to 1¼m: acts on any going: below form
when sweating/edgy: takes good hold and usually held up. *P. F. I. Cole*

STAR OF GOLD 5 b.g. Night Shift (USA) – Sure Gold 100 (Glint of Gold 128)   –
[1996 77: a7g 6.9g* 7m 8f* 8m² 1997 8d Jun 29] small, sturdy gelding: fair
handicapper at 4 yrs: tailed off only outing in 1997. *C. R. Egerton*

STAR OF GROSVENOR (IRE) 2 b.f. (Feb 16) Last Tycoon 131 – Castilian   72
Queen (USA) 82 (Diesis 133) [1997 6m 6.9m* 6.5m 7m Sep 30] rather unfurnished
filly: second foal: half-sister to 3-y-o Carmine Lake: dam 2-y-o 6f winner, daughter
of Breeders' Cup Mile winner Royal Heroine: made all in maiden at Folkestone in
August: didn't progress, though not discredited in nursery final start: likely to stay
1m: has raced only on good to firm going. *P. W. Chapple-Hyam*

STAR OF RING (IRE) 4 b.g. Taufan (USA) 119 – Karine (Habitat 134) [1996   58
–: 8.2s 1997 7g⁴ 8m 7g 10m 10.2m 8.2d Oct 8] big, good-bodied gelding: good
mover: modest performer, lightly raced: favourite on first run for a year, comfortable
winner of maiden at Thirsk in April: stiff tasks and well beaten afterwards: may prove
best short of 1m: races prominently: joined Miss G. Kelleway. *M. J. Heaton-Ellis*

STAR OF THE COURSE (USA) 2 b.f. (Feb 8) Theatrical 128 – Water Course   –
(USA) (Irish River (FR) 131) [1997 7g⁴ 7g Sep 4] IR 170,000Y: third foal: half-sister
to 3-y-o Deep Water: dam (unraced) from family of Star of Gdansk and Mt Livermore: tailed off in maidens. *P. F. I. Cole*

STAR OF THE ROAD 3 b.c. Risk Me (FR) 127 – Astrid Gilberto 75 (Runnett   47
125) [1996 49: 5m⁶ 1997 5m⁶ 5m 5d 6m⁶ 5m⁶ 5m³ 6m 6g 5f Sep 17] workmanlike
colt: poor maiden handicapper: well below form last 3 starts: stays 6f. *J. M. Carr*

STAR PRECISION 3 ch.f. Shavian 125 – Accuracy 83 (Gunner B 126) [1996   103
59: 7d 7.1v⁶ 7d⁵ 1997 10d* 13.1d* 12.1g* 12d⁶ 11.9g⁴ 12m 8d⁴ 14.6d⁶ Nov 7]
sparely-made, angular filly: has a long, round action: useful performer: won handicaps at Nottingham, Bath and Chepstow in April/May, and 3-runner minor event
(didn't have to be at best over 1m) at Leicester in October: best effort when 1¾
lengths fourth to Squeak in Lancashire Oaks at Haydock: stays 13f, pulled too hard
over 14.6f: acts on dead ground: game. *G. B. Balding*

STAR PROFILE (IRE) 3 b.f. Sadler's Wells (USA) 132 – Sandhurst Goddess   96
103 (Sandhurst Prince 128) [1996 100: 6m⁵ 6g⁵ 7g⁵ 1997 8d 7m³ 8.5d³ Jun 25] IR
200,000Y: leggy filly: second foal: half-sister to 1994 2-y-o 5f winner Lady Davenport (by Contract Law): dam Irish 5f to 7f winner: won maiden at the Curragh for
D. Weld at 2 yrs, when also fifth in Heinz 57 Phoenix Stakes at Leopardstown and
Moyglare Stud Stakes at the Curragh: not quite so good in 1997, 8 lengths last of 7 in
Poule d'Essai des Pouliches at Longchamp on reappearance and third in minor event
at Leicester: visored, tailed-off last final start: should stay 1m: yet to race on extremes
of going: joined E. Dunlop. *Saeed bin Suroor*

STAR RAGE (IRE) 7 b.g. Horage 124 – Star Bound (Crowned Prince (USA)   86
128) [1996 89: a14.8g² 1997 a12g² a16g³ 14.9m 12g⁴ 16m* 16.2d 14.8m² 16d³ 16g
16.2g⁴ 18g 14.1d Oct 30] sturdy, angular gelding: fairly useful handicapper: trained
first 3 starts by J. L. Harris: won at Redcar in August: needs thorough test at 1½m and

stays 2m: acts on the all-weather, firm and dead ground: sometimes idles, and normally held up: useful hurdler, winner twice in November: tough. *M. Johnston*

STAR SELECTION 6 b.g. Rainbow Quest (USA) 134 – Selection Board 75 (Welsh Pageant 132) [1996 105: 10g² 12.3g⁴ 10d 8.9g 1997 12.3d² 13.4s 10.9d⁵ 11.9s Oct 15] leggy, lengthy gelding: useful performer: creditable efforts at 6 yrs in minor event at Ripon and listed race (beaten 4½ lengths by Ghataas) at Ayr on first and third starts: stays 1½m: has form on firm going, but raced only on good or softer last 2 seasons: none too consistent. *J. Mackie* — 96

STAR TALENT (USA) 6 b.g. Local Talent (USA) 122 – Sedra 116 (Nebbiolo 125) [1996 87, a75: a7g* a6g⁴ a7g² a6g⁵ a7g³ 8d 7f* 8d⁵ 7g² 8g³ 7s 8.5m² 8m 7m⁴ 7f⁴ a7g² a7g⁵ 1997 a8.5f⁴ a7g² a7g³ a7g⁴ 8m* 8.1g* 8g⁶ 8d⁴ 8.5m³ 8.1d⁴ 7.6f³ 8m 7d 7.3d Sep 19] robust gelding: impresses in appearance: has reportedly had wind problems: fairly useful on turf, fair on all-weather: won claimer at Warwick (claimed out of Miss G. Kelleway's stable) and rated stakes at Sandown in April: good efforts next 5 starts, but well below form on last 3 (bolted beforehand on first of them): effective at 7f to 8.5f: acts on firm and dead ground and all-weather: visored once at 5 yrs: sometimes bandaged for former stable: suited by waiting tactics. *I. A. Balding* — 91 a74

STAR TURN (IRE) 3 ch.c. Night Shift (USA) – Ringtail 102 (Auction Ring (USA) 123) [1996 61: 6d 6f⁵ 6.9d 1997 8.2s³ 8.5m⁴ 8.2m² 8g 7g⁴ a7g³ 7g⁵ 8d² 8.2d⁵ Oct 30] strong colt: modest maiden handicapper: likely to prove best up to 1m: acts on firm and soft ground and on equitrack: consistent. *M. Bell* — 64

STAR WITNESS (IRE) 5 b.g. Contract Law (USA) 108 – Star Heading 74 (Upper Case (USA)) [1996 NR 1997 10s 10d a7g a11g⁵ Dec 8] fair form at 2 yrs: ran 6 times in Czech Republic in 1995, winning once over 11f: well held in handicaps on return to Britain. *A. G. Newcombe* — –

STATAJACK (IRE) 9 b.g. King of Clubs 124 – Statira 103 (Skymaster 126) [1996 83: a10g³ a10g 12m⁶ 10m 10.2f 10s⁴ 12m* 11.6m² 10m* 10m 9.7m⁴ a11g² 1997 10.3d 10s 8.1m 11.6m² 12d⁶ 12s³ 12m 11.7f⁵ 11.6m⁴ 10g³ 10g⁶ 12.1d² 12g²* 12m 11.8d³ 10d* a12g² a12g³ Nov 18] leggy, sparely-made gelding: fair performer: won sellers at Folkestone in September and Nottingham in November: effective at 1¼m and 1½m: acts on any turf ground and on equitrack: wears blinkers/bandages: not an easy ride (best held up), and well handled by T. Quinn. *D. R. C. Elsworth* — 66 a75

STATE APPROVAL 4 b.g. Pharly (FR) 130 – Tabeeba (Diesis 133) [1996 69, a72: 12d⁵ a12g⁴ 11.6m² 11.4d 13.1m² 16m⁵ 12m* a12g* 14d⁵ 11.5m⁶ 12m⁶ a12g³ 1997 a12g⁶ a12g a16.2g⁵ a12g* 12.1d⁶ a16.2g⁶ a12g⁵ 11.6g³ a12f* 10.8g⁵ a12g² a12g a14.8g Nov 29] small gelding: fair performer on fibresand, modest on turf: won handicaps at Wolverhampton in March and June, latter by 15 lengths: stays 13f: acts on good to firm ground, seemingly not on softer than good: front runner. *P. Eccles* — 62 a77

STATE FAIR 3 b.c. Shirley Heights 130 – Lobinda 80 (Shareef Dancer (USA) 135) [1996 92+: 6m³ 7m² 7m* 7m* 8g 1997 12.3d³ 12f 16.2m 14.8g⁴ 16m 13.4s 14.6m 16g 11.9s² Oct 15] smallish colt: has a round action: useful performer: best efforts when third in Chester Vase (beaten head and same by Panama City and Ivan Luis) and fourth in listed race at Newmarket (7½ lengths behind Three Cheers): well below form last 4 starts (beaten 20 lengths by Rainwatch in minor event at Haydock final one): stays 14.8f: acts on good to firm and dead going. *B. W. Hills* — 102

STATE GALA (IRE) 2 b.f. (Apr 24) High Estate 127 – Our Galadrial (Salmon Leap (USA) 131) [1997 6m Jun 9] IR 7,500Y: fourth foal: half-sister to 1¼m/1½m winner Westminster (by Nashamaa): dam unraced half-sister to smart middle-distance performer Boon Point: 33/1, in rear in maiden at Windsor. *M. Bell* — –

STATELY FAVOUR 2 ch.f. (Mar 16) Statoblest 120 – Dixie Favor (USA) 76 (Dixieland Band (USA)) [1997 5g 5d⁴ 6m 6.1d a6g⁴ Nov 21] smallish, useful-looking filly: first foal: dam Irish 6f (at 2 yrs) to 1m winner: modest maiden: only fourth in seller at Wolverhampton final start: likely to stay 7f: has been bandaged behind. *M. J. Camacho* — 59 a46

STATELY PRINCESS 2 b.f. (Feb 1) Robellino (USA) 127 – Affair of State (IRE) 99 (Tate Gallery (USA) 117) [1997 5m³ 5m* 5m⁶ 6g 6g Aug 30] IR 16,000Y: good-topped filly: second foal: half-sister to 3-y-o Statesman (by Doyoun), 1m winner in Sweden: dam, 2-y-o sprint winner, well beaten both starts at 3 yrs: won — 70

4-runner maiden at Newcastle in March: below that form subsequently, in blinkers final start: should stay 6f: has tended to hang left. *M. R. Channon*

STATE OF CAUTION   4 b.g. Reprimand 122 – Hithermoor Lass 75 (Red Alert 127) [1996 83: 7g² 7.5m⁴ 7g³ 7m⁴ 8m³ 8m 1997 a7g* a8g³ a7g* a8.5g a7g³ 6d⁵ 6d 6m a6g* a6g* a7g* a7g² Dec 6] useful-looking gelding: useful performer on all-weather, fairly useful on turf: in fine form in 1997, winning maiden in January and handicap in March, both at Southwell, and handicaps at Wolverhampton in September, October and November: good second to Chewit in competitive handicap on latter course final start: better at 6f/7f than 1m: goes well on fibresand, and acts on good to firm and dead ground: usually blinkered or visored. *D. Shaw*   82 a107

STATE OF GOLD (IRE)   3 b.g. High Estate 127 – Mawaal Habeebee (Northfields (USA)) [1996 –: 7g 7.6m 7g a7g⁶ 1997 a8s⁶ a8g⁴ a9.4f⁶ a8g a11g³ a11g* a12g* a12g² a10g⁵ Mar 1] modest all-weather performer: won handicap at Southwell and claimer at Wolverhampton in February: stays 1½m: acts on all-weather: tail flasher. *J. Hetherton*   60

STATISTICIAN   5 b.g. Statoblest 120 – Sharp Lady 70 (Sharpen Up 127) [1996 64: 5.2g⁴ 5f⁴ 6m 6m⁴ 6d 8f 7f² 7g 7g⁴ a7g³ a7g² a7g a7g 1997 a7g² a7g a7g a8g² a8g³ a8g⁶ a8g⁵ Mar 13] tall gelding: modest handicapper at best nowadays: stays 1m: acts on firm ground and the all-weather: tried blinkered, not in 1997. *John Berry*   50

STATORHYTHM   2 b.g. (Mar 17) Statoblest 120 – Blue Rhythm 72 (Blue Cashmere 129) [1997 5g a5g⁵ Apr 28] 12,000Y: third living foal: half-brother to 5f winner Magic Mail (by Aragon), later winner in Sweden: dam won from 5f (at 2 yrs) to 7f: behind in maiden and seller (blinkered). *T. D. Barron*   –

STATOYORK   4 b.g. Statoblest 120 – Ultimate Dream 74 (Kafu 120) [1996 80d: 6m⁵ 6f*ᵈⁱˢ 7m* 6m 7m 7m 1997 7f⁴ 7d 7f² 7d 7s⁵ 6g a5g a5g a7g Dec 18] strong gelding: fair form at best in 1997: left B. Hills after fifth start: should prove best up to 7f: acts on firm ground and probably dead, no form on fibresand: visored 2 of last 3 starts. *D. Shaw*   66 a–

STATUA (IRE)   2 b.f. (Mar 27) Statoblest 120 – Amata (USA) (Nodouble (USA)) [1997 6m⁵ 5m² 6g⁵ 6m³ 7g³ Oct 18] 18,000Y: rather leggy filly: half-sister to numerous winners, notably useful 6f (at 2 yrs) to 9f (Grade 3 in USA) winner Bluegrass Prince (by Bluebird): dam French middle-distance winner, later successful in USA: useful maiden: easily best efforts when fifth in Lowther Stakes at York third start and under 2 lengths third to Name of Love in Rockfel Stakes at Newmarket final one: never going when disappointing in Folkestone maiden in between: will stay 1m: probably needs holding up. *P. J. Makin*   98

STAYINGALIVE (USA)   2 ch.f. (Jan 25) Gone West (USA) – Lady For Two (USA) (Storm Bird (CAN) 134) [1997 6g* 6g Jul 8] $500,000Y: tall, leggy, rather unfurnished filly: sixth foal: sister to 3-y-o The West and half-sister to a minor stakes winner in USA by Seattle Slew: dam 7f winner out of smart US filly at up to 9f Very Special Lady: won maiden at Newmarket in June, though racing very freely in steadily-run race, carrying head high and giving odd swish of tail: favourite, only seventh in Cherry Hinton Stakes at same course: bred to stay 1m. *P. F. I. Cole*   95

ST BLAINE (CAN)   3 b.f. St Jovite (USA) 135 – Blaine (USA) (Lyphard's Wish (FR) 124) [1996 79p: 7g⁵ 1997 8f* 7.1m⁴ 6.9s⁴ 7g Jul 8] fairly useful performer: won maiden at Carlisle in May: blinkered, looked none too hearty on final start, carrying head awkwardly: stays 1m: acts on firm and soft ground: sent to USA. *D. R. Loder*   82

ST CLAIR SHORES (USA)   2 b.f. (Apr 17) Northern Flagship (USA) 96 – Dom Chandon (USA) (Seattle Slew (USA)) [1997 7m 7.9s 8g⁶ Oct 18] rangy, rather unfurnished filly: sixth foal: half-sister to several winners, including Grey Chandon (by Grey Dawn), listed placed in USA at 2 yrs: dam, unraced, from family of Bellypha: fair form: best effort in minor event at Kempton on debut: should stay 1m+: sold 8,000 gns in November. *M. R. Stoute*   68

STEAL 'EM   4 b.f. Efisio 120 – Eastern Ember 85 (Indian King (USA) 128) [1996 66: a5g⁶ 7.6m* 7m 7d a6g⁶ a7g 1997 a6g 6g 8.3g 10.3s⁴ 7.6m a6g Jul 21] workmanlike filly: fair form at 3 yrs, none in 1997: tried blinkered and visored. *A. Bailey*   –

STEAM ON   6 ch.g. Common Grounds 118 – Oh My Joy 57 (Grundy 137) [1996   –
NR 1997 14f Oct 3] smallish, workmanlike gelding: no form on flat: won claiming
hurdle in October. *Mrs L. C. Jewell*

STEAMROLLER STANLY   4 b.g. Shirley Heights 130 – Miss Demure 106   83
(Shy Groom (USA)) [1996 84: 10g⁶ 13.3m* 15d⁴ 14m⁶ 12g³ 18.2m⁵ 11.9g a12g*   a91
1997 a12g* a10g² a10g* 12g 12m⁴ 14.1m³ Sep 26] sturdy gelding: carries condition:
fairly useful performer: won handicap at Lingfield in January and minor event on
same course in February: creditable efforts last 2 outings: effective at 1¼m to 1¾m:
acts on good to firm and dead ground, goes well on equitrack: has carried tail
awkwardly last 3 starts. *C. A. Cyzer*

STELLAR LINE (USA)   4 ch.g. Zilzal (USA) 137 – Stellaria (USA) 98   72
(Roberto (USA) 131) [1996 72: 8f⁴ 8m⁴ 7.9g⁴ 7g⁴ 10g⁵ 1997 a10g² a10g² 8f² 10m*
10g 8m⁶ 8.5g⁴ 8d 8g a10s Nov 28] leggy, close-coupled gelding: fair performer:
made all in seller at Brighton in May on final start for D. Elsworth, winning by 13
lengths: off course 4 months before well beaten last 3 starts: stays 1¼m: acts on firm
and dead ground and on equitrack: used to be mulish at stalls, and seemed reluctant
on occasions, but did little wrong in 1997. *M. J. Polglase*

ST ENODOC (FR)   2 ch.g. (Mar 21) Sanglamore (USA) 126 – Exemina (USA)   63
(Slip Anchor 136) [1997 7g 8m⁶ 8d Oct 28] 150,000 francs Y: strong gelding: second
foal: half-brother to smart 7f (at 2 yrs) and 1½m winner St Mawes (by Shahrastani):
dam, French middle-distance winner, daughter of smart French mare El Fabulous:
modest form in maidens first 2 starts, but tailed off final one: should be suited by
further than 1m. *J. L. Dunlop*

STEPHANGEORGE   2 b.g. (Feb 22) La Grange Music 111 – Telegraph Callgirl   –
67 (Northern Tempest (USA) 120) [1997 5f 5.1m 5m 6d 6m Oct 28] 1,600Y: tall
gelding: fourth foal: dam 7f and 1m winner: signs of only a little ability. *M. Brittain*

STEPHENSONS ROCKET   6 ch.g. Music Boy 124 – Martian Princess 90   54
(Cure The Blues (USA)) [1996 60: a6g 5s 6g 5m⁵ 5g 5.1m 5m 5g² 5g 5m a6g 1997   a44
a6g 5g⁶ a5g³ 6.1g² 5.9d⁵ a6g 8f 7d 6s² 5m⁶ 6g⁴ 6m⁶ 6d 6m⁵ Sep 26] good-topped
gelding: impresses in appearance: shows knee action: modest handicapper, on a long
losing sequence: best at 5f/6f: acts on firm and soft ground, poor form at best on
fibresand: tried visored and blinkered. *R. A. Fahey*

STEP IN TO THE SUN   2 ch.f. (Mar 28) Primo Dominie 121 – June Fayre   –
(Sagaro 133) [1997 5d¹ 6m a6g Jun 7] 8,000Y: sister to 3-y-o Manhattan Diamond
and 1991 2-y-o 5f winner Hay Yuen (later winning sprinter in Italy) and half-sister to
several winners: dam twice raced: little sign of ability in sellers: blinkered final start.
R. A. Fahey

STEP N GO (IRE)   3 b.f. Alzao (USA) 117 – River Jet (USA) (Lear Fan (USA)   70
130) [1996 60+: 5.1m⁵ 5m² 5f⁶ 6g 6.1s⁴ 1997 8.3d² 10.3d* 9.9d* 10g⁵ 11.9g 10.5d
10d⁶ 10s⁶ Oct 14] robust, good-quartered filly: unimpressive mover: fair handicapper: won at Doncaster and Beverley in May: mostly well below form afterwards:
better around 1¼m than shorter: acts on good to firm and dead ground: sold 21,000
gns in December. *Mrs J. R. Ramsden*

STEP ON DEGAS   4 b.f. Superpower 113 – Vivid Impression (Cure The Blues   65
(USA)) [1996 67: 5f* 5.2m⁵ 5.1m 5m 5m a5g² 5m a5g² a6g⁵ a6g² 1997 a7g* a7g   a69
a7g³ 6m 5m 6m⁴ 6d⁵ 7m* 8d² 8m a7g a8s Nov 10] rather leggy filly: fair performer:
won handicap at Lingfield in January and minor event at Brighton in August: stays
1m: goes well on the all-weather, acts on firm and dead ground on turf: tried visored,
not in 1997: none too consistent. *M. J. Fetherston-Godley*

STERLING FELLOW   4 b.c. Pharly (FR) 130 – Favorable Exchange (USA)   –
(Exceller (USA) 129) [1996 66: a10g 12m⁶ 12d⁴ 17.2g⁵ 12.5f³ 16f* 17.2m² 14m²
14.1d⁵ 15.4g 17.9g³ 18g³ 1997 a14.8g⁴ 17.1m Apr 22] neat colt: modest staying
handicapper: well beaten in 1997: usually visored/blinkered: dead. *D. L. Williams*

STERNSINGER (USA)   2 b.c. (Jan 14) Seeking The Gold (USA) – Song Maker   67 p
(IRE) (Sadler's Wells (USA) 132) [1997 8f Oct 29] first reported foal: dam, ran once
in France, half-sister to Arc winner Sagace and Dante winner Simply Great: 12/1
from 7/1, about 8 lengths seventh to Publisher in maiden at Yarmouth, fading final
2f: should improve. *H. R. A. Cecil*

STEVIE'S WONDER (IRE)   7 ch.g. Don't Forget Me 127 – Azurai 80 (Dance   –
In Time (CAN)) [1996 –, a70d: a14.8g* a12g² a14.8g⁶ 17.2f a12g 11.8m a12g a12g
a11g³ a16.2g a12g 1997 a11g a12g⁵ a12g a14.8g Feb 12] sturdy gelding: fair performer at best: no form in 1997. *B. J. Llewellyn*

STEWARD (FR)   4 b.c. Saumarez 132 – Belle Ombre (Dancing Brave (USA)   117
140) [1996 10s³ 10g* 10m⁵ 12g² 10m* 12s⁴ 10d* 11g* 10s⁴ 1997 10d⁵ 10m⁴ 12g*
12d* 12m⁴ 12f Oct 5] smallish, sturdy colt: smart performer: won Prix d'Hedouville
at Longchamp in May and Grand Prix de Chantilly (by ¾ length from Surgeon) in
June, both 5-runner events: not best of runs when fourth to Yokohama in Prix Foy
then out of depth in the Arc at Longchamp last 2 starts: stays 1½m: acts on good to
firm and soft ground: consistent. *D. Sepulchre, France*

ST HELENSFIELD   2 ch.c. (Mar 5) Kris 135 – On Credit (FR) (No Pass No Sale   91
120) [1997 10.2f* 10d² 10m³ Nov 1] 11,000Y: strong, angular colt: has a round
action: has scope: second foal: half-brother to 3-y-o Stowaway: dam French 7f (at 2
yrs) and 10.5f winner and placed in Group 3 events: won maiden at Bath in September: fairly useful form when second of 3 to Asakir in minor event at Leicester and
third to Trigger Happy in listed race at Newmarket: will stay at least 1½m: wandered
markedly at Leicester, and looks a difficult ride. *M. Johnston*

STILETT (IRE)   3 b.c. Tirol 127 – Legal Steps (IRE) (Law Society (USA) 130)   92
[1996 8s⁶ 1997 8g 8g⁵ 8.1g* 8g³ 8g* 8m Jul 19] 24,000Y: rather leggy, quite
attractive colt: first foal: dam, Irish 12.5f winner, half-sister to a South African Grade
1-winning sprinter: fairly useful performer: won maiden at Chepstow in May and
handicap at Newmarket in July: should stay further than 1m: ran poorly on good to
firm going: sent to Malaysia. *L. M. Cumani*

STILL HERE (IRE)   4 b.g. Astronef 116 – Covey's Quick Step (Godswalk   –
(USA) 130) [1996 41, a55: a7g⁶ a10g⁴ a9.4g* 10d 9.9g 10.1f⁵ 10m a10g 8.3m
a14.8g³ 1997 a12g⁵ Jan 10] smallish, sturdy gelding: modest performer on the
all-weather, poor on turf: well beaten only 4-y-o start. *P. Bowen*

STILL WATERS   2 b.g. (Jan 9) Rainbow Quest (USA) 134 – Krill (Kris 135)   56 p
[1997 8d Oct 28] third living foal: half-brother to 4-y-o Degree: dam French 1¼m
winner: 7/2, about 11 lengths ninth to Baffin Bay in maiden at Leicester, soon niggled
along: will be suited by 1¼m+: should improve. *R. Charlton*

STINGRAY CITY (USA)   8 b.g. Raft (USA) 125 – Out of This World 76 (High   –
Top 131) [1996 NR 1997 16s 12.1d Apr 2] no longer of any account. *R. M. McKellar*

STINGRAY (IRE)   2 b.c. (May 13) Darshaan 133 – Sovereign Dona 117   74
(Sovereign Path 125) [1997 8g⁴ 8d⁵ Nov 7] IR 52,000Y: big colt: has plenty of scope:
brother to Irish 3-y-o maiden Dona Royale and half-brother to several winners,
including Irish Derby/St Leger third Foresee (by Vision) and very smart 7f to 9f
performer Royal Touch (by Tap On Wood): dam won 1¼m Prix de Psyche: much the
better effort in minor events when keeping-on last of 5 behind Derryquin at
Doncaster, beaten 8 lengths: should be suited by 1¼m+. *M. Johnston*

ST LAWRENCE (CAN)   3 gr.c. With Approval (CAN) – Mingan Isle (USA)   72
(Lord Avie (USA)) [1996 75: 7g 8f² 8m² 1997 11.5m² 13.9s Sep 3] rather leggy colt:
fair maiden, lightly raced: should prove suited by 1½m+: acts on good to firm
ground, soundly beaten on soft. *C. E. Brittain*

ST LUCIA (IRE)   2 b.f. (Mar 18) Common Grounds 118 – Scarlet Slipper (Gay   64
Mecene (USA) 128) [1997 6m 6d⁵ 5.1d 5d³ a5g Nov 15] 24,000Y: rangy filly: a?
half-sister to 2 winners, including Shimmering Scarlet (7f, and staying hurdler, by
Glint of Gold): dam, half-sister to useful 7f and 1¼m winner Golden Braid, French
1m winner: modest maiden: blinkered final 2 starts, best effort on first of them:
possibly best at 5f: sold 3,600 gns in December. *B. J. Meehan*

STOCKBROOK   4 b.g. Marju (IRE) 127 – Burning Ambition (Troy 137) [1996   –
NR 1997 11.6m 11.5s 10m⁵ Jul 25] fifth foal: half-brother to 3 winners, including
fairly useful Her Honour (up to 1½m, by Teenoso), later smart hurdler: dam well-
beaten half-sister to One In A Million: no form. *K. R. Burke*

STOCK HILL DANCER   3 ch.f. Interrex (CAN) – Stocktina 42 (Tina's Pet   58
121) [1996 56: 5m⁶ 6m 5d⁴ 1997 6d 5.3f 5.3f⁶ 6m³ 5m⁵ 6d 5.1g 6m Oct 6] modest

maiden handicapper: stays 6f: acts on good to firm ground: tried blinkered: often claimer ridden: none too consistent: sold, and joined K. Burke. *B. J. Meehan*

STOLEN KISS (IRE) 5 b. or br.m. Taufan (USA) 119 – Sweet Goodbye (Petorius 117) [1996 79: 5s* 5m⁵ 5m 5m⁵ 5g 5d 5g 1997 5m 5m 5s 5.1g 5d³ 5m 6g⁴ a5g² a6g² 5s² 5g⁵ 5m³ a5g 5g a6g Aug 15] big, workmanlike mare: poor mover: fair sprint handicapper: acts on firm and soft ground and on fibresand: blinkered/visored: has given trouble at stalls: sometimes finds little: unreliable. *M. W. Easterby* — 67 § a71 §

STOLEN MUSIC (IRE) 4 b.f. Taufan (USA) 119 – Causa Sua (Try My Best (USA) 130) [1996 –: 8.1m 8m 1997 9.9m 8g 9f 6m 8f 12.3m 7g 7g⁴ 7g 12s 8g Oct 22] short-backed filly: signs of ability but no worthwhile form: tried visored. *R. E. Barr* — –

STONE BECK 2 b.f. (Apr 10) Lapierre 119 – Dovey (Welsh Pageant 132) [1997 7.5f 8m⁴ 7.1s⁵ Oct 15] lengthy, sparely-made filly: half-sister to 1½m winner Tudor Romance (by Aragon): dam unraced: modest form in maidens, fourth at Newcastle and not knocked about other 2 starts: will be suited by at least 1¼m. *J. M. Jefferson* — 62

STONE CROSS (IRE) 5 b.g. Pennine Walk 120 – Micro Mover (Artaius (USA) 129) [1996 –: 8g⁴ a11g⁴ 15.8g 1997 8g 12.9g 9.2m Aug 18] modest form at 3 yrs: lightly raced and no form since. *Martin Todhunter* — –

STONECUTTER 4 b.g. Warning 136 – South Shore 102 (Caerleon (USA) 132) [1996 –: a8.5g 1997 a12g a14.8f* a16g 15.4m⁴ 21.6g 12g a12f 12m a16.2g Jul 25] modest performer: made all in claimer at Wolverhampton in January: left M. Channon after fifth start, W. Muir after seventh: stays 15f: acts on fibresand: visored prior to last 2 starts: inconsistent. *P. J. Makin* — 51

STONED IMACULATE (IRE) 3 ch.f. Durgam (USA) – Rose Deer (Whistling Deer 117) [1996 NR 1997 12s 14.1g³ 13.8g 17.2f* 16m* 16g* Sep 23] smallish filly: sister to 4-y-o Dr Bones: dam lightly-raced maiden: fair performer: won handicaps at Carlisle in August (maiden event) and Nottingham (2) in September, beating in-form Sipowitz by 1¼ lengths, pair clear, for final win: suited by test of stamina: acts on firm going: capable of better still. *F. Murphy* — 73 p

STONE FLOWER (USA) 3 b.f. Storm Bird (CAN) 134 – Lively Living (USA) (Key To The Mint (USA)) [1996 83: 6f⁶ 5g* 6d³ 6.1d⁵ 6.5m 6m³ 1997 8g⁴ 7g 10.4g 9g² 9m 10.3m⁵ 10d Sep 19] well-made filly: fluent mover: fairly useful performer: at least respectable efforts most starts in 1997: probably stays 1¼m: best form on good ground or firmer: has worn severe bridle. *P. W. Chapple-Hyam* — 83

STONE OF DESTINY 2 ch.c. (Mar 17) Ballad Rock 122 – Shamasiya (FR) (Vayrann 133) [1997 5g 6g² 6m² 7.3m⁴ 7g⁴ 7m⁵ 6.9d* Oct 21] 24,000Y: big, imposing colt: fourth foal: brother to 7-y-o Rock Symphony and half-brother to a winner in Hungary by Primo Dominie: dam French 1½m winner: fairly useful performer: favourite, won maiden at Folkestone decisively: keen-going sort, and will probably prove best up to 1m: yet to race on extremes of ground: very stiff task when blinkered penultimate start: has tended to edge left. *B. J. Meehan* — 87

STONE RIDGE (IRE) 5 b.g. Indian Ridge 123 – Cut In Stone (USA) 72 (Assert 134) [1996 95: 8s* 8d 8g⁵ 10.1m 8m 9m 9s⁵ 7d 1997 8m 8.1g⁵ 10.3d 8s⁶ 8d⁵ 8g Jul 8] useful-looking gelding: fairly useful handicapper: disappointing in 1997: best around 1m: acts on good to firm ground and soft (yet to race on firm): no improvement in blinkers: tends to carry head high: joined O. Sherwood. *R. Hannon* — 83

STONEY VALLEY 7 b.g. Caerleon (USA) 132 – Startino 111 (Bustino 136) [1996 NR 1997 a16g Jan 16] fair handicapper in spring of 1995: tailed off only 7-y-o start. *J. R. Jenkins* — –

STOP OUT 2 b.f. (Apr 8) Rudimentary (USA) 118 – Breakaway 98 (Song 132) [1997 5g* 5.2f 7m² 7g Aug 23] 15,000Y: tall, useful-looking filly: good walker: has a fluent, round action: fifth foal: half-sister to fairly useful 1m winner Hippy (by Damister) and winners abroad by Damister and Superlative: dam 5f winner: won maiden at Sandown in June: easily best effort when ¾-length second of 8 to Diamond White in listed race at Newmarket in August: should stay 1m: slowly away first 2 starts. *H. Morrison* — 89

STOPPES BROW 5 b.g. Primo Dominie 121 – So Bold (Never So Bold 135) [1996 81, a98: a6g a5g² 6g 7m⁴ 7.6g 7s³ 6s* 6.9m³ 5.7m 6m 6.1s³ 7g⁴ a7g² 1997 a6g — 81 a91

a5g⁶ a8g⁶ 7d⁶ 7.3g² 7m⁴ 7d 7g a7g⁴ a8g² a8g³ Dec 10] strong, lengthy gelding: poor mover: fairly useful handicapper, better on the all-weather than turf: consistent at 4 yrs, not in 1997: probably doesn't quite stay 1m: acts on firm and soft going: visored or blinkered: successful for 7-lb claimer: usually held up. *G. L. Moore*

STORIES TO TELL (USA)   3 ch.c. Shadeed (USA) 135 – Million Stories (USA) (Exclusive Native (USA)) [1996 85p: 7f² 7.5f² 1997 8v⁵ 8m Oct 22] sturdy colt: type to carry condition: fairly useful maiden at 2 yrs: well held both starts in 1997: sold 18,000 gns, and sent to Germany. *H. R. A. Cecil*   –

STORM COMMAND   3 b.g. Gildoran 123 – Summer Sky 75 (Skyliner 117) [1996 NR 1997 10g Oct 24] big gelding: fifth foal: half-brother to 4-y-o Whispering Dawn and 6-y-o Lord Sky: dam 2-y-o 5f winner: never dangerous in Newbury maiden: unimpressive to post. *D. W. P. Arbuthnot*   –

STORM CRY (USA)   2 b.c. (May 10) Hermitage (USA) – Doonesbury Lady (USA) (Doonesbury (USA)) [1997 5.7m 7d² Oct 27] 18,000 2-y-o: first foal: dam unraced: sire (by Storm Bird) unraced close relative of Sadler's Wells: absent 3 months, 1¼ lengths second to Khalas in maiden at Lingfield, clear with comfortable winner in sprint finish: should do better still. *Major D. N. Chappell*   74 p

STORM FROM THE EAST   2 b.c. (Mar 22) Formidable (USA) 125 – Callas Star (Chief Singer 131) [1997 6m 5m² 5g² 6g² 6m⁴ 6m⁴ Oct 31] IR 11,500F, IR 41,000Y: close-coupled colt: second foal: dam unraced half-sister to very smart middle-distance stayer Band: fairly useful maiden: stays 6f: raced only on good/good to firm ground: has swished tail in paddock: hung markedly third start. *R. Hannon*   80

STORMLESS   6 b.g. Silly Prices 110 – Phyl's Pet (Aberdeen 109) [1996 57: 10.9d 9g⁴ 10d² 10m* 11.1m² 10g* 10.9m³ 10.5v 1997 8.3s* 8.3s³ 8g⁴ 8.3g⁵ 10.9s⁶ 10.1g² Oct 22] tall gelding: fair handicapper: won at Hamilton in May: left P. Monteith after third start, ran well on final one: likely to prove best at 1m (given good test) to 1¼m: acts on good to firm and soft ground: consistent. *J. S. Goldie*   65

STORM RIVER (USA)   2 ch.f. (Mar 13) Riverman (USA) 131 – Storm Dove (USA) 108 (Storm Bird (CAN) 134) [1997 7m⁵ 8.1g² Sep 27] smallish, unfurnished filly: first foal: dam 6f/7f winner out of smart French winner at up to 1¼m Daeltown: fairly useful form in minor event at Kempton and maiden at Haydock, no match for 6-length winner Mohaba in latter (rather edgy): stays 1m. *H. R. A. Cecil*   81

STORM WIND (IRE)   4 ch.g. Digamist (USA) 110 – Hilton Gateway (Hello Gorgeous (USA) 128) [1996 –: 10s 13.8g 1997 a13g a14.8g⁶ a12g⁶ Feb 24] close-coupled gelding: no worthwhile form: tried visored/blinkered. *K. R. Burke*

STORMY BLUE (IRE)   2 b.c. (Jun 4) Bluebird (USA) 125 – Angel Divine (Ahonoora 122) [1997 7d Oct 14] IR 13,000Y: neat colt: fourth foal: half-brother to 3-y-o Northern Angel and 4-y-o Corniche Quest: dam unraced twin: 20/1 and very green, soon off bridle when well beaten in Leicester maiden: moved poorly to post. *S. P. C. Woods*   –

STORMY STORY (USA)   3 b.c. Storm Bird (CAN) 134 – Silver Clover (USA) (Secretariat (USA)) [1996 NR 1997 10g 10m⁵ 10g 9g⁶ Aug 20] $300,000Y: sixth foal: closely related to a winner in USA by Northern Baby and half-brother to useful 1992 2-y-o 6f and 7f winner (also third in Prix Marcel Boussac) Love of Silver (by Arctic Tern): dam won up to 9f in North America: signs of ability but no form: missed break after getting upset in stalls on final outing: sent to UAE. *J. H. M. Gosden*   –

STORY LINE   4 ch.f. In The Wings 128 – Known Line 100 (Known Fact (USA) 135) [1996 98: 10m² 11d 8d³ 12s 10.3d⁵ 1997 10.4g 11.9d 10d 13.3f 14s⁴ 16.2g 16.2v 12g³ Oct 25] sturdy, good-bodied filly: fairly useful performer: best effort of 1997 when fourth in Sandown handicap: stays 1¾m: acts on good to firm and soft ground: has worn severe noseband and been bandaged behind. *D. W. P. Arbuthnot*   83

STORYTELLER (IRE)   3 b.c. Thatching 131 – Please Believe Me 93 (Try My Best (USA) 130) [1996 NR 1997 6.9m⁵ 8f⁶ 7.5g⁴ 8m⁵ 7g⁴ 5g* 5m³ 6g 5m 6m⁶ 5m Oct 2] quite good-topped colt: first foal: dam, fairly useful 2-y-o 5f winner, out of Princess Royal Stakes winner Believer: modest handicapper: trained on debut by N. Walker: won at Doncaster in July: at least respectable efforts most starts afterwards: will prove best as a sprinter: raced only on good ground or firmer: visored last 7 starts. *Mrs J. R. Ramsden*   60

STOWAWAY   3 b.c. Slip Anchor 136 – On Credit (FR) (No Pass No Sale 120)   120 p
[1996 94p: 8m* 1997 10.3m² 12m* 11.9g* 10g⁴ Oct 18]

There can be little doubt that Godolphin will view 1997 as a disappointing year for them, particularly with their three-year-olds. They made little
impact in the classics. In the Two Thousand Guineas, Shamikh, the subject of
very favourable reports from Dubai over the winter, was well beaten and reportedly returned lame.The following day one of the best juvenile fillies of 1996,
Moonlight Paradise, finished only tenth of fifteen in the One Thousand Guineas. Godolphin's main hope in the Derby, Happy Valentine, never even made it
to the racecourse after reportedly suffering from a bad blood disorder, while
both runners in the Oaks were well beaten. Among the older horses, too, there
was little to cheer about in the major championship races, with the exception of
Swain's King George victory. After a disastrous start to the season Godolphin
was forced into a temporary shutdown, while veterinary examinations—which
revealed little—took place. The problem, concluded Godolphin's racing manager Simon Crisford, was that 'ninety percent of our horses were not good
enough and we were asking them to compete at levels that were too good for
them . . . about ten percent were not firing and were performing 3 lb to 4 lb
below their form.' Having given up any hope of a repeat trainers' championship
for Saeed bin Suroor, it was announced in June that Godolphin was planning a
clear-out of up to thirty older horses. They were to be sold, sent to America or
distributed to other trainers in Dubai and to be replaced by two-year-olds, with
the aim of concentrating on the future.

One horse who promised to reverse Godolphin's fortunes in the classics
was Stowaway, who progressed well during the season to emerge as a leading
contender for the St Leger. Stowaway had entered note-books as a horse to
follow when easily winning his only start (for Michael Jarvis) in a Newcastle
maiden in the autumn of his two-year-old season, after which he'd promptly
been snapped up by Godolphin. On returning from wintering in Dubai, Stowaway came a satisfactory second to Falak in a useful conditions event at
Doncaster in May and was only pulled out of the Derby at the forty-eight hour
declaration stage, reportedly not one-hundred percent. He returned in the Gordon Stakes at Goodwood where, sent off the 10/3 joint-favourite alongside the
horse who had beaten him at Doncaster, Falak, Stowaway showed improved
form to score a convincing victory from Poseidon, despite tending to carry his
head high and not settling particularly well. Stowaway faced a sterner test in a
typically small but select field for the Great Voltigeur Stakes at York. Among
his opponents were the short-head Derby second and ante-post favourite for the

Great Voltigeur Stakes, York—Stowaway (noseband) rallies to beat Silver Patriarch and Kingfisher Mill

St Leger, Silver Patriarch, and the King Edward VII Stakes winner Kingfisher Mill. Taken steadily to post, Stowaway settled better than on his previous runs and, after looking held under two furlongs out, found plenty under strong pressure to edge ahead of Silver Patriarch by half a length, with Kingfisher Mill another one and three quarter lengths further back in third. The victory added to Stowaway's growing reputation, and he was made the new favourite for the final classic at around 2/1, only to be found to be lame and withdrawn on the morning of the race, which went to Silver Patriarch. Stowaway made his final appearance of the year in the Champion Stakes at Newmarket. He found a mile and a quarter on the sharp side, particularly as there wasn't a strong gallop, and finished five and a half lengths fourth of seven to Pilsudski, a creditable effort in the circumstances.

		Shirley Heights	Mill Reef
	Slip Anchor	(b 1975)	Hardiemma
	(b 1982)	Sayonara	Birkhahn
Stowaway		(b 1965)	Suleika
(b.c. 1994)		No Pass No Sale	Northfields
	On Credit (FR)	(b 1982)	No Disgrace
	(ch 1988)	Noble Tiara	Vaguely Noble
		(b 1981)	Tayyara

Stowaway is the first foal of On Credit, a winner at seven furlongs at two years and twice at a mile and a quarter at three in France, where she was also placed in Group 3 races. On Credit's dam and grandam both showed smart form in France—Noble Tiara, who has bred four other winners to date, over a mile and a quarter and a mile and a half and Tayyara at up to a mile, the latter

Godolphin's "Stowaway"

winning the Prix de la Grotte. On Credit's second foal, St Helensfield, has shown fairly useful form, winning a maiden over a mile and a quarter and finishing third over the same distance in a listed event. Stowaway has been raced at up to a mile and a half, but judged on his breeding—his sire, the 1985 Epsom Derby winner Slip Anchor, is a marked influence for stamina—there is every reason to expect that he will prove at least as effective over a mile and three quarters, should he have the opportunity in the future. A tall, rather angular colt, Stowaway has yet to race on ground softer than good. He usually takes a keen hold and has a tendency to carry his head high, but seems perfectly genuine. Still lightly raced, Stowaway should train on and win more good races at a mile and a half or more. *Saeed bin Suroor*

STRACHIN   3 b.c. Salse (USA) 128 – Collage 69 (Ela-Mana-Mou 132) [1996 NR 1997 10g² 8m⁶ Oct 22] 32,000Y: third foal: half-brother to 2 winners, including 1993 2-y-o Fromage (by Formidable): dam stayed 1m: fairly useful form when second of 4 in minor event at Milan in October: only sixth in maiden at Yarmouth 11 days later: likely to prove suited by 1¼m+. *L. M. Cumani*   80

ST RADEGUND   3 b.f. Green Desert (USA) 127 – On The House (FR) 125 (Be My Guest (USA) 126) [1996 NR 1997 7g 7d* May 21] good-bodied, attractive filly: half-sister to several winners, including useful sprinter Art of War (by Machiavellian) and fairly useful miler Castel Rosselo (by Rousillon): dam, from excellent family, won 1000 Guineas and Sussex Stakes: showed promise in newcomers event at Newbury in April, and month later justified favouritism in 16-runner maiden at Goodwood in good style by 2½ lengths from Blueygreen: fractured a leg in training in June, and unlikely to race again. *G. Wragg*   85

STRAFFAN GOLD (USA)   3 b.c. Lear Fan (USA) 130 – Oro Bianco (USA) (Lyphard's Wish (FR) 124) [1996 –: 7g 8s 1997 10m 10.8s a14.8g² 17.2f⁵ 15.8m 16.1m Oct 1] quite attractive colt: modest maiden: clearly best effort on third start: left G. Wragg after next one: stays 14.8f: acts on fibresand. *Mrs M. Reveley*   – a56

STRATEGIC AIR   2 ch.g. (Apr 17) Anshan 119 – Kimbolton Katie 81 (Aragon 118) [1997 7m⁶ 8g 7m Nov 4] 3,800Y: second foal: dam 2-y-o 5f winner: modest form when sixth in maiden at Newcastle in October, but well held in similar events. *E. Weymes*   60

STRATEGIC CHOICE (USA)   6 b.h. Alleged (USA) 138 – Danlu (USA) (Danzig (USA)) [1996 124: 13.9f² 12m* 12m 12.5g* 12s³ 12f³ 1997 10.5d⁵ 12f⁴ 12s⁶ 13.3m⁴ 12f* 12m⁴ Oct 19] big, strong horse: has suffered from foot trouble: has an easy action: smart performer: won valuable event in Turkey in September: fourth in Gran Premio di Milano (behind Shantou), Geoffrey Freer Stakes at Newbury and Canadian International at Woodbine: effective at 1½m and stays 1¾m well: best form on good ground or firmer: blinkered last 2 starts: normally tracks leaders: stays in training. *P. F. I. Cole*   117

STRATHMORE CLEAR   3 b.g. Batshoof 122 – Sunflower Seed 70 (Mummy's Pet 125) [1996 75: 6s³ 7m 1997 7m* 8m* 9g² 10.1m⁶ 8s 8m 9d Sep 12] tall, close-coupled gelding: fluent mover: fairly useful performer: won maiden at Kempton in March and handicap at Warwick in April: well below best last 4 starts, including in blinkers: should stay beyond 9f: acts on good to firm going: usually races prominently: sold 20,000 gns in October, then gelded and sent to Malaysia. *G. Lewis*   89

STRAT'S LEGACY   10 b.g. Chukaroo 103 – State Romance 67 (Free State 125) [1996 46, a39: a13g a16g 12.1m 12m⁴ 12d² 12m³ 12m 12m⁴ 12d a13g a16g⁴ 1997 12g 11.5d 14m⁶ 16m 14m² 16.4g 12d 14m a16g⁶ a16g Dec 10] small, light-framed gelding: poor handicapper at best nowadays: stays 2m: acts on the all-weather and on firm and dead ground: tried blinkered: often bandaged behind: inconsistent. *D. W. P. Arbuthnot*   40 a–

STRAT'S QUEST   3 b.f. Nicholas (USA) 111 – Eagle's Quest 62 (Legal Eagle 126) [1996 61: 5.1m⁶ 6.1m⁴ 5.7m⁵ 7m⁴ 7.6m 7.3m 6.1s* a6g 1997 6.1m 6d* 6.1g 6m 8m 6d a7g 7.3d⁶ 7g Oct 24] small filly: has a quick action: fair handicapper: won at Windsor in May: mostly well below form afterwards: best form at 6f on ground softer than good: has been bandaged. *D. W. P. Arbuthnot*   65

925

STRAVANO 3 b.f. Handsome Sailor 125 – La Stravaganza 74 (Slip Anchor 136) –
[1996 –: 5m a7g 5f 5f 1997 6.1d 7.5s May 11] tall filly: no form. *B. P. J. Baugh*

STRAVSEA 2 b.f. (Mar 13) Handsome Sailor 125 – La Stravaganza 74 (Slip   48
Anchor 136) [1997 a6g 6g 6d² 6d 6.1m Aug 6] 2,600Y: leggy filly: second foal: dam,
maiden, stayed 1¼m: second in seller at Haydock in July, only form. *B. P. J. Baugh*

STRAWBERRY ROAN (IRE) 3 b.f. Sadler's Wells (USA) 132 – Doff The   113
Derby (USA) (Master Derby (USA)) [1996 103p: 7d³ 8g* 9d* 1997 10m⁴ 8d* 8d²
12d 12m⁴ 10g³ 10g Aug 16] strong, good-topped filly: half-sister to Generous: has a
quick, round action: won 5-runner listed race at Leopardstown in May: strong-
finishing length second of 10 to Classic Park in Irish 1000 Guineas at the Curragh,
and might even have won had she not been hit over head with whip around 2f out,
losing momentum and needing to be switched: creditable 8 lengths fourth of 11 to
Ebadiyla in Irish Oaks at the Curragh: 2 lengths second of 5 (demoted) to Caiseal
Ros in Meld Stakes but finished last in Royal Whip 3 weeks later, both also at the
Curragh: should be well suited by 1½m: has form on good to firm ground, goes well
on dead. *A. P. O'Brien, Ireland*

STRAZO (IRE) 4 b.g. Alzao (USA) 117 – Ministra (USA) (Deputy Minister   107
(CAN)) [1996 94: 8g⁵ 8.1d* 7m* 8m 1997 8s⁶ 10d 9f² 8m⁴ 8m 8m* 9g² 8.2d* Nov
3] good-bodied gelding: useful performer: made all in minor events at Newmarket in
October and Nottingham (beat Kala Sunrise by 3½ lengths) in November: ran well
when second to Prince of Denial in handicap at Newbury in between: best at 1m/9f:
acts on firm and dead ground: front runner: game. *Lady Herries*

STREET GENERAL 3 b.c. Generous (IRE) 139 – Hotel Street (USA) 93   94
(Alleged (USA) 138) [1996 90p: 8g² 1997 12g* 12m³ May 3] leggy colt: poor
walker: fairly useful performer, lightly raced: won maiden at Newmarket in April
despite idling: odds on, failed to improve on that on firmer ground when third of 6 to
Single Empire in minor event there following month, looking very much a stayer.
H. R. A. Cecil

STREET SINGER 2 b.c. (Jan 19) Efisio 120 – Dream Chaser 92 (Record Token –
128) [1997 5g Jun 2] half-brother to 4-y-o Catch The Lights and winning sprinters
Cradle Days (by Dance of Life) and Sister Susan (by Tate Gallery): dam suited by 6f:
25/1, last in minor event at Windsor. *Miss C. Johnsey*

STRELITZA (IRE) 3 b.f. Taufan (USA) 119 – Strident Note 89 (The Minstrel –
(CAN) 135) [1996 53: 5m 5g 5s⁶ a5g³ 7f³ 1997 a7g 8d 11.1s 8m⁶ May 28]
workmanlike filly: no form in 1997, including in blinkers: very hard ride, and one to
steer clear of. *M. W. Easterby*

STRENGTH OF VISION 3 b.g. Unfuwain (USA) 131 – Tootsiepop (USA) –
(Robellino (USA) 127) [1996 NR 1997 8m 8.3m 8m² 10g a12g Oct 27] 14,500F:
strong, lengthy gelding: third foal: dam won once and placed numerous times in
USA: little sign of ability. *C. R. Egerton*

STRETAREZ (FR) 4 b.c. Saumarez 132 – Street Opera (Sadler's Wells (USA) 117
132) [1996 12g* 12g* 12g² 10d 12.5d* 12s* 12v⁴ 1997 15.5g* 15.5d* 15.5d* 15g
15.5m⁵ 15.5d Oct 26] smart French colt, much improved: won listed race at Saint-
Cloud in March by ½ length from Philanthrop, Prix de Barbeville at Longchamp in
April by 1½ lengths from same rival and Prix Vicomtesse Vigier at Longchamp in
May by short head from Grey Shot: off course over 3 months, well held on return:
stays at least 15.5f: acts on soft ground: held up: normally consistent. *D. Sepulchre,
France*

STRETCHING (IRE) 4 br.g. Contract Law (USA) 108 – Mrs Mutton 89   57
(Dancer's Image (USA)) [1996 –: a8.5g a8.5g a10g a11g a11g² 12s⁶ a11g May 12]
only worthwhile form when staying-on second of 13 in Southwell maiden in March:
should stay 1½m: blinkered (well beaten) final start. *A. Bailey*

STRICTLY HARD 3 b.f. Reprimand 122 – Formidable Dancer 70 (Formidable –
(USA) 125) [1996 58: 6.9d 8g⁶ 8s 1997 10g 11.8g Aug 11] modest at 2 yrs: little form
in 1997: sold only 600 gns in November. *G. C. Bravery*

STRICTLY RHYTHM 2 b.c. (Apr 30) Hamas (IRE) 125§ – Halimah 56 (Be   62
My Guest (USA) 126) [1997 5m 7g 6d 6m⁵ 6m⁵ 6m Oct 6] 6,500Y, 16,000 2-y-o:
leggy, unfurnished colt: third foal: half-brother to 3-y-o 5f winner Impish (by Imp

Society): dam Irish 4-y-o 9f winner out of sister to speedy Bitty Girl and Hot Spark: modest maiden: easily best form at Catterick and Pontefract fourth and fifth starts: stays 6f. *Mrs S. A. Bramall, Ireland*

STRIDING KING 2 ch.g. (May 16) King's Signet (USA) 110 – Stride Home 78 66 (Absalom 128) [1997 5m⁶ 6m³ 6.1d³ 5.7m⁶ Jul 17] second foal: dam stayed 1½m: fair maiden, placed at Folkestone and Chepstow: appeared tenderly handled final start: stays 6f. *M. R. Channon*

STRIKE-A-POSE 7 ch.m. Blushing Scribe (USA) 107 – My Bushbaby 100 (Hul – A Hul 124) [1996 NR 1997 a16g⁵ a12g⁴ a16g⁵ Jun 6] poor and lightly raced on flat nowadays. *B. J. Llewellyn*

STRILLO 3 b.g. Safawan 118 – Silvers Era 72 (Balidar 133) [1996 NR 1997 8d 8g – May 26] 6,100F, 25,000Y: sixth foal: half-brother to 6f winners by Puissance and Tina's Pet: dam best at 5f: bought out of L. Cumani's stable 600 gns Newmarket Autumn (1996) Sales: well beaten in maidens at Doncaster and Leicester: slowly away on debut. *N. M. Babbage*

STRUGGLER 5 b.h. Night Shift (USA) – Dreamawhile 85 (Known Fact (USA) 110 135) [1996 114: 6m³ 5m⁴ 5m* 5g² 5f 5g² 5m⁶ 5.2m* 5d 6g 1997 5d⁵ 5d² 5.1m 5g* 5d 5m Sep 10] small, strong, good-bodied horse: impresses in appearance: poor mover: smart performer: ran well when neck second of 14 to Ya Malak in listed race at Sandown and when winning listed race at Deauville in August: well held in Nunthorpe Stakes at York and listed race at Doncaster last 2 starts: effective at 5f/6f: acts on firm ground and dead: visored (stumbled start, run best ignored) fifth 4-y-o start: usually held up: sold 57,000 gns in October, to stud in Florida. *D. R. Loder*

STUDIO THIRTY 5 gr.g. Rock City 120 – Chepstow Vale (USA) 97 (Key To 37 The Mint (USA)) [1996 41, a–: 10g 10m 10d 10.1m³ 10.1f a8g 11.5m⁵ 10.2g 14d 1997 a12g³ a12g² a12g Feb 18] leggy gelding: poor handicapper: stays 1½m: acts on good to firm ground and the all-weather: tried blinkered (well below form) and visored (creditable effort) once each: won twice over hurdles in December. *R. Dickin*

STUFFED 5 ch.g. Clantime 101 – Puff Pastry 78 (Reform 132) [1996 89+: 5g 5m* 79 6m⁴ 5g² 5m⁵ 6m⁴ 6m 6m 5g² 5g* 5m* 1997 5g⁶ 5g 5g Jul 11] workmanlike gelding: fair handicapper: shaped better than result suggested all 3 starts in 1997, but wasn't seen out after July: effective at 5f (best form) and 6f: acts on firm ground, hasn't raced on softer than good since early in 1994: effective blinkered or not: often apprentice ridden: reliable. *M. W. Easterby*

STURGEON (IRE) 3 ch.g. Caerleon (USA) 132 – Ridge The Times (USA) 78 71 (Riva Ridge (USA)) [1996 84: 6s 7g² 7g² 1997 8g 8g⁵ 10g³ Aug 4] smallish gelding: fair maiden: stays 1¼m: yet to race on going firmer than good: sold, and joined K. Morgan. *P. F. I. Cole*

STYLE DANCER (IRE) 3 b.g. Dancing Dissident (USA) 119 – Showing Style 81 (Pas de Seul 133) [1996 70: 5m 5g 6g 5m⁴ 5m³ 6g2 6m 6m* 1997 6g³ 6m 6g 7f³ 6d 6g² 6m 6g² 6g³ 7.1g³ 7g 7m 7m Nov 1] tall gelding: good mover: fairly useful handicapper: creditable efforts most starts in 1997: effective at 6f and 7f: acts on firm going, not discredited on dead: best efforts in visor, ran poorly only try in blinkers: usually races prominently: carries head high. *R. M. Whitaker*

STYLISH STORM (USA) 2 b.f. (May 27) Storm Bird (CAN) 134 – Purify – (USA) (Fappiano (USA)) [1997 7m Sep 22] 60,000Y: sixth foal: closely related to 5-y-o Grade 2 8.5f winner Radu Cool (by Carnivalay) and half-sister to 2 winners abroad, including French middle-distance stayer Sanzio (by Greinton): dam minor winner in USA at around 1m, half-sister to dam of Balanchine: 14/1, last in maiden at Kempton, always behind and not knocked about. *B. W. Hills*

STYLISH WAYS (IRE) 5 b.g. Thatching 131 – Style of Life (USA) (The 68 Minstrel (CAN) 135) [1996 96d: 6m⁴ 6m⁴ 6f 6m 6g 6g 5m 6f 1997 6d⁵ 6m 7g 5d 7s³ 7m Nov 1] compact gelding: fluent mover: fair handicapper at best in 1997: stays 7f: acts on good to firm and soft ground: none too consistent. *J. Pearce*

SUALTACH (IRE) 4 b.c. Marju (IRE) 127 – Astra Adastra (Mount Hagen (FR) 83 127) [1996 84§, a78§: a8.5g 7s* 7m 7.5m² 7.6g⁴ 7f a7g* a8.5g⁵ 6d⁵ 8m 7m² 9m 7d a– 8.1v 7g 1997 8m⁴ 7.6v 7m 8d⁴ 7m 8m² 7.1m³ 7.9s 8.1g⁴ 8d 8m* a8.5g⁵ Dec 26] strong, lengthy colt: has a round action: fairly useful handicapper: won 25-runner event at Redcar in October: stays 1m: acts on good to firm and soft ground and on fibresand: visored (well beaten) once: has found little and wandered: none too consistent. *R. Hollinshead*

SUBAROO SAM   3 gr.g. Arzanni 115 – Nuns Little One (Celtic Cone 116) [1996 NR 1997 a14g Dec 8] first foal: dam poor hurdler: always behind in claimer at Southwell. *J. M. Bradley*   –

SUBLIME BEAUTY (USA)   3 ch.f. Caerleon (USA) 132 – Shakela (USA) 54 (Alydar (USA)) [1996 7g³ 8d² 8g* 8m² 8g³ 1997 10f² 10d² 10g² 10g³ 12g⁵ 10f* 9g⁴ 10g Oct 27] workmanlike filly: first foal: dam (maiden) stayed 9f, half-sister to smart colts Maksud (up to 1½m) and Jendali (stayer), both by Nijinsky, and top-class miler Northjet: fairly useful performer: won minor race at Limerick in June: creditable fifth to Yashmak in Ribblesdale Stakes at Royal Ascot: stays 1½m: acts on firm ground, probably on dead: blinkered since reappearance: consistent. *J. S. Bolger, Ireland*   93

SUBTLE TOUCH (IRE)   6 b.g. Lomond (USA) 128 – Lobbino 72 (Bustino 136) [1996 NR 1997 a16.2g a10g a14g⁶ a14g⁵ 16.4s a14.8g Sep 20] ex-Irish gelding: fourth foal: half-brother to 2 winners, including fairly useful 1m to 1½m winner Lobinda (by Shareef Dancer): dam, maiden, should have stayed at least 1¼m: modest maiden at 3 yrs for L. Browne: well held here (trained first 3 starts by T. Clement), including in visor. *P. L. Gilligan*   –

SUCCESS AND GLORY (IRE)   2 b.c. (Apr 30) Alzao (USA) 117 – More Fizz (Morston (FR) 125) [1997 6d⁴ 7g³ 8d² 8m* Sep 30] 37,000F, 300,000Y: compact, attractive colt: seventh foal: half-brother to 3 winners, notably 1991 Gimcrack winner River Falls (by Aragon), later successful at 1m: dam, French 9.2f winner, from family of Zeddaan: useful colt: won maiden at Newmarket by 5 lengths from Way Out Yonder, looking better further he went: placed at York and Goodwood previously: should stay at least 1¼m. *H. R. A. Cecil*   97

SUCH BOLDNESS   3 b.c. Persian Bold 123 – Bone China (IRE) (Sadler's Wells (USA) 132) [1996 –p: 7d 1997 7g 12d² Jul 9] fair maiden: best effort, though easily brushed aside by long odds-on Taunt, in uncompetitive affair at Epsom on second start: likely to prove suited by 1¼m/1½m. *R. Akehurst*   67

SUCH PRESENCE   3 ch.g. Arzanni 115 – Marchiness Drake (Marechal Drake 101) [1996 –: 7f 10g⁶ 8s 1997 10.8s 10m 14.1s Oct 15] leggy, short-backed gelding: no form. *K. S. Bridgwater*   –

SUDDEN SPIN   7 b.g. Doulab (USA) 115 – Lightning Legacy (USA) 78 (Super Concorde (USA) 128) [1996 48, a–: a11g⁵ 16.1s⁵ 16.2m* 16.2g⁴ 13.8m 16g 1997 a16g* a16g⁵ a16g¹ 16.2m 21.6g 16m Sep 15] leggy, good-topped gelding: fair handicapper on fibresand: had hard race when winning at Southwell in January, and well beaten afterwards: stays 2m: tried visored earlier in career. *J. Norton*   – a67

SUDEST (IRE)   3 b.g. Taufan (USA) 119 – Frill (Henbit (USA) 130) [1996 67: 7.1m⁶ 6g⁶ 7m⁵ 8f 8g 1997 9g 9.7m 12.5m* 11.6s⁴ 17.2f* 11.7m* 16.2s⁴ 14m³ 17.2m² Aug 12] quite attractive gelding: fairly useful performer: won handicaps at Warwick and Bath in May and minor event at Bath in June: good efforts in frame in handicaps afterwards: effective at 1½m to 17f: acts on firm and soft going: game and consistent. *I. A. Balding*   83

SUEDORO   7 b.m. Hard Fought 125 – Bamdoro 54 (Cavo Doro 124) [1996 –: 6d 6s 5s⁴ 5m 6g 6g 1997 6m 5g 6g³ 7d³ 6.9m 6s 8g 5m³ 6g⁵ 6g⁶ 6g 5g⁴ 5f 5g* 6.1m³ 10.9d 6m Sep 26] angular mare: modest handicapper: won apprentice event at Hamilton in September: best at 5f/6f: acts on firm and dead ground: usually races prominently. *J. S. Goldie*   51

SUELLAJOY   2 ch.f. (Feb 7) Weldnaas (USA) 112 – Jeethgaya (USA) 61 (Critique (USA) 126) [1997 6.9s 8.1d³ 8m Sep 9] rangy filly: second reported foal: sister to a temperamental maiden: dam placed from 1m to 1¼m: easily best effort in maidens when 3¼ lengths third at Chepstow in August. *B. Smart*   65

SUE ME (IRE)   5 b. or br.g. Contract Law (USA) 108 – Pink Fondant (Northfields (USA)) [1996 64, a55: 5s 7d 6d a6g 7.3s⁶ 8.1d 6m 7.1s 6m⁴ a7g⁶ a6g 1997 a5g⁵ a6g 5d³ 5s³ 5d⁵ 7m 6m 5g² 5d Nov 7] quite attractive gelding: modest sprint handicapper: 64 a45

928

left W. Muir after second start: best 5-y-o efforts when placed: acts on good to firm and heavy ground, below form on fibresand: no improvement in blinkers. *D. Nicholls*

SUE'S RETURN   5 b.m. Beveled (USA) – Return To Tara (Homing 130) [1996 83: 8d⁶ 8g 8.5m 7.9g 7f² 8m⁵ 8d³ 8m* 8g 9m 1997 7.6v 8d⁵ 8m² 8d⁶ 8g⁴ 8m³ 7.1m⁴ 8d 9m Oct 4] angular mare: fairly useful handicapper: creditable efforts most starts in 1997: ideally needs further than 7f, and stays 9f: acts on firm and dead ground: usually held up: sold 9,000 gns in October. *A. P. Jarvis*   **83**

SUEZ TORNADO (IRE)   4 ch.g. Mujtahid (USA) 118 – So Stylish 77 (Great Nephew 126) [1996 7g⁶ 7d 7.8d⁴ 5g⁶ 8.5f* 8g³ 9g⁵ 1997 a8.5g⁵ 8m 11.1d 10.8m 8m 8.5d⁴ 7.3g⁴ 7g⁴ 8d* 8g⁴ 8g³ 7s⁴ 8m 7.9s 8m 8.1g⁶ 8g 8d 8s Nov 8] IR 20,000Y: lengthy, good-topped gelding: fourth foal: half-brother to 1991 2-y-o 7f winner Well Appointed (by Petorius) and a winner in Norway by Prince Rupert: dam, maiden suited by 1½m, half-sister to Cesarewitch winner Sir Michael: fair handicapper (rated 79) at 3 yrs for D. Weld in Ireland: won at Newmarket in June: ran well next 2 starts, mainly disappointing thereafter: seems ideally suited by around 1m: acts on firm and soft ground and on fibresand: effective in blinkers/visor or not: sold 6,000 gns in November. *E. J. Alston*   **76**

SUGA HAWK (IRE)   5 b.g. Pennine Walk 120 – Ishtar Abu (St Chad 120) [1996 10s⁶ a9g³ 10d⁴ 12.5f⁴ 13d⁵ 1997 a9.4g³ a8.5f a8g⁴ a11g³ a9.4g* a9.4g 10.1g⁴ 11.1d⁴ 12m³ 12m⁵ 12g² 12.3m⁴ 12m⁶ 12.3m* 15.9d³ 10d 10d⁴ Oct 28] leggy ex-Irish gelding: half-brother to several winners, mainly in Ireland, including useful 1½m to 2m performer/very smart hurdler Condor Pan (by Condorcet) and useful 6f to 1¼m winner Noora Aby (by Ahonoora): dam Irish 1½m winner: modest form (rated 59) at 4 yrs for J. Coogan: fair handicapper here, successful at Wolverhampton in March and Ripon in August: stays 13f: acts on good to firm and heavy going and on fibresand: blinkered (ran creditably) twice. *E. J. Alston*   **68**

SUGARFOOT   3 ch.c. Thatching 131 – Norpella 95 (Northfields (USA)) [1996 82: 6g⁴ 1997 7g³ 7m⁴ 10.4g 8s² 8m Jul 19] good-topped colt: fairly useful performer: best effort when ¾-length second to Right Wing in minor event at Ascot penultimate start: suited by good test at 1m, and should prove as effective back at 1¼m: acts on good to firm and soft ground. *N. Tinkler*   **92**

SUGAR MILL   7 b.g. Slip Anchor 136 – Great Tom 99 (Great Nephew 126) [1996 82: 14d⁶ 14.8m 12.3g* 12.3s** 11.9d² 11.9v* 12g³ 12s⁵ 1997 11.9s* Mar 29] tall, angular gelding: has a round action: fairly useful handicapper, generally progressive: won at Haydock in March on only 7-y-o start: finds 1½m a bare minimum and stays 14.6f: acts on good to firm and heavy ground: often soon off bridle. *Mrs M. Reveley*   **85**

SUGAR PLUM   3 br.f. Primo Dominie 121 – Ile de Danse 76 (Ile de Bourbon (USA) 133) [1996 –: 6g 1997 7m 8d 6.1g May 26] behind in maidens/handicap: sold 600 gns in October. *R. Hannon*   **–**

SUGAR REEF   3 br.g. High Kicker (USA) – Miss Poll Flinders (Swing Easy (USA) 126) [1996 NR 1997 8m Oct 22] 3,600Y: sixth foal: brother to 1994 2-y-o 5f and 7f winner Duffertoes and 1m and 1¼m winner Chilly Lad and half-brother to a 2-y-o 5f winner by Inca Chief: dam tailed off only start at 2 yrs: tailed off in Yarmouth maiden. *M. J. Ryan*   **–**

SUGGEST   2 b.c. (May 17) Midyan (USA) 124 – Awham (USA) (Lear Fan (USA) 130) [1997 5m 5f⁶ 5d 7g* 7g* 8g 7s Oct 17] smallish colt: second reported foal: dam unraced: fair performer: won claimer at Thirsk and seller at Newmarket in August: should stay beyond 7f: well beaten on extremes of ground: trained first 2 starts by Miss G. Kelleway, next (blinkered) by Martyn Meade. *W. Storey*   **65 +**

SUILE MOR   5 b.m. Satin Wood 117 – Ra Ra (Lord Gayle (USA) 124) [1996 NR 1997 10g 8.1s² 8.1m Jul 11] poor handicapper, lightly raced nowadays: stays 10.8f: acts on good to firm and soft going: has shown signs of temperament: tail swisher. *B. R. Millman*   **47**

SUITE FACTORS   3 b.g. Timeless Times (USA) 99 – Uptown Girl 65 (Caruso 112) [1996 58: 5.1m⁶ 5.1m² 5g⁴ 5m² 5.1m³ 5.1m* 6g 5f⁴ 5m⁶ 5g a5g⁴ a6g a5g 1997 a5f a5g⁴ a5g 5g 5m² 5m² 6f² 6.1s 5d 5.3f² 5.1m² 5g⁵ 5.3f³ 5g³ 5g⁴ 6g³ 5.7g⁴ 6f³ 6.9m 6.1g 7g Oct 24] rather leggy gelding: modest handicapper: creditable efforts most   **62 a41**

SUI

starts in 1997: stays 6f: ideally suited by good ground or firmer on turf, poor at best on equitrack: no improvement in visor/blinkers. *K. R. Burke*

SUITOR 4 b.g. Groom Dancer (USA) 128 – Meliora 73 (Crowned Prince (USA) – 128) [1996 52: 10g 11f 10m 15.8g³ 17.2m⁵ a13g a16g⁴ a13g a10g² 1997 a10g³ a10g⁴ a50 10m 11.6g 17.2m⁵ 16m Sep 15] big, rangy gelding: has a pronounced knee action: modest maiden: below form in 1997 after reappearance: best efforts on the all-weather at 1¼m. *S. Dow*

SUIVEZ 7 b.g. Persian Bold 123 – Butterfly Kiss 69 (Beldale Flutter (USA) 130) – [1996 –, a47: a11g⁴ 16m⁶ 1997 10.5g⁶ 11.5g 10m Aug 6] sturdy gelding: one-time modest handicapper: no form in 1997. *Mrs N. Macauley*

SUIVEZ LA TRACE 2 ch.c. (Apr 2) Shalford (IRE) 124§ – Miss Petella 77 d (Dunphy 124) [1997 5s* 6m⁵ 6.1s⁵ 6g 6s 8g 5d⁴ a5g⁶ Nov 15] 16,000Y: smallish, a? sturdy colt: good walker: fifth foal: closely related to 4-y-o Traceability and half-brother to 3-y-o Full Traceability: dam half-sister to 1000 Guineas second Meis El-Reem: fair form at best: won maiden at Pontefract in June: left R. Fahey 2 starts later, then mostly disappointing: best efforts at 5f: blinkered fourth start: sold 7,500 gns after final start. *J. J. O'Neill*

SUJUD (IRE) 5 b. or br.m. Shaadi (USA) 126 – Sit Elnaas (USA) 82 (Sir Ivor – 135) [1996 56: 17.1g³ 21.6m⁶ 16.1g⁵ 17.2m 1997 a16g Mar 3] leggy, narrow mare: modest maiden on flat: well beaten only 5-y-o start. *M. D. Hammond*

SULEIKA DANCER 4 b.f. Slip Anchor 136 – Starr Danias (USA) (Sensitive – Prince (USA)) [1996 –: a14.8g⁴ a14.8g⁶ 1997 12m 10d 10m 10f 9.7s Jul 2] quite good-topped filly: no form, including in blinkers. *S. G. Knight*

SUMBAWA (IRE) 2 ch.f. (Jan 25) Magic Ring (IRE) 115 – Tittlemouse 86 56 (Castle Keep 121) [1997 6g 7.6d⁶ 6.1m Sep 23] IR 11,000Y: fifth foal: half-sister to 1¼m/11f winner Jemima Puddleduck (by Tate Gallery) and French 1¼m winner Midy Mouse (by Midyan): dam 1¼m winner: modest form first 2 starts in maidens: will be suited by return to further than 6f. *D. Haydn Jones*

SUMMER DANCE 3 b.f. Sadler's Wells (USA) 132 – Hyabella 111 (Shirley 83 Heights 130) [1996 86p: 8g² 1997 8g* 10g Sep 18] leggy, lengthy filly: odds on, won weak maiden at Newcastle in August: favourite, similar form when tenth of 17 in handicap at Newbury only subsequent start: likely to prove suited by 1¼m+. *M. R. Stoute*

SUMMER DAY BLUES (IRE) 2 b.f. (Mar 27) Petorius 117 – Atmospheric 58 Blues (IRE) 91 (Double Schwartz 128) [1997 5g 5.1d⁴ 5g 5g Jul 9] rather leggy filly: first reported foal: dam 2-y-o 5f winner, probably stayed 7f: modest form at best: well held final start. *C. Murray*

SUMMER DEAL (USA) 2 b.f. (Feb 10) Summer Squall (USA) – Dariela 80 (USA) (Manila (USA)) [1997 5d³ 5g² 6d⁶ 7m² 7g⁶ 7m³ 8m² 7g³ a7g³ Nov 21] small filly: first foal: dam once-raced half-sister to smart French/US 1m and 1¼m performer Jeune Homme out of half-sister to Royal Academy: fairly useful maiden: better at 1m than 7f, and will stay 1¼m: acts on good to firm going and fibresand: usually races up with pace. *P. F. I. Cole*

SUMMERHILL SPECIAL (IRE) 6 b.m. Roi Danzig (USA) – Special Thanks 74 (Kampala 120) [1996 59: 12m 12s⁶ 8.5m 10m⁵ 10m⁴ 8.3g⁶ 8m 6m 10.4g 7.1f 14m 14d 12d* 1997 13.8g² 12.3m* 12g⁵ 11.1s² 13.9g 12g² 13.1g* 12m⁶ 12.3m*dis 14.6d⁶ 12.3m⁵ 12g* 12.3d⁵ 10.9d⁵ 12.1g⁵ 12s Oct 16] sturdy, good-bodied mare: fair performer: in good form for much of 1997, winning handicap at Ripon in April (also disqualified after winning ladies race there in June), minor event at Ayr in May and amateurs handicap at Catterick in August: effective at 1½m to 1¾m (when conditions aren't testing): acts on good to firm and soft going, probably on heavy: has worn blinkers, not in 1997. *D. W. Barker*

SUMMEROSA (USA) 3 ch.f. Woodman (USA) 126 – Rose Red (USA) 92 72 (Northern Dancer) [1996 78: 6m³ 5.2m⁶ 7.1s² 1997 7m⁶ 7.1d³ 8m² 7g³ 7d³ 8.5g* 8.1m Sep 17] attractive filly: fair performer: won maiden at Epsom in September: reportedly swallowed tongue when below form final outing: stays 8.5f: acts on good to firm and soft going: bandaged near-fore last 3 starts. *P. W. Chapple-Hyam*

930

SUMMER PRINCESS   4 ch.f. Prince Sabo 123 – Lafrowda 71 (Crimson Beau   –
124) [1996 –: 5.1g 5m⁶ 6.1g a6g a7g 1997 9.9m Apr 5] tall, sparely-made filly: no
form: tried visored. *G. Fierro*

SUMMER QUEEN   3 b.f. Robellino (USA) 127 – Carolside 108 (Music Maestro   80
119) [1996 62: 5m³ 5.7g⁵ a6g³ a7g⁵ 1997 7g* 7m 8d 7g 7.1m 7g Oct 24] lengthy,
sparely-made filly: fair handicapper: won at Newmarket in April: below form after
next start: stays 7f: acts on fibresand and good to firm going, possibly on dead.
S. P. C. Woods

SUMMER RIVER (IRE)   2 b.g. (Feb 6) River Falls 113 – Rose of Summer   –
(IRE) (Taufan (USA) 119) [1997 5.1m 6d a6g 7m Jul 22] 8,200Y: close-coupled
gelding: first foal: dam once-raced half-sister to smart Irish performer Lord Bud: no
form: visored last 2 starts, final one a seller: sold, and sent to Belgium. *C. Murray*

SUMMERSEAT   2 b.f. (Mar 13) Thatching 131 – Sudden Hope (FR) (Darshaan   62
133) [1997 5m⁴ a5g⁶ a5g* 6d 5s³ a8g a7g* a5g* Dec 8] 3,400Y: first foal: dam, third
at 1½m in France, half-sister to smart middle-distance filly Sudden Love: modest
form: trained by C. Fairhurst first 4 starts: won sellers at Wolverhampton in May and
November and nursery (led near finish) at Southwell in December: stays 7f: acts on
fibresand: blinkered last 2 starts. *G. Holmes*

SUMMER THYME   3 b.f. Henbit (USA) 130 – Hasty Sarah 56 (Gone Native)   –
[1996 NR 1997 12.3g 9m 10g³ Aug 9] fourth foal: half-sister to modest 1m winner
Kiss In The Dark (by Starry Night) and a winner in Hungary by Robellino: dam won
1¼m sellers: well held in maidens. *J. Berry*

SUMMER VILLA   5 b.m. Nomination 125 – Maravilla 73 (Mandrake Major   –
122) [1996 41: a8g a8g³ 7g⁴ 8.3g³ 8f⁵ 8f⁶ 6f 6.9f 1997 a11g⁶ Jan 17] neat mare:
poor performer on flat: well beaten only 5-y-o start: won over hurdles in August.
K. G. Wingrove

SUMMERVILLE WOOD   3 b.g. Nomination 125 – Four Love (Pas de Seul   61 d
133) [1996 58: 5f³ 5g 6.1m* 7f⁵ 7.1m³ 7.6m 7m³ 8.2g 7m⁴ 8g⁶ 1997 a10g⁶ 7m³ 6m*   a–
5m 6m 7d⁶ 9g⁵ a10g 10g 10g a12s a10g Dec 10] leggy, close-coupled gelding:
modest performer: clearly best 3-y-o effort when winning apprentice handicap at
Folkestone in April: needs further than 5f, and stays 1m: acts on good to firm ground:
best form in blinkers, though also successful without: inconsistent. *P. Mooney*

SUN ALERT (USA)   3 b.f. Alysheba (USA) – Sunerta (USA) 75 (Roberto (USA)   74 d
131) [1996 NR 1997 12m⁴ 12g³ 14m³ 11.9d³ 14.1m* 16.1g⁵ 14m 20m 16.4ᴍ⁴ 12d⁵
16.4g⁴ 10g 11.1m 13.8s 12m Oct 31] 10,500 2-y-o: leggy, angular filly: third living
foal: half-sister to 7f and 1m winner Solar Beam (by Majestic Light) and fairly useful
7f (at 2 yrs) and 12.5f winner Ivory Palm (by Sir Ivor): dam 7f winner at 2 yrs: fair
performer: won maiden at Yarmouth in June: well below form last 7 starts, including
in visor: stays 2m: acts on good to firm and dead going. *M. J. Polglase*

SUNBEAM DANCE (USA)   3 b.c. Gone West (USA) – Encorelle (FR) (Arctic   87
Tern (USA) 126) [1996 93: 7f* 7g⁴ 8g⁴ 8d² 1997 8g⁵ 9g 11g⁴ 9m a8f³ a8s⁶ Dec 5]
big, close-coupled, good-topped colt: easy mover: fairly useful performer at 2 yrs:
not at best in 1997, finding little when visored second start and flattered (acted as
pacemaker) when fourth of 5 to Posidonas in listed race at Newbury on third: respectable third in handicap in Dubai in November: likely to prove best up to 1¼m:
acts on firm and dead going. *Saeed bin Suroor*

SUN DANCER   2 b.g. (Apr 26) Sizzling Melody 117 – Petite Melusine (IRE) 50   –
(Fairy King (USA)) [1997 5.7m Jul 17] 5,000 2-y-o: second foal: dam placed over 5f
at 2 yrs: behind in maiden at Bath. *N. A. Smith*

SUN DANCING (IRE)   2 ch.f. (Apr 12) Magical Wonder (USA) 125 –   75
Lockwood Girl 81 (Prince Tenderfoot (USA) 126) [1997 6d⁵ a5g* a5s² Nov 28] IR
2,400Y: good-topped filly: half-sister to several winners, including fairly useful 1½m
winner Dunphy's Special (by Dunphy): dam winning sprinter: won maiden at Southwell: second in nursery at Lingfield (caught near line) fortnight later: speedy. *J. Berry*

SUNDAY MAIL TOO (IRE)   5 b.m. Fayruz 116 – Slick Chick 89 (Shiny Tenth   44
120) [1996 51: a6g 6s⁵ 5d 5s 8.1g⁴ 8.1g⁴ 6g* 5g 8.1f⁶ 6m² 6g⁴ 5m* 6m⁵ 6d 6f 5g⁴ 5m
5g 6d 6m 1997 5m⁶ 5m² 5s⁶ 6m 5g⁵ 5s⁶ 5m 6g⁶ 6g 5g 5g Sep 1] sparely-made mare:

poor handicapper: stays 6f: has form on soft going, best efforts on good to firmer: tried visored/blinkered, not in 1997: sometimes hangs. *Miss L. A. Perratt*

SUN FAIRY 3 ch.f. Hatim (USA) 121 – Petite Melusine (IRE) 50 (Fairy King (USA)) [1996 NR 1997 7m⁵ 8g³ 8g² 10s⁴ 8g⁴ 8m 9.9g³ Aug 23] leggy, unfurnished filly: first foal: dam placed at 2 yrs over 5f: poor performer, mostly campaigned in sellers: stays 1¼m: probably acts on soft ground: below form in blinkers. *J. A. Glover*   46

SUN IN THE MORNING 2 gr.f. (Mar 16) Petardia 113 – Rich Lass (Broxted 120) [1997 5.2g 5g⁵ 5g* 5m³ 5g² a5g 5.1m 5.1d⁵ 5g⁵ 5.3f⁴ Oct 1] 5,200F, 12,000Y: compact filly: dam placed at 5-y-o Able Sheriff and a fairly useful 2-y-o 6f winner by Junius: dam poor from family of smart miler Richboy: modest performer: won claimer at Leicester in May: patchy form afterwards, including in sellers: raced only at around 5f: blinkered when well beaten on fibresand. *B. J. Meehan*   61 d

SUNLEY SEEKER 2 b.f. (Mar 11) Elmaamul (USA) 125 – Sunley Sinner 93 (Try My Best (USA) 130) [1997 6m a7g* 8g 7.3d* Sep 19] close-coupled filly: has a round action: half-sister to 3 winners, including veteran Garnock Valley and 7f winner Morsun (by Aragon): dam 2-y-o 7f winner: fairly useful form: won maiden at Southwell in July and nursery at Newbury in September, staying on to beat Acid Test by 2½ lengths in latter: will stay at least 1m: seems best ridden with restraint. *M. R. Channon*   82

SUN MARK (IRE) 6 ch.g. Red Sunset 120 – Vivungi (USA) (Exbury 138) [1996 NR 1997 9.2d² 12.1d³ 12.1s* 12d 9f⁴ 12.1s⁴ 10g* 12.1g* Aug 2] modest performer: missed 1996, but in good form in 1997, winning minor event at Hamilton in May and sellers at Ripon (made most) in July and Hamilton (reportedly finished lame) in August: stays 1½m: acts on firm and soft ground: normally blinkered at 3 yrs, visored final 4-y-o start: joined Miss J. Craze. *Mrs A. Swinbank*   63

SUNNY ISLE 3 b.f. Cadeaux Genereux 131 – Highsplasher (USA) (Bucksplasher (USA)) [1996 NR 1997 8d³ 10.5g* 10.5s³ Oct 15] tall, unfurnished filly: has a round action: third reported foal: half-sister to 1993 2-y-o 7f winner Dulford Lad (by In Fijar), later useful winner in Scandinavia up to 1¾m: dam, won 6 races in USA, from family of Park Hill winner Quay Line: progressive form: won maiden at Haydock in September: edgy, under 2 lengths third of 13 to Topatori in handicap on same course following month, staying on: quite keen, but likely to stay beyond 10.5f: should improve further. *C. F. Wall*   83 p

SUN OF SPRING 7 b.g. Green Desert (USA) 127 – Unsuspected 95 (Above Suspicion 127) [1996 NR 1997 12m³ 12m* 12f 14.1g² 12d* 11.1d⁴ 12m⁴ 16.5g⁴ 12g⁴ Aug 15] smallish, sturdy gelding: modest performer: won claimer at Beverley and minor event at Musselburgh in June: ran creditably 3 of 4 starts afterwards: stays 1¾m, not 2m: acts on firm and dead going. *D. W. Chapman*   59

SUN O'TIROL (IRE) 3 b.g. Tirol 127 – Nous 76 (Le Johnstan 123) [1996 65d: 5.1g⁵ 6s 7m 6.9m* 7m⁴ 7.3m 8d 8m 1997 8d⁵ 8m 8f⁴ 8f 8.3s 8.3g 6m 7m⁵ Aug 15] workmanlike gelding: fair performer at best: became disappointing at 2 yrs, and well beaten most starts in 1997: will prove best up to 1m: acts on firm going: races keenly: tried blinkered. *J. R. Arnold*   58 d

SUNSET HARBOUR (IRE) 4 br.f. Prince Sabo 123 – City Link Pet 79 (Tina's Pet 121) [1996 51, a60: a6g² a5g³ a6g⁵ a6g³ a5g² a6g⁵ 5d 8m 7m 6m 5m³ 6g 5f* 5m⁴ 5f³ 5m 1997 5s 5g 5g⁵ 5m³ 5g* 5f⁶ 5g³ 5g⁶ 5g 5s a6g a5g² a5g⁶ Dec 12] tall filly: poor handicapper: mostly in good form in 1997, and won at Beverley in June: effective at 5f (best turf form) and 6f: acts on the all-weather and hard ground, possibly not on soft: tried blinkered at 3 yrs: has won for apprentice. *S. E. Kettlewell*   46

SUNSHINE PET (IRE) 2 b.f. (Mar 17) Petardia 113 – Faapette (Runnett 125) [1997 5d 5g 5d 5m⁴ 7f⁶ 6g 5d Sep 18] 6,000Y: good-bodied filly: seventh foal: half-sister to 3 winners, including Irish 11f winner Premier Leap (by Salmon Leap) and 1990 2-y-o 5f winner Bellerofonte (by Tate Gallery): dam Irish 2-y-o 1m winner: poor maiden: best form at 5f: blinkered penultimate start. *J. J. O'Neill*   36

SUNSTREAK 2 ch.c. (Feb 6) Primo Dominie 121 – Florentynna Bay 61 (Aragon 118) [1997 8.2d 8s Nov 8] 35,000Y: unfurnished colt: sixth foal: half-brother to 3 winners, including 4-y-o Albert The Bear: dam, 2-y-o 5f winner, half-sister to Super-   – p power: well held in maidens at Nottingham and Doncaster: should do better. *C. F. Wall*

SUPACALIFRAGILISTK   2 b.f. (Feb 20) Sabrehill (USA) 120 – Lucky Thing   57
(Green Desert (USA) 127) [1997 6d⁴ 5m 7g 7m² 8m 8m Nov 4] good-topped filly:
first foal: dam unraced daughter of sprinting half-sister to Terimon: modest maiden:
creditable efforts in nurseries fourth and final starts: stays 1m: has swished tail in
preliminaries: sold 7,000 gns in November, and joined J. Balding. *B. W. Hills*

SUPERAPPAROS   3 b.g. Superpower 113 – Ayodessa 78 (Lochnager 132) [1996   –
NR 1997 a6g⁶ a7g a8g 8.2s 6g 5g a5g 7m a7g³ a6g a6g⁴ Nov 24] third foal: a45
half-brother to fairly useful 4-y-o Antonias Melody and a winner in Norway (both by
Rambo Dancer): dam sprinter: poor maiden: stays 7f, not sure to get further: best
efforts on fibresand: tried blinkered. *S. R. Bowring*

SUPERBELLE   3 b.f. Damister (USA) 123 – Nell of The North (USA) (Canadian   58
Gil (CAN)) [1996 78: 7m³ 7f² a7g² a8.5g³ 1997 a10g* a10g⁴ 10.3m 10m 10g² 11.9g   a76
11.5m⁵ Sep 16] leggy, unfurnished filly: fair performer on the all-weather, only
modest on turf in 1997: won maiden at Lingfield in January: well below form 4 of
last 5 starts, including in blinkers: stays 1¼m. *M. A. Jarvis*

SUPER BENZ   11 ch.g. Hello Gorgeous (USA) 128 – Investiture 62 (Welsh   56
Pageant 132) [1996 84: a6g* a7g⁵ a6g* a7g* 7s* 6g* 7g 1997 7g³ 7m* May 26]
lengthy gelding: grand old campaigner, successful at least once every year since he
was a 2-y-o in 1988: still fairly useful in 1996, but finished lame on final start and
was subsequently pin-fired: only modest form in 1997, narrowly winning weak seller
at Redcar in May: effective at 6f to 1m: acts on hard soft ground and the
all-weather: tried blinkered and visored, no improvement: successful for apprentice:
game. *J. L. Eyre*

SUPERBIT   5 b.g. Superpower 113 – On A Bit 66 (Mummy's Pet 125) [1996 64,   71
a53: a8g a5g 6m 5.1m² 5m³ 6m* 5.1m³ 6.1m 5.1g⁵ 5m 5.1g* a6g³ a5g⁵ 1997 6m⁴   a–
6.1d* 5g³ 5m³ 5m 6.1g 5d⁴ 5g 5g 6.1m³ 6m 6g⁴ Oct 27] small, good-bodied gelding:
poor mover: fair handicapper: made all at Nottingham in June: best at 5f/6f: acts on
firm and dead ground, only modest form on fibresand: blinkered (finished last) once:
none too consistent. *B. A. McMahon*

SUPERCAL   3 gr.f. Environment Friend 128 – Sorayah 89 (Persian Bold 123)   106
[1996 83: 5m⁶ 6d⁶ 6m* 6m* 7m 1997 6g* 7.3g⁵ 10m⁶ 7s* 8d 7m 7d 8.1g² 8g³ 8g³
8d² 9.3f Oct 5] rather leggy, quite attractive filly: useful performer: won handicap
at Kempton in March and listed race at Lingfield in May: best efforts when placed
afterwards in Hong Kong Jockey Club Handicap at Sandown (beaten ½ length by
Hawksley Hill), Prix d'Astarte at Deauville (length third to Daneskaya), Desmond
Stakes and Matron Stakes (length second to Clerio) at the Curragh: sweating, well
beaten in Prix de l'Opera at Longchamp on final start: stays 1m: acts on good to firm
and soft going: held up. *D. R. C. Elsworth*

SUPERCHARMER   3 ch.g. Charmer 123 – Surpassing 79 (Superlative 118)   56
[1996 69: 5g 6g³ 6f⁴ 6m⁶ 7f⁴ 7g 7g⁵ 1997 a7g⁵ a7g⁴ a6g³ a6g⁶ 6.1m 6g⁴ 6g⁶ 5s⁴ 6m⁵   a62
10.8d a8.5g Sep 20] sturdy, close-coupled gelding: modest maiden: left D. Nicholls
after ninth start: stays 7f: acts on firm ground, probably on soft, and on fibresand:
tried blinkered/visored: headstrong: tends to hang. *R. T. Juckes*

SUPERCHIEF   2 b.g. (Feb 13) Precocious 126 – Rome Express (Siberian Express   78 p
(USA) 125) [1997 7g Sep 18] 1,800F: smallish, sturdy gelding: first foal: dam
unraced: 33/1, green and burly, shaped well when slow-starting ninth to Dr Fong
in maiden at Newbury, travelling strongly until short of room, not knocked about:
should do better. *Miss B. Sanders*

SUPERFRILLS   4 b.f. Superpower 113 – Pod's Daughter (IRE) 43 (Tender King   42
123) [1996 50: 5g⁴ 5m 5m² 5g⁵ 5g 5.1g 1997 5g⁶ 5.1g 5g⁴ 5m³ 5g 5d⁶ 5m⁴ 5g⁵ 5g
Oct 18] small filly: poor maiden handicapper: has raced mainly at 5f on good ground
or firmer: refused to enter stalls ninth intended outing. *Miss L. C. Siddall*

SUPER GEIL   2 b.f. (Mar 18) Superlative 118 – Mild Deception (IRE) (Glow   52
(USA)) [1997 6g⁵ a5g⁵ 6d a5g* a5g³ a6g 5d a5g² a5g³ a5g⁶ Dec 19] 3,800Y: second
foal: half-sister to 3-y-o Gresatre: dam (unraced) from good family: modest performer: won selling nursery at Southwell in September: should stay 6f: acts on fibresand:
visored last 3 starts. *C. A. Dwyer*

Daihatsu Field Marshal Stakes, Haydock—Superior Premium has the measure of Myrmidon

SUPERGOLD (IRE)   4 ch.g. Keen 116 – Superflash (Superlative 118) [1996 –: – a7g 1997 a10g a12g⁴ Jan 6] of little account. *C. Murray*

SUPER HIGH   5 b.g. Superlative 118 – Nell of The North (USA) (Canadian Gil – (CAN)) [1996 59, a87: 8m 10g a9.4g³ a8.5g³ 10g a8.5g* a9.4g³ a9.4g² 10m 10.1m³   a87 a8.5g 1997 a9.4g² a8.5f a11g* a12g a14.8g⁵ 12.3v 10g May 23] big, good-topped gelding: has a round action: fairly useful handicapper on fibresand, modest on turf: made all at Southwell in February: well beaten last 4 starts: stays 11f: usually blinkered/visored: has had tongue tied. *P. Howling*

SUPER IMPOSE   2 ch.g. (Mar 20) Superpower 113 – Sharp Lady 70 (Sharpen – Up 127) [1997 a5g Dec 22] half-brother to several winners, including 5f and 1m winner Good N'Sharp (by Mummy's Pet) and 6f winner (stays 1m) Statistician (by Statoblest): dam 6f winner: well backed, never going well when last of 8 in maiden at Lingfield. *John Berry*

SUPERIOR FORCE   4 ch.g. Superlative 118 – Gleeful 72 (Sayf El Arab (USA)   54 127) [1996 68: 7g 7f³ 7.1d⁵ 8.3m 8.3m a8g* 8m² a10g³ 10.1g⁶ 8.1m⁶ a7g 8f 8.1m*   a63 8.5m 8d 1997 a8g a8g⁴ a8g⁶ a8g⁵ 8d⁶ 8.1g 9g⁴ 8d Sep 12] smallish, workmanlike gelding: modest handicapper: disappointing in 1997 after second start, including in visor: likely to prove best over further than 1m these days: acts on firm and soft ground and on equitrack. *Miss B. Sanders*

SUPERIOR PREMIUM   3 br.c. Forzando 122 – Devils Dirge 68 (Song 132)   106 [1996 94: 5.1d* 5d² 5f² 5f⁶ 5m⁶ 5m² 5v* 5d⁵ 6g⁵ 1997 5s* 5m 6g³ 5m⁶ 6d 6s⁴ Nov 8] good-topped colt: useful performer: won listed race at Haydock in March: in frame afterwards in Ayr Gold Cup (best effort, third of 29 to Wildwood Flower) and listed race won by Snow Kid at Doncaster: stays 6f: acts on any ground: sometimes edgy in preliminaries. *R. A. Fahey*

SUPERLAO (BEL)   5 b.m. Bacalao (USA) – Princess of Import (Import 127)   45 [1996 45, a49: a6g⁶ a5g⁶ a6g a5g⁶ a5g a5g 6m 5m³ 5f³ 5f⁴ 6m 5f⁴ 5g 5m 6m⁴ 5f 1997   a39 a6g a5g⁶ a6g⁵ a6g⁶ a6g⁴ a6g³ a5g³ 5g 5g 5m³ 5d⁵ 5m⁶ 6f³ 7m 6s³ 5d* 5g 5m⁶ 6m⁶ 6m⁴ 6m 6m a7g a5g⁵ Dec 22] smallish, sturdy mare: poor handicapper: in good form for most of 1997, and won at Lingfield in June: stays 6.5f: acts on firm and soft ground and on equitrack: usually races prominently: respectable effort in visor final start: tough. *J. J. Bridger*

934

SUPERMICK　6 ch.g. Faustus (USA) 118 – Lardana 65 (Burglar 128) [1996 43: 43
10m 13.1f³ 14.1f* 12g* 12m³ a14g 12m⁵ 14s 1997 12.1m² 12.1m⁶ 11.5g² 11.9m²
12d Sep 19] angular gelding: poor handicapper: stays 1¾m: acts on firm ground and
the all-weather, below form on dead: tried visored and blinkered: joined M. Pipe, and
won over jumps in November and December. *W. R. Muir*

SUPERMODEL (GER)　2 ch.f. (Jan 29) Czaravich (USA) – Superminis (USA)　?
(Super Concorde (USA) 128) [1997 5g³ 7s⁵ 6d a7.5g³ Dec 31] seventh foal:
half-sister to minor winners in USA by Lion D'or and Fighting Fit: dam sprint winner
in USA: sire high-class 7f to 11f performer: third in newcomers event at
Baden-Baden (trained until after next start by M. Channon) and in maiden at Neuss.
U. Stoltefuss, Germany

SUPER MONARCH　3 ch.g. Cadeaux Genereux 131 – Miss Fancy That (USA)　79 §
99 (The Minstrel (CAN) 135) [1996 71p: 7d 1997 8m⁴ 7m² 8f⁵ a7g⁴ Dec 22] sturdy,
good-bodied gelding: fair maiden: trained by E. Dunlop first 3 starts, then gelded:
always behind (very slowly away) on all-weather debut: stays 1m: tends to get upset
in stalls: unreliable. *S. Dow*

SUPER PARK　5 b.g. Superpower 113 – Everingham Park 54 (Record Token 128)　43
[1996 61d: a8g 6.9m⁴ 7m 6g⁴ 7f⁴ 7.5m⁶ 7.6m³ 7f 7m 7f 8m a9.4g a8g 1997 6f 7m⁴ 7g
7.5d 7f Oct 29] strong, lengthy gelding: poor handicapper: stays 7.6f: acts on firm
and dead ground: no improvement in blinkers: inconsistent. *J. Pearce*

SUPERPRIDE　5 b.g. Superpower 113 – Lindrake's Pride (Mandrake Major 122)　60
[1996 69: 5.9d⁴ 7m 6.9g⁶ 6m³ 6m 5.9f⁴ 10m⁴ 9f 7g* 7m⁶ 7m² 7g 7g 7m 1997 7.5m
8g 7s² 7d 8m² 8.5v³ 7.5m 8g⁵ 7.9s⁶ Sep 3] good-topped gelding: modest handicapper:
effective at 7f to 8.5f: acts on any going: tried blinkered, no improvement: often front
runner: has gone early to post: inconsistent: fairly useful novice hurdler, successful 3
times. *Mrs M. Reveley*

SUPER RASCAL　2 b.c. (Mar 23) Superpower 113 – Gild The Lily 83 (Ile de　53
Bourbon (USA) 133) [1997 a5g 5m⁴ a6g³ 6s⁶ Jun 28] 4,000Y: close-coupled colt:　a68
fourth foal: dam 9f winner (later successful at 1½m in Ireland) who seemed to stay
2m, half-sister to very smart stayer Weld: in frame in maiden events at Pontefract and
Wolverhampton, best effort on latter course: will be suited by further than 6f: hung
final start. *N. P. Littmoden*

SUPER ROCKY　8 b.g. Clantime 101 – Starproof 46 (Comedy Star (USA) 121)　47
[1996 71: a5g* a5g⁴ a5g 5m⁵ 5.1g² 5m⁴ 5g a5g⁶ 5.2g³ 5m³ 5f² 5m⁶ 5m 1997 a5g⁶
5.1g⁶ 5g 6.1d 5m a5g 5g a6g a5g a5g a5g Dec 22] good-topped gelding: one-time fair
5f winner: put poor form in 1997: often blinkered. *R. Bastiman*

SUPER SAINT　3 b.g. Superpower 113 – Martyrdom (USA) (Exceller (USA)　57
129) [1996 57: 5g⁶ a5g⁵ 5f⁴ 6g⁴ 6g³ 7g⁴ 7f a8g* 1997 5m 8s a7.5g³ 9f³ 7g 6g⁵ a9.3g*
a7.5g* a8g⁵ Nov 23] tall, unfurnished gelding: modest performer: last of 10 in
claimer at Folkestone on reappearance, before winning twice at Sterrebeek: stays 9f:
best turf form on good ground, acts on equitrack: failed to handle bends on both
outings at Catterick. *Alex Vanderhaeghen, Belgium*

SUPER SCRAVELS　3 ch.f. Superlative 118 – Scravels Saran (IRE) 57 (Indian　54
King (USA) 128) [1996 37: 5m 6f³ a5g 7.5m 7.1m² 7m³ 6g⁵ 7.1m 6.9d 1997 6.9m³
10g 7.6g⁴ 8m⁴ 7g⁴ Sep 3] modest maiden: best short of 1¼m: raced mainly on good
going or firmer. *K. Mahdi*

SUPER SERENADE　8 b.g. Beldale Flutter (USA) 130 – Super Melody 72　61
(Song 132) [1996 58: 7.1g⁵ 9.7f⁴ 8.1f* 9.2m 8m⁵ 11.6d⁴ 12d 10f⁶ 1997 8.1s
10m 8.3g* 11.6m 10g Sep 3] angular gelding: modest handicapper: easily best 8-y-o
effort when winning apprentice seller at Windsor in August: effective at 1m, probably stays 11.6f: acts on firm ground, soft and equitrack: sometimes sweats: inconsistent. *G. B. Balding*

SUPER SNIP　2 ch.g. (Apr 3) Superpower 113 – Marcroft 91 (Crofthall 110) [1997　61 p
5.1s⁵ 5d Sep 5] strong, workmanlike colt: third foal: half-brother to 4-y-o Safio: dam
best at 7f to 1m: still burly, better effort when keeping-on tenth in maiden at
Haydock: completely missed break on debut: should stay at least 6f: should improve
again. *A. Bailey*

SUPERTOP   9 b. or br.g. High Top 131 – Myth 89 (Troy 137) [1996 –: 10.9m 1997   55
10g* Apr 18] leggy, workmanlike gelding: fairly useful hurdler: very lightly raced on
flat nowadays, but won 20-runner amateurs handicap at Ayr on only 9-y-o start:
should stay beyond 1¼m: acts on firm and dead going. *L. Lungo*

SUPLIZI (IRE)   6 b.h. Alzao (USA) 117 – Sphinx (GER) (Alpenkonig (GER))   –
[1996 101: 12.3g* 13.3d⁴ 1997 12g 12s Nov 8] deep-bodied horse: smart performer
in 1994, but bought out of L. Cumani's stable only 6,000 gns in 1996, and looks a
shadow of his former self. *P. Bowen*

SUPPLY AND DEMAND   3 b.g. Belmez (USA) 131 – Sipsi Fach 100 (Prince   106
Sabo 123) [1996 80+: 7m² 7m⁵ 7g⁵ 8g 8s⁶ 1997 8.5m* 8m² 9s* 10.1m² 12d 10m²
10.4g Aug 20] well-made gelding: useful performer: won maiden at Epsom in April
and handicap at Lingfield in May: good second afterwards in valuable handicaps at
Epsom and Goodwood (beaten 1½ lengths by Future Perfect): should stay 1½m: acts
on good to firm and soft ground: won juvenile hurdle in November. *G. L. Moore*

SUPREME ANGEL   2 b.f. (Feb 27) Beveled (USA) – Blue Angel (Lord Gayle   81 +
(USA) 124) [1997 5m 5.2g² 6.1g⁴ 5m² 5s² 5.2d⁶ 5s* Oct 15] angular filly: third
reported foal: sister to 7-y-o Patsy Grimes: dam never ran: fairly useful performer:
one of only handful of flat racers in yard, but won maiden at Newbury in April and
nursery at Haydock, improved form in latter, hampered start but able to pick off rivals
off strong pace: needs good test at 5f, and should be at least as effective over 6f: acts
on good to firm and soft ground. *M. P. Muggeridge*

SUPREME ILLUSION (AUS)   4 ch.f. Rory's Jester (AUS) – Counterfeit Coin   –
(AUS) (Comeram (FR) 127) [1996 –: a5g a5g 6s a7g⁴ a8g 10g⁴ a8g⁶ 7f a6g a8.5g
1997 a8g³ a8g a7g a7g a8.5g Feb 21] bad maiden on flat. *John Berry*

SUPREME MAIMOON   3 b.c. Jareer (USA) 115 – Princess Zena 96 (Habitat   –
134) [1996 70p: 6g⁶ a7g* 1997 a8g³ 7.1g 6f 7d 9.7s 7d Jul 9] good-topped colt: a77
unimpressive mover: fair performer: long way below form after reappearance: likely
to prove best up to 1m: best efforts on equitrack. *M. J. Polglase*

SUPREME SOUND   3 b.c. Superlative 118 – Sing Softly 112 (Luthier 126)   79
[1996 83p: 7g 8.1m² 10g* 1997 10m 12g 10g 12.3m³ 14.1s 10m⁴ 10m* 10.1f* 10f³
10.4d Oct 8] strong colt: has a round action: fair handicapper: had dropped considerably in the weights prior to winning at Lingfield in August and Yarmouth in
September, making all under good ride each time: stays 1¼m: acts on firm going, ran
poorly on dead and soft: front runner. *P. W. Harris*

SUPREME STAR (USA)   6 b.g. Gulch (USA) – Just A Game 108 (Tarboosh   70
(USA)) [1996 64, a–: 16m 16.4g 14m² 14m⁶ 11.6m⁶ 14m⁶ 14.4g⁶ a16g³ 1997 a13g*
a16g³ a13g* a16g Feb 11] lightly-made gelding: fair handicapper: won 2 sellers at
Lingfield in January: pulled up, reportedly lame, final start: stays 2m: acts on firm
ground, dead and the all-weather: often blinkered/visored. *P. R. Hedger*

SUPREME THOUGHT   5 b.m. Emarati (USA) 74 – Who's That Girl (Skyliner   66
117) [1996 64+: 7g⁵ 5f⁵ 6.1s 1997 6m⁵ 6d* 5g 6m 6.1s² Oct 15] tall mare: fair
handicapper, lightly raced: made all at Salisbury in August: effective at 6f/7f: acts on
firm and soft ground: sold only 3,000 gns in November. *L. G. Cottrell*

SUPREMISM   3 b.c. Be My Chief (USA) 122 – Ever Welcome 58 (Be My Guest   77
(USA) 126) [1996 77: 7g⁵ 6m³ 1997 10s 8m⁵ 8g Jun 28] good-topped colt: fair
maiden, lightly raced: should stay at least 1¼m: well beaten on soft ground: sold, and
joined Mrs D. Haine. *C. E. Brittain*

SURE QUEST   2 b.f. (May 7) Sure Blade (USA) 130 – Eagle's Quest 62 (Legal   58
Eagle 126) [1997 7d⁶ 7d⁵ Oct 27] close-coupled filly: half-sister to several winners,
including 3-y-o Strat's Quest, 5-y-o David James' Girl and 11.6f winner Quest Again
(by Then Again): dam 5f winner: modest form from mid-division in autumn maidens
at Leicester (green) and Lingfield: should stay at least 1m. *D. W. P. Arbuthnot*

SURE TO DREAM (IRE)   4 b.f. Common Grounds 118 – Hard To Stop 77   53
(Hard Fought 125) [1996 NR 1997 6m⁶ 8.3s 7m 7d a6g* a6g⁵ a5g⁴ Dec 22] 7,800Y:
lengthy, workmanlike filly: third foal: half-sister to a 7f winner in Belgium by
Aragon: dam 2-y-o 5f winner: modest form: won weak maiden at Lingfield in November: creditable efforts in handicaps on same course after: stays 6f: acts on equitrack. *R. T. Phillips*

SURF CITY   4 ch.g. Rock City 120 – Waveguide 76 (Double Form 130) [1996 61:   53
7d⁵ 7g 7.1d⁴ 7f⁶ 7.1d⁴ 6g 8m a8.5g⁴ a7g² a7g⁴ 1997 a7g⁶ a7g⁴ a7g 7m⁴ 7.5g 6.9g³
6.9m* 7.5g 7m a8g Oct 20] sturdy gelding: modest performer: won minor event at
Carlisle in August: best efforts around 7f: acted on good to firm and dead ground and
on fibresand: dead. *W. W. Haigh*

SURGEON   4 ch.c. Sharrood (USA) 124 – Suva (USA) (Northjet 136) [1996 12g³   116
12.5d 1997 12m* 12g* 12d* 12d² 12.5g* 12m⁶ Sep 14] big, strong colt: first foal:
dam, ran once, half-sister to Breeders' Cup Turf winner Tikkanen and stayer Turg-
eon: much improved in 1997: won minor events at Longchamp in March and Nancy
in April and listed race at Chantilly in May: ¾-length second of 5 to Steward in Grand
Prix de Chantilly: won 5-runner Prix Maurice de Nieuil at Maisons-Laffitte by head
from Kutta: stays 12.5f, should get further: acts on good to firm and dead ground:
consistent. *J. de Roualle, France*

SURPRESA CARA   2 ch.f. (Feb 10) Risk Me (FR) 127 – Yukosan 69 (Absalom   –
128) [1997 6d 5m 7m Oct 1] 10,500Y: good-bodied filly: third reported foal: sister to
4-y-o The Great Flood and fair 1994 2-y-o 1m winner Lochbroom Commando: dam
sprint winner: only signs of ability in minor event at Ascot and maidens at Sandown
and Salisbury. *G. Lewis*

SURPRISED   2 b.g. (Mar 16) Superpower 113 – Indigo 86 (Primo Dominie 121)   77 p
[1997 5d 5f⁴ 5g² Sep 27] big, useful-looking gelding, unfurnished at 2 yrs: third foal:
half-brother to stable's 3-y-o Bishops Court and 5-y-o Surprise Mission: dam 2-y-o
5f winner: shaped encouragingly under considerate handling in maidens, taking
second readily after winner Mrs Malaprop had gone clear at Catterick: has plenty of
scope, and looks sure to win races at 3 yrs. *Mrs J. R. Ramsden*

SURPRISE EVENT   3 b.g. Tragic Role (USA) – Eleckydo 47 (Electric 126)   –
[1996 57d: 6.1g 6.1f³ 7f³ 7f⁴ a7g⁴ 6d⁶ 1997 8f 10m Oct 23] modest maiden at best:
no form in 1997. *W. G. M. Turner*

SURPRISE MISSION   5 ch.g. Clantime 101 – Indigo 86 (Primo Dominie 121)   99
[1996 79: 5m 5d⁵ 5m³ 5g 5g 5m 5m* 5d⁴ 5g 5g 1997 5g³ 5m* 5g* 5.1v* 5g⁴ 5g⁴ 5g³
5m² 5.6m 5v⁵ 5d 5g Oct 25] leggy gelding: useful handicapper: won at Newcastle in
March, Thirsk in April and Chester (by 6 lengths) in May: below form last 4 starts:
best at 5f: acts on good to firm and heavy going: travels well and usually waited with:
sold 21,000 gns, and joined D. Vienna in USA. *Mrs J. R. Ramsden*

SURPRISE PRESENT (IRE)   2 ch.c. (Mar 19) Indian Ridge 123 – Lady   64 p
Redford (Bold Lad (IRE) 133) [1997 7g⁶ 6d Oct 17] IR 60,000Y: workmanlike colt:
first foal: dam once-raced half-sister to dam of Oscar Schindler: showed ability in
maidens at Newmarket in July and October, though taking strong hold both times,
fading into tenth behind Atuf in latter: has potential, but needs to settle. *R. Hannon*

SURTSEY   3 ch.c. Nashwan (USA) 135 – Fire And Shade (USA) 91 (Shadeed   72
(USA) 135) [1996 NR 1997 10f² 12g³ 12.3g 12.1s⁵ 15.8g Aug 15] lengthy, angular
colt: second foal: half-brother to useful 1¼m winner Freedom Flame (by Darshaan):
dam, 2-y-o 6f winner, daughter of Musidora winner Fatah Flare: fair form in small-
field maidens first 2 starts: disappointed afterwards: should stay beyond 1½m:
soundly beaten on soft ground: sold 10,000 gns in October. *M. Johnston*

SURVEYOR   2 ch.c. (Jan 28) Lycius (USA) 124 – Atacama (Green Desert (USA)   101
127) [1997 6m⁴ 6m* 6.1s² 6m* Sep 21] 26,000Y: smallish, quite attractive colt:
first foal: dam unraced granddaughter of Oaks third The Dancer: useful form: won
maiden at Lingfield by wide margin in August and nursery at Kempton in September,
beating Kennet most readily by 1½ lengths in latter, rated value 4: stays 6f: easily
best form on good to firm ground: held up, and has a useful turn of foot. *J. L. Dunlop*

SUSELJA (IRE)   6 b.m. Mon Tresor 113 – Stifen (Burslem 123) [1996 NR 1997   –
16m⁶ May 31] poor maiden handicapper: well held only 6-y-o start, though won over
hurdles in August: sold only 500 gns in November. *J. M. Jefferson*

SUSHI BAR (IRE)   6 gr.g. Petorius 117 – Sashi Woo (Rusticaro (FR) 124) [1996   48
NR 1997 14.1d a14g 13s 16.2m⁴ 18g³ 14.1g 16g* 16m 16.2d⁵ 12g* 12.1g³ 16g³
12m Oct 6] big gelding: poor handicapper nowadays: won sellers at Musselburgh
and Hamilton in the summer: finds 1½m a minimum, and stays 2m: acts on the all-
weather and firm ground. *Mrs M. Reveley*

SUSIE'S SONNY   3 ch.g. Timeless Times (USA) 99 – Pickwood Sue 74 (Right – Boy 137) [1996 NR 1997 a5g Apr 26] half-brother to several modest/fair winners, including sprinters by Workboy (2) and Morston: dam 5f winner: always behind in Wolverhampton claimer. *J. P. Leigh*

SUSSEX GORSE   6 ch.g. Arrasas (USA) 100 – Testarossa (Tower Walk 130) – [1996 –: a8g a7g a16g 12m 16.4v a10g 1997 a7g a8g 9.7m 11.5d a16.2g Jul 25] of no account. *J. E. Long*

SUVALU (USA)   5 b.g. Woodman (USA) 126 – Danlu (USA) (Danzig (USA)) – [1996 76d: a8g* a12g a8.5g 10m 8.5m 10g 1997 11.9m⁴ Aug 15] tall, close-coupled gelding: fair performer at best, disappointing since 4-y-o reappearance: broke leg over hurdles in August. *M. G. Meagher*

SWAIN (IRE)   5 b.h. Nashwan (USA) 135 – Love Smitten (CAN) (Key To   134 The Mint (USA)) [1996 125: 10.5m³ 12m* 12m² 12m* 12d⁴ 12g³ 1997 12g² 12s* 11g³ 12f Oct 5]

   Those who have campaigned for more good older horses to be kept in training in Europe must have felt they were banging their heads against a brick wall at times. The flow of top performers to stud before they've reached full maturity has continued largely unabated in recent years. However, what might have seemed a rather futile crusade at times received a considerable boost in 1997. What kind of a year would it have been without Pilsudski, Singspiel, Helissio, Bosra Sham, Spinning World and Swain, to mention but a few? Perhaps as much to the point, those horses not only provided a lot of enjoyment while winning a great deal of prize money, but they also, with the possible exception of Helissio, enhanced their reputations and in turn their value for stud. Maybe things are changing for the better, as indicated by the fact that Swain, with little left to prove, is due to race on as a six-year-old in 1998.

   Swain has a terrific record overall, having finished out of the frame only once in sixteen races. As a three-year-old, in his first season, he won his first five races, notably the Grand Prix de Deauville, and finished under three lengths third to Lammtarra in the Prix de l'Arc de Triomphe. At four, he won

King George VI And Queen Elizabeth Diamond Stakes, Ascot—
Swain (rail) shows great resolution to defeat Pilsudski, Helissio (obscured) and Singspiel

the Coronation Cup and the Prix Foy, as well as finishing second in the Grand Prix de Saint-Cloud, third in the Breeders' Cup Turf and the Prix Ganay and fourth, beaten about six lengths by Helissio, in the Arc. The impression, however, was that Swain wasn't quite out of the top drawer. Although accounting for Pentire and Singspiel for his four-year-old wins, that pair seemed better than Swain overall, as did Pilsudski (the winner of the Breeders' Cup Turf, with Singspiel second) and of course Helissio, who had taken his measure at Saint-Cloud also. At the end of that year Swain was wintered in Dubai and transferred from Andre Fabre to Saeed bin Suroor.

Swain, Pilsudski, Helissio and Singspiel all turned up in 1997 at Ascot in July for the King George VI And Queen Elizabeth Diamond Stakes. The 'race of the year' seems to come round every week nowadays, but this, apparently, was not even the 'race of the decade', nor even of 'the century'. No this was (possibly) 'the greatest horserace *ever*', according to one headline. Well, probably not, and that's not just with the benefit of hindsight. Racing enthusiasts with longer memories may well champion the likes of Sea Bird II's and Dancing Brave's Arcs and Brigadier Gerard's and El Gran Senor's Guineas, to mention just those in Europe that seemed of even more consequence beforehand and actually lived up to their promise. All the same, the 1997 King George could boast a most impressive roll call: Pilsudski had added a win in the Eclipse to his tally; Helissio a Ganay and another Grand Prix de Saint-Cloud; Singspiel a Dubai World Cup and a Coronation Cup; Shantou was a triple Group 1 winner, including of the St Leger; Predappio had mastered Pilsudski in the Hardwicke Stakes; and Strategic Choice, while possibly not in the best of form, was a multiple winner over the years, including twice in Group 1 company. What the race lacked was a top-notch three-year-old (there weren't exactly many to choose from), a good Derby or Prix du Jockey-Club winner, for instance. The sole representative of the younger generation was the easy King Edward VII Stakes winner Kingfisher Mill, facing his first major test. The build-up concentrated, naturally, on Helissio, Singspiel and Pilsudski, who went off at 11/10, 4/1 and 6/1 respectively. Swain got barely a mention in the previews after being beaten a head by the race-fit Shantou when reappearing in the Princess of Wales's Stakes at Newmarket in July. Simon Crisford, racing manager for Godolphin, seemed to sum up the general feeling when saying: 'He's one of those "nearly" horses who has a bit to find with the main contenders.' Swain, at 16/1, was preferred in the betting only to Strategic Choice.

One crucial factor in Swain's favour was the torrential rain that turned the ground from good to firm on the Friday to soft on the Saturday. Swain had already proved himself a good stayer with wins at a mile and three quarters earlier in his career. In contrast, there were slight doubts about how well some of his rivals would see out a testing mile and a half. And testing it was, Helissio and Kingfisher Mill setting a strong gallop between them for the first mile, the field swinging wide down the side of the course. Helissio got the better of the battle and looked like taking some catching approaching the home turn but Swain kept on gamely and got to him at the two-furlong marker, while Pilsudski, checked briefly and switched, was still in with every chance and Singspiel was working his way into contention wider still. Helissio went from going well to looking held in a matter of strides as Swain went on. Try as he might Pilsudski couldn't quite get to Swain, as Singspiel's run petered out. Under strong pressure, Swain kept pulling out more and reached the line a length to the good over Pilsudski, with Helissio a length and a quarter back in third and Singspiel a tired fourth; of the others, Shantou in fifth could not get into it after being hampered at halfway, Strategic Choice in sixth wasn't good enough and Predappio (seventh) and Kingfisher Mill (last of eight) didn't run up to their best. Swain's former trainer, Andre Fabre, reportedly watched the race 'with a face like thunder' and would make no comment after it.

It might not have been the race of all-time, but in winning it Swain, on the face of it at least, had put up a truly outstanding performance. Quite *how* good a performance was open to question though. Swain's other form doesn't match up to a literal interpretation of his run at Ascot. In two subsequent outings he was beaten two short heads by Posidonas and Arabian Story (when conceding weight) in the Doubleprint Arc Trial at Newbury, after looking the winner a furlong out, and officially about eight lengths (actually less than seven) into seventh by Peintre Celebre in the Prix de l'Arc de Triomphe at Longchamp. Swain suffered a bruised hoof shortly before the Arc and a quarter crack later ruled him out of the Japan Cup (he'd also been among the original entries for the Melbourne Cup). Those defeats temper our enthusiasm for Swain somewhat, but we're still prepared to give him credit for being a top-class performer under the right conditions. Let's hope he gets the chance to prove it again in 1998, though normal summer conditions might well militate against him doing so.

		Blushing Groom (ch 1974)	Red God
	Nashwan (USA) (ch 1986)		Runaway Bride
		Height of Fashion (b 1979)	Bustino
Swain (IRE) (b.h. 1992)			Highclere
		Key To The Mint (b 1969)	Graustark
	Love Smitten (CAN) (b 1981)		Key Bridge
		Square Angel (b 1970)	Quadrangle
			Nangela

With two previous essays in *Racehorses*, there's not much new to say about Swain's pedigree. Details of his promising half-brother Thief of Hearts can be found elsewhere in this publication. Love Smitten has been barren since producing that colt. Swain is a robust, attractive horse—he looked magnificent on King George day—and a relentless galloper with a fluent, rather round action. Whatever one makes of Swain's ability, it has to be emphasised that he's

Godolphin's "Swain"

an admirably game individual, something that will stand him in good stead for the tasks ahead. After winning the King George on him, jockey John Reid described him as 'the greatest battler I've ever sat on.' *Saeed bin Suroor*

SWALLOW BREEZE 3 b.f. Salse (USA) 128 – Pica 84 (Diesis 133) [1996 62+: 6.9g 7g⁵ 7f⁴ 8d³ 10m* 10g 1997 11.8d⁶ 14.1d May 9] angular filly: modest winner at 2 yrs: soundly beaten in handicaps in 1997. *Dr J. D. Scargill*   –

SWALLOW WARRIOR (IRE) 2 b.c. (May 8) Warrshan (USA) 117 – Pica 84 (Diesis 133) [1997 8.2d a8g⁶ a8.5g Dec 13] IR 7,000Y: stocky colt: second foal: half-brother to 3-y-o Swallow Breeze: dam 12.5f winner who should have stayed 2m, out of half-sister to high-class US 2-y-o filly Althea (stayed 9f) and to dam of Green Desert: only a little sign of ability in maidens. *T. J. Etherington*   –

SWAN AT WHALLEY 5 b.g. Statoblest 120 – My Precious Daisy (Sharpo 132) [1996 71: a5g⁴ a5g 5.1g³ a5g 5s 5g² 5g² 5f² 5g* 5m² 5f³ 5.1g 5m 5g 1997 5m⁵ 5d⁴ 5d* 5g 5g 5g 5.1s³ 5m 5.1g* 5d a5g Dec 8] compact gelding: fair handicapper: won at Doncaster in June and Chester in September: mostly well held otherwise in 1997: speedy and raced only at 5f: acts on firm and soft going: tailed off in visor and blinkers: tends to wander under pressure (often claimer ridden): usually a front runner, though not in strongly-run race at Chester: troublesome at stalls (4 times leading to withdrawal) and prone early to post. *R. A. Fahey*   72 a–

SWANDALE FLYER 5 ch.g. Weldnaas (USA) 112 – Misfire 56 (Gunner B 126) [1996 –: a8g a7g⁶ 10d⁴ 11.9m 8d⁶ 10.5m⁶ 10g⁵ 10.9m 12.1d⁶ 15.1s 1997 a12g⁴ a12g a12g² a16g a12g a14g May 12] big, workmanlike gelding: poor maiden handicapper: well beaten last 3 starts: best at up to 1½m. *N. Bycroft*   40

SWAN HUNTER 4 b.c. Sharrood (USA) 124 – Cache (Bustino 136) [1996 73: 11.1g* 12d² 11.6g6 14.8d⁶ 12m 1997 a12g a12g a12g⁴ 11.9g⁶ 14d² 12d 16d² 14.1s 15.8g⁵ 11.8d* 12s* a14.8g* a12g* Dec 6] leggy, angular colt: bad mover: fair performer: was becoming disappointing, but found a new lease of life towards end of year, winning claimers at Leicester and Catterick in October and handicaps at Wolverhampton in November and December: stays 2m: acts on fibresand, raced mainly on dead ground or softer on turf. *D. J. S. Cosgrove*   72 a78

SWAN ISLAND 3 ch.f. Hubbly Bubbly (USA) – Green's Cassatt (USA) 74 (Apalachee (USA) 137) [1996 62: 7g⁶ 7f 8.1s⁶ 7m² 1997 8.2m 10g⁵ a6g² a7g³ 8f 8m⁴ 7.1g 8fᵇ Sep 29] tall filly: fair handicapper. left B. Palling's stable after fifth start: stays 1m: acts on firm ground and fibresand: well beaten in blinkers: often bandaged: refused to enter stalls once at 2 yrs: none too consistent. *W. M. Brisbourne*   55 a65

SWAN LANE (USA) 3 b.f. Theatrical 128 – Fortunate Facts (USA) (Sir Ivor 135) [1996 NR 1997 8f 8.1m⁶ Jul 30] $235,000Y: third foal: half-sister to French 10.5f winner Amiral Horty (by Polish Navy) and a winner in USA by Seeking The Gold: dam, minor stakes winner in USA and placed in Grade 3 8.5f event, out of half-sister to Exceller and Capote: signs of ability but no worthwhile form: sent to UAE. *J. H. M. Gosden*   –

SWANMORE LADY (IRE) 2 b.f. (Mar 9) Forzando 122 – Steffi 67 (Precocious 126) [1997 5g 5m³ 5d 5g³ 6g⁵ a5g 6m* 5m² 6d 5.2f a5g² a5s⁵ Nov 28] 4,000Y: fourth foal: half-sister to a winner in Spain by Sharpo: dam 1m winner: modest performer: won nursery at Leicester in September: good second in similar events at Redcar and Lingfield: at least as effective at 5f as 6f: acts on good to firm ground and equitrack, well beaten on fibresand and dead ground: usually races prominently. *S. C. Williams*   57

SWAYBUS 2 ch.f. (Mar 8) Pursuit of Love 124 – Gong 84 (Bustino 136) [1997 7m⁴ 7.5g a8.5g Oct 6] 15,000Y: strong, good-bodied filly: first foal: dam 1¼m winner who stayed 1½m, half-sister to smart middle-distance stayer Waterfield: soundly beaten in maidens: has given trouble at stalls. *M. Johnston*   –

SWEET AMORET 4 b.f. Forzando 122 – Primrose Way 59 (Young Generation 129) [1996 52: 10d⁵ a9.4g* a12g⁵ a8g a8.5g 8m⁶ 7m⁶ 8m² 10m⁵ 8g 10.1m 6.9d 8g a10g² a10g⁶ a10g⁶ 1997 a13g a10g a8g a10g⁶ Feb 25] workmanlike filly: modest performer: soundly beaten in 1997. *P. Howling*   –

SWEET BETTSIE 3 b.f. Presidium 124 – Sweet And Sure (Known Fact (USA) –
135) [1996 72: 5.7d 6s⁵ 1997 6g 6s May 17] leggy filly: showed ability second start
at 2 yrs: no form in 1997. *A. G. Foster*

SWEETCHILDOFMINE 3 gr.f. Mon Tresor 113 – Sincerely Yours (Kind of –
Hush 118) [1996 NR 1997 a8g 10s⁶ 10g 10s Jun 23] 1,000Y: third foal: dam ran a
few times: signs of ability but no worthwhile form: sent to Italy. *H. Akbary*

SWEET CISEAUX (IRE) 4 b.g. Be My Guest (USA) 126 – Wild Abandon 47
(USA) (Graustark) [1996 9d 7f* 7g⁵ 7m 7.8g⁶ 7.8g⁶ 6g⁵ 1997 a8g 10.8m⁵ 8f 10g 10g
7d 12.1m Jul 25] ex-Irish gelding: half-brother to 2 winners in USA by Mr Prospector: dam, ran once in USA, half-sister to several useful winners from family of
Shareef Dancer: modest handicapper (rated 59) for D. Weld in 1996, winning at
Tipperary: poor at best in Britain (trained fourth to sixth starts by M. Heaton-Ellis):
stays 11f: acts on firm ground: tried blinkered: joined P. Bowen, and won over
hurdles (27f) in October. *B. J. Llewellyn*

SWEET CONTRALTO 3 b.f. Danehill (USA) 126 – Sweet Soprano 80 (High 89
Line 125) [1996 NR 1997 7.1d* 8s a8.5g 8g² 9m² 9g* 10d 10.3d³ Nov 7] 75,000Y:
close-coupled filly: sister to smart 1¼m and 1½m winner Alriffa and half-sister to 2
winners: dam 7f (at 2 yrs) and 11f winner: fairly useful performer: won maiden at
Haydock in May and handicap at Goodwood in August: stays 1¼m: acts on good to
firm and dead ground, poor efforts on soft and fibresand. *D. R. Loder*

SWEET DREAMS 2 b.f. (Mar 31) Selkirk (USA) 129 – Ahohoney 118 67 p
(Ahonoora 122) [1997 7.1m 7g 8.2g⁵ Sep 23] 13,000Y: well-grown, leggy filly: sister
to 3-y-o Dulcinea and half-sister to 3 winners in France, including smart 1m winner
(stays 1¼m) Amato (by Kendor): dam 6f and 1m winner here at 2 yrs, later 10.5f
winner in France: modest form in maidens, not knocked about: outpaced final 2f
when fifth to Rambling Rose at Nottingham: shapes as though will stay at least 1¼m:
swished tail in paddock on debut: should still do better. *J. L. Dunlop*

SWEET FORTUNE (USA) 3 b. or br.c. Lear Fan (USA) 130 – Sweet Delilah 92
(USA) (Super Concorde (USA) 128) [1996 NR 1997 8g³ 7g* 7g 8g* 8m Sep 21]
$90,000Y: strong colt: seventh foal: brother to Grade 3 9.5f winner Super Fan and
half-brother to 1¼m and 13f winner Naseer (by Hero's Honor): dam 1m winner in
USA: fairly useful efforts when winning maiden at Warwick in July and minor event
at Thirsk in August: no comparable time: stays 1m: sent to UAE. *M. R. Stoute*

SWEET GLOW (FR) 10 b.g. Crystal Glitters (USA) 127 – Very Sweet (Belly- –
pha 130) [1996 NR 1997 14.1m Apr 11] one-time high-class hurdler: lightly raced
and little form on flat since 1994. *M. C. Pipe*

SWEET MAGIC 6 ch.g. Sweet Monday 122 – Charm Bird 60 (Daring March 68
116) [1996 87: 6m 5m⁴ 5m⁵ 6m 5m 5.2m 1997 5g 5g 5g 5m 5g 5m³ 5s* 5m⁶ 5d 5d
Nov 7] lengthy, plain gelding: tends to look dull in coat: just a fair handicapper in
1997, and inconsistent to boot: won at Sandown in August, making virtually all:
usually races at 5f: acts on firm and soft ground: blinkered (tailed off) fifth start.
P. Howling

SWEET MATE 5 ch.g. Komaite (USA) – Be My Sweet 78 (Galivanter 131) 55
[1996 –, a62: a6g⁴ a7g* a7g² a7g⁴ a7g⁴ a6g 7g a8g 1997 a7s³ a8g a6g⁶ a6g⁴ a6g³
5.1g⁴ 6.1d* a6g* a7g a7g 6.1d a7g Jul 10] workmanlike gelding: has a round action:
modest handicapper: trained first 2 starts by Martyn Meade: won at Nottingham
(apprentices) and Southwell in May: best form at 6f/7f: acts on fibresand and on
firm and dead ground: usually wears adapted (one-eyed) blinkers: has run well when
sweating: inconsistent, and somewhat wayward. *S. R. Bowring*

SWEETNESS HERSELF 4 ch.f. Unfuwain (USA) 131 – No Sugar Baby (FR) 106
(Crystal Glitters (USA) 127) [1996 89p: 10g³ 8.3s⁴ 9.9m⁴ 10m 10m 11.8g* 14s*
12.1s* 14.1s* 16.5s* 1997 16.2s* 13.4v⁴ 13.3s³ 16g² 16.1s² 14.6m⁵ 18g 16m³
14.6d* 15v* Dec 1] tall filly: made into a useful performer in 1997, winning minor
events at Haydock in March and Doncaster in November and listed race at Maisons-
Laffitte in December: also ran well when second in Group 3 race at Baden-Baden
(1½ lengths behind Camp David) and Northumberland Plate at Newcastle (beaten a
length by Windsor Castle) and when fifth in Park Hill Stakes at Doncaster (5½

Daihatsu Conditions Stakes, Haydock—Sweetness Herself starts her season off in style

lengths behind Book At Bedtime): stays 16.5f: acts on good to firm and heavy ground: held up: game and genuine: a credit to her trainer. *M. J. Ryan*

SWEET NOTE (IRE)   3 ch.f. La Grange Music 111 – Screenable (USA) (Silent   45 d Screen (USA)) [1996 NR 1997 8.3d⁶ 7g 9.2s³ 8d 9.2m⁶ 9.2g⁶ 8.3g⁵ 8.3s 11.1g 8.3d 12.1g⁴ 9.2g⁴ 13.1s Oct 13] 5,000Y: smallish filly: half-sister to 3 winners, including 1¼m winner Barrymore (by Robellino): dam minor winner around 1m in USA: poor maiden: stays 1½m: acts on soft ground: inconsistent. *Miss L. A. Perratt*

SWEET PATOOPIE   3 b.f. Indian Ridge 123 – Patriotic 43 (Hotfoot 126) [1996   – NR 1997 6m⁵ 7s⁶ May 7] 15,000Y: leggy, quite good-topped filly: fifth foal: dam, 13.8f and 2¼m winner, half-sister to Rostova (dam of User Friendly): burly and green, some promise when fifth of 8 in maiden at Pontefract in April: got very tired when well beaten on soft ground only subsequent outing. *B. Hanbury*

SWEET REWARD   2 ch.c. (Apr 17) Beveled (USA) – Sweet Revival 41 (Claude   73 Monet (USA) 121) [1997 5.1d⁶ 5s³ 6d* 6s⁵ Jun 30] leggy colt: shows knee action: first foal: dam, 1¼m winner at 5 yrs, stayed 1½m: fair form: won maiden at Leicester in June: much stiffer task when fifth in minor event at Pontefract, wandering under pressure: will stay beyond 6f: has raced only on a good to soft/soft ground. *J. G. Smyth-Osbourne*

SWEET ROSIE (IRE)   2 b.f. (Apr 23) Petardia 113 – White's Pet (Mummy's Pet   60 125) [1997 a5g³ 5m 5g² 5g Jul 7] 2,200Y: seventh foal: closely related to 1990 2-y-o 1m winner Encore Au Bon (by Petong), later also successful in Italy, and half-sister to a winner in Italy by Mazilier: dam unraced: showed modicum of ability on debut on fibresand and when second in maiden at Lingfield: has flashed tail under pressure. *R. Boss*

943

SWEET SENORITA 2 b.f. (May 25) Young Senor (USA) 113 – Sweet N' –
Twenty 74 (High Top 131) [1997 6f⁶ 6m 7m⁵ Jul 28] first foal: dam 11.7f and
13.8f winner, also prolific winner over hurdles: no form in sellers. *M. Madgwick*

SWEET SEVENTEEN 4 gr.f. Touch of Grey 90 – Westminster Waltz (Dance In –
Time (CAN)) [1996 –: 5g 6m⁵ 5m 1997 a7g 8.5s 6.9m 8s⁵ 11.6m 8m⁴ 10g Aug 27]
workmanlike filly: bad maiden. *H. J. Collingridge*

SWEET SORROW (IRE) 2 b.f. (Apr 15) Lahib (USA) 129 – So Long Boys 71 p
(FR) (Beldale Flutter (USA) 130) [1997 6m⁵ 7m⁴ Sep 9] 15,000Y: big,
useful-looking filly: fourth foal: half-sister to 3-y-o Farewell My Love: dam, Italian
maiden possibly best up to 6f, half-sister to smart French pair Common Grounds
(over 6f/7f at 2 yrs) and Angel In My Heart (at 1m/1¼m): fair form in maidens at
Newbury and Lingfield, not knocked about once outpaced behind Jibe on latter
course: shapes as though will be suited by further than 7f: open to progress. *C. F. Wall*

SWEET SUPPOSIN (IRE) 6 b.h. Posen (USA) – Go Honey Go (General –
Assembly (USA)) [1996 –, a81d: a9.4g a8g⁵ a10g² a10g* a10g* a8g⁶ a12g* 10s a68
a9.4g* a8.5g² a9.4g⁴ a9.4g a9.4g⁶ a12g⁴ a8g⁵ a12g a9.4g 1997 a10g³ a10g* a10g
a10g⁵ a9.4g⁴ a10g* a10g⁵ a8g³ a10g⁶ a8g³ a10g³ 8g⁶ a8g⁵ a10g⁵ a10g² a10g⁴ Dec
10] lengthy horse: fair handicapper on the all-weather, lightly raced and little form
on turf nowadays: won at Lingfield in February and March: ran at least respectably
most starts after: effective at 1m to 1½m: formerly blinkered, visored nowadays: no
easy ride (normally held up) and goes well for L. Dettori. *C. A. Dwyer*

SWEET WILHELMINA 4 b.f. Indian Ridge 123 – Henpot (IRE) 68 (Alzao 80
(USA) 117) [1996 65: 8.5g 7m 8g² a7s 1997 a8g* a7g* 8s 8g* 8.5m² 8d⁴ 7g 8d² 8m³
8g Oct 18] sturdy filly: fairly useful performer: won 2 minor events at Lingfield in
February and handicap at Leicester in May: good placed efforts in handicaps at Ascot
and Newbury in September: stays 1m: acts on good to firm and dead going and the
all-weather. *Lord Huntingdon*

SWIFT 3 ch.g. Sharpo 132 – Three Terns (USA) (Arctic Tern (USA) 126) [1996 73
61: 7m 7m 5f 5m⁶ 5g* 5.2g 5g⁶ 1997 a8g² a7g³ a8.5g* 8.2m 6g³ a6g³ 6s 6m* 6g 7g*
6d⁵ 8g⁶ 7g⁶ 8g² 7m 8.5d⁶ a7g⁵ 8.2s⁴ a7g⁶ 7m Nov 1] strong, lengthy gelding: poor
mover: fair performer: won minor event at Wolverhampton in March and handicaps
at Ripon in May and Redcar in June: effective at 6f to 8.5f: acts on the all-weather
and on good to firm and dead going: has won from front but usually held up nowadays.
M. J. Polglase

SWIFT ALLIANCE 2 b.c. (Mar 2) Belong To Me (USA) – One Quick Bid 90
(USA) (Commemorate (USA)) [1997 6s 6m* 6m 6g⁶ Jul 9] 34,000Y: robust,
heavy-bodied colt: first foal: dam, winning sprinter at 4 yrs in USA, half-sister to
very smart 1¼m performer Tamayaz: sire (by Danzig) Grade 3-winning sprinter in
USA: fairly useful form: won maiden at Folkestone in May: highly tried afterwards,
better effort when under 9 lengths eighth of 15 in Coventry Stakes at Royal Ascot:
tended to hang left final start: shapes as though will be at least as effective at 7f/1m as
6f: joined Lady Herries. *R. Akehurst*

SWIFT GULLIVER (IRE) 3 ch.c. Gulch (USA) – Aminata 98 (Glenstal 110
(USA) 118) [1996 6g 8g² 7g* 7m* 8g 1997 8g³ 9s⁵ 8g* 10g 6m 7g Oct 18] big,
useful-looking colt: smart form on his nds day in 1997: won Desmond Stakes at the
Curragh in August by ¾ length from Dangerous Diva: stays 1m: blinkered last 2
starts (creditable eighth in Diadem Stakes first occasion): has got on edge, and not
easiest of rides: sent to USA. *J. S. Bolger, Ireland*

SWIFT SOVEREIGN 3 gr.g. Petong 126 – Flitteriss Park 62§ (Beldale Flutter –
(USA) 130) [1996 NR 1997 7.1d⁵ 7m Aug 21] 30,000Y: tall gelding: fifth foal:
brother to useful 1992 2-y-o 6f winner Son Pardo and half-brother to 3 winning
sprinters, including 4-y-o Atraf and 5-y-o Emerging Market: dam untrustworthy 1m
winner: always behind in maidens: sold 3,500 gns, and sent to Germany.
J. H. M. Gosden

SWIFT TIME 2 b.f. (Apr 27) Timeless Times (USA) 99 – Bustling Around 50 d
(Bustino 136) [1997 5m 5.1d 5d² 5g⁵ 5.1g 5.1g⁶ 6g Aug 22] small filly: first foal:
dam poor novice hurdler/chaser: second in seller at Doncaster in May: well held
afterwards. *M. R. Bosley*

SWIFTWAY 3 ch.g. Anshan 119 – Solemn Occasion (USA) (Secreto (USA) 128) 64
[1996 62: 7m⁶ 9f³ 10g 1997 10.3m⁵ 10m 10m⁶ 12g⁵ 12.3g² 12.3m 16.2m³ 16.1m
16.2d³ Aug 14] tall, plain gelding: modest maiden handicapper: stays 2m: acts on
firm and dead ground: inconsistent. *K. W. Hogg, Isle of Man*

SWING ALONG 2 ch.f. (Mar 23) Alhijaz 122 – So It Goes 73 (Free State 125) 86 p
[1997 6d² Oct 17] 21,000Y: strong, useful-looking filly: fourth foal: half-sister to
2-y-o 5f winners Aybeegirl and Eleuthera (both by Mazilier), and 1½m winner
Ttyfran (by Petong): dam, 2-y-o 6f winner, is half-sister to smart Italian 5f to 1m
winner Melbury Lad: 50/1, head second of 20 to Atuf in maiden at Newmarket, soon
prominent and running on strongly, though green: sure to improve and win a race.
C. F. Wall

SWING AND BRAVE (IRE) 3 b.f. Arctic Tern (USA) 126 – Sweet Snow 70
(USA) (Lyphard (USA) 132) [1996 –: 10v⁶ 1997 10g* 10m⁶ May 18] won 12-runner
maiden at Milan in April: beaten over 10 lengths in minor event there month later:
should stay beyond 1¼m. *Lord Huntingdon*

SWINGING SIXTIES (IRE) 6 b.g. Fairy King (USA) – La Bella Fontana –
(Lafontaine (USA) 117) [1996 65: 9.7s* 10d 11.1s² 1997 a13g Mar 4] tall, lengthy
gelding: fair handicapper at 5 yrs: well beaten only start in 1997. *G. L. Moore*

SWINGING THE BLUES (IRE) 3 b.c. Bluebird (USA) 125 – Winsong 66
Melody (Music Maestro 119) [1996 55+: 6m 7m 1997 8.3g⁴ 10s 8d 8.2s⁵ 10d Oct 28]
useful-looking colt: fair handicapper: well beaten last 2 outings: stays 8.3f: acts on
dead going. *R. Akehurst*

SWING SISTER 2 b.f. (Feb 22) Rock City 120 – Santa Magdalena (Hard Fought 81
125) [1997 6.1g* 7d² 7.3g⁶ 8d⁴ Nov 7] 10,000Y: close-coupled, unfurnished filly:
fifth foal: half-sister to useful stayer Ptoto (by Mtoto) and fairly useful 1¼m winner
(stayed 1¾m) Bob's Ploy (by Deploy): dam won in Belgium: fairly useful form: won
maiden at Nottingham in September: good second in minor event at Leicester
following month: stiffish tasks and not discredited final 2 starts: shapes as though
will stay 1¼m: raced only on good/dead ground: sold 19,000 gns in December.
P. R. Webber

SWINGTIME 2 ch.f. (Mar 27) Beveled (USA) – Superfina (USA) (Fluorescent –
Light (USA)) [1997 7d 7d Oct 27] sixth foal: dam unraced: well beaten in maidens at
Leicester and Lingfield. *A. G. Foster*

SWING WEST (USA) 3 b.c. Gone West (USA) – Danlu (USA) (Danzig (USA)) 65
[1996 –: 8.1s 1997 8g⁶ a7g⁵ 8g⁵ 10.8s² 11.5m³ 12g Aug 2] leggy colt: fair maiden
handicapper: stays 11.5f: acts on good to firm and soft ground: won novice hurdle in
December for P. Eccles. *P. F. I. Cole*

SWINO 3 b.g. Forzando 122 – St Helena (Monsanto (FR) 121) [1996 77: 5s³ 5g² 87 d
5g² 5g² 5.1g⁶ 5d² 5g² 5m² 5f* 6d 1997 5m⁴ 5s⁴ 5g 5.1d⁶ 5d² 6m 5d 6.1s 5.1m³ 5m
5.1s⁶ 5d 5.1g⁶ 6.1g⁶ 6s⁴ 5g* 6d 5d⁵ a6g a6g Nov 21] leggy, unfurnished gelding:
unimpressive mover: fairly useful in first half of 1997, just fair at best later: won
minor event at Redcar in October: stays 6f: acts on firm and soft going, well held on
fibresand: tried blinkered and visored, no improvement. *P. D. Evans*

SWISS COAST (IRE) 3 b.g. Mujadil (USA) 119 – Rose A Village (River 43
Beauty 105) [1996 74: 5.9g² 6m⁵ 5m³ 5f³ 6f⁴ 6m² 7f² 7.5m 1997 a8.5g 8.3d⁴ 7g⁶
7.5s⁶ 6m 6m 10m a12g Dec 26] leggy gelding: has a quick action: most disappointing
maiden, including in sellers: trained by N. Tinkler first 6 starts: tried blinkered/
visored. *R. T. Juckes*

SWISS LAW 3 b.c. Machiavellian (USA) 123 – Seductress 94 (Known Fact 108
(USA) 135) [1996 88p: 6m² 7m 1997 7m* 8g⁴ 8m 7g² 8m² 7g² Oct 25] quite
attractive colt: useful performer: won minor event at Newmarket in May: left Saeed
bin Suroor after third outing: ran well all starts for new yard, first past post in
handicap at Goodwood (demoted having hampered neck second Omaha City) on first
of them and finishing 1¾ lengths second to Jo Mell in minor event at Doncaster on
final start: likely to prove best up to 1m: yet to race on ground softer than good: has
run well when sweating. *J. H. M. Gosden*

SWITCH TO SENATE 3 b.c. Sharpo 132 – La Reine de France (Queen's –
Hussar 124) [1996 NR 1997 8.3s 10g 10s³ 9.7g Jul 9] no form. *D. J. S. Cosgrove*

SWOOSH 2 gr.g. (Apr 4) Absalom 128 – Valldemosa 81 (Music Boy 124) [1997 61
5d⁶ 5s⁴ 6g² 6.1g³ 6m Jun 2] 8,200Y: close-coupled gelding: fifth foal: brother to a
poor maiden sprinter and half-brother to 4-y-o Forzara: dam best at 5f: modest form
including in seller: stays 6f: blinkered final start. *B. J. Meehan*

SWORD ARM 3 b.g. Be My Guest (USA) 126 – Gai Bulga 110 (Kris 135) [1996 86
77: 7g⁴ 7.6d⁴ 8.2m² 1997 a8.5g* 10.3m 9g³ 8g³ 8m* 8m* 10m 8m³ 7.3d 7m 8m³ Oct
23] lengthy gelding: good mover: fairly useful performer: won maiden at Wolverhampton in March and handicap at Salisbury and minor event at Bath in May: seems
best around 1m: acts on good to firm going, below form on dead: visored 7 of last 8
starts, also successful when not: consistent: sold 28,000 gns, and joined D. Vienna in
USA. *R. Charlton*

SWORDKING (IRE) 8 ch.g. Kris 135 – Reine Mathilde (USA) 123 (Vaguely –
Noble 140) [1996 41: a14.8g a16g³ a16g³ a12g⁶ a16g³ a14.8g³ a14g² a16.2g² a16g⁵
1997 a14g⁶ a16.2g Jul 25] poor handicapper: well beaten in 1997. *J. L. Harris*

SWYNFORD CHARMER 3 ch.g. Charmer 123 – Qualitairess 49 (Kampala –
120) [1996 –: 7m a6g a7g 1997 a7g 10g 12s a7g Nov 18] plain gelding: no form,
including in sellers and blinkers: left J. Bottomley after second start. *J. Hetherton*

SWYNFORD DREAM 4 b.g. Statoblest 120 – Qualitair Dream 80 (Dreams To 84 d
Reality (USA) 113) [1996 92: 5g 5m² 5m 5m 5g 5m 5m⁶ 5.1d² 5m* 5d 5g³ 5g 1997
5g 5.1v⁶ 5g⁶ 5m 5d⁶ 5g 5m 5m 5d³ 5g 5g 5d a5g Dec 8] workmanlike gelding: fairly
useful handicapper at best: mostly below form in 1997, leaving J. Bottomley's stable
after eighth start: speedy, and raced only at 5f: acts on good to firm and dead ground:
well held only in try in blinkers: usually races prominently. *J. Hetherton*

SWYNFORD SUPREME 4 ch.g. Statoblest 120 – Comtec Princess 73 (Gulf –
Pearl 117) [1996 –: 9m⁵ 10.1m³ 10m 10g 11f a12g 1997 a16g Feb 14] big, plain
gelding: no worthwhile form: tried blinkered. *J. F. Bottomley*

SYCAMORE BOY (USA) 3 ch.g. Woodman (USA) 126 – Kafiyah (USA) 41 76
(Shadeed (USA) 135) [1996 67: 6f⁵ 1997 8.3g⁵ 8m² 8.1m⁴ 8v⁴ 10g Oct 24]
good-bodied gelding: fair maiden: easily best effort when second at Newmarket in
August: likely to prove best up to 1m: carries head high and may not be genuine. *Lord
Huntingdon*

SYCAMORE LODGE (IRE) 6 ch.g. Thatching 131 – Bell Tower 98 –
(Lyphard's Wish (FR) 124) [1996 74: 6s² 7s³ 7.5m³ 8g⁴ a8g⁴ 7m² 7g⁵ 7g³ 7.1m⁵ 8f⁶
6g* 7m⁶ 1997 6d 8.1g 8s a8g Nov 24] lengthy gelding: fair handicapper: well below
form in 1997. *M. A. Peill*

SYLPHIDE 2 b.f. (May 28) Ballet Royal (USA) – Shafayif 43 (Ela-Mana-Mou –
132) [1997 7g Aug 13] first foal: dam, poor maiden on flat, untrustworthy winning plater over hurdles: sire still running over jumps: behind in claimer.
A. J. Chamberlain

SYLVAN CLOUD 2 ch.f. (Feb 20) Sylvan Express 117 – Kept Waiting 75 –
(Tanfirion 110) [1997 5g 5m a6g³ a6g⁵ 7g 6d⁶ 5m Jul 21] 500Y: third reported foal:
half-sister to a winner in Czech Republic by Daring March: dam sprinting half-sister
to smart performer up to 9f Cloud of Dust: looks of little account. *C. W. Fairhurst*

SYLVAN DANCER (IRE) 3 b. or br.f. Dancing Dissident (USA) 119 – 60
Unspoiled (Tina's Pet 121) [1996 64: 5g² 5g³ 6m 5g 1997 5g⁵ 5d 5.1m⁴ 6d³ 6g 6.1g
6.1s a6g⁴ a7g Dec 22] modest maiden handicapper: left C. Wall after seventh start:
stays 6f: acts on good to firm and dead going and on fibresand: somewhat temperamental: none too consistent. *G. C. Bravery*

SYLVANIA LIGHTS 3 b.f. Emarati (USA) 74 – Harmony Park 55 (Music Boy – §
124) [1996 –§: a5g 5m 1997 a7g May 12] of little account. *A. G. Newcombe*

SYLVAN JUBILACION 3 b.g. Sylvan Express 117 – This Sensation 48 –
(Balidar 133) [1996 –: 7m 7d 1997 10g 11.5m 12m Aug 5] no form. *P. Mitchell*

SYLVAN PRINCESS 4 b.f. Sylvan Express 117 – Ela-Yianni-Mou 73 (Anfield 73
117) [1996 67: 11.1g⁵ 10d 8m⁶ 8f⁴ 7g³ 7.1m* 7m* 8g* 8m⁴ 8f⁸ 8f³ 8m* 7g⁶ 8m 8m
1997 8f* 8g 8m⁵ 8d² 7g 8.5m 8f² 8g a10g Jul 11] leggy filly: fair handicapper: won at
Leicester in April: inconsistent afterwards: stays 1m well: acts on firm and dead
ground: best without blinkers. *D. J. S. Cosgrove*

TAC

SYLVA PARADISE (IRE) 4 b.g. Dancing Dissident (USA) 119 – Brentsville 105
(USA) (Arctic Tern (USA) 126) [1996 98+: 8d 7f² 7g⁴ 7m³ 5f² 6f* 5m² 6m 5.6m² 6m
6m⁴ 1997 6g³ 5m 6f⁶ 5g⁶ 5d 5d 6m 5.6m 5.2g 5m Sep 28] smallish, lengthy gelding:
useful performer: best efforts when third in listed race at Newmarket (1¾ lengths
behind Monaassib) and sixth in Temple Stakes at Sandown (2 lengths behind Croft
Pool) on fourth start: mostly well held otherwise in 1997: will prove best up to 7f:
successful on dead going, very best efforts on good ground or firmer. *C. E. Brittain*

SYMONDS INN 3 ch.c. In The Wings 128 – Shining Eyes (USA) (Mr Prospector 103
(USA)) [1996 96: 6m³ 7m² 8g³ 1997 10.4g* 12g Jun 7] rangy colt: useful performer:
won minor event at York in May by 3½ lengths from Shaya, despite (not for first
time) looking tricky ride, hanging, carrying head awkwardly and flashing tail:
respectable 16½ lengths seventh of 13 to Benny The Dip in the Derby at Epsom:
not seen out afterwards: stays 1½m: raced only on good or good to firm ground.
J. G. FitzGerald

T

TAALLUF (USA) 2 b.f. (Feb 7) Hansel (USA) – Tatwij (USA) 94 (Topsider 82
(USA)) [1997 5d³ 6.1m² 5.7f² 8g⁵ Oct 24] sturdy, angular filly: has a round action:
fourth foal: half-sister to 6f winner Masafah (by Cadeaux Genereux): dam, 2-y-o 5f
winner who probably stayed 1m, half-sister to good US 2-y-o of 1987 Tejano: fairly
useful maiden: best efforts second (off course over 2 months after) and final starts:
may well prove best up to 1m. *Major W. R. Hern*

TA ARUF (USA) 2 ch.f. (Mar 1) A P Indy (USA) – Mashaarif (USA) (Mr Pros- 78
pector (USA)) [1997 8s² 8.2d⁴ Oct 30] compact filly: poor walker: fourth foal:
closely related to 5-y-o Tajar: dam unraced daughter of Larida, dam also of Magic of
Life: sire (by Seattle Slew) top-class US middle-distance performer: very much in
need of race, 1½ lengths second to Mantusis in maiden at Leicester, soon well in rear
but improving to lead penultimate furlong: below that form, again soon behind, when
fourth to wide-margin winner Almandab in similar event at Nottingham 2 weeks
later: should stay 1¼m+. *D. Morley*

TABASCO (IRE) 2 b.f. (Mar 26) Salse (USA) 128 – El Taranda 61 (Ela-Mana- 72 p
Mou 132) [1997 6m 7g⁵ Oct 18] IR 5,600F, 38,000Y: leggy, unfurnished filly: has
scope: second foal: dam maiden half-sister to very smart (up to 1½m) Young Buster:
fair form in minor event at Ascot and Redcar maiden in autumn: should do better at
1m+. *M. R. Channon*

TABASCO JAZZ 3 b.f. Salse (USA) 128 – Melody Park 104 (Music Boy 124) 65
[1996 NR 1997 7m³ 7g⁵ 7m² 7.3s 7.1g 6m 6g 7g⁴ 7g⁶ 7g 7m³ 8f⁴ 10f 10s⁶ 9.7d a9.4g⁶ a–
Dec 6] rather leggy filly: fair maiden handicapper: best at 7f/1m: acts on firm ground:
sometimes bandaged: tried blinkered: none too consistent. *B. J. Meehan*

TABERANN (IRE) 3 b.c. Doyoun 124 – Tabessa (USA) (Shahrastani (USA) 87 p
135) [1996 NR 1997 10s* Oct 14] first foal: dam Irish 7f/1m winner: 6/1, won
9-runner maiden at Ayr in October on debut by 2 lengths from Ricardo, going away at
finish: will stay 1½m: sold (to go to Australia) 88,000 gns in October. *L. M. Cumani*

TABORITE (USA) 3 gr.g. Gulch (USA) – Ziska (USA) 87 (Danzig (USA)) –
[1996 NR 1997 10.4s 10.5g⁵ 11.9s Oct 15] 6,800 3-y-o: big, long-backed gelding:
second foal: dam, 1m winner, out of champion US 2-y-o filly Heavenly Cause, later
successful in Kentucky Oaks: tailed off in maidens. *E. J. Alston*

TACHYCARDIA 5 ch.m. Weldnaas (USA) 112 – Gold Ducat 74 (Young Gene- 40
ration 129) [1996 49, a43: 5f 6m⁵ 5.3m⁴ 5f 5m a5g⁴ a6g 1997 a6g a6g a6g⁴ a6g* a47
a6g* a6g a6g³ a6g 5.3f 7m 6f 6s⁵ 5d⁴ 6m⁴ 6.9m² 5m⁵ 6f a5g⁵ a6g⁴ Dec 4] rather
sparely-made mare: poor handicapper: won at Lingfield (twice) in January: has form
at 8.5f, raced up to 7f nowadays: acts on firm and soft going: has run well for 7-lb
claimer: usually a front runner. *R. J. O'Sullivan*

947

William Hill Great St Wilfrid Handicap, Ripon—Tadeo is clear on the far side

TADEO 4 ch.g. Primo Dominie 121 – Royal Passion 78 (Ahonoora 122) [1996 105
107: 5.1g³ 5m 5f 5m⁵ 5.1m² 5m 6m 5m 5d 5s* 5d* 5g 6s⁵ 1997 5.1v 5d² 6m⁵ 6.1s 5g
5m* 5g³ 6m 5m⁴ 6m* 6s 5.6m 6g 5.1g* 5d 5g Oct 25] small, strong gelding: useful
performer: won handicaps at Newmarket in July and Ripon (Great St Wilfrid by ¾
length from Emerging Market) in August, and minor event at Nottingham (made all
to beat Crofters Ceilidh a neck) in September: effective at 5f to 6f: acts on firm and
soft going: usually front runner/races prominently. *M. Johnston*

TADWIGA 2 b.f. (Feb 25) Fairy King (USA) – Euromill (Shirley Heights 130) 98
[1997 6s³ 6g² 6.3d* 6m² 6g 7g² Oct 18] IR 25,500Y: smallish, sturdy filly: fifth foal:
sister to useful Bartok, 6f/7f winner at 2 yrs in Ireland, later successful at up to 1¼m
in Italy: dam, Irish middle-distance stayer, out of Irish and Yorkshire Oaks-placed
Green Lucia, herself half-sister to Old Vic: useful form: won Goffs £100,000
Challenge at the Curragh in June by 2 lengths from Soft Touch: much better efforts
when second in listed race at Kempton and Rockfel Stakes at Newmarket, switched
and staying on strongly to be beaten 1¼ lengths by Name of Love in latter: will stay
1m. *R. Hannon*

TAEL OF SILVER 5 b.m. Today And Tomorrow 78 – Schula 81 (Kala Shikari 51
125) [1996 70, a43: a6g a6g 5g⁵ 6.1m a6g 7g* 8m² 9m⁴ 8.2m 7m⁵ 7g 7.1s⁴ 8.2g⁶ 8.1s a–
a7g² a8g 1997 8.5m 8.3m 8f 7m⁵ 8f² a8.5g 8d⁵ 7f 8.2d² a10g Nov 25] leggy mare:
modest performer on turf: poor on all-weather: stays 9f: acts on firm and dead
ground: tried blinkered/visored: inconsistent. *A. Bailey*

TAFFS WELL 4 b.g. Dowsing (USA) 124 – Zahiah 90 (So Blessed 130) [1996 79
NR 1997 6m 6g² 6g⁴ 7.1m² 7m 7g³ Oct 24] small gelding: half-brother to several
winners, notably useful 6f to 1m performer Options Open (by Then Again): dam
2-y-o 6f winner: fair maiden: best efforts when placed in handicaps fourth and final
starts: will stay 1m: raced only on good/good to firm going: sold 21,000 gns in
October. *R. Akehurst*

TAGATAY 4 b.g. Nomination 125 – Salala 83 (Connaught 130) [1996 44: a7g⁶ 8m –
12m* a14g 1997 16s 12.3m 11f May 1] good-bodied gelding: poor handicapper at up
to 1½m in 1996: soundly beaten at 4 yrs. *M. J. Camacho*

TAHARA (IRE) 3 ch.f. Caerleon (USA) 132 – Tarwiya (IRE) 103 (Dominion –
123) [1996 NR 1997 6g 7.1m⁵ Aug 14] first foal: dam, Irish 2-y-o 5f and 7f winner,
third in Irish 1000 Guineas: signs of just a little ability in maidens at Newmarket and
Sandown: sold 17,000 gns in December. *L. M. Cumani*

TAILWIND 3 ch.g. Clantime 101 – Casbar Lady 79 (Native Bazaar 122) [1996 62
64: 5.1m⁶ 5g 5m 6g⁴ 5.2m² 5m³ 6g⁵ 7.3s 1997 6d 6m* 6f 5.9m³ a6g³ 6m a7g a8g⁴
a7g Dec 18] leggy, workmanlike gelding: modest performer: won maiden at Redcar

948

in May: ran well when in frame in handicaps and claimer afterwards: stays 1m: acts on good to firm ground and the all-weather, well below form on going softer than good: has pulled hard/tended to hang: inconsistent. *W. R. Muir*

TAIPAN (IRE)   5 b.h. Last Tycoon 131 – Alidiva 105 (Chief Singer 131)   124
[1996 108: 11.9g* 12m^2 12s* 12g* 1997 10g^3 12f^3 12g^3 12.5s* 12g* 12m^4
10d* Nov 9]

Matters European dominate the political agenda in Britain as the millennium draws near. You can be a europhobe, a eurosceptic or a europhile, it seems, depending on your opinion of EMU, the ecu and, erm, ERM. We don't know trainer John Dunlop's views on the wider picture, but in terms of racing there can be no doubt that he's firmly in the camp of the europhiles. His 'have horse, will travel' approach has reaped handsome dividends over the years and in 1997 this was nowhere better illustrated than with Taipan, who won a Group 2 race in France and Group 1 races in Germany and Italy.

Taipan has got better with each season, winning an ordinary maiden at two years, making into a fairly useful handicapper at three and landing two handicaps and a listed contest (at Lyon Parilly) at four. He had joint trouble after the last-named and it was eleven months before he reappeared in the latest season. His first three starts failed to provide another win but showed that he'd continued his improvement. Third placings in the Tattersalls Gold Cup at the Curragh, the Gran Premio di Milano and the Princess of Wales's Stakes at Newmarket marked Taipan down as a smart performer but one seemingly still a fair way removed from the top league; in the last-named he was beaten a head and four lengths by Shantou and Swain. A win in the Grand Prix de Deauville provided Taipan with a Group 2 win but proved little new; Taipan had just three opponents and didn't have to improve to win by a length from fellow British-trained challenger Camporese. Taipan's next run, in the EMS Kurierpost Europa Preis at Cologne, was just about his best effort at the time though. Taipan was opposed by the renowned globetrotter Luso and that stalwart of German pattern racing Protektor, no pushover either of them. Taipan scored a decisive success by two lengths from an admittedly below-par Luso, with Protektor a further length and a quarter away in third.

Taipan continued to keep the passport controllers busy. Next stop was Milan for the Gran Premio del Jockey-Club. Back on firmish going, Taipan finished three and a half lengths fourth to the good German horse Caitano, with

Grand Prix de Deauville—
Taipan proves too good for fellow British raiders Camporese and Lord of Men

EMS Kurierpost Europa Preis, Cologne—Taipan and Luso are too good for the home defence

Luso second. Then it was a return to Italy three weeks later for the Premio Roma. Opposed by the German Group 1 winner Oxalagu, a trio from Britain (Lord of Men, Santillana and Delilah) and four not particularly formidable home representatives, Taipan won his second Group 1. Although Oxalagu was travelling better shortly after the turn for home, Taipan forged ahead in the final

Lord Swaythling's "Taipan"

two furlongs to win by three lengths. Lord of Men was another two and a half lengths away in third and the rest were strung out on the softish going. This was a fitting finale to Taipan's season and the good news is that he remains in training in 1998. Perhaps, having proved himself in such exalted company abroad, connections will want him to try to make his mark against the best back on his home patch. Take care not to underestimate him if they do.

		Try My Best	Northern Dancer
	Last Tycoon	(b 1975)	Sex Appeal
	(b 1983)	Mill Princess	Mill Reef
Taipan (IRE)		(b 1977)	Irish Lass II
(b.h. 1992)		Chief Singer	Ballad Rock
	Alidiva	(b 1981)	Principia
	(b 1987)	Alligatrix	Alleged
		(br 1980)	Shore

Taipan is a half-brother to Ali-Royal and Sleepytime, in whose essays comments on the dam's side of the pedigree can be found, along with details of Alidiva's remarkable achievements as a broodmare. Taipan is a leggy horse with a roundish action. Although his win at a mile and a quarter on dead going in the Premio Roma is his best, his form at a mile and a half and on firm or soft going isn't far behind. He sometimes sweats but is genuine and consistent and, it scarcely needs saying, a credit to his trainer. *J. L. Dunlop*

TAJAR (USA)   5 b.g. Slew O' Gold (USA) – Mashaarif (USA) (Mr Prospector   44
(USA)) [1996 NR 1997 a7g 8s⁵ 8m 10g 12.1m* 12m² 12.3d 10m³ 10g⁴ 12m 14.6g
a12g⁶ Nov 15] poor handicapper: first start after leaving M. Dods, won amateurs
event at Chepstow in July: stays 1½m: acts on good to firm ground: blinkered twice
(below form): usually sweating: has looked none too keen. *T. Keddy*

TAJASUR (IRE)   2 ch.c. (Mar 28) Imperial Frontier (USA) 112 – Safiya (USA)   87 p
(Riverman (USA) 131) [1997 6d* Jun 29] IR 45,000F: strong, lengthy colt: fourth
foal: brother to 4-y-o Cayman Kai: dam unraced sister to smart miler Sulaafah: 2/1
joint favourite and on toes, won 4-runner minor event at Doncaster by head from
Alconleigh, leading on bit entering final 1f but running green, rider not resorting to
whip: should make useful performer if all is well with him. *J. L. Dunlop*

TAJAWUZ (IRE)   2 ch.f. (Apr 30) Kris 135 – Na-Ayim (IRE) 68 (Shirley Heights 130)   73
[1997 8.2g⁴ 7g⁴ Oct 22] first foal: dam 6f winner at 2 yrs: half-sister to dam of Rainbow Quest and excellent broodmare Slightly Dangerous: fair form in maidens at
Nottingham and Newcastle in October, racing too freely and finding little in latter:
bred to be suited by further than 1m, but needs to settle better. *Saeed bin Suroor*

TAJ MAHAL (IRE)   2 b.c. (Apr 16) High Estate 127 – Verthumna (Indian King   –
(USA) 128) [1997 6g a6g a6g Dec 6] 11,000Y: sixth foal: half-brother to 3 winners
abroad: dam maiden, ran only at 2 yrs in Ireland: no form in maidens. *C. W. Thornton*

TAJMIL (IRE)   2 ch.f. (Apr 29) Wolfhound (USA) 126 – Nouvelle Star (AUS)   70
(Luskin Star (AUS)) [1997 5.7f³ 6g⁴ 6m 7d⁴ 7.3g Oct 25] sturdy, angular filly: good
walker: has a round action: ninth foal: half-sister to 3-y-o Juwwi and 7f winner Sariah
(by Kris): dam won up to 1m in Australia and was champion older filly at 4 yrs: fair
form in maidens: wintry when well beaten in nursery final start: stays 7f: sold 25,000
gns in December. *Major W. R. Hern*

TAJREBAH (USA)   3 b.f. Dayjur (USA) 137 – Petrava (NZ) (Imposing (AUS))   70
[1996 70: 6m 7.1v 6m³ 1997 5.1m⁴ 6m³ 7.3s 6.1g⁵ 7m* 7g⁵ 7m Aug 10] good-topped
filly: fair handicapper: won at Lingfield in June: left P. Walwyn before final start:
stays 7f: best form on good to firm going. *S. P. C. Woods*

TAKE A RISK   2 ch.f. (Feb 15) Risk Me (FR) 127 – Hinari Televideo 97   60
(Caerleon (USA) 132) [1997 5f⁵ 5d 5g* 5.1g 5s⁵ Oct 15] IR 14,000Y: workmanlike
filly: poor mover: third foal: half-sister to 4-y-o Shontante: dam sprinter: modest
performer: won maiden at Musselburgh in September: some way below that form
otherwise: not sure to stay beyond 5f: has been bandaged: possibly temperamental.
M. Johnston

TAK

TAKE A TURN   2 br.g. (Mar 24) Forzando 122 – Honeychurch (USA) 93 (Bering   72
136) [1997 5g³ 6.3d 5d² 5.1m² 5.2f 6m⁵ 5.7m⁵ 7s* 8d 7v 8m Oct 22] 7,400F, IR
21,000Y: smallish gelding: has a quick action: third foal: half-brother to 4-y-o Sandblaster: dam 10.5f winner: fair performer at best: won nursery at Chester in August:
rather disappointing afterwards: stays 7f: acts on good to firm and soft ground:
visored 5 of last 6 starts: gelded at end of year. *M. R. Channon*

TAKE NOTICE   4 b.c. Warning 136 – Metair 118 (Laser Light 118) [1996 77:   –
8.3m⁴ 8.3d 8d³ 7m 6m 1997 10.3m 8.3d 5.9g 5m 6s 8g 8m May 31] close-coupled
colt: one-time fair maiden: has lost his form. *R. M. McKellar*

TAKHLID (USA)   6 b.h. Nureyev (USA) 131 – Savonnerie (USA) 108 (Irish   73
River (FR) 131) [1996 67: a7g⁴ a7g⁴ a9g⁶ 8g⁴ a8.5g 5m 6f 8s 1997 a6g⁴ a6g a6g* a6g   a79
a8g* a7g⁴ 8m 6.9m² 8.3g³ 8.9d⁵ a8.5g⁶ 7m 7.5d a8g 8g⁶ a6g* a6g 6g 8s a6s a6g³ a6g⁴
Dec 26] strong, compact horse: fair handicapper: won at Wolverhampton in March
and September and at Southwell in April, 2 of them amateurs events: effective at 6f
to 9f: acts on fibresand, firm and soft going. *D. W. Chapman*

TALAHEART   2 b.f. (Jan 21) Alnasr Alwasheek 117 – Spring In Rome (USA)   –
(Forli (ARG)) [1997 5.3f⁶ 6g⁶ a7g⁵ a6g⁶ Jul 26] 7,000Y: half-sister to numerous
winners here and in Italy, including useful 1¼m/1½m performer Cherry Hill (by
Shirley Heights): dam ran once: no worthwhile form, including in seller: blinkered
on fibresand final 2 starts. *C. N. Allen*

TALEBAN   2 b.c. (May 12) Alleged (USA) 138 – Triode (USA) 105 (Sharpen Up   88 p
127) [1997 8s* Nov 14] fourth foal: half-brother to 3-y-o Blane Water and a winner
in Germany by Storm Bird: dam 1m winner from family of smart middle-distance
filly Trillionaire: 66/10, won minor event at Milan by 2¾ lengths: will stay beyond
1m: sure to improve. *L. M. Cumani*

TALENTED TING (IRE)   8 ch.g. Hatim (USA) 121 – An Tig Gaelige (Thatch   –
(USA) 136) [1996 65d, a–: a12g a12g 10.3d 9.2d 8.3d 8.5m 8.3g² 10f² 9.2m⁵ 10m
10g 8.3f⁴ 8.3g 1997 9m 8m 9m 12.1g Aug 2] strong, lengthy gelding: one-time fair
handicapper: tried visored/blinkered: successful 7 times at Hamilton: died there in
August. *P. C. Haslam*

TALES OF BOUNTY (IRE)   2 b.g. (Apr 18) Ela-Mana-Mou 132 – Tales of   –
Wisdom 70 (Rousillon (USA) 133) [1997 8m Sep 22] 27,000Y: second foal: half-
brother to 3-y-o Mystic Quest: dam 1½m winner: 20/1, signs of ability though green
when mid-division in maiden at Kempton: may do better. *D. R. C. Elsworth*

TALES OF HEARSAY (GER)   7 gr.g. Celestial Storm (USA) 132 – Trying   –
Girl (Try My Best (USA) 130) [1996 NR 1997 10g Apr 21] ex-Irish gelding: first
living foal: dam placed in Germany: fairly useful at 3 yrs: lightly raced and probably
no longer of any account. *C. F. C. Jackson*

TALIB (USA)   3 b.g. Silver Hawk (USA) 123 – Dance For Lucy (USA) (Dance   60
Bid (USA) 114) [1996 59: 8m⁵ 8m⁶ 1997 8g⁴ 9.9d 8f Sep 18] modest maiden: should
stay beyond 1m: acts on firm going, possibly unsuited by softer than good: sold
15,000 gns in October, and joined Mrs J. Cecil. *D. Morley*

TALISMAN (IRE)   3 b.g. Silver Kite (USA) 111 – Sports Post Lady (IRE) 72 (M   55 d
Double M (USA)) [1996 55: 5m⁶ 5m⁵ 6g⁵ 7.3m 8m 1997 a7g⁵ a7g a8g³ a7g³ a8g⁴ 8f
8m a7g⁶ a8g⁴ Dec 2] useful-looking gelding: modest maiden handicapper: lost form
after fourth start: stays 1m: acts on equitrack, raced only on good going or firmer on
turf: blinkered last 2 starts. *S. Dow*

TALK BACK (IRE)   5 b.g. Bob Back (USA) 124 – Summit Talk (Head For   –
Heights 125) [1996 NR 1997 10.8m 15.4m 10m Jul 28] rather leggy gelding: second
foal: dam, Irish 7.5f winner: won maiden at Naas from 2 starts at 3 yrs: has reportedly
had a wind operation, and no sign of retaining ability at 5 yrs. *G. Lewis*

TALLULAH BELLE   4 b.f. Crowning Honors (CAN) – Fine A Leau (USA) 51   74
(Youth (USA) 135) [1996 52, a–: a6g a9.4g a6g 6.9m² 7g⁶ 8m³ 8.2m⁴ 8m 8.2f⁴ 8.3m
8f⁵ 7.6m 8m 10f³ 10g² 1997 a9.4g³ a9.4f* a10g³ a9.4g a10g* a9.4g⁵ a10g³ a10g³
a10g⁶ 10m⁵ 9.9m* 10d a8.5g 9m a9.4g⁴ 10.2d 11.9g⁵ 12m³ 11.1m* 10f² 10.4d 10m*
Oct 28] smallish filly: fair performer, much improved at 4 yrs: won maiden at
Wolverhampton, handicaps at Lingfield, Beverley and Kempton and minor event at

952

Redcar: stays 1½m: acts on the all-weather, best turf form on good going or firmer: visored once at 3 yrs: tough. *N. P. Littmoden*

TAL-Y-LLYN (IRE)   3 ch.c. Common Grounds 118 – Welsh Fantasy 104 (Welsh   77 d
Pageant 132) [1996 77: 6g⁵ 6m² 6.1s⁴ 1997 7m 7.3s* 9g⁶ 7s 8.1m 7m 8.2s Oct 15]
close-coupled colt: has a quick, unimpressive action: fair performer at best: won
minor event at Newbury in May, making most: ran poorly in handicaps afterwards:
should stay 1m: acts on good to firm and soft going. *B. W. Hills*

TAMANDU   7 b.m. Petoski 135 – Gohar (USA) (Barachois (CAN)) [1996 –: a12g⁵   –
a12g⁶ 12s 1997 a13g³ a13g Jan 30] seems of little account nowadays. *C. James*

TAMARISK (IRE)   2 b.c. (May 19) Green Desert (USA) 127 – Sine Labe   113 p
(USA) (Vaguely Noble 140) [1997 6m* 7m* 7m* 7g² Oct 18]
        'Let's be grateful to Newmarket and its sponsor for bringing our racing
out of the Dark Age' wrote Michael Tanner in *Pacemaker* in November about
the introduction of sectional timing equipment on the Rowley Mile. Sectional
times have been returned for many years in America, Hong Kong and the major
tracks in France, but rarely in Britain, where the majority of racecourses which
stage flat racing still—incredibly—lack basic electrical timing. Ironically,
Newmarket's system, installed for a reported £200,000, is more advanced than
the systems in use abroad, in that it is able to record a time not just for the leader
at any given timing point, but for every horse. The wealth of data that will
become available promises to be useful. Ongoing trials at Timeform using
video timings from the all-weather tracks at Lingfield, Southwell and Wolverhampton, as well as official times from Sha Tin and Happy Valley in Hong
Kong, suggest sectional time analysis can occasionally uncover something not
immediately apparent from standard form or time analysis. Interpreting the
fractions in the absence of any sectional standards is a skilled task, however,
requiring a thorough understanding of the effect of pace upon fatigue and the
rate of fatigue in proportion to distance, amongst other things. Sectional
timing's very complexity—and it's a good deal more complex subject than
traditional time analysis—provides, of course, its greatest potential benefit to
the intelligent punter. Worthwhile analysis is much more involved than simply
comparing one fractional time with another, which is about as far as most
published work on the subject has reached. Some of those who have enthused
about the advent of sectional timing in Britain seem to be in the dark
themselves!
        In simple terms, a good final quarter-mile time in the context of a strong
overall pace is one of the positive things to look for when analysing sectional
times, and there was one on the first day the system was trialled when Tamarisk
ran clean away with the Tattersalls Houghton Sales Conditions Stakes in
September. The overall quality of this race, restricted to horses sold at the
Houghton Sales, is dependent on the quality of the graduates at the sale; the
field of thirteen for the latest edition was by some way the smallest yet. Only
four of those started at shorter than 12/1. Tamarisk, as in his two previous races,

Tattersalls Houghton Sales Conditions Stakes, Newmarket—
Tamarisk's stable-companion Sapphire Ring is his nearest pursuer

was sent off favourite, this time at 5/4, with the Gimcrack third Headhunter next at 9/2, followed by Tamarisk's stable-companion Sapphire Ring at 7/1. Tamarisk, who had followed up his victory in a newcomers event at Goodwood in August with a six-length all-the-way win in a minor contest at Kempton, showed further improvement and turned the race into a procession. Leading or disputing the lead from the off, he drew away in the final furlong to beat Sapphire Ring by three and a half lengths. Following such an impressive performance, it came as no surprise when Tamarisk's connections decided to pay £15,000 to supplement him for the Dewhurst Stakes run over the same course and distance almost three weeks later. Tamarisk didn't let them down. Although no match for Xaar, who went past him at the furlong marker and drew seven lengths clear, the front-running Tamarisk kept on gamely to finish a clear second, confirming himself a smart colt. Interestingly, the sectional times for the Dewhurst produced different interpretations in the two trade papers, *Racing Post* headlining their story with 'A quality effort', while *The Sporting Life* stated 'Sorry but Xaar isn't quite as fast as he looks!'

		Danzig	Northern Dancer
	Green Desert (USA)	(b 1977)	Pas de Nom
	(b 1983)	Foreign Courier	Sir Ivor
Tamarisk (IRE)		(b 1979)	Courtly Dee
(b.c. May 19, 1995)		Vaguely Noble	Vienna
	Sine Labe (USA)	(b 1965)	Noble Lassie
	(ch 1986)	Trevilla	Lyphard
		(b 1981)	Trillion

Tamarisk, who cost 78,000 guineas as a yearling, is the third foal of Sine Labe, a mare who was well beaten in two outings in France as a three-year-old. Sine Labe's first foal, Grand Selection (by Cricket Ball), showed fairly useful form at up to a mile and a half. A half-sister to the Prix Saint-Alary winner Treble out of the unraced Trevilla, Sine Labe is a granddaughter of the 1978 Arc de Triomphe runner-up Trillion, dam of another top-class racemare in Triptych. The well-made Tamarisk has raced only on good or good to firm ground. Although he does race freely we think there's every chance that he'll stay a mile, and he should continue to progress and win a good race or two in 1998. *R. Charlton*

TAMARPOUR (USA) 10 b.g. Sir Ivor 135 – Tarsila (High Top 131) [1996 NR 1997 20m⁴ Jun 17] workmanlike gelding: useful hurdler: lightly raced on flat since 5 yrs: heavily bandaged, ½-length fourth of 25 to Sea Freedom in fast-run Ascot Stakes at Royal Ascot, finishing best of all: suited by thorough test of stamina: acts on good to firm ground: has run well when sweating and on edge: effective blinkered/visored: held up: has gone in snatches, and looked reluctant to race. *M. C. Pipe* — 68

TAMAYAZ (CAN) 5 b.h. Gone West – Minstrelsy (USA) (The Minstrel (CAN) 135) [1996 121: a8g* a9.9s* a10g⁵ 10d⁴ 10f³ 8m³ 10.5m* 10g⁶ a10f⁶ 1997 a9g² a10f* 9.3d⁶ 10.5m⁶ Aug 9] tall, good-topped horse: smart performer: won extremely valuable Dubai Duty Free at Nad Al Sheba in April by length from Needle Gun, best effort at 5 yrs: well below form both starts back in Europe: stayed 10.5f: acted on sand (proven in wet)/dirt and firm going, possibly not on dead: visored last 3 starts: normally raced prominently: reportedly sold to stand at Northview Stallion Station, Maryland, USA (fee $5,000, live foal). *Saeed bin Suroor* — 119

TAMBURELLO (IRE) 2 b.f. (Apr 19) Roi Danzig (USA) – Peach Melba 96 (So Blessed 130) [1997 a6g a6m 6m⁴ a6g Nov 17] half-sister to several winners, including useful performer here and in Ireland (successful up to 9.4f) Reported (by Heraldiste): dam 2-y-o 5f winner: no form in maidens: blinkered final start. *J. Berry* — –

TAMERIN BAY 2 b.c. (Mar 26) Lugana Beach 116 – Quenlyn (Welsh Pageant 132) [1997 6.1g² 5m* 7s 6m 5g 5m⁴ Aug 5] 2,800Y: leggy, narrow colt: half-brother to several winners, including 5f (at 2 yrs) to 7f winner Chilibang Bang (by Chilibang): dam ran 3 times at 2 yrs: won maiden at Pontefract in June: generally — 77 d disappointing afterwards, carrying head high in blinkers final start: stays 6f, well beaten over 7f in soft ground. *R. Boss*

TAM O'SHANTER 3 gr.g. Persian Bold 123 – No More Rosies 74 (Warpath 50
113) [1996 NR 1997 7.1s 12.1s 12.3g 13d² a14g a14g Dec 18] leggy gelding: sixth foal: brother to modest winners Eau de Cologne (up to 1½m) and Rosmarino (13f) and half-brother to 2 winners: dam, 1¼m winner from 2 starts, half-sister to Derby third Mount Athos: only form when second in 5-runner maiden handicap at Hamilton, carrying head awkwardly under pressure: off course 5 months before final start: has given trouble at stalls. *C. W. Thornton*

TAMURE (IRE) 5 b.h. Sadler's Wells (USA) 132 – Three Tails 121 (Blakeney 112
126) [1996 –: 12d 1997 10d⁴ 12d³ 10s⁵ 12m⁵ 12d² 12s² Nov 8] sturdy, lengthy horse: high-class at 3 yrs, but only smart in 1997: length second to Majorien in Prix du Conseil de Paris at Longchamp penultimate start: below form when 13 lengths second to Taufan's Melody in listed race at Doncaster final one: finds 1¼m on the sharp side, and bred to be suited by further than 1½m: acts on any going: sold 47,000 gns in December, and joined L. Cumani. *J. H. M. Gosden*

TANAASA (IRE) 3 b.c. Sadler's Wells (USA) 132 – Mesmerize (Mill Reef 106 p
(USA) 141) [1996 70p: 7m³ 1997 10d⁴ 11.5s² May 10] rangy colt: has a powerful, round action: landed odds (impressively) in maiden at Leicester in April: useful form when 7 lengths second of 5 to Silver Patriarch in strongly-run Derby Trial at Lingfield following month: withdrawn overnight, reportedly lame, from Derby: will stay 1½m: bandaged behind on debut, off-hind at Lingfield: stays in training and should do better if all is well with him. *M. R. Stoute*

TANCRED MISCHIEF 6 b.m. Northern State (USA) 91 – Mischievous Miss 40
73 (Niniski (USA) 125) [1996 28: 12.1g⁴ 14.1g⁵ 16m⁶ 17.2f⁵ 1997 16s³ 16m* 21.6g⁶ 16m⁵ 18g* 16d⁴ 15.8s² 16.2m Jul 15] small, lengthy mare: has a round action: poor handicapper: won at Musselburgh in April and Pontefract in June: ran as if something amiss final start: stays 2¼m, possibly not 21f: acts on good to firm and soft ground: held up. *D. W. Barker*

TANCRED TIMES 2 ch.f. (Apr 30) Clantime 101 – Mischievous Miss 73 (Nini-63
ski (USA) 125) [1997 5g 6g* 7g* 6d³ 6.5m 7m 7g⁵ Sep 27] 2,000Y: small, sparely-made filly: fifth foal: sister to 5-y-o Shaffishayes and half-sister to 6-y-o Tancred Mischief: dam suited by 1¾m to 2m: modest performer: won seller at Thirsk in June and nursery at Catterick in July: may well prove as effective at 6f as 7f: yet to race on extremes of ground. *D. W. Barker*

TANGERINE FLYER 2 ch.g. (Mar 30) Presidium 124 – Factuelle 43 (Known 64
Fact (USA) 135) [1997 a6g² 5m² 5.1g⁶ 5g 5m⁶ a5g a5g⁵ Dec 22] 6,400Y: good- a76 +
topped gelding: has a quick, fluent action: first foal: dam 5f winner, including at 2 yrs: fair performer: best effort since debut when winning maiden at Lingfield: speedy, but stays 6f: acts on both all-weather. *J. Berry*

TANGO KING 3 b.c. Suave Dancer (USA) 136 – Be My Queen 84 (Be My Guest 75
(USA) 126) [1996 66p: 7m 7g 8m 1997 10.8m² 14.1d* 12m⁴ 14m 14m Aug 14] unfurnished colt: has a round action: fair handicapper: justified favouritism at Nottingham in May: stays 1¾m: unraced on extremes of going: sweating and edgy final start (finished last): hurdling with Miss H. Knight. *J. L. Dunlop*

TANGO MAN (IRE) 5 ch.g. King Luthier 113 – Amour Libre (He Loves Me –
120) [1996 NR 1997 a9.4f a8.5g⁶ a14.8g Jan 22] third foal: dam maiden: no sign of ability on flat: poor winning hurdler. *R. J. Price*

TANGSHAN (CAN) 3 ch.f. Zilzal (USA) 137 – Manzanares (USA) (Sir Ivor 79
135) [1996 67p: 7f⁵ 1997 10m⁵ 8f² 8.1m⁶ 10.8m* 10.1m⁴ 10g Oct 18] fair handi-capper: made all in 5-runner event at Warwick in July, best effort: keen sort, but stays 10.8f: raced only on good going or firmer: often makes running: sold 10,500 gns in December. *M. R. Stoute*

TANIMBAR (IRE) 2 b.g. (May 6) Persian Bold 123 – Try My Rosie 93 (Try My –
Best (USA) 130) [1997 6g 6d Nov 7] IR 19,000Y: close-coupled gelding: fifth foal: half-brother to juvenile sprint winners by Tirol and Vision: dam 6f winner at 2 yrs in Ireland: well beaten in autumn maidens at Newbury and Doncaster. *D. Haydn Jones*

Moyglare Stud Stakes, the Curragh—Tarascon edges out Heed My Warning (No. 4)

TANIYAR (FR) 5 b.g. Glenstal (USA) 118 – Taeesha (Mill Reef (USA) 141) – §
[1996 52§, a39§: a13g a10g⁴ a12g a12g⁵ a7g⁴ a7g 10.8m⁵ 16.2m a11g⁵ a12g 10.4g a30 §
11.8f⁴ 10.3g³ a12g² a10g a12g⁶ 1997 a11s³ a12g⁶ a13g a8.5g⁵ 10.1g 15.8m 13.4g⁵
Sep 24] smallish gelding: poor and untrustworthy maiden: tried blinkered/visored.
R. Hollinshead

TANKERSLEY 2 ch.c. (Feb 8) Timeless Times (USA) 99 – Busted Love (Busted – p
134) [1997 7d Nov 7] 5,000F: strong, workmanlike colt: half-brother to several
winners, including 5-y-o Tessajoe: dam unraced: 33/1, burly and green, mid-field in
19-runner maiden at Doncaster, keeping on steadily: should do better. *A. Hide*

TAOISTE 4 b.c. Kris 135 – Tenue de Soiree (USA) 120 (Lyphard (USA) 132) 85
[1996 8g 5.5g* 5m 1997 7m 7d 5d⁴ 5m 6.1s 5m³ 6g 5s Aug 30] good-bodied colt:
fourth foal: half-brother to 2 winners in France, including 5-y-o Tuxedos (up to 8.5f,
by Machiavellian): dam, sprinter, closely related to smart miler Neverneyev: fairly
useful performer: trained in France at 2 and 3 yrs, winning twice from 7 starts: best
effort in Britain when close third in handicap at Sandown in July, making most: looks
a 5f performer: acts on good to firm going, seems unsuited by soft. *R. W. Armstrong*

TAOME (IRE) 3 b.f. Roi Danzig (USA) – Blue Bell Lady 75 (Dunphy 124) [1996 –
59d: 6m³ 6g 5f* 6.1m³ 1997 a6g⁶ a7g³ a8g³ a10g⁵ a8.5g⁶ Feb 19] small filly: modest
winner at 2 yrs: no form in 1997: sold, and sent to Holland. *P. D. Evans*

TAPPETO 5 b.g. Liboi (USA) 76 – Persian Carpet (FR) (Kalamoun 129) [1996 76
74: 10.8d 10m 10.8g 12g 12.1m² 11.7m³ 12m 12m 1997 12d² 12m 12s* 11.8g³ 14g³
16.1d⁶ 12m⁶ 12s Oct 16] workmanlike gelding: fair handicapper: won at Epsom in
July: ran creditably 3 of next 5 starts, including in second-time blinkers: stays 1¾m:
acts on good to firm ground and soft: has looked reluctant, and sometimes carries
head awkwardly. *H. Candy*

TARAGONA 4 b.f. Handsome Sailor 125 – Queen of Aragon 76 (Aragon 118) 45
[1996 –: 6m 1997 7.5g³ 10.3s⁵ 6m⁴ 8m a8.5g a8.5g Sep 30] poor maiden: well beaten
last 3 starts: stays 7.5f. *R. Hollinshead*

TARASCON (IRE) 2 b.f. Tirol 127 – Breyani 101 (Commanche Run 102 p
133) [1997 6m³ 7g* 6m⁵ 7d* Sep 7] second foal: dam Irish 11f to 2m winner from
family of Al Hareb: useful form: won minor event (by ½ length from Saratoga
Springs) in July and 12-runner Moyglare Stud Stakes (by head from Heed My
Warning, responding gamely to get up near line) in September, both at the Curragh:
will stay 1m+: yet to race on extremes of going: should improve further. *T. Stack,
Ireland*

TARASHAAN 2 b.g. (Mar 11) Darshaan 133 – Tarasova (USA) (Green Forest 74
(USA) 134) [1997 7f 7m⁵ 7g⁶ 8f 10g* Sep 23] 54,000Y: leggy, lengthy gelding:

fourth foal: brother to 5-y-o Wild Palm and half-brother to 4-y-o Galine: dam twice-raced half-sister to top-class French middle-distance colt Le Marmot: fair performer: favourite, improved effort to win nursery at Nottingham in September, swishing tail but holding on well under strong pressure: will stay 1½m: has given trouble in preliminaries and been slowly away. *Sir Mark Prescott*

TARATOR (USA)   4 ch.c. Green Dancer (USA) 132 – Happy Gal (FR) (Habitat   117
134) [1996 120: 10.5g³ 12.5g* 12d* 11g* 15d* 12.5g² 12m⁶ 15d* 12m⁶ 1997 15.5d⁴
Apr 27] strong, close-coupled colt: smart performer: won Prix Hubert de Chaudenay
and Prix de Lutece at Longchamp at 3 yrs: conceding weight all round, creditable 5¼
lengths fourth of 7 to Stretarez in Prix de Barbeville on return there: would have
stayed beyond 15.5f: best form on good ground or softer: developed pneumonia and
laminitis in June and was put down. *E. Lellouche, France*

TARRADALE   3 br.g. Interrex (CAN) – Encore L'Amour (USA) § (Monteverdi   44
129) [1996 –: 7d 1997 8d⁶ 8g 6m 7g 6d 10g⁶ 7.1g⁵ 8.3g⁵ 10.1g Oct 22] heavy-topped,
plain gelding: poor maiden: seems not to stay 1¼m: has hung and possibly
temperamental. *C. B. B. Booth*

TARRY   4 b.f. Salse (USA) 128 – Waitingformargaret 78 (Kris 135) [1996 60: 8g   65
11.6m⁵ 9.9m⁶ 10m⁵ 1997 12.1d* 14m 14m* 12m² 16s⁶ a13g² Dec 22] small filly: fair
performer: won claimers at Chepstow (final outing for A. Streeter) in August and
Salisbury (handicap) in October: stays 1¾m: acts on equitrack and on firm and dead
going, possibly not soft: tried blinkered/visored at 2 yrs. *Miss Gay Kelleway*

TARSKI   3 ch.g. Polish Precedent (USA) 131 – Illusory 81 (Kings Lake (USA)   94
133) [1996 91: 7.1m* 7g⁴ 1997 8m² 8.9s⁵ Sep 4] sturdy, attractive gelding: fairly
useful form when head second to Showboat in minor event at Salisbury in August,
caught near line: stiff task in listed race at York next time, never a factor: stays 1m:
acts on good to firm ground: sold 46,000 gns in October, and joined L. G. Cottrell.
H. R. A. Cecil

TART AND A HALF   5 b.m. Distant Relative 128 – Vaigrant Wind 75 (Vaigly   75 d
Great 127) [1996 83, a–: 6f 5g 5.1f² 6d 5m⁴ 5m 5m⁴ 5m 5.1m⁶ 5.2m 5g⁴ 5f 5m²   a–
6m a6g a6g 1997 5m 5g 5m³ 5v⁶ 5m⁴ 5m⁴ 5g 5m 5m 6m Oct 1] rather leggy mare:
fair handicapper at best, on a long losing run: left J. L. Eyre after eighth start: has
form at 7f, raced at 5f/6f nowadays: acts on firm ground, well beaten on going softer
than good and all-weather: usually blinkered/visored (not last 2 starts): usually races
prominently: inconsistent. *M. Pitman*

TARTAN LASS   2 b.f. (Feb 10) Selkirk (USA) 129 – Gwiffina 87 (Welsh Saint   65
126) [1997 8d 7m a7g³ Nov 15] big, angular filly: has scope: half-sister to several
winners, including 5-y-o Tedburrow and 6-y-o Bowcliffe: dam 2-y-o 6f winner,
didn't train on: fair form in maidens: third at Wolverhampton: should stay 1m.
R. Guest

TARTAN PARTY   3 gr.c. Environment Friend 128 – Northern Scene 78 (Habitat   –
134) [1996 61: 7.9g 7m 7f 10g³ 1997 10.2m 11.6s 8d 11.6g a10s a12g a16g Dec 4]
close-coupled colt: modest maiden at 2 yrs: disappointing in 1997: trained by P. Cole
first 4 starts: seems a stayer: tried blinkered/visored. *W. R. Muir*

TART (FR)   4 br.f. Warning 136 – Sharp Girl (FR) 114 (Sharpman) [1996 76: 8.2s⁴   59
10m² 10m² 11.6m³ 8g³ 10s³ 11.5m* a12g² 1997 a12g⁶ a12g a12g⁴ 8m 8d 8d 12g³   a62
10g 12g⁵ 10g 11.9g⁶ 10m* 12m⁴ a12g³ 12m Oct 31] close-coupled, workmanlike
filly: modest handicapper: won at Redcar (seller) in September for J. Pearce: suited
by 1¼m/1½m: acts on fibresand, best turf form on good to firm going. *D. Nicholls*

TARXIEN   3 b.g. Kendor (FR) 122 – Tanz (IRE) 79 (Sadler's Wells (USA) 132)   75
[1996 NR 1997 10m 10g 7.1d⁶ 10m² 11.6m² 11.9m* 12d* 13.9s⁶ 15d³ 11.8d⁴ 11.8d²
Oct 28] 1,400 2-y-o: deep-girthed gelding: poor mover: second foal: dam, 1½m
winner, from excellent middle-distance family: fair performer: won handicap at
Haydock in August and minor event at Pontefract in September, both apprentice
races: stays 15f: acts on good to firm and dead ground, probably on soft: consistent.
K. R. Burke

TASHANNAH   4 b.f. Sizzling Melody 117 – Liu Liu San (IRE) 44 (Bairn (USA)   –
126) [1996 NR 1997 6m 6d Jul 9] first foal: dam bad maiden: no sign of ability.
P. R. Hedger

957

TASHKENT   5 b.g. Thowra (FR) – Royal Bat 69 (Crowned Prince (USA) 128)   –
[1996 –: 8m 1997 7m⁶ 5m 8g Oct 7] no worthwhile form. *R. Simpson*

TASIK CHINI (USA)   3 b. or br.g. St Jovite (USA) 135 – Ten Hail Marys (USA)   74 d
(Halo (USA)) [1996 72d: 7f³ 7m⁶ 7m 8m 1997 12g* 11.8d 14.1g⁶ 12.5m⁵ 11.6s
11.9m⁶ 14m 12d 16g⁶ Sep 23] sturdy, workmanlike gelding: has a long stride: fair
handicapper: made all at Folkestone in March: largely disappointing afterwards:
stays 1½m: acts on firm ground: usually races prominently: blinkered thrice (well
beaten): has looked temperamental: inconsistent. *P. F. I. Cole*

TASSILI (IRE)   4 b.g. Old Vic 136 – Topsy 124 (Habitat 134) [1996 –: 10g⁶ 10s   63
1997 8.5m⁴ 8s 7.5m Jul 21] small gelding: modest performer: well beaten after
reappearance at 4 yrs: should be suited by 1¼m+. *Lady Herries*

TASTE OF SUCCESS   2 b.c. (Feb 5) Thatching 131 – Tastiera (USA) (Diesis   66
133) [1997 6d 6m⁴ Jul 14] first reported foal; dam unraced daughter of half-sister to
Grand Criterium winner Treizieme: better effort in maidens when running-on 4½
lengths fourth at Folkestone: should stay at least 1m. *P. W. Harris*

TASWIB (USA)   4 gr.g. Housebuster (USA) – Umbrella Rig (USA) (Jig Time
(USA)) [1996 NR 1997 10f⁶ 12m May 3] $67,000F, $175,000Y: half-brother to
minor winners in USA by Hero's Honor (sprinter) and Bet Twice (stayed 1m+): dam
minor stakes-winning sprinter: soundly beaten in maidens: sold, and sent to Sweden.
D. Morley

TATIKA   7 ch.g. Tate Gallery (USA) 117 – Independentia 68 (Home Guard (USA)   71
129) [1996 77, a90: a8g* a8g* 10.3g 8.1d⁵ 8.3g⁶ 8g 8.1m* 7.9g 7s⁵ a8g* 1997 a8g*   a90
7g a8.5g 8g⁶ Jun 12] lengthy gelding: fairly useful handicapper on the all-weather,
fair on turf: won competitive event at Lingfield in March: stays 8.5f: acts on the
all-weather, good to firm and soft ground: blinkered (below form) twice: sometimes
pulls hard: usually claimer ridden. *G. Wragg*

TATTINGER   2 b.f. (Mar 3) Prince Sabo 123 – Tight (Lochnager 132) [1997 6g   80 p
6m³ Sep 10] good-bodied filly: fifth foal: half-sister to winning sprinter Tongue Tied
(by Petong): dam non-thoroughbred half-sister to useful sprinter Clantime: much
better effort in maidens at Kempton when 4½ lengths third to useful pair Royal
Shyness and Ikhteyaar, first home on stand side: likely to improve further, and win a
race. *J. R. Fanshawe*

TAUFAN BOY   4 b.c. Taufan (USA) 119 – Lydia Maria 70 (Dancing Brave (USA)   75 d
140) [1996 81: 8m³ 10m⁶ a9.4g³ 10.3m² 10m 11.7m⁴ 12.3s⁶ 12m 11.9g⁴ 12.1s²
14.1s⁶ 1997 12m⁵ 14g 14.6d 14.4m⁴ 14.1g⁴ 13.8s³ Oct 17] quite attractive colt: has a
round action: fair handicapper: stays 1¾m: acts on fibresand, firm and soft ground:
tried visored/blinkered: has gone in snatches: sold 13,000 gns in October, and joined
G. Balding. *P. W. Harris*

TAUFAN'S MELODY   6 b.g. Taufan (USA) 119 – Glorious Fate (Northfields   114
(USA)) [1996 111: 11.5m* 11.8g² 14g⁴ 12m³ 12g² 12s² 1997 11.7g² 11.5m* 12s²
13.9g 13.4s⁴ 12g² 12g⁴ 12s* 12v* 12v⁵ᵈⁱˢ Dec 7] rather leggy, good-topped gelding:
smart performer: first past post in minor event at Lingfield in May, valuable handicap
at Ascot (beat Ridaiyma ¾ length only to be disqualified for squeezing runner-up on
home turn) in September and listed races at Doncaster (beat Tamure 13 lengths) and
Lyon Parilly (for second time) in November: probably stays 1¾m, at least when
conditions aren't testing: acts on good to firm and heavy going: genuine and
consistent. *Lady Herries*

TAUNT   3 b.c. Robellino (USA) 127 – Minute Waltz (Sadler's Wells (USA) 132)   108
[1996 82p: 7m³ 1997 10m⁶ 10g³ 10m² 12d² 12d* 12g 12v* 12s² Nov 8] well-made
colt: useful performer: won maiden at Epsom in July and handicap at Ascot in
October: good 8 lengths second of 24 to Sabadilla in November Handicap at
Doncaster final start: stays 1½m well: has form on good to firm ground, goes well
on softer than good: hung markedly right home turn at Pontefract on reappearance.
D. Morley

TAUREAN   2 b.c. (Apr 20) Dilum (USA) 115 – Herora (IRE) 98 (Heraldiste   –
(USA) 121) [1997 5m a7g 6.1m Sep 15] first foal: dam, 2-y-o sprint winner, later
suited by 7f: behind in maidens. *N. A. Graham*

TAUTEN (IRE) 7 br.m. Taufan (USA) 119 – Pitaka (Pitskelly 122) [1996 58d: –
8.3m² a8g 11.4m 10m 8.3g 11.6g⁵ 8m 8.3m⁶ 7g⁵ 12m 1997 a8.5g⁴ a12g 10g 10g
10.8g Oct 7] disappointing maiden: pulled up lame final start: tried visored.
A. J. Chamberlain

TAVERNER SOCIETY (IRE) 2 b.c. (Feb 21) Imp Society (USA) – Straw   91
Boater 89 (Thatch (USA) 136) [1997 7g⁶ 7g² 7m⁴ 8m* Sep 22] 14,000Y: strong,
close-coupled colt: has a quick action: sixth foal: half-brother to winners in Italy by
Chief Singer and Astronef: dam 9.4f winner: fairly useful form: in frame in maidens
before winning one at Kempton in September by 2 lengths from Mantusis, leading
turn and running on well, despite drifting left: stays 1m: raced only on good/good to
firm ground. *R. W. Armstrong*

TAWAFEK (USA) 4 br.c. Silver Hawk (USA) 123 – Tippy Tippy Toe (USA) 60   73
(Nureyev (USA) 131) [1996 71: 8d 8g 9m 1997 a10g* a10g⁴ 10.3m 12g⁶ 12g³
14.1m² 16.2s 14.9s³ 14m* 14m⁵ 14m³ 14.1m⁵ 16.2g 18d Oct 20] close-coupled colt:
poor mover: fair performer: won maiden at Lingfield in January and minor event at
Salisbury in July: probably stays 2m: acts on equitrack, firm and soft going:
consistent: sold 15,000 gns in October. *S. Dow*

TAWAFIJ (USA) 8 ch.g. Diesis 133 – Dancing Brownie (USA) (Nijinsky (CAN) –
138) [1996 81: 7g 7g⁶ 7g 7m⁴ 8g 8m⁶ 7m⁴ 7m 1997 7g Jun 7] good-topped, attractive
gelding: fair 7f/1m handicapper: last only outing at 8 yrs: probably acts on any going:
tried visored: held up. *M. D. Hammond*

TAWNY ARTIST 3 b.f. Pontevecchio Notte 104 – Artistic Peace (Prince of –
Peace 109) [1996 NR 1997 10m Oct 5] first foal: dam of little account over hurdles:
soon behind in maiden at Leicester. *B. R. Millman*

CIU Injured Jockeys Fund Serlby Stakes, Doncaster—
Taufan's Melody is a long way clear

TAY

TAYLOR'S PRIDE 2 b.f. (Feb 23) Nordico (USA) – Jendor 82 (Condorcet (FR)) [1997 6f 7m⁶ 7.5f Sep 17] sixth reported foal: half-sister to a 2-y-o 7f seller winner by Hard Fought and 5-y-o Highfield Fizz: dam 5f (at 2 yrs) and 1m winner who stayed 1½m: never a threat in maidens: fractious in stalls on debut. *T. D. Barron*

TAYOVULLIN (IRE) 3 ch.f. Shalford (IRE) 124§ – Fifth Quarter (Cure The Blues (USA)) [1996 61: 5.1m 5.7d⁶ 1997 a8.5g⁴ a7g* a7g³ 8f² 7f 8.3s 7g⁴ 6d a7g Oct 6] fair handicapper: won at Southwell (wandered and idled) in April: ran creditably in frame after: stays 1m: acts on fibresand, best turf form on good going or firmer: has worn bandages: visored (ran poorly) final start. *H. Morrison* — 65

TAYSEER (USA) 3 ch.g. Sheikh Albadou 128 – Millfit (USA) 62 (Blushing Groom (FR) 131) [1996 89p: 6m³ 6g⁴ 7f* 1997 7g* 7m 7d5 7g⁴ Jul 10] lightly-made gelding: has a quick action: useful performer: won 19-runner handicap (impressively) at York in May: best effort when fourth to Tumbleweed Ridge in Bunbury Cup at Newmarket (hung left) final start: will prove best up to 1m: acts on firm ground and dead: reportedly injured a leg in July: sold (to join W. Muir) only 16,000 gns in October, then gelded. *E. A. L. Dunlop* — 100

TAZIBARI 3 b.f. Barrys Gamble 102 – Jersey Maid 82 (On Your Mark 125) [1996 62: 5d² 5s* 5m⁵ 5g⁵ 1997 5g 7s 7g⁵ 7m a8g Dec 18] workmanlike filly: has a quick action: modest form at 2 yrs: only poor in 1997, leaving D. Moffat before final start: stays 7f. *J. Norton* — 45

TAZKIYA 2 ch.f. (Feb 26) King's Signet (USA) 110 – Irene's Charter 72 (Persian Bold 123) [1997 7m Sep 9] 3,000F, 26,000Y: fifth foal: half-sister to 4-y-o Smarter Charter and 5-y-o Master Charter: dam, probably best short of 1½m, won 4 races: 25/1, green and started slowly when behind in maiden at Lingfield: sold 15,000 gns in October. *C. J. Benstead* —

TE AMO (IRE) 5 b.h. Waajib 121 – Avebury Ring (Auction Ring (USA) 123) [1996 65: 10g 10.3g 8.1d 11.6m⁴ a11g 9.7m³ 11.6m² 11.8m³ 14m⁶ 11.8f* 12s⁶ 12v 1997 a10g Jan 11] small, good-bodied horse: fair performer at best in 1996: well held in claimer only outing at 5 yrs: stays 1½m: acts on good to firm and heavy ground: tried blinkered/visored. *M. C. Pipe* —

TEA PARTY (USA) 4 b.f. Night Shift (USA) – Meringue Pie (USA) (Silent Screen (USA)) [1996 76: 9m⁴ 9m⁴ 10.1g 10f⁴ 8g 8g⁴ a8.5g³ a8.5g* a9.4g² 10g³ 8s 1997 a9.4g a9.4g a10g⁵ a8g 8f⁵ 7m 7m 6.1g a7g* 7s* 7s³ 7g 6d a7g Oct 4] small, strong filly: fair handicapper: won at Wolverhampton in May and Goodwood in June: out of form last 3 starts: effective at 7f (given strong gallop) to 1¼m: acts on fibresand and soft ground, probably on good to firm: usually blinkered. *K. O. Cunningham-Brown* — 64 a68

TEAPOT ROW (IRE) 2 b.c. (Feb 7) Generous (IRE) 139 – Secrage (USA) 105 (Secreto (USA) 128) [1997 6g* 7g⁴ 7m* 8g* Sep 28] — 108 p

It's a while now since we last had cause to mention the Duke of Devonshire in connection with a good horse. One occasion was after the final race of his top-class mare Park Top, who returned with Lester Piggott to a hostile reception in the unsaddling enclosure at Longchamp after their long odds-on defeat in the Prix de Royallieu. 'We have never witnessed an uglier demonstration on a racecourse' reported *Racehorses of 1970*. 'The gesture made to the booing crowd by Park Top's owner was hardly calculated to cool the situation.' Nearly thirty years on, the Duke could have been excused for gesticulating in similar style, though this time using V for victory, after he enjoyed his most successful season as an owner since the days of Park Top. Shock July Cup winner Compton Place and promising two-year-old Teapot Row were the horses who put the Duke back in the spotlight.

A month after Compton Place had won there, Teapot Row caused something of a surprise himself at Newmarket when making a winning debut at 14/1. However, his four-length victory was gained in the style of an above-average colt and his effort against several other promising types in the Acomb Stakes at York, where he was fourth to Saratoga Springs, confirmed that impression. Granted an easier task in the Queen's Own Yorkshire Dragoons

960

Conditions Stakes at Doncaster, Teapot Row gained his second win, by a neck and the same from the inexperienced Gulland (to whom he gave 4 lb) and favourite Mahboob, getting up near the finish after having to be switched. The same race had been won by Benny The Dip the year before and Teapot Row emulated him by going on to take the Gtech Royal Lodge Stakes.

In an open-looking race at Ascot, Teapot Row opened at 16/1 and was backed to 9/1. Representatives of the bigger stables dominated the betting, headed by the runaway Sandown winner Kilimanjaro (already installed as Derby favourite) and Muhtathir, the form pick judged on his second place to Second Empire in the Prix des Chenes. Not for the first time, the smallish, leggy Teapot Row was rather overshadowed in the preliminaries, but he took the eye as usual going to post. Racing handily throughout in a race run at a true pace, Teapot Row took a while to respond once off the bit early in the straight but forged ahead inside the final furlong despite drifting quite markedly left. He had three quarters of a length to spare over the maiden Prolix, with the rest of the field (bar Muhtathir who finished a detached last) finishing close together. Kilimanjaro took fourth place but went on to disappoint when starting favourite again in the Racing Post Trophy; Teapot Row wasn't asked to run again.

Teapot Row, who was sold for 75,000 guineas at the Houghton Sales, is the only reported foal of his dam Secrage, who died of colic in 1997. Secrage, kept good company when trained in Italy as a two-year-old, beating Kingmambo in the Prix de Cabourg and finishing second to Zafonic in the Prix Morny on a couple of trips to Deauville. She also won three times at Rome, including in a seven-furlong listed race, and was then transferred to Roger Charlton's stable for a crack at the One Thousand Guineas, in which she finished ninth after running third in the Fred Darling. A serious knee problem prevented her running again and she was sold (carrying Teapot Row) for 190,000 guineas at the December Sales the following year. Secrage is the best winner to date out of Wayage, who had her only win taken away from her by the stewards after passing the post first over a mile at Maisons-Laffitte. Secrage's grandam, Waya, had no trouble winning races though; she won fourteen in all, including the Prix de Royaumont and Prix de l'Opera at three and several Grade 1 events at up to a mile and a half when transferred to the United States, earning the Eclipse Award as best older female in 1979. Waya's dam, War Path, also

961

TEA

Duke of Devonshire's "Teapot Row"

produced the Grade 1 winner Warfever and the dam of Prix Vermeille winner Walensee and the top-class French jumper World Citizen.

		Caerleon	Nijinsky
	Generous (IRE)	(b 1980)	Foreseer
	(ch 1988)	Doff The Derby	Master Derby
Teapot Row (IRE)		(b 1981)	Margarethen
(b.c. Feb 7, 1995)		Secreto	Northern Dancer
	Secrage (USA)	(b 1981)	Betty's Secret
	(b 1990)	Wayage	Mr Prospector
		(b 1984)	Waya

As well as Teapot Row, the Duke of Devonshire and his trainer James Toller have another useful two-year-old in Duck Row (the pair being named after rows of cottages on their owner's Chatsworth estate). Teapot Row is considered the Guineas prospect of the pair but he holds a Derby entry too and will stay beyond a mile; indeed he shapes as though highly likely to get the Derby trip. Teapot Row lacks the physical scope of some of those he was taking on in 1997, but he shouldn't be dismissed from the classic scene on that score alone. He's a genuine type and should continue to go the right way. *J. A. R. Toller*

TEARAWAY 2 gr.c. (Mar 20) Efisio 120 – Hoosie 75 (Niniski (USA) 125) [1997 71 6s³ 7m³ 7g³ 8g 8d² 8s⁶ Oct 13] 19,500F, IR 47,000Y: fair sort: not a good walker: first foal: dam 1¾m winner from family of Lyphard and Nobiliary: fair form in maidens and nurseries: should stay beyond 1m: acts on good to firm and soft going: often slowly away: sold 13,000 gns in October, and joined J.J.O'Neill. *J. W. Watts*

TEAR WHITE (IRE) 3 b.g. Mac's Imp (USA) 116 – Exemplary 106 (Sovereign 72 Lord 120) [1996 70§: 5g 5m³ 5g⁶ 6f⁵ 5m* 5m² 5.3f⁶ 5g⁵ 5f⁶ 5m⁵ a6g 1997 a5g³ a5g² a75 a5g⁴ 5g⁶ 5.1m⁵ a6g 6f³ 5.3f* 6f² 6d 5g⁴ 5m⁴ 6m 5m* 5m 5m 5.3f⁶ a5g³ a5g² a5g Dec 18] sturdy gelding: fair handicapper: won at Brighton in June and Goodwood in

962

August: creditable efforts most starts afterwards: effective at 5f/easy 6f: acts on firm ground (tailed off on dead) and equitrack: often used to be blinkered/visored, but only first 5 starts as 3-y-o: tends to wander, but much more amenable than in 1996: inconsistent. *T. G. Mills*

TECHNICAL MOVE (IRE) 6 br.m. Move Off 112 – Technical Merit (Gala Performance (USA)) [1996 NR 1997 11.7g Sep 8] fourth foal: dam won over hurdles: well held in maiden at Bath on debut. *G. A. Ham* –

TECHNICIAN (IRE) 2 ch.g. (May 2) Archway (IRE) 115 – How It Works (Commanche Run 133) [1997 6d 5v 5m a8g5 Dec 19] IR 11,000Y: leggy gelding: poor mover: second foal: brother to German 6f winner Running Away: dam tailed off in Irish bumper only start: only a little sign of ability in maidens. *M. A. Jarvis* –

TECHNICOLOUR (IRE) 3 b.f. Rainbow Quest (USA) 134 – Grecian Urn 123 (Ela-Mana-Mou 132) [1996 79p: 7.1s* 1997 11.4g5 Jul 16] won maiden at Chepstow only start at 2 yrs: easy to back, refused to settle when distant last in Sandown minor event only start of 1997: bred to be suited by at least 1¼m: sold 55,000 gns in December. *M. R. Stoute* –

TEDBURROW 5 b.g. Dowsing (USA) 124 – Gwiffina 87 (Welsh Saint 126) [1996 96: 6m 5d4 6m2 5m4 5g2 5m* 5m3 5m 5m 5.6m4 6m 6g 5g5 5g4 1997 5d* 6d* 6g 5d6 5.1m* 6m6 6d5 6g 5m* 5v Oct 11] leggy, workmanlike gelding: improved into smart sprinter for new stable, winning handicaps at Haydock in May and York (rated stakes) in June, £15,500 event at Chester in July and another (rated stakes) at Ascot (beat Crowded Avenue 2 lengths) in September: not well drawn final start: effective at 5f and 6f: acts on firm and dead ground: has won when sweating: usually held up: genuine: a credit to his trainer. *E. J. Alston* — 116

TEDDY'S BOW (IRE) 3 b. or br.f. Archway (IRE) 115 – Gale Force Seven (Strong Gale 116) [1996 52?: 5m5 5m4 1997 5f Sep 17] plain filly: has a round action: modest maiden at 2 yrs: soundly beaten only outing in 1997. *M. W. Easterby* –

TEDROSS 6 b. or br.h. Ardross 134 – Town Fair (Town Crier 119) [1996 NR 1997 11.6m 10g 9s5 Jun 20] second foal: dam little sign of ability: well beaten in claimer and maidens. *Jamie Poulton* –

TEE-EMM 7 b.g. Lidhame 109 – Tower Glades 90 (Tower Walk 130) [1996 40, a56: a5g5 a5g4 a5g4 5f 1997 5.1m4 5m4 5m5 Jun 4] good-topped, plain gelding: poor 5f handicapper: acts on firm ground, dead and the all-weather: blinkered once at 2 yrs and last 3 starts: usually front runner. *R. Simpson* — 40 a–

Cliveden Ruinart Champagne Rated Stakes (Handicap), Ascot—
a career-best performance from Tedburrow

TEE

TEEJAY'N'AITCH (IRE)   5 b.g. Maelstrom Lake 118 – Middle Verde (USA)   34
(Sham (USA)) [1996 44: 7.1g⁶ 7d 8d³ 11.1f³ 13.1m⁶ 8.1g 11.1m 1997 8.3d 12d⁴ 10g
16g Sep 15] lengthy gelding: good mover: poor maiden handicapper: stays 1½m:
acts on firm and dead ground: tried visored/blinkered: fair hurdler/modest chaser.
J. S. Goldie

TEEPEE (IRE)   2 b.f. (Apr 8) Indian Ridge 123 – Princess of Zurich (IRE) (Law
Society (USA) 130) [1997 6s⁴ 6m 6d Aug 28] IR 26,000Y: lengthy, unfurnished filly:
unimpressive mover: third foal: half-sister to Italian 5f winner Eco Sonoro (by
Thatching): dam, Irish 7f winner, half-sister to smart 6f/7f winner Prince Echo:
showed ability only on debut: looked none too keen in claimer final start. *W. Jarvis*

TEEPLOY GIRL   2 b.f. (Mar 5) Deploy 131 – Intoxication 73 (Great Nephew   53
126) [1997 a6g³ a7g Nov 29] 500F, 2,800Y: seventh foal: half-sister to 14.6f winner
Innerglow (by Kalaglow) and a winner in France/Spain by Never So Bold: dam,
stayed 1½m, daughter of Princess Royal winner Shebeen: better effort in sellers at
Wolverhampton in November on debut: refused to enter stalls final intended start:
should stay further than 6f. *N. P. Littmoden*

TEE TEE TOO (IRE)   5 ch.g. Hatim (USA) 121 – Scottish Welcome (Be My   –
Guest (USA) 126) [1996 –: 8m 6.9d 9.2s 7d 10f 12m 11.5m 1997 a16s⁶ Jan 1] stocky
gelding: no form for various trainers since 3 yrs. *A. W. Carroll*

TELALANJON   2 b.c. (Mar 14) Tirol 127 – Akkazao (IRE) 94 (Alzao (USA)   70 p
117) [1997 8d⁶ 8s Nov 8] 7,800Y: leggy, useful-looking colt: first foal: dam 1m to
1¼m winner: fair form from slow start in maidens at Leicester and Doncaster: will
stay 1¼m: should do better. *T. G. Mills*

TELEMANIA (IRE)   3 b.f. Mujtahid (USA) 118 – African Dance (USA) (El   87
Gran Senor (USA) 136) [1996 83p: 6.1f⁴ 6.1m* 7m³ 1997 8m⁶ 8d⁵ 8.2m 8m⁵ 7.1m²
8.1s⁶ 7m³ Sep 25] tall, lengthy filly: carries condition: fairly useful handicapper:
placed at Sandown in August and Goodwood in September: stays 1m: acts on good
to firm and soft ground: often sweating/edgy: sold 17,500 gns in December.
W. J. Haggas

TELEPHUS   8 b.g. Efisio 120 – Mrs Bizz (Status Seeker) [1996 –: a16g⁶ a13g   –
a12g a12g⁴ 1997 11.9m⁵ 10.1f Sep 17] no form since 1994. *B. J. McMath*

TELLION   3 b.g. Mystiko (USA) 124 – Salchow 116 (Niniski (USA) 125) [1996   72
NR 1997 6.1d⁴ a9.4g⁴ 10m⁶ a9.4g⁵ 10s⁴ 12m³ a14g Oct 20] 12,000 2-y-o: sixth foal:
half-brother to Meltemison, 7.5f winner Kalko (by Kalaglow) and 1m winner
Carousella (by Rousillon): dam won at 7f (at 2 yrs) and stayed 1¾m: fair performer:
barely stays 1½m: acts on good to firm going and soft: sold 10,000 gns, and joined J
Jenkins. *Major W. R. Hern*

TELLOFF   3 b.f. Reprimand 122 – La Primavera (Northfields (USA)) [1996 –: 7m   –
7g 1997 8.2m⁶ 7g Aug 6] leggy filly: signs of ability but no worthwhile form: bred to
be suited by further than 1m. *M. A. Jarvis*

TEMERAIRE (USA)   2 b.c. (Feb 22) Dayjur (USA) 137 – Key Dancer (USA)   65 p
(Nijinsky (CAN) 138) [1997 7d Nov 7] strong, quite attractive colt: seventh foal:
half-brother to 3 winners, notably 3-y-o Keyboogie: dam, good-class stakes winner
at 9.5f and 11f, out of half-sister to Ajdal and Formidable: 14/1, burly and green,
about 9 lengths ninth to High-Rise in maiden at Doncaster, outpaced from 2f out: sure
to do better. *Mrs A. J. Perrett*

TEME VALLEY   3 br.c. Polish Precedent (USA) 131 – Sudeley 65 (Dancing   80
Brave (USA) 140) [1996 NR 1997 10d² 11.5m² 12m³ Sep 22] second foal: dam,
11.5f winner, half-sister to good middle-distance performers Quiet Fling and
Peacetime and good broodmare De Stael: fairly useful maiden: placed at Ripon,
Lingfield and Kempton: stays 1½m: unraced on extremes of going: sold 26,000 gns
in October. *R. Charlton*

TEMPERING   11 b.g. Kris 135 – Mixed Applause (USA) 101 (Nijinsky (CAN)   –
138) [1996 –, a59: a11g⁴ a12g³ a11g* a12g⁵ a11g⁶ a12g* a16g² a11g³ a14g³ a12g²
a12g² a12g³ a12g 1997 a11g a11g Dec 8] prolific front-running winner (22 times) at
Southwell, all but once on fibresand: no form since early in 1996. *D. W. Chapman*

964

TEMPER LAD (USA)   2 b.c. (Feb 5) Riverman (USA) 131 – Dokki (USA) (Northern Dancer) [1997 7.1g Jun 13] fourth living foal: half-brother to smart American winner at up to 9f Sleep Easy (by Seattle Slew) and smart 6f (at 2 yrs) to 8.5f (in USA) winner Electrify (by Warning): dam unraced half-sister to US Grade 1 winners Coastal and Slew O'Gold: 33/1, in rear in maiden at Sandown. *J. H. M. Gosden*   –

TEMPTING PROSPECT   3 b.f. Shirley Heights 130 – Trying For Gold (USA) 103 (Northern Baby (CAN) 127) [1996 89p: 7m⁴ 8s* 1997 10d² 12g⁶ 12g⁵ 12m³ Nov 1] leggy, light-bodied filly: useful performer, lightly raced: placed in small-field listed events at Newbury in May and Milan in November: should stay beyond 1½m: acts on good to firm ground and soft. *Lord Huntingdon*   95

TEMPTRESS   4 br.f. Kalaglow 132 – Circe 73 (Main Reef 126) [1996 68: 10d* 12m* 11.9d⁶ 12m³ 12m 10.1m⁶ 11.4m 10d² 10f 12g³ 1997 14.1g 12m⁴ 11.9g³ 10.4g⁴ 12m⁵ 11.9d³ 12d 11.4d 10m 12s 12m a12g a10g³ a10g⁶ a13g Dec 12] lengthy filly: fair handicapper on turf (ran poorly after seventh start), modest on all-weather: stays 1½m: acts on good to firm and dead ground and equitrack: effective visored or not. *J. L. Harris*   76 d a51

TEMPUS FUGIT   2 ch.f. (Feb 23) Timeless Times (USA) 99 – Kabella (Kabour 80) [1997 5.7f 5.1g* 5d² 5.1m² 5.1f³ 5s⁶ 6g Oct 25] 2,100Y: sturdy filly: second reported foal: dam well beaten: fairly useful performer: won maiden at Nottingham in June: good second in minor events at Windsor and Chepstow following month: reportedly jarred up fourth starts, and well held after 3-month absence on return, though had stamina stretched each time: speedy and barely stays 5f: acts on dead ground and good to firm, seems unsuited by firm. *B. R. Millman*   85

TEMUJIN   2 ch.c. (Mar 26) Presidium 124 – Too Familiar 52 (Oats 126) [1997 6m May 28] 525Y: seventh foal: dam, 7f winner at 2 yrs, also successful over hurdles: last in maiden at Folkestone. *D. C. O'Brien*   –

TEN BOB (IRE)   2 br.c. (Feb 14) Bob Back (USA) 124 – Tiempo 50 (King of Spain 121) [1997 7m⁶ 8s* 8v² Nov 26] third foal: dam sprint maiden: confirmed debut promise to win maiden at Musselburgh in November readily: creditable 8 lengths second of 6 behind Eco Friendly in Prix Saint-Roman at Saint-Cloud: should stay 1¼m: acts on heavy going. *M. H. Tompkins*   91

TENDER DOLL (IRE)   2 b.f. (Mar 24) Don't Forget Me 127 – Mistress Vyne 63 (Prince Tenderfoot (USA) 126) [1997 6s⁴ 6m⁴ a7g⁵ 6g Aug 11] 1,000 2-y-o: half-sister to several winners: dam placed over 5f at 3 yrs: poor form when fourth in sellers. *C. A. Dwyer*   40

TENNYSON BAY   5 b.g. Allazzaz – Richards Folly 59 (Hotfoot 126) [1996 NR 1997 a13g Jan 7] of no account. *Jamie Poulton*   –

TEN PAST SIX   5 ch.g. Kris 135 – Tashinsky (USA) (Nijinsky (CAN) 138) [1996 93d: 9.2s² 10.3g² 10.4f⁵ 9.2g⁴ 12.4m⁶ 10.4g 10s 10.3g⁵ 12s 1997 9.2d⁶ 7.5m⁵ 10g* 11.1s 8d May 18] lengthy, good-quartered gelding: won seller at Ripon in April, making most and only worthwhile form at 5 yrs: stays 1¼m: acts on good to firm and soft ground: blinkered second start. *Martyn Wane*   60

TENSILE (IRE)   2 b.c. (Apr 10) Tenby 125 – Bonnie Isle 115 (Pitcairn 126) [1997 7g 7g⁴ 8.1d² 8f 8d Oct 17] IR 8,000F, 20,000Y: sturdy colt: has a quick action: half-brother to winners abroad by Irish River and Green Forest: dam effective at 1m and second in Oaks: fair maiden: in frame at Newmarket and Chepstow in August: below form in nurseries: will prove suited by further than 1m. *L. M. Cumani*   76

TEOFILIO (IRE)   3 ch.c. Night Shift (USA) – Rivoltade (Sir Ivor 135) [1996 87: 8m² 7.9g² 1997 8.5m* 10.3v³ 7m 8m Jun 17] good-topped colt: fairly useful performer: won Beverley maiden in April: choked next time: wore tongue strap and ran well when seventh of 28 to Fly To The Stars in Britannia Handicap at Royal Ascot final start: stays 1m: best efforts on good to firm ground: joined J. Noseda. *D. R. Loder*   93

TERAAB   3 b.g. Primo Dominie 121 – Valika 75 (Valiyar 129) [1996 –: 6f⁶ 1997 7m Mar 31] sturdy gelding: quite well bred, but no sign of ability. *J. H. M. Gosden*   –

TERDAD (USA)   4 ch.g. Lomond (USA) 128 – Istiska (FR) (Irish River (FR) 131) [1996 77: 8g² 1997 a11g³ 8g² 9.9m 10g 8.5d 8.2g⁴ 8f⁵ 7g³ 8g² 7.1d* 7s⁴ 10m⁵   66

Oct 28] big, rangy gelding: fair performer: simple task, won maiden at Musselburgh in June: left T. D. Barron after penultimate start: effective at 7f/1m: acts on firm and dead going, possibly not soft. *Mrs M. Reveley*

TEREYNA 2 gr.f. (Apr 21) Terimon 124 – Lareyna 98 (Welsh Pageant 132) [1997 8d Oct 28] half-sister to numerous winners, including smart 1¼m/1½m colt Jack Jennings (by Deploy), 7f winner at 2 yrs: dam sprint winner at 2 yrs: 25/1, under 8 lengths seventh to Baffin Bay in maiden at Leicester, slowly away but running on: should improve. *R. F. Johnson Houghton* — 58 p

TERMON 4 b.f. Puissance 110 – Alipura 74 (Anfield 117) [1996 59: 8.1g² 8.1f² 8m⁴ 8.1g* 7g 9.2m⁴ 8.3m⁵ 7.1m 8.3g³ 1997 8s 7.1m 7s⁴ 6m 7d⁵ 9.2s⁶ 8g 9.2d⁶ 8f⁵ 8m 8g a7s Nov 28] leggy filly: poor performer at best: effective at 6f to 1m: best form on good going or firmer: tried visored: inconsistent. *Miss L. A. Perratt* — 41 d

TEROOM 2 br.c. (Feb 28) Mtoto 134 – Ballad Opera (Sadler's Wells (USA) 132) [1997 7m⁵ Oct 22] 11,000F: third foal: brother to 4-y-o Totem Dancer: dam, third over 1m in France, half-sister to very smart 1m to 1¼m winner Supreme Leader from the family of Pebbles: 25/1, showed fair bit of promise in steadily-run maiden at Yarmouth, racing freely and finishing best out of pack to be over 10 lengths fifth to Misbah: should stay stay 1¼m+: sure to do better. *A. C. Stewart* — 75 p

TERRITORY (IRE) 2 b.c. (Feb 9) Common Grounds 118 – Chouette 54 (Try My Best (USA) 130) [1997 6f³ 5.1d² 5d³ 6.5v* 8v⁵ Dec 7] IR 56,000Y: first foal: dam poor maiden from family of Sayyedati: fairly useful form for G. Lewis first 3 starts: won minor race at Maisons-Laffitte in November and 3¼ lengths fifth of 7 to Smart Squall in listed race at Toulouse: stays 1m: acts on heavy going. *R. Gibson, France* — 92 ?

TERRY'S ROSE 3 br.f. Nomination 125 – Moharabuiee 60 (Pas de Seul 133) [1996 42+: 5d⁴ 6m⁶ a8.5g 6m a6s² 1997 a6g⁵ a8g⁴ a7g⁵ 6f² 6.1g² 6.1d³ a5g 8g 5.9m 8g 5.9m 6.1m 6g⁶ Sep 27] close-coupled filly: disappointing maiden: probably doesn't stay 1m: acts on firm and dead going. *R. Hollinshead* — 51 d

TERTIUM (IRE) 5 b.g. Nordico (USA) – Nouniya (Vayrann 133) [1996 93: 8d³ 8g 8.5g³ 8.5m* 10m⁴ 10.1m² 8m² 10.4m 8.1m⁵ 9.9f⁶ 7.9m 8m 8m⁶ 9m 7.9g 1997 8g 8m⁶ 8.5d 10m⁶ 8.5m² 10.1g 8m 7s² 7m⁶ 8d² 8m 8.1m² 8g⁴ 7f 8d 7m 8g Oct 18] strong, good-bodied gelding: fairly useful handicapper: generally in good form at 5 yrs until last 3 starts: effective at testing 7f to 1¼m: acts on firm and soft going: has reportedly choked on occasions, and sometimes has tongue tied: held up: joined Miss Gay Kelleway. *Martyn Wane* — 85

TESSAJOE 5 ch.g. Clantime 101 – Busted Love (Busted 134) [1996 76: 11.9g⁶ 12m* 11.9d⁴ 12f⁴ 12.4f³ 11.9m 12g² 12g* 12g⁴ 12g 1997 12g³ 12.3v⁶ 12f* 12g* 11.9g 12.3m* 12m² 11.9g 12m* 12g Oct 25] workmanlike gelding: fairly useful handicapper: better than ever at 5 yrs, winning at Thirsk (twice) in June, Ripon in July and Catterick in September: stays 1½m: acts on firm ground and soft: has been bandaged behind: usually travels long way on bridle. *M. J. Camacho* — 93

TEST THE WATER (IRE) 3 ch.c. Maelstrom Lake 118 – Baliana (CAN) (Riverman (USA) 131) [1996 89: 6m 5m² 6g² 6m² 6m³ 7d* 1997 8g⁶ 7.6d 8d⁵ 8.1s³ 8d 8v Oct 11] quite attractive colt: unimpressive mover: fairly useful handicapper: easily best effort at 3 yrs when third at Sandown in August: stays 1m well: acts on good to firm and soft ground. *R. Hannon* — 83

TETRIS (IRE) 3 b.f. Nordico (USA) – Firefly Night (Salmon Leap (USA) 131) [1996 ?: 6s² 6v⁵ 1997 8d 8.3s⁶ 8.2g Jun 18] signs of ability but little form: sent to Italy. *C. F. Wall* — –

TEULADA (USA) 3 b. or br.f. Riverman (USA) 131 – Triple Tipple (USA) 111 (Raise A Cup (USA)) [1996 NR 1997 8s⁵ 8.3g⁴ 8.3m Jul 28] half-sister to 5-y-o Zuno Flyer and useful 1m winner Triode (by Sharpen Up): dam 7f to 1m winner (later Grade 2 8.5f winner in USA) is out of half-sister to smart middle-distance filly Trillionaire: only form in maidens when fourth in steadily-run event at Windsor: will stay beyond 1m. *L. M. Cumani* — 61

TEXAS COWGIRL (IRE) 7 ch.m. Salt Dome (USA) – Cloven Dancer (USA) 86 (Hurok (USA)) [1996 9g 5.5g⁶ 6g⁵ 6d 6g 5.5g 6m 5h* 5f* 5f³ 5g³ 1997 5g² 6m³ 5s⁴ 5g² 5f² 5h² 5h² 5g* 5g² 5d² Nov 8] workmanlike mare: modest performer: ran in — 60

France/Belgium in 1996, winning 2 minor events in latter country: first outings in Britain for nearly 2 years when in frame in handicaps at Folkestone second and third starts: consistent in Belgium afterwards, winning handicap at Groenendaal in October: effective at 5f and 6f: acts on hard and soft ground and on dirt: blinkered of late. *H. Vanderdussen, Belgium*

TEXAS SCRAMBLE   8 b.g. Norwick (USA) 125 – Orange Parade (Dara   –
Monarch 128) [1996 NR 1997 14.1d Nov 3] poor maiden, very lightly raced. *B. P. J. Baugh*

TEZAAB   3 gr.g. Petong 126 – Very Nice (FR) (Green Dancer (USA) 132) [1996   51
NR 1997 7m⁵ a7g⁵ a9.4g 10s⁶ 10f 8g³ 9.7m³ 8m 8m³ 8f 10m Sep 26] 8,100F, 11,000Y: leggy gelding: half-brother to 7.5f (at 2 yrs) to 13f winner Bankroll (by Chief Singer) and a winner in Germany by Sharrood: dam, winner from 9f to 11f in France, is out of sister to Dahlia: modest maiden handicapper: stays 1¼m: acts on firm ground. *B. Hanbury*

THAHABYAH (USA)   3 b.f. Sheikh Albadou 128 – Golden Cap (USA) 76   *
(Hagley (USA)) [1996 71p: 6g⁴ 6m³ 6f* 1997 8s May 17] angular filly: progressive form at 2 yrs for H. T. Jones: tailed off only outing in 1997: stays 6f: acts on firm ground. *D. Morley*

THAHIB   3 b.c. Polish Precedent (USA) 131 – Hamama (USA) (Majestic Light   70 d
(USA)) [1996 NR 1997 12d 12d⁶ 12d⁶ 12d³ 13.8g 16m Aug 6] first foal: dam, Irish maiden third at 7f, half-sister to Quick As Lightning: fair maiden: trained by K. Prendergast in Ireland first 4 starts: no promise for new connections: stays 1½m. *J. L. Harris*

THAI MORNING   4 gr.c. Petong 126 – Bath 76 (Runnett 125) [1996 65+, a108:   –
5s 5d⁶ 6g³ 6m⁶ 5m 6m⁵ 6g 7.1f⁴ 8d a8.5g* a8g* a10s* a9.4g⁵ 1997 a8.5g³ 10m Mar   a108
31] compact, sturdy colt: has a fluent action: useful handicapper on all-weather: good third under top weight to Rambo Waltzer in £14,100 event at Wolverhampton in March: pulled too hard final start: stays 1¼m: no improvement in blinkers: sold 33,000 gns in December. *P. W. Harris*

THALEROS   7 b.g. Green Desert (USA) 127 – Graecia Magna (USA) 109   – §
(Private Account (USA)) [1996 49§, a62§: a8g² a8g² a8g⁵ 8m⁶ 8.5m⁵ 12f 1997 8d 12g a9.4g 10m a10s a14g Nov 17] big gelding: temperamental and no longer of much account. *J. S. Wainwright*

THALJANAH (IRE)   5 ch.g. In The Wings 128 – Dawn Is Breaking (Import   87
127) [1996 86: 11.9g⁵ 14m³ 18.7g 16s³ 16m 1997 18m 14.9m⁴ 18.7s³ 16s² 13.9d³ 16.1s 16m³ 16m⁴ 14.1d 16.5s Nov 8] smallish, workmanlike gelding: fairly useful handicapper: stays 18.7f: acts on good to firm ground and soft: edgy sort: possibly suited by waiting tactics. *B. Smart*

THANKSGIVING (IRE)   2 ch.f. (Feb 6) Indian Ridge 123 – Thank One's Stars   96
(Alzao (USA) 117) [1997 5.2m³ 6m³ 5m* 6g³ 5v⁵ Oct 11] good-bodied filly: fifth foal: half-sister to 3 winners, including 1995 2-y-o 5f winner Dwingeloo (by Dancing Dissident) and fairly useful 1993 2-y-o 6f and 7f winner Suris (by Taufan), later successful at up to 11f in Italy: useful form: won minor event at Folkestone in September: good third to Regal Revolution in listed race at Ayr: gone in coat and edgy, not entirely discredited in extreme conditions in Cornwallis Stakes at Ascot final start: stays 6f: acts on good to firm ground. *Major D. N. Chappell*

THANKS KEITH   2 ch.g. (Mar 6) Risk Me (FR) 127 – Nannie Annie 60 (Persian   61
Bold 123) [1997 5g⁴ a5g³ a6g 7g Sep 24] IR 4,400Y: fifth live foal: brother to a 1m to 1½m winner in Sweden: dam ran 3 times at 2 yrs: modest form in maidens at Carlisle and Southwell first 2 starts: well beaten afterwards, absent 4 months before final outing (blinkered): tends to be soon off bridle. *J. J. O'Neill*

THATCHAM ISLAND   4 ch.f. Jupiter Island 126 – Floreal 68 (Formidable   –
(USA) 125) [1996 –: 10m 10s 1997 10m a8.5g⁶ Sep 20] big, plain filly: has a round action: well beaten in maidens and handicap. *D. L. Williams*

THATCHED (IRE)   7 b.g. Thatching 131 – Shadia (USA) 53 (Naskra (USA))   55
[1996 55: 8m 8.5m 7.1g⁶ 8f³ 8f⁵ 8.1g³ 8f³ 7.5m* 8f⁵ 8.3m³ 7.5g² 8g⁴ 8.5m* 8f 8m 10g 8m* 10f 1997 7.5m 8g* 8m 8f 8g⁴ 8m⁴ 8.5v 8m 7.5m⁴ 8.5m⁵ 8m⁴ 8g 7.5g 8m 10.1g 8m⁴ 8s Nov 6] leggy gelding: has a quick action: modest handicapper: won

very strongly-run event at Carlisle in April: several good efforts after: effective at 7.5f to 1¼m: acts on hard going, not at best on soft/heavy: effective blinkered/visored or not: suitable mount for apprentice: goes well on stiff tracks: tough. *R. E. Barr*

THATCHMASTER (IRE) 6 b.g. Thatching 131 – Key Maneuver (USA) (Key To Content (USA)) [1996 65: 7m⁶ 8s⁶ 7f² 8m² 8.1m* 10g² 10g* 8g³ 1997 8m⁴ 8.1g³ 10.2m 10g* 10m⁴ 10m Oct 1] tall gelding: fair performer: won claiming handicap at Goodwood in August for second year running: unable to dictate last 2 starts, not discredited: stays 1¼m: acts on firm ground: headstrong: front runner/races prominently. *C. A. Horgan*   73

THAT MAN AGAIN 5 ch.g. Prince Sabo 123 – Milne's Way 83 (The Noble Player (USA) 126) [1996 101: 5.1g⁴ 6g 5m 5f⁴ 5m 5d⁶ 5.6m 5g 5g 1997 5.2g⁴ 5.1v⁴ 5g 5g² 5d² 5g⁶ 5m 5.2m³ 5.1g 5m⁵ a6g⁶ a6s a6g⁵ Dec 19] small, robust gelding: only fairly useful handicapper on turf, fair on all-weather, in 1997: best at 5f/easy 6f: well held on heavy ground, acts on any other turf and on the all-weather: usually races prominently: sometimes blinkered/visored. *S. C. Williams*   88 a79

THAT OLD FEELING (IRE) 5 b.g. Waajib 121 – Swift Reply (He Loves Me 120) [1996 –: 8d 1997 7m⁶ a9.4g⁴ 10m 9.2s 8m 12g 10m a8.5g Sep 30] quite good-topped gelding: fairly useful for R. Hannon at 3 yrs: very lightly raced since (bought only 2,000 gns before reappearance), and retains little ability: tried blinkered. *D. W. Chapman*   –

THEANO (IRE) 4 b.f. Thatching 131 – Akamantis 97 (Kris 135) [1996 8g* 9f* 10m³ 8m⁵ 1997 8d³ 9s² 6g 6.3d* 8g³ 6m⁶ 7m* 8s 7d⁴ 7m 8d³ Oct 12] tall filly: smart performer on her day: won valuable handicap at the Curragh (beat Ger's Royale by 4½ lengths) and minor event at Tipperary (easily) in the summer: respectable 6¾ lengths third to Ryafan in Falmouth Stakes at Newmarket on fifth start: finished lame sixth and eighth outings: useful form at 1¼m, best efforts at 6f/7f: acts on firm and soft going. *A. P. O'Brien, Ireland*   114

THE ARTFUL DODGER 2 b.g. (Mar 30) Alhijaz 122 – Madam Millie 99 (Milford 119) [1997 6.1m 6.1g Sep 28] 10,000Y: half-brother to 1½m winners Millie's Dream (by Petoski) and 4-y-o My Millie: dam sprinter: only a little sign of ability in maidens at Nottingham in September. *R. J. R. Williams*   –

THEATRE MAGIC 4 b.g. Sayf El Arab (USA) 127 – Miss Orient (Damister (USA) 123) [1996 64, a68: a7g² a8.5g² a6g⁵ 7s⁴ 8.5d² 8m⁵ 6d 6g a8g³ 8g a8g² a6g⁵ a9.4g³ 10g 7g a9.4g³ a7g³ a6g⁴ 1997 a8.5g⁶ a7g* 8.3s 6g a7g* 5m a8.5f 7.1d⁶ a7g⁴ a7g 7g a7g⁶ a6g⁵ Nov 24] close-coupled gelding: fair handicapper on all-weather, poor on turf: won at Wolverhampton in April and May: effective at 6f to 9.4f: acts on fibresand (unraced on equitrack) and dead going: effective blinkered/visored or not: takes keen hold, and races prominently. *D. Shaw*   43 a72

THEATRE OF DREAMS 2 b.f. (Apr 1) Tragic Role (USA) – Impala Lass 81 (Kampala 120) [1997 5g³ 5m⁴ 5.1m² 5m* May 2] 4,000Y: leggy filly: fifth foal: half-sister to several winners, including 3-y-o Toronto and 4-y-o Yeoman Oliver: dam 5f performer: fair form in maidens before winning 4-runner claimer at Musselburgh. *P. D. Evans*   70

THE BARNSLEY BELLE (IRE) 4 b.f. Distinctly North (USA) 115 – La Tanque (USA) (Last Raise (USA)) [1996 50, a59: 7.5g⁵ 8.1g⁶ 7g⁶ 6.9f⁵ 7.1m³ 7m² 7g a6g² a7g² a7g* a7g a8g⁵ 1997 a8g³ a7g* a8g 7m 7g 7d² 8g⁵ 7m² 7g 8s⁶ a7g³ a8g⁴ Dec 18] leggy, angular filly: modest handicapper: won at Southwell in April: bit inconsistent after: stays 1m: acts on fibresand, good to firm and dead ground: usually races prominently. *J. L. Eyre*   50 a63

THE BEAT ROLLS ON (IRE) 2 b.f. (Mar 8) Roi Danzig (USA) – Miss Pennine (IRE) (Pennine Walk 120) [1997 5m 5m* Apr 11] 1,000 2-y-o: unfurnished filly: second foal: dam Irish maiden sister to useful performer in Ireland: won seller (sold 6,600 gns) at Beverley in April: sent to Sweden. *Martyn Meade*   48

THE BLACK DUBH (IRE) 4 b.g. Classic Secret (USA) 91 – Coral Cave 79 (Ashmore (FR) 125) [1996 –: 8g 10g 1997 12m 9f May 1] of little account. *J. J. Quinn*   –

THE BLUES ACADEMY (IRE) 2 b.g. (Apr 11) Royal Academy (USA) 130 – She's The Tops 83 (Shernazar 131) [1997 7.1m⁶ 7.1g 6g⁴ Oct 22] IR 32,000Y: tall,   68 sturdy gelding: has scope: third foal: half-brother to 3-y-o Lycility: dam 1½m winner out of half-sister to Most Welcome, also the family of Teenoso: best effort in 3 runs in maidens within 5 weeks when under 4 lengths fourth to stable-companion Love Academy at Newcastle: should stay at least 1m: visored all starts. *M. Johnston*

THE BOOZING BRIEF (USA)   4 b.g. Turkoman (USA) – Evening Silk   –
(USA) (Damascus (USA)) [1996 63: 10g 11.6m 12m⁴ 11.4g⁴ 14.1f 12m⁴ a11g⁶
12.1g² 1997 10g 13s May 4] tall gelding: formerly fair maiden: no promise in 1997:
blinkered last 3 starts. *C. Parker*

THE BOY JOHN (USA)   2 b.c. (Apr 20) Groovy (USA) – La Chaux (Welsh   76
Saint 126) [1997 5m² 5m² 5d⁴ 6g² 6d⁴ 5.2d 6f² 6.9d² 6g Oct 25] 22,000Y:
close-coupled colt: fourth foal: half-brother to 2 winners in USA by Faster Than
Sound: dam Irish 2-y-o 6f winner: fair maiden: will prove best up to 1m: acts on firm
and dead ground: withdrawn after forcing way out of stalls once: sometimes edges
left: running well when brought down final start: consistent: sold 19,000 gns, and
sent to USA. *R. Hannon*

THE BUTTERWICK KID   4 ch.g. Interrex (CAN) – Ville Air 85 (Town Crier   66
119) [1996 51: 6.1d 6g 8m 7f⁴ 6m⁵ 5.9f 13.8g² 12.1g⁴ 14s⁴ 18g 1997 14.1g* 14.1d²
12.3v* 12d* 14.1f² 12g⁶ 13.1d 14.1d 16s⁴ Nov 6] workmanlike gelding: fair handicapper: won at Nottingham, Chester and Musselburgh in April/May: best effort
afterwards when fourth at Musselburgh final start, set plenty to do: stays 2m: best
form on good going or softer: tried blinkered/visored at 3 yrs: held up: genuine: won
over hurdles in December. *R. A. Fahey*

THE CANNIE ROVER   2 ch.c. (May 29) Beveled (USA) – Sister Rosarii   48
(USA) (Properantes (USA)) [1997 5s⁵ 5.9f 7g⁴ 5m 7m 7.9s 7m 6m Oct 6] 4,000Y:
tall colt: has a round action: brother to 2 winners abroad and half-brother to 3
winners, including ungenuine miler Royal Interval (by Interrex): dam unraced: poor
maiden on balance. *M. W. Easterby*

THECOMEBACKKING   2 ch.c. (Jan 20) Mystiko (USA) 124 – Nitouche 68   53
(Scottish Reel 123) [1997 5.1m 6g 6m 7.5f⁶ 8m⁴ 8d a8.5g⁵ Nov 1] 7,200Y: un-   a?
furnished colt: first foal: dam 5f (at 2 yrs) and 7f winner: modest maiden at best:
probably better at 1m than shorter. *S. C. Williams*

THE DEEJAY (IRE)   3 ch.g. Desse Zenny (USA) – White Jasmin 53 (Jalmood   66
(USA) 126) [1996 64: 5m 7m² 5.9f² 7m² 7m* 7m³ 8m 8m 7f⁶ 1997 10.3m³ 10g 14m
Aug 21] smallish, workmanlike gelding: fair handicapper: easily best effort at 3 yrs
on reappearance: should stay 1½m: raced only on good going or firmer: visored (out
of form) once: usually races prominently. *Mrs Merrita Jones*

THE DILETTANTI (USA)   4 br.g. Red Ransom (USA) – Rich Thought (USA)   97
(Rich Cream (USA)) [1996 90: 8d² 8m⁴ 8g* 10.4m 8m 10m⁴ 10.4m 1997 10.1m⁴
10m* 10.1g 10m³ 9m 12d Oct 16] sturdy colt: carries condition: fluent mover: useful
handicapper: won at Newmarket in May: best subsequent effort when third at
Windsor in July: stays 1¼m: acts on good to firm and dead ground: front runner/races
prominently. *J. A. R. Toller*

THE DOWNTOWN FOX   2 br.c. (Mar 14) Primo Dominie 121 – Sara Sprint   82
(Formidable (USA) 125) [1997 6m⁶ 6d³ 6.1g⁵ 6d² 6.1d³ Oct 30] 7,800F, 16,500Y:
leggy, rather unfurnished colt: unimpressive mover: fifth foal: half-brother to 3-y-o
Sheraton Girl: dam Italian 6f (at 2 yrs) and 7f winner, half-sister to very smart 1m/
1¼m performer Radetzky: fairly useful maiden: good efforts in Newmarket nursery
and Nottingham minor event (made most) last 2 starts: likely to hung left second start:
to prove best short of 1m. *B. A. McMahon*

THE DRUIDESS (IRE)   2 b.f. (Mar 16) Distinctly North (USA) 115 – Moody   –
Lover (Jalmood (USA) 126) [1997 5m 5m 6.1g 7d a5g⁶ a6g a7g a7g Dec 18] 2,000Y:
third living foal: half-sister to a winner in Italy by Pennine Walk: dam unraced
granddaughter of Oaks third Moonlight Night: little sign of ability. *G. C. Bravery*

THE DUBIOUS GOOSE   3 b.g. Yaheeb (USA) 95§ – Dunnington (Risk Me   43
(FR) 127) [1996 –: 5f 6m 8.2g 1997 8m 7.1g⁴ 7.1g Sep 15] small gelding: has a round
action: only worthwhile form when fourth in 7f handicap at Musselburgh in August.
Mrs J. R. Ramsden

THE EXECUTOR 7 ch.g. Vaigly Great 127 – Fee 111 (Mandamus 120) [1996 66
NR 1997 8m⁴ 8s³ 10s² 9.7m⁵ a8.5g³ 8m* 10g⁵ 8.1g² Sep 11] workmanlike gelding:
fair performer: unraced on flat between 1993 and 1997: justified favouritism in
17-runner seller at Bath in August: effective at 1m/1¼m: acts on good to firm and
soft going (below best on fibresand): tends to carry head awkwardly. *R. J. O'Sullivan*

THE FARAWAY TREE 3 b.f. Suave Dancer (USA) 136 – Sassalya (Sassafras 113
(FR) 135) [1996 85p: 6m* 1997 10g 10.2m⁵ 10g³ 11.9d² 14.6m² 14g* 16f⁵ Oct 4]
angular filly: made into a smart performer: gained deserved success in 3-runner
minor event at Haydock in September, beating Poltarf a short head: best efforts when
runner-up in Galtres Stakes at York (3 lengths behind Kaliana) and Park Hill Stakes
at Doncaster (neck behind Book At Bedtime) previous 2 starts: stays 14.6f (finished
tired in 2m Jockey Club Cup final start): acts on dead ground, probably firm.
G. Wragg

THE FED 7 ch.g. Clantime 101 – Hyde Princess 75 (Touch Paper 113) [1996 43: 36
a6g³ a6g a6g⁶ a5g 5.1g 5m 6.1m 1997 5g 6f a5g a5g⁴ Dec 22] small, strong gelding:
poor 5f handicapper: acts on all-weather, firm and dead ground: best efforts at 5 yrs
in visor, tried only once since: usually races prominently. *J. L. Eyre*

THE FLY 3 gr.c. Pharly (FR) 130 – Nelly Do Da 78 (Derring-Do 131) [1996 119
95p: 7g 7d* 8m* 8m⁴ 1997 10.4g* 12g⁵ 12d 14.6m³ 12f³ Oct 3]
    The decision to deviate occasionally from a policy which has served her
so well, that of buying only grey fillies, has paid off handsomely for Mrs
Corbett in recent years. The grey gelding Morceli, a smart chaser, has carried
her colours with distinction in National Hunt races, while the grey colt The Fly,
an 11,000-guinea yearling, has already earned over £80,000 in prize money on
the flat.
    The Fly, the winner of two of his four races as a two-year-old, devel-
oped into a decidedly smart performer in the latest season. Allowed to take his
chance in the Derby after a very smooth success in a rated stakes handicap at
York in May on his seasonal reappearance, The Fly acquitted himself with
credit in finishing fifth to Benny The Dip, beaten eleven and a half lengths.
Held up at the back of the field, as at York, The Fly was still travelling strongly
when pulled to the outside in the straight but couldn't reach a challenging
position after being checked. The Fly failed by a long way to give his running
when forcing the pace in the Irish Derby on his next start, beating only one
home, so it came as no surprise to see waiting tactics readopted when he reappeared almost three months later in the St Leger at Doncaster. The Fly, who
once again travelled strongly, was still in last place around three lengths behind
the favourite Silver Patriarch when the pair began to make a forward move
early in the straight, and when the latter came through to press for the lead over
two furlongs out The Fly was on his heels. Whereas Silver Patriarch continued
to run on strongly, going on to win by three lengths, The Fly was unable to
sustain his effort and passed the post in third, a neck behind Vertical Speed.

		Lyphard	Northern Dancer
	Pharly (FR)	(b 1969)	Goofed
	(ch 1974)	Comely	Boran
The Fly		(ch 1966)	Princess Comnene
(gr.c. 1994)		Derring-Do	Darius
	Nelly Do Da	(br 1961)	Sipsey Bridge
	(gr 1977)	Flying Nelly	Nelcius
		(gr 1970)	Flying By

    The Fly's grandam, Flying Nelly, is the dam of Further Flight and five
other winners, among them the quite useful mile-and-a-half performer Bustling
Nelly, herself the dam of Busy Flight, a smart winner of five races at that trip.
Further Flight and Busy Flight are stable-companions of The Fly and, like him,
are sons of Pharly, who was a top-class racehorse at up to a mile and a quarter.
The Fly's dam, Nelly Do Da, successful over a trip just short of six furlongs
on her only outing as a two-year-old but well beaten at three, has produced

THE

Mrs J. M. Corbett's "The Fly"

six other winners, including the useful stayer Retouch (by Touching Wood). A leggy individual and a good mover, The Fly won on dead ground as a two-year-old but has shown his best form on good and good to firm. He ran several pounds below his St Leger form on firm going on his final outing of the season, when third of four in a listed event at Newmarket won by Mons, though that was a falsely-run race which wouldn't have suited The Fly, who was again held up. The Fly is well capable of winning a pattern race and he'll be an interesting runner if he turns up at York's May meeting again, this time for the Yorkshire Cup. As far as staying two miles goes, it may be best to see him at a mile and three quarters again before being adamant either way. Clearly his pedigree gives him every chance of getting the trip, and although he failed to sustain his run in the closing stages of the St Leger, it might be premature to assume he'll never stay two miles. After all, the effort of closing on Silver Patriarch in the early part of the straight at Doncaster was bound to have taken something out of him. *B. W. Hills*

THE FLYING PHANTOM 6 gr.g. Sharrood (USA) 124 – Miss Flossa (FR) 69
(Big John (FR) 125) [1996 NR 1997 18.7s 14.1m⁴ 18g Oct 18] useful performer at 4 yrs: fair form at best in 1997: last of 31 in Cesarewitch at Newmarket final start: stays 18.7f: acts on firm and soft going: sometimes a front runner. *M. H. Tompkins*

THE FOUR ISLES 3 b.g. Never So Bold 135 – Far Claim (USA) 35 (Far North –
(CAN) 120) [1996 53: 5d³ 6m 5.1m⁶ 5g⁶ 5m⁴ 6f⁵ 6m⁶ 6d 7s 1997 8.1g Aug 3] workmanlike gelding: modest form at 2 yrs: showed nothing only outing at 3 yrs. *D. J. Wintle*

THE FRISKY FARMER 4 b.g. Emarati (USA) 74 – Farceuse (Comedy Star 56
(USA) 121) [1996 63d: a7g⁶ a6g a6g² a6g a6g² a6g⁵ 6s* a6g² 6.1g 6.1m³ 5.1g³ 6.1m⁵
6d⁵ 6m a6g a7g⁴ 1997 a7g³ a7g⁵ a6g a6g³ a6g 6m⁴ 7g⁴ 6f⁴ 6m 7m 6d⁴ 6g⁵ 6m* 6m⁶
Sep 22] leggy gelding: modest performer: made all in seller at Brighton in August:
stays easy 7f: acts on firm ground, soft and the all-weather: effective visored/
blinkered or not. *W. G. M. Turner*

THE FUELOLOGIST 2 b.g. (Apr 12) Skyliner 117 – Munequita (Marching On –
101) [1997 5g a5g 5f Sep 17] sixth foal: brother to winning 2-y-o sprinters Monkey's
Wedding (in 1993, later successful in Scandinavia) and Monkey Adel (in 1994) and
half-brother to a winning sprinter by Rambling River: dam ran once at 2 yrs: well
beaten in maidens and a seller: visored final start. *Miss J. F. Craze*

THE FUGATIVE 4 b,f. Nicholas (USA) 111 – Miss Runaway 73 (Runnett 125) 70
[1996 58d: 8m 7f⁵ a7g² a8s a10g 1997 a7g 6m 5m² 5m 6d* 5s* 5g* 5g⁵ 6g⁵ 5g 6m
5m 5.3f a7g Oct 27] small filly: fair handicapper: rattled off quick hat-trick at Epsom
and Folkestone (2) in June/July: well beaten last 4 starts: stays 7f: best form on good
going or softer on turf, seems to act on equitrack: often slowly away: sold only 2,800
gns in October. *P. Mitchell*

THE FULLBANGLADESH 4 ch.f. Hubbly Bubbly (USA) – Oakhurst § –
(Mandrake Major 122) [1996 –: a6g a8g a7g⁶ 11.1g⁵ 12g⁶ 12g⁴ 1997 a11g Feb 17]
little worthwhile form. *J. L. Eyre*

THE GAY FOX 3 gr.c. Never So Bold 135 – School Concert 80 (Music Boy 124) 95
[1996 50: 5g³ 5d² 5s⁴ 6.1m² 6m⁵ 6m 6.1s 1997 6m⁶ 5m⁴ 7m* 7g 6m 6d⁴ 5s* 6g 5.1m*
6m 6g 6s⁴ 6g 5d² Oct 16] good-topped colt: useful handicapper: won at Warwick
in May, Newmarket in June and Chester in July: best effort when short-headed by
The Puzzler at Newmarket final start: effective at 5f to 7f: acts on good to firm and
soft ground: has had tongue tied: has been heavily bandaged: races prominently.
B. A. McMahon

THE GENE GENIE 2 b.c. (Feb 3) Syrtos 106 – Sally Maxwell (Roscoe Blake 90
120) [1997 7g² 7.1g² 8d⁴ 10m⁴ Nov 1] 1,000F: good-topped, rangy colt: has scope:
second reported foal: dam second in NH Flat race: fairly useful form: ran well in
listed events at Pontefract and Newmarket final 2 starts, swallowed up over 1f out
after dictating pace in race won by Trigger Happy in latter: keen-going sort, but stays
1¼m: should win a race. *M. J. Heaton-Ellis*

THE GLOW-WORM (IRE) 2 b.c. (Apr 9) Doyoun 124 – Shakanda (IRE) 95 p
(Shernazar 131) [1997 7d* 7m³ 7g⁶ 8f³ 8d* Oct 17] 23,000F, 50,000Y: lengthy colt:
second foal: half-brother to 3-y-o Shadiann: dam Irish 1½m winner, half-sister to
dam of Prix Vermeille winner Sharaya: useful and progressive performer: won
maiden in June and nursery in October, both at Newmarket, latter 28-runner event by
neck from Noble Demand: should be well suited by 1¼m/1½m: should do well in
good-class handicaps in 1998. *B. W. Hills*

THE GREAT FLOOD 4 ch.g. Risk Me (FR) 127 – Yukosan 69 (Absalom 128) 63
[1996 55: 8d 7.5m⁴ 10g⁶ 12.1g⁴ a7g⁵ a8.5g⁴ 1997 a14.8g* a16g⁵ Jan 21] plain
gelding: modest handicapper: won at Wolverhampton (by 5 lengths) in January: stays
15f. *C. A. Dwyer*

THE GREEN GREY 3 gr.g. Environment Friend 128 – Pea Green 98 (Try My 53
Best (USA) 130) [1996 59: 6m⁶ 7.1m 6m⁶ 7.1m 10f⁵ 8d 11.4m a10g 10m 7g² 8f* 8.2d a48
a8s⁶ a10g Nov 25] big, workmanlike gelding: good mover: modest handicapper: won
17-runner apprentice maiden event at Bath in September: seems best around 1m:
acts on firm going, poor form on dead and equitrack: visored (not discredited) once.
W. R. Muir

THE GROVELLER 2 b.c. (Mar 27) Prince Sabo 123 – Estonia (Kings Lake 75
(USA) 133) [1997 6f⁴ 5.1g⁴ 6g⁴ 6d³ 7g a7g* 6.1s³ 6d Sep 2] 10,500 2-y-o: strong, a77
useful-looking colt: has round action: third foal: half-brother to 11f winner Cry Baby
(by Bairn): dam Irish 11f winner, also successful over hurdles: fair performer: won
maiden at Wolverhampton in August: stays 7f: acts on soft going and fibresand.
P. D. Evans

THE HAPPY FOX (IRE) 5 ch.g. Ballad Rock 122 – Amanzi 94 (African Sky 77
124) [1996 83d: 6s 5.1g⁵ 6m 6f 6g 5m⁵ 6m 5g² 5m⁴ 5m³ 6f 5.1g 5g 6.1s⁶ a6s³ 1997 a93
a5g* a5g* 6m⁵ 5g⁶ a6g⁴ 5.1m a6f* 6g⁴ 6m⁴ 6g 6m 5g² 5g 5m⁴ 6.1g a6g⁶ a6g* a6g*

Nov 21] lengthy gelding: fairly useful on all-weather, fair on turf: won handicaps at Wolverhampton in February, March and June and claimers at Southwell and Wolverhampton in November: effective at 5f/6f: acts on firm ground (below form on soft), best on fibresand: usually blinkered, effective when not: tends to hang left: inconsistent on turf: sent to Sweden. *B. A. McMahon*

THE HOBBY LOBBY (IRE) 2 b.g. (Apr 11) Shalford (IRE) 124§ – Chepstow   44 +
House (USA) 56 (Northern Baby (CAN) 127) [1997 5.1m6 a5g 6f4 7m5 6m5 5.1g 6m4 7g Sep 3] IR 16,500Y: fourth foal: dam third at 5f from 2 starts at 2 yrs: poor maiden on balance: trained first 4 starts by M. Channon: stays 6f: below form on fibresand: visored fourth outing. *Miss K. M. George*

THE HONORABLE LADY 2 b.f. (Mar 13) Mystiko (USA) 124 – Mrs   56 ?
Thatcher (Law Society (USA) 130) [1997 5d 6g2 6m 7g3 7m* 7g 7m 7g3 8g 7m Oct 23] IR 9,200Y: lengthy filly: third foal: half-sister to Italian 1½m and 1¾m winner Hyakutake (by Environment Friend): dam unraced daughter of half-sister to Shirley Heights: modest performer: won seller at Yarmouth in July: creditable efforts in nurseries at Catterick next 2 starts, but well below form final 2: should stay at least 1m: acts on good to firm ground. *M. R. Channon*

THE IMPOSTER (IRE) 2 ch.c. (Apr 12) Imp Society (USA) – Phoenix Dancer   44
(IRE) (Gorytus (USA) 132) [1997 6.1s6 6m3 5d4 Jul 17] first reported foal: dam, ran twice in Ireland, half-sister to useful miler Absheer, from an excellent middle-distance family: poor form when in frame in sellers. *D. J. G. Murray Smith*

THE IN-LAWS (IRE) 3 ch.f. Be My Guest (USA) 126 – Amboselli 73 (Raga   90
Navarro (ITY) 119) [1996 83: 6.9m* 8m 8.3g 7g4 7g3 1997 7m6 8g5 9m3 10m 10g3 Oct 18] leggy, unfurnished filly: fairly useful handicapper: third at Goodwood in September and Redcar in October: stays 1¼m well: yet to race on extremes of ground: sold 33,000 gns, and joined O. Sherwood. *Sir Mark Prescott*

THE INSTITUTE BOY 7 b.g. Fairy King (USA) – To Oneiro 69 (Absalom   –
128) [1996 53, a66: a5g2 a5g6 a5g* a6g3 a5g2 a5g4 a6g* a6g4 6d3 a5g 5g3 6g 5m 5g2   a71
5m5 5g* 5g4 5m2 5m 1997 a5g4 a6g2 a6g3 a5g5 a6g Feb 4] smallish, strong gelding: poor mover: fair handicapper on the all-weather, modest on turf: effective at 5f and 6f: goes well on the all-weather, acts on firm and dead ground: effective in blinkers/visor (not tried since 1995). *Miss J. F. Craze*

THE LAMBTON WORM 3 b.g. Superpower 113 – Springwell 73 (Miami   77 d
Springs 121) [1996 80: 5m2 6m2 6m3 6m* 6m4 6d6 5m 1997 6m 6d2 6g5 6g 6s4 6d4 6g 7s 7d Sep 19] strong, well-made gelding: fair handicapper: good efforts 4 of first 5 starts in 1997, well below form afterwards: should stay 7f: acts on good to firm and soft ground: showed signs of temperament when blinkered fourth start: gelded after final one. *Denys Smith*

THE LIMPING CAT (IRE) 2 b.c. (Mar 25) Emarati (USA) 74 – Little Madam   86 +
66 (Habat 127) [1997 5.1g5 5.1m* 5g3 Aug 20] 10,000Y: sturdy, close-coupled colt: poor walker: half-brother to 6f winner Monsieur Petong (by Petong) and 1988 2-y-o 5f seller winner Alo'Niko (by Mansingh): dam 5f winner: won maiden at Nottingham in July most decisively, soon leading: fairly useful effort when 5¾ lengths third to Bay Prince in listed race at York: likely to prove a sprinter: may do better yet. *B. C. Morgan*

THELONIUS (IRE) 2 ch.c. (Mar 31) Statoblest 120 – Little Sega (FR)   67
(Bellypha 130) [1997 5m5 6g 7d2 7.9s5 6m5 Sep 21] 8,000Y: leggy, quite good-topped colt: third reported foal: dam French 11f winner, granddaughter of Poule d'Essai des Pouliches and Prix de Diane winner La Sega: fair maiden: second at Warwick in August: stays 1m: acts on soft ground. *J. G. Smyth-Osbourne*

THE MAGISTRATE (IRE) 2 br.c. (Apr 24) Case Law 113 – Bel Ria (Gay Fan-   68
dango (USA) 132) [1997 6m6 7.1g5 7g5 6.9d4 Oct 21] 13,000Y: workmanlike colt: half-brother to a 2-y-o 7f seller winner by Magical Strike and Irish 1m winner Municipal (by Common Grounds): dam maiden half-sister to very smart middle-distance performer Topanoora: fair form in maidens: likely to stay 1m. *M. Blanshard*

THEME ARENA 4 b.f. Tragic Role (USA) – Sea Siesta (Vaigly Great 127) [1996   61
–: a9.4g5 11.5m 14m 1997 a12g6 16.1g* 16s* 16g 16s Nov 6] sparely-made filly: winning hurdler: modest handicapper: won at Warwick and Nottingham in October:

stiffer tasks and unable to dominate last 2 starts: stays 2m well: acts on soft ground: visored last 4 starts: front runner. *M. C. Pipe*

THE MERRY MONK 6 ch.g. Balidar 133 – Floret 49 (Monsanto (FR) 121) [1996 NR 1997 a8g⁶ Dec 2] no sign of ability in 2 runs. *D. Morris*

THEME TUNE 2 b.f. (Apr 28) Dilum (USA) 115 – Souadah (USA) (General Holme (USA) 128) [1997 7g 7g² 7g Sep 4] 8,000Y: fifth foal: half-sister to 3-y-o Blue Ridge and 5f (at 2 yrs) to 7f winner Make The Break (by Dominion): dam unraced daughter of speedy Bitty Girl: only form when 4 lengths second in maiden at Yarmouth in July. *Dr J. D. Scargill*   57

THE MUNRO'S 3 b.c. Safawan 118 – Some Cherry 41 (Some Hand 119) [1996 NR 1997 7m 9.2g 10s⁵ Oct 14] 2,200Y: fourth reported living foal: half-brother to a NH Flat race winner by Escapism: dam won 1m seller: no promise in maidens. *J. S. Goldie*   –

THE NEGOTIATOR 3 ch.g. Nebos (GER) 129 – Baie Des Anges (Pas de Seul 133) [1996 NR 1997 7m² 8.5m⁵ 8d 8.2g 8.2s⁴ 8.2m 10m⁴ 10d Nov 3] 14,000Y: tall, unfurnished gelding: second foal: dam won in Belgium: fair form on debut, generally disappointing after: headstrong, and unlikely to stay much beyond 1m: seems to act on good to firm and soft going. *M. J. Heaton-Ellis*   73 d

THE NOBLE OAK (IRE) 9 ch.g. The Noble Player (USA) 126 – Sea Palace (Huntercombe 133) [1996 –: 5m 5m 6m 5m⁴ 5g 5m 8f 1997 5.7d May 19] small gelding: sprint handicapper: little form since 1995. *M. J. Bolton*   –

THENORTHERNPLAYBOY (IRE) 4 gr.g. Distinctly North (USA) 115 – Monetary Wish (Wishing Star 117) [1996 –: a7g a12g 1997 10.3s⁶ Jun 25] poor maiden: tried blinkered: dead. *T. Wall*   –

THE ODDFELLOW 4 b.g. Efisio 120 – Agnes Jane (Sweet Monday 122) [1996 –: a8g⁶ 10s⁴ 1997 a11s a8g Jan 13] lightly raced, and no form: dead. *N. Bycroft*   –

THE ORRAMAN (IRE) 3 b.g. Taufan (USA) 119 – Miss Pennine (IRE) (Pennine Walk 120) [1996 –: 5m 6d 1997 10v⁶ 15g 12.1g Sep 1] no form. *J. J. O'Neill*   –

THE OTHER RISK 2 b.g. (Feb 1) Risk Me (FR) 127 – First Fastnet (Ahonoora 122) [1997 5m 8.3g 5d Oct 17] fourth foal: brother to French 1¼m winner Je Reve and Italian 7f winner Votfebrar: dam 5f winner at 4 yrs: probably of little account. *D. A. Nolan*   64

THE PRINCE 3 b.g. Machiavellian (USA) 123 – Mohican Girl 112 (Dancing Brave (USA) 140) [1996 NR 1997 8g⁴ 8m² 8m* 10.4d⁵ 7.9d⁴ 8m Sep 21] well-made colt: has a quick action: first foal: dam, winner at up to 11f, half-sister to Yorkshire Oaks winners Sally Brown and Untold: fairly useful performer: landed odds (easily) in maiden at Newmarket in May: creditable efforts in handicaps last 2 starts: stays 1m: acts on good to firm and dead ground. *G. Wragg*   93

THE PRUSSIAN QUEEN 2 b.f. (Apr 18) Dilum (USA) 115 – Dewberry 68 (Bay Express 132) [1997 5m Jun 4] 5,400Y: half-sister to several winners, including 2-y-o 5f winners by Monsanto, Swing Easy and Lugana Beach: dam 6f winner: tailed off in minor event at Beverley. *C. Smith*   –

THE PUZZLER (IRE) 6 br.g. Sharpo 132 – Enigma 87 (Ahonoora 122) [1996 109§: 6s² 6g³ 5g 5f⁶ 6s* 6.1s⁵ 6s 1997 6s 6f 6s 5.6m 5d* 6g 6s Nov 8] leggy, useful-looking gelding: bad mover: useful performer on his day: easily best effort at 6 yrs when winning handicap at Newmarket in October by short head from The Gay Fox: stays 7f: acts on good to firm (not firm) and heavy going: usually bandaged: has gone lame while racing on several occasions, and cannot be relied on. *B. W. Hills*   106 §

THE REAL MCCOY 3 b.g. Deploy 131 – Mukhayyalah (Dancing Brave (USA) 140) [1996 –: 6m 8g 6v 1997 8.2m Jul 25] no sign of ability. *I. P. Williams*   –

THERE BE DEMONS (USA) 2 b.c. (Feb 18) Devil's Bag (USA) – Krisalya 98 (Kris 135) [1997 8f⁶ Oct 29] 35,000Y: fourth foal: half-brother to 3-y-o Egoli, 1994 2-y-o 7f winner Crystal Cavern (by Be My Guest), later winner in USA, and 6-y-o Conic Hill (formerly fair 1m/1¼m winner): dam 10.4f winner from good family: 8/1, shaped better than bare result when about 6 lengths sixth to Publisher in maiden at Yarmouth, stumbling early on but closing up strongly until outpaced and not knocked about final 2f: will be suited by 1¼m+: sure to improve. *G. Wragg*   72 p

THERHEA (IRE) 4 b.g. Pennine Walk 120 – Arab Art (Artaius (USA) 129) 87
[1996 89d: 6s⁴ 8d* 7.9f 8f 8.1v 10s 1997 8m 8.1g 8d 10s 8g⁶ 8g² 8.2g* 8d² 8.1d²
7.9g² 8.1g⁴ 7.9s* 8d 8m⁴ 8g Oct 18] close-coupled, good-bodied gelding: takes the
eye: fairly useful handicapper: won at Nottingham in June and York in September:
suited by around 1m: acts on good to firm and soft ground: twice blinkered, including
when below form third 4-y-o start: genuine and consistent. *B. R. Millman*

THE RICH MAN (IRE) 2 b.c. (Feb 8) Last Tycoon 131 – Diavolina (USA) 85
(Lear Fan (USA) 130) [1997 5.1d³ 6.1m³ 6.1d³ 6s* 7g* 7m Aug 2] 19,000Y: strong,
good-topped colt: has plenty of scope: fourth foal: half-brother to useful French 3-y-o
1¼m winner Go Boldly (by Sadler's Wells) and useful 6f (at 2 yrs) and 7f winner
Polish Spring (by Polish Precedent): dam French 1¼m winner from family of
Lyphard: fairly useful performer: won minor event at Pontefract and nursery at Ayr
in the summer: seemed ill-at-ease on good to firm going at Goodwood final start:
needs testing conditions at 6f and will stay 1m: acts on soft ground: resolute galloper:
sent to Hong Kong. *B. W. Hills*

THE ROBE 2 b.f. (Mar 19) Robellino (USA) 127 – Outward's Gal 78 (Ashmore 54
(FR) 125) [1997 8m⁴ 8s a6g⁶ a7g⁴ a7g⁴ Dec 12] 3,200Y: sturdy filly: half-sister to a51
useful 5f (at 2 yrs) to 7.5f winner Abbey's Gal (by Efisio) and unreliable 1m winner
Princess of Orange (by Master Willie): dam poor maiden: modest maiden: stays 1m.
B. J. Meehan

THE ROUNDSILLS 3 ch.g. Handsome Sailor 125 – Eye Sight 67 (Roscoe 60
Blake 120) [1996 –: 7f⁶ 8.2g a8g⁵ 1997 10g 10.8m³ 12g* 16m 12d⁴ 14.1g Oct 4]
unfurnished gelding: modest handicapper: won at Catterick in July: best form at
1½m: acts on dead going. *R. F. Johnson Houghton*

THE STAGER (IRE) 5 b.g. Danehill (USA) 126 – Wedgewood Blue (USA) 87 –
(Sir Ivor 135) [1996 77: 6.9f² 7g* 7m³ 10f⁶ 8g⁶ 1997 8m 8g⁶ Oct 7] tall, lengthy colt:
good mover, with a long stride: fair handicapper: well below form in 1997: best at 7f/
1m: acts on firm ground: blinkered last 2 starts at 3 yrs: takes good hold. *J. R. Jenkins*

THE THRUSTER 2 b.g. (Feb 4) Elmaamul (USA) 125 – Moon Spin 83 (Night 63
Shift (USA)) [1997 6m a6g⁶ 7.6d 8m² Sep 25] lengthy, useful-looking gelding: first
foal: dam 1m to 1½m winner: modest form first and final starts, blinkered when
¾-length second to Rico Suave in nursery at Goodwood, clear most of way: bred to
stay beyond 1m, but rather headstrong. *Major W. R. Hern*

THE TIG 3 b.g. Tigani 120 – The Ranee (Royal Palace 131) [1996 –: 8m 8g 1997 –
8g 8m May 2] little sign of ability. *L. R. Lloyd-James*

THE VALE (IRE) 5 b.g. Satco (FR) 114 – Lady Kasbah (Lord Gayle (USA) 124) –
[1996 NR 1997 6.9g 10m⁴ 8g 11.1m Aug 18] leggy, plain gelding: eighth foal:
half-brother to fairly useful 6f/7f winner Teanarco (by Kafu) and fair 1m winner
Lady Donaro (by Ardoon): dam unraced: no form. *R. M. McKellar*

THE WAD 4 b.g. Emarati (USA) 74 – Fair Melys (FR) 81 (Welsh Pageant 132) 67
[1996 73: a8.5g⁶ a7g⁴ a8g a7g⁴ a6g² a6g 6.1g* 6g³ 6g⁴ 6.1m² 6m 7s⁴ 6m* 6f⁴ 5f 6m
1997 5g 6.9g 6s 5.1m³ 6d 5m 5m² 6g* 5m 5d 5g³ 5d³ 5m 5d Sep 18] leggy,
good-topped gelding: poor mover: fair performer: won claimer at Catterick in July:
stays 6f: acts on firm ground, dead and fibresand: blinkered (pulled too hard) once at
2 yrs: sometimes hangs under pressure: none too consistent. *D. Nicholls*

THE WEST (USA) 3 ch.c. Gone West (USA) – Lady For Two (USA) (Storm –
Bird (CAN) 134) [1996 107+: 6m* 6m³ 7m² 7g 1997 7g⁵ Apr 19] big, rangy, imposing colt: has scope: not the best of walkers: useful 2-y-o, second in Prix de la
Salamandre at Longchamp: refused to settle when disappointing in Greenham Stakes
at Newbury only outing at 3 yrs: should stay 1m, but needs to become much more
tractable. *P. F. I. Cole*

THE WILD WIDOW 3 gr.f. Saddlers' Hall (IRE) 126 – No Cards 109 (No 79
Mercy 126) [1996 NR 1997 8s² Oct 13] half-sister to several winners, including 1¼m
performer Tell No Lies (by High Line): dam won at up to 1m: 66/1, second of 5 to
Right Wing in minor event at Ayr on belated debut, held up last and staying on well.
J. M. P. Eustace

THE WOODCOCK 2 b.g. (Mar 11) Handsome Sailor 125 – Game Germaine –
(Mummy's Game 120) [1997 6.1g Oct 4] first foal: dam ran twice: 25/1, never a
threat in maiden at Nottingham. *B. W. Hills*

THEWRIGHTONE (IRE) 3 b.f. Fayruz 116 – Vote Barolo (Nebbiolo 125) –
[1996 –: 5g 5m 6f 5f⁵ 5f³ 5f a5g 5m⁵ 6g 5s a7g 1997 a6g 6m 5.9f 7g⁶ a8g Nov 17] of
little account. *G. R. Oldroyd*

THE WYANDOTTE INN 3 ch.g. Ballacashtal (CAN) – Carolynchristensen 58   69
(Sweet Revenge 129) [1996 57, a68: 5g a6g⁵ a6g³ 7g a5g² a6g³ 6.1s 5m² a5g² a5g³   a81
a6g² a6g² a6g* 1997 a6g⁴ a7g² a6g* a7g* a6g² 7m⁵ 7.5m² 7.5m 7m 7m 6g⁴ a7g² a7g
a8.5g⁶ Aug 8] plain, quite good-topped gelding: carries condition: poor mover: fairly
useful handicapper on the all-weather, fair on turf: won at Wolverhampton and
Lingfield early in year: trained until after tenth start by R. Hollinshead: stays 7.5f:
acts on good to firm ground: joined K. Burke. *Mrs N. Macauley*

THICK AS THIEVES 5 b.g. Shavian 125 – Vivienda 93 (Known Fact (USA)   39
135) [1996 –: a6g⁵ a7g a6g 6.1g 6d 5g⁶ 5f 7.5m 5m a7g 1997 a6g² a6g² a6g a5g³ a6g   a46
a5g⁴ a5g⁶ 6g 5d 5m⁵ 5f⁴ 5g 5f Aug 27] strong, workmanlike gelding: poor sprint
handicapper: acts on firm ground, dead and the all-weather: visored (below form)
once. *Ronald Thompson*

THIEF OF HEARTS (IRE) 2 b.c. (Apr 8) In The Wings 128 – Love Smitten   112 p
(CAN) (Key To The Mint (USA)) [1997 7.5g* 8m⁴ 9m* Oct 4]

    Thief of Hearts was a notable absentee from the Criterium de Saint-
Cloud. Had he taken part he'd almost certainly have been involved in the finish
and quite possibly would have won the race. In his absence it went to Special
Quest with Daymarti beaten about half a length in third, that pair having
finished a length or so behind Thief of Hearts when placed in the Prix de Conde
at Longchamp four weeks earlier. Now run on the Saturday of the Arc meeting,
the nine-furlong Prix de Conde at Longchamp serves as a good trial for the
Group 1 Criterium de Saint-Cloud over a furlong further. Thief of Hearts gave
the impression he'd have been suited by the longer trip at Saint-Cloud when
winning the Conde. The blinkered Special Quest set a sound pace racing keenly
in front, with Thief of Hearts held up sixth of the seven runners. Once into the
straight Thief of Hearts was produced with a run on the outside and asserted in
good style inside the last. Special Quest kept on well to deprive Daymarti of
second, with the favourite Silic a close fourth and the rest well beaten. Fifth
home Quel Senor was another who did the Conde form no harm, winning a
listed race at Longchamp later in October. The Prix de Conde was Thief of
Hearts's third race. He had made a promising debut when narrowly defeating
more experienced rivals in the opening race of Deauville's August meeting, a
minor event over seven and a half furlongs, and had then started second
favourite for the Prix des Chenes at Longchamp. Still seeming green, Thief of
Hearts finished over ten lengths behind the impressive winner Second Empire
in fourth, held up going well but unable to quicken when ridden and staying on
at one pace.

		Sadler's Wells	Northern Dancer
	In The Wings	(b 1981)	Fairy Bridge
	(b 1986)	High Hawk	Shirley Heights
Thief of Hearts (IRE)		(b 1980)	Sunbittern
(b.c. Apr 8, 1995)		Key To The Mint	Graustark
	Love Smitten (CAN)	(b 1969)	Key Bridge
	(b 1981)	Square Angel	Quadrangle
		(b 1970)	Nangela

    Thief of Hearts's pedigree was another reason for thinking he'd have
been well suited by a step up to a mile and a quarter, but now with his three-
year-old campaign in mind he's likely to prove well suited by at least a mile and
a half. By In The Wings, the sire of Singspiel and the Fabre stable's Irish Derby
winner Winged Love, Thief of Hearts is out of Love Smitten who's already
produced the top-class middle-distance stayer Swain (by Nashwan) and the
smart French mile-and-a-quarter and twelve-and-a-half-furlong winner Water
Poet (by In The Wings's sire, Sadler's Wells). Thief of Hearts is Love Smitten's
fifth live foal; her other one to race, Starstruck (by Soviet Star), was also a

Prix de Conde, Longchamp—Swain's half-brother Thief of Hearts continues on the upgrade

winner, over nine furlongs in the French Provinces. Thief of Hearts has already achieved more than either Swain or Water Poet at the same stage, in fact he's the first of his dam's foals to see a racecourse as a two-year-old. Love Smitten was a late developer herself, gaining her most important wins as a five-year-old, including the Grade 1 Apple Blossom Handicap over eight and a half furlongs. This is a fine North American family, further details of which may be found in Swain's entry in *Racehorses of 1995*. A close-coupled, good-topped colt, the best of Thief of Hearts almost certainly remains to be seen and he seems likely to make up into a very smart performer. Races like the Prix Noailles and/or Prix Hocquart would seem likely starting points for him in 1998. *A. Fabre, France*

THINK AGAIN (IRE) 3 b.g. Long Pond 113 – Either Or (Boreen (FR) 123) –
[1996 NR 1997 12s⁵ 10m 12g 10f 6g Jun 17] 1,500Y: first foal: dam, unraced, from quite good NH family: only a little sign of ability: bred for stamina. *R. Craggs*

THIRD COUSIN (IRE) 2 b.c. (May 15) Distant Relative 128 – Queen Caroline 80
(USA) 67 (Chief's Crown (USA)) [1997 6m a6g³ 5d* 6.1d⁴ Nov 3] IR 14,000Y: second foal: half-brother to 3-y-o Regal Reprimand: dam maiden (stayed 10.5f) half-sister to smart 1986 2-y-o Glory Forever, later third in Poule d'Essai des Poulains: fairly useful form: won maiden at Folkestone in October decisively: similar form when fourth in nursery at Nottingham: showed promise on fibresand: looks a sprinter. *M. J. Heaton-Ellis*

THIRD PARTY 3 gr.f. Terimon 124 – Party Game 70 (Red Alert 127) [1996 62: 63
5f³ 5g⁴ 5m⁴ 6f³ 1997 6m⁶ 5g 6f* 6f⁴ 6s 6m 6m⁶ 6.1m⁴ 6.1m⁴ Sep 23] modest performer: won maiden at Brighton in June: likely to stay 7f: acts on firm ground. *S. Dow*

THISONESFORALICE 9 b.g. Lochnager 132 – Bamdoro 54 (Cavo Doro 124) 47
[1996 –: 8.1g 1997 10.9d⁵ 10.3d⁶ 10.9g³ 11.1g⁴ 15g² 12m³ Aug 20] leggy gelding: poor handicapper: stays 15f: acts on good to firm and soft ground: tried visored: didn't go through with effort once. *J. S. Goldie*

THISTLE PARK 2 ch.g. (Apr 16) Selkirk (USA) 129 – Kimberley Park 72 (Try 70
My Best (USA) 130) [1997 5g³ 6d³ 6d Sep 18] 17,000Y: second foal: dam 7f winner: fair form in maidens: third at Thirsk and Ripon in August: not knocked about final start: should stay beyond 6f. *T. D. Barron*

THOMAS O'MALLEY 2 ch.c. (Mar 28) Wing Park 104 – Martini Time 90 –
(Ardoon 124) [1997 5.7m 6d 6g a6g Oct 6] unfurnished colt: half-brother to several winners, including 5f performer Anytime Anywhere (by Daring March): dam,

THO

5f performer, ran only at 2 yrs: little sign of ability in maidens and a seller. *R. J. O'Sullivan*

THORDIS 4 b.g. Mazilier (USA) 107 – Doppio 62 (Dublin Taxi) [1996 78: 6m² 70 6f⁵ 6.1m⁴ 7f⁵ 6m 7g* a7g 1997 a7g a6g² a6g⁶ a7g² a6g* Oct 4] quite good-topped gelding: fair handicapper: made all at Wolverhampton: effective at 6f/7f: acts on firm ground, dead and fibresand (below best only start on equitrack): effective visored or not: sold 6,100 gns in November. *P. J. Makin*

THORNBY PARK 3 b.f. Unfuwain (USA) 131 – Wantage Park 104 (Pas de Seul 88 133) [1996 72p: 8.2g 8g⁶ 1997 10d⁴ 12.3d² 14s* 14d² 14m⁴ 14g⁴ 16.2g 16.2v⁵ 14d⁶ Oct 17] lengthy filly: fairly useful handicapper: won at Goodwood in June: creditable efforts most starts afterwards: stayed 2m: acted on good to firm and heavy ground: tried blinkered, no improvement: sometimes bandaged: stud. *J. L. Dunlop*

THORNIWAMA 6 b.m. Hadeer 118 – Hidden Asset (Hello Gorgeous (USA) – 128) [1996 –, a45: a10g a12g a8g⁵ a7g⁴ a10g³ a10g* 9.7m 11.7g a11g 10f 11.6m 1997 a12g a10g Jan 25] leggy mare: poor handicapper: well beaten at 6 yrs: usually blinkered/visored. *J. J. Bridger*

THORNTOUN BELLE (IRE) 2 b.f. (May 8) Rainbows For Life (CAN) – – Manzala (USA) (Irish River (FR) 131) [1997 6g⁶ Jun 20] 7,400Y: first foal: dam Irish 1m winner out of half-sister to Poule d'Essai des Pouliches winner Masarika: well held in maiden at Ayr. *J. S. Goldie*

THORNTOUN ESTATE (IRE) 4 b.g. Durgam (USA) – Furry Friend (USA) – (Bold Bidder) [1996 59, a62: a10g³ a10g* a11g a10g³ a12g² 12s⁴ 12.1d⁴ 12d 13s a49 14.6m 1997 a12g⁵ a14.8g² 16s⁶ 13d 21.6g⁴ Apr 28] leggy gelding: poor performer: probably stays 15f: acts on all-weather, no form on turf at 4 yrs: sometimes blinkered: inconsistent, and possibly temperamental. *Martin Todhunter*

THORNTOUN HOUSE (IRE) 4 b.g. Durgam (USA) – Commanche Song 48 – (Commanche Run 133) [1996 –: 10g⁵ 15.8m⁴ 1997 a14.8g 16s Mar 27] no sign of ability. *J. S. Goldie*

THORNTOUN JEWEL (IRE) 4 b.f. Durgam (USA) – Blue Bouquet (Cure – The Blues (USA)) [1996 –: a6g 6m⁵ 7m 6m 7.1f⁶ 5.9f 1997 8m 7g 6.9m Aug 4] smallish filly: no form since 2 yrs. *Miss Z. A. Green*

THOR'S PHANTOM 4 ch.g. Weldnaas (USA) 112 – La Carlotta (Ela-Mana- – Mou 132) [1996 –: 8.3d 7d 9g 1997 12f Jun 10] seems of little account. *M. D. I. Usher*

THRASHING 2 b.c. (Feb 1) Kahyasi 130 – White-Wash 94 (Final Straw 127) – p [1997 7g Jul 8] 10,000F, 54,000Y: fourth foal: half-brother to French 1m winner Kalwhite (by Kaldoun) and French 1½m winner Clean Slate (by Bikala): dam, best at 1¼m, half-sister to smart though ultimately temperamental 1¼m/1½m winner Torchon: 33/1, never a factor in steadily-run maiden at Newmarket: showed a round action: should do better at 1¼m+. *C. E. Brittain*

THREADNEEDLE (USA) 4 b.g. Danzig Connection (USA) – Sleeping Beauty 77 87 (Mill Reef (USA) 141) [1996 81p: 8.2d 8m* 8d 1997 a9.4g⁴ Dec 13] workmanlike gelding: fair performer, lightly raced: fourth in handicap at Wolverhampton, only start in 1997: stays 9.4f. *Lord Huntingdon*

THREE ANGELS (IRE) 2 b.g. (Mar 23) Houmayoun (FR) 114 – Mullaghroe 60 (Tarboosh (USA)) [1997 7f⁶ 6.9d² 7.1s³ Nov 6] IR 4,200Y: half-brother to Irish 1m and 1¼m winner Queen of Finns (by Viking), 6f winner Puck's Boss (by Fairy King) and a winner abroad by Carmelite House: dam unraced: sire (by Shernazar) won Italian Derby: modest form in maidens, placed at Folkestone and Musselburgh late in year: will stay at least 1m. *M. H. Tompkins*

THREE ARCH BRIDGE 5 ch.m. Sayf El Arab (USA) 127 – Alanood 85 79 (Northfields (USA)) [1996 71: 8m 8.3s³ 8.3s⁵ 6.9g³ 9.2g⁶ 7.5m* a9.4g² 7.5f³ 8f* 8f 8.1g 8.3m 8.5m⁴ 8f a7g a9.4g a7s⁶ a8g⁴ 1997 a8g⁴ a8g² a8g* a8g⁵ a8g* a7g a9.4g⁴ a7g 7g⁶ 7m* 7.5m 8g 8m 8.3s 8.5s* 8m* 8m 8.5m⁴ a8g a8.5g Dec 26] quite good-topped mare: fair handicapper: won at Southwell (twice), Newcastle, Beverley and Ripon before end of May: off course 6 months before penultimate start, fell leaving stalls final one: effective at 7f to 9.4f: acts on any going: has worn near-side pricker: wears blinkers. *M. Johnston*

Prix de Lutece, Longchamp—smart stayer Three Cheers puts up his best performance

THREE CHEERS (IRE) 3 b. or br.g. Slip Anchor 136 – Three Tails 121 (Blake- 116 p
ney 126) [1996 –: 8g 1997 11.8f³ 14m* 16.2m² 14.8g* 15m* Oct 4] smallish, sturdy
gelding: smart performer: won maiden at Newmarket (hung markedly right) in May,
listed race on same course in July and Prix de Lutece at Longchamp in October, soon
pushed along in rear but running on strongly to lead over 1f out and beat Bonapartiste
by 2 lengths at last-named: also neck second of 11 to Windsor Castle in Queen's Vase
at Royal Ascot: will prove suited by 2m+: acts on good to firm ground, yet to race on
going softer than good: blinkered or visored: probably a very smart stayer in the
making, capable of figuring prominently in the Cup races. *J. H. M. Gosden*

THREE FOR A POUND 3 b.g. Risk Me (FR) 127 – Lompoa (Lomond (USA) 68
128) [1996 58: 6g⁴ 1997 6g* 6s 6m 6g⁶ a6g 7s* 7.5m³ 7g⁶ 8.1m⁶ 8.5f⁵ 8.1m Sep
21] sturdy, lengthy gelding: fair performer: won maiden at Catterick in March and
handicap there in July: stays 8.5f: acts on firm ground and soft: looked none too keen
when blinkered only all-weather outing: consistent. *J. A. Glover*

THREEPLAY (IRE) 3 b.c. Mac's Imp (USA) 116 – Houwara (IRE) (Darshaan 57
133) [1996 64: 6m⁵ 5g⁴ 6m⁵ 5g³ 6m 6.1s a5g⁵ a5g² a6g⁶ a5g³ 1997 a5g² a5g⁵ a5g⁶ 5s
5.1g a5g Dec 12] smallish, angular colt: has a round action: modest maiden: best
form at 5f: acts on good to firm ground and the all-weather: tried visored. *J. Akehurst*

THREESOCKS 4 ch.f. Weldnaas (USA) 112 – Jeethgaya (USA) 61 (Critique 35
(USA) 126) [1996 –: a8g⁴ a11g⁴ 1997 a11g³ a14.8f⁴ a12g⁴ Jan 20] poor maiden:
somewhat temperamental: dead. *B. Smart*

THREE STAR RATED (IRE) 2 b.f. (Feb 8) Pips Pride 117 – Preponderance 79 p
(IRE) 85 (Cyrano de Bergerac 120) [1997 5m⁴ 5m² 5m 5g* Sep 15] 8,000Y: tall,
lengthy filly: has scope: first foal: dam Irish 2-y-o 5f winner: fair form: trained on
debut by C. Fairhurst: won nursery at Musselburgh by 4 lengths, going away: bolted
to post (unseating rider) previous start: will stay 6f: open to improvement and should
make fairly useful handicapper. *T. D. Barron*

THREE TENNERS 2 b.f. (Apr 27) Distinctly North (USA) 115 – Hollia 72 51
(Touch Boy 109) [1997 5m 5f 6d* 7g⁴ 7g 7g⁴ 6m 7m⁶ Sep 20] 17,000Y: smallish,
strong filly: easy mover: half-sister to three 5f winners, including 3-y-o Fredrik The
Fierce: dam 2-y-o 5f winner: modest performer: won seller at Haydock in July:
creditable efforts in large-field nurseries final 2 starts: stays 7f: acts on good to firm
and dead ground: blinkered 4 of last 5 starts: tends to be slowly away. *J. Berry*

THREE WEEKS 4 ch.g. Formidable (USA) 125 – Zilda (FR) 46§ (Zino 127)   64 d
[1996 67: 10s a8g a8g² a8g* a8.5s* 1997 a9.4g² a8.5f⁵ a9.4g a9.4g 8m 8g 10.2d a8g⁶
8m a8.5g Sep 30] lengthy gelding: unimpressive mover: modest handicapper: mostly
well below form in 1997: stays 9.4f: acts on fibresand. *W. R. Muir*

THROWER 6 b.g. Thowra (FR) – Atlantic Line (Capricorn Line 111) [1996 41:   –
a14.8g⁴ 1997 12.1d⁴ Apr 2] sparely-made gelding: poor maiden handicapper on flat:
useful hurdler for S. Brookshaw, winner 4 times (up to 2½m) in second half of year.
W. M. Brisbourne

THUMBELLINA 2 b.f. (May 3) Robellino (USA) 127 – Welwyn 92 (Welsh   – p
Saint 126) [1997 5m⁶ Aug 5] 3,000Y: half-sister to useful sprinter Welsh Mist (by
Damister) and 7f winner Bashaq (by Jalmood): dam, suited by 6f, half-sister to smart
sprinter Welshwyn: last of 6 in Folkestone minor event. *S. Dow*

THUNDERHEART 6 b.g. Celestial Storm (USA) 132 – Lorelene (FR) 97   51
(Lorenzaccio 130) [1996 NR 1997 13g⁴ 16d⁵ 16m* 16.1m 13d⁵ 16g 17.5d Sep 19]
modest handicapper: won at Musselburgh in July: stays 2m: acts on any going: below
form in blinkers final start. *R. Allan*

THUNDERING PAPOOSE 2 b.f. (Mar 18) Be My Chief (USA) 122 – Thunder   –
Bug (USA) 66 (Secreto (USA) 128) [1997 6m 7m 7.1g Sep 11] sparely-made filly:
first foal: dam 1¼m winner from good American family: soundly beaten in maidens.
A. P. James

THUNDEROUS 6 b.g. Green Desert (USA) 127 – Mixed Applause (USA) 101   –
(Nijinsky (CAN) 138) [1996 –: a7g a10g⁵ a12g 1997 a12s Nov 28] no worthwhile
form: tried blinkered. *J. J. Bridger*

THWAAB 5 b.g. Dominion 123 – Velvet Habit 89 (Habitat 134) [1996 73: a7g   73
6.9d² 7d 6.9m⁵ 6.9g 5.9f⁵ 6m* 6g³ 6m* 6g² 6m* 6m 6m² 7m⁴ 6f 1997 6m 6s⁶ 6m² 6d³
6m 6g 8m³ 7g 6m³ 6.1g 8g Oct 18] strong, good-bodied gelding: fair handicapper:
inconsistent in 1997: effective at 6f to 1m: acts on good to firm and dead ground:
effective blinkered/visored or not: usually held up. *F. Watson*

THWING 2 b.f. (May 18) Presidium 124 – Swinging Baby 73 (Swing Easy (USA)   39
126) [1997 a5g Aug 15] 4,000Y: half-sister to several maidens: dam 5f winner:
never-dangerous seventh in seller at Southwell. *M. W. Easterby*

TIAPHENA 6 b.m. Derrylin 115 – Velda 74 (Thatch (USA) 136) [1996 49: 14.1s⁵   a41
17.1g a16g² 15.8g* 18m 1997 a16.2g⁴ a14g May 12] big, workmanlike mare: poor
handicapper: stays 2m, possibly not 2¼m: acts on fibresand, best turf effort on good
ground. *J. Mackie*

TIARA 2 b.f. (Apr 22) Risk Me (FR) 127 – Dona Krista 84 (King of Spain 121)   –
[1997 5.7m⁵ 5m 6g Aug 20] 48,000Y: good-topped filly: fifth foal (all by Risk Me):
sister to sprinter Risky, smart at 2 yrs in 1993: dam 2-y-o 6f winner: well held in
maidens: sold, and sent to France. *B. J. Meehan*

TIBBI BLUES 10 b.m. Cure The Blues (USA) – Tiberly (FR) (Lyphard (USA)   40
132) [1996 –: 6.9f² 8.3m² 5g 8m 1997 10g 8.3s⁶ 5s⁵ 7s³ 8g⁵ May 30] poor handicapper: barely stays 1m: acts on soft going. *J. S. Goldie*

TICKA TICKA TIMING 4 b.g. Timeless Times (USA) 99 – Belltina 41 (Bel-   32
fort (FR) 89) [1996 –: a7g a7g a6g 1997 a7g 7g 6m a6g⁵ 5g a5g³ 5g a6g a6g⁶ Dec 4]
small, sparely-made gelding: poor handicapper: stays 6f: best effort on fibresand:
tried blinkered/visored. *B. W. Murray*

TICKNTIMA 3 ch.g. Precocious 126 – Stolon Time 80 (Good Times (ITY))   –
[1996 63: 5g⁴ 5f³ 5g⁵ 6g⁵ 1997 7g 12s Nov 6] lengthy, workmanlike gelding: modest
form at 2 yrs: well beaten in 1997. *M. D. Hammond*

TIDEWATER 3 b.f. Shirley Heights 130 – Widows Walk (Habitat 134) [1996 NR   –
1997 10d Sep 13] smallish, good-bodied filly: fifth foal: half-sister to 1¼m winner
Sadler's Walk (by Sadler's Wells) and 1¼m and 1½m winner Rainbow Walk (by
Rainbow Quest): dam once-raced daughter of 1000 Guineas winner On The House:
missed break completely when well held in maiden at Goodwood: sold 10,000 gns in
December. *R. Charlton*

TIE BREAK (IRE) 2 ch.g. (May 29) Second Set (IRE) 127 – Karayasha (Posse   75
(USA) 130) [1997 6d a5g³ Nov 14] 4,600Y: compact gelding: sixth foal: half-brother

to Irish 1989 2-y-o 1m winner Karshouni (by Nishapour) and Irish 7f and 1m winner
Karakani (by Dalsaan): dam twice-raced half-sister to very smart French performer
at up to 1¼m Kaldoun: much better effort in maidens when third at Southwell, edging
right but staying on: should stay 1m. *W. J. Haggas*

TIERRA DEL FUEGO   3 b.f. Chilibang 120 – Dolly Bevan 53 (Another Realm   –
118) [1996 NR 1997 a7g a8g Dec 2] fourth foal: half-sister to 2 winners by Efisio,
notably 6-y-o Oggi: dam, 2-y-o 6f winner, half-sister to smart sprinter Pip's Pride: no
promise in maidens at Lingfield. *H. J. Collingridge*

TIGER LAKE   4 ch.g. Nashwan (USA) 135 – Tiger Flower 103 (Sadler's Wells   –
(USA) 132) [1996 82+: 10.1g⁵ 12m* 16.2m 1997 a10f⁴ 11g a10f 12v Oct 10] lengthy,
attractive gelding: fairly useful winner at 3 yrs: no form in UAE first 3 starts in 1997,
and sold 21,000 gns in July: ran poorly only start for new yard: stays 1½m: well
beaten in blinkers. *S. Dow*

TIGGY SILVANO   2 b.f. (Mar 22) Tigani 120 – Infanta Maria 82 (King of Spain   –
121) [1997 5.7m a7g Dec 18] 3,000Y: half-sister to a 2-y-o sprint winner by Robellino and winning sprinter King Rambo (by Rambo Dancer): dam 5f performer:
behind in maiden (for M. Channon) and seller 5 months apart. *M. Quinn*

TIGHTROPE   2 b.c. (Apr 30) Alzao (USA) 117 – Circus Act (Shirley Heights   80 p
130) [1997 5.7m 6m 5.2m⁴ a7g⁴ 6m² 8m* 7v⁶ Oct 10] 44,000Y: quite good-topped
colt: fifth foal: half-brother to smart USA 3-y-o winner up to 8.5f Brave Act (by
Persian Bold), 1¼m winner and useful hurdler Circus Star (by Soviet Star) and useful
1½m/1¾m winner Jellaby Askhir (by Salse): dam unraced daughter of Lowther
winner Circus Ring: fairly useful performer: generally progressive form, heavily
backed when winning nursery at Leicester in October by 4 lengths, going away
rapidly at finish: not entirely discredited in extreme conditions next time: should
prove suited by 1¼m+: acts on good to firm ground, showed promise on fibresand:
very much type to make a useful 3-y-o, and win a decent handicap. *Sir Mark Prescott*

TIGI   2 ch.f. (May 22) Tigani 120 – Molly Brazen 51 (Risk Me (FR) 127) [1997 7m   –
5m 5g 7m Oct 7] 1,000Y: sparely-made filly: first foal: dam, third at 6f, daughter of
very smart sprinter Polly Peachum: soundly beaten in maidens and a claimer.
Mrs M. Reveley

TIGRELLO   3 ch.c. Efisio 120 – Prejudice 83 (Young Generation 129) [1996 77p: 87
5f⁵ 5.7d² 6g⁶ 1997 8m² 8g⁵ 8m* 7.9g 8m⁴ 8g⁶ 8m Jul 19] leggy, quite good-topped
colt: fairly useful performer: won maiden at Warwick in May: easily best effort
afterwards when fourth of 28 to Fly To The Stars in Britannia Handicap at Royal
Ascot, first home on far side: stays 1m: acts on good to firm and dead ground: usually
has tongue tied. *G. Lewis*

TIGULLIO (IRE)   2 b.c. (Feb 27) Rainbows For Life (CAN) – L'Americaine   –
(USA) (Verbatim (USA)) [1997 7f⁶ 8s Nov 8] 21,000 2-y-o: big, rather leggy colt:
seventh foal: half-brother to several winners in France/Belgium, including useful
3-y-o miler Libria (by Bering): dam French 9f winner out of half-sister to Alzao:
never in race in autumn maidens at Yarmouth and Doncaster. *C. F. Wall*

TIKOPIA   3 b.g. Saddlers' Hall (IRE) 126 – Shesadelight 67 (Shirley Heights   82
130) [1996 NR 1997 12m³ 12.1g² 14m⁴ 10s² 10.2g⁶ 12g⁵ 11.7g* 11.9m³ Sep 21]
65,000Y: first foal: dam (maiden), stayed 2m, sister to very smart middle-distance
filly Infamy: fairly useful performer: gained deserved success in maiden at Bath in
September: needs good test at 1¼m, and should stay beyond 1½m: game and
consistent. *I. A. Balding*

TILAAL (USA)   5 ch.h. Gulch (USA) – Eye Drop (USA) 96 (Irish River (FR)   –
131) [1996 80: 8g³ 8m 1997 10.3d 9m⁵ 9m Oct 7] strong, angular horse: tubed:
disappointing maiden: tried visored. *M. D. Hammond*

TILBURG   2 b.f. (Feb 14) High Kicker (USA) – Touch My Heart 61 (Steel Heart   –
128) [1997 a5g 5.1s 5m 5g 7d 8m 7.5f 10d a8g Nov 24] 600Y: leggy filly: half-
sister to several winners, including fairly useful Irish 1988 2-y-o 5f winner So
Tenderly (by Prince Tenderfoot): dam placed over 5f: no form, including in sellers.
Mrs N. Macauley

TILER (IRE)   5 br.g. Ballad Rock 122 – Fair Siobahn (Petingo 135) [1996 86: 6s⁵   86
7d³ 6g⁴ 6m 7g 7m 6.1m³ 6d 6m² 6f* 6m² 6m² 6m 5.6m 6m 6v 7g 6f² a6g 1997 6m

6m⁶ 6m³ 7m 6s 6s⁵ 6m* 6g⁴ 6m⁵ 6m³ 6g² 6g⁴ 5f² 6g 6.1g 7g 6g 7m³ 6m Nov 4] tall, lengthy gelding: fairly useful handicapper: in good form for most of 1997, and won at Ayr in July: effective at 5f to 7f: acts on firm and soft ground and on fibresand: blinkered once earlier in career: sometimes gives trouble at stalls, and spoiled chance by rearing on final start: tends to wander under pressure: often makes running: tough. *M. Johnston*

TILLER GIRL (IRE)   2 ch.f. (Apr 17) Mujtahid (USA) 118 – Till You (USA)   – (Exclusive Native (USA)) [1997 7g 8.2d Oct 30] 18,000Y: compact filly: half-sister to useful 1¼m winner Tillandsia (by Unfuwain) and 3 winners abroad: dam, 6f to 1m winner in USA, is half-sister to J O Tobin and Mysterious: behind in maidens at Redcar and Nottingham in October. *M. J. Camacho*

TIMBERVATI (USA)   2 br.f. (Apr 14) Woodman (USA) 126 – Never Scheme   79 p (USA) (Never Bend) [1997 7m² Oct 22] $210,000Y: half-sister to several winners, notably Breeders' Cup Sprint winner Very Subtle (by Hoist The Silver): dam unraced half-sister to CCA Oaks winner High Schemes: weak 10/1-shot and green, short-head second of 13 to Jila in maiden at Yarmouth, travelling smoothly and leading over 1f out but showing her inexperience: should stay 1m: sure to improve and win a race. *H. R. A. Cecil*

TIME ALLOWED   4 b.f. Sadler's Wells (USA) 132 – Time Charter 131   119 (Saritamer (USA) 130) [1996 113: 12g² 12m* 12m² 11.9m² 14.6m² 12g² 12d* 1997 12m* May 2]

The death of the blue-blooded Time Allowed robbed her owner-breeder Robert Barnett's Fair Winter Farm of an exciting broodmare prospect. The stud has produced a number of good horses over the years, and, among the fillies to have raced in Mr Barnett's colours, Time Allowed would have joined her dam Time Charter in the paddocks. Alas, Time Allowed fractured her off-hind pastern on the gallops during her build-up to the Coronation Cup and, after having the cast removed in August, fractured her cannon bone in the same leg and was destroyed. Time Allowed had earned a tilt at the Coronation Cup by winning the Grangewood Jockey Club Stakes at Newmarket on her reappearance in May. She'd made into a smart performer as a three-year-old, finishing second four times, including in the Park Hill Stakes and two listed events, before ending the season with a game victory in the Princess Royal Stakes at Ascot. She looked fit and well when returning for the Jockey Club Stakes and,

Grangewood Jockey Club Stakes, Newmarket—Time Allowed's final race and finest performance; Busy Flight (rail) and Mons come next

travelling smoothly in a strongly-run race, quickened to challenge inside the distance and stayed on strongly to get the better of long-time leader Busy Flight by three quarters of a length, with Mons the same distance away in third and a further two and a half lengths back to Celeric.

		Northern Dancer	Nearctic
	Sadler's Wells (USA)	(b 1961)	Natalma
	(b 1981)	Fairy Bridge	Bold Reason
Time Allowed		(b 1975)	Special
(b.f. 1993)		Saritamer	Dancer's Image
	Time Charter	(gr 1971)	Irish Chorus
	(b 1979)	Centrocon	High Line
		(ch 1973)	Centro

Considering that she was from a stoutly-bred, rather late-maturing family, it wasn't altogether surprising that Time Allowed should train on. Her dam was the top-class middle-distance performer Time Charter, who won the Oaks and Champion Stakes at three years, the King George VI and Queen Elizabeth Diamond Stakes at four, and the Coronation Cup at five. Time Allowed was her fifth foal; her previous offspring included the smart stayer Zinaad (by Shirley Heights), who himself won the Jockey Club Stakes in 1993, and his useful sister By Charter, who finished second in the 1989 Cheshire Oaks. Time Charter's sixth foal is Illusion (by Green Desert), a useful mile winner in 1997. More time will be needed before we see the best of her latest foal to race, Generous Terms (by Generous), who was down the field in a two-year-old maiden at Newmarket on his debut. Time Charter was covered by Green Desert again in 1995, and for the fourth time by Shirley Heights the following year. Time Allowed's grandam, Centrocon, was a good-class middle-distance performer (winner of the Lancashire Oaks) and a sister to the high-class stayer Nicholas Bill and the 1981 Jockey Club Cup winner Centroline. Time Allowed stayed a mile and a half. She acted on good to firm and dead ground (she was never raced on softer), and was effective ridden from the front or held up. She was very game and consistent. *M. R. Stoute*

TIME CAN TELL 3 ch.g. Sylvan Express 117 – Stellaris (Star Appeal 133) 68
[1996 71: 5g 5m 7d⁴ 8f⁶ 8.1m² 8.2g* 8m⁴ 8f⁴ 1997 a8.5g⁴ a8g³ a10g² a10g⁵ a9.4g⁴ a11g⁴ 10.3m⁵ 10m² 12.3g⁴ 10.2m³ 10.3d⁵ 11.4m⁵ 8f 8d³ 8g³ 10.5d 8.5f a12g⁵ Nov 18] big, heavy-topped gelding: fair handicapper: failed to win in 1997, but made frame 10 times: effective at 1m (ridden forcefully) to 1½m: acts on firm ground and all-weather, below form on dead: below form visored/blinkered: usually bandaged. *C. Murray*

TIME CLASH 4 b.f. Timeless Times (USA) 99 – Ash Amour 54 (Hotfoot 126) –
[1996 62d: a7g³ 7d 7m⁴ 6g a7g 7f 6.1m a7g a9.4g a7g 1997 a6s⁶ a8g Jan 13] sparely-made filly: modest handicapper at 3 yrs: well held in 1997. *B. Palling*

TIME FOR ACTION (IRE) 5 b.g. Alzao (USA) 117 – Beyond Words (Ballad 83
Rock 122) [1996 91: 10m 12m 12m* 13.9m 11.9f 12m³ 12g 10.4g³ 10s 1997 a12f⁵ 10.1m 10m 12m 10m⁶ 10g 10.3g* Oct 25] small gelding: fairly useful performer: well held on sand in Dubai on reappearance: best 5-y-o effort when winning claimer at Doncaster by 9 lengths: stays 1½m: acts on good to firm and dead ground: goes well with forcing tactics: sold (to join C. Mann) 14,000 gns after final start. *M. H. Tompkins*

TIME FOR TEA (IRE) 4 ch.f. Imperial Frontier (USA) 112 – Glowing Embers 48
107 (Nebbiolo 125) [1996 70d: 6m⁵ 6f³ 7m 6m 7g⁶ 6m 8f 10.3d³ 11.5m 6.9g a6g⁵ a8g a8g 1997 6m 6m 6.1d 6m⁶ 8f⁵ 7f³ Jun 3] sturdy filly: only poor in 1997, and still a maiden: effective at 7f, and has form over 1¼m: yet to race on soft ground, acts on any other on turf and also on equitrack. *C. A. Cyzer*

TIMEKEEPER (USA) 2 b. or br.c. (Apr 3) Exbourne (USA) 125 – Falabella 97
(Steel Heart 128) [1997 5m² 5g* 6g 7s³ 7s⁵ 7.5g* 7.5m* 7.5m² 8s³ Oct 18] 18,000Y: close-coupled colt: unimpressive mover: half-brother to 1991 2-y-o 5f winner Trattoria (by Alphabatim) and several minor winners abroad: dam maiden here and

in USA, daughter of Queen Mary winner Farfalla: useful form: won maiden at Carlisle and listed races at Milan in July and Varese in August: 4½ lengths third to Saratoga Springs in Beresford Stakes at the Curragh final start: stays 1m: acts on good to firm and soft ground: genuine and reliable. *M. Bell*

TIMELY EXAMPLE (USA) 6 ch.g. Timeless Moment (USA) – Dearest Mongo (USA) (Mongo) [1996 –: a8.5g a12g⁴ a12g⁴ a14g 8g a12g⁵ 1997 10g May 17] no longer of much account on flat. *B. R. Cambidge* —

TIME OF NIGHT (USA) 4 gr. or ro.f. Night Shift (USA) – Tihama (USA) (Sassafras (FR) 135) [1996 70: 8d 8.2m 8g² 8f³ 7.1m⁴ 7m⁶ 8.2m 8.3d³ 7g² 1997 7f 7g 8.2g 8.2g³ 10.1f⁶ 8f 8g⁴ 7m a8.5g a7g⁴ Dec 18] leggy filly: modest maiden handicapper: left R. Guest after seventh start: stays 1m: acts on firm ground, dead and fibresand: well held (raced too freely) in blinkers: inconsistent. *J. L. Eyre* 63

TIMES OF TIMES (IRE) 4 b.f. Distinctly North (USA) 115 – Lady Fandet (Gay Fandango (USA) 132) [1996 71, a–: 6m 5.7m 5.2g* 6g 5g 6m 6m 6m* 6f⁶ 6m⁵ a6g 7m 6.1m 1997 6.9m 5.3g 6.1m Sep 15] rather leggy filly: fair performer at 3 yrs for M. Ryan: little form in 1997. *G. L. Moore* —

TIME TO FLY 4 b.g. Timeless Times (USA) 99 – Dauntless Flight (Golden Mallard 103) [1996 –: 6g⁵ 5.9f 5m a5g⁶ 5g 7f a6g 1997 a7g a5g⁶ a6g⁵ a5g* 5m a5g⁵ a6g* a6g² a5g³ 5g a6g⁵ a6g² Dec 4] smallish, good-bodied gelding: fair handicapper on the all-weather, poor on turf: won at Wolverhampton in April and Southwell in June: effective at 5f and 6f: seems best in blinkers. *B. W. Murray* 47 a68

TIME TO HUNT 2 gr.c. (Apr 23) Timeless Times (USA) 99 – Hunting Gold (Sonnen Gold 121) [1997 5m 6m Sep 20] sturdy colt: fifth reported foal: dam lightly raced: behind in maidens. *B. W. Murray* 51

TIME TO TANGO 4 b.f. Timeless Times (USA) 99 – Tangalooma 56 (Hotfoot 126) [1996 73: 5g³ 5f* 5f* 5m⁶ 5f⁴ 1997 6m 5f³ 6g 6g 5g 5m 5g Aug 5] smallish, lengthy filly: fair handicapper: below form in 1997 after second start: best at 5f: yet to race on going softer than good. *G. M. Moore* 67 d

TIME TO TIME 2 ch.f. (Apr 30) Timeless Times (USA) 99 – Supergreen (Superlative 118) [1997 5.1m⁴ 5m 5d³ 6d a5g⁶ Sep 8] 1,600Y: sturdy filly: fifth reported foal: dam unraced: poor maiden: third in claimer at Beverley: sold, to go to Trinidad. *T. D. Easterby* 48

TIMISSA (IRE) 3 b.f. Kahyasi 130 – Timissara (USA) (Shahrastani (USA) 135) [1996 NR 1997 8d² 10m* 12f⁴ Jun 10] smallish filly: second foal: half-sister to fairly useful Irish 1½m winner Timidjar (by Doyoun): dam Irish 1m and 1½m winner: confirmed debut promise when winning maiden at Lingfield in May: again odds on, failed to improve as anticipated for longer trip when fourth of 7 in handicap at Salisbury following month. *L. M. Cumani* 73

TIMOTHY GEORGE (IRE) 3 b.g. Don't Forget Me 127 – Ward of Court (IRE) (Law Society (USA) 130) [1996 –: 8m 6s 7d 1997 10m 10d Oct 28] strong, lengthy gelding: no form. *G. B. Balding* —

TINA KNOWS (IRE) 2 b.f. (Mar 6) Cyrano de Bergerac 120 – Nec Precario (Krayyan 117) [1997 5m 5m Jul 15] IR 2,400Y: leggy filly: second foal: dam Irish 1m winner: behind in maidens. *J. L. Eyre* —

TINDAYA 2 b.g. (Mar 29) Polar Falcon (USA) 126 – Flitcham 57 (Elegant Air 119) [1997 5g⁵ 5.9f 6f⁶ 6d Jul 3] 2,000Y: leggy gelding: second foal: half-brother to a 2-y-o 6f seller winner by Prince Sabo: dam 13f winner at 4 yrs: little worthwhile form, including in a seller. *P. D. Evans* —

TINKERBELL 3 ch.f. Sharpo 132 – Chasing Moonbeams 99 (Final Straw 127) [1996 74, a61: 5m⁵ 6.1g⁶ a7g* 7g⁵ a7g³ a7g* 6m² a7g² 7m² 8g⁵ 7m⁶ 1997 a8.5g⁶ a7g* 7m Mar 22] angular filly: unimpressive mover: modest performer: won handicap at Wolverhampton in March: well beaten only subsequent start: stays 8.5f: acts on good to firm going and on fibresand: visored: sold, and sent to Macau. *W. R. Muir* — a63

TINKER OSMASTON 6 br.m. Dunbeath (USA) 127 – Miss Primula 81 (Dominion 123) [1996 69: 6g 5g 5.1f 6.1d² 5m 5.7m 6g⁴ 5.1m⁴ 5m 1997 5.1m⁵ 5.1d⁴ 5.7d 6.1g 6s⁴ 6d* 5m⁴ 6m⁴ 6.1d³ 5.1m⁶ 5s² 5.7g 6m 6g Oct 27] workmanlike mare: 72

fair handicapper: left M. Saunders after fourth start: won at Windsor in June: well below form form last 3 starts: effective at 5f and 6f: acts on firm and soft going: well beaten only try in visor, formerly effective in blinkers (hasn't worn them since 3 yrs): usually held up. *R. J. Hodges*

TINKER'S SURPRISE (IRE)   3 b.g. Cyrano de Bergerac 120 – Lils Fairy   53
(Fairy King (USA)) [1996 54, a57: 5s 5m⁴ 5m* 5f⁵ 5g⁵ a5g⁴ 5d⁵ 5m² 6m a5g² a6g³
5s⁴ a5g⁵ 1997 5g³ 5m³ 5m² 5g⁴ 5m 5g⁵ 5m 5g 5m Oct 2] strong, good-topped
gelding: modest 5f handicapper: best turf form on good ground or firmer, also acts on
fibresand (probably on equitrack): effective with or without blinkers: takes keen
hold: has looked none too resolute. *J. Balding*

TINKLERS FOLLY   5 ch.g. Bairn (USA) 126 – Lucky Straw 57 (Tumble Wind   58
(USA)) [1996 68: 8.3d⁴ 7.1g* 7d 7.1g 8.1g 8.1f* 6.9f* 8.1g² 7m 7g* 7.5f⁶ 7m 7f
1997 7.5m 8g 8m 8f 10m³ 8m 10g⁶ 10m 8m⁴ 9.2m a8g Oct 20] strong, sturdy
gelding: mostly disappointing in 1997: barely stays 1¼m: acts
on firm and dead ground: tried visored, no improvement. *R. M. Whitaker*

TINOS ISLAND (IRE)   2 b.f. (Apr 8) Alzao (USA) 117 – Lady Windley (Bail-   –
lamont (USA)) [1997 5g 5m 7m⁴ Jun 11] 13,500Y: leggy filly: first foal: dam
French 11f winner out of Prix de Diane winner and Arc second Northern Trick: little
worthwhile form, including in sellers. *M. H. Tompkins*

TIP IT IN   8 gr.g. Le Solaret (FR) – Alidante 65 (Sahib 114) [1996 –: a8g a14g   –
1997 a14g May 12] no worthwhile form on flat. *A. Smith*

TIPPERARY SUNSET (IRE)   3 gr.g. Red Sunset 120 – Chapter And Verse   65
(Dancer's Image (USA)) [1996 –: 5g⁶ 1997 8.3s³ 8g 8.5m⁵ a9.4g 8m* 10g* 8.3g
10s² 10d³ 9m* 8s* Nov 8] strong, close-coupled gelding: fair handicapper: won at
Pontefract and Ripon in August, Newmarket (apprentices) in October and Doncaster
(ladies race) in November: suited by testing conditions at 1m, and stays 1¼m well:
acts on good to firm and soft ground: genuine and consistent. *J. J. Quinn*

TIPPITT BOY   2 b.c. (May 6) Prince Sabo 123 – Space Travel (Dancing   106
Dissident (USA) 119) [1997 5g³ 5.1m 5m⁵ 6f* 5g* 6g⁵ 5m⁵ 5m² 5v Oct 11] IR
17,000Y: close-coupled colt: first foal: dam unraced daughter of smart 6f and 7f
winner Rocket Alert: useful performer: won minor event at Warwick in June before
landing 33/1-success in Norfolk Stakes at Royal Ascot, beating Hopping Higgins

Norfolk Stakes, Royal Ascot—
Tippitt Boy holds off the rallying Hopping Higgins (rail) and Arawak Cay

short head: confirmed that level of ability in Molecomb Stakes at Goodwood 2 starts
later and when 2½ lengths second to impressive Land of Dreams in Flying Childers
Stakes at Doncaster: stays easy 6f: acts on firm ground, well beaten on heavy: has
been early to post. *K. McAuliffe*

TIPSY CREEK (USA)   3 b.c. Dayjur (USA) 137 – Copper Creek 78 (Habitat   110
134) [1996 104: 5m* 5m* 5m⁶ 5m² 1997 5.2g 5m³ 6d Oct 17] robust, good-quartered
colt: smart performer: hobdayed at end of 2-y-o career, wintered in Dubai, and not
seen out until September after reportedly breaking bone in hock: best effort when
narrowly-beaten third of 8 to Dashing Blue in listed race at Newmarket in October,
making most: well beaten (held up over 6f) in similar event there only subsequent
outing: probably best allowed to bowl along over 5f: yet to race on extremes of going:
wears bandages: sent to UAE. *B. Hanbury*

TIRMIZI (USA)   6 b.g. Shahrastani (USA) 135 – Tikarna (FR) (Targowice (USA)   49
130) [1996 NR 1997 a16g² a14g Sep 8] brother to 1½m winner Timissara and half-
brother to 3 winners, including useful 1½m performer Timourtash (by Riverman):
dam French 1m winner: fairly useful at 3 yrs in Ireland for J. Oxx: poor nowadays:
stays 2m: acts on fibresand and heavy ground. *Mrs A. Swinbank*

TIROL'S TREASURE (IRE)   3 b.f. Tirol 127 – Lisa's Favourite (Gorytus   –
(USA) 132) [1996 –: 7f⁶ 6g 6d a8g 1997 a10g Jan 4] no form. *K. T. Ivory*

TISIMA (FR)   3 ch.f. Selkirk (USA) 129 – Georgia Stephens (USA) 64 (The   61
Minstrel (CAN) 135) [1996 –: 6m⁵ 1997 6.9m³ 8m May 5] tall filly: modest maiden,
lightly raced: reared and unseated rider in stalls final start: likely to prove best up to
1m: failed second stalls test in August. *I. A. Balding*

TISSUE OF LIES (USA)   4 b. or br.g. Ascot Knight (CAN) 130 – Choral Group   65
(CAN) (Lord Durham (CAN)) [1996 74: 10m 12.4g 8.5m³ 8.2m² 8.5m⁶ 8f⁵ 11.1m²   a71
9m² 8d 10.5v a8s* a12g³ a9.4g a8g² 1997 10g 14.1f³ 13g³ 14.6d 8m 8.1m 10m a8s⁴
a10g⁴ Dec 2] strong, rangy gelding: fair handicapper: trained by M. Johnston first 6
starts: best efforts of 1997 at Lingfield last 2: stays 1½m: acts on firm ground and the
all-weather, seems unsuited by going softer than good. *J. Akehurst*

TITAN   2 b.c. (Mar 12) Lion Cavern (USA) 117 – Sutosky 78 (Great Nephew 126)   70
[1997 7s 6.9m² 6m 7d* 7m² 7v⁵ Oct 10] 6,000Y: good-topped colt: carries condition:
fifth foal: half-brother to 3-y-o Baby Jane, 4-y-o Montecristo and 5-y-o Dancing
Sioux: dam suited by 1m to 1¼m: fair performer: won nursery at Goodwood in
September, just getting up: also ran well last 2 starts: will be suited by 1m: acts on
good to firm and heavy ground. *S. Dow*

TITANIC (IRE)   2 b.c. (Mar 3) Nashwan (USA) 135 – White Star Line (USA)   100
(Northern Dancer) [1997 5m* 5.2g* 5g⁶ 5m³ 5d⁴ Oct 27] compact, attractive colt:
easy mover with a long stride: brother to fairly useful 1m winner Puissant and half-
brother to several winners, including smart French 1m (at 2 yrs) to 13.5f winner
Whitehaven (by Top Ville): dam won 3 Grade 1 events at 8.5f to 1¼m: impressive
winner of minor events at Doncaster and Yarmouth in July: didn't go on as expected,
though showed useful form when 2¾ lengths third to impressive Land of Dreams in
Flying Childers Stakes at Doncaster in September: will stay 6f, and bred to get good
deal further: acts on good to firm ground: has been edgy at start. *J. H. M. Gosden*

TITHCAR   3 b.f. Cadeaux Genereux 131 – Miznah (IRE) 102 (Sadler's Wells   67
(USA) 132) [1996 –p: 6g 1997 7f² 7m³ 5g² 5m² 5.7g² 6.1g³ 6d Oct 21] workmanlike
filly: fair maiden: creditable efforts most starts in 1997: effective at 5f to 7f: ran
poorly only start on ground softer than good. *B. Hanbury*

TITLE BID (USA)   2 b.c. (Mar 18) Danzig (USA) – Triple Tiara (USA) (Majestic   87 p
Light (USA)) [1997 6d² 6m* 6m⁴ Oct 22] close-coupled colt: first foal: dam French
1½m winner out of US graded stakes winner (11f to 13f) Persian Tiara: fairly useful
form: won maiden at Catterick in September most decisively: creditable fourth in
minor event at Yarmouth: should stay 7f/1m: should improve. *M. R. Stoute*

TITTA RUFFO   3 b.g. Reprimand 122 – Hithermoor Lass 75 (Red Alert 127)   86
[1996 85p: 7d³ 7m⁷ 7m² 8m² 8d⁴ 10g³ 10g* 10.3d⁴ 10d⁶ 10m⁴ Oct 3] quite attractive
gelding: unimpressive mover: fairly useful handicapper: won at Goodwood in June:
respectable efforts at least afterwards: stays 1¼m: yet to race on extremes of going:
sometimes carries head high: sold 12,000 gns in October. *B. J. Meehan*

Prix du Gros-Chene, Chantilly—
Titus Livius lands the odds from Wardara (No. 5) and Hever Golf Rose

TITUS LIVIUS (FR)   4 ch.c. Machiavellian (USA) 123 – Party Doll 108 (Be My   115
Guest (USA) 126) [1996 110: 6.5g³ 5d⁴ 5f 6g² 7s⁶ 5d³ 6s⁵ 1997 5.5g³ 5d² 5m* 5d²
6.5d³ 6g⁵ 5f⁶ 8f³ Nov 19] quite attractive colt: smart performer: won Prix du
Gros-Chene at Chantilly in May by ¾ length from Wardara: good efforts 3 of next 4
starts, placed in King's Stand Stakes at Royal Ascot (probably unlucky, switched
twice before finishing strongly, neck behind Don't Worry Me) and Prix Maurice de
Gheest at Deauville (1¼ lengths behind Occupandiste), then 2½ lengths sixth to
Carmine Lake in Prix de l'Abbaye de Longchamp on final start for J. Pease in France:
third in allowance race at Hollywood Park: will prove best up to 7f: acts on firm and
soft ground: held up: genuine and consistent. *W. Dollase, USA*

TIYE   2 b.f. (Feb 27) Salse (USA) 128 – Kiya (USA) 85 (Dominion 123) [1997 7g   71
7d⁵ Sep 19] third foal: half-brother to a winner in Sweden by Sharrood: dam, suited
by 1m, half-sister to smart 1993 2-y-o Lemon Souffle who stayed 1m: better effort
when fifth in minor event at Newbury: should be suited by 1m+. *R. Hannon*

T'NIEL   6 ch.m. Librate 91 – Classy Colleen (St Paddy 133) [1996 NR 1997 10g   – §
May 17] lightly-made mare: no worthwhile form: has twice refused to race. *G. Fierro*

T·N·T EXPRESS   3 b.g. Sizzling Melody 117 – Lady Minstrel (Tudor Music 131)   –
[1996 –: 5m 6g 8.2s a7g 1997 a8g a8g a11g⁶ Jan 31] no sign of ability: tried visored:
dead. *E. J. Alston*

TOBLERSONG   2 b.c. (Feb 21) Tirol 127 – Winsong Melody (Music Maestro   93
119) [1997 6s* 6m⁶ 6m² 6m* 6g⁵ Oct 25] good-bodied colt: seventh foal: half-
brother to several winners, including useful sprinter El Yasaf (by Sayf El Arab) and
5-y-o Norsong: dam sprint maiden: fairly useful performer: won maiden at Epsom in
July and minor event at Yarmouth in October: not at all discredited in listed race at
Doncaster final start: likely to prove best short of 1m: acts on good to firm and soft
ground. *R. Akehurst*

TOCCO JEWEL   7 br.m. Reesh 117 – Blackpool Belle 70 (The Brianstan 128)   –
[1996 22: 8.3m 9.7g² 10.8m 11.6m 1997 10g 11.8g 10.8g a11g a12g 10d⁶ Sep 2]
seems of little account now. *M. J. Ryan*

TOFFOLUX   2 b.f. (Mar 17) Sharpo 132 – Coca (Levmoss 133) [1997 6d 8g Oct   –
24] 4,600 2-y-o: plain filly: half-sister to several winners, including smart 7f (at 2
yrs) and 9f winner (probably stayed 1½m) Greenwich Papillon (by Glenstal): dam
placed at 11f in France: well beaten in maidens at Newmarket and Doncaster in
October. *H. J. Collingridge*

TOI TOI (IRE) 3 b.f. In The Wings 128 – Walliser (Niniski (USA) 125) [1996   82
71p: 7.1s⁵ 7d⁴ 1997 8m⁵ 12.3s⁴ 10.2s² 11.8g⁴ 12g⁵ 16.1d² 13.9s 15d 14.1s³ 11.8d³
a14g⁴ a14g* a12g⁵ Dec 6] neat filly: unimpressive mover: fairly useful handicapper:
won amateur event at Southwell in November: needs more than 1½m and stays 2m
well: acts on fibresand and soft going: below form in visor. *D. W. P. Arbuthnot*

TOKAY 2 b.f. (May 23) Kylian (USA) – Tokyo (Mtoto 134) [1997 10s⁵ Oct 15]   57 p
first foal: dam, no worthwhile form, half-sister to smart stayer Teamster: sire (by
Sadler's Wells) unraced: 16/1 and green, running-on fifth to Wave Rock in maiden at
Nottingham: will be well suited by 1½m+: should improve. *P. F. I. Cole*

TOLEPA (IRE) 4 b.f. Contract Law (USA) 108 – Our Investment (Crofter (USA)   –
124) [1996 –: 10m 7f⁴ a8.5g 10.9m 8.3g⁴ 10.1m 1997 9.9m 7.1m 8.5s May 11]
lengthy filly: no worthwhile form. *J. J. O'Neill*

TOLL'S TIMES 2 ch.g. (May 12) Clantime 101 – Petroc Concert § (Tina's Pet   42
121) [1997 5g 5m a5g 5d 7f 6g⁶ 5m⁶ Jun 26] 4,200Y: smallish gelding: brother to a
modest sprint maiden and a winner in Norway: dam irresolute maiden plater: little
form bar penultimate start: twice blinkered. *M. W. Easterby*

TO LOVE WITH LOVE 2 ch.f. (Apr 21) Cadeaux Genereux 131 – Miss   73
Loving 89 (Northfields (USA)) [1997 5d⁶ 5.2m 5.3m* 5.3m⁴ Sep 3] 30,000Y: leggy
filly: half-sister to several winning sprinters, including 3-y-o Lucky Dip and fairly
useful Love Returned (by Taufan), and a winner abroad: dam 2-y-o 5f and 7f winner:
fair form: gambled on when winning minor event at Brighton in August: creditable
effort in nursery there final start: probably a sprinter. *W. Jarvis*

TOM 2 gr.c. (Mar 25) Petong 126 – Wanton 106 (Kris 135) [1997 5g 5m 6g 7.5f³ 8s   48
8s⁵ Nov 6] smallish, good-bodied colt: seventh foal: half-brother to several winners,
notably 3-y-o Classic Park and 1997 US Grade 2 winner Rumpipumpy (by Shirley
Heights): dam sprinter, best at 2 yrs: poor maiden: third in selling nursery at Beverley
(final start for Lord Huntingdon): stays 1m: seems to act on firm and soft ground:
visored/blinkered final 3 outings. *J. Hetherton*

TOMAL 5 b.g. King Among Kings 60 – Jacinda (Thatching 131) [1996 49: a12g³   37
a10g a13g a8g 8m² 8f⁶ 8.1m³ 10f 8.3d² 8m⁵ 10m 1997 a10g 9.7g 10g⁵ 8g⁶ May 5]
small gelding: poor handicapper: seems to stay 1¼m: acts on firm and dead ground,
has shown little on the all-weather: well beaten in blinkers. *R. Ingram*

TOMASHENKO 8 ch.g. Efisio 120 – Stockingful (Santa Claus 133) [1996 NR   –
1997 10g 8f Jun 4] no longer of any account. *T. W. Donnelly*

TOMBA 3 ch.c. Efisio 120 – Indian Love Song 68 (Be My Guest (USA) 126)   118
[1996 106: 5g⁶ 6m³ 6g* 6m² 6d* 6m⁶ 6s* 1997 6m⁵ 7d⁴ 6s* 6d* 6d* 7g⁴ 6s*
6.5d² 6.5g* 6d² 7d³ 6s³ Nov 8]
  Tomba is one of the better racehorses named after famous sportsmen,
and, while he's most unlikely to make the same impact on the racecourse as
Alberto Tomba has on the ski slopes, he'll continue to do well around six and
seven furlongs when the ground is good or softer. A winner three times as a
two-year-old, Tomba developed into a smart performer at three and finished out
of the frame only once in twelve starts, winning five times. Those victories
were gained in minor contests at Haydock and Newbury, listed races at
Haydock (a rated stakes) and Newcastle, and in a Group 3 race at Hoppegarten
in Germany. In terms of prestige and prize-money the last-named event was
the most important, but Tomba showed significantly better form in the Colonel
Porter Brown Ale Chipchase Stakes run at Newcastle in June, the manner of his
victory in ground as soft as he's encountered so far encapsulating his racing
character. Held up, he was soon off the bridle but gradually warmed to his task,
led two furlongs out and, revelling in the conditions, forged clear to win by five
lengths from Azizzi. Tomba, a tough individual, also ran some good races in
defeat, notably when third behind Royal Applause and Danetime, beaten one
and a quarter lengths and half a length, in the Haydock Park Sprint Cup on his
tenth outing. He was hampered and knocked back to last when Danetime
was brought across the stand rail early on. Following an appeal by his

connections, Tomba was promoted to second on the disqualification of Danetime six days later.

		Formidable	Forli
	Efisio	(b 1975)	Native Partner
	(b 1982)	Eldoret	High Top
Tomba		(b 1976)	Bamburi
(ch.c. 1994)		Be My Guest	Northern Dancer
	Indian Love Song	(ch 1974)	What A Treat
	(b or br 1983)	Indian Bird	Relko
		(b 1975)	Maina

Tomba, a well-made colt, is the fourth foal of Indian Love Song, who failed to win in thirty-three starts in four seasons, deteriorating and becoming ungenuine having shown fair form at up to a mile and a half in her prime. A daughter of the made-and-a-half winner Indian Bird and granddaughter of the Lancashire Oaks winner and Oaks runner-up Maina, Indian Love Song's only other winning produce to date is Indian Rhapsody (by Rock City), a modest performer at seven furlongs to a mile and a quarter. Her fifth foal Adjutant (by Batshoof), a stable-companion of Tomba, finished third twice from three starts at up to a mile in the latest season. *B. J. Meehan*

TOM DOUGAL 2 b.c. (May 28) Ron's Victory (USA) 129 – Fabulous Rina (FR) 64
(Fabulous Dancer (USA) 124) [1997 5s 5m⁵ 5s⁵ a6g⁶ 6d⁴ 7m 7d² Oct 16] 6,500
2-y-o: leggy, quite good-topped colt: sixth foal: half-brother to 7f winners Sehailah
(by Mtoto) and 4-y-o Dispol Diamond: dam, French 1¼m winner, closely related to
smart French middle-distance performer Lys River: modest maiden: neck second to
Mari-Ela in seller at Newmarket: will stay 1m: acts on good to firm and soft ground
and fibresand. *C. Smith*

TOM MI DAH 3 b.g. Superlative 118 – Queensbury Star 76 (Wishing Star 117) –
[1996 60?: 6g⁵ 5m³ 5f 6m² 7g 1997 6g 6m 8.5m 8.3d⁶ Aug 13] modest at 2 yrs, no
form in 1997. *M. D. Hammond*

TOM MORGAN 6 b.g. Faustus (USA) 118 – Pirate Maid (Auction Ring (USA) –
123) [1996 –: a7g a7g 1997 a9.4g a7g 7g Oct 24] lengthy, good-topped gelding:
lightly raced and little form since fairly useful 3-y-o. *P. T. Walwyn*

TOMMY COOPER 6 br.h. Macmillion 110 – My Charade 79 (Cawston's Clown –
113) [1996 –: 14.1d 16g 1997 14g 14m Aug 21] leggy horse: no form on flat since 4
yrs: won over hurdles in September. *Mrs Barbara Waring*

TOMMY TEMPEST 8 ch.g. Northern Tempest (USA) 120 – Silently Yours 44 d
(USA) 53 (Silent Screen (USA)) [1996 46, a38: a5g a5g a5g 5m 5.7g 5.1m a5g 5f⁶ a–
5f⁵ 5.1f⁵ a5g⁵ 5.1m⁶ 5.1m a5g 1997 5.1m³ 5m* 5g 5m a5g 6m a5g a5g Dec 8]
angular gelding: poor handicapper: won at Windsor in July: well below form after:
best at 5f: acts on firm ground and the all-weather: effective in blinkers/visor or not.
R. E. Peacock

TOMMY TORTOISE 3 b.c. Rock Hopper 124 – Wish You Well 78 (Sadler's 80 p
Wells (USA) 132) [1996 70: 8.5m² 10m⁶ 10g² 1997 11.6s 11.6s 11.9f* 14.1m³ 14.4m
16.1m* 18g Oct 18] strong colt: fairly useful form: won maiden at Brighton in June
and handicap at Newcastle (awarded race after being checked 1f out) in October: will
stay beyond 2m (stiff task when tried): acts on firm going, seemingly not on soft:
needs plenty of driving: still quite lightly raced, and should go on again at 4 yrs. *Miss
Gay Kelleway*

TOM PLADDEY 3 ch.c. Clantime 101 – Croft Original (Crofthall 110) [1996 28
55: a5g⁶ 6m⁴ 7g 6g⁶ 6.9v 1997 8.2m 7g 6g 5d⁶ 6m 7g³ 8g Oct 22] leggy colt: poor
maiden: stays 7f: soundly beaten on heavy ground: tried blinkered, no improvement.
R. Bastiman

TOM TAILOR (GER) 3 b.g. Beldale Flutter (USA) 130 – Thoughtful 86 80
(Northfields (USA)) [1996 72p: 7m 7f⁴ 6m 8g³ 1997 12m⁴ 10s* 10.8f² 12d⁶ 10.1d
11.8d Oct 13] tall gelding: fairly useful performer: won maiden at Windsor in May:
well below form last 2 starts: should stay beyond 1¼m: acts on soft going: winning
hurdler. *D. R. C. Elsworth*

Tote Chester Cup (Handicap)—Top Cees doubles his 1995 winning margin

TONIGHT'S PRIZE (IRE) 3 b.g. Night Shift (USA) – Bestow 76 (Shirley   85
Heights 130) [1996 NR 1997 10d 8m⁵ 8.1m² 8.3m² 10m² 10m² 8m* Oct 6] leggy
gelding: second foal: half-brother to fair 1¼m winner Prize Pupil (by Royal Academy): dam stayer: fairly useful form in maidens, winning at Pontefract in October:
stays 1¼m: raced mainly on good to firm ground: consistent. *C. F. Wall*

TONKA 5 b.g. Mazilier (USA) 107 – Royal Meeting 44 (Dara Monarch 128) [1996   64
64, a33: a11g³ 10g 12v* a11g 1997 10d 10d* 13.3g⁶ 10.8m⁴ 10d 12s Jul 2] small,   a–
close-coupled gelding: has a quick action: modest handicapper: won at Nottingham
in May: not at best (but won over hurdles) afterwards: stays 1½m: has won on good
to firm going, goes well on ground softer than good: tried visored earlier in career:
takes keen hold, and is held up. *P. J. Makin*

TONNERRE 5 b.g. Unfuwain (USA) 131 – Supper Time 71 (Shantung 132)   65
[1996 NR 1997 12m 16g⁶ 14.1d 14.1s⁴ 14.1f⁴ 10d* 10.3m⁶ 10g³ 10m a9.4g 10.4s²
10m Sep 15] close-coupled gelding: fair handicapper: won at Nottingham in June:
tends to pull hard, and at least as effective at 1¼m as 1¾m: acts on firm and soft
ground: none too consistent. *B. A. McMahon*

TONRIN 5 b.g. General Wade 93 – Hot Tramp (Country Retreat 91) [1996 NR   –
1997 a10s a7g Dec 22] third reported foal: dam winning hurdler: no form in seller
and maiden at Lingfield. *J. J. Bridger*

TOO LOGICAL 3 b.g. Broken Hearted 124 – Logical Lady 78 (Tina's Pet 121)   –
[1996 NR 1997 11.7g Sep 8] first foal: dam 1¼m winner: well held in Bath maiden.
P. G. Murphy

TOP 3 gr.f. Shirley Heights 130 – Whirl 79 (Bellypha 130) [1996 NR 1997 10m⁶   74
10g 10v² 12m⁶ 12g* 12.3d² 15.9g Sep 24] lengthy filly: first foal: dam, 10.6f winner,
half-sister to smart miler Dance Turn: fair handicapper: won at Thirsk in August: ran
well next time: stays 1½m: acts on heavy ground, ran poorly both starts on good to
firm: tends to swish tail: withdrawn after panicking in stalls on intended debut, and
usually fitted with rug for stalls entry afterwards: sold 15,000 gns in December.
J. R. Fanshawe

TOPAGLOW (IRE) 4 ch.g. Topanoora 118 – River Glow (River Knight (FR)   –
118) [1996 –: 16m⁵ 1997 14.9g Jul 12] small gelding: fair hurdler: lightly raced and
little form on flat since 2 yrs. *P. T. Dalton*

TOPATORI (IRE)   3 ch.f. Topanoora 118 – Partygoer (General Assembly 82 +
(USA)) [1996 69: 5g⁵ 6m² 5f² 1997 7g 9m⁴ 7m* 8m³ 7f 7.1m 8d⁶ 10d³ 10.5s* Oct
15] angular filly: fairly useful performer: won maiden at Yarmouth in June and
handicap at Haydock (best effort, smoothly) in October: better around 1¼m than
shorter: has form on firm going, goes well on dead/soft. *M. H. Tompkins*

TOPAZ   2 b.c. (May 6) Alhijaz 122 – Daisy Topper (Top Ville 129) [1997 8m Oct –
1] 5,000Y: rather leggy colt: fourth foal: half-brother to a winner in Italy by Beveled:
dam (unraced) out of half-sister to Robellino: no obvious promise in maiden at
Salisbury. *J. W. Hills*

TOP BANANA   6 ch.g. Pharly (FR) 130 – Oxslip 106 (Owen Dudley 121) [1996 88
99: 5.2d² 6m³ 5m* 6f 6f 5m³ 5.2m 6.1s² 1997 6m 6d⁴ 7m 7g 7f 6.1g 7g⁶ 6.1d Oct 30]
close-coupled, workmanlike gelding: fairly useful handicapper: well held most starts
in 1997: stays 7f: acts on firm and soft ground: blinkered (not disgraced) once in
1996. *H. Candy*

TOP CEES   7 b.g. Shirley Heights 130 – Sing Softly 112 (Luthier 126) [1996 90: 105
16.4g 14.8m* 18.7m 13.9m⁶ 1997 16g² 18.7s* 16.1s⁵ 14m⁵ 13.9g⁶ 13.1d* 18g² Oct
18] close-coupled gelding: has a round action: useful handicapper, better than ever in
1997: won Chester Cup (having also won race in 1995) by 10 lengths in May and at
Ayr in September: favourite, very good second of 31 to Turnpole in Cesarewitch at
Newmarket final start: effective at 13f, given a test, and stays 2¼m+: yet to race on
firm going, seems to act on any other: held up. *Mrs J. R. Ramsden*

TOP FLOOR (IRE)   2 ch.c. (Apr 19) Waajib 121 – Keen Note 69 (Sharpo 132) 61
[1997 5s 6m⁶ 6g⁵ 6m 6g 6d Aug 30] 10,000 2-y-o: fifth foal: half-brother to a winner
in Italy by Classic Secret: dam won in Belgium at 4 yrs: modest maiden: well below
form last 2 starts, penultimate one a seller: stays 6f. *N. Tinkler*

TOP GEAR (IRE)   2 ch.c. (Apr 5) Case Law 113 – Fleur-De-Luce (Tumble Wind –
(USA)) [1997 7m 6m Oct 31] 16,000Y: big, lengthy colt: closely related to 1991
2-y-o 5f winner Lucid (by Nashamaa), later successful in Italy, and half-brother to
Irish 6f winner Lady Be Magic (by Burslem): dam Irish 9.5f winner: bandaged, well
beaten in maidens at Newmarket in October. *P. Howling*

TOP JEM   3 b.f. Damister (USA) 123 – Sharp Top 62 (Sharpo 132) [1996 NR 1997 85
8.2m 8.2d⁵ 8g⁶ 10.1m* 10s² 10.1s* 10.2d³ 10.5s² 10.1m 10g² Oct 24] sparely-made
filly: has a round action: first foal: dam stayed 2m: fairly useful handicapper: won at
Yarmouth and Newcastle in June: good second at Haydock and Newbury (led over 3f
out, caught near finish) afterwards: will stay at least 1½m: has won on good to firm
ground, best efforts on good or softer: game. *M. J. Ryan*

TOP MAITE   2 ch.c. (May 10) Komaite (USA) – Top Yard (Teekay) [1997 6g –
6.1d⁶ 7m Aug 1] workmanlike colt: fourth foal: dam unraced: well held in maidens.
A. G. Foster

TOP OF THE FORM (IRE)   3 ch.f. Masterclass (USA) 116 – Haraabah (USA) 77
99 (Topsider (USA)) [1996 79: 5g⁴ 5f* 5g³ 5m* 5m³ 6g 5m⁴ 1997 5m 6g* 5m* 5g
5.1g 6m³ 5d 6m Nov 4] sparely-made filly: fair performer: made all in claimers at
Catterick (for M. Johnston) and Pontefract in the summer: well below form last 2
starts: has won at easy 6f, but best at 5f: raced mainly on good ground or firmer: often
makes running: tends to carry head high, but game. *R. A. Fahey*

TOP OF THE GREEN (IRE)   3 b.g. Common Grounds 118 – Grayfoot 87 –
(Grundy 137) [1996 –: 7d 6s 1997 8g 7g⁵ Jun 12] tall gelding: no worthwhile form in
maidens. *P. J. Makin*

TOP PRIZE   9 b.g. High Top 131 – Raffle 82 (Balidar 133) [1996 42d: 16.1s² 33 §
16.2m 21.6m 14.1m a16g* 14.1m a12g⁵ 16.2m a14g³ 16.2g³ 17.1m 1997 a16g 16.1g
a16g² 16.2m 21.6g 16.2s a14g⁴ 16.2m Jul 15] leggy, lengthy gelding: poor staying
handicapper: acts on firm and soft ground and on fibresand: visored nowadays: lazy,
and suited by strong handling: unreliable. *M. Brittain*

TOP SHELF   3 b.f. Warning 136 – Troy Moon (Troy 137) [1996 67: 7g 7f 8g⁵ 63
1997 a8g* 10m 10.3d³ a10g⁵ 11.4m³ 10.1m⁴ 12s 10g Aug 25] leggy filly: modest
handicapper: won 3-runner race at Lingfield in February: inconsistent afterwards:
sold out of C. Brittain's stable after seventh start: stays 11.4f: acts on good to firm
ground and equitrack. *P. J. Bevan*

TOP

TOP TITFER 3 ch.f. Cap Diamant (USA) – Top Yard (Teekay) [1996 –: 6d 7m 7g –
8f 1997 10m Apr 8] leggy filly: behind in low-class events: tried visored. *A. G. Foster*

TOPTON (IRE) 3 b.g. Royal Academy (USA) 130 – Circo 77 (High Top 131) 78
[1996 NR 1997 7.3s⁴ 8.1m³ 7g⁴ 7.1d² 7d⁴ 7m² 7m² 6d* Oct 21] rather unfurnished
gelding: fourth foal: brother to Italian 1¼m winner Setender, closely related to fair
1¾m winner Alaraby (by Caerleon), and half-brother to fairly useful sprinter Robin
Lake (by Thatching): dam, second over 1m at 2 yrs, later placed in France: fair
performer: gained deserved first win in 16-runner minor event at Folkestone: joined
P. Howling for 28,000 gns soon after: effective at 6f to 1m: acts on good to firm and
soft ground: visored last 3 starts: consistent. *I. A. Balding*

TOPUP 4 b.g. Weldnaas (USA) 112 – Daisy Topper (Top Ville 129) [1996 57?: –
7.1d 10g 8.2m³ 8m a10g 1997 a12g⁶ Jan 21] signs of a little ability in 1996: well held
only 4-y-o start. *J. W. Hills*

TORCH VERT (IRE) 5 b.g. Law Society (USA) 130 – Arctic Winter (CAN) 67
(Briartic (CAN)) [1996 –: 18s 16g 16.5s 1997 17.2f³ Sep 29] compact, attractive
gelding: lightly raced, and just a fair performer on flat nowadays: stays 17f: acts on
firm ground: tried blinkered, visored when winning over hurdles in November
(twice) and December. *M. C. Pipe*

TORIANNA (USA) 2 b.f. (Mar 20) Hermitage (USA) – The High Dancer (High 75
Line 125) [1997 6g 5g² Aug 23] $35,000Y resold 12,000Y: half-sister to 3 winners,
including smart 5f performer Boozy and 7f winner Sozzled (both by Absalom): dam
poor maiden: trained on debut by J. Berry: fair form when ¾-length second of 4 to
comfortable winner Pure Coincidence in minor event at Redcar: will be suited by
further than 5f. *D. Nicholls*

TORNADO PRINCE (IRE) 2 ch.c. (Jun 4) Caerleon (USA) 132 – Welsh – p
Flame 106 (Welsh Pageant 132) [1997 6d⁵ 8d 7m Oct 22] IR 85,000Y: half-brother
to numerous winners, notably very smart Irish 1m/1¼m filly Flame of Tara (dam of
Salsabil and Marju) and to the dam of Breeders' Cup Turf winner Northern Spur:
dam miler: behind in maidens, never on terms after slow start each time (pulled hard
final one): should do better over 1¼m+. *N. A. Callaghan*

TORONTO 3 b.g. Puissance 110 – Impala Lass 81 (Kampala 120) [1996 65d: 6d⁶ 49
5.1m² 5g⁵ 6g 5s 7g 1997 a6g 5d⁶ 5m* 5g 5m⁵ 5d 5g 5m⁶ 5d 6m Sep 22] dipped-
backed, good-quartered gelding: poor performer: won maiden at Musselburgh in
May: inconsistent afterwards: best efforts at 5f on good ground or firmer: usually
blinkered: usually a front runner: sold, and sent to Denmark. *J. Berry*

TORRENT 2 ch.c. (Feb 17) Prince Sabo 123 – Maiden Pool 85 (Sharpen Up 127) 74
[1997 6g⁶ 6s³ 6g⁴ 7g Oct 7] 13,000F, 46,000Y: strong, lengthy colt: closely related to
smart performer Rich Charlie and 7f winner Penultimation (both by Young Generation)
and half-brother to several winners: dam 5f winner: fair form in maidens: well beaten
final start: stays 6f: has raced freely. *P. F. I. Cole*

TORSO 2 b.g. (Apr 30) Rudimentary (USA) 118 – Tosara 84 (Main Reef 126) – p
[1997 7g 7.5d 8d Sep 20] 17,000Y: leggy gelding: sixth foal: half-brother to 4-y-o
Sea Danzig and 1m winner Dibloom (by Nomination): dam, 1¼m winner, half-sister
to smart French stayer Chawn: signs of just a little ability in maidens: joined Mrs J.
Ramsden: likely to do better. *J. W. Watts*

TOSHIBA TALK (IRE) 5 ch.g. Horage 124 – Court Ballet (Barrons Court) –
[1996 NR 1997 12.3m⁴ Aug 16] sturdy gelding: fair hurdler: lightly raced on flat
nowadays, last of 4 in Ripon handicap only 5-y-o start. *B. Ellison*

TOSS AND TUMBLE 3 b.f. Syrtos 106 – Breakfast In Bed 80 (Tickled Pink –
114) [1996 NR 1997 7g⁴ 8g³ a5g 7m a7g⁶ Oct 18] third reported foal: dam 6f seller
winner: no form. *W. W. Haigh*

TOTALLY YOURS (IRE) 4 b.f. Classic Music (USA) – Dominia (Derring-Do 51
131) [1996 50: 8g 8.3m 7m 10m⁵ 10f³ 12g² 12g⁴ 12.1s⁶ 1997 12.3m² Apr 9] leggy
filly: modest maiden: sweating, second in seller at Ripon only 4-y-o start: should stay
1¾m: acts on firm ground: fair winning hurdler for M. Pipe. *M. R. Channon*

TOTAL RACH (IRE) 5 b.m. Nordico (USA) – Miss Kelly (Pitskelly 122) [1996 –
52: a10g³ a10g a10g⁴ a10g² a10g 8g 8m 11.9f 9.7m 8m⁴ 8.1g⁵ 8.3g* 8m 1997 a11g

a8g a10g[6] Feb 20] close-coupled mare: modest performer: well beaten in handicaps in 1997. *A. G. Newcombe*

TOTAL TROPIX 2 b.f. (Feb 3) Saddlers' Hall (IRE) 126 – Ivana (IRE) 82 – (Taufan (USA) 119) [1997 6m 7f 8.2d a8.5g[5] Oct 18] second foal: sister to 3-y-o All In Leather: dam, placed over 7f/1m, seemed irresolute: only a little sign of ability in maidens and sellers. *W. J. Haggas*

TOTEM DANCER 4 b.f. Mtoto 134 – Ballad Opera (Sadler's Wells (USA) 132) 78 [1996 83p: 12g[3] 13.8g[3] 10m[4] 11m[2] 11.1g[2] 12m[4] 14.1m[2] 14.1m[2] 14.1g* 1997 12g 13.9g[6] 20m a16g[5] 12.1g* 18g Oct 18] sparely-made filly: has a short action: fair handicapper: won at Hamilton in September: well below form most other starts: should stay beyond 1¾m: acts on good to firm ground, yet to race on softer than good. *J. L. Eyre*

TO THE ROOF (IRE) 5 b.g. Thatching 131 – Christine Daae 74 (Sadler's Wells 107 (USA) 132) [1996 105: 6s[5] 5g* 6g[2] 6g[2] 5.1f* 6m* 5m* 6f[6] 5m 6m 5g 5d[2] 5g[2] 1997 5.2g[2] 5m[5] 6g[6] 5m[4] 6g[6] 5d[5] 6m Aug 2] big, lengthy, good-bodied gelding: impresses in appearance: has a quick action: useful performer: best efforts when fifth in Palace House Stakes at Newmarket (on second start, beaten around a length by Deep Finesse), fourth in listed race at Kempton (beaten 3¼ lengths by Almaty) and sixth in Wokingham Handicap at Royal Ascot: effective at 5f/6f: acts on firm and dead ground and on fibresand: races prominently: game and genuine. *P. W. Harris*

TOTOM 2 b.f. (Feb 2) Mtoto 134 – Lyph (USA) 78 (Lypheor 118) [1997 7.5m[2] 81 p Nov 1] 11,500Y: fourth reported foal: half-sister to 1m winner in Norway by Cadeaux Genereux and 11f winner in Italy by Highest Honor: dam 9f winner at 2 yrs here and in Italy (listed) at 3 yrs: length second of 7 (well clear) in maiden at Milan: should do better. *Lord Huntingdon*

TOUCHANOVA 2 gr.f. (May 1) Touch of Grey 90 – Mazurkanova 63 (Song 132) 46 [1997 a5g[4] 6.1m 6d 5.2f 5d a6g a6g a6g* Dec 26] fifth reported foal: half-sister to winning sprinter Matthew David (by Indian Forest): dam, 2-y-o 6f winner, stayed 7.5f: poor performer: trained by A. Hide first 5 starts: won 7-runner claimer at Wolverhampton, making most: stays 6f. *G. G. Margarson*

TOUCH'N'GO 3 b.g. Rainbow Quest (USA) 134 – Mary Martin (Be My Guest 59 + (USA) 126) [1996 –: 8.1s[6] a8.5g 1997 a9.4f[4] a8g* a10g* a11g[2] 14.1d 10f[3] Jun 10] a70 fair performer on the all-weather, modest form on turf: won maiden at Southwell in February and handicap at Lingfield in March: stays 11f: front runner: gelded after final start. *M. Johnston*

TOUCH OF COLOUR 2 b.c. (Mar 13) Weldnaas (USA) 112 – Fauve 71 – (Dominion 123) [1997 6.1g 7.1m[5] 6d 7.5f Sep 17] 2,000Y: fifth foal: half-brother to 3-y-o Masterstroke: dam, stayed 6f, best at 2 yrs: well beaten, including in a seller. *J. W. Watts*

TOUGH ACT 3 b.g. Be My Chief (USA) 122 – Forelino (USA) 62§ (Trempolino 77 (USA) 135) [1996 81: 5m[5] 7.1m[2] 7d 8g[5] 1997 10d[2] 10m[2] 10f[2] Oct 1] neat gelding: fair maiden: runner-up at Goodwood (twice) and Brighton (below best, eased): stays 1¼m: acts on good to firm and dead ground: carries head awkwardly: temperament under suspicion: fair winning hurdler. *Mrs A. J. Perrett*

TOUGH LEADER 3 b.c. Lead On Time (USA) 123 – Al Guswa 98 (Shernazar 82 131) [1996 71: 5m[2] 6g[4] 5d[4] 7m* 7.5m[3] 1997 7.5m[5] 7m May 31] robust colt: fairly useful performer: best effort in handicap at Beverley on reappearance: should stay at least 1m: yet to race on extremes of going: sold only 3,600 gns in October. *B. Hanbury*

TOUGH NELL (IRE) 2 ch.f. (Mar 25) Archway (IRE) 115 – Mousseux (IRE) 61 (Jareer (USA) 115) [1997 6.9m 5d 6g Oct 27] 8,500Y: workmanlike filly: first foal: dam unraced: best effort in maidens when ninth of 22 at Leicester final start. *Bob Jones*

TOUJOURS RIVIERA 7 ch.g. Rainbow Quest (USA) 134 – Miss Beaulieu 106 84 (Northfields (USA)) [1996 81: a10g 8m 7m 7g[6] 8g 8m[2] 8m 8.1m[4] 9d[6] 8.9g 8m 8d 8m[2] 1997 7m[3] 8.5m 10m[4] 8g[4] 8m[2] 8m* 8f[3] 8f* 8m[5] a8.5g[5] a9.4g[3] Dec 13] rangy gelding: fairly useful handicapper: in good form for most of year, gaining deserved successes at Hamilton (dictated pace) in August and Brighton (led near finish) in September: effective at 1m to 1¼m: acts on firm and dead going, probably on all-weather: game. *J. Pearce*

TOULSTON LADY (IRE) 5 b.m. Handsome Sailor 125 – Rainbow Lady 65   –
(Jaazeiro (USA) 127) [1996 52, a–: 10f⁴ 8.5m³ 8m 12g⁴ 13.8m a11g a14.8g 1997   a35
a12g³ a12g³ 16m Sep 15] strong, lengthy mare: poor maiden: stays 1½m: visored/
blinkered first 2 starts. *J. Wharton*

TOVARICH 6 b.g. Soviet Star (USA) 128 – Pretty Lucky 68 (Shirley Heights   –
130) [1996 –: a12g 1997 a11g a12g a11g³ a12g Jul 26] no longer of account. *Ronald
Thompson*

TOWNVILLE CEE CEE 2 b.f. (Apr 18) Anshan 119 – Holy Day 82 (Sallust   54
134) [1997 5s 6m⁴ 6g 7.9s 6.1m 7m 7g⁶ Oct 22] 700 2-y-o: good-bodied filly: sister
to a winner in Sweden and half-sister to 2 winners, including 7f winner (including at
2 yrs) Passion Sunday (by Bairn): dam 5f winner at 2 yrs: poor maiden on balance.
J. S. Wainwright

TOY (IRE) 2 b.f. (Feb 12) Shalford (IRE) 124§ – Advantageous (Top Ville 129)   –
[1997 6m Jun 9] 9,000Y: second foal: dam, lightly raced in Ireland, half-sister to
smart miler Luzum: in rear in maiden at Windsor. *M. R. Stoute*

TRACEABILITY 4 b.g. Puissance 110 – Miss Petella (Dunphy 124) [1996 87:   84
8m 8m⁴ 10m 10.8f* 12m 11.4d* 11.9g 11.9d 14g 11f² 1997 12g 12g⁴ 10.8m⁶ 12m⁵
10s³ 10.1d³ 10m⁴ 10m² 9.9d⁶ 10m Aug 23] tall, lengthy gelding: shows knee action:
fairly useful handicapper: mainly in good form in 1997, and won at Sandown in July:
effective at 1¼m to 1½m: acts on firm and soft going: often tongue tied: races
prominently: joined M. Hammond to go hurdling. *S. C. Williams*

TRACKING 2 ch.c. (Mar 3) Machiavellian (USA) 123 – Black Fighter (USA) 79   104
(Secretariat (USA)) [1997 6.1g* 7m* 7g² 7.1s² 7m⁴ Oct 3] stocky colt: fourth foal:
half-brother to a winning sprinter in USA by Siberian Express: dam disqualified
1m winner who stayed 1¼m: useful performer: won minor events from small fields
at Nottingham and York in June/July: better form when second in similar event at
Doncaster and Group 3 Solario Stakes at Sandown (½-length second to Little Indian)
in July/August: only fourth to Haami in listed contest at Newmarket: will stay 1m:
best efforts on good going and soft: edgy sort. *H. R. A. Cecil*

TRACKS OF MY TEARS 3 gr.f. Damister (USA) 123 – Carose (Caro 133)   47
[1996 52?: 8f⁴ 10m 10f² 1997 a12g⁴ a12g² Mar 24] angular, plain filly: poor maiden:
stays 1½m: acts on firm ground and equitrack: sent to Italy. *W. G. M. Turner*

TRADING ACES 3 b.f. Be My Chief (USA) 122 – Corn Futures 78 (Nomination   71
125) [1996 63: 5g⁴ 5f⁶ 5f⁵ 7m 7.6m 6d* 7d⁵ 1997 7m a7g* 7m³ 7g⁴ 7.3s² 8d 7g 7.9s
8d Oct 16] rather leggy filly: fair handicapper: won at Wolverhampton in April:
below best last 4 starts: should stay 1m: acts on soft and good in firm ground and on
fibresand: effective visored or not: tends to get behind: sold 46,000 gns in December.
M. Bell

TRAFALGAR LADY (USA) 4 b.f. Fairy King (USA) – Tremulous (USA) 102   –
(Gregorian (USA) 124) [1996 84: 6f⁶ 6m⁵ 7d² 7.1f⁶ 8.1v⁵ 1997 7g Mar 26] neat filly:
fairly useful handicapper at 3 yrs for R. Charlton: always behind only start in 1997:
sold 55,000 gns in December, in foal to Lycius. *J. A. Glover*

TRAILBLAZER 3 b.g. Efisio 120 – Flicker Toa Flame (USA) 85 (Empery   –
(USA) 128) [1996 81: 5m⁶ 6g³ a6g* a7g⁴ 1997 7g⁶ 6s 7.9g 7s Sep 4] fairly useful
winner at 3 yrs: well below form in 1997, running as if something amiss last 2 starts.
C. W. Thornton

TRAKELOR 2 b.f. (Mar 22) Most Welcome 131 – French Cooking 70 (Royal   –
And Regal (USA)) [1997 a6g a8g⁴ Nov 24] 3,000Y: half-sister to 1992 2-y-o 7f and
1m winner Heathyards Boy (by Sayf El Arab) and 1m winner Parc des Princes (by
Anfield): dam 2m winner: well beaten in maidens at Southwell. *R. Hollinshead*

TRAMLINE 4 b.c. Shirley Heights 130 – Tramship 110 (High Line 125) [1996   82
NR 1997 10d 8d⁵ 10.2d⁵ 14.8d* 14s⁴ 16.1g 14s Aug 30] 7,800 3-y-o: strong, lengthy
colt: fifth foal: brother to fairly useful 1½m winner Trammel and half-brother to
French provincial 1½m to 15f winner Vagrancy (by Dancing Brave) and 1¼m winner
Touring (by Sadler's Wells): dam (from good family) won Park Hill: fairly useful
performer: won minor event at Newmarket in June: easily best effort in handicaps

afterwards on next start: should be suited by 2m+: has raced only on good ground or softer. *M. Blanshard*

TRANS ISLAND 2 b.c. (Feb 10) Selkirk (USA) 129 – Khubza 86 (Green Desert (USA) 127) [1997 6m² 6g* 7f* 7s* 8g² Sep 23] 45,000F, 100,000Y: big, lengthy colt: has scope: first foal: dam lightly-raced 7f winner out of smart 6f/7f winner Breadcrumb, herself half-sister to College Chapel: useful performer: won minor event at Newbury in June, £8,100 event there in July and listed race at Deauville (by 4 lengths) in August: good neck second of 4 to Pinmix in Prix la Rochette at Chantilly final outing: stays 1m: acts on firm ground and soft: got upset in stalls on debut: front runner. *I. A. Balding*   107

TRANSOM (USA) 6 b. or br.g. Private Account (USA) – Trestle (USA) (Tom Rolfe) [1996 NR 1997 12d⁴ 16g* 16.1s 20m⁵ 18g Oct 18] neat gelding: lightly raced since 3 yrs, but still capable of fairly useful form, and won handicap at Goodwood in June: creditable ninth of 31 in Cesarewitch at Newmarket final start: stays 2½m: acts on firm and dead ground: held up. *Mrs A. J. Perrett*   86

TRANSYLVANIA 2 b.f. (May 8) Wolfhound (USA) 126 – Slava (USA) (Diesis 133) [1997 6m Aug 15] lengthy, quite attractive filly: third foal: half-sister to 1995 2-y-o 6f winner Sava River (by Lycius) and a winner abroad by In The Wings: dam French 11f winner out of close relative of Soviet Star: 14/1 and green, around 8½ lengths seventh to Shmoose in maiden at Newbury, not knocked about once weakening: should do better. *J. L. Dunlop*   70 p

TRAPPER NORMAN 5 b.g. Mazilier (USA) 107 – Free Skip 68 (Free State 125) [1996 –: a8g 8f⁶ 7f 7m 7f 14m a16g a13g 1997 a10g Jan 16] no worthwhile form. *R. Ingram*   –

TRAVELLING CLOCK 2 ch.c. (Mar 22) Deploy 131 – Travel Mystery 99 (Godswalk (USA) 130) [1997 8.2s Oct 15] 10,000Y: fourth foal: dam won Sagaro Stakes and (over hurdles) Imperial Cup: 33/1, always behind in maiden at Nottingham. *B. A. McMahon*   –

TRAVELMATE 3 b.g. Persian Bold 123 – Ustka 60 (Lomond (USA) 128) [1996 62p: 7m 1997 8.2m 8g 10g* 12g² 12d* Jun 20] lengthy, useful-looking gelding: lightly-raced but fairly useful handicapper: won at Nottingham in May and Newmarket (kicked into decisive lead over 1f out, held My Learned Friend by a neck) in June: should stay beyond 1½m: acts on dead ground (scratched to post on good to firm). *J. R. Fanshawe*   81

TREACLE JONES 2 b.g. (Apr 13) Clantime 101 – Bollin Gorgeous 60 (Hello Gorgeous (USA) 128) [1997 a6g Dec 26] 1,600F, 9,500 2-y-o: third reported foal: dam 7f winner/winning hurdler: last of 7 in claimer at Wolverhampton. *N. Tinkler*   –

TREASURE CHEST (IRE) 2 b.g. (Mar 2) Last Tycoon 131 – Sought Out (IRE) 119 (Rainbow Quest (USA) 134) [1997 8.5g⁶ 8d⁵ 10.2f³ Sep 29] fluent mover: first foal: dam won Prix du Cadran: fair form in maidens at Beverley, Goodwood and Bath, not handling bends well on last-named course: will be suited by 1½m+. *Major W. R. Hern*   79

TREASURE HILL (IRE) 3 ch.g. Roi Danzig (USA) – Grass Court (Thatch (USA) 136) [1996 6m 7g³ 7s³ 6g 8g⁵ 6g 9s 7d 1997 6m 7m 8s⁶ 8g 7s Jul 3] sturdy, close-coupled gelding: fair at best (rated 73) for K. Prendergast at 2 yrs, tried blinkered: no worthwhile form here, looking thoroughly unco-operative final start: one to leave alone. *D. W. Chapman*   – §

TREASURE ISLAND 2 b.f. (Mar 11) Rainbow Quest (USA) 134 – Cockatoo Island 99 (High Top 131) [1997 7g 7d a8g Nov 13] lengthy, sparely-made filly: sixth foal: half-sister to 7-y-o Collier Bay and 7f winner Coachella (by Warning): dam 1½m to 14.8f winner: well beaten in maidens: bred for stamina. *Sir Mark Prescott*   –

TREASURE TOUCH (IRE) 3 b.g. Treasure Kay 114 – Bally Pourri (IRE) (Law Society (USA) 130) [1996 57: 5g⁴ 6s³ 6m a7g⁶ 1997 a6g³ a6g² a6g* 6.1m* 6.1m* 6m* 5d⁵ 5d* 6d 5m³ 5g 7d 5d 6m Nov 4] tall gelding: fairly useful performer: in fine form in first half of year, winning maiden at Southwell (for G. M. Moore) and handicaps at Nottingham (2), Newmarket and Thirsk: well below form last 4 starts: effective at 5f/6f: acts on good to firm and dead ground and on fibresand: often apprentice ridden: usually a front runner. *D. Nicholls*   88

TREATY (USA)   3 b.c. Trempolino (USA) 135 – Zonda 100 (Fabulous Dancer   – §
(USA) 124) [1996 NR 1997 6m 8.5g Sep 5] first known foal: dam, 5f and 6f winner
who probably stayed 1m: slowly away and always behind on debut: refused to race
only subsequent outing. *K. Mahdi*

TREBLE TERM   2 ch.f. (Apr 2) Lion Cavern (USA) 117 – Treble Hook (IRE)   66
(Ballad Rock 122) [1997 5d 6g a6g⁶ Dec 6] 10,500F, 20,000Y: third foal: half-sister
to Italian 3-y-o 5f to 6.5f winner Ninfa of Cisterna (by Polish Patriot): dam Irish
2-y-o 6f and 7f winner: modest form in maidens: probably a sprinter. *P. J. Makin*

TREGARON (USA)   6 b.h. Lyphard (USA) 132 – Klarifi 91 (Habitat 134) [1996   108
96: 8m* 8s⁵ 8m* 8m 7.3m³ 7.9m⁴ 1997 7g² 7m* 8m 7.6f² 7d 7m⁵ Sep 27] useful-
looking horse: has a short action: useful handicapper: best effort when winning
25-runner Victoria Cup at Ascot in April by 2½ lengths from World Premier:
creditable second to Cadeaux Tryst in rated stakes at Lingfield in July: effective at 7f/
1m: acts on good to firm ground, below form on softer than good: held up: sold
46,000 gns in October, and sent to USA. *R. Akehurst*

TREMENDISTO   7 b.g. Petoski 135 – Misty Halo 93 (High Top 131) [1996 50,   –
a41: a12g⁶ a16g⁵ a16g⁴ 17.1g 14d⁶ 14.1m³ 13.1m a12g⁴ 1997 a14.8g⁵ 10g Sep 23]
plain gelding: poor maiden handicapper: well below form in 1997. *D. McCain*

TREMONNOW   2 b.f. (Mar 16) Reprimand 122 – Tree Mallow 71 (Malicious)   43
[1997 5m⁶ 6.1g⁴ 6g³ 6.1d 7g⁵ 6g⁵ 6m Sep 22] 1,800Y: sister to 1½m winner Bark 'N'
Bite and half-sister to useful 1¼m winner Flockton's Own (by Electric): dam stayer:
poor maiden: should stay beyond 6f. *J. M. Bradley*

TREMPLIN (USA)   5 gr.g. Trempolino (USA) 135 – Stresa (Mill Reef (USA)   72
141) [1996 –: 10m⁵ 10s 10.1m 8d 8g 1997 8d 8.5m 10.2m⁴ 10.5g⁵ a8g Nov 25]   a–
short-necked gelding: fair handicapper nowadays: stays 10.5f: acts on good to firm
and heavy going: blinkered final start: looks none too hearty. *N. A. Callaghan*

TREVOR MITCHELL   3 b.f. Backchat (USA) 98 – Versaillesprincess (Legend   35
of France (USA) 124) [1996 –: 6m a5g a6g a8g 1997 7m 7g 8m 8f a10g Oct 27]
sparely-made filly: poor maiden handicapper: stays 1m. *J. J. Bridger*

TRIANNA   4 b.f. General Holme (USA) 128 – Triemma (IRE) (M Double M   –
(USA)) [1996 39: 6s⁶ a9.4g⁴ 8g³ a9.4g⁶ 1997 a8g Jan 6] poor maiden: blinkered: well
beaten only 4-y-o start. *R. Brotherton*

TRIBAL MISCHIEF   3 br.f. Be My Chief (USA) 122 – Lammastide 93   44
(Martinmas 128) [1996 61: 5g³ 5s² 5m⁴ 7m⁶ 5f⁵ 5s* 7g⁶ 6m 1997 5s 7g 10g⁶ 12g 8m⁵
8.3g Sep 29] tall, leggy filly: poor handicapper: probably stays 1m: tried visored.
D. Moffatt

TRIBAL MOON (IRE)   4 b.g. Ela-Mana-Mou 132 – Silk Blend (Busted 134)   66
[1996 –: 11d 10m 1997 10g 10.8s⁵ 12m⁴ Jul 14] close-coupled gelding: fair maiden:
should stay 1½m: sold only 1,200 gns in October. *Lady Herries*

TRIBAL PEACE (IRE)   5 ch.g. Red Sunset 120 – Mirabiliary (USA) 74 (Crow   68
(FR) 134) [1996 74: a10g a10g* a10g 10g 10m a10g⁵ 1997 a10g* a9.4g⁶ a10g 9g³   a71
9s⁴ 10g⁵ 9f³ 9m* 10m 9g³ 9d⁴ 10f Sep 28] small gelding: fair handicapper: won at
Lingfield in January and Goodwood (making most) in July: stays 1¼m: acts on firm,
soft going and equitrack (probably on fibresand): consistent. *B. Gubby*

TRIBLE PET   4 b.f. Petong 126 – Fire Sprite 83 (Mummy's Game 120) [1996 49:   –
a7g⁴ a8g⁴ 1997 a7g a8g⁶ a12g Jan 30] poor maiden: well beaten in 1997. *B. Gubby*

TRIDENT (USA)   2 b.c. (Feb 26) Red Ransom (USA) – Lady di Pomadora (USA)   94 p
(Danzig Connection (USA)) [1997 7g³ 7.1m* Jul 23] $130,000Y: big, good-topped
colt: powerful galloper: first foal: dam, won up to 9f in USA, out of half-sister to
grandam of Dancing Brave: shaped well in maiden at Newmarket on debut, and
landed odds in similar event at Sandown 15 days later in smooth fashion by 2½
lengths from Silvertown: should stay at least 1¼m: presumably had set-back, but
should make a smart colt in time if all is well. *M. R. Stoute*

TRIENTA MIL   3 b.g. Prince Sabo 123 – Burmese Ruby (Good Times (ITY))   –
[1996 –: 8.2s 1997 10m Sep 9] no promise in maidens. *P. T. Dalton*

TRIGGER HAPPY (IRE)   2 ch.f. (Apr 9) Ela-Mana-Mou 132 – Happy Tidings   91 p
(Hello Gorgeous (USA) 128) [1997 8g 10m* Nov 1] IR 4,500F: leggy, workmanlike

filly: sixth reported foal: sister to useful 1996 2-y-o 1¼m winner Eldorado and half-sister to Irish 1½m to 2¼m winner Fleeting Vision (by Vision) and a winner in Spain: dam unraced half-sister to Snurge: 20/1, won listed NGK Spark Plugs Zetland Stakes at Newmarket by 1¾ lengths from Night Rule, still looking green when ridden in rear 3f out but staying on strongly to draw clear final 1f, idling towards finish: very stoutly bred, and should make a useful stayer at the least. *M. Johnston*

TRILBY   4 b.f. In The Wings 128 – Fur Hat (Habitat 134) [1996 72: 11.8m 8g⁵   65
10m⁵ 10.2f³ 10f² 12f* a16g⁴ 11.9g 12.1s⁴ 1997 13d 14.1s 15.8m⁴ 13g³ 13g² 16d*
16d² 15.9m⁴ 16.1m 15.9d⁴ 16g⁶ Sep 15] smallish filly: has a round action: fair
handicapper: in good form in the summer, and won at Musselburgh in June: stays 2m:
acts on firm and dead ground, probably on soft: often visored, blinkered once at 3
yrs: won novice hurdle in September. *G. Richards*

TRINITY REEF   2 b.f. (Apr 19) Bustino 136 – Triple Reef (Mill Reef (USA)   62 p
141) [1997 7g 7.6d⁵ 8.2g Sep 23] sister to smart 1¼m winner Talented and half-sister
to several winners, including fairly useful 13f/1¾m winner Trazl (by Zalazl): dam
unraced from excellent middle-distance staying family: considerately handled in
maidens at Leicester, Lingfield and Nottingham: should do better over 1¼m+.
J. L. Dunlop

TRIPLE CHALLENGE   3 gr.f. Norton Challenger 111 – Trois Filles (French   –
Marny) [1996 NR 1997 a9.4g 10g Jun 16] 1,150 3-y-o: fourth reported foal: dam
tailed off in selling hurdles: never dangerous in maidens, trained on debut by
K. Burke. *G. L. Moore*

TRIPLE HAY   3 ch.c. Safawan 118 – Davinia 92 (Gold Form 108) [1996 80p: 7g   97
6f² 6g* 1997 7m⁵ 7g 6g* 6d 6m 6s 7m⁴ Oct 3] tall colt: useful performer: won minor
event at Windsor in June: good efforts in handicaps at Goodwood (Stewards' Cup)
and Newmarket fifth and seventh starts: effective at 6f/7f: acts on firm ground, well
held on softer than good. *R. Hannon*

TRIPLE LEAP   4 b.c. Sadler's Wells (USA) 132 – Three Tails 121 (Blakeney   94
126) [1996 93p: 10m 10d² 10s* 1997 10.5m² Sep 21] heavy-topped colt: had a
quick action: fairly useful performer, lightly raced: second in minor event at
Haydock in September, only start of 1997: should have stayed at least 1½m: dead.
J. H. M. Gosden

TRIPLE TERM   3 br.g. Terimon 124 – Triple Reef (Mill Reef (USA) 141) [1996   –
72: 7f⁴ 7.5f 8f⁴ 10m 8g⁴ 1997 8m a9.4g Jul 25] close-coupled individual: fair form as
2-y-o for J. Dunlop: no encouragement on return. *J. G. Smyth-Osbourne*

TRISTAN'S COMET   10 br.g. Sayf El Arab (USA) 127 – Gleneagle 91 (Swing   –
Easy (USA) 126) [1996 –: a16g 1997 a16g Jan 10] no longer of any account.
J. L. Harris

TROIA (IRE)   3 b.f. Last Tycoon 131 – Dubai Lady 78 (Kris 135) [1996 54²: 7m⁵   –
a8g⁵ 1997 a8g⁶ 12f⁶ 12.5d Jun 24] modest maiden: should stay beyond 1m. *B. Smart*

TROJAN HERO (SAF)   6 ch.g. Raise A Man (USA) – Helleness (SAF)   75
(Northfields (USA)) [1996 7g⁴ 7g* 7g⁵ 7g² 7g 7g 7g 7g 1997 7g⁴ 6d⁶ 8m* 8s² 7m⁵
6g 6.9f³ 6m 8g⁶ 8s a7g³ a7g* a7s² Nov 28] workmanlike ex-South African gelding:
unimpressive walker/mover: first foal: dam 5f winner: won 6 times in South Africa
up to end of 1996: fair performer in Britain: won claimer (for B. Hills) at Leicester in
June and handicap at Wolverhampton in November: probably best at 7f/1m: acts on
the all-weather and good to firm going, below form on soft: has reportedly gone lame
on off-fore a few times: races prominently. *Mrs M. Reveley*

TROJAN RISK   4 ch.g. Risk Me (FR) 127 – Troyes 81 (Troy 137) [1996 91: 9g   79
10.2g² 9m* 10.1m² 10m³ 10.3m² 10m 8.9g² 1997 a12g 10.1m 10d⁵ 10.1g 10s⁴ 10d*
10m 11m² Oct 28] sturdy, good-bodied gelding: has reportedly had dehydration
problems: fair performer: won handicap at Sandown in July: below form in similar
event and claimer after: stays 11f: acts on good to firm and soft going: usually held
up: tried blinkered: joined Mrs M. Reveley. *G. Lewis*

TROJAN WOLF   2 ch.c. (Mar 26) Wolfhound (USA) 126 – Trojan Lady (USA)   55 p
(Irish River (FR) 131) [1997 7m Nov 4] 15,000F: third living foal: half-brother to
3-y-o Nubile and 5-y-o Zain Dancer: dam, placed twice from 5 starts in France, is out

TRO

of half-sister to Sun Princess and Saddlers' Hall: 33/1, slowly away and not given hard time when ninth of 18 in Redcar maiden: should do better. *M. H. Tompkins*

TROOPER 3 b.g. Rock Hopper 124 – Silica (USA) 66 (Mr Prospector (USA)) [1996 65: 8d 7.9g⁶ 10g⁶ 1997 9g 12m 12m² 16m² 13.1g 16g a14g² Oct 20] fair handicapper: stays 2m: acts on good to firm ground and fibresand: blinkered (well beaten) fifth start: sold 16,000 gns in October, and joined M. Hammond. *R. Akehurst*   70 §

TROPICAL BEACH 4 b.g. Lugana Beach 116 – Hitravelscene (Mansingh (USA) 120) [1996 69: a7g 7d a6g 5g⁶ 5g³ 5g* 6m 5.9f 5g³ 6m⁴ 6f* 5m* 6m⁴ 6f⁵ 5d² 5m 5m⁴ 5m 5g⁵ 5f 1997 5s³ 6d³ 5g⁶ 5m⁴ 5s² 6m 5g³ 5s³ 5g* 5m 5m 6g 6d 5m 5d Nov 7] leggy gelding: modest handicapper: won at Carlisle in July: left Jack Berry after fifteenth start: needs test at 5f, and stays 6f: acts on firm and soft ground: sometimes blinkered: tends to get behind. *J. Pearce*   64

TRUE BALLAD 5 ch.g. Ballad Rock 122 – Ajuga (USA) 102 (The Minstrel (CAN) 135) [1996 NR 1997 8m 7.1m 5s 6m Jul 11] fair maiden in Ireland at 3 yrs: no form here. *J. S. Goldie*   –

TRUE GLORY (IRE) 3 b.f. In The Wings 128 – Truly Special 116 (Caerleon (USA) 132) [1996 67p: 8g 1997 10g³ 10.3d² 12m 11m* Aug 10] sturdy filly: fairly useful performer: won 4-runner handicap at Redcar: should stay beyond 11f: acts on good to firm and dead going. *J. H. M. Gosden*   84

TRULY BAY 4 b.g. Reprimand 122 – Daymer Bay (Lomond (USA) 128) [1996 40: 7m 7m³ 7.1d 7.1m a7g⁴ a8g 1997 a7g* a8g³ a7g² a7g² Feb 24] leggy gelding: modest performer: won maiden at Southwell in January: good second in handicaps there last 2 starts: should stay at least 1m: acts on fibresand: blinkered last 3 starts. *T. D. Barron*   53

TRULYFAN (IRE) 3 b. or br.f. Taufan (USA) 119 – Whateveryousay (USA) (Verbatim (USA)) [1996 45?: 5.1m⁵ 5.1m 5g 5m⁶ 1997 a7g Apr 28] poor maiden at best: tailed off only 3-y-o start. *R. A. Fahey*   –

TRULY PARCHED (USA) 3 b.g. Known Fact (USA) 135 – Drought (IRE) 69 (Rainbow Quest (USA) 134) [1996 80p: 7g⁶ 6m 1997 6g⁵ 7.6d 8.1g⁵ 8.2s Oct 15] smallish gelding: only modest in 1997, best effort third start: sold 2,500 gns, and sent to Germany. *P. W. Chapple-Hyam*   61

TRUMP 8 b.g. Last Tycoon 131 – Fleeting Affair 98 (Hotfoot 126) [1996 NR 1997 16g⁵ Sep 15] fairly useful hurdler: poor and lightly-raced stayer on flat. *C. Parker*   38

TRUST DEED (USA) 9 ch.g. Shadeed (USA) 135 – Karelia (USA) 111 (Sir Ivor 135) [1996 NR 1997 18d⁵ Jul 5] no longer of much account on flat. *S. G. Knight*   –

TRUTH TELLER 2 ch.c. (Jan 24) Statoblest 120 – Dreams Are Free (IRE) 71 (Caerleon (USA) 132) [1997 5d 6f* 6m 5.3m 6d⁴ 8g 6f* 6g a6s³ Nov 10] 12,000Y: sturdy colt: first foal: dam 1¼m winner from family of Seattle Slew and Lomond: fair performer: won minor event at Brighton in May and 4-runner nursery there in October: good third in nursery at Lingfield final start: stays 6f: acts on firm ground and equitrack, not discredited on dead going. *R. Hannon*   68

TRYING TIMES (IRE) 4 b.g. Sadler's Wells (USA) 132 – Ozone Friendly (USA) 107 (Green Forest (USA) 134) [1996 10.5g 1997 10.1m 12.1s 9.2g² 8.3s* 11.1s 10.9g² 8m 9.2d 9.2m³ 8g 9d Sep 19] ex-French gelding: second foal: brother to 3-y-o Musalsal: dam 5.5f Prix Robert Papin winner out of a 1¼m winner: ran once before sold out of A. Fabre's stable 17,500 gns in July, 1996: modest handicapper: won maiden event at Hamilton in June: largely below form afterwards: should stay 1¼m: acts on good to firm and soft ground. *J. Berry*   56

TRY OMNIPOTENT 5 b.g. Nomination 125 – Try G'S (Hotfoot 126) [1996 NR 1997 11f May 1] poor maiden at 3 yrs for C. Allen: tailed off only start in 1997. *Mrs V. A. Aconley*   –

TSARNISTA 4 b.f. Soviet Star (USA) 128 – Princess Genista 108 (Ile de Bourbon (USA) 133) [1996 100: 8d⁶ 8m 7.6m² 8m³ 8.1g⁴ 8.1m⁴ 8g⁴ 8d⁶ 1997 9m² 8d⁶ 8m⁵ 7.6f 8m Sep 27] leggy, sparely-made filly: useful performer: best 4-y-o effort when fifth in listed race at Milan: ran poorly both subsequent starts (blinkered on first occasion): stays 9f: acts on good to firm and dead going: often sweats: sold 40,000 gns in December. *J. L. Dunlop*   98

Prix de Royallieu, Longchamp—front-running Tulipa (rails) is strongly pressed by Dame Kiri

TTYFRAN 7 b.g. Petong 126 – So It Goes 73 (Free State 125) [1996 38: 10.3m³ 14.1f³ 14.1f³ 12m³ 16m 16.2g 1997 12m 16m⁵ Apr 14] workmanlike gelding: poor handicapper nowadays: well beaten in 1997. *B. P. J. Baugh* —

TUDOR ISLAND 8 b.g. Jupiter Island 126 – Catherine Howard 68 (Tower Walk 130) [1996 86: 14d 14m² 14m³ 14.8d² 14.6m³ 16.2m 1997 14g² 14g 14m 14.8m⁴ 14.4m Sep 10] strong, close-coupled gelding: fair handicapper: disappointing in 1997 after reappearance: stays 2m: acts on good to firm ground, soft and equitrack: blinkered (best effort at the time) once at 3 yrs: sometimes hangs, but is genuine. *C. E. Brittain* 78 d

TUGELA (USA) 2 br.f. (Mar 2) Riverman (USA) 131 – Rambushka (USA) 111 (Roberto (USA) 131) [1997 7.5f⁵ 8g Oct 24] leggy filly: fifth foal: half-sister to Irish 1¼m winner Cross Question (by Alleged): dam 7f (at 2 yrs) to 1¼m winner: well held in maidens: sold 21,000 gns in December. *B. W. Hills* —

TUI 2 b.f. (Apr 26) Tina's Pet 121 – Curious Feeling (Nishapour (FR) 125) [1997 6.1d 5.7m 5.1g⁶ a5g Aug 15] 400Y: second reported foal: dam, maiden on flat, won over hurdles: no worthwhile form, including in a seller. *K. McAuliffe* —

TUIGAMALA 6 b.g. Welsh Captain 113 – Nelliellamay (Super Splash (USA) 106) [1996 –, a62: a7g⁴ a7g⁴ a7g⁵ a7g⁴ a8g* a8g⁴ a10g⁴ 10f 10g 1997 a7g a8g³ a8g² a10g a9.4g a8g 10g 11.9m⁶ Jul 24] good-topped gelding: modest performer: stays 1m: acts on equitrack, no form on turf for long time: inconsistent. *R. Ingram* a59

TULIPA (USA) 4 b.f. Alleged (USA) 138 – Black Tulip (FR) (Fabulous Dancer (USA) 124) [1996 111: 10g* 10.5g* 11v² 12m* 12m 1997 12m 12f* 11.9g² 12.5m* a11s⁴ Nov 2] good-bodied filly: smart performer: trained at 3 yrs by A. Fabre in France: won Group 3 race at Milan (by neck from Papering) in June and Prix de Royallieu at Longchamp (beat Dame Kiri short head) in October: short-head second to Squeak in Lancashire Oaks at Haydock in between: stays 1½m well: acts on any ground on turf, well beaten on (sloppy) dirt. *Saeed bin Suroor* 112

TULLICH REFRAIN 2 b.f. (Mar 22) Petardia 113 – Norfolk Serenade 83 (Blakeney 126) [1997 5m³ 5.1g 5m 7m a6g 6g⁴ Oct 25] 6,000Y: leggy, sparely-made filly: seventh foal: half-sister to 9-y-o Samsolom, useful 1m and 9f winner North Song (by Anshan) and 6f (at 2 yrs) and 2m winner Secret Serenade (by Classic Secret): dam 11.7f winner: modest form first 2 starts in maidens and in Newbury nursery final outing: should stay 1m. *W. R. Muir* 60 a?

TULSA (IRE) 3 b.g. Priolo (USA) 127 – Lagrion (USA) (Diesis 133) [1996 56?: 7m 7m 6m 1997 10s 10m⁴ 8g² 9.7s 8.3g 7d 7.6g 8m³ 9s⁵ 12g 10g 8d³ 8d⁶ Oct 28] fair performer: should stay 1¼m: no improvement in blinkers or visor: unreliable. *B. Gubby* 67 §

Ladbroke Bunbury Cup (Handicap), Newmarket—Tumbleweed Ridge sweeps into the lead as How Long, Elfland (far right) and Tayseer (blaze) fight it out for the minor placings

TUMBLEWEED HERO 2 b.c. (Feb 16) Alzao (USA) 117 – Julip 99 (Track 86 Spare 125) [1997 6g² 6g⁶ 7.1g² Sep 11] 38,000Y: good-topped, attractive colt: half-brother to several winners, notably Dee Stakes winner and Belmont Stakes runner-up My Memoirs (by Don't Forget Me) and smart miler Patriach (by London Bells): dam 2-y-o 7f winner who stayed 1¼m: fairly useful maiden: runner-up in minor event at Newbury in June (best effort) and maiden at Chepstow in September: should stay 1m: has moved short to post. *B. J. Meehan*

TUMBLEWEED PEARL 3 b.f. Aragon 118 – Billie Blue 63 (Ballad Rock 122) 96 [1996 90: 6m⁴ 5.7m* 6f* 7.3s⁵ 1997 6g* 7g⁴ 7m 8f⁶ 5.5f⁵ a8.5g⁴ Nov 16] well-made filly: useful performer: won minor event at Kempton in May: below form afterwards, leaving B. Meehan after third start: should stay 1m: acts on firm and soft going. *N. Howard, USA*

TUMBLEWEED RIDGE 4 ch.c. Indian Ridge 123 – Billie Blue 63 (Ballad 108 Rock 122) [1996 102d: 7m⁵ 8m 6m 6g 7m³ 1997 8m³ a7g⁶ 7m 6g² 7.6m² 6g 7g* 7g³ 7.3m 7g 7d⁴ 7m Sep 27] well-made colt: impresses in appearance: useful handicapper: gained first win since 2-y-o days when beating How Long by 3 lengths in Bunbury Cup at Newmarket in July: creditable effort penultimate start but ran as though something possibly amiss final one: probably best around 7f: acts on firm and dead ground, ran poorly on fibresand: usually blinkered: sometimes wears tongue strap and finds little: inconsistent. *B. J. Meehan*

TUMBLWEED PROSPECT 2 ch.g. (Feb 2) Lion Cavern (USA) 117 – Ring of 77 Pearl (Auction Ring (USA) 123) [1997 6m⁴ 7g 6g² 6d² Sep 20] 5,000F, 42,000Y: leggy gelding: seventh foal: half-brother to several winners, including 1991 2-y-o 5f winner Miss Shadowfax (by Absalom) and 5-y-o Manabar (formerly fair 1m winner): dam ran 3 times at 2 yrs: fair form: runner-up in maidens at Yarmouth and Newbury: didn't last home at 7f: gelded after final start. *B. J. Meehan*

TUNDRA (IRE) 2 b.f. (Apr 7) Common Grounds 118 – Miss Krispy (FR) – (Bellypha 130) [1997 5g 5.1m 7g Sep 3] 14,500Y: leggy filly: sixth foal: half-sister to Look And Like (by Jalmood), winner in France/Germany at up to 1m: dam French 10.5f winner, half-sister to smart French sprinter Gem Diamond: well beaten in maidens and a seller. *K. McAuliffe*

TUNING 2 ch.f. (Apr 10) Rainbow Quest (USA) 134 – Discomatic (USA) (Roberto 92 p (USA) 131) [1997 8.2g² Sep 23] fourth living foal: sister to fairly useful French 3-y-o 1½m winner Raincloud and half-sister to a 2-y-o 6.5f winner by Dowsing: dam, French 9f winner, half-sister to Digamist: 3/1, showed plenty of promise when

¾-length second to Rambling Rose in maiden at Nottingham, quickening to lead well over 2f out then rallying once headed: should stay at least 1¼m: sure to improve, and win a race. *H. R. A. Cecil*

TURF MOOR (IRE) 2 b.f. (Apr 5) Mac's Imp (USA) 116 – Tuft Hill 92 (Grundy 137) [1997 5m² 5d⁵ 5m 7g⁶ 7s³ 6.1m a6g Sep 30] 8,200Y: unfurnished filly: half-sister to Up The Mariners (untrustworthy sprint winner, by Classic Secret) and 4-y-o Lady Caroline Lamb: dam, 2-y-o 6f winner, half-sister to 10.5f Prix Corrida winner Bonshamile: modest maiden: tailed off last 2 starts, final one a seller: stays 7f. *J. J. O'Neill* 53 ? a?

TURGENEV (IRE) 8 b.g. Sadler's Wells (USA) 132 – Tilia (ITY) (Dschingis Khan) [1996 70: a12g 11.8d 12.1d⁵ 13s 13.9m³ 14d* 14d² 16.2m 1997 16.1g 13d 14s* 13.9g 14d⁵ 14.1g⁶ 14.6d⁵ 14g* 14g* 13.9g 13.9s² 16d 16s 16.5s Nov 8] deep-bodied gelding: has a fluent action: fairly useful handicapper, better at 8 yrs than at any time since 1993: won at Haydock in May and July (fifth course win) and at Sandown in August: stays 1¾m well: has form on firm going, though raced mainly on good or softer: tried visored and blinkered, but at least as effective without: usually held up: tough. *R. Bastiman* 82

TURIA 4 b.f. Slip Anchor 136 – Tura (Northfields (USA)) [1996 66: 10m⁵ 12g⁴ 11.9d⁴ 12g 1997 a13g Jan 11] small, sturdy filly: fair maiden at best, well beaten (all-weather debut) only 4-y-o start. *N. A. Graham*

TURNERS WAY 3 b.g. Precocious 126 – Murmuring 69 (Kind of Hush 118) [1996 NR 1997 6g⁴ 6g 6m³ a7s Nov 28] second foal: dam 6f winner: modest maiden: should stay beyond 6f: reported to have bled from nose second start. *S. Dow* 52

TURNPOLE (IRE) 6 br.g. Satco (FR) 114 – Mountain Chase (Mount Hagen (FR) 127) [1996 70: 13.9g⁵ 14.6g 1997 12.1d* 16d² 13.9g* 16.5m² 14.6m 15.9g² 18g* Oct 18] strong gelding: fairly useful performer: better than ever in 1997, and won minor event at Hamilton in April and handicaps at York and Newmarket in October, last-named 31-runner Tote Cesarewitch, travelling well much of way and beating Top Cees by 1¾ lengths: stays 2¼m well: acts on firm and dead going: has run well when sweating. *Mrs M. Reveley* 91

TURN TO STONE (IRE) 3 b.g. West China 107 – Marronzina (IRE) (Burslem 123) [1996 NR 1997 6.5v 8s 6d 12.1m Jul 11] IR 1,100Y: second foal: dam unplaced: no sign of ability: trained first 3 starts in Ireland by Michael Flynn. *J. Neville* –

TURRILL HOUSE 5 b.m. Charmer 123 – Mcgabucks (Buckskin (FR) 133) [1996 NR 1997 a12g a16g a13g³ 18d⁴ a14g⁶ Nov 17] fair winning hurdler: bad maiden on flat. *W. J. Musson* –

Tote Cesarewitch (Handicap), Newmarket—
the field races down the stand side, Turnpole leading the way from Top Cees

TUSCAN DAWN 7 ch.g. Clantime 101 – Excavator Lady 65 (Most Secret 119) 75
[1996 83: 5g* 5d³ 5m 5m⁶ 5m⁶ 5g⁵ 5.1d 5m* 5.1g⁴ 5g 1997 a5g⁵ 5g 5d⁵ 5m² 5m²
5m⁵ 5.1m² 5d² 5.1s⁴ 5m Sep 12] leggy, lengthy gelding: poor mover: fair handicapper: best at 5f: acts on firm and soft going, below form only equitrack outing:
sometimes spoils chance by rearing in stalls (put in last), usually makes running
otherwise. *J. Berry*

TUSSLE 2 b.c. (Feb 19) Salse (USA) 128 – Crime Ofthecentury 80 (Pharly (FR) 91 p
130) [1997 6v² 6m* Oct 31] 22,000F, 72,000Y: good-topped, attractive colt: has
scope: good walker, and has quick, fluent action: first foal: dam, 5f winner, out of
Cherry Hinton winner Crime of Passion: favourite, confirmed promise of debut
earlier in month when winning maiden at Newmarket comfortably by 2 lengths from
Baajil, dictating pace and quickening clear for hands and heels over 1f out: likeable
type, and has the makings of a useful performer, probably up to 1m. *M. Bell*

TUTANKHAMUN 2 b.c. (Mar 20) Lion Cavern (USA) 117 – Menhaad (IRE) 55 – p
(Sadler's Wells (USA) 132) [1997 8d Oct 28] first foal: dam maiden daughter of very
smart French 1m to 1¼m Reine Mathilde: 9/1, midfield in maiden at Leicester,
chasing pace 6f: should improve, probably over further than 1m. *M. R. Stoute*

TUTU SIXTYSIX 6 br.m. Petong 126 – Odielse 82 (Mummy's Pet 125) [1996 40
36: 6.1m 5.9m⁶ 6g 5g 5f⁴ 5f⁶ 7m 6m 5m 5.1m 1997 a6g⁵ a6g a6g³ a6g a5g 5m a6g³
5v 5m 5m³ 5m 6g² 6g Aug 21] leggy, sparely-made mare: poor sprint handicapper:
acts on firm and dead ground and the all-weather: no improvement visored/
blinkered: usually comes from off pace and often meets trouble in running: usually
ridden by Kim Tinkler. *Don Enrico Incisa*

TWENTYTWO BLACK 2 b.f. (Apr 12) Ron's Victory (USA) 129 – Fall About –
68 (Comedy Star (USA) 121) [1997 5d 6f³ May 29] 1,600Y: fifth reported foal: dam
1½m winner at 4 yrs, half-sister to smart middle-distance filly Ulterior Motive: well
beaten both starts: dead. *M. J. Haynes*

TWICE AS SHARP 5 ch.h. Sharpo 132 – Shadiliya 90 (Red Alert 127) [1996 97
93: 5g 5m³ 6d 6m⁶ 5m* 5m⁶ 5m⁵ 5d 5g 1997 5g⁵ 5g* 5m² 5g³ 5m 5.2m³ 5.6m
5m 5d 5g Oct 25] big, close-coupled horse: useful handicapper: creditable efforts
most starts in 1997, and made all at York in May: very best form at 5f: acts on good
to firm and dead ground (probably on soft): usually races prominently. *P. W. Harris*

TWILIGHT SLEEP (USA) 5 b.g. Shadeed (USA) 135 – Sleeping Beauty 87 83
(Mill Reef (USA) 141) [1996 –: 9s 1997 13g a12g* 12.3m² 11.8g Jul 23] fairly useful
performer: won claimer at Wolverhampton for Lord Huntingdon in June: stays 1½m:
acts on fibresand, raced mainly on good/good to firm ground on turf: won over
hurdles in August: sold only 525 gns in December. *M. C. Pipe*

TWIN CREEKS 6 b.g. Alzao (USA) 117 – Double River (USA) (Irish River 68
(FR) 131) [1996 –, a75: a8g a8g⁵ a8g* a9.4g 8m a8g a7g² 8m⁶ a8g² 7m a8.5g³ a7g* a93
a7s* 1997 a8g a7g⁵ a7g* a7g 7g⁶ 6g⁵ 7m³ 7m 7f* 6g³ 7d² 7d⁶ 6.9g³ 7.1m⁵ a6g⁴ a7g*
a8s² a7g⁶ a8g² Dec 12] compact gelding: usually impresses in appearance: fairly useful handicapper on all-weather, won at Lingfield in January and November: just fair
on turf, but won minor event at Warwick in June: effective at 6f to 9f: acts on firm
and dead ground, probably better on equitrack than fibresand. *V. Soane*

TWIN TIME 3 b.f. Syrtos 106 – Carramba (CZE) (Tumble Wind (USA)) [1996 65
NR 1997 a8g³ 8d² 8g⁵ a8g 8.2m² 8.2m⁴ 9m⁶ Oct 31] quite good-topped filly: first
reported foal in Britain: dam, out of an Irish 1m winner, bred in Czechoslovakia: fair
maiden: left M. Heaton-Ellis after sixth start: should be suited by further than 1m: yet
to race on extremes of going. *J. S. King*

TWO BILLS 3 b.g. Totem (USA) 118 – Chess Mistress (USA) 59 (Run The –
Gantlet (USA)) [1996 –p: 6.1m 6.1d⁶ 6.1m 1997 8.2m Jul 19] tall gelding: signs of
ability but no form. *A. Streeter*

TWOFORTEN 2 b.c. (Mar 23) Robellino (USA) 127 – Grown At Rowan 75 56
(Gabitat 119) [1997 6m⁶ 6g⁶ 8m Oct 1] small, strong colt: first reported foal: dam 7f
winner: modest form when sixth in maidens at Lingfield and Goodwood: should stay
beyond 6f. *M. Madgwick*

TWO ON THE BRIDGE 3 b.g. Chilibang 120 – Constant Companion 84 (Pas 63
de Seul 133) [1996 59: 5.9g⁴ 5m³ 1997 8m⁶ 6g² 6s³ 5d 6f⁶ 6g² 6g³ 6s⁵ 7g⁴ 6g² 6g 6g

7.1g² 7m Oct 7] leggy, lengthy gelding: modest maiden handicapper: creditable efforts most starts in 1997: effective at 6f, probably at 1m: acts on good to firm and soft ground: no improvement in blinkers: usually races prominently. *Denys Smith*

TWO SOCKS   4 ch.g. Phountzi (USA) 104 – Mrs Feathers 57 (Pyjama Hunt 126)   69
[1996 63: a8.5g a10g⁶ 8g⁵ 10f⁴ 12.5f² 10f² 11.5f* 11.5m 10d 10f 1997 12f⁵ 14.9s⁴ 11.8d² 11.7m² 11.5d⁶ 12d² Sep 19] leggy, unfurnished gelding: fair handicapper: stays 12.5f: acts on firm and dead going and on fibresand: blinkered (below form) once at 2 yrs: suited by waiting tactics. *J. S. King*

TWO WILLIAMS   2 b.g. (Feb 18) Polar Falcon (USA) 126 – Long View 68   84 d
(Persian Bold 123) [1997 5.9m 5s² 5v* 7.5m 7g³ 5d 6d 6d 5s 6m 7s Nov 8] 20,000Y: big, strong gelding: has a round action: has reportedly had tie-back operation and been hobdayed: sixth foal: half-brother to 3 winners, including 7f (at 2 yrs) and 1¼m winner Misty View (by Absalom) and 1¼m to 2m winner Fearless Wonder (by Formidable): dam 9f winner: fairly useful form at best: won maiden at Beverley in July by 8 lengths, getting best of ragged start (stalls not used): also ran well fifth outing, but soundly beaten last 5 starts: stays 7f: acts on heavy ground: has sweated, got on edge and given trouble start. *M. W. Easterby*

TYCOONESS (IRE)   3 b.f. Last Tycoon 131 – Smash (Busted 134) [1996 NR   80 §
1997 14m² 14m² 12.3g* 12m⁴ 13.1s⁶ 14.6g 14.1d⁵ Oct 30] IR 20,000F: tall filly: half-sister to several winners, notably very smart 1m/1¼m performer Broken Hearted (by Dara Monarch): dam once-raced daughter of half-sister to Royal Palace: fairly useful performer: won maiden at Ripon in August after unseating rider in paddock and running loose for a circuit: inconsistent in handicaps afterwards: stays 1¾m: acts on good to firm and dead ground: blinkered last 3 starts: tail flasher: often looks reluctant, and not one to trust. *M. Johnston*

TYCOON GIRL (IRE)   3 b.f. Last Tycoon 131 – Forest Berries (IRE)   74
(Thatching 131) [1996 74p: 6.1m⁵ 6m* 1997 7m 7m⁵ 8.2g⁶ 10.8f³ 10g 8.1m 7g⁵ 8g Aug 1] leggy filly: fair handicapper: inconsistent in 1997: likely to prove suited by 7f/1m: yet to race on ground softer than good: sometimes slowly away: pulled too hard in blinkers fifth start. *B. J. Meehan*

TYCOON TED   4 b.g. Starch Reduced 112 – Royal Tycoon (Tycoon II) [1996   –
NR 1997 11.9d⁵ Jul 4] second reported foal: half-brother to 3-y-o Tycoon Tina: dam winning jumper: well held in claimer at Haydock. *W. M. Brisbourne*

TYCOON TINA   3 b.f. Tina's Pet 121 – Royal Tycoon (Tycoon II) [1996 –: a6g⁵   55
8.1s a8.5g 1997 8.3d² 8.3d⁴ 12m² 8d⁶ 8d* 11.8g⁵ 9.7d 12s² a12g⁴ a14.8g Nov 29] tall filly: modest handicapper: won at Musselburgh in May: good second on same course in November: effective at 1m to 1½m: acts on good to firm and soft going: sometimes slowly away. *W. M. Brisbourne*

TYCOON TODD (USA)   3 gr.c. Cozzene (USA) – Thirty Below (USA) (It's   –
Freezing (USA) 122) [1996 98p: 6g* 1997 8m 7g⁶ 7.3m 10.3d⁵ Aug 29] leggy, useful-looking colt: promising maiden of only race at 2 yrs: well beaten in 1997, including in 2000 Guineas: trained first 2 starts by Saeed bin Suroor: sent to UAE. *D. R. Loder*

TYKEYVOR (IRE)   7 b.g. Last Tycoon 131 – Ivoronica 89 (Targowice (USA)   94
130) [1996 92: 10g⁶ 11.9m³ 12f* 12m* 1997 10g 12m² 12m⁵ 10d 12s* 12m² 14.6m 12g Sep 28] lengthy, good-topped gelding: impresses in appearance: fairly useful performer: made all in handicap at Ascot in July: good second in minor event at Newbury next time: should stay beyond 1½m (ridden too forcefully when tried): acts on firm and soft ground: visored (no improvement) 3 times. *Lady Herries*

TYMEERA   4 b.f. Timeless Times (USA) 99 – Dear Glenda 66 (Gold Song 112)   54
[1996 60, a47: 6.1d* 5d⁴ 6.1m 6.1m a6g⁴ 6m⁶ 6m² 5.1f a5g a6g 1997 a7g 6.1g 6m²   a–
5.7d 6m 6d 5g 6m⁴ 5g Aug 5] small filly: unimpressive mover: modest performer: stays 6f: acts on firm and dead ground, poor at best on the all-weather: tends to hang left: visored (well beaten) once. *B. Palling*

TYPHOON EIGHT (IRE)   5 b.h. High Estate 127 – Dance Date (IRE) (Sadler's   74
Wells (USA) 132) [1996 74: 16g 12m 10.8g² 12m 10g 12m 12g* 12v 1997 10g³ 11.4d³ 10m⁴ 12g 10s⁴ Aug 30] smallish, sturdy horse: poor mover: fair handicapper: creditable efforts most starts in 1997: stays 1½m well: acts on good to firm and soft

ground: effective blinkered or not: sold (to D. Nicholls) 7,500 gns in October. *R. W. Armstrong*

TYROLEAN DANCER (IRE) 3 b.f. Tirol 127 – Waffling 68 (Lomond (USA) – 128) [1996 49: 7f 7f⁴ 7d 1997 8s⁶ 11.9m Jul 24] poor maiden: well beaten in 1997. *S. P. C. Woods*

TYROLEAN DREAM (IRE) 3 b.g. Tirol 127 – Heavenly Hope (Glenstal 76 (USA) 118) [1996 84p: 7m 8s² 1997 10m 9.2g* 11.8d⁶ 12g Oct 25] fair performer: cracked cannon-bone in the spring: best 3-y-o effort when getting up close home in maiden at Hamilton in September: stays 9f: acts on soft going. *M. H. Tompkins*

U

U K MAGIC (IRE) 2 b.g. (May 2) Alzao (USA) 117 – Lightino (Bustino 136) 57 p [1997 8d 8.2d Oct 30] 16,500 2-y-o: workmanlike gelding: fourth foal: half-brother to 8.5f winner Alambar (by Fairy King): dam Irish maiden half-sister to very smart Italian middle-distance performer Welsh Guide: showed promise at Nottingham on second of 2 runs in October maidens, not at all knocked about: should do better. *J. E. Banks*

UKRAINE VENTURE 3 b.f. Slip Anchor 136 – Sherkraine 98 (Shergar 140) 96 [1996 NR 1997 10g* 11.5s³ 12m 10.1m⁴ 10m⁶ 10m⁶ Oct 31] workmanlike, good-topped filly: fifth foal: half-sister to 6-y-o Slasher Jack and a winner in Italy by Caerleon: dam, Irish 2-y-o 6f winner, out of Poule d'Essai des Pouliches winner Ukraine Girl: useful performer: 10-length winner of maiden at Sandown in April: contested listed/pattern races afterwards, third in Lingfield Oaks Trial next time (then out of depth in Oaks itself) and running creditably last 3 starts: best efforts at 1¼m, but should stay further. *S. P. C. Woods*

ULTIMATE SMOOTHIE 5 b.g. Highest Honor (FR) 124 – Baino Charm 76 (USA) (Diesis 133) [1996 NR 1997 14m⁵ 14m* 14m⁵ 14s 17.2f⁵ Sep 29] well-made gelding: second foal: dam ran twice at 3 yrs in France, winning over 7f: fair winner in NH Flat races and over hurdles: also fair form on flat: won weak maiden at Salisbury in July: struggled in handicaps afterwards: stays 1¾m. *M. C. Pipe*

ULTRA BEET 5 b.g. Puissance 110 – Cassiar 84 (Connaught 130) [1996 58, a71: 54 a6g⁵ a5g⁵ a6g² a6g³ a7g a7g 6d 5g 5m 7m⁶ 6m² 6f³ a6g* 6f⁴ a6g a6s³ 1997 a6g* a6g* a84 a6g² a7g⁵ a6g 6d 6f⁴ 5.9m³ 5g 5m a6g⁶ a6g a6g² Dec 13] compact gelding: fairly useful on all-weather, modest on turf: won handicap at Lingfield and claimer at Wolverhampton in January, and ran well final start: best at 5f/easy 6f: acts on firm ground and the all-weather: sometimes blinkered/visored: usually races prominently. *P. C. Haslam*

ULTRA BOY 3 b.g. Music Boy 124 – Golden Award 65 (Last Tycoon 131) [1996 74 73: 5m 6d 6f³ 6m³ 6f* 1997 a7g⁵ a7g² a7g⁵ 7m 7.5s³ 8m* 8d* 7.5m⁴ 9.2g⁴ a8.5g 8f³ a8.5f Dec 3] quite good-topped gelding: fair performer: won claimers at Ripon in May and Newmarket in June: left P. Haslam after tenth start: probably best at 7f/1m: has won on dead going, best form on good to firm/firm going and fibresand: often makes running. *T. Pinfield, USA*

UNCHANGED 5 b.m. Unfuwain (USA) 131 – Favorable Exchange (USA) 69 (Exceller (USA) 129) [1996 79: 14m² 16g⁴ 18.7g⁴ 13.1g⁵ 20f 16f⁴ 20m³ 1997 16g 16.4g 15.9d⁵ 18.2f⁴ 15.4m* Sep 26] good-topped mare: fair handicapper: made all at Folkestone: stays 2½m: acts on firm ground and dead, yet to race on soft: blinkered (trip too short) fourth 4-y-o start. *C. E. Brittain*

UNCLE DOUG 6 b.g. Common Grounds 118 – Taqa 85 (Blakeney 126) [1996 63 68: 14.1g 14.1m⁶ 16g* 16g 14.1f² 16.1g⁶ 16g² 16s* 17.5m²ᵈⁱˢ 14.1m⁴ 16.5s 1997 15.8m 13.8s² Oct 17] close-coupled gelding: modest handicapper: has form at 2½m, but at least as effective at 1¾m/2m: acts on any going: best held up: has run well when sweating: sometimes looks reluctant, and not an easy ride. *Mrs M. Reveley*

UNCLE ERROL 3 b.g. Common Grounds 118 – Saint Navarro 77 (Raga – Navarro (ITY) 119) [1996 NR 1997 10.1g⁶ 8m 7m Sep 26] 4,000Y: second foal: dam best at 5f: last in maidens and a claimer. *G. M. Moore*

UNCONDITIONAL LOVE (IRE) 4 b.f. Polish Patriot (USA) 128 – 104
Thatcherite (Final Straw 127) [1996 100: 5g³ 6m² 7g³ 7f² 7m⁴ 7m 1997 6g 8.5m
9.2g² 7m² 7.3m³ 8.1s 7f 8m 8m 10.1f² 8.2d⁵ 10.3d² a10g* Nov 25] sturdy, good sort:
carries condition: good walker/powerful mover: useful performer: best efforts when
second in listed event at Goodwood (beaten ½ length by Dazzle) and third in
Hungerford Stakes at Newbury (beaten 1¾ lengths by Decorated Hero) on fourth and
fifth starts: won minor event at Lingfield on final start by neck from Running Stag:
effective at 7f to 1¼m: acts on equitrack, firm and dead ground, possibly not soft:
active type, tends to swish tail. *M. Johnston*

UNDAWATERSCUBADIVA 5 ch.g. Keen 116 – Northern Scene 78 (Habitat –
134) [1996 –: a7g⁶ a7g a9.4g⁵ 10m a11g⁶ a12g⁵ 10g a8g 1997 a11g⁴ a11g* a11g⁴ a36
a12g⁵ a11g a14g² a14g⁵ Apr 1] leggy, sparely-made gelding: poor handicapper: won
at Southwell (amateurs) in January: stays 1¾m: acts on fibresand, little form on turf.
M. P. Bielby

UNDERCOVER AGENT (IRE) 3 b.f. Fairy King (USA) – Audenhove (GER) 84
(Marduk (GER)) [1996 79p: 6m² 7g* 6.5m 1997 7m² 7m² 8d⁴ 9m 7m 8m² 7m Nov
1] angular filly: fairly useful performer: runner-up in handicaps at Warwick and
Kempton and a minor event at Brighton: stays 1m: acts on good to firm and dead
ground, unraced on extremes: sold 28,000 gns in December. *J. L. Dunlop*

UNDERSTUDY 3 b.f. In The Wings 128 – Pipina (USA) 81 (Sir Gaylord) [1996 60
8d³ 8g 9g⁴ 1997 10v³ 10g 10m 10.1g² 10.5s a11g Nov 24] workmanlike filly:
half-sister to several winners, including smart Pipsted (up to 1½m, by Busted) and
fairly useful stayer Pipitina (by Bustino): dam, 10.5f winner, from excellent family:
in frame in maidens in French Provinces at 2 yrs: modest maiden in Britain: should
stay beyond 1¼m: none too consistent. *R. Hollinshead*

UNFORGETABLE CHARM (IRE) 3 b.f. Don't Forget Me 127 – Polynesian –
Charm (USA) (What A Pleasure (USA)) [1996 NR 1997 7g 10g 6.1m⁶ Aug 6] half-
sister to several winners, including 4-y-o Koraloona: dam half-sister to smart 1969
US 2-y-o Clover Lane: no promise in maidens: visored (carried head awkwardly)
final outing. *Mrs N. Macauley*

UNGARO (GER) 3 b.c. Goofalik (USA) 118 – Ustina (GER) (Star Appeal 133) 116
[1996 7g 7.8g* 9.5g* 1997 10g* 12f² 11g* 12g⁵ 12g⁶ 14m* Oct 5] sixth reported
foal: half-brother to 5 winners, including 4-y-o Upper Class (up to 1½m, by Konigsstuhl): dam 6f (at 2 yrs) and 1m winner in Germany: smart German colt: won maiden
at Frankfurt and listed race at Cologne (beat Caitano by a head) at 2 yrs: returned to
win Group 3 event at Frankfurt in April by ½ length from Baleno: ran a tremendously
game race when nose second of 16 to Single Empire in Derby Italiano, leading over
5f out, fighting off 2 rivals after a long battle but caught by winner's wide late thrust:
won valuable national listed race at Bremen in June and BMW Deutsches St Leger at
Dortmund by 3½ lengths from Asolo: stays 1¾m: acts on firm ground, yet to race on
softer than good. *H. Blume, Germany*

UNIFORM 2 ch.f. (May 5) Unfuwain (USA) 131 – Trachelium 65 (Formidable –
(USA) 125) [1997 6m 7g 7.5f Sep 17] angular filly: has scope: first foal: dam
(maiden) should have stayed 1m, out of smart 2-y-o 5f winner Penny Blessing: only
a little sign of ability in minor event and maidens. *Miss S. E. Hall*

UNION TOWN (IRE) 3 b.g. Generous (IRE) 139 – Exclusive Life (USA) (Ex- 99
clusive Native (USA)) [1996 88: a7g 6.1m* 7f* 7m* 8.1f⁴ 1997 10m* 10.4d² 9d³ Jun
29] rangy, good-topped gelding: has scope: useful handicapper: won at Salisbury in
May: better effort following month when second at York: stays 1¼m: acts on firm
ground and dead (showed little on fibresand on debut): gelded, and sold 45,000 gns
in October. *Sir Mark Prescott*

UNITUS (IRE) 4 b.c. Soviet Star (USA) 128 – Unite 126 (Kris 135) [1996 85p: –
8.1d⁵ 8m² 10g* 12m 1997 8g 9s May 18] good-bodied colt: lightly-raced performer:
ran as if something amiss final outing as 3-y-o: well beaten in handicaps at Newbury
in 1997: stays 1¼m. *M. R. Stoute*

UNIVERSAL LADY 2 b.f. (Feb 14) Beveled (USA) – Lady of Itatiba (BEL) 63
(King of Macedon 126) [1997 5g 5m⁵ 5m² 5.7g³ 7g² 6m 7d² 6m⁶ 7.3d Sep 19]

3,000Y: leggy filly: third foal here: half-sister to 5f winner Had A Girl (by Hadeer): dam won in Belgium: modest maiden: ran badly final outing: stays 7f. *C. James*

UNKNOWN QUEST   2 b.c. (Apr 8) Rainbow Quest (USA) 134 – Annoconnor (USA) (Nureyev (USA) 131) [1997 8.1d Aug 25] fifth foal: half-brother to a winner in USA by Woodman: dam, Grade 1 9f winner from 4 to 6 yrs, half-sister to Grand Prix de Paris and Melbourne Cup winner At Talaq: behind from halfway in maiden at Chepstow: sold 8,500 gns, and sent to Germany. *P. F. I. Cole*   –

UNKNOWN TERRITORY (IRE)   3 ch.g. Imperial Frontier (USA) 112 – Lilac Lass (Virginia Boy 106) [1996 60d: 7m⁵ 6m² 6d² 6m 10f 1997 a7g a6g⁶ Apr 1] lengthy gelding: unimpressive mover: modest form in sellers at 2 yrs: well beaten in similar events in 1997: tried visored and blinkered: sold 700 gns in May. *Ronald Thompson*   –

UN MELODIE   2 b.f. (Mar 16) Caerleon (USA) 132 – Vaguar (USA) (Vaguely Noble 140) [1997 8f³ Oct 29] third foal: dam French 1¼m winner out of half-sister to Lyphard and Nobiliary: 2/1 favourite, shaped well when about 1½ lengths third to Publisher in maiden at Yarmouth, soon disputing lead and keeping on strongly, not knocked about: will be well suited by 1¼m+: sure to improve. *Saeed bin Suroor*   77 p

U-NO-HARRY (IRE)   4 b.c. Mansooj 118 – Lady Roberta (USA) (Roberto (USA) 131) [1996 74: 5d 6.1d 6.1g 6.1m 6.1m³ 6m* 6f* 6d³ 5.1m* 6m⁴ 5g⁶ 5m 5m⁵ 1997 5d 5.1m⁵ 6d 6m 6m³ 5d 5g 5f 5.1g 5m 6.1s 6g 6g a6g a6g² a6g⁵ Dec 26] sturdy colt: poor mover: fair performer: not so good in second half of 1997 as first: should stay 7f: acts on hard ground, dead and fibresand: blinkered (ran poorly) once: sometimes sweats. *R. Hollinshead*   67 d

UNSHAKEN   3 b.c. Environment Friend 128 – Reel Foyle (USA) 77 (Irish River (FR) 131) [1996 84p: 7m 5d* 6g⁵ 1997 6s 6g 7d⁵ 8s⁶ 8m 5.1s 7.1g 7g Oct 24] strong, sturdy colt: fairly useful form at 2 yrs: no form after leaving J. Fanshawe fourth start in 1997: stays 6f: acts on dead going: tried visored. *E. J. Alston*   70 d

UNSPOKEN PRAYER   4 br.f. Inca Chief (USA) – Dancing Doll (USA) (Buckfinder (USA)) [1996 47: 8g 6m⁵ 7f 8m³ 7d a6g⁴ 1997 a7g a7g³ Jan 17] leggy filly: poor maiden handicapper up to 1m: acts on good to firm ground and probably both all-weather: blinkered final outing. *J. R. Arnold*   38

UONI   4 ch.f. Minster Son 130 – Maid of Essex 66 (Bustino 136) [1996 57d: a10g a11g³ a10g³ 10.8g² 12.5f² 12m⁶ 14.1f⁴ 14.9m 12m⁵ a12g 11.9f a10g⁵ 1997 a8g a12g³ a13g a12g a16g a12g Oct 27] lengthy filly: poor maiden handicapper: should stay further than 12.5f: acts on the all-weather: tried blinkered. *P. Butler*   46

UP AT THE TOP (IRE)   2 b.f. (Mar 5) Waajib 121 – Down The Line 74 (Brigadier Gerard 144) [1997 6m³ 6m* 7m Sep 16] IR 19,000Y: tall, leggy filly: half-sister to several winners, including 6f (at 2 yrs) to 1½m winner Euchan Glen (by Wolverlife): dam Irish 1½m winner: odds on, comfortable winner of maiden at Folkestone in September: ran poorly in nursery only subsequent start, finding little: should stay at least 7f: flashes tail, and possibly temperamental. *B. W. Hills*   74 +

UP IN FLAMES (IRE)   6 br.g. Nashamaa 113 – Bella Lucia (Camden Town 125) [1996 74: 7.5m 6g 8g 8.1d⁶ 8.5m⁵ 8.9m 8g 8.5m⁶ 8f² 8.3m 8m⁶ 1997 a8g a12g⁶ 8.5d 10g⁶ 8m 8.2g 8d 8g 8.2d³ 10.1g 8.2d* a7g a8g⁵ a9.4g* a11g² Dec 8] leggy gelding: modest handicapper: won at Nottingham in November and Wolverhampton in December: effective at 1m to 11f: acts on fibresand, probably on any turf: has had tongue tied. *S. R. Bowring*   54

UPLIFTING   2 b.f. (Mar 2) Magic Ring (IRE) 115 – Strapless 84 (Bustino 136) [1997 6m 6g² 6g³ Oct 24] 19,000Y: smallish, good-topped filly: half-sister to 4-y-o Faith Alone, useful 7f performer Polish Admiral (by Roi Danzig), also successful in USA, and a winner in Austria: dam 6f winner: fair form when placed in maidens at Goodwood and Newbury, making most when clear third of 24 to Mister Rambo on latter: likely to prove best short of 1m: should improve again. *L. G. Cottrell*   77 p

UPPER MOUNT CLAIR   7 b.m. Ela-Mana-Mou 132 – Sun Street 73 (Ile de Bourbon (USA) 133) [1996 71, a60: a16g² a16g* a16g* 18s⁴ 16g³ 17.1g* 16m⁵ 20m⁶ 18.7m⁵ 1997 18m⁴ 14.9m⁵ 21.6g 18.7s 20m 16.4g Sep 2] smallish, leggy mare: fair handicapper: ran poorly after second start: stays 2½m: best efforts on fibresand or on good going or firmer on turf: showed little in blinkers. *C. E. Brittain*   71 d

UP THE CLARETS (IRE) 2 b.g. (Mar 26) Petardia 113 – Madeira Lady (On   49
Your Mark 125) [1997 5g⁶ 6g⁶ 5m⁵ 6d 7g⁵ 8m⁴ 7m³ 8m a7g⁵ Nov 15] 4,200Y: fifth
living foal: dam Irish 2-y-o 6f winner: poor maiden: stays 1m: ran poorly in blinkers
fourth start. *J. J. O'Neill*

UP THE WALL 2 b.c. (Mar 18) Aragon 118 – Ridalia 56 (Ridan (USA)) [1997   58
6m³ 6g 6g 8m 7f² 8s 7m 8m Nov 1] 6,200 2-y-o: leggy colt: closely related to 7.5f to
9.4f winner Kelly Mac (by Precocious) and half-brother to several winners, including
fairly useful sprinter Powder Blue (by He Loves Me): dam maiden: modest maiden:
trained by I. Campbell first 2 starts, next one by R. Harris: ran poorly last 3 outings:
stays 7f: acts on firm ground. *John Berry*

URGENT REPLY (USA) 4 b.g. Green Dancer (USA) 132 – Bowl of Honey   66
(USA) (Lyphard (USA) 132) [1996 NR 1997 12m⁴ 10d 10s⁵ 14d 11.9f a12f 8.3s
12.1m* 12g* 12d² 14g² 14.4m 16g 12.1g Sep 29] $22,000Y: sturdy gelding: third
foal: half-brother to a graded stakes placed (up to 13f) winner by Affirmed: dam
unraced half-sister to Nero Zilzal (smart up to 1¼m) and granddaughter of Rose
Bowl: fair performer: won claimers at Hamilton in July and Catterick in August,
dictating pace: poor efforts in handicaps last 3 starts: stays 1¾m: acts on good to firm
and soft ground. *C. A. Dwyer*

URGENT SWIFT 4 ch.g. Beveled (USA) – Good Natured § (Troy 137) [1996   86
73: 9g⁵ 10g 9f² 9f² 10m³ 10f* 10.5v 1997 12m³ 10.8m 12m² 11.5g 14.1m³ 12g²
13.1d Sep 20] rangy gelding: fairly useful handicapper: best effort when close second
at Goodwood (idled and caught post) penultimate start: stays 1¾m: acts on firm
going, seemingly not on ground softer than good: suited by waiting tactics: hurdling
with M. Pitman, and broke blood vessel on debut in October. *A. P. Jarvis*

URSA MAJOR 3 b.c. Warning 136 – Double Entendre 81 (Dominion 123) [1996   –
81: 7g⁵ 7d⁶ 6.1s² a6g* 1997 6m 7m 6m 7d 7m 5d a6s a10g Dec 10] small colt: fairly
useful as 2-y-o: little form in handicaps at 3 yrs, stiff tasks most starts: should stay
beyond 6f: acts on equitrack and soft ground. *A. Kelleway*

UTAH (IRE) 3 b.g. High Estate 127 – Easy Romance (USA) (Northern Jove   –
(CAN)) [1996 –: 8m 7d⁵ 1997 10s⁶ 8d May 16] strong, lengthy gelding: soundly
beaten in maidens. *B. Gubby*

UTHER PENDRAGON (IRE) 2 b.g. (Apr 14) Petardia 113 – Mountain Stage   –
(IRE) (Pennine Walk 120) [1997 6g a7g Sep 20] 5,500 2-y-o: workmanlike gelding:
first foal: dam Irish 1¼m winner, also successful over hurdles. well beaten in maiden
and seller. *J. A. Bennett*

UTMOST ZEAL (USA) 4 b.g. Cozzene (USA) – Zealous Lady (USA)   56
(Highland Blade (USA)) [1996 68: 8m 8g 6m 7m 7g 6.9m* 7.5g 7m² 6.9g 7g³ a7s³
a8g 1997 6.9g 8.2m 10d 8d 10.1f Jun 5] unfurnished gelding: modest handicapper:
probably stays 1m: acts on equitrack and on good to firm ground: best forcing pace:
blinkered last 2 starts (looked moody final one, then gelded). *P. W. Harris*

V

VAGABOND CHANTEUSE 3 ch.f. Sanglamore (USA) 126 – Eclipsing (IRE)   105
93 (Baillamont (USA) 124) [1996 81: 6m³ 6m⁴ 7g* 8m³ 8m⁶ 1997 8m⁴ 10m³ 10.4g²
12m³ 12m⁶ 10g 13.4s Aug 30] tall, lengthy filly: useful performer: placed in listed
race at Newmarket (¾ length third to Siyadah), Musidora Stakes at York (11 lengths
second to Reams of Verse) and Prix de Royaumont at Chantilly (2 lengths third to
Legend Maker), all in May: disappointing last 3 starts: should stay beyond 1½m: acts
on good to firm ground, tailed off on soft: tail-flasher. *T. J. Etherington*

VAIN TEMPEST 3 b.c. Warning 136 – North Wind (IRE) 101 (Lomond (USA)   82
128) [1996 NR 1997 8m⁴ 8g* 8g 10m 11.9m⁴ 11m Nov 4] strong, lengthy colt: first
reported foal: dam 11f winner: fairly useful form: landed odds in maiden at Ripon in
June: similar form in handicaps afterwards: probably stays 1½m: raced solely on
good/good to firm going. *P. W. Chapple-Hyam*

VALAGALORE 3 b.f. Generous (IRE) 139 – Victoria Cross (USA) (Spectacular 91
Bid (USA)) [1996 74p: 8m⁴ 7d⁶ 1997 12m³ 11.4m⁴ 13.8g* 14m* 14.6m 18g Oct 18]
very tall filly: probably still weak: fairly useful performer: won maiden at Catterick
in July and handicap (best effort) at Haydock in August: below best last 2 starts:
suited by good gallop at 1¾m and should stay 2m+: yet to race on extremes of going.
B. W. Hills

VALEDICTORY 4 b.g. Slip Anchor 136 – Khandjar 77 (Kris 135) [1996 100: 103
12m³ 14m* 16.2m⁶ 14.8m⁴ 1997 12m* 12d² May 22] strong, well-made gelding:
carries plenty of condition: has a markedly round action: useful performer: reportedly jarred tendons in July, 1996: first race since when winning handicap at
Newmarket, hanging left under pressure: sweating, good second in similar event at
Goodwood later in May: should stay beyond 1¾m: acts on good to firm and dead
ground: heavily bandaged last 5 starts: genuine: won over hurdles for P. Monteith in
December. *H. R. A. Cecil*

VALES ALES 4 b.g. Dominion Royale 112 – Keep Mum 63 (Mummy's Pet 125) –
[1996 –: 6d 7m 1997 6g Aug 2] no worthwhile form. *R. M. McKellar*

VALIANT DASH 11 b.g. Valiyar 129 – Dame Ashfield 90 (Grundy 137) [1996 –: 31
15d 1997 14g 17.2m 16g² 16m 17.1g⁴ Aug 17] poor staying handicapper on flat.
J. S. Goldie

VALISE 4 b.f. Salse (USA) 128 – Secret Valentine 71 (Wollow 132) [1996 –: 10m –
13.8g⁵ 16f⁴ 1997 8.3s 10.1f 8f Jun 5] little form since 2 yrs. *G. G. Margarson*

VALSLASTCHANCE 2 b.g. (May 19) Clantime 101 – Panay 77 (Arch Sculptor –
123) [1997 5m 5d May 20] 4,200Y: compact gelding: brother to two 5f winners and
half-brother to another by Alias Smith: dam 2-y-o 5f winner: well beaten in sellers,
blinkered second time. *N. Tinkler*

VANADIUM ORE 4 b.g. Precious Metal 106 – Rockefillee (Tycoon II) [1996 59: 59
8f² 8m⁴ 11.1g² 10.5s 9m 8m a8.5s 1997 10.1g* 10m⁵ Nov 4] leggy gelding: modest
handicapper: won 19-runner event at Newcastle in October: ran well next time:
should stay beyond 11f: acts on good to firm ground, below form on soft: visored last
4 starts in 1996. *W. McKeown*

VANBOROUGH LAD 8 b.g. Precocious 126 – Lustrous 73 (Golden Act (USA)) 47
[1996 –: 8m 8.1m 7s 8m 8.1s a10s a8g⁶ 1997 8d* 8m⁵ 8.3g³ 8g³ 8.3s³ 8g² 8.3m⁴ 8.3g
Sep 29] strong, lengthy gelding: poor handicapper: won Timeform Handicap at Bath
in May for third time: generally creditable efforts afterwards: has form at 7f and
11.6f, races mainly around 1m nowadays: acts on any going. *M. J. Bolton*

VAN CHINO 3 b.c. Suave Dancer (USA) 136 – Atlantic Flyer (USA) 98 (Storm 53
Bird (CAN) 134) [1996 –p: 6d 1997 7m⁴ 8.1m⁵ 6m 5g 7g 10.4s 8.5f a8.5g² 7d⁵ Oct
13] rangy colt: modest maiden: seems effective at 7f to 8.5f: acts on good to firm and
dead going and fibresand. *B. A. McMahon*

VAN GURP 4 ch.g. Generous (IRE) 139 – Atlantic Flyer (USA) 98 (Storm Bird 87 §
(CAN) 134) [1996 96: 8m⁵ 10.4f⁴ 8.1d 8m³ 8m 8d² 7.9g* 8f 8d⁵ 1997 a8.5g 10m⁵
10.4g 7m³ 8g 7.6s 9m Oct 4] small, close-coupled gelding: fluent mover: fairly
useful handicapper: stays 1m: best form on good going or firmer: takes keen hold:
inconsistent, and not one to trust: sold only 3,200 gns in October. *B. A. McMahon*

VANISHING TRICK (USA) 3 ch.f. Gone West (USA) – Wand (IRE) 69 80
(Reference Point 139) [1996 78p: 7f⁶ 7f* 1997 10d 8.2m² 8m 10m 9m³ 10.1m³ 8m⁴
10.3d⁵ Nov 7] strong, close-coupled filly: fairly useful handicapper: stays 1¼m:
seems unsuited by good to soft going: visored/blinkered last 5 outings. *H. R. A. Cecil*

VAPORIZE 5 ch.g. Handsome Sailor 125 – Belle Appeal (Teenoso (USA) 135) –
[1996 NR 1997 5.1m 8s 7.1g Aug 3] of little account. *D. M. Hyde*

VARNISHING DAY (IRE) 5 b.g. Royal Academy (USA) 130 – Red Letter Day 57
100 (Crepello 136) [1996 NR 1997 7m 6d 8m 7m⁴ a8s Nov 10] tall gelding: lightly
raced since useful 2-y-o (has reportedly had several problems, including suspected
fractured pelvis): blinkered, fourth in claimer at Newmarket in August, only form at
5 yrs: stays 7f: form only on good going or firmer. *P. W. Chapple-Hyam*

VARXI (FR) 3 gr.c. Kaldoun (FR) 122 – Girl of France (Legend of France (USA) 105
124) [1996 116: 7.5d* 8d³ 8v* 1997 8g⁶ 9.3s³ 9d⁶ Jul 26] second foal: dam useful

French 1m winner (including at 2 yrs) out of half-sister to Prix Vermeille winner Walensee: smart colt at 2 yrs, won Prix Thomas Bryon at Saint-Cloud by 5 lengths: disappointing in 1997, best effort when 2 lengths third of 5 to Kirkwall in Prix de Guiche at Longchamp: detached last on other 2 starts: should stay 1¼m: acts on heavy ground. *D. Smaga, France*

VASARI (IRE) 3 ch.g. Imperial Frontier (USA) 112 – Why Not Glow (IRE) (Glow (USA)) [1996 94: 5g² 5.1g* 6m 5v³ 6m⁵ 6g³ 1997 5s⁵ 5d 5.1d May 6] close-coupled, useful-looking gelding: fairly useful 2-y-o: little show in 1997: rather headstrong. *M. R. Channon* —

VAX NEW WAY 4 gr.g. Siberian Express (USA) 125 – Misty Arch (Starch Reduced 112) [1996 62, a75: 5d a6g* 6g⁶ a6g² a7g a6g² 5.1m⁴ a6g 6f⁴ 6m² 1997 6m 8s 5h 7g⁵ 8g⁶ 5g a6g Nov 23] sturdy, lengthy gelding: fair sprinter for J. Spearing as 3-y-o: well below form in 1997, including at Folkestone on reappearance: usually blinkered. *Alex Vanderhaeghen, Belgium* —

VAX RAPIDE 2 ch.f. (Feb 24) Sharpo 132 – Vax Lady 98 (Millfontaine 114) [1997 5m⁵ 5m Apr 30] close-coupled filly: third foal: half-sister to 3-y-o Vax Star: dam sprinter: looked speedy when winning maiden at Warwick in March: last in minor event at Ascot only subsequent start. *J. L. Spearing* 80

VAX STAR 3 gr.f. Petong 126 – Vax Lady 98 (Millfontaine 114) [1996 96: 5g² 5g* 5f² 5m* 5m 1997 5.1m 6d 5.1m 5g⁴ 6m 5g Aug 20] smallish, sturdy filly: has a quick action: fairly useful on her day: fourth in handicap at Newcastle in July: last all other starts at 3 yrs: speedy: acts on firm ground: blinkered last 4 starts: one to treat with caution: sold 16,500 gns in December. *J. L. Spearing* 88 §

VEESEY 4 b.f. Rock City 120 – Travel On 111 (Tachypous 128) [1996 –: 6.1d 6m 1997 a6g a7g a12g 8.3d Apr 10] no longer of any account. *John Berry* —

VELVET JONES 4 b. or gr.g. Sharrood (USA) 124 – Cradle of Love (USA) 87 (Roberto (USA) 131) [1996 60: 6m 7f² 7f³ 7f⁴ 7m⁴ 8.5g⁵ 7f⁵ 7m³ 7f⁶ 8m³ 8f 1997 6m⁴ 7m 7f⁵ 8.1g 6g⁶ 7m 6m 7g 8m 10.8g Oct 7] angular gelding: poor maiden handicapper: well beaten last 5 starts: stays 1m well: acts on firm ground: blinkered (below form) once. *G. F. H. Charles-Jones* 47 d

VELVET STORY 2 ch.g. (May 26) Aragon 118 – Lucy Manette 53 (Final Straw 127) [1997 5m 5m⁶ 5m² 6g a6g Dec 6] 7,000Y: small gelding: fourth foal: half-brother to Irish 1995 2-y-o 6f winner Zalzie (by Zalazl): dam third at 6f: second in seller at Carlisle for N. Tinkler in June: well beaten after. *P. D. Evans* 48

VENDIMIA 4 b.f. Dominion 123 – Villasanta (Corvaro (USA) 124) [1996 8g 8g 10g⁶ 1997 a12g Jan 6] 4,200Y: sixth foal: half-sister to several middle-distance winners: dam maiden from good French family: modest form in maidens in Ireland in 1996: visored, last in weak event at Southwell, only start of 1997: stayed 1¼m: sold IR 18,500 gns in November, in foal to Tagula. *K. McAuliffe* —

VENETIAN SCENE 3 ch.f. Night Shift (USA) – Revisit 86 (Busted 134) [1996 58: 5m³ 7.1s 7d⁶ 1997 11.8d* Apr 26] small filly: fair performer: won handicap at Leicester on only start of 1997: will stay beyond 1½m: acts on dead going. *P. F. I. Cole* 72

VENICE BEACH 5 b.g. Shirley Heights 130 – Bold And Beautiful 105 (Bold Lad (IRE) 133) [1996 NR 1997 a8.5g⁴ a9.4g⁶ a9.4g³ 11.9f⁶ Apr 21] modest maiden: only form in 1997 when third at Wolverhampton in March: stays 1¼m: takes good hold. *C. P. E. Brooks* 54

VENI VIDI VICI (IRE) 4 b.g. Fayruz 116 – Divine Apsara (Godswalk (USA) 130) [1996 71: a8g⁵ a7g 8m* 8m* 7.1d 8.2g 1997 8g 8d² 8s² 8m 8g⁴ 7s 7.1m⁶ 8m³ 7g Oct 24] stocky gelding: unimpressive mover: fair handicapper: creditable efforts at 4 yrs when in frame: suited by 1m: acts on good to firm ground, soft and fibresand: usually held up. *M. J. Heaton-Ellis* 68

VENTURE CAPITALIST 8 ch.g. Never So Bold 135 – Brave Advance (USA) 98 (Bold Laddie (USA)) [1996 114: 5d³ 6m³ 6m² 6f* 7.1d 6m 6m² 5m² 6f³ 6m 6d 1997 6m⁵ 6g³ 6m² 5g⁶ 6m 6g² 6m 6g 5.6m 5m⁴ 6g³ 7m⁴ Oct 7] lengthy, deep-girthed gelding: unimpressive mover: smart performer in 1996, only useful at best at 8 yrs: stays 6f: probably best on good going or firmer: effective blinkered, tried only twice 100

VEN

since 1995: best coming with late challenge off strong pace: has been early to post. *D. Nicholls*

VENTURE CONNECT 3 ch.g. Interrex (CAN) – Tricata (Electric 126) [1996 61p: a6g² 1997 a9.4g³ a8.5g 12d Jun 11] fair maiden: ran poorly after third at Wolverhampton in February: stays 9.4f: acts on fibresand. *C. P. E. Brooks* — a66

VERA'S FIRST (IRE) 4 b.f. Exodal (USA) – Shades of Vera 76 (Precocious 126) [1996 –: a7g⁶ a7g 1997 a7g Feb 15] no promise since fair winner at 2 yrs. *Miss Gay Kelleway* —

VERASICA 3 b.f. Handsome Sailor 125 – Vera Musica (USA) (Stop The Music (USA)) [1996 NR 1997 6m a7g Jun 7] 1,400Y: plain filly: half-sister to 4-y-o Grand Musica and 2 winners abroad: dam 7.5f winner in Italy: tailed off in maidens. *R. Hollinshead* —

VERDANT EXPRESS 2 b.f. (Apr 30) Greensmith 121 – Ballynora (Ballacashtal (CAN)) [1997 a5g 5s² 5.1g a5g 5.3f⁵ Oct 1] first foal: dam unraced: only form in selling company second start. *W. G. M. Turner* 38

VERDI (IRE) 3 b.c. Green Desert (USA) 127 – Flying Bid 71 (Auction Ring (USA) 123) [1996 NR 1997 6m⁵ 7m⁴ 10m 13.1g 10d Oct 20] IR 40,000Y: half-brother to several winners, including useful Irish 1987 2-y-o 5f and 6f winner Flutter Away (by Lomond) and 1½m winner Rahwah (by Northern Baby): dam 1¼m winner: fair maiden handicapper: stays 7f: visored (too free) final start: sold, and sent to Germany. *K. McAuliffe* 65

VEREVA (IRE) 3 br.f. Kahyasi 130 – Vearia (Mill Reef (USA) 141) [1996 NR 1997 10d* 10d* 10.5d* 10g² Aug 23] 120

Prix de Diane winner Vereva disappeared from the scene as suddenly as she appeared on it. The Prix de la Nonette at Deauville in August should have been a relatively straightforward preparation for bigger races like the Vermeille and then the Arc but Vereva lost her unbeaten record when going down by a head to the British-trained Dust Dancer. More importantly she returned home with a back injury which brought a premature end to her season. With the Nonette coming towards the end of Deauville's busy month of racing in August, her trainer blamed the state of the track for Vereva's injury—'You can't run a good horse at Deauville; it's a track for handicappers!' Vereva's career hadn't begun ideally, either. She'd been ready to run as a two-year-old, but, with her half-brother Valanour's seeming inability to cope with soft going in mind, her trainer decided to delay her debut until the spring. She then suffered from a cough which put back her appearance still further, and by the time she did make her debut the Prix de Diane was just five weeks away. That debut was in a minor event at Chantilly at the end of April over a slightly shorter trip than the Diane. After winning there she followed up in the listed Prix de la Seine, also over a mile and a quarter, at Longchamp at the end of May.

Vereva's inexperience in the Prix de Diane Hermes wasn't reflected in her position in the betting or in her performance. She started coupled as second favourite with stable-companion Darashandeh behind the Prix Saint-Alary

Prix de Diane Hermes, Chantilly—a smooth performance from Vereva; Mousse Glacee is a clear second

winner Brilliance. Among the other more fancied runners in a field of twelve were the highly regarded Palme d'Or for the Fabre/Wildenstein combination that had won the Prix du Jockey-Club with Peintre Celebre a week before, the Poule d' Essai des Pouliches winner Always Loyal, the Prix Vanteaux winner Queen Maud, Mousse Glacee, who'd disappointed as favourite in the Pouliches, and the Marcel Boussac winner Ryafan, who'd finished fourth on her reappearance in the Irish Guineas. The last-named set the pace with Vereva travelling well, in touch towards the outer. While some of her rivals met interference, Vereva enjoyed a clear run, quickening into the lead in good style over a furlong out and having a length and a half to spare over Mousse Glacee, who ran on well once getting room. Brilliance was another two lengths back, ahead of Ryafan, who just held on to fourth.

Vereva was given an eleven-week break before returning at Deauville. Had she gone on to run in the Vermeille there's every reason to think she'd have been well suited by the step up to a mile and a half. She'd almost certainly have gone close to winning it as well. Queen Maud (who'd had the worst trouble in running in the Diane) took it in Vereva's absence, with Brilliance and Mousse Glacee beaten about a length in third and fourth.

		Ile de Bourbon	Nijinsky
	Kahyasi	(br 1975)	Roseliere
	(b 1985)	Kadissya	Blushing Groom
Vereva (IRE)		(b 1979)	Kalkeen
(br.f. 1994)		Mill Reef	Never Bend
	Vearia	(b 1968)	Milan Mill
	(b 1985)	Val Divine	Val de Loir
		(b 1971)	Pola Bella

H. H. Aga Khan's "Vereva"

1011

Vereva is the best product so far of her sire, the dual Derby winner Kahyasi, who's had to rely principally on his owner the Aga Khan for patronage and who's had only small crops to represent him—Vereva was one of just twenty-three foals in his latest batch of three-year-olds. By winning the Prix de Diane, Vereva was keeping up the family tradition of winning classics begun by her fourth dam, the One Thousand Guineas and Oaks winner Bella Paola. Vereva's great grandam, Pola Bella, won the Poule d'Essai des Pouliches and found only one too good in the Prix de Diane. Prix du Jockey-Club winner Natroun is from the same family, out of a half-sister to Vereva's dam. Vereva's feat of winning a Group 1 race on her third start meant she went one better than her half-brother Valanour (by Lomond) who took the Grand Prix de Paris on his fourth outing and added the Prix d'Harcourt and Prix Ganay at four. An update on his entry in *Racehorses of 1996* is that he's standing at Haras de la Reboursiere et de Montaigu in Normandy. By contrast, Vearia's first foal Veadari (by Alleged) is still seeking his first win—at the age of six over fences in the Provinces. Her fourth foal is the unraced two-year-old colt Varapour (by Kenmare). Vearia was twice successful over a mile and a quarter (including in a listed race) and has some notable half-brothers—Champion Stakes winner Vayrann, Queen Anne Stakes winner Valiyar and Oak Tree Invitational winner Yashgan—out of the ten and a half furlong winner Val Divine.

By way of a postscript, there were signs that Vereva's trainer had moderated his views about Deauville as he won the Prix des Reservoirs for two-year-olds there in October with the Aga Khan's filly Zalaiyka, potentially a contender for the better fillies' races herself in 1998. *A. de Royer Dupre, France*

VERGLAS (IRE) 3 gr.c. Highest Honor (FR) 124 – Rahaam (USA) 91 (Secreto 118 (USA) 128) [1996 107: 5d³ 6g* 6f* 6g³ 7g⁶ 1997 7m⁴ 8g² 12d⁶ 8g⁶ 8f* Dec 26] quite attractive colt: smart performer: ran easily best race when 3 lengths second to Desert King in Lexus Irish 2000 Guineas at the Curragh in May: well beaten in Irish Derby and Desmond Stakes at the Curragh next 2 starts (trained by K. Prendergast): first run for 4½ months and on medication, won allowance race at Santa Anita: stays 1m: acts on firm going. *C. Whittingham, USA*

VERIDIAN 4 b.g. Green Desert (USA) 127 – Alik (FR) 113 (Targowice (USA) 89 130) [1996 83: 8g⁴ 7.9m⁵ 8.3g 10m⁶ 9.7m² 11.5d* 1997 11.1d 12m 14s 12m* 11.9d⁵ 12.3m* 12s² 12g⁴ 12v⁶ 12g² Oct 25] neat gelding: fairly useful handicapper: won at Doncaster in May and Chester in July: very good second of 17 to Al Azhar at Doncaster final start: better at 1½m than shorter: acts on good to firm ground and soft: seems suited by waiting tactics and strong handling: sold 42,000 gns, and joined N. Henderson. *P. W. Harris*

VERINDER'S GIFT 3 ch.g. Chilibang 120 – A Nymph Too Far (IRE) 49 – (Precocious 126) [1996 55, a45: a6g a6g 8.2g² a8.5g 1997 a8g a8g⁴ a7g 8f 9m Oct 31] modest performer at 2 yrs: well beaten in 1997: blinkered final start: stays 1m. *Dr J. D. Scargill*

VERITY 3 ch.f. Pharly (FR) 130 – Persian Victory (IRE) (Persian Bold 123) [1996 – NR 1997 a7g Oct 18] second foal: dam unraced half-sister to several winners: tailed-off last in maiden at Wolverhampton. *Lord Huntingdon*

VEROCITY (FR) 2 b.g. (Apr 15) Groom Dancer (USA) 128 – Villella (Sadler's – Wells (USA) 132) [1997 7f Oct 29] first reported foal: dam unraced close relative of useful Irish 7f and 1m winner Chanzi from family of Nonoalco: 50/1, tailed off in Yarmouth maiden. *G. Wragg*

VERONICA FRANCO 4 b.f. Darshaan 133 – Maiden Eileen (Stradavinsky 62 121) [1996 58d: 10g⁵ 12m 11.4d 11.5m 15.4g 14m 9.7d a7g⁴ a10g 1997 14m⁶ 16.4m 16.2s 11.6m³ 12m* 12m⁶ 14m* 14.1g³ 12d² 12m⁴ Oct 31] leggy filly: modest handicapper: left R. Ingram after fourth start: won at Folkestone (maiden event) in August and Sandown in September: unlucky at Folkestone penultimate start: effective at 1½m/1¾m: acts on good to firm and dead going: has shown signs of temperament: blinkered last two 3-y-o starts. *P. R. Hedger*

VERRO (USA)   10 ch.g. Irish River (FR) 131 – Royal Rafale (USA) (Reneged)   – §
[1996 –§: a12g a13g a7g 7.1g a6g⁵ a7g⁶ a6g 1997 a6g a7g 8m Aug 12] of no account.
P. D. Purdy

VERSATILITY   4 b.f. Teenoso (USA) 135 – Gay Criselle (Decoy Boy 129) [1996   –
NR 1997 9m³ 10g 10g⁶ 10.4s 10m a10g Nov 13] leggy filly: second reported foal:
dam won 2½m hurdle: no worthwhile form. *R. F. Johnson Houghton*

VERTICAL SPEED (FR)   3 ch.c. Bering 136 – Victoire Bleue 114 (Legend   120
of France (USA) 124) [1996 NR 1997 11s* 13d* 15d* 14.6m² Sep 13]
        At a cost of £18,000 in supplementary entry fees, the French colt
Vertical Speed was a welcome addition to what could otherwise have turned
into a very one-sided St Leger. When Stowaway was withdrawn on the morning
of the race it left 7/2-chance Vertical Speed as the only one of favourite Silver
Patriarch's rivals at shorter than 10/1 in the betting. Vertical Speed was put
firmly in his place by Silver Patriarch in the end, beaten three lengths, but he
gave the favourite most to do, tracking the muddling pace for much of the way,
losing a couple of places around the turn into the home straight, challenging
again from three out and staying on once Silver Patriarch had gone clear.
        The St Leger was only the fourth race of Vertical Speed's career. He'd
had quite an easy time of it in France up to then, winning his first three starts at
odds on. He made his debut in an eleven-furlong newcomers event at Longchamp in May, followed up against three rivals in the Group 3 Prix du Lys at
Maisons-Laffitte in June over thirteen furlongs and completed the hat-trick at
the same course against four opponents in the Group 2 Prix Hubert de
Chaudenay over fifteen furlongs. In the last-named he beat the British-trained
filly (and future St Leger fourth) Book At Bedtime by a comfortable four
lengths, with his stable-companion the Prix Berteux winner New Frontier in
third. Vertical Speed had been due to contest the Prix Berteux himself but was a
late withdrawal because he was running a temperature. The Grand Prix de
Deauville was to have been Vertical Speed's next race but soft ground there
brought about a change of plan and he was sent instead to Doncaster, where
connections, not unjustifiably, had anticipated a weak field.
        Bred as he is, speed, vertical or otherwise, was never likely to be his
best attribute. His dam, Victoire Bleue, won the two-and-a-half-mile Prix du
Cadran the first time it was run as part of the Arc weekend programme. She had
an interesting career; unraced at two, once-raced at three and graduating to the
Cadran from handicap company via a win in the Prix Gladiateur at four. She
looked open to further improvement at five but disappointed when sent over for
the Sagaro Stakes at Ascot and bowed out with a win in a little race at Vichy

Prix Hubert de Chaudenay, Maisons-Laffitte—
Vertical Speed is much too good for the only British challenger Book At Bedtime

Daniel Wildenstein's "Vertical Speed"

later that year. Vertical Speed is Victoire Bleue's first foal and he's followed by the colts Vaincre Ou Mourir (a two-year-old who's yet to race, by Groom Dancer) and a yearling full brother called Vanishing World. Victoire Bleue is a daughter of the smart French ten-and-a-half furlong winner Vosges, who was third in the Prix Vermeille. Vosges' dam, Virunga, was of similar merit and gained places in the Prix de Diane (behind Allez France and Dahlia) and the Yorkshire Oaks and a win in the Prix de Malleret. Virunga, a half-sister to the Champion Stakes winner Vitiges, was the dam of some other good winners besides Vosges, namely Prix Jacques le Marois winner Vin de France, Mill Reef Stakes winner Vacarme and a noteworthy French hurdler in Video Tape.

		Arctic Tern	Sea Bird II
	Bering	(ch 1973)	Bubbling Beauty
	(ch 1983)	Beaune	Lyphard
Vertical Speed (FR)		(ch 1974)	Barbra
(ch.c. 1994)		Legend of France	Lyphard
	Victoire Bleue	(b 1980)	Lupe
	(b 1987)	Vosges	Youth
		(b 1987)	Virunga

The smallish, attractive Vertical Speed looked a good young stayer in the making, but late in the year his retirement was announced following a leg injury. He's to stand alongside the leading French jumps sire Cadoudal at the Haras de Mortree in Normandy. He acted on good to firm ground and won on soft going on his debut, although, as we said, the latter going was given as the reason for his missing the Grand Prix de Deauville. *A. Fabre, France*

VERULAM (IRE)   4 b. or br.g. Marju (IRE) 127 – Hot Curry (USA) (Sharpen Up   –
127) [1996 NR 1997 10g Aug 23] fair maiden at 2 yrs: showed nothing only outing since. *J. R. Jenkins*

VERY SIMPLE (IRE)   2 ch.f. (Apr 4) Shalford (IRE) 124§ – Whist Up (Artaius   –
(USA) 129) [1997 5m Aug 18] 3,000 2-y-o: fifth foal: dam unraced: tailed off in maiden. *J. S. Moore*

VET'S DECEIT (IRE)   2 ch.g. (May 1) Statoblest 120 – Maniusha 87 (Sallust   33
134) [1997 5m 5g⁵ Apr 23] IR 5,000Y: closely related to French 1m and 9.5f winner Anoosha (by Ahonoora) and half-brother to several winners: dam 1¼m/1½m winner: showed only modicum of ability in maiden and a seller. *Ronald Thompson*

VEUVE CLICQUOT   3 b.f. Saddlers' Hall (IRE) 126 – False Lift 75 (Grundy   –
137) [1996 NR 1997 10d 14d⁵ 12d⁶ a11g Sep 8] fifth foal: half-sister to 3 winners, including fair 7f winner Sharpening (by Sharpo): dam, 2-y-o 7f winner, from family of Bassenthwaite: well beaten in maidens and handicap. *R. W. Armstrong*

VIA DEL QUATRO (IRE)   5 b.m. Posen (USA) – Gulistan (Sharpen Up 127)   –
[1996 NR 1997 16m Sep 25] IR 4,000: half-sister to untrustworthy 7.6f winner Are You Guilty (by Runnett): dam poor daughter of smart stayer Turf: modest form in 3 races at 2 yrs: well beaten since. *J. W. Mullins*

VIA VERBANO (IRE)   3 b.f. Caerleon (USA) 132 – Closette (FR) (Fabulous   105
Dancer (USA) 124) [1996 6g* 6g⁴ 6m⁵ 6m⁴ 7m² 1997 6g⁵ 8d 6m² 7d* 8d 7g* 7m 8d* 12m 8d³ 10g⁵ 8d⁴ 9g² 9d³ 10d⁴ 8d² 10g⁵ Oct 27] smallish, sturdy filly: has a quick action: fifth foal: half-sister to 4 winners in Ireland, including Via Lombardia (by Shardari), later successful in Grade 3 1m event in USA, and useful performer at up to 1½m Via Parigi (by Entitled): dam French 3-y-o 1m winner and Irish 4-y-o 7f winner: useful Irish performer: won minor event at Naas in May and handicap at Leopardstown then minor event at the Curragh in June: twelfth in Jersey Stakes at Royal Ascot in between last 2: generally ran creditably in listed/pattern company afterwards: effective at 7f to 9f (did not stay 1½m in Irish Oaks): acts on good to firm and dead ground, yet to race on extremes: blinkered final start. *J. S. Bolger, Ireland*

VIBURNUM   3 b.f. Old Vic 136 – Burning Desire (Kalaglow 132) [1996 NR 1997   63
9s² 12g 10g⁵ 14.1s⁴ 12d Oct 21] first foal: dam unraced sister to smart 1½m to 2½m performer Warm Feeling: modest maiden: will be suited by further than 1¾m: yet to race on going firmer than good. *A. G. Foster*

VICE PRESIDENTIAL   2 ch.g. (Apr 15) Presidium 124 – Steelock 68 (Loch-   84
nager 132) [1997 5s* 5s³ 5g 5d⁶ 7d⁴ 6g⁵ 6g Sep 29] 8,200Y: close-coupled gelding: easy mover: dam placed over sprint distances at 2 yrs: fairly useful performer: won maiden at Hamilton in May: best subsequent efforts in minor event at Ripon and nursery at Goodwood fourth and fifth starts: stays 7f: raced only on good ground or softer: disappointing when sweating third start. *T. J. Etherington*

VICIOUS CIRCLE   3 b.c. Lahib (USA) 129 – Tight Spin (High Top 131) [1996   78
NR 1997 10m³ Jun 3] IR 46,000Y: lengthy, angular colt: fifth foal: half-brother to modest 6f winner Girl Next Door (by Local Suitor): dam once-raced daughter of smart 5f to 7f winner Petty Purse: 12/1 and burly, staying-on 2 lengths third in maiden at Pontefract. *L. M. Cumani*

VICKI ROMARA   3 ch.f. Old Vic 136 – Romara 105 (Bold Lad (IRE) 133)   83
[1996 75: 10m¹ 10f⁴ 1997 12s² 14m⁵ 11.9d² 16m² 15.9d* 15.8s⁴ Oct 16] small workmanlike filly: fairly useful handicapper: dictated pace when winning at Chester in August, best effort: will stay beyond 2m: acts on good to firm and soft ground: races prominently, and possibly best dominating. *M. Johnston*

VICKY JAZZ   2 ch.f. (Feb 11) Alhijaz 122 – Kinkajoo 53 (Precocious 126) [1997   –
7g 7d 8m Nov 1] IR 4,400Y: fourth foal: dam lightly raced: behind in maiden and sellers. *J. S. Moore*

VICTOR BLUM (USA)   4 b.g. Dr Blum (USA) – Victoria Elena (USA) (Gold   35
Stage (USA)) [1996 NR 1997 12m 8.5m 10s 11.6g 12.5d 11.6m⁴ 10m 12m³ 15.4m⁵ Sep 26] angular gelding: second foal: dam, ran only at 2 yrs, won 3 races in USA up

VIC

to 7f: poor maiden handicapper: stays 15f: acts on good to firm going: best efforts blinkered/visored. *C. A. Horgan*

VICTORIA HOUSE (IRE) 3 b.f. River Falls 113 – Double Grange (IRE) (Double Schwartz 128) [1996 NR 1997 7m⁶ a8g 7m 7m Oct 7] 4,400Y: angular filly: first foal: dam ran a few times: well beaten in maidens and handicap. *M. J. Heaton-Ellis*

VICTORIA SIOUX 4 ch.f. Ron's Victory (USA) 129 – Blues Indigo 103 (Music Boy 124) [1996 51d: a5g⁵ a6g a5g² a6g⁴ a7g³ a6g⁶ a6g⁶ 6.1m⁵ 6f 6f 1997 a5f a6g Jan 20] bad sprint maiden: tailed off in 1997. *J. A. Pickering*

VICTORY AT HART 3 ch.g. Ron's Victory (USA) 129 – Ceramic (USA) (Raja – Baba (USA)) [1996 –: 6f⁴ 6g⁶ 6g⁶ 6g⁶ 1997 8m 8g⁶ 10m 10.8d⁵ Jun 24] leggy gelding: no worthwhile form. *D. Morris*

VICTORY NOTE (USA) 2 b.c. (Mar 30) Fairy King (USA) – Three Piece 101 p (Jaazeiro (USA)) 127) [1997 7g² 6f* 6m⁵ 7.3g³ Oct 24] 85,000Y: big, lengthy, good-quartered colt: has plenty of scope: has a round action: closely related to 5-y-o Dance So Suite and half-brother to Irish 1990 2-y-o 6f and 7f winner Treble Hook (by Ballad Rock): dam Irish maiden: useful form: won listed race at Newbury in July by 1½ lengths from Mugello: good keeping-on third to La-Faah in Horris Hill Stakes there: on toes and free to post when never-dangerous 5¾ lengths fifth to Hayil in Middle Park Stakes at Newmarket in between: will stay 1m: bandaged behind first 2 starts: type to make a better 3-y-o. *P. W. Chapple-Hyam*

VICTORY TEAM (IRE) 5 b.g. Danehill (USA) 126 – Hogan's Sister (USA) 85 (Speak John) [1996 72, a79: a8g² a8g* a8g* 8f³ 7m⁵ 7m 6g² 7m² 7m 7f⁵ 1997 6.9g² 7f⁵ 6.9m* 7m⁴ 7.3g 6g 7d 8f² 5.7f 6.9g* 7m³ 7g* 7m a7g a8g⁶ Dec 12] strong, good-bodied gelding: good mover: fairly useful performer: won minor event at Folkestone in April and handicaps in large fields at same course in September and Newbury (apprentices) in October: suited by 7f/easy 1m: acts on firm ground and equitrack: sometimes tongue tied and fitted with crossed noseband: usually waited with. *G. B. Balding*

VIENNESE DANCER 4 b.f. Prince Sabo 123 – Harmony Park 55 (Music Boy – 124) [1996 –: 6f 7f 6.9d 1997 a6g a6g Mar 13] of no account. *R. J. R. Williams*

VIGNETTE (USA) 2 b.f. (Apr 23) Diesis 133 – Be Exclusive 110 (Be My Guest 93 p (USA) 126) [1997 7m⁵ 6m* Aug 15] leggy, quite attractive filly: third foal: half-sister to a winner in USA by Wild Again: dam French 7f (at 2 yrs) and 9f (Prix Chloe) winner, also successful at 5 yrs in USA: odds on, won maiden at Haydock easily by 4 lengths from Requestor, making all and shaken up only final 1f: bred to stay beyond 6f, but not short of speed: held lofty entries, and should do better. *J. H. M. Gosden*

VIKING DREAM (IRE) 5 b.m. Vision (USA) – Nordic Pride (Horage 124) 54 [1996 NR 1997 14m³ 12f Jun 10] fourth foal: half-sister to useful Irish 7f (at 2 yrs) to 1¼m winner Identify (by Persian Bold): dam Irish 2-y-o 6f winner: fair maiden handicapper at 3 yrs for D. Weld in Ireland: fit from hurdling, better effort in 1997 when third in very slowly-run race at Salisbury, set too much to do: probably stays 1¾m: best efforts on good going or firmer: well held both starts in blinkers. *J. C. Fox*

VILLAGE NATIVE (FR) 4 ch.g. Village Star (FR) 131 – Zedative (FR) 74 62 (Zeddaan 130) [1996 60: 6f 7m⁶ 6m 8g⁶ 8g 8m 1997 5m⁴ 5d⁶ 5m 5.5d 6d⁴ 5g a5g* a65 5.3g² 5g⁴ 6g a6g⁵ a6g⁵ a6g a5g* a5g³ a6g⁶ Dec 26] lengthy, angular gelding: fair handicapper on all-weather, modest on turf: won at Wolverhampton in August and November: best at 5f/6f: acts on firm going, dead and fibresand: usually blinkered. *K. O. Cunningham-Brown*

VILLAGE PUB (FR) 3 ch.c. Village Star (FR) 131 – Sloe Berry 82 (Sharpo 132) 46 [1996 67?: 7.1f 6m 7d 6g⁵ 6v⁴ a6g a6g⁵ 1997 5m 6d 8.3g 5g³ a5g⁴ a6g⁵ 8g³ 7v⁴ 6g 9.7d a8.5g⁶ 6s a6g a5g Dec 22] poor maiden handicapper: effective at 5f to 1m: often blinkered. *K. O. Cunningham-Brown*

VILLARICA (IRE) 3 b.f. Fairy King (USA) – Bolivia (GER) (Windwurf 76 (GER)) [1996 75p: 6m⁴ 1997 7.6m² 7g⁵ 8d² 8d² 10.5d 8.1m a8.5g* Nov 1] leggy, unfurnished filly: unimpressive mover: fair performer: won weak maiden at Wolverhampton, not needing to be anywhere near best: should stay 1¼m (had no sort of run when tried): acts on good to firm ground, dead and fibresand: has carried head high: sold 13,000 gns in December. *P. W. Chapple-Hyam*

1016

VINCENT 2 b.c. (Apr 8) Anshan 119 – Top-Anna (IRE) 71 (Ela-Mana-Mou 132) [1997 7m⁴ 8.3g⁶ Sep 1] 22,000Y: second foal: dam 1½m to 2m winner: showed a little ability though behind in maidens at Newcastle and Hamilton: should stay at least 1¼m. *J. L. Harris*   51

VINDALOO 5 ch.g. Indian Ridge 123 – Lovely Lagoon 68 (Mill Reef (USA) 141) [1996 –: 9.9f 10.4m 10m 10.1m 1997 a12g Nov 29] robust gelding: fairly useful and prolific winning handicapper from 7f to 1½m in 1995 (finished lame final start): lightly raced and no form since. *M. Johnston*   –

VINTAGE RED 7 b.g. Sulaafah (USA) 119 – Armonit 81 (Town Crier 119) [1996 NR 1997 9.2d⁵ Aug 13] no form. *G. Richards*   –

VINTAGE TAITTINGER (IRE) 5 b.g. Nordico (USA) – Kalonji (Red Alert 127) [1996 –: 13d 11.1m 1997 13s 10.9d⁶ 16d* 16m⁶ 15g⁴ Aug 9] small, plain gelding: poor handicapper: won at Musselburgh (apprentices) in June: stays 2m well: acts on good to soft going. *J. S. Goldie*   33

VIOLETTE SABO 3 b.f. Prince Sabo 123 – Kajetana (FR) (Caro 133) [1996 NR 1997 5f 6g⁵ a7g³ Nov 21] 2,000 2-y-o: half-sister to 3,000 winners, notably useful 7f to 1¼m winner K-Battery (by Gunner B): dam unraced: third at Wolverhampton, only form in maidens. *T. J. Etherington*   42

V I P CHARLIE 3 b.c. Risk Me (FR) 127 – Important Guest 53 (Be My Guest (USA) 126) [1996 56: 5m⁵ 6g 6m 7m 1997 a6g* a6g* a6g³ 6d 5d⁶ 6g 6g 7f Jul 12] tall, lengthy colt: fairly useful handicapper on all-weather, fair on turf: well backed, impressive winner at Southwell and Lingfield in February: patchy form after: best form at 6f, should prove effective at 5f: acts on the all-weather, probably on good to soft going. *J. R. Jenkins*   75 a80

VIRTUAL REALITY 6 b.g. Diamond Shoal 130 – Warning Bell 88 (Bustino 136) [1996 NR 1997 10g² 10m 9.7m² 8.5m⁴ 9f 8.5g 8f Sep 17] angular gelding: fairly useful handicapper: second at Newbury in April and Folkestone in May: fell penultimate outing: effective at 8.5f to 1¼m: seems to need good going or firmer: visored (ran creditably) once: rather a weak finisher: consistent. *J. A. R. Toller*   80

VIRTUOUS 2 b.f. (Mar 10) Exit To Nowhere (USA) 122 – Exclusive Virtue (USA) 94 (Shadeed (USA) 135) [1997 7m³ 8f⁴ 8.2g* 7g Oct 18] well-made filly: second foal: dam, 7f winner at 2 yrs who stayed 1½m, half-sister to Entrepreneur and smart middle-distance pair Dance A Dream and Sadler's Image: fairly useful form: landed odds in maiden at Nottingham in October: better efforts when fourth in May Hill Stakes at Doncaster (beaten 5½ lengths by Midnight Line) and seventh in Rockfel Stakes at Newmarket: should stay at least 1¼m. *M. R. Stoute*   92

VISCOUMTESS BRAVE (IRE) 3 b. or br.f. Law Society (USA) 130 – Vadrouille (USA) 111 (Foolish Pleasure (USA)) [1996 7.5d* 7v* 1997 10m³ 10g⁴ 12g² 10g* 10.5d⁴ Nov 16] quite good-topped filly: fairly useful performer: won minor event at Milan in October: also in frame in listed races at Milan, Newbury (beaten 2 lengths by Squeak) and Krefeld and handicap at Turin: stays 1½m: acts on good to firm and heavy ground. *Lord Huntingdon*   94

VISHNU (USA) 7 b.g. Storm Bird (CAN) 134 – Vachti (FR) 114 (Crystal Palace (FR) 132) [1996 NR 1997 a16g⁵ Mar 3] strong gelding: fairly useful middle-distance stayer at best: first start for over 2 yrs, well beaten in handicap at Southwell. *J. L. Eyre*   –

VISIMOTION (USA) 7 ch.g. Imp Society (USA) – Ditdad (USA) (Tudor Grey 119) [1996 NR 1997 a7g Jan 10] lengthy gelding: one-time fair handicapper at up to 7f: well beaten in seller first outing since 4 yrs. *Miss M. E. Rowland*   –

VISIONARY (FR) 3 gr.c. Linamix (FR) 127 – Visor (USA) (Mr Prospector (USA)) [1996 8d³ 9d* 1997 9g* 8d³ 9m⁴ 10g⁴ 9.8m³ 9.5s³ Oct 29] tall quite good-topped colt: first foal: dam, minor sprint winner in USA, out of half-sister to Kentucky Derby and Belmont winner Swale: smart performer: won listed race at Chantilly in April: ran well in pattern company afterwards, including when 4½ lengths third to Daylami in Poule d'Essai des Poulains at Longchamp on second outing, 1½ lengths fourth of 5 to Starborough in Prix Jean Prat at Chantilly on third one and 3½ lengths third to Alhaarth in Prix Dollar at Longchamp on penultimate one: should stay 1½m: acts on good to firm and soft ground. *A. Fabre, France*   115

VISTA ALEGRE 2 b.g. (Jan 14) Petong 126 – Duxyana (IRE) (Cyrano de 71
Bergerac 120) [1997 5g 5m 5d 5m a5s² Nov 10] 27,000Y: small, sturdy gelding: first a84
foal: dam unraced half-sister to dam of 3-y-o Indian Rocket: first run since being
gelded, easily best effort in maidens when head second at Lingfield, making most:
fair form on turf: probably a sprinter: acts on equitrack. *P. J. Makin*

VIVA VERDI (IRE) 3 b.f. Green Desert (USA) 127 – Vaison La Romaine 100 65
(Arctic Tern (USA) 126) [1996 70+: 7m⁴ 7f 1997 8.2m 8.2d 8.2g* 7m³ 8.2m³ 8d
Oct 13] lengthy, useful-looking filly: fair performer: won 17-runner minor event at
Nottingham in May: keen sort, but stayed 1m: acted on good to firm ground: stud.
J. L. Dunlop

VOCATION (IRE) 2 ch.f. (Mar 29) Royal Academy (USA) 130 – Petite Liqueur- 74
elle (IRE) (Shernazar 131) [1997 7m* 7m³ Sep 22] 22,000Y: 2-y-o: fourth foal: sister to
3-y-o Caviar Royale and half-sister to 2 winners, including Irish 11f winner Dancing
Bluebell (by Bluebird): dam unraced granddaughter of Poule d'Essai des Pouliches
and Irish Oaks winner Corejada: 33/1, won maiden at Lingfield by neck from Honey
Storm, quickening to lead near finish: tailed-off last in minor event at Leicester 13
days later: should stay 1m. *P. R. Webber*

VOGUE IMPERIAL (IRE) 2 b.g. (Apr 13) Imperial Frontier (USA) 112 – –
Classic Choice (Patch 129) [1997 5g 5m a7g⁵ a6g⁵ Jul 26] 10,000Y: half-brother to
1990 2-y-o 7f seller winner Classic Ring (by Auction Ring) and 2 winners abroad:
dam unraced: poor form at best: blinkered third start. *P. C. Haslam*

VOILA PREMIERE (IRE) 5 b.g. Roi Danzig (USA) – Salustrina (Sallust 134) 67
[1996 80: 10m 8m 10g³ 10.2m² 10m² 10m³ 11.9v² 11.9g* 12s 1997 12d³ 12m³
10.2g⁴ 10s⁶ 10.4s Sep 4] compact gelding: impresses in appearance: fair handicapper: left M. Tompkins after second start: stays 1½m: yet to race on firm going,
acts on any other: races prominently. *P. G. Murphy*

VOLA VIA (USA) 4 b. or br.g. Known Fact (USA) 135 – Pinking Shears (USA) 86
(Sharpen Up 127) [1996 85: 8d 9s 10.1m³ 10g 9f⁵ 10m³ 10d² 10m⁶ 10s 1997 10.8m²
10.8m² 10g 10d⁴ 9m* 10m³ 10s* 10.1d⁴ 10g⁵ Aug 2] quite good-topped gelding:
unimpressive mover: fairly useful performer: won female apprentices handicap at
Kempton in May and 4-runner minor event at Goodwood in June: stays 11f: probably
acts on any going: has flashed tail: reliable. *I. A. Balding*

VOLLEY (IRE) 4 b.f. Al Hareb (USA) 123 – Highdrive (Ballymore 123) [1996 90
86: 6m* 6g⁴ 8s 1997 8d 7g³ 7m² 7m⁴ 7m³ 7g³ 7f⁵ 7m Sep 27] rangy filly: fairly useful
performer: should stay 1m: acts on firm going, poor efforts on good to soft/soft.
Major D. N. Chappell

VOLONTIERS (FR) 2 b.c. (Mar 30) Common Grounds 118 – Senlis (USA) 101 84 p
(Sensitive Prince (USA)) [1997 7d² Nov 7] 240,000 francs Y: leggy, useful-looking
colt: good walker: fifth foal: brother to French 5f (at 2 yrs) to 1m winner Astudillo,
later Grade 3 6f winner in USA, and half-brother to winners in France by Lichine and
Fabulous Dancer: dam French 2-y-o 1m winner: 7/1 from 10/1, promising short-head
second of 18 to High-Rise in maiden at Doncaster, travelling well long way but
running green under hands and heels when brought to challenge: will stay 1m: sure
to improve, and win a race. *P. W. Harris*

VOODOO SAINT (USA) 2 ch.c. (Apr 28) St Jovite (USA) 135 – Voo Doo 88 p
Dance (USA) (Stage Door Johnny) [1997 7m³ 7m⁶ Sep 10] $50,000F, 170,000Y: tall,
useful-looking colt: eighth foal: closely related to a winner in USA by Pleasant
Colony and half-brother to several minor winners there: dam won 8 times in USA,
including minor stakes up to 1¼m: fairly useful form: 3½ lengths third of 19 to
Mahboob in maiden at Newbury in August then just under 6 lengths last of 6 to
Teapot Row in well-contested minor event at Doncaster: should be well suited
by further than 7f: looked weak at 2 yrs, and should improve and win races.
P. W. Chapple-Hyam

VOYAGERS QUEST (USA) 3 b. or br.c. Dynaformer (USA) – Orange Sickle 117
(USA) (Rich Cream (USA)) [1996 108p: 8f³ 8m* 10s⁵ 9s* 1997 10d* 12m 9s⁴ 8f³
9f² 9d Nov 30] leggy, close-coupled colt: smart performer: beat Benny The Dip and
Silver Patriarch by 1½ lengths and head in Thresher Classic Trial at Sandown in
April, going on 2f out and galloping on splendidly: quickly outpaced after disputing

Thresher Classic Trial, Sandown—Voyagers Quest takes two notable scalps;
Benny The Dip is second, Silver Patriarch (almost obscured) third

lead long way when only seventh of 14 to Peintre Celebre in Prix du Jockey-Club at Chantilly in June, final outing for P. Chapple-Hyam: in frame 3 times for new connections, notably length second to Lasting Approval in Grade 2 race at Santa Anita in November: should stay 1½m: probably acts on any going: raced on medication last 3 starts. *R. McAnally, USA*

VRENNAN 3 ch.f. Suave Dancer (USA) 136 – Advie Bridge 90§ (High Line 125) 74
[1996 NR 1997 10.5d² 12.3g⁵ 14d² 14g a14.8g³ a14.8g⁴ a12s² a12g* a13g⁴ Dec 12] plain filly: third foal: dam, 1m winner at 2 yrs stayed 1½m, not one to trust: fair handicapper: ran well all starts other than when reportedly distressed on fourth, winning at Lingfield in December for J. Fanshawe: stays 15f: acts on dead going and all-weather. *W. Jarvis*

W

WAASEF 4 b.g. Warning 136 – Thubut (USA) (Tank's Prospect (USA)) [1996 NR –
1997 8d 8.3s 8.1m 9m 10.2d Aug 25] 23,000 3-y-o: big, rangy gelding: first foal: dam unraced half-sister to 2000 Guineas second Exbourne and smart miler Top Socialite: unraced at 2 yrs and 3 yrs: some promise on debut: ran as if something amiss most subsequent starts. *Miss Gay Kelleway*

WADADA 6 b. or br.g. Adbass (USA) 102 – No Rejection (Mummy's Pet 125) –
[1996 45, a33: a12g⁴ 17.2m* 17.2f³ 16m⁶ a14.8g⁵ 1997 a12g⁶ a14.8g⁴ Jan 22] small gelding: poor handicapper: stiff tasks at 6 yrs: a stayer: acts on firm going. *D. Burchell*

WADERS DREAM (IRE) 8 b.g. Doulab (USA) 115 – Sea Mistress (Habitat 43 §
134) [1996 51§, a–§: 6m 5.2g⁵ 6m⁶ 6f² 6m⁴ 6m* 7f⁵ 6m 6.1m 7f⁶ 1997 6m 6m⁶ 6m a– §
6m 6.9f 7m⁶ 7f 7f a6g Dec 2] leggy gelding: poor handicapper: stays 7f: acts on firm going: has been blinkered, usually visored: unreliable. *Pat Mitchell*

WADI 2 b.c. (Feb 11) Green Desert (USA) 127 – Eternal (Kris 135) [1997 8.2m³ 84 p
8.2s³ Oct 15] second foal: brother to 3-y-o Furnish: dam once-raced half-sister to Derby winner Quest For Fame out of Poule d'Essai des Pouliches winner Aryenne: favourite but green, third in maidens at Nottingham in September and October: shapes as though will be suited by further than 1m: likely to make fair bit better 3-y-o. *H. R. A. Cecil*

WAFA (IRE)   3 ch.f. Kefaah (USA) 124 – Shomoose (Habitat 134) [1996 NR 1997   –
a9.4g⁵ Mar 29] fourth foal: half-sister to Derby winner Shaamit (by Mtoto): dam
unraced daughter of useful Epithet, who stayed 1½m well: weak 5/1, well held in
maiden at Wolverhampton. *W. J. Haggas*

WAFF'S FOLLY   2 b.f. (Mar 17) Handsome Sailor 125 – Shirl 52 (Shirley   –
Heights 130) [1996 6g Oct 24] sparely-made filly: second foal: dam 1½m winner:
showed only a little ability in large-field maidens at Newbury, taking strong hold on
first occasion. *G. F. H. Charles-Jones*

WAFIR (IRE)   5 b.h. Scenic 128 – Taniokey (Grundy 137) [1996 88: 9.9m⁶   88
10.3m⁴ 10m³ 12m 10.4m 10.1m⁴ 12.3g² 10v* 12g⁶ 10.5d 1997 10m 10m² 10g* 10s
10.4m 10.1m⁴ 10m 10.3m³ 10m⁵ 12s Nov 8] rangy horse: fairly useful handicapper:
won at Ayr (made most) in May: mostly creditable efforts after: stays 1½m: acts on
good to firm and heavy ground: effective blinkered at 3 yrs: has looked hard ride.
P. Calver

WAGGA MOON (IRE)   3 b.g. Mac's Imp (USA) 116 – Faapette (Runnett 125)   61
[1996 55: 5s³ 5g⁴ 6m⁵ 6g 1997 7.5m³ 6g 8m 6g⁶ 7s 5.9g³ 7g 5.9m 6m 9.9g Aug 23]
lengthy, good-bodied gelding: has a fluent, round action: modest maiden handicapper: may prove best around 7f: acts on good to firm going: tried visored/blinkered:
inconsistent. *J. J. O'Neill*

WAHAB   4 b.g. Unfuwain (USA) 131 – Mileeha (USA) 97 (Blushing Groom (FR)   –
131) [1996 –: 7m a14g 1997 a7g 7m Sep 16] no sign of ability. *R. F. Marvin*

WAHIBA SANDS   4 b.g. Pharly (FR) 130 – Lovely Noor (USA) (Fappiano   106
(USA)) [1996 94p: 10m 11.8m³ 1997 10.4g⁵ 12m 10.4m 10s⁵ 12m 14.1m² 13.1s*
11.8g* 14.6d³ Nov 7] big, good-topped gelding: has a markedly round action: useful
performer: won handicap at Ayr (best effort, gave lumps of weight away and beat
Hill Farm Blues by 4 lengths) and minor event at Leicester in October: 4½ lengths
third to Sweetness Herself in minor event at Doncaster: effective at 1½m to 1¾m:
acts on good to firm and soft ground: has been bandaged: very promising novice
hurdler. *J. L. Dunlop*

WAIKIKI BEACH (USA)   6 ch.g. Fighting Fit (USA) – Running Melody 86   70 §
(Rheingold 137) [1996 70, a82: a8g² a8.5g* 6.9f⁴ a8g³ a8.5g⁴ a8g* a8.5g⁴ a9.4g a8g²   a75 §
a10g* 1997 a8g⁵ a9.4g a8.5g² 8g 9s⁵ 8.1g² 8d 8s Nov 8] lengthy gelding: fair handicapper: effective at 1m to easy 1¼m: acts on firm going, dead and the all-weather:
below form in visor at 4 yrs: unreliable. *G. L. Moore*

WAIT FOR ROSIE   3 b.f. Reprimand 122 – Turbo Rose 81 (Taufan (USA) 119)   –
[1996 77: 5g² 5g³ 5.3f* 5m² 6s³ 6.1m⁴ 6d 1997 6m 7g Aug 1] leggy filly: fair winner
at 2 yrs: showed nothing in handicaps in 1997. *V. Soane*

WAITING GAME (IRE)   3 b.c. Reprimand 122 – Walesiana (GER) (Star Appeal   89
133) [1996 94: a7g* 8.3g² 1997 9m⁴ 10.3d Jun 29] tall colt: fairly useful performer,
lightly raced: creditable fourth in minor event at Ripon on reappearance: tailed off
in handicap 3 months later: stays 9f: sold approx. £26,000 in Dubai in November.
D. R. Loder

WAIT'N'SEE   2 b.g. (Mar 8) Komaite (USA) – Kakisa 81 (Forlorn River 124)   78 d
[1997 5g 6m 5f* 6d 5s 6m 7s Nov 8] 1,800F: workmanlike gelding: shows marked
knee action: half-brother to several winning sprinters, 3 by Tina's Pet, including
fairly useful 5f performer Lake Mistassiu: dam 5f and 6f winner: gambled on, fair
form when winning maiden at Carlisle in June (trainer subsequently fined £2,500
under 'non-triers' rule for running on second start): no other form (reportedly gurgled
next time) though when not knocked about on occasions: has worn tongue strap and
crossed noseband: has got upset in paddock. *M. W. Easterby*

WAKEEL (USA)   5 b.g. Gulch (USA) – Raahia (CAN) 91 (Vice Regent (CAN))   89
[1996 87: 8s² 8v* 8s⁴ 8m 8g⁶ 10.1m 8m³ 8d 8d 1997 8.1g 8g 8s³ 8g 8.9d 8s³ 12s⁵
11.9f* 11.8g⁵ 12g² 13.3d Sep 20] tall, attractive gelding: fairly useful handicapper:
won at Brighton in July: effective at 1m to 1½m: acts on any going: tried visored/
blinkered: inconsistent: joined M. Pitman. *S. Dow*

WAKY NAO   4 b.c. Alzao (USA) 117 – Waky Na (IRE) (Ahonoora 122) [1996   116
110: 7g* 8g² 6g* 6g* 6v* 6.5g² 6g⁵ 5s⁵ 1997 5.5g² 6f 6d 8g* 8.5s⁵ 8d⁴ Nov 9] smart
German colt: best effort to win 6-runner Oettingen-Rennen at Baden-Baden in

September by 1½ lengths from Eden Rock: stays 1m: acts on heavy going, probably not on firm: trained by H. Blume first 3 starts (blinkered last of them). *B. Schutz, Germany*

WALES 2 ch.c. (Feb 8) Caerleon (USA) 132 – Knight's Baroness 116 (Rainbow Quest (USA) 134) [1997 6g³ 7g³ 8d* 10d⁶ Nov 1] compact colt: fourth foal: half-brother to 5-y-o Riyadian: dam won Irish Oaks: useful form: won maiden at Goodwood in September: third of 12 in 7f Chesham Stakes at Royal Ascot 3 months earlier, no threat to Central Park and Cape Verdi: good sixth of 7 in Criterium de Saint-Cloud: should be suited by 1½m+: has gone freely to post. *P. F. I. Cole* 98

WALI (USA) 7 b.g. Lomond (USA) 128 – Magic Slipper 97 (Habitat 134) [1996 NR 1997 a7g a6g Feb 24] fair performer at 4 yrs: very lightly raced and no form since. *J. L. Eyre*

WALKABOUT 3 ch.g. Generous (IRE) 139 – Nomadic Pleasure 91 (Habitat 134) [1996 NR 1997 8g 10.3d 14m⁴ 11.7m⁶ 13.8s⁴ Jul 3] strong, good-topped gelding: half-brother to several winners, including smart fillies Trampship (up to 1¾m, by High Line) and Cruising Height (1½m, by Shirley Heights): dam, 9f winner, half-sister to Prix Vermeille winner Paulista: signs of ability but no form. *B. W. Hills*

WALK ON BY 3 gr.g. Terimon 124 – Try G'S (Hotfoot 126) [1996 57: 8d 10g⁴ 1997 11g 12m⁶ 11.9f⁴ 9s⁴ 10m³ Jul 19] big, workmanlike gelding: fair maiden: best efforts over 1½m: acts on firm going: joined J. King and gelded. *R. Hannon* 66

WALK THE BEAT 7 b.g. Interrex (CAN) – Plaits 93 (Thatching 131) [1996 67, a69: 5m⁶ 6m 5f* 5.1f* 5f 5m³ 5.1m 5.7m 5m⁵ a6g* a6g³ 5.1g³ 5s 1997 a5f a6g* a6g⁶ a7g* a6g* 7.6v 7m⁵ 6m⁵ 5m⁴ 6d 6m* 6m 6m⁶ 7m a6g a6g⁶ Dec 2] strong gelding: impresses in appearance: has a round action: fair performer: won at Southwell (handicap and claimer) and Wolverhampton (claimer) early in year and handicap at Lingfield in August: effective at 6f/7f: acts on firm, dead going and fibresand: below best when blinkered/visored: usually held up. *Martyn Meade* 67 a73

WALLFLOWER 2 b.f. (Jan 23) Polar Falcon (USA) 126 – Stufida (Bustino 136) [1997 5g Jul 7] eighth foal: half-sister to 3 winners, including 1989 2-y-o 6f and 7f winner Fearless Revival (by Cozzene), dam of high-class sprinter Pivotal (by Polar Falcon): dam good Italian filly, winner of 1¼m Group 3 event: towards rear in maiden at Windsor: sold 5,200 gns in December. *Sir Mark Prescott* –

WALPOLE 2 b.c. (Feb 15) High Estate 127 – Walesiana (GER) (Star Appeal 133) [1997 6g Aug 2] strong, good-bodied colt: third foal: half-brother to 3-y-o Waiting Game and 1½m winner Warluskee (by Dancing Brave): dam German 6f (at 2 yrs) to 1m (Group 2) winner: coltish, behind in maiden at Newmarket. *D. R. Loder* –

WALTON GREY (IRE) 2 gr.g. (Apr 20) Paris House 123 – Green Bonnet (FR) (Green Dancer (USA) 132) [1997 6g⁵ 7d 8m Sep 25] IR 8,500Y: leggy gelding: half-brother to a winner in Belgium by Sarab: dam French maiden: showed modicum of ability only on debut. *P. D. Evans* 44

WALWORTH WIZARD 2 b.g. (Mar 18) Presidium 124 – Mrs Magic (Magic Mirror 105) [1997 5g 5g⁶ 6m Aug 6] 7,800Y: second foal: dam unraced: probably a poor maiden. *M. Dods* 43 +

WANDERING WOLF 2 ch.c. (Mar 6) Wolfhound (USA) 126 – Circle of Chalk (FR) 74 (Kris 135) [1997 5g 5m⁴ 7m Oct 2] IR 50,000Y: smallish, lengthy colt: first foal: dam French 1¼m winner, sister to useful French 1½m winner From Beyond out of Coronation Stakes winner Magic of Life, an excellent family: best effort when fourth in maiden at Kempton in September: should stay beyond 5f: last and steadily to post final start. *R. Hannon* 75

WARHURST (IRE) 6 b.g. Nordance (USA) – Pourboire 47 (Star Appeal 133) [1996 –, a63: a8g⁴ a8g* a8.5g⁴ a11g⁶ 10.1m 1997 a7s a8g a8g a8g⁶ Mar 13] angular gelding: has reportedly had leg problems: fair performer at best: no form in 1997: tried blinkered. *D. Nicholls* –

WARM SPELL 7 b.g. Northern State (USA) 91 – Warm Wind 84 (Tumble Wind (USA)) [1996 56+: a12g 16g 15.4f⁶ 10m 12d⁴ 1997 12d² 10g⁶ a16g⁶ Aug 2] good-quartered gelding: has a round action: modest handicapper: easily best effort at 7 yrs 64

WAR

on reappearance: stays 1¾m: has form on good to firm ground and equitrack, revels on dead or softer: visored first 2 starts at 7 yrs: game. *G. L. Moore*

WARNING EXPRESS 3 b.f. Warning 136 – Ivoronica 89 (Targowice (USA) 73
130) [1996 NR 1997 8m⁴ 7.1m² 7m⁴ 6d Oct 21] 40,000Y: half-sister to several
winners, including useful sprinter Lochonica (by Lochnager) and 7-y-o Tykeyvor:
dam 2-y-o 5f winner: fair form in steadily-run maidens first 2 starts: well held
afterwards: stays 1m: sent to Australia. *R. W. Armstrong*

WARNINGFORD 3 b.c. Warning 136 – Barford Lady 93 (Stanford 121§) [1996 93
NR 1997 8g⁵ 8g⁴ 7.1g* 8.1d 8g⁶ Jul 31] lengthy, good-topped colt: third foal: dam 7f
and 1m winner: fairly useful performer: won maiden (impressively) at Sandown in
June: respectable effort final start: likely to prove best at up to 1m: ran poorly on dead
going. *J. R. Fanshawe*

WARNING REEF 4 b.g. Warning 136 – Horseshoe Reef 88 (Mill Reef (USA) 77 d
141) [1996 86: 10.5g⁴ 8.1g³ 8m⁶ 10.4m³ 10.1m 12m 11.7m² 14g² 1997 a13g 17.1m⁶
18.7s⁶ 13.3g 12m⁶ 15.9m 12.1m 15.8g Aug 15] workmanlike gelding: poor mover:
disappointing maiden: staying type. *P. Eccles*

WARNING TIME 4 b.c. Warning 136 – Ballad Island 83 (Ballad Rock 122) 104
[1996 100: 6m 6g³ 7m² 6m 7.3f⁵ 5f⁴ 1997 6m 5.2g 6m 6d⁴ a6g 6g³ 6g* 6g⁵ 8f⁴ 8f⁶
8f⁵ Nov 20] strong, workmanlike colt: has a short action: useful handicapper: won
£24,000 event at Epsom in June by ¾ length from Kira, leading inside last: very good
staying-on fifth in the Wokingham at Royal Ascot (final outing for B. Meehan): ran
well first start in USA: claimed by E. Halpern $80,000 final one: stays 1m: acts on
firm and dead ground, tailed off in blinkers only attempt on fibresand. *T. Pinfield,
USA*

WARP DRIVE (IRE) 3 ch.g. Bluebird (USA) 125 – Red Roman 87 (Solinus 41
130) [1996 –: a6g a8g⁶ 1997 a7g² a7g⁵ a8g a7g⁴ a7g a7g a8g Dec 18] poor maiden:
should stay 1m: yet to race on turf: tried blinkered. *W. R. Muir*

WARREN KNIGHT 4 b.g. Weldnaas (USA) 112 – Trigamy 112 (Tribal Chief 54
125) [1996 64: 7g⁶ 8d 8m 7m 1997 8d 9g⁵ 8m 8d Aug 8] good-quartered gelding:
modest maiden: stays 9f. *C. A. Horgan*

WARRING 3 b.g. Warrshan (USA) 117 – Emerald Ring 74 (Auction Ring (USA) 60
123) [1996 48: 7g 7.1f 7d 7m 1997 7m⁴ 8d 8f² 8f⁶ a8g 8m 7g 7g Oct 24] sturdy
gelding: modest maiden handicapper: well below form last 4 starts: stays 1m well:
acts on firm and dead ground, tailed off on equitrack. *M. S. Saunders*

WARRIOR KING (IRE) 3 b.g. Fairy King (USA) – It's All Academic (IRE) 91 56
(Mazaad 106) [1996 6g 6g 9s 1997 12g⁵ 11.9f 14.1d 10.8m⁴ 10.2m⁵ 8s 8.1s² 11.6m⁴
8g³ 8m² 8m² 7.1g* 7f 8.3g 8d 7g Oct 24] 40,000Y: ex-Irish gelding: first foal: dam
2-y-o 5f winner, second in Queen Mary Stakes: modest handicapper: trained first 8
starts by Mrs N. Dutfield: well backed, won at Musselburgh in August: should stay
beyond 1m: acts on good to firm and soft ground: tried blinkered at 2 yrs: has
wandered. *C. A. Dwyer*

WARRLIN 3 b.g. Warrshan (USA) 117 – Lahin (Rainbow Quest (USA) 134) 58
[1996 59: 6g 7m⁴ 7.5f⁴ 7.9g 10m³ 10m 1997 a11g a8g⁴ 14.1m⁵ a12g a14.8g⁴ 14g⁴ a–
17.2m 14d⁵ Jul 3] leggy gelding: has a round action: modest maiden handicapper:
stays 1¾m: acts on good to firm ground, little form on all-weather. *C. W. Fairhurst*

WAR SHANTY 4 b.f. Warrshan (USA) 117 – Daring Ditty (Daring March 116) –
[1996 66: 10.2d⁵ 1997 10m 10.2m Jul 17] very lightly raced maiden: well beaten in
1997. *Lady Herries*

WARSPITE 7 b.g. Slip Anchor 136 – Valkyrie 87 (Bold Lad (IRE) 133) [1996 38: –
12m 10g 12g 10g a11g⁴ 14d a10g⁵ 1997 a11g⁵ a12g⁶ Jan 16] poor performer: well
beaten in 1997: has looked difficult ride. *P. Mooney*

WASHM (USA) 2 b.f. (Apr 12) Diesis 133 – Jathibiyah (USA) 89 (Nureyev –
(USA) 131) [1997 6.1m 7.5g Aug 22] fourth foal: closely related to fairly useful 7f
winner (including at 2 yrs) Ashjar (by Kris) and half-sister to a minor winner in USA
by Slew o'Gold: dam 7f winner (at 2 yrs) who stayed 1¼m, closely related to Irish
1000 Guineas winner Ensconse: only a little sign of ability in maidens at Nottingham
and Beverley (pulled hard). *D. Morley*

1022

WASP RANGER (USA)   3 b.g. Red Ransom (USA) – Lady Climber (USA)   94
(Mount Hagen (FR) 127) [1996 87: 6m³ 7g⁵ 7d² 1997 7g 8d* 7g² 8m 8m⁶ 7m⁴ 7.9d
10m⁶ Sep 25] very tall gelding: easy mover: fairly useful performer: won 4-runner
maiden at Goodwood in May: good efforts in handicaps 3 of last 4 starts, including in
blinkers: probably stays 1¼m: acts on good to firm and dead ground: joined C. Mann.
P. F. I. Cole

WATCHMAN   2 b.g. (Mar 8) Mazaad 106 – High Heather (Shirley Heights 130)   ?
[1997 5.9m⁶ 7.5v³ 7.5m 7m 7.5f a6.7s* a8s* Dec 21] 1,000Y: close-coupled gelding:
third foal: half-brother to 7f winner Arawa (by Doulab): dam unraced: poor maiden
(rated 45) for T.P. Tate: sent to Sweden and won both his races at Taby in December:
stays 1m: acts on dirt. *M. Kahn, Sweden*

WATCH ME GO (IRE)   8 b.g. On Your Mark 125 – Nighty Night (Sassafras   37
(FR) 135) [1996 45: 12.3g² 10.3m a11g⁴ 11.9g² a13g³ 1997 12.3m Apr 9] poor
handicapper: not discredited only outing at 8 yrs: stays 13f: acts on firm ground, dead
and all-weather: tried visored: headstrong on occasions. *Bob Jones*

WATCH ME (IRE)   4 b.f. Green Desert (USA) 127 – Fenny Rough 114 (Home   88
Guard (USA) 129) [1996 106: 6m² 6m³ 6m⁵ 1997 6m 6g⁴ 5.1m Apr 29] well-
made filly: useful sprinter at 3 yrs: best effort in 1997 when fourth in minor event at
Thirsk in April: stays 6f: raced only on good/good to firm going. *R. Hannon*

WATCH MY LIPS   5 b.g. Vin St Benet 109 – Manor Farm Toots 70 (Royalty   –
130) [1996 NR 1997 10d⁵ Sep 2] poor maiden. *M. H. Tompkins*

WATCH THE FIRE   4 b.f. Statoblest 120 – Thulium (Mansingh (USA) 120)   68
[1996 71: 5.1g³ 6f² 6m* 6g 1997 6m 7g 7f 6s* 5.9g* 6g 6g 6.1m³ a6g 7m 6g Oct 27]
fair performer: won handicap at Pontefract in June and minor event at Carlisle in
July: ran badly last 3 starts: stays 6f: acts on firm and soft going: usually held up: sold
only 3,000 gns, and sent to Saudi Arabia. *J. E. Banks*

WATERCOLOUR (IRE)   3 b.f. Groom Dancer (USA) 128 – River Nomad 99   –
(Gorytus (USA) 132) [1996 –: 6d 6f 6.9g 1997 10.3m Mar 20] smallish, angular
filly (no oil painting): no form: blinkered only start at 3 yrs: sent to Saudi Arabia.
N. M. Babbage

WATER FLOWER   3 b.f. Environment Friend 128 – Flower Girl 108 (Pharly   71
(FR) 130) [1996 NR 1997 8g 10g 10m³ 14.1m 12m 12m* Oct 2] first reported foal:
dam 6f winner: fair performer: won claimer (gamely) at Newmarket in October, then
joined M. Pipe: stays 1½m: raced only on good/good to firm ground: has been
bandaged behind. *J. R. Fanshawe*

WATER FORCE   2 b.g. (Apr 23) River Falls 113 – Quelle Chemise 65 (Night   66
Shift (USA)) [1997 5.2m 5.7g 6.1d⁴ 7g⁵ 7d⁶ 7.3d⁶ 7v Oct 10] 16,000Y: strong,
workmanlike gelding: shows knee action: second foal: dam maiden half-sister to
Cambridgeshire winner Quinlan Terry: fair maiden: rather disappointing after fourth
start: should stay 1m: free to post last 2 starts (gelded after final one). *G. B. Balding*

WATER GARDEN   3 ch.c. Most Welcome 131 – On Show 92 (Welsh Pageant   75
132) [1996 –p: 6g 7g 1997 a7g* a7g* a8.5f⁴ 7m Aug 9] good-topped colt: fair form:
won maiden and handicap at Southwell in the spring, slowly away both times:
disappointing afterwards: should stay 1m: acts on fibresand, no form on turf: sold,
and sent to Norway. *G. Wragg*

WATER HAZARD (IRE)   5 b.g. Maelstrom Lake 118 – Simply Inch (Simply   –
Great (FR) 122) [1996 –: a12g 1997 a10g⁶ Feb 4] very lightly raced and no form
since modest handicapper at 3 yrs. *S. Dow*

WATER'S EDGE   2 b.f. (May 12) Saddlers' Hall (IRE) 126 – Irish Impulse   67 p
(USA) 50 (Irish River (FR) 131) [1997 6f 7d⁵ Oct 13] quite good-topped filly: fourth
foal: dam maiden daughter of smart 1980 staying 2-y-o Exclusively Raised: better
effort in maidens when never-dangerous fifth at Leicester: should be well suited by
1¼m+: should improve again. *G. Wragg*

WATERSPOUT (USA)   3 b.c. Theatrical 128 – Water Angel (USA) (Halo (USA))   79
[1996 75: 7.1f³ 8m⁶ 1997 8m 10m² 10g Oct 18] fair maiden: will stay 1½m: raced
only on good going or firmer: temperament under suspicion: sold 15,500 gns, and
sent to Sweden. *Mrs A. J. Perrett*

WATERWAVE (USA)   4 ch.c. Irish River (FR) 131 – Wajna (USA) 108 (Nure-   80
yev (USA) 131) [1996 NR 1997 10m 8.2g³ 10s³ Oct 14] second foal: dam won at 7f
(at 2 yrs) and 1¾m: progressive form in maidens, third at Ayr final start: will be
suited by 1½m: sold approx. £14,500 in Dubai in November. *J. H. M. Gosden*

WATHBAT LION   2 ch.c. (Apr 14) Lion Cavern (USA) 117 – Alwathba (USA)   65
100 (Lyphard (USA) 132) [1997 6d⁵ 7d⁴ 7.5m 7.3m⁵ Aug 16] strong colt: fourth foal:
half-brother to 3-y-o Wathbat Nashwan and fairly useful 1¼m winner Wathbat Mtoto
(by Mtoto): dam, 2-y-o 6f winner (suited by 1m), sister to smart 7f performer Dreams
To Reality: fair maiden: sweating and edgy, creditable effort in Newbury nursery
final start: should stay 1m: sweating and edgy: sent to UAE. *M. A. Jarvis*

WATHBAT NASHWAN   3 ch.c. Nashwan (USA) 135 – Alwathba (USA) 100   85
(Lyphard (USA) 132) [1996 66p: 8f 7g 1997 10s 10m⁴ 8m⁶ 10.5g* 10m³ 10g Aug 2]
has a round action: fairly useful handicapper: won at Haydock (apprentices) in July:
will stay further than 1¼m: acts on good to firm ground: sent to UAE. *L. M. Cumani*

WATKINS   2 ch.c. (Apr 10) King's Signet (USA) 110 – Windbound Lass 60   62
(Crofter (USA) 124) [1997 7g⁵ 7m⁴ 7m⁶ 7.9s 7.1g Sep 11] 5,000Y: first living foal:
dam stayer, also successful over hurdles: modest maiden on debut: sweating and
raced freely when below form in testing conditions over 1m: has been bandaged
behind. *F. Murphy*

WAVERLEY STAR   12 br.g. Pitskelly 122 – Quelle Blague (Red God 128§) [1996   –
–: 5g 6m 5m 6f 5m 5g 1997 a6g⁶ Feb 3] no longer of any account. *J. S. Wainwright*

WAVE ROCK   2 br.g. (Apr 13) Tragic Role (USA) – Moonscape 87 (Ribero 126)   80 p
[1997 7m 7m 8.2g⁴ 10s* Oct 15] 23,000Y: smallish, sturdy gelding: half-brother to
numerous winners, including smart Lemhill (by He Loves Me), 11f to 2m winner, and
useful 6f winner Luna Bid (by Auction Ring): dam stayer: progressive form: won
maiden at Nottingham by neck from Jamorin Dancer, running on strongly: will stay
at least 1½m: open to further progress. *J. L. Dunlop*

WAYNE LUKAS   2 b.c. (Mar 4) Don't Forget Me 127 – Modern Dance (USA)   73 p
(Nureyev (USA) 131) [1997 7m Oct 2] IR 46,000Y: useful-looking colt: easy mover:
first foal: dam, once-raced half-sister to very smart 7f and 1m winner Lord Florey
and Grade 1 1m winner Too Chic, granddaughter of Oaks winner Monade: 13/2,
twelfth of 22 to Quiet Assurance in maiden at Newmarket, tracking leaders until
outpaced 2f out and eased: will do better. *H. R. A. Cecil*

WAY OUT YONDER   2 b.c. (Feb 14) Shirley Heights 130 – Patsy Western 81   92
(Precocious 126) [1997 6m³ 8m² Sep 30] 52,000Y: strong, deep-girthed colt: fourth
foal: half-brother to 3-y-o Granny's Pet, 1¼m and 1½m winner Western Sal (by
Salse) and 6-y-o Western General: dam twice-raced 6f winner, is half-sister to Queen
Anne winner Mr Fluorocarbon: fairly useful form in Newmarket maidens 4 months
apart, leading over 6f but carrying head high and tending to hang when beaten 5
lengths by Success And Glory: bred to stay beyond 1m. *B. W. Hills*

WAYPOINT   4 b.f. Cadeaux Genereux 131 – Princess Athena 119 (Ahonoora 122)   95
[1996 77, a73: a7g* 7m⁴ 7m 7g² 8.2s a7g⁵ 1997 a6g* a6g² 7m³ 7m* 6.9s² 7m* 6m   a80
7g 7m a6g⁵ Oct 18] big, lengthy filly: useful handicapper on turf, fairly useful on
all-weather: won at Lingfield in March, Doncaster in May and Newbury in July:
effective at 6f/7f: acts on the all-weather and on good to firm ground, probably not at
best on soft: visored (not disgraced in Stewards' Cup) seventh start. *R. Charlton*

WAYTOGOMO   2 b.f. (Mar 24) Midyan (USA) 124 – Running Glimpse (IRE) 84   –
(Runnett 125) [1997 5m⁶ 6g 7g Aug 13] first foal: dam sprinter: showed little in
sellers and claimer: dead. *Miss B. Sanders*

WEDDING BAND   2 b.f. (May 16) Saddlers' Hall (IRE) 126 – Priceless Bond   40
(USA) 75 (Blushing Groom (FR) 131) [1997 6m 6.1m 7m² 8.2d Oct 30] lengthy
filly: fourth foal: half-sister to fair 1996 2-y-o 6f winner Dowry (by Rudimentary):
dam 9f winner at 2 yrs: only worthwhile form when second in seller at Brighton, final
start for R. Hannon: off track 3 months subsequently. *A. G. Foster*

WEDDING MUSIC   3 b.f. Music Boy 124 – Diamond Wedding (USA) 65   –
(Diamond Shoal 130) [1996 48, a35: a5g a5g⁵ 6g⁴ 5m² 5d 5m⁴ a5g⁵ a6g⁶ 1997 a7g⁴
Jan 11] poor maiden: well beaten only start in 1997: best form at 5f: acts on good to
firm ground: visored penultimate start at 2 yrs. *P. C. Haslam*

WEE CHRISTY (IRE)   2 gr.c. (Apr 28) Contract Law (USA) 108 – Eternal   –
Optimist (Relko 136) [1997 5m 6d 6g 7.1m^6 7g 7m 6d 8m Nov 4] 7,200Y: lengthy,
sparely-made colt: seventh foal: half-brother to 5f (at 2 yrs) to 1¼m winner Who's
Tef (by Muscatite) and 3 winners abroad: dam unraced: little worthwhile form,
including in sellers: blinkered fourth start. *W. McKeown*

WEE DRAM   3 ch.f. Most Welcome 131 – Scottish Legend (Legend of France   75
(USA) 124) [1996 67: 6m 5f^6 5.7d^4 1997 6g* 7g 7g Jul 23] small filly: fair handicapper: won maiden at Folkestone in March: below form final start, carrying head
high: barely stays 7f. *R. Hannon*

WEET A BIT (IRE)   3 b.c. Archway (IRE) 115 – Aridje 79 (Mummy's Pet 125)   –
[1996 –: 5g a7g^5 1997 a6g^6 8g^2 a9.4g 10m^6 10m 10.8g Oct 7] leggy colt: signs of
ability but no worthwhile form: blinkered final start: sold, and sent to Germany.
R. Hollinshead

WEET-A-MINUTE (IRE)   4 ro.c. Nabeel Dancer (USA) 120 – Ludovica   104
(Bustino 136) [1996 106: 9m^4 10.3g^3 12f^4 11.9g^3 10.3m^6 10.5m^6 14g 12f 11.8m^5
12s^6 a10s^4 1997 7.9g^2 8g^4 7d^4 8.9s^2 10.9d^4 8m^5 8v^3 9d^6 Oct 17] lengthy colt: fine
mover: useful performer at best: good second of 6 to Winter Romance in listed race
at York fourth start, but, as at 3 yrs, rather lost his way towards end of season: stays
1½m: acts on firm and soft ground. *R. Hollinshead*

WEET AND SEE   3 b.g. Lochnager 132 – Simply Style (Bairn (USA) 126) [1996   58
NR 1997 a7g^6 a7g^3 a9.4g^6 a8.5g^2 a8.5g* 10g^6 8.2g^4 8f^6 a9.4g a9.4g a9.4g Oct 4]   a65
second foal: brother to 4-y-o Loch Style: dam unraced from good family: fair
handicapper on all-weather, modest on turf: won at Wolverhampton in March: stays
8.5f: acts on fibresand: has given trouble in stalls. *R. Hollinshead*

WEET EES GIRL (IRE)   3 ro.f. Common Grounds 118 – Kastiliya (Kalamoun   59 d
129) [1996 75: 5.1d* 5.1g^4 6.1m^5 6.1m^3 5f^6 6.1d^6 1997 5m 5g^4 5g 6.1s 6.1m a5g 5m^6
a7g Aug 15] unfurnished filly: modest performer: lost her form: trained until after
sixth start by P. D. Evans: stays 6f. *T. Wall*

WEETMAN'S WEIGH (IRE)   4 b.c. Archway (IRE) 115 – Indian Sand   86
(Indian King (USA) 128) [1996 75: a6g* a6g^2 a7g^2 a6g* 6s* 6m^3 6.1g^3 1997 6m
a7g^5 6d^4 7m* 7m* 7f* 7s^5 7.1g^4 7g^3 7m^2 7g 7d^2 7m 7m Oct 28] useful-looking colt:
fairly useful handicapper: won handicap at Thirsk and minor event at Redcar in May
and minor event at Thirsk in June: stays 7f: acts on firm ground, soft and fibresand:
sometimes hangs left: tongue tied: consistent. *R. Hollinshead*

WELCOME HEIGHTS   3 b.g. Most Welcome 131 – Mount Ida (USA) 79   71 p
(Conquistador Cielo (USA)) [1996 –: 6m 6.9d 6g 1997 10d 8.3g a8g^2 8s^3 6.1d* 7d^3
7g* 7.1g^4 8.2s^2 8.2d a10s^2 a10g* Dec 2] good-topped, workmanlike gelding: bad
mover: steady improvement into a fair handicapper in 1997, winning at Chepstow
and Doncaster in July and Lingfield in December: should stay 1½m: acts on
equitrack, raced mainly on good going or softer on turf: type to go on again in 1998.
M. J. Fetherston-Godley

WELCOME HOME   3 b.f. Most Welcome 131 – Miss Cindy 95 (Mansingh   55
(USA) 120) [1996 –: 8.1m 8.1d 1997 8m 7.1s^3 8.2g^6 7d^4 8.2s^5 8g 10d 10.4s^5 12f^6
16s a12g* 12s Nov 6] tall, good-topped filly: modest handicapper: 33/1, made all at
Wolverhampton in October: stays 1½m: acts on soft going and fibresand. *P. T. Dalton*

WELCOME LU   4 ch.f. Most Welcome 131 – Odile (Green Dancer (USA) 132)   34
[1996 45: a8g a7g^4 a11g a8g 6f 5f 7g^3 7f^6 7g* 7.5g 7f 1997 10g 8f 6.9m 7g 16m
15.8g^3 16.1g^5 12s a14g Oct 20] strong-quartered filly: poor handicapper: seems to
stay 2m: acts on firm ground and fibresand: tried blinkered. *J. L. Harris*

WELCOME SUNSET   2 b.c. (Feb 28) Most Welcome 131 – Deanta In Eirinn   72
(Red Sunset 120) [1997 5m 5.1s* 6.1g^3 7.3d 7g Oct 25] 4,400Y: tall colt: has scope:
half-brother to 5f winner Newbury Coat (by Chilibang) and a winner in Germany by
Scottish Reel: dam ran once: fair form: won maiden at Nottingham in July: ran
creditably next start, but well beaten in nurseries final 2: should stay beyond 6f.
J. Wharton

WELLAKI (USA)   3 ch.c. Miswaki (USA) 124 – Wellomond (FR) (Lomond   81
(USA) 128) [1996 80p: 8.1s^4 8.1s* 1997 10.4d^5 10g Oct 18] sturdy colt: fairly useful
form: much better effort in handicaps in October on reappearance: stays 1¼m: raced
only on good going or softer: sold 16,000 gns in October. *J. H. M. Gosden*

WELL APPOINTED (IRE)   8 b.g. Petorius 117 – So Stylish 77 (Great Nephew   52
126) [1996 NR 1997 14.1s³ May 9] modest winning hurdler: first race on flat since
1993, third in handicap at Carlisle: stays 1¾m: acts on any going: tried blinkered/
visored. *B. Mactaggart*

WELL ARMED (IRE)   6 b.g. Moscow Society (USA) 110 – Sales Centre (Deep   –
Run 119) [1996 NR 1997 10.1m⁴ 12.1s 10m⁵ 14g⁶ 16m 17.2f Aug 27] 16,000 5-y-o:
big, strong gelding: second foal: half-brother to a winning jumper by Tale Quale:
dam unraced: winning pointer in Ireland: modest jumper: signs of ability in varied
events on flat but little form: tried in blinkers. *J. J. O'Neill*

WELLCOME INN   3 ch.g. Most Welcome 131 – Mimining 83 (Tower Walk 130)   63
[1996 –: 8f 1997 11.8f⁵ 12.1s 12d² 13.8s³ 16m 12d* 14.1g 8d 12f a12g Nov 21] big,
lengthy gelding: modest performer: trained by J. A. Harris first 2 starts: won 3-runner
minor event at Beverley in August: stiffer tasks in handicaps after: may prove best
around 1½m: acts on dead going. *J. O'Reilly*

WELL DRAWN   4 b.g. Dowsing (USA) 124 – Classic Design (Busted 134) [1996   –
84+: a8g* 1997 10.8m 10g 7.1m⁵ 8g Sep 4] won maiden on equitrack at 3 yrs: well
beaten on turf in 1997: headstrong. *H. Candy*

WELLSPRING (IRE)   3 b.f. Caerleon (USA) 132 – Marwell 133 (Habitat 134)   88
[1996 NR 1997 6g* 5g³ 6s² 6g 6m Oct 3] small filly: sister to very smart sprinter/
miler Caerwent and half-sister to 2 winners, notably very smart miler Marling (by
Lomond): dam, champion sprinter also fourth in 1000 Guineas, from excellent
family: fairly useful form: won maiden at Pontefract in May: poor efforts last 2 starts,
3 months apart: likely to prove a sprinter. *D. R. Loder*

WELL WARNED   3 b.f. Warning 136 – Well Beyond (IRE) 101 (Don't Forget   104 ?
Me 127) [1996 92: 6f² 6g³ 6m* 6m 1997 7.3g³ 7m⁴ 7m 7f⁶ 7m³ Oct 7] quite good-
topped filly: good mover: useful performer: seemingly best effort when ¼ lengths
third to Dance Parade in steadily-run Fred Darling Stakes at Newbury on
reappearance: keen type, likely to prove best short of 1m: raced only on good going
or firmer. *B. W. Hills*

WELSH MELODY   4 b.f. Merdon Melody 98 – Young Whip (Bold Owl 101)   –
[1996 –, a53: a7g² a7g² a8g⁵ a7g 1997 a8.5g Jan 8] modest winner, often visored/
blinkered: well beaten only start in 1997: sold only 900 gns in January. *K. R. Burke*

WELSH MILL (IRE)   8 b.g. Caerleon (USA) 132 – Gay Milly (FR) 74 (Mill   76
Reef (USA) 141) [1996 81: 12g² 13g* 13g⁴ 14d* 15m³ 16.1m⁴ 16.1m⁵ 1997 13.8g
14s² 14g⁶ 11.9d* 11.8d³ 14g Aug 28] close-coupled gelding: fair performer: made
heavy weather of winning claimer at Haydock in July: stayed 2m: probably acted on
any going: fell fatally over hurdles in November. *Mrs M. Reveley*

WELSH MOUNTAIN   4 b.g. Welsh Captain 113 – Miss Nelski 84 (Most Secret   47
119) [1996 68: 5d 6g 6m⁵ 5.7m 5.1m 6f 6m 1997 6.1g 10g 10m 8.3g 7g 8m* 8.2d
Nov 3] smallish, good-bodied gelding: poor handicapper: won seller at Yarmouth in
August (for M. Heaton-Ellis): stays 1m: acts on good to firm ground: sometimes
visored. *K. A. Morgan*

WELTON ARSENAL   5 b.g. Statoblest 120 – Miller's Gait 74§ (Mill Reef   94
(USA) 141) [1996 92: 8s 7g* 8d⁴ 7.6f⁵ 7g⁶ 7g 8.1s² 7m⁴ 8g 1997 8g⁴ 7g* 8.1g 7d⁶ 7g
9g 8m Nov 1] sturdy gelding: fairly useful handicapper: won at Newmarket (idled,
ridden by 5-lb claimer) in May: disappointing afterwards: effective at 7f/1m: acts
on firm and soft ground: visored once: held up: often travels well but finds little.
K. Bishop

WELVILLE   4 b.g. Most Welcome 131 – Miss Top Ville (FR) (Top Ville 129)   –
[1996 94+: 7m² 1997 7.1s⁴ May 5] rangy gelding: fairly useful performer, very
lightly raced: well held only start at 4 yrs: should stay 1m. *P. J. Makin*

WENDA (IRE)   2 ch.f. (Feb 6) Priolo (USA) 127 – Pennine Drive (IRE) (Pennine   89 p
Walk 120) [1997 5d⁶ 6m* 7g Oct 18] R 28,000Y: strong, good-bodied filly: third
living foal: sister to useful Irish 3-y-o 1½m winner Carnelly: dam Irish 1½m winner
from good French middle-distance family: won £12,000 event at Ascot in September
by a head from Atuf: last of 12 after false start in Rockfel Stakes at Newmarket
following month: should stay at least 1m: good type, and remains likely to do better
at 3 yrs. *C. E. Brittain*

WENTBRIDGE LAD (IRE)   7 b.g. Coquelin (USA) 121 – Cathryn's Song   61
(Prince Tenderfoot (USA) 126) [1996 72, a–: a7g 8m² 8g⁴ 8m 8g 7.6g³ 8g² a9.4g⁵   a–
10.3m² a9.4g 7.1g² 8g 10.3m⁶ 7m⁴ 10m 7.6m² 8m³ 8d⁵ 1997 10.3d 7.6v 8m a8.5g⁶ 8f
a8.5g 8.1m⁴ 10.5m* 10m* 10g 10.3d² 7.6s⁶ a12g⁵ 10f 10d 10.1g a12g Dec 13]
lengthy gelding: modest handicapper: left P. D. Evans after sixth start: won at
Haydock and Brighton (apprentice race) on consecutive days in August: stays 1¼m:
acts on firm ground, soft and fibresand: often wears blinkers/visor, but effective
without: normally held up: carries head high: tough. *A. Bailey*

WESLEY'S LAD (IRE)   3 b. or br.g. Classic Secret (USA) 91 – Galouga (FR)   55
(Lou Piguet (FR) 126) [1996 55+: 10.2d⁴ 8.1s a8g³ 1997 a12g 11.6s 14.1g⁴ 17.2g⁶
14.1s³ a14.8g Oct 6] modest maiden handicapper: trained by J. Neville until before
final start: best efforts at 1¾m: yet to race on going firmer than good. *D. Burchell*

WESTCOURT MAGIC   4 b.g. Emarati (USA) 74 – Magic Milly 60 (Simply   97 §
Great (FR) 122) [1996 105: 5g* 5m³ 6f 6m 6d⁵ 5m 1997 5m⁴ 6g⁶ 6g 5d⁵ 6d 6.1s² 5.1s
6m 6m 5.1s* 5.6m 6g 5g 6m Nov 4] smallish, sturdy gelding: useful handicapper on
his day: won at Chester in August, but mostly disappointing at 4 yrs: stays 6f: used to
act on firm going, goes well on soft: rather an edgy type (gave trouble in stalls final
start), and often early to post: none too reliable. *M. W. Easterby*

WESTCOURT RUBY   2 b.f. (Jan 31) Petong 126 – Red Rosein 97 (Red Sunset   – p
120) [1997 5f 5g 5d Oct 17] 17,000Y: first foal: dam, tough sprinter, won Woking
ham Handicap: signs ability first 2 starts in maidens (poorly drawn final one): should
do better. *M. W. Easterby*

WESTERN GENERAL   6 ch.g. Cadeaux Genereux 131 – Patsy Western 81   77
(Precocious 126) [1996 78: 10.3d 8g⁵ 8g 8.3g* 1997 9.2s⁵ 9.2s² 9.2m Jul 11] quite
attractive gelding: fair handicapper: second twice at Hamilton in the summer:
stays 10.5f: acts on soft ground and good to firm: effective blinkered or not.
Miss M. K. Milligan

WESTERN HOUR (USA)   3 b.f. Gone West (USA) – Out On The Town (USA)   94
(Spend A Buck (USA)) [1996 77: 7g⁶ 7m³ 1997 10m* 10g³ 12.5g 10g⁶ Aug 13] tall
filly: fairly useful performer: won maiden at Salisbury in May: stiffer tasks afterwards, best effort when close third (making most at steady pace) to Squeak in listed
race at Newbury: stays 1¼m: raced only on good/good to firm going: sent to USA.
P. W. Chapple-Hyam

WESTERN LORD   2 b.g. (May 12) Noble Patriarch 115 – Sophia Western (Steel   –
Heart 128) [1997 6s⁶ 7g 7.5m 7.9s 7.5f 8.3g⁵ 10m Oct 6] 3,400Y: half-brother to
winning platers by Daring March and Warpath: dam well beaten: seems of little
account. *C. Smith*

WESTERN PLAYBOY   5 b.g. Law Society (USA) 130 – Reine d'Beaute 97   –
(Caerleon (USA) 132) [1996 –: 10f⁵ 10.2g⁶ 11.8m 1997 a12g 14m 11.7g 14m⁶ 11.7f
Jul 23] tall gelding: no form. *R. J. Baker*

WESTERN SONATA (IRE)   4 b.f. Alzao (USA) 117 – Musique Classique   66
(USA) 100 (Exclusive Native (USA)) [1996 63: 8s⁶ 6.5v a8.5g³ 1997 a10g² 8d⁴
a10g² May 24] angular filly: fair maiden: stays 1¼m: acts on equitrack, yet to race on
good going or firmer: carried head high final start. *Lord Huntingdon*

WESTERN VENTURE (IRE)   4 ch.g. Two Timing (USA) 124 – Star Gazing   37
(IRE) (Caerleon (USA) 132) [1996 55: 7f 7.1d 7d⁶ 8f² 8.3g² 9m 8m a6g 8.1s a12g⁵
1997 8s 8m⁵ 10g 8.3s 8.3s 11.1s 9.2m³ 8m 9.2m* Aug 18] quite attractive gelding:
has a quick action: poor handicapper: left R. McKellar after seventh start: made all in
18-runner seller at Hamilton in August: stays 9f: acts on firm going: blinkered (below
form) sixth start. *Martyn Wane*

WEST HUMBLE   4 ch.f. Pharly (FR) 130 – Humble Pie 92 (Known Fact (USA)   93 d
135) [1996 93: 7m³ 7g⁵ 7m³ 1997 7s⁴ 6d 6.1s 8.3m Aug 23] leggy filly: fairly useful
performer: poor form after fourth in listed race at Lingfield: left Lady Herries before
final start: should stay beyond 7f: acts on good to firm and soft ground: has had
tongue tied. *Miss B. Sanders*

WESTMINSTER (IRE)   5 ch.g. Nashamaa 113 – Our Galadrial (Salmon Leap   66
(USA) 131) [1996 70: 10s 11.6m* 12.1f⁴ 12m 11.8m³ 12m² 1997 10m 10.5m⁵ 12g²
10.9d* 12m 12.1m⁶ 10m⁵ 10g⁵ 10.9d 12s 10m³ 12s Nov 6] angular gelding: fair

handicapper: won strongly-run race at Ayr in June: disappointing last 4 starts: stays
1½m: acts on good to firm and dead ground, no form in 5 runs on soft: has been
blinkered, usually visored nowadays: normally held up. *M. H. Tompkins*

WHACKER-DO (IRE) 2 ch.c. (Apr 19) Archway (IRE) 115 – Denowski (Mal-   56 +
inowski (USA) 123) [1997 5s 5.9f 5s⁴ 6d a6g 6m 6g 6g Oct 7] IR 3,800Y: short-
backed colt: closely related to winning Irish sprinter Donnasoo (by Mansooj)
and half-brother to a winner in Austria/Hungary by Anita's Prince: dam Irish 6f
winner: modest maiden: well beaten last 2 starts: rather headstrong, but stays 6f.
R. Hollinshead

WHAT A FUSS 4 b.g. Great Commotion (USA) 123 – Hafwah (Gorytus (USA)   64
132) [1996 –, a70: 10g 10m a9.4g³ 8m a8.5g² a7g 1997 a7g* a8g⁵ 10d⁵ 12d 9d² 9.7s²   a72
11.5g* Jul 16] good-topped gelding: fair handicapper on all-weather, modest on turf:
won at Wolverhampton (maiden) in January and Yarmouth in July: effective from 7f
to 11.5f: acts on fibresand and soft ground: sometimes sweating. *B. Hanbury*

WHATEVER'S RIGHT (IRE) 8 b.g. Doulab (USA) 115 – Souveniers (Relko   71
136) [1996 68, a71: 7m 10g 8.3m 7f* a7g* 6.9m² 7g⁴ 7m 1997 a8g³ a8g⁶ a8g 8s   a54
8.3g* 7m⁶ 10m⁶ 8g a7g⁶ 8d Sep 12] strong, workmanlike gelding: fair handicapper
on turf, modest on all-weather: won at Windsor in July, best effort of 1997: stays 1m:
acts on equitrack (yet to race on fibresand), firm and dead ground: tried blinkered.
M. D. I. Usher

WHAT HAPPENED WAS 3 b.f. Deploy 131 – Berberana 68 (Never So Bold   73
135) [1996 82?: 5.1f³ 5.2g³ 6m⁵ 6g⁴ 6m² 5f² 5m* 5.7m⁴ 7m* 1997 7.6d 9.9d 8m 8g²
8g 8.1m⁵ 8.3m 14m 11.9m⁴ 10d Sep 19] neat filly: has a quick action: fair handicapper: well beaten last 4 starts: acts on good to firm ground,
seemingly not on softer than good. *Martyn Meade*

WHAT JIM WANTS (IRE) 4 b.g. Magical Strike (USA) 114 – Sally Gone   –
(IRE) (Last Tycoon 131) [1996 39: 12.1d⁶ 12m⁴ 14.1m³ 13.8s⁴ 14.1m 15.1m⁶ 12.4m²
11.9m 18g 1997 a16s⁵ 14g 18d Oct 20] smallish gelding: bad maiden. *J. J. O'Neill*

WHAT'S THAT AMY 3 b.f. Sizzling Melody 117 – Lady Pennington 51 (Blue   –
Cashmere 129) [1996 –: 6d a7g 1997 a8g⁵ a5g a5g Apr 7] no form. *C. Smith*

WHEILDON 3 ch.g. Keen 116 – Arabian Rose (USA) (Lyphard (USA) 132)   44
[1996 NR 1997 6.9m 8g⁴ 8g 10g 12v Jun 30] 5,000Y: fifth foal: half-brother to 4
winners, including fairly useful stayer Moonlight Quest (by Nishapour): dam ran
once in France: poor maiden at best: blinkered final outing. *S. C. Williams*

WHIMOWEH 2 b.f. (May 27) Son of Shaka 119 – Hollie Dancing (Frimley Park   –
109) [1997 6f Oct 3] small filly: first known foal: dam poor maiden: soon trailing in
claimer at Lingfield. *A. P. Jarvis*

WHIPPERS DELIGHT (IRE) 9 ch.g. King Persian 107 – Crashing Juno (Crash   –
Course 128) [1996 –: a12g⁴ 1997 a13g 10s May 12] modest chaser: no longer of any
account on flat. *G. F. H. Charles-Jones*

WHIRLAWHILE (USA) 3 b.g. Silver Hawk (USA) 123 – My Turbulent Beau   69
(USA) (Beau's Eagle (USA)) [1996 62p: 8m 1997 10s⁶ 10.2d⁴ 14.8d⁵ 12s⁴ Jun 27]
fair form at best in maidens: stays 1¼m: acts on soft going. *E. A. L. Dunlop*

WHISKY MACK (IRE) 2 b.g. (Mar 21) Mac's Imp (USA) 116 – Merville   84 §
(Fairy King (USA)) [1997 5.1m³ 5g³ 5d⁴ 6d* 6g 5d⁵ Oct 17] IR 10,000Y: good-
quartered gelding: third foal: half-brother to a 6f and 1m winner in Germany by
Pennine Walk: dam Irish 2-y-o 5f winner: fairly useful form when winning nursery at
Leicester in July: showed his quirks previously (gelded after second start), and well
held last 2 outings, looking reluctant first time: stays 6f: has bolted before start, and
been taken down early: best treated with caution. *R. Hannon*

WHISPERED MELODY 4 b.f. Primo Dominie 121 – Sing Softly 112 (Luthier   62
126) [1996 60: 7d⁵ 8.2m⁵ 10.1g a9.4g⁴ 7m⁴ 6.1m⁶ 5m 1997 10.8m 8f⁴ 8f⁴ 8f* 8.3s   a68
8.5d³ 7.1m 8f a7g* a8g* Dec 4] unfurnished filly: fair handicapper on all-weather,
modest on turf: won at Brighton in June and Lingfield in November (final runner
for R. Akehurst) and December: best at 7f/1m: acts on firm ground, dead and
all-weather. *J. Akehurst*

Vodafone Group Handicap, Newbury—
very close between Whitechapel (noseband), Jaseur (visor), Etterby Park (left) and Royal Crown

WHISPERING DAWN   4 b.f. Then Again 126 – Summer Sky 75 (Skyliner 117)   67
[1996 71: 8.2g³ 8m 8d 8g⁶ 9g* 8.1s⁴ 1997 a8.5g a9.4g² 10s 8.3g 10.2m⁴ 9m 10g⁶
Aug 13] leggy filly: has a round action: fair handicapper: best around 1¼m: acted on
good to firm ground, soft and fibresand: sometimes gave trouble in stalls: usually
held up: sold 2,000 gns in December, in foal to Fraam. *C. P. E. Brooks*

WHISPER LOW (IRE)   3 ch.f. Shalford (IRE) 124§ – Idle Gossip (Runnett   44
125) [1996 63, a–: 5m 5m 5f⁴ 5d a5g a5g⁵ a6g 1997 a5g⁶ a5g 5g 8.2m 5m⁴ 5m³ Aug
20] smallish, strong filly: poor performer: best efforts at 5f. *R. Hollinshead*

WHITECHAPEL (USA)   9 b.g. Arctic Tern (USA) 126 – Christchurch (FR) 88   88
(So Blessed 130) [1996 92: 13.3m⁶ 11.9f 13.3m³ 12g 12s⁴ 1997 13d 13g 12d* 11.9g
16.2g 12v³ 16g* Oct 24] big, lengthy gelding: grand old campaigner, still capable of
fairly useful form in handicaps: won at Newbury in May and October (beat Jaseur a
neck, showing more determination): effective at 1½m to 2m: has form on fibresand,
acts on good to firm and heavy going: game. *Lord Huntingdon*

WHITE EMIR   4 b.g. Emarati (USA) 74 – White African (Carwhite 127) [1996   86
90: 6g 5g⁵ 6m⁵ 6m⁴ 5f⁵ 6g² 5.1m² 5m³ 7d 6m² 5d 1997 5.2g 6m 5g 6g⁵ 6m² 6g 5m*
5d* 5d 5m 6m 5.2m 5d² 5m 6m 5d 5d Oct 17] good-quartered gelding: fairly useful
performer: ridden by Pat Eddery, won claimer at Sandown then handicap at Salisbury
in June: well held most starts afterwards: stays 6f: acts on firm and dead going: best
in blinkers: sometimes wanders under pressure, and suited by waiting tactics.
B. J. Meehan

WHITEGATE'S SON   3 ch.g. Minster Son 130 – Whitegates Lady (Le Coq d'Or   –
101) [1996 –: 6g 6m 7f 1997 10.1g Oct 22] no sign of ability. *B. Ellison*

WHITE HARE   4 b.f. Indian Ridge 123 – Pomade 79 (Luthier 126) [1996 56: 7.1d   –
8m³ 6g 7.1s 1997 8f 8g Jul 8] smallish, lengthy filly: modest maiden: well beaten in
handicaps in 1997. *Mrs M. Reveley*

WHITELOCK QUEST   9 b.g. Rainbow Quest (USA) 134 – Sagar 74 (Habitat   –
134) [1996 –: a9.4g 1997 a8g⁶ a8g⁶ a8.5g Apr 8] poor handicapper: no worthwhile
form in 1997. *N. E. Berry*

1029

WHITE PLAINS (IRE) 4 b.g. Nordico (USA) – Flying Diva 100 (Chief Singer   83
131) [1996 77: 6s³ 7m³ 7d⁵ 7m⁵ 9.7m² 10m³ 10f* 9.9m⁴ 10m⁴ 9m* 10m 10f* 10m*   a100
10m 1997 10m* 12m 12d⁶ 12m 10.2m² 9.2d* 10m 10m 8.1g 9g⁵ 8.9s a12g a8g²
a10g* a10g* a8g³ Dec 12] good-bodied gelding: useful on all-weather, fairly useful
on turf: trained first 5 starts by M. Pipe: won handicap at Nottingham in April,
claimer at Hamilton in July and 2 handicaps (second of them amateur event by 11
lengths) at Lingfield in December: ideally suited by 1¼m: acts on firm and dead
ground and on equitrack (trip too far on fibresand): has had tongue tied: often
apprentice ridden. *K. R. Burke*

WHITE SCISSORS (USA) 2 b.c. (Feb 22) St Jovite (USA) 135 – Scissors   72 p
(USA) (Blade (USA)) [1997 7m⁶ Oct 2] IR 55,000Y: good-bodied colt: fifth foal:
half-brother to 3 minor winners in USA: dam minor stakes-placed sprinting
half-sister to 9f Hollywood Oaks winner Moment To Buy: 20/1 and on burly side, 11
lengths sixth of 22 to Quiet Assurance in maiden at Newmarket, outpaced over 2f out
and not at all knocked about: sure to do better over 1m+. *H. R. A. Cecil*

WHITE SETTLER 4 b.g. Polish Patriot (USA) 128 – Oasis (Valiyar 129) [1996   67
73+: 5.1g 10m 7m³ 7.1m* 8g² 6m³ 7g 1997 8m 7m⁴ 6g⁶ 7m⁵ 7s⁵ 6m³ 7.1m 6m
6.1m Sep 23] sturdy gelding: fair handicapper: well beaten last 3 starts, blinkered
on final one: effective at 6f to 1m: acts on good to firm going, probably on soft.
R. J. Hodges

WHITEWATER AFFAIR 4 ch.f. Machiavellian (USA) 123 – Much Too Risky   115
87 (Bustino 136) [1996 110: 8m² 8m* 10s* 12m⁶ 10m⁴ 11.9m⁵ 12.5d² 12s⁴ 1997
12g* 13.9g³ 12g³ 13.5g* 11.9g² 14d³ Sep 20] big, rangy, rather raw-boned filly: has
a powerful, round action: smart performer: won John Porter Stakes at Newbury (by
½ length from Ela-Aristokrati) in April and, after third to Celeric in Yorkshire Cup
and to Predappio in Hardwicke Stakes, Prix de Pomone at Deauville (by 1½ lengths
from Otaiti) in August: bandaged, good efforts in Yorkshire Oaks at York (¾-length
second to My Emma) and Irish St Leger at the Curragh (4½ lengths behind Oscar
Schindler) last 2 starts: stays 1¾m: acts on good to firm and soft ground: often a front
runner: splendidly genuine and consistent. *M. R. Stoute*

Lanes End John Porter Stakes, Newbury—
Whitewater Affair (rail) pulls out extra to overcome Ela-Aristokrati (left) and Kutta

Mr J. M. Greetham's "Whitewater Affair"

WHITE WILLOW   8 br.g. Touching Wood (USA) 127 – Dimant Blanche (USA) –
77 (Gummo (USA) 117) [1996 62, a–: 16.1s⁴ 1997 a16s⁴ a16g Jan 10] lightly raced
on flat nowadays: well beaten in 1997. *T. Wall*

WHITLEY GRANGE BOY   4 b.g. Hubbly Bubbly (USA) – Choir (High Top   66
131) [1996 54: a8.5g⁵ 8.5d 11m 1997 a8g a7g⁵ 10.1g⁶ 12.3m⁶ 9.9g a11g⁵ 14g 12s*
a14g* a14g³ a14g³ Dec 18] tall, sparely-made gelding: fair handicapper: won at
Catterick in October and Southwell (amateurs) in November: stays 1¾m: acts on
fibresand,easily best run on turf on soft. *J. L. Eyre*

WHITTLE ROCK   4 b.f. Rock City 120 – Lurking 69 (Formidable (USA) 125)   67 d
[1996 91: 6d 6g² 6.1g 7f 6m* 6d⁶ 6m 6m⁶ 7d* 7.6d 1997 8m 7.6g⁵ 8g² 8g 10.3s³ 8g
8g 7m⁶ 6g Aug 13] strong, lengthy filly: formerly fairly useful performer: disappointing in 1997: stays 1m: acts on good to firm and soft ground: well beaten in blinkers:
sometimes looks none too keen. *Mrs M. Reveley*

WHIZZ KID   3 b.f. Puissance 110 – Panienka (POL) 70 (Dom Racine (FR) 121)   49
[1996 59?: 5f⁶ a5g² 6s⁵ 5m* 5m³ 6m⁴ 6m 5.2m 5.3f a6g⁴ 7m⁴ 1997 a5g⁴ a6g⁴ a5g
5m⁵ 6f⁶ 5.1m⁴ 5m 5.1f³ 5m⁴ 5d⁶ 5d 5m 6m 6g 5m³ 6m 7f⁶ 6.9d a7g a6g Dec 2] tall
filly: poor handicapper: best at 5f/6f: acts on firm ground and on fibresand (probably
equitrack): blinkered last 2 starts. *J. J. Bridger*

WHO DEALT   3 ch.f. Nalchik (USA) – Lana's Secret 79 (Most Secret 119) [1996   –
NR 1997 10v a9.4g⁶ 7m a7g a8.5g Nov 1] big, angular filly: sister to a poor maiden:
dam 5f winner: no sign of ability. *R. Hollinshead*

WHO NOSE (IRE)   2 b.g. (Apr 27) Cyrano de Bergerac 120 – Epoch (Wolver   73
Hollow 126) [1997 5m⁵ 5.1m² a5g³ 5m⁶ 6f* 6g* 7s³ 6m⁵ 6d² 5g² 5m 6g⁴ 7d³ 7m 7v
6g² Oct 25] IR 5,500Y: tall, close-coupled gelding: half-brother to a winner abroad
by Kampala: dam twice-raced half-sister to smart Irish performer up to 1¼m Lord

Bud: fair performer: won sellers at Brighton (awarded race) and Leicester in May: consistent afterwards, mostly in nurseries, running particularly well when ½-length second to Beware at Newbury final start, though swerving markedly left for inexperienced claimer closing stages: needs further than 5f and stays 7f: acts on firm and soft ground, well beaten on heavy: very stiff task when visored, mostly blinkered: not an easy ride. *B. J. Meehan.*

WHO'S THAT MAN   3 gr.g. Mystiko (USA) 124 – Milne's Way 83 (The Noble   63
Player (USA) 126) [1996 NR 1997 a7g⁶ 6.9g 5m 8m³ 11.6s⁶ 10f* 10g⁵ 10f* 10m⁵ 9.9d 8.1m 10s 10.3g a10s Nov 10] 40,000Y: smallish, robust gelding: second foal: half-brother to 5-y-o That Man Again: dam 6f to 1m winner: modest handicapper: won at Redcar and Brighton (awarded race) in the summer: well beaten last 5 starts: stays 1¼m: acts on firm going, seems unsuited by ground softer than good: well beaten in blinkers. *S. C. Williams*

WHOTHEHELLISHARRY   4 ch.g. Rich Charlie 117 – Ballagarrow Girl 66   40
(North Stoke 130) [1996 –: 9f⁴ 10.1g⁶ 11f 1997 a8g³ a12g 9f 12g⁴ 14.9m 10m 10g⁶   a56
8d 10.8g⁴ 12.5m⁵ Jul 19] quite good-topped gelding: modest maiden on all-weather, poor on turf: effective at 1m to 1½m: acts on good to firm ground and fibresand, ran poorly on dead: visored (below form) once: trained on reappearance by Jack Berry, joined John Berry (no relation) after final start, and won maiden hurdle in August. *P. T. Dalton*

WHY O SIX   3 b.g. Efisio 120 – Scotch Imp 83 (Imperial Fling (USA) 116) [1996   51
51: 5m 6m 6s⁶ 6d 6m⁴ 1997 6d⁶ 8m⁴ 8g a8g 7m 7g Oct 24] strong, good-bodied gelding: modest maiden: fourth at Musselburgh in April: below form after: seems to stay 1m: acts on good to firm and soft ground: tried in visor/blinkers, no improvement. *R. A. Fahey*

WICKLOW BOY (IRE)   6 b.g. Roi Danzig (USA) – Pickety Place 83 (Prince   §§
Tenderfoot (USA) 126) [1996 §§: a16g a12g 1997 a10g⁶ 17.2d a16g May 24] arrant rogue. *R. Ingram*

WIDEYEDBUSHYTAILED   2 b.f. (Apr 8) Elmaamul (USA) 125 – Run For   –
Love 70 (Runnett 125) [1997 a5g⁶ a5g 6m Jul 11] 500F: fifth foal: half-sister to 2-y-o sprint winners by Polar Falcon (in Italy) and Music Boy: dam best at 2 yrs: no sign of ability in sellers, in visor final start. *Mrs N. Macauley*

WIGGING   2 b.f. (Mar 25) Warning 136 – Pushy 112 (Sharpen Up 127) [1997 6g   75 p
6.1m³ Sep 23] quite good-topped filly: half-sister to several winners, notably smart Bluebook (by Secretariat) and useful Myself (by Nashwan), both best at up to 7f: dam, Queen Mary winner, out of good broodmare Mrs Moss: better effort in maidens when keeping-on third of 18 to easy winner Ikhteyaar at Nottingham: pulled hard on debut: should do better again. *N. A. Graham*

WIJARA (IRE)   5 b.h. Waajib 121 – Nawara 75 (Welsh Pageant 132) [1996 108:   98
8d² 10g 8m⁴ 10s² 10s⁴ 10.3f⁴ 1997 9s² 10s⁵ 11.6m³ Aug 23] sturdy horse: impresses in appearance: powerful galloper: useful performer, lightly raced: placed in rated stakes at Newbury and minor event at Windsor in 1997: stays 11.6f: acts on good to firm and soft ground: sent to UAE. *R. Hannon*

WILAWANDER   4 ch.c. Nashwan (USA) 135 – Wilayif (USA) 75 (Danzig (USA))   107
[1996 106: 12m⁴ 12m² 12f² 16.2m⁴ 13.8g* 13.9m² 14.6m⁶ 1997 12m² 16.2m² 13.9g May 15] tall colt: fluent mover: useful performer: runner-up in minor event at Doncaster (bandaged, behind Sheer Danzig) and Sagaro Stakes at Ascot (3½ lengths behind Orchestra Stall): not disgraced when seventh in Yorkshire Cup: stays 2m well: acts on firm and dead ground. *B. W. Hills*

WILCUMA   6 b.g. Most Welcome 131 – Miss Top Ville (FR) (Top Ville 129)   102
[1996 109: 8d 8.1d⁵ 10g⁵ 10.4m* 10d² 9s* 10s* 1997 10m³ 9s 10s 10s⁶ 10.4g 10m³ 10v⁵ 9g Oct 25] sturdy gelding: useful performer, not quite so good as in 1996: third in minor events at Newmarket (over 5 lengths behind Germano) and Kempton (beaten 2 lengths by Barnum Sands): below form in handicaps on other starts in 1997: stays 10.4f: acts on good to firm and soft going: held up: has run well when sweating: blinkered last 4 starts. *P. J. Makin*

WILD CANARY   2 ch.f. (Jan 24) Groom Dancer (USA) 128 – Nest 65 (Sharpo 132) [1997 a8g Nov 24] second foal: half-sister to 1996 2-y-o 6f winner Powder

River (by Alzao), later successful in Slovakia: dam, placed up to 1m, half-sister to Sheikh Albadou: last of 8 in maiden at Southwell. *Lord Huntingdon*

WILDCAT (IRE)   2 b.g. (Feb 14) Lion Cavern (USA) 117 – Kentucky Starlet   64
(USA) 69 (Cox's Ridge (USA)) [1997 7f⁴ 7m 7g* 7.6m a7g* Sep 20] 19,000Y:
second foal: dam 7f winner: modest form: won claimer at Salisbury in August
(claimed out of R. Hannon's stable £8,000) and seller at Wolverhampton in September: should stay 1m: acts on fibresand: ran poorly second (sweating, edgy) and
fourth starts: sent to Sweden. *Miss Gay Kelleway*

WILD CITY (USA)   3 b. or br.g. Wild Again (USA) – Garvin's Gal (USA)   –
(Seattle Slew (USA)) [1996 –: 6g 1997 8.2m Apr 8] robust gelding: well beaten in
maidens. *B. Hanbury*

WILDFIRE (SWI)   6 br.g. Beldale Flutter (USA) 130 – Little White Star (Mill   –
Reef (USA) 141) [1996 56: a11g³ a10g⁴ 12v a11g⁵ a12s⁴ 1997 a11g³ a11g a11g*   a51
a12g a9.4g² a12f² 12s a9.4g³ a12g⁴ a11g⁴ a12g⁶ Dec 13] sturdy gelding: has a quick
action: modest handicapper: won at Southwell in February: mostly creditable efforts
after, placed 3 times at Wolverhampton: stays 1½m: acts on good ground and all-
weather: races prominently. *J. Akehurst*

WILD LILLY   2 b.f. (Apr 20) Elmaamul (USA) 125 – Chrisanthy 81 (So Blessed   49
130) [1997 5m 6m⁶ 5g 5.1g 6d Oct 21] 1,000Y: half-sister to several winners, including 7f (at 2 yrs) to 1¼m winners Ivan The Terrible (by Siberian Express) and Satis
Dancer (by Mashhor Dancer): dam 2-y-o 5f winner who failed to train on: signs of
ability first 2 starts but well beaten afterwards. *M. J. Ryan*

WILDMOOR   3 ch.g. Common Grounds 118 – Impropriety (Law Society (USA)   61
130) [1996 56?: 6m 7f⁶ 8.5g⁴ 10m 7m 1997 12g 9.9m⁴ 14.1d 12d⁴ 12f² 12.1s* 12g⁶
13d 12f a12g³ a11g³ a10g a12g* a12g³ Dec 19] good-topped gelding: modest
handicapper: won at Hamilton in July and (having been bought from J. Bethell after
tenth start) at Wolverhampton in December: rather headstrong, but stays 1½m: acts
on firm, soft ground and the all-weather: blinkered (well beaten) once: has worn
tongue strap. *John Berry*

WILD NETTLE   3 ch.f. Beveled (USA) – Pink Pumpkin 52 (Tickled Pink 114)   40
[1996 46: 5g 5f⁶ 5m 5.3f 6.1s⁴ 6.9v 1997 5m 6d 6.1g 6m 7g a7g a6g² a7g Dec 10]
close-coupled filly: poor maiden handicapper: should stay beyond 6f: acts on firm
ground, soft and equitrack: tends to get well behind: has been tongue tied. *J. C. Fox*

WILD PALM   5 b.g. Darshaan 133 – Tarasova (USA) (Green Forest (USA) 134)   72
[1996 76: a10g⁵ 10.8d 8m 7g⁴ 6.1m 8m 7m⁵ 7g* 8g* 7f⁴ 7g³ a8g⁵ 7g² 7.3m 7m   a59
1997 7d 8m⁶ 8d⁶ 6s³ a7g⁴ 7m⁶ 6g⁶ 7g⁶ 6d Sep 2] sturdy, useful-looking gelding:
unimpressive mover: fair handicapper on turf, modest on all-weather: effective at
stiff 6f to 1m: acts on firm and soft ground: usually blinkered/visored: has worn
severe noseband and had tongue tied: has flashed tail and found little: sold, and
joined P. Howling. *W. A. O'Gorman*

WILD PROSPECT   9 b.g. Homing 130 – Cappuccilli 111 (Lorenzaccio 130)   –
[1996 –: 7g a8g 1997 7f 5.9m Jun 25] no longer of any account. *A. Bailey*

WILD RICE   5 b.g. Green Desert (USA) 127 – On Show 92 (Welsh Pageant 132)   –
[1996 93: 7m 7f³ 7m 8m 7m⁶ 7g⁴ 1997 7g 6g Jun 2] strong, good-bodied gelding:
fairly useful handicapper at 4 yrs: well below form in 1997, blinkered final start: sold
only 2,500 gns in October. *G. Wragg*

WILD RITA   5 ch.m. Risk Me (FR) 127 – Ma Pierrette 77 (Cawston's Clown 113)   86
[1996 85: 11.6m* 12m² 12g² 11.9v 12g² 12s 1997 12m⁵ 12m 11.9g 11.8g** 12.4m²
14.8m³ 12v⁵ Oct 10] lengthy mare: fairly useful handicapper: won at Leicester in
July: stays 14.8f: acts on firm and dead ground, below form on heavy: consistent:
sold 21,000 gns in October. *W. R. Muir*

WILD SKY (IRE)   3 br.g. Warning 136 – Erwinna (USA) (Lyphard (USA) 132)   81
[1996 75: 6d³ a7s⁴ 1997 6m⁴ 8m⁵ 8d² 8s⁵ 8g² 8m⁴ 8m 7d³ 7m* Nov 1] close-coupled
gelding: fairly useful handicapper: best effort when gaining first success in 25-
runner race at Newmarket, leading final 1f: stays 1m: acts on good to firm and dead
ground (poorly drawn on soft): visored (below form) once: has had tongue tied.
M. J. Heaton-Ellis

William Hill Sprint Cup Stakes (Handicap), Goodwood—Wildwood Flower (nearest camera) will have only a short head to spare over No Extras (third left) at the line. Third-placed Grand Chapeau is between the pair

WILDWOOD FLOWER   4 b.f. Distant Relative 128 – Tolstoya (Northfields   107
(USA)) [1996 101: 6m² 6.1g⁴ 6m* 5m² 6m³ 6g* 6m⁵ 6g* 6m⁵ 6g⁵ 1997 6g 6g 6m³
6g 6s³ 6m 7g⁶ 6s 6d* 6g* 6m⁵ 6d Oct 17] small, sturdy, lengthy filly: useful handicapper, better than ever in 1997: won quite valuable event (by short head from No
Extras) at Goodwood and Ayr Gold Cup (by ¾ length from Double Action) within a
week in September: below form in listed race at Newmarket final start: best form at
6f: acts on firm and dead going, probably not on soft: game. *R. Hannon*

WILFRED SHERMAN (IRE)   2 b.g. (Mar 14) Silver Kite (USA) 111 –   35 +
Algonquin Park (High Line 125) [1997 5.1m a5g⁵ a5g* a5g⁵ 5s 6g a5g Sep 8] IR   a49
4,400Y: quite good-topped gelding: brother to French 3-y-o 7.5f (at 2 yrs) and 1¼m
winner Silver Wings and half-brother to 2 other winners: dam Irish 4-y-o 1½m
winner: poor performer: won seller at Wolverhampton in April: should stay beyond
5f: sent to Sweden. *J. Berry*

WILKINS   8 b.g. Master Willie 129 – Segos 81 (Runnymede 123) [1996 NR 1997   57
16m² 14m² Oct 1] workmanlike gelding: fair hurdler: modest and lightly raced on
flat nowadays, second in 2 handicaps in 1997: stays 2m: acts on good to firm and
heavy ground: usually races prominently. *R. J. O'Sullivan*

WILLA WOOSTER   2 b.f. (Apr 24) Sure Blade (USA) 130 – Bertrade 75   62 p
(Homeboy 114) [1997 7g⁵ Oct 27] workmanlike filly: sixth foal: half-sister to 3-y-o
Homestead and 6-y-o Winsome Wooster: dam, stayed 1¼m, sister to sprinter Bertie
Wooster: 50/1, burly and green, some promise when 15 lengths fifth of 13 to Altibr in
maiden at Leicester: should improve. *P. G. Murphy*

WILL DO   4 b.g. Weldnaas (USA) 112 – Philogyny 94 (Philip of Spain 126) [1996   67
70: 6s 6m³ 7f a5g⁵ 1997 a6g⁵ a7g³ a7g³ a6g 6.1m 6.9m 7d 7m May 15] leggy gelding:
fair maiden handicapper: ran poorly last 3 starts: probably stays 7f: acts on good to
firm ground and the all-weather. *Martyn Meade*

WILLIAM'S WELL   3 ch.g. Superpower 113 – Catherines Well 99 (Junius   63
(USA) 124) [1996 53: 6g 6m 5g 6g 8g 5f³ 5g 6m³ 5d⁴ 1997 5g 6.1m 6g 6m⁵ 5m* 5g*
5m² 6s² 6g⁶ 5g⁶ 5g⁴ 5m² 5g⁶ 5g³ 5d 5d 5d Oct 20] useful-looking gelding: modest
handicapper: in good form for most of year, and won at Catterick and Musselburgh in
June: effective at 5f and 6f: acts on firm and soft ground: not an easy ride, and best in
blinkers. *M. W. Easterby*

WILLIAM WALLACE   3 b.g. Rudimentary (USA) 118 – Irish Impulse (USA)   –
50 (Irish River (FR) 131) [1996 68: 6g 7m⁶ 7g⁶ 6m³ 1997 6f⁵ 9.9s⁶ 8s⁴ 10.8m 8.3g
8.3s Jun 25] quite good-topped gelding: fair form at 2 yrs for C. Murray: well held in
1997, including in visor. *D. Haydn Jones*

WILLIE CONQUER   5 ch.g. Master Willie 129 – Maryland Cookie (USA) 101   98
(Bold Hour) [1996 93: 10m 10g 10m² 12m* 12g* 12g⁵ 12m* 1997 12g 12m³ 13.9m²
13.9g 12g⁵ 12d 12s Nov 8] smallish, lengthy, good-bodied gelding: has a quick
action: useful handicapper: placed in Bessborough Stakes at Royal Ascot and listed

rated stakes at York on second and third starts: stays 1¾m: acts on good to firm ground: held up (has taken strong hold). *R. Akehurst*

WILLIE MILES   4 b.g. Dancing Dissident (USA) 119 – Madam Bold (Never So   –
Bold 135) [1996 78?: 6m³ 7.1d a6g 6f 1997 7m 8m 8m 6m May 27] tall gelding:
maiden, no form since debut. *D. W. Chapman*

WILLIE RUSHTON   4 ch.f. Master Willie 129 – Amberush 41 (No Rush) [1996   –
60: a8g³ a10g⁵ 10.2g 11.6m² 12m 1997 a12g a12g⁶ a10g⁵ a16g⁶ 11.9g Sep 3] lengthy
filly: modest winner: well beaten all starts at 4 yrs: sent to Germany. *G. L. Moore*

WILLOW DALE (IRE)   4 b.f. Danehill (USA) 126 – Miss Willow Bend (USA)   85
(Willow Hour (USA)) [1996 82d: 8g 6m⁵ 5m³ 6g 5f 5g 6.1s 1997 6f⁵ 6m⁵ 5g² 5d² 6g²
6m 5m³ 6g³ 6d* 6s³ 5g⁴ 5m² 5m⁶ 6m 5.2m⁴ 6g 5s Aug 30] leggy, close-coupled filly:
fairly useful handicapper: in good form for most of 1997, and won at Windsor in June
and Newbury in August: best at 5f/6f: acts on firm and soft ground: tried blinkered/
visored earlier in career: sometimes flashes tail: has been bandaged near-hind:
consistent. *D. R. C. Elsworth*

WILLSKIP (USA)   3 b.g. Minshaanshu Amad (USA) 91§ – Eighty Lady (USA)   –
(Flying Lark (USA)) [1996 –: 6m 5m⁵ 7.5m 1997 10.8m 8.3d 9.9m 9.2s⁵ May 4] of
no account. *J. Berry*

WILL TO WIN   3 b.f. Mazilier (USA) 107 – Adana (FR) (Green Dancer (USA)   55
132) [1996 54: 5g⁵ 5m⁴ 6g³ 5f³ 6m 5.1m² 5d³ 6m a5g² 6.1s a5g a7g a6s³ 1997 a6g
a5g* a6g⁴ a5g² a6g* 6d⁴ 5.7d⁴ 6m³ 6s 6g³ 6m 6d 5.1g⁴ a6g a6g Nov 1] unfurnished
filly: modest performer: won Wolverhampton sellers in February and March: well
below form 4 of last 5 starts: stays 6f: acts on firm and dead going, and on fibresand:
sometimes bandaged behind. *P. G. Murphy*

WILL YOU DANCE   3 b.f. Shareef Dancer (USA) 135 – Padelia (Thatching   83
131) [1996 79p: 7m⁶ 7.9g² 1997 10m* 12s 11.9m⁵ Aug 8] strong, lengthy filly: fairly
useful performer: won maiden at Pontefract in April: last in handicaps both
subsequent starts: stayed 1¼m: acted on good to firm ground: stud. *J. L. Dunlop*

Ladbroke (Ayr) Gold Cup (Handicap)—Wildwood Flower continues to bloom;
the other horse pictured is Blessingindisguise, third home on the stand side but only eighth overall

WILTON   2 ch.c. (Apr 6) Sharpo 132 – Poyle Amber 55 (Sharrood (USA) 124)   67
[1997 5s 5m⁶ a6g* Nov 17] 12,000Y: smallish colt: first foal: dam sprint maiden
half-sister to smart sprinter Poyle George (by Sharpo): improved to win 15-runner
maiden at Southwell by neck from Eminent: bred to be a sprinter. *J. Hetherton*

WINDBORN   3 b.f. Superpower 113 – Chablisse 69 (Radetzky 123) [1996 51,   43
a49: 5g⁶ 5g³ 5.1f⁶ 6d⁵ 5.7g 5g² 6m a6g² a6g² 7m a7g⁴ a6g³ 1997 a7g³ a7g³ a8g⁶ a6g³
a6g³ a7g⁴ a9.4g³ 7s³ 6.9m 8g a10g Jul 26] small, angular filly: unimpressive mover:
poor maiden: should stay beyond 7f: acts on the all-weather and on soft ground:
blinkered final start at 2 yrs. *C. N. Allen*

WIND CHEETAH (USA)   3 b. or br.c. Storm Cat (USA) – Won't She Tell   104
(USA) (Banner Sport (USA)) [1996 102: 6g⁶ 6m* 7g 1997 7m 7d³ 7g⁵ Jul 26] good-
topped colt: has a round action: useful performer, lightly raced: under length third to
Ramooz in Van Geest Criterion Stakes at Newmarket in June: should stay beyond 7f:
yet to race on extremes of going: tongue tied last 2 starts. *M. R. Stoute*

WIND IN THE PARK   2 ch.f. (Feb 18) Clantime 101 – She's A Breeze 35   –
(Crofthall 110) [1997 6f 5s³ 5.1g Aug 7] 1,200Y: first foal: dam poor maiden: well
held in maiden and sellers. *M. Salaman*

WINDRUSH BOY   7 br.g. Dowsing (USA) 124 – Bridge Street Lady 93 (Decoy   51
Boy 129) [1996 61, a48: 5m 5f⁵ 5.1m 5.1m⁵ 5m 5m* 5f 5.1m a5g a5g a5g a5g⁵ a5g⁵   a40
1997 a5g⁵ 5m⁶ 5g⁶ 5m³ 5g 5.1g 5m 5m 5g Oct 18] lengthy, leggy gelding: modest on
turf, poor on all-weather: best form at 5f: raced only on good going or firmer on turf:
has won when sweating. *M. R. Bosley*

WINDRUSH HOLLY   4 br.f. Gildoran 123 – Bridge Street Lady 93 (Decoy Boy   59
129) [1996 62: 7.1d⁵ 10s 6g a8.5s 1997 8g 10m 10g Jun 2] lengthy filly: modest
maiden, lightly raced: should stay 1¼m: acts on dead ground, ran poorly on good to
firm. *D. R. C. Elsworth*

WINDSOR CASTLE   3 b.c. Generous (IRE) 139 – One Way Street 119   117
(Habitat 134) [1996 91p: 9f* 10f* 1997 12m⁵ 13.9g² 16.2m* 16.1s* 15.9g³
14.6m⁵ Sep 13]
    It was a good year for Windsor Castle, not just for the Royal residence
finally restored to its former glory after suffering extensive fire damage, but
also for the racehorse of that name, who made up into a smart stayer and won
both the Queen's Vase at Royal Ascot and the 'Newcastle Brown Ale' Northumberland Plate at Newcastle.
    Windsor Castle, successful on both his starts at two, raced lazily in his
first couple of races at three and was tried in blinkers at Ascot. They, along with
the step up to two miles, brought about an improved performance from Windsor
Castle, who, having done some of his rivals no favours when switched twice

Queen's Vase, Royal Ascot—the blinkered Windsor Castle holds off the visored Three Cheers

'Newcastle Brown Ale' Northumberland Plate (Handicap)—
Windsor Castle becomes only the second three-year-old winner of the race this century;
runner-up Sweetness Herself is virtually obscured

early in the straight, quickened to lead inside the final furlong and held the strong challenge of Three Cheers by a neck. Windsor Castle was fitted with blinkers again in the Northumberland Plate, one of the season's most valuable staying handicaps, won by some notable performers in recent years. The 1996 winner Celeric, in particular, went on to even better things, winning the Gold Cup at Royal Ascot in the latest season, and it would come as no great surprise if Windsor Castle were to do the same in 1998. The still-improving Windsor Castle put up an excellent performance under an 8-lb penalty at Newcastle, his handicap mark of 104 the highest in the eighteen-runner field. A little outpaced as the race began in earnest early in the straight, where Sweetness Herself took up the running, he stayed on strongly to catch that filly close home and forge a length ahead, becoming only the second three-year-old since 1900—Orpheus in 1989 was the first—to win this historic race. Windsor Castle ran well on his two subsequent starts. Without the blinkers he finished third to Double Eclipse, one place ahead of Celeric, in the Lonsdale Stakes at York; with them he finished five lengths fifth to Silver Patriarch in the St Leger at Doncaster, disputing the lead turning for home but outpaced over two furlongs out, a steadily-run race over a distance short of two miles far from ideal for such a thorough stayer. Windsor Castle should do well again returned to two miles, and he will prove suited by the Gold Cup distance of two and a half miles.

Windsor Castle's half-brother, Red Route (by Polish Precedent), started favourite for the 1994 St Leger having impressed when winning the Geoffrey Freer Stakes on his previous start, but he ran badly, beating only one home, and

		Caerleon	Nijinsky
	Generous (IRE)	(b 1980)	Foreseer
	(ch 1988)	Doff The Derby	Master Derby
Windsor Castle		(b 1981)	Margarethen
(b.c. 1994)		Habitat	Sir Gaylord
	One Way Street	(b 1966)	Little Hut
	(b 1981)	Guillotina	Busted
		(b 1969)	Tina II

wasn't seen again. A half-brother to four other winners, Windsor Castle is also closely related to the fair stayer Usk The Way and the Grand Prix de Paris winner Grape Tree Road, both by Caerleon. Windsor Castle's relations also crop up in the pedigree of the Nunthorpe dead-heater Coastal Bluff. His half-sister, the unraced Souffle (by Zafonic), trained by Henry Cecil, has been quoted as low as 20/1 in the betting for the One Thousand Guineas (details of her and a selection of other unraced two-year-olds of 1997 appear on page 1071). Windsor Castle's dam One Way Street won four of her five outings as a three-year-old, putting up her best performance on her final one when stepped up to a mile and a half in the Princess Royal Stakes at Ascot. That was the only time One Way Street encountered ground softer than good, conditions, incidentally, that also suited her dam Guillotina. A half-sister to the Goodwood Cup winner Ovaltine, Guillotina won the Prix de Royallieu at around a mile and a half and gave the impression she would have stayed much further. Windsor Castle has raced only on good ground or firmer apart from at Newcastle, where he showed himself just as effective on soft. *P. F. I. Cole*

WINDSPEED 2 ch.g. (May 17) Sheerwind – Speed Baby (USA) 76 (Diplomat – Way) [1997 8.2g 8.2d a7g Oct 20] half-brother to winning sprinter Sir Tom and a winner in France (both by Adonijah): dam won over 5f on debut but showed little afterwards: well held in maiden and sellers. *B. P. J. Baugh*

WINDSWEPT (IRE) 4 b.f. Taufan (USA) 119 – Sutica 91 (Don 128) [1996 59: 49 8.2m 8g 7g⁶ 6m⁵ 7m² 6f 8m² 7f³ 7m 1997 8.3m 8.3m⁵ 8g a8.5g 10.8g 8g⁶ Oct 27] leggy filly: good mover: poor handicapper: left D. ffrench Davis after third start: well held for new yard: stays 1m: acts on firm going, yet to race on softer than good: tried blinkered, no improvement. *M. C. Pipe*

WINDYEDGE (USA) 4 ch.g. Woodman (USA) 126 – Abeesh (USA) 77 (Nijin- – sky (CAN) 138) [1996 61: 10.2g 10m⁶ 10m² 13.8m⁴ 11.5m 1997 12.3m a9.4g Apr 26] tall, angular gelding: modest maiden at 3 yrs for B. Hills: well held in 1997. *Mrs A. M. Naughton*

WINDY TREAT (USA) 3 b. or br.g. Shadeed (USA) 135 – Widaad (USA) 109 69 § (Mr Prospector (USA)) [1996 NR 1997 8.2d³ 8g 8g² 7m* 8f⁵ a9s Nov 13] rather leggy gelding: brother to useful Irish 7f (at 2 yrs) to 1m winner Deed of Love and fairly useful 1992 Irish 2-y-o 5f winner Tahdeed and half-brother to a winner in USA: dam won Queen Mary Stakes: looked a thorough rogue second start, virtually refusing to race after leading to straight: won claimer at Newmarket in August under fine ride from G. Carter, before sold from E. Dunlop's stable 13,500 gns: failed to finish on second start in USA: will stay 1m. *E. Truman, USA*

WINGNUT (IRE) 4 ch.f. Digamist (USA) 110 – Royal Cloak (Hardicanute 130) – [1996 46, a–: a8g a7g⁶ a6g⁶ a6g⁵ a7g⁶ 6.1g 5.1g 7f⁶ 10.8g³ 10f 8.5g² 10.1g⁵ a8g a10s 1997 a8g a12g⁵ Mar 27] poor performer: well beaten in 1997. *R. Ingram*

WING OF A PRAYER 3 b.g. Statoblest 120 – Queen Angel 88 (Anfield 117) 46 [1996 61?: 6f 6g 1997 6.9m³ a6g 6.9m 8d⁴ Jun 28] smallish gelding: poor maiden: stays 1m: acts on firm and dead ground. *W. Jarvis*

WINNEBAGO 4 b.f. Kris 135 – Siouan 78 (So Blessed 130) [1996 63: 7.9g⁵ 56 10.5d 8m 8.2s 1997 12.1d 10g 14.1m³ 13.1g² 16m 13.8g 13d⁴* 12.1m⁴ Aug 18] angular filly: has a round action: modest handicapper: gained first win at Hamilton in August: stays 2m: acts on good to firm and dead ground: front runner. *C. W. Thornton*

WINSA (USA) 2 b.f. (May 12) Riverman (USA) 131 – Wasnah (USA) 96 (Nijin- 80 p sky (CAN) 138) [1997 7g⁴ 7m² 8.1g³ 8g³ Oct 24] good-bodied filly: poor mover:

fourth foal: sister to high-class miler Bahri and half-sister to 3-y-o Bahhare: dam, maiden who should have stayed 1½m, is out of Queen Mary winner Highest Trump: fairly useful maiden: good staying-on third of 14 to Panama House in nursery at Doncaster final start: will stay 1¼m: should do better. *J. L. Dunlop*

WINSOME GEORGE   2 b.g. (Jan 26) Marju (IRE) 127 – June Moon (IRE)   80
(Sadler's Wells (USA) 132) [1997 5g⁶ 5s⁶ 6d³ 5.9f² 7g* 7m⁴ 7.5m³ 7.5d⁶ 8s 8g Oct 24] 18,000Y: compact gelding: first foal: dam unraced daughter of 1000 Guineas runner-up and smart sprinter Kerrera: fairly useful performer: won maiden at Ayr in June: ran well next 2 starts, then well below form in nurseries: should be suited by 1m+: best form on good/good to firm ground. *C. W. Fairhurst*

WINSOME WOOSTER   6 ch.m. Primo Dominie 121 – Bertrade 75 (Homeboy   71
114) [1996 67: 6d⁶ 6g⁵ 7m⁴ 8.3g 7f⁴ 7g* 6m⁶ 7f³ 5.7m⁵ 6.1m 7s 7g 1997 7.3g* 7f² 7m 7.1m* Jul 30] plain, close-coupled mare: fair handicapper: won at Newbury in May and Sandown in July: stays 7f well: acts on hard and dead ground. *P. G. Murphy*

WINSTON   4 b.g. Safawan 118 – Lady Leman 74 (Pitskelly 122) [1996 73: a8g⁵   57
8.2g* 8d³ 8g* 8d⁵ 10.1m³ 8m² 8f 8m 8g 8g 1997 a8g 8m 8.5d 10g 8g 8.5v⁵ 8m 8.1m⁵ 7.5g 8.3g³ 8.2d³ 8m 8s Nov 6] sturdy gelding: modest handicapper: should stay further than 1m: acts on good to firm and dead ground, not at best both starts on the all-weather: no improvement in blinkers: carries head awkwardly: suited by being held up in strongly-run race. *J. D. Bethell*

WINTERED OUT   3 b.f. Digamist (USA) 110 – Record Song (Indian King   –
(USA) 128) [1996 –: 6g 1997 7d 8g Jun 7] tall, angular filly: no form. *G. L. Moore*

WINTER GARDEN   3 ch.g. Old Vic 136 – Winter Queen 60 (Welsh Pageant   107
132) [1996 66p: 7d 1997 10m⁵ 12m* 12s² 14m* 16.2m⁴ 14.8g² 12m Jul 29] strong, lengthy gelding: has scope: useful performer: won maiden at Thirsk in May and minor event at Salisbury in June: good neck second of 9 to Three Cheers in listed race at Newmarket penultimate start, but not for first time did not impress with finishing effort: finished lame in Gordon Stakes final start, and subsequently gelded: stays 2m: acts on good to firm and soft ground. *L. M. Cumani*

WINTER ROMANCE   4 ch.c. Cadeaux Genereux 131 – Island Wedding (USA)   109
89 (Blushing Groom (FR) 131) [1996 106: 7.9f² 8.1d* 8f 10g 10.4m⁶ 9m³ 9g⁵ 1997 8m⁴ 7.9g⁴ 10s* 10.1d² 8.9s* 10.9d³ 10v Oct 11] good-topped colt: good mover: useful performer: won valuable handicap at Ascot (idled) in June and listed race at York (by ½ length, clear, from Weet-A-Minute) in September: creditable third to

Strensall Stakes, York—
Winter Romance (right) needs to be hard driven to shake off the outsider Weet-A-Minute

Maktoum Al Maktoum's "Winter Romance"

Ghataas in another listed event at Ayr: ran poorly final start: stays 1¼m: acts on firm ground, goes well on dead or softer: held up: tends to carry head high, and not an easy ride. *E. A. L. Dunlop*

WINTER SCOUT (USA) 9 ch.g. It's Freezing (USA) 122 – His Squaw (USA) 62
(Tom Rolfe) [1996 60: 6.1g 6m 7d 7f 5.9f* 6.9f⁴ 7.1d 7m 7g 12m 1997 5.9g³ 6g
6m⁵ 5.9f* 6.9m* 6.9g² 7m 7.1m⁶ 7m Sep 9] strong, good-bodied gelding: modest
performer: successful 4 times at Carlisle, including in claimer and handicap in 1997:
well below form last 3 starts: effective blinkered or not: acts on firm ground: usually ridden by apprentice. *R. A. Fahey*

WINTERTIME 2 b.c. (Mar 25) Robellino (USA) 127 – Naturally Fresh 91 70
(Thatching 131) [1997 7g 7m 8m⁴ᵈⁱˢ Oct 23] 24,000Y: eighth foal: half-brother to
winners abroad by Valiyar and Petoski: dam 2-y-o 5f winner: showed ability in minor
event at Salisbury and maidens at Leicester and Brighton (rider failed to weigh in):
went well long way each time and may prove best up to 1m. *G. Lewis*

WIRA (IRE) 3 ch.c. Lahib (USA) 129 – Mother Courage 67 (Busted 134) [1996 –
NR 1997 7m Mar 31] 110,000Y: leggy, workmanlike colt: third foal: half-brother
to a winner in Spain by Scottish Reel: dam, staying maiden half-sister to Dance
Machine, the dam of Halling: eighth of 9 in maiden at Kempton: gave trouble at
stalls. *P. F. I. Cole*

WISHBONE ALLEY (IRE) 2 b.g. (Apr 18) Common Grounds 118 – Dul Dul 54
(USA) (Shadeed (USA) 135) [1997 7m⁶ 7m³ 7.5d 7.1g 5.1g⁵ 6s Oct 14] 10,500Y:
second foal: dam unraced half-sister to high-class sprinter Double Schwartz: modest
maiden: best efforts second and fifth starts: probably stays 7f: well beaten on ground
softer than good. *M. Dods*

WISHING STONE (USA) 3 b.f. Dayjur (USA) 137 – Worood (USA) (Vaguely 87
Noble 140) [1996 NR 1997 7g³ 8.3g* 8.3m* 9m² 8.3m² 10g⁶ Sep 18] close-coupled,

good-quartered filly: third foal: half-sister to French 1m winner Light Fresh Air (by Rahy): dam French 1m to 1½m winner: fairly useful performer: favourite when winning maiden and handicap at Windsor in July: good efforts in handicaps all subsequent starts: stays 1¼m: yet to race on ground softer than good: sold 60,000 gns in December. *E. A. L. Dunlop*

WISTON CHEESE (USA) 2 b.c. (Apr 8) Cryptoclearance (USA) – Happy Gal (FR) (Habitat 134) [1997 6v* Oct 10] good-topped colt: has scope: sixth foal: half-brother to smart French 11f to 15f winner Tarator (by Green Dancer) and a winner in Mexico by Graustark: dam, French 9.5f winner, granddaughter of Gimcrack winner Be Careful: sire (by Fappiano) high class at up to 1½m: 8/1, won maiden at Ascot in taking style from 6 fellow newcomers, patiently ridden in extreme conditions, but quickening to lead close home when given odd slap: should be well suited by 1m+: a very good prospect, sure to win more races. *J. L. Dunlop*   94 P

WITCHFINDER (USA) 5 b.g. Diesis 133 – Colonial Witch (USA) (Pleasant Colony (USA)) [1996 NR 1997 10d⁵ 8d 8d a7g³ a7s³ a7g* Dec 22] big, good sort: has a long, round stride: modest performer: best effort of 1997 when winning maiden at Lingfield: stays 1m: acts on equitrack, raced only on good/dead ground on turf: visored last 3 starts. *Mrs L. Stubbs*   64

WITCHING HOUR (IRE) 3 b.f. Alzao (USA) 117 – Itching (IRE) (Thatching 131) [1996 88: 6d* 6m² 1997 8m⁴ Apr 30] close-coupled filly: fairly useful performer: suffered leg injury after second 2-y-o start: fourth of 5 in minor event at Ascot, only start in 1997: not sure to stay much beyond 1m. *Mrs J. Cecil*   83

WITH A WILL 3 b.g. Rambo Dancer (CAN) 107 – Henceforth 58 (Full of Hope 125) [1996 –p: 6.1d⁴ 6m 6m⁵ 1997 8g 7d³ 6.9s⁴ 8.1m* 8.1g 8.5f 8.2d Oct 30] small, good-bodied gelding: modest handicapper: won for inexperienced claimer at Chepstow in July, dictating steady pace: below form afterwards: stays 1m: acts on good to firm and soft going. *H. Candy*   64

WITHOUT FRIENDS (IRE) 3 b.g. Thatching 131 – Soha (USA) 58 (Dancing Brave (USA) 140) [1996 77: 5f* 6g* 6m²diss 6.1f* 5m 7g⁴ 1997 6g* 6f⁴ 6f³ 7m⁶ 6d 6f a7g⁴ 8f² 8.1m⁶ 8g⁶ 8m⁶ 10f⁴ 10m³ a10g⁵ a10s² a10g³ Dec 19] narrow, dipped-backed gelding: won seller at Newcastle in March: left W. Storey after next outing: only modest form after third start: stays 1¼m: acts on firm ground and equitrack: well beaten in blinkers: tends to carry head high. *J. Ffitch-Heyes*   69 d

WITH THE TEMPO (IRE) 4 b.f. Last Tycoon 131 – Starlust 79 (Sallust 134) [1996 53: 8.5m² 7f⁵ 8m 7g 12s 1997 8f⁶ a6g 6m a8.5g Sep 20] disappointing maiden: tried blinkered. *Dr J. D. Scargill*   –

WITNEY-LA-ROCHE 3 ch.g. Superlative 118 – Ever Reckless 52 (Crever 94) [1996 –: 6m 7m 1997 6.1d Apr 29] no form. *J. S. Moore*   –

WIXIM (USA) 4 ch.c. Diesis 133 – River Lullaby (USA) (Riverman (USA) 131) [1996 108: 8s² 8g* 8m* 8d³ 1997 9g² 8.1g* 9.3d² 8m⁵ 8d⁴ 8f³ 9m³ Dec 14] smallish,   120

Sandown Mile—a close finish between Wixim (blaze),
First Island (second right), Bin Rosie (blinkers), Gothenberg (rail) and Acharne

sturdy, angular colt: very smart performer: won steadily-run Sandown Mile in April by head from First Island (who gave 6 lb), leading inside final 1f: best efforts in Prix d'Ispahan at Longchamp (short-neck second of 6 to Sasuru) following month and Queen Anne Stakes at Royal Ascot (around three lengths fifth to Allied Forces): narrowly-beaten third of 14 to Val's Prince in Hong Kong International Cup at Sha Tin final start: will stay 1¼m: acts on good to firm and dead ground (shaped well on soft on debut): has been bandaged behind: genuine and consistent: stays in training. *R. Charlton*

WIZARD KING 6 b.h. Shaadi (USA) 126 – Broomstick Cottage (Habitat 134) [1996 116: 7m⁵ 7m* 7m* 7.1g* 8g² 7m² 7g* 7d* 1997 7d* 8d² 7m³ 7s* 7g* 7d* 7m* 7s⁴ 7m⁴ Dec 14] 122

In the essay on Wizard King which appeared in *Racehorses of 1994* we praised Sir Mark Prescott for the skilful placing of his horses in handicaps. Well, he's not bad at finding suitable opportunities for them in listed and pattern races either judged on Wizard King's subsequent record. The winner of six races from fifteen starts by the end of his three-year-old season, Wizard King's tally now stands at eighteen from thirty-nine, his total win and place prize money in that time having risen from just over £100,000 to virtually £295,000.

Finding the right races for Wizard King hasn't just involved searching through the British *Programme Book*, either. Far from it! Of the twenty-four races he's contested in the past three seasons, thirteen have taken place abroad. While Ireland is the only country outside Britain in which Wizard King has been successful, he has picked up good place money elsewhere, including in the latest season when finishing third in the Prix du Palais-Royal at Longchamp and, on his final start, fourth in the Hong Kong International Bowl. The latter earned his connections more prize money than for any of his wins in 1997. There were five wins in all, beginning with a listed event at Leicester in April on his reappearance. Then, in chronological order, came the Ballycorus Stakes at Leopardstown, the Thomas Lonsdale Gallagher Beeswing Stakes at New-

Sheikh Ahmed bin Saeed Al Maktoum's "Wizard King"

castle, the Aon MacDonagh Boland Stakes at the Curragh and the Coolmore Home of Champions Concorde Stakes at Tipperary, the last-named event for the second successive year. Wizard King, better than ever at the age of six, showed very smart form at both Newcastle and the Curragh. In the former he was allowed to build up a four-length lead at an early stage and won unchallenged by five lengths from How Long; in the latter he proved he was just as effective coming from behind, quickly asserting in the final furlong having had to wait for a gap and beating Snow Kid by two and a half lengths.

		Danzig	Northern Dancer
	Shaadi (USA)	(b 1977)	Pas de Nom
	(b 1986)	Unfurled	Hoist The Flag
Wizard King		(b 1974)	Lemon Souffle
(b.h. 1991)		Habitat	Sir Gaylord
	Broomstick Cottage	(b 1966)	Little Hut
	(b 1984)	Broomstick Corner	Bustino
		(b or br 1977)	Flashy

Wizard King is the last of three foals produced by the unraced Broomstick Cottage prior to her being sold for 17,000 guineas in December, 1991, and exported to Brazil. Broomstick Cottage's first foal, by Primo Dominie, won abroad, while her second was the untrustworthy ten-furlong winner Lavender Cottage (by Teenoso). The second dam, Broomstick Corner, from an excellent family, was useful over middle-distances, showing marked improvement once fitted with blinkers. Blinkers or other such aids aren't required for Wizard King, a splendidly tough, genuine and consistent individual who is effective on any ground and capable of showing his best on straight or turning tracks. While he has shown smart form and won races at a mile, he is most effective at seven furlongs and does virtually all his racing at that trip nowadays. Wizard King, a tall, lengthy individual, is an unimpressive mover in his slower paces but that counts for nothing once he starts racing, when this admirable racehorse is more than a match for most. *Sir Mark Prescott*

WOLFHUNT 2 b.c. (Feb 17) Wolfhound (USA) 126 – Vayavaig 78 (Damister (USA) 123) [1997 5d 6s² 6s⁵ 6g a6g* a6g² Dec 22] 28,000Y: smallish, good-bodied colt: first foal: dam 2-y-o 6f winner, half-sister to smart sprinter Vaigly Great: fair form on turf: improved to win maiden at Wolverhampton (by 6 lengths) in December: good second in nursery at Lingfield: will stay beyond 6f: capable of better still on all-weather. *P. J. Makin* — 72 a89 p

WOLF MOUNTAIN 3 ch.c. Selkirk (USA) 129 – Cubby Hole (Town And Country 124) [1996 92: 6m² 7f³ 7m 6g* 1997 6g* 8m 6m³ 6.5f* 8f* Nov 19] leggy, lengthy colt: has a quick, fluent action: useful performer: won minor event at Leicester in May: left R. Hannon after third start and won allowance races at Santa Anita and Hollywood Park in the autumn: stays 1m: has raced only on good ground or firmer: tends to come from off pace: raced on medication in USA. *Kathy Walsh, USA* — 104 +

WONDERBOY (IRE) 3 ch.g. Arazi (USA) 135 – Alsaaybah (USA) 73 (Diesis 133) [1996 –: 7m 1997 6m 8.3s 14m 14m Aug 14] leggy colt: modest maiden: should stay 2m. *R. Akehurst* — 54

WONTCOSTALOTBUT 3 b.f. Nicholas Bill 125 – Brave Maiden 63 (Three Legs 128) [1996 NR 1997 10d 8g 8g a12g⁵ 12g Jul 9] smallish, workmanlike filly: sixth foal: half-sister to a modest 1½m winner by Mummy's Game: dam won at 1¼m and 1½m: well held in maidens and handicaps. *M. J. Wilkinson* — –

WON'T FORGET ME (IRE) 2 br.g. (Apr 26) Don't Forget Me 127 – Lucky Realm (Realm 129) [1997 6.1g 6m 6g⁴ 7g² 6.9m* 7g* 7.6m a7g a7g Dec 18] IR 3,200Y: leggy, angular gelding: half-brother to several winners, including 1985 2-y-o Happy Breed (7.6f, by Bustino): dam Irish 5f to 7f winner: modest performer: won sellers at Folkestone in August and Brighton in September: below form in nurseries afterwards, leaving M. Tompkins after penultimate start: will stay at least 1m: raced only on good/good to firm ground on turf: visored third start. *I. Semple* — 59

WOODBECK   3 b. or br.f. Terimon 124 – Arminda (Blakeney 126) [1996 NR   90
1997 8.2d⁴ 7.5d² 7m* 7v* 8g⁴ 8g³ 10.1g Aug 25] rangy filly: has scope: fourth foal:
half-sister to 3 winners, including 4-y-o Carburton: dam unraced: fairly useful performer: won maiden at Catterick in May and handicap at Chester in June: good
efforts next 2 starts: should stay 1¼m: yet to race on firm going, acts on any other.
J. A. Glover

WOODBURY LAD (USA)   4 ch.c. Woodman (USA) 126 – Habibti 136 (Habi-   –
tat 134) [1996 76, a63: 6m 6f² 7m² 7.1d³ a7g² a7g³ 1997 a8.5g⁵ Jan 15] strong,
lengthy colt: fair maiden: well below form only 4-y-o star: sent to New Zealand.
W. R. Muir

WOODETTO (IRE)   3 b.g. Maledetto (IRE) 103 – Wood Kay (IRE) (Treasure   –
Kay 114) [1996 53: 6m 7f² 6d⁴ 5m⁵ 1997 6g 6m⁴ a6g Oct 20] close-coupled, workmanlike gelding: modest maiden: well below form in 1997. *E. Weymes*

WOODLAND MELODY (USA)   2 b.f. (Apr 28) Woodman (USA) 126 –   108 p
Eloquent Minister (USA) 109 (Deputy Minister (CAN)) [1997 6g* 7.1m* 7s*
Aug 31]

     Woodland Melody's name is one that is unlikely to be particularly
familiar to readers at present, for all that she's an unbeaten and well-connected
filly, prominent in some ante-post lists for the One Thousand Guineas and
Oaks. Her two wins in Britain came in not especially high profile affairs in July
and she wasn't seen out after landing a five-runner contest at Deauville on the
last day of August.

     Woodland Melody's claim to be considered a good horse rests on that
Deauville run in the Group 3 Prix du Calvados. It seemed a substandard edition
of the race, though Sainte Marine and Seralia had won listed races on the same
course and Uninhibited had finished third to Xaar in the Prix de Cabourg.
Woodland Melody herself had won a minor event for fillies at Haydock followed by a six-runner listed contest at Sandown, the latter by a short head from
Eloquent, staying on to lead in the final stride after proving hard to settle early
on and looking held over a furlong out. Her rivals at Deauville may not have
been among the best of the French juveniles, but Woodland Melody was
impressive all the same, tracking Sainte Marine until going on over a furlong
out and soon clear. At the line she was five lengths to the good over that filly,
with the rest strung out behind. In September it was announced that Woodland
Melody had been sold (along with the same owner's Cape Verdi, among others)
to Godolphin and would be wintered in Dubai.

     Woodland Melody is open to further improvement but still has some
way to go before she can be considered a major classic candidate. She seemed
well suited by a good test at seven furlongs at two, but her breeding suggests
she's not sure to get much beyond a mile and the One Thousand Guineas looks
a more obvious target than the Oaks. The average winning distance of Wood-

Prix du Calvados, Deauville—Woodland Melody leaves her four rivals trailing

Mr R. E. Sangster's "Woodland Melody"

man's progeny at three years plus is around nine furlongs and he himself wasn't bred to get much further than the mile he won over at two. That said, he has had a notable winner over a mile and a half in the Belmont Stakes winner Hansel and over a mile and a quarter in Bosra Sham, and he was also responsible in 1997 for the Irish Derby runner-up Dr Johnson. Woodland Melody's dam, Eloquent Minister, criss-crossed the Atlantic, winning in America and taking a listed race at Doncaster at two and returning to the States after a three-year-old career in which she won another listed race, at Tipperary. She seemed a sprinter purely and simply. When previously sent to Woodman, Eloquent Minister produced the fairly useful mile winner Code of Law. She has, however, also foaled Areciba (by Risen Star), a fairly useful juvenile six-furlong winner who later seemed to stay a mile and a quarter, and the good Japanese winner at a mile and a quarter Maruka Diesis (by Diesis). Eloquent Minister is one of many winners out of the two-year-old winner Art Talk.

		Mr Prospector	Raise A Native
	Woodman (USA)	(b 1970)	Gold Digger
	(ch 1983)	Playmate	Buckpasser
Woodland Melody (USA)		(ch 1975)	Intriguing
(b.f. Apr 28, 1995)		Deputy Minister	Vice Regent
	Eloquent Minister (USA)	(b or br 1979)	Mint Copy
	(b 1986)	Art Talk	Speak John
		(b or br 1971)	Tattooed Miss

All things told, connections did well to acquire the tall, lengthy, un-furnished Woodland Melody for 75,000 guineas at the Houghton Yearling Sales. She must have been valued a good deal more highly when sold on to Godolphin. *P. W. Chapple-Hyam*

WOODLAND NYMPH 3 gr.f. Norton Challenger 111 – Royal Meeting 44 47
(Dara Monarch 128) [1996 –: 7d 7.1s 1997 a9.4g⁵ a12g³ 14.1m² a12g a14.8g a12g⁵
12.5d Jun 24] poor maiden handicapper: well below form last 4 starts, visored on
final one: stays 1¾m: acts on good to firm and soft ground and on fibresand, yet to
race on equitrack. *D. J. G. Murray Smith*

WOODLANDS ENERGY 6 b.m. Risk Me (FR) 127 – Hallowed (Wolver
Hollow 126) [1996 –: 13.1f 10.8m 12.5f 1997 10.8d Jun 24] of no account on flat.
P. A. Pritchard

WOODLANDS LAD TOO 5 b.g. Risk Me (FR) 127 – Hallowed (Wolver –
Hollow 126) [1996 –: a8g 1997 10g May 27] of no account. *P. A. Pritchard*

WOODLANDS PRIDE (IRE) 2 ch.f. (Apr 28) Petardia 113 – Valediction 71 –
(Town Crier 119) [1997 5g 7g⁵ 7d Oct 13] 2,800 2-y-o: workmanlike filly: half-sister
to 1½m winner Fairy Wisher (by Fairy King) and 1987 Irish 2-y-o 6f winner Classic
Dilemma (by Sandhurst Prince): dam none-too-genuine middle-distance maiden:
well beaten in maidens. *M. C. Chapman*

WOODREN (USA) 4 ch.f. Woodman (USA) 126 – Whitethroat (Artaius (USA) 91
129) [1996 8s³ 10g⁶ 13g³ 12m² 16m* 14f⁶ 10g⁶ 1997 11v 9m⁵ 11.9m 12m 10.2m
14g Aug 13] IR 25,000Y: workmanlike filly: half-sister to a winner in Trinidad: dam
lightly-raced half-sister to Assert, Bikala and Eurobird: fairly useful performer:
trained by J. Oxx in Ireland at 2 and 3 yrs (rated 83): mostly faced stiff tasks in 1997,
seeming to show fairly useful form on 3 occasions: stays 2m: acts on good to firm
and soft ground: below form only try in blinkers. *R. Guest*

WOODRISING 5 b.m. Nomination 125 – Bodham 88 (Bustino 136) [1996 –: –
11.9m 1997 10m a10g⁶ 11.6m⁶ Aug 11] smallish mare: modest winner at 3 yrs:
lightly raced and no form since. *C. R. Egerton*

WOODY'S BOY (IRE) 3 gr.g. Roi Danzig (USA) – Smashing Gale (Lord 68
Gayle (USA) 124) [1996 NR 1997 10.2d 10.2m⁶ 10d⁵ 11.6g⁴ 11.6m² 13.1g³ 16g 16s
Oct 15] IR 12,000Y: useful-looking gelding: third reported foal: half-brother to 1993
2-y-o 5f winner/winning hurdler Kierchem (by Mazaad): dam Irish 1m winner: fair
maiden: ran badly last 2 starts: should be suited by 1¾m+: best efforts on good
ground or firmer: has been blanketed for stalls entry. *M. J. Heaton-Ellis*

WORLD EXPRESS (IRE) 7 b.g. Jareer (USA) 115 – Eight Mile Rock 76 – §
(Dominion 123) [1996 59§: 11.8d 12d³ 14d* 17.2m⁵ 16.4g⁶ 1997 12v Oct 10] modest
and unreliable handicapper: soundly beaten only start in 1997. *B. R. Millman*

WORLD OF JOY 2 b.f. (Mar 9) Selkirk (USA) 129 – Realisatrice (USA) (Raja –
Baba (USA)) [1997 7g 6.1m Sep 23] 21,000F, 80,000Y: sixth foal: half-sister to
French 1992 2-y-o 5f winner Infant Protege (by Theatrical): dam French maiden
daughter of high-class sprinter Reality and half-sister to dam of Ravinella: some
promise in maidens at Salisbury and Nottingham in September: sent to Saudi Arabia.
R. Charlton

WORLD PREMIER 4 b.g. Shareef Dancer (USA) 135 – Abuzz 101 (Absalom 101
128) [1996 103: 7m³ 8m 7g³ 8f 7g⁴ 8f⁵ 7m 6s 1997 a8.5g 6m³ 7m² 6g³ 6g 7d 7g
5m⁵ 6g⁴ 7g Sep 18] smallish, good-topped gelding: impresses in appearance: useful
performer: several creditable efforts in 1997, including when second to Tregaron in
Victoria Cup at Ascot in April: effective at 6f/7f (finds 5f too sharp): acts on firm
ground, seemingly not on dead or softer. *C. E. Brittain*

WORLDWIDE ELSIE (USA) 4 b.f. Java Gold (USA) – Tender Camilla 115 52
(Prince Tenderfoot (USA) 126) [1996 73, a–: 10.3d 7m⁴ a8.5g⁶ 7m⁶ a8.5g 7g⁵ a9.4g
1997 a7g⁵ a8g 9.9m⁵ 10.8m a10g³ 8f May 23] tall filly: modest handicapper: stays
1¼m: acts on firm ground and all-weather: effective blinkered or not: inconsistent:
sent to Australia. *I. Campbell*

WORLD WITHOUT END (USA) 8 ch.g. World Appeal (USA) – Mardie's 31
Bid (USA) (Raise A Bid (USA)) [1996 NR 1997 a16g⁶ a14g³ a16g⁶ a16g⁵ a12g⁴ Apr
7] poor performer: stays 2¼m: acts on soft ground and fibresand: blinkered/visored
in 1997. *M. E. Sowersby*

WORTH THE EFFORT 2 b.f. (Mar 29) Beveled (USA) – Haiti Mill 68 (Free –
State 125) [1997 6m Oct 4] rather leggy filly: sixth foal: sister to 7f winner Level Up

and half-sister to 6f and 7f winner Nigel's Lucky Girl (by Belfort): dam, maiden miler, out of sister to Petong: tailed off in maiden at Newmarket after very slow start. *M. H. Tompkins*

WOSAITA   2 b.f. (Feb 11) Generous (IRE) 139 – Eljazzi 92 (Artaius (USA) 129)   64 p
[1997 7.1g⁶ Sep 27] smallish filly: half-sister to several winners, including Prix de Diane winner Rafha (by Kris), also successful at 6f (at 2 yrs) to 11.5f, and fairly useful 1½m to 1¾m winner Sarawat (by Slip Anchor): dam 2-y-o 7f winner who stayed 1¼m: 10/1 and carrying plenty of condition, held up and not given hard race when sixth of 12 to Last Christmas in steadily-run maiden at Haydock: should be well suited by 1¼m/1½m: should improve. *J. L. Dunlop*

WOT NO FAX   4 ch.g. Sharrood (USA) 124 – Priors Dean 61 (Monsanto (FR)   –
121) [1996 96: 10f* 10.1m³ 10m⁶ 10m 10m 10.1m 1997 12m 10.3d 10g May 26] plain gelding: useful form early at 3 yrs for S. Dow: well beaten in handicaps in 1997, including in blinkers. *B. J. Meehan*

WOTTASHAMBLES   6 b. or br.g. Arrasas (USA) 100 – Manawa 81 (Man-   a69
damus 120) [1996 41, a62: a16g* a13g² a16g⁵ a13g⁴ a16g⁴ 11.8d² 12g³ 12f 12m⁶ 14m³ a16g* a16g* 1997 a16g² a13g* a16g³ a12g⁵ 14m Jul 10] leggy gelding: has a round action: fair handicapper on equitrack, successful at Lingfield in February: only poor form on turf: effective at 13f to 2m: acts on firm and soft ground: blinkered once earlier in career. *L. Montague Hall*

WREKIN PILOT   2 b.g. (Apr 6) Ron's Victory (USA) 129 – Lunaire (Try My   89
Best (USA) 130) [1997 5m⁶ 5g* 5.2g⁴ 7f² 6g² 7g 6d³ 6f⁴ Sep 18] close-coupled gelding: third foal: half-brother to 4-y-o Moonraking: dam unraced half-sister to Premio Parioli winner Lucratif: fairly useful form: won maiden at Kempton in March: improved in minor events subsequently until below form final outing: stays 7f: acts on firm ground and dead: sold 11,000 gns in October. *R. Hannon*

WREN (IRE)   2 ch.f. (May 13) Bob Back (USA) 124 – In The Rigging (USA) 78   103 p
(Topsider (USA)) [1997 6g* 6m* 8g* Oct 12] 6,400Y: second foal: half-sister to Italian 3-y-o 11.5f winner Lambaran (by Law Society): dam 1m winner out of half-sister to Light Cavalry and Fairy Footsteps: useful form: won minor event at Milan in July, listed race at La Teste in August and Premio Dormello at Milan in October, last named by 4 lengths: should stay at least 1¼m: progressive. *Lord Huntingdon*

WRN PRINCESS   3 ch.f. Handsome Sailor 125 – Sovereign Rose 116 (Sharpen   –
Up 127) [1996 –: 6g 6m 6g⁶ 1997 7m 6d 7g Jul 12] little form. *B. J. Meehan*

WROUGHT IRON (USA)   2 b. or br.f. (Apr 16) Dayjur (USA) 137 – Pris de Fer   58
(USA) (Sir Ivor 135) [1997 6.1m 7d Oct 13] strong, workmanlike filly: seventh foal: half-sister to several winners in USA, including a minor stakes winner by Gulch: dam ran 6 times in USA: modest form in maidens: moved poorly down second time. *M. Bell*

WURFTAUBE (GER)   4 ch.f. Acatenango (GER) 127 – Wurfbahn (GER)   116
(Frontal 122) [1996 119: 10g⁴ 10.5g* 11s* 11s* 12g* 11g* 14d* 1997 12g* 11f² 12g² Jul 27] smart German filly: won last 6 of 7 starts at 3 yrs, notably Deutsches St Leger at Dortmund by 11 lengths: won Group 2 event at Cologne in May by 1¾ lengths from Surako: ½-length second of 7 to Oxalagu in Group 2 event at Baden-Baden then 3 lengths second of 6 to Luso in Group 1 race at Dusseldorf: better at 1¾m than shorter: acts on firm and soft going: genuine and consistent: visits Mark of Esteem. *H. Remmert, Germany*

WUXI VENTURE   2 b.g. (Apr 26) Wolfhound (USA) 126 – Push A Button (Bold   80 +
Lad (IRE) 133) [1997 6s³ 7m³ 7m⁶ a8.5g³ 7m⁵ 8s² Nov 6] sturdy, good-bodied gelding: has a fluent, round action: half-brother to 3 winners, including Irish 1¼m winner Outside Pressure (by Shernazar): dam, Irish 2-y-o 6f winner, half-sister to Riverman: fairly useful maiden on balance of form: probably flattered in blinkers in listed event at Newmarket fifth outing: runner-up in Musselburgh maiden when visored month later: stays 1m: acts on good to firm and soft ground. *S. P. C. Woods*

WYCHWOOD SANDY   6 b.g. Mansingh (USA) 120 – Do-Run-Do (Palm Track   –
122) [1996 NR 1997 5m 6m a5g Dec 8] of little account. *H. J. Collingridge*

WYNBURY FLYER   2 ch.g. (Apr 22) Risk Me (FR) 127 – Woolcana 71 (Some   40
Hand 119) [1997 5g 7g 7g⁴ 7g 7m⁶ a8g⁶ Nov 14] 700F: close-coupled gelding:
brother to a winner in Sweden up to 1m and half-brother to several winners, including
Pullover (by Windjammer, over 7f): dam 5f winner: poor maiden. *F. Murphy*

X

XAAR   2 b.c. (Mar 14) Zafonic (USA) 130 – Monroe (USA) 102 (Sir Ivor 135)   132
[1997 6d* 6g* 6g² 7g* 7g* Oct 18]
　　　The keen form-book student's time-honoured quest for the next
season's classic winners should have taken up fewer evenings than usual over
the latest winter. The destination of the first colts' classic, the Two Thousand
Guineas, has looked a near-formality since Xaar romped home by seven lengths
in the Dewhurst Stakes, establishing himself as one of the shortest-priced
ante-post favourites for the Guineas in modern times. Newmarket billed the
revamped final day of its Houghton meeting in October as 'Champions Day'
and it couldn't have been better named. As well as staging the farewell British
appearance of Pilsudski in the Dubai Champion Stakes (which also attracted
the Derby winner), a mouth-watering international clash in the Thoroughbred
Corporation Dewhurst Stakes looked sure to settle the 'champion two-year-old'
title. What couldn't have been anticipated was that the race would reveal a
champion of such supremacy. French-trained Xaar showed himself an outstanding two-year-old, quickening really well after being held up and outclass-
ing his field to a remarkable extent. Front-running Tamarisk, who had the rest

Prix de la Salamandre, Longchamp—Xaar takes his revenge on Charge d'Affaires,
the pair followed by British challengers Speedfit Too and Greenlander

Thoroughbred Corporation Dewhurst Stakes, Newmarket—
a performance right out of the top drawer from Xaar;
Tamarisk, Impressionist and Desert Prince (noseband) are left toiling

tacked down running into the Dip, was his closest pursuer at the line, two and a half lengths ahead of Irish-trained Impressionist and the Coventry Stakes runner-up Desert Prince.

Notwithstanding the fact that the Champagne Stakes winner Daggers Drawn and the Vintage Stakes winner Central Park were both well below form, there was no room to doubt that Xaar's Dewhurst performance was right out of the top drawer. An outstanding timefigure of 1.19 fast (a rating equivalent of 130, 16 lb better than any other by a two-year-old in Britain during the year) provided confirmation of the quality of the performance. The International Classification, published in mid-January, places Xaar 12 lb ahead of Tamarisk, an assessment that is much too conservative. We have given Xaar full value for his Dewhurst victory, 19 lb by our reckoning. Of two-year-old performances in the last dozen years, only Celtic Swing's record-breaking twelve-length win in the Racing Post Trophy and Arazi's stunning victory in the Breeders' Cup Juvenile have been rated more highly. In the same period, Reference Point's seven-length win (the judge gave five) in the William Hill Futurity (the race now run as the Racing Post Trophy) earned him the same Timeform rating as Xaar. The examples of Celtic Swing and Arazi—and of others in the fairly recent past, including Tromos, Storm Bird and Diesis—illustrate that not every champion two-year-old lives up to the highest expectations at three, but, if Xaar keeps fit and well and makes average physical progress, we shall be surprised to see him beaten at Newmarket. His Dewhurst form is some way above normal Two Thousand Guineas-winning standard nowadays. No winner since the mid-'eighties has put up a performance in the Guineas worth a rating above 132.

While there seems little logic in judging the prospects of a champion two-year-old on the subsequent records of earlier title-holders, there is every reason to pay closer attention when one of those predecessors happens to be his sire. Xaar has so far followed closely in the footsteps of Zafonic, the best two-year-old of 1992, though, unlike Zafonic, he didn't end his first season unbeaten. On the third of five starts, he went down by a head to Charge d'Affaires when odds on for the Prix Morny at Deauville in August. After winning a newcomers race at Maisons-Laffitte and beating Charge d'Affaires in the Prix de Cabourg at Deauville, Xaar was headed close home in the Morny after the race turned into something of a tactical affair, the first five home covered by a couple of lengths. Zafonic had to work hard to win his Morny on soft ground and didn't really catch the imagination of a wide audience until sweeping aside the opposition in the Prix de la Salamandre in which, as when winning the Dewhurst in similarly impressive style, he encountered good to firm going. It was the longer distance of the Prix de la Salamandre, not a change in going, that suited Xaar. A strongly-run race also helped to bring the best out in him and he quickened clear in tremendous style after being pushed along to take closer order early in the home straight. Xaar won by three lengths and five from Charge d'Affaires and the British-trained Speedfit Too, putting up a display that, on form, bettered that by Zafonic in the same race, and established him as the one they would all have to beat in the Dewhurst. Further comparisons with Zafonic were inevitable after Xaar's emphatic success at Newmarket. Zafonic's four-length winning margin was the widest in the race for ten years and wasn't approached by any of the winners between him and Xaar. Xaar's exceptional performance entitles him to be regarded as a better two-year-old than Zafonic, but, whereas Zafonic always looked likely to turn into purely and simply a miler at three, Xaar races as if he might stay further. Zafonic was a real powerhouse on looks, big, strong and imposing with a powerful action, and displayed all the hallmarks of a horse whose strong suit was speed. The medium-sized, attractive Xaar is a more tractable type; also, his rider was niggling at him and seemingly getting little response approaching halfway in the Dewhurst. Trainer Andre Fabre, who has won the Dewhurst and the Two Thousand Guineas with Pennekamp as well as Zafonic in the 'nineties, describes Xaar as being 'more impressive than Zafonic, more laid-back . . . he has a good temperament and has always been easy to train.' One slightly worrying sign about Xaar's otherwise relaxed demeanour was that he swished his tail continually while waiting at the start for the Dewhurst, while those searching for another possible chink in his impressive armour might reflect that Xaar's best performances so far have come in strongly-run races. A small field for the Guineas, with the prospect of a muddling pace, might temper enthusiasm a little.

The style of Xaar's victories in the Salamandre and the Dewhurst suggest strongly that the Guineas trip will suit him even better. But how far will he stay? 'When you get a horse as good as this it makes you dream of winning the Derby,' Fabre said after the Dewhurst. Making an educated guess about Xaar's stamina potential would be a little easier if more were known about his sire's influence as a stallion—Xaar is from Zafonic's first crop—but it's fair to say that few could have envisaged Zafonic's becoming noted as a sire of Derby candidates when he took up stud duties. His sire, the Mr Prospector stallion Gone West, was best at around a mile, as was his dam the very useful Zaizafon, while his maternal grandam the smart Mofida won seven races at up to an extended seven furlongs. Zafonic's popularity at stud, incidentally, will see him covering more than a hundred mares in 1998 at a fee of £30,000 each, a rise of £5,000.

If it is hard to see Zafonic transmitting stamina, what are the influences on the distaff side of Xaar's pedigree? Well, plenty is known about his dam, Monroe, a sprinting sister by the Derby winner Sir Ivor to a couple of good two-year-olds in Malinowski and Gielgud, neither of whom won at further than a mile in their career. Xaar is Monroe's thirteenth foal and her tenth winner. She has produced two other pattern winners, both trained by Fabre, the miler Masterclass (by The Minstrel) and Diese (by Diesis) who stayed ten and a half furlongs; but none of Monroe's offspring has won over as far as a mile and a half, the wide range of stallions she has visited including those strong influ-

Mr K. Abdulla's "Xaar"

		Gone West	Mr Prospector
	Zafonic (USA)	(b 1984)	Secrettame
	(b 1990)	Zaizafon	The Minstrel
Xaar		(ch 1982)	Mofida
(b.c. Mar 14, 1995)		Sir Ivor	Sir Gaylord
	Monroe (USA)	(b 1965)	Attica
	(b 1977)	Best In Show	Traffic Judge
		(ch 1965)	Stolen Hour

ences for stamina High Line (to whom she produced the mile to mile and a quarter winner Esquire) and Ile de Bourbon (sire of her American nine-furlong stakes winner Ile de Jinsky). As with most pedigrees, however, nothing is absolutely cut and dried. Monroe's younger sister, Minnie Hauk, a winner at seven furlongs and a mile, was represented in the latest season by the Prix du Cadran winner Chief Contender. One of Monroe's half-sisters, the unraced Sex Appeal, is the dam of two Dewhurst winners, Try My Best and El Gran Senor. The latter won the Two Thousand Guineas and went on to further classic success at a mile and a half in the Irish Derby after just being touched off at Epsom. These factors, together with the presence in Xaar's extended pedigree of two other colts whose careers took in both the Guineas and the Derby, Sir Ivor and The Minstrel, provide a glimmer of hope, on pedigree, that Xaar will stay a mile and a half. His relaxed style of racing is in his favour too, as would be good going or firmer on Derby Day, placing the emphasis on finishing speed rather than stamina. Except for his debut, when the going was on the soft side,

Xaar has done all his racing so far on good ground. Interestingly, his connections maintained in the days leading up to the Dewhurst that he would not run 'if there is any reference to soft in the going description.' *A. Fabre, France*

XENOPHON OF CUNAXA (IRE)   4 b.g. Cyrano de Bergerac 120 – Annais   65 §
Nin (Dominion 123) [1996 78d: 6m 7.3s* 8.1d⁴ 7f³ 7f 5.7m a7g a7g⁶ 1997 a6g
7.3g 7.1m⁵ 7d⁴ 7m 6m 6m 6.1s a9.4g³ Dec 26] leggy gelding: fair performer on his
day: stays 9.4f: unraced on heavy going, acts on any other turf/all-weather: tried
blinkered: often slowly away: most unreliable. *B. J. Llewellyn*

X-RAY (IRE)   4 gr.g. Actinium (FR) 95 – Charter Lights (Kalaglow 132) [1996   –
NR 1997 a6g⁵ Jan 30] first known foal: dam, maiden, half-sister to smart jumper
Calapaez: no sign of ability. *J. R. Jenkins*

XWIFE (IRE)   2 b.f. (May 7) Alzao (USA) 117 – Dawning Beauty (USA) (Well   ?
Decorated (USA)) [1997 6g² 6.8s³ 6.8g² 6s* 7m Sep 30] 30,000F, 55,000Y: sixth
foal: sister to Italian 1995 2-y-o 5f and 7f winner Beauty Dancer and half-sister to
a winner in Brazil: dam Irish maiden half-sister to Bluebird: competed mainly in
Scandinavia, placed 3 times at Ovrevoll then won valuable event at Taby: well tailed
off in valuable sales race at Newmarket in September: should prove better at 7f than
6f: acts on soft going. *W. Neuroth, Norway*

XYLEM (USA)   6 ch.g. Woodman (USA) 126 – Careful (USA) (Tampa Trouble   78
(USA)) [1996 a9g⁴ a9.9g* a9.9g⁴ 10.9m³ a9.9g⁶ a9.9g² 11f³ a10g² a12f² 1997 8d 8f
8m* 12v 8d⁴ 8s Nov 8] fairly useful handicapper here in 1994 for J. Gosden: won 3
times in UAE for E. Charpy before sold 17,000 gns in July, 1997: still capable of fair
form on return, and won amateurs handicap at Newcastle in October: finds 1m a bare
minimum, and seems to stay 1½m: acts on good to firm and soft ground and on sand:
effective in blinkers/visor earlier in career. *L. M. Cumani*

Y

YAAKUM   8 b.g. Glint of Gold 128 – Nawadder 73 (Kris 135) [1996 32: 15.1f   –
15.8s 14.1f⁶ 13.1g³ 1997 15g 17.1g Aug 17] robust gelding: tailed off in 1997.
S. E. Kettlewell

YABINT EL SULTAN   3 ch.f. Safawan 118 – Dalby Dancer 71 (Bustiki) [1996   89
–: 6s a6g 1997 6m⁴ 7s⁴ 7m³ 7m² 8.2d² 8.5v³ 7.6m* 8s³ 10.3d* 10.5d⁵ 10g³ 10.5g⁵
Sep 27] angular filly: fairly useful performer: successful in maiden at Chester in July
and handicap there in August: stays 10.5f: acts on good to firm and heavy going:
tough and consistent. *B. A. McMahon*

YACHT   5 b.g. Warning 136 – Bireme 127 (Grundy 137) [1996 –: 14.4g⁶ 1997   –
a12g⁴ a14g Nov 24] tall gelding: fair performer in 1994: lightly raced and little form
since, including in blinkers/visor. *A. G. Newcombe*

YAJTAHED (IRE)   2 ch.c. (Feb 13) Mujtahid (USA) 118 – Rainstone 57 (Rain-   –
bow Quest (USA) 134) [1997 6m May 31] IR 85,000Y: second foal: half-brother to
Italian 3-y-o Holes In The Grass (by Be My Guest), 1m winner at 2 yrs: dam, placed
both starts here at 2 yrs and later won in Belgium, half-sister to speedy 1991 2-y-o
Magic Ring: 50/1, in rear in maiden at Newmarket. *J. H. M. Gosden*

YAK ALFARAJ   3 b.c. Sadler's Wells (USA) 132 – Clara Bow (USA) (Coastal   76
(USA)) [1996 NR 1997 10s⁵ 12.1g⁶ 11.5s 16.2m² 16m³ 16.1d⁴ Aug 25] angular colt:
sixth foal: half-brother to several winners, including 1m winner Zilclare (by Zilzal):
dam won from 6f to 8.5f in USA: fair maiden: creditable efforts most starts: stays
2m: very best form on good to firm ground: sold 13,000 gns in October. *M. R. Stoute*

YALAIETANEE   3 b.c. Sadler's Wells (USA) 132 – Vaigly Star 118 (Star Appeal   115
133) [1996 96p: 7m⁴ 7d* 1997 7g* 8d⁴ 8g⁴ 7g Sep 18] deep-girthed colt: impresses in
appearance: has a fluent, round action: smart performer: won Tripleprint Greenham
Stakes at Newbury in April by head from Revoque: creditable fourth to Daylami
in Poule d'Essai des Poulains at Longchamp (pulled hard, hung and carried head
awkwardly, beaten 5¼ lengths) and to Desert King in Irish 2000 Guineas at the

Tripleprint Greenham Stakes, Newbury—Yalaietanee (right) has a head to spare over Revoque

Curragh (beaten 7 lengths) next 2 starts: off course nearly 4 months before last of 11 in listed race at Newbury on final start: stays 1m: yet to race on extremes of going: probably best with waiting tactics: sent to UAE. *M. R. Stoute*

YALTA (IRE)   4 b.g. Soviet Star (USA) 128 – Gay Hellene 111 (Ela-Mana-Mou   88
132) [1996 88: 8.3g² 8.1m* 10m³ 1997 8g 8s 8m 10m⁶ 8.1m* 8d² 8.3m⁶ 8m* 8d Oct
16] strong, good-bodied gelding: has a short action: fairly useful performer: made all
in claimer at Sandown in July and handicap at Kempton in September: may prove
best around 1m: acts on good to firm and dead going: withdrawn after bolting ninth
intended start: front runner/races prominently. *R. Charlton*

YA MALAK   6 b.g. Fairy King (USA) – La Tuerta 96 (Hot Spark 126) [1996   118
108?: 5d⁵ 5m⁵ 5m⁵ 5f⁵ 5f 5.1m³ 5f⁵ 5.2m 5m⁶ 1997 5m⁵ 5d* 5g⁵ 5g* 5d 5d*
5.1m⁴ 5m 5d* Aug 21]
        Some horse races are destined to be remembered for the human
participants rather than the horses, and the 1997 Nunthorpe Stakes is surely one
example. Kevin Darley's improvisations on board the unbridled Coastal Bluff
would probably have been sufficient on their own. Making sure, the jockey
upsides him was Alex Greaves, her efforts in forcing a dead-heat on Ya Malak
providing her with a place in history as the first woman to ride a pattern
winner in Britain. More than twenty-five years had elapsed since Meriel
Tufnell became the first woman to ride a winner under Jockey Club rules, on
Scorched Earth at Kempton on May 6th, 1972. In the 'eighties and 'nineties,
women professionals such as Alex Greaves, Kim Tinkler, Dana Mellor, Emma
O'Gorman, Aimee Cook and Candy Morris have all had their moments in the
spotlight, but, until August 21st, 1997, their most publicised celebrity was still
Ms Greaves, who earned the nickname of 'Queen of the Sand' in the early years
of racing on the all-weather. On June 30th in the latest season, one hundred and
seven jockeys held full flat licences in Britain, of which seven were women.
Changing attitudes are having an effect, however, as are the increasing
difficulties of male jockeys to ride at low weights, and women can derive far
greater encouragement from the apprentice ranks in which, on the same date,

thirty-six (or 27.7 percent) from a total of one hundred and thirty-five riders were female.

Alex Greaves's early career—which yielded a 1991 Lincoln win on Amenable as well as recognition on the all-weather—was fostered by David Barron, the trainer of Coastal Bluff. Since her marriage, Greaves has ridden almost exclusively for husband David Nicholls whilst retaining her maiden name, and in normal circumstances it is his achievement in sending out a Group 1 winner that would have deserved most of the headlines. Had he never ridden another winner and never trained one, Nicholls would still have had his place in racing folklore as the rider of Soba, but twenty-two years in the saddle yielded four hundred and twenty-one winners all told in Britain, and now he has made a most impressive start to his career as a trainer. Big-money inmates have not been an option for his Thirsk stables so far, but in addition to success in the numbers game—forty-four winners in 1997 continued an upward trend set by twenty-one, twenty-six and thirty in the previous three seasons—he has gained a deal of respect, particularly for what he has achieved with second-hand material. Ya Malak is a case in point.

1997 was six-year-old Ya Malak's first season with Nicholls. Thirty-three previous races had brought six wins, but 1996 had seen him go without a victory and seemingly on the downgrade. Towards the end of that season, Ya Malak was transferred from Pip Payne's stable to that of Ian Balding; after two runs for Balding, he was sold to Nicholls for 23,000 guineas at the Doncaster October Sales. Ya Malak had apparently caught Nicholls' eye a good deal earlier than that. A view of this good-looking horse in the paddock will give one obvious reason why, but the racecourse itself had provided plenty to be struck by as well, notably his one and a half lengths second of eight to So Factual in the 1995 Nunthorpe.

To get a share of first prize in the 1997 Nunthorpe, however, Nicholls had to have Ya Malak not just back to form but better than ever. Compelling evidence that he had done it came first at Epsom on Derby Day in the listed Vodac 'Dash' Rated Stakes. Ya Malak had already won a Beverley minor event on the second of his three previous starts for his new stable, but his Epsom performance was something of a different order, as Greaves had him cantering behind the leaders before sending him through a gap on the rails over a furlong out and on to a five-length victory over Dashing Blue. Emerging at the front much sooner probably had something to do with Ya Malak's tenth of eighteen in the King's Stand at Royal Ascot, but the late challenge that mastered Struggler in a listed race at Sandown the following month showed that pattern races were still worth pursuing. The King George Stakes at Goodwood was the

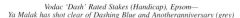

Vodac 'Dash' Rated Stakes (Handicap), Epsom—
Ya Malak has shot clear of Dashing Blue and Anotheranniversary (grey)

Nunthorpe Stakes, York—the camera can't split Ya Malak (noseband) and the luckless Coastal Bluff, who has lost his bridle

obvious target—Ya Malak had speed in abundance and was guaranteed a good lead in a sizeable field at one of Britain's fastest sprint tracks. Defeat in a minor event at Chester did nothing to dampen enthusiasm for him—he again had obviously seen too much daylight—and he lined up for the King George Stakes as 9/2 second favourite. The success that many predicted, however, did not materialise, with Ya Malak afterwards found to be suffering from a stomach problem that was at first thought to be very serious. The race that nobody could have predicted came at York twenty-three days later. Ya Malak had a race run to suit him, with fourteen rivals and a predictably strong pace. Weaving his way through, he edged ahead briefly inside the final furlong, only to be joined again by the gallant Coastal Bluff on the line.

		Northern Dancer	Nearctic
	Fairy King (USA)	(b 1961)	Natalma
	(b 1982)	Fairy Bridge	Bold Reason
Ya Malak		(b 1975)	Special
(b.g. 1991)		Hot Spark	Habitat
	La Tuerta	(ch 1972)	Garvey Girl
	(ch 1982)	Smarten Up	Sharpen Up
		(ch 1975)	L'Anguissola

A good-topped gelding and a good mover, Ya Malak has not so far shown his form on ground any more extreme than good to firm or good to soft. He was tried in blinkers once during that disappointing spell as a five-year-old and waiting tactics looked an important part of his success in 1997. He has run well when sweating. Not once has he raced over as far as six furlongs, and his dam La Tuerta did so only once herself. A winner at two and three years, showing useful form for Bill Wightman, La Tuerta has more than played her part in the good producing record of her well-known family. Ya Malak's brother, Robin Goodfellow, became her seventh winner from nine foals of racing age when he won a maiden at Catterick in October. Three of the others were fairly useful and a fifth, Dominio (by Dominion), won the St Hugh's Stakes and was runner-up in the Temple Stakes. La Tuerta's half-brother, Cadeaux Genereux, won the July Cup and Nunthorpe in 1989, and their dam, Smarten Up, was passed only by Solinus when she made most in the 1978 Nunthorpe. In ratings terms, Ya Malak is on a par with Smarten Up but at least 10 lb behind Cadeaux Genereux. The latest Nunthorpe was not a great race for quality—interestingly, the first nine were all aged at least five—but it hardly wanted for anything else. *D. Nicholls*

YANABI (USA) 2 b.f. (Apr 23) Silver Hawk (USA) 123 – Halholah (USA) 65 76 (Secreto (USA) 128) [1997 6m³ 7g⁶ 7m³ 7d² Oct 13] rangy filly: has scope: fifth foal: sister to smart 6f (at 2 yrs) to 10.5f winner Murajja and 1993 2-y-o 6f winner Tablah, and half-sister to fairly useful 7f (at 2 yrs) to 9f winner Hilaala (by Elmaamul): dam daughter of half-sister to Alydar: fair form when placed in maidens at Goodwood, Kempton and Leicester, no match for impressive La Nuit Rose on last-named course: will be suited by at least 1m: has started slowly. *P. T. Walwyn*

YANAVANAVANO (IRE) 3 b.g. Maledetto (IRE) 103 – Dublin Millennium – (Dalsaan 125) [1996 –: 5.2d 5.1g 1997 a7g 8.3g 8.5s Jul 2] of no account. *G. Lewis*

YANGTZE (IRE) 3 b.g. River Falls 113 – Sister Dympna 63 (Grundy 137) [1996 – –: 5g 7m 7.1m 1997 14.1m⁶ 11.8g 8s⁵ Jun 26] angular colt: behind in maidens and handicaps: tried blinkered. *B. R. Millman*

YANOMAMI (USA) 2 ch.f. (Apr 11) Slew O'Gold (USA) – Sunerta (USA) 75 71 (Roberto (USA) 131) [1997 7g³ 6m² Sep 26] fourth living foal: half-sister to 3 winners including fairly useful 7f (at 2 yrs) and 12.5f winner Ivory Palm (by Sir Ivor) and 3-y-o Sun Alert: dam 7f winner at 2 yrs, half-sister to Horris Hill winner Super Asset and US Grade 1 winners Bates Motel and Hatim: fair form in 4-runner maidens at Goodwood and Redcar: should prove suited by 1m+: sold 15,000 gns in December. *J. H. M. Gosden*

YANSHAN 2 b.g. (Feb 17) Anshan 119 – Joy of Freedom 57 (Damister (USA) – 123) [1997 7d 7.9s 8f⁵ Sep 18] 5,500Y: useful-looking gelding: first foal: dam 4-y-o 9.7f winner: only a little sign of ability in maidens. *Bob Jones*

YAROB (IRE) 4 ch.c. Unfuwain (USA) 131 – Azyaa 101 (Kris 135) [1996 99: 7m 96 7.1d⁴ 10.3g⁶ 10.1m² 10.4m 10m a8f⁵ 1997 11f* a10f⁵ a10f⁵ 10.1g⁴ 12d Oct 16] quite good-topped colt: useful on his day: trained by P. Rudkin first 3 starts, winning handicap at Abu Dhabi in January: ran respectably first of 2 starts on return to Britain: stays 11f: acts on firm ground, probably not on sand: edgy sort: inconsistent: sold 19,000 gns, and joined D. Loder. *R. Akehurst*

YASHMAK (USA) 3 b.f. Danzig (USA) – Slightly Dangerous (USA) 122 118 (Roberto (USA) 131) [1996 110: 6m* 7.1m² 8d² 1997 8m 10d* 12m⁴ 12g* 12m² 10f* Oct 4]

    In view of her name it's rather appropriate that Yashmak should have required a hood on occasions to help overcome a reluctance to enter the stalls, a reluctance which required her to pass a stalls test after she'd given a mulish

Ribblesdale Stakes, Royal Ascot—yet another procession at the meeting as Yashmak storms clear

Flower Bowl Invitational Handicap, Belmont Park—
Yashmak records the only overseas win of the year for the Cecil stable

display at the start of the Ribblesdale Stakes at Royal Ascot in June. It was touch and go whether Yashmak would take part in the Ribblesdale, yet once racing she showed her usual enthusiasm for the job and ran out the easiest winner of the meeting, moving smoothly into the lead three furlongs from home and going clear early in the straight to beat Akdariya by nine lengths. It was the second time Yashmak had won by this unusual margin, the first being when she'd trounced a much weaker field in the Vodafone Group Fillies' Trial Stakes at Newbury five weeks earlier. That victory put her very much into the reckoning for the Oaks at Epsom, a race for which she started second favourite behind her stable-companion Reams of Verse, a filly also in the same ownership. Yashmak acquitted herself much better in the Oaks than she'd done on her classic debut, when beating only one home over an inadequate trip in the One Thousand Guineas at Newmarket, finishing less than three lengths behind Reams of Verse in fourth. Two places behind her came Ebadiyla who was to deny Yashmak a classic victory just a few days after the latter had passed her stalls test, in the Irish Oaks at the Curragh. Yashmak again gave a deal of trouble at the start yet ran a genuine race, though unable to match Ebadiyla for pace in the final furlong. This was Yashmak's final outing on this side of the Atlantic, but she did appear once more on the racecourse, at Belmont Park in October, when she was the only three-year-old and only European challenger in an eight-runner field for the Flower Bowl Invitational Handicap. A Grade 1 event restricted to fillies and mares, it provided Yashmak with her most important success and also gave her the opportunity to confirm that there was nothing wrong with her attitude once the race had begun. One of four virtually in line a furlong out, Yashmak had to battle to get her head in front and then retain her half-length lead over the very smart fillies Maxzene and Memories of

Mr K. Abdulla's "Yashmak"

Silver. Shortly afterwards it was announced that Yashmak had been retired to stud at her owner's Juddmonte Farm in Kentucky.

		Northern Dancer	Nearctic
	Danzig (USA)	(b 1961)	Natalma
	(b 1977)	Pas de Nom	Admiral's Voyage
Yashmak (USA)		(b or br 1968)	Petitioner
(b.f. 1994)		Roberto	Hail To Reason
	Slightly Dangerous (USA)	(b 1969)	Bramalea
	(b 1979)	Where You Lead	Raise A Native
		(ch 1970)	Noblesse

Yashmak's form is virtually on a par with that shown by her dam Slightly Dangerous, but if she proves just half as successful as a broodmare then she will still be doing very well. The essay on Yashmak's younger sister, Jibe, contains full details of the stud record of Slightly Dangerous. Watch out for potential Epsom Oaks candidates among Yashmak's future progeny. This is a race which has figured prominently in the bottom line of her pedigree. Her dam and grandam both finished second in it while her great grandam Noblesse was a ten-length winner of the 1963 renewal. Yashmak, a close-coupled, quite attractive filly, was effective at a mile and a quarter and a mile and a half on ground ranging from firm to good to soft. *H. R. A. Cecil*

YAVERLAND (IRE) 5 b.h. Astronef 116 – Lautreamont (Auction Ring (USA) –
123) [1996 61: 10m⁵ 10g 10m a11g³ 1997 10g 10d 8.2d a11g Dec 8] big, strong
horse: maiden handicapper: no show in 1997. *John Berry*

YAVLENSKY (IRE) 3 b.c. Caerleon (USA) 132 – Schwanensee (USA) (Mr 102
Leader (USA)) [1996 97p: 7.5d 7.6m⁵ 8d* 9s² 1997 10d⁴ 9.9s² 12f 10s³ 10.3m⁴ 12f
Sep 21] neat colt: useful performer: best efforts when placed in minor event at
Beverley (head second to Indiscreet) in May and listed race at Milan (4 lengths third
to Jaunty Jack) in June: ran poorly last 2 starts: should stay 1½m: acts on soft going,
below form on ground firmer than good: returned to Italy. *J. L. Dunlop*

YEAST 5 b.g. Salse (USA) 128 – Orient 106 (Bay Express 132) [1996 114: 8s* 94
7m* 7.6m² 8m⁵ 10g 8m* 8g 8m* 9m 1997 8m² 7m 8m Sep 13] big, good-bodied
gelding: smart performer at 4 yrs: well below form in 1997, including when 4 lengths
second to Canyon Creek in listed race at Doncaster in March: tailed off final start:
effective at 7f to 1m: acts on good to firm and soft ground: usually front runner.
W. J. Haggas

YEATH (IRE) 5 ch.g. Exhibitioner 111 – Grain of Sand (Sandford Lad 133) –
[1996 –: a8g 9.7m 7g 1997 11.9f Apr 11] no longer of any account. *S. Dow*

YELLOW DRAGON (IRE) 4 b.g. Kefaah (USA) 124 – Veldt (High Top 131) – §
[1996 –§, a51§: a12g⁶ a10g⁶ 12f⁵ 10m a10g⁵ 10m a11g* a12g a13g 9.7g 11.6m
11.5m a10g⁴ 11.5m 1997 a12g⁶ Feb 20] temperamental handicapper: well beaten
only 4-y-o start. *B. A. Pearce*

YEOMAN OLIVER 4 b.c. Precocious 126 – Impala Lass 81 (Kampala 120) 63
[1996 73: a7g² a8g² a8g³ a8g a8.5g* a8.5g² 8.2g⁶ 10g⁶ 8m⁴ a8g* 8.1d² a9.4g a9.4g a73
a9.4g* a8.5g⁵ 7.1s⁴ 8g² 8.1s a9.4g² a9.4g a8.5s³ a9.4g 1997 a8g* a8g² a7g³ a7g a8g⁴
8.2d⁵ a9.4g⁶ a8g² Dec 18] fair handicapper on all-weather, modest on turf: won at
Southwell in January: mostly ran creditably after: stays 9.4f: acts on soft ground, best
efforts on fibresand: blinkered: usually races prominently. *B. A. McMahon*

YET AGAIN 5 ch.g. Weldnaas (USA) 112 – Brightelmstone 105 (Prince Regent 61
(FR) 129) [1996 53+: 12f 12m 10s 10d 8m³ 10m 10.8f* 9.7g 9.2g⁶ 12s a12g* 1997
a12g* a13g* 10.8m⁶ 11.9f* 11.9f⁴ 12d² 12d² 12m⁵ 11.6m⁵ 12.1g* 12.3m³ Aug 16]
compact, good-bodied gelding: modest handicapper: in good form in 1997, winning
at Lingfield (twice) in January, Brighton in April and Chepstow in August: stays 13f:
acts on firm and dead going and on equitrack: blinkered earlier in career: fairly useful
hurdler: game. *Miss Gay Kelleway*

YOKOHAMA (USA) 6 gr.h. Theatrical 128 – Griddle (ARG) (Off Shore Gamble 115
(USA)) [1996 10g* 11f 1997 12g⁵ 12d² 15d² 15g² 12m* 12f Oct 5] tall, rangy horse:
second foal: half-brother to a juvenile listed winner in USA by Herat: dam Grade 2
winner in Argentina: won 8 of 17 starts, in no better than allowance company, in
USA at 3 yrs to 5 yrs before leaving W. Mott: had run consistently in France, before
improved form when receiving good ride to win 8-runner Prix Foy at Longchamp by
length from Nothin' Leica Dane, setting steady pace then quickening: last of 18 in
Arc on same course last time: stays 15f: acts on firm and dead ground. *Mme C. Head,
France*

YO-MATE 6 b.g. Komaite (USA) – Silent Sun 90 (Blakeney 126) [1996 NR 1997 –
16d Jun 23] no sign of ability. *T. Hind*

YORKIE GEORGE 3 b.c. Efisio 120 – Petonica (IRE) 77 (Petoski 135) [1996 102
87: 6g 6g* 6s* 7s³ 1997 6m 6g 6g² 6d⁵ 7s³ 7g* 6m 8m⁴ Sep 13] sturdy, lengthy,
attractive colt: useful handicapper: won rated stakes at Yarmouth in July by 2½
lengths from Intisab: stayed 1m: acted on good to firm and soft ground: broke
near-hind pastern in late-September and was put down. *L. M. Cumani*

YORKIES BOY 2 gr.c. Clantime 101 – Slipperose 72 (Persepolis (FR) 97
127) [1997 5m 5s⁴ 5m 5m² 5.1m* 5d⁴ 5.2f⁴ 5g 5g² 5d⁴ 5.2d⁵ 6g⁴ Oct 25] 9,500Y:
leggy, useful-looking colt: fourth foal: dam 11.5f winner: useful performer: won
maiden at Chester in June: generally ran well afterwards, in frame in listed races at
York and Doncaster ninth and final starts: stays 6f: acts on firm and dead ground:
races prominently: tough and genuine. *B. A. McMahon*

YORKSHIRE (IRE) 3 ch.c. Generous (IRE) 139 – Ausherra (USA) 106 (Diesis 108
133) [1996 90p: 8d* 1997 10.4g 10.3m² 11.8d³ 12g 8s⁴ 12m² Aug 15] rangy colt:

looked good prospect only 2-y-o start: rather disappointing for much of 1997, but raced less freely and put up best effort when length second of 3 to Busy Flight in minor event at Newbury on final outing: stays 1½m: acts on good to firm and dead ground: blinkered (well held in German Derby) fourth start. *P. F. I. Cole*

YOUDONTSAY 5 ch.m. Most Welcome 131 – Fabulous Luba (Luthier 126) [1996 85: 6m⁴ 6f 5m* 5m 5g² 5m 6m 5g 1997 6s* 6g 6.1m⁵ 5d 5s⁵ 6d 7m Nov 1] workmanlike mare: fairly useful handicapper: won at Lingfield in May: effective at 5f to 7f: acts on firm and soft ground: best held up for late burst: none too consistent. *T. J. Naughton*   85

YOUNG ANNABEL (USA) 4 ch.f. Cahill Road (USA) – Only For Eve (USA) 87 (Barachois (CAN)) [1996 62, a68: 8.2d⁶ 7m 8m a7g* 7g⁵ a8g 7.9g 1997 a8g² a8g a7g³ May 12] lengthy filly: fair handicapper on all-weather, modest (not tried in 1997) on turf: stays 1m: acts on fibresand, ran poorly on equitrack. *C. A. Dwyer*   – a71

YOUNG BEN (IRE) 5 ch.g. Fayruz 116 – Jive (Ahonoora 122) [1996 41: a6g⁶ a7g a6g 5f 7.5m 5g³ 5m⁶ 5m³ 5m 5g³ 5m⁵ 6m 1997 a6g a6g 5g 5m³ 5g 5m* 5g² 6g 5g a5g 5m³ 5s 5g Oct 22] smallish gelding: modest 5f handicapper: won at Beverley in July: acts on good to firm ground, well beaten on soft and fibresand: visored or blinkered: inconsistent. *J. S. Wainwright*   55 a–

YOUNG BENSON 5 b.g. Zalazl (USA) 120 – Impala Lass 81 (Kampala 120) [1996 63: a8g⁶ a8.5g⁵ a11g³ a11g 10.8g 7m* a7g* a8.5g³ a7g a7g a9.4g⁶ 1997 8m Sep 22] workmanlike gelding: modest performer at 4 yrs: well beaten only start in 1997. *T. Wall*   –

YOUNG BIGWIG (IRE) 3 b.g. Anita's Prince 126 – Humble Mission (Shack (USA) 118) [1996 95: 5m⁴ a5g* 5g² 6m² 5.2f² 6m* 6d⁵ 6m³ 1997 6g⁵ 6d⁵ 6m 5m 6g 6s 6m 7m³ 6m a6g Dec 13] strong, lengthy gelding: useful performer at best: patchy form in 1997, sold out of Jack Berry's stable after eighth start: stays 6f: acts on firm ground and fibresand, probably dead: tried blinkered, no improvement. *D. W. Chapman*   89

YOUNG BUTT 4 ch.g. Bold Owl 101 – Cymbal 80 (Ribero 126) [1996 66: a11g⁵ 8f 8s* 10g³ 10m 1997 a12g 8d Oct 16] leggy gelding: fair handicapper, lightly raced: well beaten in 1997. *B. A. Pearce*   –

YOUNG DALESMAN 4 br.g. Teenoso (USA) 135 – Fabulous Molly (Whitstead 125) [1996 NR 1997 8.2g 10s Jul 5] workmanlike gelding: no worthwhile form on flat: winner over hurdles in August. *A. Streeter*   –

YOUNG DUKE (IRE) 9 gr.g. Double Schwartz 128 – Princess Pamela 70 (Dragonara Palace (USA) 115) [1996 80: 7m* 7f* 7.1f³ᵈⁱˢ 7.3m³ 1997 8d² Jun 25] leggy gelding: reportedly suffers from leg problems: formerly fairly useful performer: very lightly raced of late, and well below best when second in claimer at Salisbury on only 9-y-o start: stays 1m: acts on firm ground, soft and equitrack: effective in blinkers or visor, has worn neither since 1992: sometimes carries head awkwardly and wanders under pressure. *Mrs S. D. Williams*   51

YOUNG FREDERICK (IRE) 4 ch.g. Polish Patriot (USA) 128 – Notre Histoire (Habitat 134) [1996 –, a63: a7g³ a7g³ a7g⁵ 7s 8g 1997 a10g⁶ a8g⁵ a8.5g a7g 11.7m⁴ 8.3g Aug 4] poor maiden: left K. Burke after fourth start: should stay 1m: acts on the all-weather, well beaten on turf: tried blinkered and visored. *N. M. Babbage*   38

YOUNG IBNR (IRE) 2 b.g. (Mar 18) Imperial Frontier (USA) 112 – Zalatia 97 (Music Boy 124) [1997 5s 5m* 5.1d² 5.1d⁵ 5d⁶ 5m⁴ Jun 6] 12,000Y: small gelding: half-brother to several winners, including Irish 1995 2-y-o 5f winner Minzal Legend (by Primo Dominie) and 6-y-o Little Ibnr: dam 7f winner: fairly useful form at best: won maiden at Pontefract in April: good second in minor event at Nottingham later in month: long way below form final 2 starts: raced only at 5f: visored penultimate outing. *P. D. Evans*   81

YOUNG JOSH 2 b.c. (Feb 6) Warning 136 – Title Roll (IRE) 107 (Tate Gallery (USA) 117) [1997 6.1m⁶ 6g* 6g Oct 18] 20,000F: first foal: dam effective at 5f to 7f: promising colt: won maiden at Goodwood in September by neck from dead-heaters Chief Whip and Uplifting: far from discredited when short on experience and facing   84 p stiff task in Two-Year-Old Trophy at Redcar following month: should improve and make useful sprinting 3-y.-o. *J. H. M. Gosden*

YOUNG MARCIUS (USA)   3 ch.g. Green Dancer (USA) 132 – Manhatten   –
Miss 94 (Artaius (USA) 129) [1996 NR 1997 10g Jun 16] $20,000Y: tall gelding: fifth foal: half-brother to Italian 6f to 7.5f winner Black Dimention (by Sallust): dam Irish 6f winner: green when never-nearer twelfth of 24 in maiden at Windsor: moved poorly to post. *P. F. I. Cole*

YOUNG PRECEDENT   3 b.c. Polish Precedent (USA) 131 – Guyum   89
(Rousillon (USA) 133) [1996 65p: 7d⁴ 1997 7m* 8m² 8.5m⁶ 7.3m* 7m 8d Oct 16] rangy colt: fairly useful performer: won maiden at Thirsk in May and handicap at Newbury (gamely) in August: well held in competitive handicaps last 2 starts: likely to prove best at 7f/1m: acts on good to firm ground. *P. W. Harris*

YOUNG TESS   7 b.m. Teenoso (USA) 135 – Bundu (FR) 88 (Habitat 134) [1996   –
NR 1997 a16g Jan 10] well held in Southwell claimer on only flat outing since 1993: won over hurdles in March. *P. Bowen*

YOUNICO   2 b.c. (Apr 22) Nordico (USA) – Young Wilkie (Callernish) [1997 a7g   – p
Dec 10] half-brother to 1½m winners Magic Times and Yougo (both by Good Times): dam fourth both starts over hurdles: slowly away when tenth of 10 in maiden at Lingfield: bred to do better over 1m+. *M. Johnston*

YOUR MOST WELCOME   6 b.m. Most Welcome 131 – Blues Player 70   67
(Jaazeiro (USA) 127) [1996 62, a66: a10g⁶ a10g* a10g a8g a10g* 12m 9m* 10g 12g 10f⁵ a12s⁴ a10g 1997 9d⁵ 10g² 10.2m³ 10m² 10g* 10s 12m⁵ Sep 10] good-bodied mare: fair handicapper: in good form in 1997, and won at Salisbury in August: effective at 1¼m and 1½m: acted on firm ground and equitrack, below form on soft: no improvement in blinkers: held up: in foal to Beveled. *D. J. S. ffrench Davis*

YOURS IN SPORT   3 b.g. Slip Anchor 136 – Birthdays' Child (Caerleon (USA)   65 d
132) [1996 NR 1997 8m⁵ 10m 10m 11.8g 15d Sep 18] leggy, unfurnished gelding: first foal: dam, should have been suited by further tham 1m, half-sister to smart 5f to 1m winner Shasavaan: fair form on debut, modest at best afterwards: should be suited by further than 1m. *J. W. Watts*

YOUR THE LIMIT (IRE)   4 b.g. Don't Forget Me 127 – Excruciating (CAN)   39
(Bold Forbes (USA)) [1996 7v 12d 12g 10d 11d 10g 1997 8d 7.8g a8g³ 12.5g 8d a11g⁶ Dec 8] half-brother to 3 winners, notably smart Lucky Lindy (stayed 1¼m, by Trojan Fen): dam unplaced: poor maiden: trained by P. J. Flynn in Ireland prior to final start: tried blinkered. *J. Parkes*

YUPPY GIRL (IRE)   4 ch.f. Salt Dome (USA) – Sloane Ranger 84 (Sharpen Up   41 d
127) [1996 52: a7g⁴ a8.5g³ 8.1g⁵ 8m 10g 10m² 10g 10.8m⁵ a12g 10f 8m⁴ a11g⁶ 1997 a8g 8m⁶ 10g³ 10d 10.8s 11.1d 9.9g Aug 23] sparely-made filly: poor performer: well beaten most starts in 1997: stays 1¼m: acts on good to firm ground: tried visored: difficult ride and not to be trusted. *Capt. J. Wilson*

Z

ZAAHIR (IRE)   3 b.g. Marju (IRE) 127 – Abhaaj 91 (Kris 135) [1996 75p: 6g³   72
1997 7m⁶ 8g⁴ 8g⁴ 8g 10.9s Oct 13] fair form at best in maidens: sold from B. Hills after fourth start and gelded: tailed off on only outing for new yard: may prove best short of 1m. *W. Storey*

ZAALEFF (USA)   5 ch.h. Zilzal (USA) 137 – Continual (USA) (Damascus   –
(USA)) [1996 54d: 7g 14.1g a12g⁴ a12g⁵ 10m³ a9.4g 10m² 8.2m 8.3g⁴ 10f 10m 1997 10g 8d Oct 13] strong, lengthy horse: modest maiden handicapper: well held in 1997, giving impression something amiss final start. *K. Mahdi*

ZABRISKIE   3 b.c. Polish Precedent (USA) 131 – Somfas (USA) (What A   75 d
Pleasure (USA)) [1996 NR 1997 a7g 7g² 8.3s⁴ 7.1d⁴ 6m Aug 17] brother to fair 7f

winner Sombreffe, closely related to smart sprinters Russian Bond and Snaadee (both by Danzig) and half-brother to several winners, notably smart Cristofori (probably stayed 1½m, by Fappiano): dam, from excellent family, won up to 7f: easily best effort in maidens when second at Thirsk in June, hanging left: bought out of M. Stoute's stable after next start, well beaten for new connections: tried blinkered: needs treating with caution. *G. L. Moore*

ZACAROON   6 b.m. Last Tycoon 131 – Samaza (USA) 90 (Arctic Tern (USA)   51
126) [1996 –: a8g a10g 11.4d⁴ 8f 8.1s 1997 a10g³ a12g* a12g³ a12g Mar 13] lengthy mare: only modest towards end of career: won selling handicap at Lingfield in January: broke leg final start: stayed 1½m: acted on the all-weather, good to firm and dead ground: visored (ran well) once: usually held up: dead. *J. Ffitch-Heyes*

ZADA   2 b.c. (May 5) Distant Relative 128 – Handy Dancer 87 (Green God 128)   ?
[1997 7.1g 8m 7d 8s a8g⁵ a10s² Nov 28] good-topped colt: half-brother to several   a58 ?
winners, including 3-y-o Mersey Beat, smart 1m to 1½m winner Karinga Bay (by Ardross) and useful 1½m and 2m winner Roll A Dollar (by Spin of A Coin): dam 1¼m winner: modest maiden: swerved and unseated rider stalls second start: best effort second at Lingfield, forcing pace: will stay 1½m+. *G. L. Moore*

ZAFARELLI   3 gr.g. Nishapour (FR) 125 – Voltigeuse (USA) (Filiberto (USA)   61
123) [1996 –: 8g 1997 16f² 11.9f⁵ 15.4s* 16m⁶ 16.4s Aug 29] leggy gelding: modest handicapper: trained on reappearance by S. Williams: won at Folkestone in July: soundly beaten last 2 starts: stays 2m well: acts on soft going, probably on firm: refused to enter stalls second intended start. *J. R. Jenkins*

ZAFORUM   4 b.c. Deploy 131 – Beau's Delight (USA) (Lypheor 118) [1996 100:   –
12m⁶ 11.5f³ 12m 16.2m 14g⁵ 14m* 16g³ 1997 16g Apr 18] strong colt: useful performer at 3 yrs: well held only start in 1997. *L. Montague Hall*

ZAGROS (IRE)   3 b.g. Persian Heights 129 – Hana Marie 101§ (Formidable   –
(USA) 125) [1996 –: 5.9g 1997 8m 8.1m⁶ 8d Sep 2] heavy-topped gelding: no form. *T. D. Easterby*

ZAHAALIE (USA)   5 ch.g. Zilzal (USA) 137 – Bambee T T (USA) (Better Bee)   –
[1996 a7g³ a8g⁵ a9.9g a12g 1997 a12f a9.4g⁵ 8m Sep 22] close-coupled gelding: ran twice here at 2 yrs for M. Stoute: subsequently went to UAE, but well held there on reappearance and no form on flat on return to Britain, including in blinkers: won selling hurdle in December. *J. A. Pickering*

ZAHID (USA)   6 ch.g. Storm Cat (USA) – Time An' Care (USA) (Twin Time   –
(USA)) [1996 –, a64: a10g² a10g² a10g* a9.4g* a9.4g³ a10g² 9.7m a10s a10g³ a12g³   a51
a10g⁶ 1997 a12g³ a12g³ a10g² Feb 25] good-topped gelding: impresses in appearance: modest performer on all-weather (no recent form on turf): stays 1½m: effective blinkered/visored or not. *K. R. Burke*

ZAHIR (USA)   3 b.c. Riverman (USA) 131 – Manwah (USA) 72 (Lyphard (USA)   –
132) [1996 NR 1997 8m² May 2] rather leggy colt: has been fired: first foal: dam, middle-distance maiden, closely related to Unfuwain and half-sister to Nashwan: weak in market, moved poorly to post, gave trouble in stalls and proved reluctant leader when beaten 8 lengths by Mythical in 2-runner Challenge Whip at Newmarket. *Saeed bin Suroor*

ZAHRAN (IRE)   6 b.h. Groom Dancer (USA) 128 – Welsh Berry (USA) (Sir Ivor   38
135) [1996 46, a49: a8g³ a7g³ a8g a8g a8g³ 8f 8f⁴ 8g² 10m³ 9m⁵ 10.8f⁶ 8.2m⁶ 10m²   a43
9.7g⁴ 10g 10f 10m⁶ a10g a9.2f⁶ 10d 10.1m⁴ a8g³ a8g* a10s a8g³ a8g 1997 a7g² a8g a8g⁵ 8g⁴ 6.9m³ 8f⁴ 10.1f² 10d 8.1m⁴ 8m⁴ 10m 8.3g a10g⁴ Aug 9] good-topped horse: unimpressive mover: poor handicapper: effective at 7f to 1¼m: acts on firm and soft ground and on the all-weather: tried visored/blinkered earlier in career: reliable. *J. M. Bradley*

ZA-IM   3 b.c. Green Desert (USA) 127 – Al Bahathri (USA) 123 (Blushing Groom   105
(FR) 131) [1996 100p: 5.7d⁵ 6s* 1997 7g² 8m 7g² 6g* 6f 6s 6d Oct 17] smallish, good-bodied colt: useful performer: best effort when winning minor event at Haydock in July by length from Indian Spark: races freely, and best at up to 7f: possibly needs good ground or softer (unimpressive to post and probably had something amiss on good to firm in 2000 Guineas): sent to UAE. *B. W. Hills*

1062

ZAIMA (IRE)　3 b.f. Green Desert (USA) 127 – Usaylah 98 (Siberian Express　92
(USA) 125) [1996 82: 6.1f⁵ 6m⁴ 6m⁴ 7f* 8m³ 1997 7m³ 8m⁴ 7d² 7m 7s Jul 2] angular,
good-topped filly: fairly useful handicapper: clearly best effort in 1997 when second
to Captain Collins at Goodwood: effective at 7f/1m: acts on firm and dead going:
sold 12,500 gns in December. *J. L. Dunlop*

ZAIN DANCER　5 ch.g. Nabeel Dancer (USA) 120 – Trojan Lady (USA) (Irish　43 §
River (FR) 131) [1996 59: a7g⁶ 7s 7m 7g² 7.1g² 8f³ 7m⁴ 7g⁶ 7m³ 7g 1997 5s 6.1m　a55 §
5.9g a6g a7g⁴ 6g a6g* 7g 6g 6d a7g Dec 18] good-topped gelding: has a long stride:
modest handicapper: gambled on when winning strongly-run race at Southwell in
July, easily best run of year: effective at 6f to 1m: acts on firm ground and fibresand,
below form on dead going or softer: tried blinkered: very slowly away twice, and not
one to rely on. *D. Nicholls*

ZALAIYKA (FR)　2 b.f. (Apr 13) Royal Academy (USA) 130 – Zanadiyka (FR)　107 p
(Akarad (FR) 130) [1997 8d⁵ 8g* 8s* Oct 21] second foal: dam listed winner at 6.5f
and 1m and placed in numerous pattern races: won 15-runner minor event at
Chantilly in September (by 4 lengths) and 7-runner Prix des Reservoirs at Deauville
in October (by ¾ length from Insight): stays 1m: unraced on ground firmer than
good: smart performer in the making. *A. de Royer Dupre, France*

ZALITZINE (USA)　3 b.f. Zilzal (USA) 137 – Bitooh 117 (Seattle Slew (USA))　98
[1996 NR 1997 8g* 10m² 10.1d³ 10.2g³ 9g³ Oct 25] rather leggy filly: second foal:
dam, French 7f performer, won Criterium de Maisons-Laffitte at 2 yrs: useful
performer: won maiden at Kempton in May: good efforts in minor events and
handicap all starts afterwards: not sure to stay much beyond 1¼m: yet to race on
extremes of going. *M. R. Stoute*

ZALOTTO (IRE)　3 b.g. Polish Patriot (USA) 128 – Honest Penny (USA)　–
(Honest Pleasure (USA)) [1996 –: 7g 1997 6g 5s⁵ 7s 6.1d a6g² a9.4g a6g² a8g² 7.1g　a69
a8g³ a7g² a8g³ a8g² Dec 8] leggy gelding: fair maiden handicapper: runner-up 5
times at Southwell: stays 1m: acts on fibresand, little form on turf: blinkered fifth
start onwards. *T. J. Etherington*

ZAMALEK (USA)　5 b.g. Northern Baby (CAN) 127 – Chellingoua (USA)　54
(Sharpen Up 127) [1996 –: 7f 8g 12m 10m 10m a10g⁶ 8m 1997 a7g⁶ a8g a10g*
a10g³ 10m 10m* 9d⁴ 9.7s⁵ 10m 10m* 8.1g² 12m² 10m⁴ 10m 16m Sep 25] sturdy
gelding: modest handicapper: won at Lingfield in January and June and at Sandown
in July, including 2 apprentice events: stays 1½m: acts on equitrack and on good
to firm and soft ground: tried blinkered/visored: has run well when sweating.
R. M. Flower

ZAMARRA　2 ch.f. (Feb 24) Clantime 101 – Poshteen 86 (Royal Smoke 113)　59 ?
[1997 5.1m 6m 5.1g 7f Oct 3] 2,600Y: unimpressive mover: half-sister to winning
stayer Capa (by New Member) and the dam of useful sprinter Cape Merino (by
Clantime): dam 2-y-o 5f winner: signs of ability in maidens: soundly beaten in
nursery final start. *Major D. N. Chappell*

ZAMBEZI (USA)　2 b. or br.f. (Feb 20) Rahy (USA) 115 – Zonda 100 (Fabulous　75
Dancer (USA) 124) [1997 6.1m⁴ 7g² Aug 5] second foal: dam, 5f and 6f winner who
probably stayed 1m, from family of Oh So Sharp: fair form in maidens at Nottingham
and Catterick 17 days apart, tending to hang left both times: sent to France.
D. R. Loder

ZAMHAREER (USA)　6 b.g. Lear Fan (USA) 130 – Awenita (Rarity 129) [1996　40
55: 14.1m⁵ 16.1g* 16g* 16.2f⁶ 15.9m 16s 17.5m 1997 16m 12m⁴ 14g 16d³ 15.8s⁴
16g⁵ Jul 7] rather leggy gelding: poor handicapper: should stay further than 2m: best
form on good ground or softer: tried visored, no improvement: usually forces pace.
W. Storey

ZAMINDAR (USA)　3 b.c. Gone West (USA) – Zaizafon (USA) 119 (The　116
Minstrel (CAN) 135) [1996 116: 5.5d* 6g* 6g² 7m³ 1997 8m⁵ 6g² 8m⁵ Aug 17] big,
strong, good-topped colt: brother to Zafonic: smart performer: one of the leading
French 2-y-o's in 1996 (placed in Prix Morny and Prix de la Salamandre): really took
the eye and relaxed in preliminaries, unlucky not to be placed when 3 lengths fifth of
16 to Entrepreneur in strongly-run 2000 Guineas at Newmarket, set lot to do then

running on strongly from over 1f out: reported in June to be suffering from minor skin infection: below best at Deauville in Prix de Ris-Orangis (¾-length second to Monaassib) and Prix Jacques le Marois (found little): stayed 1m: unraced on extremes of going: retired to Banstead Manor Stud, near Newmarket (fee £7,000, Oct 1st). *A. Fabre, France*

ZANABAY   3 b.f. Unfuwain (USA) 131 – Chrisanthy 81 (So Blessed 130) [1996 53: 5.2d 7m⁴ 7f 6d⁴ 6m⁵ 1997 a7g⁵ 13.8m⁴ 12d 12g a10s Nov 10] modest form at 2 yrs, well held in 1997: left M. Meade after reappearance, W. Storey after fourth start. *G. Fierro*   –

ZANKLE (USA)   4 b.g. Opening Verse (USA) 126 – Capre (USA) (Seattle Slew (USA)) [1996 7.8s 6g 5m 5d 5g 8.5g* 8.5m* 10g⁶ 7m⁴ 8.5m* 1997 11d 8d* 8.5d³ 6d⁵ 9m Oct 4] rangy gelding: first foal: dam unraced half-sister to several at least useful winners, including Preakness Stakes third Fight Over: fairly useful handicapper: successful at Galway 3 times at 3 yrs: not seen out until June in 1997, improved form to win at the Curragh: good efforts afterwards, no extra final 1f after travelling well when eighth of 36 to Pasternak in Cambridgeshire at Newmarket: may prove ideally suited by around 1m: acts on good to firm and dead ground: all 4 wins from only 6 tries in blinkers, though has occasionally run well without. *D. K. Weld, Ireland*   94

ZANY LADY   2 gr.f. (May 1) Arzanni 115 – Lady Antonia 66 (Owen Anthony 102) [1997 7g⁴ Oct 7] half-sister to a winner abroad by Minster Son: dam lightly-raced maiden: 10/1 from 33/1, 5¾ lengths fourth of 14 to Red Leggings in maiden at Warwick: should do better at 1m+. *R. J. Hodges*   58 p

ZARALASKA   6 ch.g. Shernazar 131 – Eskimo Spring (USA) (Riverman   117
(USA) 131) [1996 90: 12g 12g 1997 11.9g⁵ 12m* 11.9g* 10m⁴ Jul 29]
        That rather less-than-hallowed institution the 'non-trier' produces its
share of headlines each season, the most high profile case on the flat in 1997
involving the Royal Ascot winner Zaralaska. Runner-up in the Bessborough
Handicap at the Royal meeting as a four-year-old, Zaralaska wasn't seen out
again until late the following season and was having only his third race in
nearly two years when catching the eye in a handicap at the York May meeting.
More blatant cases than Zaralaska's go unquestioned season after season but,
on this occasion, the York stewards considered that both the trainer and rider
were in breach of rule 151 (ii) (which states that every horse must be 'given a
full opportunity to win or of obtaining the best possible placing'). The rider,
5-lb claimer Royston Ffrench, was suspended for four days, and the trainer,
Luca Cumani, was fined £700 and had his attention drawn to the Jockey Club
instruction about 'schooling in public'. Furthermore, Zaralaska was suspended
from running for thirty days. That suspension ran until the Saturday before
Royal Ascot where, on the Wednesday, Zaralaska, ridden by Pat Eddery, won
the Bessborough in scintillating fashion, weaving his way through a big field
after being waited with and producing a fine turn of foot to win going away by
two and a half lengths from Nabhaan, whose trainer was quoted as saying 'It's
so annoying to be beaten by a horse you know has been cunningly handled.'
        To say that Zaralaska's win caused an uproar, particularly among
punters, would not be exaggerating, and the ramifications resulted in increased
penalties being put in place by the Jockey Club for the 1998 turf season.
Stewards will have the power to ban a jockey for up to twenty-one days (the
previous maximum was fourteen), fine a trainer up to a maximum of £3,000
(previously £2,000) and suspend a horse for up to forty days (previously thirty).
Furthermore, no horse suspended under the rule will be allowed to run its next
race in either a class A or B handicap, and any horse which wins a handicap
without previously having been in the first four will automatically have its
running referred to Portman Square (the first change appears to have been made
to prevent high-profile cases like that of Zaralaska, the second is aimed at
horses which are given three 'quiet' runs to qualify for a handicap mark).
Perhaps the Jockey Club could also use its wide-ranging powers to forbid a
suspended horse from being in the care of any licensed trainer during the period
of its ban; Zaralaska's victory in a race which may well have been his next
target anyway underlined the virtual ineffectiveness of the York punishment.

Bessborough Stakes (Handicap), Royal Ascot—
Zaralaska produces a fine turn of foot for a controversial victory;
Nabhaan and Willie Conquer are next to finish

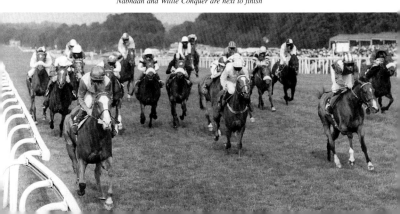

Letheby & Christopher Old Newton Cup (Handicap), Haydock—
another big win for Zaralaska; Nabhaan is again in his wake,
but this time My Learned Friend (left) and Raffles Rooster come between them

Zaralaska's performance at Royal Ascot showed him to be better than ever and he defied a much-publicised 13 lb-rise by the BHB handicapper to record another impressive win in a hotly-contested mile-and-a-half handicap, the Letheby & Christopher Old Newton Cup at Haydock in July, Eddery being able to ease him near the finish after having the race in safe keeping throughout the final furlong. Raised another 9 lb in the handicap, Zaralaska ran his final race for Cumani when an excellent fourth under 10-0 in the William Hill Cup over a mile and a quarter at Goodwood. Zaralaska remained more than able, in our view, to make his mark stepped up to listed or Group 3 company, but in late-August it was announced that he had joined David Nicholson to go hurdling. Cumani made the point that handicappers at the top of the scale who fall short of pattern standard have limited opportunities on the flat in Britain. 'We cater very well for the top-class horses and for horses rated 0-95, but those rated between 95 and 115 have very little opportunity. If an owner has an offer for a horse in that category it could be worth £100,000 to £150,000 and sadly the trainer has to tell him to sell.' Too many good quality horses are being lost to flat racing in Britain each year—a good number are campaigned abroad while others are sold for the reasons Cumani outlined—and catering for them should be a major priority. The BHB's response—to propose twenty or thirty additional rated stakes (handicaps with a limited weight range)—seems unlikely to prove an adequate solution.

		Busted	Crepello
	Shernazar	(b 1963)	Sans Le Sou
	(b 1981)	Sharmeen	Val de Loir
Zaralaska		(b 1972)	Nasreen
(ch.g. 1991)		Riverman	Never Bend
	Eskimo Spring (USA)	(b 1969)	River Lady
	(ch 1986)	Wintergrace	Northern Dancer
		(ch 1979)	Stylish Pattern

The sturdy, quite attractive Zaralaska, who has a quick action, is one of only two winners (the other in Italy) out of Eskimo Spring, an unraced half-sister to the Eclipse and Sussex Stakes winner Artaius. He is also a rare good performer sired by the middle-distance stayer Shernazar, the best of whose offspring has been the Prix Ganay winner and Arlington Million third Kartajana. Zaralaska stays a mile and a half and acts on good to firm going. He has a good turn of foot and is usually held up. *L. M. Cumani*

ZARETSKI   3 b.g. Pursuit of Love 124 – Tolstoya (Northfields (USA)) [1996 77:   **91 d**
5m 6m³ 6m⁴ 7m² 7f⁴ 6m 1997 7m* 8g⁴ 6m 7g⁵ 6d 7g 7m Oct 4] strong, good-bodied
gelding: carries condition: fairly useful performer at best: made all in maiden at
Doncaster in March: best effort when fourth to Pelham in listed race at Kempton:
disappointing afterwards: will prove best up to 1m: acts on firm ground: pulled hard
and ran poorly only try in blinkers. *C. E. Brittain*

ZATOPEK   5 b. or br.g. Reprimand 122 – Executive Lady 59 (Night Shift (USA))   **–**
[1996 65d: 6.9s³ 8d 7.3s 8m⁵ a9.4g a12g² a9.4g⁶ a12g a8g 1997 a11s⁶ a11g⁵ a12g²   **a46**
a12g³ a12g² a12g a11g⁴ 10g a11g² 11.6g a11g⁴ 12s 12.1d Aug 25] sturdy gelding:
poor maiden: will stay beyond 1½m: raced mainly on fibresand nowadays: tried
blinkered/visored. *J. Cullinan*

ZAYA   2 ch.c. (Mar 23) Zafonic (USA) 130 – Ayah (USA) 74 (Secreto (USA) 128)   **97 p**
[1997 7g* Oct 24] tall, good sort, shade unfurnished: has been fired: third foal:
half-brother to useful Irish 1995 2-y-o 7f and 1m winner Aylesbury (by Lycius): dam
thrice-raced close relative of Irish Oaks dead-heater Melodist: second favourite,
impressive debut in 12-runner maiden at Doncaster, soon in front and merely nudged
along to draw clear final 1f before eased to beat Leal Lunch by 2 lengths, rated value
6: will stay at least 1m: should go on to better things. *Saeed bin Suroor*

ZELAH (IRE)   2 b.f. (May 20) Alzao (USA) 117 – Marie Noelle (FR) 114   **71**
(Brigadier Gerard 144) [1997 5m⁴ Aug 18] 37,000Y: half-sister to several winners,
including 3-y-o Ramike, Prix Marcel Boussac winner Mary Linoa (by L'Emigrant)
and smart French 1½m to 2m winner Ming Dynasty (by Sadler's Wells): dam French
2-y-o 7.5f winner, later won up to 1¼m in USA: 14/1 from 33/1, staying-on fourth of
15 in maiden at Windsor: will be suited by 1m+. *B. Smart*

ZELANDA (IRE)   2 gr.f. (Apr 20) Night Shift (USA) – Zafadola (IRE) 112   **99**
(Darshaan 133) [1997 6g³ 6m² 6m* 6g⁶ Aug 21] sturdy, close-coupled filly: fluent
mover: third foal: dam Irish 9f and 11f winner, also third in Irish St Leger: useful
form: won maiden at Haydock in August most readily, making all: not discredited
when just over 5 lengths sixth to Cape Verdi in Lowther Stakes at York: bred to stay
further than 6f, but has plenty of speed. *J. H. M. Gosden*

ZELAYA (IRE)   4 b.f. Shaadi (USA) 126 – Zizania 77 (Ahonoora 122) [1996 45:   **45**
a7g⁶ a8g³ a7g² 1997 a7g a7g² a6g⁵ 7m Mar 27] workmanlike filly: poor maiden:
better at 7f than 6f: acts on equitrack. *G. L. Moore*

ZELDA ZONK   5 b.m. Law Society (USA) 130 – Massive Powder (Caerleon   **80**
(USA) 132) [1996 80: 8m³ 7m* 7.3s⁵ 8m 7g* 7m⁴ 7g³ 7f³ 7g² 1997 7m 7g³ 7.1g
7.1m³ 7m 7m 7m⁶ 7.1m⁴ 7m 7g 7m⁴ Oct 28] sturdy mare: fairly useful handicapper:
best 5-y-o efforts when third: effective at 7f to 1m: acts on firm and dead ground,
possibly not on soft: has been bandaged behind. *B. J. Meehan*

ZELIBA   5 br.m. Doyoun 124 – Zia (USA) 88 (Shareef Dancer (USA) 135) [1996   **–**
43, a–: a8g 11.9f 8g 9.7m³ 10m² 10g 12.5f* a12g⁵ 11.9f* 12m³ 11.9f 16m⁴ 15.4g
17.9g² 18g 14.1g⁶ a14.8g a16g 1997 16g⁵ Jul 28] smallish mare: poor handicapper:
winning hurdler, but well beaten only flat outing in 1997. *P. R. Chamings*

ZENA   2 ch.f. (Feb 3) Highest Honor (FR) 124 – Lady Lamia (USA) (Secreto   **68**
(USA) 128) [1997 6.1s³ 6.1g* 6m⁵ 7g⁶ 8d Oct 17] 8,500Y: rather leggy filly: fifth
foal: sister to German 9.5f to 1½m winner Grand Slammer and half-sister to 7-y-o
Moon Strike: dam unraced: fair form at best: won minor event at Nottingham in July,
and ran well in nursery next outing: ran poorly in blinkers final start: should stay 1m:
sold 10,000 gns in October, and joined M. Polglase. *W. Jarvis*

ZEPPO (IRE)   2 ch.c. (Apr 20) Fayruz 116 – Chase Paperchase 79 (Malinowski   **60**
(USA) 123) [1997 5g⁵ 6d 6d 6g 6g Sep 20] 3,800F, 13,000Y: close-coupled colt:
half-brother to 1990 2-y-o 6f winner Zloty (by Elegant Air) and winners abroad by
Hadeer and Red Sunset: dam sprint maiden: showed ability in maidens at Sandown
and Windsor first 2 starts: not knocked about after 3-month absence final outing:
probably a sprinter. *M. J. Heaton-Ellis*

ZEPTEPI (IRE)   2 b.f. (Apr 18) Astronef 116 – Tangle Thorn (Thatching 131)   **–**
[1997 5m 7m 8s Nov 6] 500F: first reported foal: dam French 6.5f and 1m winner: no
promise in maidens: trained first 2 starts by T. Powell. *R. Simpson*

ZERMATT (IRE) 7 b.h. Sadler's Wells (USA) 132 – Chamonis (USA) 101   64
(Affirmed (USA)) [1996 74: 10.8d⁵ 10g⁶ 12m⁴ 10.2f² 10d* 10.1m 11.6g 10m⁶ 9f⁶
1997 10m 10d 8g 10g 8.1g 8d 8.1d* 9f⁵ 7.1m 8.1g 10.2d 8g² 7.1g 8d a9.4g³ 8d a12g
a8g a9.4g⁶ a12g⁴ Dec 13] tall, strong horse: unimpressive mover: modest
handicapper: won at Chepstow in July, clear halfway: effective at 1m to easy 1½m:
acts on firm ground, soft and fibresand: has had tongue tied: blinkered last 2 starts:
inconsistent. *M. D. I. Usher*

ZERO THREE FIFTEEN (IRE) 2 b.c. (Feb 8) Archway (IRE) 115 – Sales   63
Talk (Auction Ring (USA) 123) [1997 a7g 7d⁴ 6f 6.9d Oct 21] IR 5,800Y: well-made
colt: fourth foal: dam lightly-raced maiden: best effort in maidens on second start:
sold, and sent to Sweden. *Martyn Meade*

ZERPOUR (IRE) 3 b.c. Darshaan 133 – Zerzaya 90 (Beldale Flutter (USA) 130)   100
[1996 NR 1997 12d 10g⁴ 12m* 13.9g 10m² 12g⁵ Oct 25] well-made, good sort: fifth
foal: half-brother to 3 winners in Ireland, including useful 7f winner Zabadi (by
Shahrastani) and smart 6f (at 2 yrs) and 1½m winner Zafzala (by Kahyasi): dam,
1¼m winner, is half-sister to smart performer at up to 1½m Zayyani (by Darshaan):
developed into a useful performer: won maiden at Newmarket in July: best efforts on
last 2 starts when ½-length second to Mithali in minor event at Leicester and fifth to
Al Azhar in handicap at Doncaster: stays 1½m: yet to race on extremes of going: sold
(to go to Australia) 105,000 gns in October. *L. M. Cumani*

ZEST (USA) 3 gr. or ro.f. Zilzal (USA) 137 – Toveris 91 (Homing 130) [1996 –:   –
6g 1997 7m⁶ a7g 8g⁶ Jun 13] no worthwhile form: reluctant to race on equitrack
second start. *M. Bell*

ZIBAK (USA) 3 b. or br.g. Capote (USA) – Minifah (USA) 69 (Nureyev (USA)   –
131) [1996 NR 1997 8m 8.5m⁶ Jun 5] fourth foal: half-brother to winners at around
1m by Woodman, Machiavellian and Kris: dam, maiden stayed 1½m, out of
half-sister to champion filly Chris Evert: signs of ability in maiden at Kempton on
debut: tailed off only subsequent outing. *D. Morley*

ZIBETH 3 b.f. Rainbow Quest (USA) 134 – Tiger Flower 103 (Sadler's Wells   62
(USA) 132) [1996 –p: 8f 1997 8g 10.5d³ 12m* 14d Oct 17] tall, angular filly: modest
performer: left L. Cumani after second start: only form when winning handicap at
Goodwood in September, quickening steady pace and one of only 2 brought to stand
side in straight: should stay 1¾m. *S. Dow*

ZIDAC 5 br.g. Statoblest 120 – Sule Skerry 78 (Scottish Rifle 127) [1996 82: a11g²   71
10g* 10m* 10m 1997 10m⁵ 10m 10s² 10g 10m⁴ 8.1d⁵ 10m 10g 10m³ 8.2s⁵ 10.3g Oct
25] tall gelding: fair performer: generally ran creditably most starts in 1997: effective
at 1m (given a test) to 1¼m: acts on good to firm and soft ground: sometimes flashes
tail. *P. J. Makin*

ZIELANA GORA 2 b.f. (Mar 24) Polish Precedent (USA) 131 – La Lutine 95   –
(My Swallow 134) [1997 5m 7.1m Sep 16] rather leggy, useful-looking filly: half-
sister to several winners, including Middle Park winner Mon Tresor and 10-y-o
Montendre (both by Longleat, latter formerly smart up to 7f) and 7-y-o Mondragon:
dam 5f (at 2 yrs) to 1¼m winner: soundly beaten in minor event (for S. Williams) and
maiden 5 months apart. *J. G. Smyth-Osbourne*

ZIGGY'S DANCER (USA) 6 b.h. Ziggy's Boy (USA) – My Shy Dancer   91
(USA) (Northjet 136) [1996 88: 5d⁴ 5.2d⁶ 6g 5.1g³ 5m⁶ 5d 6.1m⁵ 5m² 5.1m⁴ 5m 5m⁴
6m³ 6g 5.1d⁴ 5f² 6m 7m⁴ 5g 5m³ a6g 1997 7m 5g² a5g² 5.1v 5d 5.1m* 6m⁴ 6.1s⁴ 5g⁶
5d⁶ 5.1m³ 7m³ 6m 5m 6g 6g⁴ a6g 5g Oct 25] lengthy horse: poor mover: fairly useful
performer: won at Chester (goes well there) in June: ran at least respectably most
starts after: effective at 5f to 7f: acts on the all-weather and on firm and dead ground,
probably on soft: usually waited with: tough. *E. J. Alston*

ZIGGY STARDUST (IRE) 2 b.g. (Apr 18) Roi Danzig (USA) – Si Princess   –
(Coquelin (USA) 121) [1997 7m a8.5g Oct 6] 11,000 2-y-o: second foal: dam lightly
raced in Ireland: soundly beaten in maidens at Leicester and Wolverhampton.
Mrs A. J. Bowlby

ZIGGY'S VIOLA (IRE) 3 b.f. Roi Danzig (USA) – Olivia Jane (IRE)   53
(Ela-Mana-Mou 132) [1996 56: 7.9g 7g⁶ a8g² a8.5g 1997 14.6d⁶ 14.1m⁵ 12f⁶ 16.2m⁶
15.8g⁵ 14.1g 13.8m* 12s³ Oct 17] smallish, angular filly: modest performer: didn't

need to be at best to win seller at Catterick in September: stays 2m: acts on good
to firm and soft ground: sometimes finds little: tail swisher, and isn't an easy ride.
Mrs M. Reveley

ZIG ZAG (IRE)   2 b.f. (Jan 30) Bob Back (USA) 124 – Bebe Auction (IRE)   38
(Auction Ring (USA) 123) [1997 5d 6g³ 5.2f⁵ 7.1s Aug 30] IR 800F: angular filly:
first foal: dam unraced: poor maiden: sold, and sent to Holland. *M. H. Tompkins*

ZILLION (IRE)   2 b.g. (Feb 21) Priolo (USA) 127 – Arab Scimetar (IRE) (Sure   –
Blade (USA) 130) [1997 6m a7g 7m 7g Oct 27] 6,500Y: big gelding: third foal:
half-brother to a winner in Germany by Jareer: dam unraced: well beaten in maidens
and a nursery. *J. W. Payne*

ZIMIRI   3 ch.c. Keen 116 – Annabrianna 88 (Night Shift (USA)) [1996 75p: 7g   –
a8g* 1997 9g⁶ 8g 8m 8d Sep 12] compact, deep-bodied colt: promising juvenile, but
failed to beat a single horse in 1997, reportedly gurgled last 2 starts. *J. A. R. Toller*

ZIMZIE   2 gr.c. (May 16) Aragon 118 – Zimzizizim (Most Welcome 131) [1997   –
6m 6m 7g 8d 6m 7d Oct 16] smallish colt: first foal: dam unraced: little worthwhile
form, including in selling company: sent to Switzerland. *M. J. Haynes*

ZINE LANE   5 ch.g. Minster Son 130 – Pine (Supreme Sovereign 119) [1996 NR   38
1997 a12g³ a12g⁴ Feb 24] just a poor maiden on flat nowadays: stays 1½m: visored
both starts in 1997. *J. G. M. O'Shea*

ZINGARO (IRE)   3 b.c. Mujtahid (USA) 118 – Zia (USA) 88 (Shareef Dancer   –
(USA) 135) [1996 61: 8g⁵ 7g 1997 7g Jun 12] robust colt: modest form at 2 yrs: well
held only outing in 1997: sent to Sweden. *C. E. Brittain*

ZINGIBAR   5 b.g. Caerleon (USA) 132 – Duende 75 (High Top 131) [1996 NR   –
1997 10m Apr 16] fair on his day at 3 yrs for B. Hills: well beaten only start on flat
since: modest hurdler, winner in May. *J. M. Bradley*

ZINZARI (FR)   3 ch.c. Arctic Tern (USA) 126 – Model Girl (FR) (Lyphard   87 d
(USA) 132) [1996 70p: 8s⁵ 1997 10m² 13.9g³ 10m⁵ 12d 11.9f 13.8g⁴ 11.5m⁶ Sep 9]
useful-looking colt: fairly useful maiden: well below form last 4 starts, including in
visor: stays 1¾m: acts on good to firm going: carried head awkwardly sixth outing:
sold 16,000 gns, and sent to Kuwait. *D. R. Loder*

ZIZI (IRE)   2 b.f. (Feb 16) Imp Society (USA) – Timinala 58 (Mansingh (USA)   79
120) [1997 6f³ 5g³ 5m* 6m³ 7g 6.5m³ Sep 10] IR 3,000Y: leggy, workmanlike filly:
unimpressive mover: half-sister to fairly useful 1¼m winner Minimize (by Alzao):
dam, lightly-raced 5f performer, half-sister to smart miler Pasticcio: fair form: won
maiden at Ripon in July: good third in nurseries at Goodwood and Doncaster: should
stay 7f: raced only on good ground or firmer. *K. R. Burke*

ZOBAIDA (IRE)   2 b.f. (May 2) Green Desert (USA) 127 – Charmante (USA) 88   60 p
(Alydar (USA)) [1997 7m 7g⁶ Oct 18] rangy, unfurnished filly: half-sister to useful
Irish 7f winner Charlock (by Nureyev) and fairly useful 1¾m winner Alinova (by
Alleged): dam, 7f and 1m winner in Ireland and USA, half-sister to Zilzal: showed
promise when eighth of 22 to Quiet Assurance in maiden at Newmarket: still green
and not knocked about once held at Redcar later in month: should still do better over
1m+. *M. A. Jarvis*

ZOMARADAH   2 b.f. (Feb 21) Deploy 131 – Jawaher (IRE) 60 (Dancing Brave   76 P
(USA) 140) [1997 8s⁵ Nov 8] strong, compact filly: second foal: half-sister to 3-y-o
Nichol Fifty: dam maiden out of staying half-sister to Ribblesdale Stakes and Park
Hill Stakes winner High Hawk, dam of In The Wings: 8/1, on burly side and green,
most encouraging fifth of 22 to Eco Friendly in maiden at Doncaster, slowly away,
and soon with a lot to do, but finishing strongly despite meeting trouble, principals
very much getting first run on her: sure to do a good deal better and win races at
1¼m+. *L. M. Cumani*

ZOOM UP (IRE)   3 ch.g. Bluebird (USA) 125 – Senane 86 (Vitiges (FR) 132)   86
[1996 NR 1997 8g³ 8g* 8s⁴ 8g² 8.1m⁶ 8.1s 9d 10m⁴ 10.3g⁴ Oct 24] 18,500F, IR
24,000Y: leggy, lengthy gelding: half-brother to several winners including fairly
useful 5-y-o Crumpton Hill and ungenuine Civil Law (stayed 1½m, by Law Society):
dam, 1m winner who stayed 1½m and was possibly ungenuine, half-sister to Oaks
second Game Plan: fairly useful performer: won maiden at Warwick in May: good

efforts in handicaps (blinkered, then visored) last 2 starts: stays 1¼m: suited by good ground or firmer. *M. J. Heaton-Ellis*

ZORBA 3 b.g. Shareef Dancer (USA) 135 – Zabelina (USA) 57 (Diesis 133) [1996 68 67: 5d a6g 7m³ 7.1m³ 7.9g 7m³ 7g³ 7.1s² a8.5g⁴ 1997 a7g² a7g⁴ a8.5g² a9.4g² a11g a62 9.2g* 10g* 10.1s 7.9g 10s³ 9.2g³ 9.9d⁵ 10g 9d³ a9.4g⁶ 9s* 10.3g⁵ 8s a8g Dec 8] leggy gelding: fair performer: made all in seller at Hamilton and claimer at Redcar (final start for C. Thornton) in June, and came from last to win handicap at Ayr in October: stays 1¼m: acts on soft ground and fibresand. *J. Hetherton*

ZORRO 3 gr.g. Touch of Grey 90 – Snow Huntress 80 (Shirley Heights 130) [1996 59 –: 7m 7d a7s 1997 9.7m⁵ 10s 10.1f* 11.4g⁶ 11.5m 12d³ 9g³ a10g Dec 2] leggy, plain a– gelding: modest handicapper: best effort when winning apprentice event at Yarmouth in June: may be suited by around 1¼m: acts on firm ground, respectable effort on dead: has given trouble going to post (gelded before final start): none too consistent. *R. M. Flower*

ZUGUDI 3 b.c. Night Shift (USA) – Overdrive 99 (Shirley Heights 130) [1996 95 67+: 6m⁴ 7g 6f* 6g 7m 6g 1997 6f* 7m 7m⁴ 7m⁵ 7m 7f 7.1m 8m 6.1g 10d² 10.1m³ 10m 12s³ Nov 8] strong, heavy-topped colt: useful performer: won handicap at Yarmouth in June: best efforts when stepped up in trip in the autumn, including ¾-length second to Santillana in well-contested minor event at Newmarket: probably stays 1½m: acts on firm and soft ground: has worn a tongue strap: takes good hold and usually races prominently: blinkered (out of form) seventh and eighth starts. *K. Mahdi*

ZUHAIR 4 ch.g. Mujtahid (USA) 118 – Ghzaalh (USA) 87 (Northern Dancer) 97 [1996 NR 1997 a8.5g a6g* 6g 6g³ a6g⁶ 6g⁵ 6m³ 6m 6d² 6g 7d 6g a6g² 6.1d² 6s Nov a84 8] useful performer on turf, fairly useful on the all-weather: won amateurs claimer at Wolverhampton in May: best efforts when placed in competitive handicaps at York and Leopardstown in the summer and second (on penultimate start) to Carranita in minor event at Nottingham: better at 6f than further (yet to race at 5f): acts on good to firm and dead ground and on fibresand: well beaten only try in blinkers: wears bandages: tends to sweat: none too consistent. *D. McCain*

ZUNO FLYER (USA) 5 br.g. Lyphard (USA) 132 – Triple Tipple (USA) 111 – (Raise A Cup (USA)) [1996 47: a8g a10g³ a10g⁴ a12g⁴ a12g⁴ a10g² a9.4g a16g⁵ 11.9f⁵ 10f⁴ 14m⁶ a12g* a12g⁵ 1997 a16g a13g Jan 30] stocky gelding: poor performer: well beaten both starts in 1997. *G. L. Moore*

ZURS (IRE) 4 b.g. Tirol 127 – Needy (High Top 131) [1996 77: 8g 7m³ 8m² 7.9g³ 79 7.6m4 1997 a8g* a8.5g⁴ 8m 7g 8m 7m 7.3g 7.1m 7d 8.1m⁵ 10m⁴ 10g³ 8d⁶ 8m* 6.9m* 8v³ 7g² 7m a8g Dec 12] sturdy gelding: fair performer: won bad maiden at Lingfield in February and (having left Miss G. Kelleway after twelfth start) minor event at Leicester and apprentice handicap at Folkestone (dead-heat) in September: best at 7f/ 1m: acts on good to firm going (probably on heavy) and both all-weather: well beaten only try in blinkers: sometimes slowly away, and shows some waywardness. *Jamie Poulton*

ZURYAF (IRE) 2 .g. (Mar 17) Fayruz 116 – The Way She Moves (North Stoke 64 130) [1997 7m 7m 7.6d 7g² 7s Nov 8] 18,000Y: useful-looking gelding: half-brother to a 2-y-o 7f winner by Welsh Term and winners abroad by Skyliner and Petorius: dam no worthwhile form: modest maiden: best effort when head second to Caversfield in nursery at Leicester in October: stays 7f: blinkered last 2 starts. *B. J. Meehan*

ZYDECO (IRE) 2 b.c. (May 6) Darshaan 133 – Cajun Melody (Cajun 120) [1997 80 7g⁶ 7.6d² 7g² Oct 7] IR 42,000Y: rangy colt: fifth foal: half-brother to several winners abroad, including fairly useful French 1m/1¼m performer Danish Melody (by Danehill): dam Irish 1m winner: fairly useful maiden: trained by J. Dunlop first 2 starts: second to Sadian (beaten neck) at Lingfield then to Komistar (beaten 5 lengths) at Warwick: will stay at least 1¼m. *M. C. Pipe*

ZYGO (USA) 5 b.g. Diesis 133 – La Papagena (Habitat 134) [1996 82: 7g³ 7.3s² – 8.3m² 8m 7f⁴ 1997 8v 10g Oct 24] lengthy gelding: fairly useful maiden in 1996 for W. Jarvis: no show in 2 handicaps in October. *R. T. Phillips*

The following unraced horses appeared in ante-post lists for the 1998 classics, and are included for information purposes:

ANYTIME (IRE) 2 b.c. (Mar 27) Fairy King (USA) – Alidiva (Chief Singer 131) [1997 NR :: 1998 NR] fourth foal: half-brother to 3-y-o Sleepytime, 4-y-o Ali-Royal, and 5-y-o Taipan: dam 6f to 1m winner out of Fillies' Mile third Alligatrix: reportedly underwent surgery on a sesamoid problem early in 1997. *H. R. A. Cecil*

DREAM PURSUIT (IRE) 2 b.f. (Mar 14) Caerleon (USA) 132 – Heaven Only Knows (High Top 131) [1997 NR :: 1998 NR] 85,000F, 200,000Y: fifth foal: half-sister to winners in Italy by Alzao (listed winner, stayed 11f), Shareef Dancer (up to 1½m) and Warrshan (7f): dam lightly-raced half-sister to Kneller, Great Marquess and Northern Spur, an excellent family. *H. R. A. Cecil*

KISSOGRAM 2 b.f. (Feb 14) Caerleon (USA) 132 – Alligram (USA) 61 (Alysheba (USA)) [1997 NR :: 1998 NR] first foal: dam thrice-raced daughter of top-class miler Milligram. *L. M. Cumani*

SCORPION ORCHID (IRE) 2 gr.f. (May 2) Caerleon (USA) 132 – Negligence 66 (Roan Rocket 128) [1997 NR :: 1998 NR] IR 235,000Y: half-sister to several winners, including smart 1989 2-y-o 7f winner Negligent (by Ahonoora), later third in 1000 Guineas, and smart stayer Ala Hounak (by Sexton Blake): dam lightly raced maiden. *H. R. A. Cecil*

SINGER SARGENT (USA) 2 ch.c. (Feb 13) Kingmambo (USA) 125 – Puppet Dance (USA) 103 (Northern Dancer) [1997 NR :: 1998 NR] 880,000Y: fourth foal: half-brother to a winner in Japan by Slew O'Gold: dam French 2-y-o 5.5f winner who stayed 1m, sister to Sadler's Wells and Tate Gallery. *M. R. Stoute*

SOUFFLE 2 b.f. (Apr 4) Zafonic (USA) 130 – One Way Street 119 (Habitat 134) [1997 NR :: 1998 NR] half-sister to several winners, including 3-y-o Windsor Castle, very smart French 6.5f (at 2 yrs) to 10.5f winner Grape Tree Road (by Caerleon) and smart 1¼m to 15f winner Red Route (by Polish Precedent): dam won Princess Royal Stakes. *H. R. A. Cecil*

SPA 2 b.f. (Feb 10) Sadler's Wells (USA) 132 – Sandy Island 110 (Mill Reef (USA) 141) [1997 NR :: 1998 NR] eighth foal: sister to smart 1½m winner Sebastian and half-sister to 1995 2-y-o winner Subterfuge (by Machiavellian) and smart 7f (at 2 yrs) and 1¼m winner Sardegna (by Pharly): dam, winner of Pretty Polly Stakes and Lancashire Oaks, is closely related to Slip Anchor. *H. R. A. Cecil*

TWICKENHAM (USA) 2 ch.c. (Mar 27) Woodman (USA) 126 – Danse Royale (IRE) 112 (Caerleon (USA) 132) [1997 NR :: 1998 NR] IR 1,125,000Y: first foal: dam Irish 7f (at 2 yrs) to 1¼m winner, half-sister to Salsabil and Marju. *H. R. A. Cecil*

WEMYSS QUEST 2 b.c. (Mar 7) Rainbow Quest (USA) 134 – Wemyss Bight 121 (Dancing Brave (USA) 140) [1997 NR :: 1998 NR] first foal: dam 9f (at 2 yrs) to 1½m (including Irish Oaks) winner. *H. R. A. Cecil*

FIXTURES
1998

AYR

SCOTLAND'S PREMIER COURSE

Month	Date	Type
JANUARY	Friday 2nd	N.H.
	Saturday 31st	N.H.
FEBRUARY	Saturday 4th	N.H.
MARCH	Friday 13th	N.H.
	Saturday 14th	N.H.
APRIL	*Scottish Grand National Meeting*	
	Friday 17th	N.H.
	Saturday 18th	N.H.
MAY	Thursday 28th	FLAT
	Friday 29th	FLAT
JUNE	Friday 19th	FLAT
	Saturday 20th	FLAT
JULY	Monday 13th	FLAT
	Saturday 18th (Eve)	FLAT
	Monday 20th	FLAT
AUGUST	Tuesday 11th	FLAT
SEPTEMBER	*The Western Meeting*	
	Thursday 17th	FLAT
	Friday 18th	FLAT
	Saturday 19th	FLAT
OCTOBER	Monday 12th	FLAT
	Tuesday 13th	FLAT
NOVEMBER	Saturday 14th	N.H.
	Sunday 15th	N.H.
DECEMBER	Monday 7th	N.H.
	Saturday 26th	N.H.

How to get there

Glasgow Airport 1 Hour by Car
Prestwick Airport 10 Minutes by Car
Racecourse Landing Ground Helicopters Only
Train Service Every 30 Minutes from Glasgow

All enquiries to The Racecourse Office
2 Whitletts Road, Ayr KA8 0JE
Telephone Ayr (01292) 264179

PROMISING HORSES

All the horses in *Racehorses of 1997* thought capable of noteworthy improvement are listed below under the trainers for whom they last ran.

R. AKEHURST
Rush Off 2 b.c 65p

E. J. ALSTON
Poetry In Motion (IRE) 2 gr.f 62p

R. W. ARMSTRONG
Abusamrah (USA) 2 b.c 77p
Divvinayshan (IRE) 2 b.c 55p
Hakeem (IRE) 2 ch.c 83p
Ikhteyaar (USA) 2 b.f 103p
Jila (IRE) 2 ch.c 84p
Rachaels North (IRE) 2 gr.c 73p
Rayik 2 br.c 84p

A. BAILEY
Super Snip 2 ch.g 61p

G. B. BALDING
Bomb Alaska 2 br.g 66p
Delphic Way 2 b.f 59p
Magic Powers 2 ch.g 67p
Cugina 3 b.f 99p

I. A. BALDING
Alarming Motown 2 b.f —p
Borani 2 b.c 84p
Border Arrow 2 ch.c 97P
Celebration 2 br.f 61p
Dancing Dervish 2 b.g 58p
Double Brandy 2 ch.c 78p
Easter Ogil (IRE) 2 ch.g 71p
Ellway Prince 2 b.g 68p
Fields of Omagh (USA) 2 b.g 70p
Lucy Glitters (USA) 2 b.f 60p
Night Shot 2 br.g 85p
Pantar (IRE) 2 b.c 81p
Prime Time Girl 2 b.f 73p
Scorned (GER) 2 b.c 89p
Al Azhar 3 b.c 103p
Jorrocks (USA) 3 b.g 97p
Lochangel 3 ch.f 104p

J. E. BANKS
U K Magic (IRE) 2 b.g 57p

T. D. BARRON
Three Star Rated (IRE) 2 b.f 79p

P. BARY, FRANCE
Croco Rouge (IRE) 2 b.c 108p

M. BELL
Adeste Fideles 2 b.f 78p
Kings Arrow (IRE) 2 b.c 71p
Lord Lieutenant 2 b.g 81p
Minivet 2 b.g 78p
Tussle 2 b.c 91p
Solar Storm 3 ch.c 104p

C. J. BENSTEAD
Shaji (IRE) 2 ch.c 71p

J. BERRY
Bolshaya 2 gr.f 55p

C. E. BRITTAIN
Anna 2 b.f 69p
Cerisette (IRE) 2 b.f 94p
Circus 2 b.c 74p
Cloud Castle 2 b.f 84p
Dahomey (USA) 2 b.c 61p
La Rochelle (IRE) 2 b.f 72p
Pegnitz (USA) 2 b.c 100p
Salsette 2 b.f 73p
Thrashing 2 b.c —p
Wenda (IRE) 2 ch.f 89p

N. A. CALLAGHAN
Tornado Prince (IRE) 2 ch.c —p
Danetime (IRE) 3 b.c 119p
Plaisir d'Amour (IRE) 3 b.f 99p

M. J. CAMACHO
Lake Taal 2 ch.f 59p

H. CANDY
Fabrice 2 b.g 72p
Generous Terms 2 ch.c 66p
Grace Browning 2 b.f 84p
Inchtina 2 b.f 78p
Ritual 2 ch.g 63p

H. R. A. CECIL
Baffin Bay 2 b.c 83p
Benin (USA) 2 b.c 88P
Brimming 2 ch.c 83p
Capri 2 ch.c 75p
Chester House (USA) 2 b.c 107p
Craigsteel 2 b.c 104p
Dr Fong (USA) 2 ch.c 102p
Empire Gold (USA) 2 ch.c 67p
Fleetwood (IRE) 2 ch.c 107P
Giveaway 2 ch.c 93p
Golden Dice (USA) 2 ch.c 99p
Great Dane (IRE) 2 b.c 89p
Himself (USA) 2 b.c 88p
Jibe (USA) 2 b.f 107p
Moratorium (USA) 2 b.c 68p
Pontoon 2 br.f 89p
Porto Foricos (USA) 2 b.c —p
Sadian 2 b.c 91p
Silver Rhapsody (USA) 2 b.f 91P
Star Crystal (IRE) 2 b.f 80p
Sternsinger (USA) 2 b.c 67p
Timbervati (USA) 2 br.f 79p
Tuning 2 ch.f 92p
Wadi 2 b.c 84p

Wayne Lukas 2 b.c 73p
White Scissors (USA) 2 b.c 72p
Bina Gardens 3 b.f 106p
Carisbrooke 3 b.c 99p
Darnaway 3 b.c 92p
Fiji 3 b.f 103p
Gentilesse 3 gr.f 81p
Gingersnap 3 ch.f 83p
High Intrigue (IRE) 3 b.c 91p
Ismaros 3 b.c 106p
Light Programme 3 b.c 89p
Recourse (USA) 3 b.c 88p

MRS J. CECIL
Playgroup 2 ch.f 60p
Shaveling 2 ch.c 73p

M. R. CHANNON
Aganon 2 b.c 76p
Arctic Star 2 b.g 66p
Mansa Musa (IRE) 2 br.c 71p
Raffaello (IRE) 2 b.c 69p
Shanillo 2 gr.g 72p
Tabasco (IRE) 2 b.f 72p

MAJOR D. N. CHAPPELL
Mantello 2 ch.c —p
Storm Cry (USA) 2 b.c 74p

P. W. CHAPPLE-HYAM
Cape Verdi (IRE) 2 b.f 110p
Central Committee (IRE) 2 ch.g 82p
City Honours (USA) 2 b.c 105p
Classic Impact (IRE) 2 ch.g 73p
Connoisseur Bay (USA) 2 b.c 91p
Free As The Wind (IRE) 2 b.g 80p
Glory of Grosvenor (IRE) 2 ch.c 89p
Victory Note (USA) 2 b.c 101p
Voodoo Saint (USA) 2 ch.c 88p
Woodland Melody (USA) 2 b.f 108p

R. CHARLTON
Blue Gentian (USA) 2 b.f 96p
Conical 2 b.f —p
Derryquin 2 b.g 97p
Harmonic Way 2 ch.c 89p
Housekeeper (IRE) 2 b.f 87P
Mystic Flight (USA) 2 b.f 70p
Spanish Fern (USA) 2 b.f 89p
Still Waters 2 b.g 56p
Tamarisk (IRE) 2 b.c 113p
Ghillies Ball 3 ch.g 91p
King Alex 4 b.c 112p

P. F. I. COLE
Bintang (IRE) 2 ch.c 105p
Caernarfon Bay (IRE) 2 ch.c 67p
Carry The Flag 2 b.c 92p
Copernicus 2 b.c 78p
Courageous (IRE) 2 ch.c 79p
Courteous 2 b.c 84p
Decisive Action (USA) 2 br.c 91p
Evander (IRE) 2 ch.c 90p
Generosity 2 ch.c 75p

Golden Hawk (USA) 2 ch.c 81p
High Tension (USA) 2 b.c 74p
Tokay 2 b.f 57p
Future Perfect 3 b.g 99p
Montfort (USA) 3 b.g 96p

L. G. COTTRELL
Desert Valentine 2 b.g —p
Uplifting 2 b.f 77p
Sovereigns Court 4 ch.g 81p

L. M. CUMANI
Baajil 2 b.c 85p
Frond 2 b.f 85p
Glorosia (FR) 2 ch.f 109p
High Noon 2 b.c 67p
High-Rise (IRE) 2 b.c 84p
Lea Grande 2 ch.f 89p
Madjamila (IRE) 2 b.f 89p
Marie Loup (FR) 2 ch.f 80p
Refined (IRE) 2 b.f 95p
Salford 2 ch.g —p
Sharera (IRE) 2 b.f 65p
Slipper 2 b.f 74p
Splendid Isolation (USA) 2 b.c 80p
Taleban 2 b.c 88p
Zomaradah 2 b.f 76P
Darapour (IRE) 3 b.g 97p
Floristan (IRE) 3 b.c 75p
Geimhriuil (IRE) 3 b.c 91p
One So Wonderful 3 b.f 121p
Ridaiyma (IRE) 3 b.f 107p
Shouk 3 b.f 81p
Taberann (IRE) 3 b.c 87p
Migwar 4 b.g —p

W. S. CUNNINGHAM
Its My Pleasure 3 b.f —p

E. A. L. DUNLOP
Allgrit (USA) 2 b.c 73p
Almazhar (IRE) 2 b.c —p
Bay of Delight 2 ch.f —p
Brave Noble (USA) 2 ch.c 77p
Cool Spray (USA) 2 b.f —p
Deep Space (IRE) 2 br.c 85p
Dixie d'Oats 2 b.f 65p
Doomna (IRE) 2 b.f 93p
Foxie Lady 2 ch.f —p
Ivory Crown (IRE) 2 b.f —p
Kitoph (IRE) 2 b.f —p
Mutafarij (USA) 2 ch.c 70p
National Wish (USA) 2 ch.c 70p
Rabi (IRE) 2 b.c 105p

J. L. DUNLOP
Alcayde 2 ch.c 73p
Al-Fateh (IRE) 2 b.c 80p
Alharir (USA) 2 b.f 101p
Ashraakat (USA) 2 b.f 104p
Beauchamp Magic 2 b.g —p
Caledonian Express 2 b.f 64p
Close Up (IRE) 2 ch.c 93p
Elhayq (IRE) 2 b.c 80p

Fakhr (USA) 2 b.c 94p
Fantasy Night (IRE) 2 b.g 69p
Fiamma (IRE) 2 b.f 93p
Florazi 2 b.c 94p
Ghali (USA) 2 b.c 89p
Haami (USA) 2 b.c 106p
Herminius (IRE) 2 b.c 84p
Honest Borderer 2 b.g 74p
Indimaaj 2 b.c 79p
In The Sun (USA) 2 b.f 67p
Kahtan 2 b.c 92p
Leggera (IRE) 2 b.f 98p
Magical Colours (IRE) 2 b.f —p
Majestic Hills 2 b.c 83p
Mondschein 2 b.f 86p
Pairumani Star (IRE) 2 ch.c 68p
Persian Fantasia 2 b.f —p
Regal Patriarch (IRE) 2 br.c 70p
Ribblesdale 2 b.f 73p
Saleela (USA) 2 b.f 64p
Somayda (IRE) 2 b.c 83p
Sweet Dreams 2 b.f 67p
Tajasur (IRE) 2 ch.c 87p
Transylvania 2 b.f 70p
Trinity Reef 2 b.f 62p
Wave Rock 2 br.g 80p
Winsa (USA) 2 b.f 80p
Wiston Cheese (USA) 2 b.c 94P
Wosaita 2 b.f 64p
Elnadim (USA) 3 b.c 126p
Sheltering Sky (IRE) 3 b.c 90p

MRS P. N. DUTFIELD
Bliss (IRE) 2 b.f 75p

M. W. EASTERBY
Westcourt Ruby 2 b f —p

T. D. EASTERBY
Bollin Ann 2 b.f 60p
Bollin Ethos 2 b.c —p
Cumbrian Caruso 2 b.g 86p
Grand Estate 2 b.g 72p
Panama House 2 ch.g 78p
Simply Gifted 2 b.c 76p

C. R. EGERTON
Dangerus Precedent (IRE) 2 ch.c —p

D. R. C. ELSWORTH
Brimstone (IRE) 2 ch.c 83p
Silver Sun 2 gr.f 64p

T. J. ETHERINGTON
Piccadilly 2 ch.f 62p

J. L. EYRE
Bawsian 2 b.c 79p

A. FABRE, FRANCE
Arnaqueur (USA) 2 b.c 104p
Isle de France (USA) 2 b.f 107p
Pinmix (FR) 2 gr.c 108p
Thief of Hearts (IRE) 2 b.c 112p
Public Purse (USA) 3 b.c 110p

J. R. FANSHAWE
Ambitious 2 b.f 72p
Bryony Brind (IRE) 2 ch.f —p
Emerald Heights 2 b.c 69p
Flight For Freedom 2 b.f 60p
Mole Creek 2 gr.f 62p
Persiano 2 ch.c 73p
Publisher (USA) 2 b.c 92P
Tattinger 2 b.f 80p
Arctic Owl 3 b.g 100p
Floating Charge 3 b.g 73p

P. S. FELGATE
Gay Breeze 4 b.g 54p

M. J. FETHERSTON-GODLEY
Welcome Heights 3 b.g 71p

J. G. FITZGERALD
Jayess Elle 2 b.f 55p

J. A. GLOVER
Nunthorpe 2 ch.f 71p

J. H. M. GOSDEN
Almandab (IRE) 2 b.c 97P
Dog Watch 2 ch.g 83p
Doraid (IRE) 2 b.c 81p
Empirical (USA) 2 b.f 72p
Gandoura (USA) 2 b.f 70p
High And Mighty 2 b.g —p
Jaati (IRE) 2 b.g —p
Kilcullen (IRE) 2 b.g 81p
Laffah (USA) 2 b.c 67p
Louis Philippe (USA) 2 b.c 82p
Maazoom (IRE) 2 b.g —p
Masha-Il (IRE) 2 b.c 83p
Megned 2 b.f 72p
Mubrik (IRE) 2 b.c 86p
Niki (IRE) 2 b.f 79p
Olive The Twist (USA) 2 ch.f 70p
Pinochet (USA) 2 ch.f 65p
Plan-B 2 b.c 83p
Polska Modelle (FR) 2 ch.c —p
Riot 2 b.c 61p
Vignette (USA) 2 b.f 93p
Young Josh 2 b.c 84p
Sabadilla (USA) 3 b.c 107p
Saguaro 3 b.g 73p
Shaska 3 ch.f 90p
Three Cheers (IRE) 3 b.g 116p

N. A. GRAHAM
Mashab 2 b.c 69p
Wigging 2 b.f 75p

R. GUEST
Bedtime Story 2 b.f 42p
Mystical Song 2 ch.f 68p

W. J. HAGGAS
Internal Affair (USA) 2 b.g 67p
Shocker (IRE) 2 b.f 47p
Pen Friend 3 b.g 62p

B. HANBURY
Misbah (USA) 2 b.c 92p
Night Rule 2 b.f 89p

R. HANNON
Caversfield 2 ch.c 75p
Certain Danger (IRE) 2 b.f —p
Churlish Charm 2 b.c —p
Golden Reprimand (IRE) 2 b.c 85p
Grand Slam (IRE) 2 b.c 77p
Gurkha 2 b.c 88p
King Darius (IRE) 2 ch.c 78p
Lucky Double 2 b.c 82p
Maiella 2 ch.f —p
Miss Money Spider (IRE) 2 b.f 65p
Santone (IRE) 2 b.c 77p
Shape Shifter (IRE) 2 ch.c 69p
Surprise Present (IRE) 2 ch.c 64p

J. HANSON
Bergen (IRE) 2 b.c 78p

P. W. HARRIS
Absalom's Lad 2 gr.c 69p
Canadian Puzzler (USA) 2 gr.c 83p
Eliza Acton 2 b.f 70p
Formation Dancer 2 ch.c —p
Legal Lunch (USA) 2 b.c 84p
Mantusis (IRE) 2 ch.c 86p
Volontiers (FR) 2 b.c 84p
Northern Blessing 3 b.f 86p

MME C. HEAD, FRANCE
Loving Claim (USA) 2 b.f 110p
Special Quest (FR) 2 b.c 109p

M. J. HEATON-ELLIS
Abu Camp 2 b.c —p

MAJOR W. R. HERN
Royal Castle (IRE) 3 b.c 90p

LADY HERRIES
Act of Folly 2 b.f —p
Mowelga 3 ch.c 79p

A. HIDE
Tankersley 2 ch.c —p

B. W. HILLS
Above Board 2 b.g 67p
Almurooj 2 b.f —p
Andalish 2 b.f —p
Asyaad (USA) 2 br.c 78p
Bahr 2 ch.f 106p
Bombastic 2 ch.c 75p
Bristol Channel 2 b.f 94p
Bullion 2 b.f 85p
Chattan 2 b.c 88p
Cherokee Band (USA) 2 b.c 60p
Epsom Cyclone (USA) 2 ch.c —p
Fairy Rock (IRE) 2 b.f 73p
Genoa 2 b.f 73p
High And Low 2 b.f 78p
Incepta 2 b.c —p

Khalas 2 b.c 91p
Last Christmas 2 b.c 91p
Lido (IRE) 2 ch.c 86p
Magic of Aloha (IRE) 2 ch.f 79p
Miss Bussell 2 ch.f 65p
Mysterious Ecology 2 gr.f 72p
Penrose 2 ch.f 75p
Pure Nobility (IRE) 2 br.c 81p
Shfoug (USA) 2 b.f 85p
The Glow-Worm (IRE) 2 b.c 95p

J. W. HILLS
Cadillac Jukebox (USA) 2 b.c —p
Cold Front 2 br.c 65p
Flush (FR) 2 b.f 61p
Lemon Bridge (IRE) 2 b.c —p
Memphis Dancer 2 b.f 60p
Nocturne (IRE) 2 b.f —p
On The Right Side 2 b.g 72p

R. J. HODGES
Zany Lady 2 gr.f 58p

C. A. HORGAN
My Pledge (IRE) 2 b.c 61p

R. F. JOHNSON HOUGHTON
Bayleaf 2 ch.f 97p
Squabble 2 b.f 56p
Tereyna 2 gr.f 58p

P. HOWLING
Angelina 2 b.f 63p

LORD HUNTINGDON
Blueprint (IRE) 2 b.c 80p
Celtic Cross 2 b.f 93p
Distinctive Dance (USA) 2 b.c 88p
Eminent 2 ch.c 68p
Feel Free (IRE) 2 b.f —p
Prospectress (USA) 2 ch.f 82p
Silken Dalliance 2 b.f 67p
Smart Squall (USA) 2 b.c 97p
Stage Whisper 2 b.c 70p
Wren (IRE) 2 ch.f 103p
Rutland Chantry (USA) 3 b.g 72p

A. P. JARVIS
Emmajoun 2 b.f 69p
Ocean Line (IRE) 2 b.c 59p

M. A. JARVIS
Anemos (IRE) 2 ch.c 74p
Elbarree (IRE) 2 b.g —p
Jamorin Dancer 2 b.c 77p
Lamsaat (IRE) 2 b.f —p
Setteen 2 b.c 107p
Shohra Wa Jaah 2 b.g 61p
Zobaida (IRE) 2 b.f 60p

W. JARVIS
Absentee 2 br.f —p
Moon Gorge 2 b.f 61p
Ganga (IRE) 3 ch.f 94p

M. JOHNSTON
Alberich (IRE) 2 b.c   85p
Asset Manager 2 b.c   68p
Atlantic Viking (IRE) 2 b.c   101p
Corpus Christi (IRE) 2 b.g   63p
Double Edged 2 ch.c   85p
Fruits of Love (USA) 2 b.c   102p
Gypsy Passion 2 ch.c   87p
Kameez (IRE) 2 ch.f   69p
Lend A Hand 2 b.c   114p
Long Bond (IRE) 2 ch.c   74p
Love Academy 2 b.c   79p
Naskhi 2 b.f   82p
North Ofthe Border 2 b.c   75p
Sinon (IRE) 2 ch.c   92p
Spirit of Love (USA) 2 ch.c   —p
Trigger Happy (IRE) 2 ch.f   91p
Younico 2 b.c   —p

MISS GAY KELLEWAY
Honey Suckle 2 br.f   65p
Soviet Bureau (IRE) 2 ch.c   99p
Tommy Tortoise 3 b.c   80p

G. LEWIS
Air Attache (USA) 2 b.c   82p
Ivory League 2 b.f   —p
Right Man 3 gr.c   86p

N. P. LITTMODEN
Dryad 2 ch.c   63p

D. R. LODER
Agami (USA) 2 b.f   —p
Ambiguous 2 ch.c   —p
Beacon Blaze 2 ch.f   —p
Billionare 2 b.c   —p
Bint Kaldoun (IRE) 2 b.f   71p
Braganza (USA) 2 ch.c   67p
Captain Logan (IRE) 2 b.c   78p
Captain Tim 2 ch.c   82p
Daring Derek (USA) 2 ch.c   92P
Dashing Knight (IRE) 2 b.c   61p
Diktat 2 br.c   82p
Ethereal 2 b.c   —p
Frankie Ferrari (IRE) 2 b.c   —p
Generous Rosi 2 b.c   —p
Golden Fortune 2 ch.f   84p
Long Siege (IRE) 2 ch.c   78p
Lovers Knot 2 b.f   89p
Lucayan Indian (IRE) 2 ch.c   96p
Master Caster (IRE) 2 b.g   —p
Opening Meet 2 ch.f   74p
Paarl Rock 2 ch.c   69p
Brigand (IRE) 3 b.g   89p
Snow Kid 3 b.c   113p

P. J. MAKIN
De-Wolf 2 gr.f   74p
Ring Dancer 2 b.c   92p
Sheila-B 2 ch.f   54p
Wolfhunt 2 b.c   a89p
Always On My Mind 3 b.f   91p

B. J. MEEHAN
Dilkusha (IRE) 2 b.g   78p
Guildhall 2 b.c   79p
Imshishway (IRE) 2 b.c   82p
Midsummer Romance (IRE) 2 b.f   —p
Mister Rambo 2 b.g   87p

T. G. MILLS
Telalanjon 2 b.c   70p

P. MITCHELL
Special Person (IRE) 2 ch.f   65p

P. MOONEY
Forest Fire (SWE) 2 b.f   55p

D. MORLEY
Mahboob (IRE) 2 b.c   102p
Mudalal (USA) 2 b.c   76p

W. R. MUIR
Arry Martin 2 b.c   —p
Astrologer 2 b.c   90p
Flying Bold (IRE) 2 ch.c   66p
Danesman (IRE) 4 b.g   —p

F. MURPHY
Stoned Imaculate (IRE) 3 ch.f   73p

P. G. MURPHY
Willa Wooster 2 b.f   62p

W. J. MUSSON
Hetra Heights (USA) 2 b.f   —p

D. NICHOLLS
Euro Venture 2 b.g   70p

A. P. O'BRIEN, IRELAND
Celtic Cavalier (IRE) 2 b.c   103p
Impressionist (IRE) 2 b.c   106p
Second Empire (IRE) 2 b.c   122p

W. A. O'GORMAN
Pleasuredancer (USA) 2 gr.g   77p

J. W. PAYNE
Al Muallim (USA) 3 b.c   98p

MISS L. A. PERRATT
Ho Leng (IRE) 2 ch.g   92p
Ryefield 2 b.c   73p

MRS A. J. PERRETT
Edwardian 2 ch.c   79p
Temeraire (USA) 2 b.c   65p

K. PRENDERGAST, IRELAND
Quws 3 b.c   112p

SIR MARK PRESCOTT
Alboroda 2 gr.f   104p
Altitude (IRE) 2 b.c   —p
Confirmation 2 b.g   96p
Girlie Set (IRE) 2 b.f   47p
Grazia 2 b.f   102P
Hunt Hill (IRE) 2 b.c   —p
Liberte Bell (IRE) 2 b.f   56p

Lycian (IRE) 2 b.c 47p
Mitch Passi (IRE) 2 ch.g 78p
Mystery Guest (IRE) 2 b.g 62p
Norski Lad 2 b.c 58p
Pedro (IRE) 2 b.c 79p
Polar Mist 2 b.g 70p
Pressurise 2 ch.g —p
Primaticcio (IRE) 2 b.g —p
Rico Suave (IRE) 2 b.g 87p
Shipley Glen 2 b.c —p
Silent Warning 2 b.c —p
Splendid (IRE) 2 ch.f —p
Tightrope 2 b.c 80p
Ferny Hill (IRE) 3 b.c 98p
Rudimental 3 b.g 101p
Pasternak 4 b.c 109p

MRS J. R. RAMSDEN
Anstand 2 b.c 65p
Far Removed (IRE) 2 b.c 84p
Naviasky (IRE) 2 b.g 74p
Noble Demand (USA) 2 b.g 86p
Nordic Pirjo 2 b.f —p
Surprised 2 b.g 77p

MRS M. REVELEY
Flaxen Pride (IRE) 2 ch.f 62p
Angus-G 5 br.g 98p
Mondragon 7 b.g —p

A. DE ROYER DUPRE, FRANCE
Daymarti (IRE) 2 b.c 108p
Zalaiyka (FR) 2 b.f 107p

MISS B. SANDERS
Superchief 2 b.g 78p

B. SMART
King Slayer 2 b.c 66p

T. STACK, IRELAND
Tarascon (IRE) 2 b.f 102p

A. C. STEWART
Balaitini 2 b.f 71p
Cruinn A Bhord 2 b.f 82p
Mutamam 2 b.c 111p
Ranna 2 b.f 80p
Russian Party (IRE) 2 ch.c 69p
Teroom 2 br.c 75p
Prince Alex (IRE) 3 b.c 73p

M. R. STOUTE
Angstrom (IRE) 2 b.g 91p
Aquarela 2 b.f —p
Astrapi 2 b.f 80p
Brave Reward (USA) 2 b.c 89p
Careful Timing 2 b.f 71p
Caribbean Monarch (IRE) 2 b.c —p
Close Shave 2 b.c 79p
Confidante (USA) 2 b.f 83p
Dancing Phantom 2 b.g 91p
Double Classic (USA) 2 br.c 78p
Enchant 2 ch.f 65p
Exclusive 2 ch.f 103p

First Consul (USA) 2 ch.c 80p
Gleaming Hill (USA) 2 b.c 70p
Greek Dance (IRE) 2 b.c 88p
Highwayman (IRE) 2 b.c 82p
Jaazim (USA) 2 b.c 83p
Knife Edge (USA) 2 b.c —p
Lonesome Dude (CAN) 2 b.c 91p
Mawsoof 2 b.g 90p
Mockery 2 b.f —p
Muhib (USA) 2 b.c 76p
Peak Path (IRE) 2 b.c 84p
Prompt Delivery (USA) 2 b.c 77p
Rambling Rose 2 ch.f 96p
Sky Rocket 2 ch.c 95p
Title Bid (USA) 2 b.c 87p
Trident (USA) 2 b.c 94p
Tutankhamun 2 b.c —p
Among Men (USA) 3 b.c 119p
Greek Palace (IRE) 3 b.c 96p
Illusion 3 b.c 103p
Kayf Tara 3 b.c 103p
Tanaasa (IRE) 3 b.c 106p
Insatiable (IRE) 4 b.c 109p
Mohawk River (IRE) 4 b.c 101p

SAEED BIN SUROOR
Albarahin (USA) 2 b.c 94p
Altibr (USA) 2 ch.c 103p
Asad 2 ch.c 93p
Atuf (USA) 2 b.f 88p
Capital Prince (FR) 2 b.c 75p
Fa-Eq (IRE) 2 ch.c 86p
Fantasy Island (IRE) 2 b.c 100p
Kadir 2 b.c 70p
La Nuit Rose (FR) 2 b.f 93p
Mahab (USA) 2 b.f 70p
Meniatarra (USA) 2 ch.f 68p
Merciless 2 gr.f 94p
Methmoon (IRE) 2 b.c 65p
Muhaba (USA) 2 ch.f 96p
Opera King (USA) 2 ch.c 95p
Sea Wave (IRE) 2 b.c 73p
Un Melodie 2 b.f 77p
Zaya 2 ch.c 97p
Kahal 3 b.c 118p
Stowaway 3 b.c 120p

C. W. THORNTON
Glider (IRE) 2 b.f 48p

J. A. R. TOLLER
Duck Row (USA) 2 ch.c 104p
Teapot Row (IRE) 2 b.c 108p

M. H. TOMPKINS
Chist (USA) 2 b.c 78p
Dutch Lad 2 b.c 72p
Empire State (IRE) 2 b.g 69p
Hanuman Highway (IRE) 2 b.g 85p
Macca Luna (IRE) 2 b.f 62p
Nautical Warning 2 b.c 62p
Optimistic 2 b.f 85p
Pas de Memoires (IRE) 2 b.c 87p
Qilin (IRE) 2 b.f 92p

Trojan Wolf 2 ch.c 55p
Fantail 3 b.c 89p

A. VERDESI, ITALY
Nicole Pharly 3 b.f 107p

C. F. WALL
Carinthia (IRE) 2 br.f 63p
Jocasta 2 b.f 78p
Masamadas 2 ch.c 69p
Sunstreak 2 ch.c —p
Sweet Sorrow (IRE) 2 b.f 71p
Swing Along 2 ch.f 86p
Sunny Isle 3 b.f 83p

P. T. WALWYN
Labeq (IRE) 3 b.c 94p

J. W. WATTS
Torso 2 b.g —p

E. WEYMES
Arctic Air 2 br.f 79p

J. WHARTON
Fortune's Way (IRE) 3 b.f —p

S. C. WILLIAMS
Hobart Junction (IRE) 2 ch.c 65p
Razor 2 b.c 81p

S. P. C. WOODS
Banker Dwerry (FR) 2 b.c 79p
Benjamin Frank 2 b.g —p
Pursuit Venture 2 b.f 72p

G. WRAGG
Golden Lyric (IRE) 2 ch.c —p
Gulland 2 b.c 106p
Kimberley 2 b.c —p
Margone (USA) 2 b.f —p
Ridgeway (IRE) 2 b.c 71p
Sconced (USA) 2 ch.c 71p
Sixpence 2 b.f 67p
There Be Demons (USA) 2 b.c 72p
Water's Edge 2 b.f 67p
Fabled Light (IRE) 3 b.c 92p
Flint Knapper 3 ch.c 89p
Dantesque (IRE) 4 b.c 100p

SELECTED BIG RACES 1997

Prize money for racing abroad has been converted to £ sterling at the exchange rate current at the time of the race. The figures are correct to the nearest £. The Timeform ratings (TR) recorded by the principals in each race appear on the last line.

NAD AL SHEBA Thursday, Apr 3   FAST

1　**Dubai World Cup (L) (4yo+)** £1,464,049　　　　　　　　　　　　　1¼m

SINGSPIEL (IRE) *MRStoute,GB* 5-9-0 JDBailey.. 1
SIPHON (BRZ) *RMandella,USA* 6-9-0 DFlores.................................. 1¼ 2
SANDPIT (BRZ) *RMandella,USA* 8-9-0 CNakatani 1½ 3
Key of Luck (USA) *KPMcLaughlin,USA* 6-9-0 JCArias.................................. 2½ 4
Formal Gold (CAN) *WPerry,USA* 4-9-0 JBravo..................................... 1½ 5
Juggler (AUS) *MsGWaterhouse,Australia* 6-9-0 (b) GBoss 2½ 6
Even Top (IRE) *MHTompkins,GB* 4-9-0 RHills.. 5½ 7
Kammtarra (USA) *SaeedbinSuroor,GB* 4-9-0 LDettori............................... 2½ 8
Luso *CEBrittain,GB* 5-9-0 MJKinane 2½ 9
Flemensfirth (USA) *JHMGosden,GB* 5-9-0 GHind .... nk 10
Hokuto Vega (JPN) *TNakano,Japan* 7-8-11 NYokoyama............................ f
Bijou d'Inde *MJohnston,GB* 4-9-0 JWeaver.. bd

Sheikh Mohammed 12ran 2m01.91　　　　　TR: 132/130/127/123/122/117

LONGCHAMP Sunday, Apr 27   GOOD to SOFT

2　**Prix Ganay (Gr 1) (4yo+)** £53,023　　　　　　　　　　　　　1¼m110y

HELISSIO (FR) *ELellouche,France* 4-9-2 OPeslier................................. 3/5f 1
LE DESTIN (FR) *PHDemercastel,France* 4-9-2 TGillet 279/10 6 2
PILSUDSKI (IRE) *MRStoute,GB* 5-9-2 MJKinane 37/10 1½ 3
River Bay (USA) *JEHammond,France* 4-9-2 TJarnet 4/1 2 4
Strategic Choice (USA) *PFICole,GB* 6-9-2 TQuinn........................ 164/10 3 5
Bulington (FR) *HPantall,France* 5-9-2 CAsmussen....................... 22/1 4 6
Last Second (IRE) *SirMarkPrescott,GB* 4-8-13 GDuffield................ 103/10 2 7
Trojan Sea (USA) *DSmaga,France* 6-9-2 DBoeuf............................... 37/10 15 8

Mr E. Sarasola 8ran 2m12.10　　　　　　　TR: 129/119/116/113/107

NEWMARKET Friday, May 2   GOOD to FIRM (Rowley Mile Course)

3　**Grangewood Jockey Club Stks (A) (Gr 2) (4yo+)** £33,343　　　1½m

TIME ALLOWED *MRStoute* 4-8-6 JReid (3) 13/2 1
BUSY FLIGHT *BWHills* 4-8-9 MHills (8) .... 5/1 ¾ 2
MONS *LMCumani* 4-8-9 JWeaver (5).. 12/1 ¾ 3
Celeric *DMorley* 5-8-9 PatEddery (10) 10/1 2½ 4
1 Luso *CEBrittain,GB* 5-9-0 TQuinn (4) 4/1f 1¼ 5
Samraan (USA) *JLDunlop* 4-8-9 JCarroll (7) .... 14/1 sh 6
Persian Punch (IRE) *DRCElsworth* 4-8-9 RCochrane (6) .... 33/1 nk 7
Kutta *RWArmstrong* 5-8-9 RHills (2) .... 11/2 nk 8
Tulipa (USA) *SaeedbinSuroor* 4-8-9 LDettori (9)............................. 6/1 nk 9
Sacrament *MRStoute* 6-8-12 OPeslier (1)... 11/1 29 10

Mr R. Barnett 10ran 2m29.15　　　　　TR: 119/120/119/114+/117/113

NEWMARKET Saturday, May 3   GOOD to FIRM (Rowley Mile Course)

4　**Pertemps 2000 Guineas Stks (A) (Gr 1) (3yo c+f)** £131,832　　　1m

ENTREPRENEUR *MRStoute* 3-9-0 MJKinane (4)............................ 11/2 1
REVOQUE (IRE) *PWChapple-Hyam* 3-9-0 JReid (7) .... 10/3f ¾ 2
POTEEN (USA) *LMCumani* 3-9-0 PatEddery (1)............................ 9/1 1½ 3
Starborough *DRLoder* 3-9-0 KDarley (15)....................................... 33/1 sh 4
Zamindar (USA) *AFabre,France* 3-9-0 TJarnet (3)........................... 10/1 ¾ 5
Desert Story (IRE) *MRStoute* 3-9-0 RCochrane (12)...................... 12/1 5 6
Shii-Take *RAkehurst* 3-9-0 AClark (11) 100/1 1½ 7
Cape Cross (IRE) *JHMGosden* 3-9-0 OPeslier (9)......................... 20/1 ¾ 8
Green Card (USA) *SPCWoods* 3-9-0 WRyan (2)............................ 40/1 1½ 9
Muchea *MRChannon* 3-9-0 RHughes (16)...................................... 50/1 ¾ 10
Tycoon Todd (USA) *SaeedbinSuroor* 3-9-0 BDoyle (6)................. 50/1 3½ 11

1080

Za-Im *BWHills* 3-9-0 RHills (14) 66/1   8 12
Hidden Meadow *IABalding* 3-9-0 MHills (13) 7/1   1¼ 13
Shamikh *SaeedbinSuroor* 3-9-0 LDettori (5) 7/1   3½ 14
Putra (USA) *PFICole* 3-9-0 TQuinn (10).. 12/1   nk 15
Musical Pursuit *MHTompkins* 3-9-0 KFallon (8) .... 22/1   dist 16

Mr Michael Tabor & Mrs John Magnier 16ran 1m35.64   TR: 123/121/118/118/116

NEWMARKET Sunday, May 4   GOOD to FIRM (Rowley Mile Course)

5   **Pertemps 1000 Guineas Stks (A) (Gr 1) (3yo f) £104,730**   1m

SLEEPYTIME (IRE) *HRACecil* 3-9-0 KFallon (3)................................. 5/1   1
OH NELLIE (USA) *NACallaghan* 3-9-0 WRyan (11) 50/1   4 2
DAZZLE *MRStoute* 3-9-0 JReid (2)... 16/1   ¾ 3
Pas de Reponse (USA) *MmeCHead,France* 3-9-0 FHead (8) .... 5/2f   hd 4
Ocean Ridge (USA) *SaeedbinSuroor* 3-9-0 TJarnet (9)......................... 25/1   ¾ 5
Reams of Verse (USA) *HRACecil* 3-9-0 PatEddery (14)...................... 11/1   1½ 6
Elegant Warning (IRE) *BWHills* 3-9-0 DHolland (13) .... 50/1   ½ 7
Khassah *JHMGosden* 3-9-0 RHills (5)... 20/1   1¾ 8
Sarayir (USA) *MajorWRHern* 3-9-0 MRoberts (1)............................... 20/1   4 9
Moonlight Paradise (USA) *SaeedbinSuroor* 3-9-0 LDettori (4) .... 7/2   ½ 10
Bianca Nera *DRLoder* 3-9-0 KDarley (7) 50/1   1 11
Dance Parade (USA) *PFICole* 3-9-0 TQuinn (6)................................... 18/1   3½ 12
Rebecca Sharp *GWragg* 3-9-0 MHills (10)... 16/1   nk 13
Yashmak (USA) *HRACecil* 3-9-0 MJKinane (15).............................. 14/1   3½ 14
Reunion (IRE) *JWHills* 3-9-0 OPeslier (12).. 16/1   14 15

Greenbay Stables Ltd 15ran 1m37.66   TR: 121/113/111/111+/109/106

LONGCHAMP Sunday, May 11   GOOD to SOFT

6   **Dubai Poule d'Essai Des Pouliches (Gr 1) (3yo f) £106,044**   1m

ALWAYS LOYAL (USA) *MmeCHead,France* 3-9-0 FHead 14/10   1
SEEBE (USA) *IABalding,GB* 3-9-0 CAsmussen .... 39/10   hd 2
RED CAMELLIA *SirMarkPrescott,GB* 3-9-0 GDuffield.................... 74/10   ¾ 3
Dances With Dreams *PWChapple-Hyam,GB* 3-9-0 JReid................. 28/1   nk 4
Nightbird (IRE) *SaeedbinSuroor,GB* 3-9-0 LDettori 14/10   4 5
Mousse Glacee (FR) *JLesbordes,France* 3-9-0 VVion 1/1f   1 6
Star Profile (IRE) *SaeedbinSuroor,GB* 3-9-0 OPeslier....................... 14/10   2 7

Maktoum Al Maktoum 7ran 1m42.25   TR: 112/112/110/109/101

7   **Dubai Poule d'Essai Des Poulains (Gr 1) (3yo c) £106,044**   1m

DAYLAMI (IRE) *AdeRoyerDupre,France* 3-9-2 GMosse 16/10   1
LOUP SAUVAGE (USA) *AFabre,France* 3-9-2 OPeslier 32/10   2 2
VISIONARY (FR) *AFabre,France* 3-9-2 TJarnet............................... 71/10   2½ 3
Yalaietanee *MRStoute,GB* 3-9-2 TQuinn .... 11/10cpf   ¾ 4
Fantastic Fellow (USA) *CEBrittain,GB* 3-9-2 JReid 225/10   3 5
Bahamian Bounty *SaeedbinSuroor,GB* 3-9-2 LDettori 11/10cpf   10 6

H.H. Aga Khan 6ran 1m41.75   TR: 123/119/115/113/107+

YORK Tuesday, May 13   GOOD

8   **Tattersalls Musidora Stks (A) (Gr 3) (3yo f) £26,048**   1¼m85y

   5   REAMS OF VERSE (USA) *HRACecil* 3-8-11 KFallon (9) 11/10f   1
VAGABOND CHANTEUSE *TJEtherington* 3-8-8 TQuinn (2) 14/1   11 2
ETOILE (FR) *PWChapple-Hyam* 3-8-8 JReid (8) .... 11/1   hd 3
Entice (FR) *SaeedbinSuroor* 3-8-8 LDettori (5)..................................... 5/1   4 4
Society Rose *MRStoute* 3-8-8 MJKinane (4) 7/1   3½ 5
Alcalali (USA) *PAKelleway* 3-8-8 KDarley (1)..................................... 33/1   3½ 6
French Mist *CEBrittain* 3-8-8 BDoyle (3) 100/1   8 7
Noisette *JHMGosden* 3-8-8 RCochrane (7).. 7/1   1 8
Calypso Grant (IRE) *PWHarris* 3-8-8 PatEddery (6) 9/1   3 9
Dame Laura (IRE) *HMorrison* 3-8-8 CRutter (10) 33/1   9 10

Mr K. Abdulla 10ran 2m11.81   TR: 121/101/101

YORK Wednesday, May 14   GOOD

9   **Grosvenor Casinos Dante Stks (A) (Gr 2) (3yo) £79,190**   1¼m85y

BENNY THE DIP (USA) *JHMGosden* 3-8-11 OPeslier (4)................. 10/3f   1
   4   DESERT STORY (IRE) *MRStoute* 3-8-11 MJKinane (7)...................... 4/1   2½ 2
MUSALSAL (IRE) *BWHills* 3-8-11 MHills (9) .... 8/1   ¾ 3

Kingfisher Mill (USA) *MrsJCecil* 3-8-11 PatEddery (2) .... 15/2   nk 4
Monza (USA) *PWChapple-Hyam* 3-8-11 JReid (3) 16/1   2½ 5
Apprehension *DRLoder* 3-8-11 KDarley (5) .... 13/2   ½ 6
Yorkshire (IRE) *PFICole* 3-8-11 TQuinn (6) 6/1   5 7
Medaaly *SaeedbinSuroor* 3-8-11 LDettori (8) 6/1   8 8
Crimson Tide (IRE) *JWHills* 3-8-11 RHills (1) 12/1   4 9

Mr Landon Knight 9ran 2m11.97   TR: 116/111/110/110/104/103

YORK Thursday, May 15   GOOD

10   **Yorkshire Cup (A) (Gr 2) (4yo+) £55,339**   1m5f194y
3   CELERIC *DMorley* 5-8-9 PatEddery (2) 7/2   1
3   MONS *LMCumani* 4-8-9 JWeaver (1) .... 13/2   sh 2
    WHITEWATER AFFAIR *MRStoute* 4-8-6 MJKinane (8) .... 6/1   ¾ 3
3   Samraan (USA) *JLDunlop* 4-8-9 TQuinn (6) 14/1   1½ 4
3   Kutta *RWArmstrong* 5-8-9 RHills (4) .... 14/1   ½ 5
    Key To My Heart (IRE) *MissSEHall* 7-8-9 KFallon (5) .... 16/1   hd 6
    Wilawander *BWHills* 4-8-9 MHills (9) 25/1   7 7
3   Sacrament *MRStoute* 6-8-12 KDarley (7) .... 33/1   nk 8
    Classic Cliche (IRE) *SaeedbinSuroor* 5-9-0 LDettori (3) 1/1f   18 9

Mr Christopher Spence 9ran 2m59.39   TR: 117/119/115/116/113/113

NEWBURY Friday, May 16   GOOD to SOFT

11   **Juddmonte Lockinge Stks (A) (Gr 1) (4yo+) £73,321**   1m
    FIRST ISLAND (IRE) *GWragg* 5-9-0 MHills (1) 11/4   1
    ALI-ROYAL (IRE) *HRACecil* 4-9-0 KFallon (2) 9/1   1½ 2
1   EVEN TOP (IRE) *MHTompkins* 4-9-0 TQuinn (4) 9/1   5 3
    Spinning World (USA) *JEPease,France* 4-9-0 CAsmussen (7) ...... 6/4f   hd 4
    Gothenberg (IRE) *MJohnston* 4-9-0 JWeaver (9) 33/1   2 5
    Decorated Hero *JHMGosden* 5-9-0 LDettori (8) 10/1   1 6
    Acharne *CEBrittain* 4-9-0 BDoyle (5) .... 50/1   ¾ 7
    Bin Rosie *DRLoder* 5-9-0 (b) KDarley (3) .... 12/1   ¾ 8
    Beauchamp King *JLDunlop* 4-9-0 JReid (6) 40/1   8 9
    Cayman Kai (IRE) *RHannon* 4-9-0 DaneO'Neill (11) .... 25/1   sh 10

Mollers Racing 10ran 1m40.04   TR: 128/124/114/114/110/108

CURRAGH Saturday, May 24   GOOD to SOFT

12   **Airlie/Coolmore Irish 1,000 Guineas (Gr 1) (3yo f) £78,738**   1m
    CLASSIC PARK *APO'Brien,Ireland* 3-9-0 SCraine 20/1   1
    STRAWBERRY ROAN (IRE) *APO'Brien,Ireland* 3-9-0 CRoche 4/1   1 2
    CAISEAL ROS (IRE) *JSBolger,Ireland* 3-9-0 KJManning 20/1   2½ 3
    Ryafan (USA) *JHMGosden,GB* 3-9-0 LDettori .... 3/1f   sh 4
5   Oh Nellie (USA) *NACallaghan,GB* 3-9-0 MJKinane .... 9/2   ¾ 5
6   Seebe (USA) *IABalding,GB* 3-9-0 MJKinane .... 9/2   ¾ 6
    Almost Skint (IRE) *MissITOakes,Ireland* 3-9-0 NGMcCullagh 100/1   2½ 7
    Via Verbano (IRE) *JSBolger,Ireland* 3-9-0 CEverard .... 40/1   sh 8
5   Dazzle *MRStoute,GB* 3-9-0 JReid 5/1   4½ 9
    Royale (IRE) *APO'Brien,Ireland* 3-9-0 JAHeffernan .... 50/1   dist 10

Mrs Seamus Burns 10ran 1m42.20   TR: 115/113/108/108/106/104

CURRAGH Sunday, May 25   GOOD

13   **Lexus Irish 2,000 Guineas (Gr 1) (3yo c+f) £105,327**   1m
    DESERT KING (IRE) *APO'Brien,Ireland* 3-9-0 CRoche 3/1   1
    VERGLAS (IRE) *KPrendergast,Ireland* 3-9-0 WJSupple 33/1   3 2
    ROMANOV (IRE) *PWChapple-Hyam,GB* 3-9-0 RHughes 11/1   2 3
7   Yalaietanee *MRStoute,GB* 3-9-0 MJKinane 8/1   2 4
7   Fantastic Fellow (USA) *CEBrittain,GB* 3-9-0 BDoyle 33/1   2½ 5
4   Revoque (IRE) *PWChapple-Hyam,GB* 3-9-0 JReid .... 11/10f   ¾ 6
    Mosconi (IRE) *JSBolger,Ireland* 3-9-0 KJManning .... 9/1   ¾ 7
    Bob The Broker (IRE) *PJFlynn,Ireland* 3-9-0 PVGilson 200/1   3 8
    Peartree House (IRE) *WRMuir,GB* 3-9-0 DaneO'Neill 50/1   3 9
4   Musical Pursuit *MHTompkins,GB* 3-9-0 PatEddery 20/1   1 10
    Royal Amaretto (IRE) *BJMeehan,GB* 3-9-0 OPeslier 7/1   2 11
    Sharemono (USA) *APO'Brien,Ireland* 3-9-0 (b) JAHeffernan 100/1   12 12

Mr M. Tabor 12ran 1m38.30   TR: 124/118/114/112/105/103

LONGCHAMP Sunday, May 25   GOOD to SOFT

14   Prix d'Ispahan (Gr 1) (4yo+ c+f) £53,533   1m1f55y

SASURU *GWragg,GB* 4-9-2 MHills	6/5f		1
WIXIM (USA) *RCharlton,GB* 4-9-2 TJarnet	3/1	sn	2
SIMON DU DESERT (FR) *RCollet,France* 4-9-2 CHanotel	36/10	3	3
Baroud d'Honneur (FR) *JFBernard,France* 4-9-2 FBlondel	76/10	sh	4
Nero Zilzal (USA) *ELellouche,France* 4-9-2 TThulliez	14/1	3	5
Tamayaz (CAN) *SaeedbinSuroor,GB* 5-9-2 (v) SGuillot	5/1	3	6

Mr A. E. Oppenheimer 6ran 1m55.60   TR: 121/120/114/114

SANDOWN Monday, May 26   GOOD

15   Bonusprint Henry II Stks (A) (Gr 3) (4yo+) £25,240   2m78y

3	PERSIAN PUNCH (IRE) *DRCElsworth* 4-8-10 RCochrane (1)	3/1		1
10	CELERIC *DMorley* 5-9-3 LDettori (2)	7/4f	¾	2
	EVA LUNA (USA) *HRACecil* 5-8-12 MJKinane (5)	11/1	1	3
	Corradini *HRACecil* 5-8-12 KFallon (3)	11/1	¾	4
	Heron Island (IRE) *PWChapple-Hyam* 4-8-10 JReid (4)	12/1	hd	5
10	Kutta *RWArmstrong* 5-8-12 RHills (7)	10/1	2½	6
	Orchestra Stall *JLDunlop* 5-9-1 TQuinn (6)	4/1	4	7

Mr J. C. Smith 7ran 3m34.15   TR: 118/121/114/113/114/109

SANDOWN Tuesday, May 27   GOOD to FIRM

16   Brigadier Gerard Stks (A) (Gr 3) (4yo+) £18,840   1¼m7y

BOSRA SHAM (USA) *HRACecil* 4-9-0 KFallon (1)	1/5f		1
PREDAPPIO *SaeedbinSuroor* 4-9-1 LDettori (3)	12/1	½	2
CENTRE STALLS (IRE) *RFJohnsonHoughton* 4-8-10 JReid (2)	12/1	½	3
Rocky Oasis (USA) *MRStoute* 4-8-10 OPeslier (6)	50/1	½	4
Posidonas *PFICole* 5-9-1 TQuinn (5)	12/1	nk	5
Henry The Fifth *CEBrittain* 4-8-10 BDoyle (4)	100/1	14	6

Mr W. Said 6ran 2m07.87   TR: 126/126/112

CHANTILLY Sunday, Jun 1   GOOD to FIRM

17   Prix d'Abu Dhabi Airport Duty Free - Prix Jean Prat (Gr 1) (3yo c+f) 1m1f
£43,057

4	STARBOROUGH *DRLoder,GB* 3-9-2 LDettori	2/1		1
	MAMALIK (USA) *JHMGosden,GB* 3-9-2 RHills	67/10	1½	2
	KIRKWALL *AFabre,France* 3-9-2 TJarnet	6/5f	sh	3
7	Visionary (FR) *AFabre,France* 3-9-2 OPeslier	33/10	ns	4
	Cirino (USA) *MmeCHead,France* 3-9-2 FHead	63/10	2½	5

Sheikh Mohammed 5ran 1m51.70   TR: 118/115/115/115

18   United Arab Emirates Prix du Jockey-Club (Gr 1) (3yo c+f) £269,072   1½m

PEINTRE CELEBRE (USA) *AFabre,France* 3-9-2 OPeslier	31/10jf		1
OSCAR (IRE) *PBary,France* 3-9-2 SGuillot	9/1	2	2
ASTARABAD (USA) *AdeRoyerDupre,France* 3-9-2 GMosse	138/10	½	3
Fragrant Mix (IRE) *AFabre,France* 3-9-2 TJarnet	38/10	4	4
Ithaki (IRE) *JEPease,France* 3-9-2 CAsmussen	217/10	5	5
Shaka *J-CRouget,France* 3-9-2 J-RDubosc	31/10jf	¾	6
Voyagers Quest (USA) *PWChapple-Hyam,GB* 3-9-2 JReid	97/10	hd	7
Kashwan (SPA) *ELellouche,France* 3-9-2 TThulliez	504/10	sh	8
Bonapartiste (FR) *PHDemercastel,France* 3-9-2 (b) FHead	242/10	4	9
Fier Danseur (FR) *JLesbordes,France* 3-9-2 VVion	638/10	¾	10
Casey Tibbs (IRE) *DKWeld,Ireland* 3-9-2 (b) MJKinane	172/10	2	11
Arabian King (FR) *AFabre,France* 3-9-2 DBoeuf	139/10	2	12
Perfect Paradigm (IRE) *JHMGosden,GB* 3-9-2 LDettori	172/10	5	13
Speedfriend (FR) *RCollet,France* 3-9-2 CHanotel	618/10	4	14

Mr Daniel Wildenstein 14ran 2m29.60   TR: 126/122/121/115/109/108

EPSOM DOWNS Friday, Jun 6   GOOD to FIRM

19   Vodafone Coronation Cup (A) (Gr 1) (4yo+) £113,895   1½m10y

1	SINGSPIEL (IRE) *MRStoute* 5-9-0 LDettori (3)	5/4f		1
	DUSHYANTOR (USA) *HRACecil* 4-9-0 KFallon (2)	9/2	5	2
2	LE DESTIN (FR) *PHDemercastel,France* 4-9-0 TGillet (5)	14/1	½	3
	Ela-Aristokrati (IRE) *MHTompkins* 5-9-0 TQuinn (1)	14/1	4	4

Oscar Schindler (IRE) *KPrendergast,Ireland* 5-9-0 SCraine (4) 9/4 1¼ 5
Sheikh Mohammed 5ran 2m37.72   TR: 127+/120/119/112

20   **Vodafone Oaks (A) (Gr 1) (3yo f)** £182,250   1½m10y

  8   REAMS OF VERSE (USA) *HRACecil* 3-9-0 KFallon (6) 5/6f   1
        GAZELLE ROYALE (FR) *JEHammond,France* 3-9-0 JFortune (9)..... 33/1   1½ 2
        CROWN OF LIGHT *MRStoute* 3-9-0 OPeslier (8) .... 11/1   ¾ 3
  5   Yashmak (USA) *HRACecil* 3-9-0 MJKinane (7)................................. 6/1   ½ 4
  8   Etoile (FR) *PWChapple-Hyam* 3-9-0 JReid (4) .... 66/1   hd 5
        Ebadiya (IRE) *JOxx,Ireland* 3-9-0 JMurtagh (2) 15/2   1¼ 6
        Bint Baladee *SaeedbinSuroor* 3-9-0 KDarley (3)........................... 50/1   8 7
        Book At Bedtime (IRE) *CACyzer* 3-9-0 PatEddery (11) 33/1   5 8
        Imperial Scholar (IRE) *JMPEustace* 3-9-0 RCochrane (5)............. 150/1   nk 9
        Attire (FR) *CEBrittain* 3-9-0 MRoberts (12) 33/1   14 10
        Siyadah (USA) *SaeedbinSuroor* 3-9-0 (v) LDettori (10) 11/1   15 11
        Ukraine Venture *SPCWoods* 3-9-0 WRyan (1)................................. 25/1   4 12
Mr K. Abdulla 12ran 2m35.59   TR: 117+/114/112/111/111/108+

EPSOM DOWNS Saturday, Jun 7   GOOD

21   **Vodafone Derby Stks (A) (Gr 1) (3yo c+f)** £595,250   1½m10y

  9   BENNY THE DIP (USA) *JHMGosden* 3-9-0 WRyan (8)..................... 11/1   1
        SILVER PATRIARCH (IRE) *JLDunlop* 3-9-0 PatEddery (5) .... 6/1   sh 2
 13   ROMANOV (IRE) *PWChapple-Hyam* 3-9-0 JReid (7)....................... 25/1   5 3
  4   Entrepreneur *MRStoute* 3-9-0 MJKinane (13)................................ 4/6f   3½ 4
        The Fly *BWHills* 3-9-0 RCochrane (3).. 12/1   3 5
        Fahris (IRE) *BHanbury* 3-9-0 RHills (10).. 12/1   1 6
        Symonds Inn *JGFitzGerald* 3-9-0 KFallon (1) 33/1   4 7
  9   Musalsal (IRE) *BWHills* 3-9-0 MHills (6) 40/1   3½ 8
        Bold Demand *SaeedbinSuroor* 3-9-0 LDettori (2)......................... 20/1   5 9
        Cloudings (IRE) *AFabre,France* 3-9-0 OPeslier (14)...................... 12/1   12 10
        Single Empire (IRE) *PWChapple-Hyam* 3-9-0 DHarrison (4) 33/1   1¼ 11
        Crystal Hearted *HCandy* 3-9-0 AMcGlone (9) 66/1   3½ 12
        Papua *IABalding* 3-9-0 GCarter (11) 150/1   5 13
Mr Landon Knight 13ran 2m35.77   TR: 125/125/117/111/106+/104

CHANTILLY Sunday, Jun 8   GOOD to SOFT

22   **Prix de Diane Hermes (Gr 1) (3yo f)** £148,463   1¼m110y

        VEREVA (IRE) *AdeRoyerDupre,France* 3-9-0 GMosse 27/10   1
  6   MOUSSE GLACEE (FR) *JLesbordes,France* 3-9-0 TThulliez........... 97/10   1½ 2
        BRILLIANCE (FR) *PBary,France* 3-9-0 SGuillot 18/10f   2 3
 12   Ryafan (USA) *JHMGosden,GB* 3-9-0 LDettori........................... 124/10   ½ 4
        La Nana (FR) *DSepulchre,France* 3-9-0 ODoleuze .... 266/10   ns 5
  6   Always Loyal (USA) *MmeCHead,France* 3-9-0 FHead.................... 61/10   sh 6
        Golden Arches (FR) *PHDemercastel,France* 3-9-0 TGillet 341/10   1½ 7
        Anna Thea (IRE) *HBlume,Germany* 3-9-0 THellier 78/1   1 8
        Queen Maud (IRE) *JdeRoualle,France* 3-9-0 CAsmussen 97/10   1 9
        Palme d'Or (IRE) *AFabre,France* 3-9-0 OPeslier .... 57/10   ½ 10
        Darashandeh (IRE) *AdeRoyerDupre,France* 3-9-0 DBoeuf............... 27/10   3 11
  6   Dances With Dreams *PWChapple-Hyam,GB* 3-9-0 JReid.................. 311/10   1½ 12
H.H. Aga Khan 12ran 2m09.30   TR: 120/118/114/113/113/113

MILAN Sunday, Jun 15   FIRM

23   **Gran Premio di Milano (Gr 1) (3yo+)** £235,213   1½m

        SHANTOU (USA) *JHMGosden,GB* 4-9-7 LDettori................................ 1/2   1
  3   LUSO *CEBrittain,GB* 5-9-7 GaryStevens 1¼ 2
        TAIPAN (IRE) *JLDunlop,GB* 5-9-7 PatEddery .... ½ 3
  2   Strategic Choice (USA) *PFICole,GB* 6-9-7 TQuinn 1 4
        Toto Le Moko (IRE) *AVerdesi,Italy* 4-9-7 GPucciatti 8½ 5
        Needle Gun (IRE) *CEBrittain,GB* 7-9-7 BDoyle 3½ 6
Sheikh Mohammed 6ran 2m26.00   TR: 124/120/119/117

ASCOT Tuesday, Jun 17   GOOD to FIRM

24   **Queen Anne Stks (A) (Gr 2) (3yo+)** £65,080   1m (Str.)

        ALLIED FORCES (USA) *SaeedbinSuroor* 4-9-5 LDettori (11) 10/1   1
 16   CENTRE STALLS (IRE) *RFJohnsonHoughton* 4-9-2 TQuinn (4) .... 11/1   nk 2

11	ALI-ROYAL (IRE) *HRACecil* 4-9-2 KFallon (2)	9/4f	1¼	3
	Nwaamis (USA) *JLDunlop* 5-9-2 RHills (9)	11/1	1¼	4
14	Wixim (USA) *RCharlton* 4-9-5 PatEddery (3)	11/2	nk	5
11	Bin Rosie *DRLoder* 5-9-2 (b) KDarley (7)	16/1	hd	6
11	Beauchamp King *JLDunlop* 4-9-2 JReid (10)	50/1	3	7
	Amrak Ajeeb (IRE) *BHanbury* 5-9-2 MRimmer (1)	20/1	½	8
	Restructure (IRE) *MrsJCecil* 5-9-2 RCochrane (5)	20/1	nk	9
4	Hidden Meadow *IABalding* 3-8-6 MHills (8)	5/1	3	10
11	Gothenberg (IRE) *MJohnston* 4-9-5 JWeaver (6)	20/1	1	11

Godolphin 11ran 1m39.72   TR: 123/119/116/114/116/113

25 Prince of Wales's Stks (A) (Gr 2) (3yo+) £67,312   1¼m

16	BOSRA SHAM (USA) *HRACecil* 4-9-5 KFallon (1)	4/11f		1
	ALHAARTH (IRE) *SaeedbinSuroor* 4-9-6 LDettori (4)	10/1	8	2
	LONDON NEWS (SAF) *BWHills* 5-9-8 DJWhyte (5)	10/1	5	3
11	Even Top (IRE) *MHTompkins* 4-9-3 TQuinn (2)	13/2	½	4
11	Acharne *CEBrittain* 4-9-3 BDoyle (3)	66/1	½	5
	Balalaika *LMCumani* 4-9-0 JReid (7)	25/1	hd	6

Mr W. Said 6ran 2m04.16   TR: 130/118/111

26 St James's Palace Stks (A) (Gr 1) (3yo c+f) £134,680   1m (Rnd)

17	STARBOROUGH *DRLoder* 3-9-0 LDettori (5)	11/2		1
	AIR EXPRESS (IRE) *CEBrittain* 3-9-0 BDoyle (8)	20/1	1	2
7	DAYLAMI (IRE) *AdeRoyerDupre,France* 3-9-0 GMosse (7)	7/2	4	3
13	Desert King (IRE) *APO'Brien,Ireland* 3-9-0 CRoche (3)	2/1f	½	4
4	Poteen (USA) *LMCumani* 3-9-0 PatEddery (4)	7/2	2	5
	In Command (IRE) *BWHills* 3-9-0 MHills (4)	25/1	5	6
	Running Stag (USA) *PMitchell* 3-9-0 KFallon (6)	66/1	1½	7
17	Mamalik (USA) *JHMGosden* 3-9-0 RHills (1)	11/1	16	8

Sheikh Mohammed 8ran 1m39.18   TR: 126/124/115/114/110

ASCOT Wednesday, Jun 18   GOOD to FIRM

27 Coronation Stks (A) (Gr 1) (3yo f) £121,200   1m (Rnd)

5	REBECCA SHARP *GWragg* 3-9-0 MHills (3)	25/1		1
5	OCEAN RIDGE (USA) *SaeedbinSuroor* 3-9-0 GaryStevens (6)	16/1	¾	2
5	SLEEPYTIME (IRE) *HRACecil* 3-9-0 KFallon (4)	5/6f	2	3
12	Classic Park *APO'Brien,Ireland* 3-9-0 SCraine (2)	4/1	1½	4
5	Khassah *JHMGosden* 3-9-0 RHills (1)	8/1	hd	5
5	Moonlight Paradise (USA) *SaeedbinSuroor* 3 9 0 LDettori (5)	6/1	4	6

Mr A. E. Oppenheimer 6ran 1m42.04   TR: 117/115/111/108/108

ASCOT Thursday, Jun 19   GOOD

28 Gold Cup (A) (Gr 1) (4yo+) £113,556   2½m

15	CELERIC *DMorley* 5-9-2 PatEddery (2)	11/2		1
10	CLASSIC CLICHE (IRE) *SaeedbinSuroor* 5-9-2 LDettori (10)	6/1	¾	2
15	ELECTION DAY (IRE) *MRStoute* 5-9-2 (v) MJKinane (13)	25/1	1	3
15	Heron Island (IRE) *PWChapple-Hyam* 4-9-0 JReid (11)	33/1	5	4
10	Samraan (USA) *JLDunlop* 4-9-0 TQuinn (1)	10/1	9	5
	Double Eclipse (IRE) *MJohnston* 5-9-2 MRoberts (4)	14/1	hd	6
	Jiyush *EALDunlop* 4-9-0 RHills (12)	20/1	3½	7
	Double Trigger (IRE) *MJohnston* 6-9-2 (b) JWeaver (7)	9/1	4	8
	Moonax (IRE) *BWHills* 6-9-2 MHills (6)	16/1	7	9
	Camp David (GER) *AWohler,Germany* 7-9-2 AndreasBoschert (5)	25/1	10	10
	Nononito (FR) *JLesbordes,France* 6-9-2 GMosse (8)	15/2	5	11
15	Persian Punch (IRE) *DRCElsworth* 4-9-0 RCochrane (3)	9/2f	½	12
	Grey Shot *IABalding* 5-9-2 OPeslier (9)	12/1	1	13

Mr Christopher Spence 13ran 4m26.19   TR: 121/120/119/116

29 Cork And Orrery Stks (A) (Gr 3) (3yo+) £34,850   6f

	ROYAL APPLAUSE *BWHills* 4-9-3 MHills (16)	11/2f		1
	BLUE GOBLIN (USA) *LMCumani* 3-8-6 GaryStevens (4)	13/2	1½	2
	CATCH THE BLUES (IRE) *APO'Brien,Ireland* 5-9-0 (v) CRoche (21)	12/1	sh	3
	Monaassib *EALDunlop* 6-9-3 DO'Donohoe (7)	11/1	1½	4
	Indian Rocket *JLDunlop* 3-9-0 RHills (19)	33/1	nk	5
	Royale Figurine (IRE) *MJFetherston-Godley* 6-8-10 DHolland (5)	14/1	hd	6

Blue Duster (USA) *SaeedbinSuroor* 4-8-10 LDettori (14) .... 13/2 nk 7
Almushtarak (IRE) *KMahdi* 4-8-13 RPrice (11) .... 50/1 nk 8
Easy Dollar *BGubby* 5-8-13 (b) AClark (1) .... 25/1 ¾ 9
Tedburrow *EJAlston* 5-8-13 ACulhane (15).. 25/1 nk 10
Lucayan Prince (USA) *DRLoder* 4-9-3 (b) OPeslier (17) .... 9/1 ¾ 11
Connemara (IRE) *CADwyer* 3-8-3 DHarrison (2)................................... 25/1 2 12
Soviet State (USA) *PWChapple-Hyam* 3-8-6 JReid (13) 33/1 1 13
Farhana *WJarvis* 4-8-10 PatEddery (25) .... 14/1 ½ 14
Jayannpee *IABalding* 6-8-13 MartinDwyer (23) 33/1 1¼ 15
11 Cayman Kai (IRE) *RHannon* 4-8-13 RHughes (18) .... 33/1 nk 16
Burden of Proof (IRE) *CharlesO'Brien,Ireland* 5-9-3 JMurtagh (20).... 16/1 sh 17
Cyrano's Lad (IRE) *CADwyer* 8-8-13 KFallon (22) 33/1 2 18
China Girl (IRE) *PWChapple-Hyam* 3-8-3 DJWhyte (24) 50/1 3½ 19
Theano (IRE) *APO'Brien,Ireland* 4-8-10 TQuinn (9)........................... 33/1 ½ 20
Moonshine Girl (USA) *MRStoute* 3-8-3 WRyan (10)............................. 33/1 1¼ 21
Russian Music *MissGayKelleway* 4-8-13 JWeaver (12) .... 40/1 ½ 22
Ailleacht (USA) *JSBolger,Ireland* 5-8-10 MJKinane (8)....................... 25/1 2 23
Maktoum Al Maktoum 23ran 1m15.33   TR: 123/112/115/114/115/106

ASCOT Friday, Jun 20   Race 30: GOOD
   Race 31: GOOD TO SOFT

30   **Hardwicke Stks (A) (Gr 2) (4yo+)** £74,511   1½m
16 PREDAPPIO *SaeedbinSuroor* 4-8-12 GaryStevens (7) 6/1 1
 2 PILSUDSKI (IRE) *MRStoute* 5-9-0 MJKinane (3)................................. 2/1f ½ 2
10 WHITEWATER AFFAIR *MRStoute* 4-8-6 OPeslier (9) 12/1 2½ 3
Royal Court (IRE) *PWChapple-Hyam* 4-8-9 JReid (10)......................... 14/1 3½ 4
19 Ela-Aristokrati (IRE) *MHTompkins* 5-8-9 RCochrane (4) 20/1 1 5
19 Dushyantor (USA) *HRACecil* 4-8-9 WRyan (6) .... 8/1 ½ 6
King Alex *RCharlton* 4-8-9 PatEddery (8)... 6/1 1¾ 7
Mongol Warrior (USA) *LordHuntingdon* 4-8-12 DHarrison (5) 33/1 13 8
Lady Carla *HRACecil* 4-8-11 KFallon (2).. 7/1 1 9
 3 Busy Flight *BWHills* 4-8-9 MHills (1) 11/1 8 10
Godolphin 10ran 2m32.14   TR: 126/126/115/112/109/112

31   **King's Stand Stks (A) (Gr 2) (3yo+)** £73,512   5f
DON'T WORRY ME (IRE) *GHenrot,France* 5-8-13 OPeslier (4)........ 33/1 1
TITUS LIVIUS (FR) *JEPease,France* 4-9-2 CAsmussen (2) .... 7/1cf nk 2
HEVER GOLF ROSE *TJNaughton* 6-8-13 PatEddery (3) 7/1cf 1 3
Averti (IRE) *BJMeehan* 6-9-2 KFallon (8) 33/1 1 4
Easycall *BJMeehan* 3-8-10 MTebbutt (11).. 11/1 ¾ 5
Struggler *DRLoder* 5-9-2 KDarley (15)... 16/1 ½ 6
Rambling Bear *MBlanshard* 4-9-2 RCochrane (1).................................. 12/1 sh 7
Bolshoi (IRE) *JBerry* 5-9-2 (b) MJKinane (17)..................................... 10/1 hd 8
Croft Pool *JAGlover* 6-9-2 GCarter (14)... 16/1 nk 9
Ya Malak *DNicholls* 6-9-2 AlexGreaves (13) .... 8/1 ½ 10
Deep Finesse *MAJarvis* 3-8-10 (b) MRoberts (5).................................. 12/1 1¼ 11
Compton Place *JARToller* 3-8-10 SSanders (7) .... 12/1 hd 12
Cathedral (IRE) *BJMeehan* 3-8-10 TQuinn (9)..................................... 20/1 ¾ 13
Check The Band *APO'Brien,Ireland* 3-8-10 (b) CRoche (12).... .... 20/1 sh 14
Almaty (IRE) *JHMGosden* 4-9-2 GaryStevens (16) .... 7/1cf ¾ 15
Brave Edge *RHannon* 6-9-2 DaneO'Neill (18) .... 33/1 nk 16
29 Royale Figurine (IRE) *MJFetherston-Godley* 6-8-13 DHolland (6)....... 20/1 ½ 17
Sylva Paradise (IRE) *CEBrittain* 4-9-2 DJWhyte (10) 66/1 3 18
Mr J. F. Gribomont 18ran 1m01.95   TR: 113/115/109/109/104/106+

LONGCHAMP Sunday, Jun 22 SOFT

32   **Grand Prix de Paris (Gr 1) (3yo c+f)** £125,130   1¼m
18 PEINTRE CELEBRE (USA) *AFabre,France* 3-9-2 OPeslier 2/5cpf 1
18 ITHAKI (IRE) *JEPease,France* 3-9-2 CAsmussen 128/10 2 2
18 SHAKA *J-CRouget,France* 3-9-2 J-RDubosc 3/1 1 3
Alekos (USA) *CLaffon-Parias,France* 3-9-2 DBoeuf 145/10 5 4
13 Royal Amaretto (IRE) *BJMeehan,GB* 3-9-2 MTebbutt...................... 112/10 2½ 5
Zenith Rose (FR) *PLenogue,France* 3-9-2 SGuillot .... 98/10 sh 6
Super Cub (USA) *AFabre,France* 3-9-2 TJarnet 2/5cpf 20 7
Mr Daniel Wildenstein 7ran 2m08.40   TR: 119+/115/113

CURRAGH Sunday, Jun 29 GOOD to SOFT

33   **Budweiser Irish Derby (Gr 1) (3yo c+f) £362,000**   1½m

26	DESERT KING (IRE) *APO'Brien,Ireland* 3-9-0 CRoche	11/2	1
	DR JOHNSON (USA) *CharlesO'Brien,Ireland* 3-9-0 JPMurtagh	12/1	1 2
7	LOUP SAUVAGE (USA) *AFabre,France* 3-9-0 OPeslier	8/1	sh 3
	Johan Cruyff *APO'Brien,Ireland* 3-9-0 JAHeffernan	12/1	7 4
21	Silver Patriarch (IRE) *JLDunlop,GB* 3-9-0 PatEddery	5/4f	5 5
13	Verglas (IRE) *KPrendergast,Ireland* 3-9-0 WJSupple	33/1	hd 6
18	Casey Tibbs (IRE) *DKWeld,Ireland* 3-9-0 PShanahan	33/1	1 7
12	Strawberry Roan (IRE) *APO'Brien,Ireland* 3-8-11 LDettori	5/1	10 8
21	The Fly *BWHills,GB* 3-9-0 MHills	11/1	3 9
	Token Gesture (IRE) *DKWeld,Ireland* 3-8-11 MJKinane	16/1	4½ 10

Mr Michael Tabor & Mrs John Magnier 10ran 2m32.50   TR: 124/122/122/112

HOLLYWOOD PARK Sunday, Jun 29   FAST

34   **Hollywood Gold Cup (Gr 1) (3yo+) £363,636**   1¼m

	GENTLEMEN (ARG) *RMandella,USA* 5-8-12 GStevens	6/10cp	1
1	SIPHON (BRZ) *RMandella,USA* 6-8-12 DFlores		4 2
1	SANDPIT (BRZ) *RMandella,USA* 8-8-12 CNakatani		4 3
	Marlin (USA) *DWayneLukas,USA* 4-8-12 McCarron		1¼ 4
	Region (USA) *RMandella,USA* 8-8-12 LPincayjnr		6½ 5
	Talloires (USA) *RMandella,USA* 7-8-12 ASolis	6/10cp	nk 6

E. Andrea & Hubbard 6ran Time not taken   TR: 136/130/125/123

SAINT-CLOUD Sunday, Jun 29   GOOD to SOFT

35   **Grand Prix de Saint-Cloud (Gr 1) (3yo+ c+f) £124,095**   1½m

2	HELISSIO (FR) *ELellouche,France* 4-9-8 CAsmussen	1/10f	1
	MAGELLANO (USA) *AFabre,France* 3-8-8 TGillet	92/10	5 2
	RIYADIAN *PFICole,GB* 5-9-8 TQuinn	85/10	3 3
	Darazari (IRE) *AdeRoyerDupre,France* 4-9-8 GMosse	74/10	4 4

Mr E. Sarasola 4ran 2m29.50   TR: 133/123/119

SANDOWN Saturday, Jul 5   GOOD to SOFT

36   **Coral-Eclipse Stks (A) (Gr 1) (3yo+) £145,440**   1¼m7y

30	PILSUDSKI (IRE) *MRStoute* 5-9-7 MJKinane (1)	11/2	1
21	BENNY THE DIP (USA) *JHMGosden* 3-8-10 WRyan (2)	6/1	1¼ 2
25	BOSRA SHAM (USA) *HRACecil* 4-9-4 KFallon (4)	4/7f	sh 3
24	Allied Forces (USA) *SaeedbinSuroor* 4 9-7 LDettori (5)	16/1	3½ 4
14	Sasuru *GWragg* 4-9-7 MHills (3)	8/1	5 5

Lord Weinstock 5ran 2m12.51   TR: 131/127/126+/123/114

NEWMARKET Tuesday, Jul 8   GOOD (July Course)

37   **Princess of Wales's Stks (A) (Gr 2) (3yo+) £32,908**   1½m

23	SHANTOU (USA) *JHMGosden* 4-9-7 LDettori (7)	11/4	1
23	SWAIN (IRE) *SaeedbinSuroor* 5-9-7 MJKinane (5)	15/8f	hd 2
23	TAIPAN (IRE) *JLDunlop* 5-9-2 TQuinn (4)	10/1	4 3
30	Ela-Aristokrati (IRE) *MHTompkins* 5-9-2 RCochrane (6)	25/1	2½ 4
28	Celeric *DMorley* 5-9-7 PatEddery (1)	13/2	1 5
30	Dushyantor (USA) *HRACecil* 4-9-5 KFallon (2)	8/1	½ 6
30	Lady Carla *HRACecil* 4-9-4 WRyan (3)	10/1	6 7

Sheikh Mohammed 7ran 2m29.16   TR: 125/125/114/110/113/110

NEWMARKET Thursday, Jul 10   GOOD (July Course)

38   **Darley July Cup (A) (Gr 1) (3yo+) £92,270**   6f

31	COMPTON PLACE *JARToller* 3-8-13 SSanders (1)	50/1	1
29	ROYAL APPLAUSE *BWHills* 4-9-5 MHills (7)	11/10f	1¾ 2
29	INDIAN ROCKET *JLDunlop* 3-8-13 RHills (6)	9/1	3 3
7	Bahamian Bounty *SaeedbinSuroor* 3-8-13 LDettori (4)	9/2	hd 4
	Coastal Bluff *TDBarron* 5-9-5 KDarley (2)	10/1	1¼ 5
31	Easycall *BJMeehan* 3-8-13 MTebbutt (8)	33/1	nk 6
31	Rambling Bear *MBlanshard* 4-9-5 RCochrane (5)	50/1	½ 7
29	Blue Goblin (USA) *LMCumani* 3-8-13 PatEddery (3)	6/1	3½ 8
29	Lucayan Prince (USA) *DRLoder* 4-9-5 OPeslier (9)	12/1	2½ 9

Duke of Devonshire 9ran 1m12.10   TR: 125/123/113/113/112+/109

39   Kildangan Stud Irish Oaks (Gr 1) (3yo f) £101,532   1½m

20	EBADIYLA (IRE) *JOxx,Ireland* 3-9-0 JPMurtagh	9/2	1
20	YASHMAK (USA) *HRACecil,GB* 3-9-0 KFallon	6/4f	3 2
22	BRILLIANCE (FR) *PBary,France* 3-9-0 SGuillot	5/1	hd 3
33	Strawberry Roan (IRE) *APO'Brien,Ireland* 3-9-0 CRoche	6/1	5 4
	Family Tradition (IRE) *APO'Brien,Ireland* 3-9-0 (b) WJSupple	33/1	1½ 5
20	Etoile (FR) *PWChapple-Hyam,GB* 3-9-0 JReid	14/1	½ 6
12	Via Verbano (IRE) *JSBolger,Ireland* 3-9-0 KJManning	33/1	3 7
12	Caiseal Ros (IRE) *JSBolger,Ireland* 3-9-0 CEverard	25/1	4½ 8
	Aliya (IRE) *JOxx,Ireland* 3-9-0 PJSmullen	33/1	hd 9
	Shell Ginger (IRE) *APO'Brien,Ireland* 3-9-0 (b) JAHeffernan	33/1	15 10
	Absolute Glee (USA) *DKWeld,Ireland* 3-9-0 (b) MJKinane	20/1	1 11

H.H. Aga Khan 11ran 2m33.70   TR: 122/117/117/112/107/106

40   King George VI And Queen Elizabeth Diamond Stks (A) (Gr 1) (3yo+)   1½m
£294,600

37	SWAIN (IRE) *SaeedbinSuroor* 5-9-7 JReid (5)	16/1	1
36	PILSUDSKI (IRE) *MRStoute* 5-9-7 MJKinane (8)	6/1	1 2
35	HELISSIO (FR) *ELellouche,France* 4-9-7 CAsmussen (2)	11/10f	1¼ 3
19	Singspiel (IRE) *MRStoute* 5-9-7 LDettori (6)	4/1	2½ 4
37	Shantou (USA) *JHMGosden* 4-9-7 GHind (1)	16/1	4 5
23	Strategic Choice (USA) *PFICole* 6-9-7 RCochrane (4)	66/1	5 6
30	Predappio *SaeedbinSuroor* 4-9-7 GaryStevens (7)	12/1	3 7
9	Kingfisher Mill (USA) *MrsJCecil* 3-8-9 PatEddery (3)	8/1	13 8

Godolphin 8ran 2m36.45   TR: 134/132/130/126/120/113

41   Lanson Champagne Vintage Stks (A) (Gr 3) (2yo) £23,590   7f

	CENTRAL PARK (IRE) *PFICole* 2-9-0 PatEddery (1)	5/4f	1
	DOCKSIDER (USA) *JWHills* 2-8-11 MHills (5)	7/1	3 2
	LITTLE INDIAN *SPCWoods* 2-8-11 WRyan (6)	10/1	1¾ 3
	Arawak Cay (IRE) *DRLoder* 2-8-11 MJKinane (4)	11/2	½ 4
	Baltic State (USA) *HRACecil* 2-9-0 KFallon (3)	11/4	hd 5
	Lone Piper *CEBrittain* 2-8-11 MRoberts (2)	33/1	1½ 6

H.R.H. Prince Fahd Salman 6ran 1m27.26   TR: 117/105/100

42   Sussex Stks (A) (Gr 1) (3yo+) £92,775   1m

24	ALI-ROYAL (IRE) *HRACecil* 4-9-7 KFallon (3)	13/2	1
26	STARBOROUGH *DRLoder* 3-8-13 PatEddery (6)	9/4f	¾ 2
36	ALLIED FORCES (USA) *SaeedbinSuroor* 4-9-7 JReid (9)	9/2	¾ 3
	Among Men (USA) *MRStoute* 3-8-13 MJKinane (7)	9/2	1 4
27	Classic Park *APO'Brien,Ireland* 3-8-10 SCraine (8)	20/1	1¾ 5
24	Gothenberg (IRE) *MJohnston* 4-9-7 JWeaver (4)	25/1	2 6
26	Air Express (IRE) *CEBrittain* 3-8-13 BDoyle (2)	7/1	5 7
	Wolf Mountain *RHannon* 3-8-13 DaneO'Neill (5)	66/1	1¾ 8
25	Alhaarth (IRE) *SaeedbinSuroor* 4-9-7 RHills (1)	15/2	3½ 9

Greenbay Stables Ltd 9ran 1m37.98   TR: 127/123/123/119/113/114

43   Crowson Goodwood Cup (A) (Gr 2) (3yo+) £38,724   2m

28	DOUBLE TRIGGER (IRE) *MJohnston* 6-9-0 MRoberts (1)	16/1	1
28	CLASSIC CLICHE (IRE) *SaeedbinSuroor* 5-9-5 LDettori (6)	5/4f	1½ 2
28	DOUBLE ECLIPSE (IRE) *MJohnston* 5-9-0 JWeaver (3)	12/1	½ 3
28	Election Day (IRE) *MRStoute* 5-9-0 (v) OPeslier (2)	7/1	2½ 4
28	Persian Punch (IRE) *DRCElsworth* 4-9-0 RCochrane (10)	7/1	4 5
28	Samraan (USA) *JLDunlop* 4-9-0 PatEddery (9)	13/2	hd 6
	Canon Can (USA) *HRACecil* 4-9-0 AMcGlone (8)	25/1	2½ 7
28	Grey Shot *IABalding* 5-9-3 JReid (4)	20/1	2½ 8
	State Fair *BWHills* 3-7-13 TSprake (7)	50/1	5 9
15	Corradini *HRACecil* 5-9-0 KFallon (5)	12/1	dist 10

Mr R. W. Huggins 10ran 3m24.81   TR: 123/126/120/116/113/113

44 **Grosser Dallmayr Preis-Bayerisches Zuchtrennen (Gr 1) (3yo+)** £71,088   1¼m

	OXALAGU (GER) *BSchutz,Germany* 5-9-6 AStarke	29/10		1
	DANCE DESIGN (IRE) *DKWeld,Ireland* 4-9-2 MJKinane		½	2
	EDEN ROCK (GER) *BSchutz,Germany*		3	3
	Narrabeth (IRE) *UStoltefuss,Germany* 4-9-6 DHolland		1	4
	La Blue (GER) *BSchutz,Germany* 4-9-2 WNewnes		¾	5
23	Needle Gun (IRE) *CEBrittain,GB* 7-9-6 BDoyle		¾	6

Gestut Rietberg 6ran 2m04.60   TR: 123/118/113

DEAUVILLE Sunday, Aug 10   GOOD to SOFT

45 **Prix Maurice de Gheest (Gr 1) (3yo+)** £48,781   6f110y

	OCCUPANDISTE (IRE) *MmeCHead,France* 4-8-13 ODoleuze	82/10		1
29	MONAASSIB *EALDunlop,GB* 6-9-2 DJO'Donohoe	6/5f	½	2
31	TITUS LIVIUS (FR) *JEPease,France* 4-9-2 CAsmussen	6/4	¾	3
	Kahal *SaeedbinSuroor,GB* 3-8-12 RHills	6/5	1½	4
	Deadly Dudley (IRE) *RHannon,GB* 3-8-12 OPeslier	63/10	nk	5
	Winning Smile (FR) *TClout,France* 7-9-2 (b) TGillet	158/10	5	6
	Wardara *FBellenger,France* 5-8-13 (b) MDeSmyter	529/10	2	7
	Nombre Premier *AdeRoyerDupre,France* 3-8-12 GMosse	59/10	8	8

Wertheimer et Frere 8ran 1m16.70   TR: 115/117/115/111/110

DEAUVILLE Sunday, Aug 17   GOOD to FIRM

46 **Prix du Haras de Fresnay-Le-Buffard Jacques le Marois (Gr 1)** 1m
(3yo+ c+f) £101,419

11	SPINNING WORLD (USA) *JEPease,France* 4-9-4 CAsmussen	29/10		1
26	DAYLAMI (IRE) *AdeRoyerDupre,France* 3-8-11 GMosse	24/10	2	2
	NEUILLY (USA) *AFabre,France* 3-8-11 TJarnet	7/1	6	3
42	Starborough *DRLoder,GB* 3-8-11 LDettori	6/5f	3	4
4	Zamindar (USA) *AFabre,France* 3-8-11 OPeslier	49/10	½	5
	Piperi (IRE) *JEPease,France* 3-8-11 FSanchez	29/10	dist	6

Niarchos Family 6ran 1m34.40   TR: 130/124/112/107/106

GELSENKIRCHEN-HORST Sunday, Aug 17   GOOD to FIRM

47 **Aral-Pokal (Gr 1) (3yo+)** £71,917   1½m

	CAITANO *BSchutz,Germany* 3-8-8 AStarke	27/10		1
23	LUSO *CEBrittain,GB* 5-9-6 MRoberts	11/10f	1¾	2
	QUE BELLE (CAN) *HRemmert,Germany* 3-8-5 KWoodburn	18/10	sh	3
	Protektor (GER) *ALowe,Germany* 8-9-6 ASuborics	25/1	4½	4
	Night Petticoat (GER) *BSchutz,Germany* 4-9-2 TMundry	40/1	1¼	5
	Try Again (GER) *AWohler,Germany* 6-9-6 ABoschert	20/1	¾	6
	Asolo (GER) *BSchutz,Germany* 3-8-8 WNewnes	40/1	1¾	7
	Bad Bertrich Again (IRE) *ALowe,Germany* 4-9-6 GBocskai	185/10	2	8

Stall Blauer Reiter 8ran 2m29.82   TR: 125/124/119

YORK Tuesday, Aug 19   GOOD

48 **Juddmonte International Stks (A) (Gr 1) (3yo+)** £202,152   1¼m85y

40	SINGSPIEL (IRE) *MRStoute* 5-9-5 LDettori (3)	4/1		1
33	DESERT KING (IRE) *APO'Brien,Ireland* 3-8-11 MJKinane (1)	6/1	1½	2
36	BENNY THE DIP (USA) *JHMGosden* 3-8-11 WRyan (3)	9/2	1½	3
36	Bosra Sham (USA) *HRACecil* 4-9-2 PatEddery (4)	4/5f	1¼	4

Sheikh Mohammed 4ran 2m12.10   TR: 133/129/127/123

49 **Great Voltigeur Stks (A) (Gr 2) (3yo c+g)** £55,888   1m3f195y

	STOWAWAY *SaeedbinSuroor* 3-8-9 LDettori (3)	6/5f		1
33	SILVER PATRIARCH (IRE) *JLDunlop* 3-8-9 PatEddery (2)	15/8	½	2
40	KINGFISHER MILL (USA) *MrsJCecil* 3-8-12 MJKinane (5)	4/1	1¾	3
9	Apprehension *DRLoder* 3-8-9 RCochrane (1)	16/1	4	4
	Garuda (IRE) *JLDunlop* 3-8-9 JReid (4)	50/1	24	5

Godolphin 5ran 2m33.23   TR: 120/119/120/109

YORK Wednesday, Aug 20   GOOD

50 **Aston Upthorpe Yorkshire Oaks (A) (Gr 1) (3yo+ f+m)** £97,345   1m3f195y

	MY EMMA *RGuest* 4-9-4 DHolland (7)	7/1		1
30	WHITEWATER AFFAIR *MRStoute* 4-9-4 JReid (8)	7/1	¾	2

```
 20  CROWN OF LIGHT MRStoute 3-8-8 OPeslier (3) ................................. 12/1    1¾  3
 20  Reams of Verse (USA) HRACecil 3-8-8 KFallon (6) ........................... 4/7f    2  4
     Papering (IRE) LMCumani 4-9-4 PatEddery (2) ............................... 12/1    ¾  5
     Squeak JHMGosden 3-8-8 LDettori (4) .......................................... 15/2    2½  6
  8  Alcalali (USA) PAKelleway 3-8-8 JFortune (5) ............................... 100/1    7  7
 20  Attitre (FR) CEBrittain 3-8-8 MRoberts (1) .................................. 40/1    19  8
```

Matthews Breeding and Racing 8ran 2m30.59   TR: 116+/115/112/108

YORK Thursday, Aug 21   Race 51: GOOD
  Race 52: GOOD to SOFT

51 Stakis Casinos Lowther Stks (A) (Gr 2) (2yo f) £45,407   6f

```
     CAPE VERDI (IRE) PWChapple-Hyam 2-8-11 JReid (10) ................... 7/4f        1
     EMBASSY DRLoder 2-9-0 PatEddery (6) ...................................... 11/4    sh  2
     NADWAH (USA) PTWalwyn 2-9-0 RHills (1) .................................. 9/1    1½  3
     Miss Zafonic (FR) RHannon 2-8-11 DaneO'Neill (8) ......................... 6/1    3  4
     Statua (IRE) PJMakin 2-8-11 JFortune (9) ..................................... 66/1    ½  5
     Zelanda (IRE) JHMGosden 2-8-11 OPeslier (4) .............................. 10/1    nk  6
     Dazilyn Lady (USA) PWHarris 2-8-11 ACulhane (5) ......................... 25/1    1  7
     Expect To Shine BWHills (9) ..................................................... 10/1    10  8
     Shuhrah (USA) SaeedbinSuroor 2-8-11 LDettori (7) ......................... 11/2    5  9
```

Mr R. E. Sangster 9ran 1m12.48   TR: 108+/111/107/96/95

52 Nunthorpe Stks (A) (Gr 1) (2yo+) £53,110   5f

```
 38  COASTAL BLUFF TDBarron 5-9-9 KDarley (6) ............................... 6/1        1
 31  YA MALAK DNicholls 6-9-9 AlexGreaves (4) ................................ 11/1    dh  1
 31  AVERTI (IRE) WRMuir 6-9-9 KFallon (10) .................................... 10/1    hd  3
 29  Cyrano's Lad (IRE) CADwyer 8-9-9 JFortune (13) ......................... 50/1    ¾  4
     Eveningperformance HCandy 6-9-6 CRutter (1) ............................. 12/1    1  5
 31  Hever Golf Rose TJNaughton 6-9-6 JReid (16) ............................... 20/1    nk  6
     Mind Games JBerry 5-9-9 DHolland (15) ...................................... 9/1    1¼  7
 31  Bolshoi (IRE) JBerry 5-9-9 (b) EmmaO'Gorman (9) ...................... 20/1    nk  8
 31  Don't Worry Me (IRE) GHenrot,France 5-9-6 OPeslier (5) ............... 10/1    nk  9
 38  Indian Rocket JLDunlop 3-9-7 RHills (14) ..................................... 9/1    nk  10
 31  Croft Pool JAGlover 6-9-9 GCarter (11) ....................................... 40/1    2½  11
 38  Easycall BJMeehan 3-9-7 MTebbutt (12) ...................................... 12/1    ¾  12
 31  Struggler DRLoder 5-9-9 MRoberts (8) ........................................ 16/1    1  13
 38  Compton Place JARToller 3-9-7 SSanders (3) ................................ 9/2f    8  14
 31  Almaty (IRE) JHMGosden 4-9-9 LDettori (2) ................................ 10/1    1½  15
```

Mrs D. E. Sharp 15ran 59.58secs
Contrac Promotions Ltd, Consultco Ltd   TR: 118/118/117/115/109

GOODWOOD Saturday, Aug 23   GOOD

53 Tripleprint Celebration Mile (A) (Gr 2) (3yo+) £37,475   1m

Order as they passed the post: Cape Cross was disqualified and placed last for causing
interference to the third and fourth

```
  4  CAPE CROSS (IRE) JHMGosden 3-8-9 LDettori (3) ......................... 7/2        1
 42  AMONG MEN (USA) MRStoute 3-8-9 MJKinane (2) ........................ 8/11f    2½  2
     POLAR PRINCE (IRE) MAJarvis 4-9-1 RCochrane (4) ..................... 3/1    5  3
 13  Peartree House (USA) WRMuir 3-8-9 DaneO'Neill (1) ..................... 33/1    11  4
```

Mr M. Tabor & Mrs John Magnier 4ran 1m38.34   TR: 120/115+/106+

ARLINGTON Sunday, Aug 24   GOOD

54 Arlington Million (Gr 1) (3yo+) £372,671   1¼m

```
 34  MARLIN (USA) DWayneLukas,USA 4-9-0 GStevens ........................ 29/10f      1
 34  SANDPIT (BRZ) RMandella,USA 8-9-0 CMcCarron ........................ 38/10    ½  2
     PERCUTANT (FR) Jean-PierreDupuis,USA 6-9-0 (b) MJKinane ..... 308/10    1¼  3
     Awad (USA) DDonk,USA 7-9-0 (b) PDay ...................................... 31/10    nk  4
     Geri (USA) WMott,USA 5-9-0 JDBailey ........................................ 37/10    ½  5
 42  Allied Forces (USA) SaeedbinSuroor,GB 4-9-0 LDettori ................... 86/10    1¾  6
     Labeeb NDrysdale,USA 5-9-0 (b) CBlack ..................................... 14/1    3  7
     Ops Smile (USA) JWBoniface,USA 5-9-0 (b) RobbieDavis .............. 9/1    1½  8
```

Mr M. Tabor 8ran 2m02.54   TR: 124/123/121/120/119/116

DEAUVILLE Sunday, Aug 24   GOOD

55   **Prix Morny Piaget (Gr 1) (2yo c+f)** £81,132   6f

CHARGE D'AFFAIRES *AdeRoyerDupre,France* 2-9-0 GMosse 10/1   1
XAAR *AFabre,France* 2-9-0 OPeslier .... 3/5f   hd 2
HEEREMANDI (IRE) *APO'Brien,Ireland* 2-8-11 JReid 98/10   1½ 3
Khumba Mela (IRE) *AFabre,France* 2-8-11 TJarnet .... 53/10   nk 4
Desert Prince (IRE) *DRLoder,GB* 2-9-0 KFallon .... 51/10   sh 5
Roi Gironde (IRE) *MmeCHead,France* 2-9-0 PatEddery 11/1   4 6
Zelding (IRE) *RCollet,France* 2-8-11 DBoeuf 10/1   1 7

Marquesa de Moratalla 7ran 1m12.70   TR: 112/112/105/104/107

56   **Prix Kergorlay (Gr 2) (3yo+)** £30,426   1m7f

43   CLASSIC CLICHE (IRE) *SaeedbinSuroor,GB* 5-9-4 JReid 7/10f   1
15   ORCHESTRA STALL *JLDunlop,GB* 5-9-4 PatEddery 58/10   2 2
      CHIEF CONTENDER (IRE) *PWChapple-Hyam,GB* 4-9-4 OPeslier 8/1   2½ 3
      Eurynome (GER) *PBary,France* 4-9-1 SGuillot .... 22/1   ¾ 4
43   Persian Punch (IRE) *DRCElsworth,GB* 4-9-4 KFallon .... 96/10   sn 5
      Oliviero (FR) *J-YArtu,France* 4-9-4 (b) AJunk 17/1   1½ 6
      Stretarez (FR) *DSepulchre,France* 4-9-6 FSanchez 27/10   20 7

Godolphin 7ran 3m20.90   TR: 123/120/117/113/116/114

HAYDOCK Friday, Sep 5   GOOD to SOFT

57   **Haydock Park Sprint Cup (A) (Gr 1) (3yo+)** £75,292   6f

      Order as they passed the post: Danetime was disqualified and placed third for causing
      interference in the early stages

38   ROYAL APPLAUSE *BWHills* 4-9-0 MHills (9) 15/8f   1
      DANETIME (IRE) *NACallaghan* 3-8-12 MJKinane (3) 3/1   1¼ 2
      TOMBA *BJMeehan* 3-8-12 MTebbutt (6) .... 9/1   ½ 3
52   Averti (IRE) *WRMuir* 6-9-0 JReid (4) 12/1   1¼ 4
29   Tedburrow *EJAlston* 5-9-0 AAculhane (2) 50/1   2 5
4   Muchea *MRChannon* 3-8-12 JFortune (5) 25/1   3½ 6
45   Monaassib *EALDunlop* 6-9-0 DO'Donohoe (7) 14/1   6 7
52   Coastal Bluff *TDBarron* 5-9-0 KDarley (1) 9/2   1¼ 8
52   Indian Rocket *JLDunlop* 3-8-12 RHills (8) 8/1   3½ 9

Maktoum Al Maktoum 9ran 1m14.46   TR: 122+/119/118/115+/110

BADEN-BADEN Sunday, Sep 7   GOOD

58   **Mercedes Benz - Grosser Preis Von Baden (Gr 1) (3yo+)** £111,301   1½m

      BORGIA (GER) *BSchutz,Germany* 3-8-6 KFallon 39/10   1
47   LUSO *CEBrittain,GB* 5-9-6 RCochrane 1½ 2
40   PREDAPPIO *SaeedbinSuroor,GB* 4-9-6 LDettori ....   ½ 3
44   Narrabeth (IRE) *UStoltefuss,Germany* 4-9-6 KWoodburn 3½ 4
47   Caitano *BSchutz,Germany* 3-8-9 AStarke 2 5
      Ungaro (GER) *HBlume,Germany* 3-8-9 TMundry ....   sh 6
47   Night Petticoat (GER) *BSchutz,Germany* 4-9-2 NGrant 4 7
      Szarlatan (POL) *FrauDKaluba,Poland* 5-9-6 ATylicki 20 8
      Druzus (POL) *FrauDKaluba,Poland* 4-9-6 EmilZahariev 30 9

Gestut Ammerland 9ran 2m28.56   TR: 119+/121/4/120+/114

LONGCHAMP Sunday, Sep 7   GOOD to FIRM

59   **Emirates Prix du Moulin de Longchamp (Gr 1) (3yo+ c+f)** £91,463   1m

46   SPINNING WORLD (USA) *JEPease,France* 4-9-2 CAsmussen 6/4   1
40   HELISSIO (FR) *ELellouche,France* 4-9-2 OPeslier 1/1f   3 2
46   DAYLAMI (IRE) *AdeRoyerDupre,France* 3-8-11 GMosse .... 36/10   ½ 3
      Daneskaya *AFabre,France* 4-8-13 AJunk .... 306/10   sn 4
42   Classic Park *APO'Brien,Ireland* 3-8-8 JReid .... 539/10   hd 5
46   Neuilly (USA) *AFabre,France* 3-8-11 TJarnet 19/1   1 6
27   Rebecca Sharp *GWragg,GB* 3-8-8 MHills 318/10   2½ 7
1   Bijou d'Inde *MJohnston,GB* 4-9-2 JWeaver 44/1   8 8
46   Piperi (IRE) *JEPease,France* 3-8-11 FSanchez 6/4   15 9

Niarchos Family 9ran 1m37.10   TR: 125/120+/119+/115/115/116

DONCASTER Friday, Sep 12   GOOD to FIRM

60   **Laurent-Perrier Rose Champagne Stks (A) (Gr 2) (2yo c+g)** £54,912   7f

      DAGGERS DRAWN (USA) *HRACecil* 2-9-0 KFallon (4) 4/6f   1

41 DOCKSIDER (USA) *JWHills* 2-8-10 MHills (1) .... 9/1   ½ 2
    SARATOGA SPRINGS (CAN) *APO'Brien,Ireland* 2-8-10 (v)   1¾ 3
       MJKinane (2) 5/2
    Carrowkeel (IRE) *BWHills* 2-9-0 PatEddery (5) 9/1   3 4
    Stone of Destiny *BJMeehan* 2-8-10 (b) KDarley (3) 50/1   11 5

    Cliveden Stud 5ran 1m26.92   TR: 114/109/104/100

DONCASTER Saturday, Sep 13   GOOD to FIRM

61   Pertemps St Leger Stks (A) (Gr 1) (3yo c+f) £183,776   1¾m132y
49 SILVER PATRIARCH (IRE) *JLDunlop* 3-9-0 PatEddery (9) 5/4f   1
    VERTICAL SPEED (FR) *AFabre,France* 3-9-0 OPeslier (8) 7/2   3 2
33 THE FLY *BWHills* 3-9-0 MHills (3) .... 10/1   nk 3
20 Book At Bedtime (IRE) *CACyzer* 3-8-11 MRoberts (2) 14/1   1½ 4
    Windsor Castle *PFICole* 3-9-0 (b) TQuinn (7) .... 10/1   sh 5
    Panama City (USA) *PWChapple-Hyam* 3-9-0 JReid (6) 12/1   3½ 6
    Shaya *MajorWRHern* 3-9-0 RHills (10) 33/1   2½ 7
    Poseidon *MRChannon* 3-9-0 JFortune (5) 25/1   2 8
    Haltarra (USA) *SaeedbinSuroor* 3-9-0 LDettori (11) 16/1   10 9
    Besiege *HRACecil* 3-9-0 KFallon (4) 10/1   1 10

    Mr Peter S. Winfield 10ran 3m06.92   TR: 124/120/119/114/117/112

LEOPARDSTOWN Saturday, Sep 13   GOOD

62   Esat Digifone Champion Stks (Gr 1) (3yo+ c+f) £82,991   1¼m
40 PILSUDSKI (IRE) *MRStoute,GB* 5-9-4 MJKinane (1) 5/4f   1
48 DESERT KING (IRE) *APO'Brien,Ireland* 3-8-11 CRoche (2) 11/8   4½ 2
42 ALHAARTH (IRE) *SaeedbinSuroor,GB* 4-9-4 KDarley (7) 9/1   14 3
    Rayouni (IRE) *JOxx,Ireland* 3-8-11 JPMurtagh (3) 10/1   2 4
    Dangerous Diva (IRE) *APO'Brien,Ireland* 3-8-8 JAHeffernan (6) 33/1   3 5
    No Slouch (IRE) *APO'Brien,Ireland* 3-8-11 WJSupple (4) 100/1   10 6
    Swift Gulliver (IRE) *JSBolger,Ireland* 3-8-11 KJManning (5) 14/1   8 7

    Lord Weinstock 7ran 2m04.70   TR: 133+/125/105

LONGCHAMP Sunday, Sep 14   GOOD to FIRM

63   Prix Des Chenes (Gr 3) (2yo c+g) £22,821   1m
    SECOND EMPIRE (IRE) *APO'Brien,Ireland* 2-9-2 MJKinane 6/4f   1
    MUHTATHIR *JHMGosden,GB* 2-9-2 RHills 59/10   2½ 2
    TENBYSSIMO (IRE) *RFeligioni,Italy* 2-9-2 CAsmussen 76/10   5 3
    Thief of Hearts *AFabre,France* 2-9-2 OPeslier 22/5   3 4
    Milligan (FR) *JEPease,France* 2-9-2 FSanchez 12/1   2½ 5
    Chateau Country (USA) *MmeCHead,France* 2-9-2 ODoleuze .... 10/1   sh 6
55 Roi Gironde (IRE) *MmeCHead,France* 2-9-2 PatEddery .... 18/1   sn 7
    Zarco (FR) *DAllard,France* 2-9-2 AJunk 15/1   5 8
    Extravaganza (FR) *AFabre,France* 2-9-2 TJarnet 5/2   4 9
    Sweet Summertime (IRE) *RCollet,France* 2-9-2 DBoeuf 31/1   6 10

    Mr Michael Tabor & Mrs John Magnier 10ran 1m35.40   TR: 122/117/106+/102

64   Prix Vermeille (Gr 1) (3yo f) £82,988   1½m
22 QUEEN MAUD (IRE) *JdeRoualle,France* 3-9-0 OPeslier 174/10   1
20 GAZELLE ROYALE (FR) *JEHammond,France* 3-9-0 CAsmussen 59/10   1 2
39 BRILLIANCE (FR) *PBary,France* 3-9-0 SGuillot .... 43/10   ns 3
22 Mousse Glacee (FR) *JLesbordes,France* 3-9-0 GMosse .... 19/10f   ns 4
    Kaliana (IRE) *LMCumani,GB* 3-9-0 JReid 22/10   2 5
    Ridaiyma (IRE) *LMCumani,GB* 3-9-0 PCoppin 46/1   5 6
    Dust Dancer (IRE) *JLDunlop,GB* 3-9-0 PatEddery .... 86/10   hd 7
    Legend Maker (IRE) *AFabre,France* 3-9-0 TJarnet 20/1   1 8
    Silver Fun (FR) *MmeCHead,France* 3-9-0 ODoleuze .... 15/1   nk 9

    Mr Gary A. Tanaka 9ran 2m28.20   TR: 119/117/117/117/113/106+

65   Prix Niel (Gr 2) (3yo c+f) £41,493   1½m
    RAJPOUTE (FR) *FDoumen,France* 3-9-2 GMosse 57/10   1
32 PEINTRE CELEBRE (USA) *AFabre,France* 3-9-2 OPeslier .... 1/10f   nk 2
    IVAN LUIS (FR) *MBell,GB* 3-9-2 JReid 149/10   1 3
    New Frontier (IRE) *AFabre,France* 3-9-2 TJarnet 145/10   4 4
32 Ithaki (IRE) *JEPease,France* 3-9-2 CAsmussen .... 9/1   ¾ 5

    Mr John Martin 5ran 2m30.90   TR: 118/117+/115/109/108

CURRAGH Saturday, Sep 20   GOOD to SOFT

66   Jefferson Smurfit Memorial Irish St Leger (Gr 1) (3yo+) £83,774   1¾m

19	OSCAR SCHINDLER (IRE) *KPrendergast,Ireland* 5-9-8 SCraine (5) . 2/1jf	1
56	PERSIAN PUNCH (IRE) *DRCElsworth,GB* 4-9-8 JPMurtagh (4) 12/1	2 2
50	WHITEWATER AFFAIR *MRStoute,GB* 4-9-5 JReid (6) 4/1	2½ 3
39	Family Tradition (IRE) *APO'Brien,Ireland* 3-8-9 (b) CRoche (3) 20/1	6 4
	Stage Affair (USA) *DKWeld,Ireland* 3-8-12 MJKinane (1).................... 11/1	1 5
43	Samraan (USA) *JLDunlop,GB* 4-9-8 PJSmullen (2)............................. 12/1	1½ 6
56	Classic Cliche (IRE) *SaeedbinSuroor,GB* 5-9-8 LDettori (7) 2/1jf	dist 7

Mr Oliver Lehane 7ran 3m06.40   TR: 121+/118/111/104/105

LONGCHAMP Saturday, Sep 20   GOOD

67   Prix de la Salamandre (Gr 1) (2yo c+f) £41,753   7f

55	XAAR *AFabre,France* 2-9-0 OPeslier 6/5f	1
55	CHARGE D'AFFAIRES *AdeRoyerDupre,France* 2-9-0 GMosse........ 27/10	3 2
	SPEEDFIT TOO (IRE) *GGMargarson,GB* 2-9-0 GCarter 17/1	5 3
	Greenlander *CEBrittain,GB* 2-9-0 SGuillot.. 37/10	1½ 4
	Harbour Master (FR) *APO'Brien,Ireland* 2-9-0 (b) CAsmussen 52/10cp	1½ 5
	Sainte Marine (IRE) *RCollet,France* 2-8-11 TJarnet 12/1	2 6
	Chips (IRE) *DRCElsworth,GB* 2-9-0 SDrowne 24/1	6 7
	Marigot Bay (IRE) *APO'Brien,Ireland* 2-8-11 JAHeffernan 52/10cp	5 8

Mr K. Abdulla 8ran 1m20.12   TR: 122/116/106/104+/101

ASCOT Saturday, Sep 27   Race 68: GOOD to FIRM
        Race 69: GOOD

68   Racal Diadem Stks (A) (Gr 2) (3yo+) £59,430   6f

	ELNADIM (USA) *JLDunlop* 3-8-12 RHills (11) 4/1	1
57	MONAASSIB *EALDunlop* 6-9-0 DO'Donohoe (12)............................. 9/1	3 2
57	AVERTI (IRE) *WRMuir* 6-9-0 KFallon (2).. 6/1	sh 3
	Russian Revival (USA) *JHMGosden* 4-9-0 LDettori (3) 3/1f	½ 4
12	Dazzle *MRStoute* 3-8-9 JReid (15) 5/1	¾ 5
57	Muchea *MRChannon* 3-8-12 TQuinn (8) 40/1	nk 6
38	Rambling Bear *MBlanshard* 4-9-0 MRoberts (14)............................. 20/1	1 7
62	Swift Gulliver (IRE) *JSBolger,Ireland* 3-8-12 (b) KJManning (1)......... 40/1	nk 8
	Lochangel *IABalding* 3-8-9 RCochrane (13).................................... 12/1	½ 9
	Cretan Gift *NPLittmoden* 6-9-0 (b) JWeaver (16)............................ 40/1	hd 10
8	Dame Laura (IRE) *HMorrison* 3-8-9 KDarley (9)............................... 50/1	1¾ 11
	My Best Valentine *VSoane* 7-9-0 CRutter (5)................................... 16/1	hd 12
52	Cyrano's Lad (IRE) *CADwyer* 8-9-0 MJKinane (10) 20/1	10 13
	Daring Destiny *KRBurke* 6-9-1 (b) TSprake (7)................................ 50/1	hd 14

Mr Hamdan Al Maktoum 14ran 1m12.56   TR: 126/117/117/116+/111/113

69   Queen Elizabeth II Stks (A) (Gr 1) (3yo+) £187,840   1m (Rnd)

42	AIR EXPRESS (IRE) *CEBrittain* 3-8-11 OPeslier (7) 9/1	1
59	REBECCA SHARP *GWragg* 3-8-8 MHills (9)...................................... 16/1	sh 2
	FAITHFUL SON (USA) *MRStoute* 3-8-11 KFallon (8) 16/1	2 3
	Bahhare (USA) *JLDunlop* 3-8-11 RHills (4)...................................... 15/2	sh 4
59	Bijou d'Inde *MJohnston* 4-9-1 JWeaver (5)..................................... 20/1	nk 5
54	Allied Forces (USA) *SaeedbinSuroor* 4-9-1 LDettori (6)................... 9/2	½ 6
21	Entrepreneur *MRStoute* 3-8-11 MJKinane (2) 9/2	1 7
13	Revoque (IRE) *PWChapple-Hyam* 3-8-11 JReid (3)........................... 9/4f	3½ 8
24	Centre Stalls (IRE) *RFJohnsonHoughton* 4-9-1 TQuinn (1) 14/1	nk 9

Mr Mohamed Obaida 9ran 1m40.61   TR: 125/122/121/121/120/119

ASCOT Sunday, Sep 28   GOOD

70   Fillies' Mile (A) (Gr 1) (2yo f) £92,950   1m (Rnd)

	GLOROSIA (FR) *LMCumani* 2-8-10 LDettori (4) 10/1	1
	JIBE (USA) *HRACecil* 2-8-10 KFallon (7)... 2/1f	¾ 2
	EXCLUSIVE *MRStoute* 2-8-10 MJKinane (6) 5/1	2 3
51	Expect To Shine *BWHills* 2-8-10 MHills (8) 16/1	5 4
	Midnight Line (USA) *HRACecil* 2-8-10 WRyan (8) 11/4	2½ 5
	Hollow Haze (USA) *PWChapple-Hyam* 2-8-10 JReid (2) 10/1	7 6
	Alignment (IRE) *MRStoute* 2-8-10 TQuinn (5) 10/1	9 7
	Filey Brigg *WTKemp* 2-8-10 KDarley (3)... 66/1	1¾ 8

Mr Robert H. Smith 8ran 1m42.31   TR: 109/107/103

1093

COLOGNE Sunday, Sep 28 GOOD

71 **EMS Kurierpost Europa Preis (Gr 1) (3yo+)** £105,263   1½m

37	TAIPAN (IRE) *JLDunlop,GB* 5-9-6 SGuillot	19/10	1
58	LUSO *CEBrittain,GB* 5-9-6 RCochrane	2	2
47	PROTEKTOR (GER) *ALowe,Germany* 4-9-6 ABest	1¼	3
	Don't Worry (GER) *HBlume,Germany* 3-8-11 THellier	ns	4
58	Narrabeth (IRE) *UStoltefuss,Germany* 4-9-6 KWoodburn	1¼	5
	Happy Change (GER) *AWohler,Germany* 3-8-10 ABoschert	2	6

Lord Swaythling 6ran 2m31.88   TR: 120+/116/114/114/112

NEWMARKET Tuesday, Sep 30   GOOD to FIRM (Rowley Mile Course)

72 **Shadwell Stud Cheveley Park Stks (A) (Gr 1) (2yo f)** £63,262   6f

51	EMBASSY *DRLoder* 2-8-11 KFallon (3)	5/2	1
	CRAZEE MENTAL *DHaydnJones* 2-8-11 DHolland (2)	16/1	2½ 2
	ROYAL SHYNESS *GLewis* 2-8-11 PaulEddery (4)	16/1	1¼ 3
51	Cape Verdi (IRE) *PWChapple-Hyam* 2-8-11 JReid (6)	11/8f	1¼ 4
55	Heeremandi (IRE) *APO'Brien,Ireland* 2-8-11 (v) MJKinane (8)	20/1	nk 5
51	Nadwah (USA) *PTWalwyn* 2-8-11 RHills (5)	10/1	2½ 6
	Shmoose (IRE) *SaeedbinSuroor* 2-8-11 LDettori (1)	11/2	2½ 7
51	Miss Zafonic (FR) *RHannon* 2-8-11 DaneO'Neill (7)	16/1	nk 8

Sheikh Mohammed 8ran 1m12.26   TR: 114/107/104/101/100

NEWMARKET Thursday, Oct 2   GOOD to FIRM (Rowley Mile Course)

73 **Thoroughbred Corporation Middle Park Stks (A) (Gr 1) (2yo c)** £64,480   6f

	HAYIL (USA) *DMorley* 2-8-11 (b) RHills (4)	14/1	1
60	CARROWKEEL (IRE) *BWHills* 2-8-11 JReid (8)	15/2	¾ 2
	DESIGNER (USA) *JHMGosden* 2-8-11 OPeslier (7)	25/1	nk 3
	Arkadian Hero (USA) *LMCumani* 2-8-11 LDettori (2)	10/11f	1¾ 4
	Victory Note (USA) *PWChapple-Hyam* 2-8-11 JReid (1)	4/1	3 5
	Bemsha Swing (IRE) *RHannon* 2-8-11 DaneO'Neill (3)	12/1	2 6
	Captain Tim *DRLoder* 2-8-11 KFallon (6)	15/2	1¼ 7
	Celtic Pageant *RAkehurst* 2-8-11 TQuinn (5)	50/1	nk 8

Mr Hamdan Al Maktoum 8ran 1m12.39   TR: 108/106/105/99

NEWMARKET Saturday, Oct 4   GOOD to FIRM (Rowley Mile Course)

74 **Equity Financial Collections Sun Chariot Stks (A) (Gr 2) (3yo+ f+m)** £33,024   1¼m

	ONE SO WONDERFUL *LMCumani* 3-8-8 JReid (6)	5/2	1
	KOOL KAT KATIE (IRE) *DRLoder* 3-8-8 RCochrane (7)	7/2	nk 2
50	REAMS OF VERSE (USA) *HRACecil* 3-9-0 KFallon (5)	9/4f	3½ 3
	Fatefully (USA) *EALDunlop* 4-8-13 MHills (2)	20/1	3 4
	Mrs Miniver (USA) *PAKelleway* 3-8-8 JFortune (1)	100/1	2 5
20	Ukraine Venture *SPCWoods* 3-8-8 KDarley (3)	40/1	8 6
64	Dust Dancer *JLDunlop* 3-8-8 TQuinn (4)	8/1	8 7
5	Sarayir (USA) *MajorWRHern* 3-8-8 RHills (8)	8/1	5 8

Helena Springfield Ltd 8ran 2m02.38   TR: 121/120/120/108

LONGCHAMP Saturday, Oct 4   GOOD to FIRM

75 **Prix du Cadran (Gr 1) (4yo+)** £52,576   2½m

56	CHIEF CONTENDER (IRE) *PWChapple-Hyam,GB* 4-9-2 ODoleuze	114/10	1
37	CELERIC *DMorley,GB* 5-9-2 LDettori	4/5f	nk 2
66	PERSIAN PUNCH (IRE) *DRCElsworth,GB* 4-9-2 CAsmussen	27/10	¾ 3
	Always Earnest (USA) *MmeMBollack-Badel,France* 9-9-2 (b) ABadel	88/10	2 4
43	Double Trigger (IRE) *MJohnston,GB* 5-9-2 TJarnet	47/10	½ 5
	Leonard Quercus (FR) *FBedouret,Spain* 5-9-2 OPeslier	141/10	6 6
	Toba (IRE) *RMartin-Sanchez,Spain* 8-9-2 SGuillot	55/1	dist 7

Mrs J Magnier, R E Sangster, R Santulli. 7ran 4m17.39   TR: 120/118/118/114/113

76 **Prix Dollar (Gr 2) (3yo+)** £31,546   1m1f165y

62	ALHAARTH (IRE) *SaeedbinSuroor,GB* 4-9-4 (v) LDettori	8/5cp	1
	LORD CROMBY (IRE) *RCollet,France* 3-8-9 DBoeuf	122/10	1 2
17	VISIONARY (FR) *AFabre,France* 3-8-9 TJarnet	47/10	2½ 3

1094

18	Astarabad (USA) *AdeRoyerDupre,France* 3-8-9 GMosse	1/1f	½	4
9	Desert Story (IRE) *MRStoute,GB* 3-8-9 OPeslier	8/5cp	1½	5
	Handsome Ridge *JHMGosden,GB* 3-8-9 SGuillot	104/10	1½	6
	Mannenberg (IRE) *PHDemercastel,France* 3-8-9 VVion	40/1	1½	7
	Bello (ARG) *EBedouret,Spain* 5-9-0 CAsmussen	325/10	10	8

Godolphin 8ran 1m59.20 TR: 121/116/112/111/108/105

LONGCHAMP Sunday, Oct 5 FIRM

77 Prix Marcel Boussac (Criterium Des Pouliches) (Gr 1) (2yo f) £84,122 1m

	LOVING CLAIM (USA) *MmeCHead,France* 2-8-11 ODoleuze	37/10		1
	ISLE DE FRANCE (USA) *AFabre,France* 2-8-11 AJunk	118/10	1½	2
	PLAISIR DES YEUX (FR) *PHDemercastel,France* 2-8-11 TGillet	517/10	¾	3
55	Khumba Mela (IRE) *AFabre,France* 2-8-11 TJarnet	77/10	nk	4
	Desert Drama (IRE) *RCollet,France* 2-8-11 SGuillot	227/10	sh	5
	Silent Tribute (IRE) *MBell,GB* 2-8-11 LDettori	91/10	sh	6
	Ashraakat (USA) *JLDunlop,GB* 2-8-11 RHills	33/10	sh	7
	Saralea (FR) *DSmaga,France* 2-8-11 DBoeuf	162/10	4	8
	Anna Palariva (IRE) *AFabre,France* 2-8-11 OPeslier	5/2f	¾	9
	Noemie (FR) *GSandor,France* 2-8-11 (b) GGuignard	59/1	½	10

Maktoum Al Maktoum 10ran 1m37.60 TR: 110/107/105/104/104/104

78 Prix de L'Abbaye de Longchamp (Gr 1) (2yo+ c+f) £52,576 5f

	CARMINE LAKE (IRE) *PWChapple-Hyam,GB* 3-9-8 JReid	168/10		1
5	PAS DE REPONSE (USA) *MmeCHead,France* 3-9-8 ODoleuze	9/5cpf	½	2
57	ROYAL APPLAUSE *BWHills,GB* 4-9-11 MHills	122/10	ns	3
	Kistena (FR) *MmeCHead,France* 4-9-8 DBoeuf	9/5cpf	hd	4
68	Averti (IRE) *WRMuir,GB* 6-9-11 MJKinane	134/10	1½	5
45	Titus Livius (FR) *JEPease,France* 4-9-11 CAsmussen	122/10	sn	6
52	Hever Golf Rose *TJNaughton,GB* 6-9-8 JWeaver	498/10	¾	7
52	Don't Worry Me (IRE) *GHenrot,France* 5-9-8 OPeslier	98/10	½	8
55	Zelding (IRE) *RCollet,France* 2-8-5 TJarnet	219/10	1½	9
31	Deep Finesse *MAJarvis,GB* 3-9-11 MRoberts	964/10	1½	10
52	Eveningperformance *HCandy,GB* 6-9-8 CRutter	91/10		11
	Late Parade (IRE) *ARenzoni,Italy* 6-9-11 OFancera	138/10		12

Mr R. E. Sangster 12ran 56.90secs TR: 120/118/120/116+/115/115

79 Prix de L'Arc de Triomphe (Gr 1) (3yo+ c+f) £420,610 1½m

65	PEINTRE CELEBRE (USA) *AFabre,France* 3-8-11 OPeslier	22/10f		1
62	PILSUDSKI (IRE) *MRStoute,GB* 5-9-5 MJKinane	38/10	5	2
58	BORGIA (GER) *BSchutz,Germany* 3-8-8 KFallon	162/10	2½	3
66	Oscar Schindler (IRE) *KPrendergast,Ireland* 5-9-5 CAsmussen	123/10	sh	4
58	Predappio *SaeedbinSuroor,GB* 4-9-5 JReid	94/10cp	sh	5
59	Helissio (FR) *ELellouche,France* 4-9-5 DBoeuf	5/2	sn	6
40	Swain (IRE) *SaeedbinSuroor,GB* 5-9-5 LDettori	94/10cp	nk	7
47	Que Belle (CAN) *HRemmert,Germany* 3-8-8 KWoodburn	681/10	1½	8
16	Posidonas *PFICole,GB* 5-9-5 (b) TQuinn	912/10	2½	9
30	Busy Flight *BWHills,GB* 4-9-5 MHills	65/1	½	10
50	My Emma *RGuest,GB* 4-9-2 DHolland	161/10	2½	11
39	Ebadiyla (IRE) *JOxx,Ireland* 3-8-8 JPMurtagh	544/10	½	12
64	Gazelle Royale (FR) *JEHammond,France* 3-8-8 MRoberts	106/1	nk	13
	Steward (FR) *DSepulchre,France* 4-9-5 SGuillot	105/1	5	14
64	Queen Maud (IRE) *JdeRoualle,France* 3-8-8 TJarnet	315/10	1½	15
19	Le Destin (FR) *PHDemercastel,France* 4-9-5 TGillet	462/10	2½	16
	Nothin' Leica Dane (AUS) *JEHammond,France* 5-9-5 GMosse	578/10	½	17
	Yokohama (USA) *MmeCHead,France* 6-9-5 ODoleuze	437/10	1½	18

Mr Daniel Wildenstein 18ran 2m24.60 TR: 137/131/124/127/127/127

LONGCHAMP Sunday, Oct 12 SOFT

80 Grand Criterium (Gr 1) (2yo) £104,602 1m

63	SECOND EMPIRE (IRE) *APO'Brien,Ireland* 2-9-0 MJKinane	4/5f		1
67	CHARGE D'AFFAIRES *AdeRoyerDupre,France* 2-9-0 GMosse	23/10	1½	2
	ALBOOSTAN *DMorley,GB* 2-9-0 RHills	102/10	3	3
73	Carrowkeel (IRE) *BWHills,GB* 2-9-0 LDettori	33/10	3	4
	Worms (IRE) *HVandePoele,France* 2-9-0 OPeslier	109/10	2½	5

Mr Michael Tabor & Mrs John Magnier 5ran 1m47.70 TR: 118/115/108/104

NEWMARKET Saturday, Oct 18 GOOD (Rowley Mile Course)

81 Challenge Stks (A) (Gr 2) (3yo+) £53,059 7f

45	KAHAL *SaeedbinSuroor* 3-8-12 LDettori (4)	9/2		1
69	REBECCA SHARP *GWragg* 3-8-13 MHills (3)	9/2	nk	2
68	MUCHEA *MRChannon* 3-8-12 TQuinn (6)	33/1	1¾	3
68	Elnadim (USA) *JLDunlop* 3-9-2 RHills (10)	9/4f	hd	4
11	Decorated Hero *JHMGosden* 5-9-4 WRyan (12)	5/1	nk	5
5	Elegant Warning (IRE) *BWHills* 3-8-9 JReid (11)	33/1	hd	6
	Law Commission *DRCElsworth* 7-9-0 SDrowne (9)	100/1	hd	7
68	Dazzle *MRStoute* 3-8-9 KFallon (8)	13/2	1	8
29	Almushtarak (IRE) *KMahdi* 4-9-0 RCochrane (1)	25/1	1½	9
68	Swift Gulliver (IRE) *JSBolger,Ireland* 3-8-12 (b) JWeaver (2)	33/1	2	10
62	Dangerous Diva (IRE) *APO'Brien,Ireland* 3-8-9 MJKinane (7)	33/1	sh	11
45	Deadly Dudley (IRE) *RHannon* 3-8-12 OPeslier (5)	14/1	nk	12

Godolphin 12ran 1m25.38 TR: 118+/118+/112/116/115

82 Thoroughbred Corporation Dewhurst Stks (A) (Gr 1) (2yo c+f) £117,674 7f

67	XAAR *AFabre,France* 2-9-0 OPeslier (1)	11/8f		1
	TAMARISK (IRE) *RCharlton* 2-9-0 TSprake (7)	9/2	7	2
	IMPRESSIONIST (IRE) *APO'Brien,Ireland* 2-9-0 MJKinane (2)	20/1	2½	3
55	Desert Prince (IRE) *DRLoder* 2-9-0 LDettori (6)	14/1	nk	4
	Pegnitz (USA) *CEBrittain* 2-9-0 JReid (4)	50/1	2	5
60	Daggers Drawn (USA) *HRACecil* 2-9-0 KFallon (3)	3/1	9	6
41	Central Park (IRE) *PFICole* 2-9-0 TQuinn (5)	11/2	9	7

Mr K. Abdulla 7ran 1m24.81 TR: 132/113/106/105/100

83 Dubai Champion Stks (A) (Gr 1) (3yo+) £233,014 1¼m

79	PILSUDSKI (IRE) *MRStoute* 5-9-2 MJKinane (1)	1/1f		1
33	LOUP SAUVAGE (USA) *AFabre,France* 3-8-11 OPeslier (2)	6/1	2	2
69	BAHHARE (USA) *JLDunlop* 3-8-11 RHills (4)	9/1	2	3
49	Stowaway *SaeedbinSuroor* 3-8-11 LDettori (3)	8/1	1½	4
69	Revoque (IRE) *PWChapple-Hyam* 3-8-11 JReid (6)	9/2	1¼	5
48	Benny The Dip (USA) *JHMGosden* 3-8-11 WRyan (7)	7/1	¾	6
69	Bijou d'Inde *MJohnston* 4-9-2 JWeaver (5)	25/1	9	7

Lord Weinstock 7ran 2m05.46 TR: 125+/121+/117/114/112/111

LONGCHAMP Sunday, Oct 19 GOOD to SOFT

84 Prix de La Foret (Gr 1) (3yo+ c+f) £52,466 7f

45	OCCUPANDISTE (IRE) *MmeCHead,France* 4-8-13 ODoleuze	7/5f		1
42	GOTHENBERG (IRE) *MJohnston,GB* 4-9-2 DHolland	44/1	6	2
57	TOMBA *BJMeehan,GB* 3-9-0 MTebbutt	87/10	¾	3
	Keos (USA) *JEHammond,France* 3-9-0 CAsmussen	37/10	2	4
59	Daneskaya *AFabre,France* 4-8-13 AJunk	46/10cp	1	5
68	Russian Revival (USA) *JHMGosden,GB* 4-9-2 LDettori	63/10	sh	6
	Linoise (FR) *AFabre,France* 5-8-13 TJarnet	46/10cp	¾	7
	Kaldou Star *ELellouche,France* 3-9-0 TThulliez	11/1	¾	8
78	Don't Worry Me (IRE) *GHenrot,France* 5-8-13 TGillet	35/1	2¼	9
59	Classic Park *APO'Brien,Ireland* 3-8-11 SCraine	12/1	6	10

Wertheimer et Frere 10ran 1m21.40 TR: 123/114/112/108

MILAN Sunday, Oct 19 GOOD to FIRM

85 Gran Premio Del Jockey Club E Coppa d'Oro (Gr 1) (3yo+ c+f) 1½m
£148,620

58	CAITANO *BSchutz,Germany* 3-8-12 AStarke	15/2		1
71	LUSO *CEBrittain,GB* 5-9-4 MJKinane	34/10	1¾	2
10	MONS *LMCumani,GB* 4-9-4 JWeaver	48/10	½	3
71	Taipan (IRE) *JLDunlop,GB* 5-9-4 JReid	11/10f	1¼	4
	Annaba (IRE) *JHMGosden,GB* 4-9-1 FJovine	63/10	nk	5
65	Ivan Luis (FR) *MBell,GB* 3-8-12 RCochrane	77/10	1½	6
71	Don't Worry (GER) *HBlume,Germany* 3-8-12 THellier	45/1	¾	7
	War Declaration (IRE) *BGrizzetti,Italy* 3-8-12 GForte	23/1	8	8
	Honey Colour (IRE) *ACalchetti,Italy* 3-8-12 OFancera	47/1	11	9

Stall Blauer Reiter 9ran 2m26.20 TR: 125/121/120/118/114/115

WOODBINE Sunday, Oct 19 GOOD to FIRM

86 E. P. Taylor Stks (Gr 2) (3yo+) £92,583 1¼m

74	KOOL KAT KATIE (IRE) *DRLoder,GB* 3-8-6 OPeslier	24/10f		1

64	MOUSSE GLACEE (FR) *JLesbordes,France* 3-8-6 GMosse	4/1	1¼	2
	L'ANNEE FOLLE (FR) *FDoumen,France* 4-8-11 PDay	23/1	ns	3
64	Brilliance (FR) *PBary,France* 3-8-6 SGuillot	26/10	1½	4
	K Z Bay (CAN) *RobertNRyno,Canada* 5-8-11 RSabourin	296/10	2	5
	Grey Way (USA) *JLDunlop,GB* 4-8-11 TQuinn	12/1	1¼	6
	Colorful Vices (CAN) *MFrostad,Canada* 4-8-11 ERamsammy	10/1	hd	7
	Classic Wonder (CAN) *JohnPMackenzie,Canada* 5-8-11 MWalls	377/10	2¾	8
	Miss Universal (IRE) *BenCecil,USA* 4-8-11 JSantos	565/10	hd	9

Augustin Stables 9ran 2m02.00 TR: 120/118/118/115/111/109

87 **Canadian International (Gr 1) (3yo+)** £269,058 1½m

	CHIEF BEARHART (USA) *MFrostad,Canada* 4-9-0 (b) JSantos	13/20cpf		1
	DOWN THE AISLE (USA) *WMott,USA* 4-9-0 PDay	3/1	2¼	2
21	ROMANOV (IRE) *PWChapple-Hyam,GB* 3-8-7 OPeslier	5/1	3¼	3
40	Strategic Choice (USA) *PFICole,GB* 6-9-0 (b) TQuinn	59/10	8½	4
	Crown Attorney (CAN) *JohnPMackenzie,Canada* 4-9-0 TKabel	146/10	11	5
	Desert Waves (CAN) *MFrostad,Canada* 7-9-0 SHawley	13/20cpf	7	6

Sam Son Farm 6ran 2m29.00 TR: 124/120/115

DONCASTER Saturday, Oct 25 GOOD

88 **Racing Post Trophy (A) (Gr 1) (2yo c+f)** £94,096 1m (Rnd)

60	SARATOGA SPRINGS (CAN) *APO'Brien,Ireland* 2-9-0 MJKinane (4)	9/2		1
	MUDEER *SaeedbinSuroor* 2-9-0 LDettori (7)	9/2	sh	2
	MUTAMAM *ACStewart* 2-9-0 RHills (1)	13/2	1	3
	Craigsteel *HRACecil* 2-9-0 KFallon (5)	13/2	4	4
	Quiet Assurance (USA) *EALDunlop* 2-9-0 GCarter (2)	14/1	2½	5
	Kilimanjaro *MRStoute* 2-9-0 JReid (6)	7/2f	5	6
41	Little Indian *SPCWoods* 2-9-0 OPeslier (8)	6/1	¾	7
	Mountain Song *SirMarkPrescott* 2-9-0 GDuffield (3)	9/1	10	8

Mr M. Tabor & Mrs John Magnier 8ran 1m40.36 TR: 113/113/111/103/98

LONGCHAMP Sunday, Oct 26 GOOD to SOFT

89 **Prix Royal-Oak (Gr 1) (3yo+)** £41,710 1m7f110y

79	EBADIYLA (IRE) *JOxx,Ireland* 3-8-6 GMosse	7/1		1
	SNOW PRINCESS (IRE) *LordHuntingdon,GB* 5-9-1 KFallon	54/1	6	2
79	OSCAR SCHINDLER (IRE) *KPrendergast,Ireland* 5-9-4 CAsmussen	7/10f	¾	3
64	Silver Fun (FR) *MmeCHead,France* 3-8-6 ODoleuze	20/1	1½	4
43	Double Eclipse (IRE) *MJohnston,GB* 5-9-4 JWeaver	9/1	3	5
	Camporese (IRE) *PWChapple-Hyam,GB* 4-9-1 JReid	18/1	hd	6
79	Nothin' Leica Dane (AUS) *JEHammond,France* 5-9-4 TJarnet	12/1	2½	7
56	Stretarez (FR) *DSepulchre,France* 4-9-4 FSanchez	11/1	5	8
	Further Flight *BWHills,GB* 11-9-4 MHills	45/1	sh	9
43	Grey Shot *IABalding,GB* 5-9-4 JFortune	7/1	15	10
	Bahamian Knight (CAN) *RAkehurst,GB* 4-9-4 (b) OPeslier	24/1		11

H.H. Aga Khan 11ran 3m26.50 TR: 120+/111/113/110

FLEMINGTON Tuesday, Nov 4 GOOD to FIRM

90 **Foster's Melbourne Cup (Gr 1) (3yo+)** £600,840 2m

	MIGHT AND POWER (NZ) *JackDenham,Australia* 4-8-12 (b) JCassidy	7/2f		1
	DORIEMUS (NZ) *DLFreedman,Australia* 7-9-1 (b) GHall	9/1	sh	2
	MARKHAM (AUS) *CIBrown,Australia* 4-8-4 LDittman	25/1	½	3
	Harbour Dues *LadyHerries,GB* 4-8-6 RCochrane	40/1	½	4
	Linesman (NZ) *MsGWaterhouse,Australia* 6-8-4 (b) LCassidy	10/1	ns	5
	Arabian Story *LordHuntingdon,GB* 4-8-6 LDettori	25/1	2¼	6
	Skybeau (NZ) *LJSmith,Australia* 5-8-5 DDunn	16/1	¾	7
	Ebony Grosve (NZ) *GRogerson,NewZealand* 4-8-8 SDye	7/1	1¼	8
	Sapio (NZ) *MrsSLKay,NewZealand* 7-8-11 DNikolic	80/1	hd	9
	Grandmaster (NZ) *JBCummings,Australia* 4-7-11 LBeasley	33/1	4	10
	Court of Honour (IRE) *PCHayes,Australia* 5-8-9 BThomson	50/1	2	11
	Magnet Bay (NZ) *DBFrye,NewZealand* 7-8-5 CJohnson	100/1	1½	12
	Vialli (IRE) *D&PO'Sullivan,NewZealand* 6-8-9 BYork	16/1	¾	13
	Always Aloof (USA) *DLFreedman,Australia* 6-8-5 SKing	12/1	3½	14
	Scrupulous (AUS) *JSmith,Australia* 6-8-4 MCarson	200/1	3	15
	Yobro (AUS) *KRoberts,Australia* 7-8-2 GCooksley	33/1	3	16

Sunny Lane (AUS) *CGoggin,Australia* 5-7-10 BPrebble 66/1   3½ 17
Marble Halls (NZ) *DLFreedman,Australia* 4-8-4 (b) DOliver 7/1   1¼ 18
Alfa (AUS) *JBCummings,Australia* 4-8-8 DBeadman 14/1   3 19
Bonsai Pipeline (NZ) *RThomas,Australia* 6-7-13 DGauci 100/1   1 20
Crying Game (AUS) *MsACJohnson,Australia* 5-8-3 GChilds 200/1   1 21
Count Chivas (NZ) *SMorrish,Australia* 5-9-1 (b) DBrereton 50/1   5 22

Mr N. Moraitis 22ran 3m18.33   TR: 127/126/118/115/113/111

HOLLYWOOD PARK Saturday, Nov 8   Turf course: FIRM
                   Dirt course: FAST

91   **Breeders' Cup Sprint (Gr 1) (3yo+) £364,881**   6f

     ELMHURST (USA) *JenineSahadi,USA* 7-9-0 CNakatani 166/10   1
     HESABULL (USA) *MChambers,USA* 4-9-0 (b) GLStevens .... 154/10   ½ 2
     BET ON SUNSHINE (USA) *PaulMcGee,USA* 5-9-0 PDay .... 78/10   nk 3
     Exotic Wood (USA) *REllis,USA* 5-8-11 CMcCarron 67/10   1 4
     Confide (USA) *BenWPerkins,USA* 3-8-12 (b) MSmith 33/1   2 5
     Men's Exclusive (USA) *WWard,USA* 4-9-0 LPincayjnr .... 34/10f   ns 6
     Northern Afleet (USA) *DHofmans,USA* 4-9-0 JBailey 159/10   5½ 7
     Trafalger (USA) *DWayneLukas,USA* 3-8-12 KDesormeaux 158/10cp   5 8
78   Carmine Lake (IRE) *PWChapple-Hyam,GB* 3-8-9 JReid .... 158/10cp   hd 9
     Track Gal (USA) *JohnWSadler,USA* 6-8-11 DFlores 115/10   1½ 10
78   Pas de Reponse (USA) *MmeCHead,France* 3-8-9 ODoleuze .... 158/10cp   ½ 11
     Crafty Friend (USA) *WDollase,USA* 4-9-0 (b) ASolis 85/10   1¾ 12
     Richter Scale (USA) *PByrne,USA* 3-8-12 SSellers 34/10   2¾ 13
78   Royal Applause *BWHills,GB* 4-9-0 MHills 225/10   5½ 14

     Evergreen Farm 14ran 1m08.01   TR: 121/120/119/113/111/112+

92   **Breeders' Cup Mile (Gr 1) (3yo+) £340,476**   1m

59   SPINNING WORLD (USA) *JEPease,France* 4-9-0 CAsmussen 21/10f   1
54   GERI (USA) *WMott,USA* 5-9-0 JBailey 6/1   2 2
81   DECORATED HERO *JHMGosden,GB* 5-9-0 LDettori .... 40/1   nk 3
     Lucky Coin (USA) *RichardNieminski,USA* 4-9-0 RobbieDavis .... 2/1   ns 4
     Magellan (USA) *NDrysdale,USA* 4-9-0 EDelahoussaye 13/1   5 5
     El Angelo (USA) *JenineSahadi,USA* 5-9-0 ASolis .... 15/2   hd 6
     Soviet Line (IRE) *KPMcLaughlin,USA* 7-9-0 PDay 39/1   1¼ 7
13   Fantastic Fellow (USA) *DWayneLukas,USA* 3-8-11 KDesormeaux ..... 33/1   hd 8
     Wild Event (USA) *LMGoldfine,USA* 4-9-0 MGuidry .... 21/1   hd 9
     Helmsman (USA) *WDollase,USA* 5-9-0 (b) CNakatani .... 15/1   hd 10
     Pinfloron (FR) *WGreenman,USA* 3-9-0 DFlores .... 12/1   ½ 11
     Naninja (USA) *MMitchell,USA* 4-9-0 CMcCarron .... 42/1   nk 12

     Niarchos Family 12ran 1m32.77   TR: 126+/122/121/121

93   **Breeders' Cup Turf (Gr 1) (3yo+) £619,048**   1½m

87   CHIEF BEARHART (USA) *MFrostad,Canada* 4-9-0 (b) JSantos 19/10f   1
79   BORGIA (GER) *BSchutz,Germany* 3-8-7 KFallon .... 4/1   ¾ 2
     FLAG DOWN (CAN) *CClement,USA* 7-9-0 JDBailey .... 14/1   ½ 3
     Buck's Boy (USA) *PNHickey,USA* 4-9-0 MGuidry 35/1   4 4
     Big Sky Chester (USA) *BartGHone,USA* 5-9-0 GStevens .... 29/1   ½ 5
65   Rajpoute (FR) *RMcAnally,USA* 3-8-10 CMcCarron......................... 6/1   3 6
54   Ops Smile (USA) *JWBoniface,USA* 5-9-0 (b) J-LSamyn .... 15/1   nk 7
     Val's Prince (USA) *JEPicou,USA* 5-9-0 MSmith 7/1   4 8
54   Awad (USA) *DDonk,USA* 7-9-0 (b) PDay .... 7/1   hd 9
     Majorien *MmeCHead,France* 3-8-10 ODoleuze .... 11/1   ¾ 10
44   Dance Design (IRE) *DKWeld,Ireland* 4-8-11 MJKinane 27/1   4 11

     Sam Son Farm 11ran 2m23.92   TR: 124/123+/122/116/115/113

94   **Breeders' Cup Classic (Gr 1) (3yo+) £1,361,905**   1¼m

     Order as they passed the post: Whiskey Wisdom was disqualified and placed fourth for
     causing interference to the fourth

     SKIP AWAY (USA) *HHine,USA* 4-9-0 (b) MSmith 18/10f   1
     DEPUTY COMMANDER (USA) *WDollase,USA* 3-8-10 CNakatani 4/1   6 2
     WHISKEY WISDOM (CAN) *RAttfield,Canada* 4-9-0 PDay .... 11/1   ¾ 3
     Dowty (USA) *WMott,USA* 5-9-0 GStevens 46/1   3 4
     Savinio (USA) *WGreenman,USA* 7-9-0 ASolis.................................. 81/1   12 5
     Taiki Blizzard (USA) *KFujisawa,Japan* 6-9-0 (b) YOkabe.................. 32/1   2 6
     Behrens (USA) *HaroldJamesBond,USA* 3-8-10 JBailey.......................... 3/1   1 7

Honor Glide (USA) *JamesEDay,USA* 3-8-10 SSellers 76/1 12 8
Touch Gold (USA) *DHofmans,USA* 3-8-10 CMcCarron .... 2/1 nk 9

Carolyn Hine 9ran 1m59.16   TR: 131/124/122/117

ROME Sunday, Nov 9   GOOD to SOFT

95 **Premio Roma (Gr 1) (3yo+)** £193,387   1¼m

85 TAIPAN (IRE) *JLDunlop,GB* 5-9-3 JReid 14/10   1
44 OXALAGU (GER) *BSchutz,Germany* 5-9-3 AStarke 3 2
    LORD OF MEN *JHMGosden,GB* 4-9-3 OPeslier 2½ 3
    Santillana (USA) *JHMGosden,GB* 4-9-3 LDettori................................. 1½ 4
    Delilah (IRE) *MRStoute,GB* 3-8-12 (v) TQuinn 3½ 5
    Rio Napo (IRE) *LCamici,Italy* 3-9-1 VMezzatesta 4 6
    Risiat (IRE) *EBorromeo,Italy* 3-9-1 MDemuro....................................   1 7
23 Toto Le Moko (IRE) *AVerdesi,Italy* 4-9-3 MPasquale 8 8
    Backtrack *AMacchi,Italy* 4-9-3 GBietolini 20 9

Lord Swaythling 9ran 2m06.40   TR: 124/118/113/110/104

TOKYO Sunday, Nov 23   GOOD to FIRM

96 **Japan Cup (Gr 1) (3yo+)** £812,163   1½m

83 PILSUDSKI (IRE) *MRStoute,GB* 5-9-0 MJKinane 36/10   1
    AIR GROOVE (JPN) *YIto,Japan* 4-8-10 YTake..................................... 3/1 nk 2
    BUBBLE GUM FELLOW (JPN) *KFujisawa,Japan* 4-9-0 YOkabe ... 27/10f 1¼ 3
85 Caitano *BSchutz,Germany* 3-8-10 AStarke.................................... 109/10 nk 4
    Silk Justice (JPN) *MOkubo,Japan* 3-8-10 SFujita.................................... 6/1 nk 5
76 Astarabad (USA) *AdeRoyerDupre,France* 3-8-10 GMosse .... 158/10 hd 6
    Tsukuba Symphony *MIto,Japan* 4-9-0 YYoshida................................... 60/10 ½ 7
89 Oscar Schindler (IRE) *KPrendergast,Ireland* 5-9-0 CAsmussen.......... 98/10   3 8
    Rosen Kavalier (JPN) *YSuzuki,Japan* 4-9-0 NYokoyama.................. 792/10 ½ 9
85 Mons *LMCumani,GB* 4-9-0 JReid .... 423/10 ½ 10
    Royal Touch (JPN) *YIto,Japan* 4-9-0 MEbina .... 209/10 ½ 11
90 Ebony Grosve (NZ) *GRogerson,NewZealand* 4-9-0 RSDye.............. 387/10   2 12
    Snow Endeavor (JPN) *HMori,Japan* 3-8-10 ENakadate.................... 116/1 1½ 13
    Taiki Fortune (USA) *YTakahashi,Japan* 4-9-0 (b) YShibata 559/10   4 14

Lord Weinstock 14ran 2m25.80   TR: 123/118/120/121/121/121

HOLLYWOOD PARK Sunday, Nov 30   GOOD to SOFT

97 **Matriarch Stks (Gr 1) (3yo+ f+m)** £250,000   1¼m

22 RYAFAN (USA) *RFrankel,USA* 3-8-8 ASolis 2/1   1
    MAXZENE (USA) *TSkiffington,USA* 4-8-11 CAsmussen........................... hd 2
    YOKAMA (USA) *WMott,USA* 4-8-11 GStevens................................... 2¾ 3
    Luna Wells (IRE) *RMandella,USA* 4-8-11 CNakatani .... ns 4
    Chile Chatte (USA) *RMandella,USA* 4-8-11 KDesormeaux.....................   5 5
    Memories of Silver (USA) *JToner,USA* 4-8-11 JDBailey .... ns 6
    Fanjica (IRE) *BenCecil,USA* 5-8-11 CMcCarron 4½ 7
    Real Connection (USA) *MStute,USA* 6-8-11 GAlmeida........................ hd 8

Juddmonte Farms 8ran 2m05.80   TR: 121/120/115/115

SHA TIN Sunday, Dec 14   GOOD to FIRM

98 **Hong Kong International Vase (Gr 2) (3yo+)** £294,071   1½m

85 LUSO *CEBrittain,GB* 5-9-5 MJKinane 9/20f   1
79 POSIDONAS *PFICole,GB* 5-9-5 TQuinn .... 10/1 hd 2
90 SUNNY LANE (AUS) *CGoggin,Australia* 5-8-11 DNikolic 100/1 1¼ 3
    Indigenous (IRE) *IWAllan,HongKong* 4-9-0 DWhyte......................... 72/10 hd 4
    Multi-Star (NZ) *PFYiu,HongKong* 4-9-0 RFradd................................ 74/1 sh 5
    Privilege (IRE) *IWAllan,HongKong* 4-9-0 (v) BMarcus .... 26/1 sh 6
95 Oxalagu (GER) *BSchutz,Germany* 5-9-5 AStarke............................. 11/1 1¾ 7
    Mazal (IRE) *DOughton,HongKong* 5-9-0 AMunro .... 55/1 sh 8
    Citadeed (USA) *IWAllan,HongKong* 5-9-2 LDettori 34/1   9 9
90 Yobro (AUS) *KRoberts,Australia* 7-9-5 GCooksley .... 98/1 ¾ 10
71 Protektor (GER) *ALowe,Germany* 8-9-2 THellier.............................. 49/1 1¾ 11
    Eishin Sansan (JPN) *MSakaguchi,Japan* 5-8-11 (h) YTake................. 21/1 1¾ 12
90 Sapio (NZ) *MrsSLKay,NewZealand* 7-9-5 DBradley 24/1   7 13
9 Monza (USA) *LHo,HongKong* 3-8-13 JWeaver................................ 108/1   6 14

Mr Saeed Manana 14ran 2m26.30   TR: 120+/119/109/111/111/111

99   **Hong Kong International Cup (Gr 2) (3yo+) £316,693**   1m1f
93   VAL'S PRINCE (USA) *JEPicou,USA* 5-9-5 CAsmussen........................ 6/1   1
     ORIENTAL EXPRESS (IRE) *IWAllan,HongKong* 4-9-0 DWhyte .... 41/1   sh 2
24   WIXIM (USA) *RCharlton,GB* 4-9-2 MJKinane .... 7/2   ½ 3
     Batavian (NZ) *GRogerson,NewZealand* 4-9-2 RSDye........................... 34/1   1¼ 4
     Silence Suzuka (USA) *MHashida,Japan* 3-8-13 YTake .... 20/1   sh 5
     Smart Kid (NZ) *STWong,HongKong* 5-9-0 AMunro .... 84/1   hd 6
     Annus Mirabilis (FR) *SaeedbinSuroor,GB* 5-9-0 (v) LDettori............. 58/10   1¼ 7
     Seascay (NZ) *PCHayes,Australia* 7-9-5 (b) GChilds............................ 19/1   nk 8
     Foromor (AUS) *RQuinton,Australia* 4-9-0 (b) DBeadman..................... 43/1   1¼ 9
     Victory Mount (USA) *JMoore,HongKong* 3-8-13 FCoetzee 100/1   1¾ 10
     Smashing Pumpkin (AUS) *DAHayes,HongKong* 4-9-0 (b) BMarcus . 27/10f   nk 11
33   Johan Cruyff *P-LBiancone,HongKong* 3-9-1 ELegrix .... 11/2   hd 12
     Che Sara Sara (IRE) *DOughton,HongKong* 5-9-0 JMurtagh................. 51/1   3¾ 13
83   Bijou d'Inde *MJohnston,GB* 4-9-5 JWeaver...................................... 13/1   dist 14

     Robin Martin & Steven Weiner 14ran 1m47.20   TR: 116+/111/112/109/109/106

100   **Hong Kong International Bowl (Gr 2) (3yo+) £294,071**   7f
     CATALAN OPENING (NZ) *JBCummings,Australia* 5-9-5 DBeadman .. 4/1   1
84   RUSSIAN REVIVAL (USA) *JHMGosden,GB* 4-9-0 MJKinane........... 30/1   1¼ 2
     SHINKO KING (IRE) *KFujisawa,Japan* 6-9-0 (b) YTake................. 61/10   2¼ 3
     Wizard King *SirMarkPrescott,GB* 6-9-0 WWoods .... 18/1   sh 4
     Special (NZ) *DAHayes,HongKong* 4-9-0 BMarcus .... 29/10   ½ 5
92   Decorated Hero *JHMGosden,GB* 5-9-2 LDettori 19/10f   1¾ 6
     Adjareli (IRE) *JMoore,HongKong* 5-9-0 JMurtagh .... 79/1   ½ 7
     Jazzac (NZ) *CMJillings,NewZealand* 5-9-0 GCooksley .... 65/1   sh 8
     Quick Action (IRE) *IWAllan,HongKong* 6-9-0 DWhyte...................... 41/1   nk 9
     Fastest Star (IRE) *STWong,HongKong* 5-9-0 AMunro .... 24/1   hd 10
     Spartacus (AUS) *RHore-Lacy,Australia* 4-9-5 RSDye......................... 18/1   1 11
     Amarettitorun (USA) *LO'Brien,USA* 5-9-0 DHolland 40/1   1¾ 12
     Kowloon Pride (USA) *DHill,HongKong* 5-9-0 (b) PPayne 45/1   1½ 13
     Laser Star (NZ) *HFLam,HongKong* 5-9-0 DNikolic 100/1   2¾ 14

     Mr Dato Tan Chin Nam 14ran 1m22.00   TR: 124/116/109/109/108/105

INDEX TO SELECTED BIG RACES

Jiyush 28
Johan Cruyff 33[4],99
Juggler (AUS) a1[6]

Kahal 45[4],81*
Kaldou Star 84
Kaliana (IRE) 64[5]
Kammtarra (USA) a1
Kashwan (SPA) 18
Keos (USA) 84[4]
Key of Luck (USA) a1[4]
Key To My Heart (IRE) 10[6]
Khassah 5,27[5]
Khumba Mela (IRE) 55[4],77[4]
Kilimanjaro 88[6]
King Alex 30
Kingfisher Mill (USA) 9[4],40,49[3]
Kirkwall 17[3]
Kistena (FR) 78[4]
Kool Kat Katie (IRE) 74[2],86*
Kowloon Pride (USA) 100
Kutta 3,10[5],15[6]
K Z Bay (CAN) 86[5]

Labeeb 54
La Blue (GER) 44[5]
Lady Carla 30,37
La Nana (FR) 22[5]
L'Annee Folle (FR) 86[3]
Laser Star (NZ) 100
Last Second (IRE) 2
Late Parade (IRE) 78
Law Commission 81
Le Destin (FR) 22,19[3],79
Legend Maker (IRE) 64
Leonard Quercus (FR) 75[6]
Linesman (USA) 90[5]
Linoise (FR) 84
Little Indian 41[3],88
Lochangel 68
London News (SAF) 25[3]
Lone Piper 41[6]
Lord Cromby (IRE) 76[2]
Lord of Men 95[3]
Loup Sauvage (USA) 7[2],33[3],83[2]
Loving Claim (USA) 77*
Lucayan Prince (USA) 29,38
Lucky Coin (USA) 92[4]
Luna Wells (IRE) 97[4]
Luso a1,3[5],23[2],47[2],58[2],71[2],85[2],98*

Magellano (USA) 35[2]
Magellan (USA) 92[5]
Magnet Bay (NZ) 90
Majorien 93
Mamalik (USA) 17[2],26
Mannenberg (IRE) 76
Marble Halls (NZ) 90
Marigot Bay (IRE) 67
Markham (AUS) 90[3]
Marlin (USA) a34[4],54*
Maxzene (USA) 97[2]
Mazal (IRE) 98
Medaaly 9

Memories of Silver (USA) 97[6]
Men's Exclusive (USA) a91[6]
Midnight Line (USA) 70[5]
Might And Power (NZ) 90*
Milligan (FR) 63[5]
Mind Games 52
Miss Universal (IRE) 86
Miss Zafonic (FR) 51[4],72
Monaassib 29[4],45[2],57,68[2]
Mongol Warrior (USA) 30
Mons 33,10[2],85[3],96
Monza (USA) 9[5],98
Moonax (IRE) 28
Moonlight Paradise (USA) 5,27[6]
Moonshine Girl (USA) 29
Mosconi (IRE) 13
Mountain Song 88
Mousse Glacee (FR) 6[6],22[2],64[4],86[2]
Mrs Miniver (USA) 74[5]
Muchea 4,57[6],68[6],81[3]
Mudeer 88[2]
Muhtathir 63[2]
Multi-Star (NZ) 98[5]
Musalsal (IRE) 9[3],21
Musical Pursuit 4,13
Mutamam 88[3]
My Best Valentine 68
My Emma 50*,79

Nadwah (USA) 51[3],72[6]
Naninja (USA) 92
Narrabeth (IRE) 44[4],58[4],71[5]
Needle Gun (IRE) 23[6],44[6]
Nero Zilzal (USA) 14[5]
Neuilly (USA) 46[3],59[6]
New Frontier (IRE) 65[4]
Nightbird (IRE) 6[5]
Night Petticoat (GER) 47[5],58
Noemie (FR) 77
Noisette 8
Nombre Premier 45
Nononito (FR) 28
Northern Afleet (USA) a91
No Slouch (FR) 62[6]
Nothin' Leica Dane (AUS) 79,89
Nwaamis (USA) 24[4]

Occupandiste (IRE) 45*,84*
Ocean Ridge (USA) 5[5],27[2]
Oh Nellie (USA) 5[2],12[5]
Oliviero (FR) 56[6]
One So Wonderful 74*
Ops Smile (USA) 54,93
Orchestra Stall 15,56[2]
Oriental Express (IRE) 99[2]
Oscar (IRE) 18[2]
Oscar Schindler (IRE) 19[5],66*,79[4],89[3],96
Oxalagu (GER) 44*,95[2],98

Palme d'Or (IRE) 22
Panama City (USA) 61[6]
Papering (IRE) 50[5]
Papua 21

Pas de Reponse (USA) 54,78[2],a91
Peartree House (IRE) 13,53[3]
Pegnitz (USA) 82[5]
Peintre Celebre (USA) 18*,32*,65[2],79*
Percutant (FR) 54[3]
Perfect Paradigm (IRE) 18
Persian Punch (IRE) 3,15*,28,43[5],56[5],66[2],75[3]
Pilsudski (IRE) 2[3],30[2],36*,40[2],62*,79[2],83*,96*
Pinfloron (FR) 92
Piperi (IRE) 46[6],59
Plaisir Des Yeux (FR) 77[3]
Polar Prince (IRE) 53[2]
Poseidon 61
Posidonas 16[5],79,98[2]
Poteen (USA) 4[3],26[5]
Predappio 16[2],30*,40,58[3],79[5]
Privilege (IRE) 98[6]
Protektor (GER) 47[4],71[3],98
Putra (USA) 4

Que Belle (CAN) 47[3],79
Queen Maud (IRE) 22,64*,79
Quick Action (IRE) 100
Quiet Assurance (USA) 88[5]

Rajpoute (FR) 65*,93[6]
Rambling Bear 31,38,68
Rayouni (IRE) 62[4]
Real Connection (USA) 97
Reams of Verse (USA) 5[6],8*,20*,50[4],74[3]
Rebecca Sharp 5,27*,59,69[2],81[2]
Red Camellia 6[3]
Region (USA) a34[5]
Restructure (IRE) 24
Reunion (IRE) 5
Revoque (IRE) 4[2],13[6],69,83[5]
Richter Scale (USA) a91
Ridaiyma (IRE) 64[6]
Rio Napo (IRE) 95[6]
Risiat (IRE) 95
River Bay (USA) 2[4]
Riyadian 35[3]
Rocky Oasis (USA) 16[4]
Roi Gironde (IRE) 55[6],63
Romanov (IRE) 13[3],21[3],87[3]
Rosen Kavalier (JPN) 96
Royal Amaretto (IRE) 13,32[5]
Royal Applause 29*,38[2],57*,78[3],a91
Royal Court (IRE) 30[4]
Royale Figurine (IRE) 29[6],31
Royale (IRE) 12
Royal Shyness 72[3]
Royal Touch (JPN) 96
Running Stag (USA) 26
Russian Music 29
Russian Revival (USA) 68[4],84[6],100[2]
Ryafan (USA) 12[4],22[4],97*

Sacrament 3,10

Sainte Marine (IRE) 67[6]
Samraan (USA)
  3[6],10[4],28[5],43[6],66[6]
Sandpit (BRZ) a1[3],a34[3],54[2]
Santillana (USA) 95[4]
Sapio (NZ) 90,98
Saralea (FR) 77
Saratoga Springs (CAN)
  60[3],88*
Sarayir (USA) 5,74
Sasuru 14*,36[5]
Savinio (USA) a94[5]
Scrupulous (AUS) 90
Seascay (NZ) 99
Second Empire (IRE) 63*,80*
Seebe (USA) 6[2],12[6]
Shaka 18[6],32[3]
Shamikh 4
Shantou (USA) 23*,37*,40[5]
Sharemono (USA) 13
Shaya 61
Shell Ginger (IRE) 39
Shii-Take 4
Shinko King (IRE) 100[3]
Shmoose (IRE) 72
Shuhrah (USA) 51
Silence Suzuka (USA) 99[5]
Silent Tribute (IRE) 77[6]
Silk Justice (JPN) 96[5]
Silver Fun (FR) 64,89[4]
Silver Patriarch (IRE) 21[2],33[5],
  49[2],61*
Simon du Desert (FR) 14[3]
Single Empire (IRE) 21
Singspiel (IRE)
  a1*,19*,40[4],48*
Siphon (BRZ) a1[2],a34[2]
Siyadah (USA) 20
Skip Away (USA) a94*
Skybeau (NZ) 90
Sleepytime (IRE) 5*,27[3]
Smart Kid (NZ) 99[6]
Smashing Pumpkin (AUS) 99
Snow Endeavor (JPN) 96
Snow Princess (IRE) 89[2]
Society Rose 8[5]
Soviet Line (IRE) 92
Soviet State (USA) 29
Spartacus (AUS) 100
Special (NZ) 100[5]
Speedfit Too (IRE) 67[3]
Speedfriend (FR) 18
Spinning World (USA)
  11[4],46*,59*,92*
Squeak 50[6]
Stage Affair (USA) 66[5]
Starborough
  4[4],17*,26*,42[2],46[4]
Star Profile (IRE) 6
State Fair 43
Statua (IRE) 51[5]
Steward (FR) 79
Stone of Destiny 60[5]
Stowaway 49*,83[4]
Strategic Choice (USA)
  25,23[4],40[6],87[4]
Strawberry Roan (IRE) 12[2],33,

39[4]
Stretarez (FR) 56,89
Struggler 31[6],52
Sunny Lane (AUS) 90,98[3]
Super Cub (USA) 32
Swain (IRE) 37[2],40*,79
Sweet Summertime (IRE) 63
Swift Gulliver (IRE) 62,68,81
Sylva Paradise (IRE) 31
Symonds Inn 21
Szarlatan (POL) 58

Taiki Blizzard (USA) a94[6]
Taiki Fortune (USA) 96
Taipan (IRE)
  23[3],37[3],71*,85[4],95*
Talloires (USA) a34[6]
Tamarisk (IRE) 82[2]
Tamayaz (CAN) 14[6]
Tedburrow 29,57[5]
Tenbyssimo (IRE) 63[3]
Theano (IRE) 29
The Fly 21[5],33,61[3]
Thief of Hearts (IRE) 63[4]
Time Allowed 3*
Titus Livius (FR) 31[2],45[3],78[6]
Toba (IRE) 75
Token Gesture (IRE) 33
Tomba 57[2],84[3]
Toto Le Moko (IRE) 23[5],95
Touch Gold (USA) a94
Track Gal (USA) a91
Trafalger (USA) a91
Trojan Sea (USA) 2
Try Again (GER) 47[6]
Tsukuba Symphony 96
Tulipa (USA) 3
Tycoon Todd (USA) 4

Ukraine Venture 20,74[6]
Ungaro (GER) 58[6]

Vagabond Chanteuse 8[2]
Val's Prince (USA) 93,99*
Vereva (IRE) 22*
Verglas (IRE) 13[2],33[6]
Vertical Speed (FR) 61[2]
Vialli (IRE) 90
Via Verbano (IRE) 12,39
Victory Mount (USA) 99
Victory Note (USA) 73[5]
Visionary (FR) 7[3],17[4],76[3]
Voyagers Quest (USA) 18

Wardara 45
War Declaration (IRE) 85
Whiskey Wisdom (CAN) a94[4]
Whitewater Affair 10[3],30[3],50[2],
  66[3]
Wilawander 10
Wild Event (USA) 92
Windsor Castle 61[5]
Winning Smile (IRE) 45[6]
Wixim (USA) 14[2],24[5],99[3]
Wizard King 100[4]
Wolf Mountain 42
Worms (IRE) 80[5]

Xaar 55[2],67*,82*

Yalaietanee 7[4],13[4]
Ya Malak 31,52*
Yashmak (USA) 5,20[4],39[2]
Yobro (AUS) 90,98
Yokama (USA) 97[3]
Yokohama (USA) 79
Yorkshire (IRE) 9

Za-Im 4
Zamindar (USA) 4[5],46[5]
Zarco (FR) 63
Zelanda (IRE) 51[6]
Zelding (IRE) 55,78
Zenith Rose (FR) 32[6]

THE TIMEFORM 'TOP HORSES ABROAD'

This review of the year covers the major racing countries outside Britain. It includes Timeform Ratings for the top two-year-olds, three-year-olds and older horses. Horses not rated highly enough to be included in the main lists but which finished in the first three in a European pattern race during the season are included below the cut-off line. Fillies and mares are denoted by (f); * denotes the horse was trained for only a part of the season in the country concerned. Overseas customers wishing to keep in touch with Timeform's coverage of racing through the year can subscribe to Computer Timeform or Timeform Perspective for reports on all the important races. Timeform is also available on the Internet—http: // www.timeform.com

IRELAND   Aidan O'Brien dominated racing in Ireland in 1997, his horses earning more money than those of the next three stables (Oxx, Bolger, Weld) combined and managing wins in ten Irish pattern races (three of them classics) and eleven listed contests. He trained the most talked-about horse in Ireland, **King of Kings**, as well as the best, **Desert King**. His horses haven't yet raced outside Ireland all that often, but when they do they merit plenty of respect, as his two-year-olds **Harbour Master** (Coventry Stakes), **Saratoga Springs** (including the Racing Post Trophy) and the undefeated **Second Empire** (including the Grand Criterium) proved.

Overall, 1997 was quite similar in Ireland to the year before, with foreign-trained horses winning half of the twenty-two Group 3 races, but faring less well in the higher grades, picking up only one of the five Group 2 contests, and only two of the nine in the highest class. In one important respect, however, it was a noteworthy year. For the first time since 1964 the Irish kept all five classics at home, thanks to **Classic Park**, **Desert King**, **Ebadiyla** and **Oscar Schindler**. The last-named was the leading older performer for the second year running, comfortably clear of the tough international mare **Dance Design**, and he emulated Vintage Crop's achievement of winning successive Irish St Legers. Although Classic Park was rather disappointing after her Irish 1000 win, Ebadiyla's Irish Oaks was not her only Group 1 success as she came back to land the Prix Royal-Oak at Longchamp in the autumn. But pride of place must go to Desert King, who became the first since Grundy in 1975 to win both the Irish 2000 Guineas and Irish Derby, beating **Dr Johnson** (who stays in training) a length in the latter. Desert King was a high-class colt but sadly was denied a chance of becoming the first Irish triple crown winner since Windsor Slipper in 1942 (and the first since penalty clauses were removed in 1946), and, after finishing a creditable second to Pilsudski in the Irish Champion Stakes, he was retired to stud.

The two-year-olds were led by **Second Empire**, although Irish racegoers saw only his easy Leopardstown maiden win in August, as his two pattern victories came at Longchamp. Notwithstanding the massive reputation of **King of Kings**, it is Second Empire who has achieved most in terms of form. Close behind the former was the tough **Saratoga Springs**. Among the fillies, there was a very tight finish to the Moyglare Stud Stakes, with **Tarascon** edging home ahead of **Heed My Warning** in a race where barely a length covered the first five home. The only other pattern race confined to fillies went to British raider Alborada.

In general, the listed two-year-old winners did not inspire. The following youngsters had their lines cast in easier waters but may be worth looking out for in 1998: **Canzona** and **Outspoken** (both trained by John Oxx); **Hibernian Rhapsody** and **Make No Mistake** (both Darshaan colts in the care of Dermot Weld, the former a half-brother to Dance Design); **Irish Summit** and **Sabre Mountain** (both with Jim Bolger, though Sabre Mountain did finish lame on his final start); and the Kevin

Prendergast-trained pair **Diya** and **Wish Me Luck**. All of these horses' ratings can be found in the full Irish handicap in this annual.

Two-Year-Olds

122p	Second Empire
115	King of Kings
113	Saratoga Springs
108	Harbour Master
106p	Impressionist
105	Heeremandi (f)
104p	Risk Material
103p	Celtic Cavalier
103	Hopping Higgins (f)
102p	Heed My Warning (f)
102p	Sabre Mountain
102p	Tarascon (f)
102+	Lady Alexander (f)
102	Flame Violet (f)
101	Shahtoush (f)
100p	Hermitage Bay
100p	Wish Me Luck (f)
100	Mempari (f)
100	Natalis
100	Takarian
99	Danyross (f)
98+	Kincara Palace (f)
98	Hanzanar
97	Musk Lime (f)
96	Dixie Dynamo
96	Winona (f)

Three-Year-Olds

129	Desert King
122	Dr Johnson
122	Ebadiyla (f)
118	*Verglas
115	Classic Park (f)
113	Strawberry Roan (f)
113	Token Gesture (f)
112p	Quws
112	*Caiseal Ros (f)
112	*Johan Cruyff
111	Private Chapel

111	Rayouni
110	Ashley Park
110	*Casey Tibbs
110	Swift Gulliver
109p	Stage Affair
108	Poker-B
107	Bakkar
107	Family Tradition (f)
106	Buddy Marvel
106	*Mingling Glances (f)
106	Mr Lightfoot
106	Nobility
106	Spirit of Tara (f)
105+	Crown Regent
105	Alarme Belle (f)
105	Aliya (f)
105	Check The Band
105	Dangerous Diva (f)
105	Lil's Boy
105	*Olympic Majesty
105	Via Verbano (f)
105	Zafarabad
104	Beautiful Fire
104	Nordic Project
104	Pelmeny (f)
103	Akdariya (f)
103	Code of Honour
103	*Fort Morgan
103	Khairabar
103	Royal Affinity
103	Sweet Mazarine (f)
102	Azra (f)
102	Beamish Boy
102	Darbela (f)
102	Plaza de Toros
102	Royale (f)
101	Admiral Wings
101	Cardigan Bay
101	Carnelly (f)
101	Mosconi
101	*Orange Jasmine (f)

101	Tertia (f)
101	Thats Logic
100	Absolute Glee (f)
100	Chania (f)
100	No Slouch
100	Somerton Reef
100	Western Chief
96	Eternal Joy

Older Horses

127	Oscar Schindler
119	Dance Design (f)
118	Burden of Proof
115	Catch The Blues (f)
114	Theano (f)
113	Raiyoun
111	*Mohaajir
109	French Ballerina (f)
109	Ger's Royale
108	Ailleacht (f)
108	Best Before Dawn
107	Gordi
107	Kuwait Bay
107	The Bower
107	Vivo
106	Graduated
106	Munif
105	Orange Grouse (f)
105	Tout A Coup (f)
104	Damancher
104	Theatreworld
103	Gan Saru
103	Musical Mayhem
103	On Fair Stage (f)
103	Sharazan
102	Rossmore Girl (f)
102	Symboli Kildare
102	Wray
101	Sunset Reigns (f)
100	Nagnagnag (f)

FRANCE **Peintre Celebre** dominated the year in France, winning the two most valuable events, the Prix du Jockey-Club and the Prix de l'Arc de Triomphe, a spectacular display in the latter showing him overwhelmingly the best three-year-old in Europe. The two races have something else in common in that both are very much social occasions in France, and draw large crowds. Despite learning last year that *France-Galop* was to make a concerted effort to woo the public back to the courses, we were struck by how sparsely populated Longchamp seemed even for the classics in the spring and the Arc trials in the autumn. There is clearly work still to be done.

It is interesting to note the emphasis put on betting in French racing. At Longchamp on May 11th, the day of the Poule d'Essai des Poulains, Poule d'Essai des Pouliches and Prix Lupin—all Group 1 events—it was instead the Prix Rieussec, a handicap over nearly two miles, which held the punters' interest most. All the exotic bets (predicting first three, four or even five home) were on this contest, and it received the full four-page form pull-out that the 'big race of the day' always gets. In Britain we couldn't dream of The Mail On Sunday Handicap receiving prominence over the One Thousand Guineas. Perhaps there is a lesson to be learned here. If racing is seen simply as an outlet for betting, then that is perhaps all people will be interested in, and it leads to less desire actually to go to the races. At present, despite vastly lower admission charges than in Britain, France is seemingly struggling to attract racegoers to what the British would term outstanding fixtures, and it will have been disappointing to the authorities that the pari-mutuel turnover actually dropped slightly from 1996.

On the track there were many notable achievements besides Peintre Celebre's. **Helissio** was kept in training after a similarly brilliant Arc win at three, and while some will have been disappointed, Group 1 wins at a mile and a quarter, a mile and a half and a second place in the Prix du Moulin over a mile was no bad achievement at all. While he never quite matched his Arc performance, on all but one of his starts in 1997 he actually ran better than he had in any race except the Arc as a three-year-old. **Spinning World** became the world's unofficial best miler with smooth wins in France's two open-aged Group 1 events at the trip and at the Breeders' Cup. With the exception of **Occupandiste**'s win in the Prix de la Foret, that was it for really high-class performers among the three-year-old and older generations. Classic winners **Daylami**, **Always Loyal** and **Vereva** were ordinary by that standard, **Oscar**'s season was ended after his Prix du Jockey-Club second, as was **Magellano**'s after the Grand Prix de Saint-Cloud, while pattern winners **Astarabad** and **Loup Sauvage** were very smart, but still a little way below the best. There were no sprinters to compare with Anabaa a year ago, while potentially the best stayer, **Vertical Speed**, was injured late on and has been retired to stud. Peintre Celebre is still in training, which is good news, and of course the two-year-olds were led by **Xaar**, whose Salamandre–Dewhurst double was achieved stylishly and promises much for 1998, be it over a mile (a division left wide open by the retirement of Spinning World) or further.

Andre Fabre's position as champion trainer remains unchallenged, and in securing his eleventh title in a row he won approaching double the prize money of his nearest rival, who continues to be Criquette Head. Jean-Claude Rouget (who once again won more races than anyone), Alain de Royer-Dupre, Pascal Bary and Elie Lellouche maintained their earnings above the 10m franc mark, while Robert Collet improved a little to join them and John Hammond dipped just below that level. Olivier Peslier easily maintained his lead in the jockeys' race, both in number of wins and prize money, with Dominique Boeuf, Thierry Jarnet, Sylvain Guillot and Gerald Mosse the next in line. Peintre Celebre was largely responsible for lifting Daniel Wildenstein above the Aga Khan among the owners, while Jean-Luc Lagardere remains the leading breeder in terms of prizes earned. Not surprisingly Nureyev (Peintre Celebre, Spinning World) was the leading sire, but more interesting perhaps is Highest Honor finishing in the top three again without having a real headliner to represent him, relying instead on a number of useful and smart performers. Zafonic (Xaar) received all the headlines among the first-season sires, though Cardoun (a son of Kaldoun, who was himself fourth in the overall lists) was not far behind him with a far less exalted book of mares.

Two-Year-Olds

132	Xaar	107p	Isle de France (f)	104?	Desert Drama (f)
116	Charge d'Affaires	107p	Zalaiyka (f)	103	Cortona (f)
112p	Thief of Hearts	107	Fairly Grey (f)	103p	Diableneyev
110p	Loving Claim (f)	106p	Divineyevah (f)	102p	Pharatta (f)
109p	Special Quest	106	Scenery	102	Zelding
108p	Croco Rouge	105p	Fantastic Quest		
108p	Daymarti	105	Insight (f)	101	Gold Away
108p	Pinmix	105	Plaisir des Yeux (f)	99	Cyrillic (f)
108	Anna Palariva (f)	104p	Arnaqueur	97	Sainte Marine (f)
108	Silic	104	Khumba Mela (f)	96	Soeur Ti (f)
		104	Roi Gironde	95	Seralia (f)

GERMANY It was not even the end of February before it became known that Germany's 1996 Horse of the Year, Lavirco, was to be retired due to a recurring problem in his off-hind fetlock. However, strength in depth ensured Germany's 1997 pattern-race record was at least as good as the year before. Without having had a world-beater (135+), Germany is producing smart to high-class performers (110-125) in greater numbers than ever before. Thirty of the forty German pattern races were kept at home, as were four of the six Group 1 events (one better than in 1996), while German raiders also gained three Group 1 triumphs abroad. Meanwhile, **Borgia**'s honourable defeats at Longchamp and Hollywood Park in the autumn raised her country's reputation internationally more than did her compatriots' successes.

Off the track, 1997 was something of a transitional year. It was the final season as a trainer for Heinz Jentzsch. It is scarcely possible to do justice to the seventy-seven-year-old's achievements, but he was champion trainer thirty-one times between 1960 and 1994, including 1967 to 1987 inclusive, and he saddled forty-four German classic winners, including eight Derby winners. It may be invidious to pick only one, but 1993 victor Lando went on to success in the 1995 Japan Cup—a tremendous achievement. Peter Schiergen, the stable jockey (and former five-times champion) takes over. Another trainer to retire is Bruno Schutz (champion in 1992, 1995 and 1997), who had an abundance of talent in his yard in his final year with **Devil River Peek** backing up Germany's three leading money winners **Borgia**, **Caitano** and **Oxalagu**. Though only fifty-eight, he has been suffering with ill health. His son, Andreas, could hardly have hoped for a stronger hand as he takes over.

The three-year-old filly Borgia seemed to be everywhere. She won the German Derby and the Grosser Preis von Baden among five successes from nine outings, and was easily the most famous German horse in 1997, but it would be wrong to think she was head and shoulders above her contemporaries all through the year. She was beaten in the Preis der Diana (Oaks) by **Que Belle** who had also previously won the Henkel Rennen (1000 Guineas), but did not go on quite so well and finished eighth in the Arc. Borgia traded close decisions with **Baroon** in the Derby and the Europachampionat, but the bare form of those races was held down by others, and

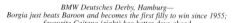

BMW Deutsches Derby, Hamburg—
Borgia just beats Baroon and becomes the first filly to win since 1955;
favourite Caitano (right) has better days ahead

injury prevented the prospective South African sire from contesting the big international events later on. And although Borgia won the 'fame stakes' hands down, her stablemate **Caitano** actually showed marginally better form (taking into account that he would have to concede a sex allowance) despite being beaten the twice they met. Both these horses have essays in the main body of this Annual. While the 1996 champion two-year-old **Eden Rock** levelled out as just a smart performer, failing to win after his reappearance, unlucky Italian Derby second **Ungaro** rebounded in October to win the German St Leger, and **March Groom** also improved in the autumn, winning Group 3 races at Baden-Baden (when trained in Hungary) and Hoppegarten.

It was disappointing that a number of the leading older horses had shortened seasons. **Artan** ran but twice, winning a Group 1 in Italy on his reappearance, before suffering injury problems. Group 2 winner **Wurftaube** had only three outings and never again got the chance to race on going softer than good. **La Blue** and **Camp David** managed to win a pattern race without making the same impact as in 1996. The most productive of the older horses were **Power Flame**, Oxalagu and Devil River Peek. Power Flame won two pattern events at Cologne in the second half of the year, though his rating suggests he's still a good way off the top international milers. Devil River Peek had a season of two halves, losing his first five races but winning his last four, including a weak Group 1 in Italy. It seems that an optimistic tilt at the Dubai World Cup is planned. Oxalagu was well campaigned to win four pattern races in Germany, but, after wearing down Dance Design to land his Group 1 at Munich in August, his season tapered off a little behind Taipan in Italy and Luso in Hong Kong.

As we have said before, German racing's policy is to give two-year-olds limited opportunity, thus discouraging the production of precocious juveniles in favour of later-developing horses. That said, it is quite possible for the leading two-year-olds to go on (Lavirco, for instance), and comfortably the best form in 1997 was shown by **El Maimoun**, a son of Royal Academy and quite a well-bred Robellino mare. Not only did he win the Group 2 race at Baden-Baden, but he took the prestigious Preis des Winterfavoriten at Cologne (scheduled to be a Group 3 race in 1998) by four lengths. He's not a certain Derby stayer, but he's bang in the frame for the Mehl-Mulhens-Rennen (2000 Guineas) at present.

Germany still has some way to go to be on a par with the top international racing countries, but it is progressing the right way and, at a time when the finances of British racing are coming under close scrutiny, some figures published in *The Sporting Life* from the International Federation of Horseracing Authorities make interesting reading. Dealing, admittedly, with figures much smaller than Britain, the following becomes apparent: Germany returns a slightly lower percentage of betting turnover to the punters than Britain (75.6% to 78%), but, after 'overhead expenses' the remaining balance is comfortably ahead 15.58% to 7.94%. However, it is after the government betting duty that the figures become startling. Whereas the Germans take 0.74%, leaving a 14.84% return of betting turnover to racing, the British takeout of 6.75% leaves just 1.19%. As we've said, in terms of gross revenue, the German figure is much smaller (around 27%), but it is clear that the German government is playing its part in helping to make Germany one of the more progressive racing nations, at least in terms of the quality of its bloodstock.

Two-Year-Olds					
110p	El Maimoun	99	Sharp Domino	117	Baroon
103	Tiger Hill			116	Ungaro
102	Angel Heart	95p	Starkey	114	Don't Worry
101	Areion	95	Evening Set (f)	114	March Groom
101	Campo			114	Saugerties
101	Ebisu	**Three-Year-Olds**		113	Eden Rock
100+	Glady Beauty (f)	125	Caitano	113	Happy Change
99	Marlowe	124	Borgia (f)	112	Ajano
		120	Que Belle (f)	112	Baleno

112	Is Tirol	118	Artan	108	Shebar
112	Lomita (f)	117	Devil River Peek	108d	Munaaji
111	Asolo	116	Camp David	107	Diktys
111	Maceo	116	Power Flame	107	Landsuitor
110	Ferrari	116	Waky Nao	107	Sachsenking
109	Anna Thea (f)	116	Wurftaube (f)	107	Sinyar
109	Lonango	114	Accento	106	Ardilan
108	Icemoon	114	Narrabeth	106	Gaelic Symphony
107	Enigma (f)	114	Protektor	106	Night Petticoat (f)
107	Genevra (f)	113	Kalatos	106	Pasolini
105	Allandro	112	Surako	106	Takin
105	Flamingo Queen (f)	111	La Blue (f)	106	Trudeau
105	Huxley	111	Zero Problemo	105	Barlovento
105	Lanelly (f)	110	Global Player	105	Bon Jovi
105	San Suru	110	Roseate Wood (f)	105	Lorado
		110	Triano	105	Lucky Power
104	Autriche (f)	109	Aristid	105	Nautiker
103	Aldino	109	Concepcion	105	Tres Hereux
102	Damus	109	Pacajas	105	Upper Class
102	Wala (f)	109	Try Again		
101	El Zulia (f)	108	Bad Bertrich Again	103	Fifire
100	Turbo Drive	108	Hondero	103	Grey Perri (f)
Older Horses		108	Lagarto	103	Jashin
123	Oxalagu	108	Sambakonig	103	Tajawall

ITALY Although there are exceptions, the rating threshold for inclusion into the main body of *Racehorses of 1997* of those European horses which didn't race in Britain is 110 for two-year-olds and 115 for three-year-olds and up. And by those criteria, Italy had only one qualifier. One!

A glance at the results of the pattern races in Italy confirms the dearth of talent. Of the twenty-five contested, no fewer than fifteen went abroad and the figures are even more dramatic when you consider only the Group 1 and 2 events. Here the score was twelve to three in the foreigners' favour, and even the 'home' wins were by horses bred in Ireland and England. There does not seem to be any immediate improvement in sight. The success story of the season was **Nicole Pharly**, who completed a Premio Regina Elena–Oaks d'Italia double most recently achieved in 1990. The bare form is only useful though, and while this progressive and game filly promised better, she was sent to join Michael Stoute and did not reappear. The two-year-old **Special Nash** won a Group 2 among five successes from seven starts but was disqualified from one of those wins, having tested positive to 'bute'; he's a game competitor, but had his limitations well and truly exposed behind Lend A Hand in the Gran Criterium. With the exception of **Armando Carpio**, the Group 3 winners were useful at best and are not going to be a threat in the top races in 1998. Whilst a couple of the two-year-old listed winners, **Green Tea** and **Fedegarcia Gioffry**, have promise, it will be a surprise if they turn out much better than smart.

That was the level reached by Italy's top-rated performer, **Kierkegaard**, when he finished second to Devil River Peek in the Group 1 Premio Vittorio di Capua in October. It was a good effort, and Nicole Pharly's Oaks win shows that Italian-trained horses can still win in the highest grade, but there's a feeling at present that it has more to do with who else turns up than anything else.

Two-Year-Olds

106	*Tenbyssimo	94	Apollo Wells	92	Blu Carillon
99	Special Nash	94p	Green Tea	92	Crisos Il Monaco
99	Della Scala	94	Luigi Ruocco	92	Diamond Snake
99	Fedegarcia Gioffry (f)	94	Slaney Squire	92	Toto Le Heros
96	Mac Black	94	Sopran Londa (f)		
95	Sergio Persico	93	Andoya (f)	**Three-Year-Olds**	
		93	Calci	112	Risiat

112	War Declaration	**Older Horses**
111	Honey Colour	115 Kierkegaard
108	Uruk (f)	114 Late Parade
107p	Nicole Pharly (f)	113 Armando Carpio
107	Gianky Gioffry	112 Coral Reef
106	She Bat (f)	112 Supreme Commander
106	Quirinale	112 Taxi de Nuit
105	Mister Rock	112 Toto Le Moko

Older Horses

115	Kierkegaard
114	Late Parade
113	Armando Carpio
112	Coral Reef
112	Supreme Commander
112	Taxi de Nuit
112	Toto Le Moko
109	*Grey Way (f)
109	Morigi
109	Ravier
109	Robins

112	War Declaration
111	Honey Colour
108	Uruk (f)
107p	Nicole Pharly (f)
107	Gianky Gioffry
106	She Bat (f)
106	Quirinale
105	Mister Rock
104	Bedside Story (f)
104	Sopran Mariduff (f)
103	Plumbird

109	Tarawa
108	Pay Me Back
107	Nil
107	Sotabrasciet
106	Toaff
105	Dancer Mitral
102	Karla Wyller (f)
100	Nenna (f)
99	Febrar

SCANDINAVIA   The quality among the horses is a good way behind the best in Europe, but racing in Scandinavia continues to make strides. Attracting international competition to the top races is a sure way of catching the attention of the racing world, and although the reintroduced Scandinavian Open Championship at Klampenborg and the Stockholm Cup at Taby both went the way of the British-trained Harbour Dues, it is only by exposure to horses from other countries that the improvement of the home stock can be gauged. As it is, only five of the listed winners in 1997 were actually bred in Scandinavia. One of those, though, had the best chance to make a real statement for Sweden, but unfortunately his biggest stage, the Stockholm Cup, turned out to be his one disappointing run of the year. His name is **Songline**.

The champion of his generation in Sweden at two and three (second in first two classics, won St Leger), Songline won all six of his races in the latest season prior to the Stockholm Cup, three of them listed contests. At Taby in June he dominated a representative field from the front and beat Inchrory comfortably. He does have an interesting quirk, racing with cotton wool plugs in his ears which tend to be pulled out on turning for home—a practice common with trotters, apparently. Songline didn't reappear after his one defeat, but is said to be staying in training, and if he's over whatever ailed him that day, he'll win more good races.

Other older horses to win listed races between nine and thirteen furlongs included the aforementioned Inchrory and Loch Bering (who won a weak race before being well beaten in Britain). Amongst the winners of the open mile events was ex-Sir Mark Prescott inmate Warming Trends, who broke a track record at Taby in September on dirt. The better sprinters included the ex-British pair Prime Match and **Options Open**, former Swedish 2000 Guineas winner Seigneur du Paus and hardy perennials **Windmachine** and **Sharp Matt** (whose Baltic Cup success was a hat-trick in the race).

The Taby Open Sprint Championship has been awarded Group 3 status in 1998, joining the Stockholm Cup, which is contested on the same day. That should help attract an even better international entry. One trainer unlikely to be backward in coming forward is Joe Naughton, who enjoyed a memorable evening in June with the 'Hever Golf' team—'Rose' winning the listed sprint and 'Glory' the equivalent of the Swedish 2000 Guineas (both ridden by Pat Eddery), the latter from subsequent Swedish Derby winner Chirac. Taby's manager, Bo Gillborg, orchestrated the whole affair with great skill, from the hospitality, to public post-race interviews and to having video tapes of the races ready on departure. Hopefully this aspect of Swedish racing will continue to prosper.

With the Scandinavian Open Championship receiving a big boost in the latest season to rival the Stockholm Cup in terms of prize money, perhaps Norway should be encouraged to upgrade, say, the Oslo Cup and then the three countries could put on a 'Scandinavian Triple Crown' with big publicity and bonuses. Perhaps that could become the target for the year 2000?

Three-Year-Old
106 River Foyle

Older Horses
110 Songline

106	Options Open
105	Blue Chief
105	Hakiki
105	Senador
105	Sharp Matt

105	Troon
105	Windmachine (f)
104	Duty Time
99	Kutbeya

DUBAI   A torrential downpour caused the Dubai World Cup to be postponed, but after the efforts to create the event to start with, and the headlines after Cigar's win in 1996, it was clear that everything would be done to prevent the elements from winning outright. Only Helissio was sent home, and the race took place five days later, with Singspiel defeating Siphon after a fine contest. At the time of writing, over eighty horses have been entered for the 1998 renewal.

Although best known for its banner race, and as a winter preparatory quarters for Godolphin's European horses, Dubai does have its own season of racing from November to April featuring several listed and 'prestige' events. At present, virtually all of the competitors are proven performers from other countries rather than home–reared stock, but the example of useful three-year-old sprinter **Ramp And Rave**, who had had only a couple of runs in America at two, may be a sign of things to come. As it is, he is the only three-year-old rated above 104.

Of the highest rated horses, World Cup fourth **Key of Luck** was injured back in the USA after his next start and has been retired, **Soviet Line** won a prestige event before taking his career earnings past £1 million with two Grade 3 successes in America and **Tamayaz** won the Dubai Duty Free (in effect the World Cup Consolation) from Needle Gun, **Magellan** and **Doreg** but ran poorly back in Europe and has been retired to stud. **Kammtarra** won two of the three legs of the Maktoum Challenge (beating **Tamhid** in the second of them) to earn a place in the World Cup but was well beaten there and in Britain and America afterwards, while **Atraf** followed a narrow win over **Rasas** in the listed sprint on the World Cup card with a Grade 3 success at Belmont before his retirement to stud. The other listed winners were **Tropicool** (nine furlongs), **Kassbaan** (mile), **Try Prospect** (six furlongs) and, at the end of the year, **Diffident**, who has been retired to stud in India.

The Dubai World Cup, which has its own web page, has quickly established itself in the international racing calendar, being granted Grade 1 status after just two years. In 1998 there will be an even better supporting cast of races, including a very valuable race on turf over a mile and a half. The international village and hospitality areas are set to be expanded as the country continues to strive to be recognised as the leisure capital of the Middle East. The focal question of course will be which horse will win the Dubai World Cup? In 1997 Richard Mandella's two runners were second and third, but we think his best was left at home! If all has gone well in his race in February, pay very close attention to Gentlemen if Mandella brings him this time. He's a very good horse.

Three-Year-Old
108 Ramp And Rave

Older Horses
123	*Key of Luck
119	*Soviet Line
119	*Tamayaz
118	*Kammtarra
116	*Atraf
116	*Magellan
116	*Tamhid
114	Doreg
113	Kalabo
113	Tropicool

111	Kassbaan
111	Rasas
111	Try Prospect
110	Bashaayeash
110	*Diffident
110	*Fahim
110	*Fatefully (f)
108	Serviable
108	Water Poet
108	Wood Magic
107	Desert Conqueror
107	Dyhim
107	Intidab
107	Wathik

107	Yazaly
106	Airport
106	Akil
106	Dahik
106	Doubleton
106	Learmont
105	Clever Cliche
105	Dancing Zena
105	Desert Shot
105	Fahal
105	Septieme Brigade
105	Yom Jameel

NORTH AMERICA   **Gentlemen** was the best horse in America in 1997. He put up the two outstanding performances of the year, giving 3 lb and a half-length beating to Skip Away in the Pimlico Special in May and then having a margin of four lengths and the same over stable-companions Siphon and Sandpit in the Hollywood Gold Cup in June. It wasn't enough to secure him the Eclipse Award among the voters, though. That 'honour' went to **Skip Away**, who repeated his Jockey Club Gold Cup win before running away with the Breeders' Cup Classic. The fact that those victories were over severely depleted fields did not seem to matter. Skip Away is a good horse, no question, but we have him behind **Formal Gold** as well. The latter began the year by beating Skip Away a length and a quarter when in receipt of 10 lb at Gulfstream in February, and ended it by beating him five and a half lengths at levels at Belmont in September. A fracture of a hind leg while being prepared for the Breeders' Cup ended his year. All three are set to race in 1998. Several of the good ones are not. **Alphabet Soup** was second to Gentlemen on his only start after his win in the Breeders' Cup Classic before a bad ankle injury forced his retirement. **Siphon** won the Santa Anita Handicap (ahead of Gentlemen) and was second to Singspiel in the Dubai World Cup before two defeats behind Gentlemen settled things in his stablemate's favour; sadly, Siphon injured himself on his final start and has been retired to stud. So, too, have **Sandpit** and **Langfuhr**. Veteran Sandpit was unable to stretch his number of seasons with a Grade 1 win to six, but continued to run with credit in the highest grade. Langfuhr was all but forgotten at the end of the year, but he'd confirmed himself a high-class horse with wins in the Carter and Metropolitan Handicaps at Belmont before injury sent him to stud. The specialist sprinters were not a great bunch. **Elmhurst** narrowly beat **Hesabull** at the Breeders' Cup but the Eclipse Award went to **Smoke Glacken**, successful in his five runs at shorter than a

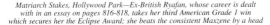

*Matriarch Stakes, Hollywood Park—Ex-British Ryafan, whose career is dealt
with in an essay on pages 816-818, takes her third American Grade 1 win
which secures her the Eclipse Award; she beats the consistent Maxzene by a head*

mile before injury forced his retirement; a speedy front runner, he might have been capable of better, but did not beat top-quality opposition. Older filly Exotic Wood had a curtailed season but her fourth at the Breeders' Cup was a good effort. **Will's Way** ran often against Skip Away and Formal Gold before injury cut short his career, for the second year running having his finest moment at Saratoga, edging past Formal Gold in the Whitney Handicap. **Louis Quatorze** won a pair of Grade 3 races with great ease but suffered an injury in the second of them and had to be retired. The former Preakness winner could well make a good stallion.

There was talk during the year about what a great group the three-year-old colts were. Nonsense. They were closely matched, and they provided some tremendous races, but in terms of merit, the best of them fell some way short of Holy Bull in 1994. The effect that a potential Triple Crown winner has on the American public is considerable. After **Silver Charm** had beaten Florida Derby winner **Captain Bodgit** by a head in the Kentucky Derby, and then defeated Santa Anita Derby winner and perennial rival **Free House** and Captain Bodgit (who was injured and has been retired) by a head and the same in a thrilling Preakness Stakes, he and his connections were featured in a host of programmes, magazines and newspapers which rarely include racing.

What was a shame was not that Silver Charm failed to win—in a race where he had every chance he was run out of it late on by **Touch Gold**—but that the general feeling was simply of let down. The precise reason why the Triple Crown has endured as a concept is because it is difficult to achieve. The excitement should come largely from having a horse with the *chance* of winning it (and the television ratings for the race were duly 71% higher than in 1996). The fact that it will be at least twenty years since Affirmed swept the board in 1978 before it is done again should only serve to heighten the sense of accomplishment for the horse who manages to emulate him.

After the Triple Crown was over, Touch Gold won the Haskell Invitational before running no sort of a race on his last two outings. **Deputy Commander** and **Behrens** were the pick of the three-year-olds at the end of the year, the pair separated by a nose in the Travers Stakes. Deputy Commander went on to win the Super Derby and finish a well-held second to Skip Away at the Breeders' Cup. Behrens won a valuable Grade 2 event at the Meadowlands before disappointing at Hollywood Park. Returning to Silver Charm, he was off the track for over six months after the Belmont, coming back on Boxing Day with an unlucky second to **Lord Grillo** (a lightly-raced ex-Argentinian also well worth keeping an eye on) in the Grade 1 Malibu Stakes over only seven furlongs. Silver Charm has had only ten races in his career, and although he will find it tougher against his elders in 1998, we may still not have seen the best of him yet.

The three-year-old fillies were up to scratch, though without an outstanding one among them. It was disappointing that Storm Song failed to train on, but **Sharp Cat** had a busy and successful campaign, winning three Grade 1 and three Grade 2 races (one of which was a walk-over). However, she failed on some of the really big occasions, losing the Kentucky Oaks to **Blushing K D** (who won six of eight starts before suffering a career-ending injury) and the Mother Goose and the Breeders' Cup Distaff to **Ajina**. Allen Paulson's Ajina took time to come to herself in 1997, being well held behind **Glitter Woman** (who went on to win the Ashland Stakes) and Blushing K D in Grade 2 company before surprising Sharp Cat in the Mother Goose. She went on to beat **Tomisue's Delight** in the CCA Oaks and, after being upset by **Runup The Colors** in the Alabama Stakes and a good second to Hidden Lake in the Beldame at Belmont, winning the Breeders' Cup Distaff. She's another who may yet come on again and do better still at four.

Breeders' Cup Juvenile, Hollywood Park—Favorite Trick maintains his sequence and easily beats Dawson's Legacy (white muzzle); doubts remain about his classic chances, though

The older fillies lacked a dominant figure. **Jewel Princess** began the year in fine style with two big wins at Santa Anita but deteriorated afterwards. **Halo America** was better than ever at seven and won the Apple Blossom but had a curtailed season. **Twice The Vice** won the Vanity Handicap, but also suffered an injury before the end of the year. One of the other leading fillies was **Hidden Lake**; away from New York she lost her first four starts, but then she reeled off four successive wins, the last 3 of them Grade 1's, including that defeat of Ajina, before disappointing at the Breeders' Cup back in California; she visits Storm Cat. Those older mares who remain in training will have their work cut out against the likes of Ajina, Runup The Colors and Sharp Cat in the coming season.

The champion two-year-old filly, overwhelmingly, was **Countess Diana** who lost a shoe in her only loss in six starts and stormed clear at the Breeders' Cup to beat **Career Collection** by over eight lengths. However, she was operated on to remove a chip in her knee in December, and with her trainer, Pat Byrne, now contracted exclusively to Frank Stronach, she will have a new stable in 1998. Other Grade 1 winners in the division included **Beautiful Pleasure** (a sister to high-class middle-distance turf horse Mecke), **Vivid Angel** and **Love Lock**, and all three were well beaten at the Breeders' Cup. Love Lock went on to beat Career Collection by eleven lengths in the Hollywood Starlet and, trained by Wayne Lukas, may well have a successful time in California early in 1998. **Silver Maiden** is a modestly-bred daughter of Silver Buck who remained undefeated when easily taking the Frizette Stakes. She contracted a virus and connections chose not to supplement her into the Breeders' Cup. Overall, though, we'd expect some new names to emerge in the coming season.

Favorite Trick went unbeaten in eight races and was landing his fifth graded stakes when taking the Breeders' Cup Juvenile by five and a half lengths to give Pat Byrne a memorable double. Favorite Trick has done everything he's been asked to do, but we'd question just how good the form actually is, and his pedigree leaves considerable room for doubt as to whether he'll stay a mile and a quarter in the classics. His new trainer will be Bill Mott. If we had to pick one horse at this early stage, it would be a colt who ran against Favorite Trick once, and was beaten by fourteen lengths! But that was the only race Shug McGaughey's **Coronado's Quest** lost, and he improved as he stepped up in distance. By Forty Niner out of a Damascus mare, Coronado's Quest has had some temperament problems, but by all accounts was more settled before landing the Grade 2 Remsen Stakes at Aqueduct in November over nine furlongs by five lengths from another interesting prospect in **Halory Hunter**. Another colt worthy of mention is Wayne Lukas' **Grand Slam**. He won a pair of

1115

*Breeders' Cup Classic, Hollywood Park—A depleted field,
and Skip Away is in top form to beat Deputy Commander (light colours) by six lengths*

Grade 1 races at Belmont before sustaining an injury on the first turn and being virtually pulled up at the Breeders' Cup.

The traffic to America of useful or smart European turf horses is staggering. The money on offer justifies it, of course, and scarcely a decent turf race goes by without several of the leading contenders being imports. What does need changing, though, is the practice of scheduled graded races on the turf being switched to the dirt track because of rain-softened going. Although racetracks in America have meetings that can last several months, the running of one race on soft turf is not going to do irreparable damage to the course. And if it is switched to dirt, then the grading committee should simply strip the race of its status. How can a field, assembled for a race on turf, be said to be up to the equivalent standard for a race on dirt? Fields are often severely depleted because the turf specialists are pulled out, and sometimes trainers enter a horse in the hope that the race will be taken off the turf. By all means cancel the claimers and the allowance races. But the switching of graded stakes is making a mockery of the system.

The American three-year-olds on turf still have a fair way to go before they can be considered top class. The top fillies on our list were all European, and to our knowledge only **Kool Kat Katie** will be racing there in 1998. She bled when winning the E P Taylor Stakes on her last start, but if she recovers from that she should have a fine future. The American males seem a little better and they may well come on again in 1998. **Honor Glide** led the way for much of the year, winning the Secretariat Stakes, but lost to **River Squall** in the Hawthorne Derby in October. Later in the autumn **Subordination** (who improved after finishing only fifth in the Secretariat) edged out **Lasting Approval** in the Hollywood Derby. **Skybound** is trained in Canada and put up a good effort when quite a close fourth against his elders in the Woodbine Mile. It's quite likely more will be heard of them: only a further 6 lb to 7 lb improvement will see them up with the best of the older turf performers.

There was not much between the top older performers. The gelding **Influent** was much improved, gaining Grade 1 wins in the Caesars International (where he beat Woodbine Mile winner and prospective stallion **Geri**) and the Man o'War Stakes (ahead of Turf Classic and Hong Kong International Cup winner **Val's Prince**) but tore a suspensory ligament and did not reappear. **Chief Bearhart** won five of his seven starts, including the Canadian International and a narrow success over Borgia in the Breeders' Cup Turf. He's due to stay in training, and is likely to be aimed at the Breeders' Cup again. **Marlin** had another fine year, winning the San Juan Capistrano Handicap (ahead of **Sunshack** and **African Dancer**) and the Arlington Million (from Sandpit) but injury forced his retirement to stud. **Always A Classic** (a half-brother to Sky Classic) progressed really well in the spring, beating **Labeeb** in the Early Times Turf Classic before a good third to **Ops Smile** and **Flag Dawn** under top weight in the Manhattan Handicap in June proved to be his last race before being retired to stud. Reliable **Awad** won the Sword Dancer Invitational Handicap and provided a good yardstick in most of the races he contested, including when second to **River Bay** in the Hollywood Turf Cup. Of the remainder, one who may come on again next year is **Lucky Coin**, a front-running miler who won seven of his nine starts and was fourth to Spinning World at the Breeders' Cup. Ex-French mare **Windsharp** was clearly the best older female on turf, but strained a tendon when winning the Beverly Hills Handicap ahead of **Different** and Gamely Handicap winner **Donna Viola**. The consistent pair **Memories of Silver** and **Maxzene** fought out a close finish to the Beverly D Stakes and were both also very smart.

Racing can ill afford headlines such as the closure of Arlington International Racecourse (chairman Richard Duchossois citing lack of support from the state of Illinois), uncertainty about the future of the *Daily Racing Form* which was up for sale for several months, a scandal about sponges being put up horses' noses before they raced, and ongoing disputes between the New York Racing Association and the state. However, the creation of the National Thoroughbred Racing Association is much more promising. The newly-formed association, which brings together all sectors of the sport, intends to promote racing from a united front, with particular emphasis on increasing television exposure both in advertising and live coverage. The task is not an easy one. Racing in America does not, currently, enjoy the image it has in Britain. However, relying on sporadic superstars, such as a Cigar or a potential Triple Crown

Pimlico Special Handicap, Pimlico—
Gentlemen gives Skip Away weight and a beating; this grand pair should meet again in 1998

winner, is not the way forward, and a campaign focussing less on gambling and more on the wider social and aesthetic qualities of a day at the races has got to be a step in the right direction. With the projected revenues and expenses for the NTRA set to grow massively in the next year, and then steadily in the four years after that, racing in America will have as good a chance at sustained growth as it has in a long time.

This could be an exciting few years in racing. Californian racecourse Del Mar has its own site on the Internet. That's not unusual these days, but for some of us to be able to sit in Timeform House late on Saturday night on August 9th and watch the Pacific Classic as it happened was extraordinary. The smooth winner that day was **Gentlemen**, our idea of the best horse in America in 1997, though the Eclipse Award voters did not see it that way. Fortunately, Gentlemen is due to continue racing in 1998 and he'll have another chance to prove himself. Don't bet against him enhancing his reputation even further.

European-trained horses who showed or reproduced their best form in North America are included in this list

† commentary in
Racehorses of 1997

Two-Year-Olds

123	Countess Diana (f)
121	Favorite Trick
119	Grand Slam
118	Coronado's Quest
118	Silver Maiden (f)
117	Love Lock (f)
116	Real Quiet
115	Artax
114	Beautiful Pleasure (f)
114	Buttons N Moes
114	Dawson's Legacy
114	Lil's Lad
113	Nationalore
113	Souvenir Copy
112	Career Collection (f)
112	Dancing With Ruth (f)
112	Johnbill
112	K. O. Punch
112	Keene Dancer
112	Ninth Inning (f)
112	Old Topper
112	Time Limit
112	Vivid Angel (f)
111	Double Honor
111	Old Trieste
109	Clark Street (f)
109	Cowboy Dan
109	Devil's Pride
109	Diamond On The Run (f)
109	Fight For M'Lady
109	Halory Hunter
109	Soft Senorita (f)
109	Well Noted

DIRT

Three-Year-Olds

127	Touch Gold
126	Silver Charm
125	Ajina (f)
125	Captain Bodgit
125	Free House
124	Behrens
124	Deputy Commander
124	Runup The Colors (f)
124	Sharp Cat (f)
122	Blushing K D (f)
121	Glitter Woman (f)
121	Lord Grillo
120	Fabulously Fast (f)
120	Smoke Glacken
120	Tomisue's Delight (f)
119	Anet
118	Dixie Flag (f)
118	Wild Rush
117	Awesome Again
117	Blazing Sword
117	I Ain't Bluffing (f)
117	Precocity
117	Pulpit
116	Crypto Star
116	Frisk Me Now
116	Kelly Kip
116	Pearl City (f)
116	Richter Scale
116	Royal Indy (f)
115	Minister's Melody (f)
115	Ordway
115	Phantom On Tour

Older Horses

136	†Gentlemen
132	†Formal Gold
131	†Skip Away
130	†Siphon
127	Sandpit
126	Alphabet Soup
125	Hidden Lake (f)
125	Jewel Princess (f)

125	Louis Quatorze
125	Will's Way
124	Langfuhr
124d	Mt Sassafras
123	Halo America (f)
123	Twice The Vice (f)
123	Unbridled's Song
122	Isitingood
122	Whiskey Wisdom
121	Atticus
121	Benchmark
121	Elmhurst
121	Tejano Run
120	Hesabull
120	Victory Speech
119	Bet On Sunshine
119	Mecke
119	Refinado Tom
119	Toga Toga Toga (f)
118	Capote Belle (f)
118	Chequer
118	Crafty Friend
118	Flat Fleet Feet (f)
118	Sir Cat
118	Track Gal (f)
118	Victor Cooley
118§	†Lucayan Prince
117	Basquejan
117	Belle's Flag (f)
117	Clear Mandate (f)
117	Devious Course
117	Miss Golden Circle (f)
117	Northern Afleet
117	†River Keen
116	†Atraf
116	City By Night
116	Dancin Renee (f)
116	Feasibility Study (f)
116	High Stakes Player
116	Listening (f)
116	Men's Exclusive
116	Prepo
116	Royal Haven
116	Stalwart Member

116	Suave Prospect	115	†Panama City	119	Helmsman
116	Western Winter	115	Rob 'n Gin	119	Labeeb
115	Ashboro (f)	115	Thesaurus	119	Ok By Me
115	Boundless Moment			119	Soviet Line
115	Diligence	**Older Horses**		119	Trail City
115	First Intent	130	†Spinning World	118	Desert Waves
115	Kid Katabatic	126	Influent	118	†L'Annee Folle (f)
115	Kingdom Found	125	Chief Bearhart	118	Same Old Wish
115	Pacific Fleet	124	Always A Classic	117	Ampulla (f)
115	Punch Line	124	Marlin	117	Devil's Cup
115	Rare Blend (f)	123	†River Bay	117	†Flyway
115	Savinio	123	Val's Prince	117	Lakeshore Road
115	Score A Birdie	123	Windsharp (f)	117	Montjoy
115	Top Rung (f)	122	Flag Down	117	Rainbow Blues
115	Tres Paraiso	122	Geri	117	Talloires
115	Why Change	121	Awad	116	Buck's Boy
		121	†Decorated Hero	116	Draw Shot
TURF		121	Lassigny	116	Escena (f)
		121	Lucky Coin	116	Expelled
Three-Year-Olds		121	Ops Smile	116	Golden Pond (f)
124	†Borgia (f)	121	Percutant	116	Magellan
121	†Ryafan (f)	121	Sunshack	116	Peckinpah's Soul
120	†Kool Kat Katie (f)	120	†Annus Mirabilis	116	Pinfloron
120	River Squall	120	Down The Aisle	116	Real Connection (f)
120	Subordination	120	Dowty	115	African Dancer
119	Honor Glide	120	El Angelo	115	Alpride (f)
119	Lasting Approval	120	Kiridashi	115	Big Sky Chester
118	†Mousse Glacee (f)	120	Maxzene (f)	115	Boyce
118	Skybound	120	Memories of Silver (f)	115	Brave Note
118	†Yashmak (f)	120	Rainbow Dancer	115	Fanjica (f)
117	†Romanov	120	Sharp Appeal	115	Joker
117	†Voyagers Quest	120	Wild Event	115	Luna Wells (f)
116	Early Colony	119	Crown Attorney	115	River Flyer
115	Auntie Mame (f)	119	Different (f)	115	Sandtrap
115	Brave Act	119	Diplomatic Jet	115	Snake Eyes
115	Famous Digger (f)	119	Donna Viola (f)	115	Toda Una Dama (f)
115	†Fantastic Fellow			115	Yokama (f)

HONG KONG For the first time, the International Classifications included a horse trained in Hong Kong, the honour falling to International Cup runner-up **Oriental Express**. Previously known as Desert Boy when trained in Britain by Peter Chapple-Hyam, Oriental Express won two races in 1997, notably the Hong Kong Derby (a race for four-year-olds over nine furlongs) in February, and also finished fourth behind London News in the Queen Elizabeth II Cup in April. On the overall balance of his form, however, Oriental Express doesn't look worth so high a rating as either the 1996/97 Hong Kong Horse of the Year, **Privilege**, runner-up behind London News but nothing like the same force late in the year, or Derby third **Indigenous**, the best horse in Hong Kong in 1997 on Timeform ratings. Indigenous improved for a mid-year switch to the Ivan Allan stable and ended 1997 with a good fourth to Luso (Privilege sixth) in the Hong Kong International Vase. Oriental Express is also rated lower by us than Irish Derby fourth **Johan Cruyff**, who gave Privilege a convincing beating over eleven furlongs at Sha Tin in November on only his second run in Hong Kong but finished down the field over a trip too short in the Hong Kong International Cup. Other horses worthy of mention are the 1996 International Cup fourth **Benji**, winner of two races early in 1997 before being injured; **Smashing Pumpkin**, a disappointing favourite for the International Cup after winning the Group 1 Stewards' Cup (Indigenous third, Privilege fourth) at Sha Tin in November but held in the highest regard; and, of the up-and-coming youngsters, the likely 1998 Derby

Hong Kong International Cup, Sha Tin—American Val's Prince (noseband) comes from well back to pip Hong Kong Derby winner Oriental Express (who was in last year's 'Racehorses' annual as Desert Boy)

favourite **Electronic Zone**, who created history in Hong Kong when he was raised 26 lb, more than any horse had been before, after winning at Sha Tin in November.

114	Indigenous	111	Oriental Express	106	Electronic Zone
113	Privilege	110	Benji	106	Smart Kid
112	Johan Cruyff	108+	Smashing Pumpkin	106	Deauville
		107	Victory Star		

Note: Timeform ratings and timefigures are now available on the internet for all meetings staged in Hong Kong (the season runs from September to June). Subscriptions are available through internet credits, full details on Timeform's website—http: //www.timeform.com

JAPAN   For many years the huge prize money for races in Japan has not been on offer to challengers from the rest of the world. There's little doubt, though, that the next decade or two is going to see Japan growing significantly as an international force. The Japan Cup, founded in 1981, stood alone for several years as the only opportunity for foreign horses to compete, but there are now eleven races open to international competition. You can be sure that as the success of the home-breds rises in these events, so more events will be opened up.

The massive investment in potential top-class stallions is no guarantee of success in the short term—but this practice has been going on for a good while now and is sure to continue to improve the quality of Japanese bloodstock. Forays abroad to race, though, have been rare—Dance Partner was beaten a short head in the 1995 Prix de la Nonette—and it is to be hoped that the fatal accident which befel Hokuto Vega at the 1997 Dubai World Cup will not deter future ventures. **Taiki Blizzard** had an excellent career in Japan, including winning the big international mile event, the Yasuda Kinen, in June ahead of **Genuine** and A Magicman. But, although Taiki Blizzard was a promising third in a Grade 3 race in California, he was disappointing in the last two editions of the Breeders' Cup Classic, perhaps not at his best on dirt. He's now been retired to stud.

As with all foreign coverage except Ireland and Hong Kong, Timeform ratings cover the top horses only. And as with Scandinavia (where the 'black type' races are covered) only those horses which raced in events open to international competition are included for Japan. Among the three-year-olds, two stood out. **Taiki Shuttle** won

1120

The Mile Championship and The Sprinters Stakes (six furlongs) towards the end of the year. Japanese Derby second **Silk Justice** followed his fifth in the Japan Cup with a win over **Marvelous Sunday** (who won the Takarazuka Kinen over eleven furlongs in July narrowly from **Bubble Gum Fellow**) and **Air Groove** in the Arima Kinen over twelve and a half furlongs in December. The filly Air Groove, named Japanese Horse of the Year, took advantage of the sex allowance to pip Bubble Gum Fellow in the Tenno Sho (Autumn) over a mile and a quarter in October, and also when the pair were placed behind Pilsudski in the Japan Cup (where **Tsukuba Symphony** was seventh).

Two Thousand Guineas and Derby equivalents winner Sunny Brian, as well as very smart stayers Mayano Top Gun and Sakura Laurel, are among those who didn't achieve anything in the international races, and have therefore not been given ratings.

Three-Year-Olds		Older Horses			
121	Silk Justice	120	Bubble Gum Fellow	118	Tsukuba Symphony
118	Taiki Shuttle	120	Marvelous Sunday	117	Genuine
		118	Air Groove (f)	117	Shinko King
		118	Taiki Blizzard	117	Sugino Hayakaze

ERRATA & ADDENDA
'Racehorses of 1996'

Easycall	line 3, P302, Flying Childers was **not** Michael Tebbutt's first pattern win (he won the Mill Reef on Princely Hush in 1994)
Hollywood Dream	line 6, below the pedigree, P435, Fresco was the **dam** of Port Merion
Lavirco	line 18, P531, Lando and Laroche were bred and owned by Gestut **Ittlingen**
Swain	line 9, Swain was **not** one of the first from Fabre's string to join Godolphin (Valley of Gold, Diffident, Tereshkova etc)
'Top Horses Abroad'	Germany – line 13, P1131 Oriental Flower was trained by Uwe Ostmann, **not** champion trainer Uwe Stoltefuss

THE FULL TIMEFORM IRISH HANDICAP

Here are listed the Timeform Ratings for every horse that ran on the flat in Ireland, plus a few who were trained there and ran abroad, during the 1997 season. † indicates that the horse appears in commentary or essay form in *Racehorses of 1997*.

Two-Year-Olds

89+	Abandonment	77p	Burgan	81	Dove Orchid
90	Absoluta	–	Caheredmond Girl	85	Dragon Triumph
–	African Nugget	–	Cairo Lady	84	Dress Design
–	After A Fashion	83p	Campo Catino	58	Dudeen
53	Aisling Beag	97p	Canzona	53	Early Fin
81	Aislo	61	Carnabrae	–	Early Memory
56	Albinella	68	Casati	57d	Electric Isle
104p	Alborada†	–	Cast A Spell	–	El Gabor
88	Aljjawarih	93	Castleross	78	Eljamil
75	Alleged Aggressor	94?	Catch The Dragon	74	Emerald Project
85p	Allegedly Yours	67p	Cavallina	73	En Retard
74	Alonzo	103p	Celtic Cavalier†	68p	Existential
74	Always Crowded	–p	Chairmanoftheboard	84	Eymir
67	Always True	84	Challenger Two	86	Fairy Flight
88	Amravati	96?	Chateau Royal	92	Family Crest
97	Andy Dufresne	95	Chenille	78	Fayrana†
97+	Another Fantasy†	69	Cheviot Indian	–	Fender Park
74p	Antrim Coast	74	Chlopa	–	Ferneyfield
84	Apache Red†	70	Christy Senior	87	Festival Song
–	April Project	59	Cincuenta	85+	Fiddler's Rock
108+	Asfurah†	74	City Imp	–	Fionnula's Rainbow
92	Attractive Crown	74	City Poser	76	First Encounter
76	Badila	–	Classic Grounds	102	Flame Violet
98p	Balla Sola	–	Class Society	68	Flatley
63	Ballyellery	82	Clewbay Pearl	68p	Foreign Love
–	Ballyvelig Lady	88	Cloudberry†	80p	Forget About It
78	Bamford Castle	85	Coconut Creek	58	Francois Laboure
–	Banahoe Boy	68	Colours To Gold†	–	Frankie's Girl
63	Banakat	59	Comeoutofthefog†	63	Frisky
–	Bayyadi	–	Commander Baker	52	Frontliner
77	Be Crafty	–	Common Verse	102p	Fruits of Love†
–	Beebeep	92?	Conectis†	87	Galahad
66p	Beldarian	–	Consider It Done	69	Gamine
–	Bella With A Zee	–	Contract Miss	–	Gay-Balina
69p	Berkeley Square	–	Cordal Island	66	Gay Paree
52	Bhutan	–	Countessmarkievicz	76p	Geisha Girl
92p	Bianconi	–	Country Day	73	Gentle Thoughts
62	Bidding Ace	51+	Covalla	71	George
69p	Bird of Prey	63	Crazy Falcon	–	Give Her Sally
78	Bismarck	64	Crown Point	59	Goldbridge
–	Black Orpheus	90	Crystal Wind	77	Golden Chimes
60?	Black Pidgeon	95	Cultural Role	94	Golden Mirage†
74	Black Rock City	65	Cunning Kate	74	Golden Rule
–	Blue Booby	–	Dame Bay	83?	Goldman
60	Blue Music	56	Dana Miya	74	Gold Radiance
81	Boat Strand	88+	Dane River	–	Goldstar
98	Boldini	99	Danyross†	–	Goldstorm
93	Bold Raparee	–	Dara Kay	–	Good Reason
68	Bombay Mix	94	Daunting Lady†	–	Great Figile
–	Brief Fling	–	Dawn Project	71	Grey Ciseaux
54	Brief Journey	78	Deilginis	69	Grey Lightning
87p	Brief Sentiment	79?	Delirious Tantrum	86p	Guscott
72p	Broken Promise	87	Desert Fox	74	Hallucination
–	Buddy And Soda	96	Dixie Dynamo	98	Hanzanar
		88p	Diya	108	Harbour Master†

– Harda Arda	– Lady's Heart	97 Musk Lime
81 Hasanat	50 La Mouette	73 Mysterious Miss
81 Have Merci	71p Latterly	61+ Mystery Dream
73 Hazarama	99 Law Library	100 Natalis
102p Heed My Warning	? Leafy Isle	– Naviglio
– Heemanela	– Leixlip Belle	59p Nazario
105 Heeremandi†	71 L'Estable Fleurie	64 Near Dunleer
66 Heffo's Army	77 Lets Clic Together	43 Nero's Dancer
65 Here On Business	73 Liffey Ballad	– Night Over Day
100p Hermitage Bay	49 Liffeydale	– Night Patrol
62 Heuston Station	86 Lightning Star	71 Night Scent
92p Hibernian Rhapsody	53 Lisa Simpson	68 Northern Royal
68 Hidden Prospect	70? Little Bella	82? Obvious Appeal
69 High Honour	74p Lizop	77 Occhi Verdi†
68 Hillside Rose	– Loyal Deed	53+ Oisin†
98+ Hoh Chi Min†	87 Maduka	61 Orient Way
78 Holly Hedge	86 Magical Baba	83p Osprey Reef
– Home Comforts	99 Magical Minty	– Our Valentine
73 Honey Storm†	78 Magical Peace	75 Out'n'about
103 Hopping Higgins†	–p Magical Shot	94p Outspoken
– Huntmore	66 Major Ballaby†	– Pacific Isle
57 Impaldi	99p Make No Mistake	75 Paradable
106p Impressionist†	– Makeyourselfathome	– Peace Prevails
– Infinity	71 Maltesse	81 Pelagius
70 Innocent Pleasures	59 Malvadilla	– Perfect Action
99p Irish Summit	90 Marigot Bay	66 Persian Isle
– Irma Dancer	79 Marilia	70 Per Tuti
73 Ishbiliya	64 Markskeepingfaith	– Petite Bold
62 Island Doy	96 Matter of Trust	93 Photogenic†
57? Ivory Isle	? Maxmix	47 Pipes of Peace
– I Will	72 Mazurka	54 Ponda Rosa
– Jackerri	– Mega Project	101 Pool Music†
91 Jacmar†	– Me Jane	59 Porcellino
– Jade Vine	– Melachrino	75 Precise Direction
58 Jadilian	54 Melette	– Prediction
– Jane's A Lady	100 Mempari	89 Prevalence
8? Jay And-A	–p Midlands Girl	– Prilora
– Jeanne d'Arc	69 Milad	111 Princely Heir†
66p Jimmy Swift	–p Mille Miglia	55 Princely Spark
86 Jimmy The Greek	68 Millie's Lily	–p Prince Minata
68 Joleah	– Miniver	74 Prince of Monaco
72 Jovine	? Mi Picasso	64? Proof Positive
70p Juinevera	84 Miquelon†	79 Prospectus
– Just As Little	– Miracle Ridge	66 Public Figure
65 Just Wondering	80 Mirror Mirror	– Queen of Fibres
80p Kalagold	66 Miss Brighton	93 Queen of Silk
74 Kananaskis	64+ Miss Chiquita	71 Queen Sarabi
94 Karakorum	76 Miss Emer	– Quintrell Downs
72 Kate Lane†	65p Missing The Beat	71 Rahika Rose
– Kearneys Arch	67 Mission Hills	81 Rainswept
54 Key Provider	– Miss Rusty	– Rapid Eagle
86p Khatani	– Miss Shannon	– Rathclarin
72 Kilbride Blues	84 Mitra	99p Remarkable Style
56 Killone Lady	75 Moonlight Truce	– Renaissance Dancer
– Killucan King	69 Moonstone†	–p Resume
98+ Kincara Palace	73p Morristown Dancer	81 Retention
115 King of Kings†	103 Mountain Song†	75p Ridgewood Ruby
– King's Colours	101 Mowbray†	72 Right Job
76p Kinnear	50 Mr Kiffups	104p Risk Material
92 Kitza	63 Mr McKen	–p Rose Petal
91 Krispy Knight†	61 Mrs Potter	97p Royal House
102+ Lady Alexander†	– Muftin	67p Rush Brook
74 Lady For Life	72 Munasib	– Rusty Image
– Lady of Guadalope	71p Musical Myth	102p Sabre Mountain

–	Sacrementum	
–	Sally Pledge	
–p	Sans Prix	
113	Saratoga Springs†	
61p	Sarayan	
65	Sarwani	
76	Say Wonderful	
?	Scandisk	
–	Scenic Squall	
65?	Scenic Way	
–	Schiphol	
86	Screen Idol	
48	Sea Birds Treasure	
–	Sea Modena	
122p	Second Empire†	
76	Seefinn	
55	Seilla	
–	Sense of Style	
59p	Shafqan	
101	Shahtoush	
67	Shalazar	
–	Shalford Song	
69	Shanko	
65p	Sharazad	
55	Sharpaten	
87p	Sharp Catch	
102	Sharp Play†	
64	Shereevagh	
–	She's Wonderful	
–	Shira-A	
–	Shoeless Joe	
–	Shvera	
–	Shyam	
95	Sideman†	
79	Silverado	
44	Silver Picean	
68	Silvery Halo	
72	Sir Cador	
–	Skatt	
–	Slew of Silver	
–	Slightly Sober	
73	Slippery Slope	
–	Smokeycove	
78?	Soft Touch†	
74	Somethingbeautiful	
–	Soviet Beam	
–	Soviet Eight	
74p	Specialist	
67	Speed Hill	
79p	Star Begonia	
–	Star To The North	
70	Stately Princess†	
–	Static Power	
–	Statoqueen	
–	Stay Alert	
61	Stellissima	
65	Sterling High	
89	Stop Out†	
91?	Stopwatch	
62	Strictly Rhythm†	
90	Strike Hard	
–	Stylish Academy	
–	Summer Scene	
70?	Summer Style	

66	Sun Lion	
81	Sunshine Street	
–	Super Passat	
88	Super Sonic Sonia	
92?	Susun Kelapa	
65	Suzy Street	
–p	Taakid	
98	Tadwiga†	
83	Taispeain	
100	Takarian	
72	Take A Turn†	
67	Take Care	
64	Taleca Son	
102p	Tarascon†	
79	Tarbaan	
51	Tasbok	
64	Technohead	
83	Ten Tricks	
–	Terrahawk	
–	The Ant	
97	The King of Cloyne	
62p	The Realtour	
–	Tifosi	
82	Tiger Haven	
–	Tiger Wings	
97	Timekeeper†	
89	Timeless Isle	
65	Tinerana Law	
80+	Tittle Tattle	
69p	Todos Santos	
70	To The Skies	
–	Touraneena	
79	Treverrick	
93	Two-Twenty-Two	
–	Untold Story	
–	Uppity	
67	Valentine Quin	
60?	Valerio's Princess	
80	Via Splendida	
90	Viola Royale	
67	Voodoo Lily	
41	Wait Your Turn	
59	Walls Lough	
56+	Whacker-Do†	
61	What A Scene	
64p	Wild Eagle	
96	Winona	
100p	Wish Me Luck	
80p	Woodwin	
80p	Yorba Linda	
58	Yulara	
–	Zeehan	
–	Zenning	
58	Zilina	

Three-Year-Olds

100	Abou Zouz†	
74	Absent Beauty	
100	Absolute Glee	
–	Acadelli	
62p	Academie Royale	
–	Act of Defiance	
–	Adirpour	
101	Admiral Wings	

88p	Afragha
66	Agent Scully
99	Air of Distinction
103	Akdariya†
105	Alarme Belle
105	Aliya
–	Aljaarif
–	All Charisma
–	Alma Latina
99	Almost Skint
79	Alparost
89	Alzaro
109	Amid Albadu†
60	Amocachi
–	Amolene
94	Angellino
70	Anid
91	Animagic
–	Animato
79	Anisata
–	Another Sally
–	Apache Chief
–	Appleton's Fancy†
78	Arc
70	Argus Gal
70	Argyle
–	Arts Project
110	Ashley Park
71	Ash Project
54	Aspen Gem
73	Astro Lines
–	Astronome
54	Audrey's Pearl
–	Avalon Accord
74	Award of Merit
95p	Ayers Rock
102	Azra
77	Babe Ruth
–	Baby Fresh
88	Back Log
–	Back To Bavaria
92	Bahamian Beauty†
107	Bakkar
83	Ballinola Lad
67	Ballylennon Mist
69	Banjala
56	Barnacranny
84	Beach Project
52	Beal Na Blath
102	Beamish Boy
104	Beautiful Fire
57d	Belike The Wind
–	Belle Project
68	Belsay
–	Better Be Sure
58	Biddy Blackhurst
–	Big Boy John
–	Bikaline du Moulin
72	Binneas
86	Bint Alsarab
68	Blind Date
70	Blue Jazz
80	Blue Ridge†
79	Blue Stocking

–	Blushing Minstrel	66	Cryptic Lady	65	Executive Choice
75+	Bobbella	69	Cryptic Pattern	87	Executive Decision
97	Bob The Broker	64	Crystal Springs	–	Experimental
–	Bohemian Belle	–	Culloville North	–	Extatic
90	Bold Hunter	–	Cumas	74	Fabricate
87	Bold Tycoon	91	Curiously	56	Fairy Oak
62	Boughtbyphone	85	Cutting Ground	66	Fallon
–	Briion	–	Cyrano Lory	107	Family Tradition
117	Brilliance†	91	Dabali	115	Fantastic Fellow†
–	Broom Street	88	Dabtara	84	Far Niente
67	Bubbly Dancer	–	Daddy's Polly	58	Fastnet View
106	Buddy Marvel†	78	Daffodil Dale	63	Faux Pas
90	Buncrana	41	Dama de Seda	53	Female Lead
74	Burnt Toast	78	Danccini	79	Figure of Fun
–	Burubako	–	Dance Tycoon	92	Fine Project
66	Bye Bold Aileen	61	Dancing Venus	77	Fizz Up
52d	By Jay†	105	Dangerous Diva†	–	Flagship Uberalles
77	Cabastro	65	Danny's Joy	72	Flags Up
63	Caduga	102	Darbela	55	Flower Hill Lad
112	Caiseal Ros	98+	Darrouzett	87	Flying Blind
67	Calamity Kate	–	Dar Zoffer	–	Flying Project
83	Call My Bluff	–	Davenport	113	Fly To The Stars†
62	Camassina	–	Davenport Silver	63	Fly Your Kite
–	Camdeno Star	111	Dazzle†	–	Forever Relic
76	Canadian Vista	110	Deadly Dudley†	–	Forlorn Point
97?	Candereli	–	Decent Project	103	Fort Morgan
74	Candide	86	Deerfield Fame	70	Frenchie
–	Cannikin	90	Delirious Moment	–	Fulminus Instar
65	Capall Farraige	69	Derringer	73	Gaelic Probe
101	Cardigan Bay	–	Derry Field	62	Galkina
95	Carhue Lass	–	Desert Ease	92	Gan Ainm
–	Carlisle Bay	129	Desert King†	92	Ganaway
101	Carnelly	45	Dicky's Rock	–	Garavogue
110	Casey Tibbs	–	Dip's Guest	75	Gardd
61	Castletubber Lady	–	Distant Affair	–	Garde Rouge
109	Catienus†	–	Distant Dancer	94	Gaultier Gale
96	Celebrity Style	–	Distinctly Noble	98	Generous Lady
66	Celtic Link	81	Distinctly West	92	Glasshouse
75	Celtic Slip	–	Doellan	66	Global Diamond
100	Chania	86p	Dona Royale	73	Glorious Encounter
84	Charita	67	Don Wattle	81	God Forbid
90	Chauncy Lane	66	Doucette	–	Gold Chaser
105	Check The Band†	–	Dragon Century	72	Golden Circle
70	Chipstead Bay†	74	Dream Project	–	Golden Lights
79	Chloe	82	Dreamworks	71	Go Thunder
76	Chu Culainn	61	Driftwood	60	Granny Kelly
96	Cinnamon Rose	122	Dr Johnson†	99p	Grass Roots
93	Ciste	–	Dromhall Lady	–	Greek Belle
89	Citizen Kane	–	Drumcooley	109	Green Card†
–	Clarecastle	71	Drumgor Prince	69	Guest Cailin
115	Classic Park†	–	Dunkip Addition	95	Gunfire
74	Classic Referendum	–	Early Present	73	Gypsy Melody
–	Classic Success	79	Eastern Project†	81	Hamamelis
108	Clerio	122	Ebadiyla†	93	Handaza
103	Code of Honour	59	Ein Tresor	–	Ha-Pa
73p	Colombian Green	–	Ela Patricia	63	Happy Flower
–	Common Currency	–	Eldorado	66	Happy Gift
–	Coolarne Lad	92	Elida	–	Harrison Hill
48	Copper Faced Jacks	–	Elinor Dashwood	–	Hassiba
–	Copper Glen	–	Encandilar	–	Hassosi
66	Corn Victor	–	En-Jay-Bee	63	Hayling Princess
–	Country Project	95	Epic Tale	81	Hayward
86	Crest of The Wave	96	Eternal Joy	–	Hazy Habit
105+	Crown Regent	111	Etoile†	69	Heroic Destiny

1129

–	Make An Effort	–	Neykari	–	Quinze
69	Malacoda	–	No Animosity	43	Quote Unquote
–	Mamdooh	61	No Avail	–	Radif
–	Manndaliy	–	Noble Shoon	38	Rainery
51	Mannoori	68	Nocksky	113	Raiyoun
–	Man of Arran	69	Nominee	109	Ramooz†
–	Manon du Source	–	Nordic Air	75	Real Guest
–	Marchaway	87	Nordic Brief	80	Realt Dhun Eibhir
–	Marinas Choice	–	Nordic Sensation	73	Reasilvia
49	Marlonette	–	Northern Bars	51	Red Tonic
36	Martha's Glimpse	–	North of Kala	–	Relic Image
–	Masalika	87	Norwegian Blue	–	Remontant
68	Mayasta	54	No Tag	96	Rescue Time
–	May Bloom	66	Notluckytochange	66	Return Again
85	Maytpleasethecourt	–	Noukari	54	Rice's Hill
87	Meglio Che Posso	34	Nymph In The Ski	65	Rince Abhann
73	Metastasio	–	Oakland Bridge	–	Rishine
–	Mettlesome Beauty	–	Oakler	48	Rising Waters
111	Midnight Escape†	61	Oakmont	–	Rita's Killaloe
93	Miltonfield†	–	Oh So Grumpy	94	Rithab
–	Minzal Legend	83	Omar	80	River Project
–	Miroswaki	59	One Man Band	73	River Valley Lady
47	Miss Hot Tamalli	68	One More Spin	75	Rizzoli
50	Miss Indonesia	103	On Fair Stage	61	Robazala
–	Miss Margate	105	Orange Grouse	83	Roblexie
43	Miss Toffee Nose	121	Orchestra Stall†	–	Roman Fever
65	Mister Munnelly	98	Oriane	102	Rossmore Girl
67	Mixed Opinion	–	Orlas Castle	29	Roundwood Rose
67	Mofasa	127	Oscar Schindler†	–	Royal Albert
111	Mohaajir	76	Osprey Ridge	–	Royal Insignia
66d	Montelacity	45	Other Options	89	Royal Midyan
66	Montelisa	70	Padashpan	–	Royal Vision
74	More Risk	–	Pajoma	24	Ruano
54	Moscow's Flame	75	Paris Model	–	Runabout
57	Mountain Rocket	79	Pas Possible	43	Run Forrest Run
94	Mount Row	–	Patience of Angels	61	Run To The Ace
–	Mt Leinster	95	Patsy Grimes†	35	Rutabaga
–	Mullaghea Lass	–	Paulas Pet	59?	Sadallah
106	Munif	52	Pegus Junior	27	Sallustar
–	Murphy's Malt	42	Peppanoora	66	Sambara
103	Musical Mayhem	97	Perfect Venue	116	Samraan†
–	Musical Sunset	64	Persian Dream	–	Sam Vaughan
–	My Blue	118	Persian Punch†	–	Sandpiper
103	My Branch†	–	Petasus	70	San Michel
–	My Niece	50	Phardy	56	Sarcastic
–	Mystical City	–	Pils Invader	79	Sarpadar
–	Mystical Valley	134	Pilsudski†	–	Satcos Princess
70	Mystic Ring	60	Playprint	57	Sauganash Song
67	My Trelawny	–	Point Luck	85	Saving Bond
75	My Trivet	–	Poison Ivy	55	Scorpio Boy
–	Naaman	115	Polar Prince†	–	Sea Idol
67	Nabeel	57	Pompier	72	Sea Leopard
100	Nagnagnag	99	Power Play	42	Sea of Dreams
–	Nahranah	–	Pray For Peace	–	Seeking Destiny
36	Na Huibheachu†	92	Premier Project	89	Sentosa Star
92	Nakayama Express	–	Premier Walk	58	Shahnaad
83	Nanda	–	Pre Ordained	77	Shahrur†
–	Nascimento	57	Pretty Beat Up	64	Shaihar
47	Nashalong†	–	Prince Mike	61	Shamartini
–	Native Chic	–	Prize of Peace	56	Shanid
99	Native-Darrig	–	Prosperous Penny	72	Shanrue
52	Native Eclipse	65	Queen Moranbon	103	Sharazan
63	Nazmi†	75	Queen of Bakla	41	Shargan
57	New Legislation	–	Queen's Flagship	54	Sharp Scotch

INTERNATIONAL CLASSIFICATIONS

The International Classifications were published on 15th January, 1998.
The leading horses are shown (* trained exclusively outside Europe).

Two-Year-Olds
127	Xaar
119	Second Empire
118	Central Park
118	Daggers Drawn
118	Embassy
116	Charge d'Affaires
116	Lend A Hand
116	Saratoga Springs
115	Mudeer
115	Tamarisk
114	Hayil
114	Muhtathir
114	Princely Heir
113	Crazee Mental
113	Loving Claim
113	Mutamam
112	Arkadian Hero
112	Bold Fact
112	Carrowkeel
112	Docksider
112	Midnight Line
112	Thief of Hearts
111	Alboostan
111	Designer
111	Glorosia
111	Halmahera
111	Harbour Master
111	King of Kings
111	Little Indian
111	Special Quest
110	Asakir
110	Asfurah
110	Daymarti
110	Desert Prince
110	El Maimoun
110	Impressionist
110	Isle de France
110	Jimmy Too
110	Lord Kintyre
110	Merlin's Ring
110	Name of Love
110	Royal Shyness
110	Tarascon
110	Teapot Row
110	Tracking
110	Woodland Melody
109	Baltic State
109	Cape Verdi
109	Croco Rouge
109	Heed My Warning
109	Jibe
109	Mijana
109	Risk Material
109	Silic
108	Anna Palariva

108	Bodyguard
108	Chester House
108	City Honours
108	Haami
108	La-Faah
108	Nadwah
108	Pinmix
108	Plaisir Des Yeux
108	Pool Music
108	Prolix
108	Regal Revolution
108	Shahtoush
108	Speedfit Too
108	Tippitt Boy
107	Alborada
107	Almutawakel
107	Arawak Cay
107	Ashraakat
107	Celtic Cavalier
107	Desert Drama
107	Fairy Grey
107	Fruits of Love
107	Greenlander
107	Gulland
107	Heeremandi
107	Khumba Mela
107	Kilimanjaro
107	Lady In Waiting
107	Linden Heights
107	Mantles Star
107	Mempari
107	Mountain Song
107	Scenery
107	Silent Tribute
107	Tenbyssimo
107	Trans Island
107	Wren
107	Zalaiyka
106	Bahr
106	Bintang
106	Craigsteel
106	Eco Friendly
106	Exclusive
106	Flawless
106	Gold Away
106	Hopping Higgins
106	Lady Alexander
106	Land of Dreams
106	Pegnitz
106	Victory Note
105	Dr Fong
105	Flame Violet
105	Insight
105	Mowbray
105	Roi Gironde
105	Sharp Domino

105	Shuhrah

Three-Year-Olds
137	Peintre Celebre
128	Desert King
126	Benny The Dip
126	Touch Gold*
125	Loup Sauvage
125	Silver Charm*
124	Captain Bodgit*
124	Entrepreneur
124	Free House*
123	Ajina*
123	Sharp Cat*
123	Silver Patriarch
122	Bahhare
122	Behrens*
122	Daylami
122	Deputy Commander*
122	Glitter Woman*
122	Revoque
122	Runup The Colors*
122	Ryafan
122	Starborough
121	Blushing K D*
121	Borgia
121	Caitano
121	Compton Place
121	Dr Johnson
121	Elnadim
120	Air Express
120	Ebadiyla
120	Fabulously Fast*
120	Oscar
120	Silk Justice*
120	Sleepytime
120	Smoke Glacken*
119	Astarabad
119	Poteen
119	Stowaway
119	Taiki Shuttle*
119	Vereva
118	Among Men
118	Anet*
118	Cape Cross
118	Dixie Flag*
118	Honor Glide*
118	Kingfisher Mill
118	Pulpit*
118	Que Belle
118	Tomisue's Delight*
118	Yashmak
118	Zamindar
117	Accelerator*
117	Awesome Again*
117	Baroon

INDEX TO PHOTOGRAPHS

PORTRAITS & SNAPSHOTS

1134

Kaliana	3 b.f. Slip Anchor – Kadissya	*John Crofts*	501
King of Kings	2 b.c. Sadler's Wells – Zummerudd	*Caroline Norris*	518
Kutta	5 b.h. Old Vic – Ardassine	*Clare Williams*	527
Loup Sauvage	3 ch.c. Riverman – Louveterie	*John Crofts*	560
Loving Claim	2 b.f. Hansel – Ville d'Amore	*Bertrand*	563
Luso	5 b.h. Salse – Lucayan Princess	*John Crofts*	568
Maylane	3 b.g. Mtoto – Possessive Dancer	*Clare Williams*	592
Midnight Line	2 ch.f. Kris S – Midnight Air	*Laurie Morton*	602
Miss Zafonic	2 b.f. Zafonic – Miss Silca Key	*Clare Williams*	613
Monaassib	6 ch.g. Cadeaux Genereux – Pluvial	*Clare Williams*	618
Nadwah	2 b.f. Shadeed – Tadwin	*Rex Coleman*	649
Occupandiste	4 b.f. Kaldoun – Only Seule	*John Crofts*	672
Oh Nellie	3 b.f. Tilt The Stars – Miss Enjoleur	*Clare Williams*	674
One So Wonderful	3 b.f. Nashwan – Someone Special	*John Crofts*	679
Orchestra Stall	5 b.g. Old Vic – Blue Brocade	*Rex Coleman*	684
Oscar	3 b.c. Sadler's Wells – Snow Day	*John Crofts*	686
Oscar Schindler	5 ch.h. Royal Academy – Saraday	*Peter Mooney*	688
Panama City	3 b.c. El Gran Senor – Obeah	*John Crofts*	694
Papering	4 b.f. Shaadi – Wrapping	*John Crofts*	696
Pas de Reponse	3 b.f. Danzig – Soundings	*John Crofts*	699
Pasternak	4 b.c. Soviet Star – Princess Pati	*Clare Williams*	703
Peintre Celebre	3 ch.c. Nureyev – Peinture Bleue	*John Crofts*	710
Pilsudski	5 b.h. Polish Precedent – Cocotte	*John Crofts*	727
Polar Prince	4 b.c. Distinctly North – Staff Approved	*John Crofts*	733
Poteen	3 b.c. Irish River – Chaleur	*John Crofts*	737
Predappio	4 b.c. Polish Precedent – Khalafiya	*John Crofts*	741
Princely Heir	2 b.c. Fairy King – Meis El-Reem	*John Crofts*	749
Puce	4 b.f. Darshaan – Souk	*John Crofts*	756
Queen Maud	3 b.f. Akarad – Modiyna	*John Crofts*	760
Ramooz	4 b.c. Rambo Dancer – My Shafy	*John Crofts*	769
Reams of Verse	3 ch.f. Nureyev – Modena	*Laurie Morton*	775
Revoque	3 b.c. Fairy King – La Bella Fontana	*John Crofts*	788
Royal Applause	4 b.c. Waajib – Flying Melody	*John Crofts*	807
Saratoga Springs	2 ch.c. El Gran Senor – Population	*Caroline Norris*	832
Sausalito Bay	3 b.c. Salse – Cantico	*Rex Coleman*	836
Second Empire	2 b.c. Fairy King – Welsh Love	*Caroline Norris*	844
Shantou	4 b.c. Alleged – Shaima	*John Crofts*	856
Silver Patriarch	3 gr.c. Saddlers' Hall – Early Rising	*John Crofts*	875
Singspiel	5 b.h. In The Wings – Glorious Song	*John Crofts*	882
Sleepytime	3 b.f. Royal Academy – Alidiva	*Laurie Morton*	889
Spinning World	4 ch.c. Nureyev – Imperfect Circle	*Bertrand*	908
Squeak	3 ch.f. Selkirk – Santa Linda	*John Crofts*	910
Starborough	3 ch.c. Soviet Star – Flamenco Wave	*John Crofts*	914
Stowaway	3 b.c. Slip Anchor – On Credit	*John Crofts*	924
Swain	5 b.h. Nashwan – Love Smitten	*John Crofts*	940
Taipan	5 b.h. Last Tycoon – Alidiva	*John Crofts*	950
Teapot Row	2 b.c. Generous – Secrage	*John Crofts*	962
The Fly	3 gr.c. Pharly – Nelly Do Da	*Rex Coleman*	971
Vereva	3 br.f. Kahyasi – Vearia	*Bertrand*	1011
Vertical Speed	3 ch.c. Bering – Victoire Bleue	*John Crofts*	1014
Whitewater Affair	4 ch.f. Machiavellian – Much Too Risky	*John Crofts*	1031
Winter Romance	4 ch.c. Cadeaux Genereux – Island Wedding	*Clare Williams*	1040
Wizard King	6 b.h. Shaadi – Broomstick Cottage	*Clare Williams*	1042
Woodland Melody	2 b.f. Woodman – Eloquent Minister	*John Crofts*	1045
Xaar	2 b.c. Zafonic – Monroe	*John Crofts*	1051
Yashmak	3 b.f. Danzig – Slightly Dangerous	*Laurie Morton*	1058
Zamindar	3 b.c. Gone West – Zaizafon	*John Crofts*	1064

RACE PHOTOGRAPHS

Great Voltigeur Stakes (York)	*John Crofts*	923
Grosvenor Casino Sheffield Conditions Stakes (York)	*Alec Russell*	131
Grosvenor Casinos Cup (Handicap) (Goodwood)	*John Crofts*	595
Grosvenor Casinos Dante Stakes (York)	*George Selwyn*	113
Grosvenor Casinos Hambleton Rated Stakes (York)	*John Crofts*	192
Gtech Royal Lodge Stakes (Ascot)	*John Crofts*	961
Hardwicke Stakes (Royal Ascot)	*John Crofts*	740
Harefield Conditions Stakes (Windsor)	*John Crofts*	520
Haydock Park July Trophy Stakes (Haydock Park)	*Alec Russell*	478
Haydock Park Sprint Cup (Haydock Park)	*Alec Russell*	806
Heinz 57 Phoenix Stakes (Leopardstown)	*Peter Mooney*	748
Hong Kong International Vase (Sha Tin)	*George Selwyn*	567
Hong Kong Jockey Club Trophy (Sandown)	*George Selwyn*	434
Japan Cup (Tokyo)	*George Selwyn*	726
Jefferson Smurfit Memorial Irish St Leger (the Curragh)	*Peter Mooney*	687
Jersey Stakes (Royal Ascot)	*Alec Russell*	61
Jockey Club of Kenya Molecomb Stakes (Goodwood)	*John Crofts*	529
John Smith's Magnet Cup (Handicap) (York)	*Alec Russell*	701
JRA Nakayama Rous Stakes (Newmarket)	*George Selwyn*	263
Juddmonte International Stakes (York)	*John Crofts*	881
Juddmonte Lockinge Stakes (Newbury)	*John Crofts*	361
Kildangan Stud Irish Oaks (the Curragh)	*Caroline Norris*	314
King Edward VII Stakes (Royal Ascot)	*John Crofts*	514
King George Stakes (Goodwood)	*John Crofts*	88
King George V Stakes (Handicap) (Royal Ascot)	*Royal Ascot*	445
King George VI And Queen Elizabeth Diamond Stakes (Ascot)	*John Crofts*	938
King's Stand Stakes (Royal Ascot)	*John Crofts*	292
Kyoto Sceptre Stakes (Doncaster)	*John Crofts*	86
Ladbroke (Ayr) Gold Cup (Handicap) (Ayr)	*Alec Russell*	1035
Ladbroke (Ayr) Silver Cup (Handicap) (Ayr)	*Alec Russell*	715
Ladbroke Bunbury Cup (Handicap) (Newmarket)	*John Crofts*	1000
Lanes End John Porter Stakes (Newbury)	*John Crofts*	1030
Lanson Champagne Vintage Stakes (Goodwood)	*John Crofts*	190
Laurent-Perrier Rose Champagne Stakes (Doncaster)	*Alec Russell*	248
Lawrence Batley Rated Stakes (Handicap) (York)	*Alec Russell*	294
Letheby & Christopher Old Newton Cup (Handicap) (Haydock)	*Alec Russell*	1066
Lexus Irish Two Thousand Guineas (the Curragh)	*John Crofts*	278
London Car Telephones Handicap (Epsom)	*John Crofts*	195
May Hill Stakes (Doncaster)	*George Selwyn*	601
Mercedes Benz Grosser Preis von Baden (Baden-Baden)	*Frank Nolting*	141
Michael Sobell Silver Tankard Handicap (York)	*Alec Russell*	414
Moyglare Stud Stakes (the Curragh)	*Peter Mooney*	956
'Newcastle Brown Ale' Northumberland Plate (Handicap) (Newcastle)	*Alec Russell*	1037
NGK Spark Plugs European Free Handicap (Newmarket)	*John Crofts*	448
Norfolk Stakes (Royal Ascot)	*John Crofts*	985
Nunthorpe Stakes (York)	*George Selwyn*	222
Nunthorpe Stakes (York)	*Alec Russell*	1055
O & K Troy Stakes (Doncaster)	*John Crofts*	159
Ormonde Stakes (Chester)	*Alec Russell*	809
Owen Brown Rockfel Stakes (Newmarket)	*George Selwyn*	650
Porcelanosa Rated Stakes (Handicap) (Doncaster)	*John Crofts*	815
Pertemps One Thousand Guineas Stakes (Newmarket)	*John Crofts*	888
Pertemps St Leger (Doncaster)	*Alec Russell*	873
Pertemps Two Thousand Guineas Stakes (Newmarket)	*John Crofts*	333
Phoenix Sprint Stakes (Leopardstown)	*Peter Mooney*	240
Polypipe plc Flying Childers Stakes (Doncaster)	*Alec Russell*	535
Portland Place Properties Jockey Club Cup (Newmarket)	*Alec Russell*	415
Prince of Wales's Stakes (Royal Ascot)	*John Crofts*	144
Princess Margaret Stakes (Ascot)	*John Crofts*	326
Princess of Wales's Stakes (Newmarket)	*John Crofts*	854

DARLEY STUD MANAGEMENT

Standing at Dalham Hall Stud, Newmarket

HALLING
1991 by Diesis - Dance Machine
Champion 4yo and 5yo in Europe - winner of **5 Group 1 races**
First Foals 1998

LION CAVERN
1989 by Mr Prospector - Secrettame
Dual **GW**, own brother to **GONE WEST**
Sire of 10 Individual winners from his First crop in 1997

MACHIAVELLIAN
1987 by Mr Prospector - Coup de Folie
Classic Sire of 16 individual Stakes Winners
REBECCA SHARP, VETTORI etc.

MARK OF ESTEEM
1993 by Darshaan - Homage
Champion Miler in Europe 1996, dual **Group 1 Winner**
Timeform Horse of the Year 1996
First Foals 1998

POLISH PRECEDENT
1986 by Danzig - Past Example
Classic Sire of PURE GRAIN and **Champion PILSUDSKI,**
PREDAPPIO, RED ROUTE, RIYADIAN

SHAREEF DANCER
1980 by Northern Dancer - Sweet Alliance
A Leading European Sire of 29 individual **GW/SWs** of 56 races

SINGSPIEL
1992 by In the Wings - Glorious Song
European Record money winner
Multiple Group 1 Winner - Retires to stud in 1998

STALLIONS for 1998

WOLFHOUND

1989 by Nureyev - Lassie Dear
Champion European Sprinter, dual **Group 1 Winner**
Sire of 6 Individual winners from his First crop in 1997

Standing at Aston Upthorpe Stud, Oxfordshire

MTOTO

1983 by Busted - Amazer
Derby Sire of SHAAMIT and **PRESENTING**
**Sire of GWs ARBATAX, BOOK AT BEDTIME, CELERIC,
MAYLANE, MDUDU, MOUSSE GLACEE**

Standing at Ragusa Stud, Co. Kildare
IN THE WINGS

1986 by Sadler's Wells - High Hawk
Classic Sire of WINGED LOVE and **European Record money
winner SINGSPIEL** and **GWs/SWs ANNABA, CENTRE STALLS,
IRISH WINGS, KAFHAR, STAGE MANNER, WINGS BASH etc**

LYCIUS

1988 by Mr Prospector - Lypatia
Sire of G1W HELLO, and **GWs MEDIA NOX** and **AYLESBURY**

PENNEKAMP

1992 by Bering - Coral Dance
Champion 2yo in Europe - 2000 Guineas Winner
multiple **Group 1 Winner**
First Foals 1998

Darley Stud Management Company Ltd.,
Dalham Hall Stud, Duchess Drive, Newmarket. CB8 9HD.
Telephone: Newmarket (01638) 730070.
Fax: (01638) 730167.

Whichever way you breed it, it has to be Airlie

Whether you're trying to breed a good horse yourself, or are looking to buy one at the sales, there's one name which should be uppermost in your mind – **Airlie Stud**.

During the 1990s, Airlie has achieved new heights with its breeding operation. As Group winner has followed Group winner, the stud's reputation as a nursery of top quality thoroughbreds has increased accordingly, while our resident stallion, **Ela-Mana-Mou**, has continued to produce runners of the highest class, as well as proving himself a highly influential broodmare sire.

We are also pleased to offer boarding facilities for mares and sales preparation for yearlings and foals at our new headquarters at Grangewilliam, so it's fair to say that Airlie Stud provides breeders with a complete service.

GRANGEWILLIAM, MAYNOOTH, Co. KILDARE.
Tel: (01) 6286336. Fax: (01) 6286674.

ELA-MANA-MOU

Sire of the winners of over **680** races and **£7** million, including
6 INDIVIDUAL GROUP 1 WINNERS and **7 OTHER INDIVIDUAL GROUP 2 WINNERS**.
His 1997 two-year-old's include the highly promising **TRIGGER HAPPY** and **SINON**.
Now also a leading broodmare sire of **19 INDIVIDUAL GROUP & STAKES WINNERS**,
including **SECOND EMPIRE** (unbeaten winner of 1997 **Gr.1** Grand Criterium).
His 1997 yearlings averaged **28,250gns** at Goffs Orby and Tattersalls October Sales.

Standing at Throckmorton Court Stud,

FORZANDO

bay 1981 by FORMIDABLE - PRINCELY MAID by King's Troop

Multiple Group Winner
Won 12 races including: Metropolitan H'cap **Gr.1**
and **5 consecutive races as a 2-year-old**

Year after year
Sire of Top, Consistent, Sound 2 Year Olds
**EASYCALL, GREAT DEEDS, HIGH PREMIUM,
MISTERIOSO, PHILIDOR, POOL MUSIC,
PURE FORMALITY, SHARPNESS IN MIND,
SUPERIOR PREMIUM, UP AND AT'EM,** etc.

Fee: £2,000 October 1st
Peter Balding, Pershore, Worcestershire WR10 2JX.
Telephone: 01386 - 462559. Fax: 01386 - 462209.

Enquiries to:
LONDON THOROUGHBRED SERVICES LTD.,
Biddlesgate Farm, Nr Cranborne, Dorset BH21 5RS.
Telephone: 01725 - 517711. Fax: 01725 - 517833.

LTS

Standing at Woodland Stud

INCHINOR

chesnut 1990 by AHONOORA - INCHMURRIN by Lomond

A Leading 7-8F Performer by AHONOORA

WON Hungerford Stakes **Gr.3**, 7f
WON Criterion Stakes **Gr.3**, 7f TRACK RECORD
WON Greenham Stakes **Gr.3**, 7f
WON Personnel Selection Stakes, 7f by 2 lengths
WON EBF Park Lodge Stakes, 6f on his debut
2nd Dewhurst Stakes **Gr.1**, 7f to Champion 2yo **ZAFONIC**
3rd Sussex Stakes **Gr.1**, 8f to **BIGSTONE** and **SAYYEDATI**

Fee: £3,000 October 1st
Successful First Season Sire in 1997

Woodland Stud, Snailwell Road, Newmarket, Suffolk. CB8 7DJ.
Telephone: Newmarket 01638 - 663081. Fax: 01638 - 663036.
Enquiries to:
LONDON THOROUGHBRED SERVICES LTD.,
Biddlesgate Farm, Nr Cranborne, Dorset BH21 5RS.
Telephone: 01725 - 517711. Fax: 01725 - 517833.

LTS

Standing at Plantation Stud

KRIS

chesnut, by SHARPEN UP - DOUBLY SURE by Reliance

Twice
CHAMPION EUROPEAN MILER

CHAMPION SIRE of Group 1 winners:
SINGLE EMPIRE, OH SO SHARP, COMMON GROUNDS, UNITE, FITNAH, FLASH OF STEEL, RAFHA, SHAVIAN, SHAMSHIR, SUDDEN LOVE,

Fee: £15,000 October 1st

Leslie Harrison, Plantation Stud, Exning, Newmarket, Suffolk CB8 7LJ.
Telephone: 01638 - 577341. Fax: 01638 - 578474.
Enquiries to:
LONDON THOROUGHBRED SERVICES LTD.,
Biddlesgate Farm, Nr Cranborne, Dorset BH21 5RS.
Telephone: 01725 - 517711. Fax: 01725 - 517833.

LTS

Standing at Plantation Stud

PURSUIT OF LOVE

bay 1989 by GROOM DANCER - DANCE QUEST by Green Dancer

Champion European 3yo Sprinter

**CHAMPION BRITISH FIRST SEASON SIRE
Sire of SWs BASSE BESOGNE,
HEAD OVER HEELS, IPPON
Musical Pursuit 2nd Dewhurst Stakes Gr.1**

Fee: £7,000 October 1st

Leslie Harrison, Plantation Stud, Exning, Newmarket, Suffolk CB8 7LJ.
Telephone: 01638 - 577341. Fax: 01638 - 578474.
Enquiries to:
LONDON THOROUGHBRED SERVICES LTD.,
Biddlesgate Farm, Nr Cranborne, Dorset BH21 5RS.
Telephone: 01725 - 517711. Fax: 01725 - 517833.

LTS

Standing at Littleton Stud

ROBELLINO

bay 1979 by ROBERTO - ISOBELLINE by Pronto
Dual Group Winner, broke course record at Ascot at 2

Proven Classic Sire of
CLASSIC PARK
Airlie/Coolmore Irish 1000 Gns **Gr.1**
MISTER BAILEYS
2000 Gns **Gr.1**

A Leading 2yo Sire in Europe

Fee: £5,000 October 1st

Standing at Littleton Stud, Winchester, Hants. S022 6QX.
Telephone: 01962 - 880210. Fax: 01962 - 882290.
Enquiries to:
LONDON THOROUGHBRED SERVICES LTD.,
Biddlesgate Farm, Nr Cranborne, Dorset BH21 5RS.
Telephone: 01725 - 517711. Fax: 01725 - 517833.

LTS

Standing at Lanwades Stud

SELKIRK

chesnut 1988 by SHARPEN UP - ANNIE EDGE by Nebbiolo

Champion European Miler 1991 and 1992

Sire of

KIRKWALL	won Prix Eugene Adam **Gr.2**, Prix de Guiche **Gr.3**
	won Prix Montenica **LR**
ORFORD NESS	won Prix de Sandringham **Gr.3**
ENTICE	won Silver Tankard S. **LR**, John Musker S. **LR**
	2nd Vodafone Nassau Stakes **Gr.2**
HIDDEN MEADOW	won Free Handicap **LR**, City of York Stakes **LR**
SQUEAK	won Lancashire Oaks **Gr.3**
	won Ballymacoll Stud Stakes **LR**
TRANS ISLAND	won Prix du Haras Huderie **LR**

Fee: £8,000 October 1st

Kirsten Rausing, Lanwades Stud, Moulton, Newmarket CB8 8QS.
Telephone: 01638 - 750222. Fax: 01638 - 751186.
Enquiries to:
LONDON THOROUGHBRED SERVICES LTD.,
Biddlesgate Farm, Nr Cranborne, Dorset BH21 5RS.
Telephone: 01725 - 517711. Fax: 01725 - 517833.

LTS

ON THE INTERNET? THEN REMEMBER THIS ADDRESS
http://www.timeform.com

Timeform

CONTENTS

- Race Cards
- Bloodstock Sales Guide
- Hong Kong Race Ratings Service
- Free Daily Racing Preview
- Racecourse maps and statistics
- News about new products
- Competitions

RACING'S MOST USEFUL SITE

When Timeform launched an internet site it was odds on that it would be an outstanding success. For over fifty years Timeform has been providing its customers with a first class service, earning an international reputation for accuracy and excellence.

Our new internet means that, instead of having to plan ahead to order early, you can get instant access to Timeform Race Cards for any meeting. That's particularly good news for overseas customers who have previously been unable to receive the information by post. There's lots of other Timeform information available too, much of it with free access, including a sample card for you to test out and some advice on how to improve your betting. Why not call in for a look?

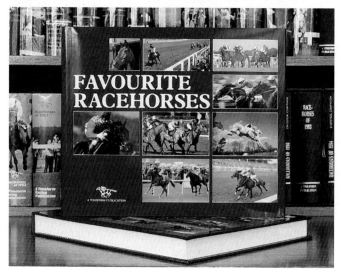

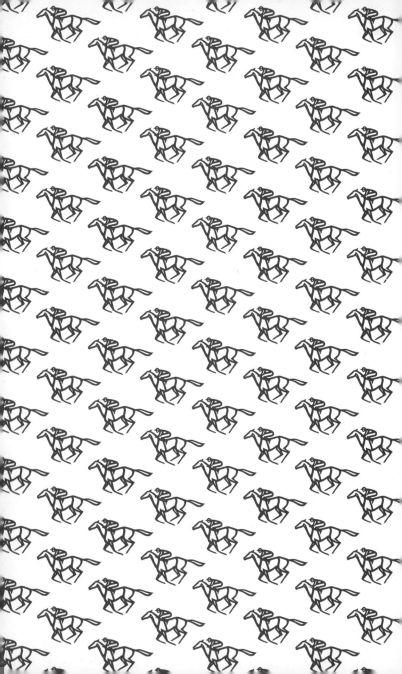